THE QUR'ĀN

حديث الثقلين

بسم اللّه الرحمن الرحيم

قال رسول اللّه ص: إني مخلِّفٌ فيكم الثقلين : كتاب اللّه، وعترتي أهل بيتي، ما إن تمسكتم بهما لن تضلوا بعدي

Inni tarekon feekom el'thakalayn, kitab'Allah
wa Itrati Ahla Bayti, ma in tamasktum bihimaa,
lan tadillu ba'adi abada.

Rasoul'Allah (saws) said:
"Indeed, I am leaving among you two that have significant weight, The Book of Allah and my family-the people of my house (Ahlul-Bayt As), if you hold fast to them, you shall not be misguided after me."

The Qur'an

Translated by
Shaykh Muhammad Sarwar

Transliteration by
M. Abdul Haleem Eliyasee

Published by
Tahrike Tarsile Qur'an, Inc.
Publishers and Distributors of the Holy Qur'an
80-08 51st Avenue
Elmhurst, New York 11373-4141
Email: read@koranusa.org
www.koranusa.org

بِسْمِ اللهِ الرَّحْمٰنِ الرَّحِيْمِ

In the name of God Most Gracious, Most Merciful

The Qur'an

Transliteration by
M. Abdul Haleem Eliyasee

Translated by
Shaykh Muhammad Sarwar

2021 Edition

ISBN: 978-1-952290-08-4

Library of Congress Control Number: 2020919401

Published by
Tahrike Tarsile Qur'an, Inc.
Publishers and Distributors of the Holy Qur'an
80-08 51st Avenue
Elmhurst, New York 11373-4141
Email: read@koranusa.org
www.koranusa.org

Printed in India

Contents

بسم الله الرحمن الرحيم

Important Disclosure

Praise be to Allah, the Cherisher and Sustainer of the worlds, Who has said in His Noble Book:
There has come to you from Allah
Light and a Perspicuous Book. (1)

And may peace and blessings be upon the Seal of the Prophets, Mohammad, who has said that:
The best among you is he who learned
The Qur'ân and then taught it. (2)

May the peace and blessings of Allah be upon him, his family and all his Companions.

The Glorious Qur'ân is the Book of Allah, the Wise and Worthy of all Praise, Who has promised to safeguard it from any violations in its purity. It becomes incumbent upon each and every person who seeks the dignity of this world and the bliss of the Hereafter to regulate his life according to it, to implement its commandments and to pay homage to the magnificence of the One Who revealed it. This can be an easy task for those favoured with guidance from Allah, especially those blessed by a understanding of Arabic, the language of the divine communication. But for those not acquainted with Arabic, their ignorance is a barrier between them and this source of guidance and illumination. A translation of the message of Allah is thus a task not to be taken lightly or performed superficially.

Before the reader begins to study the Qur'ân he must realise that unlike all other writings, this is a unique book with a supreme author, an eternal message and a universal relevance. Its contents are not confined to a particular theme or style, but contain the foundations for an entire system of life, covering a whole spectrum of issues, which range from specific articles of faith and commandments to general moral teachings, rights and obligations, crime and punishment, personal and public law, and a host of other private and social concerns. These issues are discussed in a variety of ways, such as direct stipulations, reminders of Allah's favours of His creation, admonitions and rebukes. Stories of past communities are narrated, followed by the lessons to be learned from their actions and subsequent fates.

The Qur'ân enjoys a number of characteristics unique to it alone, some of which are as follows:

1. It is the actual Word of Allah; not created but revealed for the benefit of all mankind.
   Blessed is He Who sent down the Criterion
   To His servant, that it may be
   An admonition to all creatures. (3)
2. It is complete and comprehensive. The Almighty says:
   Nothing have We omitted from the Book. (4)

   In another place we read,
   And We have sent down to thee
   The Book explaining all things. (5)
3. It is a theoretical and a practical Book, not only moralising but also defining specifically the permissible and the forbidden. The importance of understanding the message of the

---

(1) Sûrat al-Mâ'idah: 15. (2) Narrated by the six ones except Muslim. (3) Sûrat al-Furqân: 1.
(4) Sūrat al-An'âm: 38. (5) Surat an-Naḥl: 89.

Qur'ân is undeniable, but simply reciting it with the intention of seeking Allah's pleasure and reward is also an act of worship and meritorious in itself. Allah Almighty says:

So take what the Prophet gives you
And refrain from what he prohibits you. (6)

4. Allah has perfected His religion for all mankind with the revelation of this Book. He say:

This day have I perfected your religion for you,
Completed my favour upon you and have chosen
For you Islam as your religion. (7)

5. It is Allah's eternal miracle revealed to the Prophet Muhammad for all succeeding generations. In response to those who doubt the authorship of the Qur'ân, Allah Almighty has challenged the most articulate Arabs to produce a whole book, ten chapters or even one solitary chapter which can be remotely comparable to the Qur'ân. But to this day, no one has succeeded in meeting the challenge of the Almighty. The critics of the Qur'ân have been struck dumb by its ineffable eloquence and surpassing beauty.

Say, if the whole of mankind and jinns
Were to gather together to produce the
Like of this Qur'ân, they could not
Produce the like thereof; even if they
Backed up each other with help and support. (8)

The Almighty also says:

Or they may say: he forged it.
Say: Bring ye then ten chapters
Forged, like unto it and call
(To your aid) whomsoever ye can
Other than Allah, if ye speak
The truth. (9)

And again:

Or do they say: he forged it?
Say: Bring then a chapter like
Unto it and call (to your aid)
Anyone ye can besides Allah,
If it be ye speak the truth. (10)

6. It has been revealed to re-establish the sincere worship of Allah alone, without association of any partners with Him.

This is a Book with verses basic or
Fundamental (of established meaning),
Further explained in detail,-
From One who is Wise and Well-Aware.
(It teaches) that you should worship
None but Allah. (11)
And they have been commanded no more
Than this: to worship Allah,
Offering Him sincere devotion, being true

---

(6) Sûrat al-Ḥashr: 7. (7) Sûrat al-Mâ'idah: 3. (8) Sûrat Banî Isrâ'îl: 88.
(9) Sûrat Hûd: 13 (10) Sûrat Yûnus: 38 (11) Sûrat Hûd: 1-2.

In faith, to establish regular prayer
And to give Zakat, and that is
The religion Right and Straight. (12)

7. It contains a complete code which provides for all areas of life, whether spiritual, intellectual, political, social or economic. It is a code which has no boundaries of time, place or nation.

Verily this Qur'ân doth guide
To that which is most right. (13)

8. Allah Almighty has taken upon Himself the duty of preserving the Qur'ân for ever in its entirety, as He says:

We have without doubt sent down
The Message, and We will assuredly
Guard it (from corruption). (14)

So well has it been preserved, both in memory and in writing, that the Arabic text we have today is identical to the text as it was revealed to the Prophet. Not even a single letter has yielded for corruption during the passage of the centuries. And so it will remain for ever, by the consent of Allah.

Given the depth as well as the sublimity of the Qur'ânic text, a faithful translation of it into another language is virtually impossible. The various translations that exist today, however accurate they may be, cannot be designated as the Qur'ân, since they can never hope to imitate the diction or the style of the Book of Allah. But as translation is one of the few ways to export the message of the Qur'ân to allow those lacking in knowledge of Arabic to share this priceless gift, it becomes a duty for those in a position to fulfil this task.

A number of individuals have in the past ventured to translate the Qur'ân, but their works have generally been private attempts, greatly influenced by their own prejudices. In order to produce a reliable translation free from personal bias, a Royal decree (No. 19888, dated 16/8/1400 AH) was issued by the Custodian of the Two Holy Mosques, King Fahd ibn Abdul Aziz, at that time the deputy prime minister, authorising the General Presidency of the Departments of Islamic Researches, Ifta, Call and Guidance to undertake the responsibility of revising and correcting a particular translation which would be selected for this purpose and made publicly available later.

To accomplish this enormous task, a number of committees were formed, comprising scholars well-qualified both in Islamic Shari'a and the English language. Some of these scholars were associated with the General Presidency of the Departments of Islamic Researches, Ifta, Call and Guidance.

The first committee was given the task of examining the existing translations and choosing the most suitable one from among them. The committee discovered that there was no translation free from defects and so there were two options open for consideration: the first was to select the best translation available and then adopt it as a base for further works as well as a source of reference, with the objective of revising its contents and correcting any faults in view of the objections raised against it; the second was to prepare a fresh and independent translation, starting from scratch.

It became obvious from studying these translations that the second option demanded much time and efforts, neither of which were available at the time.

---

(12) Sûrat al-Bayyinah: 5. (13) Sûrat Banî Isrâ'îl: 9. (14) Sûrat al-Ḥijr: 9.

The first option was therefore considered to be more practical, since it met the existing urgent requirements and helped to achieve the desired goal in a comparatively short period of time. The translation by the late Ustadh ABDULLAH YUSUF ALI was consequently chosen for its distinguishing characteristics, such as highly elegant style, a choice of words close to the meaning of the original text, accompanied by scholarly notes and commentaries.

The committee began revising and correcting this translation with the aid of other translations available, by comparing and then adopting best expressions as well as by introducing fresh expressions where necessary. The committee was fully aware of all the criticisms that had been directed against this translation and which had been carefully brought to the notice of the presidency by a number of academic bodies and other involved parties. In the second stage, the entire work of this committee was referred to a number of individuals and organizations who then augmented any deficiencies in the work of the committee.

A third committee was set up to collate all their suggestions. It then compared all such views regarding specific issues, selected the appropriate one (s) and arrived at a text as authentic and defect-free as was humanly possible.

Finally, a fourth committee was formed to look into the findings of the second and third committees and to implement the recommendations made by them. Furthermore, this committee had to finalise the text by adopting the most accurate expression where needed, besides checking the notes vigilantly so as to clear any misconceptions regarding the articles of faith, varying juristic opinions and thoughts not in conformity with the sound Islamic point of view.

According to the Royal decree (No.12412, dated 27/10/1405 AH), this translation is printed at King Fahd Holy Qur'ân Printing Complex in Al-Madinah Al-Munawarah and also with coordination of the General Presidency of the Departments of Islamic Researches, Ifta, Call and Guidance.

To implement the directions of the Custodian of the Two Holy Mosques (May Allah preserve him) concerning the Propagation of the Book of Allah, its distribution and translation into every language spoken by Muslims the worldwide, and due to the cooperation between the General Secretariat of King Fahd Holy Qur'ân Printing Complex and the Presidency of Islamic Researches, Ifta, Call and Guidance regarding a faithful, specific and scholarly translation of the meanings of the Holy Qur'ân, we are pleased to present to all Muslims and those seeking spiritual light among English-speaking people this translation which comes as one of the Series of the translations of the meanings of the Holy Qur'ân into various languages printed by the Complex in Al-Madinah Al-Munawarah.

May Allah reward bounteously those who were behind this blessed work.

Transliteration Key of Arabic Letters

The following table shows the system which I have followed in transliterating the letters of the Arabic alphabet:

1. Alphabet

No.	Name of Arabic Letters	Arabic Letters	Latin Characters	Pronunciation
1	Hamzah	ء	’	Pronounced as *a*, *i*, *u* preceded by a very slight aspiration.
2	Bâ’	ب	b	In English like the ‘big’.
3	Tâ’	ت	t	A soft dental, as in Italian *t*.
4	Thâ’	ث	s̲	A nearly sound between *th* and *s*.
5	Jîm	ج	j	In English like the ‘judge’.
6	Ḥâ’	ح	ḥ	A strong and sustained expulsion of breath.
7	Khâ’	خ	kh	Guttural, as similar to the German ‘ach’.
8	Dâl	د	d	A soft dental, as in English ‘the’.
9	Dhâl	ذ	z̲	A sound between *ḍ* and *z*.
10	Râ’	ر	r	In English like the ‘roll’.
11	Zâ’	ز	z	In English like the ‘zone’.
12	Sîn	س	s	In English like the ‘sea’.
13	Shîn	ش	sh	In English like the ‘sheet’.
14	Ṣâd	ص	ṣ	A strongly articulated *sw*, as in English ‘swallow’.
15	Ḍâd	ض	ḍ	A strong sound between *d* and *z*, articulated as letter ‘Ṣâd’.
16	Ṭâ’	ط	ṭ	A strongly articulated palatal *t*.
17	Ẓâ’	ظ	ẓ	A strongly articulated *z*.
18	‘Ayn	ع	‘	A guttural an, the pronunciation must be learnt by an Arabic teacher.
19	Ghayn	غ	gh	A strong guttural *gh*.
20	Fâ’	ف	f	In English like the ‘foot’.
21	Qâf	ق	q	A strongly articulated semi guttural *k*.
22	Kâf	ك	k	In English like the ‘king’.
23	Lâm	ل	l	In English like the ‘love’.
24	Mîm	م	m	In English like the ‘mat’.

25	Nûn	ن	n	In English like the 'never'.
26	Hâ'	ه	h	In English like the 'happy'.
27	Wâw	و	w	In English like the 'work'.
28	Yâ'	ى	y	In English like the 'yet'.

2. Short Vowels

ـَ	Fatḥa	a	كَتَبَ	kataba
ـِ	Kasra	i	سُئِلَ	su'ila
ـُ	Ḍamma	u	يَذْهَبُ	yaẕhabu

3. Long Vowels

اَ	aa	قَالَ	qaala
اِىْ	ee	قِيْلَ	qeela
اُوْ	oo	يَقُوْلُ	yaqoolu

4. Diphthong

اَىْ	ay	كَيْفَ	kayfa
اَوْ	aw	حَوْلَ	ḥawla

5. Points to Remember

- Alif (ا) is not be confused with Hamza (ء). If it has diacritical marks (as ـَ , ـِ , ـُ) it is hamza. Alif is always followed by another letter as بَ = ba بَا = baa.
- Alif Jaazim (اْ) = å . It gives a glottal stop while reading the letter 'Alif' above which it is placed, *e.g.*, تَاْتِيَهُمْ = taåtiyahum.
- Gunna = ñ (nasal sound), as *n* is pronounced in 'uncle'.
- When silent نْ = n or Tanween (nunation) were followed by ب = b. They are pronounced like م = m with a gunna, *e.g.*, اَنْبَا = 'ambaa / خَبِيْرٌ بِمَا = khabeerum bimaa.
- Shaddah (ّ) (double letter). It is pronounced with a sustained emphasis on that letter, *e.g.*, دَلَّ = dalla.
- For Madd (~) (elongation of vowels) three symbols have been introduced: *a, i, u,* as in بَ = ba بَا = baa بَآ = baaa, بِ = bi بِىْ = bee بِىٓ = beee, بُ = bu بُوْ = boo بُوٓ = booo.
- There is only 'Mâ'roof' (known) sound in the Qur'ân as بِ = bi, بُ = bu. There is no 'Majhool' (unknown) sound in the Qur'ân except in one word: مَجْرٖىهَا 'Majrayhaa' (as in English 'ray') (P. 12, S. 11:41).

Arabic Words Explained

A comprehensive list of names, places and topics appears as an index at the end of the book. Here some oft-repeated Arabic words occurring in the translation are given with brief explanation.

ALLAH: The proper name of God in Arabic.

HAJJ: The pilgrimage to Makkah which takes place in the last month of the Islamic calendar.

IBLÎS: Satan.

ISLÂM: Literally, to submit.
The Religion of all the Prophets of Allah confirmed finally by the mission of the Prophet Muhammad ﷺ.

JINN: Invisible beings constituting a whole race like mankind.

MUHAJIR: Literally, the emigrant.
One who leaves the home town to join a Muslim community.

MUSLIM: One who professes the faith of Islam or born to a Muslim family.

QIBLA: The Ka'ba. The direction for the daily prayers of a Muslim.

QUR'ÂN: Literally, the recital.
The final revelation given to the Prophet Muhammad ﷺ in Arabic.

RAMADAN: The ninth month of the Islamic calendar during which the Muslims fast.

SÛRAH: A chapter of the Qur'ân.

ṬAGUT: Literally, a tyrant, oppresser, false god, temper to error.
Tagut is applied to any object which is worshipped besides Allah.

UMRAH: A minor form of pilgrimage to Makkah.

UMMAH: Literally, a nation but is usually applied to the Muslim Brotherhood.

YATHRIB: The name by which Madinah was known before the Prophet's migration to that city.

ZAKAT: Literally, to grow, to purify.
The third pillar of Islam.
It is a definite portion of wealth which is given to needy at the turn of the year.

List of Prostration Places in The Qur'ân

It is a good practice to prostrate at the following places while reciting the Qur'ân.

No.	Part No.	Name of Sûrah	Sûrah No.	Verse No.
1	9	Al-A'râf	7	206
2.	13	Ar-Ra'd	13	15
3.	14	An-Naḥl	16	50
4.	15	Banî Isrâ'îl	17	109
5.	16	Maryam	19	58
6.	17	Al-Ḥajj	22	18
7.	17	Al-Ḥajj	22	77
8.	19	Al-Furqân	25	60
9.	19	An-Naml	27	26
10.	21	As-Sajdah	32	15
11.	23	Ṣâd	38	24
12.	24	Ḥâ-Mîm Sajdah	41	38
13.	27	An-Najm	53	62
14.	30	Al-Inshiqâq	84	21
15.	30	Al-'Alaq	96	19

* In all, fourteen places of prostration are agreed upon by all Muslim religious scholars and '*Ulama*, while Imâm Shâf'i (R.A) suggests prostration at this place also.

The following invocation is usually recited during the prostration:

(سَجَدَ وَجْهِيَ لِلَّذِي خَلَقَهُ وَصَوَّرَهُ وَشَقَّ سَمْعَهُ وَبَصَرَهُ تَبَارَكَ اللّٰهُ أَحْسَنُ الْخَالِقِينَ)

Sajada wajhiya lillazee khalaqahoo wa ṣawwarahoo, wa shaqqa sam'ahoo wa baṣarahoo, tabaarak-Allaahu Aḥsanul-Khaaliqeen.

[*Sahih Muslim,* Vol.4, *Hadîth* No.201].

Symbols Denoting Pauses

Symbol	Extract from Verse	Sûrah Number	Verse Number
Compulsory stop			
م	وَاذْكُرْ فِي الْكِتٰبِ مَرْيَمَ م اِذِ انْتَبَذَتْ	19	16
Necessary stop			
ۖط	عَلَيْهَا صَعِيْدًا جُرُزًا ۖ	18	8
Stop vocal sound for a moment without breaking the breath			
وقفة	وَاعْفُ عَنَّا وقفة وَاغْفِرْ لَنَا وقفة وَارْحَمْنَا وقفة اَنْتَ	2	286
سكتة	كَلَّا بَلْ سكتة رَانَ	83	14
Necessary to continue, do not pause			
لا	فَاعْبُدْنِيْ لا وَاَقِمِ الصَّلٰوةَ لِذِكْرِيْ ۝	20	14
Desirable to continue, do not pause			
ز	اِلَّآ اَنْ يَّشَآءَ اللّٰهُ ز وَاذْكُرْ رَّبَّكَ	18	24
ص	حِجَابًا قف فَاَرْسَلْنَآ اِلَيْهَا رُوْحَنَا	19	17
ق	قَالُوا اتَّخَذَ اللّٰهُ وَلَدًا ق ۝ مَا لَهُمْ بِهٖ	18	4/5
صلے	وَزِدْنٰهُمْ هُدًى ۝ صلے وَّرَبَطْنَا	18	13/14
Recommended pause			
قف	وَمَلٰٓئِكَتِهٖ وَكُتُبِهٖ وَرُسُلِهٖ قف لَا نُفَرِّقُ	2	285
Optional to pause or to continue			
ج	رَبِّكَ ج لَا مُبَدِّلَ لِكَلِمٰتِهٖ ج وَلَنْ	18	27
Any two of the three verses may be read in continuity			
∴	وَقَالَ الَّذِيْنَ كَفَرُوْا لَوْلَا نُزِّلَ عَلَيْهِ الْقُرْاٰنُ جُمْلَةً وَّاحِدَةً ∴ كَذٰلِكَ ∴ لِنُثَبِّتَ بِهٖ فُؤَادَكَ وَرَتَّلْنٰهُ تَرْتِيْلًا ۝	25	32

فهرس بأسماء السُّوَر وبيان المكى والمدنى منها

Index of Sûras – Chapters
(Showing The Makki and The Madani ones)

Sûrah	No.	Page No.	Makki/ Madani	مكيّة / مدنية	رقم الصفحة	رقم السورة	اسم السورة
Al-Fâtiḥah	1	2	Madani	مكيّة	٢	١	الفاتحة
Al-Baqarah	2	4	Madani	مدنيّة	٤	٢	البقرة
Âl-'Imrân	3	53	Madani	مدنيّة	٥٣	٣	آل عمران
An-Nisâ'	4	83	Madani	مدنيّة	٨٣	٤	النّساء
Al-Mâ'idah	5	113	Madani	مدنيّة	١١٣	٥	المائدة
Al-An'âm	6	135	Makki	مكيّة	١٣٥	٦	الانعام
Al-A'râf	7	160	Makki	مكيّة	١٦٠	٧	الاعراف
Al-Anfâl	8	188	Madani	مدنيّة	١٨٨	٨	الانفال
At-Tawbah	9	199	Madani	مدنيّة	١٩٩	٩	التّوبة
Yûnus	10	220	Makki	مكيّة	٢٢٠	١٠	يونس
Hûd	11	235	Makki	مكيّة	٢٣٥	١١	هود
Yûsuf	12	250	Makki	مكيّة	٢٥٠	١٢	يوسف
Ar-Ra'd	13	265	Makki	مكيّة	٢٦٥	١٣	الرّعد
Ibrâhîm	14	272	Makki	مكيّة	٢٧٢	١٤	ابراهيم
Al-Ḥijr	15	279	Makki	مكيّة	٢٧٩	١٥	الحجر
An-Naḥl	16	286	Makki	مكيّة	٢٨٦	١٦	النّحل
Banî Isrâ'îl	17	302	Makki	مكيّة	٣٠٢	١٧	بنى اسرائيل
Al-Kahf	18	315	Makki	مكيّة	٣١٥	١٨	الكهف
Maryam	19	329	Makki	مكيّة	٣٢٩	١٩	مريم
Ṭâ-Hâ	20	337	Makki	مكيّة	٣٣٧	٢٠	طٰهٰ
Al-Anbiyâ'	21	349	Makki	مكيّة	٣٤٩	٢١	الانبياء
Al-Ḥajj	22	360	Madani	مدنيّة	٣٦٠	٢٢	الحج
Al-Mu'minûn	23	370	Makki	مكيّة	٣٧٠	٢٣	المؤمنون
An-Nûr	24	380	Madani	مدنيّة	٣٨٠	٢٤	النّور
Al-Furqân	25	391	Makki	مكيّة	٣٩١	٢٥	الفرقان
Ash-Shu'arâ'	26	399	Makki	مكيّة	٣٩٩	٢٦	الشّعراء

Sûrah	No.	Page No.	Makki/ Madani	مكية مدنية	رقم الصفحة	رقم السورة	اسم السورة
Ar-Raḥmân	55	590	Madani	مدنيّة	٥٩٠	٥٥	الرّحمٰن
Al-Wâqi'ah	56	593	Makki	مكيّة	٥٩٣	٥٦	الواقعة
Al-Ḥadîd	57	598	Madani	مدنيّة	٥٩٨	٥٧	الحديد
Al-Mujâdilah	58	603	Madani	مدنيّة	٦٠٣	٥٨	المجادلة
Al-Ḥashr	59	607	Madani	مدنيّة	٦٠٧	٥٩	الحشر
Al-Mumtaḥanah	60	610	Madani	مدنيّة	٦١٠	٦٠	الممتحنة
Aṣ-Ṣaff	61	613	Madani	مدنيّة	٦١٣	٦١	الصّف
Al-Jumu'ah	62	615	Madani	مدنيّة	٦١٥	٦٢	الجمعة
Al-Munâfiqûn	63	617	Madani	مدنيّة	٦١٧	٦٣	المنافقون
At-Taghâbun	64	618	Madani	مدنيّة	٦١٨	٦٤	التّغابن
Aṭ-Ṭalâq	65	620	Madani	مدنيّة	٦٢٠	٦٥	الطّلاق
At-Taḥrîm	66	623	Madani	مدنيّة	٦٢٣	٦٦	التّحريم
Al-Mulk	67	625	Makki	مكيّة	٦٢٥	٦٧	الملك
Al-Qālam	68	628	Makki	مكيّة	٦٢٨	٦٨	القلم
Al-Ḥâqqah	69	631	Makki	مكيّة	٦٣١	٦٩	الحاقّة
Al-Ma'ârij	70	634	Makki	مكيّة	٦٣٤	٧٠	المعارج
Nûḥ	71	636	Makki	مكيّة	٦٣٦	٧١	نوح
Al-Jinn	72	638	Makki	مكيّة	٦٣٨	٧٢	الجن
Al-Muzzammil	73	641	Makki	مكيّة	٦٤١	٧٣	المزّمّل
Al-Muddassir	74	643	Makki	مكيّة	٦٤٣	٧٤	المدّثّر
Al-Qiyâmah	75	646	Makki	مكيّة	٦٤٦	٧٥	القيامة
Ad-Dahr	76	647	Madani	مدنيّة	٦٤٧	٧٦	الدّهر
Al-Mursalât	77	650	Makki	مكيّة	٦٥٠	٧٧	المرسلات
An-Naba'	78	652	Makki	مكيّة	٦٥٢	٧٨	النّبا
An-Nâzi'ât	79	654	Makki	مكيّة	٦٥٤	٧٩	النّازعات
'Abasa	80	656	Makki	مكيّة	٦٥٦	٨٠	عبس
At-Takwîr	81	658	Makki	مكيّة	٦٥٨	٨١	التّكوير
Al-Infiṭâr	82	659	Makki	مكيّة	٦٥٩	٨٢	الانفطار
Al-Muṭaffifîn	83	660	Makki	مكيّة	٦٦٠	٨٣	المطفّفين
Al-Inshiqâq	84	661	Makki	مكيّة	٦٦١	٨٤	الانشقاق

Sûrah	No.	Page No.	Makki/ Madani	مكية مدنية	رقم الصفحة	رقم السورة	اسم السورة
Al-Burûj	85	663	Makki	مكيّة	٦٦٣	٨٥	البروج
Aṭ-Ṭâriq	86	664	Makki	مكيّة	٦٦٤	٨٦	الطّارق
Al-A‘lâ	87	665	Makki	مكيّة	٦٦٥	٨٧	الاعلىٰ
Al-Ghâshiyah	88	665	Makki	مكيّة	٦٦٥	٨٨	الغاشية
Al-Fajr	89	667	Makki	مكيّة	٦٦٧	٨٩	الفجر
Al-Balad	90	668	Makki	مكيّة	٦٦٨	٩٠	البلد
Ash-Shams	91	669	Makki	مكيّة	٦٦٩	٩١	الشّمس
Al-Layl	92	670	Makki	مكيّة	٦٧٠	٩٢	الّيل
Aḍ-Ḍuḥâ	93	670	Makki	مكيّة	٦٧٠	٩٣	الضّحىٰ
Al-Inshirâḥ	94	671	Makki	مكيّة	٦٧١	٩٤	الانشراح
At-Tîn	95	671	Makki	مكيّة	٦٧١	٩٥	التين
Al-‘Alaq	96	672	Makki	مكيّة	٦٧٢	٩٦	العلق
Al-Qadr	97	673	Makki	مكيّة	٦٧٣	٩٧	القدر
Al-Bayyinah	98	673	Madani	مدنيّة	٦٧٣	٩٨	البيّنة
Az-Zilzâl	99	674	Madani	مدنيّة	٦٧٤	٩٩	الزلزال
Al-‘Âdiyât	100	674	Makki	مكيّة	٦٧٤	١٠٠	العاديات
Al-Qâri‘ah	101	675	Makki	مكيّة	٦٧٥	١٠١	القارعة
At-Takâs̱ur	102	675	Makki	مكيّة	٦٧٥	١٠٢	التّكاثر
Al-‘Aṣr	103	676	Makki	مكيّة	٦٧٦	١٠٣	العصر
Al-Humazah	104	676	Makki	مكيّة	٦٧٦	١٠٤	الهمزة
Al-Fîl	105	676	Makki	مكيّة	٦٧٦	١٠٥	الفيل
Quraysh	106	677	Makki	مكيّة	٦٧٧	١٠٦	قريش
Al-Mâ‘ûn	107	677	Makki	مكيّة	٦٧٧	١٠٧	الماعون
Al-Kaws̱ar	108	677	Makki	مكيّة	٦٧٧	١٠٨	الكوثر
Al-Kâfirûn	109	677	Makki	مكيّة	٦٧٧	١٠٩	الكافرون
An-Naṣr	110	678	Madani	مدنيّة	٦٧٨	١١٠	النّصر
Al-Lahab	111	678	Makki	مكيّة	٦٧٨	١١١	اللّهب
Al-Ikhlâṣ	112	678	Makki	مكيّة	٦٧٨	١١٢	الاخلاص
Al-Falaq	113	678	Makki	مكيّة	٦٧٨	١١٣	الفلق
An-Nâs	114	679	Makki	مكيّة	٦٧٨	١١٤	النّاس

وَتَرْجَمَةُ مَعَانِيهِ مَعَ الْحُرُوفِ الْمَنْقُولَةِ إِلَى اللُّغَةِ الْإِنْجِلِيزِيَّة

عبد الله يوسف علي

Published by
Tahrike Tarsile Qur'an, Inc.
Publishers and Distributors of the Holy Qur'an
80-08 51st Avenue
Elmhurst, New York 11373-4141
Email: read@koranusa.org
http://www.koranusa.org
28th US Edition 2016

بسم الله الرحمن الرحيم

Al-Fatihah, The Opening

In the Name of Allah,
the Beneficent, the Merciful.

1. All praise belongs to Allah, Lord of the Universe,

2. the Beneficent, the Merciful

3. and Master of the Day of Judgment.

4. (Lord), You alone do we worship and from You alone do we seek assistance.

5. (Lord), guide us to the right path,

6. the path of those to whom You have granted blessings, who are neither subject to (Your) anger nor have gone astray.

Sûrat al-Fâtiḥa-1

(Revealed at Makkah)

Bismillaahir Raḥmaanir Raḥeem

1. Al-ḥamdu lillaahi Rabbil-'aalameen.

2. Ar-Raḥmaanir-Raḥeem.

3. Maaliki yaumid-deen.

4. Iyyaaka na'budu wa-iyyaaka nasta'een.

5. Ihdinaṣ-ṣiraaṭal mustaqeem.

6. Ṣiraaṭal lazeena an'amta 'alayhim. ghayril-maghḍoobi 'alayhim walaḍ-ḍaaalleen.

(١) سُوْرَةُ الْفَاتِحَةِ مَكِّيَّةٌ (٥)

اٰيَاتُهَا ٧ — بِسْمِ اللّٰهِ الرَّحْمٰنِ الرَّحِيْمِ — رُكُوْعَاتُهَا ١

اَلْحَمْدُ لِلّٰهِ رَبِّ الْعٰلَمِيْنَ ① المنزل الاول

الرَّحْمٰنِ الرَّحِيْمِ ②

مٰلِكِ يَوْمِ الدِّيْنِ ③

اِيَّاكَ نَعْبُدُ وَاِيَّاكَ نَسْتَعِيْنُ ④

اِهْدِنَا الصِّرَاطَ الْمُسْتَقِيْمَ ⑤

صِرَاطَ الَّذِيْنَ اَنْعَمْتَ عَلَيْهِمْ ۙ

غَيْرِ الْمَغْضُوْبِ عَلَيْهِمْ

وَلَا الضَّآلِّيْنَ ⑦ ع ٧

Al-Baqarah, The Cow

In the Name of Allah, the Beneficent, the Merciful.

1. Alif. Lam. Mim.

2. There is no doubt that this book is a guide for the pious.

3. It is the pious who believe in the unseen, attend to prayer, give in charity part of what We have granted them;

4. who have faith in what has been revealed to you (Muhammad) and others before you and have strong faith in the life hereafter.

5. It is the pious who follow the guidance of their Lord and gain lasting happiness.

6. Those who refused to accept (the faith) did not believe whether you warned them or not.

7. Allah has sealed their hearts and hearing and their vision is veiled and a great punishment awaits them.

8. There are those among people who say, "We believe in Allah and the Day of Judgment," but they are not true believers.

9. They deceive Allah and the believers. However, they have deceived no one other than themselves, but they do not realize it.

10. A sickness exists in their hearts to which Allah adds more sickness and they will suffer a painful punishment as a result of the lie which they had been speaking.

11. When they are told not to spread evil in the land, they reply, "We are only reformers."

Sûrat al-Baqarah-2

(Revealed at Madinah)

Bismillaahir Raḥmaanir Raḥeem

1. Alif-Laaam-Meeem.

2. Z̲aalikal-Kitaabu laa rayb; feeh; hudal-lilmut taqeen.

3. Allaz̲eena yu'minoona bilghaybi wa yuqeemoonaṣ-Ṣalaata wa mimmaa razaq-naahum yunfiqoon.

4. Wallaz̲eena yu'minoona bimaaa unzila ilayka wa maaa unzila min qablika wa bil-Aakhirati hum yooqinoon.

5. Ulaaa'ika 'alaa hudam-mir-Rabbihim wa ulaaa'ika humul-mufliḥoon.

6. Innal-laz̲eena kafaroo sawaaa'un 'alayhim 'a-anz̲ar-tahum am lam tunz̲irhum laa yu'minoon.

7. Khatamal-laahu 'alaa quloobihim wa 'alaa sam'ihim wa 'alaaa abṣaarihim ghishaa-watuñw-wa lahum 'az̲aabun 'aẓeem.

8. Wa minan-naasi mañy-yaqoolu aamannaa billaahi wa bil-Yawmil-Aakhiri wa maa hum bimu'mineen.

9. Yukhaadi'oonal-laaha wallaz̲eena aamanoo wa maa yakhda'oona illaaa anfusahum wa maa yash'uroon.

10. Fee quloobihim mara-ḍun fazaadahumul-laahu maraḍa; wa lahum 'az̲aabun aleemum-bimaa kaanoo yakz̲iboon.

11. Wa iz̲aa qeela lahum laa tufsidoo fil-arḍi qaalooo innamaa naḥnu muṣliḥoon.

(٢) سُورَةُ الْبَقَرَةِ مَدَنِيَّةٌ (٨٧)

آياتها ٢٨٦ — ركوعاتها ٤٠

بِسْمِ اللَّهِ الرَّحْمَٰنِ الرَّحِيمِ

الٓمٓ ١

ذَٰلِكَ الْكِتَٰبُ لَا رَيْبَ ۛ فِيهِ ۛ هُدًى

لِّلْمُتَّقِينَ ٢

الَّذِينَ يُؤْمِنُونَ بِالْغَيْبِ وَيُقِيمُونَ

الصَّلَوٰةَ وَمِمَّا رَزَقْنَٰهُمْ يُنفِقُونَ ٣

وَالَّذِينَ يُؤْمِنُونَ بِمَا أُنزِلَ

إِلَيْكَ وَمَا أُنزِلَ مِن قَبْلِكَ وَبِالْآخِرَةِ

هُمْ يُوقِنُونَ ٤

أُولَٰٓئِكَ عَلَىٰ هُدًى مِّن رَّبِّهِمْ ۖ وَأُولَٰٓئِكَ

هُمُ الْمُفْلِحُونَ ٥

إِنَّ الَّذِينَ كَفَرُوا سَوَآءٌ عَلَيْهِمْ ءَأَنذَرْتَهُمْ

أَمْ لَمْ تُنذِرْهُمْ لَا يُؤْمِنُونَ ٦

خَتَمَ اللَّهُ عَلَىٰ قُلُوبِهِمْ وَعَلَىٰ سَمْعِهِمْ ۖ

وَعَلَىٰٓ أَبْصَٰرِهِمْ غِشَٰوَةٌ ۖ وَلَهُمْ

عَذَابٌ عَظِيمٌ ٧

وَمِنَ النَّاسِ مَن يَقُولُ ءَامَنَّا بِاللَّهِ

وَبِالْيَوْمِ الْآخِرِ وَمَا هُم بِمُؤْمِنِينَ ٨

يُخَٰدِعُونَ اللَّهَ وَالَّذِينَ ءَامَنُوا وَمَا

يَخْدَعُونَ إِلَّآ أَنفُسَهُمْ وَمَا يَشْعُرُونَ ٩

فِي قُلُوبِهِم مَّرَضٌ فَزَادَهُمُ اللَّهُ مَرَضًا ۖ

وَلَهُمْ عَذَابٌ أَلِيمٌ بِمَا كَانُوا

يَكْذِبُونَ ١٠

وَإِذَا قِيلَ لَهُمْ لَا تُفْسِدُوا فِي الْأَرْضِ

قَالُوٓا إِنَّمَا نَحْنُ مُصْلِحُونَ ١١

الجزء (١) منعانقة ١ عند المتأخرين ١٢

ع — وقف لازم

12. They, certainly, do spread evil in the land but do not realize it.

12. Alaaa innahum humul-mufsidoona wa laakil-laa yash'uroon.

أَلَآ إِنَّهُمْ هُمُ الْمُفْسِدُونَ وَلَٰكِن لَّا
يَشْعُرُونَ ١٢

13. When they are told to believe as everyone else does, they say, "Should we believe as dimwitted ones do?" In fact, they are the dimwitted ones, but they do not know it.

13. Wa izaa qeela lahum aaminoo kamaaa aamanan-naasu qaalooo anu'minu kamaaa aamanas-sufahaaa'; alaaa innahum humus-sufahaaa'u wa laakil-laa ya'lamoon.

وَإِذَا قِيلَ لَهُمْ ءَامِنُوا كَمَآ ءَامَنَ النَّاسُ
قَالُوٓا أَنُؤْمِنُ كَمَآ ءَامَنَ السُّفَهَآءُ ۗ
أَلَآ إِنَّهُمْ هُمُ السُّفَهَآءُ وَلَٰكِن لَّا
يَعْلَمُونَ ١٣

14. To the believers they declare belief and in secret to their own devils they say, "We were only mocking."

14. Wa izaa laqul-lazeena aamanoo qaalooo aamannaa wa izaa khalaw ilaa shayaaṭeenihim qaalooo innaa ma'akum innamaa naḥnu mustahzi'oon.

وَإِذَا لَقُوا الَّذِينَ ءَامَنُوا قَالُوٓا ءَامَنَّا
وَإِذَا خَلَوْا إِلَىٰ شَيَٰطِينِهِمْ قَالُوٓا إِنَّا
مَعَكُمْ إِنَّمَا نَحْنُ مُسْتَهْزِءُونَ ١٤

15. Allah mocks (punishes) them and gives them time to continue blindly in their transgressions.

15. Allaahu yastahzi'u bihim wa yamudduhum fee ṭughyaanihim ya'mahoon.

اللَّهُ يَسْتَهْزِئُ بِهِمْ وَيَمُدُّهُمْ فِي
طُغْيَٰنِهِمْ يَعْمَهُونَ ١٥

16. They have traded guidance for error, but their bargain has had no profit and they have missed the true guidance.

16. Ulaaa'ikal-lazeenash-tara-wuḍ-ḍalaalata bilhudaa famaa rabiḥat-tijaaratuhum wa maa kaanoo muhtadeen.

أُولَٰٓئِكَ الَّذِينَ اشْتَرَوُا الضَّلَٰلَةَ
بِالْهُدَىٰ فَمَا رَبِحَت تِّجَٰرَتُهُمْ
وَمَا كَانُوا مُهْتَدِينَ ١٦

17. Their case is like that of one who kindles a fire and when it grows bright, Allah takes away their light leaving them in darkness (wherein) they cannot see (anything).

17. Masaluhum kamasalillazis-tawqada naaran falammaaa aḍaaa'at maa ḥawlahoo zahabal-laahu binoorihim wa tarakahum fee ẓulumaatil-laa yubṣiroon.

مَثَلُهُمْ كَمَثَلِ الَّذِي اسْتَوْقَدَ نَارًا
فَلَمَّآ أَضَآءَتْ مَا حَوْلَهُۥ ذَهَبَ اللَّهُ
بِنُورِهِمْ وَتَرَكَهُمْ فِي ظُلُمَٰتٍ
لَّا يُبْصِرُونَ ١٧

18. They are deaf, blind, and dumb and cannot regain their senses.

18. Ṣummum bukmun 'umyun fahum laa yarji'oon.

صُمٌّۢ بُكْمٌ عُمْيٌ فَهُمْ لَا يَرْجِعُونَ ١٨

19. Or it is like that of a rainstorm with darkness, thunder, and lightning approaching. They cover their ears for fear of thunder and death and Allah contains (the evil of) the unbelievers.

19. Aw kaṣayyibim-minas-samaaa'i feehi ẓulumaatuñw-wa ra'duñw-wa barq; yaj'aloona aṣaabi'ahum feee aazaanihim minaṣ-ṣawaa'iqi ḥazaral-mawt; wallaahu muḥeeṭum bilkaafireen.

أَوْ كَصَيِّبٍ مِّنَ السَّمَآءِ فِيهِ ظُلُمَٰتٌ
وَرَعْدٌ وَبَرْقٌ يَجْعَلُونَ أَصَٰبِعَهُمْ
فِيٓ ءَاذَانِهِم مِّنَ الصَّوَٰعِقِ حَذَرَ
الْمَوْتِ ۚ وَاللَّهُ مُحِيطٌۢ بِالْكَٰفِرِينَ ١٩

20. The lightning almost takes away their vision. When the lightning brightens their surroundings, they walk, and when it is dark, they stand still.

20. Yakaadul-barqu yakhṭafu abṣaarahum kullamaaa aḍaaa'a lahum mashaw feehi wa izaaa aẓlama 'alayhim qaamoo; wa law shaaa'al-laahu

يَكَادُ الْبَرْقُ يَخْطَفُ أَبْصَٰرَهُمْ ۖ
كُلَّمَآ أَضَآءَ لَهُم مَّشَوْا فِيهِ وَإِذَآ
أَظْلَمَ عَلَيْهِمْ قَامُوا ۚ وَلَوْ شَآءَ اللَّهُ

Had Allah wanted, He could have taken away their hearing and their vision. Allah has power over all things.

lazahaba bisam'ihim wa abṣaarihim; innal-laaha 'alaa kulli shay'in Qadeer.

لَذَهَبَ بِسَمْعِهِمْ وَاَبْصَارِهِمْ ؕ
اِنَّ اللّٰهَ عَلٰى كُلِّ شَىْءٍ قَدِيْرٌ ﴿٢٠﴾ ع ٣

21. People, worship your Lord Who created you and those who lived before you so that you may become pious.

21. Yaaa ayyuhan-naasu'budoo Rabbakumul-lazee khalaqakum wallazeena min qablikum la'allakum tattaqoon.

يٰۤاَيُّهَا النَّاسُ اعْبُدُوْا رَبَّكُمُ الَّذِىْ
خَلَقَكُمْ وَالَّذِيْنَ مِنْ قَبْلِكُمْ
لَعَلَّكُمْ تَتَّقُوْنَ ﴿٢١﴾

22. (Worship Allah) Who has rendered the earth as a floor for you and the sky as a dome and has sent down water from the sky to produce fruits for your sustenance. Do not knowingly set up things as equals to Allah.

22. Allazee ja'ala lakumul-arḍa firaashañw-wassamaaa'a binaaa'añw-wa anzala minassamaaa'i maaa'an fa-akhraja bihee minas-samaraati rizqal-lakum falaa taj'aloo lillaahi andaadañw-wa antum ta'lamoon.

الَّذِىْ جَعَلَ لَكُمُ الْاَرْضَ فِرَاشًا
وَّالسَّمَآءَ بِنَآءً ۖ وَّاَنْزَلَ مِنَ السَّمَآءِ
مَآءً فَاَخْرَجَ بِهٖ مِنَ الثَّمَرٰتِ
رِزْقًا لَّكُمْ ۚ فَلَا تَجْعَلُوْا لِلّٰهِ اَنْدَادًا وَّ
اَنْتُمْ تَعْلَمُوْنَ ﴿٢٢﴾

23. Should you have any doubt about what We have revealed to Our servant, present one chapter comparable to it and call (all of) your supporters, besides Allah, if your claim is true.

23. Wa in kuntum fee raybim-mimmaa nazzalnaa 'alaa 'abdinaa fa-too bi-Sooratim-mim-mislihee wad'oo shu-hadaaa'akum min doonil-laahi in kuntum ṣaadiqeen.

وَاِنْ كُنْتُمْ فِىْ رَيْبٍ مِّمَّا نَزَّلْنَا عَلٰى
عَبْدِنَا فَاْتُوْا بِسُوْرَةٍ مِّنْ مِّثْلِهٖ ۖ
وَادْعُوْا شُهَدَآءَكُمْ مِّنْ دُوْنِ اللّٰهِ
اِنْ كُنْتُمْ صٰدِقِيْنَ ﴿٢٣﴾

24. If you did not produce such a chapter and you never will, then guard yourselves against the fire, which is fueled with people and stones, and is prepared for the unbelievers.

24. Fail-lam taf'aloo wa lan taf'aloo fattaqun-Naaral-latee waqooduhan-naasu walḥijaaratu u'iddat lilkaafireen.

فَاِنْ لَّمْ تَفْعَلُوْا وَلَنْ تَفْعَلُوْا فَاتَّقُوا
النَّارَ الَّتِىْ وَقُوْدُهَا النَّاسُ وَ
الْحِجَارَةُ ۖۚ اُعِدَّتْ لِلْكٰفِرِيْنَ ﴿٢٤﴾

25. (Muhammad), tell the righteously striving believers of the happy news, that for them there are gardens wherein streams flow. Whenever they get any fruit from the gardens as food, they will say, "This is just what we had before (we came here). These fruits are produced very much alike (in quality)." They will have purified spouses and it is they who will live therein (the gardens) forever.

25. Wa bashshiril-lazeena aamanoo wa 'amiluṣ-ṣaaliḥaati anna lahum Jannaatin tajree min taḥtihal-anhaaru kullamaa ruziqoo minhaa min samaratir-rizqan qaaloo haazal-lazee ruziqnaa min qablu wa utoo bihee mutashaabihaa; wa lahum feehaaa azwaajum-muṭahharatuñw-wa hum feehaa khaalidoon.

وَبَشِّرِ الَّذِيْنَ اٰمَنُوْا وَعَمِلُوا الصّٰلِحٰتِ
اَنَّ لَهُمْ جَنّٰتٍ تَجْرِىْ مِنْ تَحْتِهَا
الْاَنْهٰرُ ؕ كُلَّمَا رُزِقُوْا مِنْهَا مِنْ
ثَمَرَةٍ رِّزْقًا ۙ قَالُوْا هٰذَا الَّذِىْ
رُزِقْنَا مِنْ قَبْلُ ۙ وَاُتُوْا بِهٖ مُتَشَابِهًا ؕ
وَلَهُمْ فِيْهَاۤ اَزْوَاجٌ مُّطَهَّرَةٌ ۙ وَّهُمْ
فِيْهَا خٰلِدُوْنَ ﴿٢٥﴾

26. Allah does not hesitate to set forth parables of anything, even a gnat. The believers know that it is the truth from their Lord, but

26. Innal-laaha laa yastaḥyeee añy-yaḍriba masalam-maa ba'ooḍa-tan famaa fawqahaa; fa-ammal-lazeena

اِنَّ اللّٰهَ لَا يَسْتَحْىٖۤ اَنْ يَّضْرِبَ مَثَلًا
مَّا بَعُوْضَةً فَمَا فَوْقَهَا ؕ فَاَمَّا الَّذِيْنَ

those who reject the truth say, "What does Allah mean by such parables?" In fact, by such parables Allah misleads and guides many. However, He only misleads the evildoers

aamanoo faya'lamoona annahul-ḥaqqu mir-Rabbihim wa ammal-lazeena kafaroo fayaqooloona maazaaa araadal-laahu bihaazaa masalaa; yuḍillu bihee kaseerañw-wa yahdee bihee kaseeraa; wa maa yuḍillu biheee illal-faasiqeen.

امنوا فيعلمون انه الحق من ربهم
واما الذين كفروا فيقولون ماذا
اراد الله بهذا مثلا يضل به وقف لازم
كثيرا ويهدي به كثيرا وما يضل
به الا الفسقين ﴿٢٦﴾

27. who break their established covenant with Allah and the relations Allah has commanded to be kept and who spread evil in the land. These are the ones who lose a great deal.

27. Allazeena yanquḍoona 'Ahdal-laahi mim ba'di meesaaqihee wa yaqṭa'oona maaa amaral-laahu biheee añy-yooṣala wa yufsidoona fil-arḍ; ulaaa'ika humul-khaasiroon.

الذين ينقضون عهد الله من بعد
ميثاقه ويقطعون ما امر الله به
ان يوصل ويفسدون في الارض
اولئك هم الخسرون ﴿٢٧﴾

28. How dare you deny the existence of Allah Who gave you life when you (initially) were dead? He then causes you to die and brings you to life again. Then you will return to His Presence.

28. Kayfa takfuroona billaahi wa kuntum amwaatan fa-aḥyaakum summa yumeetukum summa yuḥyeekum summa ilayhi turja'oon.

كيف تكفرون بالله وكنتم امواتا
فاحياكم ثم يميتكم ثم يحييكم
ثم اليه ترجعون ﴿٢٨﴾

29. It is He Who has created everything on earth for you. Then, directing His order toward the realm above, He turned it into seven heavens. He has knowledge of all things.

29. Huwal-lazee khalaqa lakum-maa fil-arḍi jamee'an summastawaaa ilas-samaaa'i fasawwaahunna sab'a samaawaat; wa Huwa bikulli shay'in 'Aleem.

هو الذي خلق لكم ما في الارض
جميعا ثم استوى الى السماء فسوىهن
سبع سموت وهو بكل شيء عليم ﴿٢٩﴾ ع ٣

30. When your Lord said to the angels, "I am appointing someone as my deputy on earth," they said (almost protesting), "Are You appointing therein one who will cause destruction and bloodshed, even though we (are the ones who) commemorate Your name and glorify You?" The Lord said, "I know that which you do not know."

30. Wa iz qaala Rabbuka lilmalaaa'ikati innee jaa'ilun filarḍi khaleefatan qaalooo ataj'alu feehaa mañy-yufsidu feehaa wa yasfikud-dimaaa'a wa naḥnu nusabbiḥu biḥamdika wa nuqaddisu laka qaala inneee a'lamu maa laa ta'lamoon.

واذ قال ربك للملئكة اني جاعل
في الارض خليفة قالوا اتجعل
فيها من يفسد فيها ويسفك الدماء
ونحن نسبح بحمدك ونقدس لك
قال اني اعلم ما لا تعلمون ﴿٣٠﴾

31. He taught Adam all the names (of mountains, oceans, valleys, plants and animals). Then He introduced (certain beings) to the angels, asking them to tell Him the names of these beings, if the angels were true to their claim (that they were more deserving to be His deputies on earth).

31. Wa 'allama Aadamalasmaaa'a kullahaa summa 'araḍahum 'alal-malaaa'ikati faqaala ambi'oonee bi-asmaaa'i haaa'ulaaa'i in kuntum ṣaadiqeen.

وعلم ادم الاسماء كلها ثم عرضهم
على الملئكة فقال انبئوني باسماء
هؤلاء ان كنتم صدقين ﴿٣١﴾

32. The angels replied, "You are glorious indeed! We do not know more than what You have taught us. You alone are All-knowing and All-wise."

32. Qaaloo subḥaanaka laa 'ilma lanaaa illaa maa 'allamtanaaa innaka Antal-'Aleemul-Ḥakeem.

قالوا سبحنك لا علم لنا الا ما علمتنا
انك انت العليم الحكيم ﴿٣٢﴾

33. The Lord said to Adam, "Tell the names of the beings to the

33. Qaala yaaa Aadamu ambi'hum bi-asmaaa'ihim falammaaa

قال يادم انبئهم باسمائهم فلما

angels." When Adam said their names, the Lord said, "Did I not tell you (angels) that I know the secrets of the heavens and the earth and all that you reveal or hide?"

amba-ahum bi-asmaaa'ihim qaala alam aqul lakum inneee a'lamu ghaybas-samaawaati wal-arḍi wa a'lamu maa tubdoona wa maa kuntum taktumoon.

اَنۢبَاَهُمْ بِاَسْمَآئِهِمْ قَالَ اَلَمْ اَقُلْ
لَّكُمْ اِنِّيْٓ اَعْلَمُ غَيْبَ السَّمٰوٰتِ وَالْاَرْضِ
وَاَعْلَمُ مَا تُبْدُوْنَ وَمَا كُنْتُمْ تَكْتُمُوْنَ ﴿۳۳﴾

34. When We told the angels to prostrate before Adam, they all obeyed except Iblis (Satan), who abstained out of arrogance, and so he became one of those who deny the truth.

34. Wa iẕ qulnaa lilmalaaa'i-katis-judoo li-Aadama fasaja-dooo illaaa Ibleesa abaa wastak-bara wa kaana minal-kaafireen.

وَاِذْ قُلْنَا لِلْمَلٰٓئِكَةِ اسْجُدُوْا لِاٰدَمَ
فَسَجَدُوْٓا اِلَّآ اِبْلِيْسَ ؕ اَبٰى وَاسْتَكْبَرَ ۫
وَكَانَ مِنَ الْكٰفِرِيْنَ ﴿۳۴﴾

35. We said, "O Adam, stay with your spouse (Eve) in the garden and enjoy the foods therein as you both wish, but do not go near this tree lest you both become of the transgressors."

35. Wa qulnaa yaaa Aadamus-kun anta wa zawjukal-Jannata wa kulaa minhaa raghadan ḥayṯu shi'tumaa wa laa taqrabaa haaẕihish-shajarata fatakoonaa minaẓ-ẓaalimeen.

وَقُلْنَا يٰٓاٰدَمُ اسْكُنْ اَنْتَ وَزَوْجُكَ
الْجَنَّةَ وَكُلَا مِنْهَا رَغَدًا حَيْثُ شِئْتُمَا ۪
وَلَا تَقْرَبَا هٰذِهِ الشَّجَرَةَ فَتَكُوْنَا
مِنَ الظّٰلِمِيْنَ ﴿۳۵﴾

36. Satan made Adam and his spouse slip and took them out of the state in which they had been living. We then told them, "Move down, you are each other's enemies. The earth will be a dwelling place for you and it will provide you with sustenance for an appointed time."

36. Fa-azallahumash-Shayṭaanu 'anhaa fa-akhrajahumaa mimmaa kaanaa feehi wa qulnah-biṭoo ba'ḍukum liba'ḍin 'aduww; wa lakum fil-arḍi mustaqarruñw-wa mataa'un ilaa ḥeen.

فَاَزَلَّهُمَا الشَّيْطٰنُ عَنْهَا فَاَخْرَجَهُمَا
مِمَّا كَانَا فِيْهِ ۪ وَقُلْنَا اهْبِطُوْا بَعْضُكُمْ
لِبَعْضٍ عَدُوٌّ ۚ وَلَكُمْ فِي الْاَرْضِ
مُسْتَقَرٌّ وَّمَتَاعٌ اِلٰى حِيْنٍ ﴿۳۶﴾

37. Adam thereafter received certain words (of prayer) from his Lord through which He granted him forgiveness; He certainly is All-forgiving and All-merciful.

37. Fatalaqqaaa Aadamu mir-Rabbihee Kalimaatin fataaba 'alayh; innahoo Huwat-Taw-waabur-Raḥeem.

فَتَلَقّٰٓى اٰدَمُ مِنْ رَّبِّهٖ كَلِمٰتٍ فَتَابَ
عَلَيْهِ ؕ اِنَّهٗ هُوَ التَّوَّابُ الرَّحِيْمُ ﴿۳۷﴾

38. We ordered them all to move out of the garden and told them that when Our guidance would come to them, those who follow it would have neither fear nor grief.

38. Qulnah-biṭoo minhaa jamee-'an fa-immaa ya-tiyan-nakum minnee hudan faman tabi'a hudaaya falaa khawfun 'alayhim wa laa hum yaḥzanoon.

قُلْنَا اهْبِطُوْا مِنْهَا جَمِيْعًا ۚ فَاِمَّا
يَاْتِيَنَّكُمْ مِّنِّيْ هُدًى فَمَنْ تَبِعَ هُدَايَ
فَلَا خَوْفٌ عَلَيْهِمْ وَلَا هُمْ يَحْزَنُوْنَ ﴿۳۸﴾

39. But those who would deny the Truth and reject Our revelations would be the companions of the Fire in which they would live forever.

39. Wallaẕeena kafaroo wa kaẕ ẕaboo bi-Aayaatinaaa ulaaa'ika Aṣḥaabun-Naari hum feehaa khaalidoon.

وَالَّذِيْنَ كَفَرُوْا وَكَذَّبُوْا بِاٰيٰتِنَآ
اُولٰٓئِكَ اَصْحٰبُ النَّارِ ۚ هُمْ فِيْهَا
خٰلِدُوْنَ ﴿۳۹﴾ ع

40. Children of Israel, recall My favors, which you enjoyed. Fulfill your covenant with Me and I shall fulfill Mine. Revere only Me.

40. Yaa Baneee Israaa'eelaẕ kuroo ni'matiyal-lateee an'amtu 'alaykum wa awfoo bi-'Ahdeee oofi bi'ahdikum wa iyyaaya farhaboon.

يٰبَنِيْٓ اِسْرَآءِيْلَ اذْكُرُوْا نِعْمَتِيَ الَّتِيْٓ
اَنْعَمْتُ عَلَيْكُمْ وَاَوْفُوْا بِعَهْدِيْٓ
اُوْفِ بِعَهْدِكُمْ ۚ وَاِيَّايَ فَارْهَبُوْنِ ﴿۴۰﴾

41. Believe in My revelations (Quran) that confirms what I

41. Wa aaminoo bimaaa anzaltu muṣaddiqal-limaa

وَاٰمِنُوْا بِمَآ اَنْزَلْتُ مُصَدِّقًا لِّمَا

revealed to you (about Prophet Muhammad in your Scripture). Do not be the first ones to deny it nor sell My revelations for a small price, but have fear of Me.

ma'akum wa laa takoonooo awwala kaafirim bihee wa laa tashtaroo bi-Aayaatee samanan qaleelañw-wa iyyaaya fattaqoon.

مَعَكُمْ وَلَا تَكُونُوٓا أَوَّلَ كَافِرٍۭ بِهِۦ ۖ
وَلَا تَشْتَرُوا بِـَٔايَٰتِى ثَمَنًا قَلِيلًا
وَإِيَّٰىَ فَٱتَّقُونِ ﴿٤١﴾

42. Do not mix truth with falsehood and do not deliberately hide the truth.

42. Wa laa talbisul-ḥaqqa bilbaaṭili wa taktumul-ḥaqqa wa antum ta'lamoon.

وَلَا تَلْبِسُوا ٱلْحَقَّ بِٱلْبَٰطِلِ
وَتَكْتُمُوا ٱلْحَقَّ وَأَنتُمْ تَعْلَمُونَ ﴿٤٢﴾

43. Be steadfast in prayer, pay the religious tax (zakat), and bow down in worship with those who do the same.

43. Wa aqeemuṣ-Ṣalaata wa aatuz-Zakaata warka'oo ma'ar-raaki'een.

وَأَقِيمُوا ٱلصَّلَوٰةَ وَءَاتُوا ٱلزَّكَوٰةَ
وَٱرْكَعُوا مَعَ ٱلرَّٰكِعِينَ ﴿٤٣﴾

44. Would you order people to do good deeds and forget to do them yourselves even though you read the Book? Why do you not think?

44. Ata-muroonan-naasa bilbirri wa tansawna anfusakum wa antum tatloonal-Kitaab; afalaa ta'qiloon.

أَتَأْمُرُونَ ٱلنَّاسَ بِٱلْبِرِّ وَتَنسَوْنَ
أَنفُسَكُمْ وَأَنتُمْ تَتْلُونَ ٱلْكِتَٰبَ ۚ
أَفَلَا تَعْقِلُونَ ﴿٤٤﴾

45. Help yourselves (in your affairs) by patience (fasting) and prayer. It (prayer) is a difficult task indeed, but not for the humble ones

45. Wasta'eenoo biṣṣabri waṣ-Ṣalaah; wa innahaa lakabeeratun illaa 'alal-khaashi'een.

وَٱسْتَعِينُوا بِٱلصَّبْرِ وَٱلصَّلَوٰةِ ۚ
وَإِنَّهَا لَكَبِيرَةٌ إِلَّا عَلَى ٱلْخَٰشِعِينَ ﴿٤٥﴾

46. who are certain of their meeting with their Lord and their return to Him.

46. Allazeena yaẓunnoona annahum mulaaqoo Rabbihim wa annahum ilayhi raaji'oon.

ٱلَّذِينَ يَظُنُّونَ أَنَّهُم مُّلَٰقُوا رَبِّهِمْ
وَأَنَّهُمْ إِلَيْهِ رَٰجِعُونَ ﴿٤٦﴾ ع

47. O children of Israel, recall My favors to you and the preference that I gave to you over all nations (of your time, then).

47. Yaa Baneee Israaa'eelaz-kuroo ni'matiyal-lateee an'amtu 'alaykum wa annee faḍḍaltukum 'alal-'aalameen.

يَٰبَنِىٓ إِسْرَٰٓءِيلَ ٱذْكُرُوا نِعْمَتِىَ
ٱلَّتِىٓ أَنْعَمْتُ عَلَيْكُمْ وَأَنِّى فَضَّلْتُكُمْ
عَلَى ٱلْعَٰلَمِينَ ﴿٤٧﴾

48. Have fear of the day when every soul will be responsible for itself. No intercession or ransom will be accepted and no one will receive help.

48. Wattaqoo Yawmal-laa tajzee nafsun 'an nafsin shay'añw-wa laa yuqbalu minhaa shafaa'atuñw-wa laa yu'khazu minhaa-'adluñw-wa laa hum yunṣaroon.

وَٱتَّقُوا يَوْمًا لَّا تَجْزِى نَفْسٌ عَن
نَّفْسٍ شَيْـًٔا وَلَا يُقْبَلُ مِنْهَا شَفَٰعَةٌ
وَلَا يُؤْخَذُ مِنْهَا عَدْلٌ وَلَا هُمْ
يُنصَرُونَ ﴿٤٨﴾

49. (Children of Israel, recall My favor) of saving you from the Pharaoh's people who afflicted you with the worst kind of cruelty, slaying your sons and sparing your women. Your suffering was indeed a great trial from your Lord.

49. Wa iz najjaynaakum min Aali Fir'awna yasoomoonakum sooo'al-'azaabi yuzabbiḥoona abnaaa'akum wa yastaḥyoona nisaaa'akum; wa fee zaalikum balaaa'um mir-Rabbikum 'aẓeem.

وَإِذْ نَجَّيْنَٰكُم مِّنْ ءَالِ فِرْعَوْنَ
يَسُومُونَكُمْ سُوٓءَ ٱلْعَذَابِ
يُذَبِّحُونَ أَبْنَآءَكُمْ وَيَسْتَحْيُونَ
نِسَآءَكُمْ ۚ وَفِى ذَٰلِكُم بَلَآءٌ مِّن
رَّبِّكُمْ عَظِيمٌ ﴿٤٩﴾

50. We parted the sea to save you and drowned Pharaoh's people before your very eyes.

50. Wa iz̲ faraqnaa bikumul-baḥra fa-anjaynaakum wa-aghraqnaaa Aala Fir'awna wa antum tanẓuroon.

وَإِذْ فَرَقْنَا بِكُمُ الْبَحْرَ فَأَنْجَيْنٰكُمْ
وَأَغْرَقْنَآ اٰلَ فِرْعَوْنَ وَأَنْتُمْ تَنْظُرُوْنَ ﴿٥٠﴾

51. When We called Moses for an appointment of forty nights. You began to worship the calf in his absence, doing wrong to yourselves.

51. Wa iz̲ waa'adnaa Moosaaa arba'eena laylatan s̲ummat-takhaz̲tumul-'ijla mim ba'dihee wa antum ẓaalimoon.

وَإِذْ وٰعَدْنَا مُوْسٰٓى أَرْبَعِيْنَ لَيْلَةً
ثُمَّ اتَّخَذْتُمُ الْعِجْلَ مِنْ بَعْدِهٖ
وَأَنْتُمْ ظٰلِمُوْنَ ﴿٥١﴾

52. Afterwards, We forgave you so that you would perhaps appreciate Our favors.

52. S̲umma 'afawnaa 'ankum mim ba'di z̲aalika la'allakum tashkuroon.

ثُمَّ عَفَوْنَا عَنْكُمْ مِّنْ بَعْدِ ذٰلِكَ
لَعَلَّكُمْ تَشْكُرُوْنَ ﴿٥٢﴾

53. We gave Moses the Book and the criteria (for discerning right from wrong) so that perhaps you would be rightly guided.

53. Wa iz̲ aataynaa Moosal Kitaaba wal-Furqaana la'allakum tahtadoon.

وَإِذْ اٰتَيْنَا مُوْسَى الْكِتٰبَ وَ
الْفُرْقَانَ لَعَلَّكُمْ تَهْتَدُوْنَ ﴿٥٣﴾

54. Moses said to his people, "My people, you have done wrong to yourselves by worshipping the calf. Seek pardon from your Lord and slay yourselves." He told them that it would be best for them in the sight of their Lord, Who might forgive them; He is All-forgiving and All-merciful.

54. Wa iz̲ qaala Moosaa liqawmihee yaa qawmi innakum ẓalamtum anfusakum bittikhaaz̲ikumul-'ijla fatoobooo ilaa Baari'ikum faqtulooo anfusakum z̲aalikum khayrul-lakum 'inda Baari'ikum fataaba 'alaykum; innahoo Huwat-Tawwaabur-Raḥeem.

وَإِذْ قَالَ مُوْسٰى لِقَوْمِهٖ يٰقَوْمِ
إِنَّكُمْ ظَلَمْتُمْ أَنْفُسَكُمْ بِاتِّخَاذِكُمُ
الْعِجْلَ فَتُوْبُوْٓا إِلٰى بَارِئِكُمْ فَاقْتُلُوْٓا
أَنْفُسَكُمْ ۭ ذٰلِكُمْ خَيْرٌ لَّكُمْ عِنْدَ
بَارِئِكُمْ ۭ فَتَابَ عَلَيْكُمْ ۭ إِنَّهٗ هُوَ
التَّوَّابُ الرَّحِيْمُ ﴿٥٤﴾

55. (Recall also) when you argued with Moses, saying that you were not ready to believe him unless you could see Allah with your own eyes. The swift wind struck you and you could do nothing but watch.

55. Wa iz̲ qultum yaa Moosaa lan nu'mina laka ḥattaa naral-laaha jahratan fa-akhaz̲at-kumuṣ-ṣaa'iqatu wa antum tanẓuroon.

وَإِذْ قُلْتُمْ يٰمُوْسٰى لَنْ نُّؤْمِنَ لَكَ
حَتّٰى نَرَى اللّٰهَ جَهْرَةً فَأَخَذَتْكُمُ
الصّٰعِقَةُ وَأَنْتُمْ تَنْظُرُوْنَ ﴿٥٥﴾

56. We then brought you back to life in the hope that you might appreciate Our favors.

56. S̲umma ba'as̲naakum mim ba'di mawtikum la'allakum tashkuroon.

ثُمَّ بَعَثْنٰكُمْ مِّنْ بَعْدِ مَوْتِكُمْ
لَعَلَّكُمْ تَشْكُرُوْنَ ﴿٥٦﴾

57. We provided you with shade from the clouds and sent down manna and quails as the best, pure sustenance for you to eat. They (children of Israel) did not wrong Us, but they wronged themselves.

57. Wa ẓallalnaa 'alaykumul-ghamaama wa anzalnaa 'alaykumul-Manna was-Salwaa kuloo min ṭayyibaati maa razaqnaakum wa maa ẓalamoonaa wa laakin kaanooo anfusahum yaẓlimoon.

وَظَلَّلْنَا عَلَيْكُمُ الْغَمَامَ وَأَنْزَلْنَا
عَلَيْكُمُ الْمَنَّ وَالسَّلْوٰى ۭ كُلُوْا مِنْ
طَيِّبٰتِ مَا رَزَقْنٰكُمْ ۭ وَمَا ظَلَمُوْنَا
وَلٰكِنْ كَانُوْٓا أَنْفُسَهُمْ يَظْلِمُوْنَ ﴿٥٧﴾

58. (Children of Israel, recall My favors) when We told you, "Enter this city, enjoy eating whatever you want therein, prostrate

58 Wa iz̲ qulnad-khuloo haazihil-qaryata fakuloo minhaa ḥays̲u shi'tum raghadañw-

وَإِذْ قُلْنَا ادْخُلُوْا هٰذِهِ الْقَرْيَةَ
فَكُلُوْا مِنْهَا حَيْثُ شِئْتُمْ رَغَدًا

yourselves and ask forgiveness when passing through the gate, and We shall forgive your sins and add to the rewards of the righteous ones."

wadkhulul-baaba sujjadañw-wa qooloo ḥiṭṭatun naghfir lakum khaṭaayaakum; wa sanazeedul-muḥsineen.

وَّادْخُلُوا الْبَابَ سُجَّدًا وَّقُوْلُوْا حِطَّةٌ نَّغْفِرْ لَكُمْ خَطٰيٰكُمْ ۚ وَسَنَزِيْدُ الْمُحْسِنِيْنَ ﴿٥٨﴾

59. The unjust ones among you changed what they were told to say. Then, We afflicted the unjust ones with a torment from the heavens for their evil deeds.

59. Fabaddalal-lazeena ẓalamoo qawlan ghayral-lazee qeela lahum fa-anzalnaa 'alal-lazeena ẓalamoo rijzamminas-samaaa'i bimaa kaanoo yafsuqoon.

فَبَدَّلَ الَّذِيْنَ ظَلَمُوْا قَوْلًا غَيْرَ الَّذِيْ قِيْلَ لَهُمْ فَاَنْزَلْنَا عَلَى الَّذِيْنَ ظَلَمُوْا رِجْزًا مِّنَ السَّمَآءِ بِمَا كَانُوْا يَفْسُقُوْنَ ﴿٥٩﴾

60. When Moses prayed for rain, We told him to strike the rock with his staff. Thereupon twelve fountains gushed out of the rock and each tribe knew their drinking place. (The Lord told them), "Eat and drink from Allah's bounties and do not abuse the earth as corrupt ones."

60. Wa izis-tasqaa Moosaa liqawmihee faqulnaḍ-rib bi'aṣaakal-ḥajar; fanfajarat minhusnataa 'ashrata 'aynan qad 'alima kullu unaasim-mashrabahum kuloo washraboo mir-rizqil-laahi wa laa ta'saw fil-arḍi mufsideen.

وَاِذِ اسْتَسْقٰى مُوْسٰى لِقَوْمِهٖ فَقُلْنَا اضْرِبْ بِّعَصَاكَ الْحَجَرَ ۖ فَانْفَجَرَتْ مِنْهُ اثْنَتَا عَشْرَةَ عَيْنًا ۖ قَدْ عَلِمَ كُلُّ اُنَاسٍ مَّشْرَبَهُمْ ۖ كُلُوْا وَاشْرَبُوْا مِنْ رِّزْقِ اللّٰهِ وَلَا تَعْثَوْا فِي الْاَرْضِ مُفْسِدِيْنَ ﴿٦٠﴾

61. When you demanded that Moses provide you with a variety of food, saying, "We no longer have patience with only one kind of food; ask your Lord to grow green herbs, cucumbers, wheat, lentils, and onions for us," Moses replied, "Would you change what is good for what is worse? Go to any town and you will get what you want." Despised and afflicted with destitution, they brought the wrath of Allah back upon themselves, for they denied the evidence (of the existence of Allah) and murdered His prophets without reason; they were disobedient transgressors.

61. Wta iz qultum yaa Moosaa lan naṣbira 'alaa ṭa'aamiñw-waaḥidin fad'u lanaa Rabbaka yukhrij lanaa mimmaa tumbitul-arḍu mimbaqlihaa wa qissaaa'ihaa wa foomihaa wa 'adasihaa wa baṣalihaa qaala atastabdiloonal-lazee huwa adnaa billazee huwa khayr; ihbiṭoo miṣran fa-inna lakum maa sa-altum; wa ḍuribat 'alayhimuz-zillatu walmaskanatu wa baaa'oo bighaḍabim-minal-laah; zaalika bi-annahum kaanoo yakfuroona bi-Aayaatil-laahi wa yaqtuloonan-Nabiyyeena bighayril-ḥaqq; zaalika bimaa 'aṣaw wa kaanoo ya'tadoon.

وَاِذْ قُلْتُمْ يٰمُوْسٰى لَنْ نَّصْبِرَ عَلٰى طَعَامٍ وَّاحِدٍ فَادْعُ لَنَا رَبَّكَ يُخْرِجْ لَنَا مِمَّا تُنْۢبِتُ الْاَرْضُ مِنْۢ بَقْلِهَا وَقِثَّآئِهَا وَفُوْمِهَا وَعَدَسِهَا وَبَصَلِهَا ۖ قَالَ اَتَسْتَبْدِلُوْنَ الَّذِيْ هُوَ اَدْنٰى بِالَّذِيْ هُوَ خَيْرٌ ۖ اِهْبِطُوْا مِصْرًا فَاِنَّ لَكُمْ مَّا سَاَلْتُمْ ۖ وَضُرِبَتْ عَلَيْهِمُ الذِّلَّةُ وَالْمَسْكَنَةُ ۖ وَبَآءُوْ بِغَضَبٍ مِّنَ اللّٰهِ ۖ ذٰلِكَ بِاَنَّهُمْ كَانُوْا يَكْفُرُوْنَ بِاٰيٰتِ اللّٰهِ وَيَقْتُلُوْنَ النَّبِيّٖنَ بِغَيْرِ الْحَقِّ ۖ ذٰلِكَ بِمَا عَصَوْا وَّكَانُوْا يَعْتَدُوْنَ ﴿٦١﴾

62. However, those who have become believers (the Muslims),

62. Innal-lazeena aamanoo wallazeena haadoo

اِنَّ الَّذِيْنَ اٰمَنُوْا وَالَّذِيْنَ هَادُوْا

and the Jews, the Christians and the Sabeans who believe in Allah and the Day of Judgment and strive righteously will receive their reward from the Lord and will have nothing to fear nor will they be grieved.

wan-Naṣaaraa waṣ-Ṣaabi'eena man aamana billaahi wal-Yawmil-Aakhiri wa 'amila ṣaaliḥan falahum ajruhum 'inda Rabbihim wa laa khawfun 'alayhim wa laa hum yaḥzanoon.

وَالنَّصٰرٰى وَالصّٰبِـِٕيْنَ مَنْ اٰمَنَ
بِاللّٰهِ وَالْيَوْمِ الْاٰخِرِ وَعَمِلَ صَالِحًا
فَلَهُمْ اَجْرُهُمْ عِنْدَ رَبِّهِمْ ۚ وَلَا
خَوْفٌ عَلَيْهِمْ وَلَا هُمْ يَحْزَنُوْنَ ﴿٦٢﴾

63. Children of Israel, recall when We made a covenant (to accept the Torah and warning) by raising Mount Tur (Sinai) above you and told you to receive earnestly what We had given to you and bear it in mind so that you could protect yourselves against evil.

63. Wa iz̲ akhaz̲naa meeṯaaqakum wa rafa'naa fawqakumuṭ-Ṭoora khuz̲oo maaa aataynaakum biquwwatiñw-waz̲kuroo maa feehi la'allakum tattaqoon.

وَاِذْ اَخَذْنَا مِيْثَاقَكُمْ وَرَفَعْنَا فَوْقَكُمُ
الطُّوْرَ ؕ خُذُوْا مَاۤ اٰتَيْنٰكُمْ بِقُوَّةٍ وَّ
اذْكُرُوْا مَا فِيْهِ لَعَلَّكُمْ تَتَّقُوْنَ ﴿٦٣﴾

64. Again you turned away. Had Allah's Grace and His Mercy not existed in your favor, you would certainly have been lost.

64. S̲umma tawallaytum mim ba'di z̲aalika falawlaa faḍlul-laahi 'alaykum wa raḥmatuhoo lakuntum minal-khaasireen.

ثُمَّ تَوَلَّيْتُمْ مِّنْ بَعْدِ ذٰلِكَ ۚ فَلَوْلَا
فَضْلُ اللّٰهِ عَلَيْكُمْ وَرَحْمَتُهٗ لَكُنْتُمْ
مِّنَ الْخٰسِرِيْنَ ﴿٦٤﴾

65. You certainly knew about those among you who were transgressors on the Sabbath. We commanded them, "Become detested apes,"

65. Wa laqad 'alimtumul-laz̲eena'-tadaw minkum fis-Sabti faqulnaa lahum koonoo qiradatan khaasi'een.

وَلَقَدْ عَلِمْتُمُ الَّذِيْنَ اعْتَدَوْا
مِنْكُمْ فِى السَّبْتِ فَقُلْنَا لَهُمْ كُوْنُوْا
قِرَدَةً خٰسِـِٕيْنَ ﴿٦٥﴾

66. in order to set an example for their contemporaries and coming generations and to make it a reminder for the pious.

66. Faja'alnaahaa nakaalal-limaa bayna yadayhaa wa maa khalfahaa wa maw'iẓatal-lilmuttaqeen.

فَجَعَلْنٰهَا نَكَالًا لِّمَا بَيْنَ يَدَيْهَا وَمَا
خَلْفَهَا وَمَوْعِظَةً لِّلْمُتَّقِيْنَ ﴿٦٦﴾

67. When Moses said to his people, "Allah commands you to sacrifice a cow," they asked, "Are you mocking us?" "Allah forbid, how would I be so ignorant," said Moses.

67. Wa iz̲ qaala Moosaa liqawmiheee innal-laaha ya-murukum an taz̲baḥoo baqaratan qaalooo atattakhiz̲unaa huzuwan qaala a'oozu billaahi an akoona minal-jaahileen.

وَاِذْ قَالَ مُوْسٰى لِقَوْمِهٖۤ اِنَّ اللّٰهَ
يَاْمُرُكُمْ اَنْ تَذْبَحُوْا بَقَرَةً ؕ قَالُوْۤا
اَتَتَّخِذُنَا هُزُوًا ؕ قَالَ اَعُوْذُ بِاللّٰهِ
اَنْ اَكُوْنَ مِنَ الْجٰهِلِيْنَ ﴿٦٧﴾

68. They demanded, "Ask your Lord to describe the kind of cow He wants us to slaughter." Moses explained, "It must be neither very old nor very young, thus do whatever you are commanded to do." Moses then told them to do as they were ordered.

68. Qaalud-'u lanaa Rabbaka yubayyil-lanaa maa hee; qaala innahoo yaqoolu innahaa baqaratul-laa faariḍuñw-wa laa bikrun 'awaanum bayna z̲aalika faf'aloo maa tu'maroon.

قَالُوا ادْعُ لَنَا رَبَّكَ يُبَيِّنْ لَّنَا مَا هِىَ ؕ
قَالَ اِنَّهٗ يَقُوْلُ اِنَّهَا بَقَرَةٌ لَّا
فَارِضٌ وَّلَا بِكْرٌ ؕ عَوَانٌۢ بَيْنَ ذٰلِكَ ؕ
فَافْعَلُوْا مَا تُؤْمَرُوْنَ ﴿٦٨﴾

69. They further demanded that Moses ask the Lord what color the cow had to be. Moses answered, "The Lord says that the cow must be yellow, a beautiful yellow."

69. Qaalud-'u lanaa Rabbaka yubayyil-lanaa maa lawnuhaa; qaala innahoo yaqoolu innahaa baqaratun ṣafraaa'u faaqi'ul-lawnuhaa tasurrunnaa-ẓireen.

قَالُوا ادْعُ لَنَا رَبَّكَ يُبَيِّنْ لَّنَا مَا
لَوْنُهَا ؕ قَالَ اِنَّهٗ يَقُوْلُ اِنَّهَا بَقَرَةٌ
صَفْرَآءُ ۙ فَاقِعٌ لَّوْنُهَا تَسُرُّ النّٰظِرِيْنَ ﴿٦٩﴾

70. They said, "We are confused about the cow, for to us all cows look alike. Ask your Lord to tell us exactly what the cow looks like, so that Allah willing, we shall have the right description."

70. Qaalud-'u lanaa Rabbaka yubayyil-lanaa maa hiya innal-baqara tashaabaha 'alaynaa wa innaaa in-shaaa'al-laahu lamuhtadoon.

قَالُوا ادْعُ لَنَا رَبَّكَ يُبَيِّنْ لَّنَا مَا هِيَ
إِنَّ الْبَقَرَ تَشٰبَهَ عَلَيْنَا ۖ وَإِنَّآ إِنْ
شَآءَ اللّٰهُ لَمُهْتَدُوْنَ ﴿٧٠﴾

71. (Moses) said, "The Lord says that it must not have even tilled the soil nor irrigated the fields and it must be free of blemishes and flaws." They said, "Now you have given us the right description." After almost failing to find it, they slaughtered the cow.

71. Qaala innahoo yaqoolu innahaa baqaratul-laa zaloolun tuseerul-arda wa laa tasqil-harsa musallamatullaa shiyata feehaa; qaalul 'aana ji'ta bilhaqq; fazabahoohaa wa maa kaadoo yaf'aloon.

قَالَ إِنَّهٗ يَقُوْلُ إِنَّهَا بَقَرَةٌ لَّا ذَلُوْلٌ
تُثِيْرُ الْأَرْضَ وَلَا تَسْقِي الْحَرْثَ ۚ
مُسَلَّمَةٌ لَّا شِيَةَ فِيْهَا ۗ قَالُوا
الْـٰٔنَ جِئْتَ بِالْحَقِّ ۚ فَذَبَحُوْهَا
وَمَا كَادُوْا يَفْعَلُوْنَ ﴿٧١﴾ ع ٨ ٨

72. When you murdered someone, each one of you tried to accuse others of being guilty. However, Allah made public what you were hiding.

72. Wa iz qataltum nafsan faddaara'tum feehaa wallaahu mukhrijum-maa kuntum taktumoon.

وَإِذْ قَتَلْتُمْ نَفْسًا فَادّٰرَءْتُمْ فِيْهَا ۗ
وَاللّٰهُ مُخْرِجٌ مَّا كُنْتُمْ تَكْتُمُوْنَ ﴿٧٢﴾

73. We said, "Strike the person slain with some part of the cow." That is how Allah brings the dead to life and shows you His miracles so that you might have understanding.

73. Faqulnad-riboohu biba'dihaa; kazaalika yuhyil-laahul-mawtaa wa yureekum Aayaatihee la'allakum ta'qiloon.

فَقُلْنَا اضْرِبُوْهُ بِبَعْضِهَا ۗ كَذٰلِكَ
يُحْيِ اللّٰهُ الْمَوْتٰى ۙ وَيُرِيْكُمْ اٰيٰتِهٖ
لَعَلَّكُمْ تَعْقِلُوْنَ ﴿٧٣﴾

74. Thereafter, your hearts turned as hard as rocks, or even harder, for some rocks give way to the streams that flow therefrom. Water comes out of some rocks when they are torn apart and others tumble down in awe before Allah. Allah does not ignore what you do.

74. Summa qasat quloobukum mim ba'di zaalika fahiya kalhijaarati aw-ashaddu qaswah; wa-inna minal-hijaarati lamaa yatafajjaru minhul-anhaar; wa-inna minhaa lamaa yash-shaqqaqu fayakhruju minhul-maaa'; wa inna minhaa lamaa yahbitu min khashyatil-laah; wa mal-laahu bighaafilin 'ammaa ta'maloon.

ثُمَّ قَسَتْ قُلُوْبُكُمْ مِّنْۢ بَعْدِ ذٰلِكَ
فَهِيَ كَالْحِجَارَةِ أَوْ أَشَدُّ قَسْوَةً ۗ
وَإِنَّ مِنَ الْحِجَارَةِ لَمَا يَتَفَجَّرُ مِنْهُ
الْأَنْهٰرُ ۗ وَإِنَّ مِنْهَا لَمَا يَشَّقَّقُ
فَيَخْرُجُ مِنْهُ الْمَآءُ ۗ وَإِنَّ مِنْهَا لَمَا
يَهْبِطُ مِنْ خَشْيَةِ اللّٰهِ ۗ وَمَا اللّٰهُ
بِغَافِلٍ عَمَّا تَعْمَلُوْنَ ﴿٧٤﴾

75. Do you, the believers in truth, desire the unbelievers to believe you? There was a group among them who would hear the word of Allah and understand it. Then they would purposely misinterpret it.

75. Afatatma'oona any-yu'minoo lakum wa qad kaana fareequm-minhum yasma'oona Kalaamal-laahi summa yuharrifoonahoo mim ba'di maa 'aqaloohu wa hum ya'lamoon.

أَفَتَطْمَعُوْنَ أَنْ يُّؤْمِنُوْا لَكُمْ
وَقَدْ كَانَ فَرِيْقٌ مِّنْهُمْ يَسْمَعُوْنَ
كَلٰمَ اللّٰهِ ثُمَّ يُحَرِّفُوْنَهٗ مِنْۢ بَعْدِ
مَا عَقَلُوْهُ وَهُمْ يَعْلَمُوْنَ ﴿٧٥﴾

76. On meeting the believers, they would declare belief but to each other they would say, "How would you (against your own interests) tell

76. Wa izaa laqul-lazeena aamanoo qaalooo aamannaa wa izaa khalaa ba'duhum ilaa ba'din

وَإِذَا لَقُوا الَّذِيْنَ اٰمَنُوْا قَالُوْٓا
اٰمَنَّا ۚ وَإِذَا خَلَا بَعْضُهُمْ إِلٰى بَعْضٍ

them (believers) about what Allah has revealed to you (in the Bible of the truthfulness of the Prophet Muhammad)? They will present it as evidence to prove you wrong before your Lord. Do you not realize it?"

qaalooo atuḥaddis̲oonahum bimaa fataḥal-laahu 'alaykum liyuḥaajjookum bihee 'inda Rabbikum; afalaa ta'qiloon.

قَالُوٓا أَتُحَدِّثُونَهُم بِمَا فَتَحَ اللَّهُ
عَلَيْكُمْ لِيُحَآجُّوكُم بِهِۦ عِندَ
رَبِّكُمْ ۚ أَفَلَا تَعْقِلُونَ ٧٦

77. Do they not know that Allah knows whatever they conceal or reveal?

77. Awalaa ya'lamoona annal-laaha ya'lamu maa yusirroona wa maa yu'linoon.

أَوَلَا يَعْلَمُونَ أَنَّ اللَّهَ يَعْلَمُ
مَا يُسِرُّونَ وَمَا يُعْلِنُونَ ٧٧

78. Certain ones of them are illiterate and have no knowledge of the Book except for what others read to them (from legends and fantasy). They are only relying on conjecture.

78. Wa minhum ummiyyoona laa ya'lamoonal-Kitaaba illaaa amaaniyya wa in hum illaa yaẓunnoon.

وَمِنْهُمْ أُمِّيُّونَ لَا يَعْلَمُونَ الْكِتٰبَ
إِلَّآ أَمَانِىَّ وَإِنْ هُمْ إِلَّا يَظُنُّونَ ٧٨

النصف

79. Woe to those who write the Book themselves and say, "This is from Allah," so that they may sell it for a small price! Woe unto them for what they have done and for what they have gained!

79. Fawaylul-lillaz̲eena yaktuboonal-kitaaba bi-aydeehim s̲umma yaqooloona haaz̲aa min 'indil-laahi liyashtaroo bihee s̲amanan qaleelan fawaylul-lahum mimmaa katabat aydeehim wa waylul-lahum mimmaa yaksiboon.

فَوَيْلٌ لِّلَّذِينَ يَكْتُبُونَ الْكِتٰبَ
بِأَيْدِيهِمْ ثُمَّ يَقُولُونَ هٰذَا مِنْ
عِندِ اللَّهِ لِيَشْتَرُوا بِهِۦ ثَمَنًا قَلِيلًا ۖ
فَوَيْلٌ لَّهُم مِّمَّا كَتَبَتْ أَيْدِيهِمْ
وَوَيْلٌ لَّهُم مِّمَّا يَكْسِبُونَ ٧٩

80. They have said, "Hellfire will never harm us except for just a few days." (Muhammad), ask them, "Have you made such agreements with Allah Who never breaks any of His agreements, or do you just ascribe to Him that which you do not know?"

80. Wa qaaloo lan tamassanan-Naaru illaaa ayyaamam ma'doodah; qul attakhaz̲tum 'indal-laahi 'ahdan falañy-yukhlifal-laahu 'ahdahooo am taqooloona 'alal-laahi maa laa ta'lamoon.

وَقَالُوا لَن تَمَسَّنَا النَّارُ إِلَّآ أَيَّامًا
مَّعْدُودَةً ۚ قُلْ أَتَّخَذْتُمْ عِندَ اللَّهِ
عَهْدًا فَلَن يُخْلِفَ اللَّهُ عَهْدَهُۥٓ ۖ أَمْ
تَقُولُونَ عَلَى اللَّهِ مَا لَا تَعْلَمُونَ ٨٠

81. There is no doubt that evildoers who are engulfed in sins are the companions of hellfire wherein they will live forever.

81. Balaa man kasaba sayyi'atañw-wa aḥaaṭat bihee khaṭeee'atuhoo fa-ulaaa'ika Aṣḥaabun-Naari hum feehaa khaalidoon.

بَلٰى مَن كَسَبَ سَيِّئَةً وَأَحَاطَتْ
بِهِۦ خَطِيٓـَٔتُهُۥ فَأُولٰٓئِكَ أَصْحٰبُ النَّارِ ۖ
هُمْ فِيهَا خٰلِدُونَ ٨١

82. As for the righteously striving believers, they will be among the people of Paradise wherein they will live forever.

82. Wallaz̲eena aamanoo wa 'amiluṣ-ṣaaliḥaati ulaaa'ika Aṣḥaabul-Jannati hum feehaa khaalidoon.

وَالَّذِينَ ءَامَنُوا وَعَمِلُوا الصّٰلِحٰتِ
أُولٰٓئِكَ أَصْحٰبُ الْجَنَّةِ ۖ هُمْ فِيهَا
خٰلِدُونَ ٨٢

ع ١١

83. We made a covenant with the children of Israel that they should not worship anyone except Me, that they should serve their parents, relatives, orphans and the destitute, that they should speak righteous words to people and that they should be steadfast in

83. Wa iz̲ akhaz̲naa mees̲aaqa Baneee Israaa'eela laa ta'budoona illal-laaha wa bilwaalidayni iḥsaanañw-wa z̲ilqurbaa walyataamaa walmasaakeeni wa qooloo linnaasi ḥusnañw-

وَإِذْ أَخَذْنَا مِيثٰقَ بَنِىٓ إِسْرَآءِيلَ
لَا تَعْبُدُونَ إِلَّا اللَّهَ وَبِالْوٰلِدَيْنِ
إِحْسَانًا وَذِى الْقُرْبٰى وَالْيَتٰمٰى
وَالْمَسٰكِينِ وَقُولُوا لِلنَّاسِ حُسْنًا

their prayers and pay the religious tax. But soon after you made this covenant, all but a few of you broke it heedlessly.

wa aqeemuṣ-Ṣalaata wa aatuz-Zakaata summa tawallaytum illaa qaleelam minkum wa antum mu'riḍoon.

وَأَقِيمُوا الصَّلَوٰةَ وَءَاتُوا الزَّكَوٰةَ ط
ثُمَّ تَوَلَّيْتُمْ إِلَّا قَلِيلًا مِّنكُمْ
وَأَنتُم مُّعْرِضُونَ ﴿٨٣﴾

84. We made a covenant with you that you should not shed each other's blood or expel each other from your homeland. You accepted and bore witness to this covenant,

84. Wa iz akhaznaa meesaa-qakum laa tasfikoona dimaa-a'akum wa laa tukhrijoona anfusakum min diyaarikum summa aqrartum wa antum tashhadoon.

وَإِذْ أَخَذْنَا مِيثَٰقَكُمْ لَا تَسْفِكُونَ
دِمَآءَكُمْ وَلَا تُخْرِجُونَ أَنفُسَكُم
مِّن دِيَٰرِكُمْ ثُمَّ أَقْرَرْتُمْ وَأَنتُمْ
تَشْهَدُونَ ﴿٨٤﴾

85. yet you murdered each other and forced a number of your people out of their homeland, helping each other to commit sin and to be hostile to one another. When you had expelled people from their homeland and later they had been made captives (of other people), you then paid their ransom (thinking that it was a righteous deed). Allah forbade you to expel these people in the first place. Do you believe in one part of the Book and not in the other? Those who behave in this way shall reap disgrace in this world and severe punishment on the Day of Resurrection. Allah is not unaware of things that you do.

85. Summa antum haaa'ulaaa'i taqtuloona anfusakum wa tukhrijoona fareeqam minkum min diyaarihim taẓaaharoona 'alayhim bil-ismi wal'udwaani wa-iñy-ya-tookum usaaraa tufaa-doohum wahuwa muḥarramun 'alaykum ikhraajuhum; afatu'-mi-noona biba'ḍil-Kitaabi wa takfuroona biba'ḍ; famaa jazaaa'u mañy-yaf'alu zaalika minkum illaa khizyun fil-ḥayaatid-dunyaa wa Yawmal-Qiyaamati yuraddoona ilaaa ashaddil-'azaab; wa mal-laahu bighaafilin 'ammaa ta'maloon.

ثُمَّ أَنتُمْ هَٰٓؤُلَآءِ تَقْتُلُونَ أَنفُسَكُمْ
وَتُخْرِجُونَ فَرِيقًا مِّنكُم مِّن دِيَٰرِهِمْ
تَظَٰهَرُونَ عَلَيْهِم بِالْإِثْمِ وَالْعُدْوَٰنِ
وَإِن يَأْتُوكُمْ أُسَٰرَىٰ تُفَٰدُوهُمْ
وَهُوَ مُحَرَّمٌ عَلَيْكُمْ إِخْرَاجُهُمْ
أَفَتُؤْمِنُونَ بِبَعْضِ الْكِتَٰبِ وَتَكْفُرُونَ
بِبَعْضٍ فَمَا جَزَآءُ مَن يَفْعَلُ ذَٰلِكَ
مِنكُمْ إِلَّا خِزْيٌ فِي الْحَيَوٰةِ الدُّنْيَا ج
وَيَوْمَ الْقِيَٰمَةِ يُرَدُّونَ إِلَىٰٓ أَشَدِّ
الْعَذَابِ وَمَا اللَّهُ بِغَٰفِلٍ عَمَّا
تَعْمَلُونَ ﴿٨٥﴾

86. They have traded the life hereafter in exchange for their worldly life. Their punishment will not be eased nor will they receive help.

86. Ulaaa'ikal-lazeenash-tarawul ḥayaatad-dunyaa bil-Aakhirati falaa yukhaffafu 'anhumul-'azaabu wa laa hum yunṣaroon.

أُولَٰٓئِكَ الَّذِينَ اشْتَرَوُا الْحَيَوٰةَ
الدُّنْيَا بِالْءَاخِرَةِ فَلَا يُخَفَّفُ عَنْهُمُ
الْعَذَابُ وَلَا هُمْ يُنصَرُونَ ﴿٨٦﴾ ع

87. We gave the Book to Moses and made the Messengers follow in his path. To Jesus, the son of Mary, We gave the miracles and supported him by the Holy Spirit. Why do you arrogantly belie some Messengers and murder others whenever they have

87. Wa laqad aataynaa Moosal-Kitaaba wa qaffaynaa mim ba'dihee bir-Rusuli wa aataynaa 'Eesab-na-Maryamal-bayyinaati wa ayyadnaahu bi-Rooḥil Qudus; afakullamaa jaaa'akum Rasoolum bimaa laa tahwaaa anfusukumus-takbartum

وَلَقَدْ ءَاتَيْنَا مُوسَى الْكِتَٰبَ وَقَفَّيْنَا
مِنۢ بَعْدِهِۦ بِالرُّسُلِ وَءَاتَيْنَا عِيسَى
ابْنَ مَرْيَمَ الْبَيِّنَٰتِ وَأَيَّدْنَٰهُ بِرُوحِ
الْقُدُسِ أَفَكُلَّمَا جَآءَكُمْ رَسُولٌۢ
بِمَا لَا تَهْوَىٰٓ أَنفُسُكُمُ اسْتَكْبَرْتُمْ ج

brought you messages that you dislike?

fafareeqan kazzabtum wa fareeqan taqtuloon.

ففريقا كذبتم وفريقا تقتلون ﴿٨٧﴾

88. They have said that their hearts cannot understand (what you, Muhammad, say). Allah has condemned them for their denial of the Truth. There are a very few of them who have faith.

88. Wa qaaloo quloobunaa ghulf; bal la‘anahumul-laahu bikufrihim faqaleelam-maa yu’minoon.

وقالوا قلوبنا غلف بل لعنهم
الله بكفرهم فقليلا ما يؤمنون ﴿٨٨﴾

89. When a Book came to them from Allah which confirmed what was with them (the fact of truthfulness of Prophet Muhammad in their Scripture), and despite the fact that they had been praying for victory over the unbelievers (by the help of the truthful Prophet), they refused to accept the Book, even though they knew it (to be the Truth). May Allah condemn those who hide the Truth!

89. Wa lammaa jaaa’ahum Kitaabum min ‘indil-laahi muṣaddiqul-limaa ma‘ahum wa kaanoo min qablu yastaftiḥoona ‘alal-lazeena kafaroo falammaa jaaa’ahum maa ‘arafoo kafaroo bih; fala‘natul-laahi ‘alal-kaafireen.

ولما جاءهم كتب من عند الله
مصدق لما معهم وكانوا من
قبل يستفتحون على الذين كفروا
فلما جاءهم ما عرفوا كفروا به
فلعنة الله على الكفرين ﴿٨٩﴾

90. Evil is that for which they have sold their souls. They have refused to accept Allah's revelations in rebellion against the servant of Allah to whom He has, by His Grace, chosen to grant His message. They have brought upon themselves Allah's wrath in addition to the wrath that they had incurred (upon themselves) for their previous sins. The unbelievers will suffer a humiliating torment.

90. Bi’samash-taraw biheee anfusahum añy-yakfuroo bimaaa anzalal-laahu baghyan añy-yunazzilal-laahu min faḍlihee ‘alaa mañy-yashaaa’u min ‘ibaadihee fabaaa’oo bighaḍabin ‘alaa ghaḍab; wa lilkaafireena ‘azaabum-muheen.

بئسما اشتروا به أنفسهم أن
يكفروا بما أنزل الله بغيا أن ينزل
الله من فضله على من يشاء من
عباده فباءو بغضب على غضب
وللكفرين عذاب مهين ﴿٩٠﴾

91. When they are told to believe in Allah's revelations, they reply, “We believe only in what Allah has revealed to us,” but they disbelieve His other true revelations, even though these revelations confirm their own (original) Scripture. (Muhammad), ask them, “Why did you murder Allah's Prophets if you were true believers?”

91. Wa izaa qeela lahum aaminoo bimaaa anzalal-laahu qaaloo nu’minu bimaaa unzila ‘alaynaa wa yakfuroona bimaa waraaa’ahoo wa huwal-ḥaqqu muṣaddiqal-limaa ma‘ahum; qul falima taqtuloona Ambiyaaa’al-laahi min qablu in kuntum mu’mineen.

وإذا قيل لهم آمنوا بما أنزل الله
قالوا نؤمن بما أنزل علينا
ويكفرون بما وراءه وهو الحق
مصدقا لما معهم قل فلم تقتلون
أنبياء الله من قبل إن كنتم
مؤمنين ﴿٩١﴾

92. (Moses) brought you certain miracles. Not very long after, you began worshipping the calf which was nothing but senseless cruelty to yourselves.

92. Wa laqad jaaa’akum Moosaa bilbayyinaati summat-takhaztumul-‘ijla mim ba‘dihee wa antum ẓaalimoon.

ولقد جاءكم موسى بالبينت ثم
اتخذتم العجل من بعده وأنتم
ظلمون ﴿٩٢﴾

93. (Children of Israel), when We made a covenant with you, raised Mount Tur (Sinai) above you, and told you to receive devotedly what We had revealed to you and to listen to it, you said that you had listened but you disobeyed. They (children of Israel) denied the truth and became totally devoted and full of love for the calf.

93. Wa iz akhaznaa meesaa-qakum wa rafa‘naa fawqa-kumuṭ-Ṭoora khuzoo maaa aataynaakum biquwwatiñw-wasma‘oo qaaloo sami‘naa wa ‘aṣaynaa wa ushriboo fee quloobihimul ‘ijla

وإذ أخذنا ميثاقكم ورفعنا
فوقكم الطور خذوا ما آتينكم
بقوة واسمعوا قالوا سمعنا
وعصينا وأشربوا في قلوبهم العجل

(Muhammad), tell these people, "If in fact you are true believers, then what your faith commands you to do is evil."

94. (Muhammad), tell them, "If your claim is true that the home with Allah in the everlasting life hereafter is for you alone, you should wish for death (for your opponents), if you are truthful (that your prayers are answered)."

95. But they can never have a longing for death because of what they have done. Allah knows the unjust well.

96. However, you will find them the greediest of all men, even more than the pagans, for life. They would each gladly live for a thousand years, but such a long life would not save them from the torment. Allah sees what they do.

97. (Muhammad), tell the people, whoever is an enemy of Gabriel who has delivered the Book to your heart as a guide and as joyful news to the believers,

98. and as a confirmation of (original) Scripture and whoever is the enemy of Allah, His angels, His Messengers, Gabriel and Michael, should know that Allah is the enemy of those who refuse to accept the Truth.

99. (Muhammad), We have given you enlightening authority. Only the wicked sinners deny it.

100. Why is it that every time they (the Jews) make a covenant, some of them abandon it? Most of them do not even believe.

100. When a Messenger of Allah came to them confirming the (original) revelation that they already had received, a group of those who had the Scripture with them threw the Book of Allah

bikufrihim; qul bi'samaa ya-murukum biheee eemaanukum in kuntum mu'mineen.

94. Qul in kaanat lakumud-Daarul-Aakhiratu 'indal-laahi khaaliṣatam-min doonin-naasi fatamannawul-mawta in kuntum ṣaadiqeen.

95. Wa lañy-yatamannawhu abadam bimaa qaddamat aydeehim; wallaahu 'aleemum biẓẓaalimeen.

96. Wa latajidannahum aḥraṣan-naasi 'alaa ḥayaah; wa minal-laz̲eena ashrakoo; yawaddu aḥaduhum law yu'ammaru alfa sanah; wa maa huwa bimuzaḥ-ziḥihee minal-'az̲aabi añy-yu'ammar; wallaahu baṣeerum bimaa ya'maloon.

97. Qul man kaana 'aduwwal-li-Jibreela fainnahoo nazzalahoo 'alaa qalbika bi-iz̲nil-laahi muṣaddiqal-limaa bayna yadayhi wa hudañw-wa bushraa lilmu'mineen.

98. Man kaana 'aduwwal-lillaahi wa malaaa'ikatihee wa Rusulihee wa Jibreela wa Meekaala fa-innal-laaha 'aduw-wul-lilkaafireen.

99. Wa laqad anzalnaaa ilayka Aayaatim bayyinaat; wa maa yakfuru bihaaa illal-faasiqoon.

100. Awa kullamaa 'aahadoo 'ahdan nabaz̲ahoo fareequm-minhum; bal aks̲aruhum laa yu'minoon.

101. Wa lammaa jaaa'ahum Rasoolum min 'indil-laahi muṣaddiqul-limaa ma'ahum nabaz̲a fareequm-minal-laz̲eena ootul-Kitaab; Kitaabal-laahi

بِكُفْرِهِمْ ۚ قُلْ بِئْسَمَا يَأْمُرُكُم بِهِۦٓ إِيمَـٰنُكُمْ
إِن كُنتُم مُّؤْمِنِينَ ﴿٩٣﴾
قُلْ إِن كَانَتْ لَكُمُ ٱلدَّارُ ٱلْـَٔاخِرَةُ
عِندَ ٱللَّهِ خَالِصَةً مِّن دُونِ ٱلنَّاسِ
فَتَمَنَّوُا۟ ٱلْمَوْتَ إِن كُنتُمْ صَـٰدِقِينَ ﴿٩٤﴾
وَلَن يَتَمَنَّوْهُ أَبَدًۢا بِمَا قَدَّمَتْ أَيْدِيهِمْ ۗ
وَٱللَّهُ عَلِيمٌۢ بِٱلظَّـٰلِمِينَ ﴿٩٥﴾
وَلَتَجِدَنَّهُمْ أَحْرَصَ ٱلنَّاسِ عَلَىٰ
حَيَوٰةٍ ۚ وَمِنَ ٱلَّذِينَ أَشْرَكُوا۟ ۚ يَوَدُّ
أَحَدُهُمْ لَوْ يُعَمَّرُ أَلْفَ سَنَةٍ ۚ وَمَا
هُوَ بِمُزَحْزِحِهِۦ مِنَ ٱلْعَذَابِ أَن
يُعَمَّرَ ۗ وَٱللَّهُ بَصِيرٌۢ بِمَا يَعْمَلُونَ ﴿٩٦﴾
قُلْ مَن كَانَ عَدُوًّا لِّجِبْرِيلَ فَإِنَّهُۥ
نَزَّلَهُۥ عَلَىٰ قَلْبِكَ بِإِذْنِ ٱللَّهِ مُصَدِّقًا
لِّمَا بَيْنَ يَدَيْهِ وَهُدًى وَبُشْرَىٰ
لِلْمُؤْمِنِينَ ﴿٩٧﴾
مَن كَانَ عَدُوًّا لِّلَّهِ وَمَلَـٰٓئِكَتِهِۦ
وَرُسُلِهِۦ وَجِبْرِيلَ وَمِيكَىٰلَ فَإِنَّ
ٱللَّهَ عَدُوٌّ لِّلْكَـٰفِرِينَ ﴿٩٨﴾
وَلَقَدْ أَنزَلْنَآ إِلَيْكَ ءَايَـٰتٍۭ بَيِّنَـٰتٍ ۖ
وَمَا يَكْفُرُ بِهَآ إِلَّا ٱلْفَـٰسِقُونَ ﴿٩٩﴾
أَوَكُلَّمَا عَـٰهَدُوا۟ عَهْدًا نَّبَذَهُۥ فَرِيقٌ
مِّنْهُم ۚ بَلْ أَكْثَرُهُمْ لَا يُؤْمِنُونَ ﴿١٠٠﴾
وَلَمَّا جَآءَهُمْ رَسُولٌ مِّنْ عِندِ ٱللَّهِ
مُصَدِّقٌ لِّمَا مَعَهُمْ نَبَذَ فَرِيقٌ
مِّنَ ٱلَّذِينَ أُوتُوا۟ ٱلْكِتَـٰبَ كِتَـٰبَ ٱللَّهِ

ربع
عند المتأخرين ١٠
ع

behind their backs as if they did not know anything about it.

waraaa'a ẓuhoorihim ka-annahum laa ya'lamoon.

وَرَآءَ ظُهُورِهِمْ كَأَنَّهُمْ لَا يَعْلَمُونَ ﴿١٠١﴾

102. They followed the incantations that the devils used against the kingdom of Solomon. Solomon did not hide the truth but the devils did. They taught magic to the people and whatever was revealed to the two angels, Harut and Marut, in Babylon. The two angels did not teach anything to anyone without saying, "Our case is a temptation for the people, so do not hide the truth."
People learned something from the two angels that could cause discord between a man and his wife. However, they could harm no one except by the permission of Allah. In fact, the (people) learned things that would harm them and render them no benefit. They knew very well that one who engaged in witchcraft would have no reward in the life hereafter. Would that they had known that they had sold their souls for that which is vile!

102. Wattaba'oo maa tatlush-Shayaaṭeenu 'alaa mulki Sulaymaana wa maa kafara Sulaymaanu wa laakinnash-Shayaaṭeena kafaroo yu'al-limoonan-naasas-siḥra wa maaa unzila 'alal-malakayni bi-Baabila Haaroota wa Maaroot; wa maa yu'allimaani min aḥadin ḥattaa yaqoolaaa innamaa naḥnu fitnatun falaa takfur fayata'al-lamoona minhumaa maa yufarriqoona bihee baynal-mar'i wa zawjih; wa maa hum biḍaarreena bihee min aḥadin illaa bi-iznillaah; wa yata'al-lamoona maa yaḍurruhum wa laa yanfa'uhum; wa laqad 'alimoo lamanish-taraahu maa lahoo fil-Aakhirati min khalaaq; wa labi'sa maa sharaw biheee anfusahum; law kaanoo ya'lamoon.

وَاتَّبَعُوا مَا تَتْلُوا الشَّيٰطِينُ عَلٰى
مُلْكِ سُلَيْمٰنَ ۚ وَمَا كَفَرَ سُلَيْمٰنُ
وَلٰكِنَّ الشَّيٰطِينَ كَفَرُوا يُعَلِّمُونَ
النَّاسَ السِّحْرَ ۗ وَمَا أُنْزِلَ عَلَى
الْمَلَكَيْنِ بِبَابِلَ هٰرُوتَ وَمٰرُوتَ ۚ
وَمَا يُعَلِّمٰنِ مِنْ أَحَدٍ حَتّٰى يَقُولَا
إِنَّمَا نَحْنُ فِتْنَةٌ فَلَا تَكْفُرْ ۖ فَيَتَعَلَّمُونَ
مِنْهُمَا مَا يُفَرِّقُونَ بِهِ بَيْنَ الْمَرْءِ
وَزَوْجِهِ ۚ وَمَا هُمْ بِضَآرِّينَ بِهِ
مِنْ أَحَدٍ إِلَّا بِإِذْنِ اللّٰهِ ۚ وَيَتَعَلَّمُونَ
مَا يَضُرُّهُمْ وَلَا يَنْفَعُهُمْ ۚ وَلَقَدْ
عَلِمُوا لَمَنِ اشْتَرٰىهُ مَا لَهُ فِي الْآخِرَةِ
مِنْ خَلٰقٍ ۚ وَلَبِئْسَ مَا شَرَوْا بِهِ
أَنْفُسَهُمْ ۚ لَوْ كَانُوا يَعْلَمُونَ ﴿١٠٢﴾

103. Would that they had known that if they had embraced the faith and avoided evil, they would have received better rewards from Allah.

103. Wa law annahum aamanoo wattaqaw lamaṯoobatum-min 'indillaahi khayr; law kaanoo ya'lamoon.

وَلَوْ أَنَّهُمْ آمَنُوا وَاتَّقَوْا لَمَثُوبَةٌ
مِنْ عِنْدِ اللّٰهِ خَيْرٌ ۚ لَوْ كَانُوا
يَعْلَمُونَ ﴿١٠٣﴾ ع

104. Believers, do not address the Prophet as raina (whereby the Jews, in their own accent, meant: Would that you would never hear), but call him unzurna (meaning: Please speak to us slowly so that we understand), and then listen. The unbelievers will face a painful torment.

104. Yaaa ayyuhal-lazeena aamanoo laa taqooloo raa'inaa wa qoolun-ẓurnaa wasma'oo; wa lilkaafireena 'azaabun aleem.

يٰٓأَيُّهَا الَّذِينَ آمَنُوا لَا تَقُولُوا
رَاعِنَا وَقُولُوا انْظُرْنَا وَاسْمَعُوا ۚ
وَلِلْكٰفِرِينَ عَذَابٌ أَلِيمٌ ﴿١٠٤﴾

105. (Muhammad), the unbelievers among the People of the Book and the pagans do not like to see anything good revealed to you from your Lord. Allah reserves His mercy for whomever He chooses. The generosity of Allah is great.

105. Maa yawaddul-lazeena kafaroo min Ahlil-Kitaabi wa lal-mushrikeena añy-yunazzala 'alaykum min khayrim-mir-Rabbikum; wallaahu yakhtaṣṣu biraḥmatihee mañy-yashaaa'; wallaahu zul-faḍlil'aẓeem.

مَا يَوَدُّ الَّذِينَ كَفَرُوا مِنْ أَهْلِ
الْكِتٰبِ وَلَا الْمُشْرِكِينَ أَنْ يُنَزَّلَ
عَلَيْكُمْ مِنْ خَيْرٍ مِنْ رَبِّكُمْ ۗ وَاللّٰهُ
يَخْتَصُّ بِرَحْمَتِهِ مَنْ يَشَآءُ ۚ وَاللّٰهُ
ذُو الْفَضْلِ الْعَظِيمِ ﴿١٠٥﴾

106. For whatever sign We change or eliminate or cause to recede into oblivion, We bring forth a better sign or one that is identical. Did you not know that Allah has power over all things?

106. Maa nansakh min Aayatin aw nunsihaa na-ti bikhayrim-minhaaa aw mislihaaa; alam ta'lam annal-laaha 'alaa kulli shay'in Qadeer.

مَا نَنْسَخْ مِنْ اٰيَةٍ اَوْ نُنْسِهَا نَاْتِ
بِخَيْرٍ مِّنْهَآ اَوْ مِثْلِهَا ؕ اَلَمْ تَعْلَمْ
اَنَّ اللّٰهَ عَلٰى كُلِّ شَیْءٍ قَدِیْرٌ ۝١٠٦

107. Did you not know that the kingdom of the heavens and the earth belongs to Allah and that no one is your guardian or helper besides Him?

107. Alam ta'lam annallaaha lahoo mulkus-samaawaati wal-arḍ; wa maa lakum min doonil-laahi miñw-waliyyiñw-wa laa naṣeer.

اَلَمْ تَعْلَمْ اَنَّ اللّٰهَ لَهٗ مُلْكُ السَّمٰوٰتِ
وَالْاَرْضِ ؕ وَمَا لَكُمْ مِّنْ دُوْنِ اللّٰهِ
مِنْ وَّلِیٍّ وَّلَا نَصِیْرٍ ۝١٠٧

108. Do you want to address the Prophet in the same manner in which Moses was addressed? Anyone who exchanges belief for disbelief has certainly gone down the wrong path.

108. Am tureedoona an tas'aloo Rasoolakum kamaa su'ila Moosaa min qabl; wa mañy-yatabaddalil-kufra bil-eemaani faqad ḍalla sawaaa'as-Sabeel.

اَمْ تُرِیْدُوْنَ اَنْ تَسْــَٔلُوْا رَسُوْلَكُمْ
كَمَا سُئِلَ مُوْسٰی مِنْ قَبْلُ ؕ وَمَنْ
یَّتَبَدَّلِ الْكُفْرَ بِالْاِیْمَانِ فَقَدْ
ضَلَّ سَوَآءَ السَّبِیْلِ ۝١٠٨

109. Once you have accepted the faith, many of the People of the Book would love, out of envy, to turn you back to disbelief, even after the Truth has become evident to them. Have forgiveness and bear with them until Allah issues His order. Allah has power over all things.

109. Wadda kaseerum-min Ahlil-Kitaabi law yaruddoo-nakum mim-ba'di eemaanikum kuffaaran ḥasadam-min 'indi anfusihim mim ba'di maa tabayyana lahumul-ḥaqq; fa'foo waṣfaḥoo ḥattaa ya-tiyallaahu bi-amrih; innal-laaha 'alaa kulli shay'in Qadeer.

وَدَّ كَثِیْرٌ مِّنْ اَهْلِ الْكِتٰبِ لَوْ یَرُدُّوْنَكُمْ
مِّنْۢ بَعْدِ اِیْمَانِكُمْ كُفَّارًا ۚۖ حَسَدًا
مِّنْ عِنْدِ اَنْفُسِهِمْ مِّنْۢ بَعْدِ مَا
تَبَیَّنَ لَهُمُ الْحَقُّ ۚ فَاعْفُوْا وَاصْفَحُوْا
حَتّٰی یَاْتِیَ اللّٰهُ بِاَمْرِهٖ ؕ اِنَّ اللّٰهَ عَلٰی
كُلِّ شَیْءٍ قَدِیْرٌ ۝١٠٩

الثّلٰثة

110. Be steadfast in your prayer and pay the religious tax. You will receive a good reward from Allah for all your good works. Allah is Well-aware of what you do.

110. Wa aqeemuṣ-Ṣalaata wa aatuz-Zakaah; wa maa tuqad-dimoo li-anfusikum min khayrin tajidoohu 'indal-laah; innal-laaha bimaa ta'maloona Baṣeer.

وَاَقِیْمُوا الصَّلٰوةَ وَاٰتُوا الزَّكٰوةَ ؕ
وَمَا تُقَدِّمُوْا لِاَنْفُسِكُمْ مِّنْ خَیْرٍ
تَجِدُوْهُ عِنْدَ اللّٰهِ ؕ اِنَّ اللّٰهَ بِمَا
تَعْمَلُوْنَ بَصِیْرٌ ۝١١٠

111. They have said that no one can ever go to Paradise except the Jews or Christians, but this is only what they hope. Ask them to prove that their claim is true.

111. Wa qaaloo lañy-yadkhulal-Jannata illaa man kaana Hoodan aw Naṣaaraa; tilka amaaniy-yuhum; qul haatoo burhaa-nakum in kuntum ṣaadiqeen.

وَقَالُوْا لَنْ یَّدْخُلَ الْجَنَّةَ اِلَّا مَنْ
كَانَ هُوْدًا اَوْ نَصٰرٰی ؕ تِلْكَ
اَمَانِیُّهُمْ ؕ قُلْ هَاتُوْا بُرْهَانَكُمْ اِنْ
كُنْتُمْ صٰدِقِیْنَ ۝١١١

112. However, one who accepts Islam in submission to Allah and does good, will have his reward with Allah. Such people will have

112. Balaa man aslama wajhahoo lillaahi wa huwa muḥsinun falahooo ajruhoo 'inda Rabbihee wa laa

بَلٰی ۚ مَنْ اَسْلَمَ وَجْهَهٗ لِلّٰهِ وَهُوَ
مُحْسِنٌ فَلَهٗۤ اَجْرُهٗ عِنْدَ رَبِّهٖ ۪ وَلَا

nothing to fear nor to grieve about.

khawfun ‘alayhim wa laa hum yaḥzanoon.

خوف عليهم ولا هم يحزنون ﴿١١٢﴾

113. The Jews accuse the Christians of having no basis for their religion and the Christians accuse the Jews of having no basis for their religion, even though both sides read the Scripture. The ignorant ones say the same thing. Allah will issue His decree about their dispute on the Day of Judgment.

113. Wa qaalatil-Yahoodu laysatin-Naṣaaraa ‘alaa shay' iñw-wa qaalatin-Naṣaaraa laysatil-Yahoodu ‘alaa shay'iñw-wa hum yatloonal-Kitaab; kaẕaalika qaalal-laẕeena laa ya‘lamoona misla qawlihim; fallaahu yaḥkumu baynahum Yawmal-Qiyaamati feemaa kaanoo feehi yakhtalifoon.

وقالت اليهود ليست النصرى
على شيء وقالت النصرى ليست
اليهود على شيء وهم يتلون الكتب
كذلك قال الذين لا يعلمون
مثل قولهم فالله يحكم بينهم يوم
القيمة فيما كانوا فيه يختلفون ﴿١١٣﴾

114. Who is more unjust than those who strive to destroy the mosques and prevent others from commemorating the name of Allah therein, and who could not enter the mosques except with fear? They (the unjust ones) will be disgraced in this life and will receive great torment in the life hereafter.

114. Wa man-aẓlamu mimmam-mana‘a masaajidal-laahi añy-yuẕkara feehas-muhoo wa sa‘aa fee kharaabihaaa; ulaaa'ika maa kaana lahum añy-yadkhuloohaaa illaa khaaa'ifeen; lahum fid-dunyaa khizyuñw-wa lahum fil-Aakhirati ‘aẕaabun ‘aẓeem.

ومن اظلم ممن منع مسجد الله
ان يذكر فيها اسمه وسعى في
خرابها اولئك ما كان لهم ان
يدخلوها الا خائفين لهم في
الدنيا خزي ولهم في الاخرة
عذاب عظيم ﴿١١٤﴾

115. The East and the West belong to Allah. Wherever you turn (in optional prayers), you are always in the presence of Allah. Allah is Munificent and Omniscient.

115. Wa lillaahil - mashriqu walmaghrib; fa-aynamaa tuwalloo fasamma Wajhullaah; innal-laaha Waasi‘un ‘Aleem.

ولله المشرق والمغرب فاينما
تولوا فثم وجه الله ان الله
واسع عليم ﴿١١٥﴾

116. They (the People of the Book), have said that Allah has taken for Himself a son. He is too glorious to have a son. To Him belongs all that is in the heavens and the earth. All pray in obedience to Him.

116. Wa qaalut-takhaẕal-laahu waladaa; Subḥaanahoo bal lahoo maa fis-samaawaati wal-arḍi kullul-lahoo qaanitoon.

وقالوا اتخذ الله ولدا سبحنه
بل له ما في السموت والارض
كل له قنتون ﴿١١٦﴾

117. Allah is the Originator of the heavens and the earth. Whenever He decides to do anything, He just commands it to exist and it comes into existence.

117. Badee‘us-samaawaati wal-arḍi wa iẕaa qaḍaaa amran fa-innamaa yaqoolu lahoo kun fayakoon.

بديع السموت والارض واذا قضى
امرا فانما يقول له كن فيكون ﴿١١٧﴾

118. The ignorant have asked, “Why does He not speak to us and why has no evidence come to show us (that He exists)?” People before them had also asked such questions. They all think in the same way. We have already made the evidence very clear for those who have certainty.

118. Wa qaalal-laẕeena laa ya‘lamoona law laa yukalli-munal-laahu aw ta-teenaaa Aayah; kaẕaalika qaalal-laẕeena min qablihim misla qawlihim; tashaabahat quloobuhum; qad bayyannal-Aayaati liqawmiñy-yooqinoon.

وقال الذين لا يعلمون لولا
يكلمنا الله او تاتينا اية كذلك
قال الذين من قبلهم مثل قولهم
تشابهت قلوبهم قد بينا الايت
لقوم يوقنون ﴿١١٨﴾

119. We have sent you (Muhammad) for a genuine purpose to proclaim glad news and warnings. You will not be blamed for the dwellers of the blazing fire.

119. Innaaa arsalnaaka bilhaqqi basheerañw-wa nazeerañw-wa laa tus'alu 'an Aṣḥaabil-Jaḥeem.

إِنَّآ أَرْسَلْنٰكَ بِالْحَقِّ بَشِيرًا وَّنَذِيرًا ۙ
وَّلَا تُسْئَلُ عَنْ أَصْحٰبِ الْجَحِيمِ ﴿١١٩﴾

120. The Jews and Christians will never be pleased with you unless you follow their faith. (Muhammad) tell them that the guidance of Allah is the only true guidance. If you follow their wishes after all the knowledge that has come to you, you will no longer have Allah as your guardian and helper."

120. Wa lan tarḍaa 'ankal-Yahoodu wa lan-Naṣaaraa ḥattaa tattabi'a millatahum; qul inna hudal-laahi huwal-hudaa; wa la'init-taba'ta ahwaaa'ahum ba'dal-lazee jaaa'aka minal-'ilmi maa laka minal-laahi miñw- waliyyiñw-wa laa naṣeer.

وَلَنْ تَرْضٰى عَنْكَ الْيَهُودُ وَلَا
النَّصٰرٰى حَتّٰى تَتَّبِعَ مِلَّتَهُمْ ۗ قُلْ
إِنَّ هُدَى اللّٰهِ هُوَ الْهُدٰى ۗ وَلَئِنِ
اتَّبَعْتَ أَهْوَآءَهُمْ بَعْدَ الَّذِي
جَآءَكَ مِنَ الْعِلْمِ ۙ مَا لَكَ مِنَ
اللّٰهِ مِنْ وَّلِيٍّ وَّلَا نَصِيرٍ ﴿١٢٠﴾

وقف منزل

121. Those (of the People of the Book) who have received Our Book (Quran), and read it thoroughly, believe in it. Those who disbelieve the Book certainly suffer a (great) loss.

121. Allazeena aataynaahumul-Kitaaba yatloonahoo ḥaqqa tilaawatiheee ulaaa'ika yu'minoona bih; wa mañy-yakfur bihee fa-ulaaa'ika humul-khaasiroon.

الَّذِينَ اٰتَيْنٰهُمُ الْكِتٰبَ يَتْلُونَهٗ حَقَّ
تِلَاوَتِهٖ ۗ أُولٰٓئِكَ يُؤْمِنُونَ بِهٖ ۗ وَمَنْ
يَّكْفُرْ بِهٖ فَأُولٰٓئِكَ هُمُ الْخٰسِرُونَ ﴿١٢١﴾ ع

122. Children of Israel, recall My favor to you and the preference that I gave to you over all the other nations (of your time then).

122. Yaa Baneee-Israaa'eelaz-kuroo ni'matiyal-lateee an'amtu 'alaykum wa annee faḍḍaltukum 'alal-'aalameen.

يٰبَنِيٓ إِسْرَآءِيلَ اذْكُرُوا نِعْمَتِيَ
الَّتِيٓ أَنْعَمْتُ عَلَيْكُمْ وَأَنِّي فَضَّلْتُكُمْ
عَلَى الْعٰلَمِينَ ﴿١٢٢﴾

123. Have fear of the day when every soul will be responsible for itself, no ransom will be accepted for it, no intercession will be of any benefit to it and no one will receive any help.

123. Wattaqoo Yawmal-laa tajzee nafsun 'an nafsin shay' añw-wa laa yuqbalu minhaa 'adluñw-wa laa tanfa'uhaa shafaa'atuñw-wa laa hum yunṣaroon.

وَاتَّقُوا يَوْمًا لَّا تَجْزِي نَفْسٌ
عَنْ نَّفْسٍ شَيْئًا وَّلَا يُقْبَلُ مِنْهَا
عَدْلٌ وَّلَا تَنْفَعُهَا شَفَاعَةٌ وَّلَا
هُمْ يُنْصَرُونَ ﴿١٢٣﴾

124. When his Lord tested Abraham's faith (by His words) and he satisfied the test, He said, "I am appointing you as the leader of mankind." Abraham asked, "Will this leadership also continue through my descendants?" The Lord replied, "The unjust do not have the right to exercise My authority."

124. Wa izib-talaaa Ibraaheema Rabbuhoo bi-Kalimaatin fa-atammahunna qaala Innee jaa'iluka linnaasi Imaaman qaala wa min zurriyyatee qaala laa yanaalu 'Ahdiz-zaalimeen.

وَإِذِ ابْتَلٰٓى إِبْرٰهٖمَ رَبُّهٗ بِكَلِمٰتٍ
فَأَتَمَّهُنَّ ۗ قَالَ إِنِّي جَاعِلُكَ لِلنَّاسِ
إِمَامًا ۗ قَالَ وَمِنْ ذُرِّيَّتِي ۗ قَالَ
لَا يَنَالُ عَهْدِي الظّٰلِمِينَ ﴿١٢٤﴾

125. We made the house (in Makkah) as a place of refuge and sanctuary for men. (People), adopt the place where Abraham stood as a place for prayer. We advised Abraham and Ishmael to keep My house clean for the pilgrims, the worshippers, and those who bow

125. Wa iz ja'alnal-Bayta masaabatal-linnaasi wa amnaa; wattakhizoo mim-Maqaami Ibraaheema muṣallaa; wa 'ahidnaaa ilaaa Ibraaheema wa Ismaa'eela an ṭahhiraa Baytiya liṭṭaaa'i-feena

وَإِذْ جَعَلْنَا الْبَيْتَ مَثَابَةً لِّلنَّاسِ
وَأَمْنًا ۗ وَاتَّخِذُوا مِنْ مَّقَامِ
إِبْرٰهٖمَ مُصَلًّى ۗ وَعَهِدْنَآ إِلٰٓى إِبْرٰهٖمَ وَ
إِسْمٰعِيلَ أَنْ طَهِّرَا بَيْتِيَ لِلطَّآئِفِينَ

down and prostrate themselves in worship.

wal'aakifeena warrukka'is-sujood.

وَالْعٰكِفِيْنَ وَالرُّكَّعِ السُّجُوْدِ ﴿١٢٥﴾

126. When Abraham prayed to the Lord saying, "Lord, make this town a place of security and provide those in the town who believe in Allah and the Day of Judgment with plenty," Allah replied, "I shall allow those who hide the truth to enjoy themselves for a while. Then I shall drive them into the torment of hellfire, a terrible destination!"

126. Wa iz qaala Ibraaheemu Rabbij-'al haazaa baladan aaminañw-warzuq ahlahoo minas-samaraati man aamana minhum billaahi wal-Yawmil Aakhiri qaala wa man kafara fa-umatti'uhoo qaleelan summa adṭarruhooo ilaa 'azaabin-Naari wa bi'sal maṣeer.

وَاِذْ قَالَ اِبْرٰهٖمُ رَبِّ اجْعَلْ هٰذَا بَلَدًا
اٰمِنًا وَّارْزُقْ اَهْلَهٗ مِنَ الثَّمَرٰتِ مَنْ
اٰمَنَ مِنْهُمْ بِاللّٰهِ وَالْيَوْمِ الْاٰخِرِ ؕ
قَالَ وَمَنْ كَفَرَ فَاُمَتِّعُهٗ قَلِيْلًا
ثُمَّ اَضْطَرُّهٗۤ اِلٰى عَذَابِ النَّارِ ؕ وَ
بِئْسَ الْمَصِيْرُ ﴿١٢٦﴾

127. While Abraham and Ishmael were raising the foundation of the house, they prayed, "Lord, accept our labor. You are All-hearing and All-knowing.

127. Wa iz yarfa'u Ibraa-heemul-qawaa'ida minal-Bayti wa Ismaa'eelu Rabbanaa taqabbal minnaaa innaka Antas-Samee'ul-'Aleem.

وَاِذْ يَرْفَعُ اِبْرٰهٖمُ الْقَوَاعِدَ مِنَ
الْبَيْتِ وَاِسْمٰعِيْلُ ؕ رَبَّنَا تَقَبَّلْ مِنَّا ؕ
اِنَّكَ اَنْتَ السَّمِيْعُ الْعَلِيْمُ ﴿١٢٧﴾

128. Lord, make us good Muslims (one who submits himself to Allah) and from our descendants make a good Muslim nation. Teach us the rules of worship and accept our repentance; You are All-forgiving and All-merciful.

128. Rabbanaa waj'alnaa muslimayni laka wa min zurriyyatinaaa ummatam-muslimatal-laka wa arinaa manaasikanaa wa tub 'alaynaaa innaka Antat-Tawwaabur-Raḥeem.

رَبَّنَا وَاجْعَلْنَا مُسْلِمَيْنِ لَكَ وَمِنْ
ذُرِّيَّتِنَاۤ اُمَّةً مُّسْلِمَةً لَّكَ ۪ وَاَرِنَا
مَنَاسِكَنَا وَتُبْ عَلَيْنَا ۚ اِنَّكَ اَنْتَ
التَّوَّابُ الرَّحِيْمُ ﴿١٢٨﴾

129. Lord, send to them (our descendants) a Messenger of their own who will recite to them Your revelations, teach them the Book, give them wisdom, and purify them. You alone are the Majestic and the Most Wise."

129. Rabbanaa wab'as feehim Rasoolam-minhum yatloo 'alayhim Aayaatika wa yu'allimuhumul-Kitaaba wal-Ḥikmata wa yuzakkeehim; innaka Antal-'Azeezul-Ḥakeem.

رَبَّنَا وَابْعَثْ فِيْهِمْ رَسُوْلًا مِّنْهُمْ
يَتْلُوْا عَلَيْهِمْ اٰيٰتِكَ وَيُعَلِّمُهُمُ
الْكِتٰبَ وَالْحِكْمَةَ وَيُزَكِّيْهِمْ ؕ اِنَّكَ
اَنْتَ الْعَزِيْزُ الْحَكِيْمُ ﴿١٢٩﴾ ع ١٥

130. No one turns away from Abraham's Tradition except one who makes a fool of himself. To Abraham We have granted distinction in this world and in the life hereafter he will be among the righteous ones.

130. Wa mañy-yarghabu 'am-Millati Ibraaheema illaa man safiha nafsah; wa laqadiṣ-ṭafaynaahu fid-dunyaa wa innahoo fil-Aakhirati laminaṣ-ṣaaliḥeen.

وَمَنْ يَّرْغَبُ عَنْ مِّلَّةِ اِبْرٰهٖمَ اِلَّا
مَنْ سَفِهَ نَفْسَهٗ ؕ وَلَقَدِ اصْطَفَيْنٰهُ
فِى الدُّنْيَا ۚ وَاِنَّهٗ فِى الْاٰخِرَةِ
لَمِنَ الصّٰلِحِيْنَ ﴿١٣٠﴾

131. When Allah commanded Abraham to submit, he replied, "I have submitted myself to the Lord of the universe."

131. Iz qaala lahoo Rabbuhooo aslim qaala aslamtu li-Rabbil-'aalameen.

اِذْ قَالَ لَهٗ رَبُّهٗۤ اَسْلِمْ ۙ قَالَ
اَسْلَمْتُ لِرَبِّ الْعٰلَمِيْنَ ﴿١٣١﴾

132. Abraham left this legacy to his sons and, in turn, so did Jacob, saying, "Allah has chosen this religion for you. You must not leave this world

132. Wa waṣṣaa bihaaa Ibraa-heemu baneehi wa Ya'qoob; yaa baniyya innal laahaṣ-ṭafaa lakumud-deena

وَوَصّٰى بِهَاۤ اِبْرٰهٖمُ بَنِيْهِ وَيَعْقُوْبُ ؕ
يٰبَنِىَّ اِنَّ اللّٰهَ اصْطَفٰى لَكُمُ الدِّيْنَ

unless you are a Muslim (submitted to the Lord of the Universe)."

falaa tamootunna illaa wa antum muslimoon.

فَلَا تَمُوتُنَّ إِلَّا وَأَنتُم مُّسْلِمُونَ ﴿١٣٢﴾

133. Were you (believers) there when death approached Jacob? When he asked his sons, "Whom will you worship after my death?" They replied, "We will worship your Lord, the Lord of your fathers, Abraham, Ishmael, and Isaac. He is the only Lord, and to Him we have submitted ourselves."

133. Am kuntum shuhadaaa'a iz̲ ḥaḍara Ya'qoobal-mawtu iz̲ qaala libaneehi maa ta'budoona mim ba'dee qaaloo na'budu ilaahaka wa ilaaha aabaaa'ika Ibraaheema wa Ismaa'eela wa Isḥaaqa Ilaahañw-waaḥidañw-wa naḥnu lahoo muslimoon.

أَمْ كُنتُمْ شُهَدَآءَ إِذْ حَضَرَ يَعْقُوبَ
الْمَوْتُ إِذْ قَالَ لِبَنِيهِ مَا تَعْبُدُونَ
مِنۢ بَعْدِي قَالُوا نَعْبُدُ إِلَٰهَكَ وَإِلَٰهَ
آبَآئِكَ إِبْرَٰهِيمَ وَإِسْمَٰعِيلَ وَإِسْحَٰقَ
إِلَٰهًا وَٰحِدًا وَنَحْنُ لَهُۥ مُسْلِمُونَ ﴿١٣٣﴾

134. That nation (children of Abraham) is gone. They have reaped what they sowed and the same applies to you. You are not responsible for their deeds.

134. Tilka ummatun qad khalat lahaa maa kasabat wa lakum maa kasabtum wa laa tus'aloona 'ammaa kaanoo ya'maloon.

تِلْكَ أُمَّةٌ قَدْ خَلَتْ لَهَا مَا كَسَبَتْ
وَلَكُم مَّا كَسَبْتُمْ وَلَا تُسْـَٔلُونَ
عَمَّا كَانُوا يَعْمَلُونَ ﴿١٣٤﴾

135. The Jews and the Christians have asked the Muslims to accept their faith to have the right guidance. (Muhammad), tell them, "We would rather follow the upright religion of Abraham who was not a pagan."

135. Wa qaaloo koonoo Hoodan aw Naṣaaraa tahtadoo; qul bal Millata Ibraaheema Ḥaneefaa; wa maa kaana minal mush-rikeen.

وَقَالُوا كُونُوا هُودًا أَوْ نَصَٰرَىٰ تَهْتَدُوا
قُلْ بَلْ مِلَّةَ إِبْرَٰهِيمَ حَنِيفًا وَمَا
كَانَ مِنَ الْمُشْرِكِينَ ﴿١٣٥﴾

136. (Muslims), say, "We believe in Allah and what He has revealed to us and to Abraham, Ishmael, Isaac, and their descendants, and what was revealed to Moses, Jesus, and the Prophets from their Lord. We make no distinction among them and to Allah we have submitted ourselves."

136. Qoolooo aamannaa billaahi wa maaa unzila ilaynaa wa maaa unzila ilaaa Ibraaheema wa Ismaa'eela wa Isḥaaqa wa Ya'qooba wal-Asbaaṭi wa maaa ootiya Moosaa wa 'Eesaa wa maaa ootiyan-Nabiyyoona mir-Rabbihim laa nufarriqu bayna aḥadim-minhum wa naḥnu lahoo muslimoon.

قُولُوٓا آمَنَّا بِاللَّهِ وَمَآ أُنزِلَ إِلَيْنَا
وَمَآ أُنزِلَ إِلَىٰٓ إِبْرَٰهِيمَ وَإِسْمَٰعِيلَ
وَإِسْحَٰقَ وَيَعْقُوبَ وَالْأَسْبَاطِ وَمَآ
أُوتِيَ مُوسَىٰ وَعِيسَىٰ وَمَآ أُوتِيَ
النَّبِيُّونَ مِن رَّبِّهِمْ لَا نُفَرِّقُ بَيْنَ
أَحَدٍ مِّنْهُمْ وَنَحْنُ لَهُۥ مُسْلِمُونَ ﴿١٣٦﴾

137. If they believe in all that you believe, they achieve the right guidance, but if they turn away, they enter in disbelief. Allah is a sufficient defender for you against them; He is All-hearing and All-knowing.

137. Fa-in aamanoo bimis̲li maaa aamantum bihee faqadih-tadaw wa-in tawallaw fa-innamaa hum fee shiqaaq; fasayakfeekahumul-laah; wa Huwas-Samee'ul-'Aleem.

فَإِنْ آمَنُوا بِمِثْلِ مَآ آمَنتُم بِهِۦ فَقَدِ
اهْتَدَوا وَّإِن تَوَلَّوْا فَإِنَّمَا هُمْ فِي
شِقَاقٍ فَسَيَكْفِيكَهُمُ اللَّهُ
وَهُوَ السَّمِيعُ الْعَلِيمُ ﴿١٣٧﴾

138. Say, "Coloring (Islam) is made by Allah. No one makes a better coloring than Allah does and we (Muslims) worship Him."

138. Ṣibghatal-laahi wa man aḥsanu minal-laahi ṣibghatañw-wa naḥnu lahoo 'aabidoon.

صِبْغَةَ اللَّهِ وَمَنْ أَحْسَنُ مِنَ اللَّهِ
صِبْغَةً وَنَحْنُ لَهُۥ عَٰبِدُونَ ﴿١٣٨﴾

139. (Muhammad), ask the People of the Book, "Why should you argue with us about Allah, Who is our Lord as well as yours,

139. Qul atuḥaaajjoonanaa fil-laahi wa Huwa Rabbunaa wa Rabbukum wa lanaaa a'maa-lunaa wa lakum

قُلْ أَتُحَآجُّونَنَا فِي اللَّهِ وَهُوَ رَبُّنَا
وَرَبُّكُمْ وَلَنَآ أَعْمَٰلُنَا وَلَكُمْ

when we are sincere in our belief in Allah?

a'maalukum wa naḥnu lahoo mukhliṣoon.

اَعۡمَالُكُمۡ‌ۚ وَنَحۡنُ لَهٗ مُخۡلِصُوۡنَ ﴿۱۳۹﴾

140. Everyone will be responsible for his own deeds. Do you (People of the Book) claim that Abraham, Ishmael, Isaac, and their descendants were Jews or Christians?" Ask them, "Who possesses greater knowledge, you or Allah? Who is more unjust than one who refuses to testify to the truth that Allah has given to him?" Allah is not unaware of what you do.

140. Am taqooloona-inna Ibraaheema wa Ismaa'eela wa Isḥaaqa wa Ya'qooba wal Asbaaṭa kaanoo Hoodan aw Naṣaaraa; qul 'a-antum a'lamu amil-laah; wa man aẓlamu mimman katama shahaadatan 'indahoo minallaah; wa mal-laahu bighaafilin 'ammaa ta'maloon.

اَمۡ تَقُوۡلُوۡنَ اِنَّ اِبۡرٰهٖمَ وَاِسۡمٰعِيۡلَ
وَاِسۡحٰقَ وَيَعۡقُوۡبَ وَالۡاَسۡبَاطَ
كَانُوۡا هُوۡدًا اَوۡ نَصٰرٰى‌ؕ قُلۡ ءَاَنۡتُمۡ
اَعۡلَمُ اَمِ اللّٰهُ‌ؕ وَمَنۡ اَظۡلَمُ مِمَّنۡ
كَتَمَ شَهَادَةً عِنۡدَهٗ مِنَ اللّٰهِ‌ؕ وَمَا
اللّٰهُ بِغَافِلٍ عَمَّا تَعۡمَلُوۡنَ ﴿۱۴۰﴾

141. That nation is gone, they have reaped what they sowed and the same applies to you. You are not responsible for their deeds.

141. Tilka ummatun qad khalat lahaa maa kasabat wa lakum maa kasabtum wa laa tus'aloona 'ammaa kaanoo ya'maloon.

تِلۡكَ اُمَّةٌ قَدۡ خَلَتۡ‌ۚ لَهَا مَا كَسَبَتۡ
وَلَكُمۡ مَّا كَسَبۡتُمۡ‌ۚ وَلَا تُسۡـَٔلُوۡنَ عَمَّا
كَانُوۡا يَعۡمَلُوۡنَ ﴿۱۴۱﴾ ع

142. Fools will soon say, "What has made them (Muslims) change the direction to which they had been facing during their prayers (the qibla)?"
(Muhammad), tell them, "Both the East and West belong to Allah and He guides (whomever He wants) to the right direction."

142. Sayaqoolus-sufahaaa'u minan-naasi maa wallaahum 'an Qiblatihimul-latee kaanoo 'alayhaa; qul lillaahil mashriqu walmaghrib; yahdee mañy-yashaaa'u ilaa Ṣiraaṭim-Mustaqeem.

سَيَقُوۡلُ السُّفَهَآءُ مِنَ النَّاسِ
مَا وَلّٰٮهُمۡ عَنۡ قِبۡلَتِهِمُ الَّتِىۡ
كَانُوۡا عَلَيۡهَا‌ؕ قُلْ لِّلّٰهِ الۡمَشۡرِقُ وَ
الۡمَغۡرِبُ‌ؕ يَهۡدِىۡ مَنۡ يَّشَآءُ اِلٰى
صِرَاطٍ مُّسۡتَقِيۡمٍ ﴿۱۴۲﴾

143. We have made you (true Muslims) a moderate nation so that you could be an example for all people and the Prophet an example for you.
The direction which you had been facing during your prayers (the qibla) was made only in order that We would know who would follow the Messenger and who would turn away.
It was a hard test, but not for those to whom Allah had given guidance. Allah did not want to make your previous prayers worthless; Allah is compassionate and All-merciful.

143. Wa kaẕaalika ja'alnaakum ummatañw-wasaṭal-litakoonoo shuhadaaa'a 'alan-naasi wa yakoonar-Rasoolu 'alaykum shaheedaa; wa maa ja'alnal-Qiblatal-latee kunta 'alayhaaa illaa lina'lama mañy-yattabi'ur-Rasoola mimmañy-yanqalibu 'alaa 'aqibayh; wa in kaanat lakabeeratan illaa 'alal-laẕeena hadal-laah; wa maa kaanal-laahu liyuḍee'a eemaanakum; innal-laaha binnaasi la-Ra'oofur-Raḥeem.

وَكَذٰلِكَ جَعَلۡنٰكُمۡ اُمَّةً وَّسَطًا
لِّتَكُوۡنُوۡا شُهَدَآءَ عَلَى النَّاسِ
وَيَكُوۡنَ الرَّسُوۡلُ عَلَيۡكُمۡ شَهِيۡدًا‌ؕ
وَمَا جَعَلۡنَا الۡقِبۡلَةَ الَّتِىۡ كُنۡتَ عَلَيۡهَآ
اِلَّا لِنَعۡلَمَ مَنۡ يَّتَّبِعُ الرَّسُوۡلَ مِمَّنۡ
يَّنۡقَلِبُ عَلٰى عَقِبَيۡهِ‌ؕ وَاِنۡ كَانَتۡ
لَكَبِيۡرَةً اِلَّا عَلَى الَّذِيۡنَ هَدَى اللّٰهُ‌ؕ
وَمَا كَانَ اللّٰهُ لِيُضِيۡعَ اِيۡمَانَكُمۡ‌ؕ اِنَّ
اللّٰهَ بِالنَّاسِ لَرَءُوۡفٌ رَّحِيۡمٌ ﴿۱۴۳﴾

144. We certainly saw you (Muhammad) often turn your face to the sky, so We shall instruct you to face a qibla that you will like.

144. Qad naraa taqalluba wajhika fis-samaaa'i falanuwalliyannaka Qiblatan tarḍaahaa; fawalli

قَدۡ نَرٰى تَقَلُّبَ وَجۡهِكَ فِى السَّمَآءِ‌ۚ
فَلَنُوَلِّيَنَّكَ قِبۡلَةً تَرۡضٰٮهَا‌ فَوَلِّ

(Muhammad), during prayer, turn your face toward the Sacred Mosque (in Makkah). Muslims, also, wherever you are, during your prayers, turn your faces toward the Sacred Mosque.
The People of the Book certainly know that this command (to change the qibla) is truly from their Lord. Allah is not unaware of what they do.

wajhaka shaṭral-Masjidil-Ḥaraam; wa ḥaysu maa kuntum fawalloo wujoohakum shaṭrah; wa innal-lazeena ootul-Kitaaba laya'lamoona annahul-ḥaqqu mir-Rabbihim; wa mal-laahu bighaafilin 'ammaa ya'maloon.

وَجْهَكَ شَطْرَ الْمَسْجِدِ الْحَرَامِ ۚ وَحَيْثُ
مَا كُنْتُمْ فَوَلُّوا وُجُوهَكُمْ شَطْرَهُ ۗ
وَإِنَّ الَّذِينَ أُوتُوا الْكِتَابَ لَيَعْلَمُونَ
أَنَّهُ الْحَقُّ مِنْ رَبِّهِمْ ۗ وَمَا اللَّهُ
بِغَافِلٍ عَمَّا يَعْمَلُونَ ﴿١٤٤﴾

145. Even if you were to bring all kinds of authoritative proof to the People of the Book, they still would not accept your qibla, nor would you accept theirs, nor would they accept each other's.
Were you to follow their desires after all the knowledge that had come to you, you would certainly be one of the unjust.

145. Wa la'in ataytal-lazeena ootul-Kitaaba bikulli Aayatim-maa tabi'oo Qiblatak; wa maaa anta bitaabi'in-Qiblatahum; wa maa ba'ḍuhum bitaabi'in Qiblata ba'ḍ; wa la'init-taba'ta ahwaaa'ahum mim ba'di maa jaaa'aka minal-'ilmi innaka izal-laminaẓ-ẓaalimeen.

وَلَئِنْ أَتَيْتَ الَّذِينَ أُوتُوا الْكِتَابَ
بِكُلِّ آيَةٍ مَا تَبِعُوا قِبْلَتَكَ ۚ وَمَا
أَنْتَ بِتَابِعٍ قِبْلَتَهُمْ ۚ وَمَا بَعْضُهُمْ
بِتَابِعٍ قِبْلَةَ بَعْضٍ ۚ وَلَئِنِ اتَّبَعْتَ
أَهْوَاءَهُمْ مِنْ بَعْدِ مَا جَاءَكَ مِنَ
الْعِلْمِ ۙ إِنَّكَ إِذًا لَمِنَ الظَّالِمِينَ ﴿١٤٥﴾ وقف لازم

146. Those, to whom We have given the Book (Bible), know you (Muhammad) just as a well as they know their sons. It is certain that some of them deliberately hide the truth.

146. Allazeena-aataynaahumul Kitaaba ya'rifoonahoo kamaa ya'rifoona abnaaa'ahum wa inna fareeqam-minhum layaktumoonal-ḥaqqa wa hum ya'lamoon.

الَّذِينَ آتَيْنَاهُمُ الْكِتَابَ يَعْرِفُونَهُ
كَمَا يَعْرِفُونَ أَبْنَاءَهُمْ ۖ وَإِنَّ فَرِيقًا
مِنْهُمْ لَيَكْتُمُونَ الْحَقَّ وَهُمْ يَعْلَمُونَ ﴿١٤٦﴾ وقف منزل

147. Never doubt that the essence of truth comes from your Lord.

147. Alḥaqqu mir-Rabbika falaa takoonanna minal-mumtareen.

الْحَقُّ مِنْ رَبِّكَ ۖ فَلَا تَكُونَنَّ مِنَ
الْمُمْتَرِينَ ﴿١٤٧﴾ ع ١٦

148. Everyone pursues his goal. Compete with each other in performing good deeds. Wherever you are, Allah will bring you all together. Allah has power over all things.

148. Wa likulliñw-wijhatun huwa muwalleehaa fastabiqul-khayraat; ayna maa takoonoo ya-ti bikumullaahu jamee'aa; innal-laaha 'alaa kulli shay'in Qadeer.

وَلِكُلٍّ وِجْهَةٌ هُوَ مُوَلِّيهَا ۖ فَاسْتَبِقُوا
الْخَيْرَاتِ ۚ أَيْنَ مَا تَكُونُوا يَأْتِ بِكُمُ
اللَّهُ جَمِيعًا ۚ إِنَّ اللَّهَ عَلَىٰ كُلِّ شَيْءٍ
قَدِيرٌ ﴿١٤٨﴾ وقف النبي صلى الله عليه وآله وسلم ١٢

149. (Muhammad), wherever you go, turn your face toward the Sacred Mosque (in Makkah). This is the truth from your Lord, who is not unaware of what you do.

149. Wa min ḥaysu kharajta fawalli wajhaka shaṭral-Masjidil-Ḥaraami wa innahoo lalḥaqqu mir-Rabbik; wa mallaahu bighaafilin 'ammaa ta'maloon.

وَمِنْ حَيْثُ خَرَجْتَ فَوَلِّ وَجْهَكَ
شَطْرَ الْمَسْجِدِ الْحَرَامِ ۖ وَإِنَّهُ لَلْحَقُّ
مِنْ رَبِّكَ ۗ وَمَا اللَّهُ بِغَافِلٍ عَمَّا
تَعْمَلُونَ ﴿١٤٩﴾

149. (Muhammad), as you come out and from wherever you come out, turn your face to the Sacred Mosque. And wherever you

150. Wa min ḥaysu kharajta fawalli wajhaka shaṭral-Masjidil-Ḥaraam; wa ḥaysu maa

وَمِنْ حَيْثُ خَرَجْتَ فَوَلِّ وَجْهَكَ
شَطْرَ الْمَسْجِدِ الْحَرَامِ ۚ وَحَيْثُ مَا

(Muslims) are, turn your faces in the same direction so that no group of people, not even the unjust among them, can have any reason against you and so that I may establish My commandments for your people to have proper guidance. (The unjust may criticize you) but do not fear them, fear only Me.

151. As We have sent a Messenger from your own people to show you evidence about Me, to purify you from sins, to teach you the Book, give you wisdom and instruct you in that which you did not know,

152. therefore, remember Me and I shall remember you. Thank Me and do not hide the truth about Me.

153. Believers, help yourselves (in your affairs) through patience (fasting) and prayer; Allah is with those who have patience.

154. Do not consider those who are slain for the cause of Allah to be dead. They are alive but you are unaware of them.

155. We shall test you through fear, hunger, loss of life, property, and crops. (Muhammad), give glad news to the people who have patience

156. and in difficulty say, "We are the servants of Allah and to Him we shall all return."

157. It is they who will receive blessings and mercy from their Lord and who follow the right guidance.

158. Safa and Marwah (names of two places in Makkah) are reminders of Allah. It is no sin for one who visits the Sacred House (in Makkah) to walk seven times between (Safa and Marwah). Whoever, willingly, does a good deed in obedience to Allah will find Allah All-knowing and Fully Appreciative.

kuntum fawalloo wujoohakum shaṭrahoo li'allaa yakoona linnaasi 'alaykum ḥujjatun illal-la<u>z</u>eena ẓalamoo minhum falaa takhshawhum wakhshawnee wa li-utimma ni'matee 'alaykum wa la'allakum tahtadoon.

151. Kamaaa arsalnaa feekum Rasoolam-minkum yatloo 'alaykum Aayaatinaa wa yuzakkeekum wa yu'allimukumul-Kitaaba wal-Ḥikmata wa yu'allimukum maa lam takoonoo ta'lamoon.

152. Fa<u>z</u>kurooneee a<u>z</u>kurkum washkuroo lee wa laa takfuroon.

153. Yaaa ayyuhal-la<u>z</u>eena aamanus-ta'eenoo biṣṣabri waṣ-Ṣalaah; innal-laaha ma'aṣ-ṣaabireen.

154. Wa laa taqooloo limañy-yuqtalu fee sabeelil-laahi amwaat; bal aḥyaaa'uñw-wa laakil-laa tash'uroon.

155. Wa lanablu-wannakum bishay'im-minal-khawfi waljoo'i wa naqṣim-minal-amwaali wal-anfusi was<u>s</u>amaraat; wa bashshiriṣ-ṣaabireen.

156. Alla<u>z</u>eena i<u>z</u>aaa aṣaabat-hum muṣeebatun qaalooo innaa lillaahi wa innaaa ilayhi raaji'oon.

157. Ulaaa'ika 'alayhim ṣalawaatum-mir-Rabbihim wa raḥmah; wa ulaaa'ika humul-muhtadoon.

158. Innaṣ-Ṣafaa wal-Marwata min sha'aaa'iril-laahi faman ḥajjal-Bayta awi'-tamara falaa junaaḥa 'alayhi añy-yaṭṭawwafa bihimaa; wa man taṭawwa'a khayran fa-innal-laaha Shaakirun 'Aleem.

كُنتُمْ فَوَلُّوا وُجُوهَكُمْ شَطْرَهُ لِئَلَّا
يَكُونَ لِلنَّاسِ عَلَيْكُمْ حُجَّةٌ
إِلَّا الَّذِينَ ظَلَمُوا مِنْهُمْ فَلَا
تَخْشَوْهُمْ وَاخْشَوْنِي وَلِأُتِمَّ نِعْمَتِي
عَلَيْكُمْ وَلَعَلَّكُمْ تَهْتَدُونَ ﴿١٥٠﴾
كَمَا أَرْسَلْنَا فِيكُمْ رَسُولًا مِّنكُمْ
يَتْلُوا عَلَيْكُمْ آيَاتِنَا وَيُزَكِّيكُمْ
وَيُعَلِّمُكُمُ الْكِتَابَ وَالْحِكْمَةَ
وَيُعَلِّمُكُم مَّا لَمْ تَكُونُوا تَعْلَمُونَ ﴿١٥١﴾
فَاذْكُرُونِي أَذْكُرْكُمْ وَاشْكُرُوا لِي
وَلَا تَكْفُرُونِ ﴿١٥٢﴾
يَا أَيُّهَا الَّذِينَ آمَنُوا اسْتَعِينُوا بِالصَّبْرِ
وَالصَّلَاةِ إِنَّ اللَّهَ مَعَ الصَّابِرِينَ ﴿١٥٣﴾
وَلَا تَقُولُوا لِمَن يُقْتَلُ فِي سَبِيلِ اللَّهِ
أَمْوَاتٌ بَلْ أَحْيَاءٌ وَلَٰكِن لَّا تَشْعُرُونَ ﴿١٥٤﴾
وَلَنَبْلُوَنَّكُم بِشَيْءٍ مِّنَ الْخَوْفِ وَالْجُوعِ
وَنَقْصٍ مِّنَ الْأَمْوَالِ وَالْأَنفُسِ
وَالثَّمَرَاتِ وَبَشِّرِ الصَّابِرِينَ ﴿١٥٥﴾
الَّذِينَ إِذَا أَصَابَتْهُم مُّصِيبَةٌ
قَالُوا إِنَّا لِلَّهِ وَإِنَّا إِلَيْهِ رَاجِعُونَ ﴿١٥٦﴾
أُولَٰئِكَ عَلَيْهِمْ صَلَوَاتٌ مِّن رَّبِّهِمْ وَ
رَحْمَةٌ وَأُولَٰئِكَ هُمُ الْمُهْتَدُونَ ﴿١٥٧﴾
إِنَّ الصَّفَا وَالْمَرْوَةَ مِن شَعَائِرِ
اللَّهِ فَمَنْ حَجَّ الْبَيْتَ أَوِ اعْتَمَرَ فَلَا
جُنَاحَ عَلَيْهِ أَن يَطَّوَّفَ بِهِمَا وَمَن
تَطَوَّعَ خَيْرًا فَإِنَّ اللَّهَ شَاكِرٌ عَلِيمٌ ﴿١٥٨﴾

عند المتاخرين ١٠ معانقة ٣ ع ١٨/٥ ٢

159. Those who hide the authoritative proofs and the guidance that We have revealed, after it has been made clear for the People of the Book, will be condemned by Allah and those who have the right to condemn.

159. Innal-lazeena yaktumoona maaa anzalnaa minal-bayyinaati walhudaa mim ba'di maa bayyannaahu linnaasi fil-Kitaab; ulaaa'ika yal'anuhumul-laahu wa yal'anuhumul-laa'inoon.

إِنَّ الَّذِينَ يَكْتُمُونَ مَا أَنزَلْنَا
مِنَ الْبَيِّنَاتِ وَالْهُدَىٰ مِن بَعْدِ
مَا بَيَّنَّاهُ لِلنَّاسِ فِي الْكِتَابِ ۙ أُولَٰئِكَ
يَلْعَنُهُمُ اللَّهُ وَيَلْعَنُهُمُ اللَّاعِنُونَ ﴿١٥٩﴾

160. However, I shall accept the repentance of those of them who repent for their sins, reform their manners, and preach the truth; I am All-forgiving and All-merciful.

160. Illal-lazeena taaboo wa aşlaḥoo wa bayyanoo fa-ulaaa'ika atoobu 'alayhim; wa Anat-Tawwaabur-Raḥeem.

إِلَّا الَّذِينَ تَابُوا وَأَصْلَحُوا وَبَيَّنُوا
فَأُولَٰئِكَ أَتُوبُ عَلَيْهِمْ ۚ وَأَنَا
التَّوَّابُ الرَّحِيمُ ﴿١٦٠﴾

161. Those who reject (Allah's revelations) and die with such attitude will be subject to the condemnation of Allah, the angels, and all people.

161. Innal-lazeena kafaroo wamaatoo wa hum kuffaarun ulaaa'ika 'alayhim la'natul-laahi walmalaaa'ikati wannaasi ajma'een.

إِنَّ الَّذِينَ كَفَرُوا وَمَاتُوا وَهُمْ
كُفَّارٌ أُولَٰئِكَ عَلَيْهِمْ لَعْنَةُ اللَّهِ
وَالْمَلَائِكَةِ وَالنَّاسِ أَجْمَعِينَ ﴿١٦١﴾

162. They will live condemned forever, have no relief from the torment, and no attention will be paid to them.

162. Khaalideena feehaa laa yukhaffafu 'anhumul-'azaabu wa laa hum yunẓaroon.

خَالِدِينَ فِيهَا ۖ لَا يُخَفَّفُ عَنْهُمُ
الْعَذَابُ وَلَا هُمْ يُنظَرُونَ ﴿١٦٢﴾

163. Your Lord is the only Lord. There is no 'llah (someone deserving to be worshipped) but He, the Beneficent and Merciful.

163. Wa ilaahukum Ilaahuñw-Waaḥid; laaa ilaaha illaa Huwar-Raḥmaanur-Raḥeem.

وَإِلَٰهُكُمْ إِلَٰهٌ وَاحِدٌ ۖ لَّا إِلَٰهَ إِلَّا
هُوَ الرَّحْمَٰنُ الرَّحِيمُ ﴿١٦٣﴾ ع

164. The creation of the heavens and the earth, the alternation of nights and days, the ships that sail in the sea for the benefit of the people, the water that Allah sends from the sky to revive the dead earth where He has scattered all kinds of animals, the winds of all directions, and the clouds rendered for service between the sky and the earth are all evidence (of His existence) for those who use their reason.

164. Inna fee khalqis-samaa-waati wal-arḍi wakhtilaafil-layli wannahaari walfulkil-latee tajree fil-baḥri bimaa yanfa'un-naasa wa maaa anzalal-laahu minas-samaaa'i mim-maaa'in fa-aḥyaa bihil-arḍa ba'da mawtihaa wa bas sa feehaa min kulli daaabbatiñw-wa taşreefir-riyaaḥi wassaḥaabil-musakh-khari baynas-samaaa'i wal-arḍi la-Aayaatil-liqawmiñy-ya'qiloon.

إِنَّ فِي خَلْقِ السَّمَاوَاتِ وَالْأَرْضِ وَ
اخْتِلَافِ اللَّيْلِ وَالنَّهَارِ وَالْفُلْكِ
الَّتِي تَجْرِي فِي الْبَحْرِ بِمَا يَنفَعُ
النَّاسَ وَمَا أَنزَلَ اللَّهُ مِنَ السَّمَاءِ
مِن مَّاءٍ فَأَحْيَا بِهِ الْأَرْضَ بَعْدَ
مَوْتِهَا وَبَثَّ فِيهَا مِن كُلِّ دَابَّةٍ
وَتَصْرِيفِ الرِّيَاحِ وَالسَّحَابِ
الْمُسَخَّرِ بَيْنَ السَّمَاءِ وَالْأَرْضِ
لَآيَاتٍ لِّقَوْمٍ يَعْقِلُونَ ﴿١٦٤﴾

165. Certain people consider other things equal to Allah and love them just as one should love Allah. However, the strongest of the believers' love is their love of Allah. Had the unjust been able to

165. Wa minan-naasi mañy-yattakhizu min doonil-laahi andaadañy-yuḥibboonahum kaḥubbil-laah; wallazeena aamanooo ashaddu ḥubbal-lillaah; wa law yaral-

وَمِنَ النَّاسِ مَن يَتَّخِذُ مِن دُونِ
اللَّهِ أَندَادًا يُحِبُّونَهُمْ كَحُبِّ اللَّهِ ۖ
وَالَّذِينَ آمَنُوا أَشَدُّ حُبًّا لِّلَّهِ ۗ وَلَوْ يَرَى

reflect upon their condition, when facing the torment, they would have had no doubt that to Allah belongs All-power and that Allah is stern in His retribution.

laz̲eena ẓalamooo iz̲ yarawnal 'az̲aab; annal-quwwata lillaahi jamee'añw-wa annallaaha shadeedul-'az̲aab.

الَّذِينَ ظَلَمُوا إِذْ يَرَوْنَ الْعَذَابَ
أَنَّ الْقُوَّةَ لِلَّهِ جَمِيعًا وَأَنَّ اللَّهَ
شَدِيدُ الْعَذَابِ ١٦٥

166. When the leaders see the torment and lose all their resources, they will denounce their followers.

166. Iz̲ tabarra-al-laz̲eenat-tubi'oo minal-laz̲eenattaba'oo wa ra-awul-'az̲aaba wa taqaṭṭa'at bihimul asbaab.

إِذْ تَبَرَّأَ الَّذِينَ اتُّبِعُوا مِنَ الَّذِينَ
اتَّبَعُوا وَرَأَوُا الْعَذَابَ وَتَقَطَّعَتْ
بِهِمُ الْأَسْبَابُ ١٦٦

167. The followers will say, "Had we had the chance we also would have denounced our leaders." That is how Allah will show them their regrettable deeds. They will not be able to escape from hellfire.

167. Wa qaalal-laz̲eenat-taba'oo law anna lanaa karratan fanatabarra-a minhum kamaa tabarra'oo minnaa; kaz̲aalika yureehimullaahu a'maalahum ḥasaraatin 'alayhim wa maa hum bikhaarijeena minan-Naar.

وَقَالَ الَّذِينَ اتَّبَعُوا لَوْ أَنَّ لَنَا
كَرَّةً فَنَتَبَرَّأَ مِنْهُمْ كَمَا تَبَرَّءُوا مِنَّا
كَذَٰلِكَ يُرِيهِمُ اللَّهُ أَعْمَالَهُمْ
حَسَرَاتٍ عَلَيْهِمْ وَمَا هُمْ بِخَارِجِينَ
مِنَ النَّارِ ١٦٧

168. People, eat of the good and lawful things on earth. Do not follow the footsteps of Satan; he is clearly your enemy.

168. Yaaa ayyuhan-naasu kuloo mimmaa fil-arḍi ḥalaalan ṭayyibañw-wa laa tattabi'oo khuṭuwaatish-Shayṭaan; innahoo lakum 'aduwwum-mubeen.

يَا أَيُّهَا النَّاسُ كُلُوا مِمَّا فِي الْأَرْضِ
حَلَالًا طَيِّبًا وَلَا تَتَّبِعُوا خُطُوَاتِ
الشَّيْطَانِ إِنَّهُ لَكُمْ عَدُوٌّ مُبِينٌ ١٦٨

169. He tries to make you do evil and shameful things and speak against Allah without knowledge.

169. Innamaa ya-murukum bissooo'i walfaḥshaaa'i wa an taqooloo 'alal-laahi maa laa ta'lamoon.

إِنَّمَا يَأْمُرُكُمْ بِالسُّوءِ وَالْفَحْشَاءِ
وَأَنْ تَقُولُوا عَلَى اللَّهِ مَا لَا تَعْلَمُونَ ١٦٩

170. When they (people) are asked to follow the revelations of Allah, they say, "We would rather follow what our fathers have followed," even though their fathers had no understanding and could not find the true guidance.

170. Wa iz̲aa qeela lahumut-tabi'oo maaa-anzalal-laahu qaaloo bal nattabi'u maaa alfaynaa 'alayhi aabaaa'anaaa; awalaw kaana aabaaa'uhum laa ya'qiloona shay'añw-wa laa yahtadoon.

وَإِذَا قِيلَ لَهُمُ اتَّبِعُوا مَا أَنْزَلَ
اللَّهُ قَالُوا بَلْ نَتَّبِعُ مَا أَلْفَيْنَا
عَلَيْهِ آبَاءَنَا أَوَلَوْ كَانَ آبَاؤُهُمْ
لَا يَعْقِلُونَ شَيْئًا وَلَا يَهْتَدُونَ ١٧٠

171. Preaching to unbelievers is like talking to someone who cannot hear anything except yells and shouts. They are deaf, dumb, and blind; they have no understanding.

171. Wa mas̲alul-laz̲eena kafaroo kamas̲alil-laz̲ee yan'iqu bimaa laa yasma'u illaa du'aaa'añw-wa nidaaa'aa; ṣummum-bukmun 'umyun fahum laa ya'qiloon.

وَمَثَلُ الَّذِينَ كَفَرُوا كَمَثَلِ
الَّذِي يَنْعِقُ بِمَا لَا يَسْمَعُ إِلَّا
دُعَاءً وَنِدَاءً صُمٌّ بُكْمٌ عُمْيٌ
فَهُمْ لَا يَعْقِلُونَ ١٧١

172. Believers, eat from the good things that We have given you and give thanks to Allah if you worship only Him.

172. Yaaa ayyuhal-laz̲eena aamanoo kuloo min ṭayyibaati maa razaqnaakum washkuroo

يَا أَيُّهَا الَّذِينَ آمَنُوا كُلُوا مِنْ
طَيِّبَاتِ مَا رَزَقْنَاكُمْ وَاشْكُرُوا

lillaahi in kuntum iyyaahu ta'budoon.

لِلّٰهِ اِنْ كُنْتُمْ اِيَّاهُ تَعْبُدُوْنَ ﴿١٧٢﴾

173. Allah has forbidden you to eat that which has not been properly slaughtered, blood, pork, and the flesh of any animal which has not been consecrated with a mention of the name of Allah. However, in an emergency, without the intention of transgression or repeating transgression, one will not be considered to have committed a sin. Allah is All-forgiving and All-merciful.

173. Innamaa ḥarrama 'alay-kumul-maytata waddama wa laḥmal-khinzeeri wa maaa uhilla bihee lighayril-laahi famaniḍ-ṭurra ghayra baaghiñw-wa laa 'aadin falaaa i<u>s</u>ma 'alayh; innal-laaha Ghafoorur-Raḥeem.

اِنَّمَا حَرَّمَ عَلَيْكُمُ الْمَيْتَةَ وَالدَّمَ
وَلَحْمَ الْخِنْزِيْرِ وَمَآ اُهِلَّ بِهٖ لِغَيْرِ
اللّٰهِ ۚ فَمَنِ اضْطُرَّ غَيْرَ بَاغٍ وَّلَا
عَادٍ فَلَآ اِثْمَ عَلَيْهِ ؕ اِنَّ اللّٰهَ
غَفُوْرٌ رَّحِيْمٌ ﴿١٧٣﴾

174. Those who receive small gains by hiding (certain facts) of the Book which Allah has revealed have, in fact, filled up their stomachs with fire. Allah will not speak with them on the Day of Judgment, nor will He purify them; instead, they will face a painful torment.

174. Innal-la<u>z</u>eena yaktu-moona maaa anzalal laahu minal-Kitaabi wa yashtaroona bihee <u>s</u>amanan qaleelan ulaaa'ika maa ya-kuloona fee buṭoonihim illan-Naara wa laa yukallimu-humul-laahu Yawmal Qiyaamati wa laa yuzakkeehim wa lahum 'a<u>z</u>aabun aleem.

اِنَّ الَّذِيْنَ يَكْتُمُوْنَ مَآ اَنْزَلَ اللّٰهُ
مِنَ الْكِتٰبِ وَيَشْتَرُوْنَ بِهٖ ثَمَنًا
قَلِيْلًا ۙ اُولٰٓئِكَ مَا يَاْكُلُوْنَ فِيْ
بُطُوْنِهِمْ اِلَّا النَّارَ وَلَا يُكَلِّمُهُمُ
اللّٰهُ يَوْمَ الْقِيٰمَةِ وَلَا يُزَكِّيْهِمْ ۚۖ
وَلَهُمْ عَذَابٌ اَلِيْمٌ ﴿١٧٤﴾

175. They have exchanged guidance for error and forgiveness for torment. What makes them seek the fire so earnestly (for they are doomed to be punished)?

175. Ulaaa'ikal-la<u>z</u>eenash-tarawuḍ-ḍalaalata bilhudaa wal'a<u>z</u>aaba bilmaghfirah; famaaa asbarahum 'alan-Naar.

اُولٰٓئِكَ الَّذِيْنَ اشْتَرَوُا الضَّلٰلَةَ
بِالْهُدٰى وَالْعَذَابَ بِالْمَغْفِرَةِ ۚ
فَمَآ اَصْبَرَهُمْ عَلَى النَّارِ ﴿١٧٥﴾

176. Allah has revealed the Book in all Truth and those who dispute it are filled with malice which has taken them far away from the truth.

176. <u>Z</u>aalika bi-annal-laaha nazzalal-Kitaaba bilḥaqq; wa innal-la<u>z</u>eenakh-talafoo fil-Kitaabi lafee shiqaaqim ba'eed.

ذٰلِكَ بِاَنَّ اللّٰهَ نَزَّلَ الْكِتٰبَ بِالْحَقِّ ؕ
وَاِنَّ الَّذِيْنَ اخْتَلَفُوْا فِى الْكِتٰبِ
لَفِيْ شِقَاقٍ بَعِيْدٍ ﴿١٧٦﴾ ع

الربع

177. Righteousness is not determined by facing East or West during prayer. Righteousness consists of the belief in Allah, the Day of Judgment, the angels, the Books of Allah, His Prophets; to give money for the love of Allah to relatives, orphans, the destitute, those who are on a journey and in urgent need of money, and beggars; to set free slaves and to be steadfast in prayer, to pay the religious tax (zakat) to fulfill one's promises, and to exercise

177. Laysal-birra an tuwalloo wujoohakum qibalal-mashriqi walmaghribi wa laakinnal birra man aamana billaahi wal-Yawmil-Aakhiri walmalaaa-'ikati wal-Kitaabi wan-Nabiy-yeena wa aatalmaala 'alaa ḥubbihee <u>z</u>awilqurbaa walyataa-maa walmasaakeena wabnas-sabeeli wassaaa'ileena wa firriqaab; wa aqaamaṣ-Ṣalaata wa aataz-Zakaata walmoofoona

لَيْسَ الْبِرَّ اَنْ تُوَلُّوْا وُجُوْهَكُمْ
قِبَلَ الْمَشْرِقِ وَالْمَغْرِبِ وَلٰكِنَّ
الْبِرَّ مَنْ اٰمَنَ بِاللّٰهِ وَالْيَوْمِ الْاٰخِرِ
وَالْمَلٰٓئِكَةِ وَالْكِتٰبِ وَالنَّبِيّٖنَ ۚ
وَاٰتَى الْمَالَ عَلٰى حُبِّهٖ ذَوِى الْقُرْبٰى
وَالْيَتٰمٰى وَالْمَسٰكِيْنَ وَابْنَ السَّبِيْلِ ۙ
وَالسَّآئِلِيْنَ وَفِى الرِّقَابِ ۚ وَاَقَامَ
الصَّلٰوةَ وَاٰتَى الزَّكٰوةَ ۚ وَالْمُوْفُوْنَ

patience in poverty, in distress, and in times of war. Such people who do these are truly righteous and pious.

bi'ahdihim izaa 'aahadoo waşşaabireena fil ba-saaa'i waddarraaa'i wa ḥeenal-ba-s; ulaaa'ikal-lazeena şadaqoo wa ulaaa'ika humul-muttaqoon.

بِعَهْدِهِمْ اِذَا عٰهَدُوْا ۚ وَالصّٰبِرِيْنَ
فِى الْبَاْسَآءِ وَالضَّرَّآءِ وَحِيْنَ الْبَاْسِ ؕ
اُولٰٓئِكَ الَّذِيْنَ صَدَقُوْا ؕ وَاُولٰٓئِكَ
هُمُ الْمُتَّقُوْنَ ﴿١٧٧﴾

178. Believers, in the case of murder the death penalty is the sanctioned retaliation: a free man for a free man, a slave for a slave, and a female for a female. However, if the convicted person receives pardon from the aggrieved party, the prescribed rules of compensation must be followed accordingly. This is a merciful alteration from your Lord. Whoever transgresses against it will face a painful punishment.

178. Yaaa ayyuhal-lazeena aamanoo kutiba 'alaykumul-qişaaşu fil-qatlaa alḥurru bilḥurri wal'abdu bil'abdi wal-unsaa bil-unsaa; faman 'ufiya lahoo min akheehi shay'un fattibaa'um-bilma'roofi wa-adaaa'un ilayhi bi-iḥsaan; zaalika takhfeefum-mir-Rabbikum wa-raḥmah; famani'-tadaa ba'da zaalika falahoo 'azaabun aleem.

يٰٓاَيُّهَا الَّذِيْنَ اٰمَنُوْا كُتِبَ عَلَيْكُمُ
الْقِصَاصُ فِى الْقَتْلٰى ؕ اَلْحُرُّ بِالْحُرِّ
وَالْعَبْدُ بِالْعَبْدِ وَالْاُنْثٰى بِالْاُنْثٰى ؕ
فَمَنْ عُفِىَ لَهٗ مِنْ اَخِيْهِ شَىْءٌ
فَاتِّبَاعٌۢ بِالْمَعْرُوْفِ وَاَدَآءٌ اِلَيْهِ
بِاِحْسَانٍ ؕ ذٰلِكَ تَخْفِيْفٌ مِّنْ
رَّبِّكُمْ وَرَحْمَةٌ ؕ فَمَنِ اعْتَدٰى
بَعْدَ ذٰلِكَ فَلَهٗ عَذَابٌ اَلِيْمٌ ﴿١٧٨﴾

179. O people of understanding, the laws of death penalty are for your life, so that perhaps you will observe piety before Allah.

179. Wa lakum fil-qişaaşi ḥayaatuñy-yaaa-ulil-albaabi la-'allakum tattaqoon.

وَلَكُمْ فِى الْقِصَاصِ حَيٰوةٌ يّٰٓاُولِى
الْاَلْبَابِ لَعَلَّكُمْ تَتَّقُوْنَ ﴿١٧٩﴾

180. If one of you facing death can leave a legacy, he should bequeath it to his parents and relatives, according to the law. This is the duty of the pious.

180. Kutiba 'alaykum izaa ḥaḍara aḥadakumul-mawtu in taraka khayranil-waşiyyatu lilwaalidayni wal-aqrabeena bilma'roofi ḥaqqan 'alal-mut-taqeen.

كُتِبَ عَلَيْكُمْ اِذَا حَضَرَ اَحَدَكُمُ
الْمَوْتُ اِنْ تَرَكَ خَيْرًا ۖۚ الْوَصِيَّةُ
لِلْوَالِدَيْنِ وَالْاَقْرَبِيْنَ بِالْمَعْرُوْفِ ۚ
حَقًّا عَلَى الْمُتَّقِيْنَ ﴿١٨٠﴾ ؕ

181. Whoever intentionally changes the will of a deceased person has committed a sin. Allah is All-hearing and All-knowing.

181. Famam-baddalahoo ba'da maa sami'ahoo fa-innamaaa ismuhoo 'alallazeena yubaddi-loonah; innallaaha Samee'un 'Aleem.

فَمَنْ بَدَّلَهٗ بَعْدَ مَا سَمِعَهٗ فَاِنَّمَآ
اِثْمُهٗ عَلَى الَّذِيْنَ يُبَدِّلُوْنَهٗ ؕ اِنَّ
اللّٰهَ سَمِيْعٌ عَلِيْمٌ ﴿١٨١﴾ ؕ

182. One who is afraid of the testator's deviations and sin and settles the matter among the parties involved has not committed a sin. Allah is All-forgiving and All-merciful.

182. Faman khaafa mim-mooşin janafan aw isman fa-aşlaḥa baynahum falaaa isma 'alayh; innal-laaha Ghafoorur-Raḥeem.

فَمَنْ خَافَ مِنْ مُّوْصٍ جَنَفًا اَوْ
اِثْمًا فَاَصْلَحَ بَيْنَهُمْ فَلَآ اِثْمَ
عَلَيْهِ ؕ اِنَّ اللّٰهَ غَفُوْرٌ رَّحِيْمٌ ﴿١٨٢﴾ ع ٢٢ ٦ ٢

183. O believers, fasting has been made mandatory for you as it was made mandatory for the people before you, so that you

183. Yaaa ayyuhal-lazeena aamanoo kutiba 'alaykumuş-Şiyaamu kamaa kutiba 'alal lazeena

يٰٓاَيُّهَا الَّذِيْنَ اٰمَنُوْا كُتِبَ عَلَيْكُمُ
الصِّيَامُ كَمَا كُتِبَ عَلَى الَّذِيْنَ

may have fear of Allah.

184. Fasting is only for a certain number of days. One who is sick or on a journey has to fast the same number of days at another time. Those who can afford redemption should feed a poor person. Good deeds performed on one's own initiative will be rewarded. However, fasting is better and will be rewarded. Would that you had known this!

185. The month of Ramadan is the month in which the Quran was revealed; a guide for the people, the most authoritative of all guidance and a criterion to discern right from wrong. Anyone of you who knows that the month of Ramadan has begun must start to fast. Those who are sick or are on a journey have to fast the same number of days at another time. Allah does not impose any hardship upon you. He wants you to have comfort so that you may complete the fast, glorify Allah for His having given you guidance, and perhaps you give Him thanks.

186. (Muhammad), if any of My servants ask you about Me, (tell them that the Lord says) "I certainly am near; I answer the prayers of those who pray." Allow My servants to ask Me for an answer to their call and believe in Me so that perhaps they may know the right direction.

187. It is made lawful for you, during the nights of fasting, to have carnal relations with your wives. They are your garments and you are their garments. Allah knew that you were deceiving yourselves. He relented toward you and forgave you. Now it is lawful for you to have carnal relations with your wives and follow what Allah has commanded. Eat and drink until

min qablikum la'allakum tattaqoon.

184. Ayyaamam-ma'doodaat; faman kaana minkum mareeḍan aw 'alaa safarin fa'iddatum-min ayyaamin ukhar; wa 'alal-lazeena yuṭeeqoonahoo fidyatun ṭa'aamu miskeenin faman taṭawwa'a khayran fahuwa khayrul-lahoo wa an taṣoomoo khayrul-lakum in kuntum ta'lamoon.

185. Shahru Ramaḍaanallazeee unzila feehil-Qur'aanu hudal-linnaasi wa bayyinaatim-minal-hudaa wal-furqaan; faman shahida minkumush-shahra falyaṣumhu wa man kaana mareeḍan aw 'alaa safarin fa'iddatum-min ayyaamin ukhar; yureedul-laahu bikumul-yusra wa laa yureedu bikumul-'usra wa litukmilul'iddata wa litukabbirul-laaha 'alaa maa hadaakum wa la'allakum tashkuroon.

186 Wa izaa sa-alaka 'ibaadee 'annee fa-innee qareeb; ujeebu da'wataddaa'i izaa da'aani falyastajeeboo lee walyu'minoo bee la'allahum yarshudoon.

187. Uḥilla lakum laylataṣ Ṣiyaamir-rafasu ilaa nisaaa'i-kum; hunna libaasullakum wa antum libaasullahunn; 'alimal-laahu annakum kuntum takhtaanoona anfusakum fataaba 'alaykum wa 'afaa 'ankum fal'aana baashiroo-hunna wabtaghoo maa katabal-laahu

مِن قَبۡلِكُمۡ لَعَلَّكُمۡ تَتَّقُونَ ١٨٣
أَيَّامٗا مَّعۡدُودَٰتٖۚ فَمَن كَانَ مِنكُم
مَّرِيضًا أَوۡ عَلَىٰ سَفَرٖ فَعِدَّةٞ مِّنۡ
أَيَّامٍ أُخَرَۚ وَعَلَى ٱلَّذِينَ يُطِيقُونَهُۥ
فِدۡيَةٞ طَعَامُ مِسۡكِينٖۖ فَمَن تَطَوَّعَ
خَيۡرٗا فَهُوَ خَيۡرٞ لَّهُۥۚ وَأَن تَصُومُواْ
خَيۡرٞ لَّكُمۡ إِن كُنتُمۡ تَعۡلَمُونَ ١٨٤
شَهۡرُ رَمَضَانَ ٱلَّذِيٓ أُنزِلَ فِيهِ
ٱلۡقُرۡءَانُ هُدٗى لِّلنَّاسِ وَبَيِّنَٰتٖ
مِّنَ ٱلۡهُدَىٰ وَٱلۡفُرۡقَانِۚ فَمَن شَهِدَ
مِنكُمُ ٱلشَّهۡرَ فَلۡيَصُمۡهُۖ وَمَن كَانَ
مَرِيضًا أَوۡ عَلَىٰ سَفَرٖ فَعِدَّةٞ مِّنۡ
أَيَّامٍ أُخَرَۗ يُرِيدُ ٱللَّهُ بِكُمُ ٱلۡيُسۡرَ
وَلَا يُرِيدُ بِكُمُ ٱلۡعُسۡرَ وَلِتُكۡمِلُواْ
ٱلۡعِدَّةَ وَلِتُكَبِّرُواْ ٱللَّهَ عَلَىٰ مَا هَدَىٰكُمۡ
وَلَعَلَّكُمۡ تَشۡكُرُونَ ١٨٥
وَإِذَا سَأَلَكَ عِبَادِي عَنِّي فَإِنِّي
قَرِيبٌۖ أُجِيبُ دَعۡوَةَ ٱلدَّاعِ إِذَا
دَعَانِۖ فَلۡيَسۡتَجِيبُواْ لِي وَلۡيُؤۡمِنُواْ بِي
لَعَلَّهُمۡ يَرۡشُدُونَ ١٨٦
أُحِلَّ لَكُمۡ لَيۡلَةَ ٱلصِّيَامِ ٱلرَّفَثُ
إِلَىٰ نِسَآئِكُمۡۚ هُنَّ لِبَاسٞ لَّكُمۡ
وَأَنتُمۡ لِبَاسٞ لَّهُنَّۗ عَلِمَ ٱللَّهُ
أَنَّكُمۡ كُنتُمۡ تَخۡتَانُونَ أَنفُسَكُمۡ
فَتَابَ عَلَيۡكُمۡ وَعَفَا عَنكُمۡۖ فَٱلۡـَٰٔنَ
بَٰشِرُوهُنَّ وَٱبۡتَغُواْ مَا كَتَبَ ٱللَّهُ

the white streak of dawn becomes distinguishable from darkness. Complete your fast, starting from dawn to dusk. It is not lawful to have carnal relations with your wives during 'itikaf (a certain form of worship) in the mosque. Such are the limits of the laws of Allah. Do not come close to transgressing them. Thus has Allah explained His evidence to men so that perhaps they will have fear of Allah.

lakum; wa kuloo washraboo ḥattaa yatabayyana lakumul-khayṭul abyaḍu minal-khayṭil-aswadi minal-fajri s̲umma atimmuṣ-Ṣiyaama ilal-layl; wa laa tubaashiroo-hunna wa antum 'aakifoona fil-masaajid; tilka ḥudoodul-laahi falaa taqraboo-haa; kaz̲aalika yubayyinul-laahu Aayaatihee linnaasi la'allahum yattaqoon.

لَكُمْ ۖ وَكُلُوْا وَاشْرَبُوْا حَتّٰى يَتَبَيَّنَ
لَكُمُ الْخَيْطُ الْاَبْيَضُ مِنَ الْخَيْطِ
الْاَسْوَدِ مِنَ الْفَجْرِ ۖ ثُمَّ اَتِمُّوا
الصِّيَامَ اِلَى الَّيْلِ ۚ وَلَا تُبَاشِرُوْهُنَّ
وَاَنْتُمْ عٰكِفُوْنَ ۙ فِي الْمَسٰجِدِ ۗ
تِلْكَ حُدُوْدُ اللّٰهِ فَلَا تَقْرَبُوْهَا ۗ
كَذٰلِكَ يُبَيِّنُ اللّٰهُ اٰيٰتِهٖ لِلنَّاسِ
لَعَلَّهُمْ يَتَّقُوْنَ ١٨٧

188. Do not use your property among yourselves in illegal ways and then deliberately bribe the rulers with your property so that you may wrongly acquire the property of (other) people.

188. Wa laa ta-kulooo amwaa-lakum baynakum bilbaaṭili wa tudloo bihaaa ilal-ḥukkaami lita-kuloo fareeqam min amwaalin-naasi bil-is̲mi wa antum ta'lamoon.

وَلَا تَاْكُلُوْٓا اَمْوَالَكُمْ بَيْنَكُمْ بِالْبَاطِلِ
وَتُدْلُوْا بِهَآ اِلَى الْحُكَّامِ لِتَاْكُلُوْا
فَرِيْقًا مِّنْ اَمْوَالِ النَّاسِ بِالْاِثْمِ
وَاَنْتُمْ تَعْلَمُوْنَ ١٨٨ ع ٢٣ ٧

189. (Muhammad), they ask you about the different phases of the moon. Tell them that they are there to indicate to people the phases of time and the pilgrimage season. It is not a righteous act to enter houses from the back. Righteousness is to be pious and enter the houses from the front door. Have fear of Allah so that perhaps you will have lasting happiness.

189. Yas'aloonaka 'anil-ahillati qul hiya mawaaqeetu linnaasi wal-Ḥajj; wa laysal-birru bi-an ta-tul-buyoota min ẓuhoorihaa wa laakinnal-birra manit-taqaa; wa-tul-buyoota min abwaa-bihaa; wattaqullaaha la'allakum tufliḥoon.

يَسْـَٔلُوْنَكَ عَنِ الْاَهِلَّةِ ۗ قُلْ هِيَ
مَوَاقِيْتُ لِلنَّاسِ وَالْحَجِّ ۗ وَلَيْسَ
الْبِرُّ بِاَنْ تَاْتُوا الْبُيُوْتَ مِنْ ظُهُوْرِهَا
وَلٰكِنَّ الْبِرَّ مَنِ اتَّقٰى ۚ وَاْتُوا الْبُيُوْتَ
مِنْ اَبْوَابِهَا ۖ وَاتَّقُوا اللّٰهَ لَعَلَّكُمْ
تُفْلِحُوْنَ ١٨٩

190. Fight, for the cause of Allah, those who fight you, but do not transgress, for Allah does not love the transgressors.

190. Wa qaatiloo fee sabeelil-laahil-laz̲eena yuqaatiloonakum wa laa ta'tadooo; innal-laaha laa yuḥibbul-mu'tadeen.

وَقَاتِلُوْا فِيْ سَبِيْلِ اللّٰهِ الَّذِيْنَ
يُقَاتِلُوْنَكُمْ وَلَا تَعْتَدُوْا ۗ اِنَّ
اللّٰهَ لَا يُحِبُّ الْمُعْتَدِيْنَ ١٩٠

191. Slay them wherever you may catch them and expel them from the place from which they expelled you. The sin of disbelief in Allah is greater than committing murder. Do not fight them in the vicinity of the Sacred Mosque in Makkah unless they start to fight. Then slay them, for it is the recompense that the

191. Waqtuloohum ḥays̲u s̲aqif-tumoohum wa akhrijoohum min ḥays̲u akhrajookum; walfitnatu ashaddu minal-qatl; wa laa tuqaatiloohum 'indal-Masjidil-Ḥaraami ḥattaa yuqaatilookum feehi fa-in qaatalookum

وَاقْتُلُوْهُمْ حَيْثُ ثَقِفْتُمُوْهُمْ
وَاَخْرِجُوْهُمْ مِّنْ حَيْثُ اَخْرَجُوْكُمْ
وَالْفِتْنَةُ اَشَدُّ مِنَ الْقَتْلِ ۚ وَلَا
تُقٰتِلُوْهُمْ عِنْدَ الْمَسْجِدِ الْحَرَامِ
حَتّٰى يُقٰتِلُوْكُمْ فِيْهِ ۚ فَاِنْ قٰتَلُوْكُمْ

unbelievers deserve.

192. If they give up disbelief and fighting, Allah is All-forgiving and All-merciful.

193. Fight them so that there will be no disbelief in Allah and Allah's religion will become dominant. If they change their behavior, there will be no hostility against anyone except the unjust.

194. A sacred month for a sacred month (if you cannot perform Umrah in this Dhil Qa'dah, you will do so in the next Dhil Qa'dah, which is also a sacred month). Sacred matters can be substituted by other sacred matters. Have fear of Allah and know that Allah supports the pious.

195. Give money for the cause of Allah but do not push yourselves into perdition. Do good; Allah loves the people who do good deeds.

196. Complete the Hajj and Umrah (two parts of the rituals of pilgrimage to Makkah) in obedience to Allah. If you are prevented from completing the duty of Hajj, offer whatever sacrifice is possible and do not shave your heads before the sacrificial animal is delivered to the prescribed place. If one of you is ill or is suffering because of some ailment in your head, you must redeem the shaving of the head by fasting, or paying money, or offering a sheep as a sacrifice. When all is well with you and you want to complete the Umrah in the Hajj season, offer whatever sacrifice is possible. If you did not find an animal, you have to fast for three days during the days of the pilgrimage rituals and seven days at home to complete the ten required fasting days. This rule is for those who did not live within (a distance of twelve miles from) the Sacred Mosque in Makkah.

faqtuloohum; kazaalika jazaaa'ul-kaafireen.

192. Fa-inintahaw fa-innal-laaha Ghafoorur-Raheem.

193. Wa qaatiloohum hattaa laa takoona fitnatuñw-wa yakoonad-deenu lillaahi fa-inin-tahaw falaa 'udwaana illaa 'alaz-zaalimeen.

194. Ash-Shahrul-Haraamu bish-Shahril-Haraami wal-hurumaatu qisaas; famani'tadaa 'alaykum fa'tadoo 'alayhi bimisli ma'-tadaa 'alaykum; wattaqul-laaha wa'lamooo annal-laaha ma'al-muttaqeen.

195. Wa anfiqoo fee sabeelil-laahi wa laa tulqoo bi-aydeekum ilat-tahlukati wa ahsinooo; innal-laaha yuhibbul-muhsi-neen.

196. Wa atimmul-Hajja wal-'Umrata lillaah; fa-in uhsirtum famas-taysara minal-hadyi walaa tahliqoo ru'oosakum hattaa yablughal-hadyu mahil-lah; faman kaana minkum mareedan aw biheee azam-mir-ra-sihee fafidyatum-min Siyaamin aw sadaqatin aw nusuk; fa-izaaa amintum faman tamatta'a bil-'Umrati ilal-Hajji famastaysara minal-hady; famal-lam yajid fa-Siyaamu salaasati ayyaamin fil-Hajji wa sab'atin izaa raja'tum; tilka 'asharatun kaamilah; zaalika limal-lam yakun ahluhoo haadiril-Masjidil-Haraam; wattaqul-laaha

فَاقْتُلُوْهُمْ كَذٰلِكَ جَزَآءُ الْكٰفِرِيْنَ ﴿١٩١﴾
فَاِنِ انْتَهَوْا فَاِنَّ اللّٰهَ غَفُوْرٌ رَّحِيْمٌ ﴿١٩٢﴾
وَقٰتِلُوْهُمْ حَتّٰى لَا تَكُوْنَ فِتْنَةٌ
وَّيَكُوْنَ الدِّيْنُ لِلّٰهِ فَاِنِ انْتَهَوْا
فَلَا عُدْوَانَ اِلَّا عَلَى الظّٰلِمِيْنَ ﴿١٩٣﴾
اَلشَّهْرُ الْحَرَامُ بِالشَّهْرِ الْحَرَامِ
وَالْحُرُمٰتُ قِصَاصٌ فَمَنِ اعْتَدٰى
عَلَيْكُمْ فَاعْتَدُوْا عَلَيْهِ بِمِثْلِ
مَا اعْتَدٰى عَلَيْكُمْ وَاتَّقُوا اللّٰهَ
وَاعْلَمُوْٓا اَنَّ اللّٰهَ مَعَ الْمُتَّقِيْنَ ﴿١٩٤﴾
وَاَنْفِقُوْا فِيْ سَبِيْلِ اللّٰهِ وَلَا تُلْقُوْا
بِاَيْدِيْكُمْ اِلَى التَّهْلُكَةِ وَاَحْسِنُوْا
اِنَّ اللّٰهَ يُحِبُّ الْمُحْسِنِيْنَ ﴿١٩٥﴾
وَاَتِمُّوا الْحَجَّ وَالْعُمْرَةَ لِلّٰهِ فَاِنْ
اُحْصِرْتُمْ فَمَا اسْتَيْسَرَ مِنَ الْهَدْيِ
وَلَا تَحْلِقُوْا رُءُوْسَكُمْ حَتّٰى يَبْلُغَ
الْهَدْيُ مَحِلَّهٗ فَمَنْ كَانَ مِنْكُمْ
مَّرِيْضًا اَوْ بِهٖٓ اَذًى مِّنْ رَّاْسِهٖ
فَفِدْيَةٌ مِّنْ صِيَامٍ اَوْ صَدَقَةٍ
اَوْ نُسُكٍ فَاِذَآ اَمِنْتُمْ فَمَنْ تَمَتَّعَ
بِالْعُمْرَةِ اِلَى الْحَجِّ فَمَا اسْتَيْسَرَ
مِنَ الْهَدْيِ فَمَنْ لَّمْ يَجِدْ فَصِيَامُ
ثَلٰثَةِ اَيَّامٍ فِي الْحَجِّ وَسَبْعَةٍ اِذَا
رَجَعْتُمْ تِلْكَ عَشَرَةٌ كَامِلَةٌ ذٰلِكَ
لِمَنْ لَّمْ يَكُنْ اَهْلُهٗ حَاضِرِي
الْمَسْجِدِ الْحَرَامِ وَاتَّقُوا اللّٰهَ

مع
عند المتقدمين ١٢٠

Have fear of Allah and know that He is stern in His retribution.

wa'lamoo annal-laaha shadee-dul-'iqaab.

وَاعْلَمُوٓا أَنَّ اللَّهَ شَدِيدُ الْعِقَابِ ﴿١٩٦﴾ ع ٢٤ ٨

197. The months of the Hajj (pilgrimage) season are well known. Whoever undertakes to complete the Hajj rituals must know that after commencing the acts of Hajj, he is not allowed to have carnal relations or to lie or to swear by the name of Allah. Allah knows all your good deeds. Supply yourselves for the journey. The best supply is piety. People of understanding, have fear of Me.

197. Al-Ḥajju ashhurum ma'-loomaat; faman faraḍa feehinnal-Ḥajja falaa rafasa wa laa fusooq; wa laa jidaala fil-Ḥajj; wa maa taf'aloo min khayriñy-ya'lamhul-laah; wa tazawwadoo fa-inna khayraz-zaadit-taqwaa; wattaqooni yaaa ulil-albaab.

الْحَجُّ أَشْهُرٌ مَّعْلُومَٰتٌ ۚ فَمَن
فَرَضَ فِيهِنَّ الْحَجَّ فَلَا رَفَثَ
وَلَا فُسُوقَ وَلَا جِدَالَ فِي الْحَجِّ ۗ
وَمَا تَفْعَلُوا مِنْ خَيْرٍ يَعْلَمْهُ اللَّهُ ۗ
وَتَزَوَّدُوا فَإِنَّ خَيْرَ الزَّادِ التَّقْوَىٰ ۚ
وَاتَّقُونِ يَٰٓأُولِي الْأَلْبَٰبِ ﴿١٩٧﴾

198. It is not a sin if you try to make a profit out of the bounty of your Lord (by trading during Hajj). When you leave Arafah, commemorate the name of your Lord in Mash'ar, the sacred reminder of Allah. Commemorate His name as He has given you guidance while prior to that you had been in error.

198. Laysa 'alaykum junaaḥun an tabtaghoo faḍlam-mir-Rabbikum; fa-izaaa afaḍtum min 'Arafaatin fazkurul-laaha 'indal-Mash'aril-Ḥaraami waz-kuroohu kamaa hadaakum wa in kuntum min qablihee laminaḍ-ḍaaalleen.

لَيْسَ عَلَيْكُمْ جُنَاحٌ أَن تَبْتَغُوا فَضْلًا
مِّن رَّبِّكُمْ ۚ فَإِذَآ أَفَضْتُم مِّنْ
عَرَفَٰتٍ فَاذْكُرُوا اللَّهَ عِندَ الْمَشْعَرِ
الْحَرَامِ ۖ وَاذْكُرُوهُ كَمَا هَدَىٰكُمْ ۚ
وَإِن كُنتُم مِّن قَبْلِهِۦ لَمِنَ الضَّآلِّينَ ﴿١٩٨﴾

199. Then, leave Mash'ar as the rest of the people do and ask forgiveness from Allah; Allah is All-forgiving and All-merciful.

199. Summa afeeḍoo min ḥaysu afaaḍan-naasu wastagh-firul-laah; innal-laaha Ghafoorur-Raḥeem.

ثُمَّ أَفِيضُوا مِنْ حَيْثُ أَفَاضَ
النَّاسُ وَاسْتَغْفِرُوا اللَّهَ ۚ إِنَّ اللَّهَ
غَفُورٌ رَّحِيمٌ ﴿١٩٩﴾

200. After you complete the acts of your Hajj, commemorate Allah also, just as you would remember your father, or even more earnestly. Some people say, "Lord, give us what we want in this life," but in the life hereafter they have no beneficial share.

200. Fa-izaa qaḍaytum manaa-sikakum fazkurul-laaha kazikrikum aabaaa'akum aw ashadda zikraa; faminannaasi mañy-yaqoolu Rabbanaaa aatinaa fiddunyaa wa maa lahoo fil-Aakhirati min khalaaq.

فَإِذَا قَضَيْتُم مَّنَٰسِكَكُمْ فَاذْكُرُوا
اللَّهَ كَذِكْرِكُمْ ءَابَآءَكُمْ أَوْ أَشَدَّ
ذِكْرًا ۗ فَمِنَ النَّاسِ مَن يَقُولُ
رَبَّنَآ ءَاتِنَا فِي الدُّنْيَا وَمَا لَهُۥ فِي
الْءَاخِرَةِ مِنْ خَلَٰقٍ ﴿٢٠٠﴾

201. Others pray, "Lord, give us good things in both this life as well as in the life hereafter and save us from the torment of the fire."

201. Wa minhum mañy-yaqoolu Rabbanaaa aatinaa fid-dunyaa ḥasanatañw-wa fil-Aakhirati ḥasanatañw-wa qinaa 'azaaban-Naar.

وَمِنْهُم مَّن يَقُولُ رَبَّنَآ ءَاتِنَا فِي
الدُّنْيَا حَسَنَةً وَفِي الْءَاخِرَةِ حَسَنَةً
وَقِنَا عَذَابَ النَّارِ ﴿٢٠١﴾

202. They will have their share of the reward for their deeds. Allah's reckoning is swift.

202. Ulaaa'ika lahum naṣee-bum-mimmaa kasaboo; wal-laahu saree'ul-ḥisaab.

أُولَٰٓئِكَ لَهُمْ نَصِيبٌ مِّمَّا كَسَبُوا ۚ
وَاللَّهُ سَرِيعُ الْحِسَابِ ﴿٢٠٢﴾ النصف

203. Commemorate (the names of) Allah in the prescribed days. For one who observes piety, it is

203. Wazkurul-laaha feee ayyaamim-ma'doodaat;

وَاذْكُرُوا اللَّهَ فِيٓ أَيَّامٍ مَّعْدُودَٰتٍ ۚ

وقف النبي صلى الله عليه وآله وسلم ١٢

not a sin to be hasty or tardy during the two days. Have fear of Allah and know that before Him you will all be raised after death.

faman ta'ajjala fee yawmayni falaaa isma 'alayhi wa man taakhkhara falaaa isma 'alayh; limanit-taqaa; wattaqul-laaha wa'lamooo annakum ilayhi tuhsharoon.

فَمَنْ تَعَجَّلَ فِيْ يَوْمَيْنِ فَلَآ اِثْمَ
عَلَيْهِ ۚ وَمَنْ تَاَخَّرَ فَلَآ اِثْمَ عَلَيْهِ ۙ
لِمَنِ اتَّقٰى ۭ وَاتَّقُوا اللّٰهَ وَاعْلَمُوْٓا
اَنَّكُمْ اِلَيْهِ تُحْشَرُوْنَ ۝٢٠٣

204. There are certain people whose words about this life may please you. They say that Allah knows what they have in their hearts. But, in fact, they are the most quarrelsome opponents.

204. Wa minan-naasi mañy-yu'jibuka qawluhoo fil hayaatid-dunyaa wa yushhidul-laaha 'alaa maa fee qalbihee wa huwa aladdulkhisaam.

وَمِنَ النَّاسِ مَنْ يُّعْجِبُكَ قَوْلُهٗ فِي
الْحَيٰوةِ الدُّنْيَا وَيُشْهِدُ اللّٰهَ عَلٰى
مَا فِيْ قَلْبِهٖ ۙ وَهُوَ اَلَدُّ الْخِصَامِ ۝٢٠٤

205. As soon as they leave you, they quickly commit evil in the land, destroying the farms (religion) and people. Allah does not love what is evil.

205. Wa izaa tawallaa sa'aa fil-ardi liyufsida feehaa wa yuhlikal-harsa wannasl; wallaahu laa yuhibbul-fasaad.

وَاِذَا تَوَلّٰى سَعٰى فِي الْاَرْضِ لِيُفْسِدَ
فِيْهَا وَيُهْلِكَ الْحَرْثَ وَالنَّسْلَ ۭ
وَاللّٰهُ لَا يُحِبُّ الْفَسَادَ ۝٢٠٥

206. When they are asked to have fear of Allah, sinful pride prevents them from paying heed to such advice. It is enough for them to have hell as a terrible dwelling place.

206. Wa izaa qeela lahuttaqil-laaha akhazathul-'izzatu bil-ismi fahasbuhoo Jahannam; wa labi'sal-mihaad.

وَاِذَا قِيْلَ لَهُ اتَّقِ اللّٰهَ اَخَذَتْهُ
الْعِزَّةُ بِالْاِثْمِ فَحَسْبُهٗ جَهَنَّمُ ۭ
وَلَبِئْسَ الْمِهَادُ ۝٢٠٦

207. There are those among people who give their lives to seek Allah's pleasure. Allah is affectionate to His servants.

207. Wa minan-naasi mañy-yashree nafsahub-tighaaa'a mardaatil-laah; wallaahu ra'oofum-bil'ibaad.

وَمِنَ النَّاسِ مَنْ يَّشْرِيْ نَفْسَهُ
ابْتِغَاۗءَ مَرْضَاتِ اللّٰهِ ۭ وَاللّٰهُ رَءُوْفٌۢ
بِالْعِبَادِ ۝٢٠٧

208. Believers, submit yourselves to the will of Allah as a whole. Do not follow the footsteps of Satan; he is your sworn enemy.

208. Yaaa ayyuhal-lazeena aamanud-khuloo fis-silmi kaaaffatañw-wa laa tattabi'oo khutuwaatish-Shaytaan; innahoo lakum 'aduwwum-mubeen.

يٰٓاَيُّهَا الَّذِيْنَ اٰمَنُوا ادْخُلُوْا فِي السِّلْمِ
كَاۗفَّةً ۠ وَّلَا تَتَّبِعُوْا خُطُوٰتِ
الشَّيْطٰنِ ۭ اِنَّهٗ لَكُمْ عَدُوٌّ مُّبِيْنٌ ۝٢٠٨

209. If you are seduced after you have received the authoritative guidance, know that Allah is Majestic and Wise.

209. Fa-in zalaltum mim ba'di maa jaaa'atkumul-bayyinaatu fa'lamoo annallaaha 'Azeezun-Hakeem.

فَاِنْ زَلَلْتُمْ مِّنْۢ بَعْدِ مَا جَاۗءَتْكُمُ
الْبَيِّنٰتُ فَاعْلَمُوْٓا اَنَّ اللّٰهَ عَزِيْزٌ حَكِيْمٌ ۝٢٠٩

210. Have they decided not to believe until Allah comes down in a shadow of clouds with the angels so that the matter is settled then? To Allah do all matters return.

210. Hal yanzuroona illaaa añy-ya-tiyahumul-laahu fee zulalim-minal-ghamaami walmalaaa'ikatu wa qudiyal-amr; wa ilal-laahi turja'ul-umoor.

هَلْ يَنْظُرُوْنَ اِلَّآ اَنْ يَّاْتِيَهُمُ اللّٰهُ
فِيْ ظُلَلٍ مِّنَ الْغَمَامِ وَالْمَلٰۗىِٕكَةُ
وَقُضِيَ الْاَمْرُ ۭ وَاِلَى اللّٰهِ تُرْجَعُ الْاُمُوْرُ ۝٢١٠ ع ٢٥ ١٤ ٩

211. (Muhammad), ask the children of Israel about how many evident miracles We have shown them. Allah is certainly

211. Sal Baneee Israaa'eela kam aataynaahum min Aayatim-bayyinah; wa mañy-yubaddil

سَلْ بَنِيْٓ اِسْرَاۗءِيْلَ كَمْ اٰتَيْنٰھُمْ
مِّنْ اٰيَةٍۢ بَيِّنَةٍ ۭ وَمَنْ يُّبَدِّلْ

stern in His retribution to those who change the bounty of Allah (His revelation), after having received His guidance.

ni'matal-laahi mim ba'di maa jaaa'athu fa-innallaaha shadeedul-'iqaab.

نعمة الله من بعد ما جاءته
فان الله شديد العقاب ٢١١

212. The worldly life is made to seem attractive to the unbelievers who scoff at the faithful, but the pious, in the life hereafter, will have a position far above them. Allah grants sustenance (without account) to anyone He wants.

212. Zuyyina lillazeena kafa-rul-ḥayaatud-dunyaa wa yaskharoona minal-lazeena aamanoo; wallazeenat-taqaw fawqahum YawmalQiyaamah; wallaahu yarzuqu mañy-yashaaa'u bighayri ḥisaab.

زين للذين كفروا الحيوة الدنيا
ويسخرون من الذين امنوا م وقف لازم
والذين اتقوا فوقهم يوم القيمة ط
والله يرزق من يشاء بغير حساب ٢١٢

213. At one time all people were only one nation. Allah sent Prophets with glad news and warnings. He sent the Book with them for a genuine purpose to provide the people with the ruling about disputed matters among them. No one disputed this matter except those who had already received evidence before. Their dispute was only because of their own hostility. To deal with this dispute, Allah, through His will, sent guidance to the believers. Allah guides to the right path whomever He wants.

213. Kaanan-naasu ummatañw-waaḥidatan faba'asal-laahun-Nabiyyeena mubashshireena wa munzireena wa anzala ma'ahumul-Kitaaba bilḥaqqi liyaḥkuma baynan-naasi feemakh-talafoo feeh; wa makh-talafa feehi 'illallazeena ootoohu mim-ba'di maa jaaa'athumul-bayyinaatu baghyam baynahum fahadal-laahul-lazeena aamanoo limakh-talafoo feehi minal-ḥaqqi bi-iznih; wallaahu yahdee mañy-yashaaa'u ilaa Ṣiraaṭim-Mustaqeem.

كان الناس امة واحدة تف فبعث
الله النبين مبشرين ومنذرين ص
وانزل معهم الكتب بالحق ليحكم
بين الناس فيما اختلفوا فيه ط
وما اختلف فيه الا الذين اوتوه
من بعد ما جاءتهم البينت بغيا
بينهم ج فهدى الله الذين امنوا
لما اختلفوا فيه من الحق باذنه ط
والله يهدي من يشاء الى صراط
مستقيم ٢١٣

214. Do you think that you can go to Paradise without experiencing the kind of suffering others have experienced before you? Distress and afflictions battered them until the Messenger and the believers said, "When will Allah send help?" Certainly Allah's help is near.

214. Am ḥasibtum an tad-khulul-Jannata wa lammaa ya-tikum masalul-lazeena khalaw min qablikum massathumul-ba-saaa'u waḍḍarraaa'u wa zulziloo ḥattaa yaqoolar-Rasoolu wallazeena aamanoo ma'ahoo mataa naṣrul-laah; alaaa inna naṣral-laahi qareeb.

ام حسبتم ان تدخلوا الجنة ولما
ياتكم مثل الذين خلوا من
قبلكم ط مستهم الباساء والضراء
وزلزلوا حتى يقول الرسول
والذين امنوا معه متى نصر الله ط
الا ان نصر الله قريب ٢١٤

215. They ask you what to spend for the cause of Allah. (Muhammad) tell them that whatever you spend, give it to your parents, the relatives, the orphans, the destitute, and those who may be in urgent need of money while on a journey.

215. Yas'aloonaka maazaa yunfiqoona qul maaa anfaqtum min khayrin falilwaalidayni wal-aqrabeena walyataamaa walmasaakeeni wabnis-sabeel; wa maa taf'aloo min

يسئلونك ماذا ينفقون ط قل ما
انفقتم من خير فللوالدين
والاقربين واليتمى والمسكين
وابن السبيل ط وما تفعلوا من

Whatever good you do, Allah certainly is aware of it.

khayrin fa-innal-laaha bihee 'Aleem

خَيْرٍ فَإِنَّ اللَّهَ بِهِ عَلِيمٌ ﴿٢١٥﴾

216. Fighting is made mandatory for you, but you dislike it. You may not like something which, in fact, is for your good and something that you may love may, in fact, be evil for you. Allah knows, but you do not know.

216. Kutiba 'alaykumul-qitaalu wa huwa kurhul-lakum wa 'asaaa an takrahoo shay'añw-wa huwa khayrul-lakum wa 'asaaa an tuḥibboo shay'añw-wa huwa sharrul-lakum; wallaahu ya'lamu wa-antum laa ta'lamoon.

كُتِبَ عَلَيْكُمُ الْقِتَالُ وَهُوَ كُرْهٌ لَّكُمْ
وَعَسَىٰ أَن تَكْرَهُوا شَيْئًا وَهُوَ
خَيْرٌ لَّكُمْ ۖ وَعَسَىٰ أَن تُحِبُّوا شَيْئًا
وَهُوَ شَرٌّ لَّكُمْ ۗ وَاللَّهُ يَعْلَمُ
وَأَنتُمْ لَا تَعْلَمُونَ ﴿٢١٦﴾

217. (Muhammad), they ask you about fighting in the sacred month. Tell them that it is a great sin. However, creating an obstacle in the way of Allah, disbelief in Him and the Sacred Mosque, and driving away the neighbors of the Sacred Mosque is an even greater sin in the sight of Allah; Disbelief in Allah is worse than committing murder. (The pagans) still try to fight you, if they can, to make you give up your religion. The deeds of those of you who give up your religion and who die unbelievers will be made void in this life as well as in the life hereafter. These people will be the dwellers of hell wherein they will remain forever.

217. Yas'aloonaka 'anish-Shahril-Ḥaraami qitaalin feeh; qul qitaalun feehi kabeer; wa ṣaddun 'an sabeelil-laahi wa kufrum-bihee wal-Masjidil-Ḥaraami wa ikhraaju ahlihee minhu akbaru 'indal-laah; walfitnatu akbaru minal-qatl; wa laa yazaaloona yuqaati-loonakum ḥattaa yaruddookum 'an deenikum inis-taṭaa'oo; wa mañy-yartadid minkum 'an deenihee fayamut wahuwa kaafirun fa-ulaaa'ika ḥabiṭat a'maaluhum fid-dunyaa wal-Aakhirati wa ulaaa'ika Aṣḥaabun-Naari hum feehaa khaalidoon.

يَسْأَلُونَكَ عَنِ الشَّهْرِ الْحَرَامِ قِتَالٍ
فِيهِ ۖ قُلْ قِتَالٌ فِيهِ كَبِيرٌ ۖ وَصَدٌّ
عَن سَبِيلِ اللَّهِ وَكُفْرٌ بِهِ وَالْمَسْجِدِ
الْحَرَامِ وَإِخْرَاجُ أَهْلِهِ مِنْهُ أَكْبَرُ
عِندَ اللَّهِ ۚ وَالْفِتْنَةُ أَكْبَرُ مِنَ
الْقَتْلِ ۗ وَلَا يَزَالُونَ يُقَاتِلُونَكُمْ
حَتَّىٰ يَرُدُّوكُمْ عَن دِينِكُمْ إِنِ
اسْتَطَاعُوا ۚ وَمَن يَرْتَدِدْ مِنكُمْ
عَن دِينِهِ فَيَمُتْ وَهُوَ كَافِرٌ
فَأُولَٰئِكَ حَبِطَتْ أَعْمَالُهُمْ فِي
الدُّنْيَا وَالْآخِرَةِ ۖ وَأُولَٰئِكَ
أَصْحَابُ النَّارِ ۖ هُمْ فِيهَا خَالِدُونَ ﴿٢١٧﴾

218. The believers and the emigrants from Makkah, who fight for the cause of Allah, indeed have hope in receiving the mercy of Allah; Allah is All-forgiving and All-merciful.

218. Innal-laẕeena aamanoo wallaẕeena haajaroo wa jaahadoo fee sabeelil-laahi ulaaa'ika yarjoona raḥmatal-laah; wallaahu Ghafoorur-Raḥeem.

إِنَّ الَّذِينَ آمَنُوا وَالَّذِينَ هَاجَرُوا
وَجَاهَدُوا فِي سَبِيلِ اللَّهِ أُولَٰئِكَ
يَرْجُونَ رَحْمَتَ اللَّهِ ۚ وَاللَّهُ غَفُورٌ رَّحِيمٌ ﴿٢١٨﴾

219. (Muhammad), they ask you about wine and gambling. Tell them that there is great sin in them. Although they have benefits for men, the sin therein is far greater than the benefit. They ask you about what they should give for the cause of Allah. Tell them, "Let it be what you can spare." This is how Allah

219. Yas'aloonaka 'anilkhamri walmaysiri qul feehimaaa iṯmun kabeeruñw-wa manaafi'u linnaasi wa iṯmuhumaaa akbaru min naf'ihimaa; wa yas 'aloonaka maaẕaa yunfiqoona qulil-'afw; kaẕaalika yubayyinul-laahu lakumul-

يَسْأَلُونَكَ عَنِ الْخَمْرِ وَالْمَيْسِرِ ۖ قُلْ
فِيهِمَا إِثْمٌ كَبِيرٌ وَمَنَافِعُ لِلنَّاسِ
وَإِثْمُهُمَا أَكْبَرُ مِن نَّفْعِهِمَا ۗ
وَيَسْأَلُونَكَ مَاذَا يُنفِقُونَ قُلِ
الْعَفْوَ ۗ كَذَٰلِكَ يُبَيِّنُ اللَّهُ لَكُمُ

explains for you His guidance so that perhaps you will think

Aayaati la'allakum tatafakkaroon.

الْاٰيٰتِ لَعَلَّكُمْ تَتَفَكَّرُوْنَ ﴿٢١٩﴾

220. about this life and the life hereafter.
They ask you about the orphans. Tell them, "The best thing to do is what is for their good. They are your brethren if you associate with them. Allah knows who is corrupt or a reformer. Had Allah wanted He would have brought upon you hardship. Allah is Majestic and All-wise.

220. Fid-dunyaa wal-Aakhirah; wa yas'aloonaka 'anil-yataamaa qul iṣlaaḥul-lahum khayr; wa in tukhaaliṭoohum fa-ikhwaanukum; wallaahu ya'lamul-mufsida minalmuṣliḥ; wa law shaaa'al-laahu la-a'natakum; innal-laaha 'Azeezun Ḥakeem.

فِى الدُّنْيَا وَالْاٰخِرَةِ ۭ وَيَسْـَٔلُوْنَكَ
عَنِ الْيَتٰمٰى ۭ قُلْ اِصْلَاحٌ لَّهُمْ خَيْرٌ ۭ
وَاِنْ تُخَالِطُوْهُمْ فَاِخْوَانُكُمْ ۭ وَاللّٰهُ
يَعْلَمُ الْمُفْسِدَ مِنَ الْمُصْلِحِ ۭ وَلَوْ شَاۗءَ
اللّٰهُ لَاَعْنَتَكُمْ ۭ اِنَّ اللّٰهَ عَزِيْزٌ حَكِيْمٌ ﴿٢٢٠﴾

221. Do not marry pagan women unless they believe in Allah. A believing slave girl is better than an idolater, even though the idolaters may attract you. Do not marry pagan men unless they believe in Allah. A believing slave is better than an idolater, even though the idolater may attract you. The pagans invite you to the fire, but Allah invites you to Paradise and forgiveness through His will. Allah shows His evidence to people so that they may take heed.

221. Wa laa tankiḥul-mushrikaati ḥattaa yu'minn; wa laamatum mu'minatun khayrum-mim-mushrikatiñw-wa law a'jabatkum; wa laa tunkiḥul-mushrikeena ḥattaa yu'minoo; wa la'abdummu'minun khayrum-mimmushrikiñw-wa law a'jabakum; ulaaa'ika yad'oona ilan-Naari wallaahu yad'ooo ilal-Jannati walmaghfirati biiznihee wa yubayyinu Aayaatihee linnaasi la'allahum yatazakkaroon.

وَلَا تَنْكِحُوا الْمُشْرِكٰتِ حَتّٰى يُؤْمِنَّ ۭ
وَلَاَمَةٌ مُّؤْمِنَةٌ خَيْرٌ مِّنْ مُّشْرِكَةٍ
وَّلَوْ اَعْجَبَتْكُمْ ۚ وَلَا تُنْكِحُوا الْمُشْرِكِيْنَ
حَتّٰى يُؤْمِنُوْا ۭ وَلَعَبْدٌ مُّؤْمِنٌ خَيْرٌ
مِّنْ مُّشْرِكٍ وَّلَوْ اَعْجَبَكُمْ ۭ اُولٰۗىِٕكَ
يَدْعُوْنَ اِلَى النَّارِ ښ وَاللّٰهُ يَدْعُوْٓا
اِلَى الْجَنَّةِ وَالْمَغْفِرَةِ بِاِذْنِهٖ ۚ
وَيُبَيِّنُ اٰيٰتِهٖ لِلنَّاسِ لَعَلَّهُمْ
يَتَذَكَّرُوْنَ ﴿٢٢١﴾ ع ٢٧ ٥

222. They ask you about women's menses. Tell them, "It is an ailment. Avoid having carnal relations with them until they are clean of menses and have taken a formal bath." Then you may have carnal relations with them according to the rules of Allah. Allah loves those who repent and those who purify themselves.

222. Wa yas'aloonaka 'anil maḥeeḍi qul huwa azan fa'tazilun-nisaaa'a fil-maḥeeḍi wa laa taqraboo-hunna ḥattaa yaṭhurna fa-izaa taṭahharna fatoohunna min ḥaysu amarakumul-laah; innallaaha yuḥibbut-Tawwaabeena wa yuḥibbul-mutaṭahhireen.

وَيَسْـَٔلُوْنَكَ عَنِ الْمَحِيْضِ ۭ قُلْ
هُوَ اَذًى ۙ فَاعْتَزِلُوا النِّسَاۗءَ فِي
الْمَحِيْضِ ۙ وَلَا تَقْرَبُوْهُنَّ حَتّٰى
يَطْهُرْنَ ۚ فَاِذَا تَطَهَّرْنَ فَاْتُوْهُنَّ
مِنْ حَيْثُ اَمَرَكُمُ اللّٰهُ ۭ اِنَّ اللّٰهَ يُحِبُّ
التَّوَّابِيْنَ وَيُحِبُّ الْمُتَطَهِّرِيْنَ ﴿٢٢٢﴾

223. Your wives are as fields for you. You may enter your fields whenever you want. Reserve something good for your souls (for the life hereafter). Have fear of Allah and know that you are going to meet Him. (Muhammad), give the glad news to the believers.

223. Nisaaa'ukum ḥarsullakum fa-too ḥarsakum annaa shi'tum wa qaddimoo li-anfusikum; wattaqul-laaha wa'lamooo annakum mulaaqooh;wa bashshirilmu'mineen.

نِسَاۗؤُكُمْ حَرْثٌ لَّكُمْ ۠ فَاْتُوْا حَرْثَكُمْ
اَنّٰى شِئْتُمْ ۡ وَقَدِّمُوْا لِاَنْفُسِكُمْ ۭ
وَاتَّقُوا اللّٰهَ وَاعْلَمُوْٓا اَنَّكُمْ مُّلٰقُوْهُ ۭ
وَبَشِّرِ الْمُؤْمِنِيْنَ ﴿٢٢٣﴾

224. Do not swear by Allah not to do good things, or have piety,

224. Wa laa taj'alul-laaha 'urḍatal-li-aymaanikum

وَلَا تَجْعَلُوا اللّٰهَ عُرْضَةً لِّاَيْمَانِكُمْ

or make peace among people. Allah is All-hearing and All-knowing.	an tabarroo wa tattaqoo wa tuṣliḥoo baynan-naas; wallaahu Samee'un-'Aleem.	اَنْ تَبَرُّوْا وَتَتَّقُوْا وَتُصْلِحُوْا بَيْنَ النَّاسِ ۭ وَاللّٰهُ سَمِيْعٌ عَلِيْمٌ ﴿٢٢٤﴾
225. Allah will not take into account your inattentive oath. However, He will question you about what your hearts have gained. Allah is All-forgiving and Lenient.	225. Laa yu'aakhi-zukumul-laahu billaghwi feee aymaa-nikum wa laakiñy-yu'aakhi-zukum bimaa kasabat quloo-bukum; wallaahu Ghafoorun Ḥaleem.	لَا يُؤَاخِذُكُمُ اللّٰهُ بِاللَّغْوِ فِيْٓ اَيْمَانِكُمْ وَلٰكِنْ يُّؤَاخِذُكُمْ بِمَا كَسَبَتْ قُلُوْبُكُمْ ۭ وَاللّٰهُ غَفُوْرٌ حَلِيْمٌ ﴿٢٢٥﴾
226. If those who swear by Allah not to ever have any carnal relations with their wives, decide to resume marital relations again within four months (they will not be punished). Allah is All-forgiving and All-merciful.	226. Lillazeena yu'loona min nisaaa'ihim tarabbuṣu arba'ati ashhurin fa-in faaa'oo fa-innal-laaha Ghafoorur-Raḥeem.	لِلَّذِيْنَ يُؤْلُوْنَ مِنْ نِّسَاۗىِٕهِمْ تَرَبُّصُ اَرْبَعَةِ اَشْهُرٍ ۚ فَاِنْ فَاۗءُوْ فَاِنَّ اللّٰهَ غَفُوْرٌ رَّحِيْمٌ ﴿٢٢٦﴾
227. If they choose divorce, Allah is All-hearing and All-knowing.	227. Wa in 'azamuṭ-ṭalaaqa fa-innal-laaha Samee'un 'Aleem	وَاِنْ عَزَمُوا الطَّلَاقَ فَاِنَّ اللّٰهَ سَمِيْعٌ عَلِيْمٌ ﴿٢٢٧﴾
228. The divorced women must wait up to three menstrual cycles before another marriage. If they believe in Allah and the Day of Judgment, it is not lawful for them to hide what Allah has created in their wombs. Within their waiting period, their husbands have the right to resume marital relations if they want reconciliation. Women have benefits as well as responsibilities. Men have a status above women. Allah is Majestic and Wise.	228. Walmutallaqaatu yatarab-baṣna bi-anfusihinna salaasata qurooo'; wa laa yaḥillu lahunna añy-yaktumna maa khalaqal-laahu feee arḥaamihinna in kunna yu'minna billaahi wal-Yawmil-Aakhir; wa bu'oola-tuhunna aḥaqqu biraddihinna fee zaalika in araadooo iṣlaaḥaa; wa lahunna mislul-lazee 'alayhinna bilma'roof; wa lirrijaali 'alayhinna darajah; wallaahu 'Azeezun Ḥakeem.	وَالْمُطَلَّقٰتُ يَتَرَبَّصْنَ بِاَنْفُسِهِنَّ ثَلٰثَةَ قُرُوْۗءٍ ۭ وَلَا يَحِلُّ لَهُنَّ اَنْ يَّكْتُمْنَ مَا خَلَقَ اللّٰهُ فِيْٓ اَرْحَامِهِنَّ اِنْ كُنَّ يُؤْمِنَّ بِاللّٰهِ وَالْيَوْمِ الْاٰخِرِ ۭ وَبُعُوْلَتُهُنَّ اَحَقُّ بِرَدِّهِنَّ فِيْ ذٰلِكَ اِنْ اَرَادُوْٓا اِصْلَاحًا ۭ وَ لَهُنَّ مِثْلُ الَّذِيْ عَلَيْهِنَّ بِالْمَعْرُوْفِ وَلِلرِّجَالِ عَلَيْهِنَّ دَرَجَةٌ ۭ وَاللّٰهُ عَزِيْزٌ حَكِيْمٌ ﴿٢٢٨﴾ ع ٢٨ ١٢
229. A marital relation can only be resumed after the first and second divorce; otherwise it must be continued with fairness or terminated with kindness. It is not lawful for you to take back from women what you have given them unless you are afraid of not being able to observe Allah's law. In this case, it would be no sin for her to pay a ransom to set herself free from the bond of marriage. These are the laws of Allah. Do	229. Aṭṭalaaqu marrataani fa-imsaakum bima'roofin aw tasreeḥum bi-iḥsaan; wa laa yaḥillu lakum an ta-khuzoo mimmaaa aataytumoohunna shay'an illaaa añy-yakhaafaaa allaa yuqeemaa ḥudoodallaah; fa-in khiftum allaa yuqeemaa ḥudoodal-laahi falaa Junaaḥa 'alayhimaa feemaf-tadat bihee tilka Ḥudoodul-laahi falaa	اَلطَّلَاقُ مَرَّتٰنِ ۠ فَاِمْسَاكٌۢ بِمَعْرُوْفٍ اَوْ تَسْرِيْحٌۢ بِاِحْسَانٍ ۭ وَلَا يَحِلُّ لَكُمْ اَنْ تَاْخُذُوْا مِمَّآ اٰتَيْتُمُوْهُنَّ شَـيْـــًٔا اِلَّآ اَنْ يَّخَافَآ اَلَّا يُقِيْمَا حُدُوْدَ اللّٰهِ ۭ فَاِنْ خِفْتُمْ اَلَّا يُقِيْمَا حُدُوْدَ اللّٰهِ ۙ فَلَا جُنَاحَ عَلَيْهِمَا فِيْمَا افْتَدَتْ بِهٖ ۭ تِلْكَ حُدُوْدُ اللّٰهِ فَلَا

not transgress against them; those who do so are unjust.

ta'tadoohaa; wa mañy-yata'adda ḥudoodal-laahi fa-ulaaa'ika humuẓẓaa-limoon.

تَعْتَدُوهَا ۚ وَمَن يَتَعَدَّ حُدُودَ
اللَّهِ فَأُولَٰئِكَ هُمُ الظَّالِمُونَ ﴿٢٢٩﴾

230. After a divorce for the third time, it is not lawful for the husband to resume marital relations with her or remarry her until she has been married and divorced by another husband. In that case, there is no sin for the former husband to marry her if they (both) think that they can abide by the law. These are the laws of Allah. He explains them for the people of knowledge.

230. Fa-in ṭallaqahaa falaa taḥillu lahoo mim ba'du ḥattaa tankiḥa zawjan ghayrah; fa-in ṭallaqahaa falaa junaaḥa 'alayhimaaa añy-yataraaja'aaa in ẓannaaa añy-yuqeemaa ḥudoodal-laah; wa tilka ḥudoodul-laahi yubayyinuhaa liqawmiñy-ya'lamoon.

فَإِن طَلَّقَهَا فَلَا تَحِلُّ لَهُ مِن بَعْدُ
حَتَّىٰ تَنكِحَ زَوْجًا غَيْرَهُ ۗ فَإِن
طَلَّقَهَا فَلَا جُنَاحَ عَلَيْهِمَا أَن
يَتَرَاجَعَا إِن ظَنَّا أَن يُقِيمَا حُدُودَ
اللَّهِ ۗ وَتِلْكَ حُدُودُ اللَّهِ يُبَيِّنُهَا
لِقَوْمٍ يَعْلَمُونَ ﴿٢٣٠﴾

231. When you divorce your wives and their waiting period has almost ended, you may resume marital relations with honor or leave them with kindness. Do not force them to live with you in suffering to satisfy your hostility. Whoever commits such transgressions has only harmed himself. Do not make jest of Allah's words.
Remember the favors that Allah has done to you and the Book and wisdom He has revealed for your guidance. Have fear of Allah and know that Allah has knowledge of all things.

231. Wa iẕaa ṭallaqtumun-nisaaa'a fabalaghna ajala-hunna fa-amsikoohunna bima'roofin aw sarriḥoo-hunna bima'roof; wa laa tumsikoo-hunna ḍiraa-rallita'tadoo; wa mañy-yaf'al ẕaalika faqad ẓalama nafsah; wa laa tattakhiẕooo Aayaatillaahi huzuwaa; waẕkuroo ni'matal-laahi 'alaykum wa maaa anzala 'alaykum minal-Kitaabi wal-Ḥikmati ya'iẓukum bih; wattaqul-laaha wa'lamooo annal-laaha bikulli shay'in 'Aleem.

وَإِذَا طَلَّقْتُمُ النِّسَاءَ فَبَلَغْنَ
أَجَلَهُنَّ فَأَمْسِكُوهُنَّ بِمَعْرُوفٍ
أَوْ سَرِّحُوهُنَّ بِمَعْرُوفٍ ۚ وَلَا
تُمْسِكُوهُنَّ ضِرَارًا لِّتَعْتَدُوا ۚ وَمَن
يَفْعَلْ ذَٰلِكَ فَقَدْ ظَلَمَ نَفْسَهُ ۚ
وَلَا تَتَّخِذُوا آيَاتِ اللَّهِ هُزُوًا ۚ
وَاذْكُرُوا نِعْمَتَ اللَّهِ عَلَيْكُمْ
وَمَا أَنزَلَ عَلَيْكُم مِّنَ الْكِتَابِ
وَالْحِكْمَةِ يَعِظُكُم بِهِ ۚ وَاتَّقُوا اللَّهَ
وَاعْلَمُوا أَنَّ اللَّهَ بِكُلِّ شَيْءٍ عَلِيمٌ ﴿٢٣١﴾

232. When the waiting period of the divorced women has ended, you (her relatives) must not prevent them from marrying their (previous) husbands again if they might reach an honorable agreement. This is an advice for those of you who believe in Allah and the Day of Judgment. It is the most beneficial and pure way of treating each other. Allah knows but you do not know.

232. Wa iẕaa ṭallaqtumun-nisaaa'a fabalaghna ajalahunna falaa ta'ḍuloo-hunna añy-yankiḥna azwaaja-hunna iẕaa taraaḍaw baynahum bilma'-roof; ẕaalika yoo'aẓu bihee man kaana minkum yu'minu billaahi walYawmil-Aakhir; ẕaalikum azkaa lakum wa aṭhar; wallaahu ya'lamu wa antum laa ta'lamoon.

وَإِذَا طَلَّقْتُمُ النِّسَاءَ فَبَلَغْنَ
أَجَلَهُنَّ فَلَا تَعْضُلُوهُنَّ أَن يَنكِحْنَ
أَزْوَاجَهُنَّ إِذَا تَرَاضَوْا بَيْنَهُم
بِالْمَعْرُوفِ ۗ ذَٰلِكَ يُوعَظُ بِهِ مَن
كَانَ مِنكُمْ يُؤْمِنُ بِاللَّهِ وَالْيَوْمِ
الْآخِرِ ۗ ذَٰلِكُمْ أَزْكَىٰ لَكُمْ وَأَطْهَرُ ۗ
وَاللَّهُ يَعْلَمُ وَأَنتُمْ لَا تَعْلَمُونَ ﴿٢٣٢﴾

233. Mothers will breastfeed their babies for two years if the

233. Walwaalidaatu yurḍi'na awlaada hunna

وَالْوَالِدَاتُ يُرْضِعْنَ أَوْلَادَهُنَّ

fathers want them to complete this term. The father has to pay them reasonable expenses. No soul is responsible for what is beyond its ability. None of the parents should suffer any loss from the other because of the baby. The heirs are responsible for looking after the children of a deceased. It is no sin for the parents to have a mutual agreement about weaning the baby. There is no sin in hiring a woman to breastfeed your children for a reasonable payment. Have fear of Allah and know that Allah is Well-aware of what you do.

ḥawlayni kaamilayni liman araada añy-yutimmar-raḍaa'ah; wa 'alal-mawloodi lahoo rizquhunna wa kiswatuhunna bilma'roof; laa tukallafu nafsun illaa wus'ahaa; laa tuḍaaarra waalidatum-biwaladihaa wa laa mawloodul-lahoo biwaladih; Wa 'alal-waarisi mislu zaalik; fa-in araadaa fiṣaalan 'an taraaḍim-minhumaa wa tashaawurin falaa junaaḥa 'alayhimaa; wa in arattum an tastarḍi'ooo awlaadakum falaa junaaḥa 'alaykum izaa sallamtum maaa aataytum bilma'roof; wattaqul-laaha wa'lamooo annal-laaha bimaa ta'maloona Baṣeer.

حَوْلَيْنِ كَامِلَيْنِ لِمَنْ أَرَادَ أَنْ
يُتِمَّ الرَّضَاعَةَ ۚ وَعَلَى الْمَوْلُودِ لَهُ
رِزْقُهُنَّ وَكِسْوَتُهُنَّ بِالْمَعْرُوفِ ۚ
لَا تُكَلَّفُ نَفْسٌ إِلَّا وُسْعَهَا ۚ
لَا تُضَارَّ وَالِدَةٌ بِوَلَدِهَا وَلَا
مَوْلُودٌ لَهُ بِوَلَدِهِ ۚ وَعَلَى الْوَارِثِ
مِثْلُ ذَٰلِكَ ۗ فَإِنْ أَرَادَا فِصَالًا عَنْ
تَرَاضٍ مِنْهُمَا وَتَشَاوُرٍ فَلَا جُنَاحَ
عَلَيْهِمَا ۗ وَإِنْ أَرَدْتُمْ أَنْ تَسْتَرْضِعُوا
أَوْلَادَكُمْ فَلَا جُنَاحَ عَلَيْكُمْ إِذَا
سَلَّمْتُمْ مَا آتَيْتُمْ بِالْمَعْرُوفِ ۗ
وَاتَّقُوا اللَّهَ وَاعْلَمُوا أَنَّ اللَّهَ بِمَا
تَعْمَلُونَ بَصِيرٌ ﴿٢٣٣﴾

234. The wives of those of you who die have to wait for a period of four months and ten days. After this appointed time, it is no sin for the relatives of the deceased to let the widows do what is reasonable. Allah knows well what you do.

234. Wallazeena yutawaffawna minkum wa yazaroona azwaajañy-yatarabbaṣna bi-anfusihinna arba'ata ashhuriñw-wa 'ashran fa-izaa balaghna ajalahunna falaa junaaḥa 'alaykum feemaa fa'alna feee anfusihinna bilma'roof; wallaahu bimaa ta'maloona Khabeer.

وَالَّذِينَ يُتَوَفَّوْنَ مِنْكُمْ وَيَذَرُونَ
أَزْوَاجًا يَتَرَبَّصْنَ بِأَنْفُسِهِنَّ
أَرْبَعَةَ أَشْهُرٍ وَعَشْرًا ۖ فَإِذَا بَلَغْنَ
أَجَلَهُنَّ فَلَا جُنَاحَ عَلَيْكُمْ فِيمَا
فَعَلْنَ فِي أَنْفُسِهِنَّ بِالْمَعْرُوفِ ۗ
وَاللَّهُ بِمَا تَعْمَلُونَ خَبِيرٌ ﴿٢٣٤﴾

235. It is not a sin if you make an indirect marriage proposal or have such an intention in your hearts. Allah knows that you will cherish their memories in your hearts. Do not have secret courtships unless you behave lawfully. Do not decide for a marriage before the appointed time is over. Know that Allah knows what is in your hearts.

235. Wa laa junaaḥa 'alaykum feemaa 'arraḍtum bihee min khiṭbatin-nisaaa'i aw aknantum feee anfusikum; 'alimal-laahu annakum satazkuroonahunna wa laakil-laa tuwaa'idoohunna sirran illaaa an taqooloo qawlamma'roofaa; wa laa ta'zimoo 'uqdatan-nikaaḥi ḥattaa yablughal-kitaabu ajalah; wa'lamooo annal-laaha ya'lamu maa

وَلَا جُنَاحَ عَلَيْكُمْ فِيمَا عَرَّضْتُمْ بِهِ
مِنْ خِطْبَةِ النِّسَاءِ أَوْ أَكْنَنْتُمْ فِي
أَنْفُسِكُمْ ۚ عَلِمَ اللَّهُ أَنَّكُمْ سَتَذْكُرُونَهُنَّ
وَلَٰكِنْ لَا تُوَاعِدُوهُنَّ سِرًّا إِلَّا أَنْ
تَقُولُوا قَوْلًا مَعْرُوفًا ۚ وَلَا تَعْزِمُوا
عُقْدَةَ النِّكَاحِ حَتَّىٰ يَبْلُغَ الْكِتَابُ
أَجَلَهُ ۚ وَاعْلَمُوا أَنَّ اللَّهَ يَعْلَمُ مَا

Have fear of Him and know that He is All-forgiving and All-merciful.

feee-anfusikum faḥẕarooh; wa'lamooo annallaaha Ghafoorun Ḥaleem

فِىٓ اَنۡفُسِكُمۡ فَاحۡذَرُوۡهُ‌ ۚ وَاعۡلَمُوۡٓا
اَنَّ اللّٰهَ غَفُوۡرٌ حَلِيۡمٌ ﴿۲۳۵﴾

236. Also, it is not a sin to divorce your wives if you did not consummate the marriage or before the fixing of the dowry. But the dowry will be due from a husband whether he is rich or poor. It is payable in a reasonable amount according to the husband's financial ability. This is an obligation for the righteous ones.

236. Laa junaaḥa 'alaykum in ṭallaqtumun-nisaaa'a maa lam tamassoohunna aw tafriḍoo lahunna fareeḍah; wa matti'oohunna 'alal-moosi'i qadaruhoo wa 'alal-muqtiri qadaruhoo mataa'am-bilma'roofi ḥaqqan 'alalmuḥsineen.

لَا جُنَاحَ عَلَيۡكُمۡ اِنۡ طَلَّقۡتُمُ النِّسَآءَ
مَا لَمۡ تَمَسُّوۡهُنَّ اَوۡ تَفۡرِضُوۡا لَهُنَّ
فَرِيۡضَةً ۖۚ وَّمَتِّعُوۡهُنَّ ۚ عَلَى
الۡمُوۡسِعِ قَدَرُهٗ وَعَلَى الۡمُقۡتِرِ قَدَرُهٗ‌ ۚ
مَتَاعًا ۢ بِالۡمَعۡرُوۡفِ‌ ۚ حَقًّا عَلَى
الۡمُحۡسِنِيۡنَ ﴿۲۳۶﴾

237. If you divorce your wives before the consummation of the marriage and the amount of dowry has been fixed, pay your wives half of the amount of their dowry, unless she or her guardians drop their demand for payment. To drop such a demand is closer to piety. Be generous to each other. Allah is Well-aware of what you do.

237. Wa in ṭallaqtumoohunna min qabli an tamassoohunna wa qad faraḍtum lahunna fareeḍatan faniṣfu maa faraḍtum illaaa añy-ya'foona aw ya'fuwallaẕee biyadihee 'uqdatunnikaaḥ; wa an ta'fooo aqrabu littaqwaa; wa laa tansawul-faḍla baynakum; innal-laaha bimaa ta'maloona Baṣeer.

وَاِنۡ طَلَّقۡتُمُوۡهُنَّ مِنۡ قَبۡلِ اَنۡ
تَمَسُّوۡهُنَّ وَقَدۡ فَرَضۡتُمۡ لَهُنَّ
فَرِيۡضَةً فَنِصۡفُ مَا فَرَضۡتُمۡ
اِلَّاۤ اَنۡ يَّعۡفُوۡنَ اَوۡ يَعۡفُوَا الَّذِىۡ
بِيَدِهٖ عُقۡدَةُ النِّكَاحِ‌ ؕ وَاَنۡ
تَعۡفُوۡٓا اَقۡرَبُ لِلتَّقۡوٰى‌ؕ وَلَا تَنۡسَوُا
الۡفَضۡلَ بَيۡنَكُمۡ‌ؕ اِنَّ اللّٰهَ بِمَا
تَعۡمَلُوۡنَ بَصِيۡرٌ ﴿۲۳۷﴾

238. Pay due attention to your prayers, especially the middle prayer, and stand up while praying, in obedience to Allah.

238. Ḥaafiẓoo 'alaṣ-Ṣalawaati waṣ-Ṣalaatil-Wusṭaa wa qoomoo lillaahi qaaniteen.

حٰفِظُوۡا عَلَى الصَّلَوٰتِ وَالصَّلٰوةِ
الۡوُسۡطٰى وَقُوۡمُوۡا لِلّٰهِ قٰنِتِيۡنَ ﴿۲۳۸﴾

239. In an emergency you may say your prayers while walking or riding; but when you are safe, remember Allah, as He has taught you what you did not know before.

239. Fa-in khiftum farijaalan aw rukbaanan fa-iẕaaa amintum faẕkurul-laaha kamaa 'allamakum maa lam takoonoo ta'lamoon.

فَاِنۡ خِفۡتُمۡ فَرِجَالًا اَوۡ رُكۡبَانًا ‌ۚ
فَاِذَآ اَمِنۡتُمۡ فَاذۡكُرُوا اللّٰهَ كَمَا
عَلَّمَكُمۡ مَّا لَمۡ تَكُوۡنُوۡا تَعۡلَمُوۡنَ ﴿۲۳۹﴾

240. Those who are about to die and leave widows behind should bequeath for their wives the expenses of one year's maintenance. The widows must not be expelled from the house for up to one year. If the widows leave the house before the appointed time, it is no sin for the relatives of the deceased to permit

240. Wallaẕeena yutawaffawna minkum wa yaẕaroona azwaajañw-waṣiyyatal-li-azwaajihim mataa'an ilal-ḥawli ghayra ikhraaj; fa-in kharajna falaa junaaḥa 'alaykum fee maa fa'alna feee anfusihinna mim

وَالَّذِيۡنَ يُتَوَفَّوۡنَ مِنۡكُمۡ وَيَذَرُوۡنَ
اَزۡوَاجًا ۖۚ وَّصِيَّةً لِّاَزۡوَاجِهِمۡ
مَّتَاعًا اِلَى الۡحَوۡلِ غَيۡرَ اِخۡرَاجٍ‌ ۚ
فَاِنۡ خَرَجۡنَ فَلَا جُنَاحَ عَلَيۡكُمۡ فِىۡ
مَا فَعَلۡنَ فِىۡٓ اَنۡفُسِهِنَّ مِنۡ

them to do what is reasonable. Allah is Majestic and Wise.	ma'roof; wallaahu 'Azeezun Ḥakeem.	مَّعْرُوفٍ ۗ وَاللّٰهُ عَزِيزٌ حَكِيمٌ ﴿٢٤٠﴾
241. The divorced women have the right to receive reasonable provisions. It is an obligation for the pious.	241. Wa lilmuṭallaqaati mataa-'um-bilma'roofi ḥaqqan 'alal-muttaqeen.	وَلِلْمُطَلَّقٰتِ مَتَاعٌۢ بِالْمَعْرُوفِ ۖ حَقًّا عَلَى الْمُتَّقِينَ ﴿٢٤١﴾
242. Thus does Allah explain His revelations to you so that perhaps you will have understanding.	242. Kaẕaalika yubayyinul-laahu lakum Aayaatihee la'allakum ta'qiloon.	كَذٰلِكَ يُبَيِّنُ اللّٰهُ لَكُمْ اٰيٰتِهٖ لَعَلَّكُمْ تَعْقِلُونَ ﴿٢٤٢﴾ ع ٣١ ١٥
243. (Muhammad), did you not see the thousands who left their homes for fear of death, who were then caused by Allah to die and brought back to life? Allah is generous to men but most people are not grateful.	243. Alam tara ilal-laẕeena kharajoo min diyaarihim wa hum uloofun ḥaẕaral-mawti faqaala lahumul-laahu mootoo ẖumma aḥyaahum; innal-laaha laẕoo faḍlin 'alannaasi wa laakinna akẖarannaasi laa yashkuroon.	اَلَمْ تَرَ اِلَى الَّذِينَ خَرَجُوا مِنْ دِيَارِهِمْ وَهُمْ اُلُوفٌ حَذَرَ الْمَوْتِ ۖ فَقَالَ لَهُمُ اللّٰهُ مُوتُوا ثُمَّ اَحْيَاهُمْ ۗ اِنَّ اللّٰهَ لَذُو فَضْلٍ عَلَى النَّاسِ وَلٰكِنَّ اَكْثَرَ النَّاسِ لَا يَشْكُرُونَ ﴿٢٤٣﴾
244. Fight for the cause of Allah and know that Allah is All-hearing and All-knowing.	244. Wa qaatiloo fee sabeelil-laahi wa'lamooo annal-laaha Samee'un 'Aleem.	وَقَاتِلُوا فِي سَبِيلِ اللّٰهِ وَاعْلَمُوٓا اَنَّ اللّٰهَ سَمِيعٌ عَلِيمٌ ﴿٢٤٤﴾
245. One who generously lends to Allah will be paid back in many multiples of the loan. It is Allah who reduces and expands things and to Him you will all return.	245. Man ẕal-laẕee yuqriḍul-laaha qarḍan ḥasanan fayuḍaa-'ifahoo lahooo aḍ'aafan kaẖee-rah; wallaahu yaqbiḍu wa yabṣuṭ; wa ilayhi turja'oon.	مَنْ ذَا الَّذِي يُقْرِضُ اللّٰهَ قَرْضًا حَسَنًا فَيُضٰعِفَهٗ لَهٗٓ اَضْعَافًا كَثِيرَةً ۗ وَاللّٰهُ يَقْبِضُ وَيَبْصُۜطُ ص وَاِلَيْهِ تُرْجَعُونَ ﴿٢٤٥﴾
246. (Muhammad), did you not see the group of the Israelites after Moses who demanded a Prophet of their own to appoint a king for them who would lead them in the fight for the cause of Allah? Their Prophet then said, "What if you are ordered to fight and you disobey?" They said, "Why should we not fight for the cause of Allah when we and our sons have been expelled from our homes?" When, however, they were ordered to fight, all refused except a few among them. Allah knows well the unjust.	246. Alam tara ilal-malai mim-Baneee Israaa'eela mim ba'di Moosaaa; iẕ qaaloo li-Nabiyyil-lahumub-'aẖ lanaa malikan nuqaatil fee sabeelillaahi qaala hal 'asaytum in kutiba 'alaykumul-qitaalu allaa tuqaatiloo qaaloo wa maa lanaaa allaa nuqaatila fee sabeelil-laahi wa qad ukhrijnaa min diyaarinaa wa abnaaa'inaa falammaa kutiba 'alayhimul-qitaalu tawallaw illaa qaleelam-minhum; wallaahu 'aleemum-biẓẓaalimeen.	اَلَمْ تَرَ اِلَى الْمَلَاِ مِنْۢ بَنِيٓ اِسْرَآءِيلَ مِنْۢ بَعْدِ مُوسٰى ۘ اِذْ قَالُوا لِنَبِيٍّ وقف لازم لَّهُمُ ابْعَثْ لَنَا مَلِكًا نُّقَاتِلْ فِي سَبِيلِ اللّٰهِ ۗ قَالَ هَلْ عَسَيْتُمْ اِنْ كُتِبَ عَلَيْكُمُ الْقِتَالُ اَلَّا تُقَاتِلُوا ۗ قَالُوا وَمَا لَنَآ اَلَّا نُقَاتِلَ فِي سَبِيلِ اللّٰهِ وَقَدْ اُخْرِجْنَا مِنْ دِيَارِنَا وَاَبْنَآئِنَا ۗ فَلَمَّا كُتِبَ عَلَيْهِمُ الْقِتَالُ تَوَلَّوْا اِلَّا قَلِيلًا مِّنْهُمْ ۗ وَاللّٰهُ عَلِيمٌۢ بِالظّٰلِمِينَ ﴿٢٤٦﴾

247. Their Prophet said, "Allah has appointed Saul as a king for you." They replied, "How can he dominate us when we deserve more to be king than he. Besides, he was not given abundant wealth." Their Prophet said, "Allah has chosen him as your ruler and has given him physical power and knowledge. Allah grants His authority to anyone whom He wants. Allah is Provident and All-knowing."

247. Wa qaala lahum Nabiy-yuhum innal-laaha qad ba'asa lakum Taaloota malikaa; qaalooo annaa yakoonu lahul-mulku 'alaynaa wa nahnu ahaqqu bilmulki minhu wa lam yu'ta sa'atamminal-maal; qaala innallaahas-tafaahu 'alaykum wa zaadahoo bastatan fil-'ilmi waljismi wallaahu yu'tee mulkahoo mañy-yashaaa'; wallaahu Waasi'un 'Aleem.

وَقَالَ لَهُمْ نَبِيُّهُمْ إِنَّ اللّٰهَ قَدْ بَعَثَ
لَكُمْ طَالُوتَ مَلِكًا ۚ قَالُوٓا أَنّٰى يَكُونُ
لَهُ الْمُلْكُ عَلَيْنَا وَنَحْنُ أَحَقُّ بِالْمُلْكِ
مِنْهُ وَلَمْ يُؤْتَ سَعَةً مِّنَ الْمَالِ ۚ
قَالَ إِنَّ اللّٰهَ اصْطَفٰهُ عَلَيْكُمْ وَزَادَهُ
بَسْطَةً فِي الْعِلْمِ وَالْجِسْمِ ۖ وَاللّٰهُ
يُؤْتِي مُلْكَهُ مَنْ يَّشَآءُ ۚ وَاللّٰهُ
وَاسِعٌ عَلِيمٌ ﴿٢٤٧﴾

248. Their Prophet further told them, "As the evidence of his authority, he will bring to you the Ark, which will be a comfort to you from your Lord and a legacy of the household of Moses and Aaron. It will be carried by the angels. This is the evidence for you if you have faith."

248. Wa qaala lahum Nabiy-yuhum inna Aayata mulkiheee añy-ya-tiyakumut-Taabootu feehi sakeenatummir-Rabbi-kum wa baqiyyatummimmaa taraka Aalu Moosaa wa Aalu Haaroona tahmiluhul-malaaa'ikah; inna fee zaalika la-Aayatal-lakum in kuntum mu'mineen.

وَقَالَ لَهُمْ نَبِيُّهُمْ إِنَّ اٰيَةَ مُلْكِهٖٓ
أَنْ يَّأْتِيَكُمُ التَّابُوتُ فِيهِ
سَكِينَةٌ مِّنْ رَّبِّكُمْ وَبَقِيَّةٌ مِّمَّا
تَرَكَ اٰلُ مُوسٰى وَاٰلُ هٰرُونَ تَحْمِلُهُ
الْمَلٰٓئِكَةُ ۚ إِنَّ فِي ذٰلِكَ لَاٰيَةً لَّكُمْ
إِنْ كُنْتُمْ مُّؤْمِنِينَ ﴿٢٤٨﴾ ع ٣٢ ٦ ١٢

249. When Saul set forth with the army he said, "Allah will test you with a river. Those who drank its water will not be of my people and those who did not even taste the water or who tasted only some of it from within the hollow of their hand, will be my friends." They all drank the water except a few of them.

When Saul and those who believed in him, crossed the river, his people said, "We do not have the strength to fight against Goliath and his army." Those who thought that (one day) they would be present before Allah said, "How often, with Allah's permission, have small groups defeated the large ones?" Allah is with those who exercise patience.

249. Falammaa fasala Taalootu biljunood; qaala innal-laaha mubtaleekum binaharin faman shariba minhu falaysa minnee wa mallam yat'amhu fa-innahoo minneee illaa manigh-tarafa ghurfatam biyadih; fashariboo minhu illaa qaleelamminhum; falammaa jaawazahoo huwa wallazeena aamanoo ma'ahoo qaaloo laa taaqata lanal-yawma bi-Jaaloota wa junoodih; qaalallazeena yazunnoona annahum mulaaqul-laahi kam min fi'atin qaleelatin ghalabat fi'atan kaseeratam bi-iznil-laah; wallaahu ma'as-saabireen.

فَلَمَّا فَصَلَ طَالُوتُ بِالْجُنُودِ ۙ
قَالَ إِنَّ اللّٰهَ مُبْتَلِيكُمْ بِنَهَرٍ ۚ
فَمَنْ شَرِبَ مِنْهُ فَلَيْسَ مِنِّي ۚ
وَمَنْ لَّمْ يَطْعَمْهُ فَإِنَّهُ مِنِّيٓ إِلَّا
مَنِ اغْتَرَفَ غُرْفَةً بِيَدِهٖ ۚ فَشَرِبُوا
مِنْهُ إِلَّا قَلِيلًا مِّنْهُمْ ۚ فَلَمَّا جَاوَزَهُ
هُوَ وَالَّذِينَ اٰمَنُوا مَعَهُ ۙ قَالُوا
لَا طَاقَةَ لَنَا الْيَوْمَ بِجَالُوتَ وَجُنُودِهٖ ۚ
قَالَ الَّذِينَ يَظُنُّونَ أَنَّهُمْ مُّلٰقُوا
اللّٰهِ ۙ كَمْ مِّنْ فِئَةٍ قَلِيلَةٍ غَلَبَتْ
فِئَةً كَثِيرَةً بِإِذْنِ اللّٰهِ ۗ وَاللّٰهُ
مَعَ الصّٰبِرِينَ ﴿٢٤٩﴾

250. Advancing towards Goliath and his army, they prayed to Allah for patience, steadfastness in battle, and for victory over the unbelievers.

250. Wa lammaa barazoo liJaaloota wa junoodihee qaaloo Rabbanaaa afrigh 'alaynaa ṣabrañw-wa s̱abbit aqdaamanaa wanṣurnaa 'alal-qawmil-kaafireen.

وَلَمَّا بَرَزُوْا لِجَالُوْتَ وَجُنُوْدِهٖ
قَالُوْا رَبَّنَآ اَفْرِغْ عَلَيْنَا صَبْرًا وَّثَبِّتْ
اَقْدَامَنَا وَانْصُرْنَا عَلَى الْقَوْمِ
الْكٰفِرِيْنَ ﴿۲۵۰﴾

251. They defeated their enemy through Allah's will. David slew Goliath and Allah granted David the kingdom and wisdom and also taught him whatever He wanted. Had Allah not made one group of people repel the other, the earth would have become full of spreading evil, but Allah is magnanimous to the worlds (His creatures).

251. Fahazamoohum bi-iẕnillaahi wa qatala Daawoodu Jaaloota wa aataahul-laahulmulka wal-Ḥikmata wa 'allamahoo mimmaa yashaaa'; wa law laa daf'ullaahin-naasa ba'ḍahum biba'ḍil-lafasadatil-arḍu wa laakinnal-laaha ẕoo faḍlin 'alal-'aalameen.

فَهَزَمُوْهُمْ بِاِذْنِ اللّٰهِ ۣ وَقَتَلَ
دَاوٗدُ جَالُوْتَ وَاٰتٰىهُ اللّٰهُ الْمُلْكَ
وَالْحِكْمَةَ وَعَلَّمَهٗ مِمَّا يَشَآءُ ؕ
وَلَوْلَا دَفْعُ اللّٰهِ النَّاسَ بَعْضَهُمْ
بِبَعْضٍ لَّفَسَدَتِ الْاَرْضُ وَلٰكِنَّ
اللّٰهَ ذُوْ فَضْلٍ عَلَى الْعٰلَمِيْنَ ﴿۲۵۱﴾

252. (Muhammad), these are the revelations which We recite to you for a genuine purpose. Certainly you are one of Our Messengers.

252. Tilka Aayaatul-laahi natloohaa 'alayka bilḥaqq; wa innaka laminal-mursaleen.

تِلْكَ اٰيٰتُ اللّٰهِ نَتْلُوْهَا عَلَيْكَ
بِالْحَقِّ ؕ وَاِنَّكَ لَمِنَ الْمُرْسَلِيْنَ ﴿۲۵۲﴾

253. We gave some of Our Messengers preference over others. To some of them Allah spoke and He raised the rank of some others. We gave authoritative proofs to Jesus, son of Mary, and supported him by the Holy Spirit. Had Allah wanted, the generations who lived after those Messengers would not have fought each other after the authority had come to them. But they differed among themselves; some of them believed in the authority and others rejected it. They would not have fought each other had Allah wanted, but Allah does as He wills.

253. Tilkar-Rusulu faḍḍalnaa ba'ḍahum 'alaa ba'ḍ; minhum man kallamal-laahu wa rafa'a ba'ḍahum darajaat; wa aataynaa 'Eesab-na-Maryamal-bayyinaati wa ayyadnaahu bi-Rooḥil-Qudus; wa law shaaa'al-laahu maqtatalal-laẕeena mim-ba'dihim mim ba'di maa jaaa'athumul-bayyinaatu wa laakinikh-talafoo faminhum man aamana wa minhum man kafar; wa law shaaa'al-laahu maq-tataloo wa laakinnallaaha yaf'alu maa yureed.

تِلْكَ الرُّسُلُ فَضَّلْنَا بَعْضَهُمْ
عَلٰى بَعْضٍ ۘ مِنْهُمْ مَّنْ كَلَّمَ اللّٰهُ
وَرَفَعَ بَعْضَهُمْ دَرَجٰتٍ ؕ وَاٰتَيْنَا
عِيْسَى ابْنَ مَرْيَمَ الْبَيِّنٰتِ وَاَيَّدْنٰهُ
بِرُوْحِ الْقُدُسِ ؕ وَلَوْ شَآءَ اللّٰهُ مَا
اقْتَتَلَ الَّذِيْنَ مِنْ بَعْدِهِمْ مِّنْ
بَعْدِ مَا جَآءَتْهُمُ الْبَيِّنٰتُ وَلٰكِنِ
اخْتَلَفُوْا فَمِنْهُمْ مَّنْ اٰمَنَ وَمِنْهُمْ
مَّنْ كَفَرَ ؕ وَلَوْ شَآءَ اللّٰهُ مَا اقْتَتَلُوْا ۣ
وَلٰكِنَّ اللّٰهَ يَفْعَلُ مَا يُرِيْدُ ﴿۲۵۳﴾ ع

الجزء الثالث (۳) وقف لازم

ع ۳۳ ۵

254. Believers, out of what We have given you, spend for the cause of Allah before the coming of the day when there will be no trading, no friendship, and no intercession. Those who deny the Truth are unjust.

254. Yaaa ayyuhal-laẕeena aamanooo anfiqoo mimmaa razaqnaakum min qabli añy-yatiya Yawmul-laa bay'un feehi wa laa khullatuñw-wa laa shafaa'ah; walkaafiroona humuẓ-ẓaalimoon.

يٰٓاَيُّهَا الَّذِيْنَ اٰمَنُوْٓا اَنْفِقُوْا مِمَّا
رَزَقْنٰكُمْ مِّنْ قَبْلِ اَنْ يَّاْتِيَ يَوْمٌ
لَّا بَيْعٌ فِيْهِ وَلَا خُلَّةٌ وَّلَا شَفَاعَةٌ ؕ
وَالْكٰفِرُوْنَ هُمُ الظّٰلِمُوْنَ ﴿۲۵۴﴾

255. Allah exists. There is no 'llah (one deserving to be worshipped) but He, the Everlasting and the Guardian of life. Drowsiness or sleep do not seize Him. To Him belongs all that is in the heavens and the earth. No one can intercede with Him for others except by His permission. He knows about people's present and past.

No one can grasp anything from His knowledge besides what He has permitted them to grasp. The heavens and the earth are under His dominion. He does not experience fatigue in preserving them both. He is the Highest and the Greatest.

255. Allaahu laaa ilaaha illaa Huwal-Ḥayyul-Qayyoom; laa ta-khuz̲uhoo sinatuñw-wa laa nawm; lahoo maa fissamaa-waati wa maa fil-arḍ; man z̲al-laz̲ee yashfa‘u ‘indahooo illaa bi-iz̲nih; ya‘lamu maa bayna aydeehim wa maa khalfahum wa laa yuḥeeṭoona bishay'im-min ‘ilmihee illaa bimaa shaaa'; wasi‘a Kursiyyuhus-samaa-waati wal-arḍa wa laa ya'oo-duhoo ḥifẓuhumaa; wa Huwal-‘Aliyyul-‘Aẓeem.

اَللّٰهُ لَاۤ اِلٰهَ اِلَّا هُوَۚ اَلۡحَىُّ الۡقَيُّوۡمُۚ
لَا تَاۡخُذُهٗ سِنَةٌ وَّلَا نَوۡمٌؕ
لَهٗ مَا فِى السَّمٰوٰتِ وَمَا فِى الۡاَرۡضِؕ
مَنۡ ذَا الَّذِىۡ يَشۡفَعُ عِنۡدَهٗۤ اِلَّا
بِاِذۡنِهٖؕ يَعۡلَمُ مَا بَيۡنَ اَيۡدِيۡهِمۡ وَمَا
خَلۡفَهُمۡۚ وَلَا يُحِيۡطُوۡنَ بِشَىۡءٍ مِّنۡ
عِلۡمِهٖۤ اِلَّا بِمَا شَآءَۚ وَسِعَ كُرۡسِيُّهُ
السَّمٰوٰتِ وَالۡاَرۡضَۚ وَلَا يَـُٔوۡدُهٗ
حِفۡظُهُمَاۚ وَهُوَ الۡعَلِىُّ الۡعَظِيۡمُ ﴿٢٥٥﴾

256. There is no compulsion in religion. Certainly, right has become clearly distinct from wrong. Whoever rejects the devil and believes in Allah has firmly taken hold of a strong handle that never breaks. Allah is All-hearing and All-knowing.

256. Laaa ikraaha fid-deeni qat-tabayyanar-rushdu minal-ghayy; famañy-yakfur biṭ-Ṭaaghooti wa yu'mim-billaahi faqadis-tamsaka bil‘urwatil-wus̲qaa lan-fiṣaama lahaa; wallaahu Samee‘un-‘Aleem.

لَاۤ اِكۡرَاهَ فِى الدِّيۡنِۙ قَد تَّبَيَّنَ الرُّشۡدُ
مِنَ الۡغَىِّۚ فَمَنۡ يَّكۡفُرۡ بِالطَّاغُوۡتِ
وَيُؤۡمِنۡۢ بِاللّٰهِ فَقَدِ اسۡتَمۡسَكَ بِالۡعُرۡوَةِ
الۡوُثۡقٰى لَا انْفِصَامَ لَهَاؕ وَاللّٰهُ
سَمِيۡعٌ عَلِيۡمٌ ﴿٢٥٦﴾

257. Allah is the Guardian of the believers and it is He who takes them out of darkness into light. The Devil is the guardian of those who deny the Truth and he leads them from light into darkness. These are the dwellers of hell wherein they will live forever.

257. Allaahu waliyyul-laz̲eena aamanoo yukhrijuhum-minaẓ-ẓulumaati ilan-noori walla-z̲eena kafarooo awli-yaaa'uhumuṭ-Ṭaaghootu yukhrijoonahum-minan-noori ilaẓ-ẓulumaat; ulaaa'ika Aṣhaabun-Naari hum feehaa khaalidoon.

اَللّٰهُ وَلِىُّ الَّذِيۡنَ اٰمَنُوۡا يُخۡرِجُهُمۡ
مِّنَ الظُّلُمٰتِ اِلَى النُّوۡرِؕ وَالَّذِيۡنَ
كَفَرُوۡۤا اَوۡلِيٰٓـئُهُمُ الطَّاغُوۡتُ ۙ
يُخۡرِجُوۡنَهُمۡ مِّنَ النُّوۡرِ اِلَى
الظُّلُمٰتِؕ اُولٰٓـئِكَ اَصۡحٰبُ النَّارِۚ
هُمۡ فِيۡهَا خٰلِدُوۡنَ ﴿٢٥٧﴾ ع ٣

258. (Muhammad), did you not see the one who argued with Abraham about his Lord for His granting him authority? Abraham said, "It is only my Lord who gives life and causes things to die." His opponent said, "I can also give life and make things die." Abraham said, "Allah causes the sun to come up from the East. You make it come from the West." Thus the unbeliever

258. Alam tara ilal-laz̲ee Ḥaaajja Ibraaheema fee Rabbiheee an aataahullaahul-mulk; iz̲ qaala Ibraaheemu Rabbiyal-laz̲ee yuḥyee wa yumeetu qaala ana uḥyee wa umeetu qaala-Ibraaheemu fa-innal-laaha ya-tee bishshamsi minal-mashriqi fa-ti bihaa minal-maghribi

اَلَمۡ تَرَ اِلَى الَّذِىۡ حَآجَّ اِبۡرٰهٖمَ
فِىۡ رَبِّهٖۤ اَنۡ اٰتٰٮهُ اللّٰهُ الۡمُلۡكَ ۘ
اِذۡ قَالَ اِبۡرٰهٖمُ رَبِّىَ الَّذِىۡ يُحۡىٖ
وَيُمِيۡتُۙ قَالَ اَنَا اُحۡىٖ وَاُمِيۡتُؕ
قَالَ اِبۡرٰهٖمُ فَاِنَّ اللّٰهَ يَاۡتِىۡ بِالشَّمۡسِ
مِنَ الۡمَشۡرِقِ فَاۡتِ بِهَا مِنَ الۡمَغۡرِبِ

وقف لازم

was confounded. Allah does not guide the unjust people.

fabuhital-lazee kafar; wallaahu laa yahdilqawmaẓ-ẓaalimeen.

فَبُهِتَ الَّذِيْ كَفَرَ ۗ وَاللّٰهُ لَا يَهْدِي
الْقَوْمَ الظّٰلِمِيْنَ ﴿٢٥٨﴾

259. (Or have you heard) of the one who, on passing through an empty and ruined town, said, "When will Allah bring it to life?" Allah caused him to die and brought him back to life after a hundred years and then asked him, "How long have you been here?" He replied, "One day or part of a day."

The Lord said, "No, you have been here for one hundred years. Look at your food and drink. They did not decay. But look at your donkey. To make your case an evidence (of the Truth) for the people, see how we bring the bones together and cover them with flesh." When he learned the whole story, he said, "Now I know that Allah has power over all things."

259. Aw kallazee marra 'alaa qaryatiñw-wa hiya khaawiyatun 'alaa 'urooshihaa qaala annaa yuḥyee haazihil-laahu ba'da mawtihaa fa-amaatahul-laahu mi'ata 'aamin summa ba'asahoo qaala kam labista qaala labistu yawman aw ba'ḍa yawmin qaala bal labista mi'ata 'aamin fanẓur ilaa ṭa'aamika wa sharaabika lam yatasannah wanẓur ilaa ḥimaarika wa linaj'alaka Aayatal-linnaasi wanẓur ilal'iẓaami kayfa nunshizuhaa summa naksoohaa laḥmaa; falammaa tabayyana lahoo qaala a'lamu annal-laaha 'alaa kulli shay'in Qadeer.

اَوْ كَالَّذِيْ مَرَّ عَلٰى قَرْيَةٍ وَّهِيَ خَاوِيَةٌ
عَلٰى عُرُوْشِهَا ۚ قَالَ اَنّٰى يُحْيٖ هٰذِهِ
اللّٰهُ بَعْدَ مَوْتِهَا ۚ فَاَمَاتَهُ اللّٰهُ
مِائَةَ عَامٍ ثُمَّ بَعَثَهٗ ۗ قَالَ كَمْ لَبِثْتَ ۗ
قَالَ لَبِثْتُ يَوْمًا اَوْ بَعْضَ يَوْمٍ ۗ
قَالَ بَلْ لَّبِثْتَ مِائَةَ عَامٍ
فَانْظُرْ اِلٰى طَعَامِكَ وَشَرَابِكَ لَمْ
يَتَسَنَّهْ ۚ وَانْظُرْ اِلٰى حِمَارِكَ ۚ وَلِنَجْعَلَكَ
اٰيَةً لِّلنَّاسِ وَانْظُرْ اِلَى الْعِظَامِ
كَيْفَ نُنْشِزُهَا ثُمَّ نَكْسُوْهَا
لَحْمًا ۚ فَلَمَّا تَبَيَّنَ لَهٗ ۙ قَالَ اَعْلَمُ
اَنَّ اللّٰهَ عَلٰى كُلِّ شَيْءٍ قَدِيْرٌ ﴿٢٥٩﴾

260. When Abraham prayed, "Lord, show me how you bring the dead back to life," the Lord said, "Did you not yet believe?" Abraham replied, "I believe but want more confidence for my heart." Allah told him, "Take four birds, induce them to come to you, cut and scatter their bodies leaving parts on every mountain top, then call them and they will swiftly come to you." Know that Allah is Majestic and Wise.

260. Wa-iz-qaala-Ibraaheemu Rabbi arinee kayfa tuḥyil-mawtaa qaala-awa lam tu'min qaala balaa wa laakil-liyaṭma'inna qalbee qaala fakhuz arba'atam-minaṭ-ṭayri faṣurhunna-ilayka summaj-'al 'alaa kulli jabalim-minhunna juz'an summad-'uhunna ya-teenaka sa'yaa; wa'lam annal-laaha 'Azeezun Ḥakeem.

وَاِذْ قَالَ اِبْرٰهٖمُ رَبِّ اَرِنِيْ كَيْفَ
تُحْيِ الْمَوْتٰى ۗ قَالَ اَوَلَمْ تُؤْمِنْ ۗ
قَالَ بَلٰى وَلٰكِنْ لِّيَطْمَئِنَّ قَلْبِيْ ۗ
قَالَ فَخُذْ اَرْبَعَةً مِّنَ الطَّيْرِ
فَصُرْهُنَّ اِلَيْكَ ثُمَّ اجْعَلْ عَلٰى
كُلِّ جَبَلٍ مِّنْهُنَّ جُزْءًا ثُمَّ
ادْعُهُنَّ يَاْتِيْنَكَ سَعْيًا ۗ وَاعْلَمْ
اَنَّ اللّٰهَ عَزِيْزٌ حَكِيْمٌ ﴿٢٦٠﴾ ٣٥ ع ٣ ٣

261. Spending money for the cause of Allah is as the seed from which seven ears may grow, each bearing one hundred grains. Allah gives in multiples to those whom He wants. Allah is Munificent and

261. Masalul-lazeena yunfi-qoona amwaalahum fee sabeelil-laahi kamasali ḥabbatin ambatat sab'a sanaabila fee kulli sumbulatim-mi'atu ḥabbah; wallaahu yuḍaa'ifu limañy-yashaaa';

مَثَلُ الَّذِيْنَ يُنْفِقُوْنَ اَمْوَالَهُمْ
فِيْ سَبِيْلِ اللّٰهِ كَمَثَلِ حَبَّةٍ اَنْۢبَتَتْ
سَبْعَ سَنَابِلَ فِيْ كُلِّ سُنْۢبُلَةٍ مِّائَةُ
حَبَّةٍ ۗ وَاللّٰهُ يُضٰعِفُ لِمَنْ يَّشَاءُ ۗ

All-knowing.

wallaahu Waasi'un-'Aleem.

وَاللّٰهُ وَاسِعٌ عَلِيْمٌ ﴿٢٦١﴾

262. Those who spend their property for the cause of Allah and do not make the recipient feel obliged or insulted shall receive their reward from Allah. They will have no fear nor will they be grieved.

262. Allazeena yunfiqoona amwaalahum fee sabeelillaahi summa laa yutbi'oona maaa anfaqoo mannañw-wa laaa azal-lahum ajruhum 'inda Rabbihim; wa laa khawfun 'alayhim wa laa hum yaḥzanoon.

اَلَّذِيْنَ يُنْفِقُوْنَ اَمْوَالَهُمْ فِيْ سَبِيْلِ
اللّٰهِ ثُمَّ لَا يُتْبِعُوْنَ مَآ اَنْفَقُوْا مَنًّا وَّلَآ
اَذًى ۙ لَّهُمْ اَجْرُهُمْ عِنْدَ رَبِّهِمْ ۚ
وَلَا خَوْفٌ عَلَيْهِمْ وَلَا هُمْ يَحْزَنُوْنَ ﴿٢٦٢﴾

263. Instructive words and forgiveness are better than charity that may cause an insult to the recipient. Allah is Rich and Forbearing.

263. Qawlum-ma'roofuñw-wa maghfiratun khayrum-min ṣadaqatiñy-yatba'uhaaa azaa; wallaahu Ghaniyyun Ḥaleem.

قَوْلٌ مَّعْرُوْفٌ وَّمَغْفِرَةٌ خَيْرٌ مِّنْ
صَدَقَةٍ يَّتْبَعُهَآ اَذًى ۗ وَاللّٰهُ غَنِيٌّ
حَلِيْمٌ ﴿٢٦٣﴾

264. Believers, do not make your charities fruitless by reproachfully reminding the recipients of your favor or making them feel insulted, like the one who spends his property to show off and who has no faith in Allah or belief in the Day of Judgment. The example of his deed is as though some soil has gathered on a rock and after a rainfall it turns hard and barren. Such people cannot benefit from what they have earned. Allah does not guide the unbelievers.

264. Yaaa ayyuhal-lazeena aamanoo laa tubṭiloo ṣadaqaatikum bilmanni wal-azaa kallazee yunfiqu maalahoo ri'aaa'an-naasi wa laa yu'minu billaahi wal-Yawmil-Aakhiri famasaluhoo kamasali ṣafwaanin 'alayhi turaabun fa-aṣaabahoo waabilun fatara-kahoo ṣaldaa; laa yaqdiroona 'alaa shay'immim-maa kasaboo; wallaahu laa yahdil-qawmal-kaafireen.

يٰٓاَيُّهَا الَّذِيْنَ اٰمَنُوْا لَا تُبْطِلُوْا
صَدَقٰتِكُمْ بِالْمَنِّ وَالْاَذٰى ۙ
كَالَّذِيْ يُنْفِقُ مَالَهٗ رِئَآءَ النَّاسِ
وَلَا يُؤْمِنُ بِاللّٰهِ وَالْيَوْمِ الْاٰخِرِ ۚ
فَمَثَلُهٗ كَمَثَلِ صَفْوَانٍ عَلَيْهِ
تُرَابٌ فَاَصَابَهٗ وَابِلٌ فَتَرَكَهٗ
صَلْدًا ۚ لَا يَقْدِرُوْنَ عَلٰى شَيْءٍ مِّمَّا
كَسَبُوْا ۚ وَاللّٰهُ لَا يَهْدِي الْقَوْمَ
الْكٰفِرِيْنَ ﴿٢٦٤﴾

265. The example of those who spend their property to please Allah out of their firm and sincere intention is as the garden on a fertile land which, after a heavy rainfall or even a drizzle, yields double produce. Allah is Well-aware of what you do.

265. Wa masalul-lazeena yunfiqoona amwaala-humubti-ghaaa'a marḍaatil-laahi wa tasbeetam-min anfusihim kamasali jannatim birabwatin aṣaabahaa waabilun fa-aatat ukulahaa ḍi'fayni fa-il-lam yuṣibhaa waabilun faṭall; wallaahu bimaa ta'maloona Baṣeer.

وَمَثَلُ الَّذِيْنَ يُنْفِقُوْنَ اَمْوَالَهُمُ ابْتِغَآءَ
مَرْضَاتِ اللّٰهِ وَتَثْبِيْتًا مِّنْ اَنْفُسِهِمْ
كَمَثَلِ جَنَّةٍ بِرَبْوَةٍ اَصَابَهَا وَابِلٌ
فَاٰتَتْ اُكُلَهَا ضِعْفَيْنِ ۚ فَاِنْ لَّمْ
يُصِبْهَا وَابِلٌ فَطَلٌّ ۗ وَاللّٰهُ بِمَا
تَعْمَلُوْنَ بَصِيْرٌ ﴿٢٦٥﴾

266. (What do you think of the case) of one of you who wishes to have a garden of palm-trees and grapes with water flowing therein and producing all kinds of fruits, especially if he is well advanced

266. Ayawaddu-aḥadukum-an takoona lahoo jannatum-min nakheeliñw-wa a'naabin tajree min taḥtihal-anhaaru lahoo feehaa min

اَيَوَدُّ اَحَدُكُمْ اَنْ تَكُوْنَ لَهٗ جَنَّةٌ
مِّنْ نَّخِيْلٍ وَّاَعْنَابٍ تَجْرِيْ مِنْ
تَحْتِهَا الْاَنْهٰرُ ۙ لَهٗ فِيْهَا مِنْ

in age and has weak children who need support, and then a hurricane with fire in it strikes the garden and burns it to the ground? This is how Allah explains to you His evidence so that you may think.

267. Believers, spend for the cause of Allah from the good things that you earn and from what We have made the earth yield for you. Do not even think of spending for the cause of Allah worthless things that you yourselves would be reluctant to accept. Know that Allah is Self-sufficient and Glorious.

268. Satan threatens you with poverty and commands you to commit sin. Allah promises you forgiveness and favors. Allah is Munificent and All-knowing.

269. Allah gives wisdom to anyone whom He wants. Whoever is given wisdom, certainly, has received much good. Only people of reason can grasp this.

270. Allah knows all about whatever you spend for His cause or any vows that you make. The unjust people have no helper.

271. It is not bad to give alms in public. However, if you give them privately to the poor, it would be better for you and an expiation for some of your sins. Allah is Well-aware of what you do.

272. (Muhammad), you do not have to guide them. Allah guides whomever He wants. Whatever you spend for the cause of Allah is

kullis-samaraati wa aṣaabahul-kibaru wa lahoo zurriyyatun ḍu'afaaa'u fa-aṣaabahaaa i'ṣaa-run feehi naarun faḥtaraqat; kazaalika yubayyinul-laahu lakumul-Aayaati la'allakum tatafakkaroon.

267. Yaaa 'ayyuhal-lazeena aamanooo anfiqoo min ṭayyi-baati maa kasabtum wa mimmaaa akhrajnaa lakum minal-arḍi wa laa tayammamul-khabeesa minhu tunfiqoona wa lastum bi-aakhizeehi illaaa an tughmiḍoo feeh; wa'lamooo annal-laaha Ghaniyyun Ḥameed.

268. Ash-Shayṭaanu ya'idu-kumul-faqra wa ya-murukum bilfaḥshaaa'i wallaahu ya'idu-kummagh-firatam-minhu wa faḍlaa; wallaahu Waasi'un 'Aleem.

269. Yu'til-Ḥikmata mañy-yashaaa'; wa mañy-yu'tal-Ḥikmata faqad ootiya khayran kaseeraa; wa maa yaz zakkaru illaaa ulul-albaab.

270. Wa maaa anfaqtum min nafaqatin aw nazartum min nazrin fa-innal-laaha ya'lamuh; wa maa lizzaalimeena min anṣaar.

271. In tubduṣ-ṣadaqaati fani-'immaa hiya wa in tukhfoohaa wa tu'toohal-fuqaraaa'a fahuwa khayrullakum; wa yukaffiru 'ankum min sayyi-aatikum; wallaahu bimaa ta'maloona Khabeer.

272. Laysa 'alayka hudaahum wa laakinnal-laaha yahdee mañy-yashaaa'; wa maa tunfiqoo

كُلِّ الثَّمَرٰتِ ۙ وَاَصَابَهُ الْكِبَرُ وَلَهٗ
ذُرِّيَّةٌ ضُعَفَآءُ ۖۚ فَاَصَابَهَآ اِعْصَارٌ
فِيْهِ نَارٌ فَاحْتَرَقَتْ ؕ كَذٰلِكَ يُبَيِّنُ
اللّٰهُ لَكُمُ الْاٰيٰتِ لَعَلَّكُمْ تَتَفَكَّرُوْنَ ﴿۲۶۶﴾
يٰۤاَيُّهَا الَّذِيْنَ اٰمَنُوْۤا اَنْفِقُوْا مِنْ
طَيِّبٰتِ مَا كَسَبْتُمْ وَمِمَّاۤ اَخْرَجْنَا
لَكُمْ مِّنَ الْاَرْضِ ۪ وَلَا تَيَمَّمُوا
الْخَبِيْثَ مِنْهُ تُنْفِقُوْنَ وَلَسْتُمْ
بِاٰخِذِيْهِ اِلَّاۤ اَنْ تُغْمِضُوْا فِيْهِ ؕ
وَاعْلَمُوْۤا اَنَّ اللّٰهَ غَنِيٌّ حَمِيْدٌ ﴿۲۶۷﴾
اَلشَّيْطٰنُ يَعِدُكُمُ الْفَقْرَ وَيَاْمُرُكُمْ
بِالْفَحْشَآءِ ۚ وَاللّٰهُ يَعِدُكُمْ مَّغْفِرَةً
مِّنْهُ وَفَضْلًا ؕ وَاللّٰهُ وَاسِعٌ عَلِيْمٌ ﴿۲۶۸﴾ ۖۙ
يُّؤْتِى الْحِكْمَةَ مَنْ يَّشَآءُ ۚ وَمَنْ يُّؤْتَ
الْحِكْمَةَ فَقَدْ اُوْتِىَ خَيْرًا كَثِيْرًا ؕ
وَمَا يَذَّكَّرُ اِلَّاۤ اُولُوا الْاَلْبَابِ ﴿۲۶۹﴾
وَمَاۤ اَنْفَقْتُمْ مِّنْ نَّفَقَةٍ اَوْ
نَذَرْتُمْ مِّنْ نَّذْرٍ فَاِنَّ اللّٰهَ
يَعْلَمُهٗ ؕ وَمَا لِلظّٰلِمِيْنَ مِنْ اَنْصَارٍ ﴿۲۷۰﴾
اِنْ تُبْدُوا الصَّدَقٰتِ فَنِعِمَّا هِىَ ۚ
وَاِنْ تُخْفُوْهَا وَتُؤْتُوْهَا الْفُقَرَآءَ
فَهُوَ خَيْرٌ لَّكُمْ ؕ وَيُكَفِّرُ عَنْكُمْ
مِّنْ سَيِّاٰتِكُمْ ؕ وَاللّٰهُ بِمَا تَعْمَلُوْنَ
خَبِيْرٌ ﴿۲۷۱﴾
لَيْسَ عَلَيْكَ هُدٰىهُمْ وَلٰكِنَّ اللّٰهَ
يَهْدِىْ مَنْ يَّشَآءُ ؕ وَمَا تُنْفِقُوْا

for your own good, provided you do not spend anything but to please Allah. For anything good that you may give for the cause of Allah, you will receive sufficient reward and no injustice will be done to you.

min khayrin fali-anfusikum; wa maa tunfiqoona illab-tighaaa'a Wajhil-laah; wa maa tunfiqoo min khayriñy-yuwaffa ilaykum wa antum laa tuẓlamoon.

مِنْ خَيْرٍ فَلِأَنفُسِكُمْ ۚ وَمَا تُنفِقُونَ
إِلَّا ابْتِغَاءَ وَجْهِ اللَّهِ ۚ وَمَا تُنفِقُوا
مِنْ خَيْرٍ يُوَفَّ إِلَيْكُمْ وَأَنتُمْ
لَا تُظْلَمُونَ ﴿٢٧٢﴾

273. (If the recipients of charity are) the poor whose poverty, because of their striving for the cause of Allah, has become an obstacle for them, and who do not have the ability to travel in the land, they seem rich compared to the ignorant, because of their modest behavior. You would know them by their faces. They would never earnestly ask people for help. Allah knows well whatever wealth you spend for the cause of Allah.

273. Lilfuqaraaa'il-lazeena uḥṣiroo fee sabeelil-laahi laa yastaṭee'oona ḍarban fil-arḍi yaḥ sabuhumul-jaahilu aghniyaaa'a minat-ta'affufi ta'rifuhum biseemaahum laa yas'aloonan-naasa ilḥaafaa; wa maa tunfiqoo min khayrin fa-innal-laaha bihee 'Aleem.

لِلْفُقَرَاءِ الَّذِينَ أُحْصِرُوا فِي سَبِيلِ
اللَّهِ لَا يَسْتَطِيعُونَ ضَرْبًا فِي الْأَرْضِ
يَحْسَبُهُمُ الْجَاهِلُ أَغْنِيَاءَ مِنَ
التَّعَفُّفِ تَعْرِفُهُم بِسِيمَاهُمْ لَا يَسْأَلُونَ
النَّاسَ إِلْحَافًا ۗ وَمَا تُنفِقُوا مِنْ
خَيْرٍ فَإِنَّ اللَّهَ بِهِ عَلِيمٌ ﴿٢٧٣﴾

274. Those who spend their property for the cause of Allah privately or in public will receive their reward from their Lord. There will be no fear for them nor will they grieve.

274. Allazeena yunfiqoona amwaalahum billayli wan-nahaari sirrañw-wa 'alaaniyatan falahum ajruhum 'inda Rabbihim wa laa khawfun 'alayhim wa laa hum yaḥzanoon.

الَّذِينَ يُنفِقُونَ أَمْوَالَهُم بِاللَّيْلِ
وَالنَّهَارِ سِرًّا وَعَلَانِيَةً فَلَهُمْ
أَجْرُهُمْ عِندَ رَبِّهِمْ وَلَا خَوْفٌ
عَلَيْهِمْ وَلَا هُمْ يَحْزَنُونَ ﴿٢٧٤﴾

275. Those who take unlawful interest will stand before Allah (on the Day of Judgment) as those who suffer from a mental imbalance because of Satan's touch; they have said that trade is just like unlawful interest. Allah has made trade lawful and has forbidden unlawful interest. One who has received advice from his Lord and has stopped committing sins will be rewarded for his previous good deeds. His affairs will be in the hands of Allah. But one who turns back to committing sins will be of the dwellers of hell wherein he will live forever.

275. Allazeena ya-kuloonar-ribaa laa yaqoomoona illaa kamaa yaqoomul-lazee yatakhab-baṭuhush-Shayṭaanu minal-mass; zaalika bi-annahum qaalooo innamal-bay'u mislur-ribaa; wa aḥallal-laahul-bay'a wa ḥarramar-ribaa; faman jaaa'ahoo maw'izatum-mir-Rabbihee fantahaa falahoo maa salaf; wa amruhooo ilal-laahi wa man 'aada fa-ulaaa'ika Aṣḥaabun-Naari hum feehaa khaalidoon.

الَّذِينَ يَأْكُلُونَ الرِّبَا لَا يَقُومُونَ
إِلَّا كَمَا يَقُومُ الَّذِي يَتَخَبَّطُهُ
الشَّيْطَانُ مِنَ الْمَسِّ ۚ ذَٰلِكَ بِأَنَّهُمْ
قَالُوا إِنَّمَا الْبَيْعُ مِثْلُ الرِّبَا ۗ
وَأَحَلَّ اللَّهُ الْبَيْعَ وَحَرَّمَ الرِّبَا ۚ
فَمَن جَاءَهُ مَوْعِظَةٌ مِّن رَّبِّهِ
فَانتَهَىٰ فَلَهُ مَا سَلَفَ وَأَمْرُهُ
إِلَى اللَّهِ ۖ وَمَنْ عَادَ فَأُولَٰئِكَ
أَصْحَابُ النَّارِ ۖ هُمْ فِيهَا خَالِدُونَ ﴿٢٧٥﴾

276. Allah makes unlawful interest devoid of all blessings and causes charity to increase. Allah does not love sinful unbelievers.

276. Yamḥaqul-laahur-ribaa wa yurbiṣ-ṣadaqaat; wallaahu laa yuḥibbu kulla kaffaarin aseem.

يَمْحَقُ اللَّهُ الرِّبَا وَيُرْبِي الصَّدَقَاتِ ۗ
وَاللَّهُ لَا يُحِبُّ كُلَّ كَفَّارٍ أَثِيمٍ ﴿٢٧٦﴾

277. The righteously striving believers, who are steadfast in

277. Innal-lazeena aamanoo wa 'amiluṣ-ṣaaliḥaati

إِنَّ الَّذِينَ آمَنُوا وَعَمِلُوا الصَّالِحَاتِ

their prayers and pay the zakat, will receive their reward from Allah. They will have no fear nor will they grieve.

wa aqaamuṣ-Ṣalaata wa aatawuz-Zakaata lahum ajruhum 'inda Rabbihim wa laa khawfun 'alayhim wa laa hum yaḥzanoon.

وَاَقَامُوا الصَّلٰوةَ وَاٰتَوُا الزَّكٰوةَ
لَهُمْ اَجْرُهُمْ عِنْدَ رَبِّهِمْ ۚ وَلَا خَوْفٌ
عَلَيْهِمْ وَلَا هُمْ يَحْزَنُوْنَ ﴿٢٧٧﴾

278. Believers, have fear of Allah and give up whatever unlawful interest you still demand from others, if you are indeed true believers.

278. Yaaa ayyuhal-lazeena aamanut-taqul-laaha wa zaroo maa baqiya minarribaaa in kuntum mu'mineen.

يٰاَيُّهَا الَّذِيْنَ اٰمَنُوا اتَّقُوا اللّٰهَ
وَذَرُوْا مَا بَقِيَ مِنَ الرِّبٰوٓا اِنْ
كُنْتُمْ مُّؤْمِنِيْنَ ﴿٢٧٨﴾

279. If you did not give up the unlawful interest which you demand, know that you are in a state of war with Allah and His Messenger. But if you repent, you will have your capital without being wronged or having done wrong to others.

279. Fa-il-lam taf'aloo fa-zanoo biḥarbim-minal-laahi wa Rasoolihee wa in tubtum falakum ru'oosu amwaalikum laa taẓlimoona wa laa tuẓlamoon.

فَاِنْ لَّمْ تَفْعَلُوْا فَاْذَنُوْا بِحَرْبٍ
مِّنَ اللّٰهِ وَرَسُوْلِهٖ ۚ وَاِنْ تُبْتُمْ فَلَكُمْ
رُءُوْسُ اَمْوَالِكُمْ ۚ لَا تَظْلِمُوْنَ
وَلَا تُظْلَمُوْنَ ﴿٢٧٩﴾

280. One who faces hardship in paying his debts must be given time until his financial condition improves. Would that you knew that waiving such a loan as charity would be better for you!

280. Wa in kaana zoo 'usratin fanaẓiratun ilaa maysarah; wa an taṣaddaqoo khayrul-lakum in kuntum ta'lamoon.

وَاِنْ كَانَ ذُوْ عُسْرَةٍ فَنَظِرَةٌ اِلٰى
مَيْسَرَةٍ ۚ وَاَنْ تَصَدَّقُوْا خَيْرٌ
لَّكُمْ اِنْ كُنْتُمْ تَعْلَمُوْنَ ﴿٢٨٠﴾

281. Safeguard yourselves against the day when you will return to Allah and every soul will be rewarded according to its deeds without being wronged.

281. Wattaqoo Yawman turja'oona feehi ilal-laahi summa tuwaffaa kullu nafsim-maa kasabat wa hum laa yuẓlamoon.

وَاتَّقُوْا يَوْمًا تُرْجَعُوْنَ فِيْهِ اِلَى
اللّٰهِ ۗ ثُمَّ تُوَفّٰى كُلُّ نَفْسٍ مَّا كَسَبَتْ
وَهُمْ لَا يُظْلَمُوْنَ ﴿٢٨١﴾ ع ٣٨

282. Believers, if you take a loan for a known period of time, have a just scribe write it down for you. The scribe should not refuse to do this as Allah has taught him. The debtor should dictate without any omission and have fear of Allah, his Lord. If the debtor is a fool, a minor, or one who is unable to dictate, his guardian should act with justice as his representative. Allow two men, or if you did not find them, one man and two women whom you choose, to bear witness to the contract so that if one of them makes a mistake the other can correct him. The witness must not refuse to testify when his testimony is needed.

282. Yaaa ayyuhal-lazeena aamanooo izaa tadaayantum bidaynin ilaaa ajalimmusam-man faktubooh; walyaktub baynakum kaatibum bil'adl; wa laa ya-ba kaatibun añy-yaktuba kamaa 'allamahullaah; falyaktub; walyumlilillazee 'alayhil-ḥaqqu walyattaqil-laaha rabbahoo wa laa yabkhas minhu shay'aa; fa-in kaanal-lazee 'alayhil-ḥaqqu safeehan aw ḍa'eefan aw laa yastaṭee'u añy-yumilla huwa falyumlil waliyyuhoo bil'adl; wastash-hidoo

يٰاَيُّهَا الَّذِيْنَ اٰمَنُوْٓا اِذَا تَدَايَنْتُمْ
بِدَيْنٍ اِلٰٓى اَجَلٍ مُّسَمًّى فَاكْتُبُوْهُ ۗ
وَلْيَكْتُبْ بَّيْنَكُمْ كَاتِبٌ بِالْعَدْلِ ۪
وَلَا يَاْبَ كَاتِبٌ اَنْ يَّكْتُبَ كَمَا عَلَّمَهُ
اللّٰهُ فَلْيَكْتُبْ ۚ وَلْيُمْلِلِ الَّذِيْ عَلَيْهِ
الْحَقُّ وَلْيَتَّقِ اللّٰهَ رَبَّهٗ وَلَا يَبْخَسْ
مِنْهُ شَيْـًٔا ۚ فَاِنْ كَانَ الَّذِيْ عَلَيْهِ
الْحَقُّ سَفِيْهًا اَوْ ضَعِيْفًا اَوْ لَا
يَسْتَطِيْعُ اَنْ يُّمِلَّ هُوَ فَلْيُمْلِلْ
وَلِيُّهٗ بِالْعَدْلِ ۚ وَاسْتَشْهِدُوْا

Do not disdain writing down a small or a large contract with all the details. A written record of the contract is more just in the sight of Allah, more helpful for the witness, and a more scrupulous way to avoid doubt. However, if everything in the contract is exchanged at the same time, there is no sin in not writing it down.

Let some people bear witness to your trade contracts, but the scribe or witness must not be harmed; it is a sin to harm them. Have fear of Allah. Allah teaches you. Allah has knowledge of all things.

shaheedayni mir-rijaalikum fa-il-lam yakoonaa rajulayni farajuluñw-wamra-ataani mimman tarḍawna minash-shuhadaaa'i an taḍilla iḥdaahumaa fatuzakkira iḥdaahumal-ukhraa; wa laa ya-bash-shuhadaaa'u izaa maa du'oo; wa laa tas'amooo an taktuboohu ṣagheeran aw kabeeran ilaaa ajalih; zaalikum aqsaṭu 'indal-laahi wa aqwamu lishshahaadati wa adnaaa allaa tartaabooo illaaa an takoona tijaaratan ḥaaḍiratan-tudeeroonahaa baynakum falaysa 'alaykum junaaḥun allaa taktuboohaa; wa ashhidooo izaa tabaaya'tum; wa laa yuḍaaarra kaatibuñw-wa laa shaheed; wa in taf'aloo fa-innahoo fusooqum-bikum; wattaqul-laaha wa yu'allimu-kumul-laah; wallaahu bikulli shay'in 'Aleem.

283. If you are on a journey and did not find a scribe, finalize your contract in the form of a deposit in which the goods are already given to the parties. If you trust each other in such a contract, let him pay back what he has entrusted you with and have fear of Allah, his Lord. Do not refuse to testify to that to which you bore witness. Whoever does so, his heart has committed a sin. Allah knows what you do.

283. Wa in kuntum 'alaa safariñw -wa lam tajidoo kaatiban farihaanum-maqboodatun fa-in amina ba'ḍukum ba'ḍan falyu'addillazi'-tumina amaa-natahoo walyattaqil-laaha Rabbah; wa laa taktumush-shahaadah; wa mañy-yaktumhaa fa-innahooo aasimun qalbuh; wallaahu bimaa ta'maloona 'Aleem.

284. To Allah belongs whatever is in the heavens and the earth. Allah will call you to account for all that you may reveal from your souls and all that you may conceal.

284. Lillaahi maa fissamaa-waati wa maa fil-arḍ; wa in tubdoo maa feee anfusikum aw tukhfoohu yuḥaasibkum bihil-laah;

شَهِيدَيْنِ مِن رِّجَالِكُمْ فَإِن لَّمْ يَكُونَا رَجُلَيْنِ فَرَجُلٌ وَّامْرَأَتَانِ مِمَّن تَرْضَوْنَ مِنَ الشُّهَدَآءِ أَن تَضِلَّ إِحْدَاهُمَا فَتُذَكِّرَ إِحْدَاهُمَا الْأُخْرَىٰ وَلَا يَأْبَ الشُّهَدَآءُ إِذَا مَا دُعُوا وَلَا تَسْـَٔمُوٓا أَن تَكْتُبُوهُ صَغِيرًا أَوْ كَبِيرًا إِلَىٰٓ أَجَلِهِ ذَٰلِكُمْ أَقْسَطُ عِندَ اللَّهِ وَأَقْوَمُ لِلشَّهَادَةِ وَأَدْنَىٰٓ أَلَّا تَرْتَابُوٓا إِلَّآ أَن تَكُونَ تِجَارَةً حَاضِرَةً تُدِيرُونَهَا بَيْنَكُمْ فَلَيْسَ عَلَيْكُمْ جُنَاحٌ أَلَّا تَكْتُبُوهَا وَأَشْهِدُوٓا إِذَا تَبَايَعْتُمْ وَلَا يُضَآرَّ كَاتِبٌ وَّلَا شَهِيدٌ وَإِن تَفْعَلُوا فَإِنَّهُ فُسُوقٌ بِكُمْ وَاتَّقُوا اللَّهَ وَيُعَلِّمُكُمُ اللَّهُ وَاللَّهُ بِكُلِّ شَيْءٍ عَلِيمٌ ۝

وَإِن كُنتُمْ عَلَىٰ سَفَرٍ وَّلَمْ تَجِدُوا كَاتِبًا فَرِهَانٌ مَّقْبُوضَةٌ فَإِنْ أَمِنَ بَعْضُكُم بَعْضًا فَلْيُؤَدِّ الَّذِي اؤْتُمِنَ أَمَانَتَهُ وَلْيَتَّقِ اللَّهَ رَبَّهُ وَلَا تَكْتُمُوا الشَّهَادَةَ وَمَن يَكْتُمْهَا فَإِنَّهُ آثِمٌ قَلْبُهُ وَاللَّهُ بِمَا تَعْمَلُونَ عَلِيمٌ ۝

لِلَّهِ مَا فِي السَّمَٰوَٰتِ وَمَا فِي الْأَرْضِ وَإِن تُبْدُوا مَا فِيٓ أَنفُسِكُمْ أَوْ تُخْفُوهُ يُحَاسِبْكُم بِهِ اللَّهُ

Allah will forgive or punish whomever He wants. Allah has power over all things.

fayaghfiru limañy-yashaaa'u wa yu'a<u>zz</u>ibu mañy-yashaaa'; wallaahu 'alaa kulli shay'in Qadeer.

فَيَغْفِرُ لِمَنْ يَّشَآءُ وَيُعَذِّبُ مَنْ
يَّشَآءُ ۗ وَاللّٰهُ عَلٰى كُلِّ شَيْءٍ قَدِيْرٌ ﴿٢٨٤﴾

285. The Messenger believed in what was revealed to him from his Lord and every one of the believers believed in Allah, His angels, His Books, and His Messengers, saying, "We find no difference among the Messengers of Allah." They also have said, "We heard Allah's commands and obeyed them. Lord, we need Your forgiveness and to You we shall return."

285. Aamanar-Rasoolu bimaaa unzila ilayhi Mir-Rabbihee walmu'minoon; kullun aamana billaahi wa Malaaa'ikatihee wa Kutubihee wa Rusulihee laa nufarriqu bayna aḥadim-mir-Rusulih; wa qaaloo sami'naa wa aṭa'naa ghufraanaka Rabbanaa wa ilaykal-maṣeer.

اٰمَنَ الرَّسُوْلُ بِمَآ اُنْزِلَ اِلَيْهِ
مِنْ رَّبِّهٖ وَالْمُؤْمِنُوْنَ ۗ كُلٌّ اٰمَنَ
بِاللّٰهِ وَمَلٰٓئِكَتِهٖ وَكُتُبِهٖ وَرُسُلِهٖ ۚ
لَا نُفَرِّقُ بَيْنَ اَحَدٍ مِّنْ رُّسُلِهٖ ۚ
وَقَالُوْا سَمِعْنَا وَاَطَعْنَا ۗ غُفْرَانَكَ
رَبَّنَا وَاِلَيْكَ الْمَصِيْرُ ﴿٢٨٥﴾

286. Allah does not impose on any soul a responsibility beyond its ability. Every soul receives whatever it gains and is liable for whatever it does.

Lord, do not hold us responsible for our forgetfulness and mistakes. Lord, do not lay upon us the burden that You laid on those who lived before us. Lord, do not lay on us what we cannot afford. Ignore and forgive our sins. Have mercy on us. You are our Lord. Help us against the unbelievers.

286. Laa yukalliful-laahu nafsan illaa wus'ahaa; lahaa maa kasabat wa 'alayhaa maktasabat; Rabbanaa laa tu'aakhi<u>z</u>naaa-in naseenaaa aw-akhṭa-naa; Rabbanaa wa laa taḥmil-'alaynaaa-iṣran kamaa ḥamaltahoo 'alalla<u>z</u>eena min qablinaa; Rabbanaa wa laa tuḥammilnaa maa laa ṭaaqata lanaa bihee wa'fu 'annaa waghfir lanaa warḥamnaaa; Anta mawlaanaa fanṣurnaa 'alal-qawmil-kaafireen.

لَا يُكَلِّفُ اللّٰهُ نَفْسًا اِلَّا وُسْعَهَا ۭ لَهَا
مَا كَسَبَتْ وَعَلَيْهَا مَا اكْتَسَبَتْ ۭ
رَبَّنَا لَا تُؤَاخِذْنَآ اِنْ نَّسِيْنَآ اَوْ
اَخْطَاْنَا ۚ رَبَّنَا وَلَا تَحْمِلْ عَلَيْنَآ
اِصْرًا كَمَا حَمَلْتَهٗ عَلَى الَّذِيْنَ
مِنْ قَبْلِنَا ۚ رَبَّنَا وَلَا تُحَمِّلْنَا مَا
لَا طَاقَةَ لَنَا بِهٖ ۚ وَاعْفُ عَنَّا ۥ
وَاغْفِرْ لَنَا ۥ وَارْحَمْنَا ۥ اَنْتَ مَوْلٰىنَا
فَانْصُرْنَا عَلَى الْقَوْمِ الْكٰفِرِيْنَ ﴿٢٨٦﴾ ع ٤٠ ٨

Al-Imran, The Imrans-3

In the Name of Allah, the Beneficent, the Merciful.

Sûrat Âl-Imrân-3

(Revealed at Madinah)

Bismillaahir Raḥmaanir Raḥeem

(٣) سُوْرَةُ اٰلِ عِمْرٰنَ مَدَنِيَّةٌ (٨٩)

اٰيَاتُهَا ٢٠٠ بِسْمِ اللّٰهِ الرَّحْمٰنِ الرَّحِيْمِ رُكُوْعَاتُهَا ٢٠

1. Alif. Lam. Mim.
2. Allah exists. He is the only Lord, the Everlasting and the Guardian of life.
3. He has sent the Book (Quran) to you (Muhammad) in all Truth. It confirms the original Bible. He revealed the Torah and the Gospel

1. Alif-Laaam-Meeem.
2. Allaahu laaa ilaaha illaa Huwal-Ḥayyul-Qayyoom.
3. Nazzala 'alaykal-Kitaaba bilḥaqqi muṣaddiqal-limaa bayna yadayhi wa anzalat-Tawraata wal-Injeel.

الٓمّٓ ﴿١﴾
اللّٰهُ لَآ اِلٰهَ اِلَّا هُوَ ۙ الْحَيُّ الْقَيُّوْمُ ﴿٢﴾
نَزَّلَ عَلَيْكَ الْكِتٰبَ بِالْحَقِّ
مُصَدِّقًا لِّمَا بَيْنَ يَدَيْهِ وَاَنْزَلَ
التَّوْرٰىةَ وَالْاِنْجِيْلَ ﴿٣﴾

4. before as a guide for the people and now He has revealed the criterion for discerning right from wrong. Those who reject the

4. Min qablu hudal-linnaasi wa anzalal-Furqaan; innalla<u>z</u>eena kafaroo bi-Aayaatil-

مِنْ قَبْلُ هُدًى لِّلنَّاسِ وَاَنْزَلَ
الْفُرْقَانَ ۛ اِنَّ الَّذِيْنَ كَفَرُوْا بِاٰيٰتِ

revelations of Allah will face the most severe torment. Allah is Majestic and capable of revenge.

laahi lahum 'azaabun shadeed; wallaahu 'azeezun zun-tiqaam.

اللّٰهِ لَهُمْ عَذَابٌ شَدِيْدٌ ۭ وَاللّٰهُ
عَزِيْزٌ ذُو انْتِقَامٍ ٤

5. Nothing in the heavens or the earth is hidden from Allah.

5. Innal-laaha laa yakhfaa 'alayhi shay'un fil-arḍi wa laa fis-samaaa'.

اِنَّ اللّٰهَ لَا يَخْفٰى عَلَيْهِ شَيْءٌ فِي
الْاَرْضِ وَلَا فِي السَّمَاۗءِ ٥

6. It is Allah who shapes you in the womb as He wills. He is the only Lord, the Majestic, and All-wise.

6. Huwal-lazee yuṣawwiru-kum fil-arḥaami kayfa yashaaa'; laaa-ilaaha-illaa Huwal 'Azeezul-Ḥakeem.

هُوَ الَّذِيْ يُصَوِّرُكُمْ فِي الْاَرْحَامِ
كَيْفَ يَشَاۗءُ ۭ لَآ اِلٰهَ اِلَّا هُوَ
الْعَزِيْزُ الْحَكِيْمُ ٦

7. It is Allah who has revealed the Book to you in which some verses are clear statements (which accept no interpretation) and these are the fundamental ideas of the Book, while other verses may have several possibilities. Those whose hearts are perverse follow the unclear statements in pursuit of their own mischievous goals by interpreting them in a way that will suit their own purpose. No one knows its true interpretation except Allah, and those who have a firm grounding in knowledge say, "We believe in it. All its verses are from our Lord." No one can grasp this fact except the people of reason.

7. Huwal-lazeee anzala 'alaykal-Kitaaba minhu Aayaatum-Muḥkamaatun hunna Ummul-Kitaabi wa ukharu Mutashaabihaatun fa-ammal-lazeena fee quloobihim zayghun fayattabi'oona maa tashaababa minhubtighaaa'al-fitnati wabtighaaa'a ta-weelih; wa maa ya'lamu ta-weelahooo illal-laah; warraasikhoona fil-'ilmi yaqooloona aamannaa bihee kullum-min 'indi Rabbinaa; wa maa yaz zakkaru illaaa ulul-albaab.

هُوَ الَّذِيْٓ اَنْزَلَ عَلَيْكَ الْكِتٰبَ
مِنْهُ اٰيٰتٌ مُّحْكَمٰتٌ هُنَّ اُمُّ
الْكِتٰبِ وَاُخَرُ مُتَشٰبِهٰتٌ ۭ فَاَمَّا
الَّذِيْنَ فِيْ قُلُوْبِهِمْ زَيْغٌ فَيَتَّبِعُوْنَ
مَا تَشَابَهَ مِنْهُ ابْتِغَاۗءَ الْفِتْنَةِ
وَابْتِغَاۗءَ تَاْوِيْلِهٖ ڱ وَمَا يَعْلَمُ
تَاْوِيْلَهٗٓ اِلَّا اللّٰهُ ڤ وَالرّٰسِخُوْنَ
فِي الْعِلْمِ يَقُوْلُوْنَ اٰمَنَّا بِهٖ ۙ كُلٌّ
مِّنْ عِنْدِ رَبِّنَا ۚ وَمَا يَذَّكَّرُ اِلَّآ
اُولُوا الْاَلْبَابِ ٧

وقف النبي صلى الله عليه وآله وسلم
وقف لازم وقف منزل

8. They say, "Lord, do not cause our hearts to deviate from Your guidance and grant us mercy. You are the Most Awarding One.

8. Rabbanaa laa tuzigh quloobanaa ba'da iz hadaytanaa wa hab lanaa milladunka raḥmah; innaka Antal-Wahhaab.

رَبَّنَا لَا تُزِغْ قُلُوْبَنَا بَعْدَ اِذْ
هَدَيْتَنَا وَهَبْ لَنَا مِنْ لَّدُنْكَ
رَحْمَةً ۚ اِنَّكَ اَنْتَ الْوَهَّابُ ٨

9. Lord, it is certain that one day You will gather all the people together. Allah does not break His promise."

9. Rabbanaaa innaka jaami-'un-naasi li-Yawmil-laa rayba feeh; innal-laaha laa yukhliful-mee'aad.

رَبَّنَآ اِنَّكَ جَامِعُ النَّاسِ لِيَوْمٍ
لَّا رَيْبَ فِيْهِ ۭ اِنَّ اللّٰهَ لَا يُخْلِفُ
الْمِيْعَادَ ٩ ع

ع ۹

10. The wealth and children of the unbelievers will never serve them (disbelievers) as a substitute for their belief in Allah. Such people will be the fuel for the fire.

10. Innal-lazeena kafaroo lan tughniya 'anhum amwaaluhum wa laaa awlaaduhum minal-laahi shay'aa; wa ulaaa'ika hum waqoodun-Naar.

اِنَّ الَّذِيْنَ كَفَرُوْا لَنْ تُغْنِيَ عَنْهُمْ
اَمْوَالُهُمْ وَلَآ اَوْلَادُهُمْ مِّنَ
اللّٰهِ شَيْـــًٔا ۭ وَاُولٰۗىِٕكَ هُمْ وَقُوْدُ النَّارِ ١٠

11. They do as the people of Pharaoh and those who lived before them did. They called Our revelations mere lies. Allah punished them for their sins. Allah is stern in His retribution.

11. Kada-bi Aali Fir'awna wallaz̲eena min qablihim; kaz̲-z̲aboo bi-Aayaatinaa fa-akhaz̲ahumul-laahu biz̲unoo-bihim; wallaahu shadeedul-'iqaab.

كَدَاْبِ اٰلِ فِرۡعَوۡنَ ۙ وَالَّذِيۡنَ
مِنۡ قَبۡلِهِمۡ ؕ كَذَّبُوۡا بِاٰيٰتِنَا ۚ
فَاَخَذَهُمُ اللّٰهُ بِذُنُوۡبِهِمۡ ؕ وَاللّٰهُ
شَدِيۡدُ الۡعِقَابِ ﴿۱۱﴾

12. (Muhammad), tell the unbelievers that they will soon be defeated and driven into hell, a terrible dwelling.

12. Qul lillaz̲eena kafaroo satughlaboona wa tuḥsharoona ilaa Jahannam; wa bi'sal-mihaad.

قُلۡ لِّلَّذِيۡنَ كَفَرُوۡا سَتُغۡلَبُوۡنَ
وَتُحۡشَرُوۡنَ اِلٰى جَهَنَّمَ ؕ وَبِئۡسَ
الۡمِهَادُ ﴿۱۲﴾

13. There, certainly, is evidence (of the existence of Allah) for you in the case of the two armies. One of them fought for the cause of Allah. The other was of the unbelievers. The unbelievers appeared to be twice the size of the believers. However, Allah supports, through His help, whomever He wants. It is a good lesson for the people of true vision.

13. Qad kaana lakum Aayatun fee fi'ataynil-taqataa fi'atun tuqaatilu fee sabeelil-laahi wa ukhraa kaafiratuñy-yarawnahum mis̲layhim ra-yal-'ayn; wallaahu yu'ayyidu binaṣrihee mañy-yashaaa'; inna fee z̲aalika la'ibratal-li-oolil-abṣaar.

قَدۡ كَانَ لَـكُمۡ اٰيَةٌ فِىۡ فِئَتَيۡنِ
الۡتَقَتَا ؕ فِئَةٌ تُقَاتِلُ فِىۡ سَبِيۡلِ
اللّٰهِ وَاُخۡرٰى كَافِرَةٌ يَّرَوۡنَهُمۡ
مِّثۡلَيۡهِمۡ رَاۡىَ الۡعَيۡنِ ؕ وَاللّٰهُ يُؤَيِّدُ
بِنَصۡرِهٖ مَنۡ يَّشَآءُ ؕ اِنَّ فِىۡ ذٰلِكَ
لَعِبۡرَةً لِّاُولِى الۡاَبۡصَارِ ﴿۱۳﴾

14. Worldly desires, wives, children, accumulated treasures of gold and silver, horses of noble breed, cattle, and farms are all made to seem attractive to men. All these are the bounties of the worldly life, but in the life to come, Allah has the best place for people to dwell.

14. Zuyyina linnaasi ḥubbush-shahawaati minannisaaa'i wal-baneena walqanaaṭeeril-muqanṭarati minaz̲-z̲ahabi walfiḍḍati walkhaylil-musawwamati wal-an'aami walḥars̲; z̲aalika mataa'ul-ḥayaatid-dunyaa wallaahu 'indahoo ḥusnul-ma-aab.

زُيِّنَ لِلنَّاسِ حُبُّ الشَّهَوٰتِ مِنَ
النِّسَآءِ وَالۡبَنِيۡنَ وَالۡقَنَاطِيۡرِ الۡمُقَنۡطَرَةِ
مِنَ الذَّهَبِ وَالۡفِضَّةِ وَالۡخَيۡلِ
الۡمُسَوَّمَةِ وَالۡاَنۡعَامِ وَالۡحَرۡثِ ؕ
ذٰلِكَ مَتَاعُ الۡحَيٰوةِ الدُّنۡيَا ۚ
وَاللّٰهُ عِنۡدَهٗ حُسۡنُ الۡمَاٰبِ ﴿۱۴﴾

15. (Muhammad), ask them, "Shall I tell you what is far superior to worldly pleasures? Those who have fear of Allah will have (as their reward) gardens wherein streams flow and wherein they will live forever with their purified spouses and with the consent of Allah. Allah knows all about His servants."

15. Qul a'unabbi'ukum bikhayrim-min z̲aalikum; lillaz̲eenat-taqaw 'inda Rabbihim Jannaatun tajree min taḥtihal-anhaaru khaalideena feehaa wa azwaajum-muṭahharatuñw-wa riḍwaanum-minal-laah; wallaahu baṣeerum bil'ibaad.

قُلۡ اَؤُنَبِّئُكُمۡ بِخَيۡرٍ مِّنۡ ذٰ لِكُمۡ ؕ
لِلَّذِيۡنَ اتَّقَوۡا عِنۡدَ رَبِّهِمۡ جَنّٰتٌ
تَجۡرِىۡ مِنۡ تَحۡتِهَا الۡاَنۡهٰرُ خٰلِدِيۡنَ
فِيۡهَا وَاَزۡوَاجٌ مُّطَهَّرَةٌ وَّرِضۡوَانٌ
مِّنَ اللّٰهِ ؕ وَاللّٰهُ بَصِيۡرٌۢ بِالۡعِبَادِ ﴿۱۵﴾

16. (Such will be the reward of) those who say, "Lord, we have believed in You. Forgive us our sins and save us from the torment of fire,"

16. Allaz̲eena yaqooloona Rabbanaaa innanaaa aamannaa faghfir lanaa z̲unoobanaa wa qinaa 'az̲aaban-Naar.

اَلَّذِيۡنَ يَقُوۡلُوۡنَ رَبَّنَاۤ اِنَّنَاۤ اٰمَنَّا
فَاغۡفِرۡ لَنَا ذُنُوۡبَنَا وَقِنَا عَذَابَ النَّارِ ﴿۱۶﴾ ۚ

17. who exercise patience, speak the truth, are devoted in prayer, spend their property for the cause of Allah, and seek forgiveness from Allah during the last part of the night.

18. Allah Himself testifies that He is the only Lord. The angels and the men of knowledge and justice testify that Allah is the only Lord, the Majestic, and All-wise.

19. In the sight of Allah, Islam is the religion. The People of the Book created differences in the matters (of religion) because of their hostility among themselves, only after knowledge had come to them. Let whoever denies the revelations of Allah know that the reckoning of Allah is swift.

20. (Muhammad), if the People of the Book argue against you, say, "I and those who follow me have submitted ourselves to Allah." Ask the People of the Book and the illiterate ones, "Have you embraced Islam?" If they embrace Islam they will find guidance, but if they turn away, your task is just to preach. Allah knows all about His servants.

21. Warn those who deny the revelations of Allah and unjustly slay the Prophets and those who call people to be just, that they will suffer a painful torment.

22. The deeds of such people are made devoid of all virtue in both this life and the life to come. There will be no one to help them.

23. (Muhammad), did you not see those who have received a share of the Book? On referring to the Book in order to judge amongst themselves, a group of them turn away with disregard

17. Aṣṣaabireena waṣṣaadiqeena walqaaniteena walmunfiqeena walmustaghfireena bil-asḥaar.

18. Shahidal-laahu annahoo laaa ilaaha illaa Huwa walmalaaa'ikatu wa ulul-'ilmi qaaa'imam bilqisṭ; laaa ilaaha illaa Huwal-'Azeezul-Ḥakeem.

19. Innad-deena 'indallaahil-Islaam; wa makhtalafal-lazeena ootul-Kitaaba illaa mim ba'di maa jaaa'ahumul-'ilmu baghyam baynahum; wa mañy-yakfur bi-Aayaatil-laahi fa-innal-laaha saree'ul-ḥisaab.

20. Fa-in ḥaaajjooka faqul aslamtu wajhiya lillaahi wa manit-taba'an; wa qul lillazeena ootul-Kitaaba wal-ummiyyeena 'a-aslamtum; fa-in aslamoo faqadih-tadaw wa in tawallaw fa-innamaa 'alaykal-balaagh; wallaahu baṣeerum bil'ibaad.

21. Innal-lazeena yakfuroona bi-Aayaatil-laahi wa yaqtuloonan-Nabiyyeena bighayri ḥaqq; wa yaqtuloonal-lazeena ya-muroona bilqisṭi minannaasi fabashshirhum bi'azaabin aleem.

22. Ulaaa'ikal-lazeena ḥabiṭat a'maaluhum fid-dunyaa wal-Aakhirati wa maa lahum min naaṣireen.

23. Alam tara ilal-lazeena ootoo naṣ eebam-minal-Kitaabi yud'awna ilaa Kitaabil-laahi liyaḥkuma baynahum summa yatawallaa fareequm-minhum wa hum mu'riḍoon.

الصّٰبِرِيْنَ وَالصّٰدِقِيْنَ وَالْقٰنِتِيْنَ
وَالْمُنْفِقِيْنَ وَالْمُسْتَغْفِرِيْنَ بِالْاَسْحَارِ ﴿١٧﴾
شَهِدَ اللّٰهُ اَنَّهٗ لَاۤ اِلٰهَ اِلَّا هُوَ ۙ وَ
الْمَلٰۤىِٕكَةُ وَاُولُوا الْعِلْمِ قَاۤىِٕمًاۢ بِالْقِسْطِ ؕ
لَاۤ اِلٰهَ اِلَّا هُوَ الْعَزِيْزُ الْحَكِيْمُ ﴿١٨﴾ النصف
اِنَّ الدِّيْنَ عِنْدَ اللّٰهِ الْاِسْلَامُ ۫
وَمَا اخْتَلَفَ الَّذِيْنَ اُوْتُوا الْكِتٰبَ
اِلَّا مِنْۢ بَعْدِ مَا جَاۤءَهُمُ الْعِلْمُ
بَغْيًاۢ بَيْنَهُمْ ؕ وَمَنْ يَّكْفُرْ بِاٰيٰتِ
اللّٰهِ فَاِنَّ اللّٰهَ سَرِيْعُ الْحِسَابِ ﴿١٩﴾
فَاِنْ حَاۤجُّوْكَ فَقُلْ اَسْلَمْتُ وَجْهِيَ
لِلّٰهِ وَمَنِ اتَّبَعَنِ ؕ وَقُلْ لِّلَّذِيْنَ
اُوْتُوا الْكِتٰبَ وَالْاُمِّيّٖنَ ءَاَسْلَمْتُمْ ؕ
فَاِنْ اَسْلَمُوْا فَقَدِ اهْتَدَوْا ۚ وَاِنْ
تَوَلَّوْا فَاِنَّمَا عَلَيْكَ الْبَلٰغُ ؕ ع ٢/١١
وَاللّٰهُ بَصِيْرٌۢ بِالْعِبَادِ ﴿٢٠﴾
اِنَّ الَّذِيْنَ يَكْفُرُوْنَ بِاٰيٰتِ اللّٰهِ
وَيَقْتُلُوْنَ النَّبِيّٖنَ بِغَيْرِ حَقٍّ ۙ
وَّيَقْتُلُوْنَ الَّذِيْنَ يَاْمُرُوْنَ بِالْقِسْطِ
مِنَ النَّاسِ ۙ فَبَشِّرْهُمْ بِعَذَابٍ اَلِيْمٍ ﴿٢١﴾
اُولٰۤىِٕكَ الَّذِيْنَ حَبِطَتْ اَعْمَالُهُمْ فِى
الدُّنْيَا وَالْاٰخِرَةِ ۫ وَمَا لَهُمْ مِّنْ نّٰصِرِيْنَ ﴿٢٢﴾
اَلَمْ تَرَ اِلَى الَّذِيْنَ اُوْتُوْا نَصِيْبًا
مِّنَ الْكِتٰبِ يُدْعَوْنَ اِلٰى كِتٰبِ اللّٰهِ
لِيَحْكُمَ بَيْنَهُمْ ثُمَّ يَتَوَلّٰى فَرِيْقٌ
مِّنْهُمْ وَهُمْ مُّعْرِضُوْنَ ﴿٢٣﴾

24. because of their belief that the fire will only touch them for a few days. This fabricated belief has deceived them in matters of their religion.

24. Zaalika bi-annahum qaaloo lan tamassanan-Naaru illaaa ayyaamam ma'doodaatiñw-wa gharrahum fee deenihim maa kaanoo yaftaroon.

ذٰلِكَ بِاَنَّهُمْ قَالُوْا لَنْ تَمَسَّنَا النَّارُ
اِلَّآ اَيَّامًا مَّعْدُوْدٰتٍ ۠ وَّغَرَّهُمْ
فِيْ دِيْنِهِمْ مَّا كَانُوْا يَفْتَرُوْنَ ۝٢٤

25. What will happen to their belief when We bring them together on the Inevitable Day when every soul will be justly recompensed for its deeds?

25. Fakayfa izaa jama'naahum li-Yawmil-laa rayba feehi wa wuffiyat kullu nafsim-maa kasabat wa hum laa yuẓlamoon.

فَكَيْفَ اِذَا جَمَعْنٰهُمْ لِيَوْمٍ لَّا رَيْبَ
فِيْهِ ۣ وَوُفِّيَتْ كُلُّ نَفْسٍ مَّا
كَسَبَتْ وَهُمْ لَا يُظْلَمُوْنَ ۝٢٥

26. (Muhammad), say, "Lord, Owner of the Kingdom, You give authority to whomever You want and take it away from whomever You want. You give honor to whomever You want and humiliate whomever You want. In Your hands is all virtue and You have power over all things.

26. Qulil-laahumma Maalikal-Mulki tu'til-mulka man tashaaa'u wa tanzi'ulmulka mimman tashaaa'u wa tu'izzu man tashaaa'u wa tuzillu man tashaaa'u biyadikal-khayr; innaka 'alaa kulli shay'in Qadeer.

قُلِ اللّٰهُمَّ مٰلِكَ الْمُلْكِ تُؤْتِي الْمُلْكَ
مَنْ تَشَاۗءُ وَتَنْزِعُ الْمُلْكَ مِمَّنْ
تَشَاۗءُ ۡ وَتُعِزُّ مَنْ تَشَاۗءُ وَتُذِلُّ
مَنْ تَشَاۗءُ ۭ بِيَدِكَ الْخَيْرُ ۭ اِنَّكَ
عَلٰي كُلِّ شَيْءٍ قَدِيْرٌ ۝٢٦

27. You cause the day to enter into the night and the night to enter into the day. You cause the living to come out of the dead and the dead to come out of the living. You give sustenance to whomever You want without keeping an account.

27. Toolijul-layla fin-nahaari wa toolijun-nahaara fil-layli wa tukhrijul-ḥayya minal-mayyiti wa tukhrijul-mayyita minal-ḥayyi wa tarzuqu man tashaaa'u bighayri ḥisaab.

تُوْلِجُ الَّيْلَ فِي النَّهَارِ وَتُوْلِجُ
النَّهَارَ فِي الَّيْلِ ۡ وَتُخْرِجُ الْحَيَّ مِنَ
الْمَيِّتِ وَتُخْرِجُ الْمَيِّتَ مِنَ الْحَيِّ ۡ
وَتَرْزُقُ مَنْ تَشَاۗءُ بِغَيْرِ حِسَابٍ ۝٢٧

28. The believers must not establish friendship with the unbelievers, out of preference to the faithful. Whoever does so has nothing to hope for from Allah unless he does it out of fear or taqiyah (fear and precaution). Allah warns you about Himself. To Allah do all things return.

28. Laa yattakhizil-mu'mi-noonal-kaafireena awliyaaa'a min doonilmu'mineena wa mañy-yaf'al zaalika falaysa minal-laahi fee shay'in illaaa an tattaqoo minhum tuqaah; wa yuḥaz zirukumul-laahu nafsah; wa ilal-laahil-maṣeer.

لَا يَتَّخِذِ الْمُؤْمِنُوْنَ الْكٰفِرِيْنَ
اَوْلِيَاۗءَ مِنْ دُوْنِ الْمُؤْمِنِيْنَ ۚ وَ
مَنْ يَّفْعَلْ ذٰلِكَ فَلَيْسَ مِنَ اللّٰهِ
فِيْ شَيْءٍ اِلَّآ اَنْ تَتَّقُوْا مِنْهُمْ
تُقٰىةً ۭ وَيُحَذِّرُكُمُ اللّٰهُ نَفْسَهٗ ۭ
وَاِلَى اللّٰهِ الْمَصِيْرُ ۝٢٨

29. (Muhammad), tell them, "Allah knows all that you may conceal in your hearts or that you may reveal. He knows all that is in the heavens and the earth. He has power over all things."

29. Qul in tukhfoo maa fee ṣudoorikum aw tubdoohu ya'lamhul-laah; wa ya'lamu maa fis-samaawaati wa maa fil-arḍ; wallaahu 'alaa kulli shay'in Qadeer.

قُلْ اِنْ تُخْفُوْا مَا فِيْ صُدُوْرِكُمْ اَوْ
تُبْدُوْهُ يَعْلَمْهُ اللّٰهُ ۭ وَيَعْلَمُ مَا
فِي السَّمٰوٰتِ وَمَا فِي الْاَرْضِ ۭ
وَاللّٰهُ عَلٰي كُلِّ شَيْءٍ قَدِيْرٌ ۝٢٩

30. On the day when every soul will see its good and bad deeds

30. Yawma tajidu kullu nafsim-maa 'amilat min

يَوْمَ تَجِدُ كُلُّ نَفْسٍ مَّا عَمِلَتْ مِنْ

right before its very eyes, it will wish for the longest period of time to separate it from its bad deeds. Allah warns you about Himself. Allah is Compassionate to His servants.

khayrim muhdaranw-wa maa 'amilat min sooo'in tawaddu law-anna baynahaa wa baynahooo amadam ba'eedaa; wa yuhazzirukumul-laahu nafsah; wallaahu ra'oofum bil'ibaad.

خَيْرٍ مُّحْضَرًا ۚ وَّمَا عَمِلَتْ مِنْ سُوْٓءٍ ۚ
تَوَدُّ لَوْ اَنَّ بَيْنَهَا وَبَيْنَهٗٓ اَمَدًۢا بَعِيْدًا ۭ
وَيُحَذِّرُكُمُ اللّٰهُ نَفْسَهٗ ۭ وَاللّٰهُ رَءُوْفٌۢ
بِالْعِبَادِ ﴿٣٠﴾

31. (Muhammad), tell them, "If you love Allah, follow me. Allah will love you and forgive your sins. Allah is All-forgiving and All-merciful."

31. Qul in kuntum tuhibboonal-laaha fattabi'oonee yuhbibkumullaahu wa yaghfir lakum zunoobakum; wallaahu Ghafoorur-Raheem.

قُلْ اِنْ كُنْتُمْ تُحِبُّوْنَ اللّٰهَ فَاتَّبِعُوْنِيْ
يُحْبِبْكُمُ اللّٰهُ وَيَغْفِرْ لَكُمْ ذُنُوْبَكُمْ ۭ
وَاللّٰهُ غَفُوْرٌ رَّحِيْمٌ ﴿٣١﴾

32. Tell them, "Obey Allah and the Messenger." If they turn away (let it be known) that Allah does not love the unbelievers.

32. Qul atee'ul-laaha war-Rasoola fa-in tawallaw fa-innal-laaha laa yuhibbul-kaafireen.

قُلْ اَطِيْعُوا اللّٰهَ وَالرَّسُوْلَ ۚ فَاِنْ تَوَلَّوْا
فَاِنَّ اللّٰهَ لَا يُحِبُّ الْكٰفِرِيْنَ ﴿٣٢﴾

33. Allah chose (and gave distinction to) Adam, Noah, the family of Abraham, and Imran over all the people of the world.

33. Innal-laahas -tafaaa Aadama wa Noohanw-wa Aala Ibraaheema wa Aala 'Imraana 'alal-'aalameen.

اِنَّ اللّٰهَ اصْطَفٰٓي اٰدَمَ وَنُوْحًا وَّاٰلَ
اِبْرٰهِيْمَ وَاٰلَ عِمْرٰنَ عَلَي الْعٰلَمِيْنَ ﴿٣٣﴾

34. They were the offspring of one another. Allah is All-hearing and All-seeing.

34 Zurriyyatam ba'duhaa mim-ba'd, wallaahu Samee'un 'Aleem.

ذُرِّيَّةًۢ بَعْضُهَا مِنْۢ بَعْضٍ ۭ وَاللّٰهُ
سَمِيْعٌ عَلِيْمٌ ﴿٣٤﴾

35. Remember when Imran's wife prayed to her Lord saying, "I have made a vow to dedicate to Your service whatever is in my womb. Lord, accept it from me. You are All-hearing and All-knowing."

35. Iz qaalatim-ra-atu 'Imraana Rabbi innee nazartu laka maa fee batneee muharraran fataqabbal minneee innaka Antas-Samee'ul-'Aleem.

اِذْ قَالَتِ امْرَاَتُ عِمْرٰنَ رَبِّ اِنِّىْ
نَذَرْتُ لَكَ مَا فِيْ بَطْنِيْ مُحَرَّرًا
فَتَقَبَّلْ مِنِّىْ ۚ اِنَّكَ اَنْتَ السَّمِيْعُ
الْعَلِيْمُ ﴿٣٥﴾

36. When the baby was born she said, "Lord, it is a female." Allah knew this. Male and female are not alike. "I have named her Mary. I pray that You will keep her and her offspring safe from Satan, the condemned one."

36. Falammaa wada'athaa qaalat Rabbi innee wada'tuhaaa unsaa wallaahu a'lamu bimaa wada'at wa laysaz-zakaru kal-unsaa wa innee sammaytuhaa Maryama wa inneee u'eezuhaa bika wa zurriyyatahaa minash-Shaytaanir-Rajeem.

فَلَمَّا وَضَعَتْهَا قَالَتْ رَبِّ اِنِّىْ
وَضَعْتُهَآ اُنْثٰى ۭ وَاللّٰهُ اَعْلَمُ بِمَا
وَضَعَتْ ۭ وَلَيْسَ الذَّكَرُ كَالْاُنْثٰى ۚ
وَاِنِّىْ سَمَّيْتُهَا مَرْيَمَ وَاِنِّىْٓ اُعِيْذُھَا
بِكَ وَذُرِّيَّتَهَا مِنَ الشَّيْطٰنِ الرَّجِيْمِ ﴿٣٦﴾

37. Her Lord graciously accepted the offer and made Mary grow up, pure and beautiful. Zachariah took custody of her. Whenever he went to visit her in her place of worship, he would find with her some food. He would ask her, "Where did this

37. Fataqabbalahaa Rabbuhaa biqaboolin hasaninw-wa ambatahaa nabaatan hasananw-wa kaffalahaa Zakariyyaa kullamaa dakhala 'alayhaa Zakariyyal-Mihraab; wajada 'indahaa rizqan qaala

فَتَقَبَّلَهَا رَبُّهَا بِقَبُوْلٍ حَسَنٍ
وَّاَنْۢبَتَهَا نَبَاتًا حَسَنًا ۙ وَّكَفَّلَهَا
زَكَرِيَّا ۚ كُلَّمَا دَخَلَ عَلَيْهَا زَكَرِيَّا
الْمِحْرَابَ ۙ وَجَدَ عِنْدَهَا رِزْقًا ۚ قَالَ

معانقة عند المتأخرين ١٢ ع ٣

food come from?" She would reply, "Allah has sent it." Allah gives sustenance to whomever He wants without keeping an account.

yaa Maryamu annaa laki haaẕaa qaalat huwa min 'indil-laah; innal-laaha yarzuqu mañy-yashaaa'u bighayri ḥisaab.

يٰمَرْيَمُ اَنّٰى لَكِ هٰذَا ؕ قَالَتْ هُوَ
مِنْ عِنْدِ اللّٰهِ ؕ اِنَّ اللّٰهَ يَرْزُقُ مَنْ
يَّشَآءُ بِغَيْرِ حِسَابٍ ﴿٣٧﴾

38. Zachariah prayed to his Lord there, saying, "Lord, grant me, by Your Grace, virtuous offspring. You hear all prayers."

38. Hunaaalika da'aa Zakariyyaa Rabbahoo qaala Rabbi hab lee mil-ladunka ẕurriyyatan ṭayyibatan innaka Samee'ud-du'aaa'.

هُنَالِكَ دَعَا زَكَرِيَّا رَبَّهٗ ۚ قَالَ
رَبِّ هَبْ لِيْ مِنْ لَّدُنْكَ ذُرِّيَّةً
طَيِّبَةً ۚ اِنَّكَ سَمِيْعُ الدُّعَآءِ ﴿٣٨﴾

39. When he was standing during prayer in his place of worship, the angels called him, saying, "Allah gives you the glad news of the birth of your son, John, who will be a confirmation of (Jesus) the Word of Allah. He will become a chaste, noble leader and one of the righteous Prophets."

39. Fanaadathul-malaaa'ikatu wa huwa qaaa'imuñy-yuṣallee fil-Miḥraab; annal-laaha yubashshiruka bi-Yaḥyaa muṣaddiqam bi-Kalimatim-minal-laahi wa sayyidañw-wa ḥaṣoorañw-wa Nabiyyam minaṣ-ṣaaliḥeen.

فَنَادَتْهُ الْمَلٰٓئِكَةُ وَهُوَ قَآئِمٌ يُّصَلِّيْ
فِي الْمِحْرَابِ ۙ اَنَّ اللّٰهَ يُبَشِّرُكَ
بِيَحْيٰى مُصَدِّقًۢا بِكَلِمَةٍ مِّنَ اللّٰهِ
وَسَيِّدًا وَّحَصُوْرًا وَّنَبِيًّا مِّنَ
الصّٰلِحِيْنَ ﴿٣٩﴾

40. He said, "How can there be a son for me when I am already senile and my wife is barren!" The angel replied, "Allah does as He wills."

40. Qaala Rabbi annaa yakoonu lee ghulaamuñw-wa qad balaghaniyal-kibaru wamra-atee 'aaqirun qaala kaẕaalikal-laahu yaf'alu maa yashaaa'.

قَالَ رَبِّ اَنّٰى يَكُوْنُ لِيْ غُلٰمٌ وَّقَدْ
بَلَغَنِيَ الْكِبَرُ وَامْرَاَتِيْ عَاقِرٌ ؕ قَالَ
كَذٰلِكَ اللّٰهُ يَفْعَلُ مَا يَشَآءُ ﴿٤٠﴾

41. Zachariah prayed to Allah saying, "Lord, show me the evidence (that it is Divine revelation)." The Lord replied, "You will not be able to speak (even though in good health) to people for three days except with gestures. Speak of your Lord often and glorify Him in the early mornings and the evenings."

41. Qaala Rabbij-'al-leee Aayatan qaala Aayatuka allaa tukalliman-naasa s̱alaas̱ata ayyaamin illaa ramzaa; waẕkur Rabbaka kas̱eerañw-wa sabbiḥ bil'ashiyyi wal-ibkaar.

قَالَ رَبِّ اجْعَلْ لِّيْٓ اٰيَةً ؕ قَالَ
اٰيَتُكَ اَلَّا تُكَلِّمَ النَّاسَ ثَلٰثَةَ
اَيَّامٍ اِلَّا رَمْزًا ؕ وَاذْكُرْ رَّبَّكَ كَثِيْرًا
وَّسَبِّحْ بِالْعَشِيِّ وَالْاِبْكَارِ ﴿٤١﴾ ع

42. "Behold," the angels told Mary, "Allah has chosen you, purified you, and given you distinction over all women.

42. Wa iẕ qaalatil-malaaa'ikatu yaa Maryamu innal-laahaṣ-ṭafaaki wa ṭahharaki waṣṭafaaki 'alaa nisaaa'il-'aalameen.

وَاِذْ قَالَتِ الْمَلٰٓئِكَةُ يٰمَرْيَمُ اِنَّ اللّٰهَ
اصْطَفٰىكِ وَطَهَّرَكِ وَاصْطَفٰىكِ
عَلٰى نِسَآءِ الْعٰلَمِيْنَ ﴿٤٢﴾

43. Mary, pray devotedly to your Lord, prostrate yourself before Him and bow down with those who bow down before Him."

43. Yaa Maryamuq-nutee li-Rabbiki wasjudee warka'ee ma'ar-raaki'een.

يٰمَرْيَمُ اقْنُتِيْ لِرَبِّكِ وَاسْجُدِيْ
وَارْكَعِيْ مَعَ الرّٰكِعِيْنَ ﴿٤٣﴾

44. (Muhammad), that was some of the news about the unseen that We have revealed to you. You were not among those who cast lots by throwing their arrows to find out who would take custody of Mary,

44. Ẕaalika min ambaaa'il-ghaybi nooḥeehi ilayk; wa maa kunta ladayhim iẕ yulqoona aqlaamahum ayyuhum yakfulu Maryama

ذٰلِكَ مِنْ اَنْۢبَآءِ الْغَيْبِ نُوْحِيْهِ
اِلَيْكَ ؕ وَمَا كُنْتَ لَدَيْهِمْ اِذْ
يُلْقُوْنَ اَقْلَامَهُمْ اَيُّهُمْ يَكْفُلُ مَرْيَمَ ص

nor were you among those who disputed the matter.

wa maa kunta ladayhim iz yakhtaşimoon.

وما كنت لديهم إذ يختصمون ﴿٤٤﴾

45. "Behold," the angels told Mary, "Allah has given you the glad news of the coming birth of a son whom He calls His Word, whose name will be Messiah, Jesus, son of Mary, who will be a man of honor in this life and the life to come, and who will be one of those nearest to Allah.

45. Iz qaalatil-malaaa'ikatu yaa Maryamu innal-laaha yubashshiruki bi-Kalimatim-minhus-muhul-Maseeḥu 'Eesab-nu-Maryama wajeehan fid-dunyaa wal-Aakhirati wa minal-muqarrabeen.

إذ قالت الملائكة يا مريم إن
الله يبشرك بكلمة منه اسمه
المسيح عيسى ابن مريم وجيها
في الدنيا والآخرة ومن
المقربين ﴿٤٥﴾

46. He will speak to the people while in his cradle and preach to them when he becomes a man. He will be one of the righteous ones.

46. Wa yukallimun-naasa filmahdi wa kahlañw-wa minas-şaaliḥeen.

ويكلم الناس في المهد وكهلا
ومن الصالحين ﴿٤٦﴾

47. (Mary) said, "How can there be a son for me when no mortal touched me?" The angel replied, "That is how Allah creates whatever He wants. When He decides to do something, He just orders it to exist and it comes into existence."

47. Qaalat Rabbi annaa yakoonu lee waladuñw-wa lam yamsasnee basharun qaala kazaalikil-laahu yakhluqu maa yashaaa'; izaa qaḍaaa amran fa-innamaa yaqoolu lahoo kun fayakoon.

قالت رب أنى يكون لي ولد ولم
يمسسني بشر قال كذلك الله
يخلق ما يشاء إذا قضى أمرا
فإنما يقول له كن فيكون ﴿٤٧﴾

48. Allah will give (Jesus) wisdom and teach him the Book, the Torah, and the Gospel.

48. Wa yu'allimuhul-Kitaaba wal-Ḥikmata wat-Tawraata wal-Injeel.

ويعلمه الكتاب والحكمة والتوراة
والإنجيل ﴿٤٨﴾

49. He will be a Messenger of Allah to the Israelites to whom he will say, "I have brought you a miracle from your Lord. I can create for you something from clay in the form of a bird. When I blow into it, it will become a real bird, by the permission of Allah. I can heal the blind and the lepers and bring the dead back to life, by the permission of Allah. I can tell you about what you eat and what you store in your homes. This is a miracle for you if you want to have faith."

49. Wa Rasoolan-ilaa Baneee Israaa'eela annee qad ji'tukum bi-Aayatim-mir-Rabbikum anneee akhluqu lakum minaṭ-ṭeeni kahay'atiṭṭayri fa-anfukhu feehi fayakoonu ṭayram bi-iznil-laahi wa ubri'ul-akmaha wal-abraşa wa-uḥyil-mawtaa bi-iznil-laahi wa unabbi'ukum bimaa ta-kuloona wa maa taddakhiroona fee buyootikum; inna fee zaalika la-Aayatal-lakum in kuntum mu'mineen.

ورسولا إلى بني إسرائيل أني
قد جئتكم بآية من ربكم
أني أخلق لكم من الطين كهيئة
الطير فأنفخ فيه فيكون طيرا
بإذن الله وأبرئ الأكمه والأبرص
وأحي الموتى بإذن الله وأنبئكم
بما تأكلون وما تدخرون
في بيوتكم إن في ذلك لآية
لكم إن كنتم مؤمنين ﴿٤٩﴾

50. "I testify to what is true in the Torah and make lawful for you some of the things that were made unlawful. I have brought you a miracle from your Lord.

50. Wa muşaddiqal-limaa bayna yadayya minat-Tawraati wa li-uḥilla lakum ba'ḍal-lazee ḥurrima 'alaykum; wa ji'tukum bi-Aayatim-mir-

ومصدقا لما بين يدي من
التوراة ولأحل لكم بعض الذي
حرم عليكم وجئتكم بآية من

Have fear of Allah and obey me.

Rabbikum fattaqul-laaha wa aṭee'oon.

رَبِّكُمْ فَاتَّقُوا اللّٰهَ وَاَطِيْعُوْنِ ۝٥٠

51. Allah is my Lord as well as yours. Worship Him, for this is the right path."

51. Innal-laaha Rabbee wa Rabbukum fa'budooh; haaẕaa Ṣiraaṭum-Mustaqeem.

اِنَّ اللّٰهَ رَبِّيْ وَرَبُّكُمْ فَاعْبُدُوْهُ ؕ
هٰذَا صِرَاطٌ مُّسْتَقِيْمٌ ۝٥١

52. When Jesus found them denying the truth, he said, "Who will help me in the cause of Allah?" The disciples replied, "We are the helpers of Allah. We believe in Him. Jesus, bear witness that we have submitted ourselves to His will."

52. Falammaaa aḥassa 'Eesaa minhumul-kufra qaala man anṣaareee ilal-laahi qaalal-Ḥawaariyyoona naḥnu anṣaarul-laahi aamannaa billaahi washhad bi-annaa muslimoon.

فَلَمَّاۤ اَحَسَّ عِيْسٰى مِنْهُمُ الْكُفْرَ
قَالَ مَنْ اَنْصَارِيْۤ اِلَى اللّٰهِ ؕ قَالَ
الْحَوَارِيُّوْنَ نَحْنُ اَنْصَارُ اللّٰهِ ۚ اٰمَنَّا
بِاللّٰهِ ۚ وَاشْهَدْ بِاَنَّا مُسْلِمُوْنَ ۝٥٢

53. They prayed, "Lord, we have believed in what You have revealed to Your Messenger and we have followed him. Write down our names with those who testify in support of the Truth."

53. Rabbanaaa aamannaa bimaaa anzalta wattaba'nar-Rasoola faktubnaa ma'ash-shaahideen.

رَبَّنَاۤ اٰمَنَّا بِمَاۤ اَنْزَلْتَ وَاتَّبَعْنَا
الرَّسُوْلَ فَاكْتُبْنَا مَعَ الشّٰهِدِيْنَ ۝٥٣

54. The unbelievers plotted and Allah planned, but Allah is a much better planner;

54. Wa makaroo wa makaral-laahu wallaahu khayrul-maakireen.

وَمَكَرُوْا وَمَكَرَ اللّٰهُ ؕ وَاللّٰهُ خَيْرُ
الْمٰكِرِيْنَ ۝٥٤ ع

55. He told Jesus, "I will save you from your enemies, raise you to Myself, keep you clean from the association with the unbelievers, and give superiority to your followers over the unbelievers until the Day of Judgment. On that day you will all return to Me and I shall resolve your dispute.

55. Iẕ qaalal-laahu yaa 'Eesaaa innee mutawaffeeka wa raafi'uka ilayya wa muṭahhiruka minal-laẕeena kafaroo wa jaa'ilul-laẕeenattaba'ooka fawqal-laẕeena kafarooo ilaa Yawmil-Qiyaamati s̱umma ilayya marji'ukum fa-aḥkumu baynakum feemaa kuntum feehi takhtalifoon.

اِذْ قَالَ اللّٰهُ يٰعِيْسٰۤى اِنِّيْ مُتَوَفِّيْكَ
وَرَافِعُكَ اِلَيَّ وَمُطَهِّرُكَ مِنَ
الَّذِيْنَ كَفَرُوْا وَجَاعِلُ الَّذِيْنَ
اتَّبَعُوْكَ فَوْقَ الَّذِيْنَ كَفَرُوْۤا اِلٰى
يَوْمِ الْقِيٰمَةِ ۚ ثُمَّ اِلَيَّ مَرْجِعُكُمْ
فَاَحْكُمُ بَيْنَكُمْ فِيْمَا كُنْتُمْ
فِيْهِ تَخْتَلِفُوْنَ ۝٥٥

56. I shall sternly punish the unbelievers in this life and in the life to come and no one will help them."

56. Fa-ammal-laẕeena kafaroo fa-u'azzibuhum 'aẕaaban shadeedan fid-dunyaa wal-Aakhirati wa maa lahum min naaṣireen.

فَاَمَّا الَّذِيْنَ كَفَرُوْا فَاُعَذِّبُهُمْ
عَذَابًا شَدِيْدًا فِي الدُّنْيَا وَالْاٰخِرَةِ
وَمَا لَهُمْ مِّنْ نّٰصِرِيْنَ ۝٥٦

57. "However, to the righteously striving believers I shall give their reward in full measure." Allah does not love the unjust.

57. Wa ammal-laẕeena aamanoo wa 'amiluṣṣaaliḥaati fayuwaffeehim ujoorahum; wallaahu laa yuḥibbuẓ-ẓaalimeen

وَاَمَّا الَّذِيْنَ اٰمَنُوْا وَعَمِلُوا الصّٰلِحٰتِ
فَيُوَفِّيْهِمْ اُجُوْرَهُمْ ؕ وَاللّٰهُ لَا يُحِبُّ
الظّٰلِمِيْنَ ۝٥٧

58. (Muhammad), what we recite to you are revelations and words of wisdom.

58. Ẕaalika natloohu 'alayka minal-Aayaati waẕ-Ẕikril-Ḥakeem.

ذٰلِكَ نَتْلُوْهُ عَلَيْكَ مِنَ الْاٰيٰتِ
وَالذِّكْرِ الْحَكِيْمِ ۝٥٨

59. To Allah the case of Jesus is as that of Adam whom He created from the earth and then said, "Exist" and Adam came into existence.

59. Inna masala 'Eesaa 'indal-laahi kamasali Aadama khalaqahoo min turaabin summa qaala lahoo kun fayakoon.

إِنَّ مَثَلَ عِيسَىٰ عِندَ ٱللَّهِ كَمَثَلِ
ءَادَمَ ۖ خَلَقَهُۥ مِن تُرَابٍ ثُمَّ قَالَ
لَهُۥ كُن فَيَكُونُ ﴿٥٩﴾

60. (Muhammad, the essence of) the Truth is from your Lord. Never have any doubt about it.

60. Al-ḥaqqu mir-Rabbika falaa takum-minal-mumtareen.

ٱلْحَقُّ مِن رَّبِّكَ فَلَا تَكُن مِّنَ
ٱلْمُمْتَرِينَ ﴿٦٠﴾

61. If anyone disputes (your prophesy) after knowledge has come to you, say, "Let each of us bring our children, women, our people, and ourselves to one place and pray to Allah to condemn the liars among us."

61. Faman ḥaaajjaka feehi mim ba'di maa jaaa'aka minal'ilmi faqul ta'aalaw nad'u abnaaa'anaa wa abnaaa'akum wa nisaaa'anaa wa nisaaa'akum wa anfusanaa wa anfusakum summa nabtahil fanaj'al la'natal-laahi 'alal-kaazibeen.

فَمَنْ حَآجَّكَ فِيهِ مِنۢ بَعْدِ مَا
جَآءَكَ مِنَ ٱلْعِلْمِ فَقُلْ تَعَالَوْا۟
نَدْعُ أَبْنَآءَنَا وَأَبْنَآءَكُمْ وَنِسَآءَنَا
وَنِسَآءَكُمْ وَأَنفُسَنَا وَأَنفُسَكُمْ
ثُمَّ نَبْتَهِلْ فَنَجْعَل لَّعْنَتَ ٱللَّهِ
عَلَى ٱلْكَٰذِبِينَ ﴿٦١﴾

62. This is the true story (of Jesus). There is no Lord but Allah. It is Allah who is Majestic and All-wise.

62. Inna haazaa lahuwal-qaṣaṣul-ḥaqq; wa maa min ilaahin illal-laah; wa innal-laaha la-Huwal-'Azeezul-Ḥakeem.

إِنَّ هَٰذَا لَهُوَ ٱلْقَصَصُ ٱلْحَقُّ ۚ وَمَا
مِنْ إِلَٰهٍ إِلَّا ٱللَّهُ ۚ وَإِنَّ ٱللَّهَ لَهُوَ
ٱلْعَزِيزُ ٱلْحَكِيمُ ﴿٦٢﴾

63. If they turn away (from the Truth, let it be known that) Allah knows well the evil-doers.

63. Fa-in tawallaw fa-innal-laaha 'aleemum bilmuf-sideen.

فَإِن تَوَلَّوْا۟ فَإِنَّ ٱللَّهَ عَلِيمٌۢ
بِٱلْمُفْسِدِينَ ﴿٦٣﴾

64. (Muhammad), say to the People of the Book, "We must come to a common term and allow ourselves to worship no one except Allah, nor consider anything equal to Him, nor regard any of us as our Lord besides Allah." However, if they turn away (from the Truth), tell them, "Bear witness that we have submitted ourselves to the will of Allah."

64. Qul yaaa Ahlal-Kitaabi ta'aalaw ilaa Kalimatin sawaaa'im baynanaa wa baynakum allaa na'buda illal-laaha wa laa nushrika bihee shay'añw-wa laa yattakhiza ba'ḍunaa ba'ḍan arbaabam-min doonil-laah; fa-in tawallaw faqoolush-hadoo bi-annaa muslimoon.

قُلْ يَٰٓأَهْلَ ٱلْكِتَٰبِ تَعَالَوْا۟ إِلَىٰ
كَلِمَةٍ سَوَآءٍۭ بَيْنَنَا وَبَيْنَكُمْ أَلَّا
نَعْبُدَ إِلَّا ٱللَّهَ وَلَا نُشْرِكَ بِهِۦ شَيْـًٔا
وَلَا يَتَّخِذَ بَعْضُنَا بَعْضًا أَرْبَابًا
مِّن دُونِ ٱللَّهِ ۚ فَإِن تَوَلَّوْا۟ فَقُولُوا۟
ٱشْهَدُوا۟ بِأَنَّا مُسْلِمُونَ ﴿٦٤﴾

65. Ask the People of the Book, "Why do you argue about Abraham? The Torah and Gospel were revealed only after him. Why do you not understand?

65. Yaaa Ahlal-Kitaabi lima tuḥaaajjoona feee Ibraaheema wa maaa unzilatit-Tawraatu wal-Injeelu illaa mim ba'dih; afalaa ta'qiloon.

يَٰٓأَهْلَ ٱلْكِتَٰبِ لِمَ تُحَآجُّونَ فِىٓ
إِبْرَٰهِيمَ وَمَآ أُنزِلَتِ ٱلتَّوْرَىٰةُ
وَٱلْإِنجِيلُ إِلَّا مِنۢ بَعْدِهِۦٓ ۚ
أَفَلَا تَعْقِلُونَ ﴿٦٥﴾

66. You even argue about what is already known to you. What can you learn from arguing about that which you have no knowledge? Allah knows, but you do not know."

66. Haaa-antum haaa'ulaaa'i ḥaajajtum feemaa lakum bihee 'ilmun falima tuḥaaajjoona feemaa laysa lakum bihee 'ilm; wallaahu ya'lamu wa antum laa ta'lamoon.

هٰۤاَنۡتُمۡ هٰۤؤُلَاۤءِ حَاجَجۡتُمۡ فِيۡمَا لَـكُمۡ
بِهٖ عِلۡمٌ فَلِمَ تُحَآجُّوۡنَ فِيۡمَا لَـيۡسَ
لَـكُمۡ بِهٖ عِلۡمٌ ؕ وَاللّٰهُ يَعۡلَمُ وَاَنۡتُمۡ
لَا تَعۡلَمُوۡنَ ﴿۶۶﴾

67. Abraham was not a Jew or a Christian. He was an upright person who had submitted himself to the will of Allah. Abraham was not a pagan.

67. Maa kaana Ibraaheemu Yahoodiyyañw-wa laa Naṣraaniyyañw-wa laakin kaana Ḥaneefam-Muslimaa; wa maa kaana minal-mushrikeen.

مَا كَانَ اِبۡرٰهِيۡمُ يَهُوۡدِيًّا وَّلَا
نَصۡرَانِيًّا وَّلٰكِنۡ كَانَ حَنِيۡفًا
مُّسۡلِمًا ؕ وَمَا كَانَ مِنَ الۡمُشۡرِكِيۡنَ ﴿۶۷﴾

68. The nearest people to Abraham, among mankind, are those who followed him, this Prophet (Muhammad) and the true believers. Allah is the Guardian of the true believers.

68. Inna awlan-naasi bi-Ibraaheema lallaẕeenat-taba-'oohu wa haaẕan-Nabiyyu wallaẕeena aamanoo; wallaahu waliyyul-mu'mineen.

اِنَّ اَوۡلَى النَّاسِ بِاِبۡرٰهِيۡمَ لَـلَّذِيۡنَ
اتَّبَعُوۡهُ وَهٰذَا النَّبِىُّ وَالَّذِيۡنَ
اٰمَنُوۡا ؕ وَاللّٰهُ وَلِىُّ الۡمُؤۡمِنِيۡنَ ﴿۶۸﴾

69. A group among the People of the Book would love to mislead you, but they mislead no one except themselves. However, they do not realize it.

69. Waddaṭ-ṭaaa'ifatum-min Ahlil-Kitaabi law yuḍil-loonakum wa maa yuḍilloona illaaa anfusahum wa maa yash'uroon.

وَدَّتۡ طَّآٮِٕفَةٌ مِّنۡ اَهۡلِ الۡكِتٰبِ
لَوۡ يُضِلُّوۡنَكُمۡ ؕ وَمَا يُضِلُّوۡنَ اِلَّاۤ
اَنۡفُسَهُمۡ وَمَا يَشۡعُرُوۡنَ ﴿۶۹﴾

70. (Muhammad), say, "People of the Book, why do you deny the revelation of Allah (the Quran) even though you know very well that it is from Allah?

70. Yaaa Ahlal-Kitaabi lima takfuroona bi-Aayaatil-laahi wa antum tashhadoon.

يٰۤاَهۡلَ الۡكِتٰبِ لِمَ تَكۡفُرُوۡنَ
بِاٰيٰتِ اللّٰهِ وَاَنۡتُمۡ تَشۡهَدُوۡنَ ﴿۷۰﴾

71. Why do you mix truth with falsehood and knowingly hide the truth?"

71. Yaaa Ahlal-Kitaabi lima talbisoonal-ḥaqqa bilbaaṭili wa taktumoonal-ḥaqqa wa antum ta'lamoon.

يٰۤاَهۡلَ الۡكِتٰبِ لِمَ تَلۡبِسُوۡنَ الۡحَـقَّ
بِالۡبَاطِلِ وَتَكۡتُمُوۡنَ الۡحَـقَّ وَاَنۡتُمۡ ع ٨
تَعۡلَمُوۡنَ ﴿۷۱﴾ ١٥

72. Some of the People of the Book say, "Believe in what is revealed to the Muslims during the day only and abandon it in the evening. Perhaps this will make them give up their religion."

72. Wa qaalaṭ-ṭaaa'ifatum-min Ahlil-Kitaabi aaminoo billaẕeee unzila 'alal-laẕeena aamanoo wajhan-nahaari wakfurooo aakhirahoo la'alla-hum yarji'oon.

وَقَالَتۡ طَّآٮِٕفَةٌ مِّنۡ اَهۡلِ الۡكِتٰبِ
اٰمِنُوۡا بِالَّذِىۡۤ اُنۡزِلَ عَلَى الَّذِيۡنَ اٰمَنُوۡا
وَجۡهَ النَّهَارِ وَاكۡفُرُوۡۤا اٰخِرَهٗ لَعَلَّهُمۡ
يَرۡجِعُوۡنَ ۚ ﴿۷۲﴾

73. They also say, "Do not believe anyone except those who follow your religion, so that no one may have what you have received or may argue with you before your Lord."

(Muhammad), tell them, "The only guidance is the

73. Wa laa tu'minooo illaa liman tabi'a deenakum qul innal-hudaa hudal-laahi añy-yu'taaa aḥadum-misla maaa ooteetum aw yuḥaaajjookum 'inda Rabbikum, qul innal-

وَلَا تُؤۡمِنُوۡۤا اِلَّا لِمَنۡ تَبِعَ دِيۡنَكُمۡ ؕ
قُلۡ اِنَّ الۡهُدٰى هُدَى اللّٰهِ ۙ اَنۡ
يُّؤۡتٰٓى اَحَدٌ مِّثۡلَ مَاۤ اُوۡتِيۡتُمۡ اَوۡ
يُحَآجُّوۡكُمۡ عِنۡدَ رَبِّكُمۡ ؕ قُلۡ اِنَّ

guidance of Allah. All favors are in the hands of Allah. He grants His favors to whomever He wants. He is Munificent and All-knowing."

faḍla biyadil-laah; yu'teehi mañy-yashaaa'; wallaahu Waasi'un 'Aleem.

الْفَضْلَ بِيَدِ اللّٰهِ ۚ يُؤْتِيْهِ مَنْ
يَّشَآءُ ۚ وَاللّٰهُ وَاسِعٌ عَلِيْمٌ ﴿٧٣﴾

74. Allah grants priority in granting mercy to whomever He wants. Allah's favors are great.

74. Yakhtaṣṣu biraḥmatihee mañy-yashaaa'; wallaahu zulfaḍlil-'aẓeem.

يَّخْتَصُّ بِرَحْمَتِهٖ مَنْ يَّشَآءُ ؕ
وَاللّٰهُ ذُو الْفَضْلِ الْعَظِيْمِ ﴿٧٤﴾

75. If you entrust some of the People of the Book with a large quantity of gold, they will return it to you, while if you entrust others among them with a small quantity of gold, they will not give it back to you unless you keep insisting on its return; for they say, "We are not bound to keep our word with the illiterate people," and they, themselves, knowingly ascribe false statements to Allah.

75. Wa min Ahlil-Kitaabi man in ta-manhu biqinṭaariñy-yu'addiheee ilayka wa minhum man in ta-manhu bideenaaril-laa yu'addiheee ilayka illaa maa dumta 'alayhi qaaa'imaa; zaalika bi-annahum qaaloo laysa 'alaynaa fil-ummiyyeena sabeel; wa yaqooloona 'alal-laahil-kaziba wa hum ya'la-moon.

وَمِنْ اَهْلِ الْكِتٰبِ مَنْ اِنْ تَاْمَنْهُ
بِقِنْطَارٍ يُّؤَدِّهٖۤ اِلَيْكَ ۚ وَمِنْهُمْ مَّنْ
اِنْ تَاْمَنْهُ بِدِيْنَارٍ لَّا يُؤَدِّهٖۤ اِلَيْكَ
اِلَّا مَا دُمْتَ عَلَيْهِ قَآئِمًا ؕ ذٰلِكَ
بِاَنَّهُمْ قَالُوْا لَيْسَ عَلَيْنَا فِى الْاُمِّيّٖنَ
سَبِيْلٌ ۚ وَيَقُوْلُوْنَ عَلَى اللّٰهِ الْكَذِبَ
وَهُمْ يَعْلَمُوْنَ ﴿٧٥﴾

76. Those who keep their promise and observe piety should know that Allah certainly loves the pious ones.

76. Balaa man awfaa bi'ahdihee wattaqaa fainnal-laaha yuḥibbul-muttaqeen.

بَلٰى مَنْ اَوْفٰى بِعَهْدِهٖ وَاتَّقٰى فَاِنَّ
اللّٰهَ يُحِبُّ الْمُتَّقِيْنَ ﴿٧٦﴾

77. Those who sell their covenant with Allah and their promises for a small price will have no share in the life hereafter. Allah will not speak to them, nor will He look at them on the Day of Judgment, nor will He purify them. They will face a painful torment.

77. Innal-lazeena yashtaroona bi-'Ahdil-laahi wa aymaanihim samanan qaleelan ulaaa'ika laa khalaaqa lahum fil-Aakhirati wa laa yukallimuhumul-laahu wa laa yanẓuru ilayhim Yawmal-Qiyaamati wa laa yuzakkeehim wa lahum 'azaabun aleem.

اِنَّ الَّذِيْنَ يَشْتَرُوْنَ بِعَهْدِ اللّٰهِ
وَاَيْمَانِهِمْ ثَمَنًا قَلِيْلًا اُولٰٓئِكَ
لَا خَلَاقَ لَهُمْ فِى الْاٰخِرَةِ وَلَا
يُكَلِّمُهُمُ اللّٰهُ وَلَا يَنْظُرُ اِلَيْهِمْ
يَوْمَ الْقِيٰمَةِ وَلَا يُزَكِّيْهِمْ ۪ وَلَهُمْ
عَذَابٌ اَلِيْمٌ ﴿٧٧﴾

78. Among the people of the Book, a group, when reading the Bible, deliberately mispronounces words in order to change their meaning. They try to show that what they have read is from the true Bible. In fact, what they have read is not from the true Bible. They say, "What we read is from Allah." In reality, it is not from Allah. They knowingly ascribe false statements to Allah.

78. Wa inna minhum lafaree-qañy-yalwoona alsinatahum bil-Kitaabi litaḥsaboohu minal-Kitaab; wa maa huwa minal-Kitaabi wa yaqooloona huwa min 'indillaahi wa maa huwa min 'indillaahi wa yaqooloona 'alal-laahilkaziba wa hum ya'lamoon.

وَاِنَّ مِنْهُمْ لَفَرِيْقًا يَّلْوٗنَ اَلْسِنَتَهُمْ
بِالْكِتٰبِ لِتَحْسَبُوْهُ مِنَ الْكِتٰبِ وَمَا
هُوَ مِنَ الْكِتٰبِ ۚ وَيَقُوْلُوْنَ هُوَ مِنْ
عِنْدِ اللّٰهِ وَمَا هُوَ مِنْ عِنْدِ اللّٰهِ ۚ
وَيَقُوْلُوْنَ عَلَى اللّٰهِ الْكَذِبَ وَهُمْ
يَعْلَمُوْنَ ﴿٧٨﴾

79. Allah would never give the Book, authority, or prophesy to

79. Maa kaana libasharin añy-yu'tiyahul-laahul-

مَا كَانَ لِبَشَرٍ اَنْ يُّؤْتِيَهُ اللّٰهُ

any person who would tell others to be his servants instead of being the servants of Allah. He (the Prophet) would rather tell them to worship Allah; they had (already) been teaching and studying the Book.

Kitaaba wal-Ḥukma wan-Nubuwwata summa yaqoola linnaasi koonoo 'ibaadal-lee min doonil-laahi wa laakin koonoo rabbaaniy-yeena bimaa kuntum tu'alli-moonal-Kitaaba wa bimaa kuntum tadrusoon.

الْكِتٰبَ وَالْحُكْمَ وَالنُّبُوَّةَ ثُمَّ يَقُوْلَ
لِلنَّاسِ كُوْنُوْا عِبَادًا لِّيْ مِنْ دُوْنِ
اللّٰهِ وَلٰكِنْ كُوْنُوْا رَبّٰنِيّٖنَ بِمَا
كُنْتُمْ تُعَلِّمُوْنَ الْكِتٰبَ وَبِمَا كُنْتُمْ
تَدْرُسُوْنَ ۙ ﴿٧٩﴾

80. A Prophet would never order you to take the angels and the Prophets as your lords. Would he order you to disbelieve after you have submitted yourselves to Allah?

80. Wa laa ya-murakum an tattakhizul-malaaa'ikata wan-Nabiyyeena arbaabaa; aya-murukum bilkufri ba'da iz antum muslimoon.

وَلَا يَاْمُرَكُمْ اَنْ تَتَّخِذُوا الْمَلٰٓئِكَةَ
وَالنَّبِيّٖنَ اَرْبَابًا ۗ اَيَاْمُرُكُمْ بِالْكُفْرِ
بَعْدَ اِذْ اَنْتُمْ مُّسْلِمُوْنَ ﴿٨٠﴾ ع ٨ ٩ ١٦

81. When Allah made a covenant with the Prophets, saying, "When I will give you the Book and wisdom and a Messenger will come to you who will testify to the guidance which you will receive from Me, you must believe in him and help him." He then asked them, "Do you affirm and accept my covenant?" They replied, "Yes, we affirm it." The Lord said, "Then bear witness to this and I shall bear witness with you.

81. Wa iz akhazal-laahu meesaaqan-Nabiyyeena lamaaa aataytukum min Kitaabiñw-wa Ḥikmatin summa jaaa'akum Rasoolum-muṣaddiqul-limaa ma'akum latu'minunna bihee wa latanṣurunnah; qaala 'a-aqrartum wa akhaztum 'alaa zaalikum iṣree qaalooo aqrarnaa; qaala fashhadoo wa anaa ma'akum minash-shaahideen.

وَاِذْ اَخَذَ اللّٰهُ مِيْثَاقَ النَّبِيّٖنَ لَمَآ
اٰتَيْتُكُمْ مِّنْ كِتٰبٍ وَّحِكْمَةٍ ثُمَّ
جَآءَكُمْ رَسُوْلٌ مُّصَدِّقٌ لِّمَا مَعَكُمْ
لَتُؤْمِنُنَّ بِهٖ وَلَتَنْصُرُنَّهٗ ۗ قَالَ ءَاَقْرَرْتُمْ
وَاَخَذْتُمْ عَلٰى ذٰلِكُمْ اِصْرِيْ ۗ قَالُوْٓا
اَقْرَرْنَا ۗ قَالَ فَاشْهَدُوْا وَاَنَا
مَعَكُمْ مِّنَ الشّٰهِدِيْنَ ﴿٨١﴾

82. After this, whoever turns away will be of the evil-doers."

82. Faman tawallaa ba'da zaalika fa ulaaa'ika humul-faasiqoon.

فَمَنْ تَوَلّٰى بَعْدَ ذٰلِكَ فَاُولٰٓئِكَ
هُمُ الْفٰسِقُوْنَ ﴿٨٢﴾

83. Do they want a religion other than the religion of Allah when all that are in the heavens and the earth have submitted themselves to His will, either by their own free will or by force? To Allah do all things return.

83. Afaghayra deenil-laahi yabghoona wa lahooo aslama man fis-samaawaati wal-arḍi ṭaw'añw-wa karhañw-wa ilayhi yurja'oon.

اَفَغَيْرَ دِيْنِ اللّٰهِ يَبْغُوْنَ وَلَهٗٓ
اَسْلَمَ مَنْ فِي السَّمٰوٰتِ وَالْاَرْضِ
طَوْعًا وَّكَرْهًا وَّاِلَيْهِ يُرْجَعُوْنَ ﴿٨٣﴾

84. (Muhammad), say, "We believe in Allah and in that which has been revealed to us and in that which was revealed to Abraham, Ishmael, Isaac, Jacob, and their descendants. We believe in that which was given to Moses, Jesus, and the Prophets by their Lord. We make no distinction between them and we have submitted ourselves to the will of Allah."

84. Qul aamannaa billaahi wa maaa unzila 'alaynaa wa maaa unzila 'alaaa Ibraaheema wa Ismaa'eela wa Isḥaaqa wa Ya'qooba wal-Asbaaṭi wa maaa ootiya Moosaa wa 'Eesaa wan-Nabiyyoona mir-Rabbihim laa nufarriqu bayna aḥadim-minhum wa naḥnu lahoo muslimoon.

قُلْ اٰمَنَّا بِاللّٰهِ وَمَآ اُنْزِلَ عَلَيْنَا
وَمَآ اُنْزِلَ عَلٰٓى اِبْرٰهِيْمَ وَاِسْمٰعِيْلَ
وَاِسْحٰقَ وَيَعْقُوْبَ وَالْاَسْبَاطِ وَمَآ
اُوْتِيَ مُوْسٰى وَعِيْسٰى وَالنَّبِيُّوْنَ
مِنْ رَّبِّهِمْ ۖ لَا نُفَرِّقُ بَيْنَ اَحَدٍ
مِّنْهُمْ ۖ وَنَحْنُ لَهٗ مُسْلِمُوْنَ ﴿٨٤﴾

85. No religion other than Islam (submission to the will of Allah) will be accepted from anyone. Whoever follows a religion other than Islam will be lost on the Day of Judgment.	85. Wa mañy-yabtaghi ghayral-Islaami deenan falañy-yuqbala minhu wa huwa fil-Aakhirati minal-khaasireen.	وَمَن يَبْتَغِ غَيْرَ الْإِسْلَامِ دِينًا فَلَن يُقْبَلَ مِنْهُ وَهُوَ فِي الْآخِرَةِ مِنَ الْخَاسِرِينَ ﴿٨٥﴾
86. Why would Allah guide a people who disbelieve after having had faith, who have found the Messenger to be truthful, and who have received authoritative evidence? Allah does not guide the unjust.	86. Kayfa yahdil-laahu qawman kafaroo ba'da eemaanihim wa shahidooo annar-Rasoola ḥaqquñw-wa jaaa'ahumul-bayyinaat; wallaahu laa yahdil-qawmaẓ-ẓaalimeen.	كَيْفَ يَهْدِي اللَّهُ قَوْمًا كَفَرُوا بَعْدَ إِيمَانِهِمْ وَشَهِدُوا أَنَّ الرَّسُولَ حَقٌّ وَجَاءَهُمُ الْبَيِّنَاتُ ۚ وَاللَّهُ لَا يَهْدِي الْقَوْمَ الظَّالِمِينَ ﴿٨٦﴾
87. What they will gain will be the condemnation of Allah, the angels, and all people,	87. Ulaaa'ika jazaaa'uhum anna 'alayhim la'natal-laahi walmalaaa'ikati wannaasi ajma'een.	أُولَٰئِكَ جَزَاؤُهُمْ أَنَّ عَلَيْهِمْ لَعْنَةَ اللَّهِ وَالْمَلَائِكَةِ وَالنَّاسِ أَجْمَعِينَ ﴿٨٧﴾
88. with which they will live forever. Their torment will not be relieved and no attention will be paid to them.	88. Khaalideena feehaa laa yukhaffafu 'anhumul-'aẕaabu wa laa hum yunẓaroon.	خَالِدِينَ فِيهَا لَا يُخَفَّفُ عَنْهُمُ الْعَذَابُ وَلَا هُمْ يُنظَرُونَ ﴿٨٨﴾
89. However, to those who repent afterwards and reform themselves, Allah is All-forgiving and All-merciful.	89. Illal-laẕeena taaboo mim ba'di ẕaalika wa aṣlaḥoo fa-innal-laaha Ghafoorur-Raḥeem.	إِلَّا الَّذِينَ تَابُوا مِن بَعْدِ ذَٰلِكَ وَأَصْلَحُوا فَإِنَّ اللَّهَ غَفُورٌ رَّحِيمٌ ﴿٨٩﴾
90. Those who disbelieve after having been believers, and increase their disbelief, are lost and their repentance will not be accepted.	90. Innal-laẕeena kafaroo ba'da eemaanihim ṯummaz-daadoo kufral-lan tuqbala tawbatuhum wa ulaaa'ika humuḍ-ḍaaalloon.	إِنَّ الَّذِينَ كَفَرُوا بَعْدَ إِيمَانِهِمْ ثُمَّ ازْدَادُوا كُفْرًا لَّن تُقْبَلَ تَوْبَتُهُمْ وَأُولَٰئِكَ هُمُ الضَّالُّونَ ﴿٩٠﴾
91. From those who have rejected the truth and died in disbelief, no ransom will be accepted even though they may pay a whole earth of gold. They will suffer a painful torment and no one will help them.	91. Innal-laẕeena kafaroo wa maatoo wa hum kuffaarun falañy-yuqbala min aḥadihim mil'ul-arḍi ẕahabañw-wa lawiftadaa bih; ulaaa'ika lahum 'aẕaabun aleemuñw-wa maa lahum min naaṣireen.	إِنَّ الَّذِينَ كَفَرُوا وَمَاتُوا وَهُمْ كُفَّارٌ فَلَن يُقْبَلَ مِنْ أَحَدِهِم مِّلْءُ الْأَرْضِ ذَهَبًا وَلَوِ افْتَدَىٰ بِهِ ۗ أُولَٰئِكَ لَهُمْ عَذَابٌ أَلِيمٌ وَمَا لَهُم مِّن نَّاصِرِينَ ﴿٩١﴾
92. You can never have extended virtue and righteousness unless you spend part of what you dearly love for the cause of Allah. Allah knows very well whatever you spend for His cause.	92. Lan tanaalul-birra ḥattaa tunfiqoo mimmaa tuḥibboon; wa maa tunfiqoo min shay'in fa-innal-laaha bihee 'Aleem.	لَن تَنَالُوا الْبِرَّ حَتَّىٰ تُنفِقُوا مِمَّا تُحِبُّونَ ۚ وَمَا تُنفِقُوا مِن شَيْءٍ فَإِنَّ اللَّهَ بِهِ عَلِيمٌ ﴿٩٢﴾
93. All food was lawful for the children of Israel except for what Israel had deemed unlawful for himself before the Torah was revealed. (Muhammad), ask them	93. Kulluṭ-ṭa'aami kaana ḥillal-li-Baneee Israaa'eela illaa maa ḥarrama Israaa'eelu 'alaa nafsihee min	كُلُّ الطَّعَامِ كَانَ حِلًّا لِّبَنِي إِسْرَائِيلَ إِلَّا مَا حَرَّمَ إِسْرَائِيلُ عَلَىٰ نَفْسِهِ مِن

ع ١١/٧ الجزء الرابع (٣)

to bring the Torah and read it, if they are true in their claim (that certain foods were unlawful for the children of Israel).

qabli an tunazzalat-Tawraah; qul fa-too bit-Tawraati fatloo-haaa in kuntum ṣaadiqeen.

قَبْلِ أَنْ تُنَزَّلَ التَّوْرٰىةُ ۗ قُلْ فَأْتُوا
بِالتَّوْرٰىةِ فَاتْلُوهَا إِنْ كُنْتُمْ صٰدِقِينَ ﴿٩٣﴾

94. Whoever ascribes falsehood to Allah despite of all the evidence is unjust.

94. Famanif-taraa 'alal-laahil-kaẕiba mim ba'di ẕaalika fa-ulaaa'ika humuẓ-ẓaalimoon.

فَمَنِ افْتَرٰى عَلَى اللّٰهِ الْكَذِبَ مِنْ
بَعْدِ ذٰلِكَ فَأُولٰٓئِكَ هُمُ الظّٰلِمُونَ ﴿٩٤﴾

95. (Muhammad), say, "Allah has spoken the Truth. Follow the upright tradition of Abraham, who was not an idolater."

95. Qul ṣadaqal-laah; fattabi'oo Millata Ibraaheema Ḥaneefaa; wa maa kaana minal-mushrikeen.

قُلْ صَدَقَ اللّٰهُ ۗ فَاتَّبِعُوا مِلَّةَ
إِبْرٰهِيمَ حَنِيفًا ۖ وَمَا كَانَ مِنَ
الْمُشْرِكِينَ ﴿٩٥﴾

وقف جبريل عليه السلام

96. The first house (of worship) that Allah assigned to men was in Bakkah (another name of Makkah). It is a blessed one and a guide for all people.

96. Inna awwala Baytiñw-wuḍi'a linnaasi lallaẕee bi-Bakkata mubaarakañw-wa hudal-lil-'aalameen.

إِنَّ أَوَّلَ بَيْتٍ وُضِعَ لِلنَّاسِ لَلَّذِي
بِبَكَّةَ مُبٰرَكًا وَهُدًى لِلْعٰلَمِينَ ﴿٩٦﴾

97. In (Bakkah), there are many clear signs (evidence of the existence of Allah). Among them is the place where Abraham stood. Whoever seeks refuge therein will be protected by the laws of amnesty. Those who have the means and ability have a duty to Allah to visit the House and perform the Hajj (pilgrimage) rituals. The unbelievers should know that Allah is Independent of all creatures.

97. Feehi Aayaatum-bayyinaa-tum-Maqaamu Ibraaheema wa man dakhalahoo kaana aaminaa; wa lillaahi 'alan-naasi Ḥijjul-Bayti manis-taṭaa'a ilayhi sabeelaa; wa man kafara fa-innal-laaha ghaniyyun 'anil-'aalameen.

فِيهِ اٰيٰتٌۢ بَيِّنٰتٌ مَّقَامُ إِبْرٰهِيمَ ۖ
وَمَنْ دَخَلَهُ كَانَ اٰمِنًا ۗ وَلِلّٰهِ عَلَى
النَّاسِ حِجُّ الْبَيْتِ مَنِ اسْتَطَاعَ
إِلَيْهِ سَبِيلًا ۚ وَمَنْ كَفَرَ فَإِنَّ اللّٰهَ
غَنِيٌّ عَنِ الْعٰلَمِينَ ﴿٩٧﴾

98. (Muhammad), ask the People of the Book, "Why do you deny the revelations of Allah when He is Well-aware of your dealings?"

98. Qul yaaa Ahlal-Kitaabi lima takfuroona bi-Aayaatillaahi wallaahu shaheedun 'alaa maa ta'maloon.

قُلْ يٰٓأَهْلَ الْكِتٰبِ لِمَ تَكْفُرُونَ بِاٰيٰتِ
اللّٰهِ ۖ وَاللّٰهُ شَهِيدٌ عَلٰى مَا تَعْمَلُونَ ﴿٩٨﴾

99. Ask them, "Why do you create obstacles in the way of Allah for those who believe in Him, trying to make His way seem crooked when you know that it is straight? Allah is not unaware of what you do.

99. Qul yaaa Ahlal-Kitaabi lima taṣuddoona 'an sabeelil-laahi man aamana tabghoonahaa 'iwajañw-wa antum shuhadaaa'; wa mallaahu bighaafilin 'ammaa ta'maloon.

قُلْ يٰٓأَهْلَ الْكِتٰبِ لِمَ تَصُدُّونَ
عَنْ سَبِيلِ اللّٰهِ مَنْ اٰمَنَ تَبْغُونَهَا
عِوَجًا وَأَنْتُمْ شُهَدَآءُ ۗ وَمَا اللّٰهُ
بِغٰفِلٍ عَمَّا تَعْمَلُونَ ﴿٩٩﴾

100. Believers, if you obey a certain group among the People of the Book, they will turn you back to disbelief.

100. Yaaa-ayyuhal-laẕeena aamanooo in tuṭee'oo fareeqam-minal-laẕeena ootul-Kitaaba yaruddookum ba'da eemaanikum kaafireen.

يٰٓأَيُّهَا الَّذِينَ اٰمَنُوٓا إِنْ تُطِيعُوا فَرِيقًا
مِنَ الَّذِينَ أُوتُوا الْكِتٰبَ يَرُدُّوكُمْ بَعْدَ
إِيمٰنِكُمْ كٰفِرِينَ ﴿١٠٠﴾

101. How could you turn back to disbelief when the words of Allah are recited to you and you have, in your midst, His Messenger? Those who seek the protection of Allah will certainly be guided to

101. Wa kayfa takfuroona wa antum tutlaa 'alaykum Aayaatul-laahi wa feekum Rasooluh; wa mañy-ya'taṣim billaahi faqad hudiya

وَكَيْفَ تَكْفُرُونَ وَأَنْتُمْ تُتْلٰى
عَلَيْكُمْ اٰيٰتُ اللّٰهِ وَفِيكُمْ رَسُولُهُ ۗ
وَمَنْ يَعْتَصِمْ بِاللّٰهِ فَقَدْ هُدِيَ

the right path.

102. Believers, have fear of Allah as you should and die only as Muslims (having submitted to the will of Allah).

103. All of you must hold fast to the rope of Allah (the Quran and His Messenger), and recall how He favored you when your hostility toward each other had torn you apart. He united your hearts in one faith and through His Grace you became brothers. You were on the verge of falling headlong into the fiery abyss, but Allah saved you. This is how Allah explains to you His revelations so that you may have the right guidance.

104. Let there be a group among you who will invite others to do good deeds, command them to obey the Law, and prohibit them from committing sins. These people will have eternal happiness.

105. Do not be like those who turned into quarreling sects after receiving clear authoritative evidence. They will suffer a great torment.

106. On the day when some faces will become white and others black, Allah will ask the people with the faces which have become black, "Why did you give up your faith? For your disbelief you must suffer the torment."

106. The people whose faces have become white will enjoy the mercy of Allah with which they will live forever.

108. Such are Allah's revelations which We explain to you, (Muhammad), for a genuine purpose. Allah does not want injustice for any of His creatures.

109. To Allah belongs all that is in the heavens and the earth and to Him do all things return.

ilaa Şiraaţim-Mustaqeem.

102. Yaaa ayyuhal-lazeena aamanut-taqul-laaha ḥaqqa tuqaatihee wa laa tamootunna illaa wa antum muslimoon.

103. Wa'taşimoo bi-Ḥablil-laahi jamee'añw-wa laa tafarraqoo; wazkuroo ni'matal-laahi 'alaykum iz kuntum a'daaa'an fa-allafa bayna quloobikum fa-aşbaḥtum bini'matiheee ikhwaanaa; wa kuntum 'alaa shafaa ḥufratim-minan-Naari fa-anqazakum minhaa; kazaalika yubayyinul-laahu lakum Aayaatihee la'allakum tahtadoon.

104. Waltakum-minkum ummatuñy-yad'oona ilal-khayri wa ya-muroona bilma'roofi wa yanhawna 'anil-munkar; wa ulaaa'ika humul-mufliḥoon.

105. Wa laa takoonoo kalla-zeena tafarraqoo wakhtalafoo mim ba'di maa jaaa'ahumul-bayyinaat; wa ulaaa'ika lahum 'azaabun 'aẓeem.

106. Yawma tabyaḍḍu wujoo-huñw-wa taswaddu wujooh; fa-ammal-lazeenas-waddat wujoohuhum akafartum ba'da eemaanikum fazooqul-'azaaba bimaa kuntum takfuroon.

107. Wa ammal-lazeenabyaḍ-ḍat wujoohuhum fafee raḥmatil-laahi hum feehaa khaalidoon.

108. Tilka Aayaatul-laahi natloohaa 'alayka bilḥaqq; wa mal-laahu yureedu ẓulmallil-'aalameen.

109. Wa lillaahi maa fissamaa-waati wa maa fil-arḍ; wa ilal-laahi turja'ul-umoor.

إِلَىٰ صِرَاطٍ مُّسْتَقِيمٍ ﴿١٠١﴾ ع ١٠
يَٰٓأَيُّهَا ٱلَّذِينَ ءَامَنُوا ٱتَّقُوا ٱللَّهَ حَقَّ
تُقَاتِهِۦ وَلَا تَمُوتُنَّ إِلَّا وَأَنتُم مُّسْلِمُونَ ﴿١٠٢﴾
وَٱعْتَصِمُوا بِحَبْلِ ٱللَّهِ جَمِيعًا وَلَا
تَفَرَّقُوا ۚ وَٱذْكُرُوا نِعْمَتَ ٱللَّهِ
عَلَيْكُمْ إِذْ كُنتُمْ أَعْدَآءً فَأَلَّفَ بَيْنَ
قُلُوبِكُمْ فَأَصْبَحْتُم بِنِعْمَتِهِۦٓ إِخْوَٰنًا
وَكُنتُمْ عَلَىٰ شَفَا حُفْرَةٍ مِّنَ ٱلنَّارِ
فَأَنقَذَكُم مِّنْهَا ۗ كَذَٰلِكَ يُبَيِّنُ ٱللَّهُ
لَكُمْ ءَايَٰتِهِۦ لَعَلَّكُمْ تَهْتَدُونَ ﴿١٠٣﴾
وَلْتَكُن مِّنكُمْ أُمَّةٌ يَدْعُونَ إِلَى
ٱلْخَيْرِ وَيَأْمُرُونَ بِٱلْمَعْرُوفِ وَيَنْهَوْنَ
عَنِ ٱلْمُنكَرِ ۚ وَأُولَٰٓئِكَ هُمُ ٱلْمُفْلِحُونَ ﴿١٠٤﴾
وَلَا تَكُونُوا كَٱلَّذِينَ تَفَرَّقُوا وَٱخْتَلَفُوا
مِنۢ بَعْدِ مَا جَآءَهُمُ ٱلْبَيِّنَٰتُ ۚ وَأُولَٰٓئِكَ
لَهُمْ عَذَابٌ عَظِيمٌ ﴿١٠٥﴾
يَوْمَ تَبْيَضُّ وُجُوهٌ وَتَسْوَدُّ وُجُوهٌ ۚ
فَأَمَّا ٱلَّذِينَ ٱسْوَدَّتْ وُجُوهُهُمْ
أَكَفَرْتُم بَعْدَ إِيمَٰنِكُمْ فَذُوقُوا
ٱلْعَذَابَ بِمَا كُنتُمْ تَكْفُرُونَ ﴿١٠٦﴾
وَأَمَّا ٱلَّذِينَ ٱبْيَضَّتْ وُجُوهُهُمْ
فَفِى رَحْمَةِ ٱللَّهِ ۖ هُمْ فِيهَا خَٰلِدُونَ ﴿١٠٧﴾
تِلْكَ ءَايَٰتُ ٱللَّهِ نَتْلُوهَا عَلَيْكَ بِٱلْحَقِّ ۗ
وَمَا ٱللَّهُ يُرِيدُ ظُلْمًا لِّلْعَٰلَمِينَ ﴿١٠٨﴾
وَلِلَّهِ مَا فِى ٱلسَّمَٰوَٰتِ وَمَا فِى ٱلْأَرْضِ ۚ
وَإِلَى ٱللَّهِ تُرْجَعُ ٱلْأُمُورُ ﴿١٠٩﴾ ع ١١

110. You are the best nation that ever existed among humanity, as long as you command people to do good, prohibit them from evil, and believe in Allah. Had the People of the Book accepted the faith (Islam), it would certainly have been better for them. Some of them have faith, but most of them are evildoers.

110. Kuntum khayra ummatin ukhrijat linnaasi ta-muroona bilma'roofi wa tanhawna 'anil-munkari wa tu'minoona billaah; wa law aamana Ahlul-Kitaabi lakaana khayral-lahum; minhumul-mu'minoona wa ak<u>s</u>aruhumul-faasiqoon.

كُنْتُمْ خَيْرَ اُمَّةٍ اُخْرِجَتْ لِلنَّاسِ
تَاْمُرُوْنَ بِالْمَعْرُوْفِ وَتَنْهَوْنَ عَنِ
الْمُنْكَرِ وَتُؤْمِنُوْنَ بِاللّٰهِ ؕ وَلَوْ اٰمَنَ
اَهْلُ الْكِتٰبِ لَكَانَ خَيْرًا لَّهُمْ ؕ مِنْهُمُ
الْمُؤْمِنُوْنَ وَاَكْثَرُهُمُ الْفٰسِقُوْنَ ﴿۱۱۰﴾

111. They can never harm you beyond annoyance. In a fight, they will turn back in defeat and they will not be helped.

111. Lañy-yaḍurrookum illaaa a<u>z</u>aa; wa iñy-yuqaatilookum yuwallookumul-adbaara <u>s</u>umma laa yunṣaroon.

لَنْ يَّضُرُّوْكُمْ اِلَّاۤ اَذًى ؕ وَاِنْ
يُّقَاتِلُوْكُمْ يُوَلُّوْكُمُ الْاَدْبَارَ قف
ثُمَّ لَا يُنْصَرُوْنَ ﴿۱۱۱﴾

112. Humiliation will strike them wherever they seek protection, except when they seek the protection of Allah and the people. They have incurred the wrath of Allah unto themselves and have been struck with destitution for their rejection of the revelations of Allah and for unjustly murdering the prophets. It is all because of their transgression and rebellion.

112. Ḍuribat 'alayhimuz<u>z</u> <u>z</u>illatu ayna maa <u>s</u>uqifooo illaa biḥablim-minal-laahi waḥablim-minan-naasi wa baaa'oo bighaḍabim-minallaahi wa ḍuribat 'alayhimul-maskanah; <u>z</u>aalika bi-annahum kaanoo yakfuroona bi-Aayaatil-laahi wa yaqtuloonal-Ambiyaaa'a bighayri ḥaqq; <u>z</u>aalika bimaa 'aṣaw wa kaanoo ya'tadoon.

ضُرِبَتْ عَلَيْهِمُ الذِّلَّةُ اَيْنَ مَا
ثُقِفُوْۤا اِلَّا بِحَبْلٍ مِّنَ اللّٰهِ وَحَبْلٍ
مِّنَ النَّاسِ وَبَآءُوْ بِغَضَبٍ مِّنَ اللّٰهِ
وَضُرِبَتْ عَلَيْهِمُ الْمَسْكَنَةُ ؕ ذٰلِكَ
بِاَنَّهُمْ كَانُوْا يَكْفُرُوْنَ بِاٰيٰتِ اللّٰهِ
وَيَقْتُلُوْنَ الْاَنْۢبِيَآءَ بِغَيْرِ حَقٍّ ؕ ذٰلِكَ
بِمَا عَصَوْا وَّكَانُوْا يَعْتَدُوْنَ ﴿۱۱۲﴾

113. The people of the Book are not all the same. Some of them are straightforward. They recite the words of Allah in prostration at night.

113. Laysoo sawaaa'aa; min Ahlil-Kitaabi ummatun qaaa'imatuñy-yatloona Aayaatil-laahi aanaaa'al-layli wa hum yasjudoon.

لَيْسُوْا سَوَآءً ؕ مِنْ اَهْلِ الْكِتٰبِ اُمَّةٌ
قَآئِمَةٌ يَّتْلُوْنَ اٰيٰتِ اللّٰهِ اٰنَآءَ الَّيْلِ
وَهُمْ يَسْجُدُوْنَ ﴿۱۱۳﴾

114. They believe in Allah and the Day of Judgment. They command people to follow good, prohibit others from committing evil and compete with each other in doing good deeds. These are the righteous ones.

114. Yu'minoona billaahi wal-Yawmil-Aakhiri wa ya-muroona bilma'roofi wa yanhawna 'anil-munkari wa yusaari'oona fil-khayraati wa ulaaa'ika minaṣ-ṣaaliḥeen.

يُؤْمِنُوْنَ بِاللّٰهِ وَالْيَوْمِ الْاٰخِرِ وَ
يَاْمُرُوْنَ بِالْمَعْرُوْفِ وَيَنْهَوْنَ
عَنِ الْمُنْكَرِ وَيُسَارِعُوْنَ فِى الْخَيْرٰتِ ؕ
وَاُولٰٓئِكَ مِنَ الصّٰلِحِيْنَ ﴿۱۱۴﴾

115. They will never be denied the rewards of their good deeds. Allah knows well about the pious.

115. Wa maa yaf'aloo min khayrin falañy-yukfarooh; wallaahu 'Aleemum bilmut-taqeen.

وَمَا يَفْعَلُوْا مِنْ خَيْرٍ فَلَنْ يُّكْفَرُوْهُ ؕ
وَاللّٰهُ عَلِيْمٌۢ بِالْمُتَّقِيْنَ ﴿۱۱۵﴾

116. The wealth and the children of the unbelievers can never make them independent of Allah. They are the dwellers of hell wherein

116. Innal-la<u>z</u>eena kafaroo lan tughniya 'anhum amwaaluhum wa laaa awlaaduhum minal-laahi

اِنَّ الَّذِيْنَ كَفَرُوْا لَنْ تُغْنِىَ عَنْهُمْ
اَمْوَالُهُمْ وَلَاۤ اَوْلَادُهُمْ مِّنَ اللّٰهِ

they will live forever.

shay'an wa ulaaa'ika Aṣḥaabun-Naar; hum feehaa khaalidoon.

شَيْـًٔا ۖ وَأُولَٰٓئِكَ أَصْحَٰبُ ٱلنَّارِ ۚ هُمْ
فِيهَا خَٰلِدُونَ ﴿١١٦﴾

117. What they spend in this life is like the freezing wind that may strike and destroy the farms of the people who have wronged themselves. Allah has not done injustice to them, but they have wronged themselves.

117. Masalu maa yunfiqoona fee haazihil-ḥayaatid-dunyaa kamasali reeḥin feehaa ṣirrun aṣaabat ḥarsa qawmin ẓalamooo anfusahum fa-ahlakath; wa maa ẓalamahumul-laahu wa laakin anfusahum yaẓlimoon.

مَثَلُ مَا يُنفِقُونَ فِى هَٰذِهِ ٱلْحَيَوٰةِ
ٱلدُّنْيَا كَمَثَلِ رِيحٍ فِيهَا صِرٌّ أَصَابَتْ
حَرْثَ قَوْمٍ ظَلَمُوٓا۟ أَنفُسَهُمْ فَأَهْلَكَتْهُ ۚ
وَمَا ظَلَمَهُمُ ٱللَّهُ وَلَٰكِنْ أَنفُسَهُمْ
يَظْلِمُونَ ﴿١١٧﴾

118. Believers, do not expose your privacy to the unbelievers. They like to mislead you and see that you are seriously harmed. Signs of animosity from their mouths have already become audible, but what they hide in their heads is even worse. We have certainly made Our evidence clear, if only you would consider it.

118. Yaaa ayyuhal-lazeena aamanoo laa tattakhizoo biṭaanatam-min doonikum laa ya-loonakum khabaalaa; waddoo maa 'anittum qad badatil-baghḍaaa'u min afwaahihim; wa maa tukhfee ṣudooruhum akbar; qad bayyannaa lakumul-Aayaati in kuntum ta'qiloon.

يَٰٓأَيُّهَا ٱلَّذِينَ ءَامَنُوا۟ لَا تَتَّخِذُوا۟ بِطَانَةً
مِّن دُونِكُمْ لَا يَأْلُونَكُمْ خَبَالًا وَدُّوا۟
مَا عَنِتُّمْ قَدْ بَدَتِ ٱلْبَغْضَآءُ مِنْ
أَفْوَٰهِهِمْ وَمَا تُخْفِى صُدُورُهُمْ
أَكْبَرُ ۚ قَدْ بَيَّنَّا لَكُمُ ٱلْءَايَٰتِ ۖ إِن
كُنتُمْ تَعْقِلُونَ ﴿١١٨﴾

119. There are people whom you love, but they do not love you, despite your belief in all the (heavenly) Books. On meeting you they proclaim belief, but in private, bite their fingers at you in anger. Tell them, "Perish in your rage!" Allah knows well what is in everyone's hearts.

119. Haaa-antum ulaaa'i tuḥibboonahum wa laa yuḥibboonakum wa tu'minoona bil-Kitaabi kullihee wa izaa laqookum qaalooo aamannaa wa izaa khalaw 'aḍḍoo 'alaykumul-anaamila minal-ghayẓ,; qul mootoo bighayẓikum; innallaaha 'aleemum bizaatiṣṣudoor.

هَٰٓأَنتُمْ أُو۟لَآءِ تُحِبُّونَهُمْ وَلَا
يُحِبُّونَكُمْ وَتُؤْمِنُونَ بِٱلْكِتَٰبِ
كُلِّهِۦ وَإِذَا لَقُوكُمْ قَالُوٓا۟ ءَامَنَّا وَإِذَا
خَلَوْا۟ عَضُّوا۟ عَلَيْكُمُ ٱلْأَنَامِلَ مِنَ
ٱلْغَيْظِ ۚ قُلْ مُوتُوا۟ بِغَيْظِكُمْ ۗ إِنَّ ٱللَّهَ
عَلِيمٌۢ بِذَاتِ ٱلصُّدُورِ ﴿١١٩﴾

120. They hate to see your success and rejoice if any misfortune befalls you. If you will be patient and pious, their plots can cause no harm to you. Allah has control over all their actions.

120. In tamsaskum ḥasanatun tasu'hum wa in tuṣibkum sayyi'atuñy-yafraḥoo bihaa wa in taṣbiroo wa tattaqoo laa yaḍurrukum kayduhum shay'aa; innallaaha bimaa ya'maloona muḥeeṭ.

إِن تَمْسَسْكُمْ حَسَنَةٌ تَسُؤْهُمْ وَإِن
تُصِبْكُمْ سَيِّئَةٌ يَفْرَحُوا۟ بِهَا ۖ وَإِن
تَصْبِرُوا۟ وَتَتَّقُوا۟ لَا يَضُرُّكُمْ كَيْدُهُمْ
شَيْـًٔا ۗ إِنَّ ٱللَّهَ بِمَا يَعْمَلُونَ مُحِيطٌ ﴿١٢٠﴾ ع ١٢

121. (Muhammad), remember the morning when you left home to show the believers their position in the battle? Allah is All-hearing and All-knowing.

121. Wa iz ghadawta min ahlika tubawwi'ul-mu'mineena maqaa'ida lilqitaal; wallaahu Samee'un 'Aleem.

وَإِذْ غَدَوْتَ مِنْ أَهْلِكَ تُبَوِّئُ
ٱلْمُؤْمِنِينَ مَقَٰعِدَ لِلْقِتَالِ ۗ
وَٱللَّهُ سَمِيعٌ عَلِيمٌ ﴿١٢١﴾

122. Two groups among you almost lost courage despite having Allah as their Guardian. The believers should always have trust in Allah.

122. Iz hammat-taaa'ifataani minkum an tafshalaa wallaahu waliyyuhumaa; wa 'alal-laahi falyatawakkalil-mu'minoon.

اِذۡ هَمَّتۡ طَّآئِفَتٰنِ مِنۡكُمۡ اَنۡ تَفۡشَلَا ۙ
وَاللّٰهُ وَلِيُّهُمَا ؕ وَعَلَى اللّٰهِ فَلۡيَتَوَكَّلِ
الۡمُؤۡمِنُوۡنَ ﴿۱۲۲﴾

123. Allah gave you victory in the battle of Badr, where your forces were much weaker than those of the enemy. Have fear of Allah so that you may give Him thanks.

123. Wa laqad naṣarakumul-laahu bi-Badriñw-wa antum azillatun fattaqul-laaha la'allakum tashkuroon.

وَلَقَدۡ نَصَرَكُمُ اللّٰهُ بِبَدۡرٍ وَّ
اَنۡتُمۡ اَذِلَّةٌ ۚ فَاتَّقُوا اللّٰهَ لَعَلَّكُمۡ
تَشۡكُرُوۡنَ ﴿۱۲۳﴾

124. Also, remember when you said to the believers, "Is it not enough that your Lord is helping you with a force of three thousand angels sent (from the heavens)?"

124. Iz taqoolu lilmu'mineena alañy-yakfiyakum añy-yumiddakum Rabbukum bisalaasati aalaafim-minal-malaaa'ikati munzaleen.

اِذۡ تَقُوۡلُ لِلۡمُؤۡمِنِيۡنَ اَلَنۡ يَّكۡفِيَكُمۡ
اَنۡ يُّمِدَّكُمۡ رَبُّكُمۡ بِثَلٰثَةِ اٰلٰفٍ
مِّنَ الۡمَلٰٓئِكَةِ مُنۡزَلِيۡنَ ﴿۱۲۴﴾ؕ

125. Certainly, if you have patience and piety, even if the enemy attacks immediately after this, Allah will help you with another force of five thousand angels, all distinctly marked (splendidly dressed).

125. Balaaa; in taṣbiroo wa tattaqoo wa ya-tookum min fawrihim haazaa yumdidkum Rabbukum bikhamsati aalaafim-minal-malaaa'ikati musawwimeen.

بَلٰٓى ۙ اِنۡ تَصۡبِرُوۡا وَتَتَّقُوۡا وَيَاۡتُوۡكُمۡ
مِّنۡ فَوۡرِهِمۡ هٰذَا يُمۡدِدۡكُمۡ
رَبُّكُمۡ بِخَمۡسَةِ اٰلٰفٍ مِّنَ الۡمَلٰٓئِكَةِ
مُسَوِّمِيۡنَ ﴿۱۲۵﴾ الربع

126. The sending of the angels is glad news from your Lord so that you will have more confidence in Him. No victory is real unless it is from Allah, the Majestic and All-wise.

126. Wa maa ja'alahul-laahu illaa bushraa lakum wa litaṭma'inna quloobukum bih; wa man-naṣru illaa min 'indil-laahil-'Azeezil-Ḥakeem.

وَمَا جَعَلَهُ اللّٰهُ اِلَّا بُشۡرٰى لَكُمۡ
وَلِتَطۡمَئِنَّ قُلُوۡبُكُمۡ بِهٖ ؕ وَمَا النَّصۡرُ
اِلَّا مِنۡ عِنۡدِ اللّٰهِ الۡعَزِيۡزِ الۡحَكِيۡمِ ﴿۱۲۶﴾ۙ

127. (They are sent) to break the power of the unbelievers or disgrace them and make them return after having lost all hope."

127. Liyaqṭa'a ṭarafam-minal-lazeena kafarooo aw yakbitahum fayanqaliboo khaaa'ibeen.

لِيَقۡطَعَ طَرَفًا مِّنَ الَّذِيۡنَ كَفَرُوۡۤا
اَوۡ يَكۡبِتَهُمۡ فَيَنۡقَلِبُوۡا خَآئِبِيۡنَ ﴿۱۲۷﴾

128. (Muhammad), it is not your concern whether He forgives them or punishes them, for they are unjust.

128. Laysa laka minal-amri shay'un aw yatooba 'alayhim aw yu'az-zibahum fa innahum ẓaalimoon.

لَيۡسَ لَكَ مِنَ الۡاَمۡرِ شَىۡءٌ اَوۡ يَتُوۡبَ
عَلَيۡهِمۡ اَوۡ يُعَذِّبَهُمۡ فَاِنَّهُمۡ ظٰلِمُوۡنَ ﴿۱۲۸﴾

129. To Allah belongs all that is in the heavens and the earth. He may forgive or punish whomever He wants. Allah is All-forgiving and All-merciful.

129. Wa lillaahi maa fissamaawaati wa maa fil-arḍ; yaghfiru limañy-yashaaa'u wa yu'az-zibu mañy-yashaaa'; wallaahu Ghafoorur-Raḥeem.

وَلِلّٰهِ مَا فِى السَّمٰوٰتِ وَمَا فِى الۡاَرۡضِ ؕ
يَغۡفِرُ لِمَنۡ يَّشَآءُ وَيُعَذِّبُ مَنۡ
يَّشَآءُ ؕ وَاللّٰهُ غَفُوۡرٌ رَّحِيۡمٌ ﴿۱۲۹﴾ ع ١٣ ٩ ٤

130. Believers, do not accept illegal interest in order to increase your wealth many times over. Have fear of Allah so that you will have everlasting happiness.

130. Yaaa ayyuhal-lazeena aamanoo laa ta-kulur-ribaaa aḍ'aafam-muḍaa'afah; wattaqul-laaha la'allakum tufliḥoon.

يٰۤاَيُّهَا الَّذِيۡنَ اٰمَنُوۡا لَا تَاۡكُلُوا
الرِّبٰٓوا اَضۡعَافًا مُّضٰعَفَةً ۖ وَّاتَّقُوا
اللّٰهَ لَعَلَّكُمۡ تُفۡلِحُوۡنَ ﴿۱۳۰﴾ۚ

131. Save yourselves from the fire which is prepared for the unbelievers.

131. Wattaqun-Naaral-lateee u‘iddat lilkaafireen.

وَاتَّقُوا النَّارَ الَّتِيٓ اُعِدَّتْ لِلْكٰفِرِيْنَ ﴿١٣١﴾

132. Obey Allah and the Messenger so that you may receive mercy.

132. Wa aṭee‘ul-laaha war-Rasoola la‘allakum turḥamoon.

وَاَطِيْعُوا اللّٰهَ وَالرَّسُوْلَ لَعَلَّكُمْ
تُرْحَمُوْنَ ﴿١٣٢﴾

133. Hasten to obtain forgiveness from your Lord and to qualify yourselves for Paradise. Paradise, vast as the heavens and the earth, is prepared for the pious

133. Wa saari‘ooo ilaa maghfiratim-mir-Rabbikum wa-Jannatin ‘arḍuhas-samaawaatu wal-arḍu u‘iddat lilmuttaqeen.

وَسَارِعُوْٓا اِلٰى مَغْفِرَةٍ مِّنْ رَّبِّكُمْ
وَجَنَّةٍ عَرْضُهَا السَّمٰوٰتُ وَالْاَرْضُ ۙ
اُعِدَّتْ لِلْمُتَّقِيْنَ ﴿١٣٣﴾ ۙ

134. who spend their property for the cause of Allah in prosperity as well as in adversity, and who also harness their anger and forgive the people. Allah loves the righteous ones.

134. Allaẕeena yunfiqoona fis-sarraaa’i waḍḍarraaa’i wal-kaaẓimeenal-ghayẓa wal-‘aafeena ‘anin-naas; wallaahu yuḥibbul-muḥsineen.

الَّذِيْنَ يُنْفِقُوْنَ فِي السَّرَّآءِ وَ
الضَّرَّآءِ وَالْكٰظِمِيْنَ الْغَيْظَ
وَالْعَافِيْنَ عَنِ النَّاسِ ؕ وَاللّٰهُ
يُحِبُّ الْمُحْسِنِيْنَ ﴿١٣٤﴾ ۚ

135. (Paradise) is also for those who, when committing a sin or doing injustice to themselves, remember Allah and ask Him to forgive their sins - Who can forgive sins besides Allah? - and who did not knowingly persist in their mistakes.

135. Wallaẕeena iẕaa fa‘aloo faaḥishatan aw ẓalamooo anfusahum ẕakarul-laaha fastaghfaroo liẕunoobihim; wa mañy-yaghfiruẕ-ẕunooba illal-laahu wa lam yuṣirroo ‘alaa maa fa‘aloo wa hum ya‘lamoon.

وَالَّذِيْنَ اِذَا فَعَلُوْا فَاحِشَةً اَوْ
ظَلَمُوْٓا اَنْفُسَهُمْ ذَكَرُوا اللّٰهَ
فَاسْتَغْفَرُوْا لِذُنُوْبِهِمْ ۠ وَمَنْ يَّغْفِرُ
الذُّنُوْبَ اِلَّا اللّٰهُ ۠ وَلَمْ يُصِرُّوْا
عَلٰى مَا فَعَلُوْا وَهُمْ يَعْلَمُوْنَ ﴿١٣٥﴾

136. Their reward will be forgiveness from their Lord and gardens wherein streams flow wherein they will live forever. How blessed is the reward of those who labor.

136. Ulaaa’ika jazaaa’uhum maghfiratum-mir-Rabbihim wa Jannaatun tajree min taḥtihal-anhaaru khaalideena feehaa; wa ni‘ma ajrul‘aamileen.

اُولٰٓئِكَ جَزَآؤُهُمْ مَّغْفِرَةٌ مِّنْ
رَّبِّهِمْ وَجَنّٰتٌ تَجْرِيْ مِنْ تَحْتِهَا
الْاَنْهٰرُ خٰلِدِيْنَ فِيْهَا ؕ وَنِعْمَ
اَجْرُ الْعٰمِلِيْنَ ﴿١٣٦﴾ ؕ

137. Different traditions existed in the past. Travel in the land and find out about the fate of those who rejected the Truth.

137. Qad khalat min qablikum sunanun faseeroo fil-arḍi fanẓuroo kayfa kaana ‘aaqibatul-mukaẕ ẕibeen

قَدْ خَلَتْ مِنْ قَبْلِكُمْ سُنَنٌ ۙ
فَسِيْرُوْا فِي الْاَرْضِ فَانْظُرُوْا
كَيْفَ كَانَ عَاقِبَةُ الْمُكَذِّبِيْنَ ﴿١٣٧﴾

138. This (Quran) is a reminder for the people and a guide and advice for the pious.

138. Haaẕaa bayaanul-linnaasi wa hudañw-wa maw‘iẓatul-lilmuttaqeen.

هٰذَا بَيَانٌ لِّلنَّاسِ وَهُدًى
وَّمَوْعِظَةٌ لِّلْمُتَّقِيْنَ ﴿١٣٨﴾

139. Do not be discouraged or grieved. You alone will have true dignity only if you are true believers.

139. Wa laa tahinoo wa laa taḥzanoo wa antumul-a‘lawna in kuntum mu’mineen.

وَلَا تَهِنُوْا وَلَا تَحْزَنُوْا وَاَنْتُمُ
الْاَعْلَوْنَ اِنْ كُنْتُمْ مُّؤْمِنِيْنَ ﴿١٣٩﴾

140. If you get hurt, certainly others have also experienced injuries. We have made people pass through the different turns of history so that Allah would know the true believers, have some of you bear witness to the people's deeds, [Allah does not love the unjust]

140. Iñy-yamsaskum qarḥun faqad massal-qawma qarḥummis̲luh; wa tilkal-ayyaamu nudaawiluhaa baynan-naasi wa liya'lamal-laahul-laz̲eena aamanoo wa yattakhiz̲a minkum shuhadaaa'; wallaahu laa yuḥibbuẓ-ẓaalimeen.

اِنْ يَّمْسَسْكُمْ قَرْحٌ فَقَدْ مَسَّ الْقَوْمَ
قَرْحٌ مِّثْلُهٗ ؕ وَتِلْكَ الْاَيَّامُ نُدَاوِلُهَا
بَيْنَ النَّاسِ ۚ وَلِيَعْلَمَ اللّٰهُ الَّذِيْنَ
اٰمَنُوْا وَيَتَّخِذَ مِنْكُمْ شُهَدَآءَ ؕ وَاللّٰهُ
لَا يُحِبُّ الظّٰلِمِيْنَ ۙ﴿۱۴۰﴾

141. test the faith of the believers, and deprive the unbelievers of (His) blessings.

141. Wa liyumaḥḥiṣal-laahul-laz̲eena aamanoo wa yamḥaqal-kaafireen.

وَلِيُمَحِّصَ اللّٰهُ الَّذِيْنَ اٰمَنُوْا
وَيَمْحَقَ الْكٰفِرِيْنَ ﴿۱۴۱﴾

142. Did you think that you could go to Paradise before proving in the world to Allah which of you fought for His cause and which of you bore patience?

142. Am ḥasibtum an tadkhulul-Jannata wa lammaa ya'lamil-laahul-laz̲eena jaahadoo minkum wa ya'lamaṣ-ṣaabireen.

اَمْ حَسِبْتُمْ اَنْ تَدْخُلُوا الْجَنَّةَ وَلَمَّا
يَعْلَمِ اللّٰهُ الَّذِيْنَ جٰهَدُوْا مِنْكُمْ
وَيَعْلَمَ الصّٰبِرِيْنَ ﴿۱۴۲﴾

143. You certainly wished to die (for the cause of Allah) before you actually faced death. Then you faced death (in the battlefield and only a few of you had the true desire to die).

143. Wa laqad kuntum tamannawnal-mawta min qabli an talqawhu faqad ra-aytumoohu wa antum tanẓuroon.

وَلَقَدْ كُنْتُمْ تَمَنَّوْنَ الْمَوْتَ مِنْ
قَبْلِ اَنْ تَلْقَوْهُ ۠ فَقَدْ رَاَيْتُمُوْهُ
وَاَنْتُمْ تَنْظُرُوْنَ ﴿۱۴۳﴾ ع ١٤ ١٤ ٥

144. Muhammad is only a Messenger. There lived other Messengers before him. Should (Muhammad) die or be slain, would you then turn back to your pre-Islamic behavior? Whoever does so can cause no harm to Allah. Allah will reward those who give thanks.

144. Wa maa Muḥammadun illaa Rasoolun qad khalat min qablihir-Rusul; afa'im-maata aw qutilan-qalabtum 'alaaa a'qaabikum; wa mañy-yanqalib 'alaa'aqibayhi falañy-yaḍurral-laaha shay'aa; wa sayajzil-laahush-shaakireen.

وَمَا مُحَمَّدٌ اِلَّا رَسُوْلٌ ۚ قَدْ خَلَتْ
مِنْ قَبْلِهِ الرُّسُلُ ؕ اَفَاۡئِنْ مَّاتَ
اَوْ قُتِلَ انْقَلَبْتُمْ عَلٰٓى اَعْقَابِكُمْ ؕ
وَمَنْ يَّنْقَلِبْ عَلٰى عَقِبَيْهِ فَلَنْ
يَّضُرَّ اللّٰهَ شَيْـًٔا ؕ وَسَيَجْزِى اللّٰهُ
الشّٰكِرِيْنَ ﴿۱۴۴﴾

145. No one can die without the permission of Allah. This is a written decree of the appointed term for life. We shall give worldly gains to whoever wants them. Those who want rewards in the life hereafter will also receive them. We reward those who give thanks.

145. Wa maa kaana linafsin an tamoota illaa bi-iz̲nillaahi kitaabam-mu'ajjalaa; wa mañy-yurid s̲awaabad-dunyaa nu'tihee minhaa wa mañy-yurid s̲awaabal-Aakhirati nu'tihee minhaa; wa sanajzish-shaakireen.

وَمَا كَانَ لِنَفْسٍ اَنْ تَمُوْتَ اِلَّا
بِاِذْنِ اللّٰهِ كِتٰبًا مُّؤَجَّلًا ؕ وَمَنْ
يُّرِدْ ثَوَابَ الدُّنْيَا نُؤْتِهٖ مِنْهَا ۚ
وَمَنْ يُّرِدْ ثَوَابَ الْاٰخِرَةِ نُؤْتِهٖ
مِنْهَا ؕ وَسَنَجْزِى الشّٰكِرِيْنَ ﴿۱۴۵﴾

146. Many godly people fought to help the Prophets in the cause of Allah. They did not lose courage, show weakness, or give

146. Wa ka-ayyim-min Nabiyyin qaatala ma'ahoo ribbiyyoona kas̲eerun famaa wahanoo limaaa

وَكَاَيِّنْ مِّنْ نَّبِيٍّ قٰتَلَ ۙ مَعَهٗ
رِبِّيُّوْنَ كَثِيْرٌ ۚ فَمَا وَهَنُوْا لِمَا

in when facing hardships in their fight for the cause of Allah. Allah loves those who have patience.

147. The only words that they spoke were, "Lord, forgive our sins and our excess in our dealings, make us steadfast (in the fight for Your cause), and grant us victory over the unbelievers."

148. Allah gave them their reward in this world and the best reward of the life to come. Allah loves the righteous ones.

149. Believers, were you to obey the unbelievers, they would turn you back to disbelief and you would become lost.

150. Believers, were you to obey the unbelievers, they would turn you back to disbelief and you would become lost.

151. We shall cause terror to enter the hearts of the faithless for their considering things equal to Allah without having received authoritative evidence. Their abode will be fire, a terrible dwelling for the unjust.

152. Allah certainly fulfilled His promise to you when you were fighting the unbelievers, by His permission. Even after We showed you what you wanted, you began to lose courage, started quarreling with each other, and disobeyed Allah's orders. Some of you want worldly gains and others of you want rewards in the hereafter. Then He let you face defeat in order to test you.

aşaabahum fee sabeelil-laahi wa maa ḍa'ufoo wa mas-takaanoo; wallaahu yuḥibbuş-şaabireen.

147. Wa maa kaana qawlahum illaaa an qaaloo Rabbanagh-fir lanaa zunoobanaa wa israafanaa feee amrinaa wa sabbit aqdaamanaa wanşurnaa 'alal-qawmil-kaafireen.

148. Fa-aataahumul-laahu sawaabad-dunyaa wa ḥusna sawaabil-Aakhirah; wallaahu yuḥibbul-muḥsineen.

149. Yaaa ayyuhal-lazeena aamanooo in tuṭee'ullazeena kafaroo yaruddookum 'alaaa a'qaabikum fatanqaliboo khaasireen.

150. Balil-laahu mawlaakum wa Huwa khayrun-naaşireen.

151. Sanulqee fee quloobil-lazeena kafarur-ru'ba bimaaa ashrakoo billaahi maa lam yunazzil bihee sulṭaanaa; wa ma-waahumun-Naar; wa bi'sa maswaẓ-ẓaalimeen.

152. Wa laqad şadaqakumul-laahu wa'dahooo iz taḥussoo-nahum bi-iznihee ḥattaaa-izaa fashiltum wa tanaaza'tum fil-amri wa 'aşaytum mim ba'di maaa araakum maa tuḥibboon; minkum mañy-yureedud-dunyaa wa minkum mañy-yureedul-Aakhirah; summa şarafakum 'anhum liyabtaliya-kum wa laqad

أَصَابَهُمْ فِي سَبِيلِ اللَّهِ وَمَا
ضَعُفُوا وَمَا اسْتَكَانُوا ۗ وَاللَّهُ
يُحِبُّ الصَّابِرِينَ ﴿١٤٦﴾
وَمَا كَانَ قَوْلَهُمْ إِلَّا أَنْ قَالُوا
رَبَّنَا اغْفِرْ لَنَا ذُنُوبَنَا وَإِسْرَافَنَا
فِي أَمْرِنَا وَثَبِّتْ أَقْدَامَنَا
وَانْصُرْنَا عَلَى الْقَوْمِ الْكَافِرِينَ ﴿١٤٧﴾
فَآتَاهُمُ اللَّهُ ثَوَابَ الدُّنْيَا وَ
حُسْنَ ثَوَابِ الْآخِرَةِ ۗ وَاللَّهُ
يُحِبُّ الْمُحْسِنِينَ ﴿١٤٨﴾ ع ١٥ ٥
يَا أَيُّهَا الَّذِينَ آمَنُوا إِنْ تُطِيعُوا
الَّذِينَ كَفَرُوا يَرُدُّوكُمْ عَلَىٰ
أَعْقَابِكُمْ فَتَنْقَلِبُوا خَاسِرِينَ ﴿١٤٩﴾
بَلِ اللَّهُ مَوْلَاكُمْ ۖ وَهُوَ خَيْرُ
النَّاصِرِينَ ﴿١٥٠﴾
سَنُلْقِي فِي قُلُوبِ الَّذِينَ كَفَرُوا
الرُّعْبَ بِمَا أَشْرَكُوا بِاللَّهِ مَا لَمْ
يُنَزِّلْ بِهِ سُلْطَانًا ۖ وَمَأْوَاهُمُ
النَّارُ ۚ وَبِئْسَ مَثْوَى الظَّالِمِينَ ﴿١٥١﴾
وَلَقَدْ صَدَقَكُمُ اللَّهُ وَعْدَهُ إِذْ
تَحُسُّونَهُمْ بِإِذْنِهِ ۖ حَتَّىٰ إِذَا فَشِلْتُمْ
وَتَنَازَعْتُمْ فِي الْأَمْرِ وَعَصَيْتُمْ
مِنْ بَعْدِ مَا أَرَاكُمْ مَا تُحِبُّونَ ۚ
مِنْكُمْ مَنْ يُرِيدُ الدُّنْيَا وَ
مِنْكُمْ مَنْ يُرِيدُ الْآخِرَةَ ۚ ثُمَّ
صَرَفَكُمْ عَنْهُمْ لِيَبْتَلِيَكُمْ ۖ وَلَقَدْ

However, He forgave you. Allah is gracious to the believers.

153. (O people, remember) when you were fleeing without even glancing to either side even though the Messengers were calling you back, Allah made you suffer sorrow upon sorrow to make you forget your grief about what you had lost and the injuries you had suffered. Allah is Well-aware of what you do.

154. After the sorrows you suffered, He sent you relief and some of you were encompassed by slumber. To some others of you, your lives were so important that you, like ignorant people, began thinking suspiciously of Allah saying, "Do we have any say in the matter?"

(Muhammad), tell them, "All matters belong to Allah." They try to hide within their souls what they do not reveal to you. They say, "Had we had the matter in our hands, we would not have been killed there."

Tell them, "Even if you had stayed in your own homes, your sworn enemies could have attacked you and slain you while you were in your beds. Allah wanted to test you and purge what existed in your hearts. Allah knows what the hearts contain.

155. Because of some of your bad deeds, those of you who ran away, when you faced the enemy, were misled by Satan. Allah forgave you for He is All-

'afaa 'ankum; wallaahu zoo faḍlin 'alal-mu'mineen.

153. Iz tuṣ'idoona wa laa talwoona 'alaaa aḥadiñw-war-Rasoolu yad'ookum feee ukhraakum fa-asaabakum ghammam bighammil-likaylaa taḥzanoo 'alaa maa faatakum wa laa maaa aṣaabakum; wallaahu khabeerum bimaa ta'maloon.

154. Summa anzala 'alaykum mim ba'dil-ghammi-amanatan nu'aasañy-yaghshaa ṭaaa'ifatam-minkum wa ṭaaa'ifatun qad ahammathum anfusuhum yaẓunnoona billaahi ghayral-ḥaqqi ẓannal-Jaahiliyyati yaqooloona hal lanaa minal-amri min shay'; qul-innal-amra kullahoo lillaah; yukhfoona feee anfusihim-maa laa yubdoona laka yaqooloona law kaana lanaa minal-amri shay'ummaa qutilnaa haahunaa; qul law kuntum fee buyootikum labarazal-lazeena kutiba 'alayhimul-qatlu ilaa maḍaaji'ihim wa liyabtaliyal-laahu maa fee ṣudoorikum wa liyumaḥḥiṣa maa fee quloobikum; wallaahu 'aleemum bizaatiṣ-ṣudoor.

155. Innal-lazeena tawallaw minkum yawmal-taqal jam'aani innamas tazallahumush-Shayṭaanu biba'ḍi maa kasaboo wa laqad 'afal-laahu 'anhum; innal-laaha

عَفَا عَنكُمْ ۗ وَاللَّهُ ذُو فَضْلٍ
عَلَى الْمُؤْمِنِينَ ﴿١٥٢﴾
إِذْ تُصْعِدُونَ وَلَا تَلْوُونَ عَلَىٰ أَحَدٍ
وَالرَّسُولُ يَدْعُوكُمْ فِي أُخْرَاكُمْ
فَأَثَابَكُمْ غَمًّا بِغَمٍّ لِّكَيْلَا تَحْزَنُوا
عَلَىٰ مَا فَاتَكُمْ وَلَا مَا أَصَابَكُمْ ۗ
وَاللَّهُ خَبِيرٌ بِمَا تَعْمَلُونَ ﴿١٥٣﴾
ثُمَّ أَنزَلَ عَلَيْكُم مِّن بَعْدِ الْغَمِّ
أَمَنَةً نُّعَاسًا يَغْشَىٰ طَائِفَةً
مِّنكُمْ ۖ وَطَائِفَةٌ قَدْ أَهَمَّتْهُمْ
أَنفُسُهُمْ يَظُنُّونَ بِاللَّهِ غَيْرَ الْحَقِّ
ظَنَّ الْجَاهِلِيَّةِ ۖ يَقُولُونَ هَل
لَّنَا مِنَ الْأَمْرِ مِن شَيْءٍ ۗ قُلْ إِنَّ
الْأَمْرَ كُلَّهُ لِلَّهِ ۗ يُخْفُونَ فِي
أَنفُسِهِم مَّا لَا يُبْدُونَ لَكَ ۖ
يَقُولُونَ لَوْ كَانَ لَنَا مِنَ الْأَمْرِ
شَيْءٌ مَّا قُتِلْنَا هَاهُنَا ۗ قُل لَّوْ
كُنتُمْ فِي بُيُوتِكُمْ لَبَرَزَ الَّذِينَ كُتِبَ
عَلَيْهِمُ الْقَتْلُ إِلَىٰ مَضَاجِعِهِمْ ۖ
وَلِيَبْتَلِيَ اللَّهُ مَا فِي صُدُورِكُمْ
وَلِيُمَحِّصَ مَا فِي قُلُوبِكُمْ ۗ
وَاللَّهُ عَلِيمٌ بِذَاتِ الصُّدُورِ ﴿١٥٤﴾
إِنَّ الَّذِينَ تَوَلَّوْا مِنكُمْ يَوْمَ
الْتَقَى الْجَمْعَانِ إِنَّمَا اسْتَزَلَّهُمُ
الشَّيْطَانُ بِبَعْضِ مَا كَسَبُوا ۖ
وَلَقَدْ عَفَا اللَّهُ عَنْهُمْ ۗ إِنَّ اللَّهَ

forgiving and Forbearing."

Ghafoorun Ḥaleem.

غَفُوْرٌ حَلِيْمٌ ﴿١٥٥﴾ ع ١٦ ٧

156. Believers, do not be like the unbelievers, who said of their brothers who traveled in the land or took part in a fight, "Had they stayed with us, they would not have died or been killed." Allah will cause only regret to enter their hearts. It is Allah who gives life and causes people to die. Allah is Well-aware of what you do.

156. Yaaa-ayyuhal-lazeena aamanoo laa takoonoo kallazeena kafaroo wa qaaloo li-ikhwaanihim-izaa ḍaraboo fil-arḍi aw kaanoo ghuzzal-law kaanoo 'indanaa maa maatoo wa maa qutiloo liyaj'alal-laahu zaalika ḥasratan fee quloobi-him; wallaahu yuḥyee wa yumeet; wallaahu bimaa ta'ma-loona Baṣeer.

يٰٓاَيُّهَا الَّذِيْنَ اٰمَنُوْا لَا تَكُوْنُوْا
كَالَّذِيْنَ كَفَرُوْا وَقَالُوْا لِاِخْوَانِهِمْ
اِذَا ضَرَبُوْا فِى الْاَرْضِ اَوْ كَانُوْا
غُزًّى لَّوْ كَانُوْا عِنْدَنَا مَا مَاتُوْا
وَمَا قُتِلُوْا ۚ لِيَجْعَلَ اللّٰهُ ذٰلِكَ
حَسْرَةً فِىْ قُلُوْبِهِمْ ۗ وَاللّٰهُ يُحْىٖ
وَيُمِيْتُ ۗ وَاللّٰهُ بِمَا تَعْمَلُوْنَ بَصِيْرٌ ﴿١٥٦﴾

157. If you were to die or to be killed for the cause of Allah, certainly, Allah's forgiveness and mercy is far better than your worldly gains.

157. Wa la'in qutiltum fee sabeelil-laahi aw muttum lamaghfiratum-minal-laahi wa raḥmatun khayrum-mimmaa yajma'oon.

وَلَئِنْ قُتِلْتُمْ فِىْ سَبِيْلِ اللّٰهِ اَوْ مُتُّمْ
لَمَغْفِرَةٌ مِّنَ اللّٰهِ وَرَحْمَةٌ خَيْرٌ
مِّمَّا يَجْمَعُوْنَ ﴿١٥٧﴾

158. If you die or are slain, certainly you will all be brought before Allah.

158. Wa la'im-muttum aw qutiltum-la-ilal-laahi tuḥsha-roon.

وَلَئِنْ مُّتُّمْ اَوْ قُتِلْتُمْ لَاِلَى اللّٰهِ
تُحْشَرُوْنَ ﴿١٥٨﴾

159. Only through the divine mercy have you (Muhammad) been able to deal with your followers so gently. If you had been stern and hard-hearted, they would all have deserted you a long time ago. Forgive them and ask Allah to forgive (their sins) and consult with them in certain matters. But, when you reach a decision, trust Allah. Allah loves those who trust Him.

159. Fabimaa raḥmatim minal-laahi linta lahum wa law kunta faẓẓan ghaleeẓal-qalbi lanfaḍḍoo min ḥawlika fa'fu 'anhum wastaghfir lahum wa shaawirhum fil-amri fa-izaa 'azamta fatawakkal 'alal-laah; innallaaha yuḥibbul-mutawak-kileen.

فَبِمَا رَحْمَةٍ مِّنَ اللّٰهِ لِنْتَ لَهُمْ ۚ
وَلَوْ كُنْتَ فَظًّا غَلِيْظَ الْقَلْبِ
لَانْفَضُّوْا مِنْ حَوْلِكَ ۖ فَاعْفُ
عَنْهُمْ وَاسْتَغْفِرْ لَهُمْ وَشَاوِرْهُمْ
فِى الْاَمْرِ ۚ فَاِذَا عَزَمْتَ فَتَوَكَّلْ عَلَى
اللّٰهِ ۗ اِنَّ اللّٰهَ يُحِبُّ الْمُتَوَكِّلِيْنَ ﴿١٥٩﴾

160. If Allah is your helper, no one can defeat you. However, if He abandons you, who would help you? The true believers trust in Allah.

160. Iñy-yanṣurkumul-laahu falaa ghaaliba lakum wa iñy-yakhzulkum faman zal-lazee yanṣurukum mim ba'dih; wa 'alal-laahi falyatawakkalil-mu'minoon.

اِنْ يَّنْصُرْكُمُ اللّٰهُ فَلَا غَالِبَ لَكُمْ ۚ
وَاِنْ يَّخْذُلْكُمْ فَمَنْ ذَا الَّذِىْ
يَنْصُرُكُمْ مِّنْۢ بَعْدِهٖ ۗ وَعَلَى اللّٰهِ
فَلْيَتَوَكَّلِ الْمُؤْمِنُوْنَ ﴿١٦٠﴾

161. No Prophet can ever be treacherous. A treacherous person will be brought before Allah on the Day of Judgment with his treacherous deeds. Then every soul will be recompensed for its

161. Wa maa kaana li-Nabiyyin añy-yaghull; wa mañy-yaghlul ya-ti bimaa ghalla Yawmal-Qiyaamah; summa tuwaffaa kullu nafsim-maa kasabat

وَمَا كَانَ لِنَبِىٍّ اَنْ يَّغُلَّ ۗ وَمَنْ
يَّغْلُلْ يَاْتِ بِمَا غَلَّ يَوْمَ الْقِيٰمَةِ ۚ
ثُمَّ تُوَفّٰى كُلُّ نَفْسٍ مَّا كَسَبَتْ

works without being wronged.

wa hum laa yuẓlamoon.

وَهُمْ لَا يُظْلَمُوْنَ ﴿١٦١﴾

162. Are those who seek Allah's pleasure equal to those who incur Allah's wrath and whose dwelling will be hell, the terrible destination?

162. Afamanit-taba'a Riḍwaa-nal-laahi kamam baaa'a bisakhaṭim-minal-laahi wa ma-waahu Jahannam; wa bi'sal-maṣeer.

اَفَمَنِ اتَّبَعَ رِضْوَانَ اللّٰهِ كَمَنْۢ بَآءَ
بِسَخَطٍ مِّنَ اللّٰهِ وَمَاْوٰىهُ جَهَنَّمُ ؕ
وَبِئْسَ الْمَصِيْرُ ﴿١٦٢﴾

163. People are of various grades in the sight of Allah. Allah is Well-aware of all that they do.

163. Hum darajaatun 'indal-laah; wallaahu baṣeerum bimaa ya'maloon.

هُمْ دَرَجٰتٌ عِنْدَ اللّٰهِ ؕ وَاللّٰهُ بَصِيْرٌۢ
بِمَا يَعْمَلُوْنَ ﴿١٦٣﴾

164. Allah granted a great favor to the believers by sending a Messenger from their own people to recite to them His revelations, to purify them of moral defects, to teach them the Book, and to give them wisdom. Before this they had lived in manifest error.

164. Laqad mannal-laahu 'alal-mu'mineena iẕ ba'aṯa feehim Rasoolam-min anfusihim yatloo 'alayhim Aayaatihee wa yuzakkeehim wa yu'allimu-humul-Kitaaba wal-Ḥikmata wa in kaanoo min qablu lafee ḍalaalim mubeen.

لَقَدْ مَنَّ اللّٰهُ عَلَى الْمُؤْمِنِيْنَ
اِذْ بَعَثَ فِيْهِمْ رَسُوْلًا مِّنْ اَنْفُسِهِمْ
يَتْلُوْا عَلَيْهِمْ اٰيٰتِهٖ وَيُزَكِّيْهِمْ
وَيُعَلِّمُهُمُ الْكِتٰبَ وَالْحِكْمَةَ ۚ وَاِنْ
كَانُوْا مِنْ قَبْلُ لَفِيْ ضَلٰلٍ مُّبِيْنٍ ﴿١٦٤﴾

النصف

165. When misfortune befell you (the believers) - your enemies had suffered twice as much (in the battle of Badr) - you asked, "Where did the misfortune come from (to cause us suffering)?" (Muhammad), tell them, "It came from yourselves. Allah has power over all things.

165. Awa lammaaa aṣaabat-kum muṣeebatun qad aṣabtum miṯlayhaa qultum annaa haaẕaa qul huwa min 'indi anfusikum; innal-laaha 'alaa kulli shay'in Qadeer.

اَوَلَمَّآ اَصَابَتْكُمْ مُّصِيْبَةٌ قَدْ اَصَبْتُمْ
مِّثْلَيْهَا ۙ قُلْتُمْ اَنّٰى هٰذَا ؕ قُلْ هُوَ
مِنْ عِنْدِ اَنْفُسِكُمْ ؕ اِنَّ اللّٰهَ عَلٰى
كُلِّ شَيْءٍ قَدِيْرٌ ﴿١٦٥﴾

166. What befell you, when the two armies confronted each other, was by the permission of Allah so that He would know who the true believers were

166. Wa maaa aṣaabakum yawmal-taqal-jam'aani fabi-iẕnil-laahi wa liya'lamal-mu'mineen.

وَمَآ اَصَابَكُمْ يَوْمَ الْتَقَى الْجَمْعٰنِ
فَبِاِذْنِ اللّٰهِ وَلِيَعْلَمَ الْمُؤْمِنِيْنَ ﴿١٦٦﴾ ۙ

167. and who were the hypocrites; the hypocrites who were asked to fight for the cause of Allah or to defend (the city)." They (hypocrites) replied, "If we knew that there was fighting (this day) we certainly would follow you." At that time they were closer to disbelief than to faith. They speak words that do not come from their hearts. Allah knows well whatever they try to hide.

167. Wa liya'lamal-laẕeena naafaqoo; wa qeela lahum ta'aalaw qaatiloo fee sabeelil-laahi awid-fa'oo qaaloo law na'lamu qitaalallat-taba'naa-kum; hum lilkufri yawma'iẕin aqrabu minhum lil-eemaan; yaqooloona bi-afwaahihim maa laysa fee quloobihim; wallaahu a'lamu bimaa yaktumoon.

وَلِيَعْلَمَ الَّذِيْنَ نَافَقُوْا ۖۚ وَقِيْلَ
لَهُمْ تَعَالَوْا قَاتِلُوْا فِيْ سَبِيْلِ اللّٰهِ
اَوِ ادْفَعُوْا ؕ قَالُوْا لَوْ نَعْلَمُ قِتَالًا لَّا
اتَّبَعْنٰكُمْ ؕ هُمْ لِلْكُفْرِ يَوْمَئِذٍ اَقْرَبُ
مِنْهُمْ لِلْاِيْمَانِ ۚ يَقُوْلُوْنَ بِاَفْوَاهِهِمْ
مَّا لَيْسَ فِيْ قُلُوْبِهِمْ ؕ وَاللّٰهُ اَعْلَمُ
بِمَا يَكْتُمُوْنَ ﴿١٦٧﴾ ۚ

168. There are those who themselves did not join the others in fighting for the cause of Allah and said about their brothers, "Had they listened to us and stayed at home, they would not have been killed." (Muhammad), tell them to save

168. Allaẕeena qaaloo li-ikhwaanihim wa qa'adoo law aṭaa'oonaa maa qutiloo; qul fadra'oo 'an

اَلَّذِيْنَ قَالُوْا لِاِخْوَانِهِمْ وَقَعَدُوْا لَوْ
اَطَاعُوْنَا مَا قُتِلُوْا ؕ قُلْ فَادْرَءُوْا عَنْ

themselves from death if they are true in their claim.	anfusikumul-mawta in kuntum ṣaadiqeen.	اَنْفُسِكُمُ الْمَوْتَ اِنْ كُنْتُمْ صٰدِقِيْنَ ﴿١٦٨﴾
169. Do not think of those slain for the cause of Allah as dead. They are alive with their Lord and receive sustenance from Him.	169. Wa laa taḥsabannal-laẕeena qutiloo fee sabeelillaahi amwaataa; bal aḥyaaa'un 'inda Rabbihim yurzaqoon.	وَلَا تَحْسَبَنَّ الَّذِيْنَ قُتِلُوْا فِيْ سَبِيْلِ اللّٰهِ اَمْوَاتًا ؕ بَلْ اَحْيَآءٌ عِنْدَ رَبِّهِمْ يُرْزَقُوْنَ ﴿١٦٩﴾
170. They are pleased with the favor from Allah, and have received the glad news that those who followed them will have no fear nor will they be grieved,	170. Fariḥeena bimaaa aataahumul-laahu min faḍlihee wa yastabshiroona billaẕeena lam yalḥaqoo bihim min khalfihim allaa khawfun 'alayhim wa laa hum yaḥzanoon.	فَرِحِيْنَ بِمَآ اٰتٰىهُمُ اللّٰهُ مِنْ فَضْلِهٖ ۙ وَيَسْتَبْشِرُوْنَ بِالَّذِيْنَ لَمْ يَلْحَقُوْا بِهِمْ مِّنْ خَلْفِهِمْ ۙ اَلَّا خَوْفٌ عَلَيْهِمْ وَلَا هُمْ يَحْزَنُوْنَ ﴿١٧٠﴾
171. that they will be rewarded with bounties and favors from Allah and that Allah will not neglect the reward of the true believers.	171. Yastabshiroona bini-'matim-minal-laahi wa faḍliñw-wa annal-laaha laa yuḍee'u ajral-mu'mineen.	يَسْتَبْشِرُوْنَ بِنِعْمَةٍ مِّنَ اللّٰهِ وَفَضْلٍ ۙ وَّاَنَّ اللّٰهَ لَا يُضِيْعُ اَجْرَ الْمُؤْمِنِيْنَ ﴿١٧١﴾
172. The righteous and pious of those who have pledged obedience to Allah and the Messenger, after injury had befallen them, will receive a great reward.	172. Allaẕeenas-tajaaboo lil-laahi war-Rasooli mim ba'di maaa aṣaabahumulqarḥ; lillaẕeena aḥsanoo minhum wattaqaw ajrun 'aẓeem.	اَلَّذِيْنَ اسْتَجَابُوْا لِلّٰهِ وَالرَّسُوْلِ مِنْۢ بَعْدِ مَآ اَصَابَهُمُ الْقَرْحُ ۛ لِلَّذِيْنَ اَحْسَنُوْا مِنْهُمْ وَاتَّقَوْا اَجْرٌ عَظِيْمٌ ﴿١٧٢﴾
173. Such people, when warned to fear those who are gathered against them, are strengthened in their faith and say, "Allah is All-sufficient as our Guardian."	173. Allaẕeena qaala lahumun-naasu innan-naasa qad jama'oo lakum fakhshawhum fazaadahum eemaanañw-wa qaaloo ḥasbunal-laahu wa ni'mal-wakeel.	اَلَّذِيْنَ قَالَ لَهُمُ النَّاسُ اِنَّ النَّاسَ قَدْ جَمَعُوْا لَكُمْ فَاخْشَوْهُمْ فَزَادَهُمْ اِيْمَانًا ۖ وَّقَالُوْا حَسْبُنَا اللّٰهُ وَنِعْمَ الْوَكِيْلُ ﴿١٧٣﴾
174. They returned with the favors and the bounties of Allah untouched by evil and followed by the pleasure of Allah. Allah's favor is great.	174. Fanqalaboo bini'matim-minal-laahi wa faḍlil-lam yamsashum sooo'uñw-wattaba'oo riḍwaanal-laah; wallaahu ẕoo faḍlin 'aẓeem.	فَانْقَلَبُوْا بِنِعْمَةٍ مِّنَ اللّٰهِ وَفَضْلٍ لَّمْ يَمْسَسْهُمْ سُوْٓءٌ ۙ وَّاتَّبَعُوْا رِضْوَانَ اللّٰهِ ؕ وَاللّٰهُ ذُوْ فَضْلٍ عَظِيْمٍ ﴿١٧٤﴾
175. It is Satan who frightens his friends. Do not be afraid of them (enemies) but have fear of Me if you truly believe.	175. Innamaa ẕaalikumush-Shayṭaanu yukhawwifu awli-yaaa'ahoo falaa takhaafoohum wa khaafooni in kuntum mu'mineen.	اِنَّمَا ذٰلِكُمُ الشَّيْطٰنُ يُخَوِّفُ اَوْلِيَآءَهٗ ۖ فَلَا تَخَافُوْهُمْ وَخَافُوْنِ اِنْ كُنْتُمْ مُّؤْمِنِيْنَ ﴿١٧٥﴾
176. (Muhammad), do not be grieved because of some people's	176. Wa laa yaḥzunkal-laẕeena yusaari'oona fil-	وَلَا يَحْزُنْكَ الَّذِيْنَ يُسَارِعُوْنَ فِي

وقف لازم

معٓ عند المتقدمين ۱۲

haste to disbelieve. They can do no harm to Allah. Allah has decided not to give them any share in the life hereafter. There will be a great torment for them.

kufr; innahum lañy-yaḍurrul-laaha shay'aa; yureedul-laahu allaa yaj'ala lahum ḥaẕẕan fil-Aakhirati wa lahum 'aẕaabun 'aẓeem.

الْكُفْرِ ۚ اِنَّهُمْ لَنْ يَّضُرُّوا اللّٰهَ شَيْـًٔا ۗ
يُرِيْدُ اللّٰهُ اَلَّا يَجْعَلَ لَهُمْ حَظًّا فِي
الْاٰخِرَةِ ۚ وَلَهُمْ عَذَابٌ عَظِيْمٌ ﴿١٧٦﴾

177. Those who have traded faith in exchange for disbelief can never do any harm to Allah. There will be a painful torment for them.

177. Innal-laẕeenash-tarawul-kufra bil-eemaani lañy-yaḍurrul-laaha shay'aa; wa lahum-'aẕaabun aleem.

اِنَّ الَّذِيْنَ اشْتَرَوُا الْكُفْرَ بِالْاِيْمَانِ
لَنْ يَّضُرُّوا اللّٰهَ شَيْـًٔا ۚ وَلَهُمْ
عَذَابٌ اَلِيْمٌ ﴿١٧٧﴾

178. The unbelievers must not think that Our respite is for their good. We only give them time to let them increase their sins. For them there will be a humiliating torment.

178. Wa laa yaḥsabannal-laẕeena kafarooo annamaa numlee lahum khayrulli-anfusihim; innamaa numlee lahum liyazdaadooo iṡmaa; wa lahum 'aẕaabum-muheen.

وَلَا يَحْسَبَنَّ الَّذِيْنَ كَفَرُوْٓا اَنَّمَا
نُمْلِيْ لَهُمْ خَيْرٌ لِّاَنْفُسِهِمْ ۗ اِنَّمَا
نُمْلِيْ لَهُمْ لِيَزْدَادُوْٓا اِثْمًا ۚ وَلَهُمْ
عَذَابٌ مُّهِيْنٌ ﴿١٧٨﴾

179. Allah left the believers in their existing state for no other reason than to distinguish the evil-doers from the virtuous ones. Allah does not inform you of the unseen. He chooses for such information any one of His Messengers that He wants. Have faith in Allah and in His Messengers. If you have faith and are pious, there will be a great reward for you.

179. Maa kaanal-laahu liyaẕa-ral-mu'mineena 'alaa maaa antum 'alayhi ḥattaa yameezal-khabeeṡa minaṭ-ṭayyib; wa maa kaanal-laahu liyuṭli'akum 'alal-ghaybi wa laakinnal-laaha yajtabee mir-Rusulihee mañy-yashaaa'u fa-aaminoo billaahi wa Rusulih; wa in tu'minoo wa tattaqoo falakum ajrun 'aẓeem.

مَا كَانَ اللّٰهُ لِيَذَرَ الْمُؤْمِنِيْنَ عَلٰى
مَآ اَنْتُمْ عَلَيْهِ حَتّٰى يَمِيْزَ الْخَبِيْثَ
مِنَ الطَّيِّبِ ۗ وَمَا كَانَ اللّٰهُ لِيُطْلِعَكُمْ
عَلَى الْغَيْبِ وَلٰكِنَّ اللّٰهَ يَجْتَبِيْ مِنْ
رُّسُلِهٖ مَنْ يَّشَآءُ ۖ فَاٰمِنُوْا بِاللّٰهِ
وَرُسُلِهٖ ۚ وَاِنْ تُؤْمِنُوْا وَتَتَّقُوْا
فَلَكُمْ اَجْرٌ عَظِيْمٌ ﴿١٧٩﴾

180. Those who are avaricious about the favors that Allah has given them should not think that this is good for them. Avarice is evil and whatever they are avaricious about will be tied to their necks on the Day of Judgment. To Allah belongs the heritage of the heavens and the earth. Allah is Well-aware of what you do.

180. Wa laa yaḥsabannal-laẕeena yabkhaloona bimaaa aataahumul-laahu min faḍlihee huwa khayral-lahum bal huwa sharrul-lahum sayuṭaw-waqoona maa bakhiloo bihee Yawmal-Qiyaamah; wa lillaahi meeraaṡus-samaawaati wal-arḍ; wallaahu bimaa ta'maloona Khabeer.

وَلَا يَحْسَبَنَّ الَّذِيْنَ يَبْخَلُوْنَ بِمَآ
اٰتٰىهُمُ اللّٰهُ مِنْ فَضْلِهٖ هُوَ خَيْرًا
لَّهُمْ ۚ بَلْ هُوَ شَرٌّ لَّهُمْ ۚ سَيُطَوَّقُوْنَ
مَا بَخِلُوْا بِهٖ يَوْمَ الْقِيٰمَةِ ۗ وَلِلّٰهِ
مِيْرَاثُ السَّمٰوٰتِ وَالْاَرْضِ ۗ وَ
اللّٰهُ بِمَا تَعْمَلُوْنَ خَبِيْرٌ ﴿١٨٠﴾ ع

181. Allah certainly has heard the words of those who said, "Allah is poor and we are wealthy." We shall write down what they have said and their murder of the Prophets without

181. Laqad sami'al-laahu qawlal-laẕeena qaalooo innal-laaha faqeeruñw-wa naḥnu aghniyaaa'; sanaktubu maa qaaloo wa qatlahumul-Ambiyaa'a

لَقَدْ سَمِعَ اللّٰهُ قَوْلَ الَّذِيْنَ قَالُوْٓا
اِنَّ اللّٰهَ فَقِيْرٌ وَّنَحْنُ اَغْنِيَآءُ ۘ
سَنَكْتُبُ مَا قَالُوْا وَقَتْلَهُمُ الْاَنْۢبِيَآءَ

وقف لازم

reason, and We shall tell them to suffer the burning torment.

bighayri ḥaqq; wa naqoolu z̲ooqoo 'az̲aabal-ḥareeq.

بِغَيْرِ حَقٍّ ۙ وَّنَقُوْلُ ذُوْقُوْا
عَذَابَ الْحَرِيْقِ ﴿١٨١﴾

182. This is only the result of their deeds. Allah is not unjust to His servants.

182. Z̲aalika bimaa qaddamat aydeekum wa annal-laaha laysa biẓallaamil-lil'abeed.

ذٰلِكَ بِمَا قَدَّمَتْ اَيْدِيْكُمْ وَاَنَّ
اللّٰهَ لَيْسَ بِظَلَّامٍ لِّلْعَبِيْدِ ﴿١٨٢﴾

183. (Muhammad), say to those who say, "Allah has commanded us not to believe any Messenger unless he offers a burnt offering;" (Muhammad) say, "Messengers came to you before me with certain miracles and with that which you had asked for (burnt offerings). Why then, did you slay them if you were true in your claim?"

183. Allaz̲eena qaalooo innal-laaha 'ahida ilaynaaa allaa nu'mina li-Rasoolin ḥattaa ya-tiyanaa biqurbaanin ta-kuluhun-naar; qul qad jaaa'akum Rusulum-min qablee bilbayyinaati wa billaz̲ee qultum falima qataltumoohum in kuntum ṣaadiqeen.

اَلَّذِيْنَ قَالُوْٓا اِنَّ اللّٰهَ عَهِدَ اِلَيْنَآ
اَلَّا نُؤْمِنَ لِرَسُوْلٍ حَتّٰى يَاْتِيَنَا
بِقُرْبَانٍ تَاْكُلُهُ النَّارُ ؕ قُلْ قَدْ جَآءَكُمْ
رُسُلٌ مِّنْ قَبْلِيْ بِالْبَيِّنٰتِ وَبِالَّذِيْ
قُلْتُمْ فَلِمَ قَتَلْتُمُوْهُمْ اِنْ
كُنْتُمْ صٰدِقِيْنَ ﴿١٨٣﴾

184. If they reject you, they had certainly rejected the Messengers who lived before you and who showed them authoritative evidence, smaller Books, and the Book of enlightenment.

184. Fa-in kaz̲ z̲abooka faqad kuz̲ z̲iba Rusulum-min qablika jaaa'oo bilbayyinaati waz-Zuburi wal-Kitaabil-Muneer.

فَاِنْ كَذَّبُوْكَ فَقَدْ كُذِّبَ رُسُلٌ
مِّنْ قَبْلِكَ جَآءُوْ بِالْبَيِّنٰتِ وَالزُّبُرِ
وَالْكِتٰبِ الْمُنِيْرِ ﴿١٨٤﴾

185. Every soul is destined to experience the agony of death. You (Muslims) will receive the recompense for your deeds on the Day of Judgment.

To be saved from the fire and admitted to Paradise is certainly a great triumph. The worldly life is no more than a deceitful possession.

185 Kullu nafsin z̲aaa'iqatul-mawt; wa innamaa tuwaffawna ujoorakum Yawmal-Qiyaamati faman zuḥziḥa 'anin-Naari wa-udkhilal-Jannata faqad faaz; wa mal-ḥayaatud-dunyaaa illaa mataa'ul-ghuroor.

كُلُّ نَفْسٍ ذَآئِقَةُ الْمَوْتِ ؕ وَاِنَّمَا
تُوَفَّوْنَ اُجُوْرَكُمْ يَوْمَ الْقِيٰمَةِ ؕ فَمَنْ
زُحْزِحَ عَنِ النَّارِ وَاُدْخِلَ الْجَنَّةَ
فَقَدْ فَازَ ؕ وَمَا الْحَيٰوةُ الدُّنْيَآ اِلَّا
مَتَاعُ الْغُرُوْرِ ﴿١٨٥﴾

186. You (believers) will certainly be tested by the loss of your property and lives and you will hear a great many grieving words from the People of the Book and the pagans. If you have patience and piety, it will be a sign of firm determination and steadfastness (in life).

186. Latublawunna feee amwaalikum wa anfusikum wa latasma'unna minal-laz̲eena ootul-Kitaaba min qablikum wa minal-laz̲eena ashrakooo az̲an kas̲eeraa; wa in taṣbiroo wa tattaqoo fa-inna z̲aalika min 'azmil-umoor.

لَتُبْلَوُنَّ فِيْٓ اَمْوَالِكُمْ وَاَنْفُسِكُمْ قف
وَلَتَسْمَعُنَّ مِنَ الَّذِيْنَ اُوْتُوا الْكِتٰبَ
مِنْ قَبْلِكُمْ وَمِنَ الَّذِيْنَ اَشْرَكُوْٓا
اَذًى كَثِيْرًا ؕ وَاِنْ تَصْبِرُوْا وَتَتَّقُوْا
فَاِنَّ ذٰلِكَ مِنْ عَزْمِ الْاُمُوْرِ ﴿١٨٦﴾

187. When Allah made a covenant with the People of the Book saying, "Tell the people about it (prophesy of Muhammad) without hiding any part therefrom," they threw it

187. Wa-iz̲-akhaz̲al-laahu mees̲aaqal -laz̲eena ootul-Kitaaba latubayyinunnahoo linnaasi wa laa taktumoonahoo fanabaz̲oohu waraaa'a ẓuhoorihim

وَاِذْ اَخَذَ اللّٰهُ مِيْثَاقَ الَّذِيْنَ
اُوْتُوا الْكِتٰبَ لَتُبَيِّنُنَّهٗ لِلنَّاسِ
وَلَا تَكْتُمُوْنَهٗ ۫ فَنَبَذُوْهُ وَرَآءَ ظُهُوْرِهِمْ

behind their backs and sold it for a very small price. What a miserable bargain!	washtaraw bihee s̲amanan qaleelan fabi'sa maa yash-taroon.	وَاشْتَرَوْا بِهٖ ثَمَنًا قَلِيْلًا ؕ فَبِئْسَ مَا يَشْتَرُوْنَ ﴿١٨٧﴾
188. Do not think that those who are happy with their possessions and positions and those who love to be praised for what they, themselves, did not do, can ever be saved from torment. For them there will be a painful punishment.	188. Laa taḥsabannal-laz̲eena yafraḥoona bimaaa ataw wa yuḥibboona añy-yuḥmadoo bimaa lam yaf'aloo falaa taḥsabannahum bimafaazatim-minal-'az̲aab; wa lahum 'az̲aabun aleem.	لَا تَحْسَبَنَّ الَّذِيْنَ يَفْرَحُوْنَ بِمَآ اَتَوْا وَّيُحِبُّوْنَ اَنْ يُّحْمَدُوْا بِمَا لَمْ يَفْعَلُوْا فَلَا تَحْسَبَنَّهُمْ بِمَفَازَةٍ مِّنَ الْعَذَابِ ۚ وَلَهُمْ عَذَابٌ اَلِيْمٌ ﴿١٨٨﴾
189. To Allah belongs all that is in the heavens and the earth, and He has power over all things.	189. Wa lillaahi mulkus-samaawaati wal-arḍ; wallaahu 'alaa kulli shay'in Qadeer.	وَلِلّٰهِ مُلْكُ السَّمٰوٰتِ وَالْاَرْضِ ؕ وَاللّٰهُ عَلٰى كُلِّ شَيْءٍ قَدِيْرٌ ﴿١٨٩﴾ ع ١٩ ٩
190. The creation of the heavens and the earth and the alternation of the day and the night are evidence (of the existence of Allah) for people of reason.	190. Inna fee khalqis-samaa-waati wal-arḍi wakhtilaafil-layli wannahaari la-Aayaatil-li-ulil-albaab.	اِنَّ فِيْ خَلْقِ السَّمٰوٰتِ وَالْاَرْضِ وَاخْتِلَافِ الَّيْلِ وَالنَّهَارِ لَاٰيٰتٍ لِّاُولِي الْاَلْبَابِ ﴿١٩٠﴾
191. It is these who speak of Allah while standing, sitting, or resting on their sides and who think about the creation of the heavens and the earth and say, "Lord, you have not created all this without reason. Glory be to you. Lord, save us from the torment of the fire.	191. Allaz̲eena yaz̲kuroonal-laaha qiyaamañw-wa qu'oodañw-wa 'alaa junoobihim wa yatafakkaroona fee khalqis-samaawaati wal-arḍi Rabbanaa maa khalaqta haaz̲aa baaṭilan Subḥaanaka-faqinaa 'az̲aaban-Naar.	الَّذِيْنَ يَذْكُرُوْنَ اللّٰهَ قِيٰمًا وَّ قُعُوْدًا وَّعَلٰى جُنُوْبِهِمْ وَيَتَفَكَّرُوْنَ فِيْ خَلْقِ السَّمٰوٰتِ وَالْاَرْضِ ۚ رَبَّنَا مَا خَلَقْتَ هٰذَا بَاطِلًا ۚ سُبْحٰنَكَ فَقِنَا عَذَابَ النَّارِ ﴿١٩١﴾
192. Lord, those whom You send to the fire are certainly disgraced. There is no helper for the unjust."	192. Rabbanaaa innaka man tudkhilin-Naara faqad akhzay-tahoo wa maa liẓẓaalimeena min anṣaar.	رَبَّنَآ اِنَّكَ مَنْ تُدْخِلِ النَّارَ فَقَدْ اَخْزَيْتَهٗ ؕ وَمَا لِلظّٰلِمِيْنَ مِنْ اَنْصَارٍ ﴿١٩٢﴾
193. "Lord, we have heard the person calling to the faith and have accepted his call. Forgive our sins, expiate our bad deeds, and let us die with the righteous ones.	193. Rabbanaaa innanaa sami'naa munaadiyañy-yunaadee lil-eemaani an aaminoo bi-Rabbikum fa-aamannaa; Rabbanaa faghfir lanaa z̲unoobanaa wa kaffir 'annaa sayyi-aatinaa wa tawaffanaa ma'al-abraar.	رَبَّنَآ اِنَّنَا سَمِعْنَا مُنَادِيًا يُّنَادِيْ لِلْاِيْمَانِ اَنْ اٰمِنُوْا بِرَبِّكُمْ فَاٰمَنَّا ۖۗ رَبَّنَا فَاغْفِرْ لَنَا ذُنُوْبَنَا وَكَفِّرْ عَنَّا سَيِّاٰتِنَا وَتَوَفَّنَا مَعَ الْاَبْرَارِ ۚ ﴿١٩٣﴾
194. Lord, grant us the victory that You have promised your Messenger and do not disgrace us on the Day of Judgment; You are the One who never ignores His promise."	194. Rabbanaa wa aatinaa maa wa'attanaa 'alaa Rusulika wa laa tukhzinaa Yawmal-Qiyaamah; innaka laa tukhliful-mee'aad.	رَبَّنَا وَاٰتِنَا مَا وَعَدْتَّنَا عَلٰى رُسُلِكَ وَلَا تُخْزِنَا يَوْمَ الْقِيٰمَةِ ؕ اِنَّكَ لَا تُخْلِفُ الْمِيْعَادَ ﴿١٩٤﴾
194. Their Lord answered their prayers saying, "I do not neglect	195. Fastajaaba lahum Rabbu-hum Annee laaa	فَاسْتَجَابَ لَهُمْ رَبُّهُمْ اَنِّيْ لَآ

anyone's labor, whether the laborer be male or female. You are all related to one another. Those who migrated from Makkah, those who were expelled from their homes, those who were tortured for My cause, and those who fought and were killed for My cause will find their sins expiated by Me and I will admit them into the gardens wherein streams flow. It will be their reward from Allah. Allah grants the best rewards."

uḍee'u 'amala 'aamilim-minkum min zakarin aw unsaa ba'ḍukum mim-ba'ḍin fal-lazeena haajaroo wa ukhrijoo min diyaarihim wa oozoo fee sabeelee wa qaataloo wa qutiloo la-ukaffiranna 'anhum sayyi-aatihim wa la-udkhilannahum Jannaatin tajree min taḥtihal-anhaaru sawaabam-min 'indil-laah; wallaahu 'indahoo ḥusnus-sawaab.

أُضِيعُ عَمَلَ عَامِلٍ مِّنكُم مِّن
ذَكَرٍ أَوْ أُنثَىٰ ۖ بَعْضُكُم مِّن
بَعْضٍ ۖ فَالَّذِينَ هَاجَرُوا وَأُخْرِجُوا
مِن دِيَارِهِمْ وَأُوذُوا فِي سَبِيلِي
وَقَاتَلُوا وَقُتِلُوا لَأُكَفِّرَنَّ عَنْهُمْ
سَيِّئَاتِهِمْ وَلَأُدْخِلَنَّهُمْ جَنَّاتٍ
تَجْرِي مِن تَحْتِهَا الْأَنْهَارُ ثَوَابًا
مِّنْ عِندِ اللَّهِ ۗ وَاللَّهُ عِندَهُ
حُسْنُ الثَّوَابِ ﴿١٩٥﴾

196. (Muhammad), do not be deceived by the changing activities of the unbelievers in different parts of the land.

196. Laa yaghurrannaka taqal-lubul-lazeena kafaroo fil-bilaad.

لَا يَغُرَّنَّكَ تَقَلُّبُ الَّذِينَ كَفَرُوا
فِي الْبِلَادِ ﴿١٩٦﴾

197. Their gains are only a means of enjoyment in this life. However, their destination is hell, the terrible dwelling.

197. Mataa'un qaleelun summa ma-waahum Jahannam; wa bi'sal-mihaad.

مَتَاعٌ قَلِيلٌ ثُمَّ مَأْوَاهُمْ جَهَنَّمُ ۚ
وَبِئْسَ الْمِهَادُ ﴿١٩٧﴾

198. For those who have fear of their Lord, there will be gardens wherein streams flow and they will live therein forever as a gift from Allah. Allah has the best reward for the virtuous people.

198. Laakinil-lazeenat-taqaw Rabbahum lahum Jannaatun tajree min taḥtihal-anhaaru khaalideena feehaa nuzulam-min 'indil-laah; wa maa 'indal-laahi khayrul-lil-abraar.

لَٰكِنِ الَّذِينَ اتَّقَوْا رَبَّهُمْ لَهُمْ جَنَّاتٌ
تَجْرِي مِن تَحْتِهَا الْأَنْهَارُ خَالِدِينَ
فِيهَا نُزُلًا مِّنْ عِندِ اللَّهِ ۗ وَمَا
عِندَ اللَّهِ خَيْرٌ لِّلْأَبْرَارِ ﴿١٩٨﴾ الثلثة

199. There are some among the People of the Book who believe in Allah and what is revealed to you and to them. They are humble before Allah and do not trade Allah's revelations for a small price. They will receive their reward from their Lord. Allah's reckoning is swift.

199. Wa inna min Ahlil-Kitaabi lamañy-yu'minu billaahi wa maaa unzila ilaykum wa maaa unzila ilayhim khaashi'eena lillaahi laa yashtaroona bi-Aayaatil-laahi samanan qaleelaa; ulaaa'ika lahum ajruhum 'inda Rabbihim; innal-laaha Saree'ul-ḥisaab.

وَإِنَّ مِنْ أَهْلِ الْكِتَابِ لَمَن يُؤْمِنُ
بِاللَّهِ وَمَا أُنزِلَ إِلَيْكُمْ وَمَا أُنزِلَ
إِلَيْهِمْ خَاشِعِينَ لِلَّهِ لَا يَشْتَرُونَ
بِآيَاتِ اللَّهِ ثَمَنًا قَلِيلًا ۗ أُولَٰئِكَ
لَهُمْ أَجْرُهُمْ عِندَ رَبِّهِمْ ۗ إِنَّ اللَّهَ
سَرِيعُ الْحِسَابِ ﴿١٩٩﴾

200. Believers, have patience, help each other with patience, establish good relations with one another, and have fear of Allah so that you may have everlasting happiness.

200. Yaaa ayyuhal-lazeena aamanuṣ-biroo wa ṣaabiroo wa raabiṭoo wattaqul-laaha la'allakum tufliḥoon.

يَا أَيُّهَا الَّذِينَ آمَنُوا اصْبِرُوا
وَصَابِرُوا وَرَابِطُوا وَاتَّقُوا اللَّهَ
لَعَلَّكُمْ تُفْلِحُونَ ﴿٢٠٠﴾ ع ٢٠ / ١١

Al-Nisa, The Women (4)

In the Name of Allah,
the Beneficent, the Merciful.

Sûrat an-Nisâ-4

(Revealed at Madinah)
Bismillaahir Raḥmaanir Raḥeem

سُوْرَةُ النِّسَآءِ مَدَنِيَّةٌ (٩٢) (٤)

آياتها ١٧٦ بِسْمِ اللّٰهِ الرَّحْمٰنِ الرَّحِيْمِ ركوعاتها ٢٤

1. People, have fear of your Lord who has created you from a single soul. From it He created the spouse of that soul and through both He populated the land with many men and women. Have fear of Allah by whose name you swear to settle your differences and have respect for your relatives. Allah certainly keeps watch over you.

1. Yaaa ayyuhan-naasut-taqoo Rabbakumul-lazee khalaqakum min nafsiñw-waaḥidatiñw-wa khalaqa minhaa zawjahaa wa bas-sa minhumaa rijaalan kaseerañw-wa nisaaa'aa; wattaqul-laahallazee tasaaa-'aloona bihee wal-arḥaam; innal-laaha kaana 'alaykum Raqeebaa.

يٰۤاَيُّهَا النَّاسُ اتَّقُوْا رَبَّكُمُ الَّذِیْ
خَلَقَكُمْ مِّنْ نَّفْسٍ وَّاحِدَةٍ وَّ
خَلَقَ مِنْهَا زَوْجَهَا وَبَثَّ مِنْهُمَا
رِجَالًا كَثِیْرًا وَّنِسَآءً ۚ وَاتَّقُوا اللّٰهَ
الَّذِیْ تَسَآءَلُوْنَ بِهٖ وَالْاَرْحَامَ ؕ
اِنَّ اللّٰهَ كَانَ عَلَیْكُمْ رَقِیْبًا ۝١

2. Give to the orphans their property. Do not exchange the pure for the filthy and do not spend the property of orphans along with your own; this would be a great sin.

2. Wa aatul-yataamaaa amwaalahum wa laa tatabad-dalul-khabeesa biṭṭayyib; wa laa ta-kulooo amwaalahum ilaaa amwaalikum; innahoo kaana ḥooban kabeeraa.

وَاٰتُوا الْیَتٰمٰۤى اَمْوَالَهُمْ وَلَا تَتَبَدَّلُوا
الْخَبِیْثَ بِالطَّیِّبِ ۪ وَلَا تَاْكُلُوْۤا
اَمْوَالَهُمْ اِلٰۤى اَمْوَالِكُمْ ؕ اِنَّهٗ كَانَ
حُوْبًا كَبِیْرًا ۝٢

3. With respect to marrying widows, if you are afraid of not being able to maintain justice with her children, marry another woman of your choice or two or three or four (who have no children). If you cannot maintain equality with more than one wife, marry only one or your slave-girl. This keeps you from acting against justice.

3. Wa-in khiftum allaa tuqsiṭoo fil-yataamaa fankiḥoo maa ṭaaba lakum minan-nisaaa'i masnaa wa sulaasa wa rubaa'a fa-in khiftum allaa ta'diloo fawaaḥidatan aw maa malakat aymaanukum; zaalika adnaaa allaa ta'ooloo.

وَاِنْ خِفْتُمْ اَلَّا تُقْسِطُوْا فِی الْیَتٰمٰى
فَانْكِحُوْا مَا طَابَ لَكُمْ مِّنَ النِّسَآءِ
مَثْنٰى وَثُلٰثَ وَرُبٰعَ ۚ فَاِنْ خِفْتُمْ
اَلَّا تَعْدِلُوْا فَوَاحِدَةً اَوْ مَا مَلَكَتْ
اَیْمَانُكُمْ ؕ ذٰلِكَ اَدْنٰۤى اَلَّا تَعُوْلُوْا ۝٣

4. Pay the women their dowry as though it were a gift. However, if they allow you to keep a part of it as a favor for you, you may spend it with pleasure.

4. Wa aatun-nisaaa'a ṣaduqaatihinna niḥlah; fa-in ṭibna lakum 'an shay'im minhu nafsan fakuloohu haneee'am-mareee'aa.

وَاٰتُوا النِّسَآءَ صَدُقٰتِهِنَّ نِحْلَةً ؕ
فَاِنْ طِبْنَ لَكُمْ عَنْ شَیْءٍ مِّنْهُ
نَفْسًا فَكُلُوْهُ هَنِیْٓـًٔا مَّرِیْٓـًٔا ۝٤

5. Do not give to people weak of understanding your property for which Allah has made you the supervisor. Feed and clothe such people and speak to them in a reasonable way.

5. Wa laa tu'tus-sufahaaa'a amwaalakumul-latee ja'alal-laahu lakum qiyaamañw-warzuqoohum feehaa waksoohum wa qooloo lahum qawlam-ma'roofaa.

وَلَا تُؤْتُوا السُّفَهَآءَ اَمْوَالَكُمُ الَّتِیْ
جَعَلَ اللّٰهُ لَكُمْ قِیٰمًا وَّارْزُقُوْهُمْ
فِیْهَا وَاكْسُوْهُمْ وَقُوْلُوْا لَهُمْ قَوْلًا
مَّعْرُوْفًا ۝٥

6. Before returning orphans' property to them, make sure that they have reached maturity. Do not consume their property

6. Wabtalul-yataamaa ḥattaaa izaa balaghun-nikaaḥa fa-in aanastum minhum rushdan fad-fa'ooo

وَابْتَلُوا الْیَتٰمٰى حَتّٰۤى اِذَا بَلَغُوا النِّكَاحَ ۚ
فَاِنْ اٰنَسْتُمْ مِّنْهُمْ رُشْدًا فَادْفَعُوْۤا

wastefully until such a time. The rich (guardian) should not take any of his ward's property. However, a poor (guardian) may use a reasonable portion. When you return their property, make sure you have witnesses. Allah is perfect in taking accounts.

ilayhim amwaalahum wa laa ta-kuloohaaa israafañw-wa bidaaran añy-yakbaroo; wa man kaana ghaniyyan falyasta'fif wa man kaana faqeeran falya-kul bilma'roof; fa-izaa dafa'tum ilayhim amwaalahum fa-ashhidoo 'alayhim; wa kafaa billaahi Ḥaseebaa.

إِلَيْهِمْ أَمْوَالَهُمْ وَلَا تَأْكُلُوهَا إِسْرَافًا
وَبِدَارًا أَنْ يَكْبَرُوا وَمَنْ كَانَ غَنِيًّا
فَلْيَسْتَعْفِفْ وَمَنْ كَانَ فَقِيرًا فَلْيَأْكُلْ
بِالْمَعْرُوفِ فَإِذَا دَفَعْتُمْ إِلَيْهِمْ
أَمْوَالَهُمْ فَأَشْهِدُوا عَلَيْهِمْ
وَكَفَىٰ بِاللَّهِ حَسِيبًا ⑥

7. Male and female are entitled to their legal share in the legacy of their parents and relatives, whether it is small or large.

7. Lirrijaali naṣeebum-mimmaa tarakal-waalidaani wal-aqraboona wa lin-nisaaa'i naṣeebum-mimmaa tarakal-waalidaani wal-aqraboona mimmaa qalla minhu aw kasur; naṣeebam-mafrooḍaa.

لِلرِّجَالِ نَصِيبٌ مِمَّا تَرَكَ الْوَالِدَانِ
وَالْأَقْرَبُونَ وَلِلنِّسَاءِ نَصِيبٌ مِمَّا
تَرَكَ الْوَالِدَانِ وَالْأَقْرَبُونَ مِمَّا قَلَّ
مِنْهُ أَوْ كَثُرَ نَصِيبًا مَفْرُوضًا ⑦

8. If relatives, orphans or destitute people, are present at the distribution of the legacy, give them something and speak kindly to them.

8. Wa izaa ḥaḍaral-qismata ulul-qurbaa walyataamaa walmasaakeenu farzuqoohum minhu wa qooloo lahum qawlam-ma'roofaa.

وَإِذَا حَضَرَ الْقِسْمَةَ أُولُو الْقُرْبَىٰ
وَالْيَتَامَىٰ وَالْمَسَاكِينُ فَارْزُقُوهُمْ مِنْهُ
وَقُولُوا لَهُمْ قَوْلًا مَعْرُوفًا ⑧

9. Those who are concerned about the welfare of their own children after their death should have fear of Allah (when dealing with the orphans) and guide them properly.

9. Walyakhshal-lazeena law tarakoo min khalfihim zurriyyatan ḍi'aafan khaafoo 'alayhim falyattaqul-laaha walyaqooloo qawlan sadeedaa.

وَلْيَخْشَ الَّذِينَ لَوْ تَرَكُوا مِنْ خَلْفِهِمْ
ذُرِّيَّةً ضِعَافًا خَافُوا عَلَيْهِمْ فَلْيَتَّقُوا
اللَّهَ وَلْيَقُولُوا قَوْلًا سَدِيدًا ⑨

10. Those who wrongfully consume the property of orphans are, in fact, consuming fire in their bellies and they will suffer the blazing fire.

10. Innal-lazeena ya-kuloona amwaalal-yataamaa ẓulman innamaa ya-kuloona fee buṭoonihim Naaraa; wa sayaṣlawna sa'eeraa.

إِنَّ الَّذِينَ يَأْكُلُونَ أَمْوَالَ الْيَتَامَىٰ
ظُلْمًا إِنَّمَا يَأْكُلُونَ فِي بُطُونِهِمْ
نَارًا وَسَيَصْلَوْنَ سَعِيرًا ⑩ ع ١٢

11. This is a commandment from Allah: After the payment of debts or anything bequeathed, let the male inherit twice as much as the female.

If there are more than two girls, they will have two-thirds of the legacy. If there is only one girl, she will inherit half of the legacy. Parents of the deceased will each inherit one-sixth of the legacy if the deceased has a surviving child. However, if no children survived the deceased, and the heirs are the parents, the mother will receive one-third of the legacy. The mother

11. Yooṣeekumul-laahu feee awlaadikum liz-zakari mislu ḥaẓẓil-unsayayn; fa-in kunna nisaaa'an fawqas-natayni falahunna sulusaa maa taraka wa in kaanat waaḥidatan falahan-niṣf; wa li-abawayhi likulli waaḥidim-minhumas-sudusu mimmaa taraka in kaana lahoo walad; fa-il-lam yakul-lahoo waladuñw-wa warisahooo abawaahu fali-ummihis-sulus;

يُوصِيكُمُ اللَّهُ فِي أَوْلَادِكُمْ لِلذَّكَرِ
مِثْلُ حَظِّ الْأُنْثَيَيْنِ فَإِنْ كُنَّ نِسَاءً
فَوْقَ اثْنَتَيْنِ فَلَهُنَّ ثُلُثَا مَا تَرَكَ
وَإِنْ كَانَتْ وَاحِدَةً فَلَهَا النِّصْفُ
وَلِأَبَوَيْهِ لِكُلِّ وَاحِدٍ مِنْهُمَا السُّدُسُ
مِمَّا تَرَكَ إِنْ كَانَ لَهُ وَلَدٌ فَإِنْ لَمْ يَكُنْ
لَهُ وَلَدٌ وَوَرِثَهُ أَبَوَاهُ فَلِأُمِّهِ الثُّلُثُ

will receive one-sixth of the legacy if the deceased has more than one surviving brother.

These are the decreed shares according to the laws of Allah. Regardless of how you feel about your parents or children, you do not know which of them is more beneficial to you. Allah is All-knowing and All-wise.

12. If your wives died without any surviving children, you will inherit half of their legacy. If they have children, you will inherit one-fourth of their legacy after the debts and things bequeathed have been excluded from the legacy.

After the payment of debts and things bequeathed has been excluded from the legacy, your wives will inherit one-fourth of your legacy if you did not have any surviving children. If you leave a child, they will inherit one eighth of your legacy.

If the deceased, either male or female, has no surviving heirs such as parents or children but has a brother or a sister, the brother or sister will each inherit one-sixth of the legacy.

If there is more than just a brother or a sister, they will share one-third of the legacy. This is after the payment of any debts and things bequeathed have been excluded from the legacy so that no one will be caused to suffer any loss. It is a guide from Allah, the All-knowing and Forbearing.

13. These are the laws of Allah. Whoever obeys Allah and His Messenger will be admitted to the gardens wherein streams flow and wherein they will live forever. This is the greatest triumph.

14. Whoever disobeys Allah and His Messenger and breaks His rules will be admitted to the fire wherein they will live forever,

fa-in kaana lahooo ikhwatun fali-ummihis-sudus; mim ba'di waṣiyyatiñy-yooṣee bihaaa aw dayn; aabaaa'ukum wa abnaaa'ukum laa tadroona ayyuhum aqrabu lakum naf'aa; fareeḍatam-minallaah; innal-laaha kaana 'Aleeman Ḥakeemaa.

12. Wa lakum niṣfu maa taraka azwaajukum il-lam yakul-lahunna walad; fa-in kaana lahunna waladun falakumur-rubu'u mimmaa tarakna mim ba'di waṣiyyatiñy-yooṣeena bihaaa aw dayn; wa lahunnar-rubu'u mimmaa taraktum il-lam yakul-lakum walad; fa-in kaana lakum waladun falahunnas-sumunu mimmaa taraktum; mim ba'di waṣiyyatin tooṣoona bihaaa aw dayn; wa in kaana rajuluñy-yoorasu kalaalatan awim-ra-atuñw-wa lahooo akhun aw ukhtun falikulli waaḥidim-minhumas-sudus; fa-in kaanooo aksara min zaalika fahum shurakaaa'u fis-sulusi mim ba'di waṣiyyatiñy-yooṣaa bihaaa aw daynin ghayra muḍaaarr; waṣiyyatam-minal-laah; wallaahu 'Aleemun Ḥaleem.

13. Tilka ḥudoodul-laah; wa mañy-yuṭi'il-laaha wa Rasoo-lahoo yudkhilhu Jannaatin tajree min taḥtihal-anhaaru khaalideena feehaa; wa zaalikal-fawzul-'aẓeem.

14. Wa mañy-ya'ṣil-laaha wa Rasoolahoo wa yata'adda ḥudoodahoo yudkhilhu Naaran khaalidan feehaa

فَإِنْ كَانَ لَهُۥٓ إِخْوَةٌ فَلِأُمِّهِ السُّدُسُ
مِنْۢ بَعْدِ وَصِيَّةٍ يُوصِى بِهَآ أَوْ دَيْنٍ ۗ
ءَابَآؤُكُمْ وَأَبْنَآؤُكُمْ لَا تَدْرُونَ أَيُّهُمْ أَقْرَبُ
لَكُمْ نَفْعًا ۚ فَرِيضَةً مِّنَ اللّٰهِ ۗ إِنَّ
اللّٰهَ كَانَ عَلِيمًا حَكِيمًا ﴿١١﴾
وَلَكُمْ نِصْفُ مَا تَرَكَ أَزْوَاجُكُمْ إِنْ
لَّمْ يَكُنْ لَّهُنَّ وَلَدٌ ۚ فَإِنْ كَانَ
لَهُنَّ وَلَدٌ فَلَكُمُ الرُّبُعُ مِمَّا تَرَكْنَ
مِنْۢ بَعْدِ وَصِيَّةٍ يُوصِينَ بِهَآ
أَوْ دَيْنٍ ۗ وَلَهُنَّ الرُّبُعُ مِمَّا تَرَكْتُمْ
إِنْ لَّمْ يَكُنْ لَّكُمْ وَلَدٌ ۚ فَإِنْ كَانَ
لَكُمْ وَلَدٌ فَلَهُنَّ الثُّمُنُ مِمَّا
تَرَكْتُمْ مِّنْۢ بَعْدِ وَصِيَّةٍ تُوصُونَ
بِهَآ أَوْ دَيْنٍ ۗ وَإِنْ كَانَ رَجُلٌ يُّورَثُ
كَلٰلَةً أَوِ امْرَأَةٌ وَّلَهُۥٓ أَخٌ أَوْ أُخْتٌ
فَلِكُلِّ وَاحِدٍ مِّنْهُمَا السُّدُسُ ۚ فَإِنْ
كَانُوٓا أَكْثَرَ مِنْ ذٰلِكَ فَهُمْ شُرَكَآءُ
فِى الثُّلُثِ مِنْۢ بَعْدِ وَصِيَّةٍ يُّوصٰى
بِهَآ أَوْ دَيْنٍ ۙ غَيْرَ مُضَآرٍّ ۚ وَصِيَّةً
مِّنَ اللّٰهِ ۗ وَاللّٰهُ عَلِيمٌ حَلِيمٌ ﴿١٢﴾
تِلْكَ حُدُودُ اللّٰهِ ۗ وَمَنْ يُّطِعِ اللّٰهَ
وَرَسُولَهُۥ يُدْخِلْهُ جَنّٰتٍ تَجْرِى مِنْ
تَحْتِهَا الْأَنْهٰرُ خٰلِدِينَ فِيهَا ۗ وَذٰلِكَ
الْفَوْزُ الْعَظِيمُ ﴿١٣﴾
وَمَنْ يَّعْصِ اللّٰهَ وَرَسُولَهُۥ وَيَتَعَدَّ
حُدُودَهُۥ يُدْخِلْهُ نَارًا خَالِدًا فِيهَا ۠

suffering a humiliating torment.

wa lahoo 'az̲aabum-muheen.

وَلَهٗ عَذَابٌ مُّهِيْنٌ ﴿١٤﴾ ع ٤ ١٣

15. Those of your women who commit fornication, let four (Muslim) witnesses testify to their act. If there is sufficient testimony, confine them to their homes until they die, or until Allah provides a way for their freedom.

15. Wallaatee ya-teenal-faaḥishata min nisaaa'ikum fastashhidoo 'alayhinna arba'atam-minkum fa-in shahidoo fa-amsikoohunna fil-buyooti ḥattaa yatawaffaa-hunnal-mawtu aw yaj'alal-laahu lahunna sabeelaa.

وَالّٰتِيْ يَاْتِيْنَ الْفَاحِشَةَ مِنْ نِّسَآئِكُمْ
فَاسْتَشْهِدُوْا عَلَيْهِنَّ اَرْبَعَةً مِّنْكُمْ ۚ
فَاِنْ شَهِدُوْا فَاَمْسِكُوْهُنَّ فِي الْبُيُوْتِ
حَتّٰى يَتَوَفّٰىهُنَّ الْمَوْتُ اَوْ يَجْعَلَ اللّٰهُ
لَهُنَّ سَبِيْلًا ﴿١٥﴾

16. If any two people commit fornication, punish them. If they repent and reform, let them go. Allah is All-forgiving and All-merciful.

16. Wallaz̲aani ya-tiyaanihaa minkum fa-aaz̲oohumaa fa-in taabaa wa aṣlaḥaa fa-a'riḍoo 'anhumaaa; innal-laaha kaana Tawwaabar-Raḥeemaa.

وَالَّذٰنِ يَاْتِيٰنِهَا مِنْكُمْ فَاٰذُوْهُمَا ۚ
فَاِنْ تَابَا وَاَصْلَحَا فَاَعْرِضُوْا عَنْهُمَا ۚ
اِنَّ اللّٰهَ كَانَ تَوَّابًا رَّحِيْمًا ﴿١٦﴾

17. Allah will only accept the repentance of those who commit evil in ignorance, if they repent immediately. Allah is All-knowing and All-wise.

17. Innamat-tawbatu 'alallaahi lillaz̲eena ya'maloonas-sooo'a bijahaalatin s̲umma yatooboona min qareebin faulaaa'ika yatoobul-laahu 'alayhim; wa kaanal-laahu 'Aleeman Ḥakeemaa.

اِنَّمَا التَّوْبَةُ عَلَى اللّٰهِ لِلَّذِيْنَ
يَعْمَلُوْنَ السُّوْٓءَ بِجَهَالَةٍ ثُمَّ
يَتُوْبُوْنَ مِنْ قَرِيْبٍ فَاُولٰٓئِكَ يَتُوْبُ
اللّٰهُ عَلَيْهِمْ ۗ وَكَانَ اللّٰهُ
عَلِيْمًا حَكِيْمًا ﴿١٧﴾

18. There is no forgiveness for those who commit sin and do not repent until the last moment of their lives or for those who die as unbelievers. For these people We have prepared a painful torment.

18. Wa laysatit-tawbatu lillaz̲eena ya'maloonas-sayyi-aati ḥattaaa iz̲aa ḥaḍara aḥadahumul-mawtu qaala innee tubtul-'aana wa lallaz̲eena yamootoona wa hum kuffaar; ulaaa'ika a'tadnaa lahum 'az̲aaban aleemaa.

وَلَيْسَتِ التَّوْبَةُ لِلَّذِيْنَ يَعْمَلُوْنَ
السَّيِّاٰتِ ۚ حَتّٰٓى اِذَا حَضَرَ اَحَدَهُمُ
الْمَوْتُ قَالَ اِنِّيْ تُبْتُ الْـٰٔنَ وَلَا
الَّذِيْنَ يَمُوْتُوْنَ وَهُمْ كُفَّارٌ ۗ
اُولٰٓئِكَ اَعْتَدْنَا لَهُمْ عَذَابًا اَلِيْمًا ﴿١٨﴾

19. Believers, it is not lawful for you to inherit women against their will as part of the legacy. Do not create difficulties for your wives in order to force them to give up part of what you had given to them to set themselves free from the bond of marriage, unless they have clearly committed adultery. Always treat them reasonably. If you dislike them, you could be disliking that which Allah has filled with

19. Yaaa ayyuhal-laz̲eena aamanoo laa yaḥillu lakum an taris̲un-nisaaa'a karhaa; wa laa ta'ḍuloohunna litaz̲haboo biba'ḍi maaa aataytumoohunna illaaa añy-ya-teena bifaaḥisha-tim-mubayyinah; wa 'aashiroo-hunna bilma'roof; fa-in karihtumoohunna fa'asaaa an takrahoo shay'añw -wa yaj'alal-

يٰٓاَيُّهَا الَّذِيْنَ اٰمَنُوْا لَا يَحِلُّ
لَكُمْ اَنْ تَرِثُوا النِّسَآءَ كَرْهًا ۗ
وَلَا تَعْضُلُوْهُنَّ لِتَذْهَبُوْا بِبَعْضِ
مَآ اٰتَيْتُمُوْهُنَّ اِلَّآ اَنْ يَّاْتِيْنَ
بِفَاحِشَةٍ مُّبَيِّنَةٍ ۚ وَعَاشِرُوْهُنَّ
بِالْمَعْرُوْفِ ۚ فَاِنْ كَرِهْتُمُوْهُنَّ
فَعَسٰٓى اَنْ تَكْرَهُوْا شَيْـًٔا وَّيَجْعَلَ

abundant good.

laahu feehi khayran kaseeraa.

اللّٰهُ فِيْهِ خَيْرًا كَثِيْرًا ﴿١٩﴾

20. If you want to divorce a woman so that you can marry another, do not take back the dowry which you had paid even if what you paid was a large amount of gold. To do this is a slanderous act and a manifest sin.

20. Wa in arattumustibdaala zawjim-makaana zawj; wa aataytum iḥdaahunna qinṭaaran falaa ta-khuzoo minhu shay'aa; ata-khuzoonahoo buhtaanañw-wa ismam-mubeenaa.

وَاِنْ اَرَدْتُّمُ اسْتِبْدَالَ زَوْجٍ مَّكَانَ
زَوْجٍ ۙ وَّاٰتَيْتُمْ اِحْدٰىهُنَّ قِنْطَارًا فَلَا
تَاْخُذُوْا مِنْهُ شَيْـًٔا ؕ اَتَاْخُذُوْنَهٗ
بُهْتَانًا وَّاِثْمًا مُّبِيْنًا ﴿٢٠﴾

21. How can you take it back when you have had intimate relations and made a solemn agreement with each other?

21. Wa kayfa ta-khuzoonahoo wa qad afḍaa ba'ḍukum ilaa ba'ḍiñw-wa akhazna minkum meesaaqan ghaleezaa.

وَكَيْفَ تَاْخُذُوْنَهٗ وَقَدْ اَفْضٰى
بَعْضُكُمْ اِلٰى بَعْضٍ وَّاَخَذْنَ
مِنْكُمْ مِّيْثَاقًا غَلِيْظًا ﴿٢١﴾

22. Do not marry, from now on, the ex-wives of your fathers, for that custom was sinful, loathsome, and abominable.

22. Wa laa tankiḥoo maa nakaḥa aabaaa'ukum minan-nisaaa'i illaa maa qad salaf; innahoo kaana faaḥishatañw-wa maqtaa; wa saaa'a sabeelaa.

وَلَا تَنْكِحُوْا مَا نَكَحَ اٰبَآؤُكُمْ مِّنَ
النِّسَآءِ اِلَّا مَا قَدْ سَلَفَ ؕ اِنَّهٗ كَانَ
فَاحِشَةً وَّمَقْتًا ؕ وَسَآءَ سَبِيْلًا ﴿٢٢﴾ ع ٨/١٤

23. You are forbidden to marry your mothers, daughters, sisters, paternal aunts, maternal aunts, nieces, your foster-mothers, your foster-sisters, your mothers-in-law, your step-daughters whom you have brought up and with whose mothers you have had carnal relations. It would not be a sin to marry her if you did not have carnal relations with her mother. You are forbidden to marry the wives of your own sons and to marry two sisters at the same time without any adverse effect to such relations of the past. Allah is All-forgiving and All-merciful.

23. Ḥurrimat 'alaykum ummahaatukum wa banaatukum wa akhawaatukum wa 'ammaatukum wa khaalaatukum wa banaatul-akhi wa banaatul-ukhti wa ummahaatu-kumul-laateee arḍa'nakum wa akhawaatu-kum-minarraḍaa'ati wa ummahaatu nisaaa'ikum wa rabaaa'ibukumul-laatee fee ḥujoorikum min nisaaa'ikumul-laatee dakhaltum-bihinna, fa-il-lam takoonoo dakhaltum bihinna falaa junaaḥa 'alaykum wa ḥalaaa'ilu abnaaa'ikumul-lazeena min aṣlaabikum wa an tajma'oo baynal-ukhtayni illaa maa qad salaf; innallaaha kaana Ghafoorar-Raḥeemaa.

حُرِّمَتْ عَلَيْكُمْ اُمَّهٰتُكُمْ وَبَنٰتُكُمْ
وَاَخَوٰتُكُمْ وَعَمّٰتُكُمْ وَخٰلٰتُكُمْ
وَبَنٰتُ الْاَخِ وَبَنٰتُ الْاُخْتِ وَ
اُمَّهٰتُكُمُ الّٰتِيْٓ اَرْضَعْنَكُمْ وَاَخَوٰتُكُمْ
مِّنَ الرَّضَاعَةِ وَاُمَّهٰتُ نِسَآئِكُمْ
وَرَبَآئِبُكُمُ الّٰتِيْ فِيْ حُجُوْرِكُمْ
مِّنْ نِّسَآئِكُمُ الّٰتِيْ دَخَلْتُمْ بِهِنَّ ؗ
فَاِنْ لَّمْ تَكُوْنُوْا دَخَلْتُمْ بِهِنَّ فَلَا
جُنَاحَ عَلَيْكُمْ ؗ وَحَلَآئِلُ اَبْنَآئِكُمُ
الَّذِيْنَ مِنْ اَصْلَابِكُمْ ۙ وَاَنْ تَجْمَعُوْا
بَيْنَ الْاُخْتَيْنِ اِلَّا مَا قَدْ سَلَفَ ؕ
اِنَّ اللّٰهَ كَانَ غَفُوْرًا رَّحِيْمًا ﴿٢٣﴾

24. You are forbidden to marry married women except your slave-girls. This is the decree of Allah. Besides these, it is lawful for you to marry other women if you pay their dower, maintain

24. Wal-muḥṣanaatu minan-nisaaa'i illaa maa malakat aymaanukum kitaabal-laahi 'alaykum; wa uḥilla lakum maa waraaa'a zaalikum

وَّالْمُحْصَنٰتُ مِنَ النِّسَآءِ اِلَّا مَا
مَلَكَتْ اَيْمَانُكُمْ ۚ كِتٰبَ اللّٰهِ
عَلَيْكُمْ ۚ وَاُحِلَّ لَكُمْ مَّا وَرَآءَ ذٰلِكُمْ

الْجُزْءُ الْخَامِسُ (٥)

chastity, and do not commit indecency. If you marry them for the appointed time you must pay their dowries. There is no harm if you reach an understanding among yourselves about Mahr (the dowry). Allah is All-knowing and All-wise.

an tabtaghoo bi-amwaalikum muḥṣineena ghayra musaa-fiḥeen; famastamta'tum bihee minhunna fa-aatoohunna ujoorahunna fareeḍah; wa laa junaaḥa 'alaykum feemaa taraaḍaytum bihee mim-ba'dil-fareeḍah; innal-laaha kaana 'Aleeman Ḥakeemaa.

ان تبتغوا باموالكم محصنين
غير مسفحين ۚ فما استمتعتم به
منهن فاتوهن اجورهن
فريضة ۚ ولا جناح عليكم فيما
تراضيتم به من بعد الفريضة ۚ
ان الله كان عليما حكيما ﴿٢٤﴾

25. If any of you did not have the means to marry a chaste believing woman, marry your believing slave-girls. Allah knows best about your faith. You have the same faith. Marry them with the permission of their masters and if they are chaste and have avoided fornication and amorous activities, give them their just dowries. If after marriage they commit adultery, they should receive half of the punishment of a free woman who has committed the same crime. This is for those who fear falling into evil. It is better for you to have self-control. Allah is All-forgiving and All-merciful.

25. Wa mal-lam yastaṭi' minkum ṭawlan añy-yankiḥal-muḥṣanaatil-mu'minaati famim-maa malakat aymaanukum min fatayaati-kumul-mu'minaat; wallaahu a'lamu bi-eemaani-kum; ba'ḍukum mim ba'ḍ; fankiḥoohunna bi-izni ahlihinna wa aatoohunna ujoorahunna bilma'roofi muḥṣanaatin ghayra musaa-fiḥ aatiñw-wa laa muttakhizaati akhdaan; fa-izaaa uḥṣinna fa-in atayna bifaaḥi-shatin fa'alay-hinna niṣfu maa 'alal-muḥṣanaati minal-'azaab; zaalika liman khashiyal- 'anata minkum; wa an taṣbiroo khayrul-lakum; wallaahu Ghafoorur-Raḥeem.

ومن لم يستطع منكم طولا ان
ينكح المحصنت المؤمنت فمن
ما ملكت ايمانكم من فتيتكم
المؤمنت ۚ والله اعلم بايمانكم ۚ
بعضكم من بعض ۚ فانكحوهن
باذن اهلهن واتوهن اجورهن
بالمعروف محصنت غير مسفحت
ولا متخذت اخدان ۚ فاذا احصن
فان اتين بفاحشة فعليهن
نصف ما على المحصنت من
العذاب ۚ ذلك لمن خشي العنت
منكم ۚ وان تصبروا خير لكم ۗ
والله غفور رحيم ﴿٢٥﴾

26. Allah wants to guide you, explain to you the customs of those who lived before you, and grant you forgiveness. He is All-knowing and All-wise.

26. Yureedul-laahu liyubay-yina lakum wa yahdiyakum sunanal-lazeena min qablikum wa yatooba 'alaykum; wallaahu 'Aleemun Ḥakeem.

يريد الله ليبين لكم ويهديكم
سنن الذين من قبلكم ويتوب
عليكم ۗ والله عليم حكيم ﴿٢٦﴾

27. Allah wants to be merciful to you, but those who follow their evil desires seek to lead you astray.

27. Wallaahu yureedu añy-yatooba 'alaykum wa yureedul-lazeena yattabi'oonash-shahawaati an tameeloo maylan 'azeemaa.

والله يريد ان يتوب عليكم
ويريد الذين يتبعون الشهوت
ان تميلوا ميلا عظيما ﴿٢٧﴾

28. Allah wants to relieve you of your burden; all human beings

28. Yureedul-laahu añy-yu-khaf-fifa 'ankum;

يريد الله ان يخفف عنكم ۚ

were created weak.

wa khuliqal-insaanu ḍa'eefaa.

وَخُلِقَ الْاِنْسَانُ ضَعِيْفًا ﴿٢٨﴾

29. Believers, do not exchange your property in wrongful ways unless it is in trade by mutual agreement. Do not kill one another. Allah is All-merciful to you.

29. Yaaa ayyuhal-lazeena aamanoo laa ta-kulooo amwaalakum baynakum bilbaaṭili 'illaaa an takoona tijaaratan 'an taraaḍimminkum; wa laa taqtulooo anfusakum; innal-laaha kaana bikum Raḥeemaa.

يٰۤاَيُّهَا الَّذِيْنَ اٰمَنُوْا لَا تَاْكُلُوْۤا
اَمْوَالَكُمْ بَيْنَكُمْ بِالْبَاطِلِ اِلَّاۤ
اَنْ تَكُوْنَ تِجَارَةً عَنْ تَرَاضٍ مِّنْكُمْ ۟
وَلَا تَقْتُلُوْۤا اَنْفُسَكُمْ ؕ اِنَّ اللّٰهَ كَانَ
بِكُمْ رَحِيْمًا ﴿٢٩﴾

30. Whoever commits murder out of animosity and injustice will be burned in hellfire. This is a very easy thing for Allah to do.

30. Wa mañy-yaf'al zaalika 'ud-waanañw-wa ẓulman fasawfa nuṣleehi Naaraa; wa kaana zaalika 'alal-laahi yaseeraa.

وَمَنْ يَّفْعَلْ ذٰلِكَ عُدْوَانًا وَّظُلْمًا
فَسَوْفَ نُصْلِيْهِ نَارًا ؕ وَكَانَ ذٰلِكَ
عَلَى اللّٰهِ يَسِيْرًا ﴿٣٠﴾

31. If you avoid violating that which has been prohibited, your (lesser) sins will be forgiven and you will be admitted into an exalted dwelling.

31. In tajtaniboo kabaaa'ira maa tunhawna 'anhu nukaffir 'ankum sayyi-aatikum wa nudkhilkum mudkhalan kareemaa.

اِنْ تَجْتَنِبُوْا كَبَآئِرَ مَا تُنْهَوْنَ عَنْهُ
نُكَفِّرْ عَنْكُمْ سَيِّاٰتِكُمْ وَنُدْخِلْكُمْ
مُّدْخَلًا كَرِيْمًا ﴿٣١﴾

32. Do not envy the favors which Allah has granted to some of you. Men and women will both be rewarded according to their deeds and pray to Allah for His favors. Allah knows all things.

32. Wa laa tatamannaw maa faḍḍalal-laahu bihee ba'ḍakum 'alaa ba'ḍ; lirrijaali naṣeebum-mimmak-tasaboo wa linnisaaa'i naṣeebum-mimmak-tasabna; was'alullaaha min faḍlih; innal-laaha kaana bikulli shay'in 'Aleemaa.

وَلَا تَتَمَنَّوْا مَا فَضَّلَ اللّٰهُ بِهٖ بَعْضَكُمْ
عَلٰى بَعْضٍ ؕ لِلرِّجَالِ نَصِيْبٌ مِّمَّا
اكْتَسَبُوْا ؕ وَلِلنِّسَآءِ نَصِيْبٌ مِّمَّا
اكْتَسَبْنَ ؕ وَسْئَلُوا اللّٰهَ مِنْ فَضْلِهٖ ؕ
اِنَّ اللّٰهَ كَانَ بِكُلِّ شَيْءٍ عَلِيْمًا ﴿٣٢﴾

33. We have chosen heirs for every legacy that parents and relatives may leave. Let those who have been promised a bequest receive their share of the legacy. Allah is Omnipresent.

33. Wa likullin ja'alnaa ma-waaliya mimmaa tarakal-waalidaani wal-aqraboon; wallazeena 'aqadat aymaanu-kum fa-aatoohum naṣeebahum; innal-laaha kaana 'alaa kulli shay'in Shaheedaa.

وَلِكُلٍّ جَعَلْنَا مَوَالِيَ مِمَّا تَرَكَ الْوَالِدٰنِ
وَالْاَقْرَبُوْنَ ؕ وَالَّذِيْنَ عَقَدَتْ
اَيْمَانُكُمْ فَاٰتُوْهُمْ نَصِيْبَهُمْ ؕ اِنَّ
اللّٰهَ كَانَ عَلٰى كُلِّ شَيْءٍ شَهِيْدًا ﴿٣٣﴾ ع ٥ ٨ ٢

34. Men are the protectors of women because of the greater preference that Allah has given to some of them and because they financially support them. Among virtuous women are those who are steadfast in prayer and dependable in keeping the secrets that Allah has protected. Admonish women who disobey

34. Arrijaalu qawwaamoona 'alan-nisaaa'i bimaa faḍ-ḍalallaahu ba'ḍahum 'alaa ba'ḍiñw-wa bimaaa-anfaqoo min amwaalihim; faṣṣaaliḥaatu qaanitaatun ḥaafiẓaatul-lil-ghaybi bimaa ḥafiẓal-laah; wallaatee takhaafoona nushoo-zahunna

اَلرِّجَالُ قَوّٰمُوْنَ عَلَى النِّسَآءِ بِمَا
فَضَّلَ اللّٰهُ بَعْضَهُمْ عَلٰى بَعْضٍ وَّبِمَآ
اَنْفَقُوْا مِنْ اَمْوَالِهِمْ ؕ فَالصّٰلِحٰتُ
قٰنِتٰتٌ حٰفِظٰتٌ لِّلْغَيْبِ بِمَا حَفِظَ
اللّٰهُ ؕ وَالّٰتِيْ تَخَافُوْنَ نُشُوْزَهُنَّ

(the laws of Allah), do not sleep with them and beat them (on the basis of judicial due process). Do not try to find faults in them if they obey (the laws of Allah). Allah is High and Supreme.

35. If there appears to be discord between a wife and her husband and if they desire reconciliation, choose arbiters from the families of both sides. Allah will bring them together; Allah is All-knowing and All-aware.

36. Worship Allah and consider no one equal to Him. Be kind to your parents, relatives, orphans, the destitute, your near and distant neighbors, your companions, wayfarers, and your slaves. Allah does not love the proud and boastful ones,

37. the stingy ones who try to make others stingy and those who hide the favors that Allah has bestowed on them. We have prepared a humiliating torment for the unbelievers,

38. those who spend their property out of a desire to show off and not because of their belief in Allah and the Day of Judgment, and (lastly) those who choose Satan for a friend; what an evil friend!

39. How could it have harmed them if they had believed in Allah and the Last Day and spent their property for the cause of Allah?

fa'izoohunna wahjuroohunna fil-madaaji'i wadriboohunna fa-in ata'nakum falaa tabghoo 'alayhinna sabeelaa; innallaaha kaana 'Aliyyan Kabeeraa.

35. Wa in khiftum shiqaaqa baynihimaa fab'asoo haka-mammin ahlihee wa hakamam-min ahlihaaa; iñy-yureedaaa işlaahañy-yuwaffiqil-laahu baynahumaaa; innal-laaha kaana 'Aleeman Khabeeraa.

36. Wa'budul-laaha wa laa tushrikoo bihee shay'añw-wa bilwaalidayni ihsaanañw-wa bizil-qurbaa walyataamaa walmasaakeeni waljaari zilqurbaa waljaaril-junubi waşşaahibi biljambi wabnis-sabeeli wa maa malakat aymaanukum; innal-laaha laa yuhibbu man kaana mukhtaalan fakhooraa.

37. Allazeena yabkhaloona wa ya-muroonan-naasa bilbukhli wa yaktumoona maaa aataahu-mullaahu min fadlih; wa-a'tadnaa lilkaafireena 'azaa-bammuheenaa.

38. Wallazeena yunfiqoona amwaalahum ri'aaa'an-naasi wa laa yu'minoona billaahi wa laa bil-Yawmil-Aakhir; wa mañy-yakunish-Shaytaanu lahoo qareenan fasaaa'a qareenaa.

39. Wa maazaa 'alayhim law aamanoo billaahi wal-Yawmil-Aakhiri wa anfaqoo mimmaa razaqahumul

فَعِظُوهُنَّ وَاهْجُرُوهُنَّ فِي الْمَضَاجِعِ
وَاضْرِبُوهُنَّ ۚ فَإِنْ أَطَعْنَكُمْ فَلَا
تَبْغُوا عَلَيْهِنَّ سَبِيلًا ۗ إِنَّ اللَّهَ
كَانَ عَلِيًّا كَبِيرًا ﴿٣٤﴾
وَإِنْ خِفْتُمْ شِقَاقَ بَيْنِهِمَا فَابْعَثُوا
حَكَمًا مِنْ أَهْلِهِ وَحَكَمًا مِنْ
أَهْلِهَا ۚ إِنْ يُرِيدَا إِصْلَاحًا
يُوَفِّقِ اللَّهُ بَيْنَهُمَا ۗ إِنَّ اللَّهَ كَانَ
عَلِيمًا خَبِيرًا ﴿٣٥﴾
وَاعْبُدُوا اللَّهَ وَلَا تُشْرِكُوا بِهِ
شَيْئًا وَبِالْوَالِدَيْنِ إِحْسَانًا وَبِذِي
الْقُرْبَىٰ وَالْيَتَامَىٰ وَالْمَسَاكِينِ وَ
الْجَارِ ذِي الْقُرْبَىٰ وَالْجَارِ الْجُنُبِ
وَالصَّاحِبِ بِالْجَنْبِ وَابْنِ السَّبِيلِ
وَمَا مَلَكَتْ أَيْمَانُكُمْ ۗ إِنَّ اللَّهَ
لَا يُحِبُّ مَنْ كَانَ مُخْتَالًا فَخُورًا ﴿٣٦﴾
الَّذِينَ يَبْخَلُونَ وَيَأْمُرُونَ
النَّاسَ بِالْبُخْلِ وَيَكْتُمُونَ مَا
آتَاهُمُ اللَّهُ مِنْ فَضْلِهِ ۗ وَأَعْتَدْنَا
لِلْكَافِرِينَ عَذَابًا مُهِينًا ﴿٣٧﴾
وَالَّذِينَ يُنْفِقُونَ أَمْوَالَهُمْ رِئَاءَ
النَّاسِ وَلَا يُؤْمِنُونَ بِاللَّهِ وَلَا
بِالْيَوْمِ الْآخِرِ ۗ وَمَنْ يَكُنِ الشَّيْطَانُ
لَهُ قَرِينًا فَسَاءَ قَرِينًا ﴿٣٨﴾
وَمَاذَا عَلَيْهِمْ لَوْ آمَنُوا بِاللَّهِ وَ
الْيَوْمِ الْآخِرِ وَأَنْفَقُوا مِمَّا رَزَقَهُمُ

Allah knows them very well.

laah; wa kaanallaahu bihim 'Aleemaa.

اللّٰهُ ؕ وَكَانَ اللّٰهُ بِهِمۡ عَلِيۡمًا ﴿٣٩﴾

40. Allah does not do even an atom's weight of injustice. A good deed is multiplied by Allah and richly rewarded.

40. Innal-laaha laa yaẓlimu mis̲qaala z̲arrah;wa in taku ḥasanatañy-yuḍaa'ifhaa wa yu'ti mil-ladunhu ajran 'aẓeemaa.

اِنَّ اللّٰهَ لَا يَظۡلِمُ مِثۡقَالَ ذَرَّةٍ ۚ وَاِنۡ
تَكُ حَسَنَةً يُّضٰعِفۡهَا وَيُؤۡتِ مِنۡ
لَّدُنۡهُ اَجۡرًا عَظِيۡمًا ﴿٤٠﴾

41. How will it be when We call for a witness from every nation and have you, (Muhammad) testify against them all?

41. Fakayfa iz̲aa ji'naa min kulli ummatim bishaheediñw-wa ji'naa bika 'alaa haaa'ulaaa'i Shaheeda.

فَكَيۡفَ اِذَا جِئۡنَا مِنۡ كُلِّ اُمَّةٍ ۭ
بِشَهِيۡدٍ وَّجِئۡنَا بِكَ عَلٰى هٰٓؤُلَآءِ
شَهِيۡدًا ﴿٤١﴾ؕ

وقف النبی صلی اللہ علیہ وآلہ وسلم

42. At that time the unbelievers who disobeyed the Messenger will wish that they could be turned into dust and they will be able to hide nothing from Allah.

42. Yawma'iz̲iñy-yawad-dullaz̲eena kafaroo wa 'aṣawur-Rasoola law tusawwaa bihimul-arḍu wa laa yaktumoonal-laaha ḥadees̲aa.

يَوۡمَئِذٍ يَّوَدُّ الَّذِيۡنَ كَفَرُوۡا وَعَصَوُا
الرَّسُوۡلَ لَوۡ تُسَوّٰى بِهِمُ الۡاَرۡضُ ؕ
وَلَا يَكۡتُمُوۡنَ اللّٰهَ حَدِيۡثًا ﴿٤٢﴾ ع

43. Believers, do not pray when you are drunk, but, instead, wait until you can understand what you say. Also, do not pray when you have experienced a seminal discharge until after you have taken a bath, unless you are on a journey. If, while sick or on a journey, you could not find any water after having defecated or after having had carnal relations, perform tayammum by touching your palms on the pure earth and wipe the (upper part of) your face and the backs of your hands. Allah is gracious and All-forgiving.

43. Yaaa ayyuhal-laz̲eena aamanoo laa taqrabuṣ-Ṣalaata wa antum sukaaraa ḥattaa ta'lamoo maa taqooloona wa laa junuban illaa 'aabiree sabeelin ḥattaa taghtasiloo; wa in kuntum marḍaaa aw 'alaa safarin aw jaaa'a aḥadum-minkum minal-ghaaa'iṭi aw laamastumun-nisaaa'a falam tajidoo maaa'an fatayam-mamoo ṣa'eedan ṭayyiban famsaḥoo biwujoohikum wa aydeekum; innal-laaha kaana 'Afuwwan Ghafooraa.

يٰۤاَيُّهَا الَّذِيۡنَ اٰمَنُوۡا لَا تَقۡرَبُوا
الصَّلٰوةَ وَاَنۡتُمۡ سُكٰرٰى حَتّٰى تَعۡلَمُوۡا
مَا تَقُوۡلُوۡنَ وَلَا جُنُبًا اِلَّا عَابِرِىۡ
سَبِيۡلٍ حَتّٰى تَغۡتَسِلُوۡا ؕ وَاِنۡ كُنۡتُمۡ
مَّرۡضٰۤى اَوۡ عَلٰى سَفَرٍ اَوۡ جَآءَ اَحَدٌ
مِّنۡكُمۡ مِّنَ الۡغَآئِطِ اَوۡ لٰمَسۡتُمُ
النِّسَآءَ فَلَمۡ تَجِدُوۡا مَآءً فَتَيَمَّمُوۡا
صَعِيۡدًا طَيِّبًا فَامۡسَحُوۡا بِوُجُوۡهِكُمۡ
وَاَيۡدِيۡكُمۡ ؕ اِنَّ اللّٰهَ كَانَ عَفُوًّا
غَفُوۡرًا ﴿٤٣﴾

44. Did you not see those who had received a portion of the Book buy misguidance and try to make you go astray too?

44. Alam tara ilal-laz̲eena ootoo naṣeebam-minal-Kitaabi yashtaroonaḍ-ḍalaalata wa yureedoona an taḍillus-sabeel.

اَلَمۡ تَرَ اِلَى الَّذِيۡنَ اُوۡتُوۡا نَصِيۡبًا
مِّنَ الۡكِتٰبِ يَشۡتَرُوۡنَ الضَّلٰلَةَ
وَيُرِيۡدُوۡنَ اَنۡ تَضِلُّوا السَّبِيۡلَ ﴿٤٤﴾ؕ

45. Allah knows who your enemies are. You need to have no guardian or helper other than Allah.

45. Wallaahu a'lamu bi-a'daaa'i-kum; wa kafaa billaahi waliyyañw-wa kafaa billaahi naṣeeraa.

وَاللّٰهُ اَعۡلَمُ بِاَعۡدَآئِكُمۡ ؕ وَكَفٰى بِاللّٰهِ
وَلِيًّا ۙ وَّكَفٰى بِاللّٰهِ نَصِيۡرًا ﴿٤٥﴾

46. Certain Jewish persons take particular words out of context and by twisting their tongues to make a

46. Minal-laz̲eena haadoo yuḥarrifoonal

مِنَ الَّذِيۡنَ هَادُوۡا يُحَرِّفُوۡنَ

jest out of the true religion, say, "We heard and (in our hearts) disobeyed. (Muhammad), raina (be kind to us)," but they intend thereby (the meaning in their own language): "Listen! May Allah turn you deaf." They should have said, "We heard and obeyed. (Muhammad), listen and consider our question." This would have been better for them and more righteous. Allah has condemned them for their disbelief. Thus no one, except a few among them, will have faith.

Kalima-'am-mawaaḍi'ihee wa yaqooloona sami'naa wa 'aṣaynaa wasma' ghayra musma'iñw-wa raa'inaa layyam bi-alsinatihim wa ṭa'nan fid-deen; wa law annahum qaaloo sami'naa wa aṭa'naa wasma' wanẓurnaa lakaana khayral-lahum wa aqwama wa laakil-la-'anahumul-laahu bikufrihim falaa yu'minoona illaa qaleela

الْكَلِمَ عَنْ مَّوَاضِعِهٖ وَيَقُوْلُوْنَ
سَمِعْنَا وَعَصَيْنَا وَاسْمَعْ غَيْرَ مُسْمَعٍ
وَّرَاعِنَا لَيًّا بِاَلْسِنَتِهِمْ وَطَعْنًا فِي
الدِّيْنِ ؕ وَلَوْ اَنَّهُمْ قَالُوْا سَمِعْنَا
وَاَطَعْنَا وَاسْمَعْ وَانْظُرْنَا لَكَانَ
خَيْرًا لَّهُمْ وَاَقْوَمَ ۙ وَلٰكِنْ لَّعَنَهُمُ اللّٰهُ
بِكُفْرِهِمْ فَلَا يُؤْمِنُوْنَ اِلَّا قَلِيْلًا ﴿٤٦﴾

47. People of the Book, have faith in the Quran that We have revealed to confirm your Book, before certain faces are changed and turned back. We shall condemn them as We did the people of the Sabbath about whom Allah's decree had decisively been ordained.

47. Yaaa ayyuhal-laz̲eena ootul-Kitaaba aaminoo bimaa nazzalnaa muṣaddiqallimaa ma'akum min qabli an naṭmisa wujoohan fanaruddahaa 'alaaa adbaarihaaa aw nal'anahum kamaa la'annaaa Aṣhaabas-Sabt; wa kaana amrul-laahi maf'oolaa.

يٰۤاَيُّهَا الَّذِيْنَ اُوْتُوا الْكِتٰبَ اٰمِنُوْا
بِمَا نَزَّلْنَا مُصَدِّقًا لِّمَا مَعَكُمْ
مِّنْ قَبْلِ اَنْ نَّطْمِسَ وُجُوْهًا
فَنَرُدَّهَا عَلٰۤى اَدْبَارِهَاۤ اَوْ نَلْعَنَهُمْ
كَمَا لَعَنَّاۤ اَصْحٰبَ السَّبْتِ ؕ وَكَانَ
اَمْرُ اللّٰهِ مَفْعُوْلًا ﴿٤٧﴾

48. Allah does not forgive the sin of considering others equal to Him, but He may choose to forgive other sins. Whoever believes in other gods besides Him has indulged in a great sin.

48. Innal-laaha laa yaghfiru añy-yushraka bihee wa yaghfiru maa doona z̲aalika limañy-yashaaa'; wa mañy-yushrik billaahi faqadif-taraaa is̲man 'aẓeemaa.

اِنَّ اللّٰهَ لَا يَغْفِرُ اَنْ يُّشْرَكَ بِهٖ
وَيَغْفِرُ مَا دُوْنَ ذٰلِكَ لِمَنْ يَّشَآءُ ۚ
وَمَنْ يُّشْرِكْ بِاللّٰهِ فَقَدِ افْتَرٰۤى
اِثْمًا عَظِيْمًا ﴿٤٨﴾

49. (Muhammad), did you not see those who try to purify themselves? They should know that Allah only purifies whomever He wants and that the slightest wrong will not be done to such people.

49. Alam tara ilal-laz̲eena yuzakkoona anfusahum; balil-laahu yuzakkee mañy-yashaaa'u wa laa yuẓlamoona fateelaa.

اَلَمْ تَرَ اِلَى الَّذِيْنَ يُزَكُّوْنَ اَنْفُسَهُمْ ؕ
بَلِ اللّٰهُ يُزَكِّيْ مَنْ يَّشَآءُ وَلَا
يُظْلَمُوْنَ فَتِيْلًا ﴿٤٩﴾

50. Consider how they create lies about Allah? This alone is a grave sin.

50. Unẓur kayfa yaftaroona 'alal-laahil-kaz̲ib; wa kafaa biheee is̲mam-mubeenaa.

اُنْظُرْ كَيْفَ يَفْتَرُوْنَ عَلَى اللّٰهِ
الْكَذِبَ ؕ وَكَفٰى بِهٖۤ اِثْمًا مُّبِيْنًا ﴿٥٠﴾ ع ٨

51. Did you not see how those who had been given a share of the Book believe in idols and Satan and who say, "The unbelievers are better guided than the believers"?

51.Alam tara-ilal-laz̲eena 'ootoo naṣeebam-minal-Kitaabi yu'minoona bil-Jibti waṭ-Ṭaaghooti wa yaqooloona lillaz̲eena kafaroo haaa-ulaaa'i ahdaa minal-laz̲eena aamanoo sabeelaa.

اَلَمْ تَرَ اِلَى الَّذِيْنَ اُوْتُوْا نَصِيْبًا مِّنَ
الْكِتٰبِ يُؤْمِنُوْنَ بِالْجِبْتِ وَالطَّاغُوْتِ
وَيَقُوْلُوْنَ لِلَّذِيْنَ كَفَرُوْا هٰۤؤُلَآءِ اَهْدٰى
مِنَ الَّذِيْنَ اٰمَنُوْا سَبِيْلًا ﴿٥١﴾

52. Allah has condemned them. No one can help one who has been condemned by Allah.

52. Ulaaa'ikal-lazeena la'ana-humul-laahu wa mañy-yal'anil-laahu falan tajida lahoo naṣeeraa.

اُولٰٓئِكَ الَّذِيْنَ لَعَنَهُمُ اللّٰهُ ۭ وَمَنْ
يَّلْعَنِ اللّٰهُ فَلَنْ تَجِدَ لَهٗ نَصِيْرًا ۝٥٢

53. Even if they had a share in the Kingdom (Divine Authority), they would not have given the smallest thing to anyone.

53. Am lahum naṣeebum-minal-mulki faizal-laa yu'too-nan-naasa naqeeraa.

اَمْ لَهُمْ نَصِيْبٌ مِّنَ الْمُلْكِ فَاِذًا
لَّا يُؤْتُوْنَ النَّاسَ نَقِيْرًا ۝٥٣

54. Are they jealous of the favors that Allah has done for certain people? We have given to the family of Abraham the Book, Wisdom, and a great Kingdom.

54. Am yaḥsudoonan-naasa 'alaa maaa aataahumul-laahu min faḍlihee faqad aataynaaa Aala Ibraaheemal-Kitaaba wal-Ḥikmata wa aataynaahum mulkan 'aẓeemaa.

اَمْ يَحْسُدُوْنَ النَّاسَ عَلٰى مَآ
اٰتٰىهُمُ اللّٰهُ مِنْ فَضْلِهٖ ۚ فَقَدْ
اٰتَيْنَآ اٰلَ اِبْرٰهِيْمَ الْكِتٰبَ وَالْحِكْمَةَ
وَاٰتَيْنٰهُمْ مُّلْكًا عَظِيْمًا ۝٥٤

55. Some have believed; others have disbelieved and tried to prevent people from believing. For these people, only the intense fire of hell is a sufficient punishment.

55. Faminhum man aamana bihee wa minhum man ṣadda 'anh; wa kafaa bi-Jahannama sa'eeraa.

فَمِنْهُمْ مَّنْ اٰمَنَ بِهٖ وَمِنْهُمْ مَّنْ
صَدَّ عَنْهُ ۭ وَكَفٰى بِجَهَنَّمَ سَعِيْرًا ۝٥٥

56. We will make those who reject Our revelations suffer in hellfire. As soon as the fire destroys their skins, We give them new skins so they may suffer more of the torment. Allah is Majestic and All-wise.

56. Innal-lazeena kafaroo bi-Aayaatinaa sawfa nuṣleehim Naaran kullamaa naḍijat julooduhum baddalnaahum juloodan ghayrahaa liyazooqul-'azaab; innallaaha kaana 'Azeezan Ḥakeemaa.

اِنَّ الَّذِيْنَ كَفَرُوْا بِاٰيٰتِنَا سَوْفَ
نُصْلِيْهِمْ نَارًا ۭ كُلَّمَا نَضِجَتْ
جُلُوْدُهُمْ بَدَّلْنٰهُمْ جُلُوْدًا غَيْرَهَا
لِيَذُوْقُوا الْعَذَابَ ۭ اِنَّ اللّٰهَ كَانَ
عَزِيْزًا حَكِيْمًا ۝٥٦

57. We will admit the righteously striving believers into the gardens wherein streams flow. They will live therein forever in a cool shade with their pure spouses.

57. Wallazeena aamanoo wa 'amiluṣ-ṣaaliḥaati sanud-khiluhum Jannaatin tajree min taḥtihal-anhaaru khaalideena feehaaa abadallahum feehaaa azwaajum-muṭahharatuñw-wa nudkhiluhum ẓillan ẓaleelaa.

وَالَّذِيْنَ اٰمَنُوْا وَعَمِلُوا الصّٰلِحٰتِ
سَنُدْخِلُهُمْ جَنّٰتٍ تَجْرِيْ مِنْ تَحْتِهَا
الْاَنْهٰرُ خٰلِدِيْنَ فِيْهَآ اَبَدًا ۭ
لَهُمْ فِيْهَآ اَزْوَاجٌ مُّطَهَّرَةٌ ۡ وَّ
نُدْخِلُهُمْ ظِلًّا ظَلِيْلًا ۝٥٧

58. Allah commands you to return that which had been entrusted to you to the rightful owners. Be just when passing judgment among people. Allah's advice is the most noble. He sees and hears everything.

58. Innal-laaha ya-murukum an tu'addul-amaanaati ilaaa ahlihaa wa izaa ḥakamtum baynan-naasi an taḥkumoo bil'adl; innal-laaha ni'immaa ya'izukum bih; innal-laaha kaana Samee'am Baṣeeraa.

اِنَّ اللّٰهَ يَاْمُرُكُمْ اَنْ تُؤَدُّوا الْاَمٰنٰتِ
اِلٰٓى اَهْلِهَا ۙ وَاِذَا حَكَمْتُمْ بَيْنَ
النَّاسِ اَنْ تَحْكُمُوْا بِالْعَدْلِ ۭ
اِنَّ اللّٰهَ نِعِمَّا يَعِظُكُمْ بِهٖ ۭ اِنَّ
اللّٰهَ كَانَ سَمِيْعًا بَصِيْرًا ۝٥٨

59. Believers, obey Allah, His Messenger, and your (qualified)

59. Yaaa-ayyuhal-lazeena aamanooo aṭee'ul-laaha

يٰٓاَيُّهَا الَّذِيْنَ اٰمَنُوْٓا اَطِيْعُوا اللّٰهَ

leaders. If you have faith in Allah and the Day of Judgment, refer to Allah and His Messenger concerning matters in which you differ. This would be a more virtuous and a better way of settling differences.

wa aṭee'ur-Rasoola wa ulil-amri minkum fain tanaaza'tum fee shay'in faruddoohu ilal-laahi war-Rasooli in kuntum tu'minoona billaahi wal-Yawmil-Aakhir; zaalika khayruñw-wa aḥsanu ta-weelaa.

وَ اَطِيْعُوا الرَّسُوْلَ وَاُولِي الْاَمْرِ
مِنْكُمْ ۚ فَاِنْ تَنَازَعْتُمْ فِيْ شَيْءٍ
فَرُدُّوْهُ اِلَى اللّٰهِ وَالرَّسُوْلِ اِنْ كُنْتُمْ
تُؤْمِنُوْنَ بِاللّٰهِ وَالْيَوْمِ الْاٰخِرِ ۭ
ذٰلِكَ خَيْرٌ وَّاَحْسَنُ تَاْوِيْلًا ۝٥٩ ع ٨ ٩ ٥

60. (Muhammad), did you not see those who thought that they had faith in what was revealed to you and to others before you, yet they choose to take their affairs to Satan for judgment even though they are commanded to deny him? Satan wants to lead them far away from the right path.

60. Alam tara-ilal-lazeena yaz'u-moona-annahum aamanoo bimaa unzila ilayka wa maaa unzila min qablika yureedoona añy-yataḥaakamooo ilaṭ-Ṭaaghooti wa qad umirooo añy-yakfuroo bih, wa yureedush-Shayṭaanu añy-yuḍillahum ḍalaalam-ba'eedaa.

اَلَمْ تَرَ اِلَى الَّذِيْنَ يَزْعُمُوْنَ اَنَّھُمْ
اٰمَنُوْا بِمَآ اُنْزِلَ اِلَيْكَ وَمَآ اُنْزِلَ مِنْ
قَبْلِكَ يُرِيْدُوْنَ اَنْ يَّتَحَاكَمُوْٓا اِلَى
الطَّاغُوْتِ وَقَدْ اُمِرُوْٓا اَنْ يَّكْفُرُوْا
بِهٖ ۭ وَيُرِيْدُ الشَّيْطٰنُ اَنْ يُّضِلَّھُمْ
ضَلٰلًۢا بَعِيْدًا ۝٦٠

61. When the (hypocrites) are told to refer to Allah's revelations and to the Messenger, they try to find excuses to stay away from you (Muhammad).

61. Wa izaa qeela lahum ta'aalaw ilaa maaa anzalallaahu wa ilar-Rasooli ra-aytal-munaafiqeena yaṣuddoona 'anka ṣudoodaa.

وَاِذَا قِيْلَ لَھُمْ تَعَالَوْا اِلٰى مَآ اَنْزَلَ
اللّٰهُ وَاِلَى الرَّسُوْلِ رَاَيْتَ الْمُنٰفِقِيْنَ
يَصُدُّوْنَ عَنْكَ صُدُوْدًا ۝٦١

62. What would happen if they were to be afflicted by a disaster brought about by their own hands? They would then come to you swearing by Allah, "We only wanted to bring about friendship and reconciliation."

62. Fakayfa izaaa aṣaabat-hum muṣeebatum bimaa qaddamat aydeehim summa jaaa'ooka yaḥlifoona billaahi in aradnaaa illaaa iḥsaanañw-wa tawfeeqaa.

فَكَيْفَ اِذَآ اَصَابَتْھُمْ مُّصِيْبَةٌۢ بِمَا
قَدَّمَتْ اَيْدِيْهِمْ ثُمَّ جَاۗءُوْكَ
يَحْلِفُوْنَ ڰ بِاللّٰهِ اِنْ اَرَدْنَآ اِلَّآ
اِحْسَانًا وَّتَوْفِيْقًا ۝٦٢

63. Allah knows what is in their hearts. (Muhammad), ignore their faults, advise them, and tell them frankly about what is in their souls.

63. Ulaaa'ikal-lazeena ya'la-mullaahu maa fee quloobihim fa-a'riḍ 'anhum wa 'iẓhum wa qul lahum feee anfusihim qawlam-baleeghaa.

اُولٰۗىِٕكَ الَّذِيْنَ يَعْلَمُ اللّٰهُ مَا فِيْ قُلُوْبِهِمْ ۤ
فَاَعْرِضْ عَنْھُمْ وَعِظْھُمْ وَقُلْ لَّھُمْ
فِيْٓ اَنْفُسِهِمْ قَوْلًۢا بَلِيْغًا ۝٦٣

64. We did not send any Messengers for any reason other than to be obeyed because of the will of Allah. If they ever do injustice to themselves and come to you (Muhammad) asking for Allah's forgiveness and if the Messenger also were to ask Allah to forgive them, they would certainly find Allah All-forgiving and All-merciful.

64. Wa maaa arsalnaa mir-Rasoolin illaa liyuṭaa'a bi-iznil-laah; wa law annahum 'iz ẓalamooo anfusahum jaaa'ooka fastaghfarul-laaha wastaghfara lahumur-Rasoolu lawajadul-laaha Tawwaabar-Raḥeemaa.

وَمَآ اَرْسَلْنَا مِنْ رَّسُوْلٍ اِلَّا لِيُطَاعَ
بِاِذْنِ اللّٰهِ ۭ وَلَوْ اَنَّھُمْ اِذْ ظَّلَمُوْٓا
اَنْفُسَھُمْ جَاۗءُوْكَ فَاسْتَغْفَرُوا اللّٰهَ
وَاسْتَغْفَرَ لَھُمُ الرَّسُوْلُ لَوَجَدُوا اللّٰهَ
تَوَّابًا رَّحِيْمًا ۝٦٤

65. I swear by your Lord that they will not be considered believers until they let you judge their disputes, and then they will find nothing in their souls to prevent them from accepting your judgment, thus submitting themselves to the will of Allah.

65. Falaa wa Rabbika laa yu'minoona ḥattaa yuḥakkimooka feemaa shajara baynahum s̲umma laa yajidoo feee anfusihim ḥarajam-mimmaa qaḍayta wa yusallimoo tasleemaa.

فَلَا وَرَبِّكَ لَا يُؤْمِنُونَ حَتّٰى
يُحَكِّمُوكَ فِيمَا شَجَرَ بَيْنَهُمْ ثُمَّ لَا
يَجِدُوا فِي أَنْفُسِهِمْ حَرَجًا مِمَّا
قَضَيْتَ وَيُسَلِّمُوا تَسْلِيمًا ﴿٦٥﴾

66. Had We commanded them to kill themselves or abandon their homes, only a few of them would have done it. If they had done what they had been advised to do, it would have strengthened their faith.

66. Wa law annaa katabnaa 'alayhim aniq-tulooo anfusakum awikh-rujoo min diyaarikum maa fa'aloohu illaa qaleelum-minhum wa law annahum fa'aloo maa yoo'aẓoona bihee lakaana khayral-lahum wa ashadda tas̲beetaa.

وَلَوْ أَنَّا كَتَبْنَا عَلَيْهِمْ أَنِ اقْتُلُوا
أَنْفُسَكُمْ أَوِ اخْرُجُوا مِنْ دِيَارِكُمْ
مَا فَعَلُوهُ إِلَّا قَلِيلٌ مِنْهُمْ ۖ وَلَوْ
أَنَّهُمْ فَعَلُوا مَا يُوعَظُونَ بِهِ لَكَانَ
خَيْرًا لَهُمْ وَأَشَدَّ تَثْبِيتًا ﴿٦٦﴾

67. We would have given them a great reward

67. Wa-iz̲al-la-aataynaahum mil-ladunnaaa-ajran 'aẓeemaa.

وَإِذًا لَآتَيْنَاهُمْ مِنْ لَدُنَّا أَجْرًا
عَظِيمًا ﴿٦٧﴾

68. and guided them to the right path.

68. Wa lahadaynaahum Ṣiraaṭam-Mustaqeemaa.

وَلَهَدَيْنَاهُمْ صِرَاطًا مُسْتَقِيمًا ﴿٦٨﴾

69. One who obeys Allah and the Messenger is a friend of the Prophets, saints, martyrs, and the righteous ones to whom Allah has granted His favors. They are the best friends that one can have.

69. Wa mañy-yuṭi'il-laaha war-Rasoola fa-ulaaa'ika ma'al-laz̲eena an'amal-laahu 'alayhim minan-Nabiyyeena waṣṣiddeeqeena washshuhadaaa'i waṣṣaaliḥeen; wa ḥasuna ulaaa'ika rafeeqaa.

وَمَنْ يُطِعِ اللّٰهَ وَالرَّسُولَ فَأُولٰئِكَ
مَعَ الَّذِينَ أَنْعَمَ اللّٰهُ عَلَيْهِمْ مِنَ
النَّبِيِّينَ وَالصِّدِّيقِينَ وَالشُّهَدَاءِ
وَالصَّالِحِينَ ۚ وَحَسُنَ أُولٰئِكَ رَفِيقًا ﴿٦٩﴾

70. The favors of Allah are such, and He knows very well (how to reward you).

70. Z̲aalikal-faḍlu minal-laah; wa kafaa billaahi 'Aleemaa.

ذٰلِكَ الْفَضْلُ مِنَ اللّٰهِ ۚ وَكَفٰى
بِاللّٰهِ عَلِيمًا ﴿٧٠﴾ ع ١١/٦

71. Believers, always be well prepared and on your guard. March in small groups or all together.

71. Yaaa ayyuhal-laz̲eena aamanoo khuz̲oo ḥiz̲rakum fanfiroo s̲ubaatin awin-firoo jamee'aa.

يَا أَيُّهَا الَّذِينَ آمَنُوا خُذُوا حِذْرَكُمْ
فَانْفِرُوا ثُبَاتٍ أَوِ انْفِرُوا جَمِيعًا ﴿٧١﴾

72. There are some among you who lag behind (in battle), and if you were to experience hardship, they would say, "It was certainly due to Allah's favors to us that we were not present with them,"

72. Wa inna minkum lamallayubaṭṭi'anna fa-in aṣaabatkum muṣeebatun qaala qad an'amal-laahu 'alayya iz̲ lam akum-ma'ahum shaheedaa.

وَإِنَّ مِنْكُمْ لَمَنْ لَيُبَطِّئَنَّ فَإِنْ
أَصَابَتْكُمْ مُصِيبَةٌ قَالَ قَدْ أَنْعَمَ اللّٰهُ
عَلَيَّ إِذْ لَمْ أَكُنْ مَعَهُمْ شَهِيدًا ﴿٧٢﴾

73. but if you were to receive a favor from Allah, they would certainly say, "(We have been ignored) as if there was no friendship among us. Would that we had been there with them for we would have had a great success."

73. Wa la'in aṣaabakum faḍlum-minal-laahi layaqoo-lanna ka-al-lam takum-baynakum wa baynahoo mawaddatuñy-yaa laytanee kuntu ma'ahum fa-afooza fawzan 'aẓeemaa.

وَلَئِنْ أَصَابَكُمْ فَضْلٌ مِنَ اللّٰهِ لَيَقُولَنَّ
كَأَنْ لَمْ تَكُنْ بَيْنَكُمْ وَبَيْنَهُ مَوَدَّةٌ
يَا لَيْتَنِي كُنْتُ مَعَهُمْ فَأَفُوزَ فَوْزًا عَظِيمًا ﴿٧٣﴾

74. Those who want to buy the life hereafter with this life should fight for the cause of Allah. We will give them a great reward whether they are killed or whether they are victorious.

74. Falyuqaatil fee sabeelil-laahil-lazeena yashroonal-ḥayaatad-dunyaa bil-Aakhirah; wa mañy-yuqaatil fee sabeelil-laahi fayuqtal aw yaghlib fasawfa nu'teehi ajran 'aẓeemaa.

فَلْيُقَاتِلْ فِى سَبِيلِ اللهِ الَّذِيْنَ يَشْرُوْنَ الْحَيٰوةَ الدُّنْيَا بِالْاٰخِرَةِ ۚ وَمَنْ يُّقَاتِلْ فِىْ سَبِيلِ اللهِ فَيُقْتَلْ اَوْ يَغْلِبْ فَسَوْفَ نُؤْتِيْهِ اَجْرًا عَظِيْمًا ۝

75. Why do you not fight for the cause of Allah or save the helpless men, women, and children who cry out, "Lord, set us free from this town of wrong doers and send us a guardian and a helper?"

75. Wa maa lakum laa tuqaatiloona fee sabeelil-laahi walmustaḍ'afeena minar-rijaali wannisaaa'i walwildaanil-lazeena yaqooloona Rabbanaaa akhrijnaa min haazihil-qarya-tiẓ-ẓaalimi ahluhaa waj-'al-lanaa milladunka waliyyañw-waj'al-lanaa mil-ladunka naṣeeraa.

وَمَا لَكُمْ لَا تُقَاتِلُوْنَ فِىْ سَبِيلِ اللهِ وَالْمُسْتَضْعَفِيْنَ مِنَ الرِّجَالِ وَالنِّسَاءِ وَالْوِلْدَانِ الَّذِيْنَ يَقُوْلُوْنَ رَبَّنَا اَخْرِجْنَا مِنْ هٰذِهِ الْقَرْيَةِ الظَّالِمِ اَهْلُهَا ۚ وَاجْعَلْ لَنَا مِنْ لَّدُنْكَ وَلِيًّا ۚ وَّاجْعَلْ لَّنَا مِنْ لَّدُنْكَ نَصِيْرًا ۝

76. The believers fight for the cause of Allah. The unbelievers fight for the cause of the Satan. So fight against the friends of Satan; the evil plans of Satan are certainly weak.

76. Allazeena aamanoo yuqaatiloona fee sabeelil-laahi wallazeena kafaroo yuqaati-loona fee sabeeliṭ-Ṭaaghoot faqaatilooo awliyaaa'ash-Shayṭaan; inna kaydash-Shayṭaani kaana ḍa'eefaa.

اَلَّذِيْنَ اٰمَنُوْا يُقَاتِلُوْنَ فِىْ سَبِيلِ اللهِ ۚ وَالَّذِيْنَ كَفَرُوْا يُقَاتِلُوْنَ فِىْ سَبِيلِ الطَّاغُوْتِ فَقَاتِلُوْا اَوْلِيَاءَ الشَّيْطٰنِ ۚ اِنَّ كَيْدَ الشَّيْطٰنِ كَانَ ضَعِيْفًا ۝

77. Did you not see those who were told to stop fighting, to say their prayers, and pay the religious tax? When they were ordered to fight, some of them feared other men as much as or more than they feared Allah and so they said, "Lord, why have you ordered us to fight? If only you would give us a little time." (Muhammad), tell them, "The pleasures of the worldly life are trivial. The life hereafter is best for the pious ones. You will not be treated the slightest bit unjustly."

77. Alam tara-ilal-lazeena qeela lahum kuffooo aydiyakum wa-aqeemuṣ-Ṣalaata wa aatuz-Zakaata falammaa kutiba-'alayhimul-qitaalu izaa faree-qum-minhum yakhshawnan-naasa kakhashyatil-laahi aw ashadda khashyah; wa qaaloo Rabbanaa lima katabta 'alaynal-qitaala law laaa akhkhartanaaa-ilaaa ajalin qareeb; qul mataa'ud-dunyaa qaleel; wal-Aakhiratu khayrul-limanit-taqaa wa laa tuẓlamoona fateelaa.

اَلَمْ تَرَ اِلَى الَّذِيْنَ قِيْلَ لَهُمْ كُفُّوْا اَيْدِيَكُمْ وَاَقِيْمُوا الصَّلٰوةَ وَاٰتُوا الزَّكٰوةَ ۚ فَلَمَّا كُتِبَ عَلَيْهِمُ الْقِتَالُ اِذَا فَرِيْقٌ مِّنْهُمْ يَخْشَوْنَ النَّاسَ كَخَشْيَةِ اللهِ اَوْ اَشَدَّ خَشْيَةً ۚ وَقَالُوْا رَبَّنَا لِمَ كَتَبْتَ عَلَيْنَا الْقِتَالَ ۚ لَوْلَا اَخَّرْتَنَا اِلَى اَجَلٍ قَرِيْبٍ ۗ قُلْ مَتَاعُ الدُّنْيَا قَلِيْلٌ ۚ وَالْاٰخِرَةُ خَيْرٌ لِّمَنِ اتَّقٰى ۚ وَلَا تُظْلَمُوْنَ فَتِيْلًا ۝

78. Wherever you are, death will find you even if you hide yourselves in firmly constructed towers. Whenever people experience good fortune they say that it is from Allah, but whenever

78. Aynamaa takoonoo yudrikkumul-mawtu wa law kuntum fee buroojim-mushay-yadah; wa-in tuṣibhum ḥasa-natuñy-yaqooloo haazihee min

اَيْنَمَا تَكُوْنُوْا يُدْرِكْكُمُ الْمَوْتُ وَلَوْ كُنْتُمْ فِىْ بُرُوْجٍ مُّشَيَّدَةٍ ۗ وَاِنْ تُصِبْهُمْ حَسَنَةٌ يَّقُوْلُوْا هٰذِهِ مِنْ

they experience misfortune, they say it is because of you, (Muhammad). Tell them, "Everything is from Allah." What is wrong with these people that they do not even try to understand?

'indil-laahi wa-in tuṣibhum sayyi'atuñy-yaqooloo haa<u>z</u>ihee min 'indik; qul kullum-min 'indillaahi famaali haaa-'ulaaa'ilqawmi laa yakaadoona yafqahoona ḥadee<u>s</u>aa.

عِنۡدِ اللّٰهِ ۚ وَاِنۡ تُصِبۡهُمۡ سَيِّئَةٌ
يَّقُوۡلُوۡا هٰذِهٖ مِنۡ عِنۡدِكَ ؕ قُلۡ كُلٌّ
مِّنۡ عِنۡدِ اللّٰهِ ؕ فَمَالِ هٰٓؤُلَآءِ الۡقَوۡمِ
لَا يَكَادُوۡنَ يَفۡقَهُوۡنَ حَدِيۡثًا ﴿۷۸﴾

79. Whatever good you may receive is certainly from Allah and whatever you suffer is from yourselves. We have sent you, (Muhammad), as a Messenger to people. Allah is a sufficient witness to your truthfulness.

79. Maaa aṣaabaka min ḥasanatin faminal-laahi wa maaa aṣaaabaka min sayyi'atin famin-nafsik; wa arsalnaaka linnaasi Rasoolaa; wa kafaa billaahi Shaheedaa.

مَاۤ اَصَابَكَ مِنۡ حَسَنَةٍ فَمِنَ اللّٰهِ ۖ
وَمَاۤ اَصَابَكَ مِنۡ سَيِّئَةٍ فَمِنۡ نَّفۡسِكَ ؕ
وَاَرۡسَلۡنٰكَ لِلنَّاسِ رَسُوۡلًا ؕ وَكَفٰى
بِاللّٰهِ شَهِيۡدًا ﴿۷۹﴾

80. One who obeys the Messenger has certainly obeyed Allah. You have not been sent to watch over those who turn away from you.

80. Mañy-yuṭi'ir-Rasoola faqad aṭaa'al-laaha wa man tawallaa famaaa arsalnaaka 'alayhim ḥafeeẓaa.

مَنۡ يُّطِعِ الرَّسُوۡلَ فَقَدۡ اَطَاعَ اللّٰهَ ۚ
وَمَنۡ تَوَلّٰى فَمَاۤ اَرۡسَلۡنٰكَ عَلَيۡهِمۡ
حَفِيۡظًا ﴿۸۰﴾

81. They proclaim obedience to you but as soon as they leave at night, a group of them make secret plans to do the contrary of what you have told them to do. Allah keeps the record of their nocturnal plans. Therefore, leave them alone and put your trust in Allah; He is Sufficient for you as your Guardian.

81. Wa yaqooloona ṭaa'atun fa-i<u>z</u>aa barazoo min 'indika bayyata ṭaaa'ifatum-minhum ghayral-la<u>z</u>ee taqoolu wallaahu yaktubu maa yubayyitoona fa-a'riḍ 'anhum wa tawakkal 'alal-laah; wa kafaa billaahi Wakeelaa.

وَيَقُوۡلُوۡنَ طَاعَةٌ فَاِذَا بَرَزُوۡا مِنۡ
عِنۡدِكَ بَيَّتَ طَآئِفَةٌ مِّنۡهُمۡ غَيۡرَ
الَّذِىۡ تَقُوۡلُ ؕ وَاللّٰهُ يَكۡتُبُ مَا يُبَيِّتُوۡنَ ۚ
فَاَعۡرِضۡ عَنۡهُمۡ وَتَوَكَّلۡ عَلَى اللّٰهِ ؕ
وَكَفٰى بِاللّٰهِ وَكِيۡلًا ﴿۸۱﴾

82. Will they not ponder on the Quran? Had it come from someone other than Allah, they would have certainly found many contradictions therein.

82. Afalaa yatadabbaroonal-Qur'aan; wa law kaana min 'indi ghayril-laahi lawajadoo fee-hikh-tilaafan ka<u>s</u>eeraa.

اَفَلَا يَتَدَبَّرُوۡنَ الۡقُرۡاٰنَ ؕ وَلَوۡ كَانَ
مِنۡ عِنۡدِ غَيۡرِ اللّٰهِ لَوَجَدُوۡا فِيۡهِ
اخۡتِلَافًا كَثِيۡرًا ﴿۸۲﴾

83. When they receive any news of peace or war, they announce it in public. Had they told it to the Messenger or to their (qualified) leaders, they could have used that information more properly. Were it not for the favor and mercy of Allah, all but a few of them would have followed Satan.

83. Wa i<u>z</u>aa jaaa'ahum amrum-minal-amni awil-khawfi a<u>z</u>aa'oo bihee wa law raddoohu ilar-Rasooli wa ilaaa ulil-amri minhum la'alimahul-la<u>z</u>eena yastambiṭoonahoo minhum; wa law laa faḍlul-laahi 'alaykum wa raḥmatuhoo lattaba'tu-mush-Shayṭaana illaa qaleelaa.

وَاِذَا جَآءَهُمۡ اَمۡرٌ مِّنَ الۡاَمۡنِ
اَوِ الۡخَوۡفِ اَذَاعُوۡا بِهٖ ؕ وَلَوۡ رَدُّوۡهُ
اِلَى الرَّسُوۡلِ وَاِلٰٓى اُولِى الۡاَمۡرِ مِنۡهُمۡ
لَعَلِمَهُ الَّذِيۡنَ يَسۡتَنۡۢبِطُوۡنَهٗ مِنۡهُمۡ ؕ
وَلَوۡلَا فَضۡلُ اللّٰهِ عَلَيۡكُمۡ وَرَحۡمَتُهٗ
لَاتَّبَعۡتُمُ الشَّيۡطٰنَ اِلَّا قَلِيۡلًا ﴿۸۳﴾

84. Thus (Muhammad), fight for the cause of Allah. You are

84. Faqaatil fee sabeelil-laahi laa tukallafu illaa

فَقَاتِلۡ فِىۡ سَبِيۡلِ اللّٰهِ ۚ لَا تُكَلَّفُ اِلَّا

84. Thus (Muhammad), fight for the cause of Allah. You are only responsible for yourself. Rouse the believers and perhaps Allah will stop the evil designs of the unbelievers. Allah's punishment and retribution are the most severe.

nafsaka wa ḥarriḍil-mu'mineena 'asallaahu añy-yakuffa ba-sallaẕeena kafaroo; wallaahu ashaddu ba-sañw-wa ashaddu tankeelaa.

نَفْسَكَ وَحَرِّضِ الْمُؤْمِنِيْنَ ۚ عَسَى
اللّٰهُ اَنْ يَّكُفَّ بَاْسَ الَّذِيْنَ كَفَرُوْا ۭ
وَاللّٰهُ اَشَدُّ بَاْسًا وَّاَشَدُّ تَنْكِيْلًا ﴿٨٤﴾

85. Whoever intercedes for a good purpose will receive his share of the reward, but the intercession for an evil purpose only adds more to one's burden. Allah has control over all things.

85. Mañy-yashfa' shafaa'atan ḥasanatañy-yakul-lahoo naṣeebum-minhaa wa mañy-yashfa' shafaa'atan sayyi'atañy-yakul-lahoo kiflum-minhaa; wa kaanal-laahu 'alaa kulli shay'im-Muqeetaa.

مَنْ يَّشْفَعْ شَفَاعَةً حَسَنَةً يَّكُنْ لَّهٗ
نَصِيْبٌ مِّنْهَا ۚ وَمَنْ يَّشْفَعْ شَفَاعَةً
سَيِّئَةً يَّكُنْ لَّهٗ كِفْلٌ مِّنْهَا ۭ وَكَانَ
اللّٰهُ عَلٰي كُلِّ شَيْءٍ مُّقِيْتًا ﴿٨٥﴾

86. Answer a greeting in kinder words than those said to you in the greeting or at least as kind. Allah keeps account of all things.

86. Wa iẕaa ḥuyyeetum bitaḥiyyatin faḥayyoo bi-aḥsana minhaaa aw ruddoohaaa; innallaaha kaana 'alaa kulli shay'in Ḥaseebaa.

وَاِذَا حُيِّيْتُمْ بِتَحِيَّةٍ فَحَيُّوْا بِاَحْسَنَ
مِنْهَآ اَوْ رُدُّوْهَا ۭ اِنَّ اللّٰهَ كَانَ عَلٰي (الربع)
كُلِّ شَيْءٍ حَسِيْبًا ﴿٨٦﴾

87. Allah exists. He is the only Lord. He will gather you all together on the Day of Judgment which will certainly come. Who is more truthful than Allah?

87. Allaahu laaa ilaaha illaa huwa layajma'annakum ilaa Yawmil-Qiyaamati laa rayba feeh; wa man aṣdaqu minallaahi ḥadeesaa.

اَللّٰهُ لَآ اِلٰهَ اِلَّا هُوَ ۭ لَيَجْمَعَنَّكُمْ اِلٰى
يَوْمِ الْقِيٰمَةِ لَا رَيْبَ فِيْهِ ۭ وَمَنْ
اَصْدَقُ مِنَ اللّٰهِ حَدِيْثًا ﴿٨٧﴾ ع

88. Why are you divided into two different parties concerning the hypocrites, when Allah Himself has turned them to disbelief because of their misdeeds? Do you want to guide those whom Allah has caused to go astray? You cannot find guidance for those whom Allah has made to err.

88. Famaa lakum filmunaafiqeena fi'atayni wallaahu arkasahum bimaa kasabooo; atureedoona an tahdoo man aḍallal-laahu wa mañy-yuḍlilil-laahu falan tajida lahoo sabeelaa.

فَمَا لَكُمْ فِي الْمُنٰفِقِيْنَ فِئَتَيْنِ
وَاللّٰهُ اَرْكَسَهُمْ بِمَا كَسَبُوْا ۭ اَتُرِيْدُوْنَ
اَنْ تَهْدُوْا مَنْ اَضَلَّ اللّٰهُ ۭ وَمَنْ
يُّضْلِلِ اللّٰهُ فَلَنْ تَجِدَ لَهٗ سَبِيْلًا ﴿٨٨﴾

89. They wish you to become unbelievers as they themselves are. Do not establish friendship with them until they have abandoned their homes for the cause of Allah. If they betray you, seize them and slay them wherever you find them. Do not establish friendship with them or seek their help

89. Waddoo law takfuroona kamaa kafaroo fatakoonoona sawaaa'an falaa tattakhiẕoo minhum awliyaaa'a ḥattaa yuhaajiroo fee sabeelil-laah; fa-in tawallaw fakhuẕoohum waqtuloohum ḥaysu wajattumoohum wa laa tattakhiẕoo minhum waliyyañw-wa laa naṣeeraa.

وَدُّوْا لَوْ تَكْفُرُوْنَ كَمَا كَفَرُوْا
فَتَكُوْنُوْنَ سَوَاۗءً فَلَا تَتَّخِذُوْا مِنْهُمْ
اَوْلِيَاۗءَ حَتّٰي يُهَاجِرُوْا فِيْ سَبِيْلِ
اللّٰهِ ۭ فَاِنْ تَوَلَّوْا فَخُذُوْهُمْ وَاقْتُلُوْهُمْ
حَيْثُ وَجَدْتُّمُوْهُمْ ۠ وَلَا تَتَّخِذُوْا
مِنْهُمْ وَلِيًّا وَّلَا نَصِيْرًا ﴿٨٩﴾

90. except with those who attach themselves to your allies or come to you with no desire to fight you or their own people. Allah could have given them power to fight you. Thus, if they

90. Illal-laẕeena yaṣiloona ilaa qawmim-baynakum wa baynahum-meesaaqun aw jaaa'ookum ḥaṣirat ṣudooruhum añy-yuqaatilookum

اِلَّا الَّذِيْنَ يَصِلُوْنَ اِلٰى قَوْمٍۢ
بَيْنَكُمْ وَبَيْنَهُمْ مِّيْثَاقٌ اَوْ جَاۗءُوْكُمْ
حَصِرَتْ صُدُوْرُهُمْ اَنْ يُّقَاتِلُوْكُمْ

أَوْ يُقَاتِلُوا قَوْمَهُمْ ۚ وَلَوْ شَاءَ اللَّهُ
لَسَلَّطَهُمْ عَلَيْكُمْ فَلَقَاتَلُوكُمْ ۚ فَإِنِ
اعْتَزَلُوكُمْ فَلَمْ يُقَاتِلُوكُمْ وَأَلْقَوْا
إِلَيْكُمُ السَّلَمَ فَمَا جَعَلَ اللَّهُ
لَكُمْ عَلَيْهِمْ سَبِيلًا ﴿٩٠﴾

aw yuqaatiloo qawmahum, wa law shaaa'al-laahu lasallaṭahum 'alaykum falaqaatalookum; fa-ini'-tazalookum falam yuqaatilookum wa alqaw ilaykumus-salama famaa ja'alal-laahu lakum 'alayhim sabeelaa.

retreated, stop fighting and come forward expressing faith in Islam. Allah will not allow you to fight them.

سَتَجِدُونَ آخَرِينَ يُرِيدُونَ
أَنْ يَأْمَنُوكُمْ وَيَأْمَنُوا قَوْمَهُمْ
كُلَّمَا رُدُّوا إِلَى الْفِتْنَةِ أُرْكِسُوا
فِيهَا ۚ فَإِنْ لَمْ يَعْتَزِلُوكُمْ وَيُلْقُوا
إِلَيْكُمُ السَّلَمَ وَيَكُفُّوا أَيْدِيَهُمْ
فَخُذُوهُمْ وَاقْتُلُوهُمْ حَيْثُ
ثَقِفْتُمُوهُمْ ۚ وَأُولَٰئِكُمْ جَعَلْنَا لَكُمْ
عَلَيْهِمْ سُلْطَانًا مُبِينًا ﴿٩١﴾ ع ١٢

91. Satajidoona aakhareena yureedoona añy-ya-manookum wa ya-manoo qawmahum kulla maa ruddooo ilal-fitnati urkisoo feehaa; fa-il-lam ya'tazilookum wa yulqooo ilaykumus-salama wa yakuffooo aydiyahum fakhuzoohum waqtuloohum ḥaysu saqiftumoohum; wa-'ulaaa'ikum ja'alnaa lakum 'alayhim sulṭaanam-mubeenaa.

91. You will soon find others who seek security from you as well as from their own people, but when they are invited to return to idol worship, they do so enthusiastically. Thus, if they did not keep away from you or come forward with a peace proposal or desist from harming you, apprehend and slay them wherever you find them, for We have given you full control over them.

وَمَا كَانَ لِمُؤْمِنٍ أَنْ يَقْتُلَ مُؤْمِنًا
إِلَّا خَطَأً ۚ وَمَنْ قَتَلَ مُؤْمِنًا خَطَأً
فَتَحْرِيرُ رَقَبَةٍ مُؤْمِنَةٍ وَدِيَةٌ
مُسَلَّمَةٌ إِلَىٰ أَهْلِهِ إِلَّا أَنْ يَصَّدَّقُوا ۚ
فَإِنْ كَانَ مِنْ قَوْمٍ عَدُوٍّ لَكُمْ وَهُوَ
مُؤْمِنٌ فَتَحْرِيرُ رَقَبَةٍ مُؤْمِنَةٍ ۖ
وَإِنْ كَانَ مِنْ قَوْمٍ بَيْنَكُمْ وَبَيْنَهُمْ
مِيثَاقٌ فَدِيَةٌ مُسَلَّمَةٌ إِلَىٰ
أَهْلِهِ وَتَحْرِيرُ رَقَبَةٍ مُؤْمِنَةٍ ۖ
فَمَنْ لَمْ يَجِدْ فَصِيَامُ شَهْرَيْنِ
مُتَتَابِعَيْنِ تَوْبَةً مِنَ اللَّهِ ۗ وَكَانَ
اللَّهُ عَلِيمًا حَكِيمًا ﴿٩٢﴾

92. Wa maa kaana limu'minin añy-yaqtula mu'minan illaa khaṭa'aa; waman qatala mu'minan khaṭa'an fataḥreeru raqabatim-mu'minatiñw-wa diyatum-musallamatun ilaaa ahliheee illaaa añy-yaṣṣaddaqoo; fa-in kaana min qawmin 'aduwwil-lakum wa huwa mu'minun fataḥreeru raqabatim mu'minah; wa in kaana min qawmim baynakum wa baynahum meesaaqun fadiyatum-musallamatun ilaaa ahlihee wa taḥreeru raqabatim-mu'minatin famal-lam yajid fa-Ṣiyaamu shahrayni mutataabi'ayni tawbatam minal-laah; wa kaanal-laahu 'Aleeman Ḥakeemaa.

92. A believer cannot slay another believer except if it may happen by mistake for which the retribution is to set free a believing slave and pay the appointed blood money to the relatives of the deceased unless the relatives wave aside the payment. If the person slain is from your enemies but himself is a believer, the penalty is to set free a believing slave. If the person slain is one of those with whom you have a peace treaty, the penalty is the same as that for a slain believer. If this was not possible, the defendant has to fast for two consecutive months, asking Allah to accept his repentance. He is All-knowing and All-wise.

وَمَنْ يَقْتُلْ مُؤْمِنًا مُتَعَمِّدًا فَجَزَاؤُهُ

93. Wa mañy-yaqtul mu'minam-muta'ammidan fajazaaa'uhoo

93. The punishment for one who purposely slays a believer will be to live in hellfire forever.

Allah is angry with him and has condemned him. He has prepared for him a great torment.

Jahannamu khaalidan feehaa wa ghaḍibal-laahu ʻalayhi wa laʻanahoo wa aʻadda lahoo ʻa̲zaaban ʻaẓeemaa.

جَهَنَّمُ خٰلِدًا فِيْهَا وَغَضِبَ اللّٰهُ عَلَيْهِ
وَلَعَنَهٗ وَاَعَدَّ لَهٗ عَذَابًا عَظِيْمًا ﴿٩٣﴾

94. Believers, if you march with arms for the cause of Allah, make sure that you know whom to fight. Do not accuse anyone who claims himself to be a Muslim of disbelief just for worldly gains. There is abundant bounty with Allah. Before, you were also like them, but Allah bestowed His favors upon you. Thus, make sure that you know whom to fight. Allah is Well-aware of what you do.

94. Yaaa ayyuhal-la̲zeena aamanooo i̲zaa ḍarabtum fee sabeelil-laahi fatabayyanoo wa laa taqooloo liman alqaaa ilaykumus-salaama lasta mu'minan tabtaghoona ʻaraḍal-ḥayaatid-dunyaa faʻindal-laahi maghaanimu ka̲seerah; ka̲zaa-lika kuntum min qablu famannal-laahu ʻalaykum fatabayyanoo; innallaaha kaana bimaa taʻmaloona Khabeeraa.

يٰۤاَيُّهَا الَّذِيْنَ اٰمَنُوْۤا اِذَا ضَرَبْتُمْ
فِيْ سَبِيْلِ اللّٰهِ فَتَبَيَّنُوْا وَلَا تَقُوْلُوْا
لِمَنْ اَلْقٰۤى اِلَيْكُمُ السَّلٰمَ لَسْتَ مُؤْمِنًا ۚ
تَبْتَغُوْنَ عَرَضَ الْحَيٰوةِ الدُّنْيَا ؗ
فَعِنْدَ اللّٰهِ مَغَانِمُ كَثِيْرَةٌ ؕ كَذٰلِكَ
كُنْتُمْ مِّنْ قَبْلُ فَمَنَّ اللّٰهُ عَلَيْكُمْ
فَتَبَيَّنُوْا ؕ اِنَّ اللّٰهَ كَانَ بِمَا
تَعْمَلُوْنَ خَبِيْرًا ﴿٩٤﴾

95. Among the believers, those who stay at home without a good reason are not equal to those who strive for the cause of Allah in person or with their property. To those who strive for His cause in person or with their property, Allah has granted a higher rank than to those who stay at home. Allah has promised that everyone will receive his proper share of the reward, but He will grant a much greater reward to those striving for His cause than to those who stay home (for no reason).

95. Laa yastawil-qaaʻidoona minal-mu'mineena ghayru ulid-ḍarari walmujaahidoona fee sabeelil-laahi bi-amwaali-him wa anfusihim; faḍḍalal-laahul-mujaahideena bi-am-waalihim wa anfusihim ʻalal-qaaʻideena darajah; wa kullañw- waʻadal-laahul-ḥusnaa; wa faḍḍalal-laahul-mujaahideena ʻalal-qaaʻideena ajran ʻaẓeemaa.

لَا يَسْتَوِى الْقٰعِدُوْنَ مِنَ الْمُؤْمِنِيْنَ
غَيْرُ اُولِى الضَّرَرِ وَالْمُجٰهِدُوْنَ فِيْ
سَبِيْلِ اللّٰهِ بِاَمْوَالِهِمْ وَاَنْفُسِهِمْ ؕ
فَضَّلَ اللّٰهُ الْمُجٰهِدِيْنَ بِاَمْوَالِهِمْ
وَاَنْفُسِهِمْ عَلَى الْقٰعِدِيْنَ دَرَجَةً ؕ
وَكُلًّا وَّعَدَ اللّٰهُ الْحُسْنٰى ؕ وَفَضَّلَ
اللّٰهُ الْمُجٰهِدِيْنَ عَلَى الْقٰعِدِيْنَ
اَجْرًا عَظِيْمًا ۙ﴿٩٥﴾

96. Allah will grant those who strive, high ranks, forgiveness, and mercy. He is All-forgiving and All-merciful.

96. Darajaatim-minhu wa maghfiratañw-wa raḥmah; wa kaanal-laahu Ghafoorar-Raḥeemaa.

دَرَجٰتٍ مِّنْهُ وَمَغْفِرَةً وَّرَحْمَةً ؕ
وَكَانَ اللّٰهُ غَفُوْرًا رَّحِيْمًا ﴿٩٦﴾ ع ١٣ ٥ ١٠

97. When the angels take away from their bodies the souls of those who have wronged themselves, they will ask them, "How did you live?" They will reply, "We lived on earth in weakness and oppression." The angels will say, "Was not Allah's land vast enough for you to go wherever you could live in peace?" The dwelling of these people will be hellfire, a terrible destination.

97. Innal-la̲zeena tawaffaa-humul-malaaa'ikatu ẓaalimeee-anfusihim qaaloo feema kuntum qaaloo kunnaa mustaḍʻafeena fil-arḍ; qaalooo alam takun arḍul-laahi waasiʻatan fatuhaajiroo feehaa; fa-ulaaa'ika ma-waahum Jahannamu wa saaa'at maṣeeraa.

اِنَّ الَّذِيْنَ تَوَفّٰىهُمُ الْمَلٰٓئِكَةُ
ظَالِمِىْۤ اَنْفُسِهِمْ قَالُوْا فِيْمَ كُنْتُمْ ؕ
قَالُوْا كُنَّا مُسْتَضْعَفِيْنَ فِى الْاَرْضِ ؕ
قَالُوْۤا اَلَمْ تَكُنْ اَرْضُ اللّٰهِ وَاسِعَةً
فَتُهَاجِرُوْا فِيْهَا ؕ فَاُولٰٓئِكَ مَاْوٰىهُمْ
جَهَنَّمُ ؕ وَسَآءَتْ مَصِيْرًا ۙ﴿٩٧﴾

98. As for the really weak and oppressed men, women, and children who were not able to find any means of obtaining their freedom or of having the right guidance,

98. Illal-mustaḍ'afeena minar-rijaali wannisaaa'i walwildaani laa yastatee'oona ḥeelatañw-wa laa yahtadoona sabeelaa.

إِلَّا الْمُسْتَضْعَفِينَ مِنَ الرِّجَالِ
وَالنِّسَاءِ وَالْوِلْدَانِ لَا يَسْتَطِيعُونَ
حِيلَةً وَلَا يَهْتَدُونَ سَبِيلًا ﴿٩٨﴾

99. perhaps Allah will forgive them; He is All-merciful and All-forgiving.

99. Fa-ulaaa'ika 'asal-laahu añy-ya'fuwa 'anhum; wa kaanal-laahu 'Afuwwan Ghafooraa.

فَأُولَٰئِكَ عَسَى اللَّهُ أَنْ يَعْفُوَ عَنْهُمْ ۚ
وَكَانَ اللَّهُ عَفُوًّا غَفُورًا ﴿٩٩﴾

100. One who abandons his home for the cause of Allah will find many places of refuge in the vast land, and one who dies, after having abandoned his home to get near to Allah and His Messenger, will receive his reward from Allah. Allah is All-forgiving and All-merciful.

100. Wa mañy-yuhaajir fee sabeelil-laahi yajid fil-arḍi muraaghaman kas̲eerañw-wa sa'ah; wa mañy-yakhruj mim baytihee muhaajiran-ilal-laahi wa Rasoolihee s̲umma yudri-khul-mawtu faqad waqa'a ajruhoo 'alal-laah; wa kaanal-laahu Ghafoorar-Raḥeemaa.

وَمَنْ يُهَاجِرْ فِي سَبِيلِ اللَّهِ يَجِدْ
فِي الْأَرْضِ مُرَاغَمًا كَثِيرًا وَسَعَةً ۚ
وَمَنْ يَخْرُجْ مِنْ بَيْتِهِ مُهَاجِرًا
إِلَى اللَّهِ وَرَسُولِهِ ثُمَّ يُدْرِكْهُ الْمَوْتُ
فَقَدْ وَقَعَ أَجْرُهُ عَلَى اللَّهِ ۗ وَكَانَ
اللَّهُ غَفُورًا رَحِيمًا ﴿١٠٠﴾ ع ١٤ / ١١

101. When you are on a journey, it is no sin to shorten your prayers if you are afraid of the mischief of the unbelievers. The unbelievers have always been your sworn enemies.

101. Wa iz̲aa ḍarabtum fil-arḍi falaysa 'alaykum junaaḥun an taqṣuroo minaṣ-Ṣalaati in khiftum añy-yaftinakumul-laz̲eena kafarooo; innal-kaafireena kaanoo lakum 'aduwwam-mubeenaa.

وَإِذَا ضَرَبْتُمْ فِي الْأَرْضِ فَلَيْسَ
عَلَيْكُمْ جُنَاحٌ أَنْ تَقْصُرُوا مِنَ
الصَّلَاةِ إِنْ خِفْتُمْ أَنْ يَفْتِنَكُمُ
الَّذِينَ كَفَرُوا ۚ إِنَّ الْكَافِرِينَ كَانُوا
لَكُمْ عَدُوًّا مُبِينًا ﴿١٠١﴾

102. (Muhammad), if you are among them (your followers during a battle) and you call them for prayer, let a group of them carry their arms during prayer. After they have made their prostration, let them go back to watch the enemy and let the other group who did not yet pray, join you, carrying their arms with due precaution. The unbelievers would love to find you neglecting your arms and property and would attack you suddenly.

102. Wa iz̲aa kunta feehim fa-aqamta lahumuṣ-Ṣalaata faltaqum ṭaaa'ifatum-minhum ma'aka walya-khuz̲ooo asliḥatahum fa-iz̲aa sajadoo fal-yakoonoo miñw-waraaa'ikum walta-ti ṭaaa'ifatun ukhraa lam yuṣalloo falyuṣalloo ma'aka walya-khuz̲oo ḥiz̲rahum wa asliḥatahum; waddal-laz̲eena kafaroo law taghfuloona 'an asliḥatikum wa amti'atikum fayameeloona 'alaykum maylatañw-waaḥidah; wa laa junaaḥa

وَإِذَا كُنْتَ فِيهِمْ فَأَقَمْتَ لَهُمُ
الصَّلَاةَ فَلْتَقُمْ طَائِفَةٌ مِنْهُمْ مَعَكَ
وَلْيَأْخُذُوا أَسْلِحَتَهُمْ فَإِذَا سَجَدُوا
فَلْيَكُونُوا مِنْ وَرَائِكُمْ وَلْتَأْتِ
طَائِفَةٌ أُخْرَىٰ لَمْ يُصَلُّوا فَلْيُصَلُّوا
مَعَكَ وَلْيَأْخُذُوا حِذْرَهُمْ
وَأَسْلِحَتَهُمْ ۗ وَدَّ الَّذِينَ كَفَرُوا
لَوْ تَغْفُلُونَ عَنْ أَسْلِحَتِكُمْ وَ
أَمْتِعَتِكُمْ فَيَمِيلُونَ عَلَيْكُمْ
مَيْلَةً وَاحِدَةً ۚ وَلَا جُنَاحَ

If rain or illness make you suffer, you may place your arms aside during prayer but still observe due precaution. Allah has prepared a humiliating torment for the unbelievers.

'alaykum in kaana bikum a<u>z</u>am-mimmaṭarin aw kuntum marḍaaa an taḍa'ooo asliḥatakum wa khu<u>z</u>oo ḥi<u>z</u>rakum; innal-laaha a'adda lilkaafireena 'a<u>z</u>aabam-muheenaa.

عَلَيْكُمْ إِن كَانَ بِكُمْ أَذًى مِّن
مَّطَرٍ أَوْ كُنتُم مَّرْضَىٰ أَن تَضَعُوا
أَسْلِحَتَكُمْ ۖ وَخُذُوا حِذْرَكُمْ ۗ إِنَّ اللَّهَ
أَعَدَّ لِلْكَافِرِينَ عَذَابًا مُّهِينًا ﴿١٠٢﴾

103. When you complete your prayer, remember Allah all the time while standing, sitting, or reclining. When you are safe, say your prayers properly. It is a constant duty of the believers.

103. Fa-i<u>z</u>aa qaḍaytumuṣ-Ṣalaata fa<u>z</u>kurul-laaha qiyaamañw-wa qu'oodañw-wa 'alaa junoobikum; fa-i<u>z</u>aṭ-ma-nantum fa-aqeemuṣ-Ṣalaah; innaṣ-Ṣalaata kaanat 'alal-mu'mineena kitaabam-mawqootaa.

فَإِذَا قَضَيْتُمُ الصَّلَاةَ فَاذْكُرُوا
اللَّهَ قِيَامًا وَقُعُودًا وَعَلَىٰ جُنُوبِكُمْ ۚ
فَإِذَا اطْمَأْنَنتُمْ فَأَقِيمُوا الصَّلَاةَ ۚ
إِنَّ الصَّلَاةَ كَانَتْ عَلَى الْمُؤْمِنِينَ
كِتَابًا مَّوْقُوتًا ﴿١٠٣﴾

104. Do not neglect the pursuit of the enemy. If you have suffered, they also have suffered, but you can, at least, expect from Allah what they can never expect. Allah is All-knowing and All-wise.

104. Wa laa tahinoo fibtighaaa'il-qawmi in takoonoo ta-lamoona fa-innahum ya-lamoona kamaa ta-lamoon; wa tarjoona minal-laahi maa laa yarjoon; wa kaanal-laahu 'Aleeman Ḥakeemaa.

وَلَا تَهِنُوا فِي ابْتِغَاءِ الْقَوْمِ ۖ إِن
تَكُونُوا تَأْلَمُونَ فَإِنَّهُمْ يَأْلَمُونَ
كَمَا تَأْلَمُونَ ۖ وَتَرْجُونَ مِنَ اللَّهِ
مَا لَا يَرْجُونَ ۗ وَكَانَ اللَّهُ ع
عَلِيمًا حَكِيمًا ﴿١٠٤﴾

105. We have revealed to you the Book in all Truth so that you can judge among people by the laws of Allah. However, never defend the treacherous ones.

105. Innaaa anzalnaaa ilaykal-Kitaaba bilḥaqqi litaḥkuma baynan-naasi bimaaa araakal-laah; wa laa takul-lilkhaaa'ineena khaṣeemaa.

إِنَّا أَنزَلْنَا إِلَيْكَ الْكِتَابَ بِالْحَقِّ
لِتَحْكُمَ بَيْنَ النَّاسِ بِمَا أَرَاكَ اللَّهُ ۚ
وَلَا تَكُن لِّلْخَائِنِينَ خَصِيمًا ﴿١٠٥﴾

106. Seek forgiveness from Allah. He is All-forgiving and All-merciful.

106. Wastaghfiril-laaha innal-laaha kaana Ghafoorar-Raḥeemaa.

وَاسْتَغْفِرِ اللَّهَ ۖ إِنَّ اللَّهَ كَانَ
غَفُورًا رَّحِيمًا ﴿١٠٦﴾

107. Do not defend those who deceive themselves; Allah does not love those who are treacherous and sinful.

107. Wa laa tujaadil 'anil-la<u>z</u>eena yakhtaanoona anfusahum; innal-laaha laa yuḥibbu man kaana khawwaanan a<u>s</u>eemaa.

وَلَا تُجَادِلْ عَنِ الَّذِينَ يَخْتَانُونَ
أَنفُسَهُمْ ۚ إِنَّ اللَّهَ لَا يُحِبُّ مَن
كَانَ خَوَّانًا أَثِيمًا ﴿١٠٧﴾

108. They hide their sins from other people but they cannot hide themselves from Allah, who is constantly with them, even when they hold nocturnal meetings, a thing which Allah does not like. Allah comprehends all that they do.

108. Yastakhfoona minannaasi wa laa yastakhfoona minal-laahi wa huwa ma'ahum <u>iz</u> yubayyitoona maa laa yarḍaa minal-qawl; wa kaanal-laahu bimaa ya'maloona muḥeeṭaa.

يَسْتَخْفُونَ مِنَ النَّاسِ وَلَا يَسْتَخْفُونَ
مِنَ اللَّهِ وَهُوَ مَعَهُمْ إِذْ يُبَيِّتُونَ
مَا لَا يَرْضَىٰ مِنَ الْقَوْلِ ۚ وَكَانَ
اللَّهُ بِمَا يَعْمَلُونَ مُحِيطًا ﴿١٠٨﴾

109. You defend them in this life but who will defend them against Allah on the Day of Judgment, and who will be their attorney?

109. Haaa-antum haaa'ulaaa'i jaadaltum 'anhum fil-ḥayaatid-dunyaa famañy-yujaadilul-laaha 'anhum Yawmal-Qiyaamati am mañy-yakoonu 'alayhim wakeelaa.

هٰٓاَنۡتُمۡ هٰٓؤُلَآءِ جٰدَلۡتُمۡ عَنۡهُمۡ فِى
الۡحَيٰوةِ الدُّنۡيَا فَمَنۡ يُّجَادِلُ
اللّٰهَ عَنۡهُمۡ يَوۡمَ الۡقِيٰمَةِ اَمۡ مَّنۡ
يَّكُوۡنُ عَلَيۡهِمۡ وَكِيۡلًا ﴿۱۰۹﴾

110. One who commits a sin or does wrong to himself and then seeks forgiveness from Allah will find Allah All-forgiving and All-merciful.

110. Wa mañy-ya'mal sooo'an aw yaẓlim nafsahoo summa yastaghfiril-laaha yajidil-laaha Ghafoorar-Raḥeemaa.

وَمَنۡ يَّعۡمَلۡ سُوۡٓءًا اَوۡ يَظۡلِمۡ
نَفۡسَهٗ ثُمَّ يَسۡتَغۡفِرِ اللّٰهَ يَجِدِ اللّٰهَ
غَفُوۡرًا رَّحِيۡمًا ﴿۱۱۰﴾

111. One who commits sins has committed them against his own soul. Allah is All-knowing and All-wise.

111. Wa mañy-yaksib isman fa-innamaa yaksibuhoo 'alaa nafsih; wa kaanal-laahu 'Aleeman Ḥakeemaa.

وَمَنۡ يَّكۡسِبۡ اِثۡمًا فَاِنَّمَا يَكۡسِبُهٗ
عَلٰى نَفۡسِهٖ ؕ وَكَانَ اللّٰهُ
عَلِيۡمًا حَكِيۡمًا ﴿۱۱۱﴾

112. One who makes a mistake or commits a sin and ascribes it to an innocent person only burdens himself with slander and a grave sin.

112. Wa mañy-yaksib kha-ṭeee'atan aw isman summa yarmi bihee bareee'an faqadiḥ-tamala buhtaanañw-wa ismam-mubeenaa.

وَمَنۡ يَّكۡسِبۡ خَطِيۡٓـئَةً اَوۡ اِثۡمًا ثُمَّ
يَرۡمِ بِهٖ بَرِيۡٓـئًا فَقَدِ احۡتَمَلَ بُهۡتَانًا
وَّاِثۡمًا مُّبِيۡنًا ﴿۱۱۲﴾ ع ٨ ١٤

113. Were it not for the favor and mercy of Allah, some of them would certainly have tried to make you (Muhammad) go astray. However, they cannot lead anyone astray but themselves nor can they harm you. Allah has revealed the Book to you, has given you wisdom, and has taught you what you did not know. Certainly Allah's favor to you has been great.

113. Wa law laa faḍlul-laahi 'alayka wa raḥmatuhoo lahammaṭ-ṭaaa'ifatum minhum añy-yuḍillooka wa maa yuḍilloona illaaa anfusahum wa maa yaḍurroonaka min shay'; wa anzalal-laahu 'alaykal-Kitaaba wal-Ḥikmata wa 'allamaka maa lam takun ta'lam; wa kaana faḍlul-laahi 'alayka 'aẓeemaa.

وَلَوۡلَا فَضۡلُ اللّٰهِ عَلَيۡكَ وَرَحۡمَتُهٗ
لَهَمَّتۡ طَّآئِفَةٌ مِّنۡهُمۡ اَنۡ يُّضِلُّوۡكَ ؕ
وَمَا يُضِلُّوۡنَ اِلَّاۤ اَنۡفُسَهُمۡ وَمَا
يَضُرُّوۡنَكَ مِنۡ شَىۡءٍ ؕ وَاَنۡزَلَ اللّٰهُ
عَلَيۡكَ الۡكِتٰبَ وَالۡحِكۡمَةَ وَعَلَّمَكَ
مَا لَمۡ تَكُنۡ تَعۡلَمُ ؕ وَكَانَ
فَضۡلُ اللّٰهِ عَلَيۡكَ عَظِيۡمًا ﴿۱۱۳﴾ الثلثة

114. There is nothing good in much of their secret talks except for that which is for charity, justice, or for reconciliation among people to seek thereby the pleasure of Allah for which We will give a great reward.

114. Laa khayra fee kaseerim-min najwaahum illaa man amara biṣadaqatin aw ma'roo-fin aw iṣlaaḥim-baynan-naas; wa mañy-yaf'al zaalikab-tighaaa'a marḍaatil-laahi fa-sawfa nu'teehi ajran 'aẓeemaa.

لَا خَيۡرَ فِىۡ كَثِيۡرٍ مِّنۡ نَّجۡوٰٮهُمۡ اِلَّا
مَنۡ اَمَرَ بِصَدَقَةٍ اَوۡ مَعۡرُوۡفٍ
اَوۡ اِصۡلَاحٍۢ بَيۡنَ النَّاسِ ؕ وَمَنۡ
يَّفۡعَلۡ ذٰلِكَ ابۡتِغَآءَ مَرۡضَاتِ اللّٰهِ
فَسَوۡفَ نُـؤۡتِيۡهِ اَجۡرًا عَظِيۡمًا ﴿۱۱۴﴾

115. Whoever gives the Messenger a difficult time, even

115. Wa mañy-yushaaqiqir-Rasoola mim ba'di

وَمَنۡ يُّشَاقِقِ الرَّسُوۡلَ مِنۡۢ بَعۡدِ

after having received clear guidance, and follows a path other than that of the believers, will be left alone. We will cast him into hell, a terrible destination.

maa tabayyana lahul-hudaa wa yattabi' ghayra sabeelil-mu'mineena nuwallihee maa tawallaa wa nuṣlihee Jahannama wa saaa'at maṣeeraa.

مَا تَبَيَّنَ لَهُ الْهُدٰى وَيَتَّبِعْ
غَيْرَ سَبِيْلِ الْمُؤْمِنِيْنَ نُوَلِّهٖ مَا تَوَلّٰى
وَنُصْلِهٖ جَهَنَّمَ ۖ وَسَآءَتْ مَصِيْرًا ﴿۱۱۵﴾ ع

116. Allah will not forgive the sin of considering something equal to Him, but He may forgive the other sins of whomever He wants. One who considers anything equal to Allah has certainly gone far away from the right path.

116. Innal-laaha laa yaghfiru añy-yushraka bihee wayaghfiru maa doona ẕaalika limañy-yashaaa'; wa mañy-yushrik billaahi faqad ḍalla ḍalaalam ba'eedaa.

اِنَّ اللّٰهَ لَا يَغْفِرُ اَنْ يُّشْرَكَ بِهٖ
وَيَغْفِرُ مَا دُوْنَ ذٰلِكَ لِمَنْ يَّشَآءُ ۗ
وَمَنْ يُّشْرِكْ بِاللّٰهِ فَقَدْ ضَلَّ
ضَلٰلًاۢ بَعِيْدًا ﴿۱۱۶﴾

117. They (the pagans) only worship idols and Satan, the persistent rebel.

117. Iñy-yad'oona min dooniheee illaaa inaasaa; wa iñy-yad'oona illaa Shayṭaanam-mareedaa.

اِنْ يَّدْعُوْنَ مِنْ دُوْنِهٖۤ اِلَّاۤ اِنٰثًا ۚ
وَاِنْ يَّدْعُوْنَ اِلَّا شَيْطٰنًا مَّرِيْدًا ﴿۱۱۷﴾ وقف لازم

118. Allah condemned Satan when he said, "I will certainly take my revenge from Your servants.

118. La'anahul-laah; wa qaala la-attakhiẕanna min 'ibaadika naṣeebam mafrooḍaa.

لَّعَنَهُ اللّٰهُ ۘ وَقَالَ لَاَتَّخِذَنَّ مِنْ
عِبَادِكَ نَصِيْبًا مَّفْرُوْضًا ﴿۱۱۸﴾

119. I will lead them astray, induce in their hearts prolonged, worldly desires, command them to pierce the ears of their animals, sacrificed for the idols, and order them to change the religion of Allah." One who accepts Satan as his guardian, instead of Allah, has certainly incurred a great loss upon himself.

119. Wa la-uḍillannahum wa la-umanniyannahum wa la-aamurannahum falayubattikunna aaẕaanal-an'aami wa la-aamurannahum falayughayyirunna khalqal-laah; wa mañy-yattakhiẕish-Shayṭaana waliyyam-min doonil-laahi faqad khasira khusraanam-mubeenaa.

وَّلَاُضِلَّنَّهُمْ وَلَاُمَنِّيَنَّهُمْ وَلَاٰمُرَنَّهُمْ
فَلَيُبَتِّكُنَّ اٰذَانَ الْاَنْعَامِ وَلَاٰمُرَنَّهُمْ
فَلَيُغَيِّرُنَّ خَلْقَ اللّٰهِ ۗ وَمَنْ يَّتَّخِذِ
الشَّيْطٰنَ وَلِيًّا مِّنْ دُوْنِ اللّٰهِ فَقَدْ
خَسِرَ خُسْرَانًا مُّبِيْنًا ﴿۱۱۹﴾

120. Satan gives them false promises and tempts them to develop longings which can never be realized.

120. Ya'iduhum wa yumanneehim wa maa ya'iduhumush-Shayṭaanu illaa ghurooraa.

يَعِدُهُمْ وَيُمَنِّيْهِمْ ۗ وَمَا يَعِدُهُمُ
الشَّيْطٰنُ اِلَّا غُرُوْرًا ﴿۱۲۰﴾

121. Such people will dwell in hellfire from which they will not be able to escape.

121. Ulaaa'ika ma-waahum Jahannamu wa laa yajidoona 'anhaa maḥeeṣaa.

اُولٰٓئِكَ مَاْوٰىهُمْ جَهَنَّمُ ز وَلَا
يَجِدُوْنَ عَنْهَا مَحِيْصًا ﴿۱۲۱﴾

122. We will admit the righteously striving believers to Paradise wherein streams flow and they will live therein forever. Allah's promise is true, for no one is more truthful than Him.

122. Wallaẕeena aamanoo wa 'amiluṣ-ṣaaliḥaati sanudkhiluhum Jannaatin tajree min taḥtihal-anhaaru khaalideena feehaaa abadaa; wa'dal-laahi ḥaqqaa; wa man aṣdaqu minal-laahi qeelaa.

وَالَّذِيْنَ اٰمَنُوْا وَعَمِلُوا الصّٰلِحٰتِ
سَنُدْخِلُهُمْ جَنّٰتٍ تَجْرِيْ مِنْ
تَحْتِهَا الْاَنْهٰرُ خٰلِدِيْنَ فِيْهَآ اَبَدًا ۗ
وَعْدَ اللّٰهِ حَقًّا ۗ وَمَنْ اَصْدَقُ
مِنَ اللّٰهِ قِيْلًا ﴿۱۲۲﴾

123. Believers and People of the Book, wishes alone can never

123. Laysa bi-amaaniyyikum wa laaa amaaniyyi Ahlil-

لَيْسَ بِاَمَانِيِّكُمْ وَلَاۤ اَمَانِيِّ اَهْلِ

provide you with salvation. Whoever commits evil will be punished accordingly and no one besides Allah will be his guardian or helper.

Kitaab; mañy-ya'mal sooo'añy-yujza bihee wa laa yajid lahoo min doonil-laahi waliyyañw-wa laa naṣeeraa.

الْكِتٰبِ ۗ مَنْ يَّعْمَلْ سُوْٓءًا يُّجْزَ بِهٖ ۙ
وَلَا يَجِدْ لَهٗ مِنْ دُوْنِ اللّٰهِ وَلِيًّا
وَّلَا نَصِيْرًا ﴿١٢٣﴾

124. Any believer, male or female, who acts righteously will enter Paradise and will not suffer the least bit of injustice.

124. Wa mañy-ya'mal minaṣ-ṣaaliḥaati min zakarin aw unsaa wa huwa mu'minun fa-ulaaa'ika yadkhuloonal-Jannata wa laa yuẓlamoona naqeeraa.

وَمَنْ يَّعْمَلْ مِنَ الصّٰلِحٰتِ مِنْ
ذَكَرٍ اَوْ اُنْثٰى وَهُوَ مُؤْمِنٌ
فَاُولٰٓئِكَ يَدْخُلُوْنَ الْجَنَّةَ وَلَا
يُظْلَمُوْنَ نَقِيْرًا ﴿١٢٤﴾

125. Whose religion is better than the one in which a person submits himself to Allah, behaves righteously, and follows the upright religion of Abraham, Allah's chosen friend?

125. Wa man aḥsanu deenam-mimman aslama wajhahoo lillaahi wa huwa muḥsinuñw-wattaba'a Millata Ibraaheema Ḥaneefaa; wattakhazal-laahu Ibraaheema khaleelaa.

وَمَنْ اَحْسَنُ دِيْنًا مِّمَّنْ اَسْلَمَ
وَجْهَهٗ لِلّٰهِ وَهُوَ مُحْسِنٌ وَّاتَّبَعَ
مِلَّةَ اِبْرٰهِيْمَ حَنِيْفًا ۗ وَاتَّخَذَ
اللّٰهُ اِبْرٰهِيْمَ خَلِيْلًا ﴿١٢٥﴾

126. To Allah belongs all that is in the heavens and the earth, and He has control over all things.

126. Wa lillaahi maa fis-samaawaati wa maa fil-arḍ; wa kaanal-laahu bikulli shay'im-muḥeeṭaa.

وَلِلّٰهِ مَا فِى السَّمٰوٰتِ وَمَا فِى الْاَرْضِ ۗ
وَكَانَ اللّٰهُ بِكُلِّ شَيْءٍ مُّحِيْطًا ﴿١٢٦﴾ ع ١٨/١١/١٥

127. (Muhammad), they ask you concerning women. Tell them, "Allah will instruct you about them, besides that which can be read in the Book, about widows with children whom you wanted to marry without giving them their due rights, and He will instruct you about the rights of the weak and oppressed children. Allah commands you to maintain justice with the orphans. Allah knows all about whatever good you do.

127. Wa yastaftoonaka finnisaaa'i qulil-laahu yufteekum feehinna wa maa yutlaa 'alaykum fil-Kitaabi fee yataaman-nisaaa'il-laatee laa tu'toonahunna maa kutiba lahunna wa targhaboona an tankiḥoohunna wal-mustaḍ'afeena minal-wildaani wa an taqoomoo lilyataamaa bilqisṭ; wa maa taf'aloo min khayrin fa-innallaaha kaana bihee 'Aleemaa.

وَيَسْتَفْتُوْنَكَ فِى النِّسَآءِ ۗ قُلِ اللّٰهُ
يُفْتِيْكُمْ فِيْهِنَّ ۙ وَمَا يُتْلٰى عَلَيْكُمْ
فِى الْكِتٰبِ فِىْ يَتٰمَى النِّسَآءِ الّٰتِىْ
لَا تُؤْتُوْنَهُنَّ مَا كُتِبَ لَهُنَّ
وَتَرْغَبُوْنَ اَنْ تَنْكِحُوْهُنَّ وَ
الْمُسْتَضْعَفِيْنَ مِنَ الْوِلْدَانِ ۙ وَاَنْ
تَقُوْمُوْا لِلْيَتٰمٰى بِالْقِسْطِ ۗ وَمَا
تَفْعَلُوْا مِنْ خَيْرٍ فَاِنَّ اللّٰهَ كَانَ
بِهٖ عَلِيْمًا ﴿١٢٧﴾

128. If a woman is afraid of her husband's ill treatment and desertion, it will be no sin for both of them to reach a reconciliation. Reconciliation is good even though men's souls are swayed by greed. If you act righteously and

128. Wa-inimra-atun khaafat mim ba'lihaa nushoozan aw i'raaḍan falaa junaaḥa 'alayhimaaa añy-yuṣliḥaa baynahumaa ṣulḥaa; waṣṣulḥu khayr; wa uḥḍiratil-anfusush-

وَاِنِ امْرَاَةٌ خَافَتْ مِنْ بَعْلِهَا
نُشُوْزًا اَوْ اِعْرَاضًا فَلَا جُنَاحَ
عَلَيْهِمَآ اَنْ يُّصْلِحَا بَيْنَهُمَا صُلْحًا ۗ
وَالصُّلْحُ خَيْرٌ ۗ وَاُحْضِرَتِ الْاَنْفُسُ

be pious, Allah is Well-aware of what you do.

129. You will never be able to maintain justice among your wives and love them all equally, no matter how hard you try. Do not give total preference to one of them, leaving the other as if in suspense. If you do bring about reconciliation and maintain piety, Allah is All-forgiving and All-merciful.

130. If the marriage is terminated, Allah will make each one of them financially independent. Allah is munificent and wise.

131. To Allah belongs all that is in the heavens and the earth. We have told you and the People of the Book to have fear of Allah. If you all refuse to believe in Him, know that to Allah belongs all that is in the heavens and the earth. Allah is self-sufficient and praiseworthy.

132. To Allah belongs all that is in the heavens and the earth. Allah is a totally sufficient guardian.

133. Had Allah wanted, He could have destroyed you all and replaced you with another people; He has the power to do so.

134. Be it known to those who want worldly rewards that Allah holds the rewards for this life as well as the life to come. Allah is All-hearing and All-seeing.

135. Believers, be the supporters of justice and testify to what you may have witnessed, for the sake of Allah, even against yourselves, parents, and relatives; whether it be against the rich or the poor.

shuḥḥ; wa in tuḥsinoo wa tattaqoo fa-innallaaha kaana bimaa ta'maloona Khabeeraa.

129. Wa lan tastaṭee'ooo an ta'diloo baynan-nisaaa'i wa law ḥaraṣtum falaa tameeloo kullal-mayli fatazaroohaa kalmu'al-laqah; wa in tuṣliḥoo wa tattaqoo fa-innal-laaha kaana Ghafoorar-Raḥeemaa.

130. Wa iñy-yatafarraqaa yugh-nil-laahu kullam-min sa'atih; wa kaanal-laahu Waasi'an Ḥakeemaa.

131. Wa lillaahi maafis-sa-maawaati wa maa fil-arḍ; wa laqad waṣṣaynal-lazeena ootul-Kitaaba min qablikum wa iyyaakum anit-taqul-laah; wa in takfuroo fainna lillaahi maa fis-samaawaati wa maa fil-arḍ; wa kaanallaahu Ghaniyyan Ḥameedaa.

132. Wa lillaahi maafis-sa-maawaati wa maa fil-arḍ; wa kafaa billaahi Wakeelaa.

133. Iñy-yasha- yuz-hibkum ayyuhan-naasu wa ya-ti bi-aakhareen; wa kaanallaahu 'alaa zaalika Qadeeraa.

134. Man kaana yureedu sawaabad-dunyaa fa'indallaahi sawaabud-dunyaa wal-Aakhi-rah; wa kaanal-laahu Samee-'am-Baṣeeraa.

135. Yaaa ayyuhal-lazeena aamanoo koonoo qawwaa-meena bilqisṭi shuhada-aa'a lillaahi wa law 'alaaa anfusikum awil-waalidayni wal-aqrabeen;

الشُّحَّ ۚ وَإِنْ تُحْسِنُوا وَتَتَّقُوا فَإِنَّ
اللَّهَ كَانَ بِمَا تَعْمَلُونَ خَبِيرًا ﴿١٢٨﴾
وَلَنْ تَسْتَطِيعُوا أَنْ تَعْدِلُوا بَيْنَ
النِّسَاءِ وَلَوْ حَرَصْتُمْ ۖ فَلَا تَمِيلُوا كُلَّ
الْمَيْلِ فَتَذَرُوهَا كَالْمُعَلَّقَةِ ۚ
وَإِنْ تُصْلِحُوا وَتَتَّقُوا فَإِنَّ اللَّهَ
كَانَ غَفُورًا رَحِيمًا ﴿١٢٩﴾
وَإِنْ يَتَفَرَّقَا يُغْنِ اللَّهُ كُلًّا مِنْ
سَعَتِهِ ۚ وَكَانَ اللَّهُ وَاسِعًا حَكِيمًا ﴿١٣٠﴾
وَلِلَّهِ مَا فِي السَّمَاوَاتِ وَمَا فِي الْأَرْضِ ۗ
وَلَقَدْ وَصَّيْنَا الَّذِينَ أُوتُوا الْكِتَابَ
مِنْ قَبْلِكُمْ وَإِيَّاكُمْ أَنِ اتَّقُوا اللَّهَ ۚ
وَإِنْ تَكْفُرُوا فَإِنَّ لِلَّهِ مَا فِي
السَّمَاوَاتِ وَمَا فِي الْأَرْضِ ۚ وَكَانَ اللَّهُ
غَنِيًّا حَمِيدًا ﴿١٣١﴾
وَلِلَّهِ مَا فِي السَّمَاوَاتِ وَمَا فِي
الْأَرْضِ ۚ وَكَفَىٰ بِاللَّهِ وَكِيلًا ﴿١٣٢﴾
إِنْ يَشَأْ يُذْهِبْكُمْ أَيُّهَا النَّاسُ
وَيَأْتِ بِآخَرِينَ ۚ وَكَانَ اللَّهُ
عَلَىٰ ذَٰلِكَ قَدِيرًا ﴿١٣٣﴾
مَنْ كَانَ يُرِيدُ ثَوَابَ الدُّنْيَا فَعِنْدَ
اللَّهِ ثَوَابُ الدُّنْيَا وَالْآخِرَةِ ۚ وَكَانَ
اللَّهُ سَمِيعًا بَصِيرًا ﴿١٣٤﴾ ع ١٩ ٨ ١٦
يَا أَيُّهَا الَّذِينَ آمَنُوا كُونُوا قَوَّامِينَ
بِالْقِسْطِ شُهَدَاءَ لِلَّهِ وَلَوْ عَلَىٰ
أَنْفُسِكُمْ أَوِ الْوَالِدَيْنِ وَالْأَقْرَبِينَ ۚ

Allah must be given preference over them. Let not your desires cause you to commit injustice. If you deviate from the truth in your testimony, or decline to give your testimony at all, know that Allah is Well-aware of what you do.

iñy-yakun ghaniyyan aw faqeeran fallaahu awlaa bihimaa falaaa tattabi‘ul hawaaa an ta‘diloo; wa in talwooo aw tu‘riḍoo fa-innallaaha kaana bimaa ta‘maloona Khabeeraa.

اِنْ يَّكُنْ غَنِيًّا اَوْ فَقِيْرًا فَاللّٰهُ اَوْلٰى
بِهِمَا قف فَلَا تَتَّبِعُوا الْهَوٰٓى اَنْ
تَعْدِلُوْا ۚ وَاِنْ تَلْوٗٓا اَوْ تُعْرِضُوْا فَاِنَّ
اللّٰهَ كَانَ بِمَا تَعْمَلُوْنَ خَبِيْرًا ﴿١٣٥﴾

136. Believers, have faith in Allah and His Messenger, the Book which is revealed to him, and the Bible which has been revealed before. Whoever refuses to believe in Allah, His angels, Books, Messengers and the Day of Judgment, has gone far away from the right path.

136. Yaaa ayyuhal-laz̲eena aamanooo aaminoo billaahi wa Rasoolihee wal-Kitaabillaz̲ee nazzala ‘alaa Rasoolihee wal-Kitaabil-laz̲eee anzala min qabl; wa mañy-yakfur billaahi wa malaaa’ikatihee wa Kutubihee wa Rusulihee wal-Yawmil-Aakhiri faqad ḍalla ḍalaalam-ba‘eedaa.

يٰٓاَيُّهَا الَّذِيْنَ اٰمَنُوْٓا اٰمِنُوْا بِاللّٰهِ
وَرَسُوْلِهٖ وَالْكِتٰبِ الَّذِيْ نَزَّلَ عَلٰى
رَسُوْلِهٖ وَالْكِتٰبِ الَّذِيْٓ اَنْزَلَ مِنْ
قَبْلُ ؕ وَمَنْ يَّكْفُرْ بِاللّٰهِ وَمَلٰٓئِكَتِهٖ
وَكُتُبِهٖ وَرُسُلِهٖ وَالْيَوْمِ الْاٰخِرِ
فَقَدْ ضَلَّ ضَلٰلًاۢ بَعِيْدًا ﴿١٣٦﴾

137. Allah would not forgive or guide to the right path those who first believe, then disbelieve, again believe and disbelieve, and then increase their disbelief.

137. Innal-laz̲eena aamanoo s̲umma kafaroo s̲umma aamanoo s̲umma kafaroo s̲ummaz-daadoo kufral-lam yakunil-laahu liyaghfira lahum wa laa liyahdiyahum sabeelaa.

اِنَّ الَّذِيْنَ اٰمَنُوْا ثُمَّ كَفَرُوْا ثُمَّ
اٰمَنُوْا ثُمَّ كَفَرُوْا ثُمَّ ازْدَادُوْا كُفْرًا
لَّمْ يَكُنِ اللّٰهُ لِيَغْفِرَ لَهُمْ وَلَا
لِيَهْدِيَهُمْ سَبِيْلًا ؕ ﴿١٣٧﴾

138. Tell the hypocrites that for them there will be a painful torment.

138. Bashshiril-munaafiqeena bi-anna lahum ‘az̲aaban aleemaa.

بَشِّرِ الْمُنٰفِقِيْنَ بِاَنَّ لَهُمْ عَذَابًا اَلِيْمَا ۙ ﴿١٣٨﴾

139. Do those who establish friendship with the unbelievers instead of the believers seek honor? Let them know that all honor belongs to Allah.

139. Allaz̲eena yattakhiz̲oo-nal-kaafireena awliyaaa’a min doonil-mu’mineen; ayabta-ghoona ‘indahumul-‘izzata fa-innal-‘izzata lillaahi jamee‘aa.

الَّذِيْنَ يَتَّخِذُوْنَ الْكٰفِرِيْنَ اَوْلِيَآءَ
مِنْ دُوْنِ الْمُؤْمِنِيْنَ ؕ اَيَبْتَغُوْنَ
عِنْدَهُمُ الْعِزَّةَ فَاِنَّ الْعِزَّةَ لِلّٰهِ
جَمِيْعًا ؕ ﴿١٣٩﴾

140. Allah has told you (believers) in the Book that when you hear people disbelieving and mocking Allah's revelations, do not sit with them unless they change the subject. You will become like them. Allah will gather all the hypocrites and the unbelievers together in hellfire.

140. Wa qad nazzala ‘alaykum fil-Kitaabi an iz̲aa sami‘tum Aayaatil-laahi yukfaru bihaa wa yustahza-u bihaa falaa taq‘udoo ma‘ahum ḥattaa yakhooḍoo fee ḥadees̲in ghayrih; innakum iz̲am-mis̲luhum; innal-laaha jaami‘ul-munaafiqeena wal-kaafireena fee Jahannama jamee‘aa.

وَقَدْ نَزَّلَ عَلَيْكُمْ فِي الْكِتٰبِ اَنْ اِذَا
سَمِعْتُمْ اٰيٰتِ اللّٰهِ يُكْفَرُ بِهَا وَيُسْتَهْزَاُ
بِهَا فَلَا تَقْعُدُوْا مَعَهُمْ حَتّٰى يَخُوْضُوْا
فِيْ حَدِيْثٍ غَيْرِهٖٓ ۖ اِنَّكُمْ اِذًا مِّثْلُهُمْ ؕ
اِنَّ اللّٰهَ جَامِعُ الْمُنٰفِقِيْنَ وَالْكٰفِرِيْنَ
فِيْ جَهَنَّمَ جَمِيْعًا ۙ ﴿١٤٠﴾

141. (The hypocrites) wait and watch. If Allah grants you victory,

141. Allaz̲eena yatarab-baṣoona bikum fa-in kaana

الَّذِيْنَ يَتَرَبَّصُوْنَ بِكُمْ ۚ فَاِنْ كَانَ

they say, "Did we not help you?" If the unbelievers are victorious, they say, "Did we not encourage you not to surrender to the believers and did we not protect you from them?" Allah will judge among you on the Day of Judgment. He will never help the unbelievers against the believers.

lakum fatḥum-minallaahi qaalooo alam nakum ma'akum wa in kaana lilkaafireena naṣeebun qaalooo alam nastaḥwiz̲ 'alaykum wa namna'kum minal-mu'mineen; fallaahu yaḥkumu baynakum Yawmal-Qiyaamah; wa lañy-yaj'alal-laahu lilkaafireena 'alal mu'mineena sabeelaa.

لَكُمْ فَتْحٌ مِّنَ اللّٰهِ قَالُوْٓا اَلَمْ نَكُنْ
مَّعَكُمْ ۖ وَاِنْ كَانَ لِلْكٰفِرِيْنَ نَصِيْبٌ ۙ
قَالُوْٓا اَلَمْ نَسْتَحْوِذْ عَلَيْكُمْ وَنَمْنَعْكُمْ
مِّنَ الْمُؤْمِنِيْنَ ؕ فَاللّٰهُ يَحْكُمُ بَيْنَكُمْ
يَوْمَ الْقِيٰمَةِ ؕ وَلَنْ يَّجْعَلَ اللّٰهُ لِلْكٰفِرِيْنَ
عَلَى الْمُؤْمِنِيْنَ سَبِيْلًا ﴿۱۴۱﴾ ع ١٧/٧

142. The hypocrites try to deceive Allah but He causes them to suffer punishment. They stand up in prayer lazily just to show that they pray, but in truth they remember Allah very little.

142. Innal-munaafiqeena yukhaadi'oonal-laaha wa huwa khaadi'uhum wa iz̲aa qaamooo ilaṣ-Ṣalaati qaamoo kusaalaa yuraaa'oonan-naasa wa laa yaz̲kuroonal-laaha illaa qaleelaa.

اِنَّ الْمُنٰفِقِيْنَ يُخٰدِعُوْنَ اللّٰهَ وَهُوَ
خَادِعُهُمْ ۚ وَاِذَا قَامُوْٓا اِلَى الصَّلٰوةِ
قَامُوْا كُسَالٰى ۙ يُرَآءُوْنَ النَّاسَ وَلَا
يَذْكُرُوْنَ اللّٰهَ اِلَّا قَلِيْلًا ﴿۱۴۲﴾

143. They are hesitant people belonging to neither side. You can find no other way for one whom Allah has caused to go astray.

143. Muz̲abz̲abeena bayna z̲aalika laaa ilaa haaa'ulaaa'i wa laaa ilaa haaa'ulaaa'; wa mañy-yuḍlilil-laahu falan tajida lahoo sabeelaa.

مُّذَبْذَبِيْنَ بَيْنَ ذٰلِكَ ۖ لَآ اِلٰى
هٰٓؤُلَآءِ وَلَآ اِلٰى هٰٓؤُلَآءِ ؕ وَمَنْ يُّضْلِلِ
اللّٰهُ فَلَنْ تَجِدَ لَهٗ سَبِيْلًا ﴿۱۴۳﴾

144. Believers, do not make unbelievers your intimate friends and supporters rather than believers. Do you want to establish clear evidence against yourselves before Allah?

144. Yaaa ayyuhal-laz̲eena aamanoo laa tattakhiz̲ul-kaafireena awliyaaa'a min doonil-mu'mineen; atureedoona an taj'aloo lillaahi 'alaykum sulṭaanam-mubeenaa.

يٰٓاَيُّهَا الَّذِيْنَ اٰمَنُوْا لَا تَتَّخِذُوا
الْكٰفِرِيْنَ اَوْلِيَآءَ مِنْ دُوْنِ الْمُؤْمِنِيْنَ ؕ
اَتُرِيْدُوْنَ اَنْ تَجْعَلُوْا لِلّٰهِ عَلَيْكُمْ
سُلْطٰنًا مُّبِيْنًا ﴿۱۴۴﴾

145. The hypocrites will be placed in the lowest level of the fire and none of you will ever find a helper for them,

145. Innal-munaafiqeena fid-darkil-asfali minan-Naari wa lan tajida lahum naṣeeraa.

اِنَّ الْمُنٰفِقِيْنَ فِى الدَّرْكِ الْاَسْفَلِ
مِنَ النَّارِ ۚ وَلَنْ تَجِدَ لَهُمْ نَصِيْرًا ﴿۱۴۵﴾

146. except those (hypocrites) who have repented, placed their trust in Allah, and sincerely followed only His religion, will live with the believers to whom Allah will give a great reward.

146. Illal-laz̲eena taaboo wa aṣlaḥoo wa'taṣamoo billaahi wa akhlaṣoo deenahum lillaahi faulaaa'ika ma'al-mu'mineena wa sawfa yu'til-laahul-mu'mineena ajran 'aẓeemaa.

اِلَّا الَّذِيْنَ تَابُوْا وَاَصْلَحُوْا وَاعْتَصَمُوْا
بِاللّٰهِ وَاَخْلَصُوْا دِيْنَهُمْ لِلّٰهِ فَاُولٰٓئِكَ
مَعَ الْمُؤْمِنِيْنَ ؕ وَسَوْفَ يُؤْتِ اللّٰهُ
الْمُؤْمِنِيْنَ اَجْرًا عَظِيْمًا ﴿۱۴۶﴾

147. Why should Allah punish you if you give thanks and believe in Him? Allah is All-rewarding and All-forgiving.

147. Maa yaf'alul-laahu bi-'az̲aabikum in shakartum wa aamantum; wa kaanallaahu Shaakiran 'Aleemaa.

مَا يَفْعَلُ اللّٰهُ بِعَذَابِكُمْ اِنْ شَكَرْتُمْ
وَاٰمَنْتُمْ ؕ وَكَانَ اللّٰهُ شَاكِرًا عَلِيْمًا ﴿۱۴۷﴾
لَا يُحِبُّ اللّٰهُ الْجَهْرَ بِالسُّوْٓءِ

148. Allah does not love public accusation unless one is truly wronged. Allah is All-hearing and All-knowing.

149. Whether you act virtuously, in public or in private, or pardon (people's) faults, Allah is All-forgiving and All-powerful.

150. Those who disbelieve in Allah and His Messengers try to create differences between Allah and His Messengers (by rejecting their message). They say, "We believe in some but not in others." Thus, they try to find a middle way

151. but, in fact, they are unbelievers, and for them We have prepared a humiliating torment.

152. As for those who believe in Allah and made no distinction between His Messengers, they will receive His reward. Allah is All-forgiving and All-merciful.

153. (Muhammad), the People of the Book ask you to make a Book descend to them from the heavens. However, they had asked Moses for things much harder to do than this, by saying, "Show us Allah in person." Thunder and lightning struck them because of their unjust demands. Despite all the evidence that had come to them, they started to worship the calf, but We forgave them for their sins and gave Moses clear authority.

154. We raised Mount (Sinai) above them because of Our solemn promise to them. Also, We told them to prostrate themselves when entering the gate (of the holy house) and not to commit transgression on the Sabbath. We made a solemn

148. Laa yuḥibbul-laahul-jahra bis-sooo'i. minal-qawli illaa man ẓulim; wa kaanallaahu Samee'an 'Aleemaa.

149. In tubdoo khayran aw tukhfoohu aw ta'foo 'an sooo'in fa-innal-laaha kaana 'Afuwwan Qadeeraa.

150. Innal-lazeena yakfuroona billaahi wa Rusulihee wa yureedoona añy-yufarriqoo baynal-laahi wa Rusulihee wa yaqooloona nu'minu biba'ḍiñw-wa nakfuru biba'ḍiñw-wa yureedoona añy-yattakhizoo bayna zaalika sabeelaa.

151. Ulaaa'ika humul-kaafiroona ḥaqqaa; wa a'tadnaa lilkaafireena 'azaabam-muheenaa.

152. Wallazeena aamanoo billaahi wa Rusulihee wa lam yufarriqoo bayna aḥadim-minhum ulaaa'ika sawfa yu'teehim ujoorahum; wa kaanal-laahu Ghafoorar-Raḥeemaa.

153. Yas'aluka-Ahlul-Kitaabi an tunazzila 'alayhim Kitaabam-minas-samaaa'i faqad sa-aloo Moosaaa akbara min zaalika faqaalooo arinal-laaha jahratan fa-akhazat-humuṣ-ṣaa'iqatu biẓulmihim; summat-takhazul-'ijla mim ba'di maa jaa'athumul-bayyinaatu fa'afawnaa 'an zaalik; wa aataynaa Moosaa sulṭaanam-mubeenaa.

154. Wa rafa'naa fawqahumuṭ-Ṭoora bimeesaaqihim wa qulnaa lahumud-khulul-baaba sujjadañw-wa qulnaa lahum laa ta'doo fis-Sabti

مِنَ الْقَوْلِ إِلَّا مَن ظُلِمَ ۚ وَكَانَ
اللَّهُ سَمِيعًا عَلِيمًا ﴿١٤٨﴾
إِن تُبْدُوا خَيْرًا أَوْ تُخْفُوهُ أَوْ تَعْفُوا
عَن سُوءٍ فَإِنَّ اللَّهَ كَانَ عَفُوًّا قَدِيرًا ﴿١٤٩﴾
إِنَّ الَّذِينَ يَكْفُرُونَ بِاللَّهِ وَرُسُلِهِ
وَيُرِيدُونَ أَن يُفَرِّقُوا بَيْنَ اللَّهِ
وَرُسُلِهِ وَيَقُولُونَ نُؤْمِنُ بِبَعْضٍ
وَنَكْفُرُ بِبَعْضٍ وَيُرِيدُونَ أَن
يَتَّخِذُوا بَيْنَ ذَٰلِكَ سَبِيلًا ﴿١٥٠﴾
أُولَٰئِكَ هُمُ الْكَافِرُونَ حَقًّا ۚ وَأَعْتَدْنَا
لِلْكَافِرِينَ عَذَابًا مُّهِينًا ﴿١٥١﴾
وَالَّذِينَ آمَنُوا بِاللَّهِ وَرُسُلِهِ وَلَمْ
يُفَرِّقُوا بَيْنَ أَحَدٍ مِّنْهُمْ أُولَٰئِكَ
سَوْفَ يُؤْتِيهِمْ أُجُورَهُمْ ۗ وَكَانَ
اللَّهُ غَفُورًا رَّحِيمًا ﴿١٥٢﴾ ع ١١
يَسْأَلُكَ أَهْلُ الْكِتَابِ أَن تُنَزِّلَ
عَلَيْهِمْ كِتَابًا مِّنَ السَّمَاءِ ۚ فَقَدْ سَأَلُوا
مُوسَىٰ أَكْبَرَ مِن ذَٰلِكَ فَقَالُوا أَرِنَا
اللَّهَ جَهْرَةً فَأَخَذَتْهُمُ الصَّاعِقَةُ
بِظُلْمِهِمْ ۚ ثُمَّ اتَّخَذُوا الْعِجْلَ
مِن بَعْدِ مَا جَاءَتْهُمُ الْبَيِّنَاتُ
فَعَفَوْنَا عَن ذَٰلِكَ ۚ وَآتَيْنَا مُوسَىٰ
سُلْطَانًا مُّبِينًا ﴿١٥٣﴾
وَرَفَعْنَا فَوْقَهُمُ الطُّورَ بِمِيثَاقِهِمْ
وَقُلْنَا لَهُمُ ادْخُلُوا الْبَابَ سُجَّدًا
وَقُلْنَا لَهُمْ لَا تَعْدُوا فِي السَّبْتِ

covenant with them.

wa akhaznaa minhum meesaa-qan ghaleezaa.

وَاَخَذْنَا مِنْهُمْ مِّيْثَاقًا غَلِيْظًا ﴿١٥٤﴾

155. However, because of their disbelief, disregard of their covenant, denial of Allah's revelations, murder of the Prophets without reason, and their saying that their hearts were covered, We sealed up their hearts. Only a few of them believe.

155. Fabimaa naqḍihim mee-saaqahum wa kufrihim bi-Aayaatil-laahi wa qatlihimul-Ambiyaaa'a bighayri ḥaqqiñw-wa qawlihim quloobunaa ghulf; bal ṭaba'allaahu 'alayhaa bikufri-him falaa yu'minoona illaa qaleelaa.

فَبِمَا نَقْضِهِمْ مِّيْثَاقَهُمْ وَكُفْرِهِمْ
بِاٰيٰتِ اللّٰهِ وَقَتْلِهِمُ الْاَنْۢبِيَآءَ بِغَيْرِ
حَقٍّ وَّقَوْلِهِمْ قُلُوْبُنَا غُلْفٌ ۭ بَلْ طَبَعَ
اللّٰهُ عَلَيْهَا بِكُفْرِهِمْ فَلَا يُؤْمِنُوْنَ
اِلَّا قَلِيْلًا ﴿١٥٥﴾

156. Their hearts were also sealed because of their lack of faith, their gravely slanderous accusation against Mary,

156. Wa bikufrihim wa qawli-him 'alaa Maryama buh-taanan 'azeemaa.

وَّبِكُفْرِهِمْ وَقَوْلِهِمْ عَلٰى مَرْيَمَ
بُهْتَانًا عَظِيْمًا ﴿١٥٦﴾

157. and their statement that they murdered Jesus, son of Mary, the Messenger of Allah, when, in fact, they could not have murdered him or crucified him. They, in fact, murdered someone else by mistake. Even those who disputed (the question of whether or not Jesus was murdered) did not have a shred of evidence. All that they knew about it was mere conjecture. They certainly could not have murdered Jesus.

157. Wa qawlihim innaa qatal-nal-Maseeḥa 'Eesab-na-Maryama Rasoolal-laahi wa maa qataloohu wa maa ṣalaboohu wa laakin shubbiha lahum; wa innal-lazeenakh-talafoo feehi lafee shakkim-minh; maa lahum bihee min 'ilmin illat-tibaa'az-ẓann; wa maa qataloohu yaqeenaa.

وَّقَوْلِهِمْ اِنَّا قَتَلْنَا الْمَسِيْحَ عِيْسَى
ابْنَ مَرْيَمَ رَسُوْلَ اللّٰهِ ۚ وَمَا قَتَلُوْهُ
وَمَا صَلَبُوْهُ وَلٰكِنْ شُبِّهَ لَهُمْ ۭ
وَاِنَّ الَّذِيْنَ اخْتَلَفُوْا فِيْهِ لَفِيْ شَكٍّ
مِّنْهُ ۭ مَا لَهُمْ بِهٖ مِنْ عِلْمٍ اِلَّا
اتِّبَاعَ الظَّنِّ ۚ وَمَا قَتَلُوْهُ يَقِيْنًا ﴿١٥٧﴾

158. Allah raised him up to Himself. Allah is Majestic and All-wise.

158. Bar-rafa'ahul-laahu ilayh; wa kaanal-laahu 'Azee-zan Ḥakeemaa.

بَلْ رَّفَعَهُ اللّٰهُ اِلَيْهِ ۭ وَكَانَ اللّٰهُ
عَزِيْزًا حَكِيْمًا ﴿١٥٨﴾

159. There will be no one among the People of the Book who will not believe in him before their deaths. On the Day of Judgment, he will testify against them.

159. Wa im-min Ahlil-Kitaabi illaa layu'minanna bihee qabla mawtihee wa Yawmal-Qiyaamati yakoonu 'alayhim shaheedaa.

وَاِنْ مِّنْ اَهْلِ الْكِتٰبِ اِلَّا لَيُؤْمِنَنَّ
بِهٖ قَبْلَ مَوْتِهٖ ۚ وَيَوْمَ الْقِيٰمَةِ
يَكُوْنُ عَلَيْهِمْ شَهِيْدًا ﴿١٥٩﴾

160. We made unlawful for the Jews certain pure things which had been lawful for them before, because of the injustice which they had committed, their obstructing many people from the way of Allah,

160. Fabiẓulmim-minalla-zeena haadoo ḥarramnaa 'alayhim ṭayyibaatin uḥillat lahum wa biṣaddihim 'an sabeelil-laahi kaseeraa.

فَبِظُلْمٍ مِّنَ الَّذِيْنَ هَادُوْا حَرَّمْنَا
عَلَيْهِمْ طَيِّبٰتٍ اُحِلَّتْ لَهُمْ وَبِصَدِّهِمْ
عَنْ سَبِيْلِ اللّٰهِ كَثِيْرًا ﴿١٦٠﴾

161. their taking usury which was prohibited for them, and their consuming people's property unjustly. For the unbelievers among them, We have prepared a painful torment.

161. Wa akhzihimur-ribaa wa qad nuhoo 'anhu wa aklihim amwaalan-naasi bilbaaṭil; wa a'tadnaa lilkaafireena minhum 'azaaban aleemaa.

وَّاَخْذِهِمُ الرِّبٰوا وَقَدْ نُهُوْا عَنْهُ
وَاَكْلِهِمْ اَمْوَالَ النَّاسِ بِالْبَاطِلِ ۭ
وَاَعْتَدْنَا لِلْكٰفِرِيْنَ مِنْهُمْ عَذَابًا
اَلِيْمًا ﴿١٦١﴾

162. However, the learned among them (the Jews) and the faithful believe in what Allah has revealed to you (Muhammad) and to the others before you, and to those who are steadfast in prayer, pay their religious tax, and believe in Allah and the Day of Judgment. They will all receive a great reward from Us.

162. Laakinir-raasikhoona fil‘ilmi minhum walmu’minoona yu’minoona bimaaa unzila ilayka wa maaa unzila min qablika walmuqeemeenaṣ-Ṣalaata walmu’toonaz-Zakaata walmu’minoona billaahi wal-Yawmil-Aakhir; ulaaa’ika sanu’teehim ajran ‘aẓeemaa.

163. (Muhammad), We have sent revelations to you just they as were sent to Noah and the Prophets who lived after him and to Abraham, Ishmael, Isaac, Jacob, his descendants, Jesus, Job, Jonah, Aaron, and Solomon. We gave the Psalms to David.

163. Innaaa awḥaynaaa ilayka kamaaa awḥaynaaa ilaa Nooḥiñw-wan-Nabiyyeena mim ba‘dih; wa awḥaynaaa ilaaa Ibraaheema wa Ismaa‘eela wa Isḥaqa wa Ya‘qooba wal Asbaaṭi wa ‘Eesaa wa Ayyooba wa Yoonusa wa Haaroona wa Sulaymaan; wa aataynaa Daawooda Zabooraa.

164. (We sent revelations to) the Messengers mentioned to you before and also to Messengers who had not been mentioned to you. Allah spoke to Moses in words.

164. Wa Rusulan qad qaṣaṣ-naahum ‘alayka min qablu wa Rusulal-lam naqṣuṣhum ‘alayk; wa kallamallaahu Moosaa takleemaa.

165. The Messengers were sent to give people the glad news (of Allah's mercy) and warn them (of His punishment) so that the human being would not have any objections against Allah, after the coming of the Messengers (that they did not have any knowledge of His mercy and punishment). Allah is Majestic and All-wise.

165. Rusulam-mubashshireena wa munzireena li’allaa yakoona linnaasi ‘alal-laahi ḥujjatum ba‘dar-Rusul; wa kaanallaahu ‘Azeezan Ḥakeemaa.

166. Allah testifies that whatever He has revealed to you (Muhammad) He has revealed it on purpose, and the angels also testify to it, but Allah's testimony alone is sufficient.

166. Laakinil-laahu yashhadu bimaaa anzala ilayka anzalahoo bi‘ilmihee wal-malaaa’ikatu yashhadoon; wa kafaa billaahi Shaheedaa.

167. Those who have rejected the faith and have obstructed people from the way of Allah have certainly gone far away from the right path.

167. Innal-lazeena kafaroo wa ṣaddoo ‘an sabeelil-laahi qad ḍalloo ḍalaalam ba‘eedaa.

168. Allah would not forgive those who have rejected the faith and committed injustice, nor will He guide them to any way

168. Innal-lazeena kafaroo wa ẓalamoo lam yakunillaahu liyaghfira lahum wa laa liyahdiyahum ṭareeqaa.

لٰكِنِ الرّٰسِخُونَ فِى الْعِلْمِ مِنْهُمْ وَالْمُؤْمِنُونَ يُؤْمِنُونَ بِمَآ اُنْزِلَ اِلَيْكَ وَمَآ اُنْزِلَ مِنْ قَبْلِكَ وَ الْمُقِيْمِيْنَ الصَّلٰوةَ وَالْمُؤْتُونَ الزَّكٰوةَ وَالْمُؤْمِنُونَ بِاللّٰهِ وَالْيَوْمِ الْاٰخِرِ ۗ اُولٰٓئِكَ سَنُؤْتِيْهِمْ اَجْرًا عَظِيْمًا ۝

اِنَّآ اَوْحَيْنَآ اِلَيْكَ كَمَآ اَوْحَيْنَآ اِلٰى نُوْحٍ وَّ النَّبِيّٖنَ مِنْ بَعْدِهٖ ۚ وَاَوْحَيْنَآ اِلٰٓى اِبْرٰهِيْمَ وَاِسْمٰعِيْلَ وَاِسْحٰقَ وَيَعْقُوْبَ وَالْاَسْبَاطِ وَعِيْسٰى وَاَيُّوْبَ وَيُوْنُسَ وَهٰرُوْنَ وَسُلَيْمٰنَ ۚ وَاٰتَيْنَا دَاوٗدَ زَبُوْرًا ۝

وَرُسُلًا قَدْ قَصَصْنٰهُمْ عَلَيْكَ مِنْ قَبْلُ وَرُسُلًا لَّمْ نَقْصُصْهُمْ عَلَيْكَ ۚ وَكَلَّمَ اللّٰهُ مُوْسٰى تَكْلِيْمًا ۝

رُسُلًا مُّبَشِّرِيْنَ وَمُنْذِرِيْنَ لِئَلَّا يَكُوْنَ لِلنَّاسِ عَلَى اللّٰهِ حُجَّةٌۢ بَعْدَ الرُّسُلِ ۗ وَكَانَ اللّٰهُ عَزِيْزًا حَكِيْمًا ۝

لٰكِنِ اللّٰهُ يَشْهَدُ بِمَآ اَنْزَلَ اِلَيْكَ اَنْزَلَهٗ بِعِلْمِهٖ ۚ وَالْمَلٰٓئِكَةُ يَشْهَدُوْنَ ۗ وَكَفٰى بِاللّٰهِ شَهِيْدًا ۝

اِنَّ الَّذِيْنَ كَفَرُوْا وَصَدُّوْا عَنْ سَبِيْلِ اللّٰهِ قَدْ ضَلُّوْا ضَلٰلًاۢ بَعِيْدًا ۝

اِنَّ الَّذِيْنَ كَفَرُوْا وَظَلَمُوْا لَمْ يَكُنِ اللّٰهُ لِيَغْفِرَ لَهُمْ وَلَا لِيَهْدِيَهُمْ طَرِيْقًا ۝

169. other than that of hell wherein they will live forever. For Allah this is not in the least bit difficult.

169. Illaa ṭareeqa Jahannama khaalideena feehaaa abadaa; wa kaana z̲aalika 'alal-laahi yaseeraa.

إلا طريق جهنم خلدين فيها
أبدا ط وكان ذلك على الله يسيرا ﴿١٦٩﴾

170. Mankind, the Messenger has come to you from your Lord in all Truth. It is for your own good to believe in him, but if you disbelieve, know that to Allah belongs all that is in the heavens and the earth. Allah is All-knowing and All-wise.

170. Yaaa ayyuhan-naasu qad jaaa'akumur-Rasoolu bilḥaqqi mir-Rabbikum fa-aaminoo khayral-lakum; wa in takfuroo fainna lillaahi maa fis-samaawaati wal-arḍ; wa kaanal-laahu 'Aleeman Ḥakeemaa.

يأيها الناس قد جاءكم الرسول
بالحق من ربكم فامنوا خيرا
لكم ط وإن تكفروا فإن لله ما في
السموت والأرض ط وكان الله
عليما حكيما ﴿١٧٠﴾

171. People of the Book, do not exceed the limits of devotion in your religion or say anything about Allah which is not the Truth. Jesus, son of Mary, is only a Messenger of Allah, His Word, and a spirit from Him whom He conveyed to Mary. So have faith in Allah and His Messengers. Do not say that there are three (gods). It is better for you to stop believing in the Trinity. Allah is only One Lord. He is free of all defects; how can He have a son? To Allah belongs all that is in the heavens and the earth. Allah alone is a sufficient guardian for all.

171. Yaaa Ahlal-Kitaabi laa taghloo fee deenikum wa laa taqooloo 'alal-laahi illalḥaqq; innamal-Maseeḥu 'Eesab-nu-Maryama Rasoolul-laahi wa Kalimatuhooo alqaahaaa ilaa Maryama wa rooḥumminhu fa-aaminoo billaahi wa Rusulihee wa laa taqooloo s̲alaas̲ah; intahoo khayrallakum; innamal-laahu Ilaahuñw-Waaḥid; Subḥaanahooo añy-yakoona lahoo walad; lahoo maa fissamaawaati wa maa fil-arḍ; wa kafaa billaahi Wakeelaa.

يأهل الكتب لا تغلوا في دينكم
ولا تقولوا على الله إلا الحق ط إنما
المسيح عيسى ابن مريم رسول الله
وكلمته ج ألقها إلى مريم وروح
منه ز فامنوا بالله ورسله قف ولا
تقولوا ثلثة ط انتهوا خيرا لكم ط
إنما الله إله وحد ط سبحنه أن
يكون له ولد م له ما في السموت
وما في الأرض ط وكفى بالله وكيلا ﴿١٧١﴾ ع

وقف لازم ع ٢٣ ٩ ٣

172. Jesus never disdained the worship of Allah nor did the nearest angels to Allah. Whoever, out of pride, disdains the worship of Allah should know that everyone will be brought before Him.

172. Lañy-yastankifal-Maseeḥu añy-yakoona 'abdal-lillaahi wa lalmalaaa'ikatul-muqarraboon; wa mañy-yastankif 'an 'ibaadatihee wa yastakbir fasayaḥshuruhum ilayhi jamee'aa.

لن يستنكف المسيح أن يكون
عبدا لله ولا الملئكة المقربون ط
ومن يستنكف عن عبادته
ويستكبر فسيحشرهم إليه جميعا ﴿١٧٢﴾

173. The righteously striving believers will receive the reward for their deeds and extra favors from Allah. But those who disdain the worship of Allah out of pride will suffer the most painful torment. They will find no guardian or helper besides Allah.

173. Fa-ammal-laz̲eena aamanoo wa 'amiluṣ-ṣaaliḥaati fayuwaffeehim ujoorahum wa yazeeduhum-min faḍlihee wa ammallaz̲eenas-tankafoo wastakbaroo fayu'az̲-z̲ibuhum 'az̲aaban aleemañw-wa laa yajidoona lahum min doonil-laahi waliyyañw-wa laa naṣeeraa.

فأما الذين ءامنوا وعملوا الصلحت
فيوفيهم أجورهم ويزيدهم من
فضله ج وأما الذين استنكفوا و
استكبروا فيعذبهم عذابا أليما ٥ لا
ولا يجدون لهم من دون الله
وليا ولا نصيرا ﴿١٧٣﴾

174. Mankind, an undeniable proof has certainly come to you and We have sent you a shining light.

174. Yaaa-ayyuhan-naasu qad jaaa'akum burhaanum-mir-Rabbikum wa anzalnaaa ilaykum Nooram-Mubeenaa.

يٰۤاَيُّهَا النَّاسُ قَدْ جَآءَكُمْ
بُرْهَانٌ مِّنْ رَّبِّكُمْ وَاَنْزَلْنَاۤ
اِلَيْكُمْ نُوْرًا مُّبِيْنًا ﴿١٧٤﴾

175. Those who believe in Allah and seek His protection will receive His mercy, favors, and guidance to the right path.

175. Fa-ammal-lazeena aamanoo billaahi wa'taṣamoo bihee fasayud-khiluhum fee raḥmatim-minhu wa faḍliñw-wa yahdeehim ilayhi Ṣiraaṭam-Mustaqeema.

فَاَمَّا الَّذِيْنَ اٰمَنُوْا بِاللّٰهِ وَاعْتَصَمُوْا
بِهٖ فَسَيُدْخِلُهُمْ فِيْ رَحْمَةٍ مِّنْهُ
وَفَضْلٍ ۙ وَّيَهْدِيْهِمْ اِلَيْهِ صِرَاطًا
مُّسْتَقِيْمًا ﴿١٧٥﴾

176. (Muhammad), they seek your verdict. Tell them, "Allah commands this concerning your kindred: If a man dies childless but has a sister, she will receive half of the legacy. If a woman died childless, her brother will receive the whole legacy. If a childless man leaves only two sisters, both together will receive two-thirds of the legacy. If the heirs are both sisters and brothers, the share of the male will be twice as much as the share of the female. Allah explains His Laws to you so that you will not go astray. Allah knows all things.

176. Yastaftoonaka qulillaahu yufteekum fil-kalaalah; inimru'un halaka laysa lahoo waladuñw-wa lahooo ukhtun falahaa niṣfu maa tarak; wa huwa yarisuhaaa il-lam yakullahaa walad; fa-in kaanatas-natayni falahumas-sulusaani mimmaa tarak; wa in kaanooo ikhwatar-rijaalañw- wa nisaaa'an faliz-zakari mislu ḥazzil-unsayayn; yubayyinullaahu lakum an taḍilloo; wallaahu bikulli shay'in 'Aleem.

يَسْتَفْتُوْنَكَ ۗ قُلِ اللّٰهُ يُفْتِيْكُمْ فِي
الْكَلٰلَةِ ۗ اِنِ امْرُؤٌا هَلَكَ لَيْسَ لَهٗ
وَلَدٌ وَّلَهٗۤ اُخْتٌ فَلَهَا نِصْفُ مَا تَرَكَ ۚ
وَهُوَ يَرِثُهَاۤ اِنْ لَّمْ يَكُنْ لَّهَا وَلَدٌ ۚ
فَاِنْ كَانَتَا اثْنَتَيْنِ فَلَهُمَا الثُّلُثٰنِ
مِمَّا تَرَكَ ۗ وَاِنْ كَانُوْۤا اِخْوَةً رِّجَالًا
وَّنِسَآءً فَلِلذَّكَرِ مِثْلُ حَظِّ الْاُنْثَيَيْنِ ۗ
يُبَيِّنُ اللّٰهُ لَكُمْ اَنْ تَضِلُّوْا ۗ
وَاللّٰهُ بِكُلِّ شَيْءٍ عَلِيْمٌ ﴿١٧٦﴾ ع ٢٤ ٥

Al-Maidah, The Table (5)

In the Name of Allah, the Beneficent, the Merciful.

Sûrat al-Mâ'idah-5

(Revealed at Madinah)

Bismillaahir Raḥmaanir Raḥeem

(٥) سُوْرَةُ الْمَآئِدَةِ مَدَنِيَّةٌ (١١٢)

آياتها ١٢٠ بِسْمِ اللّٰهِ الرَّحْمٰنِ الرَّحِيْمِ ركوعاتها ١٦

1. Believers, stand by your contracts (and obligations).

Of all animals, cattle have been made lawful for you as food with certain exceptions.

Hunting is not lawful for you during Ihrarm (a part of the formal procedure during pilgrimage). Allah decrees as He wills.

1. Yaaa-ayyuhal-lazeena aamanooo awfoo bil'uqood; uḥillat lakum baheematul-an'aami illaa maa yutlaa 'alaykum ghayra muḥilliṣ-ṣaydi wa antum ḥurum; innal-laaha yaḥkumu maa yureed.

يٰۤاَيُّهَا الَّذِيْنَ اٰمَنُوْۤا اَوْفُوْا بِالْعُقُوْدِ ۗ
اُحِلَّتْ لَكُمْ بَهِيْمَةُ الْاَنْعَامِ اِلَّا مَا يُتْلٰى
عَلَيْكُمْ غَيْرَ مُحِلِّي الصَّيْدِ وَاَنْتُمْ
حُرُمٌ ۗ اِنَّ اللّٰهَ يَحْكُمُ مَا يُرِيْدُ ﴿١﴾

2. O Believers, do not disrespect the reminders of Allah, the sacred months, the animals brought for sacrifice, or what is marked for sacrificial offering or the people heading to the precinct of the Sacred House to seek the favor and pleasure of their Lord.

2. Yaaa ayyuhal-lazeena aamanoo laa tuḥilloo sha'aaa-'iral-laahi wa lash-Shahral-Ḥaraama wa lalhadya wa lal-qalaaa'ida wa laaa aaammeenal-Baytal-Ḥaraama yabtaghoona faḍlam-mir-Rabbihim wa riḍwaanaa;

يٰۤاَيُّهَا الَّذِيْنَ اٰمَنُوْا لَا تُحِلُّوْا شَعَآئِرَ
اللّٰهِ وَلَا الشَّهْرَ الْحَرَامَ وَلَا الْهَدْيَ
وَلَا الْقَلَآئِدَ وَلَاۤ اٰمِّيْنَ الْبَيْتَ الْحَرَامَ
يَبْتَغُوْنَ فَضْلًا مِّنْ رَّبِّهِمْ وَرِضْوَانًا ۗ

Once the restrictions of Ihrarm are over, you may hunt. Do not let the hostility of a group of people keep you away from the Sacred Mosque or make you express animosity. Cooperate with each other in righteousness and piety, not in sin and hostility. Have fear of Allah; He is stern in His retribution.

wa izaa ḥalaltum faṣṭaadoo; wa laa yajrimannakum shana-aanu qawmin an ṣaddookum ʻanil-Masjidil-Ḥaraami an ta'tadoo; wa ta'aawanoo ʻalalbirri wattaqwaa; wa laa ta'aawanoo ʻalal-is̱mi wal'udwaan; wattaqul-laah; innal-laaha shadeedul-ʻiqaab.

وَاِذَا حَلَلْتُمْ فَاصْطَادُوْا ؕ وَلَا يَجْرِمَنَّكُمْ
شَنَاٰنُ قَوْمٍ اَنْ صَدُّوْكُمْ عَنِ الْمَسْجِدِ
الْحَرَامِ اَنْ تَعْتَدُوْا ۘ وَتَعَاوَنُوْا عَلَى الْبِرِّ
وَالتَّقْوٰى ۖ وَلَا تَعَاوَنُوْا عَلَى الْاِثْمِ
وَالْعُدْوَانِ ۖ وَاتَّقُوا اللّٰهَ ؕ اِنَّ اللّٰهَ
شَدِيْدُ الْعِقَابِ ۝٢

وقف لازم

الربع

3. It is unlawful for you to consume the following as food: an animal that has not been properly slaughtered, blood, pork, an animal slaughtered and consecrated in the name of someone other than Allah, an animal killed by strangulation or a violent blow, an animal killed by falling down, an animal which has been gored to death, an animal partly eaten by a wild beast before being properly slaughtered, an animal which has been sacrificed on the stone blocks (which pagans worshipped), and any flesh divided by casting superstitious and gambling arrows (a pagan tradition), which is a sin.

Today, the unbelievers have lost hope about your religion. Do not be afraid of them but have fear of Me. On this day I have perfected your religion, completed My favors to you, and have chosen Islam as your religion.

If anyone not (normally) inclined to sin is forced by hunger to eat unlawful substances instead of proper food, he may do so to spare his life. Allah is All-forgiving and All-merciful.

3 Ḥurrimat ʻalaykumul-maytatu waddamu wa laḥmul-khinzeeri wa maaa uhilla lighayril-laahi bihee walmun-khaniqatu walmawqoozatu walmutarad-diyatu wanna-ṭeeḥatu wa maaa akalas-sabu'u illaa maa zakkaytum wa maa zubiḥa ʻalan-nuṣubi wa an tastaqsimoo bil-azlaam; zaalikum fisq; alyawma ya'isal-lazeena kafaroo min deenikum falaa takhshawhum wakh-shawn; alyawma akmaltu lakum deenakum wa atmamtu ʻalaykum ni'matee wa raḍeetu lakumul-Islaama deenaa; famaniḍṭurra fee makhmaṣatin ghayra mutajaanifil-li-is̱min fa-innallaaha Ghafoorur Raḥeem.

حُرِّمَتْ عَلَيْكُمُ الْمَيْتَةُ وَالدَّمُ وَلَحْمُ
الْخِنْزِيْرِ وَمَآ اُهِلَّ لِغَيْرِ اللّٰهِ بِهٖ
وَالْمُنْخَنِقَةُ وَالْمَوْقُوْذَةُ وَالْمُتَرَدِّيَةُ
وَالنَّطِيْحَةُ وَمَآ اَكَلَ السَّبُعُ اِلَّا مَا
ذَكَّيْتُمْ ۣ وَمَا ذُبِحَ عَلَى النُّصُبِ وَاَنْ
تَسْتَقْسِمُوْا بِالْاَزْلَامِ ؕ ذٰلِكُمْ فِسْقٌ ؕ
اَلْيَوْمَ يَئِسَ الَّذِيْنَ كَفَرُوْا مِنْ دِيْنِكُمْ
فَلَا تَخْشَوْهُمْ وَاخْشَوْنِ ؕ اَلْيَوْمَ اَكْمَلْتُ
لَكُمْ دِيْنَكُمْ وَاَتْمَمْتُ عَلَيْكُمْ
نِعْمَتِيْ وَرَضِيْتُ لَكُمُ الْاِسْلَامَ دِيْنًا ؕ
فَمَنِ اضْطُرَّ فِيْ مَخْمَصَةٍ غَيْرَ مُتَجَانِفٍ
لِّاِثْمٍ ۙ فَاِنَّ اللّٰهَ غَفُوْرٌ رَّحِيْمٌ ۝٣

4. (Muhammad), they ask you what has been made lawful for them (as food). Tell them, "All pure things are made lawful for you." If you train dogs or other beasts for hunting, you should train them according to what Allah has taught you. It, then, is lawful for you to eat the animals that they hunt, provided you mention the name of Allah over the prey. Have fear of Allah. Allah's reckoning is certainly swift.

4. Yas'aloonaka maazaaa uḥilla lahum; qul uḥilla lakumuṭ-ṭayyibaatu wa maa ʻallamtum minal-jawaariḥi mukallibeena tu'allimoonahunna mimmaa ʻallamakumul-laahu fakuloo mimmaaa amsakna ʻalaykum wazkurus-mal-laahi ʻalayh; wattaqul-laah; innal-laaha saree'ul-ḥisaab.

يَسْـَٔلُوْنَكَ مَاذَآ اُحِلَّ لَهُمْ ؕ قُلْ اُحِلَّ
لَكُمُ الطَّيِّبٰتُ ۙ وَمَا عَلَّمْتُمْ مِّنَ الْجَوَارِحِ
مُكَلِّبِيْنَ تُعَلِّمُوْنَهُنَّ مِمَّا عَلَّمَكُمُ اللّٰهُ ۫
فَكُلُوْا مِمَّآ اَمْسَكْنَ عَلَيْكُمْ وَاذْكُرُوا
اسْمَ اللّٰهِ عَلَيْهِ ۖ وَاتَّقُوا اللّٰهَ ؕ اِنَّ اللّٰهَ
سَرِيْعُ الْحِسَابِ ۝٤

5. On this day, all pure things are made lawful for you (as food). The food of the People of the Book is made lawful for you and

5. Alyawma uḥilla lakumuṭ-ṭayyibaatu wa ṭa'aamullazeena ootul-Kitaaba ḥillullakum wa

اَلْيَوْمَ اُحِلَّ لَكُمُ الطَّيِّبٰتُ ؕ وَطَعَامُ
الَّذِيْنَ اُوْتُوا الْكِتٰبَ حِلٌّ لَّكُمْ ۖ وَ

your food is made lawful for them.

It is lawful for you to marry chaste believing women and chaste women of the People of the Book, provided you pay their dowry, maintain chastity, and avoid fornication or lustful relations outside of marriage. The deeds of anyone who rejects the faith, certainly, become fruitless. He, on the Day of Judgment, will be of those who suffer a great loss.

ṭa'aamukum ḥillullahum wal-muḥṣanaatu minal-mu'minaati wal-muḥṣanaatu minal-lazeena ootul-Kitaaba min qablikum izaaa aataytumoohunna ujoo-rahunna muḥṣineena ghayra musaafiḥeena wa laa mutta-khizeee akhdaan; wa mañy-yakfur bil-eemaani faqad ḥabiṭa 'amaluhoo wa huwa fil-Aakhirati minal-khaasireen.

طَعَامُكُمْ حِلٌّ لَّهُمْ ۫ وَالْمُحْصَنٰتُ مِنَ
الْمُؤْمِنٰتِ وَالْمُحْصَنٰتُ مِنَ الَّذِيْنَ
اُوْتُوا الْكِتٰبَ مِنْ قَبْلِكُمْ اِذَآ اٰتَيْتُمُوْهُنَّ
اُجُوْرَهُنَّ مُحْصِنِيْنَ غَيْرَ مُسٰفِحِيْنَ
وَلَا مُتَّخِذِيْٓ اَخْدَانٍ ؕ وَمَنْ يَّكْفُرْ
بِالْاِيْمَانِ فَقَدْ حَبِطَ عَمَلُهٗ ۡ وَهُوَ فِي
الْاٰخِرَةِ مِنَ الْخٰسِرِيْنَ ۝٥ ع ٥/٥

6. Believers, when you are about to pray, wash your face and your hands along with the elbows and wipe your head and your feet to the ankles.

If you experience a seminal discharge, manage to take (the required) bath. If you are sick, or on a journey, or have just defecated, or have had intercourse with women and could not find any water, perform a Tayammum by touching clean natural earth with both palms and wiping (the upper part of) your face and (the back of) your hands.

Allah does not want you to suffer hardship. He wants you to be purified. He wants to complete His favors to you so that perhaps you will give Him thanks.

6. Yaaa-ayyuhal-lazeena aamanooo izaa qumtum-ilaṣ-Ṣalaati faghsiloo wujoohakum wa aydiyakum ilal maraafiqi wamsaḥoo biru'oosikum wa arjulakum ilal-ka'bayn; wa-in kuntum junuban faṭṭahharoo; wa-in kuntum marḍaaa aw 'alaa safarin aw jaaa'a aḥadum-minkum minal-ghaaa'iṭi aw laamastumunnisaaa'a falam tajidoo maaa'an fatayamma-moo ṣa'eedan ṭayyiban famsa-ḥoo biwujoo-hikum wa aydee-kum-minh; maa yureedul-laahu liyaj'ala 'alaykum min ḥarajiñw-wa laakiñy-yureedu liyuṭahhira-kum wa liyutimma ni'matahoo 'alaykum la'allakum tash-kuroon.

يٰٓاَيُّهَا الَّذِيْنَ اٰمَنُوْٓا اِذَا قُمْتُمْ اِلَى
الصَّلٰوةِ فَاغْسِلُوْا وُجُوْهَكُمْ وَاَيْدِيَكُمْ
اِلَى الْمَرَافِقِ وَامْسَحُوْا بِرُءُوْسِكُمْ وَ
اَرْجُلَكُمْ اِلَى الْكَعْبَيْنِ ؕ وَاِنْ كُنْتُمْ
جُنُبًا فَاطَّهَّرُوْا ؕ وَاِنْ كُنْتُمْ مَّرْضٰٓى
اَوْ عَلٰى سَفَرٍ اَوْ جَآءَ اَحَدٌ مِّنْكُمْ مِّنَ
الْغَآئِطِ اَوْ لٰمَسْتُمُ النِّسَآءَ فَلَمْ تَجِدُوْا
مَآءً فَتَيَمَّمُوْا صَعِيْدًا طَيِّبًا فَامْسَحُوْا
بِوُجُوْهِكُمْ وَاَيْدِيْكُمْ مِّنْهُ ؕ مَا يُرِيْدُ
اللّٰهُ لِيَجْعَلَ عَلَيْكُمْ مِّنْ حَرَجٍ وَّلٰكِنْ
يُّرِيْدُ لِيُطَهِّرَكُمْ وَلِيُتِمَّ نِعْمَتَهٗ عَلَيْكُمْ
لَعَلَّكُمْ تَشْكُرُوْنَ ۝٦

7. Remember Allah's favors to you and the firm covenant that He has made with you. You said because of this covenant, "We have heard (the words of the Lord) and have obeyed Him." Have fear of Allah; He knows well all that the hearts contain.

7. Wazkuroo ni'matal-laahi 'alaykum wa meesaaqahul-lazee waasaqakum biheee iz qultum sami'naa wa aṭa'naa wattaqul-laah; innal-laaha 'aleemum-bizaatiṣ-ṣudoor.

وَاذْكُرُوْا نِعْمَةَ اللّٰهِ عَلَيْكُمْ وَمِيْثَاقَهُ
الَّذِيْ وَاثَقَكُمْ بِهٖٓ ۙ اِذْ قُلْتُمْ سَمِعْنَا
وَاَطَعْنَا ۫ وَاتَّقُوا اللّٰهَ ؕ اِنَّ اللّٰهَ
عَلِيْمٌۢ بِذَاتِ الصُّدُوْرِ ۝٧

8. Believers, be steadfast for the cause of Allah and just in bearing witness. Let not a group's hostility to you cause you to deviate from justice. Be just, for it is closer to piety. Have fear of

8. Yaaa ayyuhal-lazeena aamanoo koonoo qawwaa-meena lillaahi shuhadaaa'a bilqisṭ; wa laa yajrimannakum shana-aanu qawmin 'alaaa allaa ta'diloo; i'diloo

يٰٓاَيُّهَا الَّذِيْنَ اٰمَنُوْا كُوْنُوْا قَوّٰمِيْنَ
لِلّٰهِ شُهَدَآءَ بِالْقِسْطِ ؗ وَلَا يَجْرِمَنَّكُمْ
شَنَاٰنُ قَوْمٍ عَلٰٓى اَلَّا تَعْدِلُوْا ؕ اِعْدِلُوْا ۣ

Allah; Allah is Well-aware of what you do.

huwa aqrabu littaqwaa wattaqul-laah; innal-laaha khabeerum-bimaa ta'maloon.

هُوَ اَقْرَبُ لِلتَّقْوٰى وَاتَّقُوا اللّٰهَ
اِنَّ اللّٰهَ خَبِيْرٌۢ بِمَا تَعْمَلُوْنَ ۝٨

9. Allah has promised forgiveness and a great reward to the righteously striving believers.

9. Wa'adal-laahul-lazeena aamanoo wa 'amiluṣ-ṣaaliḥaati lahum maghfiratuñw-wa ajrun 'aẓeem.

وَعَدَ اللّٰهُ الَّذِيْنَ اٰمَنُوْا وَعَمِلُوا
الصّٰلِحٰتِ لَهُمْ مَّغْفِرَةٌ وَّاَجْرٌ
عَظِيْمٌ ۝٩

10. However, the unbelievers who have called Our revelations lies will have hell for their dwelling.

10. Wallazeena kafaroo wa kaz-zaboo bi-Aayaatinaaa ulaaa'ika Aṣḥaabul-Jaḥeem.

وَالَّذِيْنَ كَفَرُوْا وَكَذَّبُوْا بِاٰيٰتِنَآ
اُولٰٓئِكَ اَصْحٰبُ الْجَحِيْمِ ۝١٠

11. Believers, recall Allah's favors to you when a group of people were about to harm you and Allah made their evil plots against you fail. Have fear of Allah and believers, trust Allah only.

11. Yaaa ayyuhal-lazeena aamanuz-kuroo ni'matallaahi 'alaykum iz hamma qawmun añy-yabsuṭooo ilaykum aydiyahum fakaffa aydiyahum 'ankum wattaqullaah; wa 'alal-laahi falyatawak-kalil-mu'minoon.

يٰٓاَيُّهَا الَّذِيْنَ اٰمَنُوا اذْكُرُوْا
نِعْمَتَ اللّٰهِ عَلَيْكُمْ اِذْ هَمَّ قَوْمٌ
اَنْ يَّبْسُطُوْٓا اِلَيْكُمْ اَيْدِيَهُمْ فَكَفَّ
اَيْدِيَهُمْ عَنْكُمْ وَاتَّقُوا اللّٰهَ وَ
عَلَى اللّٰهِ فَلْيَتَوَكَّلِ الْمُؤْمِنُوْنَ ۝١١ ع

12. Allah certainly made a solemn covenant with the children of Israel and raised among them twelve elders. Allah said to them, "I am with you if you will be steadfast in your prayers, pay (zakat) religious tax, believe in My Messengers, support them with reverence, and give a generous loan for the cause of Allah. We shall expiate your bad deeds and admit you to the gardens wherein streams flow. Whichever of you turns to disbelief after this has certainly gone astray (from the right path)."

12. Wa laqad akhazal-laahu meesaaqa Baneee Israaa'eela wa ba'asnaa minhumus-nay'ashara naqeebaa; wa qaalal-laahu innee ma'akum la'in aqamtumuṣ-Ṣalaata wa aataytu-muz-Zakaata wa aamantum bi-Rusulee wa'azzartumoohum wa aqraḍtumul-laaha qarḍan ḥasanal-la-ukaffiranna 'ankum sayyi-aatikum wa la-udkhilan-nakum Jannaatin tajree min taḥtihal-anhaar; faman kafara ba'da zaalika minkum faqad ḍalla Sawaaa'as-Sabeel.

وَلَقَدْ اَخَذَ اللّٰهُ مِيْثَاقَ بَنِيْٓ اِسْرَآءِيْلَ
وَبَعَثْنَا مِنْهُمُ اثْنَيْ عَشَرَ نَقِيْبًا
وَقَالَ اللّٰهُ اِنِّيْ مَعَكُمْ لَئِنْ اَقَمْتُمُ
الصَّلٰوةَ وَاٰتَيْتُمُ الزَّكٰوةَ وَاٰمَنْتُمْ
بِرُسُلِيْ وَعَزَّرْتُمُوْهُمْ وَاَقْرَضْتُمُ اللّٰهَ
قَرْضًا حَسَنًا لَّاُكَفِّرَنَّ عَنْكُمْ سَيِّاٰتِكُمْ
وَلَاُدْخِلَنَّكُمْ جَنّٰتٍ تَجْرِيْ مِنْ
تَحْتِهَا الْاَنْهٰرُ فَمَنْ كَفَرَ بَعْدَ ذٰلِكَ
مِنْكُمْ فَقَدْ ضَلَّ سَوَآءَ السَّبِيْلِ ۝١٢

13. For their disregard of their solemn covenant with Allah, We condemned the Israelites and made their hearts hard as stone. Now they displace the words of Allah and have forgotten their share of the guidance that they had received. Still you receive news of the treachery of all but a few of them. Forgive and ignore

13. Fabimaa naqḍihim meesaa-qahum la'annaahum wa ja'al-naa quloobahum qaasiyah; yuḥarrifoonal-kalima 'am-mawaaḍi'ihee wa nasoo ḥaẓẓam-mimmaa zukkiroo bih; wa laa tazaalu taṭṭali'u 'alaa khaaa'inatim-minhum illaa qaleelam-minhum

فَبِمَا نَقْضِهِمْ مِّيْثَاقَهُمْ لَعَنّٰهُمْ
وَجَعَلْنَا قُلُوْبَهُمْ قٰسِيَةً يُحَرِّفُوْنَ
الْكَلِمَ عَنْ مَّوَاضِعِهٖ وَنَسُوْا حَظًّا
مِّمَّا ذُكِّرُوْا بِهٖ وَلَا تَزَالُ تَطَّلِعُ عَلٰى
خَآئِنَةٍ مِّنْهُمْ اِلَّا قَلِيْلًا مِّنْهُمْ

them. Allah loves the righteous ones.

fa'fu 'anhum waṣfaḥ; innal-laaha yuḥibbul-muḥsineen.

فَاعْفُ عَنْهُمْ وَاصْفَحْ ۭ اِنَّ اللّٰهَ
يُحِبُّ الْمُحْسِنِيْنَ ﴿١٣﴾

14. We had made a solemn covenant with those who call themselves Christians, but they forgot their share of the guidance that was sent to them. We have induced hatred and animosity among them which will remain with them until the Day of Judgment when Allah will tell them about what they had done.

14. Wa minal-lazeena qaalooo innaa Naṣaaraaa akhaznaa meesaaqahum fanasoo ḥaẓẓam-mimmaa zukkiroo bihee fa-aghraynaa baynahumul-'adaawata walbaghḍaaa'a ilaa Yawmil-Qiyaamah; wa sawfa yunabbi'uhumul-laahu bimaa kaanoo yaṣna'oon.

وَمِنَ الَّذِيْنَ قَالُوْٓا اِنَّا نَصٰرٰٓى اَخَذْنَا
مِيْثَاقَهُمْ فَنَسُوْا حَظًّا مِّمَّا ذُكِّرُوْا بِهٖ
فَاَغْرَيْنَا بَيْنَهُمُ الْعَدَاوَةَ وَالْبَغْضَاۗءَ
اِلٰى يَوْمِ الْقِيٰمَةِ ۭ وَسَوْفَ يُنَبِّئُهُمُ اللّٰهُ
بِمَا كَانُوْا يَصْنَعُوْنَ ﴿١٤﴾

15. O people of the Book, Our Messenger has come to you. He tells you about the many facts that you had been hiding of the Book and leaves many more untold.

A light and a clarifying Book has come to you from Allah

15. Yaaa Ahlal-Kitaabi qad jaaa'akum Rasoolunaa yubay-yinu lakum kaseeram-mimmaa kuntum tukhfoona minal-Kitaabi wa ya'foo 'an kaseer; qad jaaa'akum minallaahi noorunw-wa Kitaabum-Mubeen.

يٰٓاَهْلَ الْكِتٰبِ قَدْ جَاۗءَكُمْ رَسُوْلُنَا
يُبَيِّنُ لَكُمْ كَثِيْرًا مِّمَّا كُنْتُمْ تُخْفُوْنَ
مِنَ الْكِتٰبِ وَيَعْفُوْا عَنْ كَثِيْرٍ ڛ قَدْ
جَاۗءَكُمْ مِّنَ اللّٰهِ نُوْرٌ وَّكِتٰبٌ مُّبِيْنٌ ﴿١٥﴾

16. to show the way of peace to those who seek His pleasure, to bring them out of darkness into light through His will and to guide them to the right path.

16. Yahdee bihil-laahu manit-taba'a riḍwaanahoo subulas-salaami wa yukhrijuhum minaẓ-ẓulumaati ilan-noori bi-iznihee wa yahdeehim ilaa Ṣiraaṭim-Mustaqeem.

يَّهْدِيْ بِهِ اللّٰهُ مَنِ اتَّبَعَ رِضْوَانَهٗ
سُبُلَ السَّلٰمِ وَيُخْرِجُهُمْ مِّنَ
الظُّلُمٰتِ اِلَى النُّوْرِ بِاِذْنِهٖ وَيَهْدِيْهِمْ
اِلٰى صِرَاطٍ مُّسْتَقِيْمٍ ﴿١٦﴾

17. Those who have said that the Messiah, son of Mary, is Allah, have in fact committed themselves to disbelief. (Muhammad), ask them, "Who can prevent Allah from destroying the Messiah, his mother and all that is in the earth?" To Allah belongs all that is in the heavens, the earth, and all that is between them. Allah creates whatever He wants and He has power over all things.

17. Laqad kafaral-lazeena qaalooo innal-laaha Huwal-Maseeḥub-nu-Maryam; qul famañy-yamliku minal-laahi shay'an in araada añy-yuhlikal Maseeḥab-na-Maryama wa ummahoo wa man fil-arḍi jamee'aa; wa lillaahi mulkus-samaawaati wal-arḍi wa maa baynahumaa; yakhluqu maa-Yashaaa'; wallaahu 'alaa kulli shay'in Qadeer.

لَقَدْ كَفَرَ الَّذِيْنَ قَالُوْٓا اِنَّ اللّٰهَ هُوَ
الْمَسِيْحُ ابْنُ مَرْيَمَ ۭ قُلْ فَمَنْ يَّمْلِكُ
مِنَ اللّٰهِ شَيْـًٔا اِنْ اَرَادَ اَنْ يُّهْلِكَ
الْمَسِيْحَ ابْنَ مَرْيَمَ وَاُمَّهٗ وَمَنْ فِي
الْاَرْضِ جَمِيْعًا ۭ وَلِلّٰهِ مُلْكُ السَّمٰوٰتِ
وَالْاَرْضِ وَمَا بَيْنَهُمَا ۭ يَخْلُقُ
مَا يَشَاۗءُ ۭ وَاللّٰهُ عَلٰي كُلِّ شَيْءٍ قَدِيْرٌ ﴿١٧﴾

18. The Jews and Christians call themselves the beloved sons of Allah. (Muhammad), ask them, "Why does Allah punish you for your sins? In fact, you are mere human beings whom He has created. He forgives and punishes whomever He wants. To Him

18. Wa qaalatil-Yahoodu wan-Naṣaaraa naḥnu abnaaa'ullaahi wa aḥibbaaa'uh; qul falima yu'az -zibukum bizunoobikum bal antum basharum-mimman khalaq; yaghfiru limañy-yashaaa'u wa yu'az-zibu

وَقَالَتِ الْيَهُوْدُ وَالنَّصٰرٰى نَحْنُ اَبْنٰۗؤُا
اللّٰهِ وَاَحِبَّاۗؤُهٗ ۭ قُلْ فَلِمَ يُعَذِّبُكُمْ
بِذُنُوْبِكُمْ ۭ بَلْ اَنْتُمْ بَشَرٌ مِّمَّنْ
خَلَقَ ۭ يَغْفِرُ لِمَنْ يَّشَاۗءُ وَيُعَذِّبُ

belongs all that is in the heavens, the earth, and all that is between them and to Him do all things return.

mañy-yashaaa'; wa lillaahi mulkus-samaawaati wal-arḍi wa maa baynahumaa wa ilayhil-maṣeer.

مَنْ يَّشَآءُ ۭ وَلِلّٰهِ مُلْكُ السَّمٰوٰتِ
وَالْاَرْضِ وَمَا بَيْنَهُمَا ۡ وَاِلَيْهِ
الْمَصِيْرُ ﴿١٨﴾

19. O People of the Book, Our Messenger has come to you to guide you at a time when none of Our other Messengers are living among you. (We sent him) so that you will not complain about having no one to tell you of what is good or warn you of what is bad. Now a bearer of good news has come to you. Allah has power over all things.

19. Yaaa Ahlal-Kitaabi qad jaaa'akum Rasoolunaa yubayyinu lakum 'alaa fatra-tim-minar-Rusuli an taqooloo maa jaaa'anaa mim basheeriñw-wa laa naẕeerin faqad jaaa'akum basheeruñw-wa naẕeer; wallaahu 'alaa kulli shay'in Qadeer.

يٰۤاَهْلَ الْكِتٰبِ قَدْ جَآءَكُمْ رَسُوْلُنَا
يُبَيِّنُ لَكُمْ عَلٰي فَتْرَةٍ مِّنَ الرُّسُلِ
اَنْ تَقُوْلُوْا مَا جَآءَنَا مِنْۢ بَشِيْرٍ
وَّلَا نَذِيْرٍ ۡ فَقَدْ جَآءَكُمْ بَشِيْرٌ
وَّنَذِيْرٌ ۭ وَاللّٰهُ عَلٰي كُلِّ شَيْءٍ قَدِيْرٌ ﴿١٩﴾ ع ٤

20. There was a time when Moses told his people, "Recall Allah's favors to you. He made Messengers and Kings out of your own people and gave you what He had not given to others.

20. Wa iẕ qaala Moosaa liqawmihee yaa qawmiẕ kuroo ni'matal-laahi-'alaykum iẕ ja'ala feekum ambiyaaa'a wa ja'alakum mulookañw-wa aataakum maa lam yu'ti aḥadam-minal-'aalameen.

وَاِذْ قَالَ مُوْسٰي لِقَوْمِهٖ يٰقَوْمِ
اذْكُرُوْا نِعْمَةَ اللّٰهِ عَلَيْكُمْ اِذْ جَعَلَ
فِيْكُمْ اَنْۢبِيَاۗءَ وَجَعَلَكُمْ مُّلُوْكًا ڰ
وَّاٰتٰىكُمْ مَّا لَمْ يُؤْتِ اَحَدًا مِّنَ
الْعٰلَمِيْنَ ﴿٢٠﴾

21. Enter the sacred promised-land which Allah has designated for you. Do not return to disbelief lest you become lost."

21. Yaa qawmid-khulul-Arḍal-Muqaddasatal-latee katabal-laahu lakum wa laa tartaddoo 'alaaa adbaarikum fatanqaliboo khaasireen.

يٰقَوْمِ ادْخُلُوا الْاَرْضَ الْمُقَدَّسَةَ
الَّتِيْ كَتَبَ اللّٰهُ لَكُمْ وَلَا تَرْتَدُّوْا
عَلٰٓي اَدْبَارِكُمْ فَتَنْقَلِبُوْا خٰسِرِيْنَ ﴿٢١﴾

22. They said, "Moses, a giant race of people is living there. We shall never go there unless they leave the land first. If they leave it, then we will enter."

22. Qaaloo yaa Moosaaa inna feehaa qawman jabbaareena wa-innaa lan nadkhulahaa ḥattaa yakhrujoo minhaa fa-iñy-yakhrujoo minhaa fa-innaa daakhiloon.

قَالُوْا يٰمُوْسٰٓى اِنَّ فِيْهَا قَوْمًا جَبَّارِيْنَ ڰ
وَاِنَّا لَنْ نَّدْخُلَهَا حَتّٰي يَخْرُجُوْا مِنْهَا ۚ
فَاِنْ يَّخْرُجُوْا مِنْهَا فَاِنَّا دٰخِلُوْنَ ﴿٢٢﴾

23. Two God-fearing men on whom Allah had bestowed favors told them, "Proceed through the gates and when you enter the city you will be victorious. Have trust in Allah if you are true believers."

23. Qaala rajulaani minal-laẕeena yakhaafoona an'amal-laahu 'alayhimad-khuloo 'alayhimul-baab; fa-iẕaa dakhaltumoohu fa-innakum ghaaliboon; wa 'alal-laahi fatawakkalooo in kuntum mu'mineen.

قَالَ رَجُلٰنِ مِنَ الَّذِيْنَ يَخَافُوْنَ
اَنْعَمَ اللّٰهُ عَلَيْهِمَا ادْخُلُوْا عَلَيْهِمُ
الْبَابَ ۚ فَاِذَا دَخَلْتُمُوْهُ فَاِنَّكُمْ
غٰلِبُوْنَ ڬ وَعَلَي اللّٰهِ فَتَوَكَّلُوْٓا اِنْ
كُنْتُمْ مُّؤْمِنِيْنَ ﴿٢٣﴾

24. They said, "(Moses), as long as they are in the land, we shall never go there. Go with your

24. Qaaloo yaa Moosaaa innaa lan nadkhulahaaa abadam-maa daamoo feehaa faẕhab anta

قَالُوْا يٰمُوْسٰٓى اِنَّا لَنْ نَّدْخُلَهَآ
اَبَدًا مَّا دَامُوْا فِيْهَا فَاذْهَبْ اَنْتَ

Lord to fight them but we shall stay where we are."

25. (Moses) said, "Lord, I can only speak for myself and my brother; keep us away from the evil-doers."

26. The Lord said, "The land will be prohibited to them for forty years (during all such time). They will wander in the land. Do not feel sad for the evil-doing people."

27. (Muhammad), tell them the true story of the two sons of Adam (Abel and Cain). Each one of them offered a sacrifice. The sacrifice of one of them (Abel) was accepted but not that of the other (Cain), who then said to his brother, "I shall certainly kill you." (Abel) replied, "Allah only accepts the offerings of the pious ones.

28. Even if you try to kill me, I certainly shall not try to kill you. I have fear of Allah, the Lord of the creation.

29. I would prefer you to take sole responsibility for both our sins and thus become a dweller of hell; this is what an unjust person deserves."

30. (Cain's) soul prompted him to kill his own brother. In doing so he became of those who lose.

31. Allah sent down a raven which started to dig up the earth to show the killer how to bury the corpse of his brother. On seeing the raven, (Cain) said, "Woe to me! Am I less able than a raven to bury the corpse of my brother?" He became greatly remorseful.

32. For this reason, We made it a law for the children of Israel that

wa Rabbuka faqaatilaaa innaa haahunaa qaa'idoon.

25. Qaala Rabbi innee laaa amliku illaa nafsee wa akhee fafruq baynanaa wa baynal-qawmil-faasiqeen.

26. Qaala fa-innahaa muḥar-ramatun 'alayhim arba'eena sanah; yateehoona fil-arḍ; falaa ta-sa 'alal-qawmil-faasiqeen.

27. Watlu 'alayhim naba-abnay Aadama bilḥaqq; iẕ qarrabaa qurbaanan fatuqubbila min aḥadihimaa wa lam yutaqabbal minal-aakhari qaala la-aqtulannaka qaala innamaa yataqabbalul-laahu minal-muttaqeen.

28. La'im basaṭṭa ilayya yadaka litaqtulanee maaa ana bibaasiṭiñy-yadiya ilayka li-aqtulaka inneee akhaafullaaha Rabbal-'aalameen.

29. Ineee ureedu an tabooo'a bi-iṯmee wa iṯmika fatakoona min Aṣḥaabin-Naar; wa ẕaalika jazaaa'uẓ-ẓaalimeen.

30. Faṭawwa'at lahoo nafsu-hoo qatla akheehi faqatalahoo fa-aṣbaḥa minal-khaasireen.

31. Faba'aṯal-laahu ghu-raabañy-yabḥaṯu fil-arḍi liyuri-yahoo kayfa yuwaaree saw'ata akheeh; qaala yaa waylataaa a'ajaztu an akoona miṯla haaẕal-ghuraabi fa-uwaariya saw'ata akheeh; fa-aṣbaḥa minannaadimeen.

32. Min ajli ẕaalika katabnaa 'alaa Baneee

وَرَبُّكَ فَقَاتِلَآ إِنَّا هٰهُنَا قٰعِدُوْنَ ﴿٢٤﴾
قَالَ رَبِّ إِنِّيْ لَآ أَمْلِكُ إِلَّا نَفْسِيْ
وَأَخِيْ فَافْرُقْ بَيْنَنَا وَبَيْنَ الْقَوْمِ
الْفٰسِقِيْنَ ﴿٢٥﴾
قَالَ فَإِنَّهَا مُحَرَّمَةٌ عَلَيْهِمْ أَرْبَعِيْنَ
سَنَةً ۚ يَتِيْهُوْنَ فِي الْأَرْضِ ۗ فَلَا
تَأْسَ عَلَى الْقَوْمِ الْفٰسِقِيْنَ ﴿٢٦﴾ ع ٤ ، وقف لازم
وَاتْلُ عَلَيْهِمْ نَبَأَ ابْنَيْ اٰدَمَ بِالْحَقِّ ۘ
إِذْ قَرَّبَا قُرْبَانًا فَتُقُبِّلَ مِنْ أَحَدِهِمَا
وَلَمْ يُتَقَبَّلْ مِنَ الْاٰخَرِ ۗ قَالَ
لَأَقْتُلَنَّكَ ۗ قَالَ إِنَّمَا يَتَقَبَّلُ
اللّٰهُ مِنَ الْمُتَّقِيْنَ ﴿٢٧﴾ النصف
لَئِنْۢ بَسَطْتَّ إِلَيَّ يَدَكَ لِتَقْتُلَنِيْ
مَآ أَنَا بِبَاسِطٍ يَّدِيَ إِلَيْكَ لِأَقْتُلَكَ ۚ
إِنِّيْٓ أَخَافُ اللّٰهَ رَبَّ الْعٰلَمِيْنَ ﴿٢٨﴾
إِنِّيْٓ أُرِيْدُ أَنْ تَبُوْٓأَ بِإِثْمِيْ وَإِثْمِكَ
فَتَكُوْنَ مِنْ أَصْحٰبِ النَّارِ ۚ وَذٰلِكَ
جَزٰٓؤُا الظّٰلِمِيْنَ ﴿٢٩﴾
فَطَوَّعَتْ لَهٗ نَفْسُهٗ قَتْلَ أَخِيْهِ
فَقَتَلَهٗ فَأَصْبَحَ مِنَ الْخٰسِرِيْنَ ﴿٣٠﴾
فَبَعَثَ اللّٰهُ غُرَابًا يَّبْحَثُ فِي الْأَرْضِ
لِيُرِيَهٗ كَيْفَ يُوَارِيْ سَوْءَةَ أَخِيْهِ ۗ
قَالَ يٰوَيْلَتٰٓى أَعَجَزْتُ أَنْ أَكُوْنَ
مِثْلَ هٰذَا الْغُرَابِ فَأُوَارِيَ سَوْءَةَ
أَخِيْ ۚ فَأَصْبَحَ مِنَ النّٰدِمِيْنَ ﴿٣١﴾
مِنْ أَجْلِ ذٰلِكَ ۛ كَتَبْنَا عَلٰى بَنِيْٓ

وقف النبي صلى الله عليه وآله وسلم ١٢ معانقة ٥

the killing of a person for reasons other than lawful reprisal or for stopping the spread of evil in the land, is as great a sin as murdering all of mankind. However, to save a life would be as great a virtue as to save all of mankind. Our Messengers had come to them with clear authoritative evidence but many of them (Israelites), thereafter, started doing wrong in the land.

33. The only proper recompense for those who fight against Allah and His Messenger and try to spread evil in the land is to be killed, crucified, or either to have one of their hands and feet cut from the opposite side or to be sent into exile. These are to disgrace them in this life and they will suffer a great torment in the life hereafter.

34. As for those who repent before you (the legal authorities) have control over them (by proving their guilt); they should know that Allah is All-forgiving and All-merciful.

35. Believers, have fear of Allah. Find the means to reach Him and strive hard for His cause so that you may have everlasting happiness.

36. Had the unbelievers had twice as much as the wealth of the whole earth in order to ransom themselves from the torment in the life hereafter, still their ransom would not have been accepted. For them there will be a painful torment.

37. They will wish to get out of the fire but they will not have such a choice. Their torment will be

Israaa'eela annahoo man qatala nafsam bighayri nafsin aw fasaadin fil-arḍi faka-annamaa qatalan-naasa jamee'aa; wa man aḥyaahaa faka-annamaaa aḥyan-naasa jamee'aa; wa laqad jaaa'athum Rusulunaa bilbayyinaati s̲umma inna kas̲eeram-minhum ba'da z̲aalika fil-arḍi lamusrifoon.

33. Innamaa jazaaa'ul-laz̲eena yuḥaariboonal-laaha wa Rasoolahoo wa yas'awna fil-arḍi fasaadan añy-yuqattalooo aw yuṣallabooo aw tuqaṭṭa'a aydeehim wa arjuluhum min khilaafin aw yunfaw minal-arḍ; z̲aalika lahum khizyun fid-dunyaa wa lahum fil-Aakhirati 'az̲aabun 'aẓeem.

34. Illal-laz̲eena taaboo min qabli an taqdiroo 'alayhim fa'lamooo annal-laaha Ghafoorur-Raḥeem.

35. Yaaa ayyuhal-laz̲eena aamanut-taqul-laaha wabtaghooo ilayhil-waseelata wa jaahidoo fee sabeelihee la'allakum tufliḥoon.

36. Innal-laz̲eena kafaroo law anna lahum maa fil-arḍi jamee'añw-wa mis̲lahoo ma'ahoo liyaftadoo bihee min 'az̲aabi Yawmil-Qiyaamati maa tuqubbila minhum wa lahum 'az̲aabun aleem.

37. Yureedoona añy-yakhrujoo minan-Naari wa maa hum bikhaarijeena minhaa wa lahum

إِسْرَآءِيلَ أَنَّهُ مَنْ قَتَلَ نَفْسًا
بِغَيْرِ نَفْسٍ أَوْ فَسَادٍ فِي الْأَرْضِ
فَكَأَنَّمَا قَتَلَ النَّاسَ جَمِيعًا ۖ وَمَنْ
أَحْيَاهَا فَكَأَنَّمَآ أَحْيَا النَّاسَ
جَمِيعًا ۚ وَلَقَدْ جَآءَتْهُمْ رُسُلُنَا
بِالْبَيِّنٰتِ ثُمَّ إِنَّ كَثِيرًا مِّنْهُمْ
بَعْدَ ذٰلِكَ فِي الْأَرْضِ لَمُسْرِفُونَ ﴿٣٢﴾
إِنَّمَا جَزٰٓؤُا الَّذِينَ يُحَارِبُونَ اللّٰهَ
وَرَسُولَهُ وَيَسْعَوْنَ فِي الْأَرْضِ فَسَادًا
أَنْ يُّقَتَّلُوٓا أَوْ يُصَلَّبُوٓا أَوْ تُقَطَّعَ
أَيْدِيهِمْ وَأَرْجُلُهُمْ مِّنْ خِلَافٍ
أَوْ يُنْفَوْا مِنَ الْأَرْضِ ۚ ذٰلِكَ
لَهُمْ خِزْيٌ فِي الدُّنْيَا وَلَهُمْ فِي
الْاٰخِرَةِ عَذَابٌ عَظِيمٌ ﴿٣٣﴾
إِلَّا الَّذِينَ تَابُوا مِنْ قَبْلِ أَنْ
تَقْدِرُوا عَلَيْهِمْ ۚ فَاعْلَمُوٓا أَنَّ
اللّٰهَ غَفُورٌ رَّحِيمٌ ﴿٣٤﴾ ع ٨
يٰٓأَيُّهَا الَّذِينَ اٰمَنُوا اتَّقُوا اللّٰهَ
وَابْتَغُوٓا إِلَيْهِ الْوَسِيلَةَ وَجَاهِدُوا
فِي سَبِيلِهِ لَعَلَّكُمْ تُفْلِحُونَ ﴿٣٥﴾
إِنَّ الَّذِينَ كَفَرُوا لَوْ أَنَّ لَهُمْ مَّا
فِي الْأَرْضِ جَمِيعًا وَّمِثْلَهُ مَعَهُ
لِيَفْتَدُوا بِهِ مِنْ عَذَابِ يَوْمِ الْقِيٰمَةِ
مَا تُقُبِّلَ مِنْهُمْ ۚ وَلَهُمْ عَذَابٌ أَلِيمٌ ﴿٣٦﴾
يُرِيدُونَ أَنْ يَّخْرُجُوا مِنَ النَّارِ
وَمَا هُمْ بِخٰرِجِينَ مِنْهَا ۖ وَلَهُمْ

constant.

'azaabum-muqeem.

عذاب مقيم ﴿٣٧﴾

38. Cut off the hands of a male or female thief as a punishment for their deed and a lesson for them from Allah. Allah is Majestic and All-wise.

38. Wassaariqu wassaariqatu faqṭa'ooo aydiyahumaa jazaaa-'am-bimaa kasabaa nakaalam-minal-laah; wallaahu 'Azeezun Ḥakeem.

والسارق والسارقة فاقطعوا
ايديهما جزاء بما كسبا نكالا
من الله ط والله عزيز حكيم ﴿٣٨﴾

39. However, Allah will accept the repentance of whoever repents and reforms himself after committing injustice; He is All-forgiving and All-merciful.

39. Faman taaba mim ba'di ẓulmihee wa aṣlaḥa fainnal-laaha yatoobu 'alayh; innal-laaha Ghafoorur-Raḥeem.

فمن تاب من بعد ظلمه واصلح
فان الله يتوب عليه ط ان الله
غفور رحيم ﴿٣٩﴾

40. Did you not know that to Allah the Kingdom of the heavens and the earth belongs and that He punishes or forgives whomever He wants? Allah has power over all things.

40. Alam ta'lam annal-laaha lahoo mulkus-samaawaati wal-arḍi yu'az-zibu mañy-yashaa'u wa yaghfiru limañy-yashaaa'; wallaahu 'alaa kulli shay'in Qadeer.

الم تعلم ان الله له ملك
السموت والارض ط يعذب من
يشاء ويغفر لمن يشاء ط والله
على كل شيء قدير ﴿٤٠﴾

41. Messenger, do not be grieved about the people who run back to disbelief. They only say that they believe but, in fact, they had no faith in their hearts.

Certain Jewish persons knowingly listen to lies and accept the lies which come from others (Jews), who had no relation with you and who distort certain words of the Bible and say to the people, "Accept only those words which are the same as what We have told you. If you did not, then beware!"

You cannot help those whom Allah wants to try. Allah did not want to cleanse the hearts of such people. They lead a disgraceful life in this world and in the life hereafter they will suffer a great torment.

41. Yaaa-ayyuhar-Rasoolu laa yaḥzunkal-lazeena yusaa-ri'oona fil-kufri minal-lazeena qaalooo aamannaa bi-afwaahi-him wa lam tu'min quloobu-hum; wa minal-lazeena haadoo sammaa'oona lilkazibi sam-maa'oona liqawmin aakhareena lam ya-tooka yuḥarrifoonal-kalima mim ba'di mawaaḍi'i-hee yaqooloona in ooteetum haazaa fakhuzoohu wa il-lam tu'tawhu faḥzaroo; wa mañy-yuridil-laahu fitnatahoo falan tamlika lahoo minal-laahi shay'aa; ulaaa'i-kallazeena lam yuridil-laahu añy-yuṭahhira quloobahum; lahum fid-dunyaa khizyuñw-wa lahum fil-Aakhirati 'azaabun 'aẓeem.

يايها الرسول لا يحزنك الذين
يسارعون في الكفر من الذين
قالوا امنا بافواههم ولم تؤمن
قلوبهم ج ومن الذين هادوا ج
سمعون للكذب سمعون لقوم
اخرين لم ياتوك ط يحرفون
الكلم من بعد مواضعه ج يقولون
ان اوتيتم هذا فخذوه وان
لم تؤتوه فاحذروا ط ومن يرد
الله فتنته فلن تملك له من
الله شيئا ط اولئك الذين لم يرد
الله ان يطهر قلوبهم ط لهم في
الدنيا خزي ج ولهم في الاخرة
عذاب عظيم ﴿٤١﴾

42. They deliberately listen to lies (for deceitful purposes) and live on usury. If they come to you (seeking

42. Sammaa'oona lilkazibi akkaaloona lissuḥt;

سمعون للكذب اكلون للسحت ط

معٓ الوقف على الاولى اجوز عند المتقدمين ١٢

your judgment to settle their differences) you may settle their disputes or keep aloof from them.

Should you choose not to bother with them, it will not harm you in the least. If you decide to issue your decree, decide their case with justice. Allah loves those who are just.

fa-in jaaa'ooka faḥkum baynahum aw a'riḍ 'anhum wa in tu'riḍ 'anhum falañy-yaḍurrooka shay'aa; wa in ḥakamta faḥkum baynahum bilqisṭ; innal-laaha yuḥibbul-muqsiṭeen.

فَإِن جَآءُوكَ فَاحْكُم بَيْنَهُمْ أَوْ
أَعْرِضْ عَنْهُمْ ۖ وَإِن تُعْرِضْ عَنْهُمْ
فَلَن يَضُرُّوكَ شَيْـًٔا ۖ وَإِنْ حَكَمْتَ
فَاحْكُم بَيْنَهُم بِالْقِسْطِ ۚ إِنَّ اللَّهَ
يُحِبُّ الْمُقْسِطِينَ ﴿٤٢﴾

43. How can they come to you for judgment when they already have the Torah which contains the decree of Allah! It does not take them long to disregard your judgment; they are not true believers.

43. Wa kayfa yuḥak-kimoo-naka wa 'indahumut-Tawraatu feehaa ḥukmul-laahi summa yatawallawna mim ba'di zaalik; wa maaa ulaaa'ika bilmu'mi-neen.

وَكَيْفَ يُحَكِّمُونَكَ وَعِندَهُمُ
التَّوْرَىٰةُ فِيهَا حُكْمُ اللَّهِ ثُمَّ
يَتَوَلَّوْنَ مِنۢ بَعْدِ ذَٰلِكَ ۚ وَمَآ أُو۟لَـٰٓئِكَ
بِالْمُؤْمِنِينَ ﴿٤٣﴾

44. We had revealed the Torah, containing guidance and light. The Prophets, who had submitted themselves to the will of Allah, judged the Jews by the laws of the Torah. So did the godly people and the Jewish scholars who remembered some parts of the Book of Allah and bore witness to it. Mankind, do not be afraid of people but have fear of Me. Do not sell My revelations for a paltry price. Those who did not judge by the laws of Allah are unbelievers.

44. Innaaa anzalnat Tawraata feehaa hudañw-wa noor; yaḥkumu bihan-Nabiyyoonal-lazeena aslamoo lillazeena haadoo war-rabbaaniyyoona wal-aḥbaaru bimas-tuḥfiẓoo min Kitaabil-laahi wa kaanoo 'alayhi shuhadaaa'; falaa takhshawun-naasa wakhshawni wa laa tashtaroo bi-Aayaatee samanan qaleelaa; wa mal-lam yaḥkum bimaaa anzalal-laahu fa-ulaaa'ika humul-kaafiroon.

إِنَّآ أَنزَلْنَا التَّوْرَىٰةَ فِيهَا هُدًى
وَنُورٌ ۚ يَحْكُمُ بِهَا النَّبِيُّونَ
الَّذِينَ أَسْلَمُوا۟ لِلَّذِينَ هَادُوا۟
وَالرَّبَّـٰنِيُّونَ وَالْأَحْبَارُ بِمَا
اسْتُحْفِظُوا۟ مِن كِتَـٰبِ اللَّهِ وَكَانُوا۟
عَلَيْهِ شُهَدَآءَ ۚ فَلَا تَخْشَوُا۟ النَّاسَ
وَاخْشَوْنِ وَلَا تَشْتَرُوا۟ بِـَٔايَـٰتِى ثَمَنًا
قَلِيلًا ۚ وَمَن لَّمْ يَحْكُم بِمَآ أَنزَلَ
اللَّهُ فَأُو۟لَـٰٓئِكَ هُمُ الْكَـٰفِرُونَ ﴿٤٤﴾

45. In the Torah We made mandatory for the Jews these rules of retaliation: Capital punishment for the murder of a person; an eye for an eye, a nose for a nose, an ear for an ear, a tooth for a tooth, and a just compensation for a wound.

If the perpetrator is forgiven by the affected party, this will be an expiation of his crime. Those who did not judge according to what Allah has revealed are unjust.

45. Wa katabnaa 'alayhim feehaaa annan-nafsa binnafsi wal'ayna bil'ayni wal-anfa bilanfi wal-uzuna bil-uzuni wassinna bissinni waljurooḥa qiṣaaṣ; faman taṣaddaqa bihee fahuwa kaffaaratul-lah; wa mal-lam yaḥkum bimaaa anzalal-laahu fa-ulaaa'ika humuẓ-ẓaalimoon.

وَكَتَبْنَا عَلَيْهِمْ فِيهَآ أَنَّ النَّفْسَ
بِالنَّفْسِ وَالْعَيْنَ بِالْعَيْنِ وَالْأَنفَ
بِالْأَنفِ وَالْأُذُنَ بِالْأُذُنِ وَالسِّنَّ
بِالسِّنِّ وَالْجُرُوحَ قِصَاصٌ ۚ فَمَن
تَصَدَّقَ بِهِۦ فَهُوَ كَفَّارَةٌ لَّهُۥ ۚ
وَمَن لَّمْ يَحْكُم بِمَآ أَنزَلَ اللَّهُ
فَأُو۟لَـٰٓئِكَ هُمُ الظَّـٰلِمُونَ ﴿٤٥﴾

46. We made Jesus, son of Mary, follow in the footsteps (of

46. Wa qaffaynaa 'alaaa aasaarihim bi-'Eesab-ni-

وَقَفَّيْنَا عَلَىٰٓ ءَاثَـٰرِهِم بِعِيسَى ابْنِ

the earlier Prophets) and confirm what existed in the Torah in his time. We gave him the Gospel containing guidance and light, as a confirmation of the Torah and instruction and advice for the pious ones.

Maryama muṣaddiqal-limaa bayna yadayhi minat-Tawraati wa aataynaahul-Injeela feehi hudañw-wa nooruñw-wa muṣaddiqal-limaa bayna yadayhi minat-Tawraati wa hudañw-wa maw'iẓatal-lilmuttaqeen.

مَرْيَمَ مُصَدِّقًا لِّمَا بَيْنَ يَدَيْهِ مِنَ
التَّوْرٰىةِ ۖ وَاٰتَيْنٰهُ الْاِنْجِيْلَ فِيْهِ
هُدًى وَّنُوْرٌ ۙ وَّمُصَدِّقًا لِّمَا بَيْنَ
يَدَيْهِ مِنَ التَّوْرٰىةِ وَهُدًى وَّ
مَوْعِظَةً لِّلْمُتَّقِيْنَ ۗ ﴿٤٦﴾

47. The followers of the Gospels (the New Testament) must judge according to what Allah has revealed in it. Those who did not judge by the laws of Allah are evildoers.

47. Walyaḥkum Ahlul-Injeeli bimaaa anzalal-laahu feeh; wa mal-lam yaḥkum bimaaa anzalal-laahu fa-ulaaa'ika humul-faasiqoon.

وَلْيَحْكُمْ اَهْلُ الْاِنْجِيْلِ بِمَآ اَنْزَلَ
اللّٰهُ فِيْهِ ۗ وَمَنْ لَّمْ يَحْكُمْ بِمَآ اَنْزَلَ
اللّٰهُ فَاُولٰٓئِكَ هُمُ الْفٰسِقُوْنَ ﴿٤٧﴾

48. We have revealed the Book to you (Muhammad) in all Truth. It confirms the (original) Bible and has the authority to preserve or abrogate what the Bible contains. Judge among them by what Allah has revealed to you and do not follow their desires instead of the Truth which has come to you.

We have given a law and a way of life to each of you. Had Allah wanted, He could have made you into one nation, but He wanted to examine you in the matters He has given to you. Try to excel each other in righteousness. All of you will return to Allah who will tell you the truth in the matter of your differences.

48. Wa anzalnaaa ilaykal-Kitaaba bilḥaqqi muṣaddiqallimaa bayna yadayhi minal-Kitaabi wa muhayminan 'alayhi faḥkum baynahum bimaaa anzalal-laahu wa laa tattabi' ahwaaa'ahum 'ammaa jaaa'aka minal-ḥaqq; likullin ja'alnaa minkum shir'atañw-wa minhaajaa; wa law shaaa'al-laahu laja'alakum ummatañw-waaḥidatañw-wa laakil-liyablu-wakum fee maaa aataakum fastabiqul-khayraat; ilal-laahi marji'ukum jamee'an fayunab-bi'ukum bimaa kuntum feehi takhtalifoon.

وَاَنْزَلْنَآ اِلَيْكَ الْكِتٰبَ بِالْحَقِّ
مُصَدِّقًا لِّمَا بَيْنَ يَدَيْهِ مِنَ
الْكِتٰبِ وَمُهَيْمِنًا عَلَيْهِ فَاحْكُمْ
بَيْنَهُمْ بِمَآ اَنْزَلَ اللّٰهُ وَلَا تَتَّبِعْ
اَهْوَآءَهُمْ عَمَّا جَآءَكَ مِنَ الْحَقِّ ۗ
لِكُلٍّ جَعَلْنَا مِنْكُمْ شِرْعَةً وَّمِنْهَاجًا ۗ
وَلَوْ شَآءَ اللّٰهُ لَجَعَلَكُمْ اُمَّةً وَّاحِدَةً
وَّلٰكِنْ لِّيَبْلُوَكُمْ فِيْ مَآ اٰتٰىكُمْ
فَاسْتَبِقُوا الْخَيْرٰتِ ۗ اِلَى اللّٰهِ مَرْجِعُكُمْ
جَمِيْعًا فَيُنَبِّئُكُمْ بِمَا كُنْتُمْ فِيْهِ
تَخْتَلِفُوْنَ ۙ ﴿٤٨﴾

49. (Muhammad), you must judge among them by what Allah has revealed. Do not follow their desires. Beware of their mischievous deception concerning some of the matters that Allah has revealed to you. If they turn away, know that what Allah wants is to punish them for some of their sins. Many human beings are evil-doers.

49. Wa aniḥ-kum baynahum bimaaa anzalal-laahu wa laa tattabi' ahwaaa'ahum waḥzar-hum añy-yaftinooka 'am ba'ḍi maaa anzalal-laahu ilayka fa-in tawallaw fa'lam annamaa yureedul-laahu añy-yuṣeebahum biba'ḍi zunoobihim; wa inna kaseeram-minan-naasi lafaa-siqoon.

وَاَنِ احْكُمْ بَيْنَهُمْ بِمَآ اَنْزَلَ
اللّٰهُ وَلَا تَتَّبِعْ اَهْوَآءَهُمْ وَاحْذَرْهُمْ
اَنْ يَّفْتِنُوْكَ عَنْ بَعْضِ مَآ اَنْزَلَ
اللّٰهُ اِلَيْكَ ۗ فَاِنْ تَوَلَّوْا فَاعْلَمْ اَنَّمَا
يُرِيْدُ اللّٰهُ اَنْ يُّصِيْبَهُمْ بِبَعْضِ
ذُنُوْبِهِمْ ۗ وَاِنَّ كَثِيْرًا مِّنَ
النَّاسِ لَفٰسِقُوْنَ ﴿٤٩﴾

50. Do they want judgments that are issued out of ignorance? Who is a better judge for the people whose belief is based on certainty, than Allah?

50. Afaḥukmal-Jaahiliyyati yabghoon; wa man aḥsanu minal-laahi ḥukmal-liqawmiñy-yooqinoon.

أَفَحُكْمَ الْجَاهِلِيَّةِ يَبْغُونَ ۚ
وَمَنْ أَحْسَنُ مِنَ اللَّهِ حُكْمًا
لِّقَوْمٍ يُوقِنُونَ ﴿٥٠﴾

51. Believers, do not consider the Jews and Christians as your intimate friends for they are only friends with each other. Whoever does so will be considered as one of them. Allah does not guide the unjust people.

51. Yaaa-ayyuhal-lazeena aamanoo laa tattakhizul-Yahooda wan-Naṣaaraaa awliyaaa'; ba‘ḍuhum-awliyaaa'u ba‘ḍ; wa mañy-yatawallahum minkum fa-innahoo minhum; innal-laaha laa yahdil-qawmaẓ-ẓaalimeen.

يَا أَيُّهَا الَّذِينَ آمَنُوا لَا تَتَّخِذُوا
الْيَهُودَ وَالنَّصَارَىٰ أَوْلِيَاءَ ۘ بَعْضُهُمْ
أَوْلِيَاءُ بَعْضٍ ۚ وَمَن يَتَوَلَّهُم
مِّنكُمْ فَإِنَّهُ مِنْهُمْ ۗ إِنَّ اللَّهَ
لَا يَهْدِي الْقَوْمَ الظَّالِمِينَ ﴿٥١﴾

52. (Muhammad), you have seen those whose hearts are sick, running around among the people (Jews) saying, "We are afraid of being struck by disaster." But if Allah were to grant you victory or some other favors, they would then regret what they had been hiding in their souls.

52. Fataral-lazeena fee quloobihim maraḍuñy-yusaa-ri‘oona feehim yaqooloona nakhshaaa-an tuṣeebanaa daaa'irah; fa‘asallaahu añy-ya-tiya bilfatḥi aw amrim-min ‘indihee fayuṣbiḥoo ‘alaa maaa asarroo feee anfusihim naadimeen.

فَتَرَى الَّذِينَ فِي قُلُوبِهِم مَّرَضٌ
يُسَارِعُونَ فِيهِمْ يَقُولُونَ نَخْشَىٰ
أَن تُصِيبَنَا دَائِرَةٌ ۚ فَعَسَى اللَّهُ
أَن يَأْتِيَ بِالْفَتْحِ أَوْ أَمْرٍ مِّنْ
عِندِهِ فَيُصْبِحُوا عَلَىٰ مَا أَسَرُّوا فِي
أَنفُسِهِمْ نَادِمِينَ ﴿٥٢﴾

53. The believers say, "Are these the people who proclaimed themselves to be our sworn friends?" Their deeds have become devoid of all virtue and they, themselves, have become lost.

53. Wa yaqoolul-lazeena aamanooo ahaaa'ulaaa'il-lazeena aqsamoo billaahi jahda aymaanihim innahum lama-‘akum; ḥabiṭat a‘maaluhum fa-aṣbaḥoo khaasireen.

وَيَقُولُ الَّذِينَ آمَنُوا أَهَٰؤُلَاءِ
الَّذِينَ أَقْسَمُوا بِاللَّهِ جَهْدَ أَيْمَانِهِمْ ۙ
إِنَّهُمْ لَمَعَكُمْ ۚ حَبِطَتْ أَعْمَالُهُمْ
فَأَصْبَحُوا خَاسِرِينَ ﴿٥٣﴾

54. Believers, whichever of you turns away from his faith should know that Allah will soon raise a people whom He loves and who love Him, who are humble towards the believers, who are dignified to the unbelievers, who strive hard for the cause of Allah, and who have no fear of anyone's accusations. This is a favor from Allah. He bestows His favors upon whomever He wants. Allah is Munificent and All-knowing.

54. Yaaa ayyuhal-lazeena aamanoo mañy-yartadda minkum ‘an deenihee fasawfa ya-til-laahu biqawmiñy-yuḥibbuhum wa yuḥibboonahooo azillatin ‘alal-mu'mineena a‘izzatin ‘alal-kaafireena yujaahidoona fee sabeelil-laahi wa laa yakhaafoona lawmata laaa'im; zaalika faḍlul-laahi yu'teehi mañy-yashaaa'; wallaahu Waasi‘un ‘Aleem.

يَا أَيُّهَا الَّذِينَ آمَنُوا مَن يَرْتَدَّ
مِنكُمْ عَن دِينِهِ فَسَوْفَ يَأْتِي اللَّهُ
بِقَوْمٍ يُحِبُّهُمْ وَيُحِبُّونَهُ أَذِلَّةٍ
عَلَى الْمُؤْمِنِينَ أَعِزَّةٍ عَلَى الْكَافِرِينَ
يُجَاهِدُونَ فِي سَبِيلِ اللَّهِ وَلَا
يَخَافُونَ لَوْمَةَ لَائِمٍ ۚ ذَٰلِكَ
فَضْلُ اللَّهِ يُؤْتِيهِ مَن يَشَاءُ ۚ
وَاللَّهُ وَاسِعٌ عَلِيمٌ ﴿٥٤﴾

ع
وقف غفران ١٢ وقف لازم
وقف منزل عند البعض
الثلثة

55. Only Allah, His Messenger, and the true believers who are steadfast in prayer and pay alms, while they bow down during prayer, are your guardians.

55. Innamaa waliyyukumul-laahu wa Rasooluhoo wal-lazeena aamanul-lazeena yu-qeemoonaṣ-Ṣalaata wa yu'too-naz-Zakaata wa hum raaki'oon.

إِنَّمَا وَلِيُّكُمُ اللّٰهُ وَرَسُولُهٗ وَالَّذِينَ
اٰمَنُوا الَّذِينَ يُقِيمُونَ الصَّلٰوةَ
وَيُؤْتُونَ الزَّكٰوةَ وَهُمْ رٰكِعُونَ ﴿٥٥﴾

56. One whose guardians are Allah, His Messenger, and the true believers should know that Allah's party will certainly triumph.

56. Wa mañy-yatawallal-laaha wa Rasoolahoo wallazeena aamanoo fa-inna ḥizbal-laahi humul-ghaaliboon.

وَمَنْ يَّتَوَلَّ اللّٰهَ وَرَسُولَهٗ وَالَّذِينَ
اٰمَنُوا فَإِنَّ حِزْبَ اللّٰهِ هُمُ الْغٰلِبُونَ ﴿٥٦﴾ ع ٨ ١٢

57. Believers, do not consider those among the People of the Book and the unbelievers who mock at your religion and treat it as useless, as your protectors. Have fear of Allah if you are true believers.

57. Yaaa ayyuhal-lazeena aamanoo laa tattakhizul-lazeenat-takhazoo deenakum huzuwañw-wa la'ibam-minallazeena ootul-Kitaaba min qablikum walkuffaara awliyaaa'; wattaqul-laaha in kuntum mu'mineen.

يٰۤاَيُّهَا الَّذِينَ اٰمَنُوا لَا تَتَّخِذُوا
الَّذِينَ اتَّخَذُوا دِينَكُمْ هُزُوًا وَّ
لَعِبًا مِّنَ الَّذِينَ اُوتُوا الْكِتٰبَ مِنْ
قَبْلِكُمْ وَالْكُفَّارَ اَوْلِيَآءَ ۚ وَاتَّقُوا
اللّٰهَ اِنْ كُنْتُمْ مُّؤْمِنِينَ ﴿٥٧﴾

58. Because they are devoid of understanding, they ridicule your call for prayers saying that it is a useless act.

58. Wa izaa naadaytum ilaṣ-Ṣalaatit-takhazoohaa huzu-wañw-wa la'ibaa; zaalika bi-annahum qawmul-laa ya'qiloon.

وَاِذَا نَادَيْتُمْ اِلَى الصَّلٰوةِ اتَّخَذُوهَا
هُزُوًا وَّلَعِبًا ۭ ذٰلِكَ بِاَنَّهُمْ قَوْمٌ
لَّا يَعْقِلُونَ ﴿٥٨﴾

59. (Muhammad), say to the People of the Book, "Do you take revenge on us because of our belief in Allah and what He has revealed to us and to others before us? Most of you are evil-doers."

59. Qul yaaa Ahlal-Kitaabi hal tanqimoona minnaaa illaaa an aamannaa billaahi wa maaa unzila ilaynaa wa maaa unzila min qabl; wa anna aksarakum faasiqoon.

قُلْ يٰۤاَهْلَ الْكِتٰبِ هَلْ تَنْقِمُونَ
مِنَّآ اِلَّآ اَنْ اٰمَنَّا بِاللّٰهِ وَمَآ اُنْزِلَ
اِلَيْنَا وَمَآ اُنْزِلَ مِنْ قَبْلُ ۙ
وَاَنَّ اَكْثَرَكُمْ فٰسِقُونَ ﴿٥٩﴾

60. Say, "Should I tell you who will receive the worst punishment from Allah? Those whom Allah has condemned, afflicted with His anger, made apes out of them, swine, and worshippers of Satan, will have the worst dwelling and will wander far away from the right path."

60. Qul hal unabbi'ukum bisharrim-min zaalika masoo-batan 'indal-laah; malla'ana-hul-laahu wa ghaḍiba 'alayhi wa ja'ala minhumul-qiradata wal-khanaazeera wa 'abadaṭ-Ṭaaghoot; ulaaa'ika sharrum-makaanañw-wa aḍallu 'an Sawaaa'is-Sabeel.

قُلْ هَلْ اُنَبِّئُكُمْ بِشَرٍّ مِّنْ ذٰلِكَ
مَثُوبَةً عِنْدَ اللّٰهِ ۭ مَنْ لَّعَنَهُ اللّٰهُ
وَغَضِبَ عَلَيْهِ وَجَعَلَ مِنْهُمُ الْقِرَدَةَ
وَالْخَنَازِيرَ وَعَبَدَ الطَّاغُوتَ ۭ
اُولٰۤئِكَ شَرٌّ مَّكَانًا وَّاَضَلُّ عَنْ
سَوَآءِ السَّبِيلِ ﴿٦٠﴾

61. When they come to you (believers), they say, "We have accepted your faith." However, they entered into your faith as unbelievers and left it as unbelievers. Allah knows best what they were hiding.

61. Wa-izaa jaaa'ookum qaalooo aamannaa wa qad dakhaloo bilkufri wa hum qad kharajoo bih; wallaahu a'lamu bimaa kaanoo yaktumoon.

وَاِذَا جَآءُوكُمْ قَالُوْٓا اٰمَنَّا وَقَدْ
دَّخَلُوا بِالْكُفْرِ وَهُمْ قَدْ خَرَجُوا بِهٖ ۭ
وَاللّٰهُ اَعْلَمُ بِمَا كَانُوا يَكْتُمُونَ ﴿٦١﴾

62. You can see many of them compete with each other in sin, in hostility, and in taking usury. What they had been doing is certainly evil.

63. Why did the believers in the Lord and rabbis not forbid them from following their sinful words and their consuming of unlawful gains? Evil was their (rabbis and priests) profession!

64. The Jews have said, "Allah's hands are bound." May they themselves be handcuffed and condemned for what they have said! Allah's hands are free and He distributes His favors to His creatures however He wants. The rebellion and disbelief of many of them will be intensified against you because of what has been revealed to you from your Lord.

We have induced hostility and hatred among them which will remain with them until the Day of Judgment. Whenever they kindle the fire of war, Allah extinguishes it. They try to spread evil in the land but Allah does not love the evil-doers.

65. Had the People of the Book accepted the faith and observed piety, certainly We would have redeemed their bad deeds and admitted them into a blissful Paradise.

66. Had they followed the Laws of the Old and New Testaments and what was revealed to them from their Lord, they would have received Our bounties from above and below in abundance. Some of them are modest people, but many of them commit the worst sins.

67. O Messenger, proclaim what is revealed to you from your Lord. If you did not do so, it will be as though you have not

62. Wa taraa kas̱eeram-minhum yusaari'oona fil-is̱mi wal'udwaani wa aklihimus-suḥt; labi'sa maa kaanoo ya'maloon.

63. Law laa yanhaahumur-rabbaaniyyoona wal-aḥbaaru 'an qawlihimul-is̱ma wa aklihimus-suḥt; labi'sa maa kaanoo yaṣna'oon.

64. Wa qaalatil-Yahoodu Yadullaahi maghloolah; ghullat aydeehim wa lu'inoo bimaa qaaloo; bal Yadaahu mabsooṭataani yunfiqu kayfa yashaaa'; wa layazeedanna kas̱eeram-minhum-maaa unzila ilayka mir-Rabbika ṭughyaanañw-wa kufraa; wa-alqaynaa baynahumul-'adaawata wal-baghḍaaa-a'ilaa Yawmil-Qiyaamah; kullamaaa-awqadoo naaral-lilḥarbi aṭfa-ahal-laah; wa yas'awna fil-arḍi fasaadaa; wallaahu laa yuḥibbul-mufsideen.

65. Wa law anna Ahlal-Kitaabi aamanoo wattaqaw lakaffarnaa 'anhum sayyi-aatihim wa la-adkhalnaahum Jannaatin-Na'eem.

66. Wa law annahum aqaamut-Tawraata wal-Injeela wa maaa unzila ilayhim-mir-Rabbihim la-akaloo min fawqihim wa min taḥti arjulihim; minhum ummatum-muqtaṣidah; wa kas̱eerum-minhum saaa'a maa ya'maloon.

67. Yaaa ayyuhar-Rasoolu balligh maaa unzila ilayka mir-Rabbika wa il-lam taf'al famaa ballaghta

وَتَرَىٰ كَثِيرًا مِّنْهُمْ يُسَارِعُونَ فِي
الْإِثْمِ وَالْعُدْوَانِ وَأَكْلِهِمُ السُّحْتَ ۚ
لَبِئْسَ مَا كَانُوا يَعْمَلُونَ ﴿٦٢﴾
لَوْلَا يَنْهَاهُمُ الرَّبَّانِيُّونَ وَالْأَحْبَارُ
عَن قَوْلِهِمُ الْإِثْمَ وَأَكْلِهِمُ السُّحْتَ ۚ
لَبِئْسَ مَا كَانُوا يَصْنَعُونَ ﴿٦٣﴾
وَقَالَتِ الْيَهُودُ يَدُ اللَّهِ مَغْلُولَةٌ ۚ
غُلَّتْ أَيْدِيهِمْ وَلُعِنُوا بِمَا قَالُوا ۘ بَلْ
يَدَاهُ مَبْسُوطَتَانِ يُنفِقُ كَيْفَ يَشَاءُ ۚ
وَلَيَزِيدَنَّ كَثِيرًا مِّنْهُم مَّا أُنزِلَ
إِلَيْكَ مِن رَّبِّكَ طُغْيَانًا وَكُفْرًا ۚ
وَأَلْقَيْنَا بَيْنَهُمُ الْعَدَاوَةَ وَالْبَغْضَاءَ
إِلَىٰ يَوْمِ الْقِيَامَةِ ۚ كُلَّمَا أَوْقَدُوا نَارًا
لِّلْحَرْبِ أَطْفَأَهَا اللَّهُ ۚ وَيَسْعَوْنَ
فِي الْأَرْضِ فَسَادًا ۚ وَاللَّهُ لَا يُحِبُّ
الْمُفْسِدِينَ ﴿٦٤﴾
وَلَوْ أَنَّ أَهْلَ الْكِتَابِ آمَنُوا وَاتَّقَوْا
لَكَفَّرْنَا عَنْهُمْ سَيِّئَاتِهِمْ وَلَأَدْخَلْنَاهُمْ
جَنَّاتِ النَّعِيمِ ﴿٦٥﴾
وَلَوْ أَنَّهُمْ أَقَامُوا التَّوْرَاةَ وَالْإِنجِيلَ
وَمَا أُنزِلَ إِلَيْهِم مِّن رَّبِّهِمْ لَأَكَلُوا
مِن فَوْقِهِمْ وَمِن تَحْتِ أَرْجُلِهِم ۚ
مِّنْهُمْ أُمَّةٌ مُّقْتَصِدَةٌ ۖ وَكَثِيرٌ
مِّنْهُمْ سَاءَ مَا يَعْمَلُونَ ﴿٦٦﴾ ع
يَا أَيُّهَا الرَّسُولُ بَلِّغْ مَا أُنزِلَ إِلَيْكَ
مِن رَّبِّكَ ۖ وَإِن لَّمْ تَفْعَلْ فَمَا بَلَّغْتَ

وقف لازم

ع

conveyed His message. Allah protects you from men. He does not guide the unbelieving people.

68. (Muhammad), tell the People of the Book, "You have nothing unless you follow the Old and New Testaments and that which Allah has revealed to you (the Quran)." Whatever has been revealed to you (Muhammad) from your Lord will only increase their disbelief and rebellion (against you). Do not grieve for the unbelieving people.

69. The believers, Jews, Sabeans, and the Christians who believe in Allah and the Day of Judgment and who do what is right will have nothing to fear nor will they be grieved.

70. We made a covenant with the Israelites and sent Messengers to them. Whenever a Messenger came to them with a message which did not suit their desires, they would reject some of the Messengers and kill others.

71. They were blind and deaf in their pride, thinking themselves (to be the chosen nation of Allah) and thus safe from calamities. Allah forgave them but many of them, out of pride, again became blind and deaf. Allah is Well-aware of what they do.

72. Those who say that Jesus, the son of Mary, is Allah, have, in fact, turned to disbelief. Jesus said to the Israelites, "Worship Allah, my Lord and yours. Allah will deprive of paradise anyone who considers anything equal to Allah, and his dwelling will be

Risaalatah; wallaahu ya'ṣimuka minannaas; innal-laaha laa yahdilqawmal-kaafireen.

68. Qul yaaa Ahlal-Kitaabi lastum 'alaa shay'in ḥattaa tuqeemut-Tawraata wal-Injeela wa maaa unzila ilaykum-mir-Rabbikum; wa layazeedanna kaṣeeram-minhum-maaa unzila ilayka mir-Rabbika ṭughyaanañw-wa kufran falaa ta-sa'alal-qawmil-kaafireen.

69. Innal-lazeena aamanoo wallazeena haadoo waṣ-Ṣaabi'oona wan-Naṣaaraa man aamana billaahi wal-Yawmil-Aakhiri wa 'amila ṣaaliḥan falaa khawfun 'alayhim wa laa hum yaḥzanoon.

70. Laqad akhaznaa meeṣaaqa Baneee Israaa'eela wa arsal-naaa ilayhim Rusulan kullamaa jaaa'ahum Rasoolum-bimaa laa tahwaaa anfusuhum fareeqan kaz-zaboo wa fareeqañy-yaqtuloon.

71. Wa ḥasibooo allaa takoona fitnatun fa'amoo wa ṣammoo ṣumma taabal-laahu 'alayhim ṣumma 'amoo wa ṣammoo kaṣeerum-minhum; wallaahu baṣeerum-bimaa ya'maloon.

72. Laqad kafaral-lazeena qaaloo innal-laaha Huwal-Maseeḥub-nu-Maryama wa qaalal-Maseeḥu yaa Baneee Israaa'eela'-budul-laaha Rabbee wa Rabbakum innahoo mañy-yushrik billaahi faqad ḥarramal-laahu

رِسَالَتَهُ ۚ وَاللّٰهُ يَعْصِمُكَ مِنَ النَّاسِ ۗ إِنَّ اللّٰهَ لَا يَهْدِى الْقَوْمَ الْكٰفِرِينَ ۞

قُلْ يَا أَهْلَ الْكِتٰبِ لَسْتُمْ عَلٰى شَىْءٍ حَتّٰى تُقِيمُوا التَّوْرٰةَ وَالْإِنْجِيلَ وَمَا أُنْزِلَ إِلَيْكُمْ مِّنْ رَّبِّكُمْ ۗ وَلَيَزِيدَنَّ كَثِيرًا مِّنْهُمْ مَّا أُنْزِلَ إِلَيْكَ مِنْ رَّبِّكَ طُغْيَانًا وَّكُفْرًا ۖ فَلَا تَأْسَ عَلَى الْقَوْمِ الْكٰفِرِينَ ۞

إِنَّ الَّذِينَ آمَنُوا وَالَّذِينَ هَادُوا وَالصّٰبِئُونَ وَالنَّصٰرَى مَنْ آمَنَ بِاللّٰهِ وَالْيَوْمِ الْأٰخِرِ وَعَمِلَ صَالِحًا فَلَا خَوْفٌ عَلَيْهِمْ وَلَا هُمْ يَحْزَنُونَ ۞

لَقَدْ أَخَذْنَا مِيثَاقَ بَنِى إِسْرَآءِيلَ وَأَرْسَلْنَا إِلَيْهِمْ رُسُلًا ۖ كُلَّمَا جَآءَهُمْ رَسُولٌ بِمَا لَا تَهْوٰى أَنْفُسُهُمْ ۙ فَرِيقًا كَذَّبُوا وَفَرِيقًا يَّقْتُلُونَ ۞

وَحَسِبُوا أَلَّا تَكُونَ فِتْنَةٌ فَعَمُوا وَصَمُّوا ثُمَّ تَابَ اللّٰهُ عَلَيْهِمْ ثُمَّ عَمُوا وَصَمُّوا كَثِيرٌ مِّنْهُمْ ۚ وَاللّٰهُ بَصِيرٌ بِمَا يَعْمَلُونَ ۞

لَقَدْ كَفَرَ الَّذِينَ قَالُوا إِنَّ اللّٰهَ هُوَ الْمَسِيحُ ابْنُ مَرْيَمَ ۖ وَقَالَ الْمَسِيحُ يَا بَنِى إِسْرَآءِيلَ اعْبُدُوا اللّٰهَ رَبِّى وَرَبَّكُمْ ۖ إِنَّهُ مَنْ يُّشْرِكْ بِاللّٰهِ فَقَدْ حَرَّمَ اللّٰهُ

fire. The unjust people have no helpers."

73. Those who say that Allah is the third of the three, have, in fact, turned to disbelief. There is no Lord but Allah, the only One Lord. If they did not give up such belief, the unbelievers among them will suffer a painful torment.

74. Should they not repent and ask Him for forgiveness? Allah is All-forgiving and All-merciful.

75. Jesus, the son of Mary, was no more than a Messenger before whom there lived many other Messengers. His mother was a truthful woman and both of them ate earthly food. Consider how We explain the evidence (of the Truth) to them and see where they then turn.

76. (Muhammad), say to them, "Do you worship things besides Allah which can neither harm or benefit you?" It is only Allah who is All-hearing and All-knowing.

77. Say to the People of the Book, "Do not wrongly exceed the proper limit of devotion to your religion or follow the desires of the people who have erred. They have misled many others and have themselves stayed far away from the right path."

78. The unbelievers among the Israelites, because of their disobedience and transgression, were condemned by David and Jesus, the son of Mary, for their disobedience; they were transgressors.

79. They did not prevent each other from committing sins nor would they, themselves, stay

'alayhil-Jannata wa ma-waahun-Naaru wa maa lizzaalimeena min anṣaar.

73. Laqad kafaral-lazeena qaalooo innal-laaha saalisu salaasah; wa maa min ilaahin illaaa Ilaahuñw-Waaḥid; wa il-lam yantahoo 'ammaa yaqoo-loona layamas-sannallazeena kafaroo minhum 'azaabun aleem.

74. Afalaa-yatooboona ilal-laahi wa yastaghfiroonah; wallaahu Ghafoorur- Raḥeem.

75. Mal-Maseeḥub-nu-Mar-yama illaa Rasoolun qad khalat min qablihir-Rusul; wa ummu-hoo ṣiddeeqatun kaanaa ya-kulaaniṭ-ṭa'aam; unẓur kayfa nubayyinu lahumul-Aayaati summan-ẓur annaa yu'fakoon.

76. Qul ata'budoona min doonil-laahi maa laa yamliku lakum ḍarrañw-wa laa naf'aa; wallaahu Huwas-Samee'ul 'Aleem.

77. Qul yaaa Ahlal-Kitaabi laa taghloo fee deenikum ghayral-ḥaqqi wa laa tattabi-'ooo ahwaaa'a qawmin qad ḍalloo min qablu wa aḍalloo kaseerañw-wa ḍalloo 'an Sawaaa'is-Sabeel.

78. Lu'inal-lazeena kafaroo mim Baneee Israaa'eela 'alaa lisaani Daawooda wa 'Eesab-ni-Maryam; zaalika bimaa 'aṣaw wa kaanoo ya'tadoon.

79. Kaanoo laa yatanaahawna 'am-munkarin

عَلَيْهِ الْجَنَّةَ وَمَاْوٰىهُ النَّارُ ۭ وَمَا
لِلظّٰلِمِيْنَ مِنْ اَنْصَارٍ ۝٧٢
لَقَدْ كَفَرَ الَّذِيْنَ قَالُوْٓا اِنَّ
اللّٰهَ ثَالِثُ ثَلٰثَةٍ ۘ وَمَا مِنْ اِلٰهٍ
اِلَّآ اِلٰهٌ وَّاحِدٌ ۭ وَاِنْ لَّمْ يَنْتَهُوْا
عَمَّا يَقُوْلُوْنَ لَيَمَسَّنَّ الَّذِيْنَ
كَفَرُوْا مِنْهُمْ عَذَابٌ اَلِيْمٌ ۝٧٣
اَفَلَا يَتُوْبُوْنَ اِلَى اللّٰهِ وَيَسْتَغْفِرُوْنَهٗ ۭ
وَاللّٰهُ غَفُوْرٌ رَّحِيْمٌ ۝٧٤
مَا الْمَسِيْحُ ابْنُ مَرْيَمَ اِلَّا رَسُوْلٌ ۚ
قَدْ خَلَتْ مِنْ قَبْلِهِ الرُّسُلُ ۭ
وَاُمُّهٗ صِدِّيْقَةٌ ۭ كَانَا يَاْكُلٰنِ
الطَّعَامَ ۭ اُنْظُرْ كَيْفَ نُبَيِّنُ لَهُمُ
الْاٰيٰتِ ثُمَّ انْظُرْ اَنّٰى يُؤْفَكُوْنَ ۝٧٥
قُلْ اَتَعْبُدُوْنَ مِنْ دُوْنِ اللّٰهِ
مَا لَا يَمْلِكُ لَكُمْ ضَرًّا وَّلَا نَفْعًا ۭ
وَاللّٰهُ هُوَ السَّمِيْعُ الْعَلِيْمُ ۝٧٦
قُلْ يٰٓاَهْلَ الْكِتٰبِ لَا تَغْلُوْا فِيْ
دِيْنِكُمْ غَيْرَ الْحَقِّ وَلَا تَتَّبِعُوْٓا
اَهْوَاۗءَ قَوْمٍ قَدْ ضَلُّوْا مِنْ
قَبْلُ وَاَضَلُّوْا كَثِيْرًا وَّضَلُّوْا
عَنْ سَوَاۗءِ السَّبِيْلِ ۝٧٧
لُعِنَ الَّذِيْنَ كَفَرُوْا مِنْۢ بَنِيْٓ اِسْرَاۗءِيْلَ
عَلٰي لِسَانِ دَاوٗدَ وَعِيْسَى ابْنِ مَرْيَمَ ۭ
ذٰلِكَ بِمَا عَصَوْا وَّكَانُوْا يَعْتَدُوْنَ ۝٧٨
كَانُوْا لَا يَتَنَاهَوْنَ عَنْ مُّنْكَرٍ

وقف لازم

ع ١٠

away from them. Evil was what they had done!

fa'alooh; labi'sa maa kaanoo yaf'aloon.

فَعَلُوْهُ ؕ لَبِئْسَ مَا كَانُوْا يَفْعَلُوْنَ ﴿۷۹﴾

80. You have seen many of them establishing friendship with the unbelievers. Vile is what their souls have achieved! They have invoked the wrath of Allah upon themselves and they will live forever in torment.

80. Taraa kaseeram-minhum yatawallawnal-lazeena kafaroo; labi'sa maa qaddamat lahum anfusuhum an sakhiṭal-laahu 'alayhim wa fil-'azaabi hum khaalidoon.

تَرٰى كَثِيْرًا مِّنْهُمْ يَتَوَلَّوْنَ الَّذِيْنَ
كَفَرُوْا ؕ لَبِئْسَ مَا قَدَّمَتْ لَهُمْ
اَنْفُسُهُمْ اَنْ سَخِطَ اللّٰهُ عَلَيْهِمْ وَفِى
الْعَذَابِ هُمْ خٰلِدُوْنَ ﴿۸۰﴾

81. Had they had faith in Allah, the Prophet, and what was revealed to him, they would not have been the friends of the unbelievers. However, many of them are evil-doers.

81. Wa law kaanoo yu'minoona billaahi wan-Nabiyyi wa maaa unzila ilayhi mattakhazoohum awliyaaa'a wa laakinna kaseeram-minhum faasiqoon.

وَلَوْ كَانُوْا يُؤْمِنُوْنَ بِاللّٰهِ وَالنَّبِىِّ
وَمَاۤ اُنْزِلَ اِلَيْهِ مَا اتَّخَذُوْهُمْ
اَوْلِيَآءَ وَلٰكِنَّ كَثِيْرًا مِّنْهُمْ فٰسِقُوْنَ ﴿۸۱﴾

82. You find Jews and pagans among the worst of the enemies of the believers. (Of the non-believers) nearest to them (the believers) in affection you find those who say, "We are Christians," for among them are the priests and monks who are not proud.

82. Latajidanna ashad-dannaasi 'adaawatal-lillazeena aamanul-Yahooda wallazeena ashrakoo wa latajidanna aqrabahum-mawad-datallil-lazeena aamanul-lazeena qaalooo innaa Naṣaaraa; zaalika bi-anna minhum qisseeseena wa ruhbaanañw-wa annahum laa yastakbiroon.

لَتَجِدَنَّ اَشَدَّ النَّاسِ عَدَاوَةً
لِّلَّذِيْنَ اٰمَنُوا الْيَهُوْدَ وَالَّذِيْنَ
اَشْرَكُوْا ۚ وَلَتَجِدَنَّ اَقْرَبَهُمْ
مَّوَدَّةً لِّلَّذِيْنَ اٰمَنُوا الَّذِيْنَ
قَالُوْۤا اِنَّا نَصٰرٰى ؕ ذٰلِكَ بِاَنَّ
مِنْهُمْ قِسِّيْسِيْنَ وَرُهْبَانًا وَّ
اَنَّهُمْ لَا يَسْتَكْبِرُوْنَ ﴿۸۲﴾

83. When they hear what is revealed to the Messenger, you can see their eyes flood with tears, as they learn about the Truth. They say, "Lord, we believe (in this faith). Write our names down as bearing witness to it.

83. Wa izaa sami'oo maaa unzila ilar-Rasooli taraaa a'yunahum tafeeḍu minad-dam'i mimmaa 'arafoo minal-ḥaqq; yaqooloona Rabba-naaa aamannaa faktubnaa ma'ash-shaahideen.

وَاِذَا سَمِعُوْا مَاۤ اُنْزِلَ اِلَى الرَّسُوْلِ
تَرٰۤى اَعْيُنَهُمْ تَفِيْضُ مِنَ الدَّمْعِ
مِمَّا عَرَفُوْا مِنَ الْحَقِّ ۚ يَقُوْلُوْنَ رَبَّنَاۤ
اٰمَنَّا فَاكْتُبْنَا مَعَ الشّٰهِدِيْنَ ﴿۸۳﴾

اَلْجُزْءُ السَّابِعُ (۷)

84. Why should we not believe in Allah and the Truth that has come to us and hope that the Lord will admit us into the company of the righteous people?"

84. Wa maa lanaa laa nu'minu billaahi wa maa jaaa'anaa minal-ḥaqq; wa naṭma'u añy-yudkhilanaa Rabbunaa ma'al-qawmiṣ-ṣaaliḥeen.

وَمَا لَنَا لَا نُؤْمِنُ بِاللّٰهِ وَمَا جَآءَنَا
مِنَ الْحَقِّ ۙ وَنَطْمَعُ اَنْ يُّدْخِلَنَا رَبُّنَا
مَعَ الْقَوْمِ الصّٰلِحِيْنَ ﴿۸۴﴾

85. Thus, Allah has given them as their reward, gardens wherein streams flow and wherein they will live forever. Such will be the recompense of the righteous people.

85. Fa-asaabahumul-laahu bimaa qaaloo Jannaatin tajree min taḥtihal-anhaaru khaalideena feehaa; wa zaalika jazaaa'ul-muḥsineen.

فَاَثَابَهُمُ اللّٰهُ بِمَا قَالُوْا جَنّٰتٍ تَجْرِىْ
مِنْ تَحْتِهَا الْاَنْهٰرُ خٰلِدِيْنَ فِيْهَا ؕ
وَذٰلِكَ جَزَآءُ الْمُحْسِنِيْنَ ﴿۸۵﴾

86. Those who disbelieved and denied Our revelations will be the

86. Wallazeena kafaroo wa kaz-zaboo bi-Aayaatinaaa

وَالَّذِيْنَ كَفَرُوْا وَكَذَّبُوْا بِاٰيٰتِنَاۤ

dwellers of Hell.

ulaaa'ika Aṣḥaabul-Jaḥeem.

ع
أُولَٰٓئِكَ أَصْحَٰبُ ٱلْجَحِيمِ ﴿٨٦﴾

87. Believers, do not make unlawful the pure things which Allah has made lawful for you. Do not transgress; Allah does not love the transgressors.

87. Yaaa ayyuhal-lazeena aamanoo laa tuḥarrimoo ṭayyibaati maaa aḥallal-laahu lakum wa laa ta'tadooo; innal-laaha laa yuḥibbul-mu'tadeen.

يَٰٓأَيُّهَا ٱلَّذِينَ ءَامَنُوا۟ لَا تُحَرِّمُوا۟ طَيِّبَٰتِ
مَآ أَحَلَّ ٱللَّهُ لَكُمْ وَلَا تَعْتَدُوٓا۟ ۚ
إِنَّ ٱللَّهَ لَا يُحِبُّ ٱلْمُعْتَدِينَ ﴿٨٧﴾

88. Eat from the pure and lawful things that Allah has given to you. Have fear of Allah in Whom you believe.

88. Wa kuloo mimmaa razaqakumul-laahu ḥalaalan ṭayyibañw-wattaqul-laahallazeee antum bihee mu'minoon.

وَكُلُوا۟ مِمَّا رَزَقَكُمُ ٱللَّهُ حَلَٰلًا طَيِّبًا ۚ
وَٱتَّقُوا۟ ٱللَّهَ ٱلَّذِىٓ أَنتُم بِهِۦ مُؤْمِنُونَ ﴿٨٨﴾

89. Allah will not hold you responsible for your thoughtless oaths. However, He will question you about your deliberate oaths. The expiation for breaking an oath is to feed ten needy people with food, typical of that which you feed to your own people, to clothe them, or to set a slave free. One who could not pay this, he must fast for three days to expiate his oaths. Keep your oaths. Thus, does Allah explain His Laws so that you will give Him thanks.

89. Laa yu'aakhizukumullaahu billaghwi feee aymaanikum wa laakiñy-yu'aakhizukum bimaa 'aqqattumul-aymaana fakaffaaratuhooo iṭ'aamu 'asharati masaakeena min awsaṭi maa tuṭ'imoona ahleekum aw kiswatuhum aw taḥreeru raqabatin famallam yajid fa-Ṣiyaamu salaasati ayyaam; zaalika kaffaaratu aymaanikum izaa ḥalaftum; waḥfaẓooo aymaanakum; kazaalika yubayyinul-laahu lakum Aayaatihee la'allakum tashkuroon.

لَا يُؤَاخِذُكُمُ ٱللَّهُ بِٱللَّغْوِ فِىٓ أَيْمَٰنِكُمْ
وَلَٰكِن يُؤَاخِذُكُم بِمَا عَقَّدتُّمُ
ٱلْأَيْمَٰنَ ۖ فَكَفَّٰرَتُهُۥٓ إِطْعَامُ عَشَرَةِ
مَسَٰكِينَ مِنْ أَوْسَطِ مَا تُطْعِمُونَ
أَهْلِيكُمْ أَوْ كِسْوَتُهُمْ أَوْ تَحْرِيرُ رَقَبَةٍ ۖ
فَمَن لَّمْ يَجِدْ فَصِيَامُ ثَلَٰثَةِ أَيَّامٍ ۚ
ذَٰلِكَ كَفَّٰرَةُ أَيْمَٰنِكُمْ إِذَا حَلَفْتُمْ ۚ
وَٱحْفَظُوٓا۟ أَيْمَٰنَكُمْ ۚ كَذَٰلِكَ يُبَيِّنُ
ٱللَّهُ لَكُمْ ءَايَٰتِهِۦ لَعَلَّكُمْ تَشْكُرُونَ ﴿٨٩﴾

90. Believers, wine, gambling, the stone altars and arrows (that the pagans associate with certain divine characters) are all abominable acts associated with Satanic activities. Avoid them so that you may have everlasting happiness.

90. Yaaa ayyuhal-lazeena aamanooo innamal-khamru walmaysiru wal-anṣaabu wal-azlaamu rijsum-min 'amalish-shayṭaani fajtaniboohu la'allakum tufliḥoon.

يَٰٓأَيُّهَا ٱلَّذِينَ ءَامَنُوٓا۟ إِنَّمَا ٱلْخَمْرُ
وَٱلْمَيْسِرُ وَٱلْأَنصَابُ وَٱلْأَزْلَٰمُ رِجْسٌ
مِّنْ عَمَلِ ٱلشَّيْطَٰنِ فَٱجْتَنِبُوهُ
لَعَلَّكُمْ تُفْلِحُونَ ﴿٩٠﴾

91. Satan wants to induce hostility and hatred among you through wine and gambling and to prevent you from remembering Allah and prayer. Will you then avoid such things?

91. Innamaa yureedush-Shayṭaanu añy-yooqi'a baynakumul-'adaawata wal-baghḍaaa'a fil-khamri walmaysiri wa yaṣuddakum 'an zikril-laahi wa 'aniṣ-Ṣalaati fahal antum muntahoon.

إِنَّمَا يُرِيدُ ٱلشَّيْطَٰنُ أَن يُوقِعَ بَيْنَكُمُ
ٱلْعَدَٰوَةَ وَٱلْبَغْضَآءَ فِى ٱلْخَمْرِ وَٱلْمَيْسِرِ
وَيَصُدَّكُمْ عَن ذِكْرِ ٱللَّهِ وَعَنِ ٱلصَّلَوٰةِ ۖ
فَهَلْ أَنتُم مُّنتَهُونَ ﴿٩١﴾

92. Obey Allah and the Messenger and be cautious (of the harmful things). If you turn away (from Our laws), know that the duty of the Messenger is only to preach in clear words.

92. Wa aṭee'ul-laaha wa aṭee'ur-Rasoola waḥzaroo; fa-in tawallaytum fa'lamooo annamaa 'alaa Rasoolinal-balaaghul-mubeen.

وَأَطِيعُوا۟ ٱللَّهَ وَأَطِيعُوا۟ ٱلرَّسُولَ
وَٱحْذَرُوا۟ ۚ فَإِن تَوَلَّيْتُمْ فَٱعْلَمُوٓا۟
أَنَّمَا عَلَىٰ رَسُولِنَا ٱلْبَلَٰغُ ٱلْمُبِينُ ﴿٩٢﴾

93. The righteously striving believers will not be blamed for what they have eaten, if they maintain piety, do good deeds, have faith, and be charitable. Allah loves the generous people.

93. Laysa 'alal-lazeena aamanoo wa 'amiluṣ-ṣaaliḥaati junaaḥun feemaa ṭa'imooo izaa mat-taqaw wa aamanoo wa 'amiluṣ-ṣaaliḥaati summat-taqaw wa aamanoo summat-taqaw wa aḥsanoo; wallaahu yuḥibbul-muḥsineen.

لَيْسَ عَلَى الَّذِيْنَ اٰمَنُوْا وَعَمِلُوا الصّٰلِحٰتِ
جُنَاحٌ فِيْمَا طَعِمُوْۤا اِذَا مَا اتَّقَوْا
وَّاٰمَنُوْا وَعَمِلُوا الصّٰلِحٰتِ ثُمَّ اتَّقَوْا
وَّاٰمَنُوْا ثُمَّ اتَّقَوْا وَّاَحْسَنُوْا ؕ وَاللّٰهُ
يُحِبُّ الْمُحْسِنِيْنَ ۝٩٣ ع ۱۲ ۲

94. Believers, Allah will test you (to see the strength of your obedience) concerning what you hunt by hand or spear, so that He would know who has fear of Him in private. Whoever transgresses will suffer a painful torment.

94. Yaaa ayyuhal-lazeena aamanoo layabluwannakumul-laahu bishay'im-minaṣ-ṣaydi tanaaluhooo aydeekum wa rimaaḥukum liya'lamal-laahu mañy-yakhaafuhoo bilghayb; famani'-tadaa ba'da zaalika falahoo 'azaabun aleem.

يٰۤاَيُّهَا الَّذِيْنَ اٰمَنُوْا لَيَبْلُوَنَّكُمُ اللّٰهُ
بِشَيْءٍ مِّنَ الصَّيْدِ تَنَالُهٗۤ اَيْدِيْكُمْ
وَرِمَاحُكُمْ لِيَعْلَمَ اللّٰهُ مَنْ يَّخَافُهٗ
بِالْغَيْبِ ۚ فَمَنِ اعْتَدٰى بَعْدَ ذٰلِكَ
فَلَهٗ عَذَابٌ اَلِيْمٌ ۝٩٤

95. Believers, do not hunt when you are in the holy precinct. Whichever of you purposely kills game in the holy precinct has to offer, as an expiation, a sacrifice in the holy precinct which two just people among you would consider equal to the prey or food to a destitute person or has to fast (for an appointed time) to bear the burden of the penalty for his deed. Allah forgives whatever was done in the past, but He will take revenge on whoever returns to transgression, for He is Majestic and Capable of taking revenge.

95. Yaaa ayyuhal-lazeena aamanoo laa taqtuluṣ-ṣayda wa antum ḥurum; wa man qatalahoo minkummuta'am-midan fajazaaa'um mislu maa qatala minanna'ami yaḥkumu bihee zawaa 'adlim-minkum hadyam baalighal-Ka'bati aw kaffaaratun ṭa'aamu masaa-keena aw 'adlu zaalika Ṣiyaamal-liyazooqa wabaala amrih; 'afal-laahu 'ammaa salaf; wa man 'aada fayanta-qimul-laahu minh; wallaahu 'azeezun zuntiqaam.

يٰۤاَيُّهَا الَّذِيْنَ اٰمَنُوْا لَا تَقْتُلُوا الصَّيْدَ
وَاَنْتُمْ حُرُمٌ ؕ وَمَنْ قَتَلَهٗ مِنْكُمْ
مُّتَعَمِّدًا فَجَزَآءٌ مِّثْلُ مَا قَتَلَ مِنَ
النَّعَمِ يَحْكُمُ بِهٖ ذَوَا عَدْلٍ مِّنْكُمْ هَدْيًا
بٰلِغَ الْكَعْبَةِ اَوْ كَفَّارَةٌ طَعَامُ مَسٰكِيْنَ
اَوْ عَدْلُ ذٰلِكَ صِيَامًا لِّيَذُوْقَ وَبَالَ
اَمْرِهٖ ؕ عَفَا اللّٰهُ عَمَّا سَلَفَ ؕ وَمَنْ
عَادَ فَيَنْتَقِمُ اللّٰهُ مِنْهُ ؕ وَاللّٰهُ
عَزِيْزٌ ذُو انْتِقَامٍ ۝٩٥

96. It is lawful for you to hunt from the sea and to eat seafood. This is for your benefit and for the benefit of travelers. However, it is not lawful for you to hunt on land as long as you are in the sacred precinct. Have fear of Allah before whom you will all be raised.

96. Uḥilla lakum ṣaydul-baḥri wa ṭa'aamuhoo mataa'al-lakum wa lissayyaarati wa ḥurrima 'alaykum ṣaydul-barri maa dumtum ḥurumaa; wattaqul-laahal-lazeee ilayhi tuḥsharoon.

اُحِلَّ لَكُمْ صَيْدُ الْبَحْرِ وَطَعَامُهٗ
مَتَاعًا لَّكُمْ وَلِلسَّيَّارَةِ ۚ وَحُرِّمَ عَلَيْكُمْ
صَيْدُ الْبَرِّ مَا دُمْتُمْ حُرُمًا ؕ وَاتَّقُوا
اللّٰهَ الَّذِيْۤ اِلَيْهِ تُحْشَرُوْنَ ۝٩٦

97. Allah has made the Kabah, the Sacred House, the sacred months, the unmarked and marked sacrificial animals for the welfare of men and in order to inform you that Allah knows all

97. Ja'alal-laahul-Ka'batal-Baytal-Ḥaraama qiyaamal-linnaasi wash-Shahral-Ḥaraa-ma walhadya walqalaaa'id; zaalika lita'lamooo annal-laaha

جَعَلَ اللّٰهُ الْكَعْبَةَ الْبَيْتَ الْحَرَامَ
قِيٰمًا لِّلنَّاسِ وَالشَّهْرَ الْحَرَامَ وَالْهَدْيَ
وَالْقَلَآئِدَ ؕ ذٰلِكَ لِتَعْلَمُوْۤا اَنَّ اللّٰهَ

that is in the heavens and the earth. He has the knowledge of all things.

ya'lamu maa fis-samaawaati wa maa fil-arḍi wa annallaaha bikulli shay'in 'Aleem.

يَعْلَمُ مَا فِي السَّمٰوٰتِ وَمَا فِي الْأَرْضِ
وَأَنَّ اللّٰهَ بِكُلِّ شَيْءٍ عَلِيمٌ ٩٧

98. Know that Allah is stern in His retribution and He is All-forgiving and All-merciful.

98. I'lamooo annal-laaha shadeedul-'iqaabi wa annallaaha Ghafoorur-Raḥeem.

اِعْلَمُوٓا أَنَّ اللّٰهَ شَدِيدُ الْعِقَابِ
وَأَنَّ اللّٰهَ غَفُورٌ رَّحِيمٌ ٩٨

99. The duty of the Messenger is only to preach. Allah knows what you reveal or hide.

99. Maa 'alar-Rasooli illal-balaagh; wallaahu ya'lamu maa tubdoona wa maa taktumoon.

مَا عَلَى الرَّسُولِ إِلَّا الْبَلٰغُ ۗ وَاللّٰهُ
يَعْلَمُ مَا تُبْدُونَ وَمَا تَكْتُمُونَ ٩٩

100. (Muhammad), say to them, "The pure and filthy are not the same even though the abundance of filth may attract you. Men of reason, have fear of Allah so that you may have eternal happiness."

100. Qul laa yastawil-khabeesu waṭṭayyibu wa law a'jabaka kasratul-khabees; fattaqul-laaha yaaa-ulil-albaabi la'alla-kum tufliḥoon.

قُلْ لَّا يَسْتَوِي الْخَبِيثُ وَالطَّيِّبُ وَلَوْ
أَعْجَبَكَ كَثْرَةُ الْخَبِيثِ ۚ فَاتَّقُوا اللّٰهَ
يٰٓأُولِي الْأَلْبٰبِ لَعَلَّكُمْ تُفْلِحُونَ ١٠٠ ع ١٣ ٤

101. Believers, do not ask about things which, if revealed to you, would disappoint you. If you ask about such things when the Prophet is receiving revelations, they will also be revealed to you. Allah has exempted you (from the responsibilities of the things you wanted to know). He is All-forgiving and Forbearing.

101. Yaaa ayyuhal-lazeena aamanoo laa tas'aloo 'an ashyaaa'a in tubda lakum tasu'kum; wa in tas'aloo 'anhaa ḥeena yunazzalul-Qur'aanu tubda lakum; 'afallaahu 'anhaa; wallaahu Ghafoorun Ḥaleem.

يٰٓأَيُّهَا الَّذِينَ اٰمَنُوا لَا تَسْئَلُوا عَنْ
أَشْيَآءَ إِنْ تُبْدَ لَكُمْ تَسُؤْكُمْ ۚ
وَإِنْ تَسْئَلُوا عَنْهَا حِينَ يُنَزَّلُ
الْقُرْاٰنُ تُبْدَ لَكُمْ ۗ عَفَا اللّٰهُ عَنْهَا ۗ
وَاللّٰهُ غَفُورٌ حَلِيمٌ ١٠١

102. People living before you had asked about such things, but then rejected them.

102. Qad sa-alahaa qawmum min qablikum summa aṣbaḥoo bihaa kaafireen.

قَدْ سَأَلَهَا قَوْمٌ مِّنْ قَبْلِكُمْ ثُمَّ
أَصْبَحُوا بِهَا كٰفِرِينَ ١٠٢

103. Allah has not instituted the rites of Bahirah, Saibah, Wasilah, nor of Hami (names of certain animals that the pagans would offer as sacrifice). It is the pagans who have attributed falsehood to Allah. Many of them have no understanding.

103. Maa ja'alal-laahu mim baḥeeratiñw-wa laa saaa' ibatiñw-wa laa waṣeelatiñw-wa laa ḥaamiñw-wa laakinnal-lazeena kafaroo yaftaroona 'alallaahil-kazib; wa aksaruhum laa ya'qiloon.

مَا جَعَلَ اللّٰهُ مِنْ بَحِيرَةٍ وَّلَا سَآئِبَةٍ
وَّلَا وَصِيلَةٍ وَّلَا حَامٍ ۙ وَّلٰكِنَّ الَّذِينَ
كَفَرُوا يَفْتَرُونَ عَلَى اللّٰهِ الْكَذِبَ ۗ
وَأَكْثَرُهُمْ لَا يَعْقِلُونَ ١٠٣

104. When they are told to refer to the guidance of Allah and to the Messenger, they say, "The tradition of our fathers is sufficient for our guidance," even though, in fact, their fathers had neither knowledge nor proper guidance.

104. Wa izaa qeela lahum ta'aalaw ilaa maaa anzalallaahu wa ilar-Rasooli qaaloo ḥasbunaa maa wajadnaa 'alayhi aabaaa'anaaa; awa law kaana aabaaa'uhum laa ya'lamoona shay'añw-wa laa yahtadoon.

وَإِذَا قِيلَ لَهُمْ تَعَالَوْا إِلٰى مَآ
أَنْزَلَ اللّٰهُ وَإِلَى الرَّسُولِ قَالُوا
حَسْبُنَا مَا وَجَدْنَا عَلَيْهِ اٰبَآءَنَا ۗ
أَوَلَوْ كَانَ اٰبَآؤُهُمْ لَا يَعْلَمُونَ شَيْئًا
وَّلَا يَهْتَدُونَ ١٠٤

105. Believers, save your own souls, for if you have the right

105. Yaaa ayyuhal-lazeena aamanoo 'alaykum anfusakum

يٰٓأَيُّهَا الَّذِينَ اٰمَنُوا عَلَيْكُمْ أَنْفُسَكُمْ ۚ

guidance, no one who strays can harm you. You will all return to Allah, who will tell you about what you have done.

laa yaḍurrukum man ḍalla izah-tadaytum; ilal-laahi marji'ukum jamee'an fayunabbi'ukum bimaa kuntum ta'maloon.

لَا يَضُرُّكُمْ مَّنْ ضَلَّ اِذَا اهْتَدَيْتُمْ ؕ
اِلَى اللّٰهِ مَرْجِعُكُمْ جَمِيْعًا فَيُنَبِّئُكُمْ
بِمَا كُنْتُمْ تَعْمَلُوْنَ ۝١٠٥

106. Believers, when death approaches any one of you, allow two just men from your own people (Muslims) or any two other men (People of the Book), if the incident of death befalls you on a journey, bear witness to the bequest. If you have any doubts about their (others') honesty, detain them and allow them to take an oath after the prayer, each one of them saying, "I swear by Allah that my testimony is true. I am not selling the Truth for a paltry price even though the beneficiary would be one of my relatives. I do not hide the testimony which is the right of Allah, for then I would be one of the sinners."

106. Yaaa ayyuhal-lazeena aamanoo shahaadatu baynikum izaa ḥaḍara aḥadakumul-mawtu ḥeenalwaṣiyyatis-naani zawaa 'adlim-minkum aw aakharaani min ghayrikum in antum ḍarabtum fil-arḍi fa-aṣaabat-kum-muṣeebatulmawt; taḥbi-soonahumaa mim-ba'diṣ-Ṣalaati fayuqsimaani billaahi inirtabtum laa nashtaree bihee samanañw-wa law kaana zaa qurbaa wa laa naktumu shahaadatal-laahi innaaa izal-laminal-aasimeen.

يٰۤاَيُّهَا الَّذِيْنَ اٰمَنُوْا شَهَادَةُ بَيْنِكُمْ
اِذَا حَضَرَ اَحَدَكُمُ الْمَوْتُ حِيْنَ
الْوَصِيَّةِ اثْنٰنِ ذَوَا عَدْلٍ مِّنْكُمْ اَوْ
اٰخَرٰنِ مِنْ غَيْرِكُمْ اِنْ اَنْتُمْ ضَرَبْتُمْ
فِى الْاَرْضِ فَاَصَابَتْكُمْ مُّصِيْبَةُ
الْمَوْتِ ؕ تَحْبِسُوْنَهُمَا مِنْۢ بَعْدِ الصَّلٰوةِ
فَيُقْسِمٰنِ بِاللّٰهِ اِنِ ارْتَبْتُمْ لَا نَشْتَرِىْ
بِهٖ ثَمَنًا وَّلَوْ كَانَ ذَا قُرْبٰى ۙ وَلَا نَكْتُمُ
شَهَادَةَ اللّٰهِ اِنَّاۤ اِذًا لَّمِنَ الْاٰثِمِيْنَ ۝١٠٦

107. If their honesty is challenged, two others from the relatives of the deceased should swear in the same way and testify to the bequest saying, "We swear by Allah that our testimony is the true one. We do not transgress in the matter lest we become unjust ones."

107. Fa-in 'usira 'alaaa annahumas-taḥaqqaaa isman fa-aakharaani yaqoomaani maqaamahumaa minal-lazeenas-taḥaqqa 'alayhimul-awlayaani fayuqsimaani billaahi lashahaadatunaaa aḥaqqu min shahaadatihimaa wa ma'-tadaynaaa innaaa izal-laminaẓ-ẓaalimeen.

فَاِنْ عُثِرَ عَلٰۤى اَنَّهُمَا اسْتَحَقَّاۤ اِثْمًا
فَاٰخَرٰنِ يَقُوْمٰنِ مَقَامَهُمَا مِنَ الَّذِيْنَ
اسْتَحَقَّ عَلَيْهِمُ الْاَوْلَيٰنِ فَيُقْسِمٰنِ بِاللّٰهِ
لَشَهَادَتُنَاۤ اَحَقُّ مِنْ شَهَادَتِهِمَا وَمَا
اعْتَدَيْنَا ۖ اِنَّاۤ اِذًا لَّمِنَ الظّٰلِمِيْنَ ۝١٠٧

108. This will help preserve a proper testimony because the witness will be afraid of the denial of their own testimony by a second pair of witnesses. Have fear of Allah and listen (properly). Allah does not guide the evil doing people.

108. Zaalika adnaaa añy-ya-too bishshahaadati 'alaa wajhihaaa aw yakhaafooo an turadda aymaanum ba'da aymaanihim; wattaqul-laaha wasma'oo; wallaahu laa yahdil-qawmal-faasiqeen.

ذٰلِكَ اَدْنٰۤى اَنْ يَّاْتُوْا بِالشَّهَادَةِ عَلٰى
وَجْهِهَاۤ اَوْ يَخَافُوْۤا اَنْ تُرَدَّ اَيْمَانٌۢ بَعْدَ
اَيْمَانِهِمْ ؕ وَاتَّقُوا اللّٰهَ وَاسْمَعُوْا ؕ
وَاللّٰهُ لَا يَهْدِى الْقَوْمَ الْفٰسِقِيْنَ ۝١٠٨ ع ١٤ ٨

109. Have fear of the day when Allah will bring all the Messengers together and ask them, "What was the response of men to your call?" They will reply, "We have no knowledge. You are the only One who has knowledge of the unseen."

109. Yawma yajma'ul-laahur-Rusula fayaqoolu maazaaa ujibtum qaaloo laa 'ilma lanaaa innaka Anta 'Allaamul-Ghuyoob.

يَوْمَ يَجْمَعُ اللّٰهُ الرُّسُلَ فَيَقُوْلُ
مَاذَاۤ اُجِبْتُمْ ؕ قَالُوْا لَا عِلْمَ لَنَا ؕ
اِنَّكَ اَنْتَ عَلَّامُ الْغُيُوْبِ ۝١٠٩

110. When Allah said, "Jesus, son of Mary, recall My favors to you and your mother. (Recall) how I supported you by the holy

110. Iz qaalal-laahu yaa 'Eesab-na-Maryamaz-kur ni'matee 'alayka wa 'alaa waalidatik;

اِذْ قَالَ اللّٰهُ يٰعِيْسَى ابْنَ مَرْيَمَ
اذْكُرْ نِعْمَتِىْ عَلَيْكَ وَعَلٰى وَالِدَتِكَ ۘ

وقف لازم

spirit, made you speak to people from your cradle and when you grew up, taught you the Book, gave you wisdom, the Torah, and the Gospel."

"(Recall) when, by My will, you made a sculpture of a bird out of clay, blew into it, and it turned into a real bird by My Will. (Recall) how, by My will, you healed the deaf, the lepers, and raised the dead. (Recall) your coming to the Israelites with clear miracles and My saving you from their mischief, when the unbelievers among them said, 'This is obviously magic."

iz̲ ayyattuka bi-Rooḥil-Qudusi tukallimunnaasa fil-mahdi wa kahlaa; wa iz̲ 'allamtukal-Kitaaba wal-Ḥikmata wat-Tawraata wal-Injeela wa iz̲ takhluqu minaṭ-ṭeeni kahay'atiṭ-ṭayri bi-iz̲nee fatanfukhu feehaa fatakoonu ṭayram-bi-iz̲nee wa tubri'ul-akmaha wal-abraṣa bi-iz̲nee wa iz̲ tukhrijul-mawtaa bi-iz̲nee wa iz̲ kafaftu Baneee Israaa'eela 'anka iz̲ ji'tahum bil-bayyinaati fa-qaalal-laz̲eena kafaroo minhum in haaz̲aaa illaa siḥrum-mubeen.

إِذْ أَيَّدتُّكَ بِرُوحِ الْقُدُسِ
تُكَلِّمُ النَّاسَ فِي الْمَهْدِ وَكَهْلًا ۖ وَإِذْ
عَلَّمْتُكَ الْكِتَابَ وَالْحِكْمَةَ وَالتَّوْرَاةَ
وَالْإِنجِيلَ ۖ وَإِذْ تَخْلُقُ مِنَ الطِّينِ
كَهَيْئَةِ الطَّيْرِ بِإِذْنِي فَتَنفُخُ فِيهَا
فَتَكُونُ طَيْرًا بِإِذْنِي ۖ وَتُبْرِئُ الْأَكْمَهَ
وَالْأَبْرَصَ بِإِذْنِي ۖ وَإِذْ تُخْرِجُ الْمَوْتَىٰ
بِإِذْنِي ۖ وَإِذْ كَفَفْتُ بَنِي إِسْرَائِيلَ
عَنكَ إِذْ جِئْتَهُم بِالْبَيِّنَاتِ فَقَالَ
الَّذِينَ كَفَرُوا مِنْهُمْ إِنْ هَٰذَا إِلَّا
سِحْرٌ مُّبِينٌ ﴿١١٠﴾

111. "(Recall) when I inspired the disciples to have faith in Me and My Messenger. They said, 'We have accepted the faith. Lord, bear witness that we have submitted ourselves to Your will."

111. Wa iz̲ awḥaytu ilal-Ḥawaariyyeena an aaminoo bee wa bi-Rasoolee qaalooo aamannaa washhad bi-annanaa muslimoon.

وَإِذْ أَوْحَيْتُ إِلَى الْحَوَارِيِّينَ أَنْ آمِنُوا
بِي وَبِرَسُولِي قَالُوا آمَنَّا وَاشْهَدْ
بِأَنَّنَا مُسْلِمُونَ ﴿١١١﴾

112. (Recall) when the disciples said, 'Jesus, son of Mary, can your Lord send us a table full of food from heaven?' and you replied, 'Have fear of Allah if you are true believers.'

112. Iz̲ qaalal-Ḥawaariyyoona yaa 'Eesabna-Maryama hal yastaṭee'u Rabbuka añy-yunaz-zila 'alaynaa maaa'idatam-minassamaaa'i qaalat-taqul-laaha in kuntum mu'mineen.

إِذْ قَالَ الْحَوَارِيُّونَ يَا عِيسَى ابْنَ
مَرْيَمَ هَلْ يَسْتَطِيعُ رَبُّكَ أَن يُنَزِّلَ
عَلَيْنَا مَائِدَةً مِّنَ السَّمَاءِ ۖ قَالَ اتَّقُوا
اللَّهَ إِن كُنتُم مُّؤْمِنِينَ ﴿١١٢﴾

113. They said, 'We only wish to eat therefrom to comfort our hearts, to know that you have spoken the Truth to us, and to bear witness to it along with the others.'"

113. Qaaloo nureedu an na-kula minhaa wa taṭma'inna quloo-bunaa wa na'lama an qad ṣadaqtanaa wa nakoona 'alayhaa minashshaahideen.

قَالُوا نُرِيدُ أَن نَّأْكُلَ مِنْهَا وَتَطْمَئِنَّ
قُلُوبُنَا وَنَعْلَمَ أَن قَدْ صَدَقْتَنَا وَ
نَكُونَ عَلَيْهَا مِنَ الشَّاهِدِينَ ﴿١١٣﴾ الربع

114. When Jesus prayed, "Lord, send us a table full of food from heaven so that it will make a feast for us and for those who are yet to come in this world and an evidence from You. Give us sustenance, for You are the best Provider,"

114. Qaala 'Eesab-nu-Marya-mal-laahumma Rabbanaaa anzil 'alaynaa maaa'idatam-minas-samaaa'i takoonu lanaa 'eedalli-awwalinaa wa aakhi-rinaa wa Aayatam-minka warzuqnaa wa Anta khayrur-raaziqeen.

قَالَ عِيسَى ابْنُ مَرْيَمَ اللَّهُمَّ رَبَّنَا
أَنزِلْ عَلَيْنَا مَائِدَةً مِّنَ السَّمَاءِ تَكُونُ
لَنَا عِيدًا لِّأَوَّلِنَا وَآخِرِنَا وَآيَةً مِّنكَ ۖ
وَارْزُقْنَا وَأَنتَ خَيْرُ الرَّازِقِينَ ﴿١١٤﴾

115. Allah replied, "I am sending it to you, but if anyone of

115. Qaalal-laahu innee muna-zziluhaa 'alaykum famañy-

قَالَ اللَّهُ إِنِّي مُنَزِّلُهَا عَلَيْكُمْ ۖ فَمَن

you turns back to disbelief, I will make him suffer a torment that no one has ever suffered."

yakfur ba'du minkum fa-inneee u'az-zibuhoo 'azaabal-laaa u'az-zibuhooo ahadam-minal-'aalameen.

يَّكْفُرْ بَعْدُ مِنْكُمْ فَإِنِّيٓ أُعَذِّبُهٗ عَذَابًا
لَّآ أُعَذِّبُهٗٓ أَحَدًا مِّنَ الْعٰلَمِينَ ﴿١١٥﴾ ع ١٥ ٧ ٥

116. When Allah asked Jesus, son of Mary "Did you tell men to consider you and your mother as their gods besides Allah?" He replied, "Glory be to you! How could I say what I have no right to say? Had I ever said it, You would have certainly known about it. You know what is in my soul, but I do not know what is in Yours. It is You who has absolute knowledge of the unseen.

116. Wa iz qaalal-laahu yaa 'Eesab-na-Maryama 'a-anta qulta linnaasit-takhizoonee wa ummiya ilaahayni min doonil-laahi qaala Subhaanaka maa yakoonu leee an aqoola maa laysa lee bihaqq; in kuntu qultuhoo faqad 'alimtah; ta'lamu maa fee nafsee wa laaa a'lamu maa fee nafsik; innaka Anta 'Allamul-Ghuyoob.

وَإِذْ قَالَ اللّٰهُ يٰعِيسَى ابْنَ مَرْيَمَ
ءَأَنْتَ قُلْتَ لِلنَّاسِ اتَّخِذُونِي وَأُمِّيَ
إِلٰهَيْنِ مِنْ دُونِ اللّٰهِ ۗ قَالَ سُبْحٰنَكَ
مَا يَكُونُ لِيٓ أَنْ أَقُولَ مَا لَيْسَ لِي ۚ
بِحَقٍّ ۗ إِنْ كُنْتُ قُلْتُهٗ فَقَدْ عَلِمْتَهٗ ۗ
تَعْلَمُ مَا فِي نَفْسِي وَلَآ أَعْلَمُ مَا فِي
نَفْسِكَ ۗ إِنَّكَ أَنْتَ عَلَّامُ الْغُيُوبِ ﴿١١٦﴾

117. "I did not tell them anything except what You commanded me to tell them. I told them that they must worship Allah, who is everyone's Lord. I watched them as long as I was among them until You raised me to Yourself and You Yourself had also watched over them; You are Omnipresent.

117. Maa qultu lahum illaa maaa amartanee bihee ani'budul-laaha Rabbeee wa Rabbakum; wa kuntu 'alayhim shaheedam-maa dumtu feehim falammaa tawaffaytanee kunta Antar-Raqeeba 'alayhim; wa Anta 'alaa kulli shay'in Shaheed.

مَا قُلْتُ لَهُمْ إِلَّا مَآ أَمَرْتَنِي بِهٖٓ
أَنِ اعْبُدُوا اللّٰهَ رَبِّي وَرَبَّكُمْ ۚ وَكُنْتُ
عَلَيْهِمْ شَهِيدًا مَّا دُمْتُ فِيهِمْ ۚ فَلَمَّا
تَوَفَّيْتَنِي كُنْتَ أَنْتَ الرَّقِيبَ عَلَيْهِمْ ۗ
وَأَنْتَ عَلٰى كُلِّ شَيْءٍ شَهِيدٌ ﴿١١٧﴾

وقف النبي صلى الله عليه وآله وسلم ١٢

118. You may punish Your servants or forgive them for You are Majestic and Wise."

118. In tu'az-zibhum fainna-hum 'ibaaduka wa in taghfir lahum fa-innaka Antal-'Azeezul-Hakeem.

إِنْ تُعَذِّبْهُمْ فَإِنَّهُمْ عِبَادُكَ ۚ وَإِنْ
تَغْفِرْ لَهُمْ فَإِنَّكَ أَنْتَ الْعَزِيزُ الْحَكِيمُ ﴿١١٨﴾

119. Allah will say, "This is the Day when the truthful ones will benefit from their truthfulness. For them there are gardens wherein streams flow and they will live therein forever. Allah is pleased with them and they will be pleased with Allah in their supreme triumph.

119. Qaalal-laahu haazaa Yawmu yanfa'us-saadiqeena sidquhum; lahum Jannaatun tajree min tahtihal-anhaaru khaalideena feehaaa abadaa; radiyal-laahu 'anhum wa radoo 'anh; zaalikal-fawzul-'azeem.

قَالَ اللّٰهُ هٰذَا يَوْمُ يَنْفَعُ
الصّٰدِقِينَ صِدْقُهُمْ ۚ لَهُمْ جَنّٰتٌ
تَجْرِي مِنْ تَحْتِهَا الْأَنْهٰرُ خٰلِدِينَ
فِيهَآ أَبَدًا ۚ رَضِيَ اللّٰهُ عَنْهُمْ وَرَضُوا
عَنْهُ ۚ ذٰلِكَ الْفَوْزُ الْعَظِيمُ ﴿١١٩﴾

120. To Allah belongs the kingdom of the heavens and the earth and all that is between them and He has power over all things.

120. Lillaahi mulkus-samaa-waati wal-ardi wa maa feehinn; wa Huwa 'alaa kulli shay'in Qadeer.

لِلّٰهِ مُلْكُ السَّمٰوٰتِ وَالْأَرْضِ وَمَا
فِيهِنَّ ۚ وَهُوَ عَلٰى كُلِّ شَيْءٍ قَدِيرٌ ﴿١٢٠﴾ ع ١٦ ٥ ٢

Al-An'am, The Cattle (6)

In the Name of Allah, the Beneficent, the Merciful.

Sûrat al-An'âm-6

(Revealed at Makkah)

Bismillaahir Rahmaanir Raheem

(٦) سُورَةُ الْأَنْعَامِ مَكِّيَّةٌ (٥٥)

آياتها ١٦٥ — بِسْمِ اللّٰهِ الرَّحْمٰنِ الرَّحِيمِ — ركوعاتها ٢٠

1. Only Allah, Who has created the heavens, the earth,

1. Al-hamdu lillaahil-lazee khalaqas-samaawaati wal-

الْحَمْدُ لِلّٰهِ الَّذِي خَلَقَ السَّمٰوٰتِ وَ

darkness, and light, deserves all praise. The unbelievers consider other things equal to Him.

arḍa wa ja'alaẓ-ẓulumaati wannoora summal-lazeena kafaroo bi-Rabbihim ya'diloon.

الْاَرْضَ وَجَعَلَ الظُّلُمٰتِ وَالنُّوْرَ ؕ
ثُمَّ الَّذِيْنَ كَفَرُوْا بِرَبِّهِمْ يَعْدِلُوْنَ ١

2. It is He who has created you from clay to live for a lifetime and the span of your life is only known to Him. You are still suspicious!

2. Huwal-lazee khalaqakum min ṭeenin summa qaḍaaa ajalan wa ajalum musamman 'indahoo summa antum tamtaroon.

هُوَ الَّذِيْ خَلَقَكُمْ مِّنْ طِيْنٍ ثُمَّ
قَضٰٓى اَجَلًا ؕ وَاَجَلٌ مُّسَمًّى عِنْدَهٗ
ثُمَّ اَنْتُمْ تَمْتَرُوْنَ ٢

3. He is (known as) Allah in the heavens and on earth and He knows whatever you conceal, reveal, or gain.

3. Wa Huwal-laahu fissamaa-waati wa fil-arḍi ya'lamu sirrakum wa jahrakum wa ya'lamu maa taksiboon.

وَهُوَ اللّٰهُ فِي السَّمٰوٰتِ وَفِي الْاَرْضِ ؕ
يَعْلَمُ سِرَّكُمْ وَجَهْرَكُمْ وَيَعْلَمُ
مَا تَكْسِبُوْنَ ٣

4. (The unbelievers) have always turned away from the revelations and the evidence (of the Truth) that has been sent to them from time to time.

4. Wa maa ta-teehim min Aaya-tim-min Aayaati Rabbihim illaa kaanoo 'anhaa mu'riḍeen.

وَمَا تَاْتِيْهِمْ مِّنْ اٰيَةٍ مِّنْ اٰيٰتِ
رَبِّهِمْ اِلَّا كَانُوْا عَنْهَا مُعْرِضِيْنَ ٤

5. They have refused the Truth (of the message of Muhammad) that has come to them but they will soon learn the consequences of their mocking.

5. Faqad kaz-zaboo bilḥaqqi lammaa jaaa'ahum fasawfa ya-teehim ambaaa'u maa kaanoo bihee yastahzi'oon.

فَقَدْ كَذَّبُوْا بِالْحَقِّ لَمَّا جَآءَهُمْ ؕ
فَسَوْفَ يَاْتِيْهِمْ اَنْۢبٰٓؤُا مَا كَانُوْا
بِهٖ يَسْتَهْزِءُوْنَ ٥

6. Did they not consider how many generations living before them We have destroyed? We established those nations in the land with abilities far beyond those given to you. We sent down plenty of rain from the sky for them and made streams flow therein, but then, We destroyed them for their sins and established other nations after them.

6. Alam yaraw kam ahlaknaa min qablihim min qarnim-makkannaahum fil-arḍi maa lam numakkil-lakum wa arsalnas-samaaa'a 'alayhim midraarañw-wa ja'alnal-anhaara tajree min taḥtihim fa-ahlak-naahum bizunoobihim wa ansha-naa mim-ba'dihim qarnan aakhareen.

اَلَمْ يَرَوْا كَمْ اَهْلَكْنَا مِنْ قَبْلِهِمْ
مِّنْ قَرْنٍ مَّكَّنّٰهُمْ فِي الْاَرْضِ مَا لَمْ
نُمَكِّنْ لَّكُمْ وَاَرْسَلْنَا السَّمَآءَ عَلَيْهِمْ
مِّدْرَارًا ۪ وَّجَعَلْنَا الْاَنْهٰرَ تَجْرِيْ
مِنْ تَحْتِهِمْ فَاَهْلَكْنٰهُمْ بِذُنُوْبِهِمْ
وَاَنْشَاْنَا مِنْۢ بَعْدِهِمْ قَرْنًا
اٰخَرِيْنَ ٦

7. (Muhammad), had We sent you a Book on paper, the unbelievers would have touched it with their hands but would still have said, "It is no more than plain sorcery."

7. Wa law naz-zalnaa 'alayka Kitaaban fee qirṭaasin falamasoohu bi-aydeehim laqaalal-lazeena kafarooo in haazaaa illaa siḥrum-mubeen.

وَلَوْ نَزَّلْنَا عَلَيْكَ كِتٰبًا فِيْ قِرْطَاسٍ
فَلَمَسُوْهُ بِاَيْدِيْهِمْ لَقَالَ الَّذِيْنَ
كَفَرُوْٓا اِنْ هٰذَآ اِلَّا سِحْرٌ مُّبِيْنٌ ٧

8. They have said, "Why has not an angel come to him (Muhammad)?" Had We sent an angel to them, the matter would have inevitably been out of their hands, and they would have been given no more time.

8. Wa qaaloo law laaa unzila 'alayhi malak; wa law anzalna malakal-laquḍiyal-amru summa laa yunẓaroon.

وَقَالُوْا لَوْلَآ اُنْزِلَ عَلَيْهِ مَلَكٌ ؕ
وَلَوْ اَنْزَلْنَا مَلَكًا لَّقُضِيَ الْاَمْرُ ثُمَّ
لَا يُنْظَرُوْنَ ٨

9. Were We to have made him (Our Messenger) an angel, We would have made him resemble a human being and they would have again complained that the matter was as confusing to them as it is to them now.

9. Wa law ja‘alnaahu malakal-laja‘alnaahu rajulañw-wa lalabasnaa ‘alayhim maa yalbisoon.

وَلَوْ جَعَلْنٰهُ مَلَكًا لَّجَعَلْنٰهُ رَجُلًا وَّ
لَلَبَسْنَا عَلَيْهِمْ مَّا يَلْبِسُوْنَ ۝٩

10. They mocked the Messengers who lived before you (Muhammad), but those who received warnings of punishment and mocked the warnings, all suffered their torments accordingly.

10. Wa laqadis-tuhzi’a bi-Rusulim-min qablika faḥaaqa billazeena sakhiroo minhum maa kaanoo bihee yastahzi’oon.

وَلَقَدِ اسْتُهْزِئَ بِرُسُلٍ مِّنْ قَبْلِكَ
فَحَاقَ بِالَّذِيْنَ سَخِرُوْا مِنْهُمْ
مَّا كَانُوْا بِهٖ يَسْتَهْزِءُوْنَ ۝١٠ ع

11. (Muhammad), tell them to travel in the land and see what happened to those who rejected the Truth.

11. Qul seeroo fil-arḍi summan-ẓuroo kayfa kaana ‘aaqibatul-mukaz-zibeen.

قُلْ سِيْرُوْا فِي الْاَرْضِ ثُمَّ انْظُرُوْا
كَيْفَ كَانَ عَاقِبَةُ الْمُكَذِّبِيْنَ ۝١١

12. Ask them, “Who is the owner of the heavens and the earth besides Allah, the All-merciful, who will gather you all together on the Day of Judgment? That day will certainly come. Those who have lost their souls will not believe.

12. Qul limam-maa fissamaawaati wal-arḍi qul lillaah; kataba ‘alaa nafsihir-raḥmah; layajma‘annakum ilaa Yawmil-Qiyaamati laa rayba feeh; allazeena khasirooo anfusahum fahum laa yu’minoon.

قُلْ لِّمَنْ مَّا فِي السَّمٰوٰتِ وَالْاَرْضِ ؕ
قُلْ لِّلّٰهِ ؕ كَتَبَ عَلٰى نَفْسِهِ الرَّحْمَةَ ؕ
لَيَجْمَعَنَّكُمْ اِلٰى يَوْمِ الْقِيٰمَةِ لَا رَيْبَ
فِيْهِ ؕ اَلَّذِيْنَ خَسِرُوْۤا اَنْفُسَهُمْ فَهُمْ
لَا يُؤْمِنُوْنَ ۝١٢

13. To Him belongs all that rests during the night and the day. He is All-hearing and All-knowing.”

13. Wa lahoo maa sakana fillayli wannahaar; wa Huwas-Samee‘ul-‘Aleem.

وَلَهٗ مَا سَكَنَ فِي الَّيْلِ وَ النَّهَارِ ؕ
وَهُوَ السَّمِيْعُ الْعَلِيْمُ ۝١٣

14. (Muhammad), ask them, “Should I take a guardian other than Allah, the Originator of the heavens and the earth, who feeds everyone and who needs no food Himself?” Say, “I have been commanded to be the first Muslim (submitted to the will of Allah). Thus, people, do not be pagans.”

14. Qul aghayral-laahi attakhizu waliyyan faaṭiris-samaawaati wal-arḍi wa Huwa yuṭ‘imu wa laa yuṭ‘am; qul inneee umirtu an akoona awwala man aslama wa laa takoonanna minal-mushrikeen.

قُلْ اَغَيْرَ اللّٰهِ اَتَّخِذُ وَلِيًّا فَاطِرِ
السَّمٰوٰتِ وَالْاَرْضِ وَهُوَ يُطْعِمُ وَلَا
يُطْعَمُ ؕ قُلْ اِنِّيْۤ اُمِرْتُ اَنْ اَكُوْنَ
اَوَّلَ مَنْ اَسْلَمَ وَلَا تَكُوْنَنَّ مِنَ
الْمُشْرِكِيْنَ ۝١٤

15. (Muhammad), say, “It is because of the torment of the Great Day, I am afraid to disobey my Lord.”

15. Qul inneee akhaafu in ‘aṣaytu Rabbee ‘azaaba Yawmin ‘Aẓeem.

قُلْ اِنِّيْۤ اَخَافُ اِنْ عَصَيْتُ رَبِّيْ
عَذَابَ يَوْمٍ عَظِيْمٍ ۝١٥

16. One who will be saved from the torment on the Day of Judgment will certainly have received Allah's mercy and this will be a manifest triumph.

16. Mañy-yuṣraf ‘anhu Yawma’izin faqad raḥimah; wa zaalikal-fawzul-mubeen.

مَنْ يُّصْرَفْ عَنْهُ يَوْمَئِذٍ فَقَدْ
رَحِمَهٗ ؕ وَذٰلِكَ الْفَوْزُ الْمُبِيْنُ ۝١٦

17. (Muhammad), if Allah afflicts you with hardship, no one besides Him will be able to relieve you. If He bestows a favor on you, know that He has power over all things.

17. Wa iñy-yamsaskal-laahu biḍurrin falaaa kaashifa lahooo illaa Huwa wa iñy-yamsaska bikhayrin fa-Huwa ‘alaa kulli shay’in Qadeer.

وَاِنْ يَّمْسَسْكَ اللّٰهُ بِضُرٍّ فَلَا كَاشِفَ
لَهٗۤ اِلَّا هُوَ ؕ وَاِنْ يَّمْسَسْكَ بِخَيْرٍ فَهُوَ
عَلٰى كُلِّ شَيْءٍ قَدِيْرٌ ۝١٧

18. He is Wise, Well-aware, and Dominant over all His creatures.

18. Wa Huwal-Qaahiru fawqa 'ibaadih; wa Huwal-Ḩakeemul-Khabeer.

وَهُوَ الْقَاهِرُ فَوْقَ عِبَادِهٖ ؕ وَهُوَ
الْحَكِيْمُ الْخَبِيْرُ ﴿۱۸﴾

19. (Muhammad), ask them, "What is the greatest testimony? Allah testifies to my truthfulness to you. He has revealed this Quran to me to warn you and the coming generations (against disobeying Allah). Do you believe that other gods exist besides Allah? I solemnly declare that He is the only Lord and that I am not guilty of believing in what the pagans believe."

19. Qul ayyu shay'in akbaru shahaadatan qulil-laahu shaheedum baynee wa baynakum; wa ooḩiya ilayya haaẕal-Qur'aanu li-unẕirakum bihee wa mam-balagh; a'innakum latashhadoona anna ma'al-laahi aalihatan ukhraa; qul laaa ashhad; qul innamaa Huwa Ilaahuñw-Waaḩiduñw-wa innanee bareee'um-mimmaa tushrikoon.

قُلْ اَیُّ شَیْءٍ اَكْبَرُ شَهَادَةً ؕ قُلِ
اللّٰهُ ۚ شَهِيْدٌۢ بَيْنِیْ وَبَيْنَكُمْ ۚ
وَاُوْحِیَ اِلَیَّ هٰذَا الْقُرْاٰنُ لِاُنْذِرَكُمْ
بِهٖ وَمَنْۢ بَلَغَ ؕ اَئِنَّكُمْ لَتَشْهَدُوْنَ
اَنَّ مَعَ اللّٰهِ اٰلِهَةً اُخْرٰی ؕ قُلْ
لَّاۤ اَشْهَدُ ۚ قُلْ اِنَّمَا هُوَ اِلٰهٌ وَّاحِدٌ
وَّاِنَّنِیْ بَرِیْٓءٌ مِّمَّا تُشْرِكُوْنَ ﴿۱۹﴾

20. The People of the Book know him (Muhammad) just as well as they know their own children, but those who have lost their souls will not believe.

20. Allaẕeena aataynaa-humul-Kitaaba ya'rifoonahoo kamaa ya'rifoona abnaaa'a-hum; al-laẕeena khasirooo anfusahum fahum laa yu'mi-noon.

اَلَّذِيْنَ اٰتَيْنٰهُمُ الْكِتٰبَ يَعْرِفُوْنَهٗ كَمَا
يَعْرِفُوْنَ اَبْنَآءَهُمْ ۘ اَلَّذِيْنَ خَسِرُوْۤا
اَنْفُسَهُمْ فَهُمْ لَا يُؤْمِنُوْنَ ﴿۲۰﴾ ع

21. Who are more unjust than those who ascribe falsehood to Allah or reject His revelations? The unjust will certainly have no happiness.

21. Wa man aẓlamu mim-manif-taraa 'alal-laahi kaẕiban aw kaẕ-ẕaba bi-Aayaatih; innahoo laa yufliḩuẓ-ẓaa-limoon.

وَمَنْ اَظْلَمُ مِمَّنِ افْتَرٰی عَلَی اللّٰهِ
كَذِبًا اَوْ كَذَّبَ بِاٰيٰتِهٖ ؕ اِنَّهٗ
لَا يُفْلِحُ الظّٰلِمُوْنَ ﴿۲۱﴾

22. On the Day of Judgment when We will gather all people together, We will ask the pagans, "Where are those whom you believed to be your gods?"

22. Wa Yawma naḩshuruhum jamee'an s̱umma naqoolu lillaẕeena ashrakooo ayna shurakaaa'ukumul-laẕeena kuntum taz'umoon.

وَيَوْمَ نَحْشُرُهُمْ جَمِيْعًا ثُمَّ نَقُوْلُ
لِلَّذِيْنَ اَشْرَكُوْۤا اَيْنَ شُرَكَآؤُكُمُ
الَّذِيْنَ كُنْتُمْ تَزْعُمُوْنَ ﴿۲۲﴾

23. Attempting to answer, they would say, "Lord, we swear by Your Name that we were not pagans."

23. S̱umma lam takun fitnatuhum illaaa an qaaloo wallaahi Rabbinaa maa kunnaa mushrikeen.

ثُمَّ لَمْ تَكُنْ فِتْنَتُهُمْ اِلَّاۤ اَنْ قَالُوْا
وَاللّٰهِ رَبِّنَا مَا كُنَّا مُشْرِكِيْنَ ﴿۲۳﴾

24. Consider how they have lied against their own souls and have lost their gods.

24. Unẓur kayfa kaẕaboo 'alaaa anfusihim, wa ḑalla 'anhum maa kaanoo yaftaroon.

اُنْظُرْ كَيْفَ كَذَبُوْا عَلٰۤی اَنْفُسِهِمْ
وَضَلَّ عَنْهُمْ مَّا كَانُوْا يَفْتَرُوْنَ ﴿۲۴﴾

25. Some of them listen to you, but We have veiled their hearts so that they cannot understand and made them deaf. They disbelieve all the evidence (of Our existence) that they may have seen. They only come to you for

25. Wa minhum mañy-yasta-mi'u ilayka wa ja'alnaa 'alaa quloobihim akinnatan añy-yafqahoohu wa feee aaẕaani-him waqraa; wa iñy-yaraw kulla Aayatil-laa yu'minoo bihaa; ḩattaaa iẕaa jaaa'ooka

وَمِنْهُمْ مَّنْ يَّسْتَمِعُ اِلَيْكَ ۚ وَجَعَلْنَا
عَلٰی قُلُوْبِهِمْ اَكِنَّةً اَنْ يَّفْقَهُوْهُ وَفِیْۤ
اٰذَانِهِمْ وَقْرًا ؕ وَاِنْ يَّرَوْا كُلَّ اٰيَةٍ
لَّا يُؤْمِنُوْا بِهَا ؕ حَتّٰۤی اِذَا جَآءُوْكَ

وقف لازم باتفاق وقف لازم [illegible]

the sake of argument and the unbelievers say this (whatever Muhammad says) is no more than the ancient legends.

yujaadiloonaka yaqoolul-lazeena kafarooo in haazaaa illaaa asaaṭeerul-awwaleen.

يُجَادِلُوْنَكَ يَقُوْلُ الَّذِيْنَ كَفَرُوْٓا اِنْ هٰذَآ اِلَّآ اَسَاطِيْرُ الْاَوَّلِيْنَ ﴿٢٥﴾

26. They keep away from the faith and forbid others to accept it. They destroy no one except themselves, yet they do not realize it.

26. Wa hum yanhawna 'anhu wa yan'awna 'anhu wa iñy-yuhlikoona illaaa anfusahum wa maa yash'uroon.

وَهُمْ يَنْهَوْنَ عَنْهُ وَيَنْئَوْنَ عَنْهُ ۚ وَاِنْ يُّهْلِكُوْنَ اِلَّآ اَنْفُسَهُمْ وَمَا يَشْعُرُوْنَ ﴿٢٦﴾

27. If only you could see them standing in the fire saying, "Would that we could return to the worldly life. We would never reject any of our Lord's revelations and we would be true believers."

27. Wa law taraaa iz wuqifoo 'alan-Naari faqaaloo yaa laytanaa nuraddu wa laa nukaz-ziba bi-Aayaati Rabbinaa wa nakoona minal-mu'mineen.

وَلَوْ تَرٰٓى اِذْ وُقِفُوْا عَلَى النَّارِ فَقَالُوْا يٰلَيْتَنَا نُرَدُّ وَلَا نُكَذِّبَ بِاٰيٰتِ رَبِّنَا وَنَكُوْنَ مِنَ الْمُؤْمِنِيْنَ ﴿٢٧﴾

28. Whatever they had concealed will be revealed to them. If they were to return to (the worldly life), they would again worship idols, for they are liars.

28. Bal badaa lahum maa kaanoo yukhfoona min qabl; wa law ruddoo la'aadoo limaa nuhoo 'anhu wa innahum lakaaziboon.

بَلْ بَدَا لَهُمْ مَّا كَانُوْا يُخْفُوْنَ مِنْ قَبْلُ ۭ وَلَوْ رُدُّوْا لَعَادُوْا لِمَا نُهُوْا عَنْهُ وَاِنَّهُمْ لَكٰذِبُوْنَ ﴿٢٨﴾

29. They have said that this life is the only life and that there will be no Resurrection.

29. Wa qaalooo in hiya illaa ḥayaatunad-dunyaa wa maa naḥnu bimab'ooseen.

وَقَالُوْٓا اِنْ هِيَ اِلَّا حَيَاتُنَا الدُّنْيَا وَمَا نَحْنُ بِمَبْعُوْثِيْنَ ﴿٢٩﴾

30. Would that you could see them standing before their Lord, who would ask them, "Is not the Resurrection true?" They would reply, "Yes, Lord, there is a Resurrection." The Lord would then say, "For your disbelief, suffer the torment."

30. Wa law taraaa iz wuqifoo 'alaa Rabbihim; qaala alaysa haazaa bilḥaqq; qaaloo balaa wa Rabbinaa; qaala fazooqul-'azaaba bimaa kuntum takfuroon.

وَلَوْ تَرٰٓى اِذْ وُقِفُوْا عَلٰى رَبِّهِمْ ۭ قَالَ اَلَيْسَ هٰذَا بِالْحَقِّ ۭ قَالُوْا بَلٰى وَرَبِّنَا ۭ قَالَ فَذُوْقُوا الْعَذَابَ بِمَا كُنْتُمْ تَكْفُرُوْنَ ﴿٣٠﴾ ع

31. Those who do not believe in the Day of Judgment have incurred upon themselves a great loss. When the Day of Judgment suddenly comes upon them, they will sink under the burden of their sins in grief for their neglecting that day. Terrible indeed will be their burden!

31. Qad khasiral-lazeena kaz-zaboo biliqaaa'il -laahi ḥattaaa izaa jaaa'athumus-Saa'atu baghtatan qaaloo yaa ḥasra-tanaa 'alaa maa farraṭnaa feehaa wa hum yaḥmiloona awzaarahum 'alaa ẓuhoorihim; alaa saaa'a maa yaziroon.

قَدْ خَسِرَ الَّذِيْنَ كَذَّبُوْا بِلِقَآءِ اللّٰهِ ۭ حَتّٰٓى اِذَا جَآءَتْهُمُ السَّاعَةُ بَغْتَةً قَالُوْا يٰحَسْرَتَنَا عَلٰى مَا فَرَّطْنَا فِيْهَا ۙ وَهُمْ يَحْمِلُوْنَ اَوْزَارَهُمْ عَلٰى ظُهُوْرِهِمْ ۭ اَلَا سَآءَ مَا يَزِرُوْنَ ﴿٣١﴾

32. The worldly life is but useless amusement and sport (compared to) the life hereafter, which is far better and is only for the pious. Will you not then understand?

32. Wa mal-ḥayaatud-dunyaaa illaa la'ibuñw-wa lahw; wa lad-Daarul-Aakhiratu khayrul-lillazeena yattaqoon; afalaa ta'qiloon.

وَمَا الْحَيٰوةُ الدُّنْيَآ اِلَّا لَعِبٌ وَّلَهْوٌ ۭ وَلَلدَّارُ الْاٰخِرَةُ خَيْرٌ لِّلَّذِيْنَ يَتَّقُوْنَ ۭ اَفَلَا تَعْقِلُوْنَ ﴿٣٢﴾

33. We certainly know that you (Muhammad) are sad about what they (the unbelievers) say. It is not

33. Qad na'lamu innahoo layaḥzunukal-lazee

قَدْ نَعْلَمُ اِنَّهٗ لَيَحْزُنُكَ الَّذِيْ

you (alone) who has falsely been accused of lying. The unjust have always rejected Allah's revelations.

yaqooloona fa-innahum laa yukaz-ziboonaka wa laakinnaz-zaalimeena bi-Aayaatil-laahi yajhadoon.

يقولون فانهم لا يكذبونك ولكن
الظلمين بايت الله يجحدون ٣٣

34. The Messengers who lived before you were also falsely accused of lying, but they exercised patience. They were cruelly persecuted before We gave them victory. No one can change the words of Allah. You have already received news about the Messengers.

34. Wa laqad kuz-zibat Rusulum-min qablika fasabaroo 'alaa maa kuz-ziboo wa oozoo hattaaa ataahum nasrunaa; wa laa mubaddila li-Kalimaatil-laah; wa laqad jaaa'aka min-naba'il-mursaleen.

ولقد كذبت رسل من قبلك
فصبروا على ما كذبوا واوذوا حتى
اتهم نصرنا ج ولا مبدل لكلمت الله ج
ولقد جاءك من نباى المرسلين ٣٤

35. (O Muhammad), their refusal of the faith disturbs you so much that you are even willing to dig up the earth or ascend into the sky in search of further evidence to inevitably make them believe you. If Allah wants, He can certainly make them all follow the same guidance. Do not ever be unaware (of this fact).

35. Wa in kaana kabura 'alayka i'raaduhum fa-inistata'ta an tabtaghiya nafaqan fil-ardi aw sullaman fissamaaa'i fatatiyahum bi-Aayah; wa law shaaa'al-laahu lajama'ahum 'alal-hudaa; falaa takoonanna minal jaahileen.

وان كان كبر عليك اعراضهم فان
استطعت ان تبتغى نفقا فى الارض
او سلما فى السماء فتاتيهم باية ط
ولو شاء الله لجمعهم على الهدى
فلا تكونن من الجهلين ٣٥

36. Only those who have understanding will accept your faith. (Those who have no understanding) are like the dead whom Allah will resurrect and to Him will all return.

36. Innamaa yastajeebul-lazeena yasma'oon; walmawtaa yab'asuhumul-laahu summa ilayhi yurja'oon.

انما يستجيب الذين يسمعون ط
والموتى يبعثهم الله ثم اليه
يرجعون ٣٦

النصف
وقف منزل وقف غفران ١٢
عند البعض على يسمعون ١٢

37. They say, "Why have not some miracles been given to him, (Muhammad), from his Lord?" Tell them, (Muhammad), "Allah certainly has the Power to show such miracles but many of them are ignorant."

37. Wa qaaloo law laa nuzzila 'alayhi Aayatum-mir-Rabbih; qul innal-laaha qaadirun 'alaaa añy-yunazzila 'Aayatañw-wa laakinna aksarahum laa ya'lamoon.

وقالوا لولا نزل عليه اية من ربه ط
قل ان الله قادر على ان ينزل
اية ولكن اكثرهم لا يعلمون ٣٧

38. All the beasts on land and flying birds have different communities, just as you (people) do. Nothing is left without a mention in the Book. They will all be brought into the presence of their Lord.

38. Wa maa min daaabbatin fil-ardi wa laa taaa'iriñy-yateeru bijanaahayhi illaaa umamun amsaalukum; maa farratnaa fil-Kitaabi min shay'; summa ilaa Rabbihim yuhsharoon.

وما من دابة فى الارض ولا طئر
يطير بجناحيه الا امم امثالكم ط
ما فرطنا فى الكتب من شىء ثم
الى ربهم يحشرون ٣٨

39. Those who disbelieve Our revelations are, in fact, deaf and dumb. They wander in darkness. Allah leads astray or guides to the right path whomever He wants.

39. Wallazeena kaz-zaboo bi-Aayaatinaa summuñw-wa bukmun fiz-zulumaat; mañy-yasha-il-laahu yudlilh; wa mañy-yasha- yaj'alhu 'alaa Siraatim-Mustaqeem.

والذين كذبوا بايتنا صم وبكم فى
الظلمت ط من يشا الله يضلله ط ومن
يشا يجعله على صراط مستقيم ٣٩

40. (Muhammad), say to them, "You must consider, should Allah afflict you with torment, or the Day of Judgment arrive, if what you claim

40. Qul ara'aytakum in ataakum 'azaabul-laahi aw atatkumus-Saa'atu aghayrallaahi tad'oona

قل ارءيتكم ان اتكم عذاب الله
او اتتكم الساعة اغير الله تدعون ج

would be true, could you then seek help from anyone other than Allah?

in kuntum ṣaadiqeen.

إِن كُنتُمْ صَٰدِقِينَ ﴿٤٠﴾

41. You will certainly ask Him for help. He can save you from hardship if He decides to do so and you will forget all about your gods."

41. Bal iyyaahu tad'oona fayakshifu maa tad'oona ilayhi in shaaa'a wa tansawna maa tushrikoon.

بَلْ إِيَّاهُ تَدْعُونَ فَيَكْشِفُ مَا
تَدْعُونَ إِلَيْهِ إِن شَآءَ وَتَنسَوْنَ
مَا تُشْرِكُونَ ﴿٤١﴾ ع

42. We had sent (Our guidance) to the nations who lived before you and afflicted them with distress and adversity so that they might submit themselves (to the will of Allah).

42. Wa laqad arsalnaaa ilaaa umamim min qablika fa-akha͟znaahum bilba-saaa'i waḍḍarraaa'i la'allahum yata-ḍarra'oon.

وَلَقَدْ أَرْسَلْنَآ إِلَىٰٓ أُمَمٍ مِّن قَبْلِكَ
فَأَخَذْنَٰهُم بِٱلْبَأْسَآءِ وَٱلضَّرَّآءِ
لَعَلَّهُمْ يَتَضَرَّعُونَ ﴿٤٢﴾

43. Why did they not submit themselves (to Allah's will) when Our torment struck them? Instead, their hearts were hardened and Satan made their evil deeds seem attractive to them.

43. Falaw laaa i͟z jaaa'ahum ba-sunaa taḍarra'oo wa laakin qasat quloobuhum wa zayyana lahumush-Shayṭaanu maa kaanoo ya'maloon.

فَلَوْلَآ إِذْ جَآءَهُم بَأْسُنَا تَضَرَّعُوا۟
وَلَٰكِن قَسَتْ قُلُوبُهُمْ وَزَيَّنَ لَهُمُ
ٱلشَّيْطَٰنُ مَا كَانُوا۟ يَعْمَلُونَ ﴿٤٣﴾

44. When they forgot (all) the advice that they had received, We granted them all means of happiness but they were left in despair when We suddenly took Our bounties back from them.

44. Falammaa nasoo maa ͟zukkiroo bihee fataḥnaa 'alayhim abwaaba kulli shay'in ḥattaaa i͟zaa fariḥoo bimaaa ootooo akha͟znaahum baghtatan fa-i͟zaa hum mublisoon.

فَلَمَّا نَسُوا۟ مَا ذُكِّرُوا۟ بِهِۦ فَتَحْنَا عَلَيْهِمْ
أَبْوَٰبَ كُلِّ شَىْءٍ حَتَّىٰٓ إِذَا فَرِحُوا۟
بِمَآ أُوتُوٓا۟ أَخَذْنَٰهُم بَغْتَةً فَإِذَا هُم
مُّبْلِسُونَ ﴿٤٤﴾

45. Thus, the transgressing people were destroyed. It is only Allah, the Lord of creation, who deserves all praise.

45. Faquṭi'a daabirul-qawmil-la͟zeena ẓalamoo; walḥamdu lillaahi Rabbil-'aalameen.

فَقُطِعَ دَابِرُ ٱلْقَوْمِ ٱلَّذِينَ ظَلَمُوا۟ۚ
وَٱلْحَمْدُ لِلَّهِ رَبِّ ٱلْعَٰلَمِينَ ﴿٤٥﴾

46. (Muhammad), ask them, "Have you ever considered that if Allah were to disable your hearing and vision and veil your hearts, could anyone besides Him restore them?" Look at how plainly We show them the evidence (of the Truth) but they always ignore it.

46. Qul ara'aytum in akha͟zal-laahu sam'akum wa abṣaara-kum wa khatama 'alaa quloobikum man ilaahun ghay-rul-laahi ya-teekum bih; unẓur kayfa nuṣarriful-Aayaati ͟summa hum yaṣdifoon.

قُلْ أَرَءَيْتُمْ إِنْ أَخَذَ ٱللَّهُ سَمْعَكُمْ
وَأَبْصَٰرَكُمْ وَخَتَمَ عَلَىٰ قُلُوبِكُم مَّنْ
إِلَٰهٌ غَيْرُ ٱللَّهِ يَأْتِيكُم بِهِ ٱنظُرْ كَيْفَ
نُصَرِّفُ ٱلْءَايَٰتِ ثُمَّ هُمْ يَصْدِفُونَ ﴿٤٦﴾

47. Tell them, "Have you considered that if Allah's torment were to befall you suddenly or in public, would anyone else be destroyed except the unjust?"

47. Qul ara'aytakum in ataakum 'a͟zaabul-laahi baghtatan aw jahratan hal yuhlaku illal-qawmuẓ-ẓaalimoon.

قُلْ أَرَءَيْتَكُمْ إِنْ أَتَىٰكُمْ عَذَابُ
ٱللَّهِ بَغْتَةً أَوْ جَهْرَةً هَلْ يُهْلَكُ
إِلَّا ٱلْقَوْمُ ٱلظَّٰلِمُونَ ﴿٤٧﴾

48. We did not send the Messengers for any other reason than to bring (people) the glad news (of Allah's mercy) and to warn (them of the torment brought on by disobedience to Allah). Whoever accepts the faith and lives a righteous life will have nothing to fear, nor will he be grieved.

48. Wa maa nursilul-mursaleena illaa mubash-shireena wa mun͟zireena faman aamana wa aṣlaḥa falaa khawfun 'alayhim wa laa hum yaḥzanoon.

وَمَا نُرْسِلُ ٱلْمُرْسَلِينَ إِلَّا مُبَشِّرِينَ
وَمُنذِرِينَ ۖ فَمَنْ ءَامَنَ وَأَصْلَحَ فَلَا
خَوْفٌ عَلَيْهِمْ وَلَا هُمْ يَحْزَنُونَ ﴿٤٨﴾

49. Those who reject Our revelations will certainly be punished for their evil deeds.

49. Wallazeena kaz-zaboo bi-Aayaatinaa yamassuhumul-'azaabu bimaa kaanoo yafsuqoon.

وَالَّذِينَ كَذَّبُوا بِاٰيٰتِنَا يَمَسُّهُمُ الْعَذَابُ
بِمَا كَانُوا يَفْسُقُونَ ﴿٤٩﴾

50. (Muhammad), tell them, "I do not claim to have all the treasures of Allah in my hands, nor to know the unseen, nor do I claim to be an angel. I follow only what is revealed to me (from Allah)." Say to them, "Are the blind and the seeing equal?" Why then do you not think?

50. Qul laaa aqoolu lakum 'indee khazaaa'inul-laahi wa laaa a'lamul-ghayba wa laaa aqoolu lakum innee malakun in attabi'u illaa maa yooḥaaa ilayy; qul hal yastawil-a'maa walbaṣeer; afalaa tatafakkaroon.

قُلْ لَّا اَقُوْلُ لَكُمْ عِنْدِىْ خَزَآئِنُ
اللّٰهِ وَلَا اَعْلَمُ الْغَيْبَ وَلَا اَقُوْلُ
لَكُمْ اِنِّىْ مَلَكٌ ۚ اِنْ اَتَّبِعُ اِلَّا مَا يُوْحٰى
اِلَىَّ ۗ قُلْ هَلْ يَسْتَوِى الْاَعْمٰى
وَالْبَصِيْرُ ۗ اَفَلَا تَتَفَكَّرُوْنَ ﴿٥٠﴾ ع ٩ ١١

51. Preach the Quran to those who are concerned about the Day of Judgment at which time they will be brought before their Lord. Tell them that their only guardian and intercessor is Allah so that they may become pious.

51. Wa anzir bihil-lazeena yakhaafoona añy-yuḥsharooo ilaa Rabbihim laysa lahum min doonihee waliyyuñw-wa laa shafee'ul-la'allahum yattaqoon.

وَاَنْذِرْ بِهِ الَّذِيْنَ يَخَافُوْنَ اَنْ يُّحْشَرُوْٓا
اِلٰى رَبِّهِمْ لَيْسَ لَهُمْ مِّنْ دُوْنِهٖ
وَلِىٌّ وَّلَا شَفِيْعٌ لَّعَلَّهُمْ يَتَّقُوْنَ ﴿٥١﴾

52. Do not disregard those who pray to their Lord in the mornings and evenings, seeking their Lord's pleasure. You will not be held responsible for them nor will they be held responsible for you. Do not disregard them lest you become unjust.

52. Wa laa taṭrudil-lazeena yad'oona Rabbahum bilghadaati wal'ashiyyi yureedoona Wajhahoo maa 'alayka min ḥisaabihim min shay'iñw-wa maa min ḥisaabika 'alayhim min shay'in fataṭrudahum fatakoona minaẓ-ẓaalimeen.

وَلَا تَطْرُدِ الَّذِيْنَ يَدْعُوْنَ رَبَّهُمْ
بِالْغَدٰوةِ وَالْعَشِىِّ يُرِيْدُوْنَ
وَجْهَهٗ ۗ مَا عَلَيْكَ مِنْ حِسَابِهِمْ
مِّنْ شَىْءٍ وَّمَا مِنْ حِسَابِكَ
عَلَيْهِمْ مِّنْ شَىْءٍ فَتَطْرُدَهُمْ فَتَكُوْنَ
مِنَ الظّٰلِمِيْنَ ﴿٥٢﴾

53. We test some of them by the conditions of the others so that the rich and proud ones (seeing your poor and humble followers) would say, "Are these the ones from among all of us whom Allah has chosen to favor?" Does Allah not know those who give thanks (much better than others do)?

53. Wa kazaalika fatannaa ba'ḍahum biba'ḍil-liyaqoolooo ahaaa'ulaaa'i mannal-laahu 'alayhim mim bayninaaa; alaysal-laahu bia'lama bish-shaakireen.

وَكَذٰلِكَ فَتَنَّا بَعْضَهُمْ بِبَعْضٍ
لِّيَقُوْلُوْٓا اَهٰٓؤُلَآءِ مَنَّ اللّٰهُ عَلَيْهِمْ
مِّنْ بَيْنِنَا ۗ اَلَيْسَ اللّٰهُ بِاَعْلَمَ
بِالشّٰكِرِيْنَ ﴿٥٣﴾

54. When the faithful come to you, say to them, "Peace be upon you. Your Lord has decreed for Himself to be All-merciful. Anyone of you who commits a sin out of ignorance, then repents and reforms himself, will find that Allah is All-forgiving and All-merciful."

54. Wa izaa jaaa'akallazeena yu'minoona bi-Aayaatinaa faqul salaamun 'alaykum kataba Rabbukum 'alaa nafsihir-raḥmata annahoo man 'amila minkum sooo'am bijahaalatin summa taaba mim ba'dihee wa aṣlaḥa fa-annahoo Ghafoorur-Raḥeem.

وَاِذَا جَآءَكَ الَّذِيْنَ يُؤْمِنُوْنَ بِاٰيٰتِنَا
فَقُلْ سَلٰمٌ عَلَيْكُمْ كَتَبَ رَبُّكُمْ عَلٰى
نَفْسِهِ الرَّحْمَةَ ۙ اَنَّهٗ مَنْ عَمِلَ مِنْكُمْ
سُوْٓءًۢا بِجَهَالَةٍ ثُمَّ تَابَ مِنْۢ بَعْدِهٖ
وَاَصْلَحَ فَاَنَّهٗ غَفُوْرٌ رَّحِيْمٌ ﴿٥٤﴾

55. Thus do We explain Our revelations so that the sinful way

55. Wa kazaalika nufaṣṣilul Aayaati wa litastabeena

وَكَذٰلِكَ نُفَصِّلُ الْاٰيٰتِ وَلِتَسْتَبِيْنَ

can be plainly discerned.

sabeelul-mujrimeen.

سَبِيۡلُ الۡمُجۡرِمِيۡنَ ﴿۵۵﴾ ع ٥ ١٢

56. (Muhammad), tell them, "I am commanded not to worship the idols instead of Allah. I do not follow your desires lest I go astray and miss the true guidance."

56. Qul innee nuheetu an a'budal-lazeena tad'oona min doonil-laah; qul laaa attabi'u ahwaaa'akum qad dalaltu izañw-wa maaa ana minal-muhtadeen.

قُلۡ اِنِّىۡ نُهِيۡتُ اَنۡ اَعۡبُدَ الَّذِيۡنَ
تَدۡعُوۡنَ مِنۡ دُوۡنِ اللّٰهِ ؕ قُلْ لَّاۤ
اَتَّبِعُ اَهۡوَآءَكُمۡ ۙ قَدۡ ضَلَلۡتُ اِذًا
وَّمَاۤ اَنَا مِنَ الۡمُهۡتَدِيۡنَ ﴿۵۶﴾

57. Say, "I have received enough authoritative evidence from my Lord but you have rejected it. Whatever (torment Allah has warned you of due to your disbelief) and which you insist on experiencing without delay, is not in my hands. The (final) Judgment is in the hands of Allah. He reveals the Truth and He is the best Judge.

57. Qul innee 'alaa bayyinatim-mir-Rabbee wa kazzabtum bih; maa 'indee maa tasta'jiloona bih; inil-hukmu illaa lillaahi yaqussul-haqqa wa Huwa khayrul-faasileen.

قُلۡ اِنِّىۡ عَلٰى بَيِّنَةٍ مِّنۡ رَّبِّىۡ وَكَذَّبۡتُمۡ
بِهٖ ؕ مَا عِنۡدِىۡ مَا تَسۡتَعۡجِلُوۡنَ بِهٖ ؕ
اِنِ الۡحُكۡمُ اِلَّا لِلّٰهِ ؕ يَقُصُّ الۡحَقَّ
وَهُوَ خَيۡرُ الۡفٰصِلِيۡنَ ﴿۵۷﴾

58. Say, "If I had in my hands what you demand to experience without delay, the matter would have been ended altogether. Allah knows best about the unjust."

58. Qul law anna 'indee maa tasta'jiloona bihee laqudiyal-amru baynee wa baynakum; wallaahu a'lamu bizzaalimeen.

قُلْ لَّوۡ اَنَّ عِنۡدِىۡ مَا تَسۡتَعۡجِلُوۡنَ
بِهٖ لَقُضِىَ الۡاَمۡرُ بَيۡنِىۡ وَبَيۡنَكُمۡ ؕ
وَاللّٰهُ اَعۡلَمُ بِالظّٰلِمِيۡنَ ﴿۵۸﴾

59. He has with Him the keys to the unseen which no one knows besides Him. He knows all that is in the land and the sea. Not a single leaf falls of which He does not know. No single seed exists even in the darkest places of the land, nor anything in the world either wet or dry, that is not kept recorded in the self-evident Book (the tablet preserved in the heavens).

59. Wa 'indahoo mafaatihul-ghaybi laa ya'lamuhaaa illaa Hoo; wa ya'lamu maa fil-barri walbahr; wa maa tasqutu miñw-waraqatin illaa ya'lamuhaa wa laa habbatin fee zulumaatil-ardi wa laa ratbiñw-wa laa yaabisin illaa fee Kitaabim-Mubeen.

وَعِنۡدَهٗ مَفَاتِحُ الۡغَيۡبِ لَا يَعۡلَمُهَاۤ
اِلَّا هُوَ ؕ وَيَعۡلَمُ مَا فِى الۡبَرِّ وَالۡبَحۡرِ ؕ
وَمَا تَسۡقُطُ مِنۡ وَّرَقَةٍ اِلَّا يَعۡلَمُهَا
وَلَا حَبَّةٍ فِىۡ ظُلُمٰتِ الۡاَرۡضِ وَلَا
رَطۡبٍ وَّلَا يَابِسٍ اِلَّا فِىۡ كِتٰبٍ
مُّبِيۡنٍ ﴿۵۹﴾

60. It is He who keeps you alive in your sleep at night and knows all that you do during the day. He wakes you up from your sleep to complete your worldly life, after which you will all return to Him. He will let you know all about what you had done in your worldly life.

60. Wa Huwal-lazee yatawaffaakum billayli wa ya'lamu maa jarahtum binnahaari summa yab'asukum feehi liyuqdaaa ajalum-musamman summa ilayhi marji'ukum summa yunabbi'ukum bimaa kuntum ta'maloon.

وَهُوَ الَّذِىۡ يَتَوَفّٰٮكُمۡ بِالَّيۡلِ وَ
يَعۡلَمُ مَا جَرَحۡتُمۡ بِالنَّهَارِ ثُمَّ
يَبۡعَثُكُمۡ فِيۡهِ لِيُقۡضٰٓى اَجَلٌ
مُّسَمًّى ۚ ثُمَّ اِلَيۡهِ مَرۡجِعُكُمۡ ثُمَّ
يُنَبِّئُكُمۡ بِمَا كُنۡتُمۡ تَعۡمَلُوۡنَ ﴿۶۰﴾ ع ٥ ١٣

61. He is Dominant over all His creatures and He sends guards to watch over you until death approaches you. Then His angelic Messengers will, without fail,

61. Wa Huwal-Qaahiru fawqa 'ibaadihee wa yursilu 'alaykum hafazatan hattaaa izaa jaaa'a ahadakumul-mawtu tawaffathu rusulunaa

وَهُوَ الۡقَاهِرُ فَوۡقَ عِبَادِهٖ وَيُرۡسِلُ
عَلَيۡكُمۡ حَفَظَةً ؕ حَتّٰٓى اِذَا جَآءَ
اَحَدَكُمُ الۡمَوۡتُ تَوَفَّتۡهُ رُسُلُنَا

take away your souls.

wa hum laa yufarriṭoon.

وَهُمْ لَا يُفَرِّطُونَ ﴿٦١﴾

62. (After death) you will all be returned to Allah, your true Guardian. Know that judgment will be in His Hands and that His reckoning is swift.

62. S̲umma ruddooo ilallaahi mawlaahumul-ḥaqq; alaa lahul-ḥukmu wa Huwa asra‘ul-ḥaasibeen.

ثُمَّ رُدُّوا إِلَى اللَّهِ مَوْلَاهُمُ الْحَقِّ ۚ
أَلَا لَهُ الْحُكْمُ وَهُوَ أَسْرَعُ الْحَاسِبِينَ ﴿٦٢﴾

63. (Muhammad), ask them, “Who would save you from the darkness of the land and sea if you were to pray humbly and secretly saying, 'Would that we were saved from this, for we would certainly then give thanks.'”

63. Qul mañy-yunajjeekum min ẓulumaatil-barri walbaḥri tad‘oonahoo taḍarru‘añw-wa khufyatan la’in anjaanaa min haaẕihee lanakoonanna minash-shaakireen.

قُلْ مَنْ يُنَجِّيكُمْ مِنْ ظُلُمَاتِ الْبَرِّ
وَالْبَحْرِ تَدْعُونَهُ تَضَرُّعًا وَخُفْيَةً
لَئِنْ أَنْجَانَا مِنْ هَٰذِهِ لَنَكُونَنَّ
مِنَ الشَّاكِرِينَ ﴿٦٣﴾

64. Say, “It is Allah who always saves you (from such hardship) and from all kinds of distress. Even then, you consider idols equal to Allah.”

64. Qulil-laahu yunajjeekum minhaa wa min kulli karbin s̲umma antum tushrikoon.

قُلِ اللَّهُ يُنَجِّيكُمْ مِنْهَا وَمِنْ كُلِّ
كَرْبٍ ثُمَّ أَنْتُمْ تُشْرِكُونَ ﴿٦٤﴾

65. Say, “Allah has the power to send torment on you from above or below your feet, or to divide you into different groups quite hostile to one another, and make you suffer from each other's animosity.” Consider how plainly We show them a variety of evidence (of the Truth) so that they may have understanding.

65. Qul Huwal-Qaadiru ‘alaaa añy-yab‘as̲a ‘alaykum ‘aẕaa-bam-min fawqikum aw min taḥti arjulikum aw yalbisakum shiya‘añw-wa yuẕeeqa ba‘ḍa-kum ba-sa ba‘ḍ; unẓur kayfa nuṣarriful-Aayaati la‘allahum yafqahoon.

قُلْ هُوَ الْقَادِرُ عَلَىٰ أَنْ يَبْعَثَ عَلَيْكُمْ
عَذَابًا مِنْ فَوْقِكُمْ أَوْ مِنْ تَحْتِ
أَرْجُلِكُمْ أَوْ يَلْبِسَكُمْ شِيَعًا وَيُذِيقَ
بَعْضَكُمْ بَأْسَ بَعْضٍ ۗ انْظُرْ كَيْفَ
نُصَرِّفُ الْآيَاتِ لَعَلَّهُمْ يَفْقَهُونَ ﴿٦٥﴾

66. (Some of) your people have rejected the Quran, although it is the Truth. Tell them that you are not their guardian

66. Wa kaẕ-ẕaba bihee qawmuka wa huwal-ḥaqq; qul lastu ‘alaykum biwakeel.

وَكَذَّبَ بِهِ قَوْمُكَ وَهُوَ الْحَقُّ ۚ
قُلْ لَسْتُ عَلَيْكُمْ بِوَكِيلٍ ﴿٦٦﴾

67. and that for every prophecy (about you which comes from Allah) there is an appointed time (for coming true) and that they will soon experience it.

67. Likulli naba-immusta qarruñw -wa sawfa ta‘lamoon.

لِكُلِّ نَبَإٍ مُسْتَقَرٌّ ۚ وَسَوْفَ تَعْلَمُونَ ﴿٦٧﴾

68. When you see people mocking Our revelations, turn away from them so that they may change the subject. If Satan causes you to forget this, do not, when you recall, sit with the unjust people.

68. Wa iẕaa ra-aytal-laẕeena yakhooḍoona feee Aayaatinaa fa-a‘riḍ ‘anhum ḥattaa yakhoo-ḍoo fee ḥadees̲in ghayrih; wa immaa yunsiyannakash-Shayṭaanu falaa taq‘ud ba‘daẕ-ẕikraa ma‘al-qawmiẓ-ẓaali-meen.

وَإِذَا رَأَيْتَ الَّذِينَ يَخُوضُونَ فِي
آيَاتِنَا فَأَعْرِضْ عَنْهُمْ حَتَّىٰ يَخُوضُوا
فِي حَدِيثٍ غَيْرِهِ ۚ وَإِمَّا يُنْسِيَنَّكَ
الشَّيْطَانُ فَلَا تَقْعُدْ بَعْدَ الذِّكْرَىٰ
مَعَ الْقَوْمِ الظَّالِمِينَ ﴿٦٨﴾

69. And those who observe piety are not considered as committing any sin (when sitting with the unbelievers). It, however, is a reminder so that perhaps you may become pious.

69. Wa maa ‘alal-laẕeena yattaqoona min ḥisaabihim min shay’iñw-wa laakin ẕikraa la‘allahum yattaqoon.

وَمَا عَلَى الَّذِينَ يَتَّقُونَ مِنْ حِسَابِهِمْ
مِنْ شَيْءٍ وَلَٰكِنْ ذِكْرَىٰ لَعَلَّهُمْ
يَتَّقُونَ ﴿٦٩﴾

70. (Muhammad), leave alone those to whom their religion is no

70. Wa ẕaril-laẕeenat-takhaẕoo deenahum la‘ibañw-

وَذَرِ الَّذِينَ اتَّخَذُوا دِينَهُمْ لَعِبًا

more than a useless plaything and who are deceived by the lure of the worldly life. Remind them of Our revelation so that a soul will not bring about its own destruction because of its deeds. No one besides Allah is its guardian or intercessor, nor will any kind of ransom be accepted from it. Those who have entangled themselves in their evil deeds will drink boiling water and live in painful torment for their hiding the Truth.

wa lahwañw-wa ghar-rathumul-ḥayaatud-dunyaa; wa zakkir biheee an tubsala nafsum bimaa kasabat laysa lahaa min doonil-laahi waliyyuñw-wa laa shafee'; wa in ta'dil kulla 'adlil-laa yu'khaz minhaaa; ulaaa'ikal-lazeena ubsiloo bimaa kasaboo lahum sharaabum-min ḥameemiñw-wa 'azaabun aleemum bimaa kaanoo yakfuroon.

وَلَهْوًا وَّغَرَّتْهُمُ الْحَيٰوةُ الدُّنْيَا
وَذَكِّرْ بِهٖۤ اَنْ تُبْسَلَ نَفْسٌۢ بِمَا
كَسَبَتْ ۖ لَيْسَ لَهَا مِنْ دُوْنِ اللّٰهِ
وَلِيٌّ وَّلَا شَفِيْعٌ ۚ وَاِنْ تَعْدِلْ كُلَّ
عَدْلٍ لَّا يُؤْخَذْ مِنْهَا ؕ اُولٰٓئِكَ
الَّذِيْنَ اُبْسِلُوْا بِمَا كَسَبُوْا ۚ لَهُمْ شَرَابٌ
مِّنْ حَمِيْمٍ وَّعَذَابٌ اَلِيْمٌۢ بِمَا كَانُوْا
يَكْفُرُوْنَ ﴿۷۰﴾ ع ١٤

71. Say to them, "Should we, instead of asking for Allah's help, seek help from that which can neither benefit nor harm us, but would only turn us back to disbelief after Allah had granted us guidance? To do so would be to act like (those who have been) seduced by Satan, leaving them wandering aimlessly here and there, even though their friends call to them, 'Come to the right guidance that has come to us.'"

Say, "Allah's guidance is the only true guidance and we are commanded to submit ourselves to the Lord of the Universe.

71. Qul anad'oo min doonil-laahi maa laa yanfa'unaa wa laa yaḍurrunaa wa nuraddu 'alaaa a'qaabinaa ba'da iz hadaanal-laahu kallazistahwathush-Shayaaṭeenu fil-arḍi ḥayraana lahooo aṣḥaabuñy-yad'oonahooo ilalhuda'-tinaa; qul inna hudallaahi huwal-hudaa wa umirnaa linuslima li-Rabbil-'aalameen.

قُلْ اَنَدْعُوْا مِنْ دُوْنِ اللّٰهِ مَا لَا يَنْفَعُنَا
وَلَا يَضُرُّنَا وَنُرَدُّ عَلٰۤى اَعْقَابِنَا
بَعْدَ اِذْ هَدٰٮنَا اللّٰهُ كَالَّذِى اسْتَهْوَتْهُ
الشَّيٰطِيْنُ فِى الْاَرْضِ حَيْرَانَ ۖ لَهٗۤ
اَصْحٰبٌ يَّدْعُوْنَهٗۤ اِلَى الْهُدَى
ائْتِنَا ؕ قُلْ اِنَّ هُدَى اللّٰهِ هُوَ الْهُدٰى ؕ
وَاُمِرْنَا لِنُسْلِمَ لِرَبِّ الْعٰلَمِيْنَ ﴿۷۱﴾

72. Be steadfast in prayer and have fear of Allah; before Him alone will you all be brought together.

72. Wa an aqeemuṣ-Ṣalaata wattaqooh; wa Huwal-lazeee ilayhi tuḥsharoon.

وَاَنْ اَقِيْمُوا الصَّلٰوةَ وَاتَّقُوْهُ ؕ الثلثة
وَهُوَ الَّذِىْۤ اِلَيْهِ تُحْشَرُوْنَ ﴿۷۲﴾

73. It is He Who has created the heavens and the earth for a genuine purpose. When He commands the Day of Judgment to take place, it will come into existence. His Word is the Truth. The kingdom will be His alone on the day when the trumpet will be sounded. He has all knowledge of the unseen as well as the seen. He is All-wise and All-aware.

73. Wa Huwal-lazee khalaqas-samaawaati wal-arḍa bilḥaqq; wa Yawma yaqoolu kun fayakoon; Qawluhul-ḥaqq; wa lahul-mulku Yawma yunfakhu fiṣ-Ṣoor; 'Aalimul-Ghaybi wash-shahaadah; wa Huwal-Ḥakeemul-Khabeer.

وَهُوَ الَّذِىْ خَلَقَ السَّمٰوٰتِ وَالْاَرْضَ
بِالْحَقِّ ؕ وَيَوْمَ يَقُوْلُ كُنْ فَيَكُوْنُ ۚ
قَوْلُهُ الْحَقُّ ؕ وَلَهُ الْمُلْكُ يَوْمَ
يُنْفَخُ فِى الصُّوْرِ ؕ عٰلِمُ الْغَيْبِ
وَالشَّهَادَةِ ؕ وَهُوَ الْحَكِيْمُ الْخَبِيْرُ ﴿۷۳﴾

74. Consider when Abraham asked his father, Azar, "Why do you believe idols to be your gods? I do find you and your people in absolute error."

74. Wa iz qaala Ibraaheemu li-abeehi Aazara atattakhizu aṣnaaman aalihatan inneee araaka wa qawmaka fee ḍalaalim-mubeen.

وَاِذْ قَالَ اِبْرٰهِيْمُ لِاَبِيْهِ اٰزَرَ اَتَتَّخِذُ
اَصْنَامًا اٰلِهَةً ۚ اِنِّىْۤ اَرٰٮكَ وَقَوْمَكَ
فِىْ ضَلٰلٍ مُّبِيْنٍ ﴿۷۴﴾

75. Also, We showed (Abraham) the kingdom of the

75. Wa kazaalika nureee Ibraaheema malakootas-

وَكَذٰلِكَ نُرِىْۤ اِبْرٰهِيْمَ مَلَكُوْتَ

heavens and the earth to strengthen his faith.

76. When it became dark at night, he (Abraham) saw a star and said, "This is my lord." But when it disappeared, he said, "I do not love those who fade away."

77. When Abraham saw the rising moon, he said, "This is my lord." But when it faded away, he said, "If my Lord did not guide me I shall certainly go astray."

78. When he saw the rising sun, he said, "This is my Lord for it is greater (than the others)." But when this too faded away, (Abraham) said, "My people, I disavow whatever you consider equal to Allah.

79. I have submitted myself uprightly to the One who has created the heavens and the earth and I am not an idol worshipper."

80. In an argument with his people, (Abraham) asked them, "Why do you argue with me about Allah who has given me guidance? Your idols can do no harm to me unless Allah wills. Allah knows all things. Why then, do you not consider this?

81. Why should I be afraid of your idols when you are not afraid of worshipping them without having received any authority from heaven? Would that you knew which of us is more deserving to receive amnesty."

82. Those who have accepted the faith and have kept it pure from injustice have achieved security and guidance.

samaawaati wal-arḍi wa liyakoona minal-mooqineen.

76. Falammaa janna 'alayhil-laylu ra-aa kawkaban qaala haazaa Rabbee falammaaa afala qaala laaa uḥibbul-aafileen.

77. Falammaa ra-al-qamara baazighan qaala haazaa Rabbee falammaaa afala qaala la'il-lam yahdinee Rabbee la-akoonanna minal-qawmiḍ-ḍaaalleen.

78. Falammaa ra-ash-shamsa baazighatan qaala haazaa Rabbee haazaaa akbaru falammaaa afalat qaala yaa qawmi innee bareee'um-mimmaa tushrikoon.

79. Innee wajjahtu wajhiya lillazee faṭaras-samaawaati wal-arḍa Ḥaneefañw-wa maaa ana minal-mushrikeen.

80. Wa ḥaaajjahoo qawmuh; qaala atuḥaaaj-jooonnee fillaahi wa qad hadaan; wa laaa akhaafu maa tushrikoona biheee illaaa añy-yashaaa'a Rabbee shay'aa; wasi'a Rabbee kulla shay'in 'ilmaa; afalaa tatazak-karoon.

81. Wa kayfa akhaafu maaa ashraktum wa laa takhaafoona annakum ashraktum billaahi maa lam yunazzil bihee 'alaykum sulṭaanaa; fa-ayyul-fareeqayni aḥaqqu bil-amni in kuntum ta'lamoon.

82. Allazeena aamanoo wa lam yalbisooo eemaanahum bizulmin ulaaa'ika lahumul-amnu wa hum muhtadoon.

السَّمٰوٰتِ وَالْاَرْضِ وَلِيَكُوْنَ
مِنَ الْمُوْقِنِيْنَ ﴿٧٥﴾
فَلَمَّا جَنَّ عَلَيْهِ الَّيْلُ رَاٰ كَوْكَبًا ۚ
قَالَ هٰذَا رَبِّيْ ۚ فَلَمَّاۤ اَفَلَ قَالَ
لَاۤ اُحِبُّ الْاٰفِلِيْنَ ﴿٧٦﴾
فَلَمَّا رَاَ الْقَمَرَ بَازِغًا قَالَ هٰذَا رَبِّيْ ۚ
فَلَمَّاۤ اَفَلَ قَالَ لَئِنْ لَّمْ يَهْدِنِيْ
رَبِّيْ لَاَكُوْنَنَّ مِنَ الْقَوْمِ الضَّآلِّيْنَ ﴿٧٧﴾
فَلَمَّا رَاَ الشَّمْسَ بَازِغَةً قَالَ هٰذَا
رَبِّيْ هٰذَاۤ اَكْبَرُ ۚ فَلَمَّاۤ اَفَلَتْ قَالَ
يٰقَوْمِ اِنِّيْ بَرِيْٓءٌ مِّمَّا تُشْرِكُوْنَ ﴿٧٨﴾
اِنِّيْ وَجَّهْتُ وَجْهِيَ لِلَّذِيْ فَطَرَ
السَّمٰوٰتِ وَالْاَرْضَ حَنِيْفًا وَّمَاۤ اَنَا
مِنَ الْمُشْرِكِيْنَ ﴿٧٩﴾
وَحَآجَّهٗ قَوْمُهٗ ؕ قَالَ اَتُحَآجُّوْٓنِّيْ
فِي اللّٰهِ وَقَدْ هَدٰىنِ ؕ وَلَاۤ اَخَافُ
مَا تُشْرِكُوْنَ بِهٖۤ اِلَّاۤ اَنْ يَّشَآءَ
رَبِّيْ شَيْئًا ؕ وَسِعَ رَبِّيْ كُلَّ شَيْءٍ
عِلْمًا ؕ اَفَلَا تَتَذَكَّرُوْنَ ﴿٨٠﴾
وَكَيْفَ اَخَافُ مَاۤ اَشْرَكْتُمْ وَلَا
تَخَافُوْنَ اَنَّكُمْ اَشْرَكْتُمْ بِاللّٰهِ
مَا لَمْ يُنَزِّلْ بِهٖ عَلَيْكُمْ سُلْطٰنًا ؕ
فَاَيُّ الْفَرِيْقَيْنِ اَحَقُّ بِالْاَمْنِ ۚ وقف لازم
اِنْ كُنْتُمْ تَعْلَمُوْنَ ﴿٨١﴾
اَلَّذِيْنَ اٰمَنُوْا وَلَمْ يَلْبِسُوْٓا اِيْمَانَهُمْ
بِظُلْمٍ اُولٰٓئِكَ لَهُمُ الْاَمْنُ وَهُمْ

مُّهْتَدُوْنَ ۝٨٢ ع ٩/١٢ ١٥

83. Such was the authoritative reasoning that We gave Abraham over his people. We raise whomever We want to a higher rank. Your Lord is All-wise and All-knowing.

83. Wa tilka ḥujjatunaaa aataynaahaaa Ibraaheema 'alaa qawmih; narfa'u darajaatim-man nashaaa'; inna Rabbaka Ḥakeemun 'Aleem.

وَتِلْكَ حُجَّتُنَآ اٰتَيْنٰهَآ اِبْرٰهِيْمَ
عَلٰى قَوْمِهٖ ؕ نَرْفَعُ دَرَجٰتٍ مَّنْ نَّشَآءُ ؕ
اِنَّ رَبَّكَ حَكِيْمٌ عَلِيْمٌ ۝٨٣

84. We gave (Abraham) Isaac and Jacob. Both had received Our guidance. Noah received Our guidance before Abraham and so did his descendants: David, Solomon, Job, Joseph, Moses, and Aaron. Thus is the reward for the righteous people.

84. Wa wahabnaa lahooo Isḥaaqa wa ya'qoob; kullan hadaynaa; wa Nooḥan hadaynaa min qablu wa min zurriyyatihee Daawooda wa Sulaymaana wa Ayyooba wa Yoosufa wa Moosaa wa Haaroon; wa kazaalika najzil-muḥsineen.

وَوَهَبْنَا لَهٗٓ اِسْحٰقَ وَيَعْقُوْبَ ؕ كُلًّا
هَدَيْنَا ۚ وَنُوْحًا هَدَيْنَا مِنْ قَبْلُ
وَمِنْ ذُرِّيَّتِهٖ دَاوٗدَ وَسُلَيْمٰنَ وَاَيُّوْبَ
وَيُوْسُفَ وَمُوْسٰى وَهٰرُوْنَ ؕ وَكَذٰلِكَ
نَجْزِى الْمُحْسِنِيْنَ ۝٨٤

85. We also gave guidance to Zacharias, John, Jesus, and Elias, who were all pious people,

85. Wa Zakariyyaa wa Yaḥyaa wa 'Eesaa wa Ilyaasa kullum-minaṣ-ṣaaliḥeen.

وَزَكَرِيَّا وَيَحْيٰى وَعِيْسٰى وَاِلْيَاسَ ؕ
كُلٌّ مِّنَ الصّٰلِحِيْنَ ۝٨٥

86. and Ishmael, Elisha, Jonah, and Lot whom We exalted over all people.

86. Wa Ismaa'eela wal-Yasa'a wa Yoonusa wa Looṭaa; wa kullan faḍḍalnaa 'alal-'aalameen.

وَاِسْمٰعِيْلَ وَالْيَسَعَ وَيُوْنُسَ وَلُوْطًا ؕ
وَكُلًّا فَضَّلْنَا عَلَى الْعٰلَمِيْنَ ۝٨٦

87. From their fathers, descendants, and brothers, We chose (certain) people and guided them to the right path.

87. Wa min-aabaaa'ihim wa zurriyyaatihim wa ikhwaanihim wajtabaynaahum wa hadaynaahum-ilaa Ṣiraaṭim-Mustaqeem.

وَمِنْ اٰبَآئِهِمْ وَذُرِّيّٰتِهِمْ وَاِخْوَانِهِمْ ۚ
وَاجْتَبَيْنٰهُمْ وَهَدَيْنٰهُمْ اِلٰى صِرَاطٍ
مُّسْتَقِيْمٍ ۝٨٧

88. Such is the guidance of Allah by which He guides whichever of His servants He wants. If people worship idols, their deeds will be turned devoid of all virtue.

88. Zaalika hudal-laahi yahdee bihee mañy-yashaaa'u min 'ibaadih; wa law ashrakoo laḥabiṭa 'anhum maa kaanoo ya'maloon.

ذٰلِكَ هُدَى اللّٰهِ يَهْدِيْ بِهٖ مَنْ
يَّشَآءُ مِنْ عِبَادِهٖ ؕ وَلَوْ اَشْرَكُوْا لَحَبِطَ
عَنْهُمْ مَّا كَانُوْا يَعْمَلُوْنَ ۝٨٨

89. These were the people to whom We gave the Book, Authority, and Prophesy. If some people do not accept Our guidance, it should not grieve you (Muhammad), for We have made others who accept and protect Our guidance.

89. Ulaaa'ikal-lazeena aataynaahumul-Kitaaba wal-ḥukma wan-Nubuwwah; fa-iñy-yakfur bihaa haaa'ulaaa'i faqad wakkalnaa bihaa qawmal-laysoo bihaa bikaafireen.

اُولٰٓئِكَ الَّذِيْنَ اٰتَيْنٰهُمُ الْكِتٰبَ
وَالْحُكْمَ وَالنُّبُوَّةَ ۚ فَاِنْ يَّكْفُرْ بِهَا
هٰٓؤُلَآءِ فَقَدْ وَكَّلْنَا بِهَا قَوْمًا لَّيْسُوْا
بِهَا بِكٰفِرِيْنَ ۝٨٩

90. We had guided the Prophets. (Muhammad), follow their guidance and say (to the people), "I do not ask any reward for what I have preached to you. It is my duty to awaken the world."

90. Ulaaa'ikal-lazeena hadal-laahu fabihudaahumuq-tadih; qul laaa as'alukum 'alayhi ajran in huwa illaa zikraa lil'aalameen.

اُولٰٓئِكَ الَّذِيْنَ هَدَى اللّٰهُ فَبِهُدٰىهُمُ
اقْتَدِهْ ؕ قُلْ لَّآ اَسْئَلُكُمْ عَلَيْهِ اَجْرًا ؕ
اِنْ هُوَ اِلَّا ذِكْرٰى لِلْعٰلَمِيْنَ ۝٩٠ ع ٨/١٦ ١٦

91. They have no true respect of Allah when they say, "Allah has not sent anything to a mortal being." (Muhammad), tell them, "Who revealed the Book containing light and guidance for the people which Moses brought? You wrote down only some parts of the original on paper and hid much, even after having learned from it that which neither you nor your fathers knew." Tell them, "Allah has (revealed the Quran)," and then leave them alone to pursue their useless investigations.

91. Wa maa qadarul-laaha ḥaqqa qadriheee i<u>z</u> qaaloo maaa anzalal-laahu 'alaa basharim-min shay'; qul man anzalal-Kitaabal-la<u>z</u>ee jaaa'a bihee Moosaa nooranw-wa hudal-linnaasi taj'aloonahoo qaraa-ṭeesa tubdoonahaa wa tukh-foona ka<u>s</u>eeraa; wa 'ullimtum maa lam ta'lamooo antum wa laaa aabaaa'ukum qulil-laahu <u>s</u>umma <u>z</u>arhum fee khawḍihim yal'aboon

وَمَا قَدَرُوا اللّٰهَ حَقَّ قَدْرِهٖٓ اِذْ قَالُوْا
مَآ اَنْزَلَ اللّٰهُ عَلٰى بَشَرٍ مِّنْ شَيْءٍ ؕ
قُلْ مَنْ اَنْزَلَ الْكِتٰبَ الَّذِيْ جَآءَ بِهٖ
مُوْسٰى نُوْرًا وَّهُدًى لِّلنَّاسِ تَجْعَلُوْنَهٗ
قَرَاطِيْسَ تُبْدُوْنَهَا وَتُخْفُوْنَ كَثِيْرًا ۚ
وَعُلِّمْتُمْ مَّا لَمْ تَعْلَمُوْٓا اَنْتُمْ وَلَآ اٰبَآؤُكُمْ ؕ
قُلِ اللّٰهُ ۙ ثُمَّ ذَرْهُمْ فِيْ خَوْضِهِمْ يَلْعَبُوْنَ ﴿٩١﴾

92. We have blessed this Book (the Quran) and revealed it to confirm that which was revealed to the Prophets who lived before you and to warn the people of the mother land (Makkah) and those living around it. Those who believe in the Day of Judgment accept this and are steadfast in their prayers.

92. Wa haa<u>z</u>aa Kitaabun anzalnaahu Mubaarakum-muṣaddiqul-la<u>z</u>ee bayna yaday-hi wa litun<u>z</u>ira Ummal-Quraa wa man ḥawlahaa; walla<u>z</u>eena yu'minoona bil-Aakhirati yu'minoona bihee wa hum 'alaa Ṣalaatihim yuḥaa-fiẓoon.

وَهٰذَا كِتٰبٌ اَنْزَلْنٰهُ مُبٰرَكٌ مُّصَدِّقُ
الَّذِيْ بَيْنَ يَدَيْهِ وَلِتُنْذِرَ اُمَّ الْقُرٰى
وَمَنْ حَوْلَهَا ؕ وَالَّذِيْنَ يُؤْمِنُوْنَ
بِالْاٰخِرَةِ يُؤْمِنُوْنَ بِهٖ وَهُمْ عَلٰى
صَلَاتِهِمْ يُحَافِظُوْنَ ﴿٩٢﴾

93. Who are more unjust than those who ascribe lies to Allah or say that Allah has sent them revelations when nothing had been sent to them, or those who say that they can also bring down (from heaven) a book like that which Allah has revealed?

Would that you could see the unjust in the agonies of death when the angels will come forward with their hands outstretched to take their souls out of their bodies and say, "This is the day when you will face humiliating torment for the falsehood that you ascribed to Allah and for your contemptuous disregard for His revelations."

93. Wa man aẓlamu mimmanif-taraa 'alal-laahi ka<u>z</u>iban aw qaala ooḥiya ilayya wa lam yooḥa ilayhi shay'unw-wa man qaala sa-unzilu mi<u>s</u>la maaa anzalallaah; wa law taraaa i<u>z</u>iẓẓaalimoona fee ghama-raatil-mawti walmalaaa'ikatu baasiṭooo aydeehim akhrijooo anfusakum;Al-yawma tujzawna 'a<u>z</u>aabalhooni bimaa kuntum taqooloona 'alal-laahi ghayral-ḥaqqi wa kuntum 'an Aayaati-hee tastakbiroon.

وَمَنْ اَظْلَمُ مِمَّنِ افْتَرٰى عَلَى اللّٰهِ كَذِبًا
اَوْ قَالَ اُوْحِيَ اِلَيَّ وَلَمْ يُوْحَ اِلَيْهِ شَيْءٌ
وَّمَنْ قَالَ سَاُنْزِلُ مِثْلَ مَآ اَنْزَلَ اللّٰهُ ؕ
وَلَوْ تَرٰٓى اِذِ الظّٰلِمُوْنَ فِيْ غَمَرٰتِ الْمَوْتِ
وَالْمَلٰٓئِكَةُ بَاسِطُوْٓا اَيْدِيْهِمْ ۚ اَخْرِجُوْٓا
اَنْفُسَكُمْ ؕ اَلْيَوْمَ تُجْزَوْنَ عَذَابَ الْهُوْنِ
بِمَا كُنْتُمْ تَقُوْلُوْنَ عَلَى اللّٰهِ غَيْرَ الْحَقِّ
وَكُنْتُمْ عَنْ اٰيٰتِهٖ تَسْتَكْبِرُوْنَ ﴿٩٣﴾

94. Allah will say, "You have come to Us alone just as We created you at first. You have left behind all those whom We made your friends and We do not see with you any of the intercessors whom you believed to be your partners. Your relations with them have certainly been destroyed and your belief in them has left you (in the dark)."

94. Wa laqad ji'tumoonaa furaadaa kamaa khalaqnaakum awwala marratinw-wa taraktum maa khawwalnaakum waraaa'a ẓuhoorikum wa maa naraa ma'akum shufa'aaa'akumul-la<u>z</u>eena za-'amtum annahum feekum shurakaaa'; laqatta-qaṭṭa'a baynakum wa ḍalla 'ankum maa kuntum taz'umoon

وَلَقَدْ جِئْتُمُوْنَا فُرَادٰى كَمَا خَلَقْنٰكُمْ
اَوَّلَ مَرَّةٍ وَّتَرَكْتُمْ مَّا خَوَّلْنٰكُمْ وَرَآءَ
ظُهُوْرِكُمْ ۚ وَمَا نَرٰى مَعَكُمْ شُفَعَآءَكُمُ
الَّذِيْنَ زَعَمْتُمْ اَنَّهُمْ فِيْكُمْ شُرَكٰٓؤُا ؕ
لَقَدْ تَّقَطَّعَ بَيْنَكُمْ وَضَلَّ عَنْكُمْ مَّا
كُنْتُمْ تَزْعُمُوْنَ ﴿٩٤﴾ ع ١١ ١٧

95. It is Allah who makes all kinds of seeds grow, brings forth the living from the dead, and the dead from the living. It is Allah who does such things, so how can you turn away from Him?

95. Innal-laaha faaliqul-ḥabbi wannawaa yukhrijul-ḥayya minal-mayyiti wa mukhrijul-mayyiti minal-ḥayy; zaali-kumul-laahu fa-annaa tu'fa-koon.

اِنَّ اللّٰهَ فَالِقُ الْحَبِّ وَالنَّوٰى ؕ يُخْرِجُ
الْحَيَّ مِنَ الْمَيِّتِ وَمُخْرِجُ الْمَيِّتِ مِنَ
الْحَيِّ ؕ ذٰلِكُمُ اللّٰهُ فَاَنّٰى تُؤْفَكُوْنَ ﴿٩٥﴾

96. It is He who kindles the light of dawn, and has made the night for you to rest, and the sun and moon as a means of calculation. This is the design of the Majestic and All-knowing (Allah).

96. Faaliqul-iṣbaaḥi wa ja-'alal-layla sakanañw-washsh-amsa walqamara ḥusbaanaa; zaalika taqdeerul-'Azeezil-'Aleem.

فَالِقُ الْاِصْبَاحِ ۚ وَجَعَلَ الَّيْلَ سَكَنًا
وَّالشَّمْسَ وَالْقَمَرَ حُسْبَانًا ؕ ذٰلِكَ
تَقْدِيْرُ الْعَزِيْزِ الْعَلِيْمِ ﴿٩٦﴾

97. It is Allah who created the stars so that you could find your way thereby in the darkness of the land and sea. We have explained Our evidence to the people of knowledge.

97. Wa Huwal-lazee ja'ala lakumun-nujooma litahtadoo bihaa fee ẓulumaatil-barri walbaḥr; qad faṣṣalnal-Aayaati liqawmiñy-ya'lamoon.

وَهُوَ الَّذِيْ جَعَلَ لَكُمُ النُّجُوْمَ لِتَهْتَدُوْا
بِهَا فِيْ ظُلُمٰتِ الْبَرِّ وَالْبَحْرِ ؕ قَدْ فَصَّلْنَا
الْاٰيٰتِ لِقَوْمٍ يَّعْلَمُوْنَ ﴿٩٧﴾

98. It is He who has created you from a single soul. Some of you are settled (on earth) and some are still in the depository system (of their parents). We have shown the evidence (of Our existence) to the people who understand.

98. Wa Huwal-lazeee ansha-akum min nafsiñw-waaḥidatin famustaqarruñw-wa mustawda'; qad faṣṣalnal-Aayaati liqawm-iñy-yafqahoon.

وَهُوَ الَّذِيْٓ اَنْشَاَكُمْ مِّنْ نَّفْسٍ
وَّاحِدَةٍ فَمُسْتَقَرٌّ وَّمُسْتَوْدَعٌ ؕ قَدْ
فَصَّلْنَا الْاٰيٰتِ لِقَوْمٍ يَّفْقَهُوْنَ ﴿٩٨﴾

99. It is He who has sent water down from the sky to let all kinds of plants grow; the vegetables with accumulated grains; palm-trees from which appear clusters of dates within easy reach; vineyards, olive groves, and pomegranates of all types. See the fruits when they are growing and when they are ripe. This, too, is evidence (of the existence of Allah) for those who believe.

99. Wa Huwal-lazeee anzala minas-samaaa'i maaa'an fa-akhrajnaa bihee nabaata kulli shay'in fa-akhrajnaa minhu khaḍiran nukhriju minhu ḥabbam-mutaraakibaa; wa minan-nakhli min ṭal'ihaa qinwaanun daaniyatuñw-wa jannaatim-min a'naabiñw-wazzaytoona warrummaana mushtabihañw-wa ghayra muta-shaabih; unẓurooo ilaa samari-heee izaaa asmara wa yan'ih; inna fee zaalikum la-Aayaatil-liqawmiñy-yu'minoon.

وَهُوَ الَّذِيْٓ اَنْزَلَ مِنَ السَّمَآءِ مَآءً ۚ
فَاَخْرَجْنَا بِهٖ نَبَاتَ كُلِّ شَيْءٍ فَاَخْرَجْنَا
مِنْهُ خَضِرًا نُّخْرِجُ مِنْهُ حَبًّا مُّتَرَاكِبًا ۚ
وَمِنَ النَّخْلِ مِنْ طَلْعِهَا قِنْوَانٌ دَانِيَةٌ
وَّجَنّٰتٍ مِّنْ اَعْنَابٍ وَّالزَّيْتُوْنَ
وَالرُّمَّانَ مُشْتَبِهًا وَّغَيْرَ مُتَشَابِهٍ ؕ
اُنْظُرُوْٓا اِلٰى ثَمَرِهٖٓ اِذَآ اَثْمَرَ وَيَنْعِهٖ ؕ
اِنَّ فِيْ ذٰلِكُمْ لَاٰيٰتٍ لِّقَوْمٍ يُّؤْمِنُوْنَ ﴿٩٩﴾

100. (Certain) people considered the Jinn to be equal to Allah even though Allah created them and they unknowingly ascribed to Him children, both boys and girls. Allah is free of all defects and the attributes which they ascribe to Him.

100. Wa ja'aloo lillaahi shura-kaaa'al-jinna wa khalaqa-hum wa kharaqoo lahoo baneena wa banaatim bighayri 'ilm; Subḥaanahoo wa Ta'aalaa 'ammaa yaṣifoon.

وَجَعَلُوْا لِلّٰهِ شُرَكَآءَ الْجِنَّ وَخَلَقَهُمْ
وَخَرَقُوْا لَهٗ بَنِيْنَ وَبَنٰتٍۭ بِغَيْرِ عِلْمٍ ؕ
سُبْحٰنَهٗ وَتَعٰلٰى عَمَّا يَصِفُوْنَ ﴿١٠٠﴾ ع ١٢ ١٨

101. How could the One Who is the Originator of the heavens and the earth and Who had no companion, have a son? He created all things and has absolute knowledge of all things.

101. Badee'us-samaawaati wal-arḍi annaa yakoonu lahoo waladuñw-wa lam takullahoo ṣaaḥibah; wa khalaqa kulla shay'; wa Huwa bikulli shay'in 'Aleem.

بَدِيْعُ السَّمٰوٰتِ وَالْاَرْضِ ؕ اَنّٰى يَكُوْنُ لَهٗ
وَلَدٌ وَّلَمْ تَكُنْ لَّهٗ صَاحِبَةٌ ؕ وَخَلَقَ
كُلَّ شَيْءٍ ۚ وَهُوَ بِكُلِّ شَيْءٍ عَلِيْمٌ ﴿١٠١﴾

102. He is Allah your Lord. There is no Allah but He. He has created all things. Worship Him for He is the Guardian of all things.

102. Zaalikumul-laahu Rabbukum laaa ilaaha illaa Huwa khaaliqu kulli shay'in fa'budooh; wa Huwa 'alaa kulli shay'iñw-Wakeel.

ذٰلِكُمُ اللّٰهُ رَبُّكُمْ ۚ لَآ اِلٰهَ اِلَّا هُوَ ۚ خَالِقُ
كُلِّ شَیْءٍ فَاعْبُدُوْهُ ۚ وَهُوَ عَلٰی كُلِّ
شَیْءٍ وَّكِیْلٌ ﴿۱۰۲﴾

103. No mortal eyes can see Him, but He can see all eyes. He is All-kind and All-aware.

103. Laa tudrikuhul-abṣaaru wa Huwa yudrikul-abṣaara wa Huwal-Laṭeeful-Khabeer.

لَا تُدْرِكُهُ الْاَبْصَارُ ؗ وَهُوَ یُدْرِكُ الْاَبْصَارَ ۚ
وَهُوَ اللَّطِیْفُ الْخَبِیْرُ ﴿۱۰۳﴾

104. (O Muhammad), tell them, "Clear proofs have certainly come to you from your Lord. Whoever tries to understand it will gain much but those who ignore it will only harm themselves. I am not (supposed) to watch over you (all the time)."

104. Qad jaaa'akum baṣaaa'iru mir-Rabbikum faman abṣara falinafsihee wa man 'amiya fa'alayhaa; wa maaa ana 'alaykum biḥafeeẓ.

قَدْ جَآءَكُمْ بَصَآئِرُ مِنْ رَّبِّكُمْ ۚ فَمَنْ
اَبْصَرَ فَلِنَفْسِهٖ ۚ وَمَنْ عَمِیَ فَعَلَیْهَا ؕ
وَمَآ اَنَا عَلَیْكُمْ بِحَفِیْظٍ ﴿۱۰۴﴾

105. Thus do We explain Our revelations to them. Let them say, "You have learned (those statements) from other people." We want to explain Our revelations only to those who have knowledge.

105. Wa kazaalika nuṣar-riful Aayaati wa liyaqooloo darasta wa linubayyinahoo liqawmiñy-ya'lamoon.

وَكَذٰلِكَ نُصَرِّفُ الْاٰیٰتِ وَلِیَقُوْلُوْا
دَرَسْتَ وَلِنُبَیِّنَهٗ لِقَوْمٍ یَّعْلَمُوْنَ ﴿۱۰۵﴾

106. (O Muhammad), follow what has been revealed to you from your Lord; there is no Ilah (one deserving to be worshipped) but He, and stay away from pagans.

106. Ittabi' maaa ooḥiya ilayka mir-Rabbika laaa ilaaha illaa Huwa wa a'riḍ 'anil-mushrikeen.

اِتَّبِعْ مَآ اُوْحِیَ اِلَیْكَ مِنْ رَّبِّكَ ۚ لَآ اِلٰهَ
اِلَّا هُوَ ۚ وَاَعْرِضْ عَنِ الْمُشْرِكِیْنَ ﴿۱۰۶﴾

107. Had Allah wanted, they would not consider anything equal to Him. Allah has not appointed you to watch over them nor are you their guardian.

107. Wa law shaaa'al-laahu maaa ashrakoo; wa maa ja'alnaaka 'alayhim ḥafeezaa; wa maaa anta 'alayhim biwakeel.

وَلَوْ شَآءَ اللّٰهُ مَآ اَشْرَكُوْا ؕ وَمَا
جَعَلْنٰكَ عَلَیْهِمْ حَفِیْظًا ۚ وَمَآ اَنْتَ
عَلَیْهِمْ بِوَكِیْلٍ ﴿۱۰۷﴾

108. Believers, do not say bad words against the idols lest they (pagans) in their hostility and ignorance say such words against Allah. We have made every nation's deeds seem attractive to them. One day they will all return to their Lord who will inform them of all that they have done.

108. Wa laa tasubbul-lazeena yad'oona min doonil-laahi fayasubbul-laaha 'adwam bighayri 'ilm; kazaalika zayyan-naa likulli ummatin 'amalahum summa ilaa Rabbihim marji'uhum fayunabbi'uhum bimaa kaanoo ya'maloon.

وَلَا تَسُبُّوا الَّذِیْنَ یَدْعُوْنَ مِنْ دُوْنِ
اللّٰهِ فَیَسُبُّوا اللّٰهَ عَدْوًۢا بِغَیْرِ عِلْمٍ ؕ
كَذٰلِكَ زَیَّنَّا لِكُلِّ اُمَّةٍ عَمَلَهُمْ ۪
ثُمَّ اِلٰی رَبِّهِمْ مَّرْجِعُهُمْ فَیُنَبِّئُهُمْ
بِمَا كَانُوْا یَعْمَلُوْنَ ﴿۱۰۸﴾

109. The unbelievers solemnly swear by Allah that if they were to be shown some miracle, they would certainly believe. (Muhammad), tell them, "Only with Allah are all the miracles." Even if a miracle was to take place, they still would not believe.

109. Wa aqsamoo billaahi jahda aymaanihim la'in jaaa'athum Aayatul-layu'minunna bihaa; qul innamal-Aayaatu 'indal-laahi wa maa yush'irukum annahaaa izaa jaaa'at laa yu'minoon.

وَاَقْسَمُوْا بِاللّٰهِ جَهْدَ اَیْمَانِهِمْ لَئِنْ
جَآءَتْهُمْ اٰیَةٌ لَّیُؤْمِنُنَّ بِهَا ؕ قُلْ
اِنَّمَا الْاٰیٰتُ عِنْدَ اللّٰهِ وَمَا یُشْعِرُكُمْ ۙ
اَنَّهَاۤ اِذَا جَآءَتْ لَا یُؤْمِنُوْنَ ﴿۱۰۹﴾

110. We will turn their hearts and vision away (from a miracle); they did not have faith (in miracles) the first time, and We will leave them blind in their rebellion.

110. Wa nuqallibu af'idatahum wa abṣaarahum kamaa lam yu'minoo biheee awwala marratiñw-wa nazaruhum fee ṭughyaanihim ya'mahoon.

وَنُقَلِّبُ اَفْـِٕدَتَهُمْ وَاَبْصَارَهُمْ كَمَا لَمْ
یُؤْمِنُوْا بِهٖۤ اَوَّلَ مَرَّةٍ وَّنَذَرُهُمْ فِیْ

ع ١٣ — الجزء الثامن (٨)

طُغْيَانِهِمْ يَعْمَهُونَ ﴿١١٠﴾

111. Had We sent the angels to them, made the dead speak to them, and resurrected all things before their very eyes, they still would not believe unless Allah willed it to be so. But, in fact, most of them ignore (the evidence).

111. Wa law annanaa nazzalnaaa ilayhimul malaaa'ikata wa kallamahumul-mawtaa wa ḥasharnaa 'alayhim kulla shay'in qubulam-maa kaanoo liyu'minooo illaaa añy-yashaaa'al-laahu wa laakinna ak̲sarahum yajhaloon.

وَلَوْ أَنَّنَا نَزَّلْنَآ إِلَيْهِمُ الْمَلَٰٓئِكَةَ
وَكَلَّمَهُمُ الْمَوْتَىٰ وَحَشَرْنَا عَلَيْهِمْ
كُلَّ شَيْءٍ قُبُلًا مَّا كَانُوا لِيُؤْمِنُوٓا
إِلَّآ أَن يَشَآءَ اللَّهُ وَلَٰكِنَّ أَكْثَرَهُمْ
يَجْهَلُونَ ﴿١١١﴾

112. We have made devilish enemies for every Prophet from among people and jinn. They whisper attractive but deceitful words to each other. Had your Lord wanted, the devils would not have seduced people. Keep away from them and the falsehood which they invent.

112. Wa kaẕaalika ja'alnaa likulli Nabiyyin 'aduwwan Shayaaṭeenal-insi waljinni yooḥee ba'ḍuhum ilaa ba'ḍin zukhrufal-qawli ghurooraa; wa law shaaa'a Rabbuka maa fa'aloohu faẕarhum wa maa yaftaroon.

وَكَذَٰلِكَ جَعَلْنَا لِكُلِّ نَبِيٍّ عَدُوًّا
شَيَٰطِينَ الْإِنسِ وَالْجِنِّ يُوحِي
بَعْضُهُمْ إِلَىٰ بَعْضٍ زُخْرُفَ الْقَوْلِ
غُرُورًا ۚ وَلَوْ شَآءَ رَبُّكَ مَا فَعَلُوهُ
فَذَرْهُمْ وَمَا يَفْتَرُونَ ﴿١١٢﴾

113. Let those who do not believe in the Day of Judgment listen to the deceitful words with pleasure and indulge in whatever sins they want.

113. Wa litaṣghaaa ilayhi af'idatul-laẕeena laa yu'minoona bil-Aakhirati wa liyarḍawhu wa liyaqtarifoo maa hum muqtarifoon.

وَلِتَصْغَىٰٓ إِلَيْهِ أَفْـِٔدَةُ الَّذِينَ
لَا يُؤْمِنُونَ بِالْآخِرَةِ وَلِيَرْضَوْهُ
وَلِيَقْتَرِفُوا مَا هُم مُّقْتَرِفُونَ ﴿١١٣﴾

114. (Muhammad), say, "Should I seek any judge other than Allah? It is He Who has revealed this Book (Quran) to you with all its intricate details." Those to whom We have given the Bible know that the Quran has been revealed to you from your Lord in all Truth. Thus, you (people) must have no doubts about it.

114. Afaghayral-laahi abtaghee ḥakamañw-wa Huwal-laẕee anzala ilaykumul-Kitaaba mufaṣṣalaa; wallaẕeena aataynaahumul-Kitaaba ya'lamoona annahoo munazzalum-mir-Rabbika bilḥaqqi falaa takoonanna minal-mumtareen.

أَفَغَيْرَ اللَّهِ أَبْتَغِي حَكَمًا وَهُوَ
الَّذِيٓ أَنزَلَ إِلَيْكُمُ الْكِتَٰبَ
مُفَصَّلًا ۚ وَالَّذِينَ آتَيْنَٰهُمُ الْكِتَٰبَ
يَعْلَمُونَ أَنَّهُ مُنَزَّلٌ مِّن رَّبِّكَ بِالْحَقِّ
فَلَا تَكُونَنَّ مِنَ الْمُمْتَرِينَ ﴿١١٤﴾

115. (After having revealed the Quran to you) in all truth and justice, your Lord's Word has been completed. No one can change His Words. He is All-hearing and All-knowing.

115. Wa tammat Kalimatu Rabbika ṣidqañw-wa 'adlaa; laa mubaddila li-Kalimaatih; wa Huwas-Samee'ul-'Aleem.

وَتَمَّتْ كَلِمَتُ رَبِّكَ صِدْقًا وَّ
عَدْلًا ۚ لَّا مُبَدِّلَ لِكَلِمَٰتِهِ ۚ
وَهُوَ السَّمِيعُ الْعَلِيمُ ﴿١١٥﴾

116. Most of the people in the land will lead you away from Allah's guidance if you follow them; they only follow their own conjecture and preach falsehood.

116. Wa in tuṭi' ak̲sara man fil-arḍi yuḍillooka 'an sabeelil-laah; iñy-yattabi'oona illaẓ-ẓanna wa in hum illaa yakhruṣoon.

وَإِن تُطِعْ أَكْثَرَ مَن فِي الْأَرْضِ
يُضِلُّوكَ عَن سَبِيلِ اللَّهِ ۚ إِن يَتَّبِعُونَ
إِلَّا الظَّنَّ وَإِنْ هُمْ إِلَّا يَخْرُصُونَ ﴿١١٦﴾

117. Your Lord knows best those who have gone astray from His

117. Inna Rabbaka Huwa a'lamu mañy-yaḍillu

إِنَّ رَبَّكَ هُوَ أَعْلَمُ مَن يَضِلُّ

path and those who are rightly guided.

'an sabeelihee wa Huwa a'lamu bilmuhtadeen.

عَنۡ سَبِيۡلِهٖ‌ۚ وَهُوَ اَعۡلَمُ بِالۡمُهۡتَدِيۡنَ ﴿۱۱۷﴾

118. If you have faith in Allah's revelations, eat the flesh of the animal which has been slaughtered with a mention of His Name.

118. Fakuloo mimmaa zukirasmul-laahi 'alayhi in kuntum bi-Aayaatihee mu'mineen.

فَكُلُوۡا مِمَّا ذُكِرَ اسۡمُ اللّٰهِ عَلَيۡهِ اِنۡ
كُنۡتُمۡ بِاٰيٰتِهٖ مُؤۡمِنِيۡنَ ﴿۱۱۸﴾

119. Why should you not eat such flesh when Allah has told you in detail what is unlawful to eat under normal conditions.

Most people, out of ignorance, are led astray by their desires. Your Lord knows best those who transgress.

119. Wa maa lakum allaa ta-kuloo mimmaa zukirasmul-laahi 'alayhi wa qad fassala lakum maa harrama 'alaykum illaa mad-turirtum ilayh; wa inna kaseeral-layudilloona bi-ahwaaa'ihim bighayri 'ilm; inna Rabbaka Huwa a'lamu bilmu'tadeen.

وَمَا لَـكُمۡ اَلَّا تَاۡكُلُوۡا مِمَّا ذُكِرَ اسۡمُ
اللّٰهِ عَلَيۡهِ وَقَدۡ فَصَّلَ لَـكُمۡ مَّا حَرَّمَ
عَلَيۡكُمۡ اِلَّا مَا اضۡطُرِرۡتُمۡ اِلَيۡهِ‌ؕ
وَاِنَّ كَثِيۡرًا لَّيُضِلُّوۡنَ بِاَهۡوَآئِهِمۡ
بِغَيۡرِ عِلۡمٍ‌ؕ اِنَّ رَبَّكَ هُوَ اَعۡلَمُ
بِالۡمُعۡتَدِيۡنَ ﴿۱۱۹﴾

120. Stay away from both public and secret sins, for a sinner will suffer for whatever he has committed.

120. Wa zaroo zaahiral-ismi wa baatinah; innal-lazeena yaksiboonal-isma sayujzawna bimaa kaanoo yaqtarifoon.

وَذَرُوۡا ظَاهِرَ الۡاِثۡمِ وَبَاطِنَهٗ‌ؕ اِنَّ
الَّذِيۡنَ يَكۡسِبُوۡنَ الۡاِثۡمَ سَيُجۡزَوۡنَ
بِمَا كَانُوۡا يَقۡتَرِفُوۡنَ ﴿۱۲۰﴾

121. Do not eat the flesh of an animal which has been slaughtered without the name of Allah being mentioned; it is a sinful deed. Satan teaches his friends to argue with you. If you obey them, you will certainly be idol worshippers.

121. Wa laa ta-kuloo mimmaa lam yuzkaris-mullaahi 'alayhi wa innahoo lafisq; wa innash-Shayaateena layoohoona ilaaa awliyaaa'ihim liyujaadilookum wa in ata'tumoohum innakum lamushrikoon.

وَلَا تَاۡكُلُوۡا مِمَّا لَمۡ يُذۡكَرِ اسۡمُ اللّٰهِ
عَلَيۡهِ وَاِنَّهٗ لَفِسۡقٌ‌ؕ وَاِنَّ الشَّيٰطِيۡنَ
لَيُوۡحُوۡنَ اِلٰٓى اَوۡلِيٰٓـئِهِمۡ لِيُجَادِلُوۡكُمۡ‌ۚ
وَاِنۡ اَطَعۡتُمُوۡهُمۡ اِنَّكُمۡ لَمُشۡرِكُوۡنَ ﴿۱۲۱﴾

122. Can the dead to whom We have given life and light so that they may walk among the people, be considered equal to those who can never come out of darkness? The deeds of the unbelievers are made to seem attractive to them.

122. Awa man kaana maytan fa-ahyaynaahu wa ja'alnaa lahoo nooraňy-yamshee bihee fin-naasi kamam-masaluhoo fiz-zulumaati laysa bikhaarijim-minhaa; kazaalika zuyyina lilkaafireena maa kaanoo ya'maloon.

اَوَمَنۡ كَانَ مَيۡتًا فَاَحۡيَيۡنٰهُ وَجَعَلۡنَا
لَهٗ نُوۡرًا يَّمۡشِىۡ بِهٖ فِى النَّاسِ كَمَنۡ
مَّثَلُهٗ فِى الظُّلُمٰتِ لَـيۡسَ بِخَارِجٍ
مِّنۡهَا‌ؕ كَذٰلِكَ زُيِّنَ لِلۡكٰفِرِيۡنَ مَا
كَانُوۡا يَعۡمَلُوۡنَ ﴿۱۲۲﴾

123. In every town We have placed some sinful leaders who always make evil plans. These plans will only work against their own souls but they do not realize this.

123. Wa kazaalika ja'alnaa fee kulli qaryatin akaabira mujrimeehaa liyamkuroo feehaa wa maa yamkuroona illaa bi-anfusihim wa maa yash'uroon.

وَكَذٰلِكَ جَعَلۡنَا فِىۡ كُلِّ قَرۡيَةٍ اَكٰبِرَ
مُجۡرِمِيۡهَا لِيَمۡكُرُوۡا فِيۡهَا‌ؕ وَمَا
يَمۡكُرُوۡنَ اِلَّا بِاَنۡفُسِهِمۡ وَمَا يَشۡعُرُوۡنَ ﴿۱۲۳﴾

124. When a miracle is shown to them, they say, "We will not believe unless we are shown a miracle like that shown to the

124. Wa izaa jaaa'athum Aayatun qaaloo lan nu'mina hattaa nu'taa misla maaa ootiya Rusulul-laah;

وَاِذَا جَآءَتۡهُمۡ اٰيَةٌ قَالُوۡا لَنۡ نُّؤۡمِنَ
حَتّٰى نُؤۡتٰى مِثۡلَ مَاۤ اُوۡتِىَ رُسُلُ اللّٰهِ‌ؕ

messengers of Allah." Allah knows best whom to appoint as His Messenger. The sinful ones are worthless in the sight of Allah and they deserve a severe punishment for their evil plans.	Allaahu a‘lamu ḥays͟u yaj‘alu Risaalatah; sayuṣeebul-laz͟eena ajramoo ṣaghaarun ‘indal-laahi wa ‘az͟aabun shadeedum bimaa kaanoo yamkuroon.	اَللّٰهُ اَعْلَمُ حَيْثُ يَجْعَلُ رِسَالَتَهٗ ؕ سَيُصِيْبُ الَّذِيْنَ اَجْرَمُوْا صَغَارٌ عِنْدَ اللّٰهِ وَعَذَابٌ شَدِيْدٌۢ بِمَا كَانُوْا يَمْكُرُوْنَ ﴿۱۲۴﴾
125. Allah opens the hearts of whomever He wants to accept Islam, but He narrows down the chest of one whom He has led astray, as though he were climbing high up into the sky. Thus, Allah places wickedness on those who do not accept the faith.	125. Famañy-yuridil-laahu añy-yahdiyahoo yashraḥ ṣadrahoo lil-Islaami wa mañy-yurid añy-yuḍillahoo yaj‘al ṣadrahoo ḍayyiqan ḥarajan ka-annamaa yaṣṣa‘-‘adu fissamaaa’; kaz͟aalika yaj‘alul-laahur-rijsa ‘alal-laz͟eena laa yu’minoon.	فَمَنْ يُّرِدِ اللّٰهُ اَنْ يَّهْدِيَهٗ يَشْرَحْ صَدْرَهٗ لِلْاِسْلَامِ ۚ وَمَنْ يُّرِدْ اَنْ يُّضِلَّهٗ يَجْعَلْ صَدْرَهٗ ضَيِّقًا حَرَجًا كَاَنَّمَا يَصَّعَّدُ فِى السَّمَآءِ ؕ كَذٰلِكَ يَجْعَلُ اللّٰهُ الرِّجْسَ عَلَى الَّذِيْنَ لَا يُؤْمِنُوْنَ ﴿۱۲۵﴾
126. This is the path of your Lord and it is straight. We have explained Our revelations to those who take heed.	126. Wa haaz͟aa Ṣiraaṭu Rabbika Mustaqeemaa; qad faṣṣalnal-Aayaati liqawmiñy-yaz͟-z͟akkaroon.	وَهٰذَا صِرَاطُ رَبِّكَ مُسْتَقِيْمًا ؕ قَدْ فَصَّلْنَا الْاٰيٰتِ لِقَوْمٍ يَّذَّكَّرُوْنَ ﴿۱۲۶﴾
127. They will live in peace with Allah. Allah protects them as a reward for their deeds; He is their Guardian.	127. Lahum daarus-salaami ‘inda Rabbihim wa Huwa waliyyuhum bimaa kaanoo ya‘maloon.	لَهُمْ دَارُ السَّلٰمِ عِنْدَ رَبِّهِمْ وَهُوَ وَلِيُّهُمْ بِمَا كَانُوْا يَعْمَلُوْنَ ﴿۱۲۷﴾
128. On the day when everyone will be resurrected and the jinn will be told that they have made many people go astray, their friends from among people will say, "Lord, we benefited from each other until death approached us." They will be told that their dwelling will be fire wherein they will live forever unless Allah wills it to be otherwise. Your Lord is All-wise and All-knowing.	128. Wa Yawma yaḥshuruhum jamee‘aa;-yaa ma‘sharal-jinni qadistaks͟artum minal-insi wa qaala awliyaaa’uhum minal-insi Rabbanas-tamta‘a ba‘ḍunaa biba‘ḍiñw-wa balaghnaaa ajalanal-laz͟eee ajjalta lanaa; qaalan-Naaru mas͟waakum khaalideena feehaaa illaa maa shaaa’allaah; inna Rabbaka Ḥakeemun ‘Aleem.	وَيَوْمَ يَحْشُرُهُمْ جَمِيْعًا ۚ يٰمَعْشَرَ الْجِنِّ قَدِ اسْتَكْثَرْتُمْ مِّنَ الْاِنْسِ ۚ وَقَالَ اَوْلِيٰٓؤُهُمْ مِّنَ الْاِنْسِ رَبَّنَا اسْتَمْتَعَ بَعْضُنَا بِبَعْضٍ وَّبَلَغْنَآ اَجَلَنَا الَّذِىْٓ اَجَّلْتَ لَنَا ؕ قَالَ النَّارُ مَثْوٰىكُمْ خٰلِدِيْنَ فِيْهَآ اِلَّا مَا شَآءَ اللّٰهُ ؕ اِنَّ رَبَّكَ حَكِيْمٌ عَلِيْمٌ ﴿۱۲۸﴾
129. Thus do We make the unjust friends of one another because of their evil deeds.	129. Wa kaz͟aalika nuwallee ba‘ḍaẓ-ẓaalimeena ba‘ḍam bimaa kaanoo yaksiboon.	وَكَذٰلِكَ نُوَلِّىْ بَعْضَ الظّٰلِمِيْنَ بَعْضًاۢ بِمَا كَانُوْا يَكْسِبُوْنَ ﴿۱۲۹﴾ ع
130. When people and jinn are asked, "Did not Messengers from your own people come to you to convey Our revelations and to warn you of the Day of Resurrection?" They will reply,	130. Yaa ma‘sharal-jinni wal-insi alam ya-tikum Rusulum-minkum yaquṣṣoona ‘alaykum Aayaatee wa yunz͟iroonakum liqaaa’a Yawmikum	يٰمَعْشَرَ الْجِنِّ وَالْاِنْسِ اَلَمْ يَاْتِكُمْ رُسُلٌ مِّنْكُمْ يَقُصُّوْنَ عَلَيْكُمْ اٰيٰتِىْ وَيُنْذِرُوْنَكُمْ لِقَآءَ يَوْمِكُمْ

ع ۱۵ ۸ ۲

"(Yes indeed)." The worldly life deceived them. They will testify that they were unbelievers.

haaẕaa; qaaloo shahidnaa 'alaaa anfusinaa wa gharrathumul-ḥayaatuddunyaa wa shahidoo 'alaaa anfusihim annahum kaanoo kaafireen.

هٰذَا ۚ قَالُوْا شَهِدْنَا عَلٰۤى اَنْفُسِنَا
وَغَرَّتْهُمُ الْحَيٰوةُ الدُّنْيَا وَشَهِدُوْا
عَلٰۤى اَنْفُسِهِمْ اَنَّهُمْ كَانُوْا كٰفِرِيْنَ ﴿۱۳۰﴾

131. Your Lord did not want to destroy the towns, unjustly, without informing their inhabitants (of His guidance).

131. Ẕaalika al-lam yakur-Rabbuka muhlikal-quraa biẓulmiñw-wa ahluhaa ghaafiloon.

ذٰلِكَ اَنْ لَّمْ يَكُنْ رَّبُّكَ مُهْلِكَ الْقُرٰى
بِظُلْمٍ وَّاَهْلُهَا غٰفِلُوْنَ ﴿۱۳۱﴾

132. People's deeds are of different degrees and your Lord is not unaware of what people do.

132. Wa likullin darajaatum-mimmaa 'amiloo; wa maa Rabbuka bighaafilin 'ammaa ya'maloon.

وَلِكُلٍّ دَرَجٰتٌ مِّمَّا عَمِلُوْا ۚ وَمَا
رَبُّكَ بِغَافِلٍ عَمَّا يَعْمَلُوْنَ ﴿۱۳۲﴾

133. Your Lord is Self-sufficient and Merciful. Had He wanted, He could have destroyed you and replaced you by other people, just as He had created you from the offspring of others.

133. Wa Rabbukal-ghaniyyu Ẕur-raḥmah; iñy-yasha- yuẕhibkum wa yastakhlif mim ba'dikum maa yashaaa'u kamaaa ansha-akum min ẕurriyyati qawmin aakhareen.

وَرَبُّكَ الْغَنِيُّ ذُو الرَّحْمَةِ ؕ اِنْ يَّشَاْ
يُذْهِبْكُمْ وَيَسْتَخْلِفْ مِنْۢ بَعْدِكُمْ
مَّا يَشَآءُ كَمَآ اَنْشَاَكُمْ مِّنْ ذُرِّيَّةِ
قَوْمٍ اٰخَرِيْنَ ﴿۱۳۳﴾

134. Whatever you are promised will inevitably come true and you can do nothing to prevent it.

134. Inna maa too'adoona la-aatiñw-wa maaa antum bimu'jizeen.

اِنَّ مَا تُوْعَدُوْنَ لَاٰتٍ ۙ وَّمَآ اَنْتُمْ
بِمُعْجِزِيْنَ ﴿۱۳۴﴾

135. (Muhammad), tell your people, "I shall do whatever I can and you may do whatever you want, but you will soon know who will be victorious. It is certain that the unjust will never have happiness."

135. Qul yaa qawmi'-maloo 'alaa makaanatikum innee 'aamilun fasawfa ta'lamoona man takoonu lahoo 'aaqibatud-daar; innahoo laa yufliḥuẓ-ẓaalimoon.

قُلْ يٰقَوْمِ اعْمَلُوْا عَلٰى مَكَانَتِكُمْ
اِنِّيْ عَامِلٌ ۚ فَسَوْفَ تَعْلَمُوْنَ ۙ مَنْ
تَكُوْنُ لَهٗ عَاقِبَةُ الدَّارِ ؕ اِنَّهٗ
لَا يُفْلِحُ الظّٰلِمُوْنَ ﴿۱۳۵﴾

136. They set aside a share of the leftovers of their farming produce and cattle, saying, "This is for Allah and that is for the idols." Allah does not receive the share of the idols but the share of Allah is given totally to the idols. How terrible is their decision!

136. Wa ja'aloo lillaahi mimmaa ẕara-a minal-ḥars̱i walan'aami naṣeeban faqaaloo haaẕaa lillaahi biza'mihim wa haaẕaa lishurakaaa'inaa famaa kaana lishurakaaa'ihim falaa yaṣilu ilal-laahi wa maa kaana lillaahi fahuwa yaṣilu ilaa shurakaaa'ihim; saaa'a maa yaḥkumoon.

وَجَعَلُوْا لِلّٰهِ مِمَّا ذَرَاَ مِنَ الْحَرْثِ
وَالْاَنْعَامِ نَصِيْبًا فَقَالُوْا هٰذَا
لِلّٰهِ بِزَعْمِهِمْ وَهٰذَا لِشُرَكَآئِنَا ۚ فَمَا
كَانَ لِشُرَكَآئِهِمْ فَلَا يَصِلُ اِلَى
اللّٰهِ ۚ وَمَا كَانَ لِلّٰهِ فَهُوَ يَصِلُ اِلٰى
شُرَكَآئِهِمْ ؕ سَآءَ مَا يَحْكُمُوْنَ ﴿۱۳۶﴾

137. To many of the pagans, the murder of their children was made to seem attractive by the idols. This led them (the pagans) to confusion in their religion and to facing their own destruction. Had Allah wanted, they would not have murdered their

137. Wa kaẕaalika zayyana likas̱eerim-minal-mushrikeena qatla awlaadihim shurakaaa'uhum liyurdoohum wa liyalbisoo 'alayhim deenahum wa law shaaa'-

وَكَذٰلِكَ زَيَّنَ لِكَثِيْرٍ مِّنَ الْمُشْرِكِيْنَ
قَتْلَ اَوْلَادِهِمْ شُرَكَآؤُهُمْ لِيُرْدُوْهُمْ
وَلِيَلْبِسُوْا عَلَيْهِمْ دِيْنَهُمْ ۚ وَلَوْ شَآءَ

children. Keep away from them and their evil gains.

138. They (the pagans) have said that their cattle and farms are dedicated to private idols and that no one can consume (the produce) except those whom We wanted, in their opinion. They prohibited the riding of certain animals and they ate the flesh of certain animals slaughtered without a mention of the name of Allah. Instead, they ascribed falsehood to Him. They will all be given an evil recompense for their sinful invention.

139. They have also said, "Whatever exists in the wombs of these animals belongs to our people alone and it is not lawful for our women." However, if they are born dead, then everyone will have a share. Allah will give them what they deserve for (their unjust laws). Allah is All-merciful and All-knowing.

140. Those who foolishly and ignorantly murdered their children, ascribed falsehood to Allah, and made unlawful what He had given to them for their sustenance have certainly lost much. They had gone far away from the right guidance.

141. It is He who has created all kinds of gardens: those raised on trellises and those without, palm-trees and the crops of different seasons, and olives and pomegranates of all types. You may eat their fruits that they produce, but pay Allah's share on the harvest day. Do not be excessive; Allah does not love those who are excessive.

142. Allah has created animals, both small and large. Eat from what Allah has given you for your sustenance and do not follow in the footsteps of Satan. He is your sworn enemy.

143. (Assume) that there are eight pairs of cattle, two pairs of sheep, and two pairs of goats. Ask, "Which is lawful and which is not?

al-laahu maa fa'aloohu fazarhum wa maa yaftaroon.

138. Wa qaaloo haaziheee an'aamuñw-wa ḥarsun ḥijr; laa yaṭ'amuhaaa illaa man nashaaa'u biza'mihim wa an'aamun ḥurrimat ẓuhooruhaa wa an'aamul-laa yazkuroonas-mal-laahi 'alayhaf-tiraaa'an 'alayh; sayajzeehim bimaa kaanoo yaftaroon.

139. Wa qaaloo maa fee buṭooni haazihil-an'aami khaaliṣatul-lizukoorinaa wa muḥarramun 'alaaa azwaajinaa wa iñy-yakum maytatan fahum feehi shurakaaa'; sayajzeehim waṣfahum; innahoo Ḥakeemun 'Aleem.

140. Qad khasiral-lazeena qatalooo awlaadahum safaham bighayri 'ilmiñw-wa ḥarramoo maa razaqahumul-laahuf-tiraaa'an 'alal-laah; qad ḍalloo wa maa kaanoo muhtadeen.

141. Wa Huwal-lazeee ansha-a jannaatim ma'rooshaatiñw-wa ghayra ma'rooshaatiñw-wanna-khla wazzar'a mukhtalifan uku-luhoo wazzaytoona warrum-maana mutashaabi-hañw-wa ghayra mutashaabih; kuloo min samariheee izaaa asmara wa aatoo ḥaqqahoo yawma ḥaṣaa-dihee wa laa tusrifooo; innahoo laa yuḥibbul-musrifeen.

142. Wa minal-an'aami ḥamoolatañw-wa farshaa; kuloo mimmaa razaqakumul-laahu wa laa tattabi'oo khuṭuwaatish-Shayṭaan; innahoo lakum 'aduwwum-mubeen.

143. Samaaniyata azwaaj; minaḍ-ḍa-nis-nayni wa minal-ma'zis-nayn; qul 'aaazzaka-rayni

اللَّهُ مَا فَعَلُوهُ فَذَرْهُمْ وَمَا يَفْتَرُونَ ﴿١٣٧﴾
وَقَالُوا هَٰذِهِ أَنْعَامٌ وَحَرْثٌ حِجْرٌ
لَا يَطْعَمُهَا إِلَّا مَنْ نَشَاءُ بِزَعْمِهِمْ
وَأَنْعَامٌ حُرِّمَتْ ظُهُورُهَا وَأَنْعَامٌ
لَا يَذْكُرُونَ اسْمَ اللَّهِ عَلَيْهَا افْتِرَاءً
عَلَيْهِ ۚ سَيَجْزِيهِمْ بِمَا كَانُوا يَفْتَرُونَ ﴿١٣٨﴾
وَقَالُوا مَا فِي بُطُونِ هَٰذِهِ الْأَنْعَامِ
خَالِصَةٌ لِذُكُورِنَا وَمُحَرَّمٌ عَلَىٰ
أَزْوَاجِنَا ۖ وَإِنْ يَكُنْ مَيْتَةً فَهُمْ
فِيهِ شُرَكَاءُ ۚ سَيَجْزِيهِمْ وَصْفَهُمْ ۚ
إِنَّهُ حَكِيمٌ عَلِيمٌ ﴿١٣٩﴾
قَدْ خَسِرَ الَّذِينَ قَتَلُوا أَوْلَادَهُمْ
سَفَهًا بِغَيْرِ عِلْمٍ وَحَرَّمُوا مَا
رَزَقَهُمُ اللَّهُ افْتِرَاءً عَلَى اللَّهِ ۚ قَدْ
ضَلُّوا وَمَا كَانُوا مُهْتَدِينَ ﴿١٤٠﴾
وَهُوَ الَّذِي أَنْشَأَ جَنَّاتٍ مَعْرُوشَاتٍ وَغَيْرَ
مَعْرُوشَاتٍ وَالنَّخْلَ وَالزَّرْعَ مُخْتَلِفًا
أُكُلُهُ وَالزَّيْتُونَ وَالرُّمَّانَ مُتَشَابِهًا
وَغَيْرَ مُتَشَابِهٍ ۚ كُلُوا مِنْ ثَمَرِهِ إِذَا
أَثْمَرَ وَآتُوا حَقَّهُ يَوْمَ حَصَادِهِ ۖ وَلَا
تُسْرِفُوا ۚ إِنَّهُ لَا يُحِبُّ الْمُسْرِفِينَ ﴿١٤١﴾
وَمِنَ الْأَنْعَامِ حَمُولَةً وَفَرْشًا ۚ كُلُوا
مِمَّا رَزَقَكُمُ اللَّهُ وَلَا تَتَّبِعُوا خُطُوَاتِ
الشَّيْطَانِ ۚ إِنَّهُ لَكُمْ عَدُوٌّ مُبِينٌ ﴿١٤٢﴾
ثَمَانِيَةَ أَزْوَاجٍ ۖ مِنَ الضَّأْنِ اثْنَيْنِ
وَمِنَ الْمَعْزِ اثْنَيْنِ ۗ قُلْ آلذَّكَرَيْنِ

Are the two males unlawful (to eat) or the two females or those that are in the wombs of the females? If you are truthful, then, answer Me exactly."

ḥarrama amil-unsayayni ammash-tamalat ‘alayhi arḥaamul-unsayayni nabbi-’oonee bi‘ilmin in kuntum ṣaadiqeen.

حَرَّمَ اَمِ الْاُنْثَيَيْنِ اَمَّا اشْتَمَلَتْ عَلَيْهِ اَرْحَامُ الْاُنْثَيَيْنِ ۖ نَبِّئُوْنِيْ بِعِلْمٍ اِنْ كُنْتُمْ صٰدِقِيْنَ ﴿١٤٣﴾

144. "Of the two pairs of camels and cows, are the males unlawful (to eat) or the females or that which exists in the wombs of the females? Were you present when Allah commanded you to do this (prohibiting certain food and murdering your baby girls)? Who are more unjust than those who ascribe falsehood to Allah and out of ignorance make others go astray? Allah does not guide the unjust."

144. Wa minal-ibilis-nayni wa minal-baqaris-nayn; qul ’aaazzakarayni ḥarrama amil-unsayayni ammash-tamalat ‘alayhi arḥaamul-unsayayni am kuntum shuhadaaa’a iz waṣṣaakumul-laahu bihaazaa; faman aẓlamu mimmanif-taraa ‘alallaahi kazibal-liyuḍillan-naasa bighayri ‘ilm; innal-laaha laa yahdil-qawmaẓ-ẓaalimeen.

وَمِنَ الْاِبِلِ اثْنَيْنِ وَمِنَ الْبَقَرِ اثْنَيْنِ ۗ قُلْ ءٰٓالذَّكَرَيْنِ حَرَّمَ اَمِ الْاُنْثَيَيْنِ اَمَّا اشْتَمَلَتْ عَلَيْهِ اَرْحَامُ الْاُنْثَيَيْنِ ۖ اَمْ كُنْتُمْ شُهَدَآءَ اِذْ وَصّٰىكُمُ اللّٰهُ بِهٰذَا ۚ فَمَنْ اَظْلَمُ مِمَّنِ افْتَرٰى عَلَى اللّٰهِ كَذِبًا لِّيُضِلَّ النَّاسَ بِغَيْرِ عِلْمٍ ۗ اِنَّ اللّٰهَ لَا يَهْدِي الْقَوْمَ الظّٰلِمِيْنَ ﴿١٤٤﴾

145. (Muhammad), tell them, "I do not find anything which has been made unlawful to eat in what has been revealed to me except carrion, blood flowing from the body, pork [for pork is absolutely filthy] and the flesh of the animals slaughtered without the mention of the name of Allah. However, in an emergency, when one does not have any intention of rebelling or transgressing against the law, your Lord will be All-forgiving and All-merciful.

145. Qul laaa ajidu fee maaa ooḥiya ilayya muḥarraman ‘alaa ṭaa‘imiñy-yaṭ‘amuhooo illaaa añy-yakoona maytatan aw damam-masfooḥan aw laḥma khinzeerin fa-innahoo rijsun aw fisqan uhilla lighayril-laahi bih; famaniḍ-ṭurra ghayra baa-ghiñw-wa laa ‘aadin fa-inna Rabbaka Ghafoorur-Raḥeem.

قُلْ لَّآ اَجِدُ فِيْ مَآ اُوْحِيَ اِلَيَّ مُحَرَّمًا عَلٰى طَاعِمٍ يَّطْعَمُهٗٓ اِلَّآ اَنْ يَّكُوْنَ مَيْتَةً اَوْ دَمًا مَّسْفُوْحًا اَوْ لَحْمَ خِنْزِيْرٍ فَاِنَّهٗ رِجْسٌ اَوْ فِسْقًا اُهِلَّ لِغَيْرِ اللّٰهِ بِهٖ ۚ فَمَنِ اضْطُرَّ غَيْرَ بَاغٍ وَّلَا عَادٍ فَاِنَّ رَبَّكَ غَفُوْرٌ رَّحِيْمٌ ﴿١٤٥﴾

146. We made unlawful for the Jews all the claw-footed animals, fat of the cows, sheep and goats except what is found on their backs, intestines, and whatever is mixed with their bones. Thus, did We recompense them for their rebellion and We are certainly truthful.

146. Wa ‘alal-lazeena haadoo ḥarramnaa kulla zee ẓufur; wa minal-baqari walghanami ḥarramnaa ‘alayhim shu-ḥoomahumaaa illaa maa ḥamalat ẓuhooruhumaaa awil-ḥawaayaaa aw makhtalaṭa bi‘aẓm; zaalika jazaynaahum bibaghyihim wa innaa laṣaa-diqoon.

وَعَلَى الَّذِيْنَ هَادُوْا حَرَّمْنَا كُلَّ ذِيْ ظُفُرٍ ۚ وَمِنَ الْبَقَرِ وَالْغَنَمِ حَرَّمْنَا عَلَيْهِمْ شُحُوْمَهُمَآ اِلَّا مَا حَمَلَتْ ظُهُوْرُهُمَآ اَوِ الْحَوَايَآ اَوْ مَا اخْتَلَطَ بِعَظْمٍ ۗ ذٰلِكَ جَزَيْنٰهُمْ بِبَغْيِهِمْ ۖ وَاِنَّا لَصٰدِقُوْنَ ﴿١٤٦﴾

147. They reject you. (Muhammad), tell them, "Your Lord's mercy is completely over-whelming, but no one can save the sinful from His wrath."

147. Fa-in kazzabooka faqur-Rabbukum zoo raḥmatiñw-waasi‘ah; wa laa yuraddu ba-suhoo ‘anil-qawmil-mujri-meen.

فَاِنْ كَذَّبُوْكَ فَقُلْ رَّبُّكُمْ ذُوْ رَحْمَةٍ وَّاسِعَةٍ ۚ وَلَا يُرَدُّ بَاْسُهٗ عَنِ الْقَوْمِ الْمُجْرِمِيْنَ ﴿١٤٧﴾

148. The pagans will say, "Had Allah wanted, we would not have worshipped idols, nor would our fathers, nor would we have made anything unlawful." Others before them had also spoken such lies until they experienced the severity of Our wrath. (Muhammad), ask them, "Do you possess any knowledge? If so, tell us about it. You follow only conjectures and preach falsehood."

148. Sayaqoolul-laz̲eena ashrakoo law shaaa'al-laahu maaa ashraknaa wa laaa aabaaa'unaa wa laa ḥarramnaa min shay'; kaz̲aalika kaz̲ z̲abal-laz̲eena min qablihim ḥattaa z̲aaqoo ba-sanaa; qul hal 'indakum min 'ilmin fatukhrijoohu lanaaa in tattabi'oona illaẓ-ẓanna wa in antum illaa takhruṣoon.

سَيَقُوْلُ الَّذِيْنَ اَشْرَكُوْا لَوْ شَآءَ
اللّٰهُ مَآ اَشْرَكْنَا وَلَآ اٰبَآؤُنَا وَلَا
حَرَّمْنَا مِنْ شَيْءٍ ؕ كَذٰلِكَ كَذَّبَ
الَّذِيْنَ مِنْ قَبْلِهِمْ حَتّٰى ذَاقُوْا
بَاْسَنَا ؕ قُلْ هَلْ عِنْدَكُمْ مِّنْ عِلْمٍ
فَتُخْرِجُوْهُ لَنَا ؕ اِنْ تَتَّبِعُوْنَ اِلَّا
الظَّنَّ وَاِنْ اَنْتُمْ اِلَّا تَخْرُصُوْنَ ﴿١٤٨﴾

149. Say, "Final authority belongs only to Allah. Had He wanted, He would have given you all guidance."

149. Qul falillaahil-ḥujjatul-baalighatu falaw shaaa'a lahadaakum ajma'een.

قُلْ فَلِلّٰهِ الْحُجَّةُ الْبَالِغَةُ ۚ فَلَوْ شَآءَ
لَهَدٰىكُمْ اَجْمَعِيْنَ ﴿١٤٩﴾

150. Ask them to call their witness who will testify that Allah has made certain things unlawful. Even if they do testify, do not testify with them. Do not follow the desires of those who have rejected Our revelations and the pagans who do not believe in the Day of Judgment.

150. Qul halumma shuhadaaa'akumul-laz̲eena yash-hadoona annal-laaha ḥarrama haaz̲aa fa-in shahidoo falaa tashhad ma'ahum; wa laa tattabi' ahwaaa'al-laz̲eena kaz̲z̲aboo bi-Aayaatinaa wallaz̲eena laa yu'minoona bil-Aakhirati wa hum bi-Rabbihim ya'diloon.

قُلْ هَلُمَّ شُهَدَآءَكُمُ الَّذِيْنَ
يَشْهَدُوْنَ اَنَّ اللّٰهَ حَرَّمَ هٰذَا ۚ فَاِنْ
شَهِدُوْا فَلَا تَشْهَدْ مَعَهُمْ ۚ وَلَا تَتَّبِعْ
اَهْوَآءَ الَّذِيْنَ كَذَّبُوْا بِاٰيٰتِنَا وَالَّذِيْنَ
لَا يُؤْمِنُوْنَ بِالْاٰخِرَةِ وَهُمْ بِرَبِّهِمْ
يَعْدِلُوْنَ ﴿١٥٠﴾ ع ١٨ ٦ ٥

151. (Muhammad), say, "Let me tell you about what your Lord has commanded: Do not consider anything equal to Allah; Be kind to your parents; Do not murder your children out of fear of poverty for We give sustenance to you and to them. Do not even approach indecency either in public or in private. Take not a life which Allah has made sacred except by way of justice and law. Thus does He command you that you may learn wisdom.

151. Qul ta'aalaw atlu maa ḥarrama Rabbukum 'alaykum allaa tushrikoo bihee shay'añw-wa bilwaalidayni iḥsaanaa; wa laa taqtulooo awlaadakum min imlaaq; naḥnu narzuqukum wa iyyaahum wa laa taqrabul-fawaaḥisha maa ẓahara minhaa wa maa baṭana wa laa taqtulun-nafsal-latee ḥarramal-laahu illaa bilḥaqq; z̲aalikum waṣṣaakum bihee la'allakum ta'qiloon.

قُلْ تَعَالَوْا اَتْلُ مَا حَرَّمَ رَبُّكُمْ
عَلَيْكُمْ اَلَّا تُشْرِكُوْا بِهٖ شَيْئًا وَّ
بِالْوَالِدَيْنِ اِحْسَانًا ۚ وَلَا تَقْتُلُوْٓا
اَوْلَادَكُمْ مِّنْ اِمْلَاقٍ ؕ نَحْنُ نَرْزُقُكُمْ
وَاِيَّاهُمْ ۚ وَلَا تَقْرَبُوا الْفَوَاحِشَ مَا
ظَهَرَ مِنْهَا وَمَا بَطَنَ ۚ وَلَا تَقْتُلُوا
النَّفْسَ الَّتِيْ حَرَّمَ اللّٰهُ اِلَّا بِالْحَقِّ ؕ
ذٰلِكُمْ وَصّٰىكُمْ بِهٖ لَعَلَّكُمْ تَعْقِلُوْنَ ﴿١٥١﴾

152. Do not handle the property of the orphans except with a good reason until they become mature and strong. Maintain equality in your dealings by the means of measurement and balance. No

152. Wa laa taqraboo maalal-yateemi illaa billatee hiya aḥsanu ḥattaa yablugha ashuddahoo wa awful-kayla walmeezaana bilqisṭ;

وَلَا تَقْرَبُوْا مَالَ الْيَتِيْمِ اِلَّا بِالَّتِيْ
هِيَ اَحْسَنُ حَتّٰى يَبْلُغَ اَشُدَّهٗ ۚ وَ
اَوْفُوا الْكَيْلَ وَالْمِيْزَانَ بِالْقِسْطِ ۚ

soul is responsible for what is beyond its ability. Be just in your words, even if the party involved is one of your relatives, and keep your promise with Allah. Thus does your Lord guide you so that you may take heed.

153. This is My path and it is straight. Follow it and not other paths which will lead you far away from the path of Allah. Thus does Allah guide you so that you may become pious.

154. We gave Moses the Book to complete (Our favor) for the righteous ones, the Book that contained a detailed explanation of all things, a guide and a mercy so that perhaps they would have faith in the Day of Judgment.

155. This Book (Quran) which We have revealed is a blessed one. Follow its guidance and have piety so that you perhaps may receive mercy

156. and will not say that the Book was revealed only to two groups of people before you, or that you were ignorant of its knowledge,

157. or proclaim, "Had the Book been revealed to us, we would have followed its guidance better than the (Jews and Christians)." Evidence, guidance, and mercy have already come to you from your Lord.

Who are more unjust than those who reject Allah's revelations and turn away from them? We will give an evil recompense to those who turn away from Our revelations and a terrible torment for their disregard (of Our guidance).

158. Are they waiting until the angels or your Lord come to them or for some miracles to take place? On the day when some

laa nukallifu nafsan illaa wus'ahaa wa izaa qultum fa'diloo wa law kaana zaa qurbaa wa bi-'Ahdil-laahi awfoo; zaalikum waṣṣaakum bihee la'allakum tazakkaroon.

153. Wa anna haazaa Ṣiraaṭee Mustaqeeman fattabi'oohu wa laa tattabi'ussubula fatafarraqa bikum 'an sabeelih; zaalikum waṣṣaakum bihee la'allakum tattaqoon.

154. Summa aataynaa Moosal-Kitaaba tamaaman 'alal-lazeee aḥsana wa tafṣeelal-likulli shay'iñw-wa hudañw-wa raḥ-matal-la'allahum biliqaaa'i Rabbihim yu'minoon.

155. Wa haazaa Kitaabun anzalnaahu Mubaarakun fattabi'oohu wattaqoo la'al-lakum turḥamoon.

156. An taqoolooo innamaaa unzilal-Kitaabu 'alaa ṭaaa'ifatayni min qablinaa wa in kunnaa 'an diraasatihim laghaafileen.

157. Aw taqooloo law annaaa unzila 'alaynal-Kitaabu lakunnaaa ahdaa minhum; faqad jaaa'akum bayyinatum-mir-Rabbikum wa hudañw-wa raḥmah; faman aẓlamu mimman kazzaba bi-Aayaatil-laahi wa ṣadafa 'anhaa; sanajzil-lazeena yaṣdifoona 'an Aayaatinaa sooo'al-'azaabi bimaa kaanoo yaṣdifoon.

158. Hal yanẓuroona illaaa an ta-tiyahumul-malaaa'ikatu aw ya-tiya Rabbuka aw ya-tiya

لَا نُكَلِّفُ نَفْسًا اِلَّا وُسْعَهَا ۚ وَاِذَا
قُلْتُمْ فَاعْدِلُوْا وَلَوْ كَانَ ذَا قُرْبٰى ۚ
وَبِعَهْدِ اللّٰهِ اَوْفُوْا ۭ ذٰلِكُمْ وَصّٰىكُمْ
بِهٖ لَعَلَّكُمْ تَذَكَّرُوْنَ ﴿١٥٢﴾
وَاَنَّ هٰذَا صِرَاطِيْ مُسْتَقِيْمًا
فَاتَّبِعُوْهُ ۚ وَلَا تَتَّبِعُوا السُّبُلَ
فَتَفَرَّقَ بِكُمْ عَنْ سَبِيْلِهٖ ۭ ذٰلِكُمْ
وَصّٰىكُمْ بِهٖ لَعَلَّكُمْ تَتَّقُوْنَ ﴿١٥٣﴾
ثُمَّ اٰتَيْنَا مُوْسَى الْكِتٰبَ تَمَامًا
عَلَي الَّذِيْٓ اَحْسَنَ وَتَفْصِيْلًا لِّكُلِّ
شَيْءٍ وَّهُدًى وَّرَحْمَةً لَّعَلَّهُمْ بِلِقَاۗءِ
رَبِّهِمْ يُؤْمِنُوْنَ ﴿١٥٤﴾ ع ١٩
وَهٰذَا كِتٰبٌ اَنْزَلْنٰهُ مُبٰرَكٌ
فَاتَّبِعُوْهُ وَاتَّقُوْا لَعَلَّكُمْ تُرْحَمُوْنَ ﴿١٥٥﴾
اَنْ تَقُوْلُوْٓا اِنَّمَآ اُنْزِلَ الْكِتٰبُ عَلٰي
طَاۗىِٕفَتَيْنِ مِنْ قَبْلِنَا ۠ وَاِنْ كُنَّا
عَنْ دِرَاسَتِهِمْ لَغٰفِلِيْنَ ﴿١٥٦﴾
اَوْ تَقُوْلُوْا لَوْ اَنَّآ اُنْزِلَ عَلَيْنَا الْكِتٰبُ
لَكُنَّآ اَهْدٰي مِنْهُمْ ۚ فَقَدْ جَاۗءَكُمْ
بَيِّنَةٌ مِّنْ رَّبِّكُمْ وَهُدًى وَّرَحْمَةٌ ۚ
فَمَنْ اَظْلَمُ مِمَّنْ كَذَّبَ بِاٰيٰتِ
اللّٰهِ وَصَدَفَ عَنْهَا ۭ سَنَجْزِي الَّذِيْنَ
يَصْدِفُوْنَ عَنْ اٰيٰتِنَا سُوْۗءَ الْعَذَابِ
بِمَا كَانُوْا يَصْدِفُوْنَ ﴿١٥٧﴾
هَلْ يَنْظُرُوْنَ اِلَّآ اَنْ تَاْتِيَهُمُ
الْمَلٰۗىِٕكَةُ اَوْ يَاْتِيَ رَبُّكَ اَوْ يَاْتِيَ

miracles of Allah will take place, the belief of any soul will be of no avail to it unless some good deeds have been done with it, or it had been formed before the coming of such a day. (Muhammad), tell them, "Wait and we are also waiting."

ba'ḍu Aayaati Rabbik; Yawma ya-tee ba'ḍu Aayaati Rabbika laa yanfa'u nafsan eemaanuhaa lam takun aamanat min qablu aw kasabat feee eemaanihaa khayraa; qulin-taẓirooo innaa muntaẓiroon.

بَعْضُ اٰيٰتِ رَبِّكَ ؕ يَوْمَ يَاْتِيْ بَعْضُ
اٰيٰتِ رَبِّكَ لَا يَنْفَعُ نَفْسًا اِيْمَانُهَا
لَمْ تَكُنْ اٰمَنَتْ مِنْ قَبْلُ اَوْ كَسَبَتْ
فِيْٓ اِيْمَانِهَا خَيْرًا ؕ قُلِ انْتَظِرُوْٓا
اِنَّا مُنْتَظِرُوْنَ ﴿۱۵۸﴾

159. Some of those who have divided their religion into different sects are not your concern. Their affairs are in the hands of Allah Who will show them all that they have done.

159. Innal-lazeena farraqoo deenahum wa kaanoo shiya'al-lasta minhum fee shay'; innamaaa amruhum ilallaahi summa yunabbi'uhum bimaa kaanoo yaf'aloon.

اِنَّ الَّذِيْنَ فَرَّقُوْا دِيْنَهُمْ وَكَانُوْا
شِيَعًا لَّسْتَ مِنْهُمْ فِيْ شَيْءٍ ؕ اِنَّمَآ
اَمْرُهُمْ اِلَى اللّٰهِ ثُمَّ يُنَبِّئُهُمْ بِمَا
كَانُوْا يَفْعَلُوْنَ ﴿۱۵۹﴾

160. For a single good deed, one will be rewarded tenfold. But the recompense for a bad deed will be equal to that of the deed and no injustice will be done to anyone.

160. Man jaaa'a bilḥasanati falahoo 'ashru amsaalihaa wa man jaaa'a bissayyi'ati falaa yujzaaa illaa mislahaa wa hum laa yuẓlamoon.

مَنْ جَآءَ بِالْحَسَنَةِ فَلَهٗ عَشْرُ
اَمْثَالِهَا ۚ وَمَنْ جَآءَ بِالسَّيِّئَةِ فَلَا
يُجْزٰٓى اِلَّا مِثْلَهَا وَهُمْ لَا يُظْلَمُوْنَ ﴿۱۶۰﴾

161. (Muhammad), tell them, "My Lord has guided me to the right path, a well-established religion and the upright tradition of Abraham, who was not a pagan."

161. Qul innanee hadaanee Rabbeee ilaa Ṣiraaṭim-Mustaqeemin deenan qiyamam-Millata Ibraaheema Ḥaneefaa; wa maa kaana minal-mushrikeen.

قُلْ اِنَّنِيْ هَدٰىنِيْ رَبِّيْٓ اِلٰى صِرَاطٍ
مُّسْتَقِيْمٍ ۚ دِيْنًا قِيَمًا مِّلَّةَ اِبْرٰهِيْمَ
حَنِيْفًا ۚ وَمَا كَانَ مِنَ الْمُشْرِكِيْنَ ﴿۱۶۱﴾

162. Say, "My prayer, sacrifice, life, and death are all for Allah, the Lord of the Universe.

162. Qul inna Ṣalaatee wa nusukee wa maḥyaaya wa mamaatee lillaahi Rabbil 'aalameen.

قُلْ اِنَّ صَلَاتِيْ وَنُسُكِيْ وَمَحْيَايَ
وَمَمَاتِيْ لِلّٰهِ رَبِّ الْعٰلَمِيْنَ ﴿۱۶۲﴾

163. Nothing is equal to Him. Thus are the commandments which I have received and I am the first Muslim (submitted to the will of Allah)."

163. Laa shareeka lahoo wa bizaalika umirtu wa ana awwalul-muslimeen.

لَا شَرِيْكَ لَهٗ ۚ وَبِذٰلِكَ اُمِرْتُ
وَاَنَا اَوَّلُ الْمُسْلِمِيْنَ ﴿۱۶۳﴾

164. (Muhammad), tell them, "Should I take a lord besides Allah when He is the Lord of all things?" All one's evil deeds are against one's own soul. No one will be considered responsible for another's sins. You will all be returned to your Lord who will tell you what is right and wrong in disputed matters among you.

164. Qul aghayral-laahi abghee Rabbañw-wa Huwa Rabbu kulli shay'; wa laa taksibu kullu nafsin illaa 'alayhaa; wa laa taziru waaziratuñw-wizra ukhraa; summa ilaa Rabbikum marji'ukum fayunabbi'ukum bimaa kuntum feehi takhtalifoon.

قُلْ اَغَيْرَ اللّٰهِ اَبْغِيْ رَبًّا وَّهُوَ رَبُّ
كُلِّ شَيْءٍ ؕ وَلَا تَكْسِبُ كُلُّ
نَفْسٍ اِلَّا عَلَيْهَا ۚ وَلَا تَزِرُ وَازِرَةٌ
وِّزْرَ اُخْرٰى ۚ ثُمَّ اِلٰى رَبِّكُمْ مَّرْجِعُكُمْ
فَيُنَبِّئُكُمْ بِمَا كُنْتُمْ فِيْهِ تَخْتَلِفُوْنَ ﴿۱۶۴﴾

165. On earth, We have made each of your generations the successors of their predecessors; We have made some of you do good deeds of a higher degree

165. Wa Huwal-lazee ja'alakum khalaaa'ifal-arḍi wa rafa'a ba'ḍakum fawqa ba'ḍin darajaatil-

وَهُوَ الَّذِيْ جَعَلَكُمْ خَلٰٓئِفَ الْاَرْضِ
وَرَفَعَ بَعْضَكُمْ فَوْقَ بَعْضٍ دَرَجٰتٍ

than others. He will test you in this way through what He has revealed to you. Your Lord's retribution is swift and He is certainly All-forgiving and All-merciful.

Al-Araf, The Heights (7)

In the Name of Allah, the Beneficent, the Merciful

1. Alif Lam. Mim. Sad.

2. A book has been revealed to you, (Muhammad). You should not hesitate to convey its warning and its good advice to the believers.

3. (People), follow whatever is revealed to you from your Lord and do not follow other guardians besides Him. However, you pay very little attention (to Our words).

4. How many cities have We destroyed! Our wrath struck their people at night or during their midday siesta.

5. When Our wrath struck them, they could do nothing but confess to their sins.

6. We will certainly question the people and the Messengers sent to them.

7. We will tell them with absolute certainty (what they had done), for We had never been absent from them (during their lifetime).

8. (Everyone's deeds) will certainly be weighed (and evaluated) on the Day of Judgment. Those whose good deeds weigh heavier than their bad deeds will have everlasting happiness.

9. As for those whose bad deeds weigh heavier, they will lose their souls for their injustice to Our revelations.

10. We have made you inhabit the land and provided you with

liyabluwakum fee maaa aataakum; inna Rabbaka Saree‘ul-‘iqaab; wa innahoo la-Ghafoorur-Raheem.

Sûrat al-A‘râf-7

(Revealed at Makkah)

Bismillaahir Rahmaanir Raheem

1. Alif-Laaam-Meeem-Ṣaaad.

2. Kitaabun unzila ilayka falaa yakun fee ṣadrika ḥarajum-minhu litunẕira bihee wa ẕikraa lilmu’mineen.

3. Ittabi‘oo maaa unzila ilaykum mir-Rabbikum wa laa tattabi‘oo min dooniheee awliyaaa’; qaleelam-maa taẕakkaroon.

4. Wa kam min qaryatin ahlaknaahaa fajaaa’ahaa ba-sunaa bayaatan aw hum qaaa’iloon.

5. Famaa kaana da‘waahum iẕ jaaa’ahum ba-sunaaa illaaa an qaalooo innaa kunnaa ẕaalimeen.

6. Falanas’alannal-laẕeena ursila ilayhim wa lanas’alannal-mursaleen.

7. Falanaquṣṣanna-‘alayhim bi‘ilmiñw-wa maa kunnaa ghaaa’ibeen.

8. Walwaznu Yawma’iẕinil-ḥaqq; faman s̱aqulat mawaa-zeenuhoo fa-ulaaa’ika humul-mufliḥoon.

9. Wa man khaffat mawaa-zeenuhoo fa-ulaaa’ikal-laẕeena khasirooo anfusahum bimaa kaanoo bi Aayaatinaa yaẕli-moon.

10. Wa laqad makkannaakum fil-arḍi wa

لِّيَبْلُوَكُمْ فِيْ مَآ اٰتٰىكُمْ ۭ اِنَّ رَبَّكَ
سَرِيْعُ الْعِقَابِ ڮ وَاِنَّهٗ لَغَفُوْرٌ
رَّحِيْمٌ ١٦٥

(٧) سُوْرَةُ الْاَعْرَافِ مَكِّيَّةٌ (٣٩)
اٰياتها ٢٠٦ بِسْمِ اللّٰهِ الرَّحْمٰنِ الرَّحِيْمِ ركوعاتها ٢٤

الٓمّٓصٓ ١
كِتٰبٌ اُنْزِلَ اِلَيْكَ فَلَا يَكُنْ فِيْ
صَدْرِكَ حَرَجٌ مِّنْهُ لِتُنْذِرَ بِهٖ
وَذِكْرٰى لِلْمُؤْمِنِيْنَ ٢
اِتَّبِعُوْا مَآ اُنْزِلَ اِلَيْكُمْ مِّنْ رَّبِّكُمْ
وَلَا تَتَّبِعُوْا مِنْ دُوْنِهٖٓ اَوْلِيَاۗءَ ۭ
قَلِيْلًا مَّا تَذَكَّرُوْنَ ٣
وَكَمْ مِّنْ قَرْيَةٍ اَهْلَكْنٰهَا فَجَاۗءَهَا
بَاْسُنَا بَيَاتًا اَوْ هُمْ قَاۗىِٕلُوْنَ ٤
فَمَا كَانَ دَعْوٰىهُمْ اِذْ جَاۗءَهُمْ بَاْسُنَآ
اِلَّآ اَنْ قَالُوْٓا اِنَّا كُنَّا ظٰلِمِيْنَ ٥
فَلَنَسْــَٔـلَنَّ الَّذِيْنَ اُرْسِلَ اِلَيْهِمْ
وَلَنَسْــَٔـلَنَّ الْمُرْسَلِيْنَ ٦
فَلَنَقُصَّنَّ عَلَيْهِمْ بِعِلْمٍ وَّمَا كُنَّا
غَاۗىِٕبِيْنَ ٧
وَالْوَزْنُ يَوْمَىِٕذِ الْحَقُّ ۚ فَمَنْ ثَقُلَتْ
مَوَازِيْنُهٗ فَاُولٰۗىِٕكَ هُمُ الْمُفْلِحُوْنَ ٨
وَمَنْ خَفَّتْ مَوَازِيْنُهٗ فَاُولٰۗىِٕكَ
الَّذِيْنَ خَسِرُوْٓا اَنْفُسَهُمْ بِمَا كَانُوْا
بِاٰيٰتِنَا يَظْلِمُوْنَ ٩
وَلَقَدْ مَكَّنّٰكُمْ فِي الْاَرْضِ وَ

the means of sustenance. Only a few of you give thanks.

ja'alnaa lakum feehaa ma'aayish; qaleelammaa tashkuroon.

جعلنا لكم فيها معايش ۗ قليلا
ما تشكرون ﴿١٠﴾ ع ٨

11. We created and shaped you, then told the angels to prostrate themselves before Adam. All the angels obeyed except Satan, who did not.

11. Wa laqad khalaqnaakum summa sawwarnaakum summa qulnaa lilmalaaa'i-katis-judoo li-Aadama fasajadooo illaaa Ibleesa lam yakum-minas-saajideen.

ولقد خلقناكم ثم صورناكم ثم قلنا
للملائكة اسجدوا لآدم فسجدوا
إلا إبليس لم يكن من الساجدين ﴿١١﴾

12. Allah asked, "What made you disobey Me?" Satan replied, "I am better than Adam, for You have created me out of fire and Adam out of clay."

12. Qaala maa mana'aka allaa tasjuda iz amartuka qaala ana khayrum-minhu khalaqtanee min naarinw-wa khalaqtahoo min teen.

قال ما منعك ألا تسجد إذ أمرتك
قال أنا خير منه خلقتني من نار
وخلقته من طين ﴿١٢﴾

13. The Lord ordered Satan to get out (of the garden) saying, "This is no place for you to be proud. Get out of this place, for you are worthless."

13. Qaala fahbit minhaa famaa yakoonu laka an tatakabbara feehaa fakhruj innaka minas-saaghireen.

قال فاهبط منها فما يكون لك
أن تتكبر فيها فاخرج إنك
من الصاغرين ﴿١٣﴾

14. Satan asked the Lord to give him respite (keep him alive) until the Day of Resurrection.

14. Qaala anzirneee ilaa Yawmi yub'asoon.

قال أنظرني إلى يوم يبعثون ﴿١٤﴾

15. The Lord told him, "We will grant you this respite."

15. Qaala innaka minal-munzareen.

قال إنك من المنظرين ﴿١٥﴾

16. Then Satan said, "Because you have made me go astray, I shall certainly try to seduce people into straying from the right path.

16. Qaala fabimaaa aghway-tanee la-aq'udanna lahum Siraatakal-Mustaqeem

قال فبما أغويتني لأقعدن
لهم صراطك المستقيم ﴿١٦﴾

17. I shall attack them from all directions and You will not find many of them giving You thanks."

17. Summa la-aatiyannahum mim bayni aydeehim wa min khalfihim wa 'an aymaanihim wa-'an shamaaa'ilihim wa laa tajidu aksarahum shaakireen.

ثم لآتينهم من بين أيديهم
ومن خلفهم وعن أيمانهم و
عن شمائلهم ۖ ولا تجد أكثرهم
شاكرين ﴿١٧﴾

18. The Lord told Satan, "Get out of this garden, for you are banished and despised. Hell will be filled with all of those who follow you."

18. Qaalakh-ruj minhaa maz'oomam madhooraa; laman tabi'aka minhum la-amla'anna Jahannama minkum ajma'een.

قال اخرج منها مذءوما
مدحورا ۖ لمن تبعك منهم
لأملأن جهنم منكم أجمعين ﴿١٨﴾

19. Then the Lord said, "Adam, stay in the garden with your spouse and eat whatever you want therein, but do not go near this tree lest you transgress."

19. Wa yaaa Aadamus-kun anta wa zawjukal-Jannata fakulaa min haysu shi'tumaa wa laa taqrabaa haazihish-shajarata fatakoonaa minaz-zaalimeen.

ويا آدم اسكن أنت وزوجك الجنة
فكلا من حيث شئتما ولا تقربا هذه
الشجرة فتكونا من الظالمين ﴿١٩﴾

20. Satan tempted them to reveal that which was kept private

20. Fawaswasa lahumash-Shaytaanu liyubdiya lahumaa

فوسوس لهما الشيطان ليبدي لهما

from them and said, "Your Lord has not prohibited you (to eat the fruits of this tree) unless you want to be angels or immortal."

maa wooriya ‘anhumaa min saw-aatihimaa wa qaala maa nahaakumaa Rabbukumaa ‘an haa<u>z</u>ihish-shajarati illaaa an takoonaa malakayni aw takoonaa minal-khaalideen.

مَا وُرِيَ عَنْهُمَا مِنْ سَوْاٰتِهِمَا وَ
قَالَ مَا نَهٰىكُمَا رَبُّكُمَا عَنْ هٰذِهِ
الشَّجَرَةِ اِلَّآ اَنْ تَكُوْنَا مَلَكَيْنِ
اَوْ تَكُوْنَا مِنَ الْخٰلِدِيْنَ ﴿٢٠﴾

21. Satan swore before them that he was giving them good advice.

21. Wa qaasamahumaaa innee lakumaa laminan-naaṣiḥeen.

وَقَاسَمَهُمَآ اِنِّيْ لَكُمَا لَمِنَ النّٰصِحِيْنَ ﴿٢١﴾

22. Thus, he deceitfully showed them (the tree). When they had tasted (fruits) from the tree, their private parts became revealed to them and they began to cover their private parts with leaves from the garden.

Their Lord then called out to them saying, "Did I not forbid you to eat (fruits) from the tree and tell you that Satan was your sworn enemy?"

22. Fadallaahumaa bighuroor; falammaa <u>z</u>aaqash-shajarata badat lahumaa saw-aatuhumaa wa ṭafiqaa yakhṣifaani ‘alayhimaa miñw-waraqil-jannati wa naadaahumaa Rabbuhumaaa alam anhakumaa ‘an tilkumash-shajarati wa aqul lakumaaa innash-Shayṭaana lakumaa ‘aduwwum-mubeen.

فَدَلّٰىهُمَا بِغُرُوْرٍ ۚ فَلَمَّا ذَاقَا الشَّجَرَةَ
بَدَتْ لَهُمَا سَوْاٰتُهُمَا وَطَفِقَا يَخْصِفٰنِ
عَلَيْهِمَا مِنْ وَّرَقِ الْجَنَّةِ ۭ وَنَادٰىهُمَا
رَبُّهُمَآ اَلَمْ اَنْهَكُمَا عَنْ تِلْكُمَا
الشَّجَرَةِ وَاَقُلْ لَّكُمَآ اِنَّ الشَّيْطٰنَ
لَكُمَا عَدُوٌّ مُّبِيْنٌ ﴿٢٢﴾

23. They replied, "Lord, we have done injustice to our souls. If You did not forgive us and have mercy on us, we shall certainly have incurred a great loss."

23. Qaalaa Rabbanaa ẓalamnaaa anfusanaa wa illam taghfir lana wa tarḥamnaa lanakoonanna minal-khaasireen.

قَالَا رَبَّنَا ظَلَمْنَآ اَنْفُسَنَا ۫ وَ
اِنْ لَّمْ تَغْفِرْ لَنَا وَتَرْحَمْنَا لَنَكُوْنَنَّ
مِنَ الْخٰسِرِيْنَ ﴿٢٣﴾

24. The Lord told them to leave the garden as each other's enemies and go to earth to dwell and benefit from the means therein for an appointed time.

24. Qaalah-biṭoo ba‘ḍukum liba‘ḍin ‘aduww; wa lakum fil-arḍi mustaqarruñw-wa mataa‘un ilaa ḥeen.

قَالَ اهْبِطُوْا بَعْضُكُمْ لِبَعْضٍ عَدُوٌّ ۚ
وَلَكُمْ فِي الْاَرْضِ مُسْتَقَرٌّ وَّمَتَاعٌ
اِلٰى حِيْنٍ ﴿٢٤﴾

25. He told them that on earth they would live, die, and be resurrected.

25. Qaala feehaa taḥyawna wa feehaa tamootoona wa minhaa tukhrajoon.

قَالَ فِيْهَا تَحْيَوْنَ وَفِيْهَا تَمُوْتُوْنَ
وَمِنْهَا تُخْرَجُوْنَ ﴿٢٥﴾ ع ٢ ١٥ ٩

26. Children of Adam, We have given you clothing to cover your private parts and for beauty, but the robe of piety is the best. Thus is the guidance of Allah so that you may take heed.

26. Yaa Baneee Aadama qad anzalnaa ‘alaykum libaasañy-yuwaaree saw-aatikum wa reeshaa; wa libaasut-taqwaa <u>z</u>aalika khayr; <u>z</u>aalika min Aayaatil-laahi la‘allahum ya<u>z</u>-<u>z</u>akkaroon.

يٰبَنِيْٓ اٰدَمَ قَدْ اَنْزَلْنَا عَلَيْكُمْ لِبَاسًا
يُّوَارِيْ سَوْاٰتِكُمْ وَرِيْشًا ۭ وَلِبَاسُ
التَّقْوٰى ۙ ذٰلِكَ خَيْرٌ ۭ ذٰلِكَ مِنْ
اٰيٰتِ اللّٰهِ لَعَلَّهُمْ يَذَّكَّرُوْنَ ﴿٢٦﴾

27. Children of Adam, do not let Satan seduce you, as he caused your parents to be expelled from the garden and made them take off their clothes in order to show them their private parts. Satan and

27. Yaa Baneee Aadama laa yaftinannakumush-Shayṭaanu kamaaa akhraja abawaykum minal-Jannati yanzi‘u ‘anhumaa libaasahumaa liyuriyahumaa saw-aatihimaaa;

يٰبَنِيْٓ اٰدَمَ لَا يَفْتِنَنَّكُمُ الشَّيْطٰنُ كَمَآ
اَخْرَجَ اَبَوَيْكُمْ مِّنَ الْجَنَّةِ يَنْزِعُ
عَنْهُمَا لِبَاسَهُمَا لِيُرِيَهُمَا سَوْاٰتِهِمَا ۭ

those like him see you but you do not see them. We have made the Satans as friends for those who have no faith.

innahoo yaraakum huwa wa qabeeluhoo min ḥaysu laa tarawnahum; innaa ja'alnash-Shayaaṭeena awliyaaa'a lillazeena laa yu'minoon.

إِنَّهُ يَرَاكُمْ هُوَ وَقَبِيلُهُ مِنْ حَيْثُ
لَا تَرَوْنَهُمْ ۗ إِنَّا جَعَلْنَا الشَّيَاطِينَ
أَوْلِيَاءَ لِلَّذِينَ لَا يُؤْمِنُونَ ﴿٢٧﴾

28. When (the faithless) commit indecent acts they say, "We found our fathers doing this and Allah has commanded us to do the same." (Muhammad), tell them that Allah does not command anyone to commit indecency. Do you speak for Allah, saying things of which you have no knowledge?

28. Wa izaa fa'aloo faaḥishatan qaaloo wajadnaa 'alayhaaa aabaaa'anaa wallaahu amaranaa bihaa; qul innal-laaha laa ya-muru bilfaḥshaaa'i ataqooloona 'alal-laahi maa laa ta'lamoon.

وَإِذَا فَعَلُوا فَاحِشَةً قَالُوا وَجَدْنَا
عَلَيْهَا آبَاءَنَا وَاللَّهُ أَمَرَنَا بِهَا ۗ
قُلْ إِنَّ اللَّهَ لَا يَأْمُرُ بِالْفَحْشَاءِ ۖ
أَتَقُولُونَ عَلَى اللَّهِ مَا لَا تَعْلَمُونَ ﴿٢٨﴾

29. Say, "My Lord has ordered me to maintain justice. (O people), pay due attention (when worshipping Allah). Pray to Him sincerely and be devoted in your religion. Just as He gave you life, He will bring you back to life again (after you die)."

29. Qul amara Rabbee bilqisṭ; wa aqeemoo wujoohakum 'inda kulli masjidiñw-wad'oohu mukhliṣeena lahud-deen; kamaa bada-akum ta'oodoon.

قُلْ أَمَرَ رَبِّي بِالْقِسْطِ ۖ وَأَقِيمُوا
وُجُوهَكُمْ عِنْدَ كُلِّ مَسْجِدٍ وَادْعُوهُ
مُخْلِصِينَ لَهُ الدِّينَ ۚ كَمَا بَدَأَكُمْ
تَعُودُونَ ﴿٢٩﴾

30. He has guided one group (of people) and the other group is doomed to go astray; the latter group took Satan as their guardian instead of Allah and thought that they were rightly guided.

30. Fareeqan hadaa wa fareeqan ḥaqqa 'alayhimuḍ-ḍalaalah; innahumut-takhazush-Shayaaṭeena awliyaaa'a min doonil-laahi wa yaḥsaboona annahum muhtadoon.

فَرِيقًا هَدَىٰ وَفَرِيقًا حَقَّ عَلَيْهِمُ
الضَّلَالَةُ ۗ إِنَّهُمُ اتَّخَذُوا الشَّيَاطِينَ
أَوْلِيَاءَ مِنْ دُونِ اللَّهِ وَيَحْسَبُونَ
أَنَّهُمْ مُهْتَدُونَ ﴿٣٠﴾

31. Children of Adam, dress well when attending the mosques, eat and drink but do not be excessive for Allah does not love those who are excessive (in what they do).

31. Yaa Baneee Aadama khuzoo zeenatakum 'inda kulli masjidiñw-wa kuloo washraboo wa laa tusrifooo; innahoo laa yuḥibbul musrifeen.

يَا بَنِي آدَمَ خُذُوا زِينَتَكُمْ عِنْدَ
كُلِّ مَسْجِدٍ وَكُلُوا وَاشْرَبُوا وَلَا
تُسْرِفُوا ۚ إِنَّهُ لَا يُحِبُّ الْمُسْرِفِينَ ﴿٣١﴾

32. (Muhammad), ask them, "Who has made it unlawful to maintain beauty and to eat the pure foods which Allah has created for His servants? They are made for the believers in this world and are exclusively for them in the life hereafter." Thus do We explain Our revelations to the people who have knowledge.

32. Qul man ḥarrama zeenatal-laahil-lateee akhraja li'ibaadihee waṭṭayyibaati minar-rizq; qul hiya lillazeena aamanoo fil-ḥayaatid-dunyaa khaaliṣatañy-Yawmal Qiyaamah; kazaalika nufaṣṣilul-Aayaati liqawmiñy-ya'lamoon.

قُلْ مَنْ حَرَّمَ زِينَةَ اللَّهِ الَّتِي أَخْرَجَ
لِعِبَادِهِ وَالطَّيِّبَاتِ مِنَ الرِّزْقِ ۚ قُلْ
هِيَ لِلَّذِينَ آمَنُوا فِي الْحَيَاةِ الدُّنْيَا
خَالِصَةً يَوْمَ الْقِيَامَةِ ۗ كَذَٰلِكَ
نُفَصِّلُ الْآيَاتِ لِقَوْمٍ يَعْلَمُونَ ﴿٣٢﴾

33. (Muhammad), tell them, "My Lord has only prohibited indecent acts committed in public or in secret, all sins, unjust rebellion, considering things equal to Allah without having

33. Qul innamaa ḥarrama Rabbiyal-fawaaḥisha maa ẓahara minhaa wa maa baṭana wal-isma walbaghya bighayril-ḥaqqi wa an tushrikoo billaahi maa lam

قُلْ إِنَّمَا حَرَّمَ رَبِّيَ الْفَوَاحِشَ مَا
ظَهَرَ مِنْهَا وَمَا بَطَنَ وَالْإِثْمَ وَالْبَغْيَ
بِغَيْرِ الْحَقِّ وَأَنْ تُشْرِكُوا بِاللَّهِ مَا لَمْ

received any heavenly authority, and speaking for Allah without having any knowledge (of what He has said)."

yunazzil bihee sulṭaanañw-wa an taqooloo ‘alal-laahi maa laa ta‘lamoon.

يُنَزِّلْ بِهٖ سُلْطٰنًا وَّ اَنْ تَقُوْلُوْا عَلَى
اللّٰهِ مَا لَا تَعْلَمُوْنَ ﴿٣٣﴾

34. All people can live only for an appointed time. When their term ends, they will not remain (alive) even for a single hour, nor will they die before the appointed time.

34. Wa likulli ummatin ajalun fa-izaa jaaa’a ajaluhum laa yasta-khiroona saa‘atañw-wa laa yastaqdimoon.

وَلِكُلِّ اُمَّةٍ اَجَلٌ ۚ فَاِذَا جَآءَ
اَجَلُهُمْ لَا يَسْتَاْخِرُوْنَ سَاعَةً
وَّلَا يَسْتَقْدِمُوْنَ ﴿٣٤﴾

35. Children of Adam, when Messengers from among your own people come to you to preach My revelations, those who choose piety and reform themselves will have nothing to fear nor will they be grieved.

35. Yaa Baneee Aadama immaa ya-tiyannakum Rusulum-minkum yaquṣṣoona ‘alaykum Aayaatee famanit-taqaa wa aṣlaḥa falaa khawfun ‘alayhim wa laa hum yaḥzanoon.

يٰبَنِيْٓ اٰدَمَ اِمَّا يَاْتِيَنَّكُمْ رُسُلٌ
مِّنْكُمْ يَقُصُّوْنَ عَلَيْكُمْ اٰيٰتِيْ ۙ فَمَنِ
اتَّقٰى وَاَصْلَحَ فَلَا خَوْفٌ عَلَيْهِمْ وَلَا
هُمْ يَحْزَنُوْنَ ﴿٣٥﴾

36. But those who have rejected Our revelations out of pride will be the dwellers of hellfire wherein they will live forever.

36. Wallazeena kaz-zaboo bi-Aayaatinaa wastakbaroo ‘anhaaa ulaaa’ika Aṣhaabun Naari hum feehaa khaalidoon.

وَالَّذِيْنَ كَذَّبُوْا بِاٰيٰتِنَا وَاسْتَكْبَرُوْا
عَنْهَآ اُولٰٓئِكَ اَصْحٰبُ النَّارِ ۚ هُمْ
فِيْهَا خٰلِدُوْنَ ﴿٣٦﴾

37. Who are more unjust than those who invent falsehoods against Allah and reject His revelations? Such people will have their share (of torment) which is ordained for them, and when Our (angelic) Messengers come to them to cause them to die and ask them, "Where are those whom you had been worshipping besides Allah?" they will reply, "We have lost such things (and people who caused us to go astray from the path of Allah)." Thus, they will testify against their own souls by confessing their disbelief.

37. Faman azlamu mimmanif-taraa ‘alal-laahi kaziban aw kazzaba bi-Aayaatih; ulaaa’ika yanaaluhum naṣeebuhum minal-Kitaab; ḥattaaa izaa jaaa’athum rusulunaa yatawaf-fawnahum qaalooo ayna maa kuntum tad‘oona min doonil-laahi qaaloo ḍalloo ‘annaa wa shahidoo ‘alaaa anfusihim annahum kaanoo kaafireen.

فَمَنْ اَظْلَمُ مِمَّنِ افْتَرٰى عَلَى اللّٰهِ
كَذِبًا اَوْ كَذَّبَ بِاٰيٰتِهٖ ۗ اُولٰٓئِكَ
يَنَالُهُمْ نَصِيْبُهُمْ مِّنَ الْكِتٰبِ ۗ حَتّٰٓى
اِذَا جَآءَتْهُمْ رُسُلُنَا يَتَوَفَّوْنَهُمْ ۙ
قَالُوْٓا اَيْنَ مَا كُنْتُمْ تَدْعُوْنَ مِنْ
دُوْنِ اللّٰهِ ۗ قَالُوْا ضَلُّوْا عَنَّا وَشَهِدُوْا
عَلٰٓى اَنْفُسِهِمْ اَنَّهُمْ كَانُوْا كٰفِرِيْنَ ﴿٣٧﴾

38. (On the Day of Judgment) the Lord will say to them, "Join the group of jinn and people who lived before you, in hell." Each group, on entering hell, will curse the other dwellers, until all of them are brought together therein.

The last group will accuse the first, saying, "Lord, they made us go astray. Therefore, double their torment in the fire." The Lord will reply, "For every one of you there is a double torment, but you do not know it."

38. Qaalad-khuloo feee umamin qad khalat min qablikum minal-jinni wal-insi fin-Naari kullamaa dakhalat ummatul-la‘anat ukhtahaa ḥattaaa izad-daarakoo feehaa jamee‘an qaalat ukhraahum li-oolaahum Rabbanaa haaa’u-laaa’i aḍalloonaa fa-aatihim ‘azaaban ḍi‘fam-minan-Naari qaala likullin ḍi‘fuñw-wa laakil laa ta‘lamoon.

قَالَ ادْخُلُوْا فِيْٓ اُمَمٍ قَدْ خَلَتْ مِنْ
قَبْلِكُمْ مِّنَ الْجِنِّ وَالْاِنْسِ فِي النَّارِ ۗ
كُلَّمَا دَخَلَتْ اُمَّةٌ لَّعَنَتْ اُخْتَهَا ۗ
حَتّٰٓى اِذَا ادَّارَكُوْا فِيْهَا جَمِيْعًا ۙ
قَالَتْ اُخْرٰىهُمْ لِاُوْلٰىهُمْ رَبَّنَا هٰٓؤُلَآءِ
اَضَلُّوْنَا فَاٰتِهِمْ عَذَابًا ضِعْفًا مِّنَ
النَّارِ ۗ قَالَ لِكُلٍّ ضِعْفٌ وَّلٰكِنْ

لَا تَعْلَمُونَ ﴿٣٨﴾

39. The first will then say, "You are no better than us; suffer the torment as the result of your deeds."

39. Wa qaalat oolaahum li-ukhraahum famaa kaana lakum ‘alaynaa min faḍlin faz̲ooqul-‘az̲aaba bimaa kuntum taksiboon.

وَقَالَتْ أُولَاهُمْ لِأُخْرَاهُمْ فَمَا كَانَ
لَكُمْ عَلَيْنَا مِنْ فَضْلٍ فَذُوقُوا
الْعَذَابَ بِمَا كُنْتُمْ تَكْسِبُونَ ﴿٣٩﴾ ع ٨

40. For those who have rejected Our revelations out of pride, no door to the heavens will be opened, nor will they be admitted into Paradise until a camel passes through the eye of a sewing needle. Thus do We recompense the criminals.

40. Innal-laz̲eena kaz̲-z̲aboo bi-Aayaatinaa wastakbaroo ‘anhaa laa tufattaḥu lahum abwaabus-samaaa’i wa laa yadkhuloonal-jannata ḥattaa yalijal-jamalu fee sam-milkhiyaaṭ; wa kaz̲aalika najzilmujrimeen.

إِنَّ الَّذِينَ كَذَّبُوا بِآيَاتِنَا وَاسْتَكْبَرُوا
عَنْهَا لَا تُفَتَّحُ لَهُمْ أَبْوَابُ السَّمَاءِ
وَلَا يَدْخُلُونَ الْجَنَّةَ حَتَّىٰ يَلِجَ
الْجَمَلُ فِي سَمِّ الْخِيَاطِ ۚ وَكَذَٰلِكَ
نَجْزِي الْمُجْرِمِينَ ﴿٤٠﴾

41. For them, hell will be both a cradle and a blanket. Thus do We punish the unjust.

41. Lahum min jahannama mihaaduñw-wa min fawqihim ghawaash; wa kaz̲aalika najziẓ-ẓaalimeen.

لَهُمْ مِنْ جَهَنَّمَ مِهَادٌ وَمِنْ فَوْقِهِمْ
غَوَاشٍ ۚ وَكَذَٰلِكَ نَجْزِي الظَّالِمِينَ ﴿٤١﴾

42. The righteously striving believers - We do not impose on any soul that which is beyond its ability - are the dwellers of Paradise wherein they will live forever.

42. Wallaz̲eena aamanoo wa‘amiluṣ-ṣaaliḥaati laa nukal-lifu nafsan illaa wus‘ahaaa ulaaa’ika Aṣḥaabul-jannati hum feehaa khaalidoon.

وَالَّذِينَ آمَنُوا وَعَمِلُوا الصَّالِحَاتِ
لَا نُكَلِّفُ نَفْسًا إِلَّا وُسْعَهَا
أُولَٰئِكَ أَصْحَابُ الْجَنَّةِ ۖ هُمْ فِيهَا
خَالِدُونَ ﴿٤٢﴾

43. We shall remove all grudges from their hearts. They will enjoy the flowing streams in the garden and will say, "Allah, who guided us to this, deserves all praise. Had Allah not guided us, we would never have been able to find the right direction. The Messengers of our Lord came to us with the Truth." They shall be told, "This is the Paradise which you have inherited because of your good deeds."

43. Wa naza‘naa maa fee ṣudoorihim min ghillin tajree min taḥtihimul-anhaaru wa qaalul-ḥamdu lillaahil-laz̲ee hadaanaa lihaaz̲aa wa maa kunnaa linahtadiya law laaa an hadaanal-laahu laqad jaaa’at Rusulu Rabbinaa bilḥaqq; wa noodooo an tilkumul-jannatu ooris̲tumoohaa bimaa kuntum ta‘maloon.

وَنَزَعْنَا مَا فِي صُدُورِهِمْ مِنْ غِلٍّ
تَجْرِي مِنْ تَحْتِهِمُ الْأَنْهَارُ ۖ وَقَالُوا
الْحَمْدُ لِلَّهِ الَّذِي هَدَانَا لِهَٰذَا وَمَا
كُنَّا لِنَهْتَدِيَ لَوْلَا أَنْ هَدَانَا اللَّهُ
لَقَدْ جَاءَتْ رُسُلُ رَبِّنَا بِالْحَقِّ
وَنُودُوا أَنْ تِلْكُمُ الْجَنَّةُ أُورِثْتُمُوهَا
بِمَا كُنْتُمْ تَعْمَلُونَ ﴿٤٣﴾ الثلثة

44. The people of Paradise will say to the dwellers of the fire, "We have found whatever our Lord promised has come true. Have you found whatever your Lord promised you to be true?" They will reply, "Yes, we have also found it to be true." Thereupon,

44. Wa naadaaa Aṣḥaabul jannati Aṣḥaaban-Naari an qad wajadnaa maa wa‘adanaa Rabbunaa ḥaqqan fahal wajattum maa wa‘ada Rabbukum ḥaqqan qaaloo na‘am; fa-az̲z̲ana

وَنَادَىٰ أَصْحَابُ الْجَنَّةِ أَصْحَابَ
النَّارِ أَنْ قَدْ وَجَدْنَا مَا وَعَدَنَا
رَبُّنَا حَقًّا فَهَلْ وَجَدْتُمْ مَا وَعَدَ
رَبُّكُمْ حَقًّا ۖ قَالُوا نَعَمْ ۚ فَأَذَّنَ

someone will cry out, "Allah has condemned the unjust,

mu'az-zinum baynahum al-la'natul-laahi 'alaz-zaalimeen.

مُؤَذِّنٌۢ بَيْنَهُمْ اَنْ لَّعْنَةُ اللّٰهِ
عَلَى الظّٰلِمِيْنَ ﴿٤٤﴾

45. who prevented others from the way of Allah, sought to make (the path) appear crooked, and had no belief in the Day of Judgment."

45. Allazeena yasuddoona 'an sabeelil-laahi wa yabghoonahaa 'iwajaa; wa hum bil-Aakhirati kaafiroon.

الَّذِيْنَ يَصُدُّوْنَ عَنْ سَبِيْلِ
اللّٰهِ وَ يَبْغُوْنَهَا عِوَجًا ۚ وَهُمْ
بِالْاٰخِرَةِ كٰفِرُوْنَ ﴿٤٥﴾

46. There will be a barrier between the people of Paradise and hell. There will be people on the heights who know everyone by their faces and who will say to the people of Paradise, "Peace be upon you." They hoped to enter Paradise but were not yet therein.

46. Wa baynahumaa hijaab; wa 'alal-A'raafi rijaaluñy-ya'rifoona kullam biseemaahum; wa naadaw Ashaabal-Jannati an salaamun 'alaykum; lam yadkhuloohaa wa hum yatma'oon.

وَ بَيْنَهُمَا حِجَابٌ ۚ وَعَلَى الْاَعْرَافِ
رِجَالٌ يَّعْرِفُوْنَ كُلًّاۢ بِسِيْمٰهُمْ ۚ
وَ نَادَوْا اَصْحٰبَ الْجَنَّةِ اَنْ سَلٰمٌ
عَلَيْكُمْ ۟ لَمْ يَدْخُلُوْهَا وَ هُمْ
يَطْمَعُوْنَ ﴿٤٦﴾ وقف لازم باختلاف

47. When their eyes turn to the dwellers of hell, they will pray, "Lord, do not place us among the unjust."

47. Wa izaa surifat absaaruhum tilqaaa'a Ashaabin-Naari qaalo Rabbanaa laa taj'alnaa ma'al-qawmiz-zaalimeen.

وَاِذَا صُرِفَتْ اَبْصَارُهُمْ تِلْقَآءَ
اَصْحٰبِ النَّارِ ۙ قَالُوْا رَبَّنَا لَا تَجْعَلْنَا
مَعَ الْقَوْمِ الظّٰلِمِيْنَ ﴿٤٧﴾ ع ٥

48. The people of the Heights will say to those (in hell) whose faces they recognize, "Why did your supporters and your pride not help you?"

48. Wa naadaaa Ashaabul A'raafi rijaalañy-ya'rifoonahum biseemaahum qaaloo maaa aghnaa 'ankum jam'ukum wa maa kuntum tastakbiroon.

وَ نَادٰٓى اَصْحٰبُ الْاَعْرَافِ رِجَالًا
يَّعْرِفُوْنَهُمْ بِسِيْمٰهُمْ قَالُوْا مَآ
اَغْنٰى عَنْكُمْ جَمْعُكُمْ وَمَا كُنْتُمْ
تَسْتَكْبِرُوْنَ ﴿٤٨﴾

49. (They will also say), "Are these (the people of Paradise) the ones of whom you swore that they would receive no mercy from Allah?" They will continue, "People of Paradise, live therein without any fear or grief."

49. Ahaaa'ulaaa'il-lazeena aqsamtum laa yanaaluhumul-laahu birahmah; udkhulul Jannata laa khawfun 'alaykum wa laaa antum tahzanoon.

اَهٰٓؤُلَآءِ الَّذِيْنَ اَقْسَمْتُمْ لَا يَنَالُهُمُ
اللّٰهُ بِرَحْمَةٍ ؕ اُدْخُلُوا الْجَنَّةَ لَا
خَوْفٌ عَلَيْكُمْ وَلَآ اَنْتُمْ تَحْزَنُوْنَ ﴿٤٩﴾

50. The dwellers of the fire will ask the people of Paradise to give them some water or other things which Allah has granted to them. They will reply, "Allah has deprived the unbelievers of the blessings of Paradise."

50. Wa naadaaa Ashaabun Naari Ashaabal-Jannati an afeedoo 'alaynaa minalmaaa'i aw mimmaa razaqakumul-laah; qaalooo innal-laaha harramahumaa 'alal-kaafireen.

وَنَادٰٓى اَصْحٰبُ النَّارِ اَصْحٰبَ الْجَنَّةِ
اَنْ اَفِيْضُوْا عَلَيْنَا مِنَ الْمَآءِ اَوْ مِمَّا
رَزَقَكُمُ اللّٰهُ ؕ قَالُوْٓا اِنَّ اللّٰهَ
حَرَّمَهُمَا عَلَى الْكٰفِرِيْنَ ﴿٥٠﴾

51. On that Day We will neglect those who were deceived by the worldly life and who treated their religion as a useless game,

51. Allazeenat-takhazoo deenahum lahwañw-wa la'ibañw-wa gharrathumul- hayaatud-dunyaa; fal-Yawma

الَّذِيْنَ اتَّخَذُوْا دِيْنَهُمْ لَهْوًا وَّلَعِبًا
وَّغَرَّتْهُمُ الْحَيٰوةُ الدُّنْيَا ۚ فَالْيَوْمَ

because they had forgotten such a day and rejected Our revelations.

nansaahum kamaa nasoo liqaaa'a Yawmihim haazaa wa maa kaanoo bi-Aayaatinaa yajhadoon.

نَنْسٰهُمْ كَمَا نَسُوْا لِقَآءَ يَوْمِهِمْ هٰذَا ۙ
وَمَا كَانُوْا بِاٰيٰتِنَا يَجْحَدُوْنَ ﴿٥١﴾

52. We have revealed to them the Book, We know all of its details. It is guidance and mercy to believers.

52. Wa laqad ji'naahum bi-Kitaabin faṣ-ṣalnaahu ‘alaa ‘ilmin hudañw-wa raḥmatal-liqawmiñy-yu'minoon.

وَلَقَدْ جِئْنٰهُمْ بِكِتٰبٍ فَصَّلْنٰهُ عَلٰى عِلْمٍ
هُدًى وَّرَحْمَةً لِّقَوْمٍ يُّؤْمِنُوْنَ ﴿٥٢﴾

53. (Despite the clear details of Our guidance in the Book) do they still wait for further interpretations? On the Day (of Judgment) when its interpretations will be revealed, those who had ignored its guidance will confess, saying, "The Messengers of our Lord had certainly come to us with the Truth. Will anyone intercede for us or send us back (to life) so that we can act in a manner different from our manner before?" These people have certainly lost their souls, and their evil inventions (which they had used for false excuses) will vanish.

53. Hal yanẓuroona illaa ta-weelah; Yawma ya-tee ta-weeluhoo yaqoolul-lazeena nasoohu min qablu qad jaaa'at Rusulu Rabbinaa bilḥaqq; fahal-lanaa min shufa‘aaa'a fayashfa‘oo lanaaa aw nuraddu fana‘mala ghayral-lazee kunnaa na‘mal; qad khasirooo anfusahum wa ḍalla ‘anhum maa kaanoo yaftaroon.

هَلْ يَنْظُرُوْنَ اِلَّا تَاْوِيْلَهٗ ؕ يَوْمَ
يَاْتِيْ تَاْوِيْلُهٗ يَقُوْلُ الَّذِيْنَ نَسُوْهُ
مِنْ قَبْلُ قَدْ جَآءَتْ رُسُلُ رَبِّنَا
بِالْحَقِّ ۚ فَهَلْ لَّنَا مِنْ شُفَعَآءَ
فَيَشْفَعُوْا لَنَآ اَوْ نُرَدُّ فَنَعْمَلَ غَيْرَ
الَّذِيْ كُنَّا نَعْمَلُ ؕ قَدْ خَسِرُوْٓا
اَنْفُسَهُمْ وَضَلَّ عَنْهُمْ مَّا كَانُوْا
يَفْتَرُوْنَ ﴿٥٣﴾ ع

54. Your Lord is Allah, who established His dominion over the Throne (of the realm) after having created the heavens and the earth in six days (periods of time). He made the night darken the day which it pursues at a (considerable) speed, and He made the sun and the moon submissive to His command. Is it not He Who creates and governs all things? Blessed is Allah, the Cherisher of the Universe.

54. Inna Rabbakumul-laahul-lazee khalaqas-samaawaati wal-arḍa fee sittati ayyaamin summastawaa ‘alal-‘arshi yughshil-laylan-nahaara yaṭlu-buhoo ḥaseesañw-washshamsa walqamara wannujooma musakh-kharaatim bi-amrih; alaa lahul-khalqu wal-amr; tabaarakal-laahu Rabbul‘aala-meen.

اِنَّ رَبَّكُمُ اللّٰهُ الَّذِيْ خَلَقَ السَّمٰوٰتِ
وَالْاَرْضَ فِيْ سِتَّةِ اَيَّامٍ ثُمَّ اسْتَوٰى
عَلَى الْعَرْشِ ۫ يُغْشِي الَّيْلَ النَّهَارَ
يَطْلُبُهٗ حَثِيْثًا ۙ وَّالشَّمْسَ وَالْقَمَرَ
وَالنُّجُوْمَ مُسَخَّرٰتٍ بِاَمْرِهٖ ؕ اَلَا لَهُ
الْخَلْقُ وَالْاَمْرُ ؕ تَبٰرَكَ اللّٰهُ رَبُّ
الْعٰلَمِيْنَ ﴿٥٤﴾

55. Pray to your Lord humbly and privately. Allah does not love the transgressors.

55. Ud‘oo Rabbakum taḍar-ru‘añw-wa khufyah; innahoo laa yuḥibbul mu‘tadeen.

اُدْعُوْا رَبَّكُمْ تَضَرُّعًا وَّخُفْيَةً ؕ
اِنَّهٗ لَا يُحِبُّ الْمُعْتَدِيْنَ ﴿٥٥﴾ ج

56. Do not spread evil in the land after it has been well established but pray to Allah, have fear of Him, and hope to receive His mercy. Allah's mercy is close to the righteous people.

56. Wa laa tufsidoo fil-arḍi ba‘da iṣlaaḥihaa wad‘oohu khawfañw-wa ṭama‘aa; inna raḥmatal-laahi qareebum-minal-muḥsineen.

وَلَا تُفْسِدُوْا فِي الْاَرْضِ بَعْدَ اِصْلَاحِهَا
وَادْعُوْهُ خَوْفًا وَّطَمَعًا ؕ اِنَّ رَحْمَتَ
اللّٰهِ قَرِيْبٌ مِّنَ الْمُحْسِنِيْنَ ﴿٥٦﴾

57. He is the One who sends the wind bearing the glad news of His mercy. When heavy clouds are

57. Wa Huwal-lazee yursilur-riyaaḥa bushram bayna yaday raḥmatihee ḥattaaa izaaa

وَهُوَ الَّذِيْ يُرْسِلُ الرِّيٰحَ بُشْرًا ۢ
بَيْنَ يَدَيْ رَحْمَتِهٖ ؕ حَتّٰٓى اِذَآ

formed, We drive them unto a barren country and rain down on it water to cause all kinds of fruits to grow. In the same way do We bring the dead to life again. Perhaps you will take heed.

aqallat saḥaaban s̲iqaalan suqnaahu libaladim-mayyitin fa-anzalnaa bihil-maaa'a fa-akhrajnaa bihee min kullis̲-s̲amaraat; kaz̲aalika nukhrijul-mawtaa la'allakum taz̲akkaroon.

اَقَلَّتْ سَحَابًا ثِقَالًا سُقْنٰهُ لِبَلَدٍ
مَّيِّتٍ فَاَنْزَلْنَا بِهِ الْمَآءَ فَاَخْرَجْنَا
بِهٖ مِنْ كُلِّ الثَّمَرٰتِ ؕ كَذٰلِكَ نُخْرِجُ
الْمَوْتٰى لَعَلَّكُمْ تَذَكَّرُوْنَ ﴿٥٧﴾

58. A good land produces plants, by the permission of its Lord, but a wicked land produces only miserable, bitter plants. Thus do We show a variety of evidence for those who give thanks.

58. Walbaladuṭ-ṭayyibu yakhruju nabaatuhoo bi-iz̲ni Rabbihee wallaz̲ee khabus̲a laa yakhruju illaa nakidaa; kaz̲aalika nuṣarriful-Aayaati liqawmiñy-yashkuroon.

وَالْبَلَدُ الطَّيِّبُ يَخْرُجُ نَبَاتُهٗ
بِاِذْنِ رَبِّهٖ ۚ وَالَّذِىْ خَبُثَ لَا يَخْرُجُ
اِلَّا نَكِدًا ؕ كَذٰلِكَ نُصَرِّفُ الْاٰيٰتِ
لِقَوْمٍ يَّشْكُرُوْنَ ﴿٥٨﴾ ع ٥ ١٤

59. We sent Noah to his people. He told them, "Worship Allah for He is your only Lord. I am afraid of the punishment that you might suffer on the great Day (of Judgment)."

59. Laqad arsalnaa Nooḥan ilaa qawmihee faqaala yaa qawmi'-budul-laaha maa lakum min ilaahin ghayruhooo inneee akhaafu 'alaykum 'az̲aaba Yawmin 'Aẓeem.

لَقَدْ اَرْسَلْنَا نُوْحًا اِلٰى قَوْمِهٖ
فَقَالَ يٰقَوْمِ اعْبُدُوا اللّٰهَ مَا لَكُمْ
مِّنْ اِلٰهٍ غَيْرُهٗ ؕ اِنِّىْٓ اَخَافُ
عَلَيْكُمْ عَذَابَ يَوْمٍ عَظِيْمٍ ﴿٥٩﴾

60. A group of his people said to him, "You are absolutely wrong."

60. Qaalal-malau min qawmiheee innaa lanaraaka fee ḍalaalim-mubeen.

قَالَ الْمَلَاُ مِنْ قَوْمِهٖٓ اِنَّا لَنَرٰىكَ
فِىْ ضَلٰلٍ مُّبِيْنٍ ﴿٦٠﴾

61. (Noah) said, "My people, I am not in any error, rather I am a Messenger from the Lord of the Universe,

61. Qaala yaa qawmi laysa bee ḍalaalatuñw-wa laakinnee Rasoolum-mir-Rabbil'aalameen.

قَالَ يٰقَوْمِ لَيْسَ بِىْ ضَلٰلَةٌ وَّلٰكِنِّىْ
رَسُوْلٌ مِّنْ رَّبِّ الْعٰلَمِيْنَ ﴿٦١﴾

62. sent to preach to you the message of my Lord and to give you good advice. I know what you do not know about Allah.

62. Uballighukum Risaalaati Rabbee wa anṣaḥu lakum wa a'lamu minal-laahi maa laa ta'lamoon.

اُبَلِّغُكُمْ رِسٰلٰتِ رَبِّىْ وَاَنْصَحُ لَكُمْ
وَاَعْلَمُ مِنَ اللّٰهِ مَا لَا تَعْلَمُوْنَ ﴿٦٢﴾

63. Does it seem strange to you that a reminder from your Lord should be sent to a man, from among you, to warn you so that you might receive mercy?"

63. Awa'ajibtum an jaaa'akum z̲ikrum-mir-Rabbikum 'alaa rajulim-minkum liyunz̲irakum wa litattaqoo wa la'allakum turḥamoon.

اَوَعَجِبْتُمْ اَنْ جَآءَكُمْ ذِكْرٌ مِّنْ
رَّبِّكُمْ عَلٰى رَجُلٍ مِّنْكُمْ لِيُنْذِرَكُمْ
وَلِتَتَّقُوْا وَلَعَلَّكُمْ تُرْحَمُوْنَ ﴿٦٣﴾

64. They falsely accused him of telling lies. So We saved him and his companions in an ark and drowned those who called Our revelations mere lies. They were, no doubt, a blind people.

64. Fakaz̲-z̲aboohu-fa-anjaynaahu wallaz̲eena ma'ahoo fil-fulki wa aghraqnal-laz̲eena kaz̲-z̲aboo bi-Aayaatinaaa; innahum kaanoo qawman 'ameen.

فَكَذَّبُوْهُ فَاَنْجَيْنٰهُ وَالَّذِيْنَ
مَعَهٗ فِى الْفُلْكِ وَاَغْرَقْنَا
الَّذِيْنَ كَذَّبُوْا بِاٰيٰتِنَا ؕ اِنَّهُمْ
كَانُوْا قَوْمًا عَمِيْنَ ﴿٦٤﴾ ع ٦ ١٥

65. We sent Hud to his brethren, the tribe of Ad, who told

65. Wa ilaa 'Aadin akhaahum Hoodaa; qaala

وَاِلٰى عَادٍ اَخَاهُمْ هُوْدًا ؕ قَالَ

them, "My people, worship Allah for He is your only Lord. Will you not become pious?"

yaa qawmi‘-budul-laaha maa lakum min ilaahin ghayruh; afalaa tattaqoon.

يٰقَوْمِ اعْبُدُوا اللّٰهَ مَا لَكُمْ مِّنْ
اِلٰهٍ غَيْرُهٗ ؕ اَفَلَا تَتَّقُوْنَ ﴿٦٥﴾

66. A group of the unbelievers among his people said, "You look to us like a fool and we think that you are a liar."

66. Qaalal-mala-ul-lazeena kafaroo min qawmiheee innaa lanaraaka fee safaahatiñw-wa innaa lanazunnuka minal-kaazibeen.

قَالَ الْمَلَاُ الَّذِيْنَ كَفَرُوْا مِنْ
قَوْمِهٖۤ اِنَّا لَنَرٰىكَ فِيْ سَفَاهَةٍ وَّ
اِنَّا لَنَظُنُّكَ مِنَ الْكٰذِبِيْنَ ﴿٦٦﴾

67. He replied, "My people, I am not a fool but a Messenger of the Lord of the Universe.

67. Qaala yaa qawmi laysa bee safaahatuñw-wa laakinnee Rasoolum-mir-Rabbil ‘aala-meen.

قَالَ يٰقَوْمِ لَيْسَ بِيْ سَفَاهَةٌ وَّ
لٰكِنِّيْ رَسُوْلٌ مِّنْ رَّبِّ الْعٰلَمِيْنَ ﴿٦٧﴾

68. I preach the message of my Lord to you and am a trustworthy advisor for you.

68. Uballighukum Risaalaati Rabbee wa ana lakum naaṣiḥun ameen.

اُبَلِّغُكُمْ رِسٰلٰتِ رَبِّيْ وَاَنَا لَكُمْ
نَاصِحٌ اَمِيْنٌ ﴿٦٨﴾

69. Does it seem strange to you that a reminder from your Lord should be sent to a man among you so that He may warn you? Recall, that Allah appointed you as successors of the people of Noah and increased your power over other people. Give thanks to Allah for His blessings so that perhaps you will have everlasting happiness."

69. Awa ‘ajibtum an jaaa’akum zikrum-mir-Rabbikum ‘alaa rajulim-minkum liyunzirakum; wazkurooo iz ja‘alakum khulafaaa’a mim ba‘di qawmi Nooḥiñw-wa zaadakum filkhal-qi baṣṭatan fazkurooo aalaaa’al-laahi la‘allakum tufliḥoon.

اَوَعَجِبْتُمْ اَنْ جَآءَكُمْ ذِكْرٌ مِّنْ
رَّبِّكُمْ عَلٰى رَجُلٍ مِّنْكُمْ لِيُنْذِرَكُمْ ؕ
وَاذْكُرُوْۤا اِذْ جَعَلَكُمْ خُلَفَآءَ
مِنْۢ بَعْدِ قَوْمِ نُوْحٍ وَّزَادَكُمْ فِي
الْخَلْقِ بَصْۜطَةً ۚ فَاذْكُرُوْۤا
اٰلَآءَ اللّٰهِ لَعَلَّكُمْ تُفْلِحُوْنَ ﴿٦٩﴾

70. They said, "Have you come to make us worship Allah alone and give up what our fathers worshipped? If what you say is true, then you should allow the torment with which you have threatened us, to strike us."

70. Qaalooo aji’tanaa lina‘bu-dal-laaha waḥdahoo wa nazara maa kaana ya‘budu aabaaa’u-naa fa-tinaa bimaa ta‘idunaaa in kunta minaṣ-ṣaadiqeen.

قَالُوْۤا اَجِئْتَنَا لِنَعْبُدَ اللّٰهَ وَحْدَهٗ
وَنَذَرَ مَا كَانَ يَعْبُدُ اٰبَآؤُنَا ۚ
فَاْتِنَا بِمَا تَعِدُنَاۤ اِنْ كُنْتَ
مِنَ الصّٰدِقِيْنَ ﴿٧٠﴾

71. He replied, "You will certainly be afflicted by wickedness and the wrath of your Lord. Do you dispute with me about the names of that which you and your fathers have invented? Allah has given no authority to those names. Wait for Allah's decree and I, am also waiting with you."

71. Qaala qad waqa‘a ‘alaykum-mir-Rabbikum rijsuñw-wa ghaḍab; atujaadiloonanee feee asmaaa’in sammaytumoo-haaa antum wa aabaaa’ukum maa nazzalal-laahu bihaa min sulṭaan; fantaẓirooo innee ma‘akum minal-muntaẓireen.

قَالَ قَدْ وَقَعَ عَلَيْكُمْ مِّنْ رَّبِّكُمْ
رِجْسٌ وَّغَضَبٌ ؕ اَتُجَادِلُوْنَنِيْ
فِيْۤ اَسْمَآءٍ سَمَّيْتُمُوْهَاۤ اَنْتُمْ وَ
اٰبَآؤُكُمْ مَّا نَزَّلَ اللّٰهُ بِهَا مِنْ
سُلْطٰنٍ ؕ فَانْتَظِرُوْۤا اِنِّيْ مَعَكُمْ
مِّنَ الْمُنْتَظِرِيْنَ ﴿٧١﴾

72. Through Our mercy, We saved him and his companions

72. Fa-anjaynaahu wallazeena ma‘ahoo biraḥmatim-

فَاَنْجَيْنٰهُ وَالَّذِيْنَ مَعَهٗ بِرَحْمَةٍ

and destroyed those who called Our revelations mere lies and who were not believers.

minnaa wa qaṭa'naa daabiral-lazeena kaz-zaboo bi-Aayaati-naa wa maa kaanoo mu'mineen.

مِّنَّا وَقَطَعْنَا دَابِرَ الَّذِيْنَ كَذَّبُوْا
بِاٰيٰتِنَا وَمَا كَانُوْا مُؤْمِنِيْنَ ﴿٧٢﴾

ع ٨ وقف لازم

73. We sent Salih to his brethren, the tribe of Thamud, who told them, "My people, worship Allah your only Lord. Authoritative evidence has come to you from your Lord and this she-camel is the evidence for you from Allah. Let her graze in the land of Allah. Do not give her any trouble lest a painful torment strike you."

73. Wa ilaa Samooda akhaahum Ṣaaliḥaa; qaala yaa qawmi'-budul-laaha maa lakum min ilaahin ghayruhoo qad jaaa'atkum bayyinatummir-Rabbikum haazihee naaqatul-laahi lakum Aayatan fazaroohaa ta-kul feee arḍil-laahi wa laa tamassoohaa bisooo'in faya-khuzakum 'azaabun aleem.

وَاِلٰى ثَمُوْدَ اَخَاهُمْ صٰلِحًا ۘ قَالَ
يٰقَوْمِ اعْبُدُوا اللّٰهَ مَا لَكُمْ مِّنْ
اِلٰهٍ غَيْرُهٗ ؕ قَدْ جَآءَتْكُمْ بَيِّنَةٌ
مِّنْ رَّبِّكُمْ ؕ هٰذِهٖ نَاقَةُ اللّٰهِ لَكُمْ
اٰيَةً فَذَرُوْهَا تَاْكُلْ فِيْٓ اَرْضِ
اللّٰهِ وَلَا تَمَسُّوْهَا بِسُوْٓءٍ فَيَاْخُذَكُمْ
عَذَابٌ اَلِيْمٌ ﴿٧٣﴾

74. "Recall (the time) when We settled you in the land as the heirs of the tribe of Ad and how you established mansions in the plains and carved homes out of the mountains. Give thanks to Allah for His favors and do not commit evil in the land."

74. Wazkurooo iz ja'alakum khulafaaa'a mim ba'di 'Aadiñw-wa bawwa-akum fil-arḍi tattakhizoona min suhoolihaa quṣoorañw-wa tanḥitoonal jibaala buyootan fazkurooo aalaaa'al-laahi wa laa ta'saw fil-arḍi mufsideen.

وَاذْكُرُوْٓا اِذْ جَعَلَكُمْ خُلَفَآءَ مِنْۢ
بَعْدِ عَادٍ وَّبَوَّاَكُمْ فِى الْاَرْضِ
تَتَّخِذُوْنَ مِنْ سُهُوْلِهَا قُصُوْرًا
وَّتَنْحِتُوْنَ الْجِبَالَ بُيُوْتًا ۚ فَاذْكُرُوْٓا
اٰلَآءَ اللّٰهِ وَلَا تَعْثَوْا فِى الْاَرْضِ
مُفْسِدِيْنَ ﴿٧٤﴾

75. The proud ones among Salih's people asked his oppressed followers, "Do you (really) know that Salih is a Messenger of his Lord?" They replied, "We have faith in the Message which he preaches."

75. Qaalal-mala-ul-lazeenas takbaroo min qawmihee lillazeenas-tuḍ'ifoo liman aamana minhum ata'lamoona anna Ṣaaliḥam-mursalum-mir-Rabbih; qaalooo innaa bimaaa ursila bihee mu'minoon.

قَالَ الْمَلَاُ الَّذِيْنَ اسْتَكْبَرُوْا مِنْ
قَوْمِهٖ لِلَّذِيْنَ اسْتُضْعِفُوْا لِمَنْ
اٰمَنَ مِنْهُمْ اَتَعْلَمُوْنَ اَنَّ صٰلِحًا
مُّرْسَلٌ مِّنْ رَّبِّهٖ ؕ قَالُوْٓا اِنَّا بِمَآ
اُرْسِلَ بِهٖ مُؤْمِنُوْنَ ﴿٧٥﴾

76. The proud oppressors said, "We reject that which you believe in."

76.Qaalal-lazeenas-takbarooo innaa billazeee aamantum bihee kaafiroon.

قَالَ الَّذِيْنَ اسْتَكْبَرُوْٓا اِنَّا بِالَّذِىْٓ
اٰمَنْتُمْ بِهٖ كٰفِرُوْنَ ﴿٧٦﴾

77. They then slew the camel and rebelled against the orders of their Lord, saying, "Salih, if you are truly a messenger, let that torment with which you have threatened us come to pass."

77. Fa'aqarun-naaqata wa'ataw 'an amri Rabbihim wa qaaloo yaa Ṣaaliḥu'-tinaa bimaa ta'idunaaa in kunta minal-mursaleen.

فَعَقَرُوا النَّاقَةَ وَعَتَوْا عَنْ اَمْرِ
رَبِّهِمْ وَقَالُوْا يٰصٰلِحُ ائْتِنَا بِمَا
تَعِدُنَآ اِنْ كُنْتَ مِنَ الْمُرْسَلِيْنَ ﴿٧٧﴾

78. Suddenly, an earthquake jolted them, and they were left

78. Fa-akhazathumur-rajfatu fa-aṣbaḥoo fee

فَاَخَذَتْهُمُ الرَّجْفَةُ فَاَصْبَحُوْا فِىْ

motionless in their homes.

daarihim jaas-imeen.

دَارِهِمْ جٰثِمِيْنَ ۝٧٨

79. He turned away from them saying, "My people, I preached the Message of my Lord to you and gave you good advice, but you do not love advisors."

79. Fatawallaa 'anhum wa qaala yaa qawmi laqad ablaghtukum Risaalata Rabbee wa naṣaḥtu lakum wa laakil-laa tuḥibboonan-naaṣiḥeen.

فَتَوَلّٰى عَنْهُمْ وَقَالَ يٰقَوْمِ لَقَدْ
اَبْلَغْتُكُمْ رِسَالَةَ رَبِّىْ وَنَصَحْتُ
لَكُمْ وَلٰكِنْ لَّا تُحِبُّوْنَ النّٰصِحِيْنَ ۝٧٩

80. Lot told his people, "Why do you commit such indecent acts that have never been committed by anyone before?

80. Wa Looṭan iz̲ qaala liqawmiheee ata-toonal-faaḥishata maa sabaqakum bihaa min aḥadim-minal 'aalameen.

وَلُوْطًا اِذْ قَالَ لِقَوْمِهٖۤ اَتَاْتُوْنَ
الْفَاحِشَةَ مَا سَبَقَكُمْ بِهَا مِنْ
اَحَدٍ مِّنَ الْعٰلَمِيْنَ ۝٨٠

81. You engage in lustful activities with men instead of women. You have become transgressing people.

81. Innakum lata-toonar-rijaala shahwatam-min doonin-nisaaa'; bal antum qawmum-musrifoon.

اِنَّكُمْ لَتَاْتُوْنَ الرِّجَالَ شَهْوَةً مِّنْ
دُوْنِ النِّسَآءِ ؕ بَلْ اَنْتُمْ قَوْمٌ مُّسْرِفُوْنَ ۝٨١

82. His people had no answer to his remarks but to tell one another, "Expel him from our town; he and his people want to purify themselves."

82. Wa maa kaana jawaaba qawmiheee illaa an qaalooo akhrijoohum min qaryatikum innahum unaasuñy-yataṭah-haroon.

وَمَا كَانَ جَوَابَ قَوْمِهٖۤ اِلَّاۤ اَنْ
قَالُوْۤا اَخْرِجُوْهُمْ مِّنْ قَرْيَتِكُمْ ۚ اِنَّهُمْ
اُنَاسٌ يَّتَطَهَّرُوْنَ ۝٨٢

83. We saved (Lot) and his family except his wife, who remained with the rest.

83. Fa-anjaynaahu wa ahla-hooo illam-ra-atahoo kaanat minal-ghaabireen.

فَاَنْجَيْنٰهُ وَاَهْلَهٗۤ اِلَّا امْرَاَتَهٗ ۖ
كَانَتْ مِنَ الْغٰبِرِيْنَ ۝٨٣

84. We sent a torrential rain unto the (unbelievers). Consider how disastrous the end of the criminals was!

84. Wa amṭarnaa 'alayhim maṭaran fanẓur kayfa kaana 'aaqibatul-mujrimeen.

وَاَمْطَرْنَا عَلَيْهِمْ مَّطَرًا ؕ فَانْظُرْ
كَيْفَ كَانَ عَاقِبَةُ الْمُجْرِمِيْنَ ۝٨٤ ع ١٠/١٢ ١٧

85. We sent to the people of Madyan their brother Shuayb, who also told his people to worship Allah, their only Lord. He said, "Guidance has come to you from your Lord. Maintain proper measures and weights in trade. Do not cause any deficiency in people's property or spread evil in the land after it has been reformed. This is for your own good, if you have any faith.

85. Wa ilaa Madyana akhaa-hum Shu'aybaa; qaala yaa qawmi'-budul-laaha maa lakum min ilaahin ghayruhoo qad jaaa'atkum bayyinatummir-Rabbikum fa-awful-kayla walmeezaana wa laa tabkhasun-naasa ashyaaa'ahum wa laa tufsidoo fil-arḍi ba'da iṣlaaḥi-haa; z̲aalikum khayrullakum in kuntum mu'mineen.

وَاِلٰى مَدْيَنَ اَخَاهُمْ شُعَيْبًا ؕ قَالَ
يٰقَوْمِ اعْبُدُوا اللّٰهَ مَا لَكُمْ مِّنْ اِلٰهٍ
غَيْرُهٗ ؕ قَدْ جَآءَتْكُمْ بَيِّنَةٌ مِّنْ رَّبِّكُمْ
فَاَوْفُوا الْكَيْلَ وَالْمِيْزَانَ وَلَا تَبْخَسُوا
النَّاسَ اَشْيَآءَهُمْ وَلَا تُفْسِدُوْا فِى
الْاَرْضِ بَعْدَ اِصْلَاحِهَا ؕ ذٰلِكُمْ خَيْرٌ
لَّكُمْ اِنْ كُنْتُمْ مُّؤْمِنِيْنَ ۝٨٥ ۚ

86. Do not ambush the believers or hinder them from every path that leads them to Allah just because you wish to make such ways seem crooked. Recall the time when you were just a few in number and Allah

86. Wa laa taq'udoo bikulli ṣiraaṭin too'idoona wa taṣud-doona 'an sabeelil-laahi man aamana bihee wa tabghoonahaa 'iwajaa; wa

وَلَا تَقْعُدُوْا بِكُلِّ صِرَاطٍ تُوْعِدُوْنَ
وَتَصُدُّوْنَ عَنْ سَبِيْلِ اللّٰهِ مَنْ
اٰمَنَ بِهٖ وَتَبْغُوْنَهَا عِوَجًا ۚ وَ

multiplied you. Consider how terrible the end of the evil-doers was!

z̲kurooo iz̲ kuntum qaleelan fakas̲-s̲arakum wanẓuroo kayfa kaana 'aaqibatul-mufsideen.

اذْكُرُوٓا إِذْ كُنْتُمْ قَلِيلًا
فَكَثَّرَكُمْ ۖ وَانْظُرُوا كَيْفَ كَانَ
عَاقِبَةُ الْمُفْسِدِينَ ﴿٨٦﴾

87. If there are some of you who believed in the Message that I have been commanded to preach and there are others who did not, exercise patience until Allah judges among us. He is the best Judge."

87. Wa in kaana ṭaaa'ifatum-minkum aamanoo billaz̲eee ursiltu bihee wa ṭaaa'ifatul-lam yu'minoo faṣbiroo ḥattaa yaḥkumal-laahu baynanaa; wa Huwa khayrul-ḥaakimeen.

وَإِنْ كَانَ طَآئِفَةٌ مِّنْكُمْ اٰمَنُوْا
بِالَّذِيْٓ أُرْسِلْتُ بِهٖ وَطَآئِفَةٌ لَّمْ
يُؤْمِنُوْا فَاصْبِرُوْا حَتّٰى يَحْكُمَ اللّٰهُ
بَيْنَنَا ۚ وَهُوَ خَيْرُ الْحٰكِمِيْنَ ﴿٨٧﴾

88. A proud group among Shuayb's people said, "We must expel you (Shuayb) and your followers from our town unless you give up your faith and live as our own people." Shuayb asked them, "Will you use force against us?

88. Qaalal-mala-ul-laz̲eenas-takbaroo min qawmihee lanukhrijannaka yaa Shu'aybu wallaz̲eena aamanoo ma'aka min qaryatinaaa aw lata'oo-dunna fee millatinaa; qaala awa law kunnaa kaariheen.

قَالَ الْمَلَاُ الَّذِيْنَ اسْتَكْبَرُوْا مِنْ
قَوْمِهٖ لَنُخْرِجَنَّكَ يٰشُعَيْبُ وَالَّذِيْنَ
اٰمَنُوْا مَعَكَ مِنْ قَرْيَتِنَآ أَوْ لَتَعُوْدُنَّ
فِيْ مِلَّتِنَا ۚ قَالَ أَوَلَوْ كُنَّا كٰرِهِيْنَ ﴿٨٨﴾

89. We would certainly be inventing falsehoods against Allah if we were to accept your way of life when Allah has already saved us from it. We do not have to accept it nor does Allah, our Lord, will it. Our Lord's knowledge covers all things. We trust in Him and ask Him to judge among us and our people, for He is the best Judge."

89. Qadif-taraynaa 'alal-laahi kaz̲iban in 'udnaa fee millatikum ba'da iz̲ najjaanal-laahu minhaa; wa maa yakoonu lanaaa an na'ooda feehaaa illaaa añy-yashaaa'allaahu Rabbunaa; wasi'a Rabbunaa kulla shay'in 'ilmaa; 'alal-laahi tawakkalnaa; Rabbanaf-taḥ baynanaa wa bayna qawminaa bilḥaqqi wa Anta khayrul-faatiḥeen.

قَدِ افْتَرَيْنَا عَلَى اللّٰهِ كَذِبًا إِنْ عُدْنَا
فِيْ مِلَّتِكُمْ بَعْدَ إِذْ نَجّٰىنَا اللّٰهُ مِنْهَا ۚ
وَمَا يَكُوْنُ لَنَآ أَنْ نَّعُوْدَ فِيْهَآ إِلَّآ
أَنْ يَّشَآءَ اللّٰهُ رَبُّنَا ۚ وَسِعَ رَبُّنَا
كُلَّ شَيْءٍ عِلْمًا ۚ عَلَى اللّٰهِ تَوَكَّلْنَا ۚ
رَبَّنَا افْتَحْ بَيْنَنَا وَبَيْنَ قَوْمِنَا بِالْحَقِّ
وَأَنْتَ خَيْرُ الْفٰتِحِيْنَ ﴿٨٩﴾

90. A group of the unbelievers among his people told the others, "If you follow Shuayb, you will certainly lose a great deal."

90. Wa qaalal-mala-ul-laz̲eena kafaroo min qawmihee la'inittaba'tum Shu'ayban innakum iz̲al-lakhaasiroon.

وَقَالَ الْمَلَاُ الَّذِيْنَ كَفَرُوْا مِنْ قَوْمِهٖ
لَئِنِ اتَّبَعْتُمْ شُعَيْبًا إِنَّكُمْ إِذًا لَّخٰسِرُوْنَ ﴿٩٠﴾

91. Suddenly, an earthquake struck them and left them motionless in their homes.

91. Fa-akhaz̲athumur-rajfatu fa-aṣbaḥoo fee daarihim jaas̲imeen.

فَأَخَذَتْهُمُ الرَّجْفَةُ فَأَصْبَحُوْا فِيْ
دَارِهِمْ جٰثِمِيْنَ ﴿٩١﴾

92. Those who called Shuayb a liar were destroyed as though they had never existed. They certainly were the ones to lose a great deal.

92. Allaz̲eena kaz̲-z̲aboo Shu'ayban ka-al-lam yaghnaw feehaa; allaz̲eena kaz̲-z̲aboo Shu'ayban kaanoo humul-khaasireen.

الَّذِيْنَ كَذَّبُوْا شُعَيْبًا كَأَنْ لَّمْ
يَغْنَوْا فِيْهَا ۚ الَّذِيْنَ كَذَّبُوْا شُعَيْبًا
كَانُوْا هُمُ الْخٰسِرِيْنَ ﴿٩٢﴾

93. He turned away from them, saying, "My people, I preached

93. Fatawallaa 'anhum wa qaala yaa qawmi laqad

فَتَوَلّٰى عَنْهُمْ وَقَالَ يٰقَوْمِ لَقَدْ

اَبَلَّغْتُكُمْ رِسٰلٰتِ رَبِّيْ وَنَصَحْتُ لَكُمْ
فَكَيْفَ اٰسٰى عَلٰى قَوْمٍ كٰفِرِيْنَ ﴿٩٣﴾ ع ٩

ablaghtukum Risaalaati Rabbee wa naṣaḥtu lakum fakayfa aasaa 'alaa qawmin kaafireen.

the Message of my Lord to you and gave you good advice. How could I be sorry for the unbelievers?"

وَمَآ اَرْسَلْنَا فِيْ قَرْيَةٍ مِّنْ نَّبِيٍّ اِلَّآ
اَخَذْنَآ اَهْلَهَا بِالْبَاْسَآءِ وَالضَّرَّآءِ
لَعَلَّهُمْ يَضَّرَّعُوْنَ ﴿٩٤﴾

94. Wa maaa arsalnaa fee qaryatim-min-Nabiyyin illaaa akhaẕnaaa ahlahaa bilba-saaa'i waḍḍarraaa'i la'allahum yaḍ-ḍarra'oon.

94. To every town where We sent a Prophet, We tested its inhabitants through distress and adversity so that perhaps they would submit themselves to Us.

ثُمَّ بَدَّلْنَا مَكَانَ السَّيِّئَةِ الْحَسَنَةَ
حَتّٰى عَفَوْا وَّقَالُوْا قَدْ مَسَّ اٰبَآءَنَا
الضَّرَّآءُ وَالسَّرَّآءُ فَاَخَذْنٰهُمْ بَغْتَةً
وَّهُمْ لَا يَشْعُرُوْنَ ﴿٩٥﴾

95. S̱umma baddalnaa makaa-nas-sayyi'atil-ḥasanata ḥattaa 'afaw wa qaaloo qad massa aabaaa'anaḍ-ḍarraaa'u wassar-raaa'u fa-akhaẕnaahum baghta-tañw-wa hum laa yash'uroon.

95. We then replaced their misfortune with well-being until they were relieved and began saying, "Our fathers had also experienced good and bad days." Suddenly, We struck them (with torment) while they were all unaware (of what was happening).

وَلَوْ اَنَّ اَهْلَ الْقُرٰٓى اٰمَنُوْا وَاتَّقَوْا
لَفَتَحْنَا عَلَيْهِمْ بَرَكٰتٍ مِّنَ السَّمَآءِ
وَالْاَرْضِ وَلٰكِنْ كَذَّبُوْا فَاَخَذْنٰهُمْ
بِمَا كَانُوْا يَكْسِبُوْنَ ﴿٩٦﴾

96. Wa law anna ahlalquraaa aamanoo wattaqaw lafataḥnaa 'alayhim barakaatim-minas-samaaa'i wal-arḍi wa laakin kaẕ-ẕaboo fa-akhaẕnaahum bimaa kaanoo yaksiboon.

96. Had the people of the towns believed (in Our revelations) and maintained piety, We would have certainly showered on them Our blessings from the sky and the earth. But they called Our revelations lies, thus Our torment struck them for their evil deeds.

اَفَاَمِنَ اَهْلُ الْقُرٰٓى اَنْ يَّاْتِيَهُمْ
بَاْسُنَا بَيَاتًا وَّهُمْ نَآئِمُوْنَ ﴿٩٧﴾

97. Afa-amina ahlul-quraaa añy-ya-tiyahum ba-sunaa bayaatañw-wa hum naaa'imoon.

97. Did the people of the towns think themselves secure from Our wrath that could strike them at night during their sleep

اَوَاَمِنَ اَهْلُ الْقُرٰٓى اَنْ يَّاْتِيَهُمْ
بَاْسُنَا ضُحًى وَّهُمْ يَلْعَبُوْنَ ﴿٩٨﴾

98. Awa amina ahlul-quraaa añy-ya-tiyahum ba-sunaa ḍuḥañw-wa hum yal'aboon.

98. or that could seize them during their busy hours of the day?

اَفَاَمِنُوْا مَكْرَ اللّٰهِ ۚ فَلَا يَاْمَنُ
مَكْرَ اللّٰهِ اِلَّا الْقَوْمُ الْخٰسِرُوْنَ ﴿٩٩﴾ ع ٢

99. Afa-aminoo makral-laah; falaa ya-manu makral-laahi illal-qawmul khaasiroon.

99. Did they consider themselves secure from the retribution of Allah? No one can have such an attitude except those who are lost.

اَوَلَمْ يَهْدِ لِلَّذِيْنَ يَرِثُوْنَ الْاَرْضَ
مِنْ بَعْدِ اَهْلِهَآ اَنْ لَّوْ نَشَآءُ اَصَبْنٰهُمْ
بِذُنُوْبِهِمْ ۚ وَنَطْبَعُ عَلٰى قُلُوْبِهِمْ
فَهُمْ لَا يَسْمَعُوْنَ ﴿١٠٠﴾

100. Awa lam yahdi lillaẕeena yariṯoonal-arḍa mim ba'di ahlihaaa-al-law nashaaa'u aṣabnaahum biẕunoobihim; wa naṭba'u 'alaa quloobihim fahum laa yasma'oon.

100. Was it not a lesson for the successors of the past generations that had We wanted, We could have punished them for their sins, sealed their hearts, and deprived them of hearing?

تِلْكَ الْقُرٰى نَقُصُّ عَلَيْكَ مِنْ
اَنْۢبَآئِهَا ۚ وَلَقَدْ جَآءَتْهُمْ رُسُلُهُمْ
بِالْبَيِّنٰتِ ۚ فَمَا كَانُوْا لِيُؤْمِنُوْا بِمَا

101. Tilkal-quraa naquṣṣu 'alayka min ambaaa'ihaa; wa laqad jaaa'athum Rusuluhum bilbayyinaati famaa kaanoo liyu'minoo bimaa

101. (Muhammad), such were the stories of the people who lived in (different) towns in the past. We had sent Our Messengers to them with (certain) miracles but

the people still did not believe in what they had rejected before. Such is how Allah seals the hearts of the unbelievers.

kaz-zaboo min qabl; kazaalika yatba'ul-laahu 'alaa quloobil-kaafireen.

كذبوا من قبل ۚ كذلك يطبع الله على قلوب الكافرين ﴿١٠١﴾

102. We did not find many among them keeping their promises. However, We did find many evil-doers among them.

102. Wa maa wajadnaa li-aksarihim min 'ahd; wa iñw-wajadnaaa aksarahum lafaasiqeen.

وما وجدنا لأكثرهم من عهد ۖ وإن وجدنا أكثرهم لفاسقين ﴿١٠٢﴾

103. After the time of those people, We sent Moses with Our miracles to Pharaoh and his people, but they too rejected Our miracles. Consider how terrible the end of the evil-doers is!

103. Summa ba'asnaa mim ba'dihim Moosaa bi-Aayaatinaaa ilaa Fir'awna wa mala'ihee fazalamoo bihaa fanzur kayfa kaana 'aaqibatul-mufsideen.

ثم بعثنا من بعدهم موسى بآياتنا إلى فرعون وملئه فظلموا بها ۖ فانظر كيف كان عاقبة المفسدين ﴿١٠٣﴾

104. Moses told the Pharaoh, "I am a Messenger from the Lord of the Universe.

104. Wa qaala Moosaa yaa Fir'awnu innee Rasoolum-mir-Rabbil-'aalameen.

وقال موسى يا فرعون إني رسول من رب العالمين ﴿١٠٤﴾

105. I must speak only what is true about Allah. I have brought you miracles from your Lord; therefore, allow the children of Israel go free."

105. Ḥaqeequn 'alaaa al-laaa aqoola 'alal-laahi illal-ḥaqq; qad ji'tukum bibayyinatim-mir-Rabbikum fa-arsil ma'iya Baneee Israaa'eel.

حقيق على أن لا أقول على الله إلا الحق ۚ قد جئتكم ببينة من ربكم فأرسل معي بني إسرائيل ﴿١٠٥﴾

106. The Pharaoh asked Moses to show his miracles if he was telling the truth.

106. Qaala in kunta ji'ta bi-Aayatin fa-ti bihaaa in kunta minaṣ-ṣaadiqeen.

قال إن كنت جئت بآية فأت بها إن كنت من الصادقين ﴿١٠٦﴾

107. So Moses threw down his staff and suddenly it turned into a real serpent.

107. Fa-alqaa 'aṣaahu fa-izaa hiya su'baanum-mubeen.

فألقى عصاه فإذا هي ثعبان مبين ﴿١٠٧﴾

108. Then he uncovered his hand and it appeared sheer white to the onlookers.

108. Wa naza'a yadahoo fa-izaa hiya bayḍaaa'u linnaaẓireen.

ونزع يده فإذا هي بيضاء للناظرين ﴿١٠٨﴾ ع

109. Some of the Pharaoh's nobles considered him to be no more than a skillful magician

109. Qaalal-mala-u min qawmi Fir'awna inna haazaa lasaaḥirun 'aleem.

قال الملأ من قوم فرعون إن هذا لساحر عليم ﴿١٠٩﴾

110. and said, "He wants to expel you from your land." They asked (others), "What is your opinion in the matter?"

110. Yureedu añy-yukhrijakum min arḍikum fama-zaa ta-muroon.

يريد أن يخرجكم من أرضكم ۖ فماذا تأمرون ﴿١١٠﴾

111. The others suggested to hold Moses and his brother off and send, to all the cities

111. Qaalooo arjih wa akhaahu wa arsil fil-madaaa'ini ḥaashireen.

قالوا أرجه وأخاه وأرسل في المدائن حاشرين ﴿١١١﴾

112. to bring together, at the Pharaoh's court, all the skillful magicians.

112. Ya-tooka bikulli saaḥirin 'aleem.

يأتوك بكل ساحر عليم ﴿١١٢﴾

113. The magicians came to the Pharaoh and said, "We must have our reward if we are to gain a victory over him (Moses)."

113. Wa jaaa'as-saḥaratu Fir-'awna qaaloo inna lanaa la-ajran in kunnaa naḥnul-ghaalibeen.

وجاء السحرة فرعون قالوا إن لنا لأجرا إن كنا نحن الغالبين ﴿١١٣﴾

114. The Pharaoh replied, "In addition to your rewards, you will become my close friends thereafter."

114. Qaala na'am wa innakum laminal-muqarrabeen.

قال نعم وإنكم لمن المقربين ﴿١١٤﴾

115. The magicians asked Moses, "Will you throw your staff first or shall we?"

115. Qaaloo yaa Moosaaa immaaa an tulqiya wa immaaa an nakoona naḥnul-mulqeen.

قَالُوا يٰمُوسٰٓى اِمَّآ اَنْ تُلْقِيَ وَاِمَّآ اَنْ نَّكُوْنَ نَحْنُ الْمُلْقِيْنَ ﴿١١٥﴾

116. He replied, "Throw yours first." Their great magic bewitched people's eyes and terrified them.

116. Qaala alqoo falammaaa alqaw saḥarooo a'yunannaasi wastarhaboohum wa jaaa'oo bisiḥrin 'aẓeem.

قَالَ اَلْقُوْا ۚ فَلَمَّآ اَلْقَوْا سَحَرُوْٓا اَعْيُنَ النَّاسِ وَاسْتَرْهَبُوْهُمْ وَجَآءُوْ بِسِحْرٍ عَظِيْمٍ ﴿١١٦﴾

117. We revealed to Moses to throw his staff, and suddenly it began to swallow up all that the magicians had (falsely) invented.

117. Wa awḥaynaaa ilaa Moosaaa an alqi 'aṣaaka fa-izaa hiya talqafu maa ya-fikoon.

وَاَوْحَيْنَآ اِلٰى مُوْسٰٓى اَنْ اَلْقِ عَصَاكَ ۚ فَاِذَا هِيَ تَلْقَفُ مَا يَاْفِكُوْنَ ﴿١١٧﴾

118. Thus the Truth prevailed and their false art was banished.

118. Fawaqa'al-ḥaqqu wa baṭala maa kaanoo ya'maloon.

فَوَقَعَ الْحَقُّ وَبَطَلَ مَا كَانُوْا يَعْمَلُوْنَ ﴿١١٨﴾

119. The magicians who were defeated on the spot and were proved to be worthless

119. Faghuliboo hunaalika wanqalaboo ṣaaghireen.

فَغُلِبُوْا هُنَالِكَ وَانْقَلَبُوْا صٰغِرِيْنَ ﴿١١٩﴾

120. threw themselves down in prostration

120. Wa ulqiyas-saḥaratu saajideen.

وَاُلْقِيَ السَّحَرَةُ سٰجِدِيْنَ ﴿١٢٠﴾

121. saying, "We declare our belief in the Lord of the Universe,

121. Qaalooo aamannaa bi-Rabbil-'aalameen.

قَالُوْٓا اٰمَنَّا بِرَبِّ الْعٰلَمِيْنَ ﴿١٢١﴾

122. the Lord of Moses and Aaron."

122. Rabbi Moosaa wa Haaroon.

رَبِّ مُوْسٰى وَهٰرُوْنَ ﴿١٢٢﴾

123. The Pharaoh said to the magicians, "You declared your belief in him (Moses) without my permission. This is a plot to throw my people out of their city. But you will soon know.

123. Qaala Fir'awnu aamantum bihee qabla an aazana lakum; inna haazaa lamakrum-makartumoohu fil-madeenati litukhrijoo minhaaa ahlahaa fasawfa ta'lamoon.

قَالَ فِرْعَوْنُ اٰمَنْتُمْ بِهٖ قَبْلَ اَنْ اٰذَنَ لَكُمْ ۚ اِنَّ هٰذَا لَمَكْرٌ مَّكَرْتُمُوْهُ فِي الْمَدِيْنَةِ لِتُخْرِجُوْا مِنْهَآ اَهْلَهَا ۚ فَسَوْفَ تَعْلَمُوْنَ ﴿١٢٣﴾

124. I will cut off your hands and feet on the alternate sides and crucify you all."

124. La-uqaṭṭi'anna aydiyakum wa arjulakum min khilaafin summa la-uṣalliban-nakum ajma'een.

لَاُقَطِّعَنَّ اَيْدِيَكُمْ وَاَرْجُلَكُمْ مِّنْ خِلَافٍ ثُمَّ لَاُصَلِّبَنَّكُمْ اَجْمَعِيْنَ ﴿١٢٤﴾

125. The magicians said, "We will certainly return to Our Lord.

125. Qaalooo innaaa ilaa Rabbinaa munqaliboon.

قَالُوْٓا اِنَّآ اِلٰى رَبِّنَا مُنْقَلِبُوْنَ ﴿١٢٥﴾

126. You only take revenge on us because we believed in the Lord when we saw His miracles. Lord, grant us patience and let us die Muslims (submitted to Allah)."

126. Wa maa tanqimu minnaaa illaaa an aamannaa bi-Aayaati Rabbinaa lammaa jaaa'atnaa; Rabbanaaa afrigh 'alaynaa ṣabrañw-wa tawaffanaa muslimeen.

وَمَا تَنْقِمُ مِنَّآ اِلَّآ اَنْ اٰمَنَّا بِاٰيٰتِ رَبِّنَا لَمَّا جَآءَتْنَا ۚ رَبَّنَآ اَفْرِغْ عَلَيْنَا صَبْرًا وَّتَوَفَّنَا مُسْلِمِيْنَ ﴿١٢٦﴾ ع ١٨

127. Certain persons of the Pharaoh's people said, "Will you allow Moses and his people destroy the land and disregard you and your gods?" The Pharaoh

127. Wa qaalal-malau min qawmi Fir'awna atazaru Moosaa wa qawmahoo liyufsidoo fil-arḍi wa yazaraka wa aalihatak; qaala

وَقَالَ الْمَلَاُ مِنْ قَوْمِ فِرْعَوْنَ اَتَذَرُ مُوْسٰى وَقَوْمَهٗ لِيُفْسِدُوْا فِي الْاَرْضِ وَيَذَرَكَ وَاٰلِهَتَكَ ۚ قَالَ

said, "We will kill their sons and leave their women alive; they are under our domination."

sanuqattilu abnaaa'ahum wa nastaḥycc nisaaa'ahum wa innaa fawqahum qaahiroon.

سَنُقَتِّلُ اَبۡنَآءَهُمۡ وَنَسۡتَحۡیٖ نِسَآءَهُمۡ ۚ
وَاِنَّا فَوۡقَهُمۡ قٰهِرُوۡنَ ﴿۱۲۷﴾

128. Moses told his people to seek help from Allah and exercise patience. The earth belongs to Allah and He has made it the heritage of whichever of His servants He chooses. The final victory is for the pious ones.

128. Qaala Moosaa liqawmi-his-ta'eenoo billaahi waṣbiroo innal-arḍa lillaahi yoorisuhaa mañy-yashaaa'u min 'ibaadihee wal'aaqibatu lilmuttaqeen.

قَالَ مُوۡسٰی لِقَوۡمِهِ اسۡتَعِیۡنُوۡا
بِاللّٰهِ وَاصۡبِرُوۡا ۚ اِنَّ الۡاَرۡضَ لِلّٰهِ ۟ۙ
یُوۡرِثُهَا مَنۡ یَّشَآءُ مِنۡ عِبَادِهٖ ؕ
وَالۡعَاقِبَةُ لِلۡمُتَّقِیۡنَ ﴿۱۲۸﴾

129. His people said, "We suffered a great deal before you came and we are still suffering even after you have come." Moses (tried to encourage them) by saying, "There is hope that your Lord will destroy your enemies and make you (their) successors in the land. So consider how you act."

129. Qaalooo oozeenaa min qabli an ta-tiyanaa wa mim ba'di maa ji'tanaa; qaala 'asaa Rabbukum añy-yuhlika 'aduwwakum wa yastakhli-fakum fil-arḍi fayanẓura kayfa ta'maloon.

قَالُوۡۤا اُوۡذِیۡنَا مِنۡ قَبۡلِ اَنۡ تَاۡتِیَنَا وَ
مِنۡۢ بَعۡدِ مَا جِئۡتَنَا ؕ قَالَ عَسٰی رَبُّکُمۡ
اَنۡ یُّهۡلِکَ عَدُوَّکُمۡ وَیَسۡتَخۡلِفَکُمۡ
فِی الۡاَرۡضِ فَیَنۡظُرَ کَیۡفَ تَعۡمَلُوۡنَ ﴿۱۲۹﴾ ع ۱۵ ۵

130. For years We afflicted Pharaoh's people with shortages in food so that perhaps they would take heed.

130. Wa laqad akhaznaaa Aala Fir'awna bissineena wa naqṣ im-minas-samaraati la'allahum yaz-zakkaroon.

وَلَقَدۡ اَخَذۡنَاۤ اٰلَ فِرۡعَوۡنَ
بِالسِّنِیۡنَ وَنَقۡصٍ مِّنَ الثَّمَرٰتِ
لَعَلَّهُمۡ یَذَّکَّرُوۡنَ ﴿۱۳۰﴾

131. But they would always ascribe their well-being to themselves and the misfortunes that they experienced to Moses and his people. Their fate is certainly in the hands of Allah but many of them do not know.

131. Fa-izaa jaaa'athumul-ḥasanatu qaaloo lanaa haazihee wa in tuṣibhum sayyi'atuñy-yaṭṭayyaroo bi Moosaa wa mam-ma'ah; alaaa innamaa ṭaaa'iruhum 'indal-laahi wa laakinna aksarahum laa ya'lamoon.

فَاِذَا جَآءَتۡهُمُ الۡحَسَنَةُ قَالُوۡا
لَنَا هٰذِهٖ ۚ وَاِنۡ تُصِبۡهُمۡ سَیِّئَةٌ
یَّطَّیَّرُوۡا بِمُوۡسٰی وَمَنۡ مَّعَهٗ ؕ اَلَاۤ
اِنَّمَا طٰٓئِرُهُمۡ عِنۡدَ اللّٰهِ وَلٰکِنَّ
اَکۡثَرَهُمۡ لَا یَعۡلَمُوۡنَ ﴿۱۳۱﴾

132. They said to Moses, "No matter what miracle you show to bewitch us, we will not believe you."

132. Wa qaaloo mahmaa ta-tinaa bihee min Aayatil-litasḥaranaa bihaa famaa naḥnu laka bimu'mineen.

وَقَالُوۡا مَهۡمَا تَاۡتِنَا بِهٖ مِنۡ اٰیَةٍ
لِّتَسۡحَرَنَا بِهَا ۙ فَمَا نَحۡنُ لَکَ
بِمُؤۡمِنِیۡنَ ﴿۱۳۲﴾

133. We sent upon them widespread calamities: floods of locusts, lice, frogs, and blood. All were distinct miracles but these criminals, all the time, remained proud.

133. Fa-arsalnaa 'alayhimuṭ-ṭoofaana waljaraada walqum-mala waḍḍafaadi'a waddama Aayaatim-mufaṣ-ṣalaatin fas-takbaroo wa kaanoo qawmam-mujrimeen.

فَاَرۡسَلۡنَا عَلَیۡهِمُ الطُّوۡفَانَ وَالۡجَرَادَ
وَالۡقُمَّلَ وَالضَّفَادِعَ وَالدَّمَ
اٰیٰتٍ مُّفَصَّلٰتٍ ۟ فَاسۡتَکۡبَرُوۡا وَ
کَانُوۡا قَوۡمًا مُّجۡرِمِیۡنَ ﴿۱۳۳﴾

134. When the torment would strike them, they would ask Moses, "Pray for us to your Lord

134. Wa lammaa waqa'a 'alayhimur-rijzu qaaloo yaa Moosa

وَلَمَّا وَقَعَ عَلَیۡهِمُ الرِّجۡزُ قَالُوۡا یٰمُوۡسَی

through your covenant with Him. If you will save us from the torment, we will, certainly, believe in you and permit you and the children of Israel to leave."

d-'u lanaa rabbaka bimaa 'ahida 'indaka la'in kashafta 'annar-rijza lanu'minanna laka wa lanursilanna ma'aka Baneee Israaa'eel.

ادْعُ لَنَا رَبَّكَ بِمَا عَهِدَ عِنْدَكَ ۚ لَئِنْ
كَشَفْتَ عَنَّا الرِّجْزَ لَنُؤْمِنَنَّ لَكَ
وَلَنُرْسِلَنَّ مَعَكَ بَنِي إِسْرَائِيلَ ﴿١٣٤﴾

135. But when We relieved them from the torment for a given time, they again broke their promise.

135. Falammaa kashafnaa 'anhumur-rijza ilaaa ajalin hum baalighoohu i<u>z</u>aa hum yanku<u>s</u>oon.

فَلَمَّا كَشَفْنَا عَنْهُمُ الرِّجْزَ إِلَىٰ أَجَلٍ
هُمْ بَالِغُوهُ إِذَا هُمْ يَنْكُثُونَ ﴿١٣٥﴾

136. We took revenge on them for their rejecting Our miracles, by drowning them in the sea, but they were not aware of (reality).

136. Fantaqamnaa minhum fa-aghraqnaahum fil-yammi bi-annahum kaz-zaboo bi-Aayaatinaa wa kaanoo 'anhaa ghaafileen.

فَانْتَقَمْنَا مِنْهُمْ فَأَغْرَقْنَاهُمْ فِي الْيَمِّ
بِأَنَّهُمْ كَذَّبُوا بِآيَاتِنَا وَكَانُوا
عَنْهَا غَافِلِينَ ﴿١٣٦﴾

137. We gave the suppressed people the blessed eastern and western regions as their inheritance. Thus, the promises of your Lord to the children of Israel all came true because of the patience which they exercised. He destroyed all the establishments of the Pharaoh and his people.

137. Wa awrasnal-qawmal-lazeena kaanoo yustaḍ'afoona mashaariqal-arḍi wa maghaari-bahal-latee baaraknaa feehaa wa tammat Kalimatu Rabbikal-ḥusnaa 'alaa Baneee Israaa'eela bimaa ṣabaroo wa dammarnaa maa kaana yaṣna'u Fir'awnu wa qawmuhoo wa maa kaanoo ya'rishoon.

وَأَوْرَثْنَا الْقَوْمَ الَّذِينَ كَانُوا
يُسْتَضْعَفُونَ مَشَارِقَ الْأَرْضِ وَ
مَغَارِبَهَا الَّتِي بَارَكْنَا فِيهَا ۖ
وَتَمَّتْ كَلِمَتُ رَبِّكَ الْحُسْنَىٰ عَلَىٰ
بَنِي إِسْرَائِيلَ بِمَا صَبَرُوا ۖ وَ
دَمَّرْنَا مَا كَانَ يَصْنَعُ فِرْعَوْنُ
وَقَوْمُهُ وَمَا كَانُوا يَعْرِشُونَ ﴿١٣٧﴾

138. We helped the children of Israel to cross the sea. They came to a people who worshipped idols. The Israelites demanded that Moses make gods for them like those of the idol-worshippers. Moses told them, "You are an ignorant people."

138. Wa jaawaznaa bi-Baneee Israaa'eelal-baḥra fa-ataw 'alaa qawmiñy-ya'kufoona 'alaaa aṣnaamil-lahum; qaaloo yaa Moosaj'al-lanaaa ilaahan kamaa lahum aalihah; qaala innakum qawmun tajhaloon.

وَجَاوَزْنَا بِبَنِي إِسْرَائِيلَ الْبَحْرَ
فَأَتَوْا عَلَىٰ قَوْمٍ يَعْكُفُونَ عَلَىٰ
أَصْنَامٍ لَهُمْ ۚ قَالُوا يَا مُوسَى اجْعَلْ
لَنَا إِلَٰهًا كَمَا لَهُمْ آلِهَةٌ ۚ قَالَ
إِنَّكُمْ قَوْمٌ تَجْهَلُونَ ﴿١٣٨﴾

139. What these people worship is doomed to be destroyed and their deeds are based on falsehood.

139. Inna haaa'ulaaa'i mutab-barum-maa hum feehi wa baaṭilum-maa kaanoo ya'ma-loon.

إِنَّ هَٰؤُلَاءِ مُتَبَّرٌ مَا هُمْ فِيهِ وَ
بَاطِلٌ مَا كَانُوا يَعْمَلُونَ ﴿١٣٩﴾

140. "Should I choose for you a lord other than Allah, who has favored you above all other people (of your time)?" said Moses with disappointment.

140. Qaala aghayral-laahi abgheekum ilaahañw-wa Huwa faḍḍalakum 'alal 'aalameen.

قَالَ أَغَيْرَ اللَّهِ أَبْغِيكُمْ إِلَٰهًا وَ
هُوَ فَضَّلَكُمْ عَلَى الْعَالَمِينَ ﴿١٤٠﴾

141. "Children of Israel, when I saved you from the Pharaoh and his people who made you suffer

141. Wa i<u>z</u> anjaynaakum min Aali-Fir'awna yasoomoo-nakum sooo'al-'a<u>z</u>aab; yuqat-tiloona

وَإِذْ أَنْجَيْنَاكُمْ مِنْ آلِ فِرْعَوْنَ
يَسُومُونَكُمْ سُوءَ الْعَذَابِ ۚ يُقَتِّلُونَ

the worst kinds of torment, killing your sons and keeping your women alive, it was a great trial for you from your Lord."

142. We told Moses to stay with Us for thirty nights (in the mountains) but added ten nights more, so his appointment with his Lord came to an end after forty nights. Moses had appointed his brother Aaron as his deputy among his people during his absence, saying, "Try to reform them and do not follow the way of the evil-doers."

143. During the appointment, the Lord spoke to Moses. He asked the Lord to show Himself so that he could look at Him. The Lord replied, "You can never see Me. But look at the mountain. If the mountain remains firm only then will you see Me." When the Lord manifested His Glory to the mountain, He turned it into dust and Moses fell down upon his face senseless. After regaining his senses, Moses said, "Lord, You are all Holy. I repent for what I asked you to do and I am the first to believe in You."

144. The Lord said to Moses, "I have given you distinction above the people by speaking to you and giving you My Message. Receive what I have given to you and give thanks."

145. We wrote advice and laws for him on Tablets about all kinds of things, saying, "Follow them determinately and command your people to follow the good advice therein, and I will show you the dwellings of the evil-doers."

146. We will deprive those who are wrongly proud in the land of the blessing of revelations. Even if they were to see all kinds of miracles, they would not have faith; or if they were to see the

abnaaa'akum wa yastaḥyoona nisaaa'akum; wa fee zaalikum balaaa'um-mir-Rabbikum 'aẓeem.

142. Wa waa'adnaa Moosaa salaaseena laylatañw-wa atmamnaahaa bi'ashrin fatamma meeqaatu Rabbiheee arba'eena laylah; wa qaala Moosaa li-akheehi Haaroo-nakh-lufnee fee qawmee wa aṣliḥ wa laa tattabi' sabeelal-mufsideen.

143. Wa lammaa jaaa'a Moosaa limeeqaatinaa wa kallamahoo Rabbuhoo qaala Rabbi arineee anẓur ilayk; qaala lan taraanee wa laakininẓur ilal-jabali fa-inistaqarra makaanahoo fasawfa taraanee; falammaa tajallaa Rabbuhoo liljabali ja'alahoo dakkañw-wa kharra Moosaa ṣa'iqaa; falammaaa afaaqa qaala Subḥaanaka tubtu ilayka wa ana awwalul-mu'mineen.

144. Qaala yaa Moosaaa inniṣ-ṭafaytuka 'alan-naasi bi-Risaalaatee wa bi-Kalaamee fakhuz maaa aataytuka wa kum-minash-shaakireen.

145. Wa katabnaa lahoo fil-alwaaḥi min kulli shay'im-maw'iẓatañw-wa tafṣeelal-likulli shay'in fakhuzhaa biquwwatiñw-wa-mur qawmaka ya-khuzoo bi-aḥsanihaa; sa-ooreekum daaral-faasiqeen.

146. Sa-aṣrifu 'an Aayaatiyal-lazeena yatakabbaroona fil-arḍi bighayril-ḥaqq; wa iñy-yaraw kulla Aayatil-laa yu'minoo bihaa

أَبْنَآءَكُمْ وَيَسْتَحْيُونَ نِسَآءَكُمْ ۚ وَ
فِى ذَٰلِكُم بَلَآءٌ مِّن رَّبِّكُمْ عَظِيمٌ ﴿١٤١﴾ ع
وَوَٰعَدْنَا مُوسَىٰ ثَلَٰثِينَ لَيْلَةً وَ
أَتْمَمْنَٰهَا بِعَشْرٍ فَتَمَّ مِيقَٰتُ رَبِّهِۦٓ
أَرْبَعِينَ لَيْلَةً ۚ وَقَالَ مُوسَىٰ لِأَخِيهِ
هَٰرُونَ ٱخْلُفْنِى فِى قَوْمِى وَأَصْلِحْ
وَلَا تَتَّبِعْ سَبِيلَ ٱلْمُفْسِدِينَ ﴿١٤٢﴾
وَلَمَّا جَآءَ مُوسَىٰ لِمِيقَٰتِنَا وَ
كَلَّمَهُۥ رَبُّهُۥ قَالَ رَبِّ أَرِنِىٓ أَنظُرْ
إِلَيْكَ ۚ قَالَ لَن تَرَىٰنِى وَلَٰكِنِ ٱنظُرْ
إِلَى ٱلْجَبَلِ فَإِنِ ٱسْتَقَرَّ مَكَانَهُۥ
فَسَوْفَ تَرَىٰنِى ۚ فَلَمَّا تَجَلَّىٰ رَبُّهُۥ لِلْجَبَلِ
جَعَلَهُۥ دَكًّا وَخَرَّ مُوسَىٰ صَعِقًا ۚ
فَلَمَّآ أَفَاقَ قَالَ سُبْحَٰنَكَ تُبْتُ
إِلَيْكَ وَأَنَا۠ أَوَّلُ ٱلْمُؤْمِنِينَ ﴿١٤٣﴾
قَالَ يَٰمُوسَىٰٓ إِنِّى ٱصْطَفَيْتُكَ عَلَى
ٱلنَّاسِ بِرِسَٰلَٰتِى وَبِكَلَٰمِى فَخُذْ
مَآ ءَاتَيْتُكَ وَكُن مِّنَ ٱلشَّٰكِرِينَ ﴿١٤٤﴾
وَكَتَبْنَا لَهُۥ فِى ٱلْأَلْوَاحِ مِن كُلِّ
شَىْءٍ مَّوْعِظَةً وَتَفْصِيلًا لِّكُلِّ
شَىْءٍ فَخُذْهَا بِقُوَّةٍ وَأْمُرْ قَوْمَكَ
يَأْخُذُوا۟ بِأَحْسَنِهَا ۚ سَأُو۟رِيكُمْ
دَارَ ٱلْفَٰسِقِينَ ﴿١٤٥﴾
سَأَصْرِفُ عَنْ ءَايَٰتِىَ ٱلَّذِينَ
يَتَكَبَّرُونَ فِى ٱلْأَرْضِ بِغَيْرِ ٱلْحَقِّ
وَإِن يَرَوْا۟ كُلَّ ءَايَةٍ لَّا يُؤْمِنُوا۟ بِهَا ۚ

right path, they would not follow it. They would follow the rebellious way if they were to find one; in their ignorance, they have called Our revelations mere lies.

147. The deeds of those who have called Our revelations and belief in the Day of Judgment mere lies, will be turned devoid of all virtue. Can they expect to receive a reward for their deeds other than that which is the result of their deeds?

148. In Moses' absence, his people manufactured a hollow sounding calf out of their ornaments. Did they not see that it could not speak to them or provide them with any guidance? What they gained was injustice.

149. When they found that they had believed in the wrong thing, they regretfully said, "If our Lord did not have mercy on us and forgive us, we would certainly be lost."

150. When Moses returned to his people with anger and sorrow, he said, "What you have done in my absence is certainly evil. Why were you hasty about the commandments of your Lord?" He threw away the Tablets (which contained the commandments of Allah), grabbed his brother, by his head and started to pull him to himself.

His brother begged him, saying, "Son of my mother, the people suppressed me and almost killed me. Do not humiliate me before the enemies or call me unjust."

151. Moses prayed, "Lord, forgive me and my brother and admit us into Your mercy; you are the most Merciful."

152. (The Lord said), "Those who worshipped the calf will be

wa iñy-yaraw sabeelar-rushdi laa yattakhizoohu sabeelaa; wa iñy-yaraw sabeelal-ghayyi yattakhizoohu sabeelaa; zaalika bi-annahum kaz-zaboo bi-Aayaatinaa wa kaanoo 'anhaa ghaafileen.

147. Wallazeena kaz-zaboo bi-Aayaatinaa wa liqaaa'il-Aakhirati habitat a'maaluhum; hal yujzawna illaa maa kaanoo ya'maloon.

148. Wattakhaza qawmu Moosaa mim ba'dihee min huliyyihim 'ijlan jasadal-lahoo khuwaar; alam yaraw annahoo laa yukallimuhum wa laa yahdeehim sabeelaa; ittakhazoohu wa kaanoo zaalimeen.

149. Wa lammaa suqita fee-aydeehim wa ra-aw annahum qad dalloo qaaloo la'il-lam yarhamnaa Rabbunaa wa yaghfir lanaa lanakoonanna minal-khaasireen.

150. Wa lammaa raja'a Moosaaa ilaa qawmihee ghadbaana asifan qaala bi'samaa khalaftumoonee mim ba'deee a'ajiltum amra Rabbikum wa alqal-alwaaha wa akhaza bira-si akheehi yajurruhooo ilayh; qaalab-na-umma innal-qawmas tad'afoonee wa kaadoo yaqtuloonanee; falaa tushmit biyal-a'daaa'a wa laa taj'alnee ma'al-qawmiz-zaalimeen.

151. Qaala Rabbigh-fir lee wa li-akhee wa adkhilnaa fee rahmatika wa Anta arhamur-raahimeen.

152 Innal-lazeenat-takhazul-'ijla sayanaaluhum

وَإِنْ يَّرَوْا سَبِيْلَ الرُّشْدِ لَا يَتَّخِذُوْهُ
سَبِيْلًا ۚ وَإِنْ يَّرَوْا سَبِيْلَ الْغَيِّ
يَتَّخِذُوْهُ سَبِيْلًا ۚ ذٰلِكَ بِأَنَّهُمْ كَذَّبُوْا
بِاٰيٰتِنَا وَكَانُوْا عَنْهَا غٰفِلِيْنَ ﴿١٤٦﴾
وَالَّذِيْنَ كَذَّبُوْا بِاٰيٰتِنَا وَلِقَآءِ
الْاٰخِرَةِ حَبِطَتْ أَعْمَالُهُمْ ۚ هَلْ
يُجْزَوْنَ إِلَّا مَا كَانُوْا يَعْمَلُوْنَ ﴿١٤٧﴾ ع ١٧ / ٧
وَاتَّخَذَ قَوْمُ مُوْسٰى مِنْ بَعْدِهٖ مِنْ
حُلِيِّهِمْ عِجْلًا جَسَدًا لَّهٗ خُوَارٌ ۚ أَلَمْ
يَرَوْا أَنَّهٗ لَا يُكَلِّمُهُمْ وَلَا يَهْدِيْهِمْ وقف لازم
سَبِيْلًا ۘ اِتَّخَذُوْهُ وَكَانُوْا ظٰلِمِيْنَ ﴿١٤٨﴾
وَلَمَّا سُقِطَ فِيْۤ أَيْدِيْهِمْ وَرَأَوْا أَنَّهُمْ
قَدْ ضَلُّوْا ۙ قَالُوْا لَئِنْ لَّمْ يَرْحَمْنَا رَبُّنَا
وَيَغْفِرْ لَنَا لَنَكُوْنَنَّ مِنَ الْخٰسِرِيْنَ ﴿١٤٩﴾
وَلَمَّا رَجَعَ مُوْسٰۤى إِلٰى قَوْمِهٖ غَضْبَانَ
أَسِفًا ۙ قَالَ بِئْسَمَا خَلَفْتُمُوْنِيْ مِنْ
بَعْدِيْ ۚ أَعَجِلْتُمْ أَمْرَ رَبِّكُمْ ۚ وَأَلْقَى
الْأَلْوَاحَ وَأَخَذَ بِرَأْسِ أَخِيْهِ يَجُرُّهٗۤ
إِلَيْهِ ۚ قَالَ ابْنَ أُمَّ إِنَّ الْقَوْمَ
اسْتَضْعَفُوْنِيْ وَكَادُوْا يَقْتُلُوْنَنِيْ ۖ
فَلَا تُشْمِتْ بِيَ الْأَعْدَآءَ وَلَا تَجْعَلْنِيْ
مَعَ الْقَوْمِ الظّٰلِمِيْنَ ﴿١٥٠﴾
قَالَ رَبِّ اغْفِرْ لِيْ وَلِأَخِيْ وَأَدْخِلْنَا
فِيْ رَحْمَتِكَ ۖ وَأَنْتَ أَرْحَمُ
الرّٰحِمِيْنَ ﴿١٥١﴾ ع ١٨ / ٨
إِنَّ الَّذِيْنَ اتَّخَذُوا الْعِجْلَ سَيَنَالُهُمْ

afflicted by the wrath of their Lord and disgraced in their worldly life. Thus will We recompense those who invent falsehood.

ghaḍabum-mir-Rabbihim wa z̲illatun fil-ḥayaatid-dunyaa; wa kaz̲aalika najzil-muftareen.

غَضَبٌ مِّن رَّبِّهِمْ وَذِلَّةٌ فِي
الْحَيٰوةِ الدُّنْيَا ۚ وَكَذٰلِكَ نَجْزِي
الْمُفْتَرِينَ ﴿١٥٢﴾

153. To those who commit bad deeds, but then repent and believe (in Allah), Your Lord will certainly be All-forgiving and All-merciful."

153. Wallaz̲eena 'amilus-sayyi-aati s̲umma taaboo mim ba'dihaa wa aamanooo inna Rabbaka mim ba'dihaa laghafoorur-Raḥeem.

وَالَّذِينَ عَمِلُوا السَّيِّئَاتِ ثُمَّ تَابُوا مِن
بَعْدِهَا وَآمَنُوا إِنَّ رَبَّكَ مِن
بَعْدِهَا لَغَفُورٌ رَّحِيمٌ ﴿١٥٣﴾

154. When Moses' anger calmed down, he collected the Tablets. On one of them was written, "Allah's mercy and guidance are for those who have fear of Him."

154. Wa lammaa sakata 'am-Moosal-ghaḍabu akhaz̲aḷ al-waaḥa wa fee nuskhatihaa hudañw-wa raḥmatul-lillaz̲eena hum li-Rabbihim yarhaboon.

وَلَمَّا سَكَتَ عَن مُّوسَى الْغَضَبُ
أَخَذَ الْأَلْوَاحَ ۖ وَفِي نُسْخَتِهَا
هُدًى وَرَحْمَةٌ لِّلَّذِينَ هُمْ لِرَبِّهِمْ
يَرْهَبُونَ ﴿١٥٤﴾

155. Moses selected seventy men from his people to attend Our appointment. (In Our presence). When an earthquake jolted them to death, Moses said, "Lord, had You wanted to destroy them, why did You not destroy them and me before? Are You destroying us for what the fools among us have done? This (destruction) is only a trial through which You cause some to go astray and guide others. You are our Guardian. Forgive us and have mercy on us; You are the best of those who forgive."

155. Wakhtaara Moosaa qawmahoo sab'eena rajulal-limeeqaatinaa falammaaa akha-z̲athumur-rajfatu qaala Rabbi law shi'ta ahlaktahum min qablu wa iyyaaya atuhlikunaa bimaa fa'alas-sufahaaa'u minnaa in hiya illaa fitnatuka tuḍillu bihaa man tashaaa'u wa tahdee man tashaaa'u Anta waliyyunaa faghfir lanaa warḥamnaa wa Anta khayrul-ghaafireen.

وَاخْتَارَ مُوسَىٰ قَوْمَهُ سَبْعِينَ رَجُلًا
لِّمِيقَاتِنَا ۖ فَلَمَّا أَخَذَتْهُمُ الرَّجْفَةُ
قَالَ رَبِّ لَوْ شِئْتَ أَهْلَكْتَهُم
مِّن قَبْلُ وَإِيَّايَ ۖ أَتُهْلِكُنَا بِمَا
فَعَلَ السُّفَهَاءُ مِنَّا ۖ إِنْ هِيَ إِلَّا
فِتْنَتُكَ تُضِلُّ بِهَا مَن تَشَاءُ
وَتَهْدِي مَن تَشَاءُ ۖ أَنتَ وَلِيُّنَا
فَاغْفِرْ لَنَا وَارْحَمْنَا ۖ وَأَنتَ خَيْرُ
الْغَافِرِينَ ﴿١٥٥﴾

156. "Grant us well-being in this life and in the life hereafter, for we have turned ourselves to You." The Lord replied, "My torment afflicts only those whom I want to punish, but My mercy encompasses all things. I shall grant mercy to those who maintain piety, pay their religious tax, and have faith in Our revelations."

156. Waktub lanaa fee haaz̲i-hid-dunyaa ḥasanatañw-wa fil-Aakhirati innaa hudnaaa ilayk; qaala 'az̲aabeee uṣeebu bihee man ashaaa'u wa raḥmatee wasi'at kulla shay'; fasa-aktubuhaa lillaz̲eena yatta-qoona wa yu'toonaz-Zakaata wallaz̲eena hum bi-Aayaatinaa yu'minoon.

وَاكْتُبْ لَنَا فِي هَٰذِهِ الدُّنْيَا حَسَنَةً
وَفِي الْآخِرَةِ إِنَّا هُدْنَا إِلَيْكَ ۚ قَالَ
عَذَابِي أُصِيبُ بِهِ مَنْ أَشَاءُ ۖ وَرَحْمَتِي
وَسِعَتْ كُلَّ شَيْءٍ ۚ فَسَأَكْتُبُهَا
لِلَّذِينَ يَتَّقُونَ وَيُؤْتُونَ الزَّكَاةَ
وَالَّذِينَ هُم بِآيَاتِنَا يُؤْمِنُونَ ﴿١٥٦﴾

157. There are those who follow the Messenger, the illiterate

157. Allaz̲eena yattabi'oonar-Rasoolan-Nabiyyal

الَّذِينَ يَتَّبِعُونَ الرَّسُولَ النَّبِيَّ

Prophet, (not conventionally educated), whose description they find written in the Torah and the Gospel. He (the Messenger) enjoins them to do good and forbids them to do all that is unlawful, makes lawful for them all that is pure and unlawful all that is filthy, and removes their burdens and the entanglements in which they are involved. Those who believe in him, honor and help him, and follow the light which is sent down to him will have everlasting happiness.

Ummiyyal-lazee yajidoonahoo maktooban 'indahum fit-Tawraati wal-Injeeeli ya-muruhum bilma'roofi wa yanhaahum 'anil-munkari wa yuḥillu lahumuṭ-ṭayyibaati wa yuḥarrimu 'alayhimul-kha-baaa'isa wa yaḍa'u 'anhum iṣrahum wal-aghlaalal-latee kaanat 'alayhim; fallazeena aamanoo bihee wa 'azzaroohu wa naṣaroohu wattaba'un-nooral-lazeee unzila ma'ahooo ulaaa'ika humul-mufliḥoon.

الْاُمِّيَّ الَّذِيْ يَجِدُوْنَهٗ مَكْتُوْبًا
عِنْدَهُمْ فِي التَّوْرٰىةِ وَالْاِنْجِيْلِ ز
يَاْمُرُهُمْ بِالْمَعْرُوْفِ وَيَنْهٰىهُمْ عَنِ
الْمُنْكَرِ وَيُحِلُّ لَهُمُ الطَّيِّبٰتِ وَيُحَرِّمُ
عَلَيْهِمُ الْخَبٰٓئِثَ وَيَضَعُ عَنْهُمْ
اِصْرَهُمْ وَالْاَغْلٰلَ الَّتِيْ كَانَتْ عَلَيْهِمْ ط
فَالَّذِيْنَ اٰمَنُوْا بِهٖ وَعَزَّرُوْهُ
وَنَصَرُوْهُ وَاتَّبَعُوا النُّوْرَ الَّذِيْٓ
اُنْزِلَ مَعَهٗٓ اُولٰٓئِكَ هُمُ الْمُفْلِحُوْنَ ﴿١٥٧﴾ ع

158. (Muhammad), tell them, "People, I have come to you all as the Messenger of Allah, to whom the Kingdom of the heavens and the earth belongs. There is no Ilah (one deserving to be worshipped) but He. In His hands are life and death. Have faith in Allah and His Messenger, the unlettered Prophet, who believes in Allah and His words. Follow him so that perhaps you will have guidance."

158. Qul yaaa ayyuhan-naasu innee Rasoolul-laahi ilaykum jamee'an allazee lahoo mulkus-samaawaati wal-arḍi laaa ilaaha illaa huwa yuḥyee wa yumeetu fa-aaminoo billaahi wa Rasoolihin-Nabiyyil-Ummiy-yil-lazee yu'minu billaahi wa Kalimaatihee wattabi'oohu la'allakum tahtadoon.

قُلْ يٰٓاَيُّهَا النَّاسُ اِنِّيْ رَسُوْلُ اللّٰهِ
اِلَيْكُمْ جَمِيْعَا الَّذِيْ لَهٗ مُلْكُ
السَّمٰوٰتِ وَالْاَرْضِ ج لَآ اِلٰهَ اِلَّا
هُوَ يُحْيٖ وَيُمِيْتُ ص فَاٰمِنُوْا بِاللّٰهِ
وَرَسُوْلِهِ النَّبِيِّ الْاُمِّيِّ الَّذِيْ يُؤْمِنُ
بِاللّٰهِ وَكَلِمٰتِهٖ وَاتَّبِعُوْهُ لَعَلَّكُمْ
تَهْتَدُوْنَ ﴿١٥٨﴾

159. Among the people of Moses are some whose guidance and Judgment are based on the Truth.

159. Wa min qawmi Moosaaa ummatuñy-yahdoona bil-ḥaqqi wa bihee ya'diloon.

وَمِنْ قَوْمِ مُوْسٰٓى اُمَّةٌ يَّهْدُوْنَ
بِالْحَقِّ وَبِهٖ يَعْدِلُوْنَ ﴿١٥٩﴾

160. We divided the descendants of Israel into twelve tribes and told Moses to strike the rock with his staff to let twelve fountains gush out therefrom; his people had asked him to supply them with water. The twelve flowing springs were divided among them (a spring for each tribe) and each tribe knew its drinking place well. We provided them with shade from the clouds, sent down manna and quails to them for food, and told them to eat the pure things which We had given them. They did not do injustice to Us but

160. Wa qaṭṭa'naahumus-natay 'ashrata asbaaṭan umamaa; wa awḥaynaaa ilaa Moosaaa izis-tasqaahu qawmuhooo aniḍ-rib bi'aṣaakal-ḥajara fambajasat minhus-nataa 'ashrata 'aynaa; qad 'alima kullu unaasim-mashrabahum; wa ẓallalnaa 'alayhimul-ghamaama wa anzalnaa 'alayhimul-Manna was-Salwaa kuloo min ṭayyi-baati maa razaqnaakum; wa maa ẓalamoonaa

وَقَطَّعْنٰهُمُ اثْنَتَيْ عَشْرَةَ اَسْبَاطًا اُمَمًا ط
وَاَوْحَيْنَآ اِلٰى مُوْسٰٓى اِذِ اسْتَسْقٰىهُ
قَوْمُهٗٓ اَنِ اضْرِبْ بِّعَصَاكَ الْحَجَرَ ج
فَانْۢبَجَسَتْ مِنْهُ اثْنَتَا عَشْرَةَ
عَيْنًا ط قَدْ عَلِمَ كُلُّ اُنَاسٍ مَّشْرَبَهُمْ ط
وَظَلَّلْنَا عَلَيْهِمُ الْغَمَامَ وَاَنْزَلْنَا
عَلَيْهِمُ الْمَنَّ وَالسَّلْوٰى ط كُلُوْا مِنْ
طَيِّبٰتِ مَا رَزَقْنٰكُمْ ط وَمَا ظَلَمُوْنَا

they wronged themselves.

161. When they were told, "Settle down in this town, eat as you wish, seek forgiveness and enter the gate prostrating yourselves (in obedience to the Lord) and We will forgive you your sins and increase the reward of the righteous people,

162. the unjust among them changed the words which they were told to say (in the prayer). Therefore, We sent upon them torment from the sky for their wrong deeds.

163. (Muhammad), ask them about the (people of the) towns on the seashore. They had transgressed by catching fish on the Sabbath. Each Sabbath the fish came openly within their reach but not so on other days. Thus, We were testing them because of their evil deeds.

164. When a group of them questioned another group, saying, "Why do you preach to those whom Allah has decided to destroy or punish by a severe torment?" they replied, "We preach to them for we are responsible in the sight of your Lord and so that perhaps they may have fear of Allah."

165. When they (the unjust people) forgot what was preached to them, We saved the preachers from evil and afflicted the unjust for their evil deeds, with a dreadful torment.

166. When they crossed the limit of prohibition, We made them turn into detested apes.

167. (Muhammad), consider, when your Lord declared to the (Israelites) His decision to raise a people above them who would make them suffer the worst kinds

wa laakin kaanooo anfusahum yaẓlimoon.

161. Wa-iz̲ qeela lahumuskunoo haaz̲ihil-qaryata wa kuloo minhaa ḥays̲u shi'tum wa qooloo ḥiṭṭatuñw-wad-khulul-baaba sujjadan naghfir lakum khaṭeee'aatikum; sanazeedul muḥsineen.

162. Fabaddalal-laz̲eena ẓalamoo minhum qawlan ghayral-laz̲ee qeela lahum fa-arsalnaa 'alayhim rijzam-minas-samaaa'i bimaa kaanoo yaẓlimoon.

163. Was'alhum 'anil-qaryatil-latee kaanat ḥaaḍiratal-baḥr; iz̲ ya'doona fis-Sabti iz̲ ta-teehim ḥeetaanuhum yawma Sabtihim shurra'añw-wa yawma laa yasbitoona laa ta-teehim; kaz̲aalika nabloohum bimaa kaanoo yafsuqoon.

164. Wa iz̲ qaalat ummatum-minhum lima ta'iẓoona qaw-ma-nil-laahu muhlikuhum aw mu'az̲-z̲ibuhum 'az̲aaban shadeedan qaaloo ma'z̲iratan ilaa Rabbikum wa la'allahum yattaqoon.

165. Falammaa nasoo maa z̲ukkiroo biheee anjaynal-laz̲eena yanhawna 'anis-sooo'i wa akhaz̲nal-laz̲eena ẓalamoo bi'az̲aabim ba'eesim bimaa kaanoo yafsuqoon.

166. Falammaa 'ataw 'ammaa nuhoo 'anhu qulnaa lahum koonoo qiradatan khaasi'een.

167. Wa iz̲ ta-az̲-z̲ana Rabbuka layab'as̲anna 'alayhim ilaa Yawmil Qiyaamati mañy-yasoomuhum

وَلٰكِن كَانُوٓا أَنفُسَهُمۡ يَظۡلِمُونَ ﴿١٦٠﴾
وَإِذۡ قِيلَ لَهُمُ ٱسۡكُنُوا هٰذِهِ ٱلۡقَرۡيَةَ
وَكُلُوا مِنۡهَا حَيۡثُ شِئۡتُمۡ وَقُولُوا
حِطَّةٌ وَٱدۡخُلُوا ٱلۡبَابَ سُجَّدًا نَّغۡفِرۡ لَكُمۡ
خَطِيٓـَٔـٰتِكُمۡ سَنَزِيدُ ٱلۡمُحۡسِنِينَ ﴿١٦١﴾
فَبَدَّلَ ٱلَّذِينَ ظَلَمُوا مِنۡهُمۡ قَوۡلًا غَيۡرَ
ٱلَّذِي قِيلَ لَهُمۡ فَأَرۡسَلۡنَا عَلَيۡهِمۡ رِجۡزًا
مِّنَ ٱلسَّمَآءِ بِمَا كَانُوا يَظۡلِمُونَ ﴿١٦٢﴾
وَسۡـَٔلۡهُمۡ عَنِ ٱلۡقَرۡيَةِ ٱلَّتِي كَانَتۡ
حَاضِرَةَ ٱلۡبَحۡرِ إِذۡ يَعۡدُونَ فِي
ٱلسَّبۡتِ إِذۡ تَأۡتِيهِمۡ حِيتَانُهُمۡ يَوۡمَ
سَبۡتِهِمۡ شُرَّعًا وَيَوۡمَ لَا يَسۡبِتُونَ
لَا تَأۡتِيهِمۡ كَذٰلِكَ نَبۡلُوهُم
بِمَا كَانُوا يَفۡسُقُونَ ﴿١٦٣﴾
وَإِذۡ قَالَتۡ أُمَّةٌ مِّنۡهُمۡ لِمَ تَعِظُونَ
قَوۡمًا ٱللَّهُ مُهۡلِكُهُمۡ أَوۡ مُعَذِّبُهُمۡ
عَذَابًا شَدِيدًا قَالُوا مَعۡذِرَةً إِلَىٰ
رَبِّكُمۡ وَلَعَلَّهُمۡ يَتَّقُونَ ﴿١٦٤﴾
فَلَمَّا نَسُوا مَا ذُكِّرُوا بِهِۦٓ أَنجَيۡنَا
ٱلَّذِينَ يَنۡهَوۡنَ عَنِ ٱلسُّوٓءِ وَأَخَذۡنَا
ٱلَّذِينَ ظَلَمُوا بِعَذَابٍ بَـِٔيسٍ
بِمَا كَانُوا يَفۡسُقُونَ ﴿١٦٥﴾
فَلَمَّا عَتَوۡا عَن مَّا نُهُوا عَنۡهُ قُلۡنَا
لَهُمۡ كُونُوا قِرَدَةً خَٰسِـِٔينَ ﴿١٦٦﴾
وَإِذۡ تَأَذَّنَ رَبُّكَ لَيَبۡعَثَنَّ عَلَيۡهِمۡ
إِلَىٰ يَوۡمِ ٱلۡقِيَٰمَةِ مَن يَسُومُهُمۡ

وقف لازم

نصف القرآن عند المتأخرين

of torments until the Day of Judgment. Certainly your Lord's retribution is swift. He is All-forgiving and All-merciful.

168. We divided them into nations on the earth; some are righteous and others are not. We tested them with well-being and hardship so that they might return (to the right path).

169. Their descendants who inherited the Book gained (by bribery only) worthless things from the worldly life, saying, "We shall be forgiven (for what we have done)." They would have even doubled such gains if they could have received more. Was a covenant (with Allah) not made in the Book not to speak anything other than the Truth about Allah and to study its contents well? The life hereafter is much better for the pious ones. Will you not then think?

170. Those who devote themselves to the teachings of the Book and are steadfast in prayer (should know that) the reward of those who reform themselves will not be lost.

171. When We raised the mountain above them as if it were a sunshade, they thought it was about to fall upon them. We told them, "Hold firmly to what We have given to you and follow its guidance so that, perhaps, you become pious (people)."

172. (There was a time) when your Lord took from the backs of the offspring of Adam, before their birth, their descendants and made them to testify against their own souls and asked, "Am I not your Lord?" All of them testified and bore witness to their testimony that on the Day of Judgment they will not say, "We were not aware of this (fact),"

sooo'al-'azaab; inna Rabbaka lasaree'ul-'iqaab; wa innahoo la-Ghafoorur-Raḥeem.

168. Wa qaṭṭa'naahum fil-arḍi umamaa; minhumuṣ-ṣaaliḥoona wa minhum doona zaalika wa balawnaahum bilḥasanaati wassayyi-aati la'allahum yarji'oon.

169. Fakhalafa mim ba'dihim khalfuñw-warisul-Kitaaba ya-khuzoona 'araḍa haazal-adnaa wa yaqooloona sayughfaru lanaa wa iñy-ya-tihim 'araḍum-misluhoo ya-khuzooh; alam yu'khaz 'alayhim meesaaqul-Kitaabi al-laa yaqooloo 'alal-laahi illal-ḥaqqa wa darasoo maa feeh; wad-Daarul-Aakhiratu khayrul-lillazeena yattaqoon; afalaa ta'qiloon.

170. Wallazeena yumas-sikoona bil-Kitaabi wa-aqaamuṣ-Ṣalaata innaa laa nuḍee'u ajral-muṣliḥeen.

171. Wa iz nataqnal-jabala fawqahum ka-annahoo ẓulla-tuñw-wa ẓannooo annahoo waaqi'um bihim khuzoo maaa aataynaakum biquwwatiñw-wazkuroo maa feehi la'allakum tattaqoon.

172. Wa iz akhaza Rabbuka mim Baneee Aadama min ẓuhoorihim zurriyyatahum wa ash-hadahum 'alaaa anfusihim alastu bi-Rabbikum qaaloo balaa shahidnaaa; an taqooloo Yawmal-Qiyaamati innaa kunnaa 'an haazaa ghaafileen.

سُوْٓءَ الْعَذَابِ ؕ اِنَّ رَبَّكَ لَسَرِيْعُ
الْعِقَابِ ۖۚ وَاِنَّهٗ لَغَفُوْرٌ رَّحِيْمٌ ﴿۱۶۷﴾
وَقَطَّعْنٰهُمْ فِى الْاَرْضِ اُمَمًا ۚ مِنْهُمُ
الصّٰلِحُوْنَ وَمِنْهُمْ دُوْنَ ذٰلِكَ ۫
وَبَلَوْنٰهُمْ بِالْحَسَنٰتِ وَالسَّيِّاٰتِ
لَعَلَّهُمْ يَرْجِعُوْنَ ﴿۱۶۸﴾
فَخَلَفَ مِنْۢ بَعْدِهِمْ خَلْفٌ وَّرِثُوا
الْكِتٰبَ يَاْخُذُوْنَ عَرَضَ هٰذَا
الْاَدْنٰى وَيَقُوْلُوْنَ سَيُغْفَرُ لَنَا ۚ وَاِنْ
يَّاْتِهِمْ عَرَضٌ مِّثْلُهٗ يَاْخُذُوْهُ ؕ اَلَمْ
يُؤْخَذْ عَلَيْهِمْ مِّيْثَاقُ الْكِتٰبِ اَنْ
لَّا يَقُوْلُوْا عَلَى اللّٰهِ اِلَّا الْحَقَّ وَدَرَسُوْا
مَا فِيْهِ ؕ وَالدَّارُ الْاٰخِرَةُ خَيْرٌ
لِّلَّذِيْنَ يَتَّقُوْنَ ؕ اَفَلَا تَعْقِلُوْنَ ﴿۱۶۹﴾
وَالَّذِيْنَ يُمَسِّكُوْنَ بِالْكِتٰبِ وَاَقَامُوا
الصَّلٰوةَ ؕ اِنَّا لَا نُضِيْعُ اَجْرَ
الْمُصْلِحِيْنَ ﴿۱۷۰﴾
وَاِذْ نَتَقْنَا الْجَبَلَ فَوْقَهُمْ كَاَنَّهٗ
ظُلَّةٌ وَّظَنُّوْٓا اَنَّهٗ وَاقِعٌۢ بِهِمْ ۚ
خُذُوْا مَآ اٰتَيْنٰكُمْ بِقُوَّةٍ وَّاذْكُرُوْا
مَا فِيْهِ لَعَلَّكُمْ تَتَّقُوْنَ ﴿۱۷۱﴾ ع
وَاِذْ اَخَذَ رَبُّكَ مِنْۢ بَنِيْٓ اٰدَمَ
مِنْ ظُهُوْرِهِمْ ذُرِّيَّتَهُمْ وَاَشْهَدَهُمْ
عَلٰٓى اَنْفُسِهِمْ ۚ اَلَسْتُ بِرَبِّكُمْ ؕ قَالُوْا
بَلٰى ۛۚ شَهِدْنَا ۛۚ اَنْ تَقُوْلُوْا يَوْمَ
الْقِيٰمَةِ اِنَّا كُنَّا عَنْ هٰذَا غٰفِلِيْنَ ﴿۱۷۲﴾

ع ۲۱ ۹

معانقة ۱۲ عند المتاخرين

173. or say, "Our fathers worshipped idols before us and as their descendants we followed them. Will you then destroy us because of what the followers of falsehood have done?"

173. Aw taqoolooo innamaaa ashraka aabaaa'unaa min qablu wa kunnaa zurriyyatam-mim ba'dihim afatuhlikunaa bimaa fa'alal-mubṭiloon.

اَوْ تَقُوْلُوْٓا اِنَّمَآ اَشْرَكَ اٰبَآؤُنَا مِنْ
قَبْلُ وَكُنَّا ذُرِّيَّةً مِّنْ بَعْدِهِمْ ۚ
اَفَتُهْلِكُنَا بِمَا فَعَلَ الْمُبْطِلُوْنَ ﴿١٧٣﴾

174. Thus, do We explain Our revelations so that they might return to (the right path).

174. Wa kazaalika nufaṣ-ṣilul-Aayaati wa la'allahum yarji'oon.

وَكَذٰلِكَ نُفَصِّلُ الْاٰيٰتِ وَلَعَلَّهُمْ
يَرْجِعُوْنَ ﴿١٧٤﴾

175. (Muhammad), tell them the story of the person to whom We sent Our guidance, but who detached himself from it and who was then pursued by Satan until he turned into a rebel.

175. Watlu 'alayhim naba-al-lazeee aataynaahu Aayaatinaa fansalakha minhaa fa-atba'a-hush-Shayṭaanu fakaana minal-ghaaween.

وَاتْلُ عَلَيْهِمْ نَبَاَ الَّذِيْٓ اٰتَيْنٰهُ
اٰيٰتِنَا فَانْسَلَخَ مِنْهَا فَاَتْبَعَهُ
الشَّيْطٰنُ فَكَانَ مِنَ الْغٰوِيْنَ ﴿١٧٥﴾

176. Had We wanted, We could have raised him to an exalted position, but he clung to his earthly life and followed his own (evil) desires. Such person's bad habits are like those of a (lazy) dog (in a warm climate) who always has its tongue hanging out whether you chase it away or leave it alone. Such are the people who have called Our revelations mere lies. (Muhammad), tell them such stories so that perhaps they will think.

176. Wa law shi'naa larafa'naahu bihaa walaakinnahooo akhlada ilal-arḍi wattaba'a hawaah; famasaluhoo kamasalil-kalb; in taḥmil 'alayhi yalhas aw tatrukhu yalhas; zaalika masalul-qawmil-lazeena kaz-zaboo bi-Aayaatinaa; faqṣuṣil-qaṣaṣa la'allahum yatafakkaroon.

وَلَوْ شِئْنَا لَرَفَعْنٰهُ بِهَا وَلٰكِنَّهٗٓ
اَخْلَدَ اِلَى الْاَرْضِ وَاتَّبَعَ هَوٰىهُ ۚ
فَمَثَلُهٗ كَمَثَلِ الْكَلْبِ ۚ اِنْ تَحْمِلْ
عَلَيْهِ يَلْهَثْ اَوْ تَتْرُكْهُ يَلْهَثْ ؕ
ذٰلِكَ مَثَلُ الْقَوْمِ الَّذِيْنَ كَذَّبُوْا
بِاٰيٰتِنَا ۚ فَاقْصُصِ الْقَصَصَ
لَعَلَّهُمْ يَتَفَكَّرُوْنَ ﴿١٧٦﴾

177. How evil is the example of the people who have rejected Our revelations and have done injustice only to themselves!

177. Saaa'a masalanil-qawmul-lazeena kaz-zaboo bi-Aayaatinaa wa anfusahum kaanoo yaẓlimoon.

سَآءَ مَثَلَا ۟ الْقَوْمُ الَّذِيْنَ كَذَّبُوْا
بِاٰيٰتِنَا وَاَنْفُسَهُمْ كَانُوْا يَظْلِمُوْنَ ﴿١٧٧﴾

178. Those whom Allah has guided have the true guidance, but those whom He has caused to go astray are certainly lost.

178. Mañy-yahdil-laahu fahu-wal-muhtadee wa mañy-yuḍlil fa-ulaaa'ika humul-khaasiroon.

مَنْ يَّهْدِ اللّٰهُ فَهُوَ الْمُهْتَدِيْ ۚ وَمَنْ
يُّضْلِلْ فَاُولٰٓئِكَ هُمُ الْخٰسِرُوْنَ ﴿١٧٨﴾

179. We have destined many men and jinn for hell. They have hearts but do not understand, eyes but do not see. They have ears but do not hear. They are worse than lost cattle. These are the heedless ones.

179. Wa laqad zara-naa li-Jahannama kaseeram-minal-jinni wal-insi lahum quloobul-laa yafqahoona bihaa wa lahum a'yunul-laa yubṣiroona bihaa wa lahum aazaanul-laa yasma'oona bihaa; ulaaa'ika kal-an'aami bal hum aḍall; ulaaa'ika humul-ghaafiloon.

وَلَقَدْ ذَرَاْنَا لِجَهَنَّمَ كَثِيْرًا مِّنَ
الْجِنِّ وَالْاِنْسِ ۖ لَهُمْ قُلُوْبٌ لَّا
يَفْقَهُوْنَ بِهَا ز وَلَهُمْ اَعْيُنٌ
لَّا يُبْصِرُوْنَ بِهَا ز وَلَهُمْ اٰذَانٌ
لَّا يَسْمَعُوْنَ بِهَا ؕ اُولٰٓئِكَ كَالْاَنْعَامِ
بَلْ هُمْ اَضَلُّ ؕ اُولٰٓئِكَ هُمُ
الْغٰفِلُوْنَ ﴿١٧٩﴾

180. Allah has the most blessed names. You should address Him in your worship by these names and keep away from those who distort them. They will be recompensed for their (evil) deeds.

180. Wa lillaahil-Asmaaa'ul-Ḥusnaa fad‘oohu bihaa wa zarul-lazeena yulḥidoona feee Asmaaa'ih; sayujzawna maa kaanoo ya‘maloon.

وَلِلّٰهِ الْاَسْمَآءُ الْحُسْنٰى فَادْعُوْهُ
بِهَا ۪ وَذَرُوا الَّذِيْنَ يُلْحِدُوْنَ
فِيْٓ اَسْمَآئِهٖ ؕ سَيُجْزَوْنَ مَا
كَانُوْا يَعْمَلُوْنَ ﴿١٨٠﴾

181. Among Our creatures are a group who guide and judge with the Truth.

181. Wa mimman khalaqnaaa ummatuñy-yahdoona bilḥaqqi wa bihee ya‘diloon.

وَمِمَّنْ خَلَقْنَآ اُمَّةٌ يَّهْدُوْنَ
بِالْحَقِّ وَبِهٖ يَعْدِلُوْنَ ﴿١٨١﴾ ع ٢٢ ١٠ ١٢

182. We gradually lead those who have called Our revelations mere lies to destruction. Their destruction will be such that they will not even notice how it seized them.

182. Wallazeena kaz-zaboo bi-Aayaatinaa sanastad-rijuhum min ḥaysu laa ya‘lamoon.

وَالَّذِيْنَ كَذَّبُوْا بِاٰيٰتِنَا سَنَسْتَدْرِجُهُمْ
مِّنْ حَيْثُ لَا يَعْلَمُوْنَ ﴿١٨٢﴾

183. Though I have given them a respite, My plan against them is well established.

183. Wa umlee lahum; inna kaydee mateen.

وَاُمْلِيْ لَهُمْ ؕ اِنَّ كَيْدِيْ مَتِيْنٌ ﴿١٨٣﴾

184. Why did they not understand that their companion (Muhammad) is not possessed by jinn? (Muhammad) is only a (Divinely) authorized preacher.

184. Awalam yatafakkaroo maa biṣaaḥibihim min jinnah; in huwa illaa nazeerum-mubeen.

اَوَلَمْ يَتَفَكَّرُوْا ٚ مَا بِصَاحِبِهِمْ
مِّنْ جِنَّةٍ ؕ اِنْ هُوَ اِلَّا نَذِيْرٌ مُّبِيْنٌ ﴿١٨٤﴾

185. Did they not look at the Kingdom of the heavens and the earth and everything else that Allah has created? Perhaps death approaches them. In what kind of guidance can they have faith besides that of the Quran?

185. Awalam yanẓuroo fee malakootis-samaawaati wal-arḍi wa maa khalaqal-laahu min shay'iñw-wa an ‘asaaa añy-yakoona qadiqtaraba ajaluhum fabi-ayyi ḥadeesim ba‘dahoo yu'minoon.

اَوَلَمْ يَنْظُرُوْا فِيْ مَلَكُوْتِ السَّمٰوٰتِ
وَالْاَرْضِ وَمَا خَلَقَ اللّٰهُ مِنْ
شَيْءٍ ۙ وَّاَنْ عَسٰٓى اَنْ يَّكُوْنَ قَدِ
اقْتَرَبَ اَجَلُهُمْ ۚ فَبِاَيِّ حَدِيْثٍ ۢ
بَعْدَهٗ يُؤْمِنُوْنَ ﴿١٨٥﴾

186. No one can guide those whom Allah has caused to go astray and has left to continue blindly in their rebellion.

186. Mañy-yuḍlilil-laahu falaa haadiya lah; wa yazaruhum fee ṭughyaanihim ya‘mahoon.

مَنْ يُّضْلِلِ اللّٰهُ فَلَا هَادِيَ لَهٗ ؕ
وَيَذَرُهُمْ فِيْ طُغْيَانِهِمْ يَعْمَهُوْنَ ﴿١٨٦﴾

187. They ask you (Muhammad), "When will the Day of Judgment be?" Tell them, "My Lord knows best. It is He who has appointed its time. It will be a grave hour both in the heavens and on the earth. It will approach you only suddenly." They say, "It seems that you know about the coming of the Day of Judgment." Tell them, "Only Allah knows about it and most people do not know."

187. Yas'aloonaka ‘anis-Saa‘ati ayyaana mursaahaa qul innamaa ‘ilmuhaa ‘inda Rabbee laa yujalleehaa liwaqtihaaa illaa Hoo; saqulat fis-samaawaati wal-arḍ; laa ta-teekum illaa baghtah; yas'aloonaka ka-annaka ḥafiyyun ‘anhaa qul innamaa ‘ilmuhaa ‘indallaahi walaakinna aksarannaasi laa ya‘lamoon.

يَسْـَٔلُوْنَكَ عَنِ السَّاعَةِ اَيَّانَ
مُرْسٰىهَا ؕ قُلْ اِنَّمَا عِلْمُهَا عِنْدَ
رَبِّيْ ۚ لَا يُجَلِّيْهَا لِوَقْتِهَآ اِلَّا هُوَ ؕ وقف لازم / وقف منزل
ثَقُلَتْ فِي السَّمٰوٰتِ وَالْاَرْضِ ؕ لَا
تَاْتِيْكُمْ اِلَّا بَغْتَةً ؕ يَسْـَٔلُوْنَكَ كَاَنَّكَ
حَفِيٌّ عَنْهَا ؕ قُلْ اِنَّمَا عِلْمُهَا عِنْدَ
اللّٰهِ وَلٰكِنَّ اَكْثَرَ النَّاسِ لَا يَعْلَمُوْنَ ﴿١٨٧﴾

188. (Muhammad), say, "I have no control over my benefits or

188. Qul laaa amliku linafsee naf‘añw-wa laa ḍarran

قُلْ لَّآ اَمْلِكُ لِنَفْسِيْ نَفْعًا وَّلَا ضَرًّا

sufferings, without the will of Allah. Had I known about the unseen, I would have gained much good and would have faced no suffering. I am only a Warner and I preach the glad news to the believing people."

illaa maa shaaaa'al-laah; wa law kuntu a'lamul-ghayba lastaksartu minal-khayri wa maa massaniyas-soo'; in ana illaa nazeeruñw-wa basheerul-liqawmiñy-yu'minoon.

إِلَّا مَا شَاءَ اللَّهُ ۚ وَلَوْ كُنتُ أَعْلَمُ
الْغَيْبَ لَاسْتَكْثَرْتُ مِنَ الْخَيْرِ
وَمَا مَسَّنِيَ السُّوءُ ۚ إِنْ أَنَا إِلَّا
نَذِيرٌ وَبَشِيرٌ لِّقَوْمٍ يُؤْمِنُونَ ﴿١٨٨﴾ معانقة ٨ ع ٢٤ عند المتاخرين ١٠

189. It is Allah Who created you from a single soul and out of it made its spouse to bring it comfort. When he (man) engaged in carnal relations with her, she conceived a light burden which she had to carry. When the baby grew in her womb, they (husband and wife) both prayed to their Lord, "If You grant us a healthy son we shall certainly give you thanks."

189. Huwal-lazee khalaqakum min nafsiñw-waahidatiñw-wa ja'ala minhaa zawjahaa liyaskuna ilayhaa falammaa taghashshaahaa hamalat hamlan khafeefan famarrat bihee falammaaa asqalad-da'awal-laaha Rabbahumaa la'in aataytanaa saalihal-lanakoonanna minash-shaakireen.

هُوَ الَّذِي خَلَقَكُم مِّن نَّفْسٍ
وَاحِدَةٍ وَجَعَلَ مِنْهَا زَوْجَهَا
لِيَسْكُنَ إِلَيْهَا ۖ فَلَمَّا تَغَشَّاهَا
حَمَلَتْ حَمْلًا خَفِيفًا فَمَرَّتْ بِهِ ۖ
فَلَمَّا أَثْقَلَت دَّعَوَا اللَّهَ رَبَّهُمَا لَئِنْ
آتَيْتَنَا صَالِحًا لَّنَكُونَنَّ مِنَ
الشَّاكِرِينَ ﴿١٨٩﴾

190. When they were given a healthy son, they began to love him as much as they loved Allah. Allah is most exalted and is free from the defect of being loved equal to anything else.

190. Falammaaa aataahumaa saalihan ja'alaa lahoo shurakaaa'a feemaaa aataahumaa; fata'aalal-laahu 'ammaa yushrikoon.

فَلَمَّا آتَاهُمَا صَالِحًا جَعَلَا لَهُ
شُرَكَاءَ فِيمَا آتَاهُمَا ۚ فَتَعَالَى
اللَّهُ عَمَّا يُشْرِكُونَ ﴿١٩٠﴾

191. Do they (the pagans) consider things that do not create anything but are themselves created, equal to Allah?

191. A yushrikoona maa laa yakhluqu shay'añw-wa hum yukhlaqoon.

أَيُشْرِكُونَ مَا لَا يَخْلُقُ شَيْئًا
وَهُمْ يُخْلَقُونَ ﴿١٩١﴾

192. The idols are things that are not able to help others or even themselves.

192. Wa laa yastatee'oona lahum nasrañw-wa laaa anfusahum yansuroon

وَلَا يَسْتَطِيعُونَ لَهُمْ نَصْرًا وَلَا
أَنفُسَهُمْ يَنصُرُونَ ﴿١٩٢﴾

193. Believers, even if you invite them to true guidance, they will not follow you. It makes no difference whether you invite them or whether you keep quiet.

193. Wa in tad'oohum ilal-hudaa laa yattabi'ookum; sawaaa'un 'alaykum ada'awtumoohum am antum saamitoon.

وَإِن تَدْعُوهُمْ إِلَى الْهُدَىٰ لَا
يَتَّبِعُوكُمْ ۚ سَوَاءٌ عَلَيْكُمْ أَدَعَوْتُمُوهُمْ
أَمْ أَنتُمْ صَامِتُونَ ﴿١٩٣﴾

194. Those whom you (pagans) worship besides Allah, are themselves servants just like yourselves. If your claim were true, they would answer your prayers.

194. Innal-lazeena tad'oona min doonil-laahi 'ibaadun amsaalukum fad'oohum falyastajeeboo lakum in kuntum saadiqeen.

إِنَّ الَّذِينَ تَدْعُونَ مِن دُونِ
اللَّهِ عِبَادٌ أَمْثَالُكُمْ ۖ فَادْعُوهُمْ
فَلْيَسْتَجِيبُوا لَكُمْ إِن كُنتُمْ
صَادِقِينَ ﴿١٩٤﴾

195. Do they (the idols) have feet to walk, hands to hold things, eyes

195. Alahum arjuluñy-yamshoona bihaaa am lahum

أَلَهُمْ أَرْجُلٌ يَمْشُونَ بِهَا ۖ أَمْ لَهُمْ

to see, and ears to hear? (Muhammad), tell them (the pagans) to call on their idols for help and to plan against Me without delay.

aydiñy-yabṭishoona bihaaa am lahum a'yunuñy-yubṣiroona bihaaa am lahum aazaanuñy-yasma'oona bihaa; qulid-'oo shurakaaa'akum summa keedooni falaa tunẓiroon.

أَيْدٍ يَبْطِشُونَ بِهَا ۖ أَمْ لَهُمْ أَعْيُنٌ
يُبْصِرُونَ بِهَا ۖ أَمْ لَهُمْ آذَانٌ
يَسْمَعُونَ بِهَا ۗ قُلِ ادْعُوا شُرَكَاءَكُمْ
ثُمَّ كِيدُونِ فَلَا تُنْظِرُونِ ﴿١٩٥﴾

196. (Say), "My guardian is certainly Allah, who has revealed the Book and is the Guardian of the righteous ones."

196. Inna waliyyiyal-laahul-lazee nazzalal-Kitaab; wa Huwa yatawallaṣ-ṣaaliḥeen.

إِنَّ وَلِيِّيَ اللَّهُ الَّذِي نَزَّلَ
الْكِتَابَ ۖ وَهُوَ يَتَوَلَّى الصَّالِحِينَ ﴿١٩٦﴾

197. The idols which you (the pagans) worship besides Him can help neither you nor themselves.

197. Wallazeena tad'oona min doonihee laa yastaṭee'oona naṣrakum wa laaa anfusahum yanṣuroon.

وَالَّذِينَ تَدْعُونَ مِنْ دُونِهِ لَا
يَسْتَطِيعُونَ نَصْرَكُمْ وَلَا أَنْفُسَهُمْ
يَنْصُرُونَ ﴿١٩٧﴾

198. (Muhammad), if you invite them to the right guidance, they will not listen to you. You will see them looking at you but they do not really see.

198. Wa in tad'oohum ilal-hudaa laa yasma'oo wa taraahum yanẓuroona ilayka wa hum laa yubṣiroon.

وَإِنْ تَدْعُوهُمْ إِلَى الْهُدَىٰ لَا
يَسْمَعُوا ۖ وَتَرَاهُمْ يَنْظُرُونَ إِلَيْكَ
وَهُمْ لَا يُبْصِرُونَ ﴿١٩٨﴾

199. Have forgiveness, preach the truth, and keep away from the ignorant ones.

199. Khuzil-'afwa wa-mur bil'urfi wa a'riḍ 'anil-jaahileen.

خُذِ الْعَفْوَ وَأْمُرْ بِالْعُرْفِ وَأَعْرِضْ
عَنِ الْجَاهِلِينَ ﴿١٩٩﴾

200. If Satan tries to seduce you, seek refuge with Allah's (mercy). Allah is All-hearing and All-knowing.

200. Wa immaa yanzaghannaka minash-Shayṭaani nazghun fasta'iz billaah; innahoo Samee'un 'Aleem.

وَإِمَّا يَنْزَغَنَّكَ مِنَ الشَّيْطَانِ نَزْغٌ
فَاسْتَعِذْ بِاللَّهِ ۚ إِنَّهُ سَمِيعٌ عَلِيمٌ ﴿٢٠٠﴾

201. When a Satanic thought starts to bother the pious ones, they understand and see the light,

201. Innal-lazeenat-taqaw izaa massahum ṭaaa'ifum minash-Shayṭaani-tazakkaroo fa-izaa hum mubṣiroon.

إِنَّ الَّذِينَ اتَّقَوْا إِذَا مَسَّهُمْ طَائِفٌ
مِنَ الشَّيْطَانِ تَذَكَّرُوا فَإِذَا هُمْ
مُبْصِرُونَ ﴿٢٠١﴾

202. while their brethren ceaselessly try to drag them into error.

202. Wa ikhwaanuhum yamud-doonahum fil-ghayyi summa laa yuqṣiroon.

وَإِخْوَانُهُمْ يَمُدُّونَهُمْ فِي الْغَيِّ ثُمَّ
لَا يُقْصِرُونَ ﴿٢٠٢﴾

203. If you (Muhammad) did not show them a miracle, they will keep on insisting that you must show them one. Say, "I only follow what is revealed to me from my Lord. This (Quran) contains wisdom for you from your Lord. It contains guidance and mercy for those who have faith.

203. Wa izaa lam ta-tihim bi-Aayatin qaaloo law lajtabaytahaa; qul innamaaa attabi'u maa yooḥaaa ilayya mir-Rabbee; haazaa baṣaaa'iru mir-Rabbikum wa hudañw-wa raḥmatul-liqawmiñy-yu'minoon.

وَإِذَا لَمْ تَأْتِهِمْ بِآيَةٍ قَالُوا لَوْلَا
اجْتَبَيْتَهَا ۚ قُلْ إِنَّمَا أَتَّبِعُ مَا
يُوحَىٰ إِلَيَّ مِنْ رَبِّي ۚ هَٰذَا بَصَائِرُ
مِنْ رَبِّكُمْ وَهُدًى وَرَحْمَةٌ
لِقَوْمٍ يُؤْمِنُونَ ﴿٢٠٣﴾

(Bow Down)

204. Whenever the Quran is recited (to you), listen to it quietly so that you may receive mercy.

204. Wa izaa quri'al-Qur-aanu fastami'oo lahoo wa anṣitoo la'allakum turḥamoon.

وَاِذَا قُرِئَ الْقُرْاٰنُ فَاسْتَمِعُوْا لَهٗ
وَاَنْصِتُوْا لَعَلَّكُمْ تُرْحَمُوْنَ ﴿٢٠٤﴾

205. Remember your Lord deep within yourselves, humbly and privately - instead of shouting out loud - (in prayer) in the mornings and evenings and do not be of the heedless ones.

205. Wazkur-Rabbaka fee nafsika taḍarru'añw-wa kheefatañw-wa doonal-jahri minal-qawli bilghuduwwi wal-aaṣaali wa laa takum minal-ghaafileen.

وَاذْكُرْ رَّبَّكَ فِيْ نَفْسِكَ تَضَرُّعًا
وَّخِيْفَةً وَّدُوْنَ الْجَهْرِ مِنَ الْقَوْلِ
بِالْغُدُوِّ وَالْاٰصَالِ وَلَا تَكُنْ مِّنَ
الْغٰفِلِيْنَ ﴿٢٠٥﴾

206. Those who are near to your Lord do not disdain from worshipping Him. They glorify Him and prostrate themselves (in obedience to Him).

206. Innal-lazeena 'inda Rabbika laa yastakbiroona 'an 'ibaadatihee wa yusabbiḥoonahoo wa lahoo yasjudoon.

اِنَّ الَّذِيْنَ عِنْدَ رَبِّكَ لَا
يَسْتَكْبِرُوْنَ عَنْ عِبَادَتِهٖ
وَيُسَبِّحُوْنَهٗ وَلَهٗ يَسْجُدُوْنَ ﴿٢٠٦﴾ السجدة

Al-Anfal, The Spoils (8)

In the Name of Allah, the Beneficent, the Merciful.

Sûrat al-Anfâl-8

(Revealed at Madinah)

Bismillaahir Raḥmaanir Raḥeem

(٨) سُوْرَةُ الْاَنْفَالِ مَدَنِيَّةٌ (٨٨)
بِسْمِ اللّٰهِ الرَّحْمٰنِ الرَّحِيْمِ

1. They (the believers) ask you (Muhammad) about the spoils captured (from the enemies) during a war. Tell them, "They belong to Allah and the Messengers. If you have faith, have fear of Allah. Settle the disputes among yourselves and obey Allah and His Messengers."

1. Yas'aloonaka 'anil-anfaali qulil-anfaalu lillaahi-war-Rasooli fattaqul-laaha wa aṣliḥoo zaata baynikum wa aṭee'ul-laaha wa Rasoolahooo in kuntum mu'mineen.

يَسْـَٔلُوْنَكَ عَنِ الْاَنْفَالِ ؕ قُلِ الْاَنْفَالُ
لِلّٰهِ وَالرَّسُوْلِ ۚ فَاتَّقُوا اللّٰهَ وَ
اَصْلِحُوْا ذَاتَ بَيْنِكُمْ ۖ وَاَطِيْعُوا
اللّٰهَ وَرَسُوْلَهٗۤ اِنْ كُنْتُمْ مُّؤْمِنِيْنَ ﴿١﴾

2. When Allah is mentioned, the true believers begin to feel fear of Him in their hearts, and when His revelations are recited to them their faith strengthens. In their Lord alone do they trust.

2. Innamal-mu'minoonal-lazeena izaa zukiral-laahu wajilat quloobuhum wa izaa tuliyat 'alayhim Aayaatuhoo zaadat-hum eemaanañw-wa 'alaa Rabbihim yatawakkaloon.

اِنَّمَا الْمُؤْمِنُوْنَ الَّذِيْنَ اِذَا ذُكِرَ اللّٰهُ
وَجِلَتْ قُلُوْبُهُمْ وَاِذَا تُلِيَتْ عَلَيْهِمْ
اٰيٰتُهٗ زَادَتْهُمْ اِيْمَانًا وَّعَلٰى
رَبِّهِمْ يَتَوَكَّلُوْنَ ﴿٢﴾

3. They are steadfast in prayer and spend part of what We have given them for the cause of Allah.

3. Allazeena yuqeemoonaṣ-Ṣalaata wa mimmaa razaqnaahum yunfiqoon.

الَّذِيْنَ يُقِيْمُوْنَ الصَّلٰوةَ وَمِمَّا
رَزَقْنٰهُمْ يُنْفِقُوْنَ ﴿٣﴾

4. Such are the true believers. Their reward from their Lord will be high ranks, forgiveness, and a generous provision.

4. Ulaaa'ika humul-mu'minoona ḥaqqaa; lahum darajaatun 'inda Rabbihim wa maghfiratuñw-warizqun kareem.

اُولٰٓئِكَ هُمُ الْمُؤْمِنُوْنَ حَقًّا ؕ لَهُمْ
دَرَجٰتٌ عِنْدَ رَبِّهِمْ وَمَغْفِرَةٌ وَّ
رِزْقٌ كَرِيْمٌ ﴿٤﴾

5. A group among the believers dislike, (Allah's decree about the spoils captured in war) as well as His command that you come out of your home for a truthful purpose (to

5. Kamaaa akhrajaka Rabbuka mim baytika bilḥaqq; wa inna fareeqam-minal-mu'mineena

كَمَآ اَخْرَجَكَ رَبُّكَ مِنْ بَيْتِكَ
بِالْحَقِّ وَاِنَّ فَرِيْقًا مِّنَ الْمُؤْمِنِيْنَ

fight for justice).

lakaarihoon.

لَكٰرِهُوْنَ ۝٥

6. Knowing it well (that a fight in which they are to take part is about to take place), they act as though they are being driven to death which they can see before their very eyes. Despite their knowledge of the truth, they still argue with you.

6. Yujaadiloonaka fil-ḥaqqi ba'da maa tabayyana ka-annamaa yusaaqoona ilalmawti wa hum yanẕuroon.

يُجَادِلُوْنَكَ فِي الْحَقِّ بَعْدَ مَا
تَبَيَّنَ كَاَنَّمَا يُسَاقُوْنَ اِلَى الْمَوْتِ
وَهُمْ يَنْظُرُوْنَ ۝٦

7. When Allah promised to grant you (believers) victory over either one of the two groups, you wished to have control over the unarmed one. Allah decided to prove (to you) the truth of His promises and to destroy the unbelievers

7. Wa iz̲ ya'idukumul-laahu iḥdaṭ-ṭaaa'ifatayni annahaa lakum wa tawaddoona anna ghayra z̲aatish-shawkati takoonu lakum wa yureedul-laahu añy-yuḥiqqal-ḥaqqa bikalimaatihee wa yaqṭa'a daabiral-kaafireen.

وَاِذْ يَعِدُكُمُ اللّٰهُ اِحْدَى
الطَّآئِفَتَيْنِ اَنَّهَا لَكُمْ وَتَوَدُّوْنَ اَنَّ
غَيْرَ ذَاتِ الشَّوْكَةِ تَكُوْنُ لَكُمْ
وَيُرِيْدُ اللّٰهُ اَنْ يُّحِقَّ الْحَقَّ بِكَلِمٰتِهٖ
وَيَقْطَعَ دَابِرَ الْكٰفِرِيْنَ ۝٧

8. so that the truth would stand supreme and falsehood would exist no more, even though the criminals dislike it.

8. Liyuḥiqqal-ḥaqqa wa yubṭilal-baaṭila wa law karihal-mujrimoon.

لِيُحِقَّ الْحَقَّ وَيُبْطِلَ الْبَاطِلَ وَ
لَوْ كَرِهَ الْمُجْرِمُوْنَ ۝٨

9. When you (believers) begged for assistance from your Lord, He said, "I am helping you with a thousand angels, all in rows marching one after the other."

9. Iz̲ tastagheeṡoona Rabba-kum fastajaaba lakum annee mumiddukum bi-alfimminal-malaaa'ikati murdifeen.

اِذْ تَسْتَغِيْثُوْنَ رَبَّكُمْ فَاسْتَجَابَ
لَكُمْ اَنِّيْ مُمِدُّكُمْ بِاَلْفٍ مِّنَ
الْمَلٰٓئِكَةِ مُرْدِفِيْنَ ۝٩

10. Allah has sent this glad news to comfort your hearts. Victory is in the hands of Allah alone. Allah is Majestic and All-wise.

10. Wa maa ja'alahul-laahu illaa bushraa wa litaṭma'inna bihee quloobukum; wa man-naṣru-illaa min 'indil-laah; innal-laaha 'Azeezun Ḥakeem.

وَمَا جَعَلَهُ اللّٰهُ اِلَّا بُشْرٰى وَلِتَطْمَئِنَّ
بِهٖ قُلُوْبُكُمْ وَمَا النَّصْرُ اِلَّا مِنْ
عِنْدِ اللّٰهِ اِنَّ اللّٰهَ عَزِيْزٌ حَكِيْمٌ ۝١٠ ع ١٥

11. The slumber that overcame you was from Allah that brought you peace. He showered water from the sky over you to clean you, remove Satanic wickedness from you, strengthen your hearts, and grant you steadfastness.

11. Iz̲ yughashsheekumun-nu'aasa amanatam-minhu wa yunazzilu 'alaykum minas-samaaa'i maaa'al-liyuṭah-hirakum bihee wa yuz̲hiba 'ankum rijzash Shayṭaani wa liyarbiṭa 'ala quloobikum wa yuṡabbita bihil-aqdaam.

اِذْ يُغَشِّيْكُمُ النُّعَاسَ اَمَنَةً مِّنْهُ
وَيُنَزِّلُ عَلَيْكُمْ مِّنَ السَّمَآءِ مَآءً
لِّيُطَهِّرَكُمْ بِهٖ وَيُذْهِبَ عَنْكُمْ
رِجْزَ الشَّيْطٰنِ وَلِيَرْبِطَ عَلٰى
قُلُوْبِكُمْ وَيُثَبِّتَ بِهِ الْاَقْدَامَ ۝١١

12. Your Lord instructed the angels, saying, "I am with you. Encourage the believers. I shall cast terror into the hearts of the unbelievers and you will strike

12. Iz̲ yooḥee Rabbuka Ilal-malaaa'ikati annee ma'akum faṡabbitul-laz̲eena aamanoo; sa-ulqee fee quloobil-laz̲eena kafarur-ru'ba faḍriboo fawqal-a'naaqi

اِذْ يُوْحِيْ رَبُّكَ اِلَى الْمَلٰٓئِكَةِ
اَنِّيْ مَعَكُمْ فَثَبِّتُوا الَّذِيْنَ اٰمَنُوْا
سَاُلْقِيْ فِيْ قُلُوْبِ الَّذِيْنَ كَفَرُوا
الرُّعْبَ فَاضْرِبُوْا فَوْقَ الْاَعْنَاقِ

their heads and limbs;

waḍriboo minhum kulla banaan.

وَاضْرِبُوْا مِنْهُمْ كُلَّ بَنَانٍ ﴿١٢﴾

13. they have opposed Allah and His Messengers." For those who oppose Allah and His Messengers, Allah has prepared a severe retribution.

13. Zaalika bi-annahum shaaaqqul-laaha wa Rasoolah; wa mañy-yushaaqiqil-laaha wa Rasoolahoo fa-innal-laaha shadeedul-'iqaab.

ذٰلِكَ بِاَنَّهُمْ شَآقُّوا اللّٰهَ وَرَسُوْلَهٗ ۚ
وَمَنْ يُّشَاقِقِ اللّٰهَ وَرَسُوْلَهٗ فَاِنَّ
اللّٰهَ شَدِيْدُ الْعِقَابِ ﴿١٣﴾

14. We will say to them, "Endure the torment (as a consequence of your evil deeds); the unbelievers deserve nothing better than (the torment) of fire."

14. Zaalikum fazooqoohu wa anna lilkaafireena 'azaaban Naar.

ذٰلِكُمْ فَذُوْقُوْهُ وَاَنَّ لِلْكٰفِرِيْنَ
عَذَابَ النَّارِ ﴿١٤﴾

15. Believers, do not retreat when facing the marching army of the unbelievers, for no believer will turn back at that time except for strategic reasons or to join another band (the Holy Prophet or Imam).

15. Yaaa ayyuhal-lazeena aamanooo izaa laqeetumul lazeena kafaroo zaḥfan falaa tuwalloohumul-adbaar.

يٰۤاَيُّهَا الَّذِيْنَ اٰمَنُوْۤا اِذَا لَقِيْتُمُ
الَّذِيْنَ كَفَرُوْا زَحْفًا فَلَا
تُوَلُّوْهُمُ الْاَدْبَارَ ۚ ﴿١٥﴾

16. (Whoever deserts the believers) will incur the wrath of Allah and will dwell in hell, a terrible dwelling.

16. Wa mañy-yuwallihim yawma'izin duburahooo illaa mutaḥarrifal-liqitaalin aw mutaḥay-yizan ilaa fi'atin faqad baaa'a bighaḍabim minal-laahi wa ma-waahu Jahannamu wa bi'sal-maṣeer.

وَمَنْ يُّوَلِّهِمْ يَوْمَئِذٍ دُبُرَهٗۤ اِلَّا
مُتَحَرِّفًا لِّقِتَالٍ اَوْ مُتَحَيِّزًا اِلٰى
فِئَةٍ فَقَدْ بَآءَ بِغَضَبٍ مِّنَ اللّٰهِ
وَمَاْوٰىهُ جَهَنَّمُ ۖ وَبِئْسَ الْمَصِيْرُ ﴿١٦﴾

17. It was not you (believers) but Allah who slew the pagans. It was not you (Muhammad) but Allah who threw dust at them. He did this as a favorable test for the believers. Allah is All-hearing and All-knowing.

17. Falam taqtuloohum walaa-kinnal-laaha qatalahum; wa maa ramayta iz ramayta wa laakinnal-laaha ramaa; wa liyubliyal-mu'mineena minhu balaaa'an ḥasanaa; innallaaha Samee'un 'Aleem.

فَلَمْ تَقْتُلُوْهُمْ وَلٰكِنَّ اللّٰهَ قَتَلَهُمْ ۪
وَمَا رَمَيْتَ اِذْ رَمَيْتَ وَلٰكِنَّ اللّٰهَ
رَمٰى ۚ وَلِيُبْلِيَ الْمُؤْمِنِيْنَ مِنْهُ بَلَآءً
حَسَنًا ۗ اِنَّ اللّٰهَ سَمِيْعٌ عَلِيْمٌ ﴿١٧﴾

18. This is how Allah causes the (evil) plans of the unbelievers to fail.

18. Zaalikum wa annal-laaha moohinu kaydil-kaafireen.

ذٰلِكُمْ وَاَنَّ اللّٰهَ مُوْهِنُ كَيْدِ
الْكٰفِرِيْنَ ﴿١٨﴾

19. If you (the pagans) are looking for conquest, you certainly had a great chance (at the battle of Badr). But if you were to give up such a desire, it would be better for you. If you again wage war against Us, We will be ready for such a confrontation. Your man-power will be of no help to you no matter how much you have; Allah is with the believers.

19. In tastaftiḥoo faqad jaaa'akumul-fatḥu wa in tantahoo fahuwa khayrul-lakum wa in ta'oodoo na'ud wa lan tughniya 'ankum fi'atukum shay'añw-wa law kasurat wa annal-laaha ma'al-mu'mineen.

اِنْ تَسْتَفْتِحُوْا فَقَدْ جَآءَكُمُ الْفَتْحُ ۚ
وَاِنْ تَنْتَهُوْا فَهُوَ خَيْرٌ لَّكُمْ ۚ وَاِنْ
تَعُوْدُوْا نَعُدْ ۚ وَلَنْ تُغْنِيَ عَنْكُمْ
فِئَتُكُمْ شَيْئًا وَّلَوْ كَثُرَتْ ۙ وَ
اَنَّ اللّٰهَ مَعَ الْمُؤْمِنِيْنَ ﴿١٩﴾ ع ٢ ٩ ١٦

20. O believers, obey Allah and His Messengers and do not turn away from Him when you hear (His commands).

20. Yaaa ayyuhal-lazeena aamanooo aṭee'ul-laaha wa Rasoolahoo wa laa tawallaw 'anhu wa antum

يٰۤاَيُّهَا الَّذِيْنَ اٰمَنُوْۤا اَطِيْعُوا اللّٰهَ
وَرَسُوْلَهٗ وَلَا تَوَلَّوْا عَنْهُ وَاَنْتُمْ

	tasma'oon.	تَسْمَعُوْنَ ﴿٢٠﴾
21. Do not be like those who said that they have heard (the Messenger's commands) but do not pay any attention to them.	21. Wa laa takoonoo kal-lazeena qaaloo sami'naa wa hum laa yasma'oon.	وَلَا تَكُوْنُوْا كَالَّذِيْنَ قَالُوْا سَمِعْنَا وَهُمْ لَا يَسْمَعُوْنَ ﴿٢١﴾
22. The most wicked beasts in the sight of Allah are the deaf and the dumb who have no understanding.	22. Inna sharrad-dawaaabbi 'indal-laahiṣṣummul-bukmul-lazeena laa ya'qiloon.	اِنَّ شَرَّ الدَّوَآبِّ عِنْدَ اللّٰهِ الصُّمُّ الْبُكْمُ الَّذِيْنَ لَا يَعْقِلُوْنَ ﴿٢٢﴾
23. Had they possessed any virtue, Allah would certainly have made them hear. Even if Allah were to make them hear, they would still turn away (from the words of Allah).	23. Wa law'alimal-laahu feehim khayral-la-asma'ahum; wa law asma'ahum latawallaw wa hum mu'riḍoon.	وَلَوْ عَلِمَ اللّٰهُ فِيْهِمْ خَيْرًا لَّاَسْمَعَهُمْ وَلَوْ اَسْمَعَهُمْ لَتَوَلَّوْا وَّهُمْ مُّعْرِضُوْنَ ﴿٢٣﴾
24. Believers, listen to Allah and the Messengers when they call you to that which gives you life. Know that Allah is between a man and his heart and that before Him you will all be brought together.	24. Yaaa ayyuhal-lazeena aamanus-tajeeboo lillaahi wa lir-Rasooli izaa da'aakum limaa yuḥyeekum wa'lamooo annal-laaha yaḥoolu baynalmar'i wa qalbihee wa annahooo ilayhi tuḥsharoon.	يٰۤاَيُّهَا الَّذِيْنَ اٰمَنُوا اسْتَجِيْبُوْا لِلّٰهِ وَلِلرَّسُوْلِ اِذَا دَعَاكُمْ لِمَا يُحْيِيْكُمْ وَاعْلَمُوْۤا اَنَّ اللّٰهَ يَحُوْلُ بَيْنَ الْمَرْءِ وَقَلْبِهٖ وَاَنَّهٗۤ اِلَيْهِ تُحْشَرُوْنَ ﴿٢٤﴾
25. Guard yourselves against discord; it does not afflict and mislead among you the unjust alone and you must know that Allah's retribution is most severe.	25. Wattaqoo fitnatal-laa tuṣeebannal-lazeena ẓalamoo minkum khaaaṣṣah; wa'la-mooo annal-laaha shadeedul-'iqaab.	وَاتَّقُوْا فِتْنَةً لَّا تُصِيْبَنَّ الَّذِيْنَ ظَلَمُوْا مِنْكُمْ خَآصَّةً ۚ وَاعْلَمُوْۤا اَنَّ اللّٰهَ شَدِيْدُ الْعِقَابِ ﴿٢٥﴾
26. Recall the time when you (the believers) were only a few suppressed people in the land, afraid of being terrorized by the people. Allah gave you shelter, supported you with His help, and bestowed on you pure provisions so that perhaps you would give Him thanks.	26. Wazkurooo iz antum qaleelum-mustaḍ'afoona fil-arḍi takhaafoona añy-yatakhaṭ-ṭafakumun-naasu fa-aawaakum wa ayyadakum binaṣrihee wa razaqakum minaṭ-ṭayyibaati la'allakum tashkuroon.	وَاذْكُرُوْۤا اِذْ اَنْتُمْ قَلِيْلٌ مُّسْتَضْعَفُوْنَ فِى الْاَرْضِ تَخَافُوْنَ اَنْ يَّتَخَطَّفَكُمُ النَّاسُ فَاٰوٰىكُمْ وَاَيَّدَكُمْ بِنَصْرِهٖ وَ رَزَقَكُمْ مِّنَ الطَّيِّبٰتِ لَعَلَّكُمْ تَشْكُرُوْنَ ﴿٢٦﴾
27. Believers, do not be dishonest to Allah and the Messengers or knowingly abuse your trust.	27. Yaaa ayyuhal-lazeena aamanoo laa takhoonul-laaha war-Rasoola wa takhoonooo amaanaatikum wa antum ta'lamoon.	يٰۤاَيُّهَا الَّذِيْنَ اٰمَنُوْا لَا تَخُوْنُوا اللّٰهَ وَالرَّسُوْلَ وَتَخُوْنُوْۤا اَمٰنٰتِكُمْ وَاَنْتُمْ تَعْلَمُوْنَ ﴿٢٧﴾
28. You must know that even though your possessions and children are beloved to you, Allah certainly has the greatest reward (for the righteous ones).	28. Wa'lamooo annamaaa amwaalukum wa awlaadukum fitnatuñw-wa annal-laaha 'indahooo ajrun 'aẓeem.	وَاعْلَمُوْۤا اَنَّمَآ اَمْوَالُكُمْ وَاَوْلَادُكُمْ فِتْنَةٌ ۙ وَّاَنَّ اللّٰهَ عِنْدَهٗۤ اَجْرٌ عَظِيْمٌ ﴿٢٨﴾ ع ٣ ١٩ ١٧
29. Believers, if you fear Allah, He will give you guidance, will expiate your bad deeds and forgive you. Allah's favors are the	29. Yaaa-ayyuhal-lazeena aamanooo in tattaqul-laaha yaj'al-lakum furqaanañw-wa yukaffir 'ankum sayyi-aatikum wa yaghfir lakum; wallaahu	يٰۤاَيُّهَا الَّذِيْنَ اٰمَنُوْۤا اِنْ تَتَّقُوا اللّٰهَ يَجْعَلْ لَّكُمْ فُرْقَانًا وَّيُكَفِّرْ عَنْكُمْ سَيِّاٰتِكُمْ وَيَغْفِرْ لَكُمْ ؕ وَاللّٰهُ

greatest.

zul-faḍlil-‘aẓeem.

ذُو الْفَضْلِ الْعَظِيمِ ﴿٢٩﴾

30. The unbelievers planned to imprison, murder, or expel you (Muhammad) from your city. They make evil plans but Allah also plans and Allah's plans are the best.

30. Wa iz yamkuru bikallazeena kafaroo liyusbitooka aw yaqtulooka aw yukhrijook; wa yamkuroona wa yamkurul-laahu wallaahu khayrul-maakireen.

وَإِذْ يَمْكُرُ بِكَ الَّذِينَ كَفَرُوا
لِيُثْبِتُوكَ أَوْ يَقْتُلُوكَ أَوْ يُخْرِجُوكَ ۚ
وَيَمْكُرُونَ وَيَمْكُرُ اللَّهُ ۖ وَاللَّهُ
خَيْرُ الْمَاكِرِينَ ﴿٣٠﴾

31. When Our revelations are recited to them (the unbelievers), they say, “We have heard them. Had we wanted, we could also have composed such statements; they are no more than ancient legends.”

31. Wa izaa tutlaa ‘alayhim Aayaatunaa qaaloo qad sami‘-naa law nashaaa’u laqul-naa misla haazaaa in haazaaa illaaa asaaṭeerul awwaleen.

وَإِذَا تُتْلَىٰ عَلَيْهِمْ آيَاتُنَا قَالُوا قَدْ
سَمِعْنَا لَوْ نَشَاءُ لَقُلْنَا مِثْلَ هَٰذَا ۙ
إِنْ هَٰذَا إِلَّا أَسَاطِيرُ الْأَوَّلِينَ ﴿٣١﴾

32. They also say, “Lord, if this (Quran) is the Truth from you, shower down stones on us from the sky instead of rain or send us a painful punishment.”

32. Wa iz qaalul-laahumma in kaana haazaa huwal ḥaqqa min ‘indika fa-amṭir ‘alaynaa ḥijaaratam-minassamaaa’i awi’-tinaa bi‘azaabin aleem.

وَإِذْ قَالُوا اللَّهُمَّ إِنْ كَانَ
هَٰذَا هُوَ الْحَقَّ مِنْ عِنْدِكَ فَأَمْطِرْ
عَلَيْنَا حِجَارَةً مِنَ السَّمَاءِ أَوِ ائْتِنَا
بِعَذَابٍ أَلِيمٍ ﴿٣٢﴾

33. Allah would not punish them while you were among them nor while they were asking for forgiveness.

33. Wa maa kaanal-laahu liyu‘az-zibahum wa anta feehim; wa maa kaanal-laahu mu‘az-zibahum wa hum yastagh-firoon.

وَمَا كَانَ اللَّهُ لِيُعَذِّبَهُمْ وَأَنْتَ
فِيهِمْ ۚ وَمَا كَانَ اللَّهُ مُعَذِّبَهُمْ
وَهُمْ يَسْتَغْفِرُونَ ﴿٣٣﴾

34. Why should Allah not punish them when they hinder people from entering the sacred mosque? They are not its true patrons. Only the pious ones are its patrons, but most of the pagans do not know.

34. Wa maa lahum allaa yu‘az-zibahumul-laahu wa hum yaṣuddoona ‘anil-Masjidil-Ḥaraami wa maa kaanooo awliyaaa’ah; in awliyaaa’uhooo illal-muttaqoona walaakinna aksarahum laa ya‘lamoon.

وَمَا لَهُمْ أَلَّا يُعَذِّبَهُمُ اللَّهُ وَهُمْ
يَصُدُّونَ عَنِ الْمَسْجِدِ الْحَرَامِ وَمَا
كَانُوا أَوْلِيَاءَهُ ۚ إِنْ أَوْلِيَاؤُهُ إِلَّا
الْمُتَّقُونَ وَلَٰكِنَّ أَكْثَرَهُمْ لَا يَعْلَمُونَ ﴿٣٤﴾

35. Their (unbeliever's) prayer at the mosque was nothing but whistling and clapping of hands. We shall tell them, “Suffer torment for your disbelief.”

35. Wa maa kaana Ṣalaatuhum ‘indal-Bayti illaa mukaaa’añw-wa taṣdiyah; fazooqul-‘azaaba bimaa kuntum takfuroon.

وَمَا كَانَ صَلَاتُهُمْ عِنْدَ الْبَيْتِ
إِلَّا مُكَاءً وَتَصْدِيَةً ۚ فَذُوقُوا
الْعَذَابَ بِمَا كُنْتُمْ تَكْفُرُونَ ﴿٣٥﴾

36. The unbelievers spend their wealth to turn men away from the way of Allah. They will continue to spend but it will become a source of regret for them and they will be defeated (because of their evil plans). The unbelievers will

36. Innal-lazeena kafaroo yunfiqoona amwaalahum liyaṣuddoo ‘an sabeelil-laah; fasayunfiqoonahaa summa takoonu ‘alayhim ḥasratan summa yughlaboon; wal-lazeena

إِنَّ الَّذِينَ كَفَرُوا يُنْفِقُونَ
أَمْوَالَهُمْ لِيَصُدُّوا عَنْ سَبِيلِ اللَّهِ ۚ
فَسَيُنْفِقُونَهَا ثُمَّ تَكُونُ عَلَيْهِمْ
حَسْرَةً ثُمَّ يُغْلَبُونَ ۗ وَالَّذِينَ

be gathered all together in hell.

37. Allah will separate the wicked from the pure and will pile the wicked ones on top of one another to be cast into hell. They are indeed lost.

38. Muhammad, tell the unbelievers, "If you give up your evil behavior, Allah will forgive whatever you have done in the past. But if you transgress again, your fate will be the same as that of those (unbelievers) who lived before you."

39. Fight them so that idolatry will not exist anymore and Allah's religion will stand supreme. If they give up the idols, Allah will be Well-aware of what they do.

40. If the (unbelievers) turn away from the faith, Allah is your (believer's) best Guardian and best Helper.

41. Know that whatever property you may gain, one-fifth belongs to Allah, the Messenger, the kindred, orphans, the needy and those who need money while on a journey. (This is the law) if you believe in Allah and what We revealed to Our Servant on the Day of Distinction (Badr) when the armies confronted each other. Allah has power over all things.

42. Recall when your army was positioned at the less defensible brink of the valley, (the pagans') army had the more defensible higher side of the valley and the caravan was led (out of your reach) below. This situation did not take place according to your previous plans, otherwise everything would have been different.

(It was Allah's plan to place you in a vulnerable position, exposed to the enemy and it was His plan to lead the caravan out of your reach) so that His decree (that you would be granted a victory by a miracle) would become a doubtless fact; and so that those who were to be destroyed would face destruction with a clear knowledge of the Truth; and those who were to survive would also survive with a

kafarooo ilaa Jahannama yuḥsharoon.

37. Liyameezal-laahul khabee<u>s</u>a minaṭ-ṭayyibi wa yaj'alal-khabee<u>s</u>a ba'ḍahoo 'ala ba'ḍin fayarkumahoo jamee'an fayaj'alahoo fee Jahannam; ulaaa'ika humul-khaasiroon.

38. Qul-lilla<u>z</u>eena kafarooo iñy-yantahoo yughfar lahum maa qad salafa wa iñy-ya'oodoo fa-qad maḍat sunnatul-awwaleen.

39. Wa qaatiloohum ḥattaa laa takoona fitnatuñw-wa yakoo-naddeenu kulluhoo lillaah; fa-inin-tahaw fa-innallaaha bimaa ya'maloona Baṣeer.

40. Wa in tawallaw fa'lamooo annal-laaha mawlaakum; ni'mal-mawlaa wa ni'man-naṣeer.

41. Wa'lamooo annamaa gha-nimtum min shay'in fa-anna lillaahi khumusahoo wa lir-Rasooli wa li<u>z</u>il-qurbaa walya-taamaa walmasaakeeni wabnis-sabeeli in kuntum aamantum billaahi wa maaa anzalnaa 'ala 'abdinaa yawmal-Furqaani yawmaltaqal-jam'aan; wal-laahu 'alaa kulli shay'in Qadeer.

42. I<u>z</u> antum bil'udwatid-dunyaa wa hum bil'udwatil-quṣwaa warrakbu asfala minkum; wa law tawaa'attum lakhtalaftum fil-mee'aad; wa laakil-liyaqḍiyal-laahu amran kaana maf'oolaa; liyahlika man halaka 'am bayyinatiñw-wa yaḥyaa man ḥayya 'am

كَفَرُوٓا اِلٰی جَهَنَّمَ يُحْشَرُوْنَ ﴿٣٦﴾

لِيَمِيْزَ اللّٰهُ الْخَبِيْثَ مِنَ الطَّيِّبِ

وَيَجْعَلَ الْخَبِيْثَ بَعْضَهٗ عَلٰی

بَعْضٍ فَيَرْكُمَهٗ جَمِيْعًا فَيَجْعَلَهٗ

فِیْ جَهَنَّمَ ؕ اُولٰٓئِكَ هُمُ الْخٰسِرُوْنَ ﴿٣٧﴾ ع ٩ ١٨

قُلْ لِّلَّذِيْنَ كَفَرُوْٓا اِنْ يَّنْتَهُوْا يُغْفَرْ

لَهُمْ مَّا قَدْ سَلَفَ ۚ وَاِنْ يَّعُوْدُوْا

فَقَدْ مَضَتْ سُنَّتُ الْاَوَّلِيْنَ ﴿٣٨﴾

وَقَاتِلُوْهُمْ حَتّٰی لَا تَكُوْنَ فِتْنَةٌ وَّ

يَكُوْنَ الدِّيْنُ كُلُّهٗ لِلّٰهِ ۚ فَاِنِ انْتَهَوْا

فَاِنَّ اللّٰهَ بِمَا يَعْمَلُوْنَ بَصِيْرٌ ﴿٣٩﴾

وَاِنْ تَوَلَّوْا فَاعْلَمُوْٓا اَنَّ اللّٰهَ مَوْلٰىكُمْ ؕ

نِعْمَ الْمَوْلٰی وَنِعْمَ النَّصِيْرُ ﴿٤٠﴾

وَاعْلَمُوْٓا اَنَّمَا غَنِمْتُمْ مِّنْ شَیْءٍ

فَاَنَّ لِلّٰهِ خُمُسَهٗ وَلِلرَّسُوْلِ وَلِذِی

الْقُرْبٰی وَالْيَتٰمٰی وَالْمَسٰكِيْنِ وَابْنِ

السَّبِيْلِ ۙ اِنْ كُنْتُمْ اٰمَنْتُمْ بِاللّٰهِ وَمَآ

اَنْزَلْنَا عَلٰی عَبْدِنَا يَوْمَ الْفُرْقَانِ

يَوْمَ الْتَقَی الْجَمْعٰنِ ؕ وَاللّٰهُ عَلٰی

كُلِّ شَیْءٍ قَدِيْرٌ ﴿٤١﴾

اِذْ اَنْتُمْ بِالْعُدْوَةِ الدُّنْيَا وَهُمْ

بِالْعُدْوَةِ الْقُصْوٰی وَالرَّكْبُ اَسْفَلَ

مِنْكُمْ ؕ وَلَوْ تَوَاعَدْتُّمْ لَاخْتَلَفْتُمْ

فِی الْمِيْعٰدِ ۙ وَلٰكِنْ لِّيَقْضِیَ اللّٰهُ اَمْرًا

كَانَ مَفْعُوْلًا ۙ لِّيَهْلِكَ مَنْ هَلَكَ

عَنْۢ بَيِّنَةٍ وَّيَحْيٰی مَنْ حَیَّ عَنْۢ

الجزء العاشر (١٠)

clear knowledge of the Truth. Allah is All-hearing and All-knowing.

bayyinah; wa innal-laaha la-Samee'un 'Aleem.

بَيِّنَةٍ ۗ وَإِنَّ اللَّهَ لَسَمِيعٌ عَلِيمٌ ﴿٤٢﴾

43. In your dream, Allah showed (the pagans' army) as being only a few in numbers, for if He had showed them as a great number, you would have lost courage and would have started to quarrel among yourselves concerning this matter. But Allah saved you from that condition; He knows what is in your hearts.

43. Iz yureekahumul-laahu fee manaamika qaleelaa; wa law araakahum kaseeral-lafashil-tum wa latanaaza'tum fil-amri wa laakinnal-laaha sallam; innahoo 'aleemum bizaatiṣ-ṣudoor.

إِذْ يُرِيكَهُمُ اللَّهُ فِي مَنَامِكَ قَلِيلًا ۖ وَلَوْ
أَرَاكَهُمْ كَثِيرًا لَّفَشِلْتُمْ وَلَتَنَازَعْتُمْ
فِي الْأَمْرِ وَلَٰكِنَّ اللَّهَ سَلَّمَ ۗ إِنَّهُ
عَلِيمٌ بِذَاتِ الصُّدُورِ ﴿٤٣﴾

44. When you met the pagans' army, Allah made them appear fewer in your eyes and you appear fewer in their eyes so that His miracle of granting you (an incredible) victory could easily be fulfilled. To Allah do all things return.

44. Wa iz yureekumoohum izil-taqaytum feee a'yunikum qaleelañw-wa yuqallilukum feee a'yunihim liyaqḍiyal-laahu amran kaana maf'oolaa; wa ilal-laahi turja'ul-umoor.

وَإِذْ يُرِيكُمُوهُمْ إِذِ الْتَقَيْتُمْ فِي
أَعْيُنِكُمْ قَلِيلًا وَيُقَلِّلُكُمْ فِي أَعْيُنِهِمْ
لِيَقْضِيَ اللَّهُ أَمْرًا كَانَ مَفْعُولًا ۗ
وَإِلَى اللَّهِ تُرْجَعُ الْأُمُورُ ﴿٤٤﴾ ع

45. Believers, stand firm when you meet a band of your enemy and remember Allah often so that you may have everlasting happiness.

45. Yaaa ayyuhal-lazeena aamanooo izaa laqeetum fi'atan fasbutoo wazkurul-laaha kaseeral-la'allakum tufliḥoon.

يَا أَيُّهَا الَّذِينَ آمَنُوا إِذَا لَقِيتُمْ
فِئَةً فَاثْبُتُوا وَاذْكُرُوا اللَّهَ كَثِيرًا
لَّعَلَّكُمْ تُفْلِحُونَ ﴿٤٥﴾

46. Obey Allah and His messenger. Do not quarrel with each other lest you fail or lose honor. Exercise patience; Allah is with those who have patience.

46. Wa aṭee'ul-laaha wa Rasoolahoo wa laa tanaaza'oo fatafshaloo wa tazhaba reeḥu-kum waṣbiroo; innal-laaha ma'aṣ-ṣaabireen.

وَأَطِيعُوا اللَّهَ وَرَسُولَهُ وَلَا تَنَازَعُوا
فَتَفْشَلُوا وَتَذْهَبَ رِيحُكُمْ ۖ وَاصْبِرُوا ۚ
إِنَّ اللَّهَ مَعَ الصَّابِرِينَ ﴿٤٦﴾

47. Do not be like those who marched out boastfully to show off their strength to people and hinder people from the way of Allah. Allah encompasses everyone's activities.

47. Wa laa takoonoo kallazeena kharajoo min diyaarihim baṭarañw-wa ri'aaa'an-naasi wa yaṣuddoona 'an sabeelil-laah; wallaahu bimaa ya'maloona muḥeeṭ.

وَلَا تَكُونُوا كَالَّذِينَ خَرَجُوا
مِن دِيَارِهِم بَطَرًا وَرِئَاءَ النَّاسِ
وَيَصُدُّونَ عَن سَبِيلِ اللَّهِ ۚ
وَاللَّهُ بِمَا يَعْمَلُونَ مُحِيطٌ ﴿٤٧﴾

48. Satan made their (pagans') deeds seem attractive to them and said to them, "No one today is more powerful than you, and I am your supporter." But when the two armies confronted one another and the pagans were defeated, then Satan betrayed his friends, saying, "I am not with you anymore; I see what you can not see and I am afraid of Allah." Allah is severe in His retribution.

48. Wa iz-zayyana lahumush-Shayṭaanu a'maalahum wa qaala laa ghaaliba lakumul yawma minan-naasi wa innee jaarul-lakum falammaa taraaa'atil-fi'ataani nakaṣa 'alaa 'aqibayhi wa qaala innee bareee'um-minkum innee araa maa laa tarawna inneee akhaaful-laah; wallaahu sha-deedul-'iqaab.

وَإِذْ زَيَّنَ لَهُمُ الشَّيْطَانُ أَعْمَالَهُمْ
وَقَالَ لَا غَالِبَ لَكُمُ الْيَوْمَ مِنَ
النَّاسِ وَإِنِّي جَارٌ لَّكُمْ ۖ فَلَمَّا تَرَاءَتِ
الْفِئَتَانِ نَكَصَ عَلَىٰ عَقِبَيْهِ وَقَالَ
إِنِّي بَرِيءٌ مِّنكُمْ إِنِّي أَرَىٰ
مَا لَا تَرَوْنَ إِنِّي أَخَافُ اللَّهَ ۚ
وَاللَّهُ شَدِيدُ الْعِقَابِ ﴿٤٨﴾ ع

49. The hypocrites and those whose hearts are sick, say, "The (believers') religion has deceived them." Those who trust in Allah will find Allah Majestic and All-wise.

49. Iz yaqoolul-munaafiqoona wallazeena fee quloobihim maradun gharra haaa'ulaaa'i deenuhum; wa mañy-yatawak-kal 'alal-laahi fa-innal-laaha 'Azeezun Hakeem.

إِذْ يَقُولُ الْمُنٰفِقُونَ وَالَّذِينَ
فِي قُلُوبِهِمْ مَّرَضٌ غَرَّ هٰٓؤُلَآءِ
دِينُهُمْ ط وَمَنْ يَّتَوَكَّلْ عَلَى اللّٰهِ
فَإِنَّ اللّٰهَ عَزِيزٌ حَكِيمٌ ٤٩

50. Would that you could have seen the angels taking the souls of the unbelievers away from their bodies and smiting their faces and their backs, saying, "Suffer the burning torment.

50. Wa law taraaa iz yatawaf-fal-lazeena kafarul malaaa'ikatu yadriboona wujoohahum wa adbaarahum wa zooqoo 'azaa-bal-hareeq.

وَلَوْ تَرٰٓى إِذْ يَتَوَفَّى الَّذِينَ
كَفَرُوا الْمَلٰٓئِكَةُ يَضْرِبُونَ
وُجُوهَهُمْ وَأَدْبَارَهُمْ ج وَذُوقُوا
عَذَابَ الْحَرِيقِ ٥٠

51. This is the result of their deeds. Allah is not unjust to His servants."

51. Zaalika bimaa qaddamat aydeekum wa annal-laaha laysa bizallaamil-lil'abeed.

ذٰلِكَ بِمَا قَدَّمَتْ أَيْدِيكُمْ وَ
أَنَّ اللّٰهَ لَيْسَ بِظَلَّامٍ لِّلْعَبِيدِ ٥١

52. The same thing happened to the people of the Pharaoh and those who lived before them. They rejected the revelations of Allah and, because of their sins, Allah's retribution struck them. Allah is All-powerful and stern in His retribution.

52. Kada-bi Aali Fir'awna wal-lazeena min qablihim; kafaroo bi-Aayaatil-laahi fa-akhazahu-mul-laahu bizunoobihim; innal-laaha qawiyyun shadeedul-'iqaab.

كَدَأْبِ اٰلِ فِرْعَوْنَ لا وَالَّذِينَ
مِنْ قَبْلِهِمْ ط كَفَرُوا بِاٰيٰتِ اللّٰهِ
فَأَخَذَهُمُ اللّٰهُ بِذُنُوبِهِمْ ط إِنَّ اللّٰهَ
قَوِيٌّ شَدِيدُ الْعِقَابِ ٥٢

53. Allah would not change the favor that He had bestowed on a nation unless that nation changed what was in its soul. Allah is All-hearing and All-knowing.

53. Zaalika bi-annal-laaha lam yaku mughayyiran-ni'matan an'amahaa 'alaa qawmin hattaa yughayyiroo maa bi-anfusihim wa annallaaha Samee'un 'Aleem.

ذٰلِكَ بِأَنَّ اللّٰهَ لَمْ يَكُ مُغَيِّرًا
نِّعْمَةً أَنْعَمَهَا عَلٰى قَوْمٍ حَتّٰى
يُغَيِّرُوا مَا بِأَنْفُسِهِمْ لا وَأَنَّ اللّٰهَ
سَمِيعٌ عَلِيمٌ ٥٣

54. Like the people of the Pharaoh and those who lived before them, they (the unbelievers) rejected the revelations of Allah. We destroyed them for their sins and drowned the people of the Pharaoh. They were all unjust.

54. Kada-bi Aali Fir'awna wallazeena min qablihim; kaz-zaboo bi-Aayaati Rabbihim fa-ahlaknaahum bizunoobihim wa aghraqnaaa Aala Fir'awn; wa kullun kaanoo zaalimeen.

كَدَأْبِ اٰلِ فِرْعَوْنَ لا وَالَّذِينَ
مِنْ قَبْلِهِمْ ط كَذَّبُوا بِاٰيٰتِ
رَبِّهِمْ فَأَهْلَكْنٰهُمْ بِذُنُوبِهِمْ
وَأَغْرَقْنَآ اٰلَ فِرْعَوْنَ ج وَكُلٌّ
كَانُوا ظٰلِمِينَ ٥٤

55. The most wicked creatures in the sight of Allah are the unbelievers who will never have faith,

55. Inna sharrad-dawaaabbi 'indal-laahil-lazeena kafaroo fahum laa yu'minoon.

إِنَّ شَرَّ الدَّوَآبِّ عِنْدَ اللّٰهِ الَّذِينَ
كَفَرُوا فَهُمْ لَا يُؤْمِنُونَ ٥٥

56. who make promises to you but then break them every time,

56. Allazeena 'aahatta min-hum summa

الَّذِينَ عٰهَدْتَّ مِنْهُمْ ثُمَّ

and who have no piety.

yanquḍoona 'ahdahum fee kulli marratiñw-wa hum laa yattaqoon.

يَنْقُضُونَ عَهْدَهُمْ فِي كُلِّ
مَرَّةٍ وَّهُمْ لَا يَتَّقُونَ ﴿٥٦﴾

57. When you capture the (unbelievers) during a fight, teach them a lesson so that they, thereafter, will always be aware of the threat of your power.

57. Fa-immaa tas̲qafannahum fil-ḥarbi fasharrid bihim man khalfahum la'allahum yaz̲z̲akkaroon.

فَإِمَّا تَثْقَفَنَّهُمْ فِي الْحَرْبِ فَشَرِّدْ بِهِمْ
مَّنْ خَلْفَهُمْ لَعَلَّهُمْ يَذَّكَّرُونَ ﴿٥٧﴾

58. If you are afraid of the treachery of some of your allies, you may disregard your treaty with them. Allah does not love the treacherous ones.

58. Wa immaa takhaafanna min qawmin khiyaanatan fambiz̲ ilayhim 'alaa sawaaa'; innallaaha laa yuḥibbul-khaaa'ineen.

وَإِمَّا تَخَافَنَّ مِنْ قَوْمٍ خِيَانَةً
فَانْبِذْ إِلَيْهِمْ عَلَىٰ سَوَاءٍ ۚ إِنَّ
اللَّهَ لَا يُحِبُّ الْخَائِنِينَ ﴿٥٨﴾ ع

59. The unbelievers should not think that they can really escape Us or that they can never be defeated.

59. Wa laa yaḥsabannal-laz̲eena kafaroo sabaqooo; innahum laa yu'jizoon.

وَلَا يَحْسَبَنَّ الَّذِينَ كَفَرُوا سَبَقُوا ۚ
إِنَّهُمْ لَا يُعْجِزُونَ ﴿٥٩﴾

60. Mobilize your (defensive) force as much as you can to frighten the enemies of Allah and your own enemies. This also will frighten those who are behind them whom you do not know but Allah knows well. Whatever you spend for the cause of Allah, He will give you sufficient recompense with due justice.

60. Wa a'iddoo lahum mastaṭa'tum min quwwatiñw-wa mirribaaṭil-khayli turhiboona bihee 'aduwwal-laahi wa 'aduwwakum wa-aakhareena min doonihim laa ta'lamoonahum Allaahu ya'lamuhum; wa maa tunfiqoo min shay'in fee sabeelil-laahi yuwaf-failaykum wa antum laa tuẓlamoon.

وَأَعِدُّوا لَهُمْ مَا اسْتَطَعْتُمْ مِنْ
قُوَّةٍ وَمِنْ رِبَاطِ الْخَيْلِ تُرْهِبُونَ
بِهِ عَدُوَّ اللَّهِ وَعَدُوَّكُمْ وَآخَرِينَ
مِنْ دُونِهِمْ لَا تَعْلَمُونَهُمُ
اللَّهُ يَعْلَمُهُمْ ۚ وَمَا تُنْفِقُوا مِنْ
شَيْءٍ فِي سَبِيلِ اللَّهِ يُوَفَّ إِلَيْكُمْ
وَأَنْتُمْ لَا تُظْلَمُونَ ﴿٦٠﴾

61. If they (the unbelievers) propose peace, accept it and trust in Allah. Allah is All-hearing and All-knowing.

61. Wa in janaḥoo lissalmi fajnaḥ lahaa wa tawakkal 'alallaah; innahoo Huwas-Samee-'ul-'Aleem.

وَإِنْ جَنَحُوا لِلسَّلْمِ فَاجْنَحْ
لَهَا وَتَوَكَّلْ عَلَى اللَّهِ ۚ إِنَّهُ هُوَ
السَّمِيعُ الْعَلِيمُ ﴿٦١﴾

62. If they want to deceive you, Allah is All-sufficient for you. It is Allah who supported you with His own help and with that of the believers,

62. Wa iñy-yureedooo añy-yakhda'ooka fainna ḥasbakallaah; Huwal-laz̲eee ayyadaka binaṣrihee wa bilmu'mineen.

وَإِنْ يُرِيدُوا أَنْ يَخْدَعُوكَ فَإِنَّ
حَسْبَكَ اللَّهُ ۚ هُوَ الَّذِي أَيَّدَكَ
بِنَصْرِهِ وَبِالْمُؤْمِنِينَ ﴿٦٢﴾

63. among whose hearts He has placed affection and unity. If you were to spend the wealth of the whole earth, you would not be able to unite their hearts, but Allah has been able to unite them. Allah is Majestic and All-wise.

63. Wa allafa bayna quloobihim; law-anfaqta maa fil-arḍi jamee'am-maaa-allafta bayna quloobihim wa laakinnallaaha allafa baynahum; innahoo 'Azeezun Ḥakeem.

وَأَلَّفَ بَيْنَ قُلُوبِهِمْ ۚ لَوْ أَنْفَقْتَ
مَا فِي الْأَرْضِ جَمِيعًا مَا أَلَّفْتَ
بَيْنَ قُلُوبِهِمْ وَلَٰكِنَّ اللَّهَ أَلَّفَ
بَيْنَهُمْ ۚ إِنَّهُ عَزِيزٌ حَكِيمٌ ﴿٦٣﴾

64. O Prophet, Allah and those of the believers who follow you are sufficient support for you.

64. Yaaa ayyuhan-Nabiyyu ḥasbukal-laahu wa manittaba'aka minal-mu'mineen.

يَٰٓأَيُّهَا النَّبِيُّ حَسْبُكَ اللَّهُ وَمَنِ
اتَّبَعَكَ مِنَ الْمُؤْمِنِينَ ﴿٦٤﴾

65. Prophet, mobilize the believers for the battle. It will take only twenty of your men who are steadfast (in prayer) to defeat two hundred unbelieving men. Your two hundred men would defeat their two thousand; the unbelievers have no understanding.

65. Yaaa ayyuhan-Nabiyyu ḥarriḍil-mu'mineena 'alal-qitaal; iñy-yakum-minkum 'ishroona ṣaabiroona yaghliboo mi'atayn; wa iñy-yakum-minkum mi'atuñy-yaghlibooo alfam-minal-lazeena kafaroo bi-annahum qawmul-laa yafqahoon.

يَٰٓأَيُّهَا النَّبِيُّ حَرِّضِ الْمُؤْمِنِينَ عَلَى
الْقِتَالِ ۚ إِن يَكُن مِّنكُمْ عِشْرُونَ
صَٰبِرُونَ يَغْلِبُوا مِائَتَيْنِ ۚ وَإِن
يَكُن مِّنكُم مِّائَةٌ يَغْلِبُوٓا
أَلْفًا مِّنَ الَّذِينَ كَفَرُوا بِأَنَّهُمْ
قَوْمٌ لَّا يَفْقَهُونَ ﴿٦٥﴾

66. Now that Allah has eased your burden, He has found you to be weak. A hundred of your steadfast men would defeat two hundred of theirs and a thousand of yours would defeat two thousand of the unbelievers, by the will of Allah. Allah is with those who have patience.

66. Al'aana khaffafal-laahu 'ankum wa 'alima anna feekum ḍa'faa; fa-iñy-yakum-minkum mi'atun ṣaabiratuñy-yaghliboo mi'atayn; wa iñy-yakum-minkum alfuñy-yaghlibooo alfayni bi-iznil-laah; wallaahu ma'aṣ-ṣaabireen.

الْـَٰٔنَ خَفَّفَ اللَّهُ عَنكُمْ وَعَلِمَ أَنَّ
فِيكُمْ ضَعْفًا ۚ فَإِن يَكُن مِّنكُم مِّائَةٌ
صَابِرَةٌ يَغْلِبُوا مِائَتَيْنِ ۚ وَإِن
يَكُن مِّنكُمْ أَلْفٌ يَغْلِبُوٓا أَلْفَيْنِ
بِإِذْنِ اللَّهِ ۗ وَاللَّهُ مَعَ الصَّٰبِرِينَ ﴿٦٦﴾

67. The Prophet is not supposed to take any captives to strengthen his position on the earth. You want worldly gains but Allah wants the life hereafter for you. Allah is Majestic and All-wise.

67. Maa kaana li-Nabiyyin añy-yakoona lahooo asraa ḥattaa yuskhina fil-arḍ; tureedoona 'araḍad-dunyaa wallaahu yureedul-Aakhirah; wallaahu 'Azeezun Ḥakeem.

مَا كَانَ لِنَبِيٍّ أَن يَكُونَ لَهُۥٓ أَسْرَىٰ
حَتَّىٰ يُثْخِنَ فِي الْأَرْضِ ۚ تُرِيدُونَ
عَرَضَ الدُّنْيَا وَاللَّهُ يُرِيدُ
الْءَاخِرَةَ ۗ وَاللَّهُ عَزِيزٌ حَكِيمٌ ﴿٦٧﴾

68. (Had you taken captives) before being allowed by Allah's revelations, a great torment would have struck you for what you would have had done.

68. Law laa Kitaabum-minal-laahi sabaqa lamassakum feemaaa akhaztum 'azaabun 'aẓeem.

لَّوْلَا كِتَٰبٌ مِّنَ اللَّهِ سَبَقَ لَمَسَّكُمْ
فِيمَآ أَخَذْتُمْ عَذَابٌ عَظِيمٌ ﴿٦٨﴾

69. Use what you have acquired (from the battle) as your own good, lawful property. Have fear of Allah; Allah is All-forgiving and All-merciful.

69. Fakuloo mimmaa ghanimtum ḥalaalan ṭayyibañw-wattaqullaah; innal-laaha Ghafoorur-Raḥeem.

فَكُلُوا مِمَّا غَنِمْتُمْ حَلَٰلًا طَيِّبًا ۚ وَ
اتَّقُوا اللَّهَ ۚ إِنَّ اللَّهَ غَفُورٌ رَّحِيمٌ ﴿٦٩﴾

70. Prophet, tell the captives with you, "If Allah finds anything good in your hearts, He will give you a better reward than that which was taken from you and will forgive you. Allah is All-forgiving and All-merciful.

70. Yaaa ayyuhan-Nabiyyu qul liman feee aydeekum minal-asraaa iñy-ya'lamillaahu fee quloobikum khayrañy-yu'tikum khayram-mimmaaa ukhiza minkum wa yaghfir lakum; wallaahu Ghafoorur-Raḥeem.

يَٰٓأَيُّهَا النَّبِيُّ قُل لِّمَن فِيٓ أَيْدِيكُم
مِّنَ الْأَسْرَىٰٓ إِن يَعْلَمِ اللَّهُ فِي
قُلُوبِكُمْ خَيْرًا يُؤْتِكُمْ خَيْرًا
مِّمَّآ أُخِذَ مِنكُمْ وَيَغْفِرْ لَكُمْ ۗ
وَاللَّهُ غَفُورٌ رَّحِيمٌ ﴿٧٠﴾

70. Do not be surprised that they want to be dishonest with you; they have always been dishonest with Allah. However, He has power over them. Allah is All-knowing and All-wise.

71. Wa iñy-yureedoo khiyaa-nataka faqad khaanullaaha min qablu fa-amkana minhum; wallaahu 'Aleemun Ḥakeem.

وَاِنْ يُّرِيْدُوْا خِيَانَتَكَ فَقَدْ
خَانُوا اللّٰهَ مِنْ قَبْلُ فَاَمْكَنَ
مِنْهُمْ ؕ وَاللّٰهُ عَلِيْمٌ حَكِيْمٌ ﴿٧١﴾

72. The believers who left their homes and strove for the cause of Allah, through their property and in person, and those who gave refuge to them and helped them, will be each others' guardians. The believers who did not leave their homes are not your guardians until they too leave their homes. If they ask you for help in a religious cause, you must help them against their enemies unless their enemies have a peace treaty with you. Allah is Well-aware of what you do.

72. Innal-lazeena aamanoo wa haajaroo wa jaahadoo bi-amwaalihim wa anfusihim fee sabeelil-laahi wallazeena aawaw wa naṣarooo ulaaa'ika ba'ḍuhum awliyaaa'u ba'ḍ; wallazeena aamanoo wa lam yuhaajiroo maa lakum miñw-walaayatihim min shay'in ḥattaa yuhaajiroo; wa inistan-ṣarookum fid-deeni fa'alayku-munnaṣru illaa 'alaa qawmim baynakum wa baynahum meesaaq; wallaahu bimaa ta'maloona Baṣeer.

اِنَّ الَّذِيْنَ اٰمَنُوْا وَهَاجَرُوْا وَ
جٰهَدُوْا بِاَمْوَالِهِمْ وَاَنْفُسِهِمْ
فِيْ سَبِيْلِ اللّٰهِ وَالَّذِيْنَ اٰوَوْا وَّ
نَصَرُوْۤا اُولٰٓئِكَ بَعْضُهُمْ اَوْلِيَآءُ
بَعْضٍ ؕ وَالَّذِيْنَ اٰمَنُوْا وَلَمْ
يُهَاجِرُوْا مَا لَكُمْ مِّنْ وَّلَايَتِهِمْ
مِّنْ شَيْءٍ حَتّٰى يُهَاجِرُوْا ۚ وَاِنِ
اسْتَنْصَرُوْكُمْ فِي الدِّيْنِ فَعَلَيْكُمُ
النَّصْرُ اِلَّا عَلٰى قَوْمٍۢ بَيْنَكُمْ وَبَيْنَهُمْ
مِّيْثَاقٌ ؕ وَاللّٰهُ بِمَا تَعْمَلُوْنَ بَصِيْرٌ ﴿٧٢﴾

73. The unbelievers are each others' friends. If you (the believers) do not keep the same among yourselves in the land, there will come into being widespread idolatry and great evil.

73. Wallazeena kafaroo ba'ḍuhum awliyaaa'u ba'ḍ; illaa taf'aloohu takun fitnatun fil-arḍi wa fasaadun kabeer.

وَالَّذِيْنَ كَفَرُوْا بَعْضُهُمْ اَوْلِيَآءُ
بَعْضٍ ؕ اِلَّا تَفْعَلُوْهُ تَكُنْ فِتْنَةٌ
فِي الْاَرْضِ وَفَسَادٌ كَبِيْرٌ ؕ ﴿٧٣﴾

74. The believers who left their homes, and strove for the cause of Allah and those who gave them refuge and helped them, are true believers. They will have forgiveness (from their Lord) and (will be granted) honorable provisions.

74. Wallazeena aamanoo wa haajaroo wa jaahadoo fee sabeelil-laahi wallazeena aawaw wa naṣarooo ulaaa'ika humul-mu'minoona ḥaqqaa; lahum maghfiratuñw-wa rizqun kareem.

وَالَّذِيْنَ اٰمَنُوْا وَهَاجَرُوْا وَ
جٰهَدُوْا فِيْ سَبِيْلِ اللّٰهِ وَالَّذِيْنَ
اٰوَوْا وَّنَصَرُوْۤا اُولٰٓئِكَ هُمُ
الْمُؤْمِنُوْنَ حَقًّا ؕ لَهُمْ مَّغْفِرَةٌ
وَّرِزْقٌ كَرِيْمٌ ﴿٧٤﴾

75. Those who accepted the faith later, left their homes and strove with you for the cause of Allah are also your people. Relatives have priority to each other according to the Book of Allah. Allah has knowledge of all things.

75. Wallazeena aamanoo mimba'du wa haajaroo wa jaahadoo ma'akum fa-ulaaa'ika minkum; wa ulul-arḥaami ba'ḍuhum awlaa biba'ḍin fee Kitaabil-laah; innal-laaha bikulli shay'in 'Aleem.

وَالَّذِيْنَ اٰمَنُوْا مِنْۢ بَعْدُ وَهَاجَرُوْا
وَجٰهَدُوْا مَعَكُمْ فَاُولٰٓئِكَ مِنْكُمْ ؕ
وَاُولُوا الْاَرْحَامِ بَعْضُهُمْ اَوْلٰى
بِبَعْضٍ فِيْ كِتٰبِ اللّٰهِ ؕ اِنَّ اللّٰهَ
بِكُلِّ شَيْءٍ عَلِيْمٌ ﴿٧٥﴾ ع

Al-Tawbah, The Repentance (9)

In the Name of Allah, the Beneficent, the Merciful.

1. Allah and His Messenger declare the abrogation of the peace treaty that existed between them and the pagans.

2. However, during the four sacred months, they (pagans) may travel peacefully through the land. You (pagans) must know that you cannot make Allah helpless, but it is Allah who has the power to disgrace the unbelievers.

3. This Announcement from Allah and His Messenger is to be made to the people on the day of the great Pilgrimage; Allah and His Messenger have declared no amnesty for the pagans. If you (pagans) repent, it will be better for you, but if you turn away (from Allah), know that you cannot make Allah helpless.

(Muhammad) tell the unbelievers that a painful punishment has been prepared for them.

4. This does not apply to the pagans with whom you have a valid peace treaty and who had not broken it from their side or helped others against you. You (believers) must fulfill the terms of the peace treaty with them. Allah loves the pious ones.

5. When the sacred months are over, slay the pagans wherever you find them. Capture, besiege, and watch their activities. If they repent, perform prayers and pay the religious tax, set them free. Allah is All-forgiving and All-merciful.

6. If any of the pagans ask you to give them refuge, give them asylum so that they may hear the words of Allah. Then, return them to their towns, for they are an ignorant people.

Sûrat al-Taubah/Barâ'at-9

(Revealed at Madinah)

1. Baraaa'atum-minal-laahi wa Rasooliheee ilal-la<u>z</u>eena 'aahattum-minal-mushrikeen.

2. Faseeḥoo fil-arḍi arba'ata ashhuriñw-wa'lamooo annakum ghayru mu'jizil-laahi wa annal-laaha mukhzil-kaafireen.

3. Wa a<u>z</u>aanum-minal-laahi wa Rasooliheee ilan-naasi yawmal-Ḥajjil-Akbari annal-laaha bareee'um-minal-mushrikeena wa Rasooluh; fa-in tubtum fahuwa khayrullakum wa in tawallaytum fa'lamooo annakum ghayru mu'jizil-laah; wa bashshiril-la<u>z</u>eena kafaroo bi'a<u>z</u>aabin aleem.

4. Illal-la<u>z</u>eena 'aahattum minal-mushrikeena <u>s</u>umma lam yanquṣookum shay'añw-wa lam yuẓaahiroo 'alaykum aḥadan fa-atimmooo ilayhim 'ahdahum ilaa muddatihim; innal-laaha yuḥibbul-muttaqeen.

5 Fa-i<u>z</u>ansalakhal Ash-hurul Ḥurumu faqtulul-mushrikeena ḥay<u>s</u>u wajattumoohum wa khu<u>z</u>oohum waḥṣuroohum waq'udoo lahum kulla marṣad; fa-in taaboo wa aqaamuṣ-Ṣalaata wa aatawuz-Zakaata fakhalloo sabeelahum; innal-laaha Ghafoorur-Raḥeem.

6. Wa in aḥadum-minal-mushrikeenas-tajaaraka fa-ajirhu ḥattaa yasma'a Kalaa-mal-laahi <u>s</u>umma ablighhu ma-manah; <u>z</u>aalika bi-annahum qawmul-laa ya'lamoon.

(٩) سُوْرَةُ التَّوْبَةِ مَدَنِيَّةٌ (١١٣)

بَرَآءَةٌ مِّنَ اللّٰهِ وَرَسُوْلِهٖٓ اِلَى الَّذِيْنَ
عٰهَدْتُّمْ مِّنَ الْمُشْرِكِيْنَ ۝١
فَسِيْحُوْا فِى الْاَرْضِ اَرْبَعَةَ اَشْهُرٍ
وَّاعْلَمُوْٓا اَنَّكُمْ غَيْرُ مُعْجِزِى اللّٰهِ ۙ
وَاَنَّ اللّٰهَ مُخْزِى الْكٰفِرِيْنَ ۝٢
وَاَذَانٌ مِّنَ اللّٰهِ وَرَسُوْلِهٖٓ اِلَى النَّاسِ
يَوْمَ الْحَجِّ الْاَكْبَرِ اَنَّ اللّٰهَ بَرِىْٓءٌ
مِّنَ الْمُشْرِكِيْنَ ۙ وَرَسُوْلُهٗ ؕ فَاِنْ
تُبْتُمْ فَهُوَ خَيْرٌ لَّكُمْ ۚ وَاِنْ تَوَلَّيْتُمْ
فَاعْلَمُوْٓا اَنَّكُمْ غَيْرُ مُعْجِزِى اللّٰهِ ؕ
وَبَشِّرِ الَّذِيْنَ كَفَرُوْا بِعَذَابٍ اَلِيْمٍ ۝٣
اِلَّا الَّذِيْنَ عٰهَدْتُّمْ مِّنَ الْمُشْرِكِيْنَ
ثُمَّ لَمْ يَنْقُصُوْكُمْ شَيْـًٔا وَّلَمْ
يُظَاهِرُوْا عَلَيْكُمْ اَحَدًا فَاَتِمُّوْٓا اِلَيْهِمْ
عَهْدَهُمْ اِلٰى مُدَّتِهِمْ ؕ اِنَّ اللّٰهَ
يُحِبُّ الْمُتَّقِيْنَ ۝٤
فَاِذَا انْسَلَخَ الْاَشْهُرُ الْحُرُمُ فَاقْتُلُوا
الْمُشْرِكِيْنَ حَيْثُ وَجَدْتُّمُوْهُمْ
وَخُذُوْهُمْ وَاحْصُرُوْهُمْ وَاقْعُدُوْا لَهُمْ
كُلَّ مَرْصَدٍ ۚ فَاِنْ تَابُوْا وَاَقَامُوا
الصَّلٰوةَ وَاٰتَوُا الزَّكٰوةَ فَخَلُّوْا
سَبِيْلَهُمْ ؕ اِنَّ اللّٰهَ غَفُوْرٌ رَّحِيْمٌ ۝٥
وَاِنْ اَحَدٌ مِّنَ الْمُشْرِكِيْنَ اسْتَجَارَكَ
فَاَجِرْهُ حَتّٰى يَسْمَعَ كَلٰمَ اللّٰهِ ثُمَّ
اَبْلِغْهُ مَاْمَنَهٗ ؕ ذٰلِكَ بِاَنَّهُمْ

قَوۡمٌ لَّا يَعۡلَمُوۡنَ ۝٦ ع

7. How can the pagans, except those with whom you have established a peace treaty in the precinct of the Sacred Mosque, have a covenant with Allah and His Messenger? If they respect the pact, you should also follow its terms. Allah loves the pious ones.

7. Kayfa yakoonu lilmushrikeena 'ahdun 'indallaahi wa 'inda Rasooliheee illal-lazeena 'aahattum 'indal-Masjidil-Ḥaraami famas-taqaamoo lakum fastaqeemoo lahum; innallaaha yuḥibbul-muttaqeen.

كَيۡفَ يَكُوۡنُ لِلۡمُشۡرِكِيۡنَ عَهۡدٌ عِنۡدَ
اللّٰهِ وَعِنۡدَ رَسُوۡلِهٖۤ اِلَّا الَّذِيۡنَ
عٰهَدۡتُّمۡ عِنۡدَ الۡمَسۡجِدِ الۡحَـرَامِ‌ ۚ فَمَا
اسۡتَقَامُوۡا لَـكُمۡ فَاسۡتَقِيۡمُوۡا لَهُمۡ‌ ؕ
اِنَّ اللّٰهَ يُحِبُّ الۡمُتَّقِيۡنَ ۝٧

8. How could Allah and His Messenger grant them (pagans) peace when if they were to acquire superiority over you, they would respect none of the peace treaties nor their kindred relations with you! They only try to please you by paying lip-service to you, but their hearts are against you and most of them are evil-doers.

8. Kayfa wa iñy-yaẓharoo 'alaykum laa yarquboo feekum illañw-wa laa ẕimmah; yurḍoonakum bi-afwaahihim wa ta-baa quloobuhum wa akṯaruhum faasiqoon.

كَيۡفَ وَاِنۡ يَّظۡهَرُوۡا عَلَيۡكُمۡ
لَا يَرۡقُبُوۡا فِيۡكُمۡ اِلًّا وَّلَا ذِمَّةً‌ ؕ
يُرۡضُوۡنَكُمۡ بِاَفۡوَاهِهِمۡ وَتَاۡبٰى
قُلُوۡبُهُمۡ‌ ۚ وَاَكۡثَرُهُمۡ فٰسِقُوۡنَ‌ ۝٨

9. They have sold Allah's revelations for a paltry price and have created obstacles in the way of Allah. What they have done is evil.

9. Ishtaraw bi-Aayaatil-laahi ṯamanan qaleelan faṣaddoo'an sabeelih; innahum saaa'a maa kaanoo ya'maloon.

اِشۡتَرَوۡا بِاٰيٰتِ اللّٰهِ ثَمَنًا قَلِيۡلًا
فَصَدُّوۡا عَنۡ سَبِيۡلِهٖ‌ ؕ اِنَّهُمۡ
سَآءَ مَا كَانُوۡا يَعۡمَلُوۡنَ ۝٩

10. They do not respect their promises nor their family ties with the believers. They are transgressors.

10. Laa yarquboona fee mu'minin illañw-wa laa ẕimmah; wa ulaaa'ika humul mu'tadoon.

لَا يَرۡقُبُوۡنَ فِىۡ مُؤۡمِنٍ اِلًّا وَّلَا ذِمَّةً‌ ؕ
وَاُولٰٓـئِكَ هُمُ الۡمُعۡتَدُوۡنَ ۝١٠

11. If they repent, perform their prayers, and pay religious tax, they will be your brothers in the religion. We explain Our revelations to people of knowledge.

11. Fa-in taaboo wa aqaamuṣ-Ṣalaata wa aatawuz-Zakaata fa-ikhwaanukum fid-deen; wa nufaṣṣilul-Aayaati liqawmiñy-ya'lamoon.

فَاِنۡ تَابُوۡا وَاَقَامُوا الصَّلٰوةَ وَاٰتَوُا
الزَّكٰوةَ فَاِخۡوَانُكُمۡ فِى الدِّيۡنِ‌ ؕ
وَنُفَصِّلُ الۡاٰيٰتِ لِقَوۡمٍ يَّعۡلَمُوۡنَ ۝١١

12. Fight against the leaders of the unbelievers if they violate their established peace treaty with you and revile your faith, to force them to stop their aggression against you. You do not have to bind yourselves to such a treaty.

12. Wa in nakaṯooo aymaanahum mim ba'di-'ahdihim wa ṭa'anoo fee deenikum faqaatilooo a'immatal-kufri innahum laaa aymaana lahum la'allahum yantahoon.

وَاِنۡ نَّكَثُوۡۤا اَيۡمَانَهُمۡ مِّنۡۢ بَعۡدِ
عَهۡدِهِمۡ وَطَعَنُوۡا فِىۡ دِيۡنِكُمۡ
فَقَاتِلُوۡۤا اَئِمَّةَ الۡـكُفۡرِ‌ ۙ اِنَّهُمۡ لَاۤ
اَيۡمَانَ لَهُمۡ لَعَلَّهُمۡ يَنۡتَهُوۡنَ ۝١٢

13. Why will you not fight against a people who have broken their peace treaty with you, have decided to expel the Messenger (from his home town), and who were the first to disregard the peace treaty? If you are true believers, you should have fear only of Allah.

13. Alaa tuqaatiloona qawman nakaṯooo aymaanahum wa hammoo bi-ikhraajir-Rasooli wa hum bada'ookum awwala marrah; atakhshawnahum; fallaahu aḥaqqu an takhshawhu in kuntum mu'mineen.

اَلَا تُقَاتِلُوۡنَ قَوۡمًا نَّكَثُوۡۤا اَيۡمَانَهُمۡ
وَهَمُّوۡا بِاِخۡرَاجِ الرَّسُوۡلِ وَهُمۡ
بَدَءُوۡكُمۡ اَوَّلَ مَرَّةٍ‌ ؕ اَتَخۡشَوۡنَهُمۡ‌ ۚ
فَاللّٰهُ اَحَقُّ اَنۡ تَخۡشَوۡهُ اِنۡ كُنۡتُمۡ

مُّؤْمِنِينَ ﴿١٣﴾

14. Fight them. May Allah punish them by your hands, humiliate them, give you victory over them, delight the hearts of the believers

14. Qaatiloohum yu'az-zib-humul-laahu bi-aydeekum wa yukhzihim wa yanṣurkum 'alayhim wa yashfi ṣudoora qawmim mu'mineen.

قَاتِلُوهُمْ يُعَذِّبْهُمُ اللّٰهُ بِاَيْدِيكُمْ
وَيُخْزِهِمْ وَيَنْصُرْكُمْ عَلَيْهِمْ
وَيَشْفِ صُدُورَ قَوْمٍ مُّؤْمِنِينَ ﴿١٤﴾

15. and appease their anger. Allah forgives whomever He wants and He is All-knowing and All-wise.

15. Wa yuẕhib ghayẓa quloobihim; wa yatoobullaahu 'alaa mañy-yashaaa'; wallaahu 'Aleemun Ḥakeem.

وَيُذْهِبْ غَيْظَ قُلُوبِهِمْ ۗ وَيَتُوبُ
اللّٰهُ عَلٰى مَنْ يَّشَآءُ ۗ وَاللّٰهُ
عَلِيمٌ حَكِيمٌ ﴿١٥﴾

16. Do you think that Allah will not make any distinction between those of you who have fought for His cause and had relied on no one other than Allah, His Messenger, and the faithful ones, and other people? Allah is Well-aware of what you do.

16. Am ḥasibtum an tutrakoo wa lammaa ya'lamil-laahul-laẕeena jaahadoo minkum wa lam yattakhiẕoo min doonil-laahi wa laa Rasoolihee wa lalmu'mineena waleejah; wallaahu-khabeerum bimaa ta'maloon.

اَمْ حَسِبْتُمْ اَنْ تُتْرَكُوا وَلَمَّا
يَعْلَمِ اللّٰهُ الَّذِينَ جٰهَدُوا مِنْكُمْ
وَلَمْ يَتَّخِذُوا مِنْ دُونِ اللّٰهِ وَلَا
رَسُولِهٖ وَلَا الْمُؤْمِنِينَ وَلِيجَةً ۗ
وَاللّٰهُ خَبِيرٌ بِمَا تَعْمَلُونَ ﴿١٦﴾ ع ٨

17. The pagans do not have any right to establish (and patronize) the mosque of Allah while they testify against their souls to its disbelief. Their deeds are devoid of all virtue and they will live forever in hellfire.

17. Maa kaana lilmushrikeena añy-ya'muroo masaajidal-laahi shaahideena 'alaaa anfusihim bilkufr; ulaaa'ika ḥabiṭat a'maaluhum wa fin-Naari hum khaalidoon.

مَا كَانَ لِلْمُشْرِكِينَ اَنْ يَّعْمُرُوا
مَسٰجِدَ اللّٰهِ شٰهِدِينَ عَلٰٓى اَنْفُسِهِمْ
بِالْكُفْرِ ۗ اُولٰٓئِكَ حَبِطَتْ اَعْمَالُهُمْ ۚ
وَفِي النَّارِ هُمْ خٰلِدُونَ ﴿١٧﴾

18. Only those who believed in Allah and the Day of Judgment, performed their prayers, paid the religious tax, and had fear of Allah alone have the right to establish and patronize the mosque of Allah so that perhaps they will have the right guidance.

18. Innamaa ya'muru masaajidal-laahi man aamana billaahi wal-Yawmil-Aakhiri wa aqaamaṣ-Ṣalaata wa aataz-Zakaata wa lam yakhsha illal-laaha fa'asaaa ulaaa'ika añy-yakoonoo minal-muhtadeen.

اِنَّمَا يَعْمُرُ مَسٰجِدَ اللّٰهِ مَنْ اٰمَنَ
بِاللّٰهِ وَالْيَوْمِ الْاٰخِرِ وَاَقَامَ الصَّلٰوةَ
وَاٰتَى الزَّكٰوةَ وَلَمْ يَخْشَ اِلَّا
اللّٰهَ قف فَعَسٰٓى اُولٰٓئِكَ اَنْ يَّكُونُوا
مِنَ الْمُهْتَدِينَ ﴿١٨﴾

19. Do you (pagans), because you served water to the pilgrims and constructed the Sacred mosque, consider yourselves equal to those who have believed in Allah and the Day of Judgment, and have fought for the cause of Allah? In the sight of Allah you (pagans) are not equal to the believers. Allah does not guide the unjust.

19. Aja'altum siqaayatal-ḥaaajji wa 'imaaratal-Masjidil-Ḥaraami kaman aamana billaahi wal-Yawmil-Aakhiri wa jaahada fee sabeelil-laah; laa yastawoona 'indal-laah; wallaahu laa yahdil-qawmaẓ-ẓaalimeen.

اَجَعَلْتُمْ سِقَايَةَ الْحَآجِّ وَعِمَارَةَ
الْمَسْجِدِ الْحَرَامِ كَمَنْ اٰمَنَ بِاللّٰهِ
وَالْيَوْمِ الْاٰخِرِ وَجٰهَدَ فِي سَبِيلِ
اللّٰهِ ۗ لَا يَسْتَوٗنَ عِنْدَ اللّٰهِ ۗ وَاللّٰهُ
لَا يَهْدِي الْقَوْمَ الظّٰلِمِينَ ﴿١٩﴾ وقف لازم

20. To those who have believed in Allah, left their homes, and fought for His cause with their possessions and in person, Allah will grant high ranks and success.

20. Allaẕeena aamanoo wa haajaroo wa jaahadoo fee sabeelil-laahi bi-amwaalihim wa anfusihim a'ẓamu darajatan 'indal-laah; wa ulaaa'ika humul-faaa'izoon.

اَلَّذِيْنَ اٰمَنُوْا وَهَاجَرُوْا وَجٰهَدُوْا
فِيْ سَبِيْلِ اللّٰهِ بِاَمْوَالِهِمْ وَاَنْفُسِهِمْ
اَعْظَمُ دَرَجَةً عِنْدَ اللّٰهِ ؕ وَاُولٰٓئِكَ
هُمُ الْفَآئِزُوْنَ ﴿٢٠﴾

21. Their Lord will give the glad news of His granting mercy to them, His pleasure, and His admitting them to a Paradise full of everlasting bounties wherein they will live forever.

21. Yubashshiruhum Rabbuhum biraḥmatim-minhu wa riḍwaaniñw-wa Jannaatil-lahum feehaa na'eemum-muqeem.

يُبَشِّرُهُمْ رَبُّهُمْ بِرَحْمَةٍ مِّنْهُ
وَرِضْوَانٍ وَّجَنّٰتٍ لَّهُمْ فِيْهَا
نَعِيْمٌ مُّقِيْمٌ ﴿٢١﴾

22. The reward that Allah will bestow on His servants is the greatest.

22. Khaalideena feehaaa abadaa; innal-laaha 'indahooo ajrun 'aẓeem.

خٰلِدِيْنَ فِيْهَآ اَبَدًا ؕ اِنَّ اللّٰهَ
عِنْدَهٗٓ اَجْرٌ عَظِيْمٌ ﴿٢٢﴾

23. O believers, do not acknowledge your fathers and brothers as your guardians if they prefer disbelief to faith, lest you be unjust.

23. Yaaa ayyuhal-laẕeena aamanoo laa tattakhiẕooo aabaaa'akum wa ikhwaanakum awliyaaa'a inis-taḥabbul-kufra 'alal-eemaan; wa mañy-yatawallahum minkum fa-ulaaa'ika humuẓ-ẓaalimoon.

يٰٓاَيُّهَا الَّذِيْنَ اٰمَنُوْا لَا تَتَّخِذُوْٓا
اٰبَآءَكُمْ وَاِخْوَانَكُمْ اَوْلِيَآءَ اِنِ
اسْتَحَبُّوا الْكُفْرَ عَلَى الْاِيْمَانِ ؕ
وَمَنْ يَّتَوَلَّهُمْ مِّنْكُمْ فَاُولٰٓئِكَ
هُمُ الظّٰلِمُوْنَ ﴿٢٣﴾

24. (Muhammad), tell them, "If your fathers, children, brothers, spouses, relatives, the property that you possess, the trade you fear may have no profit, and the homely life are more beloved to you than Allah, His messenger, and fighting for His cause, wait until Allah fulfills His decree (of making the right distinct from the wrong). Allah does not guide the evil-doers."

24. Qul in kaana aabaaa'ukum wa abnaaa'ukum wa ikhwaanukum wa azwaajukum wa 'asheeratukum wa amwaaluniq-taraftumoohaa wa tijaaratun takhshawna kasaadahaa wa masaakinu tarḍawnahaaa aḥabba ilaykum minal-laahi wa Rasoolihee wa Jihaadin fee Sabeelihee fatarabbaṣoo ḥattaa ya-tiyallaahu bi-amrih; wallaahu laa yahdil-qawmal-faasiqeen.

قُلْ اِنْ كَانَ اٰبَآؤُكُمْ وَاَبْنَآؤُكُمْ
وَاِخْوَانُكُمْ وَاَزْوَاجُكُمْ وَعَشِيْرَتُكُمْ
وَاَمْوَالُ اقْتَرَفْتُمُوْهَا وَتِجَارَةٌ
تَخْشَوْنَ كَسَادَهَا وَمَسٰكِنُ
تَرْضَوْنَهَآ اَحَبَّ اِلَيْكُمْ مِّنَ اللّٰهِ وَ
رَسُوْلِهٖ وَجِهَادٍ فِيْ سَبِيْلِهٖ فَتَرَبَّصُوْا
حَتّٰى يَاْتِيَ اللّٰهُ بِاَمْرِهٖ ؕ وَاللّٰهُ
لَا يَهْدِي الْقَوْمَ الْفٰسِقِيْنَ ﴿٢٤﴾ ع ٨ ٩

25. Allah has helped you on many occasions including the day of Hunayn (name of a place near Makkah). When you were happy with the number of your men who proved to be of no help to you and the whole vast earth seemed to have no place to hide you (from

25. Laqad naṣarakumul-laahu fee mawaaṭina kaẖeeratiñw-wa yawma Ḥunaynin iẕ a'jabatkum kaẖratukum falam tughni 'ankum shay'añw-wa ḍaaqat 'alaykumul-arḍu bimaa

لَقَدْ نَصَرَكُمُ اللّٰهُ فِيْ مَوَاطِنَ
كَثِيْرَةٍ ۙ وَّيَوْمَ حُنَيْنٍ ۙ اِذْ اَعْجَبَتْكُمْ
كَثْرَتُكُمْ فَلَمْ تُغْنِ عَنْكُمْ شَيْئًا
وَّضَاقَتْ عَلَيْكُمُ الْاَرْضُ بِمَا

your enemies) and you turned back in retreat,

raḥubat summa wallaytum mudbireen.

رَحُبَتْ ثُمَّ وَلَّيْتُمْ مُّدْبِرِيْنَ ﴿٢٥﴾

26. Allah gave confidence to His messenger and the believers and helped them with an army which you did not see. Allah punished the unbelievers; this is the only recompense that the unbelievers deserve.

26. Summa anzalal-laahu sakeenatahoo 'alaa Rasoolihee wa 'alalmu'mineena wa anzala junoodal-lam tarawhaa wa 'azzabal-lazeena kafaroo; wa zaalika jazaaa'ul-kaafireen.

ثُمَّ اَنْزَلَ اللّٰهُ سَكِيْنَتَهٗ عَلٰى رَسُوْلِهٖ
وَعَلَى الْمُؤْمِنِيْنَ وَاَنْزَلَ جُنُوْدًا
لَّمْ تَرَوْهَا وَعَذَّبَ الَّذِيْنَ كَفَرُوْا ؕ
وَذٰلِكَ جَزَآءُ الْكٰفِرِيْنَ ﴿٢٦﴾

27. After that occasion Allah forgave those whom He wanted. Allah is All-knowing and All-merciful.

27. Summa yatoobul-laahu mim ba'di zaalika 'alaa mañy-yashaaa'; wallaahu Ghafoorur-Raḥeem.

ثُمَّ يَتُوْبُ اللّٰهُ مِنْۢ بَعْدِ ذٰلِكَ عَلٰى
مَنْ يَّشَآءُ ؕ وَاللّٰهُ غَفُوْرٌ رَّحِيْمٌ ﴿٢٧﴾

28. Believers, the pagans are filthy. Do not let them come near to the Sacred Mosque after this year. If you are afraid of poverty, He will make you rich if He wishes, by His favor. Allah is All-knowing and All-wise.

28. Yaaa ayyuhal-lazeena aamanooo innamal-mushrikoona najasun falaa yaqrabul-Masjidal-Ḥaraama ba'da 'aamihim haazaa; wa in khiftum 'aylatan fasawfa yughneekumul-laahu min faḍliheee in shaaa'; innallaaha 'Aleemun Ḥakeem.

يٰۤاَيُّهَا الَّذِيْنَ اٰمَنُوْۤا اِنَّمَا الْمُشْرِكُوْنَ
نَجَسٌ فَلَا يَقْرَبُوا الْمَسْجِدَ الْحَرَامَ
بَعْدَ عَامِهِمْ هٰذَا ۚ وَاِنْ خِفْتُمْ
عَيْلَةً فَسَوْفَ يُغْنِيْكُمُ اللّٰهُ مِنْ
فَضْلِهٖۤ اِنْ شَآءَ ؕ اِنَّ اللّٰهَ
عَلِيْمٌ حَكِيْمٌ ﴿٢٨﴾

29. Fight against those People of the Book who have no faith in Allah or the Day of Judgment, who do not consider unlawful what Allah and His messenger have made unlawful, and who do not believe in the true religion, until they humbly pay tax with their own hands.

29. Qaatilul-lazeena laa yu'minoona billaahi wa laa bil-Yawmil-Aakhiri wa laa yuḥarrimoona maa ḥarramal-laahu wa Rasooluhoo wa laa yadeenoona deenal-ḥaqqi minal-lazeena ootul-Kitaaba ḥattaa yu'ṭul-jizyata 'añy-yadiñw-wa hum ṣaaghiroon.

قَاتِلُوا الَّذِيْنَ لَا يُؤْمِنُوْنَ بِاللّٰهِ
وَلَا بِالْيَوْمِ الْاٰخِرِ وَلَا يُحَرِّمُوْنَ
مَا حَرَّمَ اللّٰهُ وَرَسُوْلُهٗ وَلَا يَدِيْنُوْنَ
دِيْنَ الْحَقِّ مِنَ الَّذِيْنَ اُوْتُوا الْكِتٰبَ
حَتّٰى يُعْطُوا الْجِزْيَةَ عَنْ يَّدٍ وَّ
هُمْ صٰغِرُوْنَ ﴿٢٩﴾ ع ٥ ١٠

30. Some of the Jews have said that Ezra is the son of Allah and Christians have said the same of Jesus. This is only what they say and it is similar to what the unbelievers who lived before them had said. May Allah destroy them wherever they exist!

30. Wa qaalatil-Yahoodu 'Uzayrunib-nul-laahi wa qaalatin-Naṣaaral-Maseeḥub-nul-laah; zaalika qawluhum bi-afwaahihim yuḍaahi'oona qawlal-lazeena kafaroo min qabl; qaatalahumul-laah; annaa yu'fakoon.

وَقَالَتِ الْيَهُوْدُ عُزَيْرُ ۨ ابْنُ اللّٰهِ
وَقَالَتِ النَّصٰرَى الْمَسِيْحُ ابْنُ اللّٰهِ ؕ
ذٰلِكَ قَوْلُهُمْ بِاَفْوَاهِهِمْ ۚ يُضَاهِـُٔوْنَ
قَوْلَ الَّذِيْنَ كَفَرُوْا مِنْ قَبْلُ ؕ
قٰتَلَهُمُ اللّٰهُ ۚ اَنّٰى يُؤْفَكُوْنَ ﴿٣٠﴾

31. They (unconditionally) obeyed the rabbis and the monks and worshipped the Messiah, son of Mary, as they should have

31. Ittakhazooo aḥbaarahum wa ruhbaanahum arbaabammin doonil-laahi wal-Maseeḥab-na-

اِتَّخَذُوْۤا اَحْبَارَهُمْ وَرُهْبَانَهُمْ
اَرْبَابًا مِّنْ دُوْنِ اللّٰهِ وَالْمَسِيْحَ ابْنَ

obeyed Allah. They were commanded to worship no one besides Allah who is the only Lord and who is most Exalted. He cannot be considered equal to any idols.

Maryama wa maaa umirooo illaa liya'budooo Ilaahañw-Waaḥidan laaa ilaaha illaa Hoo; Subḥaanahoo 'ammaa yushrikoon.

مَرْيَمَ ۚ وَمَآ اُمِرُوْٓا اِلَّا لِيَعْبُدُوْٓا
اِلٰهًا وَّاحِدًا ۚ لَآ اِلٰهَ اِلَّا هُوَ ۭ
سُبْحٰنَهٗ عَمَّا يُشْرِكُوْنَ ۝٣١

32. They would like to extinguish the light of Allah with a blow from their mouths, but even though the unbelievers may dislike it, Allah has decided to let His light shine forever.

32. Yureedoona añy-yuṭfi'oo nooral-laahi bi-afwaahihim wa ya-ballaahu illaaa añy- yutimma noorahoo wa law karihal-kaafiroon.

يُرِيْدُوْنَ اَنْ يُّطْفِـُٔوْا نُوْرَ اللّٰهِ
بِاَفْوَاهِهِمْ وَيَاْبَى اللّٰهُ اِلَّآ اَنْ
يُّتِمَّ نُوْرَهٗ وَلَوْ كَرِهَ الْكٰفِرُوْنَ ۝٣٢

33. It is Allah Who sent His messenger with guidance and a true religion that will prevail over all other religions, even though the pagans may dislike it.

33. Huwal-lazeee ar-sala Rasoolahoo bilhudaa wa deenil-ḥaqqi liyuẓhirahoo 'alad-deeni kullihee wa law karihal-mushrikoon.

هُوَ الَّذِيْٓ اَرْسَلَ رَسُوْلَهٗ بِالْهُدٰى
وَدِيْنِ الْحَقِّ لِيُظْهِرَهٗ عَلَى الدِّيْنِ
كُلِّهٖ ۙ وَلَوْ كَرِهَ الْمُشْرِكُوْنَ ۝٣٣

النصف

34. Believers, many rabbis and monks consume other people's property by false means and create obstacles in the way of Allah. Give, those who horde gold and silver and do not spend (anything out of it) for the cause of Allah, the news that their recompense will be a painful torment

34. Yaaa ayyuhal-lazeena aamanooo inna kaseeramminal-aḥbaari warruhbaani laya-kuloona amwaalan-naasi bil-baaṭili wa yaṣuddoona 'an sabeelil-laah; wallazeena yak-nizoonaz-zahaba walfiḍḍata wa laa yunfiqoonahaa fee sabeelil-laahi fabashshirhum bi'azaabin aleem.

يٰٓاَيُّهَا الَّذِيْنَ اٰمَنُوْٓا اِنَّ كَثِيْرًا
مِّنَ الْاَحْبَارِ وَالرُّهْبَانِ لَيَاْكُلُوْنَ
اَمْوَالَ النَّاسِ بِالْبَاطِلِ وَيَصُدُّوْنَ
عَنْ سَبِيْلِ اللّٰهِ ۭ وَالَّذِيْنَ يَكْنِزُوْنَ
الذَّهَبَ وَالْفِضَّةَ وَلَا يُنْفِقُوْنَهَا
فِيْ سَبِيْلِ اللّٰهِ ۙ فَبَشِّرْهُمْ
بِعَذَابٍ اَلِيْمٍ ۝٣٤

35. on the Day of Judgment and that their treasures will be heated by the fire of hell and pressed against their foreheads, sides, and back with this remark, "These are your own treasures which you hoarded for yourselves. See for yourselves what they feel like."

35. Yawma yuḥmaa 'alayhaa fee Naari Jahannama fatukwaa bihaa jibaahuhum wa junoo-buhum wa ẓuhooruhum haazaa maa kanaztum li-anfusikum fazooqoo maa kuntum takni-zoon.

يَّوْمَ يُحْمٰى عَلَيْهَا فِيْ نَارِ جَهَنَّمَ
فَتُكْوٰى بِهَا جِبَاهُهُمْ وَجُنُوْبُهُمْ
وَظُهُوْرُهُمْ ۭ هٰذَا مَا كَنَزْتُمْ
لِاَنْفُسِكُمْ فَذُوْقُوْا مَا كُنْتُمْ
تَكْنِزُوْنَ ۝٣٥

36. According to the Book of Allah, from the day He created the heavens and the earth, the number of months is twelve, four of which are sacred. (This is part of the law) of the religion. Do not commit injustice against your souls during the sacred months

36. Inna 'iddatash-shuhoori 'indal-laahis-naa 'ashara shah-ran fee Kitaabil-laahi yawma khalaqas-samaawaati wal-arḍa minhaaa arba'atun ḥurum; zaalikad-deenul-qayyim; falaa tazlimoo feehinna anfusakum;

اِنَّ عِدَّةَ الشُّهُوْرِ عِنْدَ اللّٰهِ اثْنَا
عَشَرَ شَهْرًا فِيْ كِتٰبِ اللّٰهِ يَوْمَ
خَلَقَ السَّمٰوٰتِ وَالْاَرْضَ مِنْهَآ
اَرْبَعَةٌ حُرُمٌ ۭ ذٰلِكَ الدِّيْنُ الْقَيِّمُ ڏ
فَلَا تَظْلِمُوْا فِيْهِنَّ اَنْفُسَكُمْ

but fight all the pagans just as they fight against all of you. Know that Allah is with the pious ones.

wa qaatilul-mushrikeena kaaaf-fatan kamaa yuqaatiloonakum kaaaffah; wa'lamooo annal-laaha ma'al-muttaqeen.

وَقَاتِلُوا الْمُشْرِكِينَ كَآفَّةً كَمَا
يُقَاتِلُونَكُمْ كَآفَّةً ۚ وَاعْلَمُوا أَنَّ
اللَّهَ مَعَ الْمُتَّقِينَ ﴿٣٦﴾

37. To disregard the observation of the sacred months and to observe it during the non-sacred months is to add more to one's disbelief. This causes the unbelievers to go further astray. One year they (the pagans) consider a sacred month not sacred, (and observe it during a non-sacred month) but the next year they consider it sacred at the right time. By dealing with the sacred months in such a manner, they think that they have observed the laws of Allah, but, in fact, they have changed them. Their evil deeds seem attractive to them but Allah does not guide the unbelieving people.

37. Innaman-naseee'u ziyaa-datun filkufri yuḍallu bihil-lazeena kafaroo yuḥilloonahoo 'aamañw-wa yuḥarrimoonahoo 'aamal-liyu-waaṭi'oo 'iddata maa ḥarramal-laahu fayuḥilloo maa ḥarramal-laah; zuyyina lahum sooo'u a'maalihim; wallaahu laa yahdil-qawmal-kaafireen.

إِنَّمَا النَّسِيءُ زِيَادَةٌ فِي الْكُفْرِ
يُضَلُّ بِهِ الَّذِينَ كَفَرُوا يُحِلُّونَهُ
عَامًا وَيُحَرِّمُونَهُ عَامًا لِّيُوَاطِئُوا
عِدَّةَ مَا حَرَّمَ اللَّهُ فَيُحِلُّوا مَا حَرَّمَ
اللَّهُ ۚ زُيِّنَ لَهُمْ سُوءُ أَعْمَالِهِمْ ۗ
وَاللَّهُ لَا يَهْدِي الْقَوْمَ الْكَافِرِينَ ﴿٣٧﴾ ع ٨

38. Believers, why is it that when you are told to march for the cause of Allah, you seem to linger at home. Have you given preference to the worldly life over the life hereafter? The worldly gains compared to those of the next life are but very little.

38. Yaaa ayyuhal-lazeena aamanoo maa lakum izaa qeela lakumun-firoo fee sabeelil-laahis-saaqaltum ilal-arḍ; ara-ḍeetum bilḥayaatid-dunyaa minal-Aakhirah; famaa ma-taa'ul-ḥayaatid-dunyaa fil-Aakhirati illaa qaleel.

يَا أَيُّهَا الَّذِينَ آمَنُوا مَا لَكُمْ إِذَا
قِيلَ لَكُمُ انفِرُوا فِي سَبِيلِ اللَّهِ
اثَّاقَلْتُمْ إِلَى الْأَرْضِ ۚ أَرَضِيتُم
بِالْحَيَاةِ الدُّنْيَا مِنَ الْآخِرَةِ ۚ فَمَا
مَتَاعُ الْحَيَاةِ الدُّنْيَا فِي الْآخِرَةِ
إِلَّا قَلِيلٌ ﴿٣٨﴾

39. If you do not march for His cause, He will afflict you with a painful punishment and replace you by another nation, and your (destruction) will not harm Him at all. Allah has power over all things.

39. Illaa tanfiroo yu'az-zib-kum 'azaaban aleemañw-wa yastabdil qawman ghayrakum wa laa taḍurroohu shay'aa; wal-laahu 'alaa kulli shay'in Qadeer.

إِلَّا تَنفِرُوا يُعَذِّبْكُمْ عَذَابًا أَلِيمًا
وَيَسْتَبْدِلْ قَوْمًا غَيْرَكُمْ وَلَا تَضُرُّوهُ
شَيْئًا ۗ وَاللَّهُ عَلَىٰ كُلِّ شَيْءٍ قَدِيرٌ ﴿٣٩﴾

40. If you do not help him (Muhammad), Allah has already helped him. When the unbelievers expelled him and he was one of the two people in the cave telling his companion, "Do not worry; Allah is with us," then Allah gave him confidence and supported him with an army which you did not see and He defeated the cause of the unbelievers and made His own cause stand supreme. Allah is Majestic and All-wise.

40. Illaa tanṣuroohu faqad naṣarahul-laahu iz akhrajahul-lazeena kafaroo saaniyasnayni iz humaa filghaari iz yaqoolu liṣaahibihee laa taḥzan innal-laaha ma'anaa fa-anzalallaahu sakeenatahoo 'alayhi wa ayyadahoo bijunoodil-lam ta-rawhaa wa ja'ala kalimatal-lazeena kafarus-suflaa; wa Kalimatul-laahi hiyal-'ulyaa; wallaahu 'Azeezun Ḥakeem.

إِلَّا تَنصُرُوهُ فَقَدْ نَصَرَهُ اللَّهُ إِذْ
أَخْرَجَهُ الَّذِينَ كَفَرُوا ثَانِيَ اثْنَيْنِ
إِذْ هُمَا فِي الْغَارِ إِذْ يَقُولُ
لِصَاحِبِهِ لَا تَحْزَنْ إِنَّ اللَّهَ مَعَنَا ۖ
فَأَنزَلَ اللَّهُ سَكِينَتَهُ عَلَيْهِ وَأَيَّدَهُ
بِجُنُودٍ لَّمْ تَرَوْهَا وَجَعَلَ كَلِمَةَ
الَّذِينَ كَفَرُوا السُّفْلَىٰ ۗ وَكَلِمَةُ اللَّهِ
هِيَ الْعُلْيَا ۗ وَاللَّهُ عَزِيزٌ حَكِيمٌ ﴿٤٠﴾

41. Whether unarmed or well equipped, march and fight for the cause of Allah with your possessions and in person. This would be better for you, if only you knew it.

41. Infiroo khifaafañw-wa siqaalañw-wa jaahidoo bi-amwaalikum wa anfusikum fee sabeelil-laah; zaalikum khay-rul-lakum in kuntum ta'lamoon.

انْفِرُوْا خِفَافًا وَّثِقَالًا وَّجَاهِدُوْا
بِاَمْوَالِكُمْ وَاَنْفُسِكُمْ فِيْ سَبِيْلِ
اللّٰهِ ۭ ذٰلِكُمْ خَيْرٌ لَّكُمْ اِنْ
كُنْتُمْ تَعْلَمُوْنَ ۝٤١

42. Had the gain been immediate or the journey shorter, they (hypocrites) would certainly have followed you, (Muhammad), but it was too far for them. They will swear by Allah, "Had we had the ability, we would certainly have marched with you." They destroy only themselves and Allah knows that they are lying.

42. Law kaana 'araḍan qareebañw-wa safaran qaaṣidal-lattaba'ooka wa laakim ba'udat 'alayhimush-shuqqah; wa sayaḥlifoona billaahi lawis-taṭa'naa lakharajnaa ma'akum; yuhlikoona anfusahum wal-laahu ya'lamu innahum lakaa-ziboon.

لَوْ كَانَ عَرَضًا قَرِيْبًا وَّسَفَرًا
قَاصِدًا لَّاتَّبَعُوْكَ وَلٰكِنْۢ بَعُدَتْ
عَلَيْهِمُ الشُّقَّةُ ۭ وَسَيَحْلِفُوْنَ
بِاللّٰهِ لَوِ اسْتَطَعْنَا لَخَرَجْنَا مَعَكُمْ ۚ
يُهْلِكُوْنَ اَنْفُسَهُمْ ۚ وَاللّٰهُ يَعْلَمُ
اِنَّهُمْ لَكٰذِبُوْنَ ۝٤٢ ع ٥ ١٢

43. May Allah forgive you! (Muhammad), why did you not allow them join the army so that you could discern the liars from the truthful ones?

43. 'Afal-laahu 'anka lima azinta lahum ḥattaa yatabay-yana lakal-lazeena ṣadaqoo wa ta'lamal-kaazibeen.

عَفَا اللّٰهُ عَنْكَ ۚ لِمَ اَذِنْتَ لَهُمْ
حَتّٰى يَتَبَيَّنَ لَكَ الَّذِيْنَ صَدَقُوْا
وَتَعْلَمَ الْكٰذِبِيْنَ ۝٤٣

44. Those who believe in Allah and the Day of Judgment do not ask you whether they should fight for the cause of Allah with their property and in person, or not. Allah knows all about the pious ones.

44. Laa yasta-zinukal-lazeena yu'minoona billaahi wal-Yawmil-Aakhiri añy-yujaa-hidoo bi-amwaalihim wa anfusihim; wallaahu 'Aleemum bilmuttaqeen.

لَا يَسْتَاْذِنُكَ الَّذِيْنَ يُؤْمِنُوْنَ بِاللّٰهِ
وَالْيَوْمِ الْاٰخِرِ اَنْ يُّجَاهِدُوْا
بِاَمْوَالِهِمْ وَاَنْفُسِهِمْ ۭ وَاللّٰهُ
عَلِيْمٌۢ بِالْمُتَّقِيْنَ ۝٤٤

45. Only those who do not believe in Allah and the Day of Judgment ask you such questions, because their hearts are full of doubts and they cannot make any final decisions.

45. Innamaa yasta-zinukal-lazeena laa yu'minoona billaahi wal-Yawmil-Aakhiri wartaabat quloobuhum fahum fee raybi-him yataraddadoon.

اِنَّمَا يَسْتَاْذِنُكَ الَّذِيْنَ لَا يُؤْمِنُوْنَ
بِاللّٰهِ وَالْيَوْمِ الْاٰخِرِ وَارْتَابَتْ
قُلُوْبُهُمْ فَهُمْ فِيْ رَيْبِهِمْ
يَتَرَدَّدُوْنَ ۝٤٥

46. Had they (the hypocrites) wanted to join your army, they would have prepared themselves, but Allah did not wish to motivate them, so He caused them to linger behind with those whose joining you in battle would be of no use.

46. Wa law araadul-khurooja la-a'addoo lahoo 'uddatañw-wa laakin karihal-laahum-bi'aa-sahum fasabbaṭahum wa qeelaq-'udoo ma'al-qaa'ideen.

وَلَوْ اَرَادُوا الْخُرُوْجَ لَاَعَدُّوْا لَهٗ
عُدَّةً وَّلٰكِنْ كَرِهَ اللّٰهُ انْۢبِعَاثَهُمْ
فَثَبَّطَهُمْ وَقِيْلَ اقْعُدُوْا مَعَ
الْقٰعِدِيْنَ ۝٤٦

47. Had they joined you, they would have been of no help to you

47. Law kharajoo feekum maa zaadookum illaa

لَوْ خَرَجُوْا فِيْكُمْ مَّا زَادُوْكُمْ اِلَّا

but would have just caused confusion and trouble among you by sneaking through the ranks where some of you would be ready to listen to them. Allah knows best the unjust.

khabaalañw-wa la-awḍa'oo khilaalakum yabghoona-kumul-fitnata wa feekum sammaa'oona lahum; wallaahu 'Aleemum biẓ-ẓaalimeen.

خَبَالًا وَّلَاَ اَوْضَعُوْا خِلٰلَكُمْ
يَبْغُوْنَكُمُ الْفِتْنَةَ ۚ وَفِيْكُمْ
سَمّٰعُوْنَ لَهُمْ ؕ وَاللّٰهُ عَلِيْمٌ ۢ
بِالظّٰلِمِيْنَ ﴿٤٧﴾

48. Even prior to this, they tried to cause trouble and to turn your affairs upside down until the truth came and the cause of Allah triumphed against their desires.

48. Laqadib-taghawul-fitnata min qablu wa qallaboo lakal-umoora ḥattaa jaaa'al-ḥaqqu wa ẓahara amrul-laahi wa hum kaarihoon.

لَقَدِ ابْتَغَوُا الْفِتْنَةَ مِنْ قَبْلُ
وَقَلَّبُوْا لَكَ الْاُمُوْرَ حَتّٰى جَآءَ الْحَقُّ
وَظَهَرَ اَمْرُ اللّٰهِ وَهُمْ كٰرِهُوْنَ ﴿٤٨﴾

49. Some of them ask you, "Make us exempt from taking part in the battle and do not try to tempt us by telling us what we may gain from the battle; many people have died in the battle." Hell certainly encompasses the unbelievers.

49. Wa minhum mañy-yaqoolu'-ẕal-lee wa laa taftinneee; alaa fil-fitnati saqaṭoo; wa inna Jahannama lamuḥeeṭatum bil-kaafireen.

وَمِنْهُمْ مَّنْ يَّقُوْلُ ائْذَنْ لِّيْ وَلَا
تَفْتِنِّيْ ؕ اَلَا فِي الْفِتْنَةِ سَقَطُوْا ؕ
وَاِنَّ جَهَنَّمَ لَمُحِيْطَةٌ ۢ بِالْكٰفِرِيْنَ ﴿٤٩﴾

50. If you gain success it grieves them, but if you suffer hardship they turn away from you saying, "It is good that we took our affairs into our own hands."

50. In tuṣibka ḥasanatun tasu'hum; wa in tuṣibka muṣeebatuñy-yaqooloo qad akhaẕnaaa amranaa min qablu wa yatawallaw wa hum fariḥoon.

اِنْ تُصِبْكَ حَسَنَةٌ تَسُؤْهُمْ ۚ وَاِنْ
تُصِبْكَ مُصِيْبَةٌ يَّقُوْلُوْا قَدْ
اَخَذْنَآ اَمْرَنَا مِنْ قَبْلُ وَيَتَوَلَّوْا
وَّهُمْ فَرِحُوْنَ ﴿٥٠﴾

51. (Muhammad), say, "Nothing will happen to us besides what Allah has decreed for us. He is our Guardian. In Allah alone do the believers trust."

51. Qul lañy-yuṣeebanaaa illaa maa katabal-laahu lanaa Huwa mawlaanaa; wa 'alal-laahi falyatawakkalil-mu'minoon.

قُلْ لَّنْ يُّصِيْبَنَآ اِلَّا مَا كَتَبَ
اللّٰهُ لَنَا ۚ هُوَ مَوْلٰىنَا ۚ وَعَلَى اللّٰهِ
فَلْيَتَوَكَّلِ الْمُؤْمِنُوْنَ ﴿٥١﴾

52. For us, you can anticipate nothing other than Paradise if we are killed or success if we triumph. However, what we can anticipate for you is punishment either by the hands of Allah or by ours. Wait and we are also waiting with you.

52. Qul hal tarabbaṣoona binaaa illaaa iḥdal-ḥusnayayni wa naḥnu natarabbaṣu bikum añy-yuṣeebakumul-laahu bi'aẕaabim-min 'indiheee aw bi-aydeenaa fatarabbaṣooo innaa ma'akum mutarabbiṣoon.

قُلْ هَلْ تَرَبَّصُوْنَ بِنَآ اِلَّآ اِحْدَى
الْحُسْنَيَيْنِ ؕ وَنَحْنُ نَتَرَبَّصُ بِكُمْ
اَنْ يُّصِيْبَكُمُ اللّٰهُ بِعَذَابٍ مِّنْ
عِنْدِهٖٓ اَوْ بِاَيْدِيْنَا ۖ فَتَرَبَّصُوْٓا
اِنَّا مَعَكُمْ مُّتَرَبِّصُوْنَ ﴿٥٢﴾

53. Say, "Whether you spend your wealth for the cause of Allah, willingly or reluctantly, it will never be accepted from you; you are an evildoing people."

53. Qul anfiqoo ṭaw'an aw karhal-lañy-yutaqabbala minkum innakum kuntum qawman faasiqeen.

قُلْ اَنْفِقُوْا طَوْعًا اَوْ كَرْهًا لَّنْ
يُّتَقَبَّلَ مِنْكُمْ ؕ اِنَّكُمْ كُنْتُمْ
قَوْمًا فٰسِقِيْنَ ﴿٥٣﴾

54. What prevents their offerings from being accepted is

54. Wa maa mana'ahum an tuqbala minhum

وَمَا مَنَعَهُمْ اَنْ تُقْبَلَ مِنْهُمْ

their disbelief in Allah and His messenger, their lack of interest in prayer, and their spending for the cause of Allah reluctantly.

55. Do not permit their property and children attract you; Allah wants only to punish them through their things in this life so that their souls will depart while they are unbelievers.

56. They swear by Allah that they are believers like you but they are not believers. They are a people who only cause differences.

57. They are so afraid of you that had there been a place for them to seek refuge, a cave or some entrance in which to hide themselves from you, they would have madly rushed therein.

58. They blame you about the distribution of the charity funds. They are pleased when you gave them something from it, but if they received nothing, they became angry with you.

59. Would that they had been pleased with what Allah and His messenger had given them and had said, "Allah is All-Sufficient for us. Allah and His messenger will soon do us more favors and we have hope in Allah's mercy."

60. Charity funds (zakat) are only for the poor, the destitute, the tax collectors, those whose hearts are inclined (towards Islam), the slaves, those who cannot pay their debts, for the cause of Allah, and for those who have become needy on a journey. Paying zakat is an obligation that Allah has decreed. Allah is All-knowing and All-wise.

nafaqaatuhum illaaa annahum kafaroo billaahi wa bi-Rasoolihee wa laa ya-toonaṣ-Ṣalaata illaa wa hum kusaalaa wa laa yunfiqoona illaa wa hum kaarihoon.

55. Falaa tu'jibka amwaaluhum wa laaa awlaaduhum; innamaa yureedul-laahu liyu'az-zibahum bihaa fil-ḥayaatid-dunyaa wa tazhaqa anfusuhum wa hum kaafiroon.

56. Wa yaḥlifoona billaahi innahum laminkum; wa maa hum minkum wa laakinnahum qawmuñy-yafraqoon.

57. Law yajidoona malja'an aw maghaaraatin aw mudda-khalal-lawallaw ilayhi wa hum yajmaḥoon.

58. Wa minhum mañy-yalmizuka fiṣ-ṣadaqaati fa-in u'ṭoo minhaa raḍoo wa illam yu'ṭaw minhaaa izaa hum yaskhaṭoon.

59. Wa law annahum raḍoo maaa aataahumul-laahu wa Rasooluhoo wa qaaloo ḥasbunal-laahu sayu'teenallaahu min faḍlihee wa Rasooluhooo innaaa ilallaahi raaghiboon.

60. Innamaṣ-ṣadaqaatu lilfuqaraaa'i walmasaakeeni wal-'aamileena 'alayhaa walmu'allafati quloobuhum wa fir-riqaabi-walghaarimeena wa fee sabeelil-laahi wabnis-sabeel; fareeḍatam-minal-laah; wal-laahu 'Aleemun Ḥakeem.

نَفَقٰتُهُمْ اِلَّآ اَنَّهُمْ كَفَرُوْا بِاللّٰهِ
وَبِرَسُوْلِهٖ وَلَا يَاْتُوْنَ الصَّلٰوةَ
اِلَّا وَهُمْ كُسَالٰى وَلَا يُنْفِقُوْنَ اِلَّا
وَهُمْ كٰرِهُوْنَ ﴿٥٤﴾
فَلَا تُعْجِبْكَ اَمْوَالُهُمْ وَلَآ اَوْلَادُهُمْ ؕ
اِنَّمَا يُرِيْدُ اللّٰهُ لِيُعَذِّبَهُمْ بِهَا فِى
الْحَيٰوةِ الدُّنْيَا وَتَزْهَقَ اَنْفُسُهُمْ
وَهُمْ كٰفِرُوْنَ ﴿٥٥﴾
وَيَحْلِفُوْنَ بِاللّٰهِ اِنَّهُمْ لَمِنْكُمْ ؕ
وَمَا هُمْ مِّنْكُمْ وَلٰكِنَّهُمْ قَوْمٌ
يَّفْرَقُوْنَ ﴿٥٦﴾
لَوْ يَجِدُوْنَ مَلْجَاً اَوْ مَغٰرٰتٍ اَوْ
مُدَّخَلًا لَّوَلَّوْا اِلَيْهِ وَهُمْ يَجْمَحُوْنَ ﴿٥٧﴾
وَمِنْهُمْ مَّنْ يَّلْمِزُكَ فِى الصَّدَقٰتِ ۚ
فَاِنْ اُعْطُوْا مِنْهَا رَضُوْا وَاِنْ لَّمْ
يُعْطَوْا مِنْهَآ اِذَا هُمْ يَسْخَطُوْنَ ﴿٥٨﴾
وَلَوْ اَنَّهُمْ رَضُوْا مَآ اٰتٰىهُمُ اللّٰهُ
وَرَسُوْلُهٗ ۙ وَقَالُوْا حَسْبُنَا اللّٰهُ
سَيُؤْتِيْنَا اللّٰهُ مِنْ فَضْلِهٖ وَرَسُوْلُهٗۤ ۙ
اِنَّآ اِلَى اللّٰهِ رٰغِبُوْنَ ﴿٥٩﴾ ع ١٧ ١٣
اِنَّمَا الصَّدَقٰتُ لِلْفُقَرَآءِ وَ
الْمَسٰكِيْنِ وَالْعٰمِلِيْنَ عَلَيْهَا وَ
الْمُؤَلَّفَةِ قُلُوْبُهُمْ وَفِى الرِّقَابِ
وَالْغٰرِمِيْنَ وَفِىْ سَبِيْلِ اللّٰهِ
وَابْنِ السَّبِيْلِ ؕ فَرِيْضَةً مِّنَ
اللّٰهِ ؕ وَاللّٰهُ عَلِيْمٌ حَكِيْمٌ ﴿٦٠﴾

61. Some of them speak ill of the Prophet, saying, "He listens to everything and believes what he hears." (Muhammad), tell them, "He listens only to what is good for you, believes in Allah, and has trust in the believers. He is a mercy for the believers among you. Those who speak ill of the Messenger of Allah will face a painful punishment."

61. Wa minhumul-lazeena yu'zoonan-Nabiyya wa yaqooloona huwa uzun; qul uzunu khayril-lakum yu'minu billaahi wa yu'minu lilmu'mineena wa raḥmatul-lillazeena aamanoo minkum; wallazeena yu'zoona Rasoolal-laahi lahum 'azaabun aleem.

وَمِنْهُمُ الَّذِيْنَ يُؤْذُوْنَ النَّبِيَّ
وَيَقُوْلُوْنَ هُوَ اُذُنٌ ؕ قُلْ اُذُنُ
خَيْرٍ لَّكُمْ يُؤْمِنُ بِاللّٰهِ وَيُؤْمِنُ
لِلْمُؤْمِنِيْنَ وَرَحْمَةٌ لِّلَّذِيْنَ
اٰمَنُوْا مِنْكُمْ ؕ وَالَّذِيْنَ يُؤْذُوْنَ
رَسُوْلَ اللّٰهِ لَهُمْ عَذَابٌ اَلِيْمٌ ﴿٦١﴾

62. They (hypocrites) swear by Allah in their effort to please you, but if they were true believers (they would know) that Allah and His messenger, more than anyone else, deserve to be pleased.

62. Yaḥlifoona billaahi lakum liyurḍookum wallaahu wa Rasooluhooo aḥaqqu añy-yurḍoohu in kaanoo mu'mineen.

يَحْلِفُوْنَ بِاللّٰهِ لَكُمْ لِيُرْضُوْكُمْ ۚ
وَاللّٰهُ وَرَسُوْلُهٗۤ اَحَقُّ اَنْ يُّرْضُوْهُ
اِنْ كَانُوْا مُؤْمِنِيْنَ ﴿٦٢﴾ الثلثة

63. Did they not know that for displeasing Allah and His messenger, one would be admitted to Hell wherein he would live forever? This indeed is a great humiliation.

63. Alam ya'lamooo annahoo mañy-yuḥaadidillaaha wa Rasoolahoo fa-anna lahoo Naara Jahannama khaalidan feehaa; zaalikal-khizyul-'aẓeem.

اَلَمْ يَعْلَمُوْۤا اَنَّهٗ مَنْ يُّحَادِدِ اللّٰهَ
وَرَسُوْلَهٗ فَاَنَّ لَهٗ نَارَ جَهَنَّمَ خَالِدًا
فِيْهَا ؕ ذٰلِكَ الْخِزْيُ الْعَظِيْمُ ﴿٦٣﴾

64. The hypocrites are afraid that some revelation will be revealed, thus making public what is in their hearts. (Muhammad), tell them, "Continue in your mockery; Allah will certainly allow whatever causes you worry to take place."

64. Yaḥzarul-munaafiqoona an tunaz-zala 'alayhim Sooratun tunabbi'uhum bimaa fee quloobihim; qulistahzi'oo innal-laaha mukhrijum-maa taḥzaroon.

يَحْذَرُ الْمُنٰفِقُوْنَ اَنْ تُنَزَّلَ عَلَيْهِمْ
سُوْرَةٌ تُنَبِّئُهُمْ بِمَا فِيْ قُلُوْبِهِمْ ؕ
قُلِ اسْتَهْزِءُوْا ۚ اِنَّ اللّٰهَ مُخْرِجٌ
مَّا تَحْذَرُوْنَ ﴿٦٤﴾

65. If you question them about their manners, they say, "We were arguing only for the sake of amusement." Ask them, "Were you mocking Allah, His revelations, and His messenger?"

65. Wala'in sa-altahum-layaqoolunna innamaa kunnaa nakhooḍu wa nal'ab; qul abillaahi wa Aayaatihee wa Rasoolihee kuntum tastahzi'oon.

وَلَئِنْ سَاَلْتَهُمْ لَيَقُوْلُنَّ اِنَّمَا كُنَّا
نَخُوْضُ وَنَلْعَبُ ؕ قُلْ اَبِاللّٰهِ وَاٰيٰتِهٖ
وَرَسُوْلِهٖ كُنْتُمْ تَسْتَهْزِءُوْنَ ﴿٦٥﴾

66. (You hypocrites) make no excuses. You have certainly turned back to disbelief. If We forgive one group of you, We must punish the other for they are guilty.

66. Laa ta'taziroo qad kafartum ba'da eemaanikum; in na'fu 'an ṭaaa'ifatim-minkum nu'az-zib ṭaaa'ifatam bi-annahum kaanoo mujrimeen.

لَا تَعْتَذِرُوْا قَدْ كَفَرْتُمْ بَعْدَ
اِيْمَانِكُمْ ؕ اِنْ نَّعْفُ عَنْ طَآئِفَةٍ
مِّنْكُمْ نُعَذِّبْ طَآئِفَةًۢ بِاَنَّهُمْ
كَانُوْا مُجْرِمِيْنَ ﴿٦٦﴾ ع ٧ ٨

67. Be they male or female hypocrites, they are the same. They make others commit sins, prevent them from doing good deeds, and restrain their hands (from spending for the cause of

67. Almunaafiqoona walmunaafiqaatu ba'ḍuhum mim ba'ḍ; ya-muroona bilmunkari wa yanhawna 'anil-ma'roofi wa yaqbiḍoona

اَلْمُنٰفِقُوْنَ وَالْمُنٰفِقٰتُ بَعْضُهُمْ
مِّنْۢ بَعْضٍ ۘ يَاْمُرُوْنَ بِالْمُنْكَرِ وَ
يَنْهَوْنَ عَنِ الْمَعْرُوْفِ وَيَقْبِضُوْنَ وقف لازم

Allah). They have forgotten all about Allah, who also has ignored them. The hypocrites indeed are evil-doers.

aydiyahum; nasul-laaha fanasiyahum; innal- munaafiqeena humul-faasiqoon.

أَيْدِيَهُمْ ۚ نَسُوا اللّٰهَ فَنَسِيَهُمْ ۗ إِنَّ
الْمُنٰفِقِينَ هُمُ الْفٰسِقُونَ ﴿٦٧﴾

68. For the hypocrites and the unbelievers, Allah has prepared hell wherein they will live forever. Hell is their proper punishment. Allah has condemned them and they will suffer a permanent torment

68. Wa'adal-laahul-munaafiqeena wal-munaafiqaati wal-kuffaara Naara Jahannama khaalideena feehaa; hiya ḥasbuhum; wa la'anahumul-laahu wa lahum 'a͟zaabum-muqeem.

وَعَدَ اللّٰهُ الْمُنٰفِقِينَ وَالْمُنٰفِقٰتِ
وَالْكُفَّارَ نَارَ جَهَنَّمَ خٰلِدِينَ
فِيهَا ۚ هِيَ حَسْبُهُمْ ۚ وَلَعَنَهُمُ
اللّٰهُ ۚ وَلَهُمْ عَذَابٌ مُّقِيمٌ ﴿٦٨﴾

69. like that of those who lived before you, whose power, wealth, and children were much greater than yours.

They enjoyed their share of the worldly gains and you, also, like them, have enjoyed yours. You have been sneaking among the people to cause trouble, just as they had been doing before you. Such people's deeds are devoid of all virtue both in this life and in the life hereafter. They are indeed lost.

69. Kalla͟zeena min qablikum kaanooo ashadda minkum quwwatañw-wa ak͟sara amwaalañw-wa awlaadan fastamta'oo bikhalaaqihim fastamta'tum bikhalaaqikum kamas-tamta'al-la͟zeena min qablikum bikhalaaqihim wa khuḍtum kalla͟zee khaaḍooo; ulaaa'ika ḥabiṭat a'maaluhum fid-dunyaa wal-Aakhirati wa ulaaa'ika humul-khaasiroon.

كَالَّذِينَ مِنْ قَبْلِكُمْ كَانُوا
أَشَدَّ مِنْكُمْ قُوَّةً وَّأَكْثَرَ أَمْوَالًا
وَّأَوْلَادًا ۗ فَاسْتَمْتَعُوا بِخَلَاقِهِمْ
فَاسْتَمْتَعْتُمْ بِخَلَاقِكُمْ كَمَا اسْتَمْتَعَ
الَّذِينَ مِنْ قَبْلِكُمْ بِخَلَاقِهِمْ
وَخُضْتُمْ كَالَّذِي خَاضُوا ۗ أُولٰئِكَ
حَبِطَتْ أَعْمَالُهُمْ فِي الدُّنْيَا
وَالْآخِرَةِ ۚ وَأُولٰئِكَ هُمُ الْخٰسِرُونَ ﴿٦٩﴾

70. Did they not hear the stories of the people of Noah, the tribe of Ad, Thamud, the people of Abraham, the dwellers of the city of Madyan, and those of the Subverted Cities? Allah's Messengers came to each of them with miracles. Allah did not do any injustice to them, but they wronged themselves.

70. Alam ya-tihim naba-ul-la͟zeena min qablihim qawmi Nooḥiñw-wa 'Aadiñw-wa S͟amood; wa qawmi Ibraaheema wa aṣḥaabi Madyana walmu'ta-fikaat; atathum Rusuluhum bilbayyinaati famaa kaanal-laahu liyaẓlimahum wa laakin kaanooo anfusahum yaẓlimoon.

أَلَمْ يَأْتِهِمْ نَبَأُ الَّذِينَ مِنْ قَبْلِهِمْ
قَوْمِ نُوحٍ وَّعَادٍ وَّثَمُودَ ۙ وَ
قَوْمِ إِبْرٰهِيمَ وَأَصْحٰبِ مَدْيَنَ
وَالْمُؤْتَفِكٰتِ ۗ أَتَتْهُمْ رُسُلُهُمْ
بِالْبَيِّنٰتِ ۚ فَمَا كَانَ اللّٰهُ لِيَظْلِمَهُمْ
وَلٰكِنْ كَانُوا أَنْفُسَهُمْ يَظْلِمُونَ ﴿٧٠﴾

71. The believers, both male and female, are each other's protectors. They try to make others do good, prevent them from committing sins, perform their prayers, pay the religious tax, and obey Allah and His messenger. Allah will have mercy on them; Allah is Majestic and All-wise.

71. Walmu'minoona wal-mu'minaatu ba'ḍuhum awliyaaa'u ba'ḍ; ya-muroona bil-ma'roofi wa yanhawna 'anil-munkari wa yuqeemoonaṣ-Ṣalaata wa yu'toonaz-Zakaata wa yuṭee'oonal-laaha wa Rasoolah; ulaaa'ika sayarḥamuhumul-laah; innallaaha 'Azeezun Ḥakeem.

وَالْمُؤْمِنُونَ وَالْمُؤْمِنٰتُ بَعْضُهُمْ
أَوْلِيَاءُ بَعْضٍ ۘ يَأْمُرُونَ بِالْمَعْرُوفِ
وَيَنْهَوْنَ عَنِ الْمُنْكَرِ وَيُقِيمُونَ
الصَّلٰوةَ وَيُؤْتُونَ الزَّكٰوةَ وَ
يُطِيعُونَ اللّٰهَ وَرَسُولَهُ ۗ أُولٰئِكَ
سَيَرْحَمُهُمُ اللّٰهُ ۗ إِنَّ اللّٰهَ عَزِيزٌ

وقف لازم

حَكِيمٌ ﴿٧١﴾

72. Allah has promised the male and female believers gardens wherein streams flow and wherein they will live forever in the excellent mansions of the garden of Eden. What is more important than all this for them is that Allah is pleased with them. Such is the supreme triumph.

72. Wa'adallaahul-mu'mineena walmu'minaati Jannaatin tajree min taḥtihal anhaaru khaali-deena feehaa wa masaakina ṭayyibatan fee Jannaati 'Adn; wa riḍwaanum-minal-laahi akbar; zaalika huwal-fawzul-'aẓeem.

وَعَدَ اللّٰهُ الْمُؤْمِنِيْنَ وَالْمُؤْمِنٰتِ
جَنّٰتٍ تَجْرِيْ مِنْ تَحْتِهَا الْاَنْهٰرُ
خٰلِدِيْنَ فِيْهَا وَمَسٰكِنَ طَيِّبَةً
فِيْ جَنّٰتِ عَدْنٍ ۭ وَرِضْوَانٌ مِّنَ
اللّٰهِ اَكْبَرُ ۭ ذٰلِكَ هُوَ الْفَوْزُ الْعَظِيْمُ ﴿٧٢﴾ ع ٩ ١٥

73. Prophet, fight the unbelievers (with the sword) and hypocrites (through warning and penalties) vehemently for the cause of Allah. Their dwelling is hell, a terrible destination!

73. Yaaa-ayyuhan-Nabiyyu jaahidil-kuffaara walmunaafi-qeena waghluẓ 'alayhim; wa ma-waahum Jahannam; wa bi'sal-maṣeer.

يٰٓاَيُّهَا النَّبِيُّ جَاهِدِ الْكُفَّارَ
وَالْمُنٰفِقِيْنَ وَاغْلُظْ عَلَيْهِمْ ۭ وَ
مَاْوٰىهُمْ جَهَنَّمُ ۭ وَبِئْسَ الْمَصِيْرُ ﴿٧٣﴾

74. They (the hypocrites) swear by the Name of Allah (to make others believe in what they are saying). They have spoken the testimony of disbelief and have then turned back to disbelief. They had made unsuccessful attempts to cause trouble. There is no other reason for their ungratefulness except that Allah and His messenger enriched them through their favors. If they repent, it will be better for them, but if they turn away (from the faith), Allah will make them suffer a painful punishment both in this life and in the life hereafter. They will find no guardian nor any helper in the land.

74. Yaḥlifoona billaahi maa qaaloo wa laqad qaaloo kalimatal-kufri wa kafaroo ba'da Islaamihim wa hammoo bimaa lam yanaaloo; wa maa naqamooo illaaa an aghnaa-humullaahu wa Rasooluhoo min faḍlih; faiñy- yatooboo yaku khayral-lahum wa iñy-yatawal-law yu'az-zibhumullaahu 'azaaban aleeman fiddunyaa wal-Aakhirah; wamaa lahum fil-arḍi miñw-waliyyiñw-wa laa naṣeer.

يَحْلِفُوْنَ بِاللّٰهِ مَا قَالُوْا ۭ وَ
لَقَدْ قَالُوْا كَلِمَةَ الْكُفْرِ وَ
كَفَرُوْا بَعْدَ اِسْلَامِهِمْ وَهَمُّوْا
بِمَا لَمْ يَنَالُوْا ۚ وَمَا نَقَمُوْٓا اِلَّآ
اَنْ اَغْنٰىهُمُ اللّٰهُ وَرَسُوْلُهٗ مِنْ
فَضْلِهٖ ۚ فَاِنْ يَّتُوْبُوْا يَكُ خَيْرًا
لَّهُمْ ۚ وَاِنْ يَّتَوَلَّوْا يُعَذِّبْهُمُ
اللّٰهُ عَذَابًا اَلِيْمًا ۙ فِي الدُّنْيَا وَ
الْاٰخِرَةِ ۚ وَمَا لَهُمْ فِي الْاَرْضِ
مِنْ وَّلِيٍّ وَّلَا نَصِيْرٍ ﴿٧٤﴾

75. Some of them have promised Allah that if He will favor them, they will certainly spend for His cause and be righteous ones.

75. Wa minhum man 'aaha-dal-laaha la'in aataanaa min faḍlihee lanaṣ-ṣadda-qanna wa lanakoonanna minaṣṣaaliḥeen.

وَمِنْهُمْ مَّنْ عٰهَدَ اللّٰهَ لَىِٕنْ
اٰتٰىنَا مِنْ فَضْلِهٖ لَنَصَّدَّقَنَّ
وَلَنَكُوْنَنَّ مِنَ الصّٰلِحِيْنَ ﴿٧٥﴾

76. But when His favors were bestowed on them, they became niggardly and in disregard broke their promise.

76. Falammaaa aataahum min faḍlihee bakhiloo bihee wa tawallaw wa hum mu'riḍoon.

فَلَمَّآ اٰتٰىهُمْ مِّنْ فَضْلِهٖ بَخِلُوْا
بِهٖ وَتَوَلَّوْا وَّهُمْ مُّعْرِضُوْنَ ﴿٧٦﴾

77. Allah has, for their disregard of their promise and their telling lies, placed hypocrisy in their hearts which will not

77. Fa-a'qabahum nifaaqan fee quloobihim ilaa Yawmi yalqaw-nahoo bimaaa akhlaful-laaha maa

فَاَعْقَبَهُمْ نِفَاقًا فِيْ قُلُوْبِهِمْ اِلٰى
يَوْمِ يَلْقَوْنَهٗ بِمَآ اَخْلَفُوا اللّٰهَ مَا

leave them until they face the consequences of their deeds.

wa'adoohu wa bimaa kaanoo yakziboon.

وَعَدُوهُ وَبِمَا كَانُوا يَكْذِبُونَ ﴿٧٧﴾

78. Were they not aware that Allah knows all that they hide or whisper and that Allah has absolute knowledge of the unseen?

78. Alam ya'lamooo annal-laaha ya'lamu sirrahum wa najwaahum wa annal-laaha 'Allaamul-Ghuyoob.

أَلَمْ يَعْلَمُوا أَنَّ اللَّهَ يَعْلَمُ سِرَّهُمْ وَ
نَجْوَاهُمْ وَأَنَّ اللَّهَ عَلَّامُ الْغُيُوبِ ﴿٧٨﴾

79. Allah mocks those (hypocrites) who blame and mock the rich or poor believers who donate to the welfare funds, and He has prepared a painful torment for them.

79. Allazeena yalmizoonal-muṭ-ṭawwi'eena minalmu'mi-neena fiṣ-ṣadaqaati wallazeena laa yajidoona illaa juhdahum fayaskharoona minhum sakhi-ral-laahu minhum wa lahum 'azaabun aleem.

الَّذِينَ يَلْمِزُونَ الْمُطَّوِّعِينَ مِنَ
الْمُؤْمِنِينَ فِي الصَّدَقٰتِ وَالَّذِينَ لَا
يَجِدُونَ إِلَّا جُهْدَهُمْ فَيَسْخَرُونَ
مِنْهُمْ ط سَخِرَ اللَّهُ مِنْهُمْ ز وَلَهُمْ
عَذَابٌ أَلِيمٌ ﴿٧٩﴾

80. (Muhammad), whether you ask Allah to forgive them or not, He will never do so, even if you were to beg seventy times; they have disbelieved in Allah and His messenger and Allah does not guide the evil-doers.

80. Istaghfir lahum aw laa tastaghfir lahum in tastaghfir lahum sab'eena marratan falañy-yaghfiral-laahu lahum; zaalika bi-annahum kafaroo billaahi wa Rasoolih; wallaahu laa yahdil-qawmal-faasiqeen.

اِسْتَغْفِرْ لَهُمْ أَوْ لَا تَسْتَغْفِرْ لَهُمْ ط
إِنْ تَسْتَغْفِرْ لَهُمْ سَبْعِينَ مَرَّةً
فَلَنْ يَغْفِرَ اللَّهُ لَهُمْ ط ذٰلِكَ بِأَنَّهُمْ
كَفَرُوا بِاللَّهِ وَرَسُولِهِ ط وَاللَّهُ لَا
يَهْدِي الْقَوْمَ الْفٰسِقِينَ ﴿٨٠﴾ ع ٨ ١٦

81. Those who did not take part in the battle (of Tabuk) were glad about their staying home against the order of the Messenger of Allah. They did not want to fight for the cause of Allah with their property and in person and said, "Do not march (to the battle) on the hot days." (Muhammad), tell them, "The heat of hellfire is much more severe, if only you would understand."

81. Fariḥal-mukhallafoona bimaq'adihim khilaafa Rasoo-lil-laahi wa karihooo añy-yujaa-hidoo bi-amwaalihim wa anfu-sihim fee sabeelil-laahi wa qaaloo laa tanfiroo fil-ḥarr; qul Naaru Jahannama ashaddu ḥarraa; law kaanoo yafqahoon.

فَرِحَ الْمُخَلَّفُونَ بِمَقْعَدِهِمْ خِلٰفَ
رَسُولِ اللَّهِ وَكَرِهُوا أَنْ يُجَاهِدُوا
بِأَمْوَالِهِمْ وَأَنْفُسِهِمْ فِي سَبِيلِ اللَّهِ
وَقَالُوا لَا تَنْفِرُوا فِي الْحَرِّ ط قُلْ نَارُ
جَهَنَّمَ أَشَدُّ حَرًّا ط لَوْ كَانُوا يَفْقَهُونَ ﴿٨١﴾

82. They should laugh less and weep more because of what they have gained.

82. Falyaḍḥakoo qaleelañw-walyabkoo kaseeran jazaaa'am bimaa kaanoo yaksiboon.

فَلْيَضْحَكُوا قَلِيلًا وَّلْيَبْكُوا كَثِيرًا ج
جَزَآءً بِمَا كَانُوا يَكْسِبُونَ ﴿٨٢﴾

83. When Allah brings you back safely and a group of hypocrites asks you to make them exempt from taking part in the battle, tell them, "Never march with me and never fight with us against any of the enemies (of Allah). You chose to linger behind the first time, so this time stay behind with those who are of no help in the battle."

83. Fa-ir-raja'akal-laahu ilaa ṭaaa'ifatim-minhum fasta-zanooka lilkhurooji faqul-lan takhrujoo ma'iya abadañw-wa lan tuqaatiloo ma'iya 'aduw-wan innakum raḍeetum-bilqu'oodi awwala marratin faq'udoo ma'al-khaalifeen.

فَإِنْ رَّجَعَكَ اللَّهُ إِلٰى طَآئِفَةٍ مِّنْهُمْ
فَاسْتَأْذَنُوكَ لِلْخُرُوجِ فَقُلْ لَّنْ
تَخْرُجُوا مَعِيَ أَبَدًا وَّلَنْ تُقَاتِلُوا مَعِيَ
عَدُوًّا ط إِنَّكُمْ رَضِيتُمْ بِالْقُعُودِ أَوَّلَ
مَرَّةٍ فَاقْعُدُوا مَعَ الْخٰلِفِينَ ﴿٨٣﴾

84. Should any of them die, never pray for him or stand on his

84. Wa laa tuṣalli 'alaaa aḥadim-minhum maata

وَلَا تُصَلِّ عَلٰٓى أَحَدٍ مِّنْهُمْ مَّاتَ

grave. They have disbelieved in Allah and His messenger and have died while committing evil.

abadañw-wa laa taqum 'alaa qabriheee innahum kafaroo billaahi wa Rasoolihee wa maatoo wa hum faasiqoon.

اَبَدًا وَّلَا تَقُمْ عَلٰى قَبْرِهٖ ؕ اِنَّهُمْ
كَفَرُوْا بِاللّٰهِ وَرَسُوْلِهٖ وَمَاتُوْا
وَهُمْ فٰسِقُوْنَ ۝٨٤

85. Their wealth or children should not attract you; Allah wants only to punish them through these things in this life so that they will die as unbelievers.

85. Wa laa tu'jibka amwaaluhum wa awlaaduhum; innamaa yureedul-laahu añy-yu'az-zibahum bihaa fid-dunyaa wa tazhaqa anfusuhum wa hum kaafiroon.

وَلَا تُعْجِبْكَ اَمْوَالُهُمْ وَاَوْلَادُهُمْ ؕ اِنَّمَا
يُرِيْدُ اللّٰهُ اَنْ يُّعَذِّبَهُمْ بِهَا فِى الدُّنْيَا
وَتَزْهَقَ اَنْفُسُهُمْ وَهُمْ كٰفِرُوْنَ ۝٨٥

86. When a chapter of the Quran is revealed telling them to believe in Allah and fight along with His messenger for His cause against His enemies, the healthy and rich ones of them ask you to exempt them from taking part in the battle for the cause of Allah and to let them stay home with the people who are of no help in the battle.

86. Wa izaaa unzilat Sooratun an aaminoo billaahi wa jaahidoo ma'a Rasoolihis-ta-zanaka uluttawli minhum wa qaaloo zarnaa nakum-ma'al qaa'ideen.

وَاِذَاۤ اُنْزِلَتْ سُوْرَةٌ اَنْ اٰمِنُوْا بِاللّٰهِ
وَجَاهِدُوْا مَعَ رَسُوْلِهِ اسْتَاْذَنَكَ
اُولُوا الطَّوْلِ مِنْهُمْ وَقَالُوْا ذَرْنَا
نَكُنْ مَّعَ الْقٰعِدِيْنَ ۝٨٦

87. They were happy to stay home with those who were of no help in the battle, a seal was placed on their hearts thus they were left with no understanding.

87. Radoo bi-añy-yakoonoo ma'al-khawaalifi wa tubi'a 'alaa quloobihim fahum laa yafqahoon.

رَضُوْا بِاَنْ يَّكُوْنُوْا مَعَ الْخَوَالِفِ وَطُبِعَ
عَلٰى قُلُوْبِهِمْ فَهُمْ لَا يَفْقَهُوْنَ ۝٨٧

88. But the Messenger of Allah and the believers with him fought for the cause of Allah with their possessions and in person and their reward will be all good things and everlasting happiness.

88. Laakinir-Rasoolu wal-lazeena aamanoo ma'ahoo jaahadoo bi-amwaalihim wa anfusihim; wa ulaaa'ika lahumul-khayraatu wa ulaaa'i-ka humul-muflihoon.

لٰكِنِ الرَّسُوْلُ وَالَّذِيْنَ اٰمَنُوْا مَعَهٗ
جٰهَدُوْا بِاَمْوَالِهِمْ وَاَنْفُسِهِمْ ؕ وَ
اُولٰٓئِكَ لَهُمُ الْخَيْرٰتُ ؗ وَاُولٰٓئِكَ
هُمُ الْمُفْلِحُوْنَ ۝٨٨

89. Allah has established gardens for them wherein streams flow and wherein they will live forever. This indeed is the greatest triumph.

89. A'addal-laahu lahum Jannaatin tajree min tahtihal-anhaaru khaalideena feehaa; zaalikal-fawzul 'azeem.

اَعَدَّ اللّٰهُ لَهُمْ جَنّٰتٍ تَجْرِيْ مِنْ
تَحْتِهَا الْاَنْهٰرُ خٰلِدِيْنَ فِيْهَا ؕ
ذٰلِكَ الْفَوْزُ الْعَظِيْمُ ۝٨٩ ع ١٦ ٩ ١٧

90. Some of the dwellers of the desert (who were not able to join the army) came to the Prophet seeking exemption from taking part in the battle. Those who called Allah and His messengers liars also stayed home (with those who were truly exempt). The unbelievers will soon receive a painful punishment.

90. Wa jaaa'al-mu'az-ziroona minal-A'raabi liyu'zana lahum wa qa'adal-lazeena kazabul-laaha wa Rasoolah; sayuseebul-lazeena kafaroo minhum 'azaabun aleem.

وَجَآءَ الْمُعَذِّرُوْنَ مِنَ الْاَعْرَابِ
لِيُؤْذَنَ لَهُمْ وَقَعَدَ الَّذِيْنَ كَذَبُوا
اللّٰهَ وَرَسُوْلَهٗ ؕ سَيُصِيْبُ الَّذِيْنَ
كَفَرُوْا مِنْهُمْ عَذَابٌ اَلِيْمٌ ۝٩٠

91. People who are weak or sick and those who do not have the means to take part in the fighting are exempt from this duty if their intention remains sincere about Allah and His

91. Laysa 'alad-du'afaaa'i wa laa 'alal-mardaa wa laa 'alal-lazeena laa yajidoona maa yunfiqoona harajun izaa nasahoo lillaahi wa

لَيْسَ عَلَى الضُّعَفَآءِ وَلَا عَلَى الْمَرْضٰى
وَلَا عَلَى الَّذِيْنَ لَا يَجِدُوْنَ مَا
يُنْفِقُوْنَ حَرَجٌ اِذَا نَصَحُوْا لِلّٰهِ وَ

messenger. Righteous people shall not be blamed. Allah is All-forgiving and All-merciful.

Rasoolih; maa 'alal-muḥsineena min sabeel; wallaahu Ghafoorur Raḥeem.

رَسُولِهِۦ ۚ مَا عَلَى الْمُحْسِنِينَ مِن
سَبِيلٍ ۚ وَاللَّهُ غَفُورٌ رَّحِيمٌ ﴿٩١﴾

92. Those who come to you, (Muhammad), asking to be taken to the battle, but you cannot find the necessary means for them, are exempt from the duty of fighting for the cause of Allah, even though they leave you with their eyes flooded with tears because of not being able to help the cause of Allah.

92. Wa laa 'alal-lazeena izaa maaa atawka litaḥmilahum qulta laaa ajidu maaa aḥmilu-kum 'alayhi tawallaw wa a'yunuhum tafeeḍu minad-dam'i ḥazanan allaa yajidoo maa yunfiqoon.

وَلَا عَلَى الَّذِينَ إِذَا مَآ أَتَوْكَ
لِتَحْمِلَهُمْ قُلْتَ لَآ أَجِدُ مَآ
أَحْمِلُكُمْ عَلَيْهِ تَوَلَّوا وَّأَعْيُنُهُمْ
تَفِيضُ مِنَ الدَّمْعِ حَزَنًا أَلَّا
يَجِدُوا مَا يُنفِقُونَ ﴿٩٢﴾

93. The blameworthy ones are those who ask for exemption despite their ability and who preferred to stay at home with those who are truly exempt. Allah has placed a seal on their hearts but they do not know.

93. Innamas-sabeelu 'alal-lazeena yasta-zinoonaka wa hum aghniyaaa'; raḍoo bi-añy-yakoonoo ma'al-khawaalifi wa ṭaba'al-laahu 'alaa quloobihim fahum laa ya'lamoon.

إِنَّمَا السَّبِيلُ عَلَى الَّذِينَ
يَسْتَأْذِنُونَكَ وَهُمْ أَغْنِيَآءُ ۚ
رَضُوا بِأَن يَكُونُوا مَعَ الْخَوَالِفِ
وَطَبَعَ اللَّهُ عَلَىٰ قُلُوبِهِمْ فَهُمْ لَا
يَعْلَمُونَ ﴿٩٣﴾

94. They will apologize to you on your return. Tell them, "Do not ask for pardon. We will never believe you. Allah has already told us everything about you. Allah and His messenger will soon make your deeds public, then you will return to Him who has absolute knowledge of the unseen and the seen and He will inform you of what you have done.

94. Ya'taziroona ilaykum izaa raja'tum ilayhim; qul-laa ta'taziroo lan-nu'mina lakum qad nabba-anal-laahu min akhbaarikum; wa sayaral-laahu 'amalakum wa Rasooluhoo summa turaddoona ilaa 'Aali-mil-Ghaybi washshahaadati fayunabbi'ukum bimaa kuntum ta'maloon.

يَعْتَذِرُونَ إِلَيْكُمْ إِذَا رَجَعْتُمْ
إِلَيْهِمْ ۚ قُل لَّا تَعْتَذِرُوا لَن نُّؤْمِنَ
لَكُمْ قَدْ نَبَّأَنَا اللَّهُ مِنْ أَخْبَارِكُمْ ۚ
وَسَيَرَى اللَّهُ عَمَلَكُمْ وَرَسُولُهُ ثُمَّ
تُرَدُّونَ إِلَىٰ عَالِمِ الْغَيْبِ وَالشَّهَادَةِ
فَيُنَبِّئُكُم بِمَا كُنتُمْ تَعْمَلُونَ ﴿٩٤﴾

95. When you return they will appeal to you in the Name of Allah to leave them alone. So leave them alone. They are filthy and their dwelling will be hell as a recompense for what they had gained.

95. Sayaḥlifoona billaahi lakum izanqalabtum ilayhim litu'riḍoo 'anhum fa-a'riḍoo 'anhum innahum rijsuñw-wa ma-waahum Jahannamu jazaaa-'am bimaa kaanoo yaksiboon.

سَيَحْلِفُونَ بِاللَّهِ لَكُمْ إِذَا انقَلَبْتُمْ
إِلَيْهِمْ لِتُعْرِضُوا عَنْهُمْ ۖ فَأَعْرِضُوا
عَنْهُمْ ۖ إِنَّهُمْ رِجْسٌ ۖ وَمَأْوَاهُمْ
جَهَنَّمُ جَزَآءً بِمَا كَانُوا يَكْسِبُونَ ﴿٩٥﴾

96. They swear in the Name of Allah to please you. Even if you were to be pleased with them, Allah is not pleased with evildoing people.

96. Yaḥlifoona lakum litar-ḍaw 'anhum fa-in tarḍaw 'anhum fa-innal-laaha laa yar-ḍaa 'anil-qawmil-faasiqeen.

يَحْلِفُونَ لَكُمْ لِتَرْضَوْا عَنْهُمْ ۖ فَإِن
تَرْضَوْا عَنْهُمْ فَإِنَّ اللَّهَ لَا يَرْضَىٰ
عَنِ الْقَوْمِ الْفَاسِقِينَ ﴿٩٦﴾

97. The desert-dwelling Arabs are far worse than the others in their disbelief and hypocrisy and

97. Al-A'raabu ashaddu kuf-rañw-wa nifaaqañw-wa ajdaru

الْأَعْرَابُ أَشَدُّ كُفْرًا وَنِفَاقًا وَأَجْدَرُ

الجزء الحادي عشر (١١)

have more reason to be ignorant of the revelations that Allah revealed to His messenger. Allah is All-knowing and All-wise.

allaa ya'lamoo ḥudooda maaa anzalal-laahu 'alaa Rasoolih; wallaahu 'Aleemun Ḥakeem.

أَلَّا يَعْلَمُوا حُدُودَ مَا أَنزَلَ اللَّهُ عَلَىٰ
رَسُولِهِ ۗ وَاللَّهُ عَلِيمٌ حَكِيمٌ ﴿٩٧﴾

98. Whatever some of the desert-dwelling Arabs spend for the cause of Allah, they consider it a loss to themselves. They wish to see you in trouble. Trouble has struck them already. Allah is All-hearing and All-knowing.

98. Wa minal-A'raabi mañy-yattakhizu maa yunfiqu maghramañw-wa yatarabbaṣu bikumud-dawaaa'ir; 'alayhim daaa'iratus-saw'; wallaahu Samee'un 'Aleem.

وَمِنَ الْأَعْرَابِ مَن يَتَّخِذُ مَا
يُنفِقُ مَغْرَمًا وَيَتَرَبَّصُ بِكُمُ
الدَّوَائِرَ ۚ عَلَيْهِمْ دَائِرَةُ السَّوْءِ ۗ
وَاللَّهُ سَمِيعٌ عَلِيمٌ ﴿٩٨﴾

99. Some of the desert-dwelling Arabs believe in Allah and the Day of Judgment. Whatever they spend for the cause of Allah they consider it as a means of getting nearer to Allah and have the prayers of the Messenger in their favor. This, certainly is a means to get nearer to Allah. Allah will admit them into His mercy. Allah is All-forgiving and All-merciful.

99. Wa minal-A'raabi mañy-yu'minu billaahi wal-Yawmil Aakhiri wa yattakhizu maa yunfiqu qurubaatin 'indal-laahi wa ṣalawaatir-Rasool; alaaa innahaa qurbatul-lahum; sayudkhilu-humullaahu fee raḥmatih; innallaaha Ghafoo-rur-Raḥeem.

وَمِنَ الْأَعْرَابِ مَن يُؤْمِنُ بِاللَّهِ
وَالْيَوْمِ الْآخِرِ وَيَتَّخِذُ مَا يُنفِقُ
قُرُبَاتٍ عِندَ اللَّهِ وَصَلَوَاتِ الرَّسُولِ ۚ
أَلَا إِنَّهَا قُرْبَةٌ لَّهُمْ ۚ سَيُدْخِلُهُمُ اللَّهُ
فِي رَحْمَتِهِ ۗ إِنَّ اللَّهَ غَفُورٌ رَّحِيمٌ ﴿٩٩﴾

100. Allah is well pleased with the foremost ones of those who left their homes for the cause of Allah, those who helped them after their arrival in Medina, and those who nobly followed these two groups. He has prepared gardens for them wherein streams flow and wherein they will live forever. This certainly is the supreme triumph.

100. Was-saabiqoonal awwa-loona minal-Muhaajireena wal-Anṣaari wallazeenat-taba'oo-hum bi-iḥsaanir-raḍiyal-laahu 'anhum wa raḍoo 'anhu wa a'adda lahum Jannaatin tajree taḥtahal-anhaaru khaalideena feehaaa abadaa; zaalikal-fawzul-'aẓeem.

وَالسَّابِقُونَ الْأَوَّلُونَ مِنَ الْمُهَاجِرِينَ
وَالْأَنصَارِ وَالَّذِينَ اتَّبَعُوهُم
بِإِحْسَانٍ رَّضِيَ اللَّهُ عَنْهُمْ وَ
رَضُوا عَنْهُ وَأَعَدَّ لَهُمْ جَنَّاتٍ
تَجْرِي تَحْتَهَا الْأَنْهَارُ خَالِدِينَ
فِيهَا أَبَدًا ۚ ذَٰلِكَ الْفَوْزُ الْعَظِيمُ ﴿١٠٠﴾

101. Some of the desert-dwelling Arabs around you are hypocrites, as are some of the inhabitants of Medina. They are persisting in their hypocrisies. You do not know them but We know them well and will punish them twice over. Then they will be brought to the great torment (on the Day of Judgment).

101. Wa mimman ḥawlakum minal-A'raabi munaafiqoona wa min ahlil-Madeenati maradoo 'alan-nifaaq; laa ta'lamuhum naḥnu na'lamu-hum; sanu'az-zibuhum marra-tayni summa yuraddoona ilaa 'azaabin 'aẓeem.

وَمِمَّنْ حَوْلَكُم مِّنَ الْأَعْرَابِ
مُنَافِقُونَ ۖ وَمِنْ أَهْلِ الْمَدِينَةِ ۖ
مَرَدُوا عَلَى النِّفَاقِ لَا تَعْلَمُهُمْ ۖ
نَحْنُ نَعْلَمُهُمْ ۚ سَنُعَذِّبُهُم مَّرَّتَيْنِ
ثُمَّ يُرَدُّونَ إِلَىٰ عَذَابٍ عَظِيمٍ ﴿١٠١﴾

102. Others among them have already confessed their sins and have mixed virtuous deeds with sinful ones. Perhaps Allah will forgive them. Allah is All-forgiving and All-merciful.

102. Wa aakharoona'tarafoo bizunoobihim khalaṭoo 'amalan ṣaaliḥañw-wa aakhara sayyi'aa; 'asal-laahu añy-yatooba 'alayhim; innallaaha Ghafoo-rur-Raḥeem.

وَآخَرُونَ اعْتَرَفُوا بِذُنُوبِهِمْ
خَلَطُوا عَمَلًا صَالِحًا وَآخَرَ سَيِّئًا
عَسَى اللَّهُ أَن يَتُوبَ عَلَيْهِمْ ۚ إِنَّ
اللَّهَ غَفُورٌ رَّحِيمٌ ﴿١٠٢﴾

103. Collect religious tax (zakat) from them to purify and cleanse them and pray for them; your prayers give them comfort. Allah is All-hearing and All-knowing.

103. Khuz̲ min amwaalihim ṣadaqatan tuṭahhiruhum wa tuzakkeehim bihaa wa ṣalli ‘alayhim inna ṣalaataka sakanul-lahum; wallaahu Samee‘un ‘Aleem.

خُذْ مِنْ اَمْوَالِهِمْ صَدَقَةً تُطَهِّرُهُمْ
وَتُزَكِّيْهِمْ بِهَا وَصَلِّ عَلَيْهِمْ ؕ
اِنَّ صَلٰوتَكَ سَكَنٌ لَّهُمْ ؕ وَاللّٰهُ
سَمِيْعٌ عَلِيْمٌ ﴿١٠٣﴾

104. Did they not know that it is Allah who accepts the repentance of His servants and receives charity (zakat) funds and that it is Allah who is All-forgiving and All-merciful?

104. Alam ya‘lamooo annal-laaha Huwa yaqbalut-tawbata ‘an ‘ibaadihee wa ya-khuz̲uṣ-ṣadaqaati wa annal-laaha Huwat-Tawwaabur-Raḥeem.

اَلَمْ يَعْلَمُوْۤا اَنَّ اللّٰهَ هُوَ يَقْبَلُ التَّوْبَةَ
عَنْ عِبَادِهٖ وَيَاْخُذُ الصَّدَقٰتِ وَاَنَّ
اللّٰهَ هُوَ التَّوَّابُ الرَّحِيْمُ ﴿١٠٤﴾

105. (Muhammad), tell them, “Act as you wish. Allah, His Messenger, and the believers will see your deeds. You will be brought before the One who has absolute knowledge of the unseen and the seen. He will let you know about all that you have done.

105. Wa quli‘-maloo fasayaral-laahu ‘amalakum wa Rasooluhoo walmu’minoon; wa saturaddoona ilaa ‘Aalimil-Ghaybi washshahaadati fayunabbi’ukum bimaa kuntum ta‘maloon.

وَقُلِ اعْمَلُوْا فَسَيَرَى اللّٰهُ عَمَلَكُمْ وَ
رَسُوْلُهٗ وَالْمُؤْمِنُوْنَ ؕ وَسَتُرَدُّوْنَ
اِلٰى عٰلِمِ الْغَيْبِ وَالشَّهَادَةِ فَيُنَبِّئُكُمْ
بِمَا كُنْتُمْ تَعْمَلُوْنَ ﴿١٠٥﴾ ۚ

106. Besides those who have confessed their sins, there are others who have no good deeds for which they may receive any reward or sins for which they may be punished. Their fate will be in the hands of Allah.” Allah is All-knowing and All-wise.

106. Wa aakharoona murjawna li-amril-laahi immaa yu‘az̲z̲ibuhum wa immaa yatoobu ‘alayhim;wallaahu ‘Aleemun Ḥakeem.

وَاٰخَرُوْنَ مُرْجَوْنَ لِاَمْرِ اللّٰهِ
اِمَّا يُعَذِّبُهُمْ وَاِمَّا يَتُوْبُ عَلَيْهِمْ ؕ
وَاللّٰهُ عَلِيْمٌ حَكِيْمٌ ﴿١٠٦﴾

107. The mosque which some of the hypocrites have established is only to harm people, to spread disbelief, to create discord among the believers, to wait for the one (abu Amir) who fought against Allah and His Messenger, and to make others believe that it has been established with their good intentions. But Allah testifies that they are liars.

107. Wallaz̲eenat-takhaz̲oo masjidan ḍiraarañw-wa kufrañw-wa tafreeqam baynal-mu’mineena wa irṣaadal-liman ḥaarabal-laaha wa Rasoolahoo min qabl; wa layaḥlifunna in aradnaaa illal-ḥusnaa wallaahu yashhadu innahum lakaaz̲iboon.

وَالَّذِيْنَ اتَّخَذُوْا مَسْجِدًا ضِرَارًا
وَّكُفْرًا وَّتَفْرِيْقًاۢ بَيْنَ الْمُؤْمِنِيْنَ
وَاِرْصَادًا لِّمَنْ حَارَبَ اللّٰهَ وَ
رَسُوْلَهٗ مِنْ قَبْلُ ؕ وَلَيَحْلِفُنَّ
اِنْ اَرَدْنَاۤ اِلَّا الْحُسْنٰى ؕ وَاللّٰهُ
يَشْهَدُ اِنَّهُمْ لَكٰذِبُوْنَ ﴿١٠٧﴾

108. (Muhammad), never stay in that mosque. The mosque which was established for a pious purpose and before all other mosques is more virtuous for your prayer. In this mosque, there are people who love to be purified. Allah loves those who purify themselves.

108. Laa taqum feehi abadaa; lamasjidun ussisa ‘alat-taqwaa min awwali yawmin aḥaqqu an taqooma feeh; feehi rijaaluñy-yuḥibboona añy-yataṭahharoo, wallaahu yuḥibbul-muṭṭahhireen.

لَا تَقُمْ فِيْهِ اَبَدًا ؕ لَمَسْجِدٌ اُسِّسَ عَلَى
التَّقْوٰى مِنْ اَوَّلِ يَوْمٍ اَحَقُّ اَنْ تَقُوْمَ
فِيْهِ ؕ فِيْهِ رِجَالٌ يُّحِبُّوْنَ اَنْ يَّتَطَهَّرُوْا ؕ
وَاللّٰهُ يُحِبُّ الْمُطَّهِّرِيْنَ ﴿١٠٨﴾

109. Which is better, the mosque that is founded for pious purposes and for achieving Allah's pleasure or that which is based on the brink

109. Afaman assasa bunyaanahoo ‘alaa taqwaa minal-laahi wa riḍwaanin khayrun am-man

اَفَمَنْ اَسَّسَ بُنْيَانَهٗ عَلٰى تَقْوٰى
مِنَ اللّٰهِ وَرِضْوَانٍ خَيْرٌ اَمْ مَّنْ

أَسَّسَ بُنْيَانَهُ عَلٰى شَفَا جُرُفٍ
هَارٍ فَانْهَارَ بِهِ فِي نَارِ جَهَنَّمَ ۗ وَ
اللّٰهُ لَا يَهْدِي الْقَوْمَ الظّٰلِمِينَ ﴿١٠٩﴾

assasa bunyaanahoo 'alaa shafaa jurufin haarin fanhaara bihee fee Naari Jahannam; wallaahu laa yahdil-qawmaẓ-ẓaalimeen.

of a crumbling bank and which may crumble into hell at any moment? Allah does not guide the unjust.

لَا يَزَالُ بُنْيَانُهُمُ الَّذِي بَنَوْا رِيبَةً
فِي قُلُوبِهِمْ إِلَّا أَنْ تَقَطَّعَ قُلُوبُهُمْ ۗ
وَاللّٰهُ عَلِيمٌ حَكِيمٌ ﴿١١٠﴾ ع ١١ ٣

110. Laa yazaalu bunyaanuhumul-lazee banaw reebatan fee quloobihim illaaa an taqaṭṭa'a quloobuhum; wallaahu 'Aleemun Ḥakeem.

110. The building (mosque) which they have built always motivates mischief in their hearts until (such time when) their hearts are cut into pieces. Allah is All-knowing and All-wise.

إِنَّ اللّٰهَ اشْتَرٰى مِنَ الْمُؤْمِنِينَ
أَنْفُسَهُمْ وَأَمْوَالَهُمْ بِأَنَّ لَهُمُ الْجَنَّةَ ۗ
يُقَاتِلُونَ فِي سَبِيلِ اللّٰهِ فَيَقْتُلُونَ
وَيُقْتَلُونَ ۖ وَعْدًا عَلَيْهِ حَقًّا فِي
التَّوْرٰىةِ وَالْإِنْجِيلِ وَالْقُرْاٰنِ ۗ وَمَنْ
أَوْفٰى بِعَهْدِهِ مِنَ اللّٰهِ فَاسْتَبْشِرُوا
بِبَيْعِكُمُ الَّذِي بَايَعْتُمْ بِهِ ۗ وَ
ذٰلِكَ هُوَ الْفَوْزُ الْعَظِيمُ ﴿١١١﴾

111. Innal-laahash-taraa minal-mu'mineena anfusahum wa amwaalahum bi-anna lahumul-jannah; yuqaatiloona fee sabeelillaahi fayaqtuloona wa yuqtaloon; wa'dan 'alayhi ḥaqqan fit-Tawraati wal Injeeli wal-Qur'aan; wa man awfaa bi'ahdihee minal-laah; fastabshiroo bibay'ikumullazee baaya'tum bih; wa zaalika huwal-fawzul-'aẓeem.

111. Allah has purchased the souls and property of the believers in exchange for Paradise. They fight for the cause of Allah to destroy His enemies and to sacrifice themselves. This is a true promise which He has revealed in the Torah, the Gospel, and the Quran. No one is more true to His promise than Allah. Let this bargain be glad news for them. This is indeed the supreme triumph.

اَلتَّائِبُونَ الْعٰبِدُونَ الْحٰمِدُونَ
السَّائِحُونَ الرّٰكِعُونَ السّٰجِدُونَ
الْاٰمِرُونَ بِالْمَعْرُوفِ وَالنَّاهُونَ
عَنِ الْمُنْكَرِ وَالْحٰفِظُونَ لِحُدُودِ
اللّٰهِ ۗ وَبَشِّرِ الْمُؤْمِنِينَ ﴿١١٢﴾

112.At-taaa'iboonal 'aabidoonal-ḥaamidoonas-saaa'iḥoonar-raaki'oonas-saajidoonal-aamiroona bilma'roofi wannaahoona 'anil-munkari walḥaafiẓoona liḥudoodil-laah; wa bashshiril-mu'mineen.

112. (The believers) who repent for their sins, worship Allah, praise Him, travel through the land (for pious purposes), bow down and prostrate themselves in obedience to Allah, make others do good and prevent them from sins and abide by the laws of Allah, will receive a great reward. Let this be glad news for the believer.

مَا كَانَ لِلنَّبِيِّ وَالَّذِينَ اٰمَنُوا أَنْ
يَسْتَغْفِرُوا لِلْمُشْرِكِينَ وَلَوْ كَانُوا
أُولِي قُرْبٰى مِنْ بَعْدِ مَا تَبَيَّنَ لَهُمْ
أَنَّهُمْ أَصْحٰبُ الْجَحِيمِ ﴿١١٣﴾

113. Maa kaana lin-Nabiyyi wallazeena aamanooo añy-yastaghfiroo lilmushrikeena wa law kaanooo ulee qurbaa mim ba'di maa tabayyana lahum annahum Aṣḥaabul-jaḥeem.

113. After it was made clear that the pagans are to be the dwellers of hell, the Prophet and the believers should not have sought forgiveness from Allah for them even though they may have been relatives.

وَمَا كَانَ اسْتِغْفَارُ إِبْرٰهِيمَ لِأَبِيهِ
إِلَّا عَنْ مَوْعِدَةٍ وَعَدَهَا إِيَّاهُ ۚ فَلَمَّا
تَبَيَّنَ لَهُ أَنَّهُ عَدُوٌّ لِلّٰهِ تَبَرَّأَ مِنْهُ ۗ

114. Wa maa kaanastighfaaru Ibraaheema li-abeehi illaa 'ammaw'idatiñw-wa'adahaaa iyyaahu falammaa tabayyana lahooo annahoo 'aduwwul-lillaahi tabarra-a minh;

114. There was no other reason for Abraham to seek forgiveness from Allah for his father except the promise that he had made with him. When Abraham knew that his father was an enemy of Allah, he disowned his father. Abraham

was very tender-hearted and forbearing.

115. Allah does not misguide a nation after having given them guidance until the means of piety are made known to them. Allah knows all things.

116. To Allah belongs the Kingdom of the heavens and the earth. He grants life and causes death. Allah is your only Guardian and Helper.

117. Allah pardoned the Prophet, the Emigrants, the Helpers, and those who followed them, when the hearts of some of them almost deviated (from the truth) in their hour of difficulty. Allah forgave them because of His Compassion and Mercy.

118. Allah also forgave the three people who lagged behind. Grief made them feel as though there was no place in the whole vast earth to hide them or in their souls to conceal their sorrow. They began to believe that no one could save them (from the wrath of Allah) except He Himself. Allah pardoned them so that they would also repent for their sins. Allah is All-forgiving and All-merciful.

119. Believers, have fear of Allah and always be friends with the truthful ones.

120. The inhabitants of the city of Medina and the desert Arabs dwelling around it were not to disobey the Messenger of Allah or to give priority to their own lives above that of the Prophet. Had they given priority to the life of the Messenger of Allah, whatever hardships they had experienced due to thirst, fatigue, or hunger in their struggle for the cause of Allah, or their traveling that enraged the unbelievers, and

inna Ibraaheema la-awwaahun ḥaleem.

115. Wa maa kaanal-laahu liyuḍilla qawmam ba'da iz̲ hadaahum ḥattaa yubayyina lahum-maa yattaqoon; innal-laaha bikulli shay'in 'Aleem.

116. Innal-laaha lahoo mulkus-samaawaati wal-arḍi yuḥyee wa yumeet; wa maa lakum-min doonil-laahi miñw-waliyyiñw-wa laa naṣeer.

117. Laqat-taabal-laahu 'alan-Nabiyyi wal-Muhaajireena wal-Anṣaaril-laz̲eenat-taba'oohu fee saa'atil-'usrati mim ba'di maa kaada yazeeghu quloobu fareeqim-minhum s̲umma taaba 'alayhim; innahoo bihim Ra'oofur-Raḥeem.

118. Wa 'alas̲-s̲alaas̲atil-laz̲eena khullifoo ḥattaaa iz̲aa ḍaaqat 'alayhimul-arḍu bimaa raḥubat wa ḍaaqat 'alayhim anfusuhum wa ẓannooo al-laa malja-a minal-laahi illaaa ilayhi s̲umma taaba 'alayhim liya-toobooo; innal-laaha Huwat-Tawwaabur-Raḥeem.

119. Yaaa ayyuhal-laz̲eena aamanut-taqul-laaha wa koonoo ma'aṣ-ṣaadiqeen.

120. Maa kaana li-ahlil-Madeenati wa man ḥawlahum-minal-A'raabi añy-yatakhal-lafoo 'ar-Rasoolillaahi wa laa yarghaboo bi-anfusihim 'an nafsih; z̲aalika bi-annahum laa yuṣeebuhum ẓamauñw-wa laa naṣabuñw-wa laa makhmaṣatun fee sabeelillaahi wa laa yaṭa-'oona mawṭi'añy- yagheeẓul-

إِنَّ إِبْرٰهِيمَ لَأَوَّاهٌ حَلِيمٌ ﴿١١٤﴾
وَمَا كَانَ اللّٰهُ لِيُضِلَّ قَوْمًا بَعْدَ إِذْ
هَدٰىهُمْ حَتّٰى يُبَيِّنَ لَهُمْ مَّا يَتَّقُونَ ؕ
إِنَّ اللّٰهَ بِكُلِّ شَيْءٍ عَلِيمٌ ﴿١١٥﴾
إِنَّ اللّٰهَ لَهُ مُلْكُ السَّمٰوٰتِ وَالْأَرْضِ ؕ
يُحْيِي وَيُمِيتُ ؕ وَمَا لَكُمْ مِّنْ دُونِ
اللّٰهِ مِنْ وَّلِيٍّ وَّلَا نَصِيرٍ ﴿١١٦﴾
لَقَدْ تَّابَ اللّٰهُ عَلَى النَّبِيِّ وَالْمُهٰجِرِينَ
وَالْأَنْصَارِ الَّذِينَ اتَّبَعُوهُ فِي سَاعَةِ
الْعُسْرَةِ مِنْ بَعْدِ مَا كَادَ يَزِيغُ
قُلُوبُ فَرِيقٍ مِّنْهُمْ ثُمَّ تَابَ عَلَيْهِمْ ؕ
إِنَّهُ بِهِمْ رَءُوفٌ رَّحِيمٌ ﴿١١٧﴾ ۙ
وَّعَلَى الثَّلٰثَةِ الَّذِينَ خُلِّفُوا ؕ
حَتّٰى إِذَا ضَاقَتْ عَلَيْهِمُ الْأَرْضُ
بِمَا رَحُبَتْ وَضَاقَتْ عَلَيْهِمْ أَنْفُسُهُمْ
وَظَنُّوا أَنْ لَّا مَلْجَأَ مِنَ اللّٰهِ إِلَّا
إِلَيْهِ ؕ ثُمَّ تَابَ عَلَيْهِمْ لِيَتُوبُوا ؕ
إِنَّ اللّٰهَ هُوَ التَّوَّابُ الرَّحِيمُ ﴿١١٨﴾ ع ١٤ ٨ ٣
يٰٓأَيُّهَا الَّذِينَ اٰمَنُوا اتَّقُوا اللّٰهَ وَ
كُونُوا مَعَ الصّٰدِقِينَ ﴿١١٩﴾
مَا كَانَ لِأَهْلِ الْمَدِينَةِ وَمَنْ
حَوْلَهُمْ مِّنَ الْأَعْرَابِ أَنْ يَّتَخَلَّفُوا
عَنْ رَّسُولِ اللّٰهِ وَلَا يَرْغَبُوا بِأَنْفُسِهِمْ
عَنْ نَّفْسِهِ ؕ ذٰلِكَ بِأَنَّهُمْ لَا يُصِيبُهُمْ
ظَمَأٌ وَّلَا نَصَبٌ وَّلَا مَخْمَصَةٌ فِي
سَبِيلِ اللّٰهِ وَلَا يَطَئُونَ مَوْطِئًا يَّغِيظُ

any injury they received from enemies, would have been written for them as a good deed. Allah does not ignore the reward of those who do good.

kuffaara walaa yanaaloona min 'aduwwin naylan illaa kutiba lahum bihee 'amalun ṣaaliḥ; innal-laaha laa yuḍee'u ajral-muḥsineen.

الْكُفَّارَ وَلَا يَنَالُونَ مِنْ عَدُوٍّ نَّيْلًا
إِلَّا كُتِبَ لَهُمْ بِهِ عَمَلٌ صَالِحٌ ۚ إِنَّ
اللَّهَ لَا يُضِيعُ أَجْرَ الْمُحْسِنِينَ ﴿١٢٠﴾

121. Also, they would not have spent anything, great or small, for the cause of Allah or traveled through a valley without Allah's decreeing a reward for them far better than whatever they had done.

121. Wa laa yunfiqoona nafaqatan ṣagheeratañw-wa laa kabeeratañw-wa laa yaqṭa'oona waadiyan illaa kutiba lahum liyajziyahumul-laahu aḥsana maa kaanoo ya'maloon.

وَلَا يُنْفِقُونَ نَفَقَةً صَغِيرَةً وَّلَا
كَبِيرَةً وَّلَا يَقْطَعُونَ وَادِيًا إِلَّا
كُتِبَ لَهُمْ لِيَجْزِيَهُمُ اللَّهُ أَحْسَنَ مَا
كَانُوا يَعْمَلُونَ ﴿١٢١﴾

122. Not all believers have to become specialists in religious learning (to find the true Imam). Why do not some people from each group of believers seek to become specialists in religious learning and, after completing their studies, guide their group so that they will have fear of Allah?

122. Wa maa kaanal mu'minoona liyanfiroo kaaaffah; falaw laa nafara min kulli firqatim-minhum ṭaaa'ifatul-liyatafaqqahoo fiddeeni wa liyunziroo qawmahum izaa raja'ooo ilayhim la'allahum yaḥzaroon.

وَمَا كَانَ الْمُؤْمِنُونَ لِيَنْفِرُوا كَافَّةً ۚ
فَلَوْلَا نَفَرَ مِنْ كُلِّ فِرْقَةٍ مِّنْهُمْ
طَائِفَةٌ لِّيَتَفَقَّهُوا فِي الدِّينِ
وَلِيُنْذِرُوا قَوْمَهُمْ إِذَا رَجَعُوا
إِلَيْهِمْ لَعَلَّهُمْ يَحْذَرُونَ ﴿١٢٢﴾ ع ١٥

123. Believers, fight the unbelievers near you for the cause of Allah so that they realize your strength and know that Allah is with the pious ones.

123. Yaaa ayyuhal-lazeena aamanoo qaatilul-lazeena yaloonakum minal-kuffaari walyajidoo feekum ghilẓah; wa'lamooo annal-laaha ma'al-muttaqeen.

يَا أَيُّهَا الَّذِينَ آمَنُوا قَاتِلُوا
الَّذِينَ يَلُونَكُمْ مِّنَ الْكُفَّارِ وَلْيَجِدُوا
فِيكُمْ غِلْظَةً ۚ وَاعْلَمُوا أَنَّ اللَّهَ
مَعَ الْمُتَّقِينَ ﴿١٢٣﴾ الربع

124. When a chapter (of the Quran) is revealed, some people ask others, "Whose faith among you people has received strength from this (revelation)?" It (the revelation) certainly strengthens the faith of the believers and they consider it to be glad news.

124. Wa izaa maaa unzilat Sooratun faminhum mañy-yaqoolu ayyukum zaadathu haaziheee eemaanaa; fa-ammal-lazeena aamanoo fazaadathum eemaanañw-wa hum yastabshiroon.

وَإِذَا مَا أُنْزِلَتْ سُورَةٌ فَمِنْهُمْ مَّنْ
يَّقُولُ أَيُّكُمْ زَادَتْهُ هَٰذِهِ إِيمَانًا ۚ
فَأَمَّا الَّذِينَ آمَنُوا فَزَادَتْهُمْ إِيمَانًا
وَّهُمْ يَسْتَبْشِرُونَ ﴿١٢٤﴾

125. But to those whose hearts are sick, it adds more filth to their hearts and they die as unbelievers.

125. Wa ammal-lazeena fee quloobihim maraḍun fazaadathum rijsan ilaa rijsihim wa maatoo wa hum kaafiroon.

وَأَمَّا الَّذِينَ فِي قُلُوبِهِمْ مَّرَضٌ
فَزَادَتْهُمْ رِجْسًا إِلَىٰ رِجْسِهِمْ وَمَاتُوا
وَهُمْ كَافِرُونَ ﴿١٢٥﴾

126. Do they not realize that Allah tests them once or twice a year but, nevertheless, they do not repent and give it proper thought?

126. Awalaa yarawna annahum yuftanoona fee kulli 'aamim marratan aw marratayni summa laa yatooboona wa laa hum yazzakkaroon.

أَوَلَا يَرَوْنَ أَنَّهُمْ يُفْتَنُونَ فِي كُلِّ
عَامٍ مَّرَّةً أَوْ مَرَّتَيْنِ ثُمَّ لَا يَتُوبُونَ
وَلَا هُمْ يَذَّكَّرُونَ ﴿١٢٦﴾

127. When a chapter (of the Quran) is revealed, (it upsets them). They look at one another and their eyes silently ask this question, "Has anyone noticed the disappointment on our faces?" Then they walk away. In fact, Allah has turned their hearts away (from the truth); they are a people who have no understanding.

128. A messenger from your own people has come to you. Your destruction and suffering are extremely grievous to him. He really cares about you and is very compassionate and merciful to the believers.

129. (Muhammad), if they turn away from you, say, "Allah is Sufficient (support) for me. There is no Ilah (one deserving to be worshipped) but He. In Him do I trust and He is the Owner of the Great Throne."

Yunus, Jonah (10)

In the Name of Allah,
the Beneficent, the Merciful.

1. Alif. Lam. Ra. These are the verses of the Book of wisdom.

2. Why should it seem strange to mankind that We sent revelations to a man among them, who would warn others and give to the believers the glad news of their high rank in the sight of their Lord? The unbelievers have said, "He (Muhammad) is certainly a magician."

3. Allah is your Lord who has created the heavens and the earth in six days and established His Dominion over the Throne. He maintains order over the creation. No one can intercede for others without His permission. It is Allah who is your only Lord. Worship only Him. Will you then not think?

4. (People), you will all return to Allah. The promise of Allah is true; He creates all things and (after their death) brings them to life again so that He may justly reward the righteously striving

127. Wa izaa maaa unzilat Sooratun nazara ba'ḍuhum ilaa ba'ḍ; hal yaraakum min aḥadin summan-ṣarafoo; ṣarafal-laahu quloobahum bi-annahum qaw-mul-laa yafqahoon.

128. Laqad jaaa'akum Rasoo-lum-min anfusikum 'azeezun 'alayhi maa 'anittum ḥareeṣun 'alaykum bilmu'mineena ra'oofur-raḥeem.

129. Fa-in tawallaw faqul ḥasbiyal-laahu laaa ilaaha illaa Huwa 'alayhi tawakkaltu wa Huwa Rabbul 'Arshil-'Azeem.

Sûrat Yûnus-10

(Revealed at Makkah)

Bismillaahir Raḥmaanir Raḥeem

1. Alif-Laaam-Raa; tilka Aayaatul-Kitaabil-Ḥakeem.

2. A kaana linnaasi 'ajaban an awḥaynaaa ilaa rajulim-minhum an anzirin-naasa wa bashshiril-lazeena aamanooo anna lahum qadama ṣidqin 'inda Rabbihim; qaalal-kaafi-roona inna haazaa lasaaḥirum-mubeen.

3. Inna Rabbakumul-laahul-lazee khalaqas-samaawaati wal-arḍa fee sittati ayyaamin-summas-tawaa 'alal-'Arshi yudabbirul-amra maa min shafee'in illaa mim ba'di iznih; zaalikumul-laahu Rabbukum fa'budooh; afalaa tazakkaroon.

4. Ilayhi marji'ukum jamee-'an wa'dal-laahi ḥaqqaa; inna-hoo yabda'ulkhalqa summa yu'ee-duhu liyajziyal-lazeena aamanoo wa 'amiluṣ-ṣaaliḥaati

وَاِذَا مَاۤ اُنۡزِلَتۡ سُوۡرَةٌ نَّظَرَ بَعۡضُهُمۡ
اِلٰى بَعۡضٍؕ هَلۡ يَرٰٮكُمۡ مِّنۡ اَحَدٍ
ثُمَّ انْصَرَفُوۡا ؕ صَرَفَ اللّٰهُ قُلُوۡبَهُمۡ
بِاَنَّهُمۡ قَوۡمٌ لَّا يَفۡقَهُوۡنَ ﴿۱۲۷﴾
لَقَدۡ جَآءَكُمۡ رَسُوۡلٌ مِّنۡ اَنۡفُسِكُمۡ
عَزِيۡزٌ عَلَيۡهِ مَا عَنِتُّمۡ حَرِيۡصٌ عَلَيۡكُمۡ
بِالۡمُؤۡمِنِيۡنَ رَءُوۡفٌ رَّحِيۡمٌ ﴿۱۲۸﴾
فَاِنۡ تَوَلَّوۡا فَقُلۡ حَسۡبِىَ اللّٰهُ
لَاۤ اِلٰهَ اِلَّا هُوَ ؕ عَلَيۡهِ تَوَكَّلۡتُ
وَهُوَ رَبُّ الۡعَرۡشِ الۡعَظِيۡمِ ﴿۱۲۹﴾ ع

(۱۰) سُوۡرَةُ يُوۡنُسَ مَكِّيَّةٌ (۵۱)

اٰياتها ۱۰۹ بِسۡمِ اللّٰهِ الرَّحۡمٰنِ الرَّحِيۡمِ رکوعاتها ۱۱

الۤرٰ تِلۡكَ اٰيٰتُ الۡكِتٰبِ الۡحَكِيۡمِ ﴿۱﴾
اَكَانَ لِلنَّاسِ عَجَبًا اَنۡ اَوۡحَيۡنَاۤ
اِلٰى رَجُلٍ مِّنۡهُمۡ اَنۡ اَنۡذِرِ النَّاسَ
وَبَشِّرِ الَّذِيۡنَ اٰمَنُوۡۤا اَنَّ لَهُمۡ قَدَمَ
صِدۡقٍ عِنۡدَ رَبِّهِمۡ ؕ قَالَ الۡكٰفِرُوۡنَ
اِنَّ هٰذَا لَسٰحِرٌ مُّبِيۡنٌ ﴿۲﴾
اِنَّ رَبَّكُمُ اللّٰهُ الَّذِىۡ خَلَقَ السَّمٰوٰتِ
وَالۡاَرۡضَ فِىۡ سِتَّةِ اَيَّامٍ ثُمَّ اسۡتَوٰى
عَلَى الۡعَرۡشِ يُدَبِّرُ الۡاَمۡرَ ؕ مَا مِنۡ
شَفِيۡعٍ اِلَّا مِنۡۢ بَعۡدِ اِذۡنِهٖ ؕ ذٰلِكُمُ
اللّٰهُ رَبُّكُمۡ فَاعۡبُدُوۡهُ ؕ اَفَلَا تَذَكَّرُوۡنَ ﴿۳﴾
اِلَيۡهِ مَرۡجِعُكُمۡ جَمِيۡعًا ؕ وَعۡدَ اللّٰهِ حَقًّا ؕ
اِنَّهٗ يَبۡدَؤُا الۡخَلۡقَ ثُمَّ يُعِيۡدُهٗ لِيَجۡزِىَ
الَّذِيۡنَ اٰمَنُوۡا وَعَمِلُوا الصّٰلِحٰتِ

ع ۷ / ۵

المنزل الثالث ۳

وقف النبي صلى الله عليه وآله وسلم ۱۲

believers. The unbelievers will drink boiling filthy water and suffer painful torment as a recompense for their disbelief.

bilqisṭ; wallazeena kafaroo lahum sharaabum-min ḥameemiñw-wa 'azaabun aleemum bimaa kaanoo yakfuroon.

بِالْقِسْطِ ؕ وَالَّذِيْنَ كَفَرُوْا لَهُمْ
شَرَابٌ مِّنْ حَمِيْمٍ وَّعَذَابٌ اَلِيْمٌۢ بِمَا
كَانُوْا يَكْفُرُوْنَ ۝٤

5. It is He Who has made the sun radiant and the moon luminous and has appointed for the moon certain phases so that you may compute the number of years and other reckoning. Allah has created them for a genuine purpose. He explains the evidence (of His existence) to the people of knowledge.

5. Huwal-lazee ja'alash-shamsa ḍiyaaa'añw-walqamara noorañw-wa qaddarahoo manaazila lita'lamoo 'adadas-sineena walḥisaab; maa khalaqal-laahu zaalika illaa bilḥaqq; yufaṣṣilul-Aayaati liqawmiñy-ya'lamoon.

هُوَ الَّذِيْ جَعَلَ الشَّمْسَ ضِيَآءً
وَّالْقَمَرَ نُوْرًا وَّ قَدَّرَهٗ مَنَازِلَ
لِتَعْلَمُوْا عَدَدَ السِّنِيْنَ وَالْحِسَابَ ؕ
مَا خَلَقَ اللّٰهُ ذٰلِكَ اِلَّا بِالْحَقِّ ۚ
يُفَصِّلُ الْاٰيٰتِ لِقَوْمٍ يَّعْلَمُوْنَ ۝٥

6. The alternation of the day and night and all that Allah has created in the heavens and earth are evidence (of the existence of Allah) for the pious people.

6. Inna fikh-tilaafil-layli wannahaari wa maa khalaqal-laahu fis-samaawaati wal-arḍi la-Aayaatil-liqawmiñy-yattaqoon.

اِنَّ فِي اخْتِلَافِ الَّيْلِ وَالنَّهَارِ
وَمَا خَلَقَ اللّٰهُ فِي السَّمٰوٰتِ وَالْاَرْضِ
لَاٰيٰتٍ لِّقَوْمٍ يَّتَّقُوْنَ ۝٦

7. Those who do not have hope of receiving Our mercy in the life hereafter, who are pleased and satisfied with the worldly life, and who pay no attention to Our revelations,

7. Innal-lazeena laa yarjoona liqaaa'anaa wa raḍoo bilḥayaatid-dunyaa waṭma-annoo bihaa wallazeena hum 'an Aayaatinaa ghaafiloon.

اِنَّ الَّذِيْنَ لَا يَرْجُوْنَ لِقَآءَنَا وَرَضُوْا
بِالْحَيٰوةِ الدُّنْيَا وَاطْمَاَنُّوْا بِهَا وَالَّذِيْنَ
هُمْ عَنْ اٰيٰتِنَا غٰفِلُوْنَ ۙ ۝٧

8. will all have the fire as their dwelling for that which they had done.

8. Ulaaa'ika ma-waahumun Naaru bimaa kaanoo yaksiboon.

اُولٰٓئِكَ مَاْوٰىهُمُ النَّارُ بِمَا كَانُوْا
يَكْسِبُوْنَ ۝٨

9. The righteously striving believers receive, through their faith, guidance from their Lord to the bountiful gardens wherein streams flow.

9. Innal-lazeena aamanoo wa 'amiluṣ-ṣaaliḥaati yahdeehim Rabbuhum bi-eemaanihim tajree min taḥtihimul-anhaaru fee Jannaatin-Na'eem.

اِنَّ الَّذِيْنَ اٰمَنُوْا وَعَمِلُوا الصّٰلِحٰتِ
يَهْدِيْهِمْ رَبُّهُمْ بِاِيْمَانِهِمْ ۚ تَجْرِيْ مِنْ
تَحْتِهِمُ الْاَنْهٰرُ فِيْ جَنّٰتِ النَّعِيْمِ ۝٩

10. Their prayer shall be, "Glory be to You, Lord," and their greeting, "Peace be with you," and the only other words (of worldly speech) they will speak will be, "It is Allah, Lord of the Universe, who deserves all praise."

10. Da'waahum feehaa Subḥaanakal-laahumma wa taḥiyyatuhum feehaa salaam; wa aakhiru da'waahum anil-ḥamdu lillaahi Rabbil'aalameen.

دَعْوٰىهُمْ فِيْهَا سُبْحٰنَكَ اللّٰهُمَّ وَ
تَحِيَّتُهُمْ فِيْهَا سَلٰمٌ ۚ وَاٰخِرُ دَعْوٰىهُمْ
اَنِ الْحَمْدُ لِلّٰهِ رَبِّ الْعٰلَمِيْنَ ۝١٠ ع ١ / ١٠ / ٢

11. Had Allah been as hasty to punish people as they were hasty to achieve good, their life would have already ended. We will leave those who have no hope of receiving Our mercy, in the life hereafter, to continue blindly in their transgression.

11. Wa law yu'ajjilul-laahu linnaasish-sharras-ti'jaalahum bilkhayri laquḍiya ilayhim ajaluhum fanazarul-lazeena laa yarjoona liqaaa'anaa fee ṭughyaanihim ya'mahoon.

وَلَوْ يُعَجِّلُ اللّٰهُ لِلنَّاسِ الشَّرَّ
اسْتِعْجَالَهُمْ بِالْخَيْرِ لَقُضِيَ اِلَيْهِمْ
اَجَلُهُمْ ؕ فَنَذَرُ الَّذِيْنَ لَا يَرْجُوْنَ
لِقَآءَنَا فِيْ طُغْيَانِهِمْ يَعْمَهُوْنَ ۝١١

12. When the human being is affected by hardship, he starts to pray while lying on his side, sitting or standing, but when We relieve him from hardship, he starts to act as though he had never prayed to Us to save him from the misfortune. This is how transgressors' deeds are made attractive to them.

12. Wa izaa massal-insaanaḍ-ḍurru da'aanaa lijambiheee aw qaa'idan aw qaaa'iman falammaa kashafnaa 'anhu ḍurrahoo marra ka-al-lam yad'unaaa ilaa ḍurrim-massah; kazaalika zuyyina lilmusrifeena maa kaanoo ya'maloon.

وَإِذَا مَسَّ الْإِنْسَانَ الضُّرُّ دَعَانَا
لِجَنْبِهِ أَوْ قَاعِدًا أَوْ قَائِمًا ۚ فَلَمَّا
كَشَفْنَا عَنْهُ ضُرَّهُ مَرَّ كَأَنْ لَمْ
يَدْعُنَا إِلَىٰ ضُرٍّ مَسَّهُ ۚ كَذَٰلِكَ زُيِّنَ
لِلْمُسْرِفِينَ مَا كَانُوا يَعْمَلُونَ ﴿١٢﴾

13. We destroyed certain generations who lived before you because of their injustice. Our Messengers came to them and showed them miracles, but they would not believe. Thus do We punish the criminals.

13. Wa laqad ahlaknal-quroona min qablikum lammaa ẓalamoo wa jaaa'athum Rusuluhum bil-bayyinaati wa maa kaanoo liyu'minoo; kazaalika najzil-qawmal-mujrimeen.

وَلَقَدْ أَهْلَكْنَا الْقُرُونَ مِنْ قَبْلِكُمْ
لَمَّا ظَلَمُوا ۙ وَجَاءَتْهُمْ رُسُلُهُمْ
بِالْبَيِّنَاتِ وَمَا كَانُوا لِيُؤْمِنُوا ۚ
كَذَٰلِكَ نَجْزِي الْقَوْمَ الْمُجْرِمِينَ ﴿١٣﴾

14. We have made you their successors in the land so that We could see how you behave.

14. Summa ja'alnaakum khalaaa'ifa fil-arḍi mim ba'dihim linanẓura kayfa ta'maloon.

ثُمَّ جَعَلْنَاكُمْ خَلَائِفَ فِي الْأَرْضِ مِنْ
بَعْدِهِمْ لِنَنْظُرَ كَيْفَ تَعْمَلُونَ ﴿١٤﴾

15. Whenever Our authoritative revelations are recited to those who do not wish to meet Us in the life hereafter, they say, "Bring us another book besides this one or change it." (Muhammad), tell them, "I cannot change it myself. I only follow what is revealed to me. I fear that for disobeying my Lord I shall be punished on the great (Day of Judgment)."

15. Wa izaa tutlaa 'alayhim Aayaatunaa bayyinaatin qaalal-lazeena laa yarjoona liqaaa-'ana'-ti bi-Qur'aanin ghayri haazaaa aw baddilh; qul maa yakoonu leee an ubaddilahoo min tilqaaa'i nafseee in attabi'u illaa maa yooḥaa ilayya inneee akhaafu in 'aṣaytu Rabbee 'azaaba yawmin 'aẓeem.

وَإِذَا تُتْلَىٰ عَلَيْهِمْ آيَاتُنَا بَيِّنَاتٍ ۙ
قَالَ الَّذِينَ لَا يَرْجُونَ لِقَاءَنَا ائْتِ
بِقُرْآنٍ غَيْرِ هَٰذَا أَوْ بَدِّلْهُ ۚ قُلْ مَا
يَكُونُ لِي أَنْ أُبَدِّلَهُ مِنْ تِلْقَاءِ
نَفْسِي ۖ إِنْ أَتَّبِعُ إِلَّا مَا يُوحَىٰ إِلَيَّ ۖ
إِنِّي أَخَافُ إِنْ عَصَيْتُ رَبِّي عَذَابَ
يَوْمٍ عَظِيمٍ ﴿١٥﴾

16. (Muhammad), tell them, "Had Allah wanted I would not have recited it (the Book) to you nor would I have told you anything about it (any time). I lived among you for a whole lifetime before it was revealed. Will you then not understand?

16. Qul law shaaa'al-laahu maa talawtuhoo 'alaykum wa laaa adraakum bihee faqad labistu feekum 'umuram-min qablih; afalaa ta'qiloon.

قُلْ لَوْ شَاءَ اللَّهُ مَا تَلَوْتُهُ عَلَيْكُمْ
وَلَا أَدْرَاكُمْ بِهِ ۖ فَقَدْ لَبِثْتُ فِيكُمْ
عُمُرًا مِنْ قَبْلِهِ ۚ أَفَلَا تَعْقِلُونَ ﴿١٦﴾

17. Who is more unjust than one who invents falsehood against Allah or calls His revelations lies? The criminals will certainly have no happiness.

17. Faman aẓlamu mimmanif-taraa 'alal-laahi kaziban aw kaz-zaba bi-Aayaatih; innahoo laa yufliḥul-mujrimoon.

فَمَنْ أَظْلَمُ مِمَّنِ افْتَرَىٰ عَلَى اللَّهِ
كَذِبًا أَوْ كَذَّبَ بِآيَاتِهِ ۚ إِنَّهُ لَا
يُفْلِحُ الْمُجْرِمُونَ ﴿١٧﴾

18. (Certain people) worship things other than Allah which neither harm nor benefit them. They say, "These (idols) are our

18. Wa ya'budoona min doonil-laahi maa laa yaḍurruhum wa laa yanfa'uhum wa yaqooloona

وَيَعْبُدُونَ مِنْ دُونِ اللَّهِ مَا لَا
يَضُرُّهُمْ وَلَا يَنْفَعُهُمْ وَيَقُولُونَ

intercessors before Allah." (Muhammad), tell them, "Are you trying to tell Allah about something that He does not find in the heavens or earth? Allah is free of all defects thus He cannot be considered as equal to idols."

19. All people (once) followed one belief. Then they began to follow different beliefs. Had not a word of your Lord (His decision to give every one time and free will) been decreed, Allah would already have settled their differences.

20. They (unbelievers) say, "Why has his Lord not given him some miracles to (support his claim of being His Messenger)?" Say "(The knowledge) of the unseen certainly belongs to Allah. Wait and I am also waiting with you.

21. When people are granted mercy after having suffered hardship, they begin to plot against Our revelations. Say, "Allah is the swiftest in His plans." Our messengers (from among the angels) record all that you plot.

22. It is He Who enables you to travel on land and in the sea. When you are rejoicing in a boat, with a favorable breeze, a violent storm arises with waves surrounding you from all sides. Thinking that you will not survive, you start to pray sincerely to Allah. In prayer, you say, "If You rescue us from this we shall certainly be grateful."

23. When We save you, you start to rebel unjustly in the land. People, your rebellion will only harm yourselves. You may enjoy the worldly life but to Us you will all return and We will let you

haaa'ulaaa'i shufa'aaa'unaa 'indal-laah; qul atunabbi'oonal-laaha bimaa laa ya'lamu fis-samaawaati wa laa fil-arḍ; Subḥaanahoo wa Ta'aalaa 'ammaa yushrikoon.

19. Wa maa kaanan-naasu illaaa ummatañw-waaḥidatan fakh-talafoo; wa law laa kalimatun sabaqat mir-Rabbika laquḍiya baynahum feemaa feehi yakhtalifoon.

20. Wa yaqooloona law laaa unzila 'alayhi Aayatum-mir-Rabbihee faqul innamal-ghaybu lillaahi fantaẓiroo innee ma'akum minal-muntaẓireen.

21. Wa-iẕaaa aẕaqnan-naasa raḥmatam-mim ba'di ḍarraaa'a massathum iẕaa lahum makrun feee Aayaatinaa; qulil-laahu asra'u makraa; inna rusulanaa yaktuboona maa tamkuroon.

22. Huwal-laẕee yusayyi-rukum fil-barri wal-baḥri ḥattaaa iẕaa kuntum fil-fulki wa jarayna bihim bireeḥin ṭayyibatiñw-wa fariḥoo bihaa jaaa'athaa reeḥun 'aaṣifuñw-wa jaaa'a-humul-mawju min kulli makaaniñw-wa ẓannooo anna-hum uḥeeṭa bihim da'awul-laaha mukhliṣeena lahud-deena la'in anjaytanaa min haaẕihee lanakoonanna minash-shaa-kireen.

23. Falammaaa anjaahum iẕaa hum yabghoona fil-arḍi bighayril-ḥaqq; yaaa ayyuhan-naasu innamaa baghyukum 'alaaa anfusikum-mataa'al-ḥayaatid-dunyaa

هٰٓؤُلَآءِ شُفَعَآؤُنَا عِنْدَ اللّٰهِ ؕ قُلْ
اَتُنَبِّـُٔوْنَ اللّٰهَ بِمَا لَا يَعْلَمُ فِي
السَّمٰوٰتِ وَلَا فِي الْاَرْضِ ؕ سُبْحٰنَهٗ
وَتَعٰلٰى عَمَّا يُشْرِكُوْنَ ﴿١٨﴾
وَمَا كَانَ النَّاسُ اِلَّآ اُمَّةً وَّاحِدَةً
فَاخْتَلَفُوْا ؕ وَلَوْلَا كَلِمَةٌ سَبَقَتْ
مِنْ رَّبِّكَ لَقُضِيَ بَيْنَهُمْ فِيْمَا
فِيْهِ يَخْتَلِفُوْنَ ﴿١٩﴾
وَيَقُوْلُوْنَ لَوْلَآ اُنْزِلَ عَلَيْهِ اٰيَةٌ مِّنْ
رَّبِّهٖ ۚ فَقُلْ اِنَّمَا الْغَيْبُ لِلّٰهِ فَانْتَظِرُوْا ۚ
اِنِّيْ مَعَكُمْ مِّنَ الْمُنْتَظِرِيْنَ ﴿٢٠﴾ ع ٢ ٧
وَاِذَآ اَذَقْنَا النَّاسَ رَحْمَةً مِّنْۢ
بَعْدِ ضَرَّآءَ مَسَّتْهُمْ اِذَا لَهُمْ مَّكْرٌ فِيْٓ
اٰيَاتِنَا ؕ قُلِ اللّٰهُ اَسْرَعُ مَكْرًا ؕ
اِنَّ رُسُلَنَا يَكْتُبُوْنَ مَا تَمْكُرُوْنَ ﴿٢١﴾
هُوَ الَّذِيْ يُسَيِّرُكُمْ فِي الْبَرِّ وَ
الْبَحْرِ ؕ حَتّٰىٓ اِذَا كُنْتُمْ فِي الْفُلْكِ ۚ
وَجَرَيْنَ بِهِمْ بِرِيْحٍ طَيِّبَةٍ وَّ
فَرِحُوْا بِهَا جَآءَتْهَا رِيْحٌ عَاصِفٌ
وَّجَآءَهُمُ الْمَوْجُ مِنْ كُلِّ مَكَانٍ
وَّظَنُّوْٓا اَنَّهُمْ اُحِيْطَ بِهِمْ ۙ دَعَوُا اللّٰهَ
مُخْلِصِيْنَ لَهُ الدِّيْنَ ۚ لَئِنْ اَنْجَيْتَنَا
مِنْ هٰذِهٖ لَنَكُوْنَنَّ مِنَ الشّٰكِرِيْنَ ﴿٢٢﴾
فَلَمَّآ اَنْجٰىهُمْ اِذَا هُمْ يَبْغُوْنَ فِي الْاَرْضِ
بِغَيْرِ الْحَقِّ ؕ يٰٓاَيُّهَا النَّاسُ اِنَّمَا بَغْيُكُمْ
عَلٰٓى اَنْفُسِكُمْ ۙ مَّتَاعَ الْحَيٰوةِ الدُّنْيَا ؗ

know all that you had done.

s̲umma ilaynaa marji‘ukum fanunabbi’ukum bimaa kuntum ta‘maloon.

ثُمَّ اِلَيْنَا مَرْجِعُكُمْ فَنُنَبِّئُكُمْ بِمَا
كُنْتُمْ تَعْمَلُوْنَ ﴿٢٣﴾

24. The example of the worldly life is like the water sent down from the sky which becomes mixed with the earth's produce that people and cattle consume. When the land becomes fertile and pleasant, people think that they have control over it. At Our command during the night or day, the land becomes as barren as if it had no richness the day before. Thus, do We explain the evidence (of the truth) for the people who reflect.

24. Innamaa mas̲alul ḥayaatid-dunyaa kamaaa’in anzalnaahu minas-samaaa’i fakhtalaṭa bihee nabaatul-arḍi mimmaa yakulunnaasu wal-an‘aam; ḥattaaa iz̲aaa akhaz̲atil-arḍu zukhrufahaa wazzayyanat wa ẓanna ahluhaaa annahum qaadiroona ‘alayhaaa ataahaaa amrunaa laylan aw nahaaran faja‘alnaahaa ḥaṣeedan ka-al-lam taghna bil-ams; kaz̲aalika nufaṣṣilul Aayaati liqawmiñy-yatafakkaroon.

اِنَّمَا مَثَلُ الْحَيٰوةِ الدُّنْيَا كَمَآءٍ
اَنْزَلْنٰهُ مِنَ السَّمَآءِ فَاخْتَلَطَ بِهٖ
نَبَاتُ الْاَرْضِ مِمَّا يَاْكُلُ النَّاسُ وَ
الْاَنْعَامُ ؕ حَتّٰۤى اِذَاۤ اَخَذَتِ الْاَرْضُ
زُخْرُفَهَا وَازَّيَّنَتْ وَظَنَّ اَهْلُهَاۤ
اَنَّهُمْ قٰدِرُوْنَ عَلَيْهَاۤ ۙ اَتٰىهَاۤ اَمْرُنَا
لَيْلًا اَوْ نَهَارًا فَجَعَلْنٰهَا حَصِيْدًا
كَاَنْ لَّمْ تَغْنَ بِالْاَمْسِ ؕ كَذٰلِكَ
نُفَصِّلُ الْاٰيٰتِ لِقَوْمٍ يَّتَفَكَّرُوْنَ ﴿٢٤﴾

25. Allah invites everyone to the House of Peace and guides whomever He wants to the right path.

25. Wallaahu yad‘ooo ilaa daaris-salaami wa yahdee mañy-yashaaa’u ilaa Ṣiraaṭim-Mustaqeem.

وَاللّٰهُ يَدْعُوْۤا اِلٰى دَارِ السَّلٰمِ ؕ وَيَهْدِىْ
مَنْ يَّشَآءُ اِلٰى صِرَاطٍ مُّسْتَقِيْمٍ ﴿٢٥﴾

26. The righteous will receive good reward for their deeds and more. Their faces will suffer no disgrace or ignominy. They will be the dwellers of Paradise wherein they will live forever.

26. Lillaz̲eena aḥsanul-ḥusnaa wa ziyaadatun wa laa yarhaqu wujoohahum qataruñw-wa laa z̲illah; ulaaa’ika Aṣḥaabul-jannati hum feehaa khaalidoon.

لِلَّذِيْنَ اَحْسَنُوا الْحُسْنٰى وَزِيَادَةٌ ؕ وَلَا
يَرْهَقُ وُجُوْهَهُمْ قَتَرٌ وَّلَا ذِلَّةٌ ؕ اُولٰٓئِكَ
اَصْحٰبُ الْجَنَّةِ ۚ هُمْ فِيْهَا خٰلِدُوْنَ ﴿٢٦﴾

27. The recompense for the evil deeds will be equally evil (not more) and the faces of the evildoers will suffer from disgrace. No one can protect them from the wrath of Allah. Their faces will become dark as if covered by the pitch-black darkness of night. They will be the dwellers of hell wherein they will remain forever.

27. Wallaz̲eena kasabus-sayyi-aati jazaaa’u sayyi’atim bimis̲lihaa wa tarhaquhum z̲illatun maa lahum minallaahi min ‘aaṣimin ka-annamaaa ughshiyat wujoohuhum qiṭa-‘am-minallayli muẓlimaa; ulaaa’ika Aṣḥaabun-Naari hum feeha khaalidoon.

وَالَّذِيْنَ كَسَبُوا السَّيِّاٰتِ جَزَآءُ
سَيِّئَةٍۢ بِمِثْلِهَا ۙ وَتَرْهَقُهُمْ ذِلَّةٌ ؕ
مَا لَهُمْ مِّنَ اللّٰهِ مِنْ عَاصِمٍ ۚ كَاَنَّمَاۤ
اُغْشِيَتْ وُجُوْهُهُمْ قِطَعًا مِّنَ الَّيْلِ
مُظْلِمًا ؕ اُولٰٓئِكَ اَصْحٰبُ النَّارِ ۚ
هُمْ فِيْهَا خٰلِدُوْنَ ﴿٢٧﴾

28. We will tell the pagans on the day when everyone is resurrected, “Stand with your idols wherever you are.” Then We will separate them (from their idols) and their idols will protest against them, saying, “You did not worship us.

28. Wa Yawma naḥshuruhum jamee‘an s̲umma naqoolu lillaz̲eena ashrakoo makaanakum antum wa shurakaaa’ukum; fazayyalnaa baynahum wa qaala shurakaaa’uhum maa kuntum iyyaanaa ta‘budoon.

وَيَوْمَ نَحْشُرُهُمْ جَمِيْعًا ثُمَّ نَقُوْلُ
لِلَّذِيْنَ اَشْرَكُوْا مَكَانَكُمْ اَنْتُمْ وَ
شُرَكَآؤُكُمْ ۚ فَزَيَّلْنَا بَيْنَهُمْ وَقَالَ
شُرَكَآؤُهُمْ مَّا كُنْتُمْ اِيَّانَا تَعْبُدُوْنَ ﴿٢٨﴾

29. Allah is Sufficient Witness for us that we were not aware of your worship."

29. Fakafaa billaahi shaheedam-baynanaa wa baynakum in kunnaa 'an 'ibaadatikum laghaafileen.

فَكَفٰى بِاللّٰهِ شَهِيْدًا بَيْنَنَا وَبَيْنَكُمْ
اِنْ كُنَّا عَنْ عِبَادَتِكُمْ لَغٰفِلِيْنَ ﴿٢٩﴾

30. There every soul will experience the result of all that it had done. They will be brought into the presence of Allah, their true Lord, and all that they falsely invented will vanish.

30. Hunaalika tabloo kullu nafsim-maaa aslafat; wa ruddooo ilal-laahi mawlaahumul-ḥaqqi wa ḍalla 'anhum maa kaanoo yaftaroon.

هُنَالِكَ تَبْلُوْا كُلُّ نَفْسٍ مَّاۤ اَسْلَفَتْ
وَرُدُّوْۤا اِلَى اللّٰهِ مَوْلٰىهُمُ الْحَقِّ وَضَلَّ
عَنْهُمْ مَّا كَانُوْا يَفْتَرُوْنَ ﴿٣٠﴾ ع

النصف ع ٣ ١٠ ٨

31. (Muhammad), ask them, "Who gives you sustenance from the heavens and earth, who truly possesses (your) hearing and seeing abilities, who brings the living out of the dead and the dead out of the living and who regulates the matter (the whole Universe)? They will reply, "Allah." Ask them, "Why, then, do you not have fear of Him?"

31. Qul mañy-yarzuqukum minas-samaaa'i wal-arḍi ammañy-yamlikus-sam'a wal-abṣaara wa mañy-yukhrijul-ḥayya minal-mayyiti wa yukhrijul-mayyita minal-ḥayyi wa mañy-yudabbirul amr; fasayaqooloonal-laah; faqul afalaa tattaqoon.

قُلْ مَنْ يَّرْزُقُكُمْ مِّنَ السَّمَآءِ وَ
الْاَرْضِ اَمَّنْ يَّمْلِكُ السَّمْعَ
وَالْاَبْصَارَ وَمَنْ يُّخْرِجُ الْحَيَّ
مِنَ الْمَيِّتِ وَيُخْرِجُ الْمَيِّتَ مِنَ
الْحَيِّ وَمَنْ يُّدَبِّرُ الْاَمْرَ فَسَيَقُوْلُوْنَ
اللّٰهُ ۚ فَقُلْ اَفَلَا تَتَّقُوْنَ ﴿٣١﴾

32. Thus is Allah, your true Lord. In the absence of truth there is nothing but falsehood. Then where are you turning?

32. Fazaalikumul-laahu Rabbukumul-ḥaqq; famaazaa ba'dal-ḥaqqi illaḍ-ḍalaalu faannaa tuṣrafoon.

فَذٰلِكُمُ اللّٰهُ رَبُّكُمُ الْحَقُّ ۚ فَمَاذَا بَعْدَ
الْحَقِّ اِلَّا الضَّلٰلُ ۚ فَاَنّٰى تُصْرَفُوْنَ ﴿٣٢﴾

33. The decree of your Lord that the evil-doers will not have faith has already been issued.

33. Kazaalika ḥaqqat Kalimatu Rabbika 'alallazeena fasaqooo annahum laa yu'minoon.

كَذٰلِكَ حَقَّتْ كَلِمَتُ رَبِّكَ عَلَى
الَّذِيْنَ فَسَقُوْۤا اَنَّهُمْ لَا يُؤْمِنُوْنَ ﴿٣٣﴾

34. (Muhammad), ask them, "Can any of your idols create something (cause it to die), and then bring it back to life again?" Say, "Only Allah can originate the creation and bring it to life again. Where have you strayed?"

34. Qul hal min shurakaaa'ikum mañy-yabda'ul-khalqa summa yu'eeduh; qulil-laahu yabda'ul-khalqa summa yu'eeduhoo fa-annaa tu'fakoon.

قُلْ هَلْ مِنْ شُرَكَآئِكُمْ مَّنْ يَّبْدَؤُا
الْخَلْقَ ثُمَّ يُعِيْدُهٗ ؕ قُلِ اللّٰهُ
يَبْدَؤُا الْخَلْقَ ثُمَّ يُعِيْدُهٗ فَاَنّٰى
تُؤْفَكُوْنَ ﴿٣٤﴾

35. (Muhammad), ask them, "Can any of your idols guide you to the Truth?" Say, "Only Allah guides to the Truth." Is the one who guides to the Truth a proper guide or one who himself cannot find guidance unless he is guided (by others)? What is wrong with you that you judge (so unjustly)?

35. Qul hal min shurakaaa'ikum mañy-yahdeee ilal-ḥaqq; qulil-laahu yahdee lilḥaqq; afamañy-yahdeee ilal-ḥaqqi aḥaqqu añy-yuttaba'a ammallaa yahiddeee illaaa añy-yuhdaa famaa lakum kayfa taḥkumoon.

قُلْ هَلْ مِنْ شُرَكَآئِكُمْ مَّنْ يَّهْدِيْۤ
اِلَى الْحَقِّ ؕ قُلِ اللّٰهُ يَهْدِيْ لِلْحَقِّ ؕ
اَفَمَنْ يَّهْدِيْۤ اِلَى الْحَقِّ اَحَقُّ اَنْ
يُّتَّبَعَ اَمَّنْ لَّا يَهِدِّيْۤ اِلَّاۤ اَنْ
يُّهْدٰى ۚ فَمَا لَكُمْ كَيْفَ تَحْكُمُوْنَ ﴿٣٥﴾

36. Most of the unbelievers follow only conjecture, which certainly cannot serve as a substitute for the Truth. Allah

36. Wa maa yattabi'u aksaruhum illaa ẓannaa; innaẓẓanna laa yughnee minalḥaqqi shay'aa;

وَمَا يَتَّبِعُ اَكْثَرُهُمْ اِلَّا ظَنًّا ؕ اِنَّ
الظَّنَّ لَا يُغْنِيْ مِنَ الْحَقِّ شَيْـًٔا ؕ

knows well what they do.

Innal-laaha 'aleemum bimaa yaf'aloon.

إِنَّ اللّٰهَ عَلِيْمٌ بِمَا يَفْعَلُوْنَ ﴿٣٦﴾

37. No one could have composed this Quran besides Allah. This confirms the existing Book (the Bible) and explains itself. There is no doubt that it is from the Lord of the Universe.

37. Wa maa kaana haaẕal-Qur'aanu añy-yuftaraa min doonil-laahi wa laakin taṣdee-qal-laẕee bayna yadayhi wa tafṣeelal-Kitaabi laa rayba feehi mir-Rabbil-'aalameen.

وَمَا كَانَ هٰذَا الْقُرْاٰنُ اَنْ يُّفْتَرٰى
مِنْ دُوْنِ اللّٰهِ وَلٰكِنْ تَصْدِيْقَ
الَّذِيْ بَيْنَ يَدَيْهِ وَتَفْصِيْلَ
الْكِتٰبِ لَا رَيْبَ فِيْهِ مِنْ رَّبِّ
الْعٰلَمِيْنَ ﴿٣٧﴾

38. Do they say that Muhammad has invented it? (Muhammad), tell them, "If your claim is true, compose only one chapter like it and call on anyone you can, besides Allah for help.

38. Am yaqooloonaf-taraahu qul fa-too bisooratim-mislihee wad'oo manis-taṭa'tum-min doonil-laahi in kuntum ṣaadi-qeen.

اَمْ يَقُوْلُوْنَ افْتَرٰىهُ ؕ قُلْ فَاْتُوْا
بِسُوْرَةٍ مِّثْلِهٖ وَادْعُوْا مَنِ اسْتَطَعْتُمْ
مِّنْ دُوْنِ اللّٰهِ اِنْ كُنْتُمْ صٰدِقِيْنَ ﴿٣٨﴾

39. They called a lie something that was beyond the limit of their knowledge and whose interpretation has not yet been revealed. Some people who lived before them also called Our revelations lies. Consider how terrible the end of the unjust people was!

39. Bal kaẕ- ẕaboo bimaa lam yuḥeeṭoo bi'ilmihee wa lammaa ya-tihim ta-weeluh; kaẕaalika kaẕ-ẕabal-laẕeena min qablihim fanẓur kayfa kaana 'aaqibatuẓ-ẓaalimeen.

بَلْ كَذَّبُوْا بِمَا لَمْ يُحِيْطُوْا بِعِلْمِهٖ
وَلَمَّا يَاْتِهِمْ تَاْوِيْلُهٗ ؕ كَذٰلِكَ كَذَّبَ
الَّذِيْنَ مِنْ قَبْلِهِمْ فَانْظُرْ كَيْفَ
كَانَ عَاقِبَةُ الظّٰلِمِيْنَ ﴿٣٩﴾

40. Certain ones among them believe in the Quran and others do not. Your Lord knows best the evildoers.

40. Wa minhum-mañy-yu'minu bihee wa minhum-mal-laa yu'minu bih; wa Rabbuka a'lamu bilmufsideen.

وَمِنْهُمْ مَّنْ يُّؤْمِنُ بِهٖ وَمِنْهُمْ
مَّنْ لَّا يُؤْمِنُ بِهٖ ؕ وَرَبُّكَ اَعْلَمُ
بِالْمُفْسِدِيْنَ ﴿٤٠﴾

41. If they call you a liar, tell them, "Let each one of us follow his own way. You will not be responsible for what I do and I will not be responsible for what you do."

41. Wa in kaẕ-ẕabooka faqul lee 'amalee wa lakum 'amalukum antum bareee'oona mimmaaa a'malu wa ana bareee'um-mimmaa ta'maloon.

وَاِنْ كَذَّبُوْكَ فَقُلْ لِّيْ عَمَلِيْ وَلَكُمْ
عَمَلُكُمْ ۚ اَنْتُمْ بَرِيْٓــُٔوْنَ مِمَّاۤ اَعْمَلُ
وَاَنَا بَرِيْٓءٌ مِّمَّا تَعْمَلُوْنَ ﴿٤١﴾

42. Among them are those who listen to you, but are you supposed to make the deaf hear even if they have no understanding?

42. Wa minhum-mañy-yastami-'oona ilayk; afa-anta tusmi'uṣ-ṣumma wa law kaanoo laa ya'qiloon.

وَمِنْهُمْ مَّنْ يَّسْتَمِعُوْنَ اِلَيْكَ ؕ
اَفَاَنْتَ تُسْمِعُ الصُّمَّ وَلَوْ كَانُوْا
لَا يَعْقِلُوْنَ ﴿٤٢﴾

43. Some of them will look at you, but are you supposed to guide the blind even if they have no vision?

43. Wa minhum-mañy-yanẓuru ilayk; afa-anta tahdil-'umya wa law kaanoo laa yubṣiroon.

وَمِنْهُمْ مَّنْ يَّنْظُرُ اِلَيْكَ ؕ
اَفَاَنْتَ تَهْدِي الْعُمْيَ وَلَوْ كَانُوْا
لَا يُبْصِرُوْنَ ﴿٤٣﴾

44. Allah does not do the least bit of injustice to anyone but peo-

44. Innal-laaha laa yaẓlimun-naasa shay'añw-

اِنَّ اللّٰهَ لَا يَظْلِمُ النَّاسَ شَيْـًٔا

ple wrong themselves.

wa laakin-nannaasa anfusahum yaẓlimoon.

وَّلٰكِنَّ النَّاسَ اَنْفُسَهُمْ يَظْلِمُوْنَ ﴿٤٤﴾

45. On the day when they will be resurrected, their worldly life would seem to them only as an hour of a day and they all will recognize each other. Those who called the receiving of mercy from Allah a lie are certainly lost. They did not have the right guidance.

45. Wa Yawma yaḥshuruhum ka-al-lam yalbas̲ooo illaa saa'atam-minan-nahaari yata'aarafoona baynahum; qad khasiral-laz̲eena kaz̲-z̲aboo biliqaaa'il-laahi wa maa kaanoo muhtadeen.

وَيَوْمَ يَحْشُرُهُمْ كَاَنْ لَّمْ يَلْبَثُوْٓا
اِلَّا سَاعَةً مِّنَ النَّهَارِ يَتَعَارَفُوْنَ
بَيْنَهُمْ ۭ قَدْ خَسِرَ الَّذِيْنَ كَذَّبُوْا
بِلِقَاۗءِ اللّٰهِ وَمَا كَانُوْا مُهْتَدِيْنَ ﴿٤٥﴾

46. When We show you them suffering Our retribution, or you die before their suffering (they will not be able to escape Our punishment), they will all return to Us. Allah bears witness to whatever they do.

46. Wa imma nuriyannaka ba'ḍal-laz̲ee na'iduhum aw natawaf-fayannaka fa-ilaynaa marji'uhum s̲ummal-laahu shaheedun 'alaa maa yaf'aloon.

وَاِمَّا نُرِيَنَّكَ بَعْضَ الَّذِيْ نَعِدُهُمْ
اَوْ نَتَوَفَّيَنَّكَ فَاِلَيْنَا مَرْجِعُهُمْ ثُمَّ
اللّٰهُ شَهِيْدٌ عَلٰي مَا يَفْعَلُوْنَ ﴿٤٦﴾

47. A messenger is appointed for all people. When their messenger for them came he judged among them fairly and they were not wronged.

47. Wa likulli ummatir-Rasoolun fa-iz̲aa jaaa'a Rasooluhum quḍiya baynahum bilqisṭi wa hum laa yuẓlamoon.

وَلِكُلِّ اُمَّةٍ رَّسُوْلٌ ۚ فَاِذَا جَاۗءَ
رَسُوْلُهُمْ قُضِيَ بَيْنَهُمْ بِالْقِسْطِ
وَهُمْ لَا يُظْلَمُوْنَ ﴿٤٧﴾

48. A messenger is appointed for all people. When their messenger for them came he judged among them fairly and they were not wronged.

48. Wa yaqooloona mataa haaz̲al-wa'du in kuntum ṣaadiqeen.

وَيَقُوْلُوْنَ مَتٰى هٰذَا الْوَعْدُ اِنْ
كُنْتُمْ صٰدِقِيْنَ ﴿٤٨﴾

49. (Muhammad), say, "I have no control over my suffering or benefits unless Allah wills. Every nation is destined to live for an appointed time. They can neither delay that time nor can they cause it to come sooner.

49. Qul laaa amliku linafsee ḍarrañw-wa laa naf'an illaa maa shaaa'al-laah; likulli ummatin ajalun iz̲aa jaaa'a ajaluhum falaaa yasta-khiroona saa'atañw-wa laa yastaqdimoon.

قُلْ لَّآ اَمْلِكُ لِنَفْسِيْ ضَرًّا
وَّلَا نَفْعًا اِلَّا مَا شَاۗءَ اللّٰهُ ۭ لِكُلِّ
اُمَّةٍ اَجَلٌ ۭ اِذَا جَاۗءَ اَجَلُهُمْ
فَلَا يَسْتَاْخِرُوْنَ سَاعَةً وَّلَا
يَسْتَقْدِمُوْنَ ﴿٤٩﴾

50. Ask them, "What benefit can criminals get from their demand that Allah must punish them immediately if His words are true?" Whether His punishment befalls them during the day or night (they will not be able to escape).

50. Qul ara'aytum in ataakum 'az̲aabuhoo bayaatan aw nahaaram-maaz̲aa yasta'jilu minhul-mujrimoon.

قُلْ اَرَءَيْتُمْ اِنْ اَتٰىكُمْ عَذَابُهٗ
بَيَاتًا اَوْ نَهَارًا مَّاذَا يَسْتَعْجِلُ
مِنْهُ الْمُجْرِمُوْنَ ﴿٥٠﴾

51. Besides, if He were to send them the punishment which they want to quickly experience, would they then have faith?

51. As̲umma iz̲aa maa waqa'a aamantum bih; aal'aana wa qad kuntum bihee tasta'jiloon.

اَثُمَّ اِذَا مَا وَقَعَ اٰمَنْتُمْ بِهٖ ۭ اٰۗلْــٰٔنَ
وَقَدْ كُنْتُمْ بِهٖ تَسْتَعْجِلُوْنَ ﴿٥١﴾

52. The unjust will be told, "Suffer the everlasting torment. Do you expect a recompense other than what you deserve?

52. S̲umma qeela lillaz̲eena ẓalamoo z̲ooqoo 'az̲aabal-khuld; hal tujzawna illaa bimaa kuntum taksiboon.

ثُمَّ قِيْلَ لِلَّذِيْنَ ظَلَمُوْا ذُوْقُوْا
عَذَابَ الْخُلْدِ ۚ هَلْ تُجْزَوْنَ اِلَّا
بِمَا كُنْتُمْ تَكْسِبُوْنَ ﴿٥٢﴾

53. They ask you, "Is that (punishment) true?" Tell them, "It certainly is. I swear by my Lord. You cannot escape (from Allah's retribution)."	53. Wa yastambi'oonaka aḥaqqun huwa qul ee wa Rabbeee innahoo laḥaqq; wa maaa antum bimu'jizeen.	وَيَسْتَنْۢبِـُٔوْنَكَ اَحَقٌّ هُوَ ۭ قُلْ اِيْ وَرَبِّيْٓ اِنَّهٗ لَحَقٌّ ڼ وَمَآ اَنْتُمْ بِمُعْجِزِيْنَ ۝٥٣
54. (On the Day of Judgment) to redeem oneself of one's injustice, one would gladly spend the wealth of the whole earth if it were possible. On seeing the torment one will try to hide one's regret. They will all be judged fairly and no wrong will be done to people.	54. Wa law anna likulli nafsin ẓalamat maa fil-arḍi laftadat bih; wa asarrunnadaamata lammaa ra-awul'azaab; wa quḍiya baynahum bilqisṭi wa hum laa yuẓlamoon.	وَلَوْ اَنَّ لِكُلِّ نَفْسٍ ظَلَمَتْ مَا فِي الْاَرْضِ لَافْتَدَتْ بِهٖ ۭ وَاَسَرُّوا النَّدَامَةَ لَمَّا رَاَوُا الْعَذَابَ ۚ وَقُضِيَ بَيْنَهُمْ بِالْقِسْطِ وَهُمْ لَا يُظْلَمُوْنَ ۝٥٤
55. All that is in the heavens and the earth certainly belongs to Allah and His promise is true, but many people do not know this.	55. Alaaa inna lillaahi maa fis-samaawaati wal-arḍ; alaaa inna wa'dal-laahi ḥaqquñw-walaakinna aksarahum laa ya'lamoon.	اَلَآ اِنَّ لِلّٰهِ مَا فِي السَّمٰوٰتِ وَالْاَرْضِ ۭ اَلَآ اِنَّ وَعْدَ اللّٰهِ حَقٌّ وَّلٰكِنَّ اَكْثَرَهُمْ لَا يَعْلَمُوْنَ ۝٥٥
56. It is Allah who gives life and causes things to die. To Him you will all return.	56. Huwa yuḥyee wa yumeetu wa ilayhi turja'oon.	هُوَ يُحْيٖ وَيُمِيْتُ وَاِلَيْهِ تُرْجَعُوْنَ ۝٥٦
57. People, good advice has come to you from your Lord: a (spiritual) cure, a guide and a mercy for the believers.	57. Yaaa ayyuhan-naasu qad jaaa'atkum-maw'iẓatum-mir-Rabbikum wa shifaaa'ul-limaa fiṣ-ṣudoori wa hudañw-wa raḥmatul-lilmu'mineen.	يٰٓاَيُّهَا النَّاسُ قَدْ جَاۗءَتْكُمْ مَّوْعِظَةٌ مِّنْ رَّبِّكُمْ وَشِفَاۗءٌ لِّمَا فِي الصُّدُوْرِ ڏ وَهُدًى وَّرَحْمَةٌ لِّلْمُؤْمِنِيْنَ ۝٥٧
58. (Muhammad), tell them, "To be happy with the favors and mercy of Allah is better than whatever you accumulate."	58. Qul bifaḍlil-laahi wabiraḥ-matihee fabizaalika falyaf-raḥoo huwa khayrum-mimmaa yajma'oon.	قُلْ بِفَضْلِ اللّٰهِ وَبِرَحْمَتِهٖ فَبِذٰلِكَ فَلْيَفْرَحُوْا ۭ هُوَ خَيْرٌ مِّمَّا يَجْمَعُوْنَ ۝٥٨
59. Ask them, "Have you considered that out of the sustenance which Allah has given you, you made some of it lawful and some unlawful? Did Allah permit you to do this or are you ascribing falsehood to Allah?"	59. Qul ara'aytum-maaa anzalal-laahu lakum-mirrizqin faja'altum-minhu ḥaraamañw-wa ḥalaalan qul aaallaahu azina lakum am 'alal-laahi taftaroon.	قُلْ اَرَءَيْتُمْ مَّآ اَنْزَلَ اللّٰهُ لَكُمْ مِّنْ رِّزْقٍ فَجَعَلْتُمْ مِّنْهُ حَرَامًا وَّحَلٰلًا ۭ قُلْ ءٰۗاللّٰهُ اَذِنَ لَكُمْ اَمْ عَلَي اللّٰهِ تَفْتَرُوْنَ ۝٥٩
60. What do those who ascribe falsehood to Allah think of the Day of Judgment? Allah is generous to human beings, yet many do not give thanks.	60. Wa maa ẓannul-lazeena yaftaroona 'alal-laahil-kaziba Yawmal-Qiyaamah; innallaaha lazoo faḍlin 'alan-naasi wa laakinna aksarahum laa yash-kuroon.	وَمَا ظَنُّ الَّذِيْنَ يَفْتَرُوْنَ عَلَي اللّٰهِ الْكَذِبَ يَوْمَ الْقِيٰمَةِ ۭ اِنَّ اللّٰهَ لَذُوْ فَضْلٍ عَلَي النَّاسِ وَلٰكِنَّ اَكْثَرَهُمْ لَا يَشْكُرُوْنَ ۝٦٠ ع ٧
61. (Muhammad), We observe all your affairs; whatever you	61. Wa maa takoonu fee sha-niñw-wa maa tatloo	وَمَا تَكُوْنُ فِيْ شَاْنٍ وَّمَا تَتْلُوْا

recite from the Quran and whatever you (people) do. Nothing in the heavens or the earth is hidden from your Lord, even that which is as small as the weight of atom or greater or smaller. All is recorded in the glorious Book.

minhu min Qur'aaniñw-wa laa ta'maloona min 'amalin illaa kunnaa 'alaykum shuhoodan iz tufeeḍoona feeh; wa maa ya'zubu ar-Rabbika mimmi-sqaali zarratin fil-arḍi wa laa fis-samaaa'i wa laaa aṣghara min zaalika wa laaa akbara illaa fee Kitaabim-Mubeen.

مِنْهُ مِنْ قُرْاٰنٍ وَّلَا تَعْمَلُوْنَ مِنْ
عَمَلٍ اِلَّا كُنَّا عَلَيْكُمْ شُهُوْدًا
اِذْ تُفِيْضُوْنَ فِيْهِ ؕ وَمَا يَعْزُبُ
عَنْ رَّبِّكَ مِنْ مِّثْقَالِ ذَرَّةٍ فِي
الْاَرْضِ وَلَا فِي السَّمَآءِ وَلَاۤ اَصْغَرَ
مِنْ ذٰلِكَ وَلَاۤ اَكْبَرَ اِلَّا فِيْ
كِتٰبٍ مُّبِيْنٍ ﴿٦١﴾

62. The friends of Allah will certainly have nothing to fear, nor will they be grieved.

62. Alaaa inna awliyaaa'al-laahi laa khawfun 'alayhim wa laa hum yaḥzanoon.

اَلَاۤ اِنَّ اَوْلِيَآءَ اللّٰهِ لَا خَوْفٌ
عَلَيْهِمْ وَلَا هُمْ يَحْزَنُوْنَ ﴿٦٢﴾

63. Those who have faith and fear Allah

63. Allazeena aamanoo wa kaanoo yattaqoon.

اَلَّذِيْنَ اٰمَنُوْا وَكَانُوْا يَتَّقُوْنَ ﴿٦٣﴾

64. will receive glad news both in this life and in the life hereafter. The words of Allah do not change. This alone is the supreme triumph.

64. Lahumul-bushraa filḥa-yaatid-dunyaa wa fil Aakhirah; laa tabdeela likalimaatil-laah; zaalika-huwal-fawzul-'aẓeem.

لَهُمُ الْبُشْرٰى فِي الْحَيٰوةِ الدُّنْيَا
وَفِي الْاٰخِرَةِ ؕ لَا تَبْدِيْلَ لِكَلِمٰتِ
اللّٰهِ ؕ ذٰلِكَ هُوَ الْفَوْزُ الْعَظِيْمُ ﴿٦٤﴾

65. (Muhammad), let not their words disappoint you; all dignity belongs to Allah. He is All-hearing and All-knowing.

65. Wa laa yaḥzunka qawlu-hum; innal-'izzata lillaahi jamee'aa; Huwas-Samee'ul-'Aleem.

وَلَا يَحْزُنْكَ قَوْلُهُمْ ۘ اِنَّ الْعِزَّةَ
لِلّٰهِ جَمِيْعًا ؕ هُوَ السَّمِيْعُ الْعَلِيْمُ ﴿٦٥﴾

وقف لازم

66. Does not all that is in the heavens and the earth belong to Allah? (The unbelievers) who worship the idols instead of Allah follow only conjecture. What they preach are mere lies.

66. Alaaa inna lillaahi man fis-samaawaati wa man fil-arḍ; wa maa yattabi'ullazeena yad'oona min doonillaahi shurakaaa'; iñy-yattabi'oona illaẓ-ẓanna wa in hum illaa yakhruṣoon.

اَلَاۤ اِنَّ لِلّٰهِ مَنْ فِي السَّمٰوٰتِ وَمَنْ
فِي الْاَرْضِ ؕ وَمَا يَتَّبِعُ الَّذِيْنَ
يَدْعُوْنَ مِنْ دُوْنِ اللّٰهِ شُرَكَآءَ ؕ
اِنْ يَّتَّبِعُوْنَ اِلَّا الظَّنَّ وَاِنْ هُمْ
اِلَّا يَخْرُصُوْنَ ﴿٦٦﴾

67. It is He Who has made the night for you to rest and has filled the day with light (as a means of visibility). In this there is evidence (of the existence of Allah) for the people who hear.

67. Huwal-lazee ja'ala laku-mul-layla litaskunoo feehi wannahaara mubṣiraa; inna fee zaalika la-Aayaatil-liqawmiñy-yasma'oon.

هُوَ الَّذِيْ جَعَلَ لَكُمُ الَّيْلَ لِتَسْكُنُوْا
فِيْهِ وَالنَّهَارَ مُبْصِرًا ؕ اِنَّ
فِيْ ذٰلِكَ لَاٰيٰتٍ لِّقَوْمٍ يَّسْمَعُوْنَ ﴿٦٧﴾

68. Certain people have said that Allah has begotten a son. Allah is free of all defects and of having a son. Allah is Self-sufficient and to Him belongs all that is in the heavens and the earth. In this, you (people) have

68. Qaalut-takhazal-laahu waladan Subḥaanahoo Huwal-Ghaniyyu lahoo maa fis-samaawaati wa maa fil-arḍ; in 'indakum-min

قَالُوا اتَّخَذَ اللّٰهُ وَلَدًا سُبْحٰنَهٗ ؕ
هُوَ الْغَنِيُّ ؕ لَهٗ مَا فِي السَّمٰوٰتِ
وَمَا فِي الْاَرْضِ ؕ اِنْ عِنْدَكُمْ مِّنْ

no authority. Do you ascribe to Allah things of which you have no knowledge?

sulṭaanim bihaaẕaaa; ataqooloona 'alal-laahi maa laa ta'lamoon.

سُلْطٰنٍۭ بِهٰذَا ؕ اَتَقُوْلُوْنَ عَلَى
اللّٰهِ مَا لَا تَعْلَمُوْنَ ﴿۶۸﴾

69. (Muhammad), say to them, "Those who invent falsehood against Allah will have no happiness."

69. Qul innal-laẕeena yaftaroona 'alal-laahil-kaẕiba laa yufliḥoon.

قُلْ اِنَّ الَّذِيْنَ يَفْتَرُوْنَ عَلَى
اللّٰهِ الْكَذِبَ لَا يُفْلِحُوْنَ ؕ ﴿۶۹﴾

70. They may consider it a means of enjoyment in this life but (on the Day of Judgment) they will all return to Us. Then We will cause them to suffer the most severe punishment for their disbelief.

70. Mataa'un fid-dunyaa s̱umma ilaynaa marji'uhum s̱umma nuẕeequhumul'aẕaabash-shadeeda bimaa kaanoo yakfuroon.

مَتَاعٌ فِى الدُّنْيَا ثُمَّ اِلَيْنَا مَرْجِعُهُمْ
ثُمَّ نُذِيْقُهُمُ الْعَذَابَ الشَّدِيْدَ بِمَا
كَانُوْا يَكْفُرُوْنَ ﴿۷۰﴾ ع

71. (Muhammad), tell them the story of Noah, who said to his people, "Even if my belief and my preaching of the revelation of Allah seem strange to you, I place my trust in Him. Unite yourselves and seek help from your idols. You should not regret what you want to do, but should execute your plans against me without delay

71. Watlu 'alayhim naba-a Nooḥ; iẕ qaala Iiqawmihee yaa qawmi in kaana kabura 'alaykum-maqaamee wa taẕkeeree bi-Aayaatil-laahi fa'alal-laahi tawakkaltu fa-ajmi'ooo amrakum wa shurakaaa'akum s̱umma laa yakun amrukum 'alaykum ghummatan s̱ummaq-ḍooo ilayya wa laa tunẓiroon.

وَاتْلُ عَلَيْهِمْ نَبَاَ نُوْحٍ ۘ اِذْ قَالَ
لِقَوْمِهٖ يٰقَوْمِ اِنْ كَانَ كَبُرَ عَلَيْكُمْ
مَّقَامِىْ وَتَذْكِيْرِىْ بِاٰيٰتِ اللّٰهِ
فَعَلَى اللّٰهِ تَوَكَّلْتُ فَاَجْمِعُوْۤا اَمْرَكُمْ
وَشُرَكَآءَكُمْ ثُمَّ لَا يَكُنْ اَمْرُكُمْ
عَلَيْكُمْ غُمَّةً ثُمَّ اقْضُوْۤا اِلَىَّ
وَلَا تُنْظِرُوْنِ ﴿۷۱﴾

وقف لازم

72. If you turn away from my preaching, it will not harm me; I shall receive my reward from Allah, who has commanded me to become a Muslim."

72. Fa-in tawallaytum famaa sa-altukum-min ajrin in ajriya illaa 'alal-laahi wa umirtu an akoona minal-muslimeen.

فَاِنْ تَوَلَّيْتُمْ فَمَا سَاَلْتُكُمْ مِّنْ
اَجْرٍ ؕ اِنْ اَجْرِىَ اِلَّا عَلَى اللّٰهِ ۙ
وَاُمِرْتُ اَنْ اَكُوْنَ مِنَ الْمُسْلِمِيْنَ ﴿۷۲﴾

73. They rejected Noah. Then We saved him and his people in the Ark to make them the successors of the rest. The others, who had called Our revelations lies, were drowned. Consider the fate of those who (rejected) Our warnings.

73. Fakaẕ-ẕaboohu fanajjaynaahu wa mamma'ahoo fil-fulki wa ja'alnaahum khalaaa'ifa wa aghraqnal-laẕeena kaẕ-ẕaboo bi-Aayaatinaa fanẓur kayfa kaana 'aaqibatul-munẕareen.

فَكَذَّبُوْهُ فَنَجَّيْنٰهُ وَمَنْ مَّعَهٗ فِى
الْفُلْكِ وَجَعَلْنٰهُمْ خَلٰۤئِفَ وَاَغْرَقْنَا
الَّذِيْنَ كَذَّبُوْا بِاٰيٰتِنَا ۚ فَانْظُرْ كَيْفَ
كَانَ عَاقِبَةُ الْمُنْذَرِيْنَ ﴿۷۳﴾

74. After (Noah) We sent other messengers to their people with clear authoritative evidence that proved their prophetic claims). But how could the people believe what they had previously called lies? Thus do We seal the hearts of the transgressors.

74. S̱umma ba'as̱naa mim ba'dihee Rusulan ilaa qawmihim fajaaa'oohum bilbayyinaati famaa kaanoo liyu'minoo bimaa kaẕ-ẕaboo bihee min qabl; kaẕaalika naṭba'u 'alaa quloobil-mu'tadeen.

ثُمَّ بَعَثْنَا مِنْۢ بَعْدِهٖ رُسُلًا اِلٰى
قَوْمِهِمْ فَجَآءُوْهُمْ بِالْبَيِّنٰتِ فَمَا
كَانُوْا لِيُؤْمِنُوْا بِمَا كَذَّبُوْا بِهٖ مِنْ
قَبْلُ ؕ كَذٰلِكَ نَطْبَعُ عَلٰى قُلُوْبِ
الْمُعْتَدِيْنَ ﴿۷۴﴾

75. Then We sent Moses and Aaron with Our miracles to the Pharaoh and his people. These people also proved to be arrogant. They were sinful people.

75. Summa ba'asnaa mim ba'dihim-Moosaa wa Haaroona ilaa Fir'awna wa mala'ihee bi-Aayaatinaa fastakbaroo wa kaanoo qawmam-mujrimeen.

ثُمَّ بَعَثْنَا مِنْۢ بَعْدِهِمْ مُّوْسٰى وَهٰرُوْنَ
اِلٰى فِرْعَوْنَ وَمَلَا۟ئِهٖ بِاٰيٰتِنَا
فَاسْتَكْبَرُوْا وَكَانُوْا قَوْمًا مُّجْرِمِيْنَ ﴿٧٥﴾

76. When the Truth from Us came, they called it simply magic.

76. Falammaa jaaa'ahumul-ḥaqqu min 'indinaa qaalooo inna haazaa lasiḥrum-mubeen.

فَلَمَّا جَآءَهُمُ الْحَقُّ مِنْ عِنْدِنَا قَالُوْٓا
اِنَّ هٰذَا لَسِحْرٌ مُّبِيْنٌ ﴿٧٦﴾

77. Moses asked, "Why do you call the Truth which has come to you magic? Certainly, magicians will not have happiness."

77. Qaala Moosaaa ataqooloona lilḥaqqi lammaa jaaa'akum asiḥrun haazaa wa laa yufliḥus-saaḥiroon.

قَالَ مُوْسٰٓى اَتَقُوْلُوْنَ لِلْحَقِّ لَمَّا
جَآءَكُمْ ؕ اَسِحْرٌ هٰذَا ؕ وَلَا يُفْلِحُ
السّٰحِرُوْنَ ﴿٧٧﴾

78. They asked Moses, "Have you come to turn us away from the faith of our fathers and to make yourselves the rulers in the land? We shall never accept your faith."

78. Qaalooo aji'tanaa litalfitanaa 'ammaa wajadnaa 'alayhi aabaaa'anaa wa takoona lakumal-kibriyaaa'u fil-arḍi wa maa naḥnu lakumaa bimu'mineen.

قَالُوْٓا اَجِئْتَنَا لِتَلْفِتَنَا عَمَّا
وَجَدْنَا عَلَيْهِ اٰبَآءَنَا وَتَكُوْنَ
لَكُمَا الْكِبْرِيَآءُ فِى الْاَرْضِ ؕ وَمَا
نَحْنُ لَكُمَا بِمُؤْمِنِيْنَ ﴿٧٨﴾

79. The Pharaoh ordered every skillful magician to come into his presence.

79. Wa qaala Fir'awnu'-toonee bikulli saaḥirin 'aleem.

وَقَالَ فِرْعَوْنُ ائْتُوْنِىْ بِكُلِّ
سٰحِرٍ عَلِيْمٍ ﴿٧٩﴾

80. When all the magicians were brought to his court, Moses asked them to cast down what they wanted to do.

80. Falammaa jaaa'assa-ḥaratu qaala lahum-Moosaaa alqoo maaa antum-mulqoon.

فَلَمَّا جَآءَ السَّحَرَةُ قَالَ لَهُمْ
مُّوْسٰٓى اَلْقُوْا مَآ اَنْتُمْ مُّلْقُوْنَ ﴿٨٠﴾

81. When the magicians had thrown down theirs, Moses said, "What you have performed is magic. Allah will certainly prove it to be false; Allah will not make the deeds of the evil-doers righteous deeds.

81. Falammaaa alqaw qaala Moosaa maa ji'tum bihissiḥr; innal-laaha sayubṭiluhooo innal-laaha laa yuṣliḥu 'amalal-mufsideen.

فَلَمَّآ اَلْقَوْا قَالَ مُوْسٰى مَا جِئْتُمْ بِهِ
السِّحْرُ ؕ اِنَّ اللّٰهَ سَيُبْطِلُهٗ ؕ اِنَّ
اللّٰهَ لَا يُصْلِحُ عَمَلَ الْمُفْسِدِيْنَ ﴿٨١﴾

82. Allah will make the Truth stand supreme by His words, even though the sinful people dislike it."

82. Wa yuḥiqqul-laahul-ḥaqqa bi-Kalimaatihee wa law karihal-mujrimoon.

وَيُحِقُّ اللّٰهُ الْحَقَّ بِكَلِمٰتِهٖ وَلَوْ كَرِهَ
الْمُجْرِمُوْنَ ﴿٨٢﴾ ع ٨ ١٢ ١٣

83. No one believed in Moses except some young people of his own tribe who were at the same time very afraid of the persecution of the Pharaoh and his people. The Pharaoh was certainly a tyrant and a transgressor.

83. Famaaa aamana li-Moosaaa illaa zurriyyatum-min qawmihee 'alaa khawfimmin Fir'awna wa mala'ihim añy-yaftinahum; wa inna Fir'awna la'aalin fil-arḍi wa innahoo laminal-musrifeen.

فَمَآ اٰمَنَ لِمُوْسٰٓى اِلَّا ذُرِّيَّةٌ مِّنْ
قَوْمِهٖ عَلٰى خَوْفٍ مِّنْ فِرْعَوْنَ
وَمَلَا۟ئِهِمْ اَنْ يَّفْتِنَهُمْ ؕ وَاِنَّ
فِرْعَوْنَ لَعَالٍ فِى الْاَرْضِ ۚ وَاِنَّهٗ
لَمِنَ الْمُسْرِفِيْنَ ﴿٨٣﴾

84. Moses told his people, "If you have submitted yourselves to Allah and have faith in Him, put your trust in Him."

84. Wa qaala Moosaa yaa qawmi in kuntum aamantum billaahi fa'alayhi tawakkalooo in kuntum-muslimeen.

وَقَالَ مُوْسٰى يٰقَوْمِ اِنْ كُنْتُمْ
اٰمَنْتُمْ بِاللّٰهِ فَعَلَيْهِ تَوَكَّلُوْٓا اِنْ
كُنْتُمْ مُّسْلِمِيْنَ ﴿٨٤﴾

85. They said, "In Allah do we trust. Lord, do not subject us to the persecution of the unjust ones,

85. Faqaaloo 'alal-laahi tawakkalnaa Rabbanaa laa taj'alnaa fitnatal-lilqawmiẓ-ẓaalimeen.

فَقَالُوْا عَلَى اللّٰهِ تَوَكَّلْنَا ۚ رَبَّنَا لَا
تَجْعَلْنَا فِتْنَةً لِّلْقَوْمِ الظّٰلِمِيْنَ ﴿٨٥﴾

86. Lord, save us, through Your mercy, from the disbelieving people."

86. Wa najjinaa biraḥmatika minal-qawmil-kaafireen.

وَنَجِّنَا بِرَحْمَتِكَ مِنَ الْقَوْمِ
الْكٰفِرِيْنَ ﴿٨٦﴾

87. We sent a revelation to Moses and his brother to build houses for their people in the Pharaoh's town and to build them facing one another. (We told him) that therein they should pray and that Moses should give the glad news (of Allah's mercy) to the faithful ones.

87. Wa awḥaynaaa ilaa Moosaa wa akheehi an tabaw-wa-aa liqawmikumaa bi Miṣra buyootañw-waj'aloo buyoota-kum qiblatañw-wa aqeemuṣ-Ṣa-laah; wa bashshiril-mu'mineen.

وَاَوْحَيْنَآ اِلٰى مُوْسٰى وَاَخِيْهِ
اَنْ تَبَوَّاٰ لِقَوْمِكُمَا بِمِصْرَ بُيُوْتًا
وَّاجْعَلُوْا بُيُوْتَكُمْ قِبْلَةً وَّاَقِيْمُوا
الصَّلٰوةَ ۗ وَبَشِّرِ الْمُؤْمِنِيْنَ ﴿٨٧﴾

88. Moses said, "Our Lord, You have given the Pharaoh and his people great riches and splendor in this life and this makes them stray from Your path. Our Lord, destroy their wealth and harden their hearts in disbelief so that they will suffer the most painful torment."

88. Wa qaala Moosaa Rabba-naaa innaka aatayta Fir'awna wa mala-ahoo zeenatañw-wa amwaalan filḥayaatid-dunyaa Rabbanaa liyuḍilloo 'an sabeelika Rabbanaṭ-mis 'alaaa amwaalihim washdud 'alaa quloobihim falaa yu'minoo ḥattaa yarawul-'aẕaabal-aleem.

وَقَالَ مُوْسٰى رَبَّنَآ اِنَّكَ اٰتَيْتَ
فِرْعَوْنَ وَمَلَاَهٗ زِيْنَةً وَّاَمْوَالًا
فِي الْحَيٰوةِ الدُّنْيَا ۙ رَبَّنَا لِيُضِلُّوْا
عَنْ سَبِيْلِكَ ۚ رَبَّنَا اطْمِسْ عَلٰٓى
اَمْوَالِهِمْ وَاشْدُدْ عَلٰى قُلُوْبِهِمْ فَلَا
يُؤْمِنُوْا حَتّٰى يَرَوُا الْعَذَابَ الْاَلِيْمَ ﴿٨٨﴾

89. The Lord replied, "Moses, the prayer of your brother and yourself has been heard. Both of you must be steadfast (in your faith) and must not follow the ignorant ones."

89. Qaala qad ujeebad-da'wa-tukumaa fastaqeemaa wa laa tattabi'aanni sabeelal-laẕeena laa ya'lamoon.

قَالَ قَدْ اُجِيْبَتْ دَّعْوَتُكُمَا
فَاسْتَقِيْمَا وَلَا تَتَّبِعٰٓنِّ سَبِيْلَ
الَّذِيْنَ لَا يَعْلَمُوْنَ ﴿٨٩﴾

90. We helped the children of Israel cross the sea safely. The Pharaoh and his army pursued the children of Israel with wickedness and hate until the Pharaoh was drowned. As he was drowning the Pharaoh said, "I declare that there is no Ilah (one deserving to be worshipped) but the One in whom the children of Israel believe and I have submitted to the will of Allah."

90. Wa jaawaznaa bi-Baneee Israaa'eelal-baḥra fa-atba'a-hum Fir'awnu wa junooduhoo baghyañw-wa 'adwaa; ḥattaaa iẕaaa adrakahul-gharaq; qaala aamantu annahoo laaa ilaaha illal-laẕeee aamanat bihee Banooo Israaa'eela wa ana minal-muslimeen.

وَجٰوَزْنَا بِبَنِيْٓ اِسْرَآءِيْلَ الْبَحْرَ
فَاَتْبَعَهُمْ فِرْعَوْنُ وَجُنُوْدُهٗ بَغْيًا
وَّعَدْوًا ۭ حَتّٰٓى اِذَآ اَدْرَكَهُ الْغَرَقُ ۙ
قَالَ اٰمَنْتُ اَنَّهٗ لَآ اِلٰهَ اِلَّا الَّذِيْٓ
اٰمَنَتْ بِهٖ بَنُوْٓا اِسْرَآءِيْلَ وَاَنَا
مِنَ الْمُسْلِمِيْنَ ﴿٩٠﴾

91. (Allah replied), "Now you declare belief in Me! However, before this you disobeyed as one of those who spread evil.

91. Aaal'aana wa qad 'aṣayta qablu wa kunta minal-mufsideen.

آٰلْـٰٔنَ وَقَدْ عَصَيْتَ قَبْلُ وَكُنْتَ
مِنَ الْمُفْسِدِيْنَ ﴿٩١﴾

92. We will save your body on this day so that you may become evidence (of Our existence) for the coming generations; many people are unaware of such evidence."

92. Falyawma nunajjeeka bibadanika litakoona liman khalfaka Aayah; wa inna kaseeram-minan-naasi 'an Aayaatinaa laghaafiloon.

فَالْيَوْمَ نُنَجِّيْكَ بِبَدَنِكَ لِتَكُوْنَ
لِمَنْ خَلْفَكَ اٰيَةً ۭ وَاِنَّ كَثِيْرًا
مِّنَ النَّاسِ عَنْ اٰيٰتِنَا لَغٰفِلُوْنَ ﴿٩٢﴾ ع ٩ ١٤

93. We settled the children of Israel in a blessed land and provided them with pure sustenance. They did not create differences among themselves until after the knowledge had come to them. Allah will judge their differences on the Day of Judgment.

93. Wa laqad bawwa-naa Baneee Israaa'eela mubawwa-a ṣidqiñw-wa razaqnaahum-minaṭ-ṭayyibaati famakh-talafoo ḥattaa jaaa'ahumul-'ilm; inna Rabbaka yaqḍee baynahum Yawmal-Qiyaamati feemaa kaanoo feehi yakhtalifoon.

وَلَقَدْ بَوَّاْنَا بَنِيْٓ اِسْرَاۗءِيْلَ مُبَوَّاَ
صِدْقٍ وَّرَزَقْنٰھُمْ مِّنَ الطَّيِّبٰتِ ۚ
فَمَا اخْتَلَفُوْا حَتّٰى جَاۗءَھُمُ الْعِلْمُ ۭ
اِنَّ رَبَّكَ يَقْضِيْ بَيْنَھُمْ يَوْمَ الْقِيٰمَةِ
فِيْمَا كَانُوْا فِيْهِ يَخْتَلِفُوْنَ ﴿٩٣﴾

94. If you (people) have any doubt about what We have revealed to you (about the Day of Judgment and other matters of belief), ask those who read the Book that was revealed (to the Prophets who lived) before you. The truth has certainly come to you from your Lord. Thus, do not doubt it (in your heart),

94. Fa-in kunta fee shakkim-mimmaaa anzalnaaa ilayka fas'alil-lazeena yaqra'oonal-Kitaaba min qablik; laqad jaaa'akal-ḥaqqu mir-Rabbika falaa takoonanna minal-mumtareen.

فَاِنْ كُنْتَ فِيْ شَكٍّ مِّمَّآ اَنْزَلْنَآ
اِلَيْكَ فَسْــَٔـلِ الَّذِيْنَ يَقْرَءُوْنَ
الْكِتٰبَ مِنْ قَبْلِكَ ۚ لَقَدْ جَاۗءَكَ
الْحَقُّ مِنْ رَّبِّكَ فَلَا تَكُوْنَنَّ مِنَ
الْمُمْتَرِيْنَ ﴿٩٤﴾

95. nor be of those who have called Allah's revelations lies lest you become lost.

95. Wa laa takoonanna minal-lazeena kaz-zaboo bi-Aayaatil-laahi fatakoona minal-khaasireen.

وَلَا تَكُوْنَنَّ مِنَ الَّذِيْنَ كَذَّبُوْا
بِاٰيٰتِ اللّٰهِ فَتَكُوْنَ مِنَ الْخٰسِرِيْنَ ﴿٩٥﴾

96. (Even though all kinds of miracles will be shown to them) those about whom the word of your Lord has been ordained, will not have faith

96. Innal-lazeena ḥaqqat 'alayhim Kalimatu Rabbika laa yu'minoon.

اِنَّ الَّذِيْنَ حَقَّتْ عَلَيْهِمْ كَلِمَتُ
رَبِّكَ لَا يُؤْمِنُوْنَ ﴿٩٦﴾

97. until they face the most painful torment.

97. Wa law jaaa'athum kullu Aayatin ḥattaa yarawul 'azaabal-aleem.

وَلَوْ جَاۗءَتْھُمْ كُلُّ اٰيَةٍ حَتّٰى يَرَوُا
الْعَذَابَ الْاَلِيْمَ ﴿٩٧﴾

98. Why did no one except the people of Jonah believe (in their punishment before their death) so that they could have benefited from their faith? When the people of Jonah believed, We saved them from a disgraceful torment in this life and provided them with the means of enjoyment for an appointed time.

98. Falaw laa kaanat qaryatun aamanat fanafa'ahaaa eemaanuhaaa illaa qawma Yoonus; lammaaa aamanoo kashafnaa 'anhum 'azaabal-khizyi fil-ḥayaatid-dunyaa wa matta'naahum ilaa ḥeen.

فَلَوْلَا كَانَتْ قَرْيَةٌ اٰمَنَتْ فَنَفَعَهَآ
اِيْمَانُهَآ اِلَّا قَوْمَ يُوْنُسَ ۭ لَمَّآ اٰمَنُوْا
كَشَفْنَا عَنْهُمْ عَذَابَ الْخِزْيِ
فِي الْحَيٰوةِ الدُّنْيَا وَمَتَّعْنٰهُمْ
اِلٰى حِيْنٍ ﴿٩٨﴾

99. Had your Lord wished, everyone on earth would have believed in Him. (Muhammad), do you force people to have faith?	99. Wa law shaaa'a Rabbuka la-aamana man fil-arḍi kulluhum jamee'aa; afa-anta tukrihun-naasa ḥattaa yakoonoo mu'mineen.	وَلَوْ شَآءَ رَبُّكَ لَاٰمَنَ مَنْ فِي الْاَرْضِ كُلُّهُمْ جَمِيْعًا ؕ اَفَاَنْتَ تُكْرِهُ النَّاسَ حَتّٰى يَكُوْنُوْا مُؤْمِنِيْنَ ﴿٩٩﴾
100. No one can have faith without the permission of Allah. Allah will cast down filth on those who have no understanding.	100. Wa maa kaana linafsin an tu'mina illaa bi-iznil-laah; wa yaj'alur-rijsa 'alal-lazeena laa ya'qiloon.	وَمَا كَانَ لِنَفْسٍ اَنْ تُؤْمِنَ اِلَّا بِاِذْنِ اللّٰهِ ؕ وَيَجْعَلُ الرِّجْسَ عَلَى الَّذِيْنَ لَا يَعْقِلُوْنَ ﴿١٠٠﴾
101. (Muhammad), tell them to think about things in the heavens and the earth. Miracles and warnings are of no avail to the disbelieving people.	101. Qulin-ẓuroo maazaa fis-samaawaati wal-arḍ; wa maa tughnil-Aayaatu wannuzuru 'an qawmil-laa yu'minoon.	قُلِ انْظُرُوْا مَاذَا فِي السَّمٰوٰتِ وَالْاَرْضِ ؕ وَمَا تُغْنِي الْاٰيٰتُ وَالنُّذُرُ عَنْ قَوْمٍ لَّا يُؤْمِنُوْنَ ﴿١٠١﴾
102. What can they expect other than the kind of (punishment that befell the disbelieving people) who had gone before them? (Muhammad), say to them, "You should wait and I also will wait with you."	102. Fahal yantaẓiroona illaa misla ayyaamil-lazeena khalaw min qablihim; qul fantaẓirooo innee ma'akum minal-muntaẓireen.	فَهَلْ يَنْتَظِرُوْنَ اِلَّا مِثْلَ اَيَّامِ الَّذِيْنَ خَلَوْا مِنْ قَبْلِهِمْ ؕ قُلْ فَانْتَظِرُوْٓا اِنِّيْ مَعَكُمْ مِّنَ الْمُنْتَظِرِيْنَ ﴿١٠٢﴾
103. We saved Our Messengers and those who believed; We must save the believers.	103. Summa nunajjee Rusulanaa wallazeena aamanoo; kazaalika ḥaqqan 'alaynaa nunjil-mu'mineen.	ثُمَّ نُنَجِّيْ رُسُلَنَا وَالَّذِيْنَ اٰمَنُوْا كَذٰلِكَ ۚ حَقًّا عَلَيْنَا نُنْجِ الْمُؤْمِنِيْنَ ﴿١٠٣﴾ ع ١١/١٥
104. (Muhammad), say, "People, if you have doubt about my religion, know that I, certainly, do not worship the idols which you worship instead of Allah, but I worship Allah who causes you to die. I am commanded to believe (in His existence)."	104. Qul yaaa ayyuhan-naasu in kuntum fee shakkim-min deenee falaaa a'budullazeena ta'budoona min doonil-laahi wa laakin a'budul-laahal-lazee yatawaf-faakum wa umirtu an akoona minal-mu'mineen.	قُلْ يٰٓاَيُّهَا النَّاسُ اِنْ كُنْتُمْ فِيْ شَكٍّ مِّنْ دِيْنِيْ فَلَآ اَعْبُدُ الَّذِيْنَ تَعْبُدُوْنَ مِنْ دُوْنِ اللّٰهِ وَلٰكِنْ اَعْبُدُ اللّٰهَ الَّذِيْ يَتَوَفّٰىكُمْ ۖ وَاُمِرْتُ اَنْ اَكُوْنَ مِنَ الْمُؤْمِنِيْنَ ۙ ﴿١٠٤﴾
105. (Allah has commanded me as follows), "You must have firm belief in the upright religion and do not be an idolater.	105. Wa an aqim wajhaka liddeeni Ḥaneefaa; wa laa takoonanna minal-mushrikeen.	وَاَنْ اَقِمْ وَجْهَكَ لِلدِّيْنِ حَنِيْفًا ۚ وَلَا تَكُوْنَنَّ مِنَ الْمُشْرِكِيْنَ ﴿١٠٥﴾
106. seek help from Allah but not from those who can neither benefit nor harm you, lest you become of the unjust ones."	106. Wa laa tad'u min doonil-laahi maa laa yanfa'uka wa laa yaḍurruka fa-in fa'alta fa-innaka izamminaẓ-ẓaalimeen.	وَلَا تَدْعُ مِنْ دُوْنِ اللّٰهِ مَا لَا يَنْفَعُكَ وَلَا يَضُرُّكَ ۚ فَاِنْ فَعَلْتَ فَاِنَّكَ اِذًا مِّنَ الظّٰلِمِيْنَ ﴿١٠٦﴾
107. (Muhammad), if Allah afflicts you with hardship, no one	107. Wa iñy-yamsaskal-laahu biḍurrin falaa	وَاِنْ يَّمْسَسْكَ اللّٰهُ بِضُرٍّ فَلَا

besides Him can save you. If Allah grants you a favor, no one can prevent you from receiving His favors. Allah bestows His favors upon whichever of His servants He wants. Allah is All-forgiving and All-merciful.

108. Muhammad), say, "People, truth has certainly come to you from your Lord. One who seeks guidance does so for his own good and One who goes astray will find himself lost. I am not your keeper."

109. (Muhammad), follow what is revealed to you and have patience until Allah issues His Judgment; He is the best Judge.

kaashifa lahooo illaa Huwa wa iñy-yuridka bikhayrin falaa raaadda lifaḍlih; yuṣeebu bihee mañy-yashaaa'u min 'ibaadih; wa Huwal-Ghafoorur-Raḥeem.

108. Qul yaaa ayyuhan-naasu qad jaaa'akumul-ḥaqqu mir-Rabbikum famanih-tadaa fa-innamaa yahtadee linafsihee wa man ḍalla fa-innamaa yaḍillu 'alayhaa wa maaa ana 'alaykum biwakeel.

109. Wattabi' maa yooḥaaa ilayka waṣbir ḥattaa yaḥkumal-laah; wa Huwa khayrul-ḥaakimeen.

كَاشِفَ لَهٗٓ اِلَّا هُوَ ۚ وَاِنْ يُّرِدْكَ
بِخَيْرٍ فَلَا رَآدَّ لِفَضْلِهٖ ۭ يُصِيْبُ
بِهٖ مَنْ يَّشَآءُ مِنْ عِبَادِهٖ ۭ وَهُوَ
الْغَفُوْرُ الرَّحِيْمُ ۝١٠٧
قُلْ يٰٓاَيُّهَا النَّاسُ قَدْ جَآءَكُمُ
الْحَقُّ مِنْ رَّبِّكُمْ ۚ فَمَنِ اهْتَدٰى
فَاِنَّمَا يَهْتَدِيْ لِنَفْسِهٖ ۚ وَمَنْ ضَلَّ
فَاِنَّمَا يَضِلُّ عَلَيْهَا ۚ وَمَآ اَنَا
عَلَيْكُمْ بِوَكِيْلٍ ۝١٠٨
وَاتَّبِعْ مَا يُوْحٰٓى اِلَيْكَ وَاصْبِرْ حَتّٰى
يَحْكُمَ اللّٰهُ ښ وَهُوَ خَيْرُ الْحٰكِمِيْنَ ۝١٠٩ ع ١١ ٢ ١٦

Hud, Hud (11)

In the Name of Allah,
the Beneficent, the Merciful.

Sûrat Hûd-11

(Revealed at Makkah)
Bismillaahir Raḥmaanir Raḥeem

(١١) سُوْرَةُ هُوْدٍ مَّكِّيَّةٌ (٥٢)
اٰيَاتُهَا ١٢٣ بِسْمِ اللّٰهِ الرَّحْمٰنِ الرَّحِيْمِ رُكُوْعَاتُهَا ١٠

1. Alif. Lam. Ra. This is a Book from One who is All-wise and All-aware. Its verses are well composed and distinctly arranged (from one another).

2. (It teaches), "People, do not worship anyone besides Allah. I, (Muhammad), am His Messenger sent to warn you and to give you the glad news."

3. "Seek forgiveness from your Lord and turn to Him in repentance for your sins. He will provide you good sustenance for an appointed time and will reward everyone according to his merits. I am afraid that you will suffer torment on the great Day (of Judgment) if you turn away (from Allah).

4. To Allah you will all return. Allah has power over all things."

5. (The unbelievers) cover their breasts to try to hide their disbelief from Allah, but He knows very well whatever they

1. Alif-Laaam-Raa; Kitaa-bun uḥkimat Aayaatuhoo summa fuṣṣilat mil-ladun Ḥa-keemin Khabeer.

2. Allaa ta'budooo illal-laah; innanee lakum minhu nazee-ruñw-wa basheer.

3. Wa anis-taghfiroo Rabba-kum summa toobooo ilayhi yumatti'kum mataa'an ḥasanan ilaaa ajalimmu sammañw-wa yu'ti kulla zee faḍlin faḍlahoo wa in tawallaw fa-inneee akhaa-fu 'alaykum 'azaaba Yawmin Kabeer.

4. Ilal-laahi marji'ukum wa Huwa 'alaa kulli shay'in Qadeer.

5. Alaaa innahum yasnoona ṣudoorahum liyastakhfoo minh; alaa ḥeena

الٓرٰ قف كِتٰبٌ اُحْكِمَتْ اٰيٰتُهٗ ثُمَّ
فُصِّلَتْ مِنْ لَّدُنْ حَكِيْمٍ خَبِيْرٍ ۝١
اَلَّا تَعْبُدُوْٓا اِلَّا اللّٰهَ ۭ اِنَّنِيْ لَكُمْ
مِّنْهُ نَذِيْرٌ وَّبَشِيْرٌ ۝٢
وَّاَنِ اسْتَغْفِرُوْا رَبَّكُمْ ثُمَّ تُوْبُوْٓا
اِلَيْهِ يُمَتِّعْكُمْ مَّتَاعًا حَسَنًا اِلٰٓى
اَجَلٍ مُّسَمًّى وَّيُؤْتِ كُلَّ ذِيْ
فَضْلٍ فَضْلَهٗ ۭ وَاِنْ تَوَلَّوْا فَاِنِّيْٓ
اَخَافُ عَلَيْكُمْ عَذَابَ يَوْمٍ كَبِيْرٍ ۝٣
اِلَى اللّٰهِ مَرْجِعُكُمْ ۚ وَهُوَ عَلٰي كُلِّ
شَيْءٍ قَدِيْرٌ ۝٤
اَلَآ اِنَّهُمْ يَثْنُوْنَ صُدُوْرَهُمْ
لِيَسْتَخْفُوْا مِنْهُ ۭ اَلَا حِيْنَ

conceal or reveal even when they cover themselves with their garments. Allah certainly knows the innermost (secrets) of the hearts.

6. There is no living creature on earth that does not receive sustenance from Allah. He knows its dwelling and resting place. Everything is recorded in the glorious Book.

7. Allah created the heavens and the earth in six days. His Throne existed on water so that He could test you and find out those among you who do good deeds. (Muhammad), if you were to tell them that after death they would be brought back to life again, the unbelievers would say, "This is nothing but obvious magic."

8. If We delay in afflicting them with Our punishment for an appointed time, they ask, "What is preventing it (the punishment) from taking place?" On the day when it (punishment) befalls them, no one will be able to escape from it and that which they have mocked will surround them from all sides.

9. If We grant a favor to the human being and then take it away from him. He becomes despairing and ungrateful.

10. If after his hardship, We grant him a blessing, he grows proud and rejoicing and says, "All my hardships have gone."

11. But those who exercise patience and do good works do not behave as such. They will receive forgiveness and a great reward (from the Lord).

12. Perhaps you, (Muhammad), may by chance leave (untold) a part of that which is revealed to you and feel grieved because they say,

yastaghshoona siyaabahum ya'lamu maa yusirroona wa maa yu'linoon; innahoo 'aleemum bizaatiṣ-ṣudoor.

6. Wa maa min daaabbatin fil-arḍi illaa 'alal-laahi rizquhaa wa ya'lamu mustaqarrahaa wa mustawda'ahaa; kullun fee Kitaabim-Mubeen.

7. Wa Huwal-lazee khalaqas-samaawaati wal-arḍa fee sittati ayyaamiñw-wa kaana-'Arshuhoo 'alal-maaa'i liyabluwakum ayyukum aḥsanu 'amalaa; wa la'in qulta innakum mab'oo-soona mim ba'dil-mawti layaqoolannal-lazeena kafarooo in haazaaa illaa siḥrum-mubeen.

8. Wala'in akhkharnaa 'anhumul-'azaaba ilaaa ummatim-ma'doodatil-layaqoolunna maa yaḥbisuh; alaa yawma yateehim laysa maṣroofan 'anhum wa ḥaaqa bihim-maa kaanoo bihee yastahzi'oon.

9. Wa la'in azaqnal-insaana minnaa raḥmatan summa naza'naahaa minh; innahoo laya'oosun kafoor.

10. Wala'in azaqnaahu na'-maaa'a ba'da ḍarraaa'a massat-hu layaqoolanna zahabas-sayyi-aatu 'anneee; innahoo lafariḥun fakhoor.

11. Illal-lazeena ṣabaroo wa 'amiluṣ-ṣaaliḥaati ulaaa'ika lahum-maghfiratuñw-wa ajrun kabeer.

12. Fala'allaka taarikum ba'ḍa maa yooḥaaa ilayka wa ḍaaa'iqum-bihee ṣadruka añy-

يَسْتَغْشُونَ ثِيَابَهُمْ ۙ يَعْلَمُ مَا
يُسِرُّونَ وَمَا يُعْلِنُونَ ۚ إِنَّهُ
عَلِيمٌ بِذَاتِ الصُّدُورِ ﴿٥﴾
وَمَا مِن دَابَّةٍ فِي الْأَرْضِ إِلَّا عَلَى
اللَّهِ رِزْقُهَا وَيَعْلَمُ مُسْتَقَرَّهَا وَ
مُسْتَوْدَعَهَا ۚ كُلٌّ فِي كِتَابٍ مُّبِينٍ ﴿٦﴾ الجزء الثاني عشر (١٢)
وَهُوَ الَّذِي خَلَقَ السَّمَاوَاتِ وَالْأَرْضَ
فِي سِتَّةِ أَيَّامٍ وَكَانَ عَرْشُهُ عَلَى
الْمَاءِ لِيَبْلُوَكُمْ أَيُّكُمْ أَحْسَنُ عَمَلًا ۗ
وَلَئِن قُلْتَ إِنَّكُم مَّبْعُوثُونَ مِن
بَعْدِ الْمَوْتِ لَيَقُولَنَّ الَّذِينَ كَفَرُوا
إِنْ هَٰذَا إِلَّا سِحْرٌ مُّبِينٌ ﴿٧﴾
وَلَئِنْ أَخَّرْنَا عَنْهُمُ الْعَذَابَ إِلَىٰ
أُمَّةٍ مَّعْدُودَةٍ لَّيَقُولُنَّ مَا يَحْبِسُهُ ۗ
أَلَا يَوْمَ يَأْتِيهِمْ لَيْسَ مَصْرُوفًا عَنْهُمْ
وَحَاقَ بِهِم مَّا كَانُوا بِهِ يَسْتَهْزِئُونَ ﴿٨﴾ ع ٨
وَلَئِنْ أَذَقْنَا الْإِنسَانَ مِنَّا رَحْمَةً
ثُمَّ نَزَعْنَاهَا مِنْهُ ۚ إِنَّهُ لَيَئُوسٌ
كَفُورٌ ﴿٩﴾
وَلَئِنْ أَذَقْنَاهُ نَعْمَاءَ بَعْدَ ضَرَّاءَ
مَسَّتْهُ لَيَقُولَنَّ ذَهَبَ السَّيِّئَاتُ
عَنِّي ۚ إِنَّهُ لَفَرِحٌ فَخُورٌ ﴿١٠﴾
إِلَّا الَّذِينَ صَبَرُوا وَعَمِلُوا الصَّالِحَاتِ
أُولَٰئِكَ لَهُم مَّغْفِرَةٌ وَأَجْرٌ كَبِيرٌ ﴿١١﴾
فَلَعَلَّكَ تَارِكٌ بَعْضَ مَا يُوحَىٰ
إِلَيْكَ وَضَائِقٌ بِهِ صَدْرُكَ أَن

"Why has some treasure not been sent to him or an angel sent down with him?" You (Muhammad) are only a Warner and Allah is the guardian of all things.

yaqooloo law laaa unzila 'alayhi kanzun aw jaaa'a ma'ahoo malak; innamaaa anta nazeer; wallaahu 'alaa kulli shay'iñw-wakeel.

يَقُوْلُوْا لَوْلَآ اُنْزِلَ عَلَيْهِ كَنْزٌ اَوْ
جَآءَ مَعَهٗ مَلَكٌ ؕ اِنَّمَآ اَنْتَ نَذِيْرٌ ؕ
وَاللّٰهُ عَلٰى كُلِّ شَیْءٍ وَّكِيْلٌ ؕ ﴿١٢﴾

13. Do they (the unbelievers) say that (Muhammad) has falsely ascribed (the Quran) to Allah? Ask them, "Compose ten chapters like (those of the Quran) and call on whomever you can for help besides Allah if you are true in your claim.

13. Am yaqooloonaf-taraahu qul fa-too bi'ashri Suwarim-mislihee muftarayaatiñw-wad'oo manis-tata'tum min doonil-laahi in kuntum ṣaadiqeen.

اَمْ يَقُوْلُوْنَ افْتَرٰىهُ ؕ قُلْ فَاْتُوْا بِعَشْرِ
سُوَرٍ مِّثْلِهٖ مُفْتَرَيٰتٍ وَّادْعُوْا مَنِ
اسْتَطَعْتُمْ مِّنْ دُوْنِ اللّٰهِ اِنْ كُنْتُمْ
صٰدِقِيْنَ ﴿١٣﴾

14. If they did not respond to you, then you must know that Allah has sent it with His knowledge and that He is the only Ilah (one deserving to be worshipped). Will you then become Muslims?"

14. Fa-il-lam yastajeeboo-lakum fa'lamooo annamaaa unzila bi'ilmil-laahi wa allaaa ilaaha illaa Huwa fahal antum muslimoon.

فَاِلَّمْ يَسْتَجِيْبُوْا لَكُمْ فَاعْلَمُوْٓا
اَنَّمَآ اُنْزِلَ بِعِلْمِ اللّٰهِ وَاَنْ لَّآ اِلٰهَ
اِلَّا هُوَ ۚ فَهَلْ اَنْتُمْ مُّسْلِمُوْنَ ﴿١٤﴾

15. Those who choose the worldly life and its pleasures will be given proper recompense for their deeds in this life and will not suffer any loss.

15. Man kaana yureedul-ḥayaatad-dunyaa wa zeena-tahaa nuwaffi ilayhim a'maa-lahum feehaa wa hum feehaa laa yubkhasoon.

مَنْ كَانَ يُرِيْدُ الْحَيٰوةَ الدُّنْيَا وَ
زِيْنَتَهَا نُوَفِّ اِلَيْهِمْ اَعْمَالَهُمْ
فِيْهَا وَهُمْ فِيْهَا لَا يُبْخَسُوْنَ ﴿١٥﴾

16. Such people will receive nothing in the next life except hellfire. Their deeds will be made devoid of all virtue and their efforts will be in vain.

16. Ulaaa'ikal-lazeena laysa lahum fil-Aakhirati illan-Naaru wa ḥabiṭa maa ṣana'oo feehaa wa baaṭilum-maa kaanoo ya'maloon.

اُولٰٓئِكَ الَّذِيْنَ لَيْسَ لَهُمْ فِی الْاٰخِرَةِ
اِلَّا النَّارُ ۖ ز وَحَبِطَ مَا صَنَعُوْا فِيْهَا وَ
بٰطِلٌ مَّا كَانُوْا يَعْمَلُوْنَ ﴿١٦﴾

17. He is the one (the Holy Prophet) who possesses authority from his Lord and from him (his people) a witness who is an Imam (leader) and a blessing recites it (Quran) and before it was the book of Moses. Such people do believe in this guidance (in the Quran). Those who disbelieve (in the Quran) will have hell as their dwelling place. Thus (Muhammad), have no doubt about it (the Quran). It is certainly the truth from your Lord, yet many people do not have faith.

17. Afaman kaana 'ala bayyinatim-mir-Rabbihee wa yatloohu shaahidum-minhu wa min qablihee Kitaabu Moosaaa imaamañw-wa raḥmah; ulaaa-'ika yu'minoona bih; wa mañy-yakfur bihee minal-Aḥzaabi fan-Naaru maw'iduh; falaa taku fee miryatim-minh; innahul-ḥaqqu mir-Rabbika wa laakinna aksaran-naasi laa yu'minoon.

اَفَمَنْ كَانَ عَلٰى بَيِّنَةٍ مِّنْ رَّبِّهٖ وَ
يَتْلُوْهُ شَاهِدٌ مِّنْهُ وَمِنْ قَبْلِهٖ
كِتٰبُ مُوْسٰٓى اِمَامًا وَّرَحْمَةً ؕ اُولٰٓئِكَ
يُؤْمِنُوْنَ بِهٖ ؕ وَمَنْ يَّكْفُرْ بِهٖ مِنَ
الْاَحْزَابِ فَالنَّارُ مَوْعِدُهٗ ۚ فَلَا تَكُ
فِیْ مِرْيَةٍ مِّنْهُ ۗ اِنَّهُ الْحَقُّ مِنْ رَّبِّكَ
وَلٰكِنَّ اَكْثَرَ النَّاسِ لَا يُؤْمِنُوْنَ ﴿١٧﴾

18. Who are more unjust than those who ascribe falsehood to Allah? When such people are brought into the presence of their Lord, the witness will say, "These are the ones who told lies about

18. Wa man aẓlamu mimma-nif-taraa 'alal-laahi kazibaa; ulaaa'ika yu'raḍoona 'alaa Rabbihim wa yaqoolul-ashhaa-du haaa'ulaaa'il-lazeena

وَمَنْ اَظْلَمُ مِمَّنِ افْتَرٰى عَلَى اللّٰهِ
كَذِبًا ؕ اُولٰٓئِكَ يُعْرَضُوْنَ عَلٰى رَبِّهِمْ
وَيَقُوْلُ الْاَشْهَادُ هٰٓؤُلَآءِ الَّذِيْنَ

their Lord. Certainly Allah will condemn the unjust

kazaboo 'alaa Rabbihim; alaa la'natul-laahi 'alaẓ-ẓaalimeen.

كَذَبُوا عَلَىٰ رَبِّهِمْ ۚ أَلَا لَعْنَةُ اللَّهِ
عَلَى الظَّالِمِينَ ﴿١٨﴾

19. who prevent others from the way of Allah, seek to make it appear crooked, and have no faith in the life hereafter.

19. Allazeena yaṣuddoona 'an sabeelil-laahi wa yabghoonahaa 'iwajaa; wa hum bil-Aakhirati hum kaafiroon.

الَّذِينَ يَصُدُّونَ عَن سَبِيلِ اللَّهِ
وَيَبْغُونَهَا عِوَجًا وَهُم بِالْآخِرَةِ
هُمْ كَافِرُونَ ﴿١٩﴾

20. Such people would never weaken Allah's (power) on earth nor would they find any guardian besides Allah. Their punishment will be doubled and they will not be able to hear or see.

20. Ulaaa'ika lam yakoonoo mu'jizeena fil-arḍi wa maa kaana lahum-min doonillaahi min awliyaaa'; yuḍaa'afu lahumul-'azaab; maa kaanoo yastaṭee'oonas-sam'a wa maa kaanoo yubṣiroon.

أُولَٰئِكَ لَمْ يَكُونُوا مُعْجِزِينَ فِي
الْأَرْضِ وَمَا كَانَ لَهُم مِّن دُونِ وقف لازم
اللَّهِ مِنْ أَوْلِيَاءَ ۘ يُضَاعَفُ لَهُمُ
الْعَذَابُ ۚ مَا كَانُوا يَسْتَطِيعُونَ
السَّمْعَ وَمَا كَانُوا يُبْصِرُونَ ﴿٢٠﴾

21. They have lost their souls and their false deities will turn away from them.

21. Ulaaa'ikal-lazeena khasirooo anfusahum wa ḍalla 'anhum maa kaanoo yaftaroon.

أُولَٰئِكَ الَّذِينَ خَسِرُوا أَنفُسَهُمْ وَ
ضَلَّ عَنْهُم مَّا كَانُوا يَفْتَرُونَ ﴿٢١﴾

22. Consequently, in the life to come they will certainly lose a great deal.

22. Laa jarama annahum fil-Aakhirati humul-akhsaroon.

لَا جَرَمَ أَنَّهُمْ فِي الْآخِرَةِ هُمُ
الْأَخْسَرُونَ ﴿٢٢﴾

23. The righteously striving believers who are extremely humble before their Lord, will be the dwellers of Paradise wherein they will live forever.

23. Innal-lazeena aamanoo wa 'amiluṣ-ṣaaliḥaati wa akhbatooo ilaa Rabbihim ulaaa'ika Aṣḥaabul-jannati hum feehaa khaalidoon.

إِنَّ الَّذِينَ آمَنُوا وَعَمِلُوا الصَّالِحَاتِ
وَأَخْبَتُوا إِلَىٰ رَبِّهِمْ أُولَٰئِكَ أَصْحَابُ
الْجَنَّةِ ۖ هُمْ فِيهَا خَالِدُونَ ﴿٢٣﴾

24. Can the two groups, the blind and the deaf, be considered equal to those who have vision and hearing? Will you then not take heed?

24. Masalul-fareeqayni kal-a'maa wal-aṣammi walbaṣeeri wassamee'; hal yastawiyaani masalaa; afalaa tazakkaroon.

مَثَلُ الْفَرِيقَيْنِ كَالْأَعْمَىٰ وَالْأَصَمِّ
وَالْبَصِيرِ وَالسَّمِيعِ ۚ هَلْ يَسْتَوِيَانِ
مَثَلًا ۚ أَفَلَا تَذَكَّرُونَ ﴿٢٤﴾

25. We sent Noah to his people to give them the clear warning

25. Wa laqad arsalnaa Nooḥan ilaa qawmiheee innee lakum nazeerum-mubeen.

وَلَقَدْ أَرْسَلْنَا نُوحًا إِلَىٰ قَوْمِهِ
إِنِّي لَكُمْ نَذِيرٌ مُّبِينٌ ﴿٢٥﴾

26. that they should not worship anyone besides Allah. (Noah warned them), "I am afraid that you will suffer the most painful torment."

26. Al-laa ta'budooo illal-laah; inneee akhaafu 'alaykum 'azaaba yawmin aleem.

أَن لَّا تَعْبُدُوا إِلَّا اللَّهَ ۖ إِنِّي أَخَافُ
عَلَيْكُمْ عَذَابَ يَوْمٍ أَلِيمٍ ﴿٢٦﴾

27. The unbelievers among his people said, "We do not believe that you are any better than the rest of us; we see that only the

27. Faqaalal-mala-ul-lazeena kafaroo min qawmihee maa naraaka illaa basharam-mislanaa

فَقَالَ الْمَلَأُ الَّذِينَ كَفَرُوا مِن
قَوْمِهِ مَا نَرَاكَ إِلَّا بَشَرًا مِّثْلَنَا

worthless hasty ones, the lowliest among us follow you. Thus, we do not think that you are superior to us, rather you are all liars."

wa maa naraakat-taba'aka illal-lazeena hum araazilunaa baadiyar-ra-yi wa maa naraa lakum 'alaynaa min faḍlim-bal naẓun-nukum kaazibeen.

وَمَا نَرٰىكَ اتَّبَعَكَ اِلَّا الَّذِيْنَ
هُمْ اَرَاذِلُنَا بَادِيَ الرَّاْيِ ۚ وَمَا
نَرٰى لَكُمْ عَلَيْنَا مِنْ فَضْلٍۭ بَلْ
نَظُنُّكُمْ كٰذِبِيْنَ ﴿٢٧﴾

28. Noah replied, "My people, do you think that - if my Lord has sent me a miracle and granted me mercy, but your ignorance has obscured them from your sight - we can force you to believe when you do not want to?

28. Qaala yaaqawmi ara'ay-tum in kuntu 'alaa bayyinatim-mir-Rabbee wa aataanee raḥmatam-min 'indihee fa'um-miyat 'alaykum anulzimuku-moohaa wa antum lahaa kaarihoon.

قَالَ يٰقَوْمِ اَرَءَيْتُمْ اِنْ كُنْتُ عَلٰى
بَيِّنَةٍ مِّنْ رَّبِّيْ وَاٰتٰىنِيْ رَحْمَةً مِّنْ
عِنْدِهٖ فَعُمِّيَتْ عَلَيْكُمْ ؕ اَنُلْزِمُكُمُوْهَا
وَاَنْتُمْ لَهَا كٰرِهُوْنَ ﴿٢٨﴾

29. My people, I do not ask any payment for what I preach to you. No one except Allah has to give me any reward. I do not drive away those who have faith (in my teaching); they will all receive mercy from their Lord. I know that you are ignorant people.

29. Wa yaa qawmi laaa as'alukum 'alayhi maalan in ajriya illaa 'alal-laah; wa maaa ana biṭaaridil-lazeena aama-nooo; innahum mulaaqoo Rabbihim wa laakinneee araakum qawman tajhaloon.

وَيٰقَوْمِ لَاۤ اَسْـَٔلُكُمْ عَلَيْهِ مَالًا ؕ اِنْ
اَجْرِيَ اِلَّا عَلَى اللّٰهِ وَمَاۤ اَنَا بِطَارِدِ
الَّذِيْنَ اٰمَنُوْا ؕ اِنَّهُمْ مُّلٰقُوْا رَبِّهِمْ
وَلٰكِنِّيْۤ اَرٰىكُمْ قَوْمًا تَجْهَلُوْنَ ﴿٢٩﴾

30. My people, who would protect me against Allah if I were to drive these people away? Will you then not take heed?"

30. Wa yaa qawmi mañy-yanṣurunee minal-laahi in ṭarattuhum; afalaa tazak-karoon.

وَيٰقَوْمِ مَنْ يَّنْصُرُنِيْ مِنَ اللّٰهِ اِنْ
طَرَدْتُّهُمْ ؕ اَفَلَا تَذَكَّرُوْنَ ﴿٣٠﴾

31. "I do not say that Allah's treasures belong to me, that I know the unseen, or that I am an angel. Also, I do not say about those whom you disdain, that Allah will not give them any reward; Allah knows best what is in their hearts, for then I would be unjust."

31. Wa laaa aqoolu lakum 'indee khazaa'inul-laahi wa laaa a'lamul-ghayba wa laaa aqoolu innee malakuñw-wa laaa aqoolu lillazeena tazdareee a'yunukum lañy-yu'tiyahumul-laahu khayraa; Allaahu a'lamu bimaa feee anfusihim inneee izal-laminaẓ-ẓaalimeen.

وَلَاۤ اَقُوْلُ لَكُمْ عِنْدِيْ خَزَآئِنُ اللّٰهِ
وَلَاۤ اَعْلَمُ الْغَيْبَ وَلَاۤ اَقُوْلُ اِنِّيْ
مَلَكٌ وَّلَاۤ اَقُوْلُ لِلَّذِيْنَ تَزْدَرِيْۤ
اَعْيُنُكُمْ لَنْ يُّؤْتِيَهُمُ اللّٰهُ خَيْرًا ؕ
اَللّٰهُ اَعْلَمُ بِمَا فِيْۤ اَنْفُسِهِمْ ۚۖ اِنِّيْۤ
اِذًا لَّمِنَ الظّٰلِمِيْنَ ﴿٣١﴾

32. They said, "Noah, you have argued with us a great deal. Bring down on us whatever torment with which you have been threatening us if what you say is true."

32. Qaaloo yaa Nooḥu qad jaadaltanaa fa-aksarta jidaa-lanaa fa-tinaa bimaa ta'idunaaa in kunta minaṣ-ṣaadiqeen.

قَالُوْا يٰنُوْحُ قَدْ جٰدَلْتَنَا فَاَكْثَرْتَ
جِدَالَنَا فَاْتِنَا بِمَا تَعِدُنَاۤ اِنْ كُنْتَ
مِنَ الصّٰدِقِيْنَ ﴿٣٢﴾

33. (Noah) replied, "Allah will bring torment down on you whenever He wants and you will not be able to make His (plans) fail.

33. Qaala innamaa ya-teekum bihil-laahu in shaaa'a wa maaa antum bimu'jizeen.

قَالَ اِنَّمَا يَاْتِيْكُمْ بِهِ اللّٰهُ اِنْ شَآءَ
وَمَاۤ اَنْتُمْ بِمُعْجِزِيْنَ ﴿٣٣﴾

34. My advice will be of no benefit to you if Allah wants to let

34. Wa laa yanfa'ukum nuṣḥeee in arattu

وَلَا يَنْفَعُكُمْ نُصْحِيْۤ اِنْ اَرَدْتُّ

you go astray. He is your Lord and to Him you will all return."

an anṣaḥa lakum in kaanal-laahu yureedu añy-yughwi-yakum; Huwa Rabbukum wa ilayhi turja'oon.

أَنْ أَنْصَحَ لَكُمْ إِنْ كَانَ اللَّهُ
يُرِيدُ أَنْ يُغْوِيَكُمْ ۚ هُوَ رَبُّكُمْ
وَإِلَيْهِ تُرْجَعُونَ ﴿٣٤﴾

35. Do they say that Muhammad has falsely ascribed (the Quran) to Allah? (Muhammad), tell them "Had I falsely ascribed it to Allah, I shall be responsible for my own sins. I am certainly not responsible for whatever sins you commit!"

35. Am yaqooloonaf-taraahu qul inif-taraytuhoo fa'alayya ijraamee wa ana bareee'um-mimmaa tujrimoon.

أَمْ يَقُولُونَ افْتَرَاهُ ۖ قُلْ إِنِ
افْتَرَيْتُهُ فَعَلَيَّ إِجْرَامِي وَأَنَا
بَرِيءٌ مِمَّا تُجْرِمُونَ ﴿٣٥﴾

36. It was revealed to Noah, "Besides those from your people who have already accepted the faith, no one would ever accept it. Do not be disappointed about what they have been doing,

36. Wa ooḥiya ilaa Nooḥin annahoo lañy-yu'mina min qawmika illaa man qad aamana falaa tabta'is bimaa kaanoo yaf'aloon.

وَأُوحِيَ إِلَىٰ نُوحٍ أَنَّهُ لَنْ يُؤْمِنَ
مِنْ قَوْمِكَ إِلَّا مَنْ قَدْ آمَنَ فَلَا
تَبْتَئِسْ بِمَا كَانُوا يَفْعَلُونَ ﴿٣٦﴾

37. but build the Ark under Our supervision and guidance and do not address Me with any word concerning the unjust for they are all to be drowned."

37. Waṣna'il-fulka bi-a'yunina-a wa waḥyinaa wa laa tukhaa-ṭibnee fil-lazeena ẓalamooo; innahum-mughraqoon.

وَاصْنَعِ الْفُلْكَ بِأَعْيُنِنَا وَوَحْيِنَا
وَلَا تُخَاطِبْنِي فِي الَّذِينَ ظَلَمُوا ۚ
إِنَّهُمْ مُغْرَقُونَ ﴿٣٧﴾

38. (Noah) started to build the Ark, but whenever some of his people passed by, they would mock him. He in return would reply, "Mock us, but just as you mock us, we too will mock you.

38. Wa yaṣna'ul-fulka wa kullamaa marra 'alayhi mala-um-min qawmihee sakhiroo minh; qaala in taskharoo minnaa fa-innaa naskharu minkum kamaa taskharoon.

وَيَصْنَعُ الْفُلْكَ وَكُلَّمَا مَرَّ عَلَيْهِ
مَلَأٌ مِنْ قَوْمِهِ سَخِرُوا مِنْهُ ۚ قَالَ
إِنْ تَسْخَرُوا مِنَّا فَإِنَّا نَسْخَرُ
مِنْكُمْ كَمَا تَسْخَرُونَ ﴿٣٨﴾

39. You will soon learn who will face a humiliating punishment and will be encompassed by an everlasting torment."

39. Fasawfa ta'lamoona mañy-ya-teehi 'azaabuñy-yukhzeehi wa yaḥillu 'alayhi 'azaabum-muqeem.

فَسَوْفَ تَعْلَمُونَ مَنْ يَأْتِيهِ عَذَابٌ
يُخْزِيهِ وَيَحِلُّ عَلَيْهِ عَذَابٌ مُقِيمٌ ﴿٣٩﴾

40. When at last Our decree was fulfilled, water gushed forth from the oven (in Noah's house). We told him to carry in the Ark a pair (male and female) from every species, his family - except those who were destined to perish - and the believers. No one believed in him, except a few.

40. Ḥattaaa izaa jaaa'a amrunaa wa faarat-tannooru qulnaḥ-mil feehaa min kullin zawjaynis-nayni wa ahlaka illaa man sabaqa 'alayhil-qawlu wa man aaman; wa maaa aamana ma'ahooo illaa qaleel.

حَتَّىٰ إِذَا جَاءَ أَمْرُنَا وَفَارَ التَّنُّورُ
قُلْنَا احْمِلْ فِيهَا مِنْ كُلٍّ زَوْجَيْنِ
اثْنَيْنِ وَأَهْلَكَ إِلَّا مَنْ سَبَقَ عَلَيْهِ
الْقَوْلُ وَمَنْ آمَنَ ۚ وَمَا آمَنَ مَعَهُ
إِلَّا قَلِيلٌ ﴿٤٠﴾

41. (Noah) said, "Embark in it. It will sail in the name of Allah, in His Name it will sail and in His Name it will cast anchor. My Lord is All-forgiving and All-merciful."

41. Wa qaalar-kaboo feehaa bismil-laahi majreehaa wa mursaahaa; inna Rabbee la-Ghafoorur-Raḥeem.

وَقَالَ ارْكَبُوا فِيهَا بِسْمِ اللَّهِ مَجْرَاهَا
وَمُرْسَاهَا ۚ إِنَّ رَبِّي لَغَفُورٌ رَحِيمٌ ﴿٤١﴾

42. When the Ark sailed on with them amid the mountainous

42. Wa hiya tajree bihim fee mawjin kaljibaal;

وَهِيَ تَجْرِي بِهِمْ فِي مَوْجٍ كَالْجِبَالِ

waves, Noah called out to his son who kept away from them, "My son, embark with us. Do not stay with the unbelievers."

wa naadaa Nooḥunib-nahoo wa kaana fee ma'ziliñy-yaa bunay-yarkab-ma'anaa wa laa takum ma'al-kaafireen.

وَنَادٰى نُوْحُ ۨابْنَهٗ وَكَانَ فِيْ
مَعْزِلٍ يّٰبُنَيَّ ارْكَبْ مَّعَنَا وَلَا
تَكُنْ مَّعَ الْكٰفِرِيْنَ ﴿۴۲﴾

43. His son replied, "I shall climb up a mountain and this will save me from the flood." Noah said, "No one can escape on this day from Allah's command except those on whom He has mercy." The waves separated Noah from his son, who was then drowned with the rest (of the unbelievers).

43. Qaala sa-aaweee ilaa jabaliñy-ya'ṣimunee minal-maaa'; qaala laa 'aaṣimal-yawma min amril-laahi illaa mar-raḥim; wa ḥaala baynahumal-mawju fakaana minal-mughraqeen.

قَالَ سَاٰوِيْۤ اِلٰى جَبَلٍ يَّعْصِمُنِيْ مِنَ
الْمَآءِ ؕ قَالَ لَا عَاصِمَ الْيَوْمَ مِنْ
اَمْرِ اللّٰهِ اِلَّا مَنْ رَّحِمَ ۚ وَحَالَ بَيْنَهُمَا
الْمَوْجُ فَكَانَ مِنَ الْمُغْرَقِيْنَ ﴿۴۳﴾

44. Then the earth was told to swallow up its water and the sky was ordered to stop raining. The water abated and Allah's command had been fulfilled. The Ark came to rest on Mount Judi. A voice said, "The unjust people are far away from the mercy of Allah."

44. Wa qeela yaaa arḍubla'ee maaa'aki wa yaa samaaa'u aqli'ee wa gheeḍal-maaa'u wa quḍiyal-amru wastawat 'alal-joodiyyi wa qeela bu'dal-lilqawmiẓ-ẓaalimeen.

وَقِيْلَ يٰۤاَرْضُ ابْلَعِيْ مَآءَكِ وَيٰسَمَآءُ
اَقْلِعِيْ وَغِيْضَ الْمَآءُ وَقُضِيَ الْاَمْرُ
وَاسْتَوَتْ عَلَى الْجُوْدِيِّ وَقِيْلَ بُعْدًا
لِّلْقَوْمِ الظّٰلِمِيْنَ ﴿۴۴﴾ الربع

45. Noah prayed to his Lord, saying, "Lord, my son is a member of my family. Your promise is always true and you are the best Judge."

45. Wa naadaa Nooḥur-Rabbahoo faqaala Rabbi innabnee min ahlee wa inna wa'dakal-ḥaqqu wa Anta Aḥkamul-ḥaakimeen.

وَنَادٰى نُوْحٌ رَّبَّهٗ فَقَالَ رَبِّ اِنَّ
ابْنِيْ مِنْ اَهْلِيْ وَاِنَّ وَعْدَكَ الْحَقُّ
وَاَنْتَ اَحْكَمُ الْحٰكِمِيْنَ ﴿۴۵﴾

46. His Lord replied, "He is not of your family. He is a man of unrighteous deeds. Do not ask me about that of which you have no knowledge. I advise you not to become of ignorant ones."

46. Qaala yaa Nooḥu innahoo laysa min ahlika innahoo 'amalun ghayru ṣaaliḥin falaa tas'alni maa laysa laka bihee 'ilmun inneee a'iẓuka an takoona minal-jaahileen.

قَالَ يٰنُوْحُ اِنَّهٗ لَيْسَ مِنْ اَهْلِكَ ۚ
اِنَّهٗ عَمَلٌ غَيْرُ صَالِحٍ ۖۗ فَلَا تَسْـَٔلْنِ
مَا لَيْسَ لَكَ بِهٖ عِلْمٌ ؕ اِنِّيْۤ اَعِظُكَ
اَنْ تَكُوْنَ مِنَ الْجٰهِلِيْنَ ﴿۴۶﴾

47. Noah said, "Lord, I ask You to prevent me from asking You ignorant questions and beg you for pardon and mercy or else I shall certainly be lost."

47. Qaala Rabbi inneee a'oozu bika an as'alaka maa laysa lee bihee 'ilm; wa illaa taghfir lee wa tarḥamneee akum-minal-khaasireen.

قَالَ رَبِّ اِنِّيْۤ اَعُوْذُ بِكَ اَنْ اَسْـَٔلَكَ
مَا لَيْسَ لِيْ بِهٖ عِلْمٌ ؕ وَاِلَّا تَغْفِرْ لِيْ
وَتَرْحَمْنِيْۤ اَكُنْ مِّنَ الْخٰسِرِيْنَ ﴿۴۷﴾

48. Noah was told, "Get down from the Ark. Your Lord's peace and blessings are upon you and your followers. Your Lord will grant favors to other nations and then afflict them with a painful torment."

48. Qeela yaa Nooḥuh-biṭ bisalaamim-minnaa wa bara-kaatin 'alayka wa 'alaaa umamim-mimmam-ma'ak;wa umamun sanumatti'uhum summa yamassuhum-minnaa 'azaabun aleem.

قِيْلَ يٰنُوْحُ اهْبِطْ بِسَلٰمٍ مِّنَّا وَ
بَرَكٰتٍ عَلَيْكَ وَعَلٰۤى اُمَمٍ مِّمَّنْ
مَّعَكَ ؕ وَاُمَمٌ سَنُمَتِّعُهُمْ ثُمَّ
يَمَسُّهُمْ مِّنَّا عَذَابٌ اَلِيْمٌ ﴿۴۸﴾

49. That which We have revealed to you (Muhammad) is

49. Tilka min ambaaa'il ghaybi nooḥeehaaa

تِلْكَ مِنْ اَنْۢبَآءِ الْغَيْبِ نُوْحِيْهَاۤ

news of the unseen. This was not known to you and to your people. Have patience. The pious will triumph in the end.

ilayka maa kunta ta'lamuhaaa anta wa laa qawmuka min qabli haaza faṣbir innal-'aaqibata lilmuttaqeen.

إِلَيْكَ ۖ مَا كُنتَ تَعْلَمُهَآ أَنتَ وَلَا
قَوْمُكَ مِن قَبْلِ هَـٰذَا ۖ فَاصْبِرْ ۖ
إِنَّ الْعَاقِبَةَ لِلْمُتَّقِينَ ﴿٤٩﴾

معانقة عند المتأخرين ۔ ع ٤
الوقف على فاصبر أحسن والتقي

50. To the tribe of Ad, We sent their brother Hud who told them, "Worship Allah; He is your only Lord. The idols that you worship are plainly false.

50. Wa ilaa 'Aadin akhaahum Hoodaa; qaala yaa qawmi'-budul-laaha maa lakum min ilaahin-ghayruhooo in antum illaa muftaroon.

وَإِلَىٰ عَادٍ أَخَاهُمْ هُودًا ۚ قَالَ
يَـٰقَوْمِ اعْبُدُوا اللَّهَ مَا لَكُم مِّنْ
إِلَـٰهٍ غَيْرُهُ ۖ إِنْ أَنتُمْ إِلَّا مُفْتَرُونَ ﴿٥٠﴾

51. My people, I do not ask any reward for what I have preached to you. No one can give me my reward except my Creator. Will you then not take heed?"

51. Yaa qawmi laaa as'alukum 'alayhi ajran in ajriya illaa 'alal-lazee faṭaraneee; afalaaa ta'qiloon.

يَـٰقَوْمِ لَآ أَسْـَٔلُكُمْ عَلَيْهِ أَجْرًا ۖ إِنْ
أَجْرِيَ إِلَّا عَلَى الَّذِي فَطَرَنِي ۚ
أَفَلَا تَعْقِلُونَ ﴿٥١﴾

52. "O my people, seek forgiveness from your Lord and turn to Him in repentance. He will send you abundant rain from the sky and will increase your power. Do not sinfully turn away from Him."

52. Wa yaa qawmis-taghfiroo Rabbakum summa tooboo ilayhi yursilis-samaaa'a 'alaykum-midraarañw-wa yazidkum quwwatan ilaa quwwatikum wa laa tatawallaw mujrimeen.

وَيَـٰقَوْمِ اسْتَغْفِرُوا رَبَّكُمْ ثُمَّ تُوبُوٓا
إِلَيْهِ يُرْسِلِ السَّمَآءَ عَلَيْكُم مِّدْرَارًا
وَيَزِدْكُمْ قُوَّةً إِلَىٰ قُوَّتِكُمْ وَلَا
تَتَوَلَّوْا مُجْرِمِينَ ﴿٥٢﴾

53. They said, "Hud, you have not shown us any miracles. We shall not give up our idols because of what you say and we shall not have any faith in you.

53. Qaaloo yaa Hoodu maa ji'tanaa bibayyinatiñw-wa maa naḥnu bitaarikeee aalihatinaa 'an qawlika wa maa naḥnu laka bimu'mineen.

قَالُوا يَـٰهُودُ مَا جِئْتَنَا بِبَيِّنَةٍ وَمَا
نَحْنُ بِتَارِكِيٓ ءَالِهَتِنَا عَن قَوْلِكَ وَمَا
نَحْنُ لَكَ بِمُؤْمِنِينَ ﴿٥٣﴾

54. We believe that some of our gods have afflicted you with evil." Hud said, "Allah is my witness and so are you that I have no association

54. In naqoolu illa'-taraaka ba'ḍu aalihatinaa bisooo'; qaala inneee ushhidul-laaha wash-hadooo annee bareee'um-mimmaa tushrikoon.

إِن نَّقُولُ إِلَّا اعْتَرَىٰكَ بَعْضُ ءَالِهَتِنَا
بِسُوٓءٍ ۗ قَالَ إِنِّيٓ أُشْهِدُ اللَّهَ وَاشْهَدُوٓا
أَنِّي بَرِيٓءٌ مِّمَّا تُشْرِكُونَ ﴿٥٤﴾

55. with the idols that you worship besides Allah, so plan against me without delay.

55. Min doonihee fakeedoonee jamee'an summa laa tunẓiroon.

مِن دُونِهِۦ ۖ فَكِيدُونِي جَمِيعًا ثُمَّ
لَا تُنظِرُونِ ﴿٥٥﴾

56. I trust Allah who is my Lord as well as yours. It is Allah who controls the destiny of all living creatures. It is my Lord who knows the right path.

56. Innee tawakkaltu 'alallaahi Rabbee wa Rabbikum; maa min daaabbatin illaa Huwa aakhi-zum binaaṣiyatihaaa; inna Rabbee 'alaa Ṣiraaṭim-Musta-qeem.

إِنِّي تَوَكَّلْتُ عَلَى اللَّهِ رَبِّي وَرَبِّكُم ۚ
مَّا مِن دَآبَّةٍ إِلَّا هُوَ ءَاخِذٌۢ بِنَاصِيَتِهَآ ۚ
إِنَّ رَبِّي عَلَىٰ صِرَٰطٍ مُّسْتَقِيمٍ ﴿٥٦﴾

57. If you turn away from Him, since I have already preached to you the message that I carry, my Lord will replace you with

57. Fain tawallaw faqad ablaghtukum-maaa ursiltu biheee ilaykum; wa yastakhlifu Rabbee qawman

فَإِن تَوَلَّوْا فَقَدْ أَبْلَغْتُكُم مَّآ أُرْسِلْتُ
بِهِۦٓ إِلَيْكُمْ ۚ وَيَسْتَخْلِفُ رَبِّي قَوْمًا

another nation. You cannot harm Him the least. My Lord is the Protector of all things."

ghayrakum wa laa taḍur-roonahoo shay'aa; inna Rabbee 'alaa kulli shay'in Ḥafeeẓ.

غَيْرَكُمْ ۚ وَلَا تَضُرُّوْنَهٗ شَيْـًٔا ؕ اِنَّ
رَبِّيْ عَلٰى كُلِّ شَيْءٍ حَفِيْظٌ ﴿٥٧﴾

58. When Our decree (of destroying them) was fulfilled, We mercifully saved Hud and his believing followers. We saved them from the intense torment.

58. Wa lammaa jaaa'a amrunaa najjaynaa Hoodañw-wallaz̲eena aamanoo ma'ahoo biraḥmatim-minnaa wa najjaynaahum-min 'az̲aabin ghaleeẓ.

وَلَمَّا جَآءَ اَمْرُنَا نَجَّيْنَا هُوْدًا وَّ
الَّذِيْنَ اٰمَنُوْا مَعَهٗ بِرَحْمَةٍ مِّنَّا ۚ
وَنَجَّيْنٰهُمْ مِّنْ عَذَابٍ غَلِيْظٍ ﴿٥٨﴾

59. It was the tribe of Ad who denied the miracles of their Lord, disobeyed His Messenger and followed the orders of every transgressing tyrant.

59. Wa tilka 'Aad; jaḥadoo bi-Aayaati-Rabbihim wa 'aṣaw Rusulahoo wattaba'ooo amra kulli jabbaarin 'aneed.

وَتِلْكَ عَادٌ ۟ۙ جَحَدُوْا بِاٰيٰتِ رَبِّهِمْ
وَعَصَوْا رُسُلَهٗ وَاتَّبَعُوْٓا اَمْرَ كُلِّ
جَبَّارٍ عَنِيْدٍ ﴿٥٩﴾

60. They were condemned in this life and will be condemned in the life hereafter. The tribe of Ad had certainly rejected their Lord. Allah kept the tribe of Ad, the people of Hud, away from His mercy.

60. Wa utbi'oo fee haaz̲ihid-dunyaa la'natañw-wa Yawmal-Qiyaamah; alaaa inna 'Aadan kafaroo Rabbahum; alaa bu'dal-li-'Aadin qawmi Hood.

وَاُتْبِعُوْا فِيْ هٰذِهِ الدُّنْيَا لَعْنَةً وَّ
يَوْمَ الْقِيٰمَةِ ؕ اَلَآ اِنَّ عَادًا كَفَرُوْا
رَبَّهُمْ ؕ اَلَا بُعْدًا لِّعَادٍ قَوْمِ هُوْدٍ ﴿٦٠﴾ ع ٥ وقف لازم

61. To Thamud We sent their brother Salih, who told them, "My people, worship Allah; He is your only Lord. It is He who has created you from the earth and has settled you therein. Seek forgiveness from Him and turn to Him in repentance. My Lord is certainly close to everyone and He hears all prayers."

61. Wa ilaa S̲amooda akhaa-hum Ṣaaliḥaa; qaala yaa qawmi'-budul-laaha maa lakum min ilaahin ghayruhoo Huwa ansha-akum-minal-arḍi wasta'marakum feehaa fastaghfiroohu s̲umma toobooo ilayh; inna Rabbee Qareebum-Mujeeb.

وَاِلٰى ثَمُوْدَ اَخَاهُمْ صٰلِحًا ۘ قَالَ
يٰقَوْمِ اعْبُدُوا اللّٰهَ مَا لَكُمْ مِّنْ
اِلٰهٍ غَيْرُهٗ ؕ هُوَ اَنْشَاَكُمْ مِّنَ
الْاَرْضِ وَاسْتَعْمَرَكُمْ فِيْهَا
فَاسْتَغْفِرُوْهُ ثُمَّ تُوْبُوْٓا اِلَيْهِ ؕ اِنَّ
رَبِّيْ قَرِيْبٌ مُّجِيْبٌ ﴿٦١﴾

62. They said, "Salih, we had great hope in you before this. Do you forbid us to worship that which our fathers had worshipped? We are doubtful and uncertain about what you have told us to worship."

62. Qaaloo yaa Ṣaaliḥu qad kunta feenaa marjuwwan qabla haaz̲aaa atanhaanaaa an na'bu-da maa ya'budu aabaaa'unaa wa innanaa lafee shakkim-mimmaa tad'oonaaa ilayhi mureeb.

قَالُوْا يٰصٰلِحُ قَدْ كُنْتَ فِيْنَا مَرْجُوًّا
قَبْلَ هٰذَآ اَتَنْهٰىنَآ اَنْ نَّعْبُدَ مَا
يَعْبُدُ اٰبَآؤُنَا وَاِنَّنَا لَفِيْ شَكٍّ
مِّمَّا تَدْعُوْنَآ اِلَيْهِ مُرِيْبٍ ﴿٦٢﴾

63. He said, "My people, think. I have received authoritative evidence and mercy from my Lord, so who will protect me from Allah if I disobey Him? You certainly want to destroy me.

63. Qaala yaa qawmi ara'ay-tum in kuntu 'alaa bayyinatim-mir-Rabbee wa aataanee minhu raḥmatan famañy-yanṣurunee minal-laahi in 'aṣaytuhoo famaa tazeedoonanee ghayra takhseer.

قَالَ يٰقَوْمِ اَرَءَيْتُمْ اِنْ كُنْتُ عَلٰى
بَيِّنَةٍ مِّنْ رَّبِّيْ وَاٰتٰىنِيْ مِنْهُ رَحْمَةً
فَمَنْ يَّنْصُرُنِيْ مِنَ اللّٰهِ اِنْ عَصَيْتُهٗ ۫
فَمَا تَزِيْدُوْنَنِيْ غَيْرَ تَخْسِيْرٍ ﴿٦٣﴾

64. My people, this is the she-camel of Allah, a miracle (that

64. Wa yaa qawmi haaz̲ihee naaqatul-laahi lakum

وَيٰقَوْمِ هٰذِهٖ نَاقَةُ اللّٰهِ لَكُمْ

you demanded as proof to support the truth which has been brought) to you. Leave her to graze in the land of Allah. Do not harm her with your evil deeds lest torment suddenly strike you."

Aayatan fazaroohaa ta-kul feee arḍillaahi wa laa tamassoohaa bisooo'in faya-khuzakum 'azaabun qareeb.

آيَةً فَذَرُوهَا تَأْكُلْ فِي أَرْضِ اللَّهِ وَلَا تَمَسُّوهَا بِسُوءٍ فَيَأْخُذَكُمْ عَذَابٌ قَرِيبٌ ﴿٦٤﴾

65. When they slew the she-camel, Salih told them, "You have only three days to enjoy living in your homes (before you will be struck by the torment). This is an inevitable prophecy."

65. Fa'aqaroohaa faqaala tamatta'oo fee daarikum salaasata ayyaamin zaalika wa'dun ghayru makzoob.

فَعَقَرُوهَا فَقَالَ تَمَتَّعُوا فِي دَارِكُمْ ثَلَاثَةَ أَيَّامٍ ۖ ذَٰلِكَ وَعْدٌ غَيْرُ مَكْذُوبٍ ﴿٦٥﴾

66. When Our decree came to pass. We mercifully saved Salih and his faithful followers from that day's ignominy. Your Lord is certainly Mighty and Majestic.

66. Falammaa jaaa'a amrunaa najjaynaa Ṣaaliḥañw-wallazeena aamanoo ma'ahoo biraḥmatim-minnaa wa min khizyi Yawmi'iz; inna Rabbaka Huwal-Qawiyyul-'Azeez.

فَلَمَّا جَاءَ أَمْرُنَا نَجَّيْنَا صَالِحًا وَالَّذِينَ آمَنُوا مَعَهُ بِرَحْمَةٍ مِنَّا وَمِنْ خِزْيِ يَوْمِئِذٍ ۗ إِنَّ رَبَّكَ هُوَ الْقَوِيُّ الْعَزِيزُ ﴿٦٦﴾

67. A blast struck the unjust and they were found lying motionless on their faces

67. Wa akhazal-lazeena ẓalamuṣ-ṣayḥatu fa-aṣbaḥoo fee diyaarihim jaasimeen.

وَأَخَذَ الَّذِينَ ظَلَمُوا الصَّيْحَةُ فَأَصْبَحُوا فِي دِيَارِهِمْ جَاثِمِينَ ﴿٦٧﴾

68. as though they had never existed. The people of Thamud denied the existence of their Lord. How distant from the mercy of Allah had the people of Thamud gone!

68. Ka-al-lam yaghnaw feehaaa; alaaa inna Samooda kafaroo Rabbahum; alaa bu'dal-li-Samood.

كَأَنْ لَمْ يَغْنَوْا فِيهَا ۗ أَلَا إِنَّ ثَمُودَ كَفَرُوا رَبَّهُمْ ۗ أَلَا بُعْدًا لِثَمُودَ ﴿٦٨﴾

69. Our Messengers came to Abraham with glad news. They said, "Peace be with you." He replied similarly. After a short time he presented them with roasted (meat of a) calf,

69. Wa laqad jaaa'at Rusulunaaa Ibraaheema bilbushraa qaaloo salaaman qaala salaamun famaa labisa an jaaa'a bi'ijlin ḥaneez.

وَلَقَدْ جَاءَتْ رُسُلُنَا إِبْرَاهِيمَ بِالْبُشْرَىٰ قَالُوا سَلَامًا ۖ قَالَ سَلَامٌ ۖ فَمَا لَبِثَ أَنْ جَاءَ بِعِجْلٍ حَنِيذٍ ﴿٦٩﴾

70. but when he saw that their hands did not reach out for it, he could not know who they were and became afraid of them. They said, "Do not be afraid; we are Allah's angelic Messengers sent to the people of Lot."

70. Falammaa ra-aaa aydiyahum laa taṣilu ilayhi nakirahum wa-awjasa minhum kheefah; qaaloo laa takhaf innaaa ursilnaaa ilaa qawmi Looṭ.

فَلَمَّا رَأَىٰ أَيْدِيَهُمْ لَا تَصِلُ إِلَيْهِ نَكِرَهُمْ وَأَوْجَسَ مِنْهُمْ خِيفَةً ۚ قَالُوا لَا تَخَفْ إِنَّا أُرْسِلْنَا إِلَىٰ قَوْمِ لُوطٍ ﴿٧٠﴾

71. His wife, who was standing nearby, laughed (due to suddenly experiencing menstruation). So We gave her the glad news that she would give birth to Isaac who would have a son, Jacob.

71. Wamra-atuhoo qaaa'imatun faḍaḥikat fabashsharnaahaa bi-Isḥaaq; wa miñw-waraaa'i Isḥaaqa Ya'qoob.

وَامْرَأَتُهُ قَائِمَةٌ فَضَحِكَتْ فَبَشَّرْنَاهَا بِإِسْحَاقَ وَمِنْ وَرَاءِ إِسْحَاقَ يَعْقُوبَ ﴿٧١﴾

72. She said, "Woe is me! How can I have a baby when I am so elderly and my husband is very old? This certainly is very strange."

72. Qaalat yaa waylataaa 'a-alidu wa ana 'ajoozuñw-wa haazaa ba'lee shaykhaa; inna haazaa lashay'un 'ajeeb.

قَالَتْ يَا وَيْلَتَىٰ أَأَلِدُ وَأَنَا عَجُوزٌ وَهَٰذَا بَعْلِي شَيْخًا ۖ إِنَّ هَٰذَا لَشَيْءٌ عَجِيبٌ ﴿٧٢﴾

73. They replied, "Would you be surprised at Allah's decree? People

73. Qaalooo ata'jabeena min amril-laahi raḥmatul-

قَالُوا أَتَعْجَبِينَ مِنْ أَمْرِ اللَّهِ رَحْمَتُ

of the house, may Allah's mercy and blessings be with you. Allah is Appreciative and Glorious."

74. When Abraham had controlled his fear and received the glad news, he started to plead with Us for the people of Lot;

75. Abraham was certainly a forbearing, compassionate, and tender-hearted person.

76. We said, "Abraham, avoid asking Us such questions. Your Lord's decree has already been issued and an inevitable torment will strike these people."

77. When Our Messengers came to Lot, he became sorrowful and felt totally helpless. He said, "This is indeed a distressful day."

78. His people, who had constantly indulged in evil deeds, came running to him. He said, "My people, here are my pure daughters (meaning the women of his people). Have fear of Allah and do not humiliate me before my guests. Is there no person of understanding among you?"

79. They said, "You certainly know that we have no right to your daughters and you know what we want."

81. He said, "Would that I had the power (to overcome you) or could seek strong protection."

81. Our Messengers said, "Lot, we are the Messengers of your Lord. They will never harm you. Leave the town with your family in the darkness of night and do not let any of you turn back. As for your wife, she will suffer what they (unbelievers) will suffer. Their appointed time will come at

laahi wa barakaatuhoo 'alaykum Ahlal-Bayt; innahoo Ḥameedum-Majeed.

74. Falammaa z̲ahaba 'an Ibraaheemar-raw'u wa jaaa'at-hul-bushraa yujaadilunaa fee qawmi Looṭ.

75. Inna Ibraaheema laḥaleemun awwaahum-muneeb.

76. Yaaa Ibraaheemu a'riḍ 'an haaz̲aaa innahoo qad jaaa'a amru Rabbika wa innahum aateehim 'az̲aabun ghayru mardood.

77. Wa lammaa jaaa'at Rusulunaa Looṭan seee'a bihim wa ḍaaqa bihim z̲ar'añw-wa qaala haaz̲aa yawmun 'aṣeeb.

78. Wa jaaa'ahoo qawmuhoo yuhra'oona ilayhi wa min qablu kaanoo ya'maloonas-sayyi-aat; qaala yaa qawmi haaa'ulaaa'i banaatee hunna aṭharu lakum fattaqul-laaha wa laa tukhzooni fee ḍayfeee alaysa minkum rajulur-rasheed.

79. Qaaloo laqad 'alimta maa lanaa fee banaatika min ḥaqq; wa innaka lata'lamu maa nureed.

80. Qaala law anna lee bikum quwwatan aw aaweee ilaa ruknin shadeed.

81. Qaaloo yaa Looṭu innaa Rusulu Rabbika lañy-yaṣilooo ilayka fa-asri bi-ahlika biqiṭ'im-minal-layli wa laa yaltafit minkum aḥadun illamra-ataka innahoo muṣeebuhaa maaa aṣaabahum; inna maw'idahumuṣṣubḥ;

اللّٰهِ وَبَرَكٰتُهٗ عَلَيْكُمْ اَهْلَ الْبَيْتِ ؕ
اِنَّهٗ حَمِيْدٌ مَّجِيْدٌ ﴿٧٣﴾
فَلَمَّا ذَهَبَ عَنْ اِبْرٰهِيْمَ الرَّوْعُ
وَجَآءَتْهُ الْبُشْرٰى يُجَادِلُنَا
فِيْ قَوْمِ لُوْطٍ ﴿٧٤﴾
اِنَّ اِبْرٰهِيْمَ لَحَلِيْمٌ اَوَّاهٌ مُّنِيْبٌ ﴿٧٥﴾
يٰۤاِبْرٰهِيْمُ اَعْرِضْ عَنْ هٰذَا ۚ اِنَّهٗ
قَدْ جَآءَ اَمْرُ رَبِّكَ ۚ وَاِنَّهُمْ اٰتِيْهِمْ
عَذَابٌ غَيْرُ مَرْدُوْدٍ ﴿٧٦﴾
وَلَمَّا جَآءَتْ رُسُلُنَا لُوْطًا سِيْٓءَ
بِهِمْ وَضَاقَ بِهِمْ ذَرْعًا وَّقَالَ
هٰذَا يَوْمٌ عَصِيْبٌ ﴿٧٧﴾
وَجَآءَهٗ قَوْمُهٗ يُهْرَعُوْنَ اِلَيْهِ ؕ
وَمِنْ قَبْلُ كَانُوْا يَعْمَلُوْنَ السَّيِّاٰتِ ؕ
قَالَ يٰقَوْمِ هٰٓؤُلَآءِ بَنَاتِيْ هُنَّ اَطْهَرُ
لَكُمْ فَاتَّقُوا اللّٰهَ وَلَا تُخْزُوْنِ فِيْ
ضَيْفِيْ ؕ اَلَيْسَ مِنْكُمْ رَجُلٌ رَّشِيْدٌ ﴿٧٨﴾
قَالُوْا لَقَدْ عَلِمْتَ مَا لَنَا فِيْ بَنٰتِكَ
مِنْ حَقٍّ ۚ وَاِنَّكَ لَتَعْلَمُ مَا نُرِيْدُ ﴿٧٩﴾
قَالَ لَوْ اَنَّ لِيْ بِكُمْ قُوَّةً اَوْ اٰوِيْٓ
اِلٰى رُكْنٍ شَدِيْدٍ ﴿٨٠﴾
قَالُوْا يٰلُوْطُ اِنَّا رُسُلُ رَبِّكَ لَنْ
يَّصِلُوْٓا اِلَيْكَ فَاَسْرِ بِاَهْلِكَ بِقِطْعٍ
مِّنَ الَّيْلِ وَلَا يَلْتَفِتْ مِنْكُمْ اَحَدٌ
اِلَّا امْرَاَتَكَ ؕ اِنَّهٗ مُصِيْبُهَا مَآ
اَصَابَهُمْ ؕ اِنَّ مَوْعِدَهُمُ الصُّبْحُ ؕ

dawn. Surely dawn is not far away!

82. When Our decree came to pass, We turned the town upside-down and showered unto it lumps of baked clay,

83. marked by your Lord. Such a punishment is not far away from the unjust people.

84. To the people of Madyan We sent their brother Shuayb, who told them, "My people, worship Allah; He is your only Lord. Do not be dishonest in your weighing and measuring. I can see you are safe and prosperous, but I am afraid for you of the overwhelming torment of the (appointed) day.

85. My people, be just in your weighing and measuring. Do not defraud people or spread evil in the land.

86. If you are true believers then know that the profit which Allah has left for you is better for you (than what you may gain through deceitful ways). I am not responsible for your deeds."

87. They asked him, "Shuayb, do your prayers tell you that we must give up the worship of what our fathers had worshipped and that we must not deal with our properties as we like? We still believe that you are a person of forbearance and understanding."

88. He said, "My people, do you not realize that I have received authoritative evidence from my Lord and have been granted a noble gift from Him? I do not want to oppose or ignore what I have prohibited you not to do. I only intend to reform you as much as I can. My success is in the hands of Allah. I trust Him and

alaysaṣ-ṣubḥu biqareeb.

82. Falammaa jaaa'a amrunaa ja'alnaa 'aaliyahaa saafilahaa wa amṭarnaa 'alayhaa ḥijaara-tam-min sijjeelim-manḍood.

83. Musawwamatan 'inda Rabbik; wa maa hiya minaẓ-zaalimeena bi ba'eed.

84. Wa ilaa Madyana akhaa-hum Shu'aybaa; qaala yaa qawmi'-budul-laaha maa lakum min Ilaahin ghayruhoo wa laa tanquṣul-mikyaala walmeezaan; inneee araakum bikhayriñw-wa inneee akhaafu 'alaykum 'azaaba Yawmim-muḥeeṭ.

85. Wa yaa qawmi awful-mikyaala walmeezaana bilqisṭi wa laa tabkhasunnaasa ashy-aaa'ahum wa laa ta'saw fil-arḍi mufsideen.

86. Baqiyyatul-laahi khayrul-lakum in kuntum-mu'mineen; wa maa ana 'alaykum biḥafeeẓ.

87. Qaaloo yaa Shu'aybu aṣalaatuka ta-muruka an nat-ruka maa ya'budu aabaaa'unaaa aw an naf'ala feee amwaalinaa maa nashaaa'oo innaka la-antal ḥaleemur-rasheed.

88. Qaala yaa qawmi ara'ay-tum in kuntu 'alaa bayyinatim-mir-Rabbee wa razaqanee minhu rizqan ḥasanaa; wa maaa ureedu an ukhaalifakum ilaa maaa anhaakum 'anh; in ureedu illal-iṣlaaḥa mastaṭa't; wa maa tawfeeqeee illaa billaah; 'alayhi tawakkaltu

اَلَيْسَ الصُّبْحُ بِقَرِيْبٍ ﴿٨١﴾
فَلَمَّا جَآءَ اَمْرُنَا جَعَلْنَا عَالِيَهَا
سَافِلَهَا وَاَمْطَرْنَا عَلَيْهَا حِجَارَةً
مِّنْ سِجِّيْلٍ ۙ مَّنْضُوْدٍ ﴿٨٢﴾
مُّسَوَّمَةً عِنْدَ رَبِّكَ ؕ وَمَا هِيَ
مِنَ الظّٰلِمِيْنَ بِبَعِيْدٍ ﴿٨٣﴾ ع ٣ ١٥
وَاِلٰى مَدْيَنَ اَخَاهُمْ شُعَيْبًا ؕ قَالَ
يٰقَوْمِ اعْبُدُوا اللّٰهَ مَا لَكُمْ مِّنْ
اِلٰهٍ غَيْرُهٗ ؕ وَلَا تَنْقُصُوا الْمِكْيَالَ
وَالْمِيْزَانَ اِنِّىْۤ اَرٰىكُمْ بِخَيْرٍ وَّاِنِّىْۤ اَخَافُ
عَلَيْكُمْ عَذَابَ يَوْمٍ مُّحِيْطٍ ﴿٨٤﴾
وَيٰقَوْمِ اَوْفُوا الْمِكْيَالَ وَالْمِيْزَانَ
بِالْقِسْطِ وَلَا تَبْخَسُوا النَّاسَ اَشْيَآءَهُمْ
وَلَا تَعْثَوْا فِى الْاَرْضِ مُفْسِدِيْنَ ﴿٨٥﴾
بَقِيَّتُ اللّٰهِ خَيْرٌ لَّكُمْ اِنْ كُنْتُمْ
مُّؤْمِنِيْنَ ۚ وَمَاۤ اَنَا عَلَيْكُمْ بِحَفِيْظٍ ﴿٨٦﴾
قَالُوْا يٰشُعَيْبُ اَصَلٰوتُكَ تَاْمُرُكَ اَنْ
نَّتْرُكَ مَا يَعْبُدُ اٰبَآؤُنَاۤ اَوْ اَنْ
نَّفْعَلَ فِىْۤ اَمْوَالِنَا مَا نَشٰٓؤُا ؕ اِنَّكَ
لَاَنْتَ الْحَلِيْمُ الرَّشِيْدُ ﴿٨٧﴾
قَالَ يٰقَوْمِ اَرَءَيْتُمْ اِنْ كُنْتُ عَلٰى
بَيِّنَةٍ مِّنْ رَّبِّىْ وَرَزَقَنِىْ مِنْهُ
رِزْقًا حَسَنًا ؕ وَمَاۤ اُرِيْدُ اَنْ اُخَالِفَكُمْ
اِلٰى مَاۤ اَنْهٰىكُمْ عَنْهُ ؕ اِنْ اُرِيْدُ اِلَّا
الْاِصْلَاحَ مَا اسْتَطَعْتُ ؕ وَمَا
تَوْفِيْقِىْۤ اِلَّا بِاللّٰهِ ؕ عَلَيْهِ تَوَكَّلْتُ

turn to Him in repentance.

wa ilayhi uneeb.

وَإِلَيْهِ أُنِيبُ ﴿٨٨﴾

89. My people, do not let your opposition to me lead you to commit sins or make you suffer what the people of Noah, Hud, and Salih suffered. Remember that the people of Lot were destroyed not very long ago.

89. Wa yaa qawmi laa yajri-mannakum shiqaaqeee añy-yuṣeebakum-mislu maaa aṣaaba qawma Nooḥin aw qawma Hoodin aw qawma Ṣaaliḥ; wa maa qawmu Looṭim-minkum biba'eed.

وَيٰقَوْمِ لَا يَجْرِمَنَّكُمْ شِقَاقِيٓ أَنْ
يُّصِيبَكُمْ مِّثْلُ مَآ أَصَابَ قَوْمَ نُوحٍ
أَوْ قَوْمَ هُودٍ أَوْ قَوْمَ صٰلِحٍ ۚ وَمَا
قَوْمُ لُوطٍ مِّنْكُمْ بِبَعِيدٍ ﴿٨٩﴾

90. Seek forgiveness from your Lord and turn to Him in repentance. My Lord is certainly All-merciful and Loving."

90. Wastaghfiroo Rabbakum summa toobooo ilayh; inna Rabbee Raheemuñw-Wadood.

وَاسْتَغْفِرُوا رَبَّكُمْ ثُمَّ تُوبُوٓا إِلَيْهِ ۚ
إِنَّ رَبِّي رَحِيمٌ وَّدُودٌ ﴿٩٠﴾

91. They said, "Shuayb, we do not understand much of what you say, but we know that you are weak among us. Had it not been for our respect of your tribe, we would have stoned you to death; you are not dear to us at all."

91. Qaaloo yaa Shu'aybu maa nafqahu kaseeram-mimmaa taqoolu wa innaa lanaraaka feenaa ḍa'eefaa; wa law laa rahṭuka larajamnaaka wa maaa anta 'alaynaa bi'azeez.

قَالُوا يٰشُعَيْبُ مَا نَفْقَهُ كَثِيرًا مِّمَّا
تَقُولُ وَإِنَّا لَنَرٰىكَ فِينَا ضَعِيفًا ۖ
وَلَوْلَا رَهْطُكَ لَرَجَمْنٰكَ ۖ وَمَآ أَنْتَ
عَلَيْنَا بِعَزِيزٍ ﴿٩١﴾

92. He asked them, "My people, is my tribe more respectable to you than Allah, whom you have completely ignored? My Lord certainly has full control over your deeds.

92. Qaala yaa qawmi arahṭeee a'azzu 'alaykum-minal-laahi wattakhaztumoohu waraaa'a-kum ẓihriyyan inna Rabbee bimaa ta'maloona muḥeet.

قَالَ يٰقَوْمِ أَرَهْطِيٓ أَعَزُّ عَلَيْكُمْ مِّنَ
اللّٰهِ ۖ وَاتَّخَذْتُمُوهُ وَرَآءَكُمْ ظِهْرِيًّا ۖ
إِنَّ رَبِّي بِمَا تَعْمَلُونَ مُحِيطٌ ﴿٩٢﴾

93. My people, do as you wish and I will do (as I believe). You will soon know who will suffer a humiliating torment and who was the one telling lies. Wait and I am also waiting with you."

93. Wa yaa qawmi'-maloo 'alaa makaanatikum innee 'aamilun sawfa ta'lamoona mañy-ya-teehi 'azaabuñy-yukh-zeehi wa man huwa kaazib; wartaqibooo innee ma'akum raqeeb.

وَيٰقَوْمِ اعْمَلُوا عَلٰى مَكَانَتِكُمْ إِنِّي
عَامِلٌ ۖ سَوْفَ تَعْلَمُونَ مَنْ يَأْتِيهِ
عَذَابٌ يُّخْزِيهِ وَمَنْ هُوَ كَاذِبٌ ۖ
وَارْتَقِبُوٓا إِنِّي مَعَكُمْ رَقِيبٌ ﴿٩٣﴾

94. When Our decree came to pass, We mercifully saved Shuayb and his faithful followers. A blast struck the unjust and left them in their homes, lying motionless on their faces,

94. Wa lammaa jaaa'a amru-naa najjaynaa Shu'aybañw-wal-lazeena aamanoo ma'ahoo biraḥmatim-minnaa wa akha-zatil-lazeena ẓalamuṣ-ṣayḥatu fa-aṣbaḥoo fee diyaarihim jaasimeen.

وَلَمَّا جَآءَ أَمْرُنَا نَجَّيْنَا شُعَيْبًا وَّ
الَّذِينَ آمَنُوا مَعَهُ بِرَحْمَةٍ مِّنَّا
وَأَخَذَتِ الَّذِينَ ظَلَمُوا الصَّيْحَةُ
فَأَصْبَحُوا فِي دِيَارِهِمْ جٰثِمِينَ ﴿٩٤﴾

95. as though they had never existed. How far (from the mercy of Allah) had the people of Madyan gone, just like those of Thamud?

95. Ka-al-lam yaghnaw fee-haaa; alaa bu'dal-li-Madyana kamaa ba'idat Samood.

كَأَنْ لَّمْ يَغْنَوْا فِيهَا ۗ أَلَا بُعْدًا
لِّمَدْيَنَ كَمَا بَعِدَتْ ثَمُودُ ﴿٩٥﴾ ع ٨

96. We sent Moses to the Pharaoh and his nobles with Our miracles and a clear authority.

96. Wa laqad arsalnaa Moosaa bi-Aayaatinaa wa sulṭaanim-mubeen.

وَلَقَدْ أَرْسَلْنَا مُوسٰى بِآيٰتِنَا
وَسُلْطٰنٍ مُّبِينٍ ﴿٩٦﴾

97. They followed the order of the Pharaoh but Pharaoh's orders were evil.	97. Ilaa Fir'awna wa mala'i-hee fattaba'ooo amra Fir'awna wa maaa amru Fir'awna birasheed.	إِلَىٰ فِرْعَوْنَ وَمَلَإِيْهِۦ فَاتَّبَعُوٓا أَمْرَ فِرْعَوْنَ ۖ وَمَآ أَمْرُ فِرْعَوْنَ بِرَشِيدٍ ﴿٩٧﴾
98. On the Day of Judgment he will lead his people down into the hellfire. His leadership is evil and terrible is the place to which he leads!	98. Yaqdumu qawmahoo Yawmal-Qiyaamati fa-awrada-humun-Naara wa bi'sal-wirdul-mawrood.	يَقْدُمُ قَوْمَهُۥ يَوْمَ الْقِيٰمَةِ فَأَوْرَدَهُمُ النَّارَ ۖ وَبِئْسَ الْوِرْدُ الْمَوْرُودُ ﴿٩٨﴾
99. They are condemned in this world and in the life to come. How evil is the gift and the recipient!	99. Wa utbi'oo fee haa<u>z</u>ihee la'natañw-wa Yawmal-Qiyaa-mah; bi'sar- rifdulmarfood.	وَأُتْبِعُوا فِي هٰذِهِۦ لَعْنَةً وَيَوْمَ الْقِيٰمَةِ ۚ بِئْسَ الرِّفْدُ الْمَرْفُودُ ﴿٩٩﴾
100. Such were the stories of the nations of the past which We tell to you, (Muhammad). Certain ones among them were destroyed and others have survived.	100. <u>Z</u>aalika min ambaaa'il-quraa naquṣṣuhoo 'alayka minhaa qaaa'imuñw-wa ḥaṣeed.	ذٰلِكَ مِنْ أَنۢبَآءِ الْقُرَىٰ نَقُصُّهُۥ عَلَيْكَ ۖ مِنْهَا قَآئِمٌ وَحَصِيدٌ ﴿١٠٠﴾
101. We were not unjust to them but they were unjust to themselves. The idols which they worshipped instead of Allah were of no help to them when the decree of your Lord came to pass. The idols only brought about their destruction.	101. Wa maa ẓalamnaahum wa laakin ẓalamooo anfusahum famaaa aghnat 'anhum aalihatuhumul-latee yad'oona min doonil-laahi min shay'il-lammaa jaaa'a amru Rabbik; wa maa zaadoohum ghayra tatbeeb.	وَمَا ظَلَمْنٰهُمْ وَلٰكِن ظَلَمُوٓا أَنفُسَهُمْ ۖ فَمَآ أَغْنَتْ عَنْهُمْ ءَالِهَتُهُمُ الَّتِي يَدْعُونَ مِن دُونِ اللَّهِ مِن شَيْءٍ لَّمَّا جَآءَ أَمْرُ رَبِّكَ ۖ وَمَا زَادُوهُمْ غَيْرَ تَتْبِيبٍ ﴿١٠١﴾
102. Thus was the punishment of your Lord when He punished the unjust people of the towns. The punishment of your Lord is certainly severe.	102. Wa ka<u>z</u>aalika akh<u>z</u>u Rab-bika i<u>z</u>aaa akha<u>z</u>al-quraa wa hiya ẓaalimah; inna akh<u>z</u>ahooo aleemun shadeed.	وَكَذٰلِكَ أَخْذُ رَبِّكَ إِذَآ أَخَذَ الْقُرَىٰ وَهِيَ ظٰلِمَةٌ ۚ إِنَّ أَخْذَهُۥٓ أَلِيمٌ شَدِيدٌ ﴿١٠٢﴾
103. In this there is, certainly, a lesson for those who fear the torment of the day in which all people will be gathered together; a day that is witnessed.	103. Inna fee <u>z</u>aalika la Aaya-tal-liman khaafa 'a<u>z</u>aabal-Aakhirah; <u>z</u>aalika Yawmum-majmoo'ul-lahunnaasu wa <u>z</u>aalika Yawmum-mashhood.	إِنَّ فِي ذٰلِكَ لَءَايَةً لِّمَنْ خَافَ عَذَابَ الْءَاخِرَةِ ۚ ذٰلِكَ يَوْمٌ مَّجْمُوعٌ لَّهُ النَّاسُ وَذٰلِكَ يَوْمٌ مَّشْهُودٌ ﴿١٠٣﴾
104. We have deferred this day for an appointed time.	104. Wa maa nu'akhkhiru-hooo illaa li-ajalim-ma'dood.	وَمَا نُؤَخِّرُهُۥٓ إِلَّا لِأَجَلٍ مَّعْدُودٍ ﴿١٠٤﴾
105. On the Day of Judgment no one will speak without the permission of Allah. Some will be condemned and others blessed.	105. Yawma ya-ti laa takallamu nafsun illaa bi-i<u>z</u>nih; faminhum shaqiyyuñw-wa sa'eed.	يَوْمَ يَأْتِ لَا تَكَلَّمُ نَفْسٌ إِلَّا بِإِذْنِهِۦ ۚ فَمِنْهُمْ شَقِيٌّ وَسَعِيدٌ ﴿١٠٥﴾
106. The condemned ones will live in hellfire, sighing and groaning	106. Fa-ammal-la<u>z</u>eena shaqoo fafin-Naari lahum feehaa zafeeruñw-wa shaheeq.	فَأَمَّا الَّذِينَ شَقُوا فَفِي النَّارِ لَهُمْ فِيهَا زَفِيرٌ وَشَهِيقٌ ﴿١٠٦﴾
107. for as long as the heavens and the earth exist, unless your Lord decides otherwise. Your	107. Khaalideena feehaa maa daamatis-samaawaatu wal-arḍu illaa maa shaaa'a Rabbuk; inna	خٰلِدِينَ فِيهَا مَا دَامَتِ السَّمٰوٰتُ وَالْأَرْضُ إِلَّا مَا شَآءَ رَبُّكَ ۚ إِنَّ

Lord will certainly accomplish whatever He wants.

Rabbaka fa''aalul-limaa yureed.

رَبَّكَ فَعَّالٌ لِّمَا يُرِيْدُ ﴿١٠٧﴾

108. The blessed ones will live in Paradise as long as the heavens and the earth exist, unless your Lord decides to grant endless rewards to whoever He wants.

108. Wa ammal-lazeena su'i-doo fafil-jannati-khaalideena feehaa maa daamatis-samaawaatu wal-arḍu illaa maa shaaa'a Rabbuk; 'aṭaaa'an ghayra majzooz.

وَاَمَّا الَّذِيْنَ سُعِدُوْا فَفِي الْجَنَّةِ
خٰلِدِيْنَ فِيْهَا مَا دَامَتِ السَّمٰوٰتُ
وَالْاَرْضُ اِلَّا مَا شَآءَ رَبُّكَ ؕ عَطَآءً
غَيْرَ مَجْذُوْذٍ ﴿١٠٨﴾

109. Have no doubt that these people worship (idols). They worship what their fathers had worshipped before them. We will give them the exact recompense that they deserve.

109. Falaa taku fee miryatim-mimmaa ya'budu haaa'ulaaa' maa ya'budoona illaa kamaa ya'budu aabaaa'uhum-min qabl; wa innaa lamuwaf-foohum naṣeebahum ghayra manqooṣ.

فَلَا تَكُ فِيْ مِرْيَةٍ مِّمَّا يَعْبُدُ هٰٓؤُلَآءِ ؕ
مَا يَعْبُدُوْنَ اِلَّا كَمَا يَعْبُدُ اٰبَآؤُهُمْ
مِّنْ قَبْلُ ؕ وَاِنَّا لَمُوَفُّوْهُمْ نَصِيْبَهُمْ
غَيْرَ مَنْقُوْصٍ ﴿١٠٩﴾ ع ۱۴

110. We gave the Book to Moses but people had different views about it. Had the Word of your Lord not been already ordained, He would have settled their differences (there and then). They are still in doubt about this.

110. Wa laqad aataynaa Moo-sal-Kitaaba fakhtulifa feeh; wa law laa Kalimatun sabaqat mir-Rabbika laquḍiya baynahum; wa innahum lafee shakkim-minhu mureeb.

وَلَقَدْ اٰتَيْنَا مُوْسَى الْكِتٰبَ فَاخْتُلِفَ
فِيْهِ ؕ وَلَوْلَا كَلِمَةٌ سَبَقَتْ مِنْ
رَّبِّكَ لَقُضِيَ بَيْنَهُمْ ؕ وَاِنَّهُمْ لَفِيْ
شَكٍّ مِّنْهُ مُرِيْبٍ ﴿١١٠﴾

111. Allah will certainly recompense everyone according to their deeds; He knows well all that you do.

111. Wa inna kullal-lammaa layuwaffiyannahum Rabbuka a'maalahum; innahoo bimaa ya'maloona Khabeer.

وَاِنَّ كُلًّا لَّمَّا لَيُوَفِّيَنَّهُمْ رَبُّكَ
اَعْمَالَهُمْ ؕ اِنَّهٗ بِمَا يَعْمَلُوْنَ خَبِيْرٌ ﴿١١١﴾

112. (Muhammad), be steadfast (in your faith) just as you have been commanded. Those who have turned to Allah in repentance with you, should also be steadfast in their faith. Do not indulge in rebellion. Allah is certainly aware of what you do.

112. Fastaqim kamaaa umirta wa man taaba ma'aka wa laa taṭghaw; innahoo bimaa ta'maloona Baṣeer.

فَاسْتَقِمْ كَمَآ اُمِرْتَ وَمَنْ تَابَ
مَعَكَ وَلَا تَطْغَوْا ؕ اِنَّهٗ بِمَا
تَعْمَلُوْنَ بَصِيْرٌ ﴿١١٢﴾

113. Do not be inclined towards the unjust ones lest you will be afflicted by the hellfire. Besides Allah, no one can be your protector nor will anyone be able to help you.

113. Wa laa tarkanooo ilal-lazeena ẓalamoo fatamassa-kumun-Naaru wa maa lakum-min doonil-laahi min awli-yaaa'a summa laa tunṣaroon.

وَلَا تَرْكَنُوْٓا اِلَى الَّذِيْنَ ظَلَمُوْا
فَتَمَسَّكُمُ النَّارُ ۙ وَمَا لَكُمْ مِّنْ دُوْنِ
اللّٰهِ مِنْ اَوْلِيَآءَ ثُمَّ لَا تُنْصَرُوْنَ ﴿١١٣﴾

114. Say your prayers in the morning, the last portion of the day, and at the beginning of the night. Good deeds do away with the bad deeds. This is a reminder for those who take heed.

114. Wa aqimiṣ-Ṣalaata ṭara-fayin-nahaari wa zulafam-minal-layl; innal-ḥasanaati yuzhibnas-sayyi-aat; zaalika zikraa liz zaakireen.

وَاَقِمِ الصَّلٰوةَ طَرَفَيِ النَّهَارِ وَزُلَفًا
مِّنَ الَّيْلِ ؕ اِنَّ الْحَسَنٰتِ يُذْهِبْنَ
السَّيِّاٰتِ ؕ ذٰلِكَ ذِكْرٰى لِلذّٰكِرِيْنَ ﴿١١٤﴾

115. Exercise patience; Allah does not ignore the reward of those who do good.

115. Waṣbir fa-innal-laaha laa yuḍee'u ajral-muḥsineen.

وَاصْبِرْ فَاِنَّ اللّٰهَ لَا يُضِيْعُ اَجْرَ
الْمُحْسِنِيْنَ ﴿١١٥﴾

116. Why were there no people of understanding among those people of the destroyed towns of the past except for a few, whom we saved from destruction, to prevent people from committing evil in the land? The unjust among them indulged in worldly pleasures and so became guilty.

117. Your Lord would not have destroyed those people (of the towns) for their injustice if they had tried to reform themselves.

118. Had your Lord wanted, He would have made all people one united nation. They still have different beliefs

119. except those upon whom your Lord has granted His mercy. He (Allah) has created them to receive mercy. The decree of your Lord that He will fill hell with both Jinn and human beings has already been ordained.

120. (Muhammad), We tell you all the stories of the Messengers which will strengthen your heart. In the Quran We have revealed the Truth to you with good advice and reminders for the faithful ones.

121. Say to the unbelievers, "Do as you wish and I will do as I believe.

122. Wait, and I will also be waiting with you."

123. To Allah belongs the knowledge of the unseen in the heavens and the earth and to Him do all affairs return. Worship Him and trust Him. Your Lord is not unaware of what you do.

116. Falaw laa kaana minal-qurooni min qablikum ooloo baqiyyatiny-yanhawna 'anil-fasaadi fil-arḍi illaa qaleelam-mimman anjaynaa minhum; wattaba'al-laẕeena ẓalamoo maaa utrifoo feehi wa kaanoo mujrimeen.

117. Wa maa kaana Rabbuka liyuhlikal-quraa biẓulmiñw-wa ahluhaa musliḥoon.

118. Wa law shaaa'a Rabbuka laja'alannaasa ummatañw-waa-ḥidatañw-wa laa yazaaloona mukhtalifeen.

119. Illaa mar-raḥima Rabbuk; wa liẕaalika khalaqahum; wa tammat Kalimatu Rabbika la-amla'anna Jahannama minal-jinnati wannaasi ajma'een.

120. Wa kullan-naquṣṣu 'alay-ka min ambaaa'ir-Rusuli maa nuṣabbitu bihee fu'aadak; wa jaaa'aka fee haaẕihil-ḥaqqu wa maw'iẕatuñw-wa ẕikraa lilmu'-mineen.

121. Wa qul lillaẕeena laa yu'minoona'-maloo 'alaa ma-kaanatikum innaa 'aamiloon.

122. Wantaẓiroo innaa mun-taẓiroon.

123. Wa lillaahi ghaybus-samaawaati wal-arḍi wa ilayhi yurja'ul-amru kulluhoo fa'budhu wa tawakkal 'alayh; wa maa Rabbuka bighaafilin 'ammaa ta'maloon.

فَلَوْلَا كَانَ مِنَ الْقُرُوْنِ مِنْ قَبْلِكُمْ أُولُوْا بَقِيَّةٍ يَّنْهَوْنَ عَنِ الْفَسَادِ فِي الْأَرْضِ إِلَّا قَلِيْلًا مِّمَّنْ أَنْجَيْنَا مِنْهُمْ ۚ وَاتَّبَعَ الَّذِيْنَ ظَلَمُوْا مَاۤ أُتْرِفُوْا فِيْهِ وَكَانُوْا مُجْرِمِيْنَ ۝

وَمَا كَانَ رَبُّكَ لِيُهْلِكَ الْقُرٰى بِظُلْمٍ وَّأَهْلُهَا مُصْلِحُوْنَ ۝

وَلَوْ شَاۤءَ رَبُّكَ لَجَعَلَ النَّاسَ أُمَّةً وَّاحِدَةً وَّلَا يَزَالُوْنَ مُخْتَلِفِيْنَ ۝

إِلَّا مَنْ رَّحِمَ رَبُّكَ ۚ وَلِذٰلِكَ خَلَقَهُمْ ۗ وَتَمَّتْ كَلِمَةُ رَبِّكَ لَأَمْلَأَنَّ جَهَنَّمَ مِنَ الْجِنَّةِ وَالنَّاسِ أَجْمَعِيْنَ ۝

وَكُلًّا نَّقُصُّ عَلَيْكَ مِنْ أَنْبَاۤءِ الرُّسُلِ مَا نُثَبِّتُ بِهٖ فُؤَادَكَ ۚ وَجَاۤءَكَ فِيْ هٰذِهِ الْحَقُّ وَمَوْعِظَةٌ وَّذِكْرٰى لِلْمُؤْمِنِيْنَ ۝

وَقُلْ لِّلَّذِيْنَ لَا يُؤْمِنُوْنَ اعْمَلُوْا عَلٰى مَكَانَتِكُمْ إِنَّا عٰمِلُوْنَ ۝

وَانْتَظِرُوْا إِنَّا مُنْتَظِرُوْنَ ۝

وَلِلّٰهِ غَيْبُ السَّمٰوٰتِ وَالْأَرْضِ وَإِلَيْهِ يُرْجَعُ الْأَمْرُ كُلُّهٗ فَاعْبُدْهُ وَتَوَكَّلْ عَلَيْهِ ۚ وَمَا رَبُّكَ بِغَافِلٍ عَمَّا تَعْمَلُوْنَ ۝

Yusuf, Joseph (12)

In the Name of Allah,
the Beneficent, the Merciful.

1. Alif. Lam. Ra. These are the verses of the illustrious Book.

Sûrat Yûsuf-12

(Revealed at Makkah)

Bismillaahir Raḥmaanir Raḥeem

1. Alif-Laaam-Raa; tilka Aayaatul-Kitaabil-Mubeen.

(١٢) سُوْرَةُ يُوْسُفَ مَكِّيَّةٌ (٥٣)

بِسْمِ اللّٰهِ الرَّحْمٰنِ الرَّحِيْمِ

الٓرٰ ۚ تِلْكَ اٰيٰتُ الْكِتٰبِ الْمُبِيْنِ ۝

2. We have revealed it in the Arabic language so that you (people) would understand it.

2. Innaaa anzalnaahu Qur'aanan 'Arabiyyal-la'allakum ta'qiloon.

إِنَّآ أَنزَلۡنَٰهُ قُرۡءَٰنًا عَرَبِيًّا
لَّعَلَّكُمۡ تَعۡقِلُونَ ۝٢

3. In revealing this Quran to you, We tell you the best of the stories of which you were unaware.

3. Naḥnu naquṣṣu 'alayka aḥsanal-qaṣaṣi bimaaa awḥaynaaa ilayka haazal-Qur'aana wa in kunta min qablihee laminal-ghaafileen.

نَحۡنُ نَقُصُّ عَلَيۡكَ أَحۡسَنَ ٱلۡقَصَصِ
بِمَآ أَوۡحَيۡنَآ إِلَيۡكَ هَٰذَا ٱلۡقُرۡءَانَ
وَإِن كُنتَ مِن قَبۡلِهِۦ لَمِنَ ٱلۡغَٰفِلِينَ ۝٣

4. When Joseph said, "Father, in my dream I saw eleven stars, the sun, and the moon prostrating before me,"

4. Iz qaala Yoosufu li-abeehi yaaa abati innee ra-aytu aḥada 'ashara kawkabañw-wash-shamsa walqamara ra-aytuhum lee saajideen.

إِذۡ قَالَ يُوسُفُ لِأَبِيهِ يَٰٓأَبَتِ إِنِّي
رَأَيۡتُ أَحَدَ عَشَرَ كَوۡكَبٗا وَٱلشَّمۡسَ
وَٱلۡقَمَرَ رَأَيۡتُهُمۡ لِي سَٰجِدِينَ ۝٤

5. his father said, "My son, do not tell your dream to your brothers lest they plot against you; Satan is the sworn enemy of man.

5. Qaala yaa bunayya laa taqṣuṣ ru'yaaka 'alaaa ikhwatika fayakeedoo laka kaydaa; innash-Shayṭaana lil-insaani 'aduwwum-mubeen.

قَالَ يَٰبُنَيَّ لَا تَقۡصُصۡ رُءۡيَاكَ
عَلَىٰٓ إِخۡوَتِكَ فَيَكِيدُواْ لَكَ كَيۡدًاۖ إِنَّ
ٱلشَّيۡطَٰنَ لِلۡإِنسَٰنِ عَدُوّٞ مُّبِينٞ ۝٥

6. Thus, your Lord will select you, teach you the interpretation of dreams, and grant His favors to you and the family of Jacob, just as He granted His favors to your forefathers, Abraham and Isaac. Your Lord is certainly All-knowing and All-wise."

6. Wa kazaalika yajtabeeka Rabbuka wa yu'allimuka min ta-weelil-aḥaadeesi wa yutimmu ni'matahoo 'alayka wa 'alaaa Aali Ya'qooba kamaaa atammahaa 'alaaa abawayka min qablu Ibraaheema wa Isḥaaq; inna Rabbaka 'Aleemun Ḥakeem.

وَكَذَٰلِكَ يَجۡتَبِيكَ رَبُّكَ وَيُعَلِّمُكَ
مِن تَأۡوِيلِ ٱلۡأَحَادِيثِ وَيُتِمُّ
نِعۡمَتَهُۥ عَلَيۡكَ وَعَلَىٰٓ ءَالِ يَعۡقُوبَ
كَمَآ أَتَمَّهَا عَلَىٰٓ أَبَوَيۡكَ مِن
قَبۡلُ إِبۡرَٰهِيمَ وَإِسۡحَٰقَۚ إِنَّ رَبَّكَ
عَلِيمٌ حَكِيمٞ ۝٦

7. In the story of Joseph and his brothers, there is evidence (of the truth) for those who seek to know.

7. Laqad kaana fee Yoosufa wa ikhwatiheee Aayaatul-lissaaa'ileen.

لَّقَدۡ كَانَ فِي يُوسُفَ وَإِخۡوَتِهِۦٓ
ءَايَٰتٞ لِّلسَّآئِلِينَ ۝٧

8. Joseph's brothers said to one another, "There is no doubt that Joseph and his brother are more loved by our father, even though we are all his offspring. He (our father) is certainly in manifest error."

8. Iz qaaloo la-Yoosufu wa akhoohu aḥabbu ilaaa abeenaa minnaa wa naḥnu 'uṣbah; inna abaanaa lafee ḍalaalim-mubeen.

إِذۡ قَالُواْ لَيُوسُفُ وَأَخُوهُ أَحَبُّ
إِلَىٰٓ أَبِينَا مِنَّا وَنَحۡنُ عُصۡبَةٌ
إِنَّ أَبَانَا لَفِي ضَلَٰلٖ مُّبِينٍ ۝٨

9. Certain ones among them suggested, "Let us kill Joseph or leave him somewhere far away from the presence of our father. Only then shall we receive equal treatment and thereafter become righteous people."

9. Uqtuloo Yoosufa awiṭraḥoohu arḍañy-yakhlu lakum wajhu abeekum wa takoonoo mim ba'dihee qawman ṣaaliḥeen.

ٱقۡتُلُواْ يُوسُفَ أَوِ ٱطۡرَحُوهُ أَرۡضٗا
يَخۡلُ لَكُمۡ وَجۡهُ أَبِيكُمۡ وَتَكُونُواْ
مِنۢ بَعۡدِهِۦ قَوۡمٗا صَٰلِحِينَ ۝٩

10. One of them said, "Do not kill Joseph, but if you must, throw

10. Qaala qaaa'ilum-minhum laa taqtuloo Yoosufa

قَالَ قَآئِلٞ مِّنۡهُمۡ لَا تَقۡتُلُواْ يُوسُفَ

him into a dark well so that perhaps some caravan will take him away."

11. Then they asked their father, "Why do you not trust us with Joseph? We are his well-wishers.

12. Send him with us tomorrow to play with us and (watch our cattle) graze. We shall carefully protect him."

13. Jacob replied, "I shall be grieved if you take him with you; I fear that some wild beast will harm him in your absence."

14. They said, "If some wild beast would be able to harm him, despite the presence of our strong group, it would certainly be a great loss to us."

15. When they took Joseph with them, they agreed to throw him into the well. We revealed to Joseph that (sometime) in the future at a time when they would not recognize him, he would remind them of all this.

16. In the evening they returned to their father weeping

17. and saying, "Father, we went playing and left Joseph with our belongings. A wild beast came and devoured him. We realize that you will not believe us even though we are telling the truth."

18. They presented him with a shirt stained with false blood. Jacob said, "Your souls have tempted you in this matter. Let us be patient and beg assistance from Allah if what you say is true."

19. A caravan came by and sent their water carrier out to the well. When he drew out Joseph in his bucket, he shouted, "Glad news, a

wa alqoohu fee ghayaabatil-jubbi yaltaqiṭhu ba'ḍus-sayyaarati in kuntum faa'ileen.

11. Qaaloo yaaa abaanaa maa laka laa ta-mannaa 'alaa Yoosufa wa innaa lahoo lanaaṣiḥoon.

12. Arsilhu ma'anaa ghadañy-yarta' wa yal'ab wa innaa lahoo laḥaafiẓoon.

13. Qaala innee layaḥzununeee an ta<u>z</u>haboo bihee wa akhaafu añy-ya-kulahu<u>z</u>-<u>z</u>i'bu wa antum 'anhu ghaafiloon.

14. Qaaloo la-in akalahu<u>z</u>-<u>z</u>i'bu wa naḥnu 'uṣbatun innaaa i<u>z</u>al-lakhaasiroon.

15. Falammaa <u>z</u>ahaboo bihee wa ajma'ooo añy-yaj'aloohu fee ghayaabatil-jubb; wa awḥaynaaa ilayhi latunabbi-'annahum bi-amrihim haa<u>z</u>aa wa hum laa yash'uroon.

16. Wa jaaa'ooo abaahum 'ishaaa'añy-yabkoon.

17. Qaaloo yaaa abaanaaa innaa <u>z</u>ahabnaa nastabiqu wa taraknaa Yoosufa 'inda mataa'inaa fa-akalahu<u>z</u>-<u>z</u>i'b; wa maaa anta bimu'minillanaa wa law kunnaa ṣaadiqeen.

18. Wa jaaa'oo 'alaa qameeṣihee bidamin ka<u>z</u>ib; qaala bal sawwalat lakum anfusukum amraa; faṣabrun jameel; wallaahul-musta'aanu 'alaa maa taṣifoon.

19. Wa jaaa'at sayyaaratun fa-arsaloo waaridahum fa-adlaa dalwah; qaala yaa bushraa haa<u>z</u>aa

وَأَلْقُوهُ فِي غَيَابَتِ الْجُبِّ يَلْتَقِطْهُ
بَعْضُ السَّيَّارَةِ إِن كُنتُمْ فَاعِلِينَ ﴿١٠﴾
قَالُوا يَا أَبَانَا مَا لَكَ لَا تَأْمَنَّا عَلَىٰ
يُوسُفَ وَإِنَّا لَهُ لَنَاصِحُونَ ﴿١١﴾
أَرْسِلْهُ مَعَنَا غَدًا يَرْتَعْ وَيَلْعَبْ
وَإِنَّا لَهُ لَحَافِظُونَ ﴿١٢﴾
قَالَ إِنِّي لَيَحْزُنُنِي أَن تَذْهَبُوا
بِهِ وَأَخَافُ أَن يَأْكُلَهُ الذِّئْبُ
وَأَنتُمْ عَنْهُ غَافِلُونَ ﴿١٣﴾
قَالُوا لَئِنْ أَكَلَهُ الذِّئْبُ وَنَحْنُ
عُصْبَةٌ إِنَّا إِذًا لَّخَاسِرُونَ ﴿١٤﴾
فَلَمَّا ذَهَبُوا بِهِ وَأَجْمَعُوا أَن يَجْعَلُوهُ
فِي غَيَابَتِ الْجُبِّ ۚ وَأَوْحَيْنَا إِلَيْهِ
لَتُنَبِّئَنَّهُم بِأَمْرِهِمْ هَٰذَا وَهُمْ
لَا يَشْعُرُونَ ﴿١٥﴾
وَجَاءُوا أَبَاهُمْ عِشَاءً يَبْكُونَ ﴿١٦﴾
قَالُوا يَا أَبَانَا إِنَّا ذَهَبْنَا نَسْتَبِقُ
وَتَرَكْنَا يُوسُفَ عِندَ مَتَاعِنَا فَأَكَلَهُ
الذِّئْبُ ۖ وَمَا أَنتَ بِمُؤْمِنٍ لَّنَا
وَلَوْ كُنَّا صَادِقِينَ ﴿١٧﴾ الثلثة
وَجَاءُوا عَلَىٰ قَمِيصِهِ بِدَمٍ كَذِبٍ ۚ
قَالَ بَلْ سَوَّلَتْ لَكُمْ أَنفُسُكُمْ أَمْرًا ۖ
فَصَبْرٌ جَمِيلٌ ۖ وَاللَّهُ الْمُسْتَعَانُ
عَلَىٰ مَا تَصِفُونَ ﴿١٨﴾
وَجَاءَتْ سَيَّارَةٌ فَأَرْسَلُوا وَارِدَهُمْ
فَأَدْلَىٰ دَلْوَهُ ۖ قَالَ يَا بُشْرَىٰ هَٰذَا

young boy!" The people of the caravan hid him amongst their belongings. Allah knows well what they do.

ghulaam; wa asarroohu bi-ḍaa'ah; wallaahu 'aleemum bimaa ya'maloon.

غُلٰمٌ ؕ وَاَسَرُّوْهُ بِضَاعَةً ؕ وَاللّٰهُ
عَلِيْمٌۢ بِمَا يَعْمَلُوْنَ ﴿١٩﴾

20. In selling him they (his brothers) asked for a very small price and even then they wanted to sell him very cheap.

20. Wa sharawhu bis̲amanim bakhsin daraahima ma'doodah; wa kaanoo feehi minaz-zaahideen.

وَشَرَوْهُ بِثَمَنٍۭ بَخْسٍ دَرَاهِمَ مَعْدُوْدَةٍ ۚ
وَكَانُوْا فِيْهِ مِنَ الزّٰهِدِيْنَ ﴿٢٠﴾ ع ٢ ١٤ ١٢

21. The Egyptian who bought him said to his wife, "Be kind to him, perhaps he will be of some benefit to us or we may adopt him."

Thus, We settled Joseph in the land so that We could teach him the interpretation of dreams. Allah has full control over His affairs but most people do not know.

21. Wa qaalal-laz̲ish-taraahu mim-Miṣra limra-atiheee akrimee mas̲waahu 'asaaa-añy-yanfa'anaaa aw nattakhiz̲ahoo waladaa; wa kaz̲aalika mak-kannaa li-Yoosufa fil-arḍi wa linu'allimahoo min ta-weelil-aḥaadees̲; wallaahu ghaalibun 'alaaa amrihee wa laakinna aks̲aran-naasi laa ya'lamoon.

وَقَالَ الَّذِى اشْتَرٰٮهُ مِنْ مِّصْرَ
لِامْرَاَتِهٖۤ اَكْرِمِىْ مَثْوٰٮهُ عَسٰٓى اَنْ
يَّنْفَعَنَاۤ اَوْ نَـتَّخِذَهٗ وَلَدًا ؕ وَكَذٰلِكَ
مَكَّنَّا لِيُوْسُفَ فِى الْاَرْضِ وَلِنُعَلِّمَهٗ
مِنْ تَاْوِيْلِ الْاَحَادِيْثِ ؕ وَاللّٰهُ
غَالِبٌ عَلٰٓى اَمْرِهٖ وَلٰـكِنَّ اَكْثَرَ النَّاسِ
لَا يَعْلَمُوْنَ ﴿٢١﴾

22. When he (Joseph) attained maturity, Allah gave him strength, wisdom and knowledge. Thus, do We reward those who do good.

22. Wa lammaa balagha ashuddahooo aataynaahu ḥukmañw-wa 'ilmaa; wa kaz̲aa-lika najzil-muḥsineen.

وَلَمَّا بَلَغَ اَشُدَّهٗۤ اٰتَيْنٰهُ حُكْمًا
وَّعِلْمًا ؕ وَكَذٰلِكَ نَجْزِى الْمُحْسِنِيْنَ ﴿٢٢﴾

23. His master's wife then tried to seduce him. She locked the doors and said to him, "Come on." He said, "I seek refuge in Allah who has given me a good place of shelter. The unjust will certainly have no happiness."

23. Wa raawadathul-latee huwa fee baytihaa 'an-nafsihee wa ghallaqatil abwaaba wa qaalat hayta lak; qaala ma'aaz̲al-laahi innahoo rabbeee aḥsana mas̲waay; innahoo laa yufliḥuẓ-ẓaalimoon.

وَرَاوَدَتْهُ الَّتِىْ هُوَ فِىْ بَيْتِهَا عَنْ
نَّـفْسِهٖ وَغَلَّقَتِ الْاَبْوَابَ وَقَالَتْ
هَيْتَ لَكَ ؕ قَالَ مَعَاذَ اللّٰهِ اِنَّهٗ
رَبِّىْۤ اَحْسَنَ مَثْوَاىَ ؕ اِنَّهٗ لَا يُفْلِحُ
الظّٰلِمُوْنَ ﴿٢٣﴾

24. She was determined to have him and were it not for his faith in Allah, he would certainly have yielded to her. Thus did We protect him from evil and indecency. He was certainly one of Our sincere servants.

24. Wa laqad hammat bihee wa hamma bihaa law laaa ar-ra-aa burhaana Rabbih; kaz̲aalika linaṣrifa 'anhus-sooo'a walfa-ḥshaaa'; innahoo min 'ibaadi-nal-mukhlaṣeen.

وَلَقَدْ هَمَّتْ بِهٖ ۚ وَهَمَّ بِهَا لَوْلَاۤ
اَنْ رَّاٰ بُرْهَانَ رَبِّهٖ ؕ كَذٰلِكَ لِنَصْرِفَ
عَنْهُ السُّوْۤءَ وَالْفَحْشَآءَ ؕ اِنَّهٗ مِنْ
عِبَادِنَا الْمُخْلَصِيْنَ ﴿٢٤﴾

25. She chased him to the door, grabbed him from behind, and tore off his shirt. Suddenly, they were face to face with her husband.

(Looking accusingly at Joseph) she asked her husband, "What punishment is more fitting for those who have evil desires towards your household other than

25. Wastabaqal-baaba wa qaddat qameeṣahoo min dubu-riñw-wa alfayaa sayyidahaa ladal-baab; qaalat maa jazaaa'u man araada bi-ahlika sooo'an illaaa añy-yusjana aw

وَاسْتَبَقَا الْبَابَ وَقَدَّتْ قَمِيْصَهٗ
مِنْ دُبُرٍ وَّاَلْفَيَا سَيِّدَهَا لَدَا
الْبَابِ ؕ قَالَتْ مَا جَزَآءُ مَنْ اَرَادَ
بِاَهْلِكَ سُوْۤءًا اِلَّاۤ اَنْ يُّسْجَنَ اَوْ

imprisonment and painful torment?"

26. Joseph said, "It was she who tried to seduce me." Someone from the household (a baby in a cradle) in confirmation of Joseph's statement said, "If his shirt is torn from the front, she has spoken the truth and he is lying,

27. but if his shirt is torn from behind, she is lying and he is speaking the truth."

28. When the master saw that Joseph's shirt was torn from behind, he told his wife, "This is some of your womanly guile in which you are greatly skillful.

29. Joseph, stay away from such affairs and you, woman, ask forgiveness for your sin; the guilt is yours."

30. A group of the women in the town started to gossip, saying, "The King's wife has tried to seduce her servant and has fallen madly in love with him. We think that she is in manifest error."

31. When she heard their gossiping, she invited them to her house, and gave a knife and citrus fruit to each of them. Then she told Joseph to appear before them. When they saw Joseph, they were so amazed that they cut their hands and said, "Goodness gracious! He is not a mortal but is a charming angel!"

32. She said, "This is the one on whose account you subjected me to all this blame. I tried to seduce him but he abstained. If he did not

'aẕaabun aleem.

26. Qaala hiya raawadatnee 'an-nafsee wa shahida shaahidum-min ahlihaaa in kaana qameeṣuhoo qudda min qubulin faṣadaqat wa huwa minal-kaaẕibeen.

27. Wa in kaana qameeṣuhoo qudda min duburin fakaẕabat wa huwa minaṣ-ṣaadiqeen.

28. Falammaa ra-aa qameeṣahoo qudda min duburin qaala innahoo min kaydikunna inna kaydakunna 'aẓeem.

29. Yoosufu a'riḍ 'an haaẕaa; wastaghfiree liẕambiki innaki kunti minal-khaaṭi'een.

30. Wa qaala niswatun filmadeenatim-ra-atul-'Azeezi turaawidu fataahaa 'an-nafsihee qad shaghafahaa ḥubbaa; innaa lanaraahaa fee ḍalaalim-mubeen.

31. Falammaa sami'at bimakrihinna arsalat ilayhinna wa a'tadat lahunna muttaka-añwwa aatat kulla waaḥidatim-minhunna sikkeenañw-wa qaalatikh-ruj 'alayhinna falammaa ra-aynahooo akbarnahoo wa qaṭṭa'na aydiyahunna wa qulna ḥaasha lillaahi maa haaẕaa basharaa; in haaẕaaa illaa malakun kareem.

32. Qaalat faẕaalikunnallaẕee lumtunnanee feeh; wa laqad raawattuhoo 'an-nafsihee fasta'ṣam;

عَذَابٌ اَلِيْمٌ ﴿٢٥﴾
قَالَ هِيَ رَاوَدَتْنِيْ عَنْ نَّفْسِيْ وَشَهِدَ
شَاهِدٌ مِّنْ اَهْلِهَا ۚ اِنْ كَانَ
قَمِيْصُهٗ قُدَّ مِنْ قُبُلٍ فَصَدَقَتْ
وَهُوَ مِنَ الْكٰذِبِيْنَ ﴿٢٦﴾
وَاِنْ كَانَ قَمِيْصُهٗ قُدَّ مِنْ دُبُرٍ
فَكَذَبَتْ وَهُوَ مِنَ الصّٰدِقِيْنَ ﴿٢٧﴾
فَلَمَّا رَاٰ قَمِيْصَهٗ قُدَّ مِنْ دُبُرٍ قَالَ
اِنَّهٗ مِنْ كَيْدِكُنَّ ۭ اِنَّ كَيْدَكُنَّ
عَظِيْمٌ ﴿٢٨﴾
يُوْسُفُ اَعْرِضْ عَنْ هٰذَا ۫ سكتة
وَاسْتَغْفِرِيْ لِذَنْۢبِكِ ښ اِنَّكِ كُنْتِ
مِنَ الْخٰطِـِٕيْنَ ﴿٢٩﴾ ع ٩ ١٣
وَقَالَ نِسْوَةٌ فِي الْمَدِيْنَةِ امْرَاَتُ
الْعَزِيْزِ تُرَاوِدُ فَتٰىهَا عَنْ نَّفْسِهٖ ۚ
قَدْ شَغَفَهَا حُبًّا ۭ اِنَّا لَنَرٰىهَا فِيْ
ضَلٰلٍ مُّبِيْنٍ ﴿٣٠﴾
فَلَمَّا سَمِعَتْ بِمَكْرِهِنَّ اَرْسَلَتْ
اِلَيْهِنَّ وَاَعْتَدَتْ لَهُنَّ مُتَّكَاً وَّ
اٰتَتْ كُلَّ وَاحِدَةٍ مِّنْهُنَّ سِكِّيْنًا
وَّقَالَتِ اخْرُجْ عَلَيْهِنَّ ۚ فَلَمَّا رَاَيْنَهٗٓ
اَكْبَرْنَهٗ وَقَطَّعْنَ اَيْدِيَهُنَّ وَقُلْنَ
حَاشَ لِلّٰهِ مَا هٰذَا بَشَرًا ۭ اِنْ هٰذَآ
اِلَّا مَلَكٌ كَرِيْمٌ ﴿٣١﴾
قَالَتْ فَذٰلِكُنَّ الَّذِيْ لُمْتُنَّنِيْ فِيْهِ ۭ
وَلَقَدْ رَاوَدْتُّهٗ عَنْ نَّفْسِهٖ فَاسْتَعْصَمَ ۭ

yield to me, I will order him to be locked up in prison to make him humble."

wa la'illam yaf'al maaa aamu-ruhoo layusjananna wa laya-koonam-minaṣ-ṣaaghireen.

وَلَئِن لَّمْ يَفْعَلْ مَآ ءَامُرُهُۥ لَيُسْجَنَنَّ
وَلَيَكُونًا مِّنَ ٱلصَّٰغِرِينَ ﴿٣٢﴾

33. Joseph said, "Lord, prison is dearer to me than that which women want me to do. Unless You protect me from their guile, I shall be attracted to them in my ignorance."

33. Qaala Rabbis-sijnu aḥab-bu ilayya mimmaa yad'o-onaneee ilayhi wa-illaa taṣrif 'annee kaydahunna aṣbu ilayhinna wa-akum-minal-jaahileen.

قَالَ رَبِّ ٱلسِّجْنُ أَحَبُّ إِلَيَّ مِمَّا
يَدْعُونَنِيٓ إِلَيْهِ ۖ وَإِلَّا تَصْرِفْ
عَنِّي كَيْدَهُنَّ أَصْبُ إِلَيْهِنَّ وَأَكُن
مِّنَ ٱلْجَٰهِلِينَ ﴿٣٣﴾

34. His Lord heard his prayers and protected him from their guile; He is All-hearing and All-knowing.

34. Fastajaaba lahoo Rabbu-hoo faṣarafa 'anhu kaydahunn; innahoo Huwas-Samee'ul-'Aleem.

فَٱسْتَجَابَ لَهُۥ رَبُّهُۥ فَصَرَفَ عَنْهُ
كَيْدَهُنَّ ۚ إِنَّهُۥ هُوَ ٱلسَّمِيعُ ٱلْعَلِيمُ ﴿٣٤﴾

35. Even after Joseph had been found innocent of all crime, the King and his people decided to imprison him for an appointed time (so that people might forget the incident).

35. Summa badaa lahum-mim ba'di maa ra-awul Aayaati layasjununnahoo ḥattaa ḥeen.

ثُمَّ بَدَا لَهُم مِّنۢ بَعْدِ مَا رَأَوُا۟ ٱلْءَايَٰتِ
لَيَسْجُنُنَّهُۥ حَتَّىٰ حِينٍ ﴿٣٥﴾ ع ٤ ١٤

36. Two young men were also sent to serve prison sentences (for different reasons). One of them said, "I had a dream in which I was brewing wine." The other one said, "In my dream I was carrying some bread on my head and birds were eating that bread." They asked Joseph if he would interpret their dreams. They said, "We believe you to be a righteous person."

36. Wa dakhala ma'ahussijna fatayaan; qaala aḥaduhumaaa inneee araaneee a'ṣiru khamraa; wa qaalal-aakharu inneee araaneee aḥmilu fawqa ra-see khubzan ta-kuluṭ-ṭayru minh; nabbi'naa bita-weeliheee innaa naraaka minal-muḥsineen.

وَدَخَلَ مَعَهُ ٱلسِّجْنَ فَتَيَانِ ۖ قَالَ
أَحَدُهُمَآ إِنِّيٓ أَرَىٰنِيٓ أَعْصِرُ خَمْرًا ۖ
وَقَالَ ٱلْءَاخَرُ إِنِّيٓ أَرَىٰنِيٓ أَحْمِلُ فَوْقَ
رَأْسِي خُبْزًا تَأْكُلُ ٱلطَّيْرُ مِنْهُ ۖ نَبِّئْنَا
بِتَأْوِيلِهِۦٓ ۖ إِنَّا نَرَىٰكَ مِنَ ٱلْمُحْسِنِينَ ﴿٣٦﴾

37. (Joseph) said, "(To prove that my interpretation of your dreams is true, I can tell you) what kind of food you will receive even before it comes to you. My Lord has given me such talents. I have given up the tradition of the people who do not believe in Allah and the Day of Judgment

37. Qaala laa ya-teekumaa ṭa'aamun turzaqaaniheee illaa nabba-tukumaaa bita-weelihee qabla añy-ya-tiyakumaa; zaali-kumaa mimmaa 'allamanee Rabbee; innee taraktu millata qawmil-laa yu'minoona billaahi wahum bil-Aakhirati hum kaafiroon.

قَالَ لَا يَأْتِيكُمَا طَعَامٌ تُرْزَقَانِهِۦٓ إِلَّا
نَبَّأْتُكُمَا بِتَأْوِيلِهِۦ قَبْلَ أَن يَأْتِيَكُمَا ۚ
ذَٰلِكُمَا مِمَّا عَلَّمَنِي رَبِّيٓ ۚ إِنِّي تَرَكْتُ
مِلَّةَ قَوْمٍ لَّا يُؤْمِنُونَ بِٱللَّهِ وَهُم
بِٱلْءَاخِرَةِ هُمْ كَٰفِرُونَ ﴿٣٧﴾

38. and I have embraced the religion of my fathers, Abraham, Isaac, and Jacob. We must not consider anything equal to Allah. This is part of Allah's blessing to us and the people, but most people do not give thanks.

38. Wattaba'tu Millata aa-baaa'eee Ibraaheema wa Isḥaa-qa wa Ya'qoob; maa kaana lanaaa an-nushrika billaahi min shay'; zaalika min faḍlil-laahi 'alaynaa wa 'alan-naasi wa laakinna aksaran-naasi laa yashkuroon.

وَٱتَّبَعْتُ مِلَّةَ ءَابَآءِيٓ إِبْرَٰهِيمَ
وَإِسْحَٰقَ وَيَعْقُوبَ ۚ مَا كَانَ لَنَآ
أَن نُّشْرِكَ بِٱللَّهِ مِن شَيْءٍ ۚ ذَٰلِكَ
مِن فَضْلِ ٱللَّهِ عَلَيْنَا وَعَلَى ٱلنَّاسِ
وَلَٰكِنَّ أَكْثَرَ ٱلنَّاسِ لَا يَشْكُرُونَ ﴿٣٨﴾

39. "My fellow prisoners, can many different masters be

39. Yaa ṣaaḥibayis-sijni 'a-arbaabum-mutafarriqoona

يَٰصَٰحِبَيِ ٱلسِّجْنِ ءَأَرْبَابٌ مُّتَفَرِّقُونَ

considered better than Allah who is One and All-dominant?

khayrun amil-laahul-Waaḥi-dul-Qahhaar.

خَيْرٌ اَمِ اللّٰهُ الْوَاحِدُ الْقَهَّارُ ﴿٣٩﴾

40. What you worship instead of Him are no more than empty names that you and your fathers have given to certain things. Allah has not given any authority to such names. Judgment belongs to no one but Allah. He has commanded you to worship nothing but Him. This is the only true religion, but most people do not know.

40. Maa ta'budoona min doo-niheee illaaa asmaaa'an sam-maytumoohaaa antum wa aabaaa'ukum-maaa anzalal laahu bihaa min sulṭaan; inil ḥukmu illaa lillaah; amara allaa ta'budooo illaaa iyyaah; zaali-kad-deenul-qayyimu walaakin-na aksaran-naasi laa ya'lamoon.

مَا تَعْبُدُوْنَ مِنْ دُوْنِهٖۤ اِلَّاۤ اَسْمَآءً
سَمَّيْتُمُوْهَاۤ اَنْتُمْ وَاٰبَآؤُكُمْ مَّاۤ اَنْزَلَ
اللّٰهُ بِهَا مِنْ سُلْطٰنٍ ؕ اِنِ الْحُكْمُ اِلَّا
لِلّٰهِ ؕ اَمَرَ اَلَّا تَعْبُدُوْۤا اِلَّاۤ اِيَّاهُ ؕ
ذٰلِكَ الدِّيْنُ الْقَيِّمُ وَلٰكِنَّ اَكْثَرَ
النَّاسِ لَا يَعْلَمُوْنَ ﴿٤٠﴾

41. "Fellow prisoners, your dreams tell that one of you will serve wine to his master and the other will be crucified and his head consumed by the birds. Judgment has already been passed about the meaning of the dreams that you asked about."

41. Yaa ṣaaḥibayis-sijni am-maaa aḥadukumaa fayasqee rabbahoo khamraa; wa ammal-aakharu fayuṣlabu fata-kuluṭ-ṭayru mir-ra-sih; quḍiyal-amrul-lazee feehi tastaftiyaan.

يٰصَاحِبَيِ السِّجْنِ اَمَّاۤ اَحَدُكُمَا
فَيَسْقِيْ رَبَّهٗ خَمْرًا ۚ وَاَمَّا الْاٰخَرُ
فَيُصْلَبُ فَتَاْكُلُ الطَّيْرُ مِنْ رَّاْسِهٖ ؕ
قُضِيَ الْاَمْرُ الَّذِيْ فِيْهِ تَسْتَفْتِيٰنِ ﴿٤١﴾

42. Joseph asked the one, whom he knew would not be executed, to mention his case to his master. Satan caused him (Joseph) to forget mentioning his Lord. Thus, he remained in prison for few more years.

42. Wa qaala lillazee ẓanna annahoo naajim-minhumaz kurnee 'inda rabbika fa-ansaahush-Shayṭaanu zikra Rabbihee falabisa fis-sijni biḍ'a sineen.

وَقَالَ لِلَّذِيْ ظَنَّ اَنَّهٗ نَاجٍ مِّنْهُمَا
اذْكُرْنِيْ عِنْدَ رَبِّكَ ۫ فَاَنْسٰىهُ
الشَّيْطٰنُ ذِكْرَ رَبِّهٖ فَلَبِثَ فِي السِّجْنِ
بِضْعَ سِنِيْنَ ﴿٤٢﴾ ع ٥ ١٥ ٧

43. (Sometimes later), the King dreamt that seven fat cows were eaten up by seven lean ones and that there were seven green ears of corn and seven dry ones. He asked the nobles to tell him the meaning of his dream if they were able to.

43. Wa qaalal-maliku inneee araa sab'a baqaraatin simaaniñy-ya-kuluhunna sab'un 'ijaafuñw-wa sab'a sumbulaatin khuḍriñw-wa ukhara yaabisaat; yaaa-ayyuhal-malau aftoonee fee ru'yaaya in kuntum lirru'yaa ta'buroon.

وَقَالَ الْمَلِكُ اِنِّيْۤ اَرٰى سَبْعَ
بَقَرٰتٍ سِمَانٍ يَّاْكُلُهُنَّ سَبْعٌ عِجَافٌ
وَّسَبْعَ سُنْۢبُلٰتٍ خُضْرٍ وَّاُخَرَ
يٰبِسٰتٍ ؕ يٰۤاَيُّهَا الْمَلَاُ اَفْتُوْنِيْ فِيْ
رُءْيَايَ اِنْ كُنْتُمْ لِلرُّءْيَا تَعْبُرُوْنَ ﴿٤٣﴾

44. They replied, "It is a confused dream and we do not know the meaning of such dreams."

44. Qaalooo aḍghaasu aḥlaa-m; wa maa naḥnu bita-weelil-aḥlaami bi'aalimeen.

قَالُوْۤا اَضْغَاثُ اَحْلَامٍ ۚ وَمَا نَحْنُ
بِتَاْوِيْلِ الْاَحْلَامِ بِعٰلِمِيْنَ ﴿٤٤﴾

45. The man who was in prison with Joseph and who was released, recalled after so many years Joseph's (ability to interpret dreams) and said, "I can tell you the meaning of this dream if you allow me to go (to the prison and ask the man who knows the meanings of dreams)."

45. Wa qaalal-lazee najaa minhumaa waddakara ba'da ummatin ana unabbi'ukum bita-weelihee fa-arsiloon.

وَقَالَ الَّذِيْ نَجَا مِنْهُمَا وَادَّكَرَ
بَعْدَ اُمَّةٍ اَنَا اُنَبِّئُكُمْ بِتَاْوِيْلِهٖ
فَاَرْسِلُوْنِ ﴿٤٥﴾

46. (He went to the prison) and said to Joseph, "You are a man of

46. Yoosufu ayyuhaṣ-ṣiddee-qu aftinaa fee

يُوْسُفُ اَيُّهَا الصِّدِّيْقُ اَفْتِنَا فِيْ

truth. Would you tell me the meaning of a dream in which seven fat cows are eaten up by seven lean ones and the meaning of seven green ears of corn and seven dry ones? I hope you can tell me the right meaning and people will learn about it."

sab'i baqaraatin simaaniñy-yakuluhunna sab'un 'ijaafuñw- wa sab'i sumbulaatin khuḍriñw- wa ukhara yaabisaatil-la'alleee arji'u ilan-naasi la'allahum ya'lamoon.

سَبْعٍ بَقَرٰتٍ سِمَانٍ يَّاْكُلُهُنَّ سَبْعٌ
عِجَافٌ وَّسَبْعِ سُنْۢبُلٰتٍ خُضْرٍ وَّ
اُخَرَ يٰبِسٰتٍ ۙ لَّعَلِّيْٓ اَرْجِعُ اِلَى النَّاسِ
لَعَلَّهُمْ يَعْلَمُوْنَ ﴿٤٦﴾

47. (Joseph) said, "Cultivate your lands for seven years as usual and preserve the produce in its ears each year except the little amount that you will consume.

47. Qaala tazra'oona sab'a sineena da-aban famaa ḥaṣattum faẕaroohu fee sumbuliheee illaa qaleelam-mimmaa ta-kuloon.

قَالَ تَزْرَعُوْنَ سَبْعَ سِنِيْنَ دَاَبًا ۚ
فَمَا حَصَدْتُّمْ فَذَرُوْهُ فِيْ سُنْۢبُلِهٖٓ
اِلَّا قَلِيْلًا مِّمَّا تَاْكُلُوْنَ ﴿٤٧﴾

48. After this there will ensue seven years of famine in which all the grain that you have stored will be consumed except a small quantity.

48. Summa ya-tee mim-ba'di zaalika sab'un shidaaduñy-yakulna maa qaddamtum lahunna illaa qaleelam-mimmaa tuḥṣinoon.

ثُمَّ يَاْتِيْ مِنْۢ بَعْدِ ذٰلِكَ سَبْعٌ شِدَادٌ
يَّاْكُلْنَ مَا قَدَّمْتُمْ لَهُنَّ اِلَّا قَلِيْلًا
مِّمَّا تُحْصِنُوْنَ ﴿٤٨﴾

49. Then there will be a year with plenty of rain and people will have sufficient milk and other produce."

49. Summa ya-tee mim ba'di zaalika 'aamun feehi yughaasun-naasu wa feehi ya'ṣiroon.

ثُمَّ يَاْتِيْ مِنْۢ بَعْدِ ذٰلِكَ عَامٌ فِيْهِ
يُغَاثُ النَّاسُ وَفِيْهِ يَعْصِرُوْنَ ﴿٤٩﴾ ع ٧/١٦

50. The King ordered his people to bring Joseph into his presence. When the messenger came to Joseph, he (Joseph) said, "Ask your master about the women who cut their hands. My Lord knows all about their guile."

50. Wa qaalal-maliku'-toonee bihee falammaa jaaa'ahur-rasoolu qaalar-ji' ilaa rabbika fas'alhu maa baalun-niswatil-laatee qaṭṭa'na aydiyahunn; inna Rabbee bikaydihinna 'Aleem.

وَقَالَ الْمَلِكُ ائْتُوْنِيْ بِهٖ ۚ فَلَمَّا
جَآءَهُ الرَّسُوْلُ قَالَ ارْجِعْ اِلٰى رَبِّكَ
فَسْـَٔلْهُ مَا بَالُ النِّسْوَةِ الّٰتِيْ قَطَّعْنَ
اَيْدِيَهُنَّ ؕ اِنَّ رَبِّيْ بِكَيْدِهِنَّ عَلِيْمٌ ﴿٥٠﴾

51. The King asked the women about their attempt to seduce Joseph. They replied, "Allah forbid! We do not know of any bad thing in Joseph." The wife of the King said, "Now the truth has come to light. It was I who tried to seduce Joseph. He is, certainly, a truthful man."

51. Qaala maa khaṭbukunna iz raawattunna Yoosufa 'an-nafsih; qulna ḥaasha lillaahi maa 'alimnaa 'alayhi min sooo'; qaalatim-ra-atul'Azeezil-'aana ḥaṣḥaṣal-ḥaqq; ana raawattuhoo 'an-nafsihee wa innahoo laminaṣ-ṣaadiqeen.

قَالَ مَا خَطْبُكُنَّ اِذْ رَاوَدْتُّنَّ يُوْسُفَ
عَنْ نَّفْسِهٖ ؕ قُلْنَ حَاشَ لِلّٰهِ مَا عَلِمْنَا
عَلَيْهِ مِنْ سُوْٓءٍ ؕ قَالَتِ امْرَاَتُ الْعَزِيْزِ
الْـٰٔنَ حَصْحَصَ الْحَقُّ ۫ اَنَا رَاوَدْتُّهٗ عَنْ
نَّفْسِهٖ وَاِنَّهٗ لَمِنَ الصّٰدِقِيْنَ ﴿٥١﴾

52. (Joseph said), "This proves that I was not disloyal to the King in his absence. Allah does not grant success to the efforts of disloyal people.

52. Zaalika liya'lama annee lam akhunhu bilghaybi wa annal-laaha laa yahdee kaydal-khaaa'ineen.

ذٰلِكَ لِيَعْلَمَ اَنِّيْ لَمْ اَخُنْهُ بِالْغَيْبِ
وَاَنَّ اللّٰهَ لَا يَهْدِيْ كَيْدَ الْخَآئِنِيْنَ ﴿٥٢﴾

53. I do not think that I am free from weakness; all human souls are susceptible to evil except for those to whom my Lord has granted mercy. My Lord is certainly All-forgiving and All-merciful."

53. Wa maaa ubarri'u nafseee; innan-nafsa la-ammaaratum bissooo'i illaa maa raḥima Rabbee; inna Rabbee Ghafoorur-Raḥeem.

وَمَآ اُبَرِّئُ نَفْسِيْ ۚ اِنَّ النَّفْسَ
لَاَمَّارَةٌ ۢ بِالسُّوْٓءِ اِلَّا مَا رَحِمَ
رَبِّيْ ؕ اِنَّ رَبِّيْ غَفُوْرٌ رَّحِيْمٌ ﴿٥٣﴾

54. The King ordered his men to bring Joseph before him. He wanted to grant him a high office. The King said to Joseph, "From now on you will be an honored and trusted person among us."

54. Wa qaalal-maliku'-toonee biheee astakhlişhu linafsee falammaa kallamahoo qaala innakal-yawma ladaynaa makeenun ameen.

وَقَالَ الْمَلِكُ ائْتُونِي بِهِ أَسْتَخْلِصْهُ
لِنَفْسِي ۚ فَلَمَّا كَلَّمَهُ قَالَ إِنَّكَ
الْيَوْمَ لَدَيْنَا مَكِينٌ أَمِينٌ ﴿٥٤﴾

55. Joseph said, "Put me in charge of the treasuries of the land. I know how to manage them."

55. Qaalaj-'alnee 'alaa khazaaa'inil-arḍi innee ḥafeeẓun 'aleem.

قَالَ اجْعَلْنِي عَلَىٰ خَزَائِنِ الْأَرْضِ
إِنِّي حَفِيظٌ عَلِيمٌ ﴿٥٥﴾

56. Thus, We settled Joseph in the land to live wherever he wanted. We grant a due share of Our mercy to whomever We want and We do not ignore the reward of the righteous ones.

56. Wa kazaalika makkannaa li-Yoosufa fil-arḍi yatabaw-wau-minhaa ḥaysu yashaaa'; nuṣeebu biraḥmatinaa man-nashaaa'u wa laa nuḍee'u ajral muḥsineen.

وَكَذَٰلِكَ مَكَّنَّا لِيُوسُفَ فِي الْأَرْضِ
يَتَبَوَّأُ مِنْهَا حَيْثُ يَشَاءُ ۚ نُصِيبُ
بِرَحْمَتِنَا مَنْ نَشَاءُ ۖ وَلَا نُضِيعُ
أَجْرَ الْمُحْسِنِينَ ﴿٥٦﴾

57. The reward in the next life is certainly better for the faithful ones who have observed piety in this life.

57. Wa la-ajrul-Aakhirati khayrul-lillazeena aamanoo wa kaanoo yattaqoon.

وَلَأَجْرُ الْآخِرَةِ خَيْرٌ لِلَّذِينَ
آمَنُوا وَكَانُوا يَتَّقُونَ ﴿٥٧﴾ ع ٨

58. Joseph's brothers came to him. When they entered his court, he recognized them, but they did not recognize him.

58. Wa jaaa'a ikhwatu Yoosufa fadakhaloo 'alayhi fa'arafahum wa hum lahoo munkiroon.

وَجَاءَ إِخْوَةُ يُوسُفَ فَدَخَلُوا
عَلَيْهِ فَعَرَفَهُمْ وَهُمْ لَهُ مُنْكِرُونَ ﴿٥٨﴾

59. When he had furnished them with provisions, he said, "Next time, bring me your other brother from your father. As you can see, I give each of you a certain amount of grain; I am a polite host.

59. Wa lammaa jahhazahum bijahaazihim qaala'-toonee bi-akhil-lakum-min abeekum; alaa tarawna anneee oofil-kayla wa ana khayrul-munzileen.

وَلَمَّا جَهَّزَهُمْ بِجَهَازِهِمْ قَالَ
ائْتُونِي بِأَخٍ لَكُمْ مِنْ أَبِيكُمْ ۚ
أَلَا تَرَوْنَ أَنِّي أُوفِي الْكَيْلَ وَأَنَا
خَيْرُ الْمُنْزِلِينَ ﴿٥٩﴾

60. If you did not bring him, do not come to us for we shall not give you any more grain."

60. Fa-il-lam ta-toonee bihee falaa kayla lakum 'indee wa laa taqraboon.

فَإِنْ لَمْ تَأْتُونِي بِهِ فَلَا كَيْلَ لَكُمْ
عِنْدِي وَلَا تَقْرَبُونِ ﴿٦٠﴾

61. Joseph's brothers said, "We shall try to influence his father to send him with us and we shall be successful."

61. Qaaloo sanuraawidu 'anhu abaahu wa innaa lafaa'iloon.

قَالُوا سَنُرَاوِدُ عَنْهُ أَبَاهُ وَإِنَّا
لَفَاعِلُونَ ﴿٦١﴾

62. Then Joseph told his people to put his brothers' money back into their bags so that perhaps they would recognize it, when at home, and come back to Egypt once again.

62. Wa qaala lifityaanihij-'aloo biḍaa'atahum fee riḥaalihim la'allahum ya'rifoonahaaa izan-qalabooo ilaaa ahlihim la'allahum yarji'oon.

وَقَالَ لِفِتْيَانِهِ اجْعَلُوا بِضَاعَتَهُمْ فِي
رِحَالِهِمْ لَعَلَّهُمْ يَعْرِفُونَهَا إِذَا انْقَلَبُوا
إِلَىٰ أَهْلِهِمْ لَعَلَّهُمْ يَرْجِعُونَ ﴿٦٢﴾

63. When they returned to their father, they told him, "Father, (unless we take our brother) they will refuse us one further measure of grain. Send our brother with us so

63. Falammaa raja'ooo ilaaa abeehim qaaloo yaaa abaanaa muni'a minnal-kaylu fa-arsil

فَلَمَّا رَجَعُوا إِلَىٰ أَبِيهِمْ قَالُوا
يَا أَبَانَا مُنِعَ مِنَّا الْكَيْلُ فَأَرْسِلْ

that we can obtain that measure. We shall watch over him carefully."

ma'anaaa akhaanaa naktal wa innaa lahoo lahaafizoon

مَعَنَآ اَخَانَا نَكْتَلْ وَاِنَّا لَهٗ لَحٰفِظُوْنَ ﴿٦٣﴾

64. Jacob replied, "How can I trust you after what happened to his brother before? Only Allah is the best Protector. His mercy is far greater than that of others."

64. Qaala hal aamanukum 'alayhi illaa kamaaa amintukum 'alaaa-akheehi min qabl; fal-laahu khayrun-haafizañw-wa Huwa Arhamur-raahimeen.

قَالَ هَلْ اٰمَنُكُمْ عَلَيْهِ اِلَّا كَمَآ
اَمِنْتُكُمْ عَلٰٓى اَخِيْهِ مِنْ قَبْلُ ؕ فَاللّٰهُ
خَيْرٌ حٰفِظًا ۪ وَّهُوَ اَرْحَمُ الرّٰحِمِيْنَ ﴿٦٤﴾

65. When they opened their baggage, they found that their money had been returned to them. They said, "Father, what more do we want? This is our money which has been given back to us. We can buy more provisions with this for our family. We protect our brother and will have one more camel load of grain, which is easy to get."

65. Wa lammaa fatahoo mata-a'ahum wajadoo bidaa'atahum ruddat ilayhim qaaloo yaaa-abaanaa maa nabghee; haazi-hee-bidaa'atunaa ruddat ilaynaa wa nameeru ahlanaa wa nahfazu akhaanaa wanazdaadu kayla ba'eer; zaalika kayluñy-yaseer.

وَلَمَّا فَتَحُوْا مَتَاعَهُمْ وَجَدُوْا
بِضَاعَتَهُمْ رُدَّتْ اِلَيْهِمْ ؕ قَالُوْا
يٰۤاَبَانَا مَا نَبْغِيْ ؕ هٰذِهٖ بِضَاعَتُنَا
رُدَّتْ اِلَيْنَا ۚ وَنَمِيْرُ اَهْلَنَا وَنَحْفَظُ
اَخَانَا وَنَزْدَادُ كَيْلَ بَعِيْرٍ ؕ ذٰلِكَ
كَيْلٌ يَّسِيْرٌ ﴿٦٥﴾

66. (Jacob) said, "I shall not send him with you until you solemnly promise me before Allah to return him to me unless you are prevented from doing so." When they gave their promise, he said, "Allah is the Witness of what we have said."

66. Qaala lan ursilahoo ma'akum hattaa tu'tooni mawsiqam-minal-laahi lata-tunnanee biheee illaaa añy-yuhaata bikum falammaaa aatawhu mawsiqahum qaalal-laahu'alaa maa naqoolu Wakeel.

قَالَ لَنْ اُرْسِلَهٗ مَعَكُمْ حَتّٰى تُؤْتُوْنِ
مَوْثِقًا مِّنَ اللّٰهِ لَتَاْتُنَّنِيْ بِهٖۤ اِلَّاۤ
اَنْ يُّحَاطَ بِكُمْ ۚ فَلَمَّاۤ اٰتَوْهُ مَوْثِقَهُمْ
قَالَ اللّٰهُ عَلٰى مَا نَقُوْلُ وَكِيْلٌ ﴿٦٦﴾

67. Jacob then told his sons, "Do not enter the town all together by a single gate, but each of you enter separately. I cannot help you against (the decree of) Allah. Everyone's destiny is in Allah's hands. I put my trust in Him. Whoever needs a trustee must place his trust in Him."

67. Wa qaala yaa baniyya laa tadkhuloo mim baabiñw-waa-hidiñw-wadkhuloo min abwaa-bim-mutafarriqah; wa maaa ughnee 'ankum-minal laahi min shay'; inil-hukmu-illaa lillaah; 'alayhi tawakkaltu wa 'alayhi falyatawakkalil Mutawak-kiloon.

وَقَالَ يٰبَنِيَّ لَا تَدْخُلُوْا مِنْ
بَابٍ وَّاحِدٍ وَّادْخُلُوْا مِنْ اَبْوَابٍ
مُّتَفَرِّقَةٍ ؕ وَمَاۤ اُغْنِيْ عَنْكُمْ مِّنَ
اللّٰهِ مِنْ شَيْءٍ ؕ اِنِ الْحُكْمُ اِلَّا لِلّٰهِ ؕ
عَلَيْهِ تَوَكَّلْتُ ۚ وَعَلَيْهِ فَلْيَتَوَكَّلِ
الْمُتَوَكِّلُوْنَ ﴿٦٧﴾

68. Even though they entered the town as their father had told them, it would not have been of any avail to them against the decree of Allah. It only served to satisfy Jacob's desire and judgment. He was certainly well versed by Our instruction, but most people do not know.

68. Wa lammaa dakhaloo min haysu amarahum aboohum-maa kaana yughnee 'anhum-minal-laahi min shay'in illaa haajatan fee nafsi Ya'qooba qadaahaa; wa innahoo lazoo 'ilmil-limaa 'allamnaahu wa laakinna aksaran-naasi laa ya'lamoon.

وَلَمَّا دَخَلُوْا مِنْ حَيْثُ اَمَرَهُمْ
اَبُوْهُمْ ؕ مَا كَانَ يُغْنِيْ عَنْهُمْ مِّنَ
اللّٰهِ مِنْ شَيْءٍ اِلَّا حَاجَةً فِيْ نَفْسِ
يَعْقُوْبَ قَضٰىهَا ؕ وَاِنَّهٗ لَذُوْ عِلْمٍ
لِّمَا عَلَّمْنٰهُ وَلٰكِنَّ اَكْثَرَ النَّاسِ
لَا يَعْلَمُوْنَ ﴿٦٨﴾ ع

69. When they entered Joseph's court, he gave lodging to his own brother (Benjamin) and said, "I am your brother. Do not feel sad about whatever they (half-brothers) had done."	69. Wa lammaa dakhaloo 'alaa Yoosufa aawaaa ilayhi akhaahu qaala inneee ana akhooka falaa tabta'is bimaa kaanoo ya'maloon.	وَلَمَّا دَخَلُوْا عَلٰى يُوْسُفَ اٰوٰٓى اِلَيْهِ اَخَاهُ قَالَ اِنِّيْٓ اَنَا اَخُوْكَ فَلَا تَبْتَئِسْ بِمَا كَانُوْا يَعْمَلُوْنَ ﴿٦٩﴾
70. When he had furnished them with provisions, he placed the King's drinking cup in his own brother's baggage. Then someone shouted, "People of the caravan, you are thieves!"	70. Falammaa jahhazahum bijahaazihim ja'alas-siqaayata fee raḥli akheehi s̲umma az̲-z̲ana mu'az̲z̲inun ayyatuhal-'eeru innakum lasaariqoon.	فَلَمَّا جَهَّزَهُمْ بِجَهَازِهِمْ جَعَلَ السِّقَايَةَ فِيْ رَحْلِ اَخِيْهِ ثُمَّ اَذَّنَ مُؤَذِّنٌ اَيَّتُهَا الْعِيْرُ اِنَّكُمْ لَسٰرِقُوْنَ ﴿٧٠﴾
71. Joseph's brothers turned around and asked, "What is missing?"	71. Qaaloo wa aqbaloo 'alay-him-maaz̲aa tafqidoon.	قَالُوْا وَاَقْبَلُوْا عَلَيْهِمْ مَّاذَا تَفْقِدُوْنَ ﴿٧١﴾
72. They were told, "The King's drinking cup is missing and whoever brings it will receive a camel's load of grain. I promise you and I keep my promise."	72. Qaaloo nafqidu ṣuwaa'al-maliki wa liman jaaa'a bihee ḥi-mlu ba'eeriñw-wa ana bihee za'eem.	قَالُوْا نَفْقِدُ صُوَاعَ الْمَلِكِ وَلِمَنْ جَآءَ بِهٖ حِمْلُ بَعِيْرٍ وَّاَنَا بِهٖ زَعِيْمٌ ﴿٧٢﴾
73. Joseph's brothers said, "We swear by Allah, as you know, that we have not come to spread evil in the land and that we have not committed any theft."	73. Qaaloo tallaahi laqad 'alimtum-maa ji'naa linufsida fil-arḍi wa maa kunnaa saari-qeen.	قَالُوْا تَاللّٰهِ لَقَدْ عَلِمْتُمْ مَّا جِئْنَا لِنُفْسِدَ فِي الْاَرْضِ وَمَا كُنَّا سٰرِقِيْنَ ﴿٧٣﴾
74. The Egyptians said, "What do you suggest should be the punishment of the thief, if it is proved that you are lying?"	74. Qaaloo famaa jazaaa'u-hooo in kuntum kaaz̲ibeen.	قَالُوْا فَمَا جَزَآؤُهٗٓ اِنْ كُنْتُمْ كٰذِبِيْنَ ﴿٧٤﴾
75. Joseph's brothers replied, "In whosever's baggage it is found, that person will be your bondsman. Thus is the punishment of the unjust."	75. Qaaloo jazaaa'uhoo mañw-wujida fee raḥlihee fahuwa jazaaa'uh; kaz̲aalika najziẓ-ẓaalimeen.	قَالُوْا جَزَآؤُهٗ مَنْ وُّجِدَ فِيْ رَحْلِهٖ فَهُوَ جَزَآؤُهٗ ؕ كَذٰلِكَ نَجْزِي الظّٰلِمِيْنَ ﴿٧٥﴾
76. They searched their baggage before that of Joseph's real brother where at last they found it. Thus, We showed Joseph how to plan this; he would not have been able to take his brother under the King's law unless Allah had wanted it to be so. We give a high rank to whomever We want. Over every knowledgeable person is one more knowing.	76. Fabada-a bi-aw'iyatihim qabla wi'aaa'i akheehi s̲ummas-takhrajahaa miñw-wi'aaa'i akheeh; kaz̲aalika kidnaa li-Yoosuf; maa kaana liya-khuz̲a akhaahu fee deenil-maliki illaaa añy-yashaaa'al-laah; narfa'u darajaatim-man-nashaaa'; wa fawqa kulli z̲ee 'ilmin 'Aleem.	فَبَدَاَ بِاَوْعِيَتِهِمْ قَبْلَ وِعَآءِ اَخِيْهِ ثُمَّ اسْتَخْرَجَهَا مِنْ وِّعَآءِ اَخِيْهِ ؕ كَذٰلِكَ كِدْنَا لِيُوْسُفَ ؕ مَا كَانَ لِيَاْخُذَ اَخَاهُ فِيْ دِيْنِ الْمَلِكِ اِلَّآ اَنْ يَّشَآءَ اللّٰهُ ؕ نَرْفَعُ دَرَجٰتٍ مَّنْ نَّشَآءُ ؕ وَفَوْقَ كُلِّ ذِيْ عِلْمٍ عَلِيْمٌ ﴿٧٦﴾
77. (Joseph's) brothers said, "It's no wonder that he steals; a brother of his had stolen before him." Joseph noted their remarks, but did not utter a word to them. He said (to himself), "You are in a worse position. Allah knows best what you allege."	77. Qaalooo iñy-yasriq faqad saraqa akhul-lahoo min qabl; fa-asarrahaa Yoosufu fee nafsi-hee wa lam yubdihaa lahum; qaala antum sharrum-makaanaa; wallaahu a'lamu bimaa taṣi-foon.	قَالُوْٓا اِنْ يَّسْرِقْ فَقَدْ سَرَقَ اَخٌ لَّهٗ مِنْ قَبْلُ ۚ فَاَسَرَّهَا يُوْسُفُ فِيْ نَفْسِهٖ وَلَمْ يُبْدِهَا لَهُمْ ۚ قَالَ اَنْتُمْ شَرٌّ مَّكَانًا ۚ وَاللّٰهُ اَعْلَمُ بِمَا تَصِفُوْنَ ﴿٧٧﴾

78. They said, "Noble Prince, his father is very old so please take one of us in his place. We believe you are a righteous person."

78. Qaaloo yaaa ayyuhal 'Azeezu inna lahooo aban shaykhan kabeeran fakhuz ahadanaa makaanahoo innaa naraaka minal-muhsineen.

قَالُوْا يَاَيُّهَا الْعَزِيْزُ اِنَّ لَهٗۤ اَبًا شَيْخًا كَبِيْرًا فَخُذْ اَحَدَنَا مَكَانَهٗ ۚ اِنَّا نَرٰىكَ مِنَ الْمُحْسِنِيْنَ ۝

79. He replied, "Allah forbid! How could I take someone in place of the thief? In doing so I would be committing injustice."

79. Qaala ma'aazal-laahi an na-khuza illaa mañw-wajadnaa mataa'anaa 'indahooo innaaa izal-lazaalimoon.

قَالَ مَعَاذَ اللّٰهِ اَنْ نَّأْخُذَ اِلَّا مَنْ وَّجَدْنَا مَتَاعَنَا عِنْدَهٗۤ ۙ اِنَّآ اِذًا لَّظٰلِمُوْنَ ۝

80. When they lost all hope (of convincing the Prince), they moved into a corner whispering to each other. The eldest among them said, "Did you not remember that you had solemnly promised our father, before Allah, to return Benjamin to him and that before this you had broken your promise concerning Joseph? I shall never leave this land until my father gives me permission or Allah decides for me; He is the best Judge."

80. Falammastay'asoo minhu khalasoo najiyyan qaala kabeeruhum alam ta'lamoo anna abaakum qad akhaza 'alaykum mawsiqam-minallaahi wa min qablu maa farrattum fee Yoosufa falan abrahal-arda hattaa ya-zana leee abeee aw yahkumal-laahu lee wa huwa khayrul-haakimeen.

فَلَمَّا اسْتَيْـَٔسُوْا مِنْهُ خَلَصُوْا نَجِيًّا ۚ قَالَ كَبِيْرُهُمْ اَلَمْ تَعْلَمُوْٓا اَنَّ اَبَاكُمْ قَدْ اَخَذَ عَلَيْكُمْ مَّوْثِقًا مِّنَ اللّٰهِ وَمِنْ قَبْلُ مَا فَرَّطْتُّمْ فِيْ يُوْسُفَ ۚ فَلَنْ اَبْرَحَ الْاَرْضَ حَتّٰى يَأْذَنَ لِيْ اَبِيْۤ اَوْ يَحْكُمَ اللّٰهُ لِيْ ۚ وَهُوَ خَيْرُ الْحٰكِمِيْنَ ۝

81. "Go to our father and tell him, 'Father, your son committed theft. We say only what we have seen and we have no control over the unseen.

81. Irji'ooo ilaaa abeekum faqooloo yaaa abaanaaa innabnaka saraq; wa maa shahidnaaa illaa bimaa 'alimnaa wa maa kunnaa lilghaybi haafizeen.

اِرْجِعُوْٓا اِلٰۤى اَبِيْكُمْ فَقُوْلُوْا يَاَبَانَآ اِنَّ ابْنَكَ سَرَقَ ۚ وَمَا شَهِدْنَآ اِلَّا بِمَا عَلِمْنَا وَمَا كُنَّا لِلْغَيْبِ حٰفِظِيْنَ ۝

82. You can ask the people of the town where we were and the caravan we met there. We are certainly telling the truth."

82. Was'alil-qaryatal-latee kunnaa feehaa wal'eeral-lateee aqbalnaa feehaa wa innaa lasaadiqoon.

وَسْـَٔلِ الْقَرْيَةَ الَّتِيْ كُنَّا فِيْهَا وَالْعِيْرَ الَّتِيْۤ اَقْبَلْنَا فِيْهَا ۚ وَاِنَّا لَصٰدِقُوْنَ ۝

83. (When he heard this), Jacob said, "Your souls have tempted you to make up the whole story. Allow us to honorably bear patience, for perhaps Allah will bring them all back to me. Allah is certainly All-knowing and All-wise."

83. Qaala bal sawwalat lakum anfusukum amran fasabrun jameel; 'asal-laahu añy-ya-tiyanee bihim jamee'aa; inna-hoo Huwal 'Aleemul-Hakeem.

قَالَ بَلْ سَوَّلَتْ لَكُمْ اَنْفُسُكُمْ اَمْرًا ۚ فَصَبْرٌ جَمِيْلٌ ۭ عَسَى اللّٰهُ اَنْ يَّأْتِيَنِيْ بِهِمْ جَمِيْعًا ۭ اِنَّهٗ هُوَ الْعَلِيْمُ الْحَكِيْمُ ۝

84. (Jacob) turned away from them, saying, "Alas, Joseph is lost!" He wept continuously in his grief until, in suppressing his

84. Wa tawallaa 'anhum wa qaala yaaa asafaa 'alaa Yoosufa wabyaddat 'aynaahu minal-

وَتَوَلّٰى عَنْهُمْ وَقَالَ يَاَسَفٰى عَلٰى يُوْسُفَ وَابْيَضَّتْ عَيْنٰهُ مِنَ

anger, his eyes turned white.

ḥuzni fahuwa kaẓeem.

الْحُزْنِ فَهُوَ كَظِيْمٌ ۞

85. They said, "You are always remembering Joseph. By Allah, it will either make you sick or you will die."

85. Qaaloo tallaahi tafta'u tazkuru Yoosufa ḥattaa takoona ḥaraḍan aw takoona minal-haalikeen.

قَالُوْا تَاللهِ تَفْتَؤُا تَذْكُرُ يُوْسُفَ حَتّٰى تَكُوْنَ حَرَضًا اَوْ تَكُوْنَ مِنَ الْهٰلِكِيْنَ ۞

86. He replied, "I complain of my sorrow and grief only to Allah. I know about Allah what you do not know.

86. Qaala innamaaa ashkoo baṣ-see wa ḥuzneee ilal-laahi wa a'lamu minal-laahi maa laa ta'lamoon.

قَالَ اِنَّمَاۤ اَشْكُوْا بَثِّيْ وَحُزْنِيْۤ اِلَى اللهِ وَاَعْلَمُ مِنَ اللهِ مَا لَا تَعْلَمُوْنَ ۞

87. My sons, go and search for Joseph and his brother and do not despair of receiving comfort from Allah; only the unbelievers despair of receiving comfort from Him."

87. Yaa baniyyaz-haboo fata-ḥassasoo miñy-Yoosufa wa akheehi wa laa tay'asoo mirrawḥil-laah; innahoo laa yay'asu mir-rawḥil-laahi illalqawmul-kaafiroon.

يٰبَنِيَّ اذْهَبُوْا فَتَحَسَّسُوْا مِنْ يُّوْسُفَ وَاَخِيْهِ وَلَا تَايْـَٔسُوْا مِنْ رَّوْحِ اللهِ اِنَّهٗ لَا يَايْـَٔسُ مِنْ رَّوْحِ اللهِ اِلَّا الْقَوْمُ الْكٰفِرُوْنَ ۞

88. When they entered Joseph's court, they said, "Noble Prince, hardship has struck us and our people. We have come with a little money, so give us a measure of grain and be charitable to us. Allah rewards those who give charity."

88. Falammaa dakhaloo 'alayhi qaaloo yaaa ayyuhal 'Azeezu massanaa wa ahlanaḍ-ḍurru wa ji'naa bibiḍaa'atim-muzjaatin fa-awfi lanal-kayla wa taṣaddaq 'alaynaaa innal-laaha yajzil-mutaṣaddiqeen.

فَلَمَّا دَخَلُوْا عَلَيْهِ قَالُوْا يٰۤاَيُّهَا الْعَزِيْزُ مَسَّنَا وَاَهْلَنَا الضُّرُّ وَجِئْنَا بِبِضَاعَةٍ مُّزْجٰىةٍ فَاَوْفِ لَنَا الْكَيْلَ وَتَصَدَّقْ عَلَيْنَا اِنَّ اللهَ يَجْزِى الْمُتَصَدِّقِيْنَ ۞

89. Joseph asked them, "Do you know what you did to Joseph and his brother in your ignorance?"

89. Qaala hal 'alimtum maa fa'altum bi-Yoosufa wa akhee-hi iz-antum jaahiloon.

قَالَ هَلْ عَلِمْتُمْ مَّا فَعَلْتُمْ بِيُوْسُفَ وَاَخِيْهِ اِذْ اَنْتُمْ جٰهِلُوْنَ ۞

90. Then they inquired, "Are you Joseph?" He said, "Yes, I am Joseph and this is my brother. Allah has indeed been gracious to us. One who exercises patience and observes piety should know that Allah does not ignore the reward of the righteous ones."

90. Qaalooo 'a-innaka la-anta Yoosuf; qaala ana Yoosufu wa haazaaa akhee qad mannal-laahu 'alaynaaa innahoo mañy-yattaqi wa yaṣbir fa-innal-laaha laa yuḍee'u ajral-muḥsineen.

قَالُوْۤا ءَاِنَّكَ لَاَنْتَ يُوْسُفُ قَالَ اَنَا يُوْسُفُ وَهٰذَاۤ اَخِيْ قَدْ مَنَّ اللهُ عَلَيْنَا اِنَّهٗ مَنْ يَّتَّقِ وَيَصْبِرْ فَاِنَّ اللهَ لَا يُضِيْعُ اَجْرَ الْمُحْسِنِيْنَ ۞

91. They said, "We swear by Allah that Allah has given preference to you over us and we have sinned."

91. Qaaloo tallaahi laqad aaṣarakal-laahu 'alaynaa wa in kunnaa lakhaaṭi'een.

قَالُوْا تَاللهِ لَقَدْ اٰثَرَكَ اللهُ عَلَيْنَا وَاِنْ كُنَّا لَخٰطِئِيْنَ ۞

92. (Joseph) said, "No one will blame you on this day. Allah will forgive you; He is more Merciful than others.

92. Qaala laa taṣreeba 'alay-kumul-yawm; yaghfirul-laahu lakum wa Huwa Arḥamur-raaḥimeen.

قَالَ لَا تَثْرِيْبَ عَلَيْكُمُ الْيَوْمَ يَغْفِرُ اللهُ لَكُمْ وَهُوَ اَرْحَمُ الرّٰحِمِيْنَ ۞

93. Take my shirt and place it unto my father's face. This will

93. Izhaboo biqameeṣee haa-zaa fa-alqoohu

اِذْهَبُوْا بِقَمِيْصِيْ هٰذَا فَاَلْقُوْهُ

restore his eyesight. Then bring the whole family to me."	'alaa wajhi abee ya-ti baṣeeraa; wa-toonee bi-ahlikum ajma'een.	عَلٰى وَجْهِ اَبِىْ يَاْتِ بَصِيْرًا ۚ وَاْتُوْنِىْ بِاَهْلِكُمْ اَجْمَعِيْنَ ﴿۹۳﴾ ع
94. When the caravan left the town, their father said, "I smell Joseph's scent. I hope you will not accuse me of senility."	94. Wa lammaa faṣalatil-'eeru qaala aboohum innee la-ajidu reeḥa Yoosufa law laaa-an tufannidoon.	وَلَمَّا فَصَلَتِ الْعِيْرُ قَالَ اَبُوْهُمْ اِنِّىْ لَاَجِدُ رِيْحَ يُوْسُفَ لَوْلَاۤ اَنْ تُفَنِّدُوْنِ ﴿۹۴﴾
95. His people said, "By Allah, you are still making the same old error."	95. Qaaloo tallaahi innaka lafee ḍalaalikal-qadeem.	قَالُوْا تَاللّٰهِ اِنَّكَ لَفِىْ ضَلٰلِكَ الْقَدِيْمِ ﴿۹۵﴾ الربع
96. When someone brought him the glad news, Joseph's shirt was placed on his face and his eyesight was restored, he said, "Did I not tell you that I know about Allah that which you do not know?"	96. Falammaaa an jaaa'al basheeru alqaahu 'alaa wajhihee fartadda baṣeeraa; qaala alam aqul-lakum inneee a'lamu minal-laahi maa laa ta'lamoon.	فَلَمَّاۤ اَنْ جَآءَ الْبَشِيْرُ اَلْقٰىهُ عَلٰى وَجْهِهٖ فَارْتَدَّ بَصِيْرًا ۚ قَالَ اَلَمْ اَقُلْ لَّكُمْ ۚ اِنِّىْۤ اَعْلَمُ مِنَ اللّٰهِ مَا لَا تَعْلَمُوْنَ ﴿۹۶﴾
97. They said, "Father, ask forgiveness for our sins; we have certainly sinned."	97. Qaaloo yaaa abaanastaghfir lanaa zunoobanaaa innaa kunnaa khaaṭi'een.	قَالُوْا يٰۤاَبَانَا اسْتَغْفِرْ لَنَا ذُنُوْبَنَاۤ اِنَّا كُنَّا خٰطِـِٔيْنَ ﴿۹۷﴾
98. He said, "I shall ask my Lord to forgive you; He is All-forgiving and All-merciful."	98. Qaala sawfa astaghfiru lakum Rabbeee innahoo Huwal-Ghafoorur-Raḥeem.	قَالَ سَوْفَ اَسْتَغْفِرُ لَكُمْ رَبِّىْ ؕ اِنَّهٗ هُوَ الْغَفُوْرُ الرَّحِيْمُ ﴿۹۸﴾
99. When they all came to Joseph, he welcomed his parents and said, "Enter the town (Egypt) in peace, if Allah wants it to be so."	99. Falammaa dakhaloo 'alaa Yoosufa aawaaa ilayhi abawayhi wa qaalad-khuloo Miṣra in shaaa 'al-laahu aamineen.	فَلَمَّا دَخَلُوْا عَلٰى يُوْسُفَ اٰوٰۤى اِلَيْهِ اَبَوَيْهِ وَقَالَ ادْخُلُوْا مِصْرَ اِنْ شَآءَ اللّٰهُ اٰمِنِيْنَ ﴿۹۹﴾
100. He raised his parents on the throne and they prostrated themselves before him (Joseph). He said, "This is the meaning of my dream which Allah has made come true. He has granted me many favors. He set me free from prison and brought you to me from the desert after having ended the enmity which Satan sowed between my brothers and me. My Lord is certainly kind to whomever He wants. It is He who is All-forgiving and All-wise.	100. Wa rafa'a abawayhi 'alal-'arshi wa kharroo lahoo sujjadaa; wa qaala yaaa abati haazaa ta-weelu ru'yaaya min qablu qad ja'alahaa Rabbee ḥaqqaa; wa qad aḥsana beee iz akhrajanee minas-sijni wa jaaa'a bikum-minal-badwi mim ba'di an nazaghash-Shayṭaanu baynee wa bayna ikhwateee; inna Rabbee Laṭeeful-limaa yashaaa'; innahoo Huwal 'Aleemul-Ḥakeem.	وَرَفَعَ اَبَوَيْهِ عَلَى الْعَرْشِ وَخَرُّوْا لَهٗ سُجَّدًا ۚ وَقَالَ يٰۤاَبَتِ هٰذَا تَاْوِيْلُ رُءْيَاىَ مِنْ قَبْلُ ز قَدْ جَعَلَهَا رَبِّىْ حَقًّا ؕ وَقَدْ اَحْسَنَ بِىْۤ اِذْ اَخْرَجَنِىْ مِنَ السِّجْنِ وَجَآءَ بِكُمْ مِّنَ الْبَدْوِ مِنْۢ بَعْدِ اَنْ نَّزَغَ الشَّيْطٰنُ بَيْنِىْ وَبَيْنَ اِخْوَتِىْ ؕ اِنَّ رَبِّىْ لَطِيْفٌ لِّمَا يَشَآءُ ؕ اِنَّهٗ هُوَ الْعَلِيْمُ الْحَكِيْمُ ﴿۱۰۰﴾

101. "My Lord, You have given me the kingdom and taught me the meaning of dreams. You are the Creator of the heavens and the earth. You are my Guardian in this world and in the life to come. Make me die as one who has submitted to the Will of Allah and unite me with the righteous ones."

101. Rabbi qad aataytanee minal-mulki wa 'allamtanee min ta-weelil-aḥaadees̲; faaṭiras-samaawaati wal-arḍi Anta Waliyyee fid-dunyaa wal-Aakhirah; tawaffanee musl̲imañw-wa alḥiqnee bis̤s̤aaliḥeen.

رَبِّ قَدْ اٰتَيْتَنِىْ مِنَ الْمُلْكِ وَ
عَلَّمْتَنِىْ مِنْ تَاْوِيْلِ الْاَحَادِيْثِ ۚ
فَاطِرَ السَّمٰوٰتِ وَالْاَرْضِ ۣ اَنْتَ
وَلِىّٖ فِى الدُّنْيَا وَالْاٰخِرَةِ ۚ تَوَفَّنِىْ
مُسْلِمًا وَّاَلْحِقْنِىْ بِالصّٰلِحِيْنَ ﴿١٠١﴾

102. This is some of the news of the unseen which We reveal to you, (Muhammad). You were not with them when Joseph's brothers agreed on devising their evil plans.

102. Z̲aalika min ambaaa'il-ghaybi nooḥeehi ilayka wa maa kunta ladayhim iz̲ ajma'ooo amrahum wa hum yamkuroon.

ذٰلِكَ مِنْ اَنْۢبَآءِ الْغَيْبِ نُوْحِيْهِ
اِلَيْكَ ۚ وَمَا كُنْتَ لَدَيْهِمْ اِذْ اَجْمَعُوْٓا
اَمْرَهُمْ وَهُمْ يَمْكُرُوْنَ ﴿١٠٢﴾

103. However hard you try, most people will not believe.

103. Wa maaa aks̲arun-naasi wa law ḥaraṣta bimu'mineen.

وَمَآ اَكْثَرُ النَّاسِ وَلَوْ حَرَصْتَ
بِمُؤْمِنِيْنَ ﴿١٠٣﴾

104. You do not ask any reward for your preaching (of Our guidance to them). This (Quran) is a guide for the people of the world (human beings and jinn).

104. Wa maa tas'aluhum 'alayhi min ajr; in huwa illaa z̲ikrul-lil'aalameen.

وَمَا تَسْـَٔلُهُمْ عَلَيْهِ مِنْ اَجْرٍ ؕ اِنْ
هُوَ اِلَّا ذِكْرٌ لِّلْعٰلَمِيْنَ ﴿١٠٤﴾ ع ١٠ ٥

105. There is much evidence (of the existence of Allah) in the heavens and the earth which they see, but ignore.

105. Wa ka-ayyim-min Aayatin fis-samaawaati wal-arḍi yamurroona 'alayhaa wa hum 'anhaa mu'riḍoon.

وَكَاَيِّنْ مِّنْ اٰيَةٍ فِى السَّمٰوٰتِ
وَالْاَرْضِ يَمُرُّوْنَ عَلَيْهَا وَهُمْ
عَنْهَا مُعْرِضُوْنَ ﴿١٠٥﴾

106. Most of them do not believe in Allah; they are but pagans.

106. Wa maa yu'minu aks̲aruhum billaahi illaa wa hum mushrikoon.

وَمَا يُؤْمِنُ اَكْثَرُهُمْ بِاللّٰهِ اِلَّا
وَهُمْ مُّشْرِكُوْنَ ﴿١٠٦﴾

107. Do they feel safe from Allah's overwhelming torment or of the sudden approach of the Day of Judgment while they are unaware?

107. Afa-aminooo an ta-tiyahum ghaashiyatum-min 'az̲aabil-laahi aw ta-tiyahumus-Saa'atu baghtatañw-wa hum laa yash'uroon.

اَفَاَمِنُوْٓا اَنْ تَاْتِيَهُمْ غَاشِيَةٌ مِّنْ
عَذَابِ اللّٰهِ اَوْ تَاْتِيَهُمُ السَّاعَةُ
بَغْتَةً وَّهُمْ لَا يَشْعُرُوْنَ ﴿١٠٧﴾

108. (O Muhammad), say, "This is my way. I and my followers invite you to Allah with proper understanding. Allah is free from all defects. I am not of the pagans."

108. Qul haaz̲ihee sabeeleee ad'ooo ilal-laah; 'alaa baṣeeratin ana wa manit-taba'anee wa Subḥaanal-laahi wa maaa ana minal-mushrikeen.

قُلْ هٰذِهٖ سَبِيْلِىْٓ اَدْعُوْٓا اِلَى اللّٰهِ ۣ
عَلٰى بَصِيْرَةٍ اَنَا وَمَنِ اتَّبَعَنِىْ ؕ
وَسُبْحٰنَ اللّٰهِ وَمَآ اَنَا مِنَ الْمُشْرِكِيْنَ ﴿١٠٨﴾

وقف النبي صلى الله عليه وآله وسلم ١٢

109. Whomever We sent before you were men of the people of the towns. We gave them revelations. Did they (the unbelievers) not travel sufficiently through the land to see how terrible the end

109. Wa maaa arsalnaa min qablika illaa rijaalan nooḥeee ilayhim min ahlilquraaa; afalam yaseeroo fil-arḍi fa-yanẓuroo kayfa

وَمَآ اَرْسَلْنَا مِنْ قَبْلِكَ اِلَّا رِجَالًا
نُّوْحِىْٓ اِلَيْهِمْ مِّنْ اَهْلِ الْقُرٰى ؕ اَفَلَمْ
يَسِيْرُوْا فِى الْاَرْضِ فَيَنْظُرُوْا كَيْفَ

was of those who lived before? The next life is, certainly, better for the pious ones. Will you not then take heed?

kaana 'aaqibatul-lazeena min qablihim; wa la-Daarul Aakhirati khayrul-lillazeenat-taqaw; afalaa ta'qiloon.

كَانَ عَاقِبَةُ الَّذِينَ مِن قَبْلِهِمْ ۗ
وَلَدَارُ الْآخِرَةِ خَيْرٌ لِّلَّذِينَ اتَّقَوْا ۗ
أَفَلَا تَعْقِلُونَ ﴿١٠٩﴾

110. When at last the Messengers lost all hope of achieving success in their task and thought that everyone had, falsely, called them liars, We gave them victory and saved whomever We chose to save. The guilty ones cannot escape Our wrath.

110. Ḥattaaa izas-tay'asar-Rusulu wa ẓannooo annahum qad kuziboo jaaa'ahum naṣrunaa fanujjiya man nashaaa'u wa laa yuraddu ba-sunaa 'anil-qawmil-mujrimeen.

حَتَّىٰ إِذَا اسْتَيْأَسَ الرُّسُلُ وَ
ظَنُّوا أَنَّهُمْ قَدْ كُذِبُوا جَاءَهُمْ
نَصْرُنَا فَنُجِّيَ مَن نَّشَاءُ ۖ وَلَا
يُرَدُّ بَأْسُنَا عَنِ الْقَوْمِ الْمُجْرِمِينَ ﴿١١٠﴾

111. In their story, there is a lesson for the people of understanding. It is not a legend but a confirmation of what exists (in the Torah). It (the Quran) has details about everything. It is a guide and mercy for those who have faith.

111. Laqad kaana fee qaṣaṣihim 'ibratul-li-ulil-albaab; maa kaana ḥadeesañy-yuftaraa wa laakin taṣdeeqallazee bayna yadayhi wa tafṣeela kulli shay'iñw-wa hudañw-wa raḥmatal-liqawmiñy-yu'minoon.

لَقَدْ كَانَ فِي قَصَصِهِمْ عِبْرَةٌ
لِّأُولِي الْأَلْبَابِ ۗ مَا كَانَ حَدِيثًا
يُفْتَرَىٰ وَلَٰكِن تَصْدِيقَ الَّذِي
بَيْنَ يَدَيْهِ وَتَفْصِيلَ كُلِّ شَيْءٍ
وَهُدًى وَرَحْمَةً لِّقَوْمٍ يُؤْمِنُونَ ﴿١١١﴾ ع ١٢/٧

Al-Rad, The Thunder (13)

In the Name of Allah, the Beneficent, the Merciful.

Sûrat ar-Ra'd-13

(Revealed at Madaniyyah)

Bismillaahir Raḥmaanir Raḥeem

(١٣) سُورَةُ الرَّعْدِ مَدَنِيَّةٌ (٩٦)

آياتها ٤٣ — بِسْمِ اللَّهِ الرَّحْمَٰنِ الرَّحِيمِ — ركوعاتها ٦

1. Alif. Lam. Mim. Ra. These are the verses of the Book. Whatever is revealed to you from your Lord is the Truth, but most people do not believe.

1. Alif-Laaam-Meeem-Raa; tilka Aayaatul Kitaab; wallazeee unzila ilayka mir-Rabbikal-ḥaqqu wa laakinna aksaran-naasi laa yu'minoon.

الٓمٓرٰ ۚ تِلْكَ آيَاتُ الْكِتَابِ ۗ وَالَّذِي
أُنزِلَ إِلَيْكَ مِن رَّبِّكَ الْحَقُّ
وَلَٰكِنَّ أَكْثَرَ النَّاسِ لَا يُؤْمِنُونَ ﴿١﴾

2. Allah is the One Who raised the heavens without a pillar as you can see. Then He established his control over the realm and made the sun and moon subservient to Him. Each of them will remain in motion for an appointed time. He regulates all affairs and explains the evidence (of His existence) so that perhaps you will be certain of your meeting with your Lord.

2. Allaahul-lazee rafa'as-samaawaati bighayri 'amadin tarawnahaa summas-tawaa 'alal-'Arshi wa sakhkharash-shamsa walqamar; kulluñy-yajree li-ajalim-musammaa; yudabbirul-amra yufaṣṣilul Aayaati la'allakum biliqaaa'i Rabbikum tooqinoon.

اللَّهُ الَّذِي رَفَعَ السَّمَاوَاتِ بِغَيْرِ
عَمَدٍ تَرَوْنَهَا ۖ ثُمَّ اسْتَوَىٰ عَلَى الْعَرْشِ
وَسَخَّرَ الشَّمْسَ وَالْقَمَرَ ۖ كُلٌّ
يَجْرِي لِأَجَلٍ مُّسَمًّى ۚ يُدَبِّرُ الْأَمْرَ
يُفَصِّلُ الْآيَاتِ لَعَلَّكُم بِلِقَاءِ
رَبِّكُمْ تُوقِنُونَ ﴿٢﴾

3. It is Allah who spread out the earth and fixed mountains and placed rivers therein. He made a pair of every fruit and made the night cover the day. All this is evidence (of the existence of

3. Wa Huwal-lazee maddal-arḍa wa ja'ala feehaa rawaasiya wa anhaaraa; wa min kullis-samaraati ja'ala feehaa zawjay-nis-nayni

وَهُوَ الَّذِي مَدَّ الْأَرْضَ وَجَعَلَ
فِيهَا رَوَاسِيَ وَأَنْهَارًا ۖ وَمِن كُلِّ
الثَّمَرَاتِ جَعَلَ فِيهَا زَوْجَيْنِ اثْنَيْنِ

Allah) for the people who think.

4. In the earth there are adjacent pieces of land, vineyards, farms, date-palms of single and many roots which are all watered by the same water. We have made some yield a better food than others. All this is evidence (of the existence of Allah) for the people who understand.

5. If there is anything to make you wonder, it would be the words of those who say, "When we become dust, shall we be brought back to life again?" They are unbelievers in their Lord and will wear heavy fetters around their necks. They are the dwellers of the hellfire wherein they will live forever.

6. They ask you to bring upon them punishment before they ask you for mercy. Such punishments were already brought upon the people who lived before them. Your Lord, certainly, has forgiveness for the injustice of the people. He is also stern in His retribution.

7. The unbelievers say, "Why has his Lord not sent him, (Muhammad), miracles." (Muhammad), you are only a Warner. For every nation (generation) there is a guide (Imam).

8. Allah knows well what every female conceives. He knows what the wombs spoil and dispose of. In His plans, everything has been designed proportionately.

9. He knows all the unseen and seen. He is the most Great

yughshil-laylan-nahaar; inna fee zaalika la-Aayaatil-liqawmiñy-yatafakkaroon.

4. Wa fil-arḍi qiṭa'um-mutajaawiraatuñw-wa jannaatum-min a'naabiñw-wa zar'uñw-wa nakheelun ṣinwaanuñw-wa ghayru ṣinwaaniñy-yusqaa bimaaa'iñw-waaḥid; wa nufaḍḍilu ba'ḍahaa 'alaa ba'ḍin fil-ukul; inna fee zaalika la-Aayaatil-liqawmiñy-ya'qiloon.

5. Wa in ta'jab fa'ajabun qawluhum 'a-izaa kunnaa turaaban 'a-innaa lafee khalqin jadeed; ulaaa'ikal-lazeena kafaroo bi-Rabbihim wa ulaaa'ikal-aghlaalu feee a'naaqihim wa ulaaa'ika Aṣḥaabun-Naari hum feehaa khaalidoon.

6. Wa yasta'jiloonaka bis-say-yi'ati qablal-ḥasanati wa qad khalat min qablihimul-maṣulaat; wa inna Rabbaka lazoo maghfiratil-linnaasi 'alaa ẓulmihim wa inna Rabbaka lashadeedul-'iqaab.

7. Wa yaqoolul-lazeena kafaroo law laaa unzila 'alayhi Aayatum-mir-Rabbih; innamaaa anta munziruñw-wa likulli qawmin haad.

8. Allaahu ya'lamu maa taḥmilu kullu unsaa wa maa tagheeḍul-arḥaamu wa maa tazdaad; wa kullu shay'in 'indahoo bimiq-daar.

9. 'Aalimul-Ghaybi wash-Shahaadatil-

يُغۡشِي الَّيۡلَ النَّهَارَۚ إِنَّ فِي ذٰلِكَ
لَاٰيٰتٍ لِّقَوۡمٍ يَّتَفَكَّرُوۡنَ ﴿٣﴾
وَفِي الۡاَرۡضِ قِطَعٌ مُّتَجٰوِرٰتٌ وَّجَنّٰتٌ
مِّنۡ اَعۡنَابٍ وَّزَرۡعٌ وَّنَخِيۡلٌ صِنۡوَانٌ
وَّغَيۡرُ صِنۡوَانٍ يُّسۡقٰى بِمَآءٍ وَّاحِدٍ
وَنُفَضِّلُ بَعۡضَهَا عَلٰى بَعۡضٍ فِي
الۡاُكُلِؕ اِنَّ فِيۡ ذٰلِكَ لَاٰيٰتٍ
لِّقَوۡمٍ يَّعۡقِلُوۡنَ ﴿٤﴾
وَاِنۡ تَعۡجَبۡ فَعَجَبٌ قَوۡلُهُمۡ ءَاِذَا
كُنَّا تُرٰبًا ءَاِنَّا لَفِيۡ خَلۡقٍ جَدِيۡدٍ ۬ؕ
اُولٰٓئِكَ الَّذِيۡنَ كَفَرُوۡا بِرَبِّهِمۡۚ
وَاُولٰٓئِكَ الۡاَغۡلٰلُ فِيۡۤ اَعۡنَاقِهِمۡۚ
وَاُولٰٓئِكَ اَصۡحٰبُ النَّارِۚ هُمۡ
فِيۡهَا خٰلِدُوۡنَ ﴿٥﴾
وَيَسۡتَعۡجِلُوۡنَكَ بِالسَّيِّئَةِ قَبۡلَ
الۡحَسَنَةِ وَقَدۡ خَلَتۡ مِنۡ قَبۡلِهِمُ
الۡمَثُلٰتُ ؕ وَاِنَّ رَبَّكَ لَذُوۡ مَغۡفِرَةٍ
لِّلنَّاسِ عَلٰى ظُلۡمِهِمۡۚ وَاِنَّ رَبَّكَ
لَشَدِيۡدُ الۡعِقَابِ ﴿٦﴾
وَيَقُوۡلُ الَّذِيۡنَ كَفَرُوۡا لَوۡلَاۤ اُنۡزِلَ
عَلَيۡهِ اٰيَةٌ مِّنۡ رَّبِّهٖ ؕ اِنَّمَاۤ اَنۡتَ
مُنۡذِرٌ وَّلِكُلِّ قَوۡمٍ هَادٍ ﴿٧﴾ ع
اَللّٰهُ يَعۡلَمُ مَا تَحۡمِلُ كُلُّ اُنۡثٰى
وَمَا تَغِيۡضُ الۡاَرۡحَامُ وَمَا تَزۡدَادُ ؕ
وَكُلُّ شَيۡءٍ عِنۡدَهٗ بِمِقۡدَارٍ ﴿٨﴾
عٰلِمُ الۡغَيۡبِ وَالشَّهَادَةِ

and High.

Kabeerul-Muta'aal.

الْكَبِيرُ الْمُتَعَالِ ﴿٩﴾

10. It is all the same to Him whether you speak in secret or out loud, try to hide in the darkness of night or walk in the brightness of day.

10. Sawaaa'um-minkum man asarral-qawla wa man jahara bihee wa man huwa mustakhfim-billayli wa saaribum binnahaar.

سَوَاءٌ مِّنكُم مَّنْ أَسَرَّ الْقَوْلَ وَمَن
جَهَرَ بِهِ وَمَنْ هُوَ مُسْتَخْفٍ بِاللَّيْلِ
وَسَارِبٌ بِالنَّهَارِ ﴿١٠﴾

11. Everyone is guarded and protected on all sides by the order of Allah. Allah does not change the condition of a nation unless it changes what is in its heart. When Allah wants to punish a people, there is no way to escape from it and no one besides Allah will protect them from it.

11. Lahoo mu'aqqibaatum-mim bayni yadayhi wa min khalfihee yaḥfaẓoonahoo min amril-laah; innal-laaha laa yughayyiru maa biqawmin ḥattaa yughayyiroo maa bi-anfusihim; wa izaaa araadal-laahu biqawmin sooo'an falaa maradda lah; wa maa lahum min doonihee miñw-waal.

لَهُ مُعَقِّبَاتٌ مِّن بَيْنِ يَدَيْهِ وَ
مِنْ خَلْفِهِ يَحْفَظُونَهُ مِنْ أَمْرِ
اللَّهِ ۗ إِنَّ اللَّهَ لَا يُغَيِّرُ مَا بِقَوْمٍ
حَتَّىٰ يُغَيِّرُوا مَا بِأَنفُسِهِمْ ۗ وَإِذَا
أَرَادَ اللَّهُ بِقَوْمٍ سُوءًا فَلَا مَرَدَّ لَهُ ۚ
وَمَا لَهُم مِّن دُونِهِ مِن وَالٍ ﴿١١﴾

12. It is He Who flashes lightning to frighten you and to give you hope. It is He who forms the heavy clouds.

12. Huwal-lazee yureekumul-barqa khawfañw-wa ṭama'añw-wa yunshi'us-saḥaabas-siqaal.

هُوَ الَّذِي يُرِيكُمُ الْبَرْقَ خَوْفًا وَ
طَمَعًا وَيُنشِئُ السَّحَابَ الثِّقَالَ ﴿١٢﴾

13. Both the thunder and the angels glorify Him and, out of fearing Him, always praise Him. He sends down thunderbolts to strike whomever He wants, while they are busy arguing about the existence of Allah. His punishment is stern.

13. Wa yusabbiḥur-ra'du biḥamdihee walmalaaa'ikatu min kheefatihee wa yursiluṣ-ṣawaa'iqa fayuṣeebu bihaa mañy-yashaaa'u wa hum yujaadiloona fil-laahi wa Huwa shadeedul-miḥaal.

وَيُسَبِّحُ الرَّعْدُ بِحَمْدِهِ وَالْمَلَائِكَةُ
مِنْ خِيفَتِهِ وَيُرْسِلُ الصَّوَاعِقَ
فَيُصِيبُ بِهَا مَن يَشَاءُ وَهُمْ
يُجَادِلُونَ فِي اللَّهِ ج وَهُوَ
شَدِيدُ الْمِحَالِ ﴿١٣﴾

14. Prayer to Him is the true prayer. Those to whom they pray instead of Allah will answer none of their prayers. It is as though one stretches his hands out to the water that can never reach one's mouth. The prayers of the unbelievers can have no effect but to become void.

14. Lahoo da'watul-ḥaqq; wallazeena yad'oona min doonihee laa yastajeeboona lahum bishay'in illaa kabaasiṭi kaffayhi ilal-maaa'i liyablugha faahu wa maa huwa bibaalighih; wa maa du'aaa'ul kaafireena illaa fee ḍalaal.

لَهُ دَعْوَةُ الْحَقِّ ۖ وَالَّذِينَ يَدْعُونَ
مِن دُونِهِ لَا يَسْتَجِيبُونَ لَهُم
بِشَيْءٍ إِلَّا كَبَاسِطِ كَفَّيْهِ إِلَى الْمَاءِ
لِيَبْلُغَ فَاهُ وَمَا هُوَ بِبَالِغِهِ ۚ وَمَا
دُعَاءُ الْكَافِرِينَ إِلَّا فِي ضَلَالٍ ﴿١٤﴾

(Bow Down)

15. All in the heavens and the earth prostrate themselves before Allah, either of their own free will or by force, just as do their shadows in the mornings and evenings.

15. Wa lillaahi yasjudu man fis-samaawaati wal-arḍi ṭaw-'añw-wa karhañw-wa ẓilaalu-hum bilghuduwwi wal-aaṣaal. ۩

وَلِلَّهِ يَسْجُدُ مَن فِي السَّمَاوَاتِ
وَالْأَرْضِ طَوْعًا وَكَرْهًا وَظِلَالُهُم
بِالْغُدُوِّ وَالْآصَالِ ۩ ﴿١٥﴾ السجدة

16. (Muhammad), ask them, "Who is the Lord of the heavens

16. Qul mar-Rabbus-samaa-waati wal-arḍ;

قُلْ مَن رَّبُّ السَّمَاوَاتِ وَالْأَرْضِ ۗ

and the earth?" Say, "It is Allah." Ask them, "Why then have you taken guardians other than Allah when such guardians can neither benefit nor harm themselves?" Ask them, "Are the seeing (believer) and the blind (unbeliever) equal? Is light equal to darkness?" Do they consider that their idols have created anything like that of Allah, thus, both creations appear to them to be alike?" Say, "Allah alone is the Creator of all things and He is the One, the All-Dominant."

qulillaah; qul afattakhaẕtum min dooniheee awliyaaa'a laa yamlikoona li-anfusihim naf-'añw-wa laa ḍarraa; qul hal yastawil-a'maa wal-baṣeeru am hal tastawiẓ-ẓulumaatu wannoor; am ja'aloo lillaahi shurakaaa'a khalaqoo kakhalqihee fatashaabahal-khalqu 'alayhim; qulillaahu khaaliqu kulli shay'iñw-wa Huwal-Waaḥidul-Qahhaar.

قُلِ اللّٰهُ ؕ قُلْ اَفَاتَّخَذْتُمْ مِّنْ
دُوْنِهٖۤ اَوْلِيَآءَ لَا يَمْلِكُوْنَ لِاَنْفُسِهِمْ
نَفْعًا وَّلَا ضَرًّا ؕ قُلْ هَلْ يَسْتَوِى
الْاَعْمٰى وَالْبَصِيْرُ ۙ۬ اَمْ هَلْ تَسْتَوِى
الظُّلُمٰتُ وَالنُّوْرُ ۚ۬ اَمْ جَعَلُوْا لِلّٰهِ
شُرَكَآءَ خَلَقُوْا كَخَلْقِهٖ فَتَشَابَهَ
الْخَلْقُ عَلَيْهِمْ ؕ قُلِ اللّٰهُ خَالِقُ
كُلِّ شَىْءٍ وَّهُوَ الْوَاحِدُ الْقَهَّارُ ﴿١٦﴾

17. When Allah sends down water (the truth) from the sky and floods run through the valleys (hearts), certain quantities of foam (falsehood) rise on the surface of the flood water. This is similar to that foam which rises when you expose something to the heat of a fire to manufacture ornaments or for other reasons. To Allah Truth and falsehood are like these examples. The foam disappears but what is profitable to the human being stays in the land. Thus, does Allah coin His parables.

17. Anzala minas-samaaa'i maaa'an fasaalat awdiyatum biqadarihaa faḥtamalas-saylu-zabadar-raabiyaa; wa mimmaa yooqidoona 'alayhi finnaaribtighaaa'a ḥilyatin aw mataa'in zabadum-mis̲luh; kaẕaalika yaḍribullaahul-ḥaqqa walbaaṭil; fa-ammaz-zabadu fayaẕhabu jufaaa'aa; wa ammaa maa yanfa'un-naasa fayamkus̲u filarḍ; kaẕaalika yaḍribul-laahulams̲aal.

اَنْزَلَ مِنَ السَّمَآءِ مَآءً فَسَالَتْ اَوْدِيَةٌۢ
بِقَدَرِهَا فَاحْتَمَلَ السَّيْلُ زَبَدًا
رَّابِيًا ؕ وَمِمَّا يُوْقِدُوْنَ عَلَيْهِ
فِى النَّارِ ابْتِغَآءَ حِلْيَةٍ اَوْ مَتَاعٍ
زَبَدٌ مِّثْلُهٗ ؕ كَذٰلِكَ يَضْرِبُ اللّٰهُ
الْحَقَّ وَالْبَاطِلَ ۬ؕ فَاَمَّا الزَّبَدُ
فَيَذْهَبُ جُفَآءً ۚ وَاَمَّا مَا يَنْفَعُ
النَّاسَ فَيَمْكُثُ فِى الْاَرْضِ ؕ كَذٰلِكَ
يَضْرِبُ اللّٰهُ الْاَمْثَالَ ؕ﴿١٧﴾

18. Those who answer the call of their Lord will receive good rewards. Those who did not answer the call of their Lord, whatever they offer to redeem themselves, even offering double the wealth of the whole earth, will not be accepted. They will face a terrible reckoning and their dwelling will be hell, a terrible place to rest!

18. Lillaẕeenas-tajaaboo li-Rabbihimul-ḥusnaa; wallaẕeena lam yastajeeboo lahoo law anna lahum maa fil-arḍi jamee'añw-wa mis̲lahoo ma'ahoo laftadaw bih; ulaaa'ika lahum sooo'ul-ḥisaab; wa ma-waahum Jahannamu wa bi'sal-mihaad.

لِلَّذِيْنَ اسْتَجَابُوْا لِرَبِّهِمُ الْحُسْنٰى ؕ
وَالَّذِيْنَ لَمْ يَسْتَجِيْبُوْا لَهٗ لَوْ اَنَّ
لَهُمْ مَّا فِى الْاَرْضِ جَمِيْعًا وَّمِثْلَهٗ
مَعَهٗ لَافْتَدَوْا بِهٖ ؕ اُولٰٓئِكَ لَهُمْ
سُوْٓءُ الْحِسَابِ ۙ۬ وَمَاْوٰهُمْ جَهَنَّمُ ؕ
وَبِئْسَ الْمِهَادُ ﴿١٨﴾ ع

وقف النبی صلى الله عليه وآله وسلم

ع ٢ / ١١ النصف

19. Can a person who knows that what is revealed to you from your Lord is the truth be considered equal to a blind person? Only those who have understanding take heed.

19. Afamañy-ya'lamu annamaaa unzila ilayka mir-Rabbikal-ḥaqqu kaman huwa a'maaa; innamaa yataẕakkaru - ulul-albaab.

اَفَمَنْ يَّعْلَمُ اَنَّمَآ اُنْزِلَ اِلَيْكَ
مِنْ رَّبِّكَ الْحَقُّ كَمَنْ هُوَ اَعْمٰى ؕ
اِنَّمَا يَتَذَكَّرُ اُولُوا الْاَلْبَابِ ۙ﴿١٩﴾

20. Those who fulfill their promise to, and covenant with Allah,

20. Allazeena yoofoona bi‘ahdil-laahi wa laa yanqudoonal-meesaaq.

الَّذِيْنَ يُوْفُوْنَ بِعَهْدِ اللّٰهِ وَلَا يَنْقُضُوْنَ الْمِيْثَاقَ ۙ

21. who maintain all the proper relations that Allah has commanded them to maintain, who have fear of their Lord and the hardships of the Day of Judgment,

21. Wallazeena yasiloona maaa amaral-laahu biheee añy-yoosala wa yakhshawna Rabbahum wa yakhaafoona sooo’al-hisaab.

وَالَّذِيْنَ يَصِلُوْنَ مَآ أَمَرَ اللّٰهُ بِهٖٓ أَنْ يُّوْصَلَ وَيَخْشَوْنَ رَبَّهُمْ وَيَخَافُوْنَ سُوْٓءَ الْحِسَابِ ۚ

22. who exercise patience to gain Allah's pleasure, who are steadfast in prayer, who spend for the cause of Allah privately and in public, and who keep away evil with good, will have a blissful end.

22. Wallazeena sabarub-tighaaa’a Wajhi Rabbihim wa aqaamus-Salaata wa anfaqoo mimmaa razaqnaahum sirrañw-wa-‘alaaniyataňw-wa yadra’oona bilhasanatis-sayyi’ata ulaaa’ika lahum ‘uqbad-daar.

وَالَّذِيْنَ صَبَرُوا ابْتِغَآءَ وَجْهِ رَبِّهِمْ وَأَقَامُوا الصَّلٰوةَ وَأَنْفَقُوْا مِمَّا رَزَقْنٰهُمْ سِرًّا وَّعَلَانِيَةً وَّيَدْرَءُوْنَ بِالْحَسَنَةِ السَّيِّئَةَ أُولٰٓئِكَ لَهُمْ عُقْبَى الدَّارِ ۙ

23. They will be admitted to the gardens of Eden wherein they will live forever with their righteous fathers, spouses, and offspring. The angels will come to them through every gate,

23. Jannaatu ‘Adniñy-yadkhuloonahaa wa man salaha min aabaaa’ihim wa azwaajihim wa zurriyyaatihim walmalaaa’i-katu yadkhuloona ‘alayhim min kulli baab.

جَنّٰتُ عَدْنٍ يَّدْخُلُوْنَهَا وَمَنْ صَلَحَ مِنْ اٰبَآئِهِمْ وَأَزْوَاجِهِمْ وَذُرِّيّٰتِهِمْ وَالْمَلٰٓئِكَةُ يَدْخُلُوْنَ عَلَيْهِمْ مِّنْ كُلِّ بَابٍ ۚ

24. saying, "Peace be with you for all that you have patiently endured. Blessed is the reward of Paradise."

24. Salaamun ‘alaykum bimaa sabartum; fani‘ma ‘uqbad-daar.

سَلٰمٌ عَلَيْكُمْ بِمَا صَبَرْتُمْ فَنِعْمَ عُقْبَى الدَّارِ ۗ

25. Those who disregard their covenant with Allah after He has taken such a pledge from them, who sever the proper relations that Allah has commanded them to establish, and who spread evil in the land will have Allah's condemnation instead of reward and will face the most terrible end.

25. Wallazeena yanqudoona ‘Ahdal-laahi mim ba‘di mee-saaqihee wa yaqta‘oona maaa amaral-laahu biheee añy-yoosala wa yufsidoona fil-ardi ulaaa’ika lahumul-la‘natu wa lahum sooo’ud-daar.

وَالَّذِيْنَ يَنْقُضُوْنَ عَهْدَ اللّٰهِ مِنْ بَعْدِ مِيْثَاقِهٖ وَيَقْطَعُوْنَ مَآ أَمَرَ اللّٰهُ بِهٖٓ أَنْ يُّوْصَلَ وَيُفْسِدُوْنَ فِي الْأَرْضِ أُولٰٓئِكَ لَهُمُ اللَّعْنَةُ وَلَهُمْ سُوْٓءُ الدَّارِ ۞

26. Allah gives abundant sustenance to whomever He wants and determines everyone's destiny. Some people are very happy with the worldly life. Compared to the life to come it is only a temporary means.

26. Allaahu yabsutur-rizqa limañy-yashaaa’u wa yaqdir; wa farihoo bilhayaatid-dunyaa wa mal-hayaatud-dunyaa fil-Aakhirati illaa mataa‘.

اللّٰهُ يَبْسُطُ الرِّزْقَ لِمَنْ يَّشَآءُ وَيَقْدِرُ ۗ وَفَرِحُوْا بِالْحَيٰوةِ الدُّنْيَا ۖ وَمَا الْحَيٰوةُ الدُّنْيَا فِي الْاٰخِرَةِ إِلَّا مَتَاعٌ ۞

27. The unbelievers say, "Why have not some miracles been sent to him (Muhammad) from his Lord." Say, "Allah causes whomever He wants to go astray and He guides those who turn to

27. Wa yaqoolul-lazeena kafaroo law laaa unzila ‘alayhi Aayatum-mir-Rabbih; qul innal-laaha yudillu mañy-yashaaa’u wa yahdeee

وَيَقُوْلُ الَّذِيْنَ كَفَرُوْا لَوْلَآ أُنْزِلَ عَلَيْهِ اٰيَةٌ مِّنْ رَّبِّهٖ ۗ قُلْ إِنَّ اللّٰهَ يُضِلُّ مَنْ يَّشَآءُ وَيَهْدِيْٓ

Him in repentance

ilayhi man anaab.

اِلَيْهِ مَنْ اَنَابَ ۗ۞

28. and the faithful ones whose hearts are comforted by the remembrance of Allah. Remembrance of Allah certainly brings comfort to all hearts.

28. Allazeena aamanoo wa taṭma'innu quloobuhum bizikril-laah; alaa bizikril-laahi taṭma'innul-quloob.

اَلَّذِيْنَ اٰمَنُوْا وَتَطْمَىِٕنُّ قُلُوْبُهُمْ بِذِكْرِ اللّٰهِ ۗ اَلَا بِذِكْرِ اللّٰهِ تَطْمَىِٕنُّ الْقُلُوْبُ ۞

29. The righteously striving believers will receive Tuba (the tree in the garden (paradise) and the best eternal dwelling.

29. Allazeena aamanoo wa 'amiluṣ-ṣaaliḥaati ṭoobaa lahum wa ḥusnu ma-aab.

اَلَّذِيْنَ اٰمَنُوْا وَعَمِلُوا الصّٰلِحٰتِ طُوْبٰى لَهُمْ وَحُسْنُ مَاٰبٍ ۞

30. We have sent you to a nation before whom there lived many nations so that you would read to them what We have revealed to you. They still deny the existence of the Beneficent. Say, "He is my Lord besides whom there is no other Ilah (one deserving to be worshipped). I trust Him and turn to Him in repentance."

30. Kazaalika arsalnaaka feee ummatin qad khalat min qablihaaa umamul-litatluwa 'alayhimul-lazeee-awḥaynaaa ilayka wa hum yakfuroona bir-Raḥmaan; qul Huwa Rabbee laaa ilaaha illaa Huwa 'alayhi-tawakkaltu wa ilayhi mataab.

كَذٰلِكَ اَرْسَلْنٰكَ فِيْۤ اُمَّةٍ قَدْ خَلَتْ مِنْ قَبْلِهَاۤ اُمَمٌ لِّتَتْلُوَا۟ عَلَيْهِمُ الَّذِيْۤ اَوْحَيْنَاۤ اِلَيْكَ وَهُمْ يَكْفُرُوْنَ بِالرَّحْمٰنِ ۗ قُلْ هُوَ رَبِّيْ لَاۤ اِلٰهَ اِلَّا هُوَ ۚ عَلَيْهِ تَوَكَّلْتُ وَاِلَيْهِ مَتَابِ ۞

31. Even if the Quran would make mountains move, cut the earth into pieces and make the dead able to speak, (the unbelievers still would not believe). All affairs are in the hands of Allah. Did the believers still hope that they will believe? Had Allah wanted he could have guided the whole of mankind to the right path. The unbelievers will always suffer afflictions that result from their deeds or the afflictions which occur near their homes, until Allah's promise of punishing them will be fulfilled. Allah does not disregard His promise.

31. Wa law anna Qur'aanan suyyirat bihil-jibaalu aw quṭ-ṭi'at bihil-arḍu aw kullima bihil-mawtaa; bal lillaahil-amru ja-mee'aa; afalam yay'asil-laze-na aamanooo al-law yashaaa'-ullaahu lahadan-naasa jamee-'aa; wa laa yazaalul-lazeena kafaroo tuṣeebuhum bimaa ṣana'oo qaari'atun aw taḥullu qareebam-min daarihim ḥattaa ya-tiya wa'dul-laah; innal-laaha laa yukhliful-mee'aad.

وَلَوْ اَنَّ قُرْاٰنًا سُيِّرَتْ بِهِ الْجِبَالُ اَوْ قُطِّعَتْ بِهِ الْاَرْضُ اَوْ كُلِّمَ بِهِ الْمَوْتٰى ۗ بَلْ لِّلّٰهِ الْاَمْرُ جَمِيْعًا ۗ اَفَلَمْ يَايْـَٔسِ الَّذِيْنَ اٰمَنُوْۤا اَنْ لَّوْ يَشَآءُ اللّٰهُ لَهَدَى النَّاسَ جَمِيْعًا ۗ وَلَا يَزَالُ الَّذِيْنَ كَفَرُوْا تُصِيْبُهُمْ بِمَا صَنَعُوْا قَارِعَةٌ اَوْ تَحُلُّ قَرِيْبًا مِّنْ دَارِهِمْ حَتّٰى يَاْتِيَ وَعْدُ اللّٰهِ ۗ اِنَّ اللّٰهَ لَا يُخْلِفُ الْمِيْعَادَ ۞

32. (Muhammad), people have mocked the Messengers who lived before you. I gave a respite to the unbelievers (so that they would repent, but they did not). Then I struck them with a terrible retribution.

32. Wa laqadis-tuhzi'a bi-Rusulim-min qablika fa-amlay-tu lillazeena kafaroo ṣumma akhaztuhum fakayfa kaana 'iqaab.

وَلَقَدِ اسْتُهْزِئَ بِرُسُلٍ مِّنْ قَبْلِكَ فَاَمْلَيْتُ لِلَّذِيْنَ كَفَرُوْا ثُمَّ اَخَذْتُهُمْ ۖ فَكَيْفَ كَانَ عِقَابِ ۞

33. (Can anyone be considered equal to) the One who is the Guardian of every soul and the Watcher of what it has gained? Yet, the unbelievers have considered their idols equal to

33. Afaman Huwa qaaa'imun 'alaa kulli nafsim bimaa kasabat; wa ja'aloo lillaahi shurakaaa'a qul

اَفَمَنْ هُوَ قَآئِمٌ عَلٰى كُلِّ نَفْسٍ بِمَا كَسَبَتْ ۚ وَجَعَلُوْا لِلّٰهِ شُرَكَآءَ ۗ قُلْ

Allah. Say, "Name the attributes of your idols. Are you trying to inform Him about something that does not exist on earth? Do you only mention empty names?

Evil plans have attracted the unbelievers and have misled them from the right path. No one can guide those whom Allah has caused to go astray.

sammoohum; am tunabbi'oonahoo bimaa laa ya'lamu fil-arḍi am biẓaahirim-minal-qawl; bal zuyyina lillazeena kafaroo makruhum wa ṣuddoo 'anis-sabeel; wa mañy-yuḍlilil-laahu famaa lahoo min haad.

سَمُّوْهُمْ ؕ اَمْ تُنَبِّـُٔوْنَهٗ بِمَا لَا يَعْلَمُ
فِي الْاَرْضِ اَمْ بِظَاهِرٍ مِّنَ الْقَوْلِ ؕ
بَلْ زُيِّنَ لِلَّذِيْنَ كَفَرُوْا مَكْرُهُمْ
وَصُدُّوْا عَنِ السَّبِيْلِ ؕ وَمَنْ يُّضْلِلِ
اللّٰهُ فَمَا لَهٗ مِنْ هَادٍ ۝٣٣

34. The unbelievers will face torment in this world and their punishment in the life hereafter will be even greater. No one can save them from the wrath of Allah.

34. Lahum 'azaabun fil-ḥayaatid-dunyaa wa la'azaabul-Aakhirati ashaqq; wa maa lahum minal-laahi miñw-waaq.

لَهُمْ عَذَابٌ فِي الْحَيٰوةِ الدُّنْيَا
وَلَعَذَابُ الْاٰخِرَةِ اَشَقُّ ۚ وَمَا لَهُمْ
مِّنَ اللّٰهِ مِنْ وَّاقٍ ۝٣٤

35. The gardens which have been promised to the pious have flowing streams, everlasting fruits, and perpetual shade. Such is the blissful end of the pious, but hellfire is the terrible end for the unbelievers.

35. Masalul-jannatil-latee wu'idal-muttaqoona tajree min taḥtihal-anhaar; ukuluhaa daaa'imuñw-wa ẓilluhaa; tilka 'uqbal-lazeenat-taqaw wa 'uqbal-kaafireenan-Naar.

مَثَلُ الْجَنَّةِ الَّتِيْ وُعِدَ الْمُتَّقُوْنَ ؕ
تَجْرِيْ مِنْ تَحْتِهَا الْاَنْهٰرُ ؕ اُكُلُهَا
دَآئِمٌ وَّظِلُّهَا ؕ تِلْكَ عُقْبَى الَّذِيْنَ
اتَّقَوْا ۖ وَّعُقْبَى الْكٰفِرِيْنَ النَّارُ ۝٣٥

36. The People of the Book are happy with what has been revealed to you. Among the different parties, there are some who dislike part of what has been revealed to you. (Muhammad), tell them, "I have been commanded to worship Allah alone, not to consider anything equal to Him. To Him do I pray and to Him shall I return."

36. Wallazeena aataynaahumul-Kitaaba yafraḥoona bimaaa unzila ilayka wa minal-Aḥzaabi mañy-yunkiru ba'ḍah; qul innamaaa umirtu an a'budal-laaha wa laaa ushrika bih; ilayhi ad'oo wa ilayhi ma-aab.

وَالَّذِيْنَ اٰتَيْنٰهُمُ الْكِتٰبَ يَفْرَحُوْنَ
بِمَآ اُنْزِلَ اِلَيْكَ وَمِنَ الْاَحْزَابِ
مَنْ يُّنْكِرُ بَعْضَهٗ ؕ قُلْ اِنَّمَآ اُمِرْتُ
اَنْ اَعْبُدَ اللّٰهَ وَلَآ اُشْرِكَ بِهٖ ؕ
اِلَيْهِ اَدْعُوْا وَاِلَيْهِ مَاٰبِ ۝٣٦

37. We revealed it (the Quran) as a code of conduct in the Arabic language. (Muhammad), if you follow their desires after the knowledge has been revealed to you, know that no one will be able to guard or protect you from the wrath of Allah.

37. Wa kazaalika anzalnaahu ḥukman 'Arabiyyaa; wa la'init-taba'ta ahwaaa'ahum ba'da maa jaaa'aka minal'ilmi maa laka minal-laahi miñw-waliyyiñw-wa laa waaq.

وَكَذٰلِكَ اَنْزَلْنٰهُ حُكْمًا عَرَبِيًّا ؕ
وَلَئِنِ اتَّبَعْتَ اَهْوَآءَهُمْ بَعْدَ مَا
جَآءَكَ مِنَ الْعِلْمِ ۙ مَا لَكَ مِنَ اللّٰهِ
مِنْ وَّلِيٍّ وَّلَا وَاقٍ ۝٣٧ ع ٥ ٦ ١١

38. We sent Messengers before you (Muhammad) and gave them wives and offspring. No Messenger was to show miracles without the permission of Allah.

38. Wa laqad arsalnaa Rusulam-min qablika wa ja'alnaa lahum azwaajañw-wa zurriyyah; wa maa kaana lirasoolin añy-yatiya bi-aayatin illaa bi-iznil-laah; likulli ajalin kitaab.

وَلَقَدْ اَرْسَلْنَا رُسُلًا مِّنْ قَبْلِكَ
وَجَعَلْنَا لَهُمْ اَزْوَاجًا وَّذُرِّيَّةً ؕ
وَمَا كَانَ لِرَسُوْلٍ اَنْ يَّاْتِيَ بِاٰيَةٍ اِلَّا
بِاِذْنِ اللّٰهِ ؕ لِكُلِّ اَجَلٍ كِتَابٌ ۝٣٨

39. For every event Allah has ordained His decree. Allah establishes or effaces whatever He

39. Yamḥul-laahu maa yashaaa'u wa yusbit;

يَمْحُوا اللّٰهُ مَا يَشَآءُ وَيُثْبِتُ ۖۚ

wants and with Him is the original of the Book.

wa 'indahooo Ummul-Kitaab.

وَعِنْدَهٗۤ اُمُّ الْكِتٰبِ ﴿٣٩﴾

40. Whether We show them (the unbelievers) to you facing the punishment with which We had threatened them, or make you die first (before its fulfillment), your duty is only to preach. It is up to Us to call them to account (for their deeds).

40. Wa im-maa nuriyannaka ba'ḍal-lazee na'iduhum aw natawaffayannaka fa-innamaa 'alaykal-balaaghu wa 'alaynal-ḥisaab.

وَاِنْ مَّا نُرِيَنَّكَ بَعْضَ الَّذِىْ نَعِدُهُمْ
اَوْ نَتَوَفَّيَنَّكَ فَاِنَّمَا عَلَيْكَ الْبَلٰغُ
وَعَلَيْنَا الْحِسَابُ ﴿٤٠﴾

41. Have they not considered that We have taken over the land and reduced its borders? It is Allah who issues the irreversible decree and His reckoning is swift.

41. Awalam yaraw annaa na-til-arḍa nanquṣuhaa min aṭraafihaa; wallaahu yaḥkumu laa mu'aqqiba liḥukmih; wa Huwa Saree'ul-ḥisaab.

اَوَلَمْ يَرَوْا اَنَّا نَاْتِى الْاَرْضَ نَنْقُصُهَا
مِنْ اَطْرَافِهَا ؕ وَاللّٰهُ يَحْكُمُ لَا
مُعَقِّبَ لِحُكْمِهٖ ؕ وَهُوَ سَرِيْعُ
الْحِسَابِ ﴿٤١﴾

42. Certain people who lived before plotted evil plans. However Allah has control of all plans (forms of punishments). He knows what every soul does. The unbelievers will soon learn who will achieve the blissful end.

42. Wa qad makaral-lazeena min qablihim falillaahil-makru jamee'aa; ya'lamu maa taksibu kullu nafs; wa saya'lamul-kuffaaru liman 'uqbad-daar.

وَقَدْ مَكَرَ الَّذِيْنَ مِنْ قَبْلِهِمْ فَلِلّٰهِ
الْمَكْرُ جَمِيْعًا ؕ يَعْلَمُ مَا تَكْسِبُ
كُلُّ نَفْسٍ ؕ وَسَيَعْلَمُ الْكُفّٰرُ لِمَنْ
عُقْبَى الدَّارِ ﴿٤٢﴾

43. (Muhammad), the unbelievers say, "You are not a Messenger." Say, "Allah and those who have the knowledge of the Book are sufficient witness (to my prophet-hood)."

43. Wa yaqoolul-lazeena kafaroo lasta mursalaa; qul kafaa billaahi shaheedam baynee wa baynakum wa man 'indahoo 'ilmul-Kitaab.

وَيَقُوْلُ الَّذِيْنَ كَفَرُوْا لَسْتَ مُرْسَلًا ؕ
قُلْ كَفٰى بِاللّٰهِ شَهِيْدًاۢ بَيْنِىْ وَبَيْنَكُمْ ۙ
وَمَنْ عِنْدَهٗ عِلْمُ الْكِتٰبِ ﴿٤٣﴾ ع

Ibrahim, Abraham (14)

In the Name of Allah,
the Beneficent, the Merciful.

Sûrat Ibrâhîm-14

(Revealed at Makkah)

Bismillaahir Raḥmaanir Raḥeem

(١٤) سُوْرَةُ اِبْرٰهِيْمَ مَكِّيَّةٌ (٧٢)

اٰيَاتُهَا ٥٢ بِسْمِ اللّٰهِ الرَّحْمٰنِ الرَّحِيْمِ رُكُوْعَاتُهَا ٧

1. Alif. Lam. Ra. A Book has been revealed to you, (Muhammad), so that, by the permission of their Lord, you would be able to lead people from darkness (disbelief) into light (belief) along the path of the Majestic, Praised One.

1. Alif-Laaam-Raa; Kitaa-bun anzalnaahu ilayka litukhri-jan-naasa minaẓ-ẓulumaati ilan-noori bi-izni Rabbihim ilaa ṣiraaṭil 'Azeezil-Ḥameed.

الٓرٰ ۚ كِتٰبٌ اَنْزَلْنٰهُ اِلَيْكَ لِتُخْرِجَ
النَّاسَ مِنَ الظُّلُمٰتِ اِلَى النُّوْرِ ۙ
بِاِذْنِ رَبِّهِمْ اِلٰى صِرَاطِ الْعَزِيْزِ
الْحَمِيْدِ ﴿١﴾

2. To Allah belongs whatever is in the heavens and the earth. Woe to the unbelievers; they will face the most severe punishment!

2. Allaahil-lazee lahoo maa fis-samaawaati wa maa fil-arḍ; wa waylul-lilkaafireena min 'azaabin shadeed.

اللّٰهِ الَّذِىْ لَهٗ مَا فِى السَّمٰوٰتِ وَمَا
فِى الْاَرْضِ ؕ وَوَيْلٌ لِّلْكٰفِرِيْنَ
مِنْ عَذَابٍ شَدِيْدِ ﴿٢﴾

3. It is they who have given preference to the worldly life over the life to come. They create obstacles in the way that leads to

3. Allazeena yastaḥibboo-nal-ḥayaatad-dunyaa 'alal Aakhirati wa yaṣuddoona 'an sabeelil-

الَّذِيْنَ يَسْتَحِبُّوْنَ الْحَيٰوةَ الدُّنْيَا
عَلَى الْاٰخِرَةِ وَيَصُدُّوْنَ عَنْ سَبِيْلِ

Allah and try to make it seem crooked. They are in manifest error.

laahi wa yabghoonahaa 'iwajaa; ulaaa'ika fee ḍalaalim ba'eed.

اللَّهِ وَيَبْغُونَهَا عِوَجًا ۚ أُولَٰئِكَ فِي
ضَلَالٍ بَعِيدٍ ۝٣

4. All the Messengers that We sent spoke the language of their people so that they could explain (their message to them). Allah guides or causes to go astray whomever He wants. He is Majestic and All-wise.

4. Wa maaa arsalnaa mir-Rasoolin illaa bilisaani qawmihee liyubayyina lahum fayuḍillul-laahu mañy-yashaaa'u wa yahdee mañy-yashaaa'; wa Huwal-'Azeezul-Ḥakeem

وَمَا أَرْسَلْنَا مِنْ رَسُولٍ إِلَّا بِلِسَانِ
قَوْمِهِ لِيُبَيِّنَ لَهُمْ ۖ فَيُضِلُّ اللَّهُ مَنْ
يَشَاءُ وَيَهْدِي مَنْ يَشَاءُ ۚ وَهُوَ
الْعَزِيزُ الْحَكِيمُ ۝٤

5. We sent Moses and gave him miracles in order to lead his people from darkness into light and to remind them of the days of Allah (the rise of the leader with divine authority, departure from this world and the Day of Judgment). In this there is evidence (of the truth) for those who exercise patience and give thanks.

5. Wa laqad arsalnaa-Moosaa bi-Aayaatinaaa an akhrij qawmaka minaẓ-ẓulumaati ilan-noori wa z̲akkirhum bi-ayyaamil-laah; inna fee z̲aalika la-Aayaatil-likulli ṣabbaarin shakoor.

وَلَقَدْ أَرْسَلْنَا مُوسَىٰ بِآيَاتِنَا أَنْ
أَخْرِجْ قَوْمَكَ مِنَ الظُّلُمَاتِ إِلَى النُّورِ
وَذَكِّرْهُمْ بِأَيَّامِ اللَّهِ ۚ إِنَّ فِي ذَٰلِكَ
لَآيَاتٍ لِكُلِّ صَبَّارٍ شَكُورٍ ۝٥

6. Moses told his people, "Remember the favors that Allah granted you when He saved you from the people of the Pharaoh who had punished you in the worst manner by murdering your sons and keeping your women alive. It was a great trial for you from your Lord."

6. Wa-iz̲ qaala Moosaa liqawmihiz̲-kuroo ni'matallaahi 'alaykum iz̲ anjaakum-min-Aali Fir'awna yasoomoonakum sooo'al-'az̲aabi wa yuz̲abbiḥoona abnaaa'akum wa yastaḥyoona nisaaa'akum; wafee z̲aalikum balaaa'um-mir-Rabbikum 'aẓeem.

وَإِذْ قَالَ مُوسَىٰ لِقَوْمِهِ اذْكُرُوا
نِعْمَةَ اللَّهِ عَلَيْكُمْ إِذْ أَنْجَاكُمْ
مِنْ آلِ فِرْعَوْنَ يَسُومُونَكُمْ سُوءَ
الْعَذَابِ وَيُذَبِّحُونَ أَبْنَاءَكُمْ
وَيَسْتَحْيُونَ نِسَاءَكُمْ ۚ وَفِي ذَٰلِكُمْ
بَلَاءٌ مِنْ رَبِّكُمْ عَظِيمٌ ۝٦ ع ٢ ١٤

7. "Remember when your Lord said to you, 'If you give thanks, I shall give you greater (favors), but if you deny the Truth, know that My retribution is severe.'"

7. Wa iz̲ ta-az̲-z̲ana Rabbukum la'in shakartum la-azeedannakum wa la'in kafartum inna 'az̲aabee lashadeed.

وَإِذْ تَأَذَّنَ رَبُّكُمْ لَئِنْ شَكَرْتُمْ
لَأَزِيدَنَّكُمْ ۖ وَلَئِنْ كَفَرْتُمْ إِنَّ عَذَابِي
لَشَدِيدٌ ۝٧

8. Moses told his people, "If you and everyone on the earth turn to disbelief, know that Allah is self-sufficient and praiseworthy."

8. Wa qaala Moosaaa in takfurooo antum wa man fil-arḍi jamee'an fa-innal-laaha la-Ghaniyyun Ḥameed.

وَقَالَ مُوسَىٰ إِنْ تَكْفُرُوا أَنْتُمْ
وَمَنْ فِي الْأَرْضِ جَمِيعًا فَإِنَّ
اللَّهَ لَغَنِيٌّ حَمِيدٌ ۝٨

9. Did you (believers) ever hear the news about those who lived before you, like the people of Noah, Ad, Thamud, and those who lived after them? No one knows about them except Allah. Messengers were sent to them with miracles, but they put their

9. Alam ya-tikum naba'ullaz̲eena min qablikum qawmi Nooḥiñw-wa 'Aadiñw-wa S̲amood; wallaz̲eena mim ba'dihim; laa ya'lamuhum illallaah; jaaa'at-hum Rusuluhum bilbayyinaati

أَلَمْ يَأْتِكُمْ نَبَأُ الَّذِينَ مِنْ قَبْلِكُمْ
قَوْمِ نُوحٍ وَعَادٍ وَثَمُودَ ۛ وَالَّذِينَ عند المتقدمين ١٢
مِنْ بَعْدِهِمْ ۛ لَا يَعْلَمُهُمْ إِلَّا
اللَّهُ ۚ جَاءَتْهُمْ رُسُلُهُمْ بِالْبَيِّنَاتِ مع

hands in front their (messenger's) mouths and said, "We do not believe in whatever you preach and we are also doubtful and uncertain about that to which you invite us."

faraddooo aydiyahum feee afwaahihim wa qaalooo innaa kafarnaa bimaaa ursiltum bihee wa innaa lafee shakkim-mimmaa tad'oonanaaa ilayhi mureeb.

فَرَدُّوٓا اَيۡدِيَهُمۡ فِيۡٓ اَفۡوَاهِهِمۡ
وَقَالُوۡٓا اِنَّا كَفَرۡنَا بِمَآ اُرۡسِلۡتُمۡ بِهٖ
وَاِنَّا لَفِيۡ شَكٍّ مِّمَّا تَدۡعُوۡنَنَآ
اِلَيۡهِ مُرِيۡبٍ ٩

10. The Messengers asked them, "Could there be any doubt about the existence of Allah who has created the heavens and the earth? He calls you to Himself to forgive your sins. He gives you respite only until the appointed time." They said, "You are mere mortals like us. What you want is to prevent us from worshipping that which our fathers worshipped. Show us clear proof (if what you say is true)."

10. Qaalat Rusuluhum afil-laahi shakkun Faatiris-samaa-waati wal-arḍ; yad'ookum liyaghfira lakummin zunoobi-kum wa yu'akh-khirakum ilaaa ajalim-musam-maa; qaaloo in antum illaa basharum-mislunaa tureedoona an taṣuddoonaa 'ammaa kaana ya'budu aabaaa'unaa fa-toonaa bisul-ṭaanim-mubeen.

قَالَتۡ رُسُلُهُمۡ اَفِي اللّٰهِ شَكٌّ فَاطِرِ
السَّمٰوٰتِ وَالۡاَرۡضِ ؕ يَدۡعُوۡكُمۡ
لِيَغۡفِرَ لَكُمۡ مِّنۡ ذُنُوۡبِكُمۡ وَيُؤَخِّرَكُمۡ
اِلٰٓى اَجَلٍ مُّسَمًّى ؕ قَالُوۡٓا اِنۡ اَنۡتُمۡ
اِلَّا بَشَرٌ مِّثۡلُنَا ؕ تُرِيۡدُوۡنَ اَنۡ
تَصُدُّوۡنَا عَمَّا كَانَ يَعۡبُدُ اٰبَآؤُنَا
فَاۡتُوۡنَا بِسُلۡطٰنٍ مُّبِيۡنٍ ١٠

11. The Messengers replied, "We are certainly mere mortals like you, but Allah bestows His favors on whichever of His servants He wants. We cannot bring you authority without the permission of Allah. The faithful should trust in Allah alone.

11. Qaalat lahum Rusuluhum in naḥnu illaa basharum-mislukum wa laakinnal-laaha yamunnu 'alaa mañy-yashaaa'u min 'ibaadihee wa maa kaana lanaaa an na-tiyakum bisul-ṭaanin illaa bi-iznil-laah; wa 'alal-laahi falyatawak-kalil-mu'minoon.

قَالَتۡ لَهُمۡ رُسُلُهُمۡ اِنۡ نَّحۡنُ اِلَّا
بَشَرٌ مِّثۡلُكُمۡ وَلٰـكِنَّ اللّٰهَ يَمُنُّ عَلٰى مَنۡ
يَّشَآءُ مِنۡ عِبَادِهٖ ؕ وَمَا كَانَ لَنَاۤ
اَنۡ نَّاۡتِيَكُمۡ بِسُلۡطٰنٍ اِلَّا بِاِذۡنِ اللّٰهِ ؕ
وَعَلَى اللّٰهِ فَلۡيَتَوَكَّلِ الۡمُؤۡمِنُوۡنَ ١١

12. Why should we not trust in Allah when He has shown us the right way? We shall exercise patience against the troubles with which you afflict us. Whoever needs a trustee should trust in Allah."

12. Wa maa lanaaa allaa natawakkala 'alal-laahi wa qad hadaanaa subulanaa; wa lanaṣbiranna 'alaa maaa aazay-tumoonaa; wa 'alal-laahi falya-tawakkalil-mutawak-kiloon.

وَمَا لَنَاۤ اَلَّا نَتَوَكَّلَ عَلَى اللّٰهِ وَقَدۡ
هَدٰٮنَا سُبُلَنَا ؕ وَلَنَصۡبِرَنَّ عَلٰى مَاۤ
اٰذَيۡتُمُوۡنَا ؕ وَعَلَى اللّٰهِ فَلۡيَتَوَكَّلِ
الۡمُتَوَكِّلُوۡنَ ١٢

13. The unbelievers told the Messengers, "We shall expel you from our land unless you revert to our religion." Their Lord then sent them (the messengers) a revelation, "We have decided to destroy the unjust

13. Wa qaalal-lazeena kafaroo li-Rusulihim lanukhrijanna-kum min arḍinaaa aw lata'oo-dunna fee millatinaa fa-awḥaaa ilayhim Rabbuhum lanuhlikan-naẓ-ẓaalimeen.

وَقَالَ الَّذِيۡنَ كَفَرُوۡا لِرُسُلِهِمۡ
لَنُخۡرِجَنَّكُمۡ مِّنۡ اَرۡضِنَاۤ اَوۡ لَتَعُوۡدُنَّ
فِىۡ مِلَّتِنَا ؕ فَاَوۡحٰۤى اِلَيۡهِمۡ رَبُّهُمۡ
لَنُهۡلِكَنَّ الظّٰلِمِيۡنَ ١٣

14. and settle you in the land thereafter. This is for those who are afraid of Me and of My warning."

14 Wa lanuskinan-nakumul-arḍa mim ba'dihim; zaalika liman khaafa maqaamee wa khaafa

وَلَنُسۡكِنَنَّكُمُ الۡاَرۡضَ مِنۡۢ بَعۡدِهِمۡ ؕ
ذٰ لِكَ لِمَنۡ خَافَ مَقَامِىۡ وَخَافَ

wa‘eed.

وَعِيۡدِ ﴿١٤﴾

15. They prayed for victory and the haughty transgressors were defeated.

15. Wastaftaḥoo wa khaaba kullu jabbaarin ‘aneed.

وَاسۡتَفۡتَحُوۡا وَخَابَ كُلُّ جَبَّارٍ
عَنِيۡدٍ ﴿١٥﴾

16. Thereafter they will face hellfire wherein they will drink boiling water.

16. Miñw-waraaa’ihee Jahannamu wa yusqaa mimmaaa’in ṣadeed.

مِّنۡ وَّرَآئِهٖ جَهَنَّمُ وَيُسۡقٰى مِنۡ
مَّآءٍ صَدِيۡدٍ ﴿١٦﴾

17. they sip the unpleasant water, death will approach them from all sides, but they will never die. In addition to this, they will experience the most intense torment.

17. Yatajarra‘uhoo wa laa yakaadu yuseeghuhoo wa yateehil-mawtu min kulli makaaniñw-wa maa huwa-bimayyit;- wa miñw-waraaa’ihee ‘aẕaabun ghaleeẓ.

يَّتَجَرَّعُهٗ وَلَا يَكَادُ يُسِيۡغُهٗ وَيَاۡتِيۡهِ
الۡمَوۡتُ مِنۡ كُلِّ مَكَانٍ وَّمَا هُوَ
بِمَيِّتٍ‌ؕ وَمِنۡ وَّرَآئِهٖ عَذَابٌ
غَلِيۡظٌ ﴿١٧﴾

18. The deeds of those who deny the existence of their Lord are like ashes blown about by a strong wind on a stormy day. They will achieve nothing from their deeds. (What they have done) is a manifest error.

18. Maṯalul-laẕeena kafaroo bi-Rabbihim a‘maaluhum karamaadinish-taddat bihir-reeḥu fee yawmin ‘aaṣif; laa yaqdiroona mimmaa kasaboo ‘alaa shay’; ẕaalika huwaḍ-ḍalaalul-ba‘eed.

مَثَلُ الَّذِيۡنَ كَفَرُوۡا بِرَبِّهِمۡ اَعۡمَالُهُمۡ
كَرَمَادِ ۨاشۡتَدَّتۡ بِهِ الرِّيۡحُ فِىۡ
يَوۡمٍ عَاصِفٍ‌ؕ لَا يَقۡدِرُوۡنَ مِمَّا
كَسَبُوۡا عَلٰى شَىۡءٍ‌ؕ ذٰ لِكَ هُوَ
الضَّلٰلُ الۡبَعِيۡدُ ﴿١٨﴾

19. Did you not realize that Allah has created the heavens and the earth for a genuine purpose

19. Alam tara annal-laaha khalaqas-samaawaati wal-arḍa bilḥaqq; iñy-yasha-yuẕhibkum wa ya-ti bikhalqin jadeed.

اَلَمۡ تَرَ اَنَّ اللّٰهَ خَلَقَ السَّمٰوٰتِ وَ
الۡاَرۡضَ بِالۡحَـقِّ‌ؕ اِنۡ يَّشَاۡ يُذۡهِبۡكُمۡ
وَيَاۡتِ بِخَلۡقٍ جَدِيۡدٍ ﴿١٩﴾

20. and that it is not at all difficult for Allah to replace you with another creature if He so wills?

20. Wa maa ẕaalika ‘alallaahi bi‘azeez.

وَّمَا ذٰ لِكَ عَلَى اللّٰهِ بِعَزِيۡزٍ ﴿٢٠﴾

21. (On the Day of Judgment) everyone will appear before Allah and those who have been suppressed will say to their oppressors, "We were your followers, can you do anything to rescue us from the torment of Allah?" They will reply, "Had Allah guided us, we would also have guided you. It makes no difference whether we cry for help or exercise patience; there is no escape for us."

21. Wa barazoo lillaahi jamee‘an faqaalaḍ-ḍu‘afaaa’u lillaẕeenas-takbarooo innaa kunnaa lakum taba‘an fahal antum mughnoona ‘annaa min ‘aẕaabil-laahi min shay’; qaaloo law hadaanal-laahu lahadaynaakum sawaaa’un ‘alaynaaa ajazi‘naa am ṣabarnaa maa lanaa mim maḥeeṣ.

وَبَرَزُوۡا لِلّٰهِ جَمِيۡعًا فَقَالَ الضُّعَفٰٓؤُا
لِلَّذِيۡنَ اسۡتَكۡبَرُوۡۤا اِنَّا كُنَّا لَـكُمۡ
تَبَعًا فَهَلۡ اَنۡتُمۡ مُّغۡنُوۡنَ عَنَّا مِنۡ
عَذَابِ اللّٰهِ مِنۡ شَىۡءٍ‌ؕ قَالُوۡا لَوۡ
هَدٰٮنَا اللّٰهُ لَهَدَيۡنٰكُمۡ‌ؕ سَوَآءٌ عَلَيۡنَاۤ
اَجَزِعۡنَاۤ اَمۡ صَبَرۡنَا مَا لَـنَا
مِنۡ مَّحِيۡصٍ ﴿٢١﴾ ع ٣ ٩ ١٥

22. When the decree of Allah is issued, Satan will say, "Allah's

22. Wa qaalash-Shayṭaanu lammaa quḍiyal-amru

وَقَالَ الشَّيۡطٰنُ لَمَّا قُضِىَ الۡاَمۡرُ

promise to you was true, but I, too, made a promise to you and disregarded it. I had no authority over you. I just called you and you answered. Do not blame me but blame yourselves. I cannot help you and you cannot help me. I did not agree with your belief that I was equal to Allah." The unjust will face a painful punishment.

Innallaaha wa'adakum wa'dal-ḥaqqi wa wa'attukum fa-akhlaftukum wa maa kaana liya 'alaykum-min sulṭaanin illaaa an da'awtukum fastajabtum lee falaa taloomoonee wa loomooo anfusakum maaa ana bimuṣ-rikhikum wa maaa antum bimuṣrikhiyya innee kafartu bimaaa ashraktumooni min qabl; innaẕ-ẕaalimeena lahum 'aẕaabun aleem.

إِنَّ اللَّهَ وَعَدَكُمْ وَعْدَ الْحَقِّ وَ
وَعَدْتُّكُمْ فَأَخْلَفْتُكُمْ ۖ وَمَا كَانَ
لِيَ عَلَيْكُم مِّن سُلْطَانٍ إِلَّا أَن
دَعَوْتُكُمْ فَاسْتَجَبْتُمْ لِي ۖ فَلَا تَلُومُونِي
وَلُومُوا أَنفُسَكُم ۖ مَّا أَنَا بِمُصْرِخِكُمْ
وَمَا أَنتُم بِمُصْرِخِيَّ ۖ إِنِّي كَفَرْتُ بِمَا
أَشْرَكْتُمُونِ مِن قَبْلُ ۗ إِنَّ الظَّالِمِينَ
لَهُمْ عَذَابٌ أَلِيمٌ ﴿٢٢﴾

23. The righteously striving believers will be admitted to the gardens wherein streams flow and they will live therein forever, by the permission of their Lord. Their greeting to each other will be, "Peace be with you."

23. Wa udkhilal-laẕeena aamanoo wa 'amiluṣ-ṣaaliḥaati Jannaatin tajree min taḥtihal-anhaaru khaalideena feehaa bi-iẕni Rabbihim taḥiyyatuhum feehaa salaam.

وَأُدْخِلَ الَّذِينَ آمَنُوا وَعَمِلُوا
الصَّالِحَاتِ جَنَّاتٍ تَجْرِي مِن تَحْتِهَا
الْأَنْهَارُ خَالِدِينَ فِيهَا بِإِذْنِ رَبِّهِمْ ۖ
تَحِيَّتُهُمْ فِيهَا سَلَامٌ ﴿٢٣﴾

24. Did you not consider (Muhammad) how Allah (in a parable) compares the blessed Word to that of a blessed tree (the Holy Prophet) which has firm roots and branches rising up into the sky

24. Alam tara kayfa ḍarabal-laahu maṯalan kalimatan ṭayyibatan kashajaratin ṭayyi-batin aṣluhaa ṯaabituñw-wa far'uhaa fis-samaaa'.

أَلَمْ تَرَ كَيْفَ ضَرَبَ اللَّهُ مَثَلًا
كَلِمَةً طَيِّبَةً كَشَجَرَةٍ طَيِّبَةٍ
أَصْلُهَا ثَابِتٌ وَفَرْعُهَا فِي السَّمَاءِ ﴿٢٤﴾

25. and yields fruits in every season, by the permission of its Lord? Allah sets forth parables for people so that they may take heed.

25. Tu'teee ukulahaa kulla ḥeenim bi-iẕni Rabbihaa; wa yaḍribul-laahul-amṯaala lin-naasi la'allahum yataẕak-karoon.

تُؤْتِي أُكُلَهَا كُلَّ حِينٍ بِإِذْنِ رَبِّهَا ۗ
وَيَضْرِبُ اللَّهُ الْأَمْثَالَ لِلنَّاسِ
لَعَلَّهُمْ يَتَذَكَّرُونَ ﴿٢٥﴾

26. An evil word is compared to an evil tree with no firm roots in the land and thus has no stability.

26. Wa maṯalu kalimatin kha-beeṯatin kashajaratin khabee-ṯatinij-tuṯ-ṯat min fawqil-arḍi maa lahaa min qaraar.

وَمَثَلُ كَلِمَةٍ خَبِيثَةٍ كَشَجَرَةٍ
خَبِيثَةٍ اجْتُثَّتْ مِن فَوْقِ
الْأَرْضِ مَا لَهَا مِن قَرَارٍ ﴿٢٦﴾

27. Allah strengthens the faith of the believers by the true Words in this world and in the life to come. He causes the unjust to go astray and does whatever He pleases.

27. Yuṯabbitul-laahul-laẕeena aamanoo bilqawliṯ-ṯaabiti filḥayaatid-dunyaa wa fil Aakhirati wa yuḍillul-laahuẓ-ẓaalimeen; wa yaf'alul-laahu maa yashaaa'.

يُثَبِّتُ اللَّهُ الَّذِينَ آمَنُوا بِالْقَوْلِ
الثَّابِتِ فِي الْحَيَاةِ الدُّنْيَا وَفِي
الْآخِرَةِ ۖ وَيُضِلُّ اللَّهُ الظَّالِمِينَ ۚ
وَيَفْعَلُ اللَّهُ مَا يَشَاءُ ﴿٢٧﴾ ع ٦ ١٦

28. Did you not see those who changed the Word of Allah

28. Alam tara-ilal-laẕeena baddaloo ni'matal-laahi

أَلَمْ تَرَ إِلَى الَّذِينَ بَدَّلُوا نِعْمَتَ اللَّهِ

through disbelief and led their people to destruction?

29. They will suffer in Hell. What a terrible place to stay!

30. To lead people astray, they claimed their idols were equal to Allah. (Muhammad), tell them, "Enjoy yourselves and know that the only place for you to go will be hellfire."

31. Tell My believing servants to be steadfast in prayer and to spend for the cause of their Lord, both in private and in public, out of what We have given them. Let them do this before the coming of the day when there will be no merchandising or friendship.

32. Allah is the One who created the heavens and the earth, sent down water from the sky by which He produced fruits for your sustenance, enabled you to use boats to sail on the sea, and placed the rivers at your disposal, all by His command.

33. He made the sun and moon, each following its course, and the day and the night all subservient to you.

34. He has given you everything that you asked Him for. Had you wanted to count the bounties of Allah, you would not have been able to do it. The human being is unjust and disbelieving.

35. (Muhammad), consider when Abraham prayed, "Lord, make this (Mecca) a peaceful territory and save me and my offspring from worshipping idols.

36. Lord, the idols have misled many people. Whoever follows me is my friend. As for those who disobey, You are certainly All-forgiving and All-merciful.

37. "Lord, I have settled some of my offspring in a barren valley

kufrañw-wa aḥalloo qawmahum daaral-bawaar.

29. Jahannama yaṣlawnahaa wa bi'sal-qaraar.

30. Wa ja'aloo lillaahi andaadal-liyuḍilloo 'an sabeelih; qul tamatta'oo fa-inna maṣeerakum ilan-Naar.

31. Qul-li'ibaadiyal-lazeena aamanoo yuqeemuṣ-Ṣalaata wa yunfiqoo mimmaa razaqnaahum sirrañw-wa 'alaaniyatam-min qabli añy-ya-tiya Yawmul-laa bay'un feehi wa laa khilaal.

32. Allaahul-lazee khalaqas-samaawaati wal-arḍa wa anzala minas-samaaa'i maaa'an fa-akhraja bihee minas-samaraati rizqal-lakum wa sakhkhara lakumul-fulka litajriya fil-baḥri bi-amrihee wa sakhkhara lakumul anhaar.

33. Wa sakhkhara lakumush-shamsa walqamara daaa'ibayni wa sakhkhara lakumul-layla wannahaar.

34. Wa aataakum min kulli maa sa-altumooh; wa in ta'uddoo ni'matal-laahi laa tuḥṣoohaaa; innal-insaana laẓaloomun kaffaar.

35. Wa iz qaala Ibraaheemu Rabbij-'al haazal-balada aaminañw-wajnubnee wa baniyya an na'budal-aṣnaam.

36. Rabbi innahunna aḍlalna kaseeram-minannaasi faman tabi'anee fa-innahoo minnee wa man 'aṣaanee fa-innaka Ghafoorur-Raḥeem.

37. Rabbanaaa inneee askantu min zurriyyatee

كُفْرًا وَّاَحَلُّوْا قَوْمَهُمْ دَارَ الْبَوَارِ ﴿٢٨﴾
جَهَنَّمَ ۚ يَصْلَوْنَهَا ۚ وَبِئْسَ الْقَرَارُ ﴿٢٩﴾
وَجَعَلُوْا لِلّٰهِ اَنْدَادًا لِّيُضِلُّوْا عَنْ
سَبِيْلِهٖ ۚ قُلْ تَمَتَّعُوْا فَاِنَّ مَصِيْرَكُمْ
اِلَى النَّارِ ﴿٣٠﴾
قُلْ لِّعِبَادِيَ الَّذِيْنَ اٰمَنُوْا يُقِيْمُوا
الصَّلٰوةَ وَيُنْفِقُوْا مِمَّا رَزَقْنٰهُمْ
سِرًّا وَّعَلَانِيَةً مِّنْ قَبْلِ اَنْ يَّاْتِيَ
يَوْمٌ لَّا بَيْعٌ فِيْهِ وَلَا خِلٰلٌ ﴿٣١﴾
اَللّٰهُ الَّذِيْ خَلَقَ السَّمٰوٰتِ وَالْاَرْضَ
وَاَنْزَلَ مِنَ السَّمَآءِ مَآءً فَاَخْرَجَ بِهٖ
مِنَ الثَّمَرٰتِ رِزْقًا لَّكُمْ ۚ وَسَخَّرَ لَكُمُ
الْفُلْكَ لِتَجْرِيَ فِي الْبَحْرِ بِاَمْرِهٖ ۚ
وَسَخَّرَ لَكُمُ الْاَنْهٰرَ ﴿٣٢﴾
وَسَخَّرَ لَكُمُ الشَّمْسَ وَالْقَمَرَ دَآئِبَيْنِ ۚ
وَسَخَّرَ لَكُمُ الَّيْلَ وَالنَّهَارَ ﴿٣٣﴾
وَاٰتٰىكُمْ مِّنْ كُلِّ مَا سَاَلْتُمُوْهُ ۚ وَاِنْ
تَعُدُّوْا نِعْمَتَ اللّٰهِ لَا تُحْصُوْهَا ۚ اِنَّ
الْاِنْسَانَ لَظَلُوْمٌ كَفَّارٌ ﴿٣٤﴾ ع ٥ ١٧
وَاِذْ قَالَ اِبْرٰهِيْمُ رَبِّ اجْعَلْ هٰذَا
الْبَلَدَ اٰمِنًا وَّاجْنُبْنِيْ وَبَنِيَّ اَنْ
نَّعْبُدَ الْاَصْنَامَ ﴿٣٥﴾
رَبِّ اِنَّهُنَّ اَضْلَلْنَ كَثِيْرًا مِّنَ
النَّاسِ ۚ فَمَنْ تَبِعَنِيْ فَاِنَّهٗ مِنِّيْ ۚ
وَمَنْ عَصَانِيْ فَاِنَّكَ غَفُوْرٌ رَّحِيْمٌ ﴿٣٦﴾
رَبَّنَآ اِنِّيْٓ اَسْكَنْتُ مِنْ ذُرِّيَّتِيْ

near your Sacred House so that they could be steadfast in prayer. Lord, fill the hearts of the people with love for them and produce fruits (sympathy of hearts) for their sustenance so that they may give thanks.

38. Lord, You know all that we conceal or reveal. Nothing in the heavens or the earth is hidden from Allah.

39. It is only Allah who deserves all praise. I praise Him for His giving me my sons Ishmael and Isaac during my old age. My Lord, certainly, hears all prayers.

40. Lord, make me and my offspring steadfast in prayer and accept our worship.

41. Lord, on the Day of Judgment, forgive me and my parents and all the believers."

42. (Muhammad), do not think that Allah is unaware of what the unjust people do. He only gives them a respite until the day when the eyes will remain wide open (due to fear of hell),

43. when people will hurry in fright, with their heads raised, their eyes unable to look around, and their hearts shocked due to facing hardships (which will prevail on that Day).

44. (Muhammad), warn the people of the day when torment will approach them and the unjust will say, "Lord, give us respite for a little time so that we may answer your call and follow the Messengers." (The answer to their prayer will be), "Did you not swear before that you would

biwaadin ghayri zee zar'in 'inda Baytikal-Muḥarrami Rabbanaa liyuqeemuṣ-Ṣalaata faj'al af'idatam-minan-naasi tahweee ilayhim warzuqhum-minas-samaraati la'allahum yashkuroon.

38. Rabbanaaa innaka ta'lamu maa nukhfee wa maa nu'lin; wa maa yakhfaa 'alallaahi min shay'in fil-arḍi wa laa fis-samaaa'.

39. Al-ḥamdu Iillaahil-lazee wahaba lee 'alal-kibari Ismaa-'eela wa Isḥaaq; inna Rabbee laSamee'ud-du'aaa'.

40. Rabbij-'alnee muqeemaṣ-Ṣalaati wa min zurriyyatee; Rabbanaa wa taqabbal du'aaa'.

41. Rabbanagh-fir lee wa liwaalidayya wa lilmu'mineena Yawma yaqoomul-ḥisaab.

42. Wa laa taḥsabannal-laaha ghaafilan 'ammaa ya'maluẓ-ẓaalimoon; innamaa yu'akh-khiruhum li-Yawmin tashkhaṣu feehil-abṣaar.

43. Muhṭi'eena muqni'ee ru'oosihim laa yartaddu ilayhim ṭarfuhum wa af-'idatuhum hawaaa'.

44. Wa anzirin-naasa Yawma ya-teehimul-'azaabu fayaqoo-lul-lazeena ẓalamoo Rabbanaaa akhkhirnaaa ilaaa ajalin qaree-b;-nujib da'wataka wa nattabi-'ir-Rusul; awalam takoonooo aqsamtum min qablu maa lakum

بِوَادٍ غَيْرِ ذِيْ زَرْعٍ عِنْدَ بَيْتِكَ
الْمُحَرَّمِ ۙ رَبَّنَا لِيُقِيْمُوا الصَّلٰوةَ
فَاجْعَلْ اَفْـِٕدَةً مِّنَ النَّاسِ تَهْوِيْۤ
اِلَيْهِمْ وَارْزُقْهُمْ مِّنَ الثَّمَرٰتِ
لَعَلَّهُمْ يَشْكُرُوْنَ ﴿٣٧﴾
رَبَّنَاۤ اِنَّكَ تَعْلَمُ مَا نُخْفِيْ وَمَا نُعْلِنُ ؕ
وَمَا يَخْفٰى عَلَى اللّٰهِ مِنْ شَيْءٍ فِي
الْاَرْضِ وَلَا فِي السَّمَآءِ ﴿٣٨﴾
اَلْحَمْدُ لِلّٰهِ الَّذِيْ وَهَبَ لِيْ عَلَى
الْكِبَرِ اِسْمٰعِيْلَ وَاِسْحٰقَ ؕ اِنَّ رَبِّيْ
لَسَمِيْعُ الدُّعَآءِ ﴿٣٩﴾
رَبِّ اجْعَلْنِيْ مُقِيْمَ الصَّلٰوةِ وَمِنْ
ذُرِّيَّتِيْ ۖۗ رَبَّنَا وَتَقَبَّلْ دُعَآءِ ﴿٤٠﴾
رَبَّنَا اغْفِرْ لِيْ وَلِوَالِدَيَّ وَ
لِلْمُؤْمِنِيْنَ يَوْمَ يَقُوْمُ الْحِسَابُ ﴿٤١﴾ ع ٦/١٨
وَلَا تَحْسَبَنَّ اللّٰهَ غَافِلًا عَمَّا يَعْمَلُ
الظّٰلِمُوْنَ ؕ اِنَّمَا يُؤَخِّرُهُمْ لِيَوْمٍ
تَشْخَصُ فِيْهِ الْاَبْصَارُ ﴿٤٢﴾
مُهْطِعِيْنَ مُقْنِعِيْ رُءُوْسِهِمْ لَا
يَرْتَدُّ اِلَيْهِمْ طَرْفُهُمْ ۚ وَ
اَفْـِٕدَتُهُمْ هَوَآءٌ ﴿٤٣﴾
وَاَنْذِرِ النَّاسَ يَوْمَ يَاْتِيْهِمُ
الْعَذَابُ فَيَقُوْلُ الَّذِيْنَ ظَلَمُوْا رَبَّنَاۤ
اَخِّرْنَاۤ اِلٰۤى اَجَلٍ قَرِيْبٍ ۙ نُّجِبْ
دَعْوَتَكَ وَنَتَّبِعِ الرُّسُلَ ؕ اَوَلَمْ
تَكُوْنُوْۤا اَقْسَمْتُمْ مِّنْ قَبْلُ مَا لَكُمْ

never perish?

min zawaal.

مِّنْ زَوَالٍ ﴿٤٤﴾

45. You lived in the dwellings of those who wronged themselves, even though it was made clear to you how We dealt with them. We also showed you examples."

45. Wa sakantum fee masaakinil-lazeena zalamooo anfusahum wa tabayyana lakum kayfa fa'alnaa bihim wa darabnaa lakumul-amsaal.

وَّسَكَنْتُمْ فِيْ مَسٰكِنِ الَّذِيْنَ ظَلَمُوْٓا
اَنْفُسَهُمْ وَتَبَيَّنَ لَكُمْ كَيْفَ فَعَلْنَا
بِهِمْ وَضَرَبْنَا لَكُمُ الْاَمْثَالَ ﴿٤٥﴾

46. They devised evil plans which were so sinful that even the mountains could not endure them. All these were known to Allah.

46. Wa qad makaroo makrahum wa 'indal-laahi makruhum wa in kaana makruhum litazoola minhul-jibaal.

وَقَدْ مَكَرُوْا مَكْرَهُمْ وَعِنْدَ اللّٰهِ
مَكْرُهُمْ ۭ وَاِنْ كَانَ مَكْرُهُمْ
لِتَزُوْلَ مِنْهُ الْجِبَالُ ﴿٤٦﴾

47. You must not even think that Allah will disregard His promise to His messengers. Allah is Majestic and capable of exacting His rights.

47. Falaa tahsabannal-laaha mukhlifa wa'dihee Rusulah; innal-laaha 'Azeezun zuntiqaam.

فَلَا تَحْسَبَنَّ اللّٰهَ مُخْلِفَ وَعْدِهٖ
رُسُلَهٗ ۭ اِنَّ اللّٰهَ عَزِيْزٌ ذُو انْتِقَامٍ ﴿٤٧﴾

48. On the day when the earth and the heavens will be replaced by another earth and other heavens and everyone will be brought before the One, Almighty Allah,

48. Yawma tubaddalul-ardu ghayral-ardi was-samaawaatu wa barazoo lillaahil-Waahidil Qahhaar.

يَوْمَ تُبَدَّلُ الْاَرْضُ غَيْرَ الْاَرْضِ
وَالسَّمٰوٰتُ وَبَرَزُوْا لِلّٰهِ الْوَاحِدِ
الْقَهَّارِ ﴿٤٨﴾

49. you will see the guilty ones bound in chains,

49. Wa taral-mujrimeena Yawma'izim-muqarraneena fil-asfaad.

وَتَرَى الْمُجْرِمِيْنَ يَوْمَىِٕذٍ
مُّقَرَّنِيْنَ فِي الْاَصْفَادِ ﴿٤٩﴾

50. with garments of tar and faces covered by fire.

50. Saraabeeluhum min qatiraaniñw-wa taghshaa wujoohahumun-Naar.

سَرَابِيْلُهُمْ مِّنْ قَطِرَانٍ وَّتَغْشٰى
وُجُوْهَهُمُ النَّارُ ﴿٥٠﴾

51. This is how Allah will recompense each soul for its deeds. Allah's reckoning is swift.

51. Liyajziyal-laahu kulla nafsim-maa kasabat; innallaaha Saree'ul-hisaab.

لِيَجْزِيَ اللّٰهُ كُلَّ نَفْسٍ مَّا كَسَبَتْ
اِنَّ اللّٰهَ سَرِيْعُ الْحِسَابِ ﴿٥١﴾

52. This (prophet Muhammad) is a messenger to people so that they are warned through him and know that there is only one Ilah (one deserving to be worshipped) and so that the people of understanding may take heed.

52. Haazaa balaaghul-linnaasi wa liyunzaroo bihee wa liya'lamooo annamaa Huwa Ilaahuñw-Waahiduñw-wa liyazzakkara ulul-albaab.

هٰذَا بَلٰغٌ لِّلنَّاسِ وَلِيُنْذَرُوْا بِهٖ
وَلِيَعْلَمُوْٓا اَنَّمَا هُوَ اِلٰهٌ وَّاحِدٌ
وَّلِيَذَّكَّرَ اُولُوا الْاَلْبَابِ ﴿٥٢﴾ ع ١١ ١٩

Al-Hijr, The Rocky Tract (15)

In the Name of Allah, the Beneficent, the Merciful.

Sûrat al-Ḥijr-15

(Revealed at Makkah)

Bismillaahir Rahmaanir Raheem

(١٥) سُوْرَةُ الْحِجْرِ مَكِّيَّةٌ (٥٤)

اٰيَاتُهَا ٩٩ بِسْمِ اللّٰهِ الرَّحْمٰنِ الرَّحِيْمِ رُكُوْعَاتُهَا ٦

1. Alif. Lam. Ra. These are the verses of the Book and the glorious Quran.

1. Alif-Laaam-Raa; tilka Aayaatul-Kitaabi wa Qur-aanim-Mubeen.

الۤرٰ قف تِلْكَ اٰيٰتُ الْكِتٰبِ وَقُرْاٰنٍ
مُّبِيْنٍ ﴿١﴾

2. How much will (on the Day of Judgment) the unbelievers

2. Rubamaa yawaddul-lazeena kafaroo law kaanoo

رُبَمَا يَوَدُّ الَّذِيْنَ كَفَرُوْا لَوْ

الجزء الرابع عشر (١٤)

wish to have been Muslims!

muslimeen.

كَانُوا مُسْلِمِينَ ۝٢

3. (Muhammad), leave them alone to eat and enjoy themselves and allow their desires preoccupy them; they will soon know (the Truth).

3. Z̲arhum ya-kuloo wa yatamatta'oo wa yulhihimul amalu fasawfa ya'lamoon.

ذَرْهُمْ يَأْكُلُوا وَيَتَمَتَّعُوا وَيُلْهِهِمُ
الْأَمَلُ فَسَوْفَ يَعْلَمُونَ ۝٣

4. We never destroyed any town without pre-ordaining the fate of its people.

4. Wa maaa ahlaknaa min qaryatin illaa wa lahaa kitaa-bum-ma'loom.

وَمَآ أَهْلَكْنَا مِن قَرْيَةٍ إِلَّا وَلَهَا
كِتَابٌ مَّعْلُومٌ ۝٤

5. Every nation can only live for the time appointed for it.

5. Maa tasbiqu min ummatin ajalahaa wa maa yasta-khiroon.

مَا تَسْبِقُ مِنْ أُمَّةٍ أَجَلَهَا وَمَا
يَسْتَأْخِرُونَ ۝٥

6. (The unbelievers have said), "You to whom the Quran has been revealed are insane.

6. Wa qaaloo yaaa ayyuhal laz̲ee nuzzila 'alayhiz̲-Z̲ikru innaka lamajnoon.

وَقَالُوا يَا أَيُّهَا الَّذِي نُزِّلَ عَلَيْهِ
الذِّكْرُ إِنَّكَ لَمَجْنُونٌ ۝٦

7. Why do you not bring down the angels if what you say is true."

7. Law maa ta-teenaa bil-malaaa'ikati in kunta minaṣ-ṣaadiqeen.

لَوْ مَا تَأْتِينَا بِالْمَلَائِكَةِ إِن
كُنتَ مِنَ الصَّادِقِينَ ۝٧

8. We do not send down angels except for a genuine purpose, at which time none will be given any further respite.

8. Maa nunazzilul-malaaa'i-kata illaa bilḥaqqi wa maa kaanooo iz̲am-munẓareen.

مَا نُنَزِّلُ الْمَلَائِكَةَ إِلَّا بِالْحَقِّ
وَمَا كَانُوا إِذًا مُّنظَرِينَ ۝٨

9. We Ourselves have revealed the Quran and We are its protectors.

9. Innaa Naḥnu nazzalnaz̲-Z̲ikra wa Innaa lahoo laḥaa-fiẓoon.

إِنَّا نَحْنُ نَزَّلْنَا الذِّكْرَ وَإِنَّا لَهُ
لَحَافِظُونَ ۝٩

10. We sent Messengers to the ancient people who lived before you.

10. Wa laqad arsalnaa min qablika fee shiya'il awwaleen.

وَلَقَدْ أَرْسَلْنَا مِن قَبْلِكَ فِي
شِيَعِ الْأَوَّلِينَ ۝١٠

11. No Messenger went to them whom they did not mock.

11. Wa maa ya-teehim-mir-Rasoolin illaa kaanoo biheẹ yastahzi'oon.

وَمَا يَأْتِيهِم مِّن رَّسُولٍ إِلَّا كَانُوا
بِهِ يَسْتَهْزِءُونَ ۝١١

12. This is how We cause the hearts of the guilty ones to behave.

12. Kaz̲aalika naslukuhoo fee quloobil-mujrimeen.

كَذَٰلِكَ نَسْلُكُهُ فِي قُلُوبِ الْمُجْرِمِينَ ۝١٢

13. They do not believe in the Truth and they exactly follow the tradition of the ancient (unbelievers).

13. Laa yu'minoona bihee wa qad khalat sunnatul awwaleen.

لَا يُؤْمِنُونَ بِهِ وَقَدْ خَلَتْ سُنَّةُ
الْأَوَّلِينَ ۝١٣

14. Had We opened a door for them in the sky through which they could easily pass,

14. Wa law fataḥnaa 'alayhim baabam-minas-samaaa'i faẓal-loo feehi ya'rujoon.

وَلَوْ فَتَحْنَا عَلَيْهِم بَابًا مِّنَ السَّمَاءِ
فَظَلُّوا فِيهِ يَعْرُجُونَ ۝١٤

15. they would have said, "Our eyes are bewildered and we have been affected by magic."

15. Laqaalooo innamaa sukki-rat abṣaarunaa bal naḥnu qawmum-masḥooroon.

لَقَالُوا إِنَّمَا سُكِّرَتْ أَبْصَارُنَا
بَلْ نَحْنُ قَوْمٌ مَّسْحُورُونَ ۝١٥ ع ١٥ ١

16. We made constellations in the sky and have decorated them for the onlookers.

16. Wa laqad ja'alnaa fissamaaa'i buroojañw-wa zayyannaahaa linnaaẓireen.

وَلَقَدۡ جَعَلۡنَا فِى السَّمَآءِ بُرُوۡجًا
وَّزَيَّنّٰهَا لِلنّٰظِرِيۡنَ ﴿۱۶﴾

17. We have protected them from every condemned devil,

17. Wa ḥafiẓnaahaa min kulli Shayṭaanir-rajeem.

وَحَفِظۡنٰهَا مِنۡ كُلِّ شَيۡطٰنٍ رَّجِيۡمٍ ﴿۱۷﴾

18. except for those who stealthily try to listen to the heavens, but who are chased away by a bright flame.

18. Illaa manis-taraqas-sam'a fa-atba'ahoo shihaabum-mubeen.

اِلَّا مَنِ اسۡتَرَقَ السَّمۡعَ فَاَتۡبَعَهٗ
شِهَابٌ مُّبِيۡنٌ ﴿۱۸﴾

19. We have spread out the earth, fixed mountains thereupon, and caused everything to grow to its proper weight,

19. Wal-arḍa madadnaahaa wa alqaynaa feehaa rawaasiya wa ambatnaa feehaa min kulli shay'im-mawzoon.

وَالۡاَرۡضَ مَدَدۡنٰهَا وَاَلۡقَيۡنَا فِيۡهَا
رَوَاسِىَ وَاَنۡۢبَتۡنَا فِيۡهَا مِنۡ كُلِّ شَىۡءٍ
مَّوۡزُوۡنٍ ﴿۱۹﴾

20. to provide you and those for whose sustenance you are not responsible, with the necessities of life.

20. Wa ja'alnaa lakum feehaa ma'aayisha wa mal-lastum lahoo biraaziqeen.

وَجَعَلۡنَا لَكُمۡ فِيۡهَا مَعَايِشَ وَمَنۡ
لَّسۡتُمۡ لَهٗ بِرٰزِقِيۡنَ ﴿۲۰﴾

21. With Us is the source of everything and We do not send it down without a known quantity.

21. Wa im-min shay'in illaa 'indanaa khazaaa'inuhoo wa maa nunazziluhooo illaa biqadarim-ma'loom.

وَاِنۡ مِّنۡ شَىۡءٍ اِلَّا عِنۡدَنَا
خَزَآئِنُهٗ وَمَا نُنَزِّلُهٗۤ اِلَّا بِقَدَرٍ
مَّعۡلُوۡمٍ ﴿۲۱﴾

22. We send impregnating winds and send down water from the sky for you to drink and you have no (control over its) storage.

22. Wa arsalnar-riyaaḥa lawaaqiḥa fa-anzalnaa minas-samaaa'i maaa'an fa-asqaynaakumoohu wa maaa antum lahoo bikhaazineen.

وَاَرۡسَلۡنَا الرِّيٰحَ لَوَاقِحَ فَاَنۡزَلۡنَا
مِنَ السَّمَآءِ مَآءً فَاَسۡقَيۡنٰكُمُوۡهُ ۚ وَمَاۤ
اَنۡتُمۡ لَهٗ بِخٰزِنِيۡنَ ﴿۲۲﴾

23. It is We who give life and cause things to die and We are the sole Heirs.

23. Wa innaa la-naḥnu nuḥyee wa numeetu wa naḥnul-waarisoon.

وَاِنَّا لَنَحۡنُ نُحۡىٖ وَنُمِيۡتُ وَنَحۡنُ
الۡوٰرِثُوۡنَ ﴿۲۳﴾

24. We know the people who lived before you and those who will come into existence after you.

24. Wa laqad 'alimnal-mustaq-dimeena minkum wa laqad 'alimnal-musta-khireen.

وَلَقَدۡ عَلِمۡنَا الۡمُسۡتَقۡدِمِيۡنَ مِنۡكُمۡ
وَلَقَدۡ عَلِمۡنَا الۡمُسۡتَاۡخِرِيۡنَ ﴿۲۴﴾

25. Your Lord will resurrect them all; He is All-wise and All-knowing.

25. Wa inna Rabbaka Huwa yaḥshuruhum; innahoo Ḥakeemun 'Aleem.

وَاِنَّ رَبَّكَ هُوَ يَحۡشُرُهُمۡ ؕ اِنَّهٗ
حَكِيۡمٌ عَلِيۡمٌ ﴿۲۵﴾ ع ۲

26. We have created man out of a changing, sticky clay,

26. Wa laqad khalaqnal insaana min ṣalṣaalim-min ḥama-im-masnoon.

وَلَقَدۡ خَلَقۡنَا الۡاِنۡسَانَ مِنۡ صَلۡصَالٍ
مِّنۡ حَمَاٍ مَّسۡنُوۡنٍ ﴿۲۶﴾

27. and jinn before (the human being) of smokeless fire.

27. Waljaaanna khalaqnaahu min qablu min naaris-samoom.

وَالۡجَآنَّ خَلَقۡنٰهُ مِنۡ قَبۡلُ مِنۡ
نَّارِ السَّمُوۡمِ ﴿۲۷﴾

28. At one time, your Lord said to the angels, "I will create man out of changing, sticky clay.	28. Wa-iz̲ qaala Rabbuka lilmalaaa'ikati innee khaaliqum basharam-min ṣalṣaalim-min ḥama-im-masnoon.	وَاِذْ قَالَ رَبُّكَ لِلْمَلٰٓئِكَةِ اِنِّیْ خَالِقٌۢ بَشَرًا مِّنْ صَلْصَالٍ مِّنْ حَمَاٍ مَّسْنُوْنٍ ﴿٢٨﴾
29. When it is properly shaped and I have blown My Spirit into it, you must (in his honor) bow down in prostration (before Me)."	29. Fa-iz̲aa sawwaytuhoo wa nafakhtu feehi mir-rooḥee faqa'oo lahoo saajideen.	فَاِذَا سَوَّيْتُهٗ وَنَفَخْتُ فِيْهِ مِنْ رُّوْحِیْ فَقَعُوْا لَهٗ سٰجِدِيْنَ ﴿٢٩﴾
30. All the angels prostrated in honor of Adam	30. Fasajadal-malaaa'ikatu kulluhum ajma'oon.	فَسَجَدَ الْمَلٰٓئِكَةُ كُلُّهُمْ اَجْمَعُوْنَ ﴿٣٠﴾
31. except Iblis (Satan) who refused to join with the others in prostration.	31. Illaaa Iblees; abaaa añy-Yakoona ma'as-saajideen.	اِلَّآ اِبْلِيْسَ ؕ اَبٰٓی اَنْ يَّكُوْنَ مَعَ السّٰجِدِيْنَ ﴿٣١﴾
32. Allah asked Iblis, "What made you not to join the others in prostration?"	32. Qaala yaaa Ibleesu maa laka allaa takoona ma'as-saajideen.	قَالَ يٰٓاِبْلِيْسُ مَا لَكَ اَلَّا تَكُوْنَ مَعَ السّٰجِدِيْنَ ﴿٣٢﴾
33. Iblis replied, "I did not want to prostrate in honor of a human being whom You have created out of changing, sticky clay.	33. Qaala lam akulli-asjuda libasharin khalaqtahoo min ṣalṣaalim-min ḥama-im-masnoon.	قَالَ لَمْ اَكُنْ لِّاَسْجُدَ لِبَشَرٍ خَلَقْتَهٗ مِنْ صَلْصَالٍ مِّنْ حَمَاٍ مَّسْنُوْنٍ ﴿٣٣﴾
34. Allah told him, "Get out of the garden; you are rejected	34. Qaala fakhruj minhaa fa-innaka rajeem.	قَالَ فَاخْرُجْ مِنْهَا فَاِنَّكَ رَجِيْمٌ ﴿٣٤﴾
35. and will be subjected to condemnation until the Day of Judgment."	35. Wa inna 'alaykal-la'nata ilaa Yawmid-Deen.	وَّاِنَّ عَلَيْكَ اللَّعْنَةَ اِلٰی يَوْمِ الدِّيْنِ ﴿٣٥﴾
36. Iblis prayed, "Lord, grant me respite until the Day of Judgment."	36. Qaala Rabbi fa-anẓirneee ilaa Yawmi yub'as̲oon.	قَالَ رَبِّ فَاَنْظِرْنِیْٓ اِلٰی يَوْمِ يُبْعَثُوْنَ ﴿٣٦﴾
37. The Lord said, "Your request is granted	37. Qaala fa-innaka minal-munẓareen.	قَالَ فَاِنَّكَ مِنَ الْمُنْظَرِيْنَ ﴿٣٧﴾
38. for an appointed time."	38. Ilaa Yawmil-waqtil-ma'loom.	اِلٰی يَوْمِ الْوَقْتِ الْمَعْلُوْمِ ﴿٣٨﴾
39. Iblis said, "Lord, because you have caused me to go astray, I shall make earthly things attractive to (people) and mislead all of them	39. Qaala Rabbi bimaaa aghwaytanee la-uzayyinanna lahum fil-arḍi wa la-ughwiyannahum ajma'een.	قَالَ رَبِّ بِمَآ اَغْوَيْتَنِیْ لَاُزَيِّنَنَّ لَهُمْ فِی الْاَرْضِ وَلَاُغْوِيَنَّهُمْ اَجْمَعِيْنَ ﴿٣٩﴾
40. except Your sincere servants."	40. Illaa 'ibaadaka minhumul-mukhlaṣeen.	اِلَّا عِبَادَكَ مِنْهُمُ الْمُخْلَصِيْنَ ﴿٤٠﴾
41. Allah said, "The path which leads to Me is straight	41. Qaala haaz̲aa Ṣiraaṭun 'alayya Mustaqeem.	قَالَ هٰذَا صِرَاطٌ عَلَیَّ مُسْتَقِيْمٌ ﴿٤١﴾
42. and you have no authority over My servants except the erring ones who follow you.	42. Inna 'ibaadee laysa laka 'alayhim sulṭaanun illaa manit-taba'aka minal-	اِنَّ عِبَادِیْ لَيْسَ لَكَ عَلَيْهِمْ سُلْطٰنٌ اِلَّا مَنِ اتَّبَعَكَ مِنَ

ghaaween.

الْغٰوِيْنَ ﴿٤٢﴾

43. Hell is the promised place for them all.

43. Wa inna Jahannama lamaw'iduhum ajma'een.

وَإِنَّ جَهَنَّمَ لَمَوْعِدُهُمْ أَجْمَعِيْنَ ﴿٤٣﴾

44. It has seven gates and each gate is assigned for a certain group of people.

44. Lahaa sab'atu abwaab; likulli baabim-minhum juz'um-maqsoom.

لَهَا سَبْعَةُ أَبْوَابٍ ط لِكُلِّ بَابٍ مِّنْهُمْ جُزْءٌ مَّقْسُوْمٌ ﴿٤٤﴾ ع ١٩ ٣

45. The pious will live in gardens with streams

45. Innal-muttaqeena fee Jannaatiñw-wa 'uyoon.

إِنَّ الْمُتَّقِيْنَ فِيْ جَنّٰتٍ وَّعُيُوْنٍ ط ﴿٤٥﴾

46. and they will be told to enter therein with peace and safety.

46. Udkhuloohaa bisalaamin aamineen.

اُدْخُلُوْهَا بِسَلٰمٍ اٰمِنِيْنَ ﴿٤٦﴾

47. We shall remove all hatred from their breasts and make them as brothers reclining on thrones facing one another.

47. Wa naza'naa maa fee ṣudoorihim-min ghillin ikhwaa-nan 'alaa sururim-mutaqaa-bileen.

وَنَزَعْنَا مَا فِيْ صُدُوْرِهِمْ مِّنْ غِلٍّ إِخْوَانًا عَلٰى سُرُرٍ مُّتَقٰبِلِيْنَ ﴿٤٧﴾

48. No fatigue will touch them nor will they be expelled there-from."

48. Laa yamas-suhum feehaa naṣabuñw-wa maa hum-minhaa bimukhrajeen.

لَا يَمَسُّهُمْ فِيْهَا نَصَبٌ وَّمَا هُمْ مِّنْهَا بِمُخْرَجِيْنَ ﴿٤٨﴾

49. (Muhammad), tell My servants that I am All-forgiving and All-merciful

49. Nabbi' 'ibaadeee anneee anal-Ghafoorur-Raḥeem.

نَبِّئْ عِبَادِيْٓ أَنِّيْٓ أَنَا الْغَفُوْرُ الرَّحِيْمُ ﴿٤٩﴾

50. and that My punishment is a painful one.

50. Wa anna 'az̲aabee huwal-'az̲aabul-aleem.

وَأَنَّ عَذَابِيْ هُوَ الْعَذَابُ الْأَلِيْمُ ﴿٥٠﴾ وقف لازم

51. Inform them about the guests of Abraham

51. Wa nabbi'hum 'an ḍayfi Ibraaheem.

وَنَبِّئْهُمْ عَنْ ضَيْفِ إِبْرٰهِيْمَ ﴿٥١﴾

52. who came to him saying, "Peace be with you." Abraham said, "We are afraid of you."

52. Iz̲ dakhaloo 'alayhi faqaa-loo salaaman qaala innaa minkum wajiloon.

إِذْ دَخَلُوْا عَلَيْهِ فَقَالُوْا سَلٰمًا ط قَالَ إِنَّا مِنْكُمْ وَجِلُوْنَ ﴿٥٢﴾

53. They replied, "Do not be afraid. We have brought you the glad news of (the birth) of a learned son."

53. Qaaloo laa tawjal innaa nubashshiruka bighulaamin 'aleem.

قَالُوْا لَا تَوْجَلْ إِنَّا نُبَشِّرُكَ بِغُلٰمٍ عَلِيْمٍ ﴿٥٣﴾

54. Abraham asked, "Are you giving me the glad news of a son in my old age? What reason can you give for such glad news?"

54. Qaala abash-shartu-moonee 'alaaa am-massaniyal-kibaru fabima tubashshiroon.

قَالَ أَبَشَّرْتُمُوْنِيْ عَلٰٓى أَنْ مَّسَّنِيَ الْكِبَرُ فَبِمَ تُبَشِّرُوْنَ ﴿٥٤﴾

55. They said, "We have given you the glad news for a true reason so do not despair."

55. Qaaloo bashsharnaaka bilḥaqqi falaa takum-minal-qaaniṭeen.

قَالُوْا بَشَّرْنٰكَ بِالْحَقِّ فَلَا تَكُنْ مِّنَ الْقٰنِطِيْنَ ﴿٥٥﴾

56. He said, "No one despairs of the mercy of his Lord except those who are in error.

56. Qaala wa mañy-yaqnaṭu mir-raḥmati Rabbiheee illaḍ-ḍaaalloon.

قَالَ وَمَنْ يَّقْنَطُ مِنْ رَّحْمَةِ رَبِّهٖٓ إِلَّا الضَّآلُّوْنَ ﴿٥٦﴾

57. Messengers, what is your task?"

57. Qaala famaa khaṭbukum ayyuhal-mursaloon.

قَالَ فَمَا خَطْبُكُمْ أَيُّهَا الْمُرْسَلُوْنَ ﴿٥٧﴾

58. They said, "We are sent to a people who are criminals,

58. Qaalooo innaaa ursilnaaa ilaa qawmim-mujrimeen.

قَالُوْٓا إِنَّآ أُرْسِلْنَآ إِلٰى قَوْمٍ مُّجْرِمِيْنَ ﴿٥٨﴾

59. except the family of Lot, who will all be rescued,	59. Illaaa aala Looṭ; innaa lamunaj-joohum ajma'een.	إِلَّآ ءَالَ لُوطٍ ۖ إِنَّا لَمُنَجُّوهُمْ أَجْمَعِينَ ﴿٥٩﴾
60. save his wife who is doomed to be left behind."	60. Illam-ra-atahoo qaddar-naaa innahaa laminal-ghaabi-reen.	إِلَّا ٱمْرَأَتَهُۥ قَدَّرْنَآ ۙ إِنَّهَا لَمِنَ ٱلْغَٰبِرِينَ ﴿٦٠﴾
61. When the Messengers came to the family of Lot,	61. Falammaa jaaa'a Aala Looṭinil-mursaloon.	فَلَمَّا جَآءَ ءَالَ لُوطٍ ٱلْمُرْسَلُونَ ﴿٦١﴾
62. he said, "You seem to be strangers."	62. Qaala innakum qawmum-munkaroon.	قَالَ إِنَّكُمْ قَوْمٌ مُّنكَرُونَ ﴿٦٢﴾
63. They replied, "We have come to you about the matter which the (unbelievers) have rejected.	63. Qaaloo bal ji'naaka bimaa kaanoo feehi yamtaroon.	قَالُوا۟ بَلْ جِئْنَٰكَ بِمَا كَانُوا۟ فِيهِ يَمْتَرُونَ ﴿٦٣﴾
64. We have come to you for a genuine purpose and We are true in what we say.	64. Wa ataynaaka bilḥaqqi wa innaa laṣaadiqoon.	وَأَتَيْنَٰكَ بِٱلْحَقِّ وَإِنَّا لَصَٰدِقُونَ ﴿٦٤﴾
65. Leave the town with your family sometime during the night. Walk behind them and let no one turn around. Proceed as you are commanded."	65. Fa-asri bi-ahlika biqiṭ'im-minal-layli wattabi' adbaara-hum wa laa yaltafit minkum aḥaduñw-wamḍoo ḥaysu tu'ma-roon.	فَأَسْرِ بِأَهْلِكَ بِقِطْعٍ مِّنَ ٱلَّيْلِ وَٱتَّبِعْ أَدْبَٰرَهُمْ وَلَا يَلْتَفِتْ مِنكُمْ أَحَدٌ وَٱمْضُوا۟ حَيْثُ تُؤْمَرُونَ ﴿٦٥﴾
66. We informed him that the unbelievers would be utterly destroyed toward the morning.	66. Wa qaḍaynaaa ilayhi zaalikal-amra anna daabira haaa'ulaaa'i maqṭoo'um-muṣbiḥeen.	وَقَضَيْنَآ إِلَيْهِ ذَٰلِكَ ٱلْأَمْرَ أَنَّ دَابِرَ هَٰٓؤُلَآءِ مَقْطُوعٌ مُّصْبِحِينَ ﴿٦٦﴾
67. The people of the town, in jubilation	67. Wa jaaa'a ahlul-madee-nati yastabshiroon.	وَجَآءَ أَهْلُ ٱلْمَدِينَةِ يَسْتَبْشِرُونَ ﴿٦٧﴾
68. rushed toward the house of Lot. Lot said to them, "These are my guests. Do not disgrace me.	68. Qaala inna haaa'ulaaa'i ḍayfee falaa tafḍaḥoon.	قَالَ إِنَّ هَٰٓؤُلَآءِ ضَيْفِى فَلَا تَفْضَحُونِ ﴿٦٨﴾
69. Have fear of Allah and do not humiliate me."	69. Wattaqul-laaha wa laa tukhzoon.	وَٱتَّقُوا۟ ٱللَّهَ وَلَا تُخْزُونِ ﴿٦٩﴾
70. They replied, "Did we not forbid you to bring anyone to your house?"	70. Qaalooo awalam nanhaka 'anil-'aalameen.	قَالُوٓا۟ أَوَلَمْ نَنْهَكَ عَنِ ٱلْعَٰلَمِينَ ﴿٧٠﴾
71. Lot said, "These are my daughters (meaning women of his people) if you want them."	71. Qaala haaa'ulaaa'i banaa-teee in kuntum faa'ileen.	قَالَ هَٰٓؤُلَآءِ بَنَاتِىٓ إِن كُنتُمْ فَٰعِلِينَ ﴿٧١﴾
72. By your life! In their drunkenness they were truly blind.	72. La'amruka innahum lafee sakratihim ya'mahoon.	لَعَمْرُكَ إِنَّهُمْ لَفِى سَكْرَتِهِمْ يَعْمَهُونَ ﴿٧٢﴾
73. An explosion struck them at sunrise.	73. Fa-akhazat-humuṣ-ṣay-ḥatu mushriqeen.	فَأَخَذَتْهُمُ ٱلصَّيْحَةُ مُشْرِقِينَ ﴿٧٣﴾
74. We turned the town upside down and showered on them lumps of baked clay.	74. Faja'alnaa 'aaliyahaa saa-filahaa wa amṭarnaa 'alayhim ḥijaaratam-min sijjeel.	فَجَعَلْنَا عَٰلِيَهَا سَافِلَهَا وَأَمْطَرْنَا عَلَيْهِمْ حِجَارَةً مِّن سِجِّيلٍ ﴿٧٤﴾
75. In this there is evidence (of the Truth) for the prudent ones.	75. Inna fee zaalika la-Aayaa-til-lilmutawas-simeen.	إِنَّ فِى ذَٰلِكَ لَءَايَٰتٍ لِّلْمُتَوَسِّمِينَ ﴿٧٥﴾

76. That town lies on a road which still exists.	76. Wa innahaa labisabeel-im-muqeem.	وَإِنَّهَا لَبِسَبِيلٍ مُّقِيمٍ ﴿٧٦﴾
77. In this there is evidence (of the Truth) for the believers.	77. Inna fee zaalika la Aayatal-lilmu'mineen.	إِنَّ فِي ذَٰلِكَ لَآيَةً لِّلْمُؤْمِنِينَ ﴿٧٧﴾
78. Since the People of the Forest were unjust,	78. Wa in kaana Aṣḥaabul Aykati laẓaalimeen.	وَإِن كَانَ أَصْحَابُ الْأَيْكَةِ لَظَالِمِينَ ﴿٧٨﴾
79. We afflicted them with punishment. Both people had clear (divine) authority among them.	79. Fantaqamnaa minhum; wa innahumaa labi-imaamim-mubeen.	فَانتَقَمْنَا مِنْهُمْ وَإِنَّهُمَا لَبِإِمَامٍ مُّبِينٍ ﴿٧٩﴾
80. People of Hijr rejected the Messengers.	80. Wa laqad kaẕ-ẕaba Aṣḥaabul-Ḥijril-mursaleen.	وَلَقَدْ كَذَّبَ أَصْحَابُ الْحِجْرِ الْمُرْسَلِينَ ﴿٨٠﴾
81. We showed them miracles but they ignored them.	81. Wa aataynaahum Aayaatinaa fakaanoo 'anhaa mu'riḍeen.	وَآتَيْنَاهُمْ آيَاتِنَا فَكَانُوا عَنْهَا مُعْرِضِينَ ﴿٨١﴾
82. They would carve secure houses out of the mountains.	82. Wa kaanoo yanḥitoona minal-jibaali buyootan aamineen.	وَكَانُوا يَنْحِتُونَ مِنَ الْجِبَالِ بُيُوتًا آمِنِينَ ﴿٨٢﴾
83. An explosion struck them in the morning.	83. Fa-akhaẕat-humuṣ-ṣayḥatu muṣbiḥeen.	فَأَخَذَتْهُمُ الصَّيْحَةُ مُصْبِحِينَ ﴿٨٣﴾
84. Out of what they had gained, nothing proved to be of any benefit to them.	84. Famaaa aghnaa 'anhum maa kaanoo yaksiboon.	فَمَا أَغْنَىٰ عَنْهُم مَّا كَانُوا يَكْسِبُونَ ﴿٨٤﴾
85. We have created the heavens and the earth and all that is between them, for a genuine purpose. The Day of Judgment will certainly approach, so (Muhammad) forgive them graciously.	85. Wa maa khalaqnas-samaawaati wal-arḍa wa maa baynahumaaa illaa bilhaqq; wa innas-Saa'ata la-aatiyatun faṣfaḥiṣ-ṣafḥal-jameel.	وَمَا خَلَقْنَا السَّمَاوَاتِ وَالْأَرْضَ وَمَا بَيْنَهُمَا إِلَّا بِالْحَقِّ وَإِنَّ السَّاعَةَ لَآتِيَةٌ فَاصْفَحِ الصَّفْحَ الْجَمِيلَ ﴿٨٥﴾
86. Your Lord is certainly the All-knowing Creator.	86. Inna Rabbaka Huwal-khallaaqul-'aleem.	إِنَّ رَبَّكَ هُوَ الْخَلَّاقُ الْعَلِيمُ ﴿٨٦﴾
87. (Muhammad), We have given you the seven most repeated (verses) and the great Quran.	87. Wa laqad aataynaaka sab'am-minal-maṡaanee wal-Qur-aanal-'Aẓeem.	وَلَقَدْ آتَيْنَاكَ سَبْعًا مِّنَ الْمَثَانِي وَالْقُرْآنَ الْعَظِيمَ ﴿٨٧﴾
88. Do not yearn for other people's property and wives and do not grieve (that they do not believe). Be kind to the believers.	88. Laa tamuddanna 'aynayka ilaa maa matta'naa biheee azwaajam-minhum wa laa taḥzan 'alayhim wakhfiḍ janaaḥaka lilmu'mineen.	لَا تَمُدَّنَّ عَيْنَيْكَ إِلَىٰ مَا مَتَّعْنَا بِهِ أَزْوَاجًا مِّنْهُمْ وَلَا تَحْزَنْ عَلَيْهِمْ وَاخْفِضْ جَنَاحَكَ لِلْمُؤْمِنِينَ ﴿٨٨﴾
89. Say, "Indeed, I am simply one who clearly warns."	89. Wa qul inneee anan-naẕeerul-mubeen.	وَقُلْ إِنِّي أَنَا النَّذِيرُ الْمُبِينُ ﴿٨٩﴾
90. (We have given you the Quran) as We had given (the Bible) to those who divided themselves into groups	90. Kamaaa anzalnaa 'alal-muqtasimeen.	كَمَا أَنزَلْنَا عَلَى الْمُقْتَسِمِينَ ﴿٩٠﴾
91. and also divided the Quran believing in some parts and rejecting others.	91. Allaẕeena ja'alul-Qur-aana 'iḍeen.	الَّذِينَ جَعَلُوا الْقُرْآنَ عِضِينَ ﴿٩١﴾
92. By the Lord, We will hold them all responsible	92. Fawa Rabbika lanas'al-annahum ajma'een.	فَوَرَبِّكَ لَنَسْأَلَنَّهُمْ أَجْمَعِينَ ﴿٩٢﴾

93. for what they have done.

94. Preach what you have been commanded to and stay away from the pagans.

95. We will sufficiently help you against those who deride you

96. and believe other things to be equal to Allah. They will soon know the truth.

97. We certainly know that you feel sad about what they say against you.

98. Glorify and praise your Lord and be with those who prostrate themselves before Allah.

99. Worship your Lord until ultimate certainty (death) approaches you.

93. 'Ammaa kaanoo ya'ma-loon.

94. Faṣda' bimaa tu'maru wa a'riḍ 'anil-mushrikeen.

95. Innaa kafaynaakal mus-tahzi'een.

96. Allazeena yaj'aloona ma'al-laahi ilaahan-aakhar; fasawfa ya'lamoon.

97. Wa laqad na'lamu annaka yaḍeequ ṣadruka bimaa yaqoo-loon.

98. Fasabbiḥ biḥamdi Rabbi-ka wa kum-minas-saajideen.

99. Wa'bud Rabbaka ḥattaa ya-tiyakal-yaqeen.

عَمَّا كَانُوْا يَعْمَلُوْنَ ۝

فَاصْدَعْ بِمَا تُؤْمَرُ وَاَعْرِضْ عَنِ الْمُشْرِكِيْنَ ۝

اِنَّا كَفَيْنٰكَ الْمُسْتَهْزِءِيْنَ ۙ۝

الَّذِيْنَ يَجْعَلُوْنَ مَعَ اللّٰهِ اِلٰهًا اٰخَرَ ۚ فَسَوْفَ يَعْلَمُوْنَ ۝

وَلَقَدْ نَعْلَمُ اَنَّكَ يَضِيْقُ صَدْرُكَ بِمَا يَقُوْلُوْنَ ۙ۝

فَسَبِّحْ بِحَمْدِ رَبِّكَ وَكُنْ مِّنَ السّٰجِدِيْنَ ۙ۝

وَاعْبُدْ رَبَّكَ حَتّٰى يَاْتِيَكَ الْيَقِيْنُ ۝

Al-Nahl, The Bee (16)
In the Name of Allah, the Beneficent, the Merciful.

Sûrat an-Naḥl-16
(Revealed at Makka)
Bismillaahir Raḥmaanir Raḥeem

(١٦) سُوْرَةُ النَّحْلِ مَكِّيَّةٌ (٧٠)
بِسْمِ اللّٰهِ الرَّحْمٰنِ الرَّحِيْمِ

1. Allah's help will certainly support (the believers), so pagans do not (seek) to hasten it. Allah is free of defects of being considered equal to idols.

1. Ataaa amrul-laahi falaa tasta'jilooh; Subḥaanahoo wa Ta'aalaa 'ammaa yushrikoon.

اَتٰۤى اَمْرُ اللّٰهِ فَلَا تَسْتَعْجِلُوْهُ ؕ سُبْحٰنَهٗ وَتَعٰلٰى عَمَّا يُشْرِكُوْنَ ۝

2. He sends the angels with the Spirit to carry His orders to whichever of His servants He wants so that they would warn people that He is the only Ilah (one deserving to be worshiped) and that people must have fear of Him.

2. Yunazzilul-malaaa'ikata bir-rooḥi min amrihee 'alaa mañy-yashaaa'u min 'ibaadiheee an anzirooo annahoo laaa ilaaha illaaa ana fattaqoon.

يُنَزِّلُ الْمَلٰٓئِكَةَ بِالرُّوْحِ مِنْ اَمْرِهٖ عَلٰى مَنْ يَّشَاءُ مِنْ عِبَادِهٖۤ اَنْ اَنْذِرُوْۤا اَنَّهٗ لَاۤ اِلٰهَ اِلَّاۤ اَنَا فَاتَّقُوْنِ ۝

3. He has created the heavens and the earth for a genuine purpose. He is free of defects of being considered equal to anything else.

3. Khalaqas-samaawaati wal-arḍa bilḥaqq; Ta'aalaa 'ammaa yushrikoon.

خَلَقَ السَّمٰوٰتِ وَالْاَرْضَ بِالْحَقِّ ؕ تَعٰلٰى عَمَّا يُشْرِكُوْنَ ۝

4. He created the human being from a drop of fluid but the human being openly disputes His Word.

4. Khalaqal-insaana min nuṭ-fatin fa-izaa huwa khaṣeemum-mubeen.

خَلَقَ الْاِنْسَانَ مِنْ نُّطْفَةٍ فَاِذَا هُوَ خَصِيْمٌ مُّبِيْنٌ ۝

5. He created cattle which provide you with clothes, food, and other benefits.

5. Wal-an'aama khalaqahaa lakum feehaa dif'uñw-wa manaafi'u wa minhaa ta-ku-loon.

وَالْاَنْعَامَ خَلَقَهَا لَكُمْ فِيْهَا دِفْءٌ وَّمَنَافِعُ وَمِنْهَا تَاْكُلُوْنَ ۝

6. How beautiful you find them when you bring them home and when you drive them out to graze.

6. Wa lakum feehaa jamaalun ḥeena tureeḥoona wa ḥeena tasraḥoon.

وَلَكُمْ فِيهَا جَمَالٌ حِينَ تُرِيحُونَ وَحِينَ تَسْرَحُونَ ⑥

7. They carry your heavy loads to lands which you would not have been able to reach without great difficulty. Your Lord is certainly Compassionate and All-Merciful.

7. Wa taḥmilu asqaalakum ilaa baladil-lam takoonoo baaligheehi illaa bishiqqil anfus; inna Rabbakum la-Ra'oofur-Raḥeem.

وَتَحْمِلُ أَثْقَالَكُمْ إِلَىٰ بَلَدٍ لَّمْ تَكُونُوا بَالِغِيهِ إِلَّا بِشِقِّ الْأَنفُسِ ۚ إِنَّ رَبَّكُمْ لَرَءُوفٌ رَّحِيمٌ ⑦

8. He created horses, mules, and donkeys for you to ride and as a means of beauty. He has also created things that you do not know.

8. Walkhayla walbighaala wal-ḥameera litarkaboohaa wa zeenah; wa yakhluqu maa laa ta'lamoon.

وَالْخَيْلَ وَالْبِغَالَ وَالْحَمِيرَ لِتَرْكَبُوهَا وَزِينَةً ۚ وَيَخْلُقُ مَا لَا تَعْلَمُونَ ⑧

9. Certain paths lead away from Allah but one must follow the path that leads to Allah. Had Allah wanted, he could have guided (all to the right path).

9. Wa 'alal-laahi qaṣdus-sabeeli wa minhaa jaaa'ir; wa law shaaa'a lahadaakum ajma'een.

وَعَلَى اللَّهِ قَصْدُ السَّبِيلِ وَمِنْهَا جَائِرٌ ۚ وَلَوْ شَاءَ لَهَدَاكُمْ أَجْمَعِينَ ⑨ ع ١ ٩ ٧

10. It is He Who sends down water from the sky for you to drink and produces plants as pasture for your cattle.

10. Huwal-lazeee anzala minas-samaaa'i maaa'al-lakum minhu sharaabuñw-wa minhu shajarun feehi tuseemoon.

هُوَ الَّذِي أَنزَلَ مِنَ السَّمَاءِ مَاءً ۖ لَّكُم مِّنْهُ شَرَابٌ وَمِنْهُ شَجَرٌ فِيهِ تُسِيمُونَ ⑩

11. (With this water) He causes corn, olives, palm-trees, vines, and all kinds of fruits to grow. In this there is evidence (of the existence of Allah) for the people of understanding.

11. Yumbitu lakum bihiz-zar'a wazzaytoona wanna-kheela wal a'naaba wa min kullis-samaraat; inna fee zaalika la-Aayatal-liqawmiñy-yatafakkaroon.

يُنبِتُ لَكُم بِهِ الزَّرْعَ وَالزَّيْتُونَ وَالنَّخِيلَ وَالْأَعْنَابَ وَمِن كُلِّ الثَّمَرَاتِ ۗ إِنَّ فِي ذَٰلِكَ لَآيَةً لِّقَوْمٍ يَتَفَكَّرُونَ ⑪

12. Allah has made the day and the night, the sun and the moon, and all the stars subservient to you by His command. In this there is evidence of the truth for people of understanding.

12. Wa sakhkhara lakumul-layla wannahaara wash-shamsa walqamara wannujoomu musakh-kharaatum-bi-amrih; inna fee zaalika la-Aayaatil-liqawmiñy-ya'qiloon.

وَسَخَّرَ لَكُمُ اللَّيْلَ وَالنَّهَارَ وَالشَّمْسَ وَالْقَمَرَ ۖ وَالنُّجُومُ مُسَخَّرَاتٌ بِأَمْرِهِ ۗ إِنَّ فِي ذَٰلِكَ لَآيَاتٍ لِّقَوْمٍ يَعْقِلُونَ ⑫

13. All that He has created for you on the earth are of different colors. In this there is evidence of the Truth for the people who take heed.

13. Wa maa zara-a lakum fil-arḍi mukhtalifan alwaanuh; inna fee zaalika la-Aayatal-liqawmiñy-yaz-zakkaroon.

وَمَا ذَرَأَ لَكُمْ فِي الْأَرْضِ مُخْتَلِفًا أَلْوَانُهُ ۗ إِنَّ فِي ذَٰلِكَ لَآيَةً لِّقَوْمٍ يَذَّكَّرُونَ ⑬

14. It is He Who placed the oceans at your disposal so that

14. Wa Huwal-lazee sakh-kharal-baḥra

وَهُوَ الَّذِي سَخَّرَ الْبَحْرَ

you could find therein fresh fish for food and ornaments with which to deck yourselves. You will find ships that sail for you so that you may travel in search for His bounties and give Him thanks.

lita-kuloo minhu laḥman ṭariyyañw-wa tastakhrijoo minhu ḥilyatan talbasoonahaa wa taral-fulka mawaakhira feehi wa litabtaghoo min faḍlihee wa la'allakum tashkuroon.

لِتَاْكُلُوْا مِنْهُ لَحْمًا طَرِيًّا
وَّتَسْتَخْرِجُوْا مِنْهُ حِلْيَةً
تَلْبَسُوْنَهَا ۚ وَتَرَى الْفُلْكَ مَوَاخِرَ
فِيْهِ وَلِتَبْتَغُوْا مِنْ فَضْلِهٖ
وَلَعَلَّكُمْ تَشْكُرُوْنَ ﴿١٤﴾

15. Allah has fixed the mountains on earth lest you should be hurled away when it quakes. Therein He has also made rivers and roads so that you will find your way.

15. Wa alqaa fil-arḍi rawaasiya an tameeda bikum wa anhaarañw-wa subulal-la'allakum tahtadoon.

وَاَلْقٰى فِى الْاَرْضِ رَوَاسِىَ اَنْ
تَمِيْدَ بِكُمْ وَاَنْهٰرًا وَّسُبُلًا لَّعَلَّكُمْ
تَهْتَدُوْنَ ﴿١٥﴾

16. The stars and other signs also help people to find their way.

16. Wa 'alaamaat; wa bin-najmi hum yahtadoon.

وَعَلٰمٰتٍ ۚ وَبِالنَّجْمِ هُمْ يَهْتَدُوْنَ ﴿١٦﴾

17. Is the One who can create equal to the one who cannot create anything? Why then will you not consider?

17. Afamañy-yakhluqu kamal-laa yakhluq; afalaa tazakkaroon.

اَفَمَنْ يَّخْلُقُ كَمَنْ لَّا يَخْلُقُ ۚ
اَفَلَا تَذَكَّرُوْنَ ﴿١٧﴾

18. Even if you wanted to count up all of Allah's blessings, you would not be able to. Allah is All-forgiving and All-merciful.

18. Wa in ta'uddoo ni'matal-laahi laa tuḥṣoohaaa; innal-laaha la-Ghafoorur-Raḥeem.

وَاِنْ تَعُدُّوْا نِعْمَةَ اللّٰهِ لَا تُحْصُوْهَا ۚ
اِنَّ اللّٰهَ لَغَفُوْرٌ رَّحِيْمٌ ﴿١٨﴾

19. Allah knows all that you conceal or reveal.

19. Wallaahu ya'lamu maa tusirroona wa maa tu'linoon.

وَاللّٰهُ يَعْلَمُ مَا تُسِرُّوْنَ وَمَا
تُعْلِنُوْنَ ﴿١٩﴾

20. Whatever (idols) they worship besides Allah can create nothing for they are themselves created.

20. Wallazeena yad'oona min doonil-laahi laa yakhluqoona shay'añw-wa hum yukhlaqoon.

وَالَّذِيْنَ يَدْعُوْنَ مِنْ دُوْنِ اللّٰهِ
لَا يَخْلُقُوْنَ شَيْئًا وَّهُمْ يُخْلَقُوْنَ ﴿٢٠﴾

21. They are not living but are dead. They cannot know when they will be raised.

21. Amwaatun ghayru aḥyaaa'; wa maa yash'uroona ayyaana yub'asoon.

اَمْوَاتٌ غَيْرُ اَحْيَآءٍ ۚ وَمَا يَشْعُرُوْنَ
اَيَّانَ يُبْعَثُوْنَ ﴿٢١﴾ ع ٢ ١٢ ٨

22. Your Lord is only One. The hearts of those who do not believe in the life hereafter dislike (the truth). They are puffed up with pride.

22. Ilaahukum Ilaahuñw-Waaḥid; fallazeena laa yu'minoona bil-Aakhirati quloobuhum-munkiratuñw-wa hum-mustakbiroon.

اِلٰهُكُمْ اِلٰهٌ وَّاحِدٌ ۚ فَالَّذِيْنَ لَا
يُؤْمِنُوْنَ بِالْاٰخِرَةِ قُلُوْبُهُمْ
مُّنْكِرَةٌ وَّهُمْ مُّسْتَكْبِرُوْنَ ﴿٢٢﴾

23. Allah certainly knows whatever you conceal or reveal. He does not love the proud ones.

23. Laa jarama annal-laaha ya'lamu maa yusirroona wa maa yu'linoon; innahoo laa yuḥibbul-mustakbireen.

لَا جَرَمَ اَنَّ اللّٰهَ يَعْلَمُ مَا يُسِرُّوْنَ
وَمَا يُعْلِنُوْنَ ۚ اِنَّهٗ لَا يُحِبُّ
الْمُسْتَكْبِرِيْنَ ﴿٢٣﴾

24. When they are asked, "What has your Lord revealed to

24. Wa izaa qeela lahum-maazaaa anzala

وَاِذَا قِيْلَ لَهُمْ مَّاذَآ اَنْزَلَ

you?" they say, "Only ancient legends."

Rabbukum qaalooo asaaṭeerul awwaleen.

رَبُّكُمْ ۙ قَالُوْٓا اَسَاطِيْرُ الْاَوَّلِيْنَ ﴿٢٤﴾

25. Besides their own burdens, on the Day of Judgment, they will have to carry on the burdens of those whom they have misled without knowledge. How evil that burden will be!

25. Liyaḥmilooo awzaarahum kaamilatañy-Yawmal-Qiyaamati wa min awzaaril-lazeena yuḍilloonahum bighayri 'ilm; alaa saaa'a maa yaziroon.

لِيَحْمِلُوْٓا اَوْزَارَهُمْ كَامِلَةً يَّوْمَ
الْقِيٰمَةِ ۙ وَمِنْ اَوْزَارِ الَّذِيْنَ
يُضِلُّوْنَهُمْ بِغَيْرِ عِلْمٍ ؕ اَلَا سَآءَ ع ٤
مَا يَزِرُوْنَ ﴿٢٥﴾

26. Those who went before them had also devised evil plans. Allah demolished their houses, destroying their very foundations. Their ceilings toppled on their heads and torment struck them from a direction which they had never expected.

26. Qad makaral-lazeena min qablihim fa-atal-laahu bunyaanahum-minal-qawaa'idi fa-kharra 'alayhimus-saqfu min fawqihim wa ataahumul 'azaabu min ḥaysu laa yash'uroon.

قَدْ مَكَرَ الَّذِيْنَ مِنْ قَبْلِهِمْ فَاَتَى
اللّٰهُ بُنْيَانَهُمْ مِّنَ الْقَوَاعِدِ فَخَرَّ
عَلَيْهِمُ السَّقْفُ مِنْ فَوْقِهِمْ وَاَتٰىهُمُ
الْعَذَابُ مِنْ حَيْثُ لَا يَشْعُرُوْنَ ﴿٢٦﴾

27. Allah will humiliate them on the Day of Judgment and ask them, "Where are the idols which you had considered equal to Me and which were the cause of hostility and animosity among you?" The people who were given knowledge will say, "It is the unbelievers who face disgrace and trouble on this day."

27. Summa Yawmal-Qiyaamati yukhzeehim wa yaqoolu ayna shurakaaa'iyal-lazeena kuntum tushaaaq-qoona feehim; qaalal-lazeena ootul-'ilma innal-khizyal-Yawma wassooo'a 'alal-kaafireen.

ثُمَّ يَوْمَ الْقِيٰمَةِ يُخْزِيْهِمْ وَيَقُوْلُ
اَيْنَ شُرَكَآءِيَ الَّذِيْنَ كُنْتُمْ
تُشَآقُّوْنَ فِيْهِمْ ؕ قَالَ الَّذِيْنَ اُوْتُوا
الْعِلْمَ اِنَّ الْخِزْيَ الْيَوْمَ وَالسُّوْٓءَ
عَلَى الْكٰفِرِيْنَ ﴿٢٧﴾

28. The unjust, who will be seized by the angels, will submit themselves, obey, and say, "We were not evil-doers." However, Allah certainly knows what they had been doing.

28. Allazeena tatawaf-faahumul-malaaa'ikatu ẓaalimeee anfusihim fa-alqawus-salama maa kunnaa na'malu min sooo'; balaaa innal-laaha 'aleemum bimaa kuntum ta'maloon.

الَّذِيْنَ تَتَوَفّٰىهُمُ الْمَلٰٓئِكَةُ
ظَالِمِيْٓ اَنْفُسِهِمْ ۠ فَاَلْقَوُا السَّلَمَ
مَا كُنَّا نَعْمَلُ مِنْ سُوْٓءٍ ؕ بَلٰٓى
اِنَّ اللّٰهَ عَلِيْمٌ ۢ بِمَا كُنْتُمْ تَعْمَلُوْنَ ﴿٢٨﴾

29. They will be commanded to enter hell to live therein forever. How terrible will be the place of the proud ones!

29. Fadkhulooo abwaaba Jahannama khaalideena feehaa falabi'sa maswal-mutakabbireen.

فَادْخُلُوْٓا اَبْوَابَ جَهَنَّمَ خٰلِدِيْنَ
فِيْهَا ؕ فَلَبِئْسَ مَثْوَى الْمُتَكَبِّرِيْنَ ﴿٢٩﴾

30. The pious ones will be asked, "What did your Lord reveal to you?" They will reply, "He revealed only good." The share of the righteous ones is virtue in this world and greater virtue in the life to come. How blessed will be the dwelling of the pious ones!

30. Wa qeela lillazeenat-taqaw maazaaa anzala Rabbukum; qaaloo khayraa; lillazeena aḥsanoo fee haazihid-dunyaa ḥasanah; wa la-Daarul-Aakhirati khayr; wa lani'ma daarul-muttaqeen.

وَقِيْلَ لِلَّذِيْنَ اتَّقَوْا مَاذَآ اَنْزَلَ
رَبُّكُمْ ؕ قَالُوْا خَيْرًا ؕ لِلَّذِيْنَ اَحْسَنُوْا
فِيْ هٰذِهِ الدُّنْيَا حَسَنَةٌ ؕ وَلَدَارُ
الْاٰخِرَةِ خَيْرٌ ؕ وَلَنِعْمَ دَارُ
الْمُتَّقِيْنَ ﴿٣٠﴾

31. They will be admitted into the gardens of Eden wherein

31. Jannaatu 'Adniñy-yadkhuloonahaa tajree

جَنّٰتُ عَدْنٍ يَّدْخُلُوْنَهَا تَجْرِيْ

streams flow and they will have therein whatever they want. This is how Allah will reward the pious ones.

min taḥtihal-anhaaru lahum feehaa maa yashaaa'oon; kaẕaalika yajzil-laahul-muttaqeen.

مِنْ تَحْتِهَا الْاَنْهٰرُ لَهُمْ فِيْهَا مَا
يَشَآءُوْنَ ؕ كَذٰلِكَ يَجْزِى اللّٰهُ
الْمُتَّقِيْنَ ۙ﴿۳۱﴾

32. They, being of pure birth, will be received by the angels of mercy with the greeting, "Peace be with you. Enter Paradise as a reward for your good deeds."

32. Allaẕeena tatawaf-faahumul-malaaa'ikatu ṭayyibeena yaqooloona salaamun 'alaykumud-khulul-Jannata bimaa kuntum ta'maloon.

الَّذِيْنَ تَتَوَفّٰىهُمُ الْمَلٰٓئِكَةُ طَيِّبِيْنَ ۙ
يَقُوْلُوْنَ سَلٰمٌ عَلَيْكُمُ ۙ ادْخُلُوا
الْجَنَّةَ بِمَا كُنْتُمْ تَعْمَلُوْنَ ﴿۳۲﴾

33. Are they (the unbelievers) waiting for the angels and the decree of your Lord to be fulfilled before they believe? The people who lived before them had also done the same thing. Allah did not do injustice to them, but they wronged themselves.

33. Hal yanẓuroona illaaa an tatiyahumul-malaaa'ikatu aw yatiya amru Rabbik; kaẕaalika fa'alal-laẕeena min qablihim; wa maa ẓalamahumul-laahu wa laakin kaanooo anfusahum yaẓlimoon.

هَلْ يَنْظُرُوْنَ اِلَّآ اَنْ تَاْتِيَهُمُ
الْمَلٰٓئِكَةُ اَوْ يَاْتِىَ اَمْرُ رَبِّكَ ؕ
كَذٰلِكَ فَعَلَ الَّذِيْنَ مِنْ قَبْلِهِمْ ؕ
وَمَا ظَلَمَهُمُ اللّٰهُ وَلٰكِنْ كَانُوْٓا
اَنْفُسَهُمْ يَظْلِمُوْنَ ﴿۳۳﴾

34. The evil consequences of their deeds afflicted them and they were surrounded by what they had mocked.

34. Fa-aṣaabahum sayyi-aatu maa 'amiloo wa ḥaaqa bihim maa kaanoo bihee yastahzi'oon.

فَاَصَابَهُمْ سَيِّاٰتُ مَا عَمِلُوْا وَحَاقَ
بِهِمْ مَّا كَانُوْا بِهٖ يَسْتَهْزِءُوْنَ ﴿۳۴﴾ ع

35. The pagans had said, "Had Allah wanted we would not have worshipped anything other than Him, nor would our fathers. We would not have forbidden anything without (a command from) Him." The same thing was said by the people who lived before them. Are the Messengers expected to do more than just preach clearly?

35. Wa qaalal-laẕeena ashrakoo law shaaa'al-laahu maa 'abadnaa min doonihee min shay'in-naḥnu wa laaa aabaaa'unaa wa laa ḥarramnaa min doonihee min shay'; kaẕaalika fa'alal-laẕeena min qablihim fahal 'alar-Rusuli illal-balaaghul-mubeen.

وَقَالَ الَّذِيْنَ اَشْرَكُوْا لَوْ شَآءَ اللّٰهُ
مَا عَبَدْنَا مِنْ دُوْنِهٖ مِنْ شَیْءٍ نَّحْنُ
وَلَآ اٰبَآؤُنَا وَلَا حَرَّمْنَا مِنْ دُوْنِهٖ
مِنْ شَیْءٍ ؕ كَذٰلِكَ فَعَلَ الَّذِيْنَ مِنْ
قَبْلِهِمْ ۚ فَهَلْ عَلَى الرُّسُلِ اِلَّا
الْبَلٰغُ الْمُبِيْنُ ﴿۳۵﴾

36. To every nation We sent a Messenger who told its people, "Worship Allah and stay away from Satan." Some of them were guided by Allah and others were doomed to go astray. Travel through the land and see how terrible the end was for those who rejected the truth!

36. Wa laqad ba'aṯnaa fee kulli ummatir-Rasoolan ani'budul-laaha wajtanibuṭ-Ṭaaghoota faminhum man hadal-laahu wa minhum-man ḥaqqat 'alayhiḍ-ḍalaalah; faseeroo fil-arḍi fanẓuroo kayfa kaana 'aaqibatul-mukaẕ-ẕibeen.

وَلَقَدْ بَعَثْنَا فِىْ كُلِّ اُمَّةٍ رَّسُوْلًا
اَنِ اعْبُدُوا اللّٰهَ وَاجْتَنِبُوا الطَّاغُوْتَ ۚ
فَمِنْهُمْ مَّنْ هَدَى اللّٰهُ وَمِنْهُمْ
مَّنْ حَقَّتْ عَلَيْهِ الضَّلٰلَةُ ؕ فَسِيْرُوْا
فِى الْاَرْضِ فَانْظُرُوْا كَيْفَ كَانَ
عَاقِبَةُ الْمُكَذِّبِيْنَ ﴿۳۶﴾

37. (Muhammad), even though you have a strong desire to guide

37. In taḥriṣ 'alaa hudaahum fa-innal-laaha

اِنْ تَحْرِصْ عَلٰى هُدٰىهُمْ فَاِنَّ اللّٰهَ

them, be sure that Allah will not guide (reward) those who have gone astray and no one will be able to help them.

laa yahdee mañy-yuḍillu wa maa lahum-min-naaṣireen.

لَا يَهْدِيْ مَنْ يُّضِلُّ وَمَا لَهُمْ
مِّنْ نّٰصِرِيْنَ ﴿٣٧﴾

38. They strongly swear by Allah that Allah will not bring the dead to life. Allah's promise (of the Resurrection) will certainly come true but many people do not know.

38. Wa aqsamoo billaahi jahda aymaanihim laa yab'aṣul-laahu mañy-yamoot; balaa wa'dan 'alayhi ḥaqqañw-wa laakinna akṣaran-naasi laa ya'lamoon.

وَاَقْسَمُوْا بِاللّٰهِ جَهْدَ اَيْمَانِهِمْ ۙ
لَا يَبْعَثُ اللّٰهُ مَنْ يَّمُوْتُ ؕ بَلٰى
وَعْدًا عَلَيْهِ حَقًّا وَّلٰكِنَّ اَكْثَرَ
النَّاسِ لَا يَعْلَمُوْنَ ﴿٣٨﴾

39. (Through the resurrection) Allah wants to make a clear distinction between right and wrong and make the unbelievers know that they were liars.

39. Liyubayyina lahumul-lazee yakhtalifoona feehi wa liya'lamal-lazeena kafarooo annahum kaanoo kaazibeen.

لِيُبَيِّنَ لَهُمُ الَّذِيْ يَخْتَلِفُوْنَ
فِيْهِ وَلِيَعْلَمَ الَّذِيْنَ كَفَرُوْۤا اَنَّهُمْ
كَانُوْا كٰذِبِيْنَ ﴿٣٩﴾

40. When We want to bring something into existence, Our command is, "Exist," and it comes into existence.

40. Innamaa qawlunaa lisha-y'in izaaa aradnaahu an-naqoola lahoo kun fayakoon.

اِنَّمَا قَوْلُنَا لِشَيْءٍ اِذَاۤ اَرَدْنٰهُ اَنْ
نَّقُوْلَ لَهٗ كُنْ فَيَكُوْنُ ﴿٤٠﴾ ع ٥ ١١

41. Allah settles those who leave their homes for His cause after having suffered injustice, in a prosperous dwelling in this life and greater rewards will be theirs in the life to come. Would that they knew this.

41. Wallazeena haajaroo fil-laahi mim-ba'di maa ẓulimoo lanubaw-wi'an-nahum fid-dunyaa ḥasanah; wa la-ajrul Aakhirati akbar; law kaanoo ya'lamoon.

وَالَّذِيْنَ هَاجَرُوْا فِي اللّٰهِ مِنْۢ
بَعْدِ مَا ظُلِمُوْا لَنُبَوِّئَنَّهُمْ فِي
الدُّنْيَا حَسَنَةً ؕ وَلَاَجْرُ الْاٰخِرَةِ
اَكْبَرُ ۘ لَوْ كَانُوْا يَعْلَمُوْنَ ﴿٤١﴾ وقف لازم

42. (It is they) who have exercised patience and trust in their Lord.

42. Allazeena ṣabaroo wa 'alaa Rabbihim yatawak-kaloon.

الَّذِيْنَ صَبَرُوْا وَعَلٰى رَبِّهِمْ يَتَوَكَّلُوْنَ ﴿٤٢﴾

43. Every messenger whom We sent before you were men whom We had sent with revelations, – ask the people of Al-Dhikr (those who possess divine guidance) if you do not know about this

43. Wa maaa arsalnaa min qablika illaa rijaalan-nooḥeee ilayhim; fas'alooo ahlaz-zikri in kuntum laa ta'lamoon.

وَمَاۤ اَرْسَلْنَا مِنْ قَبْلِكَ اِلَّا رِجَالًا
نُّوْحِيْۤ اِلَيْهِمْ فَسْـَٔلُوْۤا اَهْلَ الذِّكْرِ
اِنْ كُنْتُمْ لَا تَعْلَمُوْنَ ﴿٤٣﴾

44. miracles and books. We have revealed the Quran to you so that you can tell the people what has been revealed to them and so that perhaps they will think.

44. Bilbayyinaati waz-Zubur; wa anzalnaaa ilaykaz-Zikra litubayyina linnaasi maa nuzzila ilayhim wa la'allahum yatafakkaroon.

بِالْبَيِّنٰتِ وَالزُّبُرِ ؕ وَاَنْزَلْنَاۤ اِلَيْكَ
الذِّكْرَ لِتُبَيِّنَ لِلنَّاسِ مَا نُزِّلَ
اِلَيْهِمْ وَلَعَلَّهُمْ يَتَفَكَّرُوْنَ ﴿٤٤﴾ النصف

45. Can they who have devised evil plans expect to be safe from the command of Allah to the earth to swallow them up, or from a torment which might strike them from an unexpected direction?

45. Afa-aminal-lazeena ma-karus-sayyi-aati añy-yakhsifal-laahu bihimul-arḍa aw ya-tiyahumul-'azaabu min ḥayṣu laa yash'uroon.

اَفَاَمِنَ الَّذِيْنَ مَكَرُوا السَّيِّاٰتِ
اَنْ يَّخْسِفَ اللّٰهُ بِهِمُ الْاَرْضَ اَوْ
يَاْتِيَهُمُ الْعَذَابُ مِنْ حَيْثُ لَا
يَشْعُرُوْنَ ﴿٤٥﴾

46. Are they confident that Allah will not seize them whilc they are on a journey because they cannot be defeated?

47. Are they confident that He will not destroy them even when they are watchful? Your Lord is Compassionate and All-merciful.

48. Did they not see that the shadows of whatever Allah has created turn to the right and to the left in prostration and submission to Allah?

49. Whatever is in the heavens and the earth, the cattle and the angels prostrate themselves before Allah without pride.

50. They (angels) have fear of their Lord above them and fulfill His commands.

(Bow Down)

51. Allah says, "Do not worship two gods. There is only One Ilah (one deserving to be worshiped). Have fear of Me."

52. To Him belongs all that is in the heavens and the earth. His retribution is severe. Should you then have fear of anyone other than Allah?

53. Whatever bounties you have are from Allah. When hardship befalls you, you begin to cry out to Him.

54. When He saves you from the hardship, some of you start to consider other things as partners of their Lord.

55. In the end you will reject Our bounties. Enjoy yourselves; you will soon learn about (the consequences of your deeds).

56. They give to unknown images a share out of the sustenance that We gave them. By Allah, you will be questioned about that which you have falsely invented.

46. Aw ya-khuzahum fee taqallubihim famaa hum bi-mu'jizeen.

47. Aw ya-khuzahum 'alaa takhawwuf; fa-inna Rabbakum la-Ra'oofur-Raheem.

48. Awa lam yaraw ilaa maa khalaqal-laahu min shay'iñy-yatafayya'u zilaaluhoo 'anil-yameeni washshamaaa'ili sujjadal-lillaahi wa hum daakhiroon.

49. Wa lillaahi yasjudu maa fis-samaawaati wa maa fil-ardi min daaabbatiñw-walmalaaa'ikatu wa hum laa yastakbiroon.

50. Yakhaafoona Rabbahum min fawqihim wa yaf'aloona maa yu'maroon. ۩

51. Wa qaalal-laahu laa tattakhizooo ilaahaynis-nayni innamaa Huwa Ilaahuñw-Waahid; fa-iyyaaya farhaboon.

52. Wa lahoo maa fis-samaawaati wal-ardi wa lahud-deenu waasibaa; afaghayral-laahi tattaqoon.

53. Wa maa bikum-min ni'matin faminal-laahi summa izaa massakumud-durru fa-ilayhi taj'aroon.

54. Summa izaa kashafad-durra 'ankum izaa fareequm-minkum bi-Rabbihim yushrikoon.

55. Liyakfuroo bimaa aataynaahum; fatamatta'oo fasawfa ta'lamoon.

56. Wa yaj'aloona limaa laa ya'lamoona naseebam-mimmaa razaqnaahum; tallaahi latus'alunna 'ammaa kuntum taftaroon.

أَوْ يَأْخُذَهُمْ فِي تَقَلُّبِهِمْ فَمَا هُمْ
بِمُعْجِزِينَ ﴿٤٦﴾
أَوْ يَأْخُذَهُمْ عَلَىٰ تَخَوُّفٍ ۖ فَإِنَّ
رَبَّكُمْ لَرَءُوفٌ رَحِيمٌ ﴿٤٧﴾
أَوَلَمْ يَرَوْا إِلَىٰ مَا خَلَقَ اللَّهُ مِنْ
شَيْءٍ يَتَفَيَّأُ ظِلَالُهُ عَنِ الْيَمِينِ
وَالشَّمَائِلِ سُجَّدًا لِلَّهِ وَهُمْ دَاخِرُونَ ﴿٤٨﴾
وَلِلَّهِ يَسْجُدُ مَا فِي السَّمَاوَاتِ وَمَا
فِي الْأَرْضِ مِنْ دَابَّةٍ وَالْمَلَائِكَةُ
وَهُمْ لَا يَسْتَكْبِرُونَ ﴿٤٩﴾
يَخَافُونَ رَبَّهُمْ مِنْ فَوْقِهِمْ وَيَفْعَلُونَ
مَا يُؤْمَرُونَ ﴿٥٠﴾ السجدة ع
وَقَالَ اللَّهُ لَا تَتَّخِذُوا إِلَٰهَيْنِ اثْنَيْنِ
إِنَّمَا هُوَ إِلَٰهٌ وَاحِدٌ ۖ فَإِيَّايَ
فَارْهَبُونِ ﴿٥١﴾
وَلَهُ مَا فِي السَّمَاوَاتِ وَالْأَرْضِ وَلَهُ
الدِّينُ وَاصِبًا ۚ أَفَغَيْرَ اللَّهِ تَتَّقُونَ ﴿٥٢﴾
وَمَا بِكُمْ مِنْ نِعْمَةٍ فَمِنَ اللَّهِ ۖ ثُمَّ إِذَا
مَسَّكُمُ الضُّرُّ فَإِلَيْهِ تَجْأَرُونَ ﴿٥٣﴾
ثُمَّ إِذَا كَشَفَ الضُّرَّ عَنْكُمْ إِذَا
فَرِيقٌ مِنْكُمْ بِرَبِّهِمْ يُشْرِكُونَ ﴿٥٤﴾
لِيَكْفُرُوا بِمَا آتَيْنَاهُمْ ۚ فَتَمَتَّعُوا ۖ
فَسَوْفَ تَعْلَمُونَ ﴿٥٥﴾
وَيَجْعَلُونَ لِمَا لَا يَعْلَمُونَ نَصِيبًا
مِمَّا رَزَقْنَاهُمْ ۗ تَاللَّهِ لَتُسْأَلُنَّ عَمَّا
كُنْتُمْ تَفْتَرُونَ ﴿٥٦﴾

السجدة ع

57. They ascribe daughters to Allah, Allah is free of defects of having daughters, but they can have whatever they want.

57. Wa yaj'aloona lillaahil-banaati Subḥaanahoo wa lahum maa yashtahoon.

وَيَجْعَلُوْنَ لِلّٰهِ الْبَنٰتِ سُبْحٰنَهٗ ۙ
وَلَهُمْ مَّا يَشْتَهُوْنَ ﴿٥٧﴾

58. When the glad news of the birth of their daughter is brought to them, their faces turn gloomy and black with anger.

58. Wa iẕaa bushshira aḥaduhum bil-unsaa ẕalla wajhuhoo muswaddañw-wa huwa kaẓeem.

وَاِذَا بُشِّرَ اَحَدُهُمْ بِالْاُنْثٰى ظَلَّ
وَجْهُهٗ مُسْوَدًّا وَّهُوَ كَظِيْمٌ ﴿٥٨﴾

59. They try to hide themselves from the people because of the disgrace of such news. Will they keep their newborn despite the disgrace or bury it alive? How sinful is their Judgment!

59. Yatawaaraa minal-qawmi min sooo'i maa bushshira bih; ayumsikuhoo 'alaa hoonin am yadussuhoo fitturaab; alaa saaa'a maa yaḥkumoon.

يَتَوَارٰى مِنَ الْقَوْمِ مِنْ سُوْٓءِ مَا
بُشِّرَ بِهٖ ؕ اَيُمْسِكُهٗ عَلٰى هُوْنٍ اَمْ
يَدُسُّهٗ فِى التُّرَابِ ؕ اَلَا سَآءَ مَا
يَحْكُمُوْنَ ﴿٥٩﴾

60. Those who do not believe in the life to come are evil examples. To Allah belong all the exalted attributes; He is the Majestic and the All-wise.

60. Lillaẕeena laa yu'minoona bil-Aakhirati maṯalus-saw'i wa lillaahil-maṯalul-a'laa; wa Huwal-'Azeezul-Ḥakeem.

لِلَّذِيْنَ لَا يُؤْمِنُوْنَ بِالْاٰخِرَةِ
مَثَلُ السَّوْءِ ۚ وَلِلّٰهِ الْمَثَلُ الْاَعْلٰى ؕ
وَهُوَ الْعَزِيْزُ الْحَكِيْمُ ﴿٦٠﴾ ع ۱۳

61. Were Allah to seize people immediately for their injustice, no living creature would be left on earth. He gives them respite for an appointed time. When their term is over, they will not be able to change the inevitable.

61. Wa law yu'aakhiẕul-laahun-naasa biẕulmihim-maa taraka 'alayhaa min daaabbatiñw-wa laakiñy-yu'akhkhiruhum ilaaa ajalim-musamman fa-iẕaa jaaa'a ajaluhum laa yasta-khiroona saa'atañw-wa laa yastaqdimoon.

وَلَوْ يُؤَاخِذُ اللّٰهُ النَّاسَ بِظُلْمِهِمْ
مَّا تَرَكَ عَلَيْهَا مِنْ دَآبَّةٍ وَّلٰكِنْ
يُّؤَخِّرُهُمْ اِلٰٓى اَجَلٍ مُّسَمًّى ۚ
فَاِذَا جَآءَ اَجَلُهُمْ لَا يَسْتَاْخِرُوْنَ
سَاعَةً وَّلَا يَسْتَقْدِمُوْنَ ﴿٦١﴾

62. They ascribe to Allah that which even they themselves do not like and their lying tongues say that their end will be virtuous. Their share will certainly be hellfire in which they will face extremely harsh suffering.

62. Wa yaj'aloona lillaahi maa yakrahoona wa taṣifu alsinatuhumul-kaẕiba anna lahumul-ḥusnaa laa jarama anna lahumun-Naara wa annahum-mufraṭoon.

وَيَجْعَلُوْنَ لِلّٰهِ مَا يَكْرَهُوْنَ
وَتَصِفُ اَلْسِنَتُهُمُ الْكَذِبَ اَنَّ لَهُمُ
الْحُسْنٰى ؕ لَا جَرَمَ اَنَّ لَهُمُ النَّارَ
وَاَنَّهُمْ مُّفْرَطُوْنَ ﴿٦٢﴾

63. By Allah, We sent (Messengers) to nations who lived before you. Satan made their deeds seem attractive to them and, on the Day of Judgment, Satan will be their guardian. For them there will be a painful punishment.

63. Tallaahi laqad arsalnaaa ilaaa umamim-min qablika fazayyana lahumush-Shayṭaanu a'maalahum fahuwa waliyyuhumul-yawma wa lahum 'aẕaabun aleem.

تَاللّٰهِ لَقَدْ اَرْسَلْنَآ اِلٰٓى اُمَمٍ
مِّنْ قَبْلِكَ فَزَيَّنَ لَهُمُ الشَّيْطٰنُ
اَعْمَالَهُمْ فَهُوَ وَلِيُّهُمُ الْيَوْمَ
وَلَهُمْ عَذَابٌ اَلِيْمٌ ﴿٦٣﴾

64. We have sent you the Book for no other reason than to settle their differences and to be a guide

64. Wa maaa anzalnaa 'alaykal-Kitaaba illaa litubay-yina lahumul-laẕikh-talafoo feehi

وَمَآ اَنْزَلْنَا عَلَيْكَ الْكِتٰبَ اِلَّا
لِتُبَيِّنَ لَهُمُ الَّذِى اخْتَلَفُوْا فِيْهِ ۙ

and mercy for those who believe.

wa hudañw-wa raḥmatal-liqawmiñy-yu'minoon.

وَهُدًى وَّرَحْمَةً لِّقَوْمٍ يُّؤْمِنُوْنَ ﴿٦٤﴾

65. Allah has sent down water from the sky and has brought the dead earth to life. In this there is evidence (of the truth) for those who listen (carefully).

65. Wallaahu anzala minas-samaaa'i maaa'an fa-aḥyaa bihil-arḍa ba'da mawtihaaa; inna fee zaalika la-Aayatal-liqawmiñy-yasma'oon.

وَاللّٰهُ اَنْزَلَ مِنَ السَّمَآءِ مَآءً
فَاَحْيَا بِهِ الْاَرْضَ بَعْدَ مَوْتِهَا ؕ
اِنَّ فِيْ ذٰلِكَ لَاٰيَةً لِّقَوْمٍ
يَّسْمَعُوْنَ ﴿٦٥﴾ ع ٥/١٤

66. In cattle there is certainly a lesson for you. We provide you, from what is within them out of the contents of the intestines and blood, pure and delicious milk to drink.

66. Wa-inna lakum fil-an'aami la'ibrah; nusqeekum mimmaa fee buṭoonihee mim bayni farsiñw-wa damil-labanan khaaliṣan saaa'ighal-lish-shaaribeen.

وَاِنَّ لَكُمْ فِي الْاَنْعَامِ لَعِبْرَةً ؕ
نُسْقِيْكُمْ مِّمَّا فِيْ بُطُوْنِهٖ مِنْ بَيْنِ
فَرْثٍ وَّدَمٍ لَّبَنًا خَالِصًا سَآئِغًا
لِّلشّٰرِبِيْنَ ﴿٦٦﴾

67. The fruit of palm trees and vines which provide you with sugar and delicious food (raisins) also provide a lesson and evidence (of the Truth) for the people of understanding.

67. Wa min samaraatin-nakheeli wal-a'naabi tattakhizoona minhu sakarañw-wa rizqan ḥasanaa; inna fee zaalika la-Aayatal-liqawmiñy-ya'qiloon.

وَمِنْ ثَمَرٰتِ النَّخِيْلِ وَالْاَعْنَابِ
تَتَّخِذُوْنَ مِنْهُ سَكَرًا وَّ
رِزْقًا حَسَنًا ؕ اِنَّ فِيْ ذٰلِكَ لَاٰيَةً
لِّقَوْمٍ يَّعْقِلُوْنَ ﴿٦٧﴾

68. Your Lord inspired the bees, "Make hives in the mountains, in the trees, and in the trellises,

68. Wa-awḥaa Rabbuka ilannaḥli anit-takhizee minal-jibaali buyootañw-wa minash-shajari wa mimmaa ya'rishoon.

وَاَوْحٰى رَبُّكَ اِلَى النَّحْلِ اَنِ
اتَّخِذِيْ مِنَ الْجِبَالِ بُيُوْتًا
وَّمِنَ الشَّجَرِ وَمِمَّا يَعْرِشُوْنَ ﴿٦٨﴾

69. then eat of every fruit and follow the path of your Lord submissively." From out of their bellies comes a drink of different color in which there is a cure for the human being. In this there is evidence (of the truth) for the people of understanding.

69. Summa kulee min kullis-samaraati faslukee subula Rabbiki zululaa; yakhruju mim buṭoonihaa sharaabum-mukh-talifun alwaanuhoo feehi shifaaa'ul-linnaas; inna fee zaalika la-Aayatal-liqawmiñy-yatafakkaroon.

ثُمَّ كُلِيْ مِنْ كُلِّ الثَّمَرٰتِ
فَاسْلُكِيْ سُبُلَ رَبِّكِ ذُلُلًا ؕ يَخْرُجُ
مِنْ بُطُوْنِهَا شَرَابٌ مُّخْتَلِفٌ
اَلْوَانُهٗ فِيْهِ شِفَآءٌ لِّلنَّاسِ ؕ اِنَّ
فِيْ ذٰلِكَ لَاٰيَةً لِّقَوْمٍ يَّتَفَكَّرُوْنَ ﴿٦٩﴾

70. Allah has created you and He causes you to die. Some of you will grow to an extremely old age and lose your memory. Allah is All-knowing and Almighty.

70. Wallaahu khalaqakum summa yatawaffaakum; wa minkum mañy-yuraddu ilaaa arzalil 'umuri likay laa ya'lama ba'da 'ilmin shay'aa; innal-laaha 'Aleemun Qadeer.

وَاللّٰهُ خَلَقَكُمْ ثُمَّ يَتَوَفّٰىكُمْ ۫ۙ
وَمِنْكُمْ مَّنْ يُّرَدُّ اِلٰى اَرْذَلِ الْعُمُرِ
لِكَيْ لَا يَعْلَمَ بَعْدَ عِلْمٍ شَيْـًٔا ؕ
اِنَّ اللّٰهَ عَلِيْمٌ قَدِيْرٌ ﴿٧٠﴾ ع ٩/٥/١٥

71. Allah has favored some of you over the others. Those who

71. Wallaahu faḍḍala ba'ḍa-kum 'alaa ba'ḍin

وَاللّٰهُ فَضَّلَ بَعْضَكُمْ عَلٰى بَعْضٍ

are favored do not keep back their food from their dependents, thus they all equally share the food. Do they reject the bounties of Allah?

firrizq; famal-lazeena fuḍḍiloo biraaaddee rizqihim 'alaa maa malakat aymaanuhum fahum feehi sawaaa'; afabini'matil-laahi yajḥadoon.

فِي الرِّزْقِ ۚ فَمَا الَّذِينَ فُضِّلُوا
بِرَآدِّي رِزْقِهِمْ عَلَىٰ مَا مَلَكَتْ
أَيْمَانُهُمْ فَهُمْ فِيهِ سَوَآءٌ ۚ
أَفَبِنِعْمَةِ اللَّهِ يَجْحَدُونَ ﴿٧١﴾

72. Allah has created spouses for you from your own selves. He has created your sons and grandsons from your spouses and has given you pure things for your sustenance. Do they then believe in falsehood and reject the bounties of Allah?

72. Wallaahu ja'ala lakum min anfusikum azwaajañw-wa ja'ala lakum min azwaajikum baneena wa ḥafadatañw-wa razaqakum minaṭ-ṭayyibaat; afabil-baaṭili yu'minoona wa bini'matil-laahi hum yakfuroon.

وَاللَّهُ جَعَلَ لَكُم مِّنْ أَنفُسِكُمْ
أَزْوَاجًا وَجَعَلَ لَكُم مِّنْ أَزْوَاجِكُم
بَنِينَ وَحَفَدَةً وَرَزَقَكُم مِّنَ
الطَّيِّبَاتِ ۚ أَفَبِالْبَاطِلِ يُؤْمِنُونَ
وَبِنِعْمَتِ اللَّهِ هُمْ يَكْفُرُونَ ﴿٧٢﴾

73. Do they worship things other than Allah which neither provide them with any sustenance from the heavens and the earth nor have the ability to do so?

73. Wa ya'budoona min doonil-laahi maa laa yamliku lahum rizqam-minas-samaawaati wal-arḍi shay'añw-wa laa yastaṭee'oon.

وَيَعْبُدُونَ مِن دُونِ اللَّهِ مَا لَا
يَمْلِكُ لَهُمْ رِزْقًا مِّنَ السَّمَاوَاتِ
وَالْأَرْضِ شَيْئًا وَلَا يَسْتَطِيعُونَ ﴿٧٣﴾

74. Do not consider anything equal to Allah. Allah knows that which you do not know.

74. Falaa taḍriboo lillaahil amsaal; innal-laaha ya'lamu wa antum laa ta'lamoon.

فَلَا تَضْرِبُوا لِلَّهِ الْأَمْثَالَ ۚ إِنَّ
اللَّهَ يَعْلَمُ وَأَنتُمْ لَا تَعْلَمُونَ ﴿٧٤﴾

75. Allah tells a parable about a helpless servant and one to whom He has given honorable provisions and who has spent for the cause of Allah privately and in public. Can these two people be considered equal? It is only Allah who deserves all praise, but most people do not know.

75. Ḍarabal-laahu masalan 'abdam-mamlookal-laa yaqdiru 'alaa shay'iñw-wa marrazaqnaahu minnaa rizqan ḥasanan fahuwa yunfiqu minhu sirrañw-wa jahraa; hal yastawoon; alḥamdu lillaah; bal aksaruhum laa ya'lamoon.

ضَرَبَ اللَّهُ مَثَلًا عَبْدًا مَّمْلُوكًا
لَّا يَقْدِرُ عَلَىٰ شَيْءٍ وَمَن رَّزَقْنَاهُ
مِنَّا رِزْقًا حَسَنًا فَهُوَ يُنفِقُ مِنْهُ
سِرًّا وَجَهْرًا ۖ هَلْ يَسْتَوُونَ ۚ الْحَمْدُ
لِلَّهِ ۚ بَلْ أَكْثَرُهُمْ لَا يَعْلَمُونَ ﴿٧٥﴾

76. Allah tells a parable about two men. One of them is dumb and useless and a burden on his friend. Wherever he goes, he returns with nothing. Can he be considered equal to the one who maintains justice and follows the right path?

76. Wa ḍarabal-laahu masalar-rajulayni aḥaduhumaaa abkamu laa yaqdiru 'alaa shay'iñw-wa huwa kallun 'alaa mawlaahu aynamaa yuwajjihhu laa ya-ti bikhayr; hal yastawee huwa wa mañy-ya-muru bil-'adli wa huwa 'alaa Ṣiraaṭim-Mustaqeem.

وَضَرَبَ اللَّهُ مَثَلًا رَّجُلَيْنِ
أَحَدُهُمَا أَبْكَمُ لَا يَقْدِرُ عَلَىٰ شَيْءٍ
وَهُوَ كَلٌّ عَلَىٰ مَوْلَاهُ أَيْنَمَا
يُوَجِّههُّ لَا يَأْتِ بِخَيْرٍ ۖ هَلْ
يَسْتَوِي هُوَ ۙ وَمَن يَأْمُرُ بِالْعَدْلِ ۙ
وَهُوَ عَلَىٰ صِرَاطٍ مُّسْتَقِيمٍ ﴿٧٦﴾ ع ١٦

77. To Allah belong all the secrets of the heavens and the

77. Wa lillaahi ghaybus-samaawaati wal-arḍ;

وَلِلَّهِ غَيْبُ السَّمَاوَاتِ وَالْأَرْضِ ۚ

earth. It takes Allah only the blink of an eye or even less to make it the Day of Judgment. Allah has power over all things.

wa maaa amrus-Saa'ati illaa kalamḥil-baṣari aw huwa aqrab; innal-laaha 'alaa kulli shay'in Qadeer.

وَمَآ اَمۡرُ السَّاعَةِ اِلَّا كَلَمۡحِ الۡبَصَرِ
اَوۡ هُوَ اَقۡرَبُ ؕ اِنَّ اللّٰهَ عَلٰى كُلِّ
شَىۡءٍ قَدِيۡرٌ ﴿۷۷﴾

78. When Allah brought you out of your mother's wombs, you knew nothing. He gave you ears, eyes, and hearts so that perhaps you would give Him thanks.

78. Wallaahu akhrajakum mim buṭooni ummahaatikum laa ta'lamoona shay'añw-wa ja'ala lakumus-sam'a wal-abṣaara wal-af'idata la'allakum tashkuroon.

وَاللّٰهُ اَخۡرَجَكُمۡ مِّنۡۢ بُطُوۡنِ اُمَّهٰتِكُمۡ
لَا تَعۡلَمُوۡنَ شَيۡــًٔا ۙ وَّجَعَلَ لَـكُمُ
السَّمۡعَ وَالۡاَبۡصَارَ وَالۡاَفۡـِٕدَةَ ۙ
لَعَلَّكُمۡ تَشۡكُرُوۡنَ ﴿۷۸﴾

79. Did they not see the free movements of the birds high in the sky above? What keeps them aloft except Allah? In this there is evidence (of the truth) for the believing people.

79. Alam yaraw ilaṭ-ṭayri musakhkharaatin fee jawwis-samaaa'i maa yumsikuhunna illal-laah; inna fee z̲aalika la-Aayaatil-liqawmiñy-yu'minoon.

اَلَمۡ يَرَوۡا اِلَى الطَّيۡرِ مُسَخَّرٰتٍ
فِىۡ جَوِّ السَّمَآءِ ؕ مَا يُمۡسِكُهُنَّ اِلَّا
اللّٰهُ ؕ اِنَّ فِىۡ ذٰلِكَ لَاٰيٰتٍ لِّقَوۡمٍ
يُّؤۡمِنُوۡنَ ﴿۷۹﴾

80. Allah has made your house the place for you to rest. He has also made homes for you out of the skins of cattle which are easy to carry along on a journey or at a camp. He has made wool, fur, and the hair of cattle a temporary means of enjoyment for you.

80. Wallaahu ja'ala lakum mim buyootikum sakanañw-wa ja'ala lakum min juloodil an'aami buyootan tastakhif-foonahaa yawma ẓa'nikum wa yawma iqaamatikum wa min aṣwaafihaa wa awbaarihaa wa ash'aarihaaa as̲aas̲añw-wa mataa'an ilaa ḥeen.

وَاللّٰهُ جَعَلَ لَـكُمۡ مِّنۡۢ بُيُوۡتِكُمۡ
سَكَنًا وَّجَعَلَ لَـكُمۡ مِّنۡ جُلُوۡدِ
الۡاَنۡعَامِ بُيُوۡتًا تَسۡتَخِفُّوۡنَهَا يَوۡمَ
ظَعۡنِكُمۡ وَيَوۡمَ اِقَامَتِكُمۡ ۙ وَمِنۡ
اَصۡوَافِهَا وَاَوۡبَارِهَا وَاَشۡعَارِهَاۤ
اَثَاثًا وَّمَتَاعًا اِلٰى حِيۡنٍ ﴿۸۰﴾

81. Allah has provided shade for you out of what He has created and places of retreat out of mountains. He has given you garments to protect you from the heat and cover your private parts. This is how He perfects His bounties to you so that perhaps you will submit to His will.

81. Wallaahu ja'ala lakum mimmaa khalaqa ẓilaalañw-wa ja'ala lakum-minal-jibaali aknaanañw-wa ja'ala lakum saraabeela taqeekumul-ḥarra wa saraabeela taqeekum ba-sakum; kaz̲aalika yutimmu ni'matahoo 'alaykum la'alla-kum tuslimoon.

وَاللّٰهُ جَعَلَ لَـكُمۡ مِّمَّا خَلَقَ ظِلٰلًا
وَّجَعَلَ لَـكُمۡ مِّنَ الۡجِبَالِ اَكۡنَانًا
وَّجَعَلَ لَـكُمۡ سَرَابِيۡلَ تَقِيۡكُمُ
الۡحَـرَّ وَسَرَابِيۡلَ تَقِيۡكُمۡ بَاۡسَكُمۡ ؕ
كَذٰلِكَ يُتِمُّ نِعۡمَتَهٗ عَلَيۡكُمۡ
لَعَلَّكُمۡ تُسۡلِمُوۡنَ ﴿۸۱﴾

82. (Muhammad), if they turn away, your only duty is to preach clearly to them.

82. Fa-in tawallaw fa-innamaa 'alaykal-balaaghul-mubeen.

فَاِنۡ تَوَلَّوۡا فَاِنَّمَا عَلَيۡكَ الۡبَلٰغُ
الۡمُبِيۡنُ ﴿۸۲﴾

83. They recognize the bounties of Allah but they refuse them and most of them are

83. Ya'rifoona ni'matal-laahi s̲umma yunkiroonahaa

يَعۡرِفُوۡنَ نِعۡمَتَ اللّٰهِ ثُمَّ يُنۡكِرُوۡنَهَا

unbelievers.

wa aksaruhumul-kaafiroon.

وَاَكْثَرُهُمُ الْكٰفِرُوْنَ ﴿٨٣﴾ ع ١٧

84. On the day when We will call a witness (the Imam of their time) from every nation, the unbelievers will not be given permission for anything, nor will they be allowed to seek (correction).

84. Wa yawma nab'asu min kulli ummatin shaheedan summa laa yu'zanu lillazeena kafaroo wa laa hum yusta'taboon.

وَيَوْمَ نَبْعَثُ مِنْ كُلِّ اُمَّةٍ شَهِيْدًا
ثُمَّ لَا يُؤْذَنُ لِلَّذِيْنَ كَفَرُوْا وَلَا هُمْ
يُسْتَعْتَبُوْنَ ﴿٨٤﴾

85. There will be no relief for them when the torment approaches the unjust nor will they be given any respite.

85. Wa izaa ra-al-lazeena zalamul-'azaaba falaa yukhaffafu 'anhum wa laa hum yunzaroon.

وَاِذَا رَاَ الَّذِيْنَ ظَلَمُوا الْعَذَابَ فَلَا
يُخَفَّفُ عَنْهُمْ وَلَا هُمْ يُنْظَرُوْنَ ﴿٨٥﴾

86. When the idolaters see their idols, they will say, "Lord, these are the idols whom we worshipped instead of you." But the idols will say, "They are liars."

86. Wa izaa ra-al-lazeena ashrakoo shurakaaa'ahum qaaloo Rabbanaa haaa'ulaaa'i shurakaaa'unal-lazeena kunnaa nad'oo min doonika fa-alqaw ilayhimul-qawla innakum lakaaziboon.

وَاِذَا رَاَ الَّذِيْنَ اَشْرَكُوْا شُرَكَآءَهُمْ
قَالُوْا رَبَّنَا هٰٓؤُلَآءِ شُرَكَآؤُنَا الَّذِيْنَ
كُنَّا نَدْعُوْا مِنْ دُوْنِكَ ۚ فَاَلْقَوْا
اِلَيْهِمُ الْقَوْلَ اِنَّكُمْ لَكٰذِبُوْنَ ﴿٨٦﴾ الثلثة

87. (On the Day of Judgment) the unbelievers will submit themselves to Allah and whatever they had falsely invented will disappear.

87. Wa alqaw ilal-laahi yawma'izinis-salama wa dalla 'anhum-maa kaanoo yaftaroon.

وَاَلْقَوْا اِلَى اللّٰهِ يَوْمَئِذِ ۨالسَّلَمَ
وَضَلَّ عَنْهُمْ مَّا كَانُوْا يَفْتَرُوْنَ ﴿٨٧﴾

88. The unbelievers who had created obstacles in the way leading to Allah will face manifold torments as a result of their evil deeds.

88. Allazeena kafaroo wa saddoo 'an sabeelil-laahi zidnaahum 'azaaban fawqal'azaabi bimaa kaanoo yufsidoon.

اَلَّذِيْنَ كَفَرُوْا وَصَدُّوْا عَنْ سَبِيْلِ
اللّٰهِ زِدْنٰهُمْ عَذَابًا فَوْقَ الْعَذَابِ
بِمَا كَانُوْا يُفْسِدُوْنَ ﴿٨٨﴾

89. On the day when We call a witness (the Imam) against every nation from their own people, We will call you, (Muhammad), as a witness to them all (Aimmah). We have sent you the Book which clarifies all matters. It is a guide, a mercy, and glad news to the Muslims.

89. Wa yawma nab'asu fee kulli ummatin shaheedan 'alayhim-min anfusihim wa ji'naa bika shaheedan 'alaa haaa'ulaaa'; wa nazzalnaa 'alaykal-Kitaaba tibyaanal-likulli shay'iñw-wa hudañw-wa rahmatañw-wa bushraa lilmuslimeen.

وَيَوْمَ نَبْعَثُ فِيْ كُلِّ اُمَّةٍ شَهِيْدًا
عَلَيْهِمْ مِّنْ اَنْفُسِهِمْ وَجِئْنَا بِكَ
شَهِيْدًا عَلٰى هٰٓؤُلَآءِ ؕ وَنَزَّلْنَا
عَلَيْكَ الْكِتٰبَ تِبْيَانًا لِّكُلِّ
شَيْءٍ وَّهُدًى وَّرَحْمَةً وَّبُشْرٰى
لِلْمُسْلِمِيْنَ ﴿٨٩﴾ ع ١٨

90. Allah commands (people) to maintain justice, (belief in Allah) kindness (belief in His messenger), and proper relations with the relatives (of the Holy Prophet). He forbids them to commit indecency, sin, and rebellion. He commands you as such so that perhaps you will take heed.

90. Innal-laaha ya-muru bil'adli wal-ihsaani wa eetaaa'i zil-qurbaa wa yanhaa 'anil-fahshaaa'i walmunkari walbaghy; ya'izukum la'allakum tazakkaroon.

اِنَّ اللّٰهَ يَاْمُرُ بِالْعَدْلِ وَالْاِحْسَانِ
وَاِيْتَآئِ ذِى الْقُرْبٰى وَيَنْهٰى عَنِ
الْفَحْشَآءِ وَالْمُنْكَرِ وَالْبَغْيِ ۚ يَعِظُكُمْ
لَعَلَّكُمْ تَذَكَّرُوْنَ ﴿٩٠﴾

91. (He commands people) to keep their established covenants with Allah, not to disregard their

91. Wa awfoo bi 'Ahdil-laahi izaa 'aahattum wa laa

وَاَوْفُوْا بِعَهْدِ اللّٰهِ اِذَا عٰهَدْتُّمْ وَلَا

firm promise; when they have already appointed Allah as their Guarantor. Allah certainly knows what you do.

92. Do not be like the lady behind the spinning wheel who (due to dimwittedness) would break her yarn to undo her labor. You must not do the same to your established covenant by using it as means of deceit against a party that is more beneficial (pure in religion) than the other. Allah tests your faith by your oaths. He will make clear to you, on the Day of Judgment, who was right and who was wrong.

93. Had Allah wanted, He would have made you one single nation, but He guides (rewards) or causes to go astray (punishes for their disregard of their covenant) whomever He wants. You will certainly be questioned about what you have done.

94. Do not consider your covenant as a means of deceit lest you damage the firmness of your faith, suffer from evil by creating obstacles in the way that leads to Allah, and incur a great torment upon yourselves.

95. Do not sell your covenant with Allah for a small price. The reward which you will receive from Allah is better for you, if only you knew it.

96. Whatever you possess is transient and whatever is with Allah is everlasting. We will recompense those who exercise patience with their due reward and even more.

97. All righteously believing, male or female will be granted a blessed, happy life and will

tanquḍul-aymaana ba'da tawkeedihaa wa qad ja'altumul-laaha 'alaykum kafeelaa; innal-laaha ya'lamu maa taf'aloon.

92. Wa laa takoonoo kallatee naqaḍat ghazlahaa mim ba'di quwwatin ankaasaa; tattakhi-zoona aymaanakum dakhalam baynakum an takoona ummatun hiya arbaa min ummah; innamaa yablookumul-laahu bih; wa la-yubayyinanna lakum Yawmal-Qiyaamati maa kuntum feehi takhtalifoon.

93. Wa law shaaa'al-laahu laja'alakum ummatañw-waaḥi-datañw-wa laakiñy-yuḍillu mañy-yashaaa'u wa yahdee mañy-yashaaa'; wa latus'alunna 'ammaa kuntum ta'maloon.

94. Wa laa tattakhizooo aymaanakum dakhalam-bayna-kum fatazilla qadamum ba'da subootihaa wa tazooqus-sooo'a bimaa ṣadattum 'an sabeelil-laahi wa lakum 'azaabun 'aẓeem.

95. Wa laa tashtaroo bi'Ahdil-laahi samanan qaleelaa; inna-maa 'indallaahi huwa khayrul-lakum in kuntum ta'lamoon.

96. Maa 'indakum yanfadu wa maa 'indal-laahi baaq; wa lanajziyannal-lazeena ṣabarooo ajrahum bi-aḥsani maa kaanoo ya'maloon.

97. Man 'amila ṣaaliḥam-min zakarin aw unsaa wa huwa mu'minun falanuḥyiyannahoo ḥayaatan ṭayyibah;-wa lanajziyannahum

تَنْقُضُوا الْاَيْمَانَ بَعْدَ تَوْكِيْدِهَا
وَقَدْ جَعَلْتُمُ اللّٰهَ عَلَيْكُمْ كَفِيْلًا ؕ
اِنَّ اللّٰهَ يَعْلَمُ مَا تَفْعَلُوْنَ ﴿٩١﴾
وَلَا تَكُوْنُوْا كَالَّتِيْ نَقَضَتْ غَزْلَهَا
مِنْۢ بَعْدِ قُوَّةٍ اَنْكَاثًا ؕ تَتَّخِذُوْنَ
اَيْمَانَكُمْ دَخَلًاۢ بَيْنَكُمْ اَنْ تَكُوْنَ
اُمَّةٌ هِيَ اَرْبٰى مِنْ اُمَّةٍ ؕ اِنَّمَا
يَبْلُوْكُمُ اللّٰهُ بِهٖ ؕ وَلَيُبَيِّنَنَّ لَكُمْ يَوْمَ
الْقِيٰمَةِ مَا كُنْتُمْ فِيْهِ تَخْتَلِفُوْنَ ﴿٩٢﴾
وَلَوْ شَآءَ اللّٰهُ لَجَعَلَكُمْ اُمَّةً وَّاحِدَةً
وَّلٰكِنْ يُّضِلُّ مَنْ يَّشَآءُ وَيَهْدِيْ
مَنْ يَّشَآءُ ؕ وَلَتُسْـَٔلُنَّ عَمَّا كُنْتُمْ
تَعْمَلُوْنَ ﴿٩٣﴾
وَلَا تَتَّخِذُوْٓا اَيْمَانَكُمْ دَخَلًاۢ بَيْنَكُمْ
فَتَزِلَّ قَدَمٌۢ بَعْدَ ثُبُوْتِهَا وَتَذُوْقُوا
السُّوْٓءَ بِمَا صَدَدْتُّمْ عَنْ سَبِيْلِ
اللّٰهِ ۚ وَلَكُمْ عَذَابٌ عَظِيْمٌ ﴿٩٤﴾
وَلَا تَشْتَرُوْا بِعَهْدِ اللّٰهِ ثَمَنًا قَلِيْلًا ؕ
اِنَّمَا عِنْدَ اللّٰهِ هُوَ خَيْرٌ لَّكُمْ اِنْ
كُنْتُمْ تَعْلَمُوْنَ ﴿٩٥﴾
مَا عِنْدَكُمْ يَنْفَدُ وَمَا عِنْدَ اللّٰهِ
بَاقٍ ؕ وَلَنَجْزِيَنَّ الَّذِيْنَ صَبَرُوْٓا
اَجْرَهُمْ بِاَحْسَنِ مَا كَانُوْا يَعْمَلُوْنَ ﴿٩٦﴾
مَنْ عَمِلَ صَالِحًا مِّنْ ذَكَرٍ اَوْ
اُنْثٰى وَهُوَ مُؤْمِنٌ فَلَنُحْيِيَنَّهٗ
حَيٰوةً طَيِّبَةً ۚ وَلَنَجْزِيَنَّهُمْ

receive their due reward and more.

98. (Muhammad), when you recite the Quran, seek refuge in Allah from the mischief of the most wicked Satan.

99. Satan has certainly no authority over the believers who have trust in their Lord.

100. The only authority which he has is over his friends and those who consider things equal to Allah.

101. When Allah replaces one revelation with another, He knows best what to reveal. But they say, "(Muhammad), you have falsely invented it." Most people are ignorant.

102. (Muhammad), say, "The Holy Spirit has brought the Quran from your Lord, in all truth, to strengthen the faith of the believers and it is a guide and glad news for the Muslims."

103. We know that they say a mere mortal has taught it (the Quran) to him (Muhammad). The language of the person whom they think has taught it to him is not Arabic. This (the Quran) is in clear Arabic.

104. Allah will not guide those who do not believe in Allah's miracles. They will suffer a painful punishment.

105. Those who do not believe in the miracles of Allah invent lies and they are liars.

106. No one verbally denounces his faith in Allah - unless he is forced - while his heart is confident about his faith. But

ajrahum bi-ahsani maa kaanoo ya'maloon.

98. Fa-izaa qara-tal-Qur-aana fasta'iz billaahi minash-Shay-taanir-rajeem.

99. Innahoo laysa lahoo sultaanun 'alal-lazeena aama-noo wa 'alaa Rabbihim yata-wakkaloon.

100. Innamaa sultaanuhoo 'alal-lazeena yatawallawnahoo wallazeena hum biheemushri-koon.

101. Wa izaa baddalnaaa Aaya-tam-makaana Aayatiñw-wal-laahu a'lamu bimaa yunazzilu qaalooo innamaaa anta muftar; bal aksaruhum laa ya'lamoon.

102. Qul nazzalahoo Roohul-Qudusi mir-Rabbika bilhaqqi liyusabbital-lazeena aamanoo wa hudañw-wa bushraa lilmus-limeen.

103. Wa laqad na'lamu anna-hum yaqooloona innamaa yu'allimuhoo bashar; lisaanul-lazee yulhidoona ilayhi a'ja-miyyuñw-wa haazaa lisaanun 'Arabiyyum-mubeen.

104. Innal-lazeena laa yu'mi-noona bi-Aayaatil-laahi laa yahdeehimul-laahu wa lahum 'azaabun aleem.

105. Innamaa yaftaril-kazibal-lazeena laa yu'minoona bi-Aayaatil-laahi wa ulaaa'ika humul-kaaziboon.

106. Man kafara billaahi mim ba'di eemaaniheee illaa man ukriha wa qalbuhoo mut-ma'innum

أَجْرَهُم بِأَحْسَنِ مَا كَانُوا يَعْمَلُونَ ﴿٩٧﴾
فَإِذَا قَرَأْتَ الْقُرْآنَ فَاسْتَعِذْ بِاللَّهِ
مِنَ الشَّيْطَانِ الرَّجِيمِ ﴿٩٨﴾
إِنَّهُ لَيْسَ لَهُ سُلْطَانٌ عَلَى الَّذِينَ
آمَنُوا وَعَلَىٰ رَبِّهِمْ يَتَوَكَّلُونَ ﴿٩٩﴾
إِنَّمَا سُلْطَانُهُ عَلَى الَّذِينَ يَتَوَلَّوْنَهُ
وَالَّذِينَ هُم بِهِ مُشْرِكُونَ ﴿١٠٠﴾ ع ١٣ ١١ ١٩
وَإِذَا بَدَّلْنَا آيَةً مَّكَانَ آيَةٍ
وَاللَّهُ أَعْلَمُ بِمَا يُنَزِّلُ قَالُوا إِنَّمَا
أَنتَ مُفْتَرٍ ۚ بَلْ أَكْثَرُهُمْ
لَا يَعْلَمُونَ ﴿١٠١﴾
قُلْ نَزَّلَهُ رُوحُ الْقُدُسِ مِن
رَّبِّكَ بِالْحَقِّ لِيُثَبِّتَ الَّذِينَ آمَنُوا
وَهُدًى وَبُشْرَىٰ لِلْمُسْلِمِينَ ﴿١٠٢﴾
وَلَقَدْ نَعْلَمُ أَنَّهُمْ يَقُولُونَ إِنَّمَا
يُعَلِّمُهُ بَشَرٌ ۗ لِّسَانُ الَّذِي
يُلْحِدُونَ إِلَيْهِ أَعْجَمِيٌّ وَهَٰذَا
لِسَانٌ عَرَبِيٌّ مُّبِينٌ ﴿١٠٣﴾
إِنَّ الَّذِينَ لَا يُؤْمِنُونَ بِآيَاتِ
اللَّهِ لَا يَهْدِيهِمُ اللَّهُ وَلَهُمْ
عَذَابٌ أَلِيمٌ ﴿١٠٤﴾
إِنَّمَا يَفْتَرِي الْكَذِبَ الَّذِينَ
لَا يُؤْمِنُونَ بِآيَاتِ اللَّهِ ۖ وَأُولَٰئِكَ
هُمُ الْكَاذِبُونَ ﴿١٠٥﴾
مَن كَفَرَ بِاللَّهِ مِن بَعْدِ إِيمَانِهِ
إِلَّا مَنْ أُكْرِهَ وَقَلْبُهُ مُطْمَئِنٌّ

those whose breasts have become open to disbelief will be subject to the wrath of Allah and will suffer a great torment.

bil-eemaani wa laakim-man sharaḥa bilkufri ṣadran fa'alayhim ghaḍabum-minal-laahi wa lahum 'aẕaabun 'aẓeem.

بِالْاِيْمَانِ وَلٰكِنْ مَّنْ شَرَحَ
بِالْكُفْرِ صَدْرًا فَعَلَيْهِمْ غَضَبٌ مِّنَ
اللّٰهِ ۚ وَلَهُمْ عَذَابٌ عَظِيْمٌ ﴿١٠٦﴾

107. This is because they have given preference to this life over the life to come and Allah does not guide disbelieving people.

107. Ẕaalika bi-annahumus-taḥabbul-ḥayaatad-dunyaa 'alal-Aakhirati wa annallaaha laa yahdil-qawmal-kaafireen.

ذٰلِكَ بِاَنَّهُمُ اسْتَحَبُّوا الْحَيٰوةَ
الدُّنْيَا عَلَى الْاٰخِرَةِ ۙ وَاَنَّ اللّٰهَ
لَا يَهْدِى الْقَوْمَ الْكٰفِرِيْنَ ﴿١٠٧﴾

108. Allah has sealed their hearts, ears and eyes and they are not aware of it.

108. Ulaaa'ikal-laẕeena ṭaba'al-laahu 'alaa quloobihim wa sam'ihim wa abṣaarihim wa ulaaa'ika humul-ghaafiloon.

اُولٰٓئِكَ الَّذِيْنَ طَبَعَ اللّٰهُ عَلٰى
قُلُوْبِهِمْ وَسَمْعِهِمْ وَاَبْصَارِهِمْ ۚ
وَاُولٰٓئِكَ هُمُ الْغٰفِلُوْنَ ﴿١٠٨﴾

109. Consequently, on the Day of Judgment they will certainly suffer a great loss.

109. Laa jarama annahum fil-Aakhirati humul-khaasiroon.

لَا جَرَمَ اَنَّهُمْ فِى الْاٰخِرَةِ
هُمُ الْخٰسِرُوْنَ ﴿١٠٩﴾

110. Those who left their homes for the cause of Allah after they had been persecuted, strove hard for His cause, and exercised patience should know (even though they had verbally renounced their faith) that your Lord is All-forgiving and All-merciful.

110. S̱umma inna Rabbaka lillaẕeena haajaroo mim ba'di maa futinoo s̱umma jaahadoo wa ṣabarooo inna Rabbaka mim ba'dihaa la-Ghafoorur-Raḥeem.

ثُمَّ اِنَّ رَبَّكَ لِلَّذِيْنَ هَاجَرُوْا مِنْ
بَعْدِ مَا فُتِنُوْا ثُمَّ جٰهَدُوْا وَصَبَرُوْٓا ۙ
اِنَّ رَبَّكَ مِنْ بَعْدِهَا لَغَفُوْرٌ
رَّحِيْمٌ ﴿١١٠﴾

111. On the Day of Judgment every soul shall try to defend itself and every soul will be justly recompensed.

111. Yawma ta-tee kullu nafsin tujaadilu 'an-nafsihaa wa tuwaffaa kullu nafsim-maa 'amilat wa hum laa yuẓlamoon.

يَوْمَ تَاْتِىْ كُلُّ نَفْسٍ تُجَادِلُ
عَنْ نَّفْسِهَا وَتُوَفّٰى كُلُّ نَفْسٍ
مَّا عَمِلَتْ وَهُمْ لَا يُظْلَمُوْنَ ﴿١١١﴾

112. Allah tells a parable about a secure and peaceful town surrounded by abundant sustenance. Its inhabitants did not appreciate the bounties of Allah and He caused them to suffer hunger and fear as a result of their deeds.

112. Wa ḍarabal-laahu mas̱alan qaryatan kaanat aaminatam-muṭma'innatañy-ya-teehaa rizquhaa raghadam-min kulli makaanin fakafarat bi-an'umil-laahi fa-aẕaaqahal-laahu libaasal-joo'i walkhawfi bimaa kaanoo yaṣna'oon.

وَضَرَبَ اللّٰهُ مَثَلًا قَرْيَةً كَانَتْ
اٰمِنَةً مُّطْمَئِنَّةً يَّاْتِيْهَا رِزْقُهَا
رَغَدًا مِّنْ كُلِّ مَكَانٍ فَكَفَرَتْ بِاَنْعُمِ
اللّٰهِ فَاَذَاقَهَا اللّٰهُ لِبَاسَ الْجُوْعِ
وَالْخَوْفِ بِمَا كَانُوْا يَصْنَعُوْنَ ﴿١١٢﴾

113. A Messenger from their own people came to them and they called him a liar. Torment struck them because of their injustice.

113. Wa laqad jaaa'ahum Rasoolum-minhum fakaẕ-ẕaboohu fa-akhaẕahumul-'aẕaabu wa hum ẓaalimoon.

وَلَقَدْ جَآءَهُمْ رَسُوْلٌ مِّنْهُمْ
فَكَذَّبُوْهُ فَاَخَذَهُمُ الْعَذَابُ
وَهُمْ ظٰلِمُوْنَ ﴿١١٣﴾

114. (People), consume the pure and lawful sustenance which Allah has given to you and thank Allah for his bounty if you are His true worshippers.

114. Fakuloo mimmaa razaqakumul-laahu ḥalaalan ṭayyibañw-washkuroo ni'matallaahi in kuntum iyyaahu ta'budoon.

فَكُلُوا مِمَّا رَزَقَكُمُ اللَّهُ حَلَالًا
طَيِّبًا وَاشْكُرُوا نِعْمَتَ اللَّهِ
إِنْ كُنْتُمْ إِيَّاهُ تَعْبُدُونَ ﴿١١٤﴾

115. The only things which are made unlawful for you are the flesh of dead animals (not slaughtered properly), blood, pork, and that which is not consecrated with the Name of Allah. But in an emergency, without the intention of transgression and rebellion (it is not an offense for one to consume such things). Allah is certainly All-forgiving and All-merciful.

115. Innamaa ḥarrama 'alaykumul-maytata waddama wa laḥmal-khinzeeri wa maaa uhilla lighayril-laahi bihee famaniḍṭurra ghayra baaghiñw-wa laa 'aadin fa-innal-laaha Ghafoorur-Raḥeem.

إِنَّمَا حَرَّمَ عَلَيْكُمُ الْمَيْتَةَ وَالدَّمَ
وَلَحْمَ الْخِنْزِيرِ وَمَا أُهِلَّ لِغَيْرِ
اللَّهِ بِهِ فَمَنِ اضْطُرَّ غَيْرَ بَاغٍ وَلَا
عَادٍ فَإِنَّ اللَّهَ غَفُورٌ رَحِيمٌ ﴿١١٥﴾

116. (Unbelievers), do not follow whatever your lying tongues may tell you is lawful or unlawful to invent lies against Allah. Those who invent lies against Allah will have no happiness.

116. Wa laa taqooloo limaa taṣifu alsinatukumul-kaz̲iba haaz̲aa ḥalaaluñw-wa haaz̲aa ḥaraamul-litaftaroo 'alal-laahil-kaz̲ib; innal-laz̲eena yaftaroona 'alal-laahil-kaz̲iba laa yufliḥoon.

وَلَا تَقُولُوا لِمَا تَصِفُ أَلْسِنَتُكُمُ
الْكَذِبَ هَٰذَا حَلَالٌ وَهَٰذَا حَرَامٌ
لِتَفْتَرُوا عَلَى اللَّهِ الْكَذِبَ
إِنَّ الَّذِينَ يَفْتَرُونَ عَلَى اللَّهِ
الْكَذِبَ لَا يُفْلِحُونَ ﴿١١٦﴾

117. (Such an invention) will bring only a little enjoyment but will be followed by painful torment.

117. Mataa'un qaleeluñw-wa lahum 'az̲aabun aleem.

مَتَاعٌ قَلِيلٌ وَلَهُمْ عَذَابٌ
أَلِيمٌ ﴿١١٧﴾

118. We had made unlawful for the Jews all that we told you before. We did not do any wrong to them but they wronged themselves.

118. Wa 'alal-laz̲eena haadoo ḥarramnaa maa qaṣaṣnaa 'alayka min qablu wa maa ẓalamnaahum wa laakin kaanooo anfusahum yaẓlimoon.

وَعَلَى الَّذِينَ هَادُوا حَرَّمْنَا مَا
قَصَصْنَا عَلَيْكَ مِنْ قَبْلُ وَمَا
ظَلَمْنَاهُمْ وَلَٰكِنْ كَانُوا أَنْفُسَهُمْ
يَظْلِمُونَ ﴿١١٨﴾

119. To those who commit sins in their ignorance then repent and reform, your Lord is certainly All-forgiving and All-merciful.

119. S̲umma inna Rabbaka lillaz̲eena 'amilus-sooo'a bijahaalatin s̲umma taaboo mim ba'di z̲aalika wa aṣlaḥooo inna Rabbaka mim ba'dihaa la-Ghafoorur-Raḥeem.

ثُمَّ إِنَّ رَبَّكَ لِلَّذِينَ عَمِلُوا
السُّوءَ بِجَهَالَةٍ ثُمَّ تَابُوا مِنْ
بَعْدِ ذَٰلِكَ وَأَصْلَحُوا إِنَّ رَبَّكَ
مِنْ بَعْدِهَا لَغَفُورٌ رَحِيمٌ ﴿١١٩﴾ ع ١٥ ٩ ٢١

120. Abraham was, certainly, an obedient person and submissive to the will of Allah. He was not a pagan.

120. Inna Ibraaheema kaana ummatan qaanital-lillaahi Ḥaneefaa;wa lam yaku minal-mushrikeen.

إِنَّ إِبْرَاهِيمَ كَانَ أُمَّةً قَانِتًا
لِلَّهِ حَنِيفًا وَلَمْ يَكُ مِنَ
الْمُشْرِكِينَ ﴿١٢٠﴾

121. He was thankful to Allah for His bounties. Allah chose him and guided him to the right path.

121. Shaakiral-li-an'umih; ijtabaahu wa hadaahu ilaa Ṣiraaṭim-Mustaqeem.

شَاكِرًا لِأَنْعُمِهِ اجْتَبَاهُ وَهَدَاهُ

إِلَىٰ صِرَاطٍ مُّسْتَقِيمٍ ﴿١٢١﴾

122. We granted him virtue in this life and he shall be among the righteous ones in the life to come.

122. Wa aataynaahu fid-dunyaa ḥasanah; wa innahoo fil-Aakhirati laminaṣ-ṣaaliḥeen.

وَآتَيْنَاهُ فِي الدُّنْيَا حَسَنَةً ۖ وَإِنَّهُ
فِي الْآخِرَةِ لَمِنَ الصَّالِحِينَ ﴿١٢٢﴾

123. We sent you (Muhammad) a revelation that you should follow the tradition (the ten issues of discipline) of Abraham, the upright one, who was not a pagan.

123. S̲umma awḥaynaaa ilayka anit-tabi' Millata Ibraaheema Ḥaneefaa; wa maa kaana minal-mushrikeen.

ثُمَّ أَوْحَيْنَا إِلَيْكَ أَنِ اتَّبِعْ
مِلَّةَ إِبْرَاهِيمَ حَنِيفًا ۖ وَمَا كَانَ
مِنَ الْمُشْرِكِينَ ﴿١٢٣﴾

124. (The observance) of the Sabbath was sanctioned only for those who disputed it. Your Lord will certainly issue His decree about their dispute on the Day of Judgment.

124. Innamaa ju'ilas-Sabtu 'alal-laz̲eenakhtalafoo feeh; wa inna Rabbaka la-yaḥkumu baynahum Yawmal-Qiyaamati feemaa kaanoo feehi yakhtalifoon.

إِنَّمَا جُعِلَ السَّبْتُ عَلَى الَّذِينَ
اخْتَلَفُوا فِيهِ ۚ وَإِنَّ رَبَّكَ لَيَحْكُمُ
بَيْنَهُمْ يَوْمَ الْقِيَامَةِ فِيمَا كَانُوا
فِيهِ يَخْتَلِفُونَ ﴿١٢٤﴾

125. Call (the pagans) to the path of your Lord through wisdom and good advice and argue with them in the best manner. Your Lord knows well about those who stray from His path and those who seek guidance.

125. Ud'u ilaa sabeeli Rabbika bilḥikmati walmaw'iẓatil-ḥasanati wa jaadilhum billatee hiya aḥsan; inna Rabbaka Huwa a'lamu biman ḍalla 'an sabeelihee wa Huwa a'lamu bilmuhtadeen.

ادْعُ إِلَىٰ سَبِيلِ رَبِّكَ بِالْحِكْمَةِ
وَالْمَوْعِظَةِ الْحَسَنَةِ ۖ وَجَادِلْهُم
بِالَّتِي هِيَ أَحْسَنُ ۚ إِنَّ رَبَّكَ هُوَ
أَعْلَمُ بِمَن ضَلَّ عَن سَبِيلِهِ ۖ
وَهُوَ أَعْلَمُ بِالْمُهْتَدِينَ ﴿١٢٥﴾

126. If you want retaliation, let it be equal to that which you faced. But if you exercise patience it will be better for you.

126. Wa in 'aaqabtum fa'aaqiboo bimis̲li maa 'ooqibtum bih; wa la'in ṣabartum lahuwa khayrul-liṣṣaabireen.

وَإِنْ عَاقَبْتُمْ فَعَاقِبُوا بِمِثْلِ
مَا عُوقِبْتُم بِهِ ۖ وَلَئِن صَبَرْتُمْ
لَهُوَ خَيْرٌ لِّلصَّابِرِينَ ﴿١٢٦﴾

127. Exercise patience and let it be only for the cause of Allah. Do not be grieved about them nor disappointed at their evil plans.

127. Waṣbir wa maa ṣabruka illaa billaah; wa laa taḥzan 'alayhim wa laa taku fee ḍayqim-mimmaa yamkuroon.

وَاصْبِرْ وَمَا صَبْرُكَ إِلَّا بِاللَّهِ ۚ
وَلَا تَحْزَنْ عَلَيْهِمْ وَلَا تَكُ فِي
ضَيْقٍ مِّمَّا يَمْكُرُونَ ﴿١٢٧﴾

128. Allah is certainly with the pious and the righteous ones.

128. Innal-laaha ma'allaz̲ee-nat-taqaw wallaz̲eena hum-muḥsinoon.

إِنَّ اللَّهَ مَعَ الَّذِينَ اتَّقَوا
وَّالَّذِينَ هُم مُّحْسِنُونَ ﴿١٢٨﴾ ع ٢٢

Al-Isra, The Night Journey (17)

In the Name of Allah, the Beneficent, the Merciful.

Sûrat Banî Isrâ'îl

(Revealed at Makkah)

Bismillaahir Raḥmaanir Raḥeem

(١٧) سُورَةُ بَنِي إِسْرَائِيلَ مَكِّيَّةٌ (٥٠)

آياتها ١١١ بِسْمِ اللَّهِ الرَّحْمَٰنِ الرَّحِيمِ ركوعاتها ١٢

1. Allah is the Exalted One who took His servant one night for a visit from the Sacred Mosque (in Mecca) to the Aqsa Mosque (in Jerusalem). Allah has blessed the surroundings of

1. Subḥaanal-laz̲eee asraa bi'abdihee laylam-minal-Masjidil-Ḥaraami-ilal-Masjidil Aqṣa

سُبْحَانَ الَّذِي أَسْرَىٰ بِعَبْدِهِ لَيْلًا مِّنَ

the Aqsa Mosque. He took His servant on this visit to show him (miraculous) evidence of His (existence). It is He who is All-hearing and All-aware.

l-lazee baaraknaa hawlahoo linuriyahoo min Aayaatinaaa; innahoo Huwas-Samee'ul-Başeer.

المسجد الحرام الى المسجد الاقصا
الذى بركنا حوله لنريه من
ايتنا انه هو السميع البصير ﴿١﴾

2. To Moses We gave the Book and made it a guide for the children of Israel, so that they would not have anyone as their guardian other than Me.

2. Wa aataynaa Moosal-Kitaaba wa ja'alnaahu hudal-li-Baneee Israaa'eela allaa tat-takhizoo min doonee wakeelaa.

واتينا موسى الكتب وجعلنه
هدى لبنى اسراءيل الا تتخذوا
من دونى وكيلا ﴿٢﴾

3. (We made it a guide for) the offspring of those whom We carried in the Ark with Noah, a thankful servant (of Allah).

3. Zurriyyata man hamal-naa ma'a Nooh; innahoo kaana 'abdan shakooraa.

ذرية من حملنا مع نوح انه
كان عبدا شكورا ﴿٣﴾

4. We made it known to the Israelites through the Torah that they would twice commit evil in the land with great transgression and rebellion.

4. Wa qadaynaaa ilaa Ba-neee Israaa'eela fil-Kitaabi-latufsidunna fil-ardi marratayni wa lata'lunna'uluwwan ka-beeraa.

وقضينا الى بنى اسراءيل فى
الكتب لتفسدن فى الارض مرتين
ولتعلن علوا كبيرا ﴿٤﴾

5. (We told them) during your first uprising of evil We shall send to you

5. Fa-izaa jaaa'a wa'du-oolaahumaa ba'asnaaa 'alykum 'ibaadal-lanaaa ulee ba-sin shadeedin fajaasoo khilaalad-diyaar; wakaana wa'dam-maf'oolaa.

فاذا جاء وعد اولهما بعثنا عليكم
عبادا لنا اولى باس شديد فجاسوا
خلل الديار وكان وعدا مفعولا ﴿٥﴾

6. Our Mighty servants, who will chase you from house to house. This is a decree already ordained. We, then, gave you a chance to defeat your enemies with the help of increasing your wealth and offspring.

6. Summa radadnaa lakumul karrata 'alayhim wa amdad-naakumbi-amwaaliñw-wa baneena wa ja'alnaakum aksara nafeeraa.

ثم رددنا لكم الكرة عليهم و
امددنكم باموال وبنين وجعلنكم
اكثر نفيرا ﴿٦﴾

7. (We told you), "If you do good, it will be for your own benefit, but if you do bad, it will be against your souls. When the prophecy about your second transgression comes to pass, sadness will cover your faces. They (your enemies) will enter the mosque as they did the first time to bring about utter destruction.

7. In ahsantum ahsantum li-anfusikum wa in asa-tum falahaa; fa-izaa jaaa'a wa'dul-Aakhirati liyasooo'oo wujoo-hakum wa liyad-khulul masjida kamaa dakhaloohu awwala marratiñw-wa liyutabbiroo maa 'alaw tatbeeraa.

ان احسنتم احسنتم لانفسكم
وان اساتم فلها فاذا جاء وعد
الاخرة ليسوءا وجوهكم وليدخلوا
المسجد كما دخلوه اول مرة و
ليتبروا ما علوا تتبيرا ﴿٧﴾

8. Perhaps your Lord will have mercy on you. If you return to disobedience We will also punish you again. We have made hell a prison for the unbelievers."

8. 'Asaa Rabbukum añy-yarhamakum; wa in 'uttum 'udnaa; wa ja'alnaa Jahannama lilkaafireena haseeraa.

عسى ربكم ان يرحمكم وان
عدتم عدنا وجعلنا جهنم للكفرين
حصيرا ﴿٨﴾

وقف لازم

9. This Quran shows the way to that which is the most upright

9. Inna haazal-Qur'aana yahdee lillatee hiya

ان هذا القران يهدى للتى هى

and gives to the righteous believers the glad news of a great reward.

aqwamu wa yubashshirul-mu'mineenal-lazeena ya'maloonaṣ-ṣaaliḥaati anna lahum ajran kabeeraa.

اَقْوَمُ وَيُبَشِّرُ الْمُؤْمِنِيْنَ الَّذِيْنَ
يَعْمَلُوْنَ الصّٰلِحٰتِ اَنَّ لَهُمْ اَجْرًا
كَبِيْرًا ۙ﴿۹﴾

10. (It also declares) that for the unbelievers We have prepared a painful torment in the life to come.

10. Wa annal-lazeena laa yu'minoona bil-Aakhirati a'tadnaa lahum 'azaaban aleemaa.

وَّاَنَّ الَّذِيْنَ لَا يُؤْمِنُوْنَ بِالْاٰخِرَةِ
اَعْتَدْنَا لَهُمْ عَذَابًا اَلِيْمًا ﴿۱۰﴾ ع ۱

11. Man prays as earnestly against his enemies as he does for his own good. Man has always been hasty (to inflict punishment).

11. Wa yad'ul-insaanu bish-sharri du'aa'ahoo bilkhayr; wa kaanal-insaanu 'ajoolaa.

وَيَدْعُ الْاِنْسَانُ بِالشَّرِّ دُعَآءَهٗ
بِالْخَيْرِ ؕ وَكَانَ الْاِنْسَانُ عَجُوْلًا ﴿۱۱﴾

12. We have made the day and night each as evidence (of Our existence). The night is invisible and the day is visible so that you may seek favors from your Lord and determine the number of years and mark the passing of time. For everything We have given a detailed explanation.

12. Wa ja'alnal-layla wannahaara Aayatayni famaḥawnaaa Aayatal-layli wa ja'alnaaa Aayatan-nahaari mubṣiratal-litabtaghoo faḍlam-mir-Rabbikum wa lita'lamoo 'adadas-sineena walḥisaab; wa kulla shay'in faṣṣalnaahu tafṣeelaa.

وَجَعَلْنَا الَّيْلَ وَالنَّهَارَ اٰيَتَيْنِ فَمَحَوْنَآ
اٰيَةَ الَّيْلِ وَجَعَلْنَآ اٰيَةَ النَّهَارِ
مُبْصِرَةً لِّتَبْتَغُوْا فَضْلًا مِّنْ رَّبِّكُمْ
وَلِتَعْلَمُوْا عَدَدَ السِّنِيْنَ وَالْحِسَابَ ؕ
وَكُلَّ شَيْءٍ فَصَّلْنٰهُ تَفْصِيْلًا ﴿۱۲﴾

13. We have made every person's destiny (actions) cling to his neck. On the Day of Judgment, We will bring forth the record of his actions in the form of a wide open book.

13. Wa kulla insaanin alzamnaahu ṭaaa'irahoo fee 'unuqihee wa nukhriju lahoo Yawmal-Qiyaamati kitaabañy-yalqaahu manshooraa.

وَكُلَّ اِنْسَانٍ اَلْزَمْنٰهُ طٰٓئِرَهٗ
فِيْ عُنُقِهٖ ؕ وَنُخْرِجُ لَهٗ يَوْمَ الْقِيٰمَةِ
كِتٰبًا يَّلْقٰىهُ مَنْشُوْرًا ﴿۱۳﴾

14. We will tell him, "Read it and judge for yourself."

14. Iqra-kitaabak; kafaa binafsikal-Yawma 'alayka ḥaseebaa.

اِقْرَاْ كِتٰبَكَ ؕ كَفٰى بِنَفْسِكَ الْيَوْمَ
عَلَيْكَ حَسِيْبًا ؕ﴿۱۴﴾

15. One who follows guidance does so for himself and one who goes astray does so against his soul. No one will suffer for the sins of others. We have never punished anyone without sending them Our Messenger first.

15. Manihtadaa fa-innamaa yahtadee linafsihee wa man ḍalla fa-innamaa yaḍillu 'alayhaa; wa laa taziru waaziratuñw-wizra ukhraa; wa maa kunnaa mu'az-zibeena ḥattaa nab'aṣa Rasoolaa.

مَنِ اهْتَدٰى فَاِنَّمَا يَهْتَدِيْ لِنَفْسِهٖ ۚ
وَمَنْ ضَلَّ فَاِنَّمَا يَضِلُّ عَلَيْهَا ؕ وَلَا
تَزِرُ وَازِرَةٌ وِّزْرَ اُخْرٰى ؕ وَمَا كُنَّا
مُعَذِّبِيْنَ حَتّٰى نَبْعَثَ رَسُوْلًا ﴿۱۵﴾

16. When We decide to destroy a town We increase the number of tyrant ones and they spread evil therein. Thus it becomes deserving of destruction and We destroy its very foundations.

16. Wa izaaa aradnaaa an nuhlika qaryatan amarnaa mutrafeehaa fafasaqoo feehaa faḥaqqa 'alayhal-qawlu fadammarnaahaa tadmeera.

وَاِذَآ اَرَدْنَآ اَنْ نُّهْلِكَ قَرْيَةً اَمَرْنَا
مُتْرَفِيْهَا فَفَسَقُوْا فِيْهَا فَحَقَّ عَلَيْهَا
الْقَوْلُ فَدَمَّرْنٰهَا تَدْمِيْرًا ﴿۱۶﴾

17. We have destroyed many generations after the time of Noah. Your Lord is All knowing

17. Wa kam ahlaknaa minal-qurooni mim ba'di Nooḥ; wa kafaa bi-Rabbika bizunoobi

وَكَمْ اَهْلَكْنَا مِنَ الْقُرُوْنِ مِنْۢ
بَعْدِ نُوْحٍ ؕ وَكَفٰى بِرَبِّكَ بِذُنُوْبِ

and Well-aware of the sins of His servants.	‘ibaadihee Khabeeram-Baṣeeraa.	عِبَادِهٖ خَبِيْرًۢا بَصِيْرًا ﴿١٧﴾
18. Whoever desires (only) the enjoyment of this life will receive it if We want it to be so. Then We will make Hell his reward wherein he will suffer, despised and driven away from Our mercy.	18. Man kaana yureedul ‘aajilata ‘ajjalnaa lahoo feehaa maa nashaaa’u liman-nureedu summa ja‘alnaa lahoo Jahannam; yaṣlaahaa mazmoomam-madḥooraa.	مَنْ كَانَ يُرِيْدُ الْعَاجِلَةَ عَجَّلْنَا لَهٗ فِيْهَا مَا نَشَآءُ لِمَنْ نُّرِيْدُ ثُمَّ جَعَلْنَا لَهٗ جَهَنَّمَ ۚ يَصْلٰىهَا مَذْمُوْمًا مَّدْحُوْرًا ﴿١٨﴾
19. The effort of one who faithfully strives hard for the (happiness) of the life to come will be appreciated (by Allah).	19. Wa man araadal Aakhirata wa sa‘aa lahaa sa‘yahaa wa huwa mu’minun fa-ulaaa’ika kaana sa‘yuhum-mashkooraa.	وَمَنْ اَرَادَ الْاٰخِرَةَ وَسَعٰى لَهَا سَعْيَهَا وَهُوَ مُؤْمِنٌ فَاُولٰٓئِكَ كَانَ سَعْيُهُمْ مَّشْكُوْرًا ﴿١٩﴾
20. Each group will receive its share of your Lord's generosity. Your Lord's generosity is not restricted.	20. Kullan-numiddu haaa-’ulaaa’i wa haaa’ulaaa’i min ‘aṭaaa’i Rabbik; wa maa kaana ‘aṭaaa’u Rabbika maḥẓooraa.	كُلًّا نُّمِدُّ هٰٓؤُلَآءِ وَهٰٓؤُلَآءِ مِنْ عَطَآءِ رَبِّكَ ؕ وَمَا كَانَ عَطَآءُ رَبِّكَ مَحْظُوْرًا ﴿٢٠﴾
21. Consider how We have given preference to some people above others, yet the life to come has more honor and respect.	21. Unẓur kayfa faḍḍalnaa ba‘ḍahum ‘alaa ba‘ḍ; wa lal-Aakhiratu akbaru darajaatiñw-wa akbaru tafḍeelaa.	اُنْظُرْ كَيْفَ فَضَّلْنَا بَعْضَهُمْ عَلٰى بَعْضٍ ؕ وَلَلْاٰخِرَةُ اَكْبَرُ دَرَجٰتٍ وَّاَكْبَرُ تَفْضِيْلًا ﴿٢١﴾
22. Do not consider anything equal to Allah lest you become despised and neglected.	22. Laa taj‘al ma‘al-laahi ilaahan aakhara fataq‘uda mazmoomam-makhzoolaa.	لَا تَجْعَلْ مَعَ اللّٰهِ اِلٰهًا اٰخَرَ فَتَقْعُدَ مَذْمُوْمًا مَّخْذُوْلًا ﴿٢٢﴾ ع
23. Your Lord has ordained that you must not worship anything other than Him and that you must be kind to your parents. If either or both of your parents should become advanced in age, do not express to them words which show your slightest disappointment. Never dispute with them but always speak to them with kindness.	23. Wa qaḍaa Rabbuka allaa ta‘budooo illaaa iyyaahu wa bilwaalidayni iḥsaanaa; immaa yablughanna ‘indakal-kibara aḥaduhumaaa aw kilaahumaa falaa taqul-lahumaaa uffiñw-wa laa tanharhumaa wa qul-lahumaa qawlan kareemaa.	وَقَضٰى رَبُّكَ اَلَّا تَعْبُدُوْٓا اِلَّآ اِيَّاهُ وَ بِالْوَالِدَيْنِ اِحْسَانًا ؕ اِمَّا يَبْلُغَنَّ عِنْدَكَ الْكِبَرَ اَحَدُهُمَآ اَوْ كِلٰهُمَا فَلَا تَقُلْ لَّهُمَآ اُفٍّ وَّلَا تَنْهَرْهُمَا وَقُلْ لَّهُمَا قَوْلًا كَرِيْمًا ﴿٢٣﴾
24. Be humble and merciful toward them and say, “Lord, have mercy upon them as they cherished me in my childhood.”	24. Wakhfiḍ lahumaa janaa-ḥaz-zulli minar-raḥmati wa qur-Rabbir-ḥamhumaa kamaa rabbayaanee ṣagheeraa.	وَاخْفِضْ لَهُمَا جَنَاحَ الذُّلِّ مِنَ الرَّحْمَةِ وَقُلْ رَّبِّ ارْحَمْهُمَا كَمَا رَبَّيٰنِيْ صَغِيْرًا ؕ ﴿٢٤﴾
25. Your Lord knows what is in your souls. If you would be righteous, know that He is All-forgiving to those who turn to Him in repentance.	25. Rabbukum a‘lamu bimaa fee nufoosikum; in takoonoo ṣaaliḥeena fa-innahoo kaana lil-awwaabeena Ghafooraa.	رَبُّكُمْ اَعْلَمُ بِمَا فِيْ نُفُوْسِكُمْ ؕ اِنْ تَكُوْنُوْا صٰلِحِيْنَ فَاِنَّهٗ كَانَ لِلْاَوَّابِيْنَ غَفُوْرًا ﴿٢٥﴾
26. Give the relatives, (of the Holy Prophet) the destitute, and	26. Wa aati zal-qurbaa ḥaqqahoo walmiskeena	وَاٰتِ ذَا الْقُرْبٰى حَقَّهٗ وَالْمِسْكِيْنَ

those who when on a journey have become needy, their dues.	wabnas-sabeeli wa laa tubaz-zir tabzeeraa.	وَابْنَ السَّبِيلِ وَلَا تُبَذِّرْ تَبْذِيرًا ﴿٢٦﴾
27. Do not be a wasteful (unlawful) spender. Squanderers are the brothers of Satan. Satan was faithless to his Lord.	27. Innal-mubaz-zireena kaa-nooo ikhwaanash-shayaaṭeeni wa kaanash-Shayṭaanu li-Rabbihee kafooraa.	إِنَّ الْمُبَذِّرِينَ كَانُوٓا إِخْوَانَ الشَّيٰطِينِ ۖ وَكَانَ الشَّيْطٰنُ لِرَبِّهِ كَفُورًا ﴿٢٧﴾
28. If you are not able to assist them, at least speak to them in a kind manner.	28. Wa immaa tu'riḍanna 'anhumub-tighaaa'a raḥmatim-mir-Rabbika tarjoohaa faqul-lahum qawlam-maysooraa.	وَإِمَّا تُعْرِضَنَّ عَنْهُمُ ابْتِغَآءَ رَحْمَةٍ مِّنْ رَّبِّكَ تَرْجُوهَا فَقُلْ لَّهُمْ قَوْلًا مَّيْسُورًا ﴿٢٨﴾
29. Do not be stingy nor over generous lest you become empty handed and bankrupt.	29. Wa laa taj'al yadaka maghloolatan ilaa 'unuqika wa laa tabsuṭhaa kullal-basṭi fataq'uda maloomam-maḥ-sooraa.	وَلَا تَجْعَلْ يَدَكَ مَغْلُولَةً إِلٰى عُنُقِكَ وَلَا تَبْسُطْهَا كُلَّ الْبَسْطِ فَتَقْعُدَ مَلُومًا مَّحْسُورًا ﴿٢٩﴾
30. Your Lord increases and measures the sustenance of whomever He wants. He is Well-aware and watches over His servants.	30. Inna Rabbaka yabsuṭur-rizqa limañy-yashaaa'u wa yaqdir; innahoo kaana bi'ibaa-dihee Khabeeram Baṣeeraa.	إِنَّ رَبَّكَ يَبْسُطُ الرِّزْقَ لِمَنْ يَّشَآءُ وَيَقْدِرُ ۚ إِنَّهُ كَانَ بِعِبَادِهِ خَبِيرًا بَصِيرًا ﴿٣٠﴾
31. Do not kill your children for fear of poverty. We will give sustenance to all of you. To kill them is certainly a great sin.	31. Wa laa taqtulooo awlaa-dakum khashyata imlaaq; naḥnu narzuquhum wa iyyaa-kum; inna qatlahum kaana khiṭ-an kabeeraa.	وَلَا تَقْتُلُوٓا أَوْلَادَكُمْ خَشْيَةَ إِمْلَاقٍ ۖ نَحْنُ نَرْزُقُهُمْ وَإِيَّاكُمْ ۚ إِنَّ قَتْلَهُمْ كَانَ خِطْأً كَبِيرًا ﴿٣١﴾
32. Do not even approach adultery. It is indecent (unlawful) and an evil act.	32. Wa laa taqrabuz-zinaaa innahoo kaana faaḥishah; wa saaa'a sabeelaa.	وَلَا تَقْرَبُوا الزِّنٰىٓ إِنَّهُ كَانَ فَاحِشَةً ۖ وَسَآءَ سَبِيلًا ﴿٣٢﴾
33. Do not kill a soul, whose killing Allah has made unlawful, without a just cause. To the heirs of anyone who is wrongfully killed, We have given the right (to demand satisfaction or to forgive). Killing must not take place beyond lawful measures; he (victim's heir) shall certainly be supported.	33. Wa laa taqtulun-nafsal-latee ḥarramal-laahu illaa bil-ḥaqq; wa man qutila maẓloo-man faqad ja'alnaa liwaliyyihee sulṭaanan falaa yusrif-fil-qatli innahoo kaana manṣooraa.	وَلَا تَقْتُلُوا النَّفْسَ الَّتِي حَرَّمَ اللّٰهُ إِلَّا بِالْحَقِّ ۗ وَمَنْ قُتِلَ مَظْلُومًا فَقَدْ جَعَلْنَا لِوَلِيِّهِ سُلْطٰنًا فَلَا يُسْرِفْ فِّي الْقَتْلِ ۖ إِنَّهُ كَانَ مَنْصُورًا ﴿٣٣﴾
34. Do not get close to the property of the orphans (unless it is for a good reason) until he attains manhood. Keep your promise; you will (on the Day of Judgment) be questioned about it.	34. Wa laa taqraboo maalal-yateemi illaa billatee hiya aḥsa-nu ḥattaa yablugha ashuddah; wa awfoo bil'ahd; innal-'ahda kaana mas'oolaa.	وَلَا تَقْرَبُوا مَالَ الْيَتِيمِ إِلَّا بِالَّتِي هِيَ أَحْسَنُ حَتّٰى يَبْلُغَ أَشُدَّهُ ۖ وَأَوْفُوا بِالْعَهْدِ ۖ إِنَّ الْعَهْدَ كَانَ مَسْـُٔولًا ﴿٣٤﴾
35. While weighing, use proper measurements in the exchange of	35. Wa awful-kayla izaa kiltum wazinoo	وَأَوْفُوا الْكَيْلَ إِذَا كِلْتُمْ وَزِنُوا

your property. This is fair and will be better in the end.	bilqisṭaasil-mustaqeem; z̲aalika khayruñw-wa aḥsanu ta-weelaa.	بِالْقِسْطَاسِ الْمُسْتَقِيْمِ ۚ ذٰلِكَ خَيْرٌ وَّاَحْسَنُ تَاْوِيْلًا ﴿٣٥﴾
36. Do not follow (say) what you do not know; the ears, eyes, and hearts will all be held responsible for their deeds.	36. Wa laa taqfu maa laysa laka bihee 'ilm; innas-sam'a walbaṣara walfu'aada kullu ulaaa'ika kaana 'anhu mas-'oolaa.	وَلَا تَقْفُ مَا لَيْسَ لَكَ بِهٖ عِلْمٌ ۚ اِنَّ السَّمْعَ وَالْبَصَرَ وَالْفُؤَادَ كُلُّ اُولٰٓئِكَ كَانَ عَنْهُ مَسْئُوْلًا ﴿٣٦﴾
37. Do not walk proudly on the earth; your feet cannot tear apart the earth nor are you as tall as the mountains.	37. Wa laa tamshi fil-arḍi maraḥan innaka lan takhriqal-arḍa wa lan tablughal-jibaala ṭoolaa.	وَلَا تَمْشِ فِي الْاَرْضِ مَرَحًا ۚ اِنَّكَ لَنْ تَخْرِقَ الْاَرْضَ وَلَنْ تَبْلُغَ الْجِبَالَ طُوْلًا ﴿٣٧﴾
38. All such things are sins and detestable in the sight of your Lord.	38. Kullu z̲aalika kaana sayyi'uhoo 'inda Rabbika makroohaa.	كُلُّ ذٰلِكَ كَانَ سَيِّئُهٗ عِنْدَ رَبِّكَ مَكْرُوْهًا ﴿٣٨﴾
39. (Muhammad), these are words of wisdom, which your Lord has revealed to you. Do not consider anything equal to Allah lest you be thrown into hell, despised, and driven away from Allah's mercy.	39. Z̲aalika mimmaaa awḥaaa ilayka Rabbuka minal-ḥikmah; wa laa taj'al ma'allaahi ilaahan aakhara fatulqaa fee Jahannama maloomam-madḥooraa.	ذٰلِكَ مِمَّآ اَوْحٰٓى اِلَيْكَ رَبُّكَ مِنَ الْحِكْمَةِ ۗ وَلَا تَجْعَلْ مَعَ اللّٰهِ اِلٰهًا اٰخَرَ فَتُلْقٰى فِيْ جَهَنَّمَ مَلُوْمًا مَّدْحُوْرًا ﴿٣٩﴾
40. (Pagans), has your Lord given you preference over Himself by granting you sons and taking the angels as His own daughters? What you say is a monstrous utterance.	40. Afa-aṣfaakum Rabbukum bilbaneena wattakhaz̲a minal malaaa'ikati inaas̲aa; innakum lataqooloona qawlan 'aẓeemaa.	اَفَاَصْفٰىكُمْ رَبُّكُمْ بِالْبَنِيْنَ وَاتَّخَذَ مِنَ الْمَلٰٓئِكَةِ اِنَاثًا ۭ اِنَّكُمْ لَتَقُوْلُوْنَ قَوْلًا عَظِيْمًا ﴿٤٠﴾
41. We have given you various facts (about the Truth in this Quran) so that they (unbelievers) would take heed, but this has only increased their aversion (to the truth).	41. Wa laqad ṣarrafnaa fee haaz̲al-Qur'aani liyaz̲-z̲akkaroo wa maa yazeeduhum illaa nufooraa.	وَلَقَدْ صَرَّفْنَا فِيْ هٰذَا الْقُرْاٰنِ لِيَذَّكَّرُوْا ۭ وَمَا يَزِيْدُهُمْ اِلَّا نُفُوْرًا ﴿٤١﴾
42. (Muhammad), ask them, "Had there been many other gods besides Him, as they say, they would have found a way to the Lord of the Throne	42. Qul-law kaana ma'ahooo aalihatun kamaa yaqooloona iz̲al-labtaghaw ilaa z̲il-'Arshi Sabeelaa.	قُلْ لَّوْ كَانَ مَعَهٗٓ اٰلِهَةٌ كَمَا يَقُوْلُوْنَ اِذًا لَّابْتَغَوْا اِلٰى ذِي الْعَرْشِ سَبِيْلًا ﴿٤٢﴾
43. (to challenge Him). Allah is free of defects of being considered as they believe Him to be. He is the most High and Great.	43. Subḥaanahoo wa Ta'aalaa 'ammaa yaqooloona 'uluwwan kabeeraa.	سُبْحٰنَهٗ وَتَعٰلٰى عَمَّا يَقُوْلُوْنَ عُلُوًّا كَبِيْرًا ﴿٤٣﴾
44. The seven heavens, the earth, and whatever is between them all glorify Him. There is nothing that does not glorify Him	44. Tusabbiḥu lahus-samaa-waatus-sab'u wal-arḍu wa man feehinn; wa im-min shay'in illaa yusabbiḥu	تُسَبِّحُ لَهُ السَّمٰوٰتُ السَّبْعُ وَالْاَرْضُ وَمَنْ فِيْهِنَّ ۭ وَاِنْ مِّنْ شَيْءٍ اِلَّا يُسَبِّحُ

and always praise him, but you do not understand their praise and glorification. He is All-forbearing and All-forgiving.

45. When you recite the Quran, We place a curtain as a barrier between you and those who do not believe in the life to come (and the devils).

46. We place a cover over their hearts so that they cannot understand it. We deafen their ears. When you mention your Lord in this Quran as One (Supreme Being), they run away.

47. We know best what they want to hear when they listen to you. They whisper to each other and say, "You are only following a bewitched person."

48. Consider what they have called you. They have certainly gone astray and cannot find the right path.

49. The pagans say, "When we become mere bones and dust, shall we then be brought back to life as new creatures?"

50. (Muhammad), say "Yes, even if you become rocks, iron,

51. or anything that you think is harder to be brought to life." They will soon ask, "Who will bring us back to life?" Say, "The One who created you in the first place." They will shake their heads and say, "When will He bring us back to life?" Say, "Perhaps very soon.

52. On the day when He will call you, you will answer Him with praise and think that you have tarried for only a little while."

53. (Muhammad), tell My servants to say what is best. Satan

biḥamdihee wa laakil-laa tafqahoona tasbeeḥahum; innahoo kaana Ḥaleeman Ghafooraa.

45. Wa i<u>z</u>aa qara-tal Qur'aana ja'alnaa baynaka wa baynal-la<u>z</u>eena laa yu'minoona bil-Aakhirati ḥijaabam-mastooraa.

46. Wa ja'alnaa 'alaa quloobihim akinnatan añy-yafqahoohu wa feee aa<u>z</u>aanihim waqraa; wa i<u>z</u>aa <u>z</u>akarta Rabbaka fil-Qur'aani waḥdahoo wallaw 'alaaa adbaarihim nufooraa.

47. Naḥnu a'lamu bimaa yastami'oona biheee i<u>z</u> yastami'oona ilayka wa i<u>z</u> hum najwaaa i<u>z</u> yaqooluẓ-ẓaalimoona in tattabi'oona illaa rajulam-masḥooraa.

48. Unẓur kayfa ḍaraboo lakal-am<u>s</u>aala faḍalloo falaa yastaṭee'oona sabeelaa.

49. Wa qaalooo 'a-i<u>z</u>aa kunnaa 'iẓaamañw-wa rufaatan 'a-innaa lamab'oo<u>s</u>oona khalqan jadeedaa.

50. Qul koonoo ḥijaaratan aw ḥadeedaa.

51. Aw khalqam-mimmaa yakburu fee ṣudoorikum; fasayaqooloona mañy-yu'eedunaa qulil-la<u>z</u>ee faṭarakum awwala marrah; fasayunghiḍoona ilayka ru'oosahum wa yaqooloona mataa huwa qul 'asaaa añy-yakoona qareebaa.

52. Yawma yad'ookum fatastajeeboona biḥamdihee wa taẓunnoona il-labi<u>s</u>tum illaa qaleelaa.

53. Wa qul-li'ibaadee yaqoolul-latee hiya

بِحَمْدِهٖ وَلٰكِنْ لَّا تَفْقَهُوْنَ تَسْبِيْحَهُمْ
اِنَّهٗ كَانَ حَلِيْمًا غَفُوْرًا ﴿٤٤﴾
وَاِذَا قَرَاْتَ الْقُرْاٰنَ جَعَلْنَا بَيْنَكَ
وَبَيْنَ الَّذِيْنَ لَا يُؤْمِنُوْنَ بِالْاٰخِرَةِ
حِجَابًا مَّسْتُوْرًا ﴿٤٥﴾
وَّجَعَلْنَا عَلٰى قُلُوْبِهِمْ اَكِنَّةً اَنْ
يَّفْقَهُوْهُ وَفِيْٓ اٰذَانِهِمْ وَقْرًا ۚ وَاِذَا
ذَكَرْتَ رَبَّكَ فِي الْقُرْاٰنِ وَحْدَهٗ وَلَّوْا
عَلٰٓى اَدْبَارِهِمْ نُفُوْرًا ﴿٤٦﴾
نَحْنُ اَعْلَمُ بِمَا يَسْتَمِعُوْنَ بِهٖٓ اِذْ
يَسْتَمِعُوْنَ اِلَيْكَ وَاِذْ هُمْ نَجْوٰٓى
اِذْ يَقُوْلُ الظّٰلِمُوْنَ اِنْ تَتَّبِعُوْنَ
اِلَّا رَجُلًا مَّسْحُوْرًا ﴿٤٧﴾
اُنْظُرْ كَيْفَ ضَرَبُوْا لَكَ الْاَمْثَالَ
فَضَلُّوْا فَلَا يَسْتَطِيْعُوْنَ سَبِيْلًا ﴿٤٨﴾ الربع
وَقَالُوْٓا ءَاِذَا كُنَّا عِظَامًا وَّرُفَاتًا
ءَاِنَّا لَمَبْعُوْثُوْنَ خَلْقًا جَدِيْدًا ﴿٤٩﴾
قُلْ كُوْنُوْا حِجَارَةً اَوْ حَدِيْدًا ﴿٥٠﴾
اَوْ خَلْقًا مِّمَّا يَكْبُرُ فِيْ صُدُوْرِكُمْ ۚ
فَسَيَقُوْلُوْنَ مَنْ يُّعِيْدُنَا ۗ قُلِ الَّذِيْ
فَطَرَكُمْ اَوَّلَ مَرَّةٍ ۚ فَسَيُنْغِضُوْنَ
اِلَيْكَ رُءُوْسَهُمْ وَيَقُوْلُوْنَ مَتٰى
هُوَ ۗ قُلْ عَسٰٓى اَنْ يَّكُوْنَ قَرِيْبًا ﴿٥١﴾
يَوْمَ يَدْعُوْكُمْ فَتَسْتَجِيْبُوْنَ بِحَمْدِهٖ
وَتَظُنُّوْنَ اِنْ لَّبِثْتُمْ اِلَّا قَلِيْلًا ﴿٥٢﴾ ع ٥ ١٢ ٥
وَقُلْ لِّعِبَادِيْ يَقُوْلُوا الَّتِيْ هِيَ

sows dissension among them; he is the sworn enemy of human beings.

aḥsan; innash-Shayṭaana yanzaghu baynahum; innash-Shayṭaana kaana lil-insaani 'aduwwam-mubeenaa.

أَحۡسَنُ ۚ إِنَّ ٱلشَّيۡطَٰنَ يَنزَغُ بَيۡنَهُمۡ ۚ إِنَّ
ٱلشَّيۡطَٰنَ كَانَ لِلۡإِنسَٰنِ عَدُوًّا مُّبِينًا ﴿٥٣﴾

54. Your Lord knows better than you (people). He will have mercy on you or will punish you as He wills. We have not sent you to watch over them. Your Lord knows best about those in the heavens and the earth.

54. Rabbukum a'lamu-bikum iñy-yasha- yarḥamkum aw iñy-yasha- yu'az-zibkum; wa maaa arsalnaaka 'alayhim wakeelaa.

رَّبُّكُمۡ أَعۡلَمُ بِكُمۡ ۖ إِن يَشَأۡ يَرۡحَمۡكُمۡ
أَوۡ إِن يَشَأۡ يُعَذِّبۡكُمۡ ۚ وَمَآ أَرۡسَلۡنَٰكَ
عَلَيۡهِمۡ وَكِيلًا ﴿٥٤﴾

55. We have given preference to some Prophets over others and We gave the psalms to David.

55. Wa Rabbuka a'lamu-biman fis-samaawaati wal-arḍ; wa laqad faḍḍalnaa ba'ḍan-Nabiyyeena 'alaa ba'ḍiñw-wa aataynaa Daawooda Zabooraa.

وَرَبُّكَ أَعۡلَمُ بِمَن فِي ٱلسَّمَٰوَٰتِ وَ
ٱلۡأَرۡضِ ۗ وَلَقَدۡ فَضَّلۡنَا بَعۡضَ ٱلنَّبِيِّـۧنَ
عَلَىٰ بَعۡضٍ ۖ وَءَاتَيۡنَا دَاوُۥدَ زَبُورًا ﴿٥٥﴾

56. (Muhammad), tell them, "Seek help from those whom you consider equal to Allah. They are not able to remove or change your hardships."

56. Qulid-'ul-lazeena za'am-tum min doonihee falaa yamlikoona kashfaḍ-ḍurri 'ankum wa laa taḥweelaa.

قُلِ ٱدۡعُواْ ٱلَّذِينَ زَعَمۡتُم مِّن
دُونِهِۦ فَلَا يَمۡلِكُونَ كَشۡفَ ٱلضُّرِّ
عَنكُمۡ وَلَا تَحۡوِيلًا ﴿٥٦﴾

57. Those whom they worship seek to find intercessors for themselves with their Lord. (They try to find out which of the intercessors) are closer. They have hope for His mercy and fear of His punishment; the punishment of your Lord must be escaped.

57. Ulaaa'ikal-lazeena yad-'oona yabtaghoona ilaa Rabbi-himul-waseelata ayyuhum aqrabu wa yarjoona raḥmatahoo wa yakhaafoona 'azaabah; inna 'azaaba Rabbika kaana maḥzooraa.

أُوْلَٰٓئِكَ ٱلَّذِينَ يَدۡعُونَ يَبۡتَغُونَ
إِلَىٰ رَبِّهِمُ ٱلۡوَسِيلَةَ أَيُّهُمۡ أَقۡرَبُ
وَيَرۡجُونَ رَحۡمَتَهُۥ وَيَخَافُونَ عَذَابَهُۥٓ ۚ
إِنَّ عَذَابَ رَبِّكَ كَانَ مَحۡذُورًا ﴿٥٧﴾

58. The decree that all the towns were to be destroyed or afflicted with severe punishment was already written in the Book before the Day of Judgment.

58. Wa im-min qaryatin illaa Naḥnu muhlikoohaa qabla Yawmil-Qiyaamati aw mu'az-ziboohaa 'azaaban shadeedaa; kaana zaalika fil-Kitaabi mas-ṭooraa.

وَإِن مِّن قَرۡيَةٍ إِلَّا نَحۡنُ مُهۡلِكُوهَا
قَبۡلَ يَوۡمِ ٱلۡقِيَٰمَةِ أَوۡ مُعَذِّبُوهَا عَذَابًا
شَدِيدًا ۚ كَانَ ذَٰلِكَ فِي ٱلۡكِتَٰبِ
مَسۡطُورًا ﴿٥٨﴾

59. We did not abstain from sending miracles to any of Our Messengers. These miracles were called lies by the people who lived in ancient times. To the people of Thamud, We sent the she-camel as a visible miracle and they did injustice to it. We only send miracles as warnings.

59. Wa maa mana'anaaa an nursila bil-Aayaati illaaa an kaz-zaba bihal-awwaloon; wa aataynaa Samoodan-naaqata mubṣiratan faẓalamoo bihaa; wa maa nursilu bil-Aayaati illaa takhweefaa.

وَمَا مَنَعَنَآ أَن نُّرۡسِلَ بِٱلۡأٓيَٰتِ إِلَّآ
أَن كَذَّبَ بِهَا ٱلۡأَوَّلُونَ ۚ وَءَاتَيۡنَا
ثَمُودَ ٱلنَّاقَةَ مُبۡصِرَةً فَظَلَمُواْ بِهَا ۚ
وَمَا نُرۡسِلُ بِٱلۡأٓيَٰتِ إِلَّا تَخۡوِيفًا ﴿٥٩﴾

60. (Muhammad), We told you that your Lord has encompassed all mankind. We made the vision (that monkeys danced on your pulpit) which We showed you and the condemned tree, mentioned in

60. Wa iz qulnaa laka inna Rabbaka aḥaaṭa binnaas; wa maa ja'alnar-ru'yal-lateee araynaaka illaa fitnatal-linnaasi washshajaratal-mal'oonata

وَإِذۡ قُلۡنَا لَكَ إِنَّ رَبَّكَ أَحَاطَ بِٱلنَّاسِ ۚ
وَمَا جَعَلۡنَا ٱلرُّءۡيَا ٱلَّتِيٓ أَرَيۡنَٰكَ إِلَّا
فِتۡنَةً لِّلنَّاسِ وَٱلشَّجَرَةَ ٱلۡمَلۡعُونَةَ

the Quran, as a trial for the human being. Even though We warn them, it only increases their rebellion.

fil-Qur'aan; wa nukhawwifuhum famaa yazeeduhum illaa tughyaanan kabeeraa.

فِي الْقُرْاٰنِ ؕ وَنُخَوِّفُهُمْ ۙ فَمَا يَزِيْدُهُمْ
اِلَّا طُغْيَانًا كَبِيْرًا ٦٠

61. When We told the angels to prostrate before Adam, they all obeyed, except Iblis who said, "Should I prostrate before one whom You have created out of clay?"

61. Wa iz̲ qulnaa lilmalaaa'ikatis-judoo li-Aadama fasajadooo illaaa Iblees; qaala 'a-asjudu liman khalaqta ṭeenaa.

وَاِذْ قُلْنَا لِلْمَلٰٓئِكَةِ اسْجُدُوْا لِاٰدَمَ
فَسَجَدُوْٓا اِلَّآ اِبْلِيْسَ ؕ قَالَ ءَاَسْجُدُ
لِمَنْ خَلَقْتَ طِيْنًا ٦١

62. He continued, "Take notice: the one whom you have honored more than me, I shall bring him and most of his offspring under my sway if you will give me respite until the Day of Judgment."

62. Qaala ara'aytaka haaz̲al-laz̲ee karramta 'alayya la'in akhkhartani ilaa Yawmil-Qiyaamati la-aḥtanikanna z̲urriyyatahooo illaa qaleeelaa.

قَالَ اَرَءَيْتَكَ هٰذَا الَّذِيْ كَرَّمْتَ عَلَيَّ ز
لَئِنْ اَخَّرْتَنِ اِلٰى يَوْمِ الْقِيٰمَةِ لَاَحْتَنِكَنَّ
ذُرِّيَّتَهٗٓ اِلَّا قَلِيْلًا ٦٢

63. Allah said, "Go away. All those who follow you will have hell as ample recompense for their deeds.

63. Qaalaz̲-hab faman tabi'aka minhum fa-inna Jahannama jazaaa'ukum jazaaa'ammawfooraa.

قَالَ اذْهَبْ فَمَنْ تَبِعَكَ مِنْهُمْ فَاِنَّ
جَهَنَّمَ جَزَآؤُكُمْ جَزَآءً مَّوْفُوْرًا ٦٣

64. Draw any one of them you can into sin by your voice and by your cavalry and infantry, share their property and children with them and make promises to them. Your promises are all lies.

64. Wastafziz manis-taṭa'ta minhum biṣawtika wa ajlib 'alayhim bikhaylika wa rajilika wa shaarikhum fil-amwaali wal-awlaadi wa 'idhum; wa maa ya'iduhumush-Shayṭaanu illaa ghurooraa.

وَاسْتَفْزِزْ مَنِ اسْتَطَعْتَ مِنْهُمْ بِصَوْتِكَ
وَاَجْلِبْ عَلَيْهِمْ بِخَيْلِكَ وَرَجِلِكَ وَ
شَارِكْهُمْ فِي الْاَمْوَالِ وَالْاَوْلَادِ وَعِدْهُمْ ؕ
وَمَا يَعِدُهُمُ الشَّيْطٰنُ اِلَّا غُرُوْرًا ٦٤

65. You have no authority over My servants. Your Lord is a sufficient protector."

65. Inna 'ibaadee laysa laka 'alayhim sulṭaan; wa kafaa bi-Rabbika Wakeelaa.

اِنَّ عِبَادِيْ لَيْسَ لَكَ عَلَيْهِمْ
سُلْطٰنٌ ؕ وَكَفٰى بِرَبِّكَ وَكِيْلًا ٦٥

66. Your Lord who causes the ships to sail on the sea so that you may seek His bounty is certainly All-merciful to you.

66. Rabbukumul-laz̲ee yuzjee lakumul-fulka fil-baḥri litabtaghoo min faḍlih; innahoo kaana bikum Raḥeemaa.

رَبُّكُمُ الَّذِيْ يُزْجِيْ لَكُمُ الْفُلْكَ فِي
الْبَحْرِ لِتَبْتَغُوْا مِنْ فَضْلِهٖ ؕ اِنَّهٗ
كَانَ بِكُمْ رَحِيْمًا ٦٦

67. If you are afflicted by hardships in the middle of the sea, it would be an error to call anyone other than Him for help. When Allah saves you from such difficulties, you turn away from Him. The human being has always been ungrateful.

67. Wa iz̲aa massakumuḍ-ḍurru fil-baḥri ḍalla man tad'oona illaaa iyyaahu falammaa najjaakum ilal-barri a'raḍtum; wa kaanal insaanu kafooraa.

وَاِذَا مَسَّكُمُ الضُّرُّ فِي الْبَحْرِ ضَلَّ مَنْ
تَدْعُوْنَ اِلَّآ اِيَّاهُ ۚ فَلَمَّا نَجّٰىكُمْ اِلَى الْبَرِّ
اَعْرَضْتُمْ ؕ وَكَانَ الْاِنْسَانُ كَفُوْرًا ٦٧

68. Do you feel secure that We will not cause a part of the land to sink or engulf you with sand storms when you would find no one to protect you?

68. Afa-amintum añy-yakhsifa bikum jaanibal-barri aw yursila 'alaykum ḥaaṣiban s̲umma laa tajidoo lakum wakeelaa.

اَفَاَمِنْتُمْ اَنْ يَّخْسِفَ بِكُمْ جَانِبَ الْبَرِّ
اَوْ يُرْسِلَ عَلَيْكُمْ حَاصِبًا ثُمَّ لَا تَجِدُوْا
لَكُمْ وَكِيْلًا ۙ ٦٨

69. Do you feel secure that We will not drive you back to the sea,

69. Am amintum añy-yu'eedakum feehi taaratan

اَمْ اَمِنْتُمْ اَنْ يُّعِيْدَكُمْ فِيْهِ تَارَةً

send a fierce gale to you, and cause you to drown because of your disbelief when you would not be able to find anyone who would intercede for you with Us?

ukhraa fa-yursila 'alaykum qaaṣifam-minar-reeḥi fa-yugh-riqakum bimaa kafartum s̲umma laa tajidoo lakum 'alaynaa bihee tabee'aa.

اُخْرٰى فَيُرْسِلَ عَلَيْكُمْ قَاصِفًا مِّنَ
الرِّيْحِ فَيُغْرِقَكُمْ بِمَا كَفَرْتُمْ ۙ ثُمَّ لَا
تَجِدُوْا لَكُمْ عَلَيْنَا بِهٖ تَبِيْعًا ﴿٦٩﴾

70. We have honored the children of Adam, carried them on the land and the sea, given them pure sustenance, and exalted them above most of My creatures.

70. Wa laqad karramnaa Baneee Aadama wa ḥamal-naahum fil-barri walbaḥri wa razaqnaahum minaṭ-ṭayyibaati wa faḍḍalnaahum 'alaa kas̲ee-rim-mimman khalaqnaa tafḍee-laa.

وَلَقَدْ كَرَّمْنَا بَنِيْٓ اٰدَمَ وَحَمَلْنٰهُمْ
فِي الْبَرِّ وَالْبَحْرِ وَرَزَقْنٰهُمْ مِّنَ
الطَّيِّبٰتِ وَفَضَّلْنٰهُمْ عَلٰى كَثِيْرٍ
مِّمَّنْ خَلَقْنَا تَفْضِيْلًا ﴿٧٠﴾ ع ٧

71. On the day when We call every nation with their leader (Imam), those whose record of deeds are given to their right hands read the book and the least wrong is not done to them.

71. Yawma nad'oo kulla unaasim bi-imaamihim faman ootiya kitaabahoo biyamee-nihee fa-ulaaa'ika yaqra'oona kitaabahum wa laa yuẓlamoona fateelaa.

يَوْمَ نَدْعُوْا كُلَّ اُنَاسٍۢ بِاِمَامِهِمْ ۚ فَمَنْ
اُوْتِيَ كِتٰبَهٗ بِيَمِيْنِهٖ فَاُولٰٓئِكَ يَقْرَءُوْنَ
كِتٰبَهُمْ وَلَا يُظْلَمُوْنَ فَتِيْلًا ﴿٧١﴾

72. Those who are blind in this life will be blind in the life to come as well and in terrible error.

72. Wa man kaana fee haaz̲iheee a'maa fahuwa fil-Aakhirati a'maa wa aḍallu sabeelaa.

وَمَنْ كَانَ فِيْ هٰذِهٖٓ اَعْمٰى فَهُوَ فِي
الْاٰخِرَةِ اَعْمٰى وَاَضَلُّ سَبِيْلًا ﴿٧٢﴾

73. (Such blind ones) try to make you compromise in what We have revealed to you (about your successor) so that they may falsely ascribe to Us something other than the true revelation and thus establish friendship with you.

73. Wa in kaadoo la-yafti-noonaka 'anil-laz̲eee awḥay-naaa ilayka litaftariya 'alaynaa ghayrahoo wa iz̲allat-takha-z̲ooka khaleelaa.

وَاِنْ كَادُوْا لَيَفْتِنُوْنَكَ عَنِ الَّذِيْٓ
اَوْحَيْنَآ اِلَيْكَ لِتَفْتَرِيَ عَلَيْنَا غَيْرَهٗ ۖ
وَاِذًا لَّاتَّخَذُوْكَ خَلِيْلًا ﴿٧٣﴾

74. Had We not strengthened your faith you might have relied on them somehow.

74. Wa law laaa an s̲abbat-naaka laqad kitta tarkanu ilayhim shay'an qaleelaa.

وَلَوْلَآ اَنْ ثَبَّتْنٰكَ لَقَدْ كِدْتَّ تَرْكَنُ
اِلَيْهِمْ شَيْـًٔا قَلِيْلًا ﴿٧٤﴾

75. Had you done so, We would certainly have made you face double punishment in this life and after your death and you would have found none to help you.

75. Iz̲al-la-az̲aqnaaka ḍi'fal-ḥayaati wa ḍi'fal-mamaati s̲umma laa tajidu laka 'alaynaa naṣeeraa.

اِذًا لَّاَذَقْنٰكَ ضِعْفَ الْحَيٰوةِ وَضِعْفَ
الْمَمَاتِ ثُمَّ لَا تَجِدُ لَكَ عَلَيْنَا نَصِيْرًا ﴿٧٥﴾

76. They (pagans) try to annoy you so that they can expel you from the land. Had they been successful, no one would have been left behind except a few.

76. Wa in kaadoo layastafiz-zoonaka minal-arḍi liyukhri-jooka minhaa wa iz̲al-laa yalbas̲oona khilaafaka illaa qaleelaa.

وَاِنْ كَادُوْا لَيَسْتَفِزُّوْنَكَ مِنَ الْاَرْضِ
لِيُخْرِجُوْكَ مِنْهَا وَاِذًا لَّا يَلْبَثُوْنَ
خِلٰفَكَ اِلَّا قَلِيْلًا ﴿٧٦﴾

77. This was Our tradition with Our Messengers who lived before you, and you will find no change in Our tradition.

77. Sunnata man qad arsalnaa qablaka mir-Rusulinaa wa laa tajidu lisunnatinaa taḥweelaa.

سُنَّةَ مَنْ قَدْ اَرْسَلْنَا قَبْلَكَ مِنْ
رُّسُلِنَا وَلَا تَجِدُ لِسُنَّتِنَا تَحْوِيْلًا ﴿٧٧﴾ ع ٨

78. Say your prayer when the sun declines until the darkness of night and also at dawn. Dawn is certainly witnessed (by the angels

78. Aqimiṣ-Ṣalaata liduloo-kish-shamsi ilaa ghasaqil-layli wa qur'aanal-Fajri inna qur'aa-nal-Fajri

اَقِمِ الصَّلٰوةَ لِدُلُوْكِ الشَّمْسِ اِلٰى غَسَقِ
الَّيْلِ وَقُرْاٰنَ الْفَجْرِ ۗ اِنَّ قُرْاٰنَ الْفَجْرِ

of the night and day).

79. Say your special (Tahajjud) prayer during some part of the night as an additional (obligatory) prayer for you alone so that perhaps your Lord will raise you to a highly praiseworthy position.

80. (Muhammad), say, "Lord, make me enter through a path that will lead to the Truth and come out of an exit that will take me to the Truth and grant me an authoritative supporter of Your choice."

81. Say, 'Truth has come and falsehood has been banished; it is doomed to banishment.'"

82. We reveal the Quran, which is a cure and mercy for the believers but does nothing for the unjust except to lead them to perdition.

83. When We do favors to the human being, he disregards it and turns away from it. When evil afflicts him, he becomes despairing.

84. Say, "Everyone does as he intends. Your Lord knows best who has the right guidance."

85. They ask you about the Spirit. Say, "The Spirit comes by the command of my Lord. You have been given very little knowledge.

86. Had We wanted, We could have removed that which We revealed to you. Then you could not find anyone to intercede with Us for you about it

87. except by the mercy of your Lord. He has certainly bestowed great favors on you.

88. Say, "If all human beings and jinn were to come together to

kaana mashhoodaa.

79. Wa minal-layli fatahajjad bihee naafilatal-laka 'asaaa añy-yab'asaka Rabbuka Maqaamam-Maḥmoodaa.

80. Wa qur-Rabbi adkhilnee mudkhala ṣidqiñw-wa akhrijnee mukhraja ṣidqiñw-waj'al lee milladunka sulṭaanan naṣeeraa.

81. Wa qul jaaa'al-ḥaqqu wa zahaqal-baaṭil; innal-baaṭila kaana zahooqaa.

82. Wa nunazzilu minal-Qur'aani maa huwa shifaaa-'uñw- wa raḥmatul-lilmu'mineena wa laa yazeeduẓ-ẓaalimeena illaa khasaaraa.

83. Wa i**z**aaa an'amnaa 'alal-insaani a'raḍa wa na-aa bijaanibihee wa i**z**aa massahush-sharru kaana ya'oosaa.

84. Qul kulluñy-ya'malu 'alaa shaakilatihee fa-Rabbukum a'lamu biman huwa ahdaa sabeelaa.

85. Wa yas'aloonaka 'anir-Rooḥ; qulir-Rooḥu min amri Rabbee wa maaa ooteetum-minal-'ilmi illaa qaleelaa.

86. Wa la'in shi'naa lanaz-habanna billa**z**eee awḥaynaaa ilayka **s**umma laa tajidu laka bihee 'alaynaa wakeelaa.

87. Illaa raḥmatam-mir-Rabbik; inna faḍlahoo kaana 'alayka kabeeraa.

88. Qul la'inij-tama'atil-insu waljinnu

كَانَ مَشْهُوْدًا ﴿٧٨﴾
وَمِنَ الَّيْلِ فَتَهَجَّدْ بِهٖ نَافِلَةً
لَّكَ ۖ عَسٰٓى اَنْ يَّبْعَثَكَ رَبُّكَ
مَقَامًا مَّحْمُوْدًا ﴿٧٩﴾
وَقُلْ رَّبِّ اَدْخِلْنِىْ مُدْخَلَ صِدْقٍ
وَّاَخْرِجْنِىْ مُخْرَجَ صِدْقٍ وَّاجْعَلْ
لِّىْ مِنْ لَّدُنْكَ سُلْطٰنًا نَّصِيْرًا ﴿٨٠﴾
وَقُلْ جَآءَ الْحَقُّ وَزَهَقَ الْبَاطِلُ ؕ
اِنَّ الْبَاطِلَ كَانَ زَهُوْقًا ﴿٨١﴾
وَنُنَزِّلُ مِنَ الْقُرْاٰنِ مَا هُوَ
شِفَآءٌ وَّرَحْمَةٌ لِّلْمُؤْمِنِيْنَ ۙ وَلَا
يَزِيْدُ الظّٰلِمِيْنَ اِلَّا خَسَارًا ﴿٨٢﴾
وَاِذَآ اَنْعَمْنَا عَلَى الْاِنْسَانِ اَعْرَضَ
وَنَاٰ بِجَانِبِهٖ ۚ وَاِذَا مَسَّهُ الشَّرُّ كَانَ
يَئُوْسًا ﴿٨٣﴾
قُلْ كُلٌّ يَّعْمَلُ عَلٰى شَاكِلَتِهٖ ؕ فَرَبُّكُمْ
اَعْلَمُ بِمَنْ هُوَ اَهْدٰى سَبِيْلًا ﴿٨٤﴾ ع
وَيَسْــَٔلُوْنَكَ عَنِ الرُّوْحِ ؕ قُلِ الرُّوْحُ
مِنْ اَمْرِ رَبِّىْ وَمَآ اُوْتِيْتُمْ مِّنَ الْعِلْمِ
اِلَّا قَلِيْلًا ﴿٨٥﴾
وَلَئِنْ شِئْنَا لَنَذْهَبَنَّ بِالَّذِىْٓ
اَوْحَيْنَآ اِلَيْكَ ثُمَّ لَا تَجِدُ لَكَ
بِهٖ عَلَيْنَا وَكِيْلًا ﴿٨٦﴾
اِلَّا رَحْمَةً مِّنْ رَّبِّكَ ؕ اِنَّ فَضْلَهٗ
كَانَ عَلَيْكَ كَبِيْرًا ﴿٨٧﴾
قُلْ لَّئِنِ اجْتَمَعَتِ الْاِنْسُ وَالْجِنُّ

bring the equivalent of this Quran, they could not do so, even if they all were to help each other.

'alaaa añy-ya-too bimis̲li haaz̲al-Qur'aani laa ya-toona bimis̲lihee wa law kaana ba'ḍuhum liba'ḍin ẓaheeraa.

عَلٰۤى اَنْ يَّاْتُوْا بِمِثْلِ هٰذَا الْقُرْاٰنِ
لَا يَاْتُوْنَ بِمِثْلِهٖ وَلَوْ كَانَ بَعْضُهُمْ
لِبَعْضٍ ظَهِيْرًا ﴿٨٨﴾

89. We have mentioned in this Quran all kinds of examples for the human being, but most human beings turn away in disbelief.

89. Wa laqad ṣarrafnaa lin-naasi fee haaz̲al-Qur'aani min kulli mas̲alin fa-abaaa aks̲arun-naasi illaa kufooraa.

وَلَقَدْ صَرَّفْنَا لِلنَّاسِ فِيْ هٰذَا
الْقُرْاٰنِ مِنْ كُلِّ مَثَلٍ ز فَاَبٰۤى
اَكْثَرُ النَّاسِ اِلَّا كُفُوْرًا ﴿٨٩﴾

90. They have said, "We shall never believe you until you cause a spring to gush forth from the earth,

90. Wa qaaloo lan-nu'mina laka ḥattaa tafjura lanaa minal-arḍi yamboo'aa.

وَقَالُوْا لَنْ نُّؤْمِنَ لَكَ حَتّٰى تَفْجُرَ
لَنَا مِنَ الْاَرْضِ يَنْۢبُوْعًا ﴿٩٠﴾

91. or you (show) us that you have your own garden of palm trees and vines with flowing streams therein,

91. Aw takoona laka janna-tum-min nakheeliñw-wa 'inabin fatufajjiral-anhaara khilaalahaa tafjeeraa.

اَوْ تَكُوْنَ لَكَ جَنَّةٌ مِّنْ نَّخِيْلٍ وَّ
عِنَبٍ فَتُفَجِّرَ الْاَنْهٰرَ خِلٰلَهَا تَفْجِيْرًا ﴿٩١﴾

92. or cause the sky to fall into pieces on us - as you believe you can - or bring Allah and the angels face to face with us,

92. Aw tusqiṭas-samaaa'a kamaa za'amta 'alaynaa kisafan aw ta-tiya billaahi walma-laaa'ikati qabeelaa.

اَوْ تُسْقِطَ السَّمَآءَ كَمَا زَعَمْتَ عَلَيْنَا
كِسَفًا اَوْ تَاْتِيَ بِاللّٰهِ وَالْمَلٰٓئِكَةِ قَبِيْلًا ﴿٩٢﴾

93. or (show us) that you have a well-adorned house of your own, or climb into the sky. We shall never believe that you have climbed into the sky until you bring us a book that we can read." Say, "All glory belongs to my Lord. Am I more than a mortal Messenger?"

93. Aw yakoona laka baytum-min zukhrufin aw tarqaa fis-samaaa'i wa lan-nu'mina liruqiyyika ḥattaa tunazzila 'alaynaa kitaaban-naqra'ooh; qul Subḥaana Rabbee hal kuntu illaa basharar-Rasoolaa.

اَوْ يَكُوْنَ لَكَ بَيْتٌ مِّنْ زُخْرُفٍ
اَوْ تَرْقٰى فِي السَّمَآءِ ؕ وَلَنْ نُّؤْمِنَ
لِرُقِيِّكَ حَتّٰى تُنَزِّلَ عَلَيْنَا كِتٰبًا
نَّقْرَؤُهٗ ؕ قُلْ سُبْحَانَ رَبِّيْ هَلْ كُنْتُ
اِلَّا بَشَرًا رَّسُوْلًا ﴿٩٣﴾ ع ١٠

94. What keeps people from belief that guidance has come to them, and they question, "Why has Allah sent a mortal Messenger?"

94. Wa maa mana'an-naasa añy-yu'minooo iz̲ jaaa'ahumul-hudaaa illaaa an qaalooo aba-'as̲al-laahu basharar-Rasoolaa.

وَمَا مَنَعَ النَّاسَ اَنْ يُّؤْمِنُوْۤا اِذْ
جَآءَهُمُ الْهُدٰۤى اِلَّاۤ اَنْ قَالُوْۤا اَبَعَثَ
اللّٰهُ بَشَرًا رَّسُوْلًا ﴿٩٤﴾

95. (Muhammad), say, "Had the earth been inhabited by angels who would walk serenely therein, only then would We have sent to them angelic Messengers."

95. Qul law kaana fil-arḍi malaaa'ikatuñy-yamshoona muṭma'inneena lanaz-zalnaa 'alayhim-minas-samaaa'i malakar-Rasoolaa.

قُلْ لَّوْ كَانَ فِي الْاَرْضِ مَلٰٓئِكَةٌ
يَّمْشُوْنَ مُطْمَئِنِّيْنَ لَنَزَّلْنَا عَلَيْهِمْ
مِّنَ السَّمَآءِ مَلَكًا رَّسُوْلًا ﴿٩٥﴾

96. Say, "Allah is a sufficient Witness between me and you. He certainly sees and knows all about His servants.

96. Qul kafaa billaahi sha-heedam baynee wa baynakum; innahoo kaana bi'ibaadihee Khabeeram Baṣeeraa.

قُلْ كَفٰى بِاللّٰهِ شَهِيْدًاۢ بَيْنِيْ وَبَيْنَكُمْ ؕ
اِنَّهٗ كَانَ بِعِبَادِهٖ خَبِيْرًاۢ بَصِيْرًا ﴿٩٦﴾

97. Whomever Allah has guided has the proper guidance. You will

97. Wa mañy-yahdil-laahu fahuwal-muhtad; wa mañy-

وَمَنْ يَّهْدِ اللّٰهُ فَهُوَ الْمُهْتَدِ ۚ وَمَنْ

never find any guardian besides Allah for the one whom He has caused to go astray. On the Day of Judgment, We will gather them lying on their faces, blind, dumb, and deaf. Hell will be their dwelling. As hellfire abates, We will increase its blazing force.

yuḍlil falan tajida lahum awliyaaa'a min doonih; wa naḥshuruhum Yawmal-Qiyaamati 'alaa wujoohihim 'umyañw-wa bukmañw-wa ṣummaa; ma-waahum Jahannamu kullamaa khabat zidnaahum sa'eeraa.

يُضْلِلْ فَلَنْ تَجِدَ لَهُمْ اَوْلِيَآءَ مِنْ
دُوْنِهٖ ؕ وَنَحْشُرُهُمْ يَوْمَ الْقِيٰمَةِ عَلٰى
وُجُوْهِهِمْ عُمْيًا وَّبُكْمًا وَّصُمًّا ؕ مَاْوٰىهُمْ
جَهَنَّمُ ؕ كُلَّمَا خَبَتْ زِدْنٰهُمْ سَعِيْرًا ﴿٩٧﴾

98. This will be the punishment for their disbelief of Our revelations and for their saying, "Shall we be brought to life again after becoming bones and dust?"

98. Zaalika jazaaa'uhum bi-annahum kafaroo bi-Aayaatinaa wa qaalooo 'a-izaa kunnaa 'iẓaamañw-wa rufaatan 'a-innaa lamab'oosoona khalqan jadeedaa.

ذٰلِكَ جَزَآؤُهُمْ بِاَنَّهُمْ كَفَرُوْا بِاٰيٰتِنَا
وَقَالُوْٓا ءَاِذَا كُنَّا عِظَامًا وَّرُفَاتًا
ءَاِنَّا لَمَبْعُوْثُوْنَ خَلْقًا جَدِيْدًا ﴿٩٨﴾

99. Did they not see that Allah, who has created the heavens and the earth, has the power to create their like? He has given them life for an appointed time of which there is no doubt. The unjust turn away in disbelief (from Our revelation).

99. Awalam yaraw annal-laahal-lazee khalaqas-samaa-waati wal-arḍa qaadirun 'alaaa añy-yakhluqa mislahum wa ja'ala lahum ajalal-laa rayba feeh; fa-abaẓ-ẓaalimoona illaa kufooraa.

اَوَلَمْ يَرَوْا اَنَّ اللّٰهَ الَّذِيْ خَلَقَ
السَّمٰوٰتِ وَالْاَرْضَ قَادِرٌ عَلٰٓى اَنْ يَّخْلُقَ
مِثْلَهُمْ وَجَعَلَ لَهُمْ اَجَلًا لَّا رَيْبَ فِيْهِ ؕ النِّصْفُ
فَاَبَى الظّٰلِمُوْنَ اِلَّا كُفُوْرًا ﴿٩٩﴾

100. Say, "Had you owned the treasures of the Mercy of my Lord, you would have locked them up for fear of spending them. The human being has always been miserly.

100. Qul law antum tamlikoona khazaaa'ina raḥmati Rabbeee izalla-amsaktum khash-yatal-infaaq; wa kaanal-insaanu qatooraa.

قُلْ لَّوْ اَنْتُمْ تَمْلِكُوْنَ خَزَآئِنَ رَحْمَةِ
رَبِّيْٓ اِذًا لَّاَمْسَكْتُمْ خَشْيَةَ الْاِنْفَاقِ ؕ
وَكَانَ الْاِنْسَانُ قَتُوْرًا ﴿١٠٠﴾ ع ٧

101. To Moses We gave nine illustrious miracles. Ask the Israelites; Moses came to them. The Pharaoh said to him, "Moses, I believe that you are bewitched."

101. Wa laqad aataynaa Moosaa tis'a Aayaatim bayyinaatin fas'al Baneee Israaa'eela iz jaaa'ahum faqaala lahoo Fir'awnu innee la-aẓunnuka yaa Moosaa masḥooraa.

وَلَقَدْ اٰتَيْنَا مُوْسٰى تِسْعَ اٰيٰتٍۢ بَيِّنٰتٍ
فَسْئَلْ بَنِيْٓ اِسْرَآءِيْلَ اِذْ جَآءَهُمْ فَقَالَ
لَهٗ فِرْعَوْنُ اِنِّيْ لَاَظُنُّكَ يٰمُوْسٰى
مَسْحُوْرًا ﴿١٠١﴾

102. He replied, "Certainly you have come to know that these have been sent by the Lord of the heavens and the earth as lessons to people. Pharaoh, I believe that you are doomed to perdition.

102. Qaala laqad 'alimta maaa anzala haaa'ulaaa'i illaa Rab-bus-samaawaati wal-arḍi baṣaaa'ira wa innee la-aẓun-nuka yaa Fir'awnu masbooraa.

قَالَ لَقَدْ عَلِمْتَ مَآ اَنْزَلَ هٰٓؤُلَآءِ اِلَّا
رَبُّ السَّمٰوٰتِ وَالْاَرْضِ بَصَآئِرَ ۚ وَ
اِنِّيْ لَاَظُنُّكَ يٰفِرْعَوْنُ مَثْبُوْرًا ﴿١٠٢﴾

103. The Pharaoh wanted to expel the Israelites from the land so We drowned him and all who were with him.

103. Fa-araada añy-yastafiz-zahum-minal-arḍi fa-aghraq-naahu wa mamma'ahoo jamee'aa.

فَاَرَادَ اَنْ يَّسْتَفِزَّهُمْ مِّنَ الْاَرْضِ
فَاَغْرَقْنٰهُ وَمَنْ مَّعَهٗ جَمِيْعًا ﴿١٠٣﴾

104. We told the Israelites after this to settle in the land until Our second promise comes true. We will then gather them all together (on the Day of Judgment).

104. Wa qulnaa mim ba'dihee li-Baneee Israaa'eelas-kunul-arḍa fa-izaa jaaa'a wa'dul-Aakhirati ji'naa bikum lafeefaa.

وَّقُلْنَا مِنْۢ بَعْدِهٖ لِبَنِيْٓ اِسْرَآءِيْلَ
اسْكُنُوا الْاَرْضَ فَاِذَا جَآءَ وَعْدُ الْاٰخِرَةِ
جِئْنَا بِكُمْ لَفِيْفًا ﴿١٠٤﴾

105. We sent it (the Quran) in all Truth and in all Truth it came. (Muhammad), We have sent you for no other reason than to be a bearer of glad news and a Warner.

105. Wa bilḥaqqi anzalnaahu wa bilḥaqqi nazal; wa maaa arsalnaaka illaa mubash-shirañw- wa nazeeraa.

وَبِالْحَقِّ اَنْزَلْنٰهُ وَبِالْحَقِّ نَزَلَ ؕ وَمَآ
اَرْسَلْنٰكَ اِلَّا مُبَشِّرًا وَّنَذِيْرًا ﴿۱۰۵﴾

وقف لازم

106. We have divided the Quran into many segments so that you will read them to the people in gradual steps as We reveal them to you from time to time.

106. Wa Qur'aanan faraqnaahu litaqra-ahoo 'alan-naasi 'alaa mukṡiñw-wa nazzalnaahu tan-zeelaa.

وَقُرْاٰنًا فَرَقْنٰهُ لِتَقْرَاَهٗ عَلَى النَّاسِ
عَلٰى مُكْثٍ وَّنَزَّلْنٰهُ تَنْزِيْلًا ﴿۱۰۶﴾

107. Say, "It does not matter whether you believe in it or not; when it is read to those who were given the knowledge (heavenly Books) before it, they bow down and prostrate themselves before the Lord.

107. Qul aaminoo biheee aw laa tu'minooo; innallazeena ootul-'ilma min qabliheee izaa yutlaa 'alayhim yakhirroona lil-azqaani sujjadaa.

قُلْ اٰمِنُوْا بِهٖۤ اَوْ لَا تُؤْمِنُوْا ؕ اِنَّ الَّذِيْنَ
اُوْتُوا الْعِلْمَ مِنْ قَبْلِهٖۤ اِذَا يُتْلٰى عَلَيْهِمْ
يَخِرُّوْنَ لِلْاَذْقَانِ سُجَّدًا ۙ ﴿۱۰۷﴾

108. They say, "Our Lord is free of all defects of being thought of as disregarding His promise."

108. Wa yaqooloona Subḥaana Rabbinaaa in kaana wa'du Rabbinaa lamaf'oolaa.

وَّيَقُوْلُوْنَ سُبْحٰنَ رَبِّنَاۤ اِنْ كَانَ وَعْدُ
رَبِّنَا لَمَفْعُوْلًا ﴿۱۰۸﴾

(Bow Down)

109. They bow down in prostration and weep and it makes them more humble (before the Lord).

109. Wa yakhirroona lil-azqaa-ni yabkoona wa yazeeduhum khushoo'aa. ۩

وَيَخِرُّوْنَ لِلْاَذْقَانِ يَبْكُوْنَ وَ
يَزِيْدُهُمْ خُشُوْعًا ۩ ﴿۱۰۹﴾ السجدة

السجدة ٤

110. (Muhammad), tell them, "It is all the same whether you call Him Allah or the Beneficent. All the good names belong to Him." (Muhammad), do not be too loud or slow in your prayer. Choose a moderate way of praying.

110. Qulid-'ul-laaha awid'ur-Raḥmaana ayyam-maa tad'oo falahul-Asmaaa'ul-Ḥusnaa; wa laa tajhar bi-Ṣalaatika wa laa tukhaafit bihaa wabtaghi bayna zaalika sabeelaa.

قُلِ ادْعُوا اللّٰهَ اَوِ ادْعُوا الرَّحْمٰنَ ؕ
اَيًّا مَّا تَدْعُوْا فَلَهُ الْاَسْمَآءُ الْحُسْنٰى ۚ
وَلَا تَجْهَرْ بِصَلَاتِكَ وَلَا تُخَافِتْ
بِهَا وَابْتَغِ بَيْنَ ذٰلِكَ سَبِيْلًا ﴿۱۱۰﴾

111. Say, "It is only Allah who deserves all praise. He did not beget a son and had no partner in His Kingdom. He did not need any guardian to help Him in His need. Proclaim His greatness.

111. Wa qulil-ḥamdu lillaahil-lazee lam yattakhiz waladañw-wa lam yakul-lahoo shareekun fil-mulki wa lam yakul-lahoo waliyyum-minaz-zulli wa kab-birhu takbeeraa.

وَقُلِ الْحَمْدُ لِلّٰهِ الَّذِيْ لَمْ يَتَّخِذْ
وَلَدًا وَّلَمْ يَكُنْ لَّهٗ شَرِيْكٌ فِى
الْمُلْكِ وَلَمْ يَكُنْ لَّهٗ وَلِيٌّ مِّنَ
الذُّلِّ وَكَبِّرْهُ تَكْبِيْرًا ﴿۱۱۱﴾ ع

ع ١٢ / ١٢

Al-Kahf, The Cave (18)

In the Name of Allah, the Beneficent, the Merciful.

Sûrat al-Kahf-18

(Revealed at Makkah)

Bismillaahir Raḥmaanir Raḥeem

(١٨) سُوْرَةُ الْكَهْفِ مَكِّيَّةٌ (٦٩)

اٰيَاتُهَا ١١٠ — بِسْمِ اللّٰهِ الرَّحْمٰنِ الرَّحِيْمِ — رُكُوْعَاتُهَا ١٢

1. Praise be to Allah. He has sent the Book to His servant and has made it a straightforward guide (for human beings) and it is free of all crookedness

1. Al-ḥamdu lillaahil lazeee anzala 'alaa 'abdihil-Kitaaba wa lam yaj'al-lahoo 'iwajaa.

اَلْحَمْدُ لِلّٰهِ الَّذِيْۤ اَنْزَلَ عَلٰى عَبْدِهِ
الْكِتٰبَ وَلَمْ يَجْعَلْ لَّهٗ عِوَجًا ؕ ﴿۱﴾ سكتة

2. so that he can warn them of His stern retribution, give the glad news of the best and everlasting reward to the righteously striving

2. Qayyimal-liyunzira ba-san shadeedam-mil-ladunhu wa yubashshiral-mu'mineenal-lazeena ya'maloonaṣ-ṣaaliḥaati anna lahum

قَيِّمًا لِّيُنْذِرَ بَاْسًا شَدِيْدًا مِّنْ
لَّدُنْهُ وَيُبَشِّرَ الْمُؤْمِنِيْنَ الَّذِيْنَ
يَعْمَلُوْنَ الصّٰلِحٰتِ اَنَّ لَهُمْ

believers,	ajran ḥasanaa.	أَجْرًا حَسَنًا ۙ (٢)
3. wherein they shall remain forever,	3. Maakiseena feehi abadaa.	مَّاكِثِينَ فِيهِ أَبَدًا ۙ (٣)
4. and admonish those who say that Allah has begotten a son.	4. Wa yunzìral-lazeena qaalut-takhazal-laahu waladaa.	وَّيُنذِرَ الَّذِينَ قَالُوا اتَّخَذَ اللَّهُ وَلَدًا ۖ (٤)
5. Neither they nor their fathers had any knowledge of such utterance (that Allah has begotten a son). Whatever they say about (this matter) are blasphemy and plain lies.	5. Maa lahum bihee min 'ilmiñw-wa laa li-aabaaa'ihim; kaburat kalimatan takhruju min afwaahihim; iñy-yaqooloona illaa kazibaa.	مَا لَهُم بِهِ مِنْ عِلْمٍ وَلَا لِآبَائِهِمْ ۚ كَبُرَتْ كَلِمَةً تَخْرُجُ مِنْ أَفْوَاهِهِمْ ۚ إِن يَقُولُونَ إِلَّا كَذِبًا (٥)
6. Perhaps you will destroy yourself out of grief because they did not believe in this Book.	6. Fala'allaka baakhi'un nafsaka 'alaaa aasaarihim illam yu'minoo bihaazal-ḥadeesi asafaa.	فَلَعَلَّكَ بَاخِعٌ نَّفْسَكَ عَلَىٰ آثَارِهِمْ إِن لَّمْ يُؤْمِنُوا بِهَٰذَا الْحَدِيثِ أَسَفًا (٦)
7. We have caused earthly things to seem attractive so that We can see who will excel in good deeds.	7. Innaa ja'alnaa maa 'alalarḍi zeenatal-lahaa linabluwahum ayyuhum aḥsanu 'amalaa.	إِنَّا جَعَلْنَا مَا عَلَى الْأَرْضِ زِينَةً لَّهَا لِنَبْلُوَهُمْ أَيُّهُمْ أَحْسَنُ عَمَلًا (٧)
8. Let it be known that We will turn all things on earth into barren land.	8. Wa innaa lajaa'iloona maa 'alayhaa ṣa'eedan juruzaa.	وَإِنَّا لَجَاعِلُونَ مَا عَلَيْهَا صَعِيدًا جُرُزًا (٨)
9. Did you think the story of the Companions of the Cave and the Inscription was more marvelous than Our other miracles?	9. Am ḥasibta anna Aṣ-haabal-Kahfi war-Raqeemi kaanoo min Aayaatinaa 'ajabaa.	أَمْ حَسِبْتَ أَنَّ أَصْحَابَ الْكَهْفِ وَالرَّقِيمِ كَانُوا مِنْ آيَاتِنَا عَجَبًا (٩)
10. When the youth sought refuge in the cave, they prayed, "Lord, grant us mercy and help us to get out of this trouble in a righteous way."	10. Iz awal-fityatu ilal-kahfi faqaaloo Rabbanaaa aatinaa mil-ladunka raḥmatañw-wa hayyi' lanaa min amrinaa rashadaa.	إِذْ أَوَى الْفِتْيَةُ إِلَى الْكَهْفِ فَقَالُوا رَبَّنَا آتِنَا مِن لَّدُنكَ رَحْمَةً وَهَيِّئْ لَنَا مِنْ أَمْرِنَا رَشَدًا (١٠)
11. We sealed their ears in the cave for a number of years.	11. Faḍarabnaa 'alaaa aazaanihim fil-kahfi sineena 'adadaa.	فَضَرَبْنَا عَلَىٰ آذَانِهِمْ فِي الْكَهْفِ سِنِينَ عَدَدًا ۙ (١١)
12. Then We roused them to find out which of the party had the correct account of the duration of their sleep in the cave.	12. Summa ba'asnaahum lina'lama ayyul-ḥizbayni aḥṣaa limaa labisooo amadaa.	ثُمَّ بَعَثْنَاهُمْ لِنَعْلَمَ أَيُّ الْحِزْبَيْنِ أَحْصَىٰ لِمَا لَبِثُوا أَمَدًا (١٢) ع ١٢ ١٣
13. We tell you this story for a genuine purpose. They were young people who believed in their Lord and We gave them further guidance.	13. Naḥnu naquṣṣu 'alayka naba-ahum bilḥaqq; innahum fityatun aamanoo bi-Rabbihim wa zidnaahum hudaa.	نَّحْنُ نَقُصُّ عَلَيْكَ نَبَأَهُم بِالْحَقِّ ۚ إِنَّهُمْ فِتْيَةٌ آمَنُوا بِرَبِّهِمْ وَزِدْنَاهُمْ هُدًى (١٣)

14. We strengthened their hearts when they stood up against the idols and said, "Our Lord is the Lord of the heavens and the earth. We shall never worship anyone other than Him lest we commit blasphemy.

14. Wa rabaṭnaa 'alaa quloobihim iz̲ qaamoo faqaaloo Rabbunaa Rabbus-samaawaati wal-arḍi lan-nad'uwa min dooniheee ilaahal-laqad qulnaaa iz̲an shaṭaṭaa.

وَّرَبَطْنَا عَلٰى قُلُوْبِهِمْ اِذْ قَامُوْا
فَقَالُوْا رَبُّنَا رَبُّ السَّمٰوٰتِ وَالْاَرْضِ
لَنْ نَّدْعُوَا۟ مِنْ دُوْنِهٖۤ اِلٰهًا لَّقَدْ
قُلْنَاۤ اِذًا شَطَطًا ﴿١٤﴾

15. Our people have considered other things equal to Him. Why can they not present clear proof in support of their claim? Who is more unjust than one who invents falsehood against Allah?"

15. Haaa'ulaaa'i qawmunat-takhaz̲oo min dooniheee aalihatal law laa ya-toona 'alayhim bisulṭaanim bayyin; faman aẓlamu mimmaniftaraa 'alal-laahi kaz̲ibaa.

هٰۤؤُلَآءِ قَوْمُنَا اتَّخَذُوْا مِنْ دُوْنِهٖۤ
اٰلِهَةً ؕ لَوْلَا يَاْتُوْنَ عَلَيْهِمْ بِسُلْطٰنٍۭ
بَيِّنٍ ؕ فَمَنْ اَظْلَمُ مِمَّنِ افْتَرٰى
عَلَى اللّٰهِ كَذِبًا ؕ ﴿١٥﴾

16. (They were told), "Now that you have abandoned them and what they worship instead of Allah, seek refuge in the cave. Allah will, certainly, grant you mercy and provide you with help to get safely out of this trouble."

16. Wa-iz̲i'tazal-tumoohum wa maa ya'budoona illal-laaha fa-wooo ilal-kahfi yanshur lakum Rabbukum-mirraḥmatihee wa yuhayyi' lakum-min amrikum-mirfaqaa.

وَاِذِ اعْتَزَلْتُمُوْهُمْ وَمَا يَعْبُدُوْنَ اِلَّا
اللّٰهَ فَاْوٗۤا اِلَى الْكَهْفِ يَنْشُرْ لَكُمْ
رَبُّكُمْ مِّنْ رَّحْمَتِهٖ وَيُهَيِّئْ لَكُمْ
مِّنْ اَمْرِكُمْ مِّرْفَقًا ﴿١٦﴾

17. (You could see that no sunlight could reach them during their sleep in the cave). You could see the rising sun decline to the right of their cave and the setting sun move its way to the left whilst they were sleeping in an opening of the cave. This is one of the miracles of Allah. Whomever Allah guides receives the right guidance and you will never find a guardian or guide for those whom He causes to go astray.

17. Wa tarash-shamsa iz̲aa ṭala'at-tazaawaru 'an kahfihim z̲aatal-yameeni wa iz̲aa gharabat taqriḍuhum z̲aatash-shimaali wa hum fee fajwatim-minh; z̲aalika min Aayaatil-laah; mañy-yahdil-laahu fahuwal-muhtad; wa mañy-yuḍlil falan tajida lahoo waliyyam-murshidaa.

وَتَرَى الشَّمْسَ اِذَا طَلَعَتْ تَّزٰوَرُ
عَنْ كَهْفِهِمْ ذَاتَ الْيَمِيْنِ وَاِذَا
غَرَبَتْ تَّقْرِضُهُمْ ذَاتَ الشِّمَالِ
وَهُمْ فِيْ فَجْوَةٍ مِّنْهُ ؕ ذٰلِكَ مِنْ
اٰيٰتِ اللّٰهِ ؕ مَنْ يَّهْدِ اللّٰهُ فَهُوَ
الْمُهْتَدِ ۚ وَمَنْ يُّضْلِلْ فَلَنْ تَجِدَ
لَهٗ وَلِيًّا مُّرْشِدًا ﴿١٧﴾ ع

18. You might think them (the youths) awake (with their eyes wide open) while, in fact, they were sleeping. We turned their bodies from right to left and their dog stretched its front legs on the floor of the cave. Had one looked them over, he would have run away from them in dread.

18. Wa taḥsabuhum ayqaaẓañw-wa hum ruqood; wa nuqallibuhum z̲aatal-yameeni wa z̲aatash-shimaali wa kalbuhum baasiṭun z̲iraa'ayhi bilwaṣeed; lawiṭ-ṭala'ta 'alayhim lawal-layta minhum firaarañw-wa lamuli'ta minhum ru'baa.

وَتَحْسَبُهُمْ اَيْقَاظًا وَّهُمْ رُقُوْدٌ ۖۗ
وَّنُقَلِّبُهُمْ ذَاتَ الْيَمِيْنِ وَذَاتَ
الشِّمَالِ ۖۗ وَكَلْبُهُمْ بَاسِطٌ ذِرَاعَيْهِ
بِالْوَصِيْدِ ؕ لَوِ اطَّلَعْتَ عَلَيْهِمْ لَوَلَّيْتَ
مِنْهُمْ فِرَارًا وَّلَمُلِئْتَ مِنْهُمْ رُعْبًا ﴿١٨﴾

19. We roused them from their sleep so that they would question each other about their stay in the cave. One of them said, "How

19. Wa kaz̲aalika ba'as̲naahum liyatasaaa'aloo baynahum; qaala qaaa'ilum-minhum kam

وَكَذٰلِكَ بَعَثْنٰهُمْ لِيَتَسَآءَلُوْا
بَيْنَهُمْ ؕ قَالَ قَآئِلٌ مِّنْهُمْ كَمْ

long do you think we have stayed here?" They replied, "A day or part of a day." They added, "Your Lord knows better how long we have stayed here. Let us send one of us with this money to the city to get some pure food so that we might eat. He should be careful so that no one will know about us. If they were to recognize us,

labis̲tum qaaloo labis̲naa yawman aw ba'ḍa yawm; qaaloo Rabbukum a'lamu bimaa labis̲tum fab'as̲ooo aḥadakum biwariqikum haaz̲iheee ilalmadeenati falyanẓur ayyuhaaa azkaa ṭa'aaman falya-tikum birizqim-minhu walyatalaṭṭaf wa laa yush'iranna bikum aḥadaa.

لَبِثْتُمْ ۖ قَالُوا لَبِثْنَا يَوْمًا أَوْ بَعْضَ
يَوْمٍ ۚ قَالُوا رَبُّكُمْ أَعْلَمُ بِمَا
لَبِثْتُمْ فَابْعَثُوا أَحَدَكُم بِوَرِقِكُمْ
هَٰذِهِ إِلَى الْمَدِينَةِ فَلْيَنظُرْ أَيُّهَا
أَزْكَىٰ طَعَامًا فَلْيَأْتِكُم بِرِزْقٍ مِّنْهُ
وَلْيَتَلَطَّفْ وَلَا يُشْعِرَنَّ
بِكُمْ أَحَدًا ﴿١٩﴾

20. they would certainly stone us to death or force us to follow their religion. Then we shall never be able to have everlasting happiness."

20. Innahum iñy-yaẓharoo 'alaykum yarjumookum aw yu'eedookum fee millatihim wa lan tufliḥooo iz̲an abadaa.

إِنَّهُمْ إِن يَظْهَرُوا عَلَيْكُمْ
يَرْجُمُوكُمْ أَوْ يُعِيدُوكُمْ فِي مِلَّتِهِمْ
وَلَن تُفْلِحُوا إِذًا أَبَدًا ﴿٢٠﴾

21. We caused their story to become public so that people would know that Allah's promise was true and that there is no doubt about the coming of the Day of Judgment. They started to argue with each other about the matter (Resurrection) and some of them said, "Let us establish a building at the youths' sleeping place (to hide them). Their Lord knew best their intentions about them. The majority prevailed in their suggestion of the establishment of a mosque in that place.

21. Wa kaz̲aalika a's̲arnaa 'alayhim liya'lamooo anna wa'dal-laahi ḥaqquñw-wa annas-Saa'ata laa rayba feehaaa iz̲ yatanaaza'oona baynahum amrahum faqaalub-noo 'alayhim bunyaanaa; Rabbuhum a'lamu bihim; qaalal-laz̲eena ghalaboo 'alaaa amrihim lanattakhiz̲anna 'alayhim-masjidaa.

وَكَذَٰلِكَ أَعْثَرْنَا عَلَيْهِمْ لِيَعْلَمُوا
أَنَّ وَعْدَ اللَّهِ حَقٌّ وَأَنَّ السَّاعَةَ
لَا رَيْبَ فِيهَا إِذْ يَتَنَازَعُونَ بَيْنَهُمْ
أَمْرَهُمْ ۖ فَقَالُوا ابْنُوا عَلَيْهِم بُنْيَانًا ۖ
رَّبُّهُمْ أَعْلَمُ بِهِمْ ۚ قَالَ الَّذِينَ غَلَبُوا
عَلَىٰ أَمْرِهِمْ لَنَتَّخِذَنَّ عَلَيْهِم
مَّسْجِدًا ﴿٢١﴾

22. (With regard to the number of the youths) a number of people say, "There were three and the dog was the fourth one," Others say, "There were five and the dog was the sixth one." In reality, they are just feeling around in the dark. Still some of them say, "There were seven and the dog was the eighth one." (Muhammad), say, "My Lord has the best knowledge of their number. You know very little about it." Do not insist on arguing with them, but merely tell them the story as it has been revealed to you and do not ask anyone about them.

22. Sayaqooloona s̲alaas̲aturraabi'uhum kalbuhum wa yaqooloona khamsatun saadisuhum kalbuhum rajmam bilghayb; wa yaqooloona sab'atuñw-wa s̲aaminuhum kalbuhum; qur-Rabbeee a'lamu bi'iddatihim-maa ya'lamuhum illaa qaleel; falaa tumaari feehim illaa miraaa'an ẓaahirañw-wa laa tastafti feehimminhum aḥadaa.

سَيَقُولُونَ ثَلَاثَةٌ رَّابِعُهُمْ
كَلْبُهُمْ وَيَقُولُونَ خَمْسَةٌ
سَادِسُهُمْ كَلْبُهُمْ رَجْمًا بِالْغَيْبِ ۖ
وَيَقُولُونَ سَبْعَةٌ وَثَامِنُهُمْ كَلْبُهُمْ ۚ
قُل رَّبِّي أَعْلَمُ بِعِدَّتِهِم مَّا
يَعْلَمُهُمْ إِلَّا قَلِيلٌ ۗ فَلَا تُمَارِ فِيهِمْ
إِلَّا مِرَاءً ظَاهِرًا وَلَا تَسْتَفْتِ
فِيهِم مِّنْهُمْ أَحَدًا ﴿٢٢﴾

23. Never say of something, "I shall do it tomorrow,"

23. Wa laa taqoolannalishay'in innee faa'ilun

وَلَا تَقُولَنَّ لِشَيْءٍ إِنِّي فَاعِلٌ

نصف القرآن باعتبار عدد الحروف بأن التاء بعد الياء من النصف الأول واللام الثانية من النصف الأخير ١٢

ذٰلِكَ غَدًا ۝٢٣

zaalika ghadaa.

إِلَّآ أَن يَشَآءَ ٱللَّهُ ۚ وَٱذْكُر رَّبَّكَ
إِذَا نَسِيتَ وَقُلْ عَسَىٰٓ أَن يَهْدِيَنِ
رَبِّى لِأَقْرَبَ مِنْ هَٰذَا رَشَدًا ۝٢٤

24. Illaaa añy-yashaaa'al-laah; wazkur-Rabbaka izaa naseeta wa qul 'asaaa añy-yahdiyani Rabbee li-aqraba min haazaa rashadaa.

24. without adding, "if Allah wills." Recall your Lord if you forget to do something. Say, "I hope that my Lord will provide me better guidance."

وَلَبِثُوا۟ فِى كَهْفِهِمْ ثَلَٰثَ مِا۟ئَةٍ
سِنِينَ وَٱزْدَادُوا۟ تِسْعًا ۝٢٥

25. Wa labisoo fee kahfihim salaasa mi'atin sineena wazdaadoo tis'aa.

25. They, in fact, stayed in the cave for three hundred plus nine further years.

قُلِ ٱللَّهُ أَعْلَمُ بِمَا لَبِثُوا۟ ۖ لَهُۥ غَيْبُ
ٱلسَّمَٰوَٰتِ وَٱلْأَرْضِ ۖ أَبْصِرْ بِهِۦ وَ
أَسْمِعْ ۚ مَا لَهُم مِّن دُونِهِۦ مِن
وَلِىٍّ وَلَا يُشْرِكُ فِى حُكْمِهِۦٓ
أَحَدًا ۝٢٦

26. Qulil-laahu a'lamu bimaa labisoo lahoo ghaybus-samaa-waati wal-arḍi abṣir bihee wa-asmi'; maa lahum-min doonihee miñw-waliyyiñw-wa laa yushriku fee ḥukmiheee aḥadaa.

26. (Muhammad), say, "Allah knows best how long they stayed there; to Him belongs the unseen of both the heavens and the earth. How clear is His sight and how keen His hearing! No one other than Him is their guardian and no one shares His Judgment.

وَٱتْلُ مَآ أُوحِىَ إِلَيْكَ مِن
كِتَابِ رَبِّكَ ۖ لَا مُبَدِّلَ لِكَلِمَٰتِهِۦ
وَلَن تَجِدَ مِن دُونِهِۦ مُلْتَحَدًا ۝٢٧

27. Watlu maaa ooḥiya ilayka min Kitaabi Rabbika laa mubaddila li-Kalimaatihee wa lan tajida min doonihee multaḥadaa.

27. Read whatever is revealed to you from the Book of your Lord. No one can change His words and you can never find any refuge other than Him.

وَٱصْبِرْ نَفْسَكَ مَعَ ٱلَّذِينَ
يَدْعُونَ رَبَّهُم بِٱلْغَدَوٰةِ وَٱلْعَشِىِّ
يُرِيدُونَ وَجْهَهُۥ ۖ وَلَا تَعْدُ عَيْنَاكَ
عَنْهُمْ تُرِيدُ زِينَةَ ٱلْحَيَوٰةِ ٱلدُّنْيَا ۖ
وَلَا تُطِعْ مَنْ أَغْفَلْنَا قَلْبَهُۥ عَن
ذِكْرِنَا وَٱتَّبَعَ هَوَىٰهُ وَكَانَ
أَمْرُهُۥ فُرُطًا ۝٢٨ الثلثة

28. Waṣbir nafsaka ma'al-lazeena yad'oona Rabbahum bilghadaati wal'ashiyyi yuree-doona Wajhahoo wa laa ta'du 'aynaaka 'anhum tureedu zeenatal-ḥayaatiddunyaa wa laa tuṭi'man aghfalnaa qalbahoo 'an zikrinaa wattaba'a hawaahu wa kaana amruhoo furuṭaa.

28. Be patient with those who worship their Lord in the mornings and evenings to seek His pleasure. Do not overlook them to seek the worldly pleasures. Do not obey those whom We have caused to neglect Us and instead follow their own desires beyond all limits.

وَقُلِ ٱلْحَقُّ مِن رَّبِّكُمْ ۖ فَمَن شَآءَ
فَلْيُؤْمِن وَمَن شَآءَ فَلْيَكْفُرْ ۚ
إِنَّآ أَعْتَدْنَا لِلظَّٰلِمِينَ نَارًا أَحَاطَ
بِهِمْ سُرَادِقُهَا ۚ وَإِن يَسْتَغِيثُوا۟
يُغَاثُوا۟ بِمَآءٍ كَٱلْمُهْلِ يَشْوِى ٱلْوُجُوهَ ۚ

29. Wa qulil-ḥaqqu mir-Rabbikum faman shaaa'a falyu'miñw-wa man shaaa'a falyakfur; innaaa a'tadnaa liz-zaalimeena Naaran aḥaaṭa bihim suraadiquhaa; wa iñy-yastagheesoo yughaasoo bi-maaa'in kalmuhli yashwil-wujooh;

29. Say, "Truth comes from your Lord. Let people have faith or disbelieve as they choose." For the unjust We have prepared a fire which will engulf them with its (flames). Whenever they cry for help they will be answered with water as hot as the residue in boiling oil which will scald their faces. How terrible is such a drink

and such a resting place!

30. The righteously striving believers should know that We do not neglect the reward of those who do good deeds.

31. They will be admitted to the gardens of Eden wherein streams flow. They will rest on soft couches, decked with bracelets of gold and clothed in green silk garments and shining brocade. How blissful is such a reward and resting place!

32. (Muhammad), tell them the parable of the two men. To one of them We had given two gardens of vines surrounded by palm trees with a piece of farmland between them,

33. both gardens would yield fruits and did not fail, and we made a stream flow through the middle of the gardens.

34. Whatever was produced belonged to him. To his friend he exclaimed, "I have more wealth and greater man-power than you."

35. He unjustly entered his garden and said, "I do not think this (property) will ever perish

36. nor do I think that there will be a Day of Judgment. Even if I shall be brought before my Lord, I certainly deserve to have a better place than this."

37. His friend said to him, "How can you disbelieve in the One who turned clay into sperm

bi'sash-sharaab; wa saaa'at murtafaqaa.

30. Innal-lazeena aamanoo wa 'amiluṣ-ṣaaliḥaati innaa laa nuḍee'u ajra man aḥsana 'amalaa.

31. Ulaaa'ika lahum Jannaatu 'Adnin tajree min taḥtihimul-anhaaru yuḥallawna feehaa min asaawira min zahabiñw-wa yal-basoona siyaaban khuḍram-min sundusiñw-wa istabraqim-muttaki'eena feehaa 'alal-araaa'ik; ni'mas-sawaab; wa ḥasunat murtafaqaa.

32. Waḍrib lahum-masalar-rajulayni ja'alnaa li-aḥadihimaa jannatayni min a'naabiñw-wa ḥafafnaahumaa binakhliñw-wa ja'alnaa baynahumaa zar'aa.

33. Kiltal-jannatayni aatat ukulahaa wa lam taẓlim-minhu shay'añw-wa fajjarnaa khi-laala-humaa naharaa.

34. Wa kaana lahoo samarun faqaala liṣaaḥibihee wa huwa yuḥaawiruhooo ana aksaru minka maalañw-wa a'azzu nafaraa.

35. Wa dakhala jannatahoo wa huwa ẓaalimul-linafsihee qaala maaa aẓunnu an tabeeda haaziheee abadaa.

36. Wa maaa aẓunnus-Saa'ata qaaa'imatañw-wa la'ir-ruditttu ilaa Rabbee la-ajidanna khay-ram-minhaa munqalabaa.

37. Qaala lahoo ṣaaḥibuhoo wa huwa yuḥaawiruhooo akafarta billazee khalaqaka min

بِئْسَ الشَّرَابُ ۭ وَسَاۗءَتْ مُرْتَفَقًا ﴿٢٩﴾
اِنَّ الَّذِيْنَ اٰمَنُوْا وَعَمِلُوا الصّٰلِحٰتِ
اِنَّا لَا نُضِيْعُ اَجْرَ مَنْ اَحْسَنَ عَمَلًا ﴿٣٠﴾
اُولٰۗىِٕكَ لَهُمْ جَنّٰتُ عَدْنٍ تَجْرِيْ
مِنْ تَحْتِهِمُ الْاَنْهٰرُ يُحَلَّوْنَ فِيْهَا
مِنْ اَسَاوِرَ مِنْ ذَهَبٍ وَّيَلْبَسُوْنَ
ثِيَابًا خُضْرًا مِّنْ سُنْدُسٍ وَّ
اِسْتَبْرَقٍ مُّتَّكِـِٕيْنَ فِيْهَا عَلَي الْاَرَاۗىِٕكِ ۭ
نِعْمَ الثَّوَابُ ۭ وَحَسُنَتْ مُرْتَفَقًا ﴿٣١﴾ ع ٩ ١٦
وَاضْرِبْ لَهُمْ مَّثَلًا رَّجُلَيْنِ جَعَلْنَا
لِاَحَدِهِمَا جَنَّتَيْنِ مِنْ اَعْنَابٍ
وَّحَفَفْنٰهُمَا بِنَخْلٍ وَّجَعَلْنَا
بَيْنَهُمَا زَرْعًا ﴿٣٢﴾
كِلْتَا الْجَنَّتَيْنِ اٰتَتْ اُكُلَهَا
وَلَمْ تَظْلِمْ مِّنْهُ شَـيْــــًٔا ۙ وَّفَجَّرْنَا
خِلٰلَهُمَا نَهَرًا ﴿٣٣﴾
وَّكَانَ لَهٗ ثَمَرٌ ۚ فَقَالَ لِصَاحِبِهٖ
وَهُوَ يُحَاوِرُهٗٓ اَنَا اَكْثَرُ مِنْكَ
مَالًا وَّاَعَزُّ نَفَرًا ﴿٣٤﴾
وَدَخَلَ جَنَّتَهٗ وَهُوَ ظَالِمٌ لِّنَفْسِهٖ ۚ
قَالَ مَآ اَظُنُّ اَنْ تَبِيْدَ هٰذِهٖٓ اَبَدًا ﴿٣٥﴾
وَّمَآ اَظُنُّ السَّاعَةَ قَاۗىِٕمَةً ۙ وَّلَىِٕنْ
رُّدِدْتُّ اِلٰى رَبِّيْ لَاَجِدَنَّ خَيْرًا
مِّنْهَا مُنْقَلَبًا ﴿٣٦﴾
قَالَ لَهٗ صَاحِبُهٗ وَهُوَ يُحَاوِرُهٗٓ
اَكَفَرْتَ بِالَّذِيْ خَلَقَكَ مِنْ

out of which He created as a man?

turaabin s̲umma min nuṭfatin s̲umma sawwaaka rajulaa.

تُرَابٍ ثُمَّ مِنْ نُّطْفَةٍ ثُمَّ سَوّٰىكَ رَجُلًا ﴿٣٧﴾

38. I believe that He is Allah my Lord and I do not consider anything equal to Him."

38. Laakinna Huwal-laahu Rabbee wa laaa ushriku bi-Rabbeee aḥadaa.

لٰكِنَّا۠ هُوَ اللّٰهُ رَبِّيْ وَلَآ اُشْرِكُ بِرَبِّيْٓ اَحَدًا ﴿٣٨﴾

39. When entering your garden, you should have said, "This is what Allah willed; all power belongs to Allah. Even if you consider me inferior to yourself in wealth and offspring,

39. Wa law laaa iz̲ dakhalta jannataka qulta maa shaaa'al-laahu laa quwwata illaa billaah; in tarani ana aqalla minka maalañw-wa waladaa.

وَلَوْلَآ اِذْ دَخَلْتَ جَنَّتَكَ قُلْتَ مَا شَآءَ اللّٰهُ ۙ لَا قُوَّةَ اِلَّا بِاللّٰهِ ۚ اِنْ تَرَنِ اَنَا اَقَلَّ مِنْكَ مَالًا وَّوَلَدًا ﴿٣٩﴾

40. perhaps my Lord will give me a garden better than yours and strike your garden with a thunderbolt from the sky to turn it into a barren ground,

40. Fa'asaa Rabbeee añy-yu'ti-yani khayram-min jannatika wa yursila 'alayhaa ḥusbaanam-minassamaaa'i fatuṣbiḥa ṣa'eedan zalaqaa.

فَعَسٰى رَبِّيْٓ اَنْ يُّؤْتِيَنِ خَيْرًا مِّنْ جَنَّتِكَ وَيُرْسِلَ عَلَيْهَا حُسْبَانًا مِّنَ السَّمَآءِ فَتُصْبِحَ صَعِيْدًا زَلَقًا ﴿٤٠﴾

41. or cause the streams in your garden to disappear under the ground such that you will never be able to find them.

41. Aw yuṣbiḥa maaa'uhaa ghawran falan tastaṭee'a lahoo ṭalabaa.

اَوْ يُصْبِحَ مَآؤُهَا غَوْرًا فَلَنْ تَسْتَطِيْعَ لَهٗ طَلَبًا ﴿٤١﴾

42. (Sure enough the rich person's) fruits were all destroyed and he began to wring his hands in grief for all that he had invested in his garden. He found his garden tumbled to its trellises and said, "Would that I had not considered anything equal to my Lord."

42. Wa uḥeeṭa bis̲amarihee fa-aṣbaḥa yuqallibu kaffayhi 'alaa maaa anfaqa feehaa wa hiya khaawiyatun 'alaa 'urooshihaa wa yaqoolu yaalaytanee lam ushrik bi-Rabbeee aḥadaa.

وَاُحِيْطَ بِثَمَرِهٖ فَاَصْبَحَ يُقَلِّبُ كَفَّيْهِ عَلٰى مَآ اَنْفَقَ فِيْهَا وَهِيَ خَاوِيَةٌ عَلٰى عُرُوْشِهَا وَيَقُوْلُ يٰلَيْتَنِيْ لَمْ اُشْرِكْ بِرَبِّيْٓ اَحَدًا ﴿٤٢﴾

43. He had no one besides Allah to help him, nor could he himself achieve any success.

43. Wa lam takul-lahoo fi'atuñy-yanṣuroonahoo min doonil-laahi wa maa kaana muntaṣiraa.

وَلَمْ تَكُنْ لَّهٗ فِئَةٌ يَّنْصُرُوْنَهٗ مِنْ دُوْنِ اللّٰهِ وَمَا كَانَ مُنْتَصِرًا ﴿٤٣﴾

44. In such helplessness, the human being realizes that it is Allah who is the true Guardian and His rewards and recompense are the best.

44. Hunaalikal walaayatu lillaahil-ḥaqq; huwa khayrun s̲awaabañw-wa khayrun 'uqbaa.

هُنَالِكَ الْوَلَايَةُ لِلّٰهِ الْحَقِّ ۭ هُوَ خَيْرٌ ثَوَابًا وَّخَيْرٌ عُقْبًا ﴿٤٤﴾ ع ٥ ١٣ ١٧

45. (Muhammad), say to them, "The worldly life resembles the (seasonal) plants of earth that blossom by the help of the water which Allah sends from the sky.

45. Waḍrib lahum-mas̲alal-ḥayaatid-dunyaa kamaaa'in anzalnaahu minassamaaa'i

وَاضْرِبْ لَهُمْ مَّثَلَ الْحَيٰوةِ الدُّنْيَا كَمَآءٍ اَنْزَلْنٰهُ مِنَ السَّمَآءِ

After a short time all of them fade away and the winds scatter them (and turn them into dust). Allah has power over all things.

fakhtalaṭa bihee nabaatul-arḍi fa-aṣbaḥa hasheeman tazroo-hur-riyaaḥ; wa kaanal-laahu ‘alaa kulli shay’im-muqtadiraa.

فَاخْتَلَطَ بِهٖ نَبَاتُ الْاَرْضِ فَاَصْبَحَ
هَشِيْمًا تَذْرُوْهُ الرِّيٰحُ ؕ وَكَانَ
اللّٰهُ عَلٰى كُلِّ شَىْءٍ مُّقْتَدِرًا ﴿۴۵﴾

46. Children and property are the ornaments of the worldly life, but for deeds which continually produce virtue one can obtain better rewards from Allah and have greater hope in Him.

46. Al-maalu walbanoona zeenatul-ḥayaatid-dunyaa wal-baaqiyaatuṣ-ṣaaliḥaatu khayrun ‘inda Rabbika-sawaa-bañw-wa khayrun amalaa.

اَلْمَالُ وَالْبَنُوْنَ زِيْنَةُ الْحَيٰوةِ
الدُّنْيَا ۚ وَالْبٰقِيٰتُ الصّٰلِحٰتُ خَيْرٌ
عِنْدَ رَبِّكَ ثَوَابًا وَّخَيْرٌ اَمَلًا ﴿۴۶﴾

47. On the day when We will cause the mountains to travel around and the earth to turn into a leveled plain, We will also bring all human beings together. We would not leave any of them behind.

47. Wa Yawma nusayyirul jibaala wa taral-arḍa baariza-tañw-wa ḥasharnaahum falam nughaadir minhum aḥadaa.

وَيَوْمَ نُسَيِّرُ الْجِبَالَ وَتَرَى الْاَرْضَ
بَارِزَةً ۙ وَّحَشَرْنٰهُمْ فَلَمْ نُغَادِرْ
مِنْهُمْ اَحَدًا ﴿۴۷﴾

48. They will all be lined up in the presence of your Lord who will tell them, "Despite your belief that there would never be a Day of Judgment, all of you are brought in Our presence just as though We had created you for the first time. You believed that Our promise could never come true."

48. Wa ‘uriḍoo ‘alaa Rabbika ṣaffaa; laqad ji’tumoonaa kamaa khalaqnaakum awwala marrah; bal za‘amtum allan-naj‘ala lakum-maw‘idaa.

وَعُرِضُوْا عَلٰى رَبِّكَ صَفًّا ؕ لَقَدْ
جِئْتُمُوْنَا كَمَا خَلَقْنٰكُمْ اَوَّلَ مَرَّةٍ ۭ
بَلْ زَعَمْتُمْ اَلَّنْ نَّجْعَلَ لَكُمْ مَّوْعِدًا ﴿۴۸﴾

49. When the record of everyone's deeds is placed before him, you will see the criminals terrified from what the record contains. They will say, "Woe to us! What kind of record is this that has missed nothing small or great?" They will find whatever they have done right before their very eyes. Your Lord is not unjust to anyone.

49. Wa wuḍi‘al-kitaabu fata-ral-mujrimeena mushfi-qeena mimmaa feehi wa yaqooloona yaa waylatanaa maa lihaazal kitaabi laa yughaadiru ṣaghee-ratañw-wa laa kabeeratan illaaa aḥṣaahaa; wa wajadoo maa ‘amiloo ḥaaḍiraa; wa laa yaẓlimu Rabbuka aḥadaa.

وَوُضِعَ الْكِتٰبُ فَتَرَى الْمُجْرِمِيْنَ
مُشْفِقِيْنَ مِمَّا فِيْهِ وَيَقُوْلُوْنَ
يٰوَيْلَتَنَا مَالِ هٰذَا الْكِتٰبِ لَا
يُغَادِرُ صَغِيْرَةً وَّلَا كَبِيْرَةً
اِلَّاۤ اَحْصٰىهَا ۚ وَوَجَدُوْا مَا عَمِلُوْا
حَاضِرًا ؕ وَلَا يَظْلِمُ رَبُّكَ اَحَدًا ﴿۴۹﴾ ع ٦ ٥ ١٨

50. When We told the angels to prostrate in honor of Adam (before Us) they all obeyed except Iblis. He was a jinn and he sinned against the command of his Lord. Why do you (people) obey him and his offspring instead of Me, even though they are your enemies? How terrible will be the recompense that the wrong doers will receive!

50. Wa iz-qulnaa lilma-laaa’ikatis-judoo li Aadama fasajadooo illaaa Ibleesa kaana minal-jinni fafasaqa ‘an amri Rabbih; afatattakhizoonahoo wazurriyyatahooo awliyaaa’a min doonee wa hum lakum ‘aduww; bi’sa lizzaalimeena badalaa.

وَاِذْ قُلْنَا لِلْمَلٰٓئِكَةِ اسْجُدُوْا
لِاٰدَمَ فَسَجَدُوْۤا اِلَّاۤ اِبْلِيْسَ ؕ كَانَ
مِنَ الْجِنِّ فَفَسَقَ عَنْ اَمْرِ رَبِّهٖ ؕ
اَفَتَتَّخِذُوْنَهٗ وَذُرِّيَّتَهٗۤ اَوْلِيَآءَ
مِنْ دُوْنِيْ وَهُمْ لَكُمْ عَدُوٌّ ؕ
بِئْسَ لِلظّٰلِمِيْنَ بَدَلًا ﴿۵۰﴾

51. I did not call (the unjust) to witness the creation of the heavens and earth nor to witness their own creation nor did I want

51. Maaa ash-hattuhum-khalqassamaawaati wal-arḍi wa laa khalqa anfusihim wa maa

مَاۤ اَشْهَدْتُّهُمْ خَلْقَ السَّمٰوٰتِ
وَالْاَرْضِ وَلَا خَلْقَ اَنْفُسِهِمْ ۪ وَمَا

to be helped by those who lead people astray.

kuntu muttakhizal muḍilleena ‘aḍudaa.

كُنْتُ مُتَّخِذَ الْمُضِلِّيْنَ عَضُدًا ﴿٥١﴾

52. On the day when Allah asks the idolaters to seek help from their idols, they will call their idols for help, but the idols would not answer them; We shall separate the two parties from each other by a barrier.

52. Wa Yawma yaqoolu naadoo shurakaaa’i-yal-lazeena za‘amtum-fada‘aw-hum falam yastajeeboo lahum wa ja‘alnaa baynahum-maw-biqaa.

وَيَوْمَ يَقُوْلُ نَادُوْا شُرَكَآءِيَ
الَّذِيْنَ زَعَمْتُمْ فَدَعَوْهُمْ فَلَمْ
يَسْتَجِيْبُوْا لَهُمْ وَجَعَلْنَا بَيْنَهُمْ
مَّوْبِقًا ﴿٥٢﴾

53. When the criminals see hellfire, they will have no doubt about falling (headlong) therein, or having failed to find anyone to save them.

53. Wa ra-al-mujrimoonan-Naara faẓannooo annahum-muwaaqi‘oohaa wa lam yajidoo ‘anhaa maṣrifaa.

وَرَاَ الْمُجْرِمُوْنَ النَّارَ فَظَنُّوْٓا اَنَّهُمْ
مُّوَاقِعُوْهَا وَلَمْ يَجِدُوْا عَنْهَا
مَصْرِفًا ﴿٥٣﴾ ع ١٩

54. We have given various examples in this Quran for people to learn a lesson, but the human being is the most contentious creature.

54. Wa laqad ṣarrafnaa fee haazal-Qur‘aani linnaasi min kulli masal; wa kaanal insaanu aksara shay’in jadalaa.

وَلَقَدْ صَرَّفْنَا فِيْ هٰذَا الْقُرْاٰنِ
لِلنَّاسِ مِنْ كُلِّ مَثَلٍ ؕ وَكَانَ
الْاِنْسَانُ اَكْثَرَ شَيْءٍ جَدَلًا ﴿٥٤﴾

55. What prevents people from having faith when guidance comes to them or from asking for forgiveness from their Lord before they face the kind of torment that the ancient people experienced or a new form of torment.

55. Wa maa mana‘an-naasa añy-yu’minooo iz jaaa’ahumul-hudaa wa yastaghfiroo Rab-bahum illaaa an ta-tiyahum sunnatul-awwaleena aw ya-tiyahumul-‘azaabu qubulaa.

وَمَا مَنَعَ النَّاسَ اَنْ يُّؤْمِنُوْٓا اِذْ
جَآءَهُمُ الْهُدٰى وَيَسْتَغْفِرُوْا
رَبَّهُمْ اِلَّآ اَنْ تَاْتِيَهُمْ سُنَّةُ
الْاَوَّلِيْنَ اَوْ يَاْتِيَهُمُ الْعَذَابُ
قُبُلًا ﴿٥٥﴾

56. The only reason for Our sending the Messengers is to give the human being the glad news of Our mercy and to warn him about Our wrath. The unbelievers argue by false means to refute the Truth. They mock My miracles and warnings.

56. Wa maa nursilul-mursaleena illaa mubashshi-reena wa munzireen; wa yujaadilul-lazeena kafaroo bilbaaṭili liyudḥiḍoo bihil-ḥaqqa wattakhazooo Aayaatee wa maaa unziroo huzuwaa.

وَمَا نُرْسِلُ الْمُرْسَلِيْنَ اِلَّا مُبَشِّرِيْنَ
وَمُنْذِرِيْنَ ۚ وَيُجَادِلُ الَّذِيْنَ كَفَرُوْا
بِالْبَاطِلِ لِيُدْحِضُوْا بِهِ الْحَقَّ
وَاتَّخَذُوْٓا اٰيٰتِيْ وَمَآ اُنْذِرُوْا هُزُوًا ﴿٥٦﴾

57. Who are more unjust than those who are reminded of the revelations of their Lord but have disregarded them and have forgotten their deeds? We have veiled their hearts and sealed their ears so that they cannot understand. Even if you call them to the right path, they will never accept guidance.

57. Wa man aẓlamu mimman zukkira bi-Aayaati Rabbihee fa-a‘raḍa ‘anhaa wa nasiya maa qaddamat yadaah; innaa ja‘al-naa ‘alaa quloobihim akinnatan añy-yafqahoohu wa feee aazaanihim waqraa; wa in tad‘uhum ilal-hudaa falañy-yahtadooo izan abadaa.

وَمَنْ اَظْلَمُ مِمَّنْ ذُكِّرَ بِاٰيٰتِ رَبِّهٖ
فَاَعْرَضَ عَنْهَا وَنَسِيَ مَا قَدَّمَتْ
يَدٰهُ ؕ اِنَّا جَعَلْنَا عَلٰى قُلُوْبِهِمْ
اَكِنَّةً اَنْ يَّفْقَهُوْهُ وَفِيْٓ اٰذَانِهِمْ
وَقْرًا ؕ وَاِنْ تَدْعُهُمْ اِلَى الْهُدٰى
فَلَنْ يَّهْتَدُوْٓا اِذًا اَبَدًا ﴿٥٧﴾

58. Your Lord is All-forgiving and All-merciful. Had He wanted to punish them for their sins, He would have been prompt to torment them. For their punishment there is an appointed time, after which there will be no way for them to escape.

58. Wa Rabbukal-Ghafooru zur-raḥmati law yu'aakhi-zuhum bimaa kasaboo la'ajjala lahumul-'azaab; bal lahum maw'idul-lañy-yajidoo min doonihee maw'ilaa.

وَرَبُّكَ الْغَفُورُ ذُو الرَّحْمَةِ ۖ
لَوْ يُؤَاخِذُهُم بِمَا كَسَبُوا لَعَجَّلَ
لَهُمُ الْعَذَابَ ۚ بَل لَّهُم مَّوْعِدٌ
لَّن يَجِدُوا مِن دُونِهِ مَوْئِلًا ﴿٥٨﴾

59. We only destroyed the inhabitants of certain towns when they had committed injustice and did not repent before Our deadline.

59. Wa tikal-quraaa ahlak-naahum lammaa ẓalamoo wa ja'alnaa limahlikihim-maw'i-daa.

وَتِلْكَ الْقُرَىٰ أَهْلَكْنَاهُمْ لَمَّا
ظَلَمُوا وَجَعَلْنَا لِمَهْلِكِهِم
مَّوْعِدًا ﴿٥٩﴾ ع

60. (Consider) when Moses said to his young companion, "I shall continue traveling until I reach the junction of the two seas or have traveled for many years."

60. Wa iz-qaala Moosaa lifataahu laaa abraḥu ḥattaaa ablugha majma'al-baḥrayni aw amḍiya ḥuqubaa.

وَإِذْ قَالَ مُوسَىٰ لِفَتَاهُ لَا أَبْرَحُ حَتَّىٰ
أَبْلُغَ مَجْمَعَ الْبَحْرَيْنِ أَوْ أَمْضِيَ حُقُبًا ﴿٦٠﴾

61. When they reached the junction of the two seas they found out that they had forgotten all about the fish (which they had carried for food). The fish found its way into the sea.

61. Falammaa balaghaa maj-ma'a baynihimaa nasiyaa ḥootahumaa fattakhaza sabee-lahoo fil-baḥri sarabaa.

فَلَمَّا بَلَغَا مَجْمَعَ بَيْنِهِمَا نَسِيَا
حُوتَهُمَا فَاتَّخَذَ سَبِيلَهُ فِي
الْبَحْرِ سَرَبًا ﴿٦١﴾

62. Moses asked his young companion when they crossed this point, "Bring us our food; the journey has made us tired."

62. Falammaa jaawazaa qaala lifataahu aatinaa ghadaaa'anaa laqad laqeenaa min safarinaa haazaa naṣabaa.

فَلَمَّا جَاوَزَا قَالَ لِفَتَاهُ آتِنَا
غَدَاءَنَا لَقَدْ لَقِينَا مِن سَفَرِنَا
هَٰذَا نَصَبًا ﴿٦٢﴾

63. His companion replied, "Do you remember the rock on which we took rest? Satan made me forget to mention to you the story of the fish and how it amazingly made its way into the sea.

63. Qaala ara'ayta iz-away-naaa ilaṣ-ṣakhrati fa-innee naseetul-ḥoota wa maaa ansaa-neehu illash-Shayṭaanu an azkurah; wattakhaza sabeela-hoo filbaḥri 'ajabaa.

قَالَ أَرَأَيْتَ إِذْ أَوَيْنَا إِلَى الصَّخْرَةِ
فَإِنِّي نَسِيتُ الْحُوتَ وَمَا أَنسَانِيهُ
إِلَّا الشَّيْطَانُ أَنْ أَذْكُرَهُ ۚ وَاتَّخَذَ
سَبِيلَهُ فِي الْبَحْرِ ۚ عَجَبًا ﴿٦٣﴾

64. Moses said, "That is exactly what we are seeking. They followed their own footprints back (to the rock)."

64. Qaala zaalika maa kunnaa nabghi fartaddaa 'alaaa aaṣaari-himaa qaṣaṣaa.

قَالَ ذَٰلِكَ مَا كُنَّا نَبْغِ ۚ فَارْتَدَّا
عَلَىٰ آثَارِهِمَا قَصَصًا ﴿٦٤﴾

65. There they met one of Our servants who had received blessings and knowledge from Us.

65. Fawajadaa 'abdam-min 'ibaadinaaa aataynaahu Raḥma-tam-min 'indinaa wa 'allamnaa-hu mil-ladunnaa 'ilmaa.

فَوَجَدَا عَبْدًا مِّنْ عِبَادِنَا آتَيْنَاهُ
رَحْمَةً مِّنْ عِندِنَا وَعَلَّمْنَاهُ مِن
لَّدُنَّا عِلْمًا ﴿٦٥﴾

66. Moses asked him, "Can I follow you so that you will teach me the guidance that you have received?"

66. Qaala lahoo Moosaa hal attabi'uka 'alaaa an tu'allimani mimmaa 'ullimta rushdaa.

قَالَ لَهُ مُوسَىٰ هَلْ أَتَّبِعُكَ عَلَىٰ
أَن تُعَلِّمَنِ مِمَّا عُلِّمْتَ رُشْدًا ﴿٦٦﴾

67. He replied, "You will not be able to have patience with me.

67. Qaala innaka lan tastaṭee'a ma'iya ṣabraa.

قَالَ إِنَّكَ لَنْ تَسْتَطِيعَ مَعِيَ صَبْرًا ﴿٦٧﴾

68. "How can you remain patient with that of which you did not have complete information?"

68. Wa kayfa taṣbiru 'alaa maa lam tuḥiṭ bihee khubraa.

وَكَيْفَ تَصْبِرُ عَلَىٰ مَا لَمْ تُحِطْ
بِهِ خُبْرًا ﴿٦٨﴾

69. Moses said, "If Allah wishes, you will find me patient and I shall not disobey any of your orders."

69. Qaala satajiduneee in shaaa'al-laahu ṣaabirañw-wa laaa a'ṣee laka amraa.

قَالَ سَتَجِدُنِيٓ إِن شَآءَ ٱللَّهُ صَابِرًا
وَلَآ أَعْصِي لَكَ أَمْرًا ﴿٦٩﴾

70. He said to Moses, "If you follow me, do not ask me about anything until I tell you the story about it."

70. Qaala fa-init-taba'tanee falaa tas'alnee 'an shay'in ḥattaaa uḥdisa laka minhu zikraa.

قَالَ فَإِنِ ٱتَّبَعْتَنِي فَلَا تَسْـَٔلْنِي عَن
شَيْءٍ حَتَّىٰٓ أُحْدِثَ لَكَ مِنْهُ ذِكْرًا ﴿٧٠﴾ ع ١١ / ٢١

71. They started their journey and some time later they embarked in a boat in which he made a hole. Moses asked him, "Did you make the hole to drown the people on board? This is certainly very strange."

71. Fanṭalaqaa; ḥattaaa izaa rakibaa fis-safeenati kharaqahaa qaala; akharaqtahaa litughriqa ahlahaa laqad ji'ta shay'an imraa.

فَٱنطَلَقَا وقفة حَتَّىٰٓ إِذَا رَكِبَا فِي
ٱلسَّفِينَةِ خَرَقَهَا ۖ قَالَ أَخَرَقْتَهَا
لِتُغْرِقَ أَهْلَهَا لَقَدْ جِئْتَ
شَيْـًٔا إِمْرًا ﴿٧١﴾

72. He said, "Did I not tell you that you would not be able to remain patient with me?"

72. Qaala alam aqul innaka lan tastaṭee'a ma'iya ṣabraa.

قَالَ أَلَمْ أَقُلْ إِنَّكَ لَن تَسْتَطِيعَ
مَعِيَ صَبْرًا ﴿٧٢﴾

73. Moses said, "Please, forgive my forgetfulness. Do not oblige me with what is difficult for me to endure."

73. Qaala laa tu'aakhiznee bimaa naseetu wa laa turhiqnee min amree 'usraa.

قَالَ لَا تُؤَاخِذْنِي بِمَا نَسِيتُ وَلَا
تُرْهِقْنِي مِنْ أَمْرِي عُسْرًا ﴿٧٣﴾

74. They continued on their journey until they met a young boy whom he killed. Moses said, "How could you murder an innocent soul? This is, certainly, a horrifying act."

74. Fanṭalaqaa; ḥattaaa izaa laqiyaa ghulaaman faqatalahoo qaala aqatalta nafsan zakiyyatam bighayri nafs; laqad ji'ta shay'an-nukraa.

فَٱنطَلَقَا وقفة حَتَّىٰٓ إِذَا لَقِيَا غُلَٰمًا
فَقَتَلَهُۥ قَالَ أَقَتَلْتَ نَفْسًا زَكِيَّةًۢ
بِغَيْرِ نَفْسٍ لَّقَدْ جِئْتَ شَيْـًٔا نُّكْرًا ﴿٧٤﴾

75. He responded, "Did I not tell you that you would not be able to remain patient with me?"

75. Qaala alam aqul laka innaka lan tastaṭee'a ma'iya ṣabraa.

قَالَ أَلَمْ أَقُل لَّكَ إِنَّكَ لَن
تَسْتَطِيعَ مَعِيَ صَبْرًا ﴿٧٥﴾ الجزء السادس عشر (١٦)

76. Moses said, "If I ask you such questions again, abandon me; you will have enough reason to do so."

76. Qaala in sa-altuka 'an shay'im ba'dahaa falaa tuṣaaḥibnee qad balaghta milladunnee 'uzraa.

قَالَ إِن سَأَلْتُكَ عَن شَيْءٍۭ بَعْدَهَا فَلَا
تُصَٰحِبْنِي ۖ قَدْ بَلَغْتَ مِن لَّدُنِّي عُذْرًا ﴿٧٦﴾

77. They continued on their journey again until they reached a town. They asked the people there for food, but no one accepted them as their guests. They found there a wall of a house which was on the verge of tumbling to the ground. The companion of Moses repaired that wall. Moses said, "You should

77. Fanṭalaqaa; ḥattaaa izaaa atayaaa ahla qaryatinis-taṭ'amaaa ahlahaa fa-abaw añy-yuḍayyifoohumaa fawajadaa feehaa jidaarañy-yureedu añy-yanqaḍḍa fa-aqaamah; qaala

فَٱنطَلَقَا وقفة حَتَّىٰٓ إِذَآ أَتَيَآ أَهْلَ
قَرْيَةٍ ٱسْتَطْعَمَآ أَهْلَهَا فَأَبَوْا أَن
يُضَيِّفُوهُمَا فَوَجَدَا فِيهَا جِدَارًا
يُرِيدُ أَن يَنقَضَّ فَأَقَامَهُۥ ۖ قَالَ

have received some money for your labor."

law shi'ta lattakhazta 'alayhi ajraa.

لو شئت لتخذت عليه أجرا ﴿٧٧﴾

78. He replied, "This is where we should depart from one another. I shall give an explanation to you for all that I have done for which you could not remain patient.

78. Qaala haazaa firaaqu baynee wa baynik; sa-unabbi-'uka bita-weeli maa lam tastaṭi' 'alayhi ṣabraa.

قال هٰذا فراق بيني وبينك ۚ
سأنبئك بتأويل ما لم تستطع
عليه صبرا ﴿٧٨﴾

79. "The boat belonged to some destitute people who were using it as a means of their living in the sea. The king had imposed a certain amount of tax on every (undamaged) boat. I damaged it so that they would not have to pay the tax.

79. Ammas-safeenatu fakaanat limasaakeena ya'maloona fil-baḥri fa-arattu an a'eebahaa wa kaana waraaa'ahum-malikuñy-ya-khuzu kulla safeenatin ghaṣbaa.

أما السفينة فكانت لمساكين
يعملون في البحر فأردت أن
أعيبها وكان وراءهم ملك يأخذ
كل سفينة غصبا ﴿٧٩﴾

80. "The young boy had very faithful parents. We were afraid that out of love for him they would lose their faith in Allah and commit rebellion

80. Wa aammal-ghulaamu fakaana abawaahu mu'minayni fakhasheenaaa añy-yurhiqa-humaa ṭughyaanañw-wa kufraa.

وأما الغلٰم فكان أبواه مؤمنين
فخشينا أن يرهقهما طغيانا وكفرا ﴿٨٠﴾

81. so We decided that their Lord should replace him by a better and more virtuous son.

81. Fa-aradnaaa añy-yubdila-humaa Rabbuhumaa khayram-minhu zakaatañw-wa aqraba ruḥmaa.

فأردنا أن يبدلهما ربهما خيرا منه
زكٰوة وأقرب رحما ﴿٨١﴾

82. "The tumbling wall belonged to two orphans in the town whose father was a righteous person. Underneath the wall there was a treasure that belonged to them. Your Lord wanted the orphans to find the treasure through the mercy of your Lord when they mature. I did not repair the wall out of my own desire. These were the explanations of my deeds about which you could not remain patient."

82. Wa ammal-jidaaru fakaana lighulaamayni yateemayni fil-madeenati wa kaana taḥtahoo kanzul-lahumaa wa kaana aboohumaa ṣaaliḥan fa-araada Rabbuka añy-yablughaaa ashud-dahumaa wa yastakhrijaa kan-zahumaa raḥmatam-mir-Rabbik; wa maa fa'altuhoo 'an amree; zaalika ta-weelu maa lam tasṭi' 'alayhi ṣabraa.

وأما الجدار فكان لغلٰمين يتيمين
في المدينة وكان تحته كنز لهما
وكان أبوهما صالحا ۚ فأراد
ربك أن يبلغا أشدهما ويستخرجا
كنزهما ۖ رحمة من ربك ۚ وما
فعلته عن أمري ۚ ذٰلك تأويل
ما لم تسطع عليه صبرا ﴿٨٢﴾ ع ١٢

83. (Muhammad), they will ask you about Dhul-Qarnayn. Say, "I shall tell you something about him."

83. Wa yas'aloonaka 'an Zil-Qarnayni qul sa-atloo 'alay-kum- minhu zikraa.

ويسئلونك عن ذي القرنين ۖ قل
سأتلوا عليكم منه ذكرا ﴿٨٣﴾

84. We had given him great power in the land and all kinds of instructions.

84. Innaa makkannaa lahoo fil-arḍi wa aataynaahu min kulli shay'in sababaa.

إنا مكنا له في الأرض وآتينٰه
من كل شيء سببا ﴿٨٤﴾

85. With these he traveled

85. Fa-atba'a sababaa.

فأتبع سببا ﴿٨٥﴾

86. to the West where he found the sun setting into a warm source (spring) of water and a people living nearby. We said to him,

86. Ḥattaaa izaa balagha maghribash-shamsi wajadahaa taghrubu fee 'aynin ḥami'a-tiñw-wa wajada

حتى إذا بلغ مغرب الشمس وجدها
تغرب في عين حمئة ووجد

"Dhul-Qarnayn, you may punish them or treat them with kindness."

87. He replied, "I shall punish the unjust ones among them and then they will return to their Lord, who will punish them more sternly."

88. As for those who believe and do good, they will receive virtuous rewards and We will tell them to do only what they can.

89. He, with the instructions, traveled again

90. to the East where he found the sun rising upon a people whom We had exposed to its rays (did not know how to make clothes).

91. This indeed was true. We knew all that he did there.

92. He traveled

93. after this to the middle of two mountains where he found a people who could hardly understand a single word.

94. They said, "Dhul Qarnayn, Gog and Magog are ravaging this land. Would you establish a barrier between us and them if we pay you a certain tax?"

95. He replied, "The power that my Lord has granted me is better (than your tax). Help me with your man-power and I shall construct a barrier between you and Gog and Magog.

96. Bring me blocks of iron to fill up the passage between the two mountains." He told them to ply their bellows until the iron

'indahaa qawmaa; qulnaa yaa Z̲al-Qarnayni immaaa an tu'az̲-z̲iba wa immaaa an tattakhiz̲a feehim ḥusnaa.

87. Qaala ammaa man ẓalama fasawfa nu'az̲-z̲ibuhoo s̲umma yuraddu ilaa Rabbihee fayu'az̲-z̲ibuhoo 'az̲aaban-nukraa.

88. Wa ammaa man aamana wa 'amila ṣaaliḥan falahoo jazaaa'anil-ḥusnaa wa sana-qoolu lahoo min amrinaa yusraa.

89. S̲umma atba'a sababaa.

90. Ḥattaaa iz̲aa balagha maṭli'ash-shamsi wajadahaa taṭlu'u 'alaa qawmillam naj'al-lahum-min doonihaa sitraa.

91. Kaz̲aalika wa qad aḥaṭnaa bimaa ladayhi khubraa.

92. S̲umma atba'a sababaa.

93. Ḥattaaa iz̲aa balagha baynas-saddayni wajada min doonihimaa qawmal-laa yakaa-doona yafqahoona qawlaa.

94. Qaaloo yaa Z̲al-Qarnayni inna Ya-jooja wa Ma-jooja-mufsidoona fil-arḍi fahal naj'alu laka kharjan 'alaaa an taj'ala baynanaa wa baynahum saddaa.

95. Qaala maa makkannee feehi Rabbee khayrun fa-a'eenoonee biquwwatin aj'al baynakum wa baynahum radmaa.

96. Aatoonee zubaral-ḥadee-d; ḥattaaa iz̲aa saawaa baynaṣ-ṣadafayni qaalan-fukhoo

عِنْدَهَا قَوْمًا ۗ قُلْنَا يٰذَا الْقَرْنَيْنِ
اِمَّآ اَنْ تُعَذِّبَ وَاِمَّآ اَنْ تَتَّخِذَ
فِيْهِمْ حُسْنًا ﴿٨٦﴾
قَالَ اَمَّا مَنْ ظَلَمَ فَسَوْفَ نُعَذِّبُهٗ ثُمَّ
يُرَدُّ اِلٰى رَبِّهٖ فَيُعَذِّبُهٗ عَذَابًا نُّكْرًا ﴿٨٧﴾
وَاَمَّا مَنْ اٰمَنَ وَعَمِلَ صَالِحًا
فَلَهٗ جَزَآءَ ۨ الْحُسْنٰى ۚ وَسَنَقُوْلُ لَهٗ
مِنْ اَمْرِنَا يُسْرًا ؕ ﴿٨٨﴾
ثُمَّ اَتْبَعَ سَبَبًا ﴿٨٩﴾
حَتّٰٓى اِذَا بَلَغَ مَطْلِعَ الشَّمْسِ
وَجَدَهَا تَطْلُعُ عَلٰى قَوْمٍ لَّمْ نَجْعَلْ
لَّهُمْ مِّنْ دُوْنِهَا سِتْرًا ۙ ﴿٩٠﴾
كَذٰلِكَ ؕ وَقَدْ اَحَطْنَا بِمَا لَدَيْهِ خُبْرًا ﴿٩١﴾
ثُمَّ اَتْبَعَ سَبَبًا ﴿٩٢﴾
حَتّٰٓى اِذَا بَلَغَ بَيْنَ السَّدَّيْنِ وَجَدَ
مِنْ دُوْنِهِمَا قَوْمًا ۙ لَّا يَكَادُوْنَ
يَفْقَهُوْنَ قَوْلًا ﴿٩٣﴾
قَالُوْا يٰذَا الْقَرْنَيْنِ اِنَّ يَاْجُوْجَ وَ
مَاْجُوْجَ مُفْسِدُوْنَ فِى الْاَرْضِ
فَهَلْ نَجْعَلُ لَكَ خَرْجًا عَلٰٓى اَنْ
تَجْعَلَ بَيْنَنَا وَبَيْنَهُمْ سَدًّا ﴿٩٤﴾
قَالَ مَا مَكَّنِّىْ فِيْهِ رَبِّىْ خَيْرٌ
فَاَعِيْنُوْنِىْ بِقُوَّةٍ اَجْعَلْ بَيْنَكُمْ
وَبَيْنَهُمْ رَدْمًا ۙ ﴿٩٥﴾
اٰتُوْنِىْ زُبَرَ الْحَدِيْدِ ؕ حَتّٰٓى اِذَا سَاوٰى
بَيْنَ الصَّدَفَيْنِ قَالَ انْفُخُوْا ؕ

became hot as fire. Then he told them to pour on it melted brass."	ḥattaaa izaa ja'alahoo naaran qaala aatooneee ufrigh 'alayhi qiṭraa.	حَتّٰٓى إِذَا جَعَلَهٗ نَارًا ۙ قَالَ اٰتُوْنِيْٓ أُفْرِغْ عَلَيْهِ قِطْرًا ﴿٩٦﴾
97. (Thus he constructed the barrier which) neither Gog nor Magog were able to climb nor were they able to dig a tunnel through the iron and brass barrier.	97. Famas-ṭaa'ooo añy-yaẓha-roohu wa mastaṭaa'oo lahoo naqbaa.	فَمَا اسْطَاعُوْٓا أَنْ يَّظْهَرُوْهُ وَمَا اسْتَطَاعُوْا لَهٗ نَقْبًا ﴿٩٧﴾
98. Dhul-Qarnayn said, "This barrier is a blessing from my Lord but when the promise of my Lord comes to pass He will level it to the ground; the promise of my Lord always comes true."	98. Qaala haazaa raḥmatum-mir-Rabbee fa-izaa jaaa'a wa'du Rabbee ja'alahoo dak-kaaa'; wa kaana wa'du Rabbee ḥaqqaa.	قَالَ هٰذَا رَحْمَةٌ مِّنْ رَّبِّيْ ۚ فَإِذَا جَآءَ وَعْدُ رَبِّيْ جَعَلَهٗ دَكَّآءَ ۚ وَكَانَ وَعْدُ رَبِّيْ حَقًّا ﴿٩٨﴾
99. We left them (Gog and Magog) like the waves of the sea striking against each other. When the trumpet will be sounded, We will then bring them all together.	99. Wa taraknaa ba'ḍahum Yawma'iziñy-yamooju fee ba'ḍiñw-wa nufikha fiṣ-Ṣoori fajama'naahum jam'aa.	وَتَرَكْنَا بَعْضَهُمْ يَوْمَئِذٍ يَّمُوْجُ فِيْ بَعْضٍ وَّنُفِخَ فِي الصُّوْرِ فَجَمَعْنٰهُمْ جَمْعًا ﴿٩٩﴾
100. We will fully expose the view of hell on that Day to the unbelievers,	100. Wa 'araḍnaa Jahannama Yawma'izil-lilkaafireena 'arḍaa.	وَّعَرَضْنَا جَهَنَّمَ يَوْمَئِذٍ لِّلْكٰفِرِيْنَ عَرْضًا ﴿١٠٠﴾
101. whose eyes had been veiled against Our Quran and who were not able to hear (its recitation).	101. Allazeena kaanat a'yunu-hum fee ghiṭaaa'in 'an-zikree wa kaanoo laa yastaṭee'oona sam'aa.	الَّذِيْنَ كَانَتْ أَعْيُنُهُمْ فِيْ غِطَآءٍ عَنْ ذِكْرِيْ وَكَانُوْا لَا يَسْتَطِيْعُوْنَ سَمْعًا ﴿١٠١﴾ ع ١٩ ٢
102. Do the unbelievers think they can make My servants as their guardians instead of Me? We have prepared hell as a dwelling place for the unbelievers.	102. Afaḥasibal-lazeena kafa-rooo añy-yattakhizoo 'ibaadee min dooneee awliyaaa'; innaaa a'tadnaa Jahannama lilkaafi-reena nuzulaa.	أَفَحَسِبَ الَّذِيْنَ كَفَرُوْٓا أَنْ يَّتَّخِذُوْا عِبَادِيْ مِنْ دُوْنِيْٓ أَوْلِيَآءَ ۚ إِنَّآ أَعْتَدْنَا جَهَنَّمَ لِلْكٰفِرِيْنَ نُزُلًا ﴿١٠٢﴾
103. (Muhammad), Say to them, "Should I tell you who will face the greatest loss as a result of their deeds?	103. Qul hal nunabbi'ukum bilakhsareena a'maalaa.	قُلْ هَلْ نُنَبِّئُكُمْ بِالْأَخْسَرِيْنَ أَعْمَالًا ﴿١٠٣﴾
104. It will be those who labor a great deal in this life but without guidance, yet think that they are doing a great many good deeds.	104. Allazeena ḍalla sa'yuhum fil-ḥayaatiddunyaa wa hum yaḥsaboona annahum yuḥsi-noona ṣun'aa.	الَّذِيْنَ ضَلَّ سَعْيُهُمْ فِي الْحَيٰوةِ الدُّنْيَا وَهُمْ يَحْسَبُوْنَ أَنَّهُمْ يُحْسِنُوْنَ صُنْعًا ﴿١٠٤﴾
105. They have rejected the revelations of their Lord and their meeting with Him. Thus, their deeds will be made devoid of all virtue and will be of no value on the Day of Judgment.	105. Ulaaa'ikal-lazeena kafa-roo bi-Aayaati Rabbihim wa liqaaa'ihee faḥabiṭat a'maalu-hum falaa nuqeemu lahum Yawmal-Qiyaamati waznaa.	أُولٰٓئِكَ الَّذِيْنَ كَفَرُوْا بِاٰيٰتِ رَبِّهِمْ وَلِقَآئِهٖ فَحَبِطَتْ أَعْمَالُهُمْ فَلَا نُقِيْمُ لَهُمْ يَوْمَ الْقِيٰمَةِ وَزْنًا ﴿١٠٥﴾
106. For their disbelief and their mocking Our revelations and Messengers, their recompense will be hell.	106. Zaalika jazaaa'uhum Jahannamu bimaa kafaroo wattakhazooo Aayaatee wa Rusulee huzuwaa.	ذٰلِكَ جَزَآؤُهُمْ جَهَنَّمُ بِمَا كَفَرُوْا وَاتَّخَذُوْٓا اٰيٰتِيْ وَرُسُلِيْ هُزُوًا ﴿١٠٦﴾

107. The righteously striving believers will have the gardens of Paradise as their dwelling place and therein they will live forever,

108. without any desire to change their abode.

109. (Muhammad), tell them, "Had the seas been used as ink to write down the words of my Lord, they would have all been consumed before the words of my Lord could have been recorded, even though replenished with a like quantity of ink.

110. Say, "I am only a mortal like you but I have received revelation that there is only one Lord. Whoever desires to meet his Lord should strive righteously and should worship no one besides Him (do not showoff to others).

107. Innal-lazeena aamanoo wa 'amiluṣ-ṣaaliḥaati kaanat lahum Jannaatul-Firdawsi nuzulaa.

108. Khaalideena feehaa laa yabghoona 'anhaa ḥiwalaa.

109. Qul law kaanal-baḥru midaadal-li-Kalimaati Rabbee lanafidal-baḥru qabla an tanfada Kalimaatu Rabbee wa law ji'naa bimislihee madadaa.

110. Qul innamaaa ana basharum-mislukum yooḥaaa ilayya annamaaa ilaahukum Ilaahuñw-Waaḥid; faman kaana yarjoo liqaaa'a Rabbihee falya'mal 'amalan ṣaaliḥañw-wa laa yushrik bi'ibaadati Rabbiheee aḥadaa.

إِنَّ ٱلَّذِينَ ءَامَنُوا۟ وَعَمِلُوا۟ ٱلصَّٰلِحَٰتِ
كَانَتْ لَهُمْ جَنَّٰتُ ٱلْفِرْدَوْسِ نُزُلًا ﴿١٠٧﴾
خَٰلِدِينَ فِيهَا لَا يَبْغُونَ عَنْهَا حِوَلًا ﴿١٠٨﴾
قُل لَّوْ كَانَ ٱلْبَحْرُ مِدَادًا لِّكَلِمَٰتِ رَبِّى
لَنَفِدَ ٱلْبَحْرُ قَبْلَ أَن تَنفَدَ كَلِمَٰتُ
رَبِّى وَلَوْ جِئْنَا بِمِثْلِهِۦ مَدَدًا ﴿١٠٩﴾
قُلْ إِنَّمَآ أَنَا۠ بَشَرٌ مِّثْلُكُمْ يُوحَىٰٓ إِلَىَّ
أَنَّمَآ إِلَٰهُكُمْ إِلَٰهٌ وَٰحِدٌ فَمَن كَانَ يَرْجُوا۟
لِقَآءَ رَبِّهِۦ فَلْيَعْمَلْ عَمَلًا صَٰلِحًا وَلَا
يُشْرِكْ بِعِبَادَةِ رَبِّهِۦٓ أَحَدًۢا ﴿١١٠﴾ ع ١٢ ٩

Maryam, Mary (19)

In the Name of Allah,
the Beneficent, the Merciful.

Sûrat Maryam-19

(Revealed at Makkah)
Bismillaahir Raḥmaanir Raḥeem

(١٩) سُورَةُ مَرْيَمَ مَكِّيَّةٌ (٤٤)
آياتها ٩٨ بِسْمِ ٱللَّهِ ٱلرَّحْمَٰنِ ٱلرَّحِيمِ ركوعاتها ٦

1. Kaf Ha Ya Ayn Sad.

2. This is the story of the blessing of your Lord to His servant Zachariah.

3. When he quietly called his Lord

4. and said, "My Lord, my bones have become feeble and my hair has turned white with age. Yet I had never been deprived in receiving from You the answer to my prayers.

5. I am afraid of what my kinsmen will do after (my death) and my wife is barren. Lord, grant me a son

6. who will be my heir and the heir of the family of Jacob. Lord, make him a person who will please you."

7. We answered his prayers with the glad news of the birth of a son by the name of John and told him, "We had never given such a name to anyone else."

8. He said, "My Lord, how can I have a son? My wife is

1. Kaaaf-Haa-Yaa-'Ayyyn-Ṣaaad.

2. Zikru raḥmati Rabbika 'abdahoo Zakariyyaa.

3. Iz naadaa Rabbahoo nidaaa'an khafiyyaa.

4. Qaala Rabbi innee wahanal-'aẓmu minnee washta'alar-rasu shaybañw-wa lam akum bidu'aaa'ika Rabbi shaqiyyaa.

5. Wa innee khiftul-mawaaliya miñw-waraaa'ee wa kaanatim-ra-atee 'aaqiran fahab lee mil-ladunka waliyyaa.

6. Yarisunee wa yarisu min aali Ya'qoob; waj'alhu Rabbi raḍiyyaa.

7. Yaa Zakariyyaaa innaa nubashshiruka bighulaami-nismuhoo Yaḥyaa lam naj'al-lahoo min qablu samiyyaa.

8. Qaala Rabbi annaa yakoonu lee ghulaamuñw-wa

كٓهيعٓصٓ ﴿١﴾
ذِكْرُ رَحْمَتِ رَبِّكَ عَبْدَهُۥ زَكَرِيَّآ ﴿٢﴾
إِذْ نَادَىٰ رَبَّهُۥ نِدَآءً خَفِيًّا ﴿٣﴾
قَالَ رَبِّ إِنِّى وَهَنَ ٱلْعَظْمُ مِنِّى
وَٱشْتَعَلَ ٱلرَّأْسُ شَيْبًا وَلَمْ أَكُنۢ
بِدُعَآئِكَ رَبِّ شَقِيًّا ﴿٤﴾
وَإِنِّى خِفْتُ ٱلْمَوَٰلِىَ مِن وَرَآءِى
وَكَانَتِ ٱمْرَأَتِى عَاقِرًا فَهَبْ لِى
مِن لَّدُنكَ وَلِيًّا ﴿٥﴾
يَرِثُنِى وَيَرِثُ مِنْ ءَالِ يَعْقُوبَ
وَٱجْعَلْهُ رَبِّ رَضِيًّا ﴿٦﴾
يَٰزَكَرِيَّآ إِنَّا نُبَشِّرُكَ بِغُلَٰمٍ ٱسْمُهُۥ يَحْيَىٰ
لَمْ نَجْعَل لَّهُۥ مِن قَبْلُ سَمِيًّا ﴿٧﴾
قَالَ رَبِّ أَنَّىٰ يَكُونُ لِى غُلَٰمٌ وَ

barren and I have reached an extremely old (hopeless) age."

kaanatim-ra-atee 'aaqirañw-wa qad balaghtu minal-kibari 'itiyyaa.

كَانَتِ امْرَاَتِيْ عَاقِرًا وَّقَدْ بَلَغْتُ
مِنَ الْكِبَرِ عِتِيًّا ﴿٨﴾

9. (The angel) said, "This is true, but your Lord says, 'For Me it is easy; I created you when you did not exist."

9. Qaala kazaalika qaala Rabbuka huwa 'alayya hayyinuñw-wa qad khalaqtuka min qablu wa lam taku shay'aa.

قَالَ كَذٰلِكَ ۚ قَالَ رَبُّكَ هُوَ عَلَيَّ
هَيِّنٌ وَّقَدْ خَلَقْتُكَ مِنْ قَبْلُ وَلَمْ
تَكُ شَيْـًٔا ﴿٩﴾

10. Zachariah asked, "Lord, show me evidence (if this is heavenly news)." The Lord said, "The evidence for it is that you will not be able to speak, even though in good health, for three nights (and days)."

10. Qaala Rabbij-'al-leee Aayah; qaala Aayatuka allaa tukalliman-naasa salaasa layaalin sawiyyaa.

قَالَ رَبِّ اجْعَلْ لِّيْٓ اٰيَةً ۚ قَالَ اٰيَتُكَ
اَلَّا تُكَلِّمَ النَّاسَ ثَلٰثَ لَيَالٍ سَوِيًّا ﴿١٠﴾

11. Zachariah came out to his people from the place of worship and revealed to them to glorify the Lord in both the morning and the evening.

11. Fakharaja 'alaa qawmihee minal-miḥraabi fa-awḥaaa ilayhim an sabbiḥoo bukratañw- wa 'ashiyyaa.

فَخَرَجَ عَلٰى قَوْمِهٖ مِنَ الْمِحْرَابِ فَاَوْحٰٓى
اِلَيْهِمْ اَنْ سَبِّحُوْا بُكْرَةً وَّعَشِيًّا ﴿١١﴾

12. We commanded John, Zachariah's son, to follow the guidance of the Lord with due steadfastness. To John We gave knowledge and wisdom during his childhood.

12. Yaa Yaḥyaa khuzil-Kitaaba biquw-wah;-wa aataynaahul-ḥukma ṣabiyyaa.

يٰيَحْيٰى خُذِ الْكِتٰبَ بِقُوَّةٍ ۗ وَاٰتَيْنٰهُ
الْحُكْمَ صَبِيًّا ﴿١٢﴾

13. We gave him compassion and purity. He was a pious human being,

13. Wa ḥanaanam-milladunnaa wa zakaah;-wa kaana taqiyyaa.

وَّحَنَانًا مِّنْ لَّدُنَّا وَزَكٰوةً ۗ وَكَانَ تَقِيًّا ﴿١٣﴾

14. kind to his parents, not arrogant or a rebellious person.

14. Wa barram biwaalidayhi wa lam yakun jabbaaran 'aṣiyyaa.

وَّبَرًّا بِوَالِدَيْهِ وَلَمْ يَكُنْ جَبَّارًا عَصِيًّا ﴿١٤﴾

15. He was born and died in peace and will be brought back to life again in peace.

15. Wa salaamun 'alayhi yawma wulida wa yawma yamootu wa yawma yub'asu ḥayyaa.

وَسَلٰمٌ عَلَيْهِ يَوْمَ وُلِدَ وَيَوْمَ يَمُوْتُ
وَيَوْمَ يُبْعَثُ حَيًّا ﴿١٥﴾ ع ١٥ وقف لازم

16. (Muhammad), mention in the Book (the Quran) the story of Mary, how she left her family and started living in a solitary place (near a dead palm tree) toward the East

16. Wazkur fil-Kitaabi Maryam; izin-tabazat min ahlihaa makaanan sharqiyyaa.

وَاذْكُرْ فِي الْكِتٰبِ مَرْيَمَ ۘ اِذِ انْتَبَذَتْ
مِنْ اَهْلِهَا مَكَانًا شَرْقِيًّا ﴿١٦﴾

17. out of her people's sight. We sent Our Spirit to her, who stood before her in the shape of a well formed human being.

17. Fattakhazat min doonihim ḥijaaban fa-arsalnaaa ilayhaa rooḥanaa fatamassala lahaa basharan sawiyyaa.

فَاتَّخَذَتْ مِنْ دُوْنِهِمْ حِجَابًا ۫
فَاَرْسَلْنَآ اِلَيْهَا رُوْحَنَا فَتَمَثَّلَ
لَهَا بَشَرًا سَوِيًّا ﴿١٧﴾

18. Mary said, "Would that the Beneficent would protect me from you. Leave me alone if you are a God-fearing person."

18. Qaalat inneee a'oozu bir-Raḥmaani minka in kunta taqiyyaa.

قَالَتْ اِنِّيْٓ اَعُوْذُ بِالرَّحْمٰنِ مِنْكَ
اِنْ كُنْتَ تَقِيًّا ﴿١٨﴾

19. He said, "I am the Messenger of your Lord. I have come to give you a purified son."

19. Qaala innamaaa ana rasoolu Rabbiki li ahaba laki ghulaaman zakiyyaa.

قَالَ اِنَّمَآ اَنَا رَسُوْلُ رَبِّكِ ۖ لِاَهَبَ
لَكِ غُلٰمًا زَكِيًّا ﴿١٩﴾

20. She said, "How can I have a son when no mortal touched me nor was I an unchaste woman."

20. Qaalat annaa yakoonu lee ghulaamuñw-wa lam yamsasnee basharuñw-wa lam aku baghiyyaa.

قَالَتْ اَنّٰى يَكُوْنُ لِيْ غُلٰمٌ وَّلَمْ يَمْسَسْنِيْ
بَشَرٌ وَّلَمْ اَكُ بَغِيًّا ﴿٢٠﴾ الربع

21. He said, "This is true but your Lord says, "It is very easy for Me. We have decided to give you a son as evidence (of Our existence) for human beings and a mercy from Us. This is a decree already ordained."

22. She conceived the child and retreated with him to a distant and solitary place.

23. When (after nine hours) she started to experience (the pain of) childbirth labor, by the trunk of a palm tree in sadness she said, "Would that I had died long before and passed into oblivion."

24. Then she heard the baby saying, "Do not be sad. Your Lord has caused a stream to run at your feet.

25. Shake the trunk of the palm tree, it will provide you with fresh ripe dates.

26. Eat, drink, and rejoice. Should you see a person going by, tell him that on this day you have promised the Beneficent to fast and never talk to any human being."

27. She took him to her people and they, reproving her, said, "Mary, this is indeed a strange thing.

28. O Aaron's (the indecent man) sister, your father was not a bad man nor was your mother unchaste."

29. She pointed to the baby (and referred them to him for their answer). They said, "How can we talk to a baby in the cradle?"

30. He said, "I am the servant of Allah. He has given me the Book and has appointed me a Prophet.

31. He has blessed me (made benevolent) no matter where I dwell, commanded me to worship Him and pay the religious tax for as long as I live.

21. Qaala kaẕaaliki qaala Rabbuki huwa 'alayya hayyin;-wa linaj'alahooo Aayatal-linnaasi wa raḥmatam-minnaa; wa kaana amram-maqḍiyyaa.

22. Faḥamalathu fantabaẕat bihee makaanan qaṣiyyaa.

23. Fa-ajaaa'ahal-makhaaḍu ilaa jiẕ'in-nakhlati qaalat yaa laytanee mittu qabla haaẕaa wa kuntu nasyam-mansiyyaa.

24. Fanaadaahaa min taḥtihaaa allaa taḥzanee qad ja'ala Rabbuki taḥtaki sariyyaa.

25. Wa huzzeee ilayki bijiẕ-'in-nakhlati tusaaqiṭ 'alayki ruṭaban janiyyaa.

26. Fakulee washrabee wa qarree 'aynaa; fa-immaa tarayinna minal-bashari aḥadan faqooleee innee naẕartu lir-Raḥmaani ṣawman falan ukallimal-yawma insiyyaa.

27. Fa-atat bihee qawmahaa taḥmiluhoo qaaloo yaa Maryamu laqad ji'ti shay'an fariyyaa.

28. Yaaa ukhta Haaroona maa kaana abookim-ra-a saw'iñw- wa maa kaanat ummuki baghiyyaa.

29. Fa-ashaarat ilayh; qaaloo kayfa nukallimu man kaana fil-mahdi ṣabiyyaa.

30. Qaala innee 'abdullaahi aataaniyal-Kitaaba wa ja'alanee Nabiyyaa.

31. Wa ja'alanee mubaarakan ayna maa kuntu wa awṣaanee biṣ-Ṣalaati waz-Zakaati maa dumtu ḥayyaa.

قَالَ كَذٰلِكِ ۚ قَالَ رَبُّكِ هُوَ عَلَيَّ
هَيِّنٌ ۚ وَلِنَجْعَلَهُۥٓ ءَايَةً لِّلنَّاسِ وَرَحْمَةً
مِّنَّا ۚ وَكَانَ أَمْرًا مَّقْضِيًّا ﴿٢١﴾
فَحَمَلَتْهُ فَانْتَبَذَتْ بِهِۦ مَكَانًا قَصِيًّا ﴿٢٢﴾
فَأَجَآءَهَا الْمَخَاضُ إِلَىٰ جِذْعِ النَّخْلَةِ ۚ
قَالَتْ يٰلَيْتَنِى مِتُّ قَبْلَ هٰذَا وَ
كُنتُ نَسْيًا مَّنسِيًّا ﴿٢٣﴾
فَنَادٰىهَا مِن تَحْتِهَآ أَلَّا تَحْزَنِى قَدْ
جَعَلَ رَبُّكِ تَحْتَكِ سَرِيًّا ﴿٢٤﴾
وَهُزِّىٓ إِلَيْكِ بِجِذْعِ النَّخْلَةِ تُسٰقِطْ
عَلَيْكِ رُطَبًا جَنِيًّا ﴿٢٥﴾
فَكُلِى وَاشْرَبِى وَقَرِّى عَيْنًا ۖ فَإِمَّا
تَرَيِنَّ مِنَ الْبَشَرِ أَحَدًا فَقُولِىٓ إِنِّى
نَذَرْتُ لِلرَّحْمٰنِ صَوْمًا فَلَنْ أُكَلِّمَ
الْيَوْمَ إِنسِيًّا ﴿٢٦﴾
فَأَتَتْ بِهِۦ قَوْمَهَا تَحْمِلُهُۥ ۖ قَالُوا
يٰمَرْيَمُ لَقَدْ جِئْتِ شَيْـًٔا فَرِيًّا ﴿٢٧﴾
يٰٓأُخْتَ هٰرُونَ مَا كَانَ أَبُوكِ امْرَأَ
سَوْءٍ وَمَا كَانَتْ أُمُّكِ بَغِيًّا ﴿٢٨﴾
فَأَشَارَتْ إِلَيْهِ ۖ قَالُوا كَيْفَ نُكَلِّمُ
مَن كَانَ فِى الْمَهْدِ صَبِيًّا ﴿٢٩﴾
قَالَ إِنِّى عَبْدُ اللّٰهِ ءَاتٰىنِىَ الْكِتٰبَ وَ
جَعَلَنِى نَبِيًّا ﴿٣٠﴾
وَجَعَلَنِى مُبٰرَكًا أَيْنَ مَا كُنتُ وَ
أَوْصٰنِى بِالصَّلٰوةِ وَالزَّكٰوةِ مَا
دُمْتُ حَيًّا ﴿٣١﴾

32. He has commanded me to be good to my mother and did not make me an arrogant, rebellious person.

32. Wa barram biwaalidatee wa lam yaj'alnee jabbaaran shaqiyyaa.

وَبَرًّا بِوَالِدَتِي وَلَمْ يَجْعَلْنِي جَبَّارًا
شَقِيًّا ﴿٣٢﴾

33. I was born with peace and I shall die and be brought to life again with peace."

33. Wassalaamu 'alayya yawma wulittu wa yawma amootu wa yawma ub'a<u>s</u>u ḥayyaa.

وَالسَّلَامُ عَلَيَّ يَوْمَ وُلِدتُّ وَيَوْمَ
أَمُوتُ وَيَوْمَ أُبْعَثُ حَيًّا ﴿٣٣﴾

34. Such was the true story of Jesus, the son of Mary, about which they argue bitterly.

34. <u>Z</u>aalika 'Eesab-nu Maryam; qawlal-ḥaqqil-la<u>z</u>ee feehi yamtaroon.

ذَٰلِكَ عِيسَى ابْنُ مَرْيَمَ قَوْلَ الْحَقِّ
الَّذِي فِيهِ يَمْتَرُونَ ﴿٣٤﴾

35. Allah is free of all defects of having a son. When He decides to bring something into existence He need only command it to exist and it comes into existence.

35. Maa kaana lillaahi añy-yattakhi<u>z</u>a miñw-walad; Subḥaanah; i<u>z</u>aa qaḍaaa amran fa-innamaa yaqoolu lahoo kun fayakoon.

مَا كَانَ لِلَّهِ أَن يَتَّخِذَ مِن وَلَدٍ
سُبْحَانَهُ إِذَا قَضَىٰ أَمْرًا فَإِنَّمَا يَقُولُ
لَهُ كُن فَيَكُونُ ﴿٣٥﴾

36. (Baby Jesus said), "Worship Allah who is my Lord as well as yours. This is the straight path."

36. Wa innal-laaha Rabbee wa Rabbukum fa'budooh; haa<u>z</u>aa Ṣiraaṭum-Mustaqeem.

وَإِنَّ اللَّهَ رَبِّي وَرَبُّكُمْ فَاعْبُدُوهُ
هَٰذَا صِرَاطٌ مُّسْتَقِيمٌ ﴿٣٦﴾

37. (The followers of Jesus) turned themselves into quarrelling sects. The unbelievers shall face a woeful condition on the great Day (of Judgment).

37. Fakhtalafal-aḥzaabu mim baynihim fawaylul-lilla<u>z</u>eena kafaroo mim-mashhadi Yawmin 'aẓeem.

فَاخْتَلَفَ الْأَحْزَابُ مِن بَيْنِهِمْ فَوَيْلٌ
لِّلَّذِينَ كَفَرُوا مِن مَّشْهَدِ يَوْمٍ عَظِيمٍ ﴿٣٧﴾

38. (Muhammad), how clearly they will hear and see on the day when they will be brought into Our presence. Today the wrong-doers are in manifest error.

38. Asmi' bihim wa abṣir Yawma ya-toonanaa laakiniẓ-ẓaalimoonal-yawma fee ḍalaalim-mubeen.

أَسْمِعْ بِهِمْ وَأَبْصِرْ يَوْمَ يَأْتُونَنَا لَٰكِنِ
الظَّالِمُونَ الْيَوْمَ فِي ضَلَالٍ مُّبِينٍ ﴿٣٨﴾

39. Warn them of the woeful day when the final decree will be issued; they are neglectful and faithless.

39. Wa an<u>z</u>irhum Yawmal ḥasrati i<u>z</u> quḍiyal-amr; wa hum fee ghaflatiñw-wa hum laa yu'minoon.

وَأَنذِرْهُمْ يَوْمَ الْحَسْرَةِ إِذْ قُضِيَ الْأَمْرُ وقف لازم
وَهُمْ فِي غَفْلَةٍ وَهُمْ لَا يُؤْمِنُونَ ﴿٣٩﴾

40. We are the heirs of the earth and those living in it will all return to Us.

40. Innaa Naḥnu nari<u>s</u>ul -arḍa wa man 'alayhaa wa ilaynaa yurja'oon.

إِنَّا نَحْنُ نَرِثُ الْأَرْضَ وَمَنْ عَلَيْهَا
وَإِلَيْنَا يُرْجَعُونَ ﴿٤٠﴾ ع ٢٥/٢ ٥

41. Mention the story of Abraham, the truthful Prophet, in the Book (the Quran)

41. Wa<u>z</u>kur fil-Kitaabi Ibraaheem; innahoo kaana ṣiddeeqan-Nabiyyaa.

وَاذْكُرْ فِي الْكِتَابِ إِبْرَاهِيمَ إِنَّهُ
كَانَ صِدِّيقًا نَّبِيًّا ﴿٤١﴾

42. who asked his father, "Father, why do you worship something that can neither hear nor see nor help you at all?

42. I<u>z</u> qaala li-abeehi yaaa abati lima ta'budu maa laa yasma'u wa laa yubṣiru wa laa yughnee 'anka shay'aa.

إِذْ قَالَ لِأَبِيهِ يَا أَبَتِ لِمَ تَعْبُدُ
مَا لَا يَسْمَعُ وَلَا يُبْصِرُ وَلَا يُغْنِي
عَنكَ شَيْئًا ﴿٤٢﴾

43. "Father, I have received the knowledge which had not been given to you. Follow me; I shall guide you to the right path.

43. Yaaa abati innee qad jaaa'anee minal-'ilmi maa lam ya-tika fattabi'neee ahdika Ṣiraaṭan Sawiyyaa.

يَا أَبَتِ إِنِّي قَدْ جَاءَنِي مِنَ الْعِلْمِ مَا لَمْ
يَأْتِكَ فَاتَّبِعْنِي أَهْدِكَ صِرَاطًا سَوِيًّا ﴿٤٣﴾

44. Father, do not worship Satan; he has disobeyed the Beneficent.

44. Yaaa abati laa ta'budish-Shayṭaana innash-Shayṭaana kaana lir-Raḥmaani 'aṣiyyaa.

يٰٓاَبَتِ لَا تَعۡبُدِ الشَّيۡطٰنَ ؕ اِنَّ الشَّيۡطٰنَ
كَانَ لِلرَّحۡمٰنِ عَصِيًّا ﴿٤٤﴾

45. Father, I am afraid that the Beneficent Allah's torment will strike you and you will become a friend of Satan."

45. Yaaa abati inneee akhaafu añy-yamassaka 'azaabum-minar-Raḥmaani fatakoona lish-Shayṭaani waliyyaa.

يٰٓاَبَتِ اِنِّيۡۤ اَخَافُ اَنۡ يَّمَسَّكَ عَذَابٌ
مِّنَ الرَّحۡمٰنِ فَتَكُوۡنَ لِلشَّيۡطٰنِ وَلِيًّا ﴿٤٥﴾

46. His father replied, "Abraham, are you telling me to give up my gods? If you did not stop this, I shall stone you to death. Leave my house and do not come back again."

46. Qaala araaghibun anta 'an aalihatee yaaa Ibraaheemu la'il-lam tantahi la-arjumannaka wahjurnee maliyyaa.

قَالَ اَرَاغِبٌ اَنۡتَ عَنۡ اٰلِهَتِيۡ
يٰۤاِبۡرٰهِيۡمُ ۚ لَئِنۡ لَّمۡ تَنۡتَهِ لَاَرۡجُمَنَّكَ
وَاهۡجُرۡنِيۡ مَلِيًّا ﴿٤٦﴾

47. Abraham said, "Peace be with you. I shall ask my Lord to forgive you; He has been gracious to me.

47. Qaala salaamun 'alayka sa-astaghfiru laka Rabbeee innahoo kaana bee ḥafiyyaa.

قَالَ سَلٰمٌ عَلَيۡكَ ۚ سَاَسۡتَغۡفِرُ لَكَ رَبِّيۡ ؕ
اِنَّهٗ كَانَ بِيۡ حَفِيًّا ﴿٤٧﴾

48. I shall stay away from you and what you worship instead of Allah. I worship my Lord and hope that my prayers will not be ignored."

48. Wa a'tazilukum wa maa tad'oona min doonil-laahi wa ad'oo Rabbee 'asaaa allaaa akoona bidu'aa'i Rabbee shaqiyyaa.

وَاَعۡتَزِلُكُمۡ وَمَا تَدۡعُوۡنَ مِنۡ دُوۡنِ
اللّٰهِ وَاَدۡعُوۡا رَبِّيۡ ۖ عَسٰۤى اَلَّاۤ اَكُوۡنَ
بِدُعَآءِ رَبِّيۡ شَقِيًّا ﴿٤٨﴾

49. When (Abraham) rejected his people and what they worshipped instead of Allah, We gave him Isaac and Jacob and made both of them Prophets.

49. Falamma'-tazalahum wa maa ya'budoona min doonil-laahi wahabnaa lahoo Isḥaaqa wa Ya'qoob; wa kullan ja'alnaa Nabiyyaa.

فَلَمَّا اعۡتَزَلَهُمۡ وَمَا يَعۡبُدُوۡنَ مِنۡ
دُوۡنِ اللّٰهِ ۙ وَهَبۡنَا لَهٗۤ اِسۡحٰقَ وَ
يَعۡقُوۡبَ ؕ وَكُلًّا جَعَلۡنَا نَبِيًّا ﴿٤٩﴾

50. We granted them from Our mercy and made their tongues truthful and of high renown.

50. Wa wahabnaa lahum-mirraḥmatinaa wa ja'alnaa lahum lisaana ṣidqin 'aliyyaa.

وَوَهَبۡنَا لَهُمۡ مِّنۡ رَّحۡمَتِنَا وَجَعَلۡنَا
لَهُمۡ لِسَانَ صِدۡقٍ عَلِيًّا ﴿٥٠﴾ ع

51. (Muhammad), mention in the Book (the Quran) the story of Moses. Moses was a sincere person, a Messenger and a Prophet.

51. Wazkur fil-Kitaabi Moo-saaa; innahoo kaana mukhla-ṣañw-wa kaana Rasoolan-Nabiyyaa.

وَاذۡكُرۡ فِى الۡكِتٰبِ مُوۡسٰٓى ۚ اِنَّهٗ كَانَ
مُخۡلَصًا وَّكَانَ رَسُوۡلًا نَّبِيًّا ﴿٥١﴾

52. We called him from the right side of Mount Sinai and drew him close for communication.

52. Wa naadaynaahu min jaanibiṭ-Ṭooril-aymani wa qarrabnaahu najiyyaa.

وَنَادَيۡنٰهُ مِنۡ جَانِبِ الطُّوۡرِ الۡاَيۡمَنِ
وَقَرَّبۡنٰهُ نَجِيًّا ﴿٥٢﴾

53. Out of Our mercy We gave him his brother Aaron who himself was a Prophet.

53. Wa wahabnaa lahoo mirraḥmatinaaa akhaahu Haaroona Nabiyyaa.

وَوَهَبۡنَا لَهٗ مِنۡ رَّحۡمَتِنَاۤ اَخَاهُ
هٰرُوۡنَ نَبِيًّا ﴿٥٣﴾

54. Mention in the Book (the Quran) the story of Ishmael; he was true to his promise, a Messenger and a Prophet.

54. Wazkur fil-Kitaabi Ismaa-'eel; innahoo kaana ṣaadiqal-wa'di wa kaana Rasoolan-Nabiyyaa.

وَاذۡكُرۡ فِى الۡكِتٰبِ اِسۡمٰعِيۡلَ ۚ اِنَّهٗ كَانَ
صَادِقَ الۡوَعۡدِ وَكَانَ رَسُوۡلًا نَّبِيًّا ﴿٥٤﴾

55. He would order his people to worship Allah and pay the re-

55. Wa kaana ya-muru ahlahoo biṣ-Ṣalaati waz-

وَكَانَ يَاۡمُرُ اَهۡلَهٗ بِالصَّلٰوةِ وَ

ligious tax. His Lord was pleased with him.

zakaati wa kaana 'inda Rabbihee marḍiyyaa.

الزَّكٰوةِ ۖ وَكَانَ عِنْدَ رَبِّهٖ مَرْضِيًّا ﴿٥٥﴾

56. Mention in the Book (the Quran) the story of Idris (Enoch); he was a truthful Prophet.

56. Wazkur fil-Kitaabi Idrees; innahoo kaana ṣiddeeqan-Nabiyyaa.

وَاذْكُرْ فِي الْكِتٰبِ إِدْرِيسَ ۚ إِنَّهٗ
كَانَ صِدِّيقًا نَّبِيًّا ﴿٥٦﴾

57. We granted him (took to the fourth heaven where he died) a high position.

57. Wa rafa'naahu makaanan 'aliyyaa.

وَّرَفَعْنٰهُ مَكَانًا عَلِيًّا ﴿٥٧﴾

58. These were the Prophets from the offspring of Adam, from those who embarked with Noah and from the offspring of Abraham and Israel. Allah guided them and chose them for His favor. Whenever they would hear the revelations of the Beneficent they would bow down in prostration with tears.

(Bow Down)

58. Ulaaa'ikal-lazeena an'a-mal-laahu 'alayhim-minan-Nabiyyeena min zurriyyati Aadama wa mimman ḥamalnaa ma'a Nooḥiñw-wa min zurriy-yati Ibraaheema wa Israaa'eela wa mimman hadaynaa wajta-baynaaa; izaa tutlaa 'alayhim Aayaatur-Raḥmaani kharroo sujjadañw-wa bukiyyaa.

أُولٰٓئِكَ الَّذِينَ أَنْعَمَ اللّٰهُ عَلَيْهِمْ مِّنَ
النَّبِيّٖنَ مِنْ ذُرِّيَّةِ اٰدَمَ ۗ وَمِمَّنْ
حَمَلْنَا مَعَ نُوحٍ ۬ وَّمِنْ ذُرِّيَّةِ
إِبْرٰهِيمَ وَإِسْرَآءِيلَ ۬ وَمِمَّنْ هَدَيْنَا
وَاجْتَبَيْنَا ۚ إِذَا تُتْلٰى عَلَيْهِمْ اٰيٰتُ
الرَّحْمٰنِ خَرُّوا سُجَّدًا وَّبُكِيًّا ﴿٥٨﴾ السجدة

السجدة ٥

59. They were succeeded by a generation who neglected their prayers and followed their worldly desires. They will certainly be lost,

59. Fakhalafa mim ba'dihim khalfun aḍaa'uṣ-Ṣalaata wat-taba'ush-shahawaati fasawfa yalqawna ghayyaa.

فَخَلَفَ مِنْ بَعْدِهِمْ خَلْفٌ أَضَاعُوا
الصَّلٰوةَ وَاتَّبَعُوا الشَّهَوٰتِ فَسَوْفَ
يَلْقَوْنَ غَيًّا ﴿٥٩﴾

60. but those among them who repent and become righteously striving believers will be admitted to the gardens without experiencing any injustice.

60. Illaa man taaba wa aamana wa 'amila ṣaaliḥan fa-ulaaa'ika yadkhuloonal-jannata wa laa yuẓlamoona shay'aa.

إِلَّا مَنْ تَابَ وَاٰمَنَ وَعَمِلَ صَالِحًا
فَأُولٰٓئِكَ يَدْخُلُونَ الْجَنَّةَ وَلَا
يُظْلَمُونَ شَيْـًٔا ﴿٦٠﴾

61. They will be admitted to the garden of Eden which is the unseen promise of the Beneficent to His servants. His promise will certainly come true.

61. jannaati 'Adninil-latee wa'adar-Raḥmaanu 'ibaadahoo bilghayb; innahoo kaana wa'duhoo ma-tiyyaa.

جَنّٰتِ عَدْنِ ٱلَّتِي وَعَدَ الرَّحْمٰنُ عِبَادَهٗ
بِالْغَيْبِ ۗ إِنَّهٗ كَانَ وَعْدُهٗ مَأْتِيًّا ﴿٦١﴾

62. They will not hear therein any meaningless words. They will be greeted (by the angels) with "Peace be with you," and they will receive their sustenance both in the mornings and in the evenings (in paradise in this world).

62. Laa yasma'oona feehaa laghwan illaa salaamaa; wa lahum rizquhum feehaa bukra-tañw-wa 'ashiyyaa.

لَا يَسْمَعُونَ فِيهَا لَغْوًا إِلَّا سَلٰمًا ۖ
وَلَهُمْ رِزْقُهُمْ فِيهَا بُكْرَةً وَّعَشِيًّا ﴿٦٢﴾

63. Such are the gardens which We will give to Our pious servants as their inherited property.

63. Tilkal-jannatul-latee noo-risu min 'ibaadinaa man kaana taqiyyaa.

تِلْكَ الْجَنَّةُ الَّتِي نُورِثُ مِنْ عِبَادِنَا
مَنْ كَانَ تَقِيًّا ﴿٦٣﴾

64. (Muhammad), we (the angels) do not come to you without being commanded by your Lord to do so. To Him belongs all that is before us, behind us, and in between. Your Lord is not forgetful.

64. Wa maa natanazzalu illaa bi-amri Rabbika lahoo maa bayna aydeenaa wa maa khal-fanaa wa maa bayna zaalik; wa maa kaana Rabbuka nasiyyaa.

وَمَا نَتَنَزَّلُ إِلَّا بِأَمْرِ رَبِّكَ ۚ لَهٗ مَا
بَيْنَ أَيْدِينَا وَمَا خَلْفَنَا وَمَا بَيْنَ
ذٰلِكَ ۚ وَمَا كَانَ رَبُّكَ نَسِيًّا ﴿٦٤﴾

65. He is the Lord of the heavens and the earth and all that

65. Rabbus-samaawaati wal-arḍi wa maa baynahumaa

رَبُّ السَّمٰوٰتِ وَالْأَرْضِ وَمَا بَيْنَهُمَا

is between them. Worship Him and be steadfast in your worship of Him; no one is equal to Him.	fa'bud-hu waṣṭabir li'ibaadatih; hal ta'lamu lahoo samiyyaa.	فَاعْبُدْهُ وَاصْطَبِرْ لِعِبَادَتِهٖ ط هَلْ تَعْلَمُ لَهٗ سَمِيًّا ﴿٦٥﴾
66. The human being says, "Shall I be brought to life again after I die?"	66. Wa yaqoolul-insaanu 'a-izaa maa mittu lasawfa ukhraju ḥayyaa.	وَيَقُوْلُ الْاِنْسَانُ ءَاِذَا مَا مِتُّ لَسَوْفَ اُخْرَجُ حَيًّا ﴿٦٦﴾
67. Does he not remember that We created him when he did not exist?	67. Awalaa yazkurul-insaanu annaa khalaqnaahu min qablu wa lam yaku shay'aa.	اَوَلَا يَذْكُرُ الْاِنْسَانُ اَنَّا خَلَقْنٰهُ مِنْ قَبْلُ وَلَمْ يَكُ شَيْئًا ﴿٦٧﴾
68. By your Lord, We will bring them back to life with Satan and gather them around hell on their knees.	68. Fawa Rabbika lanaḥshu-rannahum wash-shayaaṭeena summa lanuḥḍirannahum ḥawla Jahannama jisiyyaa.	فَوَرَبِّكَ لَنَحْشُرَنَّهُمْ وَالشَّيٰطِيْنَ ثُمَّ لَنُحْضِرَنَّهُمْ حَوْلَ جَهَنَّمَ جِثِيًّا ﴿٦٨﴾
69. Then We will separate from every group those who were strongly rebellious against the Beneficent.	69. Summa lananzi 'anna min kulli shee'atin ayyuhum ashaddu 'alar-Raḥmaani 'itiyyaa.	ثُمَّ لَنَنْزِعَنَّ مِنْ كُلِّ شِيْعَةٍ اَيُّهُمْ اَشَدُّ عَلَى الرَّحْمٰنِ عِتِيًّا ﴿٦٩﴾
70. We know best who deserves greater suffering in hellfire.	70. Summa lanaḥnu a'lamu billazeena hum awlaa bihaa ṣiliyyaa.	ثُمَّ لَنَحْنُ اَعْلَمُ بِالَّذِيْنَ هُمْ اَوْلٰى بِهَا صِلِيًّا ﴿٧٠﴾
71. It is the inevitable decree of your Lord that every one of you will be taken to hell.	71. Wa im-minkum illaa waa-riduhaa; kaana 'alaa Rabbika ḥatmam-maqḍiyyaa.	وَاِنْ مِّنْكُمْ اِلَّا وَارِدُهَا ج كَانَ عَلٰى رَبِّكَ حَتْمًا مَّقْضِيًّا ﴿٧١﴾
72. We will save the pious ones from the hell fire and leave the unjust people therein on their knees.	72. Summa nunajjil-lazeenat-taqaw wa nazaruẓẓaalimeena feehaa jisiyyaa.	ثُمَّ نُنَجِّي الَّذِيْنَ اتَّقَوْا وَّنَذَرُ الظّٰلِمِيْنَ فِيْهَا جِثِيًّا ﴿٧٢﴾
73. When Our revelations are recited to them, the unbelievers say to the faithful ones, "Which of us is more prosperous?"	73. Wa izaa tutlaa 'alayhim Aayaatunaa bayyinaatin qaalal-lazeena kafaroo lillazeena aamanooo ayyulfareeqayni khayrum-maqaamañw-wa aḥsanu nadiyyaa.	وَاِذَا تُتْلٰى عَلَيْهِمْ اٰيٰتُنَا بَيِّنٰتٍ قَالَ الَّذِيْنَ كَفَرُوْا لِلَّذِيْنَ اٰمَنُوْٓا ۙ اَيُّ الْفَرِيْقَيْنِ خَيْرٌ مَّقَامًا وَّ اَحْسَنُ نَدِيًّا ﴿٧٣﴾
74. How many generations of greater prosperity and splendor have We destroyed before them?	74. Wa kam ahlaknaa qabla-hum-min qarnin hum aḥsanu asaasañw-wa ri'yaa.	وَكَمْ اَهْلَكْنَا قَبْلَهُمْ مِّنْ قَرْنٍ هُمْ اَحْسَنُ اَثَاثًا وَّرِءْيًا ﴿٧٤﴾
75. (Muhammad), say to them, "The Beneficent gives respite to those who have gone astray only until they face the torment with which they were threatened or the Day of Judgment. Then they will find out who will have the most miserable place and the weakest	75. Qul man kaana fiḍḍa-laalati falyamdud lahur-Raḥ-maanu maddaa; ḥattaaa izaa ra-aw maa yoo'adoona immal-'azaaba wa immas-Saa'ata fasa-ya'lamoona man huwa sharrum-	قُلْ مَنْ كَانَ فِي الضَّلٰلَةِ فَلْيَمْدُدْ لَهُ الرَّحْمٰنُ مَدًّا ۚ حَتّٰٓى اِذَا رَاَوْا مَا يُوْعَدُوْنَ اِمَّا الْعَذَابَ وَاِمَّا السَّاعَةَ ط فَسَيَعْلَمُوْنَ مَنْ هُوَ شَرٌّ

forces.

makaanañw-wa aḍ'afu jundaa.

مَكَانًا وَّاَضْعَفُ جُنْدًا ۝٧٥

76. Allah further enlightens those who seek guidance. To those who do charitable deeds which produce continuing benefits, your Lord will give a better reward and a better place in paradise.

76. Wa yazeedullaahul-lazeenah-tadaw hudaa; wal-baaqiyaatuṣṣaaliḥaatu khayrun 'inda Rabbika sawaabañw-wa khayrum-maraddaa.

وَيَزِيْدُ اللّٰهُ الَّذِيْنَ اهْتَدَوْا هُدًى ؕ
وَالْبٰقِيٰتُ الصّٰلِحٰتُ خَيْرٌ عِنْدَ
رَبِّكَ ثَوَابًا وَّخَيْرٌ مَّرَدًّا ۝٧٦

77. Consider the words of the disbeliever, "I shall certainly be given wealth and children (in paradise)."

77. Afara'aytal-lazee kafara bi-Aayaatinaa wa qaala la-ootayanna maalañw-wa waladaa.

اَفَرَءَيْتَ الَّذِيْ كَفَرَ بِاٰيٰتِنَا وَقَالَ
لَاُوْتَيَنَّ مَالًا وَّوَلَدًا ۝٧٧

78. Has he the knowledge of the unseen or has the Beneficent established such a binding agreement with Him?

78. Aṭṭala'al-ghayba amittakhaza 'indar-Raḥmaani 'ahdaa.

اَطَّلَعَ الْغَيْبَ اَمِ اتَّخَذَ عِنْدَ
الرَّحْمٰنِ عَهْدًا ۝٧٨

79. Absolutely not, We will record his words and prolong his punishment.

79. Kallaa; sanaktubu maa yaqoolu wa namuddu lahoo minal-'azaabi maddaa.

كَلَّا ؕ سَنَكْتُبُ مَا يَقُوْلُ وَنَمُدُّ لَهٗ
مِنَ الْعَذَابِ مَدًّا ۝٧٩

80. We will make, all that he speaks as his legacy, and he will come into Our presence all alone.

80. Wa narisuhoo maa yaqoolu wa ya-teenaa fardaa.

وَّنَرِثُهٗ مَا يَقُوْلُ وَيَاْتِيْنَا فَرْدًا ۝٨٠

81. They have sought honor from other gods instead of Allah.

81. Wattakhazoo min doonil-laahi aalihatal-liyakoonoo lahum 'izzaa.

وَاتَّخَذُوْا مِنْ دُوْنِ اللّٰهِ اٰلِهَةً لِّيَكُوْنُوْا
لَهُمْ عِزًّا ۝٨١

82. In fact, they can have no honor; their gods will renounce their worship of idols and will turn against them.

82. Kallaa; sa-yakfuroona bi'ibaadatihim wa yakoonoona 'alayhim ḍiddaa.

كَلَّا ؕ سَيَكْفُرُوْنَ بِعِبَادَتِهِمْ وَ
يَكُوْنُوْنَ عَلَيْهِمْ ضِدًّا ۝٨٢ ع ٧/٥

83. Did you not see that We have sent Satan to incite the unbelievers to sin (withhold Khums and zakat)?

83. Alam tara annaaa arsalnash-Shayaaṭeena 'alal-kaafireena ta'uzzuhum azzaa.

اَلَمْ تَرَ اَنَّاۤ اَرْسَلْنَا الشَّيٰطِيْنَ
عَلَى الْكٰفِرِيْنَ تَؤُزُّهُمْ اَزًّا ۝٨٣

84. (Muhammad), do not be hasty; We count it for them exactly (how many times they breathe).

84. Falaa ta'jal 'alayhim innamaa na'uddu lahum 'addaa.

فَلَا تَعْجَلْ عَلَيْهِمْ ؕ اِنَّمَا نَعُدُّ لَهُمْ
عَدًّا ۝٨٤

85. On the Day of Judgment, when the pious people will be brought in the presence of the Beneficent as the guests of honor

85. Yawma naḥshurul-muttaqeena ilar-Raḥmaani wafdaa.

يَوْمَ نَحْشُرُ الْمُتَّقِيْنَ اِلَى الرَّحْمٰنِ
وَفْدًا ۝٨٥

86. and the criminals will be driven and thrown into hell,

86. Wa nasooqul-mujrimeena ilaa Jahannama wirdaa.

وَّنَسُوْقُ الْمُجْرِمِيْنَ اِلٰى جَهَنَّمَ وِرْدًا ۝٨٦ وقف لازم

87. no one will benefit from the intercession except those who establish a covenant with the Beneficent before they die.

87. Laa yamlikoonash-shafaa'ata illaa manittakhaza 'indar-Raḥmaani 'ahdaa.

لَا يَمْلِكُوْنَ الشَّفَاعَةَ اِلَّا مَنِ اتَّخَذَ
عِنْدَ الرَّحْمٰنِ عَهْدًا ۝٨٧ وقف لازم

88. They have said that the Beneficent has given birth to a son.

88. Wa qaalut-takhazar-Raḥmaanu waladaa.

وَقَالُوا اتَّخَذَ الرَّحْمٰنُ وَلَدًا ۝٨٨

89. This is certainly a monstrous lie (unjust).

89. Laqad ji'tum shay'an iddaa.

لَقَدْ جِئْتُمْ شَيْـًٔا اِدًّا ۝٨٩

90. This would almost cause the heavens to rend apart, the earth to cleave asunder, and the mountains to crumble down in fragments,

90. Takaadus-samaawaatu yatafaṭṭarna minhu wa tanshaq-qul-arḍu wa takhirrul-jibaalu haddaa.

تَكَادُ السَّمٰوٰتُ يَتَفَطَّرْنَ مِنْهُ وَ
تَنْشَقُّ الْاَرْضُ وَتَخِرُّ الْجِبَالُ هَدًّا ﴿۹۰﴾

91. to ascribe a son to the Beneficent.

91. An da'aw lir-Raḥmaani waladaa.

اَنْ دَعَوْا لِلرَّحْمٰنِ وَلَدًا ﴿۹۱﴾

92. The Beneficent is free of all defects of having a son.

92. Wa maa yambaghee lir-Raḥmaani añy-yattakhiza waladaa.

وَمَا يَنْۢبَغِيْ لِلرَّحْمٰنِ اَنْ يَّتَّخِذَ وَلَدًا ﴿۹۲﴾

93. All that is in the heavens and the earth will return to the Beneficent as His submissive servants.

93. In kullu man fis-samaa-waati wal-arḍi illaaa aatir-Raḥmaani 'abdaa.

اِنْ كُلُّ مَنْ فِي السَّمٰوٰتِ وَالْاَرْضِ
اِلَّاۤ اٰتِي الرَّحْمٰنِ عَبْدًا ﴿۹۳﴾

94. He has counted and enumerated them one by one.

94. Laqad aḥṣaahum wa 'addahum 'addaa.

لَقَدْ اَحْصٰىهُمْ وَعَدَّهُمْ عَدًّا ﴿۹۴﴾

95. Everyone on the Day of Judgment will individually come into the presence of Allah.

95. Wa kulluhum aateehi Yawmal-Qiyaamati fardaa.

وَكُلُّهُمْ اٰتِيْهِ يَوْمَ الْقِيٰمَةِ فَرْدًا ﴿۹۵﴾

96. To the righteously striving believers the Beneficent will grant love.

96. Innal-lazeena aamanoo wa 'amiluṣ-ṣaaliḥaati sa-yaj'alu lahumur-Raḥmaanu wuddaa.

اِنَّ الَّذِيْنَ اٰمَنُوْا وَعَمِلُوا الصّٰلِحٰتِ
سَيَجْعَلُ لَهُمُ الرَّحْمٰنُ وُدًّا ﴿۹۶﴾

97. (Muhammad), We have given you the Book (the Quran) in your own language so that you can easily give the glad news to the pious ones and warn the quarrelsome ones.

97. Fa-innamaa yassarnaahu bilisaanika litubashshira bihil-muttaqeena wa tunzira bihee qawmal-luddaa.

فَاِنَّمَا يَسَّرْنٰهُ بِلِسَانِكَ لِتُبَشِّرَ بِهِ
الْمُتَّقِيْنَ وَتُنْذِرَ بِهٖ قَوْمًا لُّدًّا ﴿۹۷﴾

98. How many generations living before them did We destroy? Do you find anyone of them around or do you even hear any word (trace) from them?

98. Wa kam ahlaknaa qabla-hum-min qarnin hal tuḥissu minhum-min aḥadin aw tasma'u lahum rikzaa.

وَكَمْ اَهْلَكْنَا قَبْلَهُمْ مِّنْ قَرْنٍ ؕ هَلْ
تُحِسُّ مِنْهُمْ مِّنْ اَحَدٍ اَوْ تَسْمَعُ
لَهُمْ رِكْزًا ﴿۹۸﴾ ع

النصف ع ۱۶

Ta Ha, Ta Ha (20)

In the Name of Allah,
the Beneficent, the Merciful.

Sûrat Tâ-Hâ-20

(Revealed at Makkah)
Bismillaahir Raḥmaanir Raḥeem

(۲۰) سُوْرَةُ طٰهٰ مَكِّيَّةٌ (۴۵)
اٰياتها ۱۳۵ بِسْمِ اللّٰهِ الرَّحْمٰنِ الرَّحِيْمِ ركوعاتها ۸

1. Ta Ha.

1. Ṭaa-Haa.

طٰهٰ ﴿۱﴾

2. We have sent the Quran only as reminder

2. Maaa anzalnaa 'alaykal-Qur'aana litashqaaa.

مَاۤ اَنْزَلْنَا عَلَيْكَ الْقُرْاٰنَ لِتَشْقٰۤى ﴿۲﴾

3. for those who have fear (of disobeying Allah), not to make you, (Muhammad), miserable.

3. Illaa tazkiratal-limañy-yakhshaa.

اِلَّا تَذْكِرَةً لِّمَنْ يَّخْشٰى ﴿۳﴾

4. It is a revelation from the Creator of the earth and the high heavens.

4. Tanzeelam-mimman khalaqal-arḍa was-sama-awaatil-'ulaa.

تَنْزِيْلًا مِّمَّنْ خَلَقَ الْاَرْضَ وَالسَّمٰوٰتِ
الْعُلٰى ﴿۴﴾

5. The Beneficent (in the matters of His domination) maintains full balance (nothing is closer or farther than others to Him) over the Throne.

5. Ar-Raḥmaanu 'alal-'Arshis-tawaa.

اَلرَّحْمٰنُ عَلَى الْعَرْشِ اسْتَوٰى ﴿۵﴾

6. To Him belongs all that is in the heavens and the earth, all that lies between them, and lies below the earth.

6. Lahoo maa fis-samaa-waati wa maa fil-arḍi wa maa baynahumaa wa maa taḥtas-saraa.

لَهٗ مَا فِي السَّمٰوٰتِ وَمَا فِي الْاَرْضِ وَمَا
بَيْنَهُمَا وَمَا تَحْتَ الثَّرٰى ﴿۶﴾

7. Whether or not you express (your thoughts) in words, Allah certainly knows all silently spoken

7. Wa in tajhar bilqawli fa-innahoo ya'lamus-sirra

وَاِنْ تَجْهَرْ بِالْقَوْلِ فَاِنَّهٗ يَعْلَمُ السِّرَّ

words and what is even more difficult to find (all forgotten thoughts).	wa akhfaa.	وَأَخْفَى ٧
8. Allah is the only Lord and to Him belongs all the exalted names.	8. Allaahu laaa ilaaha illaa Huwa lahul-Asmaaa'ul Ḥusnaa.	اللَّهُ لَا إِلَٰهَ إِلَّا هُوَ ۖ لَهُ الْأَسْمَاءُ الْحُسْنَىٰ ٨
9. (Muhammad), have you heard the story of Moses?	9. Wa hal ataaka ḥadeesu Moosaaa.	وَهَلْ أَتَاكَ حَدِيثُ مُوسَىٰ ٩
10. When he saw the fire, he said to his family, "Wait here for I can see a fire. Perhaps I shall bring you a burning torch or find a way to some fire."	10. Iz ra-aa naaran faqaala li-ahlihim-kusooo inneee aanastu naaral-la'alleee aateekum minhaa biqabasin aw ajidu 'alan-naari hudaa.	إِذْ رَأَىٰ نَارًا فَقَالَ لِأَهْلِهِ امْكُثُوا إِنِّي آنَسْتُ نَارًا لَعَلِّي آتِيكُمْ مِنْهَا بِقَبَسٍ أَوْ أَجِدُ عَلَى النَّارِ هُدًى ١٠
11. When he came near the fire he was called, "Moses,	11. Falammaaa ataahaa noodiya yaa Moosaaa.	فَلَمَّا أَتَاهَا نُودِيَ يَا مُوسَىٰ ١١
12. I am your Lord. Take off your shoes (of unclean donkey-skin); you are in the Holy valley of Tuwa.	12. Inneee Ana Rabbuka fakhla' na'layka innaka bilwaadil-muqaddasi Ṭuwaa.	إِنِّي أَنَا رَبُّكَ فَاخْلَعْ نَعْلَيْكَ ۖ إِنَّكَ بِالْوَادِ الْمُقَدَّسِ طُوًى ١٢
13. I have chosen you as My Messenger. Listen to the revelation.	13. Wa anakhtartuka fastami' limaa yooḥaaa.	وَأَنَا اخْتَرْتُكَ فَاسْتَمِعْ لِمَا يُوحَىٰ ١٣
14. I Am Allah, the only Ilah (one deserving to be worshiped). Worship Me and be steadfast in prayer to have My name (always) in your mind.	14. Innaneee Anal-laahu laaa ilaaha illaaa Ana fa'budnee wa-aqimiṣ-Ṣalaata lizikree.	إِنَّنِي أَنَا اللَّهُ لَا إِلَٰهَ إِلَّا أَنَا فَاعْبُدْنِي وَأَقِمِ الصَّلَاةَ لِذِكْرِي ١٤
15. The Day of Judgment will certainly come, but I keep it (its coming) anonymous (a secret) so that every soul will receive the recompense for what it has done (on its own).	15. Innas-Saa'ata aatiyatun akaadu ukhfeehaa litujzaa kullu nafsim bimaa tas'aa.	إِنَّ السَّاعَةَ آتِيَةٌ أَكَادُ أُخْفِيهَا لِتُجْزَىٰ كُلُّ نَفْسٍ بِمَا تَسْعَىٰ ١٥
16. Let not the unbelievers who follow their vain desires make you forget the Day of Judgment, lest you perish."	16. Falaa yaṣuddannaka 'anhaa mal-laa yu'minu bihaa wattaba'a hawaahu fatardaa.	فَلَا يَصُدَّنَّكَ عَنْهَا مَنْ لَا يُؤْمِنُ بِهَا وَاتَّبَعَ هَوَاهُ فَتَرْدَىٰ ١٦
17. The Lord asked, "Moses, what is in your right hand?"	17. Wa maa tilka bi-yameenika yaa Moosaa.	وَمَا تِلْكَ بِيَمِينِكَ يَا مُوسَىٰ ١٧
18. He replied, "It is my staff. I lean on it, bring down leaves for my sheep with it, and need it for other reasons."	18. Qaala hiya 'aṣaaya atawakka'u 'alayhaa wa ahushshu bihaa 'alaa ghanamee wa liya feehaa ma-aaribu ukhraa.	قَالَ هِيَ عَصَايَ أَتَوَكَّأُ عَلَيْهَا وَأَهُشُّ بِهَا عَلَىٰ غَنَمِي وَلِيَ فِيهَا مَآرِبُ أُخْرَىٰ ١٨
19. The Lord said, "Moses, throw it on the ground."	19. Qaala alqihaa yaa Moosaa.	قَالَ أَلْقِهَا يَا مُوسَىٰ ١٩
20. Moses threw it on the ground and suddenly he saw that it was a moving serpent.	20. Fa-alqaahaa fa-izaa hiya ḥayyatun tas'aa.	فَأَلْقَاهَا فَإِذَا هِيَ حَيَّةٌ تَسْعَىٰ ٢٠
21. The Lord said, "Hold the serpent and do not be afraid; We will bring it back to its original form."	21. Qaala khuzhaa wa laa takhaf sanu'eeduhaa seeratahal-oolaa.	قَالَ خُذْهَا وَلَا تَخَفْ ۖ سَنُعِيدُهَا سِيرَتَهَا الْأُولَىٰ ٢١
22. "Now - as another Sign - place your hand under your arm and it will come out sheer white without harm (or stain).	22. Waḍmum yadaka ilaa janaaḥika takhruj bayḍaaa'a min ghayri sooo'in Aayatan ukhraa.	وَاضْمُمْ يَدَكَ إِلَىٰ جَنَاحِكَ تَخْرُجْ بَيْضَاءَ مِنْ غَيْرِ سُوءٍ آيَةً أُخْرَىٰ ٢٢

وقف لازم

23. This We have done to show you some of Our greater miracles.	23. Linuriyaka min Aayaa-tinal-Kubraa.	لِنُرِيَكَ مِنْ اٰيٰتِنَا الْكُبْرٰى ﴿٢٣﴾
24. Go to the Pharaoh; he has become a rebel."	24. Izhab ilaa Fir'awna inna-hoo ṭaghaa.	اِذْهَبْ اِلٰى فِرْعَوْنَ اِنَّهٗ طَغٰى ﴿٢٤﴾ ع ١/٢٤ ١٠
25. Moses said, "Lord, grant me courage.	25. Qaala Rabbish-raḥ lee ṣadree.	قَالَ رَبِّ اشْرَحْ لِيْ صَدْرِيْ ﴿٢٥﴾
26. Make my task easy	26. Wa yassir leee amree.	وَيَسِّرْ لِيْٓ اَمْرِيْ ﴿٢٦﴾
27. and my tongue fluent	27. Waḥlul 'uqdatam-milli-saanee.	وَاحْلُلْ عُقْدَةً مِّنْ لِّسَانِيْ ﴿٢٧﴾
28. so that they may understand me.	28. Yafqahoo qawlee.	يَفْقَهُوْا قَوْلِيْ ﴿٢٨﴾
29. Appoint a deputy (for me) from my own people.	29. Waj'al-lee wazeeram-min ahlee.	وَاجْعَلْ لِّيْ وَزِيْرًا مِّنْ اَهْلِيْ ﴿٢٩﴾
30. Let it be my brother Aaron	30. Haaroona akhee.	هٰرُوْنَ اَخِي ﴿٣٠﴾
31. to support me.	31. Ushdud biheee azree.	اشْدُدْ بِهٖٓ اَزْرِيْ ﴿٣١﴾
32. Let him be my partner in this task	32. Wa ashrik-hu feee amree.	وَاَشْرِكْهُ فِيْٓ اَمْرِيْ ﴿٣٢﴾
33. so that we may glorify	33. Kay nusabbiḥaka kaseeraa.	كَيْ نُسَبِّحَكَ كَثِيْرًا ﴿٣٣﴾
34. and remember you often.	34. Wa nazkuraka kaseeraa.	وَّنَذْكُرَكَ كَثِيْرًا ﴿٣٤﴾
35. You are Well-aware of our situation."	35. Innaka kunta binaa baṣeeraa.	اِنَّكَ كُنْتَ بِنَا بَصِيْرًا ﴿٣٥﴾
36. The Lord said, "Moses, your request is granted.	36. Qaala qad ooteeta su'laka yaa Moosaa.	قَالَ قَدْ اُوْتِيْتَ سُؤْلَكَ يٰمُوْسٰى ﴿٣٦﴾
37. It is the second time that We have bestowed upon you Our favor.	37. Wa laqad manannaa 'alayka marratan ukhraaa.	وَلَقَدْ مَنَنَّا عَلَيْكَ مَرَّةً اُخْرٰٓى ﴿٣٧﴾
38. Remember when We revealed to your mother a certain revelation	38. Iz awḥaynaaa ilaaa ummika maa yooḥaaa.	اِذْ اَوْحَيْنَآ اِلٰٓى اُمِّكَ مَا يُوْحٰٓى ﴿٣٨﴾
39. to place her child in a chest and throw it into the sea which would hurl it towards the shore. Then an enemy of Mine who was also the enemy of the child would pick it up from there. I made you attractive and loveable so that you would be reared before My own eyes.	39. Aniqzifeehi fit-Taabooti faqzifeehi fil-yammi fal-yul-qihil-yammu bis-saaḥili ya-khuzhu 'aduwwul-lee wa 'aduwwul-lah; wa alqaytu 'alayka maḥabbatam-minnee wa lituṣna'a 'alaa 'ayneee.	اَنِ اقْذِفِيْهِ فِي التَّابُوْتِ فَاقْذِفِيْهِ فِي الْيَمِّ فَلْيُلْقِهِ الْيَمُّ بِالسَّاحِلِ يَاْخُذْهُ عَدُوٌّ لِّيْ وَعَدُوٌّ لَّهٗ ۭ وَاَلْقَيْتُ عَلَيْكَ مَحَبَّةً مِّنِّيْ ۚ وَلِتُصْنَعَ عَلٰي عَيْنِيْ ﴿٣٩﴾ وقف لازم
40. Your sister went to them and said, "May I show you someone who will nurse this child?" We returned you to your mother to make her rejoice and forget her grief. You slew a man and We saved you from trouble. We tried you through various trials. Then you stayed some years with the people of Madyan (Shuayb and his family) and after that you came back to Egypt as was ordained.	40. Iz tamsheee ukhtuka fataqoolu hal adullukum 'alaa mañy-yakfuluhoo-faraja'naaka ilaaa ummika kay taqarra 'aynuhaa wa laa taḥzan; wa qatalta nafsan fanajjaynaaka minal-ghammi wa fatannaaka futoonaa; falabista sineena feee ahli Madyana summa ji'ta 'alaa qadariñy-yaa Moosaa.	اِذْ تَمْشِيْٓ اُخْتُكَ فَتَقُوْلُ هَلْ اَدُلُّكُمْ عَلٰي مَنْ يَّكْفُلُهٗ ۭ فَرَجَعْنٰكَ اِلٰٓى اُمِّكَ كَيْ تَقَرَّ عَيْنُهَا وَلَا تَحْزَنَ ۥ وَقَتَلْتَ نَفْسًا فَنَجَّيْنٰكَ مِنَ الْغَمِّ وَفَتَنّٰكَ فُتُوْنًا ۥ فَلَبِثْتَ سِنِيْنَ فِيْٓ اَهْلِ مَدْيَنَ ۥ ثُمَّ جِئْتَ عَلٰي قَدَرٍ يّٰمُوْسٰى ﴿٤٠﴾

41. I chose you for Myself."	41. Waṣṭana'tuka linafsee.	وَاصْطَنَعْتُكَ لِنَفْسِيْ ﴿٤١﴾
42. "Go with your brother. Take My miracles and do not be weak in preaching My message.	42. Izhab anta wa akhooka bi-Aayaatee wa laa taniyaa fee zikree.	اِذْهَبْ اَنْتَ وَاَخُوْكَ بِاٰيٰتِيْ وَلَا تَنِيَا فِيْ ذِكْرِيْ ﴿٤٢﴾
43. Go both of you to the Pharaoh; he has become a rebel.	43. Izhabaaa ilaa Fir'awna innahoo ṭaghaa.	اِذْهَبَآ اِلٰى فِرْعَوْنَ اِنَّهٗ طَغٰى ﴿٤٣﴾
44. Both of you must speak with him in a gentle manner so that perhaps he may come to himself and have fear (of Allah)."	44. Faqoolaa lahoo qawlal-layyinal-la'allahoo yatazakkaru aw yakhshaa.	فَقُوْلَا لَهٗ قَوْلًا لَّيِّنًا لَّعَلَّهٗ يَتَذَكَّرُ اَوْ يَخْشٰى ﴿٤٤﴾
45. They said, "Our Lord, we are afraid of his transgression and rebellion against us."	45. Qaalaa Rabbanaaa innanaa nakhaafu añy-yafruṭa 'alaynaaa aw añy-yaṭghaa.	قَالَا رَبَّنَآ اِنَّنَا نَخَافُ اَنْ يَّفْرُطَ عَلَيْنَآ اَوْ اَنْ يَّطْغٰى ﴿٤٥﴾
46. The Lord replied to them, "Do not be afraid; I am with you all the time, listening and seeing."	46. Qaala laa takhaafaaa innanee ma'akumaaa asma'u wa araa.	قَالَ لَا تَخَافَآ اِنَّنِيْ مَعَكُمَآ اَسْمَعُ وَاَرٰى ﴿٤٦﴾
47. They came to the Pharaoh and told him that they were the Messengers of his Lord and that they wanted him to let the Israelites go with them and stop afflicting the Israelites with torment. They told the Pharaoh, "We have brought miracles from your Lord. Peace be with those who follow the right guidance.	47. Fa-tiyaahu faqoolaaa innaa Rasoolaa Rabbika fa-arsil ma'anaa Baneee Israaa'eela wa laa tu'azzibhum qad ji'naaka bi-Aayatim-mir-Rabbika wassa-laamu 'alaa manit-taba'al-hudaaa.	فَاْتِيٰهُ فَقُوْلَآ اِنَّا رَسُوْلَا رَبِّكَ فَاَرْسِلْ مَعَنَا بَنِيْٓ اِسْرَآءِيْلَ ۙ۬ وَلَا تُعَذِّبْهُمْ ؕ قَدْ جِئْنٰكَ بِاٰيَةٍ مِّنْ رَّبِّكَ ؕ وَالسَّلٰمُ عَلٰى مَنِ اتَّبَعَ الْهُدٰى ﴿٤٧﴾
48. It is revealed to us that those who call our message a lie or turn away from it will face the torment."	48. Innaa qad ooḥiya ilaynaaa annal-'azaaba 'alaa man kaz-zaba wa tawallaa.	اِنَّا قَدْ اُوْحِيَ اِلَيْنَآ اَنَّ الْعَذَابَ عَلٰى مَنْ كَذَّبَ وَتَوَلّٰى ﴿٤٨﴾
49. The Pharaoh asked them, "Who is your Lord?"	49. Qaala famar-Rabbu-kumaa yaa Moosaa.	قَالَ فَمَنْ رَّبُّكُمَا يٰمُوْسٰى ﴿٤٩﴾
50. They replied, "Our Lord is the One Who has created all things and has given guidance."	50. Qaala Rabbunal-lazeee a'ṭaa kulla shay'in khalqahoo summa hadaa.	قَالَ رَبُّنَا الَّذِيْٓ اَعْطٰى كُلَّ شَيْءٍ خَلْقَهٗ ثُمَّ هَدٰى ﴿٥٠﴾
51. He then asked, "What do you know about the past generations?"	51. Qaala famaa baalul-qurooonil-oolaa.	قَالَ فَمَا بَالُ الْقُرُوْنِ الْاُوْلٰى ﴿٥١﴾
52. Moses replied, "The knowledge about it is with my Lord in the Book. My Lord is free from error and forgetfulness.	52. Qaala 'ilmuhaa 'inda Rabbee fee kitaab; laa yaḍillu Rabbee wa laa yansaa.	قَالَ عِلْمُهَا عِنْدَ رَبِّيْ فِيْ كِتٰبٍ ۚ لَا يَضِلُّ رَبِّيْ وَلَا يَنْسَى ﴿٥٢﴾
53. It is Allah who has made the earth as a cradle for you with roads for you to travel. He has sent water from the sky to produce various pairs of plants.	53. Allazee ja'ala lakumul-arḍa mahdañw-wa salaka lakum feehaa subulañw-wa anzala minas-samaaa'i maaa'an fa-akhrajnaa biheee azwaajam-min-nabaatin shattaa.	الَّذِيْ جَعَلَ لَكُمُ الْاَرْضَ مَهْدًا وَّسَلَكَ لَكُمْ فِيْهَا سُبُلًا وَّاَنْزَلَ مِنَ السَّمَآءِ مَآءً ؕ فَاَخْرَجْنَا بِهٖٓ اَزْوَاجًا مِّنْ نَّبَاتٍ شَتّٰى ﴿٥٣﴾

54. Consume them as food or for grazing your cattle. In this there is evidence (of a great deal of information about the future of the mission) for the people of reason (with divine authority to decipher)."

54. Kuloo war'aw an'aamakum; inna fee zaalika la-Aayaatil-li-ulinnuhaa.

كُلُوْا وَارْعَوْا اَنْعَامَكُمْ ؕ اِنَّ فِيْ
ذٰلِكَ لَاٰيٰتٍ لِّاُولِي النُّهٰى ٥٤ ع ٢ ١١

55. We have created you from the earth to which We will return you and will bring you back to life again.

55. Minhaa khalaqnaakum wa feehaa nu'eedukum wa minhaa nukhrijukum taaratan ukhraa.

مِنْهَا خَلَقْنٰكُمْ وَفِيْهَا نُعِيْدُكُمْ
وَمِنْهَا نُخْرِجُكُمْ تَارَةً اُخْرٰى ٥٥

56. We showed the Pharaoh all of Our miracles, but he called them lies and turned away from them.

56. Wa laqad araynaahu Aayaatinaa kullahaa fakazzaba wa abaa.

وَلَقَدْ اَرَيْنٰهُ اٰيٰتِنَا كُلَّهَا فَكَذَّبَ
وَاَبٰى ٥٦

57. He said to Moses, "Have you come to expel us from our land through your magic?

57. Qaala aji'tanaa litukhrijanaa min arḍinaa bisiḥrika yaa Moosaa.

قَالَ اَجِئْتَنَا لِتُخْرِجَنَا مِنْ اَرْضِنَا
بِسِحْرِكَ يٰمُوْسٰى ٥٧

58. We shall also answer you by magic. Let us make an appointment for a contest among us and let each of us be present at a certain time in the appointed place."

58. Falana-tiyannaka bisiḥrim-mislihee faj'al baynanaa wa baynaka maw'idal-laa nukhlifuhoo naḥnu wa laaa anta makaanan suwaa.

فَلَنَاْتِيَنَّكَ بِسِحْرٍ مِّثْلِهٖ فَاجْعَلْ
بَيْنَنَا وَبَيْنَكَ مَوْعِدًا لَّا نُخْلِفُهٗ
نَحْنُ وَلَاۤ اَنْتَ مَكَانًا سُوًى ٥٨

59. Moses said, "Let the contest take place on the Day of the Feast so that all the people can come together during the brightness of the day."

59. Qaala maw'idukum yawmuz-zeenati wa añy-yuḥsharan-naasu ḍuḥaa.

قَالَ مَوْعِدُكُمْ يَوْمُ الزِّيْنَةِ وَاَنْ
يُّحْشَرَ النَّاسُ ضُحًى ٥٩

60. The Pharaoh returned to organize his plans and then attended the appointment.

60. Fatawallaa Fir'awnu fajama'a kaydahoo summa ataa.

فَتَوَلّٰى فِرْعَوْنُ فَجَمَعَ كَيْدَهٗ ثُمَّ اَتٰى ٦٠

61. Moses told them, (the magicians) "Woe to you if you invent falsehood against Allah; you will be destroyed by the torment. Whoever invents falsehood against Allah will certainly fail."

61. Qaala lahum-Moosaa waylakum laa taftaroo 'alal-laahi kaziban fayusḥitakum bi 'azaab; wa qad khaaba maniftaraa.

قَالَ لَهُمْ مُّوْسٰى وَيْلَكُمْ لَا تَفْتَرُوْا
عَلَى اللّٰهِ كَذِبًا فَيُسْحِتَكُمْ بِعَذَابٍ ۚ
وَقَدْ خَابَ مَنِ افْتَرٰى ٦١

62. They started arguing and whispering to each other

62. Fatanaaza'ooo amrahum baynahum wa asarrun-najwaa.

فَتَنَازَعُوْۤا اَمْرَهُمْ بَيْنَهُمْ وَاَسَرُّوا
النَّجْوٰى ٦٢

63. and said, "These two people are magicians. They want to expel you from your land through their magic and to destroy your own exemplary tradition.

63. Qaalooo in haazaani lasaaḥiraani yureedaani añy-yukhrijaakum min arḍikum bisiḥrihimaa wa yazhabaa biṭareeqati-kumul-muslaa.

قَالُوْۤا اِنْ هٰذٰنِ لَسٰحِرٰنِ يُرِيْدٰنِ
اَنْ يُّخْرِجٰكُمْ مِّنْ اَرْضِكُمْ بِسِحْرِهِمَا
وَيَذْهَبَا بِطَرِيْقَتِكُمُ الْمُثْلٰى ٦٣

64. Bring together your devices and come forward in ranks; the winner will, certainly, have great happiness."

64. Fa-ajmi'oo kaydakum summa'-too ṣaffaa; wa qad aflaḥal-yawma manis-ta'laa.

فَاَجْمِعُوْا كَيْدَكُمْ ثُمَّ ائْتُوْا صَفًّا ۚ
وَقَدْ اَفْلَحَ الْيَوْمَ مَنِ اسْتَعْلٰى ٦٤

65. They said, "Moses, would you be the first to show your skill or should we be the first to throw down our devices?"

65. Qaaloo yaa Moosaaa immaaa an tulqiya wa immaaa an-nakoona awwala man alqaa.

قَالُوْا يٰمُوْسٰۤى اِمَّاۤ اَنْ تُلْقِيَ وَاِمَّاۤ
اَنْ نَّكُوْنَ اَوَّلَ مَنْ اَلْقٰى ٦٥

66. Moses said, "You throw first." When they did, their ropes and staffs through their magic seemed to be moving.

66. Qaala bal alqoo fa-izaa ḥibaaluhum wa 'iṣiyyuhum yukhayyalu ilayhi min siḥrihim annahaa tas'aa.

قَالَ بَلۡ اَلۡقُوۡا ۚ فَاِذَا حِبَالُهُمۡ وَ
عِصِيُّهُمۡ يُخَيَّلُ اِلَيۡهِ مِنۡ سِحۡرِهِمۡ
اَنَّهَا تَسۡعٰى ﴿۶۶﴾

67. Moses felt afraid within himself.

67. Fa-awjasa fee nafsihee kheefatam-Moosaa.

فَاَوۡجَسَ فِىۡ نَفۡسِهٖ خِيۡفَةً مُّوۡسٰى ﴿۶۷﴾

68. We told him, "Do not be afraid for you will be the winner.

68. Qulnaa laa takhaf innaka antal-a'laa.

قُلۡنَا لَا تَخَفۡ اِنَّكَ اَنۡتَ الۡاَعۡلٰى ﴿۶۸﴾

69. Throw down what is in your right hand and it will swallow up all that they have performed; theirs is only a magical performance. Magicians can find no happiness in whatever they do."

69. Wa alqi maa fee yameenika talqaf maa sana'ooo; innamaa ṣana'oo kaydu ṣaaḥir; wa laa yufliḥus-saaḥiru ḥaysu ataa.

وَاَلۡقِ مَا فِىۡ يَمِيۡنِكَ تَلۡقَفۡ مَا
صَنَعُوۡا ؕ اِنَّمَا صَنَعُوۡا كَيۡدُ سٰحِرٍ ؕ
وَلَا يُفۡلِحُ السّٰحِرُ حَيۡثُ اَتٰى ﴿۶۹﴾

70. The magicians bowed down in prostration saying, "We believe in the Lord of Moses and Aaron."

70. Fa-ulqiyas-saḥaratu sujjadan qaalooo aamannaa bi-Rabbi Haaroona wa Moosaa.

فَاُلۡقِىَ السَّحَرَةُ سُجَّدًا قَالُوۡۤا اٰمَنَّا
بِرَبِّ هٰرُوۡنَ وَمُوۡسٰى ﴿۷۰﴾

71. The Pharaoh said, "Since you believed in him without my permission, then Moses certainly must be your chief who has taught you magic. I shall cut your hands and feet on alternate sides and crucify you on the trunk of the palm tree. You shall certainly find which among us can afflict more severe and lasting punishment."

71. Qaala aamantum lahoo qabla an aazana lakum; innahoo lakabeerukumul-lazee 'allamakumus-siḥra fala-uqaṭṭi'anna aydiyakum wa arjulakum-min khilaafiñw-wa la-uṣallibannakum fee juzoo'in-nakhli wa lata'la-munna ayyunaaa ashaddu' azaabañw-wa abqaa.

قَالَ اٰمَنۡتُمۡ لَهٗ قَبۡلَ اَنۡ اٰذَنَ لَكُمۡ ؕ
اِنَّهٗ لَكَبِيۡرُكُمُ الَّذِىۡ عَلَّمَكُمُ السِّحۡرَ ۚ
فَلَاُقَطِّعَنَّ اَيۡدِيَكُمۡ وَاَرۡجُلَكُمۡ مِّنۡ
خِلَافٍ وَّلَاُصَلِّبَنَّكُمۡ فِىۡ جُذُوۡعِ
النَّخۡلِ ۫ وَلَتَعۡلَمُنَّ اَيُّنَاۤ اَشَدُّ
عَذَابًا وَّاَبۡقٰى ﴿۷۱﴾

72. They (the magicians) said, "We would never prefer you to the miracles that we have seen or to our Creator. Do what you want. This life is only for a short time.

72. Qaaloo lan nu'siraka 'alaa maa jaaa'anaa minal-bayyinaati wallazee faṭaranaa faqḍi maaa anta qaaḍ; innamaa taqḍee haazihil ḥayaatad-dunyaaa.

قَالُوۡا لَنۡ نُّـؤۡثِرَكَ عَلٰى مَا جَآءَنَا
مِنَ الۡبَيِّنٰتِ وَالَّذِىۡ فَطَرَنَا فَاقۡضِ
مَاۤ اَنۡتَ قَاضٍ ؕ اِنَّمَا تَقۡضِىۡ هٰذِهِ
الۡحَيٰوةَ الدُّنۡيَا ﴿۷۲﴾

73. We have faith in our Lord so that He will forgive our sins and our magical performances that you forced us to show. Allah is better than all things and His rewards last longer."

73. Innaaa aamannaa bi-Rabbinaa liyaghfira lanaa khaṭaayaanaa wa maaa akrahtanaa 'alayhi minassiḥr; wallaahu khayruñw-wa abqaaa.

اِنَّاۤ اٰمَنَّا بِرَبِّنَا لِيَـغۡفِرَ لَنَا خَطٰيٰنَا
وَمَاۤ اَكۡرَهۡتَنَا عَلَيۡهِ مِنَ السِّحۡرِ ؕ
وَاللّٰهُ خَيۡرٌ وَّاَبۡقٰى ﴿۷۳﴾ الثلثة

74. The dwelling place of one who comes into the presence of his Lord as a criminal will be hell wherein he will never die nor enjoy his life.

74. Innahoo mañy-ya-ti Rabbahoo mujriman fa-inna lahoo Jahannama laa yamootu feehaa wa laa yaḥyaa.

اِنَّهٗ مَنۡ يَّاۡتِ رَبَّهٗ مُجۡرِمًا فَاِنَّ لَهٗ
جَهَنَّمَ ؕ لَا يَمُوۡتُ فِيۡهَا وَلَا يَحۡيٰى ﴿۷۴﴾

75. One who comes into the presence of his Lord with faith

75. Wa mañy-ya-tihee mu'minan qad 'amilaṣ-ṣaaliḥaati

وَمَنۡ يَّاۡتِهٖ مُؤۡمِنًا قَدۡ عَمِلَ الصّٰلِحٰتِ

and righteous deeds

fa-ulaaa'ika lahumud-dara-jaatul-'ulaa.

فَأُولَٰٓئِكَ لَهُمُ الدَّرَجَٰتُ الْعُلَىٰ ﴿٧٥﴾

76. will be rewarded by high status in the gardens of Eden wherein streams flow. Such will be the reward of those who purify themselves.

76. Jannaatu 'Adnin tajree min taḥtihal-anhaaru khaali-deena feehaa; wa zaalika jazaaa'u man tazakkaa.

جَنَّٰتُ عَدْنٍ تَجْرِي مِن تَحْتِهَا
الْأَنْهَٰرُ خَٰلِدِينَ فِيهَا ۚ وَذَٰلِكَ
جَزَآءُ مَن تَزَكَّىٰ ﴿٧٦﴾ ع ٤ ١٢

77. We sent revelations to Moses telling him, "Travel with My servants during the night and strike a dry road across the sea (for them). Have no fear of being overtaken (by the Pharaoh) nor of anything else."

77. Wa laqad awḥaynaaa ilaa Moosaaa an asri bi'ibaadee faḍrib lahum ṭareeqan fil-baḥri yabasal-laa takhaafu darakañw-wa laa takhshaa.

وَلَقَدْ أَوْحَيْنَآ إِلَىٰ مُوسَىٰٓ أَنْ
أَسْرِ بِعِبَادِي فَاضْرِبْ لَهُمْ طَرِيقًا
فِي الْبَحْرِ يَبَسًا لَّا تَخَٰفُ دَرَكًا
وَلَا تَخْشَىٰ ﴿٧٧﴾

78. The Pharaoh and his army chased Moses and his people, but the sea overwhelmed them as it did (drowned them).

78. Fa-atba'ahum Fir'awnu bijunoodihee faghashiyahum-minal-yammi maa ghashi-yahum.

فَأَتْبَعَهُمْ فِرْعَوْنُ بِجُنُودِهِۦ
فَغَشِيَهُم مِّنَ الْيَمِّ مَا غَشِيَهُمْ ﴿٧٨﴾

79. The Pharaoh and his people had gone far away from guidance.

79. Wa aḍalla Fir'awnu qaw-mahoo wa maa hadaa.

وَأَضَلَّ فِرْعَوْنُ قَوْمَهُۥ وَمَا هَدَىٰ ﴿٧٩﴾

80. Children of Israel, We saved you from your enemy and promised to settle you on the right side of the peaceful Mount Tur (Sinai) and We sent you manna and quails.

80. Yaa Baneee Israaa'eela qad anjaynaakum-min 'aduw-wikum wa waa'adnaakum jaanibaṭ-Ṭooril-aymana wa nazzalnaa 'alaykumul-Manna was-Salwaa.

يَٰبَنِيٓ إِسْرَٰٓءِيلَ قَدْ أَنجَيْنَٰكُم مِّنْ
عَدُوِّكُمْ وَوَٰعَدْنَٰكُمْ جَانِبَ الطُّورِ
الْأَيْمَنَ وَنَزَّلْنَا عَلَيْكُمُ الْمَنَّ
وَالسَّلْوَىٰ ﴿٨٠﴾

81. I allowed you to consume the pure sustenance which We had given you but not to become rebels, lest you become subject to My wrath. Whoever becomes subject to My wrath will certainly be destroyed.

81. Kuloo min ṭayyibaati maa razaqnaakum wa laa taṭghaw feehi fa-yaḥilla 'alaykum ghaḍabee wa mañy-yaḥlil 'alayhi ghaḍabee faqad hawaa.

كُلُوا مِن طَيِّبَٰتِ مَا رَزَقْنَٰكُمْ وَلَا
تَطْغَوْا فِيهِ فَيَحِلَّ عَلَيْكُمْ غَضَبِي ۖ وَ
مَن يَحْلِلْ عَلَيْهِ غَضَبِي فَقَدْ هَوَىٰ ﴿٨١﴾

82. I am All-forgiving to the righteously striving believers who repent and follow the right guidance.

82. Wa innee la-Ghaffaarul liman taaba wa-aamana wa 'amila ṣaaliḥan summah-tadaa.

وَإِنِّي لَغَفَّارٌ لِّمَن تَابَ وَءَامَنَ
وَعَمِلَ صَٰلِحًا ثُمَّ اهْتَدَىٰ ﴿٨٢﴾

83. The Lord asked, "Moses, what made you attend your appointment with Me before your people?"

83. Wa maaa a'jalaka 'an qawmika yaa Moosaa.

وَمَآ أَعْجَلَكَ عَن قَوْمِكَ يَٰمُوسَىٰ ﴿٨٣﴾

84. Moses replied, "They are just behind me. I came earlier to seek Your pleasure."

84. Qaala hum ulaaa'i 'alaaa asaree wa 'ajiltu ilayka Rabbi litarḍaa.

قَالَ هُمْ أُولَآءِ عَلَىٰٓ أَثَرِي وَعَجِلْتُ
إِلَيْكَ رَبِّ لِتَرْضَىٰ ﴿٨٤﴾

85. The Lord said, "We tested your people after you left them and the Samiri made them go astray."

85. Qaala fa-innaa qad fa-tannaa qawmaka mim ba'dika wa aḍal-lahumus-Saamiriyy.

قَالَ فَإِنَّا قَدْ فَتَنَّا قَوْمَكَ مِنۢ
بَعْدِكَ وَأَضَلَّهُمُ السَّامِرِيُّ ﴿٨٥﴾

86. Moses, sad and angry, returned to his people saying,

86. Faraja'a Moosaaa ilaa qawmihee ghaḍbaana

فَرَجَعَ مُوسَىٰٓ إِلَىٰ قَوْمِهِۦ غَضْبَٰنَ

"My people, did your Lord not make you a gracious promise? Why did you disregard your appointment with me? Was it because of the long time or did you want to become subject to the wrath of your Lord?

asifaa; qaala yaa qawmi alam ya'idkum Rabbukum wa'dan ḥasanaa; afaṭaala 'alaykumul-'ahdu am arattum añy-yaḥilla 'alaykum ghaḍabum-mir-Rabbikum fa-akhlaftum-maw'idee.

اَسِفًا ۚ قَالَ يٰقَوۡمِ اَلَمۡ يَعِدۡكُمۡ
رَبُّكُمۡ وَعۡدًا حَسَنًا ۚ اَفَطَالَ
عَلَيۡكُمُ الۡعَهۡدُ اَمۡ اَرَدۡتُّمۡ اَنۡ
يَّحِلَّ عَلَيۡكُمۡ غَضَبٌ مِّنۡ رَّبِّكُمۡ
فَاَخۡلَفۡتُمۡ مَّوۡعِدِىۡ ﴿۸۶﴾

87. They replied, "We did not go against our promise with you out of our own accord. We were forced to carry people's ornaments. We threw them and so did the Samiri.

87. Qaaloo maaa akhlafnaa maw'idaka bimalkinaa wa laakinnaa ḥummilnaaa awzaa-ram-min zeenatil-qawmi faqaẕafnaahaa fakaẕaalika alqas-Saamiriyy.

قَالُوۡا مَاۤ اَخۡلَفۡنَا مَوۡعِدَكَ بِمَلۡكِنَا
وَلٰـكِنَّا حُمِّلۡنَاۤ اَوۡزَارًا مِّنۡ
زِيۡنَةِ الۡقَوۡمِ فَقَذَفۡنٰهَا فَكَذٰلِكَ
اَلۡقَى السَّامِرِىُّ ۙ ﴿۸۷﴾

88. Then the Samiri forged the body of a motionless calf which gave a hollow sound." The people said, "This is your Lord and the Lord of Moses whom he (Moses) forgot to mention."

88. Fa-akhraja lahum 'ijlan jasadal-lahoo khuwaarun faqaaloo haaẕaaa ilaahukum wa ilaahu Moosaa fanasiya.

فَاَخۡرَجَ لَهُمۡ عِجۡلًا جَسَدًا لَّهٗ
خُوَارٌ فَقَالُوۡا هٰذَاۤ اِلٰهُكُمۡ وَاِلٰهُ
مُوۡسٰى ۙ فَنَسِىَ ﴿۸۸﴾

89. Did they not consider that the calf could not give them any answer, nor could it harm or benefit them?

89. Afalaa yarawna allaa yarji'u ilayhim qawlañw-wa laa yamliku lahum ḍarrañw-wa laa naf'aa.

اَفَلَا يَرَوۡنَ اَلَّا يَرۡجِعُ اِلَيۡهِمۡ قَوۡلًا ۙ
وَّلَا يَمۡلِكُ لَهُمۡ ضَرًّا وَّلَا نَفۡعًا ﴿۸۹﴾ ع ۴ ۱۳ ۱۴

90. Aaron had told them before, "My people, you are deceived by the calf. Your Lord is the Beneficent. Follow me and obey my orders."

90. Wa laqad qaala lahum Haaroonu min qablu yaa qawmi innamaa futintum bihee wa inna Rabbakumur-Raḥmaanu fatta-bi'oonee wa aṭee'ooo amree.

وَلَقَدۡ قَالَ لَهُمۡ هٰرُوۡنُ مِنۡ قَبۡلُ
يٰقَوۡمِ اِنَّمَا فُتِنۡتُمۡ بِهٖ ۚ وَاِنَّ رَبَّكُمُ
الرَّحۡمٰنُ فَاتَّبِعُوۡنِىۡ وَاَطِيۡعُوۡۤا اَمۡرِىۡ ﴿۹۰﴾

91. They said, "We shall continue worshipping the calf until Moses comes back."

91. Qaaloo lan-nabraḥa 'alayhi 'aakifeena ḥattaa yarji'a ilaynaa Moosaa.

قَالُوۡا لَنۡ نَّبۡرَحَ عَلَيۡهِ عٰكِفِيۡنَ حَتّٰى
يَرۡجِعَ اِلَيۡنَا مُوۡسٰى ﴿۹۱﴾

92. Then Moses asked Aaron, "What made you not follow me when you saw them in error?

92. Qaala yaa Haaroonu maa mana'aka iẕ ra-aytahum dallooo.

قَالَ يٰهٰرُوۡنُ مَا مَنَعَكَ اِذۡ رَاَيۡتَهُمۡ
ضَلُّوۡۤا ۙ ﴿۹۲﴾

93. Did you disobey my orders?"

93. Allaa tattabi'ani afa'a-ṣayta amree.

اَلَّا تَتَّبِعَنِ ؕ اَفَعَصَيۡتَ اَمۡرِىۡ ﴿۹۳﴾

94. Aaron replied, "Son of my mother, do not seize me by my beard or head. I was afraid that you might consider me responsible for causing discord among the children of Israel and that I did not pay attention to your words."

94. Qaala yabna'umma laa ta-khuẕ biliḥyatee wa laa bira-seee innee khasheetu an taqoola farraqta bayna Baneee Israaa-'eela wa lam tarqub qawlee.

قَالَ يَبۡنَؤُمَّ لَا تَاۡخُذۡ بِلِحۡيَتِىۡ وَلَا
بِرَاۡسِىۡ ۚ اِنِّىۡ خَشِيۡتُ اَنۡ تَقُوۡلَ فَرَّقۡتَ
بَيۡنَ بَنِىۡۤ اِسۡرَآءِيۡلَ وَلَمۡ تَرۡقُبۡ قَوۡلِىۡ ﴿۹۴﴾

95. Moses asked, "Samiri, what were your motives?"

95. Qaala famaa khaṭbuka yaa Saamiriyy.

قَالَ فَمَا خَطۡبُكَ يٰسَامِرِىُّ ﴿۹۵﴾

96. He replied, "I had seen (while crossing the sea) what they did not see. I picked up a handful (of soil) from the foot-marks of the messenger (Gabriel's horse) and preserved it. Thus, my soul prompted me (to place that soil inside the golden calf that caused it to vibrate and give out a certain kind of sound).

96. Qaala baṣurtu bimaa lam yabṣuroo bihee faqabaḍtu qabḍatam-min a<u>s</u>arir-Rasooli fanabaztuhaa wa ka<u>z</u>aalika sawwalat lee nafsee

قَالَ بَصُرْتُ بِمَا لَمْ يَبْصُرُوْا بِهٖ
فَقَبَضْتُ قَبْضَةً مِّنْ اَثَرِ الرَّسُوْلِ
فَنَبَذْتُهَا وَكَذٰلِكَ سَوَّلَتْ لِيْ نَفْسِيْ ﴿٩٦﴾

97. Moses said, "Go away! Throughout your life you will not be able to let anyone touch you. This will be your punishment in this life. The time for your final punishment is inevitable. You will never be able to avoid it. Look at your god which you have been worshipping. We will burn it in the fire and scatter its ashes into the sea."

97. Qaala fa<u>z</u>hab fa-inna laka fil-ḥayaati an taqoola laa misaasa wa inna laka maw'idal-lan tukhlafahoo wanẓur ilaaa ilaahikal-la<u>z</u>ee ẓalta 'alayhi 'aakifaa; lanuḥarriqannahoo <u>s</u>umma lanansifannahoo fil-yammi nasfaa.

قَالَ فَاذْهَبْ فَاِنَّ لَكَ فِي الْحَيٰوةِ اَنْ
تَقُوْلَ لَا مِسَاسَ وَاِنَّ لَكَ مَوْعِدًا
لَّنْ تُخْلَفَهٗ وَانْظُرْ اِلٰٓى اِلٰهِكَ
الَّذِيْ ظَلْتَ عَلَيْهِ عَاكِفًا لَنُحَرِّقَنَّهٗ
ثُمَّ لَنَنْسِفَنَّهٗ فِي الْيَمِّ نَسْفًا ﴿٩٧﴾

98. Your Lord is Allah who is the only Ilah (one deserving to be worshiped) and He has the knowledge of all things.

98. Innamaaa ilaahukumul-laahul-la<u>z</u>ee laaa ilaaha illaa Hoo; wasi'a kulla shay'in 'ilmaa.

اِنَّمَآ اِلٰهُكُمُ اللّٰهُ الَّذِيْ لَآ اِلٰهَ اِلَّا
هُوَ وَسِعَ كُلَّ شَيْءٍ عِلْمًا ﴿٩٨﴾

99. Thus We tell you, (Muhammad), the stories of the past and We have given you the Quran.

99. Ka<u>z</u>aalika naquṣṣu 'alay-ka min ambaaa'i maa qad sabaq; wa qad aataynaaka mil-ladunnaa <u>Z</u>ikraa.

كَذٰلِكَ نَقُصُّ عَلَيْكَ مِنْ اَنْۢبَآءِ
مَا قَدْ سَبَقَ وَقَدْ اٰتَيْنٰكَ مِنْ
لَّدُنَّا ذِكْرًا ﴿٩٩﴾

100. Whoever disregards (the Quran) will be heavily burdened with sin on the Day of Judgment

100. Man a'raḍa 'anhu fa-innahoo yaḥmilu Yawmal-Qiyaamati wizraa.

مَنْ اَعْرَضَ عَنْهُ فَاِنَّهٗ يَحْمِلُ يَوْمَ
الْقِيٰمَةِ وِزْرًا ﴿١٠٠﴾

101. with which he will live forever. On the Day of Judgment it will be a terrible load for him to carry.

101. Khaalideena feehi wa saaa'a lahum Yawmal-Qiya-amati ḥimlaa.

خٰلِدِيْنَ فِيْهِ وَسَآءَ لَهُمْ يَوْمَ
الْقِيٰمَةِ حِمْلًا ﴿١٠١﴾

102. On the day when the trumpet will be sounded We will raise the criminals from their graves and their eyes will be turned blue and blind.

102. Yawma yunfakhu fiṣ-Ṣoori wa naḥshurul-mujrimeena Yawma'i<u>z</u>in zurqaa.

يَّوْمَ يُنْفَخُ فِي الصُّوْرِ وَنَحْشُرُ
الْمُجْرِمِيْنَ يَوْمَئِذٍ زُرْقًا ﴿١٠٢﴾

103. They will slowly talk to each other and say, "Our life on earth was as short as ten days."

103. Yatakhaafatoona bayna-hum il-labi<u>s</u>tum illaa 'ashraa.

يَّتَخَافَتُوْنَ بَيْنَهُمْ اِنْ لَّبِثْتُمْ اِلَّا
عَشْرًا ﴿١٠٣﴾

104. We know best what they say. The moderate ones among them will say, "You did not live on earth for more than a day."

104. Naḥnu a'lamu bimaa yaqooloona i<u>z</u> yaqoolu am<u>s</u>a-luhum ṭareeqatan illabi<u>s</u>tum illaa yawmaa.

نَحْنُ اَعْلَمُ بِمَا يَقُوْلُوْنَ اِذْ يَقُوْلُ
اَمْثَلُهُمْ طَرِيْقَةً اِنْ لَّبِثْتُمْ اِلَّا
يَوْمًا ﴿١٠٤﴾ ع ٥ ١٥ ١٤

105. (Muhammad), they will ask you about the mountains. Say to them, "My Lord will grind them to powder

105. Wa yas'aloonaka 'anil-jibaali faqul yansifuhaa Rabbee nasfaa.

وَيَسْـَٔلُوْنَكَ عَنِ الْجِبَالِ فَقُلْ
يَنْسِفُهَا رَبِّيْ نَسْفًا ﴿١٠٥﴾

106. and leave them so smoothly leveled

107. that you will see no depression or elevation therewith."

108. On that day they will follow their caller without deviation. Their voices will be low in the presence of the Beneficent. You will hear nothing but faint whisper.

109. On that day no one's intercession will be of any benefit unless he has received permission from the Beneficent and whose word is acceptable to Him.

110. Allah knows all that is in front of them and behind them and they cannot encompass His knowledge.

111. Faces will be humble before the Everlasting and the Self-existing Allah. Despair will strike those who are loaded with the burden of injustice.

112. The righteously striving believers should have no fear of being treated with injustice or inequity.

113. We have revealed the Quran in the Arabic language containing various warnings so that it may cause them to have fear (of Allah) or Dhikr (the advent of Al-Mahdi) take place for them.

114. Allah is the Most High and the True King. (Muhammad), do not be hasty in reading the revelation to the people before its revealing is completed. Say, "My Lord, grant me more knowledge."

115. We had commanded Adam (certain matters). He forgot Our commandment and We did not find in him the determination (to fulfill Our commandments).

116. When We told the angels to prostrate in honor of Adam (before Allah) they all obeyed except Iblis (Satan) who refused.

117. We said, "Adam, this (Satan) is your enemy and the enemy of your spouse. Let him not expel you and your spouse from the garden lest you plunge into misery.

106. Fa-yaẕaruhaa qaa'an ṣafṣafaa.

107. Laa taraa feehaa 'iwajañw-wa laaa amtaa.

108. Yawma'iziñy-yattabi'oo-nad-daa'iya laa 'iwaja lah; wa khasha'atil aṣwaatu lir-Raḥmaani falaa tasma'u illaa hamsaa.

109. Yawma'izil-laa tanfa'ush shafaa'atu illaa man aẕina lahur-Raḥmaanu wa raḍiya lahoo qawlaa

110. Ya'lamu maa bayna aydeehim wa maa khalfahum wa laa yuḥeeṭoona bihee 'ilmaa.

111. Wa 'anatil-wujoohu lil-Ḥayyil-Qayyoomi wa qad khaaba man ḥamala ẓulmaa

112. Wa mañy-ya'mal minaṣ-ṣaaliḥaati wa huwa mu'minun falaa yakhaafu ẓulmañw-wa laa haḍmaa.

113. Wa kaẕaalika anzalnaahu Qur'aanan 'Arabiyyañw-wa ṣarrafnaa feehi minal-wa'eedi la'allahum yattaqoona aw yuḥdiṯu lahum ẕikraa.

114. Fata'aalal-laahul-Malikul-Ḥaqq; wa laa ta'jal bil-Qur'aani min qabli añy-yuqḍaa ilayka waḥyuhoo waqur-Rabbi zidnee 'ilmaa.

115. Wa laqad 'ahidnaaa ilaaa Aadama min qablu fanasiya wa lam najid lahoo 'azmaa.

116. Wa iẕ qulnaa lilmalaaa'ikatis-judoo li Aadama fasajadooo illaaa Iblees; abaa.

117. Faqulnaa yaaa Aadamu inna haaẕaa 'aduwwul-laka walizawjika falaa yukhrijannakumaa minal-Jannati fatashqaa.

فَيَذَرُهَا قَاعًا صَفْصَفًا ﴿١٠٦﴾

لَّا تَرٰى فِيْهَا عِوَجًا وَّلَاۤ اَمْتًا ﴿١٠٧﴾

يَوْمَئِذٍ يَّتَّبِعُوْنَ الدَّاعِيَ لَا عِوَجَ لَهٗ ۚ

وَخَشَعَتِ الْاَصْوَاتُ لِلرَّحْمٰنِ

فَلَا تَسْمَعُ اِلَّا هَمْسًا ﴿١٠٨﴾

يَوْمَئِذٍ لَّا تَنْفَعُ الشَّفَاعَةُ اِلَّا مَنْ

اَذِنَ لَهُ الرَّحْمٰنُ وَرَضِيَ لَهٗ قَوْلًا ﴿١٠٩﴾

يَعْلَمُ مَا بَيْنَ اَيْدِيْهِمْ وَمَا

خَلْفَهُمْ وَلَا يُحِيْطُوْنَ بِهٖ عِلْمًا ﴿١١٠﴾

وَعَنَتِ الْوُجُوْهُ لِلْحَيِّ الْقَيُّوْمِ ؕ

وَقَدْ خَابَ مَنْ حَمَلَ ظُلْمًا ﴿١١١﴾

وَمَنْ يَّعْمَلْ مِنَ الصّٰلِحٰتِ وَهُوَ

مُؤْمِنٌ فَلَا يَخٰفُ ظُلْمًا وَّلَا هَضْمًا ﴿١١٢﴾

وَكَذٰلِكَ اَنْزَلْنٰهُ قُرْاٰنًا عَرَبِيًّا وَّ

صَرَّفْنَا فِيْهِ مِنَ الْوَعِيْدِ لَعَلَّهُمْ

يَتَّقُوْنَ اَوْ يُحْدِثُ لَهُمْ ذِكْرًا ﴿١١٣﴾

فَتَعٰلَى اللّٰهُ الْمَلِكُ الْحَقُّ ۚ وَلَا تَعْجَلْ

بِالْقُرْاٰنِ مِنْ قَبْلِ اَنْ يُّقْضٰۤى اِلَيْكَ

وَحْيُهٗ ۫ وَقُلْ رَّبِّ زِدْنِيْ عِلْمًا ﴿١١٤﴾

وَلَقَدْ عَهِدْنَاۤ اِلٰۤى اٰدَمَ مِنْ قَبْلُ

فَنَسِيَ وَلَمْ نَجِدْ لَهٗ عَزْمًا ﴿١١٥﴾ ع ٦ ١٥

وَاِذْ قُلْنَا لِلْمَلٰٓئِكَةِ اسْجُدُوْا

لِاٰدَمَ فَسَجَدُوْۤا اِلَّاۤ اِبْلِيْسَ ؕ اَبٰى ﴿١١٦﴾

فَقُلْنَا يٰۤاٰدَمُ اِنَّ هٰذَا عَدُوٌّ لَّكَ

وَلِزَوْجِكَ فَلَا يُخْرِجَنَّكُمَا مِنَ

الْجَنَّةِ فَتَشْقٰى ﴿١١٧﴾

118. In the garden (Paradise) you will experience no hunger, nakedness,	118. Inna laka allaa tajoo'a feeha wa laa ta'raa.	إِنَّ لَكَ أَلَّا تَجُوعَ فِيهَا وَلَا تَعْرَىٰ ﴿١١٨﴾
119. thirst, or exposure to the hot sun."	119. Wa annaka laa taẓma'u feehaa wa laa taḍḥaa.	وَأَنَّكَ لَا تَظْمَؤُا فِيهَا وَلَا تَضْحَىٰ ﴿١١٩﴾
120. Satan, trying to seduce him, said, "Adam, do you want me to show you the Tree of Eternity and the Everlasting Kingdom?"	120. Fawaswasa ilayhish-Shayṭaanu qaala yaaa Aadamu hal adulluka 'alaa shajaratil-khuldi wa mulkil-laa yablaa.	فَوَسْوَسَ إِلَيْهِ الشَّيْطٰنُ قَالَ يٰٓاٰدَمُ هَلْ أَدُلُّكَ عَلٰى شَجَرَةِ الْخُلْدِ وَمُلْكٍ لَّا يَبْلٰى ﴿١٢٠﴾
121. Adam and his wife ate (fruits) from the tree and found themselves naked. Then they started to cover themselves with the leaves from the garden. Adam disobeyed his Lord and went astray.	121. Fa-akalaa minhaa fabadat lahumaa saw-aatuhumaa wa ṭafiqaa yakhṣifaani 'alayhimaa miñw-waraqil-jannah; wa 'aṣaaa Aadamu Rabbahoo faghawaa.	فَأَكَلَا مِنْهَا فَبَدَتْ لَهُمَا سَوْاٰتُهُمَا وَطَفِقَا يَخْصِفٰنِ عَلَيْهِمَا مِنْ وَّرَقِ الْجَنَّةِ ز وَعَصٰٓى اٰدَمُ رَبَّهٗ فَغَوٰى ﴿١٢١﴾
122. His Lord forgave him, accepted his repentance, and gave him guidance.	122. Summaj-tabaahu Rabbuhoo fataaba 'alayhi wa hadaa.	ثُمَّ اجْتَبٰهُ رَبُّهٗ فَتَابَ عَلَيْهِ وَهَدٰى ﴿١٢٢﴾
123. Allah then told them, "Get out of here all of you; you are each other's enemies. When My guidance comes to you, those who follow it will not go astray nor will they endure any misery.	123. Qaalah-biṭaa minhaa jamee'am ba'ḍukum liba'ḍin 'aduww; fa-immaa ya-tiyannakum-minnee hudan famanit-taba'a hudaaya falaa yaḍillu wa laa yashqaa.	قَالَ اهْبِطَا مِنْهَا جَمِيعًا بَعْضُكُمْ لِبَعْضٍ عَدُوٌّ ج فَإِمَّا يَأْتِيَنَّكُمْ مِّنِّىْ هُدًى ۵ فَمَنِ اتَّبَعَ هُدَاىَ فَلَا يَضِلُّ وَلَا يَشْقٰى ﴿١٢٣﴾
124. Whoever ignores My guidance will live a destitute life and on the Day of Judgment We will raise him blind (unable to see paradise).	124. Wa man a'raḍa 'an Zikree fa-inna lahoo ma'eeshatan ḍankañw-wa naḥshuruhoo Yawmal-Qiyaamati a'maa.	وَمَنْ أَعْرَضَ عَنْ ذِكْرِىْ فَإِنَّ لَهٗ مَعِيْشَةً ضَنْكًا وَّنَحْشُرُهٗ يَوْمَ الْقِيٰمَةِ أَعْمٰى ﴿١٢٤﴾
125. He will say, "My Lord, why have you brought me back to life blind; when before I could see?"	125. Qaala Rabbi lima ḥashartaneee a'maa wa qad kuntu baṣeeraa.	قَالَ رَبِّ لِمَ حَشَرْتَنِىْٓ أَعْمٰى وَقَدْ كُنْتُ بَصِيْرًا ﴿١٢٥﴾
126. The Lord will say, "This is true, but just as you forgot Our revelations that had come to you, so, also, are you forgotten on this day."	126. Qaala kazaalika atatka Aayaatunaa fanaseetahaa wa kazaalikal-Yawma tunsaa.	قَالَ كَذٰلِكَ أَتَتْكَ اٰيٰتُنَا فَنَسِيْتَهَا ج وَكَذٰلِكَ الْيَوْمَ تُنْسٰى ﴿١٢٦﴾
127. Thus We recompense those who are unjust and had no faith in the revelations of his Lord. The torment in the life to come will be more severe and of extended duration.	127. Wa kazaalika najzee man asrafa wa lam yu'mim bi-Aayaati-Rabbih; wa la'azaabul-Aakhirati ashaddu wa abqaaa.	وَكَذٰلِكَ نَجْزِىْ مَنْ أَسْرَفَ وَلَمْ يُؤْمِنْ بِاٰيٰتِ رَبِّهٖ ط وَلَعَذَابُ الْاٰخِرَةِ أَشَدُّ وَأَبْقٰى ﴿١٢٧﴾
128. Was it not a warning for them to see how many	128. Afalam yahdi lahum kam ahlaknaa	أَفَلَمْ يَهْدِ لَهُمْ كَمْ أَهْلَكْنَا

generations living before them We destroyed and how they are now walking in their ruins? In this there is the evidence (of the Truth) for the people of reason.

qablahum-minal-qurooni yamshoona fee masaakinihim; inna fee zaalika la-Aayaatil-li-ulinnuhaa.

قَبْلَهُمْ مِّنَ الْقُرُوْنِ يَمْشُوْنَ فِيْ
مَسٰكِنِهِمْ ؕ اِنَّ فِيْ ذٰلِكَ لَاٰيٰتٍ
لِّاُولِي النُّهٰى ﴿۱۲۸﴾ ع ١٣ ١٦

129. Had not the word of your Lord been decreed (otherwise), the unbelievers deserved immediate punishment. The appointed time for their punishment will inevitably come.

129. Wa law laa Kalimatun sabaqat mir-Rabbika lakaana lizaamañw-wa ajalum-musammaa.

وَلَوْلَا كَلِمَةٌ سَبَقَتْ مِنْ رَّبِّكَ
لَكَانَ لِزَامًا وَّاَجَلٌ مُّسَمًّى ﴿۱۲۹﴾

130. (Muhammad), have patience with what they say, glorify your Lord, and always praise Him before sunrise, sunset, in some hours of the night, and at both the beginning and end of the day, so that perhaps you will please your Lord.

130. Faṣbir ‘alaa maa yaqooloona wa sabbiḥ biḥamdi Rabbika qabla ṭuloo‘ish-shamsi wa qabla ghuroobihaa wa min aanaaa’il-layli fasabbiḥ wa aṭraafan-nahaari la‘allaka tarḍaa.

فَاصْبِرْ عَلٰى مَا يَقُوْلُوْنَ وَسَبِّحْ
بِحَمْدِ رَبِّكَ قَبْلَ طُلُوْعِ الشَّمْسِ وَ
قَبْلَ غُرُوْبِهَا ۚ وَمِنْ اٰنَآئِ الَّيْلِ
فَسَبِّحْ وَاَطْرَافَ النَّهَارِ لَعَلَّكَ تَرْضٰى ﴿۱۳۰﴾

131. Do not be envious of what We have given to some people as means of enjoyment, spouses and worldly delight. Such means are a trial for them, but the reward that you will receive from your Lord will be far better and everlasting.

131. Wa laa tamuddanna ‘aynayka ilaa maa matta‘naa biheee azwaajam-minhum zahratal-ḥayaatid-dunyaa linaftinahum feeh; wa rizqu Rabbika khayruñw-wa abqaa.

وَلَا تَمُدَّنَّ عَيْنَيْكَ اِلٰى مَا مَتَّعْنَا
بِهٖۤ اَزْوَاجًا مِّنْهُمْ زَهْرَةَ الْحَيٰوةِ
الدُّنْيَا ۙ لِنَفْتِنَهُمْ فِيْهِ ؕ وَرِزْقُ
رَبِّكَ خَيْرٌ وَّاَبْقٰى ﴿۱۳۱﴾

132. Instruct your family to pray and to be steadfast in their worship. We do not ask any sustenance from you; it is We who give you sustenance. Know that piety will have a happy end.

132. Wa-mur ahlaka biṣ-Ṣalaati waṣṭabir ‘alayhaa laa nas’aluka rizqaa; Naḥnu narzuquk; wal‘aaqibatu littaqwaa.

وَاْمُرْ اَهْلَكَ بِالصَّلٰوةِ وَاصْطَبِرْ
عَلَيْهَا ؕ لَا نَسْئَلُكَ رِزْقًا ؕ نَحْنُ
نَرْزُقُكَ ؕ وَالْعَاقِبَةُ لِلتَّقْوٰى ﴿۱۳۲﴾

133. They have said, “Why did he (Muhammad) not bring some miracle from his Lord?” Have they not received the previously revealed heavenly Books as the evidence of the Truth?

133. Wa qaaloo law laa yateenaa bi-Aayatim-mir-Rabbih; awalam ta-tihim bayyinatu maa fiṣ-ṣuḥufil-oolaa.

وَقَالُوْا لَوْلَا يَاْتِيْنَا بِاٰيَةٍ مِّنْ
رَّبِّهٖ ؕ اَوَلَمْ تَاْتِهِمْ بَيِّنَةُ مَا فِي
الصُّحُفِ الْاُوْلٰى ﴿۱۳۳﴾

134. Had We destroyed them with a torment before the coming of Muhammad they would have said, “Lord, would that you had sent us a Messenger so that we could have followed Your revelations before being humiliated and disgraced.”

134. Wa law annaaa ahlaknaahum bi‘azaabim-min qablihee laqaaloo Rabbanaa law laaa arsalta ilaynaa Rasoolan fanattabi‘a Aayaatika min qabli an-nazilla wa nakhzaa.

وَلَوْ اَنَّآ اَهْلَكْنٰهُمْ بِعَذَابٍ مِّنْ
قَبْلِهٖ لَقَالُوْا رَبَّنَا لَوْلَاۤ اَرْسَلْتَ
اِلَيْنَا رَسُوْلًا فَنَتَّبِعَ اٰيٰتِكَ مِنْ
قَبْلِ اَنْ نَّذِلَّ وَنَخْزٰى ﴿۱۳۴﴾

135. (Muhammad), tell them, “Everyone is waiting. Wait and you shall know very soon who will be the followers of the right path with the right guidance.”

135. Qul kullum-mutarabbiṣun fatarabbaṣoo fasata‘lamoona man Aṣḥaabuṣ-Ṣiraaṭis-Sawiyyi wa manih-tadaa.

قُلْ كُلٌّ مُّتَرَبِّصٌ فَتَرَبَّصُوْا ۚ
فَسَتَعْلَمُوْنَ مَنْ اَصْحٰبُ الصِّرَاطِ
السَّوِيِّ وَمَنِ اهْتَدٰى ﴿۱۳۵﴾ ع ٨ ١٧

Al-Anbiya, The Prophets (21)

In the Name of Allah, the Beneficent, the Merciful.

Sûrat al-Anbiyâ'-21

(Revealed at Makkah)

Bismillaahir Raḥmaanir Raḥeem

(٢١) سُورَةُ الْأَنبِيَاءِ مَكِّيَّةٌ (٧٣)

آياتها ١١٢ بِسْمِ اللَّهِ الرَّحْمَٰنِ الرَّحِيمِ ركوعاتها ٧

1. The people's day of reckoning is drawing closer, yet they are heedlessly neglectful.

1. Iqtaraba linnaasi ḥisaabuhum wa hum fee ghaflatim-mu'riḍoon.

اقْتَرَبَ لِلنَّاسِ حِسَابُهُمْ وَهُمْ فِي
غَفْلَةٍ مُّعْرِضُونَ ١

2. Whenever a new revelation comes to them from their Lord, they listen to it in a playful manner,

2. Maa ya-teehim-min Zikrim-mir-Rabbihim-muḥdasin illas-tama'oohu wa hum yal'aboon.

مَا يَأْتِيهِم مِّن ذِكْرٍ مِّن رَّبِّهِم مُّحْدَثٍ
إِلَّا اسْتَمَعُوهُ وَهُمْ يَلْعَبُونَ ٢

3. and their hearts are preoccupied with trivial matters. The unjust ones whisper to each other and say, "Is he (Muhammad) more than a mere mortal like you? How can you follow that which you know is only magic?"

3. Laahiyatan quloobuhum; wa asarrun-najwal-lazeena ẓalamoo hal-haazaaa illaa basharum-mislukum afatatoonas-siḥra wa antum tubṣiroon.

لَاهِيَةً قُلُوبُهُمْ وَأَسَرُّوا النَّجْوَى
الَّذِينَ ظَلَمُوا هَلْ هَٰذَا إِلَّا بَشَرٌ
مِّثْلُكُمْ أَفَتَأْتُونَ السِّحْرَ وَأَنتُمْ
تُبْصِرُونَ ٣

4. The Lord said, "Tell them (Muhammad), 'My Lord knows all that is said in the heavens and the earth. He is All-hearing and All-knowing.'"

4. Qaala Rabbee ya'lamul qawla fis-samaaa'i wal-arḍi wa Huwas-Samee'ul-'Aleem.

قَالَ رَبِّي يَعْلَمُ الْقَوْلَ فِي السَّمَاءِ
وَالْأَرْضِ وَهُوَ السَّمِيعُ الْعَلِيمُ ٤

5. They have said, "It (the Quran) is only the result of some confused dreams. He is only a poet. He should show us some miracles, as the ancient Prophets had done."

5. Bal qaalooo aḍghaasu aḥlaamim balif-taraahu bal huwa shaa'irun falya-tinaa bi-Aayatin kamaaa ursilal awwaloon.

بَلْ قَالُوا أَضْغَاثُ أَحْلَامٍ بَلِ افْتَرَاهُ
بَلْ هُوَ شَاعِرٌ فَلْيَأْتِنَا بِآيَةٍ
كَمَا أُرْسِلَ الْأَوَّلُونَ ٥

6. The people of the town whom We had destroyed also had no faith. Will these people then believe (in Allah)?

6. Maaa aamanat qablahum min qaryatin ahlaknaahaaa afahum yu'minoon.

مَا آمَنَتْ قَبْلَهُم مِّن قَرْيَةٍ
أَهْلَكْنَاهَا أَفَهُمْ يُؤْمِنُونَ ٦

7. The messengers that We had sent before you were only men to whom We had given revelation. Ask the people of Al-Dhikr (family of the Holy Prophet) if you do not know.

7. Wa maaa arsalnaa qablaka illaa rijaalan-nooḥeee ilayhim fas'alooo ahlaz-zikri in kuntum laa ta'lamoon.

وَمَا أَرْسَلْنَا قَبْلَكَ إِلَّا رِجَالًا
نُّوحِي إِلَيْهِمْ فَاسْأَلُوا أَهْلَ
الذِّكْرِ إِن كُنتُمْ لَا تَعْلَمُونَ ٧

8. We had not made them such bodies that would not eat any food nor were they immortal.

8. Wa maa ja'alnaahum jasadal-laa ya-kuloonaṭ-ṭa'aama wa maa kaanoo khaalideen.

وَمَا جَعَلْنَاهُمْ جَسَدًا لَّا يَأْكُلُونَ
الطَّعَامَ وَمَا كَانُوا خَالِدِينَ ٨

9. Our promise to them came true and We saved them and those whom We wanted, but destroyed the unjust people.

9. Summa ṣadaqnaahumul-wa'da fa-anjaynaahum wa man nashaaa'u wa ahlaknal-musrifeen.

ثُمَّ صَدَقْنَاهُمُ الْوَعْدَ فَأَنجَيْنَاهُمْ
وَمَن نَّشَاءُ وَأَهْلَكْنَا الْمُسْرِفِينَ ٩

10. We have sent a Book, (the Quran), which is an honor for you. Will you then not understand?

10. Laqad anzalnaaa ilaykum Kitaaban feehi zikrukum afalaa ta'qiloon.

لَقَدْ أَنزَلْنَا إِلَيْكُمْ كِتَابًا فِيهِ
ذِكْرُكُمْ أَفَلَا تَعْقِلُونَ ١٠

الجزء السابع عشر (١٧)

ع ١

11. How many unjust towns did We destroy and replace with other nations?

11. Wa kam qaṣamnaa min qaryatin kaanat ẓaalimatañw-wa ansha-naa ba'dahaa qawman aakhareen.

وَكَمْ قَصَمْنَا مِنْ قَرْيَةٍ كَانَتْ
ظَالِمَةً وَّأَنْشَأْنَا بَعْدَهَا قَوْمًا
آخَرِينَ ١١

12. When they found Our torment approaching them they started to run away from the town.

12. Falammaaa aḥassoo ba-sanaaa iz̲aa hum-minhaa yarkuḍoon.

فَلَمَّآ أَحَسُّوا بَأْسَنَآ إِذَا هُمْ
مِّنْهَا يَرْكُضُونَ ١٢

13. We told them, "Do not run away. Come back to your luxuries and your houses so that you can be questioned."

13. Laa tarkuḍoo warji'ooo ilaa maaa utriftum feehi wa masaakinikum la'allakum tus'aloon.

لَا تَرْكُضُوا وَارْجِعُوٓا إِلَىٰ مَآ أُتْرِفْتُمْ
فِيهِ وَمَسٰكِنِكُمْ لَعَلَّكُمْ تُسْـَٔلُونَ ١٣

14. They said, "Woe to us! We have been unjust."

14. Qaaloo yaa waylanaaa innaa kunnaa ẓaalimeen.

قَالُوا يٰوَيْلَنَآ إِنَّا كُنَّا ظٰلِمِينَ ١٤

15. Such was what they continued to say until We mowed them down and made them completely extinct.

15. Famaa zaalat tilka da'waahum ḥattaa ja'alnaahum ḥaṣeedan khaamideen.

فَمَا زَالَتْ تِّلْكَ دَعْوٰىهُمْ حَتّٰى
جَعَلْنٰهُمْ حَصِيدًا خٰمِدِينَ ١٥

16. We did not create the heavens and the earth just for fun.

16. Wa maa khalaqnas-samaaa'a wal-arḍa wa maa baynahumaa laa'ibeen.

وَمَا خَلَقْنَا السَّمَآءَ وَالْأَرْضَ وَمَا
بَيْنَهُمَا لٰعِبِينَ ١٦

17. Had We wanted to play games, We could have certainly done so with things at hand.

17. Law aradnaaa an-nattakhiz̲a lahwal-lat-takhaz̲naahu mil-ladunnaaa in kunnaa faa'ileen.

لَوْ أَرَدْنَآ أَنْ نَّتَّخِذَ لَهْوًا لَّاتَّخَذْنٰهُ
مِنْ لَّدُنَّآ إِنْ كُنَّا فٰعِلِينَ ١٧

18. We bring forward the Truth to crush and destroy falsehood; it is doomed to be banished. Woe to you for your way of thinking about Allah!

18. Bal naqz̲ifu bilḥaqqi 'alal-baaṭili fa-yadmaghuhoo fa-iz̲aa huwa zaahiq; wa lakumul-waylu mimmaa taṣifoon.

بَلْ نَقْذِفُ بِالْحَقِّ عَلَى الْبَاطِلِ
فَيَدْمَغُهُ فَإِذَا هُوَ زَاهِقٌ وَلَكُمُ
الْوَيْلُ مِمَّا تَصِفُونَ ١٨

19. To Him belong all those who are in the heavens and the earth. Those who are closer to Him are not arrogant to worship Him, nor do they get tired of worshipping.

19. Wa lahoo man fissamaa-waati wal-arḍ; wa man 'indahoo laa yastakbiroona 'an 'ibaadatihee wa laa yastaḥsiroon.

وَلَهُ مَنْ فِي السَّمٰوٰتِ وَالْأَرْضِ
وَمَنْ عِنْدَهُ لَا يَسْتَكْبِرُونَ عَنْ
عِبَادَتِهِ وَلَا يَسْتَحْسِرُونَ ١٩

20. They glorify Him day and night without fail.

20. Yusabbiḥoonal-layla wannahaara laa yafturoon.

يُسَبِّحُونَ الَّيْلَ وَالنَّهَارَ لَا يَفْتُرُونَ ٢٠

21. Have they chosen deities from earth? Can such deities give life to anyone?

21. Amit-takhaz̲ooo aalihatam-minal-arḍi hum yunshiroon.

أَمِ اتَّخَذُوٓا آلِهَةً مِّنَ الْأَرْضِ
هُمْ يُنْشِرُونَ ٢١

22. Had there been other deities in the heavens and the earth besides Allah, both the heavens and the earth would have been destroyed. Allah, the Lord of the Throne, is free of all defects of what they think He is.

22. Law kaana feehimaaa aalihatun illal-laahu lafasadataa; fa-Subḥaanallaahi Rabbil-'Arshi 'ammaa yaṣifoon.

لَوْ كَانَ فِيهِمَآ آلِهَةٌ إِلَّا اللهُ
لَفَسَدَتَا فَسُبْحٰنَ اللهِ رَبِّ
الْعَرْشِ عَمَّا يَصِفُونَ ٢٢

23. He will not be questioned about anything He does, but all people will be questioned about their deeds.

23. Laa yus'alu 'ammaa yaf'alu wa hum yus'aloon.

لَا يُسْـَٔلُ عَمَّا يَفْعَلُ وَهُمْ يُسْـَٔلُونَ ﴿٢٣﴾

24. Have they chosen other gods besides Allah? (Muhammad), ask them, "Show the proof (in support of such belief). This is (the Quran) which tells us about the (beliefs of the people) in my time and those who lived before me." Most of them do not know. Moreover, the truth is that they neglect (the question of belief altogether).

24. Amit-takhazoo min dooniheee aalihatan qul haatoo burhaanakum haazaa zikru mam-ma'iya wa zikru man qablee; bal aksaruhum laa ya'lamoonal-ḥaqqa fahum-mu'riḍoon.

أَمِ اتَّخَذُوا مِنْ دُونِهِ آلِهَةً ۖ قُلْ
هَاتُوا بُرْهَانَكُمْ ۖ هَٰذَا ذِكْرُ مَنْ
مَعِيَ وَذِكْرُ مَنْ قَبْلِي ۗ بَلْ أَكْثَرُهُمْ
لَا يَعْلَمُونَ الْحَقَّ ۖ فَهُمْ مُعْرِضُونَ ﴿٢٤﴾

25. To all the Messengers that were sent before you We revealed that I Am the only Ilah (one deserving to be worshiped) so worship Me alone.

25. Wa maaa arsalnaa min qablika mir-Rasoolin illaa nooḥeee ilayhi annahoo laaa ilaaha illaaa Ana fa'budoon.

وَمَا أَرْسَلْنَا مِنْ قَبْلِكَ مِنْ رَسُولٍ
إِلَّا نُوحِي إِلَيْهِ أَنَّهُ لَا إِلَٰهَ إِلَّا
أَنَا فَاعْبُدُونِ ﴿٢٥﴾

26. They said, "The Beneficent has given birth to a son. He is free of all defects of giving birth to a son." (Those whom they think are Allah's sons) are only His honorable servants.

26. Wa qaalut-takhazar-Raḥmaanu waladan-Subḥaanah; bal 'ibaadum-mukramoon.

وَقَالُوا اتَّخَذَ الرَّحْمَٰنُ وَلَدًا ۗ سُبْحَانَهُ ۚ
بَلْ عِبَادٌ مُكْرَمُونَ ﴿٢٦﴾

27. These servants do not speak before He speaks. They simply act according to His orders.

27. Laa yasbiqoonahoo bil-qawli wa hum bi-amrihee ya'maloon.

لَا يَسْبِقُونَهُ بِالْقَوْلِ وَهُمْ بِأَمْرِهِ
يَعْمَلُونَ ﴿٢٧﴾

28. He knows all that is in front of them and all that is behind them. (These servants of Allah) will not intercede with Him for anyone without His permission and they tremble in awe (before His greatness).

28. Ya'lamu maa bayna aydeehim wa maa khalfahum wa laa yashfa'oona illaa limanir-taḍaa wa hum-min khash-yatihee mushfiqoon.

يَعْلَمُ مَا بَيْنَ أَيْدِيهِمْ وَمَا خَلْفَهُمْ
وَلَا يَشْفَعُونَ إِلَّا لِمَنِ ارْتَضَىٰ
وَهُمْ مِنْ خَشْيَتِهِ مُشْفِقُونَ ﴿٢٨﴾

29. We will punish in hell anyone of them who would say that he is the Lord instead of Allah; thus do We punish the unjust ones.

29. Wa mañy-yaqul minhum inneee ilaahum-min doonihee fazaalika najzeehi Jahannam; kazaalika najziẓ-ẓaalimeen.

وَمَنْ يَقُلْ مِنْهُمْ إِنِّي إِلَٰهٌ مِنْ
دُونِهِ فَذَٰلِكَ نَجْزِيهِ جَهَنَّمَ ۚ
كَذَٰلِكَ نَجْزِي الظَّالِمِينَ ﴿٢٩﴾ ع ١٩ ٢

30. Did the unbelievers not see that the heavens and the earth were one piece and that We tore them apart from one another? From water We have created all living things. Will they then have no faith?

30. Awalam yaral-lazeena kafarooo annas-samaawaati wal-arḍa kaanataa ratqan fafataqnaahumaa wa ja'alnaa minal-maaa'i kulla shay'in ḥayyin afalaa yu'minoon.

أَوَلَمْ يَرَ الَّذِينَ كَفَرُوا أَنَّ
السَّمَاوَاتِ وَالْأَرْضَ كَانَتَا رَتْقًا
فَفَتَقْنَاهُمَا ۖ وَجَعَلْنَا مِنَ الْمَاءِ
كُلَّ شَيْءٍ حَيٍّ ۖ أَفَلَا يُؤْمِنُونَ ﴿٣٠﴾

31. We placed firm mountains on earth lest it shake them away. We made wide roads for them so that they might have the right guidance.

31. Wa ja'alnaa fil-arḍi rawaasiya an tameeda bihim wa ja'alnaa feehaa fijaajan subulal-la'allahum yahtadoon.

وَجَعَلْنَا فِي الْأَرْضِ رَوَاسِيَ أَنْ
تَمِيدَ بِهِمْ وَجَعَلْنَا فِيهَا فِجَاجًا
سُبُلًا لَعَلَّهُمْ يَهْتَدُونَ ﴿٣١﴾

32. We made the sky above them as a well-guarded ceiling, but they

32. Wa ja'alnas-samaaa'a saqfam-maḥfooẓañw-

وَجَعَلْنَا السَّمَاءَ سَقْفًا مَحْفُوظًا ۖ

have neglected the evidence (of Our existence) therein.	wa hum 'an Aayaatihaa mu'riḍoon.	وَّهُمْ عَنْ اٰيٰتِهَا مُعْرِضُوْنَ ﴿٣٢﴾
33. It is Allah who has created the night, the day, the Sun, and Moon and has made them swim in a certain orbit.	33. Wa Huwal-lazee khalaqal-layla wannahaara washshamsa walqamara kullun fee falakiñy-yasbaḥoon.	وَهُوَ الَّذِىْ خَلَقَ الَّيْلَ وَالنَّهَارَ وَالشَّمْسَ وَالْقَمَرَ ؕ كُلٌّ فِىْ فَلَكٍ يَّسْبَحُوْنَ ﴿٣٣﴾
34. We made no mortal before you immortal. Will they become immortal after you die?	34. Wa maa ja'alnaa libasharim-min qablikal-khuld; afa'im-mitta fahumul-khaalidoon.	وَمَا جَعَلْنَا لِبَشَرٍ مِّنْ قَبْلِكَ الْخُلْدَ ؕ اَفَا۟ئِنْ مِّتَّ فَهُمُ الْخٰلِدُوْنَ ﴿٣٤﴾
35. Every soul has to experience the taste of death. We test you with both hardships and blessings. In the end you will all return to Us.	35. Kullu nafsin zaaa'iqatul-mawt; wa nablookum bish-sharri walkhayri fitnah; wa ilaynaa turja'oon.	كُلُّ نَفْسٍ ذَآئِقَةُ الْمَوْتِ ؕ وَنَبْلُوْكُمْ بِالشَّرِّ وَالْخَيْرِ فِتْنَةً ؕ وَاِلَيْنَا تُرْجَعُوْنَ ﴿٣٥﴾
36. (Muhammad), whenever the unbelievers see you, they think that you deserve nothing more than to be mocked. They say, "Is it he, (Muhammad), who speaks against your gods?" However, they themselves have no faith in the Beneficent at all.	36. wa izaa ra-aakal-lazeena kafarooo iñy-yattakhizoonaka illa huzuwaa; ahaazal-lazee yazkuru aalihatakum wa hum bi-zikrir-Raḥmaani hum kaafiroon.	وَاِذَا رَاٰكَ الَّذِيْنَ كَفَرُوْٓا اِنْ يَّتَّخِذُوْنَكَ اِلَّا هُزُوًا ؕ اَهٰذَا الَّذِىْ يَذْكُرُ اٰلِهَتَكُمْ ۚ وَهُمْ بِذِكْرِ الرَّحْمٰنِ هُمْ كٰفِرُوْنَ ﴿٣٦﴾
37. The human being is created to behave in haste. Tell them, "Do not behave in haste; Allah will soon show you the evidence of His existence."	37. Khuliqal-insaanu min 'ajal; sa-ureekum Aayaatee falaa tasta'jiloon.	خُلِقَ الْاِنْسَانُ مِنْ عَجَلٍ ؕ سَاُورِيْكُمْ اٰيٰتِىْ فَلَا تَسْتَعْجِلُوْنِ ﴿٣٧﴾
38. They say, "When shall the Day of Judgment come to pass if you are true in your claim?"	38. Wa yaqooloona mataa haazal-wa'du in kuntum ṣaadiqeen.	وَيَقُوْلُوْنَ مَتٰى هٰذَا الْوَعْدُ اِنْ كُنْتُمْ صٰدِقِيْنَ ﴿٣٨﴾
39. Would that the unbelievers had known that no one would protect their faces and backs against the fire, nor would they be helped.	39. Law ya'lamul-lazeena kafaroo ḥeena laa yakuffoona 'añw-wujoohihimun-Naara wa laa 'an ẓuhoorihim wa laa hum yunṣaroon.	لَوْ يَعْلَمُ الَّذِيْنَ كَفَرُوْا حِيْنَ لَا يَكُفُّوْنَ عَنْ وُّجُوْهِهِمُ النَّارَ وَلَا عَنْ ظُهُوْرِهِمْ وَلَا هُمْ يُنْصَرُوْنَ ﴿٣٩﴾
40. The fire will suddenly strike and confound them. They will not be able to repel it, nor will they receive any attention.	40. Bal ta-teehim baghtatan fatabhatuhum falaa yasta-ṭee'oona raddahaa wa laa hum yunẓaroon.	بَلْ تَاْتِيْهِمْ بَغْتَةً فَتَبْهَتُهُمْ فَلَا يَسْتَطِيْعُوْنَ رَدَّهَا وَلَا هُمْ يُنْظَرُوْنَ ﴿٤٠﴾
41. They mocked the Messengers who were sent before you; thus, the torment which they had ridiculed encompassed them all.	41. Wa laqadis-tuhzi'a bi-Rusulim-min qablika faḥaaqa billazeena sakhiroo minhum-maa kaanoo bihee yastahzi'oon.	وَلَقَدِ اسْتُهْزِئَ بِرُسُلٍ مِّنْ قَبْلِكَ فَحَاقَ بِالَّذِيْنَ سَخِرُوْا مِنْهُمْ مَّا كَانُوْا بِهٖ يَسْتَهْزِءُوْنَ ﴿٤١﴾

42. Ask them, "Who can protect them from (the wrath of) the Beneficent Allah during the night and day?" Yet they are neglectful about their Lord.

42. Qul mañy-yakla'ukum billayli wannahaari minar-Raḥmaan; bal hum 'an zikri Rabbihim-mu'riḍoon.

قُلْ مَنْ يَّكْلَؤُكُمْ بِالَّيْلِ وَ
النَّهَارِ مِنَ الرَّحْمٰنِ ؕ بَلْ هُمْ عَنْ
ذِكْرِ رَبِّهِمْ مُّعْرِضُوْنَ ﴿٤٢﴾

43. Can their gods protect them against Us? Their gods have no power even to help themselves, nor are they safe from Our retribution.

43. Am lahum aalihatun tamna'uhum-min dooninaa; laa yastaṭee'oona naṣra anfusihim wa laa hum-minnaa yuṣ-ḥaboon.

اَمْ لَهُمْ اٰلِهَةٌ تَمْنَعُهُمْ مِّنْ دُوْنِنَا ؕ
لَا يَسْتَطِيْعُوْنَ نَصْرَ اَنْفُسِهِمْ وَلَا
هُمْ مِّنَّا يُصْحَبُوْنَ ﴿٤٣﴾

44. We have been providing these men and their fathers with the means of enjoyment for a long time. Have they not ever considered that We populated the earth and then caused many of the inhabitants to pass away? Can they have any success (in their wickedness)?

44. Bal matta'naa haaa'u-laaa'i wa aabaaa'ahum ḥattaa ṭaala 'alayhimul-'umur; afalaa yarawna annaa na-til-arḍa nanquṣuhaa min aṭraafihaaa; afahumul-ghaaliboon.

بَلْ مَتَّعْنَا هٰٓؤُلَآءِ وَاٰبَآءَهُمْ حَتّٰى
طَالَ عَلَيْهِمُ الْعُمُرُ ؕ اَفَلَا يَرَوْنَ اَنَّا
نَاْتِى الْاَرْضَ نَنْقُصُهَا مِنْ اَطْرَافِهَا ؕ
اَفَهُمُ الْغٰلِبُوْنَ ﴿٤٤﴾

45. (Muhammad), tell them, "I am warning you by revelation alone." The deaf do not hear any call when they are warned.

45. Qul innamaaa unzirukum bilwaḥy; wa laa yasma'uṣ-ṣummud-du'aaa'a izaa maa yunzaroon

قُلْ اِنَّمَآ اُنْذِرُكُمْ بِالْوَحْىِ ۖ ز
وَلَا يَسْمَعُ الصُّمُّ الدُّعَآءَ اِذَا
مَا يُنْذَرُوْنَ ﴿٤٥﴾

46. If a blast of the torment of your Lord strikes them, they will say, "Woe to us! We have been unjust people."

46. Wa la'im-massat-hum nafḥatum-min 'azaabi Rabbika la-yaqoolunna yaawaylanaaa innaa kunnaa ẓaalimeen.

وَلَئِنْ مَّسَّتْهُمْ نَفْحَةٌ مِّنْ عَذَابِ
رَبِّكَ لَيَقُوْلُنَّ يٰوَيْلَنَآ اِنَّا
كُنَّا ظٰلِمِيْنَ ﴿٤٦﴾

47. We shall maintain proper justice on the Day of Judgment. No soul will be wronged the least. For a deed even as small as a mustard seed one will be duly recompensed. We are efficient in maintaining the account.

47. Wa naḍa'ul-mawaazeenal-qisṭa li-Yawmil-Qiyaamati falaa tuẓlamu nafsun shay'aa; wa-in-kaana misqaala-ḥabba-tim-min khardalin ataynaa bihaa; wa kafaa binaa ḥaasi-been.

وَنَضَعُ الْمَوَازِيْنَ الْقِسْطَ لِيَوْمِ
الْقِيٰمَةِ فَلَا تُظْلَمُ نَفْسٌ شَيْئًا ؕ
وَاِنْ كَانَ مِثْقَالَ حَبَّةٍ مِّنْ خَرْدَلٍ
اَتَيْنَا بِهَا ؕ وَكَفٰى بِنَا حٰسِبِيْنَ ﴿٤٧﴾

48. To Moses and Aaron We granted the criteria of discerning right from wrong, and We gave them the light and a reminder to the pious ones

48. Wa laqad aataynaa Moosaa wa Haaroonal-Furqaa-na wa ḍiyaa'añw-wa zikral-lilmut-taqeen.

وَلَقَدْ اٰتَيْنَا مُوْسٰى وَهٰرُوْنَ
الْفُرْقَانَ وَضِيَآءً وَّذِكْرًا
لِّلْمُتَّقِيْنَ ﴿٤٨﴾

49. who fear their unseen Lord and are anxious about the Day of Judgment.

49. Allazeena yakhshawna Rabbahum bilghaybi wa hum-minas-Saa'ati mushfiqoon.

الَّذِيْنَ يَخْشَوْنَ رَبَّهُمْ بِالْغَيْبِ
وَهُمْ مِّنَ السَّاعَةِ مُشْفِقُوْنَ ﴿٤٩﴾

50. This (Quran) which We have revealed is a blessed reminder. Will you then deny it?

50. Wa haazaa Zikrum-Mubaarakun anzalnaah; afa-antum lahoo munkiroon.

وَهٰذَا ذِكْرٌ مُّبٰرَكٌ اَنْزَلْنٰهُ ؕ اَفَاَنْتُمْ

51. To Abraham We gave the right guidance and We knew him very well.

52. Abraham asked his father and his people, "What are these statues which you worship?"

53. They replied, "We found our fathers worshipping them."

54. He said, "Both you and your fathers have certainly been in error."

55. They exclaimed, "Have you brought the Truth or are you joking?"

56. He said. "Your Lord is the Lord of the heavens and the earth. It was He who created them and I testify to this fact."

57. Abraham said to himself, "By Allah! I will devise a plan against their idols when they are away."

58. He broke all the idols into pieces, except the biggest among them so that perhaps people would refer to it.

59. (When the people came to the temple and saw the broken idols) they asked each other, "Who has done this to our gods? He certainly is an unjust person."

60. Some of them said, "We heard a youth called Abraham speaking against the idols."

61. Their chiefs said, "Bring him before the eyes of the people and let them testify that he has spoken against the idols."

62. They asked, "Abraham, did you do this to our idols?"

63. He replied, "I think the biggest among them has broken the smaller ones. Ask them if they

51. Wa laqad aataynaaa Ibraaheema rushdahoo min qablu wa kunnaa bihee 'aalimeen.

52. Iz qaala li-abeehi wa qawmihee maa haazihit-tamaaseelul-latee antum lahaa 'aakifoon.

53. Qaaloo wajadnaaa aabaaa'anaa lahaa 'aabideen.

54. Qaala laqad kuntum antum wa aabaaa'ukum fee ḍalaalim-mubeen.

55. Qaalooo aji'tanaa bil-ḥaqqi am anta minal-laa'ibeen.

56. Qaala bar-Rabbukum Rabbus-samaawaati wal-arḍil-lazee faṭarahunna wa ana 'alaa zaalikum-minash-shaahideen.

57. Wa tallaahi la-akeedanna aṣnaamakum ba'da an tuwalloo mudbireen.

58. Faja'alahum juzaazan illaa kabeeral-lahum la'allahum ilayhi yarji'oon.

59. Qaaloo man fa'ala haazaa bi-aalihatinaaa innahoo laminaẓ-ẓaalimeen.

60. Qaaloo sami'naa fatañy-yazkuruhum yuqaalu lahooo Ibraaheem.

61. Qaaloo fa-too bihee 'alaaa a'yunin-naasi la'allahum yash-hadoon.

62. Qaalooo 'a-anta fa'alta haazaa bi-aalihatinaa yaaa Ibraaheem.

63. Qaala bal fa'alahoo kabeeruhum haazaa

لَهٗ مُنْكِرُوْنَ ٥٠ ع
وَلَقَدْ اٰتَيْنَآ اِبْرٰهِيْمَ رُشْدَهٗ مِنْ
قَبْلُ وَكُنَّا بِهٖ عٰلِمِيْنَ ٥١
اِذْ قَالَ لِاَبِيْهِ وَقَوْمِهٖ مَا هٰذِهِ
التَّمَاثِيْلُ الَّتِيْٓ اَنْتُمْ لَهَا عٰكِفُوْنَ ٥٢
قَالُوْا وَجَدْنَآ اٰبَآءَنَا لَهَا عٰبِدِيْنَ ٥٣
قَالَ لَقَدْ كُنْتُمْ اَنْتُمْ وَاٰبَآؤُكُمْ
فِيْ ضَلٰلٍ مُّبِيْنٍ ٥٤
قَالُوْٓا اَجِئْتَنَا بِالْحَقِّ اَمْ اَنْتَ
مِنَ اللّٰعِبِيْنَ ٥٥
قَالَ بَلْ رَّبُّكُمْ رَبُّ السَّمٰوٰتِ
وَالْاَرْضِ الَّذِيْ فَطَرَهُنَّ ۖ وَاَنَا
عَلٰى ذٰلِكُمْ مِّنَ الشّٰهِدِيْنَ ٥٦
وَتَاللّٰهِ لَاَكِيْدَنَّ اَصْنَامَكُمْ
بَعْدَ اَنْ تُوَلُّوْا مُدْبِرِيْنَ ٥٧
فَجَعَلَهُمْ جُذٰذًا اِلَّا كَبِيْرًا لَّهُمْ
لَعَلَّهُمْ اِلَيْهِ يَرْجِعُوْنَ ٥٨
قَالُوْا مَنْ فَعَلَ هٰذَا بِاٰلِهَتِنَآ اِنَّهٗ
لَمِنَ الظّٰلِمِيْنَ ٥٩
قَالُوْا سَمِعْنَا فَتًى يَّذْكُرُهُمْ يُقَالُ
لَهٗٓ اِبْرٰهِيْمُ ٦٠
قَالُوْا فَاْتُوْا بِهٖ عَلٰٓى اَعْيُنِ النَّاسِ
لَعَلَّهُمْ يَشْهَدُوْنَ ٦١
قَالُوْٓا ءَاَنْتَ فَعَلْتَ هٰذَا بِاٰلِهَتِنَا
يٰٓاِبْرٰهِيْمُ ٦٢
قَالَ بَلْ فَعَلَهٗ ۖ كَبِيْرُهُمْ هٰذَا

are able to speak."	fas'aloohum in kaanoo yanṭiqoon.	فَسْـَٔلُوهُمْ إِن كَانُوا۟ يَنطِقُونَ ﴿٦٣﴾
64. Thereupon they realized their own foolishness and said, "We ourselves are wrong-doers."	64. Faraja'ooo ilaaa anfusihim faqaalooo innakum antumuẓ-ẓaalimoon.	فَرَجَعُوٓا۟ إِلَىٰٓ أَنفُسِهِمْ فَقَالُوٓا۟ إِنَّكُمْ أَنتُمُ ٱلظَّـٰلِمُونَ ﴿٦٤﴾
65. With their heads cast down they said, "Abraham, you know that idols do not speak. How then can you ask such a question?"	65. <u>S</u>umma nukisoo 'alaa ru'oosihim laqad 'alimta maa haaa'ulaaa'i yanṭiqoon.	ثُمَّ نُكِسُوا۟ عَلَىٰ رُءُوسِهِمْ لَقَدْ عَلِمْتَ مَا هَـٰٓؤُلَآءِ يَنطِقُونَ ﴿٦٥﴾
66. He said, "Do you, instead of Allah, worship things that can neither harm nor benefit you?"	66. Qaala afata'budoona min doonil-laahi maa laa yanfa'ukum shay'añw-wa laa yaḍurrukum.	قَالَ أَفَتَعْبُدُونَ مِن دُونِ ٱللَّهِ مَا لَا يَنفَعُكُمْ شَيْـًٔا وَلَا يَضُرُّكُمْ ﴿٦٦﴾
67. Woe to you for what you worship instead of Allah. Have you no understanding?"	67. Uffil-lakum wa limaa ta'budoona min doonil-laah; afalaa ta'qiloon.	أُفٍّ لَّكُمْ وَلِمَا تَعْبُدُونَ مِن دُونِ ٱللَّهِ ۖ أَفَلَا تَعْقِلُونَ ﴿٦٧﴾
68. They said, "Burn him to ashes if you want to help your gods."	68. Qaaloo ḥarriqoohu wanṣurooo aalihatakum in kuntum faa'ileen.	قَالُوا۟ حَرِّقُوهُ وَٱنصُرُوٓا۟ ءَالِهَتَكُمْ إِن كُنتُمْ فَـٰعِلِينَ ﴿٦٨﴾
69. We said to the fire, "Be cool and peaceful (with Abraham)."	69. Qulnaa yaa naaru koonee bardañw-wa salaaman 'alaaa Ibraaheem.	قُلْنَا يَـٰنَارُ كُونِى بَرْدًا وَسَلَـٰمًا عَلَىٰٓ إِبْرَٰهِيمَ ﴿٦٩﴾
70. They had devised an evil plan (against Abraham), but We turned it into failure."	70. Wa araadoo bihee kaydan faja'alnaahumul akhsareen.	وَأَرَادُوا۟ بِهِۦ كَيْدًا فَجَعَلْنَـٰهُمُ ٱلْأَخْسَرِينَ ﴿٧٠﴾
71. We took Abraham and Lot safely to the land in which We had sent blessings to the worlds.	71. Wa najjaynaahu wa Looṭan ilal-arḍil-latee baaraknaa feehaa lil'aalameen.	وَنَجَّيْنَـٰهُ وَلُوطًا إِلَى ٱلْأَرْضِ ٱلَّتِى بَـٰرَكْنَا فِيهَا لِلْعَـٰلَمِينَ ﴿٧١﴾
72. We granted him Isaac and Jacob as a gift and helped both of them to become righteous people.	72. Wa wahabnaa lahooo Isḥaaq; wa Ya'qooba naafilah; wa kullan ja'alnaa ṣaaliḥeen.	وَوَهَبْنَا لَهُۥٓ إِسْحَـٰقَ وَيَعْقُوبَ نَافِلَةً ۖ وَكُلًّا جَعَلْنَا صَـٰلِحِينَ ﴿٧٢﴾
73. We appointed them as leaders to guide the people through Our command and sent them revelation to strive for good deeds, worship their Lord, and pay religious tax. Both of them were Our worshipping servants.	73. Waja'alnaahum a'immatañy-yahdoona bi-amrinaa wa awḥaynaaa ilayhim fi'lal khayraati wa iqaamaṣ-Ṣalaati wa eetaaa'az-Zakaati wa kaanoolanaa 'aabideen.	وَجَعَلْنَـٰهُمْ أَئِمَّةً يَهْدُونَ بِأَمْرِنَا وَأَوْحَيْنَآ إِلَيْهِمْ فِعْلَ ٱلْخَيْرَٰتِ وَإِقَامَ ٱلصَّلَوٰةِ وَإِيتَآءَ ٱلزَّكَوٰةِ ۖ وَكَانُوا۟ لَنَا عَـٰبِدِينَ ﴿٧٣﴾
74. To Lot We gave knowledge and wisdom and saved him from the people of the town who were committing indecent (filthy) acts. They were certainly a bad and	74. Wa Looṭan aataynaahu ḥukmañw-wa 'ilmañw-wa najjaynaahu minal-qaryatil-latee kaanat-ta'malul-khabaaa'i<u>s</u>; innahum kaanoo	وَلُوطًا ءَاتَيْنَـٰهُ حُكْمًا وَعِلْمًا وَنَجَّيْنَـٰهُ مِنَ ٱلْقَرْيَةِ ٱلَّتِى كَانَت تَّعْمَلُ ٱلْخَبَـٰٓئِثَ ۚ إِنَّهُمْ كَانُوا۟

sinful people.

Qawma saw'in faasiqeen.

قَوْمَ سَوْءٍ فٰسِقِيْنَ ﴿٧٤﴾

75. We encompassed him in Our mercy; he was a righteous man.

75. Wa adkhalnaahu fee raḥmatinaaa innahoo minaṣ-ṣaaliḥeen.

وَاَدْخَلْنٰهُ فِيْ رَحْمَتِنَا ؕ اِنَّهٗ مِنَ
الصّٰلِحِيْنَ ﴿٧٥﴾ ع ٥ ٢٥ ٥

76. We answered the prayer of Noah who had prayed to Us before and saved him and his followers from the great disaster.

76. Wa Nooḥan iz naadaa min qablu fastajabnaa lahoo fanajjaynaahu wa ahlahoo minal-karbil-'aẓeem.

وَنُوْحًا اِذْ نَادٰى مِنْ قَبْلُ فَاسْتَجَبْنَا
لَهٗ فَنَجَّيْنٰهُ وَاَهْلَهٗ مِنَ الْكَرْبِ
الْعَظِيْمِ ﴿٧٦﴾

77. We helped him against the people who said Our revelations were mere lies. They were a bad people and We drowned them all.

77. Wa naṣarnaahu minal-qawmil-lazeena kaz-zaboo bi Aayaatinaaa; innahum kaanoo qawma saw'in fa-aghraqnaahum ajma'een.

وَنَصَرْنٰهُ مِنَ الْقَوْمِ الَّذِيْنَ
كَذَّبُوْا بِاٰيٰتِنَا ؕ اِنَّهُمْ كَانُوْا قَوْمَ
سَوْءٍ فَاَغْرَقْنٰهُمْ اَجْمَعِيْنَ ﴿٧٧﴾

78. David and Solomon were trying to settle the case of the people's sheep that grazed in a cornfield at night and destroyed it. We witnessed their decree in that matter.

78. Wa Daawooda wa Sulaymaana iz yaḥkumaani fil-ḥarsi iz nafashat feehi ghanamul-qawmi wa kunnaa liḥukmihim shaahideen.

وَدَاوٗدَ وَسُلَيْمٰنَ اِذْ يَحْكُمٰنِ فِي
الْحَرْثِ اِذْ نَفَشَتْ فِيْهِ غَنَمُ
الْقَوْمِ ۚ وَكُنَّا لِحُكْمِهِمْ شٰهِدِيْنَ ﴿٧٨﴾

79. We made Solomon understand the law about the case and gave both David and Solomon knowledge and wisdom. We made the mountains and birds glorify the Lord along with David. We had also done to him such favors before.

79. Fafahhamnaahaa Sulaymaan; wa kullan aataynaa ḥukmañw-wa 'ilmañw-wa sakhkharnaa ma'a Daawoodal-jibaala yusabbiḥna waṭṭayr; wa kunnaa faa'ileen.

فَفَهَّمْنٰهَا سُلَيْمٰنَ ۚ وَكُلًّا اٰتَيْنَا
حُكْمًا وَّعِلْمًا ؗ وَّسَخَّرْنَا مَعَ دَاوٗدَ
الْجِبَالَ يُسَبِّحْنَ وَالطَّيْرَ ؕ وَكُنَّا
فٰعِلِيْنَ ﴿٧٩﴾

80. We taught him the art of making coats of mail so that you could protect yourselves during a war. Will you then give thanks?

80. Wa 'allamnaahu ṣan'ata laboosil-lakum lituḥṣinakum mim ba-sikum fahal antum shaakiroon.

وَعَلَّمْنٰهُ صَنْعَةَ لَبُوْسٍ لَّكُمْ
لِتُحْصِنَكُمْ مِّنْۢ بَاْسِكُمْ ۚ فَهَلْ
اَنْتُمْ شٰكِرُوْنَ ﴿٨٠﴾

81. We made subservient to Solomon the swift wind that blew on his command to the land in which We had sent blessings. We have the knowledge of all things.

81. Wa li-Sulaymaanar-reeḥa 'aaṣifatan tajree bi-amriheee ilal-arḍil-latee baaraknaa feehaa; wa kunnaa bikulli shay'in 'aalimeen.

وَلِسُلَيْمٰنَ الرِّيْحَ عَاصِفَةً تَجْرِيْ
بِاَمْرِهٖۤ اِلَى الْاَرْضِ الَّتِيْ بٰرَكْنَا فِيْهَا ؕ
وَكُنَّا بِكُلِّ شَيْءٍ عٰلِمِيْنَ ﴿٨١﴾

82. We subdued the devils who would dive into the sea for him and perform other tasks for Solomon. We kept them in his service.

82. Wa minash-Shayaaṭeeni mañy-yaghooṣoona lahoo wa ya'maloona 'amalan doona zaalika wa kunnaa lahum ḥaafiẓeen.

وَمِنَ الشَّيٰطِيْنِ مَنْ يَّغُوْصُوْنَ لَهٗ
وَيَعْمَلُوْنَ عَمَلًا دُوْنَ ذٰلِكَ ۚ وَكُنَّا
لَهُمْ حٰفِظِيْنَ ﴿٨٢﴾

83. When Job prayed, "O Lord, I have been afflicted with hardships. Have mercy on me; You are the

83. Wa Ayyooba iz naadaa Rabbahooo annee massaniyaḍ-

وَاَيُّوْبَ اِذْ نَادٰى رَبَّهٗۤ اَنِّيْ مَسَّنِيَ

Most Merciful of those who have mercy,"

ḍurru wa Anta arḥamur-raaḥimeen.

الضُّرُّ وَأَنْتَ أَرْحَمُ الرّٰحِمِينَ ٨٣

84. We answered his prayer, relieved him from his hardships, brought his family (back to him), and gave him twice as much property as that (which was destroyed). It was a mercy from Us and a reminder for the worshippers.

84. Fastajabnaa lahoo fakashafnaa maa bihee min ḍurriñw-wa-aataynaahu ahlahoo wa mis̲lahum-ma'ahum raḥmatam-min 'indinaa wa z̲ikraa lil'aabideen.

فَاسْتَجَبْنَا لَهُ فَكَشَفْنَا مَا بِهِ مِنْ
ضُرٍّ وَآتَيْنٰهُ أَهْلَهُ وَمِثْلَهُمْ مَعَهُمْ
رَحْمَةً مِنْ عِنْدِنَا وَذِكْرٰى
لِلْعٰبِدِينَ ٨٤

85. Ishmael, Idris, and Dhul Kifl all were people of great patience.

85. Wa Ismaa'eela wa Idreesa wa Z̲al-kifli kullum-minaṣ-ṣaabireen.

وَإِسْمٰعِيلَ وَإِدْرِيسَ وَذَا الْكِفْلِ
كُلٌّ مِنَ الصّٰبِرِينَ ٨٥

86. We encompassed them in Our mercy; they were righteous people.

86. Wa adkhalnaahum fee raḥmatinaaa innahum-minaṣ-ṣaaliḥeen.

وَأَدْخَلْنٰهُمْ فِي رَحْمَتِنَا إِنَّهُمْ
مِنَ الصّٰلِحِينَ ٨٦

87. Dhan Nun (Jonah, the companion of the Whale) went away angry (over the deeds of his people) and thought that We would never apply Our measures upon him, but in darkness he cried, "Lord, You are the Only Lord whom I glorify. Indeed I have been of those who do wrong to themselves, (so forgive me)."

87. Wa Z̲an-Nooni-iz̲-z̲ahaba mughaaḍiban faẓaanna al-lan naqdira 'alayhi fanaadaa fiẓ-ẓulumaati al-laaa ilaaha illaaa Anta Subḥaanaka innee kuntu minaẓ-ẓaalimeen.

وَذَا النُّونِ إِذْ ذَهَبَ مُغٰضِبًا
فَظَنَّ أَنْ لَنْ نَقْدِرَ عَلَيْهِ فَنَادٰى
فِي الظُّلُمٰتِ أَنْ لَا إِلٰهَ إِلَّا
أَنْتَ سُبْحٰنَكَ إِنِّي كُنْتُ مِنَ
الظّٰلِمِينَ ٨٧

88. We answered his prayer and saved him from his grief. Thus We save the faithful ones.

88. Fastajabnaa lahoo wa najjaynaahu minal-ghamm; wa kaz̲aalika nunjil mu'mineen.

فَاسْتَجَبْنَا لَهُ وَنَجَّيْنٰهُ مِنَ
الْغَمِّ وَكَذٰلِكَ نُنْجِي الْمُؤْمِنِينَ ٨٨

89. Zachariah prayed, "Lord, do not leave me alone without offspring, although you are the best heir."

89. Wa Zakariyyaaa iz̲ naadaa Rabbahoo Rabbi laa taz̲arnee fardañw-wa Anta khayrul-waaris̲een.

وَزَكَرِيَّا إِذْ نَادٰى رَبَّهُ رَبِّ
لَا تَذَرْنِي فَرْدًا وَأَنْتَ خَيْرُ
الْوٰرِثِينَ ٨٩

90. We answered his prayer and granted him his son, John, by making his wife fruitful (made her menstrual system function again). They were people who would compete with each other in good deeds and pray to Us with love and reverence. With Us they were all humble people.

90. Fastajabnaa lahoo wa wahabnaa lahoo Yaḥyaa wa aṣlaḥnaa lahoo zawjah; innahum kaanoo yusaari'oona fil-khayraati wa yad'oonanaa raghabañw-wa rahabaa; wa kaanoo lanaa khaashi'een.

فَاسْتَجَبْنَا لَهُ وَوَهَبْنَا لَهُ يَحْيٰى
وَأَصْلَحْنَا لَهُ زَوْجَهُ إِنَّهُمْ
كَانُوا يُسٰرِعُونَ فِي الْخَيْرٰتِ وَ
يَدْعُونَنَا رَغَبًا وَرَهَبًا وَكَانُوا
لَنَا خٰشِعِينَ ٩٠

91. Into the woman who maintained her chastity We breathed Our Spirit and made her

91. Wallateee aḥṣanat farjahaa fanafakhnaa feehaa mir-rooḥinaa wa ja'alnaahaa

وَالَّتِي أَحْصَنَتْ فَرْجَهَا فَنَفَخْنَا
فِيهَا مِنْ رُوحِنَا وَجَعَلْنٰهَا

and her son a miracle for all people.	wabnahaaa Aayatal-lil'aalameen.	وَابْنَهَآ اٰيَةً لِّلْعٰلَمِيْنَ ۝٩١
92. People, you are one nation and I am your Lord. Worship Me.	92. Inna haaẕiheee ummatukum ummatañw-waaḥidatañw-wa Ana Rabbukum fa'budoon.	اِنَّ هٰذِهٖٓ اُمَّتُكُمْ اُمَّةً وَّاحِدَةً ۖ وَّاَنَا رَبُّكُمْ فَاعْبُدُوْنِ ۝٩٢
93. People have divided themselves into many sects, but all will return to Us.	93. Wa taqaṭṭa'ooo amrahum baynahum kullun ilaynaa raaji'oon.	وَتَقَطَّعُوْٓا اَمْرَهُمْ بَيْنَهُمْ ۭ كُلٌّ اِلَيْنَا رٰجِعُوْنَ ۝٩٣ ع ١٨
94. The reward of the righteously striving believers will not be neglected (annulled). We are keeping the record of their good deeds.	94. Famañy-ya'mal minaṣ-ṣaaliḥaati wa huwa mu'minun falaa kufraana lisa'yihee wa-innaa lahoo kaatiboon.	فَمَنْ يَّعْمَلْ مِنَ الصّٰلِحٰتِ وَهُوَ مُؤْمِنٌ فَلَا كُفْرَانَ لِسَعْيِهٖ ۚ وَاِنَّا لَهٗ كٰتِبُوْنَ ۝٩٤
95. The people whom We destroyed can never return to this world	95. Wa ḥaraamun 'alaa qaryatin ahlaknaahaaa annahum laa yarji'oon.	وَحَرٰمٌ عَلٰى قَرْيَةٍ اَهْلَكْنٰهَآ اَنَّهُمْ لَا يَرْجِعُوْنَ ۝٩٥
96. until Gog and Magog are let loose to rush down from the hills.	96. Ḥattaaa iẕaa futiḥat Ya-jooju wa Ma-jooju wa hum-min kulli ḥadabiñy-yansiloon.	حَتّٰٓى اِذَا فُتِحَتْ يَاْجُوْجُ وَمَاْجُوْجُ وَهُمْ مِّنْ كُلِّ حَدَبٍ يَّنْسِلُوْنَ ۝٩٦
97. The Day of Judgment will then draw near and the unbelievers will stare amazedly and cry, "Woe to us! We had neglected this day. We have done injustice to ourselves."	97. Waqtarabal-wa'dul-ḥaqqu fa-iẕaa hiya shaakhiṣatun abṣaarul-laẕeena kafaroo yaa waylanaa qad kunnaa fee ghaflatim-min haaẕaa bal kunnaa ẓaalimeen.	وَاقْتَرَبَ الْوَعْدُ الْحَقُّ فَاِذَا هِىَ شَاخِصَةٌ اَبْصَارُ الَّذِيْنَ كَفَرُوْا ۭ يٰوَيْلَنَا قَدْ كُنَّا فِيْ غَفْلَةٍ مِّنْ هٰذَا بَلْ كُنَّا ظٰلِمِيْنَ ۝٩٧
98. They will be told, "You and what you had worshipped instead of Allah will be thrown in hellfire."	98. Innakum wa maa ta'budoona min doonil-laahi ḥaṣabu Jahannama antum lahaa waaridoon.	اِنَّكُمْ وَمَا تَعْبُدُوْنَ مِنْ دُوْنِ اللّٰهِ حَصَبُ جَهَنَّمَ ۭ اَنْتُمْ لَهَا وٰرِدُوْنَ ۝٩٨
99. Had the idols been true lords, they would not have gone to hell. "All of you will live therein forever."	99. Law kaana haaa'ulaaa'i aalihatam-maa waradoohaa wa kullun feehaa khaalidoon.	لَوْ كَانَ هٰٓؤُلَاۗءِ اٰلِهَةً مَّا وَرَدُوْهَا ۭ وَكُلٌّ فِيْهَا خٰلِدُوْنَ ۝٩٩
100. They will groan in pain therein, but no one will listen to them.	100. Lahum feehaa zafeeruñw-wa hum feehaa laa yasma'oon.	لَهُمْ فِيْهَا زَفِيْرٌ وَّهُمْ فِيْهَا لَا يَسْمَعُوْنَ ۝١٠٠
101. However, those (Jesus and angels) to whom We have already promised blessings will be far away from hell.	101. Innal-laẕeena sabaqat lahum-minnal-ḥusnaaa ulaaa'ika 'anhaa mub'adoon.	اِنَّ الَّذِيْنَ سَبَقَتْ لَهُمْ مِّنَّا الْحُسْنٰٓى ۙ اُولٰۗىِٕكَ عَنْهَا مُبْعَدُوْنَ ۝١٠١
102. They will not even hear the slightest sound from it while	102. Laa yasma'oona ḥaseesahaa wa hum fee	لَا يَسْمَعُوْنَ حَسِيْسَهَا ۚ وَهُمْ فِيْ

enjoying the best that they can wish for in their everlasting life.

mash-tahat anfusuhum khaali-doon.

مَا اشْتَهَتْ اَنْفُسُهُمْ خٰلِدُوْنَ ﴿١٠٢﴾

103. They will not be affected by the great terror. The angels will come to them with this glad news: "This is your day which was promised to you."

103. Laaa yaḥzunuhumul-faza'ul-akbaru wa tatalaq-qaahumul-malaaa'ikatu haaz̲aa Yawmu-kumul-laz̲ee kuntum too'adoon.

لَا يَحْزُنُهُمُ الْفَزَعُ الْاَكْبَرُ وَ
تَتَلَقّٰهُمُ الْمَلٰٓئِكَةُ ؕ هٰذَا يَوْمُكُمُ
الَّذِيْ كُنْتُمْ تُوْعَدُوْنَ ﴿١٠٣﴾

104. (This will happen) on the day when We roll up (destroy and turn them into smoke) the heavens as if it were a written scroll and bring it back into existence just as though We had created it for the first time. This is what We have promised and We have always been true to Our promise.

104. Yawma naṭwis-samaaa'a kaṭayyis-sijilli lilkutub; kamaa bada-naaa awwala khalqin-nu'eeduh; wa'dan 'alaynaaa; innaa kunnaa faa'ileen.

يَوْمَ نَطْوِي السَّمَآءَ كَطَيِّ السِّجِلِّ
لِلْكُتُبِ ؕ كَمَا بَدَاْنَآ اَوَّلَ خَلْقٍ
نُّعِيْدُهٗ ؕ وَعْدًا عَلَيْنَا ؕ اِنَّا
كُنَّا فٰعِلِيْنَ ﴿١٠٤﴾

105. We have written in the psalms, which We had revealed after the book (Torah), that the earth will be given to Our righteous servants (Al-Mahdi and his people) as their inheritance.

105. Wa laqad katabnaa fiz Zaboori mim ba'diz-z̲ikri annal-arḍa yaris̲uhaa 'ibaadi-yaṣ-ṣaaliḥoon.

وَلَقَدْ كَتَبْنَا فِي الزَّبُوْرِ مِنْۢ
بَعْدِ الذِّكْرِ اَنَّ الْاَرْضَ يَرِثُهَا
عِبَادِيَ الصّٰلِحُوْنَ ﴿١٠٥﴾

106. This is a lesson for those who worship (Allah).

106. Inna fee haaz̲aa labalaa-ghal-liqawmin 'aabideen.

اِنَّ فِيْ هٰذَا لَبَلٰغًا لِّقَوْمٍ
عٰبِدِيْنَ ﴿١٠٦﴾

107. (Muhammad), We have sent you for no other reason but to be a mercy for mankind.

107. Wa maaa arsalnaaka illaa raḥmatal-lil'aalameen.

وَمَآ اَرْسَلْنٰكَ اِلَّا رَحْمَةً لِّلْعٰلَمِيْنَ ﴿١٠٧﴾

108. Say, "It is revealed to me that there is only one Lord. Will you then submit yourselves to His will?"

108. Qul innamaa yooḥaaa ilayya annamaaa ilaahukum Ilaahuñw-Waaḥid; fahal antum muslimoon.

قُلْ اِنَّمَا يُوْحٰٓى اِلَيَّ اَنَّمَآ اِلٰهُكُمْ
اِلٰهٌ وَّاحِدٌ ۚ فَهَلْ اَنْتُمْ مُّسْلِمُوْنَ ﴿١٠٨﴾

109. If they turn away, tell them, "I have warned every one of you equally. I do not know when the torment which you have to suffer will take place.

109. Fa-in tawallaw faqul aaz̲antukum 'alaa sawaaa'; wa in adreee aqareebun am ba'eedum-maa too' adoon.

فَاِنْ تَوَلَّوْا فَقُلْ اٰذَنْتُكُمْ عَلٰى
سَوَآءٍ ؕ وَاِنْ اَدْرِيْٓ اَقَرِيْبٌ اَمْ
بَعِيْدٌ مَّا تُوْعَدُوْنَ ﴿١٠٩﴾

110. Allah knows well all that is spoken aloud and all that you hide.

110. Innahoo ya'lamul-jahra minal-qawli wa ya'lamu maa taktumoon.

اِنَّهٗ يَعْلَمُ الْجَهْرَ مِنَ الْقَوْلِ
وَيَعْلَمُ مَا تَكْتُمُوْنَ ﴿١١٠﴾

111. I do not know (why Allah has commanded me to warn you of the torment). It, perhaps, is a trial for you and a respite for an appointed time."

111. Wa in adree la'allahoo fitnatul-lakum wa mataa'un ilaa ḥeen.

وَاِنْ اَدْرِيْ لَعَلَّهٗ فِتْنَةٌ لَّكُمْ
وَّمَتَاعٌ اِلٰى حِيْنٍ ﴿١١١﴾

112. He also said, "Lord, judge (us) with Truth. Our Lord is the Beneficent. One must seek His help against the blasphemous things you say about Him."

112. Qaala Rabbiḥ-kum bil-ḥaqq; wa Rabbunar-Raḥmaa-nul-musta'aanu 'alaa maa taṣifoon.

قٰلَ رَبِّ احْكُمْ بِالْحَقِّ ؕ وَرَبُّنَا
الرَّحْمٰنُ الْمُسْتَعَانُ عَلٰى مَا
تَصِفُوْنَ ﴿١١٢﴾ النصف ع ١٩

Al-Hajj, The Pilgrimage (22)

In the Name of Allah,
the Beneficent, the Merciful.

1. People, have fear of your Lord; the quake (of the physical realm) at the Hour of Doom will be terribly violent.

2. The day that hour comes, you will see every breast-feeding mother drop her baby out of fear and every pregnant female will cast off her burden (give birth). You will see the people behaving as though they were drunk, while, in fact, they are not drunk. They only will look as such because of the severity of Allah's torment.

3. There are those among people who argue about Allah without knowledge and follow every filthy Satan.

4. It has been decided that Satan will mislead and submit anyone who establishes friendship with him to the torment of the burning fire.

5. People, if you have doubts about the Resurrection, you must know that We created you from clay that was turned into a living germ. This was developed into a clot, which was then made into flesh with blood or dead for not having enough blood. This is how We show you that resurrection is not more difficult for Us than your creation. We cause whatever We want to stay in the womb for an appointed time, We then take you out of the womb as a baby, so that you may grow up to manhood. There are those of you who may then die and others may grow to a very old age and lose your memory. You may see the earth as a barren land, but when we send rain, it starts to stir and

Sûrat al-Ḥajj-22

(Revealed at Madinah)

Bismillaahir Raḥmaanir Raḥeem

1. Yaaa ayyuhan-naasuttaqoo Rabbakum; inna zalzalatas-Saa'ati shay'un 'aẓeem.

2. Yawma tarawnahaa taẕhalu kullu murḍi'atin 'ammaaa arḍa'at wa taḍa'u kullu ẕaati ḥamlin ḥamlahaa wa tarannaasa sukaaraa wa maa hum bisu-kaaraa wa laakinna 'azaabal-laahi shadeed.

3. Wa minan-naasi mañy-yujaadilu fil-laahi bighayri 'ilmiñw-wa yattabi'u kullaa shayṭaanim-mareed.

4. Kutiba 'alayhi annahoo man tawallaahu fa-annahoo yuḍil-luhoo wa yahdeehi ilaa 'aẓaa-bis-sa'eer.

5. Yaaa-ayyuhan-naasu-in kuntum fee raybim-minal-ba'ṡi fa-innaa khalaqnaakum-min turaabin ṡumma min nuṭfatin ṡumma min 'alaqatin ṡumma mim-muḍghatim-mukhal-laqatiñw-wa ghayri mukhalla-qatil-linubayyina lakum; wa nuqirru fil-arḥaami maa nashaaa'u ilaaa ajalim-musam-man ṡumma nukhrijukum ṭiflan ṡumma litablughooo ashud-dakum wa minkum-mañy-yutawaffaa wa minkum-mañy-yuraddu ilaaa arẕalil-'umuri likaylaa ya'lama mim ba'di 'ilmin shay'aa; wa taral-arḍa

(٢٢) سُوْرَةُ الْحَجِّ مَدَنِيَّةٌ (١٠٣)

اٰيَاتُهَا ٧٨ بِسْمِ اللّٰهِ الرَّحْمٰنِ الرَّحِيْمِ رُكُوْعَاتُهَا ١٠

يٰۤاَيُّهَا النَّاسُ اتَّقُوْا رَبَّكُمْۚ اِنَّ
زَلْزَلَةَ السَّاعَةِ شَيْءٌ عَظِيْمٌ ۝١
يَوْمَ تَرَوْنَهَا تَذْهَلُ كُلُّ مُرْضِعَةٍ
عَمَّاۤ اَرْضَعَتْ وَتَضَعُ كُلُّ ذَاتِ
حَمْلٍ حَمْلَهَا وَتَرَى النَّاسَ
سُكٰرٰى وَمَا هُمْ بِسُكٰرٰى وَلٰكِنَّ
عَذَابَ اللّٰهِ شَدِيْدٌ ۝٢
وَمِنَ النَّاسِ مَنْ يُّجَادِلُ فِي اللّٰهِ
بِغَيْرِ عِلْمٍ وَّيَتَّبِعُ كُلَّ شَيْطٰنٍ
مَّرِيْدٍ ۝٣
كُتِبَ عَلَيْهِ اَنَّهٗ مَنْ تَوَلَّاهُ
فَاَنَّهٗ يُضِلُّهٗ وَيَهْدِيْهِ اِلٰى
عَذَابِ السَّعِيْرِ ۝٤
يٰۤاَيُّهَا النَّاسُ اِنْ كُنْتُمْ فِيْ
رَيْبٍ مِّنَ الْبَعْثِ فَاِنَّا خَلَقْنٰكُمْ
مِّنْ تُرَابٍ ثُمَّ مِنْ نُّطْفَةٍ ثُمَّ مِنْ
عَلَقَةٍ ثُمَّ مِنْ مُّضْغَةٍ مُّخَلَّقَةٍ
وَّغَيْرِ مُخَلَّقَةٍ لِّنُبَيِّنَ لَكُمْؕ وَ
نُقِرُّ فِي الْاَرْحَامِ مَا نَشَاۤءُ اِلٰۤى اَجَلٍ
مُّسَمًّى ثُمَّ نُخْرِجُكُمْ طِفْلًا ثُمَّ
لِتَبْلُغُوْۤا اَشُدَّكُمْۚ وَمِنْكُمْ مَّنْ
يُّتَوَفّٰى وَمِنْكُمْ مَّنْ يُّرَدُّ اِلٰۤى
اَرْذَلِ الْعُمُرِ لِكَيْلَا يَعْلَمَ مِنْۢ
بَعْدِ عِلْمٍ شَيْـًٔاؕ وَتَرَى الْاَرْضَ

swell and produce various pairs of attractive herbs.

haamidatan fa-i<u>z</u>aaa anzalnaa 'alayhal-maaa'ah-tazzat wa rabat wa ambatat min kulli zawjim baheej.

هَامِدَةً فَإِذَآ أَنزَلْنَا عَلَيْهَا
الْمَآءَ اهْتَزَّتْ وَرَبَتْ وَأَنۢبَتَتْ
مِن كُلِّ زَوْجٍۭ بَهِيجٍ ٥

6. This is because Allah is the Supreme Truth who gives life to the dead and who has power over all things.

6. <u>Z</u>aalika bi-annal-laaha Huwal-ḥaqqu wa annahoo yuḥyil-mawtaa wa annahoo 'alaa kulli shay'in Qadeer.

ذَٰلِكَ بِأَنَّ اللَّهَ هُوَ الْحَقُّ وَأَنَّهُۥ
يُحْيِ الْمَوْتَىٰ وَأَنَّهُۥ عَلَىٰ كُلِّ شَيْءٍ
قَدِيرٌ ٦

7. There is no doubt about the coming of the Hour of Doom and that Allah will raise everyone from their graves.

7. Wa annas-Saa'ata aatiya-tul-laa rayba feehaa wa annal-laaha yab'a<u>s</u>u man fil-quboor.

وَأَنَّ السَّاعَةَ ءَاتِيَةٌ لَّا رَيْبَ فِيهَا
وَأَنَّ اللَّهَ يَبْعَثُ مَن فِي الْقُبُورِ ٧

8. There are people who argue about Allah without knowledge, guidance, and an enlightening Book.

8. Wa minan-naasi mañy-yujaadilu fil-laahi bighayri 'ilmiñw-wa laa hudañw-wa laa Kitaabim-Muneer.

وَمِنَ النَّاسِ مَن يُجَادِلُ فِي
اللَّهِ بِغَيْرِ عِلْمٍ وَلَا هُدًى وَلَا
كِتَٰبٍ مُّنِيرٍ ٨

9. They turn away (from the Truth) to lead people away from the path of Allah. Their share in this world will be disgrace and on the Day of Judgment We will cause them to feel the burning torment.

9. <u>S</u>aaniya 'iṭfihee liyuḍilla 'an sabeelil-laahi lahoo fiddun-yaa khizyuñw-wa nu<u>z</u>eequhoo Yawmal-Qiyaamati 'a<u>z</u>aabal-ḥareeq.

ثَانِيَ عِطْفِهِۦ لِيُضِلَّ عَن سَبِيلِ اللَّهِ
لَهُۥ فِي الدُّنْيَا خِزْيٌ وَنُذِيقُهُۥ
يَوْمَ الْقِيَٰمَةِ عَذَابَ الْحَرِيقِ ٩

10. (They will be told), "This is the result of what your hands have wrought. Allah is certainly not unjust to His servants."

10. <u>Z</u>aalika bimaa qaddamat yadaaka wa annal-laaha laysa bi<u>z</u>allaamil-lil'abeed.

ذَٰلِكَ بِمَا قَدَّمَتْ يَدَاكَ وَأَنَّ اللَّهَ
لَيْسَ بِظَلَّٰمٍ لِّلْعَبِيدِ ١٠ ع ٨

11. Of people there are those who worship Allah on the basis of doubt (to achieve worldly gains). They are confident when they are prosperous, but when they face hardships they turn away (from worship). They are lost in this life and will be lost in the life to come. Such loss is indeed destructive.

11. Wa minan-naasi mañy-ya'budul-laaha 'alaa ḥarfin fa-in aṣaabahoo khayruniṭ-ma-anna bihee wa in aṣaabat-hu fitnatunin-qalaba 'alaa wajhi-hee khasirad-dunyaa wal-Aakhirah; <u>z</u>aalika huwal-khusraanul-mubeen.

وَمِنَ النَّاسِ مَن يَعْبُدُ اللَّهَ عَلَىٰ
حَرْفٍ فَإِنْ أَصَابَهُۥ خَيْرٌ اطْمَأَنَّ
بِهِۦ وَإِنْ أَصَابَتْهُ فِتْنَةٌ انقَلَبَ
عَلَىٰ وَجْهِهِۦ خَسِرَ الدُّنْيَا وَالْآخِرَةَ
ذَٰلِكَ هُوَ الْخُسْرَانُ الْمُبِينُ ١١

12. They worship things instead of Allah which can neither harm them nor benefit them. This is indeed to stray far away from the right path.

12. Yad'oo min doonil-laahi maa laa yaḍurruhoo wa maa laa yanfa'uh; <u>z</u>aalika huwaḍ-ḍalaalul-ba'eed.

يَدْعُوا مِن دُونِ اللَّهِ مَا لَا يَضُرُّهُۥ
وَمَا لَا يَنفَعُهُۥ ذَٰلِكَ هُوَ الضَّلَٰلُ
الْبَعِيدُ ١٢

13. Their worship of such things, in which there is no hope for any benefit, can only harm them. How terrible is such a guardian and companion!

13. Yad'oo laman ḍarruhooo aqrabu min-naf'ih; labi'sal-mawlaa wa labi'sal-'asheer.

يَدْعُوا لَمَن ضَرُّهُۥٓ أَقْرَبُ مِن نَّفْعِهِۦ
لَبِئْسَ الْمَوْلَىٰ وَلَبِئْسَ الْعَشِيرُ ١٣

14. Allah will admit the righteously striving believers to the gardens wherein streams flow. Allah has all the power to do whatever He wants.

14. Innal-laaha yudkhilul la*z*eena aamanoo wa 'amiluṣ-ṣaaliḥaati Jannaatin tajree min taḥtihal-anhaar; innal-laaha yaf'alu maa yureed.

إِنَّ اللَّهَ يُدْخِلُ الَّذِينَ آمَنُوا وَعَمِلُوا
الصَّالِحَاتِ جَنَّاتٍ تَجْرِي مِنْ
تَحْتِهَا الْأَنْهَارُ ۚ إِنَّ اللَّهَ يَفْعَلُ
مَا يُرِيدُ ﴿١٤﴾

15. If there is one who doubts that Allah will never grant him help (reward) in this world nor in the life hereafter, he should find an instruction and guide (between himself and Allah) then find a distinction in the facts he finds and see if this plan removes his doubts.

15. Man kaana yaẓunnu allañy-yanṣurahul-laahu fiddunyaa wal-Aakhirati fal-yamdud bisababin ilassamaaa'i *s*ummal-yaqṭa' falyanẓur hal yuẓhibanna kayduhoo maa yagheeẓ.

مَنْ كَانَ يَظُنُّ أَنْ لَنْ يَنْصُرَهُ اللَّهُ
فِي الدُّنْيَا وَالْآخِرَةِ فَلْيَمْدُدْ بِسَبَبٍ
إِلَى السَّمَاءِ ثُمَّ لْيَقْطَعْ فَلْيَنْظُرْ
هَلْ يُذْهِبَنَّ كَيْدُهُ مَا يَغِيظُ ﴿١٥﴾

16. We have revealed the Quran, which contains authoritative verses. Allah guides only those whom He wants.

16. Wa ka*z*aalika anzalnaahu Aayaatim bayyinaatiñw-wa annal-laaha yahdee mañy-yureed.

وَكَذَٰلِكَ أَنْزَلْنَاهُ آيَاتٍ بَيِّنَاتٍ وَأَنَّ
اللَّهَ يَهْدِي مَنْ يُرِيدُ ﴿١٦﴾

17. Allah will make truth and falsehood clearly distinct from each other to the believers, the Jews, the Sabeans, the Christian, the Zoroastrians, and the Pagans on the Day of Judgment. Allah is a Witness to all things.

17. Innal-la*z*eena aamanoo walla*z*eena haadoo waṣ-Ṣaabi'eena wan-Naṣaaraa wal-Majoosa walla*z*eena ashrakooo innal-laaha yafṣilu baynahum Yawmal-Qiyaamah; innal-laaha 'alaa kulli shay'in Shaheed.

إِنَّ الَّذِينَ آمَنُوا وَالَّذِينَ هَادُوا
وَالصَّابِئِينَ وَالنَّصَارَىٰ وَالْمَجُوسَ وَ
الَّذِينَ أَشْرَكُوا إِنَّ اللَّهَ يَفْصِلُ
بَيْنَهُمْ يَوْمَ الْقِيَامَةِ ۚ إِنَّ اللَّهَ عَلَىٰ
كُلِّ شَيْءٍ شَهِيدٌ ﴿١٧﴾

18. Did you not see that those in the heavens and the earth, the Sun, the Moon, the Stars, the mountains, the trees, the animals, and many people, all bow down to Allah? There are many who are subject to His torment. No one can give honor to whomever Allah has insulted. Allah has all the power to do what He wants.

(Bow Down)

18. Alam tara-annal-laaha yasjudu lahoo man fis-samaawaati wa man fil-arḍi wash-shamsu walqamaru wan-nujoomu wal-jibaalu wash-shajaru wad-dawaaabbu wa ka*s*eerum-minan-naasi wa ka*s*eerun ḥaqqa 'alayhil-'a*z*aab; wa mañy-yuhinil-laahu famaa lahoo mim-mukrim; innallaaha yaf'alu maa yashaaa'.

أَلَمْ تَرَ أَنَّ اللَّهَ يَسْجُدُ لَهُ مَنْ فِي
السَّمَاوَاتِ وَمَنْ فِي الْأَرْضِ وَ
الشَّمْسُ وَالْقَمَرُ وَالنُّجُومُ وَالْجِبَالُ
وَالشَّجَرُ وَالدَّوَابُّ وَكَثِيرٌ مِنَ
النَّاسِ ۖ وَكَثِيرٌ حَقَّ عَلَيْهِ الْعَذَابُ ۗ
وَمَنْ يُهِنِ اللَّهُ فَمَا لَهُ مِنْ مُكْرِمٍ ۚ
إِنَّ اللَّهَ يَفْعَلُ مَا يَشَاءُ ۩ ﴿١٨﴾ السجدة ٦

19. These are two groups who dispute with each other about their Lord. For the unbelievers the garment of fire has already been prepared. Boiling water will be poured upon their heads.

19. Haa*z*aani khaṣmaanikh-taṣamoo fee Rabbihim fal-la*z*eena kafaroo quṭṭi'at lahum *s*iyaabum-min-naar; yuṣabbu min fawqi ru'oosihimul-ḥameem.

هَٰذَانِ خَصْمَانِ اخْتَصَمُوا فِي رَبِّهِمْ ۖ
فَالَّذِينَ كَفَرُوا قُطِّعَتْ لَهُمْ ثِيَابٌ
مِنْ نَارٍ يُصَبُّ مِنْ فَوْقِ
رُءُوسِهِمُ الْحَمِيمُ ﴿١٩﴾

20. It will melt their skins and all that is in their bellies.	20. Yuṣharu bihee maa fee buṭoonihim waljulood.	يُصْهَرُ بِهٖ مَا فِيْ بُطُوْنِهِمْ وَالْجُلُوْدُ ۝٢٠
21. They will be subdued by iron rods.	21. Wa lahum-maqaami'u min ḥadeed.	وَلَهُمْ مَّقَامِعُ مِنْ حَدِيْدٍ ۝٢١
22. Whenever in anguish they will try to come out of hell; they will be returned therein to suffer the burning torment.	22. Kullamaaa araadooo añy-yakhrujoo minhaa min ghammin u'eedoo feehaa wa zooqoo 'azaabal-ḥareeq.	كُلَّمَآ اَرَادُوْٓا اَنْ يَّخْرُجُوْا مِنْهَا مِنْ غَمٍّ اُعِيْدُوْا فِيْهَا ۗ وَذُوْقُوْا عَذَابَ الْحَرِيْقِ ۝٢٢ ع ٢ ٩
23. Allah will admit the righteously striving believers to the gardens wherein streams flow. There they will be decked with gold bracelets, pearls, and garments of silk,	23. Innal-laaha yudkhilul-lazeena aamanoo wa 'amiluṣ-ṣaaliḥaati Jannaatin tajree min taḥtihal-anhaaru yuḥallawna feehaa min asaawira min zahabiñw-wa lu'lu'aa; wa libaasuhum feehaa ḥareer.	اِنَّ اللّٰهَ يُدْخِلُ الَّذِيْنَ اٰمَنُوْا وَ عَمِلُوا الصّٰلِحٰتِ جَنّٰتٍ تَجْرِيْ مِنْ تَحْتِهَا الْاَنْهٰرُ يُحَلَّوْنَ فِيْهَا مِنْ اَسَاوِرَ مِنْ ذَهَبٍ وَّلُؤْلُؤًا ۭ وَلِبَاسُهُمْ فِيْهَا حَرِيْرٌ ۝٢٣
24. for they were guided to speak the noblest words and follow the praiseworthy path.	24. Wa hudooo ilaṭ-ṭayyibi minal-qawli wa hudooo ilaa ṣiraaṭil-ḥameed.	وَهُدُوْٓا اِلَى الطَّيِّبِ مِنَ الْقَوْلِ ښ وَهُدُوْٓا اِلٰى صِرَاطِ الْحَمِيْدِ ۝٢٤
25. A painful torment awaits the pagans who create obstacles in the way that leads to Allah and the Sacred Mosque - which We have made for those who dwell nearby and foreigners alike - and those who commit evil and injustice therein.	25. Innal-lazeena kafaroo wa yaṣuddoona 'an sabeelil-laahi wal-Masjidil-Ḥaraamil-lazee ja'alnaahu linnaasi-sawaaa'a-nil-'aakifu feehi walbaad; wa mañy-yurid feehi bi-ilḥaadim biẓulmin-nuziqhu min 'azaabin aleem.	اِنَّ الَّذِيْنَ كَفَرُوْا وَيَصُدُّوْنَ عَنْ سَبِيْلِ اللّٰهِ وَالْمَسْجِدِ الْحَرَامِ الَّذِيْ جَعَلْنٰهُ لِلنَّاسِ سَوَاۗءَ الْعَاكِفُ فِيْهِ وَالْبَادِ ۭ وَمَنْ يُّرِدْ فِيْهِ بِاِلْحَادٍۢ بِظُلْمٍ نُّذِقْهُ مِنْ عَذَابٍ اَلِيْمٍ ۝٢٥ ع ٣ ١٠
26. When We prepared for Abraham the place to build the Sacred House, We told him not to consider anything equal to Me and to keep the House clean for those walking around it, those standing, bowing down, and prostrating in prayer.	26. Wa iz bawwa-naa li-Ibraaheema makaanal-Bayti al-laa tushrik bee shay'añw-wa ṭahhir Baytiya liṭṭaaa'ifeena walqaaa'imeena warrukka'is-sujood.	وَاِذْ بَوَّاْنَا لِاِبْرٰهِيْمَ مَكَانَ الْبَيْتِ اَنْ لَّا تُشْرِكْ بِيْ شَيْـــًٔا وَّطَهِّرْ بَيْتِيَ لِلطَّاۗىِٕفِيْنَ وَالْقَاۗىِٕمِيْنَ وَالرُّكَّعِ السُّجُوْدِ ۝٢٦
27. (We commanded Abraham), "Call people for Hajj (an act of worship accomplished by visiting the sacred sites in Mecca)." They will come on foot and on lean camels from all the distant quarters	27. Wa azzin fin-naasi bil-Ḥajji ya-tooka rijaalañw-wa 'alaa kulli ḍaamiriñy-ya-teena min kulli fajjin 'ameeq.	وَاَذِّنْ فِي النَّاسِ بِالْحَجِّ يَاْتُوْكَ رِجَالًا وَّعَلٰي كُلِّ ضَامِرٍ يَّاْتِيْنَ مِنْ كُلِّ فَجٍّ عَمِيْقٍ ۝٢٧
28. to observe their benefits, commemorate the name of Allah	28. Li-yashhadoo manaafi'a lahum wa yazkurus-	لِّيَشْهَدُوْا مَنَافِعَ لَهُمْ وَيَذْكُرُوا

during the appointed days, and offer the sacrifice of the cattle that Allah has given them. They themselves should consume part of the sacrificial flesh and give the rest to the destitute and needy people.

29. Let the pilgrims then neatly dress themselves, fulfill their vows, and walk seven times around the Kabah.

30. Such are the regulations of Hajj. To respect the prohibitions of Allah is a virtuous deed in the sight of one's Lord. Consuming the flesh of certain animals is made lawful for you. Stay away from wickedness, idols, and false words.

31. As the upright servants of Allah, do not consider anything equal to Allah. To consider things equal to Allah is like one falling from the sky, who is snatched away by the birds or carried away by a strong wind to a far distant place.

32. To respect the symbols of Allah is the sign of a pious heart.

33. There are benefits for you in the (sacrificial offerings) of Allah until the appointed time when you slaughter them as your offering near the Ancient House.

34. To every nation We have given certain sacrificial rituals. Let them consecrate their sacrificial animals with His Name. Your Ilah (Lord) is One Ilah and you must submit yourselves to His will. (Muhammad), give the glad news (of Allah's mercy) to the devoted servants of Allah:

35. Those whose hearts are filled with awe on hearing about Allah, who exercise patience in hardships, who are steadfast in prayer, and who spend their

mal-laahi feee ayyaamim-ma'loomaatin 'alaa maa razaqahum-mim baheematil-an'aami fakuloo minhaa wa aṭ'imul-baaa'isal-faqeer.

29. Summal-yaqḍoo tafasa-hum wal-yoofoo nuzoorahum wal-yaṭṭawwafoo bil-Baytil-'Ateeq.

30. Zaalika wa mañy-yu'aẓẓim ḥurumaatil-laahi fahuwa khayrul-lahoo 'inda Rabbih; wa uḥillat lakumul-an'aamu illaa maa yutlaa 'alaykum fajtanibur-rijsa minal-awsaani wajtaniboo qawlaz-zoor.

31. Ḥunafaaa'a lillaahi ghayra mushrikeena bih; wa mañy-yushrik billaahi faka-annamaa-kharra minas-samaaa'i fatakh-ṭafuhuṭ-ṭayru aw tahwee bihir-reeḥu fee makaanin saḥeeq.

32. Zaalika wa mañy- yu'aẓẓim sha'aaa'iral-laahi fa-innahaa min taqwal-quloob.

33. Lakum feehaa manaafi'u ilaaa ajalim-musamman summa maḥilluhaaa ilal-Baytil-'Ateeq.

34. Wa likulli ummatin ja'alnaa mansakal-liyazkurus-mal-laahi 'alaa maa razaqahum mim baheematil-an'aam; fa-ilaahukum Ilaahuñw-Waaḥidun falahooo aslimoo; wa bash-shiril-mukhbiteen.

35. Allazeena izaa zukiral-laahu wajilat quloobuhum waṣṣaabireena 'alaa maaa aṣaabahum walmuqeemiṣ-Ṣalaati

اسْمَ اللّٰهِ فِيْٓ اَيَّامٍ مَّعْلُوْمٰتٍ
عَلٰى مَا رَزَقَهُمْ مِّنْۢ بَهِيْمَةِ
الْاَنْعَامِ ۚ فَكُلُوْا مِنْهَا وَاَطْعِمُوا
الْبَآئِسَ الْفَقِيْرَ ﴿٢٨﴾
ثُمَّ لْيَقْضُوْا تَفَثَهُمْ وَلْيُوْفُوْا نُذُوْرَهُمْ
وَلْيَطَّوَّفُوْا بِالْبَيْتِ الْعَتِيْقِ ﴿٢٩﴾
ذٰلِكَ ۗ وَمَنْ يُّعَظِّمْ حُرُمٰتِ اللّٰهِ
فَهُوَ خَيْرٌ لَّهٗ عِنْدَ رَبِّهٖ ۗ وَاُحِلَّتْ
لَكُمُ الْاَنْعَامُ اِلَّا مَا يُتْلٰى عَلَيْكُمْ
فَاجْتَنِبُوا الرِّجْسَ مِنَ الْاَوْثَانِ
وَاجْتَنِبُوْا قَوْلَ الزُّوْرِ ﴿٣٠﴾
حُنَفَآءَ لِلّٰهِ غَيْرَ مُشْرِكِيْنَ بِهٖ ۗ
وَمَنْ يُّشْرِكْ بِاللّٰهِ فَكَاَنَّمَا خَرَّ مِنَ
السَّمَآءِ فَتَخْطَفُهُ الطَّيْرُ اَوْ تَهْوِيْ
بِهِ الرِّيْحُ فِيْ مَكَانٍ سَحِيْقٍ ﴿٣١﴾
ذٰلِكَ ۗ وَمَنْ يُّعَظِّمْ شَعَآئِرَ اللّٰهِ
فَاِنَّهَا مِنْ تَقْوَى الْقُلُوْبِ ﴿٣٢﴾
لَكُمْ فِيْهَا مَنَافِعُ اِلٰٓى اَجَلٍ مُّسَمًّى
ثُمَّ مَحِلُّهَآ اِلَى الْبَيْتِ الْعَتِيْقِ ﴿٣٣﴾ ع ٨ ١١
وَلِكُلِّ اُمَّةٍ جَعَلْنَا مَنْسَكًا لِّيَذْكُرُوا
اسْمَ اللّٰهِ عَلٰى مَا رَزَقَهُمْ مِّنْۢ بَهِيْمَةِ
الْاَنْعَامِ ۗ فَاِلٰهُكُمْ اِلٰهٌ وَّاحِدٌ فَلَهٗٓ
اَسْلِمُوْا ۗ وَبَشِّرِ الْمُخْبِتِيْنَ ﴿٣٤﴾
الَّذِيْنَ اِذَا ذُكِرَ اللّٰهُ وَجِلَتْ
قُلُوْبُهُمْ وَالصّٰبِرِيْنَ عَلٰى مَآ
اَصَابَهُمْ وَالْمُقِيْمِي الصَّلٰوةِ ۙ

property for the cause of Allah.

wa mimmaa razaqnaahum yunfiqoon.

وَمِمَّا رَزَقْنٰهُمْ يُنْفِقُوْنَ ﴿٣٥﴾

36. For you We have made the sacrificial camel one of the reminders of Allah. It also has other benefits for you. Consecrate it with the Name of Allah when it is steadily standing. When it is slaughtered, consume its flesh and give part of it to the needy who do and those do not ask for help from others. Thus We have made the camel subservient to you so that perhaps you may give thanks.

36. Walbudna ja'alnaahaa lakum-min sha'aa'iril-laahi lakum feehaa khayrun fazkurusmal-laahi 'alayhaa ṣawaaff; fa-izaa wajabat junoobuhaa fakuloo minhaa wa aṭ'imul-qaani'a walmu'tarr; kazaalika sakhkhar-naahaa lakum la'allakum tashkuroon.

وَالْبُدْنَ جَعَلْنٰهَا لَكُمْ مِّنْ شَعَآئِرِ
اللّٰهِ لَكُمْ فِيْهَا خَيْرٌ ۖ فَاذْكُرُوا اسْمَ
اللّٰهِ عَلَيْهَا صَوَآفَّ ۚ فَاِذَا وَجَبَتْ
جُنُوْبُهَا فَكُلُوْا مِنْهَا وَاَطْعِمُوا
الْقَانِعَ وَالْمُعْتَرَّ ؕ كَذٰلِكَ سَخَّرْنٰهَا
لَكُمْ لَعَلَّكُمْ تَشْكُرُوْنَ ﴿٣٦﴾

37. It is not the flesh and blood of your sacrifice that pleases Allah. What pleases Allah is your piety. Allah has made subservient to you the sacrificial animals so that perhaps you will glorify Him; He is guiding you. (Muhammad), give the glad news (of Allah's mercy) to the righteous people.

37. Lañy-yanaalal-laaha luḥoomuhaa wa laa dimaaa'uhaa wa laakiñy-yanaaluhut-taqwaa minkum; kazaalika sakhkharahaa lakum litukabbirul-laaha 'alaa maa hadaakum; wa bashshiril-muḥsineen.

لَنْ يَّنَالَ اللّٰهَ لُحُوْمُهَا وَلَا
دِمَآؤُهَا وَلٰكِنْ يَّنَالُهُ التَّقْوٰى
مِنْكُمْ ؕ كَذٰلِكَ سَخَّرَهَا لَكُمْ
لِتُكَبِّرُوا اللّٰهَ عَلٰى مَا هَدٰىكُمْ ؕ
وَبَشِّرِ الْمُحْسِنِيْنَ ﴿٣٧﴾

38. Allah defends the believers but He does not love any of the treacherous, ungrateful ones.

38. Innal-laaha yudaafi'u 'anil-lazeena aamanooo; innal-laaha laa yuḥibbu kulla khawwaanin kafoor.

اِنَّ اللّٰهَ يُدٰفِعُ عَنِ الَّذِيْنَ اٰمَنُوْا ؕ اِنَّ
اللّٰهَ لَا يُحِبُّ كُلَّ خَوَّانٍ كَفُوْرٍ ﴿٣٨﴾ ع

39. Permission to take up arms is hereby granted to those who are attacked; they have suffered injustice. Allah has all the power to give victory

39. Uzina lillazeena yuqaataloona bi-annahum ẓulimoo; wa innal-laaha 'alaa naṣrihim la-Qadeer.

اُذِنَ لِلَّذِيْنَ يُقٰتَلُوْنَ بِاَنَّهُمْ ظُلِمُوْا ؕ
وَاِنَّ اللّٰهَ عَلٰى نَصْرِهِمْ لَقَدِيْرُ ۙ ﴿٣٩﴾

40. to those who were unjustly expelled from their homes only because they said, "Allah is our Lord." Had it not been for Allah's repelling some people through the might of the others, the monasteries, churches, synagogues, and mosques in which Allah is very often worshipped would have been utterly destroyed. Allah shall certainly help those who help Him. He is All-powerful and Majestic.

40. Allazeena ukhrijoo min diyaarihim bighayri ḥaqqin illaaa añy-yaqooloo Rabbunal-laah; wa law laa daf'ul-laahin-naasa ba'ḍahum biba'ḍil-lahuddimat ṣawaami'u wa biya'uñw-wa ṣalawaatuñw-wa masaajidu yuzkaru feehasmul-laahi kaseeraa; wa layanṣuran-nallaahu mañy-yanṣuruh; innallaaha la-Qawiyyun 'Azeez.

الَّذِيْنَ اُخْرِجُوْا مِنْ دِيَارِهِمْ بِغَيْرِ
حَقٍّ اِلَّآ اَنْ يَّقُوْلُوْا رَبُّنَا اللّٰهُ ؕ
وَلَوْلَا دَفْعُ اللّٰهِ النَّاسَ بَعْضَهُمْ
بِبَعْضٍ لَّهُدِّمَتْ صَوَامِعُ وَبِيَعٌ
وَّصَلَوٰتٌ وَّمَسٰجِدُ يُذْكَرُ فِيْهَا
اسْمُ اللّٰهِ كَثِيْرًا ؕ وَلَيَنْصُرَنَّ
اللّٰهُ مَنْ يَّنْصُرُهٗ ؕ اِنَّ اللّٰهَ
لَقَوِيٌّ عَزِيْزٌ ﴿٤٠﴾

41. He will certainly help those who, if given power in the land, will worship Allah through prayer, pay the religious tax,

41. Allazeena immakkannaahum fil-arḍi aqaamuṣ-Ṣalaata wa-aatawuz-Zakaata

الَّذِيْنَ اِنْ مَّكَّنّٰهُمْ فِى الْاَرْضِ
اَقَامُوا الصَّلٰوةَ وَاٰتَوُا الزَّكٰوةَ

رکوع ٥ / ١٢

enjoin others do good, and prevent them from committing evil. The consequence of all things is in the hands of Allah.

wa amaroo bilma'roofi wa nahaw 'anilmunkar; wa lillaahi 'aaqibatul-umoor.

وَأَمَرُوا بِالْمَعْرُوفِ وَنَهَوْا عَنِ
الْمُنكَرِ ۗ وَلِلَّهِ عَاقِبَةُ الْأُمُورِ ﴿٤١﴾

42. If they have called you, (Muhammad), a liar, (remember that) the people of Noah, Ad, Thamud,

42. Wa iñy-yukazzibooka faqad kaz-zabat qablahum qawmu Noohiñw-wa 'Aaduñw-wa Samood.

وَإِن يُكَذِّبُوكَ فَقَدْ كَذَّبَتْ
قَبْلَهُمْ قَوْمُ نُوحٍ وَعَادٌ وَثَمُودُ ﴿٤٢﴾

43. and the people of Abraham, Lot,

43. Wa qawmu Ibraaheema wa qawmu Loot.

وَقَوْمُ إِبْرَاهِيمَ وَقَوْمُ لُوطٍ ﴿٤٣﴾

44. Madyan, and Moses had also called their Prophets liars. I gave respite to the unbelievers, then seized them with torment. How terrible was that torment!

44. Wa as-haabu Madyana wa kuzziba Moosaa fa-amlaytu lilkaafireena summa akhaztu-hum fakayfa kaana nakeer.

وَأَصْحَابُ مَدْيَنَ ۖ وَكُذِّبَ مُوسَىٰ
فَأَمْلَيْتُ لِلْكَافِرِينَ ثُمَّ أَخَذْتُهُمْ
فَكَيْفَ كَانَ نَكِيرِ ﴿٤٤﴾

45. How many were the unjust dwellers of the towns that We destroyed. From their trellises to their lofty mansions, all were toppled and their wells were abandoned.

45. Faka-ayyim-min qaryatin ahlaknaahaa wa hiya zaali-matun fahiya khaawiyatun 'ala 'urooshihaa wa bi'-rimmu'at-talatiñw-wa qasrim-masheed.

فَكَأَيِّن مِّن قَرْيَةٍ أَهْلَكْنَاهَا
وَهِيَ ظَالِمَةٌ فَهِيَ خَاوِيَةٌ
عَلَىٰ عُرُوشِهَا وَبِئْرٍ مُّعَطَّلَةٍ وَ
قَصْرٍ مَّشِيدٍ ﴿٤٥﴾

46. Did they not travel (sufficiently) in the land to have understanding hearts and listening ears? It is their hearts which are blind, not their ears.

46. Afalam yaseeroo fil-ardi fatakoona lahum quloobuñy-ya'qiloona bihaaa aw aazaa-nuñy-yasma'oona bihaa fa-innahaa laa ta'mal-absaaru wa laakin ta'mal-quloobul-latee fis-sudoor.

أَفَلَمْ يَسِيرُوا فِي الْأَرْضِ فَتَكُونَ
لَهُمْ قُلُوبٌ يَعْقِلُونَ بِهَا أَوْ آذَانٌ
يَسْمَعُونَ بِهَا ۖ فَإِنَّهَا لَا تَعْمَى
الْأَبْصَارُ وَلَٰكِن تَعْمَى الْقُلُوبُ
الَّتِي فِي الصُّدُورِ ﴿٤٦﴾

47. They want you to bring upon them their punishment without delay. Allah never disregards His promise. One day for Allah is equal to a thousand years for you.

47. Wa yasta'jiloonaka bil-'azaabi wa lañy-yukhlifal-laahu wa'dah; wa inna yawman 'inda-Rabbika ka-alfi sanatim-mimmaa ta'uddoon.

وَيَسْتَعْجِلُونَكَ بِالْعَذَابِ وَ
لَن يُخْلِفَ اللَّهُ وَعْدَهُ ۚ وَإِنَّ
يَوْمًا عِندَ رَبِّكَ كَأَلْفِ سَنَةٍ
مِّمَّا تَعُدُّونَ ﴿٤٧﴾

48. To how many unjust towns have We given respite and then sized with torment. To Me do all things return.

48. Wa ka-ayyim-min qarya-tin amlaytu lahaa wa hiya zaalimatun summa akhaztuhaa wa ilayyal-maseer.

وَكَأَيِّن مِّن قَرْيَةٍ أَمْلَيْتُ لَهَا
وَهِيَ ظَالِمَةٌ ثُمَّ أَخَذْتُهَا
وَإِلَيَّ الْمَصِيرُ ﴿٤٨﴾ ع ٦ ١٠ ١٣

49. (Muhammad), tell them, "People, I am giving you a clear warning.

49. Qul yaaa ayyuhan-naasu innamaaa ana lakum nazeerum-mubeen.

قُلْ يَا أَيُّهَا النَّاسُ إِنَّمَا أَنَا
لَكُمْ نَذِيرٌ مُّبِينٌ ﴿٤٩﴾

50. The righteously striving believers will receive forgiveness and honorable sustenance.

50. Fallazeena aamanoo wa 'amiluṣ-ṣaaliḥaati lahum-maghfiratuñw-wa rizqun kareem.

فَالَّذِيْنَ اٰمَنُوْا وَعَمِلُوا الصّٰلِحٰتِ
لَهُمْ مَّغْفِرَةٌ وَّرِزْقٌ كَرِيْمٌ ۝٥٠

51. Those who try to challenge Our miracles will be the dwellers of hell."

51. Wallazeena sa'aw feee Aayaatinaa mu'aajizeena ulaaa'ika Aṣ-ḥaabul-jaḥeem.

وَالَّذِيْنَ سَعَوْا فِيْٓ اٰيٰتِنَا مُعٰجِزِيْنَ
اُولٰٓئِكَ اَصْحٰبُ الْجَحِيْمِ ۝٥١

52. Satan would try to tamper with the desires of every Prophet or Messenger whom We sent. Then Allah would remove Satan's temptations and strengthen His revelations. Allah is All-knowing and All-wise.

52. Wa maaa arsalnaa min qablika mir-Rasooliñw-wa laa Nabiyyin illaaa izaa tamannaaa alqash-Shayṭaanu feee umniyyatihee fa-yansakhul-laahu maa yulqish-Shayṭaanu summa yuḥkimul-laahu Aayaatih; wallaahu 'Aleemun Ḥakeem.

وَمَآ اَرْسَلْنَا مِنْ قَبْلِكَ مِنْ رَّسُوْلٍ
وَّلَا نَبِيٍّ اِلَّآ اِذَا تَمَنّٰٓى اَلْقَى
الشَّيْطٰنُ فِيْٓ اُمْنِيَّتِهٖ ۚ فَيَنْسَخُ
اللّٰهُ مَا يُلْقِي الشَّيْطٰنُ ثُمَّ يُحْكِمُ
اللّٰهُ اٰيٰتِهٖ ۭ وَاللّٰهُ عَلِيْمٌ حَكِيْمٌ ۝٥٢

53. He would make Satan's temptations a trial for those whose hearts are hard and sick. The wrong-doers are far away from the Lord,

53. Liyaj'ala maa yulqish-Shayṭaanu fitnatal-lillazeena fee quloobihim-maraḍuñw-walqaasiyati quloobuhum; wa innaẓ-ẓaalimeena lafee shiqaaqim-ba'eed.

لِّيَجْعَلَ مَا يُلْقِي الشَّيْطٰنُ
فِتْنَةً لِّلَّذِيْنَ فِيْ قُلُوْبِهِمْ مَّرَضٌ
وَّالْقَاسِيَةِ قُلُوْبُهُمْ ۭ وَاِنَّ الظّٰلِمِيْنَ
لَفِيْ شِقَاقٍۢ بَعِيْدٍ ۝٥٣

54. so that those who have received knowledge would know and believe that whatever happens with the Prophets and Messengers is the Truth from their Lord and will believe it. This will cause their hearts to become filled with awe. Allah guides the believers to the right path.

54. Wa liya'lamal-lazeena ootul-'ilma annahul-ḥaqqu mir-Rabbika fayu'minoo bihee fatukhbita lahoo quloobuhum; wa innal-laaha lahaadil-lazeena aamanooo ilaa Ṣiraaṭim-Mustaqeem.

وَّلِيَعْلَمَ الَّذِيْنَ اُوْتُوا الْعِلْمَ
اَنَّهُ الْحَقُّ مِنْ رَّبِّكَ فَيُؤْمِنُوْا
بِهٖ فَتُخْبِتَ لَهٗ قُلُوْبُهُمْ ۭ وَاِنَّ
اللّٰهَ لَهَادِ الَّذِيْنَ اٰمَنُوْٓا اِلٰى
صِرَاطٍ مُّسْتَقِيْمٍ ۝٥٤

55. The unbelievers will continue to doubt the Quran until the Hour of Doom suddenly siezes them or the torment of the last day strikes them.

55. Wa laa yazaalul-lazeena kafaroo fee miryatim-minhu ḥattaa ta-tiyahumus-Saa'atu baghtatan aw ya-tiyahum 'azaabu Yawmin 'aqeem.

وَلَا يَزَالُ الَّذِيْنَ كَفَرُوْا فِيْ
مِرْيَةٍ مِّنْهُ حَتّٰى تَاْتِيَهُمُ
السَّاعَةُ بَغْتَةً اَوْ يَاْتِيَهُمْ عَذَابُ
يَوْمٍ عَقِيْمٍ ۝٥٥

56. On that day it is Allah who will be the Absolute King and Judge of (mankind). The righteously striving believers will go to Paradise

56. Almulku Yawma'izil-lillaahi yaḥkumu baynahum; fallazeena aamanoo wa 'amiluṣ-ṣaaliḥaati fee Jannaatin-Na'eem.

اَلْمُلْكُ يَوْمَىِٕذٍ لِّلّٰهِ ۭ يَحْكُمُ
بَيْنَهُمْ ۭ فَالَّذِيْنَ اٰمَنُوْا وَعَمِلُوا
الصّٰلِحٰتِ فِيْ جَنّٰتِ النَّعِيْمِ ۝٥٦

57. and the unbelievers who called Our revelations lies will

57. Wallazeena kafaroo wa kazzaboo bi-Aayaatinaa

وَالَّذِيْنَ كَفَرُوْا وَكَذَّبُوْا بِاٰيٰتِنَا

suffer humiliating torment.

58. Those who abandoned their homes for the cause of Allah and who then died or were murdered will receive honorable sustenance from Allah; He is the Most Generous and Munificent.

59. Allah will certainly admit them to a pleasant dwelling. Allah is All-knowing and Forbearing.

60. One who is wronged and who retaliates by that which is equal to his suffering, Allah will certainly help him; He is All-pardoning and All-forgiving.

61. Allah causes the night to enter the day and the day to enter the night. He is All-hearing and All-aware.

62. Allah is the Supreme Truth and whatever they worship instead of Him is falsehood. Allah is most Exalted and most Great.

63. Did you not see that Allah has sent water from the sky and has made the earth green all over? He is Kind and All-aware.

64. To Him belongs all that is in the heavens and the earth. Allah is Self-sufficient and Praiseworthy.

65. Did you not see that Allah, through His command, has made all that is in the earth and the ships that sail on the sea subservient to you? He prevents the sky from falling on the earth unless He decides otherwise. Allah is Compassionate and Merciful to mankind.

fa-ulaaa'ika lahum 'a<u>z</u>aabum-muheen.

58. Walla<u>z</u>eena haajaroo fee sabeelil-laahi <u>s</u>umma qutilooo aw maatoo la-yarzuqan-nahumul-laahu rizqan ḥasanaa; wa innallaaha la-Huwa khayrur-raaziqeen.

59. La-yudkhilan-nahum-mud-khalañy-yarḍawnah; wa innal-laaha la-'Aleemun Ḥaleem.

60. <u>Z</u>aalika wa man 'aaqaba bimi<u>s</u>li maa 'ooqiba bihee-<u>s</u>umma bughiya 'alayhi la-yanṣurannahul-laah; innal-laaha la-'Afuwwun Ghafoor.

61. <u>Z</u>aalika bi-annal-laaha yoolijul-layla fin-nahaari wa yoolijun-nahaara fil-layli wa annal-laaha Samee'um-Baṣeer.

62. <u>Z</u>aalika bi-annal-laaha Huwal-Ḥaqqu wa anna maa yad'oona min doonihee huwal-baaṭilu wa annal-laaha Huwal-'Aliyyul-Kabeer.

63. Alam tara annal-laaha anzala minas-samaaa'i maaa'an fatuṣbiḥul-arḍu mukhḍarrah; innal-laaha Laṭeefun Khabeer.

64. Lahoo maa fis-samaa-waati wa maa fil-arḍ; wa innal-laaha la-Huwal-Ghaniyyul-Ḥameed.

65. Alam tara-annal-laaha sakhkhara lakum-maa fil-arḍi walfulka tajree fil-baḥri bi-amrihee wa yumsikus-samaaa'a an taqa'a 'alal-arḍi illaa bi-<u>i</u>znih; innal-laaha binnaasi la-Ra'oofur-Raḥeem.

فَاُولٰٓئِكَ لَهُمْ عَذَابٌ مُّهِيْنٌ ﴿٥٧﴾ ع ٩ ١٤
وَالَّذِيْنَ هَاجَرُوْا فِيْ سَبِيْلِ اللّٰهِ
ثُمَّ قُتِلُوْٓا اَوْ مَاتُوْا لَيَرْزُقَنَّهُمُ
اللّٰهُ رِزْقًا حَسَنًا ؕ وَاِنَّ اللّٰهَ لَهُوَ
خَيْرُ الرّٰزِقِيْنَ ﴿٥٨﴾
لَيُدْخِلَنَّهُمْ مُّدْخَلًا يَّرْضَوْنَهٗ ؕ
وَاِنَّ اللّٰهَ لَعَلِيْمٌ حَلِيْمٌ ﴿٥٩﴾
ذٰلِكَ ۚ وَمَنْ عَاقَبَ بِمِثْلِ مَا
عُوْقِبَ بِهٖ ثُمَّ بُغِيَ عَلَيْهِ لَيَنْصُرَنَّهُ
اللّٰهُ ؕ اِنَّ اللّٰهَ لَعَفُوٌّ غَفُوْرٌ ﴿٦٠﴾
ذٰلِكَ بِاَنَّ اللّٰهَ يُوْلِجُ الَّيْلَ فِي
النَّهَارِ وَيُوْلِجُ النَّهَارَ فِي الَّيْلِ
وَاَنَّ اللّٰهَ سَمِيْعٌۢ بَصِيْرٌ ﴿٦١﴾
ذٰلِكَ بِاَنَّ اللّٰهَ هُوَ الْحَقُّ وَاَنَّ مَا
يَدْعُوْنَ مِنْ دُوْنِهٖ هُوَ الْبَاطِلُ
وَاَنَّ اللّٰهَ هُوَ الْعَلِيُّ الْكَبِيْرُ ﴿٦٢﴾
اَلَمْ تَرَ اَنَّ اللّٰهَ اَنْزَلَ مِنَ السَّمَآءِ
مَآءً ۫ فَتُصْبِحُ الْاَرْضُ مُخْضَرَّةً ؕ
اِنَّ اللّٰهَ لَطِيْفٌ خَبِيْرٌ ﴿٦٣﴾
لَهٗ مَا فِي السَّمٰوٰتِ وَمَا فِي الْاَرْضِ ؕ
وَاِنَّ اللّٰهَ لَهُوَ الْغَنِيُّ الْحَمِيْدُ ﴿٦٤﴾ ع ٧ ١٥
اَلَمْ تَرَ اَنَّ اللّٰهَ سَخَّرَ لَكُمْ مَّا فِي
الْاَرْضِ وَالْفُلْكَ تَجْرِيْ فِي الْبَحْرِ
بِاَمْرِهٖ ؕ وَيُمْسِكُ السَّمَآءَ اَنْ تَقَعَ
عَلَى الْاَرْضِ اِلَّا بِاِذْنِهٖ ؕ اِنَّ
اللّٰهَ بِالنَّاسِ لَرَءُوْفٌ رَّحِيْمٌ ﴿٦٥﴾

66. It is He who has given you life, He will make you die and will make you live again. Surely the human being is ungrateful.

66. Wa Huwal-lazeee aḥyaa-kum summa yumeetukum summa yuḥyeekum; innal-insaana lakafoor.

وَهُوَ الَّذِیٓ اَحۡیَاکُمۡ ز ثُمَّ
یُمِیۡتُکُمۡ ثُمَّ یُحۡیِیۡکُمۡ ط اِنَّ
الۡاِنۡسَانَ لَکَفُوۡرٌ ﴿۶۶﴾

67. We enjoined every nation with certain acts of worship which they perform. The unbelievers must not dispute with you about the manner of your worship. Invite them to follow the right path of the Lord.

67. Likulli ummatin ja'alnaa mansakan hum naasikoohu falaa yunaazi'unnaka fil-amr; wad'u ilaa Rabbika innaka la'alaa hudam-mustaqeem.

لِکُلِّ اُمَّۃٍ جَعَلۡنَا مَنۡسَکًا هُمۡ
نَاسِکُوۡهُ فَلَا یُنَازِعُنَّکَ فِی الۡاَمۡرِ
وَادۡعُ اِلٰی رَبِّکَ ط اِنَّکَ لَعَلٰی
هُدًی مُّسۡتَقِیۡمٍ ﴿۶۷﴾

68. If they still dispute with you about your worship, tell them, "Allah knows best what you do.

68. Wa in jaadalooka faqulil-laahu a'lamu bimaa ta'maloon.

وَاِنۡ جٰدَلُوۡکَ فَقُلِ اللّٰهُ اَعۡلَمُ
بِمَا تَعۡمَلُوۡنَ ﴿۶۸﴾

69. He will issue His decree about your differences on the Day of Judgment."

69. Allaahu yaḥkumu bayna-kum Yawmal-Qiyaamati fee-maa kuntum feehi takhtalifoon.

اَللّٰهُ یَحۡکُمُ بَیۡنَکُمۡ یَوۡمَ الۡقِیٰمَۃِ فِیۡمَا
کُنۡتُمۡ فِیۡهِ تَخۡتَلِفُوۡنَ ﴿۶۹﴾

70. Did you not know that Allah knows all that is in the heavens and the earth? His decree is already recorded in the Book and issuing such a Judgment is not difficult for Him at all.

70. Alam ta'lam annal-laaha ya'lamu maa fis-samaaa'i wal-arḍ; inna zaalika fee kitaab; inna zaalika 'alal-laahi yaseer.

اَلَمۡ تَعۡلَمۡ اَنَّ اللّٰهَ یَعۡلَمُ مَا فِی
السَّمَآءِ وَالۡاَرۡضِ ط اِنَّ ذٰلِکَ فِیۡ
کِتٰبٍ ط اِنَّ ذٰلِکَ عَلَی اللّٰهِ یَسِیۡرٌ ﴿۷۰﴾

71. They worship things instead of Allah that had received no authority (from the heavens) nor have they any knowledge of such authority. The unjust people will have no one to help them.

71. Wa ya'budoona min doonil-laahi maa lam yunazzil bihee sulṭaanañw-wa maa laysa lahum bihee 'ilm; wa maa liẓẓaalimeena min-naṣeer.

وَیَعۡبُدُوۡنَ مِنۡ دُوۡنِ اللّٰهِ مَا لَمۡ
یُنَزِّلۡ بِهٖ سُلۡطٰنًا وَّمَا لَیۡسَ لَهُمۡ
بِهٖ عِلۡمٌ ط وَمَا لِلظّٰلِمِیۡنَ مِنۡ نَّصِیۡرٍ ﴿۷۱﴾

72. When Our authoritative revelations are recited to the unbelievers, you can clearly read the dislike on their faces. They almost attack those who read Our revelations to them. Say to them, "Should I tell you about what is the worst thing for you than these revelations? It is the fire which Allah has prepared for the unbelievers. What a terrible destination!"

72. Wa izaa tutlaa 'alayhim Aayaatunaa bayyinaatin ta'rifu fee wujoohil-lazeena kafarul-munkara yakaadoona yasṭoona bil-lazeena yatloona 'alayhim Aayaatinaa; qul afa-unab-bi'ukum bisharrim-min zaali-kum; an-Naaru wa'adahal-laahul-lazeena kafaroo wa bi'sal-maṣeer.

وَاِذَا تُتۡلٰی عَلَیۡهِمۡ اٰیٰتُنَا بَیِّنٰتٍ
تَعۡرِفُ فِیۡ وُجُوۡهِ الَّذِیۡنَ کَفَرُوا
الۡمُنۡکَرَ ط یَکَادُوۡنَ یَسۡطُوۡنَ بِالَّذِیۡنَ
یَتۡلُوۡنَ عَلَیۡهِمۡ اٰیٰتِنَا ط قُلۡ
اَفَاُنَبِّئُکُمۡ بِشَرٍّ مِّنۡ ذٰلِکُمۡ ط اَلنَّارُ ط
وَعَدَهَا اللّٰهُ الَّذِیۡنَ کَفَرُوۡا ط
وَبِئۡسَ الۡمَصِیۡرُ ﴿۷۲﴾ ع ۹ ۸ ۱۲

73. People, listen to this parable: Those whom you worship instead of Allah do not have the power to create even a

73. Yaaa ayyuhan-naasu ḍuriba maṣalun fastami'oo lah; innal-lazeena tad'oona

یٰۤاَیُّهَا النَّاسُ ضُرِبَ مَثَلٌ
فَاسۡتَمِعُوۡا لَهٗ ط اِنَّ الَّذِیۡنَ تَدۡعُوۡنَ

fly, even though all of them would come together for the task. If the fly was to snatch something from them they would not be able to rescue it from the fly. How feeble are such worshippers and that which they worship.

min doonil-laahi lañy-yakhluqoo zubaabañw-wa lawijtama'oo lahoo wa iñy-yaslubhumuz-zubaabu shay'al-laa yastan-qizoohu minh; ḍa'ufaṭ-ṭaalibu walmaṭloob.

مِنْ دُونِ اللّٰهِ لَنْ يَّخْلُقُوْا ذُبَابًا وَّلَوِ اجْتَمَعُوْا لَهٗ ۗ وَاِنْ يَّسْلُبْهُمُ الذُّبَابُ شَيْـًٔا لَّا يَسْتَنْقِذُوْهُ مِنْهُ ۗ ضَعُفَ الطَّالِبُ وَالْمَطْلُوْبُ ﴿٧٣﴾

74. They have not revered Allah properly. Allah is All-powerful and Majestic.

74. Maa qadarul-laaha ḥaqqa qadrih; innal-laaha la-Qawiyyun 'Azeez.

مَا قَدَرُوا اللّٰهَ حَقَّ قَدْرِهٖ ۗ اِنَّ اللّٰهَ لَقَوِيٌّ عَزِيْزٌ ﴿٧٤﴾

75. Allah chooses Messengers from both angels and human beings. Allah is All-hearing and All-aware.

75. Allaahu yaṣṭafee minal-malaaa'ikati Rusulañw-wa minan-naas; innal-laaha Samee'um Baṣeer.

اَللّٰهُ يَصْطَفِيْ مِنَ الْمَلٰٓئِكَةِ رُسُلًا وَّمِنَ النَّاسِ ۗ اِنَّ اللّٰهَ سَمِيْعٌۢ بَصِيْرٌ ﴿٧٥﴾

76. Allah knows all that they have and all that is behind them, and to Him do all things return.

76. Ya'lamu maa bayna aydeehim wa maa khalfahum; wa ilal-laahi turja'ul-umoor.

يَعْلَمُ مَا بَيْنَ اَيْدِيْهِمْ وَمَا خَلْفَهُمْ ۗ وَاِلَى اللّٰهِ تُرْجَعُ الْاُمُوْرُ ﴿٧٦﴾

(Bow Down)

77. Believers, worship your Lord, bow down and prostrate yourselves before Him and do virtuous deeds so that perhaps you will have everlasting happiness.

77. Yaaa ayyuhal-lazeena aamanur-ka'oo wasjudoo wa'budoo Rabbakum waf'alul-khayra la'allakum tufliḥoon.

يٰٓاَيُّهَا الَّذِيْنَ اٰمَنُوا ارْكَعُوْا وَاسْجُدُوْا وَاعْبُدُوْا رَبَّكُمْ وَافْعَلُوا الْخَيْرَ لَعَلَّكُمْ تُفْلِحُوْنَ ﴿٧٧﴾ السجدة

السجدة عند الامام الشافعي رحمه الله تعالى ١٢

78. Strive steadfastly for the Cause of Allah. He has chosen you but has not imposed on you hardship in your religion, the noble religion of your father, Abraham. Allah named you Muslims before and in this Book, so that the Messenger will witness (your actions) and will be the witness over mankind. Be steadfast in your prayer, pay the religious tax, and seek protection from Allah; He is your Guardian, a gracious Guardian and Helper.

78. Wa jaahidoo fil-laahi ḥaqqa jihaadih; Huwaj-tabaakum wa maa ja'ala 'alaykum fid-deeni min ḥaraj; Millata abeekum Ibraaheem; Huwa sammaakumul-muslimeena min qablu wa fee haazaa li-yakoonar-Rasoolu shaheedan 'alaykum wa takoonoo shuhadaaa'a 'alan-naas; fa-aqeemuṣ-Ṣalaata wa aatuz-Zakaata wa'taṣimoo billaahi Huwa mawlaakum fani'mal-mawlaa wa ni'man-naṣeer.

وَجَاهِدُوْا فِى اللّٰهِ حَقَّ جِهَادِهٖ ۗ هُوَ اجْتَبٰىكُمْ وَمَا جَعَلَ عَلَيْكُمْ فِى الدِّيْنِ مِنْ حَرَجٍ ۗ مِلَّةَ اَبِيْكُمْ اِبْرٰهِيْمَ ۗ هُوَ سَمّٰىكُمُ الْمُسْلِمِيْنَ ۙ مِنْ قَبْلُ وَفِيْ هٰذَا لِيَكُوْنَ الرَّسُوْلُ شَهِيْدًا عَلَيْكُمْ وَتَكُوْنُوْا شُهَدَآءَ عَلَى النَّاسِ ۚ فَاَقِيْمُوا الصَّلٰوةَ وَاٰتُوا الزَّكٰوةَ وَاعْتَصِمُوْا بِاللّٰهِ ۗ هُوَ مَوْلٰىكُمْ ۚ فَنِعْمَ الْمَوْلٰى وَنِعْمَ النَّصِيْرُ ﴿٧٨﴾

Al-Muminun, The Believers (23)
In the Name of Allah, the Beneficent, the Merciful.

Sûrat al-Mu'-minûn-23
(Revealed at Makkah)
Bismillaahir Raḥmaanir Raḥeem

(٢٣) سُوْرَةُ الْمُؤْمِنُوْنَ مَكِّيَّةٌ (٧٤)

اياتها ١١٨ — بِسْمِ اللّٰهِ الرَّحْمٰنِ الرَّحِيْمِ — ركوعاتها ٦

1. Triumphant indeed are the believers,

1. Qad aflaḥal-mu'minoon.

قَدْ اَفْلَحَ الْمُؤْمِنُوْنَ ۙ ﴿١﴾

الجزء الثامن عشر (١٨)

2. who are submissive to Allah in their prayers,	2. Allazeena hum fee Ṣalaatihim khaashi'oon.	الَّذِيْنَ هُمْ فِيْ صَلَاتِهِمْ خٰشِعُوْنَ ۝٢
3. who avoid impious talks,	3. Wallazeena hum 'anil-laghwi mu'riḍoon.	وَالَّذِيْنَ هُمْ عَنِ اللَّغْوِ مُعْرِضُوْنَ ۝٣
4. pay their religious tax	4. Wallazeena hum liz-Zakaati faa'iloon.	وَالَّذِيْنَ هُمْ لِلزَّكٰوةِ فٰعِلُوْنَ ۝٤
5. and restrain their carnal desires	5. Wallazeena hum lifuroo-jihim ḥaafiẓoon.	وَالَّذِيْنَ هُمْ لِفُرُوْجِهِمْ حٰفِظُوْنَ ۝٥
6. except with their spouses and slave-girls for which they are not blamed,	6. Illaa 'alaaa azwaajihim aw maa malakat aymaanuhum fa-innahum ghayru maloomeen.	اِلَّا عَلٰٓى اَزْوَاجِهِمْ اَوْ مَا مَلَكَتْ اَيْمَانُهُمْ فَاِنَّهُمْ غَيْرُ مَلُوْمِيْنَ ۝٦
7. those who desire to go beyond such limits are transgressors -	7. Famanib-taghaa waraaa'a zaalika fa-ulaaa'ika humul-'aadoon.	فَمَنِ ابْتَغٰى وَرَآءَ ذٰلِكَ فَاُولٰٓئِكَ هُمُ الْعٰدُوْنَ ۝٧
8. those who are true to their trust,	8. Wallazeena hum li-amaanaatihim wa 'ahdihim raa'oon.	وَالَّذِيْنَ هُمْ لِاَمٰنٰتِهِمْ وَعَهْدِهِمْ رٰعُوْنَ ۝٨
9. to their promise,	9. Wallazeena hum 'alaa Ṣalawaatihim yuḥaafiẓoon.	وَالَّذِيْنَ هُمْ عَلٰى صَلَوٰتِهِمْ يُحَافِظُوْنَ ۝٩
10. and who are steadfast in their prayer,	10. Ulaaa'ika humul waari-soon.	اُولٰٓئِكَ هُمُ الْوٰرِثُوْنَ ۝١٠
11. these are the heirs of Paradise wherein they will live forever.	11. Allazeena yarisoonal-Firdawsa hum feehaa khaali-doon.	الَّذِيْنَ يَرِثُوْنَ الْفِرْدَوْسَ ؕ هُمْ فِيْهَا خٰلِدُوْنَ ۝١١
12. We have created the human being from an extract of clay	12. Wa laqad khalaqnal insaana min sulaalatim-min ṭeen.	وَلَقَدْ خَلَقْنَا الْاِنْسَانَ مِنْ سُلٰلَةٍ مِّنْ طِيْنٍ ۝١٢
13. which was then turned into a living germ and placed in safe depository.	13. Summa ja'alnaahu nuṭ-fatan fee qaraarim-makeen.	ثُمَّ جَعَلْنٰهُ نُطْفَةً فِيْ قَرَارٍ مَّكِيْنٍ ۝١٣
14. The living germ, then, was turned into a shapeless lump, which was then turned into a chunk of meat, which was turned into bones. The bones, then, were covered with flesh. At this stage, We caused it to become another creature. All blessings belong to Allah, the best Creator.	14. Summa khalaqnan-nuṭfata 'alaqatan fakhalaqnal-'alaqata muḍghatan fakhalaq-nal-muḍghata 'iẓaaman fakasawnal-'iẓaama laḥman summa ansha-naahu khalqan aakhar; fatabaarakal-laahu aḥsanul-khaaliqeen.	ثُمَّ خَلَقْنَا النُّطْفَةَ عَلَقَةً فَخَلَقْنَا الْعَلَقَةَ مُضْغَةً فَخَلَقْنَا الْمُضْغَةَ عِظٰمًا فَكَسَوْنَا الْعِظٰمَ لَحْمًا ۗ ثُمَّ اَنْشَاْنٰهُ خَلْقًا اٰخَرَ ؕ فَتَبٰرَكَ اللّٰهُ اَحْسَنُ الْخٰلِقِيْنَ ۝١٤
15. Thereafter you will certainly die	15. Summa innakum ba'da zaalika la-mayyitoon.	ثُمَّ اِنَّكُمْ بَعْدَ ذٰلِكَ لَمَيِّتُوْنَ ۝١٥
16. and you will be brought back to life again on the Day of Resurrection.	16. Summa innakum Yaw-mal-Qiyaamati tub'asoon.	ثُمَّ اِنَّكُمْ يَوْمَ الْقِيٰمَةِ تُبْعَثُوْنَ ۝١٦

وقف لازم

17. We have created seven heavens above you and have never been neglectful to Our Creation.

17. Wa laqad khalaqnaa fawqakum sab'a ṭaraaa'iq; wa maa kunnaa 'anil-khalqi ghaafileen.

وَلَقَدْ خَلَقْنَا فَوْقَكُمْ سَبْعَ طَرَآئِقَ ۖ وَمَا
كُنَّا عَنِ الْخَلْقِ غٰفِلِيْنَ ﴿١٧﴾

18. We have sent a measure of water from the sky to stay on earth and We have the power to take it away.

18. Wa anzalnaa minas-samaaa'i maaa'am biqadarin fa-askannaahu fil-arḍi wa innaa 'alaa zahaabim bihee laqaa-diroon

وَاَنْزَلْنَا مِنَ السَّمَآءِ مَآءًۢ بِقَدَرٍ
فَاَسْكَنّٰهُ فِى الْاَرْضِ ۖ وَاِنَّا عَلٰى
ذَهَابٍۢ بِهٖ لَقٰدِرُوْنَ ﴿١٨﴾

19. We have established for you gardens of palm trees and vineyards with this water with many fruits for you to consume.

19. Fa-ansha-naa lakum bihee Jannaatim-min-nakheeliñw-wa a'naab; lakum feehaa fawaa-kihu kaseeratuñw-wa minhaa ta-kuloon.

فَاَنْشَاْنَا لَكُمْ بِهٖ جَنّٰتٍ مِّنْ نَّخِيْلٍ
وَّاَعْنَابٍ ۘ لَكُمْ فِيْهَا فَوَاكِهُ كَثِيْرَةٌ
وَّمِنْهَا تَاْكُلُوْنَ ﴿١٩﴾

وقف لازم

20. We have also created for you the tree that grows on Mount Sinai which produces oil and relish for those who use it.

20. Wa shajaratan takhruju min Ṭoori Saynaaa'a tambutu bidduhni wa ṣibghillil aakileen.

وَشَجَرَةً تَخْرُجُ مِنْ طُوْرِ سَيْنَآءَ
تَنْۢبُتُ بِالدُّهْنِ وَصِبْغٍ لِّلْاٰكِلِيْنَ ﴿٢٠﴾

21. There is a lesson for you concerning cattle. We provide you with drink from their bellies and many other benefits. You can consume them as meat.

21. Wa inna lakum fil-an'aami la'ibrah; nusqeekum-mimmaa fee buṭoonihaa wa lakum feehaa manaafi'u kaseeratuñw-wa minhaa ta-kuloon.

وَاِنَّ لَكُمْ فِى الْاَنْعَامِ لَعِبْرَةً ؕ نُسْقِيْكُمْ
مِّمَّا فِىْ بُطُوْنِهَا وَلَكُمْ فِيْهَا مَنَافِعُ
كَثِيْرَةٌ وَّمِنْهَا تَاْكُلُوْنَ ﴿٢١﴾

22. You are carried by the animals on land and by the ships in the sea.

22. Wa 'alayhaa wa 'alal-fulki tuḥmaloon.

وَعَلَيْهَا وَعَلَى الْفُلْكِ تُحْمَلُوْنَ ﴿٢٢﴾ ع

ع ٢٢

23. We sent Noah to his people who said, "My people, worship Allah for He is your only Lord. Will you then not have fear of Him?"

23. Wa laqad arsalnaa Nooḥan ilaa qawmihee faqaala yaa qawmi'-budullaaha maa lakum min ilaahin ghayruhoo afalaa tattaqoon.

وَلَقَدْ اَرْسَلْنَا نُوْحًا اِلٰى قَوْمِهٖ فَقَالَ
يٰقَوْمِ اعْبُدُوا اللّٰهَ مَا لَكُمْ مِّنْ اِلٰهٍ
غَيْرُهٗ ؕ اَفَلَا تَتَّقُوْنَ ﴿٢٣﴾

24. The chiefs of the unbelievers said to the others, "He is a mere mortal like you. He wants only to be superior to you. Had Allah wanted He would have sent the angels (instead of him). We have never heard from our fathers anything like what he says.

24. Faqaalal-mala'ul-lazeena kafaroo min qawmihee maa haazaaa illaa basharum-mislukum yureedu añy-yatafaḍḍala 'alaykum wa law shaaa'al-laahu la-anzala malaaa'ikatam-maa sami'naa bihaazaa feee aabaaa'inal awwaleen.

فَقَالَ الْمَلَؤُا الَّذِيْنَ كَفَرُوْا مِنْ قَوْمِهٖ
مَا هٰذَآ اِلَّا بَشَرٌ مِّثْلُكُمْ ۙ يُرِيْدُ
اَنْ يَّتَفَضَّلَ عَلَيْكُمْ ؕ وَلَوْ شَآءَ اللّٰهُ
لَاَنْزَلَ مَلٰٓئِكَةً ۖۚ مَّا سَمِعْنَا بِهٰذَا فِىْٓ
اٰبَآئِنَا الْاَوَّلِيْنَ ﴿٢٤﴾

25. He is only an insane person. Wait for some time. Perhaps he will come to his senses."

25. In huwa illaa rajulum bihee jinnatun fatarabbaṣoo bihee ḥattaa ḥeen.

اِنْ هُوَ اِلَّا رَجُلٌۢ بِهٖ جِنَّةٌ فَتَرَبَّصُوْا
بِهٖ حَتّٰى حِيْنٍ ﴿٢٥﴾

26. Noah prayed, "Lord, help me; they have called me a liar."

26. Qaala Rabbin-ṣurnee bimaa kazzaboon.

قَالَ رَبِّ انْصُرْنِىْ بِمَا كَذَّبُوْنِ ﴿٢٦﴾

27. We inspired him, saying, "Build the Ark before Our eyes

27. Fa-awḥaynaaa ilayhi aniṣ-na'il-fulka

فَاَوْحَيْنَآ اِلَيْهِ اَنِ اصْنَعِ الْفُلْكَ

and by the instruction of Our revelation. When our decree comes to pass and water comes forth from the Oven, embark in the Ark with a pair of every kind of animals and your family except those already doomed (to perish). Do not plead with Me for the unjust; they will be drowned."

bi-a'yuninaa wa waḥyinaa fa-izaa jaaa'a amrunaa wa faarat-tannooru fasluk feehaa min kullin zawjaynis-nayni wa ahlaka illaa man sabaqa 'alayhil-qawlu minhum wa laa tukhaaṭibnee fil-lazeena ẓalamooo innahum-mughraqoon.

بِأَعْيُنِنَا وَوَحْيِنَا فَإِذَا جَآءَ أَمْرُنَا
وَفَارَ التَّنُّوْرُ ۙ فَاسْلُكْ فِيْهَا مِنْ كُلٍّ
زَوْجَيْنِ اثْنَيْنِ وَأَهْلَكَ إِلَّا مَنْ سَبَقَ
عَلَيْهِ الْقَوْلُ مِنْهُمْ ۚ وَلَا تُخَاطِبْنِيْ
فِي الَّذِيْنَ ظَلَمُوْا ۚ إِنَّهُمْ مُّغْرَقُوْنَ ﴿٢٧﴾

28. When all of you settle in the Ark, say, "Only Allah, Who has saved us from the unjust people, deserves all praise."

28. Fa-izas-tawayta anta wa mam-ma'aka 'alal-fulki faqulil-ḥamdu lillaahil-lazee najjaanaa minal-qawmiẓ-ẓaalimeen.

فَإِذَا اسْتَوَيْتَ أَنْتَ وَمَنْ مَّعَكَ
عَلَى الْفُلْكِ فَقُلِ الْحَمْدُ لِلّٰهِ الَّذِيْ
نَجّٰىنَا مِنَ الْقَوْمِ الظّٰلِمِيْنَ ﴿٢٨﴾

29. Say, "Lord, grant us a blessed landing from the Ark; You are the One who provides the safest landing."

29. Wa qur-Rabbi anzilnee munzalam-mubaarakañw-wa Anta khayrul-munzileen.

وَقُلْ رَّبِّ أَنْزِلْنِيْ مُنْزَلًا مُّبٰرَكًا وَّ
أَنْتَ خَيْرُ الْمُنْزِلِيْنَ ﴿٢٩﴾

30. In this story there is enough evidence (of the Truth); thus do We try (mankind).

30. Inna fee zaalika la-Aayaatiñw-wa in kunnaa lamubtaleen.

إِنَّ فِيْ ذٰلِكَ لَاٰيٰتٍ وَّإِنْ كُنَّا
لَمُبْتَلِيْنَ ﴿٣٠﴾

31. We brought another generation into existence after the people of Noah.

31. Summa ansha-naa mim ba'dihim qarnan aakhareen.

ثُمَّ أَنْشَأْنَا مِنْ بَعْدِهِمْ قَرْنًا اٰخَرِيْنَ ﴿٣١﴾

32. We sent to them a Messenger from among their own people who told them, "Worship Allah; He is your only Lord. Will you then not have fear of Him?"

32. Fa-arsalnaa feehim Rasoolam-minhum ani'budul-laaha maa lakum-min ilaahin ghayruhooo afalaa tattaqoon.

فَأَرْسَلْنَا فِيْهِمْ رَسُوْلًا مِّنْهُمْ أَنِ
اعْبُدُوا اللّٰهَ مَا لَكُمْ مِّنْ إِلٰهٍ غَيْرُهٗ ۭ
أَفَلَا تَتَّقُوْنَ ﴿٣٢﴾ ع

33. A group of his people who disbelieved him and had called the Day of Judgment a lie and whom We had made prosperous in this life, said, "He is a mere mortal like you. He eats and drinks as you do.

33. Wa qaalal-mala-u min qawmihil-lazeena kafaroo wa kazzaboo biliqaaa'il-Aakhirati wa atrafnaahum fil-ḥayaatid-dunyaa maa haazaaa illaa basharum-mislukum ya-kulu mimmaa ta-kuloona minhu wa yashrabu mimmaa tashraboon.

وَقَالَ الْمَلَأُ مِنْ قَوْمِهِ الَّذِيْنَ كَفَرُوْا
وَكَذَّبُوْا بِلِقَآءِ الْاٰخِرَةِ وَأَتْرَفْنٰهُمْ
فِي الْحَيٰوةِ الدُّنْيَا ۙ مَا هٰذَآ إِلَّا بَشَرٌ
مِّثْلُكُمْ ۙ يَأْكُلُ مِمَّا تَأْكُلُوْنَ مِنْهُ
وَيَشْرَبُ مِمَّا تَشْرَبُوْنَ ﴿٣٣﴾

34. If you follow a mortal like yourselves you will certainly be lost.

34. Wa la'in aṭ'atum basharam-mislakum innakum izal-lakhaasiroon.

وَلَئِنْ أَطَعْتُمْ بَشَرًا مِّثْلَكُمْ إِنَّكُمْ
إِذًا لَّخٰسِرُوْنَ ﴿٣٤﴾

35. Does he promise you that after you die and become dust and bones you will be brought back to life again?

35. Aya'idukum annakum izaa mittum wa kuntum turaabañw-wa 'iẓaaman annakum-mukhrajoon.

أَيَعِدُكُمْ أَنَّكُمْ إِذَا مِتُّمْ وَكُنْتُمْ تُرَابًا
وَّعِظَامًا أَنَّكُمْ مُّخْرَجُوْنَ ﴿٣٥﴾

36. Such a promise will never come true.

36. Hayhaata hayhaata limaa too'adoon.

هَيْهَاتَ هَيْهَاتَ لِمَا تُوْعَدُوْنَ ﴿٣٦﴾

37. This is our only life. We live and will die but we will never be brought back to life again.

37. In hiya illaa ḥayaatunad-dunyaa namootu wa naḥyaa wa maa naḥnu bimab'oo<u>s</u>een.

إِنْ هِيَ إِلَّا حَيَاتُنَا الدُّنْيَا نَمُوتُ وَ
نَحْيَا وَمَا نَحْنُ بِمَبْعُوثِينَ ﴿٣٧﴾

38. He is only a man who invents lies against Allah, so have no faith in him."

38. In huwa illaa rajulunif-taraa 'alal-laahi ka<u>z</u>ibañw-wa maa naḥnu lahoo bimu'mineen.

إِنْ هُوَ إِلَّا رَجُلٌ افْتَرَىٰ عَلَى اللَّهِ
كَذِبًا وَمَا نَحْنُ لَهُ بِمُؤْمِنِينَ ﴿٣٨﴾

39. The Messenger prayed, "Lord, help me; they have called me a liar."

39. Qaala Rabbin-ṣurnee bimaa ka<u>zz</u>aboon.

قَالَ رَبِّ انْصُرْنِي بِمَا كَذَّبُونِ ﴿٣٩﴾

40. Allah replied, "After a very short time they will certainly regret their deeds."

40. Qaala 'ammaa qaleelil-la-yuṣbiḥunna naadimeen.

قَالَ عَمَّا قَلِيلٍ لَيُصْبِحُنَّ نَادِمِينَ ﴿٤٠﴾

41. A blast struck them for a just cause, and We made them look like withered leaves. Allah keeps the unjust people away from His mercy.

41. Fa-akha<u>z</u>at-humuṣ-ṣay-ḥatu bilḥaqqi faja'alnaahum ghu<u>s</u>aaa'aa; fabu'dal-lilqaw-miẓ-ẓaalimeen.

فَأَخَذَتْهُمُ الصَّيْحَةُ بِالْحَقِّ فَجَعَلْنَاهُمْ
غُثَاءً ۚ فَبُعْدًا لِلْقَوْمِ الظَّالِمِينَ ﴿٤١﴾

42. After them We brought another generation into existence.

42. <u>S</u>umma ansha-naa mim ba'dihim quroonan aakhareen.

ثُمَّ أَنْشَأْنَا مِنْ بَعْدِهِمْ قُرُونًا
آخَرِينَ ﴿٤٢﴾

43. Every nation has an appointed life span.

43. Maa tasbiqu min ummatin ajalahaa wa maa yasta-khiroon.

مَا تَسْبِقُ مِنْ أُمَّةٍ أَجَلَهَا وَمَا
يَسْتَأْخِرُونَ ﴿٤٣﴾

44. We sent Our messengers one after the other but whenever a Messenger would come to a nation, its people would call him a liar and We would destroy one nation after the other, thus, only their stories were left behind them. Allah keeps the unbelievers far away from His Mercy.

44. <u>S</u>umma arsalnaa Rusu-lanaa tatraa kullamaa jaaa'a ummatar-Rasooluhaa ka<u>z</u>-<u>z</u>abooh; fa-atba'naa ba'ḍahum ba'ḍañw-wa ja'alnaahum aḥaadee<u>s</u>; fabu'dal-liqawmil-laa yu'minoon.

ثُمَّ أَرْسَلْنَا رُسُلَنَا تَتْرَا ۖ كُلَّمَا
جَاءَ أُمَّةً رَسُولُهَا كَذَّبُوهُ ۚ فَأَتْبَعْنَا
بَعْضَهُمْ بَعْضًا وَجَعَلْنَاهُمْ أَحَادِيثَ ۚ
فَبُعْدًا لِقَوْمٍ لَا يُؤْمِنُونَ ﴿٤٤﴾

45. Then We sent Moses and his brother Aaron with Our miracles and clear authority

45. <u>S</u>umma arsalnaa Moosaa wa akhaahu Haaroona bi Aayaatinaa wa sulṭaanim-mu-been.

ثُمَّ أَرْسَلْنَا مُوسَىٰ وَأَخَاهُ هَارُونَ
بِآيَاتِنَا وَسُلْطَانٍ مُبِينٍ ﴿٤٥﴾

46. to the Pharaoh and his nobles. But they behaved proudly and thought themselves superior people.

46. Ilaa Fir'awna wa mala'i-hee fastakbaroo wa kaanoo qawman 'aaleen.

إِلَىٰ فِرْعَوْنَ وَمَلَئِهِ فَاسْتَكْبَرُوا وَ
كَانُوا قَوْمًا عَالِينَ ﴿٤٦﴾

47. They said, "Should we believe in two mere mortals who are like ourselves and whose people are our slaves?"

47. Faqaalooo anu'minu libasharayni mi<u>s</u>linaa wa qawmuhumaa lanaa 'aabidoon.

فَقَالُوا أَنُؤْمِنُ لِبَشَرَيْنِ مِثْلِنَا
وَقَوْمُهُمَا لَنَا عَابِدُونَ ﴿٤٧﴾

48. They called them liars and consequently were destroyed.

48. Faka<u>zz</u>aboohumaa fa-kaanoo minal-muhlakeen.

فَكَذَّبُوهُمَا فَكَانُوا مِنَ الْمُهْلَكِينَ ﴿٤٨﴾

49. We gave the Book to Moses so that perhaps they may have guidance.

49. Wa laqad aataynaa Moosal-Kitaaba la'allahum yahtadoon.

وَلَقَدْ آتَيْنَا مُوسَى الْكِتَابَ لَعَلَّهُمْ
يَهْتَدُونَ ﴿٤٩﴾

50. We made the son of Mary and his mother a miracle and

50. Wa ja'alnab-na Maryama wa ummahooo Aayatañw-wa

وَجَعَلْنَا ابْنَ مَرْيَمَ وَأُمَّهُ آيَةً وَ

settled them on a high land, quite secure and watered by a spring.

aawaynaahumaaa ilaa rabwatin zaati qaraariñw-wa ma'een.

وَاٰوَيْنٰهُمَآ اِلٰى رَبْوَةٍ ذَاتِ قَرَارٍ وَّمَعِيْنٍ ۝٥٠

51. I told them, "Messengers, eat from the pure things and act righteously; I know all that you do.

51. Yaaa ayyuhar-Rusulu kuloo minaṭ-ṭayyibaati wa'maloo ṣaaliḥan innee bimaa ta'maloona 'Aleem.

يٰٓاَيُّهَا الرُّسُلُ كُلُوْا مِنَ الطَّيِّبٰتِ وَاعْمَلُوْا صَالِحًا ۭ اِنِّيْ بِمَا تَعْمَلُوْنَ عَلِيْمٌ ۝٥١

52. Your religion is one and I am your Lord. Have fear of Me."

52. Wa inna haaziheee ummatukum ummatañw-waaḥidatañw-wa Ana Rabbukum fattaqoon.

وَاِنَّ هٰذِهٖٓ اُمَّتُكُمْ اُمَّةً وَّاحِدَةً وَّاَنَا رَبُّكُمْ فَاتَّقُوْنِ ۝٥٢

53. The people divided themselves into many sects, each with their own book and each happy with whatever they had.

53. Fataqaṭṭa'ooo amrahum baynahum zuburaa; kullu ḥizbim bimaa ladayhim fariḥoon.

فَتَقَطَّعُوْٓا اَمْرَهُمْ بَيْنَهُمْ زُبُرًا ۭ كُلُّ حِزْبٍۢ بِمَا لَدَيْهِمْ فَرِحُوْنَ ۝٥٣

54. (Muhammad), leave them alone in their dark ignorance for an appointed time.

54. Fazarhum fee ghamratihim ḥattaa ḥeen.

فَذَرْهُمْ فِيْ غَمْرَتِهِمْ حَتّٰى حِيْنٍ ۝٥٤

55. Do they think that We are helping them by giving them children and property?

55. A-yaḥsaboona annamaa numidduhum bihee mimmaa-liñw-wa baneen.

اَيَحْسَبُوْنَ اَنَّمَا نُمِدُّهُمْ بِهٖ مِنْ مَّالٍ وَّبَنِيْنَ ۝٥٥

56. We provide them with the means of competing with each other in virtuous deeds, but they do not realize this.

56. Nusaari'u lahum fil-khayraat; bal laa yash'uroon.

نُسَارِعُ لَهُمْ فِي الْخَيْرٰتِ ۭ بَلْ لَّا يَشْعُرُوْنَ ۝٥٦

57. Only those who are, out of fear of Him, humble before their Lord,

57. Innal-lazeena hum-min khashyati Rabbihim-mushfiqoon.

اِنَّ الَّذِيْنَ هُمْ مِّنْ خَشْيَةِ رَبِّهِمْ مُّشْفِقُوْنَ ۝٥٧

58. who believe in the revelations of their Lord,

58. Wallazeena hum bi-Aayaati Rabbihim yu'minoon.

وَالَّذِيْنَ هُمْ بِاٰيٰتِ رَبِّهِمْ يُؤْمِنُوْنَ ۝٥٨

59. who consider nothing equal to their Lord,

59. Wallazeena hum bi-Rabbihim laa yushrikoon.

وَالَّذِيْنَ هُمْ بِرَبِّهِمْ لَا يُشْرِكُوْنَ ۝٥٩

60. who spend their property for the cause of Allah, and whose hearts are afraid of their return

60. Wallazeena yu'toona maaa aataw-wa quloobuhum wajilatun annahum ilaa Rabbihim raaji'oon.

وَالَّذِيْنَ يُؤْتُوْنَ مَآ اٰتَوْا وَّقُلُوْبُهُمْ وَجِلَةٌ اَنَّهُمْ اِلٰى رَبِّهِمْ رٰجِعُوْنَ ۝٦٠

61. to Allah, these are the ones who really compete with each other in virtuous deeds and are the foremost ones in the task.

61. Ulaaa'ika yusaari'oona fil-khayraati wa hum lahaa saabiqoon.

اُولٰۗىِٕكَ يُسٰرِعُوْنَ فِي الْخَيْرٰتِ وَهُمْ لَهَا سٰبِقُوْنَ ۝٦١

62. We do not impose on any soul what is beyond its capacity. We have the Book, which speaks the truth and no injustice will be done to it.

62. Wa laa nukallifu nafsan illaa wus'ahaa wa ladaynaa kitaabuñy-yanṭiqu bilḥaqqi wa hum la yuẓlamoon.

وَلَا نُكَلِّفُ نَفْسًا اِلَّا وُسْعَهَا وَلَدَيْنَا كِتٰبٌ يَّنْطِقُ بِالْحَقِّ وَهُمْ لَا يُظْلَمُوْنَ ۝٦٢

63. In fact, the hearts of the unbelievers are in the dark

63. Bal quloobuhum fee ghamratim-min haazaa

بَلْ قُلُوْبُهُمْ فِيْ غَمْرَةٍ مِّنْ هٰذَا

because of their ignorance of real virtue; they act against it.

wa lahum a'maalum-min dooni zaalika hum lahaa 'aamiloon.

وَلَهُمْ أَعْمَالٌ مِّن دُونِ ذَٰلِكَ هُمْ لَهَا عَامِلُونَ ﴿٦٣﴾

64. But when We will strike with torment those (unbelievers) who are rich, they will start to cry for help.

64. Ḥattaaa izaaa akhaznaa mutrafeehim bil'azaabi izaa hum yaj'aroon.

حَتَّىٰٓ إِذَآ أَخَذْنَا مُتْرَفِيهِم بِالْعَذَابِ إِذَا هُمْ يَجْـَٔرُونَ ﴿٦٤﴾

65. We shall tell them, "Do not cry for help on this day; you will receive none from Us."

65. Laa taj'arul-yawma innakum-minnaa laa tunṣaroon.

لَا تَجْـَٔرُوا الْيَوْمَ ۖ إِنَّكُم مِّنَّا لَا تُنصَرُونَ ﴿٦٥﴾

66. Our revelations had certainly been recited to you, but you turned your backs to them

66. Qad kaanat Aayaatee tutlaa 'alaykum fakuntum 'alaaa a'qaabikum tankiṣoon.

قَدْ كَانَتْ ءَايَٰتِى تُتْلَىٰ عَلَيْكُمْ فَكُنتُمْ عَلَىٰٓ أَعْقَٰبِكُمْ تَنكِصُونَ ﴿٦٦﴾

67. and arrogantly mocked and reviled them.

67. Mustakbireena bihee saamiran tahjuroon

مُسْتَكْبِرِينَ بِهِۦ سَٰمِرًا تَهْجُرُونَ ﴿٦٧﴾

68. Was it that you did not give any thought to it (the Quran)? Was it different from what was revealed to your fathers?

68. Afalam yaddabbarul-qawla am jaaa'ahum-maa lam ya-ti aabaaa'ahumul awwaleen.

أَفَلَمْ يَدَّبَّرُوا الْقَوْلَ أَمْ جَآءَهُم مَّا لَمْ يَأْتِ ءَابَآءَهُمُ الْأَوَّلِينَ ﴿٦٨﴾

69. Or did you not recognize your Messenger and thus, denied him (Muhammad)

69. Am lam ya'rifoo Rasoolahum fahum lahoo munkiroon.

أَمْ لَمْ يَعْرِفُوا رَسُولَهُمْ فَهُمْ لَهُۥ مُنكِرُونَ ﴿٦٩﴾

70. or you said that he is possessed by Satan? In fact, he has brought you the truth, but most of you dislike it.

70. Am yaqooloona bihee jinnah; bal jaaa'ahum bilḥaqqi wa aksaruhum lil-ḥaqqi kaarihoon.

أَمْ يَقُولُونَ بِهِۦ جِنَّةٌۢ ۚ بَلْ جَآءَهُم بِالْحَقِّ وَأَكْثَرُهُمْ لِلْحَقِّ كَٰرِهُونَ ﴿٧٠﴾

71. Had the truth followed their desires, the heavens and the earth and all that is in them would have been destroyed. We sent them the Quran but they ignored it.

71. Wa lawit-taba'al-ḥaqqu ahwaaa'ahum lafasadatis-samaawaatu wal-arḍu wa man feehinn; bal ataynaahum bizikrihim fahum 'an zikrihim-mu'riḍoon.

وَلَوِ اتَّبَعَ الْحَقُّ أَهْوَآءَهُمْ لَفَسَدَتِ السَّمَٰوَٰتُ وَالْأَرْضُ وَمَن فِيهِنَّ ۚ بَلْ أَتَيْنَٰهُم بِذِكْرِهِمْ فَهُمْ عَن ذِكْرِهِم مُّعْرِضُونَ ﴿٧١﴾

72. (Do they disbelieve because) you asked them for payment? The reward that you will receive from your Lord is the best. He is the best Provider.

72. Am tas'aluhum kharjan fakharaaju Rabbika khayruñw-wa Huwa khayrur-raaziqeen.

أَمْ تَسْـَٔلُهُمْ خَرْجًا فَخَرَاجُ رَبِّكَ خَيْرٌ ۖ وَهُوَ خَيْرُ الرَّٰزِقِينَ ﴿٧٢﴾

73. (Muhammad), you certainly have called them to the right path,

73. Wa innaka latad'oohum ilaa Ṣiraaṭim-Mustaqeem.

وَإِنَّكَ لَتَدْعُوهُمْ إِلَىٰ صِرَٰطٍ مُّسْتَقِيمٍ ﴿٧٣﴾ الربع

74. but those who disbelieve the life hereafter deviate from the right path.

74. Wa innal-lazeena laa yu'minoona bil-Aakhirati 'aniṣ-ṣiraati lanaakiboon.

وَإِنَّ الَّذِينَ لَا يُؤْمِنُونَ بِالْءَاخِرَةِ عَنِ الصِّرَٰطِ لَنَٰكِبُونَ ﴿٧٤﴾

75. Even if We were to grant them mercy and rescue them from

75. Wa law raḥimnaahum wa kashafnaa maa bihim-min ḍurril-

وَلَوْ رَحِمْنَٰهُمْ وَكَشَفْنَا مَا بِهِم مِّن ضُرٍّ

hardship, they would still blindly persist in their rebellion.

lalajjoo fee ṭughyaanihim ya'mahoon.

لَّلَجُّوا فِي طُغْيَانِهِمْ يَعْمَهُونَ ﴿٧٥﴾

76. We struck them with torment (hunger, fear and death), but they did not submit themselves to their Lord, nor did they make themselves humble

76. Wa laqad akhaz̲naahum bil'az̲aabi famastakaanoo li-Rabbihim wa maa yataḍarra'oon.

وَلَقَدْ أَخَذْنَاهُم بِالْعَذَابِ فَمَا
اسْتَكَانُوا لِرَبِّهِمْ وَمَا يَتَضَرَّعُونَ ﴿٧٦﴾

77. until We opened the gate of greater torment (death) and they suddenly found themselves in despair.

77. Ḥattaaa iz̲aa fataḥnaa 'alayhim baaban z̲aa 'az̲aabin shadeedin iz̲aa hum feehi mublisoon.

حَتَّىٰ إِذَا فَتَحْنَا عَلَيْهِم بَابًا ذَا عَذَابٍ
شَدِيدٍ إِذَا هُمْ فِيهِ مُبْلِسُونَ ﴿٧٧﴾

78. It is He who has created ears, eyes, and hearts for you. Little are the thanks that you give.

78. Wa Huwal-laz̲eee ansha-a-lakumus-sam'a wal-abṣaara wal-af'idah; qaleelam-maa tashkuroon.

وَهُوَ الَّذِي أَنشَأَ لَكُمُ السَّمْعَ وَالْأَبْصَارَ
وَالْأَفْئِدَةَ ۚ قَلِيلًا مَّا تَشْكُرُونَ ﴿٧٨﴾

79. It is He who has settled you on the earth and before Him you will all be assembled.

79. Wa Huwal-laz̲ee z̲ara-akum fil-arḍi wa ilayhi tuḥsharoon.

وَهُوَ الَّذِي ذَرَأَكُمْ فِي الْأَرْضِ
وَإِلَيْهِ تُحْشَرُونَ ﴿٧٩﴾

80. It is He who gives life and causes death and it is He who alternates night and day. Will you not then understand?

80. Wa Huwal-laz̲ee yuḥyee wa yumeetu wa lahukhtilaaful-layli wannahaar; afalaa ta'qiloon.

وَهُوَ الَّذِي يُحْيِي وَيُمِيتُ وَلَهُ
اخْتِلَافُ اللَّيْلِ وَالنَّهَارِ ۚ أَفَلَا
تَعْقِلُونَ ﴿٨٠﴾

81. They say exactly the same thing as the people who lived before.

81. Bal qaaloo mis̲la maa qaalal-awwaloon.

بَلْ قَالُوا مِثْلَ مَا قَالَ الْأَوَّلُونَ ﴿٨١﴾

82. They say, "When we die and become dust and bones, shall we then be raised up again?

82. Qaalooo 'a-iz̲aa mitnaa wa kunnaa turaabañw-wa 'iẓaaman 'a-innaa lamab-'oos̲oon.

قَالُوا أَإِذَا مِتْنَا وَكُنَّا تُرَابًا وَعِظَامًا
أَإِنَّا لَمَبْعُوثُونَ ﴿٨٢﴾

83. We and our fathers have been given such promises before. These are no more than ancient legends."

83. Laqad wu'idnaa naḥnu wa aabaaa'unaa haaz̲aa min qablu in haaz̲aaa illaaa asaaṭeerul-awwaleen.

لَقَدْ وُعِدْنَا نَحْنُ وَآبَاؤُنَا هَٰذَا
مِن قَبْلُ إِنْ هَٰذَا إِلَّا أَسَاطِيرُ
الْأَوَّلِينَ ﴿٨٣﴾

84. (Muhammad), say to them, "Tell me, if you know, to whom does the earth and its contents belong?"

84. Qul limanil-arḍu wa man feehaaa in kuntum ta'lamoon.

قُل لِّمَنِ الْأَرْضُ وَمَن فِيهَا إِن
كُنتُمْ تَعْلَمُونَ ﴿٨٤﴾

85. They will quickly reply, "They belongs to Allah." Say, "Will you then not take heed?"

85. Sa-yaqooloona lillaah; qul afalaa taz̲akkaroon.

سَيَقُولُونَ لِلَّهِ ۚ قُلْ أَفَلَا تَذَكَّرُونَ ﴿٨٥﴾

86. Ask them, "Who is the Lord of the seven heavens and the Great Throne?"

86. Qul mar-Rabbus-samaa-waatis-sab'i wa Rabbul-'Arshil-'Aẓeem.

قُلْ مَن رَّبُّ السَّمَاوَاتِ السَّبْعِ وَرَبُّ
الْعَرْشِ الْعَظِيمِ ﴿٨٦﴾

87. They will quickly say, "It is Allah." Say, "Will you then not have fear of Him?"

87. Sa-yaqooloona lillaah; qul afalaa tattaqoon.

سَيَقُولُونَ لِلَّهِ ۚ قُلْ أَفَلَا تَتَّقُونَ ﴿٨٧﴾

88. Ask them, "Do you have any knowledge, in whose hands is the ownership of all things? Who is the one who gives protection and yet He Himself is never protected?"

88. Qul mam bi-yadihee malakootu kulli shay'iñw-wa Huwa yujeeru wa laa yujaaru 'alayhi in kuntum ta'lamoon.

قُلْ مَن بِيَدِهِ مَلَكُوتُ كُلِّ شَيْءٍ وَهُوَ
يُجِيرُ وَلَا يُجَارُ عَلَيْهِ إِن كُنتُمْ

		تَعْلَمُوْنَ ﴿٨٨﴾
89. They will reply spontaneously, "It is Allah." Ask them, "Why has falsehood bewitched you?"	89. Sa-yaqooloona lillaah; qul fa-annaa tusḥaroon.	سَيَقُوْلُوْنَ لِلّٰهِ ۭ قُلْ فَاَنّٰى تُسْحَرُوْنَ ﴿٨٩﴾
90. We have sent them the truth and they, certainly, are liars.	90. Bal ataynaahum bil-ḥaqqi wa innahum lakaazi̱boon.	بَلْ اَتَيْنٰهُمْ بِالْحَقِّ وَاِنَّهُمْ لَكٰذِبُوْنَ ﴿٩٠﴾
91. Allah has never given birth to a son and there is no Ilah (one deserving to be worshipped as a creator) besides Him. Were it as such, each Ilah would have taken away his creatures and claimed superiority over the others. Allah is free of all defects of what they believe He is.	91. Mat-takhaza̱l-laahu miñw-waladiñw-wa maa kaana ma'ahoo min ilaah; iza̱l-laza̱haba kullu ilaahim bimaa khalaqa wa la'alaa ba'ḍuhum 'alaa ba'ḍ; Subḥaanal-laahi 'ammaa yaṣifoon.	مَا اتَّخَذَ اللّٰهُ مِنْ وَّلَدٍ وَّمَا كَانَ مَعَهٗ مِنْ اِلٰهٍ اِذًا لَّذَهَبَ كُلُّ اِلٰهٍۢ بِمَا خَلَقَ وَلَعَلَا بَعْضُهُمْ عَلٰي بَعْضٍ ۭ سُبْحٰنَ اللّٰهِ عَمَّا يَصِفُوْنَ ﴿٩١﴾
92. He has the knowledge of all seen and unseen things. He, the Most High, is free of all such defects that they ascribe (to Him).	92. Aalimil-Ghaybi wash-shahaadati fata'aalaa 'ammaa yushrikoon.	عٰلِمِ الْغَيْبِ وَالشَّهَادَةِ فَتَعٰلٰى عَمَّا يُشْرِكُوْنَ ﴿٩٢﴾ ع ١٥ ٥
93. Say, "Lord, if you will afflict them with punishment,	93. Qur-Rabbi immaa turiyannee maa yoo'adoon.	قُلْ رَّبِّ اِمَّا تُرِيَنِّيْ مَا يُوْعَدُوْنَ ﴿٩٣﴾
94. exclude me from the unjust people."	94. Rabbi falaa taj'alnee fil-qawmiẓ-ẓaalimeen.	رَبِّ فَلَا تَجْعَلْنِيْ فِي الْقَوْمِ الظّٰلِمِيْنَ ﴿٩٤﴾
95. We have the Power to strike them with torment before your very eyes.	95. Wa innaa 'alaaa an-nuri-yaka maa na'iduhum laqaa-diroon.	وَاِنَّا عَلٰٓي اَنْ نُّرِيَكَ مَا نَعِدُهُمْ لَقٰدِرُوْنَ ﴿٩٥﴾
96. Respond to the injustice (done to you) with the better deed. We know best what they attribute to Allah.	96. Idfa' billatee hiya aḥsa-nus-sayyi'ah; Naḥnu a'lamu bimaa yaṣifoon.	اِدْفَعْ بِالَّتِيْ هِىَ اَحْسَنُ السَّيِّئَةَ ۭ نَحْنُ اَعْلَمُ بِمَا يَصِفُوْنَ ﴿٩٦﴾
97. Say, "Lord, I seek your protection against the strong temptations of the devils.	97. Wa qur-Rabbi a'oozu̱ bika min hamazaatish-Shayaaṭeen.	وَقُلْ رَّبِّ اَعُوْذُ بِكَ مِنْ هَمَزٰتِ الشَّيٰطِيْنِ ﴿٩٧﴾
98. I seek your protection should they approach me."	98. Wa a'oozu̱ bika Rabbi añy-yaḥḍuroon.	وَاَعُوْذُ بِكَ رَبِّ اَنْ يَّحْضُرُوْنِ ﴿٩٨﴾
99. When death approaches one of the unbelievers, he says, "Lord, send me back again	99. Ḥattaaa iza̱a jaaa'a aḥada-humul-mawtu qaala Rabbir-ji'oon.	حَتّٰٓي اِذَا جَاۗءَ اَحَدَهُمُ الْمَوْتُ قَالَ رَبِّ ارْجِعُوْنِ ﴿٩٩﴾
100. so that perhaps I shall act righteously for the rest of my life." Although he says so, his wish will never come true. After death they will be behind a barrier until the day of their resurrection.	100. La'alleee a'malu ṣaaliḥan feemaa taraktu kallaaa; innahaa kalimatun huwa qaaa'iluhaa wa miñw-waraaa'ihim barzakhun ilaa Yawmi yub'as̱oon.	لَعَلِّيْٓ اَعْمَلُ صَالِحًا فِيْمَا تَرَكْتُ كَلَّا ۭ اِنَّهَا كَلِمَةٌ هُوَ قَاۗىِٕلُهَا ۭ وَمِنْ وَّرَاۗىِٕهِمْ بَرْزَخٌ اِلٰى يَوْمِ يُبْعَثُوْنَ ﴿١٠٠﴾
101. After the trumpet sounds there will be no kindred relations nor any opportunity to ask about others or seek their assistance.	101. Fa-iza̱a nufikha fiṣ-Ṣoori falaaa ansaaba baynahum Yawma'iziñw-wa laa yata-saaa'aloon.	فَاِذَا نُفِخَ فِي الصُّوْرِ فَلَآ اَنْسَابَ بَيْنَهُمْ يَوْمَىِٕذٍ وَّلَا يَتَسَاۗءَلُوْنَ ﴿١٠١﴾

102. If the side of one's good deeds weighs heavier on a scale, he will have everlasting happiness,

102. Faman s̲aqulat mawaazeenuhoo fa-ulaaa'ika humul-mufliḥoon.

فَمَنْ ثَقُلَتْ مَوَازِيْنُهٗ فَاُولٰٓئِكَ هُمُ الْمُفْلِحُوْنَ ﴿١٠٢﴾

103. but if it weighs less, one will be lost forever in hell.

103. Wa man khaffat mawaazeenuhoo fa-ulaaa'ikal-laz̲eena khasirooo anfusahum fee Jahannama khaalidoon.

وَمَنْ خَفَّتْ مَوَازِيْنُهٗ فَاُولٰٓئِكَ الَّذِيْنَ خَسِرُوْٓا اَنْفُسَهُمْ فِيْ جَهَنَّمَ خٰلِدُوْنَ ﴿١٠٣﴾

104. The flame of the fire will strike their faces and they (their mouths wide open) will be groaning therein in pain.

104. Talfaḥu wujoohahumun-Naaru wa hum feehaa kaaliḥoon.

تَلْفَحُ وُجُوْهَهُمُ النَّارُ وَهُمْ فِيْهَا كٰلِحُوْنَ ﴿١٠٤﴾

105. (They will be told), "Were Our revelations not recited to you and did you not call them lies?"

105. Alam takun Aayaatee tutlaa 'alaykum fakuntum bihaa tukaz̲ z̲iboon.

اَلَمْ تَكُنْ اٰيٰتِيْ تُتْلٰى عَلَيْكُمْ فَكُنْتُمْ بِهَا تُكَذِّبُوْنَ ﴿١٠٥﴾

106. They will reply, "Lord, our hard-heartedness overcame us and we went astray.

106. Qaaloo Rabbanaa ghalabat 'alaynaa shiqwatunaa wa kunnaa qawman ḍaaalleen.

قَالُوْا رَبَّنَا غَلَبَتْ عَلَيْنَا شِقْوَتُنَا وَكُنَّا قَوْمًا ضَآلِّيْنَ ﴿١٠٦﴾

107. Lord, take us out of this and if we sin again, we shall certainly be unjust."

107. Rabbanaaa akhrijnaa minhaa fa-in 'udnaa fa-innaa ẓaalimoon.

رَبَّنَآ اَخْرِجْنَا مِنْهَا فَاِنْ عُدْنَا فَاِنَّا ظٰلِمُوْنَ ﴿١٠٧﴾

108. He will say, "Be quiet and say nothing."

108. Qaalakh-sa'oo feehaa wa laa tukallimoon.

قَالَ اخْسَئُوْا فِيْهَا وَلَا تُكَلِّمُوْنِ ﴿١٠٨﴾

109. There was a group of my servants among you who always prayed: Lord, forgive us and grant us mercy; You are the best of those who show mercy.

109. Innahoo kaana fareequm-min 'ibaadee yaqooloona Rabbanaaa aamannaa faghfir lanaa warḥamnaa wa Anta khayrur-raaḥimeen.

اِنَّهٗ كَانَ فَرِيْقٌ مِّنْ عِبَادِيْ يَقُوْلُوْنَ رَبَّنَآ اٰمَنَّا فَاغْفِرْ لَنَا وَارْحَمْنَا وَاَنْتَ خَيْرُ الرّٰحِمِيْنَ ﴿١٠٩﴾

110. "You mocked and laughed at them until you forgot all about Me.

110. Fattakhaz̲tumoohum sikhriyyan ḥattaaa ansawkum z̲ikree wa kuntum-minhum taḍḥakoon.

فَاتَّخَذْتُمُوْهُمْ سِخْرِيًّا حَتّٰىٓ اَنْسَوْكُمْ ذِكْرِيْ وَكُنْتُمْ مِّنْهُمْ تَضْحَكُوْنَ ﴿١١٠﴾

111. On this day I have given them their reward for their exercising patience and it is they who have triumphed."

111. Innee jazaytuhumul-Yawma bimaa ṣabarooo annahum humul-faaa'izoon.

اِنِّيْ جَزَيْتُهُمُ الْيَوْمَ بِمَا صَبَرُوْٓا اَنَّهُمْ هُمُ الْفَآئِزُوْنَ ﴿١١١﴾

112. He (Allah) will ask them, "How many years did you live in your graves?"

112. Qaala kam labis̲tum fil-arḍi 'adada sineen.

قٰلَ كَمْ لَبِثْتُمْ فِي الْاَرْضِ عَدَدَ سِنِيْنَ ﴿١١٢﴾

113. They will reply. "We remained for about a day or part of it, but ask those who have kept count (the angels)."

113. Qaaloo labis̲naa yawman aw ba'ḍa yawmin fas'alil-'aaaddeen.

قَالُوْا لَبِثْنَا يَوْمًا اَوْ بَعْضَ يَوْمٍ فَسْئَلِ الْعَآدِّيْنَ ﴿١١٣﴾

114. He (Allah) will say, "You indeed remained there for a short time, were you to have proper knowledge about it.

114. Qaala il-labis̲tum illaa qaleelal-law annakum kuntum ta'lamoon.

قٰلَ اِنْ لَّبِثْتُمْ اِلَّا قَلِيْلًا لَّوْ اَنَّكُمْ كُنْتُمْ تَعْلَمُوْنَ ﴿١١٤﴾

115. Did you think that We had created you for a playful purpose and that you were not to return to Us?"

116. Allah is the most exalted King and the Supreme Truth. He is the only Ilah (one deserving to be worshipped) and the Lord of the Gracious Throne.

117. One who worships things besides Allah has no proof of the authority of such things. His Lord is certainly keeping the record of his deeds. The unbelievers will not have everlasting happiness.

118. (Muhammad), say, "Lord, forgive me and grant me mercy; You are the best of the merciful ones.

Al-Nur, The Light (24)

In the Name of Allah, the Beneficent, the Merciful.

1. This is a chapter which We have revealed to you and made obligatory for you to follow its guidance. We have revealed clear verses in it so that perhaps you may take heed.

2. Flog the fornicating woman and the fornicator with a hundred lashes each. Do not be reluctant (sympathetic) in enforcing the laws of Allah, if you have faith in Allah and the Day of Judgment. It (punishment) must be executed in the presence (and by) a group of believers.

3. No one should marry a fornicator except a fornicating man or a pagan woman. No one should marry a fornicating woman except a fornicator or a pagan man. Such (marriage) is unlawful to the believers.

4. Those who accuse married women of committing adultery - but were not able to prove their accusation by producing four witnesses - must be flogged eighty lashes. Never accept their testimony thereafter; they are sinful,

115. Afaḥasibtum annamaa khalaqnaakum 'abasañw-wa annakum ilaynaa laa turja'oon.

116. Fata'aalal-laahul-Malikul-Ḥaqq; laaa ilaaha illaa Huwa Rabbul-'Arshil-Kareem.

117. Wa mañy-yad'u ma'allaahi ilaahan aakhara laa-burhaana lahoo bihee fa-innamaa ḥisaabuhoo 'inda Rabbih; innahoo laa yufliḥul-kaafiroon.

118. Wa qur-Rabbigh-fir warḥam wa Anta khayrur-raaḥimeen.

Sûrat an-Nûr-24

(Revealed at Madinah)

Bismillaahir Raḥmaanir Raḥeem

1. Sooratun anzalnaahaa wa faraḍnaahaa wa anzalnaa feehaaa Aayaatim-bayyinaatil-la'allakum taẕakkaroon.

2. Azzaaniyatu wazzaanee fajlidoo kulla waaḥidim-minhumaa mi'ata jaldatiñw-wa laa ta-khuẕkum bihimaa ra-fatun fee deenil-laahi in kuntum tu'minoona billaahi wal-Yawmil-Aakhiri wal-yashhad 'aẕaabahumaa ṭaaa'ifatum-minal-mu'mineen.

3. Azzaanee laa yankiḥu illaa zaaniyatan aw mushrikatañw-wazzaaniyatu laa yankiḥuhaaa illaa zaanin aw mushrik; wa ḥurrima ẕaalika 'alal-mu'mineen.

4. Wallaẕeena yarmoonal-muḥṣanaati s̱umma lam ya-too bi-arba'ati shuhadaaa'a fajlidoohum s̱amaaneena jaldatañw-wa laa taqbaloo lahum shahaadatan abadaa; wa ulaaa'ika humul-faasiqoon.

أَفَحَسِبْتُمْ أَنَّمَا خَلَقْنَٰكُمْ عَبَثًا
وَأَنَّكُمْ إِلَيْنَا لَا تُرْجَعُونَ ﴿١١٥﴾
فَتَعَٰلَى ٱللَّهُ ٱلْمَلِكُ ٱلْحَقُّ لَآ إِلَٰهَ إِلَّا
هُوَ رَبُّ ٱلْعَرْشِ ٱلْكَرِيمِ ﴿١١٦﴾
وَمَن يَدْعُ مَعَ ٱللَّهِ إِلَٰهًا ءَاخَرَ لَا
بُرْهَٰنَ لَهُۥ بِهِۦ فَإِنَّمَا حِسَابُهُۥ عِندَ
رَبِّهِۦٓ إِنَّهُۥ لَا يُفْلِحُ ٱلْكَٰفِرُونَ ﴿١١٧﴾
وَقُل رَّبِّ ٱغْفِرْ وَٱرْحَمْ وَأَنتَ
خَيْرُ ٱلرَّٰحِمِينَ ﴿١١٨﴾ ع

(٢٤) سُورَةُ ٱلنُّورِ مَدَنِيَّةٌ (١٠٢)

آياتها ٦٤ بِسْمِ ٱللَّهِ ٱلرَّحْمَٰنِ ٱلرَّحِيمِ ركوعاتها ٩

سُورَةٌ أَنزَلْنَٰهَا وَفَرَضْنَٰهَا وَأَنزَلْنَا
فِيهَآ ءَايَٰتٍۭ بَيِّنَٰتٍ لَّعَلَّكُمْ تَذَكَّرُونَ ﴿١﴾
ٱلزَّانِيَةُ وَٱلزَّانِى فَٱجْلِدُوا۟ كُلَّ وَٰحِدٍ
مِّنْهُمَا مِا۟ئَةَ جَلْدَةٍ وَلَا تَأْخُذْكُم
بِهِمَا رَأْفَةٌ فِى دِينِ ٱللَّهِ إِن كُنتُمْ
تُؤْمِنُونَ بِٱللَّهِ وَٱلْيَوْمِ ٱلْءَاخِرِ وَلْيَشْهَدْ
عَذَابَهُمَا طَآئِفَةٌ مِّنَ ٱلْمُؤْمِنِينَ ﴿٢﴾
ٱلزَّانِى لَا يَنكِحُ إِلَّا زَانِيَةً أَوْ مُشْرِكَةً
وَٱلزَّانِيَةُ لَا يَنكِحُهَآ إِلَّا زَانٍ
أَوْ مُشْرِكٌ وَحُرِّمَ ذَٰلِكَ عَلَى
ٱلْمُؤْمِنِينَ ﴿٣﴾
وَٱلَّذِينَ يَرْمُونَ ٱلْمُحْصَنَٰتِ ثُمَّ لَمْ
يَأْتُوا۟ بِأَرْبَعَةِ شُهَدَآءَ فَٱجْلِدُوهُمْ
ثَمَٰنِينَ جَلْدَةً وَلَا تَقْبَلُوا۟ لَهُمْ شَهَٰدَةً
أَبَدًا وَأُو۟لَٰٓئِكَ هُمُ ٱلْفَٰسِقُونَ ﴿٤﴾

5. except that of those who afterwards repent and reform themselves; Allah is All-forgiving and All-merciful.

5. Illal-la<u>z</u>eena taaboo mim ba‘di <u>z</u>aalika wa aṣlaḥoo fa-innal-laaha Ghafoorur Raḥeem.

إِلَّا الَّذِينَ تَابُوا مِنْ بَعْدِ ذَٰلِكَ
وَأَصْلَحُوا فَإِنَّ اللَّهَ غَفُورٌ رَحِيمٌ ﴿٥﴾

6. Those who accuse their spouses of committing adultery but had no witness except themselves, should testify four times saying, "Allah is my witness that I am telling the truth."

6. Walla<u>z</u>eena yarmoona azwaajahum wa lam yakul-lahum shuhadaaa'u illaaa anfusuhum fashahaadatu aḥadihim arba‘u shahaadaatim billaahi innahoo laminaṣ-ṣaadiqeen.

وَالَّذِينَ يَرْمُونَ أَزْوَاجَهُمْ وَلَمْ
يَكُنْ لَهُمْ شُهَدَاءُ إِلَّا أَنْفُسُهُمْ
فَشَهَادَةُ أَحَدِهِمْ أَرْبَعُ شَهَادَاتٍ
بِاللَّهِ إِنَّهُ لَمِنَ الصَّادِقِينَ ﴿٦﴾

7. They should say on the fifth time, "Let Allah's curse be upon me if I am a liar."

7. Wal-khaamisatu anna la‘natal-laahi ‘alayhi in kaana minal-kaa<u>z</u>ibeen.

وَالْخَامِسَةُ أَنَّ لَعْنَتَ اللَّهِ عَلَيْهِ
إِنْ كَانَ مِنَ الْكَاذِبِينَ ﴿٧﴾

8. The spouse will be acquitted of the punishment if she challenges his testimony by saying four times, "Allah is my witness that he is a liar."

8. Wa yadra'u ‘anhal-‘a<u>z</u>aaba an tashhada arba‘a shahaadaatim billaahi innahoo laminal-kaa<u>z</u>ibeen.

وَيَدْرَؤُا عَنْهَا الْعَذَابَ أَنْ تَشْهَدَ
أَرْبَعَ شَهَادَاتٍ بِاللَّهِ إِنَّهُ لَمِنَ
الْكَاذِبِينَ ﴿٨﴾

9. On the fifth time she must say, "Let the curse of Allah be upon me if what he says is true."

9. Wal-khaamisata anna ghaḍabal-laahi ‘alayhaaa in kaana minaṣ-ṣaadiqeen.

وَالْخَامِسَةَ أَنَّ غَضَبَ اللَّهِ عَلَيْهَا
إِنْ كَانَ مِنَ الصَّادِقِينَ ﴿٩﴾

10. Had it not been for Allah's favors and mercy upon you (your life would have been in chaos). Allah accepts repentance and He is All-wise.

10. Wa law laa faḍlul-laahi ‘alaykum wa raḥmatuhoo wa annal-laaha Tawwaabun Ḥakeem.

وَلَوْلَا فَضْلُ اللَّهِ عَلَيْكُمْ وَرَحْمَتُهُ
وَأَنَّ اللَّهَ تَوَّابٌ حَكِيمٌ ﴿١٠﴾ ع ١٠/٧

11. Those who brought forward the false report (against Aishah, or Mary, the Coptic) were of a certain party amongst you. You must not think it will harm you. Rather, it will benefit you. Each one of you will face the result of his sin. The one among the group who was the chief instigator will face a great torment.

11. Innal-la<u>z</u>eena jaaa'oo bil-ifki ‘uṣbatum-minkum; laa taḥsaboohu sharral-lakum bal huwa khayrul-lakum; likul-limri'im-minhum-mak-tasaba minal-i<u>s</u>m; walla<u>z</u>ee tawallaa-kibrahoo minhum lahoo ‘a<u>z</u>aabun ‘aẓeem.

إِنَّ الَّذِينَ جَاءُو بِالْإِفْكِ عُصْبَةٌ
مِنْكُمْ لَا تَحْسَبُوهُ شَرًّا لَكُمْ بَلْ هُوَ
خَيْرٌ لَكُمْ لِكُلِّ امْرِئٍ مِنْهُمْ مَا
اكْتَسَبَ مِنَ الْإِثْمِ وَالَّذِي تَوَلَّىٰ
كِبْرَهُ مِنْهُمْ لَهُ عَذَابٌ عَظِيمٌ ﴿١١﴾

12. Would that on your hearing this report, the believing men and woman among you had a favorable attitude toward it, and said, "This report is clearly false."

12. Law laaa i<u>z</u> sami‘tumoohu ẓannal-mu'minoona walmu-'minaatu bi-anfusihim khay-rañw-wa qaaloo haa<u>z</u>aaa ifkum-mubeen.

لَوْلَا إِذْ سَمِعْتُمُوهُ ظَنَّ الْمُؤْمِنُونَ
وَالْمُؤْمِنَاتُ بِأَنْفُسِهِمْ خَيْرًا وَقَالُوا
هَٰذَا إِفْكٌ مُبِينٌ ﴿١٢﴾

13. Would that they had brought four witness to testify to their report. Since they brought none, they are liars before Allah.

13. Law laa jaaa'oo ‘alayhi bi-arba‘ati shuhadaaa'; fa-i<u>z</u> lam ya-too bishshuhadaaa'i fa-ulaaa'ika ‘indal-laahi humul-kaa<u>z</u>iboon.

لَوْلَا جَاءُو عَلَيْهِ بِأَرْبَعَةِ شُهَدَاءَ
فَإِذْ لَمْ يَأْتُوا بِالشُّهَدَاءِ فَأُولَٰئِكَ
عِنْدَ اللَّهِ هُمُ الْكَاذِبُونَ ﴿١٣﴾

14. Were it not for the favors and mercy of Allah upon you, in this world and in the life to come, a great torment would strike you for your involvement in this false report.

14. Wa law laa faḍlul-laahi 'alaykum wa raḥmatuhoo fiddunyaa wal-Aakhirati lamassakum fee maaa-afaḍtum feehi 'az̲aabun 'aẓeem.

وَلَوْلَا فَضْلُ اللّٰهِ عَلَيْكُمْ وَرَحْمَتُهٗ
فِي الدُّنْيَا وَالْاٰخِرَةِ لَمَسَّكُمْ فِيْ مَاۤ
اَفَضْتُمْ فِيْهِ عَذَابٌ عَظِيْمٌ ﴿١٤﴾

15. Your tongues moved and your mouths spoke of something of which you had no knowledge. You thought it to be a trivial matter, while in the eyes of Allah it is blasphemy.

15. Iz̲ talaqqawnahoo bi-alsinatikum wa taqooloona bi-afwaahikum-maa laysa lakum bihee 'ilmuñw-wa taḥsaboo-nahoo hayyinañw-wa huwa 'indal-laahi 'aẓeem.

اِذْ تَلَقَّوْنَهٗ بِاَلْسِنَتِكُمْ وَتَقُوْلُوْنَ
بِاَفْوَاهِكُمْ مَّا لَيْسَ لَكُمْ بِهٖ عِلْمٌ
وَّتَحْسَبُوْنَهٗ هَيِّنًا ۖ وَّهُوَ عِنْدَ
اللّٰهِ عَظِيْمٌ ﴿١٥﴾

16. Would that on hearing this report, you had said, "We have nothing to say about it. Allah forbid! It is a serious accusation."

16. Wa law laaa iz̲ sami'tu-moohu qultum-maa yakoonu lanaaa an-natakallama bihaaz̲aa Subḥaanaka haaz̲aa buhtaanun 'aẓeem.

وَلَوْلَاۤ اِذْ سَمِعْتُمُوْهُ قُلْتُمْ مَّا يَكُوْنُ
لَنَاۤ اَنْ نَّتَكَلَّمَ بِهٰذَا ۖ سُبْحٰنَكَ
هٰذَا بُهْتَانٌ عَظِيْمٌ ﴿١٦﴾

17. Allah advises you never to do such things again if you have any faith.

17. Ya'iẓukumul-laahu an ta'oodoo limis̲liheee abadan in kuntum-mu'mineen.

يَعِظُكُمُ اللّٰهُ اَنْ تَعُوْدُوْا لِمِثْلِهٖۤ اَبَدًا
اِنْ كُنْتُمْ مُّؤْمِنِيْنَ ﴿١٧﴾

18. Allah explains to you His revelations. Allah is All-knowing and All-wise.

18. Wa yubayyinul-laahu lakumul-Aayaat; wallaahu 'Aleemun Ḥakeem.

وَيُبَيِّنُ اللّٰهُ لَكُمُ الْاٰيٰتِ ۗ وَاللّٰهُ
عَلِيْمٌ حَكِيْمٌ ﴿١٨﴾

19. Those who like to publicize indecency among the believers will face painful torment in this world and in the life to come. Allah knows what you do not know.

19. Innal-laz̲eena yuḥibboona an tashee'al-faaḥishatu fil-laz̲eena aamanoo lahum 'az̲aabun aleemun fid-dunyaa wal-Aakhirah; wallaahu ya'la-mu wa antum laa ta'lamoon.

اِنَّ الَّذِيْنَ يُحِبُّوْنَ اَنْ تَشِيْعَ الْفَاحِشَةُ
فِي الَّذِيْنَ اٰمَنُوْا لَهُمْ عَذَابٌ اَلِيْمٌ ۙ
فِي الدُّنْيَا وَالْاٰخِرَةِ ۗ وَاللّٰهُ يَعْلَمُ
وَاَنْتُمْ لَا تَعْلَمُوْنَ ﴿١٩﴾

20. Were it not for the favor and mercy of Allah upon you (you would face painful punishment in this world and the life to come). Allah is Compassionate and Merciful.

20. Wa law laa faḍlul-laahi 'alaykum wa raḥmatuhoo wa annal-laaha Ra'oofur-Raḥeem.

وَلَوْلَا فَضْلُ اللّٰهِ عَلَيْكُمْ وَرَحْمَتُهٗ
وَاَنَّ اللّٰهَ رَءُوْفٌ رَّحِيْمٌ ﴿٢٠﴾ ع ٢ ٨

21. Believers, do not follow the footsteps of Satan; whoever does so will be made by Satan to commit indecency and sin. Were it not for the favor and mercy of Allah, none of you would ever have been purified. Allah purifies whomever He wants. Allah is All-hearing and All-knowing.

21. Yaaa ayyuhal-laz̲eena aamanoo laa tattabi'oo khuṭuwaatish-Shayṭaan; wa mañy-yattabi' khuṭuwaatish-Shayṭaani fa-innahoo ya-muru bilfaḥshaaa'i walmunkar; wa law laa faḍlul-laahi 'alaykum wa raḥmatuhoo maa zakaa minkum-min aḥadin abadañw-wa laakinnal-laaha yuzakkee mañy-yashaaa';

يٰۤاَيُّهَا الَّذِيْنَ اٰمَنُوْا لَا تَتَّبِعُوْا خُطُوٰتِ
الشَّيْطٰنِ ۗ وَمَنْ يَّتَّبِعْ خُطُوٰتِ
الشَّيْطٰنِ فَاِنَّهٗ يَاْمُرُ بِالْفَحْشَآءِ
وَالْمُنْكَرِ ۗ وَلَوْلَا فَضْلُ اللّٰهِ عَلَيْكُمْ
وَرَحْمَتُهٗ مَا زَكٰى مِنْكُمْ مِّنْ اَحَدٍ
اَبَدًا ۙ وَّلٰكِنَّ اللّٰهَ يُزَكِّيْ مَنْ يَّشَآءُ ۗ

wallaahu Samee'un 'Aleem.

وَاللّٰهُ سَمِيْعٌ عَلِيْمٌ ﴿٢١﴾

22. The well-to-do and the rich among you should not fail to give to relatives, the destitute, and Emigrants for the cause of Allah. Be considerate and forgiving. Do you not want Allah to forgive you? Allah is All-forgiving and All-merciful.

22. Wa laa ya-tali ulul-faḍli minkum wassa'ati añy-yu-tooo ulil-qurbaa walmasaakeena walmuhaajireena fee sabeelillaahi walya'foo walyaṣfaḥooo; alaa tuḥibboona añy-yaghfiral-laahu lakum; wallaahu Ghafoorur-Raḥeem.

وَلَا يَأْتَلِ اُولُوا الْفَضْلِ مِنْكُمْ
وَالسَّعَةِ اَنْ يُّؤْتُوْٓا اُولِي الْقُرْبٰى
وَالْمَسٰكِيْنَ وَالْمُهٰجِرِيْنَ فِيْ سَبِيْلِ
اللّٰهِ ۖ وَلْيَعْفُوْا وَلْيَصْفَحُوْا ۭ اَلَا
تُحِبُّوْنَ اَنْ يَّغْفِرَ اللّٰهُ لَكُمْ ۭ وَاللّٰهُ
غَفُوْرٌ رَّحِيْمٌ ﴿٢٢﴾

23. Those who slander the unaware but chaste and believing women (of committing unlawful carnal relations) are condemned in this life and in the life hereafter. They will suffer a great punishment

23. Innal-lazeena yarmoonal-muḥṣanaatil-ghaafilaatil-mu'minaati lu'inoo fid-dunyaa wal-Aakhirati wa lahum 'azaabun 'aẓeem.

اِنَّ الَّذِيْنَ يَرْمُوْنَ الْمُحْصَنٰتِ
الْغٰفِلٰتِ الْمُؤْمِنٰتِ لُعِنُوْا فِي الدُّنْيَا
وَالْاٰخِرَةِ ۠ وَلَهُمْ عَذَابٌ عَظِيْمٌ ﴿٢٣﴾

24. on the day when their tongues, hands, and feet will testify to what they had done.

24. Yawma tashhadu 'alayhim alsinatuhum wa aydeehim wa arjuluhum bimaa kaanoo ya'maloon.

يَّوْمَ تَشْهَدُ عَلَيْهِمْ اَلْسِنَتُهُمْ
وَاَيْدِيْهِمْ وَاَرْجُلُهُمْ بِمَا كَانُوْا
يَعْمَلُوْنَ ﴿٢٤﴾

25. On that day Allah will give them due recompense and they will know that Allah is the Supreme Judge.

25. Yawma'iziñy-yuwaffeehimul-laahu deenahumul-ḥaqqa wa ya'lamoona annal-laaha Huwal-Ḥaqqul-Mubeen.

يَوْمَىِٕذٍ يُّوَفِّيْهِمُ اللّٰهُ دِيْنَهُمُ الْحَقَّ
وَيَعْلَمُوْنَ اَنَّ اللّٰهَ هُوَ الْحَقُّ الْمُبِيْنُ ﴿٢٥﴾

26. Indecent woman (in words and deeds) are for indecent men and indecent men are for indecent woman. Decent women are for decent men and decent men are for decent women. The decent people are innocent of what people allege. They will receive mercy and honorable sustenance.

26. Alkhabeesaatu lilkhabeeseena walkhabeesoona lilkhabeesaati waṭṭayyibaatu liṭṭayyibeena waṭṭayyiboona liṭṭayyibaat; ulaaa'ika mubarra'oona mimmaa yaqooloon; lahum-maghfiratuñw-wa rizqun kareem.

اَلْخَبِيْثٰتُ لِلْخَبِيْثِيْنَ وَالْخَبِيْثُوْنَ
لِلْخَبِيْثٰتِ ۚ وَالطَّيِّبٰتُ لِلطَّيِّبِيْنَ
وَالطَّيِّبُوْنَ لِلطَّيِّبٰتِ ۚ اُولٰۗىِٕكَ مُبَرَّءُوْنَ
مِمَّا يَقُوْلُوْنَ ۭ لَهُمْ مَّغْفِرَةٌ وَّرِزْقٌ
كَرِيْمٌ ﴿٢٦﴾ ع ٣ ٦ ٩

27. O believers, do not enter each other's houses until you have asked permission and have greeted the people therein. This is best for you so that perhaps you may remember (Allah's guidance).

27. Yaaa ayyuhal-lazeena aamanoo laa tadkhuloo buyootan ghayra buyootikum ḥattaa tasta-nisoo wa tusallimoo 'allaa ahlihaa; zaalikum khayrul-lakum la'allakum tazakkaroon.

يٰٓاَيُّهَا الَّذِيْنَ اٰمَنُوْا لَا تَدْخُلُوْا
بُيُوْتًا غَيْرَ بُيُوْتِكُمْ حَتّٰى تَسْتَاْنِسُوْا
وَتُسَلِّمُوْا عَلٰٓي اَهْلِهَا ۭ ذٰلِكُمْ خَيْرٌ
لَّكُمْ لَعَلَّكُمْ تَذَكَّرُوْنَ ﴿٢٧﴾

28. If you did not find anyone therein, do not enter until you are given permission. If you are told to go away, do so; this is more

28. Fa-il-lam tajidoo feehaaa aḥadan falaa tadkhuloohaa ḥattaa yu'zana lakum wa in

فَاِنْ لَّمْ تَجِدُوْا فِيْهَآ اَحَدًا فَلَا
تَدْخُلُوْهَا حَتّٰى يُؤْذَنَ لَكُمْ ۚ وَاِنْ

decent of you. Allah knows all that you do.

qeela lakumurji‘oo farji‘oo huwa azkaa lakum; wallaahu bimaa ta‘maloona ‘Aleem.

قِيْلَ لَكُمُ ارْجِعُوْا فَارْجِعُوْا هُوَ اَزْكٰى
لَكُمْ ۭ وَاللّٰهُ بِمَا تَعْمَلُوْنَ عَلِيْمٌ ۝٢٨

29. There is no harm for you to enter non-dwelling houses (public places) where you have some goods. Allah knows whatever you reveal or hide.

29. Laysa ‘alaykum junaaḥun an tadkhuloo buyootan ghayra maskoonatin feehaa mataa‘ul-lakum; wallaahu ya‘lamu maa tubdoona wa maa taktumoon.

لَيْسَ عَلَيْكُمْ جُنَاحٌ اَنْ تَدْخُلُوْا
بُيُوْتًا غَيْرَ مَسْكُوْنَةٍ فِيْهَا مَتَاعٌ
لَّكُمْ ۭ وَاللّٰهُ يَعْلَمُ مَا تُبْدُوْنَ وَمَا
تَكْتُمُوْنَ ۝٢٩

30. (Muhammad), tell the believing men to cast down their eyes and guard their carnal desires; this will make them more pure. Allah is certainly aware of what they do.

30. Qul lilmu’mineena yaghuḍḍoo min abṣaarihim wa yaḥfaẓoo furoojahum; ẕaalika azkaa lahum; innallaaha khabeerum bimaa yaṣna‘oon.

قُلْ لِّلْمُؤْمِنِيْنَ يَغُضُّوْا مِنْ اَبْصَارِهِمْ
وَيَحْفَظُوْا فُرُوْجَهُمْ ۭ ذٰلِكَ اَزْكٰى
لَهُمْ ۭ اِنَّ اللّٰهَ خَبِيْرٌۢ بِمَا يَصْنَعُوْنَ ۝٣٠

31. Tell the believing woman to cast down their eyes, guard their chastity, and not to show off their beauty except what is permitted by the law. Let them cover their breasts with their veils. They must not show off their beauty to anyone other than their husbands, fathers, father-in-laws, sons, step-sons, brothers, sons of brothers and sisters, women of their kind, their slaves, people of the household who were not of the age of carnal desires (being very young or very old). They must not stamp their feet to show off their hidden ornaments. All of you believers, turn to Allah in repentance so that perhaps you will have everlasting happiness.

31. Wa qul lilmu’minaati yaghḍuḍna min abṣaarihinna wa yaḥfaẓna furoojahunna wa laa yubdeena zeenatahunna illaa maa ẓahara minhaa walyaḍribna bikhumurihinna ‘alaa juyoobihinna wa laa yubdeena zeenatahunna illaa libu‘oolatihinna aw aabaaa’i-hinna aw aabaaa’i bu‘oolati-hinna aw abnaaa’ihinna aw abnaaa’i bu‘oolatihinna aw ikhwaanihinna aw baneee ikhwaanihinna aw baneee akhawaatihinna aw nisaaa’i-hinna aw maa malakat aymaanuhunna awit-taabi‘eena ghayri ulil-irbati minar-rijaali awiṭ-ṭiflillaẕeena lam yaẓharoo ‘alaa ‘awraatin-nisaaa’i wa laa yaḍribna bi-arjulihinna liyu‘lama maa yukhfeena min zeenatihinn; wa tooboo ilallaahi jamee‘an ayyuhal mu’minoona la‘allakum tufliḥoon.

وَقُلْ لِّلْمُؤْمِنٰتِ يَغْضُضْنَ مِنْ
اَبْصَارِهِنَّ وَيَحْفَظْنَ فُرُوْجَهُنَّ
وَلَا يُبْدِيْنَ زِيْنَتَهُنَّ اِلَّا مَا ظَهَرَ
مِنْهَا وَلْيَضْرِبْنَ بِخُمُرِهِنَّ عَلٰي
جُيُوْبِهِنَّ ۠ وَلَا يُبْدِيْنَ زِيْنَتَهُنَّ
اِلَّا لِبُعُوْلَتِهِنَّ اَوْ اٰبَاۗىِٕهِنَّ اَوْ
اٰبَاۗءِ بُعُوْلَتِهِنَّ اَوْ اَبْنَاۗىِٕهِنَّ اَوْ اَبْنَاۗءِ
بُعُوْلَتِهِنَّ اَوْ اِخْوَانِهِنَّ اَوْ بَنِيْٓ
اِخْوَانِهِنَّ اَوْ بَنِيْٓ اَخَوٰتِهِنَّ اَوْ
نِسَاۗىِٕهِنَّ اَوْ مَا مَلَكَتْ اَيْمَانُهُنَّ
اَوِ التّٰبِعِيْنَ غَيْرِ اُولِي الْاِرْبَةِ
مِنَ الرِّجَالِ اَوِ الطِّفْلِ الَّذِيْنَ لَمْ
يَظْهَرُوْا عَلٰي عَوْرٰتِ النِّسَاۗءِ ۠ وَلَا
يَضْرِبْنَ بِاَرْجُلِهِنَّ لِيُعْلَمَ مَا يُخْفِيْنَ
مِنْ زِيْنَتِهِنَّ ۭ وَتُوْبُوْٓا اِلَى اللّٰهِ
جَمِيْعًا اَيُّهَ الْمُؤْمِنُوْنَ لَعَلَّكُمْ
تُفْلِحُوْنَ ۝٣١

32. Marry the single people among you and the righteous slaves and slave-girls. If you are poor, Allah will make you rich through His favor; He is Bountiful and All-knowing.

32. Wa ankiḥul-ayaamaa minkum waṣ-ṣaaliḥeena min ‘ibaadikum wa imaa’ikum; iñy-yakoonoo fuqaraaa’a yughni-himul-laahu min faḍlih; wal-laahu Waasi‘un ‘Aleem.

وَأَنكِحُوا الْأَيَامَىٰ مِنكُمْ وَالصَّالِحِينَ
مِنْ عِبَادِكُمْ وَإِمَائِكُمْ ۚ إِن يَكُونُوا
فُقَرَاءَ يُغْنِهِمُ اللَّهُ مِن فَضْلِهِ ۗ
وَاللَّهُ وَاسِعٌ عَلِيمٌ ﴿٣٢﴾

33. Let those who cannot find someone to marry maintain chastity until Allah makes them rich through His favors. Let the slaves who want to buy their freedom have an agreement with you in writing if you find them to be virtuous. Give them money out of Allah's property which He has given to you. Do not force your girls into prostitution to make money even if they do not want to be chaste (get married). If they have been compelled to do so, Allah will be All-merciful and All-forgiving to them.

33. Wal-yasta‘fifil-lazeena laa yajidoona nikaaḥan ḥattaa yughniyahumul-laahu min faḍlih; wallazeena yabta-ghoonal-kitaaba mimmaa malakat aymaanukum fakaati-boohum in ‘alimtum feehim khayrañw-wa aatoohum-mim-maalil-laahil-lazeee aataakum; wa laa tukrihoo fatayaatikum ‘alal-bighaaa’i in aradna taḥaṣṣunal-litabtaghoo ‘araḍal-ḥayaatid-dunyaa; wa mañy-yukrihhunna fa-innal-laaha mim ba‘di ikraahihinna Ghafoorur-Raḥeem.

وَلْيَسْتَعْفِفِ الَّذِينَ لَا يَجِدُونَ
نِكَاحًا حَتَّىٰ يُغْنِيَهُمُ اللَّهُ مِن
فَضْلِهِ ۗ وَالَّذِينَ يَبْتَغُونَ الْكِتَابَ
مِمَّا مَلَكَتْ أَيْمَانُكُمْ فَكَاتِبُوهُمْ إِنْ
عَلِمْتُمْ فِيهِمْ خَيْرًا ۖ وَآتُوهُم مِّن
مَّالِ اللَّهِ الَّذِي آتَاكُمْ ۚ وَلَا تُكْرِهُوا
فَتَيَاتِكُمْ عَلَى الْبِغَاءِ إِنْ أَرَدْنَ تَحَصُّنًا
لِّتَبْتَغُوا عَرَضَ الْحَيَاةِ الدُّنْيَا ۚ وَمَن
يُكْرِههُّنَّ فَإِنَّ اللَّهَ مِن بَعْدِ
إِكْرَاهِهِنَّ غَفُورٌ رَّحِيمٌ ﴿٣٣﴾

34. We have revealed to you illustrious revelations, stories of the past generations, and good advice for the pious people.

34. Wa laqad anzalnaaa ilaykum Aayaatim-mubay-yinaatiñw-wa masalam-minal-lazeena khalaw min qablikum wa maw‘iẓatal-lilmuttaqeen.

وَلَقَدْ أَنزَلْنَا إِلَيْكُمْ آيَاتٍ مُّبَيِّنَاتٍ
وَمَثَلًا مِّنَ الَّذِينَ خَلَوْا مِن
قَبْلِكُمْ وَمَوْعِظَةً لِّلْمُتَّقِينَ ﴿٣٤﴾ ع ٤ / ١٠

35. Allah is the light of the heavens and the earth. A metaphor for His light is a niche in which there is a lamp placed in a glass. The glass is like a shining star which is lit from a blessed olive tree that is neither eastern nor western. Its oil almost lights up even though it has not been touched by the fire. It is light upon light. Allah guides to His light whomever He wants. Allah uses various metaphors. He has the knowledge of all things.

35. Allaahu noorus-samaa-waati wal-arḍ; masalu noorihee kamishkaatin feehaa miṣbaaḥ; almiṣbaaḥu fee zujaajatin azzujaajatu-ka-annahaa kawkabun durriyyuñy-yooqadu min shajaratim-mubaarakatin zaytoonatil-laa sharqiyyatiñw-wa laa gharbiyyatiñy-yakaadu zaytuhaa yuḍeee’u wa law lam tamsashu naar; noorun ‘alaa noor; yahdil-laahu linoorihee mañy-yashaaa’; wa yaḍribul-laahul-amsaala linnaas; wallaahu bikulli

اللَّهُ نُورُ السَّمَاوَاتِ وَالْأَرْضِ ۚ مَثَلُ
نُورِهِ كَمِشْكَاةٍ فِيهَا مِصْبَاحٌ ۖ
الْمِصْبَاحُ فِي زُجَاجَةٍ ۖ الزُّجَاجَةُ
كَأَنَّهَا كَوْكَبٌ دُرِّيٌّ يُوقَدُ مِن شَجَرَةٍ
مُّبَارَكَةٍ زَيْتُونَةٍ لَّا شَرْقِيَّةٍ وَلَا
غَرْبِيَّةٍ يَكَادُ زَيْتُهَا يُضِيءُ وَلَوْ لَمْ
تَمْسَسْهُ نَارٌ ۚ نُّورٌ عَلَىٰ نُورٍ ۗ يَهْدِي
اللَّهُ لِنُورِهِ مَن يَشَاءُ ۚ وَيَضْرِبُ
اللَّهُ الْأَمْثَالَ لِلنَّاسِ ۗ وَاللَّهُ بِكُلِّ

shay'in 'Aleem.

شَىْءٍ عَلِيْمٌ ۞

36. (This niche) is in the houses (of the prophets) that Allah has declared to be highly respected and His name is mentioned therein in glory in the morning and evening

36. Fee buyootin azinal-laahu an turfa'a wa yuzkara feehasmuhoo yusabbihu lahoo feehaa bilghuduwwi wal-aaṣaal.

فِىْ بُيُوتٍ اَذِنَ اللّٰهُ اَنْ تُرْفَعَ وَيُذْكَرَ فِيْهَا اسْمُهٗ ۙ يُسَبِّحُ لَهٗ فِيْهَا بِالْغُدُوِّ وَالْاٰصَالِ ۞

37. by people who can be diverted neither by merchandise nor bargaining from worshipping Allah, saying their prayers and paying religious tax. They do these things, for they are afraid of the day when all hearts and eyes will undergo terrible unrest and crisis.

37. Rijaalul-laa tulheehim tijaaratuñw-wa laa bay'un 'an zikril-laahi wa iqaamiṣ-Ṣalaati wa eetaaa'iz-Zakaati yakhaafoona Yawman tataqallabu feehil-quloobu wal-abṣaar.

رِجَالٌ ۙ لَّا تُلْهِيْهِمْ تِجَارَةٌ وَّلَا بَيْعٌ عَنْ ذِكْرِ اللّٰهِ وَاِقَامِ الصَّلٰوةِ وَاِيْتَاءِ الزَّكٰوةِ ۙ يَخَافُوْنَ يَوْمًا تَتَقَلَّبُ فِيْهِ الْقُلُوْبُ وَالْاَبْصَارُ ۞

38. (They worship Him) so that Allah will reward their best deeds and give them more through His favors. Allah gives sustenance to whomever He wants without account.

38. Liyajziyahumul-laahu aḥsana maa 'amiloo wa yazeedahum-min faḍlih; wallaahu yarzuqu mañy-yashaaa'u bighayri ḥisaab.

لِيَجْزِيَهُمُ اللّٰهُ اَحْسَنَ مَا عَمِلُوْا وَيَزِيْدَهُمْ مِّنْ فَضْلِهٖ ۗ وَاللّٰهُ يَرْزُقُ مَنْ يَّشَاءُ بِغَيْرِ حِسَابٍ ۞

39. The deeds of the unbelievers are like a mirage which a thirsty man thinks is water until he went near and found nothing. Instead he finds Allah who gives him his due recompense. Allah's reckoning is swift.

39. Wallazeena kafarooo a'maaluhum kasaraabim biqee'atiñy-yaḥsabuhuẓ-ẓamaanu maaa'an ḥattaaa izaa jaaa'ahoo lam yajidhu shay'-añw-wa wajadal-laaha 'indahoo fawaffaahu ḥisaabah; wallaahu saree'ul ḥisaab.

وَالَّذِيْنَ كَفَرُوْا اَعْمَالُهُمْ كَسَرَابٍ بِقِيْعَةٍ يَّحْسَبُهُ الظَّمْاٰنُ مَاءً ۗ حَتّٰى اِذَا جَاءَهٗ لَمْ يَجِدْهُ شَيْئًا وَّوَجَدَ اللّٰهَ عِنْدَهٗ فَوَفّٰىهُ حِسَابَهٗ ۗ وَاللّٰهُ سَرِيْعُ الْحِسَابِ ۞

40. Or they (the deeds of the unbelievers) are like the darkness of a deep, stormy sea with layers of giant waves, covered by dark clouds. It is darkness upon darkness whereby even if one stretches out his hands he could not see them. One can have no light unless Allah gave him light.

40. Aw kaẓulumaatin fee baḥril-lujjiyyiñy-yaghshaahu mawjum-min fawqihee mawjum-min fawqihee saḥaab; ẓulumaatum ba'ḍuhaa fawqa ba'ḍin izaaa akhraja yadahoo lam yakad yaraahaa wa mal-lam yaj'alil-laahu lahoo nooran famaa lahoo min-noor.

اَوْ كَظُلُمَاتٍ فِىْ بَحْرٍ لُّجِّيٍّ يَّغْشَاهُ مَوْجٌ مِّنْ فَوْقِهٖ مَوْجٌ مِّنْ فَوْقِهٖ سَحَابٌ ۗ ظُلُمَاتٌ بَعْضُهَا فَوْقَ بَعْضٍ ۗ اِذَا اَخْرَجَ يَدَهٗ لَمْ يَكَدْ يَرٰىهَا ۗ وَمَنْ لَّمْ يَجْعَلِ اللّٰهُ لَهٗ نُوْرًا فَمَا لَهٗ مِنْ نُّوْرٍ ۞

41. Did you not see that all that is between the heavens and the earth glorifies Allah and that the birds spread their wings in the air, having learned their prayer and Tasbih (Allah is free of all defects), glorify Allah? He knows everyone's prayers and praising; Allah has absolute knowledge of what they do.

41. Alam tara annal-laaha yusabbihu lahoo man fissamaawaati wal-arḍi waṭ-ṭayru ṣaaaffaatin kullun qad 'alima Ṣalaatahoo wa tasbeeḥah; wallaahu 'Aleemum bimaa yaf'aloon.

اَلَمْ تَرَ اَنَّ اللّٰهَ يُسَبِّحُ لَهٗ مَنْ فِى السَّمٰوٰتِ وَالْاَرْضِ وَالطَّيْرُ صٰٓفّٰتٍ ۗ كُلٌّ قَدْ عَلِمَ صَلَاتَهٗ وَتَسْبِيْحَهٗ ۗ وَاللّٰهُ عَلِيْمٌ بِمَا يَفْعَلُوْنَ ۞

42. To Allah belongs the kingdom of the heavens and the earth, and to Him do all things return.

42. Wa lillaahi mulkus-samaawaati wal-arḍ; wa ilallaahil-maṣeer.

وَلِلّٰهِ مُلْكُ السَّمٰوٰتِ وَالْاَرْضِ ۚ
وَاِلَى اللّٰهِ الْمَصِيْرُ ﴿٤٢﴾

43. Did you not see that Allah moves the clouds gently, brings them together, piles them up, and then you can see the rain coming from them? He sends down hailstones from the mountains in the sky. With them He strikes or protects from them whomever He wants. The lightening can almost take away sight.

43. Alam tara annal-laaha yuzjee saḥaaban summa yu'allifu baynahoo summa yaj'aluhoo rukaaman fataral-wadqa yakhruju min khilaalihee wa yunazzilu minas-samaaa'i min jibaalin feehaa mim baradin fa-yuṣeebu bihee mañy-yashaaa'u wa yaṣrifuhoo 'am-mañy-yashaaa'u yakaadu sanaa barqihee yazhabu bil-abṣaar.

اَلَمْ تَرَ اَنَّ اللّٰهَ يُزْجِيْ سَحَابًا ثُمَّ
يُؤَلِّفُ بَيْنَهٗ ثُمَّ يَجْعَلُهٗ رُكَامًا فَتَرَى
الْوَدْقَ يَخْرُجُ مِنْ خِلٰلِهٖ ۚ وَيُنَزِّلُ
مِنَ السَّمَآءِ مِنْ جِبَالٍ فِيْهَا مِنْۢ
بَرَدٍ فَيُصِيْبُ بِهٖ مَنْ يَّشَآءُ وَيَصْرِفُهٗ
عَنْ مَّنْ يَّشَآءُ ؕ يَكَادُ سَنَا بَرْقِهٖ
يَذْهَبُ بِالْاَبْصَارِ ؕ ﴿٤٣﴾

44. Allah alternates the night and the day. In this there is a lesson for the people of understanding.

44. Yuqallibul-laahul-layla wannahaar; inna fee zaalika la'ibratal-li-ulil-abṣaar.

يُقَلِّبُ اللّٰهُ الَّيْلَ وَالنَّهَارَ ؕ اِنَّ
فِيْ ذٰلِكَ لَعِبْرَةً لِّاُولِى الْاَبْصَارِ ﴿٤٤﴾

45. Allah has created every living being from water: Some of them creep on their bellies; some walk on two feet, and some of them walk on four legs. Allah creates whatever He wants. He has power over all things.

45. Wallaahu khalaqa kulla daaabbatim-mim-maaa'in faminhum-mañy-yamshee 'alaa baṭnihee wa minhum-mañy-yamshee 'alaa rijlayni wa minhum-mañy-yamshee 'alaaa arba'; yakhluqul-laahu maa yashaaa'; innal-laaha 'alaa kulli shay'in Qadeer.

وَاللّٰهُ خَلَقَ كُلَّ دَآبَّةٍ مِّنْ مَّآءٍ ۚ
فَمِنْهُمْ مَّنْ يَّمْشِيْ عَلٰى بَطْنِهٖ ۚ
وَمِنْهُمْ مَّنْ يَّمْشِيْ عَلٰى رِجْلَيْنِ ۚ
وَمِنْهُمْ مَّنْ يَّمْشِيْ عَلٰۤى اَرْبَعٍ ؕ يَخْلُقُ
اللّٰهُ مَا يَشَآءُ ؕ اِنَّ اللّٰهَ عَلٰى كُلِّ
شَيْءٍ قَدِيْرٌ ﴿٤٥﴾

46. We have revealed illustrious revelations. Allah guides to the right path whomever He wants.

46. Laqad anzalnaaa Aayaatim-mubayyinaat; wallaahu yahdee mañy-yashaaa'u ilaa Ṣiraaṭim-Mustaqeem.

لَقَدْ اَنْزَلْنَاۤ اٰيٰتٍ مُّبَيِّنٰتٍ ؕ وَاللّٰهُ
يَهْدِيْ مَنْ يَّشَآءُ اِلٰى صِرَاطٍ
مُّسْتَقِيْمٍ ﴿٤٦﴾

47. They say, "We have believed in Allah and the Messenger and we have obeyed them." Then a group of them turn away from their (belief). They are not believers.

47. Wa yaqooloona aamannaa billaahi wa bir-Rasooli wa aṭa'naa summa yatawallaa fareequm-minhum-mim ba'di zaalik; wa maaa ulaaa'ika bilmu'mineen.

وَيَقُوْلُوْنَ اٰمَنَّا بِاللّٰهِ وَبِالرَّسُوْلِ
وَاَطَعْنَا ثُمَّ يَتَوَلّٰى فَرِيْقٌ مِّنْهُمْ
مِّنْۢ بَعْدِ ذٰلِكَ ؕ وَمَاۤ اُولٰٓئِكَ
بِالْمُؤْمِنِيْنَ ﴿٤٧﴾

48. When they are called to Allah and His Messenger so that they will judge among them, suddenly, some of them turn away.

48. Wa izaa du'ooo ilal-laahi wa Rasoolihee li-yaḥkuma baynahum izaa fareequm-minhum-mu'riḍoon.

وَاِذَا دُعُوْۤا اِلَى اللّٰهِ وَرَسُوْلِهٖ لِيَحْكُمَ
بَيْنَهُمْ اِذَا فَرِيْقٌ مِّنْهُمْ مُّعْرِضُوْنَ ﴿٤٨﴾

49. If right were on their side, they would come quickly.

49. Wa iñy-yakul-lahumul ḥaqqu ya-tooo ilayhi muz-'ineen.

وَإِنْ يَكُنْ لَّهُمُ الْحَقُّ يَأْتُوا إِلَيْهِ مُذْعِنِينَ ۝

50. Are their hearts sick? Do they have doubts or are they afraid that Allah and His Messenger may do injustice to them? In fact, they, themselves, are unjust.

50. Afee quloobihim-ma-raḍun amirtaabooo am yakhaafoona añy-yaḥeefallaahu 'alayhim wa Rasooluh; bal ulaaa'ika humuẓ-ẓaalimoon.

أَفِي قُلُوبِهِمْ مَرَضٌ أَمِ ارْتَابُوا أَمْ يَخَافُونَ أَنْ يَحِيفَ اللّٰهُ عَلَيْهِمْ وَرَسُولُهُ ۚ بَلْ أُولٰئِكَ هُمُ الظّٰلِمُونَ ۝

51. When the believers are called to Allah and His Messenger to be judged, their only words are, "We have listened and obeyed." They will have everlasting happiness.

51. Innamaa kaana qawlal-mu'mineena iẓaa du'ooo ilal-laahi wa Rasoolihee li-yaḥkuma baynahum añy-yaqooloo sami'naa wa ata'naa; wa ulaaa'ika humul-mufliḥoon.

إِنَّمَا كَانَ قَوْلَ الْمُؤْمِنِينَ إِذَا دُعُوا إِلَى اللّٰهِ وَرَسُولِهِ لِيَحْكُمَ بَيْنَهُمْ أَنْ يَقُولُوا سَمِعْنَا وَأَطَعْنَا ۚ وَأُولٰئِكَ هُمُ الْمُفْلِحُونَ ۝

52. Those who obey Allah and His Messenger, who are humble before Allah, and who have fear of Him will, certainly, be successful.

52. Wa mañy-yuṭi'il-laaha wa Rasoolahoo wa yakhshal-laaha wa yattaqhi fa-ulaaa'ika humul-faaa'izoon.

وَمَنْ يُطِعِ اللّٰهَ وَرَسُولَهُ وَيَخْشَ اللّٰهَ وَيَتَّقْهِ فَأُولٰئِكَ هُمُ الْفَائِزُونَ ۝

53. They strongly swear by Allah that they would march to fight (for the cause of Allah) if you were to order them to. Tell them, "You do not need to swear; fighting for the cause of Allah is a virtuous deed and Allah is Well-aware of what you do."

53. Wa aqsamoo billaahi jahda aymaanihim la-'in amartahum la-yakhrujunna qul laa tuqsimoo ṭaa'atum-ma'roofah; innal-laaha khabee-rum bimaa ta'maloon.

وَأَقْسَمُوا بِاللّٰهِ جَهْدَ أَيْمَانِهِمْ لَئِنْ أَمَرْتَهُمْ لَيَخْرُجُنَّ ۖ قُلْ لَّا تُقْسِمُوا ۖ طَاعَةٌ مَّعْرُوفَةٌ ۚ إِنَّ اللّٰهَ خَبِيرٌ بِمَا تَعْمَلُونَ ۝

54. Say to them, "Obey Allah and His Messenger. If you turn away, they are responsible for their own obligations. If you follow the Messenger, you will have the right guidance. The responsibility of the Messenger is only to preach clearly."

54. Qul aṭee'ul-laaha wa aṭee'ur-Rasoola fa-in tawallaw fa-innamaa 'alayhi maa ḥummila wa 'alaykum-maa ḥummiltum wa in tuṭee'oohu tahtadoo; wa maa 'alar-Rasooli illal-balaaghul-mubeen.

قُلْ أَطِيعُوا اللّٰهَ وَأَطِيعُوا الرَّسُولَ ۖ فَإِنْ تَوَلَّوْا فَإِنَّمَا عَلَيْهِ مَا حُمِّلَ وَعَلَيْكُمْ مَّا حُمِّلْتُمْ ۖ وَإِنْ تُطِيعُوهُ تَهْتَدُوا ۚ وَمَا عَلَى الرَّسُولِ إِلَّا الْبَلَاغُ الْمُبِينُ ۝

55. Allah has promised the righteously striving believers to appoint them as His deputies on earth, as He had appointed those who lived before. He will make the religion that He has chosen for them to stand supreme. He will replace their fear with peace and security so that they will worship Allah alone and consider no one equal to Him. Whoever becomes

55. Wa'adal-laahul-lazeena aamanoo minkum wa 'amiluṣ-ṣaaliḥaati la-yastakhlifan-nahum fil-arḍi kamastakh-lafal-lazeena min qablihim wa la-yumakkinanna lahum deenahumul-lazir taḍaa lahum wa la-yubaddilannahum-mim ba'di khawfihim amnaa; ya'budoonanee laa

وَعَدَ اللّٰهُ الَّذِينَ آمَنُوا مِنْكُمْ وَعَمِلُوا الصّٰلِحَاتِ لَيَسْتَخْلِفَنَّهُمْ فِي الْأَرْضِ كَمَا اسْتَخْلَفَ الَّذِينَ مِنْ قَبْلِهِمْ وَلَيُمَكِّنَنَّ لَهُمْ دِينَهُمُ الَّذِي ارْتَضَى لَهُمْ وَلَيُبَدِّلَنَّهُمْ مِّنْ بَعْدِ خَوْفِهِمْ أَمْنًا ۚ يَعْبُدُونَنِي لَا

an unbeliever after this will be a sinful person.

56. Be steadfast in prayer, pay the religious tax, and obey the Messenger so that perhaps you will receive mercy.

57. The unbelievers should not think that they can defeat (Allah) on earth. Their dwelling will be hell, the most terrible abode.

58. Believers, your slaves and the immature people are required to ask your permission three times a day before entering your house: before the morning prayer, at noon time, and after the late evening prayer; these are most private times. After your permission has been granted, there is no harm if they come into your presence from time to time. This is how Allah explains His revelations to you. Allah is All-knowing and All-wise.

59. When your children become mature, they must ask your permission before entering your house, as the rest of the mature people do. Thus does Allah explain to you His revelations. Allah is All-knowing and All-wise.

60. Elderly women who have no hope of getting married are allowed not to wear the kind of clothing that young woman must wear, as long as they do not show off their beauty. It is better for them to maintain chastity. Allah is All-hearing and All-knowing.

yushrikoona bee shay'aa; wa man kafara ba'da zaalika fa-ulaaa'ika humul-faasiqoon.

56. Wa aqeemuṣ-Ṣalaata wa aatuz-Zakaata wa aṭee'ur-Rasoola la'allakum turḥamoon.

57. Laa taḥsabannal-lazeena kafaroo mu'jizeena fil-arḍ; wa ma-waahumun-Naaru wa la-bi'sal-maṣeer.

58. Yaaa ayyuhal-lazeena aamanoo li-yasta-zinkumul-lazeena malakat aymaanukum wallazeena lam yablughul-ḥuluma minkum salaasa marraat; min qabli Ṣalaatil-Fajri wa ḥeena taḍa'oona siyaa-bakum-minaz-zaheerati wa mim-ba'di Ṣalaatil-'Ishaaa'; salaasu 'awraatil-lakum; laysa 'alaykum wa laa 'alayhim junaaḥum ba'dahunn; ṭawwaa-foona 'alaykum ba'ḍukum 'alaa ba'ḍ; kazaalika yubayyinul-laahu lakumul-Aaayaati wallaahu 'Aleemun Ḥakeem.

59. Wa izaa balaghal-aṭfaalu minkumul-ḥuluma fal-yasta-zinoo kamas-ta-zanallazeena min qablihim; kazaalika yubay-yinul-laahu lakum Aayaatih; wallaahu 'Aleemun Ḥakeem.

60. Walqawaa'idu minan-nisaaa'il-laatee laa yarjoona nikaaḥan falaysa 'alayhinna junaaḥun añy-yaḍa'na siyaa-bahunna ghayra mutabar-rijaatim bizeenah; wa añy-yasta'fifna khayrul-lahunn; wallaahu Samee'un 'Aleem.

يُشْرِكُوْنَ بِيْ شَيْـئًا ۗ وَمَنْ كَفَرَ بَعْدَ ذٰلِكَ فَاُولٰٓئِكَ هُمُ الْفٰسِقُوْنَ ۝

وَاَقِيْمُوا الصَّلٰوةَ وَاٰتُوا الزَّكٰوةَ وَاَطِيْعُوا الرَّسُوْلَ لَعَلَّكُمْ تُرْحَمُوْنَ ۝

لَا تَحْسَبَنَّ الَّذِيْنَ كَفَرُوْا مُعْجِزِيْنَ فِى الْاَرْضِ ۚ وَمَاْوٰىهُمُ النَّارُ ۗ وَلَبِئْسَ الْمَصِيْرُ ۝

يٰٓاَيُّهَا الَّذِيْنَ اٰمَنُوا لِيَسْتَاْذِنْكُمُ الَّذِيْنَ مَلَكَتْ اَيْمَانُكُمْ وَالَّذِيْنَ لَمْ يَبْلُغُوا الْحُلُمَ مِنْكُمْ ثَلٰثَ مَرّٰتٍ ۗ مِنْ قَبْلِ صَلٰوةِ الْفَجْرِ وَحِيْنَ تَضَعُوْنَ ثِيَابَكُمْ مِّنَ الظَّهِيْرَةِ وَمِنْ بَعْدِ صَلٰوةِ الْعِشَاۤءِ ۗ ثَلٰثُ عَوْرٰتٍ لَّكُمْ ۗ لَيْسَ عَلَيْكُمْ وَلَا عَلَيْهِمْ جُنَاحٌ بَعْدَهُنَّ ۗ طَوّٰفُوْنَ عَلَيْكُمْ بَعْضُكُمْ عَلٰى بَعْضٍ ۗ كَذٰلِكَ يُبَيِّنُ اللّٰهُ لَكُمُ الْاٰيٰتِ ۗ وَاللّٰهُ عَلِيْمٌ حَكِيْمٌ ۝

وَاِذَا بَلَغَ الْاَطْفَالُ مِنْكُمُ الْحُلُمَ فَلْيَسْتَاْذِنُوْا كَمَا اسْتَاْذَنَ الَّذِيْنَ مِنْ قَبْلِهِمْ ۗ كَذٰلِكَ يُبَيِّنُ اللّٰهُ لَكُمْ اٰيٰتِهٖ ۗ وَاللّٰهُ عَلِيْمٌ حَكِيْمٌ ۝

وَالْقَوَاعِدُ مِنَ النِّسَاۤءِ الّٰتِيْ لَا يَرْجُوْنَ نِكَاحًا فَلَيْسَ عَلَيْهِنَّ جُنَاحٌ اَنْ يَّضَعْنَ ثِيَابَهُنَّ غَيْرَ مُتَبَرِّجٰتٍ بِزِيْنَةٍ ۗ وَاَنْ يَّسْتَعْفِفْنَ خَيْرٌ لَّهُنَّ ۗ وَاللّٰهُ سَمِيْعٌ عَلِيْمٌ ۝

61. It is not a sin (not to segregate the table) for the blind, the lame, the sick ones, and yourselves to eat at your own homes, or the homes of your father, mothers, brothers, sisters, your paternal and maternal uncles, aunts, or at the homes of your friends, and the homes with which you are entrusted. It makes no difference whether you eat all together or one person at a time. When you enter a house, say the blessed greeting which Allah has instructed you to say. Thus does Allah explain to you His revelations so that perhaps you will understand.

61. Laysa 'alal-a'maa ḥarajuñw-wa laa 'alal-a'raji ḥarajuñw-wa laa 'alal-mareeḍi ḥarajuñw-wa laa 'alaaa anfusikum an ta-kuloo mim buyootikum aw buyooti aabaaa'ikum aw buyooti ummahaatikum aw buyooti ikhwaanikum aw buyooti akhawaatikum aw buyooti a'maamikum aw buyooti 'ammaatikum aw buyooti akhwaalikum aw buyooti khaalaatikum aw maa malaktum-mafaatiḥahooo aw ṣadeeqikum; laysa 'alaykum junaaḥun an ta-kuloo jamee'an aw ashtaataa; fa-izaa dakhaltum buyootan fasallimoo 'alaaa anfusikum taḥiyyatam-min 'indil-laahi mubaarakatan ṭayyibah; kazaalika yubay-yinul-laahu lakumul-Aayaati la'allakum ta'qiloon.

لَيْسَ عَلَى الْاَعْمٰى حَرَجٌ وَّلَا عَلَى
الْاَعْرَجِ حَرَجٌ وَّلَا عَلَى الْمَرِيْضِ
حَرَجٌ وَّلَا عَلٰٓى اَنْفُسِكُمْ اَنْ تَاْكُلُوْا
مِنْۢ بُيُوْتِكُمْ اَوْ بُيُوْتِ اٰبَآئِكُمْ
اَوْ بُيُوْتِ اُمَّهٰتِكُمْ اَوْ بُيُوْتِ
اِخْوَانِكُمْ اَوْ بُيُوْتِ اَخَوٰتِكُمْ
اَوْ بُيُوْتِ اَعْمَامِكُمْ اَوْ بُيُوْتِ
عَمّٰتِكُمْ اَوْ بُيُوْتِ اَخْوَالِكُمْ اَوْ
بُيُوْتِ خٰلٰتِكُمْ اَوْ مَا مَلَكْتُمْ
مَّفَاتِحَهٗٓ اَوْ صَدِيْقِكُمْ ؕ لَيْسَ
عَلَيْكُمْ جُنَاحٌ اَنْ تَاْكُلُوْا جَمِيْعًا
اَوْ اَشْتَاتًا ؕ فَاِذَا دَخَلْتُمْ بُيُوْتًا
فَسَلِّمُوْا عَلٰٓى اَنْفُسِكُمْ تَحِيَّةً مِّنْ
عِنْدِ اللّٰهِ مُبٰرَكَةً طَيِّبَةً ؕ
كَذٰلِكَ يُبَيِّنُ اللّٰهُ لَكُمُ الْاٰيٰتِ
لَعَلَّكُمْ تَعْقِلُوْنَ ﴿٦١﴾ ع

62. The true believers are those who have faith in Allah and His Messenger and when they are dealing with the Messenger in important matters, they did not leave without his permission. (Muhammad), those who ask your permission believe in Allah and His Messenger. When they ask your leave to attend to their affairs, you may give permission to anyone of them you choose and ask forgiveness for them from Allah. Allah is All-forgiving and All-merciful.

62. Innamal-mu'minoonal-lazeena aamanoo billaahi wa Rasoolihee wa-izaa kaanoo ma'ahoo 'alaaa amrin jaami'il-lam yazhaboo ḥattaa yasta-zinooh; innal-lazeena yasta-zinoonaka ulaaa'ikal-lazeena yu'minoona billaahi wa Rasoolih; fa-izas-ta-zanooka liba'ḍi sha-nihim fa-zal-liman shi'ta minhum wastaghfir lahumul-laah; innal-laaha Ghafoorur-Raḥeem.

اِنَّمَا الْمُؤْمِنُوْنَ الَّذِيْنَ اٰمَنُوْا
بِاللّٰهِ وَرَسُوْلِهٖ وَاِذَا كَانُوْا مَعَهٗ
عَلٰٓى اَمْرٍ جَامِعٍ لَّمْ يَذْهَبُوْا حَتّٰى
يَسْتَاْذِنُوْهُ ؕ اِنَّ الَّذِيْنَ يَسْتَاْذِنُوْنَكَ
اُولٰٓئِكَ الَّذِيْنَ يُؤْمِنُوْنَ بِاللّٰهِ وَ
رَسُوْلِهٖ ۚ فَاِذَا اسْتَاْذَنُوْكَ لِبَعْضِ
شَاْنِهِمْ فَاْذَنْ لِّمَنْ شِئْتَ
مِنْهُمْ وَاسْتَغْفِرْ لَهُمُ اللّٰهَ ؕ اِنَّ
اللّٰهَ غَفُوْرٌ رَّحِيْمٌ ﴿٦٢﴾

63. Do not address the Messenger as you would call each

63. Laa taj'aloo du'aaa'ar-Rasooli baynakum

لَا تَجْعَلُوْا دُعَآءَ الرَّسُوْلِ بَيْنَكُمْ

other. Allah knows those who secretly walk away from you and hide themselves. Those who oppose the Messengers should beware, lest misfortune or a painful torment should befall them.

kadu'aaa'i ba'ḍikum ba'ḍaa; qad ya'lamul-laahul-lazeena yatasallaloona minkum liwaazaa; fal-yaḥzaril-lazeena yukhaalifoona 'an amriheee an tuṣeebahum fitnatun aw yuṣeebahum 'azaabun aleem.

كدعاء بعضكم بعضا ۚ قد يعلم
الله الذين يتسللون منكم لواذا ۚ
فليحذر الذين يخالفون عن أمره
أن تصيبهم فتنة أو يصيبهم
عذاب أليم ﴿٦٣﴾

64. The heavens and the earth, certainly, belong to Allah. He surely knows all about you in this life. On the day when you return to Him, He will tell you all about whatever you have done. Allah has the knowledge of all things.

64. Alaaa inna lillaahi maa fis-samaawaati wal-arḍi qad ya'lamu maaa antum 'alayhi wa Yawma yurja'oona ilayhi fayunabbi'uhum bimaa 'amiloo; wallaahu bikulli shay'in 'Aleem.

ألا إن لله ما في السموت و
الأرض ۖ قد يعلم ما أنتم عليه ۖ
ويوم يرجعون إليه فينبئهم بما
عملوا ۗ والله بكل شيء عليم ﴿٦٤﴾ ع ٣ ١٥

Al-Furqan, Discernment (25)

In the Name of Allah, the Beneficent, the Merciful.

Sûrat al-Furqân-25

(Revealed at Makkah)

Bismillaahir Raḥmaanir Raḥeem

(٢٥) سورة الفرقان مكية (٤٢)

اياتها ٧٧ بسم الله الرحمن الرحيم ركوعاتها ٦

1. Blessed is He who has revealed the criteria (for discerning truth from falsehood) to His servant so that He could warn mankind.

1. Tabaarakal-lazee nazzalal-Furqaana 'alaa 'abdihee li-yakoona lil'aalameena nazeeraa.

تبرك الذي نزل الفرقان على
عبده ليكون للعلمين نذيرا ﴿١﴾

2. To Him belongs the kingdom of the heavens and the earth. He did not beget any sons, nor did He have any partner in His kingdom. He has created all things with precisely accurate planning.

2. Allazee lahoo mulkus-samaawaati wal-arḍi wa lam yattakhiz waladañw-wa lam yakul-lahoo shareekun filmulki wa khalaqa kulla shay'in faqaddarahoo taqdeeraa.

الذي له ملك السموت والأرض
ولم يتخذ ولدا ولم يكن له
شريك في الملك وخلق كل
شيء فقدره تقديرا ﴿٢﴾

3. Yet they have chosen for themselves other deities besides Him, who do not create anything but rather are themselves created, who have no power over their own benefits, or trouble, and who have no control over life, death, and resurrection.

3. Wattakhazoo min dooniheee aalihatal-laa yakhluqoona shay'añw-wa hum yukhlaqoona wa laa yamlikoona li-anfusihim ḍarrañw-wa laa naf'añw-wa laa yamlikoona mawtañw-wa laa ḥayaatañw-wa laa nushooraa.

واتخذوا من دونه آلهة لا
يخلقون شيئا وهم يخلقون
ولا يملكون لأنفسهم ضرا و
لا نفعا ولا يملكون موتا ولا
حيوة ولا نشورا ﴿٣﴾

4. The unbelievers say, "This (Quran) is no more than forged statements which he (Muhammad), with the help of some other people, has falsely invented." Certainly, what they say is unjust and sinful.

4. Wa qaalal-lazeena kafarooo in haazaaa illaaa ifkunif-taraahu wa a'aanahoo 'alayhi qawmun aakharoona faqad jaaa'oo ẓulmañw-wa zooraa.

وقال الذين كفروا إن هذا
إلا إفك افترىه وأعانه عليه
قوم آخرون ۛ فقد جاءو
ظلما وزورا ﴿٤﴾ ۚ

معانقة ١٠ عند المتأخرين ١٢٠

5. They have also said, "It (the Quran) contains ancient legends, which were written down while they were dictated to him in the mornings and the evenings."

6. (Muhammad), tell them, "The One who knows all the secrets of the heavens and the earth has sent it down; He is All-forgiving and All-merciful."

7. They say, "Why does this Messenger eat food, and walk in the streets? Why has not an angel been sent to him so that they could preach the message together?

8. Why has a treasure not been laid out for him or a garden from which he could eat been given to him?" The unjust ones say, "You are merely following a bewitched person."

9. Consider their various views about you. They have gone astray and are not able to find the right path.

10. Blessed is He who could give you palaces and gardens wherein streams would flow, far better than what they want you to have.

11. They deny the Hour of Doom so We have prepared for them a burning fire.

12. When it (fire) will see them from a distant place, they can hear it raging and roaring.

13. When they will be thrown, tied down, into a narrow place therein, then only will they wish for their death (destruction).

5. Wa qaalooo asaaṭeerul awwaleenak-tatabahaa fahiya tumlaa ‘alayhi bukratañw-wa aṣeelaa.

6. Qul anzalahul-laz̲ee ya‘lamussirra fis-samaawaati wal-arḍ; innahoo kaana Ghafoorar-Raḥeemaa.

7. Wa qaaloo maa li-haaz̲ar-Rasooli ya-kuluṭ-ṭa‘aama wa yamshee fil-aswaaq; law laaa unzila ilayhi malakun fa-yakoona ma‘ahoo naz̲eeraa.

8. Aw yulqaaa ilayhi kanzun aw takoonu lahoo jannatuñy-ya-kulu minhaa; wa qaalaẓ-ẓaalimoona in tattabi‘oona illaa rajulam-masḥooraa.

9. Unẓur kayfa ḍaraboo lakal ams̲aala faḍalloo falaa yastaṭee‘oona sabeelaa.

10. Tabaarakal-laz̲eee in shaaa'a ja‘ala laka khayram-min z̲aalika Jannaatin tajree min taḥtihal-anhaaru wa yaj‘al-laka quṣooraa.

11. Bal kaz̲z̲aboo bis-Saa‘ati wa a‘tadnaa liman kaz̲z̲aba bis-Saa‘ati sa‘eeraa.

12. Iz̲aa ra-athum-mim-ma-kaanim ba‘eedin sami‘oo lahaa taghayyuẓañw-wa zafeeraa.

13. Wa iz̲aaa ulqoo minhaa makaanan ḍayyiqam-muqar-raneena da‘aw hunaalika s̲ubooraa.

وَقَالُوْٓا اَسَاطِيْرُ الْاَوَّلِيْنَ
اكْتَتَبَهَا فَهِيَ تُمْلٰى عَلَيْهِ
بُكْرَةً وَّاَصِيْلًا ۝٥
قُلْ اَنْزَلَهُ الَّذِيْ يَعْلَمُ السِّرَّ فِي
السَّمٰوٰتِ وَالْاَرْضِ ؕ اِنَّهٗ كَانَ
غَفُوْرًا رَّحِيْمًا ۝٦
وَقَالُوْا مَالِ هٰذَا الرَّسُوْلِ يَاْكُلُ
الطَّعَامَ وَيَمْشِيْ فِي الْاَسْوَاقِ ؕ
لَوْلَآ اُنْزِلَ اِلَيْهِ مَلَكٌ فَيَكُوْنَ
مَعَهٗ نَذِيْرًا ۝٧
اَوْ يُلْقٰٓى اِلَيْهِ كَنْزٌ اَوْ تَكُوْنُ لَهٗ
جَنَّةٌ يَّاْكُلُ مِنْهَا ؕ وَقَالَ الظّٰلِمُوْنَ
اِنْ تَتَّبِعُوْنَ اِلَّا رَجُلًا مَّسْحُوْرًا ۝٨
اُنْظُرْ كَيْفَ ضَرَبُوْا لَكَ الْاَمْثَالَ
فَضَلُّوْا فَلَا يَسْتَطِيْعُوْنَ سَبِيْلًا ۝٩ ع ٩ ١٦
تَبٰرَكَ الَّذِيْٓ اِنْ شَآءَ جَعَلَ
لَكَ خَيْرًا مِّنْ ذٰلِكَ جَنّٰتٍ
تَجْرِيْ مِنْ تَحْتِهَا الْاَنْهٰرُ ۙ
وَيَجْعَلْ لَّكَ قُصُوْرًا ۝١٠
بَلْ كَذَّبُوْا بِالسَّاعَةِ ۣ وَاَعْتَدْنَا
لِمَنْ كَذَّبَ بِالسَّاعَةِ سَعِيْرًا ۝١١
اِذَا رَاَتْهُمْ مِّنْ مَّكَانٍۢ بَعِيْدٍ
سَمِعُوْا لَهَا تَغَيُّظًا وَّزَفِيْرًا ۝١٢
وَاِذَآ اُلْقُوْا مِنْهَا مَكَانًا ضَيِّقًا
مُّقَرَّنِيْنَ دَعَوْا هُنَالِكَ ثُبُوْرًا ۝١٣
لَا تَدْعُوا الْيَوْمَ ثُبُوْرًا وَّاحِدًا

14. They will be told, "Do not pray to die only once but pray to die many times."

15. (Muhammad), ask them, "Is what you want better, or the eternal garden promised to the pious ones as their reward and dwelling?

16. Therein they will eternally have whatever they want. This is a binding promise from your Lord."

17. On the day when the unbelievers and whatever they had been worshipping besides Allah will be resurrected, He will ask the idols, "Did you mislead My servants or did they themselves go astray from the right path?"

18. They will reply, "Lord, You alone deserve all glory! We were not supposed to choose any guardian other than you. Since you have been benevolent to these people and their fathers, they forgot Your guidance and, thus, became subject to perdition."

19. Allah will say (to the idolaters), "Your idols have rejected your faith. You cannot avoid their rejection nor can you find any help. Any one of you who commits injustice will be made to suffer a great torment."

20. All the Messengers whom We sent before, certainly, ate food and walked through the streets. We have made some of you (people) a trial for the others. Would you then exercise patience? Your Lord is All-aware.

14. Laa tad'ul-yawma <u>s</u>ubooraañw-waaḥidañw-wad'oo <u>s</u>ubooran ka<u>s</u>eeraa.

15. Qul a<u>z</u>aalika khayrun am Jannatul-khuldil-latee wu'idal-muttaqoon; kaanat lahum jazaaa'añw-wa maṣeeraa.

16. Lahum feehaa maa yashaaa'oona khaalideen; kaana 'alaa Rabbika wa'dam-mas'oolaa.

17. Wa Yawma yaḥshuruhum wa maa ya'budoona min doonil-laahi fa-yaqoolu 'a-antum aḍlaltum 'ibaadee haaa'ulaaa'i am hum ḍallus-sabeel.

18. Qaaloo Subḥaanaka maa kaana yambaghee lanaaa an-nattakhi<u>z</u>a min doonika min awliyaaa'a wa laakim-mat-ta'tahum wa aabaaa'ahum ḥattaa nasu<u>z</u>-<u>z</u>ikra wa kaanoo qawmam booraa.

19. Faqad ka<u>z</u>-<u>z</u>abookum bimaa taqooloona famaa tastaṭee'oona ṣarfañw-wa laa naṣraa; wa mañy-ya<u>z</u>lim-minkum nu<u>z</u>iqhu 'a<u>z</u>aaban kabeeraa.

20. Wa maaa arsalnaa qablaka minal-mursaleena illaaa innahum la-ya-kuloonaṭ-ṭa'aama wa yamshoona fil-aswaaq; wa ja'alnaa ba'ḍakum liba'ḍin fitnatan ataṣbiroon; wa kaana Rabbuka Baṣeeraa.

وَّادْعُوْا ثُبُوْرًا كَثِيْرًا ﴿١٤﴾
قُلْ اَذٰلِكَ خَيْرٌ اَمْ جَنَّةُ الْخُلْدِ
الَّتِيْ وُعِدَ الْمُتَّقُوْنَ ؕ كَانَتْ
لَهُمْ جَزَآءً وَّ مَصِيْرًا ﴿١٥﴾
لَهُمْ فِيْهَا مَا يَشَآءُوْنَ خٰلِدِيْنَ ؕ
كَانَ عَلٰى رَبِّكَ وَعْدًا مَّسْـُٔوْلًا ﴿١٦﴾
وَ يَوْمَ يَحْشُرُهُمْ وَمَا يَعْبُدُوْنَ
مِنْ دُوْنِ اللّٰهِ فَيَقُوْلُ ءَاَنْتُمْ
اَضْلَلْتُمْ عِبَادِيْ هٰٓؤُلَآءِ اَمْ
هُمْ ضَلُّوا السَّبِيْلَ ؕ ﴿١٧﴾
قَالُوْا سُبْحٰنَكَ مَا كَانَ يَنْۢبَغِيْ
لَنَآ اَنْ نَّتَّخِذَ مِنْ دُوْنِكَ
مِنْ اَوْلِيَآءَ وَلٰكِنْ مَّتَّعْتَهُمْ وَ
اٰبَآءَهُمْ حَتّٰى نَسُوا الذِّكْرَ ۚ وَ
كَانُوْا قَوْمًۢا بُوْرًا ﴿١٨﴾
فَقَدْ كَذَّبُوْكُمْ بِمَا تَقُوْلُوْنَ ۙ
فَمَا تَسْتَطِيْعُوْنَ صَرْفًا وَّلَا نَصْرًا ۚ
وَمَنْ يَّظْلِمْ مِّنْكُمْ نُذِقْهُ عَذَابًا
كَبِيْرًا ﴿١٩﴾
وَمَآ اَرْسَلْنَا قَبْلَكَ مِنَ الْمُرْسَلِيْنَ
اِلَّآ اِنَّهُمْ لَيَاْكُلُوْنَ الطَّعَامَ وَ
يَمْشُوْنَ فِي الْاَسْوَاقِ ؕ وَجَعَلْنَا
بَعْضَكُمْ لِبَعْضٍ فِتْنَةً ؕ اَتَصْبِرُوْنَ ۚ
وَكَانَ رَبُّكَ بَصِيْرًا ﴿٢٠﴾ ع
وَقَالَ الَّذِيْنَ لَا يَرْجُوْنَ لِقَآءَنَا
لَوْلَآ اُنْزِلَ عَلَيْنَا الْمَلٰٓئِكَةُ اَوْ نَرٰى

ع ٢ ١٧ الجزء التاسع عشر (١٩)

21. Those who have no desire to meet Us have said, "Would that the angels had been sent to us or that we could see our Lord." They are really filled with pride and have committed the greatest and worst kind of rebellion and hostility.

21. Wa qaalal-lazeena laa yarjoona liqaaa'anaa law laaa unzila 'alaynal-malaaa'ikatu aw naraa Rabbanaa; laqadistakb-aroo feee anfusihim wa 'ataw 'utuwwan kabeeraa.

رَبَّنَا ۚ لَقَدِ اسْتَكْبَرُوْا فِيْٓ اَنْفُسِهِمْ
وَعَتَوْ عُتُوًّا كَبِيْرًا ﴿٢١﴾

22. On the day when the criminals see the angels, there will, certainly, be no rejoicing for them. Rather, they will say, "A measure against us is already taken."

22. Yawma yarawnal malaaa-'ikata laa bushraa Yawma'izil-lilmujrimeena wa yaqooloona ḥijram-maḥjooraa.

يَوْمَ يَرَوْنَ الْمَلٰٓئِكَةَ لَا بُشْرٰى
يَوْمَئِذٍ لِّلْمُجْرِمِيْنَ وَيَقُوْلُوْنَ حِجْرًا
مَّحْجُوْرًا ﴿٢٢﴾

23. We shall call their deeds into Our presence and scatter them into the air as dust (something devoid of all virtue).

23. Wa qadimnaaa ilaa maa 'amiloo min 'amalin faja'al-naahu habaaa'am-mansooraa.

وَقَدِمْنَآ اِلٰى مَا عَمِلُوْا مِنْ عَمَلٍ فَجَعَلْنٰهُ
هَبَآءً مَّنْثُوْرًا ﴿٢٣﴾

24. The dwellers of Paradise on that day will have the best residence and resting place.

24. Aṣ-ḥaabul-Jannati Yaw-ma'izin khayrum-mus-taqar-rañw-wa aḥsanu maqeelaa.

اَصْحٰبُ الْجَنَّةِ يَوْمَئِذٍ خَيْرٌ مُّسْتَقَرًّا
وَّاَحْسَنُ مَقِيْلًا ﴿٢٤﴾

25. The day when the sky will be rent asunder along with clouds, and the angels descend in groups

25. Wa Yawma tashaqqaqus-samaaa'u bilghamaami wa nuzzilal-malaaa'ikatu tan-zeelaa.

وَيَوْمَ تَشَقَّقُ السَّمَآءُ بِالْغَمَامِ وَنُزِّلَ
الْمَلٰٓئِكَةُ تَنْزِيْلًا ﴿٢٥﴾

26. absolute kingdom (ownership of all things) will belong to the Beneficent. It will be a hard day for the unbelievers.

26. Almulku Yawma'i-zinil-ḥaqqu lir-Raḥmaan; wa kaana Yawman'alal-kaafireena 'asee-raa.

اَلْمُلْكُ يَوْمَئِذِ ِۨ الْحَقُّ لِلرَّحْمٰنِ ۚ
وَكَانَ يَوْمًا عَلَى الْكٰفِرِيْنَ عَسِيْرًا ﴿٢٦﴾

27. It will be a day when the unjust will bite their fingers, (regretfully) saying, "Would that I had followed the path with the Messenger.

27. Wa Yawma ya'aḍḍuẓ-ẓaalimu 'alaa yadayhi yaqoolu yaa-laytanit-takhaztu ma'ar-Rasooli sabeelaa.

وَيَوْمَ يَعَضُّ الظَّالِمُ عَلٰى يَدَيْهِ
يَقُوْلُ يٰلَيْتَنِي اتَّخَذْتُ مَعَ الرَّسُوْلِ
سَبِيْلًا ﴿٢٧﴾

28. Woe is me! I wish I had not been friends with so and so.

28. Yaa waylataa laytanee lam attakhiz fulaanan khaleelaa.

يٰوَيْلَتٰى لَيْتَنِيْ لَمْ اَتَّخِذْ فُلَانًا
خَلِيْلًا ﴿٢٨﴾

29. He led me away from the true guidance after it had come to me. Satan is deceitful to people."

29. Laqad aḍallanee 'aniz-zikri ba'da iz jaaa'anee; wa kaanash-Shayṭaanu lil-insaani khazoolaa.

لَقَدْ اَضَلَّنِيْ عَنِ الذِّكْرِ بَعْدَ اِذْ
جَآءَنِيْ ۗ وَكَانَ الشَّيْطٰنُ لِلْاِنْسَانِ
خَذُوْلًا ﴿٢٩﴾

30. The Messenger will say, "Lord, my people had abandoned this Quran."

30. Wa qaalar-Rasoolu yaa Rabbi inna qawmit-takhazoo haazal-Qur-aana mahjooraa.

وَقَالَ الرَّسُوْلُ يٰرَبِّ اِنَّ قَوْمِي
اتَّخَذُوْا هٰذَا الْقُرْاٰنَ مَهْجُوْرًا ﴿٣٠﴾

31. Thus, from the sinful people We made enemies for every Prophet. Your Lord is a Sufficient Guide and Helper.

31. Wa kazaalika ja'alnaa likulli Nabiyyin 'aduwwam-minal-mujrimeen; wa kafaa bi-Rabbika haadiyañw-wa naṣeeraa.

وَكَذٰلِكَ جَعَلْنَا لِكُلِّ نَبِيٍّ عَدُوًّا مِّنَ
الْمُجْرِمِيْنَ ۗ وَكَفٰى بِرَبِّكَ هَادِيًا
وَّنَصِيْرًا ﴿٣١﴾

32. The unbelievers have said, "Why was the whole Quran not revealed to him at once?" We have revealed it to you in gradual steps to strengthen your hearts and give you explanations.

32. Wa qaalal-lazeena kafaroo law laa nuzzila 'alayhil-Qur-aanu jumlatañw-waaḥidah; kazaalika linusabbita bihee fu'aadaka wa rattalnaahu tarteelaa.

وَقَالَ الَّذِيْنَ كَفَرُوْا لَوْلَا نُزِّلَ عَلَيْهِ الْقُرْاٰنُ جُمْلَةً وَّاحِدَةً ۚۛ كَذٰلِكَ ۚۛ لِنُثَبِّتَ بِهٖ فُؤَادَكَ وَرَتَّلْنٰهُ تَرْتِيْلًا ﴿٣٢﴾

33. We will support you with the Truth and the best interpretation whenever the infidels argue against you.

33. Wa laa ya-toonaka bimasalin illaa ji'naaka bilḥaqqi wa aḥsana tafseeraa.

وَلَا يَاْتُوْنَكَ بِمَثَلٍ اِلَّا جِئْنٰكَ بِالْحَقِّ وَاَحْسَنَ تَفْسِيْرًا ؕ ﴿٣٣﴾

34. Those who will be driven headlong into hell will have a terrible dwelling and a path far away from the right destination.

34. Allazeena yuḥsharoona 'alaa wujoohihim ilaa Jahannama ulaaa'ika sharrum-makaanañw-wa aḍallu sabeelaa.

اَلَّذِيْنَ يُحْشَرُوْنَ عَلٰى وُجُوْهِهِمْ اِلٰى جَهَنَّمَ ۙ اُولٰٓئِكَ شَرٌّ مَّكَانًا وَّاَضَلُّ سَبِيْلًا ﴿٣٤﴾

مع ٧ عند المتقدمين ١٢ — ع ٣

35. We gave the Book to Moses and made his brother Aaron his Minister.

35. Wa laqad aataynaa Moosal-Kitaaba wa ja'alnaa ma'ahooo akhaahu Haaroona wazeeraa.

وَلَقَدْ اٰتَيْنَا مُوْسَى الْكِتٰبَ وَجَعَلْنَا مَعَهٗٓ اَخَاهُ هٰرُوْنَ وَزِيْرًا ۚ ﴿٣٥﴾

36. We told them, "Both of you go to the people who have rejected Our revelations." We completely destroyed those unbelievers.

36. Faqulnaz-habaaa ilal-qawmil-lazeena kazzaboo bi-Aayaatinaa fadammarnaahum tadmeeraa.

فَقُلْنَا اذْهَبَآ اِلَى الْقَوْمِ الَّذِيْنَ كَذَّبُوْا بِاٰيٰتِنَا ؕ فَدَمَّرْنٰهُمْ تَدْمِيْرًا ؕ ﴿٣٦﴾

37. We drowned the people of Noah because of their rejection of the Messengers and made them evidence of the Truth for mankind. We have prepared a painful torment for the unjust ones.

37. Wa qawma Nooḥil-lammaa kazzabur-Rusula aghraqnaahum wa ja'al-naahum linnaasi Aayah; wa a'tadnaa liẓẓaalimeena 'azaaban aleemaa.

وَقَوْمَ نُوْحٍ لَّمَّا كَذَّبُوا الرُّسُلَ اَغْرَقْنٰهُمْ وَجَعَلْنٰهُمْ لِلنَّاسِ اٰيَةً ؕ وَاَعْتَدْنَا لِلظّٰلِمِيْنَ عَذَابًا اَلِيْمًا ۚ ﴿٣٧﴾

38. To each of the tribes of Ad, Thamud, Ashab Al-Rass (females having carnal relations with each other) and many generations in between

38. Wa 'Aadañw-wa Samooda wa Aṣḥaabar-Rassi wa-quroonam bayna zaalika kaseeraa.

وَّعَادًا وَّثَمُوْدَا۠ وَاَصْحٰبَ الرَّسِّ وَقُرُوْنًا بَيْنَ ذٰلِكَ كَثِيْرًا ﴿٣٨﴾

39. We gave guidance and drove each to destruction (broke into pieces).

39. Wa kullan ḍarabnaa lahul-amsaala wa kullan tabbarnaa tatbeeraa.

وَكُلًّا ضَرَبْنَا لَهُ الْاَمْثَالَ ۫ وَكُلًّا تَبَّرْنَا تَتْبِيْرًا ﴿٣٩﴾

40. Our Messengers came into the town which was struck by a fatal rain. Did they (unbelievers) not see what had happened to this town? In fact, they had no faith in the Resurrection.

40. Wa laqad ataw 'alal-qaryatil-lateee umṭirat maṭaras-saw'; afalam yakoonoo yarawnahaa; bal kaanoo laa yarjoona nushooraa.

وَلَقَدْ اَتَوْا عَلَى الْقَرْيَةِ الَّتِيْٓ اُمْطِرَتْ مَطَرَ السَّوْءِ ؕ اَفَلَمْ يَكُوْنُوْا يَرَوْنَهَا ۚ بَلْ كَانُوْا لَا يَرْجُوْنَ نُشُوْرًا ﴿٤٠﴾

41. (Muhammad), when they see you, they will only mock you and say, "Has Allah really sent him as a messenger?

41. Wa izaa ra-awka iñy-yattakhizoonaka illaa huzuwan ahaazal-lazee ba'asal-laahu Rasoolaa.

وَاِذَا رَاَوْكَ اِنْ يَّتَّخِذُوْنَكَ اِلَّا هُزُوًا ؕ اَهٰذَا الَّذِيْ بَعَثَ اللّٰهُ رَسُوْلًا ﴿٤١﴾

42. Had we not been steadfast he would almost have led us away from our gods." On facing torment they will soon know who

42. In kaada la-yuḍillunaa 'an aalihatinaa law laaa an ṣabarnaa 'alayhaa; wa sawfa ya'lamoona

اِنْ كَادَ لَيُضِلُّنَا عَنْ اٰلِهَتِنَا لَوْلَآ اَنْ صَبَرْنَا عَلَيْهَا ؕ وَسَوْفَ يَعْلَمُوْنَ

had really gone astray.

ḥeena yarawnal ‘azaaba man aḍallu sabeelaa.

حِيْنَ يَرَوْنَ الْعَذَابَ مَنْ اَضَلُّ
سَبِيْلًا ﴿٤٢﴾

43. How can you be the guardian of those who have chosen their own desires as their Lord?

43. Ara’ayta manit-takhaza ilaahahoo hawaahu afa-anta takoonu ‘alayhi wakeelaa.

اَرَءَيْتَ مَنِ اتَّخَذَ اِلٰهَهٗ هَوٰىهُ ط
اَفَاَنْتَ تَكُوْنُ عَلَيْهِ وَكِيْلًا ﴿٤٣﴾

44. Do you think that most of them listen and understand? They are like cattle or even more, straying and confused.

44. Am taḥsabu anna aksa-rahum yasma‘oona aw ya‘qi-loon; in hum illaa kal-an‘aami bal hum aḍallu sabeelaa

اَمْ تَحْسَبُ اَنَّ اَكْثَرَهُمْ يَسْمَعُوْنَ
اَوْ يَعْقِلُوْنَ ط اِنْ هُمْ اِلَّا كَالْاَنْعَامِ
بَلْ هُمْ اَضَلُّ سَبِيْلًا ﴿٤٤﴾ ع ١٠ ٢

45. Did you not see how your Lord has stretched the shadow (the time from dawn to sunset)? Had He wanted He would have made it stationary. Then We made the sun its guiding indicator,

45. Alam tara ilaa Rabbika kayfa maddaẓ-ẓilla wa law shaaa’a laja‘alahoo saakinan summa ja‘alnash-shamsa ‘alayhi daleelaa.

اَلَمْ تَرَ اِلٰى رَبِّكَ كَيْفَ مَدَّ الظِّلَّ ج
وَلَوْ شَآءَ لَجَعَلَهٗ سَاكِنًا ج ثُمَّ جَعَلْنَا
الشَّمْسَ عَلَيْهِ دَلِيْلًا ﴿٤٥﴾

46. then We reduced it toward Us a little.

46. Summa qabaḍnaahu ilay-naa qabḍañy-yaseeraa.

ثُمَّ قَبَضْنٰهُ اِلَيْنَا قَبْضًا يَّسِيْرًا ﴿٤٦﴾

47. It is He who has made the night as a covering for you, sleep as a rest for you, and the day for you to rise again.

47. Wa Huwal-lazee ja‘ala lakumul-layla libaasañw-wannawma subaatañw-wa ja‘alan-nahaara nushooraa.

وَهُوَ الَّذِيْ جَعَلَ لَكُمُ الَّيْلَ لِبَاسًا وَّ
النَّوْمَ سُبَاتًا وَّجَعَلَ النَّهَارَ نُشُوْرًا ﴿٤٧﴾

48. It is He who sends the winds to you with the glad news of His mercy and who sends purifying rain from the sky

48. Wa Huwal-lazeee arsalar-riyaaḥa bushram bayna yaday raḥmatih; wa anzalnaa minas-samaaa’i maaa’an ṭahooraa.

وَهُوَ الَّذِيْٓ اَرْسَلَ الرِّيٰحَ بُشْرًاۢ بَيْنَ
يَدَيْ رَحْمَتِهٖ ج وَاَنْزَلْنَا مِنَ السَّمَآءِ
مَآءً طَهُوْرًا ﴿٤٨﴾

49. to revive the barren land and provide water for many creatures, cattle, and people.

49. Linuḥyiya bihee balda-tam-maytañw-wa nusqiyahoo mimmaa khalaqnaaa an‘aa-mañw-wa anaasiyya kaseeraa.

لِنُحْيِۦَ بِهٖ بَلْدَةً مَّيْتًا وَّنُسْقِيَهٗ مِمَّا
خَلَقْنَآ اَنْعَامًا وَّاَنَاسِيَّ كَثِيْرًا ﴿٤٩﴾

50. We send them rain from time to time so that they may take heed. Many people have responded, but ungratefully.

50. Wa laqad ṣarrafnaahu baynahum li-yazzakkaroo fa-abaaa aksarun-naasi illaa kufooraa.

وَلَقَدْ صَرَّفْنٰهُ بَيْنَهُمْ لِيَذَّكَّرُوْا ۖ
فَاَبٰٓى اَكْثَرُ النَّاسِ اِلَّا كُفُوْرًا ﴿٥٠﴾

51. Had We wanted We could have sent a Prophet to every town.

51. Wa law shi’naa laba‘asnaa fee kulli qar-yatin-nazeeraa.

وَلَوْ شِئْنَا لَبَعَثْنَا فِيْ كُلِّ قَرْيَةٍ
نَّذِيْرًا ﴿٥١﴾

52. Do not yield to the unbelievers but launch a great campaign against them with the help of the Quran.

52. Falaa tuṭi‘il-kaafireena wa jaahidhum bihee jihaadan kabeeraa.

فَلَا تُطِعِ الْكٰفِرِيْنَ وَجَاهِدْهُمْ بِهٖ
جِهَادًا كَبِيْرًا ﴿٥٢﴾

53. It is He who has joined the two seas, one palatable and sweet, the other bitterly salty, and has established a barrier between

53. Wa Huwal-lazee marajal baḥrayni haazaa ‘azbun furaatuñw-wa haazaa milḥun ujaaj; wa ja‘ala

وَهُوَ الَّذِيْ مَرَجَ الْبَحْرَيْنِ هٰذَا عَذْبٌ
فُرَاتٌ وَّهٰذَا مِلْحٌ اُجَاجٌ ج وَجَعَلَ

بَيْنَهُمَا بَرْزَخًا وَّحِجْرًا مَّحْجُوْرًا ﴿٥٣﴾

baynahumaa barzakhañw-wa ḥijram-maḥjooraa.

them as a partition.

وَهُوَ الَّذِيْ خَلَقَ مِنَ الْمَآءِ بَشَرًا فَجَعَلَهٗ نَسَبًا وَّصِهْرًا ۗ وَكَانَ رَبُّكَ قَدِيْرًا ﴿٥٤﴾

54. Wa Huwal-lazee khalaqa minal-maaa'i basharan fa-ja'alahoo nasabañw-wa ṣihraa; wa kaana Rabbuka Qadeeraa.

54. It is He who has created the human being from water to have relationships of both lineage and wedlock. Your Lord has all power.

وَيَعْبُدُوْنَ مِنْ دُوْنِ اللّٰهِ مَا لَا يَنْفَعُهُمْ وَلَا يَضُرُّهُمْ ۗ وَكَانَ الْكَافِرُ عَلٰى رَبِّهٖ ظَهِيْرًا ﴿٥٥﴾

55. Wa ya'budoona min doonil-laahi maa laa yanfa-'uhum wa laa yaḍurruhum; wa kaanal-kaafiru 'alaa Rabbihee ẓaheeraa.

55. They worship besides Allah things that can neither benefit nor harm them. The unbelievers are defiant against their Lord.

وَمَآ اَرْسَلْنٰكَ اِلَّا مُبَشِّرًا وَّنَذِيْرًا ﴿٥٦﴾

56. Wa maa arsalnaaka illaa mubashshirañw-wa nazeeraa.

56. We have sent you for no other reason but to be a bearer of glad news and warning.

قُلْ مَآ اَسْئَلُكُمْ عَلَيْهِ مِنْ اَجْرٍ اِلَّا مَنْ شَآءَ اَنْ يَّتَّخِذَ اِلٰى رَبِّهٖ سَبِيْلًا ﴿٥٧﴾

57. Qul maaa as'alukum 'alayhi min ajrin illaa man shaaa'a añy-yattakhiza ilaa Rabbihee sabeelaa.

57. Tell them, "I ask no recompense for my preaching to you, except the fact that whoever wants should choose the way of his Lord."

وَتَوَكَّلْ عَلَى الْحَيِّ الَّذِيْ لَا يَمُوْتُ وَسَبِّحْ بِحَمْدِهٖ ۚ وَكَفٰى بِهٖ بِذُنُوْبِ عِبَادِهٖ خَبِيْرًا ﴿٥٨﴾

58. Wa tawakkal 'alal-Ḥayyil-lazee laa yamootu wa sabbiḥ biḥamdih; wa kafaa bihee bizunoobi 'ibaadihee khabeeraa.

58. Also trust in the Living One who never dies and glorify Him with His praise. He has sufficient knowledge of the sins of His servants.

مع عند المتقدمين ١٢

الَّذِيْ خَلَقَ السَّمٰوٰتِ وَالْاَرْضَ وَمَا بَيْنَهُمَا فِيْ سِتَّةِ اَيَّامٍ ثُمَّ اسْتَوٰى عَلَى الْعَرْشِ ۚ اَلرَّحْمٰنُ فَسْئَلْ بِهٖ خَبِيْرًا ﴿٥٩﴾

59. Allazee khalaqas-samaa-waati wal-arḍa wa maa baynahumaa fee sittati ayyaa-min summastawaa 'alal-'Arsh; ar-Raḥmaanu fas'al bihee khabeeraa.

59. It is He who created the heavens and the earth and all that is between them in six days and then He established His domination over the Throne. He is the Beneficent. Refer to Him as the final authority.

(Bow Down)

وَاِذَا قِيْلَ لَهُمُ اسْجُدُوْا لِلرَّحْمٰنِ قَالُوْا وَمَا الرَّحْمٰنُ ۗ اَنَسْجُدُ لِمَا تَاْمُرُنَا وَزَادَهُمْ نُفُوْرًا ۩ ﴿٦٠﴾

60. Wa izaa qeela lahumus-judoo lir-Raḥmaani qaaloo wa mar-Raḥmaanu anasjudu limaa ta-murunaa wa zaadahum nufooraa.

60. When they are told to prostrate themselves before the Beneficent, they say, "Who is the Beneficent? Why should we prostrate ourselves before the one whom you have commanded us to?" This only increases their rebelliousness.

تَبٰرَكَ الَّذِيْ جَعَلَ فِي السَّمَآءِ بُرُوْجًا وَّجَعَلَ فِيْهَا سِرٰجًا وَّقَمَرًا مُّنِيْرًا ﴿٦١﴾

61. Tabaarakal-lazee ja'ala fis-samaaa'i buroojañw-wa ja'ala feehaa siraajañw-wa qamaram-muneeraa.

61. Blessed is He who has established constellations in the sky and made therein a lamp and a shining moon.

وَهُوَ الَّذِيْ جَعَلَ الَّيْلَ وَالنَّهَارَ خِلْفَةً لِّمَنْ اَرَادَ اَنْ يَّذَّكَّرَ اَوْ اَرَادَ شُكُوْرًا ﴿٦٢﴾

62. Wa Huwal-lazee ja'alal-layla wannahaara khilfatal-liman araada añy-yaz-zakkara aw araada shukooraa.

62. It is He who has made the night and the day, one proceeding the other, for whoever wants to take heed or give thanks (make up for the prayers missed in one of them during the other one).

وَعِبَادُ الرَّحْمٰنِ الَّذِيْنَ يَمْشُوْنَ عَلَى الْاَرْضِ هَوْنًا وَّاِذَا خَاطَبَهُمُ

63. Wa 'ibaadur-Raḥmaanil-lazeena yamshoona 'alal-arḍi hawnañw-wa izaa khaaṭa-bahumul-

63. (Among) the servants of the Beneficent are those who walk on earth in fear and when addressed by the ignorant ones, their only

response is, "Peace be with you."

64. They are those who spend the night worshipping their Lord, prostrating, and standing,

65. who pray, "Lord, protect us from the torment of hell; it is a great loss

66. it is a terrible abode and an evil station,"

67. (It is such servants of Allah) who in their spending were neither extravagant nor stingy but maintain moderation,

68. who do not worship idols besides Allah, nor without a just cause murder a soul to whom Allah has granted amnesty, and who do not commit fornication, for those who do so will arrive in Atham (a place in hell) for this sin

69. and on the Day of Judgment their torment will be double. They will suffer forever in disgrace.

70. But only those who repent and believe and act righteously will have their sins replaced with virtue; Allah is All-forgiving and All-merciful.

71. Those who repent and act righteously should truly returned to Allah and must not commit that sin again,

72. those who do not attend gathering for unlawful songs and when they come across something impious, pass it by nobly,

73. who, when reminded of the revelations of their Lord, did not try to ignore them as though deaf and blind. Rather, they try to understand and think about them.

74. They pray, "Our Lord, make our spouses and children to be the delight of our eyes and (for) us (appoint) an Imam (leader) of

jaahiloona qaaloo salaamaa.

64. Wallazeena yabeetoona li-Rabbihim sujjadañw-wa qiyaamaa.

65. Wallazeena yaqooloona Rabbanaṣ-rif 'annaa 'azaaba Jahannama inna 'azaabahaa kaana gharaamaa.

66. Innahaa saaa'at mustaqarrañw-wa muqaamaa.

67. Wallazeena izaaa anfaqoo lam yusrifoo wa lam yaqturoo wa-kaana bayna zaalika qawaamaa.

68. Wallazeena laa yad'oona ma'al-laahi ilaahan aakhara wa laa yaqtuloonan-nafsal-latee ḥarramal-laahu illaa bilḥaqqi wa laa yaznoon; wa mañyyaf'al zaalika yalqa asaamaa.

69. Yuḍaa'af lahul-'azaabu Yawmal-Qiyaamati wa yakhlud feehee muhaanaa.

70. Illaa man taaba wa aamana wa 'amila 'amalan ṣaaliḥan fa-ulaaa'ika yubaddilul-laahu sayyi-aatihim ḥasanaat;wa kaanal-laahu Ghafoorar-Raḥeemaa.

71. Wa man taaba wa 'amila ṣaaliḥan fa-innahoo yatoobu ilal-laahi mataabaa.

72. Wallazeena laa yashhadoonaz-zoora wa izaa marroo billaghwi marroo kiraamaa.

73. Wallazeena izaa zukkiroo bi-Aayaati Rabbihim lam yakhirroo 'alayhaa ṣummañw-wa 'umyaanaa.

74. Wallazeena yaqooloona Rabbanaa hab lanaa min azwaajinaa wa zurriyyaatinaa qurrata a'yuniñw-wa

الْجٰهِلُوْنَ قَالُوْا سَلٰمًا ﴿٦٣﴾
وَالَّذِيْنَ يَبِيْتُوْنَ لِرَبِّهِمْ سُجَّدًا
وَّقِيَامًا ﴿٦٤﴾
وَالَّذِيْنَ يَقُوْلُوْنَ رَبَّنَا اصْرِفْ عَنَّا
عَذَابَ جَهَنَّمَ ۖ اِنَّ عَذَابَهَا كَانَ
غَرَامًا ﴿٦٥﴾
اِنَّهَا سَآءَتْ مُسْتَقَرًّا وَّمُقَامًا ﴿٦٦﴾
وَالَّذِيْنَ اِذَآ اَنْفَقُوْا لَمْ يُسْرِفُوْا وَلَمْ
يَقْتُرُوْا وَكَانَ بَيْنَ ذٰلِكَ قَوَامًا ﴿٦٧﴾
وَالَّذِيْنَ لَا يَدْعُوْنَ مَعَ اللّٰهِ اِلٰهًا
اٰخَرَ وَلَا يَقْتُلُوْنَ النَّفْسَ الَّتِيْ حَرَّمَ
اللّٰهُ اِلَّا بِالْحَقِّ وَلَا يَزْنُوْنَ ۚ وَمَنْ
يَّفْعَلْ ذٰلِكَ يَلْقَ اَثَامًا ﴿٦٨﴾
يُّضٰعَفْ لَهُ الْعَذَابُ يَوْمَ الْقِيٰمَةِ
وَيَخْلُدْ فِيْهٖ مُهَانًا ﴿٦٩﴾
اِلَّا مَنْ تَابَ وَاٰمَنَ وَعَمِلَ عَمَلًا صَالِحًا
فَاُولٰٓئِكَ يُبَدِّلُ اللّٰهُ سَيِّاٰتِهِمْ حَسَنٰتٍ ۗ
وَكَانَ اللّٰهُ غَفُوْرًا رَّحِيْمًا ﴿٧٠﴾
وَمَنْ تَابَ وَعَمِلَ صَالِحًا فَاِنَّهٗ يَتُوْبُ
اِلَى اللّٰهِ مَتَابًا ﴿٧١﴾
وَالَّذِيْنَ لَا يَشْهَدُوْنَ الزُّوْرَ ۙ وَاِذَا
مَرُّوْا بِاللَّغْوِ مَرُّوْا كِرَامًا ﴿٧٢﴾
وَالَّذِيْنَ اِذَا ذُكِّرُوْا بِاٰيٰتِ رَبِّهِمْ
لَمْ يَخِرُّوْا عَلَيْهَا صُمًّا وَّعُمْيَانًا ﴿٧٣﴾
وَالَّذِيْنَ يَقُوْلُوْنَ رَبَّنَا هَبْ لَنَا مِنْ
اَزْوَاجِنَا وَذُرِّيّٰتِنَا قُرَّةَ اَعْيُنٍ وَّ

the pious ones."

j'alnaa lilmuttaqeena Imaamaa.

اجْعَلْنَا لِلْمُتَّقِينَ إِمَامًا ﴿٧٤﴾

75. They will all receive paradise as their reward for their forbearance and patience, where they will be greeted with, "Peace be with you."

75. Ulaaa'ika yujzawnal-ghurfata bimaa ṣabaroo wa yulaqqawna feehaa taḥiyya-tañw-wa salaamaa.

أُولَٰٓئِكَ يُجْزَوْنَ الْغُرْفَةَ بِمَا صَبَرُوا وَيُلَقَّوْنَ فِيهَا تَحِيَّةً وَسَلَٰمًا ﴿٧٥﴾

76. They will live therein forever, the best abode and place of rest.

76. Khaalideena feehaa; ḥasunat mustaqarrañw-wa muqaamaa.

خَٰلِدِينَ فِيهَا ۚ حَسُنَتْ مُسْتَقَرًّا وَمُقَامًا ﴿٧٦﴾

77. (Muhammad), say (to the disbeliever) "It does not matter to my Lord whether you worship Him or not. You have rejected His guidance and your punishment is inevitable."

77. Qul maa ya'ba'u bikum Rabbee law laa du'aaa'ukum faqad kazzabtum fasawfa yakoonu lizaamaa.

قُلْ مَا يَعْبَؤُا بِكُمْ رَبِّي لَوْلَا دُعَآؤُكُمْ ۖ فَقَدْ كَذَّبْتُمْ فَسَوْفَ يَكُونُ لِزَامًا ﴿٧٧﴾

الربع ع ٦

Al-Shuara, The Poets (26)

In the Name of Allah, the Beneficent, the Merciful.

Sûrat ash-Shu'arâ'-26

(Revealed at Makkah)

Bismillaahir Raḥmaanir Raḥeem

(٢٦) سُورَةُ الشُّعَرَآءِ مَكِّيَّةٌ (٤٧)

آياتها ٢٢٧ ركوعاتها ١١

بِسْمِ اللَّهِ الرَّحْمَٰنِ الرَّحِيمِ

1. Ta Sin. Mim.

1. Ṭaa-Seeen-Meeem.

طسٓمٓ ﴿١﴾

2. These are the verses of the illustrious Book.

2. Tilka Aayaatul-Kitaabil-Mubeen.

تِلْكَ ءَايَٰتُ الْكِتَٰبِ الْمُبِينِ ﴿٢﴾

3. You will perhaps devastate yourself in distress because they are not accepting the faith.

3. La'allaka baakhi'un-naf-saka allaa yakoonoo mu'mi-neen.

لَعَلَّكَ بَٰخِعٌ نَّفْسَكَ أَلَّا يَكُونُوا مُؤْمِنِينَ ﴿٣﴾

4. Had We wanted, We would have sent them a miracle from the sky to make their heads hang down in submission.

4. In-nasha- nunazzil 'alayhim minas-samaaa'i Aayatan faẓallat a'naaquhum lahaa khaaḍi'een.

إِن نَّشَأْ نُنَزِّلْ عَلَيْهِم مِّنَ السَّمَآءِ ءَايَةً فَظَلَّتْ أَعْنَٰقُهُمْ لَهَا خَٰضِعِينَ ﴿٤﴾

5. Whenever a new message comes to them from the Beneficent Allah, they turn away from it.

5. Wa maa ya-teehim-min zikrim-minar-Raḥmaani muḥdasin illaa kaanoo 'anhu mu'riḍeen.

وَمَا يَأْتِيهِم مِّن ذِكْرٍ مِّنَ الرَّحْمَٰنِ مُحْدَثٍ إِلَّا كَانُوا عَنْهُ مُعْرِضِينَ ﴿٥﴾

6. They have called (our revelation) lies. They will soon learn the consequences of what they mocked.

6. Faqad kazzaboo fasaya-teehim ambaaa'u maa kaanoo bihee yastahzi'oon.

فَقَدْ كَذَّبُوا فَسَيَأْتِيهِمْ أَنۢبَٰٓؤُا مَا كَانُوا بِهِۦ يَسْتَهْزِءُونَ ﴿٦﴾

7. Did they not seen the earth in which We have made gracious plants grow?

7. Awa lam yaraw ilal-arḍi kam ambatnaa feehaa min kulli zawjin kareem.

أَوَلَمْ يَرَوْا إِلَى الْأَرْضِ كَمْ أَنۢبَتْنَا فِيهَا مِن كُلِّ زَوْجٍ كَرِيمٍ ﴿٧﴾

8. In this there is, certainly, evidence (of the Truth). But most of them have no faith.

8. Inna fee zaalika la-Aayah; wa maa kaana aksaruhum mu'mineen.

إِنَّ فِي ذَٰلِكَ لَءَايَةً ۖ وَمَا كَانَ أَكْثَرُهُم مُّؤْمِنِينَ ﴿٨﴾

9. Your Lord is the Majestic and the All-merciful.

9. Wa inna Rabbaka la-Huwal 'Azeezur-Raḥeem.

وَإِنَّ رَبَّكَ لَهُوَ الْعَزِيزُ الرَّحِيمُ ﴿٩﴾

ع ٩ ٥

10. When Your Lord told Moses to go to the unjust people of the Pharaoh

10. Wa iz naadaa Rabbuka Moosaaa ani'-til-qawmaẓ-ẓaalimeen.

وَإِذْ نَادَىٰ رَبُّكَ مُوسَىٰٓ أَنِ ائْتِ الْقَوْمَ الظَّٰلِمِينَ ﴿١٠﴾

11. and ask them, "Why do you not fear Allah?"	11. Qawma Fir'awn; alaa yattaqoon.	قَوْمَ فِرْعَوْنَ ؕ اَلَا يَتَّقُوْنَ ﴿١١﴾
12. he replied, "Lord, I am afraid that they will call me a liar.	12. Qaala Rabbi inneee akhaafu añy-yukazziboon.	قَالَ رَبِّ اِنِّيْۤ اَخَافُ اَنْ يُّكَذِّبُوْنِؕ ﴿١٢﴾
13. I feel nervous and my tongue is not fluent, so send Aaron with me.	13. Wa yaḍeequ ṣadree wa laa yanṭaliqu lisaanee fa-arsil ilaa Haaroon.	وَيَضِيْقُ صَدْرِيْ وَلَا يَنْطَلِقُ لِسَانِيْ فَاَرْسِلْ اِلٰى هٰرُوْنَ ﴿١٣﴾
14. They have charged me with a crime for which I am afraid they will kill me."	14. Wa lahum 'alayya zambun fa-akhaafu añy-yaqtuloon.	وَلَهُمْ عَلَيَّ ذَنْۢبٌ فَاَخَافُ اَنْ يَّقْتُلُوْنِ ﴿١٤﴾
15. The Lord said, "Have no fear, both of you go with Our miracles. We shall listen closely to you."	15. Qaala kallaa fazhabaa bi-Aayaatinaaa innaa ma'akum mustami'oon.	قَالَ كَلَّا ۚ فَاذْهَبَا بِاٰيٰتِنَاۤ اِنَّا مَعَكُمْ مُّسْتَمِعُوْنَ ﴿١٥﴾
16. They came to the Pharaoh and said, "We are the Messengers of the Lord of the Universe.	16. Fa-tiyaa Fir'awna faqoolaaa innaa Rasoolu Rabbil-'aalameen.	فَاْتِيَا فِرْعَوْنَ فَقُوْلَاۤ اِنَّا رَسُوْلُ رَبِّ الْعٰلَمِيْنَۙ ﴿١٦﴾
17. Send the Israelites with us."	17. An arsil ma'anaa Baneee Israaa'eel.	اَنْ اَرْسِلْ مَعَنَا بَنِيْۤ اِسْرَآءِيْلَؕ ﴿١٧﴾
18. The Pharaoh said, "Did we not bring you up in our home as an infant and did you not live with us for many years?	18. Qaala alam nurabbika feenaa waleedañw-wa labista feenaa min 'umurika sineen.	قَالَ اَلَمْ نُرَبِّكَ فِيْنَا وَلِيْدًا وَّلَبِثْتَ فِيْنَا مِنْ عُمُرِكَ سِنِيْنَۙ ﴿١٨﴾
19. And you did the deed which you did. You are certainly ungrateful."	19. Wa fa'alta fa'latakal-latee fa'alta wa anta minal-kaafireen.	وَفَعَلْتَ فَعْلَتَكَ الَّتِيْ فَعَلْتَ وَاَنْتَ مِنَ الْكٰفِرِيْنَ ﴿١٩﴾
20. Moses said, "I did do it and I (did not think he would die and) made a mistake.	20. Qaala fa'altuhaaa izañw-wa ana minaḍ-ḍaaalleen.	قَالَ فَعَلْتُهَاۤ اِذًا وَّاَنَا مِنَ الضَّآلِّيْنَؕ ﴿٢٠﴾
21. Then I ran away from you in fear, but my Lord granted me the law and has appointed me as a Messenger.	21. Fafarartu minkum lammaa khiftukum fawahaba lee Rabbee ḥukmañw-wa ja'alanee minal-mursaleen.	فَفَرَرْتُ مِنْكُمْ لَمَّا خِفْتُكُمْ فَوَهَبَ لِيْ رَبِّيْ حُكْمًا وَّجَعَلَنِيْ مِنَ الْمُرْسَلِيْنَ ﴿٢١﴾
22. And this is the favor with which you oblige me: You have made the Israelites your slaves."	22. Wa tilka ni'matun tamunnuhaa 'alayya an 'abbatta Baneee Israaa'eel.	وَتِلْكَ نِعْمَةٌ تَمُنُّهَا عَلَيَّ اَنْ عَبَّدْتَّ بَنِيْۤ اِسْرَآءِيْلَؕ ﴿٢٢﴾
23. The Pharaoh asked, "Who is the Lord of the Universe?"	23. Qaala Fir'awnu wa maa Rabbul-'aalameen.	قَالَ فِرْعَوْنُ وَمَا رَبُّ الْعٰلَمِيْنَؕ ﴿٢٣﴾
24. Moses replied, "The Lord of the heavens and the earth and all that is between them, if you want to be certain."	24. Qaala Rabbus-samaawaati wal-arḍi wa maa baynahumaaa in kuntum-mooqineen	قَالَ رَبُّ السَّمٰوٰتِ وَالْاَرْضِ وَمَا بَيْنَهُمَا ؕ اِنْ كُنْتُمْ مُّوْقِنِيْنَ ﴿٢٤﴾
25. The Pharaoh said to the people around him, "Did you hear that?"	25. Qaala liman ḥawlahooo alaa tastami'oon.	قَالَ لِمَنْ حَوْلَهٗۤ اَلَا تَسْتَمِعُوْنَ ﴿٢٥﴾
26. Moses continued, "He is the Lord and the Lord of your forefathers."	26. Qaala Rabbukum wa Rabbu aabaaa'ikumul awwaleen.	قَالَ رَبُّكُمْ وَرَبُّ اٰبَآئِكُمُ الْاَوَّلِيْنَ ﴿٢٦﴾
27. The Pharaoh said, "The Messenger who has been sent to	27. Qaala inna Rasoolakumul-lazeee ursila	قَالَ اِنَّ رَسُوْلَكُمُ الَّذِيْۤ اُرْسِلَ

you is certainly insane."	ilaykum lamajnoon.	إِلَيْكُمْ لَمَجْنُونٌ ٢٧
28. Moses continued, "He is the Lord of the East and West and all that is between them, if only you would think."	28. Qaala Rabbul-mashriqi walmaghribi wa maa bayna-humaaa in kuntum ta'qiloon.	قَالَ رَبُّ الْمَشْرِقِ وَالْمَغْرِبِ وَمَا بَيْنَهُمَا ۖ إِن كُنتُمْ تَعْقِلُونَ ٢٨
29. Pharaoh said, "If you put forward any Ilah (one deserving to be worshiped) other than me, I will surely imprison you."	29. Qaala la'init-takhazta ilaahan ghayree la-aj'alannaka minal-masjooneen.	قَالَ لَئِنِ اتَّخَذْتَ إِلَٰهًا غَيْرِي لَأَجْعَلَنَّكَ مِنَ الْمَسْجُونِينَ ٢٩
30. Moses asked, "What if I were to bring you clear proof (of the existence of Allah)?"	30. Qaala awalaw ji'tuka bishay'im-mubeen.	قَالَ أَوَلَوْ جِئْتُكَ بِشَيْءٍ مُّبِينٍ ٣٠
31. The Pharaoh replied, "Bring it, if you are telling the truth."	31. Qaala fa-ti biheee in kunta minaṣ-ṣaadiqeen.	قَالَ فَأْتِ بِهِ إِن كُنتَ مِنَ الصَّادِقِينَ ٣١
32. Moses threw his staff and suddenly it became a serpent.	32. Fa-alqaa 'aṣaahu fa-izaa hiya su'baanum-mubeen.	فَأَلْقَىٰ عَصَاهُ فَإِذَا هِيَ ثُعْبَانٌ مُّبِينٌ ٣٢
33. Then he uncovered his hand and it was sheer white to the onlookers.	33. Wa naza'a yadahoo fa-izaa hiya bayḍaaa'u linnaa-ẓireen.	وَنَزَعَ يَدَهُ فَإِذَا هِيَ بَيْضَاءُ لِلنَّاظِرِينَ ٣٣
34. The Pharaoh said to the people around him, "He is certainly a skillful magician.	34. Qaala lilmala'i ḥawlahooo inna haazaa lasaaḥirun 'aleem.	قَالَ لِلْمَلَإِ حَوْلَهُ إِنَّ هَٰذَا لَسَاحِرٌ عَلِيمٌ ٣٤
35. He wants to expel you from your land through his magic. What is your opinion?"	35. Yureedu añy-yukhrijakum min arḍikum bisiḥrihee famaa-zaa ta-muroon.	يُرِيدُ أَن يُخْرِجَكُم مِّنْ أَرْضِكُم بِسِحْرِهِ فَمَاذَا تَأْمُرُونَ ٣٥
36. They said, "Hold him and his brother off for a while	36. Qaalooo arjih wa akhaahu wab'as filmadaaa'ini ḥaashi-reen.	قَالُوا أَرْجِهْ وَأَخَاهُ وَابْعَثْ فِي الْمَدَائِنِ حَاشِرِينَ ٣٦
37. and summon every skillful magician from all the cities."	37. Ya-tooka bikulli saḥ-ḥaarin 'aleem.	يَأْتُوكَ بِكُلِّ سَحَّارٍ عَلِيمٍ ٣٧
38. So all the magicians were gathered together	38. Fajumi'as-saḥaratu li-meeqaati Yawmim-ma'loom.	فَجُمِعَ السَّحَرَةُ لِمِيقَاتِ يَوْمٍ مَّعْلُومٍ ٣٨
39. at the appointed time	39. Wa qeela linnaasi hal antum-mujtami'oon.	وَقِيلَ لِلنَّاسِ هَلْ أَنتُم مُّجْتَمِعُونَ ٣٩
40. and the people were asked, "Will you all be there so that we may follow the magicians if they become victorious?"	40. La'allanaa nattabi'us-saḥarata in kaanoo humul-ghaalibeen..	لَعَلَّنَا نَتَّبِعُ السَّحَرَةَ إِن كَانُوا هُمُ الْغَالِبِينَ ٤٠
41. When the magicians came, they asked the Pharaoh, "Will	41. Falammaa jaaa'as-saḥa-ratu qaaloo li-Fir'awna	فَلَمَّا جَاءَ السَّحَرَةُ قَالُوا لِفِرْعَوْنَ

there be any reward for us if we win?"	a'inna lanaa la-ajran in kunnaa naḥnul-ghaalibeen.	أَئِنَّ لَنَا لَأَجْرًا إِنْ كُنَّا نَحْنُ الْغٰلِبِيْنَ ﴿٤١﴾
42. He replied, "You will then be my closest associates."	42. Qaala na'am wa innakum izal-laminal-muqarrabeen.	قَالَ نَعَمْ وَإِنَّكُمْ إِذًا لَّمِنَ الْمُقَرَّبِيْنَ ﴿٤٢﴾
43. (Moses) said to the magicians, "Cast down what you want to."	43. Qaala lahum-Moosaaa alqoo maaa antum-mulqoon.	قَالَ لَهُمْ مُّوْسٰٓى أَلْقُوْا مَآ أَنْتُمْ مُّلْقُوْنَ ﴿٤٣﴾
44. So they cast down their ropes and staffs saying, "By the honor of the Pharaoh we shall certainly become the winners."	44. Fa-alqaw ḥibaalahum wa 'iṣiyyahum wa qaaloo bi'izzati Fir'awna innaa lanaḥnul-ghaaliboon.	فَأَلْقَوْا حِبَالَهُمْ وَعِصِيَّهُمْ وَقَالُوْا بِعِزَّةِ فِرْعَوْنَ إِنَّا لَنَحْنُ الْغٰلِبُوْنَ ﴿٤٤﴾
45. Then Moses cast down his staff and suddenly it swallowed up what they had falsely invented.	45. Fa-alqaa Moosaa 'aṣaahu fa-izaa hiya talqafu maa ya-fikoon.	فَأَلْقٰى مُوْسٰى عَصَاهُ فَإِذَا هِيَ تَلْقَفُ مَا يَأْفِكُوْنَ ﴿٤٥﴾
46. The magicians fell down in adoration	46. Fa-ulqiyas-saḥaratu saajideen.	فَأُلْقِيَ السَّحَرَةُ سٰجِدِيْنَ ﴿٤٦﴾
47. saying, "We believe in the Lord of the Universe	47. Qaalooo aamannaa bi-Rabbil-'aalameen.	قَالُوْٓا اٰمَنَّا بِرَبِّ الْعٰلَمِيْنَ ﴿٤٧﴾
48. and the Lord of Moses and Aaron."	48. Rabbi Moosaa wa Haaroon.	رَبِّ مُوْسٰى وَهٰرُوْنَ ﴿٤٨﴾
49. The Pharaoh said, "Is it that you believed without my permission? He seems to be your chief who has taught you magic, but you will soon know (the result of what you have done) I shall certainly cut off your hands and feet on opposite sides and crucify you all together."	49. Qaala aamantum lahoo qabla an aazana lakum innahoo lakabeerukumul-lazee 'allamakumus-siḥra falasawfa ta'lamoon; la-uqaṭṭi'anna aydiyakum wa arjulakum-min khilaafiñw-wa la-uṣallibannakum ajma'een.	قَالَ اٰمَنْتُمْ لَهٗ قَبْلَ أَنْ اٰذَنَ لَكُمْ إِنَّهٗ لَكَبِيْرُكُمُ الَّذِيْ عَلَّمَكُمُ السِّحْرَ فَلَسَوْفَ تَعْلَمُوْنَ لَأُقَطِّعَنَّ أَيْدِيَكُمْ وَأَرْجُلَكُمْ مِّنْ خِلَافٍ وَّلَأُصَلِّبَنَّكُمْ أَجْمَعِيْنَ ﴿٤٩﴾
50. They said, "It does not matter. We shall be returning to our Lord	50. Qaaloo laa ḍayra innaaa ilaa Rabbinaa munqaliboon.	قَالُوْا لَا ضَيْرَ إِنَّآ إِلٰى رَبِّنَا مُنْقَلِبُوْنَ ﴿٥٠﴾
51. We hope that our Lord will forgive us for our sins; we were not believers at first."	51. Innaa naṭma'u añy-yaghfira lanaa Rabbunaa khaṭaayaanaaa an kunnaaa awwalal-mu'mineen.	إِنَّا نَطْمَعُ أَنْ يَّغْفِرَ لَنَا رَبُّنَا خَطٰيٰنَآ أَنْ كُنَّآ أَوَّلَ الْمُؤْمِنِيْنَ ﴿٥١﴾ ع ٤/١٨
52. We sent a revelation to Moses telling him to leave with our servants during the night; they would be pursued (by the Pharaoh).	52. Wa awḥaynaaa ilaa Moosaaa an asri bi'ibaadeee innakum-muttaba'oon.	وَأَوْحَيْنَآ إِلٰى مُوْسٰٓى أَنْ أَسْرِ بِعِبَادِيْٓ إِنَّكُمْ مُّتَّبَعُوْنَ ﴿٥٢﴾
53. The Pharaoh sent word to all the cities saying,	53. Fa-arsala Fir'awnu fil-madaaa'ini ḥaashireen.	فَأَرْسَلَ فِرْعَوْنُ فِي الْمَدَآئِنِ حٰشِرِيْنَ ﴿٥٣﴾
54. "These are a small group of people	54. Inna haaa'ulaaa'i lashirzimatun qaleeloon.	إِنَّ هٰٓؤُلَآءِ لَشِرْذِمَةٌ قَلِيْلُوْنَ ﴿٥٤﴾
55. who have enraged us greatly."	55. Wa-innahum-lanaa la-ghaaa'iẓoon.	وَإِنَّهُمْ لَنَا لَغَآئِظُوْنَ ﴿٥٥﴾
56. "We are warning all of you about them."	56. Wa innaa lajamee'un ḥaaziroon.	وَإِنَّا لَجَمِيْعٌ حٰذِرُوْنَ ﴿٥٦﴾

57. We deprived them (the unbelievers) of gardens, springs,	57. Fa-akhrajnaahum-min Jannaatiñw-wa ‘uyoon.	فَأَخْرَجْنَٰهُم مِّن جَنَّٰتٍ وَعُيُونٍ ۝٥٧
58. treasures, and graceful dwellings.	58. Wa kunooziñw-wa maqaamin kareem.	وَكُنُوزٍ وَمَقَامٍ كَرِيمٍ ۝٥٨
59. Thus we allowed the Israelites to inherit them all.	59. Kazaalika wa awrasnaahaa Baneee Israaa’eel.	كَذَٰلِكَ وَأَوْرَثْنَٰهَا بَنِىٓ إِسْرَٰٓءِيلَ ۝٥٩
60. The people of the Pharaoh pursued them at sunrise	60. Fa-atba‘oohum-mushriqeen.	فَأَتْبَعُوهُم مُّشْرِقِينَ ۝٦٠
61. When the two groups came close to each other, the companions of Moses said, “We will be caught.”	61. Falammaa taraaa’al-jam‘aani qaala aṣḥaabu Moosaaa innaa lamudrakoon.	فَلَمَّا تَرَٰٓءَا ٱلْجَمْعَانِ قَالَ أَصْحَٰبُ مُوسَىٰٓ إِنَّا لَمُدْرَكُونَ ۝٦١
62. Moses said, “Certainly not. My Lord is with me and He will certainly save me.”	62. Qaala kallaaa inna ma‘iya Rabbee sa-yahdeen.	قَالَ كَلَّآ ۖ إِنَّ مَعِىَ رَبِّى سَيَهْدِينِ ۝٦٢
63. We sent a revelation to Moses saying, “Strike the sea with your staff.” The sea was rent asunder and each side stood high up like a huge mountain.	63. Fa-awḥaynaaa ilaa Moosaaa aniḍrib bi‘aṣaakal-baḥra fanfalaqa fakaana kullu firqin kaṭṭawdil-‘aẓeem.	فَأَوْحَيْنَآ إِلَىٰ مُوسَىٰٓ أَنِ ٱضْرِب بِّعَصَاكَ ٱلْبَحْرَ ۖ فَٱنفَلَقَ فَكَانَ كُلُّ فِرْقٍ كَٱلطَّوْدِ ٱلْعَظِيمِ ۝٦٣
64. Then We brought the two parties closer.	64. Wa azlafnaa sammal-aakhareen.	وَأَزْلَفْنَا ثَمَّ ٱلْءَاخَرِينَ ۝٦٤
65. We saved Moses and all the people with him	65. Wa anjaynaa Moosaa wa mam-ma‘ahooo ajma‘een.	وَأَنجَيْنَا مُوسَىٰ وَمَن مَّعَهُۥٓ أَجْمَعِينَ ۝٦٥
66. then drowned the other party.	66. Summa aghraqnal-aakhareen.	ثُمَّ أَغْرَقْنَا ٱلْءَاخَرِينَ ۝٦٦
67. In this there was certainly evidence (of the Truth), but most of them did not have any faith.	67. Inna fee zaalika la-Aayaah; wa maa kaana aksaruhum-mu’mineen.	إِنَّ فِى ذَٰلِكَ لَءَايَةً ۖ وَمَا كَانَ أَكْثَرُهُم مُّؤْمِنِينَ ۝٦٧
68. Your Lord is certainly Majestic and All-merciful.	68. Wa inna Rabbaka la-Huwal-‘Azeezur-Raḥeem.	وَإِنَّ رَبَّكَ لَهُوَ ٱلْعَزِيزُ ٱلرَّحِيمُ ۝٦٨
69. Explain to them the story of Abraham,	69. Watlu ‘alayhim naba-a Ibraaheem.	وَٱتْلُ عَلَيْهِمْ نَبَأَ إِبْرَٰهِيمَ ۝٦٩
70. when he asked his father and others, “What do you worship?”	70. Iz qaala li-abeehi wa qawmihee maa ta‘budoon.	إِذْ قَالَ لِأَبِيهِ وَقَوْمِهِۦ مَا تَعْبُدُونَ ۝٧٠
71. They replied, “We worship idols and shall continue to worship them.”	71. Qaaloo na‘budu aṣnaaman fanaẓallu lahaa ‘aakifeen.	قَالُوا۟ نَعْبُدُ أَصْنَامًا فَنَظَلُّ لَهَا عَٰكِفِينَ ۝٧١
72. He asked them, “Can the idols hear you when you pray to them	72. Qaala hal yasma‘oonakum iz tad‘oon.	قَالَ هَلْ يَسْمَعُونَكُمْ إِذْ تَدْعُونَ ۝٧٢
73. or can they benefit or harm you?”	73. Aw yanfa‘oonakum aw yaḍurroon.	أَوْ يَنفَعُونَكُمْ أَوْ يَضُرُّونَ ۝٧٣
74. They said, “But our fathers worshipped them.”	74. Qaaloo bal wajadnaaa aabaaa’anaa kazaalika yaf‘aloon.	قَالُوا۟ بَلْ وَجَدْنَآ ءَابَآءَنَا كَذَٰلِكَ يَفْعَلُونَ ۝٧٤
75. (Abraham) said, “Do you know that what you worship	75. Qaala afara’aytum-maa kuntum ta‘budoon.	قَالَ أَفَرَءَيْتُم مَّا كُنتُمْ تَعْبُدُونَ ۝٧٥

ع ٤ وقف لازم

76. and what your forefathers worshipped	76. Antum wa aabaaa'ukumul-aqdamoon.	أَنتُمْ وَآبَاؤُكُمُ الْأَقْدَمُونَ ﴿٧٦﴾
77. are my enemies except the Lord of the universe?	77. Fa-innahum 'aduwwulleee illaa Rabbal-'aalameen	فَإِنَّهُمْ عَدُوٌّ لِّي إِلَّا رَبَّ الْعَالَمِينَ ﴿٧٧﴾
78. It is He who created me and He will guide me.	78. Allazee khalaqanee fa-Huwa yahdeen.	الَّذِي خَلَقَنِي فَهُوَ يَهْدِينِ ﴿٧٨﴾
79. It is He who gives me food and drink	79. Wallazee Huwa yuṭ'imunee wa yasqeen.	وَالَّذِي هُوَ يُطْعِمُنِي وَيَسْقِينِ ﴿٧٩﴾
80. and heals me when I am sick.	80. Wa izaa mariḍtu fahuwa yashfeen.	وَإِذَا مَرِضْتُ فَهُوَ يَشْفِينِ ﴿٨٠﴾
81. He will cause me to die and will bring me back to life	81. Wallazee yumeetunee summa yuḥyeen.	وَالَّذِي يُمِيتُنِي ثُمَّ يُحْيِينِ ﴿٨١﴾
82. It is He whom I expect to forgive my sins on the Day of Judgment.	82. Wallazeee aṭma'u añy-yaghfira lee khaṭeee'atee Yawmad-Deen.	وَالَّذِي أَطْمَعُ أَن يَغْفِرَ لِي خَطِيئَتِي يَوْمَ الدِّينِ ﴿٨٢﴾
83. Lord, grant me authority. Join me with the righteous ones.	83. Rabbi hab lee ḥukmañw-wa alḥiqnee biṣ-ṣaaliḥeen.	رَبِّ هَبْ لِي حُكْمًا وَأَلْحِقْنِي بِالصَّالِحِينَ ﴿٨٣﴾
84. Make my words come true in the future.	84. Waj'al-lee lisaana ṣidqin fil-aakhireen.	وَاجْعَل لِّي لِسَانَ صِدْقٍ فِي الْآخِرِينَ ﴿٨٤﴾
85. Make me inherit the bountiful Paradise.	85. Waj'alnee miñw-warasati Jannatin-Na'eem.	وَاجْعَلْنِي مِن وَرَثَةِ جَنَّةِ النَّعِيمِ ﴿٨٥﴾
86. Forgive my father. He has gone astray.	86. Waghfir li-abeee innahoo kaana minḍḍaaalleen.	وَاغْفِرْ لِأَبِي إِنَّهُ كَانَ مِنَ الضَّالِّينَ ﴿٨٦﴾
87. Do not betray me on the Day of Judgment	87. Wa laa tukhzinee Yawma yub'asoon.	وَلَا تُخْزِنِي يَوْمَ يُبْعَثُونَ ﴿٨٧﴾
88. when neither wealth nor children will be of any benefit	88. Yawma laa yanfa'u maaluñw-wa laa banoon.	يَوْمَ لَا يَنفَعُ مَالٌ وَلَا بَنُونَ ﴿٨٨﴾
89. except what is done in obedience to Allah with a submissive heart."	89. Illaa man atal-laaha biqalbin saleem.	إِلَّا مَنْ أَتَى اللَّهَ بِقَلْبٍ سَلِيمٍ ﴿٨٩﴾
90. On the Day of Judgment Paradise will be brought near	90. Wa uzlifatil-Jannatu lilmuttaqeen.	وَأُزْلِفَتِ الْجَنَّةُ لِلْمُتَّقِينَ ﴿٩٠﴾
91. the pious and hell will be left open for the rebellious ones	91. Wa burrizatil-Jaḥeemu lilghaaween.	وَبُرِّزَتِ الْجَحِيمُ لِلْغَاوِينَ ﴿٩١﴾
92. who will be asked, "What did you worship	92. Wa qeela lahum aynamaa kuntum ta'budoon.	وَقِيلَ لَهُمْ أَيْنَمَا كُنتُمْ تَعْبُدُونَ ﴿٩٢﴾
93. besides Allah? Will the idols help you? Can they help themselves?"	93. Min doonil-laahi hal yanṣuroonakum aw yantaṣiroon	مِن دُونِ اللَّهِ هَلْ يَنصُرُونَكُمْ أَوْ يَنتَصِرُونَ ﴿٩٣﴾
94. The idol worshippers, the idols, the rebellious ones,	94. Fakubkiboo feehaa hum walghaawoon.	فَكُبْكِبُوا فِيهَا هُمْ وَالْغَاوُونَ ﴿٩٤﴾
95. and the army of Satan will all be thrown headlong into hell.	95. Wa junoodu Ibleesa ajma'oon.	وَجُنُودُ إِبْلِيسَ أَجْمَعُونَ ﴿٩٥﴾
96. Quarrelling therein with each other,	96. Qaaloo wa hum feehaa yakhtaṣimoon.	قَالُوا وَهُمْ فِيهَا يَخْتَصِمُونَ ﴿٩٦﴾
97. they will say, "By Allah, we were in clear error	97. Tallaahi in kunnaa lafee ḍalaalim-mubeen.	تَاللَّهِ إِن كُنَّا لَفِي ضَلَالٍ مُّبِينٍ ﴿٩٧﴾

98. when we considered you equal to the Lord of the Universe.	98. Iz nusawweekum bi-Rabbil-‘aalameen.	إِذْ نُسَوِّيكُم بِرَبِّ الْعٰلَمِينَ ﴿٩٨﴾
99. Only the sinful ones made us go astray.	99. Wa maaa aḍallanaaa illal-mujrimoon.	وَمَآ أَضَلَّنَآ إِلَّا الْمُجْرِمُونَ ﴿٩٩﴾
100. We neither have anyone to intercede for us before Allah	100. Famaa lanaa min shaa-fi‘een.	فَمَا لَنَا مِن شٰفِعِينَ ﴿١٠٠﴾
101. nor a loving friend.	101. Wa laa ṣadeeqin ḥameem.	وَلَا صَدِيقٍ حَمِيمٍ ﴿١٠١﴾
102. Would that we could have a chance to live again so that we might become believers.”	102. Falaw anna lanaa karratan fanakoona minal-mu’mineen.	فَلَوْ أَنَّ لَنَا كَرَّةً فَنَكُونَ مِنَ الْمُؤْمِنِينَ ﴿١٠٢﴾
103. In this there is evidence (of the truth), but many of them do not have any faith.	103. Inna fee zaalika la-Aayah; wa maa kaana aksaruhum mu’mineen.	إِنَّ فِي ذٰلِكَ لَءَايَةً ۖ وَمَا كَانَ أَكْثَرُهُم مُّؤْمِنِينَ ﴿١٠٣﴾
104. Your Lord is certainly Majestic and All-merciful.	104. Wa inna Rabbaka la-Huwal-‘Azeezur-Raḥeem.	وَإِنَّ رَبَّكَ لَهُوَ الْعَزِيزُ الرَّحِيمُ ﴿١٠٤﴾
105. The people of Noah rejected the Messengers.	105. Kazzabat qawmu Noo-ḥinil-mursaleen.	كَذَّبَتْ قَوْمُ نُوحٍ الْمُرْسَلِينَ ﴿١٠٥﴾
106. Their brother Noah asked them, “Why do you not fear Allah?”	106. Iz qaala lahum akhoohum Nooḥun alaa tattaqoon.	إِذْ قَالَ لَهُمْ أَخُوهُمْ نُوحٌ أَلَا تَتَّقُونَ ﴿١٠٦﴾
107. “I am a trustworthy Messenger sent to you.	107. Innee lakum Rasoolun ameen.	إِنِّي لَكُمْ رَسُولٌ أَمِينٌ ﴿١٠٧﴾
108. Have fear of Allah and obey me.	108. Fattaqullaaha wa aṭee-‘oon.	فَاتَّقُوا اللّٰهَ وَأَطِيعُونِ ﴿١٠٨﴾
109. I ask no payment from you for my preaching. The Lord of the Universe will give me my reward.	109. Wa maaa as’alukum ‘alayhi min ajrin in ajriya illaa ‘alaa Rabbil-‘aalameen.	وَمَآ أَسْـَٔلُكُمْ عَلَيْهِ مِنْ أَجْرٍ ۖ إِنْ أَجْرِيَ إِلَّا عَلٰى رَبِّ الْعٰلَمِينَ ﴿١٠٩﴾
110. Have fear of Allah and obey me.”	110. Fattaqul-laaha wa aṭee-‘oon.	فَاتَّقُوا اللّٰهَ وَأَطِيعُونِ ﴿١١٠﴾
111. They said, “Should we believe in you when no one has followed you except the lowest ones?”	111. Qaalooo anu’minu laka wattaba‘akal-arzaloon.	قَالُوٓا أَنُؤْمِنُ لَكَ وَاتَّبَعَكَ الْأَرْذَلُونَ ﴿١١١﴾
112. (Noah) said, “I have no knowledge of their deeds.	112. Qaala wa maa ‘ilmee bimaa kaanoo ya‘maloon.	قَالَ وَمَا عِلْمِي بِمَا كَانُوا يَعْمَلُونَ ﴿١١٢﴾
113. only you would realize, their account is with my Lord.	113. In ḥisaabuhum illaa ‘alaa Rabbee law tash‘uroon.	إِنْ حِسَابُهُمْ إِلَّا عَلٰى رَبِّي ۖ لَوْ تَشْعُرُونَ ﴿١١٣﴾
114. I do not drive away the believers.	114. Wa maaa ana biṭaaridil-mu’mineen.	وَمَآ أَنَا بِطَارِدِ الْمُؤْمِنِينَ ﴿١١٤﴾
115. I am only to warn you clearly.	115. In ana illaa nazeerum-mubeen.	إِنْ أَنَا إِلَّا نَذِيرٌ مُّبِينٌ ﴿١١٥﴾
116. They said, “Noah, if you did not desist, you will, certainly, be stoned to death.”	116. Qaaloo la’il-lam tantahi yaa Nooḥu latakoonanna minal-marjoomeen.	قَالُوا لَئِن لَّمْ تَنتَهِ يٰنُوحُ لَتَكُونَنَّ مِنَ الْمَرْجُومِينَ ﴿١١٦﴾

النصف

117. Then Noah said, "Lord, my people have rejected me.
118. Allow Your judgment to take place between me and these people and save me and the believers with me."
119. We saved him and those who were with him in a fully prepared Ark,
120. and drowned the others.
121. In this there is evidence (of the truth) but most of them do not have any faith.
122. Your Lord is Majestic and All-merciful.
123. The tribe of Ad rejected the Messengers.
124. Their brother Hud asked them, "Why do you not have fear (of Allah)?
125. I am a trustworthy Messenger sent to you.
126. Have fear of Allah and obey me.
127. I do not ask for any payment for my preaching. I shall receive my reward from the Lord of the universe.
128. "Do you build useless monuments on every road
129. and raise strong mansions as if you were to live forever?
130. When you attack, you attack as tyrants do.
131. Have fear of Allah and obey me.
132. Have fear of the One who has bestowed upon you all that you know.
133. He has given you cattle, children,
134. gardens, and springs.
135. I am afraid that you will suffer the torment of the great day (the Day of Judgment)."

117. Qaala Rabbi inna qawmee kazzaboon.
118. Faftaḥ baynee wa baynahum fatḥañw-wa najjinee wa mam-ma'iya minal-mu'mineen.
119. Fa-anjaynaahu wa mam-ma'ahoo fil-fulkil-mashḥoon.
120. Summa aghraqnaa ba'dul-baaqeen.
121. Inna fee zaalika la-Aayaah; wa maa kaana aksaru-hum-mu'mineen.
122. Wa inna Rabbaka la-Huwal-'Azeezur-Raḥeem.
123. Kazzabat 'Aadunil-mursaleen.
124. Iz qaala lahum akhoohum Hoodun alaa tattaqoon.
125. Innee lakum Rasoolun ameen.
126. Fattaqullaaha wa aṭee'oon.
127. Wa maaa as'alukum 'alayhi min ajrin in ajriya illaa 'alaa Rabbil-'aalameen.
128. Atabnoona bikulli ree'in aayatan ta'basoon.
129. Wa tattakhizoona maṣaa-ni'a la'allakum takhludoon.
130. Wa izaa baṭashtum ba-ṭashtum jabbaareen.
131. Fattaqul-laaha wa aṭee-'oon.
132. Wattaqul-lazeee amad-dakum bimaa ta'lamoon.
133. Amaddakum bi-an'aa-miñw-wa baneen.
134. Wa jannaatiñw-wa'uyoon.
135. Inneee akhaafu 'alaykum 'azaaba Yawmin 'azeem.

قَالَ رَبِّ اِنَّ قَوۡمِىۡ كَذَّبُوۡنِ ۖۚ ﴿١١٧﴾
فَافۡتَحۡ بَيۡنِىۡ وَبَيۡنَهُمۡ فَتۡحًا وَّنَجِّنِىۡ
وَمَنۡ مَّعِىَ مِنَ الۡمُؤۡمِنِيۡنَ ﴿١١٨﴾
فَاَنۡجَيۡنٰهُ وَمَنۡ مَّعَهٗ فِى الۡفُلۡكِ
الۡمَشۡحُوۡنِ ﴿١١٩﴾
ثُمَّ اَغۡرَقۡنَا بَعۡدُ الۡبٰقِيۡنَ ﴿١٢٠﴾
اِنَّ فِىۡ ذٰلِكَ لَاٰيَةً ؕ وَمَا كَانَ
اَكۡثَرُهُمۡ مُّؤۡمِنِيۡنَ ﴿١٢١﴾
وَاِنَّ رَبَّكَ لَهُوَ الۡعَزِيۡزُ الرَّحِيۡمُ ﴿١٢٢﴾ ع ٦ ١٨
كَذَّبَتۡ عَادُ ۨالۡمُرۡسَلِيۡنَ ۖۚ ﴿١٢٣﴾
اِذۡ قَالَ لَهُمۡ اَخُوۡهُمۡ هُوۡدٌ اَلَا
تَتَّقُوۡنَ ۚ ﴿١٢٤﴾
اِنِّىۡ لَـكُمۡ رَسُوۡلٌ اَمِيۡنٌ ۙ ﴿١٢٥﴾
فَاتَّقُوا اللّٰهَ وَاَطِيۡعُوۡنِ ۚ ﴿١٢٦﴾
وَمَاۤ اَسۡـئَلُكُمۡ عَلَيۡهِ مِنۡ اَجۡرٍ ۚ اِنۡ
اَجۡرِىَ اِلَّا عَلٰى رَبِّ الۡعٰلَمِيۡنَ ؕ ﴿١٢٧﴾
اَتَبۡنُوۡنَ بِكُلِّ رِيۡعٍ اٰيَةً تَعۡبَثُوۡنَ ۙ ﴿١٢٨﴾
وَتَتَّخِذُوۡنَ مَصَانِعَ لَعَلَّكُمۡ
تَخۡلُدُوۡنَ ۚ ﴿١٢٩﴾
وَاِذَا بَطَشۡتُمۡ بَطَشۡتُمۡ جَبَّارِيۡنَ ۚ ﴿١٣٠﴾
فَاتَّقُوا اللّٰهَ وَاَطِيۡعُوۡنِ ۚ ﴿١٣١﴾
وَاتَّقُوا الَّذِىۡۤ اَمَدَّكُمۡ بِمَا تَعۡلَمُوۡنَ ۚ ﴿١٣٢﴾
اَمَدَّكُمۡ بِاَنۡعَامٍ وَّبَنِيۡنَ ۚۙ ﴿١٣٣﴾
وَجَنّٰتٍ وَّعُيُوۡنٍ ۚ ﴿١٣٤﴾
اِنِّىۡۤ اَخَافُ عَلَيۡكُمۡ عَذَابَ
يَوۡمٍ عَظِيۡمٍ ؕ ﴿١٣٥﴾

136. They said, "Whether you preached to us or not,	136. Qaaloo sawaaa'un 'alay-naaa awa-'aẓta am lam takum-minal-waa'iẓeen.	قَالُوْا سَوَآءٌ عَلَيْنَآ اَوَعَظْتَ اَمْ لَمْ تَكُنْ مِّنَ الْوٰعِظِيْنَ ﴿١٣٦﴾
137. your preaching consists of nothing but ancient legends	137. In haa<u>z</u>aaa illaa khuluqul-awwaleen.	اِنْ هٰذَآ اِلَّا خُلُقُ الْاَوَّلِيْنَ ﴿١٣٧﴾
138. and we shall not face any torment."	138. Wa maa naḥnu bimu'a<u>z</u><u>z</u>abeen.	وَمَا نَحْنُ بِمُعَذَّبِيْنَ ﴿١٣٨﴾
139. They rejected him and We destroyed them. In this there is evidence (of the Truth), yet most of them do not have any faith.	139. Fakaz<u>z</u>aboohu fa-ahlaknaahum; inna fee <u>z</u>aalika la-Aayah; wa maa kaana ak<u>s</u>aruhum-mu'mineen.	فَكَذَّبُوْهُ فَاَهْلَكْنٰهُمْ ؕ اِنَّ فِيْ ذٰلِكَ لَاٰيَةً ؕ وَمَا كَانَ اَكْثَرُهُمْ مُّؤْمِنِيْنَ ﴿١٣٩﴾
140. Your Lord is Majestic and All-merciful.	140. Wa inna Rabbaka la-Huwal-'Azeezur-Raḥeem.	وَاِنَّ رَبَّكَ لَهُوَ الْعَزِيْزُ الرَّحِيْمُ ﴿١٤٠﴾ ع ١٨ / ١١
141. The tribe of Thamud rejected the Messengers.	141. Kaz<u>z</u>abat <u>S</u>amoodul-mursaleen.	كَذَّبَتْ ثَمُوْدُ الْمُرْسَلِيْنَ ﴿١٤١﴾
142. Their brother Salih asked them, "Why do you not fear (Allah)?	142. I<u>z</u> qaala lahum akhoohum Ṣaaliḥun alaa tattaqoon.	اِذْ قَالَ لَهُمْ اَخُوْهُمْ صٰلِحٌ اَلَا تَتَّقُوْنَ ﴿١٤٢﴾
143. I am a trustworthy Messenger sent to you.	143. Innee lakum Rasoolun ameen.	اِنِّيْ لَكُمْ رَسُوْلٌ اَمِيْنٌ ﴿١٤٣﴾
144. Have fear of Allah and obey me.	144. Fattaqul-laaha wa aṭee-'oon.	فَاتَّقُوا اللّٰهَ وَاَطِيْعُوْنِ ﴿١٤٤﴾
145. I do not ask for any payment for my preaching. I shall receive my reward from the Lord of the universe."	145. Wa maaa as'alukum 'alayhi min ajrin in ajriya illaa 'alaa Rabbil 'aalameen.	وَمَآ اَسْـَٔلُكُمْ عَلَيْهِ مِنْ اَجْرٍ ۚ اِنْ اَجْرِيَ اِلَّا عَلٰى رَبِّ الْعٰلَمِيْنَ ﴿١٤٥﴾
146. "Do you think that you will remain here peacefully forever	146. Atutrakoona fee maa haahunaaa aamineen.	اَتُتْرَكُوْنَ فِيْ مَا هٰهُنَآ اٰمِنِيْنَ ﴿١٤٦﴾
147. amidst the gardens, springs,	147. Fee jannaatiñw-wa 'uyoon.	فِيْ جَنّٰتٍ وَّعُيُوْنٍ ﴿١٤٧﴾
148. farms, and palm-trees in thick groves,	148. Wa zuroo'iñw-wa nakhlin ṭal'uhaa haḍeem.	وَّزُرُوْعٍ وَّنَخْلٍ طَلْعُهَا هَضِيْمٌ ﴿١٤٨﴾
149. carving comfortable houses out of the mountains?	149. Wa tanḥitoona minal-jibaali buyootan faariheen.	وَتَنْحِتُوْنَ مِنَ الْجِبَالِ بُيُوْتًا فٰرِهِيْنَ ﴿١٤٩﴾
150. Have fear of Allah and obey me.	150. Fattaqul-laaha wa aṭee-'oon.	فَاتَّقُوا اللّٰهَ وَاَطِيْعُوْنِ ﴿١٥٠﴾
151. Do not obey the orders of the transgressors	151. Wa laa tuṭee'ooo amral-musrifeen.	وَلَا تُطِيْعُوْٓا اَمْرَ الْمُسْرِفِيْنَ ﴿١٥١﴾
152. who spread evil in the land with no reform."	152. Alla<u>z</u>eena yufsidoona fil-arḍi wa laa yuṣliḥoon.	الَّذِيْنَ يُفْسِدُوْنَ فِي الْاَرْضِ وَلَا يُصْلِحُوْنَ ﴿١٥٢﴾
153. They said, "You are only of the bewitched ones.	153. Qaalooo innamaaa anta minal-musaḥḥareen.	قَالُوْٓا اِنَّمَآ اَنْتَ مِنَ الْمُسَحَّرِيْنَ ﴿١٥٣﴾
154. You are but a mere mortal like us. Show us a miracle if you are telling the Truth."	154. Maaa anta illaa basharum-mi<u>s</u>lunaa fa-ti bi-Aayatin in kunta minaṣ-ṣaadiqeen.	مَآ اَنْتَ اِلَّا بَشَرٌ مِّثْلُنَا ۚ فَاْتِ بِاٰيَةٍ اِنْ كُنْتَ مِنَ الصّٰدِقِيْنَ ﴿١٥٤﴾

155. He said, "This is a she-camel. She will have her share of water as you have your share, each on a certain day.

155. Qaala haaz̲ihee naaqatul-lahaa shirbuñw-wa lakum shir-bu yawmim-ma‘loom.

قَالَ هٰذِهٖ نَاقَةٌ لَّهَا شِرْبٌ وَّلَكُمْ شِرْبُ يَوْمٍ مَّعْلُوْمٍ ۚ ﴿١٥٥﴾

156. Do not cause her to suffer lest you become subject to the torment of the great day (of Judgment)."

156. Wa laa tamassoohaa bisooo'in faya-khuz̲akum ‘az̲aabu Yawmin ‘Aẓeem.

وَلَا تَمَسُّوْهَا بِسُوْٓءٍ فَيَاْخُذَكُمْ عَذَابُ يَوْمٍ عَظِيْمٍ ﴿١٥٦﴾

157. They slew the she-camel, but later became regretful

157. Fa‘aqaroohaa fa-aṣbaḥoo naadimeen.

فَعَقَرُوْهَا فَاَصْبَحُوْا نٰدِمِيْنَ ۙ ﴿١٥٧﴾

158. and torment struck them. In this there is evidence of the Truth, yet many people do not have any faith.

158. Fa-akhaz̲ahumul-‘az̲aab; inna fee z̲aalika la-Aayah; wa maa kaana aks̲aruhum-mu'mi-neen.

فَاَخَذَهُمُ الْعَذَابُ ؕ اِنَّ فِيْ ذٰلِكَ لَاٰيَةً ؕ وَمَا كَانَ اَكْثَرُهُمْ مُّؤْمِنِيْنَ ﴿١٥٨﴾

159. Your Lord is Majestic and All-merciful.

159. Wa inna Rabbaka la-Huwal-‘Azeezur-Raḥeem.

وَاِنَّ رَبَّكَ لَهُوَ الْعَزِيْزُ الرَّحِيْمُ ﴿١٥٩﴾ ع ١٩ ١٢

160. The people of Lot rejected the Messengers.

160. Kaz̲z̲abat qawmu Looṭi-nil-mursaleen.

كَذَّبَتْ قَوْمُ لُوْطِ ِۨ الْمُرْسَلِيْنَ ﴿١٦٠﴾

161. Their brother Lot asked them, "Why do you not have fear (of Allah)?

161. Iz̲ qaala lahum akhoohum Looṭun alaa tattaqoon.

اِذْ قَالَ لَهُمْ اَخُوْهُمْ لُوْطٌ اَلَا تَتَّقُوْنَ ﴿١٦١﴾

162. I am a trustworthy Messenger.

162. Innee lakum Rasoolun ameen.

اِنِّيْ لَكُمْ رَسُوْلٌ اَمِيْنٌ ۙ ﴿١٦٢﴾

163. Have fear of Allah and obey me.

163. Fattaqullaaha wa aṭee-‘oon.

فَاتَّقُوا اللّٰهَ وَاَطِيْعُوْنِ ۚ ﴿١٦٣﴾

164. I do not ask any payment for my preaching. I shall receive my reward from the Lord of the universe.

164. Wa maaa as'alukum ‘alayhi min ajrin in ajriya illaa ‘alaa Rabbil-‘aalameen.

وَمَآ اَسْـَٔلُكُمْ عَلَيْهِ مِنْ اَجْرٍ ۚ اِنْ اَجْرِيَ اِلَّا عَلٰى رَبِّ الْعٰلَمِيْنَ ؕ ﴿١٦٤﴾

165. Do you, in the world, want to have carnal relations with males

165. Ata-toonaz̲-z̲ukraana minal-‘aalameen.

اَتَاْتُوْنَ الذُّكْرَانَ مِنَ الْعٰلَمِيْنَ ۙ ﴿١٦٥﴾

166. instead of your wives, whom your Lord has created especially for you? You are a transgressing people."

166. Wa taz̲aroona maa khalaqa lakum Rabbukum-min azwaaji-kum; bal antum qawmun ‘aadoon.

وَتَذَرُوْنَ مَا خَلَقَ لَكُمْ رَبُّكُمْ مِّنْ اَزْوَاجِكُمْ ؕ بَلْ اَنْتُمْ قَوْمٌ عٰدُوْنَ ﴿١٦٦﴾

167. They said, "Lot, if you did not give up preaching, you will certainly be expelled (from this town)."

167. Qaaloo la'il-lam tantahi yaa Looṭu latakoonanna minal-mukhrajeen.

قَالُوْا لَئِنْ لَّمْ تَنْتَهِ يٰلُوْطُ لَتَكُوْنَنَّ مِنَ الْمُخْرَجِيْنَ ﴿١٦٧﴾

168. He said, "I certainly hate what you practice.

168. Qaala innee li‘amalikum-minal-qaaleen.

قَالَ اِنِّيْ لِعَمَلِكُمْ مِّنَ الْقَالِيْنَ ؕ ﴿١٦٨﴾

169. Lord, save me and my family from their deeds."

169. Rabbi najjinee wa ahlee mimmaa ya‘maloon.

رَبِّ نَجِّنِيْ وَاَهْلِيْ مِمَّا يَعْمَلُوْنَ ﴿١٦٩﴾

170. We saved him and all of his family

170. Fanajjaynaahu wa ahla-hooo ajma‘een.

فَنَجَّيْنٰهُ وَاَهْلَهٗٓ اَجْمَعِيْنَ ۙ ﴿١٧٠﴾

171. except an old woman who remained behind.

171. Illaa ‘ajoozan filghaa-bireen.

اِلَّا عَجُوْزًا فِي الْغٰبِرِيْنَ ۚ ﴿١٧١﴾

172. We then destroyed the others

172. S̲umma dammarnal-aa-khareen.

ثُمَّ دَمَّرْنَا الْاٰخَرِيْنَ ۚ ﴿١٧٢﴾

173. by pouring upon them a terrible shower of rain. How evil was the rain for those who had been warned!

173. Wa amṭarnaa ‘alayhim-maṭaran fasaaa'a maṭarul-munz̲areen.

وَاَمْطَرْنَا عَلَيْهِمْ مَّطَرًا ۚ فَسَآءَ مَطَرُ الْمُنْذَرِيْنَ ﴿١٧٣﴾

174. In this there is an evidence of the Truth, but many of them did not have any faith.	174. Inna fee <u>z</u>aalika la-Aayah; wa maa kaana ak<u>s</u>aruhum mu'mineen.	إِنَّ فِي ذَٰلِكَ لَآيَةً ۖ وَمَا كَانَ أَكْثَرُهُمْ مُؤْمِنِينَ ﴿١٧٤﴾
175. Your Lord is Majestic and All-merciful.	175. Wa inna Rabbaka la-Huwal-'Azeezur-Raḥeem.	وَإِنَّ رَبَّكَ لَهُوَ الْعَزِيزُ الرَّحِيمُ ﴿١٧٥﴾ ع ٩ ٢٦ ١٣
176. The dwellers of the forest also rejected the Messengers.	176. Ka<u>zz</u>aba Aṣ-ḥaabul Ayka-til-mursaleen.	كَذَّبَ أَصْحَابُ لْـَٔيْكَةِ الْمُرْسَلِينَ ﴿١٧٦﴾
177. Shuayb asked them, "Why do you not have fear (of Allah)?	177. I<u>z</u> qaala lahum Shu'aybun alaa tattaqoon.	إِذْ قَالَ لَهُمْ شُعَيْبٌ أَلَا تَتَّقُونَ ﴿١٧٧﴾
178. I am a trustworthy Messenger.	178. Innee lakum Rasoolun ameen.	إِنِّي لَكُمْ رَسُولٌ أَمِينٌ ﴿١٧٨﴾
179. Have fear of Allah and obey me.	179. Fattaqul-laaha wa aṭee-'oon.	فَاتَّقُوا اللَّهَ وَأَطِيعُونِ ﴿١٧٩﴾
180. I do not ask any payment for my preaching. I shall receive my reward from the Lord of the universe."	180. Wa maaa as'alukum 'alayhi min ajrin in ajriya illaa 'alaa Rabbil-'aalameen.	وَمَا أَسْأَلُكُمْ عَلَيْهِ مِنْ أَجْرٍ ۖ إِنْ أَجْرِيَ إِلَّا عَلَىٰ رَبِّ الْعَالَمِينَ ﴿١٨٠﴾
181. "Maintain just measure in your business and do not cause loss to others.	181. Awful-kayla wa laa ta-koonoo minal-mukhsireen.	أَوْفُوا الْكَيْلَ وَلَا تَكُونُوا مِنَ الْمُخْسِرِينَ ﴿١٨١﴾
182. Weigh your goods with proper balance	182. Wazinoo bilqisṭaasil-mustaqeem.	وَزِنُوا بِالْقِسْطَاسِ الْمُسْتَقِيمِ ﴿١٨٢﴾
183. and do not defraud people in their property or spread evil in the land.	183. Wa laa tabkhasun-naasa ashyaaa'ahum wa laa ta'<u>s</u>aw fil-arḍi mufsideen.	وَلَا تَبْخَسُوا النَّاسَ أَشْيَاءَهُمْ وَلَا تَعْثَوْا فِي الْأَرْضِ مُفْسِدِينَ ﴿١٨٣﴾
184. Have fear of the One who has created you and the generations that lived before you."	184. Wattaqul-la<u>z</u>ee khalaqa-kum waljibillatal-awwaleen.	وَاتَّقُوا الَّذِي خَلَقَكُمْ وَالْجِبِلَّةَ الْأَوَّلِينَ ﴿١٨٤﴾
185. They said, "You are only of the bewitched ones	185. Qaalooo innamaaa anta minal-musaḥḥareen.	قَالُوا إِنَّمَا أَنْتَ مِنَ الْمُسَحَّرِينَ ﴿١٨٥﴾
186. and you are but a mere mortal like us. We think you are a liar.	186. Wa maaa anta illaa basharum-mi<u>s</u>lunaa wa in-naẓunnuka laminal-kaa<u>z</u>ibeen.	وَمَا أَنْتَ إِلَّا بَشَرٌ مِثْلُنَا وَإِنْ نَظُنُّكَ لَمِنَ الْكَاذِبِينَ ﴿١٨٦﴾
187. Let a part of the sky fall on us if what you say is true."	187. Fa-asqiṭ 'alaynaa kisa-fam-minas-samaaa'i in kunta minaṣ-ṣaadiqeen.	فَأَسْقِطْ عَلَيْنَا كِسَفًا مِنَ السَّمَاءِ إِنْ كُنْتَ مِنَ الصَّادِقِينَ ﴿١٨٧﴾
188. He said, "My Lord knows all that you do."	188. Qaala Rabbeee a'lamu bimaa ta'maloon.	قَالَ رَبِّي أَعْلَمُ بِمَا تَعْمَلُونَ ﴿١٨٨﴾
189. They rejected him and then the torment of the hot day (and winds) struck them. It was certainly a great torment.	189. Faka<u>zz</u>aboohu fa-akha-<u>z</u>ahum 'a<u>z</u>aabu Yawmiẓ-ẓullah; innahoo kaana 'a<u>z</u>aaba Yawmin 'Aẓeem.	فَكَذَّبُوهُ فَأَخَذَهُمْ عَذَابُ يَوْمِ الظُّلَّةِ ۚ إِنَّهُ كَانَ عَذَابَ يَوْمٍ عَظِيمٍ ﴿١٨٩﴾
190. In this there is an evidence of the Truth, but many of them did	190. Inna fee <u>z</u>aalika la-Aayah; wa maa kaana	إِنَّ فِي ذَٰلِكَ لَآيَةً ۖ وَمَا كَانَ

not have any faith.	ak<u>s</u>aruhum-mu‘mineen.	أَكْثَرُهُم مُّؤْمِنِينَ ١٩٠
191. Your Lord is Majestic and All-merciful.	191. Wa inna Rabbaka la-Huwal-‘Azeezur-Raḥeem.	وَإِنَّ رَبَّكَ لَهُوَ الْعَزِيزُ الرَّحِيمُ ١٩١
192. This (Quran) is certainly the revelation from the Lord of the universe.	192. Wa innahoo latanzeelu-Rabbil ‘aalameen.	وَإِنَّهُ لَتَنزِيلُ رَبِّ الْعَالَمِينَ ١٩٢
193. It has been revealed through the trustworthy Spirit	193. Nazala bihir-Rooḥul Ameen.	نَزَلَ بِهِ الرُّوحُ الْأَمِينُ ١٩٣
194. to your heart, so that you will warn (the people of the dangers of disobeying Allah).	194. ‘Alaa qalbika litakoona minal-mun<u>z</u>ireen.	عَلَىٰ قَلْبِكَ لِتَكُونَ مِنَ الْمُنذِرِينَ ١٩٤
195. It has been revealed in plain Arabic.	195. Bilisaanin ‘Arabiyyim-mubeen.	بِلِسَانٍ عَرَبِيٍّ مُّبِينٍ ١٩٥
196. Its news was also mentioned in the ancient Books (of the prophets).	196. Wa innahoo lafee Zuburil-awwaleen.	وَإِنَّهُ لَفِي زُبُرِ الْأَوَّلِينَ ١٩٦
197. Was it not sufficient evidence for them (pagans) of the truthfulness (of the Quran) that the Israelite scholars already knew (about the Quran through their Book)?	197. Awalam yakul-lahum Aayatan añy-ya‘lamahoo ‘ulamaaa’u Baneee Israaa’eel.	أَوَلَمْ يَكُن لَّهُمْ آيَةً أَن يَعْلَمَهُ عُلَمَاءُ بَنِي إِسْرَائِيلَ ١٩٧
198. Had We revealed it to a non-Arab	198. Wa law nazzalnaahu ‘alaa ba‘ḍil-a‘jameen.	وَلَوْ نَزَّلْنَاهُ عَلَىٰ بَعْضِ الْأَعْجَمِينَ ١٩٨
199. who read it to them, they (pagans) would not have believed in it.	199. Faqara-ahoo ‘alayhim maa kaanoo bihee mu’mineen.	فَقَرَأَهُ عَلَيْهِم مَّا كَانُوا بِهِ مُؤْمِنِينَ ١٩٩
200. Thus it passes through the hearts of the criminals.	200. Ka<u>z</u>aalika salaknaahu fee quloobil-mujrimeen.	كَذَٰلِكَ سَلَكْنَاهُ فِي قُلُوبِ الْمُجْرِمِينَ ٢٠٠
201. They will not believe in it until they suffer the painful torment.	201. Laa yu’minoona bihee ḥattaa yarawul-‘a<u>z</u>aabal-aleem.	لَا يُؤْمِنُونَ بِهِ حَتَّىٰ يَرَوُا الْعَذَابَ الْأَلِيمَ ٢٠١
202. The torment will strike them suddenly without their knowledge.	202. Faya-tiyahum baghtatañw-wa hum laa yash‘uroon.	فَيَأْتِيَهُم بَغْتَةً وَهُمْ لَا يَشْعُرُونَ ٢٠٢
203. They will say, "Can we be granted any respite?"	203. Fa-yaqooloo hal naḥnu munẓaroon.	فَيَقُولُوا هَلْ نَحْنُ مُنظَرُونَ ٢٠٣
204. Do they want to hasten Our torment?	204. Afabi-‘a<u>z</u>aabinaa yasta‘jiloon.	أَفَبِعَذَابِنَا يَسْتَعْجِلُونَ ٢٠٤
205. Do you not see that even if We give them respite for years	205. Afara’ayta im-mat-ta‘naahum sineen.	أَفَرَأَيْتَ إِن مَّتَّعْنَاهُمْ سِنِينَ ٢٠٥
206. and then Our torment will strike them,	206. <u>S</u>umma jaaa’ahum-maa kaanoo yoo‘adoon.	ثُمَّ جَاءَهُم مَّا كَانُوا يُوعَدُونَ ٢٠٦
207. none of their luxuries will be able to save them from the torment?	207. Maaa aghnaa ‘anhum-maa kaanoo yumatta‘oon.	مَا أَغْنَىٰ عَنْهُم مَّا كَانُوا يُمَتَّعُونَ ٢٠٧
208. We never destroyed any town without first sending to them warning and guidance.	208. Wa maaa ahlaknaa min qaryatin illaa lahaa mun<u>z</u>iroon.	وَمَا أَهْلَكْنَا مِن قَرْيَةٍ إِلَّا لَهَا مُنذِرُونَ ٢٠٨
209. We have never been unjust to anyone.	209. <u>Z</u>ikraa wa maa kunnaa ẓaalimeen.	ذِكْرَىٰ وَمَا كُنَّا ظَالِمِينَ ٢٠٩
210. The Satans have not revealed the Quran;	210. Wa maa tanazzalat bihish-Shayaaṭeen.	وَمَا تَنَزَّلَتْ بِهِ الشَّيَاطِينُ ٢١٠
211. they are not supposed to do so. Nor do they have the ability for such a task.	211. Wa maa yambaghee lahum wa maa yastaṭee‘oon.	وَمَا يَنبَغِي لَهُمْ وَمَا يَسْتَطِيعُونَ ٢١١
212. The Satans are barred from listening to anything from the heavens.	212. Innahum ‘anis-sam‘i lama‘zooloon.	إِنَّهُمْ عَنِ السَّمْعِ لَمَعْزُولُونَ ٢١٢

ع ١٠/١٤

مع عند المتقدمين ١٠

213. (Muhammad), do not worship anything besides Allah lest you suffer the punishment.	213. Falaa tad'u ma'al-laahi ilaahan aakhara fatakoona minal-mu'azzabeen.	فَلَا تَدۡعُ مَعَ اللّٰهِ اِلٰهًا اٰخَرَ فَتَكُوۡنَ مِنَ الۡمُعَذَّبِيۡنَ ۚ ﴿۲۱۳﴾
214. Warn your close relatives	214. Wa anzir 'asheeratakal - aqrabeen.	وَاَنۡذِرۡ عَشِيۡرَتَكَ الۡاَقۡرَبِيۡنَ ۙ ﴿۲۱۴﴾
215. and be kind to your believing followers.	215. Wakhfiḍ janaaḥaka lima-nit-taba'aka minal-mu'mineen.	وَاخۡفِضۡ جَنَاحَكَ لِمَنِ اتَّبَعَكَ مِنَ الۡمُؤۡمِنِيۡنَ ۚ ﴿۲۱۵﴾
216. If they disobey you, tell them, "I condemn your disobedient deeds."	216. Fa-in 'aṣawka faqul innee bareee'um-mimmaa ta'maloon.	فَاِنۡ عَصَوۡكَ فَقُلۡ اِنِّىۡ بَرِىۡٓءٌ مِّمَّا تَعۡمَلُوۡنَ ۚ ﴿۲۱۶﴾
217. Have trust in the Majestic and All-merciful,	217. Wa tawakkal alal 'Azee-zir-Raḥeem.	وَتَوَكَّلۡ عَلَى الۡعَزِيۡزِ الرَّحِيۡمِ ۙ ﴿۲۱۷﴾
218. who can see you when standing	218. Allazee yaraaka ḥeena taqoom.	الَّذِىۡ يَرٰٮكَ حِيۡنَ تَقُوۡمُ ۙ ﴿۲۱۸﴾
219. or changing your condition during your prostration among those who prostrate (in the backs of your forefathers, the prophets).	219. Wa taqallubaka fis-saaji-deen.	وَتَقَلُّبَكَ فِى السّٰجِدِيۡنَ ﴿۲۱۹﴾
220. He is All-hearing and All-knowing."	220. Innahoo Huwas-Samee'ul-'Aleem.	اِنَّهٗ هُوَ السَّمِيۡعُ الۡعَلِيۡمُ ﴿۲۲۰﴾
221. Should I tell you to whom the Satans come?	221. Hal unabbi'ukum 'alaa man tanazzalush-Shayaaṭeen.	هَلۡ اُنَبِّئُكُمۡ عَلٰى مَنۡ تَنَزَّلُ الشَّيٰطِيۡنُ ؕ ﴿۲۲۱﴾
222. They come to every sinful liar.	222. Tanazzalu 'alaa kulli affaakin aseem.	تَنَزَّلُ عَلٰى كُلِّ اَفَّاكٍ اَثِيۡمٍ ۙ ﴿۲۲۲﴾
223. The Satans try to listen to the heavens but many of them are liars.	223. Yulqoonas-sam'a wa aksaruhum kaaziboon.	يُّلۡقُوۡنَ السَّمۡعَ وَاَكۡثَرُهُمۡ كٰذِبُوۡنَ ؕ ﴿۲۲۳﴾
224. Only the erring people follow the poets (people who invent false religions).	224. Washshu'araaa'u yattabi-'uhumul-ghaawoon.	وَالشُّعَرَآءُ يَتَّبِعُهُمُ الۡغَاوٗنَ ﴿۲۲۴﴾
225. Did you not see them wandering and bewildered in every valley (come up with false arguments to support their false religion)	225. Alam tara annahum fee kulli waadiñy-yaheemoon.	اَلَمۡ تَرَ اَنَّهُمۡ فِىۡ كُلِّ وَادٍ يَّهِيۡمُوۡنَ ۙ ﴿۲۲۵﴾
226. and preaching what they themselves never practice?	226. Wa annahum yaqooloona maa laa yaf'aloon.	وَاَنَّهُمۡ يَقُوۡلُوۡنَ مَا لَا يَفۡعَلُوۡنَ ۙ ﴿۲۲۶﴾
227. This does not include the righteously striving believers among them who remember Allah very often and use their talent to seek help after they have been wronged. The unjust will soon know how terrible their end will be.	227. Illal-lazeena aamanoo wa 'amiluṣ-ṣaaliḥaati wa zakarul-laaha kaseerañw-wantaṣaroo mim ba'di maa ẓulimoo; wa sa-ya'lamul-lazeena ẓalamooo ayya munqalabiñy-yanqali-boon.	اِلَّا الَّذِيۡنَ اٰمَنُوۡا وَعَمِلُوا الصّٰلِحٰتِ وَذَكَرُوا اللّٰهَ كَثِيۡرًا وَّانْتَصَرُوۡا مِنۡۢ بَعۡدِ مَا ظُلِمُوۡا ؕ وَسَيَعۡلَمُ الَّذِيۡنَ ظَلَمُوۡۤا اَىَّ مُنۡقَلَبٍ يَّنۡقَلِبُوۡنَ ﴿۲۲۷﴾ ع ۱۱ ۱۵

Al-Naml, The Ant (27) In the Name of Allah, the Beneficent, the Merciful.	**Sûrat an-Naml-27** (Revealed at Makkah) **Bismillaahir Raḥmaanir Raḥeem**	(۲۷) سُوۡرَةُ النَّمۡلِ مَكِّيَّةٌ (۴۸) اٰيَاتُهَا ۹۳ بِسۡمِ اللّٰهِ الرَّحۡمٰنِ الرَّحِيۡمِ رُكُوۡعَاتُهَا ۷
1. Ta. Sin. These are the verses of the Quran and of the illustrious Book.	1. Ṭaa-Seeen;tilka Aayaatul-Qur-aani wa Kitaabim-Mu-been.	طٰسٓ ۚ تِلۡكَ اٰيٰتُ الۡقُرۡاٰنِ وَكِتَابٍ مُّبِيۡنٍ ۙ ﴿۱﴾

2. They are glad news and guidance for the believers

2. Hudañw-wa bushraa lil-mu'mineen.

هُدًى وَّبُشْرٰى لِلْمُؤْمِنِيْنَ ۝٢

3. who are steadfast in prayer, who pay the religious tax, and who have strong faith in the life hereafter.

3. Allazeena yuqeemoonaṣ-Ṣalaata wa yu'toonaz-Zakaata wa hum bil-Aakhirati hum yooqinoon.

الَّذِيْنَ يُقِيْمُوْنَ الصَّلٰوةَ وَيُؤْتُوْنَ
الزَّكٰوةَ وَهُمْ بِالْاٰخِرَةِ هُمْ يُوْقِنُوْنَ ۝٣

4. We have made the deeds of those who do not believe in the life to come attractive to them, and they wander about blindly.

4. Innal-lazeena laa yu'minoona bil-Aakhirati zayyannaa lahum a'maalahum fahum ya'mahoon.

اِنَّ الَّذِيْنَ لَا يُؤْمِنُوْنَ بِالْاٰخِرَةِ زَيَّنَّا
لَهُمْ اَعْمَالَهُمْ فَهُمْ يَعْمَهُوْنَ ۝٤

5. They will suffer the worst kind of torment and will be lost in the life to come.

5. Ulaaa'ikal-lazeena lahum sooo'ul-'azaabi wa hum fil-Aakhirati humul-akhsaroon.

اُولٰٓئِكَ الَّذِيْنَ لَهُمْ سُوْٓءُ الْعَذَابِ
وَهُمْ فِي الْاٰخِرَةِ هُمُ الْاَخْسَرُوْنَ ۝٥

6. (Muhammad), you have certainly received the Quran from the All-wise and All-knowing One.

6. Wa innaka latulaqqal-Qur'aana mil-ladun Ḥakeemin 'Aleem.

وَاِنَّكَ لَتُلَقَّى الْقُرْاٰنَ مِنْ لَّدُنْ
حَكِيْمٍ عَلِيْمٍ ۝٦

الثلثة

7. Moses said to his family, "I have seen fire. I shall bring you some news about it or some fire so that you can warm yourselves."

7. Iz qaala Moosaa li-ahliheee inneee aanastu naaran sa-aateekum-minhaa bikhabarin aw aateekum bishihaabin qabasil-la'allakum taṣṭaloon.

اِذْ قَالَ مُوْسٰى لِاَهْلِهٖٓ اِنِّيْٓ اٰنَسْتُ
نَارًا ؕ سَاٰتِيْكُمْ مِّنْهَا بِخَبَرٍ اَوْ اٰتِيْكُمْ
بِشِهَابٍ قَبَسٍ لَّعَلَّكُمْ تَصْطَلُوْنَ ۝٧

8. When he approached the fire, he was told, "Blessed is the one in the fire and around it. All glory belongs to Allah, the Lord of the universe.

8. Falammaa jaaa'ahaa noodiya am boorika man finnaari wa man ḥawlahaa wa Sub-ḥaanal-laahi Rabbil-'aalameen.

فَلَمَّا جَآءَهَا نُوْدِيَ اَنْۢ بُوْرِكَ مَنْ
فِي النَّارِ وَمَنْ حَوْلَهَا ؕ وَسُبْحٰنَ
اللّٰهِ رَبِّ الْعٰلَمِيْنَ ۝٨

9. Moses, I am Allah, the Majestic and All-wise."

9. Yaa Moosaaa innahooo Anal-laahul-'Azeezul-Ḥakeem.

يٰمُوْسٰٓى اِنَّهٗٓ اَنَا اللّٰهُ الْعَزِيْزُ الْحَكِيْمُ ۝٩

10. "Throw down your staff." When Moses saw his staff on the ground moving like a living creature, he stepped back and did not come forward again. The Lord said, "Moses, do not be afraid. Messengers do not become afraid in My presence,

10. Wa alqi 'aṣaak; falammaa ra-aahaa tahtazzu ka-annahaa jaaannuñw-wallaa mudbirañw-wa lam yu'aqqib; yaa Moosaa laa takhaf innee laa yakhaafu ladayyal-mursaloon.

وَاَلْقِ عَصَاكَ ؕ فَلَمَّا رَاٰهَا تَهْتَزُّ
كَاَنَّهَا جَآنٌّ وَّلّٰى مُدْبِرًا وَّلَمْ
يُعَقِّبْ ؕ يٰمُوْسٰى لَا تَخَفْ ۫ اِنِّيْ
لَا يَخَافُ لَدَيَّ الْمُرْسَلُوْنَ ۝١٠

11. not even the unjust people become afraid in My presence. (For the unjust ones), who then replace their bad deeds by good ones, I am All-forgiving and All-merciful.

11. Illaa man ẓalama ṡumma baddala ḥusnam ba'da sooo'in fa-innee Ghafoorur-Raḥeem.

اِلَّا مَنْ ظَلَمَ ثُمَّ بَدَّلَ حُسْنًۢا بَعْدَ
سُوْٓءٍ فَاِنِّيْ غَفُوْرٌ رَّحِيْمٌ ۝١١

12. Place your hand into your pocket. It will come out sheer white but unharmed. This is one of the nine miracles which shall be shown to the Pharaoh and his people; they are truly wicked men."

12. Wa adkhil yadaka fee jaybika takhruj bayḍaaa'a min ghayri sooo'in fee tis'i Aayaatin ilaa Fir'awna wa qawmih; innahum kaanoo qawman faasiqeen.

وَاَدْخِلْ يَدَكَ فِيْ جَيْبِكَ تَخْرُجْ
بَيْضَآءَ مِنْ غَيْرِ سُوْٓءٍ ۫ فِيْ تِسْعِ اٰيٰتٍ
اِلٰى فِرْعَوْنَ وَقَوْمِهٖ ؕ اِنَّهُمْ كَانُوْا
قَوْمًا فٰسِقِيْنَ ۝١٢

13. When Our miracles were visibly shown to them, they said, "It is plain magic."

13. Falammaa jaaa'at-hum Aayaatunaa mubṣiratan qaaloo haazaa siḥrum-mubeen.

فَلَمَّا جَآءَتْهُمْ اٰيٰتُنَا مُبْصِرَةً قَالُوْا هٰذَا سِحْرٌ مُّبِيْنٌ ﴿١٣﴾

14. They rejected the evidence because of their arrogance and injustice, although their souls knew it to be true. Think how terrible the end of the sinful ones was!

14. Wa jaḥadoo bihaa wastay-qanat-haaa anfusuhum ẓul-mañw-wa 'uluwwaa; fanẓur kayfa kaana 'aaqibatul-muf-sideen.

وَجَحَدُوْا بِهَا وَاسْتَيْقَنَتْهَآ اَنْفُسُهُمْ ظُلْمًا وَّعُلُوًّا ۗ فَانْظُرْ كَيْفَ كَانَ عَاقِبَةُ الْمُفْسِدِيْنَ ﴿١٤﴾ ع ٤ ١٦

15. We granted knowledge to David and Solomon. They said, "It is only Allah who deserves all praise. He has exalted us above many of His believing servants."

15. Wa laqad aataynaa Daawooda wa Sulaymaana 'ilmaa; wa qaalal-ḥamdulil-laahil-lazee faḍḍalanaa 'alaa kaseerim-min 'ibaadihil-mu'mineen.

وَلَقَدْ اٰتَيْنَا دَاوٗدَ وَسُلَيْمٰنَ عِلْمًا ۚ وَقَالَا الْحَمْدُ لِلّٰهِ الَّذِيْ فَضَّلَنَا عَلٰى كَثِيْرٍ مِّنْ عِبَادِهِ الْمُؤْمِنِيْنَ ﴿١٥﴾

16. Solomon became the heir to David. He said, "People, we have been taught the language of the birds and have been granted a share of everything. This indeed is a manifest favor (from Allah)."

16. Wa warisa Sulaymaanu Daawooda wa qaala yaaa ayyuhan-naasu 'ullimnaa manṭiqaṭ-ṭayri wa ooteenaa min kulli shay'in inna haazaa lahuwal-faḍlul-mubeen.

وَوَرِثَ سُلَيْمٰنُ دَاوٗدَ وَقَالَ يٰٓاَيُّهَا النَّاسُ عُلِّمْنَا مَنْطِقَ الطَّيْرِ وَاُوْتِيْنَا مِنْ كُلِّ شَيْءٍ ۗ اِنَّ هٰذَا لَهُوَ الْفَضْلُ الْمُبِيْنُ ﴿١٦﴾

17. Solomon's army, consisting of human beings, jinn, and birds were gathered together in his presence in ranks.

17. Wa ḥushira li-Sulaymaana junooduhoo minal-jinni wal-insi waṭṭayri fahum yooza'oon.

وَحُشِرَ لِسُلَيْمٰنَ جُنُوْدُهٗ مِنَ الْجِنِّ وَالْاِنْسِ وَالطَّيْرِ فَهُمْ يُوْزَعُوْنَ ﴿١٧﴾

18. When they arrived in the valley of the ants, one ant said to the others, "Enter your dwellings lest you be carelessly crushed by Solomon and his army."

18. Ḥattaaa izaaa ataw 'alaa waadin-namli qaalat namla-tuñy-yaaa ayyuhan-namlud-khuloo masaakinakum laa yaḥṭiman-nakum Sulaymaanu wa ju-nooduhoo wa hum laa yash'uroon.

حَتّٰىٓ اِذَآ اَتَوْا عَلٰى وَادِ النَّمْلِ ۙ قَالَتْ نَمْلَةٌ يّٰٓاَيُّهَا النَّمْلُ ادْخُلُوْا مَسٰكِنَكُمْ ۚ لَا يَحْطِمَنَّكُمْ سُلَيْمٰنُ وَجُنُوْدُهٗ ۙ وَهُمْ لَا يَشْعُرُوْنَ ﴿١٨﴾

19. (Solomon) smiled at the ant's remarks and said, "Lord, inspire me to thank you for Your favors to me and my parents and to act righteously so as to please you. Admit me, by Your mercy into the company of Your righteous servants."

19. Fatabassama ḍaaḥikam-min qawlihaa wa qaala Rabbi awzi'neee an ashkura ni'mata-kal-lateee an'amta 'alayya wa 'alaa waalidayya wa an a'mala ṣaaliḥan tarḍaahu wa adkhilnee biraḥmatika fee 'ibaadikaṣ-ṣaaliḥeen.

فَتَبَسَّمَ ضَاحِكًا مِّنْ قَوْلِهَا وَقَالَ رَبِّ اَوْزِعْنِيْٓ اَنْ اَشْكُرَ نِعْمَتَكَ الَّتِيْٓ اَنْعَمْتَ عَلَيَّ وَعَلٰى وَالِدَيَّ وَاَنْ اَعْمَلَ صَالِحًا تَرْضٰىهُ وَاَدْخِلْنِيْ بِرَحْمَتِكَ فِيْ عِبَادِكَ الصّٰلِحِيْنَ ﴿١٩﴾

20. (Solomon) inspected the birds and said, "How is it that I

20. Wa tafaqqadaṭ-ṭayra faqaala maa liya laaa aral-

وَتَفَقَّدَ الطَّيْرَ فَقَالَ مَا لِيَ لَآ اَرَى

cannot see the hoopoe. Is he absent?	hudhud; am kaana minal-ghaaa'ibeen.	الْهُدْهُدَ ۖ أَمْ كَانَ مِنَ الْغَائِبِينَ ٢٠
21. I shall certainly punish him severely or slaughter him unless he has a good reason for his absence."	21. Lau'azzibannahoo 'azaaban shadeedan aw la-azbaḥannahooo aw laya-tiyannee bisulṭaanim-mubeen.	لَأُعَذِّبَنَّهُ عَذَابًا شَدِيدًا أَوْ لَأَذْبَحَنَّهُ أَوْ لَيَأْتِيَنِّي بِسُلْطَانٍ مُّبِينٍ ٢١
22. Not long after, the hoopoe came forward and said, "I have information, which you did not have. I have come from the land of Sheba with a true report.	22. Famakasa ghayra ba'eedin faqaala aḥaṭtu bimaa lam tuḥiṭ bihee wa ji'tuka min Saba-im binaba-iñy-yaqeen.	فَمَكَثَ غَيْرَ بَعِيدٍ فَقَالَ أَحَطتُّ بِمَا لَمْ تُحِطْ بِهِ وَجِئْتُكَ مِن سَبَإٍ بِنَبَإٍ يَقِينٍ ٢٢
23. I found a woman ruling the people there and she possessed all things (almost everything) and a great throne.	23. Innee wajattum-ra-atan tamlikuhum wa ootiyat min kulli shay'iñw-wa lahaa 'arshun 'aẓeem.	إِنِّي وَجَدتُّ امْرَأَةً تَمْلِكُهُمْ وَأُوتِيَتْ مِن كُلِّ شَيْءٍ وَلَهَا عَرْشٌ عَظِيمٌ ٢٣
24. I found her and her people prostrating before the sun instead of Allah. Satan has made their deeds attractive to them. He has kept them away from the right path and they have no guidance.	24. Wajattuhaa wa qawmahaa yasjudoona lishshamsi min doonil-laahi wa zayyana lahumush-Shayṭaanu a'maalahum faṣaddahum 'anis-sabeeli fahum laa yahtadoon.	وَجَدتُّهَا وَقَوْمَهَا يَسْجُدُونَ لِلشَّمْسِ مِن دُونِ اللَّهِ وَزَيَّنَ لَهُمُ الشَّيْطَانُ أَعْمَالَهُمْ فَصَدَّهُمْ عَنِ السَّبِيلِ فَهُمْ لَا يَهْتَدُونَ ٢٤
25. (Satan has done this) so that they will not prostrate (worship) Allah who brings forth whatever is hidden in the heavens (water) and the earth (plants) and knows whatever you conceal or reveal.	25. Allaa yasjudoo lillaahillazee yukhrijul-khab'a fis-samaawaati wal-arḍi wa ya'lamu maa tukhfoona wa maa tu'linoon.	أَلَّا يَسْجُدُوا لِلَّهِ الَّذِي يُخْرِجُ الْخَبْءَ فِي السَّمَاوَاتِ وَالْأَرْضِ وَيَعْلَمُ مَا تُخْفُونَ وَمَا تُعْلِنُونَ ٢٥
26. Allah is the only Lord and master of the Great Throne."	26. Allaahu laaa ilaaha illaa Huwa Rabbul-'Arshil 'Aẓeem. ۩	اللَّهُ لَا إِلَٰهَ إِلَّا هُوَ رَبُّ الْعَرْشِ الْعَظِيمِ ۩ ٢٦
27. Solomon said, "We shall see whether you are truthful or a liar.	27. Qaala sananẓuru aṣadaqta am kunta minal-kaazibeen.	قَالَ سَنَنظُرُ أَصَدَقْتَ أَمْ كُنتَ مِنَ الْكَاذِبِينَ ٢٧
28. Take this letter of mine and deliver it to them, then return and see what their reply will be."	28. Izhab bikitaabee haazaa fa-alqih ilayhim summa tawalla 'anhum fanẓur maazaa yarji'oon.	اذْهَب بِّكِتَابِي هَٰذَا فَأَلْقِهْ إِلَيْهِمْ ثُمَّ تَوَلَّ عَنْهُمْ فَانظُرْ مَاذَا يَرْجِعُونَ ٢٨
29. (The Queen of Sheba) said to her officials, "A gracious (sealed) letter has been dropped before me.	29. Qaalat yaaa ayyuhal-mala'u inneee ulqiya ilayya kitaabun kareem.	قَالَتْ يَا أَيُّهَا الْمَلَأُ إِنِّي أُلْقِيَ إِلَيَّ كِتَابٌ كَرِيمٌ ٢٩
30. It reads, 'From Solomon: In the Name of Allah, the Beneficent and the Merciful.	30. Innahoo min Sulaymaana wa innahoo bismil-laahir-Raḥmaanir-Raḥeem.	إِنَّهُ مِن سُلَيْمَانَ وَإِنَّهُ بِسْمِ اللَّهِ الرَّحْمَٰنِ الرَّحِيمِ ٣٠

(Bow Down)

السجدة ٨

31. You must not consider yourselves superior to me but come to me as Muslims (in submission) without being arrogant."'

32. She said, "My officials, what are your views on this matter? I will not decide until I have your views."

33. They replied, "We have great power and valor. You are the commander, so decide as you like."

34. She said, "When Kings enter a town they do destroy it and disrespect its honorable people." That, indeed, is what they do.

35. "I will send a gift and we shall see what response the Messengers will bring." She declared.

36. When her Messengers came to Solomon, he said, "Have you brought me wealth? What Allah has given to me is far better than what He has given to you, but you are happy with your gifts.

37. Go back to your people and we shall soon come there with an army which they will not be able to face (withstand). We shall drive them from their town, humble and disgraced."

38. Solomon asked his people, "Who among you can bring her throne before (the queen of Sheba) comes to me submissively?"

39. A monstrous jinn said, "I can bring it before you even stand up. I am powerful and trustworthy."

40. The one who had knowledge from the Book said, "I can bring it to you before you even blink your eye." When Solomon saw the

31. Allaa ta'loo 'alayya wa-toonee muslimeen.

32. Qaalat yaaa ayyuhal-mala'u aftoonee feee amree maa kuntu qaaṭi'atan amran ḥattaa tashhadoon.

33. Qaaloo naḥnu ooloo quw-watiñw-wa ooloo ba-sin shadee-d; wal-amru ilayki fanẓuree maaẕaa ta-mureen.

34. Qaalat innal-mulooka iẕaa dakhaloo qaryatan afsadoohaa wa ja'alooo a'izzata ahlihaaa aẕillah; wa kaẕaalika yaf-'aloon.

35. Wa innee mursilatun ilayhim bihadiyyatin fanaa-ẓiratum bima yarji'ul-mursa-loon.

36. Falammaa jaaa'a Sulay-maana qaala atumiddoonani bimaalin famaaa aataaniyal-laahu khayrum-mimmaaa aataakum bal antum bihadiy-yatikum tafraḥoon.

37. Irji' ilayhim falana-tiyan-nahum bijunoodil-laa qibala lahum bihaa wa lanukhri-jannahum-minhaaa aẕillatañw-wa hum ṣaaghiroon.

38. Qaala yaaa ayyuhal-mala'u ayyukum ya-teenee bi'arshihaa qabla añy-ya-toonee muslimeen.

39. Qaala 'ifreetum-minal-jinni ana aateeka bihee qabla an taqooma mimmaqaamika wa innee 'alayhi laqawiyyun ameen.

40. Qaalal-laẕee 'indahoo 'ilmum-minal-Kitaabi ana aateeka bihee qabla añy-yar-tadda ilayka

أَلَّا تَعْلُوا عَلَيَّ وَأْتُونِي مُسْلِمِينَ ﴿٣١﴾
قَالَتْ يَا أَيُّهَا الْمَلَأُ أَفْتُونِي فِي
أَمْرِي مَا كُنتُ قَاطِعَةً أَمْرًا
حَتَّىٰ تَشْهَدُونِ ﴿٣٢﴾
قَالُوا نَحْنُ أُولُو قُوَّةٍ وَأُولُو
بَأْسٍ شَدِيدٍ وَالْأَمْرُ إِلَيْكِ
فَانظُرِي مَاذَا تَأْمُرِينَ ﴿٣٣﴾
قَالَتْ إِنَّ الْمُلُوكَ إِذَا دَخَلُوا
قَرْيَةً أَفْسَدُوهَا وَجَعَلُوا أَعِزَّةَ
أَهْلِهَا أَذِلَّةً وَكَذَٰلِكَ يَفْعَلُونَ ﴿٣٤﴾
وَإِنِّي مُرْسِلَةٌ إِلَيْهِم بِهَدِيَّةٍ
فَنَاظِرَةٌ بِمَ يَرْجِعُ الْمُرْسَلُونَ ﴿٣٥﴾
فَلَمَّا جَاءَ سُلَيْمَانَ قَالَ أَتُمِدُّونَنِ
بِمَالٍ فَمَا آتَانِيَ اللَّهُ خَيْرٌ مِّمَّا
آتَاكُم بَلْ أَنتُم بِهَدِيَّتِكُمْ
تَفْرَحُونَ ﴿٣٦﴾
ارْجِعْ إِلَيْهِمْ فَلَنَأْتِيَنَّهُم بِجُنُودٍ
لَّا قِبَلَ لَهُم بِهَا وَلَنُخْرِجَنَّهُم
مِّنْهَا أَذِلَّةً وَهُمْ صَاغِرُونَ ﴿٣٧﴾
قَالَ يَا أَيُّهَا الْمَلَأُ أَيُّكُمْ يَأْتِينِي
بِعَرْشِهَا قَبْلَ أَن يَأْتُونِي مُسْلِمِينَ ﴿٣٨﴾
قَالَ عِفْرِيتٌ مِّنَ الْجِنِّ أَنَا آتِيكَ
بِهِ قَبْلَ أَن تَقُومَ مِن مَّقَامِكَ
وَإِنِّي عَلَيْهِ لَقَوِيٌّ أَمِينٌ ﴿٣٩﴾
قَالَ الَّذِي عِندَهُ عِلْمٌ مِّنَ الْكِتَابِ
أَنَا آتِيكَ بِهِ قَبْلَ أَن يَرْتَدَّ إِلَيْكَ

throne placed before him, he said, "This is a favor from my Lord by which He wants to test whether I am grateful or ungrateful. Whoever thanks Allah does so for his own good. Whoever is ungrateful to Allah should know that my Lord is Self-sufficient and Benevolent."

41. Then he said, "Make a few changes to her throne and let us see whether she will recognize it or not."

42. When she came she was asked, "Is your throne like this?" She replied, "It seems that this is it. We had received the knowledge before this and were submissive (to Solomon's power)."

43. Her idols prevented her from believing in Allah and she was one of the unbelievers.

44. She was told to enter the palace. When she saw it, she thought that it was a pool and raised her clothes up to her legs. Solomon said, "This is a palace constructed with glass." She said, "My Lord, indeed I have wronged myself and I submit myself with Solomon to the will of Allah, the Lord of the universe."

45. We sent to the tribe of Thamud their brother Salih so that they would worship Allah, but they became two quarrelling groups.

46. Salih said, "My people, why do you commit sins so quickly before doing good? Would that you ask forgiveness from Allah so that perhaps He will have mercy upon you."

47. They said, "We have an ill omen about you and your

ṭarfuk; falammaa ra-aahu mustaqirran 'indahoo qaala haazaa min faḍli Rabbee li-yabluwaneee 'a-ashkuru am akfuru wa man shakara fa-innamaa yashkuru linafsihee wa man kafara fa-inna Rabbee Ghaniyyun Kareem.

41. Qaala nakkiroo lahaa 'arshahaa nanẓur atahtadeee am takoonu minal-lazeena laa yahtadoon.

42. Falammaa jaaa'at qeela ahaakazaa 'arshuki qaalat ka-annahoo hoo; wa ooteenal-'ilma min qablihaa wa kunnaa muslimeen.

43. Wa ṣaddahaa maa kaanat ta'budu min doonil-laahi innahaa kaanat min qawmin kaafireen.

44. Qeela lahad-khuliṣ-ṣarḥa falammaa ra-at-hu ḥasibat-hu lujjatañw-wa kashafat 'an saaqayhaa; qaala innahoo ṣarḥum-mumarradum-min qawaareer; qaalat Rabbi innee ẓalamtu nafsee wa aslamtu ma'a Sulaymaana lillaahi Rabbil-'aalameen.

45. Wa laqad arsalnaaa ilaa Samooda akhaahum Ṣaaliḥan ani'-budul-laaha fa-izaa hum fareeqaani yakhtaṣimoon.

46. Qaala yaa qawmi lima tasta'jiloona bissayyi'ati qab-lal-ḥasanati law laa tas-taghfiroonal-laaha la'allakum turḥamoon.

47. Qaaluṭ-ṭayyarnaa bika wa bimam-ma'ak;

طَرْفُكَ ۚ فَلَمَّا رَاٰهُ مُسْتَقِرًّا عِنْدَهٗ
قَالَ هٰذَا مِنْ فَضْلِ رَبِّیْ ۖ
لِيَبْلُوَنِيْٓ ءَاَشْكُرُ اَمْ اَكْفُرُ ۗ وَمَنْ
شَكَرَ فَاِنَّمَا يَشْكُرُ لِنَفْسِهٖ ۚ وَمَنْ
كَفَرَ فَاِنَّ رَبِّیْ غَنِیٌّ كَرِيْمٌ ﴿۴۰﴾
قَالَ نَكِّرُوْا لَهَا عَرْشَهَا نَنْظُرْ
اَتَهْتَدِیْٓ اَمْ تَكُوْنُ مِنَ الَّذِيْنَ
لَا يَهْتَدُوْنَ ﴿۴۱﴾
فَلَمَّا جَآءَتْ قِيْلَ اَهٰكَذَا عَرْشُكِ ۚ
قَالَتْ كَاَنَّهٗ هُوَ ۚ وَاُوْتِيْنَا الْعِلْمَ
مِنْ قَبْلِهَا وَكُنَّا مُسْلِمِيْنَ ﴿۴۲﴾
وَصَدَّهَا مَا كَانَتْ تَّعْبُدُ مِنْ دُوْنِ
اللّٰهِ ۚ اِنَّهَا كَانَتْ مِنْ قَوْمٍ كٰفِرِيْنَ ﴿۴۳﴾
قِيْلَ لَهَا ادْخُلِی الصَّرْحَ ۚ فَلَمَّا
رَاَتْهُ حَسِبَتْهُ لُجَّةً وَّكَشَفَتْ عَنْ
سَاقَيْهَا ۚ قَالَ اِنَّهٗ صَرْحٌ مُّمَرَّدٌ
مِّنْ قَوَارِيْرَ ۗ قَالَتْ رَبِّ اِنِّیْ ظَلَمْتُ
نَفْسِیْ وَاَسْلَمْتُ مَعَ سُلَيْمٰنَ لِلّٰهِ
رَبِّ الْعٰلَمِيْنَ ﴿۴۴﴾ ع ۳ ۱۸
وَلَقَدْ اَرْسَلْنَآ اِلٰی ثَمُوْدَ اَخَاهُمْ
صٰلِحًا اَنِ اعْبُدُوا اللّٰهَ فَاِذَا
هُمْ فَرِيْقٰنِ يَخْتَصِمُوْنَ ﴿۴۵﴾
قَالَ يٰقَوْمِ لِمَ تَسْتَعْجِلُوْنَ
بِالسَّيِّئَةِ قَبْلَ الْحَسَنَةِ ۚ لَوْلَا
تَسْتَغْفِرُوْنَ اللّٰهَ لَعَلَّكُمْ تُرْحَمُوْنَ ﴿۴۶﴾
قَالُوا اطَّيَّرْنَا بِكَ وَبِمَنْ مَّعَكَ ۚ

followers." Salih replied, Allah has made your ill-fortune await you. You are a people on trial."

qaala ṭaaa'irukum 'indal-laahi bal antum qawmun tuftanoon.

قَالَ طٰٓئِرُكُمْ عِنْدَ اللّٰهِ بَلْ
اَنْتُمْ قَوْمٌ تُفْتَنُوْنَ ﴿٤٧﴾

48. There were nine tribes in the city spreading evil without any reform in the land.

48. Wa kaana fil-madeenati tis'atu rahṭiñy-yufsidoona fil-arḍi wa laa yuṣliḥoon.

وَكَانَ فِى الْمَدِيْنَةِ تِسْعَةُ رَهْطٍ
يُّفْسِدُوْنَ فِى الْاَرْضِ وَلَا يُصْلِحُوْنَ ﴿٤٨﴾

49. They said, "Let us swear by Allah to do away with him and his family during the night, then tell his guardian that we did not see how he and his family had been destroyed, and we shall be telling the truth."

49. Qaaloo taqaasamoo billaahi lanubayyitannahoo wa ahlahoo summa lanaqoolanna liwaliyyihee maa shahidnaa mahlika ahlihee wa innaa laṣaadiqoon.

قَالُوْا تَقَاسَمُوْا بِاللّٰهِ لَنُبَيِّتَنَّهٗ
وَاَهْلَهٗ ثُمَّ لَنَقُوْلَنَّ لِوَلِيِّهٖ
مَا شَهِدْنَا مَهْلِكَ اَهْلِهٖ وَاِنَّا
لَصٰدِقُوْنَ ﴿٤٩﴾

50. They plotted and We planned without their knowledge. Consider the result of their plot.

50. Wa makaroo makrañw-wa makarnaa makrañw-wa hum laa yash'uroon.

وَمَكَرُوْا مَكْرًا وَّمَكَرْنَا مَكْرًا
وَّهُمْ لَا يَشْعُرُوْنَ ﴿٥٠﴾

51. We destroyed them and their people altogether.

51. Fanẓur kayfa kaana 'aaqibatu makrihim annaa dammarnaahum wa qawmahum ajma'een.

فَانْظُرْ كَيْفَ كَانَ عَاقِبَةُ مَكْرِهِمْ ۙ
اَنَّا دَمَّرْنٰهُمْ وَقَوْمَهُمْ اَجْمَعِيْنَ ﴿٥١﴾

52. Those are their empty houses which We ruined because of their injustice. In this there is evidence (of the truth) for the people of knowledge.

52. Fatilka buyootuhum khaawiyatam bimaa ẓalamooo; inna fee ẕaalika la-Aayatal-liqawmiñy-ya'lamoon.

فَتِلْكَ بُيُوْتُهُمْ خَاوِيَةًۢ بِمَا
ظَلَمُوْا ؕ اِنَّ فِىْ ذٰلِكَ لَاٰيَةً لِّقَوْمٍ
يَّعْلَمُوْنَ ﴿٥٢﴾

53. We saved the believers who maintained piety.

53. Wa anjaynal-laẕeena aamanoo wa kaanoo yattaqoon.

وَاَنْجَيْنَا الَّذِيْنَ اٰمَنُوْا وَكَانُوْا
يَتَّقُوْنَ ﴿٥٣﴾

54. Lot asked his people, "Do you intentionally commit indecency?

54. Wa Looṭan iẕ qaala liqawmiheee ata-toonal-faaḥishata wa antum tubṣiroon.

وَلُوْطًا اِذْ قَالَ لِقَوْمِهٖٓ اَتَاْتُوْنَ
الْفَاحِشَةَ وَاَنْتُمْ تُبْصِرُوْنَ ﴿٥٤﴾

55. Do you have carnal relations with men rather than women? You are ignorant people."

55. A'innakum lata-toonar-rijaala shahwatam-min doonin-nisaaa'; bal antum qawmun tajhaloon.

اَئِنَّكُمْ لَتَاْتُوْنَ الرِّجَالَ شَهْوَةً مِّنْ
دُوْنِ النِّسَآءِ ؕ بَلْ اَنْتُمْ قَوْمٌ
تَجْهَلُوْنَ ﴿٥٥﴾

56. His people had no answer but to say, "Expel Lot and his family from the town for they want to be pure."

56. Famaa kaana jawaaba qawmiheee illaaa an qaalooo akhrijooo aala Looṭim-min qaryatikum innahum unaasuñy-yataṭahharoon.

فَمَا كَانَ جَوَابَ قَوْمِهٖٓ اِلَّآ اَنْ
قَالُوْٓا اَخْرِجُوْٓا اٰلَ لُوْطٍ مِّنْ
قَرْيَتِكُمْ ۚ اِنَّهُمْ اُنَاسٌ يَّتَطَهَّرُوْنَ ﴿٥٦﴾

57. We saved (Lot) and his family except his wife who was

57. Fa-anjaynaahu wa ahlahooo illam-ra-atahoo

فَاَنْجَيْنٰهُ وَاَهْلَهٗٓ اِلَّا امْرَاَتَهٗ ز

destined to remain behind.

58. We sent to them a terrible rainstorm. How horrible was the rain for the people who had already received warning?

59. (O Muhammad), say, "It is only Allah who deserves all praise. Peace be upon His chosen servants. Which is better, Allah or the idols?

60. "(Are the idols worthier or) the One who has created the heavens and the earth, who has sent water from the sky for you, who has established delightful gardens and you could not even plant one tree? Is there any Lord besides Allah? In fact, the unbelievers are the ones who deviate from the right path.

61. "(Are the idols worthier or) the One who has made the earth a resting place, the rivers flow from its valleys, the mountains as anchors and a barrier between the two seas? Is there any lord besides Allah? In fact, most people do not know.

62. "(Are the idols worthier or) the One who answers the prayers of the distressed ones, removes their hardship, and makes you the successors in the land? Is there any Lord besides Allah? In fact, you take very little heed."

63. "(Are the idols worthier or) the One who guides you in the darkness of the land and sea and sends the winds bearing the glad news of His mercy? Is there any Lord besides Allah? Allah is free of all defects of being considered equal to anything else."

64. "(Are the idols worthier or) the One who began the creation and who will turn it back, who gives you sustenance from the heavens and the earth? Is there any Lord besides Allah? Say, 'Bring your proof if what you say is true.'"

qaddarnaahaa minal-ghaabireen.

58. Wa amṭarnaa 'alayhim-maṭaran fasaaa'a maṭarul-munẕareen.

59. Quli-ḥamdu lillaahi wa salaamun 'alaa 'ibaadihil-lazeenaṣ-ṭafaaa; Aaallaahu khayrun ammaa yushrikoon.

60. Amman khalaqas-samaawaati wal-arḍa wa anzala lakum-minas-samaaa'i maaa'an fa-ambatnaa bihee ḥadaaa'iqa ẕaata bahjah; maa kaana lakum an tumbitoo shajarahaaa; 'a-ilaahum-ma'al-laah; bal hum qawmuñy-ya'diloon.

61. Amman ja'alal-arḍa qaraarañw-wa ja'ala khilaalahaaa anhaarañw-wa ja'ala lahaa rawaasiya wa ja'ala baynal-baḥrayni ḥaajizaa; 'a-ilaahum-ma'allaah; bal akẖaruhum laa ya'lamoon.

62. Ammañy-yujeebul-muḍṭarra iẕaa da'aahu wa yakshifus-sooo'a wa yaj'alukum khulafaaa'al-arḍi 'a-ilaahum-ma'al-laahi qaleelam-maa taẕakkaroon.

63. Ammañy-yahdeekum fee ẓulumaatil-barri wal-baḥri wa mañy-yursilur-riyaaḥa bushram bayna yaday raḥmatih; 'a-ilaahum-ma'al-laah; Ta'aalal-laahu 'ammaa yushrikoon.

64. Ammañy-yabda'ul-khalqa ẖumma yu'eeduhoo wa mañy-yarzuqukum-minas-samaaa'i wal-arḍ; 'a-ilaahum-ma'allaah; qul haatoo burhaanakum in kuntum ṣaadiqeen.

قَدَّرْنٰهَا مِنَ الْغٰبِرِيْنَ ﴿٥٧﴾
وَاَمْطَرْنَا عَلَيْهِمْ مَّطَرًا ۚ فَسَآءَ
مَطَرُ الْمُنْذَرِيْنَ ﴿٥٨﴾ ع
قُلِ الْحَمْدُ لِلّٰهِ وَسَلٰمٌ عَلٰى
عِبَادِهِ الَّذِيْنَ اصْطَفٰى ؕ آٰللّٰهُ
خَيْرٌ اَمَّا يُشْرِكُوْنَ ﴿٥٩﴾
اَمَّنْ خَلَقَ السَّمٰوٰتِ وَالْاَرْضَ
وَاَنْزَلَ لَكُمْ مِّنَ السَّمَآءِ مَآءً ۚ فَاَنْۢبَتْنَا
بِهٖ حَدَآئِقَ ذَاتَ بَهْجَةٍ ۚ مَا كَانَ
لَكُمْ اَنْ تُنْۢبِتُوْا شَجَرَهَا ؕ ءَاِلٰهٌ مَّعَ
اللّٰهِ ؕ بَلْ هُمْ قَوْمٌ يَّعْدِلُوْنَ ﴿٦٠﴾
اَمَّنْ جَعَلَ الْاَرْضَ قَرَارًا وَّجَعَلَ
خِلٰلَهَاۤ اَنْهٰرًا وَّجَعَلَ لَهَا رَوَاسِيَ
وَجَعَلَ بَيْنَ الْبَحْرَيْنِ حَاجِزًا ؕ ءَاِلٰهٌ
مَّعَ اللّٰهِ ؕ بَلْ اَكْثَرُهُمْ لَا يَعْلَمُوْنَ ﴿٦١﴾
اَمَّنْ يُّجِيْبُ الْمُضْطَرَّ اِذَا دَعَاهُ
وَيَكْشِفُ السُّوْٓءَ وَيَجْعَلُكُمْ خُلَفَآءَ
الْاَرْضِ ؕ ءَاِلٰهٌ مَّعَ اللّٰهِ ؕ قَلِيْلًا
مَّا تَذَكَّرُوْنَ ﴿٦٢﴾
اَمَّنْ يَّهْدِيْكُمْ فِيْ ظُلُمٰتِ الْبَرِّ
وَالْبَحْرِ وَمَنْ يُّرْسِلُ الرِّيٰحَ بُشْرًا
بَيْنَ يَدَيْ رَحْمَتِهٖ ؕ ءَاِلٰهٌ مَّعَ
اللّٰهِ ؕ تَعٰلَى اللّٰهُ عَمَّا يُشْرِكُوْنَ ﴿٦٣﴾
اَمَّنْ يَّبْدَؤُا الْخَلْقَ ثُمَّ يُعِيْدُهٗ وَمَنْ
يَّرْزُقُكُمْ مِّنَ السَّمَآءِ وَالْاَرْضِ ؕ ءَاِلٰهٌ
مَّعَ اللّٰهِ ؕ قُلْ هَاتُوْا بُرْهَانَكُمْ اِنْ

الجزء العشرون (٢٠)

كُنْتُمْ صٰدِقِيْنَ ﴿٦٤﴾

65. (Muhammad) say, "No one in the heavens or the earth knows the unseen except Allah, and no one realizes when they will be resurrected.

65. Qul laa ya'lamu man fis-samaawaati wal-arḍil-ghayba illal-laah; wa maa yash'uroona ayyaana yub'asoon.

قُلْ لَّا يَعْلَمُ مَنْ فِي السَّمٰوٰتِ
وَالْاَرْضِ الْغَيْبَ اِلَّا اللّٰهُ ؕ وَمَا
يَشْعُرُوْنَ اَيَّانَ يُبْعَثُوْنَ ﴿٦٥﴾

66. In the next life they will fully comprehend it (resurrection) but (in the worldly life) they are in doubt about it, in fact they are blind about it."

66. Balid-daaraka 'ilmuhum fil-Aakhirah; bal hum fee shakkim-minhaa bal hum-minhaa 'amoon.

بَلِ ادّٰرَكَ عِلْمُهُمْ فِي الْاٰخِرَةِ ۫ بَلْ هُمْ
فِيْ شَكٍّ مِّنْهَا ۫ بَلْ هُمْ مِّنْهَا عَمُوْنَ ﴿٦٦﴾ ع ٥ ٨

67. The unbelievers have said, "Shall we and our fathers be brought out of the graves after we become dust?

67. Wa qaalal-lazeena kafarooo 'a-izaa kunnaa turaabañw-wa aabaaa'unaaa a'innaa lamukhrajoon.

وَقَالَ الَّذِيْنَ كَفَرُوْٓا ءَاِذَا كُنَّا تُرٰبًا
وَّاٰبَآؤُنَآ اَئِنَّا لَمُخْرَجُوْنَ ﴿٦٧﴾

68. This was promised to us and to our fathers before us. It is only of the ancient legends (false stories)."

68. Laqad wu'idnaa haazaa naḥnu wa aabaaa'unaa min qablu in haazaaa illaaa asaaṭeerul-awwaleen.

لَقَدْ وُعِدْنَا هٰذَا نَحْنُ وَاٰبَآؤُنَا مِنْ
قَبْلُ ۙ اِنْ هٰذَآ اِلَّآ اَسَاطِيْرُ الْاَوَّلِيْنَ ﴿٦٨﴾

69. Say, "Travel through the land and see how terrible was the end of the criminal ones."

69. Qul seeroo fil-arḍi fanẓuroo kayfa kaana 'aaqibatul-mujrimeen.

قُلْ سِيْرُوْا فِي الْاَرْضِ فَانْظُرُوْا كَيْفَ
كَانَ عَاقِبَةُ الْمُجْرِمِيْنَ ﴿٦٩﴾

70. (Muhammad), do not be grieved (about their disbelief) nor distressed about their evil plans against you.

70. Wa laa taḥzan 'alayhim wa laa takun fee ḍayqim-mimmaa yamkuroon.

وَلَا تَحْزَنْ عَلَيْهِمْ وَلَا تَكُنْ فِيْ ضَيْقٍ
مِّمَّا يَمْكُرُوْنَ ﴿٧٠﴾

71. They ask, "When will the Day of Judgment come, if it is true at all?"

71. Wa yaqooloona mataa haazal-wa'du in kuntum ṣaadiqeen.

وَيَقُوْلُوْنَ مَتٰى هٰذَا الْوَعْدُ اِنْ
كُنْتُمْ صٰدِقِيْنَ ﴿٧١﴾

72. Say, "Perhaps some of the things which you wish to experience immediately are very close to you."

72. Qul 'asaaa añy-yakoona radifa lakum ba'ḍul-lazee tasta'jiloon.

قُلْ عَسٰٓى اَنْ يَّكُوْنَ رَدِفَ لَكُمْ بَعْضُ
الَّذِيْ تَسْتَعْجِلُوْنَ ﴿٧٢﴾

73. Your Lord has many favors for mankind but most of them are ungrateful.

73. Wa inna Rabbaka lazoo faḍlin 'alan-naasi wa laakinna aksarahum laa yashkuroon.

وَاِنَّ رَبَّكَ لَذُوْ فَضْلٍ عَلَى النَّاسِ
وَلٰكِنَّ اَكْثَرَهُمْ لَا يَشْكُرُوْنَ ﴿٧٣﴾

74. Your Lord certainly knows whatever their hearts conceal or reveal.

74. Wa-inna Rabbaka la-ya'-lamu maa tukinnu ṣudooruhum wa maa yu'linoon.

وَاِنَّ رَبَّكَ لَيَعْلَمُ مَا تُكِنُّ صُدُوْرُهُمْ
وَمَا يُعْلِنُوْنَ ﴿٧٤﴾

75. All the secrets in the heavens and earth are recorded in the illustrious Book.

75. Wa maa min ghaaa'ibatin fis-samaaa'i wal-arḍi illaa fee kitaabim-mubeen.

وَمَا مِنْ غَآئِبَةٍ فِي السَّمَآءِ وَالْاَرْضِ
اِلَّا فِيْ كِتٰبٍ مُّبِيْنٍ ﴿٧٥﴾

76. This Quran tells the Israelites most of the matters about which they had disputes among themselves.

76. Inna haazal-Qur'aana yaquṣṣu 'alaa Baneee Israaa-'eela aksaral-lazee hum feehi yakhtalifoon.

اِنَّ هٰذَا الْقُرْاٰنَ يَقُصُّ عَلٰى بَنِيْٓ
اِسْرَآءِيْلَ اَكْثَرَ الَّذِيْ هُمْ فِيْهِ

يَخْتَلِفُوْنَ ﴿٧٦﴾

77. It is a guide and mercy for the believers.

77. Wa innahoo lahudañw-wa raḥmatul-lilmu'mineen.

وَاِنَّهٗ لَهُدًى وَّرَحْمَةٌ لِّلْمُؤْمِنِيْنَ ﴿٧٧﴾

78. Your Lord will judge among them according to His own decree. He is Majestic and All-knowing.

78. Inna Rabbaka yaqḍi baynahum biḥukmih; wa Huwal-'Azeezul-'Aleem.

اِنَّ رَبَّكَ يَقْضِيْ بَيْنَهُمْ بِحُكْمِهٖ ۚ
وَهُوَ الْعَزِيْزُ الْعَلِيْمُ ﴿٧٨﴾

79. Trust in Allah; you follow the manifest truth.

79. Fatawakkal 'alal-laahi innaka 'alal-ḥaqqil-mubeen.

فَتَوَكَّلْ عَلَى اللّٰهِ ؕ اِنَّكَ عَلَى الْحَقِّ
الْمُبِيْنِ ﴿٧٩﴾

80. You cannot make the dead listen and the deaf are unable to hear calls. Thus, they turn back on their heels.

80. Innaka laa tusmi'ul-mawtaa wa laa tusmi'uṣ-ṣummad-du'aaa'a izaa wallaw mudbireen.

اِنَّكَ لَا تُسْمِعُ الْمَوْتٰى وَلَا تُسْمِعُ
الصُّمَّ الدُّعَآءَ اِذَا وَلَّوْا مُدْبِرِيْنَ ﴿٨٠﴾

81. You cannot guide the straying blind ones. You can only make hear those who believe in Our revelations submissively.

81. Wa maaa anta bihaadil 'umyi 'an ḍalaalatihim in tusmi'u illaa mañy-yu'minu bi-Aayaatinaa fahum-muslimoon.

وَمَآ اَنْتَ بِهٰدِى الْعُمْيِ عَنْ ضَلٰلَتِهِمْ ؕ
اِنْ تُسْمِعُ اِلَّا مَنْ يُّؤْمِنُ بِاٰيٰتِنَا
فَهُمْ مُّسْلِمُوْنَ ﴿٨١﴾

82. When the word about them comes true We shall make a creature appear to them on earth who will tell them that people had no faith in Our revelations.

82. Wa izaa waqa'al-qawlu 'alayhim akhrajnaa lahum daaabbatam-minal-arḍi tukallimuhum annan-naasa kaanoo bi-Aayaatinaa laa yooqinoon.

وَاِذَا وَقَعَ الْقَوْلُ عَلَيْهِمْ اَخْرَجْنَا
لَهُمْ دَآبَّةً مِّنَ الْاَرْضِ تُكَلِّمُهُمْ ۙ
اَنَّ النَّاسَ كَانُوْا بِاٰيٰتِنَا لَا يُوْقِنُوْنَ ﴿٨٢﴾ ع

83. On the day when We resurrect from every nation a group from among those who had rejected Our revelations, they will be kept confined in ranks.

83. Wa Yawma naḥshuru min kulli ummatin fawjam-mimmañy-yukaz-zibu bi-Aayaatinaa fahum yooza'oon.

وَيَوْمَ نَحْشُرُ مِنْ كُلِّ اُمَّةٍ فَوْجًا مِّمَّنْ
يُّكَذِّبُ بِاٰيٰتِنَا فَهُمْ يُوْزَعُوْنَ ﴿٨٣﴾

84. When they are brought into the presence of Allah, He will ask them, "Did you reject My revelations without fully understanding them? What did you know about them if you had any knowledge at all?"

84. Ḥattaaa izaa jaaa'oo qaala akaz-zabtum bi-Aayaatee wa lam tuḥeeṭoo bihaa 'ilman ammaazaa kuntum ta'maloon.

حَتّٰٓى اِذَا جَآءُوْ قَالَ اَكَذَّبْتُمْ بِاٰيٰتِيْ
وَلَمْ تُحِيْطُوْا بِهَا عِلْمًا اَمَّاذَا
كُنْتُمْ تَعْمَلُوْنَ ﴿٨٤﴾

85. They will become subject to punishment because of their injustice. Thus, they will not speak.

85. Wa waqa'al-qawlu 'alayhim bimaa ẓalamoo fahum laa yanṭiqoon.

وَوَقَعَ الْقَوْلُ عَلَيْهِمْ بِمَا ظَلَمُوْا
فَهُمْ لَا يَنْطِقُوْنَ ﴿٨٥﴾

86. Did they not see that We have created the night for them to rest and the day for them to see? In this there is evidence for the believing people.

86. Alam yaraw annaa ja'alnal-layla li-yaskunoo feehi wannahaara mubṣiraa; inna fee zaalika la-Aayaatil-liqawmiñy-yu'minoon.

اَلَمْ يَرَوْا اَنَّا جَعَلْنَا الَّيْلَ لِيَسْكُنُوْا
فِيْهِ وَالنَّهَارَ مُبْصِرًا ؕ اِنَّ فِيْ ذٰلِكَ
لَاٰيٰتٍ لِّقَوْمٍ يُّؤْمِنُوْنَ ﴿٨٦﴾

87. Everyone in the heavens and earth will be terrified on the day when the trumpet will be sounded except those whom

87. Wa Yawma yunfakhu fiṣ-Ṣoori fafazi'a man fis samaawaati wa man fil-arḍi illaa

وَيَوْمَ يُنْفَخُ فِي الصُّوْرِ فَفَزِعَ مَنْ
فِي السَّمٰوٰتِ وَمَنْ فِي الْاَرْضِ اِلَّا

Allah will save. Everyone will meekly come into the presence of Allah.

man shaaa'al-laah; wa kullun atawhu daakhireen.

مَنْ شَآءَ اللّٰهُ ؕ وَكُلٌّ اَتَوْهُ دٰخِرِيْنَ ﴿٨٧﴾

88. You think the mountains are solid. In fact, they move like clouds. It is Allah's technique which has established everything perfect (strong). He is Well-aware of what you do.

88. Wa taral-jibaala taḥsabuhaa jaamidatañw-wa hiya tamurru marras-saḥaab; ṣun'al-laahil-la<u>z</u>eee atqana kulla shay'; innahoo khabeerum bimaa taf'aloon.

وَتَرَى الْجِبَالَ تَحْسَبُهَا جَامِدَةً وَّهِيَ تَمُرُّ مَرَّ السَّحَابِ ؕ صُنْعَ اللّٰهِ الَّذِيْٓ اَتْقَنَ كُلَّ شَيْءٍ ؕ اِنَّهٗ خَبِيْرٌۢ بِمَا تَفْعَلُوْنَ ﴿٨٨﴾

89. Whoever does a good deed will receive a better reward (ten-fold) than what he has done. He will be secure from the terror of the Day of Judgment.

89. Man jaaa'a bilḥasanati falahoo khayrum-minhaa wa hum-min faza'iñy-Yawma'izin aaminoon.

مَنْ جَآءَ بِالْحَسَنَةِ فَلَهٗ خَيْرٌ مِّنْهَا ۚ وَهُمْ مِّنْ فَزَعٍ يَّوْمَئِذٍ اٰمِنُوْنَ ﴿٨٩﴾

90. Those who commit evil will be thrown headlong into hellfire. (It will be said to them) can you expect any recompense other than what you deserve for your deeds?

90. Wa man jaaa'a bissayyi'ati fakubbat wujoohuhum fin-Naari hal tujzawna illaa maa kuntum ta'maloon.

وَمَنْ جَآءَ بِالسَّيِّئَةِ فَكُبَّتْ وُجُوْهُهُمْ فِي النَّارِ ؕ هَلْ تُجْزَوْنَ اِلَّا مَا كُنْتُمْ تَعْمَلُوْنَ ﴿٩٠﴾

91. I am commanded to worship the Lord of this town (Makkah) which He has made sacred. To Him belong all things. I am commanded to be a Muslim

91. Innamaaa umirtu an a'buda Rabba haa<u>z</u>ihil-baldatil-la<u>z</u>ee ḥarramahaa wa lahoo kullu shay'iñw-wa umirtu an akoona minal-muslimeen.

اِنَّمَآ اُمِرْتُ اَنْ اَعْبُدَ رَبَّ هٰذِهِ الْبَلْدَةِ الَّذِيْ حَرَّمَهَا وَلَهٗ كُلُّ شَيْءٍ ؗ وَّاُمِرْتُ اَنْ اَكُوْنَ مِنَ الْمُسْلِمِيْنَ ﴿٩١﴾

92. and recite the Quran. Whoever seeks guidance will find it for his own soul. Say to whoever goes astray, "I am only a Warner."

92. Wa an atluwal-Qur'aana famanih-tadaa fa-innamaa yahtadee linafsihee wa man ḍalla faqul innamaaa ana minal-mun<u>z</u>ireen.

وَاَنْ اَتْلُوَا الْقُرْاٰنَ ۚ فَمَنِ اهْتَدٰى فَاِنَّمَا يَهْتَدِيْ لِنَفْسِهٖ ۚ وَمَنْ ضَلَّ فَقُلْ اِنَّمَآ اَنَا مِنَ الْمُنْذِرِيْنَ ﴿٩٢﴾

93. Say, "It is only He who deserves all praise. He will soon show you His signs and you will recognize them. Your Lord is not unaware of what you do."

93. Wa qulil-ḥamdu lillaahi sa-yureekum Aayaatihee fata'rifoonahaa; wa maa Rabbuka bighaafilin 'ammaa ta'maloon

وَقُلِ الْحَمْدُ لِلّٰهِ سَيُرِيْكُمْ اٰيٰتِهٖ فَتَعْرِفُوْنَهَا ؕ وَمَا رَبُّكَ بِغَافِلٍ عَمَّا تَعْمَلُوْنَ ﴿٩٣﴾ ع

Al-Qasas, The Story (28)

In the Name of Allah, the Beneficent, the Merciful.

Sûrat al-Qaṣaṣ-28

(Revealed at Makkah)

Bismillaahir Raḥmaanir Raḥeem

(٢٨) سُوْرَةُ الْقَصَصِ مَكِّيَّةٌ (٤٩)

اٰيَاتُهَا ٨٨ — بِسْمِ اللّٰهِ الرَّحْمٰنِ الرَّحِيْمِ — رُكُوْعَاتُهَا ٩

1. Ta Sin. Mim.

1. Ṭaa-Seeen-Meeem.

طٰسٓمّٓ ﴿١﴾

2. These are the verses of the illustrious Book.

2. Tilka Aayaatul-Kitaabil-mubeen.

تِلْكَ اٰيٰتُ الْكِتٰبِ الْمُبِيْنِ ﴿٢﴾

3. We recite to you some of the story of Moses and the Pharaoh for a genuine purpose, and for the benefit of the believing people.

3. Natloo 'alayka min-naba-i Moosaa wa Fir'awna bilḥaqqi liqawmiñy-yu'minoon.

نَتْلُوْا عَلَيْكَ مِنْ نَّبَاِ مُوْسٰى وَفِرْعَوْنَ بِالْحَقِّ لِقَوْمٍ يُّؤْمِنُوْنَ ﴿٣﴾

4. The Pharaoh dominated the land and divided its inhabitants into different groups, suppressing one group by killing their sons and keeping their women alive. He was certainly an evil-doer.

4. Inna Fir'awna 'alaa fil-arḍi wa ja'ala ahlahaa shiya'añy-yastaḍ'ifu ṭaaa'ifatam-minhum yuẕabbiḥu abnaaa'ahum wa yastaḥyee nisaaa'ahum; innahoo kaana minal-mufsideen.

إِنَّ فِرْعَوْنَ عَلَا فِي الْأَرْضِ وَجَعَلَ
أَهْلَهَا شِيَعًا يَسْتَضْعِفُ طَآئِفَةً
مِّنْهُمْ يُذَبِّحُ أَبْنَآءَهُمْ وَيَسْتَحْيِ نِسَآءَهُمْ
إِنَّهُ كَانَ مِنَ الْمُفْسِدِينَ ④

5. We, however, have decided to grant a favor to the suppressed ones in the land by appointing them leaders and heirs of thereof,

5. Wa nureedu an-namunna 'alal-laẕeenas-tuḍ'ifoo fil-arḍi wa naj'alahum a'immatañw-wa naj'alahumul-waariṡeen.

وَنُرِيدُ أَن نَّمُنَّ عَلَى الَّذِينَ
اسْتُضْعِفُوا فِي الْأَرْضِ وَنَجْعَلَهُمْ
أَئِمَّةً وَنَجْعَلَهُمُ الْوَارِثِينَ ⑤

6. giving them power in the land, and making the Pharaoh, Haman (his Minister), and their armies to experience from their victims what they feared most.

6. Wa numakkina lahum fil-arḍi wa nuriya Fir'awna wa Haamaana wa junoodahumaa minhum-maa kaanoo yaḥẕaroon.

وَنُمَكِّنَ لَهُمْ فِي الْأَرْضِ وَنُرِيَ
فِرْعَوْنَ وَهَامَانَ وَجُنُودَهُمَا
مِنْهُم مَّا كَانُوا يَحْذَرُونَ ⑥

7. We inspired Moses' mother, saying, "Breast-feed your son. When you become afraid for his life, throw him into the sea. Do not be afraid or grieved for We shall return him to you and make him one of the Messengers."

7. Wa-awḥaynaaa ilaaa-ummi Moosaaa an arḍi'eehi fa-iẕaa khifti 'alayhi fa-alqeehi filyammi wa laa takhaafee wa laa taḥzaneee innaa raaaddoohu ilayki wa jaa'iloohu minal-mursaleen.

وَأَوْحَيْنَا إِلَىٰ أُمِّ مُوسَىٰ أَنْ أَرْضِعِيهِ
فَإِذَا خِفْتِ عَلَيْهِ فَأَلْقِيهِ فِي الْيَمِّ
وَلَا تَخَافِي وَلَا تَحْزَنِي إِنَّا رَآدُّوهُ
إِلَيْكِ وَجَاعِلُوهُ مِنَ الْمُرْسَلِينَ ⑦

8. The people of the Pharaoh picked him up (without realizing) that he would become their enemy and a source of their sorrow. The Pharaoh, Haman, and their army were sinful people.

8. Faltaqatahooo Aalu Fir'awna li-yakoona lahum 'aduwwañw-wa ḥazanaa; inna Fir'awna wa Haamaana wa junoodahumaa kaanoo khaaṭi'een.

فَالْتَقَطَهُ آلُ فِرْعَوْنَ لِيَكُونَ لَهُمْ
عَدُوًّا وَحَزَنًا إِنَّ فِرْعَوْنَ وَهَامَانَ
وَجُنُودَهُمَا كَانُوا خَاطِئِينَ ⑧

9. The Pharaoh's wife said, "He, (Moses), is the delight of my eyes as well as yours. Do not kill him. Perhaps he will benefit us or we may adopt him." They were unaware of the future.

9. Wa qaalatim-ra-atu Fir'awna qurratu 'aynil-lee wa lak; laa taqtuloohu 'asaaa añy-yanfa'anaaa aw nattakhiẕahoo waladañw-wa hum laa yash'uroon.

وَقَالَتِ امْرَأَتُ فِرْعَوْنَ قُرَّتُ عَيْنٍ
لِّي وَلَكَ لَا تَقْتُلُوهُ عَسَىٰ أَن
يَنفَعَنَا أَوْ نَتَّخِذَهُ وَلَدًا وَهُمْ
لَا يَشْعُرُونَ ⑨

10. The heart of Moses' mother was relieved and confident. However, she would almost have made the whole matter public had We not strengthened her heart with faith.

10. Wa aṣbaḥa fu'aadu ummi Moosaa faarighan in kaadat latubdee bihee law laaa ar-rabaṭnaa 'alaa qalbihaa lita-koona minal-mu'mineen.

وَأَصْبَحَ فُؤَادُ أُمِّ مُوسَىٰ فَارِغًا إِن
كَادَتْ لَتُبْدِي بِهِ لَوْلَا أَن رَّبَطْنَا
عَلَىٰ قَلْبِهَا لِتَكُونَ مِنَ الْمُؤْمِنِينَ ⑩

11. She told Moses' sister to follow her brother. His sister watched him from one side and the people of the Pharaoh did not notice her presence.

11. Wa qaalat li-ukhtihee quṣṣeehi fabaṣurat bihee 'an junubiñw-wa hum laa yash'uroon.

وَقَالَتْ لِأُخْتِهِ قُصِّيهِ فَبَصُرَتْ بِهِ
عَن جُنُبٍ وَهُمْ لَا يَشْعُرُونَ ⑪

12. We had decreed that he (Moses) must not be breast-fed by any nurse (besides his mother). His sister said to the people of the Pharaoh, "May I show you a family who can nurse him for you with kindness?"

12. Wa ḥarramnaa 'alayhil-maraaḍi'a min qablu faqaalat hal adullukum 'alaaa ahli baytiñy-yakfuloonahoo lakum wa hum lahoo naaṣiḥoon.

وَحَرَّمْنَا عَلَيْهِ الْمَرَاضِعَ مِنْ
قَبْلُ فَقَالَتْ هَلْ أَدُلُّكُمْ عَلَىٰ
أَهْلِ بَيْتٍ يَكْفُلُونَهُ لَكُمْ وَهُمْ
لَهُ نَاصِحُونَ ﴿١٢﴾

13. Thus did We return Moses to his mother that We would delight her eyes, relieve her sorrows, and let her know that the promise of Allah was true, but many people do not know.

13. Faradadnaahu ilaaa um-mihee kay taqarra 'aynuhaa wa laa taḥzana wa lita'lama anna wa'dal-laahi ḥaqquñw-wa laa-kinna aksarahum laa ya'la-moon.

فَرَدَدْنَاهُ إِلَىٰ أُمِّهِ كَيْ تَقَرَّ عَيْنُهَا
وَلَا تَحْزَنَ وَلِتَعْلَمَ أَنَّ وَعْدَ اللَّهِ
حَقٌّ وَلَٰكِنَّ أَكْثَرَهُمْ لَا يَعْلَمُونَ ﴿١٣﴾

14. When he matured and grew to manhood, We granted him wisdom and knowledge. Thus do We reward the righteous ones.

14. Wa lammaa balagha ashuddahoo wastawaaa aatay-naahu ḥukmañw-wa 'ilmaa; wa kaẕaalika najzil-muḥsineen.

وَلَمَّا بَلَغَ أَشُدَّهُ وَاسْتَوَىٰ آتَيْنَاهُ حُكْمًا
وَعِلْمًا ۚ وَكَذَٰلِكَ نَجْزِي الْمُحْسِنِينَ ﴿١٤﴾

15. He entered the city without the knowledge of its inhabitants and found two men fighting each other. One was his follower and the other his enemy. His follower asked him for help against his enemies. Moses struck his enemy to death, but later said, "It was the work of Satan; he is the sworn enemy of the human being and wants to mislead him."

15. Wa dakhalal-madeenata 'alaa ḥeeni ghaflatim-min ahlihaa fawajada feehaa raju-layni yaqtatilaani haaẕaa min shee'atihee wa haaẕaa min 'aduwwihee fastaghaasahul-laẕee min shee'atihee 'alal-laẕee min 'aduwwihee fawakazahoo Moosaa faqaḍaa 'alayhi qaala haaẕaa min 'amalish-Shayṭaani innahoo 'aduwwum-muḍillum-mubeen.

وَدَخَلَ الْمَدِينَةَ عَلَىٰ حِينِ غَفْلَةٍ
مِنْ أَهْلِهَا فَوَجَدَ فِيهَا رَجُلَيْنِ
يَقْتَتِلَانِ هَٰذَا مِنْ شِيعَتِهِ وَهَٰذَا
مِنْ عَدُوِّهِ ۖ فَاسْتَغَاثَهُ الَّذِي مِنْ
شِيعَتِهِ عَلَى الَّذِي مِنْ عَدُوِّهِ فَوَكَزَهُ
مُوسَىٰ فَقَضَىٰ عَلَيْهِ ۖ قَالَ هَٰذَا مِنْ
عَمَلِ الشَّيْطَانِ ۖ إِنَّهُ عَدُوٌّ مُضِلٌّ
مُبِينٌ ﴿١٥﴾

16. (Moses) said, "My Lord, I have wronged myself. Forgive me!" The Lord forgave him; He is All-forgiving and All-merciful.

16. Qaala Rabbi innee ẓalam-tu nafsee faghfir lee faghafara lah; innahoo Huwal-Ghafoorur-Raḥeem.

قَالَ رَبِّ إِنِّي ظَلَمْتُ نَفْسِي فَاغْفِرْ لِي
فَغَفَرَ لَهُ ۚ إِنَّهُ هُوَ الْغَفُورُ الرَّحِيمُ ﴿١٦﴾

17. He said, "Lord, in appreciation for Your favor to me I shall never support the criminals."

17. Qaala Rabbi bimaaa an'amta 'alayya falan akoona ẓaheeral-lilmujrimeen.

قَالَ رَبِّ بِمَا أَنْعَمْتَ عَلَيَّ فَلَنْ
أَكُونَ ظَهِيرًا لِلْمُجْرِمِينَ ﴿١٧﴾

18. He remained in the city but very afraid and watchful. Suddenly the person who asked him for help the previous day asked him for help again. Moses said, "You are certainly a mischievous person."

18. Fa-aṣbaḥa fil-madeenati khaaa'ifañy-yataraqqabu fa-iẕal-laẕis-tanṣarahoo bil-amsi yastaṣrikhuh; qaala lahoo Moosaaa innaka laghawiyyum-mubeen.

فَأَصْبَحَ فِي الْمَدِينَةِ خَائِفًا يَتَرَقَّبُ
فَإِذَا الَّذِي اسْتَنْصَرَهُ بِالْأَمْسِ
يَسْتَصْرِخُهُ ۚ قَالَ لَهُ مُوسَىٰ إِنَّكَ
لَغَوِيٌّ مُبِينٌ ﴿١٨﴾

19. When Moses was about to attack their enemy, he said,

19. Falammaaa an araada añy-yabṭisha billaẕee

فَلَمَّا أَنْ أَرَادَ أَنْ يَبْطِشَ بِالَّذِي

"Moses, do you want to kill me as you slew a soul the other day? You want nothing else but to become a tyrant in the land and not a reformer."

huwa 'aduwwul-lahumaa qaala yaa Moosaaa atureedu an taqtulanee kamaa qatalta nafsam bil-amsi in tureedu illaaa an takoona jabbaaran fil-arḍi wa maa tureedu an takoona minal-muṣliḥeen.

هُوَ عَدُوٌّ لَّهُمَا ۙ قَالَ يٰمُوۡسٰۤى اَتُرِيۡدُ
اَنۡ تَقۡتُلَنِىۡ كَمَا قَتَلۡتَ نَفۡسًۢا
بِالۡاَمۡسِ ۖ اِنۡ تُرِيۡدُ اِلَّاۤ اَنۡ تَكُوۡنَ
جَبَّارًا فِى الۡاَرۡضِ وَمَا تُرِيۡدُ اَنۡ
تَكُوۡنَ مِنَ الۡمُصۡلِحِيۡنَ ﴿١٩﴾

20. A man came running from the farthest part of the city saying, "Moses, people are planning to kill you. I sincerely advise you to leave the city."

20. Wa jaaa'a rajulum-min aqṣal-madeenati yas'aa qaala yaa Moosaaa innal-mala-a ya-tamiroona bika liyaqtulooka fakhruj innee laka minan-naaṣiḥeen.

وَجَآءَ رَجُلٌ مِّنۡ اَقۡصَا الۡمَدِيۡنَةِ
يَسۡعٰى قَالَ يٰمُوۡسٰۤى اِنَّ الۡمَلَاَ يَاۡتَمِرُوۡنَ
بِكَ لِيَقۡتُلُوۡكَ فَاخۡرُجۡ اِنِّىۡ لَـكَ
مِنَ النّٰصِحِيۡنَ ﴿٢٠﴾

21. So he left the city afraid and cautious, saying, "Lord, protect me against the unjust people."

21. Fakharaja minhaa khaaa-'ifañy-yataraqqab; qaala Rabbi najjinee minal-qawmiẓ-ẓaali-meen.

فَخَرَجَ مِنۡهَا خَآئِفًا يَّتَرَقَّبُ قَالَ
رَبِّ نَجِّنِىۡ مِنَ الۡقَوۡمِ الظّٰلِمِيۡنَ ﴿٢١﴾ ع ٨ ٥

22. When he started his journey to Madian he said, "Perhaps my Lord will show me the right path."

22. Wa lammaa tawajjaha tilqaaa'a Madyana qaala 'asaa Rabbeee añy-yahdiyanee Sa-waaa'as-Sabeel.

وَلَمَّا تَوَجَّهَ تِلۡقَآءَ مَدۡيَنَ قَالَ عَسٰى
رَبِّىۡۤ اَنۡ يَّهۡدِيَنِىۡ سَوَآءَ السَّبِيۡلِ ﴿٢٢﴾

23. When he arrived at the well of Madian, he found some people watering (their sheep) and two women keeping the sheep away from the others. He asked the two women, "What is the matter with you?" They replied, "We cannot water our sheep until all the shepherds have driven away their flocks. Our father is an old man."

23. Wa lammaa warada maaa'a Madyana wajada 'alayhi ummatam-minannaasi yasqoona wa wajada min doonihimum-ra-atayni taẕoo-daani qaala maa khaṭbukumaa qaalataa laa nasqee ḥattaa yuṣdirarri'aaa'u wa aboonaa shaykhun kabeer.

وَلَمَّا وَرَدَ مَآءَ مَدۡيَنَ وَجَدَ عَلَيۡهِ
اُمَّةً مِّنَ النَّاسِ يَسۡقُوۡنَ ۖ وَوَجَدَ
مِنۡ دُوۡنِهِمُ امۡرَاَتَيۡنِ تَذُوۡدٰنِ ۚ
قَالَ مَا خَطۡبُكُمَا ؕ قَالَتَا لَا نَسۡقِىۡ
حَتّٰى يُصۡدِرَ الرِّعَآءُ ٚ وَاَبُوۡنَا
شَيۡخٌ كَبِيۡرٌ ﴿٢٣﴾

24. Moses watered their flocks and then sought shelter under a shadow praying, "Lord, I need the means to preserve (the power) that You have granted me."

24. Fasaqaa lahumaa s̲umma tawallaaa ilaẓ-ẓilli faqaala Rabbi innee limaaa anzalta ilayya min khayrin faqeer.

فَسَقٰى لَهُمَا ثُمَّ تَوَلّٰۤى اِلَى الظِّلِّ
فَقَالَ رَبِّ اِنِّىۡ لِمَاۤ اَنۡزَلۡتَ اِلَىَّ مِنۡ
خَيۡرٍ فَقِيۡرٌ ﴿٢٤﴾

25. One of the women, walking bashfully, came to Moses and said, "My father calls you and wants to pay you for your watering our flocks." When Moses came to the woman's father and told him his whole story, he said, "Do not be afraid.

25. Fajaaa'at-hu iḥdaahumaa tamshee 'alas-tiḥyaaa'in qaalat inna abee yad'ooka li-yajziyaka ajra maa saqayta lanaa; falammaa jaaa'ahoo wa qaṣṣa 'alayhil-qaṣaṣa

فَجَآءَتۡهُ اِحۡدٰٮهُمَا تَمۡشِىۡ عَلَى
اسۡتِحۡيَآءٍ ۚ قَالَتۡ اِنَّ اَبِىۡ يَدۡعُوۡكَ
لِيَجۡزِيَكَ اَجۡرَ مَا سَقَيۡتَ لَنَا ؕ فَلَمَّا
جَآءَهٗ وَقَصَّ عَلَيۡهِ الۡقَصَصَ ۙ

Now you are secure from the unjust people."

qaala laa takhaf najawta minal-qawmiẓ-ẓaalimeen.

قَالَ لَا تَخَفْ نَجَوْتَ مِنَ الْقَوْمِ
الظّٰلِمِيْنَ ﴿٢٥﴾

26. One of the women said to her father, "Father, hire him; the best whom you may hire is a strong and trustworthy one."

26. Qaalat iḥdaahumaa yaaa abatis-ta-jirhu inna khayra manis-ta-jartal-qawiyyul-ameen.

قَالَتْ اِحْدٰىهُمَا يٰٓاَبَتِ اسْتَاْجِرْهُ اِنَّ
خَيْرَ مَنِ اسْتَاْجَرْتَ الْقَوِيُّ الْاَمِيْنُ ﴿٢٦﴾

27. He (Shuayb) said to (Moses), "I want to give one of my daughters to you in marriage on the condition that you will work for me for eight years, but you may continue for two more years only out of your own accord. I do not want it to become a burden for you. Allah willing, you will find me a righteous person."

27. Qaala inneee ureedu-an unkiḥaka iḥdab-natayya haatayni 'alaaa an ta-juranee s̱amaaniya ḥijaj; fa-in atmamta 'ashran famin 'indika wa maaa ureedu an ashuqqa 'alayk; satajiduneee-in shaaa'al-laahu minaṣ-ṣaaliḥeen.

قَالَ اِنِّيْٓ اُرِيْدُ اَنْ اُنْكِحَكَ اِحْدَى
ابْنَتَيَّ هٰتَيْنِ عَلٰٓى اَنْ تَاْجُرَنِيْ ثَمٰنِيَ
حِجَجٍ ۚ فَاِنْ اَتْمَمْتَ عَشْرًا فَمِنْ
عِنْدِكَ ۚ وَمَآ اُرِيْدُ اَنْ اَشُقَّ عَلَيْكَ
سَتَجِدُنِيْٓ اِنْ شَاۗءَ اللّٰهُ مِنَ الصّٰلِحِيْنَ ﴿٢٧﴾

28. (Moses) said, "Let it be a binding contract between us and I shall be free to serve for any of the said terms. Allah will bear witness to our agreement."

28. Qaala ẕaalika baynee wa baynaka ayyamal-ajalayni qaḍaytu falaa 'udwaana 'alayya wallaahu 'alaa maa naqoolu Wakeel.

قَالَ ذٰلِكَ بَيْنِيْ وَبَيْنَكَ ۭ اَيَّمَا
الْاَجَلَيْنِ قَضَيْتُ فَلَا عُدْوَانَ عَلَيَّ ۭ
وَاللّٰهُ عَلٰى مَا نَقُوْلُ وَكِيْلٌ ﴿٢٨﴾

29. When Moses completed the term of the contract and departed from his employer with his family, he saw a fire (on his way) on one side of the Mount (Sinai). He asked his wife, "Stay here. I can see some fire. Perhaps I will be able to bring some news of it or some fire for you to warm yourselves."

29. Falammaa qaḍaa Moosal-ajala wa saara bi-ahliheee aanasa min jaanibiṭ-Ṭoori naaran qaala li-ahlihim-kus̱ooo inneee aanastu naaral-la'alleee aateekum-minhaa bikhabarin aw jaẕwatim-minannaari la-'allakum taṣṭaloon.

فَلَمَّا قَضٰى مُوْسَى الْاَجَلَ وَسَارَ
بِاَهْلِهٖٓ اٰنَسَ مِنْ جَانِبِ الطُّوْرِ
نَارًا ۚ قَالَ لِاَهْلِهِ امْكُثُوْٓا اِنِّيْٓ
اٰنَسْتُ نَارًا لَّعَلِّيْٓ اٰتِيْكُمْ مِّنْهَا
بِخَبَرٍ اَوْ جَذْوَةٍ مِّنَ النَّارِ
لَعَلَّكُمْ تَصْطَلُوْنَ ﴿٢٩﴾

30. He was called from a tree of the blessed spot on the bank of the right side of the valley when he approached it, "Moses, I am Allah, the Lord of the Universe.

30. Falammaaa ataahaa noodiya min shaaṭi'il waadil-aymani fil-buq'atil-mubaarakati minash-shajarati añy-yaa Moosaaa inneee Anal-laahu Rabbul'aalameen.

فَلَمَّآ اَتٰىهَا نُوْدِيَ مِنْ شَاطِئِ الْوَادِ
الْاَيْمَنِ فِي الْبُقْعَةِ الْمُبٰرَكَةِ
مِنَ الشَّجَرَةِ اَنْ يّٰمُوْسٰٓى اِنِّيْٓ اَنَا
اللّٰهُ رَبُّ الْعٰلَمِيْنَ ﴿٣٠﴾

31. Throw down your staff." When Moses saw his staff moving on the ground like a living being he moved back and did not step forward. He was told, "Moses, step forward. Do not be afraid; you will be safe and secure."

31. Wa-an alqi 'aṣaaka falammaa ra-aahaa tahtazzu ka-annahaa jaaannuñw-wallaa mudbirañw-wa lam yu'aqqib; yaa Moosaaa aqbil wa laa takhaf innaka minal-aamineen.

وَاَنْ اَلْقِ عَصَاكَ ۭ فَلَمَّا رَاٰهَا تَهْتَزُّ
كَاَنَّهَا جَاۗنٌّ وَّلّٰى مُدْبِرًا وَّلَمْ
يُعَقِّبْ ۭ يٰمُوْسٰٓى اَقْبِلْ وَلَا تَخَفْ
اِنَّكَ مِنَ الْاٰمِنِيْنَ ﴿٣١﴾

32. "Place your hand in your pocket; it will come out sheer white but not sick. Be humble for fear of Allah and show these two miracles of your Lord to the Pharaoh and his officials; they are an evil-doing people."

32. Usluk yadaka fee jaybika takhruj bayḍaaa'a min ghayri sooo'iñw-waḍmum ilayka janaaḥaka minar-rahbi faẕaanika burhaanaani mir-Rabbika ilaa Fir'awna wa mala'ih; innahum kaanoo qawman faasiqeen.

اُسْلُكْ يَدَكَ فِيْ جَيْبِكَ تَخْرُجْ بَيْضَآءَ
مِنْ غَيْرِ سُوْٓءٍ ز وَّاضْمُمْ اِلَيْكَ
جَنَاحَكَ مِنَ الرَّهْبِ فَذٰنِكَ بُرْهَانٰنِ
مِنْ رَّبِّكَ اِلٰى فِرْعَوْنَ وَمَلَا۟ئِهٖ ط
اِنَّهُمْ كَانُوْا قَوْمًا فٰسِقِيْنَ ﴿٣٢﴾

33. (Moses) said, "Lord, I have killed a man from their people and I am afraid that they will kill me.

33. Qaala Rabbi innee qataltu minhum nafsan fa-akhaafu añy-yaqtuloon.

قَالَ رَبِّ اِنِّيْ قَتَلْتُ مِنْهُمْ نَفْسًا
فَاَخَافُ اَنْ يَّقْتُلُوْنِ ﴿٣٣﴾

34. My brother Aaron is more fluent then I am. Send him with me to assist me and express my truthfulness; I am afraid they will reject me."

34. Wa-akhee Haaroonu huwa afṣaḥu minnee lisaanan fa-arsilhu ma'iya rid-añy-yuṣaddiquneee inneee akhaafu añy-yukaẕ-ẕiboon.

وَاَخِيْ هٰرُوْنُ هُوَ اَفْصَحُ مِنِّيْ لِسَانًا
فَاَرْسِلْهُ مَعِيَ رِدْاً يُّصَدِّقُنِيْٓ ز
اِنِّيْٓ اَخَافُ اَنْ يُّكَذِّبُوْنِ ﴿٣٤﴾

35. The Lord said, "We will support you by your brother and will grant you such prestige that no one will dare to approach any one of you. By the help of Our miracles both you and your followers will certainly triumph."

35. Qaala sanashuddu 'aḍudaka bi-akheeka wa naj'alu lakumaa sulṭaanan falaa yaṣiloona ilaykumaa; bi-Aayaatinaa antumaa wa manit-taba'akumal-ghaaliboon.

قَالَ سَنَشُدُّ عَضُدَكَ بِاَخِيْكَ
وَنَجْعَلُ لَكُمَا سُلْطٰنًا فَلَا
يَصِلُوْنَ اِلَيْكُمَا ۚ بِاٰيٰتِنَآ ۚ اَنْتُمَا
وَمَنِ اتَّبَعَكُمَا الْغٰلِبُوْنَ ﴿٣٥﴾

معانقة ١٢ عند المتاخرين ١٢٠

36. When Moses came to them with Our miracles, they said, "These are only invented magic. We have never heard of such things from our fathers."

36. Falammaa jaaa'ahum-Moosaa bi-Aayaatinaa bayyinaatin qaaloo maa haaẕaaa illaa siḥrum-muftarañw-wa maa sami'naa bihaaẕaa feee aabaaa-'inal awwaleen.

فَلَمَّا جَآءَهُمْ مُّوْسٰى بِاٰيٰتِنَا بَيِّنٰتٍ
قَالُوْا مَا هٰذَآ اِلَّا سِحْرٌ مُّفْتَرًى
وَّمَا سَمِعْنَا بِهٰذَا فِيْٓ اٰبَآئِنَا
الْاَوَّلِيْنَ ﴿٣٦﴾

37. Moses said, "My Lord knows best who has received guidance from Him and who will achieve a happy end. The unjust ones certainly will have no happiness."

37. Wa qaala Moosaa Rabbeee a'lamu biman jaaa'a bilhudaa min 'indihee wa man takoonu lahoo 'aaqibatud-daari innahoo laa yufliḥuẓ-ẓaalimoon.

وَقَالَ مُوْسٰى رَبِّيْٓ اَعْلَمُ بِمَنْ جَآءَ
بِالْهُدٰى مِنْ عِنْدِهٖ وَمَنْ تَكُوْنُ
لَهٗ عَاقِبَةُ الدَّارِ ط اِنَّهٗ لَا يُفْلِحُ
الظّٰلِمُوْنَ ﴿٣٧﴾

38. The Pharaoh said, "My people, I know no one who could be your Lord besides myself. Haman, construct for me a tower of baked bricks so that I may climb on it and see the Ilah (one deserving to be worshiped) of

38. Wa qaala Fir'awnu yaaa ayyuhal-mala-u maa 'alimtu lakum-min ilaahin ghayree fa-awqid lee yaa Haamaanu 'alaṭ-ṭeeni faj'al-lee ṣarḥal-la'alleee aṭṭali'u ilaaa ilaahi Moosaa

وَقَالَ فِرْعَوْنُ يٰٓاَيُّهَا الْمَلَاُ مَا عَلِمْتُ
لَكُمْ مِّنْ اِلٰهٍ غَيْرِيْ ج فَاَوْقِدْ لِيْ
يٰهَامٰنُ عَلَى الطِّيْنِ فَاجْعَلْ لِّيْ
صَرْحًا لَّعَلِّيْٓ اَطَّلِعُ اِلٰٓى اِلٰهِ مُوْسٰى

Moses; I think he is a liar."

wa innee la-aẓunnuhoo minal-kaazibeen.

وَإِنِّي لَأَظُنُّهُ مِنَ الْكَٰذِبِينَ ٣٨

39. The Pharaoh and his army were puffed-up with pride in the land for no true cause. They thought that they would never return to Us.

39. Wastakbara huwa wa junooduhoo fil-arḍi bighayril-ḥaqqi wa ẓannooo annahum ilaynaa laa yurja'oon.

وَاسْتَكْبَرَ هُوَ وَجُنُودُهُ فِي الْأَرْضِ
بِغَيْرِ الْحَقِّ وَظَنُّوا أَنَّهُمْ إِلَيْنَا
لَا يُرْجَعُونَ ٣٩

40. We seized him and his army and threw them into the sea. See how terrible was the end of the unjust people!

40. Fa-akhaznaahu wa junoodahoo-fanabaznaahum fil-yammi fanẓur kayfa kaana 'aaqibatuẓ-ẓaalimeen.

فَأَخَذْنَٰهُ وَجُنُودَهُ فَنَبَذْنَٰهُمْ فِي الْيَمِّ
فَانْظُرْ كَيْفَ كَانَ عَٰقِبَةُ الظَّٰلِمِينَ ٤٠

41. We made them the kinds of (Aimmah) leaders who would invite people to the fire and who would receive no help on the Day of Judgment.

41. Wa ja'alnaahum a'immatañy-yad'oona ilan-Naari wa Yawmal-Qiyaamati laa yunṣaroon.

وَجَعَلْنَٰهُمْ أَئِمَّةً يَدْعُونَ إِلَى
النَّارِ وَيَوْمَ الْقِيَٰمَةِ لَا يُنْصَرُونَ ٤١

42. We made them to be mentioned with condemnation in this life and they will be disgraced on the Day of Judgment.

42. Wa atba'naahum fee haazihid-dunyaa la'nah; wa Yawmal-Qiyaamati hum-minal-maqbooḥeen.

وَأَتْبَعْنَٰهُمْ فِي هَٰذِهِ الدُّنْيَا
لَعْنَةً وَيَوْمَ الْقِيَٰمَةِ هُمْ مِنَ
الْمَقْبُوحِينَ ٤٢

43. After destroying the people of the ancient towns We gave the Book to Moses to be a source of knowledge, guidance, and mercy for mankind so that perhaps they would take heed.

43. Wa laqad aataynaa Moosal-Kitaaba mim ba'di maaa ahlaknal-quroonal-oolaa baṣaaa'ira linnaasi wa hudañw-wa raḥmatal-la'allahum yatazak-karoon.

وَلَقَدْ آتَيْنَا مُوسَى الْكِتَٰبَ مِنْ بَعْدِ
مَا أَهْلَكْنَا الْقُرُونَ الْأُولَىٰ بَصَائِرَ
لِلنَّاسِ وَهُدًى وَرَحْمَةً لَعَلَّهُمْ
يَتَذَكَّرُونَ ٤٣

44. (Muhammad), you were not present at the west bank to witness when We informed Moses about the commandments.

44. Wa maa kunta bijaanibil gharbiyyi iz qaḍaynaaa ilaa Moosal-amra wa maa kunta minash-shaahideen.

وَمَا كُنْتَ بِجَانِبِ الْغَرْبِيِّ إِذْ
قَضَيْنَا إِلَىٰ مُوسَى الْأَمْرَ وَمَا
كُنْتَ مِنَ الشَّٰهِدِينَ ٤٤

45. We raised many generations after Moses and they lived for many years. You did not dwell with the people of Madian reciting Our revelations to them, but We had certainly sent Messengers to them.

45. Wa laakinnaaa ansha-naa quroonan fataṭaawala 'alay-himul-'umur; wa maa kunta saawiyan feee ahli Madyana tatloo 'alayhim Aayaatinaa wa laakinnaa kunnaa mursileen.

وَلَٰكِنَّا أَنْشَأْنَا قُرُونًا فَتَطَاوَلَ
عَلَيْهِمُ الْعُمُرُ وَمَا كُنْتَ ثَاوِيًا فِي
أَهْلِ مَدْيَنَ تَتْلُوا عَلَيْهِمْ آيَٰتِنَا
وَلَٰكِنَّا كُنَّا مُرْسِلِينَ ٤٥

46. You had not been present at the side of the Mount (Sinai) when We called Moses (from the tree). However, as a mercy from your Lord We told you his story so that you might warn the people to whom no Warner had been sent that perhaps they might take heed,

46. Wa maa kunta bijaanibiṭ-Ṭoori iz naadaynaa wa laakir-raḥmatam-mir-Rabbika litunzira qawmam-maaa ataahum-min-nazeerim-min qablika la'allahum yatazakkaroon.

وَمَا كُنْتَ بِجَانِبِ الطُّورِ إِذْ نَادَيْنَا
وَلَٰكِنْ رَحْمَةً مِنْ رَبِّكَ لِتُنْذِرَ
قَوْمًا مَا أَتَٰهُمْ مِنْ نَذِيرٍ مِنْ
قَبْلِكَ لَعَلَّهُمْ يَتَذَكَّرُونَ ٤٦

47. and that, on experiencing afflictions because of their own deeds, they might not say, "Lord, would that You had sent to us a Messenger so that we could follow Your revelations and become believers."

47. Wa law laaa an tuṣeebahum-muṣeebatum bimaa qaddamat aydeehim fa-yaqooloo Rabbanaa law laaa arsalta ilaynaa Rasoolan fanattabi'a Aayaatika wa nakoona minal-mu'mineen.

وَلَوْلَآ اَنْ تُصِيْبَهُمْ مُّصِيْبَةٌ بِمَا
قَدَّمَتْ اَيْدِيْهِمْ فَيَقُوْلُوْا رَبَّنَا
لَوْلَآ اَرْسَلْتَ اِلَيْنَا رَسُوْلًا فَنَتَّبِعَ
اٰيٰتِكَ وَنَكُوْنَ مِنَ الْمُؤْمِنِيْنَ ﴿٤٧﴾

48. When the Truth from Us came to them they said, "Would that he (Muhammad) had received what was given to Moses (by his Lord)." Did they not reject what Moses had brought to them saying, "These two, Moses and Aaron, are two magicians who support each other? We do not have any faith in them."

48. Falammaa jaaa'ahumul-ḥaqqu min 'indinaa qaaloo law laaa ootiya mis̱la maaa ootiya Moosaaa; awalam yakfuroo bimaaa ootiya Moosaa min qablu qaaloo siḥraani taẓaaharaa wa qaalooo innaa bikullin kaafiroon.

فَلَمَّا جَآءَهُمُ الْحَقُّ مِنْ عِنْدِنَا قَالُوْا
لَوْلَآ اُوْتِيَ مِثْلَ مَآ اُوْتِيَ مُوْسٰى ؕ
اَوَلَمْ يَكْفُرُوْا بِمَآ اُوْتِيَ مُوْسٰى مِنْ
قَبْلُ ۚ قَالُوْا سِحْرٰنِ تَظَاهَرَا ۟ وَ
قَالُوْٓا اِنَّا بِكُلٍّ كٰفِرُوْنَ ﴿٤٨﴾

49. (Muhammad), tell them, "Bring a Book if you are able to, from Allah, better in its guidance than the Torah and the Quran; I shall follow it."

49. Qul fa-too bi-Kitaabim-min 'indil-laahi huwa ahdaa minhumaaa attabi'hu in kuntum ṣaadiqeen.

قُلْ فَاْتُوْا بِكِتٰبٍ مِّنْ عِنْدِ اللّٰهِ
هُوَ اَهْدٰى مِنْهُمَآ اَتَّبِعْهُ اِنْ كُنْتُمْ
صٰدِقِيْنَ ﴿٤٩﴾

50. If they could not meet such a challenge, know that they are only following their (evil) desires. Who strays more than one who follows his desires without guidance from Allah? Allah does not guide the unjust people.

50. Fa-il-lam yastajeeboo laka fa'lam annamaa yattabi'oona ahwaaa'ahum; wa man aḍallu mimmanit-taba'a hawaahu bighayri hudam-minal-laah; innal-laaha laa yahdil-qawmaẓ-ẓaalimeen.

فَاِنْ لَّمْ يَسْتَجِيْبُوْا لَكَ فَاعْلَمْ اَنَّمَا
يَتَّبِعُوْنَ اَهْوَآءَهُمْ ؕ وَمَنْ اَضَلُّ
مِمَّنِ اتَّبَعَ هَوٰىهُ بِغَيْرِ هُدًى
مِّنَ اللّٰهِ ؕ اِنَّ اللّٰهَ لَا يَهْدِي
الْقَوْمَ الظّٰلِمِيْنَ ﴿٥٠﴾ ع ٥/٨

51. We sent Our guidance to them so that perhaps they might take heed.

51. Wa laqad waṣṣalnaa lahumul-qawla la'allahum yataẕakkaroon.

وَلَقَدْ وَصَّلْنَا لَهُمُ الْقَوْلَ لَعَلَّهُمْ
يَتَذَكَّرُوْنَ ﴿٥١﴾

52. (Some of) the followers of the Bible believe in the Quran.

52. Allaẕeena aataynaahumul-Kitaaba min qablihee hum bihee yu'minoon.

اَلَّذِيْنَ اٰتَيْنٰهُمُ الْكِتٰبَ مِنْ قَبْلِهٖ
هُمْ بِهٖ يُؤْمِنُوْنَ ﴿٥٢﴾ النصف

53. When it is recited to them, they say, "We believe in it. It is the Truth from our Lord. We were Muslims before it was revealed."

53. Wa iẕaa yutlaa 'alayhim qaaloo aamannaa biheee innahul-ḥaqqu mir-Rabbinaaa innaa kunnaa min qablihee muslimeen.

وَاِذَا يُتْلٰى عَلَيْهِمْ قَالُوْٓا اٰمَنَّا بِهٖٓ
اِنَّهُ الْحَقُّ مِنْ رَّبِّنَآ اِنَّا كُنَّا مِنْ
قَبْلِهٖ مُسْلِمِيْنَ ﴿٥٣﴾

54. They will receive double reward for their forbearance, replacing evil by virtue, and for

54. Ulaaa'ika yu'tawna ajrahum-marratayni bimaa ṣabaroo wa yadra'oona bilḥasanatis

اُولٰٓئِكَ يُؤْتَوْنَ اَجْرَهُمْ مَّرَّتَيْنِ
بِمَا صَبَرُوْا وَيَدْرَءُوْنَ بِالْحَسَنَةِ

their spending for the cause of Allah.

sayyi'ata wa mimmaa razaq-naahum yunfiqoon.

السَّيِّئَةَ وَمِمَّا رَزَقْنٰهُمْ يُنْفِقُوْنَ ﴿٥٤﴾

55. When they hear impious words (lies), they keep away from them, saying, "We shall be responsible for our deeds and you will be responsible for yours. Peace be with you. We do not want to become ignorant."

55. Wa izaa sami'ul-laghwa a'raḍoo 'anhu wa qaaloo lanaaa a'maalunaa wa lakum a'maa-lukum salaamun 'alaykum laa nabtaghil-jaahileen.

وَاِذَا سَمِعُوا اللَّغْوَ اَعْرَضُوْا عَنْهُ
وَقَالُوْا لَنَآ اَعْمَالُنَا وَلَكُمْ اَعْمَالُكُمْ ز
سَلٰمٌ عَلَيْكُمْ لَا نَبْتَغِي الْجٰهِلِيْنَ ﴿٥٥﴾

56. (Muhammad), you cannot guide whomever you love, but Allah guides whomever He wants and knows best those who seek guidance.

56. Innaka laa tahdee man aḥbabta wa laakinnal-laaha yahdee mañy-yashaaa'; wa Huwa a'lamu bilmuhtadeen.

اِنَّكَ لَا تَهْدِيْ مَنْ اَحْبَبْتَ وَ
لٰكِنَّ اللّٰهَ يَهْدِيْ مَنْ يَّشَآءُ ۚ وَهُوَ
اَعْلَمُ بِالْمُهْتَدِيْنَ ﴿٥٦﴾

57. They (the pagans) say, "If we were to follow your guidance we would be snatched away from our land." Had We not given them the secure, holy precinct wherein all types of fruits are brought to them as a sustenance from Us? However, many of them do not know it.

57. Wa qaalooo in-nattabi'il-hudaa ma'aka nutakhaṭṭaf min arḍinaaa; awalam numakkil-lahum ḥaraman aaminañy-yujbaaa ilayhi samaraatu kulli shay'ir-rizqam-mil-ladunnaa wa laakinna aksarahum laa ya'lamoon.

وَقَالُوْٓا اِنْ نَّتَّبِعِ الْهُدٰى مَعَكَ
نُتَخَطَّفْ مِنْ اَرْضِنَا ؕ اَوَلَمْ نُمَكِّنْ
لَّهُمْ حَرَمًا اٰمِنًا يُّجْبٰٓى اِلَيْهِ
ثَمَرٰتُ كُلِّ شَيْءٍ رِّزْقًا مِّنْ لَّدُنَّا
وَلٰكِنَّ اَكْثَرَهُمْ لَا يَعْلَمُوْنَ ﴿٥٧﴾

58. How many nations, who had enjoyed great prosperity, had We destroyed? Those are their homes which were not inhabited thereafter except for a short time. Only We were their heirs.

58. Wa kam ahlaknaa min qaryatim baṭirat ma'eeshatahaa fatilka masaakinuhum lam tuskam-mim ba'dihim illaa qaleela; wa kunnaa Naḥnul-waariseen.

وَكَمْ اَهْلَكْنَا مِنْ قَرْيَةٍ ۢ بَطِرَتْ
مَعِيْشَتَهَا ۚ فَتِلْكَ مَسٰكِنُهُمْ لَمْ تُسْكَنْ
مِّنْ ۢ بَعْدِهِمْ اِلَّا قَلِيْلًا ؕ وَكُنَّا نَحْنُ
الْوٰرِثِيْنَ ﴿٥٨﴾

59. Your Lord did not destroy the people of the towns without first sending a Messenger to the mother town who would recite His revelations to them. We did not want to destroy the towns if the people therein were not unjust.

59. Wa maa kaana Rabbuka muhlikal-quraa ḥattaa yab'asa feee ummihaa Rasoolañy-yatloo 'alayhim Aayaatinaa; wa maa kunnaa muhlikil-quraaa illaa wa ahluhaa ẓaalimoon.

وَمَا كَانَ رَبُّكَ مُهْلِكَ الْقُرٰى
حَتّٰى يَبْعَثَ فِيْٓ اُمِّهَا رَسُوْلًا يَّتْلُوْا
عَلَيْهِمْ اٰيٰتِنَا ۚ وَمَا كُنَّا مُهْلِكِي
الْقُرٰٓى اِلَّا وَاَهْلُهَا ظٰلِمُوْنَ ﴿٥٩﴾

60. Whatever you (people) have been given is only the means for enjoyment and beauty in the worldly life, but the means for enjoyment (which you will receive from Allah) in the life to come will be better and everlasting. Will you then not take heed?

60. Wa maaa ooteetum-min shay'in famataa'ul-ḥayaatid-dunyaa wa zeenatuhaa; wa maa 'indal-laahi khayruñw-wa abqaaa; afalaa ta'qiloon.

وَمَآ اُوْتِيْتُمْ مِّنْ شَيْءٍ فَمَتَاعُ
الْحَيٰوةِ الدُّنْيَا وَزِيْنَتُهَا ۚ وَمَا عِنْدَ
اللّٰهِ خَيْرٌ وَّاَبْقٰى ؕ اَفَلَا تَعْقِلُوْنَ ﴿٦٠﴾ ع

61. Is the case of those to whom We have promised good things - which they will certainly receive in the life to come - equal to the case of those to whom We have granted the means of enjoyment in the worldly life and who will certainly be questioned about them in the life to come?

61. Afamañw-wa'adnaahu wa'dan ḥasanan fahuwa laa-qeehi kamam-matta'naahu mataa'al-ḥayaatid-dunyaa summa huwa Yawmal-Qiyaa-mati minal-muḥḍareen.

اَفَمَنْ وَّعَدْنٰهُ وَعْدًا حَسَنًا
فَهُوَ لَاقِيْهِ كَمَنْ مَّتَّعْنٰهُ مَتَاعَ
الْحَيٰوةِ الدُّنْيَا ثُمَّ هُوَ يَوْمَ الْقِيٰمَةِ

مِنَ الْمُحْضَرِينَ ﴿٦١﴾

62. One day He will ask them, "Where are those whom you had considered equal to Me?"

62. Wa Yawma yunaadeehim fa-yaqoolu ayna shurakaaa-'iyal-lazeena kuntum taz'u-moon.

وَيَوْمَ يُنَادِيهِمْ فَيَقُولُ أَيْنَ شُرَكَائِيَ
الَّذِينَ كُنتُمْ تَزْعُمُونَ ﴿٦٢﴾

63. Those who have become subject to punishment will say, "Lord, they seduced us." Their idols will say, "We seduced them but we renounce their worshipping us for it was not us whom they worshipped."

63. Qaalal-lazeena ḥaqqa 'alayhimul-qawlu Rabbanaa haaa'ulaaa'il-lazeena aghway-naaa aghwaynaahum kamaa ghawaynaa tabarra-naaa ilayka maa kaanooo iyyaanaa ya'bu-doon.

قَالَ الَّذِينَ حَقَّ عَلَيْهِمُ الْقَوْلُ رَبَّنَا
هَٰؤُلَاءِ الَّذِينَ أَغْوَيْنَا أَغْوَيْنَاهُمْ
كَمَا غَوَيْنَا تَبَرَّأْنَا إِلَيْكَ مَا كَانُوا
إِيَّانَا يَعْبُدُونَ ﴿٦٣﴾

64. They will be told to call their idols. They called them but did not receive any answer. They will see the torment approaching and wish that they had sought guidance.

64. Wa qeelad-'oo shura-kaaa'akum fada'awhum falam yastajeeboo lahum wa ra-awul-'azaab; law annahum kaanoo yahtadoon.

وَقِيلَ ادْعُوا شُرَكَاءَكُمْ فَدَعَوْهُمْ
فَلَمْ يَسْتَجِيبُوا لَهُمْ وَرَأَوُا الْعَذَابَ ۚ
لَوْ أَنَّهُمْ كَانُوا يَهْتَدُونَ ﴿٦٤﴾

65. On the day when Allah will call them and ask them, "What answer did you give to (Our) messengers?"

65. Wa Yawma yunaadeehim fa-yaqoolu maazaaa ajabtumul mursaleen.

وَيَوْمَ يُنَادِيهِمْ فَيَقُولُ مَاذَا
أَجَبْتُمُ الْمُرْسَلِينَ ﴿٦٥﴾

66. The door to all answers will be closed to them and they will not even be able to ask one another.

66. Fa'amiyat 'alayhimul ambaaa'u Yawma'izin fahum laa yatasaaa'aloon.

فَعَمِيَتْ عَلَيْهِمُ الْأَنبَاءُ يَوْمَئِذٍ
فَهُمْ لَا يَتَسَاءَلُونَ ﴿٦٦﴾

67. However, those who have repented and have become righteously striving believers will perhaps have everlasting happiness.

67. Fa-ammaa man taaba wa aamana wa 'amila ṣaaliḥan fa'asaaa añy-yakoona minal-mufliḥeen.

فَأَمَّا مَن تَابَ وَآمَنَ وَعَمِلَ صَالِحًا
فَعَسَىٰ أَن يَكُونَ مِنَ الْمُفْلِحِينَ ﴿٦٧﴾

68. Your Lord creates and chooses (to grant mercy) to whomever He wants. (In matters of guidance) they (unbelievers) do not have the choice to choose whatever they want. Allah is free of all defects of being considered equal to anything else.

68. Wa Rabbuka yakhluqu maa yashaaa'u wa yakhtaar; maa kaana lahumul-khiyarah; Subḥaanal-laahi wa ta'aalaa 'ammaa yushrikoon.

وَرَبُّكَ يَخْلُقُ مَا يَشَاءُ وَيَخْتَارُ ۗ
مَا كَانَ لَهُمُ الْخِيَرَةُ ۚ سُبْحَانَ
اللَّهِ وَتَعَالَىٰ عَمَّا يُشْرِكُونَ ﴿٦٨﴾

69. Your Lord knows all that their hearts hide or reveal.

69. Wa Rabbuka ya'lamu maa tukinnu ṣudooruhum wa maa yu'linoon.

وَرَبُّكَ يَعْلَمُ مَا تُكِنُّ صُدُورُهُمْ
وَمَا يُعْلِنُونَ ﴿٦٩﴾

70. He is Allah, the only Ilah (one deserving to be worshiped) and it is only He who deserves to be given thanks in this world and in the life to come. Judgment is in His hands and to Him you will all return.

70. Wa Huwal-laahu laaa ilaaha illaa Hoo; lahul-ḥamdu fil-oolaa wal Aakhirah; wala-hul-ḥukmu wa ilayhi turja'oon.

وَهُوَ اللَّهُ لَا إِلَٰهَ إِلَّا هُوَ ۖ لَهُ
الْحَمْدُ فِي الْأُولَىٰ وَالْآخِرَةِ ۖ وَلَهُ
الْحُكْمُ وَإِلَيْهِ تُرْجَعُونَ ﴿٧٠﴾

71. (Muhammad), ask them, "Think, if Allah were to cause the night to continue until the Day of Judgment, which Lord besides

71. Qul ara'aytum in ja'alal laahu 'alaykumul-layla sarma-dan ilaa Yawmil-Qiyaamati man

قُلْ أَرَأَيْتُمْ إِن جَعَلَ اللَّهُ عَلَيْكُمُ
اللَّيْلَ سَرْمَدًا إِلَىٰ يَوْمِ الْقِيَامَةِ مَنْ

Allah could bring you light? Will you then not listen to (His revelations)?"

ilaahun ghayrul-laahi ya-teckum biḍiyaaa'in afalaa tasma'oon.

إِلٰهٌ غَيْرُ اللّٰهِ يَأْتِيْكُمْ بِضِيَآءٍ ؕ
أَفَلَا تَسْمَعُوْنَ ﴿٧١﴾

72. Say, "Do you not think that if Allah were to cause the day to continue until the Day of Judgment, which Lord besides Allah could bring you the night to rest? Do you not see (His signs)?"

72. Qul ara'aytum in ja'alal-laahu 'alaykumun-nahaara sarmadan ilaa Yawmil-Qiyaamati man ilaahun ghayrul-laahi ya-teekum bilaylin taskunoona feehi afalaa tubṣiroon.

قُلْ أَرَءَيْتُمْ إِنْ جَعَلَ اللّٰهُ عَلَيْكُمُ
النَّهَارَ سَرْمَدًا إِلٰى يَوْمِ الْقِيٰمَةِ
مَنْ إِلٰهٌ غَيْرُ اللّٰهِ يَأْتِيْكُمْ بِلَيْلٍ
تَسْكُنُوْنَ فِيْهِ ؕ أَفَلَا تُبْصِرُوْنَ ﴿٧٢﴾

73. Out of His mercy He has made the night and day for you to rest, seek His favor and perhaps you will give Him thanks.

73. Wa mir-raḥmatihee ja'ala lakumul-layla wannahaara litaskunoo feehi wa litabtaghoo min faḍlihee wa la'allakum tashkuroon.

وَمِنْ رَّحْمَتِهٖ جَعَلَ لَكُمُ الَّيْلَ
وَالنَّهَارَ لِتَسْكُنُوْا فِيْهِ وَلِتَبْتَغُوْا
مِنْ فَضْلِهٖ وَلَعَلَّكُمْ تَشْكُرُوْنَ ﴿٧٣﴾

74. He (Allah) will call the unbelievers on the Day of Judgment and ask them, "Where are your idols in which you had faith?

74. Wa Yawma yunaadeehim fa-yaqoolu ayna shurakaaa'iyal-lazeena kuntum taz'umoon.

وَيَوْمَ يُنَادِيْهِمْ فَيَقُوْلُ أَيْنَ
شُرَكَآءِيَ الَّذِيْنَ كُنْتُمْ تَزْعُمُوْنَ ﴿٧٤﴾

75. We shall call from every nation a witness and shall ask them to bring proof (in support of their belief). They will know that truth belongs to Allah and that whatever they had falsely invented has abandoned them.

75. Wa naza'naa min kulli ummatin shaheedan faqulnaa haatoo burhaanakum fa'ali-mooo annal-ḥaqqa lillaahi wa ḍalla 'anhum-maa kaanoo yaftaroon.

وَنَزَعْنَا مِنْ كُلِّ أُمَّةٍ شَهِيْدًا
فَقُلْنَا هَاتُوْا بُرْهَانَكُمْ فَعَلِمُوْٓا
أَنَّ الْحَقَّ لِلّٰهِ وَضَلَّ عَنْهُمْ مَّا
كَانُوْا يَفْتَرُوْنَ ﴿٧٥﴾ ع ١٥ ١٠

76. Korah was a man from the people of Moses. This man rebelled against them. We had given him so much treasure that the keys of the stores of his treasures could hardly even be carried by a group of strong people (ten to nineteen people). His people told him, "Do not be proud of your wealth; Allah does not love those who are happy (for their wealth).

76. Inna Qaaroona kaana min qawmi Moosaa fabaghaa 'alayhim wa aataynaahu minal-kunoozi maaa inna mafaati-ḥahoo latanooo'u bil'uṣbati ulil-quwwati iz qaala lahoo qawmuhoo laa tafraḥ innal-laaha laa yuḥibbul-fariḥeen.

إِنَّ قَارُوْنَ كَانَ مِنْ قَوْمِ
مُوْسٰى فَبَغٰى عَلَيْهِمْ ۪ وَاٰتَيْنٰهُ
مِنَ الْكُنُوْزِ مَآ إِنَّ مَفَاتِحَهٗ
لَتَنُوْٓأُ بِالْعُصْبَةِ أُولِي الْقُوَّةِ ۗ
إِذْ قَالَ لَهٗ قَوْمُهٗ لَا تَفْرَحْ إِنَّ اللّٰهَ
لَا يُحِبُّ الْفَرِحِيْنَ ﴿٧٦﴾

77. Seek the gains of the life to come through your wealth without ignoring your share of this life. Do favors to others just as Allah has done favors to you. Do not commit evil in the land, for Allah does not love the evil-doers."

77. Wabtaghi feemaaa aataa-kal-laahud-Daaral Aakhirata wa laa tansa naṣeebaka minad-dunyaa wa aḥsin kamaaa aḥsanal-laahu ilayka wa laa tabghil-fasaada fil-arḍi innal-laaha laa yuḥibbul-mufsideen.

وَابْتَغِ فِيْمَآ اٰتٰىكَ اللّٰهُ الدَّارَ
الْاٰخِرَةَ وَلَا تَنْسَ نَصِيْبَكَ مِنَ
الدُّنْيَا وَأَحْسِنْ كَمَآ أَحْسَنَ اللّٰهُ
إِلَيْكَ وَلَا تَبْغِ الْفَسَادَ فِي الْأَرْضِ ؕ
إِنَّ اللّٰهَ لَا يُحِبُّ الْمُفْسِدِيْنَ ﴿٧٧﴾

78. He said, "I have received this wealth because of my knowledge." Did he not know that Allah had destroyed many generations that lived before him who were stronger than him in power and people? (Those who lived before) will not be questioned about these criminals' sins.

78. Qaala innamaaa ootee-tuhoo 'alaa 'ilmin 'indeee; awalam ya'lam annal-laaha qad ahlaka min qablihee minal-qurooni man huwa ashaddu minhu quwwatañw-wa ak̲saru jam'aa; wa laa yus'alu 'an z̲unoobihimul-mujrimoon.

قَالَ إِنَّمَآ أُوتِيتُهُۥ عَلَىٰ عِلْمٍ
عِندِىٓ ۚ أَوَلَمْ يَعْلَمْ أَنَّ ٱللَّهَ
قَدْ أَهْلَكَ مِن قَبْلِهِۦ مِنَ ٱلْقُرُونِ
مَنْ هُوَ أَشَدُّ مِنْهُ قُوَّةً وَ
أَكْثَرُ جَمْعًا ۚ وَلَا يُسْـَٔلُ عَن
ذُنُوبِهِمُ ٱلْمُجْرِمُونَ ﴿٧٨﴾

79. Korah would bedeck himself (in colorful garments) to show off his wealth. Those who wanted worldly gains would say, "Would that we were given that which Korah has received. He has certainly received a great share."

79. Fakharaja 'alaa qawmihee fee zeenatih; qaalal-laz̲eena yureedoonal-ḥayaatad-dunyaa yaalayta lanaa mis̲la maaa ootiya Qaaroonu innahoo laz̲oo ḥaẓẓin 'aẓeem.

فَخَرَجَ عَلَىٰ قَوْمِهِۦ فِى زِينَتِهِۦ ۖ
قَالَ ٱلَّذِينَ يُرِيدُونَ ٱلْحَيَوٰةَ
ٱلدُّنْيَا يَـٰلَيْتَ لَنَا مِثْلَ مَآ أُوتِىَ
قَـٰرُونُ إِنَّهُۥ لَذُو حَظٍّ عَظِيمٍ ﴿٧٩﴾

80. The people who had received knowledge would tell them, "Woe to you! The reward of Allah is far better for the righteously striving believers. No one can receive such reward except those who exercise patience."

80. Wa qaalal-laz̲eena ootul-'ilma waylakum s̲awaabul-laahi khayrul-liman aamana wa 'amila ṣaaliḥaa; wa laa yulaq-qaahaaa illaṣ-ṣaabiroon.

وَقَالَ ٱلَّذِينَ أُوتُوا۟ ٱلْعِلْمَ
وَيْلَكُمْ ثَوَابُ ٱللَّهِ خَيْرٌ لِّمَنْ
ءَامَنَ وَعَمِلَ صَـٰلِحًا ۚ وَلَا يُلَقَّىٰهَآ
إِلَّا ٱلصَّـٰبِرُونَ ﴿٨٠﴾

81. We caused the earth to swallow up him and his home. No one besides Allah could help him nor could he himself achieve victory.

81. Fakhasafnaa bihee wa bidaarihil-arḍa fama kaana lahoo min fi'atiñy-yanṣuroo-nahoo min doonillaahi wa maa kaana minal-muntaṣireen.

فَخَسَفْنَا بِهِۦ وَبِدَارِهِ ٱلْأَرْضَ
فَمَا كَانَ لَهُۥ مِن فِئَةٍ يَنصُرُونَهُۥ
مِن دُونِ ٱللَّهِ وَمَا كَانَ مِنَ
ٱلْمُنتَصِرِينَ ﴿٨١﴾

82. The people who the other day had wished to be like him, began saying, "Woe to us! Allah gives abundant wealth only to those of His servants whom He wants and He determines everyone's share. Had it not been for Allah's favor to us, He would have caused the earth to swallow us up. Woe to the unbelievers who will have no happiness."

82. Wa aṣbaḥal-laz̲eena ta-mannaw makaanahoo bil-amsi yaqooloona wayka-annal-laaha yabsuṭur-rizqa limañy-ya-shaaa'u min 'ibaadihee wa yaqdiru law laaa am-mannal-laahu 'alaynaa lakhasafa binaa wayka-annahoo laa yufliḥul-kaafiroon.

وَأَصْبَحَ ٱلَّذِينَ تَمَنَّوْا۟ مَكَانَهُۥ
بِٱلْأَمْسِ يَقُولُونَ وَيْكَأَنَّ ٱللَّهَ
يَبْسُطُ ٱلرِّزْقَ لِمَن يَشَآءُ مِنْ
عِبَادِهِۦ وَيَقْدِرُ ۖ لَوْلَآ أَن مَّنَّ ٱللَّهُ
عَلَيْنَا لَخَسَفَ بِنَا ۖ وَيْكَأَنَّهُۥ لَا
يُفْلِحُ ٱلْكَـٰفِرُونَ ﴿٨٢﴾ ع ٨ ١١

83. There is the life hereafter which We have prepared for those who do not want to impose their superiority over the others in the land nor commit evil (indulgence in women's affairs) therein.

83. Tilkad-Daarul Aaakhiratu naj'aluhaa lillaz̲eena laa yureedoona 'uluwwan fil-arḍi

تِلْكَ ٱلدَّارُ ٱلْـَٔاخِرَةُ نَجْعَلُهَا
لِلَّذِينَ لَا يُرِيدُونَ عُلُوًّا فِى ٱلْأَرْضِ

The happy end certainly belongs to the pious ones.

84. The reward for a good deed will be greater than the deed itself and the recompense for an evil deed will be equivalent to the deed.

85. (Muhammad), Allah, Who has commanded you to follow the guidance of the Quran, will certainly return you victoriously to your place of birth. Say, “My Lord knows best who has brought guidance and who is in plain error.”

86. You had no hope of receiving the Book except by the mercy of your Lord. Do not be a supporter of the unbelievers (addressed to the Holy Prophet but people are meant thereby).

87. You must not allow them to prevent you from following the revelations of Allah after they are revealed to you. Call (mankind) to your Lord and do not be a pagan.

88. Do not worship anything besides Allah. He is the only Ilah (one deserving to be worshiped). Everything will be destroyed except the face of Allah (the messengers and people who possess divine authority). To Him belongs Judgment and to Him you will all return.

Al-Ankabut, The Spider (29)

In the Name of Allah, the Beneficent, the Merciful.

1. Alif. Lam. Mim.

2. Do people think they will not be tested because they say, “We have faith?”

3. We had certainly tried those who lived before them to make sure who were truthful in their

wa laa fasaadaa; wal‘aaqibatu lilmuttaqeen.

84. Man jaaa’a bilḥasanati falahoo khayrum-minhaa wa man jaaa’a bissayyi’ati falaa yujzal-lazeena ‘amilus-sayyi-’aati illaa maa kaanoo ya‘maloon.

85. Innal-lazee faraḍa ‘alaykal-Qur’aana laraaadduka ilaa ma‘aad; qur-Rabbeee a‘lamu man jaaa’a bil-hudaa wa man huwa fee ḍalaalim-mubeen.

86. Wa maa kunta tarjooo añy-yulqaaa ilaykal-Kitaabu illaa raḥmatam-mir-Rabbika falaa takoonanna zaheeral-lilkaa-fireen.

87. Wa laa yaṣuddunnaka ‘an Aayaatil-laahi ba‘da iz unzilat ilayka wad‘u ilaa Rabbika wa laa takoonanna minal-mush-rikeen.

88. Wa laa tad‘u ma‘al-laahi ilaahan aakhar; laaa ilaaha illaa Hoo; kullu shay’in haalikun illaa Wajhah; lahul-ḥukmu wa ilayhi turja‘oon.

Sûrat al-‘Ankabût-29

(Revealed at Makkah)

Bismillaahir Raḥmaanir Raḥeem

1. Alif-Laaam-Meeem.

2. Aḥasiban-naasu añy-yutra-kooo añy-yaqoolooo aamannaa wa hum laa yuftanoon.

3. Wa laqad fatannal-lazeena min qablihim fala-ya‘laman-nallaahul-lazeena ṣadaqoo

وَلَا فَسَادًا ۚ وَالْعَاقِبَةُ لِلْمُتَّقِينَ ﴿٨٣﴾
مَنْ جَاءَ بِالْحَسَنَةِ فَلَهُ خَيْرٌ
مِّنْهَا ۚ وَمَنْ جَاءَ بِالسَّيِّئَةِ فَلَا
يُجْزَى الَّذِينَ عَمِلُوا السَّيِّئَاتِ
إِلَّا مَا كَانُوا يَعْمَلُونَ ﴿٨٤﴾
إِنَّ الَّذِي فَرَضَ عَلَيْكَ الْقُرْآنَ
لَرَادُّكَ إِلَىٰ مَعَادٍ ۚ قُلْ رَّبِّي
أَعْلَمُ مَنْ جَاءَ بِالْهُدَىٰ وَمَنْ
هُوَ فِي ضَلَالٍ مُّبِينٍ ﴿٨٥﴾
وَمَا كُنْتَ تَرْجُو أَنْ يُلْقَىٰ
إِلَيْكَ الْكِتَابُ إِلَّا رَحْمَةً مِّنْ رَّبِّكَ
فَلَا تَكُونَنَّ ظَهِيرًا لِّلْكَافِرِينَ ﴿٨٦﴾
وَلَا يَصُدُّنَّكَ عَنْ آيَاتِ اللَّهِ بَعْدَ
إِذْ أُنْزِلَتْ إِلَيْكَ ۖ وَادْعُ إِلَىٰ رَبِّكَ
وَلَا تَكُونَنَّ مِنَ الْمُشْرِكِينَ ﴿٨٧﴾ وقف لازم
وَلَا تَدْعُ مَعَ اللَّهِ إِلَٰهًا آخَرَ ۘ لَا
إِلَٰهَ إِلَّا هُوَ ۚ كُلُّ شَيْءٍ هَالِكٌ
إِلَّا وَجْهَهُ ۚ لَهُ الْحُكْمُ وَإِلَيْهِ
تُرْجَعُونَ ﴿٨٨﴾ ع القصص

(٢٩) سُورَةُ الْعَنْكَبُوتِ مَكِّيَّةٌ (٨٥)

آياتها ٦٩ بِسْمِ اللَّهِ الرَّحْمَٰنِ الرَّحِيمِ ركوعاتها ٧

الم ﴿١﴾
أَحَسِبَ النَّاسُ أَنْ يُتْرَكُوا أَنْ
يَقُولُوا آمَنَّا وَهُمْ لَا يُفْتَنُونَ ﴿٢﴾
وَلَقَدْ فَتَنَّا الَّذِينَ مِنْ قَبْلِهِمْ
فَلَيَعْلَمَنَّ اللَّهُ الَّذِينَ صَدَقُوا

faith and who were liars.

4. Do the evildoers think they can escape Us? How terrible is their judgment?

5. Those who have the desire to be in the presence of Allah on the Day of Judgment must know that their day will certainly be coming. Allah is All-Hearing and All-knowing.

6. Whoever strives hard should know that it is for his own good. Allah is independent of the whole world.

7. We shall expiate the sins of the righteously striving believers and shall reward them better than their deeds.

8. We have advised the human being, "Be kind to your parents. Do not obey them if they force you to consider equal to Me things which you do not know are such." You will all return (to Me) and I shall show all that you have done.

9. We shall admit the righteously striving believers into the company of the pious ones.

10. Some people say, "We have faith in Allah." However, when they face some hardship for Allah's cause, they begin to consider the persecution that they have experienced from people as a torment from Allah. When your Lord grants you a victory, they say, "We were with you." Does Allah not know best what is in the hearts of every creature?

11. Allah certainly knows all about the believers and the hypocrites.

12. The unbelievers say to the believers. "Follow our way. We

wa la-ya'lamannal-kaazibeen.

4. Am ḥasibal-lazeena ya'maloonas-sayyi-aati añy-yasbiqoonaa; saaa'a maa yaḥkumoon.

5. Man kaana yarjoo liqaaa-'allaahi fa-inna-ajalal-laahi la-aat; wa Huwas-Samee'ul-'Aleem.

6. Wa man jaahada fa-innamaa yujaahidu linafsih; innal-laaha laghaniyyun 'anil 'aalameen.

7. Wallazeena aamanoo wa 'amiluṣ-ṣaaliḥaati lanukaf-firanna 'anhum sayyi-aatihim wa lanajziyan-nahum aḥsanal-lazee kaanoo ya'maloon.

8. Wa waṣṣaynal-insaana biwaalidayhi ḥusnaa; wa in jaahadaaka litushrika bee maa laysa laka bihee 'ilmun falaa tuṭi'humaaa; ilayya marji'ukum fa-unabbi'ukum bimaa kuntum ta'maloon.

9. Wallazeena aamanoo wa 'amiluṣ-ṣaaliḥaati lanudkhilan-nahum fiṣ-ṣaaliḥeen.

10. Wa minan-naasi mañy-yaqoolu aamannaa billaahi fa-izaaa ooziya fil-laahi ja'ala fitnatan-naasi ka'azaabil-laahi wa la'in jaaa'a naṣrum-mir-Rabbika la-yaqoolunna innaa kunnaa ma'akum; awa-laysallaahu bi-a'lama bimaa fee ṣudooril-'aalameen.

11. Wa la-ya'lamannal-laahul-lazeena aamanoo wa laya-'lamannal-munaafiqeen.

12. Wa qaalal-lazeena kafa-roo lillazeena aamanut-

وَلَيَعْلَمَنَّ الْكٰذِبِيْنَ ٣
اَمْ حَسِبَ الَّذِيْنَ يَعْمَلُوْنَ السَّيِّاٰتِ
اَنْ يَّسْبِقُوْنَا ۚ سَآءَ مَا يَحْكُمُوْنَ ٤
مَنْ كَانَ يَرْجُوْا لِقَآءَ اللّٰهِ فَاِنَّ اَجَلَ
اللّٰهِ لَاٰتٍ ۚ وَهُوَ السَّمِيْعُ الْعَلِيْمُ ٥
وَمَنْ جَاهَدَ فَاِنَّمَا يُجَاهِدُ لِنَفْسِهٖ ۚ
اِنَّ اللّٰهَ لَغَنِيٌّ عَنِ الْعٰلَمِيْنَ ٦
وَالَّذِيْنَ اٰمَنُوْا وَعَمِلُوا الصّٰلِحٰتِ
لَنُكَفِّرَنَّ عَنْهُمْ سَيِّاٰتِهِمْ وَلَنَجْزِيَنَّهُمْ
اَحْسَنَ الَّذِيْ كَانُوْا يَعْمَلُوْنَ ٧
وَوَصَّيْنَا الْاِنْسَانَ بِوَالِدَيْهِ
حُسْنًا ۚ وَاِنْ جَاهَدٰكَ لِتُشْرِكَ بِيْ
مَا لَيْسَ لَكَ بِهٖ عِلْمٌ فَلَا تُطِعْهُمَا ۚ
اِلَيَّ مَرْجِعُكُمْ فَاُنَبِّئُكُمْ بِمَا كُنْتُمْ
تَعْمَلُوْنَ ٨
وَالَّذِيْنَ اٰمَنُوْا وَعَمِلُوا الصّٰلِحٰتِ
لَنُدْخِلَنَّهُمْ فِي الصّٰلِحِيْنَ ٩
وَمِنَ النَّاسِ مَنْ يَّقُوْلُ اٰمَنَّا بِاللّٰهِ
فَاِذَآ اُوْذِيَ فِي اللّٰهِ جَعَلَ فِتْنَةَ
النَّاسِ كَعَذَابِ اللّٰهِ ۗ وَلَئِنْ جَآءَ
نَصْرٌ مِّنْ رَّبِّكَ لَيَقُوْلُنَّ اِنَّا كُنَّا
مَعَكُمْ ۗ اَوَلَيْسَ اللّٰهُ بِاَعْلَمَ بِمَا فِيْ
صُدُوْرِ الْعٰلَمِيْنَ ١٠
وَلَيَعْلَمَنَّ اللّٰهُ الَّذِيْنَ اٰمَنُوْا
وَلَيَعْلَمَنَّ الْمُنٰفِقِيْنَ ١١
وَقَالَ الَّذِيْنَ كَفَرُوْا لِلَّذِيْنَ اٰمَنُوْا

shall take the responsibility for your sins." They cannot take responsibility for any of their sins. They are only liars.

tabi'oo sabeelanaa walnaḥmil khaṭaayaakum wa maa hum biḥaamileena min khaṭaa-yaahum-min shay'in innahum lakaaẕiboon.

اتَّبِعُوْا سَبِيْلَنَا وَلْنَحْمِلْ خَطٰيٰكُمْ ۭ وَمَا
هُمْ بِحٰمِلِيْنَ مِنْ خَطٰيٰهُمْ مِّنْ
شَيْءٍ ۭ اِنَّهُمْ لَكٰذِبُوْنَ ⑫

13. Besides the other burdens that they will have to carry, they will certainly be loaded with the burden of their own sins. They will be questioned on the Day of Judgment about what they had falsely invented.

13. Wa la-yaḥmilunna aṯqaa-lahum wa aṯqaalam-ma'a aṯqaalihim wa la-yus'alunna Yawmal-Qiyaamati 'ammaa kaanoo yaftaroon.

وَلَيَحْمِلُنَّ اَثْقَالَهُمْ وَاَثْقَالًا مَّعَ
اَثْقَالِهِمْ ۡ وَلَيُسْـَٔلُنَّ يَوْمَ الْقِيٰمَةِ
عَمَّا كَانُوْا يَفْتَرُوْنَ ⑬ ع ١ ١٣ ١٣

14. We sent Noah to his people and he lived with them for nine hundred and fifty years, then the flood engulfed them for their injustice.

14. Wa laqad arsalnaa Nooḥan ilaa qawmihee falabiṯa feehim alfa sanatin illaa khamseena 'aaman fa-akhaẕahumuṭ-ṭoofaanu wa hum ẕaalimoon.

وَلَقَدْ اَرْسَلْنَا نُوْحًا اِلٰى قَوْمِهٖ
فَلَبِثَ فِيْهِمْ اَلْفَ سَنَةٍ اِلَّا خَمْسِيْنَ
عَامًا ۭ فَاَخَذَهُمُ الطُّوْفَانُ وَهُمْ
ظٰلِمُوْنَ ⑭

15. We saved Noah and the people in the Ark and made (their case) a miracle for the world.

15. Fa-anjaynaahu wa aṣ-ḥaa-bas-safeenati wa ja'alnaahaaa Aayatal-lil'aalameen.

فَاَنْجَيْنٰهُ وَاَصْحٰبَ السَّفِيْنَةِ
وَجَعَلْنٰهَآ اٰيَةً لِّلْعٰلَمِيْنَ ⑮

16. Abraham told his people, "Worship Allah and have fear of Him. It is better for you, if only you knew it.

16. Wa Ibraaheema iẕ qaala liqawmihi'-budul-laaha watta-qoohu ẕaalikum khayrul-lakum in kuntum ta'lamoon.

وَاِبْرٰهِيْمَ اِذْ قَالَ لِقَوْمِهِ اعْبُدُوا
اللّٰهَ وَاتَّقُوْهُ ۭ ذٰلِكُمْ خَيْرٌ لَّكُمْ اِنْ
كُنْتُمْ تَعْلَمُوْنَ ⑯

17. You worship idols besides Allah but you create falsehood (by honoring and respecting lies). Whatever you worship besides Him cannot provide you with anything for your sustenance. Seek your sustenance from the bounties of Allah. Worship Him. Give Him thanks. To Him you will all return."

17. Innamaa ta'budoona min doonil-laahi awṯaanañw-wa takhluqoona ifkaa; innal-laẕeena ta'budoona min doonil-laahi laa yamlikoona lakum rizqan fabtaghoo 'indal-laahir-rizqa wa'budoohu washkuroo lahooo ilayhi turja'oon.

اِنَّمَا تَعْبُدُوْنَ مِنْ دُوْنِ اللّٰهِ
اَوْثَانًا وَّتَخْلُقُوْنَ اِفْكًا ۭ اِنَّ
الَّذِيْنَ تَعْبُدُوْنَ مِنْ دُوْنِ اللّٰهِ
لَا يَمْلِكُوْنَ لَكُمْ رِزْقًا فَابْتَغُوْا
عِنْدَ اللّٰهِ الرِّزْقَ وَاعْبُدُوْهُ وَاشْكُرُوْا
لَهٗ ۭ اِلَيْهِ تُرْجَعُوْنَ ⑰

18. If you (pagans) call our (revelations) lies, certainly many generations living before you have also done the same thing. The duty of a Messenger is only to preach clearly.

18. Wa in tukaẕẕiboo faqad kaẕẕaba umamum-min qablikum wa maa 'alar-Rasooli illal-balaaghul-mubeen.

وَاِنْ تُكَذِّبُوْا فَقَدْ كَذَّبَ اُمَمٌ مِّنْ
قَبْلِكُمْ ۭ وَمَا عَلَى الرَّسُوْلِ اِلَّا
الْبَلٰغُ الْمُبِيْنُ ⑱

19. Did they not see how Allah begins the creation and then turns it back? This is not difficult at all for Allah.

19. Awa lam yaraw kayfa yubdi'ul-laahul-khalqa ṯumma yu'eeduh; inna ẕaalika 'alal-laahi yaseer.

اَوَلَمْ يَرَوْا كَيْفَ يُبْدِئُ اللّٰهُ
الْخَلْقَ ثُمَّ يُعِيْدُهٗ ۭ اِنَّ ذٰلِكَ

عَلَى اللّٰهِ يَسِيْرٌ ﴿١٩﴾

20. (Muhammad), say to them, "Travel through the land and see how He has begun the creation and how Allah will invent the next life. Allah has power over all things.

20. Qul seeroo fil-arḍi fanẓuroo kayfa bada-al-khalq; s̲ummal-laahu yunshi'un-nash-atal-Aakhirah; innallaaha 'alaa kulli shay'in Qadeer.

قُلْ سِيْرُوْا فِي الْاَرْضِ فَانْظُرُوْا
كَيْفَ بَدَاَ الْخَلْقَ ثُمَّ اللّٰهُ يُنْشِئُ
النَّشْاَةَ الْاٰخِرَةَ ط اِنَّ اللّٰهَ عَلٰى
كُلِّ شَيْءٍ قَدِيْرٌ ﴿٢٠﴾

21. He punishes or grants mercy to whomever He wants and to Him you will all return."

21. Yu'az̲z̲ibu mañy-yashaaa'u wa yarḥamu mañy-yashaaa', wa ilayhi tuqlaboon.

يُعَذِّبُ مَنْ يَّشَآءُ وَيَرْحَمُ مَنْ
يَّشَآءُ ج وَاِلَيْهِ تُقْلَبُوْنَ ﴿٢١﴾

22. You cannot challenge Allah in the heavens or in the earth. No one besides Allah is your guardian or helper.

22. Wa maaa antum bimu-'jizeena fil-arḍi wa laa fis-samaaa'i wa maa lakum-min doonil-laahi miñw-waliyyiñw-wa laa naṣeer.

وَمَآ اَنْتُمْ بِمُعْجِزِيْنَ فِي الْاَرْضِ
وَلَا فِي السَّمَآءِ ز وَمَا لَكُمْ مِّنْ
دُوْنِ اللّٰهِ مِنْ وَّلِيٍّ وَّلَا نَصِيْرٍ ﴿٢٢﴾ ع ٩ ١٤

23. Those who have rejected Allah's revelations have no hope in receiving His mercy. They will face a painful torment.

23. Wallaz̲eena kafaroo bi-Aayaatil-laahi wa liqaaa'iheee ulaaa'ika ya'isoo mir-raḥmatee wa ulaaa'ika lahum 'az̲aabun aleem.

وَالَّذِيْنَ كَفَرُوْا بِاٰيٰتِ اللّٰهِ وَلِقَآئِهٖٓ
اُولٰٓئِكَ يَئِسُوْا مِنْ رَّحْمَتِيْ وَ
اُولٰٓئِكَ لَهُمْ عَذَابٌ اَلِيْمٌ ﴿٢٣﴾

24. (Abraham's) people had no answer except suggesting, "Kill him or burn him." However, Allah saved him from the fire. In this there is evidence (of truth) for the believing people.

24. Famaa kaana jawaaba qawmiheee illaaa an qaaluq-tuloohu aw ḥarriqoohu fa-anjaahul-laahu minan-naar; inna fee z̲aalika la-Aayaatil-liqawmiñy-yu'minoon.

فَمَا كَانَ جَوَابَ قَوْمِهٖٓ اِلَّآ اَنْ
قَالُوا اقْتُلُوْهُ اَوْ حَرِّقُوْهُ فَاَنْجٰىهُ
اللّٰهُ مِنَ النَّارِ ط اِنَّ فِيْ ذٰلِكَ
لَاٰيٰتٍ لِّقَوْمٍ يُّؤْمِنُوْنَ ﴿٢٤﴾

25. Abraham said, "You believe in idols besides Allah only out of worldly love, but on the Day of Judgment you will denounce and condemn each other. Your dwelling will be fire and no one will help you."

25. Wa qaala innamat-takhaz̲-tum-min doonil-laahi aws̲aa-nam-mawaddata baynikum fil-ḥayaatid-dunyaa s̲umma Yaw-mal-Qiyaamati yakfuru ba'ḍu-kum biba'ḍiñw-wa yal'anu ba'ḍukum ba'ḍañw-wa ma-waakumun-Naaru wa maa lakum-min-naaṣireen.

وَقَالَ اِنَّمَا اتَّخَذْتُمْ مِّنْ دُوْنِ
اللّٰهِ اَوْثَانًا لا مَّوَدَّةَ بَيْنِكُمْ فِي
الْحَيٰوةِ الدُّنْيَا ج ثُمَّ يَوْمَ الْقِيٰمَةِ
يَكْفُرُ بَعْضُكُمْ بِبَعْضٍ وَّيَلْعَنُ
بَعْضُكُمْ بَعْضًا ز وَّمَاْوٰىكُمُ النَّارُ
وَمَا لَكُمْ مِّنْ نّٰصِرِيْنَ ﴿٢٥﴾ وقف لازم

26. Only Lot believed in (Abraham) and said, "I seek refuge in my Lord, for He is Majestic and All-wise."

26. Fa-aamana lahoo Looṭ; wa qaala innee muhaajirun ilaa Rabbeee innahoo Huwal 'Azeezul-Ḥakeem.

فَاٰمَنَ لَهٗ لُوْطٌ م وَقَالَ اِنِّيْ
مُهَاجِرٌ اِلٰى رَبِّيْ ط اِنَّهٗ هُوَ الْعَزِيْزُ
الْحَكِيْمُ ﴿٢٦﴾

27. We granted Isaac and Jacob to Abraham and We bestowed upon his offspring prophet-hood and the Book. We gave him his reward in this world, and in the next life he will be among the pious ones.

27. Wa wahabnaa lahooo Is-ḥaaqa wa Ya'qooba wa ja'alnaa fee zurriyyatihin-Nubuwwata wal-Kitaaba wa aataynaahu ajrahoo fid-dunyaa wa innahoo fil-Aakhirati laminaṣ-ṣaali-ḥeen.

وَوَهَبْنَا لَهٗٓ اِسْحٰقَ وَيَعْقُوْبَ
وَجَعَلْنَا فِيْ ذُرِّيَّتِهِ النُّبُوَّةَ
وَالْكِتٰبَ وَاٰتَيْنٰهُ اَجْرَهٗ فِي
الدُّنْيَا ۚ وَاِنَّهٗ فِي الْاٰخِرَةِ لَمِنَ
الصّٰلِحِيْنَ ﴿٢٧﴾

28. Lot said to his people, "You are certainly committing the kind of indecency which no one in the world has committed before.

28. Wa Looṭan iz qaala liqawmiheee innakum lata-toonal-faaḥishata maa saba-qakum-bihaa min aḥadim-minal-'aalameen.

وَلُوْطًا اِذْ قَالَ لِقَوْمِهٖٓ اِنَّكُمْ
لَتَاْتُوْنَ الْفَاحِشَةَ ۘ مَا سَبَقَكُمْ
بِهَا مِنْ اَحَدٍ مِّنَ الْعٰلَمِيْنَ ﴿٢٨﴾

29. Do you engage in carnal relations with men, rob the travelers, and commit evil in your gatherings?" His people had no answer but to say, "Bring upon us the torment of Allah if you are truthful."

29. A'innakum lata-toonar-rijaala wa taqṭa'oonas-sabeela wa ta-toona fee naadeekumul-munkara famaa kaana jawaaba qawmiheee illaaa an qaalu'-tinaa bi'azaabil-laahi in kunta minaṣ-ṣaadiqeen.

اَئِنَّكُمْ لَتَاْتُوْنَ الرِّجَالَ وَتَقْطَعُوْنَ
السَّبِيْلَ ۙ وَتَاْتُوْنَ فِيْ نَادِيْكُمُ
الْمُنْكَرَ ۭ فَمَا كَانَ جَوَابَ قَوْمِهٖٓ
اِلَّآ اَنْ قَالُوا ائْتِنَا بِعَذَابِ اللّٰهِ
اِنْ كُنْتَ مِنَ الصّٰدِقِيْنَ ﴿٢٩﴾

30. He prayed, "Lord help me against the evil-doing people."

30. Qaala Rabbin-ṣurnee 'alal-qawmil-mufsideen.

قَالَ رَبِّ انْصُرْنِيْ عَلَى الْقَوْمِ
الْمُفْسِدِيْنَ ﴿٣٠﴾ ع ٣ ٨ ع ١٥

31. When Our angelic Messengers brought glad news to Abraham, they told him, "We are about to destroy the people of this town for their injustice."

31. Wa lammaa jaaa'at Rusu-lunaaa Ibraaheema bil-bushraa qaalooo innaa muhlikooo ahli haazihil-qaryati inna ahlahaa kaanoo ẓaalimeen.

وَلَمَّا جَآءَتْ رُسُلُنَآ اِبْرٰهِيْمَ
بِالْبُشْرٰى ۙ قَالُوْٓا اِنَّا مُهْلِكُوْٓا
اَهْلِ هٰذِهِ الْقَرْيَةِ ۚ اِنَّ اَهْلَهَا
كَانُوْا ظٰلِمِيْنَ ﴿٣١﴾

32. Abraham said, "Lot is there in that town!" They said, "We know everyone there. We shall certainly save him and his family except his wife who will remain behind."

32. Qaala inna feehaa Looṭaa; qaaloo naḥnu a'lamu biman feehaa lanunajjiyan-nahoo wa ahlahooo illam-ra-atahoo kaa-nat minal-ghaabireen.

قَالَ اِنَّ فِيْهَا لُوْطًا ۭ قَالُوْا نَحْنُ
اَعْلَمُ بِمَنْ فِيْهَا ۫ لَنُنَجِّيَنَّهٗ
وَاَهْلَهٗٓ اِلَّا امْرَاَتَهٗ ۫ كَانَتْ
مِنَ الْغٰبِرِيْنَ ﴿٣٢﴾

33. When Our angelic Messengers came to Lot, he was grieved and depressed to see them. They told him, "Do not be afraid or grieved. We will rescue you and your family except your

33. Wa lammaaa an jaaa'at Rusulunaa Looṭan seee'a bihim wa ḍaaqa bihim zar'añw-wa qaaloo laa takhaf wa laa taḥzan innaa

وَلَمَّآ اَنْ جَآءَتْ رُسُلُنَا لُوْطًا
سِيْٓءَ بِهِمْ وَضَاقَ بِهِمْ ذَرْعًا وَّ
قَالُوْا لَا تَخَفْ وَلَا تَحْزَنْ ۣ اِنَّا

wife who will remain behind.

munajjooka wa ahlaka illam-ra-ataka kaanat minal-ghaabireen.

مُنَجُّوكَ وَأَهْلَكَ إِلَّا امْرَأَتَكَ كَانَتْ
مِنَ الْغٰبِرِينَ ﴿٣٣﴾

34. We will bring torment from the sky on this town, because of the evil deeds of its inhabitants."

34. Innaa munziloona 'alaaa ahli haazihil-qaryati rijzam-minas-samaaa'i bimaa kaanoo yafsuqoon.

إِنَّا مُنزِلُونَ عَلَىٰ أَهْلِ هٰذِهِ
الْقَرْيَةِ رِجْزًا مِّنَ السَّمَاءِ بِمَا
كَانُوا يَفْسُقُونَ ﴿٣٤﴾

35. We left manifest evidence (of the truth) there for the people of understanding.

35. Wa laqat-taraknaa min-haaa Aayatam-bayyinatal-liqawmiñy-ya'qiloon.

وَلَقَد تَّرَكْنَا مِنْهَا آيَةً بَيِّنَةً
لِّقَوْمٍ يَعْقِلُونَ ﴿٣٥﴾

36. We sent to the people of Madian their brother Shuayb. He told them, "Worship Allah. Have hope in the life to come. Do not spread evil in the land."

36. Wa ilaa Madyana akhaa-hum Shu'ayban faqaala yaa qawmi'-budul-laaha warjul-Yawmal-Aakhira wa laa ta'saw fil-arḍi mufsideen.

وَإِلَىٰ مَدْيَنَ أَخَاهُمْ شُعَيْبًا
فَقَالَ يٰقَوْمِ اعْبُدُوا اللَّهَ وَارْجُوا
الْيَوْمَ الْآخِرَ وَلَا تَعْثَوْا فِي الْأَرْضِ
مُفْسِدِينَ ﴿٣٦﴾

37. They rejected him so We jolted them with a violent earthquake and they were left motionless in their houses.

37. Fakaz̲z̲aboohu fa-akha-z̲at-humur-rajfatu fa-aṣbaḥoo fee daarihim jaas̲imeen.

فَكَذَّبُوهُ فَأَخَذَتْهُمُ الرَّجْفَةُ
فَأَصْبَحُوا فِي دَارِهِمْ جٰثِمِينَ ﴿٣٧﴾

38. How the people of Ad and Thamud were destroyed is evident to you from their homes. Satan made their deeds seem attractive to them and prevented them from the right path, even though they had visions.

38. Wa 'Aadañw-wa S̲amooda wa qat-tabayyana lakum-mim-masaakinihim wa zayyana lahumush-Shayṭaanu a'maala-hum faṣaddahum 'anis-sabeeli wa kaanoo mustabṣireen.

وَعَادًا وَثَمُودَا وَقَد تَّبَيَّنَ لَكُم
مِّن مَّسٰكِنِهِمْ وَزَيَّنَ لَهُمُ
الشَّيْطٰنُ أَعْمٰلَهُمْ فَصَدَّهُمْ عَنِ
السَّبِيلِ وَكَانُوا مُسْتَبْصِرِينَ ﴿٣٨﴾

39. Korah, the Pharaoh, and Haman were also destroyed. Moses had brought them illustrious miracles, but they were puffed-up with pride in the land and they could not defeat Us.

39. Wa Qaaroona wa Fir-'awna wa Haamaana wa laqad jaaa'ahum-Moosaa bilbay-yinaati fastakbaroo fil-arḍi wa maa kaanoo saabiqeen.

وَقٰرُونَ وَفِرْعَوْنَ وَهٰمٰنَ
وَلَقَدْ جَاءَهُم مُّوسَىٰ بِالْبَيِّنٰتِ
فَاسْتَكْبَرُوا فِي الْأَرْضِ وَمَا
كَانُوا سٰبِقِينَ ﴿٣٩﴾

40. We punished all of these people because of their sin. Some of them were struck by a violent sand-storm, some by a blast of sound, others were swallowed up by the earth, and some were drowned (in the sea). Allah did not do injustice to them, but they

40. Fakullan akhaz̲naa biz̲am-bihee faminhum-man arsalnaa 'alayhi ḥaaṣibaa; wa minhum-man akhaz̲at-huṣ-ṣayḥatu wa minhum-man khasafnaa bihil-arḍa wa minhum-man aghraq-naa; wamaa kaanal-laahu

فَكُلًّا أَخَذْنَا بِذَنۢبِهِ فَمِنْهُم مَّن
أَرْسَلْنَا عَلَيْهِ حَاصِبًا وَمِنْهُم
مَّنْ أَخَذَتْهُ الصَّيْحَةُ وَمِنْهُم مَّن
خَسَفْنَا بِهِ الْأَرْضَ وَمِنْهُم
مَّنْ أَغْرَقْنَا وَمَا كَانَ اللَّهُ

had wronged themselves.

li-yaẓlimahum wa laakin kaanoo anfusahum yaẓlimoon.

لِيَظْلِمَهُمْ وَلٰكِنْ كَانُوْٓا اَنْفُسَهُمْ
يَظْلِمُوْنَ ﴿٤٠﴾

41. The belief of considering other things as one's guardians besides Allah is as feeble as a spider's web. The spider's web is the frailest of all dwellings, if only they knew it.

41. Masalul-lazeenat-takhazoo min doonil-laahi awliyaaa'a kamasalil 'ankabootit-takhazat baytaa; wa inna awhanal-buyooti la-baytul-'ankaboot; law kaanoo ya'lamoon.

مَثَلُ الَّذِيْنَ اتَّخَذُوْا مِنْ دُوْنِ
اللّٰهِ اَوْلِيَآءَ كَمَثَلِ الْعَنْكَبُوْتِ ج
اِتَّخَذَتْ بَيْتًا ط وَاِنَّ اَوْهَنَ
الْبُيُوْتِ لَبَيْتُ الْعَنْكَبُوْتِ م لَوْ
كَانُوْا يَعْلَمُوْنَ ﴿٤١﴾

وقف لازم

42. Allah knows whatever they worship besides Him; He is the Majestic and All-wise.

42. Innal-laaha ya'lamu maa yad'oona min doonihee min shay'; wa Huwal-'Azeezul-Ḥakeem.

اِنَّ اللّٰهَ يَعْلَمُ مَا يَدْعُوْنَ
مِنْ دُوْنِهٖ مِنْ شَيْءٍ ط وَهُوَ
الْعَزِيْزُ الْحَكِيْمُ ﴿٤٢﴾

43. These are parables which We tell to human beings, but only the learned ones understand them.

43. Wa tilkal-amsaalu naḍribuhaa linnaasi wa maa ya'qiluhaaa illal-'aalimoon.

وَتِلْكَ الْاَمْثَالُ نَضْرِبُهَا لِلنَّاسِ ج
وَمَا يَعْقِلُهَآ اِلَّا الْعٰلِمُوْنَ ﴿٤٣﴾

44. Allah has created the heavens and the earth for a genuine purpose. In this there is evidence (of the truth) for the believers.

44. Khalaqal-laahus-samaawaati wal-arḍa bilḥaqq; inna fee zaalika la-Aayatal-lilmu'mineen.

خَلَقَ اللّٰهُ السَّمٰوٰتِ وَالْاَرْضَ
بِالْحَقِّ ط اِنَّ فِيْ ذٰلِكَ لَاٰيَةً
لِّلْمُؤْمِنِيْنَ ﴿٤٤﴾ ع

45. (Muhammad), recite to them what has been revealed to you in the Book and be steadfast in prayer; prayer (speaking of Allah) keeps one away from indecency and sins. Allah's paying attention to the worshipper is (indeed) the greatest (reward for worshipping Allah). Allah knows what you do.

45. Utlu maaa ooḥiya ilayka minal-Kitaabi wa aqimiṣ-Ṣalaat; innaṣ-Ṣalaata tanhaa 'anil-faḥshaaa'i wal munkar; wa lazikrul-laahi akbar; wal-laahu ya'lamu maa taṣna'oon.

اُتْلُ مَآ اُوْحِيَ اِلَيْكَ مِنَ الْكِتٰبِ وَ
اَقِمِ الصَّلٰوةَ ط اِنَّ الصَّلٰوةَ تَنْهٰى
عَنِ الْفَحْشَآءِ وَالْمُنْكَرِ ط وَلَذِكْرُ اللّٰهِ
اَكْبَرُ ط وَاللّٰهُ يَعْلَمُ مَا تَصْنَعُوْنَ ﴿٤٥﴾

الجزء الحادي والعشرون (٢١)

46. Do not argue with the People of the Book except only by the best manner, (the Quran) except the unjust among them. Tell them, "We believe in what is revealed to us and to you. Our Lord and your Lord is one. We have submitted ourselves to His will."

46. Wa laa tujaadilooo Ahlal-Kitaabi illaa billatee hiya aḥsanu illal-lazeena ẓalamoo minhum wa qoolooo aamannaa billazeee unzila ilaynaa wa unzila ilaykum wa Ilaahunaa wa Ilaahukum Waaḥiduñw-wa naḥnu lahoo muslimoon.

وَلَا تُجَادِلُوْٓا اَهْلَ الْكِتٰبِ اِلَّا بِالَّتِيْ
هِيَ اَحْسَنُ ق اِلَّا الَّذِيْنَ ظَلَمُوْا
مِنْهُمْ وَقُوْلُوْٓا اٰمَنَّا بِالَّذِيْٓ اُنْزِلَ اِلَيْنَا
وَاُنْزِلَ اِلَيْكُمْ وَاِلٰهُنَا وَاِلٰهُكُمْ
وَاحِدٌ وَّنَحْنُ لَهٗ مُسْلِمُوْنَ ﴿٤٦﴾

47. We have revealed the Book to you. People to whom We have given the Book (the Holy Prophet and his family) believe in it. Also of

47. Wa kazaalika anzalnaaa ilaykal-Kitaab; fallazeena aataynaahumul-Kitaaba yu'minoona bihee

وَكَذٰلِكَ اَنْزَلْنَآ اِلَيْكَ الْكِتٰبَ ط
فَالَّذِيْنَ اٰتَيْنٰهُمُ الْكِتٰبَ يُؤْمِنُوْنَ بِهٖ

these (Muslims) there are those who believe in the Book (the Quran). No one rejects Our revelations except the unbelievers.

wa min haaa’ulaaa’i mañy-yu’minu bih; wa maa yajḥadu bi-Aayaatinaaa illal-kaafiroon.

وَمِنْ هٰٓؤُلَآءِ مَنْ يُّؤْمِنُ بِهٖ ۭ وَمَا
يَجْحَدُ بِاٰيٰتِنَآ اِلَّا الْكٰفِرُوْنَ ﴿٤٧﴾

48. You were not able to read or write before the Quran was revealed to you; otherwise, the followers of falsehood would have tried to confuse the matter.

48. Wa maa kunta tatloo min qablihee min kitaabiñw-wa laa takhuṭṭuhoo bi-yameenika izal-lartaabal-mubṭiloon.

وَمَا كُنْتَ تَتْلُوْا مِنْ قَبْلِهٖ مِنْ
كِتٰبٍ وَّلَا تَخُطُّهٗ بِيَمِيْنِكَ اِذًا لَّارْتَابَ
الْمُبْطِلُوْنَ ﴿٤٨﴾

49. In fact, the Quran consists of illustrious verses that exist in the hearts of those who have knowledge. No one rejects Our revelations except the unjust ones.

49. Bal huwa Aayaatum bayyinaatun fee ṣudooril-lazee-na ootul-‘ilm; wa maa yajḥadu bi-Aayaatinaaa illaẓ-ẓaali-moon.

بَلْ هُوَ اٰيٰتٌۢ بَيِّنٰتٌ فِيْ صُدُوْرِ
الَّذِيْنَ اُوْتُوا الْعِلْمَ ۭ وَمَا يَجْحَدُ
بِاٰيٰتِنَآ اِلَّا الظّٰلِمُوْنَ ﴿٤٩﴾

50. They say, “Why is a miracle not sent to him from his Lord?” Say, “Miracles are in the hands of Allah. I am simply a Warner.”

50. Wa qaaloo law laaa unzila ‘alayhi Aayaatum-mir-Rabbi-hee qul innamal-Aayaatu ‘indal-laahi wa innamaaa ana nazee-rum-mubeen.

وَقَالُوْا لَوْلَآ اُنْزِلَ عَلَيْهِ اٰيٰتٌ
مِّنْ رَّبِّهٖ ۭ قُلْ اِنَّمَا الْاٰيٰتُ
عِنْدَ اللّٰهِ ۭ وَاِنَّمَآ اَنَا نَذِيْرٌ مُّبِيْنٌ ﴿٥٠﴾

51. Was it not enough for them that We have revealed the Book to you to be recited to them? It is a mercy and a reminder for the believers.

51. Awa lam yakfihim annaaa anzalnaa ‘alaykal-Kitaaba yut-laa ‘alayhim; inna fee zaalika laraḥmatañw-wa zikraa liqaw-miñy-yu’minoon.

اَوَلَمْ يَكْفِهِمْ اَنَّآ اَنْزَلْنَا عَلَيْكَ
الْكِتٰبَ يُتْلٰى عَلَيْهِمْ ۭ اِنَّ فِيْ ذٰلِكَ
لَرَحْمَةً وَّذِكْرٰى لِقَوْمٍ يُّؤْمِنُوْنَ ﴿٥١﴾ ع ٥ ٧

52. Say, “Allah is sufficient as a witness between me and you. He knows all that is in the heavens and the earth.” Those who have faith in falsehood and disbelieve in Allah are certainly lost.

52. Qul kafaa billaahi baynee wa baynakum shaheedaa; ya‘lamu maa fis-samaawaati wal-arḍ; wallazeena aamanoo bil-baaṭili wa kafaroo billaahi ulaaa’ika humul-khaasiroon.

قُلْ كَفٰى بِاللّٰهِ بَيْنِيْ وَبَيْنَكُمْ شَهِيْدًا ۚ
يَعْلَمُ مَا فِي السَّمٰوٰتِ وَالْاَرْضِ ۭ
وَالَّذِيْنَ اٰمَنُوْا بِالْبَاطِلِ وَكَفَرُوْا
بِاللّٰهِ ۙ اُولٰۗىِٕكَ هُمُ الْخٰسِرُوْنَ ﴿٥٢﴾

53. They demand that you bring upon them torment immediately. Had not the time been fixed, the torment would certainly have approached them. It would have come to them suddenly and they would not have even realized how it came.

53. Wa yasta‘jiloonaka bil-‘azaab; wa law laaa ajalum-mu-sammal-lajaaa’ahumul-‘azaab; wa la-ya-tiyannahum baghta-tañw-wa hum laa yash‘uroon.

وَيَسْتَعْجِلُوْنَكَ بِالْعَذَابِ ۭ وَلَوْلَآ
اَجَلٌ مُّسَمًّى لَّجَاۗءَهُمُ الْعَذَابُ ۭ
وَلَيَاْتِيَنَّهُمْ بَغْتَةً وَّهُمْ لَا يَشْعُرُوْنَ ﴿٥٣﴾

54. They demand that you bring upon them the torment immediately. Hell will certainly engulf the unbelievers.

54. Yasta‘jiloonaka bil‘azaab; wa inna Jahannama lamuḥee-ṭatum bilkaafireen.

يَسْتَعْجِلُوْنَكَ بِالْعَذَابِ ۭ وَاِنَّ
جَهَنَّمَ لَمُحِيْطَةٌۢ بِالْكٰفِرِيْنَ ﴿٥٤﴾

55. They will be told on the Day of Judgment, when the torment will surround them from all sides, “Suffer the consequences of your deeds.”

55. Yawma yaghshaahumul ‘azaabu min fawqihim wa min taḥti arjulihim wa yaqoolu zooqoo maa kuntum ta‘maloon.

يَوْمَ يَغْشٰىهُمُ الْعَذَابُ مِنْ فَوْقِهِمْ
وَمِنْ تَحْتِ اَرْجُلِهِمْ وَيَقُوْلُ ذُوْقُوْا
مَا كُنْتُمْ تَعْمَلُوْنَ ﴿٥٥﴾

56. My believing servants, My land is vast. Worship Me alone.

56. Yaa 'ibaadiyal-lazeena aamanooo inna ardee waasi-'atun fa-iyyaaya fa'budoon.

يٰعِبَادِيَ الَّذِينَ آمَنُوا إِنَّ أَرْضِي
وَاسِعَةٌ فَإِيَّايَ فَاعْبُدُونِ ﴿٥٦﴾

57. Every soul will experience the agony of death and to Me you will all return.

57. Kullu nafsin zaaa'iqatul-mawt; summa ilaynaa tur-ja'oon.

كُلُّ نَفْسٍ ذَائِقَةُ الْمَوْتِ ثُمَّ
إِلَيْنَا تُرْجَعُونَ ﴿٥٧﴾

58. We shall give mansions in Paradise wherein streams flow to the righteously striving believers and therein they will live forever. How blessed is the reward of the hard-working people

58. Wallazeena aamanoo wa 'amiluṣ-ṣaaliḥaati la-nubawwi-'annahum-minal-Jannati ghura-fan tajree min taḥtihal-anhaaru khaalideena feehaa; ni'ma ajrul 'aamileen.

وَالَّذِينَ آمَنُوا وَعَمِلُوا الصّٰلِحٰتِ
لَنُبَوِّئَنَّهُمْ مِنَ الْجَنَّةِ غُرَفًا تَجْرِي
مِنْ تَحْتِهَا الْأَنْهٰرُ خٰلِدِينَ فِيهَا
نِعْمَ أَجْرُ الْعٰمِلِينَ ﴿٥٨﴾

59. who have exercised patience and who have had trust in their Lord.

59. Allazeena ṣabaroo wa 'alaa Rabbihim yatawakkaloon.

الَّذِينَ صَبَرُوا وَعَلٰى رَبِّهِمْ
يَتَوَكَّلُونَ ﴿٥٩﴾

60. There are many living creatures which do not carry their sustenance, but Allah provides them and you with sustenance. He is All-hearing and All-knowing.

60. Wa ka-ayyim-min daaab-batil-laa taḥmilu rizqahaa; Al-laahu yarzuquhaa wa iyyaakum; wa Huwas-Samee'ul 'Aleem.

وَكَأَيِّنْ مِنْ دَابَّةٍ لَا تَحْمِلُ رِزْقَهَا
اللّٰهُ يَرْزُقُهَا وَإِيَّاكُمْ وَهُوَ
السَّمِيعُ الْعَلِيمُ ﴿٦٠﴾

61. If you ask them, "Who has created the heavens and the earth and has subdued the sun and moon?" They will say, "Allah has done it." So why are they wandering about!?

61. Wa la'in sa-altahum-man khalaqas-samaawaati wal-arḍa wa sakhkharash-shamsa wal-qamara la-yaqoolunnal-laahu fa-annaa yu'fakoon.

وَلَئِنْ سَأَلْتَهُمْ مَنْ خَلَقَ السَّمٰوٰتِ
وَالْأَرْضَ وَسَخَّرَ الشَّمْسَ وَالْقَمَرَ
لَيَقُولُنَّ اللّٰهُ فَأَنّٰى يُؤْفَكُونَ ﴿٦١﴾

62. Allah increases the sustenance of whichever of His servants He wants and He determines their share. Allah has the knowledge of all things.

62. Allaahu yabsuṭur-rizqa limañy-yashaaa'u min 'ibaadi-hee wa yaqdiru lah; innal-laaha bikulli shay'in 'Aleem.

اللّٰهُ يَبْسُطُ الرِّزْقَ لِمَنْ يَشَاءُ
مِنْ عِبَادِهِ وَيَقْدِرُ لَهُ إِنَّ اللّٰهَ
بِكُلِّ شَيْءٍ عَلِيمٌ ﴿٦٢﴾

63. When you ask them as to who has sent down water from the sky to revive the dead earth? They will say, "Allah has done it." Say, "It is only Allah who deserves all praise, but many of them do not understand."

63. Wa la'in sa-altahum-man-nazzala minas-samaaa'i maaa-'an fa-aḥyaa bihil-arḍa mim ba'di mawtihaa la-yaqoolunnal-laah; qulil-ḥamdu-lillaah; bal aksaruhum laa ya'qiloon.

وَلَئِنْ سَأَلْتَهُمْ مَنْ نَزَّلَ مِنَ
السَّمَاءِ مَاءً فَأَحْيَا بِهِ الْأَرْضَ مِنْ
بَعْدِ مَوْتِهَا لَيَقُولُنَّ اللّٰهُ قُلِ
الْحَمْدُ لِلّٰهِ بَلْ أَكْثَرُهُمْ
لَا يَعْقِلُونَ ﴿٦٣﴾ ع ١٢ ٦

64. The worldly life is not more than a childish game. It is the life hereafter which will be the real life (without death), if only they

64. Wa maa haazihil-ḥayaa-tud-dunyaaa illaa lahwuñw-wa la'ib; wa innad-Daaral-Aakhi-rata la-hiyal-

وَمَا هٰذِهِ الْحَيٰوةُ الدُّنْيَا إِلَّا لَهْوٌ
وَلَعِبٌ وَإِنَّ الدَّارَ الْآخِرَةَ لَهِيَ

knew it.

65. When they sail in a boat, they sincerely pray to Allah with pure faith. However, when We bring them safely to land, they start considering things equal to Allah.

66. Let them be ungrateful for what We have granted them. Let them enjoy themselves, but they will soon know (the consequences of their deeds).

67. Did the (pagans) not see that We have made the holy precinct a safe place while all the people around are suffering terror? Do they believe in falsehood and disbelieve in Allah's bounties?

68. Who is more unjust than one who invents falsehood against Allah or rejects the Truth after it has come to him? Is not hell the dwelling for the unbeliever?

69. We shall certainly guide, those who strive for Our cause (with patience), to Our path (keep them on it well protected). Allah is certainly with the righteous ones.

Al-Rum, The Romans (30)

In the Name of Allah,
the Beneficent, the Merciful.

1. Alif. Lam. Mim.

2. The Romans have been defeated (by the Persians) in a nearby land, and they (the Persians) after their (victory)

3. will be defeated (by the Muslims)

4. within a few years.
All matters of the past (to command) and future (to judge) are in the hands of Allah. The believers will enjoy the help of Allah on that day (of victory over the Persians).

5. He helps whomever He wants. He is Majestic and All-merciful.

ḥayawaan; law kaanoo ya'lamoon.

65. Fa-iz̲aa rakiboo fil-fulki da'awul-laaha mukhliṣeena lahud-deena falammaa najjaa-hum ilal-barri iz̲aa hum yush-rikoon.

66. Li-yakfuroo bimaaa aa-taynaahum wa li-yatamatta'oo fasawfa ya'lamoon.

67. Awalam yaraw annaa ja'alnaa ḥaraman aaminañw-wa yutakhaṭṭafun-naasu min ḥaw-lihim; afabil-baaṭili yu'minoo-na wa bini'matil-laahi yakfu-roon.

68. Wa man aẓlamu mimma-nif-taraa 'alal-laahi kaz̲iban aw kaz̲z̲aba bilḥaqqi lammaa jaaa'ah; alaysa fee Jahannama maṡwal-lil-kaafireen.

69. Wallaz̲eena jaahadoo feenaa lanahdiyannahum subu-lanaa; wa innal-laaha lama'al-muḥsineen

Sûrat ar-Rûm-30

(Revealed at Makkah)
Bismillaahir Raḥmaanir Raḥeem

1. Alif-Laaam-Meeem.

2. Ghulibatir-Room.

3. Feee adnal-arḍi wa hum-mim ba'di ghalabihim sa-yaghliboon.

4. Fee biḍ'i sineen; lillaahil amru min qablu wa mim ba'd; wa yawma'iz̲iñy-yafraḥul-mu'-minoon.

5. Binaṣril-laah'. yanṣuru mañy-yashaaa'u wa Huwal-'Azeezur-Raḥeem.

وقف لازم

الْحَيَوَانُ ۘ لَوْ كَانُوا يَعْلَمُونَ ﴿٦٤﴾
فَإِذَا رَكِبُوا فِي الْفُلْكِ دَعَوُا اللَّهَ
مُخْلِصِينَ لَهُ الدِّينَ ۚ فَلَمَّا نَجَّاهُمْ
إِلَى الْبَرِّ إِذَا هُمْ يُشْرِكُونَ ﴿٦٥﴾
لِيَكْفُرُوا بِمَا آتَيْنَاهُمْ ۙ وَلِيَتَمَتَّعُوا ۖ
فَسَوْفَ يَعْلَمُونَ ﴿٦٦﴾
أَوَلَمْ يَرَوْا أَنَّا جَعَلْنَا حَرَمًا آمِنًا
وَيُتَخَطَّفُ النَّاسُ مِنْ حَوْلِهِمْ ۚ
أَفَبِالْبَاطِلِ يُؤْمِنُونَ وَبِنِعْمَةِ
اللَّهِ يَكْفُرُونَ ﴿٦٧﴾
وَمَنْ أَظْلَمُ مِمَّنِ افْتَرَىٰ عَلَى اللَّهِ
كَذِبًا أَوْ كَذَّبَ بِالْحَقِّ لَمَّا جَاءَهُ ۚ
أَلَيْسَ فِي جَهَنَّمَ مَثْوًى لِلْكَافِرِينَ ﴿٦٨﴾
وَالَّذِينَ جَاهَدُوا فِينَا لَنَهْدِيَنَّهُمْ
سُبُلَنَا ۚ وَإِنَّ اللَّهَ لَمَعَ الْمُحْسِنِينَ ﴿٦٩﴾ ع ٦/٣

(٣٠) سُورَةُ الرُّومِ مَكِّيَّةٌ (٨٤)

آياتها ٦٠ بِسْمِ اللَّهِ الرَّحْمَٰنِ الرَّحِيمِ ركوعاتها ٦

الم ﴿١﴾
غُلِبَتِ الرُّومُ ﴿٢﴾
فِي أَدْنَى الْأَرْضِ وَهُمْ مِنْ بَعْدِ
غَلَبِهِمْ سَيَغْلِبُونَ ﴿٣﴾
فِي بِضْعِ سِنِينَ ۗ لِلَّهِ الْأَمْرُ مِنْ
قَبْلُ وَمِنْ بَعْدُ ۚ وَيَوْمَئِذٍ يَفْرَحُ
الْمُؤْمِنُونَ ﴿٤﴾
بِنَصْرِ اللَّهِ ۚ يَنْصُرُ مَنْ يَشَاءُ ۖ وَهُوَ
الْعَزِيزُ الرَّحِيمُ ﴿٥﴾

6. This is the promise of Allah. Allah does not ignore His promise, but many people do not know.

6. Wa'dal-laahi laa yukhliful-laahu wa'dahoo wa laakinna aks̱aran-naasi laa ya'lamoon.

وَعْدَ اللّٰهِ ۭ لَا يُخْلِفُ اللّٰهُ وَعْدَهٗ
وَلٰكِنَّ اَكْثَرَ النَّاسِ لَا يَعْلَمُوْنَ ۝٦

7. They only know the superficial realities of the worldly life and they are unaware of the life to come.

7. Ya'lamoona ẓaahiram-minal-ḥayaatid-dunyaa wa hum 'anil-Aakhirati hum ghaafiloon.

يَعْلَمُوْنَ ظَاهِرًا مِّنَ الْحَيٰوةِ الدُّنْيَا ښ
وَهُمْ عَنِ الْاٰخِرَةِ هُمْ غٰفِلُوْنَ ۝٧

8. Had they not thought in their own souls that Allah has not created the heavens and the earth and all that is between them but for a genuine purpose to exist for an appointed term? Many people do not believe in their meeting with their Lord.

8. Awalam yatafakkaroo feee anfusihim; maa khalaqal-laahus-samaawaati wal-arḍa wa maa baynahumaaa illaa bil-ḥaqqi wa ajalim-musammaa; wa inna-kas̱eeram-minan-naasi biliqaaa'i Rabbihim lakaafiroon.

اَوَلَمْ يَتَفَكَّرُوْا فِيْٓ اَنْفُسِهِمْ ۣ مَا
خَلَقَ اللّٰهُ السَّمٰوٰتِ وَالْاَرْضَ وَمَا
بَيْنَهُمَآ اِلَّا بِالْحَقِّ وَاَجَلٍ مُّسَمًّى ۭ
وَاِنَّ كَثِيْرًا مِّنَ النَّاسِ بِلِقَاۗئِ
رَبِّهِمْ لَكٰفِرُوْنَ ۝٨

9. Did they not travel through the land to see how terrible was the end of the people who lived before them? The people who lived before them were stronger than them in might, in tilling, and in developing the earth. Our Messengers came to them with clear miracles. Allah did not do an injustice to them but they wronged themselves.

9. Awalam yaseeroo fil-arḍi fa-yanẓuroo kayfa kaana 'aaqibatul-laẕeena min qablihim; kaanooo-ashadda minhum quwwatañw-wa as̱aarul-arḍa wa 'amaroohaaa aks̱ara mimmaa 'amaroohaa wa jaaa'athum Rusuluhum bil-bayyinaati famaa kaanal-laahu li-yaẓlimahum wa laakin kaanooo anfusahum yaẓlimoon.

اَوَلَمْ يَسِيْرُوْا فِي الْاَرْضِ فَيَنْظُرُوْا
كَيْفَ كَانَ عَاقِبَةُ الَّذِيْنَ مِنْ
قَبْلِهِمْ ۭ كَانُوْٓا اَشَدَّ مِنْهُمْ قُوَّةً
وَّاَثَارُوا الْاَرْضَ وَعَمَرُوْهَآ اَكْثَرَ
مِمَّا عَمَرُوْهَا وَجَاۗءَتْهُمْ رُسُلُهُمْ
بِالْبَيِّنٰتِ ۭ فَمَا كَانَ اللّٰهُ لِيَظْلِمَهُمْ
وَلٰكِنْ كَانُوْٓا اَنْفُسَهُمْ يَظْلِمُوْنَ ۝٩

10. The end of the evil-doers was terrible, for they had rejected the revelations of Allah and mocked them.

10. S̱umma kaana 'aaqibatal-laẕeena asaaa'us-sooo-aaa an kaẕẕaboo bi-Aayaatil-laahi wa kaanoo bihaa yastahzi'oon.

ثُمَّ كَانَ عَاقِبَةَ الَّذِيْنَ اَسَاۗءُوا
السُّوْۗآٰى اَنْ كَذَّبُوْا بِاٰيٰتِ اللّٰهِ
وَكَانُوْا بِهَا يَسْتَهْزِءُوْنَ ۝١٠ ع

11. Allah begins the creation then causes it to turn back, and to Him you will all return.

11. Allaahu yabda'ul-khalqa s̱umma yu'eeduhoo s̱umma ilayhi turja'oon.

اَللّٰهُ يَبْدَؤُا الْخَلْقَ ثُمَّ يُعِيْدُهٗ ثُمَّ
اِلَيْهِ تُرْجَعُوْنَ ۝١١

12. On the day when the Hour of Doom comes, the criminals will despair.

12. Wa Yawma taqoomus-Saa'atu yublisul-mujrimoon.

وَيَوْمَ تَقُوْمُ السَّاعَةُ يُبْلِسُ
الْمُجْرِمُوْنَ ۝١٢

13. None of the idols could intercede for them and they will reject their idols.

13. Wa lam yakul-lahum-min shurakaaa'ihim shufa'aaa'u wa kaanoo bishurakaaa'ihim kaafireen.

وَلَمْ يَكُنْ لَّهُمْ مِّنْ شُرَكَاۗىِٕهِمْ شُفَعٰۗؤُا
وَكَانُوْا بِشُرَكَاۗىِٕهِمْ كٰفِرِيْنَ ۝١٣

14. When that day comes, (people) will be separated from one another (by sending one group to paradise and one to hell).

14. Wa Yawma taqoomus-Saa'atu Yawma'iẕiñy-yatafarraqoon.

وَيَوْمَ تَقُوْمُ السَّاعَةُ يَوْمَىِٕذٍ

يَتَفَرَّقُوْنَ ﴿١٤﴾

15. The righteously striving believers will happily live (receive honor) in paradise.

15. Fa-ammal-lazeena aamanoo wa 'amiluṣ-ṣaaliḥaati fa-hum fee rawḍatiñy-yuḥbaroon.

فَاَمَّا الَّذِيْنَ اٰمَنُوْا وَعَمِلُوا الصّٰلِحٰتِ
فَهُمْ فِيْ رَوْضَةٍ يُّحْبَرُوْنَ ﴿١٥﴾

16. However, the unbelievers, who called Our revelations and the Day of Judgment lies, will be brought into torment.

16. Wa ammal-lazeena kafaroo wa kazzaboo bi-Aayaatinaa wa liqaaa'il Aakhirati fa-ulaaa'ika fil'azaabi muḥḍaroon.

وَاَمَّا الَّذِيْنَ كَفَرُوْا وَكَذَّبُوْا بِاٰيٰتِنَا
وَلِقَآئِ الْاٰخِرَةِ فَاُولٰٓئِكَ فِي
الْعَذَابِ مُحْضَرُوْنَ ﴿١٦﴾

17. Glory belongs to Allah when you find yourselves in the evening and in the morning.

17. Fa-Subḥaanal-laahi ḥeena tumsoona wa ḥeena tuṣbiḥoon.

فَسُبْحٰنَ اللّٰهِ حِيْنَ تُمْسُوْنَ وَحِيْنَ
تُصْبِحُوْنَ ﴿١٧﴾

18. To Him belongs all the thanksgiving which takes place in the heavens and the earth, in the evenings and the noontime.

18. Wa lahul-ḥamdu fissamaawaati wal-arḍi wa 'ashiyyañw-wa ḥeena tuẓhiroon.

وَلَهُ الْحَمْدُ فِي السَّمٰوٰتِ وَ
الْاَرْضِ وَعَشِيًّا وَّحِيْنَ تُظْهِرُوْنَ ﴿١٨﴾

19. He brings forth the living from the dead, takes out the dead from the living, and revives the earth from its death. Thus, you will all be brought back to life again.

19. Yukhrijul-ḥayya minal-mayyiti wa yukhrijul-mayyita minal-ḥayyi wa yuḥyil-arḍa ba'da mawtihaa; wa kazaalika tukhrajoon.

يُخْرِجُ الْحَيَّ مِنَ الْمَيِّتِ وَيُخْرِجُ
الْمَيِّتَ مِنَ الْحَيِّ وَيُحْيِ الْاَرْضَ
بَعْدَ مَوْتِهَا ؕ وَكَذٰلِكَ تُخْرَجُوْنَ ﴿١٩﴾ ع ٩ ٥

20. Of the evidence of His existence is His creating you from clay, and from that you became human beings scattered all around;

20. Wa min Aayaatiheee an khalaqakum-min turaabin summa izaaa antum basharun tantashiroon.

وَمِنْ اٰيٰتِهٖٓ اَنْ خَلَقَكُمْ مِّنْ تُرَابٍ
ثُمَّ اِذَآ اَنْتُمْ بَشَرٌ تَنْتَشِرُوْنَ ﴿٢٠﴾

21. His creating spouses for you out of yourselves so that you might take comfort in them; and His creating love and mercy among you. In this there is evidence (of the truth) for the people who (carefully) think.

21. Wa min Aayaatiheee an khalaqa lakum-min-anfusikum azwaajal-litaskunooo ilayhaa wa ja'ala baynakum-mawad-datañw-wa raḥmah; inna fee zaalika la-Aayaatil-liqawmiñy-yatafakkaroon.

وَمِنْ اٰيٰتِهٖٓ اَنْ خَلَقَ لَكُمْ مِّنْ
اَنْفُسِكُمْ اَزْوَاجًا لِّتَسْكُنُوْٓا اِلَيْهَا
وَجَعَلَ بَيْنَكُمْ مَّوَدَّةً وَّرَحْمَةً ؕ
اِنَّ فِيْ ذٰلِكَ لَاٰيٰتٍ لِّقَوْمٍ يَّتَفَكَّرُوْنَ ﴿٢١﴾

22. Other evidence of His existence is the creation of the heavens and the earth and the differences of languages and colors. In this there is evidence (of the truth) for the knowledgeable ones (mankind).

22. Wa min Aayaatihee khalqus-samaawaati wal-arḍi wakhtilaafu alsinatikum wa alwaanikum; inna fee zaalika la-Aayaatil-lil-'aalimeen.

وَمِنْ اٰيٰتِهٖ خَلْقُ السَّمٰوٰتِ وَالْاَرْضِ
وَاخْتِلَافُ اَلْسِنَتِكُمْ وَاَلْوَانِكُمْ ؕ
اِنَّ فِيْ ذٰلِكَ لَاٰيٰتٍ لِّلْعٰلِمِيْنَ ﴿٢٢﴾

23. Your sleeping during the night and in the day your seeking His favors are evidence (of the truth) for the people who have hearing.

23. Wa min Aayaatihee manaamukum billayli wannahaari wabtighaaa'ukum-min faḍlih; inna fee zaalika la-Aayaatil-liqawmiñy-yasma'oon.

وَمِنْ اٰيٰتِهٖ مَنَامُكُمْ بِالَّيْلِ وَالنَّهَارِ
وَابْتِغَآؤُكُمْ مِّنْ فَضْلِهٖ ؕ اِنَّ فِيْ
ذٰلِكَ لَاٰيٰتٍ لِّقَوْمٍ يَّسْمَعُوْنَ ﴿٢٣﴾

24. Also within the evidence of His existence is His showing you lightning which gives you fear

24. Wa min Aayaatihee yureekumul-barqa khawfañw-

وَمِنْ اٰيٰتِهٖ يُرِيْكُمُ الْبَرْقَ خَوْفًا

and hope and His sending water down from the sky which revives the earth after its death. In this there is evidence (of the truth) for the people of understanding.

wa ṭama'añw-wa yunazzilu minas-samaaa'i maaa'an fa-yuḥyee bihil-arḍa ba'da mawtihaaa inna fee zaalika la-Aayaatil-liqawmiñy-ya'qiloon.

وَّطَمَعًا وَّيُنَزِّلُ مِنَ السَّمَآءِ مَآءً
فَيُحْيٖ بِهِ الْاَرْضَ بَعْدَ مَوْتِهَا ؕ
اِنَّ فِيْ ذٰلِكَ لَاٰيٰتٍ لِّقَوْمٍ
يَّعْقِلُوْنَ ﴿٢٤﴾

25. Of other evidence of His existence is that both the heavens and the earth stand firm at His command. When He calls you from the earth, you will start to come out.

25. Wa min Aayaatiheee an taqoomas-samaaa'u wal-arḍu bi-amrih; summa izaa da'aakum da'watam-minal-arḍi izaaa antum takhrujoon.

وَمِنْ اٰيٰتِهٖۤ اَنْ تَقُوْمَ السَّمَآءُ وَ
الْاَرْضُ بِاَمْرِهٖ ؕ ثُمَّ اِذَا دَعَاكُمْ
دَعْوَةً ۖۗ مِّنَ الْاَرْضِ ۖۗ اِذَاۤ
اَنْتُمْ تَخْرُجُوْنَ ﴿٢٥﴾

26. Everyone in the heavens and the earth belongs to Him and is subservient to Him.

26. Wa lahoo man fissamaawaati wal-arḍi kullul-lahoo qaanitoon.

وَلَهٗ مَنْ فِي السَّمٰوٰتِ وَالْاَرْضِ ؕ
كُلٌّ لَّهٗ قٰنِتُوْنَ ﴿٢٦﴾

27. It is He who begins the creation, then turns it back. For Him this is very easy. All the exalted attributes in the heavens and the earth belong to Him. He is the Majestic and All-wise.

27. Wa Huwal-lazee yabda'ul-khalqa summa yu'eeduhoo wa huwa ahwanu 'alayh; wa lahul-masalul-a'laa fissamaawaati wal-arḍ; wa Huwal-'Azeezul-Ḥakeem.

وَهُوَ الَّذِيْ يَبْدَؤُا الْخَلْقَ ثُمَّ
يُعِيْدُهٗ وَهُوَ اَهْوَنُ عَلَيْهِ ؕ وَلَهُ
الْمَثَلُ الْاَعْلٰى فِي السَّمٰوٰتِ وَالْاَرْضِ ۚ
وَهُوَ الْعَزِيْزُ الْحَكِيْمُ ﴿٢٧﴾ ع

ركوع ٣ ع ٨ ٦

28. Allah has told you this parable about yourselves: Could your slaves share your wealth equally with you and could you fear them as you fear yourselves? Thus do We clarify the evidence (of the truth) for the people of understanding.

28. Ḍaraba lakum-masalam-min anfusikum hal lakum-mim-maa malakat aymaanukum-min shurakaaa'a fee maa razaqnaakum fa-antum feehi sawaaa'un takhaafoonahum kakheefatikum anfusakum; kazaalika nufaṣṣilul-Aayaati liqawmiñy-ya'qiloon.

ضَرَبَ لَكُمْ مَّثَلًا مِّنْ اَنْفُسِكُمْ ؕ هَلْ
لَّكُمْ مِّنْ مَّا مَلَكَتْ اَيْمَانُكُمْ مِّنْ
شُرَكَآءَ فِيْ مَا رَزَقْنٰكُمْ فَاَنْتُمْ فِيْهِ
سَوَآءٌ تَخَافُوْنَهُمْ كَخِيْفَتِكُمْ اَنْفُسَكُمْ ؕ
كَذٰلِكَ نُفَصِّلُ الْاٰيٰتِ لِقَوْمٍ
يَّعْقِلُوْنَ ﴿٢٨﴾

29. In fact, the unjust have followed their desires without knowledge. Who will guide those whom Allah has caused to go astray? No one will be their helper.

29. Balit-taba'al-lazeena ẓalamooo ahwaaa'ahum bighayri 'ilmin famañy-yahdee man aḍallal-laahu wa maa lahum min-naaṣireen.

بَلِ اتَّبَعَ الَّذِيْنَ ظَلَمُوْۤا اَهْوَآءَهُمْ
بِغَيْرِ عِلْمٍ ۚ فَمَنْ يَّهْدِيْ مَنْ اَضَلَّ
اللّٰهُ ؕ وَمَا لَهُمْ مِّنْ نّٰصِرِيْنَ ﴿٢٩﴾

30. (Muhammad), you must be devoted to the upright (pure) religion. It is in agreement with the nature which Allah has designed for people. The design of Allah cannot be altered. Thus is

30. Fa-aqim wajhaka liddeeni Ḥaneefaa; fiṭratal-laahil-latee faṭaran-naasa 'alayhaa; laa tabdeela likhalqil-laah; zaalikad-deenul-

فَاَقِمْ وَجْهَكَ لِلدِّيْنِ حَنِيْفًا ؕ فِطْرَتَ
اللّٰهِ الَّتِيْ فَطَرَ النَّاسَ عَلَيْهَا ؕ
لَا تَبْدِيْلَ لِخَلْقِ اللّٰهِ ؕ ذٰلِكَ الدِّيْنُ

the upright religion, but many people do not know.	qayyimu wa laakinna akṣaran-naasi laa ya'lamoon.	الْقَيِّمُ ۙ وَلٰكِنَّ أَكْثَرَ النَّاسِ لَا يَعْلَمُونَ ﴿٣٠﴾
31. Turn in repentance to Him. Have fear of Him. Be steadfast in your prayer. Do not be like the pagans	31. Muneebeena ilayhi wat-taqoohu wa aqeemuṣ-Ṣalaata wa laa takoonoo minal-mush-rikeen.	مُنِيبِينَ إِلَيْهِ وَاتَّقُوهُ وَأَقِيمُوا الصَّلٰوةَ وَلَا تَكُونُوا مِنَ الْمُشْرِكِينَ ﴿٣١﴾
32. who have divided themselves into various religious sects, each one happy with his own belief.	32. Minal-lazeena farraqoo deenahum wa kaanoo shiya'an kullu ḥizbim bimaa ladayhim fariḥoon.	مِنَ الَّذِينَ فَرَّقُوا دِينَهُمْ وَكَانُوا شِيَعًا ۖ كُلُّ حِزْبٍ بِمَا لَدَيْهِمْ فَرِحُونَ ﴿٣٢﴾
33. When people face hardship, they begin praying to their Lord and turn in repentance to Him. When they receive mercy from Him, a group of them begin to consider things equal to Allah,	33. Wa izaa massan-naasa ḍurrun da'aw Rabbahum-muneebeena ilayhi summa izaaa azaaqahum-minhu raḥmatan izaa fareequm-min-hum bi-Rabbihim yushrikoon.	وَإِذَا مَسَّ النَّاسَ ضُرٌّ دَعَوْا رَبَّهُمْ مُنِيبِينَ إِلَيْهِ ثُمَّ إِذَا أَذَاقَهُمْ مِنْهُ رَحْمَةً إِذَا فَرِيقٌ مِنْهُمْ بِرَبِّهِمْ يُشْرِكُونَ ﴿٣٣﴾
34. because of their ingratitude for what We have given them. Let them enjoy themselves, but they will soon know (the consequences of their deeds).	34. Li-yakfuroo bimaaa aatay-naahum; fatamatta'oo fasawfa ta'lamoon.	لِيَكْفُرُوا بِمَا آتَيْنَاهُمْ ۚ فَتَمَتَّعُوا فَسَوْفَ تَعْلَمُونَ ﴿٣٤﴾
35. Have We sent them any authority to speak in support of their idols?	35. Am anzalnaa 'alayhim sulṭaanan fahuwa yatakallamu bimaa kaanoo bihee yushri-koon.	أَمْ أَنْزَلْنَا عَلَيْهِمْ سُلْطَانًا فَهُوَ يَتَكَلَّمُ بِمَا كَانُوا بِهِ يُشْرِكُونَ ﴿٣٥﴾
36. When people receive mercy, they are happy with it. However, when hardship befalls them because of their own deeds, they despair.	36. Wa izaaa azaqnan-naasa raḥmatan fariḥoo bihaa wa in tuṣibhum sayyi'atum bimaa qaddamat aydeehim izaa hum yaqnaṭoon.	وَإِذَا أَذَقْنَا النَّاسَ رَحْمَةً فَرِحُوا بِهَا ۖ وَإِنْ تُصِبْهُمْ سَيِّئَةٌ بِمَا قَدَّمَتْ أَيْدِيهِمْ إِذَا هُمْ يَقْنَطُونَ ﴿٣٦﴾
37. Did they not see how Allah increases the livelihood of whomever He wants and determines his share? In this there is evidence (of the truth) for the believing people.	37. Awalam yaraw annallaaha yabsuṭur-rizqa limañy-ya-shaaa'u wa yaqdir; inna fee zaalika la-Aayaatil-liqawmiñy-yu'minoon.	أَوَلَمْ يَرَوْا أَنَّ اللَّهَ يَبْسُطُ الرِّزْقَ لِمَنْ يَشَاءُ وَيَقْدِرُ ۚ إِنَّ فِي ذٰلِكَ لَآيَاتٍ لِقَوْمٍ يُؤْمِنُونَ ﴿٣٧﴾
38. Give the relatives, the destitute, and the needy travelers their share (of charity). It is better for those who want to please Allah and they will have ever-lasting happiness.	38. Fa-aati zal-qurbaa ḥaqqa-hoo walmiskeena wabnas-sabeel; zaalika khayrul-lil-lazeena yureedoona Wajhal-laahi wa ulaaa'ika humul-muf-liḥoon.	فَآتِ ذَا الْقُرْبَىٰ حَقَّهُ وَالْمِسْكِينَ وَابْنَ السَّبِيلِ ۚ ذٰلِكَ خَيْرٌ لِلَّذِينَ يُرِيدُونَ وَجْهَ اللَّهِ ۖ وَأُولٰئِكَ هُمُ الْمُفْلِحُونَ ﴿٣٨﴾
39. Allah will not allow to increase whatever illegal interest	39. Wa maaa aataytum-mir-ribal-li-yarbuwa feee	وَمَا آتَيْتُمْ مِنْ رِبًا لِيَرْبُوَ فِي

you try to receive in order to increase your wealth at the expense of people's property. Whatever amount of zakat you give to please Allah will be doubled (for you).

amwaalin-naasi falaa yarboo 'indal-laahi wa maaa aataytum-min Zakaatin tureedoona Wajhal-laahi fa-ulaaa'ika humul-muḍ'ifoon.

اَمْوَالِ النَّاسِ فَلَا يَرْبُوْا عِنْدَ اللّٰهِ ۚ
وَمَآ اٰتَيْتُمْ مِّنْ زَكٰوةٍ تُرِيْدُوْنَ وَجْهَ
اللّٰهِ فَاُولٰٓئِكَ هُمُ الْمُضْعِفُوْنَ ﴿٣٩﴾

40. It is Allah who has created you and given you sustenance. He will make you die and will bring you back to life. Can any of your idols do such things? Allah is free from all defects of being considered equal to anything else.

40. Allaahul-lazee khalaqa-kum summa razaqakum summa yumeetukum summa yuḥ-yee-kum hal min shurakaaa'ikum mañy-yaf'alu min zaalikum-min shay'; Subḥaanahoo wa Ta'aalaa 'ammaa yushrikoon.

اَللّٰهُ الَّذِيْ خَلَقَكُمْ ثُمَّ رَزَقَكُمْ
ثُمَّ يُمِيْتُكُمْ ثُمَّ يُحْيِيْكُمْ ۭ هَلْ مِنْ
شُرَكَاۗىِٕكُمْ مَّنْ يَّفْعَلُ مِنْ ذٰلِكُمْ
مِّنْ شَيْءٍ ۭ سُبْحٰنَهٗ وَتَعٰلٰى عَمَّا
يُشْرِكُوْنَ ﴿٤٠﴾ ع ١٣ ٤

41. Evil has spread over the land and the sea because of human deeds and through these Allah will cause some people to suffer so that perhaps they will return to Him.

41. Ẓaharal-fasaadu fil-barri wal-baḥri bimaa kasabat aydin-naasi li-yuzeeqahum ba'ḍal-lazee 'amiloo la'allahum yarji'oon.

ظَهَرَ الْفَسَادُ فِي الْبَرِّ وَالْبَحْرِ بِمَا
كَسَبَتْ اَيْدِي النَّاسِ لِيُذِيْقَهُمْ
بَعْضَ الَّذِيْ عَمِلُوْا لَعَلَّهُمْ يَرْجِعُوْنَ ﴿٤١﴾

42. (Muhammad), tell them, "Travel through the land to see how terrible the end of those who lived before was. Many of them were pagans.

42. Qul seeroo fil-arḍi fanẓu-roo kayfa kaana 'aaqibatul-lazeena min qabl; kaana aksaru-hum-mushrikeen.

قُلْ سِيْرُوْا فِي الْاَرْضِ فَانْظُرُوْا
كَيْفَ كَانَ عَاقِبَةُ الَّذِيْنَ مِنْ
قَبْلُ ۭ كَانَ اَكْثَرُهُمْ مُّشْرِكِيْنَ ﴿٤٢﴾

43. Be devoted to the upright religion before the coming of the inevitable day when no one can escape from Allah and people will be sent either to Paradise or hell."

43. Fa-aqim wajhaka lid-dee-nil-qayyimi min qabli añy-ya-tiya Yawmul-laa maradda lahoo minal-laahi Yawma'iziñy-yaṣ-ṣadda'oon.

فَاَقِمْ وَجْهَكَ لِلدِّيْنِ الْقَيِّمِ مِنْ
قَبْلِ اَنْ يَّاْتِيَ يَوْمٌ لَّا مَرَدَّ لَهٗ
مِنَ اللّٰهِ يَوْمَىِٕذٍ يَّصَّدَّعُوْنَ ﴿٤٣﴾

44. Those who disbelieve do so against their own souls. Those who do good pave the way for their own benefit.

44. Man kafara fa'alayhi kufruhoo wa man 'amila ṣaa-liḥan fali-anfusihim yamha-doon.

مَنْ كَفَرَ فَعَلَيْهِ كُفْرُهٗ ۚ وَمَنْ عَمِلَ
صَالِحًا فَلِاَنْفُسِهِمْ يَمْهَدُوْنَ ﴿٤٤﴾

45. Allah will reward the righteously striving believers through His favor. He does not love the unbelievers.

45. Li-yajziyal-lazeena aama-noo wa 'amiluṣ-ṣaaliḥaati min faḍlih; innahoo laa yuḥibbul-kaafireen.

لِيَجْزِيَ الَّذِيْنَ اٰمَنُوْا وَعَمِلُوا
الصّٰلِحٰتِ مِنْ فَضْلِهٖ ۭ اِنَّهٗ لَا
يُحِبُّ الْكٰفِرِيْنَ ﴿٤٥﴾

46. Of the evidence of His existence is His sending the glad-news-bearing winds so that He can allow you to receive His mercy, cause the ships to sail by His command, and let you seek His favor so that perhaps you will give Him thanks.

46. Wa min Aayaatiheee añy-yursilar-riyaaḥa mubashshi-raatiñw-wa li-yuzeeqakum-mir-raḥmatihee wa litajriyal-fulku bi-amrihee wa litabtaghoo min faḍlihee wa la'allakum tashku-roon.

وَمِنْ اٰيٰتِهٖٓ اَنْ يُّرْسِلَ الرِّيَاحَ
مُبَشِّرٰتٍ وَّلِيُذِيْقَكُمْ مِّنْ رَّحْمَتِهٖ
وَلِتَجْرِيَ الْفُلْكُ بِاَمْرِهٖ وَلِتَبْتَغُوْا
مِنْ فَضْلِهٖ وَلَعَلَّكُمْ تَشْكُرُوْنَ ﴿٤٦﴾

47. (Muhammad), We had sent before you Our Messengers to their people. They (Messengers) showed them clear miracles and We subjected those committing crimes to Our reprisal. It was necessary for Us to help the believers.

47. Wa laqad arsalnaa min qablika Rusulan ilaa qawmihim fajaaa'oohum bil-bayyinaati fantaqamnaa minal-lazeena ajramoo wa kaana ḥaqqan 'alaynaa naṣrul-mu'mineen.

وَلَقَدْ اَرْسَلْنَا مِنْ قَبْلِكَ رُسُلًا اِلٰى
قَوْمِهِمْ فَجَآءُوْهُمْ بِالْبَيِّنٰتِ فَانْتَقَمْنَا
مِنَ الَّذِيْنَ اَجْرَمُوْا ؕ وَكَانَ حَقًّا
عَلَيْنَا نَصْرُ الْمُؤْمِنِيْنَ ﴿٤٧﴾

48. It is Allah who sends the winds to raise the clouds. He spreads them in the sky as He wants, then He intensifies them, and then you can see the rain coming down from the cloud. When He sends it down upon whichever of His servants He wants, they rejoice.

48. Allaahul-lazee yursilur-riyaaḥa fatuseeru saḥaaban fa-yabsuṭuhoo fis-samaaa'i kayfa yashaaa'u wa yaj'aluhoo kisa-fan fataral-wadqa yakhruju min khilaalihee fa-izaaa aṣaaba bi-hee mañy-yashaaa'u min 'ibaa-diheee izaa hum yastabshiroon.

اَللّٰهُ الَّذِىْ يُرْسِلُ الرِّيٰحَ فَتُثِيْرُ
سَحَابًا فَيَبْسُطُهٗ فِى السَّمَآءِ كَيْفَ
يَشَآءُ وَيَجْعَلُهٗ كِسَفًا فَتَرَى الْوَدْقَ
يَخْرُجُ مِنْ خِلٰلِهٖ ۚ فَاِذَآ اَصَابَ
بِهٖ مَنْ يَّشَآءُ مِنْ عِبَادِهٖۤ اِذَا
هُمْ يَسْتَبْشِرُوْنَ ﴿٤٨﴾

49. (They rejoice the rainfall), although prior to that (rainfall) upon them they lived in despair.

49. Wa in kaanoo min qabli añy-yunazzala 'alayhim-min qablihee lamubliseen.

وَاِنْ كَانُوْا مِنْ قَبْلِ اَنْ يُّنَزَّلَ
عَلَيْهِمْ مِّنْ قَبْلِهٖ لَمُبْلِسِيْنَ ﴿٤٩﴾

50. Look at the traces of the mercy of Allah, how He has revived the dead earth. Allah revives the dead; He has power over all things.

50. Fanẓur ilaaa aasaari raḥ-matil-laahi kayfa yuḥ-il-arḍa ba'da mawtihaaa; inna zaalika lamuḥyil-mawtaa wa Huwa 'alaa kulli shay'in Qadeer.

فَانْظُرْ اِلٰٓى اٰثٰرِ رَحْمَتِ اللّٰهِ كَيْفَ
يُحْىِ الْاَرْضَ بَعْدَ مَوْتِهَا ؕ اِنَّ
ذٰلِكَ لَمُحْىِ الْمَوْتٰى ۚ وَهُوَ عَلٰى كُلِّ
شَىْءٍ قَدِيْرٌ ﴿٥٠﴾

51. Even if We had sent the wind and caused (the plants) to turn yellow and to fade away, they (unbelievers) would still have remained in disbelief.

51. Wa la'in arsalnaa reeḥan fara-awhu muṣfarral-laẓalloo mim ba'dihee yakfuroon.

وَلَئِنْ اَرْسَلْنَا رِيْحًا فَرَاَوْهُ مُصْفَرًّا
لَّظَلُّوْا مِنْ بَعْدِهٖ يَكْفُرُوْنَ ﴿٥١﴾

52. You cannot make the dead listen, nor do the deaf hear. Thus, they (the unbelievers) turn away on their heels.

52. Fa-innaka laa tusmi'ul-mawtaa wa laa tusmi'uṣ-ṣum-mad-du'aaa'a izaa wallaw mudbireen.

فَاِنَّكَ لَا تُسْمِعُ الْمَوْتٰى وَلَا تُسْمِعُ
الصُّمَّ الدُّعَآءَ اِذَا وَلَّوْا مُدْبِرِيْنَ ﴿٥٢﴾

53. You cannot guide the straying blind. You can make no one listen except those who believe in Our revelations and are Muslims.

53. Wa maaa anta bihaadil-'umyi 'an ḍalaalatihim in tus-mi'u illaa mañy-yu'minu bi-Aa-yaatinaa fahum-muslimoon.

وَمَآ اَنْتَ بِهٰدِ الْعُمْىِ عَنْ ضَلٰلَتِهِمْ ؕ
اِنْ تُسْمِعُ اِلَّا مَنْ يُّؤْمِنُ بِاٰيٰتِنَا
فَهُمْ مُّسْلِمُوْنَ ﴿٥٣﴾ ع ٥ ١٣

54. It is Allah who has created you weak, then, given you strength after your weakness and caused you to become weak and old after being strong. He creates whatever He wants. He is All-

54. Allaahul-lazee khalaqa-kum-min ḍu'fin summa ja'ala mim ba'di ḍu'fin quwwatan summa ja'ala mim ba'di quw-watin ḍu'fañw-

اَللّٰهُ الَّذِىْ خَلَقَكُمْ مِّنْ ضُعْفٍ
ثُمَّ جَعَلَ مِنْ بَعْدِ ضُعْفٍ قُوَّةً
ثُمَّ جَعَلَ مِنْ بَعْدِ قُوَّةٍ ضُعْفًا

قرء حفص بضم الضاد وفتحها في الثلاثة لكن الضم مختارة ١٢

knowing and All-powerful.

wa shaybah; yakhluqu maa yashaaa'u wa Huwal 'Aleemul-Qadeer.

وَّ شَيۡبَةً ؕ يَخۡلُقُ مَا يَشَآءُ ۚ وَهُوَ
الۡعَلِيۡمُ الۡقَدِيۡرُ ﴿۵۴﴾

55. On the day when the Hour of Doom comes, the criminals will swear that they have remained (in their graves) for no more than an hour. They had been inventing lies in this way.

55. Wa Yawma taqoomus-Saa'atu yuqsimul-mujrimoona maa labisoo ghayra saa'ah; kazaalika kaanoo yu'fakoon.

وَيَوۡمَ تَقُوۡمُ السَّاعَةُ يُقۡسِمُ
الۡمُجۡرِمُوۡنَ ۙ مَا لَبِثُوۡا غَيۡرَ سَاعَةٍ ؕ
كَذٰلِكَ كَانُوۡا يُؤۡفَكُوۡنَ ﴿۵۵﴾

56. Those who have received knowledge and have faith, according to the Book of Allah, will say, "You have remained up to the Day of Resurrection. This is the Day of Resurrection, but you did not know."

56. Wa qaalal-lazeena ootul-'ilma wal-eemaana laqad labistum fee kitaabil-laahi ilaa yawmil-ba'si fahaazaa yawmul-ba'si wa laakinnakum kuntum laa ta'lamoon.

وَقَالَ الَّذِيۡنَ اُوۡتُوا الۡعِلۡمَ وَالۡاِيۡمَانَ
لَقَدۡ لَبِثۡتُمۡ فِىۡ كِتٰبِ اللّٰهِ اِلٰى
يَوۡمِ الۡبَعۡثِ ۫ فَهٰذَا يَوۡمُ الۡبَعۡثِ
وَلٰكِنَّكُمۡ كُنۡتُمۡ لَا تَعۡلَمُوۡنَ ﴿۵۶﴾

57. The excuses of the unjust on this day will be of no avail to them and they will not be given any chance to correct themselves.

57. Fa-Yawma'izil-laa yanfa-'ul-lazeena zalamoo ma'ziratu-hum wa laa hum yusta'taboon.

فَيَوۡمَئِذٍ لَّا يَنۡفَعُ الَّذِيۡنَ ظَلَمُوۡا
مَعۡذِرَتُهُمۡ وَلَا هُمۡ يُسۡتَعۡتَبُوۡنَ ﴿۵۷﴾

58. We have told people various parables in this Quran. Even if you had shown them a miracle, the unbelievers would have said, "You are only the followers of falsehood."

58. Wa laqad darabnaa linnaasi fee haazal-Qur'aani min kulli masal; wa la'in ji'tahum bi-Aayatil-la-yaqoolannal-lazeena kafarooo in antum illaa mubtiloon.

وَلَقَدۡ ضَرَبۡنَا لِلنَّاسِ فِىۡ هٰذَا الۡقُرۡاٰنِ
مِنۡ كُلِّ مَثَلٍ ؕ وَلَئِنۡ جِئۡتَهُمۡ بِاٰيَةٍ
لَّيَـقُوۡلَنَّ الَّذِيۡنَ كَفَرُوۡۤا اِنۡ
اَنۡتُمۡ اِلَّا مُبۡطِلُوۡنَ ﴿۵۸﴾

59. Thus does Allah seal the hearts of those who do not know.

59. Kazaalika yatba'ul-laahu 'alaa quloobil-lazeena laa ya'lamoon.

كَذٰلِكَ يَطۡبَعُ اللّٰهُ عَلٰى قُلُوۡبِ
الَّذِيۡنَ لَا يَعۡلَمُوۡنَ ﴿۵۹﴾

60. You must exercise patience. The promise of Allah is certainly true. Do not allow the faithless to make you (angry) despair.

60. Fasbir inna wa'dal-laahi haqquñw-wa laa yastakhif-fannakal-lazeena laa yooqinoon.

فَاصۡبِرۡ اِنَّ وَعۡدَ اللّٰهِ حَقٌّ وَّلَا ع ٦ ٧ ٩
يَسۡتَخِفَّنَّكَ الَّذِيۡنَ لَا يُوۡقِنُوۡنَ ﴿۶۰﴾

Luqman, Luqman (31)
In the Name of Allah, the Beneficent, the Merciful.

Sûrat Luqmân-31
(Revealed at Makkah)
Bismillaahir Rahmaanir Raheem

(٣١) سُوۡرَةُ لُقۡمٰنَ مَكِّيَّةٌ (٥٧)
اٰياتها ٣٤ بِسۡمِ اللّٰهِ الرَّحۡمٰنِ الرَّحِيۡمِ رُكُوعاتها ٤

1. Alif. Lam. Mim.

1. Alif-Laaam-Meeem.

الٓمّٓ ۚ ﴿۱﴾

2. These are the verses of the Book of wisdom.

2. Tilka Aayaatul-Kitaabil-Hakeem.

تِلۡكَ اٰيٰتُ الۡكِتٰبِ الۡحَكِيۡمِ ۙ ﴿۲﴾

3. A guidance and mercy for the righteous

3. Hudañw-wa rahmatal-lilmuhsineen.

هُدًى وَّرَحۡمَةً لِّلۡمُحۡسِنِيۡنَ ۙ ﴿۳﴾

4. people who are steadfast in prayer, pay the religious tax, and have firm belief in the life to come.

4. Allazeena yuqeemoonas-Salaata wa yu'toonaz-Zakaata wa hum bil-Aakhirati hum yooqinoon.

الَّذِيۡنَ يُقِيۡمُوۡنَ الصَّلٰوةَ وَيُؤۡتُوۡنَ
الزَّكٰوةَ وَهُمۡ بِالۡاٰخِرَةِ هُمۡ

5. They follow the (expressed) guidance of their Lord and they will have everlasting happiness.

6. There are people who pay for worthless tales (or activities) that deviates them from the path of Allah without their realizing such bad results. They treat the signs of Allah with ridicule. It is such people who will suffer a humiliating torment.

7. When Our revelations are recited to them, they turn back on their heels out of pride as if they did not hear them or their ears had been sealed off. Give them the news of their facing painful torment.

8. The righteously striving believers will enter blissful paradise

9. wherein they will live forever. It is the true promise of Allah. He is Majestic and All-wise.

10. He has created the heavens without any visible pillar as you can see, fixed the mountains on earth so that it may not shake you away, and settled therein all types of living creatures. We have sent down water from the sky and made all kinds of plants grow in gracious pairs.

11. This is the creature of Allah. Show me what those whom you consider equal to Allah have created. In fact, the unjust ones are in plain error.

12. We gave wisdom to Luqman so that he would give thanks to Allah. Those who give thanks to Allah do so for their own good. Those who are ungrateful should know that Allah is Self-sufficient and Praiseworthy.

5. Ulaaa'ika 'alaa hudam-mir-Rabbihim wa ulaaa'ika humul-mufliḥoon.

6. Wa minan-naasi mañy-yashtaree lahwal-ḥadeeṡi li-yuḍilla 'an sabeelil-laahi bighayri 'ilmiñw-wa yattakhiẕahaa huzuwaa; ulaaa'ika lahum 'aẕaabum-muheen.

7. Wa iẕaa tutlaa 'alayhi Aayaatunaa wallaa mustakbiran ka-allam yasma'haa ka-anna feee uẕunayhi waqran fabash-shirhu bi'aẕaabin aleem.

8. Innal-laẕeena aamanoo wa 'amiluṣ-ṣaaliḥaati lahum Jannaatun-Na'eem.

9. Khaalideena feehaa wa'dal-laahi ḥaqqaa; wa Huwal-'Azeezul-Ḥakeem.

10. Khalaqas-samaawaati bighayri 'amadin tarawnahaa wa alqaa fil-arḍi rawaasiya an tameeda bikum wa bassa feehaa min kulli daaabbah; wa anzalnaa minas-samaaa'i maaa'an fa-ambatnaa feehaa min kulli zawjin kareem.

11. Haaẕaa khalqul-laahi fa-aroonee maaẕaa khalaqal-laẕeena min doonih; baliẓ-ẓaa-limoona fee ḍalaalim Mubeen.

12. Wa laqad aataynaa Luqmaanal-ḥikmata anishkur lil-laah; wa mañy-yashkur fa-innamaa yashkuru linafsihee wa man kafara fa-innal-laaha Ghaniyyun Ḥameed.

يُوقِنُونَ ③
أُولٰٓئِكَ عَلٰى هُدًى مِّنْ رَّبِّهِمْ
وَأُولٰٓئِكَ هُمُ الْمُفْلِحُونَ ⑤
وَمِنَ النَّاسِ مَنْ يَّشْتَرِيْ لَهْوَ
الْحَدِيْثِ لِيُضِلَّ عَنْ سَبِيْلِ اللّٰهِ
بِغَيْرِ عِلْمٍ ۖ وَّيَتَّخِذَهَا هُزُوًا ۗ
أُولٰٓئِكَ لَهُمْ عَذَابٌ مُّهِيْنٌ ⑥
وَإِذَا تُتْلٰى عَلَيْهِ اٰيٰتُنَا وَلّٰى
مُسْتَكْبِرًا كَأَنْ لَّمْ يَسْمَعْهَا
كَأَنَّ فِيْٓ أُذُنَيْهِ وَقْرًا ۚ فَبَشِّرْهُ
بِعَذَابٍ أَلِيْمٍ ⑦
إِنَّ الَّذِيْنَ اٰمَنُوْا وَعَمِلُوا الصّٰلِحٰتِ
لَهُمْ جَنّٰتُ النَّعِيْمِ ⑧
خٰلِدِيْنَ فِيْهَا ۗ وَعْدَ اللّٰهِ حَقًّا ۗ
وَهُوَ الْعَزِيْزُ الْحَكِيْمُ ⑨
خَلَقَ السَّمٰوٰتِ بِغَيْرِ عَمَدٍ تَرَوْنَهَا
وَأَلْقٰى فِي الْأَرْضِ رَوَاسِيَ أَنْ
تَمِيْدَ بِكُمْ وَبَثَّ فِيْهَا مِنْ كُلِّ
دَآبَّةٍ ۗ وَأَنْزَلْنَا مِنَ السَّمَآءِ مَآءً
فَأَنْۢبَتْنَا فِيْهَا مِنْ كُلِّ زَوْجٍ كَرِيْمٍ ⑩
هٰذَا خَلْقُ اللّٰهِ فَأَرُوْنِيْ مَاذَا خَلَقَ
الَّذِيْنَ مِنْ دُوْنِهٖ ۗ بَلِ الظّٰلِمُوْنَ
فِيْ ضَلٰلٍ مُّبِيْنٍ ⑪ ع ١١
وَلَقَدْ اٰتَيْنَا لُقْمٰنَ الْحِكْمَةَ أَنِ
اشْكُرْ لِلّٰهِ ۗ وَمَنْ يَّشْكُرْ فَإِنَّمَا
يَشْكُرُ لِنَفْسِهٖ ۚ وَمَنْ كَفَرَ فَإِنَّ

اللّٰهَ غَنِيٌّ حَمِيْدٌ ﴿١٢﴾

13. Luqman advised his son, telling him, "My son, do not consider anything equal to Allah, for it is the greatest injustice."

13. Wa iz̲ qaala Luqmaanu libnihee wa huwa ya'iẓuhoo yaa bunayya laa tushrik billaahi innash-shirka laẓulmun 'aẓeem.

وَاِذْ قَالَ لُقْمٰنُ لِابْنِهٖ وَهُوَ يَعِظُهٗ
يٰبُنَيَّ لَا تُشْرِكْ بِاللّٰهِ ۗ اِنَّ الشِّرْكَ
لَظُلْمٌ عَظِيْمٌ ﴿١٣﴾

14. (Concerning his parents), We advised the man, whose mother bears him with great pain (weakness after weakness) and breast-feeds him for two years, to give thanks to Me first and then to them; to Me all things proceed.

14. Wa waṣṣaynal-insaana biwaalidayhi ḥamalathu ummuhoo wahnan 'alaa wahniñw-wa fiṣaaluhoo fee 'aamayni anishkur lee waliwaalidayka ilayyal-maṣeer.

وَوَصَّيْنَا الْاِنْسَانَ بِوَالِدَيْهِ ۚ حَمَلَتْهُ
اُمُّهٗ وَهْنًا عَلٰى وَهْنٍ وَّفِصٰلُهٗ
فِيْ عَامَيْنِ اَنِ اشْكُرْ لِيْ وَلِوَالِدَيْكَ ۗ
اِلَيَّ الْمَصِيْرُ ﴿١٤﴾

وقف النبي صلى الله عليه وآله وسلم ١٢ النصف

15. If they try to force you to consider things equal to Me, of which you have no knowledge, do not obey them. Maintain lawful relations with them in this world and follow the path of those who turn in repentance to Me. To Me you will all return and I shall tell you all that you have done.

15. Wa in jaahadaaka 'alaaa an tushrika bee maa laysa laka bihee 'ilmun falaa tuṭi'humaa wa ṣaaḥib-humaa fid-dunyaa ma'roofañw-wattabi' sabeela man anaaba ilayy; s̲umma ilayya marji'ukum fa-unabbi'ukum bimaa kuntum ta'maloon.

وَاِنْ جَاهَدٰكَ عَلٰٓى اَنْ تُشْرِكَ بِيْ
مَا لَيْسَ لَكَ بِهٖ عِلْمٌ فَلَا تُطِعْهُمَا
وَصَاحِبْهُمَا فِي الدُّنْيَا مَعْرُوْفًا ۡ
وَّاتَّبِعْ سَبِيْلَ مَنْ اَنَابَ اِلَيَّ ۚ ثُمَّ
اِلَيَّ مَرْجِعُكُمْ فَاُنَبِّئُكُمْ بِمَا كُنْتُمْ
تَعْمَلُوْنَ ﴿١٥﴾

16. "My son, Allah brings forth items of sustenance, even if they are as small as a grain of mustard seed, hidden in a rock or in the heavens or the earth. Allah is subtle and All-aware.

16. Yaa bunayya innahaaa in taku mis̲qaala ḥabbatim-min khardalin fatakun fee ṣakhratin aw fis-samaawaati aw fil-arḍi ya-ti bihal-laah; innal-laaha Laṭeefun Khabeer.

يٰبُنَيَّ اِنَّهَآ اِنْ تَكُ مِثْقَالَ حَبَّةٍ
مِّنْ خَرْدَلٍ فَتَكُنْ فِيْ صَخْرَةٍ اَوْ
فِي السَّمٰوٰتِ اَوْ فِي الْاَرْضِ يَاْتِ
بِهَا اللّٰهُ ۗ اِنَّ اللّٰهَ لَطِيْفٌ خَبِيْرٌ ﴿١٦﴾

17. My son, be steadfast in prayer. Make others do good. Prevent them from doing evil. Be patient in hardship. Patience comes from faith and determination.

17. Yaa bunayya aqimiṣ-Ṣalaata wa-mur bilma'roofi wanha 'anil-munkari waṣbir-'alaa maaa aṣaabaka inna z̲aalika min 'azmil-umoor.

يٰبُنَيَّ اَقِمِ الصَّلٰوةَ وَاْمُرْ بِالْمَعْرُوْفِ
وَانْهَ عَنِ الْمُنْكَرِ وَاصْبِرْ عَلٰى
مَآ اَصَابَكَ ۗ اِنَّ ذٰلِكَ مِنْ
عَزْمِ الْاُمُوْرِ ﴿١٧﴾

18. Do not show people that you are an inferior person. Do not walk around puffed-up with pride; Allah does not love arrogant and boastful people.

18. Wa laa tuṣa'-'ir khaddaka linnaasi wa laa tamshi fil-arḍi maraḥan innal-laaha laa yuḥibbu kulla mukhtaalin fakhoor.

وَلَا تُصَعِّرْ خَدَّكَ لِلنَّاسِ وَلَا
تَمْشِ فِي الْاَرْضِ مَرَحًا ۗ اِنَّ
اللّٰهَ لَا يُحِبُّ كُلَّ مُخْتَالٍ فَخُوْرٍ ﴿١٨﴾

19. Be moderate (slower) in your walking and your talking.

19. Waqṣid fee mashyika waghḍuḍ

وَاقْصِدْ فِيْ مَشْيِكَ وَاغْضُضْ

The most unpleasant sound is the braying of donkeys."	min şawtik; inna ankaral-aşwaati laşawtul-ḥameer.	مِنْ صَوْتِكَ ۚ إِنَّ أَنكَرَ الْأَصْوَاتِ لَصَوْتُ الْحَمِيرِ ﴿١٩﴾ ع ٨ ١١
20. Did you not see that Allah has made all that is in the heavens and the earth subservient to you (human beings), and has extended and perfected for you His apparent and unseen bounties (the Holy prophet and his family)? Some people argue about Allah without knowledge, guidance, or an enlightening book.	20. Alam taraw annal-laaha sakhkhara lakum-maa fis-samaawaati wa maa fil-arḍi wa asbagha 'alaykum ni'amahoo ẓaahiratañw-wa baaṭinah; wa minan-naasi mañy-yujaadilu fil-laahi bighayri 'ilmiñw-wa laa hudañw-wa laa Kitaabim-muneer.	أَلَمْ تَرَوْا أَنَّ اللَّهَ سَخَّرَ لَكُم مَّا فِي السَّمَاوَاتِ وَمَا فِي الْأَرْضِ وَأَسْبَغَ عَلَيْكُمْ نِعَمَهُ ظَاهِرَةً وَبَاطِنَةً ۗ وَمِنَ النَّاسِ مَن يُجَادِلُ فِي اللَّهِ بِغَيْرِ عِلْمٍ وَلَا هُدًى وَلَا كِتَابٍ مُّنِيرٍ ﴿٢٠﴾
21. When they are told to follow what Allah has revealed to them, they say, "We shall only follow our father's way of life." Will they follow it even if it is Satan who is calling them to the burning torment?	21. Wa iẕaa qeela lahumut-tabi'oo maaa anzalal-laahu qaaloo bal nattabi'u maa wajadnaa 'alayhi aabaaa'anaaa; awalaw kaanash-Shayṭaanu yad'oohum ilaa 'aẕaabis-sa'eer.	وَإِذَا قِيلَ لَهُمُ اتَّبِعُوا مَا أَنزَلَ اللَّهُ قَالُوا بَلْ نَتَّبِعُ مَا وَجَدْنَا عَلَيْهِ آبَاءَنَا ۚ أَوَلَوْ كَانَ الشَّيْطَانُ يَدْعُوهُمْ إِلَىٰ عَذَابِ السَّعِيرِ ﴿٢١﴾
22. Whoever submits himself to the will of Allah in righteousness has certainly achieved a stronghold. The end of all things is in the hands of Allah.	22. Wa mañy-yuslim wajhahooo ilal-laahi wa huwa muḥsinun faqadistamsaka bil'ur-watil-wusqaa; wa ilal-laahi 'aaqibatul-umoor.	وَمَن يُسْلِمْ وَجْهَهُ إِلَى اللَّهِ وَهُوَ مُحْسِنٌ فَقَدِ اسْتَمْسَكَ بِالْعُرْوَةِ الْوُثْقَىٰ ۗ وَإِلَى اللَّهِ عَاقِبَةُ الْأُمُورِ ﴿٢٢﴾
23. (Muhammad), do not allow the unbelievers grieve you. To Us they will all return and We shall tell them all about what they have done. Allah knows best what is in everyone's hearts.	23. Wa man kafara falaa yaḥzunka kufruh; ilaynaa marji'uhum fanunab-bi'uhum bimaa 'amilooo; innal-laaha 'aleemum biẕaatiş-şudoor.	وَمَن كَفَرَ فَلَا يَحْزُنكَ كُفْرُهُ ۚ إِلَيْنَا مَرْجِعُهُمْ فَنُنَبِّئُهُم بِمَا عَمِلُوا ۚ إِنَّ اللَّهَ عَلِيمٌ بِذَاتِ الصُّدُورِ ﴿٢٣﴾
24. We shall allow them to enjoy themselves for a short while, then force them into severe torment.	24. Numatti'uhum qaleelan summa naḍṭarruhum ilaa 'aẕaabin ghaleeẓ.	نُمَتِّعُهُمْ قَلِيلًا ثُمَّ نَضْطَرُّهُمْ إِلَىٰ عَذَابٍ غَلِيظٍ ﴿٢٤﴾
25. If you ask them, "Who has created the heavens and the earth," they will certainly say, "Allah has created them." Say, "It is only Allah who deserves all praise, but most of them do not know."	25. Wa la'in sa-altahum-man khalaqas-samaawaati wal-arḍa la-yaqoolunnal-laah; qulil-ḥamdu-lillaah; bal aksaruhum laa ya'lamoon.	وَلَئِن سَأَلْتَهُم مَّنْ خَلَقَ السَّمَاوَاتِ وَالْأَرْضَ لَيَقُولُنَّ اللَّهُ ۚ قُلِ الْحَمْدُ لِلَّهِ ۚ بَلْ أَكْثَرُهُمْ لَا يَعْلَمُونَ ﴿٢٥﴾
26. To Allah belongs all that is in the heavens and the earth. Allah is self-sufficient and praiseworthy.	26. Lillaahi maa fis-samaawaati wal-arḍ; innallaaha Huwal-Ghaniyyul-Ḥameed.	لِلَّهِ مَا فِي السَّمَاوَاتِ وَالْأَرْضِ ۚ إِنَّ اللَّهَ هُوَ الْغَنِيُّ الْحَمِيدُ ﴿٢٦﴾

27. If all the trees in the earth were pens and the ocean, with seven more oceans, were ink, still these could not suffice to record all the Words of Allah. Allah is Majestic and All-wise.

27. Wa law anna maa fil-arḍi min shajaratin aqlaamuñw-wal baḥru yamudduhoo mim ba'dihee sab'atu-abḥurim-maa nafidat Kalimaatul-laah; innallaaha 'Azeezun Ḥakeem.

وَلَوْ أَنَّ مَا فِي الْأَرْضِ مِنْ شَجَرَةٍ
أَقْلَامٌ وَّالْبَحْرُ يَمُدُّهُ مِنْ بَعْدِهِ
سَبْعَةُ أَبْحُرٍ مَّا نَفِدَتْ كَلِمٰتُ
اللّٰهِ ۭ إِنَّ اللّٰهَ عَزِيزٌ حَكِيمٌ ﴿٢٧﴾

28. For Allah your creation and your resurrection are only like the creation and resurrection of one soul. Allah is All-hearing and All-seeing.

28. Maa khalqukum wa laa ba'ṯukum illaa kanafsiñw-waaḥidah; innal-laaha Samee'um Baṣeer.

مَا خَلْقُكُمْ وَلَا بَعْثُكُمْ إِلَّا كَنَفْسٍ
وَّاحِدَةٍ ۭ إِنَّ اللّٰهَ سَمِيعٌ بَصِيرٌ ﴿٢٨﴾

29. Did you not see that Allah causes the night to enter into the day and the day into the night? He has made the sun and moon subservient (to Himself). Each moves (in an orbit) for an appointed time. Allah is certainly All-aware of what you do.

29. Alam tara annal-laaha yoolijul-layla fin-nahaari wa yoolijun-nahaara fil-layli wa sakhkharash-shamsa wal-qamara kulluñy-yajreee ilaaa ajalim-musammañw-wa annal-laaha bimaa ta'maloona Khabeer.

أَلَمْ تَرَ أَنَّ اللّٰهَ يُولِجُ الَّيْلَ فِي
النَّهَارِ وَيُولِجُ النَّهَارَ فِي الَّيْلِ وَ
سَخَّرَ الشَّمْسَ وَالْقَمَرَ ۡ كُلٌّ يَّجْرِيٓ
إِلٰٓى أَجَلٍ مُّسَمًّى وَّأَنَّ اللّٰهَ بِمَا
تَعْمَلُونَ خَبِيرٌ ﴿٢٩﴾

30. This is because Allah is the supreme Truth and whatever they worship besides Him is falsehood. Allah is the Most High and the Most Great.

30. Ẕaalika bi-annal-laaha Huwal-Ḥaqqu wa anna maa yad'oona min doonihil-baaṭilu wa annal-laaha Huwal-'Aliyyul-Kabeer.

ذٰلِكَ بِأَنَّ اللّٰهَ هُوَ الْحَقُّ وَأَنَّ
مَا يَدْعُونَ مِنْ دُونِهِ الْبٰطِلُ
وَأَنَّ اللّٰهَ هُوَ الْعَلِيُّ الْكَبِيرُ ﴿٣٠﴾ ع ۳ ۱۱ ۱۲

31. Did you not see the ships sail in the ocean through the bounty of Allah so that He may show you the evidence (of His existence)? There is evidence (of the truth) in this for every forbearing and grateful one.

31. Alam tara annal-fulka tajree fil-baḥri bini'matil-laahi li-yuriyakum-min Aayaatih; inna fee ẕaalika la-Aayaatil-likulli ṣabbaarin shakoor.

أَلَمْ تَرَ أَنَّ الْفُلْكَ تَجْرِي فِي
الْبَحْرِ بِنِعْمَتِ اللّٰهِ لِيُرِيَكُمْ مِّنْ
اٰيٰتِهِ ۭ إِنَّ فِي ذٰلِكَ لَاٰيٰتٍ لِّكُلِّ
صَبَّارٍ شَكُورٍ ﴿٣١﴾

32. When the waves cover them like shadows, they pray to Allah with sincerity in their religion, but when We bring them safely to land, only some of them follow the right path (as virtuous people). No one rejects Our revelations except the treacherous ungrateful ones.

32. Wa iẕaa ghashiyahum-mawjun kaẓẓulali da'awullaaha mukhliṣeena lahud-deena falammaa najjaahum ilal-barri faminhum-muqtaṣid; wa maa yajḥadu bi-Aayaatinaaa illaa kullu khattaarin kafoor.

وَإِذَا غَشِيَهُمْ مَّوْجٌ كَالظُّلَلِ
دَعَوُا اللّٰهَ مُخْلِصِينَ لَهُ الدِّينَ ۚ
فَلَمَّا نَجّٰىهُمْ إِلَى الْبَرِّ فَمِنْهُمْ
مُّقْتَصِدٌ ۭ وَمَا يَجْحَدُ بِاٰيٰتِنَآ إِلَّا
كُلُّ خَتَّارٍ كَفُورٍ ﴿٣٢﴾

33. Mankind, have fear of your Lord and the day when a father will be of no avail to his son, nor will a son carry any part of the burden of his father. The promise of Allah is true. Do not allow the

33. Yaaa ayyuhan-naasut-taqoo Rabbakum wakhshaw Yawmal-laa yajzee waalidun 'añw-waladihee wa laa mawloodun huwa

يٰٓأَيُّهَا النَّاسُ اتَّقُوا رَبَّكُمْ
وَاخْشَوْا يَوْمًا لَّا يَجْزِي وَالِدٌ
عَنْ وَّلَدِهِ ز وَلَا مَوْلُودٌ هُوَ

جَازٍ عَنْ وَّالِدِهٖ شَيْـًٔا ؕ اِنَّ
وَعْدَ اللّٰهِ حَقٌّ فَلَا تَغُرَّنَّكُمُ
الْحَيٰوةُ الدُّنْيَا ٙ وَلَا يَغُرَّنَّكُمْ
بِاللّٰهِ الْغَرُوْرُ ﴿۳۳﴾

jaazin 'añw-waalidihee shay-'aa; inna wa'dal-laahi ḥaqqun falaa taghurran-nakumul-ḥayaatud-dunyaa wa laa yaghurrannakum billaahil-gharoor.

worldly life deceive you nor permit your pride deceive you about Allah.

اِنَّ اللّٰهَ عِنْدَهٗ عِلْمُ السَّاعَةِ ۚ
وَيُنَزِّلُ الْغَيْثَ ۚ وَيَعْلَمُ مَا فِى
الْاَرْحَامِ ؕ وَمَا تَدْرِىْ نَفْسٌ مَّا
ذَا تَكْسِبُ غَدًا ؕ وَمَا تَدْرِىْ
نَفْسٌۢ بِاَىِّ اَرْضٍ تَمُوْتُ ؕ اِنَّ
اللّٰهَ عَلِيْمٌ خَبِيْرٌ ﴿۳۴﴾ ع ١٤

34. Innal-laaha 'indahoo 'il-mus-Saa'ati wa yunazzilul-ghaysa wa ya'lamu maa fil-arḥaami wa maa tadree nafsum-maazaa taksibu ghadaa; wa maa tadree nafsum bi-ayyi arḍin tamoot; innallaaha 'Aleemun Khabeer.

34. Only Allah has the knowledge of the coming of the Hour of Doom. He sends down the rain and knows what is in the wombs. No soul is aware of what it will achieve tomorrow and no soul knows in which land it will die. Allah is All-knowing and All-aware.

(۳۲) سُوْرَةُ السَّجْدَةِ مَكِّيَّةٌ (۷۵)
آياتها ٣٠ — بِسْمِ اللّٰهِ الرَّحْمٰنِ الرَّحِيْمِ — ركوعاتها ٣

Sûrat as-Sajdah-32

(Revealed at Makkah)

Bismillaahir Raḥmaanir Raḥeem

Al-Sajdah, The Prostration (32)

In the Name of Allah, the Beneficent, the Merciful.

الٓمّٓ ﴿۱﴾

1. Alif-Laaam-Meeem.

1. Alif. Lam. Mim.

تَنْزِيْلُ الْكِتٰبِ لَا رَيْبَ فِيْهِ مِنْ
رَّبِّ الْعٰلَمِيْنَ ﴿۲﴾

2. Tanzeelul-Kitaabi laa rayba feehi mir-Rabbil 'aalameen.

2. There is no doubt that this Book is revealed by the Lord of the universe.

اَمْ يَقُوْلُوْنَ افْتَرٰىهُ ۚ بَلْ هُوَ الْحَقُّ
مِنْ رَّبِّكَ لِتُنْذِرَ قَوْمًا مَّآ اَتٰىهُمْ
مِّنْ نَّذِيْرٍ مِّنْ قَبْلِكَ لَعَلَّهُمْ
يَهْتَدُوْنَ ﴿۳﴾

3. Am yaqooloonaf-taraah; bal huwal-ḥaqqu mir-Rabbika litunzira qawmam-maaa ataahum-min-nazeerim-min qablika la'allahum yahtadoon.

3. Do they say that he, (Muhammad), has invented it? No, it is the truth from your Lord so that you will warn the people who have not received a warning before you. Perhaps they will seek guidance.

اَللّٰهُ الَّذِىْ خَلَقَ السَّمٰوٰتِ وَالْاَرْضَ
وَمَا بَيْنَهُمَا فِىْ سِتَّةِ اَيَّامٍ ثُمَّ
اسْتَوٰى عَلَى الْعَرْشِ ؕ مَا لَكُمْ مِّنْ
دُوْنِهٖ مِنْ وَّلِىٍّ وَّلَا شَفِيْعٍ ؕ
اَفَلَا تَتَذَكَّرُوْنَ ﴿۴﴾

4. Allaahul-lazee khalaqas-samaawaati wal-arḍa wa maa baynahumaa fee sittati ayyaamin summas-tawaa 'alal-'Arshi maa lakum-min doonihee miñw-waliyyiñw-wa laa shafee'; afalaa tatazakkaroon.

4. Allah is the one who created the heavens and the earth and all that is between them in six days, then He established His dominion over the Throne. No one besides Him is your guardian or intercessor. Will you then not take heed?

يُدَبِّرُ الْاَمْرَ مِنَ السَّمَآءِ اِلَى
الْاَرْضِ ثُمَّ يَعْرُجُ اِلَيْهِ فِىْ

5. Yudabbirul-amra minas-samaaa'i ilal-arḍi summa ya'ruju ilayhi fee

5. He sends the regulation of the affairs from the heavens to the earth, then on the day which is equal to one thousand years of

yours, it will ascend to Him.

yawmin kaana miqdaaruhooo alfa sanatim-mimmaa ta'ud-doon.

يَوْمٍ كَانَ مِقْدَارُهٗۤ اَلْفَ سَنَةٍ
مِّمَّا تَعُدُّوْنَ ۝٥

6. He knows the unseen and the seen. He is Majestic and All-merciful.

6. Zaalika 'Aalimul-Ghaybi wash-shahaadatil-'Azeezur-Raḥeem.

ذٰلِكَ عٰلِمُ الْغَيْبِ وَالشَّهَادَةِ
الْعَزِيْزُ الرَّحِيْمُ ۝٦

7. It is He Who created everything in the best manner and began the creation of the human being from clay.

7. Allazeee aḥsana kulla shay'in khalaqahoo wa bada-a khalqal-insaani min ṭeen.

الَّذِيْۤ اَحْسَنَ كُلَّ شَيْءٍ خَلَقَهٗ
وَبَدَاَ خَلْقَ الْاِنْسَانِ مِنْ طِيْنٍ ۝٧

8. He made His offspring come into existence from an extract of insignificant fluid,

8. Summa ja'ala naslahoo min sulaalatim-mim-maaa'im-maheen.

ثُمَّ جَعَلَ نَسْلَهٗ مِنْ سُلٰلَةٍ مِّنْ
مَّآءٍ مَّهِيْنٍ ۝٨

9. then He gave it proper shape and blew His spirit into it. He made ears, eyes and hearts for you, but you give Him very little thanks.

9. Summa sawwaahu wa nafakha feehi mir-rooḥihee wa ja'ala lakumus-sam'a wal-abṣaara wal-af'idah; qaleelam-maa tashkuroon.

ثُمَّ سَوّٰىهُ وَنَفَخَ فِيْهِ مِنْ رُّوْحِهٖ
وَجَعَلَ لَكُمُ السَّمْعَ وَالْاَبْصَارَ
وَالْاَفْـِٕدَةَ ؕ قَلِيْلًا مَّا تَشْكُرُوْنَ ۝٩

10. They have said, "How can we be brought to life again after we have been lost in the earth?" In fact, they have no faith in meeting their Lord (brought in His presence on the Day of Judgment).

10. Wa qaalooo 'a-izaa ḍalalnaa fil-arḍi 'a-innaa lafee khalqin jadeed; bal hum biliqaaa'i Rabbihim kaafiroon.

وَقَالُوْۤا ءَاِذَا ضَلَلْنَا فِي الْاَرْضِ
ءَاِنَّا لَفِيْ خَلْقٍ جَدِيْدٍ ؕ بَلْ هُمْ
بِلِقَآئِ رَبِّهِمْ كٰفِرُوْنَ ۝١٠

11. (Muhammad), say, "The angel of death, who is appointed over every one of you, will cause you to die and to your Lord you will all return."

11. Qul yatawaf-faakum-Malakul-Mawtil-lazee wukkila bikum summa ilaa Rabbikum turja'oon.

قُلْ يَتَوَفّٰىكُمْ مَّلَكُ الْمَوْتِ
الَّذِيْ وُكِّلَ بِكُمْ ثُمَّ اِلٰى
رَبِّكُمْ تُرْجَعُوْنَ ۝١١ ع ١١ ١٤

12. Would that you could see (on the Day of Judgment) that criminals, with their heads hanging down before their Lord, say, "Our Lord, we have seen and heard. Send us back to act righteously. Now we have strong faith."

12. Wa law taraaa izil-mujrimoona naakisoo ru'oosihim 'inda Rabbihim Rabbanaaa abṣarnaa wa sami'naa farji'naa na'mal ṣaaliḥan innaa mooqinoon.

وَلَوْ تَرٰۤى اِذِ الْمُجْرِمُوْنَ نَاكِسُوْا
رُءُوْسِهِمْ عِنْدَ رَبِّهِمْ ؕ رَبَّنَاۤ
اَبْصَرْنَا وَسَمِعْنَا فَارْجِعْنَا نَعْمَلْ
صَالِحًا اِنَّا مُوْقِنُوْنَ ۝١٢

13. Had We wanted, We could have given guidance (that would not allow him to fail) to every soul, but My decree, that hell will be filled-up with jinn and people, has already been executed.

13. Wa law shi'naa la-aataynaa kulla nafsin hudaahaa wa laakin ḥaqqal-qawlu minnee la-amla'anna Jahannama minal-jinnati wannaasi ajma'een.

وَلَوْ شِئْنَا لَاٰتَيْنَا كُلَّ نَفْسٍ
هُدٰىهَا وَلٰكِنْ حَقَّ الْقَوْلُ
مِنِّيْ لَاَمْلَئَنَّ جَهَنَّمَ مِنَ الْجِنَّةِ
وَالنَّاسِ اَجْمَعِيْنَ ۝١٣

14. They will be told, "Suffer on this Day of Judgment. For your

14. Fazooqoo bimaa naseetum liqaaa'a Yawmikum

فَذُوْقُوْا بِمَا نَسِيْتُمْ لِقَآءَ يَوْمِكُمْ

having ignored it (the meeting), We have ignored you (left you to yourselves). Suffer everlasting torment for your evil deeds."	haaz̲aaa innaa naseenaakum wa z̲ooqoo 'az̲aabal-khuldi bimaa kuntum ta'maloon.	هٰذَا ۚ اِنَّا نَسِيْنٰكُمْ وَذُوْقُوْا عَذَابَ الْخُلْدِ بِمَا كُنْتُمْ تَعْمَلُوْنَ ﴿١٤﴾
15. The only people who believe in Our revelations are those who, when reminded about them, bow down in prostration and glorify their Lord with His praise without pride.	15. Innamaa yu'minu bi-Aayaatinal-laz̲eena iz̲aa z̲ukkiroo bihaa kharroo sujjadañw-wa sabbaḥoo biḥamdi Rabbihim wa hum laa yastakbiroon. ۩	اِنَّمَا يُؤْمِنُ بِاٰيٰتِنَا الَّذِيْنَ اِذَا ذُكِّرُوْا بِهَا خَرُّوْا سُجَّدًا وَّسَبَّحُوْا بِحَمْدِ رَبِّهِمْ وَهُمْ لَا يَسْتَكْبِرُوْنَ ۩ ﴿١٥﴾
16. Their sides give up rest in beds in order to pray before their Lord in fear and hope. They spend for the cause of Allah out of what we have given them	16. Tatajaafaa junoobuhum 'anil-maḍaaji'i yad'oona Rabbahum khawfañw-wa ṭama'añw-wa mimmaa razaqnaahum yunfiqoon.	تَتَجَافٰى جُنُوْبُهُمْ عَنِ الْمَضَاجِعِ يَدْعُوْنَ رَبَّهُمْ خَوْفًا وَّطَمَعًا ۫ وَّمِمَّا رَزَقْنٰهُمْ يُنْفِقُوْنَ ﴿١٦﴾
17. No soul knows what delight awaits them as the reward for their deeds.	17. Falaa ta'lamu nafsum-maaa ukhfiya lahum-min qurrati a'yunin jazaaa'am bimaa kaanoo ya'maloon.	فَلَا تَعْلَمُ نَفْسٌ مَّآ اُخْفِيَ لَهُمْ مِّنْ قُرَّةِ اَعْيُنٍ ۚ جَزَآءًۢ بِمَا كَانُوْا يَعْمَلُوْنَ ﴿١٧﴾
18. Is a believer equal to an evil-doer? They are not equal at all.	18. Afaman kaana mu'minan kaman kaana faasiqaa; laa yastawoon.	اَفَمَنْ كَانَ مُؤْمِنًا كَمَنْ كَانَ فَاسِقًا ؕ لَا يَسْتَوٗنَ ﴿١٨﴾
19. The righteously striving believers will have Paradise for their dwelling as the reward of their good deeds.	19. Ammal-laz̲eena aamanoo wa 'amiluṣ-ṣaaliḥaati falahum Jannaatul-ma-waa nuzulam bimaa kaanoo ya'maloon.	اَمَّا الَّذِيْنَ اٰمَنُوْا وَعَمِلُوا الصّٰلِحٰتِ فَلَهُمْ جَنّٰتُ الْمَاْوٰى ۫ نُزُلًۢا بِمَا كَانُوْا يَعْمَلُوْنَ ﴿١٩﴾
20. However, the dwelling of the sinful ones will be hellfire. Each time they try to come out, they will be turned back with this remark, "Suffer the torment of the fire which you had called a lie."	20. Wa ammal-laz̲eena fasaqoo fama-waahumun-Naaru kullamaaa araadooo añy-yakhrujoo minhaaa u'eedoo feehaa wa qeela lahum z̲ooqoo 'az̲aaban-Naaril-laz̲ee kuntum bihee tukaz̲z̲iboon.	وَاَمَّا الَّذِيْنَ فَسَقُوْا فَمَاْوٰىهُمُ النَّارُ ؕ كُلَّمَآ اَرَادُوْٓا اَنْ يَّخْرُجُوْا مِنْهَآ اُعِيْدُوْا فِيْهَا وَقِيْلَ لَهُمْ ذُوْقُوْا عَذَابَ النَّارِ الَّذِيْ كُنْتُمْ بِهٖ تُكَذِّبُوْنَ ﴿٢٠﴾
21. We shall certainly make them suffer worldly torment before suffering the great torment so that perhaps they may return to Us.	21. Wa lanuz̲eeqan-nahum minal-'az̲aabil-adnaa doonal 'az̲aabil-akbari la'allahum yarji'oon.	وَلَنُذِيْقَنَّهُمْ مِّنَ الْعَذَابِ الْاَدْنٰى دُوْنَ الْعَذَابِ الْاَكْبَرِ لَعَلَّهُمْ يَرْجِعُوْنَ ﴿٢١﴾
22. Who are more unjust than those who are reminded of the revelation of their Lord, but have ignored it? We will subject the	22. Wa man aẓlamu mim-man z̲ukkira bi-Aayaati Rabbihee s̲umma a'raḍa 'anhaaa; innaa minal-	وَمَنْ اَظْلَمُ مِمَّنْ ذُكِّرَ بِاٰيٰتِ رَبِّهٖ ثُمَّ اَعْرَضَ عَنْهَا ؕ اِنَّا مِنَ

السَّجْدَة ٩

وقف غفران

وقف غفران

criminals to Our retribution.

mujrimeena muntaqimoon.

الْمُجْرِمِينَ مُنْتَقِمُونَ ﴿٢٢﴾ ع

23. We gave the Book to Moses - do not have any doubt about the Day of Judgment - and made it a guide for the children of Israel.

23. Wa laqad aataynaa Moo-sal-Kitaaba falaa takun fee miryatim-mil-liqaaa'ihee wa ja'alnaahu hudal-li-Baneee Israaa'eel.

وَلَقَدْ آتَيْنَا مُوسَى الْكِتَابَ فَلَا
تَكُنْ فِي مِرْيَةٍ مِّنْ لِّقَائِهِ
وَجَعَلْنَاهُ هُدًى لِّبَنِي إِسْرَائِيلَ ﴿٢٣﴾

24. We appointed some of the Israelites as leaders for their exercising patience to guide the others to Our commands. They had firm belief in Our revelations.

24. Wa ja'alnaa minhum a'immatañy-yahdoona bi-amri-naa lammaa ṣabaroo wa kaanoo bi-Aayaatinaa yooqinoon.

وَجَعَلْنَا مِنْهُمْ أَئِمَّةً يَهْدُونَ
بِأَمْرِنَا لَمَّا صَبَرُوا ۖ وَكَانُوا
بِآيَاتِنَا يُوقِنُونَ ﴿٢٤﴾

25. Your Lord will issue His decree about their (believers' and disbelievers') differences on the Day of Judgment.

25. Inna Rabbaka Huwa yafṣilu baynahum Yawmal-Qiyaamati feemaa kaanoo feehi yakhtalifoon.

إِنَّ رَبَّكَ هُوَ يَفْصِلُ بَيْنَهُمْ يَوْمَ
الْقِيَامَةِ فِيمَا كَانُوا فِيهِ يَخْتَلِفُونَ ﴿٢٥﴾

26. Was it not a lesson for them (the unbelievers), that We destroyed the many generations living before them among whose ruined dwellings they are now walking? In this there is much evidence (of the truth). Will they then not listen?

26. Awalam yahdi lahum kam ahlaknaa min qablihim-minal-qurooni yamshoona fee masaa-kinihim; inna fee zaalika la-Aayaat afalaa yasma'oon.

أَوَلَمْ يَهْدِ لَهُمْ كَمْ أَهْلَكْنَا مِنْ
قَبْلِهِمْ مِّنَ الْقُرُونِ يَمْشُونَ فِي
مَسَاكِنِهِمْ ۚ إِنَّ فِي ذَٰلِكَ لَآيَاتٍ ۖ
أَفَلَا يَسْمَعُونَ ﴿٢٦﴾

27. Did they not seen that We drive the water to the barren land and cause crops to grow which they and their cattle consume? Why then will they not see?

27. Awalam yaraw annaa nasooqul-maaa'a ilal-arḍil-juruzi fanukhriju bihee zar'an ta-kulu minhu an'aamuhum wa anfusuhum afalaa yubṣiroon.

أَوَلَمْ يَرَوْا أَنَّا نَسُوقُ الْمَاءَ إِلَى
الْأَرْضِ الْجُرُزِ فَنُخْرِجُ بِهِ زَرْعًا
تَأْكُلُ مِنْهُ أَنْعَامُهُمْ وَأَنْفُسُهُمْ ۖ
أَفَلَا يُبْصِرُونَ ﴿٢٧﴾ الثلاثة

28. They say, "If what you say is true, when will the final triumph come?"

28. Wa yaqooloona mataa haazal-fatḥu in kuntum ṣaadi-qeen.

وَيَقُولُونَ مَتَىٰ هَٰذَا الْفَتْحُ إِنْ
كُنْتُمْ صَادِقِينَ ﴿٢٨﴾

29. (Muhammad), say, "On the day of the final triumph, the faith of the unbelievers will be of no avail to them, nor will they be given any respite."

29. Qul Yawmal-fatḥi laa yanfa'ul-lazeena kafarooo eemaanuhum wa laa hum yunẓaroon.

قُلْ يَوْمَ الْفَتْحِ لَا يَنْفَعُ الَّذِينَ
كَفَرُوا إِيمَانُهُمْ وَلَا هُمْ يُنْظَرُونَ ﴿٢٩﴾

30. Turn away from them and wait. They are also waiting.

30. Fa-a'riḍ 'anhum wantaẓir innahum-muntaẓiroon.

فَأَعْرِضْ عَنْهُمْ وَانْتَظِرْ إِنَّهُمْ
مُّنْتَظِرُونَ ﴿٣٠﴾ ع

Al-Ahzab, The Confederates (33)

In the Name of Allah, the Beneficent, the Merciful.

Sûrat al-Aḥzâb-33

(Revealed at Madinah)

Bismillaahir Raḥmaanir Raḥeem

(٣٣) سُورَةُ الْأَحْزَابِ مَدَنِيَّةٌ (٩٠)

آياتها ٧٣ بِسْمِ اللَّهِ الرَّحْمَٰنِ الرَّحِيمِ ركوعاتها ٩

1. O prophet, have fear of Allah and do not yield to the infidels and hypocrites

1. Yaaa ayyuhan-Nabiy-yuttaqil-laaha wa laa tuṭi'il-

يَا أَيُّهَا النَّبِيُّ اتَّقِ اللَّهَ وَلَا تُطِعِ

(one of the examples in the Quran where the Holy Prophet is addressed but people are meant thereby). Allah is All-knowing and All-wise.

kaafireena wal-munaafiqeen; innal-laaha kaana 'Aleeman Ḥakeemaa.

الْكٰفِرِيْنَ وَالْمُنٰفِقِيْنَ ۭ اِنَّ اللّٰهَ كَانَ
عَلِيْمًا حَكِيْمًا ①

2. Follow what has been revealed to you from your Lord. Allah is All-aware of what you do.

2. Wattabi' maa yooḥaaa ilayka mir-Rabbik; innallaaha kaana bimaa ta'maloona Khabeeraa.

وَّاتَّبِعْ مَا يُوْحٰٓى اِلَيْكَ مِنْ رَّبِّكَ ۭ
اِنَّ اللّٰهَ كَانَ بِمَا تَعْمَلُوْنَ خَبِيْرًا ②

3. Trust in Allah and be sure that He is a Sufficient Guardian.

3. Wa tawakkal'alal-laah; wa kafaa billaahi Wakeelaa.

وَّتَوَكَّلْ عَلَى اللّٰهِ ۭ وَكَفٰى بِاللّٰهِ
وَكِيْلًا ③

4. Allah has not created two hearts inside any one human being. Allah does not consider your wives whom you renounce by zihar as your mothers nor those whom you adopt as your sons. These are only words of your mouth. Allah tells the Truth and shows the right path.

4. Maa ja'alal-laahu lirajulim-min qalbayni fee jawfih; wa maa ja'ala azwaajakumullaaa'i tuẓaahiroona minhunna ummahaatikum; wa maa ja'ala ad'iyaaa'akum abnaaa'akum; ẕaalikum qawlukum bi-afwaahikum wallaahu yaqoolulḥaqqa wa Huwa yahdis-sabeel.

مَا جَعَلَ اللّٰهُ لِرَجُلٍ مِّنْ قَلْبَيْنِ
فِيْ جَوْفِهٖ ۚ وَمَا جَعَلَ اَزْوَاجَكُمُ
الّٰۗـِٔيْ تُظٰهِرُوْنَ مِنْهُنَّ اُمَّهٰتِكُمْ ۚ
وَمَا جَعَلَ اَدْعِيَاۗءَكُمْ اَبْنَاۗءَكُمْ ۭ
ذٰلِكُمْ قَوْلُكُمْ بِاَفْوَاهِكُمْ ۭ وَاللّٰهُ
يَقُوْلُ الْحَقَّ وَهُوَ يَهْدِي السَّبِيْلَ ④

5. Call them sons of their own fathers. It is more just in the eyes of Allah. If you did not know their fathers, they are your brothers and friends in religion. You will not be responsible for your mistakes, but you will be responsible for what you do intentionally. Allah is All-forgiving and All-merciful.

5. Ud'oohum li-aabaaa'ihim huwa aqsaṭu 'indal-laah; fa-illam ta'lamooo aabaaa'ahum fa-ikhwaanukum fid-deeni wa mawaaleekum; wa laysa 'alaykum junaaḥun feemaaa akhṭatum bihee wa laakim-maa ta'ammadat quloobukum; wa kaanal-laahu Ghafoorar-Raḥeemaa.

اُدْعُوْهُمْ لِاٰبَاۗىِٕهِمْ هُوَ اَقْسَطُ
عِنْدَ اللّٰهِ ۚ فَاِنْ لَّمْ تَعْلَمُوْٓا اٰبَاۗءَهُمْ
فَاِخْوَانُكُمْ فِي الدِّيْنِ وَمَوَالِيْكُمْ ۭ
وَلَيْسَ عَلَيْكُمْ جُنَاحٌ فِيْمَآ اَخْطَاْتُمْ
بِهٖ ۙ وَلٰكِنْ مَّا تَعَمَّدَتْ قُلُوْبُكُمْ ۭ
وَكَانَ اللّٰهُ غَفُوْرًا رَّحِيْمًا ⑤

6. The Prophet has more authority over the believers than themselves. His wives are their mothers. The relatives, according to the Book of Allah, are closer to each other than the believers and the emigrants. However, you may show kindness to your guardians. This, also, is written in the Book.

6. An-Nabiyyu awlaa bilmu'mineena min anfusihim wa azwaajuhooo ummahaatuhum; wa ulul-arḥaami ba'ḍuhum awlaa biba'ḍin fee Kitaabillaahi minal-mu'mineena wal-Muhaajireena illaaa an taf'alooo ilaaa awliyaaa'ikum-ma'roofaa; kaana ẕaalika fil-Kitaabi masṭooraa.

اَلنَّبِيُّ اَوْلٰى بِالْمُؤْمِنِيْنَ مِنْ
اَنْفُسِهِمْ وَاَزْوَاجُهٗٓ اُمَّهٰتُهُمْ ۭ
وَاُولُوا الْاَرْحَامِ بَعْضُهُمْ اَوْلٰى
بِبَعْضٍ فِيْ كِتٰبِ اللّٰهِ مِنَ
الْمُؤْمِنِيْنَ وَالْمُهٰجِرِيْنَ اِلَّآ اَنْ تَفْعَلُوْٓا
اِلٰٓى اَوْلِيٰۗىِٕكُمْ مَّعْرُوْفًا ۭ كَانَ ذٰلِكَ
فِي الْكِتٰبِ مَسْطُوْرًا ⑥

7. We had a solemn covenant with you (Muhammad), and the

7. Wa iẕ akhaẕnaa minan-Nabiyyeena meeṡaaqahum

وَاِذْ اَخَذْنَا مِنَ النَّبِيّٖنَ مِيْثَاقَهُمْ

Prophets: Noah, Abraham, Moses, and Jesus, the son of Mary.

wa minka wa min-Nooḥiñw-wa Ibraaheema wa Moosaa wa 'Eesab-ni-Maryama wa-akhaẕ-naa minhum-meesaaqan gha-leeẓaa.

وَمِنكَ وَمِن نُّوحٍ وَإِبْرَٰهِيمَ
وَمُوسَىٰ وَعِيسَى ٱبْنِ مَرْيَمَ ۖ
وَأَخَذْنَا مِنْهُم مِّيثَٰقًا غَلِيظًا ﴿٧﴾

8. This was a firm agreement. Allah will ask the truthful ones about their truthfulness and prepare a painful torment for the unbelievers.

8. Liyas'alaṣ-ṣaadiqeena 'an ṣidqihim; wa a'adda lilkaa-fireena 'aẕaaban aleemaa.

لِّيَسْـَٔلَ ٱلصَّٰدِقِينَ عَن صِدْقِهِمْ ۚ
وَأَعَدَّ لِلْكَٰفِرِينَ عَذَابًا أَلِيمًا ﴿٨﴾

9. Believers, recall Allah's favor to you when the army attacked you. We sent a wind and the armies, which you did not see, to support you. Allah sees all that you do.

9. Yaaa ayyuhal-laẕeena aamanuẕ-kuroo ni'matallaahi 'alaykum iẕ jaaa'atkum junoo-dun fa-arsalnaa 'alayhim reeḥañw-wa junoodal-lam tarawhaa; wa kaanal-laahu bimaa ta'maloona Baṣeeraa.

يَٰٓأَيُّهَا ٱلَّذِينَ ءَامَنُوا۟ ٱذْكُرُوا۟ نِعْمَةَ
ٱللَّهِ عَلَيْكُمْ إِذْ جَآءَتْكُمْ جُنُودٌ
فَأَرْسَلْنَا عَلَيْهِمْ رِيحًا وَجُنُودًا
لَّمْ تَرَوْهَا ۚ وَكَانَ ٱللَّهُ بِمَا تَعْمَلُونَ
بَصِيرًا ﴿٩﴾

10. Eyes became dull and hearts almost reached the throat when they attacked you from above and below and you started to think of Allah with suspicion.

10. Iẕ jaaa'ookum-min fawqi-kum wa min asfala minkum wa iẕ zaaghatil-abṣaaru wa bala-ghatil-quloobul-ḥanaajira wa taẓunnoona billaahiẓ-ẓunoo-naa.

إِذْ جَآءُوكُم مِّن فَوْقِكُمْ وَمِنْ
أَسْفَلَ مِنكُمْ وَإِذْ زَاغَتِ ٱلْأَبْصَٰرُ
وَبَلَغَتِ ٱلْقُلُوبُ ٱلْحَنَاجِرَ وَتَظُنُّونَ
بِٱللَّهِ ٱلظُّنُونَا۠ ﴿١٠﴾

11. There the believers were tested and tremendously shaken.

11. Hunaalikab-tuliyal-mu'-minoona wa zulziloo zilzaalan shadeedaa.

هُنَالِكَ ٱبْتُلِىَ ٱلْمُؤْمِنُونَ وَزُلْزِلُوا۟
زِلْزَالًا شَدِيدًا ﴿١١﴾

12. It was there that the hypocrites and those whose hearts were sick, said, "The promise of Allah and His messenger has proved to be nothing but deceit."

12. Wa-iẕ yaqoolul-munaafi-qoona wallaẕeena fee quloo-bihim-maraḍum-maa wa'ada-nal-laahu wa Rasooluhooo illaa ghurooraa.

وَإِذْ يَقُولُ ٱلْمُنَٰفِقُونَ وَٱلَّذِينَ فِى
قُلُوبِهِم مَّرَضٌ مَّا وَعَدَنَا ٱللَّهُ
وَرَسُولُهُۥٓ إِلَّا غُرُورًا ﴿١٢﴾

13. It was there that a group of them said, "People of Yathrib, turn back for there is no place for you to stay." Another group, asking for the Prophet's permis-sion, said, "Our homes are defenseless." In fact, they were not defenseless. They only wanted to run away.

13. Wa-iẕ qaalaṭ-ṭaaa'ifatum-minhum yaaa ahla Yasriba laa muqaama lakum farji'oo; wa yasta-ẕinu fareequm-minhu-mun-Nabiyya yaqooloona inna buyootanaa 'awrah; wa maa hiya bi'awratin iñy-yureedoona illaa firaaraa.

وَإِذْ قَالَت طَّآئِفَةٌ مِّنْهُمْ يَٰٓأَهْلَ
يَثْرِبَ لَا مُقَامَ لَكُمْ فَٱرْجِعُوا۟ ۚ
وَيَسْتَـْٔذِنُ فَرِيقٌ مِّنْهُمُ ٱلنَّبِىَّ
يَقُولُونَ إِنَّ بُيُوتَنَا عَوْرَةٌ وَمَا هِىَ
بِعَوْرَةٍ ۖ إِن يُرِيدُونَ إِلَّا فِرَارًا ﴿١٣﴾

14. Had the army of the enemies invaded their homes and asked them to give up their religion, they would have yielded

14. Wa law dukhilat 'alayhim-min aqṭaarihaa summa su'ilul-fitnata la-aatawhaa wa maa

وَلَوْ دُخِلَتْ عَلَيْهِم مِّنْ أَقْطَارِهَا
ثُمَّ سُئِلُوا۟ ٱلْفِتْنَةَ لَءَاتَوْهَا وَمَا

to them without delay.

15. They had certainly promised Allah that they would not turn away. To promise Allah is certainly a (great) responsibility.

16. (Muhammad), tell them, "Running away will never be of any benefit to you even if you run away from death or being killed. Still you would not be able to enjoy yourselves except for a short while."

17. Say, "Who can prevent Allah from punishing you or granting you mercy? They will not find anyone besides Allah as their guardian or helper."

18. Allah certainly knows those among you who create obstacles (on the way that leads to Allah) and those who say to their brothers, "Come quickly to us" and very rarely take part in the fighting.

19. They are niggardly in spending for you. When fear comes, you can see them looking at you, their eyes rolling about as if to faint because of the agony of death. When their fear subsides, they start to bite you with their sharp tongues. They are miserly in spending for a virtuous cause and had no faith. Allah has turned their deeds devoid of all virtue. This was not at all difficult for Allah.

20. They think that the allied tribes had not yet gone. If the allied tribes were to attack them, they wish to be left alone among the Bedouin Arabs where they would only follow the news about you. Even if they were with you, only a few of them would take

talabbasoo bihaaa illaa yaseeraa.

15. Wa laqad kaanoo 'aahadul-laaha min qablu laa yuwal-loonal-adbaar; wa kaana 'ah-dul-laahi mas'oolaa.

16. Qul lañy-yanfa'akumul-firaaru in farartum-minal mawti awil-qatli wa i̱zal-laa tumat-ta'oona illaa qaleelaa.

17. Qul man ẕal-laẕee ya'ṣi-mukum-minal-laahi in araada bikum sooo'an aw araada bi-kum raḥmah; wa laa yajidoona lahum-min doonil-laahi wali-yyañw-wa laa naṣeeraa.

18. Qad ya'lamul-laahul-mu'awwiqeena minkum wal-qaaa'ileena li-ikhwaanihim halumma ilaynaa, wa laa ya-toonal-ba-sa illaa qaleelaa.

19. Ashiḥḥatan 'alaykum fa-izaa jaaa'al-khawfu ra-aytahum yanẓuroona ilayka tadooru a'yunuhum kallaẕee yughshaa 'alayhi minal-mawti fa-izaa ẕahabal-khawfu salaqookum bi-alsinatin ḥidaadin ashiḥḥatan 'alal khayr; ulaaa'ika lam yu'minoo fa-aḥbaṭal-laahu a'maalahum; wa kaana ẕaalika 'alal-laahi yaseeraa.

20. Yaḥsaboonal-Aḥzaaba lam yaẕhaboo wa iñy-ya-til-Aḥzaa-bu yawaddoo law annahum baadoona fil-A'raabi yas-aloona 'an ambaaa'ikum wa law kaanoo feekum-

تَلَبَّثُوا بِهَا إِلَّا يَسِيرًا ﴿١٤﴾
وَلَقَدْ كَانُوا عَاهَدُوا اللَّهَ مِنْ
قَبْلُ لَا يُوَلُّونَ الْأَدْبَارَ ۚ وَكَانَ عَهْدُ
اللَّهِ مَسْئُولًا ﴿١٥﴾
قُلْ لَنْ يَنْفَعَكُمُ الْفِرَارُ إِنْ فَرَرْتُمْ
مِنَ الْمَوْتِ أَوِ الْقَتْلِ وَإِذًا
لَا تُمَتَّعُونَ إِلَّا قَلِيلًا ﴿١٦﴾
قُلْ مَنْ ذَا الَّذِي يَعْصِمُكُمْ مِنَ
اللَّهِ إِنْ أَرَادَ بِكُمْ سُوءًا أَوْ أَرَادَ
بِكُمْ رَحْمَةً ۚ وَلَا يَجِدُونَ لَهُمْ
مِنْ دُونِ اللَّهِ وَلِيًّا وَلَا نَصِيرًا ﴿١٧﴾
قَدْ يَعْلَمُ اللَّهُ الْمُعَوِّقِينَ مِنْكُمْ
وَالْقَائِلِينَ لِإِخْوَانِهِمْ هَلُمَّ إِلَيْنَا ۖ
وَلَا يَأْتُونَ الْبَأْسَ إِلَّا قَلِيلًا ﴿١٨﴾
أَشِحَّةً عَلَيْكُمْ ۖ فَإِذَا جَاءَ الْخَوْفُ
رَأَيْتَهُمْ يَنْظُرُونَ إِلَيْكَ تَدُورُ
أَعْيُنُهُمْ كَالَّذِي يُغْشَىٰ عَلَيْهِ
مِنَ الْمَوْتِ ۖ فَإِذَا ذَهَبَ الْخَوْفُ
سَلَقُوكُمْ بِأَلْسِنَةٍ حِدَادٍ أَشِحَّةً
عَلَى الْخَيْرِ ۚ أُولَٰئِكَ لَمْ يُؤْمِنُوا
فَأَحْبَطَ اللَّهُ أَعْمَالَهُمْ ۚ وَكَانَ ذَٰلِكَ
عَلَى اللَّهِ يَسِيرًا ﴿١٩﴾
يَحْسَبُونَ الْأَحْزَابَ لَمْ يَذْهَبُوا ۖ
وَإِنْ يَأْتِ الْأَحْزَابُ يَوَدُّوا لَوْ
أَنَّهُمْ بَادُونَ فِي الْأَعْرَابِ يَسْأَلُونَ
عَنْ أَنْبَائِكُمْ ۖ وَلَوْ كَانُوا فِيكُمْ

part in the fight.

maa qaatalooo illaa qaleelaa.

مَا قٰتَلُوْٓا اِلَّا قَلِيْلًا ؏ ٢٠ ع ٢ ١٢ ١٨

21. The Messenger of Allah is certainly a good example for those of you who have hope in Allah and in the Day of Judgment and who remember Allah very often.

21. Laqad kaana lakum fee Rasoolil-laahi uswatun ḥasanatul-liman kaana yarjullaaha wal-Yawmal-Aakhira wa zakaral-laaha kaseeraa.

لَقَدْ كَانَ لَكُمْ فِيْ رَسُوْلِ اللّٰهِ
اُسْوَةٌ حَسَنَةٌ لِّمَنْ كَانَ يَرْجُوا اللّٰهَ
وَالْيَوْمَ الْاٰخِرَ وَذَكَرَ اللّٰهَ كَثِيْرًا ٢١

22. On seeing the allied tribes, the believers said, "This is what Allah and His messenger had promised us. The promise of Allah and His messenger is true." This only strengthens their faith and their desire of submission to the will of Allah.

22. Wa lammaa ra-almu'minoonal-Aḥzaab; qaaloo haazaa maa wa'adanal-laahu wa Rasooluhoo wa ṣadaqal-laahu wa Rasooluh; wa maa zaadahum illaaa eemaanañw-wa tasleemaa.

وَلَمَّا رَاَ الْمُؤْمِنُوْنَ الْاَحْزَابَ ۙ قَالُوْا
هٰذَا مَا وَعَدَنَا اللّٰهُ وَرَسُوْلُهٗ
وَصَدَقَ اللّٰهُ وَرَسُوْلُهٗ ۡ وَمَا
زَادَهُمْ اِلَّآ اِيْمَانًا وَّتَسْلِيْمًا ٢٢

23. Among the believers there are people who are true in their promise to Allah (do not run away from battle field). There are those of them who have already passed away and others of them are waiting. They never yield to any change.

23. Minal-mu'mineena rijaalun ṣadaqoo maa 'aahadul-laaha 'alayhi faminhum-man qaḍaa naḥbahoo wa minhum-mañyyantaẓiru wa maa baddaloo tabdeelaa.

مِنَ الْمُؤْمِنِيْنَ رِجَالٌ صَدَقُوْا
مَا عَاهَدُوا اللّٰهَ عَلَيْهِ ۚ فَمِنْهُمْ مَّنْ
قَضٰى نَحْبَهٗ وَمِنْهُمْ مَّنْ يَّنْتَظِرُ ۖ
وَمَا بَدَّلُوْا تَبْدِيْلًا ۙ ٢٣

24. Allah will certainly reward the truthful ones for their truthfulness and punish or pardon the hypocrites as He wishes. Allah is All-forgiving and All-merciful.

24. Li-yajziyal-laahuṣ-ṣaadiqeena biṣidqihim wa yu'azzibal-munaafiqeena in shaaa'a aw yatooba 'alayhim; innal-laaha kaana Ghafoorar-Raḥeemaa.

لِّيَجْزِيَ اللّٰهُ الصّٰدِقِيْنَ بِصِدْقِهِمْ
وَيُعَذِّبَ الْمُنٰفِقِيْنَ اِنْ شَآءَ اَوْ
يَتُوْبَ عَلَيْهِمْ ۭ اِنَّ اللّٰهَ كَانَ
غَفُوْرًا رَّحِيْمًا ۚ ٢٤

25. Allah repelled the unbelievers in their rage. They could not achieve anything good. Allah rendered sufficient support to the believers in fighting. Allah is All-powerful and Majestic.

25. Wa raddal-laahul-lazeena kafaroo bighayẓihim lam yanaaloo khayraa; wa kafal-laahul-mu'mineenal-qitaal; wa kaanal-laahu Qawiyyan 'Azeezaa.

وَرَدَّ اللّٰهُ الَّذِيْنَ كَفَرُوْا بِغَيْظِهِمْ لَمْ
يَنَالُوْا خَيْرًا ۭ وَكَفَى اللّٰهُ الْمُؤْمِنِيْنَ
الْقِتَالَ ۭ وَكَانَ اللّٰهُ قَوِيًّا عَزِيْزًا ۚ ٢٥

26. Allah brought down those among the people of the Book who had supported the allied tribes from their castles and struck their hearts with terror. You did away with some of them and captured the others.

26. Wa anzalal-lazeena ẓaaharoohum-min Ahlil-Kitaabi min ṣayaaṣeehim wa qazafa fee quloobihimur-ru'ba fareeqan taqtuloona wa ta-siroona fareeqaa.

وَاَنْزَلَ الَّذِيْنَ ظَاهَرُوْهُمْ مِّنْ
اَهْلِ الْكِتٰبِ مِنْ صَيَاصِيْهِمْ
وَقَذَفَ فِيْ قُلُوْبِهِمُ الرُّعْبَ فَرِيْقًا
تَقْتُلُوْنَ وَتَاْسِرُوْنَ فَرِيْقًا ۚ ٢٦

27. Allah made you inherit their land, houses, property, and a land on which you had never walked. Allah has power over all things.

27. Wa awrasakum arḍahum wa diyaarahum wa amwaalahum wa arḍal-lam taṭa'oohaa; wa kaanal-laahu 'alaa kulli shay'in Qadeeraa.

وَاَوْرَثَكُمْ اَرْضَهُمْ وَدِيَارَهُمْ
وَاَمْوَالَهُمْ وَاَرْضًا لَّمْ تَطَـُٔوْهَا ۭ
وَكَانَ اللّٰهُ عَلٰى كُلِّ شَيْءٍ قَدِيْرًا ؏ ٢٧ ع ٣ ٧ ١٩

28. Prophet, tell your wives, "If you want the worldly life and its beauty, I shall allow you to enjoy it and set you free in an honorable manner,

28. Yaaa ayyuhan-Nabiyyu qul li-azwaajika in kuntunna turidnal-ḥayaatad-dunyaa wa zeenatahaa-fata'aalayna umatti'kunna-wa-usarriḥkunna saraa-ḥan-jameelaa.

يٰٓاَيُّهَا النَّبِيُّ قُلْ لِّاَزْوَاجِكَ اِنْ
كُنْتُنَّ تُرِدْنَ الْحَيٰوةَ الدُّنْيَا
وَزِيْنَتَهَا فَتَعَالَيْنَ اُمَتِّعْكُنَّ
وَاُسَرِّحْكُنَّ سَرَاحًا جَمِيْلًا ﴿٢٨﴾

29. but if you want the pleasure of Allah, His messenger, and the life hereafter, you must know that Allah has prepared a great reward for the righteous ones among you."

29. Wa in kuntunna turidnal laaha wa Rasoolahoo wad Daaral-Aakhirata fa-innal-laaha-a'adda lilmuḥsinaati min-kunna ajran 'aẓeemaa.

وَاِنْ كُنْتُنَّ تُرِدْنَ اللّٰهَ وَرَسُوْلَهٗ
وَالدَّارَ الْاٰخِرَةَ فَاِنَّ اللّٰهَ اَعَدَّ
لِلْمُحْسِنٰتِ مِنْكُنَّ اَجْرًا عَظِيْمًا ﴿٢٩﴾

30. O wives of the Prophet, if anyone among you commits evident indecency, her torment will be double. This is not at all difficult for Allah.

30. Yaa nisaaa'an-Nabiyyi mañy-ya-ti minkunna bifaa-ḥishatim-mubayyinatiñy-yuḍaa-'af lahal-'azaabu ḍi'fayn; wa kaana zaalika 'alal-laahi yaseeraa.

يٰنِسَآءَ النَّبِيِّ مَنْ يَّاْتِ مِنْكُنَّ
بِفَاحِشَةٍ مُّبَيِّنَةٍ يُّضٰعَفْ لَهَا
الْعَذَابُ ضِعْفَيْنِ ؕ وَكَانَ ذٰلِكَ
عَلَى اللّٰهِ يَسِيْرًا ﴿٣٠﴾

31. To those of you who obey Allah and His messenger and act righteously, We will give double reward and an honorable sustenance.

31. Wa mañy-yaqnut minku-nna lillaahi wa Rasoolihee wa ta'mal ṣaaliḥan nu'tihaaa ajra-haa marratayni wa a'tadnaa lahaa rizqan kareemaa.

وَمَنْ يَّقْنُتْ مِنْكُنَّ لِلّٰهِ وَرَسُوْلِهٖ
وَتَعْمَلْ صَالِحًا نُّؤْتِهَآ اَجْرَهَا
مَرَّتَيْنِ ۙ وَاَعْتَدْنَا لَهَا رِزْقًا كَرِيْمًا ﴿٣١﴾

32. Wives of the Prophet, you are not like other women. If you have fear of Allah, do not be tender in your speech lest people whose hearts are sick may lust after you. Speak to people in a normal manner.

32. Yaa nisaaa'an-Nabiyyi lastunna ka-aḥadim minan-nisaaa'; init-taqaytunna falaa takhḍa'na bilqawli fayaṭma'al lazee fee qalbihee maraḍuñw-wa qulna qawlam-ma'roofaa.

يٰنِسَآءَ النَّبِيِّ لَسْتُنَّ كَاَحَدٍ مِّنَ
النِّسَآءِ اِنِ اتَّقَيْتُنَّ فَلَا تَخْضَعْنَ
بِالْقَوْلِ فَيَطْمَعَ الَّذِيْ فِيْ قَلْبِهٖ
مَرَضٌ وَّقُلْنَ قَوْلًا مَّعْرُوْفًا ۚ ﴿٣٢﴾

33. You must stay in your homes and do not display yourselves after the manner of the (pre-Islamic) age of darkness. Be steadfast in the prayer, pay the religious tax, and obey Allah and His messenger. O People of the house, Allah wants to remove all kinds of uncleanness from you and to purify you thoroughly.

33. Wa qarna fee buyoo-tikunna wa laa tabarrajna tabarrujal-Jaahiliyyatil-oolaa wa aqimnaṣ-Ṣalaata wa aateenaz-Zakaata wa aṭi'nal-laaha wa Rasoolah; innamaa yureedul-laahu liyuzhiba 'ankumur-rijsa Ahlal-Bayti wa yuṭahhirakum taṭheeraa.

وَقَرْنَ فِيْ بُيُوْتِكُنَّ وَلَا تَبَرَّجْنَ
تَبَرُّجَ الْجَاهِلِيَّةِ الْاُوْلٰى وَاَقِمْنَ
الصَّلٰوةَ وَاٰتِيْنَ الزَّكٰوةَ وَاَطِعْنَ
اللّٰهَ وَرَسُوْلَهٗ ؕ اِنَّمَا يُرِيْدُ اللّٰهُ
لِيُذْهِبَ عَنْكُمُ الرِّجْسَ اَهْلَ الْبَيْتِ
وَيُطَهِّرَكُمْ تَطْهِيْرًا ۚ ﴿٣٣﴾

34. Wives of the Prophet, remember the revelations of Allah and Words of wisdom that are recited in your homes. Allah is

34. Wazkurna maa yutlaa fee buyootikunna min Aayaatil-laahi wal-Ḥikmah; innallaaha

وَاذْكُرْنَ مَا يُتْلٰى فِيْ بُيُوْتِكُنَّ
مِنْ اٰيٰتِ اللّٰهِ وَالْحِكْمَةِ ؕ اِنَّ اللّٰهَ

Most Kind and All-aware.

35. Allah has promised forgiveness and great rewards to the Muslim men and the Muslim women, the believing men and the believing women, the obedient men and the obedient women, the truthful men and the truthful women, the forbearing men and the forbearing women, the humble men and the humble women, the alms-giving men and the alms-giving women, the fasting men and the fasting women, the chaste men and the chaste women, and the men and women who remember Allah very often.

36. The believing men and women must not feel free to do something in their affairs other than that which has been already decided for them by Allah and His messenger. One who disobeys Allah and His messenger is in plain error.

37. (Muhammad), when you said to the person to whom you and Allah have granted favor, "Keep your wife and have fear of Allah. You hide within yourself what Allah wants to make public. You are afraid of people while it is Allah whom one should fear." When Zayd set her (his wife) free, We gave her in marriage to you so that the believers would not face difficulties about the wives of their adopted sons when they are divorced. Allah's decree has already been issued.

38. The Prophet cannot be blamed for carrying out the commands of Allah. It was the tradition of Allah with those who

---

kaana Laṭeefan Khabeeraa.

35. Innal-muslimeena wal-muslimaati walmu'mineena walmu'minaati walqaaniteena walqaanitaati waṣṣaadiqeena waṣṣaadiqaati waṣṣaabireena waṣṣaabiraati walkhaashi'eena walkhaashi'aati walmutaṣad-diqeena walmutaṣaddiqaati waṣṣaaa'imeena waṣṣaaa'i-maati walḥaafiẓeena furoojahum walḥaafiẓaati waz-zaaki-reenal-laaha kaseerañw-waz-zaakiraati a'addal-laahu lahum-maghfiratañw-wa ajran 'aẓee-maa.

36. Wa maa kaana limu'mi-niñw-wa laa mu'minatin izaa qaḍal-laahu wa Rasooluhooo amran añy-yakoona lahumul-khiyaratu min amrihim; wa mañy-ya'ṣil-laaha wa Rasoo-lahoo faqad ḍalla ḍalaalam-mubeenaa.

37. Wa iz taqoolu lillazeee an'amal-laahu 'alayhi wa an'amta 'alayhi amsik 'alayka zawjaka wattaqillaaha wa tukhfee fee nafsika mal-laahu mubdeehi wa takhshan-naasa wallaahu aḥaqqu an takhshaah; falammaa qaḍaa Zaydum-minhaa waṭaran zawwajnaa-kahaa likay laa yakoona 'alal-mu'mineena ḥarajun feee azwaaji ad'iyaaa'ihim izaa qaḍaw minhunna waṭaraa; wa kaana amrul-laahi maf'oolaa.

38. Maa kaana 'alan-Nabiyyi min ḥarajin feemaa faraḍal-laahu lahoo sunnatal-laahi fil-

---

كَانَ لَطِيْفًا خَبِيْرًا ۞

إِنَّ الْمُسْلِمِيْنَ وَالْمُسْلِمٰتِ وَالْمُؤْمِنِيْنَ وَالْمُؤْمِنٰتِ وَالْقٰنِتِيْنَ وَالْقٰنِتٰتِ وَالصّٰدِقِيْنَ وَالصّٰدِقٰتِ وَالصّٰبِرِيْنَ وَالصّٰبِرٰتِ وَالْخٰشِعِيْنَ وَالْخٰشِعٰتِ وَالْمُتَصَدِّقِيْنَ وَالْمُتَصَدِّقٰتِ وَالصَّآئِمِيْنَ وَالصّٰئِمٰتِ وَالْحٰفِظِيْنَ فُرُوْجَهُمْ وَالْحٰفِظٰتِ وَالذّٰكِرِيْنَ اللّٰهَ كَثِيْرًا وَّالذّٰكِرٰتِ ۙ اَعَدَّ اللّٰهُ لَهُمْ مَّغْفِرَةً وَّاَجْرًا عَظِيْمًا ۞

وَمَا كَانَ لِمُؤْمِنٍ وَّلَا مُؤْمِنَةٍ اِذَا قَضَى اللّٰهُ وَرَسُوْلُهٗۤ اَمْرًا اَنْ يَّكُوْنَ لَهُمُ الْخِيَرَةُ مِنْ اَمْرِهِمْ ۗ وَمَنْ يَّعْصِ اللّٰهَ وَرَسُوْلَهٗ فَقَدْ ضَلَّ ضَلٰلًا مُّبِيْنًا ۞

وَاِذْ تَقُوْلُ لِلَّذِيْۤ اَنْعَمَ اللّٰهُ عَلَيْهِ وَاَنْعَمْتَ عَلَيْهِ اَمْسِكْ عَلَيْكَ زَوْجَكَ وَاتَّقِ اللّٰهَ وَتُخْفِيْ فِيْ نَفْسِكَ مَا اللّٰهُ مُبْدِيْهِ وَتَخْشَى النَّاسَ ۚ وَاللّٰهُ اَحَقُّ اَنْ تَخْشٰهُ ۗ فَلَمَّا قَضٰى زَيْدٌ مِّنْهَا وَطَرًا زَوَّجْنٰكَهَا لِكَيْ لَا يَكُوْنَ عَلَى الْمُؤْمِنِيْنَ حَرَجٌ فِيْۤ اَزْوَاجِ اَدْعِيَآئِهِمْ اِذَا قَضَوْا مِنْهُنَّ وَطَرًا ۗ وَكَانَ اَمْرُ اللّٰهِ مَفْعُوْلًا ۞

مَا كَانَ عَلَى النَّبِيِّ مِنْ حَرَجٍ فِيْمَا فَرَضَ اللّٰهُ لَهٗ ۗ سُنَّةَ اللّٰهِ فِى

lived before. The command of Allah has already been decreed and ordained.

lazeena khalaw min qabl; wa kaana amrul-laahi qadaram-maqdooraa.

الَّذِينَ خَلَوْا مِن قَبْلُ ۚ وَكَانَ أَمْرُ
اللَّهِ قَدَرًا مَّقْدُورًا ﴿٣٨﴾

39. Those who preach the message of Allah and are humble before Him should not be afraid of anyone besides Allah. Allah is Sufficient in keeping the account.

39. Allazeena yuballighoona Risaalaatil-laahi wa yakhshaw-nahoo wa laa yakhshawna aḥadan illal-laah; wa kafaa billaahi Ḥaseebaa.

الَّذِينَ يُبَلِّغُونَ رِسٰلٰتِ اللَّهِ وَ
يَخْشَوْنَهُ وَلَا يَخْشَوْنَ أَحَدًا إِلَّا
اللَّهَ ۗ وَكَفَىٰ بِاللَّهِ حَسِيبًا ﴿٣٩﴾

40. Muhammad is not the father of any of your males. He is the Messenger of Allah and the last Prophet. Allah has the knowledge of all things.

40. Maa kaana Muḥammadun abaaa aḥadim-mir-rijaalikum wa laakir-Rasoolal-laahi wa Khaataman-Nabiyyeen; wa kaanal-laahu bikulli shay'in 'Aleemaa.

مَّا كَانَ مُحَمَّدٌ أَبَا أَحَدٍ مِّن رِّجَالِكُمْ
وَلٰكِن رَّسُولَ اللَّهِ وَخَاتَمَ النَّبِيِّينَ ۗ
وَكَانَ اللَّهُ بِكُلِّ شَيْءٍ عَلِيمًا ﴿٤٠﴾ ع

41. O believers, remember Allah very often

41. Yaaa ayyuhal-lazeena aamanuz-kurul-laaha zikran kaseeraa.

يٰأَيُّهَا الَّذِينَ آمَنُوا اذْكُرُوا اللَّهَ
ذِكْرًا كَثِيرًا ﴿٤١﴾

42. and glorify Him both in the mornings and in the evenings.

42. Wa sabbiḥoohu bukra-tañw-wa aṣeelaa.

وَّسَبِّحُوهُ بُكْرَةً وَّأَصِيلًا ﴿٤٢﴾

43. It is He who forgives you and His angels pray for you so that He will take you out of darkness into light. Allah is All-merciful to the believers.

43. Huwal-lazee yuṣallee 'alaykum wa malaaa'ikatuhoo liyukhrijakum-minaẓẓulumaati ilan-noor; wa kaana bilmu'-mineena Raḥeemaa.

هُوَ الَّذِي يُصَلِّي عَلَيْكُمْ وَمَلٰئِكَتُهُ
لِيُخْرِجَكُم مِّنَ الظُّلُمٰتِ إِلَى النُّورِ ۚ
وَكَانَ بِالْمُؤْمِنِينَ رَحِيمًا ﴿٤٣﴾

44. On the day when they will be brought into the presence of their Lord, their greeting to each other will be, "Peace be with you." Allah has prepared an honorable reward for them.

44. Taḥiyyatuhum Yawma yalqawnahoo salaamuñw-wa a'adda lahum ajran kareemaa.

تَحِيَّتُهُمْ يَوْمَ يَلْقَوْنَهُ سَلٰمٌ ۚ وَأَعَدَّ
لَهُمْ أَجْرًا كَرِيمًا ﴿٤٤﴾

45. O Prophet, We have sent you as a witness, a bearer of glad news, a Warner,

45. Yaaa ayyuhan-Nabiyyu innaaa arsalnaaka shaahidañw-wa mubashshirañw-wa nazee-raa.

يٰأَيُّهَا النَّبِيُّ إِنَّا أَرْسَلْنٰكَ شٰهِدًا
وَّمُبَشِّرًا وَّنَذِيرًا ﴿٤٥﴾

46. a preacher for Allah by His permission and as a shining torch.

46. Wa daa'iyan ilal-laahi bi-iznihee wa siraajam-muneeraa.

وَّدَاعِيًا إِلَى اللَّهِ بِإِذْنِهِ وَسِرَاجًا
مُّنِيرًا ﴿٤٦﴾

47. Give glad news to the believers of their receiving great favor from Allah.

47. Wa bashshiril-mu'mi-neena bi-anna lahum-minal-laahi faḍlan kabeeraa.

وَبَشِّرِ الْمُؤْمِنِينَ بِأَنَّ لَهُم مِّنَ
اللَّهِ فَضْلًا كَبِيرًا ﴿٤٧﴾

48. Do not yield to the unbelievers or the hypocrites. Ignore their annoying you. Trust in Allah. Allah is your All-sufficient Protector.

48. Wa laa tuṭi'il-kaafireena walmunaafiqeena wa da' azaahum wa tawakkal 'alallaah; wa kafaa billaahi Wakeelaa.

وَلَا تُطِعِ الْكٰفِرِينَ وَالْمُنٰفِقِينَ وَدَعْ
أَذٰىهُمْ وَتَوَكَّلْ عَلَى اللَّهِ ۚ وَكَفَىٰ
بِاللَّهِ وَكِيلًا ﴿٤٨﴾

49. Believers, if you marry believing women and then

49. Yaaa ayyuhal-lazeena aamanooo izaa nakaḥtumul-

يٰأَيُّهَا الَّذِينَ آمَنُوا إِذَا نَكَحْتُمُ

الْمُؤْمِنٰتِ ثُمَّ طَلَّقْتُمُوْهُنَّ مِنْ
قَبْلِ اَنْ تَمَسُّوْهُنَّ فَمَا لَكُمْ
عَلَيْهِنَّ مِنْ عِدَّةٍ تَعْتَدُّوْنَهَا ۚ
فَمَتِّعُوْهُنَّ وَسَرِّحُوْهُنَّ سَرَاحًا
جَمِيْلًا ﴿٤٩﴾

mu'minaati summa ṭallaqtu-moohunna min qabli an tamas-soohunna famaa lakum 'alay-hinna min 'iddatin ta'taddoona-haa famatti'oohunna wa sarri-ḥoohunna saraaḥan jameelaa.

divorce them before the consummation of the marriage, they do not have to observe the waiting period. Give them their provisions and set them free in an honorable manner.

يٰٓاَيُّهَا النَّبِيُّ اِنَّآ اَحْلَلْنَا لَكَ اَزْوَاجَكَ
الّٰتِيْٓ اٰتَيْتَ اُجُوْرَهُنَّ وَمَا مَلَكَتْ
يَمِيْنُكَ مِمَّآ اَفَآءَ اللّٰهُ عَلَيْكَ وَبَنٰتِ
عَمِّكَ وَبَنٰتِ عَمّٰتِكَ وَبَنٰتِ خَالِكَ
وَبَنٰتِ خٰلٰتِكَ الّٰتِيْ هَاجَرْنَ مَعَكَ ۫
وَامْرَاَةً مُّؤْمِنَةً اِنْ وَّهَبَتْ نَفْسَهَا
لِلنَّبِيِّ اِنْ اَرَادَ النَّبِيُّ اَنْ يَّسْتَنْكِحَهَا ۗ
خَالِصَةً لَّكَ مِنْ دُوْنِ الْمُؤْمِنِيْنَ ؕ
قَدْ عَلِمْنَا مَا فَرَضْنَا عَلَيْهِمْ فِيْٓ
اَزْوَاجِهِمْ وَمَا مَلَكَتْ اَيْمَانُهُمْ لِكَيْلَا
يَكُوْنَ عَلَيْكَ حَرَجٌ ؕ وَكَانَ اللّٰهُ
غَفُوْرًا رَّحِيْمًا ﴿٥٠﴾

50. Yaaa ayyuhan-Nabiyyu innaaa aḥlalnaa laka azwaa-jakal-laateee aatayta ujoora-hunna wa maa malakat yamee-nuka mimmaaa afaaa'al-laahu 'alayka wa banaati 'ammika wa banaati 'ammaatika wa banaati khaalika wa banaati khaalaa-tikal-laatee haajarna ma'aka wamra-atam-mu'minatan iñw-wahabat nafsahaa lin-Nabiyyi in araadan-Nabiyyu añy-yastan-kiḥahaa khaaliṣatal-laka min doonil-mu'mineen; qad 'alim-naa maa faraḍnaa 'alayhim feee azwaajihim wa maa malakat aymaanuhum likaylaa yakoona 'alayka ḥaraj; wa kaanal-laahu Ghafoorar-Raḥeemaa.

50. Prophet, We have made lawful for you your wives whom you have given their dowry, slave girls whom Allah has given to you as gifts, the daughters of your uncles and aunts, both paternal and maternal, who have migrated with you.

The believing woman, who has offered herself to the Prophet and whom the Prophet may want to marry, will be specially for him, not for other believers. We knew what to make obligatory for them concerning their wives and slave girls so that you would face no hardship (because we have given distinction to you over the believers). Allah is All-forgiving and All-merciful.

تُرْجِيْ مَنْ تَشَآءُ مِنْهُنَّ وَتُـْٔوِيْٓ
اِلَيْكَ مَنْ تَشَآءُ ؕ وَمَنِ ابْتَغَيْتَ
مِمَّنْ عَزَلْتَ فَلَا جُنَاحَ عَلَيْكَ ؕ
ذٰلِكَ اَدْنٰٓى اَنْ تَقَرَّ اَعْيُنُهُنَّ وَلَا
يَحْزَنَّ وَيَرْضَيْنَ بِمَآ اٰتَيْتَهُنَّ
كُلُّهُنَّ ؕ وَاللّٰهُ يَعْلَمُ مَا فِيْ قُلُوْبِكُمْ ؕ
وَكَانَ اللّٰهُ عَلِيْمًا حَلِيْمًا ﴿٥١﴾

51. Turjee man tashaaa'u minhunna wa tu'weee ilayka man tashaaa'u wa manibta-ghayta mimman 'azalta falaa junaaḥa 'alayk; zaalika adnaaa an taqarra a'yunuhunna wa laa yaḥzanna wa yarḍayna bimaaa aataytahunna kulluhunn; wal-laahu ya'lamu maa fee quloo-bikum; wa kaanal-laahu 'Aleeman Ḥaleemaa.

51. You may refuse whichever (of the women who offer themselves to you) as you want and accept whichever of them you wish. There is no blame on you if you marry one whom you had refused previously. This would be more delightful for them. They should not be grieved but should be happy with whatever you have given to every one of them. Allah knows what is in your hearts. Allah is All-knowing and All-forbearing.

لَا يَحِلُّ لَكَ النِّسَآءُ مِنْۢ بَعْدُ وَلَآ
اَنْ تَبَدَّلَ بِهِنَّ مِنْ اَزْوَاجٍ وَّلَوْ

52. Laa yaḥillu lakan-nisaaa'u mim ba'du wa laaa an tabaddala bihinna min azwaajiñw-wa law

52. Besides these, other women are not lawful for you to marry nor is it lawful for you to exchange your wives for the

wives of others (except for the slave girls), even though they may seem attractive to you. Allah is watchful over all things.

a'jabaka ḥusnuhunna illaa maa malakat yameenuk; wa kaanal-laahu 'alaa kulli shay'ir-Raqeebaa.

اَعْجَبَكَ حُسْنُهُنَّ اِلَّا مَا مَلَكَتْ
يَمِيْنُكَ ؕ وَكَانَ اللّٰهُ عَلٰى كُلِّ
شَیْءٍ رَّقِيْبًا ﴿۵۲﴾ ع

53. O believers, do not enter the houses of the Prophet for a meal without permission. If you are invited, you may enter, but be punctual (so that you will not be waiting while the meal is being prepared).

When you have finished eating, leave his home. Do not sit around chatting among yourselves. This will annoy the Prophet but he will feel embarrassed to tell you. Allah does not feel embarrassed to tell you the truth.

When you want to ask something from the wives of the Prophet, ask them from behind the curtain. This would be more proper for you and for them. You must not trouble the Messenger of Allah or ever marry his wives after his death, for this would be a grave offense in the sight of Allah.

53. Yaaa ayyuhal-lazeena aamanoo laa tadkhuloo buyoo-tan-Nabiyyi illaaa añy-yu'zana lakum ilaa ṭa'aamin ghayra naaẓireena inaahu wa laakin izaa du'eetum fadkhuloo fa-izaa ṭa'imtum fantashiroo wa laa musta-niseena liḥadees; inna zaalikum kaana yu'zin-Nabiyya fa-yastaḥyee minkum wallaahu laa yastaḥyee minal-ḥaqq; wa izaa sa-altumoohunna mataa'an fas'aloohunna miñw-waraaa'i ḥijaab; zaalikum aṭharu liquloobikum wa quloobihinn; wa maa kaana lakum an tu'zoo Rasoolal-laahi wa laaa an tankiḥooo azwaajahoo mim ba'diheee abadaa; inna zaa-likum kaana 'indal-laahi 'aẓeemaa.

يٰۤاَيُّهَا الَّذِيْنَ اٰمَنُوْا لَا تَدْخُلُوْا بُيُوْتَ
النَّبِیِّ اِلَّاۤ اَنْ يُّؤْذَنَ لَكُمْ اِلٰى طَعَامٍ
غَيْرَ نٰظِرِيْنَ اِنٰىهُ ۙ وَلٰكِنْ اِذَا
دُعِيْتُمْ فَادْخُلُوْا فَاِذَا طَعِمْتُمْ
فَانْتَشِرُوْا وَلَا مُسْتَاْنِسِيْنَ لِحَدِيْثٍ ؕ
اِنَّ ذٰلِكُمْ كَانَ يُؤْذِی النَّبِیَّ فَيَسْتَحْیٖ
مِنْكُمْ ۫ وَاللّٰهُ لَا يَسْتَحْیٖ مِنَ الْحَقِّ ؕ
وَاِذَا سَاَلْتُمُوْهُنَّ مَتَاعًا فَسْــَٔلُوْهُنَّ
مِنْ وَّرَآءِ حِجَابٍ ؕ ذٰلِكُمْ اَطْهَرُ
لِقُلُوْبِكُمْ وَقُلُوْبِهِنَّ ؕ وَمَا كَانَ
لَكُمْ اَنْ تُؤْذُوْا رَسُوْلَ اللّٰهِ وَلَاۤ اَنْ
تَنْكِحُوْۤا اَزْوَاجَهٗ مِنْۢ بَعْدِهٖۤ اَبَدًا ؕ
اِنَّ ذٰلِكُمْ كَانَ عِنْدَ اللّٰهِ عَظِيْمًا ﴿۵۳﴾

54. Whether you reveal something or hid it, Allah has the knowledge of all things.

54. In tubdoo shay'an aw tukhfoohu fa-innal-laaha kaana bikulli shay'in 'Aleemaa.

اِنْ تُبْدُوْا شَيْـًٔا اَوْ تُخْفُوْهُ فَاِنَّ اللّٰهَ
كَانَ بِكُلِّ شَیْءٍ عَلِيْمًا ﴿۵۴﴾

55. It will not be an offense for the wives of the Prophet (not to observe the modest dress) in the presence of their fathers, sons, brothers, sons of their brothers and sisters, their own women, and their slave girls. They should have fear of Allah. Allah witnesses all things.

55. Laa junaaḥa 'alayhinna feee aabaaa'ihinna wa laaa abnaaa'ihinna wa laaa ikhwaa-nihinna wa laaa abnaaa'i ikhwaanihinna wa laaa abnaaa'i akhawaatihinna wa laa nisaaa'i-hinna wa laa maa malakat aymaanuhunn; wattaqeenal-laah; innal-laaha kaana 'alaa kulli shay'in-Shaheedaa.

لَا جُنَاحَ عَلَيْهِنَّ فِیْۤ اٰبَآئِهِنَّ وَلَا
اَبْنَآئِهِنَّ وَلَاۤ اِخْوَانِهِنَّ وَلَاۤ اَبْنَآءِ
اِخْوَانِهِنَّ وَلَاۤ اَبْنَآءِ اَخَوٰتِهِنَّ
وَلَا نِسَآئِهِنَّ وَلَا مَا مَلَكَتْ
اَيْمَانُهُنَّ ۚ وَاتَّقِيْنَ اللّٰهَ ؕ اِنَّ اللّٰهَ
كَانَ عَلٰى كُلِّ شَیْءٍ شَهِيْدًا ﴿۵۵﴾

56. Allah purifies and adorns the Prophet, and His angels praise him. O believers, pray for the Prophet (acknowledge his possessing divine authority) and greet him (as your guardian and as the messenger of Allah) with, the greeting of peace submissively."

56. Innal-laaha wa malaaa'i-katahoo yuṣalloona 'alan-Nabiyy; yaaa ayyuhal-lazeena aamanoo ṣalloo 'alayhi wa sallimoo tasleemaa.

اِنَّ اللّٰهَ وَمَلٰٓئِكَتَهٗ يُصَلُّوْنَ عَلَى
النَّبِیِّ ؕ يٰۤاَيُّهَا الَّذِيْنَ اٰمَنُوْا صَلُّوْا

57. Those who annoy Allah and His messenger will be condemned by Allah in this life and in the life to come. He has prepared for them a humiliating torment.

58. Those who annoy the believing men and women without reason will bear the sin for a false accusation, a manifest offense.

59. Prophet, tell your wives, daughters, and the wives of the believers to cover their bosoms and breasts. This will make them distinguishable from others and protect them from being annoyed. Allah is All-forgiving and All-merciful.

60. If the hypocrites, those whose hearts are sick and those who encourage the spread of evil in the city, did not desist, We shall arouse you against them and they will be allowed to be your neighbors for only a short while.

61. They will be condemned wherever they are and will be seized and done away with for good.

62. This was the tradition of Allah with those who lived before. There will never be any change in the tradition of Allah.

63. (Muhammad), people ask you about the Day of Judgment. Say, "Only Allah has knowledge about it. Perhaps the Hour of Doom will soon come to pass."

64. Allah has condemned the unbelievers and prepared for them a burning torment

65. wherein they will live forever without being able to find any guardian or helper.

57. Innal-lazeena yu'zoonal-laaha wa Rasoolahoo la'ana-humul-laahu fid-dunyaa wal-Aakhirati wa a'adda lahum 'azaabam-muheenaa.

58. Wallazeena yu'zoonal-mu'mineena walmu'minaati bighayri mak-tasaboo faqadiḥ-tamaloo buhtaanañw-wa is-mam-mubeenaa.

59. Yaaa ayyuhan-Nabiyyu qul li-azwaajika wa banaatika wa nisaaa'il-mu'mineena yud-neena 'alayhinna min jalaabee-bihinn; zaalika adnaaa añy-yu'rafna falaa yu'zayn; wa kaanal-laahu Ghafoorar-Raḥee-maa.

60. La'il-lam yantahil-munaa-fiqoona wallazeena fee quloo-bihim-maraḍuñw-walmur-jifoona fil-madeenati lanughri-yannaka bihim summa laa yujaawiroonaka feehaaa illaa qaleelaa.

61. Mal'ooneena aynamaa suqifooo ukhizoo wa quttiloo taqteelaa.

62. Sunnatal-laahi fil-lazeena khalaw min qablu wa lan tajida lisunnatil-laahi tabdeelaa.

63. Yas'alukan-naasu 'anis-Saa'ati qul innamaa 'ilmuhaa 'indal-laah; wa maa yudreeka la'allas-Saa'ata takoonu qaree-baa.

64. Innal-laaha la'anal-kaafi-reena wa a'adda lahum sa'ee-raa.

65. Khaalideena feehaaa aba-daa; laa yajidoona waliyyañw-wa laa naṣeeraa.

عَلَيۡهِ وَسَلِّمُوۡا تَسۡلِيۡمًا ﴿۵۶﴾
اِنَّ الَّذِيۡنَ يُؤۡذُوۡنَ اللّٰهَ وَرَسُوۡلَهٗ
لَعَنَهُمُ اللّٰهُ فِى الدُّنۡيَا وَالۡاٰخِرَةِ
وَاَعَدَّ لَهُمۡ عَذَابًا مُّهِيۡنًا ﴿۵۷﴾
وَالَّذِيۡنَ يُؤۡذُوۡنَ الۡمُؤۡمِنِيۡنَ وَالۡمُؤۡمِنٰتِ
بِغَيۡرِ مَا اكۡتَسَبُوۡا فَقَدِ احۡتَمَلُوۡا ع ٧
بُهۡتَانًا وَّاِثۡمًا مُّبِيۡنًا ﴿۵۸﴾
يٰۤاَيُّهَا النَّبِىُّ قُلۡ لِّاَزۡوَاجِكَ وَبَنٰتِكَ
وَنِسَآءِ الۡمُؤۡمِنِيۡنَ يُدۡنِيۡنَ عَلَيۡهِنَّ
مِنۡ جَلَابِيۡبِهِنَّ ؕ ذٰلِكَ اَدۡنٰٓى اَنۡ
يُّعۡرَفۡنَ فَلَا يُؤۡذَيۡنَ ؕ وَكَانَ اللّٰهُ
غَفُوۡرًا رَّحِيۡمًا ﴿۵۹﴾
لَئِنۡ لَّمۡ يَنۡتَهِ الۡمُنٰفِقُوۡنَ وَالَّذِيۡنَ
فِىۡ قُلُوۡبِهِمۡ مَّرَضٌ وَّالۡمُرۡجِفُوۡنَ فِى
الۡمَدِيۡنَةِ لَنُغۡرِيَنَّكَ بِهِمۡ ثُمَّ لَا
يُجَاوِرُوۡنَكَ فِيۡهَاۤ اِلَّا قَلِيۡلًا ۛ ﴿۶۰﴾ معانقة ١٢ عند المتاخرين
مَّلۡعُوۡنِيۡنَ ۛ اَيۡنَمَا ثُقِفُوۡۤا اُخِذُوۡا
وَقُتِّلُوۡا تَقۡتِيۡلًا ﴿۶۱﴾
سُنَّةَ اللّٰهِ فِى الَّذِيۡنَ خَلَوۡا مِنۡ قَبۡلُ ۚ
وَلَنۡ تَجِدَ لِسُنَّةِ اللّٰهِ تَبۡدِيۡلًا ﴿۶۲﴾ الربع
يَسۡـَٔلُكَ النَّاسُ عَنِ السَّاعَةِ ؕ قُلۡ اِنَّمَا
عِلۡمُهَا عِنۡدَ اللّٰهِ ؕ وَمَا يُدۡرِيۡكَ لَعَلَّ
السَّاعَةَ تَكُوۡنُ قَرِيۡبًا ﴿۶۳﴾
اِنَّ اللّٰهَ لَعَنَ الۡكٰفِرِيۡنَ وَاَعَدَّ لَهُمۡ
سَعِيۡرًا ۙ ﴿۶۴﴾
خٰلِدِيۡنَ فِيۡهَاۤ اَبَدًا ۚ لَا يَجِدُوۡنَ وَلِيًّا

66. On the day when their faces will be turned from side to side on the fire, they will say, "Would that we had obeyed Allah and the Messenger!"

67. They will say, "Lord, we obeyed our chiefs and elders and they caused us to go astray.

68. Lord, make them to suffer double torment and subject them to the greatest condemnation."

69. O believers, do not be like those who annoyed Moses. Allah proved him to be innocent of what they had said about him. Moses was an honorable person in the sight of Allah.

70. O believers, have fear of Allah and speak righteous (correct) words.

71. Allah will reform your deeds and forgive your sins. One who obeys Allah and His messenger will certainly achieve a great success.

72. We offered Our Trust (Our deputation) to the heavens, to the earth, and to the mountains, but they could not bear this burden and were afraid to accept it. Mankind was able to accept this offer but he was unjust to himself and ignorant of the significance of this Trust.

73. (As a result of this) Allah will punish the hypocrites and the pagans, but He will accept the repentance of the believers. Allah is All-forgiving and All-merciful.

66. Yawma tuqallabu wujoohuhum fin-Naari yaqooloona yaa laytanaaa aṭa'nal-laaha wa aṭa'nar-Rasoolaa.

67. Wa qaaloo Rabbanaaa innaaa aṭa'naa saadatanaa wa kubaraaa'anaa fa-aḍalloonas-sabeelaa.

68. Rabbanaaa aatihim ḍi'fayni minal-'aẕaabi wal'anhum la'nan kabeeraa.

69. Yaaa ayyuhal-laẕeena aamanoo laa takoonoo kallaẕeena aaẕaw Moosaa fa-barra-ahul-laahu mimmaa qaaloo; wa kaana 'indal-laahi wajeehaa.

70. Yaaa ayyuhal-laẕeena aamanut-taqul-laaha wa qooloo qawlan sadeedaa.

71. Yuṣliḥ lakum a'maalakum wa yaghfir lakum ẕunoobakum; wa mañy-yuṭi'il-laaha wa Rasoolahoo faqad faaza fawzan 'aẓeemaa.

72. Innaa 'araḍnal-amaanata 'alas-samaawaati walarḍi wal-jibaali fa-abayna añy-yaḥmilnahaa wa ashfaqna minhaa wa ḥamalahal-insaan; innahoo kaana ẓalooman jahoolaa.

73. Liyu'aẕẕibal-laahul-munaafiqeena walmunaafiqaati walmushrikeena walmushrikaati wa yatoobal-laahu 'alal-mu'mineena walmu'minaat; wa kaanal-laahu Ghafoorar-Raḥeema.

وَلَا نَصِيرًا ﴿٦٥﴾
يَوْمَ تُقَلَّبُ وُجُوهُهُمْ فِي النَّارِ يَقُولُونَ
يَا لَيْتَنَا أَطَعْنَا اللَّهَ وَأَطَعْنَا الرَّسُولَا ﴿٦٦﴾
وَقَالُوا رَبَّنَا إِنَّا أَطَعْنَا سَادَتَنَا
وَكُبَرَاءَنَا فَأَضَلُّونَا السَّبِيلَا ﴿٦٧﴾
رَبَّنَا آتِهِمْ ضِعْفَيْنِ مِنَ الْعَذَابِ
وَالْعَنْهُمْ لَعْنًا كَبِيرًا ﴿٦٨﴾ ع ٨ / ٥
يَا أَيُّهَا الَّذِينَ آمَنُوا لَا تَكُونُوا
كَالَّذِينَ آذَوْا مُوسَىٰ فَبَرَّأَهُ اللَّهُ مِمَّا
قَالُوا ۚ وَكَانَ عِنْدَ اللَّهِ وَجِيهًا ﴿٦٩﴾
يَا أَيُّهَا الَّذِينَ آمَنُوا اتَّقُوا اللَّهَ
وَقُولُوا قَوْلًا سَدِيدًا ﴿٧٠﴾
يُصْلِحْ لَكُمْ أَعْمَالَكُمْ وَيَغْفِرْ لَكُمْ
ذُنُوبَكُمْ ۗ وَمَنْ يُطِعِ اللَّهَ وَرَسُولَهُ
فَقَدْ فَازَ فَوْزًا عَظِيمًا ﴿٧١﴾
إِنَّا عَرَضْنَا الْأَمَانَةَ عَلَى السَّمَاوَاتِ
وَالْأَرْضِ وَالْجِبَالِ فَأَبَيْنَ أَنْ
يَحْمِلْنَهَا وَأَشْفَقْنَ مِنْهَا وَحَمَلَهَا
الْإِنْسَانُ ۖ إِنَّهُ كَانَ ظَلُومًا جَهُولًا ﴿٧٢﴾
لِيُعَذِّبَ اللَّهُ الْمُنَافِقِينَ وَالْمُنَافِقَاتِ
وَالْمُشْرِكِينَ وَالْمُشْرِكَاتِ وَيَتُوبَ
اللَّهُ عَلَى الْمُؤْمِنِينَ وَالْمُؤْمِنَاتِ ۗ
وَكَانَ اللَّهُ غَفُورًا رَحِيمًا ﴿٧٣﴾ ع ٩ / ٦

Saba, Sheba (34)

In the Name of Allah, the Beneficent, the Merciful.

1. It is only Allah who deserves all praise. To Him belongs all that is

Sûrat Saba'-34

(Revealed at Makkah)

Bismillaahir Raḥmaanir Raḥeem

1. Al-ḥamdu lillaahil-laẕee lahoo maa fis-samaawaati

(٣٤) سُورَةُ سَبَإٍ مَكِّيَّةٌ (٥٨)

آياتها ٥٤ بِسْمِ اللَّهِ الرَّحْمَٰنِ الرَّحِيمِ ركوعاتها ٦

الْحَمْدُ لِلَّهِ الَّذِي لَهُ مَا فِي السَّمَاوَاتِ

in the heavens and the earth and it is only He who deserves to be praised in the life to come (in the end). He is All-wise and All-aware.

wa maa fil-arḍi wa lahul-ḥamdu fil-Aakhirah; wa Huwal-Ḥakeemul-Khabeer.

وَمَا فِي الْأَرْضِ وَلَهُ الْحَمْدُ فِي الْآخِرَةِ ۚ
وَهُوَ الْحَكِيمُ الْخَبِيرُ ﴿١﴾

2. He knows all that enters the earth, all that comes out of it (plants), all that descends from the sky (rain), and all that ascends to it (people's deeds). He is All-merciful and All-forgiving.

2. Ya'lamu maa yaliju fil-arḍi wa maa yakhruju minhaa wa maa yanzilu minas-samaaa'i wa maa ya'ruju feehaa; wa Huwar-Raḥeemul-Ghafoor.

يَعْلَمُ مَا يَلِجُ فِي الْأَرْضِ وَمَا يَخْرُجُ
مِنْهَا وَمَا يَنْزِلُ مِنَ السَّمَاءِ وَمَا
يَعْرُجُ فِيهَا ۚ وَهُوَ الرَّحِيمُ الْغَفُورُ ﴿٢﴾

3. The unbelievers have said, "There will be no Hour of Doom." Say, "By my Lord, it certainly will come upon you. My Lord knows the unseen. Not even an atom's weight in the heavens or the earth remains hidden from Him. Nothing exists greater or smaller than this without its record in the illustrious Book.

3. Wa qaalal-lazeena kafaroo laa ta-teenas-Saa'ah; qul balaa wa Rabbee lata-tiyannakum 'Aalimil-Ghayb; laa ya'zubu 'anhu misqaalu zarratin fis-samaawaati wa laa fil-arḍi wa laaa aṣgharu min zaalika wa laaa akbaru illaa fee kitaabim-mubeen.

وَقَالَ الَّذِينَ كَفَرُوا لَا تَأْتِينَا
السَّاعَةُ ۖ قُلْ بَلَىٰ وَرَبِّي لَتَأْتِيَنَّكُمْ
عَالِمِ الْغَيْبِ ۖ لَا يَعْزُبُ عَنْهُ مِثْقَالُ
ذَرَّةٍ فِي السَّمَاوَاتِ وَلَا فِي الْأَرْضِ وَلَا
أَصْغَرُ مِنْ ذَٰلِكَ وَلَا أَكْبَرُ إِلَّا فِي
كِتَابٍ مُبِينٍ ﴿٣﴾

4. Allah will certainly reward the righteously striving believers. These are the ones who will receive forgiveness and honorable sustenance.

4. Liyajziyal-lazeena aamanoo wa 'amiluṣ-ṣaaliḥaat; ulaaa'ika lahum-maghfiratuñw-wa rizqun kareem.

لِيَجْزِيَ الَّذِينَ آمَنُوا وَعَمِلُوا الصَّالِحَاتِ ۚ
أُولَٰئِكَ لَهُمْ مَغْفِرَةٌ وَرِزْقٌ كَرِيمٌ ﴿٤﴾

5. However, those who try to challenge Our revelations will face the most painful torment."

5. Wallazeena sa'aw feee Aayaatinaa mu'aajizeena ulaaa-'ika lahum 'azaabum-mir-rijzin aleem.

وَالَّذِينَ سَعَوْا فِي آيَاتِنَا مُعَاجِزِينَ أُولَٰئِكَ
لَهُمْ عَذَابٌ مِنْ رِجْزٍ أَلِيمٌ ﴿٥﴾

6. Those who have been given knowledge will see that whatever has been revealed to you from your Lord is the truth and that it guides to the straight path of the Majestic and Praiseworthy One.

6. Wa yaral-lazeena utul-'Ilmal-lazeee unzila ilayka mir-Rabbika huwal-ḥaqq; wa yahdeee ilaa ṣiraaṭil-'Azeezil-Ḥameed.

وَيَرَى الَّذِينَ أُوتُوا الْعِلْمَ الَّذِي
أُنْزِلَ إِلَيْكَ مِنْ رَبِّكَ هُوَ الْحَقَّ
وَيَهْدِي إِلَىٰ صِرَاطِ الْعَزِيزِ
الْحَمِيدِ ﴿٦﴾

7. The unbelievers have said, "Should we tell you about a man who says that you will be brought back to life again after you having been completely disintegrated?

7. Wa qaalal-lazeena kafaroo hal nadullukum 'alaa rajuliñy-yunabbi'ukum izaa muzziqtum kulla mumazzaq; innakum lafee khalqin jadeed.

وَقَالَ الَّذِينَ كَفَرُوا هَلْ نَدُلُّكُمْ
عَلَىٰ رَجُلٍ يُنَبِّئُكُمْ إِذَا مُزِّقْتُمْ كُلَّ
مُمَزَّقٍ إِنَّكُمْ لَفِي خَلْقٍ جَدِيدٍ ﴿٧﴾

8. Has he invented this falsehood against Allah or is he possessed by jinn?" However, those who do not have any faith in the life to come will suffer torment and stray far away from the right path.

8. Aftaraa 'alal-laahi kaziban am bihee jinnah; balil-lazeena laa yu'minoona bil-Aakhirati fil-'azaabi waḍḍalaalil-ba'eed.

أَفْتَرَىٰ عَلَى اللَّهِ كَذِبًا أَمْ بِهِ جِنَّةٌ ۗ
بَلِ الَّذِينَ لَا يُؤْمِنُونَ بِالْآخِرَةِ فِي
الْعَذَابِ وَالضَّلَالِ الْبَعِيدِ ﴿٨﴾

9. Did they not see the heavens and the earth in front and

9. Afalam yaraw ilaa maa bayna aydeehim wa maa

أَفَلَمْ يَرَوْا إِلَىٰ مَا بَيْنَ أَيْدِيهِمْ وَمَا

behind them? Had We wanted, We could have caused the earth to swallow them up or made a part of the sky fall upon them. In this there is evidence (of the truth) for every repenting person.

10. We granted David a favor by commanding the mountains and birds to sing Our praise along with him, and softened iron for him

11. so that he could make coats of mail and properly measure their rings. We told him and his people to act righteously. We are well-aware of what you do.

12. (We made subservient to) Solomon the wind that traveled a month's journey in the morning and a month's journey in the evening. We made a stream of brass flow for him and some of the jinn worked for him by his Lord's command. We would make whichever of them (jinn) who turned away from Our command to suffer a burning torment.

13. They would make for him anything that he wanted such as fortresses, statues, large basins like reservoirs, and huge immovable cooking pots. It was said, "Family of David, worship and act gratefully. Only few of my servants are grateful."

14. When We decreed that Solomon should die, no one made it (his death) public other than a creeping creature of the earth that ate up his staff. When he fell down, then it became clear to (man) that if the jinn had known the unseen, they (the jinn) would not have remained in such a humiliating torment for so long.

15. There was evidence (of the truth) for the people of Sheba in their homeland. (We gave them) two gardens, one on the left and one on the right, and (told them),

khalfahum-minas-samaaa'i wal-arḍ; in-nasha-nakhsif bihimul-arḍa aw nusqiṭ 'alayhim kisafam-minassamaaa'; inna fee zaalika la-Aayatal-likulli 'abdim-muneeb.

10. Wa laqad aataynaa Daawooda minnaa faḍlaa; yaa jibaalu awwibee ma'ahoo waṭṭayra wa alannaa lahul-ḥadeed.

11. Ani'mal saabighaatiñw-wa qaddir fis-sardi wa'maloo ṣaaliḥan innee bimaa ta'maloona Baṣeer.

12. Wa li-Sulaymaanar-reeḥa ghuduwwuhaa shahruñw-wa rawaaḥuhaa shahr; wa asal-naa lahoo 'aynal-qiṭr; wa minal-jinni mañy-ya'malu bayna yadayhi bi-izni Rabbih; wa mañy-yazigh minhum 'an amrinaa nuziqhu min 'azaabis-sa'eer.

13. Ya'maloona lahoo maa yashaaa'u mim-maḥaareeba wa tamaaseela wa jifaanin kal-jawaabi wa qudoorir-raasiyaat; i'malooo aala Daawooda shukraa; wa qaleelum-min 'ibaadiyash-shakoor.

14. Falammaa qaḍaynaa 'alayhil-mawta maa dallahum 'alaa mawtiheee illaa daaab-batul-arḍi ta-kulu minsa-atahoo falammaa kharra tabayyanatil-jinnu al-law kaanoo ya'la-moonal-ghayba maa labisoo fil-'azaabil-muheen.

15. Laqad kaana li-Saba-in fee maskanihim Aayatun janna-taani 'añy-yameeniñw-wa shimaalin kuloo

خَلْفَهُم مِّنَ السَّمَآءِ وَالْأَرْضِ ۚ إِن
نَّشَأْ نَخْسِفْ بِهِمُ الْأَرْضَ أَوْ نُسْقِطْ
عَلَيْهِمْ كِسَفًا مِّنَ السَّمَآءِ ۚ إِنَّ فِي
ذَٰلِكَ لَآيَةً لِّكُلِّ عَبْدٍ مُّنِيبٍ ﴿٩﴾ ع ٩/٧
وَلَقَدْ آتَيْنَا دَاوُودَ مِنَّا فَضْلًا ۖ
يَا جِبَالُ أَوِّبِي مَعَهُ وَالطَّيْرَ ۖ وَأَلَنَّا
لَهُ الْحَدِيدَ ﴿١٠﴾
أَنِ اعْمَلْ سَابِغَاتٍ وَقَدِّرْ فِي السَّرْدِ ۖ
وَاعْمَلُوا صَالِحًا ۖ إِنِّي بِمَا تَعْمَلُونَ
بَصِيرٌ ﴿١١﴾
وَلِسُلَيْمَانَ الرِّيحَ غُدُوُّهَا شَهْرٌ
وَرَوَاحُهَا شَهْرٌ ۖ وَأَسَلْنَا لَهُ عَيْنَ
الْقِطْرِ ۖ وَمِنَ الْجِنِّ مَن يَعْمَلُ بَيْنَ
يَدَيْهِ بِإِذْنِ رَبِّهِ ۖ وَمَن يَزِغْ مِنْهُمْ
عَنْ أَمْرِنَا نُذِقْهُ مِنْ عَذَابِ السَّعِيرِ ﴿١٢﴾
يَعْمَلُونَ لَهُ مَا يَشَاءُ مِن مَّحَارِيبَ
وَتَمَاثِيلَ وَجِفَانٍ كَالْجَوَابِ وَقُدُورٍ
رَّاسِيَاتٍ ۚ اعْمَلُوا آلَ دَاوُودَ شُكْرًا ۚ
وَقَلِيلٌ مِّنْ عِبَادِيَ الشَّكُورُ ﴿١٣﴾
فَلَمَّا قَضَيْنَا عَلَيْهِ الْمَوْتَ مَا دَلَّهُمْ
عَلَىٰ مَوْتِهِ إِلَّا دَابَّةُ الْأَرْضِ تَأْكُلُ
مِنسَأَتَهُ ۖ فَلَمَّا خَرَّ تَبَيَّنَتِ الْجِنُّ
أَن لَّوْ كَانُوا يَعْلَمُونَ الْغَيْبَ مَا لَبِثُوا
فِي الْعَذَابِ الْمُهِينِ ﴿١٤﴾
لَقَدْ كَانَ لِسَبَإٍ فِي مَسْكَنِهِمْ آيَةٌ ۖ
جَنَّتَانِ عَن يَمِينٍ وَشِمَالٍ ۖ كُلُوا

"Consume the sustenance which your Lord has given to you and give Him thanks. You have a blessed land and an All-forgiving Lord."

mir-rizqi Rabbikum washkuroo lah; baldatun ṭayyibatuñw-wa Rabbun Ghafoor.

مِنْ رِّزْقِ رَبِّكُمْ وَاشْكُرُوْا لَهٗ ؕ بَلْدَةٌ
طَيِّبَةٌ وَّرَبٌّ غَفُوْرٌ ﴿۱۵﴾

16. They ignored (the evidence) and We sent to them a flood, arising from a broken dam. Nothing was left in their gardens but bitter fruits, few tamarisks, and a few lotus trees.

16. Fa-a'raḍoo fa-arsalnaa 'alayhim Saylal-'Arimi wa baddalnaahum bijannatayhim jannatayni zawaatay ukulin khamṭiñw-wa asliñw-wa shay-'im-min sidrin qaleel.

فَاَعْرَضُوْا فَاَرْسَلْنَا عَلَيْهِمْ سَيْلَ
الْعَرِمِ وَبَدَّلْنٰهُمْ بِجَنَّتَيْهِمْ جَنَّتَيْنِ
ذَوَاتَیْ اُكُلٍ خَمْطٍ وَّاَثْلٍ وَّشَیْءٍ
مِّنْ سِدْرٍ قَلِيْلٍ ﴿۱۶﴾

17. This was how We recompensed them for their ungratefulness and thus do We recompense the ungrateful ones.

17. Zaalika jazaynaahum bimaa kafaroo wa hal nujaazeee illal-kafoor.

ذٰلِكَ جَزَيْنٰهُمْ بِمَا كَفَرُوْا ؕ وَهَلْ نُجٰزِیْۤ
اِلَّا الْكَفُوْرَ ﴿۱۷﴾

18. We established between them and the town that We had blessed, other towns nearby, and thus made it easier to travel. We told them, "Travel there safely day and night."

18. Wa ja'alnaa baynahum wa baynal-qural-latee baaraknaa feeha quran ẓaahiratañw-wa qaddarnaa feehas-sayr; seeroo feehaa la-yaaliya wa ayyaaman aamineen.

وَجَعَلْنَا بَيْنَهُمْ وَبَيْنَ الْقُرَى
الَّتِیْ بٰرَكْنَا فِيْهَا قُرًى ظَاهِرَةً وَّ
قَدَّرْنَا فِيْهَا السَّيْرَ ؕ سِيْرُوْا فِيْهَا
لَيَالِیَ وَاَيَّامًا اٰمِنِيْنَ ﴿۱۸﴾

19. They said, "Lord, make the distances of our journeys longer." They did injustice to themselves and We turned their existence into ancient tales by making them disintegrate totally. In this there is evidence (of the truth) for every forbearing and grateful person.

19. Faqaaloo Rabbanaa baa-'id bayna asfaarinaa wa ẓalamooo anfusahum faja'alnaahum aḥaadeesa wa mazzaqnaahum kulla mumazzaq; inna fee zaalika la-Aayaatil-likulli ṣabbaarin-shakoor.

فَقَالُوْا رَبَّنَا بٰعِدْ بَيْنَ اَسْفَارِنَا
وَظَلَمُوْۤا اَنْفُسَهُمْ فَجَعَلْنٰهُمْ اَحَادِيْثَ
وَمَزَّقْنٰهُمْ كُلَّ مُمَزَّقٍ ؕ اِنَّ فِیْ ذٰلِكَ
لَاٰيٰتٍ لِّكُلِّ صَبَّارٍ شَكُوْرٍ ﴿۱۹﴾

20. Iblis (Satan) made his judgment about them to come true. They all followed them except a believing group among them.

20. Wa laqad ṣaddaqa 'alayhim Ibleesu ẓannahoo fattaba'oohu illaa fareeqam-minal-mu'mineen.

وَلَقَدْ صَدَّقَ عَلَيْهِمْ اِبْلِيْسُ ظَنَّهٗ
فَاتَّبَعُوْهُ اِلَّا فَرِيْقًا مِّنَ الْمُؤْمِنِيْنَ ﴿۲۰﴾

21. He did not have any authority over them except to the extent that would allow Us to know who had faith in the life to come and who had doubts about it. Your Lord is a Guard over all things.

21. Wa maa kaana lahoo 'alayhim-min sulṭaanin illaa lina'lama mañy-yu'minu bil-Aakhirati mimman huwa minhaa fee shakk; wa Rabbuka 'alaa kulli shay'in Ḥafeeẓ.

وَمَا كَانَ لَهٗ عَلَيْهِمْ مِّنْ سُلْطٰنٍ اِلَّا
لِنَعْلَمَ مَنْ يُّؤْمِنُ بِالْاٰخِرَةِ مِمَّنْ
هُوَ مِنْهَا فِیْ شَكٍّ ؕ وَرَبُّكَ عَلٰى كُلِّ
شَیْءٍ حَفِيْظٌ ﴿۲۱﴾ ع ۱۲ ۸

22. (Muhammad), say to them, "Ask help from those whom you worship besides Allah. They do not possess an atom's weight in the heavens and the earth, have no share therein, nor will any of their idols be able to support them."

22. Qulid-'ul-lazeena za'amtum-min doonil-laahi laa yamlikoona misqaala zarratin fis-samaawaati wa laa fil-arḍi wa maa lahum feehimaa min shirkiñw-wa maa lahoo minhum- min ẓaheer.

قُلِ ادْعُوا الَّذِيْنَ زَعَمْتُمْ مِّنْ دُوْنِ
اللّٰهِ ۚ لَا يَمْلِكُوْنَ مِثْقَالَ ذَرَّةٍ فِی
السَّمٰوٰتِ وَلَا فِی الْاَرْضِ وَمَا لَهُمْ
فِيْهِمَا مِنْ شِرْكٍ وَّمَا لَهٗ مِنْهُمْ

23. No intercession with Him will be of any benefit except that of those whom He has granted permission. Fear vanishes from their heart when (they receive a message from their Lord). They ask each other, "What did your Lord say?" Others answer, "He spoke the Truth. He is the Most High and the Most Great."

24. Say, "Who provides you with sustenance from the heavens and the earth?" Say, "It is Allah. Only one group among us has the true guidance. The others must certainly be in plain error."

25. Say, "You will not be questioned about our sins nor shall we about your deeds."

26. Say, "Our Lord will gather us all together and issue the true Judgment about our differences. He is the Best Judge and All-knowing."

27. Say, "Show me those whom you have related to Allah as His partner. He is free of all defects of having any partners. He is the Majestic and All-wise Allah."

28. We have sent you as a bearer of glad news and a Warner to the whole of mankind, but most people do not know.

29. They say, "When will the Day of Judgment be if what you say is true?"

30. Say, "That day has already been decreed for you and you cannot change the time of its coming even by a single hour."

31. The unbelievers have said, "We shall never believe in this Quran nor in the Bible." If you see the unjust halted in the presence of their Lord, you find them exchanging words among themselves. The oppressed among them say to their oppressors, "Had it not been for

23. Wa laa tanfa'ush-shafaa'atu 'indahooo illaa liman a<u>z</u>ina lah; ḥattaaa i<u>z</u>aa fuzzi'a 'an quloobihim qaaloo maa<u>z</u>aa qaala Rabbukum; qaalul-ḥaqq; wa Huwal-'Aliyyul-Kabeer.

24. Qul mañy-yarzuqukum-minas-samaawaati wal-arḍi qulil-laahu wa innaaa aw iyyaakum la'alaa hudan aw fee ḍalaalim-mubeen.

25. Qul laa tus'aloona 'ammaaa ajramnaa wa laa nus'alu 'ammaa ta'maloon.

26. Qul yajma'u baynanaa Rabbunaa <u>s</u>umma yaftaḥu baynanaa bilḥaqq; wa Huwal-Fattaaḥul-'Aleem.

27. Qul arooniyal-la<u>z</u>eena alḥaqtum bihee shurakaaa'a kallaa; bal Huwal-laahul 'Azeezul-Ḥakeem.

28. Wa maaa arsalnaaka illaa kaaaffatal-linnaasi basheerañw-wa na<u>z</u>eerañw-wa laakinna ak<u>s</u>aran-naasi laa ya'lamoon.

29. Wa yaqooloona mataa haa<u>z</u>al-wa'du in kuntum ṣaadiqeen.

30. Qul lakum-mee'aadu Yawmil-laa tasta-khiroona 'anhu saa'atañw-wa laa tastaqdimoon.

31. Wa qaalal-la<u>z</u>eena kafaroo lan-nu'mina bihaa<u>z</u>al-Qur'aani wa laa billa<u>z</u>ee bayna yadayh; wa law taraaa iziẓ-ẓaalimoona mawqoofoona 'inda Rabbihim yarji'u ba'ḍuhum ilaa ba'ḍinil qawla yaqoolul-la<u>z</u>eenas-tuḍ'ifoo

مِّن ظَهِيرٍ ﴿٢٢﴾
وَلَا تَنفَعُ الشَّفَاعَةُ عِندَهُ إِلَّا لِمَنْ
أَذِنَ لَهُ حَتَّىٰ إِذَا فُزِّعَ عَن
قُلُوبِهِمْ قَالُوا مَاذَا قَالَ رَبُّكُمْ قَالُوا
الْحَقَّ وَهُوَ الْعَلِيُّ الْكَبِيرُ ﴿٢٣﴾
قُلْ مَن يَرْزُقُكُم مِّنَ السَّمَاوَاتِ وَالْأَرْضِ
قُلِ اللَّهُ وَإِنَّا أَوْ إِيَّاكُمْ لَعَلَىٰ هُدًى
أَوْ فِي ضَلَالٍ مُّبِينٍ ﴿٢٤﴾
قُل لَّا تُسْأَلُونَ عَمَّا أَجْرَمْنَا وَلَا
نُسْأَلُ عَمَّا تَعْمَلُونَ ﴿٢٥﴾
قُلْ يَجْمَعُ بَيْنَنَا رَبُّنَا ثُمَّ يَفْتَحُ بَيْنَنَا
بِالْحَقِّ وَهُوَ الْفَتَّاحُ الْعَلِيمُ ﴿٢٦﴾
قُلْ أَرُونِيَ الَّذِينَ أَلْحَقْتُم بِهِ شُرَكَاءَ
كَلَّا بَلْ هُوَ اللَّهُ الْعَزِيزُ الْحَكِيمُ ﴿٢٧﴾
وَمَا أَرْسَلْنَاكَ إِلَّا كَافَّةً لِّلنَّاسِ
بَشِيرًا وَنَذِيرًا وَلَٰكِنَّ أَكْثَرَ النَّاسِ
لَا يَعْلَمُونَ ﴿٢٨﴾
وَيَقُولُونَ مَتَىٰ هَٰذَا الْوَعْدُ إِن
كُنتُمْ صَادِقِينَ ﴿٢٩﴾
قُل لَّكُم مِّيعَادُ يَوْمٍ لَّا تَسْتَأْخِرُونَ
عَنْهُ سَاعَةً وَلَا تَسْتَقْدِمُونَ ﴿٣٠﴾ ع
وَقَالَ الَّذِينَ كَفَرُوا لَن نُّؤْمِنَ بِهَٰذَا
الْقُرْآنِ وَلَا بِالَّذِي بَيْنَ يَدَيْهِ وَلَوْ
تَرَىٰ إِذِ الظَّالِمُونَ مَوْقُوفُونَ عِندَ
رَبِّهِمْ يَرْجِعُ بَعْضُهُمْ إِلَىٰ بَعْضٍ
الْقَوْلَ يَقُولُ الَّذِينَ اسْتُضْعِفُوا

لِلَّذِينَ اسْتَكْبَرُوا لَوْلَا أَنتُمْ
لَكُنَّا مُؤْمِنِينَ ٣١

lillazeenas-takbaroo law laaa antum lakunnaa mu'mineen.

you, we would certainly have been believers."

قَالَ الَّذِينَ اسْتَكْبَرُوا لِلَّذِينَ
اسْتُضْعِفُوا أَنَحْنُ صَدَدْنَاكُمْ عَنِ
الْهُدَىٰ بَعْدَ إِذْ جَاءَكُم ۖ بَلْ كُنتُم
مُّجْرِمِينَ ٣٢

32. Qaalal-lazeenas-takbaroo lillazeenas-tuḍ'ifooo anaḥnu ṣadadnaakum 'anil-hudaa ba'da iz jaaa'akum bal kuntum-mujrimeen.

32. The oppressing ones will say to the oppressed ones, "Did we prevent you from having guidance after it had come to you? In fact, you yourselves were criminals."

وَقَالَ الَّذِينَ اسْتُضْعِفُوا لِلَّذِينَ
اسْتَكْبَرُوا بَلْ مَكْرُ اللَّيْلِ وَالنَّهَارِ إِذْ
تَأْمُرُونَنَا أَن نَّكْفُرَ بِاللَّهِ وَنَجْعَلَ
لَهُ أَندَادًا ۚ وَأَسَرُّوا النَّدَامَةَ لَمَّا
رَأَوُا الْعَذَابَ ۚ وَجَعَلْنَا الْأَغْلَالَ
فِي أَعْنَاقِ الَّذِينَ كَفَرُوا ۚ هَلْ
يُجْزَوْنَ إِلَّا مَا كَانُوا يَعْمَلُونَ ٣٣

33. Wa qaalal-lazeenastuḍ'ifoo lillazeenas-takbaroo bal makrul-layli wannahaari iz ta-muroonanaaa an-nakfura billaahi wa naj'ala lahooo andaadaa; wa asarrun-nadaamata lammaa ra-awul-'azaab; wa ja'alnal-aghlaala feee a'naaqil-lazeena kafaroo; hal yujzawna illaa maa kaanoo ya'maloon.

33. The oppressed ones will say to them, "It was you who planned night and day, ordering us to disbelieve Allah, and consider other things equal to Him." They will hide their regret on seeing their torment. We shall chain the necks of the unbelievers. Can they be recompensed with other than what they deserved for their deeds?

وَمَا أَرْسَلْنَا فِي قَرْيَةٍ مِّن نَّذِيرٍ إِلَّا
قَالَ مُتْرَفُوهَا إِنَّا بِمَا أُرْسِلْتُم
بِهِ كَافِرُونَ ٣٤

34. Wa maaa arsalnaa fee qaryatim-min-nazeerin illaa qaala mutrafoohaaa innaa bimaaa ursiltum bihee kaafiroon.

34. Every time We sent a Warner to a town, the rich ones therein said (to Our Messenger), "We have no faith in what you have brought (to us).

وَقَالُوا نَحْنُ أَكْثَرُ أَمْوَالًا وَأَوْلَادًا
وَمَا نَحْنُ بِمُعَذَّبِينَ ٣٥

35. Wa qaaloo naḥnu aksaru amwaalañw-wa awlaadañw-wa maa naḥnu bimu'az-zabeen.

35. We are the ones who have more wealth and children and we shall suffer no punishment."

قُلْ إِنَّ رَبِّي يَبْسُطُ الرِّزْقَ لِمَن
يَشَاءُ وَيَقْدِرُ وَلَٰكِنَّ أَكْثَرَ النَّاسِ
لَا يَعْلَمُونَ ٣٦

36. Qul inna Rabbee yabsuṭur-rizqa limañy-yashaaa'u wa yaqdiru wa laakinna aksaran-naasi laa ya'lamoon.

36. Say, "My Lord increases and measures the sustenance of whomever He wants, but most people do not know."

وَمَا أَمْوَالُكُمْ وَلَا أَوْلَادُكُم بِالَّتِي
تُقَرِّبُكُمْ عِندَنَا زُلْفَىٰ إِلَّا مَنْ آمَنَ
وَعَمِلَ صَالِحًا فَأُولَٰئِكَ لَهُمْ جَزَاءُ
الضِّعْفِ بِمَا عَمِلُوا وَهُمْ فِي الْغُرُفَاتِ
آمِنُونَ ٣٧

37. Wa maaa amwaalukum wa laaa awlaadukum billatee tuqarribukum 'indanaa zulfaaa illaa man aamana wa 'amila ṣaaliḥan fa-ulaaa'ika lahum jazaaa'uḍ-ḍi'fi bimaa 'amiloo wa hum fil-ghurufaati aaminoon.

37. Your property and children cannot bring you closer to Us. Only those who believe and act righteously will have double reward for their deeds and will live in secure mansions.

38. Those who try to challenge Our revelations will be driven into torment.

38. Walla<u>z</u>eena yas'awna feee Aayaatinaa mu'aajizeena ulaaa'ika fil-'a<u>z</u>aabi muḥḍaroon.

وَالَّذِينَ يَسْعَوْنَ فِيٓ ءَايَٰتِنَا مُعَٰجِزِينَ
أُولَٰٓئِكَ فِي الْعَذَابِ مُحْضَرُونَ ﴿٣٨﴾

39. Say, "It is my Lord who increases and measures the sustenance of whomever of His servants He wants. He will replace whatever you spend for His cause and He is the best Provider."

39. Qul inna Rabbee yabsuṭur-rizqa limañy-yashaaa'u min 'ibaadihee wa yaqdiru lah; wa maaa anfaqtum-min shay'in fahuwa yukhlifuhoo wa Huwa khayrur-raaziqeen.

قُلْ إِنَّ رَبِّي يَبْسُطُ الرِّزْقَ لِمَن يَشَآءُ
مِنْ عِبَادِهِ وَيَقْدِرُ لَهُ وَمَآ أَنفَقْتُم
مِّن شَيْءٍ فَهُوَ يُخْلِفُهُ وَهُوَ
خَيْرُ الرَّٰزِقِينَ ﴿٣٩﴾

40. On the day when Allah will raise them all together and ask the angels, "Had these people been worshipping you?"

40. Wa Yawma yaḥshuruhum jamee'an <u>s</u>umma yaqoolu lilmalaaa'ikati a-haaa'ulaaa'i iyyaakum kaanoo ya'budoon.

وَيَوْمَ يَحْشُرُهُمْ جَمِيعًا ثُمَّ يَقُولُ
لِلْمَلَٰٓئِكَةِ أَهَٰٓؤُلَآءِ إِيَّاكُمْ كَانُوا
يَعْبُدُونَ ﴿٤٠﴾

41. They will reply, "All glory belongs to you. You are our Guardian, not they. They had been worshipping the jinn and most of them had strong faith."

41. Qaaloo Subḥaanaka Anta waliyyunaa min doonihim bal kaanoo ya'budoonal-jinna ak<u>s</u>aruhum bihim-mu'minoon.

قَالُوا سُبْحَٰنَكَ أَنتَ وَلِيُّنَا مِن
دُونِهِم بَلْ كَانُوا يَعْبُدُونَ
الْجِنَّ أَكْثَرُهُم بِهِم مُّؤْمِنُونَ ﴿٤١﴾

42. None of them can help or harm each other on this day. We shall tell the unjust ones, "Suffer the torment of the fire which you had called a lie."

42. Fal-Yawma laa yamliku ba'ḍukum liba'ḍin-naf'añw-wa laa ḍarraa; wa naqoolu lilla<u>z</u>eena ẓalamoo <u>z</u>ooqoo 'a<u>z</u>aaban-Naaril-latee kuntum bihaa tuka<u>z</u>-<u>z</u>iboon.

فَالْيَوْمَ لَا يَمْلِكُ بَعْضُكُمْ لِبَعْضٍ
نَّفْعًا وَلَا ضَرًّا وَنَقُولُ لِلَّذِينَ
ظَلَمُوا ذُوقُوا عَذَابَ النَّارِ الَّتِي كُنتُم
بِهَا تُكَذِّبُونَ ﴿٤٢﴾

43. When Our illustrious revelations are recited to them, they say, "This man only wants to prevent you from worshipping what your fathers had worshipped." They have said, "This (the Quran) is nothing but an invented lie." The unbelievers have said about the truth when it came to them, "This only is plain magic."

43. Wa i<u>z</u>aa tutlaa 'alayhim Aayaatunaa bayyinaatin qaaloo maa haa<u>z</u>aaa illaa rajuluñy-yureedu añy-yaṣuddakum 'ammaa kaana ya'budu aabaaa'ukum wa qaaloo maa haa<u>z</u>aaa illaaa ifkum-muftaraa; wa qaalal-la<u>z</u>eena kafaroo lilḥaqqi lammaa jaaa'ahum in haa<u>z</u>aaa illaa siḥrum-mubeen.

وَإِذَا تُتْلَىٰ عَلَيْهِمْ ءَايَٰتُنَا بَيِّنَٰتٍ قَالُوا
مَا هَٰذَآ إِلَّا رَجُلٌ يُرِيدُ أَن يَصُدَّكُمْ
عَمَّا كَانَ يَعْبُدُ ءَابَآؤُكُمْ وَقَالُوا
مَا هَٰذَآ إِلَّآ إِفْكٌ مُّفْتَرًى وَقَالَ
الَّذِينَ كَفَرُوا لِلْحَقِّ لَمَّا جَآءَهُمْ
إِنْ هَٰذَآ إِلَّا سِحْرٌ مُّبِينٌ ﴿٤٣﴾

44. We did not send to them (the pagans) any books to study nor a Messenger to warn them, and those who lived before them had rejected the Truth.

44. Wa maaa aataynaahum min Kutubiñy-yadrusoonahaa wa maaa arsalnaaa ilayhim qablaka min-na<u>z</u>eer.

وَمَآ ءَاتَيْنَٰهُم مِّن كُتُبٍ يَدْرُسُونَهَا
وَمَآ أَرْسَلْنَآ إِلَيْهِمْ قَبْلَكَ مِن
نَّذِيرٍ ﴿٤٤﴾

45. People who lived before refused to accept what Our messengers preached to them although those

45. Wa ka<u>z</u><u>z</u>abal-la<u>z</u>eena min qablihim wa maa

وَكَذَّبَ الَّذِينَ مِن قَبْلِهِمْ وَمَا

messengers had not received from Us even one tenth of what we have given to them (Prophet Muhammad and his people). They, however, rejected Our messengers. Thus, how strong was Our condemnation against them.

balaghoo mi'shaara maaa aataynaahum fakazzaboo Rusulee; fakayfa kaana nakeer.

بَلَغُوا مِعْشَارَ مَا آتَيْنَاهُمْ فَكَذَّبُوا
رُسُلِي ۖ فَكَيْفَ كَانَ نَكِيرِ ﴿٤٥﴾ ع ٥ ١١

46. Say, "I advise you to believe only in One and you must worship Allah individually or two people together." Think carefully; your companion is not possessed by jinn. He is only warning you of the coming severe torment.

46. Qul innamaaa a'izukum biwaahidatin an taqoomoo lillaahi masnaa wa furaadaa summa tatafakkaroo; maa bisaahibikum-min jinnah; in huwa illaa nazeerul-lakum bayna yaday 'azaabin shadeed.

قُلْ إِنَّمَا أَعِظُكُمْ بِوَاحِدَةٍ ۖ أَنْ
تَقُومُوا لِلَّهِ مَثْنَىٰ وَفُرَادَىٰ ثُمَّ
تَتَفَكَّرُوا ۚ مَا بِصَاحِبِكُمْ مِنْ جِنَّةٍ ۚ
إِنْ هُوَ إِلَّا نَذِيرٌ لَكُمْ بَيْنَ يَدَيْ
عَذَابٍ شَدِيدٍ ﴿٤٦﴾

47. Say, "Whatever reward I ask you (for my preaching) will be for your own good. No one can reward me except Allah. He is the Witness over all things."

47. Qul maa sa-altukum-min ajrin fahuwa lakum in ajriya illaa 'alal-laahi wa Huwa 'alaa kulli shay'in Shaheed.

قُلْ مَا سَأَلْتُكُمْ مِنْ أَجْرٍ فَهُوَ لَكُمْ ۖ
إِنْ أَجْرِيَ إِلَّا عَلَى اللَّهِ ۖ وَهُوَ عَلَىٰ
كُلِّ شَيْءٍ شَهِيدٌ ﴿٤٧﴾

48. Say, "My Lord speaks the Truth. He has the knowledge of the unseen."

48. Qul inna Rabbee yaqzifu bilhaqq; 'Allaamul-Ghuyoob.

قُلْ إِنَّ رَبِّي يَقْذِفُ بِالْحَقِّ ۚ
عَلَّامُ الْغُيُوبِ ﴿٤٨﴾

49. Say, "The truth has come. Falsehood has vanished and it will not come back again."

49. Qul jaaa'al-haqqu wa maa yubdi'ul-baatilu wa maa yu'eed.

قُلْ جَاءَ الْحَقُّ وَمَا يُبْدِئُ الْبَاطِلُ
وَمَا يُعِيدُ ﴿٤٩﴾

50. Say, "If I go astray it will only be against my own soul, but if I receive guidance, it will be through my Lord's revelations." He is All-hearing and Omnipresent.

50. Qul in dalaltu fa-innamaaa adillu 'alaa nafsee wa inihtadaytu fabimaa yooheee ilayya Rabbeee; innahoo Samee'un Qareeb.

قُلْ إِنْ ضَلَلْتُ فَإِنَّمَا أَضِلُّ عَلَىٰ
نَفْسِي ۖ وَإِنِ اهْتَدَيْتُ فَبِمَا يُوحِي
إِلَيَّ رَبِّي ۚ إِنَّهُ سَمِيعٌ قَرِيبٌ ﴿٥٠﴾

51. Would that you could see how the unbelievers will be terrified by death from which they cannot escape. They will be seized from a nearby place

51. Wa law taraaa iz fazi'oo falaa fawta wa ukhizoo mim-makaanin qareeb.

وَلَوْ تَرَىٰ إِذْ فَزِعُوا فَلَا فَوْتَ وَأُخِذُوا
مِنْ مَكَانٍ قَرِيبٍ ﴿٥١﴾

52. and then they will say, "We have faith in the Quran." How can they have any guidance through ways that never provide any guidance when the ways that did provide them guidance were ignored?

52. Wa qaaloo aamannaa bihee wa annaa lahumut-tanaawushu mim-makaanim ba'eed.

وَقَالُوا آمَنَّا بِهِ ۚ وَأَنَّىٰ لَهُمُ التَّنَاوُشُ
مِنْ مَكَانٍ بَعِيدٍ ﴿٥٢﴾

53. They had rejected it in their worldly life and expressed disbelief in the unseen (Day of Judgment), considering it less than a remote possibility.

53. Wa qad kafaroo bihee min qablu wa yaqzifoona bilghaybi mim-makaanim ba'eed.

وَقَدْ كَفَرُوا بِهِ مِنْ قَبْلُ ۖ وَيَقْذِفُونَ
بِالْغَيْبِ مِنْ مَكَانٍ بَعِيدٍ ﴿٥٣﴾

54. A gulf will exist between them and their desires on the Day of Judgment like the similar people who lived before. They, also, had lived in doubt and uncertainty (about the life hereafter).

54. Wa heela baynahum wa bayna maa yashtahoona kamaa fu'ila bi-ashyaa'ihim-min qabl; innahum kaanoo fee shakkim-mureeb.

وَحِيلَ بَيْنَهُمْ وَبَيْنَ مَا يَشْتَهُونَ كَمَا
فُعِلَ بِأَشْيَاعِهِمْ مِنْ قَبْلُ ۚ إِنَّهُمْ
كَانُوا فِي شَكٍّ مُرِيبٍ ﴿٥٤﴾ ع ٦ ١٢

Al-Fatir, The Originator (35)

In the Name of Allah,
the Beneficent, the Merciful.

Sûrat Fâṭir-35

(Revealed at Makkah)
Bismillaahir Raḥmaanir Raḥeem

سُوۡرَةُ فَاطِرٍ مَكِّيَّةٌ (٣٥) (٤٣)
(اٰيَاتُهَا ٤٥) بِسۡمِ اللّٰهِ الرَّحۡمٰنِ الرَّحِيۡمِ (رُكُوۡعَاتُهَا ٥)

1. All praise belongs to Allah, the creator of the heavens and the earth, who has made the angels Messengers of two or three or four wings. He increases the creation as He wills. Allah has power over all things.

1. Al-ḥamdu lillaahi faaṭiris-samaawaati wal-arḍi jaa'ilil-malaaa'ikati rusulan uleee ajniḥatim-masnaa wa sulaasa wa rubaa'; yazeedu fil-khalqi maa yashaaa'; innal-laaha 'alaa kulli shay'in Qadeer.

الۡحَمۡدُ لِلّٰهِ فَاطِرِ السَّمٰوٰتِ وَالۡاَرۡضِ
جَاعِلِ الۡمَلٰٓـئِكَةِ رُسُلًا اُولِىۡۤ اَجۡنِحَةٍ
مَّثۡنٰى وَثُلٰثَ وَرُبٰعَ ؕ يَزِيۡدُ فِى الۡخَـلۡقِ
مَا يَشَآءُ ؕ اِنَّ اللّٰهَ عَلٰى كُلِّ شَىۡءٍ قَدِيۡرٌ ﴿١﴾

2. No one can withhold whatever mercy Allah grants to the human being, nor can one release whatever He withholds. He is Majestic and All-wise.

2. Maa yaftaḥil-laahu lin-naasi mir-raḥmatin falaa mumsika lahaa wa maa yumsik falaa mursila lahoo mimba'dih; wa Huwal-'Azeezul-Ḥakeem.

مَا يَفۡتَحِ اللّٰهُ لِلنَّاسِ مِنۡ رَّحۡمَةٍ
فَلَا مُمۡسِكَ لَهَا ۚ وَمَا يُمۡسِكۡ ۙ
فَلَا مُرۡسِلَ لَهٗ مِنۡۢ بَعۡدِهٖ ؕ وَهُوَ
الۡعَزِيۡزُ الۡحَكِيۡمُ ﴿٢﴾

3. People, remember the bounty of Allah that He has granted to you. Is there any creator besides Allah who could provide you with sustenance from the heavens and the earth? He is the only Ilah (one deserving to be worshiped). Where then can you turn away?

3. Yaaa ayyuhan-naasuz-kuroo ni'matal-laahi 'alaykum; hal min khaaliqin ghayrul-laahi yarzuqukum-minas-samaaa'i wal-arḍ; laaa ilaaha illaa Huwa fa-annaa tu'fakoon.

يٰۤاَيُّهَا النَّاسُ اذۡكُرُوۡا نِعۡمَتَ اللّٰهِ
عَلَيۡكُمۡ ؕ هَلۡ مِنۡ خَالِقٍ غَيۡرُ اللّٰهِ
يَرۡزُقُكُمۡ مِّنَ السَّمَآءِ وَالۡاَرۡضِ ؕ لَاۤ
اِلٰهَ اِلَّا هُوَ ۖ فَاَنّٰى تُؤۡفَكُوۡنَ ﴿٣﴾

4. If they reject you, other messengers had certainly been rejected before you. All decisions are in the hands of Allah.

4. Wa iñy-yukazzibooka faqad kuzzibat Rusulum-min qablik; wa ilal-laahi turja'ul-umoor.

وَاِنۡ يُّكَذِّبُوۡكَ فَقَدۡ كُذِّبَتۡ
رُسُلٌ مِّنۡ قَبۡلِكَ ؕ وَاِلَى اللّٰهِ تُرۡجَعُ
الۡاُمُوۡرُ ﴿٤﴾

5. People, the promise of Allah is true. Let not the worldly life deceive you. Let not the devil deceive you about Allah.

5. Yaaa ayyuhan-naasu inna wa'dal-laahi ḥaqqun falaa taghurrannakumul-ḥayaatud-dunyaa: wa laa yaghurran-nakum billaahil-gharoor.

يٰۤاَيُّهَا النَّاسُ اِنَّ وَعۡدَ اللّٰهِ حَقٌّ
فَلَا تَغُرَّنَّكُمُ الۡحَيٰوةُ الدُّنۡيَا ٚ وَلَا
يَغُرَّنَّكُمۡ بِاللّٰهِ الۡغَرُوۡرُ ﴿٥﴾

6. Satan is your enemy. Thus, consider him as your enemy. His party only calls you to make you the dwellers in the burning fire.

6. Innash-Shayṭaana lakum 'aduwwun fattakhizoohu 'aduwwaa; innamaa yad'oo ḥizbahoo liyakoonoo min aṣḥaabis-sa'eer.

اِنَّ الشَّيۡطٰنَ لَـكُمۡ عَدُوٌّ فَاتَّخِذُوۡهُ
عَدُوًّا ؕ اِنَّمَا يَدۡعُوۡا حِزۡبَهٗ لِيَكُوۡنُوۡا
مِنۡ اَصۡحٰبِ السَّعِيۡرِ ؕ ﴿٦﴾

7. The unbelievers will suffer a severe torment, but the righteously striving believers will receive forgiveness and a great reward.

7. Allazeena kafaroo lahum 'azaabun shadeed; wallazeena aamanoo wa 'amiluṣ-ṣaaliḥaati lahum-maghfiratuñw-wa ajrun kabeer.

اَلَّذِيۡنَ كَفَرُوۡا لَهُمۡ عَذَابٌ
شَدِيۡدٌ ؕ وَالَّذِيۡنَ اٰمَنُوۡا وَعَمِلُوا
الصّٰلِحٰتِ لَهُمۡ مَّغۡفِرَةٌ وَّاَجۡرٌ كَبِيۡرٌ ﴿٧﴾ ع

8. Can one whose evil deeds seem attractive and virtuous to him (be compared to a truly righteous person)? Allah guides or causes to go astray whomever He wants. (Muhammad), do not be grieved because of their disbelief. Allah knows well whatever they do.

8. Afaman zuyyina lahoo sooo'u 'amalihee fara-aahu ḥasanaa; fa-innal-laaha yuḍillu mañy-yashaaa'u wa yahdee mañy-yashaaa'u falaa taẕhab nafsuka 'alayhim ḥasaraat; innal-laaha 'aleemum bimaa yaṣna'oon.

اَفَمَنْ زُيِّنَ لَهٗ سُوْٓءُ عَمَلِهٖ فَرَاٰهُ
حَسَنًا ۭ فَاِنَّ اللّٰهَ يُضِلُّ مَنْ يَّشَاۗءُ
وَيَهْدِيْ مَنْ يَّشَاۗءُ ڮ فَلَا تَذْهَبْ
نَفْسُكَ عَلَيْهِمْ حَسَرٰتٍ ۭ اِنَّ اللّٰهَ
عَلِيْمٌۢ بِمَا يَصْنَعُوْنَ ﴿٨﴾

9. It is Allah who sends the winds to raise the clouds. We then drive them unto barren areas and revive the dead earth. (The Resurrection) will also be executed in the same way.

9. Wallaahul-laẕeee arsalar-riyaaḥa fatuṯeeru saḥaaban fasuqnaahu ilaa baladim-mayyitin fa-aḥyaynaa bihil-arḍa ba'da mawtihaa; kaẕaa-likan-nushoor.

وَاللّٰهُ الَّذِيْٓ اَرْسَلَ الرِّيٰحَ فَتُثِيْرُ
سَحَابًا فَسُقْنٰهُ اِلٰى بَلَدٍ مَّيِّتٍ
فَاَحْيَيْنَا بِهِ الْاَرْضَ بَعْدَ مَوْتِهَا ۭ
كَذٰلِكَ النُّشُوْرُ ﴿٩﴾

10. Whoever seeks honor should know that all honor belongs to Allah. Good words (worship) will be presented before Him and He will accept good deeds. Those who make evil plans will suffer intense torment. Their evil plans are doomed to destruction.

10. Man kaana yureedul 'izzata falillaahil-'izzatu jamee'aa; ilayhi yaṣ'aḍul-kalimuṭ-ṭayyibu wal'amaluṣ-ṣaaliḥu yarfa'uh; wallaẕeena yamkuroonas-sayyi-aati lahum 'aẕaabun shadeed; wa makru ulaaa'ika huwa yaboor.

مَنْ كَانَ يُرِيْدُ الْعِزَّةَ فَلِلّٰهِ الْعِزَّةُ
جَمِيْعًا ۭ اِلَيْهِ يَصْعَدُ الْكَلِمُ
الطَّيِّبُ وَالْعَمَلُ الصَّالِحُ يَرْفَعُهٗ ۭ
وَالَّذِيْنَ يَمْكُرُوْنَ السَّيِّاٰتِ لَهُمْ
عَذَابٌ شَدِيْدٌ ۭ وَمَكْرُ اُولٰۗىِٕكَ
هُوَ يَبُوْرُ ﴿١٠﴾

11. Allah created you from clay which He then turned into a living germ and made you into pairs. No female conceives or delivers without His knowledge. No one grows older nor can anything be reduced from one's life without having its record in the Book. This is not at all difficult for Allah.

11. Wallaahu khalaqakum-min turaabin ṯumma min-nuṭfatin ṯumma ja'alakum azwaajaa; wa maa taḥmilu min unṯaa wa laa taḍa'u illaa bi'ilmih; wa maa yu'ammaru mim-mu'ammariñw-wa laa yunqaṣu min 'umuriheee illaa fee kitaab; inna ẕaalika 'alal-laahi yaseer.

وَاللّٰهُ خَلَقَكُمْ مِّنْ تُرَابٍ ثُمَّ مِنْ
نُّطْفَةٍ ثُمَّ جَعَلَكُمْ اَزْوَاجًا ۭ وَمَا
تَحْمِلُ مِنْ اُنْثٰى وَلَا تَضَعُ اِلَّا
بِعِلْمِهٖ ۭ وَمَا يُعَمَّرُ مِنْ مُّعَمَّرٍ وَّلَا
يُنْقَصُ مِنْ عُمُرِهٖٓ اِلَّا فِيْ كِتٰبٍ ۭ
اِنَّ ذٰلِكَ عَلَي اللّٰهِ يَسِيْرٌ ﴿١١﴾

12. The two oceans, one sweet and the other salty, are not alike. From each you can eat fresh meat and obtain ornaments to use. You can see ships go back and forth in the ocean so that you may seek His favor and give Him thanks.

12. Wa maa yastawil-baḥraani haaẕaa 'aẕbun furaatun saaa'ighun sharaabuhoo wa haaẕaa milḥun ujaaj; wa min kullin ta-kuloona laḥman ṭariyyañw-wa tastakhrijoona ḥilyatan talbasoonahaa wa taral-fulka feehi mawaakhira litabtaghoo

وَمَا يَسْتَوِي الْبَحْرٰنِ ڰ هٰذَا عَذْبٌ
فُرَاتٌ سَاۗىِٕغٌ شَرَابُهٗ وَهٰذَا مِلْحٌ
اُجَاجٌ ۭ وَمِنْ كُلٍّ تَاْكُلُوْنَ لَحْمًا طَرِيًّا
وَّتَسْتَخْرِجُوْنَ حِلْيَةً تَلْبَسُوْنَهَا ۚ وَ
تَرَى الْفُلْكَ فِيْهِ مَوَاخِرَ لِتَبْتَغُوْا

min faḍlihee wa la'allakum tashkuroon.

مِنْ فَضْلِهٖ وَلَعَلَّكُمْ تَشْكُرُوْنَ ﴿١٢﴾

13. He causes the night to enter into the day and the day to enter into the night. He has made subservient to Himself the sun and moon, each moving in an orbit for an appointed time. Such is Allah, your Lord, to whom belongs the kingdom. Those whom you worship besides Him do not possess even a single straw.

13. Yoolijul-layla fin-nahaari wa yoolijun-nahaara fil-layli wa sakhkharash-shamsa wal-qamara kulluñy-yajree li-ajalim-musamma; zaalikumul-laahu Rabbukum lahul-mulk; wallazeena tad'oona min doonihee maa yamlikoona min qiṭmeer.

يُوْلِجُ الَّيْلَ فِي النَّهَارِ وَيُوْلِجُ النَّهَارَ فِي الَّيْلِ ۙ وَسَخَّرَ الشَّمْسَ وَالْقَمَرَ ۖ كُلٌّ يَّجْرِيْ لِاَجَلٍ مُّسَمًّى ۭ ذٰلِكُمُ اللّٰهُ رَبُّكُمْ لَهُ الْمُلْكُ ۭ وَالَّذِيْنَ تَدْعُوْنَ مِنْ دُوْنِهٖ مَا يَمْلِكُوْنَ مِنْ قِطْمِيْرٍ ۭ ﴿١٣﴾

14. They will not listen to your prayers if you pray to them. Even if they would listen, they would not be able to answer you. On the Day of Judgment they will reject your worship of them. Not even an expert reporter can tell you the truth in the way that Allah can.

14. In tad'oohum laa yasma'oo du'aaa'akum wa law sami'oo mas-tajaaboo lakum; wa Yawmal-Qiyaamati yakfuroona bishirkikum; wa laa yunabbi'uka mislu khabeer.

اِنْ تَدْعُوْهُمْ لَا يَسْمَعُوْا دُعَاۗءَكُمْ ۚ وَلَوْ سَمِعُوْا مَا اسْتَجَابُوْا لَكُمْ ۭ وَيَوْمَ الْقِيٰمَةِ يَكْفُرُوْنَ بِشِرْكِكُمْ ۭ وَلَا يُنَبِّئُكَ مِثْلُ خَبِيْرٍ ﴿١٤﴾

15. People, you are always in need of Allah and Allah is Self-sufficient and Praiseworthy.

15. Yaaa ayyuhan-naasu antumul-fuqaraaa'u ilallaahi wallaahu Huwal-Ghaniyyul-Ḥameed.

يٰٓاَيُّهَا النَّاسُ اَنْتُمُ الْفُقَرَاۗءُ اِلَى اللّٰهِ ۚ وَاللّٰهُ هُوَ الْغَنِيُّ الْحَمِيْدُ ﴿١٥﴾

16. He could replace you by a new creation if He decided to.

16. Iñy-yasha-yuzhibkum wa ya-ti bikhalqin jadeed.

اِنْ يَّشَاْ يُذْهِبْكُمْ وَيَاْتِ بِخَلْقٍ جَدِيْدٍ ۚ ﴿١٦﴾

17. This would not cost Allah dearly at all.

17. Wa maa zaalika 'alal-laahi bi'azeez.

وَمَا ذٰلِكَ عَلَى اللّٰهِ بِعَزِيْزٍ ﴿١٧﴾

18. No one will bear the burden of another. Even if an overburdened soul should ask another to bear a part of his burden, no one will do so, not even if he is a relative. (Muhammad), you can only warn those who have fear of their Lord without seeing Him and who are steadfast in prayer. Whoever purifies himself, does so for his own good. To Allah do all things return.

18. Wa laa taziru waaziratuñw-wizra ukhraa; wa in tad'u musqalatun ilaa ḥimlihaa laa yuḥmal minhu shay'uñw-wa law kaana zaa qurbaa; innamaa tunzirul-lazeena yakhshawna Rabbahum bilghaybi wa aqaamuṣ-Ṣalaah; wa man tazakkaa fa-innamaa yatazakkaa linafsih; wa ilal-laahil-maṣeer.

وَلَا تَزِرُ وَازِرَةٌ وِّزْرَ اُخْرٰى ۭ وَاِنْ تَدْعُ مُثْقَلَةٌ اِلٰى حِمْلِهَا لَا يُحْمَلْ مِنْهُ شَيْءٌ وَّلَوْ كَانَ ذَا قُرْبٰى ۭ اِنَّمَا تُنْذِرُ الَّذِيْنَ يَخْشَوْنَ رَبَّهُمْ بِالْغَيْبِ وَاَقَامُوا الصَّلٰوةَ ۭ وَمَنْ تَزَكّٰى فَاِنَّمَا يَتَزَكّٰى لِنَفْسِهٖ ۭ وَاِلَى اللّٰهِ الْمَصِيْرُ ﴿١٨﴾

19. The blind and the seeing are not alike

19. Wa maa yastawil-a'maa wal-baṣeer.

وَمَا يَسْتَوِي الْاَعْمٰى وَالْبَصِيْرُ ﴿١٩﴾

20. nor are darkness and light

20. Wa laz-zulumaatu wa lan-noor.

وَلَا الظُّلُمٰتُ وَلَا النُّوْرُ ﴿٢٠﴾

21. nor shade and heat

21. Wa laz-zillu wa lal-ḥaroor.

وَلَا الظِّلُّ وَلَا الْحَرُوْرُ ۚ ﴿٢١﴾

22. nor the living and the dead. Allah makes to listen whomever He wants. (Muhammad), you cannot make people in the graves to listen.

22. Wa maa yastawil aḥyaaa'u wa lal-amwaat; innal-laaha yusmi'u mañy-yashaaa'u wa maaa anta bimusmi'im-man fil-quboor.

وَمَا يَسْتَوِي الْأَحْيَاءُ وَلَا الْأَمْوَاتُ ۚ
إِنَّ اللَّهَ يُسْمِعُ مَنْ يَشَاءُ ۖ وَمَا أَنْتَ
بِمُسْمِعٍ مَنْ فِي الْقُبُورِ ﴿٢٢﴾

23. You are simply a Warner.

23. In anta illaa naẕeer.

إِنْ أَنْتَ إِلَّا نَذِيرٌ ﴿٢٣﴾

24. We have sent you in all truth as a bearer of glad news and a Warner. No nation who lived before was left without a Warner.

24. Innaaa arsalnaaka bil-ḥaqqi basheerañw-wa naẕeeraa; wa im-min ummatin illaa khalaa feehaa naẕeer.

إِنَّا أَرْسَلْنَاكَ بِالْحَقِّ بَشِيرًا وَنَذِيرًا ۚ
وَإِنْ مِنْ أُمَّةٍ إِلَّا خَلَا فِيهَا نَذِيرٌ ﴿٢٤﴾

25. If they reject you, (know that) others who lived before them had also rejected their Messengers, Messengers who had brought them miracles, scriptures, and the enlightening Book,

25. Wa iñy-yukaẕẕibooka faqad kaẕẕabal-laẕeena min qablihim jaaa'athum Rusuluhum bilbayyinaati wa biz-Zuburi wa bil-Kitaabil-Muneer.

وَإِنْ يُكَذِّبُوكَ فَقَدْ كَذَّبَ الَّذِينَ مِنْ
قَبْلِهِمْ ۚ جَاءَتْهُمْ رُسُلُهُمْ بِالْبَيِّنَاتِ
وَبِالزُّبُرِ وَبِالْكِتَابِ الْمُنِيرِ ﴿٢٥﴾

26. so I seized the unbelievers and how terrible was their torment.

26. Summa akhaẕtul-laẕeena kafaroo fakayfa kaana nakeer.

ثُمَّ أَخَذْتُ الَّذِينَ كَفَرُوا
فَكَيْفَ كَانَ نَكِيرِ ﴿٢٦﴾ ع ٣ ١٢ ١٥

27. Did you not see that Allah has sent water down from the sky, has produced fruits of various colors, and has made streaks of various colors in the mountains, white, red, and intense black?

27. Alam tara annal-laaha anzala minas-samaaa'i maaa'an fa-akhrajnaa bihee samaraatim-mukhtalifan alwaanuhaa; wa minal-jibaali judadum bee-ḍuñw-wa ḥumrum-mukhtalifun al-waanuhaa wa gharaa-beebu sood.

أَلَمْ تَرَ أَنَّ اللَّهَ أَنْزَلَ مِنَ السَّمَاءِ
مَاءً ۚ فَأَخْرَجْنَا بِهِ ثَمَرَاتٍ مُخْتَلِفًا
أَلْوَانُهَا ۚ وَمِنَ الْجِبَالِ جُدَدٌ بِيضٌ
وَحُمْرٌ مُخْتَلِفٌ أَلْوَانُهَا وَغَرَابِيبُ
سُودٌ ﴿٢٧﴾

28. He has also created people, beasts, and cattle of various colors. Only Allah's knowledgeable servants fear Him. Allah is Majestic and All-pardoning.

28. Wa minan-naasi wadda-waaabbi wal-an'aami mukh-talifun alwaanuhoo kaẕaalik; innamaa yakhshal-laaha min 'ibaadihil-'ulamaaa'; innal-laaha 'Azeezun Ghafoor.

وَمِنَ النَّاسِ وَالدَّوَابِّ وَالْأَنْعَامِ
مُخْتَلِفٌ أَلْوَانُهُ كَذَٰلِكَ ۗ إِنَّمَا يَخْشَى
اللَّهَ مِنْ عِبَادِهِ الْعُلَمَاءُ ۗ إِنَّ اللَّهَ
عَزِيزٌ غَفُورٌ ﴿٢٨﴾

29. Those who recite the Book of Allah, who are steadfast in prayer and who spend out of what We have given them for the cause of Allah, both in public and in private, have hope in an indestructible bargain

29. Innal-laẕeena yatloona Kitaabal-laahi wa aqaamuṣ-Ṣalaata wa anfaqoo mimmaa razaqnaahum sirrañw-wa 'alaa-niyatañy-yarjoona tijaaratallan taboor.

إِنَّ الَّذِينَ يَتْلُونَ كِتَابَ اللَّهِ وَأَقَامُوا
الصَّلَاةَ وَأَنْفَقُوا مِمَّا رَزَقْنَاهُمْ سِرًّا
وَعَلَانِيَةً يَرْجُونَ تِجَارَةً لَنْ تَبُورَ ﴿٢٩﴾

30. and in receiving their reward from Allah and in further favors. He is All-forgiving and All-appreciating.

30. Liyuwaffiyahum ujoo-rahum wa yazeedahum-min faḍlih; innahoo Ghafoorun Shakoor.

لِيُوَفِّيَهُمْ أُجُورَهُمْ وَيَزِيدَهُمْ مِنْ
فَضْلِهِ ۚ إِنَّهُ غَفُورٌ شَكُورٌ ﴿٣٠﴾

31. Whatever We have revealed to you from the Book is

31. Wallaẕeee awḥaynaaa ilayka minal-Kitaabi

وَالَّذِي أَوْحَيْنَا إِلَيْكَ مِنَ الْكِتَابِ

all truth. It confirms what was revealed before. Allah sees His servants and is All-aware of them.

32. We gave the Book as an inheritance to Our chosen servants, among whom some are unjust against their souls, some are moderate, and some are exceedingly virtuous by the permission of Allah. This is indeed a great favor.

33. They will enter the gardens of Eden wherein they will be decked with bracelets of gold and pearls, and silk garments.

34. They will say, "It is only Allah who deserves all praise. He has removed all of our suffering. Our Lord is certainly All-forgiving and All-appreciating.

35. It is He who has granted us, through His favor, an everlasting dwelling wherein we shall not experience fatigue or weakness."

36. The unbelievers will dwell in hell. It will not be decreed for them to die nor will their torment be relieved. Thus do We recompense the ungrateful ones.

37. Therein they will cry out, "Lord, take us out of here. We shall act righteously and behave differently from what we did before." They will be told, "Did We not allow you to live long enough for you to seek guidance? Did We not send a Warner to you? Suffer (the torment). There is no one to help the unjust."

38. Allah has knowledge of whatever is unseen in the heavens and the earth. He knows best what the hearts contain.

huwal-ḥaqqu muṣaddiqal-limaa bayna yadayh; innal-laaha bi'ibaadihee la-Khabeerum Baṣeer.

32. S̲umma awras̲nal-Kitaabal-laz̲eenaṣ-ṭafaynaa min 'ibaadinaa faminhum ẓaalimul-linafsihee wa minhum-muqtaṣid; wa minhum saabiqum bilkhayraati bi-iz̲nil-laah; z̲aalika huwal-faḍlul-kabeer.

33. Jannaatu 'Adniñy-yadkhuloonahaa yuḥallawna feehaa min asaawira min z̲ahabiñw-wa lu'lu'aa; wa libaasuhum feehaa ḥareer.

34. Wa qaalul-ḥamdu lillaahil-laz̲eee az̲haba 'annal-ḥazan; inna Rabbanaa la-Ghafoorun Shakoor.

35. Allaz̲eee aḥallanaa daaral-muqaamati min faḍlihee laa yamassunaa feehaa naṣabuñw-wa laa yamassunaa feehaa lughoob.

36. Wallaz̲eena kafaroo lahum Naaru Jahannama laa yuqḍaa 'alayhim fayamootoo wa laa yukhaffafu 'anhum-min 'az̲aabihaa; kaz̲aalika najzee kulla kafoor.

37. Wa hum yaṣṭarikhoona feehaa Rabbanaaa akhrijnaa na'mal ṣaaliḥan ghayral-laz̲ee kunnaa na'mal; awa lam nu'ammirkum-maa yataz̲akkaru feehi man taz̲akkara wa jaaa'akumun-naz̲eeru faz̲ooqoo famaa liẓẓaalimeena min naṣeer.

38. Innal-laaha 'aalimu ghaybis-samaawaati wal-arḍ; innahoo 'aleemum biz̲aatiṣ-ṣudoor.

هُوَ الْحَقُّ مُصَدِّقًا لِّمَا بَيْنَ يَدَيْهِ ؕ
إِنَّ اللّٰهَ بِعِبَادِهٖ لَخَبِيْرٌۢ بَصِيْرٌ ﴿٣١﴾
ثُمَّ أَوْرَثْنَا الْكِتٰبَ الَّذِيْنَ اصْطَفَيْنَا
مِنْ عِبَادِنَا ۚ فَمِنْهُمْ ظَالِمٌ لِّنَفْسِهٖ ۚ
وَمِنْهُمْ مُّقْتَصِدٌ ۚ وَمِنْهُمْ سَابِقٌۢ
بِالْخَيْرٰتِ بِإِذْنِ اللّٰهِ ؕ ذٰلِكَ هُوَ
الْفَضْلُ الْكَبِيْرُ ﴿٣٢﴾ ؕ
جَنّٰتُ عَدْنٍ يَّدْخُلُوْنَهَا يُحَلَّوْنَ
فِيْهَا مِنْ أَسَاوِرَ مِنْ ذَهَبٍ وَّلُؤْلُؤًا ۚ
وَلِبَاسُهُمْ فِيْهَا حَرِيْرٌ ﴿٣٣﴾
وَقَالُوا الْحَمْدُ لِلّٰهِ الَّذِيْٓ أَذْهَبَ عَنَّا
الْحَزَنَ ؕ إِنَّ رَبَّنَا لَغَفُوْرٌ شَكُوْرٌ ﴿٣٤﴾
الَّذِيْٓ أَحَلَّنَا دَارَ الْمُقَامَةِ مِنْ
فَضْلِهٖ ۚ لَا يَمَسُّنَا فِيْهَا نَصَبٌ وَّلَا
يَمَسُّنَا فِيْهَا لُغُوْبٌ ﴿٣٥﴾
وَالَّذِيْنَ كَفَرُوْا لَهُمْ نَارُ جَهَنَّمَ ۚ لَا
يُقْضٰى عَلَيْهِمْ فَيَمُوْتُوْا وَلَا يُخَفَّفُ
عَنْهُمْ مِّنْ عَذَابِهَا ؕ كَذٰلِكَ نَجْزِيْ
كُلَّ كَفُوْرٍ ﴿٣٦﴾ ۚ
وَهُمْ يَصْطَرِخُوْنَ فِيْهَا ۚ رَبَّنَآ أَخْرِجْنَا
نَعْمَلْ صَالِحًا غَيْرَ الَّذِيْ كُنَّا
نَعْمَلُ ؕ أَوَلَمْ نُعَمِّرْكُمْ مَّا يَتَذَكَّرُ
فِيْهِ مَنْ تَذَكَّرَ وَجَآءَكُمُ النَّذِيْرُ ؕ
فَذُوْقُوْا فَمَا لِلظّٰلِمِيْنَ مِنْ نَّصِيْرٍ ﴿٣٧﴾ ع ١٢/١٦
إِنَّ اللّٰهَ عٰلِمُ غَيْبِ السَّمٰوٰتِ وَالْأَرْضِ ؕ
إِنَّهٗ عَلِيْمٌۢ بِذَاتِ الصُّدُوْرِ ﴿٣٨﴾

39. It is He who has made you each other's successors on earth. Whoever disbelieves, does so against his own self. The disbelief of the unbelievers will only increase the anger of their Lord and will only cause them greater loss.

39. Huwal-lazee ja'alakum khalaaa'ifa fil-arḍ; faman kafara fa'alayhi kufruh; wa laa yazeedul-kaafireena kufruhum 'inda Rabbihim illaa maqtaa; wa laa yazeedul-kaafireena kufruhum illaa khasaaraa.

هُوَ الَّذِىۡ جَعَلَكُمۡ خَلٰٓئِفَ فِى
الۡاَرۡضِ ؕ فَمَنۡ كَفَرَ فَعَلَيۡهِ كُفۡرُهٗ ؕ
وَلَا يَزِيۡدُ الۡكٰفِرِيۡنَ كُفۡرُهُمۡ عِنۡدَ
رَبِّهِمۡ اِلَّا مَقۡتًا ۚ وَلَا يَزِيۡدُ الۡكٰفِرِيۡنَ
كُفۡرُهُمۡ اِلَّا خَسَارًا ﴿٣٩﴾

39. (Muhammad), ask them, "Think about the idols which you worship besides Allah. Show me what part of the earth they have created. Do they have any share in the heavens? Has Allah sent them a Book to confirm their authority? In fact, whatever the unjust promise each other is nothing but deceit."

40. Qul ara'aytum shurakaaa'a kumul-lazeena tad'oona min doonil-laah; aroonee maazaa khalaqoo minal-arḍi am lahum shirkun fis-samaawaati am aataynaahum Kitaaban fahum 'alaa bayyinatim-minh; bal iñy-ya'iduẓ-ẓaalimoona ba'ḍuhum ba'ḍan illaa ghurooraa.

قُلۡ اَرَءَيۡتُمۡ شُرَكَآءَكُمُ الَّذِيۡنَ
تَدۡعُوۡنَ مِنۡ دُوۡنِ اللّٰهِ ؕ اَرُوۡنِىۡ مَاذَا
خَلَقُوۡا مِنَ الۡاَرۡضِ اَمۡ لَهُمۡ شِرۡكٌ
فِى السَّمٰوٰتِ ۚ اَمۡ اٰتَيۡنٰهُمۡ كِتٰبًا فَهُمۡ
عَلٰى بَيِّنَتٍ مِّنۡهُ ۚ بَلۡ اِنۡ يَّعِدُ
الظّٰلِمُوۡنَ بَعۡضُهُمۡ بَعۡضًا اِلَّا غُرُوۡرًا ﴿٤٠﴾

41. Allah prevents the heavens and the earth from falling apart. If they do fall apart, then no one besides Him can restore them. He is All-forbearing and All-forgiving.

41. Innal-laaha yumsikus-samaawaati wal-arḍa an tazoolaa; wa la'in zaalataaa in amsakahumaa min aḥadim-mim ba'dih; innahoo kaana Ḥaleeman Ghafooraa.

اِنَّ اللّٰهَ يُمۡسِكُ السَّمٰوٰتِ وَالۡاَرۡضَ
اَنۡ تَزُوۡلَا ۚ وَلَئِنۡ زَالَتَاۤ اِنۡ اَمۡسَكَهُمَا
مِنۡ اَحَدٍ مِّنۡۢ بَعۡدِهٖ ؕ اِنَّهٗ كَانَ
حَلِيۡمًا غَفُوۡرًا ﴿٤١﴾

42. They solemnly swear that if a Warner were to come to them, they would certainly have been better guided than any other nation. However, when a Warner came to them, it only increased their hatred

42. Wa aqsamoo billaahi jahda aymaanihim la'in jaaa'ahum nazeerul-layakoonunna ahdaa min iḥdal-umami falammaa jaaa'ahum nazeerum-maa zaadahum illaa nufooraa.

وَاَقۡسَمُوۡا بِاللّٰهِ جَهۡدَ اَيۡمَانِهِمۡ لَئِنۡ
جَآءَهُمۡ نَذِيۡرٌ لَّيَكُوۡنُنَّ اَهۡدٰى مِنۡ
اِحۡدَى الۡاُمَمِ ۚ فَلَمَّا جَآءَهُمۡ نَذِيۡرٌ
مَّا زَادَهُمۡ اِلَّا نُفُوۡرَا ۙ ﴿٤٢﴾

43. because of their pride in the land and their evil plots. Evil plots only affect the plotters. Do they expect anything other than (Allah's) tradition (torment) with those who lived before? You will never find any change in the tradition of Allah nor will you find any alteration in it.

43. Istikbaaran fil-arḍi wa makras-sayyi'; wa laa yaḥeequl-makrus-sayyi'u illaa bi-ahlih; fahal yanẓuroona illaa sunnatal-awwaleen; falan tajida lisunnatil-laahi tabdeelaa; wa lan tajida lisunnatil-laahi taḥweelaa.

اۨسۡتِكۡبَارًا فِى الۡاَرۡضِ وَمَكۡرَ السَّيِّـئِ ؕ
وَلَا يَحِيۡقُ الۡمَكۡرُ السَّيِّـئُ اِلَّا بِاَهۡلِهٖ ؕ
فَهَلۡ يَنۡظُرُوۡنَ اِلَّا سُنَّتَ الۡاَوَّلِيۡنَ ۚ
فَلَنۡ تَجِدَ لِسُنَّتِ اللّٰهِ تَبۡدِيۡلًا ۚ وَ
لَنۡ تَجِدَ لِسُنَّتِ اللّٰهِ تَحۡوِيۡلًا ﴿٤٣﴾

44. Had they not traveled (sufficiently) through the land to see how terrible was the end of the mightier people who lived before

44. Awalam yaseeroo fil-arḍi fayanẓuroo kayfa kaana 'aaqibatul-lazeena min

اَوَلَمۡ يَسِيۡرُوۡا فِى الۡاَرۡضِ فَيَنۡظُرُوۡا
كَيۡفَ كَانَ عَاقِبَةُ الَّذِيۡنَ مِنۡ

them? Nothing in the heavens or the earth can challenge Allah. Allah is All-knowing and All-powerful.

45. Were Allah to punish people for their deeds immediately, not one creature would have survived on earth. However, He has given them a respite for an appointed time and when their term comes to an end, let it be known that Allah watches over His servants.

qablihim wa kaanooo ashadda minhum quwwah; wa maa kaanal-laahu liyu'jizahoo min shay'in fis-samaawaati wa laa fil-arḍ; innahoo kaana 'Aleeman Qadeeraa.

45. Wa law yu'aakhizul-laahun-naasa bimaa kasaboo maa taraka 'alaa ẓahrihaa min daaabbatiñw-wa laakiñy-yu'akh-khiruhum ilaaa ajalim-musamman fa-izaa jaaa'a ajaluhum fa-innal-laaha kaana bi'ibaadihee Baṣeeraa.

قَبْلِهِمْ وَكَانُوْٓا اَشَدَّ مِنْهُمْ قُوَّةً ؕ
وَمَا كَانَ اللّٰهُ لِيُعْجِزَهٗ مِنْ شَیْءٍ فِی
السَّمٰوٰتِ وَلَا فِی الْاَرْضِ ؕ اِنَّهٗ كَانَ
عَلِیْمًا قَدِیْرًا ﴿٤٤﴾
وَلَوْ یُؤَاخِذُ اللّٰهُ النَّاسَ بِمَا
كَسَبُوْا مَا تَرَكَ عَلٰی ظَهْرِهَا مِنْ
دَآبَّةٍ وَّلٰكِنْ یُّؤَخِّرُهُمْ اِلٰٓی اَجَلٍ
مُّسَمًّی ۚ فَاِذَا جَآءَ اَجَلُهُمْ فَاِنَّ
اللّٰهَ كَانَ بِعِبَادِهٖ بَصِیْرًا ﴿٤٥﴾ ع ٨ ١٧

Ya Sin, Ya Sin (36)
In the Name of Allah, the Beneficent, the Merciful.

Sûrat Yâ-Sin-36
(Revealed at Makkah)
Bismillaahir Raḥmaanir Raḥeem

(٣٦) سُوْرَةُ یٰسٓ مَكِّیَّةٌ (٤١)
اٰیَاتُهَا ٨٣ بِسْمِ اللّٰهِ الرَّحْمٰنِ الرَّحِیْمِ رُكُوْعَاتُهَا ٥

1. (I swear by) Ya Sin
2. and the Quran, the Book of wisdom
3. that you (Muhammad) are a Messenger
4. and that you follow the right path.
5. This (Quran) is a revelation sent down from the Majestic and All-merciful
6. so that you may warn a people who are unaware because their fathers were not warned.
7. (I swear) that most of them are doomed to be punished. They will not accept the faith.
8. We have enchained their necks up to their chins. Thus, they cannot bend their heads (to find their way).
9. We have set up a barrier in front of and behind them and have made them blind (in seeing right guidance). Thus, they cannot see.
10. Whether you warn them or not, they will not believe.

1. Yaa-Seeen.
2. Wal-Qur'aanil-Ḥakeem.
3. Innaka laminal-mursaleen.
4. 'Alaa Ṣiraaṭim-Musta-qeem.
5. Tanzeelal-'Azeezir-Raḥeem.
6. Litunzira qawmam-maaa unzira aabaaa'uhum fahum ghaafiloon.
7. Laqad ḥaqqal-qawlu 'alaaa aksarihim fahum laa yu'minoon.
8. Innaa ja'alnaa feee a'naaqihim aghlaalan fahiya ilal-azqaani fahum-muqmaḥoon.
9. Wa ja'alnaa mim bayni aydeehim saddañw-wa min khalfihim saddan fa-aghshaynaahum fahum laa yubṣiroon.
10. Wa sawaaa'un 'alayhim 'a-anzartahum am lam

یٰسٓ ﴿١﴾
وَالْقُرْاٰنِ الْحَكِیْمِ ﴿٢﴾
اِنَّكَ لَمِنَ الْمُرْسَلِیْنَ ﴿٣﴾
عَلٰی صِرَاطٍ مُّسْتَقِیْمٍ ﴿٤﴾
تَنْزِیْلَ الْعَزِیْزِ الرَّحِیْمِ ﴿٥﴾
لِتُنْذِرَ قَوْمًا مَّآ اُنْذِرَ اٰبَآؤُهُمْ فَهُمْ
غٰفِلُوْنَ ﴿٦﴾
لَقَدْ حَقَّ الْقَوْلُ عَلٰٓی اَكْثَرِهِمْ فَهُمْ
لَا یُؤْمِنُوْنَ ﴿٧﴾
اِنَّا جَعَلْنَا فِیْٓ اَعْنَاقِهِمْ اَغْلٰلًا فَهِیَ
اِلَی الْاَذْقَانِ فَهُمْ مُّقْمَحُوْنَ ﴿٨﴾
وَجَعَلْنَا مِنْ بَیْنِ اَیْدِیْهِمْ سَدًّا
وَّمِنْ خَلْفِهِمْ سَدًّا فَاَغْشَیْنٰهُمْ
فَهُمْ لَا یُبْصِرُوْنَ ﴿٩﴾
وَسَوَآءٌ عَلَیْهِمْ ءَاَنْذَرْتَهُمْ اَمْ لَمْ

tunzirhum laa yu'minoon.

تُنْذِرْهُمْ لَا يُؤْمِنُوْنَ ﴿١٠﴾

11. You should warn only those who follow Al-Dhikr (the Quran) and have fear of the Beneficent without seeing Him. Give them the glad news of their receiving forgiveness and an honorable reward (from Allah).

11. Innamaa tunziru manit-taba'az-Zikra wa khashiyar-Raḥmaana bilghayb; fabash-shirhu bimaghfiratiñw-wa ajrin kareem.

إِنَّمَا تُنْذِرُ مَنِ اتَّبَعَ الذِّكْرَ وَخَشِيَ
الرَّحْمٰنَ بِالْغَيْبِ ۚ فَبَشِّرْهُ بِمَغْفِرَةٍ
وَّأَجْرٍ كَرِيْمٍ ﴿١١﴾

12. It is We who bring the dead to life and record the deeds of human beings and their consequences (of continual effects). We keep everything recorded in an illustrious Book.

12. Innaa Naḥnu nuḥyil mawtaa wa naktubu maa qaddamoo wa aasaarahum; wa kulla shay'in aḥṣaynaahu feee Imaamim-Mubeen.

إِنَّا نَحْنُ نُحْيِ الْمَوْتٰى وَنَكْتُبُ مَا قَدَّمُوْا
وَآثَارَهُمْ ۚ وَكُلَّ شَيْءٍ أَحْصَيْنٰهُ فِيْٓ
إِمَامٍ مُّبِيْنٍ ﴿١٢﴾

13. Tell them the story of the people of the town to whom Messengers came.

13. Waḍrib lahum-masalan Aṣḥaabal-Qaryah; iz jaaa'a-hal-mursaloon.

وَاضْرِبْ لَهُمْ مَّثَلًا أَصْحٰبَ الْقَرْيَةِ ۘ
إِذْ جَآءَهَا الْمُرْسَلُوْنَ ﴿١٣﴾

14. We sent them two Messengers whom they rejected. We supported them by sending a third one who told the people, "We are the Messengers (of Allah) who have been sent to you."

14. Iz arsalnaaa ilayhimus-nayni fakazzaboohumaa fa'azzaznaa bisaalisin faqaa-looo innaaa ilaykum-mursaloon.

إِذْ أَرْسَلْنَآ إِلَيْهِمُ اثْنَيْنِ فَكَذَّبُوْهُمَا
فَعَزَّزْنَا بِثَالِثٍ فَقَالُوْٓا إِنَّآ إِلَيْكُمْ
مُّرْسَلُوْنَ ﴿١٤﴾

15. The people said, "You are mere mortals like us and the Beneficent has sent nothing. You are only liars."

15. Qaaloo maaa antum illaa basharum-mislunaa wa maaa anzalar-Raḥmaanu min shay'in in antum illaa takziboon.

قَالُوْا مَآ أَنْتُمْ إِلَّا بَشَرٌ مِّثْلُنَا ۙ وَمَآ
أَنْزَلَ الرَّحْمٰنُ مِنْ شَيْءٍ ۙ إِنْ أَنْتُمْ
إِلَّا تَكْذِبُوْنَ ﴿١٥﴾

16. They said, "Our Lord knows that We are Messengers

16. Qaaloo Rabbunaa ya'lamu innaaa ilaykum lamursaloon.

قَالُوْا رَبُّنَا يَعْلَمُ إِنَّآ إِلَيْكُمْ لَمُرْسَلُوْنَ ﴿١٦﴾

17. who have been sent to you. Our only duty is to preach clearly to you."

17. Wa maa 'alaynaaa illal-balaaghul-mubeen.

وَمَا عَلَيْنَآ إِلَّا الْبَلٰغُ الْمُبِيْنُ ﴿١٧﴾

18. The people said, "We have ill omens about you (your names). If you did not desist, we shall stone you and make you suffer a painful torment."

18. Qaalooo innaa taṭayyarnaa bikum la'il-lam tantahoo lanar-jumannakum wa layamassan-nakum-minnaa 'azaabun aleem.

قَالُوْٓا إِنَّا تَطَيَّرْنَا بِكُمْ ۚ لَئِنْ لَّمْ
تَنْتَهُوْا لَنَرْجُمَنَّكُمْ وَلَيَمَسَّنَّكُمْ مِّنَّا
عَذَابٌ أَلِيْمٌ ﴿١٨﴾

19. The Messengers said, "This ill omen lies within yourselves. Will you then take heed? In fact, you are a transgressing people."

19. Qaaloo ṭaaa'irukum-ma'akum; a'in zukkirtum; bal antum qawmum-musrifoon.

قَالُوْا طَآئِرُكُمْ مَّعَكُمْ ۚ أَئِنْ ذُكِّرْتُمْ ۚ
بَلْ أَنْتُمْ قَوْمٌ مُّسْرِفُوْنَ ﴿١٩﴾

20. A man came running from the farthest part of the city saying, "My people, follow the Messengers.

20. Wa jaaa'a min aqṣal-madeenati rajuluñy-yas'aa qaala yaa qawmit-tabi'ul-mursaleen.

وَجَآءَ مِنْ أَقْصَا الْمَدِيْنَةِ رَجُلٌ يَّسْعٰى
قَالَ يٰقَوْمِ اتَّبِعُوا الْمُرْسَلِيْنَ ﴿٢٠﴾

21. Follow those who do not ask you for any reward and who are rightly guided."

21. Ittabi'oo mal-laa yas'alu-kum ajrañw-wa hum-muhta-doon.

اتَّبِعُوْا مَنْ لَّا يَسْـَٔلُكُمْ أَجْرًا وَّهُمْ
مُّهْتَدُوْنَ ﴿٢١﴾

وقف غفران ع ١ ٣ وقف لازم

22. "Why should I not worship Allah who has created me? To him you will all return.

22. Wa maa liya laaa a'budul-lazee faṭaranee wa ilayhi turja'oon.

وَمَا لِيَ لَآ أَعْبُدُ الَّذِي فَطَرَنِي
وَإِلَيْهِ تُرْجَعُونَ ٢٢

23. Should I worship other gods besides Him? If the Beneficent were to afflict me with hardship, the intercession of the idols could be of no benefit to me nor could it rescue me from hardship.

23. 'A-attakhizu min dooniheee aalihatan iñy-yuridnir-Raḥmaanu biḍurril-laa tughni 'annee shafaa'atuhum shay' añw-wa laa yunqizoon.

ءَأَتَّخِذُ مِن دُونِهِۦٓ ءَالِهَةً إِن يُرِدْنِ
الرَّحْمَٰنُ بِضُرٍّ لَّا تُغْنِ عَنِّي شَفَٰعَتُهُمْ
شَيْـًٔا وَلَا يُنقِذُونِ ٢٣

24. (Had I worshipped things besides Allah, I would have been in manifest error).

24. Inneee izal-lafee ḍalaa-lim-mubeen.

إِنِّيٓ إِذًا لَّفِي ضَلَٰلٍ مُّبِينٍ ٢٤

25. Messengers, listen to me. I believe in your Lord."

25. Inneee aamantu bi-Rabbikum fasma'oon.

إِنِّيٓ ءَامَنتُ بِرَبِّكُمْ فَاسْمَعُونِ ٢٥

26. (Having been murdered by the unbelievers) he was told to enter paradise

26. Qeelad-khulil-Jannah; qaala yaa layta qawmee ya'lamoon.

قِيلَ ادْخُلِ الْجَنَّةَ ۖ قَالَ يَٰلَيْتَ
قَوْمِي يَعْلَمُونَ ٢٦

27. (wherein he said), "Would that people knew how my Lord has granted me forgiveness and honor."

27. Bimaa ghafara lee Rabbee wa ja'alanee minal-mukra-meen.

بِمَا غَفَرَ لِي رَبِّي وَجَعَلَنِي مِنَ
الْمُكْرَمِينَ ٢٧

28. We did not send an army against his people from the heaven after his death nor did We need to send one.

28. Wa maaa anzalnaa 'alaa qawmihee mim ba'dihee min jundim-minas-samaaa'i wa maa kunnaa munzileen.

وَمَآ أَنزَلْنَا عَلَىٰ قَوْمِهِۦ مِنۢ بَعْدِهِۦ مِن
جُندٍ مِّنَ السَّمَآءِ وَمَا كُنَّا مُنزِلِينَ ٢٨

29. It was only a single blast which made them extinct (dead).

29. In kaanat illaa ṣayḥatañw-waaḥidatan fa-izaa hum khaamidoon.

إِن كَانَتْ إِلَّا صَيْحَةً وَٰحِدَةً فَإِذَا
هُمْ خَٰمِدُونَ ٢٩

30. Woe to human beings! Whenever a Messenger came to them, they mocked him.

30. Yaa ḥasratan 'alal-'ibaad; maa ya-teehim-mir Rasoolin illaa kaanoo bihee yastahzi'oon.

يَٰحَسْرَةً عَلَى الْعِبَادِ ۚ مَا يَأْتِيهِم مِّن
رَّسُولٍ إِلَّا كَانُوا۟ بِهِۦ يَسْتَهْزِءُونَ ٣٠

31. Did they not see how many generations, living before them, We had destroyed and they cannot ever come back to them?

31. Alam yaraw kam ahlak-naa qablahum-minal-qurooni annahum ilayhim laa yarji'oon.

أَلَمْ يَرَوْا۟ كَمْ أَهْلَكْنَا قَبْلَهُم مِّنَ
الْقُرُونِ أَنَّهُمْ إِلَيْهِمْ لَا يَرْجِعُونَ ٣١

32. They will all be brought into Our presence together.

32. Wa in kullul-lammaa jamee'ul-ladaynaa muḥḍaroon.

وَإِن كُلٌّ لَّمَّا جَمِيعٌ لَّدَيْنَا مُحْضَرُونَ ٣٢ ع

33. Evidence (of the truth) for them is how We revived the dead earth

33. Wa Aayatul-lahumul arḍul-maytatu aḥyaynaahaa wa akhrajnaa minhaa ḥabban faminhu ya-kuloon.

وَءَايَةٌ لَّهُمُ الْأَرْضُ الْمَيْتَةُ
أَحْيَيْنَٰهَا وَأَخْرَجْنَا مِنْهَا حَبًّا
فَمِنْهُ يَأْكُلُونَ ٣٣

34. and produced therein grains from which they eat and established therein gardens of palm trees and vineyards and have made streams flow therein

34. Wa ja'alnaa feehaa jannaatim-min nakheeliñw-wa a'naabiñw-wa fajjarnaa feehaa minal-'uyoon.

وَجَعَلْنَا فِيهَا جَنَّٰتٍ مِّن نَّخِيلٍ وَ
أَعْنَٰبٍ وَفَجَّرْنَا فِيهَا مِنَ الْعُيُونِ ٣٤

35. so that they may consume the fruits and whatever their

35. Liya-kuloo min samari-hee wa maa 'amilathu

لِيَأْكُلُوا۟ مِن ثَمَرِهِۦ وَمَا عَمِلَتْهُ

hands prepare. Will they not then be grateful?

aydeehim; afalaa yashkuroon.

أَيْدِيهِمْ ۖ أَفَلَا يَشْكُرُونَ ٣٥

36. All glory belongs to the One Who has created pairs out of what grows from the earth, out of their soul and out of that which they do not know.

36. Subḥaanal-lazee khalaqal azwaaja kullahaa mimmaa tumbitul-arḍu wa min anfusihim wa mimmaa laa ya'lamoon.

سُبْحَٰنَ الَّذِي خَلَقَ الْأَزْوَاجَ كُلَّهَا
مِمَّا تُنْبِتُ الْأَرْضُ وَمِنْ أَنْفُسِهِمْ
وَمِمَّا لَا يَعْلَمُونَ ٣٦

37. Of the signs for them is how We separated the day from the night and thus they remained in darkness;

37. Wa Aayatul-lahumul-laylu naslakhu minhunnahaara fa-izaa hum-muẓlimoon.

وَآيَةٌ لَهُمُ اللَّيْلُ ۚ نَسْلَخُ مِنْهُ النَّهَارَ
فَإِذَا هُمْ مُظْلِمُونَ ٣٧

38. how the sun moves in its orbit and this is the decree of the Majestic and All-knowing Allah;

38. Wash-shamsu tajree limustaqarril-lahaa; zaalika taqdeerul-'Azeezil-'Aleem.

وَالشَّمْسُ تَجْرِي لِمُسْتَقَرٍّ لَهَا ۚ ذَٰلِكَ
تَقْدِيرُ الْعَزِيزِ الْعَلِيمِ ٣٨

39. how We ordained the moon to pass through certain phases until it seems eventually to be like a bent down twig;

39. Walqamara qaddarnaahu manaazila ḥattaa 'aada kal'urjoonil-qadeem.

وَالْقَمَرَ قَدَّرْنَاهُ مَنَازِلَ حَتَّىٰ عَادَ
كَالْعُرْجُونِ الْقَدِيمِ ٣٩

40. how the sun is not supposed to catch up with the moon, nor is the night to precede the day and all of them are to float in a certain orbit;

40. Lash-shamsu yambaghee lahaaa an tudrikal-qamara wa lal-laylu saabiqun-nahaar; wa kullun fee falakiñy-yasbaḥoon.

لَا الشَّمْسُ يَنْبَغِي لَهَا أَنْ تُدْرِكَ
الْقَمَرَ وَلَا اللَّيْلُ سَابِقُ النَّهَارِ ۚ وَ
كُلٌّ فِي فَلَكٍ يَسْبَحُونَ ٤٠

41. how We carried them and their offspring inside the loaded Ark

41. Wa-Aayatul-lahum-annaa ḥamalnaa zurriyyatahum fil-fulkil-mashḥoon.

وَآيَةٌ لَهُمْ أَنَّا حَمَلْنَا ذُرِّيَّتَهُمْ
فِي الْفُلْكِ الْمَشْحُونِ ٤١

42. and created for them similar things to ride.

42. Wa khalaqnaa lahum-mim-mislihee maa yarkaboon.

وَخَلَقْنَا لَهُمْ مِنْ مِثْلِهِ مَا يَرْكَبُونَ ٤٢

43. Had We wanted, We could have drowned them and nothing would have been able to help or rescue them

43. Wa in nasha- nughriqhum falaa ṣareekha lahum wa laa hum yunqazoon.

وَإِنْ نَشَأْ نُغْرِقْهُمْ فَلَا صَرِيخَ لَهُمْ
وَلَا هُمْ يُنْقَذُونَ ٤٣

44. except Our mercy which could enable them to enjoy themselves for an appointed time.

44. Illaa raḥmatam-minnaa wa mataa'an ilaa ḥeen.

إِلَّا رَحْمَةً مِنَّا وَمَتَاعًا إِلَىٰ حِينٍ ٤٤

45. Whenever they are told to guard themselves against sin and the forthcoming torment so that perhaps they could receive mercy,

45. Wa izaa qeela lahumut-taqoo maa bayna aydeekum wa maa khalfakum la'allakum turḥamoon.

وَإِذَا قِيلَ لَهُمُ اتَّقُوا مَا بَيْنَ
أَيْدِيكُمْ وَمَا خَلْفَكُمْ لَعَلَّكُمْ
تُرْحَمُونَ ٤٥

46. and whenever a revelation out of their Lord's revelations comes to them, they ignore it.

46. Wa maa ta-teehim-min Aayatim-min Aayaati Rabbihim illaa kaanoo 'anhaa mu'riḍeen.

وَمَا تَأْتِيهِمْ مِنْ آيَةٍ مِنْ آيَاتِ
رَبِّهِمْ إِلَّا كَانُوا عَنْهَا مُعْرِضِينَ ٤٦

47. When they are told to spend for the cause of Allah out of what He has provided for them for their sustenance, the unbelievers say to

47. Wa izaa qeela lahum anfiqoo mimmaa razaqakumul-laahu qaalallazeena kafaroo lillazeena aamanooo

وَإِذَا قِيلَ لَهُمْ أَنْفِقُوا مِمَّا رَزَقَكُمُ
اللَّهُ قَالَ الَّذِينَ كَفَرُوا لِلَّذِينَ آمَنُوا

the believers, "Should we feed those whom Allah has decided to feed? You are in plain error."	anuṭ'imu mal-law yashaaa'ul-laahu aṭ'amahooo in antum illaa fee ḍalaalim-mubeen.	أَنُطْعِمُ مَنْ لَّوْ يَشَآءُ اللّٰهُ أَطْعَمَهٗٓ ۖ إِنْ أَنْتُمْ إِلَّا فِي ضَلٰلٍ مُّبِينٍ ﴿٤٧﴾
48. The unbelievers say, "When will the Day of Judgment come if what you say is at all true?"	48. Wa yaqooloona mataa haazal-wa'du in kuntum ṣaadiqeen.	وَيَقُولُونَ مَتٰى هٰذَا الْوَعْدُ إِنْ كُنْتُمْ صٰدِقِينَ ﴿٤٨﴾
49. They will not have to wait long. When the Day of Judgment comes, it will take only a single blast of sound to strike them while they are quarrelling with one another.	49. Maa yanẓuroona illaa ṣayḥatañw-waaḥidatan ta-khuzuhum wa hum yakhiṣ-ṣimoon.	مَا يَنْظُرُونَ إِلَّا صَيْحَةً وَّاحِدَةً تَأْخُذُهُمْ وَهُمْ يَخِصِّمُونَ ﴿٤٩﴾
50. Then they will not be able to make a will or return to their families.	50. Falaa yastaṭee'oona taw-ṣiyatañw-wa laaa ilaaa ahlihim yarji'oon.	فَلَا يَسْتَطِيعُونَ تَوْصِيَةً وَّلَآ إِلٰٓى أَهْلِهِمْ يَرْجِعُونَ ﴿٥٠﴾ ع
51. When the trumpet is sounded, they will be driven out of their grave into the presence of their Lord.	51. Wa nufikha fiṣ-Ṣoori fa-izaa hum-minal-ajdaasi ilaa Rabbihim yansiloon.	وَنُفِخَ فِي الصُّورِ فَإِذَا هُمْ مِّنَ الْأَجْدَاثِ إِلٰى رَبِّهِمْ يَنْسِلُونَ ﴿٥١﴾
52. They will say, "Woe to us! Who has raised us up from our graves?" (The angels will say), "This is what the Beneficent had promised and the messengers had also spoken the truth."	52. Qaaloo yaa waylanaa mam ba'asanaa mim-marqa-dinaa; haazaa maa wa'adar-Raḥmaanu wa ṣadaqal-mursa-loon.	قَالُوا يٰوَيْلَنَا مَنْۢ بَعَثَنَا مِنْ مَّرْقَدِنَا ۜ هٰذَا مَا وَعَدَ الرَّحْمٰنُ وَصَدَقَ الْمُرْسَلُونَ ﴿٥٢﴾
53. After only a single blast of sound, they will all be brought into Our presence.	53. In kaanat illaa ṣayḥatañw-waaḥidatan fa-izaa hum jamee'ul-ladaynaa muḥḍaroon.	إِنْ كَانَتْ إِلَّا صَيْحَةً وَّاحِدَةً فَإِذَا هُمْ جَمِيعٌ لَّدَيْنَا مُحْضَرُونَ ﴿٥٣﴾
54. No soul will be in the least bit wronged on that Day and no one will receive any recompense other than what he deserves for his deeds.	54. Fal-Yawma laa tuẓlamu naf-sun shay'añw-wa laa tujzawna illaa maa kuntum ta'maloon.	فَالْيَوْمَ لَا تُظْلَمُ نَفْسٌ شَيْـًٔا وَّلَا تُجْزَوْنَ إِلَّا مَا كُنْتُمْ تَعْمَلُونَ ﴿٥٤﴾
55. The dwellers of Paradise on that day will enjoy themselves.	55. Inna Aṣḥaabal-Jannatil-Yawma fee shughulin faaki-hoon.	إِنَّ أَصْحٰبَ الْجَنَّةِ الْيَوْمَ فِي شُغُلٍ فٰكِهُونَ ﴿٥٥﴾
56. They and their spouses will recline on couches in the shade	56. Hum wa azwaajuhum fee ẓilaalin 'alal-araaa'iki mutta-ki'oon.	هُمْ وَأَزْوٰجُهُمْ فِي ظِلٰلٍ عَلَى الْأَرَآئِكِ مُتَّكِـُٔونَ ﴿٥٦﴾
57. therein. They will have fruits and whatever they desire.	57. Lahum feehaa faakiha-tuñw-wa lahum-maa yadda'oon.	لَهُمْ فِيهَا فٰكِهَةٌ وَّلَهُمْ مَّا يَدَّعُونَ ﴿٥٧﴾
58. "Peace be with you," will be a greeting for them from the Merciful Lord.	58. Salaamun qawlam-mir-Rabbir-Raḥeem.	سَلٰمٌ ۟ قَوْلًا مِّنْ رَّبٍّ رَّحِيمٍ ﴿٥٨﴾
59. (The Lord will command), "Criminals, stand away from the others on this day."	59. Wamtaazul-Yawma ayyu-hal-mujrimoon.	وَامْتَازُوا الْيَوْمَ أَيُّهَا الْمُجْرِمُونَ ﴿٥٩﴾
60. Children of Adam, did We not command you not to worship	60. Alam a'had ilaykum yaa Baneee Aadama	أَلَمْ أَعْهَدْ إِلَيْكُمْ يٰبَنِيٓ اٰدَمَ

وقف منزل وقف غفران
وقف لازم

Satan? He was your sworn enemy.	al-laa ta'budush-Shayṭaana innahoo lakum 'aduwwum-mubeen.	أَنْ لَّا تَعْبُدُوا الشَّيْطٰنَ ۚ إِنَّهُ لَكُمْ عَدُوٌّ مُّبِينٌ ﴿٦٠﴾ وقف غفران ۱۲
61. Did We not command you to worship Me and tell you that this is the straight path?	61. Wa-ani'-budoonee; haa<u>z</u>aa Ṣiraaṭum-Mustaqeem.	وَّأَنِ اعْبُدُونِي ۚ هٰذَا صِرَاطٌ مُّسْتَقِيمٌ ﴿٦١﴾
62. Satan misled a great multitude of you. Did you not have any understanding?	62. Wa laqad aḍalla minkum jibillan ka<u>s</u>eeraa; afalam takoonoo ta'qiloon.	وَلَقَدْ أَضَلَّ مِنْكُمْ جِبِلًّا كَثِيرًا ۖ أَفَلَمْ تَكُونُوا تَعْقِلُونَ ﴿٦٢﴾
63. This is hell with which you were threatened.	63. Haa<u>z</u>ihee Jahannamul-latee kuntum too'adoon.	هٰذِهٖ جَهَنَّمُ الَّتِي كُنْتُمْ تُوعَدُونَ ﴿٦٣﴾
64. Suffer its heat therein on this day for your disbelief.	64. Iṣlawhal-Yawma bimaa kuntum takfuroon.	اِصْلَوْهَا الْيَوْمَ بِمَا كُنْتُمْ تَكْفُرُونَ ﴿٦٤﴾
65. We shall seal their mouths on that Day, allow their hands speak to us and their feet testify to what they had achieved.	65. Al-Yawma nakhtimu 'alaaa afwaahihim wa tukallimunaaa aydeehim wa tashhadu arjuluhum bimaa kaanoo yaksiboon.	اَلْيَوْمَ نَخْتِمُ عَلٰٓى أَفْوَاهِهِمْ وَتُكَلِّمُنَآ أَيْدِيهِمْ وَتَشْهَدُ أَرْجُلُهُمْ بِمَا كَانُوا يَكْسِبُونَ ﴿٦٥﴾
66. We could have blinded them had We wanted. Then they would have raced along to cross the bridge but how could they have seen (their way)?	66. Wa law nashaaa'u laṭamasnaa 'alaaa a'yunihim fastabaquṣ-ṣiraaṭa fa-annaa yubṣiroon.	وَلَوْ نَشَآءُ لَطَمَسْنَا عَلٰٓى أَعْيُنِهِمْ فَاسْتَبَقُوا الصِّرَاطَ فَأَنّٰى يُبْصِرُونَ ﴿٦٦﴾
67. Had We wanted We could have turned them into other creatures (metamorphosed) in their worldly lives and they could not have been able to proceed or turn back.	67. Wa law nashaaa'u lamasakhnaahum 'alaa makaanatihim famas-taṭaa'oo muḍiyyañw-wa laa yarji'oon.	وَلَوْ نَشَآءُ لَمَسَخْنٰهُمْ عَلٰى مَكَانَتِهِمْ فَمَا اسْتَطَاعُوا مُضِيًّا وَّلَا يَرْجِعُونَ ﴿٦٧﴾ ع ٤ ١٧
68. The physical growth of those whom We grant a long life will be reversed. Will you then not understand?	68. Wa man-nu'ammirhu nunakkishu fil-khalq; afalaa ya'qiloon.	وَمَنْ نُّعَمِّرْهُ نُنَكِّسْهُ فِي الْخَلْقِ ۖ أَفَلَا يَعْقِلُونَ ﴿٦٨﴾
69. We did not teach him (Muhammad) poetry, nor was he supposed to be a poet. It is only the word (of Allah) and the illustrious Quran	69. Wa maa 'allamnaahush-shi'ra wa maa yambaghee lah; in huwa illaa <u>z</u>ikruñw-wa Qur'aanum-Mubeen.	وَمَا عَلَّمْنٰهُ الشِّعْرَ وَمَا يَنْۢبَغِي لَهُ ۖ إِنْ هُوَ إِلَّا ذِكْرٌ وَّقُرْاٰنٌ مُّبِينٌ ﴿٦٩﴾
70. by which he may warn those who are living and may allow the words of Allah to come true against the unbelievers.	70. Liyun<u>z</u>ira man kaana ḥayyañw-wa yaḥiqqal-qawlu 'alal-kaafireen.	لِّيُنْذِرَ مَنْ كَانَ حَيًّا وَّيَحِقَّ الْقَوْلُ عَلَى الْكٰفِرِينَ ﴿٧٠﴾
71. Did they not see that We have created from the labor of Our own hands cattle and they own them?	71. Awalam yaraw annaa khalaqnaa lahum-mimmaa 'amilat aydeenaaa an'aaman fahum lahaa maalikoon.	أَوَلَمْ يَرَوْا أَنَّا خَلَقْنَا لَهُمْ مِّمَّا عَمِلَتْ أَيْدِينَآ أَنْعَامًا فَهُمْ لَهَا مٰلِكُونَ ﴿٧١﴾
72. We have made the cattle subservient to them so they can ride and consume them.	72. Wa <u>z</u>allalnaahaa lahum faminhaa rakoobuhum wa minhaa ya-kuloon.	وَذَلَّلْنٰهَا لَهُمْ فَمِنْهَا رَكُوبُهُمْ وَمِنْهَا يَأْكُلُونَ ﴿٧٢﴾

73. From cattle they get milk and other benefits. Will they not then give thanks?

73. Wa lahum feehaa manaafi‘u wa mashaarib; afalaa yashkuroon.

وَلَهُمْ فِيهَا مَنَافِعُ وَمَشَارِبُ ط
أَفَلَا يَشْكُرُونَ ﴿٧٣﴾

74. They chose idols besides Allah in the hope of receiving help from them,

74. Wattakhazoo min doonil-laahi aalihatal-la‘allahum yunṣaroon.

وَاتَّخَذُوا مِن دُونِ اللَّهِ آلِهَةً
لَّعَلَّهُمْ يُنصَرُونَ ﴿٧٤﴾

75. but they will not be able to help them. Instead, the unbelievers will be brought into the presence of Allah as the soldiers of the idols.

75. Laa yastaṭee‘oona naṣrahum wa hum lahum jundum-muḥḍaroon.

لَا يَسْتَطِيعُونَ نَصْرَهُمْ وَهُمْ
لَهُمْ جُندٌ مُّحْضَرُونَ ﴿٧٥﴾

76. Muhammad, do not allow their words sadden you. We certainly know whatever they conceal or reveal.

76. Falaa yaḥzunka qawluhum; innaa na‘lamu maa yusirroona wa maa yu‘linoon.

فَلَا يَحْزُنكَ قَوْلُهُمْ م إِنَّا نَعْلَمُ
مَا يُسِرُّونَ وَمَا يُعْلِنُونَ ﴿٧٦﴾

وقف لازم

77. Did the human being not consider that We have created him from a drop of fluid? He is openly quarrelsome.

77. Awalam yaral-insaanu annaa khalaqnaahu min-nuṭfatin fa-izaa huwa khaṣeemum-mubeen.

أَوَلَمْ يَرَ الْإِنسَانُ أَنَّا خَلَقْنَاهُ مِن
نُّطْفَةٍ فَإِذَا هُوَ خَصِيمٌ مُّبِينٌ ﴿٧٧﴾

78. He questions Our Resurrection of him, but has forgotten his own creation. He has said, "Who will give life to the bones which have become ashes?"

78. Wa ḍaraba lanaa masalañw-wa nasiya khalqahoo qaala mañy-yuḥyil-‘iẓaama wa hiya rameem.

وَضَرَبَ لَنَا مَثَلًا وَنَسِيَ خَلْقَهُ ط قَالَ
مَن يُحْيِ الْعِظَامَ وَهِيَ رَمِيمٌ ﴿٧٨﴾

79. (Muhammad), tell him, "He who gave them life in the first place will bring them back to life again. He has the best knowledge of all creatures.

79. Qul yuḥyeehal-lazeee ansha-ahaaa awwala marrah; wa Huwa bikulli khalqin ‘Aleem.

قُلْ يُحْيِيهَا الَّذِي أَنشَأَهَا أَوَّلَ
مَرَّةٍ ط وَهُوَ بِكُلِّ خَلْقٍ عَلِيمٌ ﴿٧٩﴾

80. He has created fire for you out of the green tree from which you can kindle other fires.

80. Allazee ja‘ala lakum-minash-shajaril-akhḍari naaran fa-izaaa antum-minhu tooqidoon.

الَّذِي جَعَلَ لَكُم مِّنَ الشَّجَرِ الْأَخْضَرِ
نَارًا فَإِذَا أَنتُم مِّنْهُ تُوقِدُونَ ﴿٨٠﴾

81. Is the One who has created the heavens and the earth not able to create another creature like the human being? He certainly has the power to do so. He is the Supreme Creator and is All-knowing.

81. Awa laysal-lazee khalaqas-samaawaati wal-arḍa biqaadirin ‘alaaa añy-yakhluqa mislahum; balaa wa Huwal-Khallaaqul-‘Aleem.

أَوَلَيْسَ الَّذِي خَلَقَ السَّمَاوَاتِ
وَالْأَرْضَ بِقَادِرٍ عَلَىٰ أَن يَخْلُقَ
مِثْلَهُم بَلَىٰ وَهُوَ الْخَلَّاقُ الْعَلِيمُ ﴿٨١﴾

82. Whenever He decides to create something He has only to say, "Exist," and it comes into existence.

82. Innamaaa amruhooo izaaa araada shay'an añy-yaqoola lahoo kun fayakoon.

إِنَّمَا أَمْرُهُ إِذَا أَرَادَ شَيْئًا أَن يَقُولَ
لَهُ كُن فَيَكُونُ ﴿٨٢﴾

وقف غفران ١٢

83. All glory belongs to the One in whose hands is the control of all things. To Him you will all return.

83. Fa-Subḥaanal-lazee biyadihee malakootu kulli shay'iñw-wa ilayhi turja‘oon.

فَسُبْحَانَ الَّذِي بِيَدِهِ مَلَكُوتُ كُلِّ
شَيْءٍ وَإِلَيْهِ تُرْجَعُونَ ﴿٨٣﴾ ع

ع ٤ / ٥

Al-Saffat, The Ranks (37)

In the Name of Allah, the Beneficent, the Merciful.

Sûrat Ṣâffât-37

(Revealed at Makkah)

Bismillaahir Raḥmaanir Raḥeem

(٣٧) سُورَةُ الصَّافَّاتِ مَكِّيَّةٌ (٥٦)

آياتها ١٨٢ — بِسْمِ اللَّهِ الرَّحْمَٰنِ الرَّحِيمِ — ركوعاتها ٥

1. I swear by (the angels and the prophets) who stand in ranks (in worship),

1. Waṣṣaaaffaati ṣaffaa.

وَالصَّافَّاتِ صَفًّا ﴿١﴾

المنزل السادس (٦)

2. by those who drive away the devil (to protect Our revelation),	2. Fazzaajiraati zajraa.	فَالزّٰجِرٰتِ زَجۡرًا ۝٢
3. and by those who recite Our revelations,	3. Fattaaliyaati Zikraa.	فَالتّٰلِيٰتِ ذِكۡرًا ۝٣
4. that your Lord is the only Lord.	4. Inna Ilaahakum la-Waaḥid.	اِنَّ اِلٰهَكُمۡ لَوَاحِدٌ ۝٤
5. He is the Lord of the heavens and the earth and all that is between them, the Lord of the Eastern regions.	5. Rabbus-samaawaati wal-arḍi wa maa baynahumaa wa Rabbul-mashaariq.	رَبُّ السَّمٰوٰتِ وَالۡاَرۡضِ وَمَا بَيۡنَهُمَا وَرَبُّ الۡمَشَارِقِ ۝٥
6. We have decked the lower heavens with stars	6. Innaa zayyannas-samaaa-'ad-dunyaa bizeenatinil-kawaa-kib.	اِنَّا زَيَّنَّا السَّمَآءَ الدُّنۡيَا بِزِيۡنَةِ اۨلۡكَوَاكِبِ ۝٦
7. to protect them from the wicked Satan.	7. Wa ḥifẓam-min kulli Shayṭaanim-maarid.	وَحِفۡظًا مِّنۡ كُلِّ شَيۡطٰنٍ مَّارِدٍ ۝٧
8. The devils cannot hear those high above. They would be struck from all sides	8. Laa yassamma'oona ilal-mala-il-a'laa wa yuqzafoona min kulli jaanib.	لَا يَسَّمَّعُوۡنَ اِلَى الۡمَلَاِ الۡاَعۡلٰى وَيُقۡذَفُوۡنَ مِنۡ كُلِّ جَانِبٍ ۝٨
9. and driven away to suffer the necessary torment.	9. Duḥoorañw-wa lahum 'azaabuñw-waaṣib.	دُحُوۡرًا وَّلَهُمۡ عَذَابٌ وَّاصِبٌ ۝٩
10. Some of them who stealthily steal words from the heavens are pursued by a glistening flame.	10. Illaa man khaṭifal-khaṭfata fa-atba'ahoo shihaabun saaqib.	اِلَّا مَنۡ خَطِفَ الۡخَطۡفَةَ فَاَتۡبَعَهٗ شِهَابٌ ثَاقِبٌ ۝١٠
11. (Muhammad), ask them, "Have they (people) been created stronger than what We have created?" We have created them from sticky clay.	11. Fastaftihim ahum ashaddu khalqan am-man khalaqnaaa; innaa khalaqnaahum-min ṭeenil-laazib.	فَاسۡتَفۡتِهِمۡ اَهُمۡ اَشَدُّ خَلۡقًا اَمۡ مَّنۡ خَلَقۡنَا ؕ اِنَّا خَلَقۡنٰهُمۡ مِّنۡ طِيۡنٍ لَّازِبٍ ۝١١
12. (Muhammad), you will be surprised that they still mock (Allah's revelations).	12. Bal 'ajibta wa yaskharoon.	بَلۡ عَجِبۡتَ وَيَسۡخَرُوۡنَ ۝١٢
13. They pay no attention when they are reminded	13. Wa izaa zukkiroo laa yazkuroon.	وَاِذَا ذُكِّرُوۡا لَا يَذۡكُرُوۡنَ ۝١٣
14. and when they see a miracle, they mock	14. Wa izaa ra-aw Aayatañy-yastaskhiroon.	وَاِذَا رَاَوۡا اٰيَةً يَّسۡتَسۡخِرُوۡنَ ۝١٤
15. it and say, "It is only plain magic."	15. Wa qaalooo in haazaaa illaa siḥrum-mubeen.	وَقَالُوۡۤا اِنۡ هٰذَاۤ اِلَّا سِحۡرٌ مُّبِيۡنٌ ۝١٥
16. They say, "Shall we be brought to life again after we die and turn into dust and bones?	16. 'A-izaa mitnaa wa kunnaa turaabañw-wa 'iẓaaman 'a-innaa lamab'oosoon.	ءَاِذَا مِتۡنَا وَكُنَّا تُرَابًا وَّعِظَامًا ءَاِنَّا لَمَبۡعُوۡثُوۡنَ ۝١٦
17. Will our forefathers also be brought to life again?"	17. Awa aabaaa'unal awwa-loon.	اَوَ اٰبَآؤُنَا الۡاَوَّلُوۡنَ ۝١٧
18. Say, "Yes, you will certainly be (thrown in the fire) in disgrace."	18. Qul na'am wa antum daakhiroon.	قُلۡ نَعَمۡ وَاَنۡتُمۡ دَاخِرُوۡنَ ۝١٨
19. The Day of Judgment will come within a single roar and they will remain gazing at it.	19. Fa-innamaa hiya zajra-tuñw-waaḥidatun fa-izaa hum yanẓuroon.	فَاِنَّمَا هِىَ زَجۡرَةٌ وَّاحِدَةٌ فَاِذَا هُمۡ يَنۡظُرُوۡنَ ۝١٩

20. They will say, "Woe to us!" (They will be told), "This is the day of receiving recompense."

20. Wa qaaloo yaa waylanaa haaz̲aa Yawmud-Deen.

وَقَالُوا يٰوَيْلَنَا هٰذَا يَوْمُ الدِّيْنِ ﴿٢٠﴾

21. This, indeed, is the Day of Judgment in which you disbelieved.

21. Haaz̲aa Yawmul-Faṣlil-laz̲ee kuntum bihee tukaz̲ z̲iboon.

هٰذَا يَوْمُ الْفَصْلِ الَّذِيْ كُنْتُمْ بِهٖ تُكَذِّبُوْنَ ﴿٢١﴾ ع

22. (Allah will command the angels), "Gather together the unjust, their spouses, and what they had worshipped

22. Uḥshurul-laz̲eena ẓalamoo wa azwaajahum wa maa kaanoo ya'budoon.

اُحْشُرُوا الَّذِيْنَ ظَلَمُوْا وَاَزْوَاجَهُمْ وَمَا كَانُوْا يَعْبُدُوْنَ ﴿٢٢﴾

23. besides Allah, and call them to the way (leading) to hell.

23. Min doonil-laahi fahdoohum ilaa ṣiraaṭil-Jaḥeem.

مِنْ دُوْنِ اللّٰهِ فَاهْدُوْهُمْ اِلٰى صِرَاطِ الْجَحِيْمِ ﴿٢٣﴾

24. Stop them. They must be questioned."

24. Wa qifoohum innahum-mas'ooloon.

وَقِفُوْهُمْ اِنَّهُمْ مَّسْئُوْلُوْنَ ﴿٢٤﴾

25. They will be asked, "Why do you not help each other?"

25. Maa lakum laa tanaaṣaroon.

مَا لَكُمْ لَا تَنَاصَرُوْنَ ﴿٢٥﴾

26. In fact, on that day they will be submissive.

26. Bal humul-Yawma mustaslimoon.

بَلْ هُمُ الْيَوْمَ مُسْتَسْلِمُوْنَ ﴿٢٦﴾

27. They will turn to each other saying,

27. Wa aqbala ba'ḍuhum 'alaa ba'ḍiñy-yatasaaa'aloon.

وَاَقْبَلَ بَعْضُهُمْ عَلٰى بَعْضٍ يَّتَسَآءَلُوْنَ ﴿٢٧﴾

28. "It was you who tried to mislead us from righteousness."

28. Qaalooo innakum kuntum ta-toonanaa 'anil-yameen.

قَالُوْٓا اِنَّكُمْ كُنْتُمْ تَاْتُوْنَنَا عَنِ الْيَمِيْنِ ﴿٢٨﴾

29. Others will respond, "It was you who did not want to have any faith.

29. Qaaloo bal lam takoonoo mu'mineen.

قَالُوْا بَلْ لَّمْ تَكُوْنُوْا مُؤْمِنِيْنَ ﴿٢٩﴾

30. We had no authority over you, in fact you were a rebellious people.

30. Wa maa kaana lanaa 'alaykum-min sulṭaanim bal kuntum qawman ṭaagheen.

وَمَا كَانَ لَنَا عَلَيْكُمْ مِّنْ سُلْطٰنٍ بَلْ كُنْتُمْ قَوْمًا طٰغِيْنَ ﴿٣٠﴾

31. Thus, the words of Our Lord about us have come true and now we are suffering the torment.

31. Faḥaqqa 'alaynaa qawlu Rabbinaaa innaa laz̲aaa'iqoon.

فَحَقَّ عَلَيْنَا قَوْلُ رَبِّنَآ اِنَّا لَذَآئِقُوْنَ ﴿٣١﴾

32. We misled you and we ourselves had also gone astray."

32. Fa-aghwaynaakum innaa kunnaa ghaaween.

فَاَغْوَيْنٰكُمْ اِنَّا كُنَّا غٰوِيْنَ ﴿٣٢﴾

33. On that day they will all commonly suffer the torment.

33. Fa-innahum Yawma'iz̲in fil-'az̲aabi mushtarikoon.

فَاِنَّهُمْ يَوْمَئِذٍ فِي الْعَذَابِ مُشْتَرِكُوْنَ ﴿٣٣﴾

34. This is how We deal with the criminals.

34. Innaa kaz̲aalika naf'alu bil-mujrimeen.

اِنَّا كَذٰلِكَ نَفْعَلُ بِالْمُجْرِمِيْنَ ﴿٣٤﴾

35. They were the ones, who on being told, "There is no Ilah (one deserving to be worshiped) except Allah," became arrogant

35. Innahum kaanooo iz̲aa qeela lahum laaa ilaaha illallaahu yastakbiroon.

اِنَّهُمْ كَانُوْٓا اِذَا قِيْلَ لَهُمْ لَآ اِلٰهَ اِلَّا اللّٰهُ يَسْتَكْبِرُوْنَ ﴿٣٥﴾

36. and said, "Should we give up our idols for the sake of an insane poet (possessed by Jinn)."

36. Wa yaqooloona a'innaa lataarikooo aalihatinaa lishaa'i-rim-majnoon.

وَيَقُوْلُوْنَ اَئِنَّا لَتَارِكُوْٓا اٰلِهَتِنَا لِشَاعِرٍ مَّجْنُوْنٍ ﴿٣٦﴾

37. In fact, he had brought them the truth and had acknowledged the Messengers (who were sent before him).

37. Bal jaaa'a bilḥaqqi wa ṣaddaqal-mursaleen.

بَلْ جَآءَ بِالْحَقِّ وَصَدَّقَ الْمُرْسَلِيْنَ ﴿٣٧﴾

38. (They will be told), "You will certainly suffer the painful torment	38. Innakum lazaaa'iqul-'azaabil-aleem.	إِنَّكُمْ لَذَآئِقُوا الْعَذَابِ الْأَلِيمِ ۝٣٨
39. and will be recompensed only for what you deserve.	39. Wa maa tujzawna illaa maa kuntum ta'maloon.	وَمَا تُجْزَوْنَ إِلَّا مَا كُنتُمْ تَعْمَلُونَ ۝٣٩
40. However, the sincere servants of Allah	40. Illaa'ibaadal-laahil-mukh-laṣeen.	إِلَّا عِبَادَ اللَّهِ الْمُخْلَصِينَ ۝٤٠
41. will have their determined sustenance	41. Ulaaa'ika lahum rizqum-ma'loom.	أُولَٰٓئِكَ لَهُمْ رِزْقٌ مَّعْلُومٌ ۝٤١
42. and fruits while they are honored.	42. Fawaakihu wa hum-muk-ramoon.	فَوَاكِهُ ۖ وَهُم مُّكْرَمُونَ ۝٤٢
43. (They will live) in the bountiful gardens,	43. Fee Jannaatin-Na'eem.	فِي جَنَّاتِ النَّعِيمِ ۝٤٣
44. on couches facing each other.	44. 'Alaa- sururim-mutaqaa-bileen.	عَلَىٰ سُرُرٍ مُّتَقَابِلِينَ ۝٤٤
45. They will be served with a cup full of crystal clear wine,	45. Yuṭaafu 'alayhim bika-sim-mim-ma'een.	يُطَافُ عَلَيْهِم بِكَأْسٍ مِّن مَّعِينٍ ۝٤٥
46. delicious to those who drink it,	46. Bayḍaaa'a laz-zatil-lish-shaaribeen.	بَيْضَآءَ لَذَّةٍ لِّلشَّارِبِينَ ۝٤٦
47. but not harmful (spoiling) or intoxicating.	47. Laa feehaa ghawluñw-wa laa hum 'anhaa yunzafoon.	لَا فِيهَا غَوْلٌ وَلَا هُمْ عَنْهَا يُنزَفُونَ ۝٤٧
48. They will have with them loving ones with big black and white eyes	48. Wa 'indahum qaaṣiraatuṭ-ṭarfi'een.	وَعِندَهُمْ قَاصِرَاتُ الطَّرْفِ عِينٌ ۝٤٨
49. who are as chaste as sheltered eggs.	49. Ka-annahunna bayḍum-maknoon.	كَأَنَّهُنَّ بَيْضٌ مَّكْنُونٌ ۝٤٩
50. They will turn to each other and ask questions.	50. Fa-aqbala ba'ḍuhum 'alaa ba'ḍiñy-yatasaaa'aloon.	فَأَقْبَلَ بَعْضُهُمْ عَلَىٰ بَعْضٍ يَتَسَآءَلُونَ ۝٥٠
51. One of them will say, "I had a companion who asked me,	51. Qaala qaaa'ilum-minhum innee kaana lee qareen.	قَالَ قَآئِلٌ مِّنْهُمْ إِنِّي كَانَ لِي قَرِينٌ ۝٥١
52. 'Do you believe in the Day of Judgment?	52. Yaqoolu a'innaka laminal-muṣaddiqeen.	يَقُولُ أَإِنَّكَ لَمِنَ الْمُصَدِّقِينَ ۝٥٢
53. Shall we be recompensed for our deeds after we die and become bones and dust?	53. 'A-izaa mitnaa wa kunnaa turaabañw-wa 'izaaman 'a-innaa lamadeenoon.	أَإِذَا مِتْنَا وَكُنَّا تُرَابًا وَعِظَامًا أَإِنَّا لَمَدِينُونَ ۝٥٣
54. Do you want to see him?"'	54. Qaala hal antum-muṭṭa-li'oon.	قَالَ هَلْ أَنتُم مُّطَّلِعُونَ ۝٥٤
55. He will look down and see him in (the middle of) hell.	55. Faṭṭala'a fara-aahu fee sawaaa'il-Jaḥeem.	فَاطَّلَعَ فَرَآهُ فِي سَوَآءِ الْجَحِيمِ ۝٥٥
56. He will say to his friend in hell, "By Allah, you almost destroyed me.	56. Qaala tallaahi in kitta laturdeen.	قَالَ تَاللَّهِ إِن كِدتَّ لَتُرْدِينِ ۝٥٦
57. Had I not the guidance of my Lord, I would certainly have been brought into torment."	57. Wa law laa ni'matu Rab-bee lakuntu minal-muḥḍareen.	وَلَوْلَا نِعْمَةُ رَبِّي لَكُنتُ مِنَ الْمُحْضَرِينَ ۝٥٧
58. He will ask his (worldly) companion, "Did you not say that there would be only one death	58. Afamaa naḥnu bimayyi-teen.	أَفَمَا نَحْنُ بِمَيِّتِينَ ۝٥٨
59. and that we would not be punished?"	59. Illa mawtatanal-oolaa wa maa naḥnu bimu'azzabeen.	إِلَّا مَوْتَتَنَا الْأُولَىٰ وَمَا نَحْنُ

		بِمُعَذَّبِيْنَ ﴿٥٩﴾
60. This is certainly the greatest triumph	60. Inna haaẕaa lahuwal-fawzul-'aẓeem.	اِنَّ هٰذَا لَهُوَ الْفَوْزُ الْعَظِيْمُ ﴿٦٠﴾
61. for which one must strive hard.	61. Limiṯli haaẕaa falya'malil-'aamiloon.	لِمِثْلِ هٰذَا فَلْيَعْمَلِ الْعٰمِلُوْنَ ﴿٦١﴾
62. Is this not a better reward than the tree of Al-Zaqqum	62. Aẕaalika khayrun-nuzulan am shajaratuz-Zaqqoom.	اَذٰلِكَ خَيْرٌ نُّزُلًا اَمْ شَجَرَةُ الزَّقُّوْمِ ﴿٦٢﴾
63. which We have made as a torment for the unjust?	63. Innaa ja'alnaahaa fitnatal-liẓẓaalimeen.	اِنَّا جَعَلْنٰهَا فِتْنَةً لِّلظّٰلِمِيْنَ ﴿٦٣﴾
64. (Al-Zaqqum) is a tree which grows from the deepest part of hell,	64. Innahaa shajaratun takhruju feee aṣlil-Jaḥeem.	اِنَّهَا شَجَرَةٌ تَخْرُجُ فِيْٓ اَصْلِ الْجَحِيْمِ ﴿٦٤﴾
65. and its fruits are like the heads of devils.	65. Ṭal'uhaa ka-annahoo ru'oosush-Shayaaṭeen.	طَلْعُهَا كَاَنَّهٗ رُءُوْسُ الشَّيٰطِيْنِ ﴿٦٥﴾
66. The dwellers of hell will eat that fruit and fill-up their bellies.	66. Fa-innahum la-aakiloona minhaa famaali'oona minhal-buṭoon.	فَاِنَّهُمْ لَاٰكِلُوْنَ مِنْهَا فَمَالِـُٔوْنَ مِنْهَا الْبُطُوْنَ ﴿٦٦﴾
67. Then they will have, on top of it, the torment of boiling water.	67. S̱umma inna lahum 'alayhaa lashawbam-min ḥameem.	ثُمَّ اِنَّ لَهُمْ عَلَيْهَا لَشَوْبًا مِّنْ حَمِيْمٍ ﴿٦٧﴾
68. They can only return to hell.	68. S̱umma inna marji'ahum la-ilal-Jaḥeem.	ثُمَّ اِنَّ مَرْجِعَهُمْ لَاِلَى الْجَحِيْمِ ﴿٦٨﴾
69. They found their fathers going astray	69. Innahum alfaw aabaaa'ahum ḍaaalleen.	اِنَّهُمْ اَلْفَوْا اٰبَآءَهُمْ ضَآلِّيْنَ ﴿٦٩﴾
70. and rushed to follow them.	70. Fahum 'alaaa aas̱aarihim yuhra'oon.	فَهُمْ عَلٰٓى اٰثٰرِهِمْ يُهْرَعُوْنَ ﴿٧٠﴾
71. Most of the ancient people had also gone astray.	71. Wa laqad ḍalla qablahum aks̱arul-awwaleen.	وَلَقَدْ ضَلَّ قَبْلَهُمْ اَكْثَرُ الْاَوَّلِيْنَ ﴿٧١﴾
72. We had certainly sent many a Warner to them.	72. Wa laqad arsalnaa feehim-munẕireen.	وَلَقَدْ اَرْسَلْنَا فِيْهِمْ مُّنْذِرِيْنَ ﴿٧٢﴾
73. See how terrible the end of those who were warned was.	73. Fanẓur kayfa kaana 'aaqibatul-munẕareen.	فَانْظُرْ كَيْفَ كَانَ عَاقِبَةُ الْمُنْذَرِيْنَ ﴿٧٣﴾
74. Only Our sincere servants were saved.	74. Illaa 'ibaadal-laahil-mukhlaṣeen.	اِلَّا عِبَادَ اللّٰهِ الْمُخْلَصِيْنَ ﴿٧٤﴾ ع ٥٣ ٢
75. Noah called for help. How blessed was the answer which he received.	75. Wa laqad naadaanaa Nooḥun falani'mal-mujeeboon.	وَلَقَدْ نَادٰىنَا نُوْحٌ فَلَنِعْمَ الْمُجِيْبُوْنَ ﴿٧٥﴾
76. We rescued him and his people from the greatest affliction	76. Wa najjaynaahu wa ahlahoo minal-karbil-'aẓeem.	وَنَجَّيْنٰهُ وَاَهْلَهٗ مِنَ الْكَرْبِ الْعَظِيْمِ ﴿٧٦﴾
77. and We made his offspring the only survivors (with truth and guidance).	77. Wa ja'alnaa ẕurriyyatahoo humul-baaqeen.	وَجَعَلْنَا ذُرِّيَّتَهٗ هُمُ الْبٰقِيْنَ ﴿٧٧﴾
78. We perpetuated his praise in later generations.	78. Wa taraknaa 'alayhi fil-aakhireen.	وَتَرَكْنَا عَلَيْهِ فِي الْاٰخِرِيْنَ ﴿٧٨﴾
79. Peace be with Noah among all men in the worlds.	79. Salaamun 'alaa Nooḥin fil-'aalameen.	سَلٰمٌ عَلٰى نُوْحٍ فِي الْعٰلَمِيْنَ ﴿٧٩﴾

80. Thus do We reward the righteous ones.	80. Innaa kaẕaalika najzil-muḥsineen.	إِنَّا كَذَٰلِكَ نَجْزِي الْمُحْسِنِينَ ٨٠
81. He was one of Our believing servants.	81. Innahoo min ‘ibaadinal-mu’mineen.	إِنَّهُ مِنْ عِبَادِنَا الْمُؤْمِنِينَ ٨١
82. We drowned all the others (besides Noah and his people).	82. S̲umma aghraqnal-aakhareen.	ثُمَّ أَغْرَقْنَا الْآخَرِينَ ٨٢
83. Abraham was one of his followers.	83. Wa inna min shee‘atihee la-Ibraaheem.	وَإِنَّ مِنْ شِيعَتِهِ لَإِبْرَاهِيمَ ٨٣
84. He turned to his Lord with a sound (submissive) heart	84. Iẕ jaaa’a Rabbahoo biqalbin saleem.	إِذْ جَاءَ رَبَّهُ بِقَلْبٍ سَلِيمٍ ٨٤
85. and asked his father and his people, “What is that you worship?	85. Iẕ qaala li-abeehi wa qawmihee maaẕaa ta‘budoon.	إِذْ قَالَ لِأَبِيهِ وَقَوْمِهِ مَاذَا تَعْبُدُونَ ٨٥
86. Do you want to worship false idols as your lords besides Allah?	86. A’ifkan aalihatan doonal-laahi tureedoon.	أَئِفْكًا آلِهَةً دُونَ اللَّهِ تُرِيدُونَ ٨٦
87. What do you think about the Lord of the universe?”	87. Famaa ẓannukum bi-Rabbil-‘aalameen.	فَمَا ظَنُّكُمْ بِرَبِّ الْعَالَمِينَ ٨٧
88. (The people invited him to attend their feast). Then he looked at the stars	88. Fanaẓara naẓratan finnu-joom.	فَنَظَرَ نَظْرَةً فِي النُّجُومِ ٨٨
89. and said, “I am sick!”	89. Faqaala innee saqeem.	فَقَالَ إِنِّي سَقِيمٌ ٨٩
90. All the people turned away from him	90. Fatawallaw ‘anhu mudbi-reen.	فَتَوَلَّوْا عَنْهُ مُدْبِرِينَ ٩٠
91. and he turned to their idols and asked them, “Do you eat?	91. Faraagha ilaaa aalihatihim faqaala alaa ta-kuloon.	فَرَاغَ إِلَىٰ آلِهَتِهِمْ فَقَالَ أَلَا تَأْكُلُونَ ٩١
92. Why do you not speak?”	92. Maa lakum laa tanṭiqoon.	مَا لَكُمْ لَا تَنْطِقُونَ ٩٢
93. He struck them with his right hand.	93. Faraagha ‘alayhim ḍar-bam bilyameen.	فَرَاغَ عَلَيْهِمْ ضَرْبًا بِالْيَمِينِ ٩٣
94. Thereupon the people came running to him.	94. Fa-aqbalooo ilayhi yazif-foon.	فَأَقْبَلُوا إِلَيْهِ يَزِفُّونَ ٩٤
95. He said, “How can you worship what you yourselves have carved	95. Qaala ata‘budoona maa tanḥitoon.	قَالَ أَتَعْبُدُونَ مَا تَنْحِتُونَ ٩٥
96. even though Allah created both you and that which you have made?”	96. Wallaahu khalaqakum wa maa ta‘maloon.	وَاللَّهُ خَلَقَكُمْ وَمَا تَعْمَلُونَ ٩٦
97. They said, “Allow us to build a fire and throw him into the flames.”	97. Qaalub-noo lahoo bun-yaanan fa-alqoohu fil-Jaḥeem.	قَالُوا ابْنُوا لَهُ بُنْيَانًا فَأَلْقُوهُ فِي الْجَحِيمِ ٩٧
98. They plotted against him, but We brought humiliation upon them.	98. Fa-araadoo bihee kaydan faja‘alnaahumul-asfaleen.	فَأَرَادُوا بِهِ كَيْدًا فَجَعَلْنَاهُمُ الْأَسْفَلِينَ ٩٨
99. (Abraham) said, “I will go to my Lord who will guide me.”	99. Wa qaala innee ẕaahibun ilaa Rabbee sa-yahdeen.	وَقَالَ إِنِّي ذَاهِبٌ إِلَىٰ رَبِّي سَيَهْدِينِ ٩٩
100. Abraham prayed, “Lord, grant me a righteous son.”	100. Rabbi hab lee minaṣ-ṣaaliḥeen.	رَبِّ هَبْ لِي مِنَ الصَّالِحِينَ ١٠٠

وقف لازم

101. We gave him the glad news of the birth of a forbearing son.	101. Fabashsharnaahu bighulaamin ḥaleem.	فَبَشَّرْنٰهُ بِغُلٰمٍ حَلِيْمٍ ﴿١٠١﴾
102. When his son was old enough to work with him, he said, "My son, I have had a dream that I must sacrifice you. What do you think of this?" He replied, "Father, fulfill whatever you are commanded to do and you will find me patient, by the will of Allah."	102. Falammaa balagha ma'ahus-sa'ya qaala yaa bunayya inneee araa fil-manaami anneee aẕbaḥuka fanẓur maaẕaa taraa; qaala yaaa abatif-'al maa tu'maru satajiduneee in shaaa'-allaahu minaṣ-ṣaabireen.	فَلَمَّا بَلَغَ مَعَهُ السَّعْيَ قَالَ يٰبُنَيَّ اِنِّيْٓ اَرٰى فِي الْمَنَامِ اَنِّيْٓ اَذْبَحُكَ فَانْظُرْ مَاذَا تَرٰى ؕ قَالَ يٰٓاَبَتِ افْعَلْ مَا تُؤْمَرُ ؗ سَتَجِدُنِيْٓ اِنْ شَآءَ اللّٰهُ مِنَ الصّٰبِرِيْنَ ﴿١٠٢﴾
103. When they both agreed and Abraham had lain down his son on the side of his face (for slaughtering),	103. Falammaaa aslamaa wa tallahoo liljabeen.	فَلَمَّآ اَسْلَمَا وَتَلَّهٗ لِلْجَبِيْنِ ﴿١٠٣﴾
104. We called to him, "Abraham,	104. Wa naadaynaahu añy-yaaa Ibraaheem.	وَنَادَيْنٰهُ اَنْ يّٰٓاِبْرٰهِيْمُ ﴿١٠٤﴾
105. you have fulfilled what you were commanded to do in your dream." Thus do We reward the righteous ones.	105. Qad ṣaddaqtar-ru'yaa; innaa kaẕaalika najzil-muḥsineen.	قَدْ صَدَّقْتَ الرُّءْيَا ۚ اِنَّا كَذٰلِكَ نَجْزِي الْمُحْسِنِيْنَ ﴿١٠٥﴾
106. It was certainly an open trial.	106. Inna haaẕaa lahuwal-balaaa'ul-mubeen	اِنَّ هٰذَا لَهُوَ الْبَلٰٓؤُا الْمُبِيْنُ ﴿١٠٦﴾
107. We ransomed his son with a great sacrifice	107. Wa fadaynaahu biẕibḥin 'aẓeem.	وَفَدَيْنٰهُ بِذِبْحٍ عَظِيْمٍ ﴿١٠٧﴾
108. and perpetuated his praise in later generations.	108. Wa taraknaa 'alayhi fil-aakhireen.	وَتَرَكْنَا عَلَيْهِ فِي الْاٰخِرِيْنَ ﴿١٠٨﴾
109. Peace be with Abraham.	109. Salaamun 'alaaa Ibraaheem.	سَلٰمٌ عَلٰٓى اِبْرٰهِيْمَ ﴿١٠٩﴾
110. Thus do We reward the righteous ones.	110. Kaẕaalika najzil-muḥsineen.	كَذٰلِكَ نَجْزِي الْمُحْسِنِيْنَ ﴿١١٠﴾
111. He was one of Our believing servants.	111. Innahoo min 'ibaadinal-mu'mineen.	اِنَّهٗ مِنْ عِبَادِنَا الْمُؤْمِنِيْنَ ﴿١١١﴾
112. We gave him the glad news of the birth of Isaac, one of the righteous Prophets.	112. Wa bashsharnaahu bi-Isḥaaqa Nabiyyam-minaṣ-ṣaaliḥeen.	وَبَشَّرْنٰهُ بِاِسْحٰقَ نَبِيًّا مِّنَ الصّٰلِحِيْنَ ﴿١١٢﴾
113. We had blessed him and Isaac. Some of their offspring were righteous and others were openly unjust to themselves.	113. Wa baaraknaa 'alayhi wa 'alaaa Isḥaaq; wa min ẕurriyyatihimaa muḥsinuñw-wa ẓaalimul-Iinafsihee mubeen.	وَبٰرَكْنَا عَلَيْهِ وَعَلٰٓى اِسْحٰقَ ؕ وَمِنْ ذُرِّيَّتِهِمَا مُحْسِنٌ وَّظَالِمٌ لِّنَفْسِهٖ مُبِيْنٌ ﴿١١٣﴾
114. We certainly bestowed Our favor upon Moses and Aaron	114. Wa laqad manannaa 'alaa Moosaa wa Haaroon.	وَلَقَدْ مَنَنَّا عَلٰى مُوْسٰى وَهٰرُوْنَ ﴿١١٤﴾
115. and saved them and their people from great suffering.	115. Wa najjaynaahumaa wa qawmahumaa minal-karbil-'aẓeem.	وَنَجَّيْنٰهُمَا وَقَوْمَهُمَا مِنَ الْكَرْبِ الْعَظِيْمِ ﴿١١٥﴾
116. We helped them and they were victorious.	116. Wa naṣarnaahum fakaanoo humul-ghaalibeen.	وَنَصَرْنٰهُمْ فَكَانُوْا هُمُ الْغٰلِبِيْنَ ﴿١١٦﴾
117. We gave them the enlightening Book,	117. Wa aataynaahumal-Kitaabal-mustabeen.	وَاٰتَيْنٰهُمَا الْكِتٰبَ الْمُسْتَبِيْنَ ﴿١١٧﴾

118. guided them to the right path,	118. Wa hadaynaahumaṣ-Ṣiraaṭal-Mustaqeem.	وَهَدَيْنٰهُمَا الصِّرَاطَ الْمُسْتَقِيْمَ ﴿١١٨﴾
119. and perpetuated their praise in later generations.	119. Wa taraknaa 'alayhimaa fil-aakhireen.	وَتَرَكْنَا عَلَيْهِمَا فِي الْاٰخِرِيْنَ ﴿١١٩﴾
120. Peace be with Moses and Aaron.	120. Salaamun 'alaa Moosaa wa Haaroon.	سَلٰمٌ عَلٰى مُوْسٰى وَهٰرُوْنَ ﴿١٢٠﴾
121. Thus do We reward the righteous ones.	121. Innaa kazaalika najzil-muḥsineen.	اِنَّا كَذٰلِكَ نَجْزِي الْمُحْسِنِيْنَ ﴿١٢١﴾
122. They were two of Our believing servants.	122. Innahumaa min 'ibaadi-nal-mu'mineen.	اِنَّهُمَا مِنْ عِبَادِنَا الْمُؤْمِنِيْنَ ﴿١٢٢﴾
123. Elias was certainly of the Messengers.	123. Wa inna Ilyaasa laminal-mursaleen.	وَاِنَّ اِلْيَاسَ لَمِنَ الْمُرْسَلِيْنَ ﴿١٢٣﴾
124. He told his people, "Why do you not have fear of Allah?	124. Iz qaala liqawmiheee alaa tattaqoon.	اِذْ قَالَ لِقَوْمِهٖٓ اَلَا تَتَّقُوْنَ ﴿١٢٤﴾
125. Do you worship Baal and abandon the Best Creator,	125. Atad'oona Ba'lañw-wa tazaroona aḥsanal-khaaliqeen.	اَتَدْعُوْنَ بَعْلًا وَّتَذَرُوْنَ اَحْسَنَ الْخٰلِقِيْنَ ﴿١٢٥﴾
126. Allah, who is your Lord and the Lord of your forefathers?"	126. Allaaha Rabbakum wa Rabba aabaaa'ikumul-awwaleen.	اللّٰهَ رَبَّكُمْ وَرَبَّ اٰبَآئِكُمُ الْاَوَّلِيْنَ ﴿١٢٦﴾
127. They called him a liar. Thus, all of them (unbelievers) will suffer torment	127. Fakaz-zaboohu fa-innahum lamuḥḍaroon.	فَكَذَّبُوْهُ فَاِنَّهُمْ لَمُحْضَرُوْنَ ﴿١٢٧﴾
128. except the sincere servants of Allah.	128. Illaa 'ibaadal-laahil-mukhlaṣeen.	اِلَّا عِبَادَ اللّٰهِ الْمُخْلَصِيْنَ ﴿١٢٨﴾
129. We perpetuated his praise in the later generations.	129. Wa taraknaa 'alayhi fil-aakhireen.	وَتَرَكْنَا عَلَيْهِ فِي الْاٰخِرِيْنَ ﴿١٢٩﴾
130. Peace be with Elyasin (Muhammad and his family).	130. Salaamun 'alaaa Ilyaa-seen.	سَلٰمٌ عَلٰٓى اِلْ يَاسِيْنَ ﴿١٣٠﴾
131. In this way do We reward the righteous ones.	131. Innaa kazaalika najzil-muḥsineen.	اِنَّا كَذٰلِكَ نَجْزِي الْمُحْسِنِيْنَ ﴿١٣١﴾
132. He was one of Our believing servants.	132. Innahoo min 'ibaadinal-mu'mineen.	اِنَّهٗ مِنْ عِبَادِنَا الْمُؤْمِنِيْنَ ﴿١٣٢﴾
133. Lot was certainly of the Messengers.	133. Wa inna Looṭal-laminal-mursaleen.	وَاِنَّ لُوْطًا لَّمِنَ الْمُرْسَلِيْنَ ﴿١٣٣﴾
134. We rescued him and his whole family,	134. Iz najjaynaahu wa ahla-hooo ajma'een.	اِذْ نَجَّيْنٰهُ وَاَهْلَهٗٓ اَجْمَعِيْنَ ﴿١٣٤﴾
135. except for an old woman who remained behind.	135. Illaa 'ajoozan fil-ghaa-bireen.	اِلَّا عَجُوْزًا فِي الْغٰبِرِيْنَ ﴿١٣٥﴾
136. Then We totally destroyed the others.	136. Summa dammarnal aakha-reen.	ثُمَّ دَمَّرْنَا الْاٰخَرِيْنَ ﴿١٣٦﴾
137. You pass by (their ruined town) in the morning and at night.	137. Wa innakum latamurroona 'alayhim-muṣbiḥeen.	وَاِنَّكُمْ لَتَمُرُّوْنَ عَلَيْهِمْ مُّصْبِحِيْنَ ﴿١٣٧﴾
138. Will you then not understand?	138. Wa billayl; afalaa ta'qi-loon.	وَبِالَّيْلِ اَفَلَا تَعْقِلُوْنَ ﴿١٣٨﴾ ع ٤٥ ٨
139. Jonah was certainly one of the Messengers.	139. Wa inna Yoonusa laminal-mursaleen.	وَاِنَّ يُوْنُسَ لَمِنَ الْمُرْسَلِيْنَ ﴿١٣٩﴾
140. He fled toward a loaded ship	140. Iz abaqa ilal-fulkil-mashḥoon.	اِذْ اَبَقَ اِلَى الْفُلْكِ الْمَشْحُوْنِ ﴿١٤٠﴾
141. wherein people cast lots whereby he was of those to be thrown into the water.	141. Fasaahama fakaana minal-mudḥaḍeen.	فَسَاهَمَ فَكَانَ مِنَ الْمُدْحَضِيْنَ ﴿١٤١﴾
142. The fish swallowed him up and he deserved (all this).	142. Faltaqamahul-ḥootu wa huwa muleem.	فَالْتَقَمَهُ الْحُوْتُ وَهُوَ مُلِيْمٌ ﴿١٤٢﴾

النّصف

143. Had he not glorified Allah,	143. Falaw laaa annahoo kaana minal-musabbiḥeen.	فَلَوْلَآ أَنَّهُۥ كَانَ مِنَ الْمُسَبِّحِينَ ﴿١٤٣﴾
144. he would certainly have remained inside the fish until the Day of Resurrection.	144. Lalabis̲a fee baṭniheee ilaa Yawmi yub'as̲oon.	لَلَبِثَ فِي بَطْنِهِۦٓ إِلَىٰ يَوْمِ يُبْعَثُونَ ﴿١٤٤﴾
145. We cast him out of the fish unto dry land and he was sick.	145. Fanabaz̲naahu bil'araaa'i wa huwa saqeem.	فَنَبَذْنٰهُ بِالْعَرَآءِ وَهُوَ سَقِيمٌ ﴿١٤٥﴾
146. We made a plant of gourd grow up for him.	146. Wa ambatnaa 'alayhi shajaratam-miñy-yaqṭeen.	وَأَنۢبَتْنَا عَلَيْهِ شَجَرَةً مِّنْ يَّقْطِينٍ ﴿١٤٦﴾
147. We sent him to a hundred thousand or more people.	147. Wa arsalnaahu ilaa mi'ati alfin aw yazeedoon.	وَأَرْسَلْنٰهُ إِلَىٰ مِائَةِ أَلْفٍ أَوْ يَزِيدُونَ ﴿١٤٧﴾
148. They believed in him so We granted them enjoyment for an appointed time.	148. Fa-aamanoo famatta'-naahum ilaa ḥeen.	فَاٰمَنُوا فَمَتَّعْنٰهُمْ إِلَىٰ حِينٍ ﴿١٤٨﴾
149. (Muhammad), ask them, "Do daughters belong to your Lord and sons to them?"	149. Fastaftihim ali-Rabbikal-banaatu wa lahumul-banoon.	فَاسْتَفْتِهِمْ أَلِرَبِّكَ الْبَنَاتُ وَلَهُمُ الْبَنُونَ ﴿١٤٩﴾
150. Have We created the angels as females before their very eyes?	150. Am khalaqnal-malaaa'i-kata inaas̲añw-wa hum shaahi-doon.	أَمْ خَلَقْنَا الْمَلٰٓئِكَةَ إِنٰثًا وَّهُمْ شٰهِدُونَ ﴿١٥٠﴾
151. It is only because of their false invention that they say,	151. Alaaa innahum-min ifki-him la-yaqooloon	أَلَآ إِنَّهُمْ مِّنْ إِفْكِهِمْ لَيَقُولُونَ ﴿١٥١﴾
152. "Allah has begotten a son." They are certainly liars.	152. Waladal-laahu wa inna-hum lakaaz̲iboon.	وَلَدَ اللّٰهُ وَإِنَّهُمْ لَكٰذِبُونَ ﴿١٥٢﴾
153. Has He chosen daughters in preference to sons?	153. Aṣṭafal-banaati 'alal-ba-neen.	أَصْطَفَى الْبَنَاتِ عَلَى الْبَنِينَ ﴿١٥٣﴾
154. Woe to you! How terrible is your Judgment.	154. Maa lakum kayfa taḥku-moon.	مَا لَكُمْ كَيْفَ تَحْكُمُونَ ﴿١٥٤﴾
155. Do you not understand?	155. Afalaa taz̲akkaroon.	أَفَلَا تَذَكَّرُونَ ﴿١٥٥﴾
156. Do you have clear authority?	156. Am lakum sulṭaanum-mubeen.	أَمْ لَكُمْ سُلْطٰنٌ مُّبِينٌ ﴿١٥٦﴾
157. Bring your book if what you say is true.	157. Fa-too bi-Kitaabikum in kuntum ṣaadiqeen.	فَأْتُوا بِكِتٰبِكُمْ إِنْ كُنْتُمْ صٰدِقِينَ ﴿١٥٧﴾
158. They have said that there is a kinship between Him and the jinn. The jinn certainly know that they will all be brought to suffer torment.	158. Wa ja'aloo baynahoo wa baynal-jinnati nasabaa; wa laqad 'alimatil-jinnatu innahum lamuḥḍaroon.	وَجَعَلُوا بَيْنَهُۥ وَبَيْنَ الْجِنَّةِ نَسَبًا ۚ وَلَقَدْ عَلِمَتِ الْجِنَّةُ إِنَّهُمْ لَمُحْضَرُونَ ﴿١٥٨﴾
159. Allah is free of all defects of being described as they describe Him	159. Subḥaanal-laahi 'ammaa yaṣifoon.	سُبْحٰنَ اللّٰهِ عَمَّا يَصِفُونَ ﴿١٥٩﴾
160. except the sincere servants of Allah, (who do not describe Him as the unbelievers do).	160. Illaa 'ibaadal-laahil-mukhlaṣeen.	إِلَّا عِبَادَ اللّٰهِ الْمُخْلَصِينَ ﴿١٦٠﴾
161. You and whatever you worship	161. Fa-innakum wa maa ta'bu-doon.	فَإِنَّكُمْ وَمَا تَعْبُدُونَ ﴿١٦١﴾
162. cannot mislead anyone	162. Maaa antum 'alayhi bifaa-tineen.	مَآ أَنْتُمْ عَلَيْهِ بِفٰتِنِينَ ﴿١٦٢﴾
163. except those who are doomed to enter hell.	163. Illaa man huwa ṣaalil-Jaḥeem.	إِلَّا مَنْ هُوَ صَالِ الْجَحِيمِ ﴿١٦٣﴾
164. The angels say, "Each of us has an appointed place.	164. Wa maa minnaaa illaa lahoo maqaamum-ma'loom.	وَمَا مِنَّآ إِلَّا لَهُۥ مَقَامٌ مَّعْلُومٌ ﴿١٦٤﴾

165. We stand in ranks (for prayer)	165. Wa innaa lanaḥnuṣ-ṣaaaffoon.	وَإِنَّا لَنَحْنُ الصَّافُّونَ ﴿١٦٥﴾
166. and we glorify Allah."	166. Wa innaa lanaḥnul-musabbiḥoon.	وَإِنَّا لَنَحْنُ الْمُسَبِّحُونَ ﴿١٦٦﴾
167. Even though they (unbelievers) say,	167. Wa in kaanoo layaqooloon.	وَإِنْ كَانُوا لَيَقُولُونَ ﴿١٦٧﴾
168. "Had we received guidance from the people living before us,	168. Law anna 'indanaa zikram-minal-awwaleen.	لَوْ أَنَّ عِنْدَنَا ذِكْرًا مِنَ الْأَوَّلِينَ ﴿١٦٨﴾
169. we would have certainly been sincere servants of Allah."	169. Lakunnaa 'ibaadal-laahil-mukhlaṣeen.	لَكُنَّا عِبَادَ اللَّهِ الْمُخْلَصِينَ ﴿١٦٩﴾
170. They have rejected the Quran. They will soon learn about the consequences (of their disbelief).	170. Fakafaroo bihee fasawfa ya'lamoon.	فَكَفَرُوا بِهِ فَسَوْفَ يَعْلَمُونَ ﴿١٧٠﴾
171. We decreed that Our Messenger servants	171. Wa laqad sabaqat Kalimatunaa li'ibaadinal-mursaleen.	وَلَقَدْ سَبَقَتْ كَلِمَتُنَا لِعِبَادِنَا الْمُرْسَلِينَ ﴿١٧١﴾
172. will certainly be victorious	172. Innahum lahumul-manṣooroon.	إِنَّهُمْ لَهُمُ الْمَنْصُورُونَ ﴿١٧٢﴾
173. and that Our army will be triumphant.	173. Wa inna jundanaa lahumul-ghaaliboon.	وَإِنَّ جُنْدَنَا لَهُمُ الْغَالِبُونَ ﴿١٧٣﴾
174. (Muhammad), stay away from them for a while	174. Fatawalla 'anhum ḥatta ḥeen.	فَتَوَلَّ عَنْهُمْ حَتَّىٰ حِينٍ ﴿١٧٤﴾
175. and watch them. They, too, will watch.	175. Wa abṣirhum fasawfa yubṣiroon.	وَأَبْصِرْهُمْ فَسَوْفَ يُبْصِرُونَ ﴿١٧٥﴾
176. Do they want to suffer Our torment immediately?	176. Afabi'azaabinaa yasta'jiloon.	أَفَبِعَذَابِنَا يَسْتَعْجِلُونَ ﴿١٧٦﴾
177. When it descends into their place, it will be terrible for those who have already been warned.	177. Fa-izaa nazala bisaaḥatihim fasaaa'a Ṣabaaḥul-munzareen.	فَإِذَا نَزَلَ بِسَاحَتِهِمْ فَسَاءَ صَبَاحُ الْمُنْذَرِينَ ﴿١٧٧﴾
178. Stay away from them for a while	178. Wa tawalla 'anhum ḥattaa ḥeen.	وَتَوَلَّ عَنْهُمْ حَتَّىٰ حِينٍ ﴿١٧٨﴾
179. and watch. They, also, will watch.	179. Wa abṣir fasawfa yubṣiroon.	وَأَبْصِرْ فَسَوْفَ يُبْصِرُونَ ﴿١٧٩﴾
180. Your Lord, the Lord of Honor, is free of all defects of being considered as they describe Him.	180. Subḥaana Rabbika Rabbil-'izzati 'ammaa yaṣifoon.	سُبْحَانَ رَبِّكَ رَبِّ الْعِزَّةِ عَمَّا يَصِفُونَ ﴿١٨٠﴾
181. Peace be with the Messengers (of Allah).	181. Wa salaamun 'alal-mursaleen.	وَسَلَامٌ عَلَى الْمُرْسَلِينَ ﴿١٨١﴾
182. It is only Allah, the Lord of the universe, who deserves all praise.	182. Wal-ḥamdu lillaahi Rabbil-'aalameen.	وَالْحَمْدُ لِلَّهِ رَبِّ الْعَالَمِينَ ﴿١٨٢﴾ ع

Sad, Sad (38) In the Name of Allah, the Beneficent, the Merciful.	**Sûrat Ṣâd-38** (Revealed at Makkah) **Bismillaahir Raḥmaanir Raḥeem**	(٣٨) سُورَةُ صٓ مَكِّيَّةٌ (٣٨) آياتها ٨٨　بِسْمِ اللَّهِ الرَّحْمَٰنِ الرَّحِيمِ　ركوعاتها ٥
1. Sad, I swear by the Quran, which is full of reminders of Allah, (that you are a Messenger).	1. Ṣaaad; wal-Qur'aani zizzikr.	صٓ ۚ وَالْقُرْآنِ ذِي الذِّكْرِ ﴿١﴾
2. In fact, the unbelievers are the ones who in their disbelief are boastful and quarrelsome.	2. Balil-lazeena kafaroo fee 'izzatiñw-wa shiqaaq.	بَلِ الَّذِينَ كَفَرُوا فِي عِزَّةٍ وَشِقَاقٍ ﴿٢﴾
3. How many ancient generations did We destroy? (On facing Our	3. Kam ahlaknaa min qablihim-min qarnin	كَمْ أَهْلَكْنَا مِنْ قَبْلِهِمْ مِنْ قَرْنٍ

torment) they cried out for help, but it was quite late for them to flee.	fanaadaw wa laata ḥeena manaaṣ.	فَنَادَوْا وَّلَاتَ حِيْنَ مَنَاصٍ ۝٣
4. It seems strange to the pagans that a man from their own people should come to them as a Prophet. The unbelievers have said, "He is only a lying magician."	4. Wa 'ajibooo an jaaa'a-hum-munzirum-minhum wa qaalal-kaafiroona haazaa saaḥi-run kazzaab.	وَعَجِبُوْٓا اَنْ جَآءَهُمْ مُّنْذِرٌ مِّنْهُمْ وَقَالَ الْكٰفِرُوْنَ هٰذَا سٰحِرٌ كَذَّابٌ ۝٤
5. They say, "Has he condemned all other gods but One? This, certainly, is strange."	5. Aja'alal-aalihata Ilaa-hañw-waaḥidan inna haazaa lashay-'un 'ujaab.	اَجَعَلَ الْاٰلِهَةَ اِلٰهًا وَّاحِدًا ۚ اِنَّ هٰذَا لَشَیْءٌ عُجَابٌ ۝٥
6. A group of the pagans walked out of a meeting with the Prophet and told the others, "Let us walk away. Be steadfast in the worship of your gods. This man wants to dominate you.	6. Wanṭalaqal-mala-u min-hum animshoo waṣbiroo 'alaaa aalihatikum inna haazaa lashay'uñy-yuraad.	وَانْطَلَقَ الْمَلَاُ مِنْهُمْ اَنِ امْشُوْا وَاصْبِرُوْا عَلٰٓى اٰلِهَتِكُمْ ۚ اِنَّ هٰذَا لَشَیْءٌ يُّرَادُ ۝٦
7. We have heard nothing like this in the latest religion. This is only his false invention.	7. Maa sami'naa bihaazaa fil-millatil-aakhirati in haazaa illakh-tilaaq.	مَا سَمِعْنَا بِهٰذَا فِی الْمِلَّةِ الْاٰخِرَةِ ۚ اِنْ هٰذَآ اِلَّا اخْتِلَاقٌ ۝٧
8. Can it be that he alone has received the Quran?" In fact, they have doubts about My Quran and this is because they have not yet faced (My) torment.	8. 'A-unzila 'alayhiz-zikru mim bayninaa; bal hum fee shakkim-min Zikree bal lammaa yazooqoo 'azaab.	ءَاُنْزِلَ عَلَيْهِ الذِّكْرُ مِنْۢ بَيْنِنَا ۚ بَلْ هُمْ فِیْ شَكٍّ مِّنْ ذِكْرِیْ ۚ بَلْ لَّمَّا يَذُوْقُوْا عَذَابِ ۝٨
9. Do they possess the treasures of the mercy of your (Muhammad's), Lord, the Majestic and Munificent Allah?	9. Am 'indahum khazaaa'inu raḥmati Rabbikal-'Azeezil-Wahhaab.	اَمْ عِنْدَهُمْ خَزَآئِنُ رَحْمَةِ رَبِّكَ الْعَزِيْزِ الْوَهَّابِ ۝٩
10. Do they own the heavens and the earth and all that is between them? Let them try on their own to block (the ways of the heavens so that Our revelations cannot come to you).	10. Am lahum-mulkus-samaa-waati wal-arḍi wa maa bayna-humaa falyartaqoo fil-asbaab.	اَمْ لَهُمْ مُّلْكُ السَّمٰوٰتِ وَالْاَرْضِ وَمَا بَيْنَهُمَا ۟ فَلْيَرْتَقُوْا فِی الْاَسْبَابِ ۝١٠
11. They are only a small band among the defeated allied tribes.	11. Jundum-maa hunaalika mahzoomum-minal-Aḥzaab.	جُنْدٌ مَّا هُنَالِكَ مَهْزُوْمٌ مِّنَ الْاَحْزَابِ ۝١١
12. The people of Noah, Ad and the dominating Pharaoh had rejected Our revelations.	12. Kazzabat qablahum qaw-mu Nooḥiñw-wa 'Aaduñw-wa Fir'awnu zul-awtaad.	كَذَّبَتْ قَبْلَهُمْ قَوْمُ نُوْحٍ وَّعَادٌ وَّفِرْعَوْنُ ذُو الْاَوْتَادِ ۝١٢
13. So also did the people of Thamud, Lot, and the dwellers of the Forest and those parties.	13. Wa Samoodu wa qawmu Looṭiñw-wa Aṣḥaabul-'Aykah; ulaaa'ikal-Aḥzaab.	وَثَمُوْدُ وَقَوْمُ لُوْطٍ وَّاَصْحٰبُ لْـَٔيْكَةِ ۭ اُولٰٓئِكَ الْاَحْزَابُ ۝١٣
14. Each of them who rejected the Messenger became subject to Our punishment.	14. In kullun illaa kaz zabar-Rusula faḥaqqa 'iqaab.	اِنْ كُلٌّ اِلَّا كَذَّبَ الرُّسُلَ فَحَقَّ عِقَابِ ۝١٤ ع ١٠
15. They had only to wait for the single inevitable blast	15. Wa maa yanẓuru haaa-ulaaa'i illaa ṣayḥatañw-	وَمَا يَنْظُرُ هٰٓؤُلَآءِ اِلَّا صَيْحَةً

whereby there is no relief.	waaḥidatam-maa lahaa min fawaaq.	وَّاحِدَةً مَّا لَهَا مِنْ فَوَاقٍ ﴿١٥﴾
16. They scornfully said, "Lord, show us our share of torment before the day when everyone must present the account of their deeds."	16. Wa qaaloo Rabbanaa 'ajjil lanaa qiṭṭanaa qabla Yawmil-Ḥisaab.	وَقَالُوْا رَبَّنَا عَجِّلْ لَّنَا قِطَّنَا قَبْلَ يَوْمِ الْحِسَابِ ﴿١٦﴾
17. (Muhammad), bear patiently what they say and recall Our servant, David, who had strong hands and who was most repentant.	17. Iṣbir 'alaa maa yaqooloona wazkur 'abdanaa Daawooda zal-ayd; innahooo awwaab.	اِصْبِرْ عَلٰى مَا يَقُوْلُوْنَ وَاذْكُرْ عَبْدَنَا دَاوٗدَ ذَا الْاَيْدِ ۚ اِنَّهٗٓ اَوَّابٌ ﴿١٧﴾
18. We made the mountains join him in glorifying Us in the evening and in the morning.	18. Innaa sakhkharnal-jibaala ma'ahoo yusabbiḥna bil'ashiyyi wal-ishraaq.	اِنَّا سَخَّرْنَا الْجِبَالَ مَعَهٗ يُسَبِّحْنَ بِالْعَشِيِّ وَالْاِشْرَاقِ ﴿١٨﴾
19. We made the birds assemble around him in flocks.	19. Waṭṭayra maḥshoorah; kullul-lahooo awwaab.	وَالطَّيْرَ مَحْشُوْرَةً ۗ كُلٌّ لَّهٗٓ اَوَّابٌ ﴿١٩﴾
20. We strengthened his kingdom, giving him wisdom and the power of sound Judgment.	20. Wa shadadnaa mulkahoo wa aataynaahul-Ḥikmata wa faṣlal-khiṭaab.	وَشَدَدْنَا مُلْكَهٗ وَاٰتَيْنٰهُ الْحِكْمَةَ وَفَصْلَ الْخِطَابِ ﴿٢٠﴾
21. Have you heard the news of the disputing parties who climbed down the walls of the prayer room	21. Wa hal ataaka naba'ul-khaṣmi iz tasawwarul-miḥraab.	وَهَلْ اَتٰىكَ نَبَؤُا الْخَصْمِ ۘ اِذْ تَسَوَّرُوا الْمِحْرَابَ ﴿٢١﴾
22. and entered where David was (praying)? He was frightened, so they said, "Do not be afraid. We are only two disputing parties of which one of us has transgressed against the other. Judge between us with truth and justice and guide us to the right path."	22. Iz dakhaloo 'alaa Daawooda fafazi'a minhum qaaloo laa takhaf khaṣmaani baghaa ba'ḍunaa 'alaa ba'ḍin faḥkum baynanaa bilḥaqqi wa laa tushṭiṭ wahdinaaa ilaa Sawaaa'iṣ-Ṣiraaṭ.	اِذْ دَخَلُوْا عَلٰى دَاوٗدَ فَفَزِعَ مِنْهُمْ قَالُوْا لَا تَخَفْ ۚ خَصْمٰنِ بَغٰى بَعْضُنَا عَلٰى بَعْضٍ فَاحْكُمْ بَيْنَنَا بِالْحَقِّ وَلَا تُشْطِطْ وَاهْدِنَآ اِلٰى سَوَآءِ الصِّرَاطِ ﴿٢٢﴾
23. One of them said, "This is my brother who has ninety-nine ewes when I have only one. He has demanded me to place that one in his custody; he had the stronger argument."	23. Inna haazaaa akhee lahoo tis'uñw-wa tis'oona na'jatañw-wa liya na'jatuñw-waaḥidah; faqaala akfilneehaa wa 'azzanee fil-khiṭaab.	اِنَّ هٰذَآ اَخِيْ لَهٗ تِسْعٌ وَّتِسْعُوْنَ نَعْجَةً وَّلِيَ نَعْجَةٌ وَّاحِدَةٌ فَقَالَ اَكْفِلْنِيْهَا وَعَزَّنِيْ فِي الْخِطَابِ ﴿٢٣﴾
24. David said, "He has certainly been unjust in demanding your ewe from you. Most partners transgress against each other except for the righteously striving believers who are very few." David realized that it was a test from Us so he asked forgiveness from his Lord and bowed down before Him in repentance.	24. Qaala laqad ẓalamaka bisu'aali na'jatika ilaa ni'aajihee wa inna kaseeram-minal-khulaṭaaa'i layabghee ba'ḍuhum 'alaa ba'ḍin illallazeena aamanoo wa 'amiluṣ-ṣaaliḥaati wa qaleelum-maa hum; wa ẓanna Daawoodu annamaa fatannaahu fastaghfara Rabbahoo wa kharra raaki'añw-wa-anaab.	قَالَ لَقَدْ ظَلَمَكَ بِسُؤَالِ نَعْجَتِكَ اِلٰى نِعَاجِهٖ ۗ وَاِنَّ كَثِيْرًا مِّنَ الْخُلَطَآءِ لَيَبْغِيْ بَعْضُهُمْ عَلٰى بَعْضٍ اِلَّا الَّذِيْنَ اٰمَنُوْا وَعَمِلُوا الصّٰلِحٰتِ وَقَلِيْلٌ مَّا هُمْ ۗ وَظَنَّ دَاوٗدُ اَنَّمَا فَتَنّٰهُ فَاسْتَغْفَرَ رَبَّهٗ وَخَرَّ رَاكِعًا وَّاَنَابَ ﴿٢٤﴾ السجدة
25. We forgave him for this. In Our eyes he certainly has a good	25. Faghafarnaa lahoo zaalik; wa-inna lahoo 'indanaa	فَغَفَرْنَا لَهٗ ذٰلِكَ ۗ وَاِنَّ لَهٗ عِنْدَنَا

(Bow Down)

وقف لازم

السجدة ١٠

position and the best share (of the world to come).

lazulfaa wa ḥusna ma-aab.

لَزُلْفٰى وَحُسْنَ مَاٰبٍ ٢٥

26. We told him. "David, We have appointed you as Our deputy on earth so judge among the people with truth. Do not follow (worldly) desires lest you go astray from the way of Allah. Those who go astray from the way of Allah will suffer severe torment for forgetting the Day of Reckoning.

26. Yaa Daawoodu innaa ja'alnaaka khaleefatan fil-arḍi faḥkum baynan-naasi bilḥaqqi wa laa tattabi'il-hawaa fayuḍil-laka 'an sabeelil-laah; innal-lazeena yaḍilloona 'an sabeelil-laah; lahum 'azaabun shadee-dum bimaa nasoo Yawmal-Ḥisaab.

يٰدَاوٗدُ اِنَّا جَعَلْنٰكَ خَلِيْفَةً فِى
الْاَرْضِ فَاحْكُمْ بَيْنَ النَّاسِ بِالْحَقِّ
وَلَا تَتَّبِعِ الْهَوٰى فَيُضِلَّكَ عَنْ
سَبِيْلِ اللّٰهِ ؕ اِنَّ الَّذِيْنَ يَضِلُّوْنَ
عَنْ سَبِيْلِ اللّٰهِ لَهُمْ عَذَابٌ شَدِيْدٌۢ
بِمَا نَسُوْا يَوْمَ الْحِسَابِ ٢٦ ع ١٢ ٢

27. We have not created the heavens and the earth and all that is between them without purpose, even though this is the belief of the unbelievers. Woe to the unbelievers; they will suffer the torment of fire.

27. Wa maa khalaqnas-samaaa'a wal-arḍa wa maa baynahumaa baaṭilaa; zaalika ẓannul-lazeena kafaroo; faway-lul-lillazeena kafaroo minan-Naar.

وَمَا خَلَقْنَا السَّمَآءَ وَالْاَرْضَ وَمَا
بَيْنَهُمَا بَاطِلًا ؕ ذٰلِكَ ظَنُّ الَّذِيْنَ
كَفَرُوْا ۚ فَوَيْلٌ لِّلَّذِيْنَ كَفَرُوْا مِنَ
النَّارِ ٢٧

28. Do We consider the righteously striving believers equal to the evil-doers in the land? Are the pious ones equal to those who openly commit sin?

28. Am naj'alul-lazeena aamanoo wa 'amiluṣṣaaliḥaati kalmufsideena fil-arḍi am naj'alul-muttaqeena kalfujjaar.

اَمْ نَجْعَلُ الَّذِيْنَ اٰمَنُوْا وَعَمِلُوا
الصّٰلِحٰتِ كَالْمُفْسِدِيْنَ فِى الْاَرْضِ ۫
اَمْ نَجْعَلُ الْمُتَّقِيْنَ كَالْفُجَّارِ ٢٨

29. It is a blessed Book which We have revealed for you so that you will reflect upon its verses and so the people of understanding will take heed.

29. Kitaabun anzalnaahu ilayka mubaarakul-liyaddabbarooo Aayaatihee wa liyatazakkara ulul-albaab.

كِتٰبٌ اَنْزَلْنٰهُ اِلَيْكَ مُبٰرَكٌ لِّيَدَّبَّرُوْٓا
اٰيٰتِهٖ وَلِيَتَذَكَّرَ اُولُوا الْاَلْبَابِ ٢٩

30. We granted Solomon to David, a blessed servant of Ours and certainly the most repentant person.

30. Wa wahabnaa li-Daawooda Sulaymaan; ni'mal-'abd; innahooo awwaab.

وَوَهَبْنَا لِدَاوٗدَ سُلَيْمٰنَ ؕ نِعْمَ الْعَبْدُ ؕ
اِنَّهٗٓ اَوَّابٌ ٣٠

31. When the noble galloping horses were displayed to him one evening,

31. Iz 'uriḍa 'alayhi bil'ashiy-yiṣ-ṣaafinaatul-jiyaad.

اِذْ عُرِضَ عَلَيْهِ بِالْعَشِىِّ الصّٰفِنٰتُ
الْجِيَادُ ٣١

32. he said, "My love of horses for the cause of Allah has made me continue watching them until sunset, thus making me miss my prayer."

32. Faqaala inneee aḥbabtu ḥubbal-khayri 'an zikri Rabbee ḥattaa tawaarat bilḥijaab.

فَقَالَ اِنِّىْٓ اَحْبَبْتُ حُبَّ الْخَيْرِ عَنْ
ذِكْرِ رَبِّىْ ۚ حَتّٰى تَوَارَتْ بِالْحِجَابِ ٣٢ وقفة

33. He said, "Bring them back to me." Then he started to rub their legs and necks.

33. Ruddoohaa 'alayya faṭafiqa masḥam bissooqi wal-a'naaq.

رُدُّوْهَا عَلَىَّ ؕ فَطَفِقَ مَسْحًۢا بِالسُّوْقِ
وَالْاَعْنَاقِ ٣٣

34. We tested Solomon by (causing death to his son) and leaving his body on Solomon's chair. Then he turned to Us in repentance,

34. Wa laqad fatannaa Sulay-maana wa alqaynaa 'alaa kursiyyihee jasadan summa anaab.

وَلَقَدْ فَتَنَّا سُلَيْمٰنَ وَاَلْقَيْنَا عَلٰى
كُرْسِيِّهٖ جَسَدًا ثُمَّ اَنَابَ ٣٤

35. saying, "Lord, forgive me and grant me a kingdom of which no one after me can have the like. You are All-munificent."

35. Qaala Rabbigh-fir lee wa hab lee mulkal-laa yambaghee li-aḥadim-mim ba'dee innaka Antal Wahhaab.

قَالَ رَبِّ اغْفِرْ لِي وَهَبْ لِي مُلْكًا لَّا
يَنبَغِي لِأَحَدٍ مِّنْ بَعْدِي ۖ إِنَّكَ أَنتَ
الْوَهَّابُ ﴿٣٥﴾

36. We made the wind subservient to him, to blow gently wherever he desired at his command

36. Fasakhkharnaa lahur-reeḥa tajree bi-amrihee rukhaaa'an ḥaysu aṣaab.

فَسَخَّرْنَا لَهُ الرِّيحَ تَجْرِي بِأَمْرِهِ رُخَاءً
حَيْثُ أَصَابَ ﴿٣٦﴾

37. and all the devils that built and dived for him.

37. Wash-Shayaaṭeena kulla bannaaa'iñw-wa ghawwaaṣ.

وَالشَّيَاطِينَ كُلَّ بَنَّاءٍ وَغَوَّاصٍ ﴿٣٧﴾

38. The rest of the devils were bound in chains.

38. Wa aakhareena muqarraneena fil-aṣfaad.

وَآخَرِينَ مُقَرَّنِينَ فِي الْأَصْفَادِ ﴿٣٨﴾

39. We told him, "This is Our gift to you so give them away freely or keep them as you like without any questions asked."

39. Haazaa 'aṭaaa'unaa famnun aw amsik bighayri ḥisaab.

هَٰذَا عَطَاؤُنَا فَامْنُنْ أَوْ أَمْسِكْ
بِغَيْرِ حِسَابٍ ﴿٣٩﴾

40. He, in Our eyes, certainly has a high position and the best place to which to return.

40. Wa inna lahoo 'indanaa lazulfaa wa ḥusna ma-aab.

وَإِنَّ لَهُ عِندَنَا لَزُلْفَىٰ وَحُسْنَ
مَآبٍ ﴿٤٠﴾ ع

41. (Muhammad), recall Our servant Job. When he prayed to his Lord saying, "Satan has afflicted me with hardship and torment,"

41. Wazkur 'abdanaaa Ayyoob; iz naadaa Rabbahooo annee massaniyash-Shayṭaanu binuṣbiñw-wa 'azaab.

وَاذْكُرْ عَبْدَنَا أَيُّوبَ إِذْ نَادَىٰ وقف لازم
رَبَّهُ أَنِّي مَسَّنِيَ الشَّيْطَانُ بِنُصْبٍ
وَعَذَابٍ ﴿٤١﴾

42. (We answered his prayer, healed his sickness, and told him), "Run on your feet. This is cool water (for you) to wash and drink."

42. Urkuḍ birijlika haazaa mughtasalum baariduñw-wa sharaab.

ارْكُضْ بِرِجْلِكَ ۖ هَٰذَا مُغْتَسَلٌ
بَارِدٌ وَشَرَابٌ ﴿٤٢﴾

43. We gave him back his family and doubled their number as a blessing from Us and as a reminder to the people of understanding.

43. Wa wahabnaa lahooo ahlahoo wa mislahum-ma'ahum raḥmatam-minnaa wa zikraa liulil-albaab.

وَوَهَبْنَا لَهُ أَهْلَهُ وَمِثْلَهُم مَّعَهُمْ
رَحْمَةً مِّنَّا وَذِكْرَىٰ لِأُولِي الْأَلْبَابِ ﴿٤٣﴾

44. We told him, "Take a handful of straw (a hundred stems). Strike your wife with it to comply with your oath." We found him to be patient. What an excellent servant he was. He was certainly most repenting.

44. Wa khuz biyadika ḍighsan faḍrib bihee wa laa taḥnas, innaa wajadnaahu ṣaabiraa; ni'mal-'abd; innahooo awwaab.

وَخُذْ بِيَدِكَ ضِغْثًا فَاضْرِب بِّهِ
وَلَا تَحْنَثْ ۗ إِنَّا وَجَدْنَاهُ صَابِرًا ۚ
نِّعْمَ الْعَبْدُ ۖ إِنَّهُ أَوَّابٌ ﴿٤٤﴾

45. (Muhammad), recall Our servants Abraham, Isaac, and Jacob, all of whom possessed virtuous hands (power) and clear visions.

45. Wazkur 'ibaadanaaa Ibraaheema wa Isḥaaqa wa Ya'qooba ulil-aydee wal-abṣaar.

وَاذْكُرْ عِبَادَنَا إِبْرَاهِيمَ وَإِسْحَاقَ وَ
يَعْقُوبَ أُولِي الْأَيْدِي وَالْأَبْصَارِ ﴿٤٥﴾

46. We gave them this pure distinction because of their continual remembrance of the Day of Judgment.

46. Innaaa akhlaṣnaahum bikhaaliṣatin zikrad-daar.

إِنَّا أَخْلَصْنَاهُم بِخَالِصَةٍ ذِكْرَى
الدَّارِ ﴿٤٦﴾

47. In Our eyes they were of the chosen, virtuous people.

47. Wa innahum 'indanaa laminal-muṣṭafaynal-Akhyaar.

وَإِنَّهُمْ عِندَنَا لَمِنَ الْمُصْطَفَيْنَ

		الْاَخْيَارِ ۝٤٧
48. Recall Ishmael, Elisha, and Dhulkifl (Ezekiel), who were all virtuous people.	48. Wazkur Ismaa'eela wal-yasa'a wa Zal-Kifli wa kullum-minal-akhyaar.	وَاذْكُرْ اِسْمٰعِيْلَ وَالْيَسَعَ وَذَا الْكِفْلِ ؕ وَكُلٌّ مِّنَ الْاَخْيَارِ ۝٤٨
49. Such is their noble story. The pious ones will certainly have the best place to which to return.	49. Haazaa zikr; wa inna lilmuttaqeena lahusna ma-aab.	هٰذَا ذِكْرٌ ؕ وَاِنَّ لِلْمُتَّقِيْنَ لَحُسْنَ مَاٰبٍ ۝٤٩
50. They will enter gardens of Eden with their gates open for them.	50. Jannaati 'Adnim-mufat-tahatal-lahumul-abwaab.	جَنّٰتِ عَدْنٍ مُّفَتَّحَةً لَّهُمُ الْاَبْوَابُ ۝٥٠
51. They will be resting therein and will be able to ask for many kinds of fruit and drink.	51. Muttaki'eena feehaa yad-'oona feehaa bifaakihatin kaseeratiñw-wa sharaab.	مُتَّكِـِٕيْنَ فِيْهَا يَدْعُوْنَ فِيْهَا بِفَاكِهَةٍ كَثِيْرَةٍ وَّشَرَابٍ ۝٥١
52. They will have bashful ones of equal age with them.	52. Wa 'indahum qaasiraatut tarfi atraab.	وَعِنْدَهُمْ قٰصِرٰتُ الطَّرْفِ اَتْرَابٌ ۝٥٢
53. This is what you were promised for the Day of Judgment.	53. Haazaa maa too'adoona li-Yawmil-Hisaab.	هٰذَا مَا تُوْعَدُوْنَ لِيَوْمِ الْحِسَابِ ۝٥٣
54. Our provision (for you) will never be exhausted.	54. Inna haazaa larizqunaa maa lahoo min-nafaad.	اِنَّ هٰذَا لَرِزْقُنَا مَا لَهٗ مِنْ نَّفَادٍ ۝٥٤
55. However, the rebellious ones will have the worst place to which to return.	55. Haazaa; wa inna littaa-gheena lasharra ma-aab.	هٰذَا ؕ وَاِنَّ لِلطّٰغِيْنَ لَشَرَّ مَاٰبٍ ۝٥٥
56. They will suffer in hell. What a terrible dwelling!	56. Jahannama yaslawnahaa fabi'sal-mihaad.	جَهَنَّمَ ۚ يَصْلَوْنَهَا ۚ فَبِئْسَ الْمِهَادُ ۝٥٦
57. (They will be told), "This is your recompense. Taste the scalding water and Ghassaq (name of a valley in hell),	57. Haazaa falyazooqoohu hameemuñw-wa ghassaaq.	هٰذَا ۙ فَلْيَذُوْقُوْهُ حَمِيْمٌ وَّغَسَّاقٌ ۝٥٧
58. and other similar things in pairs."	58. Wa aakharu min shak-liheee azwaaj.	وَّاٰخَرُ مِنْ شَكْلِهٖۤ اَزْوَاجٌ ۝٥٨
59. Their leaders will be told, "This band will also be thrown headlong with you into hell." Their leaders will exclaim, "May condemnation fall upon them! Let them suffer by the heat of (the torment) fire."	59. Haazaa fawjum-muqta-himum-ma'akum laa marhabam bihim; innahum saalun-Naar.	هٰذَا فَوْجٌ مُّقْتَحِمٌ مَّعَكُمْ ۚ لَا مَرْحَبًۢا بِهِمْ ؕ اِنَّهُمْ صَالُوا النَّارِ ۝٥٩
60. Their followers will say, "In fact, it is you who deserve condemnation. It was you who led us to hell, a terrible dwelling."	60. Qaaloo bal antum laa mar-habam bikum; antum qad-damtumoohu lanaa fabi'sal-qaraar.	قَالُوْا بَلْ اَنْتُمْ ۟ لَا مَرْحَبًۢا بِكُمْ ؕ اَنْتُمْ قَدَّمْتُمُوْهُ لَنَا ۚ فَبِئْسَ الْقَرَارُ ۝٦٠
61. They will continue saying, "Lord, double the torment of fire for those who led us into this.	61. Qaaloo Rabbanaa man qaddama lanaa haazaa fazidhu 'azaaban di'fan fin-Naar.	قَالُوْا رَبَّنَا مَنْ قَدَّمَ لَنَا هٰذَا فَزِدْهُ عَذَابًا ضِعْفًا فِي النَّارِ ۝٦١
62. However, why is it that we cannot see men whom we had considered as wicked	62. Wa qaaloo maa lanaa laa naraa rijaalan kunnaa na'uddu-hum-minal-ashraar.	وَقَالُوْا مَا لَنَا لَا نَرٰى رِجَالًا كُنَّا نَعُدُّهُمْ مِّنَ الْاَشْرَارِ ۝٦٢
63. and whom we mocked? Have they been rescued or can our eyes not find them?"	63. Attakhaznaahum sikh-riyyan am zaaghat 'anhumul-absaar.	اَتَّخَذْنٰهُمْ سِخْرِيًّا اَمْ زَاغَتْ عَنْهُمُ الْاَبْصَارُ ۝٦٣
64. Such disputes will certainly take place among the dwellers of hellfire.	64. Inna zaalika lahaqqun takhaasumu Ahlin-Naar.	اِنَّ ذٰلِكَ لَحَقٌّ تَخَاصُمُ اَهْلِ النَّارِ ۝٦٤ ع

الثلثة

65. (Muhammad) say, "I am only a Warner. The only Lord is Allah, the Almighty.	65. Qul innamaaa ana munzi-ruñw-wa maa min ilaahin illal-laahulWaaḥidul-Qahhaar.	قُلْ إِنَّمَآ أَنَا مُنْذِرٌ ۖ وَّمَا مِنْ إِلٰهٍ إِلَّا اللّٰهُ الْوَاحِدُ الْقَهَّارُ ﴿٦٥﴾
66. He is the Lord of the heavens, the earth, and all that is between them, the Majestic and All-forgiving.	66. Rabbus-samaawaati wal-arḍi wa maa baynahumal 'Azeezul-Ghaffaar.	رَبُّ السَّمٰوٰتِ وَالْأَرْضِ وَمَا بَيْنَهُمَا الْعَزِيْزُ الْغَفَّارُ ﴿٦٦﴾
67. Say, "It (khilafat, deputy-ship of the Holy prophet) is the greatest news,	67. Qul huwa naba'un 'aẓeem.	قُلْ هُوَ نَبَؤٌا عَظِيْمٌ ﴿٦٧﴾
68. you have turned away from it.	68. Antum 'anhu mu'riḍoon.	أَنْتُمْ عَنْهُ مُعْرِضُوْنَ ﴿٦٨﴾
69. I have no knowledge of the dispute among the angels (concerning their attitude towards Adam).	69. Maa kaana liya min 'ilmim bilmala-il-a'laaa iz yakhtaṣimoon.	مَا كَانَ لِيَ مِنْ عِلْمٍ بِالْمَلَإِ الْأَعْلٰى إِذْ يَخْتَصِمُوْنَ ﴿٦٩﴾
70. I have only received revelation to give you plain warning.	70. Iñy-yooḥaaa ilayya illaaa annamaaa ana naẕeerum-mubeen.	إِنْ يُّوْحٰى إِلَيَّ إِلَّآ أَنَّمَآ أَنَا نَذِيْرٌ مُّبِيْنٌ ﴿٧٠﴾
71. When your Lord told the angels, "I will create a mortal out of clay,	71. Iẕ qaala Rabbuka lilma-laaa'ikati innee khaaliqum basharam-min ṭeen.	إِذْ قَالَ رَبُّكَ لِلْمَلٰٓئِكَةِ إِنِّيْ خَالِقٌۢ بَشَرًا مِّنْ طِيْنٍ ﴿٧١﴾
72. and when I give it proper shape and blow My spirit into it, bow down in prostration (in his honor)."	72. Fa-iẕaa sawwaytuhoo wa nafakhtu feehi mir-rooḥee faqa'oo lahoo saajideen.	فَإِذَا سَوَّيْتُهُ وَنَفَخْتُ فِيْهِ مِنْ رُّوْحِيْ فَقَعُوْا لَهُ سٰجِدِيْنَ ﴿٧٢﴾
73. All the angels then prostrated themselves	73. Fasajadal-malaaa'ikatu kulluhum ajma'oon.	فَسَجَدَ الْمَلٰٓئِكَةُ كُلُّهُمْ أَجْمَعُوْنَ ﴿٧٣﴾
74. except Iblis, who puffed himself up with pride and became a disbeliever.	74. Illaaa Iblees; istakbara wa kaana minal-kaafireen.	إِلَّآ إِبْلِيْسَ ۗ اِسْتَكْبَرَ وَكَانَ مِنَ الْكٰفِرِيْنَ ﴿٧٤﴾
75. The Lord said, "Iblis, what prevented you from prostrating before what I have created with My own hands? Was it because of your pride or are you truly exalted?"	75. Qaala yaaa Ibleesu maa mana'aka an tasjuda limaa khalaqtu biyadayy; astakbarta am kunta minal-'aaleen.	قَالَ يٰٓإِبْلِيْسُ مَا مَنَعَكَ أَنْ تَسْجُدَ لِمَا خَلَقْتُ بِيَدَيَّ ۗ أَسْتَكْبَرْتَ أَمْ كُنْتَ مِنَ الْعَالِيْنَ ﴿٧٥﴾
76. He said, "I am better than he is. You have created me from fire and him out of clay."	76. Qaala-ana khayrum-minh; khalaqtanee min-naariñw-wa khalaqtahoo min ṭeen.	قَالَ أَنَا خَيْرٌ مِّنْهُ ۗ خَلَقْتَنِيْ مِنْ نَّارٍ وَّخَلَقْتَهُ مِنْ طِيْنٍ ﴿٧٦﴾
77. The Lord said, "Get out of here. You deserve to be stoned!	77. Qaala fakhruj minhaa fa-innaka rajeem.	قَالَ فَاخْرُجْ مِنْهَا فَإِنَّكَ رَجِيْمٌ ﴿٧٧﴾
78. My condemnation will be with you until the Day of Judgment!"	78. Wa-inna 'alayka la'nateee ilaa Yawmid-Deen.	وَّإِنَّ عَلَيْكَ لَعْنَتِيْٓ إِلٰى يَوْمِ الدِّيْنِ ﴿٧٨﴾
79. He said, "Lord, grant me respite until the Day of Resurrection."	79. Qaala Rabbi fa-anẓirneee ilaa Yawmi yub'asoon.	قَالَ رَبِّ فَأَنْظِرْنِيْٓ إِلٰى يَوْمِ يُبْعَثُوْنَ ﴿٧٩﴾

80. The Lord said, "You will only be given a respite	80. Qaala fa-innaka minal-munẓareen.	قَالَ فَإِنَّكَ مِنَ الْمُنظَرِينَ ﴿٨٠﴾
81. for an appointed time."	81. Ilaa Yawmil-waqtil-ma'loom.	إِلَىٰ يَوْمِ الْوَقْتِ الْمَعْلُومِ ﴿٨١﴾
82. He said, "By Your Glory, I shall seduce all of them (children of Adam)	82. Qaala fabi'izzatika la-ughwiyannahum ajma'een.	قَالَ فَبِعِزَّتِكَ لَأُغْوِيَنَّهُمْ أَجْمَعِينَ ﴿٨٢﴾
83. except Your sincere servants among them."	83. Illaa 'ibaadaka minhumul-mukhlaṣeen.	إِلَّا عِبَادَكَ مِنْهُمُ الْمُخْلَصِينَ ﴿٨٣﴾
84. The Lord said, "I swear by the Truth - and I speak the Truth -	84. Qaala falḥaqq; walḥaqqa aqool.	قَالَ فَالْحَقُّ وَالْحَقَّ أَقُولُ ﴿٨٤﴾
85. that I shall certainly fill hell with you and your followers all together."	85. La-amla'anna Jahannama minka wa mimman tabi'aka minhum ajma'een.	لَأَمْلَأَنَّ جَهَنَّمَ مِنكَ وَمِمَّن تَبِعَكَ مِنْهُمْ أَجْمَعِينَ ﴿٨٥﴾
86. (Muhammad), say, "I do not ask any reward for my preaching to you for I am not a pretender.	86. Qul maaa as'alukum 'alayhi min ajriñw-wa maaa ana minal-mutakallifeen.	قُلْ مَا أَسْأَلُكُمْ عَلَيْهِ مِنْ أَجْرٍ وَمَا أَنَا مِنَ الْمُتَكَلِّفِينَ ﴿٨٦﴾
87. It (the Quran) is but a reminder (good advice) for all creatures.	87. In huwa illaa zikrul lil'aalameen.	إِنْ هُوَ إِلَّا ذِكْرٌ لِّلْعَالَمِينَ ﴿٨٧﴾
88. You will certainly know its truthfulness after a certain time."	88. Wa lata'lamunna naba-ahoo ba'da ḥeen.	وَلَتَعْلَمُنَّ نَبَأَهُ بَعْدَ حِينٍ ﴿٨٨﴾ ع

Al-Zumar, The Hordes (39)

In the Name of Allah, the Beneficent, the Merciful.

Sûrat az-Zumar-39

(Revealed at Makkah)

Bismillaahir Raḥmaanir Raḥeem

(٣٩) سُورَةُ الزُّمَرِ مَكِّيَّةٌ (٥٩)

آياتها ٧٥ — بِسْمِ اللَّهِ الرَّحْمَٰنِ الرَّحِيمِ — ركوعاتها ٨

1. This Book is a revelation from Allah, the Majestic and All-Wise.	1. Tanzeelul-Kitaabi minal-laahil-'Azeezil-Ḥakeem.	تَنزِيلُ الْكِتَابِ مِنَ اللَّهِ الْعَزِيزِ الْحَكِيمِ ﴿١﴾
2. We have revealed the Book to you in all truth. Worship Allah and be devoted to His religion.	2. Innaaa anzalnaaa ilaykal-Kitaaba bilḥaqqi fa'budillaaha mukhliṣal-lahud-deen.	إِنَّا أَنزَلْنَا إِلَيْكَ الْكِتَابَ بِالْحَقِّ فَاعْبُدِ اللَّهَ مُخْلِصًا لَّهُ الدِّينَ ﴿٢﴾
3. The religion of Allah is certainly pure. Concerning those whom they consider as their guardians besides Allah, they say, "We only worship them so that they may make our positions nearer to Allah." Allah will certainly issue His decree about their differences. Allah does not guide the liars and the unbelievers.	3. Alaa lillaahid-deenul-khaaliṣ; wallazeenat-takhazoo min dooniheee awliyaaa'; maa na'buduhum illaa liyuqar-riboonaaa ilal-laahi zulfaaa innal-laaha yaḥkumu bayna-hum fee maa hum feehi yakhtalifoon; innal-laaha laa yahdee man huwa kaazibun kaffaar.	أَلَا لِلَّهِ الدِّينُ الْخَالِصُ ۚ وَالَّذِينَ اتَّخَذُوا مِن دُونِهِ أَوْلِيَاءَ مَا نَعْبُدُهُمْ إِلَّا لِيُقَرِّبُونَا إِلَى اللَّهِ زُلْفَىٰ إِنَّ اللَّهَ يَحْكُمُ بَيْنَهُمْ فِي مَا هُمْ فِيهِ يَخْتَلِفُونَ ۗ إِنَّ اللَّهَ لَا يَهْدِي مَنْ هُوَ كَاذِبٌ كَفَّارٌ ﴿٣﴾ وقف لازم
4. Had Allah wanted to have a son, He would have chosen one from His creatures according to His will. Allah is free of all defects of having a son. He is One and Almighty.	4. Law araadal-laahu añy-yattakhiza waladal-laṣṭafaa mimmaa yakhluqu maa yashaaa'; Subḥaanahoo Huwal-laahul-Waaḥidul-Qahhaar.	لَّوْ أَرَادَ اللَّهُ أَن يَتَّخِذَ وَلَدًا لَّاصْطَفَىٰ مِمَّا يَخْلُقُ مَا يَشَاءُ ۚ سُبْحَانَهُ ۖ هُوَ اللَّهُ الْوَاحِدُ الْقَهَّارُ ﴿٤﴾

5. He has created the heavens and the earth for a genuine purpose. He covers the night with the day and the day with the night and has subdued the sun and the moon, each of which floats for an appointed time. Allah is certainly Majestic and All-Forgiving.

5. Khalaqas-samaawaati wal-arḍa bilḥaqq; yukawwirul-layla 'alan-nahaari wa yukawwirun-nahaara 'alal-layli wa sakhkharash-shamsa walqamara kulluñy-yajree li-ajalim-musammaa; alaa Huwal-'Azeezul-Ghaffaar.

خَلَقَ السَّمٰوٰتِ وَالْاَرْضَ بِالْحَقِّ ۚ
يُكَوِّرُ الَّيْلَ عَلَى النَّهَارِ وَيُكَوِّرُ
النَّهَارَ عَلَى الَّيْلِ وَسَخَّرَ الشَّمْسَ
وَالْقَمَرَ ۭ كُلٌّ يَّجْرِيْ لِاَجَلٍ
مُّسَمًّى ۭ اَلَا هُوَ الْعَزِيْزُ الْغَفَّارُ ۝٥

6. He has created you from a single soul. Out of this He created your spouse. He created for you eight pairs of cattle. He creates you in successive creations in the wombs of your mothers behind three curtains of darkness. Allah is your Lord to whom belongs the Kingdom. He is the only Lord. Where then will you turn away?

6. Khalaqakum min nafsiñw-waaḥidatin summa ja'ala minhaa zawjahaa wa anzala lakum minal-an'aami samaaniyata azwaaj; yakhluqukum fee buṭooni ummahaatikum khalqammim ba'di khalqin fee ẓulumaatin salaas; zaalikumul-laahu Rabbukum lahul-mulku laaa ilaaha illaa Huwa fa-annaa tuṣrafoon.

خَلَقَكُمْ مِّنْ نَّفْسٍ وَّاحِدَةٍ ثُمَّ جَعَلَ
مِنْهَا زَوْجَهَا وَاَنْزَلَ لَكُمْ مِّنَ
الْاَنْعَامِ ثَمٰنِيَةَ اَزْوَاجٍ ۭ يَخْلُقُكُمْ
فِيْ بُطُوْنِ اُمَّهٰتِكُمْ خَلْقًا مِّنْۢ بَعْدِ
خَلْقٍ فِيْ ظُلُمٰتٍ ثَلٰثٍ ۭ ذٰلِكُمُ اللّٰهُ
رَبُّكُمْ لَهُ الْمُلْكُ ۭ لَآ اِلٰهَ اِلَّا هُوَ ۚ
فَاَنّٰى تُصْرَفُوْنَ ۝٦

7. If you disbelieve, know that Allah is certainly independent of you. He does not want disbelief (ungratefulness) for His servants. If you give thanks, He will accept it from you. No one will be responsible for the sins of others. To your Lord you will all return and He will tell you about what you have done. He knows best what the hearts contain.

7. In takfuroo fa-innal-laaha ghaniyyun 'ankum wa laa yarḍaa li'ibaadihil-kufra wa in tashkuroo yarḍahu lakum; wa laa taziru waaziratuñw-wizra ukhraa; summa ilaa Rabbikum marji'ukum fayunabbi'ukum bimaa kuntum ta'maloon; innahoo 'aleemum bizaatiṣ-ṣudoor.

اِنْ تَكْفُرُوْا فَاِنَّ اللّٰهَ غَنِيٌّ عَنْكُمْ ۣ
وَلَا يَرْضٰى لِعِبَادِهِ الْكُفْرَ ۚ وَاِنْ تَشْكُرُوْا
يَرْضَهُ لَكُمْ ۭ وَلَا تَزِرُ وَازِرَةٌ وِّزْرَ
اُخْرٰى ۭ ثُمَّ اِلٰى رَبِّكُمْ مَّرْجِعُكُمْ
فَيُنَبِّئُكُمْ بِمَا كُنْتُمْ تَعْمَلُوْنَ ۭ اِنَّهٗ
عَلِيْمٌۢ بِذَاتِ الصُّدُوْرِ ۝٧

8. When the human being is afflicted with hardship, he starts to pray to his Lord and turns to Him in repentance. When Allah grants him a favor, he forgets the hardship about which he had prayed to Allah and starts to consider equal to Allah things that lead him astray from His path. (Muhammad), tell him, "You can only enjoy in your disbelief for a short time. You will certainly be a dweller of hellfire."

8. Wa izaa massal-insaana ḍurrun da'aa Rabbahoo muneeban ilayhi summa izaa khawwalahoo ni'matam-minhu nasiya maa kaana yad'ooo ilayhi min qablu wa ja'ala lillaahi andaadal-liyuḍilla 'an sabeelih; qul tamatta' bikufrika qaleelan innaka min Aṣḥaabin-Naar.

وَاِذَا مَسَّ الْاِنْسَانَ ضُرٌّ دَعَا رَبَّهٗ
مُنِيْبًا اِلَيْهِ ثُمَّ اِذَا خَوَّلَهٗ نِعْمَةً
مِّنْهُ نَسِيَ مَا كَانَ يَدْعُوْٓا اِلَيْهِ مِنْ
قَبْلُ وَجَعَلَ لِلّٰهِ اَنْدَادًا لِّيُضِلَّ
عَنْ سَبِيْلِهٖ ۭ قُلْ تَمَتَّعْ بِكُفْرِكَ
قَلِيْلًا ڰ اِنَّكَ مِنْ اَصْحٰبِ النَّارِ ۝٨

9. Can this one be considered equal to one who worships Allah during the night, prostrating and standing, who has fear of the Day

9. Amman huwa qaanitun aanaaa'al-layli saajidañw-wa qaaa'imañy-yaḥzarul Aakhirata wa yarjoo

اَمَّنْ هُوَ قَانِتٌ اٰنَاۗءَ الَّيْلِ سَاجِدًا
وَّقَاۗىِٕمًا يَّحْذَرُ الْاٰخِرَةَ وَيَرْجُوْا

of Judgment, and who has hope in the mercy of his Lord? Say, "Are those who know equal to those who do not know? Only the people of reason take heed."

raḥmata Rabbih; qul hal yastawil-lazeena ya'lamoona wallazeena laa ya'lamoon; innamaa yatazakkaru ulul-albaab.

رَحْمَةَ رَبِّهٖ ؕ قُلْ هَلْ يَسْتَوِي الَّذِيْنَ
يَعْلَمُوْنَ وَالَّذِيْنَ لَا يَعْلَمُوْنَ ؕ اِنَّمَا
يَتَذَكَّرُ اُولُوا الْاَلْبَابِ ﴿٩﴾ ع ٩ ١٥

10. Say to My believing servants, "Have fear of your Lord. Those who act righteously in this life will receive a good reward. The land of Allah is vast. He will recompense the deeds of those who have exercised patience, without keeping an account."

10. Qul yaa 'ibaadil-lazeena aamanut-taqoo Rabbakum; lillazeena aḥsanoo fee haazihid-dunyaa ḥasanah; wa arḍul-laahi waasi'ah; innamaa yuwaffaṣ-ṣaabiroona ajrahum bighayri ḥisaab.

قُلْ يٰعِبَادِ الَّذِيْنَ اٰمَنُوا اتَّقُوْا
رَبَّكُمْ ؕ لِلَّذِيْنَ اَحْسَنُوْا فِيْ
هٰذِهِ الدُّنْيَا حَسَنَةٌ ؕ وَاَرْضُ
اللّٰهِ وَاسِعَةٌ ؕ اِنَّمَا يُوَفَّى الصّٰبِرُوْنَ
اَجْرَهُمْ بِغَيْرِ حِسَابٍ ﴿١٠﴾

11. Say, "I am commanded to worship Allah and be devoted to His religion

11. Qul inneee umirtu an a'budal-laaha mukhliṣal-lahud-deen.

قُلْ اِنِّيْٓ اُمِرْتُ اَنْ اَعْبُدَ اللّٰهَ
مُخْلِصًا لَّهُ الدِّيْنَ ﴿١١﴾

12. and I am commanded to be the first Muslim."

12. Wa umirtu li-an akoona awwalal-muslimeen.

وَاُمِرْتُ لِاَنْ اَكُوْنَ اَوَّلَ الْمُسْلِمِيْنَ ﴿١٢﴾

13. Say, "I am afraid that for disobeying my Lord I shall suffer the torment of the great day."

13. Qul inneee akhaafu in 'aṣaytu Rabbee 'azaaba Yawmin 'azeem.

قُلْ اِنِّيْٓ اَخَافُ اِنْ عَصَيْتُ رَبِّيْ
عَذَابَ يَوْمٍ عَظِيْمٍ ﴿١٣﴾

14. Say, "I worship Allah alone and devote myself to His religion.

14. Qulil-laaha a'budu mukh-liṣal-lahoo deenee.

قُلِ اللّٰهَ اَعْبُدُ مُخْلِصًا لَّهٗ دِيْنِيْ ﴿١٤﴾

15. Worship besides Him whatever you want. The greatest losers are those whose souls and family members will be lost on the Day of Judgment for this is certainly an obvious loss."

15. Fa'budoo maa shi'tum min doonih; qul innal-khaasireenal-lazeena khasirooo anfusahum wa ahleehim Yawmal-Qiyaamah; alaa zaalika huwal-khusraanul-mubeen.

فَاعْبُدُوْا مَا شِئْتُمْ مِّنْ دُوْنِهٖ ؕ
قُلْ اِنَّ الْخٰسِرِيْنَ الَّذِيْنَ خَسِرُوْٓا
اَنْفُسَهُمْ وَاَهْلِيْهِمْ يَوْمَ الْقِيٰمَةِ ؕ
اَلَا ذٰلِكَ هُوَ الْخُسْرَانُ الْمُبِيْنُ ﴿١٥﴾

16. Above and below them there will be shadows of fire. This is how Allah frightens His servants. My servants have fear of Me.

16. Lahum min fawqihim ẓulalum-minan-Naari wa min taḥtihim ẓulal; zaalika yukhaw-wiful-laahu bihee 'ibaadah; yaa 'ibaadi fattaqoon.

لَهُمْ مِّنْ فَوْقِهِمْ ظُلَلٌ مِّنَ النَّارِ
وَمِنْ تَحْتِهِمْ ظُلَلٌ ؕ ذٰلِكَ يُخَوِّفُ
اللّٰهُ بِهٖ عِبَادَهٗ ؕ يٰعِبَادِ فَاتَّقُوْنِ ﴿١٦﴾

17. Those who have avoided worshipping idols and have turned in repentance to Allah will receive the glad news.

17. Wallazeenaj-tanabuṭ-Ṭaaghoota añy-ya'budoohaa wa anaabooo ilal-laahi lahumul-bushraa; fabashshir 'ibaad.

وَالَّذِيْنَ اجْتَنَبُوا الطَّاغُوْتَ اَنْ
يَّعْبُدُوْهَا وَاَنَابُوْٓا اِلَى اللّٰهِ لَهُمُ
الْبُشْرٰى ۚ فَبَشِّرْ عِبَادِ ﴿١٧﴾

18. (Muhammad), give the glad news to those of My servants who listen to the words and follow only the best ones. Tell them that they are

18. Allazeena yastami'oonal-qawla fayattabi'oona aḥsanah; ulaaa'ikal-lazeena hadaahumul-

الَّذِيْنَ يَسْتَمِعُوْنَ الْقَوْلَ فَيَتَّبِعُوْنَ
اَحْسَنَهٗ ؕ اُولٰٓئِكَ الَّذِيْنَ هَدٰىهُمُ

those whom Allah has guided. They are the people of understanding.

19. How can you rescue the one who is destined to suffer the torment?

20. Those who have fear of their Lord will have lofty mansions built upon mansions beneath which streams flow. It is the promise of Allah. Allah does not disregard His promise.

21. Did you not see that Allah has sent down water from the sky and made it flow as springs out of the earth? He makes crops of different colors grow with this water and flourish, which then turn yellow and wither away. In this there is a reminder for the people of understanding.

22. One whose chest (heart and mind) is left open for Islam (submission to His will) shall receive light from his Lord. Woe to those whose hearts have become like stone against the remembrance of Allah. They are clearly in error.

23. Allah has revealed the best reading material in the form of a Book with similar passages which refer to each other and make the skins of those who fear their Lord shiver. Then their skins and hearts incline to the remembrance of Allah. This is the guidance of Allah. He guides whomever He wants. No one can guide those whom Allah has caused to go astray.

24. Is there anyone who protects his face from the torment of the Day of Judgment when the unjust will be told, "Suffer the result of your deeds?"

laahu wa ulaaa'ika hum ulul-albaab.

19. Afaman ḥaqqa 'alayhi kalimatul-'azaab; afa-anta tunqizu man fin-Naar.

20. Laakinil-lazeenat-taqaw Rabbahum lahum ghurafum-min fawqihaa ghurafum-mabniyyatun tajree min taḥti-hal-anhaaru wa'dal-laahi laa yukhliful-laahul-mee'aad.

21. Alam tara annal-laaha anzala minas-samaaa'i maaa'an fasalakahoo yanaabee'a fil-arḍi summa yukhriju bihee zar'am-mukhtalifan alwaanuhoo summa yaheeju fataraahu muṣfarran summa yaj'aluhoo ḥuṭaamaa; inna fee zaalika lazikraa li-ulil-albaab.

22. Afaman sharaḥal-laahu ṣadrahoo lil-Islaami fahuwa 'alaa noorim-mir-Rabbih; fa-waylul-lilqaasiyati quloobu-hum min zikril-laah; ulaaa'ika fee ḍalaalim-mubeen.

23. Allaahu nazzala aḥsanal-ḥadeesi Kitaabam-mutashaa-biham-masaaniya taqsha'irru minhu juloodul-lazeena yakh-shawna Rabbahum summa taleenu julooduhum wa quloo-buhum ilaa zikril-laah; zaalika hudal-laahi yahdee bihee mañy-yashaaa'; wa mañy-yuḍlilil-laahu famaa lahoo min haad.

24. Afamañy-yattaqee biwaj-hihee sooo'al-'azaabi Yawmal-Qiyaamah; wa qeela lizzaali-meena zooqoo maa kuntum taksiboon.

اللّٰهُ وَاُولٰٓئِكَ هُمْ اُولُوا الْاَلْبَابِ ﴿١٨﴾
اَفَمَنْ حَقَّ عَلَيْهِ كَلِمَةُ الْعَذَابِ ؕ
اَفَاَنْتَ تُنْقِذُ مَنْ فِي النَّارِ ﴿١٩﴾
لٰكِنِ الَّذِيْنَ اتَّقَوْا رَبَّهُمْ لَهُمْ غُرَفٌ
مِّنْ فَوْقِهَا غُرَفٌ مَّبْنِيَّةٌ ۙ تَجْرِيْ
مِنْ تَحْتِهَا الْاَنْهٰرُ ؕ وَعْدَ اللّٰهِ ؕ لَا
يُخْلِفُ اللّٰهُ الْمِيْعَادَ ﴿٢٠﴾
اَلَمْ تَرَ اَنَّ اللّٰهَ اَنْزَلَ مِنَ السَّمَآءِ
مَآءً فَسَلَكَهٗ يَنَابِيْعَ فِي الْاَرْضِ ثُمَّ
يُخْرِجُ بِهٖ زَرْعًا مُّخْتَلِفًا اَلْوَانُهٗ ثُمَّ
يَهِيْجُ فَتَرٰىهُ مُصْفَرًّا ثُمَّ يَجْعَلُهٗ
حُطَامًا ؕ اِنَّ فِيْ ذٰلِكَ لَذِكْرٰى
لِاُولِي الْاَلْبَابِ ﴿٢١﴾ ع ١٢
اَفَمَنْ شَرَحَ اللّٰهُ صَدْرَهٗ لِلْاِسْلَامِ
فَهُوَ عَلٰى نُوْرٍ مِّنْ رَّبِّهٖ ؕ فَوَيْلٌ
لِّلْقٰسِيَةِ قُلُوْبُهُمْ مِّنْ ذِكْرِ
اللّٰهِ ؕ اُولٰٓئِكَ فِيْ ضَلٰلٍ مُّبِيْنٍ ﴿٢٢﴾
اَللّٰهُ نَزَّلَ اَحْسَنَ الْحَدِيْثِ كِتٰبًا
مُّتَشَابِهًا مَّثَانِيَ ۖ تَقْشَعِرُّ مِنْهُ
جُلُوْدُ الَّذِيْنَ يَخْشَوْنَ رَبَّهُمْ ۚ ثُمَّ
تَلِيْنُ جُلُوْدُهُمْ وَقُلُوْبُهُمْ اِلٰى ذِكْرِ
اللّٰهِ ؕ ذٰلِكَ هُدَى اللّٰهِ يَهْدِيْ بِهٖ
مَنْ يَّشَآءُ ؕ وَمَنْ يُّضْلِلِ اللّٰهُ فَمَا
لَهٗ مِنْ هَادٍ ﴿٢٣﴾
اَفَمَنْ يَّتَّقِيْ بِوَجْهِهٖ سُوْٓءَ الْعَذَابِ
يَوْمَ الْقِيٰمَةِ ؕ وَقِيْلَ لِلظّٰلِمِيْنَ ذُوْقُوْا

25. Those who lived before them had also rejected Our revelations. Thus, the torment struck them and they did not even realize where it came from.

26. Allah made them suffer humiliation in this life. Would that they knew that the torment for them in the next life will be even greater.

27. We have given all kinds of examples for human beings in this Quran so that perhaps they may take heed.

28. This Quran is a flawless reading text in the Arabic language. Perhaps they will have fear (of Allah).

29. Allah tells a parable in which there is a company of horrific querulous people and only one of them is well disciplined. Can they be considered as equal? It is only Allah who deserves all praise. In fact, most of them do not know.

30. (Muhammad), you will die and all of them will also die.

31. Then, on the Day of Judgment, all of you will present your disputes before your Lord.

32. Who is more unjust than one who invents falsehood against Allah and rejects the truth after it has come to them? Is not hell a dwelling for the unbelievers?

33. Those who have brought the truth and have acknowledged it are those who have fear (of Allah).

34. They will receive whatever they want from their Lord. Thus is the reward of the righteous ones.

35. Allah will certainly expiate their bad deeds and reward them

25. Kaz-zabal-lazeena min qablihim fa-ataahumul 'azaabu min haysu laa yash'uroon.

26. Fa-azaaqahumul-laahul-khizya fil-hayaatid-dunyaa wa la'azaabul-Aakhirati akbar; law kaanoo ya'lamoon.

27. Wa laqad darabnaa lin-naasi fee haazal-Qur'aani min kulli masalil-la'allahum yata-zakkaroon.

28. Qur'aanan 'Arabiyyan ghayra zee 'iwajil-la'allahum yattaqoon.

29. Ḍarabal-laahu masalar-rajulan feehi shurakaaa'u mutashaakisoona wa rajulan salamal-lirajulin hal yastawi-yaani masalaa; al-ḥamdu lillaah; bal aksaruhum laa ya'lamoon.

30. Innaka mayyituñw-wa innahum mayyitoon.

31. Summa innakum Yaw-mal-Qiyaamati 'inda Rabbikum takhtaṣimoon.

32. Faman aẓlamu mimman kazaba 'alal-laahi wa kaz-zaba biṣṣidqi iz jaaa'ah; alaysa fee Jahannama maswal-lilkaafireen.

33. Wallazee jaaa'a biṣṣidqi wa ṣaddaqa biheee ulaaa'ika humul-muttaqoon.

34. Lahum maa yashaaa'oona 'inda Rabbihim; zaalika jazaaa'ul-muḥsineen.

35. Liyukaffiral-laahu 'anhum aswa-allazee 'amiloo

مَا كُنْتُمْ تَكْسِبُوْنَ ﴿٢٤﴾
كَذَّبَ الَّذِيْنَ مِنْ قَبْلِهِمْ فَاَتٰىهُمُ
الْعَذَابُ مِنْ حَيْثُ لَا يَشْعُرُوْنَ ﴿٢٥﴾
فَاَذَاقَهُمُ اللّٰهُ الْخِزْيَ فِي الْحَيٰوةِ
الدُّنْيَا ۚ وَلَعَذَابُ الْاٰخِرَةِ اَكْبَرُ ۘ وقف لازم
لَوْ كَانُوْا يَعْلَمُوْنَ ﴿٢٦﴾
وَلَقَدْ ضَرَبْنَا لِلنَّاسِ فِيْ هٰذَا
الْقُرْاٰنِ مِنْ كُلِّ مَثَلٍ لَّعَلَّهُمْ
يَتَذَكَّرُوْنَ ﴿٢٧﴾
قُرْاٰنًا عَرَبِيًّا غَيْرَ ذِيْ عِوَجٍ
لَّعَلَّهُمْ يَتَّقُوْنَ ﴿٢٨﴾
ضَرَبَ اللّٰهُ مَثَلًا رَّجُلًا فِيْهِ شُرَكَاۤءُ
مُتَشٰكِسُوْنَ وَرَجُلًا سَلَمًا لِّرَجُلٍ ۭ
هَلْ يَسْتَوِيٰنِ مَثَلًا ۭ اَلْحَمْدُ لِلّٰهِ ۚ
بَلْ اَكْثَرُهُمْ لَا يَعْلَمُوْنَ ﴿٢٩﴾
اِنَّكَ مَيِّتٌ وَّاِنَّهُمْ مَّيِّتُوْنَ ﴿٣٠﴾
ثُمَّ اِنَّكُمْ يَوْمَ الْقِيٰمَةِ عِنْدَ رَبِّكُمْ
تَخْتَصِمُوْنَ ﴿٣١﴾ ع
فَمَنْ اَظْلَمُ مِمَّنْ كَذَبَ عَلَى اللّٰهِ
وَكَذَّبَ بِالصِّدْقِ اِذْ جَاۤءَهٗ ۭ اَلَيْسَ
فِيْ جَهَنَّمَ مَثْوًى لِّلْكٰفِرِيْنَ ﴿٣٢﴾
وَالَّذِيْ جَاۤءَ بِالصِّدْقِ وَصَدَّقَ بِهٖٓ
اُولٰۗىِٕكَ هُمُ الْمُتَّقُوْنَ ﴿٣٣﴾
لَهُمْ مَّا يَشَاۤءُوْنَ عِنْدَ رَبِّهِمْ ۭ ذٰلِكَ
جَزٰۗؤُا الْمُحْسِنِيْنَ ﴿٣٤﴾ ۚ
لِيُكَفِّرَ اللّٰهُ عَنْهُمْ اَسْوَاَ الَّذِيْ عَمِلُوْا

much more for what they have done.

wa yajziyahum ajrahum bi-aḥsanil-lazee kaanoo ya'maloon.

وَيَجْزِيَهُمْ أَجْرَهُم بِأَحْسَنِ الَّذِي
كَانُوا يَعْمَلُونَ ﴿٣٥﴾

36. Is Allah not sufficient (support) for His servants? They frighten you with what they worship besides Allah. Who can guide one whom Allah has caused to go astray?

36. Alaysal-laahu bikaafin 'abdahoo wa yukhawwifoonaka billazeena min doonih; wa mañy-yuḍlilil-laahu famaa lahoo min haad.

أَلَيْسَ اللَّهُ بِكَافٍ عَبْدَهُ ۖ وَيُخَوِّفُونَكَ
بِالَّذِينَ مِن دُونِهِ ۚ وَمَن يُضْلِلِ اللَّهُ
فَمَا لَهُ مِنْ هَادٍ ﴿٣٦﴾

37. Who can mislead one whom Allah has guided? Is Allah not Majestic and capable to exact retribution?

37. Wa mañy-yahdil-laahu famaa lahoo mim-muḍill; alaysal-laahu bi'azeezin-zintiqaam.

وَمَن يَهْدِ اللَّهُ فَمَا لَهُ مِن مُّضِلٍّ ۗ
أَلَيْسَ اللَّهُ بِعَزِيزٍ ذِي انتِقَامٍ ﴿٣٧﴾

38. If you ask them, "Who has created the heavens and the earth," they will certainly say, "Allah has created them." Ask them, "Do you think that you can rescue me from the punishment of Allah with which He may afflict me? Can you prevent His mercy if He wants to grant it to me?" Say, "Allah is Sufficient (support) for me. In Him alone one must trust."

38. Wa la'in sa-altahum man khalaqas-samaawaati wal-arḍa layaqoolunnal-laah; qul afara'aytum maa tad'oona min doonil-laahi in araadaniyal-laahu biḍurrin hal hunna kaashifaatu ḍurriheee aw araadanee biraḥmatin hal hunna mumsikaatu raḥmatih; qul ḥasbiyal-laahu 'alayhi yatawakkalul-mutawakkiloon.

وَلَئِن سَأَلْتَهُم مَّنْ خَلَقَ السَّمَاوَاتِ
وَالْأَرْضَ لَيَقُولُنَّ اللَّهُ ۚ قُلْ أَفَرَأَيْتُم
مَّا تَدْعُونَ مِن دُونِ اللَّهِ إِنْ أَرَادَنِيَ
اللَّهُ بِضُرٍّ هَلْ هُنَّ كَاشِفَاتُ ضُرِّهِ أَوْ
أَرَادَنِي بِرَحْمَةٍ هَلْ هُنَّ مُمْسِكَاتُ
رَحْمَتِهِ ۚ قُلْ حَسْبِيَ اللَّهُ ۖ عَلَيْهِ يَتَوَكَّلُ
الْمُتَوَكِّلُونَ ﴿٣٨﴾

39. Say, "My people, act as you wish. I shall do as I like and you will soon know

39. Qul yaa qawmi'-maloo 'alaa makaanatikum innee 'aamilun fasawfa ta'lamoon.

قُلْ يَا قَوْمِ اعْمَلُوا عَلَىٰ مَكَانَتِكُمْ إِنِّي
عَامِلٌ ۖ فَسَوْفَ تَعْلَمُونَ ﴿٣٩﴾

40. who will face the humiliating torment and suffer everlasting retribution."

40. Mañy-ya-teehi 'azaabuñy-yukhzeehi wa yaḥillu 'alayhi 'azaabum-muqeem.

مَن يَأْتِيهِ عَذَابٌ يُخْزِيهِ وَيَحِلُّ
عَلَيْهِ عَذَابٌ مُّقِيمٌ ﴿٤٠﴾

41. (Muhammad), We have revealed the Book to you for mankind in all truth. Whoever seeks guidance does so for his own good. Whosoever goes astray goes against his own soul. You are not their representative.

41. Innaaa anzalnaa 'alaykal-Kitaaba linnaasi bilḥaqq; famanih-tadaa falinafsihee wa man ḍalla fa-innamaa yaḍillu 'alayhaa wa maaa anta 'alayhim biwakeel.

إِنَّا أَنزَلْنَا عَلَيْكَ الْكِتَابَ لِلنَّاسِ
بِالْحَقِّ ۖ فَمَنِ اهْتَدَىٰ فَلِنَفْسِهِ ۖ وَمَن
ضَلَّ فَإِنَّمَا يَضِلُّ عَلَيْهَا ۖ وَمَا أَنتَ
عَلَيْهِم بِوَكِيلٍ ﴿٤١﴾ ع

42. Allah preserves the souls when they die as well as those which did not die during people's sleep. He withholds those souls which He has decreed to die and releases the others for an appointed time. In this there is evidence (of the Truth) for the

42. Allaahu yatawaffal-anfusa ḥeena mawtihaa wallatee lam tamut fee manaamihaa fa-yumsikul-latee qaḍaa 'alayhal-mawta wa yursilul-ukhraaa ilaaa ajalim-musammaa; inna fee

اللَّهُ يَتَوَفَّى الْأَنفُسَ حِينَ مَوْتِهَا وَ
الَّتِي لَمْ تَمُتْ فِي مَنَامِهَا ۖ فَيُمْسِكُ
الَّتِي قَضَىٰ عَلَيْهَا الْمَوْتَ وَيُرْسِلُ
الْأُخْرَىٰ إِلَىٰ أَجَلٍ مُّسَمًّى ۚ إِنَّ فِي

thoughtful people.

43. Have they chosen intercessors besides Allah? Say, "Would you choose them as your intercessors even though they do not possess anything and have no understanding?"

44. Say, "All forms of intercession belongs to Allah. To Him belong the heavens and the earth and to Him you will all return."

45. When Allah alone is mentioned, the hearts of those who do not believe in the Day of Judgment begin to shrink, but when the idols are mentioned, they rejoice.

46. Say, "Lord, the Creator of the heavens and the earth, knowing the seen and unseen, it is You who will issue Your decree about the differences of Your servants."

47. Had the unjust possessed double the amount of the wealth of the whole earth, they would certainly have liked to offer it on the Day of Resurrection as redemption from the torment of Our scourge when Allah makes public what they had never expected.

48. Their bad deeds will become public and they will be surrounded by the torment, which they had mocked during their worldly life.

49. When the human being is afflicted with hardship, he cries out to us for help. When We grant him a favor, he says, "I knew that I deserved it." In fact, it is only a test for him, but most people do not know this.

50. People who lived before them had also said, "Our wealth has been earned by our own merits." What they had earned was of no benefit to them.

51. They were afflicted by the terrible result of whatever they

z̲aalika la-Aayaatil-liqawmiñy-yatafakkaroon.

43. Amit-takhaz̲oo min doonillaahi shufa'aaa'; qul awalaw kaanoo laa yamlikoona shay'añw-wa laa ya'qiloon.

44. Qul lillaahish-shafaa'atu jamee'an lahoo mulkus-samaawaati wal-arḍi s̲umma ilayhi turja'oon.

45. Wa iz̲aa z̲ukiral-laahu waḥdahush-ma-azzat quloobul-laz̲eena laa yu'minoona bil-Aakhirati wa iz̲aa z̲ukiral-laz̲eena min dooniheee iz̲aa hum yastabshiroon.

46. Qulil-laahumma faaṭiras samaawaati wal-arḍi 'Aalimal-Ghaybi washshahaadati Anta taḥkumu bayna 'ibaadika fee maa kaanoo feehi yakhtalifoon.

47. Wa law anna lillaz̲eena ẓalamoo maa fil-arḍi jamee'añw-wa mis̲lahoo ma'ahoo laftadaw bihee min sooo'il-'az̲aabi Yawmal-Qiyaamah; wa badaa lahum minal-laahi maa lam yakoonoo yaḥtasiboon.

48. Wa badaa lahum sayyi-aatu maa kasaboo wa ḥaaqa bihim maa kaanoo bihee yastahzi'oon.

49. Fa-iz̲aa massal-insaana ḍurrun da'aanaa s̲umma iz̲aa khawwalnaahu ni'matam-minnaa qaala innamaaa ooteetuhoo 'alaa 'ilm; bal hiya fitnatuñw-wa laakinna aks̲arahum laa ya'lamoon.

50. Qad qaalahal-laz̲eena min qablihim famaaa aghnaa 'anhum maa kaanoo yaksiboon.

51. Fa-aṣaabahum sayyi-aatu maa kasaboo; wallaz̲eena

ذٰلِكَ لَاٰيٰتٍ لِّقَوْمٍ يَّتَفَكَّرُوْنَ ﴿٤٢﴾
اَمِ اتَّخَذُوْا مِنْ دُوْنِ اللّٰهِ شُفَعَآءَ ؕ
قُلْ اَوَلَوْ كَانُوْا لَا يَمْلِكُوْنَ شَيْـًٔا وَّلَا
يَعْقِلُوْنَ ﴿٤٣﴾
قُلْ لِّلّٰهِ الشَّفَاعَةُ جَمِيْعًا ؕ لَهٗ مُلْكُ
السَّمٰوٰتِ وَالْاَرْضِ ؕ ثُمَّ اِلَيْهِ تُرْجَعُوْنَ ﴿٤٤﴾
وَاِذَا ذُكِرَ اللّٰهُ وَحْدَهُ اشْمَاَزَّتْ
قُلُوْبُ الَّذِيْنَ لَا يُؤْمِنُوْنَ بِالْاٰخِرَةِ ۚ
وَاِذَا ذُكِرَ الَّذِيْنَ مِنْ دُوْنِهٖۤ اِذَا
هُمْ يَسْتَبْشِرُوْنَ ﴿٤٥﴾
قُلِ اللّٰهُمَّ فَاطِرَ السَّمٰوٰتِ وَالْاَرْضِ عٰلِمَ
الْغَيْبِ وَالشَّهَادَةِ اَنْتَ تَحْكُمُ بَيْنَ
عِبَادِكَ فِيْ مَا كَانُوْا فِيْهِ يَخْتَلِفُوْنَ ﴿٤٦﴾
وَلَوْ اَنَّ لِلَّذِيْنَ ظَلَمُوْا مَا فِي الْاَرْضِ
جَمِيْعًا وَّمِثْلَهٗ مَعَهٗ لَافْتَدَوْا بِهٖ
مِنْ سُوْٓءِ الْعَذَابِ يَوْمَ الْقِيٰمَةِ ؕ وَبَدَا
لَهُمْ مِّنَ اللّٰهِ مَا لَمْ يَكُوْنُوْا يَحْتَسِبُوْنَ ﴿٤٧﴾
وَبَدَا لَهُمْ سَيِّاٰتُ مَا كَسَبُوْا وَحَاقَ
بِهِمْ مَّا كَانُوْا بِهٖ يَسْتَهْزِءُوْنَ ﴿٤٨﴾
فَاِذَا مَسَّ الْاِنْسَانَ ضُرٌّ دَعَانَا ز ثُمَّ
اِذَا خَوَّلْنٰهُ نِعْمَةً مِّنَّا ۙ قَالَ اِنَّمَآ
اُوْتِيْتُهٗ عَلٰى عِلْمٍ ؕ بَلْ هِيَ فِتْنَةٌ
وَّلٰكِنَّ اَكْثَرَهُمْ لَا يَعْلَمُوْنَ ﴿٤٩﴾
قَدْ قَالَهَا الَّذِيْنَ مِنْ قَبْلِهِمْ فَمَآ
اَغْنٰى عَنْهُمْ مَّا كَانُوْا يَكْسِبُوْنَ ﴿٥٠﴾
فَاَصَابَهُمْ سَيِّاٰتُ مَا كَسَبُوْا ؕ وَالَّذِيْنَ

gained. Besides this affliction, the unjust among them will also suffer the consequence of their deeds. They will not be able to challenge Allah.

ẓalamoo min haaa'ulaaa'i sayuṣeebuhum sayyi-aatu maa kasaboo wa maa hum bimu'jizeen.

ظَلَمُوا مِنْ هٰٓؤُلَآءِ سَيُصِيبُهُمْ سَيِّاٰتُ
مَا كَسَبُوا ۙ وَمَا هُمْ بِمُعْجِزِينَ ۝٥١

52. Did they not know that Allah measures and increases the sustenance of whomever He wants? In this there is evidence (of the truth) for the believing people.

52. Awalam ya'lamooo annal-laaha yabsuṭur-rizqa limañy-yashaaa'u wa yaqdir; inna fee zaalika la-Aayaatil-liqawmiñy-yu'minoon.

أَوَلَمْ يَعْلَمُوٓا أَنَّ اللّٰهَ يَبْسُطُ الرِّزْقَ
لِمَنْ يَّشَآءُ وَيَقْدِرُ ۭ إِنَّ فِى ذٰلِكَ
لَاٰيٰتٍ لِّقَوْمٍ يُّؤْمِنُونَ ۝٥٢ ٥ ع ١١ ٢

53. (Muhammad), tell my servants who have committed injustice to themselves, "Do not despair of the mercy of Allah. Allah certainly forgives all sins. He is All-forgiving and All-merciful."

53. Qul yaa 'ibaadiyal-lazeena asrafoo 'alaaa anfusihim laa taqnaṭoo mirraḥmatil-laah; innal-laaha yaghfiruz-zunooba jamee'aa; innahoo Huwal-Ghafoorur-Raḥeem.

قُلْ يٰعِبَادِىَ الَّذِينَ أَسْرَفُوا عَلٰٓى
أَنْفُسِهِمْ لَا تَقْنَطُوا مِنْ رَّحْمَةِ اللّٰهِ ۭ
إِنَّ اللّٰهَ يَغْفِرُ الذُّنُوبَ جَمِيعًا ۭ إِنَّهٗ
هُوَ الْغَفُورُ الرَّحِيمُ ۝٥٣

54. Turn in repentance to your Lord and submit to His will before you are afflicted with the torment after which you can receive no help.

54. Wa aneebooo ilaa Rabbikum wa aslimoo lahoo min qabli añy-ya-tiyakumul'azaabu summa laa tunṣaroon.

وَأَنِيبُوٓا إِلٰى رَبِّكُمْ وَأَسْلِمُوا لَهٗ مِنْ
قَبْلِ أَنْ يَّأْتِيَكُمُ الْعَذَابُ ثُمَّ
لَا تُنْصَرُونَ ۝٥٤

55. Follow the best of what is revealed to you from your Lord before the torment suddenly approaches you and you do not realize how it came about.

55. Wattabi'ooo aḥsana maaa unzila ilaykum mir-Rabbikum min qabli añy-ya-tiyakumul-'azaabu baghtatañw-wa antum laa tash'uroon.

وَاتَّبِعُوٓا أَحْسَنَ مَآ أُنْزِلَ إِلَيْكُمْ مِّنْ
رَّبِّكُمْ مِّنْ قَبْلِ أَنْ يَّأْتِيَكُمُ الْعَذَابُ
بَغْتَةً وَّأَنْتُمْ لَا تَشْعُرُونَ ۝٥٥

56. Turn to Allah in repentance before a soul says, "Woe to me because of my failure to fulfill my duties to Allah. Woe to me for mocking Allah's guidance!"

56. An taqoola nafsuñy-yaa ḥasrataa 'alaa maa farraṭtu fee jambil-laahi wa in kuntu laminas-saakhireen.

أَنْ تَقُولَ نَفْسٌ يّٰحَسْرَتٰى عَلٰى مَا
فَرَّطْتُّ فِى جَنْبِ اللّٰهِ وَإِنْ كُنْتُ
لَمِنَ السّٰخِرِينَ ۝٥٦

57. Or before the soul says, "Had Allah guided me, I could have been a pious man."

57. Aw taqoola law annal-laaha hadaanee lakuntu minal-muttaqeen.

أَوْ تَقُولَ لَوْ أَنَّ اللّٰهَ هَدٰىنِى لَكُنْتُ
مِنَ الْمُتَّقِينَ ۝٥٧

58. Or, on seeing the torment, it would say, "Had I the opportunity, this time I would certainly become a person of good deeds."

58. Aw taqoola ḥeena taral-'azaaba law anna lee karratan fa-akoona minal muḥsineen.

أَوْ تَقُولَ حِينَ تَرَى الْعَذَابَ لَوْ
أَنَّ لِى كَرَّةً فَأَكُونَ مِنَ الْمُحْسِنِينَ ۝٥٨

59. Allah will reply to the soul, "My revelations had certainly come to you but you rejected them. You sought arrogance and became an unbeliever."

59. Balaa qad jaaa'atka Aayaatee fakaz-zabta bihaa wastakbarta wa kunta minal kaafireen.

بَلٰى قَدْ جَآءَتْكَ اٰيٰتِى فَكَذَّبْتَ بِهَا
وَاسْتَكْبَرْتَ وَكُنْتَ مِنَ الْكٰفِرِينَ ۝٥٩

60. On the Day of Judgment you will see the faces of those who had invented falsehood against Allah blackened. Is not

60. Wa Yawmal-Qiyaamati taral-lazeena kazaboo 'alallaahi wujoohuhum muswaddah; alaysa fee

وَيَوْمَ الْقِيٰمَةِ تَرَى الَّذِينَ كَذَبُوا عَلَى
اللّٰهِ وُجُوهُهُمْ مُّسْوَدَّةٌ ۭ أَلَيْسَ فِى

hell the dwelling of the arrogant ones?

61. Allah will save the pious ones because of their virtuous deeds. No hardship will touch them nor will they be grieved.

62. Allah is the Creator and Guardian of all things.

63. In His hands are the keys of the treasures of the heavens and the earth. Those who reject Allah's revelations will be lost.

64. (Muhammad), say, "Ignorant ones, do you command me to worship things other than Allah

65. (even though Allah has said), "It has been revealed to you and to those who lived before you that if you consider other things equal to Allah, your deeds will be made devoid of all virtue and you will certainly be lost?"

66. (Muhammad), You must worship Allah alone and give Him thanks.

67. They have not paid due respect to Allah. The whole earth will be in the grip of His hands (power) on the Day of Judgment and the heavens will be just like a scroll in His right hand (power). Allah is free of all defects of being considered equal to their idols.

68. When the trumpet is sounded everyone in the heavens and the earth will faint in terror except for those whom Allah will save. They will all stand up and wait when the trumpet sounds for the second time.

69. The earth will become bright from the light of its Lord. The Book of Records will be presented and the Prophets and witnesses will be summoned. All will be judged with justice and no wrong will be done to anyone.

70. Every soul will be recompensed for its deeds. Allah knows best whatever they have done.

Jahannama masawal-lilmuta-kabbireen.

61. Wa yunajjil-laahul-lazee-nat-taqaw bimafaazatihim laa yamassuhumus-sooo'u wa laa hum yaḥzanoon.

62. Allaahu Khaaliqu kulli shay'iñw-wa Huwa 'alaa kulli shay'iñw-Wakeel.

63. Lahoo maqaaleedus-sa-maawaati wal-arḍ; wallazeena kafaroo bi-Aayaatil-laahi ulaaa'ika humul-khaasiroon.

64. Qul afaghayral-laahi ta-murooonneee a'budu ayyuhal-jaahiloon.

65. Wa laqad ooḥiya ilayka wa ilal-lazeena min qablika la-in ashrakta layaḥbaṭanna 'amalu-ka wa latakoonanna minal-khaasireen.

66. Balil-laaha fa'bud wa kum-minash-shaakireen.

67. Wa maa qadarul-laaha ḥaqqa qadrihee wal-arḍu jamee-'an qabḍatuhoo Yawmal-Qiyaamati was-samaawaatu maṭwiyyaatum biyameenih; Subḥaanahoo wa Ta'aalaa 'ammaa yushrikoon.

68. Wa nufikha fiṣ-Ṣoori faṣa'iqa man fis-samaawaati wa man fil-arḍi illaa man shaaa'al-laahu summa nufikha feehi ukhraa fa-izaa hum qiyaamuñy-yanzuroon.

69. Wa-ashraqatil-arḍu binoori Rabbihaa wa wuḍi'al-Kitaabu wa jeee'a bin-Nabiyyeena wash-shuhadaaa'i wa quḍiya baynahum bilḥaqqi wa hum laa yuẓlamoon.

70. Wa wuffiyat kullu naf-simmaa 'amilat wa Huwa a'lamu bimaa yaf'aloon.

جَهَنَّمَ مَثْوًى لِّلْمُتَكَبِّرِيْنَ ﴿٦٠﴾
وَيُنَجِّي اللّٰهُ الَّذِيْنَ اتَّقَوْا بِمَفَازَتِهِمْ
لَا يَمَسُّهُمُ السُّوْٓءُ وَلَا هُمْ يَحْزَنُوْنَ ﴿٦١﴾
اَللّٰهُ خَالِقُ كُلِّ شَيْءٍ وَّهُوَ عَلٰى كُلِّ
شَيْءٍ وَّكِيْلٌ ﴿٦٢﴾
لَهٗ مَقَالِيْدُ السَّمٰوٰتِ وَالْاَرْضِ وَالَّذِيْنَ
كَفَرُوْا بِاٰيٰتِ اللّٰهِ اُولٰٓئِكَ هُمُ الْخٰسِرُوْنَ ﴿٦٣﴾
قُلْ اَفَغَيْرَ اللّٰهِ تَاْمُرُوْٓنِّيْٓ اَعْبُدُ اَيُّهَا
الْجٰهِلُوْنَ ﴿٦٤﴾
وَلَقَدْ اُوْحِيَ اِلَيْكَ وَاِلَى الَّذِيْنَ مِنْ
قَبْلِكَ لَئِنْ اَشْرَكْتَ لَيَحْبَطَنَّ عَمَلُكَ
وَلَتَكُوْنَنَّ مِنَ الْخٰسِرِيْنَ ﴿٦٥﴾
بَلِ اللّٰهَ فَاعْبُدْ وَكُنْ مِّنَ الشّٰكِرِيْنَ ﴿٦٦﴾
وَمَا قَدَرُوا اللّٰهَ حَقَّ قَدْرِهٖ وَالْاَرْضُ
جَمِيْعًا قَبْضَتُهٗ يَوْمَ الْقِيٰمَةِ وَ
السَّمٰوٰتُ مَطْوِيّٰتٌ بِيَمِيْنِهٖ سُبْحٰنَهٗ
وَتَعٰلٰى عَمَّا يُشْرِكُوْنَ ﴿٦٧﴾
وَنُفِخَ فِي الصُّوْرِ فَصَعِقَ مَنْ فِي
السَّمٰوٰتِ وَمَنْ فِي الْاَرْضِ اِلَّا مَنْ
شَآءَ اللّٰهُ ثُمَّ نُفِخَ فِيْهِ اُخْرٰى فَاِذَا
هُمْ قِيَامٌ يَّنْظُرُوْنَ ﴿٦٨﴾
وَاَشْرَقَتِ الْاَرْضُ بِنُوْرِ رَبِّهَا وَوُضِعَ
الْكِتٰبُ وَجِايْٓءَ بِالنَّبِيّٖنَ وَالشُّهَدَآءِ
وَقُضِيَ بَيْنَهُمْ بِالْحَقِّ وَهُمْ لَا يُظْلَمُوْنَ ﴿٦٩﴾
وَوُفِّيَتْ كُلُّ نَفْسٍ مَّا عَمِلَتْ وَهُوَ
اَعْلَمُ بِمَا يَفْعَلُوْنَ ﴿٧٠﴾

71. The unbelievers will be driven to hell in hordes. Its gates will be opened when they are brought nearby and the keepers will ask them, "Did messengers from your own people not come to you to recite your Lord's revelations and to warn you about this day?" They will reply, "Yes, the Messengers did come to us, but the unbelievers were doomed to face the torment."

71. Wa seeqal-lazeena kafa-rooo ilaa Jahannama zumaraa; ḥattaaa izaa jaaa'oohaa futiḥat abwaabuhaa wa qaala lahum khazanatuhaaa alam ya-tikum Rusulum-minkum yatloona 'alaykum Aayaati Rabbikum wa yunziroonakum liqaaa'a Yawmikum haazaa; qaaloo balaa wa laakin ḥaqqat kali-matul-'azaabi 'alal-kaafireen.

وَسِيقَ الَّذِينَ كَفَرُوا إِلَىٰ جَهَنَّمَ
زُمَرًا ۖ حَتَّىٰ إِذَا جَاءُوهَا فُتِحَتْ
أَبْوَابُهَا وَقَالَ لَهُمْ خَزَنَتُهَا أَلَمْ
يَأْتِكُمْ رُسُلٌ مِنْكُمْ يَتْلُونَ عَلَيْكُمْ
آيَاتِ رَبِّكُمْ وَيُنْذِرُونَكُمْ لِقَاءَ يَوْمِكُمْ
هَٰذَا ۚ قَالُوا بَلَىٰ وَلَٰكِنْ حَقَّتْ كَلِمَةُ
الْعَذَابِ عَلَى الْكَافِرِينَ ﴿٧١﴾

72. They will be told, "Enter the gates of hell to live therein forever. What a terrible dwelling for the arrogant ones!"

72. Qeelad-khulooo abwaaba Jahannama khaalideena feehaa fabi'sa maswal-mutakabbireen.

قِيلَ ادْخُلُوا أَبْوَابَ جَهَنَّمَ خَالِدِينَ
فِيهَا ۖ فَبِئْسَ مَثْوَى الْمُتَكَبِّرِينَ ﴿٧٢﴾

73. The pious ones will be led to Paradise in large groups. Its gates will be opened to them when they are brought nearby and its keepers will say, "Peace be with you indeed you were pure (born of proper wedlock). Enter the gates of Paradise to live therein forever."

73. Wa seeqal-lazeenat-taqaw Rabbahum ilal-Jannati zumaraa; ḥattaaa izaa jaaa'oohaa wa futiḥat abwaabuhaa wa qaala lahum khazanatuhaa salaamun 'alaykum ṭibtum fadkhuloohaa khaalideen.

وَسِيقَ الَّذِينَ اتَّقَوْا رَبَّهُمْ إِلَى الْجَنَّةِ
زُمَرًا ۖ حَتَّىٰ إِذَا جَاءُوهَا وَفُتِحَتْ
أَبْوَابُهَا وَقَالَ لَهُمْ خَزَنَتُهَا سَلَامٌ
عَلَيْكُمْ طِبْتُمْ فَادْخُلُوهَا خَالِدِينَ ﴿٧٣﴾

74. They will say, "It is only Allah who deserves all praise. He has made His promise come true and has given the earth as an inheritance to us. Now we live in the gardens as we wish. Blessed is the reward of those who labor.

74. Wa qaalul-ḥamdu-lillaa-hil-lazee ṣadaqanaa wa'dahoo wa awrasanal-arḍa natabaw-wau- minal-Jannati ḥaysu na-shaaa'u fani'ma ajrul-'aami-leen.

وَقَالُوا الْحَمْدُ لِلَّهِ الَّذِي صَدَقَنَا
وَعْدَهُ وَأَوْرَثَنَا الْأَرْضَ نَتَبَوَّأُ
مِنَ الْجَنَّةِ حَيْثُ نَشَاءُ ۖ فَنِعْمَ
أَجْرُ الْعَامِلِينَ ﴿٧٤﴾

75. (Muhammad), on that day you will see the angels circling around the Throne, glorifying and praising their Lord. Judgment with justice will be decreed between the people of Paradise and hell and it will be said, "It is only Allah, Lord of the Universe, who deserves all praise."

75. Wa taral-malaaa'ikata ḥaaaffeena min ḥawlil-'Arshi yusabbiḥoona biḥamdi Rabbi-him wa quḍiya bay-nahum bilḥaqqi wa qeelal-ḥamdu lillaahi Rabbil'aalameen.

وَتَرَى الْمَلَائِكَةَ حَافِّينَ مِنْ
حَوْلِ الْعَرْشِ يُسَبِّحُونَ بِحَمْدِ رَبِّهِمْ ۖ
وَقُضِيَ بَيْنَهُمْ بِالْحَقِّ وَقِيلَ الْحَمْدُ
لِلَّهِ رَبِّ الْعَالَمِينَ ﴿٧٥﴾

Al-Ghafir, The Forgiver (40)

In the Name of Allah, the Beneficent, the Merciful.

Sûrat al-Mu'min-40

(Revealed at Makkah)

Bismillaahir Raḥmaanir Raḥeem

(٤٠) سُورَةُ الْمُؤْمِنِ مَكِّيَّةٌ (٦٠)

آياتها ٨٥ — بِسْمِ اللَّهِ الرَّحْمَٰنِ الرَّحِيمِ — ركوعاتها ٩

1. Ha. Mim.

1. Ḥaa-Meeem.

حم ﴿١﴾

2. This Book is a revelation from Allah, the Majestic and All-knowing,

2. Tanzeelul-Kitaabi minal-laahil-'Azeezil-'Aleem.

تَنْزِيلُ الْكِتَابِ مِنَ اللَّهِ الْعَزِيزِ
الْعَلِيمِ ﴿٢﴾

3. who forgives sins, who accepts repentance, whose punishment is severe, and whose bounty is universal. He is the only Ilah (one deserving to be worshiped) and to Him all things proceed.

3. Ghaafiriz-zambi wa qaabilit-tawbi shadeedil 'iqaab; zit-ṭawli laaa ilaaha illaa Huwa ilayhil-maṣeer.

غَافِرِ الذَّنْۢبِ وَقَابِلِ التَّوْبِ شَدِيْدِ
الْعِقَابِ ذِي الطَّوْلِ لَآ اِلٰهَ اِلَّا
هُوَ اِلَيْهِ الْمَصِيْرُ (3)

4. No one disputes the revelations of the Lord except the unbelievers. Let not their activities in the land deceive you.

4. Maa yujaadilu feee Aayaatil-laahi illal-lazeena kafaroo falaa yaghrurka taqallubuhum fil-bilaad.

مَا يُجَادِلُ فِيْٓ اٰيٰتِ اللّٰهِ اِلَّا الَّذِيْنَ
كَفَرُوْا فَلَا يَغْرُرْكَ تَقَلُّبُهُمْ
فِي الْبِلَادِ (4)

5. The people of Noah who lived before and the Confederate tribes who lived after them rejected Our revelations. Every nation schemed against its Messengers to seize them and disputed against them to defeat the truth. However, I seized them and how terrible was their punishment!

5. Kazzabat qablahum qawmu Nooḥiñw-wal-Aḥzaabu mim ba'dihim wa hammat kullu ummatim bi-Rasoolihim liyakhuzoohu wa jaadaloo bilbaaṭili liyudḥiḍoo bihil-ḥaqqa fa-akhaztuhum fakayfa kaana 'iqaab.

كَذَّبَتْ قَبْلَهُمْ قَوْمُ نُوْحٍ وَّالْاَحْزَابُ
مِنْۢ بَعْدِهِمْ وَهَمَّتْ كُلُّ اُمَّةٍۢ
بِرَسُوْلِهِمْ لِيَاْخُذُوْهُ وَجٰدَلُوْا
بِالْبَاطِلِ لِيُدْحِضُوْا بِهِ الْحَقَّ
فَاَخَذْتُهُمْ فَكَيْفَ كَانَ عِقَابِ (5)

6. The word of your Lord that the unbelievers will be the dwellers in hellfire has already been decreed.

6. Wa kazaalika ḥaqqat Kalimatu Rabbika 'alal-lazeena kafarooo annahum Aṣḥaabun-Naar.

وَكَذٰلِكَ حَقَّتْ كَلِمَتُ رَبِّكَ عَلَى
الَّذِيْنَ كَفَرُوْٓا اَنَّهُمْ اَصْحٰبُ النَّارِ (6)

7. The bearers of the Throne and those around it glorify their Lord with His praise. They believe in Him and ask Him to forgive the believers. They say, "Our Lord, Your mercy and knowledge encompass all things. Forgive those who turn to You in repentance and follow Your path. Lord, save them from the torment of hell.

7. Allazeena yaḥmiloonal-'Arsha wa man ḥawlahoo yusabbiḥoona biḥamdi Rabbihim wa yu'minoona bihee wa yastaghfiroona lillazeena aamanoo Rabbanaa wasi'ta kulla shay'ir-raḥmatañw-wa 'ilman faghfir lillazeena taaboo wattaba'oo sabeelaka waqihim 'azaabal-Jaḥeem.

اَلَّذِيْنَ يَحْمِلُوْنَ الْعَرْشَ وَمَنْ حَوْلَهٗ
يُسَبِّحُوْنَ بِحَمْدِ رَبِّهِمْ وَيُؤْمِنُوْنَ
بِهٖ وَيَسْتَغْفِرُوْنَ لِلَّذِيْنَ اٰمَنُوْا رَبَّنَا
وَسِعْتَ كُلَّ شَيْءٍ رَّحْمَةً وَّعِلْمًا فَاغْفِرْ
لِلَّذِيْنَ تَابُوْا وَاتَّبَعُوْا سَبِيْلَكَ وَقِهِمْ
عَذَابَ الْجَحِيْمِ (7)

8. Lord, admit them and their fathers, spouses, and offspring who have reformed themselves to the gardens of Eden which You have promised them. You are Majestic and All-wise.

8. Rabbanaa wa adkhilhum Jannaati 'Adninil-latee wa'attahum wa man ṣalaḥa min aabaaa'ihim wa azwaajihim wa zurriyyaatihim; innaka Antal-'Azeezul-Ḥakeem.

رَبَّنَا وَاَدْخِلْهُمْ جَنّٰتِ عَدْنِ الَّتِيْ
وَعَدْتَّهُمْ وَمَنْ صَلَحَ مِنْ اٰبَآئِهِمْ
وَاَزْوَاجِهِمْ وَذُرِّيّٰتِهِمْ اِنَّكَ اَنْتَ
الْعَزِيْزُ الْحَكِيْمُ (8)

9. Lord, keep them away from evil deeds. Whomever You save from evil on the Day of Judgment has certainly been granted Your mercy and this is the greatest triumph.

9. Waqihimus-sayyi-aat; wa man taqis-sayyi-aati Yawma'izin faqad raḥimtah; wa zaalika huwal-fawzul-'aẓeem.

وَقِهِمُ السَّيِّاٰتِ وَمَنْ تَقِ السَّيِّاٰتِ
يَوْمَئِذٍ فَقَدْ رَحِمْتَهٗ وَذٰلِكَ هُوَ
الْفَوْزُ الْعَظِيْمُ (9) ع

10. The unbelievers will be told, "Allah's abhorrence towards you is much greater than your hatred of your own selves. You were called to the faith but you disbelieved."

10. Innal-lazeena kafaroo yunaadawna lamaqtul-laahi akbaru mim-maqtikum anfusakum iz tud'awna ilal eemaani fatakfuroon.

إِنَّ الَّذِينَ كَفَرُوا يُنَادَوْنَ لَمَقْتُ اللَّهِ
أَكْبَرُ مِن مَّقْتِكُمْ أَنفُسَكُمْ إِذْ
تُدْعَوْنَ إِلَى الْإِيمَانِ فَتَكْفُرُونَ ١٠

11. They say, "Lord, You have caused us to die twice and You have brought us back to life twice. We have confessed our sins, so is there any way out of this (hell)?"

11. Qaaloo Rabbanaaa amattanas-natayni wa aḥyaytanas-natayni fa'tarafnaa bizunoobinaa fahal ilaa khuroojim-min sabeel.

قَالُوا رَبَّنَا أَمَتَّنَا اثْنَتَيْنِ وَأَحْيَيْتَنَا
اثْنَتَيْنِ فَاعْتَرَفْنَا بِذُنُوبِنَا فَهَلْ
إِلَىٰ خُرُوجٍ مِّن سَبِيلٍ ١١

12. They will be answered, "Your suffering is only because you disbelieved when Allah alone was mentioned. When other things were considered equal to Him, you believed in them. Judgment belongs to Allah, the Most High, the Most Great.

12. Zaalikum bi-annahooo izaa du'iyal-laahu waḥdahoo kafartum wa iñy-yushrak bihee tu'minoo; falḥukmu lillaahil 'Aliyyil-Kabeer.

ذَٰلِكُم بِأَنَّهُ إِذَا دُعِيَ اللَّهُ وَحْدَهُ
كَفَرْتُمْ ۖ وَإِن يُشْرَكْ بِهِ تُؤْمِنُوا ۚ
فَالْحُكْمُ لِلَّهِ الْعَلِيِّ الْكَبِيرِ ١٢

13. It is He who has shown you the evidence of His existence and has sent you sustenance from the sky, yet only those who turn to Allah in repentance take heed.

13. Huwal-lazee yureekum Aayaatihee wa yunazzilu lakum minas-samaaa'i rizqaa; wa maa yatazakkaru illaa mañy-yuneeb.

هُوَ الَّذِي يُرِيكُمْ آيَاتِهِ وَيُنَزِّلُ لَكُم
مِّنَ السَّمَاءِ رِزْقًا ۚ وَمَا يَتَذَكَّرُ
إِلَّا مَن يُنِيبُ ١٣

14. Worship Allah and be devoted to His religion even though the unbelievers dislike this.

14. Fad'ul-laaha mukhlișeena lahud-deena wa law karihal-kaafiroon.

فَادْعُوا اللَّهَ مُخْلِصِينَ لَهُ الدِّينَ
وَلَوْ كَرِهَ الْكَافِرُونَ ١٤

15. Allah is the promoter of His servants and the owner of the Throne. He sends the Spirit (Ruh Al-Qudus) by His command to whichever of His servants He wants; to warn them of the day of the meeting (of the inhabitants of the heavens and earth) on the Day of Judgment.

15. Rafee'ud-darajaati zul-'Arshi yulqir-rooḥa min amrihee 'alaa mañy-yashaaa'u min 'ibaadihee liyunzira yawmat-talaaq.

رَفِيعُ الدَّرَجَاتِ ذُو الْعَرْشِ يُلْقِي
الرُّوحَ مِنْ أَمْرِهِ عَلَىٰ مَن يَشَاءُ مِنْ
عِبَادِهِ لِيُنذِرَ يَوْمَ التَّلَاقِ ١٥

16. Nothing will remain hidden from Allah concerning them on the day when they appear before Allah (from their graves). (It will be asked), "To whom does the kingdom belong on this Day?" (It will be answered), "The kingdom belongs to the Almighty, One Allah."

16. Yawma hum baarizoona laa yakhfaa 'alal-laahi minhum shay'; limanil-mulkul-Yawma lillaahil-Waaḥidil-Qahhaar.

يَوْمَ هُم بَارِزُونَ ۖ لَا يَخْفَىٰ عَلَى
اللَّهِ مِنْهُمْ شَيْءٌ ۚ لِّمَنِ الْمُلْكُ
الْيَوْمَ ۖ لِلَّهِ الْوَاحِدِ الْقَهَّارِ ١٦

17. Every soul will be recompensed for its deeds on this Day. There will be no injustice. Certainly Allah's reckoning is swift.

17. Al-Yawma tujzaa kullu nafsim bimaa kasabat; laa ẓulmal-Yawm; innal-laaha saree'ul-ḥisaab.

الْيَوْمَ تُجْزَىٰ كُلُّ نَفْسٍ بِمَا
كَسَبَتْ ۚ لَا ظُلْمَ الْيَوْمَ ۚ إِنَّ اللَّهَ
سَرِيعُ الْحِسَابِ ١٧

18. (Muhammad), warn them of the approaching day (Day of Judgment) when because of hardship and frustration their hearts will almost reach up to their throats. The unjust will have no friends nor any intercessor who will be heard.

18. Wa anzirhum yawmal-aazifati izil-quloobu ladal-ḥanaajiri kaaẓimeen; maa lizzaalimeena min ḥameemiñw-wa laa shafee'iñy-yuṭaa'.

وَأَنذِرْهُمْ يَوْمَ الْآزِفَةِ إِذِ الْقُلُوبُ
لَدَى الْحَنَاجِرِ كَاظِمِينَ ۚ مَا
لِلظَّالِمِينَ مِنْ حَمِيمٍ وَلَا شَفِيعٍ

19. Allah knows the disloyalty of the eyes and what the hearts conceal.

20. Allah judges with Truth but those whom they worship besides Allah can have no Judgment. Allah is certainly All-hearing and All-aware.

21. Did they not travel through the land to see the terrible end of those who lived before them? They had been mightier than them in power and in leaving their traces on earth. Allah punished them for their sins. They had no one to protect them from torment (created by Allah).

22. Messengers had come to them with illustrious miracles but they disbelieved and thus Allah struck them with His torment. He is Mighty and Severe in His retribution.

23. We sent Moses with Our miracles and clear authority

24. to the Pharaoh, Haman, and Korah, who said, "He is only a lying magician."

25. When We sent him to them for a genuine purpose, they said, "Kill the sons of those who have believed in him but keep their women alive." The plots of the unbelievers can only result in failure.

26. The Pharaoh said, "Let me kill Moses and let him call for help from his Lord. I am afraid that he will change your religion or spread evil throughout the land."

19. Ya'lamu khaaa'inatal a'yuni wa maa tukhfiṣ-ṣudoor.

20. Wallaahu yaqḍee bilḥaqq; wallazeena yad'oona min doonihee laa yaqḍoona bishay'; innal-laaha Huwas-Samee'ul-Baṣeer.

21. Awalam yaseeroo fil-arḍi fayanẓuroo kayfa kaana 'aaqibatul-lazeena kaanoo min qablihim; kaanoo hum ashadda minhum quwwatañw-wa aasaa-ran fil-arḍi fa-akhazahumul-laahu bizunoobihim wa maa kaana lahum minal-laahi miñw-waaq.

22. Zaalika bi-annahum kaa-nat ta-teehim Rusuluhum bilbayyinaati fakafaroo fa-akhazahumul-laah; innahoo qawiyyun shadeedul-'iqaab.

23. Wa laqad arsalnaa Moosaa bi-Aayaatinaa wa sulṭaanim-mubeen.

24. Ilaa Fir'awna wa Haamaa-na wa Qaaroona faqaaloo saaḥirun kaz-zaab.

25. Falamma jaaa'ahum-bil-ḥaqqi min 'indinaa qaaluq-tulooo abnaaa'al-lazeena aamanoo ma'ahoo wastaḥyoo-nisaaa'ahum; wa maa kaydul kaafireena illaa fee ḍalaal.

26. Wa qaala Fir'awnu zaroo-neee aqtul Moosaa walyad'u Rabbahooo inneee akhaafu añy-yubaddila deenakum aw añy- yuẓhira fil-arḍil-fasaad.

يُطَاعُ ﴿١٨﴾
يَعْلَمُ خَآئِنَةَ الْاَعْيُنِ وَمَا تُخْفِي
الصُّدُوْرُ ﴿١٩﴾
وَاللّٰهُ يَقْضِيْ بِالْحَقِّ ۭ وَالَّذِيْنَ
يَدْعُوْنَ مِنْ دُوْنِهٖ لَا يَقْضُوْنَ بِشَيْءٍ ۭ ع ٢ / ١١ / ٧
اِنَّ اللّٰهَ هُوَ السَّمِيْعُ الْبَصِيْرُ ﴿٢٠﴾
اَوَلَمْ يَسِيْرُوْا فِي الْاَرْضِ فَيَنْظُرُوْا
كَيْفَ كَانَ عَاقِبَةُ الَّذِيْنَ كَانُوْا مِنْ
قَبْلِهِمْ ۭ كَانُوْا هُمْ اَشَدَّ مِنْهُمْ قُوَّةً
وَّاٰثَارًا فِي الْاَرْضِ فَاَخَذَهُمُ اللّٰهُ
بِذُنُوْبِهِمْ ۭ وَمَا كَانَ لَهُمْ مِّنَ اللّٰهِ
مِنْ وَّاقٍ ﴿٢١﴾
ذٰلِكَ بِاَنَّهُمْ كَانَتْ تَّاْتِيْهِمْ رُسُلُهُمْ
بِالْبَيِّنٰتِ فَكَفَرُوْا فَاَخَذَهُمُ اللّٰهُ ۭ
اِنَّهٗ قَوِيٌّ شَدِيْدُ الْعِقَابِ ﴿٢٢﴾
وَلَقَدْ اَرْسَلْنَا مُوْسٰى بِاٰيٰتِنَا وَ
سُلْطٰنٍ مُّبِيْنٍ ﴿٢٣﴾
اِلٰى فِرْعَوْنَ وَهَامٰنَ وَقَارُوْنَ فَقَالُوْا
سٰحِرٌ كَذَّابٌ ﴿٢٤﴾
فَلَمَّا جَآءَهُمْ بِالْحَقِّ مِنْ عِنْدِنَا قَالُوا
اقْتُلُوْٓا اَبْنَآءَ الَّذِيْنَ اٰمَنُوْا مَعَهٗ
وَاسْتَحْيُوْا نِسَآءَهُمْ ۭ وَمَا كَيْدُ
الْكٰفِرِيْنَ اِلَّا فِيْ ضَلٰلٍ ﴿٢٥﴾
وَقَالَ فِرْعَوْنُ ذَرُوْنِيْٓ اَقْتُلْ
مُوْسٰى وَلْيَدْعُ رَبَّهٗ ۚ اِنِّيْٓ اَخَافُ اَنْ
يُّبَدِّلَ دِيْنَكُمْ اَوْ اَنْ يُّظْهِرَ فِي

27. Moses said, "I seek protection of your and my Lord against every arrogant person who has no faith in the Day of Judgment."

28. A believing person from the people of the Pharaoh who concealed his faith said, "Would you kill a man just because he says Allah is my Lord? He has brought you illustrious miracles from your Lord. If he speaks lies, it will only harm him, but if he speaks the Truth, some of his warnings may affect you. Allah does not guide a transgressing liar."

29. "My people, today you have the kingdom and the power on earth but who will help us against the wrath of Allah if it befalls us?"

The Pharaoh said, "I show you only what I think is proper and guide you only to the right direction."

30. The believing man said, "I am afraid that you will face a (terrible) day like that of the groups:

31. people of Noah, Ad, Thamud, and those after them. Allah did not want injustice for His servants.

32. My people, I am afraid for you on (the Day of Judgment), when people will cry for help.

33. On that day you will run away, but no one will be able to protect you from Allah (His Judgment). No one can guide one whom Allah has caused to go astray."

27. Wa qaala Moosaaa innee-'uztu bi-Rabbee wa Rabbikum min kulli mutakabbiril-laa yu'minu bi-Yawmil-Ḥisaab.

28. Wa qaala rajulum mu'mi-num-min Aali Fir'awna yaktumu eemaanahooo ataqtu-loona rajulan añy-yaqoola Rabbiyal-laahu wa qad jaaa'akum bil-bayyinaati mir-Rabbikum wa iñy-yaku kaaziban fa'alayhi kazibuhoo wa iñy-yaku ṣaadiqañy-yuṣibkum ba'ḍul-lazee ya'idu-kum, innal-laaha laa yahdee man huwa musrifun kaz-zaab.

29. Yaa qawmi lakumul mulkul-yawma ẓaahireena fil-arḍi famañy-yanṣurunaa mim ba-sil-laahi in jaaa'anaa; qaala Fir'awnu maaa ureekum illaa maaa araa wa maaa ahdeekum illaa sabeelar-rashaad.

30. Wa qaalal-lazeee aamana yaa qawmi inneee akhaafu 'alaykum misla yawmil-Aḥzaab.

31. Misla da-bi qawmi Noo-ḥiñw-wa 'Aadiñw-wa Samooda wallazeena mim ba'dihim; wa mal-laahu yureedu ẓulmal-lil 'ibaad.

32. Wa yaa qawmi inneee akhaafu 'alaykum yawmat tanaad.

33. Yawma tuwalloona mud-bireena maa lakum minal-laahi min 'aaṣim; wa mañy-yuḍlilil-laahu famaa lahoo min haad.

الْاَرْضِ الْفَسَادَ ﴿٢٦﴾
وَقَالَ مُوْسٰىٓ اِنِّيْ عُذْتُ بِرَبِّيْ وَرَبِّكُمْ
مِّنْ كُلِّ مُتَكَبِّرٍ لَّا يُؤْمِنُ بِيَوْمِ
الْحِسَابِ ﴿٢٧﴾ ع ٣ ٨
وَقَالَ رَجُلٌ مُّؤْمِنٌ ۖ مِّنْ اٰلِ
فِرْعَوْنَ يَكْتُمُ اِيْمَانَهٗٓ اَتَقْتُلُوْنَ
رَجُلًا اَنْ يَّقُوْلَ رَبِّيَ اللّٰهُ وَقَدْ
جَآءَكُمْ بِالْبَيِّنٰتِ مِنْ رَّبِّكُمْ ؕ وَاِنْ
يَّكُ كَاذِبًا فَعَلَيْهِ كَذِبُهٗ ۚ وَاِنْ
يَّكُ صَادِقًا يُّصِبْكُمْ بَعْضُ الَّذِيْ
يَعِدُكُمْ ؕ اِنَّ اللّٰهَ لَا يَهْدِيْ مَنْ
هُوَ مُسْرِفٌ كَذَّابٌ ﴿٢٨﴾
يٰقَوْمِ لَكُمُ الْمُلْكُ الْيَوْمَ ظٰهِرِيْنَ
فِي الْاَرْضِ ۫ فَمَنْ يَّنْصُرُنَا مِنْۢ بَاْسِ
اللّٰهِ اِنْ جَآءَنَا ؕ قَالَ فِرْعَوْنُ مَآ
اُرِيْكُمْ اِلَّا مَآ اَرٰى وَمَآ اَهْدِيْكُمْ
اِلَّا سَبِيْلَ الرَّشَادِ ﴿٢٩﴾
وَقَالَ الَّذِيْٓ اٰمَنَ يٰقَوْمِ اِنِّيْٓ اَخَافُ
عَلَيْكُمْ مِّثْلَ يَوْمِ الْاَحْزَابِ ﴿٣٠﴾
مِثْلَ دَاْبِ قَوْمِ نُوْحٍ وَّعَادٍ وَّثَمُوْدَ
وَالَّذِيْنَ مِنْۢ بَعْدِهِمْ ؕ وَمَا اللّٰهُ
يُرِيْدُ ظُلْمًا لِّلْعِبَادِ ﴿٣١﴾
وَيٰقَوْمِ اِنِّيْٓ اَخَافُ عَلَيْكُمْ يَوْمَ
التَّنَادِ ﴿٣٢﴾
يَوْمَ تُوَلُّوْنَ مُدْبِرِيْنَ ۚ مَا لَكُمْ مِّنَ
اللّٰهِ مِنْ عَاصِمٍ ۚ وَمَنْ يُّضْلِلِ اللّٰهُ

34. Joseph came to you before with illustrious evidence but you still have doubts about what he brought. When he passed away, you said, "Allah will never send any messenger after him." Thus does Allah cause to go astray the skeptical, transgressing people,

35. those who dispute the revelations of Allah without having received clear authority (proper proof). This act greatly angers Allah and the believers. Thus does Allah seal the hearts of every arrogant oppressor."

36. Pharaoh said, "Haman, build a tower (of baked bricks) for me so that I shall have access (find instructions)

37. to the heavens and be able to climb up to the Lord of Moses. I think that Moses is lying." Thus, Pharaoh's evil deeds seemed attractive to him and prevented him from the right path. The Pharaoh's plots only led him to his own destruction.

38. The believing man said, "My people, follow me and I shall show you the right guidance.

39. My people, this worldly life is only the means (to an end), but the life hereafter will be the everlasting abode.

40. Whoever commits evil deeds will be recompensed to the same degree. The righteously striving believer, male or female, will enter Paradise wherein they will receive their sustenance

34. Wa laqad jaaa'akum Yoosufu min qablu bil-bayyinaati famaa ziltum fee shakkim-mimmaa jaaa'akum bihee ḥattaaa iẕaa halaka qultum lañy-yab'aṯal-laahu mim ba'dihee Rasoolaa; kaẕaalika yuḍillul-laahu man huwa musrifum-murtaab.

35. Allaẕeena yujaadiloona feee Aaayaatil-laahi bighayri sulṭaanin ataahum kabura maqtan 'indal-laahi wa 'indal-laẕeena aamanoo; kaẕaalika yaṭba'ul-laahu'alaa kulli qalbi mutakabbirin jabbaar.

36. Wa qaala Fir'awnu yaa Haamaanub-ni lee ṣarḥal-la'alleee ablughul-asbaab.

37. Asbaabas-samaawaati fa-aṭṭali'a ilaaa ilaahi Moosaa wa innee la-aẓunnuhoo kaaẕibaa; wa kaẕaalika zuyyina li-Fir'awna sooo'u 'amalihee wa ṣudda 'anis-sabeel; wa maa kaydu Fir'awna illaa fee tabaab.

38. Wa qaalal-laẕeee aamana yaa qawmit-tabi'ooni ahdikum sabeelar-rashaad.

39. Yaa qawmi innamaa haaẕihil-ḥayaatud-dunyaa mataa'uñw-wa innal Aakhirata hiya daarul-qaraar.

40. Man 'amila sayyi'atan falaa yujzaaa illaa miṯlahaa wa man 'amila ṣaaliḥam-min ẕakarin aw unṯaa wa huwa mu'minun fa-ulaaa'ika

فَمَا لَهُ مِنْ هَادٍ ﴿٣٣﴾
وَلَقَدْ جَاءَكُمْ يُوسُفُ مِنْ قَبْلُ
بِالْبَيِّنٰتِ فَمَا زِلْتُمْ فِي شَكٍّ مِمَّا
جَاءَكُمْ بِهٖ ۖ حَتّٰى إِذَا هَلَكَ قُلْتُمْ
لَنْ يَبْعَثَ اللّٰهُ مِنْ بَعْدِهٖ رَسُولًا ۚ
كَذٰلِكَ يُضِلُّ اللّٰهُ مَنْ هُوَ مُسْرِفٌ
مُرْتَابٌ ﴿٣٤﴾
الَّذِينَ يُجَادِلُونَ فِي آيٰتِ اللّٰهِ
بِغَيْرِ سُلْطٰنٍ أَتٰهُمْ ۖ كَبُرَ مَقْتًا عِنْدَ
اللّٰهِ وَعِنْدَ الَّذِينَ آمَنُوا ۚ كَذٰلِكَ
يَطْبَعُ اللّٰهُ عَلٰى كُلِّ قَلْبِ مُتَكَبِّرٍ
جَبَّارٍ ﴿٣٥﴾
وَقَالَ فِرْعَوْنُ يٰهَامٰنُ ابْنِ لِي
صَرْحًا لَعَلِّي أَبْلُغُ الْأَسْبَابَ ﴿٣٦﴾
أَسْبَابَ السَّمٰوٰتِ فَأَطَّلِعَ إِلٰى إِلٰهِ
مُوسٰى وَإِنِّي لَأَظُنُّهُ كَاذِبًا ۚ وَكَذٰلِكَ
زُيِّنَ لِفِرْعَوْنَ سُوءُ عَمَلِهٖ وَصُدَّ عَنِ
السَّبِيلِ ۚ وَمَا كَيْدُ فِرْعَوْنَ إِلَّا
فِي تَبَابٍ ﴿٣٧﴾ ع
وَقَالَ الَّذِي آمَنَ يٰقَوْمِ اتَّبِعُونِ
أَهْدِكُمْ سَبِيلَ الرَّشَادِ ﴿٣٨﴾
يٰقَوْمِ إِنَّمَا هٰذِهِ الْحَيٰوةُ الدُّنْيَا
مَتَاعٌ ۫ وَإِنَّ الْآخِرَةَ هِيَ دَارُ الْقَرَارِ ﴿٣٩﴾
مَنْ عَمِلَ سَيِّئَةً فَلَا يُجْزٰى إِلَّا
مِثْلَهَا ۚ وَمَنْ عَمِلَ صَالِحًا مِنْ
ذَكَرٍ أَوْ أُنْثٰى وَهُوَ مُؤْمِنٌ فَأُولٰئِكَ

without any account being kept.

yadkhuloonal-Jannata yurzaqoona feehaa bighayri ḥisaab.

يَدۡخُلُوۡنَ الۡجَـنَّةَ يُرۡزَقُوۡنَ فِيۡهَا
بِغَيۡرِ حِسَابٍ ﴿٤٠﴾

41. My people, "How strange is it that I invite you to salvation when you invite me to the fire.

41. Wa yaa qawmi maa leee ad'ookum ilan-najaati wa tad'oonaneee ilan-Naar.

وَيٰقَوۡمِ مَا لِىۡۤ اَدۡعُوۡكُمۡ اِلَى النَّجٰوةِ
وَتَدۡعُوۡنَنِىۡۤ اِلَى النَّارِ ﴿٤١﴾

النصف

42. You call me to disbelieve in Allah and to believe other things equal to Him about which I have no knowledge. I call you to the Majestic and All-forgiving One.

42. Tad'oonanee li-akfura billaahi wa ushrika bihee maa laysa lee bihee 'ilmuñw-wa ana ad'ookum ilal'Azeezil-Ghaffaar.

تَدۡعُوۡنَنِىۡ لِاَكۡفُرَ بِاللّٰهِ وَاُشۡرِكَ
بِهٖ مَا لَـيۡسَ لِىۡ بِهٖ عِلۡمٌ وَّاَنَا
اَدۡعُوۡكُمۡ اِلَى الۡعَزِيۡزِ الۡغَفَّارِ ﴿٤٢﴾

43. It is certain that the idols to which you invite me surely have no claim to be deities in this world or in the life to come. Our return is to Allah and the transgressors will be the dwellers in hellfire.

43. Laa jarama annamaa tad'oonaneee ilayhi laysa lahoo da'watun fid-dunyaa wa laa fil-Aakhirati wa anna maraddanaaa ilal-laahi wa annal-musrifeena hum Aṣḥaabun-Naar.

لَا جَرَمَ اَنَّمَا تَدۡعُوۡنَنِىۡۤ اِلَيۡهِ
لَـيۡسَ لَهٗ دَعۡوَةٌ فِى الدُّنۡيَا وَلَا فِى
الۡاٰخِرَةِ وَاَنَّ مَرَدَّنَاۤ اِلَى اللّٰهِ
وَاَنَّ الۡمُسۡرِفِيۡنَ هُمۡ اَصۡحٰبُ النَّارِ ﴿٤٣﴾

44. You will soon recall what I have told you. I entrust Allah with my affairs. Allah is Well-Aware of His servants."

44. Fasatazkuroona maaa aqoolu lakum; wa ufawwiḍu amreee ilal-laah; innal-laaha Baṣeerum bil'ibaad.

فَسَتَذۡكُرُوۡنَ مَاۤ اَقُوۡلُ لَـكُمۡ ؕ وَاُفَوِّضُ
اَمۡرِىۡۤ اِلَى اللّٰهِ ؕ اِنَّ اللّٰهَ بَصِيۡرٌۢ
بِالۡعِبَادِ ﴿٤٤﴾

45. Allah protected him against their evil plans and the people of the Pharaoh were struck by the most horrible torment.

45. Fawaqaahul-laahu sayyi-aati maa makaroo wa ḥaaqa bi-Aali-Fir'awna sooo'ul-'azaab.

فَوَقٰٮهُ اللّٰهُ سَيِّاٰتِ مَا مَكَرُوۡا
وَحَاقَ بِاٰلِ فِرۡعَوۡنَ سُوۡٓءُ الۡعَذَابِ ۚ ﴿٤٥﴾

46. They will be exposed to the fire in the mornings and the evenings, (in this world) and on the Day of Judgment they will be told, "People of the Pharaoh, suffer the most severe torment."

46. An-Naaru yu'raḍoona 'alayhaa ghuduwwañw-wa 'ashiyyaa; wa Yawma taqoomus-Saa'atu adkhilooo Aala Fir'awna ashaddal'azaab.

اَلنَّارُ يُعۡرَضُوۡنَ عَلَيۡهَا غُدُوًّا وَّعَشِيًّا ۚ
وَيَوۡمَ تَقُوۡمُ السَّاعَةُ اَدۡخِلُوۡۤا
اٰلَ فِرۡعَوۡنَ اَشَدَّ الۡعَذَابِ ﴿٤٦﴾

47. During a dispute in the fire, the suppressed ones will say to those who had dominated them, "We were your followers. Can you now relieve us of our suffering in the fire?"

47. Wa iz yataḥaaajjoona fin Naari fayaqooluḍ-ḍu'afaaa'u lillazeenas-takbarooo innaa kunnaa lakum taba'an fahal antum mughnoona 'annaa naṣeebam-minan-Naar.

وَاِذۡ يَتَحَآجُّوۡنَ فِى النَّارِ فَيَقُوۡلُ
الضُّعَفٰٓؤُا لِلَّذِيۡنَ اسۡتَكۡبَرُوۡۤا اِنَّا كُنَّا
لَـكُمۡ تَبَعًا فَهَلۡ اَنۡتُمۡ مُّغۡنُوۡنَ
عَنَّا نَصِيۡبًا مِّنَ النَّارِ ﴿٤٧﴾

48. The ones who had dominated them will say, "All of us are now in hell. Allah has already issued His Judgment of His servants (and no one can change this)."

48. Qaalal-lazeenas-takbarooo innaa kullun feehaaa innal-laaha qad ḥakama baynal-'ibaad.

قَالَ الَّذِيۡنَ اسۡتَكۡبَرُوۡۤا اِنَّا كُلٌّ
فِيۡهَاۤ اِنَّ اللّٰهَ قَدۡ حَكَمَ بَيۡنَ الۡعِبَادِ ﴿٤٨﴾

49. The dwellers in hellfire will ask its keepers, "Pray to your

49. Wa qaalal-lazeena fin-Naari likhazanati

وَقَالَ الَّذِيۡنَ فِى النَّارِ لِخَزَنَةِ

Lord to relieve us from the torment at least for one day."

Jahannamad-'oo Rabbakum yukhaffif 'annaa yawmam-minal-'azaab.

جَهَنَّمَ ادْعُوْا رَبَّكُمْ يُخَفِّفْ عَنَّا
يَوْمًا مِّنَ الْعَذَابِ ۝٤٩

50. The keepers will ask them, "Did your Messengers not come to you with illustrious evidence (of the Truth)? They will reply, "Yes, they did." The keepers will then say, "You may pray but the prayer of the unbelievers will be void (remain without an answer)."

50. Qaalooo awalam taku tateekum Rusulukum bilbayyinaati qaaloo balaa; qaaloo fad'oo; wa maa du'aa'ul-kaafireena illaa fee ḍalaal.

قَالُوْٓا اَوَلَمْ تَكُ تَاْتِيْكُمْ رُسُلُكُمْ
بِالْبَيِّنٰتِ ؕ قَالُوْا بَلٰى ؕ قَالُوْا فَادْعُوْا ۚ
وَمَا دُعٰٓؤُا الْكٰفِرِيْنَ اِلَّا فِيْ ضَلٰلٍ ۝٥٠ ع ٥ ١٠

51. We shall help Our messengers and the believers, in this life and on the day when the witness will come forward.

51. Innaa lananṣuru Rusulanaa wallazeena aamanoo fil-ḥayaatid-dunyaa wa Yawma yaqoomul-ashhaad.

اِنَّا لَنَنْصُرُ رُسُلَنَا وَالَّذِيْنَ اٰمَنُوْا فِي
الْحَيٰوةِ الدُّنْيَا وَيَوْمَ يَقُوْمُ الْاَشْهَادُ ۙ۝٥١

52. The excuses of the unjust will be of no benefit to them on that day. They will be condemned to live in a most terrible abode.

52. Yawma laa yanfa'uẓ-ẓaalimeena ma'ziratuhum wa lahumul-la'natu wa lahum sooo'ud-daar.

يَوْمَ لَا يَنْفَعُ الظّٰلِمِيْنَ مَعْذِرَتُهُمْ
وَلَهُمُ اللَّعْنَةُ وَلَهُمْ سُوْٓءُ الدَّارِ ۝٥٢

53. To Moses We had given guidance and to the children of Israel We had given the Book as their inheritance

53. Wa laqad aataynaa Moosal-hudaa wa awrasnaa Baneee Israaa'eelal-Kitaab.

وَلَقَدْ اٰتَيْنَا مُوْسَى الْهُدٰى وَ
اَوْرَثْنَا بَنِيْٓ اِسْرَآءِيْلَ الْكِتٰبَ ۙ۝٥٣

54. and as a guide and a reminder to the people of understanding.

54. Hudañw-wa zikraa li-ulil albaab.

هُدًى وَّذِكْرٰى لِاُولِي الْاَلْبَابِ ۝٥٤

55. (Muhammad), exercise patience. The promise of Allah is true. Seek forgiveness for your sins and glorify your Lord with His praise in the evenings and in the early mornings.

55. Faṣbir inna wa'dal-laahi ḥaqquñw-wastaghfir lizambika wa sabbiḥ biḥamdi Rabbika bil'ashiyyi wal ibkaar.

فَاصْبِرْ اِنَّ وَعْدَ اللّٰهِ حَقٌّ وَّاسْتَغْفِرْ
لِذَنْۢبِكَ وَسَبِّحْ بِحَمْدِ رَبِّكَ بِالْعَشِيِّ
وَالْاِبْكَارِ ۝٥٥

56. Those who dispute the revelations of Allah without having received any authority (proper proof) do so because of their arrogance, but their arrogance cannot bring them any success. Seek protection of Allah for He is All-hearing and All-aware.

56. Innal-lazeena yujaadiloona feee Aayaatillaahi bighayri sulṭaanin ataahum in fee ṣudoorihim illaa kibrum-maa hum bibaaligheeh; fasta'iz billaahi innahoo Huwas-Samee'ul Baṣeer.

اِنَّ الَّذِيْنَ يُجَادِلُوْنَ فِيْٓ اٰيٰتِ اللّٰهِ
بِغَيْرِ سُلْطٰنٍ اَتٰىهُمْ ۙ اِنْ فِيْ
صُدُوْرِهِمْ اِلَّا كِبْرٌ مَّا هُمْ
بِبَالِغِيْهِ ۚ فَاسْتَعِذْ بِاللّٰهِ ؕ اِنَّهٗ هُوَ
السَّمِيْعُ الْبَصِيْرُ ۝٥٦

57. The creation of the heavens and the earth is certainly greater than the creation of mankind, but most people do not know.

57. Lakhalqus-samaawaati wal-arḍi akbaru min khalqin-naasi wa laakinna aksarannaasi laa ya'lamoon.

لَخَلْقُ السَّمٰوٰتِ وَالْاَرْضِ اَكْبَرُ مِنْ
خَلْقِ النَّاسِ وَلٰكِنَّ اَكْثَرَ النَّاسِ
لَا يَعْلَمُوْنَ ۝٥٧

58. Just as the blind and the seeing are not equal, so are the righteously striving believers and the sinners not equal. How little you pay attention to this.

58. Wa maa yastawil-a'maa walbaṣeeru wallazeena aamanoo wa 'amiluṣ-ṣaaliḥaati wa lal-musee'; qaleelam-maa tatazakkaroon.

وَمَا يَسْتَوِي الْاَعْمٰى وَالْبَصِيْرُ ۙ۬
وَالَّذِيْنَ اٰمَنُوْا وَعَمِلُوا الصّٰلِحٰتِ
وَلَا الْمُسِيْٓءُ ؕ قَلِيْلًا مَّا تَتَذَكَّرُوْنَ ۝٥٨

59. The Hour of Doom will inevitably come, but most people do not have faith.	59. Innas-Saa'ata la-aatiyatul-laa rayba feehaa wa laakinna aks̲aran-naasi laa yu'minoon.	ان الساعة لاتية لا ريب فيها ولكن اكثر الناس لا يؤمنون ٥٩
60. Your Lord has said, "Pray to Me for I shall answer your prayers. Those who are too proud to worship Me will soon go to hell in disgrace."	60. Wa qaala Rabbukumud-'ooneee astajib lakum; innal-laz̲eena yastakbiroona 'an 'ibaadatee sayad-khuloona Jahannama daakhireen.	وقال ربكم ادعوني استجب لكم ان الذين يستكبرون عن عبادتي سيدخلون جهنم دخرين ٦٠
61. It is Allah Who has made the night for you to rest and the day for you to see. Allah is Benevolent to the human being, but most people do not give Him due thanks.	61. Allaahul-laz̲ee ja'ala lakumul-layla litaskunoo feehi wannahaara mubṣiraa; innal-laaha laz̲oo-faḍlin 'alan-naasi wa laakinna aks̲aran-naasi laa yashkuroon.	الله الذي جعل لكم اليل لتسكنوا فيه والنهار مبصرا ط ان الله لذو فضل على الناس ولكن اكثر الناس لا يشكرون ٦١
62. It is Allah, your Lord, Who has created all things. He is the only Lord. Why then do you turn away from His worship to the worshipping of idols?	62. Z̲aalikumul-laahu Rabbukum Khaaliqu kulli shay'; laaa ilaaha illaa Huwa fa-annaa tu'fakoon.	ذلكم الله ربكم خالق كل شيء لا اله الا هو فانى تؤفكون ٦٢
63. Thus, indeed, are those who have rejected the revelations of Allah.	63. Kaz̲aalika yu'fakul laz̲ee-na kaanoo bi-Aayaatillaahi yajḥadoon.	كذلك يؤفك الذين كانوا بايت الله يجحدون ٦٣
64. It is Allah who has created the earth as a place for you to live and the sky as a dome above you. He has shaped you in the best form and has provided you with pure sustenance. This is Allah, your Lord. Blessed is Allah, the Lord of the Universe.	64. Allaahul-laz̲ee ja'ala lakumul-arḍa qaraarañw-wassamaaa'a binaaa'añw-wa ṣawwarakum fa-aḥsana ṣuwarakum wa razaqakum minaṭ-ṭayyibaat; z̲aalikumul-laahu Rabbukum fatabaarakal-laahu Rabbul-'aalameen.	الله الذي جعل لكم الارض قرارا والسماء بناء وصوركم فاحسن صوركم ورزقكم من الطيبت ط ذلكم الله ربكم فتبرك الله رب العلمين ٦٤
65. He is the Everlasting and the only Lord. So worship Him and be devoted to His religion. It is only Allah, the Lord of the universe, who deserves all praise.	65. Huwal-Ḥayyu laaa ilaaha illaa Huwa fad'oohu mukh-liṣeena lahud-deen; al-ḥamdu lillaahi Rabbil-'aalameen.	هو الحي لا اله الا هو فادعوه مخلصين له الدين ط الحمد لله رب العلمين ٦٥
66. (Muhammad) say, "I have been forbidden to worship whatever you worship besides Allah after receiving clear evidence from my Lord. I have been commanded to submit myself to the will of the Lord of the universe."	66. Qul innee nuheetu an a'budal-laz̲eena tad'oona min doonil-laahi lammaa jaaa'a-niyal-bayyinaatu mir-Rabbee wa umirtu an uslima li-Rabbil-'aalameen.	قل اني نهيت ان اعبد الذين تدعون من دون الله لما جاءني البينت من ربي ز وامرت ان اسلم لرب العلمين ٦٦
67. It is He Who created you from clay, turning it into a living	67. Huwal-laz̲ee khalaqakum min turaabin s̲umma	هو الذي خلقكم من تراب ثم

germ, then into a clot of blood, and then brought you forth as a child. He then made you grow into manhood and become old. He causes some of you to live for the appointed time and some of you to die before, so that perhaps you may have understanding.

min nuṭfatin summa min 'alaqatin summa yukhrijukum ṭiflan summa litablughooo ashuddakum summa litakoonoo shuyookhaa; wa minkum mañy-yutawaffaa min qablu wa litablughooo ajalam-musam-mañw-wa la'allakum ta'qiloon.

مِنْ نُّطْفَةٍ ثُمَّ مِنْ عَلَقَةٍ ثُمَّ
يُخْرِجُكُمْ طِفْلًا ثُمَّ لِتَبْلُغُوٓا
اَشُدَّكُمْ ثُمَّ لِتَكُوْنُوْا شُيُوْخًا ۚ
وَمِنْكُمْ مَّنْ يُّتَوَفّٰى مِنْ قَبْلُ
وَلِتَبْلُغُوٓا اَجَلًا مُّسَمًّى وَّلَعَلَّكُمْ
تَعْقِلُوْنَ ﴿٦٧﴾

68. It is He Who gives life and causes things to die. When He decides to do something, He only says, "Exist," and it comes into existence.

68. Huwal-lazee yuḥyee wa yumeetu fa-izaa qaḍaaa amran fa-innamaa yaqoolu lahoo kun fa-yakoon.

هُوَ الَّذِيْ يُحْيٖ وَيُمِيْتُ ۚ فَاِذَا
قَضٰٓى اَمْرًا فَاِنَّمَا يَقُوْلُ لَهٗ كُنْ
فَيَكُوْنُ ﴿٦٨﴾ ع ٨

69. Did you not see how those who dispute the revelations of Allah, turn away from Truth to falsehood?

69. Alam tara ilal-lazeena yujaadiloona feee Aayaatillaahi annaa yuṣrafoon.

اَلَمْ تَرَ اِلَى الَّذِيْنَ يُجَادِلُوْنَ
فِيْٓ اٰيٰتِ اللّٰهِ ؕ اَنّٰى يُصْرَفُوْنَ ﴿٦٩﴾

70. Those who rejected the Book and the message which was given to Our Messenger will soon know (the consequences of their evil deeds)

70. Allazeena kaz-zaboo bil-Kitaabi wa bimaaa arsalnaa bihee Rusulanaa fasawfa ya'lamoon.

الَّذِيْنَ كَذَّبُوْا بِالْكِتٰبِ وَبِمَآ اَرْسَلْنَا
بِهٖ رُسُلَنَا ۛ فَسَوْفَ يَعْلَمُوْنَ ﴿٧٠﴾

71. when fetters will be placed around their necks and chains will drag them

71. Izil-aghlaalu feee a'naaqi-him wassalaasilu yusḥaboon.

اِذِ الْاَغْلٰلُ فِيْٓ اَعْنَاقِهِمْ وَالسَّلٰسِلُ
يُسْحَبُوْنَ ﴿٧١﴾

72. into boiling water and then they will be burned in the fire.

72. Fil-ḥameemi summa fin-Naari yusjaroon.

فِي الْحَمِيْمِ ثُمَّ فِي النَّارِ يُسْجَرُوْنَ ﴿٧٢﴾

73. Then they will be asked, "Where are the idols which you worshipped besides Allah?"

73. Summa qeela lahum-ayna maa kuntum tushrikoon.

ثُمَّ قِيْلَ لَهُمْ اَيْنَ مَا كُنْتُمْ
تُشْرِكُوْنَ ﴿٧٣﴾

74. They will reply, "They have abandoned us. In fact, we had worshipped nothing." Thus does Allah cause the unbelievers to go astray.

74. Min doonil-laah; qaaloo ḍalloo 'annaa bal-lam nakun nad'oo min qablu shay'aa; kazaalika yuḍillul-laahul-kaafireen.

مِنْ دُوْنِ اللّٰهِ ؕ قَالُوْا ضَلُّوْا عَنَّا
بَلْ لَّمْ نَكُنْ نَّدْعُوْا مِنْ قَبْلُ شَيْـًٔا ؕ
كَذٰلِكَ يُضِلُّ اللّٰهُ الْكٰفِرِيْنَ ﴿٧٤﴾

75. They will be told, "This (torment) is the result of your unreasonable happiness on the earth and of your propagation of falsehood.

75. Zaalikum bimaa kuntum tafraḥoona fil-arḍi bighayril-ḥaqqi wa bimaa kuntum tamraḥoon.

ذٰلِكُمْ بِمَا كُنْتُمْ تَفْرَحُوْنَ فِي الْاَرْضِ
بِغَيْرِ الْحَقِّ وَبِمَا كُنْتُمْ تَمْرَحُوْنَ ﴿٧٥﴾

76. Enter the gates of hell to live therein forever. How terrible is the dwelling of the arrogant ones.

76. Udkhulooo abwaaba Jahannama khaalideena feehaa fabi'sa maswal-mutakabbireen.

اُدْخُلُوْٓا اَبْوَابَ جَهَنَّمَ خٰلِدِيْنَ
فِيْهَا ۚ فَبِئْسَ مَثْوَى الْمُتَكَبِّرِيْنَ ﴿٧٦﴾

77. (Muhammad), exercise patience. The promise of Allah is true.

77. Faṣbir inna wa'dal-laahi ḥaqq; fa-immaa

فَاصْبِرْ اِنَّ وَعْدَ اللّٰهِ حَقٌّ ۚ فَاِمَّا

معانقة ١٣ عند المتاخرين ١٢٠

Whether We let you witness the suffering with which they were threatened or because of your death (you do not see their suffering), We shall still punish them when they return to Us (on the Day of Judgment).

nuriyannaka ba'ḍal-lazee na'i-duhum aw natawaffayannaka fa-ilaynaa yurja'oon.

نُرِيَنَّكَ بَعْضَ الَّذِي نَعِدُهُمْ أَوْ
نَتَوَفَّيَنَّكَ فَإِلَيْنَا يُرْجَعُونَ ﴿٧٧﴾

78. We have told you the stories of some of Our messengers whom We had sent before you and We had not told you the stories of some others. A messenger is not supposed to show a miracle without the permission of Allah. When Allah's decree of punishment comes to pass, He will judge truthfully and the supporters of the falsehood will perish (fail).

78. Wa laqad arsalnaa Rusulam-min qablika minhum man qaṣaṣnaa 'alayka wa minhum mal-lam naqṣuṣ 'alayk; wa maa kaana li-Rasoolin añy-ya-tiya bi-Aayatin illaa bi-iznil-laah; fa-izaa jaaa'a amrul-laahi quḍiya bilḥaqqi wa khasira hunaalikal-mubṭiloon.

وَلَقَدْ أَرْسَلْنَا رُسُلًا مِّن قَبْلِكَ
مِنْهُم مَّن قَصَصْنَا عَلَيْكَ وَمِنْهُم
مَّن لَّمْ نَقْصُصْ عَلَيْكَ ۗ وَمَا كَانَ
لِرَسُولٍ أَن يَأْتِيَ بِآيَةٍ إِلَّا بِإِذْنِ
اللَّهِ ۚ فَإِذَا جَاءَ أَمْرُ اللَّهِ قُضِيَ بِالْحَقِّ
وَخَسِرَ هُنَالِكَ الْمُبْطِلُونَ ﴿٧٨﴾ ع ٨ ١٠ ١٣

79. It is Allah Who has created cattle for you to ride and to consume as food.

79. Allaahul-lazee ja'ala lakumul-an'aama litarkaboo minhaa wa minhaa ta-kuloon.

اللَّهُ الَّذِي جَعَلَ لَكُمُ الْأَنْعَامَ
لِتَرْكَبُوا مِنْهَا وَمِنْهَا تَأْكُلُونَ ﴿٧٩﴾

80. You may also obtain other benefits from them. You may ride them to seek whatever you need or be carried by them as ships carry you by sea.

80. Wa lakum feehaa manaafi'u wa litablughoo 'alayhaa ḥaajatan fee ṣudoorikum wa 'alayhaa wa 'alal-fulki tuḥma-loon.

وَلَكُمْ فِيهَا مَنَافِعُ وَلِتَبْلُغُوا عَلَيْهَا
حَاجَةً فِي صُدُورِكُمْ وَعَلَيْهَا وَ
عَلَى الْفُلْكِ تُحْمَلُونَ ﴿٨٠﴾

81. Allah shows you His evidence (of His existence). How can you then deny such evidence?

81. Wa yureekum Aayaatihee fa-ayya Aayaatillaahi tunki-roon.

وَيُرِيكُمْ آيَاتِهِ فَأَيَّ آيَاتِ
اللَّهِ تُنكِرُونَ ﴿٨١﴾

82. Did they not travel through the land to see the terrible end of those who lived before them? They were far mightier in both number and power and in what they had established. Their (worldly) gains were of no benefit to them.

82. Afalam yaseeroo fil-arḍi fayanẓuroo kayfa kaana 'aaqibatul-lazeena min qabli-him; kaanooo aksara minhum wa ashadda quwwatañw-wa aasaaran fil-arḍi famaaa aghnaa 'anhum maa kaanoo yaksiboon.

أَفَلَمْ يَسِيرُوا فِي الْأَرْضِ فَيَنظُرُوا
كَيْفَ كَانَ عَاقِبَةُ الَّذِينَ مِن
قَبْلِهِمْ ۚ كَانُوا أَكْثَرَ مِنْهُمْ وَأَشَدَّ
قُوَّةً وَآثَارًا فِي الْأَرْضِ فَمَا أَغْنَىٰ
عَنْهُم مَّا كَانُوا يَكْسِبُونَ ﴿٨٢﴾

83. They were far too content with their own knowledge (to pay attention to the Messengers) when Our Messengers came to them with illustrious evidence. They were encompassed by the torment for mocking Our guidance.

83. Falammaa jaaa'athum Rusuluhum bilbayyinaati fariḥoo bimaa 'indahum minal-'ilmi wa ḥaaqa bihim maa kaanoo bihee yastahzi'oon.

فَلَمَّا جَاءَتْهُمْ رُسُلُهُم بِالْبَيِّنَاتِ
فَرِحُوا بِمَا عِندَهُم مِّنَ الْعِلْمِ وَحَاقَ
بِهِم مَّا كَانُوا بِهِ يَسْتَهْزِئُونَ ﴿٨٣﴾

84. They said, "We believe in Allah alone and disbelieve in whatever we had considered equal to Him," but only when they experienced Our might.

84. Falammaa ra-aw ba-sanaa qaalooo aamannaa billaahi waḥdahoo wa kafarnaa bimaa kunnaa bihee mushrikeen.

فَلَمَّا رَأَوْا بَأْسَنَا قَالُوا آمَنَّا بِاللَّهِ
وَحْدَهُ وَكَفَرْنَا بِمَا كُنَّا بِهِ مُشْرِكِينَ ﴿٨٤﴾

85. Their faith proved to be of no benefit to them when they

85. Falam yaku yanfa'uhum eemaanuhum lammaa ra-aw

فَلَمْ يَكُ يَنفَعُهُمْ إِيمَانُهُمْ لَمَّا رَأَوْا

became subject to Our power (that brought them suffering). Such was Allah's prevailing tradition among His servants in the past. Thus were the unbelievers destroyed.	ba-sanaa sunnatal-laahil-latee qad khalat fee 'ibaadihee wa khasira hunaalikal-kaafiroon.	بَأْسَنَا ۖ سُنَّتَ اللَّهِ الَّتِي قَدْ خَلَتْ فِي عِبَادِهِ ۖ وَخَسِرَ هُنَالِكَ الْكَافِرُونَ ﴿٨٥﴾ ع ٧/١٤
Al-Fussilat, Expounded Revelations (41) In the Name of Allah, the Beneficent, the Merciful.	**Sûrat Ḥâ Mîm as-Sajdah-41** (Revealed at Makkah) **Bismillaahir Raḥmaanir Raḥeem**	(٤١) سُورَةُ حمٓ السَّجْدَةِ مَكِّيَّةٌ (٦١) آياتها ٥٤ ركوعاتها ٦ بِسْمِ اللَّهِ الرَّحْمَٰنِ الرَّحِيمِ
1. Ha Mim	1. Ḥaa-Meeem.	حمٓ ﴿١﴾
2. This is the revelation from the Beneficent, the Merciful.	2. Tanzeelum Minar-Raḥmaanir-Raḥeem.	تَنزِيلٌ مِّنَ الرَّحْمَٰنِ الرَّحِيمِ ﴿٢﴾
3. The verses (the laws) of this Book have been fully expounded. It is a reading in the Arabic language for the people of knowledge.	3. Kitaabun fuṣṣilat Aayaatuhoo Qur'aanan 'Arabiyyal-liqawmiñy-ya'lamoon.	كِتَابٌ فُصِّلَتْ آيَاتُهُ قُرْآنًا عَرَبِيًّا لِّقَوْمٍ يَعْلَمُونَ ﴿٣﴾
4. It contains glad news and warnings (for the people), but most of them have ignored it (the Quran) and do not listen.	4. Basheerañw-wa naẕeeran fa-a'raḍa akṡaruhum fahum laa yasma'oon.	بَشِيرًا وَنَذِيرًا فَأَعْرَضَ أَكْثَرُهُمْ فَهُمْ لَا يَسْمَعُونَ ﴿٤﴾
5. They say, "Our hearts are covered against and our ears are deaf to whatever you (Muhammad) invite us to. There is a barrier between us and you. So act as you please and we shall act as we please."	5. Wa qaaloo quloobunaa feee akinnatim-mimmaa tad'oonaaa ilayhi wa feee aaẕaaninaa waqruñw-wa mim bayninaa wa baynika ḥijaabun fa'mal innanaa 'aamiloon.	وَقَالُوا قُلُوبُنَا فِي أَكِنَّةٍ مِّمَّا تَدْعُونَا إِلَيْهِ وَفِي آذَانِنَا وَقْرٌ وَمِن بَيْنِنَا وَبَيْنِكَ حِجَابٌ فَاعْمَلْ إِنَّنَا عَامِلُونَ ﴿٥﴾ الثلثة
6. (O Muhammad) say, "I am a human being like you. I have received a revelation saying that your Lord is the only One. So be upright and obedient to Him and seek forgiveness from Him.	6. Qul innamaaa anaa basharum-miṡlukum yooḥaaa ilayya annamaaa ilaahukum Ilaahuñw-Waaḥidun fastaqeemooo ilayhi wastaghfirooh; wa waylul-lil-mushrikeen.	قُلْ إِنَّمَا أَنَا بَشَرٌ مِّثْلُكُمْ يُوحَىٰ إِلَيَّ أَنَّمَا إِلَٰهُكُمْ إِلَٰهٌ وَاحِدٌ فَاسْتَقِيمُوا إِلَيْهِ وَاسْتَغْفِرُوهُ ۗ وَوَيْلٌ لِّلْمُشْرِكِينَ ﴿٦﴾
7. Woe to the pagans, who do not pay Zakat and have no faith in the life to come.	7. Allaẕeena laa yu'toonaz-Zakaata wa hum bil-Aakhirati hum kaafiroon.	الَّذِينَ لَا يُؤْتُونَ الزَّكَاةَ وَهُم بِالْآخِرَةِ هُمْ كَافِرُونَ ﴿٧﴾
8. The righteously striving believers will have a never-ending reward (without being obliged)."	8. Innal-laẕeena aamanoo wa 'amiluṣ-ṣaaliḥaati lahum ajrun ghayru mamnoon.	إِنَّ الَّذِينَ آمَنُوا وَعَمِلُوا الصَّالِحَاتِ لَهُمْ أَجْرٌ غَيْرُ مَمْنُونٍ ﴿٨﴾ ع ٨/١٥
9. Say, "Do you really disbelieve in the One Who created the earth in two days? Do you consider things equal to Him? He is the Lord of the Universe.	9. Qul a'innakum latakfuroona billaẕee khalaqal-arḍa fee yawmayni wa taj'aloona lahooo andaadaa; ẕaalika Rabbul'aalameen.	قُلْ أَئِنَّكُمْ لَتَكْفُرُونَ بِالَّذِي خَلَقَ الْأَرْضَ فِي يَوْمَيْنِ وَتَجْعَلُونَ لَهُ أَندَادًا ۚ ذَٰلِكَ رَبُّ الْعَالَمِينَ ﴿٩﴾

10. In four days He placed the mountains on it, blessed it, and equally measured out sustenance for those who seek sustenance.

10. Wa ja‘ala feehaa rawaasiya min fawqihaa wa baaraka feehaa wa qaddara feehaaa aqwaatahaa feee arba‘ati ayyaamin sawaaa’al-lissaaa’ileen.

وَجَعَلَ فِيْهَا رَوَاسِيَ مِنْ فَوْقِهَا
وَبٰرَكَ فِيْهَا وَقَدَّرَ فِيْهَآ اَقْوَاتَهَا
فِيْٓ اَرْبَعَةِ اَيَّامٍ ؕ سَوَآءً لِّلسَّآئِلِيْنَ ﴿١٠﴾

11. He established His dominance over the sky, which (for that time) was like smoke. Then He told (planed and created) the heavens and the earth, 'Take your shape either willingly or by force.' They said, 'We willingly obey.'"

11. Summas-tawaaa ilas-samaaa’i wa hiya dukhaanun faqaala lahaa wa lil-arḍi’-tiyaa ṭaw‘an aw karhaa; qaalataaa ataynaa ṭaaa’i‘een.

ثُمَّ اسْتَوٰٓى اِلَى السَّمَآءِ وَهِيَ
دُخَانٌ فَقَالَ لَهَا وَلِلْاَرْضِ
ائْتِيَا طَوْعًا اَوْ كَرْهًا ؕ قَالَتَآ
اَتَيْنَا طَآئِعِيْنَ ﴿١١﴾

12. He formed (created) the seven heavens in two days (periods of time) and revealed to each one its task. He decked the sky above the earth with torches (stars) and protected it (from intruders). This is how the design of the Majestic and All-knowing Allah is.

12. Faqaḍaahunna sab‘a samaawaatin fee yawmayni wa awḥaa fee kulli samaaa’in amrahaa; wa zayyannassamaaa’ad-dunyaa bimaṣaabeeḥa wa ḥifẓaa; zaalika taqdeerul-‘Azeezil-‘Aleem.

فَقَضٰىهُنَّ سَبْعَ سَمٰوٰتٍ فِيْ
يَوْمَيْنِ وَاَوْحٰى فِيْ كُلِّ سَمَآءٍ
اَمْرَهَا ؕ وَزَيَّنَّا السَّمَآءَ الدُّنْيَا
بِمَصَابِيْحَ ۖۗ وَحِفْظًا ؕ ذٰلِكَ
تَقْدِيْرُ الْعَزِيْزِ الْعَلِيْمِ ﴿١٢﴾

13. If they ignore (your message), tell them, "I have warned you against a destructive blast of sound like that which struck the people of Ad and Thamud.

13. Fa-in a‘raḍoo faqul anzartukum ṣaa‘iqatam-misla ṣaa‘iqati ‘Aadiñw-wa Samood.

فَاِنْ اَعْرَضُوْا فَقُلْ اَنْذَرْتُكُمْ
صٰعِقَةً مِّثْلَ صٰعِقَةِ عَادٍ وَّثَمُوْدَ ؕ ﴿١٣﴾

14. When Messengers from all sides came to them saying, 'Do not worship anything besides Allah,' they said, 'Had our Lord wanted, He would have sent us angels as messengers. We do not believe in your message.'"

14. Iz jaaa’at-humur-Rusulu mim bayni aydeehim wa min khalfihim allaa ta‘budooo illal-laah; qaaloo law shaaa’a Rabbunaa la-anzala malaaa’ikatan fa-innaa bimaaa ursiltum bihee kaafiroon.

اِذْ جَآءَتْهُمُ الرُّسُلُ مِنْۢ بَيْنِ اَيْدِيْهِمْ
وَمِنْ خَلْفِهِمْ اَلَّا تَعْبُدُوْٓا اِلَّا اللّٰهَ ؕ
قَالُوْا لَوْ شَآءَ رَبُّنَا لَاَنْزَلَ مَلٰٓئِكَةً
فَاِنَّا بِمَآ اُرْسِلْتُمْ بِهٖ كٰفِرُوْنَ ﴿١٤﴾

15. The people of Ad, unjustly seeking dominance on earth, said, "Who is more powerful than us?" Did they not consider that Allah created them and that He is more powerful than they are? They rejected Our revelations.

15. Fa-ammaa ‘Aadun fastakbaroo fil-arḍi bighayril-ḥaqqi wa qaaloo man ashaddu minnaa quwwatan awalam yaraw annal-laahal-lazee khalaqahum Huwa ashaddu minhum quwwah; wa kaanoo bi-Aayaatinaa yajḥadoon.

فَاَمَّا عَادٌ فَاسْتَكْبَرُوْا فِي الْاَرْضِ
بِغَيْرِ الْحَقِّ وَقَالُوْا مَنْ اَشَدُّ مِنَّا
قُوَّةً ؕ اَوَلَمْ يَرَوْا اَنَّ اللّٰهَ الَّذِيْ
خَلَقَهُمْ هُوَ اَشَدُّ مِنْهُمْ قُوَّةً ؕ وَ
كَانُوْا بِاٰيٰتِنَا يَجْحَدُوْنَ ﴿١٥﴾

16. We sent upon them a violent (cold) wind during a few ill-fated days to make them suffer a disgraceful torment in this life. Their torment in the life to come

16. Fa-arsalnaa ‘alayhim reeḥan ṣarṣaran feee ayyaamin naḥisaatil-linuzeeqahum ‘azaabal-khizyi fil-ḥayaatid-dunyaa wa

فَاَرْسَلْنَا عَلَيْهِمْ رِيْحًا صَرْصَرًا فِيْٓ
اَيَّامٍ نَّحِسَاتٍ لِّنُذِيْقَهُمْ عَذَابَ
الْخِزْيِ فِي الْحَيٰوةِ الدُّنْيَا ؕ وَ

will be even more disgraceful and they will not receive any help.

la'az̲aabul-Aakhirati akhzaa wa hum laa yunṣaroon.

لَعَذَابُ الْاٰخِرَةِ اَخْزٰى وَهُمْ
لَا يُنْصَرُوْنَ ﴿١٦﴾

17. We sent guidance to the people of Thamud but they preferred blindness to guidance so a humiliating blast of torment struck them for their evil deeds.

17. Wa ammaa S̲amoodu fahadaynaahum fastaḥabbul-'amaa 'alal-hudaa fa-akhaz̲at-hum ṣaa'iqatul-'az̲aabil-hooni bimaa kaanoo yaksiboon.

وَاَمَّا ثَمُوْدُ فَهَدَيْنٰهُمْ فَاسْتَحَبُّوا
الْعَمٰى عَلَى الْهُدٰى فَاَخَذَتْهُمْ
صٰعِقَةُ الْعَذَابِ الْهُوْنِ بِمَا
كَانُوْا يَكْسِبُوْنَ ﴿١٧﴾

18. We rescued only the believers who had fear (of Allah).

18. Wa najjaynal-laz̲eena aamanoo wa kaanoo yattaqoon.

وَنَجَّيْنَا الَّذِيْنَ اٰمَنُوْا وَكَانُوْا
يَتَّقُوْنَ ﴿١٨﴾ ع ٢ ١٦

19. There will be the day when the enemies of Allah will be made to surge toward the fire and spurred on

19. Wa Yawma yuḥsharu a'daaa'ul-laahi ilan-Naari fa-hum yooza'oon.

وَيَوْمَ يُحْشَرُ اَعْدَآءُ اللّٰهِ اِلَى
النَّارِ فَهُمْ يُوْزَعُوْنَ ﴿١٩﴾

20. until (on the brink of it) their eyes, ears, and skin will testify to their deeds.

20. Ḥattaaa iz̲aa maa jaaa'oo-haa shahida 'alayhim sam'u-hum wa abṣaaruhum wa juloo-duhum bimaa kaanoo ya'ma-loon.

حَتّٰٓى اِذَا مَا جَآءُوْهَا شَهِدَ عَلَيْهِمْ
سَمْعُهُمْ وَاَبْصَارُهُمْ وَجُلُوْدُهُمْ بِمَا
كَانُوْا يَعْمَلُوْنَ ﴿٢٠﴾

21. They will ask their own skin, "Why did you testify against us?" They will reply, "Allah, who has made everything speak, made us also speak. It was He Who created you in the first place and to Him you have returned.

21. Wa qaaloo lijuloodihim lima shahittum 'alaynaa qaalooo anṭaqanal-laahul-laz̲eee anṭaqa kulla shay'iñw-wa Huwa khalaqakum awwala marratiñw-wa ilayhi turja'oon.

وَقَالُوْا لِجُلُوْدِهِمْ لِمَ شَهِدْتُّمْ عَلَيْنَا
قَالُوْٓا اَنْطَقَنَا اللّٰهُ الَّذِيْٓ اَنْطَقَ كُلَّ
شَيْءٍ وَّهُوَ خَلَقَكُمْ اَوَّلَ مَرَّةٍ وَّ
اِلَيْهِ تُرْجَعُوْنَ ﴿٢١﴾

22. You did not (think) to hide your deeds from your ears, eyes, and skin (private parts) and you felt that Allah would not know all that you had been doing.

22. Wa maa kuntum tastati-roona añy-yashhada 'alaykum sam'ukum wa laaa abṣaarukum wa laa juloodukum wa laakin ẓanantum annal-laaha laa ya'lamu kas̲eeram-mimmaa ta'maloon.

وَمَا كُنْتُمْ تَسْتَتِرُوْنَ اَنْ يَّشْهَدَ
عَلَيْكُمْ سَمْعُكُمْ وَلَآ اَبْصَارُكُمْ وَلَا
جُلُوْدُكُمْ وَلٰكِنْ ظَنَنْتُمْ اَنَّ اللّٰهَ لَا
يَعْلَمُ كَثِيْرًا مِّمَّا تَعْمَلُوْنَ ﴿٢٢﴾

23. This was how you considered your Lord, but He knows you better than you know yourselves. Thus, you are suffering loss."

23. Wa z̲aalikum ẓannuku-mul-laz̲ee ẓanantum bi-Rabbi-kum ardaakum fa-aṣbaḥtum minal-khaasireen.

وَذٰلِكُمْ ظَنُّكُمُ الَّذِيْ ظَنَنْتُمْ بِرَبِّكُمْ
اَرْدٰىكُمْ فَاَصْبَحْتُمْ مِّنَ الْخٰسِرِيْنَ ﴿٢٣﴾

24. Even if they were to exercise patience, their dwelling would still be hellfire (in total loss and humiliation). Even if they were to seek for a chance to correct themselves they would receive none.

24. Fa-iñy-yaṣbiroo fan-Naaru mas̲wal-lahum wa iñy-yasta'tiboo famaa hum minal mu'tabeen.

فَاِنْ يَّصْبِرُوْا فَالنَّارُ مَثْوًى لَّهُمْ
وَاِنْ يَّسْتَعْتِبُوْا فَمَا هُمْ مِّنَ
الْمُعْتَبِيْنَ ﴿٢٤﴾

25. We assigned for them companions who would make their past and present (deeds) seem attractive to them. Thus, they became subject to what the jinn and human beings before were destined to suffer. They indeed were lost (and failed).

25. Wa qayyaḍnaa lahum quranaaa'a fazayyanoo lahum maa bayna aydeehim wa maa khalfahum wa ḥaqqa 'alay-himul-qawlu feee umamin qad khalat min qablihim minal-jinni wal-insi innahum kaanoo khaasireen.

وَقَيَّضْنَا لَهُمْ قُرَنَآءَ فَزَيَّنُوا لَهُمْ
مَّا بَيْنَ اَيْدِيهِمْ وَمَا خَلْفَهُمْ
وَحَقَّ عَلَيْهِمُ الْقَوْلُ فِيٓ اُمَمٍ قَدْ
خَلَتْ مِنْ قَبْلِهِمْ مِّنَ الْجِنِّ وَ
الْاِنْسِ ۚ اِنَّهُمْ كَانُوا خٰسِرِيْنَ ﴿٢٥﴾ ع ١٧

26. The unbelievers say, "Do not listen to this Quran but make a lot of unnecessary noise while it is being read so that perhaps you will overcome (its challenge)."

26. Wa qaalal-lazeena kafaroo laa tasma'oo lihaazal-Qur'aani walghaw feehi la'allakum taghliboon.

وَقَالَ الَّذِيْنَ كَفَرُوْا لَا تَسْمَعُوْا
لِهٰذَا الْقُرْاٰنِ وَالْغَوْا فِيْهِ لَعَلَّكُمْ
تَغْلِبُوْنَ ﴿٢٦﴾

27. We shall certainly make the unbelievers suffer severe torment and will punish them for their evil deeds.

27. Falanuzeeqannal-lazeena kafaroo 'azaaban shadeedañw-wa lanajziyannahum aswa-allazee kaanoo ya'maloon.

فَلَنُذِيْقَنَّ الَّذِيْنَ كَفَرُوْا عَذَابًا
شَدِيْدًا ۙ وَّلَنَجْزِيَنَّهُمْ اَسْوَاَ الَّذِيْ
كَانُوْا يَعْمَلُوْنَ ﴿٢٧﴾

28. The recompense of the enemies of Allah for their rejection of Our revelations will be fire as their eternal dwelling.

28. Zaalika jazaaa'u a'daaa'il-laahin-Naaru lahum feehaa daarul-khuld; jazaaa'am bimaa kaanoo bi Aayaatinaa yajḥa-doon.

ذٰلِكَ جَزَآءُ اَعْدَآءِ اللّٰهِ النَّارُ ۚ
لَهُمْ فِيْهَا دَارُ الْخُلْدِ ۖ جَزَآءًۢ بِمَا
كَانُوْا بِاٰيٰتِنَا يَجْحَدُوْنَ ﴿٢٨﴾

29. The unbelievers will say, "Lord, show us the human beings and jinn who caused us to go astray. We shall place them under our feet to lower them."

29. Wa qaalal-lazeena kafaroo Rabbanaaa arinal-lazayni aḍal-laanaa minal-jinni wal-insi naj'alhumaa taḥta aqdaaminaa liyakoonaa minal-asfaleen.

وَقَالَ الَّذِيْنَ كَفَرُوْا رَبَّنَآ اَرِنَا
الَّذَيْنِ اَضَلّٰنَا مِنَ الْجِنِّ وَالْاِنْسِ
نَجْعَلْهُمَا تَحْتَ اَقْدَامِنَا لِيَكُوْنَا
مِنَ الْاَسْفَلِيْنَ ﴿٢٩﴾

30. To those who have said, "Allah is our Lord," and who have remained steadfast in their belief, the angels will descend (at the time of their death), saying, "Do not be afraid or grieved. Receive the glad news of the Paradise which was promised to you.

30. Innal-lazeena qaaloo Rab-bunal-laahu summas-taqaamoo tatanazzalu 'alayhimul malaaa-'ikatu allaa takhaafoo wa laa taḥzanoo wa abshiroo bil-Jannatil-latee kuntum too'a-doon.

اِنَّ الَّذِيْنَ قَالُوْا رَبُّنَا اللّٰهُ ثُمَّ
اسْتَقَامُوْا تَتَنَزَّلُ عَلَيْهِمُ الْمَلٰٓئِكَةُ
اَلَّا تَخَافُوْا وَلَا تَحْزَنُوْا وَاَبْشِرُوْا
بِالْجَنَّةِ الَّتِيْ كُنْتُمْ تُوْعَدُوْنَ ﴿٣٠﴾

31. We were your protectors (against Satan) in this world and in the life to come (at the time of your death and onwards), where you will have whatever you call for,

31. Naḥnu awliyaaa'ukum fil-ḥayaatid-dunyaa wa fil-Aakhi-rati wa lakum feehaa maa tashtaheee anfusukum wa lakum feehaa maa tadda'oon.

نَحْنُ اَوْلِيٰٓؤُكُمْ فِي الْحَيٰوةِ الدُّنْيَا
وَفِي الْاٰخِرَةِ ۚ وَلَكُمْ فِيْهَا مَا
تَشْتَهِيْٓ اَنْفُسُكُمْ وَلَكُمْ فِيْهَا مَا
تَدَّعُوْنَ ﴿٣١﴾

ع ۷ ۱۸

32. a hospitable welcome from the All-forgiving and All-merciful Allah."

32. Nuzulam-min Ghafoorir-Raḥeem.

نُزُلًا مِّنْ غَفُوْرٍ رَّحِيْمٍ ﴿٣٢﴾

33. Who speaks better than one who invites human beings to Allah, acts righteously, and says, "I am a Muslim?"

33. Wa man aḥsanu qawlam-mimman da'aaa ilal-laahi wa 'amila ṣaaliḥañw-wa qaala innanee minal-muslimeen.

وَمَنْ اَحْسَنُ قَوْلًا مِّمَّنْ دَعَآ اِلَى
اللّٰهِ وَعَمِلَ صَالِحًا وَّقَالَ اِنَّنِيْ
مِنَ الْمُسْلِمِيْنَ ﴿٣٣﴾

34. Virtue and evil are not equal. If you replace evil habits by virtuous ones, you will certainly find that your enemies will become your intimate friends.

34. Wa laa tastawil-ḥasanatu wa las-sayyi'ah; idfa' billatee hiya aḥsanu fa-izal-lazee baynaka wa baynahoo 'adaawatun ka-annahoo waliyyun ḥameem.

وَلَا تَسْتَوِى الْحَسَنَةُ وَلَا السَّيِّئَةُ ؕ
اِدْفَعْ بِالَّتِيْ هِيَ اَحْسَنُ فَاِذَا الَّذِيْ
بَيْنَكَ وَبَيْنَهٗ عَدَاوَةٌ كَاَنَّهٗ
وَلِيٌّ حَمِيْمٌ ﴿٣٤﴾

35. Only those who exercise patience and who have been granted a great share of Allah's favor can find such an opportunity.

35. Wa maa yulaqqaahaaa illal-lazeena ṣabaroo wa maa yulaqqaahaaa illaa zoo ḥaẓẓin 'aẓeem.

وَمَا يُلَقّٰىهَآ اِلَّا الَّذِيْنَ صَبَرُوْا ۚ
وَمَا يُلَقّٰىهَآ اِلَّا ذُوْ حَظٍّ عَظِيْمٍ ﴿٣٥﴾

36. (Muhammad), seek Allah's protection if Satan's temptation grieves you, for Allah is All-hearing and All-knowing.

36. Wa immaa yanzaghannaka minash-Shayṭaani nazghun fasta'iz billaahi innahoo Huwas-Samee'ul-'Aleem.

وَاِمَّا يَنْزَغَنَّكَ مِنَ الشَّيْطٰنِ نَزْغٌ
فَاسْتَعِذْ بِاللّٰهِ ؕ اِنَّهٗ هُوَ السَّمِيْعُ
الْعَلِيْمُ ﴿٣٦﴾

37. (Of the evidence of His existence) are the night, day, sun, and moon. Do not prostrate before the sun and the moon, but prostrate before Allah Who has created them if you want to worship Him alone.

37. Wa min Aayaatihil-laylu wannahaaru washshamsu walqamar; laa tasjudoo lish-shamsi wa laa lilqamari wasjudoo lillaahil-lazee khalaqahunna in kuntum iyyaahu ta'budoon.

وَمِنْ اٰيٰتِهِ الَّيْلُ وَالنَّهَارُ وَالشَّمْسُ
وَالْقَمَرُ ؕ لَا تَسْجُدُوْا لِلشَّمْسِ وَلَا
لِلْقَمَرِ وَاسْجُدُوْا لِلّٰهِ الَّذِيْ خَلَقَهُنَّ
اِنْ كُنْتُمْ اِيَّاهُ تَعْبُدُوْنَ ﴿٣٧﴾

(Bow Down)

38. However, if people are very arrogant to prostrate before your Lord, allow them to know that Allah's other creatures glorify Him both day and night without fatigue.

38. Fa-inis-takbaroo fallazeena 'inda Rabbika yusabbiḥoona lahoo billayli wannahaari wa hum laa yas'amoon.

فَاِنِ اسْتَكْبَرُوْا فَالَّذِيْنَ عِنْدَ
رَبِّكَ يُسَبِّحُوْنَ لَهٗ بِالَّيْلِ وَالنَّهَارِ
وَهُمْ لَا يَسْئَمُوْنَ ﴿٣٨﴾ السجدة

السجدة ١١

39. Further evidence is that (at times) you find the earth to be calm and humble (barren). When We send upon it water, it moves and swells (to let the plants grow). The One who brings it back to life will also bring the dead back to life. He has power over all things.

39. Wa min Aayaatiheee annaka taral-arḍa khaashi'atan fa-izaaa anzalnaa 'alayhal-maaa'ahtazzat wa rabat; innal-lazeee aḥyaahaa lamuḥyil-mawtaa; innahoo 'alaa kulli shay'in Qadeer.

وَمِنْ اٰيٰتِهٖٓ اَنَّكَ تَرَى الْاَرْضَ
خَاشِعَةً فَاِذَآ اَنْزَلْنَا عَلَيْهَا الْمَآءَ
اهْتَزَّتْ وَرَبَتْ ؕ اِنَّ الَّذِيْٓ اَحْيَاهَا
لَمُحْيِ الْمَوْتٰى ؕ اِنَّهٗ عَلٰى كُلِّ شَيْءٍ
قَدِيْرٌ ﴿٣٩﴾

40. Those who reject Our revelations are not hidden from

40. Innal-lazeena yulḥidoona feee Aayaatinaa

اِنَّ الَّذِيْنَ يُلْحِدُوْنَ فِيْٓ اٰيٰتِنَا

Us. Is the one who will be thrown into hellfire better than the one who will be brought safely into the presence of Allah on the Day of Judgment? Act as you wish; Allah is Well-aware of whatever you do.

laa yakhfawna 'alaynaa; afamañy-yulqaa fin-Naari khayrun am mañy-ya-teee aaminañy-Yawmal-Qiyaamah; i'maloo maa shi'tum innahoo bimaa ta'maloona Başeer.

لَا يَخْفَوْنَ عَلَيْنَا ۗ اَفَمَنْ يُّلْقٰى
فِي النَّارِ خَيْرٌ اَمْ مَّنْ يَّاْتِيْٓ اٰمِنًا
يَّوْمَ الْقِيٰمَةِ ۗ اِعْمَلُوْا مَا شِئْتُمْ ۙ
اِنَّهٗ بِمَا تَعْمَلُوْنَ بَصِيْرٌ ﴿٤٠﴾

41. There are those who disbelieved in Al-Dhikr (the Quran) when it was sent to them, but it certainly is a glorious Book.

41. Innal lazeena kafaroo biz-Zikri lammaa jaa'ahum wa innahoo la-Kitaabun 'Azeez.

اِنَّ الَّذِيْنَ كَفَرُوْا بِالذِّكْرِ لَمَّا
جَآءَهُمْ ۚ وَاِنَّهٗ لَكِتٰبٌ عَزِيْزٌ ﴿٤١﴾

42. Falsehood cannot reach it from any direction. It is the revelation from the All-wise, Praiseworthy One.

42. Laa ya-teehil-baaţilu mim bayni yadayhi wa laa min khalfihee tanzeelum-min Ḥakeemin Ḥameed.

لَّا يَاْتِيْهِ الْبَاطِلُ مِنْۢ بَيْنِ يَدَيْهِ
وَلَا مِنْ خَلْفِهٖ ۗ تَنْزِيْلٌ مِّنْ
حَكِيْمٍ حَمِيْدٍ ﴿٤٢﴾

43. Nothing has been said to you which was not said to the Messengers who lived before you. Your Lord is certainly All-forgiving, but stern in His retribution.

43. Maa yuqaalu laka illaa maa qad qeela lir-Rusuli min qablik; inna Rabbaka lazoo maghfiratiñw-wa zoo 'iqaabin aleem.

مَا يُقَالُ لَكَ اِلَّا مَا قَدْ قِيْلَ لِلرُّسُلِ
مِنْ قَبْلِكَ ۗ اِنَّ رَبَّكَ لَذُوْ مَغْفِرَةٍ
وَّذُوْ عِقَابٍ اَلِيْمٍ ﴿٤٣﴾

44. Had We sent down this Quran in a non-Arabic language, they would have said, "Why have its verses not been well expounded?" A non-Arabic book and an Arabic speaking person! (O Muhammad), say, "It is a guide and a cure for the believers. As for those who do not believe, they are deaf and blind. It is as though they had been called from a distant place."

44. Wa law ja'alnaahu Qur'aa-nan A'jamiyyal-laqaaloo law laa fuşşilat Aayaatuhooo 'A-a'jamiyyuñw-wa 'Arabiyy; qul huwa lillazeena aamanoo hudañw-wa shifaaa'; wallazeena laa yu'minoona feee aazaanihim waqruñw-wa huwa 'alayhim 'amaa; ulaaa'ika yunaadawna mim-makaanim ba'eed.

وَلَوْ جَعَلْنٰهُ قُرْاٰنًا اَعْجَمِيًّا لَّقَالُوْا
لَوْلَا فُصِّلَتْ اٰيٰتُهٗ ۗ ءَاَعْجَمِيٌّ وَّ
عَرَبِيٌّ ۗ قُلْ هُوَ لِلَّذِيْنَ اٰمَنُوْا هُدًى
وَّشِفَآءٌ ۗ وَالَّذِيْنَ لَا يُؤْمِنُوْنَ فِيْٓ
اٰذَانِهِمْ وَقْرٌ وَّهُوَ عَلَيْهِمْ عَمًى ۗ
اُولٰٓئِكَ يُنَادَوْنَ مِنْ مَّكَانٍۢ بَعِيْدٍ ﴿٤٤﴾

45. We had given the Book to Moses about which people greatly disagreed. Had the word of your Lord not been decreed, He would have certainly settled their differences (there and then). They were greatly suspicious and doubtful about the Book of Moses.

45. Wa laqad aataynaa Moosal-Kitaaba fakhtulifa feeh; wa law laa Kalimatun sabaqat mir-Rabbika laquḍiya baynahum; wa innahum lafee shakkim-minhu mureeb.

وَلَقَدْ اٰتَيْنَا مُوْسَى الْكِتٰبَ فَاخْتُلِفَ
فِيْهِ ۗ وَلَوْلَا كَلِمَةٌ سَبَقَتْ مِنْ
رَّبِّكَ لَقُضِيَ بَيْنَهُمْ ۗ وَاِنَّهُمْ لَفِيْ
شَكٍّ مِّنْهُ مُرِيْبٍ ﴿٤٥﴾

46. Whoever acts righteously does so for his own good and whoever commits evil does so against his soul. Your Lord is not unjust to His servants.

46. Man 'amila şaaliḥan falinafsihee wa man asaaa'a fa'alayhaa; wamaa Rabbuka bizallaamil-lil'abeed.

مَنْ عَمِلَ صَالِحًا فَلِنَفْسِهٖ ۚ وَمَنْ
اَسَآءَ فَعَلَيْهَا ۗ وَمَا رَبُّكَ بِظَلَّامٍ
لِّلْعَبِيْدِ ﴿٤٦﴾

اِلَيْهِ يُرَدُّ عِلْمُ السَّاعَةِ ۗ وَمَا

قرء حفص بتسهيل الهمزة الثانية ١٢

ع ٢ ٥

الجزء الخامس والعشرون (٢٥)

47. It is He who has the knowledge of the Hour of Doom and the fruits that will come out of their covering. He knows what the females conceive and deliver. On the day when the unbelievers will be asked, "Where are the idols which you considered equal to Allah?" they will reply, "We informed you that none of us have seen them."

48. Whatever they had worshipped before will disappear and they will then know that there is no way for them to escape.

49. The human being never tires of asking for good, but if he is afflicted by hardship, he despairs and gives up all hope.

50. When We grant him mercy after his suffering, he (boldly) says, "This is what I deserved. I do not think that there will ever be a Day of Judgment. Even if I will be returned to my Lord, I shall still deserve to receive better rewards from Him." We shall certainly tell the unbelievers about their deeds and cause them to suffer a severe punishment.

51. When We grant the human being a favor, he ignores it and turns away, but when he is afflicted by hardship, he starts lengthy prayers.

52. Say, "Think, if the (Quran) is from Allah and you have rejected it, then who has gone farther astray than the one who has wandered far from the truth?

52. We shall (continue to) show them Our evidence in the world and within their souls until it becomes clear that He is the Truth. Was it not sufficient for

47. Ilayhi yuraddu 'ilmus-Saaa'ah; wa maa takhruju min samaraatim-min akmaamihaa wa maa taḥmilu min unsaa wa laa taḍa'u illaa bi'ilmih; wa Yawma yunaadeehim ayna shurakaaa'ee qaalooo aazannaaka maa minnaa min shaheed.

48. Wa ḍalla 'anhum maa kaanoo yad'oona min qablu wa ẓannoo maa lahum mimmaḥeeṣ.

49. Laa yas'amul-insaanu min du'aaa'il-khayri wa immassahush-sharru faya'oosun qanooṭ.

50. Wa la-in azaqnaahu raḥmatam-minnaa mim ba'di ḍarraaa'a massathu la-yaqoolanna haazaa lee wa maaa aẓunnus-Saa'ata qaaa'imatañw-wa la'in-ruji'tu ilaa Rabbeee inna lee 'indahoo lalḥusnaa; falanunabbi'annal-lazeena kafaroo bimaa 'amiloo wa lanuzeeqannahum min 'azaabin ghaleeẓ.

51. Wa izaaa an'amnaa 'alal-insaani a'raḍa wa na-aa bijaanibihee wa izaa massahush-sharru fazoo du'aaa'in 'areeḍ.

52. Qul ara'aytum in kaana min 'indil-laahi summa kafartum bihee man aḍallu mimman huwa fee shiqaaqim ba'eed.

53. Sanureehim Aayaatinaa fil-aafaaqi wa feee anfusihim ḥattaa yatabayyana lahum annahul-ḥaqq; awa lam yakfi bi-Rabbika annahoo

تَخْرُجُ مِنْ ثَمَرٰتٍ مِّنْ اَكْمَامِهَا
وَمَا تَحْمِلُ مِنْ اُنْثٰى وَلَا تَضَعُ
اِلَّا بِعِلْمِهٖ ؕ وَيَوْمَ يُنَادِيْهِمْ
اَيْنَ شُرَكَآءِىْ ۙ قَالُوْٓا اٰذَنّٰكَ ۙ
مَا مِنَّا مِنْ شَهِيْدٍ ﴿٤٧﴾
وَضَلَّ عَنْهُمْ مَّا كَانُوْا يَدْعُوْنَ
مِنْ قَبْلُ وَظَنُّوْا مَا لَهُمْ مِّنْ
مَّحِيْصٍ ﴿٤٨﴾
لَا يَسْـَٔمُ الْاِنْسَانُ مِنْ دُعَآءِ الْخَيْرِ ؗ
وَاِنْ مَّسَّهُ الشَّرُّ فَيَـُٔوْسٌ قَنُوْطٌ ﴿٤٩﴾
وَلَئِنْ اَذَقْنٰهُ رَحْمَةً مِّنَّا مِنْۢ بَعْدِ
ضَرَّآءَ مَسَّتْهُ لَيَقُوْلَنَّ هٰذَا لِىْ ۙ
وَمَآ اَظُنُّ السَّاعَةَ قَآئِمَةً ۙ وَّلَئِنْ
رُّجِعْتُ اِلٰى رَبِّىْٓ اِنَّ لِىْ عِنْدَهٗ
لَلْحُسْنٰى ۚ فَلَنُنَبِّئَنَّ الَّذِيْنَ كَفَرُوْا
بِمَا عَمِلُوْا ؗ وَلَنُذِيْقَنَّهُمْ مِّنْ
عَذَابٍ غَلِيْظٍ ﴿٥٠﴾
وَاِذَآ اَنْعَمْنَا عَلَى الْاِنْسَانِ اَعْرَضَ
وَنَاٰ بِجَانِبِهٖ ۚ وَاِذَا مَسَّهُ الشَّرُّ فَذُوْ
دُعَآءٍ عَرِيْضٍ ﴿٥١﴾
قُلْ اَرَءَيْتُمْ اِنْ كَانَ مِنْ عِنْدِ
اللّٰهِ ثُمَّ كَفَرْتُمْ بِهٖ مَنْ اَضَلُّ
مِمَّنْ هُوَ فِىْ شِقَاقٍۢ بَعِيْدٍ ﴿٥٢﴾
سَنُرِيْهِمْ اٰيٰتِنَا فِى الْاٰفَاقِ وَفِىْٓ
اَنْفُسِهِمْ حَتّٰى يَتَبَيَّنَ لَهُمْ اَنَّهُ
الْحَقُّ ؕ اَوَلَمْ يَكْفِ بِرَبِّكَ اَنَّهٗ

you that your Lord witnesses all things?

'alaa kulli shay'in Shaheed.

عَلٰى كُلِّ شَيْءٍ شَهِيْدٌ ﴿٥٣﴾

54. They are certainly doubtful about their meeting with their Lord. Allah indeed encompasses all things.

54. Alaaa innahum fee miryatim-mil-liqaaa'i Rabbihim; alaaa innahoo bikulli shay'im-muḥeeṭ.

اَلَآ اِنَّهُمْ فِيْ مِرْيَةٍ مِّنْ لِّقَآءِ
رَبِّهِمْ ۗ اَلَآ اِنَّهٗ بِكُلِّ شَيْءٍ مُّحِيْطٌ ﴿٥٤﴾ ع ١٠/٢

Al-Shura, The Counsel (42)

In the Name of Allah, the Beneficent, the Merciful.

Sûrat ash-Shûrâ

(Revealed at Makkah)

Bismillaahir Rah&maanir Rah&eem

(٤٢) سُوْرَةُ الشُّوْرٰى مَكِّيَّةٌ (٦٢)

اٰیاتُها ٥٣ بِسْمِ اللّٰهِ الرَّحْمٰنِ الرَّحِيْمِ رُکوعاتُها ٥

1. Ha. Mim

1. Ḥaa-Meeem.

حٰمٓ ﴿١﴾

2. Ayn. Sin. Qaf

2. 'Ayyyn-Seeen-Qaaaf.

عٓسٓقٓ ﴿٢﴾

3. (Muhammad), this is how Allah, the Majestic and All-wise, sends revelations to you and sent them to those who lived before you.

3. Kaẕaalika yooḥeee ilayka wa ilal-laẕeena min qablikal-laahul-'Azeezul-Ḥakeem.

كَذٰلِكَ يُوْحِيْٓ اِلَيْكَ وَاِلَى الَّذِيْنَ
مِنْ قَبْلِكَ ۙ اللّٰهُ الْعَزِيْزُ الْحَكِيْمُ ﴿٣﴾

4. To Him belongs all that is in the heavens and the earth. He is the Most High and the Most Great.

4. Lahoo maa fis-samaawaati wa maa fil-arḍi wa Huwal 'Aliyyul-'Aẓeem.

لَهٗ مَا فِي السَّمٰوٰتِ وَمَا فِي الْاَرْضِ ۭ
وَهُوَ الْعَلِيُّ الْعَظِيْمُ ﴿٤﴾

5. (When the revelation passes through) the heavens, they almost break apart. At that time the angels glorify their Lord with His praise and seek forgiveness for those who live on earth. Allah is certainly All-forgiving and All-merciful.

5. Takaadus-samaawaatu yatafaṭṭarna min fawqihinna walmalaaa'ikatu yusabbiḥoona biḥamdi Rabbihim wa yastaghfiroona liman fil-arḍ; alaaa innal-laaha Huwal-Ghafoorur-Raḥeem.

تَكَادُ السَّمٰوٰتُ يَتَفَطَّرْنَ مِنْ
فَوْقِهِنَّ وَالْمَلٰۗىِٕكَةُ يُسَبِّحُوْنَ
بِحَمْدِ رَبِّهِمْ وَيَسْتَغْفِرُوْنَ لِمَنْ
فِي الْاَرْضِ ۭ اَلَآ اِنَّ اللّٰهَ هُوَ
الْغَفُوْرُ الرَّحِيْمُ ﴿٥﴾

6. Allah is the guardian of even those who have chosen others (idols) besides Him as their guardians, (Muhammad), you will not have to answer for them.

6. Wallaẕeenat-takhaẕoo min dooniheee awliyaaa'al-laahu Ḥafeeẓun 'alayhim wa maaa anta 'alayhim biwakeel.

وَالَّذِيْنَ اتَّخَذُوْا مِنْ دُوْنِهٖٓ
اَوْلِيَاۗءَ اللّٰهُ حَفِيْظٌ عَلَيْهِمْ ڮ وَمَآ
اَنْتَ عَلَيْهِمْ بِوَكِيْلٍ ﴿٦﴾

7. We have revealed the Quran to you in the Arabic language so that you could warn the people of the Mother Town (Makkah) and those around it of the inevitable Day of Resurrection when some will go to Paradise and others to burning (hell).

7. Wa kaẕaalika awḥaynaaa ilayka Qur'aanan 'Arabiyyal-litunẕira Ummal-Quraa wa man ḥawlahaa wa tunẕira Yawmal-Jam'i laa rayba feeh; fareequn fil-Jannati wa fareequn fis-sa'eer.

وَكَذٰلِكَ اَوْحَيْنَآ اِلَيْكَ قُرْاٰنًا
عَرَبِيًّا لِّتُنْذِرَ اُمَّ الْقُرٰى وَمَنْ
حَوْلَهَا وَتُنْذِرَ يَوْمَ الْجَمْعِ لَا رَيْبَ
فِيْهِ ۭ فَرِيْقٌ فِي الْجَنَّةِ وَفَرِيْقٌ
فِي السَّعِيْرِ ﴿٧﴾

8. Had Allah wanted, He could have made them all one single nation (infallible like angels), but He grants His mercy

8. Wa law shaaa'al-laahu laja'alahum ummatañw-waaḥidatañw-walaakiñy-yudkhilu mañy-yashaaa'u

وَلَوْ شَاۗءَ اللّٰهُ لَجَعَلَهُمْ اُمَّةً
وَّاحِدَةً وَّلٰكِنْ يُّدْخِلُ مَنْ يَّشَاۗءُ

to whomever He wills. The unjust will have no guardian or helper.

fee raḥmatih; waẓ-ẓaalimoona maa lahum miñw-waliyyiñw-wa laa naṣeer.

فِىْ رَحْمَتِهٖ ؕ وَالظّٰلِمُوْنَ مَا لَهُمْ
مِّنْ وَّلِىٍّ وَّلَا نَصِيْرٍ ﴿٨﴾

9. Have they chosen other guardians besides Him? Allah is the real Guardian and it is He who will bring the dead back to life. He has power over all things.

9. Amit-takhazoo min dooniheee awliyaaa'a fallaahu Huwal-Waliyyu wa Huwa yuḥyil-mawtaa wa Huwa 'alaa kulli shay'in Qadeer.

اَمِ اتَّخَذُوْا مِنْ دُوْنِهٖۤ اَوْلِيَآءَ ۚ
فَاللّٰهُ هُوَ الْوَلِىُّ وَهُوَ يُحْىِ الْمَوْتٰى ؗ
وَهُوَ عَلٰى كُلِّ شَىْءٍ قَدِيْرٌ ﴿٩﴾ ع ٩ ٢

10. Whatever differences you may have about the Quran, the final decision (to be made on the Day of Judgment) rests with Allah. This is how Allah my Lord decides. In Him do I trust and to Him do I turn in repentance.

10. Wa makh-talaftum feehi min shay'in faḥukmuhooo ilal-laah; zaalikumul-laahu Rabbee 'alayhi tawakkaltu wa ilayhi uneeb.

وَمَا اخْتَلَفْتُمْ فِيْهِ مِنْ شَىْءٍ
فَحُكْمُهٗۤ اِلَى اللّٰهِ ؕ ذٰلِكُمُ اللّٰهُ رَبِّىْ
عَلَيْهِ تَوَكَّلْتُ ۖۗ وَاِلَيْهِ اُنِيْبُ ﴿١٠﴾

11. He is the Originator of the heavens and the earth. He has made you and the cattle in pairs and has multiplied you by His creation. There is certainly nothing like Him. He is All-hearing and All-aware.

11. Faaṭirus-samaawaati wal-arḍ; ja'ala lakum min anfusikum azwaajañw-wa minal-an'aami azwaajaa; yazra'ookum feeh; laysa kamislihee shay'; wa Huwas-Samee'ul-Baṣeer.

فَاطِرُ السَّمٰوٰتِ وَالْاَرْضِ ؕ جَعَلَ
لَكُمْ مِّنْ اَنْفُسِكُمْ اَزْوَاجًا وَّمِنَ
الْاَنْعَامِ اَزْوَاجًا ۚ يَذْرَؤُكُمْ
فِيْهِ ؕ لَيْسَ كَمِثْلِهٖ شَىْءٌ ۚ وَهُوَ
السَّمِيْعُ الْبَصِيْرُ ﴿١١﴾

12. In His hands are the keys of the heavens and the earth. He increases and measures the sustenance of whomever He wants. He has the knowledge of all things.

12. Lahoo maqaaleedus-samaawaati wal-arḍi yabsuṭur rizqa limañy-yashaaa'u wa yaqdir; innahoo bikulli shay'in 'Aleem.

لَهٗ مَقَالِيْدُ السَّمٰوٰتِ وَالْاَرْضِ ۚ
يَبْسُطُ الرِّزْقَ لِمَنْ يَّشَآءُ وَيَقْدِرُ ؕ
اِنَّهٗ بِكُلِّ شَىْءٍ عَلِيْمٌ ﴿١٢﴾

13. He has plainly clarified the religion which is revealed to you and that which Noah, Abraham, Moses, and Jesus were commanded to follow, (He has explained it) so that you will learn the laws of the religion and remain united about the issues therein. What you call the pagans to is extremely grave for them. Allah attracts to (the religion) whomever He wants and guides to it whoever turns to Him in repentance.

13. Shara'a lakum minad-deeni maa waṣṣaa bihee Nooḥañw-wallazeee aw-ḥaynaaa ilayka wa maa waṣṣaynaa biheee Ibraaheema wa Moosaa wa 'Eesaaa an aqeemud-deena walaa tatafarraqoo feeh; kabura 'alal-mushrikeena maa tad'oohum ilayh; Allaahu yajtabeee ilayhi mañy-yashaaa'u wa yahdeee ilayhi mañy-yuneeb.

شَرَعَ لَكُمْ مِّنَ الدِّيْنِ مَا وَصّٰى بِهٖ
نُوْحًا وَّالَّذِىْۤ اَوْحَيْنَاۤ اِلَيْكَ
وَمَا وَصَّيْنَا بِهٖۤ اِبْرٰهِيْمَ وَمُوْسٰى
وَعِيْسٰۤى اَنْ اَقِيْمُوا الدِّيْنَ
وَلَا تَتَفَرَّقُوْا فِيْهِ ؕ كَبُرَ عَلَى
الْمُشْرِكِيْنَ مَا تَدْعُوْهُمْ اِلَيْهِ ؕ
اَللّٰهُ يَجْتَبِىْۤ اِلَيْهِ مَنْ يَّشَآءُ
وَيَهْدِىْۤ اِلَيْهِ مَنْ يُّنِيْبُ ﴿١٣﴾

14. Only after receiving the knowledge did people divide themselves into different groups because of rebellion among

14. Wa maa tafarraqooo illaa mim ba'di maa jaaa'ahumul-'ilmu baghyam baynahum; wa law laa

وَمَا تَفَرَّقُوْۤا اِلَّا مِنْۢ بَعْدِ مَا
جَآءَهُمُ الْعِلْمُ بَغْيًاۢ بَيْنَهُمْ ؕ وَلَوْلَا

themselves. Had it not been for your Lord's giving them respite for an appointed time, He would certainly have settled their differences once and for all. Those who inherited the Book from their (quarrelsome) predecessors also were in doubt and in suspicion about it.

Kalimatun sabaqat mir-Rabbika ilaaa ajalim musammal-laquḍiya baynahum; wa innal-lazeena oorisul-Kitaaba mim ba'dihim lafee shakkim minhu mureeb.

كَلِمَةٌ سَبَقَتْ مِن رَّبِّكَ إِلَىٰٓ
أَجَلٍ مُّسَمًّى لَّقُضِيَ بَيْنَهُمْ ۚ وَإِنَّ
الَّذِينَ أُورِثُوا الْكِتَـٰبَ مِن بَعْدِهِمْ
لَفِي شَكٍّ مِّنْهُ مُرِيبٍ ﴿١٤﴾

15. Thus, (Muhammad), preach (My revelation) to the people and be steadfast (in your faith) as you have been commanded. Do not follow their desires but say, "I believe in the Book which Allah has sent down and I have been commanded to exercise justice among you. Allah is our Lord and your Lord. Each of us will be responsible for his deeds. Let there be no disputes among us. Allah will bring us all together and to Him we shall all return."

15. Falizaalika fad'u wastaqim kamaaa umirta wa laa tattabi' ahwaaa'ahum wa qul aamantu bimaaa anzalal-laahu min Kitaab; wa umirtu li-a'dila baynakum Allaahu Rabbunaa wa Rabbukum lanaaa a'maalunaa wa lakum a'maalukum laa ḥujjata baynanaa wa baynakum; Allaahu yajma'u baynanaa wa ilayhil-maṣeer.

فَلِذَٰلِكَ فَادْعُ ۖ وَاسْتَقِمْ كَمَآ
أُمِرْتَ ۖ وَلَا تَتَّبِعْ أَهْوَآءَهُمْ ۖ وَقُلْ
ءَامَنتُ بِمَآ أَنزَلَ اللَّهُ مِن كِتَـٰبٍ ۖ
وَأُمِرْتُ لِأَعْدِلَ بَيْنَكُمُ ۖ اللَّهُ رَبُّنَا
وَرَبُّكُمْ ۖ لَنَآ أَعْمَـٰلُنَا وَلَكُمْ أَعْمَـٰلُكُمْ ۖ
لَا حُجَّةَ بَيْنَنَا وَبَيْنَكُمُ ۖ اللَّهُ يَجْمَعُ
بَيْنَنَا ۖ وَإِلَيْهِ الْمَصِيرُ ﴿١٥﴾

16. The argument of those who quarrel about Allah, after pledging obedience to Him, is void in the eyes of their Lord. Such people will be subject to His wrath and will suffer a severe torment.

16. Wallazeena yuḥaaajjoona fil-laahi mim ba'di mastujeeba lahoo ḥujjatuhum daahiḍatun 'inda Rabbihim wa 'alayhim ghaḍabuñw-wa lahum 'azaabun shadeed.

وَالَّذِينَ يُحَآجُّونَ فِي اللَّهِ مِنۢ
بَعْدِ مَا اسْتُجِيبَ لَهُۥ حُجَّتُهُمْ
دَاحِضَةٌ عِندَ رَبِّهِمْ وَعَلَيْهِمْ
غَضَبٌ وَلَهُمْ عَذَابٌ شَدِيدٌ ﴿١٦﴾

17. It is Allah who revealed the Book and the Balance for a truthful purpose. You never know. Perhaps the Hour of Doom is close at hand.

17. Allaahul-lazeee anzalal Kitaaba bilḥaqqi wal-Meezaan; wa maa yudreeka la'allas-Saa'ata qareeb.

اللَّهُ الَّذِيٓ أَنزَلَ الْكِتَـٰبَ بِالْحَقِّ
وَالْمِيزَانَ ۗ وَمَا يُدْرِيكَ لَعَلَّ
السَّاعَةَ قَرِيبٌ ﴿١٧﴾

18. The unbelievers want you to show them the Day of Judgment immediately while the believers are afraid of it for they know it to be the truth. Those who insist on arguing about the Hour of Doom are certainly in plain error.

18. Yasta'jilu bihal-lazeena laa yu'minoona bihaa wallazeena aamanoo mushfiqoona minhaa wa ya'lamoona annahal-ḥaqq; alaaa innal-lazeena yumaaroona fis-Saa'ati lafee ḍalaalim ba'eed.

يَسْتَعْجِلُ بِهَا الَّذِينَ لَا يُؤْمِنُونَ
بِهَا ۖ وَالَّذِينَ ءَامَنُوا مُشْفِقُونَ
مِنْهَا وَيَعْلَمُونَ أَنَّهَا الْحَقُّ ۗ أَلَآ
إِنَّ الَّذِينَ يُمَارُونَ فِي السَّاعَةِ
لَفِي ضَلَـٰلٍ بَعِيدٍ ﴿١٨﴾

19. Allah is kind to His servants. He gives sustenance to whomever He wants. He is All-powerful and Majestic.

19. Allaahu Laṭeefum bi'ibaadihee yarzuqu mañy-yashaaa'u wa Huwal Qawiyyul-'Azeez.

اللَّهُ لَطِيفٌۢ بِعِبَادِهِۦ يَرْزُقُ مَن
يَشَآءُ ۖ وَهُوَ الْقَوِيُّ الْعَزِيزُ ﴿١٩﴾ ع ١٠ ٣

20. We shall increase the harvest of those who seek a good

20. Man kaana yureedu ḥarsal-Aakhirati

مَن كَانَ يُرِيدُ حَرْثَ الْـَٔاخِرَةِ

harvest (reward) in the life hereafter. However, those who want to have their harvest in this life will be given it, but will have no share in the hereafter.

nazid lahoo fee ḥarsihee wa man kaana yureedu ḥarsad-dunyaa nu'tihee minhaa wa maa lahoo fil-Aakhirati min naṣeeb.

نَزِدْ لَهٗ فِيْ حَرْثِهٖ ۚ وَمَنْ كَانَ
يُرِيْدُ حَرْثَ الدُّنْيَا نُؤْتِهٖ مِنْهَا ۙ
وَمَا لَهٗ فِي الْاٰخِرَةِ مِنْ نَّصِيْبٍ ﴿٢٠﴾

21. Do they have idols who have established a religion without having had the permission of Allah? Had it not been for your Lord's word, giving them respite for an appointed time, He would certainly have settled their differences once and for all. The unjust will certainly suffer a painful torment.

21. Am lahum shurakaaa'u shara'oo lahum minad-deeni maa lam ya-zam bihil-laah; wa law laa Kalimatul-faṣli laquḍiya baynahum; wa innaẓ-ẓaalimeena lahum 'azaabun aleem.

اَمْ لَهُمْ شُرَكٰٓؤُا شَرَعُوْا لَهُمْ مِّنَ
الدِّيْنِ مَا لَمْ يَاْذَنْ بِهِ اللّٰهُ ؕ وَلَوْلَا
كَلِمَةُ الْفَصْلِ لَقُضِيَ بَيْنَهُمْ ؕ
وَاِنَّ الظّٰلِمِيْنَ لَهُمْ عَذَابٌ اَلِيْمٌ ﴿٢١﴾

22. You can see that the unjust are afraid of the consequences of their deeds which will inevitably strike them. However, the righteously striving believers will live in the gardens wherein they will have whatever they want from their Lord. This is certainly the greatest reward.

22. Taraẓ-ẓaalimeena mushfiqeena mimmaa kasaboo wa huwa waaqi'um bihim; wallazeena aamanoo wa 'amiluṣ-ṣaaliḥaati fee rawḍaatil-Jannaati lahum maa yashaaa'oona 'inda Rabbihim; zaalika huwal-faḍlul-kabeer.

تَرَى الظّٰلِمِيْنَ مُشْفِقِيْنَ مِمَّا
كَسَبُوْا وَهُوَ وَاقِعٌۢ بِهِمْ ؕ وَالَّذِيْنَ
اٰمَنُوْا وَعَمِلُوا الصّٰلِحٰتِ فِيْ رَوْضٰتِ
الْجَنّٰتِ ۚ لَهُمْ مَّا يَشَآءُوْنَ عِنْدَ
رَبِّهِمْ ؕ ذٰلِكَ هُوَ الْفَضْلُ الْكَبِيْرُ ﴿٢٢﴾

23. This is the glad news which Allah gives to His servants, the righteously striving believers. (Muhammad), say, "I do not ask you for any payment for my preaching to you except (your) love of (my near) relatives." Whoever achieves virtue will have its merit increased. Allah is All-forgiving and Appreciating.

23. Zaalikal-lazee yubashshirul-laahu 'ibaadahul lazeena aamanoo wa 'amiluṣ-ṣaaliḥaat; qul laaa as'alukum 'alayhi ajran illal-mawaddata fil-qurbaa; wa mañy-yaqtarif ḥasanatan nazid lahoo feehaa ḥusnaa; innal-laaha Ghafoorun Shakoor.

ذٰلِكَ الَّذِيْ يُبَشِّرُ اللّٰهُ عِبَادَهُ
الَّذِيْنَ اٰمَنُوْا وَعَمِلُوا الصّٰلِحٰتِ ؕ
قُلْ لَّاۤ اَسْـَٔلُكُمْ عَلَيْهِ اَجْرًا اِلَّا
الْمَوَدَّةَ فِي الْقُرْبٰى ؕ وَمَنْ يَّقْتَرِفْ
حَسَنَةً نَّزِدْ لَهٗ فِيْهَا حُسْنًا ؕ اِنَّ
اللّٰهَ غَفُوْرٌ شَكُوْرٌ ﴿٢٣﴾

24. Do they say that he, (Muhammad), has invented falsehood against Allah? Had Allah wanted, He could have sealed up your heart. Allah causes falsehood to vanish (become void) and, by His words, firmly establishes the truth. He has full knowledge of what the hearts contain.

24. Am yaqooloonaf-taraa 'alal-laahi kaziban fa-iñy-yasha-illaahu yakhtim 'alaa qalbik; wa yamḥul-laahul baaṭila wa yuḥiqqul-ḥaqqa bi Kalimaatih; innahoo 'Aleemum bizaatiṣ-ṣudoor.

اَمْ يَقُوْلُوْنَ افْتَرٰى عَلَى اللّٰهِ كَذِبًا ۚ
فَاِنْ يَّشَاِ اللّٰهُ يَخْتِمْ عَلٰى قَلْبِكَ ؕ
وَيَمْحُ اللّٰهُ الْبَاطِلَ وَيُحِقُّ
الْحَقَّ بِكَلِمٰتِهٖ ؕ اِنَّهٗ عَلِيْمٌ
بِذَاتِ الصُّدُوْرِ ﴿٢٤﴾

25. It is He who accepts the repentance of His servants, forgives their evil deeds, and knows all about what you do.

25. Wa Huwal-lazee yaqbalut-tawbata 'an 'ibaadihee wa ya'foo 'anis-sayyi-aati wa ya'lamu maa taf'aloon.

وَهُوَ الَّذِيْ يَقْبَلُ التَّوْبَةَ عَنْ
عِبَادِهٖ وَيَعْفُوْا عَنِ السَّيِّاٰتِ وَ
يَعْلَمُ مَا تَفْعَلُوْنَ ﴿٢٥﴾

26. He answers the prayers of the righteously striving believers and grants them increasing favors. The unbelievers will suffer a severe punishment.

26. Wa yastajeebul-lazeena aamanoo wa 'amiluṣ-ṣaaliḥaati wa yazeeduhum min faḍlih; wal kaafiroona lahum 'azaabun shadeed.

وَيَسْتَجِيبُ الَّذِينَ اٰمَنُوا وَعَمِلُوا
الصّٰلِحٰتِ وَيَزِيدُهُم مِّن فَضْلِهٖ ۚ
وَالْكٰفِرُونَ لَهُمْ عَذَابٌ شَدِيدٌ ﴿٢٦﴾

27. Had Allah given abundant sustenance to His servants, they would have certainly rebelled on earth, but He sends them a known measure of sustenance as He wills. He is All-aware of His servants and watches over them all.

27. Wa law basaṭal-laahur-rizqa li'ibaadihee labaghaw fil-arḍi walaakiñy-yunazzilu biqadarim-maa yashaaa'; innahoo bi'ibaadihee Khabeerum Baṣeer.

وَلَوْ بَسَطَ اللّٰهُ الرِّزْقَ لِعِبَادِهٖ لَبَغَوْا
فِي الْاَرْضِ وَلٰكِن يُّنَزِّلُ بِقَدَرٍ مَّا
يَشَآءُ ۚ اِنَّهٗ بِعِبَادِهٖ خَبِيرٌۢ بَصِيرٌ ﴿٢٧﴾

28. It is He who sends down the rain after they have lost hope and spreads out His mercy. He is the Guardian and the Most Praiseworthy.

28. Wa Huwal-lazee yunazzilul-ghaysa mim ba'di maa qanaṭoo wa yanshuru raḥmatah; wa Huwal Waliyyul-Ḥameed.

وَهُوَ الَّذِي يُنَزِّلُ الْغَيْثَ مِنۢ بَعْدِ
مَا قَنَطُوا وَيَنشُرُ رَحْمَتَهٗ ۚ وَهُوَ
الْوَلِيُّ الْحَمِيدُ ﴿٢٨﴾

29. Of the evidence (of His existence) is His creation of the heavens and the earth and the beasts which inhabit it. He has all the power to bring them together if He wishes this to be so.

29. Wa min Aayaatihee khalqus-samaawaati wal-arḍi wa maa bassa feehimaa min daaabbah; wa Huwa 'alaa jam'ihim izaa yashaaa'u Qadeer.

وَمِنْ اٰيٰتِهٖ خَلْقُ السَّمٰوٰتِ وَالْاَرْضِ
وَمَا بَثَّ فِيهِمَا مِن دَآبَّةٍ ۚ وَهُوَ
عَلٰى جَمْعِهِمْ اِذَا يَشَآءُ قَدِيرٌ ﴿٢٩﴾ ع

30. Whatever hardship befalls you is the result of your own deeds. Allah pardons many of your sins.

30. Wa maaa aṣaabakum mim-muṣeebatin fabimaa kasabat aydeekum wa ya'foo 'an kaseer.

وَمَا اَصَابَكُم مِّن مُّصِيبَةٍ فَبِمَا
كَسَبَتْ اَيْدِيكُمْ وَيَعْفُوا عَن كَثِيرٍ ﴿٣٠﴾

31. You cannot challenge Allah on earth and you will have no one besides Allah as your guardian or helper.

31. Wa maaa antum bimu'jizeena fil-arḍi wa maa lakum min doonil-laahi miñw-waliyyiñw- wa laa naṣeer.

وَمَا اَنتُم بِمُعْجِزِينَ فِي الْاَرْضِ ۚ
وَمَا لَكُم مِّن دُونِ اللّٰهِ مِن وَّلِيٍّ
وَّلَا نَصِيرٍ ﴿٣١﴾

32. Further evidence (of His existence) are the ships which stand as mountains in the sea.

32. Wa min Aayaatihil jawaari fil-baḥri kal-a'laam.

وَمِنْ اٰيٰتِهِ الْجَوَارِ فِي الْبَحْرِ
كَالْاَعْلٰمِ ﴿٣٢﴾

33. Had He wanted, He could have stopped the wind and let the ships remain motionless on the surface of the sea. In this there is evidence (of the Truth) for all those who are patient and grateful.

33. Iñy-yasha-yuskinir-reeḥa fa-yaẓlalna rawaakida 'alaa ẓahrih; inna fee zaalika la-Aayaatil-likulli ṣabbaarin shakoor.

اِن يَّشَاْ يُسْكِنِ الرِّيحَ فَيَظْلَلْنَ رَوَاكِدَ
عَلٰى ظَهْرِهٖ ۚ اِنَّ فِي ذٰلِكَ لَاٰيٰتٍ
لِّكُلِّ صَبَّارٍ شَكُورٍ ﴿٣٣﴾

34. Or, He could have destroyed them as punishment for the human being's deeds. However, Allah pardons many sins.

34. Aw yoobiqhunna bimaa kasaboo wa ya'fu 'an kaseer.

اَوْ يُوبِقْهُنَّ بِمَا كَسَبُوا وَيَعْفُ
عَن كَثِيرٍ ﴿٣٤﴾

35. He knows all those who dispute His revelations. They will find no way to escape (from His torment).

35. Wa ya'lamal-lazeena yujaadiloona feee Aayaatinaa maa lahum mim-maheeṣ.

وَّيَعْلَمَ الَّذِينَ يُجَادِلُونَ فِي اٰيٰتِنَا ۚ
مَا لَهُم مِّن مَّحِيصٍ ﴿٣٥﴾

36. Whatever you have received is just a means of enjoyment for this life but the reward of Allah for the believers and those who trust in their Lord will be better and everlasting.

36. Famaaa ooteetum min shay'in famataa'ul-ḥayaatid-dunyaa wa maa 'indal-laahi khayruñw-wa abqaa lillaẕeena aamanoo wa 'alaa Rabbihim yatawakkaloon.

فَمَآ أُوتِيتُم مِّن شَيْءٍ فَمَتَاعُ
الْحَيَوٰةِ الدُّنْيَا ۖ وَمَا عِندَ اللَّهِ خَيْرٌ
وَأَبْقَىٰ لِلَّذِينَ آمَنُوا وَعَلَىٰ رَبِّهِمْ
يَتَوَكَّلُونَ ﴿٣٦﴾

37. (This reward will be for) those who keep away from major sins and indecency, who forgive when they are made angry,

37. Wallaẕeena yajtaniboona kabaaa'iral-is̲mi wal-fawaa-ḥisha wa iẕaa maa ghaḍiboo hum yaghfiroon.

وَالَّذِينَ يَجْتَنِبُونَ كَبَٰٓئِرَ الْإِثْمِ
وَالْفَوَاحِشَ وَإِذَا مَا غَضِبُوا هُمْ
يَغْفِرُونَ ﴿٣٧﴾

38. who have pledged their obedience to their Lord, who are steadfast in prayer, who conduct their affairs with consultation among themselves, who spend for the cause of Allah out of what We have given them,

38. Wallaẕeenas-tajaaboo li-Rabbihim wa aqaamuṣ-Ṣalaata wa amruhum shooraa bayna-hum wa mimmaa razaqnaahum yunfiqoon.

وَالَّذِينَ اسْتَجَابُوا لِرَبِّهِمْ وَأَقَامُوا
الصَّلَوٰةَ وَأَمْرُهُمْ شُورَىٰ بَيْنَهُمْ
وَمِمَّا رَزَقْنَٰهُمْ يُنفِقُونَ ﴿٣٨﴾

39. and those who, when suffering a great injustice, seek to defend themselves.

39. Wallaẕeena iẕaaa aṣaa-bahumul-baghyu hum yanta-ṣiroon.

وَالَّذِينَ إِذَآ أَصَابَهُمُ الْبَغْيُ هُمْ
يَنتَصِرُونَ ﴿٣٩﴾

40. The recompense for evil will be equivalent to the deed. He who pardons (the evil done to him) and reforms himself, will receive his reward from Allah. He certainly does not love the unjust.

40. Wa jazaaa'u sayyi'atin sayyi'atum-mis̲luhaa faman 'afaa wa aṣlaḥa fa-ajruhoo 'alal-laah; innahoo laa yuḥib-buẓ-ẓaalimeen.

وَجَزَٰٓؤُا سَيِّئَةٍ سَيِّئَةٌ مِّثْلُهَا ۖ
فَمَنْ عَفَا وَأَصْلَحَ فَأَجْرُهُ عَلَى
اللَّهِ ۚ إِنَّهُ لَا يُحِبُّ الظَّٰلِمِينَ ﴿٤٠﴾

41. Those who successfully defend themselves after being wronged will not be questioned.

41. Wa lamanin-taṣara ba'da ẓulmihee fa-ulaaa'ika maa 'alayhim min sabeel.

وَلَمَنِ انتَصَرَ بَعْدَ ظُلْمِهِ فَأُولَٰٓئِكَ
مَا عَلَيْهِم مِّن سَبِيلٍ ﴿٤١﴾

42. Only those who do injustice to people and commit rebellion on earth for no reason will be questioned. They will suffer a painful torment.

42. Innamas-sabeelu 'alal-laẕeena yaẓlimoonan-naasa wa yabghoona fil-arḍi bighayril-ḥaqq; ulaaa'ika lahum 'aẕaabun aleem.

إِنَّمَا السَّبِيلُ عَلَى الَّذِينَ يَظْلِمُونَ
النَّاسَ وَيَبْغُونَ فِي الْأَرْضِ بِغَيْرِ
الْحَقِّ ۚ أُولَٰٓئِكَ لَهُمْ عَذَابٌ أَلِيمٌ ﴿٤٢﴾

43. To exercise patience and forgive (the wrong done to one) is the proof of genuine determination.

43. Wa laman ṣabara wa ghafara inna ẕaalika lamin 'azmil-umoor.

وَلَمَن صَبَرَ وَغَفَرَ إِنَّ ذَٰلِكَ لَمِنْ
عَزْمِ الْأُمُورِ ﴿٤٣﴾ ع ٤ ١٤ ٥

44. Whomever Allah has caused to go astray will find no guardian after this. You will see the unjust, on facing the torment, say, "Is there any way to turn back (to the worldly life)?"

44. Wa mañy-yuḍlilillaahu famaa lahoo miñw-waliyyim-mim ba'dih; wa taraẓ-ẓaalimeena lammaa ra-awul-'aẕaaba yaqooloona hal ilaa maraddim-min sabeel.

وَمَن يُضْلِلِ اللَّهُ فَمَا لَهُ مِن وَلِيٍّ
مِّن بَعْدِهِ ۗ وَتَرَى الظَّٰلِمِينَ لَمَّا
رَأَوُا الْعَذَابَ يَقُولُونَ هَلْ إِلَىٰ
مَرَدٍّ مِّن سَبِيلٍ ﴿٤٤﴾

45. You will see them exposed to the fire, subdued in humiliation, looking sideways at it pleadingly. However, at the same time, the believers will say, "The true losers are those who will lose their souls and families on the Day of Judgment. The unjust will certainly suffer everlasting torment.

46. They will have no guardian or helper besides Allah. Whoever Allah has caused to go astray will never find the right direction."

47. You must pledge obedience to your Lord before the coming of the inevitable Day when you will find no refuge to escape from (the power of) Allah and no one to defend you.

48. (Muhammad), if they turn away from your message, know that We have not sent you as their keeper. Your duty is only to deliver the message. When We grant mercy to the human being, he becomes joyous, but when he is afflicted by evil as a result of his own deeds, he proves to be ungrateful.

49. To Allah belong the heavens and the earth. He creates whatever He wants. He grants male or female offspring to whomever He wants as He wants.

50. He pairs-up male and female and causes whomever He wants to be childless. He is All-knowing and All-powerful.

51. To no human being does Allah speak but through revelation, from behind a curtain, or by sending a Messenger who

45. Wa taraahum yu‘raḍoona ‘alayhaa khaashi‘eena minaz-zulli yanẓuroona min ṭarfin khafiyy; wa qaalal-lazeena aamanooo innal-khaasireenal-lazeena khasirooo anfusahum wa ahleehim Yawmal-Qiyaa-mah; alaaa innaẓ-ẓaalimeena fee ‘azaabim-muqeem.

46. Wa maa kaana lahum min awliyaaa’a yanṣuroonahum min doonil-laah; wa mañy-yuḍlilil-laahu famaa lahoo min sabeel.

47. Istajeeboo li-Rabbikum min qabli añy-ya-tiya Yawmul-laa maradda lahoo minal-laah; maa lakum mim-malja-iñy-Yawma’iziñw-wa maa lakum min nakeer.

48. Fa-in a‘raḍoo famaaa arsalnaaka ‘alayhim ḥafeeẓaa; in ‘alayka illal-balaagh; wa innaaa izaaa azaqnal insaana minnaa raḥmatan fariḥa bihaa wa in tuṣibhum sayyi’atum bimaa qaddamat aydeehim fa-innal-insaana kafoor.

49. Lillaahi mulkus-samaa-waati wal-arḍ; yakhluqu maa yashaaa’; yahabu limañy-yashaaa’u inaaṣañw-wa yahabu limañy-yashaaa’uz-zukoor.

50. Aw yuzawwijuhum zuk-raanañw- wa inaaṣaa; wa yaj‘alu mañy-yashaaa’u ‘aqeemaa; innahoo ‘Aleemun Qadeer.

51. Wa maa kaana libasharin añy-yukallimahul-laahu illaa waḥyan aw miñw-waraaa’i ḥijaabin aw

وَتَرَاهُمْ يُعْرَضُوْنَ عَلَيْهَا خَاشِعِيْنَ مِنَ الذُّلِّ يَنْظُرُوْنَ مِنْ طَرْفٍ خَفِيٍّ ۗ وَقَالَ الَّذِيْنَ اٰمَنُوْۤا اِنَّ الْخٰسِرِيْنَ الَّذِيْنَ خَسِرُوْۤا اَنْفُسَهُمْ وَاَهْلِيْهِمْ يَوْمَ الْقِيٰمَةِ ۗ اَلَاۤ اِنَّ الظّٰلِمِيْنَ فِيْ عَذَابٍ مُّقِيْمٍ ۝

وَمَا كَانَ لَهُمْ مِّنْ اَوْلِيَآءَ يَنْصُرُوْنَهُمْ مِّنْ دُوْنِ اللّٰهِ ۗ وَمَنْ يُّضْلِلِ اللّٰهُ فَمَا لَهٗ مِنْ سَبِيْلٍ ۝

اِسْتَجِيْبُوْا لِرَبِّكُمْ مِّنْ قَبْلِ اَنْ يَّاْتِيَ يَوْمٌ لَّا مَرَدَّ لَهٗ مِنَ اللّٰهِ ۗ مَا لَكُمْ مِّنْ مَّلْجَاٍ يَّوْمَئِذٍ وَّمَا لَكُمْ مِّنْ نَّكِيْرٍ ۝

فَاِنْ اَعْرَضُوْا فَمَاۤ اَرْسَلْنٰكَ عَلَيْهِمْ حَفِيْظًا ۗ اِنْ عَلَيْكَ اِلَّا الْبَلٰغُ ۗ وَاِنَّاۤ اِذَاۤ اَذَقْنَا الْاِنْسَانَ مِنَّا رَحْمَةً فَرِحَ بِهَا ۗ وَاِنْ تُصِبْهُمْ سَيِّئَةٌ ۢبِمَا قَدَّمَتْ اَيْدِيْهِمْ فَاِنَّ الْاِنْسَانَ كَفُوْرٌ ۝

لِلّٰهِ مُلْكُ السَّمٰوٰتِ وَالْاَرْضِ ۗ يَخْلُقُ مَا يَشَآءُ ۗ يَهَبُ لِمَنْ يَّشَآءُ اِنَاثًا وَّيَهَبُ لِمَنْ يَّشَآءُ الذُّكُوْرَ ۝

اَوْ يُزَوِّجُهُمْ ذُكْرَانًا وَّاِنَاثًا ۗ وَّيَجْعَلُ مَنْ يَّشَآءُ عَقِيْمًا ۗ اِنَّهٗ عَلِيْمٌ قَدِيْرٌ ۝

وَمَا كَانَ لِبَشَرٍ اَنْ يُّكَلِّمَهُ اللّٰهُ اِلَّا وَحْيًا اَوْ مِنْ وَّرَآئِ حِجَابٍ اَوْ

reveals, by His permission, whatever He pleases. He is the Most High and the All-wise.

yursila Rasoolan fayoohiya bi-iznihee maa yashaaa'; innahoo 'Aliyyun Hakeem.

يُرْسِلَ رَسُوْلًا فَيُوْحِيَ بِاِذْنِهٖ
مَا يَشَآءُ ؕ اِنَّهٗ عَلِيٌّ حَكِيْمٌ ﴿۵۱﴾

52. Thus, We have revealed a Spirit (Ruh Al-Qudus) to you, (Muhammad), by Our command. Before, you did not even know what a Book or Faith was, but We have made the Quran as a light by which We guide whichever of Our servants We want. You certainly guide (people) to the right path,

52. Wa kazaalika awhaynaaa ilayka rooham-min amrinaa; maa kunta tadree mal-Kitaabu wa lal-eemaanu wa laakin ja'alnaahu nooran nahdee bihee man nashaaa'u min 'ibaadinaa; wa innaka latahdeee ilaa Siraatim Mustaqeem.

وَكَذٰلِكَ اَوْحَيْنَآ اِلَيْكَ رُوْحًا مِّنْ
اَمْرِنَا ؕ مَا كُنْتَ تَدْرِيْ مَا الْكِتٰبُ
وَلَا الْاِيْمَانُ وَلٰكِنْ جَعَلْنٰهُ نُوْرًا
نَّهْدِيْ بِهٖ مَنْ نَّشَآءُ مِنْ عِبَادِنَا ؕ
وَاِنَّكَ لَتَهْدِيْٓ اِلٰى صِرَاطٍ مُّسْتَقِيْمٍ ﴿۵۲﴾

53. the path of Allah (people who possess divine authority) who is the owner of all that is in the heavens and the earth. To Allah certainly do all matters return.

53. Siraatil-laahil-lazee lahoo maa fis-samaawaati wa maa fil-ard; alaaa ilal-laahi taseerul-umoor.

صِرَاطِ اللّٰهِ الَّذِيْ لَهٗ مَا فِي السَّمٰوٰتِ
وَمَا فِي الْاَرْضِ ؕ اَلَآ اِلَى اللّٰهِ
تَصِيْرُ الْاُمُوْرُ ﴿۵۳﴾ ع ۵

Al-Zukhruf, The Ornaments (43)
In the Name of Allah, the Beneficent, the Merciful.

Sûrat az-Zukhruf-43
(Revealed at Makkah)
Bismillaahir Rahmaanir Raheem

(۴۳) سُوْرَةُ الزُّخْرُفِ مَكِّيَّةٌ (۶۳)
اٰيَاتُهَا ۸۹ بِسْمِ اللّٰهِ الرَّحْمٰنِ الرَّحِيْمِ رُكُوْعَاتُهَا ۷

1. Ha. Mim

1. Haa-Meeem.

حٰمٓ ﴿۱﴾

2. I swear by the illustrious Book.

2. Wal-Kitaabil-Mubeen.

وَالْكِتٰبِ الْمُبِيْنِ ﴿۲﴾ مع

3. We have made it an Arabic reading text so that perhaps you may understand.

3. Innaa ja'alnaahu Qur'aanan 'Arabiyyal-la'allakum ta'qiloon.

اِنَّا جَعَلْنٰهُ قُرْءٰنًا عَرَبِيًّا لَّعَلَّكُمْ
تَعْقِلُوْنَ ﴿۳﴾ عند المتقدمين ۱۰

4. It (the Quran) exists in the original Book with Us, which is certainly Most Exalted, full of wisdom, and (beyond linguistic structures).

4. Wa innahoo feee Ummil-Kitaabi ladaynaa la'aliyyun hakeem.

وَاِنَّهٗ فِيْٓ اُمِّ الْكِتٰبِ لَدَيْنَا
لَعَلِيٌّ حَكِيْمٌ ﴿۴﴾

5. Can We ignore sending you the Quran just because you are a transgressing people?

5. Afanadribu 'ankumuz-Zikra safhan an kuntum qawmam-musrifeen.

اَفَنَضْرِبُ عَنْكُمُ الذِّكْرَ صَفْحًا اَنْ
كُنْتُمْ قَوْمًا مُّسْرِفِيْنَ ﴿۵﴾

6. How many Messengers did We send to the ancient people?

6. Wa kam arsalnaa min-Nabiyyin fil-awwaleen.

وَكَمْ اَرْسَلْنَا مِنْ نَّبِيٍّ فِي الْاَوَّلِيْنَ ﴿۶﴾

7. No Prophet came to them whom they did not mock.

7. Wa maa ya-teehim min Nabiyyin illaa kaanoo bihee yastahzi'oon.

وَمَا يَاْتِيْهِمْ مِّنْ نَّبِيٍّ اِلَّا كَانُوْا
بِهٖ يَسْتَهْزِءُوْنَ ﴿۷﴾

8. We destroyed those who were stronger than them (Quraysh) in power. The stories of the ancient people have already been mentioned.

8. Fa-ahlaknaaa ashadda minhum batshanw-wa madaa masalul-awwaleen.

فَاَهْلَكْنَآ اَشَدَّ مِنْهُمْ بَطْشًا وَّمَضٰى
مَثَلُ الْاَوَّلِيْنَ ﴿۸﴾

9. (Muhammad), if you ask them, "Who has created the heavens

9. Wa la'in sa-altahum man khalaqas-samaawaati

وَلَئِنْ سَاَلْتَهُمْ مَّنْ خَلَقَ السَّمٰوٰتِ

and the earth?" They will certainly say, "The Majestic and All-knowing Allah has created them."

wal-arḍa layaqoolunna khalaqahunnal-'Azeezul-'Aleem.

وَالْاَرْضَ لَيَقُوْلُنَّ خَلَقَهُنَّ الْعَزِيْزُ
الْعَلِيْمُ ﴿٩﴾

10. It is He who has made the earth for you as a cradle and has made roads therein so that you will perhaps seek guidance.

10. Allaz̲ee ja'ala lakumul-arḍa mahdañw-wa ja'ala lakum feehaa subulal-la'allakum tahtadoon.

الَّذِیْ جَعَلَ لَكُمُ الْاَرْضَ مَهْدًا
وَّجَعَلَ لَكُمْ فِيْهَا سُبُلًا لَّعَلَّكُمْ
تَهْتَدُوْنَ ﴿١٠﴾

11. It is He who has sent down water from the sky in a known measure by which He has given life to the dead earth. In the same way will you also be resurrected.

11. Wallaz̲ee nazzala minas-samaaa'i maaa'am biqadar; fa-ansharnaa bihee baldatam-maytaa; kaz̲aalika tukhrajoon.

وَالَّذِیْ نَزَّلَ مِنَ السَّمَآءِ مَآءًۢ بِقَدَرٍ
فَاَنْشَرْنَا بِهٖ بَلْدَةً مَّيْتًا كَذٰلِكَ
تُخْرَجُوْنَ ﴿١١﴾

12. It is He who has created everything in pairs. He created the ships and cattle for you to ride

12. Wallaz̲ee khalaqal-azwaaja kullahaa wa ja'ala lakum minal-fulki wal-an'aami maa tarkaboon.

وَالَّذِیْ خَلَقَ الْاَزْوَاجَ كُلَّهَا
وَجَعَلَ لَكُمْ مِّنَ الْفُلْكِ وَالْاَنْعَامِ
مَا تَرْكَبُوْنَ ﴿١٢﴾

13. so that perhaps when you ride them, you will recall the bounties of your Lord. And when you establish your control over it you will say, "Glory belongs to Him who has made it subservient to us when we would not have been able to do so ourselves.

13. Litastawoo 'alaa ẓuhoorihee s̲umma taz̲kuroo ni'mata Rabbikum iz̲astawaytum 'alayhi wa taqooloo Subḥaanal-laz̲ee sakhkhara lanaa haaz̲aa wa maa kunnaa lahoo muqrineen.

لِتَسْتَوٗا عَلٰى ظُهُوْرِهٖ ثُمَّ تَذْكُرُوْا
نِعْمَةَ رَبِّكُمْ اِذَا اسْتَوَيْتُمْ عَلَيْهِ
وَتَقُوْلُوْا سُبْحٰنَ الَّذِیْ سَخَّرَ لَنَا هٰذَا
وَمَا كُنَّا لَهٗ مُقْرِنِيْنَ ﴿١٣﴾

14. To our Lord we shall all return."

14. Wa innaaa ilaa Rabbinaa lamunqaliboon.

وَاِنَّاۤ اِلٰى رَبِّنَا لَمُنْقَلِبُوْنَ ﴿١٤﴾

15. The pagans have considered some of His servants as His children. There is no doubt that the human being is simply ungrateful.

15. Wa ja'aloo lahoo min 'ibaadihee juz'aa; innal insaana lakafoorum-mubeen.

وَجَعَلُوْا لَهٗ مِنْ عِبَادِهٖ جُزْءًا
اِنَّ الْاِنْسَانَ لَكَفُوْرٌ مُّبِيْنٌ ﴿١٥﴾ ع ١٥ ٧

16. Has Allah chosen some of His own creatures as daughters for Himself and given you the preference of having sons?

16. Amit-takhaz̲a mimmaa yakhluqu banaatiñw-wa aṣfaakum bilbaneen.

اَمِ اتَّخَذَ مِمَّا يَخْلُقُ بَنٰتٍ وَّ
اَصْفٰكُمْ بِالْبَنِيْنَ ﴿١٦﴾

17. When one of them is given the glad news of the birth of a daughter, which they believe to be the only kind of child that the Beneficent can have, his face blackens with anger.

17. Wa iz̲aa bushshira aḥaduhum bimaa ḍaraba lir-Raḥmaani mas̲alan ẓalla wajhuhoo muswaddañw-wa huwa kaẓeem.

وَاِذَا بُشِّرَ اَحَدُهُمْ بِمَا ضَرَبَ
لِلرَّحْمٰنِ مَثَلًا ظَلَّ وَجْهُهٗ مُسْوَدًّا
وَّهُوَ كَظِيْمٌ ﴿١٧﴾

18. Does Allah choose for Himself the kind of children who grow up wearing ornaments and who are not strong enough to defend their rights?

18. Awa mañy-yunashsha'u fil-ḥilyati wa huwa filkhiṣaami ghayru mubeen.

اَوَمَنْ يُّنَشَّؤُا فِی الْحِلْيَةِ وَهُوَ
فِی الْخِصَامِ غَيْرُ مُبِيْنٍ ﴿١٨﴾

19. Do they say that the angels, who are the servants of the Beneficent, are females? Have they witnessed

19. Wa ja'alul-malaaa'ikatal-laz̲eena hum 'ibaadur-

وَجَعَلُوا الْمَلٰٓئِكَةَ الَّذِيْنَ هُمْ عِبٰدُ

their creation? Their words as such will be recorded and they will be questioned for it.

Raḥmaani inaasaa; ashahidoo khalqahum satuktabu shahaadatuhum wa yus'aloon.

الرَّحْمٰنِ اِنَاثًا ؕ اَشَهِدُوْا خَلْقَهُمْ ؕ
سَتُكْتَبُ شَهَادَتُهُمْ وَيُسْـَٔلُوْنَ ﴿١٩﴾

20. The pagans say, "Had the Beneficent wanted, we would not have worshipped them (idols)." Whatever they say is not based on knowledge. It is only a false conjecture (argument).

20. Wa qaaloo law shaaa'ar-Raḥmaanu maa 'abadnaahum; maa lahum bizaalika min 'ilmin in hum illaa yakhruṣoon.

وَقَالُوْا لَوْ شَآءَ الرَّحْمٰنُ مَا عَبَدْنٰهُمْ ؕ
مَا لَهُمْ بِذٰلِكَ مِنْ عِلْمٍ ۗ اِنْ هُمْ اِلَّا
يَخْرُصُوْنَ ﴿٢٠﴾

21. Had We, before sending the Quran, given them a book to which they now refer as an authority?

21. Am aataynaahum Kitaabam-min qablihee fahum bihee mustamsikoon.

اَمْ اٰتَيْنٰهُمْ كِتٰبًا مِّنْ قَبْلِهٖ فَهُمْ
بِهٖ مُسْتَمْسِكُوْنَ ﴿٢١﴾

22. In fact, they say, "We found our fathers following a certain belief and we now follow in their footsteps for our guidance."

22. Bal qaalooo innaa wajadnaaa aabaaa'anaa 'alaaa ummatiñw-wa innaa 'alaaa aasaarihim muhtadoon.

بَلْ قَالُوْٓا اِنَّا وَجَدْنَآ اٰبَآءَنَا عَلٰٓى
اُمَّةٍ وَّاِنَّا عَلٰٓى اٰثٰرِهِمْ مُّهْتَدُوْنَ ﴿٢٢﴾

23. In the same way, whenever We had sent a messenger before you to warn a town, the rich ones therein said, "We found our fathers following a certain belief and we follow in their footsteps."

23. Wa kazaalika maaa arsalnaa min qablika fee qaryatim-min nazeerin illaa qaala mutrafoohaaa innaa wajadnaaa aabaaa'anaa 'alaaa ummatiñw-wa innaa 'alaaa aasaarihim muqtadoon.

وَكَذٰلِكَ مَآ اَرْسَلْنَا مِنْ قَبْلِكَ فِىْ
قَرْيَةٍ مِّنْ نَّذِيْرٍ اِلَّا قَالَ مُتْرَفُوْهَآ ۙ
اِنَّا وَجَدْنَآ اٰبَآءَنَا عَلٰٓى اُمَّةٍ وَّاِنَّا
عَلٰٓى اٰثٰرِهِمْ مُّقْتَدُوْنَ ﴿٢٣﴾

24. A messenger would say, "Would you still follow in the footsteps of your fathers even if I were to bring you better guidance?" They would say, "We have no faith in your message."

24. Qaala awa law ji'tukum bi-ahdaa mimmaa wajattum 'alayhi aabaaa'akum qaalooo innaa bimaaa ursiltum bihee kaafiroon.

قٰلَ اَوَلَوْ جِئْتُكُمْ بِاَهْدٰى مِمَّا
وَجَدْتُّمْ عَلَيْهِ اٰبَآءَكُمْ ؕ قَالُوْٓا اِنَّا
بِمَآ اُرْسِلْتُمْ بِهٖ كٰفِرُوْنَ ﴿٢٤﴾

25. We exacted retribution on them. See how terrible the end of those who rejected (Our revelations) was!

25. Fantaqamnaa minhum fanẓur kayfa kaana 'aaqibatul-mukaz-zibeen.

فَانْتَقَمْنَا مِنْهُمْ فَانْظُرْ كَيْفَ
كَانَ عَاقِبَةُ الْمُكَذِّبِيْنَ ﴿٢٥﴾ ع النصف ١٠ ٨

26. When Abraham said to his father and his people, "I boldly renounce what you worship

26. Wa iz qaala Ibraaheemu liabeehi wa qawmiheee innanee baraaa'um-mimmaa ta'budoon.

وَاِذْ قَالَ اِبْرٰهِيْمُ لِاَبِيْهِ وَقَوْمِهٖٓ
اِنَّنِىْ بَرَآءٌ مِّمَّا تَعْبُدُوْنَ ﴿٢٦﴾ ۙ

27. except for the One who has created me and will guide me."

27. Illal-lazee faṭaranee fainnahoo sa-yahdeen.

اِلَّا الَّذِىْ فَطَرَنِىْ فَاِنَّهٗ سَيَهْدِيْنِ ﴿٢٧﴾

28. Allah made (belief in Allah) an everlasting task for his successors, so that perhaps they would return (to Him).

28. Wa ja'alahaa Kalimatam baaqiyatan fee 'aqibihee la'allahum yarji'oon.

وَجَعَلَهَا كَلِمَةًۢ بَاقِيَةً فِىْ عَقِبِهٖ
لَعَلَّهُمْ يَرْجِعُوْنَ ﴿٢٨﴾

29. In fact, We allowed them and their fathers to enjoy themselves until the Truth and a strong Messenger came to them.

29. Bal matta'tu haaa'ulaaa'i wa aabaaa'ahum ḥattaa jaaa'ahumul-ḥaqqu wa Rasoolum-mubeen.

بَلْ مَتَّعْتُ هٰٓؤُلَآءِ وَاٰبَآءَهُمْ حَتّٰى
جَآءَهُمُ الْحَقُّ وَرَسُوْلٌ مُّبِيْنٌ ﴿٢٩﴾

30. When the Truth came to them, they said, "This is magic and we have no faith in it."

30. Wa lammaa jaaa'ahumul-ḥaqqu qaaloo haazaa siḥruñw-wa innaa bihee kaafiroon.

وَلَمَّا جَآءَهُمُ الْحَقُّ قَالُوْا هٰذَا سِحْرٌ

31. Then they said, “Why had this Quran not been revealed to a man from either of the two great towns.”

32. Do they distribute the mercy of your Lord (prophet-hood and Quran)? It is We who have distributed their sustenance in this world and raised the positions of a number of them above the others (in matters of children and property) so that they take advantage of each other's labor. The mercy of your Lord is better than what they can amass.

33. Were it not for the fact that all people would become one (in disbelief), We would have made for the unbelievers in the Beneficent, ceilings out of silver and ladders by which they would climb up,

34. doors for their houses, couches on which to recline,

35. and ornament (of gold). All these are only the means of enjoyment in this world, but the pious will receive their reward from your Lord in the life hereafter.

36. We shall make Satan the companion of whoever turns blind toward the remembrance of the Beneficent.

37. Satan will prevent them from the right path while they think that they have the right guidance.

38. When he returns to us, he will say (to Satan), “Would that there had been as long a distance between me and you as that between the East and West. What a terrible companion you have been.”

39. They will be told on the Day of Judgment, “Regret will never be of any benefit to you. You have done injustice to your souls and you will share the torment.”

31. Wa qaaloo law laa nuzzila haazal-Qur’aanu ‘alaa rajulim-minal-qaryatayni ‘azeem.

32. Ahum yaqsimoona raḥmata Rabbik; Naḥnu qasamnaa baynahum ma‘eeshatahum fil-ḥayaatid-dunyaa wa rafa‘naa ba‘ḍahum fawqa ba‘ḍin darajaatil-liyattakhiza ba‘ḍuhum ba‘ḍan sukhriyyaa; wa raḥmatu Rabbika khayrum-mimmaa yajma‘oon.

33. Wa law laaa añwy-yakoonan-naasu ummatañw-waaḥidatal-laja‘alnaa limañy-yakfuru bir-Raḥmaani libuyootihim suqufam-min fiḍḍatiñw-wa ma‘aarija ‘alayhaa yaẓharoon.

34. Wa libuyootihim abwaabañw-wa sururan ‘alayhaa yattaki’oon.

35. Wa zukhrufaa; wa in kullu zaalika lammaa mataa‘ul-ḥayaatid-dunyaa; wal-Aakhiratu ‘inda Rabbika lilmuttaqeen.

36. Wa mañy-ya‘shu ‘an zikrir-Raḥmaani nuqayyiḍ lahoo Shayṭaanan fahuwa lahoo qareen.

37. Wa innahum la-yaṣuddoonahum ‘anis-sabeeli wa yaḥsaboona annahum muhtadoon.

38. Ḥattaaa izaa jaaa’anaa qaala yaa layta baynee wa baynaka bu‘dal-mashriqayni fabi’sal-qareen.

39. Wa lañy-yanfa‘akumul Yawma iẓ-ẓalamtum annakum fil-‘azaabi mushtarikoon.

وَاِنَّا بِهٖ كٰفِرُوْنَ ﴿٣٠﴾
وَقَالُوْا لَوْلَا نُزِّلَ هٰذَا الْقُرْاٰنُ عَلٰى
رَجُلٍ مِّنَ الْقَرْيَتَيْنِ عَظِيْمٍ ﴿٣١﴾
اَهُمْ يَقْسِمُوْنَ رَحْمَتَ رَبِّكَ ۭ نَحْنُ
قَسَمْنَا بَيْنَهُمْ مَّعِيْشَتَهُمْ فِي الْحَيٰوةِ
الدُّنْيَا وَرَفَعْنَا بَعْضَهُمْ فَوْقَ بَعْضٍ
دَرَجٰتٍ لِّيَتَّخِذَ بَعْضُهُمْ بَعْضًا سُخْرِيًّا ۭ
وَرَحْمَتُ رَبِّكَ خَيْرٌ مِّمَّا يَجْمَعُوْنَ ﴿٣٢﴾
وَلَوْلَآ اَنْ يَّكُوْنَ النَّاسُ اُمَّةً وَّاحِدَةً
لَّجَعَلْنَا لِمَنْ يَّكْفُرُ بِالرَّحْمٰنِ لِبُيُوْتِهِمْ
سُقُفًا مِّنْ فِضَّةٍ وَّمَعَارِجَ عَلَيْهَا
يَظْهَرُوْنَ ﴿٣٣﴾
وَلِبُيُوْتِهِمْ اَبْوَابًا وَّسُرُرًا عَلَيْهَا
يَتَّكِـُٔوْنَ ﴿٣٤﴾
وَزُخْرُفًا ۭ وَاِنْ كُلُّ ذٰلِكَ لَمَّا
مَتَاعُ الْحَيٰوةِ الدُّنْيَا ۭ وَالْاٰخِرَةُ
عِنْدَ رَبِّكَ لِلْمُتَّقِيْنَ ﴿٣٥﴾ ع ٣
وَمَنْ يَّعْشُ عَنْ ذِكْرِ الرَّحْمٰنِ نُقَيِّضْ
لَهٗ شَيْطٰنًا فَهُوَ لَهٗ قَرِيْنٌ ﴿٣٦﴾
وَاِنَّهُمْ لَيَصُدُّوْنَهُمْ عَنِ السَّبِيْلِ
وَيَحْسَبُوْنَ اَنَّهُمْ مُّهْتَدُوْنَ ﴿٣٧﴾
حَتّٰٓى اِذَا جَاۗءَنَا قَالَ يٰلَيْتَ بَيْنِيْ
وَبَيْنَكَ بُعْدَ الْمَشْرِقَيْنِ فَبِئْسَ
الْقَرِيْنُ ﴿٣٨﴾
وَلَنْ يَّنْفَعَكُمُ الْيَوْمَ اِذْ ظَّلَمْتُمْ
اَنَّكُمْ فِي الْعَذَابِ مُشْتَرِكُوْنَ ﴿٣٩﴾

40. (Muhammad), can you make the deaf hear or guide the blind or the one who is clearly in error?

40. Afa-anta tusmi'uṣ-ṣumma aw tahdil-'umya wa man kaana fee ḍalaalim-mubeen.

أَفَأَنتَ تُسْمِعُ الصُّمَّ أَوْ تَهْدِي الْعُمْيَ
وَمَن كَانَ فِي ضَلَالٍ مُّبِينٍ ﴿٤٠﴾

41. We shall exact retribution upon them either after your death

41. Fa-immaa naẕhabanna bika fa-innaa minhum muntaqimoon.

فَإِمَّا نَذْهَبَنَّ بِكَ فَإِنَّا مِنْهُم
مُّنتَقِمُونَ ﴿٤١﴾

42. or show them to you suffering the torment with which We had threatened them. We are certainly dominant over them all.

42. Aw nuriyannakal-laẕee wa'adnaahum fa-innaa 'alayhim muqtadiroon.

أَوْ نُرِيَنَّكَ الَّذِي وَعَدْنَاهُمْ فَإِنَّا
عَلَيْهِم مُّقْتَدِرُونَ ﴿٤٢﴾

43. Follow devotedly that which is revealed to you. You are certainly on the right path.

43. Fastamsik billaẕeee ooḥiya ilayka innaka 'alaa Ṣiraaṭim-Mustaqeem.

فَاسْتَمْسِكْ بِالَّذِي أُوحِيَ إِلَيْكَ
إِنَّكَ عَلَىٰ صِرَاطٍ مُّسْتَقِيمٍ ﴿٤٣﴾

44. The Quran is a reminder to you and to your people and you will soon be asked for guidance.

44. Wa innahoo laẕikrul-laka wa liqawmika wa sawfa tus'aloon.

وَإِنَّهُ لَذِكْرٌ لَّكَ وَلِقَوْمِكَ وَسَوْفَ
تُسْأَلُونَ ﴿٤٤﴾

45. You can ask Our Messengers whom We sent before you if We had commanded them to worship other gods besides the Beneficent."

45. Was'al man arsalnaa min qablika mir-Rusulinaaa aja-'alnaa min doonir-Raḥmaani aalihatañy- yu'badoon.

وَاسْأَلْ مَنْ أَرْسَلْنَا مِن قَبْلِكَ مِن
رُّسُلِنَا أَجَعَلْنَا مِن دُونِ الرَّحْمَٰنِ
آلِهَةً يُعْبَدُونَ ﴿٤٥﴾

46. We sent Moses to the Pharaoh and his nobles with Our miracles and he said, "I am the Messenger of the Lord of the universe."

46. Wa laqad arsalnaa Moosaa bi-Aayaatinaaa ilaa Fir'awna wa mala'ihee faqaala innee Rasoolu Rabbil-'aalameen.

وَلَقَدْ أَرْسَلْنَا مُوسَىٰ بِآيَاتِنَا إِلَىٰ
فِرْعَوْنَ وَمَلَئِهِ فَقَالَ إِنِّي رَسُولُ
رَبِّ الْعَالَمِينَ ﴿٤٦﴾

47. When he showed them Our miracles, they started to laugh at them.

47. Falammaa jaaa'ahum bi-Aayaatinaaa iẕaa hum minhaa yaḍḥakoon.

فَلَمَّا جَاءَهُم بِآيَاتِنَا إِذَا هُم مِّنْهَا
يَضْحَكُونَ ﴿٤٧﴾

48. Of all the miracles which We showed to them the latter ones were greater than the former. We struck them with torment so that perhaps they would return to Us.

48. Wa maa nureehim min Aayatin illaa hiya akbaru min ukhtihaa wa akhaẕnaahum bil'aẕaabi la'allahum yarji'oon.

وَمَا نُرِيهِم مِّنْ آيَةٍ إِلَّا هِيَ أَكْبَرُ
مِنْ أُخْتِهَا وَأَخَذْنَاهُم بِالْعَذَابِ
لَعَلَّهُمْ يَرْجِعُونَ ﴿٤٨﴾

49. They said, "O Magician, (learned one) pray to your Lord for us through your covenant with Him (If he saves us from the torment), we shall certainly seek guidance."

49. Wa qaaloo yaaa ayyuhas-saaḥirud-'u lanaa Rabbaka bimaa 'ahida 'indaka innanaa lamuhtadoon.

وَقَالُوا يَا أَيُّهَ السَّاحِرُ ادْعُ لَنَا رَبَّكَ
بِمَا عَهِدَ عِندَكَ إِنَّنَا لَمُهْتَدُونَ ﴿٤٩﴾

50. When We relieved them from the torment they suddenly turned back on their heels.

50. Falammaa kashafnaa 'anhumul-'aẕaaba iẕaa hum yankusoon.

فَلَمَّا كَشَفْنَا عَنْهُمُ الْعَذَابَ إِذَا
هُمْ يَنكُثُونَ ﴿٥٠﴾

51. The Pharaoh shouted to his people, "My people, is the

51. Wa naadaa Fir'awnu fee qawmihee qaala yaa qawmi

وَنَادَىٰ فِرْعَوْنُ فِي قَوْمِهِ قَالَ يَا قَوْمِ

kingdom of Egypt not mine and can you not see that the streams flow from beneath my palace?

alaysa lee mulku Miṣra wa haazihil-anhaaru tajree min taḥteee afalaa tubṣiroon.

أَلَيْسَ لِي مُلْكُ مِصْرَ وَهَٰذِهِ الْأَنْهَارُ
تَجْرِي مِنْ تَحْتِي ۖ أَفَلَا تُبْصِرُونَ ﴿٥١﴾

52. Am I not better than this lowly man who can barely express himself?

52. Am anaa khayrum-min haazal-lazee huwa maheenuñw-wa laa yakaadu yubeen.

أَمْ أَنَا خَيْرٌ مِنْ هَٰذَا الَّذِي هُوَ
مَهِينٌ وَلَا يَكَادُ يُبِينُ ﴿٥٢﴾

53. Why have bracelets of gold not been given to him and why have angels not accompanied him?"

53. Falaw laaa ulqiya 'alayhi aswiratum-min zahabin aw jaaa'a ma'ahul-malaaa'ikatu muqtarineen.

فَلَوْلَا أُلْقِيَ عَلَيْهِ أَسْوِرَةٌ مِنْ ذَهَبٍ
أَوْ جَاءَ مَعَهُ الْمَلَائِكَةُ مُقْتَرِنِينَ ﴿٥٣﴾

54. Thus, he made dimwits out of his people and they followed him. They, certainly, were a sinful people. When they invoked Our anger,

54. Fastakhaffa qawmahoo fa-aṭaa'ooh; innahum kaanoo qawman faasiqeen.

فَاسْتَخَفَّ قَوْمَهُ فَأَطَاعُوهُ ۚ إِنَّهُمْ
كَانُوا قَوْمًا فَاسِقِينَ ﴿٥٤﴾

55. We brought them to justice by drowning them all together.

55. Falammaaa aasafoonan-taqamnaa minhum fa-aghraq-naahum ajma'een.

فَلَمَّا آسَفُونَا انْتَقَمْنَا مِنْهُمْ
فَأَغْرَقْنَاهُمْ أَجْمَعِينَ ﴿٥٥﴾

56. We made them become of the people of the past and an example for the coming generations.

56. Faja'alnaahum salafañw-wa masalal-lil-aakhireen.

فَجَعَلْنَاهُمْ سَلَفًا وَمَثَلًا لِلْآخِرِينَ ﴿٥٦﴾ ع ٥ ١١

57. When the son of Mary was mentioned as an example, your people cried out in protest, saying,

57. Wa lammaa ḍuribab-nu Maryama masalan izaa qawmu-ka minhu yaṣiddoon.

وَلَمَّا ضُرِبَ ابْنُ مَرْيَمَ مَثَلًا إِذَا قَوْمُكَ
مِنْهُ يَصِدُّونَ ﴿٥٧﴾

58. "Are our gods any better than Jesus for (according to Muhammad), if our gods go to hell so also will Jesus." What they say is only a false argument. In fact, they are a quarrelsome people.

58. Waqaalooo'a-aalihatunaa khayrun am hoo; maa ḍara-boohu laka illaa jadalaa; bal hum qawmun khaṣimoon.

وَقَالُوا أَآلِهَتُنَا خَيْرٌ أَمْ هُوَ ۚ مَا
ضَرَبُوهُ لَكَ إِلَّا جَدَلًا ۚ بَلْ هُمْ
قَوْمٌ خَصِمُونَ ﴿٥٨﴾

59. Jesus was only a servant of Ours to whom We had granted favors and whom We made as an example for the Israelites.

59. In huwa illaa 'abdun an'amnaa 'alayhi wa ja'alnaahu masalal-li-Baneee Israaa'eel.

إِنْ هُوَ إِلَّا عَبْدٌ أَنْعَمْنَا عَلَيْهِ وَجَعَلْنَاهُ
مَثَلًا لِبَنِي إِسْرَائِيلَ ﴿٥٩﴾

60. Had We wanted, We could have made the angels as your successors on the earth.

60. Wa law nashaaa'u laja'al-naa minkum malaaa'ikatan fil-arḍi yakhlufoon.

وَلَوْ نَشَاءُ لَجَعَلْنَا مِنْكُمْ مَلَائِكَةً
فِي الْأَرْضِ يَخْلُفُونَ ﴿٦٠﴾

61. (Muhammad), tell them, "Jesus is a sign of the Hour of Doom. Have no doubt about it and follow me; this is the straight path.

61. Wa innahoo la'ilmul-lis-Saa'ati falaa tamtarunna bihaa wattabi'oon; haazaa Ṣiraaṭum-Mustaqeem.

وَإِنَّهُ لَعِلْمٌ لِلسَّاعَةِ فَلَا تَمْتَرُنَّ بِهَا
وَاتَّبِعُونِ ۚ هَٰذَا صِرَاطٌ مُسْتَقِيمٌ ﴿٦١﴾

62. Do not allow Satan to prevent you from the right path. He is your sworn enemy."

62. Wa laa yaṣuddan-naku-mush-Shayṭaanu innahoo la-kum 'aduwwum-mubeen.

وَلَا يَصُدَّنَّكُمُ الشَّيْطَانُ ۖ إِنَّهُ لَكُمْ
عَدُوٌّ مُبِينٌ ﴿٦٢﴾

63. When Jesus came with clear proof (in support of his truthfulness), he said, "I have come to you with wisdom to clarify for you some of the

63. Wa lammaa jaaa'a 'Eesaa bilbayyinaati qaala qad ji'tu-kum bil-Ḥikmati wa li-ubay-yina lakum

وَلَمَّا جَاءَ عِيسَىٰ بِالْبَيِّنَاتِ قَالَ قَدْ
جِئْتُكُمْ بِالْحِكْمَةِ وَلِأُبَيِّنَ لَكُمْ

matters in which you have disputes. Have fear of Allah and obey me.

ba'ḍal-lazee takhtalifoona feeh; fattaqul-laaha wa aṭee'oon.

بَعۡضَ الَّذِیۡ تَخۡتَلِفُوۡنَ فِیۡهِ‌ۚ فَاتَّقُوا
اللّٰهَ وَاَطِيۡعُوۡنِ ﴿۶۳﴾

64. Allah is your Lord and my Lord, so worship Him. This is the right path."

64. Innal-laaha Huwa Rabbee wa Rabbukum fa'budooh; haazaa Ṣiraaṭum-Mustaqeem.

اِنَّ اللّٰهَ هُوَ رَبِّىۡ وَرَبُّكُمۡ فَاعۡبُدُوۡهُ‌ؕ
هٰذَا صِرَاطٌ مُّسۡتَقِيۡمٌ ﴿۶۴﴾

65. However, certain groups created differences among themselves. Woe to the unjust. They will face a painful torment.

65. Fakhtalafal-aḥzaabu mim baynihim fawaylul-lillazeena ẓalamoo min 'azaabi Yawmin aleem.

فَاخۡتَلَفَ الۡاَحۡزَابُ مِنۡۢ بَيۡنِهِمۡ‌ۚ
فَوَيۡلٌ لِّلَّذِيۡنَ ظَلَمُوۡا مِنۡ عَذَابِ
يَوۡمٍ اَلِيۡمٍ ﴿۶۵﴾

66. Are they waiting for the Hour of Doom when the torment will suddenly strike them and they will not even realize from where it came?

66. Hal yanẓuroona illas-Saa'ata an ta-tiyahum baghtatañw-wa hum laa yash'uroon.

هَلۡ يَنۡظُرُوۡنَ اِلَّا السَّاعَةَ اَنۡ
تَاۡتِيَهُمۡ بَغۡتَةً وَّهُمۡ لَا يَشۡعُرُوۡنَ ﴿۶۶﴾

67. All intimate friends on that day will become each other's enemies except for the pious,

67. Al-akhillaaa'u Yawma'izim ba'ḍuhum liba'ḍin 'aduwwun illal-muttaqeen.

اَلۡاَخِلَّاۤءُ يَوۡمَئِذٍۢ بَعۡضُهُمۡ لِبَعۡضٍ
عَدُوٌّ اِلَّا الۡمُتَّقِيۡنَ ﴿۶۷﴾ ع ٦/١٢

68. whom Allah will tell, "My servants, you need have no fear on this day, nor will you be grieved."

68. Yaa 'ibaadi laa khawfun 'alaykumul-Yawma wa laaa antum taḥzanoon.

يٰعِبَادِ لَا خَوۡفٌ عَلَيۡكُمُ الۡيَوۡمَ وَلَاۤ
اَنۡتُمۡ تَحۡزَنُوۡنَ‌ۚ ﴿۶۸﴾

69. Those who have faith in Our revelations and have submitted themselves to Our will,

69. Allazeena aamanoo bi-Aayaatinaa wa kaanoo muslimeen.

اَلَّذِيۡنَ اٰمَنُوۡا بِاٰيٰتِنَا وَكَانُوۡا
مُسۡلِمِيۡنَ‌ۚ ﴿۶۹﴾

70. will be told, "Enter Paradise with your spouses in delight.

70. Udkhulul-Jannata antum wa azwaajukum tuḥbaroon.

اُدۡخُلُوا الۡجَـنَّةَ اَنۡتُمۡ وَاَزۡوَاجُكُمۡ
تُحۡبَرُوۡنَ ﴿۷۰﴾

71. Golden dishes and cups will be passed among them. All that the souls may desire and that may delight their eyes will be available therein. You will live therein forever.

71. Yuṭaafu 'alayhim biṣiḥaafim-min zahabiñw-wa akwaab; wa feehaa maa tashtaheehil-anfusu wa talaz-zul-a'yunu wa antum feehaa khaalidoon.

يُطَافُ عَلَيۡهِمۡ بِصِحَافٍ مِّنۡ ذَهَبٍ
وَّاَكۡوَابٍ‌ۚ وَفِيۡهَا مَا تَشۡتَهِيۡهِ
الۡاَنۡفُسُ وَتَلَذُّ الۡاَعۡيُنُ‌ۚ وَاَنۡتُمۡ فِيۡهَا
خٰلِدُوۡنَ‌ۚ ﴿۷۱﴾

72. This is the Paradise which you have received as your inheritance by virtue of what you have done (good deeds).

72. Wa tilkal-Jannatul-lateee ooristumoohaa bimaa kuntum ta'maloon.

وَتِلۡكَ الۡجَـنَّةُ الَّتِىۡۤ اُوۡرِثۡتُمُوۡهَا بِمَا
كُنۡتُمۡ تَعۡمَلُوۡنَ ﴿۷۲﴾

73. You will have abundant fruits therein to consume."

73. Lakum feehaa faakihatun kaseeratum-minhaa ta-kuloon.

لَـكُمۡ فِيۡهَا فَاكِهَةٌ كَثِيۡرَةٌ مِّنۡهَا
تَاۡكُلُوۡنَ ﴿۷۳﴾

74. The sinful ones will live forever in the torment of hell. Their torment will not be relieved and they will lose all hope of receiving anything good.

74. Innal-mujrimeena fee 'azaabi Jahannama khaalidoon.

اِنَّ الۡمُجۡرِمِيۡنَ فِىۡ عَذَابِ جَهَنَّمَ

75. We had not done any injustice to them but they had wronged themselves.

76. They will cry out, "O guard, your Lord should cause us to die."

77. The guarding angel will say, "You will have to stay.

78. We brought you the truth but most of you disliked it."

79. If the unbelievers persist in their disbelief, We shall also persist in punishing them.

80. Do they think that We do not hear their secrets and whispers? We certainly can hear them and Our Messengers who are with them, record it all.

81. (O Muhammad), say, "The Beneficent never had a son; I was the first worshipper (creature to know Him).

82. The Lord of the heavens and the earth and the Throne is free of all defects of being described in the way they describe Him.

83. Leave them (to indulge) in their desires and play around until they face that day which has been promised to them.

84. It is Allah who is the Lord of the heavens and is the Lord on earth. He is All-wise and All-knowing.

85. Blessed is He to whom belong the heavens, the earth and all that is between them and who has the knowledge of the Hour of Doom. To Him you will all return.

86. Those whom they worship besides Allah are not able to intercede, except for those among them who believe in the Truth (Allah) and who know whom to intercede for.

75. Laa yufattaru 'anhum wa hum feehi mublisoon.

76. Wa maa ẓalamnaahum walaakin kaanoo humuẓ-ẓaalimeen.

77. Wa naadaw yaa Maaliku liyaqḍi 'alaynaa Rabbuka qaala innakum maaki<u>s</u>oon.

78. Laqad ji'naakum bilḥaqqi wa laakinna ak<u>s</u>arakum lilḥaqqi kaarihoon.

79. Am abramooo amran fa-innaa mubrimoon.

80. Am yaḥsaboona annaa laa nasma'u sirrahum wa najwaa-hum; balaa wa Rusulunaa ladayhim yaktuboon.

81. Qul in kaana lir-Raḥmaani walad; fa-ana awwalul-'aabideen.

82. Subḥaana Rabbis-samaa-waati wal-arḍi Rabbil 'Arshi 'ammaa yaṣifoon.

83. Fa<u>z</u>arhum yakhooḍoo wa-yal'aboo ḥattaa yulaaqoo Yawmahumul-la<u>z</u>ee yoo'a-doon.

84. Wa Huwal-la<u>z</u>ee fissa-maaa'i Ilaahuñw-wa fil-arḍi Ilaah; wa Huwal-Ḥakeemul 'Aleem.

85. Wa tabaarakal-la<u>z</u>ee lahoo mulkus-samaawaati wal-arḍi wa maa baynahumaa wa 'indahoo 'ilmus-Saa'ati wa ilayhi turja'oon.

86. Wa laa yamlikul-la<u>z</u>eena yad'oona min doonihish-shafaa'ata illaa man shahida bilḥaqqi wa hum ya'lamoon.

خٰلِدُوْنَ ﴿٧٤﴾
لَا يُفَتَّرُ عَنْهُمْ وَهُمْ فِيْهِ مُبْلِسُوْنَ ﴿٧٥﴾
وَمَا ظَلَمْنٰهُمْ وَلٰكِنْ كَانُوْا هُمُ
الظّٰلِمِيْنَ ﴿٧٦﴾
وَنَادَوْا يٰمٰلِكُ لِيَقْضِ عَلَيْنَا رَبُّكَ
قَالَ اِنَّكُمْ مّٰكِثُوْنَ ﴿٧٧﴾
لَقَدْ جِئْنٰكُمْ بِالْحَقِّ وَلٰكِنَّ اَكْثَرَكُمْ
لِلْحَقِّ كٰرِهُوْنَ ﴿٧٨﴾
اَمْ اَبْرَمُوْٓا اَمْرًا فَاِنَّا مُبْرِمُوْنَ ﴿٧٩﴾
اَمْ يَحْسَبُوْنَ اَنَّا لَا نَسْمَعُ سِرَّهُمْ
وَنَجْوٰىهُمْ ۭ بَلٰى وَرُسُلُنَا لَدَيْهِمْ
يَكْتُبُوْنَ ﴿٨٠﴾
قُلْ اِنْ كَانَ لِلرَّحْمٰنِ وَلَدٌ ڰ فَاَنَا اَوَّلُ
الْعٰبِدِيْنَ ﴿٨١﴾
سُبْحٰنَ رَبِّ السَّمٰوٰتِ وَالْاَرْضِ رَبِّ
الْعَرْشِ عَمَّا يَصِفُوْنَ ﴿٨٢﴾
فَذَرْهُمْ يَخُوْضُوْا وَيَلْعَبُوْا حَتّٰى
يُلٰقُوْا يَوْمَهُمُ الَّذِيْ يُوْعَدُوْنَ ﴿٨٣﴾
وَهُوَ الَّذِيْ فِي السَّمَاۗءِ اِلٰهٌ وَّفِي
الْاَرْضِ اِلٰهٌ ۭ وَهُوَ الْحَكِيْمُ الْعَلِيْمُ ﴿٨٤﴾
وَتَبٰرَكَ الَّذِيْ لَهٗ مُلْكُ السَّمٰوٰتِ
وَالْاَرْضِ وَمَا بَيْنَهُمَا ۚ وَعِنْدَهٗ
عِلْمُ السَّاعَةِ ۚ وَاِلَيْهِ تُرْجَعُوْنَ ﴿٨٥﴾
وَلَا يَمْلِكُ الَّذِيْنَ يَدْعُوْنَ مِنْ
دُوْنِهِ الشَّفَاعَةَ اِلَّا مَنْ شَهِدَ
بِالْحَقِّ وَهُمْ يَعْلَمُوْنَ ﴿٨٦﴾

87. (Muhammad), if you ask them, “Who created the idols?” They will certainly say, “Allah has created them.” Why do you then turn away from Allah?

88. (Allah has knowledge of Muhammad's words when he complains to Him), “My Lord, these, my people, do not believe.”

89. We have told him, “Ignore them and say to them 'with peace.' They will soon know the consequences of their deeds.

Al-Dukhan, The Smoke (44)

In the Name of Allah, the Beneficent, the Merciful.

1. Ha. Mim.

2. I swear by the illustrious Book

3. that We have revealed the Quran on a blessed night to warn mankind.

4. On this night, every absolute command coming from Us becomes distinguishable;

5. the command that is from Us which We have been sending

6. as a mercy (for the human being), from your Lord. Your Lord is All-hearing and All-knowing.

7. He is the Lord of the heavens and the earth and all that is between them, if only you would have strong faith.

8. There is only One Lord. It is He who gives life and causes things to die. He is your Lord and the Lord of your forefathers.

9. In fact, the unbelievers have doubts because of excessive involvement in worldly affairs.

10. Wait for the day (which will come before the Day of Judgment) when the sky will give out dense smoke

11. which will smother the people. They will say, “This is a painful torment.

12. Lord, remove this torment from us for we are believers.”

87. Wa la'in sa-altahum man khalaqahum la-yaqoolun-nallaahu fa-annaa yu'fakoon.

88. Wa qeelihee yaa Rabbi inna haaa'ulaaa'i qawmul-laa yu'minoon.

89. Faṣfaḥ ‘anhum wa qul salaam; fasawfa ya‘lamoon.

Sûrat ad-Dukhân-44

(Revealed at Makkah)

Bismillaahir Raḥmaanir Raḥeem

1. Ḥaa-Meeem.

2. Wal-Kitaabil-Mubeen.

3. Innaaa anzalnaahu fee laylatim-mubaarakatin innaa kunnaa munẕireen.

4. Feehaa yufraqu kullu amrin ḥakeem.

5. Amram-min ‘indinaa; innaa kunnaa mursileen.

6. Raḥmatam-mir-Rabbik; innahoo Huwas-Samee‘ul-‘Aleem.

7. Rabbis-samaawaati wal-arḍi wa maa baynahumaa; in kuntum mooqineen.

8. Laaa ilaaha illaa Huwa yuḥyee wa yumeetu Rabbukum wa Rabbu aabaaa'ikumul-awwaleen.

9. Bal hum fee shakkiñy-yal‘aboon.

10. Fartaqib Yawma ta-tis samaaa'u bidukhaanim-mubeen.

11. Yaghshan-naasa haaẕaa ‘aẕaabun aleem.

12. Rabbanak-shif ‘annal ‘aẕaaba innaa mu'minoon.

وَلَئِن سَأَلْتَهُم مَّنْ خَلَقَهُمْ لَيَقُولُنَّ
اللَّهُ فَأَنَّىٰ يُؤْفَكُونَ ﴿٨٧﴾
وَقِيلِهِ يَا رَبِّ إِنَّ هَٰؤُلَاءِ قَوْمٌ لَّا
يُؤْمِنُونَ ﴿٨٨﴾ وقف لازم
فَاصْفَحْ عَنْهُمْ وَقُلْ سَلَامٌ فَسَوْفَ
يَعْلَمُونَ ﴿٨٩﴾ ع ٢٢/٢٤

سُورَةُ الدُّخَانِ مَكِّيَّةٌ (٤٤) (٦٤)

آياتها ٥٩ بِسْمِ اللَّهِ الرَّحْمَٰنِ الرَّحِيمِ ركوعاتها ٣

حم ﴿١﴾
وَالْكِتَابِ الْمُبِينِ ﴿٢﴾ مع ١٢ عند المتقدمين ١٠
إِنَّا أَنزَلْنَاهُ فِي لَيْلَةٍ مُّبَارَكَةٍ إِنَّا
كُنَّا مُنذِرِينَ ﴿٣﴾
فِيهَا يُفْرَقُ كُلُّ أَمْرٍ حَكِيمٍ ﴿٤﴾
أَمْرًا مِّنْ عِندِنَا إِنَّا كُنَّا مُرْسِلِينَ ﴿٥﴾
رَحْمَةً مِّن رَّبِّكَ إِنَّهُ هُوَ السَّمِيعُ
الْعَلِيمُ ﴿٦﴾
رَبِّ السَّمَاوَاتِ وَالْأَرْضِ وَمَا بَيْنَهُمَا وقف لازم
إِن كُنتُم مُّوقِنِينَ ﴿٧﴾
لَا إِلَٰهَ إِلَّا هُوَ يُحْيِي وَيُمِيتُ رَبُّكُمْ
وَرَبُّ آبَائِكُمُ الْأَوَّلِينَ ﴿٨﴾
بَلْ هُمْ فِي شَكٍّ يَلْعَبُونَ ﴿٩﴾
فَارْتَقِبْ يَوْمَ تَأْتِي السَّمَاءُ بِدُخَانٍ
مُّبِينٍ ﴿١٠﴾
يَغْشَى النَّاسَ هَٰذَا عَذَابٌ أَلِيمٌ ﴿١١﴾
رَبَّنَا اكْشِفْ عَنَّا الْعَذَابَ إِنَّا
مُؤْمِنُونَ ﴿١٢﴾

13. How could this punishment bring them to their senses when a Messenger evidently had come to them	13. Annaa lahumuz-zikraa wa qad jaaa'ahum Rasoolum-mubeen.	أَنَّىٰ لَهُمُ الذِّكْرَىٰ وَقَدْ جَاءَهُمْ رَسُولٌ مُّبِينٌ ﴿١٣﴾
14. and they turned away, saying, "He is a trained and possessed (insane) person."	14. Summa tawallaw 'anhu wa qaaloo mu'allamum-majnoon.	ثُمَّ تَوَلَّوْا عَنْهُ وَقَالُوا مُعَلَّمٌ مَّجْنُونٌ ﴿١٤﴾
15. We shall remove the torment for a while but you will revert to your old ways.	15. Innaa kaashiful-'azaabi qaleelaa; innakum 'aaa'idoon.	إِنَّا كَاشِفُوا الْعَذَابِ قَلِيلًا إِنَّكُمْ عَائِدُونَ ﴿١٥﴾
16. However, We shall certainly bring them to justice on the day when the great seizure takes place.	16. Yawma nabṭishul-baṭshatal-kubraaa innaa muntaqimoon.	يَوْمَ نَبْطِشُ الْبَطْشَةَ الْكُبْرَىٰ إِنَّا مُنتَقِمُونَ ﴿١٦﴾
17. We had certainly tested the people of the Pharaoh before those to whom a noble Messenger had come, saying,	17. Wa laqad fatannaa qablahum qawma Fir'awna wa jaaa'ahum Rasoolun kareem.	وَلَقَدْ فَتَنَّا قَبْلَهُمْ قَوْمَ فِرْعَوْنَ وَجَاءَهُمْ رَسُولٌ كَرِيمٌ ﴿١٧﴾
18. "Send the servants of Allah with me. I am a trustworthy Messenger sent to you.	18. An addooo ilayya 'ibaadal-laahi innee lakum Rasoolun ameen.	أَنْ أَدُّوا إِلَيَّ عِبَادَ اللَّهِ إِنِّي لَكُمْ رَسُولٌ أَمِينٌ ﴿١٨﴾
19. Do not consider yourselves above Allah. I shall show you a manifest authority (in support of my truthfulness).	19. Wa al-laa ta'loo 'alal-laahi inneee aateekum bisulṭaanim-mubeen.	وَأَن لَّا تَعْلُوا عَلَى اللَّهِ إِنِّي آتِيكُم بِسُلْطَانٍ مُّبِينٍ ﴿١٩﴾
20. I seek protection of my Lord and your Lord from your decision of stoning me.	20. Wa innee 'uztu bi-Rabbee wa Rabbikum an tarjumoon.	وَإِنِّي عُذْتُ بِرَبِّي وَرَبِّكُمْ أَن تَرْجُمُونِ ﴿٢٠﴾
21. If you did not believe, leave me alone."	21. Wa il-lam tu'minoo lee fa'taziloon.	وَإِن لَّمْ تُؤْمِنُوا لِي فَاعْتَزِلُونِ ﴿٢١﴾
22. Moses addressed his Lord, saying, "Lord, these people are sinners."	22. Fada'aa Rabbahooo anna haaa'ulaaa'i qawmum-mujrimoon.	فَدَعَا رَبَّهُ أَنَّ هَٰؤُلَاءِ قَوْمٌ مُّجْرِمُونَ ﴿٢٢﴾
23. We told him, "Leave the city with My servants during the night. You will be pursued.	23. Fa-asri bi'ibaadee laylan innakum muttaba'oon.	فَأَسْرِ بِعِبَادِي لَيْلًا إِنَّكُم مُّتَّبَعُونَ ﴿٢٣﴾
24. Cross the sea by cutting a path through it. Pharaoh's army will be drowned therein.	24. Watrukil-baḥra rahwan innahum jundum-mughraqoon.	وَاتْرُكِ الْبَحْرَ رَهْوًا إِنَّهُمْ جُندٌ مُّغْرَقُونَ ﴿٢٤﴾
25. How many were the gardens, springs,	25. Kam tarakoo min jannaatiñw-wa 'uyoon.	كَمْ تَرَكُوا مِن جَنَّاتٍ وَعُيُونٍ ﴿٢٥﴾
26. cornfields, gracious mansions,	26. Wa zuroo'iñw-wa maqaamin kareem.	وَزُرُوعٍ وَمَقَامٍ كَرِيمٍ ﴿٢٦﴾
27. and other bounties which they enjoyed yet left behind!	27. Wa na'matin kaanoo feehaa faakiheen.	وَنَعْمَةٍ كَانُوا فِيهَا فَاكِهِينَ ﴿٢٧﴾
28. We gave these as an inheritance to other people."	28. Kazaalika wa awrasnaahaa qawman aakhareen.	كَذَٰلِكَ وَأَوْرَثْنَاهَا قَوْمًا آخَرِينَ ﴿٢٨﴾

وقف لازم

وقف لازم

الثلثة

29. "Neither the sky nor the earth cried for them, nor were they given respite.	29. Famaa bakat 'alayhimus-samaaa'u wal-arḍu wa maa kaanoo munẓareen.	فَمَا بَكَتْ عَلَيْهِمُ السَّمَآءُ وَالْاَرْضُ وَمَا كَانُوْا مُنْظَرِيْنَ ﴿٢٩﴾ ع ٢٩ ١٤
30. We rescued the Israelites from the humiliating torment	30. Wa laqad najjaynaa Baneee Israaa'eela minal 'aẕaa-bil-muheen.	وَلَقَدْ نَجَّيْنَا بَنِيْٓ اِسْرَآءِيْلَ مِنَ الْعَذَابِ الْمُهِيْنِ ﴿٣٠﴾
31. and from the Pharaoh. He was the chief of the transgressors.	31. Min Fir'awn; innahoo kaana 'aaliyam-minal musri-feen.	مِنْ فِرْعَوْنَ ؕ اِنَّهٗ كَانَ عَالِيًا مِّنَ الْمُسْرِفِيْنَ ﴿٣١﴾
32. We gave preference to the Israelites over the other people with Our knowledge	32. Walaqadikh-tarnaahum 'alaa 'ilmin 'alal-'aalameen.	وَلَقَدِ اخْتَرْنٰهُمْ عَلٰى عِلْمٍ عَلَى الْعٰلَمِيْنَ ﴿٣٢﴾
33. and sent them revelations of which some were a clear trial for them."	33. Wa aataynaahum minal-Aayaati maa feehi balaaa'um-mubeen.	وَاٰتَيْنٰهُمْ مِّنَ الْاٰيٰتِ مَا فِيْهِ بَلٰٓؤٌا مُّبِيْنٌ ﴿٣٣﴾
34. These people say,	34. Inna haaa'ulaaa'i la-ya-qooloon.	اِنَّ هٰٓؤُلَآءِ لَيَقُوْلُوْنَ ﴿٣٤﴾
35. "After we die, we shall never be raised to life again.	35. In hiya illaa mawtatunal-oolaa wa maa naḥnu bimun-shareen.	اِنْ هِيَ اِلَّا مَوْتَتُنَا الْاُوْلٰى وَمَا نَحْنُ بِمُنْشَرِيْنَ ﴿٣٥﴾
36. Bring back to life our fathers if what you say is true."	36. Fa-too bi-aabaaa'inaaa in kuntum ṣaadiqeen.	فَاْتُوْا بِاٰبَآئِنَآ اِنْ كُنْتُمْ صٰدِقِيْنَ ﴿٣٦﴾
37. Are they better than the tribe of Tubba (name of a Yemenite tribal chief) and those who lived before them? We destroyed them. They were criminals.	37. Ahum khayrun am qawmu Tubba'iñw-wallaẕeena min qablihim; ahlaknaahum innahum kaanoo mujrimeen.	اَهُمْ خَيْرٌ اَمْ قَوْمُ تُبَّعٍ ۙ وَّالَّذِيْنَ مِنْ قَبْلِهِمْ ؕ اَهْلَكْنٰهُمْ ۫ اِنَّهُمْ كَانُوْا مُجْرِمِيْنَ ﴿٣٧﴾
38. We have not created the heavens and the earth and all that is between them for Our own amusement.	38. Wa maa khalaqnas-samaawaati wal-arḍa wa maa bayna-humaa laa'ibeen.	وَمَا خَلَقْنَا السَّمٰوٰتِ وَالْاَرْضَ وَمَا بَيْنَهُمَا لٰعِبِيْنَ ﴿٣٨﴾
39. We have created them for a genuine purpose, but most people do not know.	39. Maa khalaqnaahumaaa illaa bilḥaqqi wa laakinna akṡarahum laa ya'lamoon.	مَا خَلَقْنٰهُمَآ اِلَّا بِالْحَقِّ وَلٰكِنَّ اَكْثَرَهُمْ لَا يَعْلَمُوْنَ ﴿٣٩﴾
40. The appointed time for all of them will be the Day of Judgment	40. Inna Yawmal-Faṣli mee-qaatuhum ajma'een.	اِنَّ يَوْمَ الْفَصْلِ مِيْقَاتُهُمْ اَجْمَعِيْنَ ﴿٤٠﴾
41. (when wrong will be distinguished from right). On this day friends will be of no benefit to one another, nor will they receive any help	41. Yawma laa yughnee mawlan 'am-mawlan shay'añw-wa laa hum yunṣaroon.	يَوْمَ لَا يُغْنِيْ مَوْلًى عَنْ مَّوْلًى شَيْـًٔا وَّلَا هُمْ يُنْصَرُوْنَ ﴿٤١﴾
42. except for those to whom Allah grants mercy. He is	42. Illaa mar-raḥimal-laah; innahoo Huwal-'Azeezur-	اِلَّا مَنْ رَّحِمَ اللّٰهُ ؕ اِنَّهٗ هُوَ الْعَزِيْزُ

Majestic and All-merciful.	Raḥeem.	الرَّحِيْمُ ﴿٤٢﴾
43. The tree of Al-Zaqqum	43. Inna shajarataz-Zaqqoom.	اِنَّ شَجَرَتَ الزَّقُّوْمِ ﴿٤٣﴾
44. is food for the sinner.	44. Ṭa'aamul-aseem.	طَعَامُ الْاَثِيْمِ ﴿٤٤﴾
45. It will be like melted brass, which will boil in the bellies	45. Kalmuhli yaghlee filbuṭoon.	كَالْمُهْلِ ۚ يَغْلِيْ فِي الْبُطُوْنِ ﴿٤٥﴾
46. like water.	46. Kaghalyil-ḥameem.	كَغَلْيِ الْحَمِيْمِ ﴿٤٦﴾
47. (It will be said to the guards of such sinners), "Seize, press and drag them into the middle of hell.	47. Khuzoohu fa'tiloohu ilaa sawaaa'il-Jaḥeem.	خُذُوْهُ فَاعْتِلُوْهُ اِلٰى سَوَآءِ الْجَحِيْمِ ﴿٤٧﴾
48. Then pour onto their heads the boiling water to torment them."	48. Summa ṣubboo fawqa rasihee min 'azaabil-ḥameem.	ثُمَّ صُبُّوْا فَوْقَ رَاْسِهٖ مِنْ عَذَابِ الْحَمِيْمِ ﴿٤٨﴾
49. They will be told, "Suffer the torment. You had thought yourselves to be majestic and honorable.	49. Zuq innaka antal 'azeezul-kareem.	ذُقْ ۚ اِنَّكَ اَنْتَ الْعَزِيْزُ الْكَرِيْمُ ﴿٤٩﴾
50. This is the torment that you persistently doubted."	50. Inna haazaa maa kuntum bihee tamtaroon.	اِنَّ هٰذَا مَا كُنْتُمْ بِهٖ تَمْتَرُوْنَ ﴿٥٠﴾
51. The pious ones will be in a secure place	51. Innal-muttaqeena fee maqaamin ameen.	اِنَّ الْمُتَّقِيْنَ فِيْ مَقَامٍ اَمِيْنٍ ﴿٥١﴾
52. amid gardens and springs,	52. Fee Jannaatiñw-wa 'uyoon.	فِيْ جَنّٰتٍ وَّعُيُوْنٍ ﴿٥٢﴾
53. clothed in fine silk and rich brocade, sitting face to face with one another.	53. Yalbasoona min sundusiñw-wa istabraqim-mutaqaabileen.	يَّلْبَسُوْنَ مِنْ سُنْدُسٍ وَّ اِسْتَبْرَقٍ مُّتَقٰبِلِيْنَ ﴿٥٣﴾
54. We shall pair them up with maidens with big black and white lovely eyes.	54. Kazaalika wa zawwajnaahum biḥoorin'een.	كَذٰلِكَ ۗ وَزَوَّجْنٰهُمْ بِحُوْرٍ عِيْنٍ ﴿٥٤﴾
55. They will be offered all kinds of fruits, in peace and security.	55. Yad'oona feehaa bikulli faakihatin aamineen.	يَدْعُوْنَ فِيْهَا بِكُلِّ فَاكِهَةٍ اٰمِنِيْنَ ﴿٥٥﴾
56. They will not experience any death other than that which they have already been through.	56. Laa yazooqoona feehal-mawta illal-mawtatal-oolaa wa waqaahum 'azaabal Jaḥeem.	لَا يَذُوْقُوْنَ فِيْهَا الْمَوْتَ اِلَّا الْمَوْتَةَ الْاُوْلٰى ۚ وَوَقٰهُمْ عَذَابَ الْجَحِيْمِ ﴿٥٦﴾
57. Allah will protect them from the torment of hell as a favor from your Lord. (Muhammad), this is certainly the greatest triumph.	57. Faḍlam-mir-Rabbik; zaalika huwal-fawzul-'aẓeem.	فَضْلًا مِّنْ رَّبِّكَ ۚ ذٰلِكَ هُوَ الْفَوْزُ الْعَظِيْمُ ﴿٥٧﴾
58. We have made it (blessings of Paradise) for you easy (to reach) so that perhaps they may take heed.	58. Fa-innamaa yassarnaahu bilisaanika la'allahum yatazakkaroon.	فَاِنَّمَا يَسَّرْنٰهُ بِلِسَانِكَ لَعَلَّهُمْ يَتَذَكَّرُوْنَ ﴿٥٨﴾
59. Wait (for Allah's decree) and they also will be waiting.	59. Fartaqib innahum murtaqiboon.	فَارْتَقِبْ اِنَّهُمْ مُّرْتَقِبُوْنَ ﴿٥٩﴾

Al-Jathiyah, The Kneeling (45)

In the Name of Allah,
the Beneficent, the Merciful.

1. Ha. Mim

2. This Book is revealed from Allah, the Majestic and All-wise.

3. In the heavens and the earth there is evidence (of the Truth) for the believers.

4. In your creation and in that of the beasts living on earth there is evidence of the Truth for the people who have strong faith.

5. In the alternation of the night and the day, the sustenance which Allah has sent down from the sky to revive the barren earth, and in the changing of the direction of the winds there is evidence of the truth for the people of understanding.

6. These are the revelations of Allah which We recite to you for a genuine purpose. In what statements other than Allah's and His revelations will they then believe?

7. Woe to every sinful liar!

8. He hears the revelations of Allah which are recited to him, then persists in his arrogance as if he had not even heard them. Tell him that he will suffer a painful torment.

9. When he learns (sees) any one of Our revelations, he scorns them. Such people will suffer a humiliating torment.

10. Hell is awaiting them and none of their deeds will be of any benefit to them, and so also will be the guardians whom they have chosen besides Allah. They will

Sûrat al-Jâsiyah-45

(Revealed at Makkah)
Bismillaahir Raḥmaanir Raḥeem

1. Ḥaa-Meeem.

2. Tanzeelul Kitaabi minal-laahil-'Azeezil Ḥakeem.

3. Inna fis-samaawaati wal-arḍi la-Aayaatil-lilmu'mineen.

4. Wa fee khalqikum wa maa yabus̲s̲u min daaabbatin Aayaatul-liqawmiñy-yooq-inoon.

5. Wakhtilaafil-layli wanna-haari wa maaa anzalal laahu minas-samaaa'i mir-rizqin fa-aḥyaa bihil-arḍa ba'da mawti-haa wa taṣreefir-riyaaḥi Aayaatul-liqawmiñy-ya'qiloon.

6. Tilka Aayaatul-laahi nat-loohaa 'alayka bilḥaqq; fabi-ayyi ḥadees̲im ba'dallaahi wa Aayaatihee yu'minoon.

7. Waylul-likulli affaakin as̲eem.

8. Yasma'u Aayaatil-laahi tutlaa 'alayhi s̲umma yuṣirru mustakbiran ka-al-lam yasma'-haa fabashshirhu bi'az̲aabin aleem.

9. Wa iz̲aa 'alima min Aayaatinaa shay'anit-takhaz̲a-haa huzuwaa; ulaaa'ika lahum 'az̲aabum muheen.

10. Miñw-waraaa'ihim Ja-hannamu wa laa yughnee 'anhum maa kasaboo shay'añw-wa laa mat-takhaz̲oo min doonil-laahi awliyaaa'a wa

(٤٥) سُوْرَةُ الْجَاثِيَةِ مَكِّيَّةٌ (٦٥)

آياتها ٣٧ بِسْمِ اللّٰهِ الرَّحْمٰنِ الرَّحِيْمِ رکوعاتها ٤

حٰمٓ ﴿١﴾
تَنْزِيْلُ الْكِتٰبِ مِنَ اللّٰهِ الْعَزِيْزِ
الْحَكِيْمِ ﴿٢﴾
اِنَّ فِي السَّمٰوٰتِ وَالْاَرْضِ لَاٰيٰتٍ
لِّلْمُؤْمِنِيْنَ ﴿٣﴾
وَفِيْ خَلْقِكُمْ وَمَا يَبُثُّ مِنْ
دَآبَّةٍ اٰيٰتٌ لِّقَوْمٍ يُّوْقِنُوْنَ ﴿٤﴾
وَاخْتِلَافِ الَّيْلِ وَالنَّهَارِ وَمَآ
اَنْزَلَ اللّٰهُ مِنَ السَّمَآءِ مِنْ رِّزْقٍ
فَاَحْيَا بِهِ الْاَرْضَ بَعْدَ مَوْتِهَا
وَتَصْرِيْفِ الرِّيٰحِ اٰيٰتٌ لِّقَوْمٍ
يَّعْقِلُوْنَ ﴿٥﴾
تِلْكَ اٰيٰتُ اللّٰهِ نَتْلُوْهَا عَلَيْكَ
بِالْحَقِّ فَبِاَيِّ حَدِيْثٍ بَعْدَ اللّٰهِ
وَاٰيٰتِهٖ يُؤْمِنُوْنَ ﴿٦﴾
وَيْلٌ لِّكُلِّ اَفَّاكٍ اَثِيْمٍ ﴿٧﴾
يَّسْمَعُ اٰيٰتِ اللّٰهِ تُتْلٰى عَلَيْهِ ثُمَّ
يُصِرُّ مُسْتَكْبِرًا كَاَنْ لَّمْ يَسْمَعْهَا
فَبَشِّرْهُ بِعَذَابٍ اَلِيْمٍ ﴿٨﴾
وَاِذَا عَلِمَ مِنْ اٰيٰتِنَا شَيْئًا اتَّخَذَهَا
هُزُوًا اُولٰٓئِكَ لَهُمْ عَذَابٌ مُّهِيْنٌ ﴿٩﴾
مِنْ وَّرَآئِهِمْ جَهَنَّمُ وَلَا يُغْنِيْ
عَنْهُمْ مَّا كَسَبُوْا شَيْئًا وَّلَا مَا
اتَّخَذُوْا مِنْ دُوْنِ اللّٰهِ اَوْلِيَآءَ وَ

لَهُمْ عَذَابٌ عَظِيمٌ ﴿١٠﴾

lahum 'azaabun 'azeem.

suffer a great torment.

هَٰذَا هُدًى ۚ وَالَّذِينَ كَفَرُوا بِآيَاتِ رَبِّهِمْ لَهُمْ عَذَابٌ مِّن رِّجْزٍ أَلِيمٌ ﴿١١﴾ ع ١١/١٧

11. Haazaa hudaa; wallazeena kafaroo bi-Aayaati Rabbihim lahum 'azaabum mir-rijzin aleem.

11. This (Quran) is guidance. Those who reject the revelations of their Lord will suffer the most painful punishment.

اللَّهُ الَّذِي سَخَّرَ لَكُمُ الْبَحْرَ لِتَجْرِيَ الْفُلْكُ فِيهِ بِأَمْرِهِ وَلِتَبْتَغُوا مِن فَضْلِهِ وَلَعَلَّكُمْ تَشْكُرُونَ ﴿١٢﴾

12. Allaahul-lazee sakhkhara lakumul-baḥra litajriyal-fulku feehi bi-amrihee wa litabtaghoo min faḍlihee wa la'allakum tashkuroon.

12. Allah has made the sea subservient to you so that ships sail on by His command and you seek His favors. Perhaps you will be grateful.

وَسَخَّرَ لَكُم مَّا فِي السَّمَاوَاتِ وَمَا فِي الْأَرْضِ جَمِيعًا مِّنْهُ ۚ إِنَّ فِي ذَٰلِكَ لَآيَاتٍ لِّقَوْمٍ يَتَفَكَّرُونَ ﴿١٣﴾

13. Wa sakhkhara lakum maa fis-samaawaati wa maa fil-arḍi jameeam-minh; inna fee zaalika la-Aayaatil-liqawmiñy-yatafakkaroon.

13. He has also made subservient to you all that is in the heavens and the earth. In this there is evidence (of the Truth) for those who use their minds.

قُل لِّلَّذِينَ آمَنُوا يَغْفِرُوا لِلَّذِينَ لَا يَرْجُونَ أَيَّامَ اللَّهِ لِيَجْزِيَ قَوْمًا بِمَا كَانُوا يَكْسِبُونَ ﴿١٤﴾

14. Qul lillazeena aamanoo yaghfiroo lillazeena laa yarjoona ayyaamal-laahi liyajziya qawmam bimaa kaanoo yaksiboon.

14. Tell the believers to forgive those who do not have faith in the days of Allah (Day of Judgment) and Resurrection. Allah will give due recompense to all the people for their deeds.

مَنْ عَمِلَ صَالِحًا فَلِنَفْسِهِ ۖ وَمَنْ أَسَاءَ فَعَلَيْهَا ۖ ثُمَّ إِلَىٰ رَبِّكُمْ تُرْجَعُونَ ﴿١٥﴾

15. Man 'amila ṣaaliḥan falinafsihee wa man asaaa'a fa'alayhaa summa ilaa Rabbikum turja'oon.

15. One who acts righteously does so for his own benefit and one who commits evil does so against his own soul. To your Lord you will all return.

وَلَقَدْ آتَيْنَا بَنِي إِسْرَائِيلَ الْكِتَابَ وَالْحُكْمَ وَالنُّبُوَّةَ وَرَزَقْنَاهُم مِّنَ الطَّيِّبَاتِ وَفَضَّلْنَاهُمْ عَلَى الْعَالَمِينَ ﴿١٦﴾

16. Wa laqad aataynaa Baneee Israaa'eelal-Kitaaba wal-Ḥukma wan-Nubuwwata wa razaqnaahum minaṭ-ṭayyibaati wa faḍḍalnaahum 'alal- 'aalameen.

16. We gave the Book to the Israelites, the commandments, and prophecy, granted them pure sustenance, and gave them preference above all people (of their time).

وَآتَيْنَاهُم بَيِّنَاتٍ مِّنَ الْأَمْرِ ۖ فَمَا اخْتَلَفُوا إِلَّا مِن بَعْدِ مَا جَاءَهُمُ الْعِلْمُ بَغْيًا بَيْنَهُمْ ۚ إِنَّ رَبَّكَ يَقْضِي بَيْنَهُمْ يَوْمَ الْقِيَامَةِ فِيمَا كَانُوا فِيهِ يَخْتَلِفُونَ ﴿١٧﴾

17. Wa aataynaahum bayyinaatim-minal-amri famakhtalafooo illaa mim ba'di maa jaaa'ahumul-'ilmu baghyam baynahum; inna Rabbaka yaqḍee baynahum Yawmal-Qiyaamati feemaa kaanoo feehi yakhtalifoon.

17. We also gave them clear evidence in support of the true religion. Only after having received knowledge did they create differences among themselves because of their rebelliousness. Your Lord will issue His decree concerning their differences on the Day of Judgment.

ثُمَّ جَعَلْنَاكَ عَلَىٰ شَرِيعَةٍ مِّنَ الْأَمْرِ

18. Summa ja'alnaaka 'alaa sharee'atim-minal-amri

18. We have established for you a code of conduct and a religion. Follow it and do not follow the

desires of the ignorant people. (It is another example where the Holy Prophet is addressed but his followers are meant thereby).

19. They will never be sufficient (protection) for you in place of Allah. The unjust are each other's friends, but Allah is the Guardian of the pious ones.

20. This (Quran) is enlightenment for the people and a guide and mercy for the people who have strong faith.

21. Do the people who commit evil think that We shall make their life and death like that of the righteously striving believers? How terrible is their Judgment!

22. Allah has created the heavens and the earth for a genuine purpose so that every soul will be duly recompensed for its deeds without being wronged.

23. Have you seen the one who has chosen his desires as his lord? Allah has knowingly caused him to go astray, sealed his ears and heart and veiled his vision. Who besides Allah can guide him? Will they, then, not take heed?

24. They have said, "The only life is this worldly life and here we shall live and die. It is only time which will destroy us." They have no knowledge about this. It is only their guesswork.

25. When Our enlightening revelations are recited to them, their only argument against them is, "Bring our forefathers back to

fattabi'haa wa laa tattabi' ahwaaa'al-lazeena laa ya'la-moon.

19. Innahum lañy-yughnoo 'anka minal-laahi shay'aa; wa-innaẓ-ẓaalimeena ba'ḍuhum awliyaaa'u ba'ḍ; wallaahu waliyyul-muttaqeen.

20. Haazaa baṣaaa'iru lin-naasi wa hudañw-wa raḥmatul-liqawmiñy-yooqinoon.

21. Am ḥasibal-lazeenaj-tara-ḥus-sayyi-aati an naj'alahum kallazeena aamanoo wa 'amiluṣ-ṣaaliḥaati sawaaa'am maḥyaahum wa mamaatuhum; saaa'a maa yaḥkumoon.

22. Wa khalaqal-laahus-sa-maawaati wal-arḍa bilḥaqqi wa litujzaa kullu nafsim bimaa kasabat wa hum laa yuẓlamoon.

23. Afara'ayta manit-takhaza ilaahahoo hawaahu wa aḍal-lahul-laahu 'alaa 'ilmiñw-wa khatama 'alaa sam'ihee wa qalbihee wa ja'ala 'alaa baṣa-rihee ghishaawatan famañy-yahdeehi mim ba'dil-laah; afalaa tazakkaroon.

24. Wa qaaloo maa hiya illaa ḥayaatunad-dunyaa namootu wa naḥyaa wa maa yuhlikunaaa illad-dahr; wa maa lahum bizaalika min 'ilmin in hum illaa yaẓunnoon.

25. Wa izaa tutlaa 'alayhim Aayaatunaa bayyinaatim-maa kaana ḥujjatahum illaaa an

فَاتَّبِعْهَا وَلَا تَتَّبِعْ اَهْوَآءَ الَّذِيْنَ
لَا يَعْلَمُوْنَ ﴿۱۸﴾
اِنَّهُمْ لَنْ يُّغْنُوْا عَنْكَ مِنَ اللّٰهِ
شَيْـًٔا ؕ وَاِنَّ الظّٰلِمِيْنَ بَعْضُهُمْ
اَوْلِيَآءُ بَعْضٍ ۚ وَاللّٰهُ وَلِيُّ
الْمُتَّقِيْنَ ﴿۱۹﴾
هٰذَا بَصَآئِرُ لِلنَّاسِ وَهُدًى
وَّرَحْمَةٌ لِّقَوْمٍ يُّوْقِنُوْنَ ﴿۲۰﴾
اَمْ حَسِبَ الَّذِيْنَ اجْتَرَحُوا السَّيِّاٰتِ
اَنْ نَّجْعَلَهُمْ كَالَّذِيْنَ اٰمَنُوْا
وَعَمِلُوا الصّٰلِحٰتِ ۙ سَوَآءً مَّحْيَاهُمْ
وَمَمَاتُهُمْ ؕ سَآءَ مَا يَحْكُمُوْنَ ﴿۲۱﴾ ع ۲ ۱۸
وَخَلَقَ اللّٰهُ السَّمٰوٰتِ وَالْاَرْضَ
بِالْحَقِّ وَلِتُجْزٰى كُلُّ نَفْسٍ
بِمَا كَسَبَتْ وَهُمْ لَا يُظْلَمُوْنَ ﴿۲۲﴾
اَفَرَءَيْتَ مَنِ اتَّخَذَ اِلٰهَهٗ هَوٰىهُ
وَاَضَلَّهُ اللّٰهُ عَلٰى عِلْمٍ وَّخَتَمَ
عَلٰى سَمْعِهٖ وَقَلْبِهٖ وَجَعَلَ عَلٰى
بَصَرِهٖ غِشٰوَةً ؕ فَمَنْ يَّهْدِيْهِ
مِنْ بَعْدِ اللّٰهِ ؕ اَفَلَا تَذَكَّرُوْنَ ﴿۲۳﴾
وَقَالُوْا مَا هِيَ اِلَّا حَيَاتُنَا الدُّنْيَا
نَمُوْتُ وَنَحْيَا وَمَا يُهْلِكُنَآ اِلَّا
الدَّهْرُ ۚ وَمَا لَهُمْ بِذٰلِكَ مِنْ
عِلْمٍ ۚ اِنْ هُمْ اِلَّا يَظُنُّوْنَ ﴿۲۴﴾
وَاِذَا تُتْلٰى عَلَيْهِمْ اٰيٰتُنَا بَيِّنٰتٍ
مَّا كَانَ حُجَّتَهُمْ اِلَّآ اَنْ

life if what you say is true."

qaalu'-too bi-aabaaa'inaaa in kuntum ṣaadiqeen.

قَالُوا ائْتُوْا بِاٰبَآئِنَآ اِنْ كُنْتُمْ
صٰدِقِيْنَ ﴿٢٥﴾

26. (Muhammad), say, "It is Allah who gives you life and causes you to die. He will bring you together on the inevitable Day of Judgment," but most people do not know.

26. Qulil-laahu yuḥyeekum s̲umma yumeetukum s̲umma yajma'ukum ilaa Yawmil Qiyaamati laa rayba feehi wa laakinna aks̲aran-naasi laa ya'lamoon.

قُلِ اللّٰهُ يُحْيِيْكُمْ ثُمَّ يُمِيْتُكُمْ
ثُمَّ يَجْمَعُكُمْ اِلٰى يَوْمِ الْقِيٰمَةِ
لَا رَيْبَ فِيْهِ وَلٰكِنَّ اَكْثَرَ
النَّاسِ لَا يَعْلَمُوْنَ ﴿٢٦﴾ ع ٣ ٥ ١٩

27. To Allah belongs the kingdom of the heavens and the earth. On the day when the Hour of Doom arrives, the followers of falsehood will suffer much loss.

27. Wa lillaahi mulkus-samaa-waati wal-arḍ; wa Yawma taqoomus-Saa'atu Yawma 'iz̲iñy-yakhsarul-mubṭiloon.

وَلِلّٰهِ مُلْكُ السَّمٰوٰتِ وَالْاَرْضِ ط
وَيَوْمَ تَقُوْمُ السَّاعَةُ يَوْمَئِذٍ
يَّخْسَرُ الْمُبْطِلُوْنَ ﴿٢٧﴾

28. You will see all the people kneeling down. Everyone will be summoned to the Book (containing the record of their deeds). They will be told, "On this day you will be recompensed for what you have done."

28. Wa taraa kulla ummatin jaas̲iyah; kullu ummatin tud'aaa ilaa kitaabihaa; al-Yawma tujzaw-na maa kuntum ta'maloon.

وَتَرٰى كُلَّ اُمَّةٍ جَاثِيَةً قف كُلُّ
اُمَّةٍ تُدْعٰى اِلٰى كِتٰبِهَا ط اَلْيَوْمَ
تُجْزَوْنَ مَا كُنْتُمْ تَعْمَلُوْنَ ﴿٢٨﴾

29. This (Muhammad) is Our Book that speaks to you the truth. We have made a copy of all that you have done.

29. Haaz̲aa kitaabunaa yanṭi-qu 'alaykum bilḥaqq; innaa kunnaa nastansikhu maa kuntum ta'maloon.

هٰذَا كِتٰبُنَا يَنْطِقُ عَلَيْكُمْ
بِالْحَقِّ ط اِنَّا كُنَّا نَسْتَنْسِخُ
مَا كُنْتُمْ تَعْمَلُوْنَ ﴿٢٩﴾

30. The Lord will admit the righteously striving, believing people into His mercy. This is certainly a clear victory.

30. Fa-ammal-laz̲eena aama-noo wa 'amiluṣ-ṣaaliḥaati fa-yudkhiluhum Rabbuhum fee raḥmatih; z̲aalika huwal-fawzul-mubeen.

فَاَمَّا الَّذِيْنَ اٰمَنُوْا وَعَمِلُوا
الصّٰلِحٰتِ فَيُدْخِلُهُمْ رَبُّهُمْ فِيْ
رَحْمَتِهٖ ط ذٰلِكَ هُوَ الْفَوْزُ الْمُبِيْنُ ﴿٣٠﴾

31. To the unbelievers the Lord will say, "Were not Our revelations recited to you and did not you arrogantly reject them? You were a sinful people."

31. Wa ammal-laz̲eena kafa-roo afalam takun Aayaatee tutlaa 'alaykum fastakbartum wa kuntum qawmam-mujri-meen.

وَاَمَّا الَّذِيْنَ كَفَرُوْا قف اَفَلَمْ تَكُنْ
اٰيٰتِيْ تُتْلٰى عَلَيْكُمْ فَاسْتَكْبَرْتُمْ
وَكُنْتُمْ قَوْمًا مُّجْرِمِيْنَ ﴿٣١﴾

32. When it was said that the promise of Allah is true and that the Hour would inevitably come, you said, "We do not know what the Hour of Doom is, we are suspicious about it, and we are not convinced."

32. Wa iz̲aa qeela inna wa'dal-laahi ḥaqquñw-was Saa'atu laa rayba feehaa qultum maa nadree mas-Saa'atu in naẓunnu illaa ẓannañw-wa maa naḥnu bimustayqineen.

وَاِذَا قِيْلَ اِنَّ وَعْدَ اللّٰهِ حَقٌّ
وَّالسَّاعَةُ لَا رَيْبَ فِيْهَا قُلْتُمْ مَّا
نَدْرِيْ مَا السَّاعَةُ لا اِنْ نَّظُنُّ اِلَّا
ظَنًّا وَّمَا نَحْنُ بِمُسْتَيْقِنِيْنَ ﴿٣٢﴾

33. Their evil deeds will be revealed to them and (the

33. Wa badaa lahum sayyi-aatu maa 'amiloo wa ḥaaqa

وَبَدَا لَهُمْ سَيِّاٰتُ مَا عَمِلُوْا وَحَاقَ

torment) which they had mocked will surround them.

bihim maa kaanoo bihee yastahzi'oon.

بِهِم مَّا كَانُوا بِهِ يَسْتَهْزِءُونَ ٣٣

34. They will be told, "On this day We shall forget you in the same way that you had forgotten your coming into Our presence. Your dwelling will be hellfire and no one will help you.

34. Wa qeelal-Yawma nansaakum kamaa naseetum liqaaa'a Yawmikum haaẕaa wa ma-waakumun-Naaru wa maa lakum min naaṣireen.

وَقِيلَ الْيَوْمَ نَنسَاكُمْ كَمَا نَسِيتُمْ
لِقَاءَ يَوْمِكُمْ هَٰذَا وَمَأْوَاكُمُ النَّارُ
وَمَا لَكُم مِّن نَّاصِرِينَ ٣٤

35. This is only because you had mocked the revelations of Allah and the worldly life had deceived you. On this day they will not be taken out of hell, nor will they be granted any chance for correction.

35. Ẕaalikum bi-annakumut takhaẕtum Aayaatil-laahi huzuwañw-wa gharrat-kumul ḥayaatud-dunyaa; fal-Yawma laa yukhrajoona minhaa wa laa hum yusta'taboon.

ذَٰلِكُم بِأَنَّكُمُ اتَّخَذْتُمْ آيَاتِ اللَّهِ
هُزُوًا وَغَرَّتْكُمُ الْحَيَاةُ الدُّنْيَا
فَالْيَوْمَ لَا يُخْرَجُونَ مِنْهَا وَلَا
هُمْ يُسْتَعْتَبُونَ ٣٥

36. It is only Allah, Lord of the heavens and the earth and Lord of the universe, who deserves all praise.

36. Falillaahil-ḥamdu Rabbis-samaawaati wa Rabbil-arḍi Rabbil-'aalameen.

فَلِلَّهِ الْحَمْدُ رَبِّ السَّمَاوَاتِ وَرَبِّ
الْأَرْضِ رَبِّ الْعَالَمِينَ ٣٦

37. It is His greatness (power) that dominates the heavens and the earth. He is the Majestic and All-wise.

37. Wa lahul-kibriyaaa'u fissamaawaati wal-arḍi wa Huwal-'Azeezul-Ḥakeem.

وَلَهُ الْكِبْرِيَاءُ فِي السَّمَاوَاتِ
وَالْأَرْضِ وَهُوَ الْعَزِيزُ الْحَكِيمُ ٣٧

ع ٤

Al-Ahqaf, The Ahqaf (46)

In the Name of Allah, the Beneficent, the Merciful.

Sûrat al-Aḥqâf-46

(Revealed at Makkah)

Bismillaahir Raḥmaanir Raḥeem

سُورَةُ الْأَحْقَافِ مَكِّيَّةٌ (٤٦) (٦٦)

آياتها ٣٥ بِسْمِ اللَّهِ الرَّحْمَٰنِ الرَّحِيمِ ركوعاتها ٤

1. Ha. Mim

1. Ḥaa-Meeem.

حم ١

2. This Book is revealed from Allah the Majestic and All-wise.

2. Tanzeelul-Kitaabi minal-laahil-'Azeezil-Ḥakeem.

تَنزِيلُ الْكِتَابِ مِنَ اللَّهِ الْعَزِيزِ
الْحَكِيمِ ٢

3. We have created the heavens and the earth and all that is between them for only a genuine purpose and an appointed time. The unbelievers (people of Quraysh) ignore that of which they have been warned.

3. Maa khalaqnas-samaa-waati wal-arḍa wa maa bayna-humaaa illaa bilḥaqqi wa ajalim-musammaa; wallaẕeena kafaroo 'ammaaa unẕiroo mu'riḍoon.

مَا خَلَقْنَا السَّمَاوَاتِ وَالْأَرْضَ وَمَا
بَيْنَهُمَا إِلَّا بِالْحَقِّ وَأَجَلٍ مُّسَمًّى
وَالَّذِينَ كَفَرُوا عَمَّا أُنذِرُوا
مُعْرِضُونَ ٣

4. (Muhammad), ask them, "Have you thought about what you worship besides Allah? Show me which part of the earth they have created. Do they have a share in the creation of the heavens? Bring me a Book, revealed before this Quran, or any other proof based on knowledge, to support your belief, if indeed you are truthful."

4. Qul ara'aytum maa tad'oona min doonil-laahi aroonee maaẕaa khalaqoo minal-arḍi am lahum shirkun fis-samaawaati i-toonee bi-Kitaabim-min qabli haaẕaaa aw aṡaaratim min 'ilmin in kuntum ṣaadiqeen.

قُلْ أَرَأَيْتُم مَّا تَدْعُونَ مِن دُونِ
اللَّهِ أَرُونِي مَاذَا خَلَقُوا مِنَ
الْأَرْضِ أَمْ لَهُمْ شِرْكٌ فِي السَّمَاوَاتِ
ائْتُونِي بِكِتَابٍ مِّن قَبْلِ هَٰذَا أَوْ
أَثَارَةٍ مِّنْ عِلْمٍ إِن كُنتُمْ صَادِقِينَ ٤

الجزء السادس والعشرون (٢٦)

5. Who is more astray than one who prays to things besides Allah; things that would not be able to answer his prayers even if he would wait until the Day of Judgment. They are not even aware of his prayers.

5. Wa man aḍallu mimmañy-yad'oo min doonil-laahi mallaa yastajeebu lahooo ilaa Yawmil-Qiyaamati wa hum 'an du'aa'ihim ghaafiloon.

وَمَنْ اَضَلُّ مِمَّنْ يَّدْعُوْا مِنْ
دُوْنِ اللّٰهِ مَنْ لَّا يَسْتَجِيْبُ
لَهٗۤ اِلٰى يَوْمِ الْقِيٰمَةِ وَهُمْ عَنْ
دُعَآئِهِمْ غٰفِلُوْنَ ۝٥

6. When people will be resurrected, such gods will become their enemies and will reject their worship.

6. Wa iz̲aa ḥushiran-naasu kaanoo lahum a'daaa'añw-wa kaanoo bi'ibaadatihim kaafireen.

وَاِذَا حُشِرَ النَّاسُ كَانُوْا لَهُمْ اَعْدَآءً
وَّكَانُوْا بِعِبَادَتِهِمْ كٰفِرِيْنَ ۝٦

7. When Our enlightening revelations are recited to them, the unbelievers of the truth which has come to them, say, "This is plain magic."

7. Wa iz̲aa tutlaa 'alayhim Aayaatunaa bayyinaatin qaalal-laz̲eena kafaroo lilḥaqqi lammaa jaaa'ahum haaz̲aa siḥrum-mubeen.

وَاِذَا تُتْلٰى عَلَيْهِمْ اٰيٰتُنَا بَيِّنٰتٍ
قَالَ الَّذِيْنَ كَفَرُوْا لِلْحَقِّ لَمَّا
جَآءَهُمْ ۙ هٰذَا سِحْرٌ مُّبِيْنٌ ۝٧

8. Or they say, "(Muhammad) has invented it (Quran) by himself." Say, "Had I invented it, you would not be able to rescue me from Allah. He knows best what you say about it. He is our witness and He is All-forgiving and All-merciful."

8. Am yaqooloonaf-taraahu qul inif-taraytuhoo falaa tamlikoona lee minal-laahi shay'an Huwa a'lamu bimaa tufeeḍoona feehi kafaa bihee shaheedam baynee wa baynakum wa Huwal Ghafoorur-Raḥeem.

اَمْ يَقُوْلُوْنَ افْتَرٰىهُ ؕ قُلْ اِنِ افْتَرَيْتُهٗ
فَلَا تَمْلِكُوْنَ لِيْ مِنَ اللّٰهِ شَيْـًٔا ؕ
هُوَ اَعْلَمُ بِمَا تُفِيْضُوْنَ فِيْهِ ؕ كَفٰى
بِهٖ شَهِيْدًاۢ بَيْنِيْ وَبَيْنَكُمْ ؕ وَهُوَ
الْغَفُوْرُ الرَّحِيْمُ ۝٨

9. Say, "I am not the first Messenger. I do not know what will be done to me or to you. I follow only what has been revealed to me. I am one who gives clear warning only."

9. Qul maa kuntu bid'am-minar-Rusuli wa maaa adree maa yuf'alu bee wa laa bikum in attabi'u illaa maa yooḥaaa ilayya wa maaa anaa illaa naz̲eerum-mubeen.

قُلْ مَا كُنْتُ بِدْعًا مِّنَ الرُّسُلِ
وَمَآ اَدْرِيْ مَا يُفْعَلُ بِيْ وَلَا
بِكُمْ ؕ اِنْ اَتَّبِعُ اِلَّا مَا يُوْحٰۤى
اِلَيَّ وَمَآ اَنَا اِلَّا نَذِيْرٌ مُّبِيْنٌ ۝٩

10. Say, "What do you think will happen if this Quran is from Allah and you have rejected it? Besides, a witness from among the Israelites has testified to the divinity of a Book like it and believed in it (Quran) while you have arrogantly denied it. Allah does not guide the unjust.

10. Qul ara'aytum in kaana min 'indil-laahi wa kafartum bihee wa shahida shaahidum-mim Baneee Israaa'eela 'alaa mis̲lihee fa-aamana wastakbartum innal-laaha laa yahdil-qawmaẓ-ẓaalimeen.

قُلْ اَرَءَيْتُمْ اِنْ كَانَ مِنْ عِنْدِ
اللّٰهِ وَكَفَرْتُمْ بِهٖ وَشَهِدَ شَاهِدٌ
مِّنْۢ بَنِيْۤ اِسْرَآءِيْلَ عَلٰى مِثْلِهٖ
فَاٰمَنَ وَاسْتَكْبَرْتُمْ ؕ اِنَّ اللّٰهَ لَا
يَهْدِى الْقَوْمَ الظّٰلِمِيْنَ ۝١٠ ع ١

11. The unbelievers have said about the believers, "Had there been anything good in it (Quran), they could not have accepted it before us." Since they did not benefit from its guidance, they say, "It (Quran) is only a

11. Wa qaalal-laz̲eena kafaroo lillaz̲eena aamanoo law kaana khayram-maa sabaqoonaaa ilayh; wa iz̲ lam yahtadoo bihee fasayaqooloona

وَقَالَ الَّذِيْنَ كَفَرُوْا لِلَّذِيْنَ اٰمَنُوْا
لَوْ كَانَ خَيْرًا مَّا سَبَقُوْنَآ اِلَيْهِ ؕ
وَاِذْ لَمْ يَهْتَدُوْا بِهٖ فَسَيَقُوْلُوْنَ

fabricated legend."

haazaaa ifkun qadeem.

هٰذَآ اِفْكٌ قَدِيْمٌ ﴿١١﴾

12. Before this (Quran), the Book of Moses was a guide and a blessing. This Book confirms the Torah. It is in the Arabic language so that it may warn the unjust people, and give glad news to the righteous ones.

12. Wa min qablihee Kitaabu Moosaaa imaamañw-wa raḥmah; wa haazaa Kitaabum-muṣaddiqul-lisaanan 'Arabiyyal-liyunzìral-lazeena ẓalamoo wa bushraa lilmuḥsineen.

وَمِنْ قَبْلِهٖ كِتٰبُ مُوْسٰٓى اِمَامًا
وَّرَحْمَةً ؕ وَهٰذَا كِتٰبٌ مُّصَدِّقٌ
لِّسَانًا عَرَبِيًّا لِّيُنْذِرَ الَّذِيْنَ ظَلَمُوْا ۖۗ
وَبُشْرٰى لِلْمُحْسِنِيْنَ ﴿١٢﴾

13. Those who have said, "Our Lord is Allah," and are steadfast in their belief need have no fear or be grieved.

13. Innal-lazeena qaaloo Rab-bunal-laahu summas-taqaamoo falaa khawfun 'alayhim wa laa hum yaḥzanoon.

اِنَّ الَّذِيْنَ قَالُوْا رَبُّنَا اللّٰهُ ثُمَّ
اسْتَقَامُوْا فَلَا خَوْفٌ عَلَيْهِمْ وَلَا
هُمْ يَحْزَنُوْنَ ﴿١٣﴾

14. They will be the dwellers of Paradise wherein they will live forever as a reward for what they have done.

14. Ulaaa'ika Aṣḥaabul- Jannati khaalideena feehaa jazaaa'am bimaa kaanoo ya'maloon.

اُولٰٓئِكَ اَصْحٰبُ الْجَنَّةِ خٰلِدِيْنَ فِيْهَا ۚ
جَزَآءًۢ بِمَا كَانُوْا يَعْمَلُوْنَ ﴿١٤﴾

15. We have advised the human being to be kind to his parents; his mother bore him with hardship and delivered him while suffering a great deal of pain. The period in which his mother bore and weaned him lasted for thirty months. When he grew up to manhood and became forty years old, he then said, "Lord, inspire me to give You thanks for the bounties you have granted to me and my parents, and to act righteously to please You. Lord, make my offspring virtuous. Lord I turn to you in repentance; I am a Muslim."

15. Wa waṣṣaynal-insaana biwaalidayhi iḥsaanan ḥamalat-hu ummuhoo kurhañw-wa waḍa'athu kurhañw-wa ḥamluhoo wa fiṣaaluhoo salaasoona shahraa; ḥattaaa izaa balagha ashuddahoo wa balagha arba'eena sanatan qaala Rabbi awzi'neee an ashkura ni'matakal-lateee an'amta 'alayya wa 'alaa waalidayya wa an a'mala ṣaaliḥan tarḍaahu wa aṣliḥ lee fee zurriyyateee innee tubtu ilayka wa innee minal-muslimeen.

وَوَصَّيْنَا الْاِنْسَانَ بِوَالِدَيْهِ
اِحْسٰنًا ؕ حَمَلَتْهُ اُمُّهٗ كُرْهًا وَّ
وَضَعَتْهُ كُرْهًا ؕ وَحَمْلُهٗ وَفِصٰلُهٗ
ثَلٰثُوْنَ شَهْرًا ؕ حَتّٰٓى اِذَا بَلَغَ اَشُدَّهٗ
وَبَلَغَ اَرْبَعِيْنَ سَنَةً ۙ قَالَ رَبِّ
اَوْزِعْنِىْٓ اَنْ اَشْكُرَ نِعْمَتَكَ الَّتِىْٓ
اَنْعَمْتَ عَلَىَّ وَعَلٰى وَالِدَىَّ وَاَنْ
اَعْمَلَ صَالِحًا تَرْضٰىهُ وَاَصْلِحْ
لِىْ فِىْ ذُرِّيَّتِىْ ۚ اِنِّىْ تُبْتُ
اِلَيْكَ وَاِنِّىْ مِنَ الْمُسْلِمِيْنَ ﴿١٥﴾

16. These are the ones from whom We accept righteous deeds and ignore their bad deeds. They will be among the dwellers of Paradise. It is the true promise which was given to them.

16. Ulaaa'ikal-lazeena nata-qabbalu 'anhum aḥsana maa 'amiloo wa natajaawazu 'an sayyi-aatihim feee Aṣḥaabil-Jannati wa'daṣ-ṣidqil-lazee kaanoo yoo'adoon.

اُولٰٓئِكَ الَّذِيْنَ نَتَقَبَّلُ عَنْهُمْ اَحْسَنَ
مَا عَمِلُوْا وَنَتَجَاوَزُ عَنْ سَيِّاٰتِهِمْ فِىْٓ
اَصْحٰبِ الْجَنَّةِ ؕ وَعْدَ الصِّدْقِ الَّذِىْ
كَانُوْا يُوْعَدُوْنَ ﴿١٦﴾

17. There are people who say to their parents, "Fie upon you! Are you telling us that we shall be raised from our graves? So many people have died before us and

17. Wallazee qaala liwaali-dayhi uffil-lakumaaa ata'i-daanineee an ukhraja wa qad khalatil-

وَالَّذِىْ قَالَ لِوَالِدَيْهِ اُفٍّ لَّكُمَآ
اَتَعِدٰنِنِىْٓ اَنْ اُخْرَجَ وَقَدْ خَلَتِ

(none of them have been raised)." Their parents plead to Allah and say to their child, "Woe to you! Have faith; the promise of Allah is certainly true." He replies, "What you say is only of the ancient legends."

quroonu min qablee wa humaa yastagheesaanil-laaha waylaka aamin inna wa'dal-laahi ḥaqq; fa-yaqoolu maa haazaaa illaaa asaaṭeerul-awwaleen.

الْقُرُونُ مِنْ قَبْلِي ۚ وَهُمَا يَسْتَغِيثَانِ
اللّٰهَ وَيْلَكَ اٰمِنْ ۖ إِنَّ وَعْدَ اللّٰهِ
حَقٌّ ۚ فَيَقُولُ مَا هٰذَآ إِلَّآ أَسَاطِيرُ
الْاَوَّلِينَ ﴿١٧﴾

18. Such people will be subject to the punishment of Allah, which was also decreed for many human beings and jinn before them. These people are certainly lost.

18. Ulaaa'ikal-lazeena ḥaqqa 'alayhimul-qawlu feee umamin qad khalat min qablihim minal-jinni wal insi innahum kaanoo khaasireen.

أُولٰٓئِكَ الَّذِينَ حَقَّ عَلَيْهِمُ الْقَوْلُ
فِيٓ أُمَمٍ قَدْ خَلَتْ مِنْ قَبْلِهِمْ مِّنَ
الْجِنِّ وَالْإِنْسِ ۖ إِنَّهُمْ كَانُوا خٰسِرِينَ ﴿١٨﴾

19. Everyone will have a position proportionate to the degree of his deeds. Finally, Allah will recompense them for their deeds and they will not be wronged.

19. Wa likullin darajaatum mimmaa 'amiloo wa liyuwaf-fiyahum a'maalahum wa hum laa yuẓlamoon.

وَلِكُلٍّ دَرَجٰتٌ مِّمَّا عَمِلُوا ۖ وَلِيُوَفِّيَهُمْ
أَعْمَالَهُمْ وَهُمْ لَا يُظْلَمُونَ ﴿١٩﴾

20. On the day when the unbelievers will be exposed to the fire, they will be told, "You have spent your happy days during your worldly life and enjoyed them. On this day you will suffer a humiliating torment (thirst) for your unreasonably arrogant manners on earth and for the evil deeds which you have committed."

20. Wa Yawma yu'raḍul-lazeena kafaroo 'alan-Naari azhabtum ṭayyibaatikum fee ḥayaatikumud-dunyaa wasta-mta'tum bihaa fal Yawma tujzawna 'azaabal-hooni bimaa kuntum tastakbiroona fil-arḍi bighayril-ḥaqqi wa bimaa kuntum tafsuqoon.

وَيَوْمَ يُعْرَضُ الَّذِينَ كَفَرُوا عَلَى
النَّارِ ۖ أَذْهَبْتُمْ طَيِّبٰتِكُمْ فِي
حَيَاتِكُمُ الدُّنْيَا وَاسْتَمْتَعْتُمْ بِهَا ۚ
فَالْيَوْمَ تُجْزَوْنَ عَذَابَ الْهُوْنِ
بِمَا كُنْتُمْ تَسْتَكْبِرُونَ فِي الْأَرْضِ
بِغَيْرِ الْحَقِّ وَبِمَا كُنْتُمْ تَفْسُقُونَ ﴿٢٠﴾ ع ٢

21. (Muhammad), recall the brother of the people of Ad, when he warned his people in the valley of Al-Ahqaf saying, "There existed many Warners before and after him. Do not worship anything other than Allah. I am afraid for you about the torment of the great Day."

21. Wazkur akhaa 'Aad; iz anzara qawmahoo bil-Aḥqaafi wa qad khalatin nuzuru mim bayni yadayhi wa min khalfiheee allaa ta'budooo illal-laah; inneee akhaafu 'alaykum 'azaaba Yawmin 'aẓeem.

وَاذْكُرْ أَخَا عَادٍ ۖ إِذْ أَنْذَرَ قَوْمَهُ
بِالْأَحْقَافِ وَقَدْ خَلَتِ النُّذُرُ
مِنْ بَيْنِ يَدَيْهِ وَمِنْ خَلْفِهِٓ أَلَّا
تَعْبُدُوٓا إِلَّا اللّٰهَ ۖ إِنِّيٓ أَخَافُ عَلَيْكُمْ
عَذَابَ يَوْمٍ عَظِيمٍ ﴿٢١﴾

22. They said, "Have you come to turn us away from our gods? Show us that (torment) with which you threaten us if you are truthful."

22. Qaalooo aji'tanaa lita-fikanaa 'an aalihatinaa fa-tinaa bimaa ta'idunaaa in kunta minaṣ-ṣaadiqeen.

قَالُوٓا أَجِئْتَنَا لِتَأْفِكَنَا عَنْ اٰلِهَتِنَا ۚ
فَأْتِنَا بِمَا تَعِدُنَآ إِنْ كُنْتَ مِنَ
الصّٰدِقِينَ ﴿٢٢﴾

23. He said, "Only Allah has the knowledge (of the coming of such torment. I preach to you the message that I have brought, but I can see that you are an ignorant people."

23. Qaala innamal-'ilmu 'indal-laahi wa uballighukum maaa ursiltu bihee wa laakin-neee araakum qawman tajha-loon.

قَالَ إِنَّمَا الْعِلْمُ عِنْدَ اللّٰهِ ۖ
وَأُبَلِّغُكُمْ مَّآ أُرْسِلْتُ بِهِ وَلٰكِنِّيٓ
أَرٰىكُمْ قَوْمًا تَجْهَلُونَ ﴿٢٣﴾

24. When they saw the torment as a cloud proceeding to their valleys, they said, "This cloud will bring us rain." He said, "No, it is the torment which you wanted to suffer immediately. It is a wind bearing painful torment.

24. Falammaa ra-awhu 'aariḍam-mustaqbila awdiyatihim qaaloo haaẕaa 'aariḍum-mumṭirunaa; bal huwa masta'jaltum bihee reeḥun feehaa 'aẕaabun aleem.

فَلَمَّا رَاَوْهُ عَارِضًا مُّسْتَقْبِلَ اَوْ
دِيَتِهِمْ ۙ قَالُوْا هٰذَا عَارِضٌ مُّمْطِرُنَا ؕ
بَلْ هُوَ مَا اسْتَعْجَلْتُمْ بِهٖ ؕ رِيْحٌ فِيْهَا
عَذَابٌ اَلِيْمٌ ﴿٢٤﴾

25. It will destroy everything by the will of its Lord (one example of general world applied to certain individuals, i.e. certain things were destroyed not everything)." (Not very long after) nothing could be seen of them except their dwellings. Thus do We recompense the sinful people.

25. Tudammiru kulla shay'im bi-amri Rabbihaa fa-aṣbaḥoo laa yuraaa illaa masaakinuhum; kaẕaalika najzil-qawmal-mujrimeen.

تُدَمِّرُ كُلَّ شَيْءٍۢ بِاَمْرِ رَبِّهَا
فَاَصْبَحُوْا لَا يُرٰٓى اِلَّا مَسٰكِنُهُمْ ؕ
كَذٰلِكَ نَجْزِى الْقَوْمَ الْمُجْرِمِيْنَ ﴿٢٥﴾

26. We had established them more firmly in the land than you are. We had given them ears, eyes, and hearts but none of their ears, eyes, and hearts proved to be of any benefit to them; they rejected the revelations of Allah and the torment which they mocked brought upon them utter destruction.

26. Wa laqad makkannaahum feemaaa im-makkannaakum feehi wa ja'alnaa lahum sam'añw-wa abṣaarañw-wa af'idatan famaaa aghnaa 'anhum sam'u-hum wa laaa abṣaaruhum wa laaa af'idatuhum min shay'in iẕ kaanoo yajḥadoona bi Aayaatil-laahi wa ḥaaqa bihim maa kaanoo bihee yastahzi'oon.

وَلَقَدْ مَكَّنّٰهُمْ فِيْمَآ اِنْ مَّكَّنّٰكُمْ
فِيْهِ وَجَعَلْنَا لَهُمْ سَمْعًا وَّاَبْصَارًا
وَّاَفْـِٕدَةً ۖ فَمَآ اَغْنٰى عَنْهُمْ سَمْعُهُمْ
وَلَآ اَبْصَارُهُمْ وَلَآ اَفْـِٕدَتُهُمْ
مِّنْ شَيْءٍ اِذْ كَانُوْا يَجْحَدُوْنَ ۙ
بِاٰيٰتِ اللّٰهِ وَحَاقَ بِهِمْ مَّا كَانُوْا
بِهٖ يَسْتَهْزِءُوْنَ ﴿٢٦﴾ ع ٣

27. We destroyed certain towns around you and explained for you the evidence (of the Truth) so that perhaps you would turn (to Allah)

27. Wa laqad ahlaknaa maa ḥawlakum minal-quraa wa ṣarrafnal-Aayaati la'allahum yarji'oon.

وَلَقَدْ اَهْلَكْنَا مَا حَوْلَكُمْ مِّنَ الْقُرٰى
وَصَرَّفْنَا الْاٰيٰتِ لَعَلَّهُمْ يَرْجِعُوْنَ ﴿٢٧﴾

28. Why did the idols, whom they worshipped as a means of pleasing Allah, not help them? In fact, they proved to be the cause of their going astray and it was lies which they had falsely invented.

28. Falaw laa naṣarahumul-laẕeenat-takhaẕoo min doonil-laahi qurbaanan aalihah; bal ḍalloo 'anhum; wa ẕaalika ifkuhum wa maa kaanoo yaftaroon.

فَلَوْلَا نَصَرَهُمُ الَّذِيْنَ اتَّخَذُوْا مِنْ
دُوْنِ اللّٰهِ قُرْبَانًا اٰلِهَةً ؕ بَلْ
ضَلُّوْا عَنْهُمْ ۚ وَذٰلِكَ اِفْكُهُمْ
وَمَا كَانُوْا يَفْتَرُوْنَ ﴿٢٨﴾

29. We turned a party of jinn towards you to listen to the Quran. When they attended a Quranic recitation, they said to each other, "Be silent," and, when it was over, they turned back to their people, in warning,

29. Wa iẕ ṣarafnaaa ilayka nafaram-minal-jinni yastami'oo-nal-Qur'aana falammaa ḥaḍaroo-hu qaalooo anṣitoo falammaa quḍiya wallaw ilaa qawmihim munẕireen.

وَاِذْ صَرَفْنَآ اِلَيْكَ نَفَرًا مِّنَ الْجِنِّ
يَسْتَمِعُوْنَ الْقُرْاٰنَ ۚ فَلَمَّا حَضَرُوْهُ
قَالُوْٓا اَنْصِتُوْا ۚ فَلَمَّا قُضِيَ وَلَّوْا
اِلٰى قَوْمِهِمْ مُّنْذِرِيْنَ ﴿٢٩﴾

30. and said, "Our people, we have listened to the recitation of a Book revealed after Moses. It

30. Qaaloo yaa qawmanaaa innaa sami'naa Kitaaban unzila mim ba'di Moosaa muṣaddiqal-

قَالُوْا يٰقَوْمَنَآ اِنَّا سَمِعْنَا كِتٰبًا
اُنْزِلَ مِنْ بَعْدِ مُوْسٰى مُصَدِّقًا

confirms the Books revealed before and guides to the Truth and the right path.

limaa bayna yadayhi yahdeee ilal-ḥaqqi wa ilaa Ṭareeqim Musta-qeem.

لِّمَا بَيْنَ يَدَيْهِ يَهْدِيْٓ اِلَى الْحَقِّ
وَاِلٰى طَرِيْقٍ مُّسْتَقِيْمٍ ۝٣٠

31. Our people, respond favorably to the Messenger of Allah and believe in Him. He will forgive your sins and rescue you from the painful torment.

31. Yaa qawmanaaa ajeeboo daa'iyal-laahi wa aaminoo bihee yaghfir lakum min zunoobikum wa yujirkum min 'azaabin aleem.

يٰقَوْمَنَآ اَجِيْبُوْا دَاعِيَ اللّٰهِ وَاٰمِنُوْا
بِهٖ يَغْفِرْ لَكُمْ مِّنْ ذُنُوْبِكُمْ
وَيُجِرْكُمْ مِّنْ عَذَابٍ اَلِيْمٍ ۝٣١

32. Those who do not favorably respond to the Messenger of Allah should know that they cannot challenge Allah on earth and will not have anyone as their guardian besides Him. Such people are in plain error."

32. Wa mal-laa yujib daa'iyal-laahi falaysa bimu'jizin fil-arḍi wa laysa lahoo min dooniheee awliyaaa'; ulaaa'ika fee ḍalaalim mubeen.

وَمَنْ لَّا يُجِبْ دَاعِيَ اللّٰهِ فَلَيْسَ
بِمُعْجِزٍ فِي الْاَرْضِ وَلَيْسَ لَهٗ
مِنْ دُوْنِهٖٓ اَوْلِيَآءُ ۭ اُولٰۗىِٕكَ فِيْ
ضَلٰلٍ مُّبِيْنٍ ۝٣٢

33. Did they not see that Allah has created the heavens and the earth and that He experienced no fatigue in doing this? He has the power to bring the dead back to life. Certainly He has power over all things.

33. Awalam yaraw annal-laahal-lazee khalaqas-samaawaati wal-arḍa wa lam ya'ya bikhal-qihinna biqaadirin'alaaa añy-yuḥyiyal-mawtaa; balaaa inna-hoo 'alaa kulli shay'in Qadeer.

اَوَلَمْ يَرَوْا اَنَّ اللّٰهَ الَّذِيْ خَلَقَ
السَّمٰوٰتِ وَالْاَرْضَ وَلَمْ يَعْيَ
بِخَلْقِهِنَّ بِقٰدِرٍ عَلٰٓي اَنْ يُّحْيِۦَ
الْمَوْتٰى ۭ بَلٰٓى اِنَّهٗ عَلٰي كُلِّ
شَيْءٍ قَدِيْرٌ ۝٣٣

34. On the day when the unbelievers will be exposed to the fire, they will be asked, "Is this not real?" They will say, "Yes, Our Lord, it is real." He will say, "Suffer the torment for your disbelief."

34. Wa Yawma yu'raḍul-lazeena kafaroo 'alan-Naari alaysa haazaa bilḥaqq; qaaloo balaa wa Rabbinaa; qaala fazooqul-'azaaba bimaa kuntum takfuroon.

وَيَوْمَ يُعْرَضُ الَّذِيْنَ كَفَرُوْا عَلَي
النَّارِ ۭ اَلَيْسَ هٰذَا بِالْحَقِّ ۭ
قَالُوْا بَلٰى وَرَبِّنَا ۭ قَالَ فَذُوْقُوا
الْعَذَابَ بِمَا كُنْتُمْ تَكْفُرُوْنَ ۝٣٤

35. (Muhammad), exercise patience as did the steadfast messengers. Do not try to make them suffer the torment immediately; on the day when they will see the torment with which they were threatened, they will think that they had lived no more than an hour. The message has been delivered. No one else will be destroyed except the evildoing people.

35. Faṣbir kamaa ṣabara ulul'azmi minar-Rusuli wa laa tasta'jil-lahum; ka-annahum Yawma yarawna maa yoo'a-doona lam yalbasooo illaa saa'atam min nahaar; balaagh; fahal yuhlaku illal-qawmul-faasiqoon.

فَاصْبِرْ كَمَا صَبَرَ اُولُوا الْعَزْمِ
مِنَ الرُّسُلِ وَلَا تَسْتَعْجِلْ لَّهُمْ ۭ
كَاَنَّهُمْ يَوْمَ يَرَوْنَ مَا يُوْعَدُوْنَ ۙ لَمْ
يَلْبَثُوْٓا اِلَّا سَاعَةً مِّنْ نَّهَارٍ ۭ بَلٰغٌ ۚ
فَهَلْ يُهْلَكُ اِلَّا الْقَوْمُ الْفٰسِقُوْنَ ۝٣٥

Muhammad, Muhammad (47)

In the Name of Allah,
the Beneficent, the Merciful.

Sûrat Muḥammad-47

(Revealed at Madinah)

Bismillaahir Raḥmaanir Raḥeem

(٤٧) سُوْرَةُ مُحَمَّدٍ مَّدَنِيَّةٌ (٩٥)

اٰيَاتُهَا ٣٨ بِسْمِ اللّٰهِ الرَّحْمٰنِ الرَّحِيْمِ رُكُوْعَاتُهَا ٤

1. Allah has made devoid of all virtue the deeds of those who have

1. Allazeena kafaroo wa ṣaddoo 'an sabeelil-

اَلَّذِيْنَ كَفَرُوْا وَصَدُّوْا عَنْ سَبِيْلِ

turned to disbelief and prevented others from the way of Allah.

laahi aḍalla a'maalahum.

اللّٰهِ اَضَلَّ اَعْمَالَهُمْ ۝١

2. Allah forgives the sins and reforms the hearts of the righteously striving believers who have faith in what is revealed to Muhammad - which is the Truth from his Lord.

2. Wallazeena aamanoo wa 'amiluṣ-ṣaaliḥaati wa aamanoo bimaa nuzzila 'alaa Muḥam-madiñw-wa huwal ḥaqqu mir-Rabbihim kaffara 'anhum sayyi-aatihim wa aṣlaḥa baala-hum.

وَالَّذِيْنَ اٰمَنُوْا وَعَمِلُوا الصّٰلِحٰتِ
وَاٰمَنُوْا بِمَا نُزِّلَ عَلٰى مُحَمَّدٍ وَّهُوَ
الْحَقُّ مِنْ رَّبِّهِمْ ۙ كَفَّرَ عَنْهُمْ
سَيِّاٰتِهِمْ وَاَصْلَحَ بَالَهُمْ ۝٢

3. This is because the unbelievers have followed falsehood and the believers have followed the Truth from their Lord. Thus Allah explains to the human being his own prospects.

3. Zaalika bi-annal-lazeena kafarut-taba'ul-baaṭila wa annal-lazeena aamanut-taba'ul-ḥaqqa mir-Rabbihim; kazaalika yaḍribul-laahu linnaasi amsaa-lahum.

ذٰلِكَ بِاَنَّ الَّذِيْنَ كَفَرُوا اتَّبَعُوا
الْبَاطِلَ وَاَنَّ الَّذِيْنَ اٰمَنُوا اتَّبَعُوا
الْحَقَّ مِنْ رَّبِّهِمْ ۗ كَذٰلِكَ يَضْرِبُ
اللّٰهُ لِلنَّاسِ اَمْثَالَهُمْ ۝٣

4. If you encounter the unbelievers in a battle, strike-off their heads (one example of a general term, but is addressed to individuals, i.e. the prophet or his successor). Take them as captives when they are defeated. Then you may set them free as a favor to them, with or without a ransom, when the battle is over. This is the Law. Had Allah wanted, He could have granted them (unbelievers) victory, but He wants to test you through each other. The deeds of those who are killed for the cause of Allah will never be without virtuous results.

4. Fa-izaa laqeetumul-lazeena kafaroo faḍarbar-riqaab; ḥattaaa izaa askhan-tumoohum fashuddul wasaaq; fa-immaa mannam ba'du wa immaa fidaaa'an ḥattaa taḍa'al-ḥarbu awzaarahaa; zaalika wa law yashaaa'ul-laahu lantaṣara minhum wa laakil-liyabluwa ba'ḍakum biba'ḍ; wallazeena qutiloo fee sabeelil-laahi falañy-yuḍilla a'maalahum.

فَاِذَا لَقِيْتُمُ الَّذِيْنَ كَفَرُوْا فَضَرْبَ
الرِّقَابِ ۗ حَتّٰٓى اِذَآ اَثْخَنْتُمُوْهُمْ فَشُدُّوا
الْوَثَاقَ ۖ فَاِمَّا مَنًّۢا بَعْدُ وَاِمَّا فِدَآءً
حَتّٰى تَضَعَ الْحَرْبُ اَوْزَارَهَا ۛ
ذٰلِكَ ۛ وَلَوْ يَشَآءُ اللّٰهُ لَانْتَصَرَ
مِنْهُمْ ۙ وَلٰكِنْ لِّيَبْلُوَا۟ بَعْضَكُمْ
بِبَعْضٍ ۗ وَالَّذِيْنَ قُتِلُوْا فِيْ
سَبِيْلِ اللّٰهِ فَلَنْ يُّضِلَّ اَعْمَالَهُمْ ۝٤

5. Allah will lead them to everlasting happiness and improve their condition.

5. Sayahdeehim wa yuṣliḥu baalahum.

سَيَهْدِيْهِمْ وَيُصْلِحُ بَالَهُمْ ۝٥

6. He will admit them into the Paradise which He has made known to them.

6. Wa yudkhiluhumul-Jannata 'arrafahaa lahum.

وَيُدْخِلُهُمُ الْجَنَّةَ عَرَّفَهَا لَهُمْ ۝٦

7. Believers, if you help Allah, He will help you and make you steadfast (in your faith).

7. Yaaa ayyuhal-lazeena aamanooo in tanṣurul-laaha yanṣurkum wa yusabbit aqdaa-makum.

يٰٓاَيُّهَا الَّذِيْنَ اٰمَنُوْٓا اِنْ تَنْصُرُوا
اللّٰهَ يَنْصُرْكُمْ وَيُثَبِّتْ اَقْدَامَكُمْ ۝٧

8. The fate of the unbelievers will be to stumble and their deeds will have no virtuous results;

8. Wallazeena kafaroo fata's al-lahum wa aḍalla a'maala-hum.

وَالَّذِيْنَ كَفَرُوْا فَتَعْسًا لَّهُمْ وَاَضَلَّ
اَعْمَالَهُمْ ۝٨

9. they have hated Allah's revelation, and thus He has made their deeds devoid of all virtue.

9. Zaalika bi-annahum kari-hoo maaa anzalal-laahu fa-aḥbaṭa a'maalahum.

ذٰلِكَ بِاَنَّهُمْ كَرِهُوْا مَآ اَنْزَلَ اللّٰهُ
فَاَحْبَطَ اَعْمَالَهُمْ ۝٩

10. Did they not travel through the land and see the terrible end of

10. Afalam yaseeroo fil-arḍi fayanẓuroo

اَفَلَمْ يَسِيْرُوْا فِي الْاَرْضِ فَيَنْظُرُوْا

وقد بينت ان قول ذٰلك ط ولكن حسن اتصاله بما قبله ويوقف علٰى ذٰلك ط ١٢ مع ٤ عند المتقدمين ١٢٠

those who lived before them? Allah brought upon them utter destruction and the unbelievers will also face similar perdition.

kayfa kaana 'aaqibatul-lazeena min qablihim; dammaral-laahu 'alayhim wa lilkaafireena amsaaluhaa.

كَيۡفَ كَانَ عَاقِبَةُ الَّذِيۡنَ مِنۡ قَبۡلِهِمۡ
دَمَّرَ اللّٰهُ عَلَيۡهِمۡ وَلِلۡكٰفِرِيۡنَ
اَمۡثَالُهَا ﴿١٠﴾

11. Allah is the Guardian of the believers, but the unbelievers have no guardian.

11. Zaalika bi-annal-laaha mawlal-lazeena aamanoo wa annal-kaafireena laa mawlaa lahum.

ذٰلِكَ بِاَنَّ اللّٰهَ مَوۡلَى الَّذِيۡنَ اٰمَنُوۡا
وَاَنَّ الۡكٰفِرِيۡنَ لَا مَوۡلٰى لَهُمۡ ﴿١١﴾ ع ١١ ٥

12. Allah will admit the righteously striving believers into the gardens wherein streams flow. However, the unbelievers who enjoyed themselves and ate like cattle (overate) will have for their dwelling hellfire.

12. Innal-laaha yudkhilul-lazeena aamanoo wa 'amiluṣ-ṣaaliḥaati Jannaatin tajree min taḥtihal-anhaar; wallazeena kafaroo yatamatta'oona wa ya-kuloona kamaa ta-kulul an'aamu wan-Naaru maswal-lahum.

اِنَّ اللّٰهَ يُدۡخِلُ الَّذِيۡنَ اٰمَنُوۡا
وَعَمِلُوا الصّٰلِحٰتِ جَنّٰتٍ تَجۡرِىۡ
مِنۡ تَحۡتِهَا الۡاَنۡهٰرُ ؕ وَالَّذِيۡنَ كَفَرُوۡا
يَتَمَتَّعُوۡنَ وَيَاۡكُلُوۡنَ كَمَا تَاۡكُلُ
الۡاَنۡعَامُ وَالنَّارُ مَثۡوًى لَّهُمۡ ﴿١٢﴾

13. (Muhammad), how many towns, much more powerful than the one from which you have been expelled, have We destroyed and left helpless?

13. Wa ka-ayyim-min qarya-tin hiya ashaddu quwwatam-min qaryatikal-lateee akhra-jatka ahlaknaahum falaa naaṣira lahum.

وَكَاَيِّنۡ مِّنۡ قَرۡيَةٍ هِىَ اَشَدُّ
قُوَّةً مِّنۡ قَرۡيَتِكَ الَّتِىۡۤ اَخۡرَجَتۡكَ ۚ
اَهۡلَكۡنٰهُمۡ فَلَا نَاصِرَ لَهُمۡ ﴿١٣﴾

14. Can the one who follows the authority of his Lord be considered equal to the one whose evil deeds are made to seem attractive to him and who follows his own desires?

14. Afaman kaana 'alaa bayyinatim-mir-Rabbihee kaman zuyyina lahoo sooo'u 'amalihee wattaba'ooo ah-waaa'ahum.

اَفَمَنۡ كَانَ عَلٰى بَيِّنَةٍ مِّنۡ رَّبِّهٖ
كَمَنۡ زُيِّنَ لَهٗ سُوۡٓءُ عَمَلِهٖ وَاتَّبَعُوۡۤا
اَهۡوَآءَهُمۡ ﴿١٤﴾

15. The garden, which is promised to the pious, is like one in which there are streams of unpolluted water, streams of milk of unchanged taste, streams of delicious wine, and streams of crystal clear honey. Therein they will have all kinds of fruits and forgiveness from their Lord. On the other hand (can these people be considered like) those who will live forever in hellfire and will drink boiling water which will rip their intestines to bits?

15. Masalul-Jannatil-latee wu'idal-muttaqoon; feehaaa anhaarum-mim-maaa'in ghayri aasinin wa anhaarum mil-labanil-lam yataghayyar ṭa'mu-hoo wa anhaarum-min khamril-lazzatil-lishshaaribeena wa anhaarum-min 'asalim muṣaf-faa; wa lahum feehaa min kullis-samaraati wa maghfiratum-mir-Rabbihim kaman huwa khaali-dun fin-Naari wa suqoo maaa'an ḥameeman faqaṭṭa'a am'aaa'ahum.

مَثَلُ الۡجَنَّةِ الَّتِىۡ وُعِدَ الۡمُتَّقُوۡنَ ؕ
فِيۡهَاۤ اَنۡهٰرٌ مِّنۡ مَّآءٍ غَيۡرِ اٰسِنٍ ۚ
وَاَنۡهٰرٌ مِّنۡ لَّبَنٍ لَّمۡ يَتَغَيَّرۡ طَعۡمُهٗ ۚ
وَاَنۡهٰرٌ مِّنۡ خَمۡرٍ لَّذَّةٍ لِّلشّٰرِبِيۡنَ ۚ
وَاَنۡهٰرٌ مِّنۡ عَسَلٍ مُّصَفًّى ؕ وَلَهُمۡ
فِيۡهَا مِنۡ كُلِّ الثَّمَرٰتِ وَمَغۡفِرَةٌ
مِّنۡ رَّبِّهِمۡ ؕ كَمَنۡ هُوَ خَالِدٌ فِى النَّارِ
وَسُقُوۡا مَآءً حَمِيۡمًا فَقَطَّعَ اَمۡعَآءَهُمۡ ﴿١٥﴾

16. (Muhammad), some of them listen to you, but when they leave you they ask those who have received knowledge, "What

16. Wa minhum mañy-yasta-mi'u ilayka ḥattaaa izaa khara-joo min 'indika qaaloo lilla-zeena

وَمِنۡهُمۡ مَّنۡ يَّسۡتَمِعُ اِلَيۡكَ ۚ حَتّٰۤى اِذَا
خَرَجُوۡا مِنۡ عِنۡدِكَ قَالُوۡا لِلَّذِيۡنَ

did he say a few moments ago?" Allah has sealed the hearts of such people who have followed their worldly desires.

ootul-'ilma maazaa qaala aanifaa; ulaaa'ikal lazeena ṭaba'al-laahu 'alaa quloobihim wattaba'ooo ahwaaa'ahum.

أُوتُوا الْعِلْمَ مَاذَا قَالَ آنِفًا ۚ
أُولَٰئِكَ الَّذِينَ طَبَعَ اللَّهُ عَلَىٰ
قُلُوبِهِمْ وَاتَّبَعُوا أَهْوَاءَهُمْ ﴿١٦﴾

17. Allah will increase the guidance and piety of those who seek guidance.

17. Wallazeenah-tadaw zaadahum hudañw-wa aataahum taqwaahum.

وَالَّذِينَ اهْتَدَوْا زَادَهُمْ هُدًى
وَآتَاهُمْ تَقْوَاهُمْ ﴿١٧﴾

18. Are they waiting for the Hour of Doom to suddenly approach them? Its signs have already appeared. How will they then come to their senses when the Hour itself will approach them?

18. Fahal yanẓuroona illas-Saa'ata an ta-tiyahum baghtatan faqad jaaa'a ashraaṭuhaa; fa-annaa lahum izaa jaaa'at-hum zikraahum.

فَهَلْ يَنْظُرُونَ إِلَّا السَّاعَةَ أَنْ
تَأْتِيَهُمْ بَغْتَةً ۖ فَقَدْ جَاءَ
أَشْرَاطُهَا ۚ فَأَنَّىٰ لَهُمْ إِذَا جَاءَتْهُمْ
ذِكْرَاهُمْ ﴿١٨﴾

19. Know that Allah is the only Lord. Ask forgiveness for your sins and for the sins of the believing men and women. Allah knows when you move and when you rest.

19. Fa'lam annahoo laaa ilaaha illal-laahu wastaghfir lizambika wa lilmu'mineena walmu'minaat; wallaahu ya'lamu mutaqallabakum wa maswaakum.

فَاعْلَمْ أَنَّهُ لَا إِلَٰهَ إِلَّا اللَّهُ وَاسْتَغْفِرْ
لِذَنْبِكَ وَلِلْمُؤْمِنِينَ وَالْمُؤْمِنَاتِ ۗ
وَاللَّهُ يَعْلَمُ مُتَقَلَّبَكُمْ وَمَثْوَاكُمْ ﴿١٩﴾ ٢ع٨ ٢

20. The believers say, "Why is a chapter about jihad - fighting for the cause of Allah - not revealed?" However, when such a chapter, with clear commands and a mention of jihad, is revealed, you will see those whose hearts are sick look at you as if suffering the agony of death. One can expect nothing better from them!

20. Wa yaqoolul-lazeena aamanoo law laa nuzzilat Sooratun fa-izaaa unzilat Sooratum-Muḥkamatuñw-wa zukira feehal-qitaalu ra-aytallazeena fee quloobihim maraḍuñy-yanẓuroona ilayka naẓaral-maghshiyyi 'alayhi minal-mawt; fa-awlaa lahum.

وَيَقُولُ الَّذِينَ آمَنُوا لَوْلَا نُزِّلَتْ
سُورَةٌ ۖ فَإِذَا أُنْزِلَتْ سُورَةٌ مُحْكَمَةٌ
وَذُكِرَ فِيهَا الْقِتَالُ ۙ رَأَيْتَ الَّذِينَ
فِي قُلُوبِهِمْ مَرَضٌ يَنْظُرُونَ إِلَيْكَ
نَظَرَ الْمَغْشِيِّ عَلَيْهِ مِنَ الْمَوْتِ ۖ
فَأَوْلَىٰ لَهُمْ ﴿٢٠﴾

21. Since they have (pledged) Us obedience and to speak reasonably, it would be more proper for them, when it is decided (that everyone must take part in the battle), to remain true (in their pledge to Allah).

21. Ṭaa'atuñw-wa qawlum ma'roof; fa-izaa 'azamal amru falaw ṣadaqul-laaha lakaana khayral-lahum.

طَاعَةٌ وَقَوْلٌ مَعْرُوفٌ ۚ فَإِذَا عَزَمَ
الْأَمْرُ فَلَوْ صَدَقُوا اللَّهَ لَكَانَ
خَيْرًا لَهُمْ ﴿٢١﴾

22. If you ignore the commands of Allah would you then also spread evil in the land and sever the ties of kinship?

22. Fahal 'asaytum in tawallaytum an tufsidoo fil-arḍi wa tuqaṭṭi'ooo arḥaamakum.

فَهَلْ عَسَيْتُمْ إِنْ تَوَلَّيْتُمْ أَنْ تُفْسِدُوا
فِي الْأَرْضِ وَتُقَطِّعُوا أَرْحَامَكُمْ ﴿٢٢﴾

23. Allah has condemned these people and made them deaf, dumb, and blind.

23. Ulaaa'ikal-lazeena la'anahumul-laahu fa-aṣammahum wa a'maaa abṣaarahum.

أُولَٰئِكَ الَّذِينَ لَعَنَهُمُ اللَّهُ فَأَصَمَّهُمْ
وَأَعْمَىٰ أَبْصَارَهُمْ ﴿٢٣﴾

24. Is it that they do not think about the Quran or are their hearts

24. Afalaa yatadabbaroonal-Qur'aana am 'alaa

أَفَلَا يَتَدَبَّرُونَ الْقُرْآنَ أَمْ عَلَىٰ

sealed?

Quloobin aqfaaluhaa.

قُلُوبٍ أَقْفَالُهَا ﴿٢٤﴾

25. Those who have reverted to disbelief after guidance has become manifest to them, have been seduced and given false hopes by Satan.

25. Innal-lazeenar-taddoo ‘alaaa adbaarihim mim ba‘di maa tabayyana lahumul-hudash-Shayṭaanu sawwala lahum wa amlaa lahum.

إِنَّ الَّذِينَ ارْتَدُّوا عَلَىٰ أَدْبَارِهِم
مِّن بَعْدِ مَا تَبَيَّنَ لَهُمُ الْهُدَى ۙ
الشَّيْطَانُ سَوَّلَ لَهُمْ وَأَمْلَىٰ لَهُمْ ﴿٢٥﴾

26. This is because they have said to those who hate Allah's revelation, “We shall obey you in some matters.” However, Allah knows all their secrets.

26. Zaalika bi-annahum qaaloo lillazeena karihoo maa nazzalal-laahu sanuṭee‘ukum fee ba‘ḍil-amri wallaahu ya‘lamu israa-rahum.

ذَٰلِكَ بِأَنَّهُمْ قَالُوا لِلَّذِينَ كَرِهُوا
مَا نَزَّلَ اللَّهُ سَنُطِيعُكُمْ فِي بَعْضِ
الْأَمْرِ ۖ وَاللَّهُ يَعْلَمُ إِسْرَارَهُمْ ﴿٢٦﴾

27. How terrible it will be for them when the angels take away their souls by striking their faces and their backs

27. Fakayfa izaa tawaffat-humul-malaaa’ikatu yaḍri-boona wujoohahum wa adbaa-rahum.

فَكَيْفَ إِذَا تَوَفَّتْهُمُ الْمَلَائِكَةُ
يَضْرِبُونَ وُجُوهَهُمْ وَأَدْبَارَهُمْ ﴿٢٧﴾

28. for their following that which had incurred Allah's anger, and their hatred to please Allah. Thus, Allah has made their deeds devoid of all virtue.

28. Zaalika bi-annahumut-taba‘oo maaa askhaṭal-laaha wa karihoo riḍwaanahoo fa-aḥbaṭa a‘maalahum.

ذَٰلِكَ بِأَنَّهُمُ اتَّبَعُوا مَا أَسْخَطَ
اللَّهَ وَكَرِهُوا رِضْوَانَهُ فَأَحْبَطَ
أَعْمَالَهُمْ ﴿٢٨﴾ ع

29. Do those whose hearts are sick think that Allah will never make their malice public?

29. Am ḥasibal-lazeena fee quloobihim maraḍun al-lañy-yukhrijal-laahu aḍghaanahum.

أَمْ حَسِبَ الَّذِينَ فِي قُلُوبِهِم
مَّرَضٌ أَن لَّن يُخْرِجَ اللَّهُ أَضْغَانَهُمْ ﴿٢٩﴾

30. Had We wanted, We could have made you recognize their faces. You will certainly recognize them by the tone of their speech. Allah knows all your deeds.

30. Wa law nashaaa’u la-araynaakahum fala‘araftahum biseemaahum; wa lata‘rifannahum fee laḥnilqawl; wallaahu ya‘lamu a‘maalakum.

وَلَوْ نَشَاءُ لَأَرَيْنَاكَهُمْ فَلَعَرَفْتَهُم
بِسِيمَاهُمْ ۚ وَلَتَعْرِفَنَّهُمْ فِي لَحْنِ الْقَوْلِ ۚ
وَاللَّهُ يَعْلَمُ أَعْمَالَكُمْ ﴿٣٠﴾

30. We shall certainly test you until We know those who strive hard for the cause of Allah and those who exercise patience. We will also examine your deeds.

31. Wa lanabluwannakum ḥattaa na‘lamal-mujaahideena minkum waṣṣaabireena wa nabluwa akhbaarakum.

وَلَنَبْلُوَنَّكُمْ حَتَّىٰ نَعْلَمَ الْمُجَاهِدِينَ
مِنكُمْ وَالصَّابِرِينَ وَنَبْلُوَ
أَخْبَارَكُمْ ﴿٣١﴾

32. The unbelievers who prevent others from the way of Allah and give the Messengers a hard time - even after guidance has been made clear to them - will never be able to cause any harm to Allah, and He will turn their deeds devoid of all virtue.

32. Innal-lazeena kafaroo wa ṣaddoo ‘an sabeelil-laahi wa shaaaqqur-Rasoola mim ba‘di maa tabayyana lahumul-hudaa lañy-yaḍurrul-laaha shay’aa; wa sa-yuḥbiṭu a‘maalahum.

إِنَّ الَّذِينَ كَفَرُوا وَصَدُّوا عَن
سَبِيلِ اللَّهِ وَشَاقُّوا الرَّسُولَ مِن
بَعْدِ مَا تَبَيَّنَ لَهُمُ الْهُدَىٰ
لَن يَضُرُّوا اللَّهَ شَيْئًا وَسَيُحْبِطُ
أَعْمَالَهُمْ ﴿٣٢﴾

33. Believers, obey Allah and the Messenger and do not

33. Yaaa ayyuhal-lazeena aamanoo aṭee‘ul-laaha

يَا أَيُّهَا الَّذِينَ آمَنُوا أَطِيعُوا اللَّهَ

invalidate your deeds.

34. Allah will never forgive the unbelievers who prevent others from the way of Allah and who die as unbelievers.

35. Do not be weak-hearted and do not appeal for an (unjust) settlement; you have the upper hand. Allah is with you and He will never reduce (the reward for) your deeds.

36. The worldly life is only a childish game. If you have faith and piety, you will receive your rewards and Allah will not ask you to pay for them.

37. If He asks for your possessions He finds you to be niggardly; being hard for you to give. Thus, He makes your malice become public.

38. It is you who are asked to spend for the cause of Allah, but some of you behave in a niggardly way. Whoever behaves in a miserly way does so against his own soul. Allah is Self-sufficient and you are poor. If you were to turn away from Him, He would just replace you with another people, who would not be like you.

Al-Fath, The Victory (48)

In the Name of Allah, the Beneficent, the Merciful.

1. We have granted to you, (Muhammad), a manifest victory,

2. so that Allah will redeem the sins (which the pagans think you have committed against them) in the past or (you will commit) in the future. He will complete His favors to you, guide you to the right path,

3. and grant you a majestic triumph.

---

wa aṭee'ur-Rasoola wa laa tubṭilooo a'maalakum.

34. Innal-lazeena kafaroo wa ṣaddoo 'an sabeelil-laahi summa maatoo wahum kuffaarun falañy-yaghfira-llaahu lahum.

35. Falaa tahinoo wa tad'ooo ilas-salmi wa antumul-a'lawna wallaahu ma'akum wa lañy-yatirakum a'maalakum.

36. Innamal-ḥayaatud-dunyaa la'ibuñw-wa lahw; wa in to'minoo wa tattaqoo yu'tikum ujoorakum wa laa yas'alkum amwaalakum.

37. Iñy-yas'alkumoohaa fa-yuḥfikum tabkhaloo wa yukhrij aḍghaanakum.

38. Haaa antum haaa ulaaa'i tud'awna litunfiqoo fee sabee-lillaahi faminkum mañy-yab-khalu wa mañy-yabkhal fa-innamaa yabkhalu 'an nafsih; wallaahul Ghaniyyu wa antumul-fuqaraaa'; wa-in tatawallaw yastabdil qawman ghayrakum summa laa yakoonooo amsaalakum.

Sûrat al-Fatḥ-48

(Revealed at Madinah)

Bismillaahir Raḥmaanir Raḥeem

1. Innaa fataḥnaa laka Fat-ḥam-Mubeenaa.

2. Liyaghfira lakal-laahu maa taqaddama min zambika wa maa ta-akhkhara wa yutimma ni'matahoo 'alayka wa yahdi-yaka Ṣiraaṭam Mustaqeemaa.

3. Wa yanṣurakal-laahu naṣran 'azeezaa.

وَأَطِيعُوا الرَّسُولَ وَلَا تُبْطِلُوا
أَعْمَالَكُمْ ﴿٣٣﴾
إِنَّ الَّذِينَ كَفَرُوا وَصَدُّوا عَن
سَبِيلِ اللَّهِ ثُمَّ مَاتُوا وَهُمْ كُفَّارٌ
فَلَن يَغْفِرَ اللَّهُ لَهُمْ ﴿٣٤﴾
فَلَا تَهِنُوا وَتَدْعُوا إِلَى السَّلْمِ
وَأَنتُمُ الْأَعْلَوْنَ وَاللَّهُ مَعَكُمْ وَلَن
يَتِرَكُمْ أَعْمَالَكُمْ ﴿٣٥﴾
إِنَّمَا الْحَيَاةُ الدُّنْيَا لَعِبٌ وَلَهْوٌ
وَإِن تُؤْمِنُوا وَتَتَّقُوا يُؤْتِكُمْ
أُجُورَكُمْ وَلَا يَسْأَلْكُمْ أَمْوَالَكُمْ ﴿٣٦﴾
إِن يَسْأَلْكُمُوهَا فَيُحْفِكُمْ تَبْخَلُوا
وَيُخْرِجْ أَضْغَانَكُمْ ﴿٣٧﴾
هَا أَنتُمْ هَٰؤُلَاءِ تُدْعَوْنَ لِتُنفِقُوا
فِي سَبِيلِ اللَّهِ فَمِنكُم مَّن يَبْخَلُ
وَمَن يَبْخَلْ فَإِنَّمَا يَبْخَلُ عَن
نَّفْسِهِ وَاللَّهُ الْغَنِيُّ وَأَنتُمُ الْفُقَرَاءُ
وَإِن تَتَوَلَّوْا يَسْتَبْدِلْ قَوْمًا غَيْرَكُمْ
ثُمَّ لَا يَكُونُوا أَمْثَالَكُم ﴿٣٨﴾ ع ٨

(٤٨) سُورَةُ الْفَتْحِ مَدَنِيَّةٌ (١١١)

آياتها ٢٩ بِسْمِ اللَّهِ الرَّحْمَٰنِ الرَّحِيمِ ركوعاتها ٤

إِنَّا فَتَحْنَا لَكَ فَتْحًا مُّبِينًا ﴿١﴾
لِّيَغْفِرَ لَكَ اللَّهُ مَا تَقَدَّمَ مِن ذَنبِكَ
وَمَا تَأَخَّرَ وَيُتِمَّ نِعْمَتَهُ عَلَيْكَ
وَيَهْدِيَكَ صِرَاطًا مُّسْتَقِيمًا ﴿٢﴾
وَيَنصُرَكَ اللَّهُ نَصْرًا عَزِيزًا ﴿٣﴾

4. It is Allah who has given confidence to the hearts of the believers to increase and strengthen their faith - to Allah belong the armies of the heavens and the earth and He is All-knowing and All-wise -

4. Huwal-lazeee anzalas-sakeenata fee quloobil-mu'mineena liyazdaadooo eemaanam-ma'a eemaanihim; wa lillaahi junoodus-samaawaati wal-arḍ; wa kaanal-laahu 'Aleeman Ḥakeemaa.

هُوَ الَّذِيْٓ اَنْزَلَ السَّكِيْنَةَ فِيْ قُلُوْبِ
الْمُؤْمِنِيْنَ لِيَزْدَادُوْٓا اِيْمَانًا مَّعَ
اِيْمَانِهِمْ ۭ وَلِلّٰهِ جُنُوْدُ السَّمٰوٰتِ
وَالْاَرْضِ ۭ وَكَانَ اللّٰهُ عَلِيْمًا
حَكِيْمًا ۝

5. so that He will admit the believers (both male and female) in the gardens wherein streams flow, to live therein forever and He will redeem their sins. This is the greatest triumph in the sight of Allah,

5. Liyudkhilal-mu'mineena walmu'minaati Jannaatin tajree min taḥtihal-anhaaru khaalideena feehaa wa yukaffira 'anhum sayyi-aatihim; wa kaana zaalika 'indal-laahi fawzan 'aẓeemaa.

لِّيُدْخِلَ الْمُؤْمِنِيْنَ وَالْمُؤْمِنٰتِ جَنّٰتٍ
تَجْرِيْ مِنْ تَحْتِهَا الْاَنْهٰرُ خٰلِدِيْنَ
فِيْهَا وَيُكَفِّرَ عَنْهُمْ سَيِّاٰتِهِمْ ۭ وَكَانَ
ذٰلِكَ عِنْدَ اللّٰهِ فَوْزًا عَظِيْمًا ۝

6. that He will punish the hypocrites and the pagans who have evil suspicions about Allah. It is they who are surrounded by evil and have become subject to the wrath and condemnation of Allah. He has prepared for them hell, a terrible place to live.

6. Wa yu'az-zibal-munaafiqeena walmunaafiqaati wal-mushrikeena walmushrikaatiẓ-ẓaaanneena billaahi ẓannas-saw'; 'alayhim daaa'iratus-saw'i wa ghaḍibal laahu 'alayhim wa la'anahum wa a'adda lahum Jahannama wa saaa'at maṣeeraa.

وَّيُعَذِّبَ الْمُنٰفِقِيْنَ وَالْمُنٰفِقٰتِ
وَالْمُشْرِكِيْنَ وَالْمُشْرِكٰتِ الظَّاۗنِّيْنَ
بِاللّٰهِ ظَنَّ السَّوْءِ ۭ عَلَيْهِمْ دَاۗىِٕرَةُ
السَّوْءِ ۚ وَغَضِبَ اللّٰهُ عَلَيْهِمْ وَلَعَنَهُمْ
وَاَعَدَّ لَهُمْ جَهَنَّمَ ۭ وَسَاۗءَتْ
مَصِيْرًا ۝

7. To Allah belong the armies of the heavens and the earth. Allah is Majestic and All-wise.

7. Wa lillaahi junoodus-samaawaati wal-arḍ; wa kaanal-laahu 'Azeezan Ḥakeemaa.

وَلِلّٰهِ جُنُوْدُ السَّمٰوٰتِ وَالْاَرْضِ ۭ
وَكَانَ اللّٰهُ عَزِيْزًا حَكِيْمًا ۝

8. We have sent you as a witness, a bearer of glad news, and a Warner,

8. Innaaa arsalnaaka shaahidañw-wa mubashshirañw-wa nazeeraa.

اِنَّآ اَرْسَلْنٰكَ شَاهِدًا وَّمُبَشِّرًا
وَّنَذِيْرًا ۝

9. so that you (people) may believe in Allah and His Messenger, help and respect Allah and glorify Him in the morning and the evening.

9. Litu'minoo billaahi wa Rasoolihee wa tu'azziroohu watuwaqqiroohu watusabbiḥoohu bukratañw-wa aṣeelaa.

لِّتُؤْمِنُوْا بِاللّٰهِ وَرَسُوْلِهٖ وَتُعَزِّرُوْهُ
وَتُوَقِّرُوْهُ ۭ وَتُسَبِّحُوْهُ بُكْرَةً
وَّاَصِيْلًا ۝

10. Those who pledge obedience to you are, in fact, pledging obedience to Allah. The hands of Allah are above their hands. As for those who disregard their pledge, they do so only against their own souls. Those who fulfill their promise to Allah

10. Innal-lazeena yubaayi'oonaka innamaa yubaayi'oonal-laaha Yadullaahi fawqa aydeehim; faman nakasa fa innamaa yankusu 'alaa nafsihee wa man awfaa bimaa 'aahada 'alayhul-

اِنَّ الَّذِيْنَ يُبَايِعُوْنَكَ اِنَّمَا يُبَايِعُوْنَ
اللّٰهَ ۭ يَدُ اللّٰهِ فَوْقَ اَيْدِيْهِمْ ۚ
فَمَنْ نَّكَثَ فَاِنَّمَا يَنْكُثُ عَلٰي
نَفْسِهٖ ۚ وَمَنْ اَوْفٰى بِمَا عٰهَدَ عَلَيْهُ

will receive a great reward.

laaha fasayu'teehi ajran 'aẓeemaa.

الله فسيؤتيه أجرا عظيما ﴿١٠﴾

11. The Bedouins who lag behind in taking part in the battle say to you, "Ask forgiveness for us; we were busy with our property and household." They speak what is not in their hearts. (Muhammad), tell them, "Who will help you against Allah if He intends to harm you and who will prevent Him from benefiting you? In fact, Allah is Well-aware of whatever you do."

11. Sa-yaqoolu lakal-mukhal-lafoona minal-A'raabi shaghalatnaaa amwaalunaa wa ahloonaa fastaghfir lanaa; yaqooloona bi-alsinatihim maa laysa fee quloobihim; qul famañy-yamliku lakum-minal-laahi shay'an in araada bikum ḍarran aw araada bikum naf'aa; bal kaanal-laahu bimaa ta'maloona Khabeeraa.

سيقول لك المخلفون من
الأعراب شغلتنا أموالنا وأهلونا
فاستغفر لنا ۚ يقولون بألسنتهم
ما ليس في قلوبهم ۚ قل فمن
يملك لكم من الله شيئا إن أراد
بكم ضرا أو أراد بكم نفعا ۚ بل
كان الله بما تعملون خبيرا ﴿١١﴾

12. You thought the Messenger and the believers would never, ever return to their families and this attracted your hearts and caused you to develop evil suspicions. You are a wrong doing people.

12. Bal ẓanantum al-lañy-yanqalibar-Rasoolu walmu'mi-noona ilaaa ahleehim abadañw-wa zuyyina ẕaalika fee quloobikum wa ẓanantum ẓannas-saw'i wa kuntum qawmam booraa.

بل ظننتم أن لن ينقلب الرسول
والمؤمنون إلى أهليهم أبدا
وزين ذلك في قلوبكم
وظننتم ظن السوء وكنتم
قوما بورا ﴿١٢﴾

13. Those who did not believe in Allah and His Messenger should know that We have prepared hell for the unbelievers.

13. Wa mal-lam yu'mim billaahi wa Rasoolihee fa-innaaa a'tadnaa lilkaafireena sa'eeraa.

ومن لم يؤمن بالله ورسوله
فإنا أعتدنا للكافرين سعيرا ﴿١٣﴾

14. To Allah belongs the kingdom of the heavens and the earth. He forgives or punishes whomever He wants. Allah is All-forgiving and All-merciful.

14. Wa lillaahi mulkus-samaa-waati wal-arḍ; yaghfiru limañy-yashaaa'u wa yu'aẕ-ẕibu mañy-yashaaa'; wa kaanallaahu Ghafoorar-Raḥeemaa.

ولله ملك السماوات والأرض ۚ
يغفر لمن يشاء ويعذب من
يشاء ۚ وكان الله غفورا رحيما ﴿١٤﴾

15. The laggardly Bedouins will say, "When you leave to collect the spoils, allow us follow you." They want to alter the command of Allah (saying that only the participating believers are entitled to such benefits). Tell them, "You can never follow us for such a purpose. Allah has said before and He will say again (what type of people you are). In fact, you are jealous of us." The truth is that they understand very little.

15. Sa-yaqoolul-mukhalla-foona iẕan-ṭalaqtum ilaa maghaanima lita-khuẕoohaa ẕaroonaa nattabi'kum yureedoona añy-yubaddiloo Kalaamal-laah; qul lan tattabi'oonaa kaẕaalikum qaalal-laahu min qablu fasayaqooloona bal taḥsu-doonanaa; bal kaanoo laa yafqa-hoona illaa qaleelaa.

سيقول المخلفون إذا انطلقتم
إلى مغانم لتأخذوها ذرونا
نتبعكم ۖ يريدون أن يبدلوا
كلام الله ۚ قل لن تتبعونا
كذلكم قال الله من قبل ۖ
فسيقولون بل تحسدوننا ۚ بل
كانوا لا يفقهون إلا قليلا ﴿١٥﴾

16. Tell the laggardly Bedouins, "You will be called to

16. Qul lilmukhallafeena minal A'raabi

قل للمخلفين من الأعراب

face strong people whom you will fight right to the end or who will submit to you. If you obey the Messenger, Allah will give you a good reward. However, if you turn away as you did before, Allah will make you suffer a painful torment.

satud ‘awna ilaa qawmin ulee ba-sin shadeedin tuqaatiloonahum aw yuslimoona fa-in tuṭee‘oo yu’tikumul-laahu ajran ḥasanaa; wa-in tatawallaw kamaa tawallaytum min qablu yu‘az̲ z̲ibkum ‘az̲aaban aleemaa.

سَتُدْعَوْنَ إِلَىٰ قَوْمٍ أُولِي بَأْسٍ
شَدِيدٍ تُقَاتِلُونَهُمْ أَوْ يُسْلِمُونَ
فَإِنْ تُطِيعُوا يُؤْتِكُمُ اللَّهُ أَجْرًا
حَسَنًا وَإِنْ تَتَوَلَّوْا كَمَا تَوَلَّيْتُمْ
مِنْ قَبْلُ يُعَذِّبْكُمْ عَذَابًا أَلِيمًا ١٦

17. It is not an offense for the blind, the lame, or the sick not to take part in the battle. Whoever obeys Allah and His Messenger will be admitted to the gardens wherein streams flow. Allah will make whoever turns away suffer a painful torment.

17. Laysa ‘alal-a‘maa ḥarajuñw-wa laa ‘alal-a‘raji ḥarajuñw-wa laa ‘alal-mareeḍi ḥaraj; wa mañy-yuṭi‘il-laaha wa Rasoolahoo yudkhilhu Jannaatin tajree min taḥtihal anhaaru wa mañy-yatawalla yu‘az̲-z̲ibhu ‘az̲aaban aleemaa.

لَيْسَ عَلَى الْأَعْمَىٰ حَرَجٌ وَلَا عَلَى
الْأَعْرَجِ حَرَجٌ وَلَا عَلَى الْمَرِيضِ
حَرَجٌ وَمَنْ يُطِعِ اللَّهَ وَرَسُولَهُ
يُدْخِلْهُ جَنَّاتٍ تَجْرِي مِنْ تَحْتِهَا
الْأَنْهَارُ وَمَنْ يَتَوَلَّ يُعَذِّبْهُ
عَذَابًا أَلِيمًا ١٧ ع

18. Allah is pleased with the believers for their pledging obedience to you under the tree. He knew whatever was in their hearts, thus, He granted them confidence and rewarded them with an immediate victory

18. Laqad raḍiyal-laahu ‘anil-mu’mineena iz̲ yubaayi‘oonaka taḥtash-shajarati fa‘alima maa fee quloobihim fa-anzalas-sakeenata ‘alayhim wa as̲aabahum fatḥan qareebaa.

لَقَدْ رَضِيَ اللَّهُ عَنِ الْمُؤْمِنِينَ إِذْ
يُبَايِعُونَكَ تَحْتَ الشَّجَرَةِ فَعَلِمَ
مَا فِي قُلُوبِهِمْ فَأَنْزَلَ السَّكِينَةَ
عَلَيْهِمْ وَأَثَابَهُمْ فَتْحًا قَرِيبًا ١٨

19. and the spoils which they received from it (the Battle). Allah is Majestic and All-wise.

19. Wa maghaanima kas̲eerata-tañy-ya-khuz̲oonahaa; wa kaanal-laahu ‘Azeezan Ḥakeemaa.

وَمَغَانِمَ كَثِيرَةً يَأْخُذُونَهَا وَكَانَ
اللَّهُ عَزِيزًا حَكِيمًا ١٩

20. Allah has promised that you will receive ample spoils. He has enabled you to receive this at this time and has protected you from enemies to make it an evidence (of the Truth) for the believers. He will guide you to the right path.

20. Wa‘adakumul-laahu maghaanima kas̲eeratan ta-khuz̲oonahaa fa‘ajjala lakum haaz̲ihee wa kaffa aydiyan-naasi ‘ankum wa litakoona Aayatal-lilmu’mineena wa yahdiyakum Ṣiraaṭam Mustaqeemaa.

وَعَدَكُمُ اللَّهُ مَغَانِمَ كَثِيرَةً
تَأْخُذُونَهَا فَعَجَّلَ لَكُمْ هَٰذِهِ
وَكَفَّ أَيْدِيَ النَّاسِ عَنْكُمْ
وَلِتَكُونَ آيَةً لِلْمُؤْمِنِينَ وَيَهْدِيَكُمْ
صِرَاطًا مُسْتَقِيمًا ٢٠

21. Besides these, there were other gains which you could not receive, but Allah has full control over them. Allah has power over all things.

21. Wa ukhraa lam taqdiroo ‘alayhaa qad aḥaaṭal-laahu bihaa; wa kaanal-laahu ‘alaa kulli shay’in Qadeeraa.

وَأُخْرَىٰ لَمْ تَقْدِرُوا عَلَيْهَا قَدْ
أَحَاطَ اللَّهُ بِهَا وَكَانَ اللَّهُ عَلَىٰ
كُلِّ شَيْءٍ قَدِيرًا ٢١

22. Had the unbelievers fought against you, they would have run

22. Wa law qaatalakumul-laz̲eena kafaroo lawallawul-

وَلَوْ قَاتَلَكُمُ الَّذِينَ كَفَرُوا لَوَلَّوُا

away from the battle and would have found no guardian or helper.

adbaara summa laa yajidoona waliyyañw-wa laa naṣeeraa.

الْاَدْبَارَ ثُمَّ لَا يَجِدُوْنَ وَلِيًّا
وَّلَا نَصِيْرًا ﴿٢٢﴾

23. This is the tradition of Allah which existed before, and you will never find any change in His tradition.

23. Sunnatal-laahil-latee qad khalat min qablu wa lan tajida lisunnatil-laahi tabdeelaa.

سُنَّةَ اللّٰهِ الَّتِيْ قَدْ خَلَتْ مِنْ
قَبْلُ ۚ وَلَنْ تَجِدَ لِسُنَّةِ اللّٰهِ
تَبْدِيْلًا ﴿٢٣﴾

24. It is He who (protected you against them (pagans of Makkah) and prevented you from fighting them) kept peace between you and the people of the valley of Makkah after having given you a victory over them. Allah is Well-aware of what you do.

24. Wa Huwal-lazee kaffa aydiyahum 'ankum wa aydiyakum 'anhum bibaṭni Makkata mim ba'di an azfa-rakum 'alayhim; wa kaanal-laahu bimaa ta'maloona Baṣeeraa.

وَهُوَ الَّذِيْ كَفَّ اَيْدِيَهُمْ عَنْكُمْ
وَاَيْدِيَكُمْ عَنْهُمْ بِبَطْنِ مَكَّةَ
مِنْۢ بَعْدِ اَنْ اَظْفَرَكُمْ عَلَيْهِمْ ۭ
وَكَانَ اللّٰهُ بِمَا تَعْمَلُوْنَ بَصِيْرًا ﴿٢٤﴾

25. It was the unbelievers who kept you from the Sacred Mosque and prevented your sacrificial offering from reaching its proper place. Allah would not have kept you from fighting the unbelievers, had there not been believing men and women (among them) whom you did not know and whom you might have unknowingly harmed. Allah did this because He grants mercy to whomever He wants. Had they (believers) all moved out of Makkah We would certainly have punished them (pagans) with a painful torment.

25. Humul-lazeena kafaroo wa ṣaddookum 'anil-Masjidil-Ḥaraami walhadya ma'koofan añy-yablugha maḥillah; wa law laa rijaalum-mu'minoona wa nisaaa'um-mu'minaatul lam ta'lamoohum an taṭa'oohum fatuṣeebakum minhum ma'ar-ratum bighayri 'ilmin liyud-khilal-laahu fee raḥmatihee mañy-yashaaa'; law tazayyaloo la'az-zabnallazeena kafaroo minhum 'azaaban aleemaa.

هُمُ الَّذِيْنَ كَفَرُوْا وَصَدُّوْكُمْ عَنِ
الْمَسْجِدِ الْحَرَامِ وَالْهَدْيَ مَعْكُوْفًا
اَنْ يَّبْلُغَ مَحِلَّهٗ ۭ وَلَوْلَا رِجَالٌ
مُّؤْمِنُوْنَ وَنِسَاۗءٌ مُّؤْمِنٰتٌ لَّمْ
تَعْلَمُوْهُمْ اَنْ تَطَـُٔوْهُمْ فَتُصِيْبَكُمْ
مِّنْهُمْ مَّعَرَّةٌۢ بِغَيْرِ عِلْمٍ ۚ لِيُدْخِلَ
اللّٰهُ فِيْ رَحْمَتِهٖ مَنْ يَّشَاۗءُ ۚ لَوْ
تَزَيَّلُوْا لَعَذَّبْنَا الَّذِيْنَ كَفَرُوْا
مِنْهُمْ عَذَابًا اَلِيْمًا ﴿٢٥﴾

26. Since the unbelievers held zealous ignorance in their hearts, like that of the pre-Islamic age of darkness, Allah gave confidence to His Messenger and to the believers, binding them to the principle of piety which they deserve. Allah has the knowledge of all things.

26. Iz ja'alal-lazeena kafaroo fee quloobihimul-ḥamiyyata ḥamiyyatal-Jaahiliyyati fa-anzalal-laahu sakeenatahoo 'alaa Rasoolihee wa 'alal-mu'mineena wa alzamahum kalimatat-taqwaa wa kaanooo aḥaqqa bihaa wa ahlahaa; wa kaanal-laahu bikulli shay'in 'Aleemaa.

اِذْ جَعَلَ الَّذِيْنَ كَفَرُوْا فِيْ
قُلُوْبِهِمُ الْحَمِيَّةَ حَمِيَّةَ الْجَاهِلِيَّةِ
فَاَنْزَلَ اللّٰهُ سَكِيْنَتَهٗ عَلٰي رَسُوْلِهٖ
وَعَلَي الْمُؤْمِنِيْنَ وَاَلْزَمَهُمْ كَلِمَةَ
التَّقْوٰى وَكَانُوْٓا اَحَقَّ بِهَا وَاَهْلَهَا ۭ
وَكَانَ اللّٰهُ بِكُلِّ شَيْءٍ عَلِيْمًا ﴿٢٦﴾ ع ٣ ٩ ١١

27. Allah made the dream of His Messenger come true for a genuine purpose. (In this he was told), "If Allah wills, you

27. Laqad ṣadaqal-laahu Rasoolahur-ru'yaa bilḥaqq; latadkhulunnal-Masjidal-Ḥaraa-ma

لَقَدْ صَدَقَ اللّٰهُ رَسُوْلَهُ الرُّءْيَا
بِالْحَقِّ ۚ لَتَدْخُلُنَّ الْمَسْجِدَ الْحَرَامَ

(believers) will enter the Sacred Mosque, in security, with your heads shaved, nails cut, and without any fear in your hearts." He knew what you did not know. Besides this victory, He will give you another immediate victory."

28. "It is He who has sent His messenger with guidance and the true religion to make it prevail over all other religions (with the coming of Al-Mahdi). Allah is a sufficient witness to this Truth."

29. Muhammad is the Messenger of Allah and those with him are stern to the unbelievers yet kind among themselves. You can see them bowing and prostrating before Allah, seeking His favors and pleasure. Their faces (foreheads) are marked due to the effect of their frequent prostration. That is their description in the Torah, and in the Gospel they are mentioned as the seed which shoots out its stalk then becomes stronger, harder, and stands firm on its stumps, attracting the farmers. Thus Allah has described the believers to enrage the unbelievers. Allah has promised forgiveness and a great reward to the righteously striving believers.

in shaaa'al-laahu aamineena muḥalliqeena ru'oosakum wa muqaṣṣireena laa takhaafoona fa'alima maa lam ta'lamoo faja'ala min dooni zaalika fatḥan qareebaa.

28. Huwal-lazeee arsala Rasoolahoo bilhudaa wa deenil-ḥaqqi liyuẓhirahoo 'alad-deeni kullih; wa kafaa billaahi Shaheedaa.

29. Muḥammadur-Rasoolul-laah; wallazeena ma'ahooo ashiddaaa'u 'alal-kuffaari ruḥamaaa'u baynahum taraahum rukka'an sujjadañy-yabtaghoona faḍlam-minallaahi wa riḍwaanaa; seemaahum fee wujoohihim min asaris-sujood; zaalika masaluhum fit-Tawraah; wa masaluhum fil-Injeel; kazar'in akhraja shaṭ-'ahoo fa-aazarahoo fastaghlaẓa fastawaa 'alaa sooqihee yu'jibuz-zurraa'a liyagheeẓa bihimul-kuffaar; wa'adallaahul-lazeena aamanoo wa'amiluṣ-ṣaaliḥaati minhum maghfiratañw-wa ajran 'aẓeemaa.

إِن شَآءَ ٱللَّهُ ءَامِنِينَ مُحَلِّقِينَ
رُءُوسَكُمْ وَمُقَصِّرِينَ لَا تَخَافُونَ
فَعَلِمَ مَا لَمْ تَعْلَمُوا فَجَعَلَ مِن
دُونِ ذَٰلِكَ فَتْحًا قَرِيبًا ﴿٢٧﴾
هُوَ ٱلَّذِىٓ أَرْسَلَ رَسُولَهُۥ بِٱلْهُدَىٰ
وَدِينِ ٱلْحَقِّ لِيُظْهِرَهُۥ عَلَى ٱلدِّينِ
كُلِّهِۦ ۚ وَكَفَىٰ بِٱللَّهِ شَهِيدًا ﴿٢٨﴾
مُّحَمَّدٌ رَّسُولُ ٱللَّهِ ۚ وَٱلَّذِينَ مَعَهُۥٓ
أَشِدَّآءُ عَلَى ٱلْكُفَّارِ رُحَمَآءُ بَيْنَهُمْ
تَرَىٰهُمْ رُكَّعًا سُجَّدًا يَبْتَغُونَ فَضْلًا
مِّنَ ٱللَّهِ وَرِضْوَٰنًا ۖ سِيمَاهُمْ فِى
وُجُوهِهِم مِّنْ أَثَرِ ٱلسُّجُودِ ۚ ذَٰلِكَ
مَثَلُهُمْ فِى ٱلتَّوْرَىٰةِ ۚ وَمَثَلُهُمْ
فِى ٱلْإِنجِيلِ كَزَرْعٍ أَخْرَجَ شَطْـَٔهُۥ
فَـَٔازَرَهُۥ فَٱسْتَغْلَظَ فَٱسْتَوَىٰ عَلَىٰ
سُوقِهِۦ يُعْجِبُ ٱلزُّرَّاعَ لِيَغِيظَ بِهِمُ
ٱلْكُفَّارَ ۗ وَعَدَ ٱللَّهُ ٱلَّذِينَ ءَامَنُوا
وَعَمِلُوا ٱلصَّٰلِحَٰتِ مِنْهُم مَّغْفِرَةً
وَأَجْرًا عَظِيمًۢا ﴿٢٩﴾

Al-Hujarat, The Chambers (49)

In the Name of Allah, the Beneficent, the Merciful.

Sûrat al-Ḥujurât-49

(Revealed at Madaniyyah)

Bismillaahir Raḥmaanir Raḥeem

(٤٩) سُورَةُ الحُجُرٰتِ مَدَنِيَّةٌ (١٠٦)

آياتها ١٨ بِسْمِ ٱللَّهِ ٱلرَّحْمَٰنِ ٱلرَّحِيمِ ركوعاتها ٢

1. O believers, do not be presumptuous with the Messenger of Allah (in your deeds and in your words). Have fear of Allah; He is All-hearing and All-knowing.

2. Believers, do not raise your voices above the voice of the Prophet; do not be too loud in speaking to him [as you may have

1. Yaa ayyuhal-lazeena aamanoo laa tuqaddimoo bayna yadayil-laahi wa Rasoolihee wattaqul-laah; innal-laaha Samee'un 'Aleem.

2. Yaaa ayyuhal-lazeena aamanoo laa tarfa'ooo aṣwaatakum fawqa ṣawtin Nabiyyi wa laa

يَٰٓأَيُّهَا ٱلَّذِينَ ءَامَنُوا لَا تُقَدِّمُوا
بَيْنَ يَدَىِ ٱللَّهِ وَرَسُولِهِۦ ۖ وَٱتَّقُوا
ٱللَّهَ ۚ إِنَّ ٱللَّهَ سَمِيعٌ عَلِيمٌ ﴿١﴾
يَٰٓأَيُّهَا ٱلَّذِينَ ءَامَنُوا لَا تَرْفَعُوٓا
أَصْوَٰتَكُمْ فَوْقَ صَوْتِ ٱلنَّبِىِّ وَلَا

been to one another], lest your deeds will be made devoid of all virtue without your realizing it.

tajharoo lahoo bilqawli kajahri ba'ḍikum liba'ḍin an taḥbaṭa a'maalukum wa antum laa tash'uroon.

تجهروا له بالقول كجهر بعضكم
لبعض أن تحبط أعمالكم
وأنتم لا تشعرون ٢

3. The hearts of those who lower their voices in the presence of the Messenger of Allah are tested by Allah through piety. They will have forgiveness and a great reward.

3. Innal-lazeena yaghuḍḍoona aṣwaatahum 'inda Rasoolil-laahi ulaaa'ikal-lazeenam-taḥ anal-laahu quloobahum littaqwaa; lahum-maghfiratuñw-wa ajrun 'aẓeem.

إن الذين يغضون أصواتهم
عند رسول الله أولئك الذين
امتحن الله قلوبهم للتقوى
لهم مغفرة وأجر عظيم ٣

4. Most of those who call you from behind the private chambers do not have any understanding.

4. Innal-lazeena yunaadoonaka miñw-waraaa'il-ḥujuraati aksaruhum laa ya'qiloon.

إن الذين ينادونك من وراء
الحجرات أكثرهم لا يعقلون ٤

5. Had they exercised patience until you came out, it would have been better for them. Allah is All-forgiving and All-merciful.

5. Wa law annahum ṣabaroo ḥattaa takhruja ilayhim lakaana khayral-lahum; wallaahu Ghafoorur-Raḥeem.

ولو أنهم صبروا حتى تخرج
إليهم لكان خيرا لهم والله
غفور رحيم ٥

6. Believers, if one who publicly commits sins brings you any news, ascertain its truthfulness carefully, lest you harm people through ignorance and then regret what you have done.

6. Yaaa ayyuhal-lazeena aamanooo in jaaa'akum faasiqum binaba-in fatabayyanooo an tuṣeeboo qawmam bijahaalatin fatuṣbiḥoo 'alaa maa fa'altum naadimeen.

يا أيها الذين آمنوا إن جاءكم
فاسق بنبإ فتبينوا أن تصيبوا
قوما بجهالة فتصبحوا على ما
فعلتم ندمين ٦

7. Know that the Messenger of Allah is with you. Had he yielded to you on many of the matters, you would have been in great trouble. However, Allah has endeared the faith to you and has made it attractive to your hearts. He has made disbelief, evil deeds and disobedience hateful to you. Such people will have the right guidance

7. Wa'lamooo anna feekum Rasoolal-laah; law yuṭee'ukum fee kaseerim-minal-amri la'anittum walaakinnal-laaha ḥabbaba ilaykumul-eemaana wa zayyanahoo fee quloobikum wa karraha ilaykumul-kufra walfusooqa wal'iṣyaan; ulaaa'ika humur-raashidoon.

واعلموا أن فيكم رسول الله
لو يطيعكم في كثير من الأمر
لعنتم ولكن الله حبب إليكم
الإيمان وزينه في قلوبكم وكره
إليكم الكفر والفسوق والعصيان
أولئك هم الرشدون ٧

8. as a favor and a blessing from Allah. Allah is All-knowing and All-wise.

8. Faḍlam-minal-laahi wa ni'mah; wallaahu 'Aleemun Ḥakeem.

فضلا من الله ونعمة والله
عليم حكيم ٨

9. If two parties among the believers start to fight against each other, restore peace among them. If one party rebels against

9. Wa in ṭaaa'ifataani minal-mu'mineenaq-tataloo fa-aṣliḥoo baynahumaa fa-im

وإن طائفتان من المؤمنين
اقتتلوا فأصلحوا بينهما فإن

9. If two parties among the believers start to fight against each other, restore peace among them. If one party rebels against

baghat iḥdaahumaa ‘alal-ukhraa faqaatilul-latee tabghee ḥattaa tafeee’a ilaaa amril-laah; fa-in faaa’at fa-aṣliḥoo bay-nahumaa bil‘adli wa aqsiṭooo innal-laaha yuḥibbul-muq-siṭeen.

بَغَتْ اِحْدٰىهُمَا عَلَى الْاُخْرٰى
فَقَاتِلُوا الَّتِيْ تَبْغِيْ حَتّٰى تَفِيْٓءَ اِلٰٓى
اَمْرِ اللّٰهِ ۚ فَاِنْ فَآءَتْ فَاَصْلِحُوْا
بَيْنَهُمَا بِالْعَدْلِ وَاَقْسِطُوْا ؕ
اِنَّ اللّٰهَ يُحِبُّ الْمُقْسِطِيْنَ ﴿٩﴾

10. Believers are each other's brothers. Restore peace among your brothers. Have fear of Allah so that perhaps you will receive mercy.

10. Innamal-mu’minoona ikhwatun fa-aṣliḥoo bayna akhawaykum wattaqul-laaha la‘allakum turḥamoon

اِنَّمَا الْمُؤْمِنُوْنَ اِخْوَةٌ فَاَصْلِحُوْا
بَيْنَ اَخَوَيْكُمْ وَاتَّقُوا اللّٰهَ لَعَلَّكُمْ
تُرْحَمُوْنَ ﴿١٠﴾ ع

11. Believers, let not a group of you mock another. Perhaps they are better than you. Let not women mock each other; perhaps one is better than the other. Let not one of you find faults in another nor let anyone of you defame another. How terrible is the defamation after having true faith. Those who did not repent are certainly unjust.

11. Yaaa ayyuhal-lazeena aamanoo laa yaskhar qawmum min qawmin ‘asaaa añy-yakoonoo khayram minhum wa laa nisaaa’um min nisaaa’in ‘asaaa añy-yakunna khayram-minhunna wa laa talmizooo anfusakum wa laa tanaabazoo bil-alqaab; bi’sa-lismul-fusooqu ba‘dal eemaan; wa mal-lam yatub fa ulaaa’ika humuẓ-ẓaalimoon.

يٰٓاَيُّهَا الَّذِيْنَ اٰمَنُوْا لَا يَسْخَرْ
قَوْمٌ مِّنْ قَوْمٍ عَسٰٓى اَنْ يَّكُوْنُوْا
خَيْرًا مِّنْهُمْ وَلَا نِسَآءٌ مِّنْ نِّسَآءٍ
عَسٰٓى اَنْ يَّكُنَّ خَيْرًا مِّنْهُنَّ ۚ
وَلَا تَلْمِزُوْٓا اَنْفُسَكُمْ وَلَا تَنَابَزُوْا
بِالْاَلْقَابِ ؕ بِئْسَ الِاسْمُ الْفُسُوْقُ
بَعْدَ الْاِيْمَانِ ۚ وَمَنْ لَّمْ يَتُبْ
فَاُولٰٓئِكَ هُمُ الظّٰلِمُوْنَ ﴿١١﴾

12. Believers, stay away from conjecture; acting upon some conjecture may lead to sin. Do not spy on one another or back-bite. Would any of you like to eat the disgusting dead flesh of your brother? Have fear of Allah; Allah accepts repentance and is All-merciful.

12. Yaaa ayyuhal-lazeena aamanuj-taniboo kaseeram-minaẓ-ẓanni inna ba‘ḍaẓ-ẓanni ismuñw- wa laa tajassasoo wa laa yaghtab ba‘ḍukum ba‘ḍaa; ayuḥibbu aḥadukum añy-ya-kula laḥma akheehi maytan fakarihtumooh; wattaqul-laah;innal-laaha Tawwaabur-Raḥeem.

يٰٓاَيُّهَا الَّذِيْنَ اٰمَنُوا اجْتَنِبُوْا
كَثِيْرًا مِّنَ الظَّنِّ ۫ اِنَّ بَعْضَ
الظَّنِّ اِثْمٌ وَّلَا تَجَسَّسُوْا وَلَا
يَغْتَبْ بَّعْضُكُمْ بَعْضًا ؕ اَيُحِبُّ
اَحَدُكُمْ اَنْ يَّاْكُلَ لَحْمَ اَخِيْهِ
مَيْتًا فَكَرِهْتُمُوْهُ ؕ وَاتَّقُوا اللّٰهَ ؕ
اِنَّ اللّٰهَ تَوَّابٌ رَّحِيْمٌ ﴿١٢﴾

13. People, We have created you all male and female and have made you nations and tribes so that you would recognize each other. The most honorable among you in the sight of Allah is the

13. Yaaa ayyuhan-naasu innaa khalaqnaakum min zakariñw-wa unsaa wa ja‘alnaakum shu‘oobañw-wa qabaaa’ila lita‘aarafooo inna akramakum

يٰٓاَيُّهَا النَّاسُ اِنَّا خَلَقْنٰكُمْ مِّنْ
ذَكَرٍ وَّاُنْثٰى وَجَعَلْنٰكُمْ شُعُوْبًا
وَّقَبَآئِلَ لِتَعَارَفُوْا ؕ اِنَّ اَكْرَمَكُمْ

most pious of you. Allah is All-knowing and All-aware.

'indal laahi atqaakum innal-laaha 'Aleemun Khabeer

عِنْدَ اللّٰهِ اَتْقٰىكُمْ ؕ اِنَّ اللّٰهَ
عَلِيْمٌ خَبِيْرٌ ﴿۱۳﴾

14. The Bedouin Arabs have said, "We are believers." Tell them, "You did not believe, but you should say that you have submitted (by the sword). In fact, belief has not yet entered your hearts. If you obey Allah and His Messenger, nothing will be reduced from your deeds. Allah is All-forgiving and All-merciful.

14. Qaalatil A'raabu aamannaa qul lam tu'minoo wa laakin qoolooo aslamnaa wa lamma yadkhulil eemaanu fee quloobikum wa in tuṭee'ul-laaha wa Rasoolahoo laa yalitkum min a'maalikum shay'aa; innal-laaha Ghafoorur-Raḥeem.

قَالَتِ الْاَعْرَابُ اٰمَنَّا ؕ قُلْ لَّمْ
تُؤْمِنُوْا وَلٰكِنْ قُوْلُوْٓا اَسْلَمْنَا
وَلَمَّا يَدْخُلِ الْاِيْمَانُ فِيْ قُلُوْبِكُمْ ؕ
وَاِنْ تُطِيْعُوا اللّٰهَ وَرَسُوْلَهٗ لَا
يَلِتْكُمْ مِّنْ اَعْمَالِكُمْ شَيْـًٔا ؕ
اِنَّ اللّٰهَ غَفُوْرٌ رَّحِيْمٌ ﴿۱۴﴾

15. The believers are those who believe in Allah and His Messenger, who did not change their belief into doubt, and who strive hard for the cause of Allah with their property and persons. They are the truthful ones."

15. Innamal-mu'minoonal-lazeena aamanoo billaahi wa Rasoolihee summa lam yartaaboo wa jaahadoo bi-amwaalihim wa anfusihim fee sabeelil-laah; ulaaa'ika humuṣ-ṣaadiqoon.

اِنَّمَا الْمُؤْمِنُوْنَ الَّذِيْنَ اٰمَنُوْا بِاللّٰهِ
وَرَسُوْلِهٖ ثُمَّ لَمْ يَرْتَابُوْا وَجٰهَدُوْا
بِاَمْوَالِهِمْ وَاَنْفُسِهِمْ فِيْ سَبِيْلِ
اللّٰهِ ؕ اُولٰٓئِكَ هُمُ الصّٰدِقُوْنَ ﴿۱۵﴾

16. (Muhammad), say, "Do you teach Allah about your religion? Allah knows whatever is in the heavens and the earth. Allah has the knowledge of all things."

16. Qul atu'allimoonal-laaha bideenikum wallaahu ya'lamu maa fis-samaawaati wa maa fil-arḍ; wallaahu bikulli shay'in 'Aleem.

قُلْ اَتُعَلِّمُوْنَ اللّٰهَ بِدِيْنِكُمْ ؕ وَاللّٰهُ
يَعْلَمُ مَا فِي السَّمٰوٰتِ وَمَا فِي
الْاَرْضِ ؕ وَاللّٰهُ بِكُلِّ شَيْءٍ عَلِيْمٌ ﴿۱۶﴾

17. (The Bedouins tell you that) you owe them (a great deal) for their embracing Islam. Tell them, "You are not doing me any favors by embracing Islam. In fact, it is Allah to whom you owe a great deal. He has guided you to the faith. You are not of the truthful people.

17. Yamunnoona 'alayka an aslamoo qul laa tamunnoo 'alayya Islaamakum balillaahu yamunnu 'alaykum an hadaakum lil-eemaani in kuntum ṣaadiqeen.

يَمُنُّوْنَ عَلَيْكَ اَنْ اَسْلَمُوْا ؕ قُلْ
لَّا تَمُنُّوْا عَلَيَّ اِسْلَامَكُمْ ۚ بَلِ
اللّٰهُ يَمُنُّ عَلَيْكُمْ اَنْ هَدٰىكُمْ
لِلْاِيْمَانِ اِنْ كُنْتُمْ صٰدِقِيْنَ ﴿۱۷﴾

18. Allah knows whatever is unseen in the heavens and in the earth. He is Well-aware of what you do."

18. Innal-laaha ya'lamu ghaybas-samaawaati wal-arḍ; wallaahu Baṣeerum bimaa ta'maloon.

اِنَّ اللّٰهَ يَعْلَمُ غَيْبَ السَّمٰوٰتِ
وَالْاَرْضِ ؕ وَاللّٰهُ بَصِيْرٌۢ بِمَا
تَعْمَلُوْنَ ﴿۱۸﴾ ع ٢ ٨

Qaf, Qaf (50)

In the Name of Allah, the Beneficent, the Merciful.

Sûrat Qâf-50

(Revealed at Makkah)

Bismillaahir Raḥmaanir Raḥeem

(۵۰) سُوْرَةُ قٓ مَكِّيَّةٌ (۳۴)

اٰيَاتُهَا ۴۵ — بِسْمِ اللّٰهِ الرَّحْمٰنِ الرَّحِيْمِ — رُكُوْعَاتُهَا ۳

1. (I swear) by Qaf and the glorious Quran, (you are the Messenger of Allah).

1. Qaaaf; wal Qur-aanil Majeed.

قٓ ۚ وَالْقُرْاٰنِ الْمَجِيْدِ ﴿۱﴾

2. In fact, it seems odd to them (pagans) that a Warner from their

2. Bal 'ajibooo an jaaa'ahum munzirum-

بَلْ عَجِبُوْٓا اَنْ جَآءَهُمْ مُّنْذِرٌ

own people has come to them. The unbelievers have said, "It is very strange

minhum faqaalal-kaafiroona haazaa shay'un 'ajeeb.

مِّنْهُمْ فَقَالَ الْكٰفِرُوْنَ هٰذَا
شَيْءٌ عَجِيْبٌ ﴿٢﴾

3. that after we die and become dust, we shall be brought back to life again. This seems far from reality."

3. 'A-izaa mitnaa wa kunnaa turaaban zaalika raj'um ba'eed.

ءَاِذَا مِتْنَا وَكُنَّا تُرَابًا ۚ ذٰلِكَ
رَجْعٌۢ بَعِيْدٌ ﴿٣﴾

4. We already know how much of them (of their bodies) the earth will consume. With Us there is a Book that contains all records.

4. Qad 'alimnaa maa tanqușul-arḍu minhum wa 'indanaa Kitaabun Ḥafeeẓ.

قَدْ عَلِمْنَا مَا تَنْقُصُ الْاَرْضُ
مِنْهُمْ ۚ وَعِنْدَنَا كِتٰبٌ حَفِيْظٌ ﴿٤﴾

5. In fact, they have rejected the truth that has come to them, thus they live in confusion.

5. Bal kaz-zaboo bilḥaqqi lammaa jaaa'ahum fahum feee amrim-mareej.

بَلْ كَذَّبُوْا بِالْحَقِّ لَمَّا جَآءَهُمْ
فَهُمْ فِيْٓ اَمْرٍ مَّرِيْجٍ ﴿٥﴾

6. Did they not look how We have established the sky above them and decked it without gaps and cracks?

6. Afalam yanẓurooo ilassamaaa'i fawqahum kayfa banaynaahaa wa zayyannaahaa wa maa lahaa min furooj.

اَفَلَمْ يَنْظُرُوْٓا اِلَى السَّمَآءِ فَوْقَهُمْ
كَيْفَ بَنَيْنٰهَا وَزَيَّنّٰهَا وَمَا لَهَا مِنْ
فُرُوْجٍ ﴿٦﴾

7. (Have they not seen) how We have spread out the earth, placed on it firm mountains and made all kinds of flourishing pairs of plants grow?

7. Wal-arḍa madadnaahaa wa alqaynaa feehaa rawaasiya wa ambatnaa feehaa min kulli zawjim baheej.

وَالْاَرْضَ مَدَدْنٰهَا وَاَلْقَيْنَا فِيْهَا
رَوَاسِيَ وَاَنْۢبَتْنَا فِيْهَا مِنْ كُلِّ
زَوْجٍۢ بَهِيْجٍ ﴿٧﴾

8. This is a reminder and it sharpens the insight of every servant of Allah who turns to Him in repentance.

8. Tabșirataňw-wa zikraa likulli 'abdim-muneeb.

تَبْصِرَةً وَّذِكْرٰى لِكُلِّ عَبْدٍ
مُّنِيْبٍ ﴿٨﴾

9. We have sent blessed water down from the sky to grow gardens, harvestable crops,

9. Wa nazzalnaa minassamaaa'i maaa'am mubaarakan fa-ambatnaa bihee jannaatiňw-wa ḥabbal-ḥașeed.

وَنَزَّلْنَا مِنَ السَّمَآءِ مَآءً مُّبٰرَكًا
فَاَنْۢبَتْنَا بِهٖ جَنّٰتٍ وَّحَبَّ الْحَصِيْدِ ﴿٩﴾

10. and tall palm-trees with clusters of dates

10. Wannakhla baasiqaatil-lahaa ṭal'un-naḍeed.

وَالنَّخْلَ بٰسِقٰتٍ لَّهَا طَلْعٌ نَّضِيْدٌ ﴿١٠﴾

11. as sustenance for My servants. With this We have brought the dead land back to life. Thus will also be your resurrection.

11. Rizqal-lil'ibaad; wa aḥyaynaa bihee baldatam maytaa; kazaalikal-khurooj.

رِّزْقًا لِّلْعِبَادِ ۙ وَاَحْيَيْنَا بِهٖ بَلْدَةً
مَّيْتًا ۗ كَذٰلِكَ الْخُرُوْجُ ﴿١١﴾

12. The people of Noah, dwellers of Al-Rass, Thamud,

12. Kaz-zabat qablahum qawmu Nooḥiňw-wa Așḥaabur-Rassi wa Samood.

كَذَّبَتْ قَبْلَهُمْ قَوْمُ نُوْحٍ وَّاَصْحٰبُ
الرَّسِّ وَثَمُوْدُ ﴿١٢﴾

13. Ad, the Pharaoh, brethren (in kind) of Lot,

13. Wa 'Aaduňw-wa Fir'awnu wa ikhwaanu Looṭ.

وَعَادٌ وَّفِرْعَوْنُ وَاِخْوَانُ لُوْطٍ ﴿١٣﴾

14. dwellers of the forest, and the people of Tubba had all rejected the Prophets. Thus, they became subject to Our torment.

14. Wa Așḥaabul-Aykati wa qawmu Tubba'; kullun kaz-zabar-Rusula faḥaqqa wa'eed.

وَّاَصْحٰبُ الْاَيْكَةِ وَقَوْمُ تُبَّعٍ ۗ كُلٌّ
كَذَّبَ الرُّسُلَ فَحَقَّ وَعِيْدِ ﴿١٤﴾

15. Did We fail (experienced fatigue) to accomplish the first creation? (Of course, We did not; We have all power over all things). So they remain confused about a new creation.

15. Afa'ayeenaa bilkhalqil-awwal; bal hum fee labsim-min khalqin jadeed.

أَفَعَيِينَا بِالْخَلْقِ الْأَوَّلِ ۚ بَلْ هُمْ
فِي لَبْسٍ مِّنْ خَلْقٍ جَدِيدٍ ﴿١٥﴾ ع ١٥/١٥

16. We swear that We have created the human being and We know what his soul whispers to him. We are closer to him than even his jugular vein.

16. Wa laqad khalaqnal-insaana wa na'lamu maa tuwaswisu bihee nafsuhoo wa Naḥnu aqrabu ilayhi min ḥablil-wareed.

وَلَقَدْ خَلَقْنَا الْإِنسَانَ وَنَعْلَمُ
مَا تُوَسْوِسُ بِهِ نَفْسُهُ ۖ وَنَحْنُ أَقْرَبُ
إِلَيْهِ مِنْ حَبْلِ الْوَرِيدِ ﴿١٦﴾

17. Since the two scribes are sitting on each of his shoulders,

17. Iz̲ yatalaqqal-mutalaqqiyaani 'anil-yameeni wa 'anish-shimaali qa'eed.

إِذْ يَتَلَقَّى الْمُتَلَقِّيَانِ عَنِ الْيَمِينِ
وَعَنِ الشِّمَالِ قَعِيدٌ ﴿١٧﴾

18. he does not utter a word which is not recorded immediately by the watchful scribes, Raqib and Atid.

18. Maa yalfiẓu min qawlin illaa ladayhi raqeebun 'ateed.

مَا يَلْفِظُ مِن قَوْلٍ إِلَّا لَدَيْهِ
رَقِيبٌ عَتِيدٌ ﴿١٨﴾

19. The agony of death will reach the human being as a matter of all truth and he (the human being) will be told, "This is what you had been trying to run away from."

19. Wa jaaa'at sakratul-mawti bilḥaqq; z̲aalika maa kunta minhu taḥeed.

وَجَاءَتْ سَكْرَةُ الْمَوْتِ بِالْحَقِّ ۖ
ذَٰلِكَ مَا كُنتَ مِنْهُ تَحِيدُ ﴿١٩﴾

20. The trumpet will certainly be sounded. This will be the day (you were) threatened about.

20. Wa nufikha fiṣ-Ṣoor; z̲aalika yawmul-wa'eed.

وَنُفِخَ فِي الصُّورِ ۚ ذَٰلِكَ يَوْمُ
الْوَعِيدِ ﴿٢٠﴾

21. Every soul will be accompanied by one to drive him and another as a witness.

21. Wa jaaa'at kullu nafsim-ma'ahaa saaa'iquñw-wa shaheed.

وَجَاءَتْ كُلُّ نَفْسٍ مَّعَهَا سَائِقٌ
وَشَهِيدٌ ﴿٢١﴾

22. (He will be told), "You were completely heedless of this day. We have removed the veil from your eyes and your vision will now be sharp and strong."

22. Laqad kunta fee ghaflatim-min haaz̲aa fakashafnaa 'anka ghiṭaaa'aka fabaṣarukal-Yawma ḥadeed.

لَّقَدْ كُنتَ فِي غَفْلَةٍ مِّنْ هَٰذَا
فَكَشَفْنَا عَنكَ غِطَاءَكَ فَبَصَرُكَ
الْيَوْمَ حَدِيدٌ ﴿٢٢﴾

23. His companion (Satan) will say, "This is that which I have ready."

23. Wa qaala qareenuhoo haaz̲aa maa ladayya 'ateed.

وَقَالَ قَرِينُهُ هَٰذَا مَا لَدَيَّ
عَتِيدٌ ﴿٢٣﴾

24. O you, the two of you (the Holy Prophet and his successor), "Throw into hell every persistent unbeliever,

24. Alqiyaa fee Jahannama kulla kaffaarin 'aneed.

أَلْقِيَا فِي جَهَنَّمَ كُلَّ كَفَّارٍ
عَنِيدٍ ﴿٢٤﴾

25. hinderer of good, a doubter transgressor,

25. Mannaa'il-lilkhayri mu'-tadim-mureeb.

مَّنَّاعٍ لِّلْخَيْرِ مُعْتَدٍ مُّرِيبٍ ﴿٢٥﴾

26. who considers something as his Ilah (one deserving to be worshiped) besides Allah. Thus the two of you throw him into severe torment."

26. Allaz̲ee ja'ala ma'al-laahi ilaahan aakhara fa-alqiyaahu fil-'az̲aabish-shadeed.

الَّذِي جَعَلَ مَعَ اللَّهِ إِلَٰهًا آخَرَ
فَأَلْقِيَاهُ فِي الْعَذَابِ الشَّدِيدِ ﴿٢٦﴾

27. His companion (Satan) will say, "Our Lord, I did not mislead

27. Qaala qareenuhoo Rab-banaa maaa aṭghaytuhoo

قَالَ قَرِينُهُ رَبَّنَا مَا أَطْغَيْتُهُ

him, but he himself went astray far away from the right path."

wa laakin kaana fee ḍalaalim ba'eed.

وَلَٰكِن كَانَ فِي ضَلَٰلٍ بَعِيدٍ ﴿٢٧﴾

28. The Lord will say, "Do not argue in My presence; I had certainly sent you a warning.

28. Qaala laa takhtaṣimoo ladayya wa qad qaddamtu ilaykum bilwa'eed.

قَالَ لَا تَخْتَصِمُوا لَدَيَّ وَقَدْ قَدَّمْتُ إِلَيْكُم بِالْوَعِيدِ ﴿٢٨﴾

29. No word is to be exchanged in My presence. I am not unjust to My servants."

29. Maa yubaddalul-qawlu ladayya wa maaa anaa biẓal-laamil-lil'abeed.

مَا يُبَدَّلُ الْقَوْلُ لَدَيَّ وَمَا أَنَا بِظَلَّٰمٍ لِّلْعَبِيدِ ﴿٢٩﴾ ع ٢ ١٤ ١٦

30. On that day We shall ask hell, "Are you full?" It will say, "There is no room for more."

30. Yawma naqoolu li-Jahannama halim-tala-ti wa taqoolu hal mim-mazeed.

يَوْمَ نَقُولُ لِجَهَنَّمَ هَلِ امْتَلَأْتِ وَتَقُولُ هَلْ مِن مَّزِيدٍ ﴿٣٠﴾

31. Paradise will be beautified quickly for the pious ones

31. Wa uzlifatil-Jannatu lil-muttaqeena ghayra ba'eed.

وَأُزْلِفَتِ الْجَنَّةُ لِلْمُتَّقِينَ غَيْرَ بَعِيدٍ ﴿٣١﴾

32. (and they will be told), "This is what you were promised. It is for everyone who turned in repentance to Allah, kept his promise,

32. Haaẕaa maa too'adoona likulli awwaabin ḥafeeẓ.

هَٰذَا مَا تُوعَدُونَ لِكُلِّ أَوَّابٍ حَفِيظٍ ﴿٣٢﴾

33. feared the Beneficent in secret, and turned to Him with a repenting heart."

33. Man khashiyar-Raḥmaana bilghaybi wa jaaa'a biqalbim-muneeb.

مَّنْ خَشِيَ الرَّحْمَٰنَ بِالْغَيْبِ وَجَآءَ بِقَلْبٍ مُّنِيبٍ ﴿٣٣﴾

34. (They will be told), "Enter Paradise in peace and therein you will live forever."

34. Udkhuloohaa bisalaamin ẕaalika yawmul-khulood.

ادْخُلُوهَا بِسَلَٰمٍ ذَٰلِكَ يَوْمُ الْخُلُودِ ﴿٣٤﴾

35. They will have therein whatever they want and will receive from Us more rewards.

35. Lahum maa yashaaa'oona feehaa wa ladaynaa mazeed.

لَهُم مَّا يَشَآءُونَ فِيهَا وَلَدَيْنَا مَزِيدٌ ﴿٣٥﴾

36. How many an ancient town that were much stronger than they (unbelievers) did We destroy? (You should) pass by (different) lands but do you find any place of escape (from Our torment)?

36. Wa kam ahlaknaa qabla-hum min qarnin hum ashaddu minhum baṭshan fanaqqaboo fil-bilaad; hal mim-maḥeeṣ.

وَكَمْ أَهْلَكْنَا قَبْلَهُم مِّن قَرْنٍ هُمْ أَشَدُّ مِنْهُم بَطْشًا فَنَقَّبُوا فِي الْبِلَٰدِ هَلْ مِن مَّحِيصٍ ﴿٣٦﴾

37. This is a reminder for everyone who understands, listens, and sees.

37. Inna fee ẕaalika laẕikraa liman kaana lahoo qalbun aw alqas-sam'a wa huwa shaheed.

إِنَّ فِي ذَٰلِكَ لَذِكْرَىٰ لِمَن كَانَ لَهُ قَلْبٌ أَوْ أَلْقَى السَّمْعَ وَهُوَ شَهِيدٌ ﴿٣٧﴾

38. We created the heavens, the earth, and all that is between them in six days without experiencing any fatigue.

38. Wa laqad khalaqnas-samaawaati wal-arḍa wa maa baynahumaa fee sittati ayyaa-miñw-wa maa massanaa mil-lughoob.

وَلَقَدْ خَلَقْنَا السَّمَٰوَٰتِ وَالْأَرْضَ وَمَا بَيْنَهُمَا فِي سِتَّةِ أَيَّامٍ وَمَا مَسَّنَا مِن لُّغُوبٍ ﴿٣٨﴾

39. (Muhammad), exercise patience against what they say. Glorify your Lord with His praise before sunrise and sunset.

39. Faṣbir 'alaa maa yaqoo-loona wa sabbiḥ biḥamdi Rabbika qabla ṭuloo'ish-shamsi

فَاصْبِرْ عَلَىٰ مَا يَقُولُونَ وَسَبِّحْ بِحَمْدِ رَبِّكَ قَبْلَ طُلُوعِ الشَّمْسِ

wa qablal-ghuroob.

وَقَبۡلَ الۡغُرُوۡبِ ۝٣٩

40. Glorify Him during the night and also glorify Him after prostration.

40. Wa minal-layli fasabbiḥhu wa adbaaras-sujood.

وَمِنَ الَّيۡلِ فَسَبِّحۡهُ وَاَدۡبَارَ السُّجُوۡدِ ۝٤٠

41. Wait for the day when the trumpet will be sounded from a nearby place.

41. Wastami' Yawma yunaa-dil-munaadi mim-makaanin qareeb.

وَاسۡتَمِعۡ يَوۡمَ يُنَادِ الۡمُنَادِ مِنۡ مَّكَانٍ قَرِيۡبٍ ۝٤١

42. On that day they will certainly hear the sound of the trumpet in all truth and that will be the Day of Resurrection.

42. Yawma yasma'oonaṣ-ṣayḥata bilḥaqq; zaalika yawmul-khurooj.

يَّوۡمَ يَسۡمَعُوۡنَ الصَّيۡحَةَ بِالۡحَقِّ ؕ ذٰلِكَ يَوۡمُ الۡخُرُوۡجِ ۝٤٢

43. We give life and cause things to die. To Us all things will return.

43. Innaa Naḥnu nuḥyee wa numeetu wa ilaynal-maṣeer.

اِنَّا نَحۡنُ نُحۡىٖ وَنُمِيۡتُ وَاِلَيۡنَا الۡمَصِيۡرُ ۝٤٣

44. On the day when the earth is rent asunder, they will quickly come out of their graves. This is how easy it is for Us to bring about the Day of Resurrection.

44. Yawma tashaqqaqul-arḍu 'anhum siraa'aa; zaalika ḥash-run 'alaynaa yaseer.

يَوۡمَ تَشَقَّقُ الۡاَرۡضُ عَنۡهُمۡ سِرَاعًا ؕ ذٰلِكَ حَشۡرٌ عَلَيۡنَا يَسِيۡرٌ ۝٤٤

45. We know best what they say and you cannot compel them. Remind, by way of the Quran, those who have fear of My warnings.

45. Naḥnu a'lamu bimaa yaqooloona wa maaa anta 'alayhim bijabbaar; fazakkir bil-Qur'aani mañy-yakhaafu wa'eed.

نَحۡنُ اَعۡلَمُ بِمَا يَقُوۡلُوۡنَ وَمَاۤ اَنۡتَ عَلَيۡهِمۡ بِجَبَّارٍ فَذَكِّرۡ بِالۡقُرۡاٰنِ مَنۡ يَّخَافُ وَعِيۡدِ ۝٤٥ ع ٢ ١٧

Al-Dhariyat, The Winds (51)

In the Name of Allah, the Beneficent, the Merciful.

Sûrat az-Zâriyât-51

(Revealed at Makkah)

Bismillaahir Raḥmaanir Raḥeem

(٥١) سُوۡرَةُ الذّٰرِيٰتِ مَكِّيَّةٌ (٦٧)

بِسۡمِ اللّٰهِ الرَّحۡمٰنِ الرَّحِيۡمِ

1. By the winds which carry dust particles,

1. Waz zaariyaati zarwaa.

وَالذّٰرِيٰتِ ذَرۡوًا ۝١

2. by the clouds which are heavily loaded with water,

2. Falḥaamilaati wiqraa.

فَالۡحٰمِلٰتِ وِقۡرًا ۝٢

3. by the ships which smoothly sail on the oceans,

3. Faljaariyaati yusraa.

فَالۡجٰرِيٰتِ يُسۡرًا ۝٣

4. by the angels which distribute the affairs,

4. Falmuqassimaati amraa.

فَالۡمُقَسِّمٰتِ اَمۡرًا ۝٤

5. that whatever you are promised is certainly true

5. Innamaa too'adoona la-ṣaadiq.

اِنَّمَا تُوۡعَدُوۡنَ لَصَادِقٌ ۝٥

6. and the Day of Judgment will inevitably take place.

6. Wa innad-deena lawaaqi'.

وَّاِنَّ الدِّيۡنَ لَوَاقِعٌ ۝٦

7. By the beautiful heavens,

7. Wassamaaa'i zaatil-ḥu-buk.

وَالسَّمَآءِ ذَاتِ الۡحُبُكِ ۝٧

8. your ideas are different.

8. Innakum lafee qawlim-mukhtalif.

اِنَّكُمۡ لَفِىۡ قَوۡلٍ مُّخۡتَلِفٍ ۝٨

9. Let whoever wishes, turn away from him.

9. Yu'faku 'anhu man ufik.

يُّؤۡفَكُ عَنۡهُ مَنۡ اُفِكَ ۝٩

10. Condemned are those who conjecture their religion without authority,

10. Qutilal-kharraaṣoon.

قُتِلَ الۡخَرّٰصُوۡنَ ۝١٠

11. and who have lost the right path and are oblivious (of Allah).	11. Allaz̲eena hum fee ghamratin saahoon.	الَّذِيْنَ هُمْ فِيْ غَمْرَةٍ سَاهُوْنَ ﴿١١﴾
12. They ask, "When will it be the Day of Judgment?"	12. Yas'aloona ayyaana Yawmud-Deen	يَسْـَٔلُوْنَ اَيَّانَ يَوْمُ الدِّيْنِ ﴿١٢﴾
13. On the Day of Judgment they will be punished by the fire	13. Yawma hum 'alan-Naari yuftanoon.	يَوْمَ هُمْ عَلَى النَّارِ يُفْتَنُوْنَ ﴿١٣﴾
14. and will be told, "Suffer that (torment) which you wanted to experience immediately."	14. Z̲ooqoo fitnatakum haaz̲al-laz̲ee kuntum bihee tasta'jiloon.	ذُوْقُوْا فِتْنَتَكُمْ ؕ هٰذَا الَّذِيْ كُنْتُمْ بِهٖ تَسْتَعْجِلُوْنَ ﴿١٤﴾
15. The pious ones will live amidst gardens and springs,	15. Innal-muttaqeena fee Jannaatiñw-wa 'uyoon.	اِنَّ الْمُتَّقِيْنَ فِيْ جَنّٰتٍ وَّعُيُوْنٍ ﴿١٥﴾
16. receiving their reward from their Lord. They had been righteous people before the Day of Judgment.	16. Aakhiz̲eena maaa aataahum Rabbuhum; innahum kaanoo qabla z̲aalika muḥsineen.	اٰخِذِيْنَ مَاۤ اٰتٰىهُمْ رَبُّهُمْ ؕ اِنَّهُمْ كَانُوْا قَبْلَ ذٰلِكَ مُحْسِنِيْنَ ﴿١٦﴾
17. They slept very little during the night	17. Kaanoo qaleelam-minal-layli maa yahja'oon.	كَانُوْا قَلِيْلًا مِّنَ الَّيْلِ مَا يَهْجَعُوْنَ ﴿١٧﴾
18. and asked for forgiveness in the early morning.	18. Wa bil-asḥaari hum yastaghfiroon.	وَبِالْاَسْحَارِ هُمْ يَسْتَغْفِرُوْنَ ﴿١٨﴾
19. They assigned a share of their property for the needy and the deprived.	19. Wa feee amwaalihim ḥaqqul-lissaaa'ili walmaḥroom.	وَفِيْۤ اَمْوَالِهِمْ حَقٌّ لِّلسَّآئِلِ وَالْمَحْرُوْمِ ﴿١٩﴾
20. In the earth there is evidence (of the Truth) for those who have strong faith.	20. Wa fil-arḍi Aayaatul-lilmooqineen.	وَفِي الْاَرْضِ اٰيٰتٌ لِّلْمُوْقِنِيْنَ ﴿٢٠﴾
21. There is also evidence of the Truth within your own selves. Will you then not see?	21. Wa feee anfusikum; afalaa tubṣiroon.	وَفِيْۤ اَنْفُسِكُمْ ؕ اَفَلَا تُبْصِرُوْنَ ﴿٢١﴾
22. In the heavens there is your sustenance and that (the advent of Al-Mahdi) which you are promised.	22. Wa fis-samaaa'i rizqukum wa maa too'adoon.	وَفِي السَّمَآءِ رِزْقُكُمْ وَمَا تُوْعَدُوْنَ ﴿٢٢﴾
23. This, by the Lord of the heavens and the earth, is as certain as your ability to speak.	23. Fawa Rabbis-samaaa'i wal-arḍi innahoo laḥaqqum-mis̲la maaa annakum tanṭiqoon.	فَوَرَبِّ السَّمَآءِ وَالْاَرْضِ اِنَّهٗ لَحَقٌّ مِّثْلَ مَاۤ اَنَّكُمْ تَنْطِقُوْنَ ﴿٢٣﴾
24. Have you heard the story of the honorable guests of Abraham?	24. Hal ataaka ḥadees̲u ḍayfi Ibraaheemal-mukrameen.	هَلْ اَتٰىكَ حَدِيْثُ ضَيْفِ اِبْرٰهِيْمَ الْمُكْرَمِيْنَ ﴿٢٤﴾
25. When they came to him saying, "Peace be with you," he replied to their greeting in the same manner and said to himself, "These are a strange people."	25. Iz̲ dakhaloo 'alayhi faqaaloo salaaman qaala salaamun qawmum-munkaroon.	اِذْ دَخَلُوْا عَلَيْهِ فَقَالُوْا سَلٰمًا ؕ قَالَ سَلٰمٌ ۚ قَوْمٌ مُّنْكَرُوْنَ ﴿٢٥﴾
26. He went quietly to his wife and returned to his guests with a fat, roasted calf.	26. Faraagha ilaaa ahlihee fajaaa'a bi'ijlin sameen.	فَرَاغَ اِلٰۤى اَهْلِهٖ فَجَآءَ بِعِجْلٍ سَمِيْنٍ ﴿٢٦﴾
27. He placed it before them. Then he asked, "Why are you not eating?"	27. Faqarrabahooo ilayhim qaala alaa ta-kuloon.	فَقَرَّبَهٗۤ اِلَيْهِمْ قَالَ اَلَا تَاْكُلُوْنَ ﴿٢٧﴾
28. He began to feel afraid. They said, "Do not be afraid," and then gave him the glad news of the birth of a knowledgeable son.	28. Fa-awjasa minhum kheefatan qaaloo laa takhaf wa bashsharoohu bighulaamin 'aleem.	فَاَوْجَسَ مِنْهُمْ خِيْفَةً ؕ قَالُوْا لَا تَخَفْ ؕ وَبَشَّرُوْهُ بِغُلٰمٍ عَلِيْمٍ ﴿٢٨﴾
29. His wife came forward in a group, crying and covering her	29. Fa-aqbalatim-ra-atuhoo fee ṣarratin faṣakkat	فَاَقْبَلَتِ امْرَاَتُهٗ فِيْ صَرَّةٍ فَصَكَّتْ

ع ۳ ۱۸

وقف لازم

face, saying, "I am an old barren woman!"	wajhahaa wa qaalat 'ajoozun 'aqeem.	وَجْهَهَا وَقَالَتْ عَجُوزٌ عَقِيمٌ ٢٩
30. They said, "This is true but your Lord has said (that you will have a son); He is All-wise and All-knowing."	30. Qaaloo kaẕaaliki qaala Rabbuki innahoo Huwal-Ḥakeemul-'Aleem.	قَالُوا كَذٰلِكِ ۙ قَالَ رَبُّكِ ۖ إِنَّهُ هُوَ الْحَكِيمُ الْعَلِيمُ ٣٠
31. Abraham asked, "Messengers, what is your task?"	31. Qaala famaa khaṭbukum ayyuhal-mursaloon.	قَالَ فَمَا خَطْبُكُمْ أَيُّهَا الْمُرْسَلُونَ ٣١
32. They replied, "We have been sent to a sinful people	32. Qaalooo innaaa ursilnaaa ilaa qawmimmujrimeen.	قَالُوا إِنَّا أُرْسِلْنَا إِلَىٰ قَوْمٍ مُجْرِمِينَ ٣٢
33. to bring down upon them showers of marked lumps of clay.	33. Linursila 'alayhim ḥijaa-ratam-min ṭeen.	لِنُرْسِلَ عَلَيْهِمْ حِجَارَةً مِنْ طِينٍ ٣٣
34. They are transgressors in the presence of your Lord."	34. Musawwamatan 'inda Rabbika lilmusrifeen.	مُسَوَّمَةً عِنْدَ رَبِّكَ لِلْمُسْرِفِينَ ٣٤
35. We saved the believers among them,	35. Fa-akhrajnaa man kaana feehaa minal-mu'mineen.	فَأَخْرَجْنَا مَنْ كَانَ فِيهَا مِنَ الْمُؤْمِنِينَ ٣٥
36. but We found only one Muslim house.	36. Famaa wajadnaa feehaa ghayra baytim-minal-musli-meen.	فَمَا وَجَدْنَا فِيهَا غَيْرَ بَيْتٍ مِنَ الْمُسْلِمِينَ ٣٦
37. We left therein evidence for those who fear the painful torment.	37. Wa taraknaa feehaaa Aayatal-lillaẕeena yakhaafoo-nal-'aẕaabal-aleem.	وَتَرَكْنَا فِيهَا آيَةً لِلَّذِينَ يَخَافُونَ الْعَذَابَ الْأَلِيمَ ٣٧
38. There is also evidence (of the Truth) in the story of Moses when We sent him to the Pharaoh with clear authority.	38. Wa fee Moosaaa iẕ arsal-naahu ilaa Fir'awna bisulṭaa-nim-mubeen.	وَفِي مُوسَىٰ إِذْ أَرْسَلْنَاهُ إِلَىٰ فِرْعَوْنَ بِسُلْطَانٍ مُبِينٍ ٣٨
39. The Pharaoh and his forces turned away from him, saying, "He is either a magician or an insane person."	39. Fatawallaa biruknihee wa qaala saaḥirun aw majnoon.	فَتَوَلَّىٰ بِرُكْنِهِ وَقَالَ سَاحِرٌ أَوْ مَجْنُونٌ ٣٩
40. We seized him and his army and threw them into the sea. He himself was to be blamed.	40. Fa-akhaẕnaahu wa junoo-dahoo fanabaẕnaahum fil-yammi wa huwa muleem.	فَأَخَذْنَاهُ وَجُنُودَهُ فَنَبَذْنَاهُمْ فِي الْيَمِّ وَهُوَ مُلِيمٌ ٤٠
41. There is also evidence of the Truth in the story of Ad, whom We struck with a violent wind	41. Wa fee 'Aadin iẕ arsalnaa 'alayhimur-reeḥal 'aqeem.	وَفِي عَادٍ إِذْ أَرْسَلْنَا عَلَيْهِمُ الرِّيحَ الْعَقِيمَ ٤١
42. which turned everything it approached into dust.	42. Maa taẕaru min shay'in atat 'alayhi illaa ja'alat-hu karrameem.	مَا تَذَرُ مِنْ شَيْءٍ أَتَتْ عَلَيْهِ إِلَّا جَعَلَتْهُ كَالرَّمِيمِ ٤٢
43. There is also evidence (of the Truth) in the story of Thamud, who were told to enjoy themselves for an appointed time (three days).	43. Wa fee S̱amooda iẕ qeela lahum tamatta'oo ḥattaa ḥeen.	وَفِي ثَمُودَ إِذْ قِيلَ لَهُمْ تَمَتَّعُوا حَتَّىٰ حِينٍ ٤٣
44. They transgressed against the command of their Lord. So a blast of sound struck them and they were unable to do anything but stare.	44. Fa'ataw 'an amri Rabbi-him fa-akhaẕat-humuṣ-ṣaa'iqatu wa hum yanẓuroon.	فَعَتَوْا عَنْ أَمْرِ رَبِّهِمْ فَأَخَذَتْهُمُ

الجزء السابع والعشرون (٢٧)

45. They were unable to stand up, nor were they helped.

46. The people of Noah who lived before them were also evil-doing people.

47. We have made the heavens with Our own hands (power) and We expand it.

48. We have spread out the earth and how brilliantly it is spread!

49. We have created everything in pairs so that perhaps you may take heed.

50. (Muhammad), tell them, "Seek refuge with Allah (perform Hajj). I have been sent from Him to warn you plainly.

51. Do not choose other gods besides Him. I have been sent from Him to warn you plainly."

52. In the same way no messenger came to those who lived before them without his people calling him a magician or an insane person.

53. Have they inherited such dealings with the Prophets from their predecessors or are they a rebellious people?

54. (Muhammad), leave them alone and you will not be blamed.

55. Keep on reminding them. This benefits the believers.

56. We have created jinn and human beings only that they might worship Me (follow My laws).

57. I do not expect to receive any sustenance from them or that they should feed Me.

58. It is Allah Who is the Sustainer and the Lord of invincible strength.

59. The unjust will bear a burden like that of their unjust predecessors. Let them not make Me bring immediate punishment upon them.

60. Woe to the unbelievers when the day with which they have been threatened comes!

45. Famas-taṭaa'oo min qiyaamiñw-wa maa kaanoo muntaṣireen.

46. Wa qawma Nooḥim-min qablu innahum kaanoo qawman faasiqeen.

47. Wassamaaa'a banaynaa-haa bi-aydiñw-wa innaa lamoo-si'oon.

48. Wal-arḍa farashnaahaa fani'mal-maahidoon.

49. Wa min kulli shay'in khalaqnaa zawjayni la'allakum taẕakkaroon.

50. Fafirrooo ilal-laahi innee lakum minhu naẕeerum-mubeen.

51. Wa laa taj'aloo ma'allaahi ilaahan aakhara innee lakum minhu naẕeerum mubeen.

52. Kaẕaalika maaa atalla-ẕeena min qablihim-mir-Rasoo-lin illaa qaaloo saaḥirun aw majnoon.

53. Atawaaṣaw bih; bal hum qawmun ṭaaghoon.

54. Fatawalla 'anhum famaaa anta bimaloom.

55. Wa ẕakkir fa-innaẕ-ẕikraa tanfa'ul-mu'mineen.

56. Wa maa khalaqtul-jinna wal-insa illaa liya'budoon.

57. Maaa ureedu minhum mir-rizqiñw-wa maaa ureedu añy-yuṭ'imoon.

58. Innal-laaha Huwar-Raz-zaaqu Ẕul-Quwwatil-Mateen.

59. Fa-inna lillaẕeena ẓala-moo ẕanoobam-misla ẕanoobi aṣḥaabihim falaa yasta'jiloon.

60. Fawaylul-lillaẕeena kafa-roo miñy-Yawmihimul- laẕee yoo'adoon.

الصّٰعِقَةُ وَهُمْ يَنْظُرُوْنَ ﴿٤٤﴾
فَمَا اسْتَطَاعُوْا مِنْ قِيَامٍ وَّمَا كَانُوْا
مُنْتَصِرِيْنَ ﴿٤٥﴾
وَقَوْمَ نُوْحٍ مِّنْ قَبْلُ ۭ اِنَّهُمْ كَانُوْا
قَوْمًا فٰسِقِيْنَ ﴿٤٦﴾ ع ٢ ٤٣
وَالسَّمَآءَ بَنَيْنٰهَا بِاَيْىدٍ وَّاِنَّا لَمُوْسِعُوْنَ ﴿٤٧﴾
وَالْاَرْضَ فَرَشْنٰهَا فَنِعْمَ الْمٰهِدُوْنَ ﴿٤٨﴾
وَمِنْ كُلِّ شَيْءٍ خَلَقْنَا زَوْجَيْنِ
لَعَلَّكُمْ تَذَكَّرُوْنَ ﴿٤٩﴾
فَفِرُّوْا اِلَى اللّٰهِ ۭ اِنِّيْ لَكُمْ مِّنْهُ
نَذِيْرٌ مُّبِيْنٌ ﴿٥٠﴾
وَلَا تَجْعَلُوْا مَعَ اللّٰهِ اِلٰـهًا اٰخَرَ ۭ
اِنِّيْ لَكُمْ مِّنْهُ نَذِيْرٌ مُّبِيْنٌ ﴿٥١﴾
كَذٰلِكَ مَآ اَتَى الَّذِيْنَ مِنْ قَبْلِهِمْ مِّنْ
رَّسُوْلٍ اِلَّا قَالُوْا سَاحِرٌ اَوْ مَجْنُوْنٌ ﴿٥٢﴾
اَتَوَاصَوْا بِهٖ ۚ بَلْ هُمْ قَوْمٌ طَاغُوْنَ ﴿٥٣﴾
فَتَوَلَّ عَنْهُمْ فَمَآ اَنْتَ بِمَلُوْمٍ ﴿٥٤﴾
وَّذَكِّرْ فَاِنَّ الذِّكْرٰى تَنْفَعُ الْمُؤْمِنِيْنَ ﴿٥٥﴾
وَمَا خَلَقْتُ الْجِنَّ وَالْاِنْسَ اِلَّا
لِيَعْبُدُوْنِ ﴿٥٦﴾
مَآ اُرِيْدُ مِنْهُمْ مِّنْ رِّزْقٍ وَّمَآ اُرِيْدُ
اَنْ يُّطْعِمُوْنِ ﴿٥٧﴾
اِنَّ اللّٰهَ هُوَ الرَّزَّاقُ ذُو الْقُوَّةِ الْمَتِيْنُ ﴿٥٨﴾
فَاِنَّ لِلَّذِيْنَ ظَلَمُوْا ذَنُوْبًا مِّثْلَ ذَنُوْبِ
اَصْحٰبِهِمْ فَلَا يَسْتَعْجِلُوْنِ ﴿٥٩﴾
فَوَيْلٌ لِّلَّذِيْنَ كَفَرُوْا مِنْ يَّوْمِهِمُ

Al-Tur, Mount Sinai (52)

In the Name of Allah,
the Beneficent, the Merciful.

1. By the Mount (Sinai),
2. by the written book
3. on parchment for distribution,
4. by the established House (in the fourth heaven),
5. by the high ceiling (sky),
6. and by the swelling ocean,
7. the torment of your Lord will inevitably take place
8. and no one will be able to prevent it.
9. On the day when the heavens will breathe
10. and the mountains quickly move,
11. woe will be on that day to those who rejected the Truth
12. and who indulged in sinful disputes against (Allah's revelations).
13. On that day they will be left to the fire without fail
14. and they will be told, "This is the fire which you called a lie.
15. Is it magic or do you not still see?
16. Burn in its heat. It is all the same for you whether you dare to bear it or not; this is the recompense for your deeds."
17. The pious will live in bountiful Paradise,
18. talking of what they have received from their Lord and of how their Lord has saved them from the torment of hell.
19. They will be told, "Eat and drink to your heart's delight for what you have done."

Sûrat aṭ-Ṭûr-52

(Revealed at Makkah)

Bismillaahir Raḥmaanir Raḥeem

1. Waṭ-Ṭoor.
2. Wa Kitaabim-masṭoor.
3. Fee raqqim-manshoor.
4. Wal-Baytil-Ma'moor.
5. Wassaqfil-marfoo'.
6. Wal-baḥril-masjoor.
7. Inna 'aẕaaba Rabbika lawaaqi'.
8. Maa lahoo min daafi'.
9. Yawma tamoorus samaaa'u mawraa.
10. Wa taseerul-jibaalu sayraa.
11. Fawayluñy-Yawma'iẕil-lilmukaẕ-ẕibeen.
12. Allaẕeena hum fee khawḍiñy-yal'aboon.
13. Yawma yuda'-'oona ilaa Naari Jahannama da'-'aa.
14. Haaẕihin-Naarul-latee kuntum bihaa tukaẕ-ẕiboon.
15. Afasiḥrun haaẕaaa am antum laa tubṣiroon.
16. Iṣlawhaa faṣbirooo aw laa taṣbiroo sawaaa'un 'alaykum innamaa tujzawna maa kuntum ta'maloon.
17. Innal-muttaqeena fee Jannaatiñw-wa na'eem.
18. Faakiheena bimaaa aataahum Rabbuhum wa waqaahum Rabbuhum 'aẕaabal-Jaḥeem.
19. Kuloo washraboo haneee-'am bimaa kuntum ta'maloon.

الَّذِي يُوعَدُونَ (٦٠) ع ٣/٤

(٥٢) سُورَةُ الطُّورِ مَكِّيَّةٌ (٧٦)

آياتها ٤٩ بِسْمِ اللّٰهِ الرَّحْمٰنِ الرَّحِيْمِ ركوعاتها ٢

وَالطُّوْرِ (١)
وَكِتٰبٍ مَّسْطُوْرٍ (٢)
فِيْ رَقٍّ مَّنْشُوْرٍ (٣)
وَّالْبَيْتِ الْمَعْمُوْرِ (٤)
وَالسَّقْفِ الْمَرْفُوْعِ (٥)
وَالْبَحْرِ الْمَسْجُوْرِ (٦)
اِنَّ عَذَابَ رَبِّكَ لَوَاقِعٌ (٧)
مَّا لَهٗ مِنْ دَافِعٍ (٨)
يَّوْمَ تَمُوْرُ السَّمَآءُ مَوْرًا (٩)
وَّتَسِيْرُ الْجِبَالُ سَيْرًا (١٠)
فَوَيْلٌ يَّوْمَئِذٍ لِّلْمُكَذِّبِيْنَ (١١)
الَّذِيْنَ هُمْ فِيْ خَوْضٍ يَّلْعَبُوْنَ (١٢) وقف لازم
يَوْمَ يُدَعُّوْنَ اِلٰى نَارِ جَهَنَّمَ دَعًّا (١٣)
هٰذِهِ النَّارُ الَّتِيْ كُنْتُمْ بِهَا
تُكَذِّبُوْنَ (١٤)
اَفَسِحْرٌ هٰذَآ اَمْ اَنْتُمْ لَا تُبْصِرُوْنَ (١٥)
اِصْلَوْهَا فَاصْبِرُوْٓا اَوْ لَا تَصْبِرُوْا ۚ
سَوَآءٌ عَلَيْكُمْ ۖ اِنَّمَا تُجْزَوْنَ مَا
كُنْتُمْ تَعْمَلُوْنَ (١٦)
اِنَّ الْمُتَّقِيْنَ فِيْ جَنّٰتٍ وَّنَعِيْمٍ (١٧)
فٰكِهِيْنَ بِمَآ اٰتٰهُمْ رَبُّهُمْ ۚ وَوَقٰهُمْ
رَبُّهُمْ عَذَابَ الْجَحِيْمِ (١٨)
كُلُوْا وَاشْرَبُوْا هَنِيْٓـًٔا بِمَا كُنْتُمْ

		تَعْمَلُوْنَ ﴿١٩﴾
20. They will recline on couches arranged in rows and We shall couple them with maidens with large, lovely eyes.	20. Muttaki'eena 'alaa sururim-maṣfoofah; wa zawwajnaahum biḥoorin 'een.	مُتَّكِـِٕيْنَ عَلٰى سُرُرٍ مَّصْفُوْفَةٍ ۚ وَ زَوَّجْنٰهُمْ بِحُوْرٍ عِيْنٍ ﴿٢٠﴾
21. (The bountiful paradise is for the pious ones) and for the believers and their offspring who have followed them (their parents) in belief, whom We shall join with their parents therein. We shall reduce nothing from their deeds. Everyone will be responsible for his own actions.	21. Wallazeena aamanoo wattaba'at-hum zurriyyatuhum bi-eemaanin alḥaqnaa bihim zurriyyatahum wa maaa alatnaahum min 'amalihim min shay'; kullum-ri'im bimaa kasaba raheen.	وَالَّذِيْنَ اٰمَنُوْا وَاتَّبَعَتْهُمْ ذُرِّيَّتُهُمْ بِاِيْمَانٍ اَلْحَقْنَا بِهِمْ ذُرِّيَّتَهُمْ وَمَا اَلَتْنٰهُمْ مِّنْ عَمَلِهِمْ مِّنْ شَيْءٍ ۚ كُلُّ امْرِئٍۭ بِمَا كَسَبَ رَهِيْنٌ ﴿٢١﴾
22. We shall provide them with fruits and the meat of the kind which they desire.	22. Wa amdadnaahum bifaakihatiñw-wa laḥmim-mimmaa yashtahoon.	وَاَمْدَدْنٰهُمْ بِفَاكِهَةٍ وَّلَحْمٍ مِّمَّا يَشْتَهُوْنَ ﴿٢٢﴾
23. They will pass to one another cups of un-intoxicating wine that is free of sins.	23. Yatanaaza'oona feehaa ka-sal-laa laghwun feehaa wa laa ta-seem.	يَتَنَازَعُوْنَ فِيْهَا كَاْسًا لَّا لَغْوٌ فِيْهَا وَلَا تَاْثِيْمٌ ﴿٢٣﴾
24. They will be served by youths who will be as beautiful as (protected) pearls.	24. Wa yaṭoofu 'alayhim ghilmaanul-lahum ka-annahum lu'lu'um-maknoon.	وَيَطُوْفُ عَلَيْهِمْ غِلْمَانٌ لَّهُمْ كَاَنَّهُمْ لُؤْلُؤٌ مَّكْنُوْنٌ ﴿٢٤﴾
25. They will turn to one another and ask questions,	25. Wa aqbala ba'ḍuhum 'alaa ba'ḍiñy-yatasaaa'aloon.	وَاَقْبَلَ بَعْضُهُمْ عَلٰى بَعْضٍ يَّتَسَآءَلُوْنَ ﴿٢٥﴾
26. saying, "We were afraid while in the world.	26. Qaalooo innaa kunnaa qablu feee ahlinaa mushfiqeen.	قَالُوْٓا اِنَّا كُنَّا قَبْلُ فِيْٓ اَهْلِنَا مُشْفِقِيْنَ ﴿٢٦﴾
27. However, Allah has granted us favors and saved us from the scorching heat of the torment.	27. Famannal-laahu 'alaynaa wa waqaanaa 'azaabas-samoom.	فَمَنَّ اللّٰهُ عَلَيْنَا وَوَقٰنَا عَذَابَ السَّمُوْمِ ﴿٢٧﴾
28. We had prayed to Him; He is Kind and All-merciful."	28. Innaa kunnaa min qablu nad'oohu innahoo Huwal-Barrur-Raḥeem.	اِنَّا كُنَّا مِنْ قَبْلُ نَدْعُوْهُ ۭ اِنَّهٗ هُوَ الْبَرُّ الرَّحِيْمُ ﴿٢٨﴾ ع ٢٨ ٣
29. (Muhammad), remind them, by the Grace of Your Lord, that you are neither a soothsayer nor a possessed (insane) person.	29. Fazakkir famaaa anta bini'mati Rabbika bikaahiniñw-wa laa majnoon.	فَذَكِّرْ فَمَآ اَنْتَ بِنِعْمَتِ رَبِّكَ بِكَاهِنٍ وَّلَا مَجْنُوْنٍ ﴿٢٩﴾
30. Do they say, "He is only a poet and we are waiting to see him die?"	30. Am yaqooloona shaa'irun natarabbaṣu bihee raybal-manoon.	اَمْ يَقُوْلُوْنَ شَاعِرٌ نَّتَرَبَّصُ بِهٖ رَيْبَ الْمَنُوْنِ ﴿٣٠﴾
31. Say, "Wait, I am also waiting with you."	31. Qul tarabbaṣoo fa-innee ma'akum minal-Mutarabbiṣeen.	قُلْ تَرَبَّصُوْا فَاِنِّيْ مَعَكُمْ مِّنَ

		الْمُتَرَبِّصِينَ ﴿٣١﴾
32. Does their reason tell them to say this or is it because they are a rebellious people?	32. Am ta-muruhum aḥlaamu-hum bihaa**z**aaa am hum qaw-mun ṭaaghoon.	أَمْ تَأْمُرُهُمْ أَحْلَامُهُم بِهَٰذَا ۚ أَمْ هُمْ قَوْمٌ طَاغُونَ ﴿٣٢﴾
33. Do they say, "He has falsely invented it (the Quran)?" In fact, they themselves have no faith.	33. Am yaqooloona taqaw-walah; bal laa yu'minoon.	أَمْ يَقُولُونَ تَقَوَّلَهُ ۚ بَل لَّا يُؤْمِنُونَ ﴿٣٣﴾
34. Let them produce a discourse (a man from Allah) like it if they are true in their claim.	34. Falya-too biḥadeesim-misliheee in kaanoo ṣaadiqeen.	فَلْيَأْتُوا بِحَدِيثٍ مِّثْلِهِ إِن كَانُوا صَادِقِينَ ﴿٣٤﴾
35. Have they been created from nothing or are they themselves their own creators?	35. Am khuliqoo min ghayri shay'in am humul-khaaliqoon.	أَمْ خُلِقُوا مِنْ غَيْرِ شَيْءٍ أَمْ هُمُ الْخَالِقُونَ ﴿٣٥﴾
36. Have they created the heavens and the earth? In fact, they have no strong faith.	36. Am khalaqus-samaawaati wal-arḍ; bal laa yooqinoon.	أَمْ خَلَقُوا السَّمَاوَاتِ وَالْأَرْضَ ۚ بَل لَّا يُوقِنُونَ ﴿٣٦﴾
37. Do they own the treasures of your Lord? Have they any authority over Allah?	37. Am 'indahum khazaaa'inu Rabbika am humul-muṣay-ṭiroon.	أَمْ عِندَهُمْ خَزَائِنُ رَبِّكَ أَمْ هُمُ الْمُصَيْطِرُونَ ﴿٣٧﴾
38. Do they have a ladder (by which they can climb up to the heavens) and listen (to the angels) and come back to the rest of the people with clear authority?	38. Am lahum sullamuñy-yastami'oona feehi falya-ti mustami'uhum bisulṭaanim mubeen.	أَمْ لَهُمْ سُلَّمٌ يَسْتَمِعُونَ فِيهِ ۖ فَلْيَأْتِ مُسْتَمِعُهُم بِسُلْطَانٍ مُّبِينٍ ﴿٣٨﴾
39. Do the daughters belong to Him and the sons to you?	39. Am lahul-banaatu wa lakumul-banoon.	أَمْ لَهُ الْبَنَاتُ وَلَكُمُ الْبَنُونَ ﴿٣٩﴾
40. Do you (Muhammad) ask them for any payment (for your preaching) which they cannot afford?	40. Am tas'aluhum ajran fahum mim-maghramim mus-qaloon.	أَمْ تَسْأَلُهُمْ أَجْرًا فَهُم مِّن مَّغْرَمٍ مُّثْقَلُونَ ﴿٤٠﴾
41. Do they have knowledge of the unseen, so they are able to predict (the future)?	41. Am 'indahumul-ghaybu fahum yaktuboon.	أَمْ عِندَهُمُ الْغَيْبُ فَهُمْ يَكْتُبُونَ ﴿٤١﴾
42. Do they design evil plans? The unbelievers themselves will be snared by their evil plots.	42. Am yureedoona kaydan fallazeena kafaroo humul makeedoon.	أَمْ يُرِيدُونَ كَيْدًا ۖ فَالَّذِينَ كَفَرُوا هُمُ الْمَكِيدُونَ ﴿٤٢﴾
43. Do they have another Ilah (one deserving to be worshiped) besides Allah? Allah is free of all defects of being considered equal to the idols.	43. Am lahum ilaahun ghay-rul-laah; Subḥaanal-laahi 'am-maa yushrikoon.	أَمْ لَهُمْ إِلَٰهٌ غَيْرُ اللَّهِ ۚ سُبْحَانَ اللَّهِ عَمَّا يُشْرِكُونَ ﴿٤٣﴾
44. Even if they were to see a part of the heavens falling down upon them, they would say, "It is only dense cloud."	44. Wa iñy-yaraw kisfammi-nassamaaa'i saaqiṭañy-yaqo-oloo saḥaabum-markoom.	وَإِن يَرَوْا كِسْفًا مِّنَ السَّمَاءِ سَاقِطًا يَقُولُوا سَحَابٌ مَّرْكُومٌ ﴿٤٤﴾
45. So leave them alone until they face the day when they will be struck dead from terror	45. Fazarhum ḥattaa yulaaqoo Yawmahumul-lazee feehi yuṣ'aqoon.	فَذَرْهُمْ حَتَّىٰ يُلَاقُوا يَوْمَهُمُ الَّذِي فِيهِ يُصْعَقُونَ ﴿٤٥﴾

46. and when their evil plans will be of no benefit to them nor will they be helped.	46. Yawma laa yughnee 'anhum kayduhum shay'añw-wa laa hum yunṣaroon.	يَوْمَ لَا يُغْنِي عَنْهُمْ كَيْدُهُمْ شَيْـًٔا وَّلَا هُمْ يُنْصَرُوْنَ ۝٤٦
47. The unjust will suffer other torments besides this but most of them do not know.	47. Wa inna lillaẕeena ẓalamoo 'aẕaaban doona ẕaalika wa laakinna akṡarahum laa ya'lamoon.	وَإِنَّ لِلَّذِيْنَ ظَلَمُوْا عَذَابًا دُوْنَ ذٰلِكَ وَلٰكِنَّ أَكْثَرَهُمْ لَا يَعْلَمُوْنَ ۝٤٧
48. Wait patiently for the command of your Lord. We are watching over you (you are under Our protection). Glorify your Lord when you rise during the night (for tahajjud)	48. Waṣbir liḥukmi Rabbika fa-innaka bia'yuninaa wa sabbiḥ biḥamdi Rabbika ḥeena taqoom.	وَاصْبِرْ لِحُكْمِ رَبِّكَ فَإِنَّكَ بِأَعْيُنِنَا وَسَبِّحْ بِحَمْدِ رَبِّكَ حِيْنَ تَقُوْمُ ۝٤٨
49. and glorify Him after the setting of the stars.	49. Wa minal-layli fasabbiḥhu wa idbaaran-nujoom.	وَمِنَ الَّيْلِ فَسَبِّحْهُ وَإِدْبَارَ النُّجُوْمِ ۝٤٩ ع

Al-Najm, The Star (53)

In the Name of Allah, the Beneficent, the Merciful.

Sûrat an-Najm-53

(Revealed at Makkah)

Bismillaahir Raḥmaanir Raḥeem

(٥٣) سُوْرَةُ النَّجْمِ مَكِّيَّةٌ (٢٣)

آياتها ٦٢ — بِسْمِ اللّٰهِ الرَّحْمٰنِ الرَّحِيْمِ — ركوعاتها ٣

1. By the star, when descending (in space),	1. Wannajmi iẕaa hawaa.	وَالنَّجْمِ إِذَا هَوٰى ۝١
2. your companion (Muhammad) is not in error nor has he deviated.	2. Maa ḍalla ṣaaḥibukum wa maa ghawaa.	مَا ضَلَّ صَاحِبُكُمْ وَمَا غَوٰى ۝٢
3. He does not speak out of his own desires.	3. Wa maa yanṭiqu 'anil-hawaa.	وَمَا يَنْطِقُ عَنِ الْهَوٰى ۝٣
4. It (whatever he says) is a revelation which has been revealed to him.	4. In huwa illaa Waḥyuñy-yooḥaa.	إِنْ هُوَ إِلَّا وَحْيٌ يُّوْحٰى ۝٤
5. The great, mighty one taught him,	5. 'Allamahoo shadeedul-quwaa.	عَلَّمَهٗ شَدِيْدُ الْقُوٰى ۝٥
6. the possessor of intense power (taught him), so he became well balanced,	6. Ẕoo mirratin fastawaa.	ذُوْ مِرَّةٍ فَاسْتَوٰى ۝٦
7. while he (the Holy Prophet) was on the uppermost horizon.	7. Wa huwa bil-ufuqil-a'laa.	وَهُوَ بِالْأُفُقِ الْأَعْلٰى ۝٧
8. He (the Holy Prophet) then drew near (the curtain of light)	8. Ṡumma danaa fatadallaa.	ثُمَّ دَنَا فَتَدَلّٰى ۝٨
9. (then looked down toward the dominion of earth) and it seemed as close as the distance of two bows, or even less.	9. Fakaana qaaba qawsayni aw adnaa.	فَكَانَ قَابَ قَوْسَيْنِ أَوْ أَدْنٰى ۝٩
10. He (Allah) then revealed to His servant whatever He wanted to reveal.	10. Fa-awḥaaa ilaa 'abdihee maaa awḥaa.	فَأَوْحٰى إِلٰى عَبْدِهٖ مَا أَوْحٰى ۝١٠
11. His (Muhammad's) heart did not lie about what he had witnessed.	11. Maa kaẕabal-fu'aadu maa ra-aa.	مَا كَذَبَ الْفُؤَادُ مَا رَأٰى ۝١١
12. Do you then argue with him even about what he observes (and sees)?	12. Afatumaaroonahoo 'alaa maa yaraa.	أَفَتُمٰرُوْنَهٗ عَلٰى مَا يَرٰى ۝١٢
13. He certainly saw it (revelation) during his other descent	13. Wa laqad ra-aahu nazlatan ukhraa.	وَلَقَدْ رَاٰهُ نَزْلَةً أُخْرٰى ۝١٣
14. to the Lotus tree (in the seven heavens)	14. 'Inda Sidratil-Muntahaa.	عِنْدَ سِدْرَةِ الْمُنْتَهٰى ۝١٤
15. near which is Al-Mawa Paradise.	15. 'Indahaa Jannatul-Ma-waa.	عِنْدَهَا جَنَّةُ الْمَأْوٰى ۝١٥
16. Even though, a covering covers the Lotus-tree,	16. Iẕ yaghshas-Sidrata maa yaghshaa.	إِذْ يَغْشَى السِّدْرَةَ مَا يَغْشٰى ۝١٦
17. (Muhammad's) eyes did not turn blind, nor did they lead him to falsehood.	17. Maa zaaghal-baṣaru wa maa ṭaghaa.	مَا زَاغَ الْبَصَرُ وَمَا طَغٰى ۝١٧

18. He certainly saw some of the greatest signs (of the creation) of his Lord.	18. Laqad ra-aa min Aayaati Rabbihil-Kubraa.	لَقَدْ رَاٰى مِنْ اٰيٰتِ رَبِّهِ الْكُبْرٰى ﴿١٨﴾
19. (Can anything as such be considered true) of Al-Lat, Al-Uzza,	19. Afara'aytumul-Laata wal'Uzzaa.	اَفَرَءَيْتُمُ اللّٰتَ وَالْعُزّٰى ﴿١٩﴾
20. and your third idol Al-Manat (whom you considered as Allah's daughters)?	20. Wa Manaatas-saalisatal-ukhraa.	وَمَنٰوةَ الثَّالِثَةَ الْاُخْرٰى ﴿٢٠﴾
21. Do sons belong to you and daughters to Allah?	21. Alakumuz-zakaru wa lahul-unsaa.	اَلَكُمُ الذَّكَرُ وَلَهُ الْاُنْثٰى ﴿٢١﴾
22. This indeed is a defective distribution!	22. Tilka izan qismatun deezaa.	تِلْكَ اِذًا قِسْمَةٌ ضِيْزٰى ﴿٢٢﴾
23. These are only names given by yourselves and your fathers. Allah has not given them any authority. They, (unbelievers), only follow mere conjecture and the desires of their souls, even though guidance has already come to them from their Lord.	23. In hiya illaaa asmaaa'un sammaytumoohaaa antum wa aabaaa'ukum maaa anzalal-laahu bihaa min sulṭaan; iñy-yattabi'oona illaz-zanna wa maa tahwal-anfusu wa laqad jaaa'ahum-mir-Rabbihimul-hudaa.	اِنْ هِىَ اِلَّاۤ اَسْمَآءٌ سَمَّيْتُمُوْهَاۤ اَنْتُمْ وَاٰبَآؤُكُمْ مَّاۤ اَنْزَلَ اللّٰهُ بِهَا مِنْ سُلْطٰنٍ ؕ اِنْ يَّتَّبِعُوْنَ اِلَّا الظَّنَّ وَمَا تَهْوَى الْاَنْفُسُ ۚ وَلَقَدْ جَآءَهُمْ مِّنْ رَّبِّهِمُ الْهُدٰى ﴿٢٣﴾
24. Can the human being have whatever he wishes?	24. Am lil-insaani maa taman-naa.	اَمْ لِلْاِنْسَانِ مَا تَمَنّٰى ﴿٢٤﴾
25. All that is in the life to come and all that is in this life belongs only to Allah.	25. Falillaahil-Aakhiratu wal-oolaa.	فَلِلّٰهِ الْاٰخِرَةُ وَالْاُوْلٰى ﴿٢٥﴾ ع ٢٥ ٥
26. There are many angels in the heavens whose intercession will be of no benefit unless Allah grants such permission to whichever of them He wants.	26. Wa kam mim-malakin fis-samaawaati laa tughnee shafaa'atuhum shay'an illaa mim ba'di añy-ya-zanal-laahu limañy- yashaaa'u wa yarḍaa.	وَكَمْ مِّنْ مَّلَكٍ فِى السَّمٰوٰتِ لَا تُغْنِىْ شَفَاعَتُهُمْ شَيْــًٔا اِلَّا مِنْۢ بَعْدِ اَنْ يَّاْذَنَ اللّٰهُ لِمَنْ يَّشَآءُ وَيَرْضٰى ﴿٢٦﴾
27. Only those who do not believe in the life hereafter call the angels females.	27. Innal-lazeena laa yu'mi-noona bil-Aakhirati la-yusam-moonal-malaaa'ikata tasmi-yatal-unsaa.	اِنَّ الَّذِيْنَ لَا يُؤْمِنُوْنَ بِالْاٰخِرَةِ لَيُسَمُّوْنَ الْمَلٰٓئِكَةَ تَسْمِيَةَ الْاُنْثٰى ﴿٢٧﴾
28. They have no knowledge about it. They only follow mere conjecture which can never sufficiently replace the Truth.	28. Wa maa lahum bihee min 'ilmin iñy-yattabi'oona illaz-zanna wa inna-zzanna laa yughnee minal-ḥaqqi shay'aa.	وَمَا لَهُمْ بِهٖ مِنْ عِلْمٍ ؕ اِنْ يَّتَّبِعُوْنَ اِلَّا الظَّنَّ ۚ وَاِنَّ الظَّنَّ لَا يُغْنِىْ مِنَ الْحَقِّ شَيْــًٔا ﴿٢٨﴾
29. (Muhammad), stay away from those who turned away from Our guidance and who did not desire anything except the worldly life.	29. Fa-a'riḍ 'am-man tawallaa 'an zikrinaa wa lam yurid illal-ḥayaatad-dunyaa.	فَاَعْرِضْ عَنْ مَّنْ تَوَلّٰى ۙ عَنْ ذِكْرِنَا وَلَمْ يُرِدْ اِلَّا الْحَيٰوةَ الدُّنْيَا ﴿٢٩﴾
30. This is what the extent of their knowledge amounts to. Your Lord knows best who has gone astray from His path and who has been rightly guided.	30. Zaalika mablaghuhum mi-nal'ilm; inna Rabbaka Huwa a'lamu biman ḍalla 'an sabee-lihee wa Huwa a'lamu bimanih-tadaa.	ذٰلِكَ مَبْلَغُهُمْ مِّنَ الْعِلْمِ ؕ اِنَّ رَبَّكَ هُوَ اَعْلَمُ بِمَنْ ضَلَّ عَنْ سَبِيْلِهٖ ۙ وَهُوَ اَعْلَمُ بِمَنِ اهْتَدٰى ﴿٣٠﴾ الربع
31. To Allah belongs whatever is in the heavens and the earth. In	31. Wa lillaahi maa fissa-maawaati wa maa fil-arḍi	وَلِلّٰهِ مَا فِى السَّمٰوٰتِ وَمَا فِى الْاَرْضِ ۙ

the end Allah will recompense the evildoers for their deeds and reward the righteous ones for their deeds.	liyajziyal-lazeena asaaa'oo bimaa 'amiloo wa yajziyal-lazeena aḥsanoo bilḥusnaa.	لِيَجْزِيَ الَّذِينَ أَسَاءُوا بِمَا عَمِلُوا وَيَجْزِيَ الَّذِينَ أَحْسَنُوا بِالْحُسْنَى ﴿٣١﴾
32. Those who stay away from grave sins and indecency (should know that) in matters of minor sins your Lord's forgiveness is vast (if you ask for pardon). He knows best about you from when He created you from the earth and when you were embryos in your mothers' wombs. Do not consider yourselves very great. Allah knows best, who is the most righteous person.	32. Allazeena yajtaniboona kabaaa'iral-ismi walfawaa-ḥisha illal-lamam; inna Rabbaka waasi'ul maghfirah; Huwa a'lamu bikum iz ansha-akum minal arḍi wa iz antum ajinnatun fee buṭooni umma-haatikum falaa tuzakkooo anfu-sakum Huwa a'lamu bimanit-taqaa.	الَّذِينَ يَجْتَنِبُونَ كَبَائِرَ الْإِثْمِ وَالْفَوَاحِشَ إِلَّا اللَّمَمَ ۚ إِنَّ رَبَّكَ وَاسِعُ الْمَغْفِرَةِ ۚ هُوَ أَعْلَمُ بِكُمْ إِذْ أَنْشَأَكُمْ مِنَ الْأَرْضِ وَإِذْ أَنْتُمْ أَجِنَّةٌ فِي بُطُونِ أُمَّهَاتِكُمْ ۖ فَلَا تُزَكُّوا أَنْفُسَكُمْ ۖ هُوَ أَعْلَمُ بِمَنِ اتَّقَىٰ ﴿٣٢﴾
33. (Muhammad), have you ever seen the one who has turned away (from guidance),	33. Afara'aytal-lazee tawallaa.	أَفَرَأَيْتَ الَّذِي تَوَلَّىٰ ﴿٣٣﴾
34. and grudgingly spends very little for the cause of Allah?	34. Wa a'ṭaa qaleelañw-wa akdaa.	وَأَعْطَىٰ قَلِيلًا وَأَكْدَىٰ ﴿٣٤﴾
35. Does he possess the knowledge of the unseen, thus he can see (all things)?	35. A'indahoo 'ilmul-ghaybi fahuwa yaraa.	أَعِنْدَهُ عِلْمُ الْغَيْبِ فَهُوَ يَرَىٰ ﴿٣٥﴾
36. Was he not informed of the contents of the Book of Moses	36. Am lam yunabba-bimaa fee Ṣuḥufi Moosaa.	أَمْ لَمْ يُنَبَّأْ بِمَا فِي صُحُفِ مُوسَىٰ ﴿٣٦﴾
37. and about Abraham who fulfilled his duty (to Allah)?	37. Wa Ibraaheemal-lazee waffaaa.	وَإِبْرَاهِيمَ الَّذِي وَفَّىٰ ﴿٣٧﴾
38. Certainly no one will bear the responsibility of the sins of another,	38. Allaa taziru waaziratuñw-wizra ukhraa.	أَلَّا تَزِرُ وَازِرَةٌ وِزْرَ أُخْرَىٰ ﴿٣٨﴾
39. nor can man achieve anything without hard labor.	39. Wa al-laysa lil-insaani illaa maa sa'aa.	وَأَنْ لَيْسَ لِلْإِنْسَانِ إِلَّا مَا سَعَىٰ ﴿٣٩﴾
40. He will certainly see the result of his labor	40. Wa anna sa'yahoo sawfa yuraa.	وَأَنَّ سَعْيَهُ سَوْفَ يُرَىٰ ﴿٤٠﴾
41. and will be fully recompensed for his deeds.	41. Summa yujzaahul-jazaaa'al-awfaa.	ثُمَّ يُجْزَاهُ الْجَزَاءَ الْأَوْفَىٰ ﴿٤١﴾
42. To your Lord will all things eventually return.	42. Wa anna ilaa Rabbikal-muntahaa.	وَأَنَّ إِلَىٰ رَبِّكَ الْمُنْتَهَىٰ ﴿٤٢﴾
43. It is He who causes laughter and weeping.	43. Wa annahoo Huwa aḍḥaka wa abkaa.	وَأَنَّهُ هُوَ أَضْحَكَ وَأَبْكَىٰ ﴿٤٣﴾
44. It is He who causes death and gives life.	44. Wa annahoo Huwa amaata wa aḥyaa.	وَأَنَّهُ هُوَ أَمَاتَ وَأَحْيَا ﴿٤٤﴾
45. It is He who has created spouses, male and female,	45. Wa annahoo khalaqaz-zawjayniz-zakara wal-unsaa.	وَأَنَّهُ خَلَقَ الزَّوْجَيْنِ الذَّكَرَ وَالْأُنْثَىٰ ﴿٤٥﴾
46. from a discharged living germ	46. Min nuṭfatin izaa tumnaa.	مِنْ نُطْفَةٍ إِذَا تُمْنَىٰ ﴿٤٦﴾
47. and on Him depends the life hereafter.	47. Wa anna 'alayhin-nash-atal-ukhraa.	وَأَنَّ عَلَيْهِ النَّشْأَةَ الْأُخْرَىٰ ﴿٤٧﴾
48. It is He who grants people temporary and durable wealth.	48. Wa annahoo Huwa aghnaa wa aqnaa.	وَأَنَّهُ هُوَ أَغْنَىٰ وَأَقْنَىٰ ﴿٤٨﴾
49. It is He who is the Lord of Sirius.	49. Wa annahoo Huwa Rab-bush-Shi'raa.	وَأَنَّهُ هُوَ رَبُّ الشِّعْرَىٰ ﴿٤٩﴾

(Bow Down)

50. It is He who utterly destroyed the ancient tribes of Ad,	50. Wa annahooo ahlaka 'Aadanil-oolaa.	وَاَنَّهٗۤ اَهۡلَكَ عَادَاۨ الۡاُوۡلٰى ﴿٥٠﴾
51. Thamud who are no more,	51. Wa Samooda famaaa abqaa.	وَثَمُوۡدَا۟ فَمَاۤ اَبۡقٰى ﴿٥١﴾
52. and the people of Noah; they were the most unjust and rebellious people.	52. Wa qawma Nooḥim-min qablu innahum kaanoo hum aẓlama wa aṭghaa.	وَقَوۡمَ نُوۡحٍ مِّنۡ قَبۡلُ ؕ اِنَّهُمۡ كَانُوۡا هُمۡ اَظۡلَمَ وَاَطۡغٰى ﴿٥٢﴾
53. It is He who turned upside down the people of Lot	53. Walmu'tafikata ahwaa.	وَالۡمُؤۡتَفِكَةَ اَهۡوٰى ﴿٥٣﴾
54. and covered them with torment.	54. Faghashshaahaa maa ghashshaa.	فَغَشّٰٮهَا مَا غَشّٰى ﴿٥٤﴾
55. About which of the bounties of your Lord can they persistently dispute?	55. Fabi-ayyi aalaaa'i Rabbika tatamaaraa.	فَبِاَىِّ اٰلَاۤءِ رَبِّكَ تَتَمَارٰى ﴿٥٥﴾
56. This is a (Prophet) like that of the ancient Warners (prophets).	56. Haaẕaa naẕeerum-minan-nuẕuril-oolaa.	هٰذَا نَذِيۡرٌ مِّنَ النُّذُرِ الۡاُوۡلٰى ﴿٥٦﴾
57. The Day of Judgment is drawing nearer.	57. Azifatil-aazifah.	اَزِفَتِ الۡاٰزِفَةُ ﴿٥٧﴾
58. No one besides Allah can rescue a soul from hardship.	58. Laysa lahaa min doonil-laahi kaashifah.	لَيۡسَ لَهَا مِنۡ دُوۡنِ اللّٰهِ كَاشِفَةٌ ﴿٥٨﴾
59. Does this statement seem strange to them	59. Afamin haaẕal-ḥadeesi ta'jaboon.	اَفَمِنۡ هٰذَا الۡحَدِيۡثِ تَعۡجَبُوۡنَ ﴿٥٩﴾
60. so they laugh instead of weeping,	60. Wa taḍḥakoona wa laa tabkoon.	وَتَضۡحَكُوۡنَ وَلَا تَبۡكُوۡنَ ﴿٦٠﴾
61. indulging in carelessly idle games?	61. Wa antum saamidoon.	وَاَنۡتُمۡ سٰمِدُوۡنَ ﴿٦١﴾
62. So prostrate yourselves before Allah and worship him.	62. Fasjudoo lillaahi wa'budoo.۩	فَاسۡجُدُوۡا لِلّٰهِ وَاعۡبُدُوۡا ۩ ﴿٦٢﴾

السجدة ع ١٢

Al-Qamar, The Moon (54) In the Name of Allah, the Beneficent, the Merciful.	**Sûrat al-Qamar-54** (Revealed at Makkah) **Bismillaahir Raḥmaanir Raḥeem**	(٥٤) سُوۡرَةُ الۡقَمَرِ مَكِّيَّةٌ (٣٧) اٰياتها ٥٥ — بِسۡمِ اللّٰهِ الرَّحۡمٰنِ الرَّحِيۡمِ — ركوعاتها ٣
1. The Hour of Doom is drawing near and the moon is rent asunder.	1. Iqtarabatis-Saa'atu wan-shaqqal-qamar.	اِقۡتَرَبَتِ السَّاعَةُ وَانۡشَقَّ الۡقَمَرُ ﴿١﴾
2. Whenever they see a miracle, they turn away from it and say, "This is just a powerful magic."	2. Wa iñy-yaraw Aayatañy-yu'riḍoo wa yaqooloo siḥrum-mustamirr.	وَاِنۡ يَّرَوۡا اٰيَةً يُّعۡرِضُوۡا وَيَقُوۡلُوۡا سِحۡرٌ مُّسۡتَمِرٌّ ﴿٢﴾
3. They rejected it and followed their own desires, but all matters will be settled (by Allah).	3. Wa kaẕ-ẕaboo wattaba'ooo ahwaaa'ahum; wa kullu Am-rim-mustaqirr.	وَكَذَّبُوۡا وَاتَّبَعُوۡۤا اَهۡوَآءَهُمۡ وَكُلُّ اَمۡرٍ مُّسۡتَقِرٌّ ﴿٣﴾
4. They certainly received the kind of news in which there were lessons and strong words of wisdom,	4. Wa laqad jaaa'ahum minal-ambaaa'i maa feehi muzdajar.	وَلَقَدۡ جَآءَهُمۡ مِّنَ الۡاَنۡۢبَآءِ مَا فِيۡهِ مُزۡدَجَرٌ ﴿٤﴾
5. but the warnings had no effect on them.	5. Ḥikmatum baalighatun famaa tughnin-nuẕur.	حِكۡمَةٌ ۢ بَالِغَةٌ فَمَا تُغۡنِ النُّذُرُ ﴿٥﴾
6. (Muhammad), leave them alone. One day a caller will call to a terrible thing.	6. Fatawalla 'anhum; Yawma yad'ud-daa'i ilaa shay'in nukur.	فَتَوَلَّ عَنۡهُمۡ ۘ يَوۡمَ يَدۡعُ الدَّاعِ اِلٰى شَىۡءٍ نُّكُرٍ ﴿٦﴾

وقف لازم

7. With their eyes extremely humbled they will come out of their graves, as locusts rushing about.	7. Khushsha'an abṣaaruhum yakhrujoona minal-ajdaas̲i ka-annahum jaraadum-muntashir.	خُشَّعًا أَبْصَارُهُمْ يَخْرُجُونَ مِنَ الْأَجْدَاثِ كَأَنَّهُمْ جَرَادٌ مُّنتَشِرٌ ﴿٧﴾
8. Rushing dreadfully toward the caller the unbelievers will say, "This is a hard day."	8. Muhṭi'eena ilad-daa'i yaqoolul-kaafiroona haaz̲aa yawmun 'asir.	مُّهْطِعِينَ إِلَى الدَّاعِ ۖ يَقُولُ الْكَافِرُونَ هَٰذَا يَوْمٌ عَسِرٌ ﴿٨﴾
9. The people of Noah, who lived before them, had also rejected (Our guidance). They rejected Our servant and said, "He is an insane person so allow us drive him away."	9. Kaz̲-z̲abat qablahum qawmu Nooḥin fakaz̲-z̲aboo 'abdanaa wa qaaloo majnoonũw-wazdujir.	كَذَّبَتْ قَبْلَهُمْ قَوْمُ نُوحٍ فَكَذَّبُوا عَبْدَنَا وَقَالُوا مَجْنُونٌ وَازْدُجِرَ ﴿٩﴾
10. Noah prayed, "Lord, help me; I am defeated."	10. Fada'aa Rabbahooo annee maghloobun fantaṣir.	فَدَعَا رَبَّهُ أَنِّي مَغْلُوبٌ فَانتَصِرْ ﴿١٠﴾
11. We opened the gates of the sky and water started to pour down.	11. Fafataḥnaaa abwaabas-samaaa'i bimaaa'im-munhamir.	فَفَتَحْنَا أَبْوَابَ السَّمَاءِ بِمَاءٍ مُّنْهَمِرٍ ﴿١١﴾
12. We caused the earth to burst forth with springs so that the waters could come together for a predestined purpose.	12. Wa fajjarnal-arḍa 'uyoonan-faltaqal-maaa'u 'alaaa amrin qad qudir.	وَفَجَّرْنَا الْأَرْضَ عُيُونًا فَالْتَقَى الْمَاءُ عَلَىٰ أَمْرٍ قَدْ قُدِرَ ﴿١٢﴾
13. We carried him, (Noah), on a vessel built with boards fixed together with nails, (ropes)	13. Wa ḥamalnaahu 'alaa z̲aati alwaaḥiñw-wa dusur.	وَحَمَلْنَاهُ عَلَىٰ ذَاتِ أَلْوَاحٍ وَدُسُرٍ ﴿١٣﴾
14. which floated on the water before Our very eyes. The flood was a recompense for the deeds of the unbelievers.	14. Tajree bia'yuninaa jazaaa-'al-liman kaana kufir.	تَجْرِي بِأَعْيُنِنَا جَزَاءً لِّمَن كَانَ كُفِرَ ﴿١٤﴾
15. We made (the story of Noah) as evidence of the Truth. However, was there anyone who would take heed?	15. Wa laqat-taraknaahaaa Aayatan fahal mimmuddakir.	وَلَقَد تَّرَكْنَاهَا آيَةً فَهَلْ مِن مُّدَّكِرٍ ﴿١٥﴾
16. How terrible was My torment and the result of (their disregard) of My warning?	16. Fakayfa kaana 'az̲aabee wa nuz̲ur.	فَكَيْفَ كَانَ عَذَابِي وَنُذُرِ ﴿١٦﴾
17. We have made the Quran easy to understand (remember), but is there anyone who will pay attention?	17. Wa laqad yassarnal Qur-aana liz̲-z̲ikri fahal mim-muddakir.	وَلَقَدْ يَسَّرْنَا الْقُرْآنَ لِلذِّكْرِ فَهَلْ مِن مُّدَّكِرٍ ﴿١٧﴾
18. The people of Ad rejected Our guidance. How terrible was My torment and the result (of their disregard) of My warning?	18. kaz̲-z̲abat 'Aadun fakayfa kaana 'az̲aabee wa nuz̲ur.	كَذَّبَتْ عَادٌ فَكَيْفَ كَانَ عَذَابِي وَنُذُرِ ﴿١٨﴾
19. On an unfortunate day We sent upon them a continuous cold wind	19. Innaaa arsalnaa 'alayhim reeḥan ṣarṣaran fee Yawmi naḥsim-mustamirr.	إِنَّا أَرْسَلْنَا عَلَيْهِمْ رِيحًا صَرْصَرًا فِي يَوْمِ نَحْسٍ مُّسْتَمِرٍّ ﴿١٩﴾
20. which hurled people around like uprooted trunks of palm-trees.	20. Tanzi'un-naasa ka-annahum a'jaazu nakhlim-munqa'ir.	تَنزِعُ النَّاسَ كَأَنَّهُمْ أَعْجَازُ نَخْلٍ مُّنقَعِرٍ ﴿٢٠﴾
21. How terrible was Our torment and the result of (their disregard) of Our warning?	21. Fakayfa kaana 'az̲aabee wa nuz̲ur.	فَكَيْفَ كَانَ عَذَابِي وَنُذُرِ ﴿٢١﴾
22. We have made the Quran easy to understand (remember),	22. wa laqad yassarnal-Qur-aana liz̲-z̲ikri	وَلَقَدْ يَسَّرْنَا الْقُرْآنَ لِلذِّكْرِ

ع ٢٢ ٨

but is there anyone who will pay attention?	fahal mim-muddakir.	فَهَلْ مِنْ مُّدَّكِرٍ ﴿٢٢﴾ ع
24. The people of Thamud rejected Our warnings.	23. Kaz-zabat Samoodu binnuzur.	كَذَّبَتْ ثَمُوْدُ بِالنُّذُرِ ﴿٢٣﴾
24. They said, "Should we follow only one person among us. We shall be clearly in error and in trouble (if we do so).	24. Faqaalooo abasharam-minnaa waaḥidan natta-bi'uhooo innaaa izal-lafee ḍalaaliñw-wa su'ur.	فَقَالُوْٓا اَبَشَرًا مِّنَّا وَاحِدًا نَّتَّبِعُهٗٓ ۙ اِنَّآ اِذًا لَّفِيْ ضَلٰلٍ وَّسُعُرٍ ﴿٢٤﴾
25. How is it that he has received guidance? In fact, he is the most untruthful and arrogant person."	25. 'A-ulqiyaz-zikru 'alayhi mim bayninaa bal huwa kaz-zaabun ashir.	ءَاُلْقِيَ الذِّكْرُ عَلَيْهِ مِنْۢ بَيْنِنَا بَلْ هُوَ كَذَّابٌ اَشِرٌ ﴿٢٥﴾
26. (We told Salih), "Tomorrow they will know who the most arrogant liar is.	26. Sa-ya'lamoona ghadam-manil-kaz-zaabul-ashir.	سَيَعْلَمُوْنَ غَدًا مَّنِ الْكَذَّابُ الْاَشِرُ ﴿٢٦﴾
27. We are sending the she-camel to them to test them. So watch them and be patient.	27. Innaa mursilun-naaqati fitnatal-lahum fartaqibhum waṣṭabir.	اِنَّا مُرْسِلُوا النَّاقَةِ فِتْنَةً لَّهُمْ فَارْتَقِبْهُمْ وَاصْطَبِرْ ﴿٢٧﴾
28. Tell them that each one of them has the right to have a certain share of water."	28. Wa nabbi'hum annal-maaa'a qismatum baynahum kullu shirbim-muḥtaḍar.	وَنَبِّئْهُمْ اَنَّ الْمَآءَ قِسْمَةٌۢ بَيْنَهُمْ ۚ كُلُّ شِرْبٍ مُّحْتَضَرٌ ﴿٢٨﴾
29. They called together their companions and agreed to slay the she-camel.	29. Fanaadaw ṣaaḥibahum fata'aaṭaa fa'aqar.	فَنَادَوْا صَاحِبَهُمْ فَتَعَاطٰى فَعَقَرَ ﴿٢٩﴾
30. How terrible was My punishment and warning.	30. Fakayfa kaana 'azaabee wa nuzur.	فَكَيْفَ كَانَ عَذَابِيْ وَنُذُرِ ﴿٣٠﴾
31. We sent upon them a single blast of sound and they were left like hay to be used by the cattle.	31. Innaaa arsalnaa 'alayhim ṣayḥatañw-waaḥidatan faka-anoo kahasheemil-muḥtaẓir.	اِنَّآ اَرْسَلْنَا عَلَيْهِمْ صَيْحَةً وَّاحِدَةً فَكَانُوْا كَهَشِيْمِ الْمُحْتَظِرِ ﴿٣١﴾
32. We made the Quran easy to understand, but is there anyone who would take heed?	32. Wa laqad yassarnal-Qur-aana liz-zikri fahal mim-muddakir.	وَلَقَدْ يَسَّرْنَا الْقُرْاٰنَ لِلذِّكْرِ فَهَلْ مِنْ مُّدَّكِرٍ ﴿٣٢﴾
33. The people of Lot rejected Our warning.	33. Kaz-zabat qawmu Looṭim binnuzur.	كَذَّبَتْ قَوْمُ لُوْطٍۢ بِالنُّذُرِ ﴿٣٣﴾
34. We sent down upon them a violent sandstorm (which destroyed them all) except for the family of Lot, whom We saved in the early morning	34. Innaaa arsalnaa 'alayhim ḥaaṣiban illaaa aala Looṭ; najjaynaahum bisaḥar.	اِنَّآ اَرْسَلْنَا عَلَيْهِمْ حَاصِبًا اِلَّآ اٰلَ لُوْطٍ ۭ نَجَّيْنٰهُمْ بِسَحَرٍ ﴿٣٤﴾
35. as a favor from Us. Thus do We recompense the grateful ones.	35. Ni'matam-min 'indinaa; kazaalika najzee man shakar.	نِّعْمَةً مِّنْ عِنْدِنَا ۭ كَذٰلِكَ نَجْزِيْ مَنْ شَكَرَ ﴿٣٥﴾
36. Lot warned them against Our torment, but they persistently disputed it.	36. Wa laqad anzarahum baṭ-shatanaa fatamaaraw binnuzur.	وَلَقَدْ اَنْذَرَهُمْ بَطْشَتَنَا فَتَمَارَوْا بِالنُّذُرِ ﴿٣٦﴾
37. They demanded that he turn over his guests to them.	37. Wa laqad raawadoohu 'an ḍayfihee faṭamasnaaa a'yu-nahum fazooqoo 'azaabee wa nuzur.	وَلَقَدْ رَاوَدُوْهُ عَنْ ضَيْفِهٖ فَطَمَسْنَآ اَعْيُنَهُمْ فَذُوْقُوْا عَذَابِيْ وَنُذُرِ ﴿٣٧﴾

38. We struck their faces, blinded them, and said, "Suffer Our torment of which you were warned."	38. Wa laqad ṣabbaḥahum bukratan 'azaabum-mustaqirr.	وَلَقَدْ صَبَّحَهُمْ بُكْرَةً عَذَابٌ مُّسْتَقِرٌّ ﴿٣٨﴾
39. One early morning, Our torment brought upon them utter destruction. We said, "Suffer Our torment of which you were warned."	39. Fazooqoo 'azaabee wa nuzur:	فَذُوقُوا عَذَابِي وَنُذُرِ ﴿٣٩﴾
40. We have made the Quran easy to understand (remember), but is there anyone who will pay attention?	40. Wa laqad yassarnal-Qur-aana liz-zikri fahal mim-muddakir.	وَلَقَدْ يَسَّرْنَا الْقُرْآنَ لِلذِّكْرِ فَهَلْ مِنْ مُّدَّكِرٍ ﴿٤٠﴾ ع
41. The Pharaoh and his people had also received Our warning,	41. Wa laqad jaaa'a Aala Fir-'awnan-nuzur.	وَلَقَدْ جَاءَ آلَ فِرْعَوْنَ النُّذُرُ ﴿٤١﴾
42. but they rejected all Our miracles. So We seized them in the way that a Majestic and All-powerful One would.	42. Kaz-zaboo bi-Aayaatinaa kullihaa fa-akhaznaahum akhza 'azeezim-muqtadir.	كَذَّبُوا بِآيَاتِنَا كُلِّهَا فَأَخَذْنَاهُمْ أَخْذَ عَزِيزٍ مُّقْتَدِرٍ ﴿٤٢﴾
43. Are you unbelievers (of Quraysh) mightier than those of the nations which We destroyed before, or have you received amnesty through the ancient Scriptures?	43. Akuffaarukum khayrum-min ulaaa'ikum am lakum baraaa'atun fiz-Zubur.	أَكُفَّارُكُمْ خَيْرٌ مِّنْ أُولَٰئِكُمْ أَمْ لَكُمْ بَرَاءَةٌ فِي الزُّبُرِ ﴿٤٣﴾
44. Do they say, "We shall be victorious because we are united?"	44. Am yaqooloona naḥnu jamee'um-muntaṣir.	أَمْ يَقُولُونَ نَحْنُ جَمِيعٌ مُّنْتَصِرٌ ﴿٤٤﴾
45. (Let them know that) this united group will soon run away in defeat.	45. Sa-yuhzamul-jam'u wa yuwalloonad-dubur.	سَيُهْزَمُ الْجَمْعُ وَيُوَلُّونَ الدُّبُرَ ﴿٤٥﴾
46. In fact, the Hour of Doom is the time for them to suffer. The suffering of this hour is the most calamitous and the most bitter (of all suffering).	46. Balis-Saa'atu maw'iduhum was-Saa'atu adhaa wa amarr.	بَلِ السَّاعَةُ مَوْعِدُهُمْ وَالسَّاعَةُ أَدْهَىٰ وَأَمَرُّ ﴿٤٦﴾
47. The sinful ones will face the blazing torment of hell	47. Innal-mujrimeena fee ḍalaaliñw-wa su'ur.	إِنَّ الْمُجْرِمِينَ فِي ضَلَالٍ وَسُعُرٍ ﴿٤٧﴾
48. when they are dragged on their faces into the fire and told, "Feel the touch of hell."	48. Yawma yusḥaboona fin-Naari 'alaa wujoohihim zooqoo massa saqar.	يَوْمَ يُسْحَبُونَ فِي النَّارِ عَلَىٰ وُجُوهِهِمْ ذُوقُوا مَسَّ سَقَرَ ﴿٤٨﴾
49. We have created everything with a certain measure (to fulfill the intended purpose).	49. Innaa kulla shay'in kha-laqnaahu biqadar.	إِنَّا كُلَّ شَيْءٍ خَلَقْنَاهُ بِقَدَرٍ ﴿٤٩﴾
50. It takes only a single command from Us (to bring the Day of Judgment) and that can be achieved within the blink of an eye.	50. Wa maaa amrunaaa illaa waaḥidatun kalamḥim bilbaṣar.	وَمَا أَمْرُنَا إِلَّا وَاحِدَةٌ كَلَمْحٍ بِالْبَصَرِ ﴿٥٠﴾
51. We destroyed their (unbelievers) idol worshipping followers, but is there anyone who takes heed (of Our warning)?	51. Wa laqad ahlaknaaa ash-yaa'akum fahal mim-muddakir.	وَلَقَدْ أَهْلَكْنَا أَشْيَاعَكُمْ فَهَلْ مِنْ مُّدَّكِرٍ ﴿٥١﴾
52. Whatever they have done has been recorded in the Books (records of the deeds).	52. Wa kullu shay'in fa'aloo-hu fiz-Zubur.	وَكُلُّ شَيْءٍ فَعَلُوهُ فِي الزُّبُرِ ﴿٥٢﴾
53. Every small or great deed is written down (for the record).	53. Wa kullu ṣagheeriñw-wa kabeerim-mustaṭar.	وَكُلُّ صَغِيرٍ وَكَبِيرٍ مُّسْتَطَرٌ ﴿٥٣﴾
54. The pious ones will live in Paradise wherein streams flow,	54. Innal-muttaqeena fee Jannaatiñw-wa nahar.	إِنَّ الْمُتَّقِينَ فِي جَنَّاتٍ وَنَهَرٍ ﴿٥٤﴾
55. honorably seated in the presence of the All-dominant King.	55. Fee maq'adi ṣidqin 'inda Maleekim-Muqtadir.	فِي مَقْعَدِ صِدْقٍ عِنْدَ مَلِيكٍ مُّقْتَدِرٍ ﴿٥٥﴾ ع

ع ١٨/٢ ٩

وقف لازم

ع ١٥/٣ ١٠

Al-Rahman, The Beneficent (55)

In the Name of Allah,
the Beneficent, the Merciful.

Sûrat ar-Raḥmân-55

(Revealed at Madinah)
Bismillaahir Raḥmaanir Raḥeem

(٥٥) سُوْرَةُ الرَّحْمٰنِ مَدَنِيَّةٌ (٩٧)

اٰيَاتُهَا ٧٨ — بِسْمِ اللّٰهِ الرَّحْمٰنِ الرَّحِيْمِ — رُكُوْعَاتُهَا ٣

1. The Beneficent (Allah)	1. Ar-Raḥmaan.	اَلرَّحْمٰنُ ۙ﴿١﴾
2. has taught the Quran to (Muhammad).	2. 'Allamal-Qur-aan.	عَلَّمَ الْقُرْاٰنَ ؕ﴿٢﴾
3. He created the human being	3. Khalaqal-insaan.	خَلَقَ الْاِنْسَانَ ۙ﴿٣﴾
4. and taught him intelligible speech.	4. 'Allamahul-bayaan.	عَلَّمَهُ الْبَيَانَ ﴿٤﴾
5. The sun and moon rotate in a predestined orbit.	5. Ashshamsu walqamaru biḥusbaan.	اَلشَّمْسُ وَ الْقَمَرُ بِحُسْبَانٍ ۙ﴿٥﴾
6. The plants and trees prostrate before Him.	6. Wannajmu washshajaru yasjudaan.	وَّالنَّجْمُ وَالشَّجَرُ يَسْجُدٰنِ ﴿٦﴾
7. He raised the heavens and set up everything in balance,	7. Wassamaaa'a rafa'ahaa wa waḍa'al-Meezaan.	وَالسَّمَآءَ رَفَعَهَا وَوَضَعَ الْمِيْزَانَ ۙ﴿٧﴾
8. so that you would maintain justice in balancing matters.	8. Allaa taṭghaw fil-meezaan.	اَلَّا تَطْغَوْا فِى الْمِيْزَانِ ﴿٨﴾
9. Therefore, maintain just measure and do not transgress against the Balance.	9. Wa aqeemul-wazna bil-qisṭi wa laa tukhsirul-meezaan.	وَاَقِيْمُوا الْوَزْنَ بِالْقِسْطِ وَلَا تُخْسِرُوا الْمِيْزَانَ ﴿٩﴾
10. He spread out the earth for the people.	10. Wal-arḍa waḍa'ahaa lil-anaam.	وَالْاَرْضَ وَضَعَهَا لِلْاَنَامِ ۙ﴿١٠﴾
11. There exist all kinds of fruits, palm-trees with sheathed blossoms,	11. Feehaa faakihatuñw-wannakhlu ẕaatul-akmaam.	فِيْهَا فَاكِهَةٌ ۙ وَّالنَّخْلُ ذَاتُ الْاَكْمَامِ ۖ﴿١١﴾
12. grain with its husks, and aromatic herbs.	12. Walḥabbu ẕul-'aṣfi war-Rayḥaan.	وَالْحَبُّ ذُو الْعَصْفِ وَالرَّيْحَانُ ۚ﴿١٢﴾
13. (Mankind and Jinn), which of the favors of your Lord do you deny?	13. Fabi-ayyi aalaaa'i Rabbi-kumaa tukaẕ ẕibaan.	فَبِاَىِّ اٰلَآءِ رَبِّكُمَا تُكَذِّبٰنِ ﴿١٣﴾
14. He created the human being from clay like that used for pottery	14. Khalaqal-insaana min ṣalṣaalin kalfakhkhaar.	خَلَقَ الْاِنْسَانَ مِنْ صَلْصَالٍ كَالْفَخَّارِ ۙ﴿١٤﴾
15. and jinn from the many colored flames of fire.	15. Wa khalaqal-jaaanna mim-maarijim-min-Naar.	وَخَلَقَ الْجَآنَّ مِنْ مَّارِجٍ مِّنْ نَّارٍ ۚ﴿١٥﴾
16. (Mankind and Jinn), which of the favors of your Lord do you deny?	16. Fabi-ayyi aalaaa'i Rabbi-kumaa tukaẕ ẕibaan.	فَبِاَىِّ اٰلَآءِ رَبِّكُمَا تُكَذِّبٰنِ ﴿١٦﴾
17. He is the Lord of the two East (one in winter and one in summer) and two West (through all seasons).	17. Rabbul-mashriqayni wa Rabbul-maghribayn.	رَبُّ الْمَشْرِقَيْنِ وَرَبُّ الْمَغْرِبَيْنِ ۚ﴿١٧﴾
18. (Mankind and Jinn), which of the favors of your Lord do you deny?	18. Fabi-ayyi aalaaa'i Rabbi-kumaa tukaẕ ẕibaan.	فَبِاَىِّ اٰلَآءِ رَبِّكُمَا تُكَذِّبٰنِ ﴿١٨﴾
19. He has made the two oceans meet each other,	19. Marajal-baḥrayni yalta-qiyaan.	مَرَجَ الْبَحْرَيْنِ يَلْتَقِيٰنِ ۙ﴿١٩﴾
20. but has created a barrier between them so that they will not merge totally.	20. Baynahumaa barzakhul-laa yabghiyaan.	بَيْنَهُمَا بَرْزَخٌ لَّا يَبْغِيٰنِ ۚ﴿٢٠﴾
21. (Mankind and Jinn), which of the favors of your Lord do you deny?	21. Fabi-ayyi aalaaa'i Rabbi-kumaa tukaẕ ẕibaan.	فَبِاَىِّ اٰلَآءِ رَبِّكُمَا تُكَذِّبٰنِ ﴿٢١﴾

22. From the two oceans come pearls and coral.	22. Yakhruju minhumal-lu'lu'u walmarjaan.	يَخْرُجُ مِنْهُمَا اللُّؤْلُؤُ وَالْمَرْجَانُ ﴿٢٢﴾
23. (Mankind and Jinn), which of the favors of your Lord do you deny?	23. Fabi-ayyi aalaaa'i Rabbi-kumaa tukaz zibaan.	فَبِأَيِّ آلَاءِ رَبِّكُمَا تُكَذِّبَانِ ﴿٢٣﴾
24. By His command, the ships with raised masts sail on the sea like lighthouses.	24. Wa lahul-jawaaril-mun-sha'aatu fil-baḥri kala'laam.	وَلَهُ الْجَوَارِ الْمُنْشَآتُ فِي الْبَحْرِ كَالْأَعْلَامِ ﴿٢٤﴾
25. (Mankind and Jinn), which of the favors of your Lord do you deny?	25. Fabi-ayyi aalaaa'i Rabbi-kumaa tukaz zibaan.	فَبِأَيِّ آلَاءِ رَبِّكُمَا تُكَذِّبَانِ ﴿٢٥﴾
26. Everyone on earth is destined to die.	26. Kullu man 'alayhaa faan.	كُلُّ مَنْ عَلَيْهَا فَانٍ ﴿٢٦﴾
27. Only the face (Supreme Essence) of your Glorious and Gracious Lord will remain forever.	27. Wa yabqaa Wajhu Rabbika Zul-Jalaali wal-Ikraam.	وَيَبْقَىٰ وَجْهُ رَبِّكَ ذُو الْجَلَالِ وَالْإِكْرَامِ ﴿٢٧﴾
28. (Mankind and Jinn), which of the favors of your Lord do you deny?	28. Fabi-ayyi aalaaa'i Rabbi-kumaa tukaz zibaan.	فَبِأَيِّ آلَاءِ رَبِّكُمَا تُكَذِّبَانِ ﴿٢٨﴾
29. Everyone in the heavens and the earth depends on Him. His task in preserving His creation is continuous.	29. Yas'aluhoo man fis-samaawaati wal-arḍ; kulla yawmin Huwa fee sha-n.	يَسْأَلُهُ مَنْ فِي السَّمَاوَاتِ وَالْأَرْضِ ۚ كُلَّ يَوْمٍ هُوَ فِي شَأْنٍ ﴿٢٩﴾
30. (Mankind and Jinn), which of the favors of your Lord do you deny?	30. Fabi-ayyi aalaaa'i Rabbi-kumaa tukaz zibaan.	فَبِأَيِّ آلَاءِ رَبِّكُمَا تُكَذِّبَانِ ﴿٣٠﴾
31. Mankind and Jinn, We shall certainly settle your accounts.	31. Sanafrughu lakum ayyu-has-saqalaan.	سَنَفْرُغُ لَكُمْ أَيُّهَ الثَّقَلَانِ ﴿٣١﴾
32. (Mankind and Jinn), which of the favors of your Lord do you deny?	32. Fabi-ayyi aalaaa'i Rabbi-kumaa tukaz zibaan.	فَبِأَيِّ آلَاءِ رَبِّكُمَا تُكَذِّبَانِ ﴿٣٢﴾
33. Mankind and Jinn, if you can penetrate the diameters of the heavens and the earth, do so, but you cannot do so without power and authority.	33. Yaa ma'sharal-jinni wal-insi inis-taṭa'tum an tanfuzoo min aqṭaaris-samaawaati wal-arḍi fanfuzoo; laa tanfuzoona illaa bisulṭaan.	يَا مَعْشَرَ الْجِنِّ وَالْإِنْسِ إِنِ اسْتَطَعْتُمْ أَنْ تَنْفُذُوا مِنْ أَقْطَارِ السَّمَاوَاتِ وَالْأَرْضِ فَانْفُذُوا ۚ لَا تَنْفُذُونَ إِلَّا بِسُلْطَانٍ ﴿٣٣﴾
34. (Mankind and Jinn), which of the favors of your Lord do you deny?	34. Fabi-ayyi aalaaa'i Rabbi-kumaa tukaz zibaan.	فَبِأَيِّ آلَاءِ رَبِّكُمَا تُكَذِّبَانِ ﴿٣٤﴾
35. Flames of fire and melted brass will be released against you and you will not be able to protect yourselves.	35. Yursalu 'alaykumaa shu-waaẓum-min naariñw-wa nu-ḥaasun falaa tantaṣiraan.	يُرْسَلُ عَلَيْكُمَا شُوَاظٌ مِنْ نَارٍ وَنُحَاسٌ فَلَا تَنْتَصِرَانِ ﴿٣٥﴾
36. (Mankind and Jinn), which of the favors of your Lord do you deny?	36. Fabi-ayyi aalaaa'i Rabbi-kumaa tukaz zibaan.	فَبِأَيِّ آلَاءِ رَبِّكُمَا تُكَذِّبَانِ ﴿٣٦﴾
37. (On the Day of Judgment) when the heavens are rent asunder they will have a flowery color as if painted as such.	37. Fa-izan shaqqatis-sa-maaa'u fakaanat wardatan kaddihaan.	فَإِذَا انْشَقَّتِ السَّمَاءُ فَكَانَتْ وَرْدَةً كَالدِّهَانِ ﴿٣٧﴾
38. (Mankind and Jinn), which of the favors of your Lord do you deny?	38. Fabi-ayyi aalaaa'i Rabbi-kumaa tukaz zibaan.	فَبِأَيِّ آلَاءِ رَبِّكُمَا تُكَذِّبَانِ ﴿٣٨﴾
39. On that Day (certain) jinn and human beings will not be	39. Fa-yawma'izil-laa yus'alu 'an zambiheee insuñw-	فَيَوْمَئِذٍ لَا يُسْأَلُ عَنْ ذَنْبِهِ إِنْسٌ

questioned about their sins.	wa laa jaaann.	وَلَا جَآنٌّ ﴿٣٩﴾
40. (Mankind and Jinn), which of the favors of your Lord do you deny?	40. Fabi-ayyi aalaaa'i Rabbikumaa tukaz̲z̲ibaan.	فَبِأَيِّ آلَآءِ رَبِّكُمَا تُكَذِّبَانِ ﴿٤٠﴾
41. The guilty ones will be recognized by their faces and will be seized by their forelocks and feet.	41. Yu'raful-mujrimoona biseemaahum fa-yu'khaẕu binnawaaṣi wal-aqdaam.	يُعْرَفُ الْمُجْرِمُونَ بِسِيمٰهُمْ فَيُؤْخَذُ بِالنَّوَاصِي وَالْأَقْدَامِ ﴿٤١﴾
42. (Mankind and Jinn), which of the favors of your Lord do you deny?	42. Fabi-ayyi aalaaa'i Rabbikumaa tukaz̲z̲ibaan.	فَبِأَيِّ آلَآءِ رَبِّكُمَا تُكَذِّبَانِ ﴿٤٢﴾
43. (The guilty ones will be told), "This is hell which the sinful ones called a lie."	43. Haaẕihee Jahannamullatee yukaẕẕibu bihal-mujrimoon.	هٰذِهِ جَهَنَّمُ الَّتِي يُكَذِّبُ بِهَا الْمُجْرِمُونَ ﴿٤٣﴾ وقف لازم
44. They will (moaning and groaning) run around in blazing fire and boiling water.	44. Yaṭoofoona baynahaa wa bayna ḥameemin aan.	يَطُوفُونَ بَيْنَهَا وَبَيْنَ حَمِيمٍ اٰنٍ ﴿٤٤﴾
45. (Mankind and Jinn), which of the favors of your Lord do you deny?	45. Fabi-ayyi aalaaa'i Rabbikumaa tukaz̲z̲ibaan.	فَبِأَيِّ آلَآءِ رَبِّكُمَا تُكَذِّبَانِ ﴿٤٥﴾ ع ٢
46. Those who fear of the status of their Lord have two gardens.	46. Wa liman khaafa maqaama Rabbihee Jannataan.	وَلِمَنْ خَافَ مَقَامَ رَبِّهِ جَنَّتٰنِ ﴿٤٦﴾
47. (Mankind and Jinn), which of the favors of your Lord do you deny?	47. Fabi-ayyi aalaaa'i Rabbikumaa tukaz̲z̲ibaan.	فَبِأَيِّ آلَآءِ رَبِّكُمَا تُكَذِّبَانِ ﴿٤٧﴾
48. They (the two gardens) are full of various trees.	48. Z̲awaataaa afnaan.	ذَوَاتَآ أَفْنَانٍ ﴿٤٨﴾
49. (Mankind and Jinn), which of the favors of your Lord do you deny?	49. Fabi-ayyi aalaaa'i Rabbikumaa tukaz̲z̲ibaan.	فَبِأَيِّ آلَآءِ رَبِّكُمَا تُكَذِّبَانِ ﴿٤٩﴾
50. In the two gardens there are two flowing springs.	50. Feehimaa 'aynaani tajriyaan.	فِيهِمَا عَيْنٰنِ تَجْرِيَانِ ﴿٥٠﴾
51. (Mankind and Jinn), which of the favors of your Lord do you deny?	51. Fabi-ayyi aalaaa'i Rabbikumaa tukaz̲z̲ibaan.	فَبِأَيِّ آلَآءِ رَبِّكُمَا تُكَذِّبَانِ ﴿٥١﴾
52. In them (the two gardens) there are pairs of each kind of fruit.	52. Feehimaa min kulli faakihatin zawjaan.	فِيهِمَا مِنْ كُلِّ فَاكِهَةٍ زَوْجٰنِ ﴿٥٢﴾
53. (Mankind and Jinn), which of the favors of your Lord do you deny?	53. Fabi-ayyi aalaaa'i Rabbikumaa tukaz̲z̲ibaan.	فَبِأَيِّ آلَآءِ رَبِّكُمَا تُكَذِّبَانِ ﴿٥٣﴾
54. (The dwellers of Paradise) recline on couches lined with silk brocade and it is easy to reach the ripe fruits from the two gardens.	54. Muttaki'eena 'alaa furushim baṭaaa'inuhaa min istabraq; wa janal-jannatayni daan.	مُتَّكِـِٔينَ عَلٰى فُرُشٍۢ بَطَآئِنُهَا مِنْ إِسْتَبْرَقٍ ؕ وَجَنَا الْجَنَّتَيْنِ دَانٍ ﴿٥٤﴾
55. (Mankind and Jinn), which of the favors of your Lord do you deny?	55. Fabi-ayyi aalaaa'i Rabbikumaa tukaz̲z̲ibaan.	فَبِأَيِّ آلَآءِ رَبِّكُمَا تُكَذِّبَانِ ﴿٥٥﴾
56. There are bashful maidens untouched by mankind or jinn before them.	56. Feehinna qaaṣiraatuṭ-ṭarfi lam yaṭmis̲hunna insun qablahum wa laa jaaann.	فِيهِنَّ قٰصِرٰتُ الطَّرْفِ لَمْ يَطْمِثْهُنَّ إِنْسٌ قَبْلَهُمْ وَلَا جَآنٌّ ﴿٥٦﴾
57. (Mankind and Jinn), which of the favors of your Lord do you deny?	57. Fabi-ayyi aalaaa'i Rabbikumaa tukaz̲z̲ibaan.	فَبِأَيِّ آلَآءِ رَبِّكُمَا تُكَذِّبَانِ ﴿٥٧﴾
58. They (maidens) are as beautiful as rubies and pearls.	58. Ka-annahunnal-yaaqootu walmarjaan.	كَأَنَّهُنَّ الْيَاقُوتُ وَالْمَرْجَانُ ﴿٥٨﴾
59. (Mankind and Jinn), which of the favors of your Lord do you deny?	59. Fabi-ayyi aalaaa'i Rabbikumaa tukaz̲z̲ibaan.	فَبِأَيِّ آلَآءِ رَبِّكُمَا تُكَذِّبَانِ ﴿٥٩﴾
60. Can anything else be a response to a favor but a favor?	60. Hal jazaaa'ul-iḥsaani illal-iḥsaan.	هَلْ جَزَآءُ الْإِحْسَانِ إِلَّا الْإِحْسَانُ ﴿٦٠﴾

61. (Mankind and Jinn), which of the favors of your Lord do you deny?	61. Fabi-ayyi aalaaa'i Rabbi-kumaa tukaz zibaan.	فَبِاَيِّ اٰلَآءِ رَبِّكُمَا تُكَذِّبٰنِ ﴿٦١﴾
62. Besides this, there are two other gardens.	62. Wa min doonihimaa Jannataan.	وَمِنْ دُوْنِهِمَا جَنَّتٰنِ ﴿٦٢﴾
63. (Mankind and Jinn), which of the favors of your Lord do you deny?	63. Fabi-ayyi aalaaa'i Rabbi-kumaa tukaz zibaan.	فَبِاَيِّ اٰلَآءِ رَبِّكُمَا تُكَذِّبٰنِ ﴿٦٣﴾
64. (The other two gardens) are dark green in color.	64. Mudhaaammataan.	مُدْهَآمَّتٰنِ ﴿٦٤﴾
65. (Mankind and Jinn), which of the favors of your Lord do you deny?	65. Fabi-ayyi aalaaa'i Rabbi-kumaa tukaz zibaan.	فَبِاَيِّ اٰلَآءِ رَبِّكُمَا تُكَذِّبٰنِ ﴿٦٥﴾
66. In these there also are two springs gushing forth.	66. Feehimaa 'aynaani nad-daakhataan.	فِيْهِمَا عَيْنٰنِ نَضَّاخَتٰنِ ﴿٦٦﴾
67. (Mankind and Jinn), which of the favors of your Lord do you deny?	67. Fabi-ayyi aalaaa'i Rabbi-kumaa tukaz zibaan.	فَبِاَيِّ اٰلَآءِ رَبِّكُمَا تُكَذِّبٰنِ ﴿٦٧﴾
68. In both gardens there are fruits, palm-trees, and pomegranates.	68. Feehimaa faakihatuñw-wa nakhluñw-wa rummaan.	فِيْهِمَا فَاكِهَةٌ وَّنَخْلٌ وَّرُمَّانٌ ﴿٦٨﴾
69. (Mankind and Jinn), which of the favors of your Lord do you deny?	69. Fabi-ayyi aalaaa'i Rabbi-kumaa tukaz zibaan.	فَبِاَيِّ اٰلَآءِ رَبِّكُمَا تُكَذِّبٰنِ ﴿٦٩﴾
70. There are well-disciplined, beautiful maidens.	70. Feehinna khayraatun hisaan.	فِيْهِنَّ خَيْرٰتٌ حِسَانٌ ﴿٧٠﴾
71. (Mankind and Jinn), which of the favors of your Lord do you deny?	71. Fabi-ayyi aalaaa'i Rabbi-kumaa tukaz zibaan.	فَبِاَيِّ اٰلَآءِ رَبِّكُمَا تُكَذِّبٰنِ ﴿٧١﴾
72. They (maidens) have big, black and white beautiful eyes and dwell in tents.	72. Hoorum-maqsooraatun fil-khiyaam.	حُوْرٌ مَّقْصُوْرٰتٌ فِي الْخِيَامِ ﴿٧٢﴾
73. (Mankind and Jinn), which of the favors of your Lord do you deny?	73. Fabi-ayyi aalaaa'i Rabbi-kumaa tukaz zibaan.	فَبِاَيِّ اٰلَآءِ رَبِّكُمَا تُكَذِّبٰنِ ﴿٧٣﴾
74. No jinn or man had touched them before them.	74. Lam yatmishunna insun qablahum wa laa jaaann.	لَمْ يَطْمِثْهُنَّ اِنْسٌ قَبْلَهُمْ وَلَا جَآنٌّ ﴿٧٤﴾
75. (Mankind and Jinn), which of the favors of your Lord do you deny?	75. Fabi-ayyi aalaaa'i Rabbi-kumaa tukaz zibaan.	فَبِاَيِّ اٰلَآءِ رَبِّكُمَا تُكَذِّبٰنِ ﴿٧٥﴾
76. They (maidens) recline on plain green and beautifully printed cushions.	76. Muttaki'eena 'alaa rafrafin khudriñw-wa 'abqariyyin hisaan.	مُتَّكِـِٕيْنَ عَلٰى رَفْرَفٍ خُضْرٍ وَّعَبْقَرِيٍّ حِسَانٍ ﴿٧٦﴾
77. (Mankind and Jinn), which of the favors of your Lord do you deny?	77. Fabi-ayyi aalaaa'i Rabbi-kumaa tukaz zibaan.	فَبِاَيِّ اٰلَآءِ رَبِّكُمَا تُكَذِّبٰنِ ﴿٧٧﴾
78. Blessed is the name of your Lord, the Lord of Glory and Grace.	78. Tabaarakasmu Rabbika Zil-Jalaali wal-Ikraam.	تَبٰرَكَ اسْمُ رَبِّكَ ذِي الْجَلٰلِ وَالْاِكْرَامِ ﴿٧٨﴾ ع ٣

Al-Waqiah, The Event (56)

In the Name of Allah, the Beneficent, the Merciful.

Sûrat al-Wâqi‘ah-56

(Revealed at Makkah)

Bismillaahir Rahmaanir Raheem

(٥٦) سُوْرَةُ الْوَاقِعَةِ مَكِّيَّةٌ (٤٦)

اٰيَاتُهَا ٩٦ — بِسْمِ اللّٰهِ الرَّحْمٰنِ الرَّحِيْمِ — رُكُوْعَاتُهَا ٣

1. When the inevitable event comes,	1. Izaa waqa'atil-waaqi'ah.	اِذَا وَقَعَتِ الْوَاقِعَةُ ﴿١﴾
2. no soul will deny its coming.	2. Laysa liwaq'atihaa kaazi-bah.	لَيْسَ لِوَقْعَتِهَا كَاذِبَةٌ ﴿٢﴾
3. It will abase some (sinful ones) and exalt others (people of good deeds).	3. Khaafidatur-raafi'ah.	خَافِضَةٌ رَّافِعَةٌ ﴿٣﴾
4. When the earth is violently shaken	4. Izaa rujjatil-ardu rajjaa.	اِذَا رُجَّتِ الْاَرْضُ رَجًّا ﴿٤﴾

وقف لازم

5. and the mountains crumbled,	5. Wa bussatil-jibaalu bassaa.	وَّبُسَّتِ الْجِبَالُ بَسًّا ۙ﴿٥﴾
6. they will become like dust scattered around.	6. Fakaanat habaaa'am-mumbassaa.	فَكَانَتْ هَبَآءً مُّنْۢبَثًّا ۙ﴿٦﴾
7. On that Day, you (mankind) will be divided into three groups:	7. Wa kuntum azwaajan salaasah.	وَّكُنْتُمْ اَزْوَاجًا ثَلٰثَةً ؕ﴿٧﴾
8. The people of the right hand - those whose books of records will be placed in their right hands. How happy they will be!	8. Fa-Aṣḥaabul-Maymanati maaa Aṣḥaabul-Maymanah.	فَاَصْحٰبُ الْمَيْمَنَةِ ۙ۬ مَاۤ اَصْحٰبُ الْمَيْمَنَةِ ؕ﴿٨﴾
9. The people of the left hand - those whose books of records will be placed in their left hands. How miserable they will be!	9. Wa Aṣḥaabul-Mash'amati maaa Aṣḥaabul-Mash'amah.	وَاَصْحٰبُ الْمَشْـَٔمَةِ ۙ۬ مَاۤ اَصْحٰبُ الْمَشْـَٔمَةِ ؕ﴿٩﴾
10. The foremost ones (in faith and virtue) - the foremost ones in receiving their reward.	10. Wassaabiqoonas-saabiqoon.	وَالسّٰبِقُوْنَ السّٰبِقُوْنَ ۚ﴿١٠﴾
11. (The foremost ones) will be the nearest ones to Allah	11. Ulaaa'ikal-muqarraboon.	اُولٰٓئِكَ الْمُقَرَّبُوْنَ ۚ﴿١١﴾
12. in the beautiful Paradise.	12. Fee Jannaatin-Na'eem.	فِيْ جَنّٰتِ النَّعِيْمِ ﴿١٢﴾
13. Many of them will be from (followers of) the ancient (prophets) people	13. Sullatum-minal awwaleen.	ثُلَّةٌ مِّنَ الْاَوَّلِيْنَ ۙ﴿١٣﴾
14. and only a few of them from the later generations (followers of Prophet Muhammad).	14. Wa qaleelum-minal-aakhireen.	وَقَلِيْلٌ مِّنَ الْاٰخِرِيْنَ ؕ﴿١٤﴾
15. They will recline on installed couches	15. 'Alaa sururim-mawḍoonah.	عَلٰى سُرُرٍ مَّوْضُوْنَةٍ ۙ﴿١٥﴾
16. facing one another.	16. Muttaki'eena 'alayhaa mutaqaabileen.	مُّتَّكِـِٕيْنَ عَلَيْهَا مُتَقٰبِلِيْنَ ﴿١٦﴾
17. Immortal (cheerful) youths will serve them	17. Yaṭoofu 'alayhim wildaanum-mukhalladoon.	يَطُوْفُ عَلَيْهِمْ وِلْدَانٌ مُّخَلَّدُوْنَ ۙ﴿١٧﴾
18. with goblets, jugs, and cups of crystal clear wine	18. Bi-akwaabiñw-wa abaareeq; wa ka-sim-mim ma'een.	بِاَكْوَابٍ وَّاَبَارِيْقَ ۙ۬ وَكَاْسٍ مِّنْ مَّعِيْنٍ ۙ﴿١٨﴾
19. which will not cause them any intoxication or illness.	19. Laa yuṣadda'oona 'anhaa wa laa yunzifoon.	لَّا يُصَدَّعُوْنَ عَنْهَا وَلَا يُنْزِفُوْنَ ۙ﴿١٩﴾
20. Also, they will be served with the fruits of their choice	20. Wa faakihatim-mimmaa yatakhay-yaroon.	وَفَاكِهَةٍ مِّمَّا يَتَخَيَّرُوْنَ ۙ﴿٢٠﴾
21. and the flesh of birds, as they desire.	21. Wa laḥmi ṭayrim-mimmaa yashtahoon.	وَلَحْمِ طَيْرٍ مِّمَّا يَشْتَهُوْنَ ؕ﴿٢١﴾
22. They will have maidens with large, lovely black and white eyes,	22. Wa ḥoorun 'een.	وَحُوْرٌ عِيْنٌ ۙ﴿٢٢﴾
23. like pearls preserved in their shells,	23. Ka-amsaalil-lu'lu'il-maknoon.	كَاَمْثَالِ اللُّؤْلُؤِ الْمَكْنُوْنِ ۚ﴿٢٣﴾
24. as reward for their deeds.	24. Jazaaa'am bimaa kaanoo ya'maloon.	جَزَآءًۢ بِمَا كَانُوْا يَعْمَلُوْنَ ﴿٢٤﴾
25. They will not hear any unnecessary or sinful talk	25. Laa yasma'oona feehaa laghwañw-wa laa ta-seemaa.	لَا يَسْمَعُوْنَ فِيْهَا لَغْوًا وَّلَا تَاْثِيْمًا ۙ﴿٢٥﴾
26. except each other's greetings of, "Peace be with you."	26. Illaa qeelan salaaman salaamaa.	اِلَّا قِيْلًا سَلٰمًا سَلٰمًا ﴿٢٦﴾
27. As for the people of the right hand, how happy they will be!	27. Wa Aṣḥaabul-Yameeni maaa Aṣḥaabul-Yameen.	وَاَصْحٰبُ الْيَمِيْنِ ۙ۬ مَاۤ اَصْحٰبُ

28. They will live amid the lotus trees without thorns

29. and banana trees,

30. with fruits piled up one on the other,

31. and amid the extended shade

32. near to flowing water

33. and abundant fruits,

34. undiminished and never denied,

35. and the noble maidens

36. that We have created (for the people of the right hand).

37. We have made them virgins,

38. loving and of equal age.

39. These (people of the right hand) consist of many from the ancient

40. and many from the later generations.

41. As for the people on the left hand, how miserable they will be!

42. They will live amid the scorching heat,

43. scalding water and under a shadow of black smoke,

44. neither cold nor graceful in shape.

45. They had lived in luxury before this

46. and persisted in heinous, great sins.

47. It was they who said, "Shall we be resurrected after we die and have turned into dust and bones?

48. Will our ancient forefathers be resurrected also?"

49. (Muhammad), say, "All the ancient and later generations

28. Fee sidrim-makhḍood.

29. Wa ṭalḥim-manḍood.

30. Wa ẓillim-mamdood.

31. Wa maaa'im-maskoob.

32. Wa faakihatin kaṯeerah.

33. Laa maqṭoo'atiñw-wa laa mamnoo'ah.

34. Wa furushim-marfoo'ah.

35. Innaaa ansha-naahunna inshaaa'aa.

36. Faja'alnaahunna abkaaraa.

37. 'Uruban atraabaa.

38. Li-Aṣḥaabil-Yameen.

39. S̲ullatum-minal awwaleen.

40. Wa s̲ullatum-minal aakhireen.

41. Wa Aṣḥaabush-Shimaali maaa Aṣḥaabush-Shimaal.

42. Fee samoomiñw-wa ḥameem.

43. Wa ẓillim-miñy-yaḥmoom.

44. Laa baaridiñw-wa laa kareem.

45. Innahum kaanoo qabla z̲aalika mutrafeen.

46. Wa kaanoo yuṣirroona 'alal-ḥins̲il-'aẓeem.

47. Wa kaanoo yaqooloona a'iz̲aa mitnaa wa kunnaa turaabañw-wa 'iẓaaman 'a-innaa lamab'oos̲oon.

48. Awa aabaaa'unal-awwaloon.

49. Qul innal-awwaleena wal-aakhireen.

الْيَمِينِ ﴿٢٧﴾
فِي سِدْرٍ مَّخْضُودٍ ﴿٢٨﴾
وَطَلْحٍ مَّنضُودٍ ﴿٢٩﴾
وَظِلٍّ مَّمْدُودٍ ﴿٣٠﴾
وَمَاءٍ مَّسْكُوبٍ ﴿٣١﴾
وَفَاكِهَةٍ كَثِيرَةٍ ﴿٣٢﴾
لَّا مَقْطُوعَةٍ وَلَا مَمْنُوعَةٍ ﴿٣٣﴾
وَفُرُشٍ مَّرْفُوعَةٍ ﴿٣٤﴾
إِنَّا أَنشَأْنَاهُنَّ إِنشَاءً ﴿٣٥﴾
فَجَعَلْنَاهُنَّ أَبْكَارًا ﴿٣٦﴾
عُرُبًا أَتْرَابًا ﴿٣٧﴾
لِّأَصْحَابِ الْيَمِينِ ﴿٣٨﴾ ع ٣٨ ١٤
ثُلَّةٌ مِّنَ الْأَوَّلِينَ ﴿٣٩﴾
وَثُلَّةٌ مِّنَ الْآخِرِينَ ﴿٤٠﴾
وَأَصْحَابُ الشِّمَالِ مَا أَصْحَابُ
الشِّمَالِ ﴿٤١﴾
فِي سَمُومٍ وَحَمِيمٍ ﴿٤٢﴾
وَظِلٍّ مِّن يَحْمُومٍ ﴿٤٣﴾
لَّا بَارِدٍ وَلَا كَرِيمٍ ﴿٤٤﴾
إِنَّهُمْ كَانُوا قَبْلَ ذَٰلِكَ مُتْرَفِينَ ﴿٤٥﴾
وَكَانُوا يُصِرُّونَ عَلَى الْحِنثِ
الْعَظِيمِ ﴿٤٦﴾
وَكَانُوا يَقُولُونَ أَئِذَا مِتْنَا وَكُنَّا
تُرَابًا وَعِظَامًا أَإِنَّا لَمَبْعُوثُونَ ﴿٤٧﴾
أَوَآبَاؤُنَا الْأَوَّلُونَ ﴿٤٨﴾
قُلْ إِنَّ الْأَوَّلِينَ وَالْآخِرِينَ ﴿٤٩﴾

50. will be brought together for an appointment on an appointed day.	50. Lamajmoo‘oona ilaa meeqaati Yawmim-ma‘loom.	لَمَجْمُوعُونَ إِلَىٰ مِيقَاتِ يَوْمٍ مَّعْلُومٍ ٥٠
51. Then you people who had gone astray and rejected the Truth	51. Summa innakum ayyu-haḍ-ḍaaalloonal mukaz-ziboon.	ثُمَّ إِنَّكُمْ أَيُّهَا الضَّالُّونَ الْمُكَذِّبُونَ ٥١
52. will eat from the fruit of the tree of Al-Zaqqum,	52. La-aakiloona min shaja-rim-min Zaqqoom.	لَآكِلُونَ مِن شَجَرٍ مِّن زَقُّومٍ ٥٢
53. filling your bellies with it,	53. Famaali’oona minhal-buṭoon.	فَمَالِئُونَ مِنْهَا الْبُطُونَ ٥٣
54. and on top of this you will drink boiling water	54. Fashaariboona ‘alayhi minal-ḥameem.	فَشَارِبُونَ عَلَيْهِ مِنَ الْحَمِيمِ ٥٤
55. like a thirsty camel.”	55. Fashaariboona shurbal-ḥeem.	فَشَارِبُونَ شُرْبَ الْهِيمِ ٥٥
56. Such will be their dwelling on the Day of Judgment.	56. Haazaa nuzuluhum Yawmad-Deen.	هَٰذَا نُزُلُهُمْ يَوْمَ الدِّينِ ٥٦
57. It is We who have created you. Why then did you not testify to the Truth?	57. Naḥnu khalaqnaakum fa-law laa tuṣaddiqoon.	نَحْنُ خَلَقْنَاكُمْ فَلَوْلَا تُصَدِّقُونَ ٥٧
58. Have you seen sperm?	58. Afara’aytum maa tum-noon.	أَفَرَأَيْتُم مَّا تُمْنُونَ ٥٨
59. Do you create it or is it We who create it?	59. ’A-antum takhluqoo-nahooo am Naḥnul-khaaliqoon.	ءَأَنتُمْ تَخْلُقُونَهُ أَمْ نَحْنُ الْخَالِقُونَ ٥٩
60. We have destined death for you and no one can challenge Us	60. Naḥnu qaddarnaa bayna-kumul-mawta wa maa Naḥnu bimasbooqeen.	نَحْنُ قَدَّرْنَا بَيْنَكُمُ الْمَوْتَ وَمَا نَحْنُ بِمَسْبُوقِينَ ٦٠
61. in replacing you with another creation like you, changing you into a form which you do not know.	61. ‘Alaaa an nubaddila amsaalakum wa nunshi’akum fee maa laa ta‘lamoon.	عَلَىٰ أَن نُّبَدِّلَ أَمْثَالَكُمْ وَنُنشِئَكُمْ فِي مَا لَا تَعْلَمُونَ ٦١
62. You certainly knew about (your) first development. Why do you not take heed?	62. Wa laqad ‘alimtumun-nash-atal-oolaa falaw laa tazakkaroon.	وَلَقَدْ عَلِمْتُمُ النَّشْأَةَ الْأُولَىٰ فَلَوْلَا تَذَكَّرُونَ ٦٢
63. Have you seen what you sow?	63. Afara’aytum maa taḥru-soon.	أَفَرَأَيْتُم مَّا تَحْرُثُونَ ٦٣
64. Do you make it grow or is it We who make it grow?	64. ’A-antum tazra‘oonahooo am Naḥnuz-zaari‘ooon.	ءَأَنتُمْ تَزْرَعُونَهُ أَمْ نَحْنُ الزَّارِعُونَ ٦٤
65. Had We wanted, We could have crushed it to bits and you would have been left to lament,	65. Law nashaaa’u laja‘al-naahu ḥuṭaaman faẓaltum tafakkahoon.	لَوْ نَشَاءُ لَجَعَلْنَاهُ حُطَامًا فَظَلْتُمْ تَفَكَّهُونَ ٦٥
66. crying, “We have been left to suffer loss.	66. Innaa lamughramoon.	إِنَّا لَمُغْرَمُونَ ٦٦
67. Surely, we have been deprived (of the benefits).”	67. Bal naḥnu maḥroomoon.	بَلْ نَحْنُ مَحْرُومُونَ ٦٧
68. Have you seen the water which you drink?	68. Afara’aytumul-maaa’al-lazee tashraboon.	أَفَرَأَيْتُمُ الْمَاءَ الَّذِي تَشْرَبُونَ ٦٨
69. Is it you who sent it down from the clouds or is it We who have sent it down?	69. ’A-antum anzaltumoohu minal-muzni am Naḥnul-munziloon.	ءَأَنتُمْ أَنزَلْتُمُوهُ مِنَ الْمُزْنِ أَمْ نَحْنُ الْمُنزِلُونَ ٦٩

70. Had We wanted, We could have made it salty. Why then do you not give thanks?	70. Law nashaaa'u ja'alnaahu ujaajan falaw laa tashkuroon.	لَوْ نَشَآءُ جَعَلْنٰهُ اُجَاجًا فَلَوْلَا تَشْكُرُوْنَ ﴿٧٠﴾
71. Have you seen the fire which you kindle?	71. Afara'aytumun-naaral-latee tooroon.	اَفَرَءَيْتُمُ النَّارَ الَّتِيْ تُوْرُوْنَ ﴿٧١﴾
72. Is it you who have produced its tree or is it We who have produced it?	72. 'A-antum ansha-tum shajaratahaaa am Naḥnul-munshi'oon.	ءَاَنْتُمْ اَنْشَاْتُمْ شَجَرَتَهَآ اَمْ نَحْنُ الْمُنْشِـُٔوْنَ ﴿٧٢﴾
73. It is We who have made it as a reminder and a means of comfort for the people.	73. Naḥnu ja'alnaahaa tazkira-tañw-wa mataa'al-lilmuqween.	نَحْنُ جَعَلْنٰهَا تَذْكِرَةً وَّمَتَاعًا لِّلْمُقْوِيْنَ ﴿٧٣﴾
74. (Muhammad), glorify your Lord, the Great One.	74. Fasabbiḥ bismi-Rabbikal-'aẓeem.	فَسَبِّحْ بِاسْمِ رَبِّكَ الْعَظِيْمِ ﴿٧٤﴾
75. I swear by the setting of the stars	75. Falaaa uqsimu bimawaa-qi'in-nujoom.	فَلَآ اُقْسِمُ بِمَوٰقِعِ النُّجُوْمِ ﴿٧٥﴾
76. - which is indeed a great oath if only you knew it -	76. Wa innahoo laqasamul-law ta'lamoona 'aẓeem.	وَاِنَّهٗ لَقَسَمٌ لَّوْ تَعْلَمُوْنَ عَظِيْمٌ ﴿٧٦﴾
77. that this is an honorable Quran	77. Innahoo la-Qur-aanun Kareem.	اِنَّهٗ لَقُرْاٰنٌ كَرِيْمٌ ﴿٧٧﴾
78. preserved in a hidden Book which	78. Fee kitaabim-maknoon.	فِيْ كِتٰبٍ مَّكْنُوْنٍ ﴿٧٨﴾
79. no one can touch except the purified ones.	79. Laa yamassuhooo illal-muṭahharoon.	لَّا يَمَسُّهٗٓ اِلَّا الْمُطَهَّرُوْنَ ﴿٧٩﴾
80. (This Quran) is a revelation from the Lord of the universe.	80. Tanzeelum-mir-Rabbil 'aalameen.	تَنْزِيْلٌ مِّنْ رَّبِّ الْعٰلَمِيْنَ ﴿٨٠﴾
81. Do you say that this statement is a lie?	81. Afabihaazal-ḥadeesi an-tum mudhinoon.	اَفَبِهٰذَا الْحَدِيْثِ اَنْتُمْ مُّدْهِنُوْنَ ﴿٨١﴾
82. Do you turn your sustenance into disbelief (appreciation into rejection)?	82. Wa taj'aloona rizqakum annakum tukaz ziboon.	وَتَجْعَلُوْنَ رِزْقَكُمْ اَنَّكُمْ تُكَذِّبُوْنَ ﴿٨٢﴾
83. Why can you not help a soul dying	83. Falaw laaa izaa balaghatil-ḥulqoom.	فَلَوْلَآ اِذَا بَلَغَتِ الْحُلْقُوْمَ ﴿٨٣﴾
84. right before your very eyes?	84. Wa antum ḥeena'izin tanẓuroon.	وَاَنْتُمْ حِيْنَئِذٍ تَنْظُرُوْنَ ﴿٨٤﴾
85. We are closer to him than you, but you cannot see.	85. Wa Naḥnu aqrabu ilayhi minkum wa laakil-laa tubṣi-roon.	وَنَحْنُ اَقْرَبُ اِلَيْهِ مِنْكُمْ وَلٰكِنْ لَّا تُبْصِرُوْنَ ﴿٨٥﴾
86. If you are true to your claim that there is no Day of Judgment,	86. Falaw laaa in kuntum ghayra madeeneen.	فَلَوْلَآ اِنْ كُنْتُمْ غَيْرَ مَدِيْنِيْنَ ﴿٨٦﴾
87. why can you not bring it (the soul) back (to life)?	87. Tarji'oonahaaa in kuntum ṣaadiqeen.	تَرْجِعُوْنَهَآ اِنْ كُنْتُمْ صٰدِقِيْنَ ﴿٨٧﴾
88. (If a dying soul) is of those near to Allah,	88. Fa-ammaaa in kaana minal-muqarrabeen.	فَاَمَّآ اِنْ كَانَ مِنَ الْمُقَرَّبِيْنَ ﴿٨٨﴾
89. it will have rest, happiness, (in his grave) and a beautiful Paradise.	89. Farawḥuñw-wa rayḥaa-nuñw-wa Jannatu Na'eem.	فَرَوْحٌ وَّرَيْحَانٌ ۙ وَّجَنَّتُ نَعِيْمٍ ﴿٨٩﴾
90. If it is of the people of the right hand,	90. Wa ammaaa in kaana min-Aṣḥaabil-Yameen.	وَاَمَّآ اِنْ كَانَ مِنْ اَصْحٰبِ الْيَمِيْنِ ﴿٩٠﴾
91. it will be with the people of the right hand, living in peace and security.	91. Fasalaamul-laka min Aṣ-ḥaabil-Yameen.	فَسَلٰمٌ لَّكَ مِنْ اَصْحٰبِ الْيَمِيْنِ ﴿٩١﴾

92. If it is of those who have rejected the Truth and have gone astray,

92. Wa ammaaa in kaana minal-mukaz-zibeenaḍ-ḍaal-leen.

وَأَمَّآ إِن كَانَ مِنَ ٱلْمُكَذِّبِينَ
ٱلضَّآلِّينَ ﴿٩٢﴾

93. its dwelling will be boiling water

93. Fanuzulum-min ḥameem.

فَنُزُلٌ مِّنْ حَمِيمٍ ﴿٩٣﴾

94. and the heat of hellfire.

94. Wa taṣliyatu Jaḥeem.

وَتَصْلِيَةُ جَحِيمٍ ﴿٩٤﴾

95. This is the absolute Truth and certainty.

95. Inna haazaa lahuwa ḥaq-qul-yaqeen.

إِنَّ هَٰذَا لَهُوَ حَقُّ ٱلْيَقِينِ ﴿٩٥﴾

96. So glorify the name of your Lord, the Great One.

96. Fasabbiḥ bismi Rabbikal 'aẓeem.

فَسَبِّحْ بِٱسْمِ رَبِّكَ ٱلْعَظِيمِ ﴿٩٦﴾ ع ٣ ٢٢ ١٦

Al-Hadid, The Iron (57)

In the Name of Allah, the Beneficent, the Merciful.

Sûrat al-Ḥadîd-57

(Revealed at Madinah)

Bismillaahir Raḥmaanir Raḥeem

(٥٧) سُورَةُ ٱلْحَدِيدِ مَدَنِيَّةٌ (٩٤)

آياتها ٢٩ بِسْمِ ٱللَّهِ ٱلرَّحْمَٰنِ ٱلرَّحِيمِ ركوعاتها ٤

1. All that is in the heavens and the earth glorify Allah. He is Majestic and All-wise.

1. Sabbaḥa lillaahi maa fis-samaawaati wal-arḍi wa Huwal-'Azeezul-Ḥakeem.

سَبَّحَ لِلَّهِ مَا فِى ٱلسَّمَٰوَٰتِ وَٱلْأَرْضِ ۖ
وَهُوَ ٱلْعَزِيزُ ٱلْحَكِيمُ ﴿١﴾

2. To Him belongs the Kingdom of the heavens and the earth. He gives life and causes things to die. He has power over all things.

2. Lahoo mulkus-samaa-waati wal-arḍi yuḥyee wa yumeetu wa Huwa 'alaa kulli shay'in Qadeer.

لَهُۥ مُلْكُ ٱلسَّمَٰوَٰتِ وَٱلْأَرْضِ ۖ يُحْىِۦ وَ
يُمِيتُ ۖ وَهُوَ عَلَىٰ كُلِّ شَىْءٍ قَدِيرٌ ﴿٢﴾

3. He is the First, the Last, the Manifest, and the Unseen and He knows all things.

3. Huwal-Awwalu wal-Aakhiru waẓ-Ẓaahiru wal-Baaṭinu wa Huwa bikulli shay'in 'Aleem.

هُوَ ٱلْأَوَّلُ وَٱلْءَاخِرُ وَٱلظَّٰهِرُ وَ
ٱلْبَاطِنُ ۖ وَهُوَ بِكُلِّ شَىْءٍ عَلِيمٌ ﴿٣﴾

4. It is He who created the heavens and the earth in six days (periods) and then established His Dominion over the Throne. He knows whatever enters into the earth, what comes out of it, what descends from the sky, and what ascends to it. He is with you wherever you may be and He is Well-aware of what you do.

4. Huwal-lazee khalaqas-samaawaati wal-arḍa fee sittati ayyaamin summas tawaa 'alal-'Arsh; ya'lamu maa yaliju fil-arḍi wa maa yakhruju minhaa wa maa yanzilu minas-samaaa'i wa maa ya'ruju feehaa wa Huwa ma'akum ayna maa kuntum; wallaahu bimaa ta'maloona Baṣeer.

هُوَ ٱلَّذِى خَلَقَ ٱلسَّمَٰوَٰتِ وَٱلْأَرْضَ
فِى سِتَّةِ أَيَّامٍ ثُمَّ ٱسْتَوَىٰ عَلَى
ٱلْعَرْشِ ۚ يَعْلَمُ مَا يَلِجُ فِى ٱلْأَرْضِ
وَمَا يَخْرُجُ مِنْهَا وَمَا يَنزِلُ مِنَ
ٱلسَّمَآءِ وَمَا يَعْرُجُ فِيهَا ۖ وَهُوَ
مَعَكُمْ أَيْنَ مَا كُنتُمْ ۚ وَٱللَّهُ
بِمَا تَعْمَلُونَ بَصِيرٌ ﴿٤﴾

5. To Him belong the heavens and the earth and to Him all things return.

5. Lahoo mulkus-samaa-waati wal-arḍ; wa ilal-laahi turja'ul-umoor.

لَهُۥ مُلْكُ ٱلسَّمَٰوَٰتِ وَٱلْأَرْضِ ۚ
وَإِلَى ٱللَّهِ تُرْجَعُ ٱلْأُمُورُ ﴿٥﴾

6. He causes night to enter into day and day into night. He knows best what all hearts contain.

6. Yoolijul-layla fin-nahaari wa yoolijun-nahaara fil-layl; wa Huwa 'Aleemum bizaatiṣ-ṣudoor.

يُولِجُ ٱلَّيْلَ فِى ٱلنَّهَارِ وَيُولِجُ
ٱلنَّهَارَ فِى ٱلَّيْلِ ۚ وَهُوَ عَلِيمٌۢ
بِذَاتِ ٱلصُّدُورِ ﴿٦﴾

7. Have faith in Allah and His Messenger and spend for His cause out of what is entrusted to you. Those who believe and spend for the cause of Allah will have a great reward.

7. Aaminoo billaahi wa Rasoolihee wa anfiqoo mimmaa ja‘alakum mustakhlafeena feehi fallazeena aamanoo minkum wa anfaqoo lahum ajrun kabeer.

آمنوا بالله ورسوله وأنفقوا مما
جعلكم مستخلفين فيه فالذين
آمنوا منكم وأنفقوا لهم أجر كبير ٧

8. If you are true indeed to this covenant, why do you not believe in Allah, when His Messenger invites you to believe in your Lord with whom you have made a solemn covenant?

8. Wa maa lakum laa tu’minoona billaahi war-Rasoolu yad‘ookum litu’minoo bi-Rabbikum wa qad akhaza meesaaqakum in kuntum mu’mineen.

وما لكم لا تؤمنون بالله و
الرسول يدعوكم لتؤمنوا بربكم
وقد أخذ ميثاقكم إن كنتم
مؤمنين ٨

9. It is He who sends illustrious revelations to His servant to take you out of darkness to light. Allah is Compassionate and All-merciful to you.

9. Huwal-lazee yunazzilu ‘alaa ‘abdiheee Aayaatim bayyinaatil-liyukhrijakum minaẓ-ẓulumaati ilan-noor; wa innal-laaha bikum la Ra’oofur-Raḥeem.

هو الذي ينزل على عبده آيات
بينات ليخرجكم من الظلمات
إلى النور وإن الله بكم لرءوف
رحيم ٩

10. Why do you not spend for the cause of Allah, in fact, to Allah belong the legacy of the heavens and the earth? Those among you who spent for the cause of Allah and fought before victory (retaking of Makkah) will not be equal (with others). Their status is of greater position than those who spent for the cause of Allah and fought for it after victory. However, to both parties Allah has promised good rewards. Allah is Well-aware of what you do.

10. Wa maa lakum allaa tunfiqoo fee sabeelil-laahi wa lillaahi meeraasus-samaawaati wal-arḍ; laa yastawee minkum man anfaqa min qablil-Fatḥi wa qaatal; ulaaa’ika a‘ẓamu darajatam-minal-lazeena anfaqoo mim ba‘du wa qaataloo; wa kullañw-wa‘adallaahul-ḥusnaa; wallaahu bimaa ta‘maloona Khabeer.

وما لكم ألا تنفقوا في سبيل الله
ولله ميراث السماوات والأرض
لا يستوي منكم من أنفق من قبل
الفتح وقاتل أولئك أعظم درجة
من الذين أنفقوا من بعد و
قاتلوا وكلا وعد الله الحسنى
والله بما تعملون خبير ١٠ ع ١٧

11. Whoever gives a virtuous loan to Allah will receive double from Him in addition to an honorable reward.

11. Man zal-lazee yuqriḍul-laaha qarḍan ḥasanan fa-yuḍaa‘ifahoo lahoo wa lahooo ajrun kareem.

من ذا الذي يقرض الله قرضا
حسنا فيضاعفه له وله أجر
كريم ١١

12. On the Day of Judgment you will see the believers, male and female, with their light shining in front of them and to their right. They will be told, “Paradise wherein streams flow is the glad news for you today. You will live therein forever. This is the greatest triumph.”

12. Yawma taral-mu’mineena walmu’minaati yas‘aa nooruhum bayna aydeehim wa bi-aymaanihim bushraakumul-Yawma Jannaatun tajree min taḥtihal-anhaaru khaalideena feehaa; zaalika huwal-fawzul-‘aẓeem.

يوم ترى المؤمنين والمؤمنات
يسعى نورهم بين أيديهم وبأيمانهم
بشراكم اليوم جنات تجري من
تحتها الأنهار خالدين فيها
ذلك هو الفوز العظيم ١٢

13. On the Day the hypocrites, male and female, will say to the believers, "Please wait for us so that we might benefit from your light." They will be told, "Go back and search for your own light." A barrier with a door will be placed between them. Inside it there will be mercy but outside of it there will be torment.

13. Yawma yaqoolul-munaafiqoona walmunaafiqaatu lillazeena aamanun-zuroonaa naqtabis min noorikum qeelarji'oo waraaa'akum faltamisoo nooran faduriba baynahum bisooril-lahoo baab; baatinuhoo feehir-rahmatu wa zaahiruhoo min qibalihil-'azaab.

يَوۡمَ يَقُوۡلُ الۡمُنٰفِقُوۡنَ وَالۡمُنٰفِقٰتُ
لِلَّذِيۡنَ اٰمَنُوا انۡظُرُوۡنَا نَقۡتَبِسۡ مِنۡ
نُّوۡرِكُمۡ ۚ قِيۡلَ ارۡجِعُوۡا وَرَآءَكُمۡ
فَالۡتَمِسُوۡا نُوۡرًا ؕ فَضُرِبَ بَيۡنَهُمۡ بِسُوۡرٍ
لَّهٗ بَابٌ ؕ بَاطِنُهٗ فِيۡهِ الرَّحۡمَةُ وَ
ظَاهِرُهٗ مِنۡ قِبَلِهِ الۡعَذَابُ ؕ ﴿۱۳﴾

14. (Those outside) will call out, "Were we not with you?" (Those inside) will reply, "Yes, you were with us but you spent your life in disbelief and hypocrisy, wished death to (Muhammad), had doubts about his message and let your longings deceive you until the decree of Allah came to pass. The devil deceived you about the mercy of Allah.

14. Yunaadoonahum alam nakum-ma'akum qaaloo balaa walaakinnakum fatantum anfusakum wa tarabbastum wartabtum wa gharratkumul-amaaniyyu hattaa jaaa'a amrullaahi wa gharrakum billaahil-gharoor.

يُنَادُوۡنَهُمۡ اَلَمۡ نَكُنۡ مَّعَكُمۡ ؕ قَالُوۡا
بَلٰى وَلٰكِنَّكُمۡ فَتَنۡتُمۡ اَنۡفُسَكُمۡ
وَتَرَبَّصۡتُمۡ وَارۡتَبۡتُمۡ وَغَرَّتۡكُمُ
الۡاَمَانِىُّ حَتّٰى جَآءَ اَمۡرُ اللّٰهِ وَغَرَّكُمۡ
بِاللّٰهِ الۡغَرُوۡرُ ﴿۱۴﴾

15. So on this day no ransom will be accepted from you nor from the unbelievers. Your dwelling will be fire. It will be what you deserve and a terrible end."

15. Fal-Yawma laa yu'khazu minkum fidyatuñw-wa laa minallazeena kafaroo; ma-waakumun-Naaru hiya maw-laakum wa bi'sal-maseer.

فَالۡيَوۡمَ لَا يُؤۡخَذُ مِنۡكُمۡ فِدۡيَةٌ وَّلَا
مِنَ الَّذِيۡنَ كَفَرُوۡا ؕ مَاۡوٰٮكُمُ النَّارُ ؕ
هِىَ مَوۡلٰٮكُمۡ ؕ وَبِئۡسَ الۡمَصِيۡرُ ﴿۱۵﴾

16. Was it not necessary for the hearts of the believers to become humbled by the remembrance of Allah and by the Truth which has been revealed so that they will not be like the followers of the Bible who lived before them and whose hearts have become hard like stone through the long years? Many of them are evildoers.

16. Alam ya-ni lillazeena aamanooo an takhsha'a quloobuhum lizikril-laahi wa maa nazala minal-haqq; wa laa yakoonoo kallazeena ootul-Kitaaba min qablu fataala 'alayhimul-amadu faqasat quloobuhum wa kaseerum-minhum faasiqoon.

اَلَمۡ يَاۡنِ لِلَّذِيۡنَ اٰمَنُوۡۤا اَنۡ
تَخۡشَعَ قُلُوۡبُهُمۡ لِذِكۡرِ اللّٰهِ وَمَا نَزَلَ
مِنَ الۡحَقِّ ۙ وَلَا يَكُوۡنُوۡا كَالَّذِيۡنَ
اُوۡتُوا الۡكِتٰبَ مِنۡ قَبۡلُ فَطَالَ
عَلَيۡهِمُ الۡاَمَدُ فَقَسَتۡ قُلُوۡبُهُمۡ ؕ
وَكَثِيۡرٌ مِّنۡهُمۡ فٰسِقُوۡنَ ﴿۱۶﴾

17. You must know that Allah brings the dead earth back to life. We have explained Our revelations to you so that you may perhaps have understanding.

17. I'lamooo annal-laaha yuhyil-arda ba'da mawtihaa; qad bayyannaa lakumul Aayaati la'allakum ta'qiloon.

اِعۡلَمُوۡۤا اَنَّ اللّٰهَ يُحۡىِ الۡاَرۡضَ
بَعۡدَ مَوۡتِهَا ؕ قَدۡ بَيَّنَّا لَكُمُ
الۡاٰيٰتِ لَعَلَّكُمۡ تَعۡقِلُوۡنَ ﴿۱۷﴾

18. The charitable men and women who give a virtuous loan to Allah will receive double from Him in addition to their honorable reward.

18. Innal-mussaddiqeena wal-mussaddiqaati wa aqradul-laaha qardan hasanañy-yudaa'afu lahum wa lahum ajrun kareem.

اِنَّ الۡمُصَّدِّقِيۡنَ وَالۡمُصَّدِّقٰتِ
وَاَقۡرَضُوا اللّٰهَ قَرۡضًا حَسَنًا يُّضٰعَفُ
لَهُمۡ وَلَهُمۡ اَجۡرٌ كَرِيۡمٌ ﴿۱۸﴾

19. Those who believe in Allah and His Messenger are the truthful ones and are witness (to the deeds of others) before their Lord. They will have their reward and their light. Those who disbelieve and reject Our revelations shall be the dwellers of hell.

19. Wallazeena aamanoo billaahi wa Rusuliheee ulaaa'ika humuṣ-ṣiddeeqoona washshuhadaaa'u 'inda Rabbihim lahum ajruhum wa nooruhum wallazeena kafaroo wa kaz-zaboo bi-Aayaatinaaa ulaaa'ika Aṣḥaabul-Jaḥeem.

والَّذِيْنَ اٰمَنُوْا بِاللّٰهِ وَرُسُلِهٖۤ اُولٰٓئِكَ هُمُ الصِّدِّيْقُوْنَ ۖ وَالشُّهَدَآءُ عِنْدَ رَبِّهِمْ لَهُمْ اَجْرُهُمْ وَنُوْرُهُمْ ؕ وَالَّذِيْنَ كَفَرُوْا وَكَذَّبُوْا بِاٰيٰتِنَاۤ اُولٰٓئِكَ اَصْحٰبُ الْجَحِيْمِ ۞

20. You must know that the worldly life is only a game, a temporary attraction, a means of boastfulness among yourselves and a place for multiplying your wealth and children. It is like the rain which produces plants that are attractive to the unbelievers. These plants flourish, turn yellow, and then become crushed bits of straw. In the life hereafter there will be severe torment or forgiveness and mercy from Allah. The worldly life is only means of causing neglectfulness.

20. I'lamooo annamal-ḥayaa-tud-dunyaa la'ibuñw-wa lahwuñw-wa zeenatuñw-wa tafaakhurum baynakum wa takaaṣurun fil-amwaali wal awlaad; kamaṣali ghaysin a'jabal-kuffaara nabaatuhoo ṣumma yaheeju fataraahu muṣfarran ṣumma yakoonu ḥuṭaamaa; wa fil-Aakhirati 'azaabun shadeed; wa magh-firatum-minal-laahi wa riḍ-waan; wa mal-ḥayaatud-dun-yaaa illaa mataa'ul-ghuroor.

اِعْلَمُوْۤا اَنَّمَا الْحَيٰوةُ الدُّنْيَا لَعِبٌ وَّلَهْوٌ وَّزِيْنَةٌ وَّتَفَاخُرٌۢ بَيْنَكُمْ وَتَكَاثُرٌ فِي الْاَمْوَالِ وَالْاَوْلَادِ ؕ كَمَثَلِ غَيْثٍ اَعْجَبَ الْكُفَّارَ نَبَاتُهٗ ثُمَّ يَهِيْجُ فَتَرٰىهُ مُصْفَرًّا ثُمَّ يَكُوْنُ حُطَامًا ؕ وَفِي الْاٰخِرَةِ عَذَابٌ شَدِيْدٌ ۙ وَّ مَغْفِرَةٌ مِّنَ اللّٰهِ وَرِضْوَانٌ ؕ وَمَا الْحَيٰوةُ الدُّنْيَاۤ اِلَّا مَتَاعُ الْغُرُوْرِ ۞

21. Compete with one another to achieve forgiveness from your Lord and to reach Paradise, which is as vast as the heavens and the earth, and is prepared for those who believe in Allah and His messengers. This is the blessing of Allah and He grants it to whomever He wants. The blessings of Allah are great.

21. Saabiqooo ilaa magh-firatim-mir-Rabbikum wa Jannatin 'arḍuhaa ka'arḍis-samaaa'i wal-arḍi u'iddat lillazeena aamanoo billaahi wa Rusulih; zaalika faḍlul-laahi yu'teehi mañy-yashaaa'; wallaahu zul-faḍlil-'azeem.

سَابِقُوْۤا اِلٰى مَغْفِرَةٍ مِّنْ رَّبِّكُمْ وَجَنَّةٍ عَرْضُهَا كَعَرْضِ السَّمَآءِ وَالْاَرْضِ ۙ اُعِدَّتْ لِلَّذِيْنَ اٰمَنُوْا بِاللّٰهِ وَرُسُلِهٖ ؕ ذٰلِكَ فَضْلُ اللّٰهِ يُؤْتِيْهِ مَنْ يَّشَآءُ ؕ وَاللّٰهُ ذُو الْفَضْلِ الْعَظِيْمِ ۞

22. Whatever hardships you face on earth and in your souls are written in the Book (knowledge of Allah, His prophets and their Awṣiya, successors) before its emergence. This (having such knowledge) is certainly easy for Allah

22. Maaa aṣaaba mim-muṣee-batin fil-arḍi wa laa feee anfusikum illaa fee kitaabim-min qabli an nabra-ahaa; inna zaalika 'alal-laahi yaseer.

مَاۤ اَصَابَ مِنْ مُّصِيْبَةٍ فِي الْاَرْضِ وَلَا فِيْۤ اَنْفُسِكُمْ اِلَّا فِيْ كِتٰبٍ مِّنْ قَبْلِ اَنْ نَّبْرَاَهَا ؕ اِنَّ ذٰلِكَ عَلَى اللّٰهِ يَسِيْرٌ ۙ ۞

23. so that you would not grieve over what you have lost nor become very happy about what Allah has granted to you.

23. Likaylaa ta-saw 'alaa maa faatakum wa laa tafraḥoo bimaaa aataakum; wallaahu

لِّكَيْلَا تَاْسَوْا عَلٰى مَا فَاتَكُمْ وَلَا تَفْرَحُوْا بِمَاۤ اٰتٰىكُمْ ؕ وَاللّٰهُ

Allah does not love the arrogant boastful ones

24. who are niggardly and who try to make other people also niggardly. Those who turn away (from guidance) should know that Allah is Self-sufficient and Praiseworthy.

25. We sent Our Messengers with clear evidence (to support their truthfulness), and sent with them the Book and the Balance (the Imam) so that people can maintain justice. We sent down iron - in which there is strong power and benefit for the people - so that Allah would know who would help Him and His Messenger without seeing the unseen. Allah is All-powerful and Majestic.

26. We sent Noah and Abraham and placed prophethood and the Book among their offspring, some of whom have the right guidance. However, many of them are evildoers.

27. Then We sent Our other Messengers to follow their traditions. After them We sent Jesus, the son of Mary, to whom We gave the Gospel. In the hearts of his followers We placed compassion and mercy. We did not command them to lead the monastic life. This was their own method of seeking the pleasure of Allah. Despite this intention, they did not properly observe it (the monastic life). To the believers among them, We gave their reward but many of them are evil-doers.

28. Believers, have fear of Allah and believe in His Messenger. Allah will grant you a

laa yuḥibbu kulla mukhtaalin fakhoor.

24. Allazeena yabkhaloona wa ya-muroonan-naasa bil-bukhl; wa mañy-yatawalla fa-innal-laaha Huwal Ghaniyyul-Ḥameed.

25. Laqad arsalnaa Rusulanaa bilbayyinaati wa anzalnaa ma'ahumul-Kitaaba wal-Meezaana liyaqooman-naasu bilqist; wa anzalnal-ḥadeeda feehi ba-sun shadeeduñw-wa manaafi'u linnaasi wa liya'la-mal-laahu mañy-yanṣuruhoo wa Rusulahoo bilghayb; innal-laaha Qawiyyun 'Azeez.

26. Wa laqad arsalnaa Noohañw-wa Ibraaheema wa ja'alnaa fee zurriyyatihiman-Nubuwwata wal-Kitaaba faminhum muhtad; wa kaseerum-minhum faasiqoon.

27. Summa qaffaynaa 'alaaa aasaarihim bi-Rusulinaa wa qaffaynaa bi-'Eesab-ni-Maryama wa aataynaahul-Injeela wa ja'alnaa fee quloobil-lazeenat-taba'oohu ra-fatañw-wa raḥmah; wa rahbaaniyyata-nibtada'oohaa maa katabnaahaa 'alayhim illabtighaaa'a riḍw-aanil-laahi famaa ra'awhaa ḥaqqa ri'aayatihaa fa-aataynal-lazeena aamanoo minhum ajrahum wa kaseerum-minhum faasiqoon.

28. Yaaa ayyuhal-lazeena aamanuttaqul-laaha wa-aaminoo bi-Rasoolihee yu'tikum kiflayni

لَا يُحِبُّ كُلَّ مُخْتَالٍ فَخُوْرِۨ ۟

اَلَّذِيْنَ يَبْخَلُوْنَ وَيَأْمُرُوْنَ النَّاسَ بِالْبُخْلِ ؕ وَمَنْ يَّتَوَلَّ فَاِنَّ اللّٰهَ هُوَ الْغَنِيُّ الْحَمِيْدُ ۟

لَقَدْ اَرْسَلْنَا رُسُلَنَا بِالْبَيِّنٰتِ وَ اَنْزَلْنَا مَعَهُمُ الْكِتٰبَ وَ الْمِيْزَانَ لِيَقُوْمَ النَّاسُ بِالْقِسْطِ ۚ وَ اَنْزَلْنَا الْحَدِيْدَ فِيْهِ بَأْسٌ شَدِيْدٌ وَّمَنَافِعُ لِلنَّاسِ وَلِيَعْلَمَ اللّٰهُ مَنْ يَّنْصُرُهٗ وَرُسُلَهٗ بِالْغَيْبِ ؕ اِنَّ اللّٰهَ قَوِيٌّ عَزِيْزٌ ۟

وَلَقَدْ اَرْسَلْنَا نُوْحًا وَّ اِبْرٰهِيْمَ وَجَعَلْنَا فِيْ ذُرِّيَّتِهِمَا النُّبُوَّةَ وَالْكِتٰبَ فَمِنْهُمْ مُّهْتَدٍ ۚ وَكَثِيْرٌ مِّنْهُمْ فٰسِقُوْنَ ۟

ثُمَّ قَفَّيْنَا عَلٰۤى اٰثَارِهِمْ بِرُسُلِنَا وَقَفَّيْنَا بِعِيْسَى ابْنِ مَرْيَمَ وَاٰتَيْنٰهُ الْاِنْجِيْلَ ۙ وَجَعَلْنَا فِيْ قُلُوْبِ الَّذِيْنَ اتَّبَعُوْهُ رَأْفَةً وَّرَحْمَةً ؕ وَرَهْبَانِيَّةَ اۨبْتَدَعُوْهَا مَا كَتَبْنٰهَا عَلَيْهِمْ اِلَّا ابْتِغَآءَ رِضْوَانِ اللّٰهِ فَمَا رَعَوْهَا حَقَّ رِعَايَتِهَا ۚ فَاٰتَيْنَا الَّذِيْنَ اٰمَنُوْا مِنْهُمْ اَجْرَهُمْ ۚ وَكَثِيْرٌ مِّنْهُمْ فٰسِقُوْنَ ۟

يٰۤاَيُّهَا الَّذِيْنَ اٰمَنُوا اتَّقُوا اللّٰهَ وَاٰمِنُوْا بِرَسُوْلِهٖ يُؤْتِكُمْ كِفْلَيْنِ

double share of mercy, (safety from hell and admission to Paradise) a light (Imam) whereby you can walk, and forgive your sins. Allah is All-forgiving and All-merciful.

mir raḥmatihee wa yaj'al lakum nooran tamshoona bihee wa yaghfir lakum; wallaahu Ghafoorur-Raḥeem.

مِن رَّحْمَتِهِۦ وَيَجْعَل لَّكُمْ نُورًا
تَمْشُونَ بِهِۦ وَيَغْفِرْ لَكُمْ ۚ وَٱللَّهُ
غَفُورٌ رَّحِيمٌ ﴿٢٨﴾

29. (Have fear of Allah and believe in His Messenger) so that the followers of the Bible will know that they can receive no reward from Allah. They should know that all favors are in the hands of Allah. He grants them to whomever He wants. The favors of Allah are great.

29. Li'allaa ya'lama Ahlul-kitaabi allaa yaqdiroona 'alaa shay'im-min faḍlil-laahi wa annal-faḍla bi-Yadillaahi yu'teehi mañy-yashaaa'; wallaahu zul-faḍlil-'aẓeem.

لِّئَلَّا يَعْلَمَ أَهْلُ ٱلْكِتَٰبِ أَلَّا يَقْدِرُونَ
عَلَىٰ شَىْءٍ مِّن فَضْلِ ٱللَّهِ ۙ وَأَنَّ ٱلْفَضْلَ
بِيَدِ ٱللَّهِ يُؤْتِيهِ مَن يَشَآءُ ۚ وَٱللَّهُ
ذُو ٱلْفَضْلِ ٱلْعَظِيمِ ﴿٢٩﴾ ع

Al-Mujadilah, She Pleaded (58)

In the Name of Allah,
the Beneficent, the Merciful.

Sûrat al-Mujâdalah-58

(Revealed at Madinah)
Bismillaahir Raḥmaanir Raḥeem

(٥٨) سُورَةُ ٱلْمُجَادَلَةِ مَدَنِيَّةٌ (١٠٥)
آياتها ٢٢ بِسْمِ ٱللَّهِ ٱلرَّحْمَٰنِ ٱلرَّحِيمِ ركوعاتها ٣

1. Allah has certainly heard the words of the woman who disputed with you about her husband and who (after not having received a favorable response from you) complained to Allah. Allah was listening to your argument. Allah is All-hearing and All-aware.

1. Qad sami'al-laahu qawlal-latee tujaadiluka fee zawjihaa wa tashtakeee ilal-laahi wallaa-hu yasma'u taḥaawurakumaa; innal-laaha Samee'um Baṣeer.

قَدْ سَمِعَ ٱللَّهُ قَوْلَ ٱلَّتِى تُجَٰدِلُكَ
فِى زَوْجِهَا وَتَشْتَكِىٓ إِلَى ٱللَّهِ وَ
ٱللَّهُ يَسْمَعُ تَحَاوُرَكُمَآ ۚ إِنَّ ٱللَّهَ
سَمِيعٌۢ بَصِيرٌ ﴿١﴾

2. Those who renounce their wives by calling them to be as their mothers should know that their wives could never become their mothers. Their mothers are those who have given birth to them. The words that they speak are certainly detestable and sinful. However, Allah is Pardoning and All-forgiving.

2. Allazeena yuẓaahiroona minkum min nisaaa'ihim maa hunna ummahaatihim in ummahaatuhum illal-laaa'ee waladnahum; wa innahum la-yaqooloona munkaram-minal-qawli wa zooraa; wa innal-laaha la-'Afuwwun Ghafoor.

ٱلَّذِينَ يُظَٰهِرُونَ مِنكُم مِّن نِّسَآئِهِم
مَّا هُنَّ أُمَّهَٰتِهِمْ ۖ إِنْ أُمَّهَٰتُهُمْ إِلَّا
ٱلَّٰٓـِٔى وَلَدْنَهُمْ ۚ وَإِنَّهُمْ لَيَقُولُونَ
مُنكَرًا مِّنَ ٱلْقَوْلِ وَزُورًا ۚ وَإِنَّ ٱللَّهَ
لَعَفُوٌّ غَفُورٌ ﴿٢﴾

3. Those who renounce their wives by calling them mothers and then change their minds about what they have said will have to set free a slave as a ransom and only then will their carnal relations be lawful. This is what you have been commanded. Allah is Well-aware of whatever you do.

3. Wallazeena yuẓaahiroona min nisaaa'ihim summa ya'oodoona limaa qaaloo fataḥreeru raqabatim-min qabli añy-yatamaaas-saa; zaalikum too'aẓoona bih; wallaahu bimaa ta'maloona Khabeer.

وَٱلَّذِينَ يُظَٰهِرُونَ مِن نِّسَآئِهِمْ ثُمَّ
يَعُودُونَ لِمَا قَالُوا۟ فَتَحْرِيرُ رَقَبَةٍ مِّن
قَبْلِ أَن يَتَمَآسَّا ۚ ذَٰلِكُمْ تُوعَظُونَ
بِهِۦ ۚ وَٱللَّهُ بِمَا تَعْمَلُونَ خَبِيرٌ ﴿٣﴾

4. If one could not set free a slave, he must fast for two consecutive months, and only then can he have lawful carnal relations. If this was also not possible, he must feed sixty destitute people. This is the command of Allah, so that perhaps you will have faith in Allah and His Messenger. Such are the Laws of Allah, and those

4. Famal-lam yajid fa-ṣiyaa-mu shahrayni mutataabi'ayni min qabli añy-yatamaaas-saa famal-lam yastaṭi' fa-iṭ'aamu sitteena miskeenaa; zaalika litu'minoo billaahi wa Rasoolih;

فَمَن لَّمْ يَجِدْ فَصِيَامُ شَهْرَيْنِ
مُتَتَابِعَيْنِ مِن قَبْلِ أَن يَتَمَآسَّا ۖ
فَمَن لَّمْ يَسْتَطِعْ فَإِطْعَامُ سِتِّينَ
مِسْكِينًا ۚ ذَٰلِكَ لِتُؤْمِنُوا۟ بِٱللَّهِ وَرَسُولِهِۦ

الجزء الثامن والعشرون (٢٨)

who disbelieve them will suffer a painful torment.

wa tilka ḥudoodul-laah; wa lilkaafireena ‘azaabun aleem.

وَتِلْكَ حُدُوْدُ اللّٰهِ ۗ وَلِلْكٰفِرِيْنَ
عَذَابٌ اَلِيْمٌ ﴿٤﴾

5. Those who oppose Allah and His Messenger will be humiliated as were those who lived before. We have sent illustrious revelations and those who disbelieve will suffer a humiliating torment.

5. Innal-lazeena yuḥaaad-doonal-laaha wa Rasoolahoo kubitoo kamaa kubital-lazeena min qablihim; wa qad anzalnaaa Aayaatim bayyinaat; wa lilkaa-fireena ‘azaabum-muheen.

اِنَّ الَّذِيْنَ يُحَآدُّوْنَ اللّٰهَ وَرَسُوْلَهٗ
كُبِتُوْا كَمَا كُبِتَ الَّذِيْنَ مِنْ قَبْلِهِمْ
وَقَدْ اَنْزَلْنَآ اٰيٰتٍۢ بَيِّنٰتٍ ۗ وَلِلْكٰفِرِيْنَ
عَذَابٌ مُّهِيْنٌ ﴿٥﴾

6. On the day when everyone will be resurrected, Allah will tell them about their deeds which He has recorded in their entirety - while they themselves have forgotten them. Allah is the witness over all things.

6. Yawma yab‘asuhumul-laahu jamee‘an fa-yunabbi'u-hum bimaa ‘amiloo; aḥṣaahul-laahu wa nasooh; wallaahu ‘alaa kulli shay'in Shaheed.

يَوْمَ يَبْعَثُهُمُ اللّٰهُ جَمِيْعًا فَيُنَبِّئُهُمْ
بِمَا عَمِلُوْا ۗ اَحْصٰىهُ اللّٰهُ وَنَسُوْهُ ۗ
وَاللّٰهُ عَلٰى كُلِّ شَيْءٍ شَهِيْدٌ ﴿٦﴾ ع ٢

7. Did you not consider that Allah knows all that is in the heavens and the earth? There is not a single place wherein any secret counsel can take place between any three people without Allah being the fourth, nor five people without His being the sixth, nor any gathering of more or fewer people, wherever it may be, without His being with them. On the Day of Judgment, He will tell them about their deeds. Allah has the knowledge of all things.

7. Alam tara annal-laaha ya‘lamu maa fis-samaawaati wa maa fil-arḍi maa yakoonu min najwaa salaasatin illaa Huwa raabi‘uhum wa laa khamsatin illaa Huwa saadisuhum wa laaa adnaa min zaalika wa laaa aksara illaa Huwa ma‘ahum ayna maa kaanoo summa yunabbi'uhum bimaa ‘amiloo Yawmal-Qiyaamah; innal-laaha bikulli shay'in ‘Aleem.

اَلَمْ تَرَ اَنَّ اللّٰهَ يَعْلَمُ مَا فِى السَّمٰوٰتِ
وَمَا فِى الْاَرْضِ ۗ مَا يَكُوْنُ مِنْ نَّجْوٰى
ثَلٰثَةٍ اِلَّا هُوَ رَابِعُهُمْ وَلَا خَمْسَةٍ اِلَّا
هُوَ سَادِسُهُمْ وَلَآ اَدْنٰى مِنْ ذٰلِكَ
وَلَآ اَكْثَرَ اِلَّا هُوَ مَعَهُمْ اَيْنَ مَا كَانُوْا ۚ
ثُمَّ يُنَبِّئُهُمْ بِمَا عَمِلُوْا يَوْمَ الْقِيٰمَةِ ۗ
اِنَّ اللّٰهَ بِكُلِّ شَيْءٍ عَلِيْمٌ ﴿٧﴾

8. Did you not see those who have been forbidden to have secret counsels violate this prohibition and resume their secret counsels for sinful and hostile purposes, and to disobey the Messenger? When they come to you (Muhammad), they greet you with (pre-Islamic) a greeting with which Allah did not greet you and say to themselves, "Why has Allah not punished us for what we say (if he is a true Prophet)?" The heat of hell is a sufficient torment for them. This is the most terrible fate.

8. Alam tara ilal-lazeena nuhoo ‘anin-najwaa summa ya‘oodoona limaa nuhoo ‘anhu wa yatanaajawna bil-ismi wal‘udwaani wa ma‘ṣiyatir-Rasooli wa izaa jaaa'ooka ḥayyawka bimaa lam yuḥay-yika bihil-laahu wa yaqooloona feee anfusihim law laa yu‘az-zibunal-laahu bimaa naqool; ḥasbuhum Jahannamu yaṣlaw-nahaa fabi'sal-maṣeer.

اَلَمْ تَرَ اِلَى الَّذِيْنَ نُهُوْا عَنِ النَّجْوٰى
ثُمَّ يَعُوْدُوْنَ لِمَا نُهُوْا عَنْهُ وَيَتَنٰجَوْنَ
بِالْاِثْمِ وَالْعُدْوَانِ وَمَعْصِيَتِ
الرَّسُوْلِ ۖ وَاِذَا جَآءُوْكَ حَيَّوْكَ بِمَا لَمْ
يُحَيِّكَ بِهِ اللّٰهُ ۙ وَيَقُوْلُوْنَ فِيْٓ اَنْفُسِهِمْ
لَوْلَا يُعَذِّبُنَا اللّٰهُ بِمَا نَقُوْلُ ۗ حَسْبُهُمْ
جَهَنَّمُ ۚ يَصْلَوْنَهَا ۚ فَبِئْسَ الْمَصِيْرُ ﴿٨﴾

9. Believers, when you hold a secret counsel, let it not be for a sinful, hostile purpose or to disobey the Messenger, but let your counsel take place for virtuous and pious reasons. Have fear of Allah in whose presence you

9. Yaaa ayyuhal-lazeena aamanooo izaa tanaajaytum falaa tatanaajaw bil-ismi wal‘udwaani wa ma‘ṣiyatir-Rasooli wa tanaajaw bilbirri

يٰٓاَيُّهَا الَّذِيْنَ اٰمَنُوْٓا اِذَا تَنَاجَيْتُمْ فَلَا
تَتَنَاجَوْا بِالْاِثْمِ وَالْعُدْوَانِ وَ
مَعْصِيَتِ الرَّسُوْلِ وَتَنَاجَوْا بِالْبِرِّ

will all be brought together.

wattaqwaa wattaqul-laahal-lazeee ilayhi tuhsharoon.

وَالتَّقْوٰى ۭ وَاتَّقُوا اللّٰهَ الَّذِيْٓ اِلَيْهِ
تُحْشَرُوْنَ ۝٩

10. Holding secret counsels for (evil purposes) is a work of Satan to cause grief to the believers, but he can do no harm to them except by the will of Allah. Believers must trust Allah.

10. Innaman-najwaa minash-Shayṭaani liyaḥzunal-la<u>z</u>eena aamanoo wa laysa biḍaaarrihim shay'an illaa bi-i<u>z</u>nil-laah; wa 'alal-laahi falyatawakkalil-mu'minoon.

اِنَّمَا النَّجْوٰى مِنَ الشَّيْطٰنِ لِيَحْزُنَ
الَّذِيْنَ اٰمَنُوْا وَلَيْسَ بِضَاۗرِّهِمْ شَيْــــًٔا
اِلَّا بِاِذْنِ اللّٰهِ ۭ وَعَلَي اللّٰهِ فَلْيَتَوَكَّلِ
الْمُؤْمِنُوْنَ ۝١٠

11. Believers, when you are told to make room in a meeting for others, do so. Allah will then make room for you. If you are told to stand up, you then must do so. Allah will raise the position of the believers among you and of those who have received knowledge. Allah is Well-aware of what you do.

11. Yaaa ayyuhal-la<u>z</u>eena aamanooo i<u>z</u>aa qeela lakum tafassaḥoo fil-majaalisi fafsaḥoo yafsaḥil-laahu lakum wa i<u>z</u>aa qeelan-shuzoo fanshuzoo yarfa'il-laahul-la<u>z</u>eena aamanoo minkum walla<u>z</u>eena ootul-'ilma darajaat; wallaahu bimaa ta'maloona Khabeer.

يٰٓاَيُّهَا الَّذِيْنَ اٰمَنُوْٓا اِذَا قِيْلَ لَكُمْ
تَفَسَّحُوْا فِي الْمَجٰلِسِ فَافْسَحُوْا
يَفْسَحِ اللّٰهُ لَكُمْ ۚ وَاِذَا قِيْلَ انْشُزُوْا
فَانْشُزُوْا يَرْفَعِ اللّٰهُ الَّذِيْنَ اٰمَنُوْا
مِنْكُمْ ۙ وَالَّذِيْنَ اُوْتُوا الْعِلْمَ دَرَجٰتٍ ۭ
وَاللّٰهُ بِمَا تَعْمَلُوْنَ خَبِيْرٌ ۝١١

12. Believers, whenever you consult (ask a question from) the Prophet, offer charity before your consultation. This will be better for you and more pure. However, if you did not find anything to give in charity, then Allah is All-forgiving and All-merciful.

12. Yaaa-ayyuhal-la<u>z</u>eena aamanooo i<u>z</u>aa naajaytumur-Rasoola faqaddimoo bayna yaday najwaakum ṣadaqah; <u>z</u>aalika khayrul-lakum wa aṭhar; fa-il-lam tajidoo fa-innal-laaha Ghafoorur-Raḥeem.

يٰٓاَيُّهَا الَّذِيْنَ اٰمَنُوْٓا اِذَا نَاجَيْتُمُ
الرَّسُوْلَ فَقَدِّمُوْا بَيْنَ يَدَيْ
نَجْوٰىكُمْ صَدَقَةً ۭ ذٰلِكَ خَيْرٌ لَّكُمْ
وَاَطْهَرُ ۭ فَاِنْ لَّمْ تَجِدُوْا فَاِنَّ اللّٰهَ
غَفُوْرٌ رَّحِيْمٌ ۝١٢

13. Were you afraid that giving in charity before your consultation would make you poor? Since you did not offer such charity, Allah forgave you for this. At least be steadfast in prayer, pay the religious tax, and obey Allah and His Messenger. Allah is Well-aware of what you do.

13. 'A-ashfaqtum an tuqad-dimoo bayna yaday najwaakum ṣadaqaat; fa-i<u>z</u> lam taf'aloo wa taabal-laahu 'alaykum fa-aqeemuṣ-Ṣalaata wa aatuz-Zakaata wa aṭee'ul-laaha wa Rasoolah; wallaahu Khabeerum bimaa ta'maloon.

ءَاَشْفَقْتُمْ اَنْ تُقَدِّمُوْا بَيْنَ يَدَيْ
نَجْوٰىكُمْ صَدَقٰتٍ ۭ فَاِذْ لَمْ تَفْعَلُوْا
وَتَابَ اللّٰهُ عَلَيْكُمْ فَاَقِيْمُوا الصَّلٰوةَ
وَاٰتُوا الزَّكٰوةَ وَاَطِيْعُوا اللّٰهَ وَرَسُوْلَهٗ ۭ
وَاللّٰهُ خَبِيْرٌۢ بِمَا تَعْمَلُوْنَ ۝١٣ ع

14. Did you not see those who have established friendship with the people who are subject to the wrath of Allah? They do not belong to you nor do you to them, yet they knowingly try to prove their point by using false oaths.

14. Alam tara ilal-la<u>z</u>eena tawallaw qawman ghaḍibal-laahu 'alayhim maa hum minkum wa laa minhum wa yaḥlifoona 'alal-ka<u>z</u>ibi wa hum ya'lamoon.

اَلَمْ تَرَ اِلَى الَّذِيْنَ تَوَلَّوْا قَوْمًا
غَضِبَ اللّٰهُ عَلَيْهِمْ ۭ مَا هُمْ مِّنْكُمْ
وَلَا مِنْهُمْ ۙ وَيَحْلِفُوْنَ عَلَي الْكَذِبِ
وَهُمْ يَعْلَمُوْنَ ۝١٤

15. Allah has prepared a severe torment for them. What an evil deed they have committed!

15. A‘addal-laahu lahum-‘azaaban shadeedan innahum saaa‘a maa kaanoo ya‘maloon.

اَعَدَّ اللهُ لَهُمْ عَذَابًا شَدِيْدًا ۖ اِنَّهُمْ سَآءَ مَا كَانُوْا يَعْمَلُوْنَ ۝

16. They have made their oaths as a shield to obstruct others from the way of Allah. They will suffer a humiliating torment.

16. Ittakhazooo aymaanahum junnatan faṣaddoo ‘an sabeelil-laahi falahum ‘azaabum-muheen.

اِتَّخَذُوْا اَيْمَانَهُمْ جُنَّةً فَصَدُّوْا عَنْ سَبِيْلِ اللهِ فَلَهُمْ عَذَابٌ مُّهِيْنٌ ۝

17. Neither their wealth nor their children will be able to protect them against Allah. They will be the dwellers of hellfire wherein they will live forever.

17. Lan tughniya ‘anhum am-waaluhum wa laaa awlaaduhum minal-laahi shay‘aa; ulaaa’ika Aṣhaabun-Naari hum feehaa khaalidoon.

لَنْ تُغْنِيَ عَنْهُمْ اَمْوَالُهُمْ وَلَا اَوْلَادُهُمْ مِّنَ اللهِ شَيْئًا ۚ اُولٰٓئِكَ اَصْحٰبُ النَّارِ ۚ هُمْ فِيْهَا خٰلِدُوْنَ ۝

18. On the Day when Allah will resurrect them all together, they will swear to Him as they swore to you and they will think that they have a good case, but they are certainly liars.

18. Yawma yab‘asuhumul-laahu jamee‘an fa-yaḥlifoona lahoo kamaa yaḥlifoona lakum wa yaḥsaboona annahum ‘alaa shay’; alaaa innahum humul-kaaziboon.

يَوْمَ يَبْعَثُهُمُ اللهُ جَمِيْعًا فَيَحْلِفُوْنَ لَهٗ كَمَا يَحْلِفُوْنَ لَكُمْ وَ يَحْسَبُوْنَ اَنَّهُمْ عَلٰى شَيْءٍ ۚ اَلَآ اِنَّهُمْ هُمُ الْكٰذِبُوْنَ ۝

19. Satan has dominated them and has made them forget the guidance of Allah. They are Satan's party and the party of Satan will certainly suffer a great loss.

19. Istaḥwaza ‘alayhimush-Shayṭaanu fa-ansaahum zikral-laah; ulaaa’ika ḥizbush-Shayṭaan; alaaa inna ḥizbash-Shayṭaani humul-khaasiroon.

اِسْتَحْوَذَ عَلَيْهِمُ الشَّيْطٰنُ فَاَنْسٰهُمْ ذِكْرَ اللهِ ۚ اُولٰٓئِكَ حِزْبُ الشَّيْطٰنِ ۚ اَلَآ اِنَّ حِزْبَ الشَّيْطٰنِ هُمُ الْخٰسِرُوْنَ ۝

20. Disgrace will strike those who oppose Allah and His Messenger.

20. Innal-lazeena yuḥaaad-doonal-laaha wa Rasoolahooo ulaaa’ika fil azalleen.

اِنَّ الَّذِيْنَ يُحَآدُّوْنَ اللهَ وَرَسُوْلَهٗ اُولٰٓئِكَ فِي الْاَذَلِّيْنَ ۝

21. Allah has decreed, "I and My Messenger shall certainly triumph." Allah is All-powerful and Majestic.

21. Katabal-laahu la-aghli-banna anaa wa Rusulee; innal-laaha Qawiyyun ‘Azeez.

كَتَبَ اللهُ لَاَغْلِبَنَّ اَنَا وَرُسُلِيْ ۚ اِنَّ اللهَ قَوِيٌّ عَزِيْزٌ ۝

22. You will not find any people of faith in Allah and the Day of Judgment who would establish friendship with those who oppose Allah and His Messenger, even if it would be in the interest of their fathers, sons, brothers, and kinsmen. Allah has established faith in their hearts and supported them by a Spirit (Ruh Al-Qudus) from Himself.

He will admit them in Paradise wherein streams flow, to live therein forever. Allah is pleased with them and they are pleased with Allah. These are members of the party of Allah and the party of Allah

22. Laa tajidu qawmañy-yu’mi-noona billaahi wal-Yawmil-Aakhiri yuwaaaddoona man ḥaaaddal-laaha wa Rasoolahoo wa law kaanooo aabaaa’ahum aw abnaaa’ahum aw ikhwaa-nahum aw ‘asheeratahum; ulaaa’ika kataba fee quloobihi-mul-eemaana wa ayyadahum biroohim-minhu wa yudkhilu-hum Jannaatin tajree min taḥtihal-anhaaru khaalideena feehaa; radiyallaahu ‘anhum wa radoo ‘anh; ulaaa’ika ḥizbul-

لَا تَجِدُ قَوْمًا يُّؤْمِنُوْنَ بِاللهِ وَالْيَوْمِ الْاٰخِرِ يُوَآدُّوْنَ مَنْ حَآدَّ اللهَ وَ رَسُوْلَهٗ وَلَوْ كَانُوْا اٰبَآءَهُمْ اَوْ اَبْنَآءَهُمْ اَوْ اِخْوَانَهُمْ اَوْ عَشِيْرَتَهُمْ ۚ اُولٰٓئِكَ كَتَبَ فِيْ قُلُوْبِهِمُ الْاِيْمَانَ وَاَيَّدَهُمْ بِرُوْحٍ مِّنْهُ ۚ وَيُدْخِلُهُمْ جَنّٰتٍ تَجْرِيْ مِنْ تَحْتِهَا الْاَنْهٰرُ خٰلِدِيْنَ فِيْهَا ۚ رَضِيَ اللهُ عَنْهُمْ وَرَضُوْا عَنْهُ ۚ اُولٰٓئِكَ حِزْبُ

will certainly have everlasting happiness.

Al-Hashr, The Exile (59)

In the Name of Allah, the Beneficent, the Merciful.

1. All that is in the heavens and the earth glorifies Allah. He is the Majestic and All-wise.

2. It is He who drove the unbelievers among the followers of the Book (Torah) out of their homes (in the Arabian Peninsula) as soon as they were surrounded. You did not think that they would leave their homes and they thought that their fortresses would save them from Allah. The decree of Allah came upon them in a way that even they did not expect. He caused such terror to enter their hearts that they started to destroy their own homes by their own hands and by those of the believers. People of vision, learn from this a lesson.

3. Had Allah not decreed exile for them, He certainly would have punished them (in some other way). In this life and in the next life they would have suffered the torment of hellfire.

4. This is because they opposed Allah and His Messenger and whoever opposes Allah should know that Allah's retribution is severe.

5. All the productive palm trees (of the Jews hostile to you) which you cut down or left untouched were by the permission of Allah to bring disgrace upon the evil-doers.

6. Since you did not have to exhaust your horses and camels (or even fight), Allah granted to His Messenger their property. Allah gives authority to His Messenger over whomever He wants. Allah has power over all things.

laah; alaaa inna ḥizbal-laahi humul-mufliḥoon.

Sûrat al-Ḥashr-59

(Revealed at Madinah)

Bismillaahir Raḥmaanir Raḥeem

1. Sabbaḥa lillaahi maa fissa-maawaati wa maa fil-arḍi wa Huwal-'Azeezul-Ḥakeem.

2. Huwal-lazeee akhrajal-lazeena kafaroo min Ahlil-Kitaabi min diyaarihim li-awwalil-Ḥashr; maa ẓanantum añy-yakhrujoo wa ẓannooo annahum maa ni'atuhum ḥuṣoonuhum minal-laahi fa-ataahumul-laahu min ḥaysu lam yaḥtasiboo wa qazafa fee quloobihimur-ru'b; yukhriboona buyootahum bi-aydeehim wa aydil-mu'mineena fa'tabiroo yaaa ulil-abṣaar.

3. Wa law laaa an katabal-laahu 'alayhimul-jalaaa'a la'az-zabahum fid-dunyaa wa lahum fil-Aakhirati 'azaabun-Naar.

4. Zaalika bi-annahum shaaaq-qul-laaha wa Rasoolahoo wa mañy-yushaaaqqil-laaha fa-innal-laaha shadeedul-'iqaab.

5. Maa qaṭa'tum mil-leenatin aw taraktumoohaa qaaa'imatan 'alaaa uṣoolihaa fabi-iznil-laahi wa liyukhziyal-faasiqeen.

6. Wa maaa afaaa'al-laahu 'alaa Rasoolihee minhum famaaa awjaftum 'alayhi min khayliñw-wa laa rikaabiñw-wa laakinnal-laaha yusalliṭu Rusulahoo 'alaa mañy-yashaaa'; wallaahu 'alaa kulli shay'in Qadeer.

اللّٰهِ ۭ اَلَآ اِنَّ حِزْبَ اللّٰهِ هُمُ الْمُفْلِحُوْنَ ﴿٢٢﴾ ع

(٥٩) سُوْرَةُ الْحَشْرِ مَدَنِيَّةٌ (١٠١)

اٰيَاتُهَا ٢٤ بِسْمِ اللّٰهِ الرَّحْمٰنِ الرَّحِيْمِ رُكُوْعَاتُهَا ٣

سَبَّحَ لِلّٰهِ مَا فِي السَّمٰوٰتِ وَمَا فِي
الْاَرْضِ ۚ وَهُوَ الْعَزِيْزُ الْحَكِيْمُ ﴿١﴾
هُوَ الَّذِيْٓ اَخْرَجَ الَّذِيْنَ كَفَرُوْا مِنْ
اَهْلِ الْكِتٰبِ مِنْ دِيَارِهِمْ لِاَوَّلِ
الْحَشْرِ ۭ مَا ظَنَنْتُمْ اَنْ يَّخْرُجُوْا وَظَنُّوْٓا
اَنَّهُمْ مَّانِعَتُهُمْ حُصُوْنُهُمْ مِّنَ اللّٰهِ
فَاَتٰىهُمُ اللّٰهُ مِنْ حَيْثُ لَمْ يَحْتَسِبُوْا
وَقَذَفَ فِيْ قُلُوْبِهِمُ الرُّعْبَ يُخْرِبُوْنَ
بُيُوْتَهُمْ بِاَيْدِيْهِمْ وَاَيْدِي الْمُؤْمِنِيْنَ ۤ
فَاعْتَبِرُوْا يٰٓاُولِي الْاَبْصَارِ ﴿٢﴾
وَلَوْلَآ اَنْ كَتَبَ اللّٰهُ عَلَيْهِمُ الْجَلَاۗءَ
لَعَذَّبَهُمْ فِي الدُّنْيَا ۭ وَلَهُمْ فِي الْاٰخِرَةِ
عَذَابُ النَّارِ ﴿٣﴾
ذٰلِكَ بِاَنَّهُمْ شَاۗقُّوا اللّٰهَ وَرَسُوْلَهٗ ۚ
وَمَنْ يُّشَاۗقِّ اللّٰهَ فَاِنَّ اللّٰهَ شَدِيْدُ
الْعِقَابِ ﴿٤﴾
مَا قَطَعْتُمْ مِّنْ لِّيْنَةٍ اَوْ تَرَكْتُمُوْهَا
قَاۗىِٕمَةً عَلٰٓي اُصُوْلِهَا فَبِاِذْنِ اللّٰهِ وَ
لِيُخْزِيَ الْفٰسِقِيْنَ ﴿٥﴾
وَمَآ اَفَاۗءَ اللّٰهُ عَلٰي رَسُوْلِهٖ مِنْهُمْ فَمَآ
اَوْجَفْتُمْ عَلَيْهِ مِنْ خَيْلٍ وَّلَا رِكَابٍ
وَّلٰكِنَّ اللّٰهَ يُسَلِّطُ رُسُلَهٗ عَلٰي مَنْ
يَّشَاۗءُ ۭ وَاللّٰهُ عَلٰي كُلِّ شَيْءٍ قَدِيْرٌ ﴿٦﴾

ع ٣ ۹

وقف النبي صلى الله عليه وآله وسلم ١٢

7. Whatever Allah grants to His Messenger (out of the property) of the people of the towns, belongs to Allah, the Messenger, the kinsfolk, the orphans, the destitute and those who may become needy while on a journey, so that it will not circulate only in the hands of rich ones among you. Take only what the Messenger gives to you and desist from what he forbids you. Have fear of Allah; Allah is severe in His retribution.

7. Maaa afaaa'al-laahu 'alaa Rasoolihee min ahlil-quraa falillaahi wa lir-Rasooli wa lizil-qurbaa walyataamaa walmasaakeeni wabnissabeeli kay laa yakoona doolatam baynal-aghniyaaa'i minkum; wa maaa aataakumur-Rasoolu fakhuzoohu wa maa nahaakum 'anhu fantahoo; wattaqul-laaha innal-laaha shadeedul-'iqaab.

مَآ أَفَآءَ اللّٰهُ عَلٰى رَسُوْلِهٖ مِنْ أَهْلِ
الْقُرٰى فَلِلّٰهِ وَلِلرَّسُوْلِ وَلِذِى الْقُرْبٰى
وَالْيَتٰمٰى وَالْمَسٰكِيْنِ وَابْنِ السَّبِيْلِ
كَىْ لَا يَكُوْنَ دُوْلَةًۢ بَيْنَ الْأَغْنِيَآءِ
مِنْكُمْ ۚ وَمَآ اٰتٰىكُمُ الرَّسُوْلُ فَخُذُوْهُ
وَمَا نَهٰىكُمْ عَنْهُ فَانْتَهُوْا ۚ وَاتَّقُوا وقف لازم
اللّٰهَ ۖ إِنَّ اللّٰهَ شَدِيْدُ الْعِقَابِ ۝٧

8. The poor immigrants who were deprived of their homes and property, who seek favors and pleasures from Allah, and who help Him and His Messenger will also have (a share in the said property). These people are the truthful ones.

8. Lilfuqaraaa'il-Muhaajireenal-lazeena ukhrijoo min diyaarihim wa amwaalihim yabtaghoona faḍlam-minal-laahi wa riḍwaanañw-wa yanṣuroonal-laaha wa Rasoolah; ulaaa'ika humuṣ-ṣaadiqoon.

لِلْفُقَرَآءِ الْمُهٰجِرِيْنَ الَّذِيْنَ أُخْرِجُوْا
مِنْ دِيَارِهِمْ وَأَمْوَالِهِمْ يَبْتَغُوْنَ
فَضْلًا مِّنَ اللّٰهِ وَرِضْوَانًا وَّ
يَنْصُرُوْنَ اللّٰهَ وَرَسُوْلَهٗ ۚ أُولٰٓئِكَ
هُمُ الصّٰدِقُوْنَ ۝٨

9. Those who established a community center and embraced the faith before the arrival of the immigrants love those who have come to their town. They are not jealous of what is given to the immigrants. They give preference to them over themselves - even concerning the things that they themselves urgently need. Whoever controls his greed will have everlasting happiness.

9. Wallazeena tabawwa'ud-daara wal-eemaana min qablihim yuḥibboona man haajara ilayhim wa laa yajidoona fee ṣudoorihim ḥaajatam-mimmaaa ootoo wa yu'siroona 'alaa anfusihim wa law kaana bihim khaṣaaṣah; wa mañy-yooqa shuḥḥa nafsihee fa-ulaaa'ika humul-mufliḥoon.

وَالَّذِيْنَ تَبَوَّءُو الدَّارَ وَالْإِيْمَانَ
مِنْ قَبْلِهِمْ يُحِبُّوْنَ مَنْ هَاجَرَ
إِلَيْهِمْ وَلَا يَجِدُوْنَ فِىْ صُدُوْرِهِمْ
حَاجَةً مِّمَّآ أُوْتُوْا وَيُؤْثِرُوْنَ عَلٰٓى
أَنْفُسِهِمْ وَلَوْ كَانَ بِهِمْ خَصَاصَةٌ ۚ
وَمَنْ يُّوْقَ شُحَّ نَفْسِهٖ فَأُولٰٓئِكَ
هُمُ الْمُفْلِحُوْنَ ۝٩

10. Those who migrated later (to Medina) say, "Lord, forgive us and our brothers who preceded us in the faith, and clear our hearts of any ill will against the believers. Lord, You are Compassionate and All-merciful."

10. Wallazeena Jaa'oo mim ba'dihim yaqooloona Rabbanagh-fir lanaa wa li-ikhwaaninal-lazeena sabaqoonaa bil-eemaani wa laa taj'al fee quloobinaa ghillallil-lazeena aamanoo Rabbanaaa innaka Ra'oofur-Raheem.

وَالَّذِيْنَ جَآءُوْ مِنْۢ بَعْدِهِمْ يَقُوْلُوْنَ
رَبَّنَا اغْفِرْ لَنَا وَلِإِخْوَانِنَا الَّذِيْنَ
سَبَقُوْنَا بِالْإِيْمَانِ وَلَا تَجْعَلْ فِىْ
قُلُوْبِنَا غِلًّا لِّلَّذِيْنَ اٰمَنُوْا رَبَّنَآ إِنَّكَ
رَءُوْفٌ رَّحِيْمٌ ۝١٠ الربع

11. Did you not see the hypocrites who say to their disbelieving brothers among the People of the Book, "If you are

11. Alam tara ilal-lazeena naafaqoo yaqooloona li-ikhwaanihimul-lazeena kafaroo min

أَلَمْ تَرَ إِلَى الَّذِيْنَ نَافَقُوْا يَقُوْلُوْنَ
لِإِخْوَانِهِمُ الَّذِيْنَ كَفَرُوْا مِنْ

driven out, we shall, also, leave the town with you and we shall never obey whoever seeks to harm you; if you are attacked, we shall help you"? Allah testifies that they are liars.

Ahlil-Kitaabi la'in ukhrijtum lanakhrujanna ma'akum wa laa nuṭee'u feekum aḥadan abadañw-wa-in qootiltum lananṣuran-nakum wallaahu yashhadu innahum lakaa-ziboon.

اَهۡلِ الۡكِتٰبِ لَـئِنۡ اُخۡرِجۡتُمۡ لَنَخۡرُجَنَّ
مَعَكُمۡ وَلَا نُطِيۡعُ فِيۡكُمۡ اَحَدًا
اَبَدًا ۙ وَّاِنۡ قُوۡتِلۡتُمۡ لَنَـنۡصُرَنَّكُمۡ ؕ
وَاللّٰهُ يَشۡهَدُ اِنَّهُمۡ لَـكٰذِبُوۡنَ ﴿۱۱﴾

12. If they were to be expelled, they would not go with them. If they were to be attacked they would not help them. Even if they were to help them, they would run away from the battle and leave them helpless.

12. La'in ukhrijoo laa yakhru-joona ma'ahum wa la'in qoo-tiloo laa yanṣuroonahum wa la'in naṣaroohum la-yuwallun-nal-adbaar; summa laa yunṣa-roon.

لَـئِنۡ اُخۡرِجُوۡا لَا يَخۡرُجُوۡنَ مَعَهُمۡ ۚ
وَلَـئِنۡ قُوۡتِلُوۡا لَا يَنۡصُرُوۡنَهُمۡ ۚ وَلَـئِنۡ
نَّصَرُوۡهُمۡ لَيُوَلُّنَّ الۡاَدۡبَارَ ۙ ثُمَّ لَا
يُنۡصَرُوۡنَ ﴿۱۲﴾

13. They are more afraid of you than of Allah. They are a people who lack understanding.

13. La-antum ashaddu rahba-tan fee ṣudoorihim minal-laah; zaalika bi-annahum qawmul-laa yafqahoon.

لَاَنۡتُمۡ اَشَدُّ رَهۡبَةً فِىۡ صُدُوۡرِهِمۡ مِّنَ
اللّٰهِ ؕ ذٰلِكَ بِاَنَّهُمۡ قَوۡمٌ لَّا يَفۡقَهُوۡنَ ﴿۱۳﴾

14. They will not fight you united except with the protection of fortified towns or from behind walls. They are strong among themselves. You think that they are united, but in fact, their hearts are divided. They are a people who have no understanding.

14. Laa yuqaatiloonakum ja-mee'an illaa fee quram-muḥaṣ-ṣanatin aw miñw-waraaa'i judur; ba-suhum baynahum shadeed; taḥsabuhum jamee-'añw-wa quloobuhum shattaa; zaalika bi-annahum qawmul-laa ya'qiloon.

لَا يُقَاتِلُوۡنَكُمۡ جَمِيۡعًا اِلَّا فِىۡ قُرًى
مُّحَصَّنَةٍ اَوۡ مِنۡ وَّرَآءِ جُدُرٍ ؕ
بَاۡسُهُمۡ بَيۡنَهُمۡ شَدِيۡدٌ ؕ تَحۡسَبُهُمۡ
جَمِيۡعًا وَّقُلُوۡبُهُمۡ شَتّٰى ؕ ذٰلِكَ
بِاَنَّهُمۡ قَوۡمٌ لَّا يَعۡقِلُوۡنَ ﴿۱۴﴾

15. They are like those who, a short time before, suffered the consequences of their deeds. They, too, will suffer a painful torment.

15. Kamasalil-lazeena min qablihim qareeban zaaqoo wabaala amrihim wa lahum 'azaabun aleem.

كَمَثَلِ الَّذِيۡنَ مِنۡ قَبۡلِهِمۡ قَرِيۡبًا ذَاقُوۡا
وَبَالَ اَمۡرِهِمۡ ۚ وَلَهُمۡ عَذَابٌ اَلِيۡمٌ ﴿۱۵﴾

16. They are like Satan who said to people, "Reject the faith," but when the people rejected the faith he said, "I have nothing to do with you. I fear the Lord of the universe."

16. Kamasalish-Shayṭaani iz qaala lil insaanik-fur falammaa kafara qaala innee bareee'um-minka inneee akhaaful-laaha Rabbal-'aalameen.

كَمَثَلِ الشَّيۡطٰنِ اِذۡ قَالَ لِلۡاِنۡسَانِ
اكۡفُرۡ ۚ فَلَمَّا كَفَرَ قَالَ اِنِّىۡ بَرِىۡٓءٌ مِّنۡكَ
اِنِّىۡۤ اَخَافُ اللّٰهَ رَبَّ الۡعٰلَمِيۡنَ ﴿۱۶﴾

17. The fate of both of them will be hellfire wherein they will live forever. Thus will be the recompense for the unjust.

17. Fakaana 'aaqibatahumaaa annahumaa fin-Naari khaali-dayni feehaa; wa zaalika jazaaa-'uẓ-ẓaalimeen.

فَكَانَ عَاقِبَتَهُمَاۤ اَنَّهُمَا فِى النَّارِ
خَالِدَيۡنِ فِيۡهَا ؕ وَذٰلِكَ جَزٰٓؤُا
الظّٰلِمِيۡنَ ﴿۱۷﴾ ع ٥

18. Believers, have fear of Allah. A soul must see what it has done for the future. Have fear of Allah for Allah is All-aware of what you do.

18. Yaaa ayyuhal-lazeena aamanut-taqul-laaha waltanẓur nafsum-maa qaddamat lighad; wattaqul-laah; innal-laaha Khabeerum bimaa ta'maloon.

يٰۤاَيُّهَا الَّذِيۡنَ اٰمَنُوا اتَّقُوا اللّٰهَ
وَلۡتَنۡظُرۡ نَفۡسٌ مَّا قَدَّمَتۡ لِغَدٍ ۚ
وَاتَّقُوا اللّٰهَ ؕ اِنَّ اللّٰهَ خَبِيۡرٌۢ بِمَا

تَعۡمَلُوۡنَ ﴿١٨﴾

19. Do not be like those who forget about Allah. He will make them forget themselves. These are the sinful people.

19. Wa laa takoonoo kallazeena nasul-laaha fa-ansaahum anfusahum; ulaaa'ika humul-faasiqoon.

وَلَا تَكُوۡنُوۡا كَالَّذِيۡنَ نَسُوا اللّٰهَ فَاَنۡسٰهُمۡ
اَنۡفُسَهُمۡ ؕ اُولٰٓئِكَ هُمُ الۡفٰسِقُوۡنَ ﴿١٩﴾

20. The people of Paradise and hell are not alike; the people of Paradise are the successful ones.

20. Laa yastaweee Aṣḥaabun-Naari wa Aṣḥaabul-Jannah; Aṣḥaabul-Jannati humul-faaa'izoon.

لَا يَسۡتَوِىۡۤ اَصۡحٰبُ النَّارِ وَاَصۡحٰبُ
الۡجَنَّةِ ؕ اَصۡحٰبُ الۡجَنَّةِ هُمُ الۡفَآئِزُوۡنَ ﴿٢٠﴾

21. Had We sent down this Quran on a mountain, you would have seen it humbled and rent asunder for fear of Allah. These are parables which We tell to people so that perhaps they will think.

21. Law anzalnaa haazal-Qur-aana 'alaa jabalil-lara-aytahoo khaashi'am-muta-ṣaddi'am-min khashyatillaah; wa tilkal-amsaalu naḍribuhaa linnaasi la'allahum yatafakkaroon.

لَوۡ اَنۡزَلۡنَا هٰذَا الۡقُرۡاٰنَ عَلٰى جَبَلٍ
لَّرَاَيۡتَهٗ خَاشِعًا مُّتَصَدِّعًا مِّنۡ
خَشۡيَةِ اللّٰهِ ؕ وَتِلۡكَ الۡاَمۡثَالُ
نَضۡرِبُهَا لِلنَّاسِ لَعَلَّهُمۡ يَتَفَكَّرُوۡنَ ﴿٢١﴾

22. He is Allah, the only Lord, Who knows the unseen and the seen. He is the Beneficent and All-merciful One.

22. Huwal-laahul-lazee laaa Ilaaha illaa Hoo; 'Aalimul-Ghaybi wash-shahaadah; Huwar-Raḥmaanur-Raḥeem.

هُوَ اللّٰهُ الَّذِىۡ لَاۤ اِلٰهَ اِلَّا هُوَ ۚ
عٰلِمُ الۡغَيۡبِ وَالشَّهَادَةِ ۚ هُوَ
الرَّحۡمٰنُ الرَّحِيۡمُ ﴿٢٢﴾

23. He is Allah, the only Lord, the King, the Holy, Al-Qudus (free from things that cause ignorance) the Peace, the Forgiver, the Watchful Guardian, the Majestic, the Dominant, and the Exalted. Allah is free from all defects of having any partner.

23. Huwal-laahul-lazee laaa Ilaaha illa Hoo; al-Malikul-Quddoosus-Salaamul-Mu'minul-Muhayminul-'Azeezul-Jabbaarul-Mutakabbir; Subḥaanal-laahi 'ammaa yushrikoon.

هُوَ اللّٰهُ الَّذِىۡ لَاۤ اِلٰهَ اِلَّا هُوَ ۚ اَلۡمَلِكُ
الۡقُدُّوۡسُ السَّلٰمُ الۡمُؤۡمِنُ الۡمُهَيۡمِنُ
الۡعَزِيۡزُ الۡجَبَّارُ الۡمُتَكَبِّرُ ؕ سُبۡحٰنَ
اللّٰهِ عَمَّا يُشۡرِكُوۡنَ ﴿٢٣﴾

24. He is Allah, the Creator, the Designer, the Modeler, and to Him belong all beautiful names. All that is in the heavens and the earth glorify Him. He is All-majestic and All-wise.

24. Huwal-laahul-Khaaliqul-Baari'ul-Muṣawwiru lahul-Asmaaa'ul-Ḥusnaa; yusabbiḥu lahoo maa fissamaawaati wal-arḍi wa Huwal-'Azeezul-Ḥakeem.

هُوَ اللّٰهُ الۡخَالِقُ الۡبَارِئُ الۡمُصَوِّرُ
لَهُ الۡاَسۡمَآءُ الۡحُسۡنٰى ؕ يُسَبِّحُ لَهٗ
مَا فِى السَّمٰوٰتِ وَالۡاَرۡضِ ۚ وَهُوَ
الۡعَزِيۡزُ الۡحَكِيۡمُ ﴿٢٤﴾ ع ٣ ٧ ٦

Al-Mumtahinah, The Females Verified (60)

In the Name of Allah, the Beneficent, the Merciful.

Sûrat al-Mumtaḥinah-60

(Revealed at Madaniyyah)

Bismillaahir Raḥmaanir Raheem

(٦٠) سُوۡرَةُ الۡمُمۡتَحِنَةِ مَدَنِيَّةٌ (٩١)

اٰياتها ١٣ بِسۡمِ اللّٰهِ الرَّحۡمٰنِ الرَّحِيۡمِ ركوعاتها ٢

1. Believers, do not choose My enemies and your own enemies for friends, and offer them strong love. They have rejected the Truth which has come to you and have expelled the Messenger and you from your homes because of your belief in

1. Yaaa ayyuhal-lazeena aamanoo laa tattakhizoo 'aduwwee wa 'aduwwakum awliyaaa'a tulqoona ilayhim bilmawaddati wa qad kafaroo bimaa jaaa'akum minal ḥaqq; yukhrijoonar-

يٰۤاَيُّهَا الَّذِيۡنَ اٰمَنُوۡا لَا تَتَّخِذُوۡا
عَدُوِّىۡ وَعَدُوَّكُمۡ اَوۡلِيَآءَ تُلۡقُوۡنَ
اِلَيۡهِمۡ بِالۡمَوَدَّةِ وَقَدۡ كَفَرُوۡا بِمَا
جَآءَكُمۡ مِّنَ الۡحَقِّ ۚ يُخۡرِجُوۡنَ

Allah, your Lord. When you go to fight for My cause and seek My pleasure, you secretly express your love of them. I know best what you reveal or conceal. Whichever of you does this has indeed gone astray from the right path.

Rasoola wa iyyaakum an tu'minoo billahi Rabbikum in kuntum kharajtum jihaadan fee sabeelee wabtighaaa'a marḍaatee; tusirroona ilayhim bilmawaddati wa anaa a'lamu bimaaa akhfaytum wa maaa a'lantum; wa mañy-yaf'alhu minkum faqad ḍalla Sawaaa'as-Sabeel.

الرَّسُولَ وَإِيَّاكُمْ أَنْ تُؤْمِنُوا بِاللَّهِ
رَبِّكُمْ إِنْ كُنْتُمْ خَرَجْتُمْ جِهَادًا فِي
سَبِيلِي وَابْتِغَاءَ مَرْضَاتِي تُسِرُّونَ
إِلَيْهِمْ بِالْمَوَدَّةِ وَأَنَا أَعْلَمُ بِمَا
أَخْفَيْتُمْ وَمَا أَعْلَنْتُمْ وَمَنْ يَفْعَلْهُ
مِنْكُمْ فَقَدْ ضَلَّ سَوَاءَ السَّبِيلِ ١

2. If they find an opportunity to turn against you, they will become your enemies and will stretch out their hands and tongues at you with evil intent. They would love to see you turn away from your faith.

2. Iñy-yas̲qafookum yakoonoo lakum a'daaa'añw-wa yabsuṭooo ilaykum aydiyahum wa alsinatahum bissooo'i wa waddoo law takfuroon.

إِنْ يَثْقَفُوكُمْ يَكُونُوا لَكُمْ أَعْدَاءً
وَيَبْسُطُوا إِلَيْكُمْ أَيْدِيَهُمْ وَأَلْسِنَتَهُمْ
بِالسُّوءِ وَوَدُّوا لَوْ تَكْفُرُونَ ٢

3. Your relatives and children will never be of any benefit to you on the Day of Judgment. Allah will separate you from them. He is All-aware of what you do.

3. Lan tanfa'akum arḥaamukum wa laaa awlaadukum; Yawmal-Qiyaamati yafṣilu baynakum; wallaahu bimaa ta'maloona Baṣeer.

لَنْ تَنْفَعَكُمْ أَرْحَامُكُمْ وَلَا أَوْلَادُكُمْ
يَوْمَ الْقِيَامَةِ يَفْصِلُ بَيْنَكُمْ وَاللَّهُ
بِمَا تَعْمَلُونَ بَصِيرٌ ٣

معانقہ ۱۲ اتباع الوقف علی القیمۃ عند المتاخرین ۱۲۰

4. Abraham and those with him are the best examples for you to follow. They told the people, "We have nothing to do with you and with those whom you worship besides Allah. We have rejected you. Enmity and hatred will separate us forever unless you believe in Allah alone." Abraham told his father, "I shall ask forgiveness for you only, but I shall not be of the least help to you

4. Qad kaanat lakum uswatun ḥasanatun feee Ibraaheema wallaz̲eena ma'ahoo iz̲ qaaloo liqawmihim innaa bura'aaa'u minkum wa mimmaa ta'budoona min doonil-laahi kafarnaa bikum wa badaa baynanaa wa baynakumul-'adaawatu wal-baghḍaaa'u abadan ḥattaa tu'minoo billaahi waḥdahooo illaa qawla Ibraaheema liabeehi la-astaghfiranna laka wa maaa amliku laka minal-laahi min shay'in Rabbanaa 'alayka tawakkalnaa wa ilayka anabnaa wa ilaykal-maṣeer.

قَدْ كَانَتْ لَكُمْ أُسْوَةٌ حَسَنَةٌ فِي
إِبْرَاهِيمَ وَالَّذِينَ مَعَهُ إِذْ قَالُوا
لِقَوْمِهِمْ إِنَّا بُرَآءُ مِنْكُمْ وَمِمَّا
تَعْبُدُونَ مِنْ دُونِ اللَّهِ كَفَرْنَا بِكُمْ
وَبَدَا بَيْنَنَا وَبَيْنَكُمُ الْعَدَاوَةُ
وَالْبَغْضَاءُ أَبَدًا حَتَّى تُؤْمِنُوا بِاللَّهِ
وَحْدَهُ إِلَّا قَوْلَ إِبْرَاهِيمَ لِأَبِيهِ
لَأَسْتَغْفِرَنَّ لَكَ وَمَا أَمْلِكُ لَكَ مِنَ
اللَّهِ مِنْ شَيْءٍ رَبَّنَا عَلَيْكَ تَوَكَّلْنَا
وَإِلَيْكَ أَنَبْنَا وَإِلَيْكَ الْمَصِيرُ ٤

5. They prayed, "Lord, we have trust in You, turned to You in repentance, and to You we shall all return. Lord, save us from the evil intentions of the unbelievers. Our Lord, forgive us. You are Majestic and All-wise."

5. Rabbanaa laa taj'alnaa fitnatal-lillaz̲eena kafaroo waghfir lanaa Rabbanaa innaka Antal-'Azeezul-Ḥakeem.

رَبَّنَا لَا تَجْعَلْنَا فِتْنَةً لِلَّذِينَ
كَفَرُوا وَاغْفِرْ لَنَا رَبَّنَا إِنَّكَ
أَنْتَ الْعَزِيزُ الْحَكِيمُ ٥

6. They are the best examples for those who have hope in Allah

6. Laqad kaana lakum feehim uswatun

لَقَدْ كَانَ لَكُمْ فِيهِمْ أُسْوَةٌ

and the Day of Judgment. Whoever turns away should know that Allah is Self-sufficient and Praiseworthy.

ḥasanatul-liman kaana yarjul-laaha wal-Yawmal-Aakhir; wa mañy-yatawalla fa-innal-laaha Huwal-Ghaniyyul-Ḥameed.

حَسَنَةٌ لِّمَنْ كَانَ يَرْجُوا اللّٰهَ وَ
الْيَوْمَ الْاٰخِرَ ۭ وَمَنْ يَّتَوَلَّ فَاِنَّ
اللّٰهَ هُوَ الْغَنِيُّ الْحَمِيْدُ ۝٦ ع ١ ٢ ٧

7. Allah will perhaps bring about love between you and those of the unbelievers with whom you were enemies. Allah is All-powerful, All-merciful, and All-forgiving.

7. 'Asal-laahu añy-yaj'ala baynakum wa baynal-lazeena 'aadaytum minhum mawaddah; Wallaahu Qadeer; Wallaahu Ghafoorur-Raḥeem.

عَسَى اللّٰهُ اَنْ يَّجْعَلَ بَيْنَكُمْ وَبَيْنَ
الَّذِيْنَ عَادَيْتُمْ مِّنْهُمْ مَّوَدَّةً ۭ وَ
اللّٰهُ قَدِيْرٌ ۭ وَاللّٰهُ غَفُوْرٌ رَّحِيْمٌ ۝٧

8. Allah does not forbid you to deal kindly and justly with those who did not fight against you about the religion nor did they expel you from your homes. Allah does not love the unjust people.

8. Laa yanhaakumul-laahu 'anil-lazeena lam yuqaati-lookum fid-deeni wa lam yukhrijookum-min diyaarikum an tabarroohum wa tuqsiṭooo ilayhim; innal-laaha yuḥibbul-muqsiṭeen.

لَا يَنْهٰىكُمُ اللّٰهُ عَنِ الَّذِيْنَ لَمْ
يُقَاتِلُوْكُمْ فِي الدِّيْنِ وَلَمْ يُخْرِجُوْكُمْ
مِّنْ دِيَارِكُمْ اَنْ تَبَرُّوْهُمْ وَتُقْسِطُوْٓا
اِلَيْهِمْ ۭ اِنَّ اللّٰهَ يُحِبُّ الْمُقْسِطِيْنَ ۝٨

9. He only forbids you to be friends with those who have fought against you about the religion, expelled you from your homes, or supported others in expelling you. Whoever love these people are unjust.

9. Innamaa yanhaakumul-laahu 'anil-lazeena qaataloo-kum fid-deeni wa akhrajookum min diyaarikum wa ẓaaharoo 'alaa ikhraajikum an tawallaw-hum; wa mañy-yatawallahum fa-ulaaa'ika humuẓ-ẓaalimoon.

اِنَّمَا يَنْهٰىكُمُ اللّٰهُ عَنِ الَّذِيْنَ
قٰتَلُوْكُمْ فِي الدِّيْنِ وَاَخْرَجُوْكُمْ
مِّنْ دِيَارِكُمْ وَظٰهَرُوْا عَلٰٓى
اِخْرَاجِكُمْ اَنْ تَوَلَّوْهُمْ ۚ وَمَنْ
يَّتَوَلَّهُمْ فَاُولٰۗىِٕكَ هُمُ الظّٰلِمُوْنَ ۝٩

10. Believers, when believing immigrant women come to you, test them. Allah knows best about their faith. If you know that they are believers, do not return them to the unbelievers. Such women are not lawful for them and unbelievers are not lawful for such women. Give the unbelievers whatever they have spent (on such women for their dowry). There is no offense for you to marry them if you agree to give them their dowry. Do not hold on to your disbelieving wives; you may get back what you have spent on them for their dowry and the unbelievers may also ask for what they have spent. This is the command of Allah by which He judges you. Allah is All-Knowing and All-Wise.

10. Yaaa ayyuhal-lazeena aamanoo izaa jaaa'akumul-mu'minaatu muhaajiraatin famtaḥinoohunna Allaahu a'lamu bi-eemaanihinna fa-in 'alimtumoohunna mu'mi-naatin falaa tarji'oohunna ilal-kuffaar; laa hunna ḥillul-lahum wa laa hum yaḥilloona lahunna wa aatoohum maaa anfaqoo wa laa junaaḥa 'alaykum an tankiḥoohunna izaaa aatay-tumoohunna ujoorahunna wa laa tumsikoo bi'iṣamil-kawaafiri was'aloo maaa anfaqtum walyas'aloo maaa anfaqoo zaalikum ḥukmul-laahi yaḥkumu baynakum wallaahu 'Aleemun Ḥakeem.

يٰٓاَيُّهَا الَّذِيْنَ اٰمَنُوْٓا اِذَا جَاۗءَكُمُ
الْمُؤْمِنٰتُ مُهٰجِرٰتٍ فَامْتَحِنُوْهُنَّ ۭ
اَللّٰهُ اَعْلَمُ بِاِيْمَانِهِنَّ ۚ فَاِنْ عَلِمْتُمُوْهُنَّ
مُؤْمِنٰتٍ فَلَا تَرْجِعُوْهُنَّ اِلَى الْكُفَّارِ ۭ
لَا هُنَّ حِلٌّ لَّهُمْ وَلَا هُمْ يَحِلُّوْنَ
لَهُنَّ ۭ وَاٰتُوْهُمْ مَّآ اَنْفَقُوْا ۭ وَلَا
جُنَاحَ عَلَيْكُمْ اَنْ تَنْكِحُوْهُنَّ اِذَآ
اٰتَيْتُمُوْهُنَّ اُجُوْرَهُنَّ ۭ وَلَا تُمْسِكُوْا
بِعِصَمِ الْكَوَافِرِ وَسْـَٔـلُوْا مَآ اَنْفَقْتُمْ
وَلْيَسْـَٔـلُوْا مَآ اَنْفَقُوْا ۭ ذٰلِكُمْ حُكْمُ اللّٰهِ ۭ
يَحْكُمُ بَيْنَكُمْ ۭ وَاللّٰهُ عَلِيْمٌ حَكِيْمٌ ۝١٠

11. If your wives go away from you to unbelievers who will not give you back the dowry which you spent on them, allow the Muslims to pay back such dowry from the property of the unbelievers which may come into their hands. Have fear of Allah in whom you believe.

11. Wa in faatakum shay'um-min azwaajikum ilal-kuffaari fa'aaqabtum fa-aatul-laz̲eena z̲ahabat azwaajuhum mis̲la maaa anfaqoo; wattaqul-laahal-laz̲eee antum bihee mu'minoon.

وَاِنْ فَاتَكُمْ شَيْءٌ مِّنْ اَزْوَاجِكُمْ
اِلَى الْكُفَّارِ فَعَاقَبْتُمْ فَاٰتُوا
الَّذِيْنَ ذَهَبَتْ اَزْوَاجُهُمْ مِّثْلَ مَا
اَنْفَقُوْا ؕ وَاتَّقُوا اللّٰهَ الَّذِيْٓ اَنْتُمْ
بِهٖ مُؤْمِنُوْنَ ﴿١١﴾

12. Prophet, when believing women come to you to express their allegiance they must pledge not to consider anything equal to Allah, not to steal, or to commit fornication, not to kill their children, or to bring false charges against anyone (such as ascribing others' children to their husbands), and not to disobey you in lawful matters, accept their pledge, and ask forgiveness for them from Allah. Allah is All-Forgiving and All-Merciful.

12. Yaaa ayyuhan-Nabiyyu iz̲aa jaaa'akal-mu'minaatu yu-baayi'naka 'alaaa allaa yushrik-na billaahi shay'añw-wa laa yasriqna wa laa yazneena wa laa yaqtulna awlaadahunna wa laa ya-teena bibuhtaaniñy-yaftaree-nahoo bayna aydeehinna wa arjulihinna wa laa ya'ṣeenaka fee ma'roofin fabaayi'hunna wastaghfir lahunnal-laaha innal-laaha Ghafoorur Raḥeem.

يٰۤاَيُّهَا النَّبِيُّ اِذَا جَآءَكَ الْمُؤْمِنٰتُ
يُبَايِعْنَكَ عَلٰٓى اَنْ لَّا يُشْرِكْنَ
بِاللّٰهِ شَيْـًٔا وَّلَا يَسْرِقْنَ وَلَا يَزْنِيْنَ
وَلَا يَقْتُلْنَ اَوْلَادَهُنَّ وَلَا يَاْتِيْنَ
بِبُهْتَانٍ يَّفْتَرِيْنَهٗ بَيْنَ اَيْدِيْهِنَّ وَ
اَرْجُلِهِنَّ وَلَا يَعْصِيْنَكَ فِيْ مَعْرُوْفٍ
فَبَايِعْهُنَّ وَاسْتَغْفِرْ لَهُنَّ اللّٰهَ ؕ اِنَّ
اللّٰهَ غَفُوْرٌ رَّحِيْمٌ ﴿١٢﴾

13. Believers, do not establish friendship with the people who have become subject to the wrath of Allah. They do not have any hope in the life to come, just as the unbelievers have no hope in those who are in their graves.

13. Yaaa ayyuhal-laz̲eena aamanoo laa tatawallaw qawman ghaḍibal-laahu 'alayhim qad ya'isoo minal-Aakhirati kamaa ya'isal-kuffaaru min Aṣḥaabil-quboor.

يٰۤاَيُّهَا الَّذِيْنَ اٰمَنُوْا لَا تَتَوَلَّوْا قَوْمًا
غَضِبَ اللّٰهُ عَلَيْهِمْ قَدْ يَئِسُوْا مِنَ
الْاٰخِرَةِ كَمَا يَئِسَ الْكُفَّارُ مِنْ
اَصْحٰبِ الْقُبُوْرِ ﴿١٣﴾

Al-Saff, The Ranks (61)

In the Name of Allah, the Beneficent, the Merciful.

Sûrat aṣ-Ṣaff-61

(Revealed at Madinah)

Bismillaahir Raḥmaanir Raḥeem

(٦١) سُوْرَةُ الصَّفِّ مَدَنِيَّةٌ (١٠٩)

اٰيَاتُهَا ١٤ — بِسْمِ اللّٰهِ الرَّحْمٰنِ الرَّحِيْمِ — رُكُوْعَاتُهَا ٢

1. All that is in the heavens and the earth glorifies Allah. He is the Majestic and All-Wise.

1. Sabbaḥa lillaahi maa fis-samaawaati wa maa fil-arḍi wa Huwal-'Azeezul-Ḥakeem.

سَبَّحَ لِلّٰهِ مَا فِي السَّمٰوٰتِ وَمَا فِي الْاَرْضِ ۚ
وَهُوَ الْعَزِيْزُ الْحَكِيْمُ ﴿١﴾

2. Believers, why do you preach what you do not practice?

2. Yaaa ayyuhal-laz̲eena aamanoo lima taqooloona maa laa taf'aloon.

يٰۤاَيُّهَا الَّذِيْنَ اٰمَنُوْا لِمَ تَقُوْلُوْنَ
مَا لَا تَفْعَلُوْنَ ﴿٢﴾

3. It is most hateful in the sight of Allah if you say something and do not practice it.

3. Kabura maqtan 'indal-laahi an taqooloo maa laa taf'aloon.

كَبُرَ مَقْتًا عِنْدَ اللّٰهِ اَنْ تَقُوْلُوْا
مَا لَا تَفْعَلُوْنَ ﴿٣﴾

4. Allah loves those who fight for His cause in ranks firm as an

4. Innal-laaha yuḥibbul-laz̲eena yuqaatiloona

اِنَّ اللّٰهَ يُحِبُّ الَّذِيْنَ يُقَاتِلُوْنَ

unbreakable wall.

fee sabeelihee ṣaffan ka-annahum bunyaanum-marṣooṣ.

فِي سَبِيلِهِ صَفًّا كَأَنَّهُمْ بُنْيَانٌ
مَّرْصُوصٌ ④

5. Moses said to his people, "Why do you create difficulties for me when you know that I am Allah's Messenger to you?" When they deviated (doubted the right path), Allah made their hearts to doubt. Allah does not guide the evil-doing people.

5. Wa iz̲ qaala Moosaa li-qawmihee yaa qawmi lima tu'z̲oonanee wa qat-ta'lamoona annee Rasoolul-laahi ilaykum falammaa zaaghooo azaaghal-laahu quloobahum; wallaahu laa yahdil-qawmal-faasiqeen.

وَإِذْ قَالَ مُوسَىٰ لِقَوْمِهِ يَٰقَوْمِ لِمَ
تُؤْذُونَنِي وَقَد تَّعْلَمُونَ أَنِّي رَسُولُ
اللَّهِ إِلَيْكُمْ ۖ فَلَمَّا زَاغُوا أَزَاغَ اللَّهُ
قُلُوبَهُمْ ۚ وَاللَّهُ لَا يَهْدِي الْقَوْمَ
الْفَٰسِقِينَ ⑤

6. Jesus, son of Mary, said to the Israelites, "I am the Messenger of Allah sent to you. I confirm the Torah which is in existence and give you the glad news of the coming of a Messenger who will come after me named Ahmad." When this Messenger came to them with all the proofs (to support his truthfulness), they said, "He is only a magician."

6. Wa-iz̲ qaala 'Eesab-nu-Maryama yaa Baneee Israa-'eela innee Rasoolul-laahi ilaykum-muṣaddiqal-limaa bayna yadayya minat-Tawraati wa mubashshiram bi-Rasooliñy-ya-tee mim ba'dis-muhoo Aḥmad; falammaa jaaa'ahum bil-bayyinaati qaaloo haaz̲aa siḥrum mubeen.

وَإِذْ قَالَ عِيسَى ابْنُ مَرْيَمَ يَٰبَنِي
إِسْرَٰءِيلَ إِنِّي رَسُولُ اللَّهِ إِلَيْكُم
مُّصَدِّقًا لِّمَا بَيْنَ يَدَيَّ مِنَ
التَّوْرَىٰةِ وَمُبَشِّرًا بِرَسُولٍ يَأْتِي مِن
بَعْدِي اسْمُهُ أَحْمَدُ ۖ فَلَمَّا جَاءَهُم
بِالْبَيِّنَٰتِ قَالُوا هَٰذَا سِحْرٌ مُّبِينٌ ⑥

7. Who is more unjust than one who creates falsehood against Allah when he has already been invited to Islam? Allah does not guide the unjust people.

7. Wa man aẓlamu mimmanif-taraa 'alal-laahil-kaz̲iba wa huwa yud'aaa ilal-Islaam; wallaahu laa yahdil-qawmaẓ-ẓaalimeen.

وَمَنْ أَظْلَمُ مِمَّنِ افْتَرَىٰ عَلَى اللَّهِ
الْكَذِبَ وَهُوَ يُدْعَىٰ إِلَى الْإِسْلَٰمِ ۚ
وَاللَّهُ لَا يَهْدِي الْقَوْمَ الظَّٰلِمِينَ ⑦

8. They want to put out the light of Allah with their mouths, but Allah will certainly make His light shine forever - even though the unbelievers may dislike this.

8. Yureedoona liyuṭfi'oo nooral-laahi bi-afwaahihim wallaahu mutimmu noorihee wa law karihal-kaafiroon.

يُرِيدُونَ لِيُطْفِئُوا نُورَ اللَّهِ
بِأَفْوَٰهِهِمْ وَاللَّهُ مُتِمُّ نُورِهِ
وَلَوْ كَرِهَ الْكَٰفِرُونَ ⑧

9. It is He who has sent His Messenger with guidance and the true religion to stand supreme over all religions, even though the pagans may dislike it.

9. Huwal-laz̲ee arsala Rasoolahoo bilhudaa wa deenil-ḥaqqi liyuẓhirahoo 'alad-deeni kullihee wa law karihal-mushrikoon.

هُوَ الَّذِي أَرْسَلَ رَسُولَهُ بِالْهُدَىٰ
وَدِينِ الْحَقِّ لِيُظْهِرَهُ عَلَى الدِّينِ
كُلِّهِ وَلَوْ كَرِهَ الْمُشْرِكُونَ ⑨

10. Believers, shall I show you a bargain, which will save you from the painful torment?

10. Yaaa ayyuhal-laz̲eena aamanoo hal adullukum 'alaa tijaaratin tunjeekum min 'az̲aabin aleem.

يَٰأَيُّهَا الَّذِينَ ءَامَنُوا هَلْ أَدُلُّكُمْ عَلَىٰ
تِجَٰرَةٍ تُنجِيكُم مِّنْ عَذَابٍ أَلِيمٍ ⑩

11. Have faith in Allah and His Messenger and strive hard for His cause with your wealth and in person. This is better for you if

11. Tu'minoona billaahi wa Rasoolihee wa tujaahidoona fee sabeelil-laahi bi-amwaalikum wa anfusikum;

تُؤْمِنُونَ بِاللَّهِ وَرَسُولِهِ وَتُجَٰهِدُونَ
فِي سَبِيلِ اللَّهِ بِأَمْوَٰلِكُمْ وَأَنفُسِكُمْ ۚ

only you knew it.

12. Allah will forgive your sins and admit you into Paradise wherein streams flow, and you will live in the lofty mansions of the Garden of Eden. This is indeed the greatest triumph.

13. (Besides forgiveness) you will receive other favors, which you will love: help from Allah and an immediate victory (Muhammad), give such glad news to the believers.

14. Believers, be the helpers of Allah just as when Jesus, the son of Mary, asked the disciples, "Who will be my helpers for the cause of Allah?" and the disciples replied, "We are the helpers of Allah." A group of the Israelites believed in him and others rejected him. We helped the believers against their enemies and they became victorious.

zaalikum khayrul-lakum in kuntum ta'lamoon.

12. Yaghfir lakum zunoobakum wa yudkhilkum Jannaatin tajree min taḥtihal anhaaru wa masaakina ṭayyibatan fee Jannaati 'Adn; zaalikal-fawzul-'aẓeem.

13. Wa-ukhraa tuḥibboonahaa naṣrum-minal-laahi wa fatḥun qareeb; wa bashshiril mu'mineen.

14. Yaaa ayyuhal-lazeena aamanoo koonooo anṣaaral-laahi kamaa qaala 'Eesab-nu Maryama lil-Ḥawaariyyeena man anṣaareee ilal-laahi qaalal-Ḥawaariyyoona naḥnu anṣaa-rul-laahi fa-aamanat ṭaaa'ifatum-mim Baneee Israaa'eela wa kafarat ṭaaa'ifatun fa-ayyadnal-lazeena aamanoo 'alaa 'aduwwihim fa-aṣbaḥoo ẓaahireen.

ذٰلِكُمْ خَيْرٌ لَّكُمْ إِنْ كُنتُمْ تَعْلَمُونَ ﴿١١﴾
يَغْفِرْ لَكُمْ ذُنُوبَكُمْ وَيُدْخِلْكُمْ
جَنّٰتٍ تَجْرِي مِن تَحْتِهَا الْأَنْهٰرُ
وَمَسٰكِنَ طَيِّبَةً فِي جَنّٰتِ عَدْنٍ ۚ
ذٰلِكَ الْفَوْزُ الْعَظِيمُ ﴿١٢﴾
وَأُخْرَىٰ تُحِبُّونَهَا ۖ نَصْرٌ مِّنَ اللَّهِ وَ
فَتْحٌ قَرِيبٌ ۗ وَبَشِّرِ الْمُؤْمِنِينَ ﴿١٣﴾
يٰٓأَيُّهَا الَّذِينَ آمَنُوا كُونُوٓا أَنصَارَ
اللَّهِ كَمَا قَالَ عِيسَى ابْنُ مَرْيَمَ
لِلْحَوَارِيِّينَ مَنْ أَنصَارِيٓ إِلَى اللَّهِ ۖ
قَالَ الْحَوَارِيُّونَ نَحْنُ أَنصَارُ اللَّهِ
فَآمَنَت طَّآئِفَةٌ مِّنۢ بَنِيٓ إِسْرَآءِيلَ
وَكَفَرَت طَّآئِفَةٌ ۖ فَأَيَّدْنَا الَّذِينَ
آمَنُوا عَلَىٰ عَدُوِّهِمْ فَأَصْبَحُوا ظٰهِرِينَ ﴿١٤﴾ ع ٥ ١٠

Al-Jumuah, Day of Assembly (62)

In the Name of Allah, the Beneficent, the Merciful.

1. All that is in the heavens and the earth glorifies Allah, the King, Al-Quddus (free from the matters that can lead one to ignorance) the Majestic and the All-Wise.

2. It is He who has sent to the illiterate (people without a heavenly book) a messenger from among their own people to recite to them His revelations and purify them. He will teach the Book to them and wisdom, even though before this they had been in plain error,

3. and to others, who have not yet joined, (accepted the faith). He (Allah) is Majestic and All-Wise.

4. Such is the favor of Allah, which He grants to whomever He

Sûrat al-Jumu'ah-62

(Revealed at Madinah)

Bismillaahir Raḥmaanir Raḥeem

1. Yusabbiḥu lillaahi maa fis-samaawaati wa maa fil-arḍil-Malikil-Quddoosil-'Azeezil-Ḥakeem.

2. Huwal-lazee ba'asa fil-ummiyyeena Rasoolam-minhum yatloo 'alayhim Aayaatihee wa yuzakkeehim wa yu'allimuhumul-Kitaaba wal-Ḥikmata wa in kaanoo min qablu lafee ḍalaalim Mubeen.

3. Wa aakhareena minhum lammaa yalḥaqoo bihim wa Huwal-'Azeezul-Ḥakeem.

4. Zaalika faḍlul-laahi yu'teehi mañy-yashaaa';

(٦٢) سُورَةُ الْجُمُعَةِ مَدَنِيَّةٌ (١١٠)

آياتها ١١ بِسْمِ اللَّهِ الرَّحْمٰنِ الرَّحِيمِ ركوعاتها ٢

يُسَبِّحُ لِلَّهِ مَا فِي السَّمٰوٰتِ وَمَا فِي
الْأَرْضِ الْمَلِكِ الْقُدُّوسِ الْعَزِيزِ
الْحَكِيمِ ﴿١﴾
هُوَ الَّذِي بَعَثَ فِي الْأُمِّيِّينَ رَسُولًا
مِّنْهُمْ يَتْلُوا عَلَيْهِمْ آيٰتِهِ وَيُزَكِّيهِمْ
وَيُعَلِّمُهُمُ الْكِتٰبَ وَالْحِكْمَةَ ۚ وَإِن
كَانُوا مِن قَبْلُ لَفِي ضَلٰلٍ مُّبِينٍ ﴿٢﴾
وَآخَرِينَ مِنْهُمْ لَمَّا يَلْحَقُوا بِهِمْ ۚ وَ
هُوَ الْعَزِيزُ الْحَكِيمُ ﴿٣﴾
ذٰلِكَ فَضْلُ اللَّهِ يُؤْتِيهِ مَن يَشَآءُ ۚ

wants. Allah's favor is great.

Wallaahu zul-faḍlil-‘aẓeem.

وَاللّٰهُ ذُو الْفَضْلِ الْعَظِيْمِ ﴿٤﴾

5. Those who were to carry the responsibility of the Torah but ignored it, are like donkeys laden with books. How terrible is the example of the people who reject the revelations of Allah. Allah does not guide the unjust.

5. Maṯalul-laẕeena ḥummilut Tawraata ṯumma lam yaḥmiloohaa kamaṯalil-ḥimaari yaḥmilu asfaaraa; bi'sa maṯalul-qawmil-laẕeena kaẕ ẕaboo bi-Aayaatil-laah; wallaahu laa yahdil-qawmaẓẓaalimeen.

مَثَلُ الَّذِيْنَ حُمِّلُوا التَّوْرٰىةَ ثُمَّ
لَمْ يَحْمِلُوْهَا كَمَثَلِ الْحِمَارِ يَحْمِلُ
اَسْفَارًا ۭ بِئْسَ مَثَلُ الْقَوْمِ الَّذِيْنَ
كَذَّبُوْا بِاٰيٰتِ اللّٰهِ ۭ وَاللّٰهُ لَا يَهْدِي
الْقَوْمَ الظّٰلِمِيْنَ ﴿٥﴾

6. (Muhammad), ask the Jews, "If you believe that you are the chosen people of Allah to the exclusion of all other people, wish for death if you are truthful."

6. Qul yaaa ayyuhal-laẕeena haadooo in za‘amtum annakum awliyaaa'u lillaahi min doonin-naasi fatamannawul-mawta in kuntum ṣaadiqeen.

قُلْ يٰٓاَيُّهَا الَّذِيْنَ هَادُوْٓا اِنْ
زَعَمْتُمْ اَنَّكُمْ اَوْلِيَاۗءُ لِلّٰهِ مِنْ
دُوْنِ النَّاسِ فَتَمَنَّوُا الْمَوْتَ اِنْ
كُنْتُمْ صٰدِقِيْنَ ﴿٦﴾

7. They will never wish for death because of what they have done! Allah knows best about the unjust people.

7. Wa laa yatamannawnahooo abadam bimaa qaddamat aydeehim; wallaahu ‘aleemum bizẓaalimeen.

وَلَا يَتَمَنَّوْنَهٗٓ اَبَدًاۢ بِمَا قَدَّمَتْ
اَيْدِيْهِمْ ۭ وَاللّٰهُ عَلِيْمٌۢ بِالظّٰلِمِيْنَ ﴿٧﴾

8. (Muhammad), tell them, "The death from which you run away will certainly approach you. Then you will be returned to the One who knows the unseen and the seen, and He will tell you what you have done."

8. Qul innal-mawtal-laẕee tafirroona minhu fa-innahoo mulaaqeekum ṯumma turaddoona ilaa ‘Aalimil-ghaybi washshahaadati fayunabbi'ukum bimaa kuntum ta‘maloon.

قُلْ اِنَّ الْمَوْتَ الَّذِيْ تَفِرُّوْنَ مِنْهُ
فَاِنَّهٗ مُلٰقِيْكُمْ ثُمَّ تُرَدُّوْنَ اِلٰى عٰلِمِ
الْغَيْبِ وَالشَّهَادَةِ فَيُنَبِّئُكُمْ بِمَا
كُنْتُمْ تَعْمَلُوْنَ ﴿٨﴾ ع ٨/١١

9. Believers, on Friday when the call for prayer is made, try to prepare yourselves to attend prayer (remembering Allah) and leave off all business. This would be better for you if only you knew it.

9. Yaaa ayyuhal-laẕeena aamanooo iẕaa noodiya liṣ-Ṣalaati miñy-Yawmil-Jumu‘ati fas‘aw ilaa ẕikril-laahi wa ẕarul-bay‘; ẕaalikum khayrul-lakum in kuntum ta‘lamoon.

يٰٓاَيُّهَا الَّذِيْنَ اٰمَنُوْٓا اِذَا نُوْدِيَ
لِلصَّلٰوةِ مِنْ يَّوْمِ الْجُمُعَةِ فَاسْعَوْا
اِلٰى ذِكْرِ اللّٰهِ وَذَرُوا الْبَيْعَ ۭ ذٰلِكُمْ
خَيْرٌ لَّكُمْ اِنْ كُنْتُمْ تَعْلَمُوْنَ ﴿٩﴾

10. When the prayer ends, disperse through the land and seek the favor of Allah. Remember Allah often so that perhaps you will have everlasting happiness.

10. Fa-iẕaa quḍiyatiṣ-Ṣalaatu fantashiroo fil-arḍi wabtaghoo min faḍlil-laahi waẕkurul-laaha kaṯeeral-la‘allakum tufliḥoon.

فَاِذَا قُضِيَتِ الصَّلٰوةُ فَانْتَشِرُوْا فِي
الْاَرْضِ وَابْتَغُوْا مِنْ فَضْلِ اللّٰهِ وَ
اذْكُرُوا اللّٰهَ كَثِيْرًا لَّعَلَّكُمْ تُفْلِحُوْنَ ﴿١٠﴾

11. When they see a merchandise or sport, they rush toward it and leave you standing alone. Say, "(Allah's rewards for good deeds) are better than merriment (game) or merchandise; Allah is the best

11. Wa iẕaa ra-aw tijaaratan aw lahwanin-faḍḍooo ilayhaa wa tarakooka qaa'imaa; qul maa ‘indal-laahi khayrum-minal-lahwi wa minat-

وَاِذَا رَاَوْا تِجَارَةً اَوْ لَهْوَا ِۨ انْفَضُّوْٓا
اِلَيْهَا وَتَرَكُوْكَ قَاۗىِٕمًا ۭ قُلْ مَا
عِنْدَ اللّٰهِ خَيْرٌ مِّنَ اللَّهْوِ وَمِنَ

Sustainer."

Al-Munafiqun, The Hypocrites (63)
In the Name of Allah,
the Beneficent, the Merciful.

1. When the hypocrites come to you, they say, "We testify that you are the Messenger of Allah." Allah knows that you are His Messenger. Allah testifies that the hypocrites are liars.

2. They have chosen their oaths as a shield for them to obstruct others from the way of Allah. How terrible is what they do!

3. This is because they accepted the faith and then rejected it. Their hearts are sealed, thus they do not have any understanding.

4. When you see them, their physical appearance attracts you, and when they speak, you carefully listen to them. In fact, they are like propped-up hollow trunks of wood (do not hear and understand). (They are so cowardly) they think that every cry (they hear) is against them. They are the enemy, so beware of them, may Allah condemn them. Where are they turning to, leaving behind the Truth?

5. When they are told, "Come and let the Prophet of Allah seek forgiveness for you," they shake their heads and you can see them arrogantly turning away.

6. It is all the same whether you sought forgiveness for them or not; Allah will never forgive them. Allah does not guide the evil-doing people.

7. It is they who say, "Give nothing to those who are around the Messenger of Allah so that they will desert him." To Allah belong the treasures of the heavens and the

tijaarah; wallaahu khayrur-raaziqeen.

Sûrat al-Munâfiqûn-63
(Revealed at Madinah)
Bismillaahir Raḥmaanir Raḥeem

1. Izaa jaaa'akal-munaafiqoona qaaloo nashhadu innaka la-Rasoolul-laah; wallaahu ya'lamu innaka la-Rasooluhoo wallaahu yashhadu innal-munaafiqeena lakaaziboon.

2. Ittakhazooo aymaanahum junnatan faṣaddoo 'an sabeelil-laah; innahum saaa'a maa kaanoo ya'maloon.

3. Zaalika bi-annahum aamanoo summa kafaroo faṭubi'a 'alaa quloobihim fahum laa yafqahoon.

4. Wa izaa ra-aytahum tu'jibuka ajsaamuhum wa-iñy-yaqooloo tasma' liqawlihim ka-annahum khushubum musannadah; yaḥsaboona kulla ṣayḥatin 'alayhim; humul-'aduwwu faḥzarhum; qaatalahumul-laahu annaa yu'fakoon.

5. Wa izaa qeela lahum ta'aalaw yastaghfir lakum Rasoolul-laahi lawwaw ru'oosahum wa ra-aytahum yaṣuddoona wa hum mustakbiroon.

6. Sawaaa'un 'alayhim astaghfarta lahum am lam tastaghfir lahum lañy-yaghfiral-laahu lahum; innal-laaha laa yahdil-qawmal-faasiqeen.

7. Humul-lazeena yaqooloona laa tunfiqoo 'alaa man 'inda Rasoolil-laahi ḥattaa yanfaḍḍoo;

التِّجَارَةِ ۭ وَاللّٰهُ خَيْرُ الرّٰزِقِيْنَ ﴿١١﴾ ع

(٦٣) سُوْرَةُ الْمُنٰفِقُوْنَ مَدَنِيَّةٌ (١٠٤)
آياتها ١١ بِسْمِ اللّٰهِ الرَّحْمٰنِ الرَّحِيْمِ ركوعاتها ٢

اِذَا جَآءَكَ الْمُنٰفِقُوْنَ قَالُوْا نَشْهَدُ
اِنَّكَ لَرَسُوْلُ اللّٰهِ ۘ وَاللّٰهُ يَعْلَمُ
اِنَّكَ لَرَسُوْلُهٗ ۭ وَاللّٰهُ يَشْهَدُ اِنَّ
الْمُنٰفِقِيْنَ لَكٰذِبُوْنَ ﴿١﴾
اِتَّخَذُوْٓا اَيْمَانَهُمْ جُنَّةً فَصَدُّوْا
عَنْ سَبِيْلِ اللّٰهِ ۭ اِنَّهُمْ سَاۗءَ مَا
كَانُوْا يَعْمَلُوْنَ ﴿٢﴾
ذٰلِكَ بِاَنَّهُمْ اٰمَنُوْا ثُمَّ كَفَرُوْا فَطُبِعَ
عَلٰي قُلُوْبِهِمْ فَهُمْ لَا يَفْقَهُوْنَ ﴿٣﴾
وَاِذَا رَاَيْتَهُمْ تُعْجِبُكَ اَجْسَامُهُمْ ۭ
وَاِنْ يَّقُوْلُوْا تَسْمَعْ لِقَوْلِهِمْ ۭ كَاَنَّهُمْ
خُشُبٌ مُّسَنَّدَةٌ ۭ يَحْسَبُوْنَ كُلَّ صَيْحَةٍ
عَلَيْهِمْ ۭ هُمُ الْعَدُوُّ فَاحْذَرْهُمْ ۭ
قٰتَلَهُمُ اللّٰهُ ۡ اَنّٰى يُؤْفَكُوْنَ ﴿٤﴾
وَاِذَا قِيْلَ لَهُمْ تَعَالَوْا يَسْتَغْفِرْ لَكُمْ
رَسُوْلُ اللّٰهِ لَوَّوْا رُءُوْسَهُمْ وَرَاَيْتَهُمْ
يَصُدُّوْنَ وَهُمْ مُّسْتَكْبِرُوْنَ ﴿٥﴾
سَوَاۗءٌ عَلَيْهِمْ اَسْتَغْفَرْتَ لَهُمْ
اَمْ لَمْ تَسْتَغْفِرْ لَهُمْ ۭ لَنْ يَّغْفِرَ
اللّٰهُ لَهُمْ ۭ اِنَّ اللّٰهَ لَا يَهْدِي
الْقَوْمَ الْفٰسِقِيْنَ ﴿٦﴾
هُمُ الَّذِيْنَ يَقُوْلُوْنَ لَا تُنْفِقُوْا عَلٰي
مَنْ عِنْدَ رَسُوْلِ اللّٰهِ حَتّٰى يَنْفَضُّوْا ۭ

ع ١٤ ٢
وقف لازم

earth, but the hypocrites have no understanding.

wa lillaahi khazaaa'inus-samaawaati wal-arḍi wa laakinnal-munaafiqeena laa yafqahoon.

وَلِلّٰهِ خَزَآئِنُ السَّمٰوٰتِ وَالْاَرْضِ
وَلٰكِنَّ الْمُنٰفِقِيْنَ لَا يَفْقَهُوْنَ ⑦

8. They say, "When we return to Medina, the honorable ones will certainly drive out the mean ones." Honor belongs to Allah, His Messenger and the believers, but the hypocrites do not know.

8. Yaqooloona la'ir-raja'naaa ilal-Madeenati la-yukhrijannal-a'azzu minhal-azall; wa lillaahil'izzatu wa li-Rasoolihee wa lilmu'mineena wa laakinnal-munaafiqeena laa ya'lamoon.

يَقُوْلُوْنَ لَئِنْ رَّجَعْنَآ اِلَى الْمَدِيْنَةِ
لَيُخْرِجَنَّ الْاَعَزُّ مِنْهَا الْاَذَلَّ ؕ وَ
لِلّٰهِ الْعِزَّةُ وَلِرَسُوْلِهٖ وَلِلْمُؤْمِنِيْنَ
وَلٰكِنَّ الْمُنٰفِقِيْنَ لَا يَعْلَمُوْنَ ⑧ ع ١ ٨ ١٣

9. Believers, do not let your wealth and children divert you from remembering Allah. Whoever is diverted will suffer a great loss.

9. Yaaa ayyuhal-lazeena aamanoo laa tulhikum amwaalukum wa laaa awlaadukum 'an zikril-laah; wa mañy-yaf'al-zaalika fa-ulaaa'ika humul-khaasiroon.

يٰۤاَيُّهَا الَّذِيْنَ اٰمَنُوْا لَا تُلْهِكُمْ
اَمْوَالُكُمْ وَلَاۤ اَوْلَادُكُمْ عَنْ
ذِكْرِ اللّٰهِ ۚ وَمَنْ يَّفْعَلْ ذٰلِكَ
فَاُولٰٓئِكَ هُمُ الْخٰسِرُوْنَ ⑨

10. Spend for the cause of Allah out of what We have given you before death approaches you, and say, "Lord, would that you would give me respite for a short time so that I could spend for Your cause and become one of those who do good."

10. Wa anfiqoo mim-maa razaqnaakum min qabli añy-yatiya aḥadakumul-mawtu fa-yaqoola Rabbi law laaa akhkhartaneee ilaaa ajalin qareeb; fa-aṣṣaddaqa wa akum-minaṣ-ṣaaliḥeen.

وَاَنْفِقُوْا مِنْ مَّا رَزَقْنٰكُمْ مِّنْ
قَبْلِ اَنْ يَّاْتِيَ اَحَدَكُمُ الْمَوْتُ
فَيَقُوْلَ رَبِّ لَوْلَاۤ اَخَّرْتَنِيْۤ اِلٰۤى
اَجَلٍ قَرِيْبٍ ۙ فَاَصَّدَّقَ وَاَكُنْ
مِّنَ الصّٰلِحِيْنَ ⑩

11. Allah will never grant respite to any soul when its appointed time has come. Allah is Well-aware of what you do.

11. Wa lañy-yu'akhkhiral-laahu nafsan izaa jaaa'a ajaluhaa; wallaahu Khabeerum bimaa ta'maloon.

وَلَنْ يُّؤَخِّرَ اللّٰهُ نَفْسًا اِذَا جَآءَ اَجَلُهَا ؕ
وَاللّٰهُ خَبِيْرٌۢ بِمَا تَعْمَلُوْنَ ⑪ ع ٢ ٣ ١٤

Al-Taghabun, Cheating (64)
In the Name of Allah,
the Beneficent, the Merciful.

Sûrat at-Taghâbun-64

(Revealed at Madinah)

Bismillaahir Raḥmaanir Raḥeem

(٦٤) سُوْرَةُ التَّغَابُنِ مَدَنِيَّةٌ (١٠٨)
اٰيَاتُهَا ١٨ بِسْمِ اللّٰهِ الرَّحْمٰنِ الرَّحِيْمِ رُكُوْعَاتُهَا ٢

1. All that is in the heavens and the earth glorifies Allah. To Him belong the Kingdom and all praise. He has power over all things.

1. Yusabbiḥu lillaahi maa fis-samaawaati wa maa fil-arḍi lahul-mulku wa lahul-ḥamd; wa Huwa 'alaa kulli shay'in Qadeer.

يُسَبِّحُ لِلّٰهِ مَا فِي السَّمٰوٰتِ وَمَا فِي
الْاَرْضِ ۚ لَهُ الْمُلْكُ وَلَهُ الْحَمْدُ ۫
وَهُوَ عَلٰى كُلِّ شَيْءٍ قَدِيْرٌ ①

2. It is He who has created you all but some of you have accepted the faith and some of you have not. Allah is Well-aware of what you do.

2. Huwal-lazee khalaqakum faminkum kaafiruñw-wa minkum mu'min; wallaahu bimaa ta'maloona Baṣeer.

هُوَ الَّذِيْ خَلَقَكُمْ فَمِنْكُمْ كَافِرٌ
وَّمِنْكُمْ مُّؤْمِنٌ ؕ وَاللّٰهُ بِمَا
تَعْمَلُوْنَ بَصِيْرٌ ②

3. He has created the heavens and the earth for a genuine

3. Khalaqas-samaawaati wal-arḍa bilḥaqqi

خَلَقَ السَّمٰوٰتِ وَالْاَرْضَ بِالْحَقِّ

وَصَوَّرَكُمْ فَأَحْسَنَ صُوَرَكُمْ
وَإِلَيْهِ الْمَصِيرُ ③

wa ṣawwarakum fa-aḥsana ṣuwarakum wa ilayhil-maṣeer.

purpose and has formed you in the best shape. To Him all things return.

يَعْلَمُ مَا فِي السَّمٰوٰتِ وَالْأَرْضِ
وَيَعْلَمُ مَا تُسِرُّونَ وَمَا تُعْلِنُونَ
وَاللّٰهُ عَلِيمٌ بِذَاتِ الصُّدُورِ ④

4. Ya'lamu maa fis-samaawaati wal-arḍi wa ya'lamu maa tusirroona wa maa tu'linoon; wallaahu 'Aleemum bizaatiṣ-ṣudoor.

4. He knows all that is in the heavens and the earth and all that you reveal or conceal. Allah knows best whatever the hearts contain.

أَلَمْ يَأْتِكُمْ نَبَؤُا الَّذِينَ كَفَرُوا مِنْ
قَبْلُ فَذَاقُوا وَبَالَ أَمْرِهِمْ وَ
لَهُمْ عَذَابٌ أَلِيمٌ ⑤

5. Alam ya-tikum naba'ul-lazeena kafaroo min qablu fazaaqoo wabaala amrihim wa lahum 'azaabun aleem.

5. Did you not receive the news about the unbelievers living before you who suffered the consequences of their deeds and will suffer a painful torment?

ذٰلِكَ بِأَنَّهُ كَانَتْ تَأْتِيهِمْ رُسُلُهُمْ
بِالْبَيِّنٰتِ فَقَالُوا أَبَشَرٌ يَهْدُونَنَا
فَكَفَرُوا وَتَوَلَّوْا وَاسْتَغْنَى اللّٰهُ
وَاللّٰهُ غَنِيٌّ حَمِيدٌ ⑥

6. Zaalika bi-annahoo kaanat ta-teehim Rusuluhum bilbayyinaati faqaalooo abasharuñy-yahdoonanaa fakafaroo wa tawallaw; wastaghnal-laah; wallaahu Ghaniyyun Ḥameed.

6. This was because their messengers came to them with clear proof (to support their prophethood) and they said, "Can mere mortals provide us with guidance?" They rejected the Messengers and turned away. Allah does not need the worship of anyone. Allah is self-sufficient and praiseworthy.

زَعَمَ الَّذِينَ كَفَرُوا أَنْ لَنْ يُبْعَثُوا
قُلْ بَلَىٰ وَرَبِّي لَتُبْعَثُنَّ ثُمَّ لَتُنَبَّؤُنَّ
بِمَا عَمِلْتُمْ وَذٰلِكَ عَلَى اللّٰهِ يَسِيرٌ ⑦

7. Za'amal-lazeena kafarooo al-lañy-yub'asoo; qul balaa wa Rabbee latub'asunna summa latunabba'unna bimaa 'amiltum; wa zaalika 'alal-laahi yaseer.

7. The unbelievers have thought that they would never be resurrected (Muhammad). Say, "I swear by my Lord that you will certainly be resurrected and will be told about all that you have done." All this is certainly very easy for Allah.

فَآمِنُوا بِاللّٰهِ وَرَسُولِهِ وَالنُّورِ الَّذِي
أَنْزَلْنَا وَاللّٰهُ بِمَا تَعْمَلُونَ خَبِيرٌ ⑧

8. Fa-aaminoo billaahi wa Rasoolihee wannooril-lazeee anzalnaa; wallaahu bimaa ta'maloona Khabeer.

8. Thus, have faith in Allah, His Messenger, and the Light, which We have sent down. Allah is Well-aware of what you do.

يَوْمَ يَجْمَعُكُمْ لِيَوْمِ الْجَمْعِ ذٰلِكَ
يَوْمُ التَّغَابُنِ وَمَنْ يُؤْمِنْ بِاللّٰهِ
وَيَعْمَلْ صَالِحًا يُكَفِّرْ عَنْهُ
سَيِّئَاتِهِ وَيُدْخِلْهُ جَنّٰتٍ تَجْرِي
مِنْ تَحْتِهَا الْأَنْهٰرُ خٰلِدِينَ فِيهَا
أَبَدًا ذٰلِكَ الْفَوْزُ الْعَظِيمُ ⑨

9. Yawma yajma'ukum liyawmil-jam'i zaalika yawmut-taghaabun; wa mañy-yu'mim billaahi wa ya'mal ṣaaliḥañy-yukaffir 'anhu sayyi-aatihee wa yudkhilhu Jannaatin tajree min taḥtihal-anhaaru khaalideena feehaaa abadaa; zaalikal-fawzul-'aẓeem.

9. On the day when We shall gather you all together (for the Day of Judgment), all cheating will be exposed. One who believes in Allah and acts righteously will receive forgiveness for his sins. He (Allah) will admit him into Paradise wherein streams flow and he will live forever. This, certainly, is the greatest triumph.

وَالَّذِينَ كَفَرُوا وَكَذَّبُوا بِآيٰتِنَا
أُولٰئِكَ أَصْحٰبُ النَّارِ خٰلِدِينَ
فِيهَا وَبِئْسَ الْمَصِيرُ ⑩

10. Wallazeena kafaroo wa kaz zaboo bi-Aayaatinaaa ulaaa'ika Aṣḥaabun-Naari khaalideena feehaa wa bi'sal maṣeer.

10. As for those who have disbelieved and rejected Our revelations, they will dwell forever in hell-fire, a terrible fate.

11. No one will be afflicted with any hardship without it being the will of Allah. The hearts of whoever believed in Allah will receive guidance (acknowledge the presence of Allah). Allah has the knowledge of all things.

11. Maaa aṣaaba mim-muṣeebatin illaa bi-iznil-laah; wa mañy-yu'mim billaahi yahdi qalbah; wallaahu bikulli shay'in 'Aleem.

مَآ اَصَابَ مِنْ مُّصِيْبَةٍ اِلَّا بِاِذْنِ
اللّٰهِ ۭ وَمَنْ يُّؤْمِنْ بِاللّٰهِ يَهْدِ قَلْبَهٗ ۭ
وَاللّٰهُ بِكُلِّ شَيْءٍ عَلِيْمٌ ⑪

12. Obey Allah and the Messenger, but if you turn away, know that the only duty of Our Messenger is to preach clearly.

12. Wa aṭee'ul-laaha wa aṭee'ur-Rasool; fa-in tawallaytum fa-innamaa 'alaa Rasoolinal-balaaghul mubeen.

وَاَطِيْعُوا اللّٰهَ وَاَطِيْعُوا الرَّسُوْلَ ۚ
فَاِنْ تَوَلَّيْتُمْ فَاِنَّمَا عَلٰي رَسُوْلِنَا
الْبَلٰغُ الْمُبِيْنُ ⑫

13. Allah is the only Lord and in Allah the believers should trust.

13. Allaahu laaa ilaaha illaa Hoo; wa 'alal-laahi falyatawakkalil-mu'minoon.

اَللّٰهُ لَآ اِلٰهَ اِلَّا هُوَ ۭ وَعَلَي اللّٰهِ
فَلْيَتَوَكَّلِ الْمُؤْمِنُوْنَ ⑬

14. Believers, some of your wives and children may prove to be your enemies so beware of them. However, if you would pardon, ignore, and forgive, know that Allah is All-forgiving and All-merciful.

14. Yaaa ayyuhal-lazeena aamanooo inna min azwaajikum wa awlaadikum 'aduwwal-lakum faḥzaroohum; wa in ta'foo wa taṣfaḥoo wa taghfiroo fa-innallaaha Ghafoorur-Raḥeem.

يٰٓاَيُّهَا الَّذِيْنَ اٰمَنُوْٓا اِنَّ مِنْ
اَزْوَاجِكُمْ وَاَوْلَادِكُمْ عَدُوًّا لَّكُمْ
فَاحْذَرُوْهُمْ ۚ وَاِنْ تَعْفُوْا وَتَصْفَحُوْا
وَتَغْفِرُوْا فَاِنَّ اللّٰهَ غَفُوْرٌ رَّحِيْمٌ ⑭

15. Your property and children are a trial (a matter of love) for you, but the reward (which one may receive from Allah) is great.

15. Innamaaa amwaalukum wa awlaadukum fitnah; wallaahu 'indahooo ajrun 'aẓeem.

اِنَّمَآ اَمْوَالُكُمْ وَاَوْلَادُكُمْ
فِتْنَةٌ ۭ وَاللّٰهُ عِنْدَهٗٓ اَجْرٌ عَظِيْمٌ ⑮

16. You must have as much fear of Allah as you can. Listen to the Messenger, obey him, and spend, for your own sake, good things for the cause of Allah. Those who control their greed will have everlasting happiness.

16. Fattaqul-laaha mastaṭa'tum wasma'oo wa aṭee'oo wa-anfiqoo khayral li-anfusikum; wa mañy-yooqa shuḥḥa nafsihee fa-ulaaa'ika humul-mufliḥoon.

فَاتَّقُوا اللّٰهَ مَا اسْتَطَعْتُمْ وَاسْمَعُوْا
وَاَطِيْعُوْا وَاَنْفِقُوْا خَيْرًا لِّاَنْفُسِكُمْ ۭ
وَمَنْ يُّوْقَ شُحَّ نَفْسِهٖ فَاُولٰۗىِٕكَ
هُمُ الْمُفْلِحُوْنَ ⑯

17. If you give a virtuous loan to Allah, He will pay back double and forgive your sins. Allah is the Most Appreciating and the Most Forbearing.

17. In tuqriḍul-laaha qarḍan ḥasanañy-yuḍaa'ifhu lakum wa yaghfir lakum; wallaahu Shakoorun Ḥaleem.

اِنْ تُقْرِضُوا اللّٰهَ قَرْضًا حَسَنًا
يُّضٰعِفْهُ لَكُمْ وَيَغْفِرْ لَكُمْ ۭ
وَاللّٰهُ شَكُوْرٌ حَلِيْمٌ ⑰

18. He knows the unseen and the seen. He is the Majestic and All-wise.

18. 'Aalimul-Ghaybi wash-shahaadatil-'Azeezul-Ḥakeem.

عٰلِمُ الْغَيْبِ وَالشَّهَادَةِ الْعَزِيْزُ
الْحَكِيْمُ ⑱ ٢ ع ٨ ١٦

Al-Talaq, The Divorce (65)

In the Name of Allah,
the Beneficent, the Merciful.

Sûrat aṭ-Ṭalâq-65

(Revealed at Madinah)

Bismillaahir Raḥmaanir Raḥeem

(٦٥) سُوْرَةُ الطَّلَاقِ مَدَنِيَّةٌ (٩٩)

اٰياتها ١٢ — بِسْمِ اللّٰهِ الرَّحْمٰنِ الرَّحِيْمِ — ركوعاتها ٢

1. O Prophet and believers, if you want to divorce your wives, you should

1. Yaaa ayyuhan-Nabiyyu izaa ṭallaqtumun-nisaaa'a

يٰٓاَيُّهَا النَّبِيُّ اِذَا طَلَّقْتُمُ النِّسَاۗءَ

do so at a time after which they can start their waiting period. Allow them keep an account of the number of the days in the waiting period. Have fear of Allah, your Lord. (It is one of the examples where it is addressed to the Holy Prophet but people are meant thereby).

(During their waiting period) do not expel them from their homes and they also must not go out of their homes, unless they commit proven indecency. These are the laws of Allah. Whoever transgresses against the laws of Allah has certainly wronged himself. You never know, perhaps Allah will bring about some new situation.

faṭalliqoohunna li'iddatihinna wa aḥṣul-'iddata wattaqul laaha Rabbakum laa tukhri-joohunna mim buyootihinna wa laa yakhrujna illaaa añy-ya-teena bifaaḥishatim-mubayyinah; wa tilka ḥudoodul-laah; wa mañy-yata'adda ḥudoodal-laahi faqad ẓalama nafsah; laa tadree la'allal-laaha yuḥdis̲u ba'da z̲aalika amraa.

فَطَلِّقُوهُنَّ لِعِدَّتِهِنَّ وَأَحْصُوا
الْعِدَّةَ ۖ وَاتَّقُوا اللَّهَ رَبَّكُمْ ۖ لَا
تُخْرِجُوهُنَّ مِنْ بُيُوتِهِنَّ وَلَا
يَخْرُجْنَ إِلَّا أَنْ يَأْتِينَ بِفَاحِشَةٍ
مُبَيِّنَةٍ ۚ وَتِلْكَ حُدُودُ اللَّهِ ۚ
وَمَنْ يَتَعَدَّ حُدُودَ اللَّهِ فَقَدْ
ظَلَمَ نَفْسَهُ ۚ لَا تَدْرِي لَعَلَّ اللَّهَ
يُحْدِثُ بَعْدَ ذَٰلِكَ أَمْرًا ﴿١﴾

2. When their waiting period is about to end, keep them or separate from them lawfully. Allow two just people witness the divorce and allow them bear witness for the sake of Allah. Thus does Allah command those who have faith in Him and the Day of Judgment.

2. Fa-iz̲aa balaghna ajala-hunna fa-amsikoohunna bima'-roofin aw faariqoohunna bima'roofiñw-wa ashhidoo z̲away 'adlim-minkum wa aqeemush-shahaadata lillah; z̲aalikum yoo'aẓu bihee man kaana yu'minu billaahi wal-Yawmil Aakhir; wa mañy-yattaqil-laaha yaj'al lahoo makhrajaa.

فَإِذَا بَلَغْنَ أَجَلَهُنَّ فَأَمْسِكُوهُنَّ
بِمَعْرُوفٍ أَوْ فَارِقُوهُنَّ بِمَعْرُوفٍ
وَأَشْهِدُوا ذَوَيْ عَدْلٍ مِنْكُمْ
وَأَقِيمُوا الشَّهَادَةَ لِلَّهِ ۚ ذَٰلِكُمْ
يُوعَظُ بِهِ مَنْ كَانَ يُؤْمِنُ بِاللَّهِ
وَالْيَوْمِ الْآخِرِ ۚ وَمَنْ يَتَّقِ اللَّهَ
يَجْعَلْ لَهُ مَخْرَجًا ﴿٢﴾

3. Allah will make a way (out of difficulty) for one who has fear of Him and will provide him with sustenance in a way that he will not even notice. Allah is Sufficient for the needs of whoever trusts in Him. Allah has full access to whatever He wants. Allah has prescribed a due measure for everything.

3. Wa yarzuqhu min ḥays̲u laa yaḥtasib; wa mañy-yatawakkal 'alal-laahi fahuwa ḥasbuh; innal-laaha baalighu amrih; qad ja'alal-laahu likulli shay'in qadraa.

وَيَرْزُقْهُ مِنْ حَيْثُ لَا يَحْتَسِبُ ۚ
وَمَنْ يَتَوَكَّلْ عَلَى اللَّهِ فَهُوَ حَسْبُهُ ۚ
إِنَّ اللَّهَ بَالِغُ أَمْرِهِ ۚ قَدْ جَعَلَ
اللَّهُ لِكُلِّ شَيْءٍ قَدْرًا ﴿٣﴾

4. If you have any doubt whether your wives have reached the stage of menopause, the waiting period will be three months. This will also be the same for those who did not experience menstruation. The end of the waiting period for a pregnant woman is the delivery. Allah will make the affairs of one who fears Him easy.

4. Wallaaa'ee ya'isna minal-maḥeeḍi min nisaaa'ikum inir-tabtum fa'iddatuhunna s̲alaas̲atu ashhuriñw-wallaaa'ee lam yaḥiḍn; wa oolaatul-aḥmaali ajaluhunna añy-yaḍa'na ḥamlahunn; wa mañy-yattaqil-laaha yaj'al-lahoo min armrihee yusraa

وَاللَّائِي يَئِسْنَ مِنَ الْمَحِيضِ مِنْ
نِسَائِكُمْ إِنِ ارْتَبْتُمْ فَعِدَّتُهُنَّ
ثَلَاثَةُ أَشْهُرٍ وَاللَّائِي لَمْ يَحِضْنَ ۚ
وَأُولَاتُ الْأَحْمَالِ أَجَلُهُنَّ أَنْ
يَضَعْنَ حَمْلَهُنَّ ۚ وَمَنْ يَتَّقِ اللَّهَ
يَجْعَلْ لَهُ مِنْ أَمْرِهِ يُسْرًا ﴿٤﴾

5. This is the command of Allah, which He has sent down to you. Allah will expiate the evil

5. Z̲aalika amrul-laahi anzalahoo ilaykum; wa mañy-

ذَٰلِكَ أَمْرُ اللَّهِ أَنْزَلَهُ إِلَيْكُمْ ۚ وَمَنْ

deeds of those who fear Him and will increase their rewards.

yattaqil-laaha yukaffir ʻanhu sayyi-aatihee wa yuʻẓim lahoo ajraa.

يَتَّقِ اللّٰهَ يُكَفِّرْ عَنْهُ سَيِّاٰتِهٖ وَ
يُعْظِمْ لَهٗۤ اَجْرًا ۝٥

6. Lodge them (your wives) as you lived before if you can afford it. Do not annoy them so as to make life intolerable for them. If they are pregnant, provide them with maintenance until their delivery. Pay their wage if they breast-feed your children and settle your differences lawfully. If you are unable to settle them, let another person breast-feed the child.

6. Askinoohunna min ḥaysu sakantum miñw-wujdikum wa laa tuḍaaarroohunna lituḍay-yiqoo ʻalayhinn wa-in kunna oolaati ḥamlin fa-anfiqoo ʻalayhinna ḥattaa yaḍaʻna ḥamlahunn ; fa-in arḍaʻna lakum fa-aatoohunna ujoorahunna wa-tamiroo baynakum bimaʻroof; wa-in taʻaasartum fasaturḍiʻu lahooo ukhraa.

اَسْكِنُوْهُنَّ مِنْ حَيْثُ سَكَنْتُمْ مِّنْ
وُّجْدِكُمْ وَلَا تُضَآرُّوْهُنَّ لِتُضَيِّقُوْا
عَلَيْهِنَّ ؕ وَاِنْ كُنَّ اُولَاتِ حَمْلٍ
فَاَنْفِقُوْا عَلَيْهِنَّ حَتّٰى يَضَعْنَ
حَمْلَهُنَّ ۚ فَاِنْ اَرْضَعْنَ لَكُمْ
فَاٰتُوْهُنَّ اُجُوْرَهُنَّ ۚ وَاْتَمِرُوْا
بَيْنَكُمْ بِمَعْرُوْفٍ ۚ وَاِنْ تَعَاسَرْتُمْ
فَسَتُرْضِعُ لَهٗۤ اُخْرٰى ؕ۝٦

7. Let the well-to-do people spend abundantly (for the mother and the child) and let the poor spend from what Allah has given them. Allah does not impose on any soul that which he cannot afford. Allah will bring about ease after hardship.

7. Liyunfiq zoo saʻatim-min saʻatihee wa man qudira ʻalayhi rizquhoo falyunfiq mimmaaa aataahul-laah; laa yukalliful-laahu nafsan illaa maaa aataahaa; sa-yajʻalul-laahu baʻda ʻusriñy-yusraa.

لِيُنْفِقْ ذُوْ سَعَةٍ مِّنْ سَعَتِهٖ ؕ وَمَنْ
قُدِرَ عَلَيْهِ رِزْقُهٗ فَلْيُنْفِقْ مِمَّاۤ
اٰتٰىهُ اللّٰهُ ؕ لَا يُكَلِّفُ اللّٰهُ نَفْسًا اِلَّا
مَاۤ اٰتٰىهَا ؕ سَيَجْعَلُ اللّٰهُ بَعْدَ
عُسْرٍ يُّسْرًا ۝٧ ع ١٧/٧

8. How many a town has disobeyed its Lord and His Messenger! For them Our questioning was strict and Our punishment severe.

8. Wa ka-ayyim-min qarya-tin ʻatat ʻan amri Rabbihaa wa Rusulihee faḥaasabnaahaa ḥisaaban shadeedañw- wa ʻaz-zabnaahaa ʻazaaban nukraa.

وَكَاَيِّنْ مِّنْ قَرْيَةٍ عَتَتْ عَنْ اَمْرِ
رَبِّهَا وَرُسُلِهٖ فَحَاسَبْنٰهَا حِسَابًا
شَدِيْدًا ۙ وَّعَذَّبْنٰهَا عَذَابًا نُّكْرًا ۝٨

9. They suffered the consequences of their deeds and their end was perdition.

9. Fazaaqat wabaala amri-haa wa kaana ʻaaqibatu amri-haa khusraa.

فَذَاقَتْ وَبَالَ اَمْرِهَا وَكَانَ
عَاقِبَةُ اَمْرِهَا خُسْرًا ۝٩

10. a Messenger who recites to you the illustrious revelations of Allah, to bring the righteously striving believers out of darkness into light.

10. Aʻaddal-laahu lahum ʻazaaban shadeedan fattaqul-laaha yaaa ulil-albaab; allazeena aamanoo; qad anzalal-laahu ilaykum zikraa.

اَعَدَّ اللّٰهُ لَهُمْ عَذَابًا شَدِيْدًا ۙ
فَاتَّقُوا اللّٰهَ يٰۤاُولِى الْاَلْبَابِ ۛۚ مع ١٤
الَّذِيْنَ اٰمَنُوْا ۛ قَدْ اَنْزَلَ اللّٰهُ عند المتقدمين ١٠
اِلَيْكُمْ ذِكْرًا ۙ۝١٠

11. Allah will admit those who believe in Him and act righteously to Paradise wherein streams flow, and they will live

11. Rasoolañy-yatloo ʻalay-kum Aayaatil-laahi mubayyi-naatil-liyukhrijal-lazeena aa-manoo

رَّسُوْلًا يَّتْلُوْا عَلَيْكُمْ اٰيٰتِ اللّٰهِ
مُبَيِّنٰتٍ لِّيُخْرِجَ الَّذِيْنَ اٰمَنُوْا

therein forever. Allah will provide them with excellent sustenance.

wa 'amiluṣ-ṣaaliḥaati minaẓ-ẓulumaati ilan-noor; wa mañy-yu'mim billaahi wa ya'mal ṣaaliḥañy-yudkhilhu Jannaatin tajree min taḥtihal-anhaaru khaalideena feehaa abadaa; qad aḥsanal-laahu lahoo rizqaa.

وَعَمِلُوا الصّٰلِحٰتِ مِنَ الظُّلُمٰتِ
إِلَى النُّوْرِ ۚ وَمَنْ يُّؤْمِنْ بِاللّٰهِ
وَيَعْمَلْ صَالِحًا يُّدْخِلْهُ
جَنّٰتٍ تَجْرِيْ مِنْ تَحْتِهَا الْاَنْهٰرُ
خٰلِدِيْنَ فِيْهَآ اَبَدًا ۖ قَدْ اَحْسَنَ
اللّٰهُ لَهٗ رِزْقًا ﴿١١﴾

12. It is Allah who has created the seven heavens and a like number of earths. His commandments are sent between them, so that you will know that Allah has power over all things and that His knowledge encompasses all things.

12. Allaahul-lazee khalaqa Sab'a Samaawaatiñw-wa minal-arḍi mislahunna yatanazzalul-amru baynahunna lita'lamooo annal-laaha 'alaa kulli shay'in Qadeeruñw-wa annal-laaha qad aḥaaṭa bikulli shay'in 'ilmaa.

اَللّٰهُ الَّذِيْ خَلَقَ سَبْعَ سَمٰوٰتٍ
وَّمِنَ الْاَرْضِ مِثْلَهُنَّ ۖ يَتَنَزَّلُ
الْاَمْرُ بَيْنَهُنَّ لِتَعْلَمُوْٓا اَنَّ اللّٰهَ
عَلٰى كُلِّ شَيْءٍ قَدِيْرٌ ۙ وَّاَنَّ اللّٰهَ قَدْ
اَحَاطَ بِكُلِّ شَيْءٍ عِلْمًا ﴿١٢﴾ ع ٢ ٥ ١٨

Al-Tahrim, Prohibition (66)

In the Name of Allah, the Beneficent, the Merciful.

Sûrat at-Taḥrîm-66

(Revealed at Madinah)

Bismillaahir Raḥmaanir Raḥeem

(٦٦) سُوْرَةُ التَّحْرِيْمِ مَدَنِيَّةٌ (١٠٧)
اٰيَاتُهَا ١٢ بِسْمِ اللّٰهِ الرَّحْمٰنِ الرَّحِيْمِ رُكُوْعَاتُهَا ٢

1. Prophet, in seeking the pleasure of your wives, why do you make unlawful that which Allah has made lawful? Allah is All-forgiving and All-merciful.

1. Yaaa ayyuhan-Nabiyyu lima tuḥarrimu maaa aḥallal-laahu laka tabtaghee marḍaata azwaajik; wallaahu Ghafoorur-Raḥeem.

يٰٓاَيُّهَا النَّبِيُّ لِمَ تُحَرِّمُ مَآ اَحَلَّ
اللّٰهُ لَكَ ۚ تَبْتَغِيْ مَرْضَاتَ اَزْوَاجِكَ ۗ
وَاللّٰهُ غَفُوْرٌ رَّحِيْمٌ ﴿١﴾

2. Allah has shown you how to absolve yourselves of your oaths. He is your Guardian and is All-knowing and All-wise.

2. Qad faraḍal-laahu lakum taḥillata aymaanikum; wallaahu mawlaakum wa Huwal-'Aleemul-Ḥakeem.

قَدْ فَرَضَ اللّٰهُ لَكُمْ تَحِلَّةَ
اَيْمَانِكُمْ ۚ وَاللّٰهُ مَوْلٰىكُمْ ۚ وَهُوَ
الْعَلِيْمُ الْحَكِيْمُ ﴿٢﴾

3. The Prophet told a secret to one of his wives, (telling her not to mention it to anyone else). When she divulged it, Allah informed His Prophet about this. The Prophet told his wife part of the information which he had received from Allah and ignored the rest. Then she asked, "Who informed you about this?" He replied, "The All-aware and All-knowing one has told me."

3. Wa-iz-asarran-Nabiyyu ilaa ba'ḍi azwaajihee ḥadeesan falammaa nabba-at bihee wa aẓharahul-laahu 'alayhi 'arrafa ba'ḍahoo wa a'raḍa 'am ba'ḍin falammaa nabba-ahaa bihee qaalat man amba-aka haazaa qaala nabba-aniyal-'Aleemul-Khabeer.

وَاِذْ اَسَرَّ النَّبِيُّ اِلٰى بَعْضِ اَزْوَاجِهٖ
حَدِيْثًا ۚ فَلَمَّا نَبَّاَتْ بِهٖ وَاَظْهَرَهُ
اللّٰهُ عَلَيْهِ عَرَّفَ بَعْضَهٗ وَاَعْرَضَ
عَنْۢ بَعْضٍ ۚ فَلَمَّا نَبَّاَهَا بِهٖ قَالَتْ
مَنْ اَنْۢبَاَكَ هٰذَا ۖ قَالَ نَبَّاَنِيَ
الْعَلِيْمُ الْخَبِيْرُ ﴿٣﴾

4. Would that you two (wives of the Prophet) had turned to

4. In tatoobaaa ilal-laahi faqad ṣaghat

اِنْ تَتُوْبَآ اِلَى اللّٰهِ فَقَدْ صَغَتْ

Allah in repentance. Your hearts have sinned. If you conspire with each other against him, know that Allah is his Guardian. Gabriel, the righteous (ones) among the believers, and the angels will all support him.

quloobukumaa wa in taẓaaharaa 'alayhi fa innal-laaha Huwa mawlaahu wa Jibreelu wa ṣaaliḥul-mu'mineen; walmalaaa'ikatu ba'da z̲aalika ẓaheer.

قُلُوبُكُمَا ۚ وَإِنْ تَظٰهَرَا عَلَيْهِ
فَإِنَّ اللّٰهَ هُوَ مَوْلٰىهُ وَجِبْرِيلُ
وَصَالِحُ الْمُؤْمِنِينَ ۚ وَالْمَلٰٓئِكَةُ
بَعْدَ ذٰلِكَ ظَهِيرٌ ۴

5. If he divorces you, perhaps his Lord will replace you with better wives, who will be Muslims: believers, faithful, obedient, repentant, and devout in prayer and fasting either widows or virgins.

5. 'Asaa Rabbuhooo in ṭallaqakunna añy-yubdilahooo azwaajan khayram-minkunna muslimaatim-mu'minaatin qaanitaatin taaa'ibaatin 'aabidaatin saaa'iḥaatin s̲ayyibaatiñw-wa abkaaraa.

عَسٰى رَبُّهٗٓ إِنْ طَلَّقَكُنَّ أَنْ يُّبْدِلَهٗٓ
أَزْوَاجًا خَيْرًا مِّنْكُنَّ مُسْلِمٰتٍ
مُّؤْمِنٰتٍ قٰنِتٰتٍ تٰٓئِبٰتٍ عٰبِدٰتٍ
سٰٓئِحٰتٍ ثَيِّبٰتٍ وَّأَبْكَارًا ۵

6. Believers, save yourselves and your families from the fire, which is fueled with people and stones and is guarded by stern angels who do not disobey Allah's commands and who do whatever they are ordered to do.

6. Yaaa ayyuhal-laz̲eena aamanoo qoo anfusakum wa ahleekum Naarañw-waqooduhan-naasu walḥijaaratu 'alayha malaaa'ikatun ghilaaẓun shidaadul-laa ya'ṣoonal-laaha maaa amarahum wa yaf'aloona maa yu'maroon.

يٰٓأَيُّهَا الَّذِينَ اٰمَنُوا قُوٓا أَنْفُسَكُمْ
وَأَهْلِيكُمْ نَارًا وَّقُودُهَا النَّاسُ
وَالْحِجَارَةُ عَلَيْهَا مَلٰٓئِكَةٌ
غِلَاظٌ شِدَادٌ لَّا يَعْصُونَ اللّٰهَ مَآ
أَمَرَهُمْ وَيَفْعَلُونَ مَا يُؤْمَرُونَ ۶

7. Unbelievers (will be told on the Day of Judgment), "Do not make any excuses on this day; you are only receiving recompense for what you have done."

7. Yaaa ayyuhal-laz̲eena kafaroo laa ta'taz̲irul-Yawma innamaa tujzawna maa kuntum ta'maloon.

يٰٓأَيُّهَا الَّذِينَ كَفَرُوا لَا تَعْتَذِرُوا
الْيَوْمَ ۖ إِنَّمَا تُجْزَوْنَ مَا كُنْتُمْ
تَعْمَلُونَ ۷ ع ۷/۱۹

8. Believers, turn to Allah in repentance with the intention of never repeating the same sin. Perhaps your Lord will expiate your evil deeds and admit you to Paradise wherein streams flow. On the Day of Judgment, Allah will not disgrace the Prophet and those who have believed in him. Their lights will shine in front of them and to their right. They will say, "Our Lord, perfect our light for us and forgive our sins. You have power over all things."

8. Yaaa ayyuhal-laz̲eena aamanoo tooboo ilal-laahi tawbatan-naṣooḥaa; 'asaa Rabbukum añy-yukaffira 'ankum sayyi-aatikum wa yudkhilakum Jannaatin tajree min taḥtihal-anhaaru Yawma laa yukhzil-laahun-Nabiyya wallaz̲eena aamanoo ma'hoo nooruhum yas'aa bayna aydeehim wa bi-aymaanihim yaqooloona Rabbanaaa atmim lanaa nooranaa waghfir lanaa innaka 'alaa kulli shay'in Qadeer.

يٰٓأَيُّهَا الَّذِينَ اٰمَنُوا تُوبُوٓا إِلَى
اللّٰهِ تَوْبَةً نَّصُوحًا ۖ عَسٰى رَبُّكُمْ
أَنْ يُّكَفِّرَ عَنْكُمْ سَيِّاٰتِكُمْ
وَيُدْخِلَكُمْ جَنّٰتٍ تَجْرِي مِنْ
تَحْتِهَا الْأَنْهٰرُ ۙ يَوْمَ لَا يُخْزِي
اللّٰهُ النَّبِيَّ وَالَّذِينَ اٰمَنُوا مَعَهٗ ۚ
نُورُهُمْ يَسْعٰى بَيْنَ أَيْدِيهِمْ وَ
بِأَيْمَانِهِمْ يَقُولُونَ رَبَّنَآ أَتْمِمْ
لَنَا نُورَنَا وَاغْفِرْ لَنَا ۚ إِنَّكَ عَلٰى
كُلِّ شَيْءٍ قَدِيرٌ ۸

9. Prophet, fight against the unbelievers and the hypocrites and be stern against them. Their dwelling will be hellfire, the most terrible fate.

9. Yaaa ayyuhan-Nabiyyu jaahidil-kuffaara walmunaa-fiqeena waghluẓ 'alayhim; wa ma-waahum Jahannam; wa bi'sal-maṣeer.

يٰۤاَيُّهَا النَّبِيُّ جَاهِدِ الْكُفَّارَ
وَالْمُنٰفِقِيْنَ وَاغْلُظْ عَلَيْهِمْ ۭ وَ
مَاْوٰىهُمْ جَهَنَّمُ ۭ وَبِئْسَ الْمَصِيْرُ ۝٩

10. Allah has told the unbelievers the story of the wives of Noah and Lot as a parable. They were married to two of Our righteous servants but were unfaithful to them. Nothing could protect them from the (wrath) of Allah and they were told to enter hell-fire with the others.

10. Ḍarabal-laahu masalal-lillazeena kafarum-ra-ata Nooḥiñw-wamra-ata Looṭ; kaanataa taḥta 'abdayni min 'ibaadinaa ṣaaliḥayni fakha-anataahumaa falam yughniyaa 'anhumaa minal-laahi shay'añw-wa qeelad-khulan-Naara ma'ad-daakhileen.

ضَرَبَ اللّٰهُ مَثَلًا لِّلَّذِيْنَ كَفَرُوا
امْرَاَتَ نُوْحٍ وَّامْرَاَتَ لُوْطٍ ۭ
كَانَتَا تَحْتَ عَبْدَيْنِ مِنْ عِبَادِنَا
صَالِحَيْنِ فَخَانَتٰهُمَا فَلَمْ يُغْنِيَا
عَنْهُمَا مِنَ اللّٰهِ شَيْـًٔا وَّقِيْلَ
ادْخُلَا النَّارَ مَعَ الدّٰخِلِيْنَ ۝١٠

11. To the believers, as a parable, Allah has told the story of the wife of Pharaoh who said, "Lord, establish for me a house in Paradise in your presence. Rescue me from the Pharaoh and his deeds and save me from the unjust people."

11. Wa ḍarabal-laahu masa-lal-lillazeena aamanumra-ata Fir'awn; iz qaalat Rabbibni lee 'indaka baytan fil-Jannati wa najjinee min Fir'awna wa 'amalihee wa najjinee minal-qawmiẓ-ẓaalimeen.

وَضَرَبَ اللّٰهُ مَثَلًا لِّلَّذِيْنَ اٰمَنُوا
امْرَاَتَ فِرْعَوْنَ ۘ اِذْ قَالَتْ رَبِّ
ابْنِ لِيْ عِنْدَكَ بَيْتًا فِي الْجَنَّةِ
وَنَجِّنِيْ مِنْ فِرْعَوْنَ وَعَمَلِهٖ وَ
نَجِّنِيْ مِنَ الْقَوْمِ الظّٰلِمِيْنَ ۝١١

وقف لازم

12. He has also told, as a parable, the story of Mary, daughter of Imran who protected her privacy (did not look at it) and into whose womb We breathed Our spirit. She made the words of her Lord and the predictions in His Books come true. She was an obedient woman.

12. Wa Maryamab-nata 'Imraanal-lateee aḥṣanat farjahaa fanafakhnaa feehi mir-rooḥinaa wa ṣaddaqat bikali-maati Rabbihaa wa kutubihee wa kaanat minal-qaaniteen.

وَمَرْيَمَ ابْنَتَ عِمْرٰنَ الَّتِيْٓ اَحْصَنَتْ
فَرْجَهَا فَنَفَخْنَا فِيْهِ مِنْ رُّوْحِنَا
وَصَدَّقَتْ بِكَلِمٰتِ رَبِّهَا وَكُتُبِهٖ
وَكَانَتْ مِنَ الْقٰنِتِيْنَ ۝١٢

ع

Al-Mulk, The Kingdom (67)

In the Name of Allah, the Beneficent, the Merciful.

Sûrat al-Mulk-67

(Revealed at Makkah)

Bismillaahir Raḥmaanir Raḥeem

(٦٧) سُوْرَةُ الْمُلْكِ مَكِّيَّةٌ (٧٧)

اٰياتها ٣٠ بِسْمِ اللّٰهِ الرَّحْمٰنِ الرَّحِيْمِ ركوعاتها ٢

1. Blessed is He in whose hands is the Kingdom and who has power over all things.

1. Tabaarakal-lazee biyadi-hil-mulku wa Huwa 'alaa kulli shay'in Qadeer.

تَبٰرَكَ الَّذِيْ بِيَدِهِ الْمُلْكُ ۡ وَهُوَ
عَلٰى كُلِّ شَيْءٍ قَدِيْرُ ۝١

2. It is He who has created death and life (destined them) to put you to the test and see which of you is most virtuous in your deeds. He is Majestic and All-forgiving.

2. Allazee khalaqal-mawta walḥayaata liyabluwakum ayyukum aḥsanu 'amalaa; wa Huwal-'Azeezul-Ghafoor.

الَّذِيْ خَلَقَ الْمَوْتَ وَالْحَيٰوةَ
لِيَبْلُوَكُمْ اَيُّكُمْ اَحْسَنُ عَمَلًا ۭ
وَهُوَ الْعَزِيْزُ الْغَفُوْرُ ۝٢

الجزء التاسع والعشرون (٢٩)

3. It is He who has created seven heavens, one above the

3. Allazee khalaqa Sab'a samaawaatin ṭibaaqaa;-maa

الَّذِيْ خَلَقَ سَبْعَ سَمٰوٰتٍ طِبَاقًا ۭ مَا

other (in levels). You can see no flaw in the creation of the Beneficent. Look again. Can you see faults?

4. Look twice (and keep on looking), your eyes will only become dull and tired.

5. We have decked the lowest heavens with torches. With these torches We have stoned the devils and We have prepared for them the torment of hell.

6. For those who have disbelieved in their Lord, there is the torment of hell, the most terrible place to which to return.

7. When they are thrown into hell, they will hear its roaring while it boils.

8. It almost explodes in rage. Whenever a group is thrown into it, its keepers will ask them, "Did no one come to warn you?"

9. They will say, "Yes, someone did come to warn us, but we rejected him saying, 'Allah has revealed nothing. You are in great error.'"

10. They will also say, "Had We listened or used our minds, we would not have become the dwellers of hell."

11. They will confess to their sins, but the dwellers of hell will be far away from Allah's (mercy).

12. Those who fear their Lord in secret will receive forgiveness and a great reward.

13. Whether you conceal what you say or reveal it, Allah knows best all that the hearts contain.

14. Does the One Who is Subtle, All-aware, and Who created all things not know all about them?

taraa fee khalqir-Raḥmaani min tafaawut; farji'il-baṣara hal taraa min fuṭoor.

4. Summar-ji'il-baṣara karratayni yanqalib ilaykal baṣaru khaasi'añw-wa huwa ḥaseer.

5. Wa laqad zayyannas-samaaa'ad-dunyaa bimaṣaa-beeḥa wa ja'alnaahaa rujoomal-lish-Shayaaṭeeni wa a'tadnaa lahum 'azaabas-sa'eer.

6. Wa lillazeena kafaroo bi-Rabbihim 'azaabu Jahannama wa bi'sal-maṣeer.

7. Izaaa ulqoo feeha sami-'oo lahaa shaheeqañw-wa hiya tafoor.

8. Takaadu tamayyazu minal-ghayzi kullamaaa ulqiya feehaa fawjun sa-alahum khazanatuhaaa alam ya-tikum nazeer.

9. Qaaloo balaa qad jaaa'anaa nazeerun fakaz zab-naa wa qulnaa maa nazzalal-laahu min shay'in in antum illaa fee ḍalaalin kabeer.

10. Wa qaaloo law kunnaa nasma'u aw na'qilu maa kunnaa feee Aṣḥaabis-sa'eer.

11. Fa'tarafoo bizambihim fasuḥqal-li-Aṣḥaabis-sa'eer.

12. Innal-lazeena yakh-shawna Rabbahum bilghaybi lahum maghfiratuñw-wa ajrun kabeer.

13. Wa asirroo qawlakum awijharoo bih; innahoo 'Aleemum bizaatiṣ-ṣudoor.

14. Alaa ya'lamu man khalaq; wa Huwal-Laṭeeful Khabeer.

تَرٰى فِىْ خَلْقِ الرَّحْمٰنِ مِنْ تَفٰوُتٍ ؕ
فَارْجِعِ الْبَصَرَ ۙ هَلْ تَرٰى مِنْ فُطُوْرٍ ﴿۳﴾
ثُمَّ ارْجِعِ الْبَصَرَ كَرَّتَيْنِ يَنْقَلِبْ
اِلَيْكَ الْبَصَرُ خَاسِئًا وَّهُوَ حَسِيْرٌ ﴿۴﴾
وَلَقَدْ زَيَّنَّا السَّمَآءَ الدُّنْيَا بِمَصَابِيْحَ
وَجَعَلْنٰهَا رُجُوْمًا لِّلشَّيٰطِيْنِ وَاَعْتَدْنَا
لَهُمْ عَذَابَ السَّعِيْرِ ﴿۵﴾
وَلِلَّذِيْنَ كَفَرُوْا بِرَبِّهِمْ عَذَابُ
جَهَنَّمَ ؕ وَبِئْسَ الْمَصِيْرُ ﴿۶﴾
اِذَآ اُلْقُوْا فِيْهَا سَمِعُوْا لَهَا شَهِيْقًا
وَّهِىَ تَفُوْرُ ۙ ﴿۷﴾
تَكَادُ تَمَيَّزُ مِنَ الْغَيْظِ ؕ كُلَّمَآ اُلْقِىَ
فِيْهَا فَوْجٌ سَاَلَهُمْ خَزَنَتُهَآ اَلَمْ
يَاْتِكُمْ نَذِيْرٌ ﴿۸﴾
قَالُوْا بَلٰى قَدْ جَآءَنَا نَذِيْرٌ ۙ
فَكَذَّبْنَا وَقُلْنَا مَا نَزَّلَ اللّٰهُ مِنْ
شَىْءٍ ۖۚ اِنْ اَنْتُمْ اِلَّا فِىْ ضَلٰلٍ كَبِيْرٍ ﴿۹﴾
وَقَالُوْا لَوْ كُنَّا نَسْمَعُ اَوْ نَعْقِلُ مَا
كُنَّا فِىْٓ اَصْحٰبِ السَّعِيْرِ ﴿۱۰﴾
فَاعْتَرَفُوْا بِذَنْۢبِهِمْ ۚ فَسُحْقًا
لِّاَصْحٰبِ السَّعِيْرِ ﴿۱۱﴾
اِنَّ الَّذِيْنَ يَخْشَوْنَ رَبَّهُمْ بِالْغَيْبِ
لَهُمْ مَّغْفِرَةٌ وَّاَجْرٌ كَبِيْرٌ ﴿۱۲﴾
وَاَسِرُّوْا قَوْلَكُمْ اَوِ اجْهَرُوْا بِهٖ ؕ اِنَّهٗ
عَلِيْمٌ ۢ بِذَاتِ الصُّدُوْرِ ﴿۱۳﴾
اَلَا يَعْلَمُ مَنْ خَلَقَ ؕ وَهُوَ اللَّطِيْفُ

15. It is He who has made the earth a floor for you. You walk through its vast valleys and eat of its sustenance. Before Him you will all be resurrected.

16. Do you feel secure that the One in the heavens will not cause you to sink into the earth when it is violently shaking?

17. Do you feel secure that the One in the heavens will not strike you with a sandstorm? You will soon know, with the coming of the torment, how serious Our warning was.

18. Those who lived before them had also rejected the warning, and how terrible was the retribution!

19. Did they not see the birds above them, stretching out, and flapping their wings. No one keeps them up in the sky except the Beneficent. He certainly watches over all things.

20. This, which is your army; does it help you instead of the Beneficent? The unbelievers are certainly deceived (by Satan).

21. Is there anyone who would provide you with sustenance if Allah were to deny you sustenance? In fact, they obstinately persist in their transgression and hatred.

22. Can one who walks with his head hanging down be better guided that one who walks with his head upright on the right path?

23. (Muhammad), say, "It is Allah who has brought you into being and made ears, eyes, and hearts for you, but you give very little thanks."

24. Say, "It is Allah who has settled you on the earth, and to Him you will be resurrected."

15. Huwal-lazee ja'ala lakumul-arḍa zaloolan famshoo fee manaakibihaa wa kuloo mirrizqihee wa ilayhin-nushoor.

16. 'A-amintum man fissamaaa'i añy-yakhsifa bikumul-arḍa fa-izaa hiya tamoor.

17. Am amintum man fissamaa'i añy-yursila 'alaykum ḥaaṣiban fasata'lamoona kayfa nazeer.

18. Wa laqad kaz-zabal-lazeena min qablihim fakayfa kaana nakeer.

19. Awalam yaraw ilaṭ-ṭayri fawqahum ṣaaaffaatiñw-wa yaqbiḍn; maa yumsikuhunna illar-Raḥmaan; innahoo bikulli shay'im Baṣeer.

20. Amman haazal-lazee huwa jundul-lakum yanṣurukum min doonir Raḥmaan; inilkaafiroona illaa fee ghuroor.

21. Amman haazal-lazee yarzuqukum in amsaka rizqah; bal lajjoo fee 'utuwwiñw-wa nufoor.

22. Afamañy-yamshee mukibban 'alaa wajhiheee ahdaaa ammañy-yamshee sawiyyan 'alaa Ṣiraaṭim-Mustaqeem.

23. Qul Huwal-lazee anshaakum wa ja'ala lakumus-sam'a wal abṣaara wal-af'idata qaleelam-maa tashkuroon.

24. Qul Huwal-lazee zaraakum fil-arḍi wa ilayhi tuḥsharoon.

الْخَبِيرُ ﴿١٤﴾ ع ١٤
هُوَ الَّذِي جَعَلَ لَكُمُ الْأَرْضَ ذَلُولًا
فَامْشُوا فِي مَنَاكِبِهَا وَكُلُوا مِن
رِّزْقِهِ ۖ وَإِلَيْهِ النُّشُورُ ﴿١٥﴾
أَأَمِنتُم مَّن فِي السَّمَاءِ أَن يَخْسِفَ
بِكُمُ الْأَرْضَ فَإِذَا هِيَ تَمُورُ ﴿١٦﴾
أَمْ أَمِنتُم مَّن فِي السَّمَاءِ أَن يُرْسِلَ
عَلَيْكُمْ حَاصِبًا ۖ فَسَتَعْلَمُونَ
كَيْفَ نَذِيرِ ﴿١٧﴾
وَلَقَدْ كَذَّبَ الَّذِينَ مِن قَبْلِهِمْ
فَكَيْفَ كَانَ نَكِيرِ ﴿١٨﴾
أَوَلَمْ يَرَوْا إِلَى الطَّيْرِ فَوْقَهُمْ صَافَّاتٍ
وَيَقْبِضْنَ ۚ مَا يُمْسِكُهُنَّ إِلَّا الرَّحْمَٰنُ ۚ وقف لازم
إِنَّهُ بِكُلِّ شَيْءٍ بَصِيرٌ ﴿١٩﴾
أَمَّنْ هَٰذَا الَّذِي هُوَ جُندٌ لَّكُمْ
يَنصُرُكُم مِّن دُونِ الرَّحْمَٰنِ ۚ إِنِ
الْكَافِرُونَ إِلَّا فِي غُرُورٍ ﴿٢٠﴾
أَمَّنْ هَٰذَا الَّذِي يَرْزُقُكُمْ إِنْ أَمْسَكَ
رِزْقَهُ ۚ بَل لَّجُّوا فِي عُتُوٍّ وَنُفُورٍ ﴿٢١﴾
أَفَمَن يَمْشِي مُكِبًّا عَلَىٰ وَجْهِهِ
أَهْدَىٰ أَمَّن يَمْشِي سَوِيًّا عَلَىٰ
صِرَاطٍ مُّسْتَقِيمٍ ﴿٢٢﴾
قُلْ هُوَ الَّذِي أَنشَأَكُمْ وَجَعَلَ
لَكُمُ السَّمْعَ وَالْأَبْصَارَ وَالْأَفْئِدَةَ ۖ
قَلِيلًا مَّا تَشْكُرُونَ ﴿٢٣﴾
قُلْ هُوَ الَّذِي ذَرَأَكُمْ فِي الْأَرْضِ

25. They say, "When will this torment take place if what you say is true?"

26. Say, "Allah knows best. I am only one who gives warning."

27. When they see it [him] approaching, the faces of the unbelievers will blacken and they will be told, "This is what you wanted to be called (Amir al-Mu'minin)."

28. (Muhammad), say, "Have you ever considered; Allah destroys or grants mercy to me and my followers, but who will protect the unbelievers from a painful torment?

29. Say, "He is the Beneficent One in whom we have faith and trust. You will soon know who is in manifest error."

30. Say, "Consider, were your water to dry up, who would bring you water from the spring?"

Al-Qalam, The Pen (68)

In the Name of Allah,
the Beneficent, the Merciful.

1. Nun. By the pen and by what they write,

2. (Muhammad), you are not possessed by jinn, thanks to the bounty of your Lord.

3. You will certainly receive a never-ending reward (without being obliged the least).

4. You have attained a great moral standard (religion).

5. You will see and they will also see

6. which of you has been afflicted by insanity.

7. Your Lord knows best who has gone astray from His path and who is rightly guided.

8. Do not yield to those who reject the Truth.

25. Wa yaqooloona mataa haazal-wa'du in kuntum ṣaadiqeen.

26. Qul innamal-'ilmu 'indal-laahi wa innamaaa anaa nazeerum-mubeen.

27. Falammaa ra-awhu zulfatan seee'at wujoohul-lazeena kafaroo wa qeela haazal-lazee kuntum bihee tadda'oon.

28. Qul ara'aytum in ahlakaniyal-laahu wa mam-ma'iya aw raḥimanaa famañy-yujeerul-kaafireena min 'azaabin aleem.

29. Qul Huwar-Raḥmaanu aamannaa bihee wa 'alayhi tawakkalnaa fasata'lamoona man huwa fee ḍalaalim-mubeen.

30. Qul ara'aytum in aṣbaḥa maaa'ukum ghawran famañy-ya-teekum bimaaa'im-ma'een.

Sûrat al-Qalam-68

(Revealed at Makkah)

Bismillaahir Raḥmaanir Raḥeem

1. Nooon; walqalami wa maa yasṭuroon.

2. Maa anta bini'mati Rabbika bimajnoon.

3. Wa inna laka la ajran ghayra mamnoon.

4. Wa innaka la'alaa khuluqin 'aẓeem.

5. Fasatubṣiru wa yubṣiroon.

6. Bi-ayyikumul-maftoon.

7. Inna Rabbaka Huwa a'lamu biman ḍalla 'an sabeelihee wa Huwa a'lamu bilmuhtadeen.

8. Falaa tuṭi'il-mukaz zibeen.

والیه تحشرون ﴿٢٤﴾
ویقولون متی هذا الوعد إن
کنتم صدقین ﴿٢٥﴾
قل إنما العلم عند الله وإنما
أنا نذیر مبین ﴿٢٦﴾
فلما رأوه زلفة سیئت وجوه
الذین کفروا وقیل هذا الذی
کنتم به تدعون ﴿٢٧﴾
قل أرءیتم إن أهلکنی الله ومن
معی أو رحمنا فمن یجیر
الکفرین من عذاب ألیم ﴿٢٨﴾
قل هو الرحمن ءامنا به وعلیه
توکلنا فستعلمون من هو فی
ضلل مبین ﴿٢٩﴾
قل أرءیتم إن أصبح ماؤکم غورا
فمن یأتیکم بماء معین ﴿٣٠﴾

(٦٨) سورة القلم مکیة (٢)

بسم الله الرحمن الرحیم

ن والقلم وما یسطرون ﴿١﴾
ما أنت بنعمة ربك بمجنون ﴿٢﴾
وإن لك لأجرا غیر ممنون ﴿٣﴾
وإنك لعلی خلق عظیم ﴿٤﴾
فستبصر ویبصرون ﴿٥﴾
بأییکم المفتون ﴿٦﴾
إن ربك هو أعلم بمن ضل عن
سبیله وهو أعلم بالمهتدین ﴿٧﴾

9. They would like you to relent to them so that they could also relent toward you.

10. Do not yield to one persistent in swearing,

11. back-biting, gossiping,

12. obstructing virtues, a sinful transgressor,

13. ill-mannered, and morally corrupt or just because he may possess wealth and children.

14. When Our revelations are recited to him,

15. he says, "These are ancient legends."

16. We shall place a mark on his nose.

17. We have tested them in the same way as we tested the dwellers of the garden (in Yemen) when they swore to pluck all the fruits of the garden in the morning,

18. without saying, "if Allah so wills."

19. A visitor from your Lord circled around the garden during the night while they were asleep

20. and the garden, in the morning, was found burned down all together.

21. In the morning they called out to one another,

22. "Go early to your farms, if you want to pluck the fruits."

23. They all left, whispering to one another,

24. "Let no beggar come to the garden."

25. They were resolved to repel the beggars.

26. When they saw the garden, they said, "Surely we have lost our way.

27. (No, we are not lost.) In fact, we have been deprived of everything."

28. A reasonable one among them said, "Did I not tell you that you should glorify Allah?"

9. Waddoo law tudhinu fayudhinoon.

10. Wa laa tuti' kulla ḥallaa-fim-maheen.

11. Hammaazim mash-shaaa'im binameem.

12. Mannaa'il-lilkhayri mu'-tadin a̲seem.

13. 'Utullim ba'da z̲aalika zaneem.

14. An kaana z̲aa maaliñw-wa baneen.

15. Iz̲aa tutlaa 'alayhi Aayaatunaa qaala asaaṭeerul-awwaleen.

16. Sanasimuhoo 'alal-khur-ṭoom.

17. Innaa balawnaahum ka-maa balawnaaa Aṣḥaabal-jannati iz̲ aqsamoo layaṣri-munnahaa muṣbiḥeen.

18. Wa laa yastas̲noon.

19. Faṭaafa 'alayhaa ṭaaa'i-fum-mir-Rabbika wa hum naaa'imoon.

20. Fa-aṣbaḥat kaṣṣareem.

21. Fatanaadaw muṣbiḥeen.

22. Anighdoo 'alaa ḥars̲ikum in kuntum ṣaarimeen.

23. Fanṭalaqoo wa hum yata-khaafatoon.

24. Al-laa yadkhulannahal-yawma 'alaykum-miskeen.

25. Wa ghadaw 'alaa ḥardin qaadireen.

26. Falammaa ra-awhaa qaa-looo innaa laḍaaalloon.

27. Bal naḥnu maḥroomoon.

28. Qaala awsaṭuhum alam aqul lakum law laa tusabbiḥoon.

فَلَا تُطِعِ الْمُكَذِّبِيْنَ (٨)

وَدُّوْا لَوْ تُدْهِنُ فَيُدْهِنُوْنَ (٩)

وَلَا تُطِعْ كُلَّ حَلَّافٍ مَّهِيْنٍ (١٠)

هَمَّازٍ مَّشَّآءٍ بِنَمِيْمٍ (١١)

مَّنَّاعٍ لِّلْخَيْرِ مُعْتَدٍ اَثِيْمٍ (١٢)

عُتُلٍّ بَعْدَ ذٰلِكَ زَنِيْمٍ (١٣)

اَنْ كَانَ ذَا مَالٍ وَّبَنِيْنَ (١٤)

اِذَا تُتْلٰى عَلَيْهِ اٰيٰتُنَا قَالَ اَسَاطِيْرُ

الْاَوَّلِيْنَ (١٥)

سَنَسِمُهٗ عَلَى الْخُرْطُوْمِ (١٦)

اِنَّا بَلَوْنٰهُمْ كَمَا بَلَوْنَآ اَصْحٰبَ الْجَنَّةِ

اِذْ اَقْسَمُوْا لَيَصْرِمُنَّهَا مُصْبِحِيْنَ (١٧)

وَلَا يَسْتَثْنُوْنَ (١٨)

فَطَافَ عَلَيْهَا طَآئِفٌ مِّنْ رَّبِّكَ

وَهُمْ نَآئِمُوْنَ (١٩)

فَاَصْبَحَتْ كَالصَّرِيْمِ (٢٠)

فَتَنَادَوْا مُصْبِحِيْنَ (٢١)

اَنِ اغْدُوْا عَلٰى حَرْثِكُمْ اِنْ

كُنْتُمْ صٰرِمِيْنَ (٢٢)

فَانْطَلَقُوْا وَهُمْ يَتَخَافَتُوْنَ (٢٣)

اَنْ لَّا يَدْخُلَنَّهَا الْيَوْمَ عَلَيْكُمْ

مِّسْكِيْنٌ (٢٤)

وَّغَدَوْا عَلٰى حَرْدٍ قٰدِرِيْنَ (٢٥)

فَلَمَّا رَاَوْهَا قَالُوْا اِنَّا لَضَآلُّوْنَ (٢٦)

بَلْ نَحْنُ مَحْرُوْمُوْنَ (٢٧)

قَالَ اَوْسَطُهُمْ اَلَمْ اَقُلْ لَّكُمْ

29. They said, "All glory belongs to Allah. We have certainly been unjust."

30. Certain ones among them started to blame others.
31. They said, "Woe to us. We have been arrogant.
32. Perhaps our Lord will replace it with a better garden. We turn in repentance to our Lord."

33. Such is the torment; if only they knew that the torment in the life hereafter will certainly be greater.
34. The pious ones will receive a beautiful Paradise from their Lord.

35. Shall We treat the Muslims like criminals?
36. What is the matter with you? How could you judge this to be so?
37. Do you have a book from which you study
38. that tells you to do whatever you want?
39. Do you have a covenant with Us, which allows you to do whatever you want until the Day of Judgment?
40. (Muhammad), ask which of them can guarantee that on the Day of Judgment
41. they will receive the same thing that the Muslims will? Do they have any witness to such an agreement? Let them bring out such a witness, if they are truthful.
42. On the day when secrets become public, they will be told to prostrate, but they will not be able to do it.
43. Their eyes will be lowered and disgrace will cover them. They had certainly been told to prostrate (before Allah) when they were safe and sound.

44. Leave those who reject the Quran to Me and I shall lead them step by step to destruction, without their being aware of it.

29. Qaaloo Subḥaana Rabbinaa innaa kunnaa ẓaalimeen.
30. Fa-aqbala ba'ḍuhum 'alaa ba'ḍiñy-yatalaawamoon.
31. Qaaloo yaa waylanaaa innaa kunnaa ṭaagheen.
32. 'Asaa Rabbunaaa añy-yubdilanaa khayram-minhaaa innaaa ilaa Rabbinaa Raaghiboon.
33. Kaẕaalikal-'aẕaab; wa la'aẕaabul-Aakhirati akbar; law kaanoo ya'lamoon.
34. Inna lilmuttaqeena 'inda Rabbihim Jannaatin-Na'eem.
35. Afanaj'alul-muslimeena kalmujrimeen.
36. Maa lakum kayfa taḥkumoon.
37. Am lakum Kitaabun feehi tadrusoon.
38. Inna lakum feehi lamaa takhayyaroon.
39. Am lakum aymaanun 'alaynaa baalighatun ilaa Yawmil-Qiyaamati inna lakum lamaa taḥkumoon.
40. Salhum ayyuhum biẕaalika za'eem.
41. Am lahum shurakaaa'u falya-too bishurakaaa'ihim in kaanoo ṣaadiqeen.
42. Yawma yukshafu 'an saaqiñw-wa yud'awna ilas-sujoodi falaa yastaṭee'oon.
43. Khaashi'atan abṣaaruhum tarhaquhum ẕillah; wa qad kaanoo yud'awna ilas-sujoodi wa hum saalimoon.
44. Faẕarnee wa mañy-yukaẕẕibu bihaaẕal ḥadeesi sanastadrijuhum min ḥaysu laa ya'lamoon.

لَوۡلَا تُسَبِّحُونَ ﴿٢٨﴾
قَالُوا سُبۡحَٰنَ رَبِّنَآ إِنَّا كُنَّا ظَٰلِمِينَ ﴿٢٩﴾
فَأَقۡبَلَ بَعۡضُهُمۡ عَلَىٰ بَعۡضٖ يَتَلَٰوَمُونَ ﴿٣٠﴾
قَالُوا يَٰوَيۡلَنَآ إِنَّا كُنَّا طَٰغِينَ ﴿٣١﴾
عَسَىٰ رَبُّنَآ أَن يُبۡدِلَنَا خَيۡرٗا مِّنۡهَآ
إِنَّآ إِلَىٰ رَبِّنَا رَٰغِبُونَ ﴿٣٢﴾
كَذَٰلِكَ ٱلۡعَذَابُۖ وَلَعَذَابُ ٱلۡأٓخِرَةِ
أَكۡبَرُۚ لَوۡ كَانُوا يَعۡلَمُونَ ﴿٣٣﴾ وقف لازم
إِنَّ لِلۡمُتَّقِينَ عِندَ رَبِّهِمۡ جَنَّٰتِ
ٱلنَّعِيمِ ﴿٣٤﴾
أَفَنَجۡعَلُ ٱلۡمُسۡلِمِينَ كَٱلۡمُجۡرِمِينَ ﴿٣٥﴾
مَا لَكُمۡ كَيۡفَ تَحۡكُمُونَ ﴿٣٦﴾
أَمۡ لَكُمۡ كِتَٰبٞ فِيهِ تَدۡرُسُونَ ﴿٣٧﴾
إِنَّ لَكُمۡ فِيهِ لَمَا تَخَيَّرُونَ ﴿٣٨﴾
أَمۡ لَكُمۡ أَيۡمَٰنٌ عَلَيۡنَا بَٰلِغَةٌ إِلَىٰ
يَوۡمِ ٱلۡقِيَٰمَةِ إِنَّ لَكُمۡ لَمَا تَحۡكُمُونَ ﴿٣٩﴾
سَلۡهُمۡ أَيُّهُم بِذَٰلِكَ زَعِيمٌ ﴿٤٠﴾ عند المتقدمين
أَمۡ لَهُمۡ شُرَكَآءُ فَلۡيَأۡتُوا بِشُرَكَآئِهِمۡ
إِن كَانُوا صَٰدِقِينَ ﴿٤١﴾
يَوۡمَ يُكۡشَفُ عَن سَاقٖ وَيُدۡعَوۡنَ
إِلَى ٱلسُّجُودِ فَلَا يَسۡتَطِيعُونَ ﴿٤٢﴾
خَٰشِعَةً أَبۡصَٰرُهُمۡ تَرۡهَقُهُمۡ ذِلَّةٞۖ
وَقَدۡ كَانُوا يُدۡعَوۡنَ إِلَى ٱلسُّجُودِ
وَهُمۡ سَٰلِمُونَ ﴿٤٣﴾
فَذَرۡنِي وَمَن يُكَذِّبُ بِهَٰذَا ٱلۡحَدِيثِۖ
سَنَسۡتَدۡرِجُهُم مِّنۡ حَيۡثُ لَا يَعۡلَمُونَ ﴿٤٤﴾

45. I shall give them respite; however, My plan is so strong that they will never be able to escape from it.	45. Wa umlee lahum; inna kaydee mateen.	وأملي لهم ۚ إن كيدي متين ﴿٤٥﴾
46. (Muhammad), do you ask for your preaching any recompense that is too heavy a price for them to pay?	46. Am tas'aluhum ajran fahum mim-maghramim musqaloon.	أم تسألهم أجرا فهم من مغرم مثقلون ﴿٤٦﴾
47. Do they possess the knowledge of the unseen, which confirms the truthfulness of their belief?	47. Am 'indahumul-ghaybu fahum yaktuboon.	أم عندهم الغيب فهم يكتبون ﴿٤٧﴾
48. Exercise patience until the promise of your Lord (to punish the unbelievers) comes true. Do not be like Jonah who left his people sad and depressed,	48. Faṣbir liḥukmi Rabbika wa laa takun kaṣaaḥibil-ḥoot; iz naadaa wa huwa makẓoom.	فاصبر لحكم ربك ولا تكن كصاحب الحوت إذ نادى وهو مكظوم ﴿٤٨﴾ وقف لازم
49. and who cried (to his Lord for help, while imprisoned and helpless inside the fish). Had it not been for a favor from his Lord, he would have been left out in the open, and blamed.	49. Law laaa an tadaarakahoo ni'matum-mir-Rabbihee lanubiza bil 'araaa'i wa huwa mazmoom.	لولا أن تداركه نعمة من ربه لنبذ بالعراء وهو مذموم ﴿٤٩﴾
50. But his Lord chose him as His Prophet and made him one of the righteous ones.	50. Fajtabaahu Rabbuhoo faja'alahoo minaṣ-ṣaaliḥeen.	فاجتباه ربه فجعله من الصالحين ﴿٥٠﴾
51. When the unbelievers listen to you reciting the Quran they almost try to destroy you with their piercing eyes. Then they say, "He is certainly insane."	51. Wa iñy-yakaadul-lazeena kafaroo la-yuzliqoonaka bi-abṣaarihim lammaa sami'uz-Zikra wa yaqooloona innahoo lamajnoon.	وإن يكاد الذين كفروا ليزلقونك بأبصارهم لما سمعوا الذكر ويقولون إنه لمجنون ﴿٥١﴾ وقف لازم
52. It (the Quran) is only a reminder from Allah to mankind.	52. Wa maa huwa illaa zikrul-lil'aalameen.	وما هو إلا ذكر للعالمين ﴿٥٢﴾ ع

Al-Haqqah, The Torment! (69) In the Name of Allah, the Beneficent, the Merciful.	**Sûrat al-Ḥâqqah-69** (Revealed at Makkah) **Bismillaahir Raḥmaanir Raḥeem**	(٦٩) سورة الحاقة مكية (٧٨) آياتها ٥٢ بسم الله الرحمن الرحيم ركوعاتها ٢
1. The torment!	1. Al-ḥaaaqqah.	الحاقة ﴿١﴾
2. What is the torment?	2. Mal-ḥaaaqqah.	ما الحاقة ﴿٢﴾
3. What do you think the torment is?	3. Wa maaa adraaka mal-ḥaaaqqah.	وما أدراك ما الحاقة ﴿٣﴾
4. The people of Thamud and Ad denied the Day of Judgment.	4. Kaz-zabat Samoodu wa 'Aadum bilqaari'ah.	كذبت ثمود وعاد بالقارعة ﴿٤﴾
5. Thamud was destroyed by a violent blast of sound.	5. Fa-ammaa Samoodu fa-uhlikoo biṭṭaaghiyah.	فأما ثمود فأهلكوا بالطاغية ﴿٥﴾
6. Ad was destroyed by a wind which was cold and came out in excess of the amount commanded to come out	6. Wa ammaa 'Aadun fa-uhlikoo bireeḥin ṣarṣarin 'aatiyah.	وأما عاد فأهلكوا بريح صرصر عاتية ﴿٦﴾
7. and continued to strike them for seven nights and eight days and you could see the people lying dead like the hollow trunks	7. Sakhkharahaa 'alayhim sab'a layaaliñw-wa samaaniyata ayyaamin ḥusooman fataral-qawma feehaa	سخرها عليهم سبع ليال وثمانية أيام حسوما فترى القوم فيها

of uprooted palm-trees.	ṣar‘aa ka-annahum a‘jaazu nakhlin khaawiyah.	صَرْعٰى كَاَنَّهُمْ اَعْجَازُ نَخْلٍ خَاوِيَةٍ ۝٧
8. Can you see any of their survivors?	8. Fahal taraa lahum mim baaqiyah.	فَهَلْ تَرٰى لَهُمْ مِّنْ بَاقِيَةٍ ۝٨
9. The Pharaoh, those who lived before him and the people of the Subverted Cities all persisted in doing evil.	9. Wa jaaa’a Fir‘awnu wa man qablahoo wal-mu’tafikaatu bilkhaaṭi’ah.	وَجَآءَ فِرْعَوْنُ وَمَنْ قَبْلَهٗ وَ الْمُؤْتَفِكٰتُ بِالْخَاطِئَةِ ۝٩
9. They disobeyed the Messenger of their Lord and He seized them with torment, which increased with time.	10. Fa‘aṣaw Rasoola Rabbihim fa akhaz̲ahum akhz̲atarraabiyah.	فَعَصَوْا رَسُوْلَ رَبِّهِمْ فَاَخَذَهُمْ اَخْذَةً رَّابِيَةً ۝١٠
10. When the flood rose high and covered the whole land, We carried you in the Ark,	11. Innaa lammaa ṭaghalmaaa’u ḥamalnaakum filjaariyah.	اِنَّا لَمَّا طَغَا الْمَآءُ حَمَلْنٰكُمْ فِي الْجَارِيَةِ ۝١١
12. to make it a lesson for you, but only attentive ears will retain it.	12. Linaj‘alahaa lakum taz̲kiratañw-wa ta‘iyahaaa uz̲unuñwwaa‘iyah.	لِنَجْعَلَهَا لَكُمْ تَذْكِرَةً وَّتَعِيَهَآ اُذُنٌ وَّاعِيَةٌ ۝١٢
13. With (the first) single blast of sound from the trumpet,	13. Fa-iz̲aa nufikha fiṣ-Ṣoori nafkhatuñw-waaḥidah.	فَاِذَا نُفِخَ فِي الصُّوْرِ نَفْخَةٌ وَّاحِدَةٌ ۝١٣
14. the earth and mountains will be raised up high and crushed all together.	14. Wa ḥumilatil-arḍu wal jibaalu fadukkataa dakkatañwwaaḥidah.	وَّحُمِلَتِ الْاَرْضُ وَالْجِبَالُ فَدُكَّتَا دَكَّةً وَّاحِدَةً ۝١٤
15. On that day, the inevitable event will take place	15. Fa-yawma’iz̲iñw-waqa‘atil-waaqi‘ah.	فَيَوْمَئِذٍ وَّقَعَتِ الْوَاقِعَةُ ۝١٥
16. and the heavens will be rent asunder,	16. Wanshaqqatis-samaaa’u fahiya Yawma’iz̲iñwwaahiyah.	وَانْشَقَّتِ السَّمَآءُ فَهِيَ يَوْمَئِذٍ وَّاهِيَةٌ ۝١٦
17. and it will become void. The angels will be around the heavens and on that day eight people will carry the Throne (knowledge) of your Lord above all the creatures.	17. Walmalaku ‘alaaa arjaa’ihaa; wa yaḥmilu ‘Arsha Rabbika fawqahum Yawma’iz̲in s̲amaaniyah.	وَّالْمَلَكُ عَلٰٓى اَرْجَآئِهَا ۚ وَيَحْمِلُ عَرْشَ رَبِّكَ فَوْقَهُمْ يَوْمَئِذٍ ثَمٰنِيَةٌ ۝١٧
18. On that day all your secrets will be exposed.	18. Yawma’iz̲in tu‘raḍoona laa takhfaa minkum khaafiyah.	يَوْمَئِذٍ تُعْرَضُوْنَ لَا تَخْفٰى مِنْكُمْ خَافِيَةٌ ۝١٨
19. Those who will receive the books of the records of their deeds in their right hands will say, “Come and read my record.	19. Fa-ammaa man ootiya kitaabahoo biyameenihee fayaqoolu haaa’umuq-ra’oo kitaabiyah.	فَاَمَّا مَنْ اُوْتِيَ كِتٰبَهٗ بِيَمِيْنِهٖ فَيَقُوْلُ هَآؤُمُ اقْرَءُوْا كِتٰبِيَهْ ۝١٩
20. I was sure that the record of my deeds would be shown to me.”	20. Innee ẓanantu annee mulaaqin ḥisaabiyah.	اِنِّيْ ظَنَنْتُ اَنِّيْ مُلٰقٍ حِسَابِيَهْ ۝٢٠
21. So he will have a pleasant life	21. Fahuwa fee ‘eeshatir raaḍiyah.	فَهُوَ فِيْ عِيْشَةٍ رَّاضِيَةٍ ۝٢١
22. in an exalted garden	22. Fee Jannatin ‘aaliyah.	فِيْ جَنَّةٍ عَالِيَةٍ ۝٢٢
23. with fruits within easy reach.	23. Quṭoofuhaa daaniyah.	قُطُوْفُهَا دَانِيَةٌ ۝٢٣

24. Such people will be told, "Eat and drink with pleasure as the reward for what you did in the past."	24. Kuloo washraboo haneee-'am bimaaa aslaftum fil-ayyaamil-khaaliyah.	كُلُوا وَاشْرَبُوا هَنِيٓـًٔا بِمَآ أَسْلَفْتُمْ فِي الْأَيَّامِ الْخَالِيَةِ ﴿٢٤﴾
25. However, one who will receive the books of the records of his deeds in his left hand will say, "I wish that this record had never been given to me	25. Wa ammaa man ootiya kitaabahoo bishimaalihee faya-qoolu yaalaytanee lam oota kitaabiyah.	وَأَمَّا مَنْ أُوتِيَ كِتٰبَهٗ بِشِمَالِهٖ ۙ فَيَقُولُ يٰلَيْتَنِي لَمْ أُوتَ كِتٰبِيَهْ ﴿٢٥﴾
26. and that I had never known what my records contained.	26. Wa lam adri maa ḥisaa-biyah.	وَلَمْ أَدْرِ مَا حِسَابِيَهْ ﴿٢٦﴾
27. I wish death had taken me away for good.	27. Yaa laytahaa kaanatil-qaaḍiyah.	يٰلَيْتَهَا كَانَتِ الْقَاضِيَةَ ﴿٢٧﴾
28. My wealth has been of no benefit to me	28. Maaa aghnaa 'annee maaliyah.	مَآ أَغْنٰى عَنِّي مَالِيَهْ ﴿٢٨﴾
29. and my belief has destroyed me."	29. Halaka 'annee sulṭaa-niyah.	هَلَكَ عَنِّي سُلْطٰنِيَهْ ﴿٢٩﴾
30. The angels will be told, "Seize and chain him,	30. Khuẕoohu faghullooh.	خُذُوهُ فَغُلُّوهُ ﴿٣٠﴾
31. then throw him into hell to feel the heat therein.	31. S̱ummal-Jaḥeema ṣallooh.	ثُمَّ الْجَحِيمَ صَلُّوهُ ﴿٣١﴾
32. Fasten a chain to him - seventy cubits long -	32. S̱umma fee silsilatin ẕar-'uhaa sab'oona ẕiraa'an faslu-kooh.	ثُمَّ فِي سِلْسِلَةٍ ذَرْعُهَا سَبْعُونَ ذِرَاعًا فَاسْلُكُوهُ ﴿٣٢﴾
33. he did not believe in the great Allah,	33. Innahoo kaana laa yu'mi-nu billaahil-'aẓeem.	إِنَّهٗ كَانَ لَا يُؤْمِنُ بِاللّٰهِ الْعَظِيمِ ﴿٣٣﴾
34. nor was he concerned with feeding the destitute.	34. Wa laa yaḥuḍḍu 'alaa ṭa'aamil-miskeen.	وَلَا يَحُضُّ عَلٰى طَعَامِ الْمِسْكِينِ ﴿٣٤﴾
35. On this day, he will have no friends	35. Falaysa lahul-Yawma haahunaa ḥameem.	فَلَيْسَ لَهُ الْيَوْمَ هٰهُنَا حَمِيمٌ ﴿٣٥﴾
36. and no food except perspiration of unbelievers	36. Wa laa ṭa'aamun illaa min ghisleen.	وَلَا طَعَامٌ إِلَّا مِنْ غِسْلِينٍ ﴿٣٦﴾
37. which only the sinners eat."	37. Laa ya-kuluhooo illal-khaaṭi'oon.	لَا يَأْكُلُهٗٓ إِلَّا الْخٰطِـُٔونَ ﴿٣٧﴾ ع ٣٧ ٥
38. I swear by what you see	38. Falaaa uqsimu bimaa tubṣiroon	فَلَآ أُقْسِمُ بِمَا تُبْصِرُونَ ﴿٣٨﴾
39. and what you do not see,	39. Wa maa laa tubṣiroon.	وَمَا لَا تُبْصِرُونَ ﴿٣٩﴾
40. it (the Quran) is certainly the word of a reverent messenger.	40. Innahoo laqawlu Rasoo-lin Kareem.	إِنَّهٗ لَقَوْلُ رَسُولٍ كَرِيمٍ ﴿٤٠﴾
41. It is not the word of a poet but only a few of you have faith,	41. Wa maa huwa biqawli shaa'ir; qaleelam-maa tu'mi-noon.	وَمَا هُوَ بِقَوْلِ شَاعِرٍ ۚ قَلِيلًا مَّا تُؤْمِنُونَ ﴿٤١﴾
42. nor is it the work of a soothsayer but only a few of you take heed.	42. Wa laa biqawli kaahin; qaleelam-maa taẕakkaroon.	وَلَا بِقَوْلِ كَاهِنٍ ۚ قَلِيلًا مَّا تَذَكَّرُونَ ﴿٤٢﴾
43. It is a revelation from the Lord of the universe.	43. Tanzeelum-mir-Rabbil-'aalameen.	تَنْزِيلٌ مِّنْ رَّبِّ الْعٰلَمِينَ ﴿٤٣﴾
44. Had Muhammad invented some words against Us,	44. Wa law taqawwala 'alay-naa ba'ḍal-aqaaweel.	وَلَوْ تَقَوَّلَ عَلَيْنَا بَعْضَ الْأَقَاوِيلِ ﴿٤٤﴾

45. We would have caught hold of him by the right hand (power)	45. La-akhaznaa minhu bilyameen.	لَاَخَذْنَا مِنْهُ بِالْيَمِيْنِ ﴿٤٥﴾
46. and cut-off the vein in his spine.	46. Summa laqata‘naa minhulwateen.	ثُمَّ لَقَطَعْنَا مِنْهُ الْوَتِيْنَ ﴿٤٦﴾
47. None of you could prevent Us from doing this to him.	47. Famaa minkum min ahadin ‘anhu haajizeen.	فَمَا مِنْكُمْ مِّنْ اَحَدٍ عَنْهُ حٰجِزِيْنَ ﴿٤٧﴾
48. This (the Quran) is certainly a reminder for the pious ones.	48. Wa innahoo latazkiratul-lilmuttaqeen.	وَاِنَّهُ لَتَذْكِرَةٌ لِّلْمُتَّقِيْنَ ﴿٤٨﴾
49. We know that some of you are rejecters	49. Wa innaa lana‘lamu anna minkum mukazzibeen.	وَاِنَّا لَنَعْلَمُ اَنَّ مِنْكُمْ مُّكَذِّبِيْنَ ﴿٤٩﴾
50. and (on the Day of Judgment) he will be a great source of regret for the unbelievers.	50. Wa innahoo lahasratun ‘alal-kaafireen	وَاِنَّهُ لَحَسْرَةٌ عَلَى الْكٰفِرِيْنَ ﴿٥٠﴾
51. He is the Truth beyond any doubt.	51. Wa innahoo lahaqqul yaqeen.	وَاِنَّهُ لَحَقُّ الْيَقِيْنِ ﴿٥١﴾
52. (Muhammad), glorify the name of your Lord, the Great One.	52. Fasabbih bismi Rabbikal ‘Azeem.	فَسَبِّحْ بِاسْمِ رَبِّكَ الْعَظِيْمِ ﴿٥٢﴾ ع ١٥/٢

Al-Maarij, High Ranks (70) / Sûrat al-Ma‘ârij-70 / (٧٠) سُوْرَةُ الْمَعَارِجِ مَكِّيَّةٌ (٧٩)

In the Name of Allah, the Beneficent, the Merciful.

(Revealed at Makkah)

Bismillaahir Rahmaanir Raheem

آياتها ٤٤ — بِسْمِ اللّٰهِ الرَّحْمٰنِ الرَّحِيْمِ — ركوعاتها ٢

1. Someone has (needlessly) demanded to experience the torment (of Allah),	1. Sa-ala saaa’ilum bi‘azaabiñw-waaqi‘.	سَاَلَ سَآئِلٌ بِعَذَابٍ وَّاقِعٍ ﴿١﴾
2. which will inevitably seize the unbelievers.	2. Lilkaafireena laysa lahoo daafi‘.	لِّلْكٰفِرِيْنَ لَيْسَ لَهُ دَافِعٌ ﴿٢﴾
3. No one can defend him against Allah, the Lord of the exalted positions.	3. Minal - laahi zil-ma‘aarij.	مِّنَ اللّٰهِ ذِي الْمَعَارِجِ ﴿٣﴾
4. The angels and the Spirit will ascend to Him on the Day (of Judgment), as long as fifty thousand years.	4. Ta‘rujul-malaaa’ikatu war-Roohu ilayhi fee yawmin kaana miqdaaruhoo khamseena alfa sanah.	تَعْرُجُ الْمَلٰٓئِكَةُ وَالرُّوْحُ اِلَيْهِ فِيْ يَوْمٍ كَانَ مِقْدَارُهُ خَمْسِيْنَ اَلْفَ سَنَةٍ ﴿٤﴾
5. (Muhammad), exercise patience with no complaints.	5. Fasbir sabran jameelaa.	فَاصْبِرْ صَبْرًا جَمِيْلًا ﴿٥﴾
6. They think that it (the Day of Judgment) is far away	6. Innahum yarawnahoo ba‘eedaa.	اِنَّهُمْ يَرَوْنَهُ بَعِيْدًا ﴿٦﴾
7. but We see it to be very near.	7. Wa naraahu qareebaa.	وَّنَرٰىهُ قَرِيْبًا ﴿٧﴾
8. On the day when the heavens become like melted brass	8. Yawma takoonus-samaa-’u kalmuhl.	يَوْمَ تَكُوْنُ السَّمَآءُ كَالْمُهْلِ ﴿٨﴾
9. and the mountains become like wool,	9. Wa takoonul-jibaalu kal-‘ihn.	وَتَكُوْنُ الْجِبَالُ كَالْعِهْنِ ﴿٩﴾
10. even intimate friends will not inquire about their friends,	10. Wa laa yas’alu hameemun hameemaa.	وَلَا يَسْئَلُ حَمِيْمٌ حَمِيْمًا ﴿١٠﴾
11. though they may see each other. A sinner will wish that he could save himself from the torment of that day by sacrificing his children,	11. Yubassaroonahum; yaw-addul-mujrimu law yaftadee min ‘azaabi Yawmi’izim bibaneeh.	يُّبَصَّرُوْنَهُمْ ؕ يَوَدُّ الْمُجْرِمُ لَوْ يَفْتَدِيْ مِنْ عَذَابِ يَوْمِئِذٍ بِبَنِيْهِ ﴿١١﴾
12. his wife, his brother,	12. Wa saahibatihee wa akheeh.	وَصَاحِبَتِهِ وَاَخِيْهِ ﴿١٢﴾
13. his mother who gave birth to him,	13. Wa faseelatihil-latee tu’-weeh.	وَفَصِيْلَتِهِ الَّتِيْ تُـْٔوِيْهِ ﴿١٣﴾

14. and all those on earth.	14. Wa man fil-arḍi jamee'an s̲umma yunjeeh.	وَمَنْ فِي الْأَرْضِ جَمِيعًا ثُمَّ يُنْجِيهِ ﴿١٤﴾
15. It is raging flames of fire that	15. kallaa innahaa laẓaa.	كَلَّا ۖ إِنَّهَا لَظَىٰ ﴿١٥﴾
16. will strip off the flesh (turns one blind and blackens the skin)	16. Nazzaa'atal lishshawaa.	نَزَّاعَةً لِلشَّوَىٰ ﴿١٦﴾
17. and drag into it anyone who had turned away (from obeying Allah),	17. Tad'oo man adbara wa tawallaa.	تَدْعُو مَنْ أَدْبَرَ وَتَوَلَّىٰ ﴿١٧﴾
18. and who accumulated wealth without spending it for a good purpose.	18. Wa jama'a fa-aw'aa.	وَجَمَعَ فَأَوْعَىٰ ﴿١٨﴾
19. Human beings are created greedy.	19. Innal-insaana khuliqa haloo'aa.	إِنَّ الْإِنْسَانَ خُلِقَ هَلُوعًا ﴿١٩﴾
20. When they are afflicted, they complain,	20. Iz̲aa massahush-sharru jazoo'aa.	إِذَا مَسَّهُ الشَّرُّ جَزُوعًا ﴿٢٠﴾
21. but when they are fortunate, they become niggardly	21. Wa iz̲aa massahul-khay-ru manoo'aa.	وَإِذَا مَسَّهُ الْخَيْرُ مَنُوعًا ﴿٢١﴾
22. except those who are steadfast	22. Illal-muṣalleen.	إِلَّا الْمُصَلِّينَ ﴿٢٢﴾
23. and constant in their prayers.	23. Allaz̲eena hum 'alaa Ṣalaatihim daaa'imoon.	الَّذِينَ هُمْ عَلَىٰ صَلَاتِهِمْ دَائِمُونَ ﴿٢٣﴾
24. They are those who assign a certain share of their property	24. Wallaz̲eena feee amwaa-lihim ḥaqqum-ma'loom.	وَالَّذِينَ فِي أَمْوَالِهِمْ حَقٌّ مَعْلُومٌ ﴿٢٤﴾
25. for the needy and the deprived,	25. Lissaaa'ili walmaḥroom.	لِلسَّائِلِ وَالْمَحْرُومِ ﴿٢٥﴾
26. who acknowledge the Day of Judgment,	26. Wallaz̲eena yuṣaddiqoo-na bi-Yawmid-Deen.	وَالَّذِينَ يُصَدِّقُونَ بِيَوْمِ الدِّينِ ﴿٢٦﴾
27. who are afraid of the torment of their Lord,	27. Wallaz̲eena hum min 'az̲aabi Rabbihim mushfiqoon.	وَالَّذِينَ هُمْ مِنْ عَذَابِ رَبِّهِمْ مُشْفِقُونَ ﴿٢٧﴾
28. the punishment of their Lord is not something for them to feel secure of,	28. Inna 'az̲aaba Rabbihim ghayru ma-moon.	إِنَّ عَذَابَ رَبِّهِمْ غَيْرُ مَأْمُونٍ ﴿٢٨﴾
29. who guard their carnal desires	29. Wallaz̲eena hum lifuroo-jihim ḥaafiẓoon.	وَالَّذِينَ هُمْ لِفُرُوجِهِمْ حَافِظُونَ ﴿٢٩﴾
30. except from their wives and slave girls, in which case they are not to be blamed,	30. Illaa 'alaaa azwaajihim aw maa malakat aymaanuhum fa-innahum ghayru maloomeen.	إِلَّا عَلَىٰ أَزْوَاجِهِمْ أَوْ مَا مَلَكَتْ أَيْمَانُهُمْ فَإِنَّهُمْ غَيْرُ مَلُومِينَ ﴿٣٠﴾
31. but whoever goes beyond this is a transgressor;	31. Famanib-taghaa waraaa'a z̲aalika fa-ulaaa'ika humul-'aadoon.	فَمَنِ ابْتَغَىٰ وَرَاءَ ذَٰلِكَ فَأُولَٰئِكَ هُمُ الْعَادُونَ ﴿٣١﴾
32. who honor their trust and promises,	32. Wallaz̲eena hum li-amaa-naatihim wa 'ahdihim raa'oon.	وَالَّذِينَ هُمْ لِأَمَانَاتِهِمْ وَعَهْدِهِمْ رَاعُونَ ﴿٣٢﴾
33. who testify to what they have witnessed,	33. wallaz̲eena hum bisha-haadaatihim qaaa'imoon.	وَالَّذِينَ هُمْ بِشَهَادَاتِهِمْ قَائِمُونَ ﴿٣٣﴾
34. and (finally) who do not miss their daily prayers at the prescribed times;	34. Wallaz̲eena hum 'alaa Ṣalaatihim yuḥaafiẓoon.	وَالَّذِينَ هُمْ عَلَىٰ صَلَاتِهِمْ يُحَافِظُونَ ﴿٣٤﴾

35. such people will receive due honor in Paradise.
36. What is the matter with the unbelievers who in your presence (O Muhammad) worthlessly sit
37. on the left and right?
38. Does every one of them desire to enter the bountiful Paradise?
39. By no means! For they know very well out of what We have created them.
40. I swear by the Lord of the Eastern regions (of winter and summer seasons) and Western regions that We have certainly all the power
41. to replace them by a better people and none can challenge Our power.
42. (Muhammad), leave them alone to dispute and play until they face the Day with which they have been threatened:
43. the Day when they rush out of their graves as if racing toward a caller,
44. with their eyes cast down and covered by disgrace; the day about which they were warned.

35. Ulaaa'ika fee Jannaatim-mukramoon.
36. Famaalil-lazeena kafaroo qibalaka muhṭi'een.
37. 'Anil-yameeni wa 'anish-shimaali 'izeen.
38. Ayaṭma'u kullum-ri'im minhum añy-yudkhala jannata Na'eem.
39. Kallaaa innaa khalaqnaahum-mimmaa ya'lamoon.
40. Falaaa uqsimu bi-Rabbil-mashaariqi wal-maghaaribi innaa laqaadiroon.
41. 'Alaaa an nubaddila khayram-minhum wa maa Naḥnu bimasbooqeen.
42. Fazarhum yakhooḍoo wa yal'aboo ḥattaa yulaaqoo Yawmahumul-lazee yoo'adoon.
43. Yawma yakhrujoona minal-ajdaasi siraa'an ka-annahum ilaa nuṣubiñy-yoofiḍoon.
44. Khaashi'atan abṣaaruhum tarhaquhum zillah; zaalikal Yawmul-lazee kaanoo yoo'adoon.

اُولٰٓئِكَ فِیْ جَنّٰتٍ مُّكْرَمُوْنَ ﴿٣٥﴾ ع ٣٥ ٧
فَمَالِ الَّذِیْنَ كَفَرُوْا قِبَلَكَ
مُهْطِعِیْنَ ﴿٣٦﴾
عَنِ الْیَمِیْنِ وَعَنِ الشِّمَالِ عِزِیْنَ ﴿٣٧﴾
اَیَطْمَعُ كُلُّ امْرِیٍٔ مِّنْهُمْ اَنْ یُّدْخَلَ
جَنَّةَ نَعِیْمٍ ﴿٣٨﴾
كَلَّاؕ اِنَّا خَلَقْنٰهُمْ مِّمَّا یَعْلَمُوْنَ ﴿٣٩﴾
فَلَاۤ اُقْسِمُ بِرَبِّ الْمَشٰرِقِ وَالْمَغٰرِبِ
اِنَّا لَقٰدِرُوْنَ ﴿٤٠﴾
عَلٰۤى اَنْ نُّبَدِّلَ خَیْرًا مِّنْهُمْ ۙ وَمَا
نَحْنُ بِمَسْبُوْقِیْنَ ﴿٤١﴾
فَذَرْهُمْ یَخُوْضُوْا وَیَلْعَبُوْا حَتّٰى
یُلٰقُوْا یَوْمَهُمُ الَّذِیْ یُوْعَدُوْنَ ﴿٤٢﴾
یَوْمَ یَخْرُجُوْنَ مِنَ الْاَجْدَاثِ سِرَاعًا
كَاَنَّهُمْ اِلٰى نُصُبٍ یُّوْفِضُوْنَ ﴿٤٣﴾
خَاشِعَةً اَبْصَارُهُمْ تَرْهَقُهُمْ ذِلَّةٌ ؕ
ذٰلِكَ الْیَوْمُ الَّذِیْ كَانُوْا یُوْعَدُوْنَ ﴿٤٤﴾ ع ٩ ٨

Nuh, Noah (71)

In the Name of Allah,
the Beneficent, the Merciful.

1. We sent Noah to his people telling him, "Warn your people before a painful torment approaches them."
2. Noah said, "My people, I am warning you plainly.
3. Worship Allah, have fear of Him, and obey me.
4. He will forgive your sins and give you a respite for an appointed time. When the time which Allah has appointed arrives, none will be

Sûrat Nûḥ-71

(Revealed at Makkah)
Bismillaahir Raḥmaanir Raḥeem

1. Innaaa arsalnaa Nooḥan ilaa qawmiheee an anzir qawmaka min qabli añy-yatiyahum 'azaabun aleem.
2. Qaala yaa qawmi innee lakum nazeerum-mubeen.
3. Ani'budul-laaha wattaqoohu wa aṭee'oon.
4. Yaghfir lakum min zunoobikum wa yu'akhkhirkum ilaaa ajalim-musammaa; inna ajalal laahi izaa

(٧١) سُوْرَةُ نُوْحٍ مَّكِّيَّةٌ (٧١)
آیاتها ٢٨ بِسْمِ اللّٰهِ الرَّحْمٰنِ الرَّحِیْمِ رکوعاتها ٢
اِنَّاۤ اَرْسَلْنَا نُوْحًا اِلٰى قَوْمِهٖۤ اَنْ
اَنْذِرْ قَوْمَكَ مِنْ قَبْلِ اَنْ یَّاْتِیَهُمْ
عَذَابٌ اَلِیْمٌ ﴿١﴾
قَالَ یٰقَوْمِ اِنِّیْ لَكُمْ نَذِیْرٌ مُّبِیْنٌ ﴿٢﴾
اَنِ اعْبُدُوا اللّٰهَ وَاتَّقُوْهُ وَاَطِیْعُوْنِ ﴿٣﴾
یَغْفِرْ لَكُمْ مِّنْ ذُنُوْبِكُمْ وَیُؤَخِّرْكُمْ
اِلٰۤى اَجَلٍ مُّسَمًّى ؕ اِنَّ اَجَلَ اللّٰهِ اِذَا

able to postpone it. Would that you knew this."	jaaa'a laa yu'akhkhar; law kuntum ta'lamoon.	جَآءَ لَا يُؤَخَّرُ لَوْ كُنْتُمْ تَعْلَمُوْنَ ﴿٤﴾
5. Noah said, "My Lord, I have been preaching to my people, night and day,	5. Qaala Rabbi innee da'awtu qawmee laylañw-wa nahaaraa.	قَالَ رَبِّ اِنِّيْ دَعَوْتُ قَوْمِيْ لَيْلًا وَّنَهَارًا ﴿٥﴾
6. but it has had no effect on them except to make them run away.	6. Falam yazidhum du'aaa-'eee illaa firaaraa.	فَلَمْ يَزِدْهُمْ دُعَآءِيْٓ اِلَّا فِرَارًا ﴿٦﴾
7. Every time I invite them to Your (guidance) so that You can forgive them, they put their fingers into their ears, cover their heads with their clothes, persist in their disbelief, and display extreme arrogance."	7. Wa innee kullamaa da-'awtuhum litaghfira lahum ja'a-looo aṣaabi'ahum feee aazaani-him wastaghshaw siyaabahum wa aṣarroo wastakbarus-tik-baaraa.	وَاِنِّيْ كُلَّمَا دَعَوْتُهُمْ لِتَغْفِرَ لَهُمْ جَعَلُوْٓا اَصَابِعَهُمْ فِيْٓ اٰذَانِهِمْ وَاسْتَغْشَوْا ثِيَابَهُمْ وَاَصَرُّوْا وَاسْتَكْبَرُوا اسْتِكْبَارًا ﴿٧﴾
8. "I preached to them aloud, in public.	8. Summa innee da'aw-tuhum jihaaraa.	ثُمَّ اِنِّيْ دَعَوْتُهُمْ جِهَارًا ﴿٨﴾
9. Then I conveyed the message to them, again, both in public and in complete privacy,	9. Summa inneee a'lantu la-hum wa asrartu lahum israaraa.	ثُمَّ اِنِّيْٓ اَعْلَنْتُ لَهُمْ وَاَسْرَرْتُ لَهُمْ اِسْرَارًا ﴿٩﴾
10. and told them, 'Ask forgiveness from your Lord; He is All-forgiving.	10. Faqultus-taghfiroo Rab-bakam innahoo kaana Ghaf-faaraa.	فَقُلْتُ اسْتَغْفِرُوْا رَبَّكُمْ اِنَّهٗ كَانَ غَفَّارًا ﴿١٠﴾
11. He will send you abundant rain from the sky,	11. Yursilis-samaaa'a 'alay-kum midraaraa.	يُّرْسِلِ السَّمَآءَ عَلَيْكُمْ مِّدْرَارًا ﴿١١﴾
12. strengthen you by (providing) you wealth and children, and make gardens and streams for you.	12. Wa yumdidkum bi-am-waaliñw-wa baneena wa yaj'al lakum Jannaatiñw-wa yaj'al lakum anhaaraa.	وَّيُمْدِدْكُمْ بِاَمْوَالٍ وَّبَنِيْنَ وَيَجْعَلْ لَّكُمْ جَنّٰتٍ وَّيَجْعَلْ لَّكُمْ اَنْهٰرًا ﴿١٢﴾
13. What is the matter with you that you do not have any consideration for the greatness of Allah	13. Maa lakum laa tarjoona lillaahi waqaaraa.	مَا لَكُمْ لَا تَرْجُوْنَ لِلّٰهِ وَقَارًا ﴿١٣﴾
14. who has created you in several stages?'"	14. Wa qad khalaqakam aṭ-waaraa.	وَقَدْ خَلَقَكُمْ اَطْوَارًا ﴿١٤﴾
15. "Did you not see that Allah has created the seven heavens one above the other	15. Alam taraw kayfa khala-qal-laahu Sab'a samaawaatin-ṭibaaqaa.	اَلَمْ تَرَوْا كَيْفَ خَلَقَ اللّٰهُ سَبْعَ سَمٰوٰتٍ طِبَاقًا ﴿١٥﴾
16. and placed therein the moon as a light	16. Wa ja'alal-qamara fee-hinna noorañw-wa ja'alash shamsa siraajaa.	وَّجَعَلَ الْقَمَرَ فِيْهِنَّ نُوْرًا وَّجَعَلَ الشَّمْسَ سِرَاجًا ﴿١٦﴾
17. and the sun as a torch?	17. Wallaahu ambatakum minal-arḍi nabaataa.	وَاللّٰهُ اَنْۢبَتَكُمْ مِّنَ الْاَرْضِ نَبَاتًا ﴿١٧﴾
18. Allah made you grow from the earth. He will make you return to it and then take you out of it again.	18. Summa yu'eedukum. fee-haa wa yukhrijukum ikhraajaa.	ثُمَّ يُعِيْدُكُمْ فِيْهَا وَيُخْرِجُكُمْ اِخْرَاجًا ﴿١٨﴾
19. Allah has spread out the earth	19. Wallaahu ja'ala lakumul-arḍa bisaaṭaa.	وَاللّٰهُ جَعَلَ لَكُمُ الْاَرْضَ بِسَاطًا ﴿١٩﴾

وقف لازم

20. for you, so that you may walk along its wide roads."

21. Noah said, "Lord, they have disobeyed me and followed those whose wealth and children would only bring about destruction for them.

22. They have arrogantly plotted great evil plans against me,

23. and have said to each other, 'Do not give-up your idols. Do not renounce Wadd, Suwa, Yaghuth, Yauq, and Nasr (names of certain idols).'

24. They have misled many and the unjust will achieve nothing but more error."

25. Because of their sins, they were drowned and made to enter a fire. They could find no one to help them besides Allah.

26. Noah said, "Lord, do not leave a single disbeliever on earth;

27. if You do, they will mislead Your servants and will only give birth to ungrateful sinners.

28. Lord, forgive me, my parents, the believers who have entered my home and all believing men and women. Give nothing to the unjust but destruction.

20. Litaslukoo minhaa subulan fijaajaa.

21. Qaala Nooḥur-Rabbi innahum 'aṣawnee wattaba'oo mallam yazidhu maaluhoo wa waladuhooo illaa khasaaraa.

22. Wa makaroo makran kubbaaraa.

23. Wa qaaloo laa taẕarunna aalihatakum wa laa taẕarunna Waddañw-wa laa Suwaa'añw-wa laa Yaghooṡa wa Ya'ooqa wa Nasraa.

24. Wa qad aḍalloo kaṡeeraa; wa laa tazidiẓ-ẓaalimeena illaa ḍalaalaa.

25. Mimmaa khaṭeee'aatihim ughriqoo fa-udkhiloo Naaran falam yajidoo lahum min doonil-laahi anṣaaraa.

26. Wa qaala Nooḥur-Rabbi laa taẕar 'alal-arḍi minal-kaafireena dayyaaraa.

27. Innaka in taẕarhum yuḍilloo 'ibaadaka wa laa yalidooo illaa faajiran kaffaaraa.

28. Rabbigh-fir lee wa liwaalidayya wa liman dakhala baytiya mu'minañw-wa lilmu'mineena walmu'minaati wa laa tazidiẓ-ẓaalimeena illaa tabaaraa.

لِتَسْلُكُوا مِنْهَا سُبُلًا فِجَاجًا ﴿٢٠﴾
قَالَ نُوحٌ رَّبِّ إِنَّهُمْ عَصَوْنِي وَ
اتَّبَعُوا مَن لَّمْ يَزِدْهُ مَالُهُ وَ
وَلَدُهُ إِلَّا خَسَارًا ﴿٢١﴾
وَمَكَرُوا مَكْرًا كُبَّارًا ﴿٢٢﴾
وَقَالُوا لَا تَذَرُنَّ آلِهَتَكُمْ وَلَا
تَذَرُنَّ وَدًّا وَلَا سُوَاعًا ۥ وَلَا
يَغُوثَ وَيَعُوقَ وَنَسْرًا ﴿٢٣﴾
وَقَدْ أَضَلُّوا كَثِيرًا ۥ وَلَا تَزِدِ
الظَّالِمِينَ إِلَّا ضَلَالًا ﴿٢٤﴾
مِّمَّا خَطِيئَاتِهِمْ أُغْرِقُوا فَأُدْخِلُوا
نَارًا ۥ فَلَمْ يَجِدُوا لَهُم مِّن
دُونِ اللَّهِ أَنصَارًا ﴿٢٥﴾
وَقَالَ نُوحٌ رَّبِّ لَا تَذَرْ عَلَى
الْأَرْضِ مِنَ الْكَافِرِينَ دَيَّارًا ﴿٢٦﴾
إِنَّكَ إِن تَذَرْهُمْ يُضِلُّوا عِبَادَكَ
وَلَا يَلِدُوا إِلَّا فَاجِرًا كَفَّارًا ﴿٢٧﴾
رَّبِّ اغْفِرْ لِي وَلِوَالِدَيَّ وَلِمَن
دَخَلَ بَيْتِيَ مُؤْمِنًا وَلِلْمُؤْمِنِينَ
وَالْمُؤْمِنَاتِ ۖ وَلَا تَزِدِ الظَّالِمِينَ
إِلَّا تَبَارًا ﴿٢٨﴾

Al-Jinn, The Jinn (72)

In the Name of Allah, the Beneficent, the Merciful.

1. (Muhammad), say, "It has been revealed to me that a party of jinn has listened (to the recitation) of the Quran and has told (their people), 'We heard an amazing reading

Sûrat al-Jinn-72

(Revealed at Makkah)

Bismillaahir Raḥmaanir Raḥeem

1. Qul ooḥiya ilayya annahus-tama'a nafarum-minal-jinni faqaalooo innaa sami'na Qur-aanan 'ajabaa.

(٧٢) سُورَةُ الْجِنِّ مَكِّيَّةٌ (٤٠)

آياتها ٢٨ بِسْمِ اللَّهِ الرَّحْمَٰنِ الرَّحِيمِ ركوعاتها ٢

قُلْ أُوحِيَ إِلَيَّ أَنَّهُ اسْتَمَعَ نَفَرٌ مِّنَ
الْجِنِّ فَقَالُوا إِنَّا سَمِعْنَا قُرْآنًا
عَجَبًا ﴿١﴾

2. which guides people to the right path and we believe in it. We shall never consider anyone equal to our Lord;

2. Yahdeee ilar-rushdi fa-aamannaa bihee wa lan nushrika bi-Rabbinaaa aḥadaa.

يَّهْدِيْٓ اِلَى الرُّشْدِ فَاٰمَنَّا بِهٖ ۗ
وَلَنْ نُّشْرِكَ بِرَبِّنَآ اَحَدًا ۝٢

3. our Lord is by far exalted above having either a wife or son.'"

3. Wa annahoo Ta'aalaa jaddu Rabbinaa mat-takhaza ṣaaḥibatañw-wa laa waladaa.

وَّاَنَّهٗ تَعٰلٰى جَدُّ رَبِّنَا مَا اتَّخَذَ
صَاحِبَةً وَّلَا وَلَدًا ۝٣

4. "The dimwit one (the devil) among us has been telling unjust things about Allah.

4. Wa annahoo kaana ya-qoolu safeehunaa 'alal-laahi shaṭaṭaa

وَّاَنَّهٗ كَانَ يَقُوْلُ سَفِيْهُنَا عَلَى
اللّٰهِ شَطَطًا ۝٤

5. We thought that no man or jinn could ever tell lies about Allah."

5. Wa annaa ẓanannaaa al-lan taqoolal-insu waljinnu 'alal-laahi kazibaa.

وَّاَنَّا ظَنَنَّآ اَنْ لَّنْ تَقُوْلَ الْاِنْسُ
وَالْجِنُّ عَلَى اللّٰهِ كَذِبًا ۝٥

6. "Certain human beings sought refuge with certain jinn and this increased their loss and failures.

6. Wa annahoo kaana rijaa-lum-minal-insi ya'oozoona birijaalim-minal-jinni fazaa-doohum rahaqaa.

وَّاَنَّهٗ كَانَ رِجَالٌ مِّنَ الْاِنْسِ
يَعُوْذُوْنَ بِرِجَالٍ مِّنَ الْجِنِّ
فَزَادُوْهُمْ رَهَقًا ۝٦

7. Those people, like you, thought that Allah would never send down a messenger."

7. Wa annahum ẓannoo kamaa ẓanantum al-lañy-yab-'asal-laahu aḥadaa.

وَّاَنَّهُمْ ظَنُّوْا كَمَا ظَنَنْتُمْ اَنْ لَّنْ
يَّبْعَثَ اللّٰهُ اَحَدًا ۝٧

8. "We went near the heavens but found it to be full of strong guards and shooting flames.

8. Wa annaa lamasnas-sa-maaa'a fawajadnaahaa muli'at ḥarasan shadeedañw-wa shuhu-baa.

وَّاَنَّا لَمَسْنَا السَّمَآءَ فَوَجَدْنٰهَا مُلِئَتْ
حَرَسًا شَدِيْدًا وَّشُهُبًا ۝٨

9. We used to sit nearby and try to listen to the heavens, but shooting flames now await those who try to do that.

9. Wa annaa kunnaa naq-'udu minhaa maqaa'ida lis-sam'i famañy-yastami'il-aana yajid lahoo shihaabar-raṣadaa.

وَّاَنَّا كُنَّا نَقْعُدُ مِنْهَا مَقَاعِدَ
لِلسَّمْعِ ۗ فَمَنْ يَّسْتَمِعِ الْاٰنَ يَجِدْ
لَهٗ شِهَابًا رَّصَدًا ۝٩

10. We do not know whether by this arrangement Allah intends benefit and guidance for the people of the earth or only wickedness."

10. Wa annaa laa nadreee asharrun ureeda biman fil-arḍi am araada bihim Rabbuhum rashadaa.

وَّاَنَّا لَا نَدْرِيْٓ اَشَرٌّ اُرِيْدَ بِمَنْ فِى
الْاَرْضِ اَمْ اَرَادَ بِهِمْ رَبُّهُمْ رَشَدًا ۝١٠

11. "As for us, some of us are righteous and others are not. We have all followed different ways.

11. Wa annaa minnaṣ-ṣaali-ḥoona wa minnaa doona zaalika kunnaa ṭaraaa'iqa qidadaa.

وَّاَنَّا مِنَّا الصّٰلِحُوْنَ وَمِنَّا دُوْنَ
ذٰلِكَ ۗ كُنَّا طَرَآئِقَ قِدَدًا ۝١١

12. We knew that we could never challenge Allah whether we stayed on earth or fled elsewhere.

12. Wa annaa ẓanannaaa al-lan nu'jizal-laaha fil-arḍi wa lan nu'jizahoo harabaa.

وَّاَنَّا ظَنَنَّآ اَنْ لَّنْ نُّعْجِزَ اللّٰهَ فِى
الْاَرْضِ وَلَنْ نُّعْجِزَهٗ هَرَبًا ۝١٢

13. Now that we have listened to the guidance, we believe in it. Whoever believes in his Lord does not need to fear loss or

13. Wa annaa lammaa sami'-nal-hudaaa aamannaa bihee famañy-yu'mim bi-Rabbihee falaa yakhaafu

وَّاَنَّا لَمَّا سَمِعْنَا الْهُدٰٓى اٰمَنَّا بِهٖ ۗ
فَمَنْ يُّؤْمِنْ بِرَبِّهٖ فَلَا يَخَافُ

oppression."

bakhsañw-wa laa rahaqaa.

بَخۡسًا وَّلَا رَهَقًا ﴿١٣﴾

14. "Certain ones among us are Muslims and some of us have deviated from the Truth. Whoever has embraced Islam has followed the right guidance.

14. Wa annaa minnal-muslimoona wa minnal-qaasiṭoona faman aslama fa-ulaaa'ika taḥarraw rashadaa.

وَّاَنَّا مِنَّا الۡمُسۡلِمُوۡنَ وَمِنَّا
الۡقٰسِطُوۡنَ ؕ فَمَنۡ اَسۡلَمَ فَاُولٰٓئِكَ
تَحَرَّوۡا رَشَدًا ﴿١٤﴾

15. However, the deviators from the Truth will be the fuel for hell."

15. Wa ammal-qaasiṭoona fakaanoo li-Jahannama ḥaṭabaa.

وَاَمَّا الۡقٰسِطُوۡنَ فَكَانُوۡا لِجَهَنَّمَ
حَطَبًا ﴿١٥﴾

16. Had they (jinn and mankind) remained steadfast in their religion (Islam), We would certainly have given them abundant water to drink

16. Wa allawis-taqaamoo 'alaṭ-ṭareeqati la-asqaynaahum maa'an ghadaqaa.

وَّاَنۡ لَّوِ اسۡتَقَامُوۡا عَلَى الطَّرِيۡقَةِ
لَاَسۡقَيۡنٰهُمۡ مَّآءً غَدَقًا ﴿١٦﴾

17. as a trial for them. Allah will make those who disregard the guidance from their Lord suffer increasing torment.

17. Linaftinahum feeh; wa mañy-yu'riḍ 'an ẕikri Rabbihee yaslukhu 'aẕaaban ṣa'adaa.

لِّنَفۡتِنَهُمۡ فِيۡهِ ؕ وَمَنۡ يُّعۡرِضۡ عَنۡ
ذِكۡرِ رَبِّهٖ يَسۡلُكۡهُ عَذَابًا صَعَدًا ﴿١٧﴾

18. All the parts of the body to be placed on the ground during prostration belong to Allah. Do not prostrate before anyone other than Allah.

18. Wa annal-masaajida lillaahi falaa tad'oo ma'al-laahi aḥadaa.

وَّاَنَّ الۡمَسٰجِدَ لِلّٰهِ فَلَا تَدۡعُوۡا مَعَ
اللّٰهِ اَحَدًا ﴿١٨﴾

19. When the servant of Allah (Muhammad) preached (his message) the jinn would all crowd around him.

19. Wa annahoo lammaa qaama 'abdul-laahi yad'oohu kaadoo yakoonoona 'alayhi libadaa.

وَّاَنَّهٗ لَمَّا قَامَ عَبۡدُ اللّٰهِ يَدۡعُوۡهُ
كَادُوۡا يَكُوۡنُوۡنَ عَلَيۡهِ لِبَدًا ﴿١٩﴾ ع ١٩ ١١

20. (Muhammad), say, "I worship only my Lord and do not consider anyone as His partner."

20. Qul innamaaa ad'oo Rabbee wa laaa ushriku biheee aḥadaa.

قُلۡ اِنَّمَاۤ اَدۡعُوۡا رَبِّىۡ وَلَاۤ اُشۡرِكُ
بِهٖۤ اَحَدًا ﴿٢٠﴾

21. Say, "I do not possess any power to harm or benefit you."

21. Qul innee laaa amliku lakum ḍarrañw-wa laa rashadaa.

قُلۡ اِنِّىۡ لَاۤ اَمۡلِكُ لَكُمۡ ضَرًّا
وَّلَا رَشَدًا ﴿٢١﴾

22. Say, "No one can protect me from Allah, nor can I find any place of refuge but with him.

22. Qul innee lañy-yujeeranee minal-laahi aḥad; wa lan ajida min doonihee multaḥadaa.

قُلۡ اِنِّىۡ لَنۡ يُّجِيۡرَنِىۡ مِنَ اللّٰهِ اَحَدٌ ۙ
وَّلَنۡ اَجِدَ مِنۡ دُوۡنِهٖ مُلۡتَحَدًا ﴿٢٢﴾

23. My only (means of protection) is to convey the message of Allah. Whoever disobeys Allah and His Messenger will go to hell, wherein he will live forever."

23. Illaa balaagham-minal-laahi wa Risaalaatih; wa mañy-ya'ṣil-laaha wa Rasoolahoo fa-inna lahoo Naara Jahannama khaalideena feehaaa abadaa.

اِلَّا بَلٰغًا مِّنَ اللّٰهِ وَرِسٰلٰتِهٖ ؕ وَ
مَنۡ يَّعۡصِ اللّٰهَ وَرَسُوۡلَهٗ فَاِنَّ لَهٗ
نَارَ جَهَنَّمَ خٰلِدِيۡنَ فِيۡهَاۤ اَبَدًا ﴿٢٣﴾

24. (On the Day of Judgment) when the unbelievers witness that with which they have been threatened, they will then know whose helpers are weaker and fewer in number.

24. Ḥattaaa iẕaa ra-aw maa yoo'adoona fasaya'lamoona man aḍ'afu naaṣirañw-wa aqallu 'adadaa.

حَتّٰٓى اِذَا رَاَوۡا مَا يُوۡعَدُوۡنَ فَسَيَعۡلَمُوۡنَ
مَنۡ اَضۡعَفُ نَاصِرًا وَّاَقَلُّ عَدَدًا ﴿٢٤﴾

25. (Muhammad), say, "I do not know whether that with which you have been threatened is close by or

25. Qul in adreee aqareebum-maa too'adoona

قُلۡ اِنۡ اَدۡرِىۡۤ اَقَرِيۡبٌ مَّا تُوۡعَدُوۡنَ

whether my Lord will prolong the time of its coming.	am yaj'alu lahoo Rabbeee amadaa.	اَمْ يَجْعَلُ لَهٗ رَبِّيْٓ اَمَدًا ﴿٢٥﴾
26. He knows the unseen and He does not allow anyone to know His secrets	26. 'Aalimul-Ghaybi falaa yuẕhiru'alaa ghaybiheee aḥadaa.	عٰلِمُ الْغَيْبِ فَلَا يُظْهِرُ عَلٰى غَيْبِهٖٓ اَحَدًا ﴿٢٦﴾
27. except those of His messengers whom He chooses in whose case He provides him knowledge for his present needs and a reserve (of knowledge) for his future needs,	27. Illaa manir-taḍaa mir Rasoolin fa-innahoo yasluku mim bayni yadayhi wa min khalfihee raṣadaa.	اِلَّا مَنِ ارْتَضٰى مِنْ رَّسُوْلٍ فَاِنَّهٗ يَسْلُكُ مِنْۢ بَيْنِ يَدَيْهِ وَمِنْ خَلْفِهٖ رَصَدًا ﴿٢٧﴾
28. so that He will know that they have conveyed the messages of their Lord. He encompasses all that is with them and He keeps a precise account of all things."	28. Liya'lama an qad ablaghoo Risaalaati Rabbihim wa aḥaaṭa bimaa ladayhim wa aḥṣaa kulla shay'in 'adadaa.	لِّيَعْلَمَ اَنْ قَدْ اَبْلَغُوْا رِسٰلٰتِ رَبِّهِمْ وَاَحَاطَ بِمَا لَدَيْهِمْ وَاَحْصٰى كُلَّ شَيْءٍ عَدَدًا ﴿٢٨﴾ ع ٢ ١٢

Al-Muzzammil, The Mantled (73)

In the Name of Allah, the Beneficent, the Merciful.

Sûrat al-Muzzammil-73

(Revealed at Makkah)

Bismillaahir Raḥmaanir Raḥeem

(٧٣) سُوْرَةُ الْمُزَّمِّلِ مَكِّيَّةٌ (٣)

اٰياتها ٢٠ — بِسْمِ اللّٰهِ الرَّحْمٰنِ الرَّحِيْمِ — ركوعاتها ٢

1. You who have wrapped yourself up with a mantle	1. Yaaa ayyuhal-muzzammil.	يٰٓاَيُّهَا الْمُزَّمِّلُ ﴿١﴾
2. worship (Allah) for a few hours at night.	2. Qumil-layla illaa qaleelaa.	قُمِ الَّيْلَ اِلَّا قَلِيْلًا ﴿٢﴾
3. (Worship Him) for more or less than half of the night	3. Niṣfahooo awinquṣ minhu qaleelaa.	نِّصْفَهٗٓ اَوِ انْقُصْ مِنْهُ قَلِيْلًا ﴿٣﴾
4. and recite the Quran in a distinct tone;	4. Aw zid 'alayhi wa rattilil-Qur-aana tarteelaa.	اَوْ زِدْ عَلَيْهِ وَرَتِّلِ الْقُرْاٰنَ تَرْتِيْلًا ﴿٤﴾
5. We will send upon you a heavy word (Tahajjud prayer).	5. Innaa sanulqee 'alayka qawlan s̱aqeelaa.	اِنَّا سَنُلْقِيْ عَلَيْكَ قَوْلًا ثَقِيْلًا ﴿٥﴾
6. Prayer at night leaves the strongest impression on one's soul and the words spoken are more consistent and truthful.	6. Inna naashi'atal-layli hiya ashaddu waṭ-añw-wa aq-wamu qeelaa.	اِنَّ نَاشِئَةَ الَّيْلِ هِيَ اَشَدُّ وَطْاً وَّاَقْوَمُ قِيْلًا ﴿٦﴾
7. During the day, you are preoccupied with many activities.	7. Inna laka fin-nahaari sabḥan ṭaweelaa.	اِنَّ لَكَ فِي النَّهَارِ سَبْحًا طَوِيْلًا ﴿٧﴾
8. Speak of the name of your Lord, raise your hands with index finger moving to express humbleness before Him,	8. Waẕkuris-ma Rabbika wa tabattal ilayhi tabteelaa.	وَاذْكُرِ اسْمَ رَبِّكَ وَتَبَتَّلْ اِلَيْهِ تَبْتِيْلًا ﴿٨﴾
9. and the Lord of the east and west, with due sincerity. He is the only Lord, so choose Him as your Guardian.	9. Rabbul-mashriqi wal-maghribi laaa ilaaha illaa Huwa fattakhiẕhu Wakeelaa.	رَبُّ الْمَشْرِقِ وَالْمَغْرِبِ لَآ اِلٰهَ اِلَّا هُوَ فَاتَّخِذْهُ وَكِيْلًا ﴿٩﴾
10. Bear patiently whatever they (pagans) say, do not yield to them and keep on preaching decently to them.	10. Waṣbir 'alaa maa yaqooloona wahjurhum hajran jameelaa.	وَاصْبِرْ عَلٰى مَا يَقُوْلُوْنَ وَاهْجُرْهُمْ هَجْرًا جَمِيْلًا ﴿١٠﴾
11. Leave the prosperous unbelievers to Me and give them	11. Wa ẕarnee walmukaẕ ẕibeena ulin-na'mati	وَذَرْنِيْ وَالْمُكَذِّبِيْنَ اُولِي النَّعْمَةِ

respite for a little while;

12. We have prepared for them fetters, flaming fire,

13. food which chokes (them), and a painful torment.

14. On that day, the earth and the mountains will be violently shaken, and the mountains will be turned into heaps of moving sand.

15. We have sent you a messenger, who will witness your deeds, just as We sent a Messenger to the Pharaoh.

16. However, the Pharaoh disobeyed the Messenger and We seized him with a severe retribution.

17. If you disbelieve, how will you be able to protect yourselves from the hardships of the day which would even turn children grey-headed?

18. On that day, the heavens will be rent asunder. This is the decree of Allah which has already been ordained.

19. This is a reminder so that anyone who wants to seek guidance from his Lord can do so.

20. Your Lord knows that you and a group of those who are with you get up for prayer sometimes for less than two-thirds of the night, sometimes half and sometimes one-third of it. Allah determines the duration of the night and day. He knew that it would be hard for you to keep an exact account of the timing of the night prayers, so He turned to you with forgiveness. Thus, recite from the Quran as much as possible. He knew that some of you would be sick, others would travel in the land to seek Allah's favors, and still others would fight for the cause of Allah. Thus, recite from the Quran as much as

wa mahhilhum qaleelaa.

12. Inna ladaynaaa ankaalañw-wa Jaḥeemaa.

13. Wa ṭa'aaman zaa ghuṣṣa-tiñw-wa 'azaaban aleemaa.

14. Yawma tarjuful-arḍu waljibaalu wa kaanatil-jibaalu kaseebam-maheelaa.

15. Innaaa arsalnaaa ilaykum Rasoolan shaahidan 'alaykum kamaaa arsalnaa ilaa Fir'awna Rasoolaa.

16. Fa'aṣaa Fir'awnur-Rasoola fa-akhaznaahu akhzañw-wabeelaa.

17. Fakayfa tattaqoona in kafartum Yawmañy-yaj'alul-wildaana sheebaa.

18. Assamaaa'u munfaṭirum bih; kaana wa'duhoo maf-'oolaa.

19. Inna haazihee tazkiratun faman shaaa'at-takhaza ilaa Rabbihee sabeelaa.

20. Inna Rabbaka ya'lamu annaka taqoomu adnaa min sulusa-yil-layli wa niṣfahoo wa sulusahoo wa ṭaaa'ifatum-minnal-lazeena ma'ak; wal-laahu yuqaddirul-layla wanna-haar; 'alima al-lan tuḥṣoohu fataaba 'alaykum faqra'oo maa tayassara minal-Qur-aan; 'alima an sayakoonu minkum marḍaa wa aakharoona yaḍri-boona fil-arḍi yabtaghoona min faḍlil-laahi wa aakharoona yu-qaatiloona fee sabeelil-laahi faqra'oo

وَمَهِّلْهُمْ قَلِيلًا ﴿١١﴾
إِنَّ لَدَيْنَآ أَنكَالًا وَّجَحِيمًا ﴿١٢﴾
وَطَعَامًا ذَا غُصَّةٍ وَّعَذَابًا أَلِيمًا ﴿١٣﴾
يَوْمَ تَرْجُفُ الْأَرْضُ وَالْجِبَالُ وَ
كَانَتِ الْجِبَالُ كَثِيبًا مَّهِيلًا ﴿١٤﴾
إِنَّآ أَرْسَلْنَآ إِلَيْكُمْ رَسُولًا
شَاهِدًا عَلَيْكُمْ كَمَآ أَرْسَلْنَآ إِلَىٰ
فِرْعَوْنَ رَسُولًا ﴿١٥﴾
فَعَصَىٰ فِرْعَوْنُ الرَّسُولَ فَأَخَذْنَٰهُ
أَخْذًا وَبِيلًا ﴿١٦﴾
فَكَيْفَ تَتَّقُونَ إِن كَفَرْتُمْ يَوْمًا
يَجْعَلُ الْوِلْدَانَ شِيبًا ﴿١٧﴾
السَّمَآءُ مُنفَطِرٌ بِهِۦ كَانَ وَعْدُهُۥ
مَفْعُولًا ﴿١٨﴾
إِنَّ هَٰذِهِۦ تَذْكِرَةٌ فَمَن شَآءَ
اتَّخَذَ إِلَىٰ رَبِّهِۦ سَبِيلًا ﴿١٩﴾ ع ١٩ ١٣
إِنَّ رَبَّكَ يَعْلَمُ أَنَّكَ تَقُومُ أَدْنَىٰ
مِن ثُلُثَيِ الَّيْلِ وَنِصْفَهُۥ وَثُلُثَهُۥ
وَطَآئِفَةٌ مِّنَ الَّذِينَ مَعَكَ ۚ وَاللَّهُ
يُقَدِّرُ الَّيْلَ وَالنَّهَارَ ۚ عَلِمَ أَن
لَّن تُحْصُوهُ فَتَابَ عَلَيْكُمْ
فَاقْرَءُوا مَا تَيَسَّرَ مِنَ الْقُرْآنِ ۚ
عَلِمَ أَن سَيَكُونُ مِنكُم مَّرْضَىٰ ۙ
وَآخَرُونَ يَضْرِبُونَ فِي الْأَرْضِ
يَبْتَغُونَ مِن فَضْلِ اللَّهِ ۙ وَآخَرُونَ
يُقَاتِلُونَ فِي سَبِيلِ اللَّهِ ۖ فَاقْرَءُوا

possible, be steadfast in prayer, pay the zakat, and give virtuous loans to Allah. Whatever good deeds you save for the next life, you will certainly find them with Allah. This is the best investment, and for this you will find the greatest reward. Ask forgiveness from Allah. Allah is All-forgiving and All-merciful.	maa tayassara minh; wa aqeemuṣ-Ṣalaata wa aatuz-Zakaata wa aqriḍul-laaha qarḍan ḥasanaa; wa maa tuqaddimoo li-anfusikum min khayrin tajidoohu 'indal-laahi huwa khayrañw-wa a'ẓama ajraa; wastaghfirul-laah; innal-laaha Ghafoorur-Raḥeem.	مَا تَيَسَّرَ مِنْهُ ۙ وَأَقِيمُوا الصَّلَوٰةَ وَآتُوا الزَّكَوٰةَ وَأَقْرِضُوا اللَّهَ قَرْضًا حَسَنًا ۚ وَمَا تُقَدِّمُوا لِأَنْفُسِكُمْ مِّنْ خَيْرٍ تَجِدُوهُ عِنْدَ اللَّهِ هُوَ خَيْرًا وَّأَعْظَمَ أَجْرًا ۚ وَاسْتَغْفِرُوا اللَّهَ ۖ إِنَّ اللَّهَ غَفُورٌ رَّحِيمٌ ﴿٢٠﴾ ع ١٤
Al-Muddaththir, The Cloaked One (74) In the Name of Allah, the Beneficent, the Merciful.	**Sûrat al-Muddassir-74** (Revealed at Makkah) **Bismillaahir Raḥmaanir Raḥeem**	(٧٤) سُورَةُ الْمُدَّثِّرِ مَكِّيَّةٌ (٤) آياتها ٥٦ بِسْمِ اللَّهِ الرَّحْمَٰنِ الرَّحِيمِ ركوعاتها ٢
1. O Cloaked one,	1. Yaaa ayyuhal-muddas sir.	يَا أَيُّهَا الْمُدَّثِّرُ ﴿١﴾
2. stand up, deliver your warning,	2. Qum fa-anzir.	قُمْ فَأَنْذِرْ ﴿٢﴾
3. proclaim the greatness of your Lord,	3. Wa Rabbaka fakabbir.	وَرَبَّكَ فَكَبِّرْ ﴿٣﴾
4. cleanse your clothes,	4. Wa siyaabaka faṭahhir.	وَثِيَابَكَ فَطَهِّرْ ﴿٤﴾
5. stay away from filthy matters (sins),	5. Warrujza fahjur.	وَالرُّجْزَ فَاهْجُرْ ﴿٥﴾
6. and do not oblige (anyone) for worldly gains.	6. Wa laa tamnun tastaksir.	وَلَا تَمْنُنْ تَسْتَكْثِرُ ﴿٦﴾
7. Exercise patience to please your Lord.	7. Wa li-Rabbika faṣbir.	وَلِرَبِّكَ فَاصْبِرْ ﴿٧﴾
8. When the trumpet is sounded,	8. Fa-izaa nuqira fin-naaqoor.	فَإِذَا نُقِرَ فِي النَّاقُورِ ﴿٨﴾
9. it will be a hard day	9. Fazaalika Yawma'iziñy-yawmun 'aseer.	فَذَٰلِكَ يَوْمَئِذٍ يَّوْمٌ عَسِيرٌ ﴿٩﴾
10. and for the unbelievers, in particular, it will not be at all easy.	10. 'Alal-kaafireena ghayru yaseer.	عَلَى الْكَافِرِينَ غَيْرُ يَسِيرٍ ﴿١٠﴾
11. Leave to Me the one, whom I have created from a single parent,	11. Zarnee wa man khalaqtu waḥeedaa.	ذَرْنِي وَمَنْ خَلَقْتُ وَحِيدًا ﴿١١﴾
12. and to whom I have granted abundant wealth	12. Wa ja'altu lahoo maalam-mamdoodaa.	وَّجَعَلْتُ لَهُ مَالًا مَّمْدُودًا ﴿١٢﴾
13. and children who testified to a false testimony	13. Wa baneena shuhoodaa.	وَّبَنِينَ شُهُودًا ﴿١٣﴾
14. whose life I have made run smoothly	14. Wa mahhattu lahoo tamheedaa.	وَّمَهَّدْتُّ لَهُ تَمْهِيدًا ﴿١٤﴾
15. and who still desires more.	15. Summa yaṭma'u an azeed.	ثُمَّ يَطْمَعُ أَنْ أَزِيدَ ﴿١٥﴾
16. Never will he receive more. He has been hostile to Our revelations.	16. Kallaa innahoo kaana li-Aayaatinaa 'aneedaa.	كَلَّا ۖ إِنَّهُ كَانَ لِآيَاتِنَا عَنِيدًا ﴿١٦﴾
17. I shall hasten him to suffer by climbing the slope (of Mount Saud in hell).	17. Sa-urhiquhoo ṣa'oodaa.	سَأُرْهِقُهُ صَعُودًا ﴿١٧﴾
18. He planned and plotted.	18. Innahoo fakkara wa qaddar.	إِنَّهُ فَكَّرَ وَقَدَّرَ ﴿١٨﴾

19. May he be condemned!

20. What an evil plan he has made!

21. May he be condemned again for his schemes! He looked around,

22. frowned and scowled,

23. then turned back, and, swelling up with arrogance,

24. said, "This (the Quran) is nothing but magic whereby greatness is sought.

25. There is nothing in this other than the words of a mere mortal."

26. I shall make him suffer the torment of Saqar (hell).

27. What does it tell you Saqar (hell) is?

28. It leaves and spares no one and nothing.

29. It scorches people's skin

30. and it has nineteen keepers (angels).

31. We have made only angels as the keepers of the fire (for they are the strongest in carrying out Our commands). Our informing (people) of the numbers of these angels is a trial for the unbelievers. It gives more certainty to the people of the Book and strengthens the faith of the believers. The people of the Book and the believers have no doubt about it. We have fixed the number to make the unbelievers and those whose hearts are sick say, "What does Allah mean by such a parable?" Thus, Allah guides and causes to go astray whomever He wants. No one knows about the army of your Lord except He Himself. This parable is a reminder for mankind.

32. By the moon,

33. by the retreating night,

---

19. Faqutila kayfa qaddar.

20. Summa qutila kayfa qaddar.

21. Summa naẓar.

22. Summa 'abasa wa basar.

23. Summa adbara wastakbar.

24. Faqaala in haazaaa illaa siḥruny-yu'ṣar.

25. In haazaaa illaa qawlul-bashar.

26. Sa-uṣleehi saqar.

27. Wa maaa adraaka maa saqar.

28. Laa tubqee wa laa tazar.

29. Lawwaaḥatul-lilbashar.

30. 'Alayhaa tis'ata 'ashar.

31. Wa maa ja'alnaaa Aṣḥaa-ban-Naari illaa malaaa'ikatañw-wa maa ja'alnaa 'iddatahum illaa fitnatal-lillazeena kafaroo liyastayqinal-lazeena ootul-Kitaaba wa yazdaadal-lazeena aamanooo eemaanañw-wa laa yartaabal-lazeena ootul-Ki-taaba walmu'minoona wa liyaqoolal-lazeena fee quloo-bihim maraḍuñw-walkaafiroona maazaaa araadal-laahu bihaa-zaa maṣalaa; kazaalika yuḍillul-laahu mañy-yashaaa'u wa yahdee mañy-yashaaa'; wa maa ya'lamu junooda Rabbika illaa Hoo; wa maa hiya illaa zikraa lil-bashar.

32. Kallaa walqamar.

33. Wallayli iz adbar.

فَقُتِلَ كَيْفَ قَدَّرَ ۟

ثُمَّ قُتِلَ كَيْفَ قَدَّرَ ۟

ثُمَّ نَظَرَ ۟

ثُمَّ عَبَسَ وَبَسَرَ ۟

ثُمَّ اَدْبَرَ وَاسْتَكْبَرَ ۟

فَقَالَ اِنْ هٰذَآ اِلَّا سِحْرٌ يُّؤْثَرُ ۟

اِنْ هٰذَآ اِلَّا قَوْلُ الْبَشَرِ ۟

سَاُصْلِيْهِ سَقَرَ ۟

وَمَآ اَدْرٰىكَ مَا سَقَرُ ۟

لَا تُبْقِيْ وَلَا تَذَرُ ۟

لَوَّاحَةٌ لِّلْبَشَرِ ۟

عَلَيْهَا تِسْعَةَ عَشَرَ ۟

وَمَا جَعَلْنَآ اَصْحٰبَ النَّارِ اِلَّا مَلٰٓئِكَةً ۖ وَّمَا جَعَلْنَا عِدَّتَهُمْ اِلَّا فِتْنَةً لِّلَّذِيْنَ كَفَرُوْا ۙ لِيَسْتَيْقِنَ الَّذِيْنَ اُوْتُوا الْكِتٰبَ وَيَزْدَادَ الَّذِيْنَ اٰمَنُوْآ اِيْمَانًا وَّلَا يَرْتَابَ الَّذِيْنَ اُوْتُوا الْكِتٰبَ وَ الْمُؤْمِنُوْنَ ۙ وَلِيَقُوْلَ الَّذِيْنَ فِيْ قُلُوْبِهِمْ مَّرَضٌ وَّالْكٰفِرُوْنَ مَاذَآ اَرَادَ اللّٰهُ بِهٰذَا مَثَلًا ۚ كَذٰلِكَ يُضِلُّ اللّٰهُ مَنْ يَّشَآءُ وَيَهْدِيْ مَنْ يَّشَآءُ ۚ وَمَا يَعْلَمُ جُنُوْدَ رَبِّكَ اِلَّا هُوَ ۚ وَمَا هِيَ اِلَّا ذِكْرٰى لِلْبَشَرِ ۟

كَلَّا وَالْقَمَرِ ۟

وَالَّيْلِ اِذْ اَدْبَرَ ۟

34. by the brightening dawn,	34. Waṣṣubḥi izaaa asfar.	وَالصُّبۡحِ اِذَاۤ اَسۡفَرَ ﴿٣٤﴾
35. it (the army of your Lord) is certainly one of the greatest.	35. Innahaa la-iḥdal-kubar.	اِنَّهَا لَاِحۡدَى الۡكُبَرِ ﴿٣٥﴾
36. It is a warning for mankind	36. Nazeeral-lilbashar.	نَذِيۡرًا لِّلۡبَشَرِ ﴿٣٦﴾
37. whether one steps forward to embrace the faith or one turns away from it.	37. Liman shaaa'a minkum añy-yataqaddama aw yata-akhkhar.	لِمَنۡ شَآءَ مِنۡكُمۡ اَنۡ يَّتَقَدَّمَ اَوۡ يَتَاَخَّرَ ﴿٣٧﴾
38. Every soul will be a captive of its deeds	38. Kullu nafsim bimaa kasabat raheenah.	كُلُّ نَفۡسٍ بِمَا كَسَبَتۡ رَهِيۡنَةٌ ﴿٣٨﴾
39. except the people of the right hand	39. Illaaa Aṣḥaabal-Yameen.	اِلَّاۤ اَصۡحٰبَ الۡيَمِيۡنِ ﴿٣٩﴾
40. who will be in Paradise	40. Fee Jannaat; yatasaaa'aloon.	فِىۡ جَنّٰتٍ يَتَسَآءَلُوۡنَ ﴿٤٠﴾
41. and will ask of the criminals,	41. 'Anil-mujrimeen.	عَنِ الۡمُجۡرِمِيۡنَ ﴿٤١﴾
42. "what led you into hell?"	42. Maa salakakum fee saqar.	مَا سَلَكَكُمۡ فِىۡ سَقَرَ ﴿٤٢﴾
43. They will reply, "We did not pray,	43. Qaaloo lam naku minal-muṣalleen.	قَالُوۡا لَمۡ نَكُ مِنَ الۡمُصَلِّيۡنَ ﴿٤٣﴾
44. nor did we feed the destitute.	44. Wa lam naku nuṭ'imul-miskeen.	وَلَمۡ نَكُ نُطۡعِمُ الۡمِسۡكِيۡنَ ﴿٤٤﴾
45. We indulged and persisted in useless disputes,	45. Wa kunnaa nakhooḍu ma'al-khaaa'iḍeen.	وَكُنَّا نَخُوۡضُ مَعَ الۡخَآئِضِيۡنَ ﴿٤٥﴾
46. and rejected the Day of Judgment	46. Wa kunnaa nukaz zibu bi Yawmid-Deen.	وَكُنَّا نُكَذِّبُ بِيَوۡمِ الدِّيۡنِ ﴿٤٦﴾
47. until death approached us."	47. Ḥattaaa ataanal-yaqeen.	حَتّٰۤى اَتٰىنَا الۡيَقِيۡنُ ﴿٤٧﴾
48. The intercession of the intercessors will be of no benefit to them.	48. Famaa tanfa'uhum shafaa'atush-shaafi'een.	فَمَا تَنۡفَعُهُمۡ شَفَاعَةُ الشّٰفِعِيۡنَ ﴿٤٨﴾
49. If such will be the Day of Judgment, what is the matter with them? Why do they run away from guidance,	49. Famaa lahum 'anit-tazkirati mu'riḍeen.	فَمَا لَهُمۡ عَنِ التَّذۡكِرَةِ مُعۡرِضِيۡنَ ﴿٤٩﴾
50. like frightened donkeys	50. Ka-annahum ḥumurum-mustanfirah.	كَاَنَّهُمۡ حُمُرٌ مُّسۡتَنۡفِرَةٌ ﴿٥٠﴾
51. running away from a lion?	51. Farrat min qaswarah.	فَرَّتۡ مِنۡ قَسۡوَرَةٍ ﴿٥١﴾
52. Is it that every one of them wants to receive a heavenly book addressed to him personally?	52. Bal yureedu kullum-ri'-im-minhum añy-yu'taa ṣuḥufam-munashsharah.	بَلۡ يُرِيۡدُ كُلُّ امۡرِئٍ مِّنۡهُمۡ اَنۡ يُّؤۡتٰى صُحُفًا مُّنَشَّرَةً ﴿٥٢﴾
53. This will certainly never be the case! In fact, they are not afraid of the Day of Judgment.	53. Kallaa bal laa yakhaafoonal-aakhirah.	كَلَّا بَلۡ لَّا يَخَافُوۡنَ الۡاٰخِرَةَ ﴿٥٣﴾
54. There is no doubt that the Quran is a guide.	54. Kallaaa innahoo tazkirah.	كَلَّاۤ اِنَّهٗ تَذۡكِرَةٌ ﴿٥٤﴾
55. Thus anyone who seeks guidance may do so.	55. Faman shaaa'a zakarah.	فَمَنۡ شَآءَ ذَكَرَهٗ ﴿٥٥﴾
56. No one will seek guidance unless Allah wills it. He alone is worthy of being feared and it befits Him to forgive.	56. Wa maa yazkuroona illaaa añy-yashaaa'al laah; Huwa Ahlut-taqwaa wa Ahlul-maghfirah.	وَمَا يَذۡكُرُوۡنَ اِلَّاۤ اَنۡ يَّشَآءَ اللّٰهُ هُوَ اَهۡلُ التَّقۡوٰى وَاَهۡلُ الۡمَغۡفِرَةِ ﴿٥٦﴾

مع ١٦ عند المتقدمين ١٢

ع ٢ ٤٥

Al-Qiyamah, Resurrection (75)	Sûrat al-Qiyâmah-75	(٧٥) سُوۡرَةُ الۡقِيٰمَةِ مَكِّيَّةٌ (٣١)
In the Name of Allah, the Beneficent, the Merciful.	(Revealed at Makkah) **Bismillaahir Raḥmaanir Raḥeem**	اٰياتها ٤٠ بِسۡمِ اللّٰهِ الرَّحۡمٰنِ الرَّحِيۡمِ ركوعاتها ٢
1. I swear by the Day of Resurrection	1. Laaa uqsimu bi-Yawmil-Qiyaamah.	لَاۤ اُقۡسِمُ بِيَوۡمِ الۡقِيٰمَةِ ۙ‏ ﴿۱﴾
2. and by the self-accusing soul (that you will certainly be resurrected).	2. We laaa uqsimu bin-nafsil-lawwaamah.	وَلَاۤ اُقۡسِمُ بِالنَّفۡسِ اللَّوَّامَةِ ؕ‏ ﴿۲﴾
3. Do men think that We shall never be able to assemble their bones?	3. Ayaḥsabul-insaanu al-lan najma'a 'iẓaamah.	اَيَحۡسَبُ الۡاِنۡسَانُ اَلَّنۡ نَّجۡمَعَ عِظَامَهٗ ؕ‏ ﴿۳﴾
4. We certainly have the power to restore them, even (the very tips of) their fingers.	4. Balaa qaadireena 'alaaa an nusawwiya banaanah.	بَلٰى قٰدِرِيۡنَ عَلٰٓى اَنۡ نُّسَوِّىَ بَنَانَهٗ‏ ﴿۴﴾
5. In fact, people want to commit sins and send them ahead (without repentance).	5. Bal yureedul insaanu liyafjura amaamah.	بَلۡ يُرِيۡدُ الۡاِنۡسَانُ لِيَفۡجُرَ اَمَامَهٗ ۚ‏ ﴿۵﴾
6. He asks, "When will be the Day of Judgment?"	6. Yas'alu ayyaana Yawmul-Qiyaamah.	يَسۡـَٔلُ اَيَّانَ يَوۡمُ الۡقِيٰمَةِ ؕ‏ ﴿۶﴾
7. When the eye is bewildered,	7. Fa-izaa bariqal-baṣar.	فَاِذَا بَرِقَ الۡبَصَرُ ۙ‏ ﴿۷﴾
8. the moon is eclipsed,	8. Wa khasafal-qamar.	وَخَسَفَ الۡقَمَرُ ۙ‏ ﴿۸﴾
9. and the sun and the moon are brought together,	9. Wa jumi'ash-shamsu wal-qamar.	وَجُمِعَ الشَّمۡسُ وَالۡقَمَرُ ۙ‏ ﴿۹﴾
10. people will say, "Is there anywhere to run away?"	10. Yaqoolul-insaanu Yawma'izin aynal-mafarr.	يَقُوۡلُ الۡاِنۡسَانُ يَوۡمَٮِٕذٍ اَيۡنَ الۡمَفَرُّ ۚ‏ ﴿۱۰﴾
11. Certainly not! There will be no place of refuge.	11. Kallaa laa wazar.	كَلَّا لَا وَزَرَ ؕ‏ ﴿۱۱﴾
12. The only place of refuge on that Day will be with Allah.	12. Ilaa Rabbika Yawma-'izinil-mustaqarr.	اِلٰى رَبِّكَ يَوۡمَٮِٕذِ اۨلۡمُسۡتَقَرُّ ؕ‏ ﴿۱۲﴾
13. On that Day, people will be informed of all that they had done and all that they were supposed to do.	13. Yunabba'ul-insaanu Yawma'izim bimaa qaddama wa akhkhar.	يُنَبَّؤُا الۡاِنۡسَانُ يَوۡمَٮِٕذٍۢ بِمَا قَدَّمَ وَاَخَّرَ ؕ‏ ﴿۱۳﴾
14. In fact, people are well-aware of their own soul	14. Balil-insaanu 'alaa naf-sihee baṣeerah.	بَلِ الۡاِنۡسَانُ عَلٰى نَفۡسِهٖ بَصِيۡرَةٌ ۙ‏ ﴿۱۴﴾
15. even though they make excuses.	15. Wa law alqaa ma'aazee-rah.	وَّلَوۡ اَلۡقٰى مَعَاذِيۡرَهٗ ؕ‏ ﴿۱۵﴾
16. (Muhammad), do not move your tongue too quickly to recite the Quran.	16. Laa tuḥarrik bihee lisaa-naka lita'jala bih.	لَا تُحَرِّكۡ بِهٖ لِسَانَكَ لِتَعۡجَلَ بِهٖ ؕ‏ ﴿۱۶﴾
17. We shall be responsible for its collection and its recitation.	17. Inna 'alaynaa jam'ahoo wa qur'aanah.	اِنَّ عَلَيۡنَا جَمۡعَهٗ وَقُرۡاٰنَهٗ ۖۚ‏ ﴿۱۷﴾
18. When We recite it, follow its recitation by Us.	18. Fa-izaa qara-naahu fatta-bi' qur-aanah.	فَاِذَا قَرَاۡنٰهُ فَاتَّبِعۡ قُرۡاٰنَهٗ ۚ‏ ﴿۱۸﴾
19. We shall be responsible for its explanation.	19. Summa inna 'alaynaa bayaanah.	ثُمَّ اِنَّ عَلَيۡنَا بَيَانَهٗ ؕ‏ ﴿۱۹﴾
20. (You human beings certainly do not want to pay much attention to the Quran) but in fact, you love the worldly life	20. Kallaa bal tuḥibboonal-'aajilah.	كَلَّا بَلۡ تُحِبُّوۡنَ الۡعَاجِلَةَ ۙ‏ ﴿۲۰﴾
21. and neglect the life to come.	21. Wa tazaroonal-Aakhirah.	وَتَذَرُوۡنَ الۡاٰخِرَةَ ؕ‏ ﴿۲۱﴾
22. On the Day of Judgment some faces will be bright,	22. Wujoohuñy-Yawma'izin naaḍirah.	وُجُوۡهٌ يَّوۡمَٮِٕذٍ نَّاضِرَةٌ ۙ‏ ﴿۲۲﴾

23. and look forward to receiving mercy from their Lord.	23. Ilaa Rabbihaa naaẓirah.	إِلَىٰ رَبِّهَا نَاظِرَةٌ ﴿٢٣﴾
24. Others will be despondent,	24. Wa wujoohuñy-yawma'i-zim baasirah.	وَوُجُوهٌ يَوْمَئِذٍ بَاسِرَةٌ ﴿٢٤﴾
25. due to being certain of facing a great calamity.	25. Taẓunnu añy-yuf'ala bihaa faaqirah.	تَظُنُّ أَنْ يُفْعَلَ بِهَا فَاقِرَةٌ ﴿٢٥﴾
26. (Some people, certainly, may not believe in it), but when a person's soul reaches up to his throat	26. kallaaa izaa balaghatit-taraaqee.	كَلَّآ إِذَا بَلَغَتِ التَّرَاقِيَ ﴿٢٦﴾
27. and it is said, "Who is able to provide a curing charm,"	27. Wa qeela man raaq.	وَقِيلَ مَنْ ۜ رَاقٍ ﴿٢٧﴾
28. he will then realize that it is time to leave this world.	28. Wa ẓanna annahul firaaq.	وَظَنَّ أَنَّهُ الْفِرَاقُ ﴿٢٨﴾
29. When legs (the worldly and the hereafter) are intertwined with each other,	29. Waltaffatis-saaqu bissaaq.	وَالْتَفَّتِ السَّاقُ بِالسَّاقِ ﴿٢٩﴾
30. that will be the time to be driven to one's Lord.	30. Ilaa Rabbika Yawma'i-zinil-masaaq.	إِلَىٰ رَبِّكَ يَوْمَئِذٍ الْمَسَاقُ ﴿٣٠﴾ ع ١ ٣٠ ١٧
31. He never acknowledged the faith nor did he ever pray.	31. Falaa ṣaddaqa wa laa ṣallaa.	فَلَا صَدَّقَ وَلَا صَلَّىٰ ﴿٣١﴾
32. He rejects the faith, turns away	32. Wa laakin kaz zaba wa tawallaa.	وَلَٰكِنْ كَذَّبَ وَتَوَلَّىٰ ﴿٣٢﴾
33. and haughtily went to his people.	33. Summa zahaba ilaaa ahlihee yatamaṭṭaa.	ثُمَّ ذَهَبَ إِلَىٰ أَهْلِهِ يَتَمَطَّىٰ ﴿٣٣﴾
34. Woe to you!	34. Awlaa laka fa-awlaa.	أَوْلَىٰ لَكَ فَأَوْلَىٰ ﴿٣٤﴾
35. Woe to you! A human being of such behavior, will certainly deserve it.	35. Summa awlaa laka fa-awlaa.	ثُمَّ أَوْلَىٰ لَكَ فَأَوْلَىٰ ﴿٣٥﴾
36. Does the human being think that he will be left uncontrolled?	36. Ayaḥsabul-insaanu añy-yutraka sudaa.	أَيَحْسَبُ الْإِنْسَانُ أَنْ يُتْرَكَ سُدًى ﴿٣٦﴾
37. Was he not once just a drop of discharged sperm?	37. Alam yaku nuṭfatam-mim-maniyyiñy-yumnaa.	أَلَمْ يَكُ نُطْفَةً مِنْ مَنِيٍّ يُمْنَىٰ ﴿٣٧﴾
38. Was he not turned into a clot of blood? He (Allah) then formed him and gave him proper shape.	38. Summa kaana 'alaqatan fakhalaqa fasawwaa.	ثُمَّ كَانَ عَلَقَةً فَخَلَقَ فَسَوَّىٰ ﴿٣٨﴾
39. From the human being, He (Allah) made males and females in pairs.	39. Faja'ala minhuz-zawjay-niz-zakara wal-unsaa.	فَجَعَلَ مِنْهُ الزَّوْجَيْنِ الذَّكَرَ وَالْأُنْثَىٰ ﴿٣٩﴾
40. Does He then not have the power to bring the dead back to life?	40. Alaysa zaalika biqaadirin 'alaaa añy-yuḥyiyal-mawtaa.	أَلَيْسَ ذَٰلِكَ بِقَادِرٍ عَلَىٰ أَنْ يُحْيِيَ الْمَوْتَىٰ ﴿٤٠﴾ ع ٢ ١٠ ١٨

Al-Insan, Human Being (76) In the Name of Allah, the Beneficent, the Merciful.	**Sûrat ad-Dahr; or al-Insân-76** (Revealed at Madinah) **Bismillaahir Raḥmaanir Raḥeem**	(٧٦) سُورَةُ الدَّهْرِ مَدَنِيَّةٌ (٩٨) آيَاتُهَا ٣١ بِسْمِ اللَّهِ الرَّحْمَٰنِ الرَّحِيمِ رُكُوعَاتُهَا ٢
1. Had there ever been a certain time when there was no mention of the human being?	1. Hal ataa 'alal-insaani ḥeenum-minad-dahri lam yakun shay'am mazkooraa.	هَلْ أَتَىٰ عَلَى الْإِنْسَانِ حِينٌ مِنَ الدَّهْرِ لَمْ يَكُنْ شَيْئًا مَذْكُورًا ﴿١﴾
2. We created the human being from a mixed seed (the union of sperm and egg) to test him. We gave him hearing and vision.	2. Innaa khalaqnal-insaana min-nuṭfatin amshaaj; nabta-leehi faja'alnaahu samee'am baṣeeraa.	إِنَّا خَلَقْنَا الْإِنْسَانَ مِنْ نُطْفَةٍ أَمْشَاجٍ ۖ نَبْتَلِيهِ فَجَعَلْنَاهُ سَمِيعًا

		بَصِيْرًا ﴿٢﴾
3. We showed him the right path whether he would be grateful or ungrateful.	3. Inna hadaynaahus-sabeela immaa shaakirañw-wa immaa kafooraa.	اِنَّا هَدَيْنٰهُ السَّبِيْلَ اِمَّا شَاكِرًا وَّاِمَّا كَفُوْرًا ﴿٣﴾
4. We have prepared chains, shackles, and flaming fire (for the unbelievers).	4. Innaaa a'tadnaa lilkaafireena salaasilaa wa aghlaalañw-wa sa'eeraa.	اِنَّآ اَعْتَدْنَا لِلْكٰفِرِيْنَ سَلٰسِلَاۡ وَاَغْلٰلًا وَّسَعِيْرًا ﴿٤﴾
5. The virtuous ones will drink from a cup containing an admixture of camphor.	5. Innal-abraara yashraboona min ka-sin kaana mizaajuhaa kaafooraa.	اِنَّ الْاَبْرَارَ يَشْرَبُوْنَ مِنْ كَاْسٍ كَانَ مِزَاجُهَا كَافُوْرًا ﴿٥﴾
6. It is a spring from which the servants of Allah drink. (It is the spring that) they make flow as they like.	6. 'Aynañy-yashrabu bihaa 'ibaadul-laahi yufajjiroonahaa tafjeeraa.	عَيْنًا يَّشْرَبُ بِهَا عِبَادُ اللّٰهِ يُفَجِّرُوْنَهَا تَفْجِيْرًا ﴿٦﴾
7. The servants of Allah fulfill their vows and are afraid of the day in which there will be great widespread horror.	7. Yoofoona binnaẕri wa yakhaafoona yawman kaana sharruhoo mustaṭeeraa.	يُوْفُوْنَ بِالنَّذْرِ وَيَخَافُوْنَ يَوْمًا كَانَ شَرُّهٗ مُسْتَطِيْرًا ﴿٧﴾
8. They feed the destitute, orphans, and captives for the love of Allah, saying,	8. Wa yuṭ'imoonaṭ-ṭa'aama 'alaa ḥubbihee miskeenañw-wa yateemañw-wa aseeraa.	وَيُطْعِمُوْنَ الطَّعَامَ عَلٰى حُبِّهٖ مِسْكِيْنًا وَّيَتِيْمًا وَّاَسِيْرًا ﴿٨﴾
9. "We only feed you for the sake of Allah and we do not want any reward or thanks from you.	9. Innamaa nuṭ'imukum liwajhil-laahi laa nureedu minkum jazaaa'añw-wa laa shukooraa.	اِنَّمَا نُطْعِمُكُمْ لِوَجْهِ اللّٰهِ لَا نُرِيْدُ مِنْكُمْ جَزَآءً وَّلَا شُكُوْرًا ﴿٩﴾
10. We are afraid of our Lord and the intensely distressful day."	10. Innaa nakhaafu mir-Rabbinaa Yawman 'aboosan qamṭareeraa.	اِنَّا نَخَافُ مِنْ رَّبِّنَا يَوْمًا عَبُوْسًا قَمْطَرِيْرًا ﴿١٠﴾
11. Allah will certainly rescue them from the terror of that day and will meet them with joy and pleasure.	11. Fawaqaahumul-laahu sharra ẕaalikal-Yawmi wa laqqaahum naḍratañw-wa suroorаa.	فَوَقٰىهُمُ اللّٰهُ شَرَّ ذٰلِكَ الْيَوْمِ وَ لَقّٰىهُمْ نَضْرَةً وَّسُرُوْرًا ﴿١١﴾
12. For their patience, He will reward them with Paradise and silk.	12. Wa jazaahum bimaa ṣabaroo Jannatañw-wa ḥareeraa.	وَجَزٰىهُمْ بِمَا صَبَرُوْا جَنَّةً وَّحَرِيْرًا ﴿١٢﴾
13. They will recline therein on couches and they will find neither excessive heat nor cold.	13. Muttaki'eena feehaa 'alal-araaa'iki laa yarawna feehaa shamsañw-wa laa zamhareeraa.	مُّتَّكِـِٕيْنَ فِيْهَا عَلَى الْاَرَآئِكِ ۚ لَا يَرَوْنَ فِيْهَا شَمْسًا وَّلَا زَمْهَرِيْرًا ﴿١٣﴾
14. The shades of the garden will be closely spread over them and it will be easy for them to reach the fruits.	14. Wa daaniyatan 'alayhim ẕilaaluhaa wa ẕullilat quṭoofuhaa taẕleelaa.	وَدَانِيَةً عَلَيْهِمْ ظِلٰلُهَا وَذُلِّلَتْ قُطُوْفُهَا تَذْلِيْلًا ﴿١٤﴾
15. They will be served with silver dishes and crystal clear goblets.	15. Wa yuṭaafu 'alayhim biaaniyatim-min fiḍḍatiñw-wa akwaabin kaanat qawaareeraa.	وَيُطَافُ عَلَيْهِمْ بِاٰنِيَةٍ مِّنْ فِضَّةٍ وَّاَكْوَابٍ كَانَتْ قَوَارِيْرَا۠ ﴿١٥﴾

قرء حفص بغير الالف في الوصل فيهما ووقف على الاول بالالف وعلى الثاني بغير الالف ١٢

16. Also there will be crystal clear goblets of silver containing the exact measure of drink which they desire.	16. Qawaareera min fiḍḍatin qaddaroohaa taqdeeraa.	قَوَارِيْرَا۟ مِنْ فِضَّةٍ قَدَّرُوْهَا تَقْدِيْرًا ﴿١٦﴾
17. They will drink cups containing (soft flowing) sparkling water	17. Wa yusqawna feehaa kasan kaana mizaajuhaa zanjabeelaa.	وَيُسْقَوْنَ فِيْهَا كَاْسًا كَانَ مِزَاجُهَا زَنْجَبِيْلًا ﴿١٧﴾
18. from a spring named Salsabil.	18. 'Aynan feehaa tusammaa salsabeelaa.	عَيْنًا فِيْهَا تُسَمّٰى سَلْسَبِيْلًا ﴿١٨﴾
19. They will be served by immortal youths who look like scattered pearls.	19. Wa yaṭoofu 'alayhim wildaanum-mukhalladoona izaa ra-aytahum ḥasibtahum lu'lu'am-mansooraa.	وَيَطُوْفُ عَلَيْهِمْ وِلْدَانٌ مُّخَلَّدُوْنَ ۚ اِذَا رَاَيْتَهُمْ حَسِبْتَهُمْ لُؤْلُؤًا مَّنْثُوْرًا ﴿١٩﴾
20. If you were to see it, you would find it to be a great kingdom with great bounty.	20. Wa izaa ra-ayta samma ra-ayta na'eemañw-wa mulkan kabeeraa.	وَاِذَا رَاَيْتَ ثَمَّ رَاَيْتَ نَعِيْمًا وَّ مُلْكًا كَبِيْرًا ﴿٢٠﴾
21. They will have fine green silk and brocade, and they will be decked with bracelets of silver. Their Lord will provide them with a drink of pure wine.	21. 'Aaliyahum siyaabu sundusin khuḍruñw-wa istabraq; wa ḥullooo asaawira min fiḍḍah; wa saqaahum Rabbuhum sharaaban ṭahooraa.	عٰلِيَهُمْ ثِيَابُ سُنْدُسٍ خُضْرٌ وَّ اِسْتَبْرَقٌ ۫ وَّحُلُّوْٓا اَسَاوِرَ مِنْ فِضَّةٍ ۚ وَسَقٰىهُمْ رَبُّهُمْ شَرَابًا طَهُوْرًا ﴿٢١﴾
22. This will be their reward and their efforts will be appreciated.	22. Inna haazaa kaana lakum jazaaa'añw-wa kaana sa'yukum mashkooraa.	اِنَّ هٰذَا كَانَ لَكُمْ جَزَآءً وَّكَانَ سَعْيُكُمْ مَّشْكُوْرًا ﴿٢٢﴾ ع ٢٢ ١٩
23. (Muhammad), We have revealed the Quran to you in gradual steps.	23. Innaa Naḥnu nazzalnaa 'alaykal-Qur-aana tanzeelaa.	اِنَّا نَحْنُ نَزَّلْنَا عَلَيْكَ الْقُرْاٰنَ تَنْزِيْلًا ﴿٢٣﴾
24. So wait patiently for the command of your Lord and do not yield to any sinful or disbelieving person among them (people).	24. Faṣbir liḥukmi Rabbika wa laa tuṭi' minhum aasiman aw kafooraa.	فَاصْبِرْ لِحُكْمِ رَبِّكَ وَلَا تُطِعْ مِنْهُمْ اٰثِمًا اَوْ كَفُوْرًا ﴿٢٤﴾
25. Mention the Name of your Lord, mornings and evenings.	25. Wazkuris-ma Rabbika bukratañw-wa aṣeelaa.	وَاذْكُرِ اسْمَ رَبِّكَ بُكْرَةً وَّاَصِيْلًا ﴿٢٥﴾
26. Prostrate before Him and glorify Him extensively during the night.	26. Wa minal-layli fasjud lahoo wa sabbiḥhu laylan ṭaweelaa.	وَمِنَ الَّيْلِ فَاسْجُدْ لَهٗ وَسَبِّحْهُ لَيْلًا طَوِيْلًا ﴿٢٦﴾
27. These people (unbelievers) love the worldly life and neglect the terrifying day behind them which will come.	27. Inna haaa'ulaaa'i yuḥibboonal-'aajilata wa yazaroona waraaa'ahum Yawman saqeelaa.	اِنَّ هٰٓؤُلَآءِ يُحِبُّوْنَ الْعَاجِلَةَ وَ يَذَرُوْنَ وَرَآءَهُمْ يَوْمًا ثَقِيْلًا ﴿٢٧﴾
28. We have created them and have given them strength. Had We wanted, We could have replaced them with another people like them.	28. Naḥnu khalaqnaahum wa shadadnaaa asrahum wa izaa shi'naa baddalnaaa amsaalahum tabdeelaa.	نَحْنُ خَلَقْنٰهُمْ وَشَدَدْنَآ اَسْرَهُمْ ۚ وَاِذَا شِئْنَا بَدَّلْنَآ اَمْثَالَهُمْ تَبْدِيْلًا ﴿٢٨﴾

29. This (chapter) is a reminder. Those who want to seek guidance from their Lord may do so.	29. Inna haazihee tazkiratun faman shaaa'at-takhaza ilaa Rabbihee sabeelaa.	إِنَّ هَٰذِهِۦ تَذْكِرَةٌ ۖ فَمَن شَآءَ ٱتَّخَذَ إِلَىٰ رَبِّهِۦ سَبِيلًا ﴿٢٩﴾
30. (The virtuous ones mentioned in this chapter) want only what Allah wants. Allah is All-knowing and All-wise.	30. Wa maa tashaaa'oona illaaa añy-yashaaa'al-laah; innal-laaha kaana 'Aleeman Ḥakeema.	وَمَا تَشَآءُونَ إِلَّآ أَن يَشَآءَ ٱللَّهُ ۚ إِنَّ ٱللَّهَ كَانَ عَلِيمًا حَكِيمًا ﴿٣٠﴾
31. He admits to His mercy whomever He wants. For the unjust He has prepared a painful punishment.	31. Yudkhilu mañy-yashaaa'u fee raḥmatih; waẓẓaalimeena a'adda lahum 'azaaban aleemaa.	يُدْخِلُ مَن يَشَآءُ فِى رَحْمَتِهِۦ ۚ وَٱلظَّٰلِمِينَ أَعَدَّ لَهُمْ عَذَابًا أَلِيمًۢا ﴿٣١﴾

Al-Mursalat, Angels Sent (77)	**Sûrat al-Mursalât-77**	(٧٧) سُورَةُ ٱلْمُرْسَلَٰتِ مَكِّيَّةٌ (٣٣)
In the Name of Allah, the Beneficent, the Merciful.	(Revealed at Makkah) **Bismillaahir Raḥmaanir Raḥeem**	آياتها ٥٠ بِسْمِ ٱللَّهِ ٱلرَّحْمَٰنِ ٱلرَّحِيمِ ركوعاتها ٢

1. (I swear) by (My) continuously sent forth signs,	1. Wal-mursalaati 'urfaa.	وَٱلْمُرْسَلَٰتِ عُرْفًا ﴿١﴾
2. by (the angels) as swift as blowing winds,	2. Fal-'aaṣifaati 'aṣfaa.	فَٱلْعَٰصِفَٰتِ عَصْفًا ﴿٢﴾
3. by (the angels) spreading (the words of Allah) far and wide,	3. Wannaashiraati nashraa.	وَٱلنَّٰشِرَٰتِ نَشْرًا ﴿٣﴾
4. by (the angels) who make a clear distinction between right and wrong,	4. Fal-faariqaati farqaa.	فَٱلْفَٰرِقَٰتِ فَرْقًا ﴿٤﴾
5. and by those who reveal revelations (to the prophets)	5. Fal-mulqiyaati zikraa.	فَٱلْمُلْقِيَٰتِ ذِكْرًا ﴿٥﴾
6. to provide excuses for some and to give warnings to others;	6. 'Uzran aw nuzraa.	عُذْرًا أَوْ نُذْرًا ﴿٦﴾
7. that whatever with which you have been warned will inevitably come to pass.	7. Innamaa too'adoona lawaaqi'.	إِنَّمَا تُوعَدُونَ لَوَٰقِعٌ ﴿٧﴾
8. Then the stars will lose their light.	8. Fa-izan-nujoomu ṭumisat.	فَإِذَا ٱلنُّجُومُ طُمِسَتْ ﴿٨﴾
9. Heavens will rent asunder.	9. Wa izas-samaaa'u furijat.	وَإِذَا ٱلسَّمَآءُ فُرِجَتْ ﴿٩﴾
10. The mountains will be blown away as dust.	10. Wa izal-jibaalu nusifat.	وَإِذَا ٱلْجِبَالُ نُسِفَتْ ﴿١٠﴾
11. The Messengers will receive their appointments.	11. Wa izar-Rusulu uqqitat.	وَإِذَا ٱلرُّسُلُ أُقِّتَتْ ﴿١١﴾
12. If one asks, "To which day have such calamitous events been postponed?"	12. Li-ayyi Yawmin ujjilat.	لِأَىِّ يَوْمٍ أُجِّلَتْ ﴿١٢﴾
13. one will be told, "To the Day of Distinction."	13. Li-Yawmil-Faṣl.	لِيَوْمِ ٱلْفَصْلِ ﴿١٣﴾
14. What does it tell you the Day of distinction (Judgment) is?	14. Wa maaa adraaka maa Yawmul-Faṣl.	وَمَآ أَدْرَىٰكَ مَا يَوْمُ ٱلْفَصْلِ ﴿١٤﴾
15. On that day, woe will be to those who have rejected Allah's revelations!	15. Wayluñy-Yawma'izil-lilmukaz zibeen.	وَيْلٌ يَوْمَئِذٍ لِّلْمُكَذِّبِينَ ﴿١٥﴾
16. Did We not destroy the ancient people	16. Alam nuhlikil-awwaleen.	أَلَمْ نُهْلِكِ ٱلْأَوَّلِينَ ﴿١٦﴾
17. and make others settle after them in their land?	17. Summa nutbi'uhumul-aakhireen.	ثُمَّ نُتْبِعُهُمُ ٱلْءَاخِرِينَ ﴿١٧﴾
18. Thus do We deal with the sinful ones.	18. Kazaalika naf'alu bilmujrimeen.	كَذَٰلِكَ نَفْعَلُ بِٱلْمُجْرِمِينَ ﴿١٨﴾

19. On that day, woe upon those who have rejected Allah's revelations!	19. Wayluñy-Yawma'iz̲il-lil-mukaz̲z̲ibeen.	وَيْلٌ يَّوْمَئِذٍ لِّلْمُكَذِّبِيْنَ ﴿١٩﴾
20. Did We not create you from an insignificant drop of fluid	20. Alam nakhluqkum mim-maaa'im-maheen.	اَلَمْ نَخْلُقْكُّمْ مِّنْ مَّآءٍ مَّهِيْنٍ ﴿٢٠﴾
21. and place it in a secure place	21. Faja'alnaahu fee qaraa-rim-makeen.	فَجَعَلْنٰهُ فِيْ قَرَارٍ مَّكِيْنٍ ﴿٢١﴾
22. for an appointed time?	22. Ilaa qadarim-ma'loom.	اِلٰى قَدَرٍ مَّعْلُوْمٍ ﴿٢٢﴾
23. Thus did We plan and how excellent is Our planning!	23. Faqadarnaa fani'mal-qaadiroon.	فَقَدَرْنَا ۖ فَنِعْمَ الْقٰدِرُوْنَ ﴿٢٣﴾
24. On that day, woe will be upon those who have rejected the revelations of Allah!	24. Wayluñy-Yawma'iz̲il-lilmukaz̲z̲ibeen.	وَيْلٌ يَّوْمَئِذٍ لِّلْمُكَذِّبِيْنَ ﴿٢٤﴾
25. Did We not make the earth as a dwelling place	25. Alam naj'alil-arḍa kifaataa.	اَلَمْ نَجْعَلِ الْاَرْضَ كِفَاتًا ﴿٢٥﴾
26. for the living and the dead,	26. Aḥyaaa'añw-wa amwaataa.	اَحْيَآءً وَّاَمْوَاتًا ﴿٢٦﴾
27. place on it high mountains, and provide you with fresh water?	27. Wa ja'alnaa feehaa ra-waasiya shaamikhaatiñw-wa asqaynaakum maaa'an furaataa.	وَّجَعَلْنَا فِيْهَا رَوَاسِيَ شٰمِخٰتٍ وَّ اَسْقَيْنٰكُمْ مَّآءً فُرَاتًا ﴿٢٧﴾
28. that Day (of Judgment) woe will be upon those who have rejected Allah's revelations!	28. Wayluñy-Yawma'iz̲il-lilmukaz̲z̲ibeen.	وَيْلٌ يَّوْمَئِذٍ لِّلْمُكَذِّبِيْنَ ﴿٢٨﴾
29. Proceed to that (Day of Judgment) which you have rejected.	29. Inṭaliqooo ilaa maa kuntum bihee tukaz̲z̲iboon.	اِنْطَلِقُوْٓا اِلٰى مَا كُنْتُمْ بِهٖ تُكَذِّبُوْنَ ﴿٢٩﴾
30. Proceed to that shadow, rising in three columns	30. Inṭaliqooo ilaa ẓillin z̲ee s̲alaas̲i shu'ab.	اِنْطَلِقُوْٓا اِلٰى ظِلٍّ ذِيْ ثَلٰثِ شُعَبٍ ﴿٣٠﴾
31. which neither gives shade nor protects one from the flames.	31. Laa ẓaleeliñw-wa laa yughnee minal-lahab.	لَّا ظَلِيْلٍ وَّلَا يُغْنِيْ مِنَ اللَّهَبِ ﴿٣١﴾
32. The fire will shoot out sparks as big as huge towers	32. Innahaa tarmee bishararin kalqaṣr.	اِنَّهَا تَرْمِيْ بِشَرَرٍ كَالْقَصْرِ ﴿٣٢﴾
33. and black camels.	33. Ka-annahoo jimaalatun ṣufr.	كَاَنَّهٗ جِمٰلَتٌ صُفْرٌ ﴿٣٣﴾
34. On that day, woe will be upon those who have rejected Allah's revelations!	34. Wayluñy-Yawma'iz̲il-lilmukaz̲z̲ibeen.	وَيْلٌ يَّوْمَئِذٍ لِّلْمُكَذِّبِيْنَ ﴿٣٤﴾
35. On that day they will not be able to speak,	35. Haaz̲aa Yawmu laa yanṭi-qoon.	هٰذَا يَوْمُ لَا يَنْطِقُوْنَ ﴿٣٥﴾
36. nor will they be permitted to offer any excuses.	36. Wa laa yu'z̲anu lahum fa-ya'taz̲iroon.	وَلَا يُؤْذَنُ لَهُمْ فَيَعْتَذِرُوْنَ ﴿٣٦﴾
37. On that day, woe will be upon those who have rejected Allah's revelations!	37. Wayluñy-Yawma'iz̲il-lilmukaz̲z̲ibeen.	وَيْلٌ يَّوْمَئِذٍ لِّلْمُكَذِّبِيْنَ ﴿٣٧﴾
38. That is the Day of Judgment. We will bring you together with all the ancient peoples.	38. Haaz̲aa Yawmul-Faṣli jama'naakum wal-awwaleen.	هٰذَا يَوْمُ الْفَصْلِ ۚ جَمَعْنٰكُمْ وَ الْاَوَّلِيْنَ ﴿٣٨﴾
39. If you have any plans, use them.	39. Fa-in kaana lakum kay-dun fakeedoon.	فَاِنْ كَانَ لَكُمْ كَيْدٌ فَكِيْدُوْنِ ﴿٣٩﴾
40. On that day, woe will be upon those who have rejected Allah's revelations!	40. Wayluñy-Yawma'iz̲il-lilmukaz̲z̲ibeen.	وَيْلٌ يَّوْمَئِذٍ لِّلْمُكَذِّبِيْنَ ﴿٤٠﴾ ع ١ ٤٠ ٢١
41. The pious ones will rest amid the shade, springs,	41. Innal-muttaqeena fee ẓilaaliñw-wa 'uyoon.	اِنَّ الْمُتَّقِيْنَ فِيْ ظِلٰلٍ وَّعُيُوْنٍ ﴿٤١﴾
42. and fruits of the kind which they desire.	42. Wa fawaakiha mimmaa yashtahoon.	وَّفَوَاكِهَ مِمَّا يَشْتَهُوْنَ ﴿٤٢﴾

43. (They will be told), "Eat and drink in good health as a reward for what you have done."	43. Kuloo washraboo haneee-'am bimaa kuntum ta'maloon.	كُلُوْا وَاشْرَبُوْا هَنِيْٓـًٔا بِمَا كُنْتُمْ تَعْمَلُوْنَ ﴿۴۳﴾
44. Thus do We reward the righteous ones.	44. Innaa kaẕaalika najzil-muḥsineen.	اِنَّا كَذٰلِكَ نَجْزِي الْمُحْسِنِيْنَ ﴿۴۴﴾
45. On that day, woe will be upon those who have rejected Allah's revelations!	45. Wayluñy-Yawma'iẕil-lilmukaẕẕibeen.	وَيْلٌ يَّوْمَئِذٍ لِّلْمُكَذِّبِيْنَ ﴿۴۵﴾
46. (Unbelievers), eat and enjoy yourselves for a little while. You are certainly sinful ones.	46. Kuloo wa tamatta'oo qaleelan innakum mujrimoon.	كُلُوْا وَتَمَتَّعُوْا قَلِيْلًا اِنَّكُمْ مُّجْرِمُوْنَ ﴿۴۶﴾
47. On that day, woe will be upon those who have rejected Allah's revelations!	47. Wayluñy-Yawma'iẕil-lilmukaẕẕibeen.	وَيْلٌ يَّوْمَئِذٍ لِّلْمُكَذِّبِيْنَ ﴿۴۷﴾
48. When they are told to say their prayers, they do not bow down (in prayer).	48. Wa iẕaa qeela lahumur-ka'oo laa yarka'oon.	وَاِذَا قِيْلَ لَهُمُ ارْكَعُوْا لَا يَرْكَعُوْنَ ﴿۴۸﴾
49. On that day, woe will be upon those who have rejected Allah's revelations!	49. Wayluñy-Yawma'iẕil-lilmukaẕẕibeen.	وَيْلٌ يَّوْمَئِذٍ لِّلْمُكَذِّبِيْنَ ﴿۴۹﴾
50. In which word other than the Quran will they believe?	50. Fabi-ayyi ḥadeeṡim ba'-dahoo yu'minoon.	فَبِاَيِّ حَدِيْثٍۭ بَعْدَهٗ يُؤْمِنُوْنَ ﴿۵۰﴾ ع ٢ ٢٢
Al-Naba, The News (78) In the Name of Allah, the Beneficent, the Merciful.	**Sûrat an-Naba'-78** (Revealed at Makkah) **Bismillaahir Raḥmaanir Raḥeem**	(۷۸) سُوْرَةُ النَّبَاِ مَكِّيَّةٌ (۸۰) بِسْمِ اللّٰهِ الرَّحْمٰنِ الرَّحِيْمِ
1. What is it that they quarrel about?	1. 'Amma yatasaaa'aloon.	عَمَّ يَتَسَآءَلُوْنَ ﴿۱﴾
2. They quarrel about the great news (Imam Ali)	2. 'Anin-naba-il-'aẓeem.	عَنِ النَّبَاِ الْعَظِيْمِ ﴿۲﴾
3. concerning which they have disputes.	3. Allaẕee hum feehi mukh-talifoon.	الَّذِيْ هُمْ فِيْهِ مُخْتَلِفُوْنَ ﴿۳﴾
4. (What they think is certainly despicable!) They will soon come to know (the reality).	4. Kallaa sa-ya'lamoon.	كَلَّا سَيَعْلَمُوْنَ ﴿۴﴾
5. Yes, indeed, before long they will learn all about it.	5. S̲umma kallaa sa-ya'la-moon.	ثُمَّ كَلَّا سَيَعْلَمُوْنَ ﴿۵﴾
6. Did We not make the earth as a place to rest	6. Alam naj'alil-arḍa mi-haadaa.	اَلَمْ نَجْعَلِ الْاَرْضَ مِهٰدًا ﴿۶﴾
7. and the mountains as pegs (to anchor the earth)?	7. Waljibaala awtaadaa.	وَّالْجِبَالَ اَوْتَادًا ﴿۷﴾
8. Have We not created you in pairs,	8. Wa khalaqnaakum az-waajaa.	وَّخَلَقْنٰكُمْ اَزْوَاجًا ﴿۸﴾
9. made sleep for you to rest,	9. Wa ja'alnaa nawmakum subaataa.	وَّجَعَلْنَا نَوْمَكُمْ سُبَاتًا ﴿۹﴾
10. made the night as a covering,	10. Wa ja'alnal-layla libaa-saa.	وَّجَعَلْنَا الَّيْلَ لِبَاسًا ﴿۱۰﴾
11. and the day as time (for you) to make a living?	11. Wa ja'alnan-nahaara ma'aashaa.	وَّجَعَلْنَا النَّهَارَ مَعَاشًا ﴿۱۱﴾
12. Have We not made seven strong heavens above you,	12. Wa banaynaa fawqakum sab'an shidaadaa.	وَّبَنَيْنَا فَوْقَكُمْ سَبْعًا شِدَادًا ﴿۱۲﴾
13. (the sun) as a shining torch,	13. Wa ja'alnaa siraajañw-wahhaajaa.	وَّجَعَلْنَا سِرَاجًا وَّهَّاجًا ﴿۱۳﴾
14. and sent down heavy rains from the clouds with hurricanes	14. Wa anzalnaa minal-mu'-ṣiraati maaa'an s̲ajjaajaa.	وَّاَنْزَلْنَا مِنَ الْمُعْصِرٰتِ مَآءً ثَجَّاجًا ﴿۱۴﴾

الجزء الثلثون (٣٠)

15. to make the seeds, plants,	15. Linukhrija bihee ḥabbañw-wa nabaataa.	لِّنُخْرِجَ بِهٖ حَبًّا وَّنَبَاتًا ﴿١٥﴾
16. and thick gardens grow?	16. Wa jannaatin alfaafaa.	وَّجَنّٰتٍ اَلْفَافًا ﴿١٦﴾
17. The Day of Judgment will certainly be the final appointment.	17. Inna Yawmal-Faṣli kaana meeqaataa.	اِنَّ يَوْمَ الْفَصْلِ كَانَ مِيْقَاتًا ﴿١٧﴾
18. On that day the trumpet will be sounded and you will come (to Us) in huge groups.	18. Yawma yunfakhu fiṣ-Ṣoori fata-toona afwaajaa.	يَّوْمَ يُنْفَخُ فِي الصُّوْرِ فَتَاْتُوْنَ اَفْوَاجًا ﴿١٨﴾
19. The heavens will have openings like doors.	19. Wa futiḥatis-samaaa'u fakaanat abwaabaa.	وَّفُتِحَتِ السَّمَآءُ فَكَانَتْ اَبْوَابًا ﴿١٩﴾
20. The mountains will be driven away and become like mirages.	20. Wa suyyiratil-jibaalu fakaanat saraabaa.	وَّسُيِّرَتِ الْجِبَالُ فَكَانَتْ سَرَابًا ﴿٢٠﴾
21. Hell will lie in wait (for its prey).	21. Inna Jahannama kaanat mirṣaadaa.	اِنَّ جَهَنَّمَ كَانَتْ مِرْصَادًا ﴿٢١﴾
22. It will be a place of return for the rebellious ones	22. Liṭṭaagheena ma-aabaa.	لِّلطّٰغِيْنَ مَاٰبًا ﴿٢٢﴾
23. and they will live therein for ages.	23. Laabiseena feehaaa aḥqaabaa.	لّٰبِثِيْنَ فِيْهَآ اَحْقَابًا ﴿٢٣﴾
24. They will not feel cold nor taste any drink	24. Laa yazooqoona feehaa bardañw-wa laa sharaabaa.	لَا يَذُوْقُوْنَ فِيْهَا بَرْدًا وَّلَا شَرَابًا ﴿٢٤﴾
25. except boiling water and pus,	25. Illaa ḥameemañw-wa ghas-saaqaa.	اِلَّا حَمِيْمًا وَّغَسَّاقًا ﴿٢٥﴾
26. as a fitting recompense for their deeds.	26. Jazaaa'añw-wifaaqaa.	جَزَآءً وِّفَاقًا ﴿٢٦﴾
27. They did not expect such a Judgment	27. Innahum kaanoo laa yarjoona ḥisaabaa.	اِنَّهُمْ كَانُوْا لَا يَرْجُوْنَ حِسَابًا ﴿٢٧﴾
28. and persistently rejected Our revelations.	28. Wa kaz zaboo bi-Aayaatinaa kiz zaabaa.	وَّكَذَّبُوْا بِاٰيٰتِنَا كِذَّابًا ﴿٢٨﴾
29. However, We have recorded everything in a book.	29. Wa kulla shay'in aḥṣaynaahu kitaabaa.	وَكُلَّ شَيْءٍ اَحْصَيْنٰهُ كِتٰبًا ﴿٢٩﴾
30. (They will be told), "Suffer, We shall only increase the torment for you."	30. Fazooqoo falan nazeedakum illaa 'azaabaa.	فَذُوْقُوْا فَلَنْ نَّزِيْدَكُمْ اِلَّا عَذَابًا ﴿٣٠﴾ ع
31. The pious ones will be triumphant.	31. Inna lilmuttaqeena mafaazaa.	اِنَّ لِلْمُتَّقِيْنَ مَفَازًا ﴿٣١﴾
32. They will have gardens and vineyards,	32. Ḥadaaa'iqa wa a'naabaa.	حَدَآئِقَ وَاَعْنَابًا ﴿٣٢﴾
33. maidens with pear-shaped breasts who are of equal age (to their spouses),	33. Wa kawaa'iba atraabaa.	وَّكَوَاعِبَ اَتْرَابًا ﴿٣٣﴾
34. and cups full of (clean) wine.	34. Wa ka-san dihaaqaa.	وَّكَاْسًا دِهَاقًا ﴿٣٤﴾
35. They will not hear therein any unnecessary words or lies.	35. Laa yasma'oona feehaa laghwañw-wa laa kiz zaabaa.	لَا يَسْمَعُوْنَ فِيْهَا لَغْوًا وَّلَا كِذّٰبًا ﴿٣٥﴾
36. This will be their reward from your Lord, a favor from Him and a recompense for their deeds.	36. Jazaaa'am-mir-Rabbika 'aṭaaa'an ḥisaabaa.	جَزَآءً مِّنْ رَّبِّكَ عَطَآءً حِسَابًا ﴿٣٦﴾
37. He is the Lord of the heavens and the earth and all that is between them. He is the Beneficent and no one will be able to address Him.	37. Rabbis-samaawaati wal-arḍi wa maa baynahumar-Raḥmaani laa yamlikoona minhu khiṭaabaa.	رَّبِّ السَّمٰوٰتِ وَالْاَرْضِ وَمَا بَيْنَهُمَا الرَّحْمٰنِ لَا يَمْلِكُوْنَ مِنْهُ خِطَابًا ﴿٣٧﴾
38. On that day, the Spirit and the angels who stand in lines will	38. Yawma yaqoomur-Rooḥu wal-malaaa'ikatu ṣaffal-	يَوْمَ يَقُوْمُ الرُّوْحُ وَالْمَلٰٓئِكَةُ صَفًّا

not speak except those whom the Beneficent has permitted, and he will speak the right words.

laa yatakallamoona illaa man azina lahur-Raḥmaanu wa qaala ṣawaabaa.

لَا يَتَكَلَّمُونَ إِلَّا مَنْ أَذِنَ لَهُ الرَّحْمٰنُ
وَقَالَ صَوَابًا ﴿٣٨﴾

39. That will be the Day of the Truth. So let those who want seek refuge with their Lord's (mercy).

39. Zaalikal-Yawmul-Ḥaqq; faman shaaa'at-takhaza ilaa Rabbihee ma-aabaa.

ذٰلِكَ الْيَوْمُ الْحَقُّ ۚ فَمَنْ شَاءَ اتَّخَذَ
إِلٰى رَبِّهٖ مَاٰبًا ﴿٣٩﴾

40. We have warned you of the approaching torment. On that day, a person will see what his hands have committed. A disbeliever will say, "Would that I had been dust."

40. Innaaa anzarnaakum 'azaaban qareebañy-Yawma yanẓurul-mar'u maa qaddamat yadaahu wa yaqoolul-kaafiru yaa laytanee kuntu turaabaa.

إِنَّا أَنْذَرْنٰكُمْ عَذَابًا قَرِيبًا ۚ يَوْمَ يَنْظُرُ
الْمَرْءُ مَا قَدَّمَتْ يَدٰهُ وَيَقُولُ الْكٰفِرُ
يٰلَيْتَنِي كُنْتُ تُرٰبًا ﴿٤٠﴾ ع

Al-Naziat, Soul-Snatchers (79)

In the Name of Allah, the Beneficent, the Merciful.

Sûrat an-Nâzi'ât-79

(Revealed at Makkah)

Bismillaahir Raḥmaanir Raḥeem

(٧٩) سُورَةُ النّٰزِعٰتِ مَكِّيَّةٌ (٨١)

آياتها ٤٦ بِسْمِ اللّٰهِ الرَّحْمٰنِ الرَّحِيمِ ركوعاتها ٢

1. (I swear) by those who violently tear-out (the souls of the unbelievers from their bodies),

1. Wannaazi'aati gharqaa.

وَالنّٰزِعٰتِ غَرْقًا ﴿١﴾

2. by those who gently release (the souls of the believers),

2. Wannaashiṭaati nashṭaa.

وَالنّٰشِطٰتِ نَشْطًا ﴿٢﴾

3. by those who float (in the heavens by the will of Allah),

3. Wassaabiḥaati sabḥaa.

وَالسّٰبِحٰتِ سَبْحًا ﴿٣﴾

4. by those who hasten along

4. Fassaabiqaati sabqaa.

فَالسّٰبِقٰتِ سَبْقًا ﴿٤﴾

5. and by those who regulate the affairs,

5. Falmudabbiraati amraa.

فَالْمُدَبِّرٰتِ أَمْرًا ﴿٥﴾ وقف لازم

6. (You will see) the Day the shaker will shake (the earth)

6. Yawma tarjufur-raajifah.

يَوْمَ تَرْجُفُ الرَّاجِفَةُ ﴿٦﴾

7. followed by the second blast of sound,

7. Tatba'uhar-raadifah.

تَتْبَعُهَا الرَّادِفَةُ ﴿٧﴾

8. hearts on that Day will undergo terrible trembling,

8. Quloobuñy-Yawma'iziñw-waajifah.

قُلُوبٌ يَوْمَئِذٍ وَّاجِفَةٌ ﴿٨﴾ وقف لازم

9. and eyes (of such hearts) will be humbly cast down.

9. Abṣaaruhaa khaashi'ah.

أَبْصٰرُهَا خٰشِعَةٌ ﴿٩﴾

10. (The unbelievers) say, "Shall we be brought back to life again

10. Yaqooloona 'a-innaa la-mardoodoona fil-ḥaafirah.

يَقُولُونَ ءَإِنَّا لَمَرْدُودُونَ فِي الْحَافِرَةِ ﴿١٠﴾ وقف لازم

11. after we have become bones and dust?"

11. 'A -izaa kunnaa 'iẓaaman nakhirah.

ءَإِذَا كُنَّا عِظٰمًا نَّخِرَةً ﴿١١﴾

12. They have said, "Such a resurrection will certainly be a great loss."

12. Qaaloo tilka izan karra-tun khaasirah.

قَالُوا تِلْكَ إِذًا كَرَّةٌ خٰسِرَةٌ ﴿١٢﴾ وقف لازم

13. However, it will take only a single blast

13. Fa-innamaa hiya zajratuñw-waaḥidah.

فَإِنَّمَا هِيَ زَجْرَةٌ وّٰحِدَةٌ ﴿١٣﴾

14. to bring them out of their graves and back to life on the earth's surface.

14. Fa-izaa hum bissaahirah.

فَإِذَا هُمْ بِالسَّاهِرَةِ ﴿١٤﴾ وقف لازم

15. (Muhammad), have you heard the story of Moses

15. Hal ataaka ḥadeesu Moosaa.

هَلْ أَتٰىكَ حَدِيثُ مُوسٰى ﴿١٥﴾

16. when his Lord called him in the holy valley of Tuwa,

16. Iz naadaahu Rabbuhoo bilwaadil-muqaddasi Ṭuwaa.

إِذْ نَادٰىهُ رَبُّهٗ بِالْوَادِ الْمُقَدَّسِ
طُوًى ﴿١٦﴾

17. saying, "Go to the Pharaoh. He has transgressed beyond all bounds."	17. Izhab ilaa Fir'awna innahoo taghaa.	اِذْهَبْ اِلٰى فِرْعَوْنَ اِنَّهٗ طَغٰى ۫ۖ ﴿۱۷﴾
18. And say to him, "Would you like to reform yourself?	18. Faqul hal laka ilaaa an tazakkaa.	فَقُلْ هَلْ لَّكَ اِلٰۤى اَنْ تَزَكّٰى ۙ ﴿۱۸﴾
19. I shall guide you to your Lord so that you may perhaps have fear of Him."	19. Wa ahdiyaka ilaa Rabbika fatakhshaa.	وَ اَهْدِيَكَ اِلٰى رَبِّكَ فَتَخْشٰى ۚ ﴿۱۹﴾
20. Moses showed him the great miracle	20. Fa-araahul-Aayatal-Kubraa.	فَاَرٰىهُ الْاٰيَةَ الْكُبْرٰى ۫ۖ ﴿۲۰﴾
21. but the Pharaoh rejected it and disobeyed (Moses).	21. Fakazzaba wa 'asaa.	فَكَذَّبَ وَ عَصٰى ۫ۖ ﴿۲۱﴾
22. Then he turned away in a hurry,	22. Summa adbara yas'aa.	ثُمَّ اَدْبَرَ يَسْعٰى ۫ۖ ﴿۲۲﴾
23. and gathered his people together	23. Fahashara fanaadaa.	فَحَشَرَ فَنَادٰى ۫ۖ ﴿۲۳﴾
24. saying, "I am your supreme lord."	24. Faqaala anaa Rabbukumul-A'laa.	فَقَالَ اَنَا رَبُّكُمُ الْاَعْلٰى ۫ۖ ﴿۲۴﴾
25. So Allah struck him with the torment of this life and the life hereafter.	25. Fa-akhazahul-laahu nakaalal-Aakhirati wal-oolaa.	فَاَخَذَهُ اللّٰهُ نَكَالَ الْاٰخِرَةِ وَ الْاُوْلٰى ؕ ﴿۲۵﴾
26. In this there is a lesson for those who have fear of Allah.	26. Inna fee zaalika la'ibratal-limany-yakhshaa.	اِنَّ فِیْ ذٰلِكَ لَعِبْرَةً لِّمَنْ یَّخْشٰى ؕ ﴿۲۶﴾ ع
27. (People), is your creation harder for Allah than that of the heavens, which He created, raised, and established	27. 'A-antum ashaddu khalqan amis-samaaa'; banaahaa.	ءَاَنْتُمْ اَشَدُّ خَلْقًا اَمِ السَّمَآءُ ؕ بَنٰىهَا ﴿۲۷﴾
28. high above?	28. Rafa'a samkahaa fasawwaahaa.	رَفَعَ سَمْكَهَا فَسَوّٰىهَا ۙ ﴿۲۸﴾
29. He has made its nights dark and its days bright.	29. Wa aghtasha laylahaa wa akhraja duhaahaa.	وَ اَغْطَشَ لَیْلَهَا وَ اَخْرَجَ ضُحٰىهَا ﴿۲۹﴾
30. After this, He spread out the earth,	30. Wal-arda ba'da zaalika dahaahaa.	وَ الْاَرْضَ بَعْدَ ذٰلِكَ دَحٰىهَا ؕ ﴿۳۰﴾
31. produced water and grass therefrom,	31. Akhraja minhaa maaa'ahaa wa mar'aahaa.	اَخْرَجَ مِنْهَا مَآءَهَا وَ مَرْعٰىهَا ﴿۳۱﴾
32. then firmly set up the mountains.	32. Waljibaala arsaahaa.	وَ الْجِبَالَ اَرْسٰىهَا ۙ ﴿۳۲﴾
33. All this was done as a means of enjoyment for you and your cattle.	33. Mataa'al-lakum wa li-an'aamikum.	مَتَاعًا لَّكُمْ وَ لِاَنْعَامِكُمْ ؕ ﴿۳۳﴾
34. On the day when the great calamity comes,	34. Fa-izaa jaaa'atit-taaammatul-kubraa.	فَاِذَا جَآءَتِ الطَّآمَّةُ الْكُبْرٰى ۫ۖ ﴿۳۴﴾
35. the human being will recall whatever he has done.	35. Yawma yatazakkarul-insaanu maa sa'aa.	یَوْمَ یَتَذَكَّرُ الْاِنْسَانُ مَا سَعٰى ۙ ﴿۳۵﴾
36. Hellfire will become visible for those who would see it.	36. Wa burrizatil-Jaheemu limany-yaraa.	وَ بُرِّزَتِ الْجَحِیْمُ لِمَنْ یَّرٰى ﴿۳۶﴾
37. Those who have rebelled	37. Fa-ammaa man taghaa.	فَاَمَّا مَنْ طَغٰى ۙ ﴿۳۷﴾
38. and preferred the worldly life,	38. Wa aasaral-hayaatad-dunyaa.	وَ اٰثَرَ الْحَیٰوةَ الدُّنْیَا ۙ ﴿۳۸﴾
39. hell will be their dwelling.	39. Fa-innal-Jaheema hiyal-ma-waa.	فَاِنَّ الْجَحِیْمَ هِیَ الْمَاْوٰى ؕ ﴿۳۹﴾
40. However, those who had feared their Lord and restrained their souls from acting according to its desires,	40. Wa ammaa man khaafa maqaama Rabbihee wa nahannafsa 'anil-hawaa.	وَ اَمَّا مَنْ خَافَ مَقَامَ رَبِّهٖ وَ نَهَى النَّفْسَ عَنِ الْهَوٰى ۙ ﴿۴۰﴾

41. Paradise will be their dwelling.	41. Fa innal-Jannata hiyal-ma-waa.	فَاِنَّ الْجَنَّةَ هِيَ الْمَاْوٰى ﴿٤١﴾
42. (Muhammad), they ask you, "When will the Hour of Doom come?"	42. Yas'aloonaka 'anis-Saa-'ati ayyaana mursaahaa.	يَسْـَٔلُوْنَكَ عَنِ السَّاعَةِ اَيَّانَ مُرْسٰىهَا ﴿٤٢﴾
43. (Muhammad), you do not know (when and how) it will come.	43. Feema anta min zikraa-haa.	فِيْمَ اَنْتَ مِنْ ذِكْرٰىهَا ﴿٤٣﴾
44. This matter is in the hands of your Lord.	44. Ilaa Rabbika muntahaa-haa.	اِلٰى رَبِّكَ مُنْتَهٰىهَا ﴿٤٤﴾
45. You are only a Warner for those who fear such a day.	45. Innamaaa anta munziru mañy-yakhshaahaa.	اِنَّمَاۤ اَنْتَ مُنْذِرُ مَنْ يَّخْشٰىهَا ﴿٤٥﴾
46. On the day when they see it, it would seem to them as though they had only lived in the world for a morning and an afternoon.	46. Ka-annahum Yawma yarawnahaa lam yalbasooo illaa 'ashiyyatan aw ḍuḥaahaa.	كَاَنَّهُمْ يَوْمَ يَرَوْنَهَا لَمْ يَلْبَثُوْۤا اِلَّا عَشِيَّةً اَوْ ضُحٰىهَا ﴿٤٦﴾ ع ٢

Al-Abasa, He Frowned (80)

In the Name of Allah, the Beneficent, the Merciful.

Sûrat 'Abasa-80

(Revealed at Makkah)

Bismillaahir Raḥmaanir Raḥeem

سُوْرَةُ عَبَسَ مَكِّيَّةٌ (٨٠) (٢٤)

اٰياتها ٤٢ بِسْمِ اللّٰهِ الرَّحْمٰنِ الرَّحِيْمِ ركوعها ١

1. He (the rich man) frowned and then turned away	1. 'Abasa wa tawallaaa.	عَبَسَ وَتَوَلّٰۤى ﴿١﴾
2. because a blind man came to him (the Holy Prophet).	2. An jaaa'ahul-a'maa.	اَنْ جَآءَهُ الْاَعْمٰى ﴿٢﴾
3. What do you know? Perhaps he (the blind man) wanted to purify himself,	3. Wa maa yudreeka la'al-lahoo yaz zakkaaa.	وَمَا يُدْرِيْكَ لَعَلَّهٗ يَزَّكّٰۤى ﴿٣﴾
4. or upon receiving advice, benefit thereby.	4. Aw yaz-zakkaru fatan-fa'ahuz-zikraa.	اَوْ يَذَّكَّرُ فَتَنْفَعَهُ الذِّكْرٰى ﴿٤﴾
5. One who is rich	5. Ammaa manis-taghnaa.	اَمَّا مَنِ اسْتَغْنٰى ﴿٥﴾
6. you deal with seriously,	6. Fa-anta lahoo taṣaddaa.	فَاَنْتَ لَهٗ تَصَدّٰى ﴿٦﴾
7. regardless, he (the rich one) is serious or not.	7. Wa maa 'alayka allaa yazzakkaa.	وَمَا عَلَيْكَ اَلَّا يَزَّكّٰى ﴿٧﴾
8. One who comes to you earnestly (striving for guidance)	8. Wa ammaa man jaaa'aka yas'aa.	وَاَمَّا مَنْ جَآءَكَ يَسْعٰى ﴿٨﴾
9. and who has fear of Allah,	9. Wa huwa yakhshaa.	وَهُوَ يَخْشٰى ﴿٩﴾
10. you entertain (turn to him).	10. Fa-anta 'anhu talahhaa.	فَاَنْتَ عَنْهُ تَلَهّٰى ﴿١٠﴾
11. These verses are a reminder,	11. Kallaaa innahaa tazkirah.	كَلَّاۤ اِنَّهَا تَذْكِرَةٌ ﴿١١﴾
12. so those who want to follow its guidance should do so.	12. Faman shaaa'a zakarah.	فَمَنْ شَآءَ ذَكَرَهٗ ﴿١٢﴾ وقف لازم
13. They (these verses) are also recorded in honorable books,	13. Fee ṣuḥufim-mukarramah.	فِيْ صُحُفٍ مُّكَرَّمَةٍ ﴿١٣﴾
14. exalted, purified,	14. Marfoo'atim-muṭahha-rah.	مَّرْفُوْعَةٍ مُّطَهَّرَةٍ ﴿١٤﴾
15. by the hands of the noble, virtuous,	15. Bi-aydee safarah.	بِاَيْدِيْ سَفَرَةٍ ﴿١٥﴾
16. and scribes (from the angels).	16. Kiraamim bararah.	كِرَامٍ بَرَرَةٍ ﴿١٦﴾
17. May (the disbelieving) human being be condemned! What makes him disbelieve?	17. Qutilal-insaanu maaa akfarah.	قُتِلَ الْاِنْسَانُ مَاۤ اَكْفَرَهٗ ﴿١٧﴾

18. From what has Allah created him?	18. Min ayyi shay'in khalaqah.	مِنْ اَيِّ شَيْءٍ خَلَقَهٗ ﴿١٨﴾
19. He created him from a living germ. He determined his fate	19. Min nuṭfatin khalaqahoo faqaddarah.	مِنْ نُّطْفَةٍ ؕ خَلَقَهٗ فَقَدَّرَهٗ ﴿١٩﴾
20. and made the path of guidance easy for him to follow.	20. S̲ummas-sabeela yassarah.	ثُمَّ السَّبِيْلَ يَسَّرَهٗ ﴿٢٠﴾
21. Then He causes him to die and be buried	21. S̲umma amaatahoo faaqbarah.	ثُمَّ اَمَاتَهٗ فَاَقْبَرَهٗ ﴿٢١﴾
22. and He will resurrect him whenever He wants.	22. S̲umma iz̲aa shaaa'a ansharah.	ثُمَّ اِذَا شَآءَ اَنْشَرَهٗ ﴿٢٢﴾
23. Certainly, he has not duly fulfilled His commands.	23. Kallaa lammaa yaqḍi maaa amarah.	كَلَّا لَمَّا يَقْضِ مَآ اَمَرَهٗ ﴿٢٣﴾
24. Human beings should think about (how We produce) his food.	24. Falyanẓuril-insaanu ilaa ṭa'aamih.	فَلْيَنْظُرِ الْاِنْسَانُ اِلٰى طَعَامِهٖ ﴿٢٤﴾
25. We send down abundant water,	25. Annaa ṣababnal-maaa'a ṣabbaa.	اَنَّا صَبَبْنَا الْمَآءَ صَبًّا ﴿٢٥﴾
26. and allow the earth break open	26. S̲umma shaqaqnal-arḍa shaqqaa.	ثُمَّ شَقَقْنَا الْاَرْضَ شَقًّا ﴿٢٦﴾
27. to yield therein corn,	27. Fa-ambatnaa feehaa ḥabbaa.	فَاَنْۢبَتْنَا فِيْهَا حَبًّا ﴿٢٧﴾
28. grapes, vegetables,	28. Wa 'inabañw-wa qaḍbaa.	وَّعِنَبًا وَّقَضْبًا ﴿٢٨﴾
29. olives, dates,	29. Wa zaytoonañw-wa nakhlaa.	وَّزَيْتُوْنًا وَّنَخْلًا ﴿٢٩﴾
30. thickly planted gardens,	30. Wa ḥadaaa'iqa ghulbaa.	وَّحَدَآئِقَ غُلْبًا ﴿٣٠﴾
31. fruits, and grass,	31. Wa faakihatañw-wa abbaa.	وَّفَاكِهَةً وَّاَبًّا ﴿٣١﴾
32. to be the of means of enjoyment for you and your cattle.	32. Mataa'al-lakum wa lian'aamikum.	مَّتَاعًا لَّكُمْ وَلِاَنْعَامِكُمْ ﴿٣٢﴾
33. When the Day of Judgment comes,	33. Fa-iz̲aa jaaa'atiṣ-ṣaaakhkhah.	فَاِذَا جَآءَتِ الصَّآخَّةُ ﴿٣٣﴾
34. it will be such a day when a person will run away from his brother,	34. Yawma yafirrul-mar'u min akheeh.	يَوْمَ يَفِرُّ الْمَرْءُ مِنْ اَخِيْهِ ﴿٣٤﴾
35. mother, father,	35. Wa ummihee wa abeeh.	وَاُمِّهٖ وَاَبِيْهِ ﴿٣٥﴾
36. wife and sons,	36. Wa ṣaaḥibatihee wa baneeh.	وَصَاحِبَتِهٖ وَبَنِيْهِ ﴿٣٦﴾
37. on that day everyone will be completely engrossed in his own concerns.	37. Likullim-ri-'im-minhum Yawma'iz̲in sha-nuñy-yughneeh.	لِكُلِّ امْرِئٍ مِّنْهُمْ يَوْمَئِذٍ شَاْنٌ يُّغْنِيْهِ ﴿٣٧﴾
38. Some faces on that day will be radiant,	38. Wujoohuñy-Yawma'iz̲im-musfirah.	وُجُوْهٌ يَّوْمَئِذٍ مُّسْفِرَةٌ ﴿٣٨﴾
39. laughing, and joyous	39. Ḍaaḥikatum-mustabshirah.	ضَاحِكَةٌ مُّسْتَبْشِرَةٌ ﴿٣٩﴾
40. but others will be gloomy	40. Wawujoohuñy-Yawma'i-z̲in 'alayhaa ghabarah.	وَوُجُوْهٌ يَّوْمَئِذٍ عَلَيْهَا غَبَرَةٌ ﴿٤٠﴾
41. and covered by darkness.	41. Tarhaquhaa qatarah.	تَرْهَقُهَا قَتَرَةٌ ﴿٤١﴾
42. These will be the faces of the sinful unbelievers.	42. Ulaaa'ika humul-kafaratul-fajarah.	اُولٰٓئِكَ هُمُ الْكَفَرَةُ الْفَجَرَةُ ﴿٤٢﴾ ع ٤٢ ٥

Al-Takwir, The Cessation (81)	Sûrat at-Takwîr-81	(٨١) سُوْرَةُ التَّكْوِيْرِ مَكِّيَّةٌ (٧)
In the Name of Allah, the Beneficent, the Merciful.	(Revealed at Makkah) **Bismillaahir Raḥmaanir Raḥeem**	آياتها ٢٩ بِسْمِ اللّٰهِ الرَّحْمٰنِ الرَّحِيْمِ ركوعاتها ١
1. (On the day) when the sun is made to cease shining,	1. Iz̲ash-shamsu kuwwirat.	إِذَا الشَّمْسُ كُوِّرَتْ ﴿١﴾
2. the stars are made to fade away,	2. Wa iz̲an-nujoomun-kadarat.	وَإِذَا النُّجُوْمُ انْكَدَرَتْ ﴿٢﴾
3. the mountains are scattered about as dust,	3. Wa iz̲al-jibaalu suyyirat.	وَإِذَا الْجِبَالُ سُيِّرَتْ ﴿٣﴾
4. the young-bearing camels are abandoned,	4. Wa iz̲al-'ishaaru 'uṭṭilat.	وَإِذَا الْعِشَارُ عُطِّلَتْ ﴿٤﴾
5. the wild beasts are herded together,	5. Wa iz̲al-wuḥooshu ḥushirat.	وَإِذَا الْوُحُوْشُ حُشِرَتْ ﴿٥﴾
6. the oceans are brought to a boil,	6. Wa iz̲al-biḥaaru sujjirat.	وَإِذَا الْبِحَارُ سُجِّرَتْ ﴿٦﴾
7. souls are reunited with their bodies,	7. Wa iz̲an-nufoosu zuwwijat.	وَإِذَا النُّفُوْسُ زُوِّجَتْ ﴿٧﴾
8. questions are asked about the baby girls buried alive,	8. Wa iz̲al-maw'oodatu su'ilat.	وَإِذَا الْمَوْءٗدَةُ سُئِلَتْ ﴿٨﴾
9. such as, "For what crime were they murdered?"	9. Bi-ayyi z̲ambin qutilat.	بِأَيِّ ذَنْۢبٍ قُتِلَتْ ﴿٩﴾
10. the records of deeds are made public,	10. Wa iz̲aṣ-ṣuḥufu nushirat.	وَإِذَا الصُّحُفُ نُشِرَتْ ﴿١٠﴾
11. the heavens are unveiled (made void),	11. Wa iz̲as-samaaa'u kushiṭat.	وَإِذَا السَّمَآءُ كُشِطَتْ ﴿١١﴾
12. hell is made to blaze,	12. Wa iz̲al-Jaḥeemu su'-'irat.	وَإِذَا الْجَحِيْمُ سُعِّرَتْ ﴿١٢﴾
13. and Paradise is brought near,	13. Wa iz̲al-Jannatu uzlifat.	وَإِذَا الْجَنَّةُ أُزْلِفَتْ ﴿١٣﴾
14. then every soul will discover the consequence of its deeds.	14. 'Alimat nafsum-maaa aḥḍarat.	عَلِمَتْ نَفْسٌ مَّآ أَحْضَرَتْ ﴿١٤﴾
15. I swear by Al-Khunnas (certain star)	15. Falaaa uqsimu bilkhunnas.	فَلَآ أُقْسِمُ بِالْخُنَّسِ ﴿١٥﴾
16. which fades away from sight during the day,	16. Aljawaaril-kunnas.	الْجَوَارِ الْكُنَّسِ ﴿١٦﴾
17. by the darkening night	17. Wallayli iz̲aa 'as'as.	وَالَّيْلِ إِذَا عَسْعَسَ ﴿١٧﴾
18. and brightening morning,	18. Waṣṣubḥi iz̲aa tanaffas.	وَالصُّبْحِ إِذَا تَنَفَّسَ ﴿١٨﴾
19. that it (the Quran) is the word of the honorable,	19. Innahoo laqawlu rasoolin kareem.	إِنَّهٗ لَقَوْلُ رَسُوْلٍ كَرِيْمٍ ﴿١٩﴾
20. mighty Messenger who is of great privilege in the presence of the Lord of the Throne.	20. Z̲ee quwwatin 'inda Z̲il-'Arshi makeen.	ذِيْ قُوَّةٍ عِنْدَ ذِي الْعَرْشِ مَكِيْنٍ ﴿٢٠﴾
21. He is obeyed by (all creatures) and is faithful to his trust.	21. Muṭaa'in s̲amma ameen.	مُّطَاعٍ ثَمَّ أَمِيْنٍ ﴿٢١﴾
22. Your companion (Muhammad) does not suffer from any mental illness.	22. Wa maa ṣaaḥibukum bimajnoon.	وَمَا صَاحِبُكُمْ بِمَجْنُوْنٍ ﴿٢٢﴾
23. He certainly saw him (Gabriel) high up on the horizon (in his original form).	23. Wa laqad ra-aahu bilufuqil-mubeen	وَلَقَدْ رَاٰهُ بِالْأُفُقِ الْمُبِيْنِ ﴿٢٣﴾
24. He is not parsimonious of the unseen.	24. Wa maa huwa 'alal-ghaybi-biḍaneen.	وَمَا هُوَ عَلَى الْغَيْبِ بِضَنِيْنٍ ﴿٢٤﴾

25. It (the Quran) is not the word of condemned Satan.	25. Wa maa huwa biqawli Shayṭaanir-rajeem.	وَمَا هُوَ بِقَوْلِ شَيْطٰنٍ رَّجِيْمٍ ﴿٢٥﴾
26. Where then will you go?	26. Fa-ayna tazhaboon.	فَاَيْنَ تَذْهَبُوْنَ ﴿٢٦﴾
27. This is certainly the guidance for all (jinn and mankind).	27. In huwa illaa zikrul-lil-'aalameen.	اِنْ هُوَ اِلَّا ذِكْرٌ لِّلْعٰلَمِيْنَ ﴿٢٧﴾
28. So those who want to choose the right guidance should do so.	28. Liman shaaa'a minkum añy-yastaqeem.	لِمَنْ شَآءَ مِنْكُمْ اَنْ يَّسْتَقِيْمَ ﴿٢٨﴾
29. However, you will not be able to choose anything unless Allah, Lord of the universe, wills it to be so.	29. Wa maa tashaaa'oona illaaa añy-yashaaa'allaahu Rabbul- 'Aalameen.	وَمَا تَشَآءُوْنَ اِلَّآ اَنْ يَّشَآءَ اللّٰهُ رَبُّ الْعٰلَمِيْنَ ﴿٢٩﴾ ع ٢٩ ١ ٢

Al-Infitar, The Cataclysm (82) In the Name of Allah, the Beneficent, the Merciful.	**Sûrat al-Infiṭâr-82** (Revealed at Makkah) **Bismillaahir Raḥmaanir Raḥeem**	(٨٢) سُوْرَةُ الْاِنْفِطَارِ مَكِّيَّةٌ (٨٢) اٰيَاتُهَا ١٩ بِسْمِ اللّٰهِ الرَّحْمٰنِ الرَّحِيْمِ رُكُوْعُهَا ١
1. When the heavens are rent asunder,	1. Izas-samaaa'un-faṭarat.	اِذَا السَّمَآءُ انْفَطَرَتْ ﴿١﴾
2. the stars are dispersed,	2. Wa izal-kawaakibun-tasa-rat.	وَاِذَا الْكَوَاكِبُ انْتَثَرَتْ ﴿٢﴾
3. the oceans are turned into fire	3. Wa izal-biḥaaru fujjirat.	وَاِذَا الْبِحَارُ فُجِّرَتْ ﴿٣﴾
4. and the graves are turned inside out,	4. Wa izal-qubooru bu'sirat.	وَاِذَا الْقُبُوْرُ بُعْثِرَتْ ﴿٤﴾
5. every soul will see the result of its deeds - those recorded before his death and those which will produce either virtue or evil after his death.	5. 'Alimat nafsum-maa qaddamat wa akhkharat.	عَلِمَتْ نَفْسٌ مَّا قَدَّمَتْ وَاَخَّرَتْ ﴿٥﴾
6. Human being, what evil has deceived you about your Gracious Lord?	6. Yaaa ayyuhal-insaanu maa gharraka bi-Rabbikal-kareem.	يٰۤاَيُّهَا الْاِنْسَانُ مَا غَرَّكَ بِرَبِّكَ الْكَرِيْمِ ﴿٦﴾
7. Who created you proportionately and fashioned you	7. Allazee khalaqaka fasaw-waaka fa'adalak.	الَّذِيْ خَلَقَكَ فَسَوّٰىكَ فَعَدَلَكَ ﴿٧﴾
8. in whatever composition He wanted?	8. Feee ayye ṣooratim-maa shaaa'a rakkabak.	فِيْۤ اَيِّ صُوْرَةٍ مَّا شَآءَ رَكَّبَكَ ﴿٨﴾
9. Despite this, you deny the Day of Judgment,	9. Kallaa bal tukaz-ziboona bid-deen.	كَلَّا بَلْ تُكَذِّبُوْنَ بِالدِّيْنِ ﴿٩﴾
10. but you should know that there are angelic guards	10. Wa Inna 'alaykum laḥaa-fizeen.	وَاِنَّ عَلَيْكُمْ لَحٰفِظِيْنَ ﴿١٠﴾
11. watching over you	11. Kiraaman kaatibeen.	كِرَامًا كَاتِبِيْنَ ﴿١١﴾
12. and these honorable scribes know whatever you do.	12. Ya'lamoona maa taf'a-loon.	يَعْلَمُوْنَ مَا تَفْعَلُوْنَ ﴿١٢﴾
13. The virtuous ones will live in bliss	13. Innal-abraara lafee Na'eem.	اِنَّ الْاَبْرَارَ لَفِيْ نَعِيْمٍ ﴿١٣﴾
14. and the evil-doers will be in hell,	14. Wa innal-fujjaara lafee Jaheem.	وَّاِنَّ الْفُجَّارَ لَفِيْ جَحِيْمٍ ﴿١٤﴾
15. which they will enter on the Day of Judgment	15. Yaṣlawnahaa Yawmad-Deen.	يَّصْلَوْنَهَا يَوْمَ الدِّيْنِ ﴿١٥﴾
16. to burn therein.	16. Wa maa hum 'anhaa bighaaa'ibeen.	وَمَا هُمْ عَنْهَا بِغَآئِبِيْنَ ﴿١٦﴾
17. They will never be able to escape from it. What does it tell you the Day of Judgment is?	17. Wa maaa adraaka maa Yawmud-Deen.	وَمَاۤ اَدْرٰىكَ مَا يَوْمُ الدِّيْنِ ﴿١٧﴾

18. Then what does it tell you the Day of Judgment is?	18. S̲umma maaa adraaka maa Yawmud-Deen.	ثُمَّ مَآ أَدْرٰىكَ مَا يَوْمُ الدِّينِ ﴿١٨﴾
19. On that day, no soul will be of any benefit to any other soul. On that day, all affairs will be in the hands of Allah.	19. Yawma laa tamliku nafsul-linafsin shay'aa; wal-amru Yawma'iz̲il-lillaah.	يَوْمَ لَا تَمْلِكُ نَفْسٌ لِّنَفْسٍ شَيْـًٔا ۖ وَالْأَمْرُ يَوْمَئِذٍ لِّلّٰهِ ﴿١٩﴾

Al-Mutaffifin, The Defrauders (83) In the Name of Allah, the Beneficent, the Merciful.	**Sûrat al-Muṭaffifn-83** (Revealed at Makkah) **Bismillaahir Raḥmaanir Raḥeem**	سُورَةُ الْمُطَفِّفِينَ مَكِّيَّةٌ (٨٣) (٨٦) بِسْمِ اللّٰهِ الرَّحْمٰنِ الرَّحِيمِ
1. Woe to those who are fraudulent in (weighing and measuring),	1. Waylul-lil-muṭaffifeen.	وَيْلٌ لِّلْمُطَفِّفِينَ ﴿١﴾
2. those who demand a full measure from others	2. Allaz̲eena iz̲ak-taaloo 'alan-naasi yastawfoon.	الَّذِينَ إِذَا اكْتَالُوا عَلَى النَّاسِ يَسْتَوْفُونَ ﴿٢﴾
3. but when they measure or weigh, give less.	3. Wa iz̲aa kaaloohum aw wazanoohum yukhsiroon.	وَإِذَا كَالُوهُمْ أَو وَّزَنُوهُمْ يُخْسِرُونَ ﴿٣﴾
4. Do they not realize that they will be resurrected	4. Alaa yaẓunnu ulaaa'ika annahum mab'oos̲oon.	أَلَا يَظُنُّ أُولٰٓئِكَ أَنَّهُم مَّبْعُوثُونَ ﴿٤﴾
5. on a great day	5. Li-Yawmin 'Aẓeem.	لِيَوْمٍ عَظِيمٍ ﴿٥﴾
6. when mankind will stand before the Lord of the universe?	6. Yawma yaqoomun-naasu li-Rabbil 'aalameen.	يَوْمَ يَقُومُ النَّاسُ لِرَبِّ الْعٰلَمِينَ ﴿٦﴾
7. Woe to them! Allow them to know that the records of the sinner's deeds are in Sijin.	7. Kallaaa inna kitaabal-fujjaari lafee Sijjeen.	كَلَّآ إِنَّ كِتٰبَ الْفُجَّارِ لَفِي سِجِّينٍ ﴿٧﴾
8. What does it tell you Sijin is?	8. Wa maa adraaka maa Sijjeen.	وَمَآ أَدْرٰىكَ مَا سِجِّينٌ ﴿٨﴾
9. It is a comprehensively written Book (of records).	9. Kitaabum-marqoom.	كِتٰبٌ مَّرْقُومٌ ﴿٩﴾
10. Woe, on that day, to those who have rejected (Allah's revelations)	10. Wayluñy-Yawma'iz̲il-lil-mukaz̲-z̲ibeen.	وَيْلٌ يَوْمَئِذٍ لِّلْمُكَذِّبِينَ ﴿١٠﴾
11. and those who have rejected the Day of Judgment.	11. Allaz̲eena yukaz̲-z̲iboona bi-Yawmid-Deen.	الَّذِينَ يُكَذِّبُونَ بِيَوْمِ الدِّينِ ﴿١١﴾
12. No one rejects it except the sinful transgressors	12. Wa maa yukaz̲-z̲ibu bi-heee illaa kullu mu'tadin as̲eem.	وَمَا يُكَذِّبُ بِهِۦٓ إِلَّا كُلُّ مُعْتَدٍ أَثِيمٍ ﴿١٢﴾
13. who, when listening to Our revelations, say, "These are only ancient legends."	13. Iz̲aa tutlaa 'alayhi Aayaa-tunaa qaala asaaṭeerul-awwa-leen.	إِذَا تُتْلٰى عَلَيْهِ ءَايٰتُنَا قَالَ أَسٰطِيرُ الْأَوَّلِينَ ﴿١٣﴾
14. They will never have faith. In fact, their hearts are stained from their deeds.	14. Kallaa bal; raana 'alaa quloobihim maa kaanoo yaksi-boon.	كَلَّا ۖ بَلْ ۜ رَانَ عَلٰى قُلُوبِهِم مَّا كَانُوا يَكْسِبُونَ ﴿١٤﴾
15. On the Day of Judgment, they will certainly be barred from the mercy of their Lord.	15. Kallaaa innahum 'ar-Rabbihim Yawma'iz̲il-lamaḥ-jooboon.	كَلَّآ إِنَّهُمْ عَن رَّبِّهِمْ يَوْمَئِذٍ لَّمَحْجُوبُونَ ﴿١٥﴾
16. They will suffer the heat of fire	16. S̲umma innahum laṣaa-lul-Jaḥeem.	ثُمَّ إِنَّهُمْ لَصَالُوا الْجَحِيمِ ﴿١٦﴾
17. and will be told, "This is what you had called a lie."	17. S̲umma yuqaalu haaz̲al laz̲ee kuntum bihee	ثُمَّ يُقَالُ هٰذَا الَّذِي كُنتُم بِهِۦ

	tukaz ziboon.	تُكَذِّبُونَ ﴿١٧﴾
18. However, the records of the deeds of the virtuous ones will certainly be in Illiyin.	18. Kallaaa inna kitaabal-abraari lafee 'Illiyyeen.	كَلَّآ إِنَّ كِتٰبَ الْأَبْرَارِ لَفِي عِلِّيِّينَ ﴿١٨﴾
19. What does it tell you Illiyin is?	19. Wa maaa adraaka maa 'Illiyyoon.	وَمَآ أَدْرٰىكَ مَا عِلِّيُّونَ ﴿١٩﴾
20. It is a comprehensively written Book (of records).	20. Kitaabum-marqoom.	كِتٰبٌ مَّرْقُومٌ ﴿٢٠﴾
21. The ones nearest to Allah will bring it to the public.	21. Yashhaduhul-muqarra-boon.	يَشْهَدُهُ الْمُقَرَّبُونَ ﴿٢١﴾
22. The virtuous will live in bliss,	22. Innal-abraara lafee Na'eem.	إِنَّ الْأَبْرَارَ لَفِي نَعِيمٍ ﴿٢٢﴾
23. reclining on couches, reviewing (the bounties given to them).	23. 'Alal-araaa'iki yanzuroon.	عَلَى الْأَرَآئِكِ يَنْظُرُونَ ﴿٢٣﴾
24. You can trace on their faces the joy of their bliss.	24. Ta'rifu fee wujoohihim nadratan-na'eem.	تَعْرِفُ فِي وُجُوهِهِمْ نَضْرَةَ النَّعِيمِ ﴿٢٤﴾
25. They will be given pure wine out of sealed containers	25. Yusqawna mir-raheeqim-makhtoom.	يُسْقَوْنَ مِنْ رَّحِيقٍ مَّخْتُومٍ ﴿٢٥﴾
26. which have the fragrance of musk. This is the kind of place for which one should really aspire.	26. Khitaamuhoo misk; wa fee zaalika falyatanaafasil Mutanaafisoon.	خِتٰمُهُ مِسْكٌ وَفِي ذٰلِكَ فَلْيَتَنَافَسِ الْمُتَنٰفِسُونَ ﴿٢٦﴾
27. With the wine is a drink from Tasnim,	27. Wa mizaajuhoo min Tas-neem.	وَمِزَاجُهُ مِنْ تَسْنِيمٍ ﴿٢٧﴾
28. a spring, and the nearest ones to Allah will drink from it.	28. 'Aynañy-yashrabu bihal-muqarraboon.	عَيْنًا يَشْرَبُ بِهَا الْمُقَرَّبُونَ ﴿٢٨﴾
29. The sinners had been laughing at the believers.	29. Innal-lazeena ajramoo kaanoo minal-lazeena aamanoo yadhakoon.	إِنَّ الَّذِينَ أَجْرَمُوا كَانُوا مِنَ الَّذِينَ آمَنُوا يَضْحَكُونَ ﴿٢٩﴾
30. When passing by them, they would wink at one another	30. Wa izaa marroo bihim yataghaamazoon.	وَإِذَا مَرُّوا بِهِمْ يَتَغَامَزُونَ ﴿٣٠﴾
31. and, on returning to their people, boast about what they had done.	31. Wa izan-qalabooo ilaaa ahlihimun-qalaboo fakiheen.	وَإِذَا انْقَلَبُوٓا إِلٰٓى أَهْلِهِمُ انْقَلَبُوا فَكِهِينَ ﴿٣١﴾
32. On seeing the believers, they would say, "These people have gone astray."	32. Wa izaa ra-awhum qaa-looo inna haaa'ulaaa'i ladaaal loon.	وَإِذَا رَأَوْهُمْ قَالُوٓا إِنَّ هٰٓؤُلَآءِ لَضَآلُّونَ ﴿٣٢﴾
33. No one has appointed them to watch over the believers.	33. Wa maaa ursiloo 'alay-him haafizeen.	وَمَآ أُرْسِلُوا عَلَيْهِمْ حٰفِظِينَ ﴿٣٣﴾
34. On the Day of Judgment, the believers will laugh at the unbelievers	34. Fal-Yawmal-lazeena aa-manoo minal-kuffaari yadha-koon.	فَالْيَوْمَ الَّذِينَ آمَنُوا مِنَ الْكُفَّارِ يَضْحَكُونَ ﴿٣٤﴾
35. while reclining on couches and reviewing (the bounties given to them).	35. 'Alal-araaa'iki yanzu-roon.	عَلَى الْأَرَآئِكِ يَنْظُرُونَ ﴿٣٥﴾
36. Will not the unbelievers then be duly recompensed for their laughing at the believers?	36. Hal suwwibal-kuffaaru maa kaanoo yaf'aloon.	هَلْ ثُوِّبَ الْكُفَّارُ مَا كَانُوا يَفْعَلُونَ ﴿٣٦﴾

Al-Inshiqaq, (Heavens) Rendered Apart (84)

In the Name of Allah, the Beneficent, the Merciful.

Sûrat al-Inshiqâq-84

(Revealed at Makkah)

Bismillaahir Rahmaanir Raheem

(٨٤) سُورَةُ الْانْشِقَاقِ مَكِّيَّةٌ (٨٣)

آياتها ٢٥ بِسْمِ اللّٰهِ الرَّحْمٰنِ الرَّحِيمِ ركوعها ١

1. When the heaven is rent asunder	1. Izas-samaaa'un-shaqqat.	إِذَا السَّمَآءُ انْشَقَّتْ ﴿١﴾

2. It will obey the commands of its Lord which are incumbent on it,	2. Wa a<u>z</u>inat li-Rabbihaa wa buqqat.	وَاَذِنَتۡ لِرَبِّهَا وَحُقَّتۡ ۙ﴿٢﴾
3. when the earth is stretched out	3. Wa i<u>z</u>al-arḍu muddat.	وَاِذَا الۡاَرۡضُ مُدَّتۡ ۙ﴿٣﴾
4. and it throws out of itself all that it contains	4. Wa alqat maa feehaa wa takhallat.	وَاَلۡقَتۡ مَا فِيۡهَا وَتَخَلَّتۡ ۙ﴿٤﴾
5. in obedience to the commands of its Lord which are incumbent on it, (the human being will receive due recompense for his deeds).	5. Wa a<u>z</u>inat li-Rabbihaa wa ḥuqqat.	وَاَذِنَتۡ لِرَبِّهَا وَحُقَّتۡ ؕ﴿٥﴾
6. Human being, you strive hard to get closer to your Lord, and so you will certainly receive the recompense (of your deeds).	6. Yaaa ayyuhal-insaanu innaka kaadiḥun ilaa Rabbika kadḥan famulaaqeeh.	يٰۤاَيُّهَا الۡاِنۡسَانُ اِنَّكَ كَادِحٌ اِلٰى رَبِّكَ كَدۡحًا فَمُلٰقِيۡهِ ۚ﴿٦﴾
7. The reckoning of those whose Book of records will be given into their right hands	7. Fa-ammaa man ootiya kitaabahoo biyameenih.	فَاَمَّا مَنۡ اُوۡتِىَ كِتٰبَهٗ بِيَمِيۡنِهٖ ۙ﴿٧﴾
8. will be easy,	8. Fasawfa yuḥaasabu ḥisaabañy-yaseeraa.	فَسَوۡفَ يُحَاسَبُ حِسَابًا يَّسِيۡرًا ۙ﴿٨﴾
9. and they will return to their people, delighted.	9. Wa yanqalibu ilaaa ahlihee masrooraa.	وَّيَنۡقَلِبُ اِلٰٓى اَهۡلِهٖ مَسۡرُوۡرًا ؕ﴿٩﴾
10. However, as for those whose Book of records will be given behind their backs,	10. Wa ammaa man ootiya kitaabahoo waraaa'a ẓahrih.	وَاَمَّا مَنۡ اُوۡتِىَ كِتٰبَهٗ وَرَآءَ ظَهۡرِهٖ ۙ﴿١٠﴾
11. they will say, "Woe to us!"	11. Fasawfa yad'oo <u>s</u>ubooraa.	فَسَوۡفَ يَدۡعُوۡا ثُبُوۡرًا ۙ﴿١١﴾
12. They will suffer the heat of hellfire.	12. Wa yaṣlaa sa'eeraa.	وَّيَصۡلٰى سَعِيۡرًا ؕ﴿١٢﴾
13. They lived among their people joyfully	13. Innahoo kaana feee ahlihee masrooraa.	اِنَّهٗ كَانَ فِىۡۤ اَهۡلِهٖ مَسۡرُوۡرًا ؕ﴿١٣﴾
14. and thought that they would never be brought back to life again.	14. Innahoo ẓanna al-lañy-yaḥoor.	اِنَّهٗ ظَنَّ اَنۡ لَّنۡ يَّحُوۡرَ ۛۚ﴿١٤﴾
15. This is a fact. Their Lord is Well-aware of (all that they do).	15. Balaaa inna Rabbahoo kaana bihee baṣeeraa.	بَلٰٓى ۛۚ اِنَّ رَبَّهٗ كَانَ بِهٖ بَصِيۡرًا ؕ﴿١٥﴾
16. I swear by the sunset,	16. Falaaa uqsimu bishshafaq.	فَلَاۤ اُقۡسِمُ بِالشَّفَقِ ۙ﴿١٦﴾
17. by the night in which things all come together to rest,	17. Wallayli wa maa wasaq.	وَالَّيۡلِ وَمَا وَسَقَ ۙ﴿١٧﴾
18. and by the moon when it is full,	18. Walqamari i<u>z</u>at-tasaq.	وَالۡقَمَرِ اِذَا اتَّسَقَ ۙ﴿١٨﴾
19. that you will certainly pass through one stage after another.	19. Latarkabunna ṭabaqan 'an-ṭabaq.	لَتَرۡكَبُنَّ طَبَقًا عَنۡ طَبَقٍ ؕ﴿١٩﴾
20. What is the matter with them? Why do they not believe?	20. Famaa lahum laa yu'minoon.	فَمَا لَهُمۡ لَا يُؤۡمِنُوۡنَ ۙ﴿٢٠﴾
21. Why, when the Quran is recited to them, do they not prostrate themselves?	21. Wa i<u>z</u>aa quri'a 'alayhimul-Qur-aanu laa yasjudoon.۩	وَاِذَا قُرِئَ عَلَيۡهِمُ الۡقُرۡاٰنُ لَا يَسۡجُدُوۡنَ ؕ۩﴿٢١﴾
22. In fact, they reject the Quran,	22. Balil-la<u>z</u>eena kafaroo yuka<u>z</u><u>z</u>iboon.	بَلِ الَّذِيۡنَ كَفَرُوۡا يُكَذِّبُوۡنَ ۖ﴿٢٢﴾
23. but Allah knows best whatever they accumulate in their hearts.	23. Wallaahu a'lamu bimaa yoo'oon.	وَاللّٰهُ اَعۡلَمُ بِمَا يُوۡعُوۡنَ ۖ﴿٢٣﴾
24. (Muhammad), tell them that they will all suffer a painful torment	24. Fabashshirhum bi'a<u>z</u>aabin aleem.	فَبَشِّرۡهُمۡ بِعَذَابٍ اَلِيۡمٍ ۙ﴿٢٤﴾
25. except the righteously striving believers, who will	25. Illal-la<u>z</u>eena aamanoo wa 'amiluṣ-ṣaaliḥaati	اِلَّا الَّذِيۡنَ اٰمَنُوۡا وَعَمِلُوا الصّٰلِحٰتِ

(Bow Down)

معانقة عند المتأخرين ١٢٠

السجدة ١٣

receive a never-ending reward.

lahum ajrun ghayru mamnoon.

لَهُمْ أَجْرٌ غَيْرُ مَمْنُونٍ ﴿٢٥﴾

ع ٢٥ ٩

Al-Buruj, The Constellations (85)

In the Name of Allah, the Beneficent, the Merciful.

Sûrat al-Burûj-85

(Revealed at Makkah)

Bismillaahir Raḥmaanir Raḥeem

(٨٥) سُورَةُ الْبُرُوجِ مَكِّيَّةٌ (٢٧)

بِسْمِ اللَّهِ الرَّحْمَٰنِ الرَّحِيمِ

1. By the heavens with constellations,

1. Wassamaaa'i zaatil-burooj.

وَالسَّمَاءِ ذَاتِ الْبُرُوجِ ﴿١﴾

2. by the promised day,

2. Wal-Yawmil-Maw'ood.

وَالْيَوْمِ الْمَوْعُودِ ﴿٢﴾

3. and by the witness (Muhammad) and that which is witnessed (the Day of Judgment),

3. Wa Shaahidiñw-wa Mashhood.

وَشَاهِدٍ وَمَشْهُودٍ ﴿٣﴾

4. may the people be condemned who tortured (the believers) in ditches

4. Qutila Aṣḥaabul-Ukhdood.

قُتِلَ أَصْحَابُ الْأُخْدُودِ ﴿٤﴾

5. by a burning fire

5. Annaari zaatil-waqood.

النَّارِ ذَاتِ الْوَقُودِ ﴿٥﴾

6. while they themselves sat around it

6. Iz hum 'alayhaa qu'ood.

إِذْ هُمْ عَلَيْهَا قُعُودٌ ﴿٦﴾

7. witnessing what they were doing.

7. Wa hum 'alaa maa yaf'aloona bilmu'mineena shuhood.

وَهُمْ عَلَىٰ مَا يَفْعَلُونَ بِالْمُؤْمِنِينَ
شُهُودٌ ﴿٧﴾

8. The only reason for which they tormented the believers was the latter's belief in Allah, the Majestic, and Praiseworthy

8. Wa maa naqamoo minhum illaaa añy-yu'minoo billaahil 'Azeezil-Ḥameed.

وَمَا نَقَمُوا مِنْهُمْ إِلَّا أَنْ يُؤْمِنُوا
بِاللَّهِ الْعَزِيزِ الْحَمِيدِ ﴿٨﴾

9. and the One to whom belong the heavens and the earth. Allah is the Witness of all things.

9. Allazee lahoo mulkus-samaawaati wal-arḍ; wallaahu 'alaa kulli shay'in Shaheed.

الَّذِي لَهُ مُلْكُ السَّمَاوَاتِ وَالْأَرْضِ ۚ وَ
اللَّهُ عَلَىٰ كُلِّ شَيْءٍ شَهِيدٌ ﴿٩﴾

10. Those who persecute the believing men and women, then, did not repent, will suffer the torment of hell and that of the burning fire.

10. Innal-lazeena fatanul-mu'mineena wal-mu'minaati summa lam yatooboo falahum 'azaabu Jahannama wa lahum 'azaabul-ḥareeq.

إِنَّ الَّذِينَ فَتَنُوا الْمُؤْمِنِينَ وَالْمُؤْمِنَاتِ
ثُمَّ لَمْ يَتُوبُوا فَلَهُمْ عَذَابُ جَهَنَّمَ وَلَهُمْ
عَذَابُ الْحَرِيقِ ﴿١٠﴾

11. The righteously striving believers will live in Paradise wherein streams flow. This is the greatest triumph.

11. Innal-lazeena aamanoo wa 'amiluṣ-ṣaaliḥaati lahum Jannaatun tajree min taḥtihal-anhaar; zaalikal-fawzul-kabeer.

إِنَّ الَّذِينَ آمَنُوا وَعَمِلُوا الصَّالِحَاتِ لَهُمْ
جَنَّاتٌ تَجْرِي مِنْ تَحْتِهَا الْأَنْهَارُ ۚ
ذَٰلِكَ الْفَوْزُ الْكَبِيرُ ﴿١١﴾

12. The retribution of Allah is terribly severe.

12. Inna baṭsha Rabbika lashadeed.

إِنَّ بَطْشَ رَبِّكَ لَشَدِيدٌ ﴿١٢﴾

13. It is He who creates all things and causes them to return.

13. Innahoo Huwa yubdi'u wa yu'eed.

إِنَّهُ هُوَ يُبْدِئُ وَيُعِيدُ ﴿١٣﴾

14. He is the All-forgiving, the Most Loving One,

14. Wa Huwal-Ghafoorul-Wadood.

وَهُوَ الْغَفُورُ الْوَدُودُ ﴿١٤﴾

15. the Owner of the Throne, the Glorious One,

15. Zul-'Arshil-Majeed.

ذُو الْعَرْشِ الْمَجِيدُ ﴿١٥﴾

16. and the Most Effective in His decision.

16. Fa'-'aalul-limaa yureed.

فَعَّالٌ لِمَا يُرِيدُ ﴿١٦﴾

17. Have you not heard about the stories of the armies	17. Hal ataaka ḥadeesul-junood.	هَلْ أَتَاكَ حَدِيثُ الْجُنُودِ ﴿١٧﴾
18. of the Pharaoh and Thamud?	18. Fir'awna wa Samood.	فِرْعَوْنَ وَثَمُودَ ﴿١٨﴾
19. In fact, the unbelievers had always rejected (Our revelations).	19. Balil-lazeena kafaroo fee takzeeb.	بَلِ الَّذِينَ كَفَرُوا فِي تَكْذِيبٍ ﴿١٩﴾
20. However, Allah encompassed their activities.	20. Wallaahu miñw-waraaa'ihim-muḥeeṭ.	وَاللَّهُ مِن وَرَائِهِم مُّحِيطٌ ﴿٢٠﴾
21. What is revealed to you is certainly a glorious Quran	21. Bal huwa Qur-aanum-Majeed.	بَلْ هُوَ قُرْآنٌ مَّجِيدٌ ﴿٢١﴾
22. that exists in a well-guarded tablet.	22. Fee Lawḥim-Maḥfooẓ.	فِي لَوْحٍ مَّحْفُوظٍ ﴿٢٢﴾ ع ٢٢ ١

Al-Tariq, The Nightly Star (86)

In the Name of Allah, the Beneficent, the Merciful.

Sûrat aṭ-Ṭâriq-86

(Revealed at Makkah)

Bismillaahir Raḥmaanir Raḥeem

(٨٦) سُورَةُ الطَّارِقِ مَكِّيَّةٌ (٣٦)

آياتها ١٧ بِسْمِ اللَّهِ الرَّحْمَٰنِ الرَّحِيمِ ركوعها ١

1. (I swear) by the heaven and Al-Tariq.	1. Wassamaaa'i waṭṭaariq.	وَالسَّمَاءِ وَالطَّارِقِ ﴿١﴾
2. What does it tell you Al-Tariq is?	2. Wa maaa adraaka maṭ-ṭaariq.	وَمَا أَدْرَاكَ مَا الطَّارِقُ ﴿٢﴾
3. (It is) the (nightly) radiant star.	3. Annajmus saaqib.	النَّجْمُ الثَّاقِبُ ﴿٣﴾
4. There is no soul which is not guarded (by the two angels who record all of its deeds).	4. In kullu nafsil-lammaa 'alayhaa ḥaafiẓ.	إِن كُلُّ نَفْسٍ لَّمَّا عَلَيْهَا حَافِظٌ ﴿٤﴾
5. The human being must reflect to find out from what he has been created.	5. Fal-yanẓuril-insaanu mimma khuliq.	فَلْيَنظُرِ الْإِنسَانُ مِمَّ خُلِقَ ﴿٥﴾
6. He has been created from an ejected drop of fluid	6. Khuliqa mim-maaa'in daafiq.	خُلِقَ مِن مَّاءٍ دَافِقٍ ﴿٦﴾
7. which comes out of the loins and ribs.	7. Yakhruju mim bayniṣ-ṣulbi wat-taraaa'ib.	يَخْرُجُ مِن بَيْنِ الصُّلْبِ وَالتَّرَائِبِ ﴿٧﴾
8. Allah has all power to resurrect him.	8. Innahoo 'alaa raj'ihee laqaadir.	إِنَّهُ عَلَىٰ رَجْعِهِ لَقَادِرٌ ﴿٨﴾
9. On the day when all secrets will be made public,	9. Yawma tublas-saraaa'ir.	يَوْمَ تُبْلَى السَّرَائِرُ ﴿٩﴾
10. he will have no power, nor anyone to help him.	10. Famaa lahoo min quwwatiñw-wa laa naaṣir.	فَمَا لَهُ مِن قُوَّةٍ وَلَا نَاصِرٍ ﴿١٠﴾
11. By the raining sky	11. Wassamaaa'i zaatir-raj'.	وَالسَّمَاءِ ذَاتِ الرَّجْعِ ﴿١١﴾
12. and the replenishing earth,	12. Wal-arḍi zaatiṣ-ṣad'.	وَالْأَرْضِ ذَاتِ الصَّدْعِ ﴿١٢﴾
13. the Quran is the final word,	13. Innahoo laqawlun faṣl.	إِنَّهُ لَقَوْلٌ فَصْلٌ ﴿١٣﴾
14. and it is certainly not a jest.	14. Wa maa huwa bilhazl.	وَمَا هُوَ بِالْهَزْلِ ﴿١٤﴾
15. They (unbelievers) plot every evil plan,	15. Innahum yakeedoona kaydaa.	إِنَّهُمْ يَكِيدُونَ كَيْدًا ﴿١٥﴾
16. but I also plan against them.	16. Wa akeedu kaydaa.	وَأَكِيدُ كَيْدًا ﴿١٦﴾
17. Give respite to the unbelievers and leave them alone for a while.	17. Famah-hilil-kaafireena amhilhum ruwaydaa.	فَمَهِّلِ الْكَافِرِينَ أَمْهِلْهُمْ رُوَيْدًا ﴿١٧﴾ ع ١٧ ١

Al-Ala, The Most High (87) In the Name of Allah, the Beneficent, the Merciful.	Sûrat al-A'lâ-87 (Revealed at Makkah) Bismillaahir Raḥmaanir Raḥeem	(٨٧) سُوْرَةُ الْاَعْلٰى مَكِّيَّةٌ (٨) اٰيَاتُهَا ١٩ بِسْمِ اللّٰهِ الرَّحْمٰنِ الرَّحِيْمِ رُكُوْعُهَا ١
18. (Muhammad), glorify the name of your lord, the Most High,	1. Sabbiḥis-ma Rabbikal-A'laa.	سَبِّحِ اسْمَ رَبِّكَ الْاَعْلَى ۙ ﴿١﴾
19. Who has created (all things) proportionately,	2. Allazee khalaqa fasaw-waa.	الَّذِیْ خَلَقَ فَسَوّٰى ۪ۙ ﴿٢﴾
3. decreed their destinies, and provided them with guidance.	3. Wallazee qaddara fahadaa.	وَالَّذِیْ قَدَّرَ فَهَدٰى ۪ۙ ﴿٣﴾
4. It is He who has caused the grass to grow,	4. Wallazeee akhrajal mar'aa.	وَالَّذِیْۤ اَخْرَجَ الْمَرْعٰى ۪ۙ ﴿٤﴾
5. then caused it to wither away.	5. Faja'alahoo ghusaaa'an aḥwaa.	فَجَعَلَهٗ غُثَآءً اَحْوٰى ؕ ﴿٥﴾
6. We shall teach you (the Quran) and you will not forget it	6. Sanuqri'uka falaa tansaaa.	سَنُقْرِئُكَ فَلَا تَنْسٰۤى ۙ ﴿٦﴾
7. unless Allah wills it to be otherwise. He knows all that is made public and all that remains hidden.	7. Illaa maa shaaa'al-laah; innahoo ya'lamul-jahra wa maa yakhfaa.	اِلَّا مَا شَآءَ اللّٰهُ ؕ اِنَّهٗ يَعْلَمُ الْجَهْرَ وَمَا يَخْفٰى ؕ ﴿٧﴾
8. We shall make all your tasks easy.	8. Wa nuyassiruka lilyusraa.	وَنُيَسِّرُكَ لِلْيُسْرٰى ۚۖ ﴿٨﴾
9. Therefore, keep on preaching as long as it is of benefit.	9. Fazakkir in nafa'atiz zikraa.	فَذَكِّرْ اِنْ نَّفَعَتِ الذِّكْرٰى ؕ ﴿٩﴾
10. Those who have fear of Allah will benefit	10. Sa-yaz zakkaru mañy-yakhshaa.	سَيَذَّكَّرُ مَنْ يَّخْشٰى ۙ ﴿١٠﴾
11. but the reprobate will turn away	11. Wa yatajannabuhal ashqaa.	وَيَتَجَنَّبُهَا الْاَشْقَى ۙ ﴿١١﴾
12. and suffer the heat of the great fire	12. Allazee yaṣlan-Naaral-kubraa.	الَّذِیْ يَصْلَى النَّارَ الْكُبْرٰى ۚ ﴿١٢﴾
13. wherein they will neither live nor die.	13. Summa laa yamootu feehaa wa laa yaḥyaa.	ثُمَّ لَا يَمُوْتُ فِيْهَا وَلَا يَحْيٰى ؕ ﴿١٣﴾
14. Lasting happiness will be for those who purify themselves,	14. Qad aflaḥa man tazakkaa.	قَدْ اَفْلَحَ مَنْ تَزَكّٰى ۙ ﴿١٤﴾
15. remember the name of the Lord, and pray to Him.	15. Wa zakaras-ma Rabbihee faṣallaa.	وَذَكَرَ اسْمَ رَبِّهٖ فَصَلّٰى ؕ ﴿١٥﴾
16. However, (the unbelievers) prefer the worldly life	16. Bal tu'siroonal-ḥayaa-tad-dunyaa.	بَلْ تُؤْثِرُوْنَ الْحَيٰوةَ الدُّنْيَا ۖ ﴿١٦﴾
17. even though the life hereafter will be better and will last forever.	17. Wal-Aakhiratu khay-ruñw-wa abqaa.	وَالْاٰخِرَةُ خَيْرٌ وَّاَبْقٰى ؕ ﴿١٧﴾
18. This is what is written in the ancient heavenly Books,	18. Inna haazaa lafiṣ-Ṣuḥu-fil-oolaa.	اِنَّ هٰذَا لَفِى الصُّحُفِ الْاُوْلٰى ۙ ﴿١٨﴾
19. the Scriptures of Abraham and Moses.	19. Ṣuḥufi Ibraaheema wa Moosaa.	صُحُفِ اِبْرٰهِيْمَ وَمُوْسٰى ۧ ﴿١٩﴾ ع ١٩ ١٢

Al-Ghashiyah, The Overwhelming Event (88) In the Name of Allah, the Beneficent, the Merciful.	Sûrat al-Ghâshiyah-88 (Revealed at Makkah) Bismillaahir Raḥmaanir Raḥeem	(٨٨) سُوْرَةُ الْغَاشِيَةِ مَكِّيَّةٌ (٦٨) اٰيَاتُهَا ٢٦ بِسْمِ اللّٰهِ الرَّحْمٰنِ الرَّحِيْمِ رُكُوْعُهَا ١
1. Have you heard the story of the overwhelming event (the Day of Judgment)?	1. Hal ataaka ḥadeesul-ghaashiyah.	هَلْ اَتٰىكَ حَدِيْثُ الْغَاشِيَةِ ؕ ﴿١﴾
2. On that day the faces of some people will be humbly cast down,	2. Wujoohuñy-Yawma'izin khaashi'ah.	وُجُوْهٌ يَّوْمَئِذٍ خَاشِعَةٌ ۙ ﴿٢﴾

3. troubled and tired (as a result of their deeds in the past).	3. ‘Aamilatun-naaṣibah.	عَامِلَةٌ نَّاصِبَةٌ ﴿٣﴾
4. They will suffer the heat of the blazing fire	4. Taṣlaa Naaran ḥaamiyah.	تَصْلٰى نَارًا حَامِيَةً ﴿٤﴾
5. and will be made to drink from a fiercely boiling spring.	5. Tusqaa min ‘aynin aaniyah.	تُسْقٰى مِنْ عَيْنٍ اٰنِيَةٍ ﴿٥﴾
6. They will have no food other than bitter and thorny fruit	6. Laysa lahum ṭa‘aamun illaa min ḍaree‘.	لَيْسَ لَهُمْ طَعَامٌ اِلَّا مِنْ ضَرِيْعٍ ﴿٦﴾
7. which will neither fatten them nor satisfy them.	7. Laa yusminu wa laa yughnee min joo‘.	لَّا يُسْمِنُ وَلَا يُغْنِيْ مِنْ جُوْعٍ ﴿٧﴾
8. However, on that day the faces of other people will be happy	8. Wujoohuñy-Yawma’iz̲in naa‘imah.	وُجُوْهٌ يَّوْمَئِذٍ نَّاعِمَةٌ ﴿٨﴾
9. and pleased with the result of their deeds in the past.	9. Lisa‘yihaa raaḍiyah.	لِّسَعْيِهَا رَاضِيَةٌ ﴿٩﴾
10. They will live in an exalted garden	10. Fee Jannatin ‘aaliyah.	فِيْ جَنَّةٍ عَالِيَةٍ ﴿١٠﴾
11. wherein they will not hear any vain talk.	11. Laa tasma‘u feehaa laaghiyah.	لَّا تَسْمَعُ فِيْهَا لَاغِيَةً ﴿١١﴾
12. Therein will be a flowing spring,	12. Feehaa ‘aynun jaariyah.	فِيْهَا عَيْنٌ جَارِيَةٌ ﴿١٢﴾ وقف لازم
13. raised couches,	13. Feehaa sururum marfoo‘ah.	فِيْهَا سُرُرٌ مَّرْفُوْعَةٌ ﴿١٣﴾
14. well-arranged goblets,	14. Wa akwaabum-mawḍoo‘ah.	وَّاَكْوَابٌ مَّوْضُوْعَةٌ ﴿١٤﴾
15. well-placed cushions,	15. Wa namaariqu maṣfoofah.	وَّنَمَارِقُ مَصْفُوْفَةٌ ﴿١٥﴾
16. and well-spread carpets.	16. Wa zaraabiyyu mabs̲oos̲ah.	وَّزَرَابِيُّ مَبْثُوْثَةٌ ﴿١٦﴾
17. Have they not looked at how the camel is created,	17. Afalaa yanẓuroona ilal-ibili kayfa khuliqat.	اَفَلَا يَنْظُرُوْنَ اِلَى الْاِبِلِ كَيْفَ خُلِقَتْ ﴿١٧﴾
18. how the heavens are raised up high,	18. Wa ilas-samaaa’i kayfa rufi‘at.	وَاِلَى السَّمَآءِ كَيْفَ رُفِعَتْ ﴿١٨﴾
19. how the mountains are set firm,	19. Wa ilal-jibaali kayfa nuṣibat.	وَاِلَى الْجِبَالِ كَيْفَ نُصِبَتْ ﴿١٩﴾
20. and how the earth is spread out?	20. Wa ilal-arḍi kayfa suṭiḥat.	وَاِلَى الْاَرْضِ كَيْفَ سُطِحَتْ ﴿٢٠﴾
21. (Muhammad), preach; you are only a preacher,	21. Faz̲akkir innamaaa anta Muz̲akkir.	فَذَكِّرْ اِنَّمَآ اَنْتَ مُذَكِّرٌ ﴿٢١﴾
22. even though you do not have full control over them, (yet effects of preaching are favorable),	22. Lasta ‘alayhim bimuṣayṭir.	لَسْتَ عَلَيْهِمْ بِمُصَيْطِرٍ ﴿٢٢﴾
23. except those who turn away and disbelieve,	23. Illaa man tawallaa wa kafar.	اِلَّا مَنْ تَوَلّٰى وَكَفَرَ ﴿٢٣﴾
24. Allah will punish them with the greatest torment.	24. Fayu‘az̲ z̲ibuhul-laahul-‘az̲aabal-akbar.	فَيُعَذِّبُهُ اللّٰهُ الْعَذَابَ الْاَكْبَرَ ﴿٢٤﴾
25. To Us they will all return.	25. Inna ilaynaaa iyaabahum.	اِنَّ اِلَيْنَآ اِيَابَهُمْ ﴿٢٥﴾
26. In Our hands are their accounts.	26. S̲umma inna ‘alaynaa ḥisaabahum.	ثُمَّ اِنَّ عَلَيْنَا حِسَابَهُمْ ﴿٢٦﴾ ع النصف

Al-Fajr, The Dawn (89) In the Name of Allah, the Beneficent, the Merciful.	Sûrat al-Fajr-89 (Revealed at Makkah) **Bismillaahir Raḥmaanir Raḥeem**	(٨٩) سُوْرَةُ الْفَجْرِ مَكِّيَّةٌ (١٠) اٰياتها ٣٠ — بِسْمِ اللّٰهِ الرَّحْمٰنِ الرَّحِيْمِ — ركوعها ١
1. (I swear) by the dawn,	1. Wal-Fajr.	وَالْفَجْرِ ۝١
2. by the ten (secret) nights, (of the month of Dhil-hajj)	2. Wa layaalin 'ashr.	وَلَيَالٍ عَشْرٍ ۝٢
3. by the even and odd (names of certain prayers)	3. Wash-shaf'i wal-watr.	وَّالشَّفْعِ وَالْوَتْرِ ۝٣
4. and by the night when it moves toward daybreak.	4. Wallayli iẕaa yasr.	وَالَّيْلِ اِذَا يَسْرِ ۝٤
5. Is this not a sufficient oath for intelligent people?	5. Hal fee ẕaalika qasamul-liẕee ḥijr.	هَلْ فِيْ ذٰلِكَ قَسَمٌ لِّذِيْ حِجْرٍ ۝٥
6. (Muhammad), did you not see how your Lord dealt with the tribe of Ad,	6. Alam tara kayfa fa'ala Rabbuka bi'aad.	اَلَمْ تَرَ كَيْفَ فَعَلَ رَبُّكَ بِعَادٍ ۝٦
7. the people of the huge column city of Eram	7. Irama ẕaatil-'imaad.	اِرَمَ ذَاتِ الْعِمَادِ ۝٧
8. whose like was not created in any other land?	8. Allatee lam yukhlaq miṣluhaa fil-bilaad.	الَّتِيْ لَمْ يُخْلَقْ مِثْلُهَا فِي الْبِلَادِ ۝٨
9. (Also consider how He dealt with) the Thamud, who carved their houses out of the rocks in the valley.	9. Wa Ṣamoodal-laẕeena jaabuṣ-ṣakhra bilwaad.	وَثَمُوْدَ الَّذِيْنَ جَابُوا الصَّخْرَ بِالْوَادِ ۝٩
10. (Also consider the people of) the Pharaoh who victimized people by driving stakes into their hands and legs,	10. Wa Fir'awna ẕil-awtaad.	وَفِرْعَوْنَ ذِي الْاَوْتَادِ ۝١٠
11. led rebellious lives,	11. Allaẕeena ṭaghaw fil-bilaad.	الَّذِيْنَ طَغَوْا فِي الْبِلَادِ ۝١١
12. and spread much evil in the land.	12. Fa-akṣaroo feehal-fasaad.	فَاَكْثَرُوْا فِيْهَا الْفَسَادَ ۝١٢
13. Thus, your Lord afflicted them with torment;	13. Faṣabba 'alayhim Rabbuka sawṭa 'aẕaab.	فَصَبَّ عَلَيْهِمْ رَبُّكَ سَوْطَ عَذَابٍ ۝١٣
14. your Lord keeps an eye on (all evil-doing people).	14. Inna Rabbaka labil-mirṣaad.	اِنَّ رَبَّكَ لَبِالْمِرْصَادِ ۝١٤
15. When his Lord tests the human being, honors, and grants him bounty, he says, "Allah has honored me."	15. Fa-ammal insaanu iẕaa mab-talaahu Rabbuhoo fa-akramahoo wa na'-'amahoo fayaqoolu Rabbeee akraman.	فَاَمَّا الْاِنْسَانُ اِذَا مَا ابْتَلٰىهُ رَبُّهٗ فَاَكْرَمَهٗ وَنَعَّمَهٗ ۙ فَيَقُوْلُ رَبِّيْۤ اَكْرَمَنِ ۝١٥
16. However, when his Lord tests him by a measured amount of sustenance, he says, "Allah has disgraced me."	16. Wa ammaaa iẕaa mabta-laahu faqadara 'alayhi rizqahoo fayaqoolu Rabbee ahaanan.	وَاَمَّاۤ اِذَا مَا ابْتَلٰىهُ فَقَدَرَ عَلَيْهِ رِزْقَهٗ ۙ فَيَقُوْلُ رَبِّيْۤ اَهَانَنِ ۝١٦
17. Indeed you do not show kindness to the orphans,	17. kallaa bal laa tukrimoo-nal-yateem.	كَلَّا بَلْ لَّا تُكْرِمُوْنَ الْيَتِيْمَ ۝١٧
18. or urge one another to feed the destitute.	18. Wa laa taḥaaaḍḍoona 'alaa ṭa'aamil- miskeen.	وَلَا تَحٰٓضُّوْنَ عَلٰى طَعَامِ الْمِسْكِيْنِ ۝١٨
19. Why do you take away the inheritance of others indiscriminately	19. Wa ta-kuloonat-turaaṣa aklal-lammaa.	وَتَاْكُلُوْنَ التُّرَاثَ اَكْلًا لَّمًّا ۝١٩
20. and why do you have an excessive love of riches?	20. Wa tuḥibboonal-maala ḥubban jammaa.	وَّتُحِبُّوْنَ الْمَالَ حُبًّا جَمًّا ۝٢٠
21. (It is certain) when the earth is crushed into small pieces	21. kallaaa iẕaa dukkatil-arḍu dakkan dakkaa.	كَلَّاۤ اِذَا دُكَّتِ الْاَرْضُ دَكًّا دَكًّا ۝٢١
22. and (when you find yourself) in the presence of your Lord and the rows and rows of angels, (your greed for riches will be of no avail to you).	22. Wa jaaa'a Rabbuka wal-malaku ṣaffan ṣaffaa.	وَّجَآءَ رَبُّكَ وَالْمَلَكُ صَفًّا صَفًّا ۝٢٢

23. On that day, hell will be brought closer and the human being will come to his senses, but this will be of no avail to him.	23. Wa jeee'a Yawma'izim bi-Jahannam; Yawma'iziñy-yatazak-karul-insaanu wa annaa lahuz-zikraa.	وَجِايْٓءَ يَوْمَئِذٍۭ بِجَهَنَّمَ ۙ يَوْمَئِذٍ يَّتَذَكَّرُ الْاِنْسَانُ وَاَنّٰى لَهُ الذِّكْرٰى ؕ٢٣
24. He will say, "Would that I had done some good deeds for this life."	24. Yaqoolu yaa laytanee qaddamtu liḥayaatee.	يَقُوْلُ يٰلَيْتَنِيْ قَدَّمْتُ لِحَيَاتِيْ ۚ٢٤
25. On that day the punishment of Allah and His detention will be unparalleled.	25. Fa-Yawma'izil-laa yu'azzibu 'azaabahooo aḥad.	فَيَوْمَئِذٍ لَّا يُعَذِّبُ عَذَابَهٗٓ اَحَدٌ ۙ٢٥
26. And His bonds will be such as none other can bind.	26. Wa laa yoosiqu wasaaqa-hooo aḥad.	وَّلَا يُوْثِقُ وَثَاقَهٗٓ اَحَدٌ ؕ٢٦
27. O serene soul,	27. Yaaa ayyatuhan-nafsul-muṭma'innah.	يٰٓاَيَّتُهَا النَّفْسُ الْمُطْمَئِنَّةُ ۖ٢٧
28. return to your Lord well pleased with him and He will be pleased with you.	28. Irji'eee ilaa Rabbiki raaḍiyatam-marḍiyyah.	ارْجِعِيْٓ اِلٰى رَبِّكِ رَاضِيَةً مَّرْضِيَّةً ۚ٢٨
29. Enter among My servants	29. Fadkhulee fee 'ibaadee.	فَادْخُلِيْ فِيْ عِبٰدِيْ ۙ٢٩
30. into My Paradise.	30. Wadkhulee Jannatee.	وَادْخُلِيْ جَنَّتِيْ ع ٣٠

Al-Balad, The Town (90)

In the Name of Allah, the Beneficent, the Merciful.

Sûrat al-Balad-90

(Revealed at Makkah)

Bismillaahir Raḥmaanir Raḥeem

(٩٠) سُوْرَةُ الْبَلَدِ مَكِّيَّةٌ (٣٥)

اٰيَاتُهَا ٢٠ بِسْمِ اللّٰهِ الرَّحْمٰنِ الرَّحِيْمِ رُكُوْعُهَا ١

1. I swear by this town (Makkah,	1. Laaa uqsimu bihaazal-balad.	لَآ اُقْسِمُ بِهٰذَا الْبَلَدِ ۙ١
2. considered a sanctuary for all, even by the pagans, but only) you are violated therein,	2. Wa anta ḥillum bihaazal-balad.	وَاَنْتَ حِلٌّۢ بِهٰذَا الْبَلَدِ ۙ٢
3. by the father (Adam) and his son (prophets and their successors)	3. Wa waalidiñw-wa maa walad.	وَوَالِدٍ وَّمَا وَلَدَ ۙ٣
4. that We have created human beings capable to face a great deal of hardship.	4. Laqad khalaqnal-insaana fee kabad.	لَقَدْ خَلَقْنَا الْاِنْسَانَ فِيْ كَبَدٍ ؕ٤
5. Does He think that no one will ever have control over him?	5. Ayaḥsabu al-lañy-yaqdira 'alayhi aḥad.	اَيَحْسَبُ اَنْ لَّنْ يَّقْدِرَ عَلَيْهِ اَحَدٌ ۘ٥
6. He (boasts and shows off and) says, "I have spent a great deal of money (to oppose Allah's religion)."	6. Yaqoolu ahlaktu maalal-lubadaa.	يَقُوْلُ اَهْلَكْتُ مَالًا لُّبَدًا ؕ٦
7. Does he think that no one had seen him (the wickedness in his soul)?	7. Ayaḥsabu al-lam yara-hooo aḥad.	اَيَحْسَبُ اَنْ لَّمْ يَرَهٗٓ اَحَدٌ ؕ٧
8. Did We not give him two eyes,	8. Alam naj'al lahoo 'ay-nayn.	اَلَمْ نَجْعَلْ لَّهٗ عَيْنَيْنِ ۙ٨
9. a tongue, and two lips?	9. Wa lisaanañw-wa shafa-tayn.	وَلِسَانًا وَّشَفَتَيْنِ ۙ٩
10. Have We not shown him the ways of good and evil?	10. Wa hadaynaahun-naj-dayn.	وَهَدَيْنٰهُ النَّجْدَيْنِ ۚ١٠
11. He has not yet entered into Al-Aqaba.	11. Falaq-taḥamal-'aqabah.	فَلَا اقْتَحَمَ الْعَقَبَةَ ۖ١١
12. What does it tell you Al-Aqaba is?	12. Wa maaa adraaka mal'a-qabah.	وَمَآ اَدْرٰىكَ مَا الْعَقَبَةُ ؕ١٢
13. It is the setting free of a slave	13. Fakku raqabah.	فَكُّ رَقَبَةٍ ۙ١٣
14. or, in a day of famine, the feeding of	14. Aw iṭ'aamun fee yawmin zee masghabah.	اَوْ اِطْعٰمٌ فِيْ يَوْمٍ ذِيْ مَسْغَبَةٍ ۙ١٤
15. an orphaned relative	15. Yateeman zaa maqrabah.	يَّتِيْمًا ذَا مَقْرَبَةٍ ۙ١٥

ربع ١٤

وقف لازم

16. or a downtrodden destitute person, (so that he would be of)	16. Aw miskeenan zaa matrabah.	أَوْ مِسْكِينًا ذَا مَتْرَبَةٍ ﴿١٦﴾
17. the believers who cooperate with others in patience (steadfastness) and kindness.	17. Summa kaana minal-lazeena aamanoo wa tawaaṣaw bissabri wa tawaaṣaw bil-marḥamah.	ثُمَّ كَانَ مِنَ الَّذِينَ آمَنُوا وَتَوَاصَوْا بِالصَّبْرِ وَتَوَاصَوْا بِالْمَرْحَمَةِ ﴿١٧﴾
18. These are the people of the right hand.	18. Ulaaa'ika Aṣḥaabul-Maymanah.	أُولَٰئِكَ أَصْحَابُ الْمَيْمَنَةِ ﴿١٨﴾
19. Those who disbelieve in Our revelations are the people of the left	19. Wallazeena kafaroo bi-Aayaatinaa hum Aṣḥaabul-Mash'amah.	وَالَّذِينَ كَفَرُوا بِآيَاتِنَا هُمْ أَصْحَابُ الْمَشْأَمَةِ ﴿١٩﴾
20. who will be engulfed in the fire.	20. 'Alayhim Naarum-mu'ṣadah.	عَلَيْهِمْ نَارٌ مُؤْصَدَةٌ ﴿٢٠﴾ ع ١٥

Al-Shams, The Sun (91)

In the Name of Allah, the Beneficent, the Merciful.

Sûrat ash-Shams-91

(Revealed at Makkah)

Bismillaahir Raḥmaanir Raḥeem

(٩١) سُورَةُ الشَّمْسِ مَكِّيَّةٌ (٢٦)

آياتها ١٥ بِسْمِ اللَّهِ الرَّحْمَٰنِ الرَّحِيمِ ركوعها ١

1. (I swear) by the sun and its noon-time brightness,	1. Wash-shamsi wa ḍuḥaa-haa.	وَالشَّمْسِ وَضُحَاهَا ﴿١﴾
2. by the moon when it follows the sun,	2. Wal-qamari izaa talaa-haa.	وَالْقَمَرِ إِذَا تَلَاهَا ﴿٢﴾
3. by the day when it brightens the earth,	3. Wannahaari izaa jallaa-haa.	وَالنَّهَارِ إِذَا جَلَّاهَا ﴿٣﴾
4. by the night when it covers the earth with darkness,	4. Wallayli izaa yaghshaa-haa.	وَاللَّيْلِ إِذَا يَغْشَاهَا ﴿٤﴾
5. by the heavens and that (Power) which established them,	5. Wassamaaa'i wa maa banaahaa.	وَالسَّمَاءِ وَمَا بَنَاهَا ﴿٥﴾
6. by the earth and that (Power) which spread it out	6. Wal-arḍi wa maa ṭaḥaa-haa.	وَالْأَرْضِ وَمَا طَحَاهَا ﴿٦﴾
7. and by the soul and that (Power) which designed it	7. Wa nafsiñw-wa maa sawwaahaa.	وَنَفْسٍ وَمَا سَوَّاهَا ﴿٧﴾
8. and inspired it with knowledge of evil and piety,	8. Fa-alhamahaa fujoorahaa wa taqwaahaa.	فَأَلْهَمَهَا فُجُورَهَا وَتَقْوَاهَا ﴿٨﴾
9. those who purify their souls will certainly have everlasting happiness	9. Qad aflaḥa man zakkaa-haa.	قَدْ أَفْلَحَ مَنْ زَكَّاهَا ﴿٩﴾
10. and those who corrupt their souls will certainly be deprived (of happiness).	10. Wa qad khaaba man dassaahaa.	وَقَدْ خَابَ مَنْ دَسَّاهَا ﴿١٠﴾
11. The people of Thamud rejected (the truth) as a result of their rebelliousness	11. Kaz zabat Samoodu biṭaghwaahaaa.	كَذَّبَتْ ثَمُودُ بِطَغْوَاهَا ﴿١١﴾
12. when the most corrupt of them incited them (to commit evil).	12. Izim ba'asa ashqaahaa.	إِذِ انْبَعَثَ أَشْقَاهَا ﴿١٢﴾
13. The Messenger of Allah told them, "This is a she-camel, belonging to Allah. Do not deprive her of her share of water."	13. Faqaala lahum Rasoolul-laahi naaqatal-laahi wa suqyaa-haa.	فَقَالَ لَهُمْ رَسُولُ اللَّهِ نَاقَةَ اللَّهِ وَسُقْيَاهَا ﴿١٣﴾
14. However, they rejected him and slew her. So their Lord suddenly destroyed them and their city for their sins.	14. Fakaz-zaboohu fa'aqa-roohaa fadamdama 'alayhim Rabbuhum bizambihim fasaw-waahaa.	فَكَذَّبُوهُ فَعَقَرُوهَا فَدَمْدَمَ عَلَيْهِمْ رَبُّهُمْ بِذَنْبِهِمْ فَسَوَّاهَا ﴿١٤﴾
15. (Allah) is not afraid of the result of what He has decreed.	15. Wa laa yakhaafu 'uqbaahaa.	وَلَا يَخَافُ عُقْبَاهَا ﴿١٥﴾ ع ١٥ ١٦

Al-Layl, The Night (92)	Sûrat al-Layl-92	(٩٢) سُوْرَةُ الَّيْلِ مَكِّيَّةٌ (٩)
In the Name of Allah, the Beneficent, the Merciful.	(Revealed at Makkah) **Bismillaahir Raḥmaanir Raḥeem**	آياتها ٢١ بِسْمِ اللّٰهِ الرَّحْمٰنِ الرَّحِيْمِ ركوعها ١
1. (I swear) by the night when it covers the day,	1. Wallayli izaa yaghshaa.	وَالَّيْلِ إِذَا يَغْشٰى ﴿١﴾
2. by the day when it appears brightened,	2. Wannahaari izaa tajallaa.	وَالنَّهَارِ إِذَا تَجَلّٰى ﴿٢﴾
3. and by that (Power) which created the male and female,	3. Wa maa khalaqaz-zakara wal-unsaaa.	وَمَا خَلَقَ الذَّكَرَ وَالْأُنْثٰى ﴿٣﴾
4. you strive in various ways.	4. Inna sa'yakum lashattaa.	إِنَّ سَعْيَكُمْ لَشَتّٰى ﴿٤﴾
5. We shall facilitate the path to bliss	5. Fa ammaa man a'ṭaa wattaqaa.	فَأَمَّا مَنْ أَعْطٰى وَاتَّقٰى ﴿٥﴾
6. for those who spend for the cause of Allah,	6. Wa ṣaddaqa bil-ḥusnaa.	وَصَدَّقَ بِالْحُسْنٰى ﴿٦﴾
7. observe piety, and believe in receiving rewards from Allah.	7. Fasanuyassiruhoo lil-yusraa.	فَسَنُيَسِّرُهٗ لِلْيُسْرٰى ﴿٧﴾
8. However, for those who niggardly, amass their wealth,	8. Wa ammaa mam bakhila wastaghnaa.	وَأَمَّا مَنْ بَخِلَ وَاسْتَغْنٰى ﴿٨﴾
9. and have no faith in receiving rewards (from Allah),	9. Wa kaz zaba bil-ḥusnaa.	وَكَذَّبَ بِالْحُسْنٰى ﴿٩﴾
10. We shall facilitate the path to affliction	10. Fasanuyassiruhoo lil-'usraa.	فَسَنُيَسِّرُهٗ لِلْعُسْرٰى ﴿١٠﴾
11. and their wealth will be of no benefit to them when they face destruction.	11. Wa maa yughnee 'anhu maaluhooo izaa taraddaa.	وَمَا يُغْنِيْ عَنْهُ مَالُهٗٓ إِذَا تَرَدّٰى ﴿١١﴾
12. Certainly, in Our hands is guidance,	12. Inna 'alaynaa lal-hudaa.	إِنَّ عَلَيْنَا لَلْهُدٰى ﴿١٢﴾
13. and to Us belong the hereafter and the worldly life.	13. Wa inna lanaa lal-Aakhirata wal-oolaa.	وَإِنَّ لَنَا لَلْاٰخِرَةَ وَالْأُوْلٰى ﴿١٣﴾
14. I have warned you about the fiercely blazing fire	14. Fa-anzartukum Naaran talaẓẓaa.	فَأَنْذَرْتُكُمْ نَارًا تَلَظّٰى ﴿١٤﴾
15. in which no one will suffer forever	15. Laa yaṣlaahaaa illal-ash-qaa.	لَا يَصْلٰىهَآ إِلَّا الْأَشْقَى ﴿١٥﴾
16. except the wicked ones who have rejected the (Truth) and have turned away from it.	16. Allazee kaz-zaba wa tawallaa.	الَّذِيْ كَذَّبَ وَتَوَلّٰى ﴿١٦﴾
17. The pious ones who spend for the cause of Allah	17. Wa sayujannabuhal-atqaa.	وَسَيُجَنَّبُهَا الْأَتْقَى ﴿١٧﴾
18. and purify themselves will be safe from this fire.	18. Allazee yu'tee maalahoo yatazakkaa.	الَّذِيْ يُؤْتِيْ مَالَهٗ يَتَزَكّٰى ﴿١٨﴾
19. They do not expect any reward	19. Wa maa li-aḥadin 'inda-hoo min ni'matin tujzaaa.	وَمَا لِأَحَدٍ عِنْدَهٗ مِنْ نِّعْمَةٍ تُجْزٰٓى ﴿١٩﴾
20. except the pleasure of their Lord, the Most High,	20. Illabtighaaa'a Wajhi Rabbihil-A'laa.	إِلَّا ابْتِغَآءَ وَجْهِ رَبِّهِ الْأَعْلٰى ﴿٢٠﴾
21. and the reward (of their Lord) will certainly make them happy.	21. Wa lasawfa yarḍaa.	وَلَسَوْفَ يَرْضٰى ﴿٢١﴾ ع ٢١ ١٧
Al-Duha, Daylight (93)	**Sûrat aḍ-Ḍuḥâ-93**	(٩٣) سُوْرَةُ الضُّحٰى مَكِّيَّةٌ (١١)
In the Name of Allah, the Beneficent, the Merciful.	(Revealed at Makkah) **Bismillaahir Raḥmaanir Raḥeem**	آياتها ١١ بِسْمِ اللّٰهِ الرَّحْمٰنِ الرَّحِيْمِ ركوعها ١
1. (I swear) by the midday brightness	1. Waḍḍuḥaa.	وَالضُّحٰى ﴿١﴾

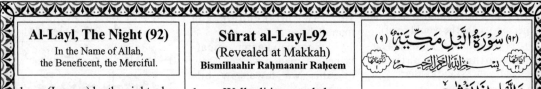

2. and by the night, when it is dark.	2. Wallayli izaa sajaa.	وَالَّيْلِ اِذَا سَجٰى ۙ (٢)
3. (Muhammad), your Lord has not abandoned you (by not sending you His revelation), nor is He displeased with you.	3. Maa wadda'aka Rabbuka wa maa qalaa.	مَا وَدَّعَكَ رَبُّكَ وَمَا قَلٰى ۗ (٣)
4. The reward in the next life will certainly be better for you than worldly gains.	4. Wa lal-Aakhiratu khay-rul-laka minal-oolaa.	وَلَلْاٰخِرَةُ خَيْرٌ لَّكَ مِنَ الْاُوْلٰى ۗ (٤)
5. Your Lord will soon grant you sufficient favors to please you.	5. Walasawfa yu'ṭeeka Rabbuka fatarḍaa.	وَلَسَوْفَ يُعْطِيْكَ رَبُّكَ فَتَرْضٰى ۗ (٥)
6. Did He not find you as an orphan and give you shelter?	6. Alam yajidka yateeman fa-aawaa.	اَلَمْ يَجِدْكَ يَتِيْمًا فَاٰوٰى ۠ (٦)
7. Did He not find you unknown (to people); did He not give guidance (to people to know you)?	7. Wa wajadaka ḍaaallan fahadaa.	وَوَجَدَكَ ضَآلًّا فَهَدٰى ۠ (٧)
8. And did He not find you with a great deal of dependents and make you rich (with revelation for their guidance)?	8. Wa wajadaka 'aaa'ilan fa-aghnaa.	وَوَجَدَكَ عَآئِلًا فَاَغْنٰى ۗ (٨)
9. Do not oppress the orphans	9. Fa-ammal-yateema falaa taqhar.	فَاَمَّا الْيَتِيْمَ فَلَا تَقْهَرْ ۗ (٩)
10. and do not reject the beggars,	10. Wa ammas-saaa'ila falaa tanhar.	وَاَمَّا السَّآئِلَ فَلَا تَنْهَرْ ۗ (١٠)
11. (one more example where the Holy Prophet is addressed but people are meant thereby) and proclaim the bounties of your Lord.	11. Wa ammaa bini'mati Rabbika faḥaddis.	وَاَمَّا بِنِعْمَةِ رَبِّكَ فَحَدِّثْ ۧ (١١) ع ١١ ١٨

Al-Nashrah, The Comfort (94) In the Name of Allah, the Beneficent, the Merciful.	**Sûrat al-Inshirâh-94** (Revealed at Makkah) **Bismillaahir Raḥmaanir Raḥeem**	(٩٤) سُوْرَةُ الْاِنْشِرَاحِ مَكِّيَّةٌ (١٢) اٰيَاتُهَا ٨ بِسْمِ اللّٰهِ الرَّحْمٰنِ الرَّحِيْمِ رُكُوْعُهَا ١
1. (Muhammad), did We not comfort your heart,	1. Alam nashraḥ laka ṣadrak.	اَلَمْ نَشْرَحْ لَكَ صَدْرَكَ ۙ (١)
2. relieve you of the burden	2. Wa waḍa'naa 'anka wizrak.	وَوَضَعْنَا عَنْكَ وِزْرَكَ ۙ (٢)
3. which had been a heavy weight upon your back (by creating Ali ibn abu Talib to help you against your atrocious enemies),	3. Allazeee anqaḍa ẓahrak.	الَّذِيْٓ اَنْقَضَ ظَهْرَكَ ۙ (٣)
4. and grant you an exalted reputation?	4. Wa rafa'naa laka zikrak.	وَرَفَعْنَا لَكَ ذِكْرَكَ ۗ (٤)
5. After every difficulty there is relief.	5. Fa-inna ma'al-'usri yusraa.	فَاِنَّ مَعَ الْعُسْرِ يُسْرًا ۙ (٥)
6. Certainly, after every difficulty there comes relief.	6. Inna ma'al-'usri yusraa	اِنَّ مَعَ الْعُسْرِ يُسْرًا ۗ (٦)
7. When you are free (from your farewell pilgrimage), appoint (your successor)	7. Fa-izaa faraghta fanṣab.	فَاِذَا فَرَغْتَ فَانْصَبْ ۙ (٧)
8. and commit yourself to be in the presence of your Lord.	8. Wa ilaa Rabbika farghab.	وَاِلٰى رَبِّكَ فَارْغَبْ ۧ (٨) ع ٨ ١٩

Al-Tin, The Fig (95) In the Name of Allah, the Beneficent, the Merciful.	**Sûrat at-Tîn-95** (Revealed at Makkah) **Bismillaahir Raḥmaanir Raḥeem**	(٩٥) سُوْرَةُ التِّيْنِ مَكِّيَّةٌ (٢٨) اٰيَاتُهَا ٨ بِسْمِ اللّٰهِ الرَّحْمٰنِ الرَّحِيْمِ رُكُوْعُهَا ١
1. (I swear) by the fig, by the olive,	1. Watteeni wazzaytoon.	وَالتِّيْنِ وَالزَّيْتُوْنِ ۙ (١)
2. by Mount Sinai,	2. Wa Ṭoori Seeneen.	وَطُوْرِ سِيْنِيْنَ ۙ (٢)
3. and by this inviolable city, Makkah,	3. Wa haazal-baladil-ameen.	وَهٰذَا الْبَلَدِ الْاَمِيْنِ ۙ (٣)
4. We have created the human being in the best form	4. Laqad khalaqnal-insaana feee aḥsani	لَقَدْ خَلَقْنَا الْاِنْسَانَ فِيْٓ اَحْسَنِ

	taqweem.	تَقْوِيْمٍ ﴿٤﴾
5. and We shall make him the lowest of low	5. S̲umma radadnaahu as-fala saafileen.	ثُمَّ رَدَدْنٰهُ اَسْفَلَ سٰفِلِيْنَ ﴿٥﴾
6. except the righteously striving believers who will have a never-ending reward.	6. Illal-laz̲eena aamanoo wa ‘amiluṣ-ṣaaliḥaati falahum ajrun ghayru mamnoon.	اِلَّا الَّذِيْنَ اٰمَنُوْا وَعَمِلُوا الصّٰلِحٰتِ فَلَهُمْ اَجْرٌ غَيْرُ مَمْنُوْنٍ ﴿٦﴾
7. After (knowing) this, what makes you still disbelieve in the Day of Judgment?	7. Famaa yukaz̲-z̲ibuka ba‘du bid-Deen.	فَمَا يُكَذِّبُكَ بَعْدُ بِالدِّيْنِ ﴿٧﴾
8. Is Allah not the best of the Judges?	8. Alaysal-laahu bi-Aḥka-mil-ḥaakimeen.	اَلَيْسَ اللّٰهُ بِاَحْكَمِ الْحٰكِمِيْنَ ﴿٨﴾ ع ٨

Al-Alaq, The Clot of Blood (96)

In the Name of Allah, the Beneficent, the Merciful.

Sûrat al-‘Alaq-96

(Revealed at Makkah)

Bismillaahir Raḥmaanir Raḥeem

(٩٦) سُوْرَةُ الْعَلَقِ مَكِّيَّةٌ (١)

اٰيَاتُهَا ١٩ — رُكُوْعُهَا ١

بِسْمِ اللّٰهِ الرَّحْمٰنِ الرَّحِيْمِ

1. (Muhammad), read in the name of your Lord who created (all things).	1. Iqra-bismi Rabbikal-laz̲ee khalaq.	اِقْرَاْ بِاسْمِ رَبِّكَ الَّذِيْ خَلَقَ ﴿١﴾
2. He created man from a clot of blood.	2. Khalaqal-insaana min ‘alaq	خَلَقَ الْاِنْسَانَ مِنْ عَلَقٍ ﴿٢﴾
3. Recite! Your Lord is the most Honorable One,	3. Iqra-wa Rabbukal-Akram.	اِقْرَاْ وَرَبُّكَ الْاَكْرَمُ ﴿٣﴾
4. who, by the pen, taught the human being:	4. Allaz̲ee ‘allama bil-qalam.	الَّذِيْ عَلَّمَ بِالْقَلَمِ ﴿٤﴾
5. He taught the human being what he did not know.	5. ‘Allamal-insaana maa lam ya‘lam.	عَلَّمَ الْاِنْسَانَ مَا لَمْ يَعْلَمْ ﴿٥﴾
6. Despite this, the human being still tends to rebel	6. Kallaaa innal-insaana la-yaṭghaaa.	كَلَّآ اِنَّ الْاِنْسَانَ لَيَطْغٰٓى ﴿٦﴾
7. because he thinks that he is independent.	7. Ar-ra-aahus-taghnaa.	اَنْ رَّاٰهُ اسْتَغْنٰى ﴿٧﴾
8. However, (all things) will return to your Lord.	8. Inna ilaa Rabbikar-ruj‘aa.	اِنَّ اِلٰى رَبِّكَ الرُّجْعٰى ﴿٨﴾
9. Have you seen the one who prohibits	9. Ara’aytal-laz̲ee yanhaa.	اَرَءَيْتَ الَّذِيْ يَنْهٰى ﴿٩﴾
10. a servant of Ours from prayer?	10. ‘Abdan iz̲aa ṣallaa.	عَبْدًا اِذَا صَلّٰى ﴿١٠﴾
11. What will happen if the praying person is rightly guided	11. Ara’ayta in kaana ‘alal-hudaaa.	اَرَءَيْتَ اِنْ كَانَ عَلَى الْهُدٰٓى ﴿١١﴾
12. or if he commands others to maintain piety?	12. Aw amara bittaqwaa.	اَوْ اَمَرَ بِالتَّقْوٰى ﴿١٢﴾
13. What will happen if the prohibiting person rejects the Truth and turns away from it?	13. Ara’ayta in kaz̲-z̲aba wa tawallaa.	اَرَءَيْتَ اِنْ كَذَّبَ وَتَوَلّٰى ﴿١٣﴾
14. Did he not realize that Allah sees him?	14. Alam ya‘lam bi-annal-laaha yaraa.	اَلَمْ يَعْلَمْ بِاَنَّ اللّٰهَ يَرٰى ﴿١٤﴾
15. He must know that if he did not desist, We shall certainly drag him by his forelocks,	15. Kallaa la-’il-lam yantahi lanasfa‘am binnaaṣiyah.	كَلَّا لَئِنْ لَّمْ يَنْتَهِ ۙ لَنَسْفَعًا بِالنَّاصِيَةِ ﴿١٥﴾
16. his lying sinful forelock.	16. Naaṣiyatin kaaz̲ibatin khaaṭi’ah.	نَاصِيَةٍ كَاذِبَةٍ خَاطِئَةٍ ﴿١٦﴾
17. Let him call on his associates for help	17. Falyad‘u naadiyah.	فَلْيَدْعُ نَادِيَهٗ ﴿١٧﴾
18. and We too will call the stern and angry keepers of hell.	18. Sanad‘uz-zabaaniyah.	سَنَدْعُ الزَّبَانِيَةَ ﴿١٨﴾

19. (Muhammad), never yield to him! Prostrate yourself and try to come closer to Allah.

19. Kallaa laa tuṭi'hu wasjud waqtarib.

كَلَّا لَا تُطِعْهُ وَاسْجُدْ وَاقْتَرِبْ ۩

Al-Qadr, Destiny (97)
In the Name of Allah,
the Beneficent, the Merciful.

Sûrat al-Qadr-97
(Revealed at Makkah)
Bismillaahir Raḥmaanir Raḥeem

سُوْرَةُ الْقَدْرِ مَكِّيَّةٌ (٩٧) (٢٥)

بِسْمِ اللهِ الرَّحْمٰنِ الرَّحِيْمِ

1. We revealed the Quran on the Night of Destiny.

1. Innaaa anzalnaahu fee Laylatil-Qadr.

اِنَّا اَنْزَلْنٰهُ فِيْ لَيْلَةِ الْقَدْرِ ۚ

2. What does it tell you the Night of Destiny is?

2. Wa maaa adraaka maa Laylatul-Qadr.

وَمَا اَدْرٰىكَ مَا لَيْلَةُ الْقَدْرِ ۚ

3. (Worship) on the Night of Destiny is better than (worship) for a thousand months.

3. Laylatul-Qadri khayrum-min alfi shahr.

لَيْلَةُ الْقَدْرِ ۙ خَيْرٌ مِّنْ اَلْفِ شَهْرٍ ۚ

4. On this night, the angels and the spirit descend by the permission of their Lord with His decree (to determine everyone's destiny).

4. Tanazzalul-malaaa'ikatu war-Rooḥu feehaa bi-izni Rabbihim min kulli amr.

تَنَزَّلُ الْمَلٰٓئِكَةُ وَالرُّوْحُ فِيْهَا بِاِذْنِ رَبِّهِمْ مِّنْ كُلِّ اَمْرٍ ۚ

5. This night is all peace until the break of dawn.

5. Salaam; hiya ḥattaa maṭla'il-Fajr.

سَلٰمٌ ۗ هِيَ حَتّٰى مَطْلَعِ الْفَجْرِ ۚ

Al-Bayyinah, The Testimony (98)
In the Name of Allah,
the Beneficent, the Merciful.

Sûrat al-Bayyinah-98
(Revealed at Madinah)
Bismillaahir Raḥmaanir Raḥeem

سُوْرَةُ الْبَيِّنَةِ مَدَنِيَّةٌ (٩٨) (١٠٠)

بِسْمِ اللهِ الرَّحْمٰنِ الرَّحِيْمِ

1. The unbelievers among the people of the Book and the pagans disbelieved (in Islam) only after receiving divine testimony:

1. Lam yakunil-lazeena kafaroo min Ahlil-Kitaabi wal-mushrikeena munfakkeena ḥattaa ta-tiyahumul-bayyinah.

لَمْ يَكُنِ الَّذِيْنَ كَفَرُوْا مِنْ اَهْلِ الْكِتٰبِ وَالْمُشْرِكِيْنَ مُنْفَكِّيْنَ حَتّٰى تَاْتِيَهُمُ الْبَيِّنَةُ ۙ

2. a Messenger (Muhammad) from Allah, reciting to them parts of the purified,

2. Rasoolum-minal-laahi yatloo ṣuḥufam-muṭahharah.

رَسُوْلٌ مِّنَ اللهِ يَتْلُوْا صُحُفًا مُّطَهَّرَةً ۙ

3. holy Book which contain eternal laws of guidance.

3. Feehaa kutubun qayyimah.

فِيْهَا كُتُبٌ قَيِّمَةٌ ؕ

4. Nor did the people of the Book disagree among themselves until after receiving the ancient divine testaments.

4. Wa maa tafarraqal-lazeena ootul-Kitaaba illaa mim ba'di maa jaaa'at-humul-bayyinah.

وَمَا تَفَرَّقَ الَّذِيْنَ اُوْتُوا الْكِتٰبَ اِلَّا مِنْ بَعْدِ مَا جَآءَتْهُمُ الْبَيِّنَةُ ؕ

5. They were commanded to worship Allah only, be clean of sins, steadfast in prayer, and pay the zakat. This is truly the eternal religion.

5. Wa maaa umirooo illaa liya'budul-laaha mukhliṣeena lahud-deena ḥunafaaa'a wa yuqeemuṣ-Ṣalaata wa yu'tuz-Zakaata wa zaalika deenul-qayyimah.

وَمَا اُمِرُوْٓا اِلَّا لِيَعْبُدُوا اللهَ مُخْلِصِيْنَ لَهُ الدِّيْنَ ۙ حُنَفَآءَ وَيُقِيْمُوا الصَّلٰوةَ وَيُؤْتُوا الزَّكٰوةَ وَذٰلِكَ دِيْنُ الْقَيِّمَةِ ؕ

6. The unbelievers among the people of the Book and the pagans will dwell forever in hell; they are the worst of all creatures.

6. Innal-lazeena kafaroo min Ahlil-Kitaabi wal-mushrikeena fee Naari Jahannama khaalideena feehaa; ulaa'ika hum sharrul-bariyyah.

اِنَّ الَّذِيْنَ كَفَرُوْا مِنْ اَهْلِ الْكِتٰبِ وَالْمُشْرِكِيْنَ فِيْ نَارِ جَهَنَّمَ خٰلِدِيْنَ فِيْهَا ؕ اُولٰٓئِكَ هُمْ شَرُّ الْبَرِيَّةِ ؕ

7. The righteously striving believers are the best of all creatures.

7. Innal-lazeena aamanoo wa 'amiluṣ-ṣaaliḥaati ulaaa'ika hum-khayrul-bariyyah.

اِنَّ الَّذِيْنَ اٰمَنُوْا وَعَمِلُوا الصّٰلِحٰتِ ۙ اُولٰٓئِكَ هُمْ خَيْرُ الْبَرِيَّةِ ؕ

8. Their reward from their Lord will be the gardens of Eden wherein streams flow and wherein they will live forever. Allah will be pleased with them and they will be pleased with Him. This (reward) is for those who fear their Lord.

8. Jazaaa'uhum 'inda Rabbihim Jannaatu 'Adnin tajree min taḥtihal-anhaaru khaalideena feehaaa abadaa; raḍiyal-laahu 'anhum wa raḍoo 'anh; zaalika liman khashiya Rabbah.

جَزَآؤُهُمْ عِنْدَ رَبِّهِمْ جَنّٰتُ عَدْنٍ
تَجْرِيْ مِنْ تَحْتِهَا الْاَنْهٰرُ خٰلِدِيْنَ
فِيْهَآ اَبَدًا ؕ رَضِيَ اللّٰهُ عَنْهُمْ وَرَضُوْا
عَنْهُ ؕ ذٰلِكَ لِمَنْ خَشِيَ رَبَّهٗ ۝٨ ع ٨ ٢٣

Al-Zilzal, The Earthquake (99)

In the Name of Allah, the Beneficent, the Merciful.

1. When the earth is shaken by a terrible quake
2. and it throws out its burden,
3. the human being will say, "What is happening to it?"
4. On that day the earth will declare all (the activities of the human being) which have taken place on it,
5. having been inspired by your Lord.
6. On that day, people will come out of their graves in different groups to see (the results of) their own deeds.
7. Whoever has done an atom's weight of good
8. will see it, and whoever has done an atom's weight of evil will also see it.

Sûrat az-Zilzâl-99

(Revealed at Madinah)

Bismillaahir Raḥmaanir Raḥeem

1. Izaa zulzilatil-arḍu zilzaalahaa.
2. Wa akhrajatil-arḍu asqaalahaa.
3. Wa qaalal-insaanu maa lahaa.
4. Yawma'izin tuḥaddisu akhbaarahaa.
5. Bi-anna Rabbaka awḥaa lahaa.
6. Yawma'iziñy-yaṣdurun-naasu ashtaatal-liyuraw a'maalahum.
7. Famañy-ya'mal misqaala zarratin khayrañy-yarah.
8. Wa mañy-ya'mal misqaala zarratin sharrañy-yarah.

سُوْرَةُ الزِّلْزَالِ مَدَنِيَّةٌ (٩٩) (٩٣)
اٰيَاتُهَا ٨ بِسْمِ اللّٰهِ الرَّحْمٰنِ الرَّحِيْمِ رُكُوْعُهَا ١

اِذَا زُلْزِلَتِ الْاَرْضُ زِلْزَالَهَا ۝١
وَاَخْرَجَتِ الْاَرْضُ اَثْقَالَهَا ۝٢
وَقَالَ الْاِنْسَانُ مَا لَهَا ۝٣
يَوْمَئِذٍ تُحَدِّثُ اَخْبَارَهَا ۝٤
بِاَنَّ رَبَّكَ اَوْحٰى لَهَا ۝٥
يَوْمَئِذٍ يَّصْدُرُ النَّاسُ اَشْتَاتًا ۙ لِّيُرَوْا
اَعْمَالَهُمْ ۝٦
فَمَنْ يَّعْمَلْ مِثْقَالَ ذَرَّةٍ خَيْرًا يَّرَهٗ ۝٧
وَمَنْ يَّعْمَلْ مِثْقَالَ ذَرَّةٍ شَرًّا يَّرَهٗ ۝٨ ع ٨ ٢٤

Al-Adiyat, The Chargers (100)

In the Name of Allah, the Beneficent, the Merciful.

1. (I swear) by the snorting chargers (of the warriors), whose
2. and produce sparks
3. while running during a raid at dawn,
4. and leave behind a cloud of dust,
5. then reach the midst of the crowd (the enemy).
6. The human being is certainly ungrateful to his Lord.
7. He himself knows this very well.
8. He certainly has a strong love for wealth and riches.
9. Did he not know that on the day when those in the graves are resurrected

Sûrat al-'Âdiyâ-100

(Revealed at Makkah)

Bismillaahir Raḥmaanir Raḥeem

1. Wal-'aadiyaati ḍabḥaa.
2. Fal-mooriyaati qadḥaa.
3. Fal-mugheeraati ṣubḥaa.
4. Fa-asarna bihee naq'aa.
5. Fawasaṭna bihee jam'aa.
6. Innal-insaana li-Rabbihee lakanood.
7. Wa innahoo 'alaa zaalika lashaheed.
8. Wa innahoo liḥubbil-khayri lashadeed.
9. Afalaa ya'lamu izaa bu'sira maa fil-

سُوْرَةُ الْعٰدِيٰتِ مَكِّيَّةٌ (١٠٠) (١٤)
اٰيَاتُهَا ١١ بِسْمِ اللّٰهِ الرَّحْمٰنِ الرَّحِيْمِ رُكُوْعُهَا ١

وَالْعٰدِيٰتِ ضَبْحًا ۝١
فَالْمُوْرِيٰتِ قَدْحًا ۝٢
فَالْمُغِيْرٰتِ صُبْحًا ۝٣
فَاَثَرْنَ بِهٖ نَقْعًا ۝٤
فَوَسَطْنَ بِهٖ جَمْعًا ۝٥
اِنَّ الْاِنْسَانَ لِرَبِّهٖ لَكَنُوْدٌ ۝٦
وَاِنَّهٗ عَلٰى ذٰلِكَ لَشَهِيْدٌ ۝٧
وَاِنَّهٗ لِحُبِّ الْخَيْرِ لَشَدِيْدٌ ۝٨
اَفَلَا يَعْلَمُ اِذَا بُعْثِرَ مَا فِي

	Quboor.	الْقُبُورِ ۙ ٩
10. and all that is in the hearts is made public,	10. Wa ḥuṣṣila maa fiṣ-ṣudoor.	وَحُصِّلَ مَا فِي الصُّدُورِ ۙ ١٠
11. their Lord will examine his deeds?	11. Inna Rabbahum bihim Yawma'izil-lakhabeer.	إِنَّ رَبَّهُمْ بِهِمْ يَوْمَئِذٍ لَّخَبِيرٌ ١١ ع ع ١١ ٢٥

Al-Qariah, The Crash (101)

In the Name of Allah, the Beneficent, the Merciful.

Sûrat al-Qâri‘ah-101

(Revealed at Makkah)

Bismillaahir Raḥmaanir Raḥeem

(١٠١) سُورَةُ الْقَارِعَةِ مَكِّيَّةٌ (٣٠)
آياتها ١١ بِسْمِ اللَّهِ الرَّحْمَٰنِ الرَّحِيمِ ركوعها ١

1. The (unprecedented) crash!	1. Al-qaari‘ah.	الْقَارِعَةُ ۙ ١
2. What is the crash?	2. Mal-qaari‘ah.	مَا الْقَارِعَةُ ۚ ٢
3. What does it tell you the crash is?	3. Wamaaa adraaka mal-qaari‘ah.	وَمَا أَدْرَاكَ مَا الْقَارِعَةُ ۚ ٣
4. On that day, people will be like scattered moths	4. Yawma yakoonun-naasu kal-faraashil-mabsoos.	يَوْمَ يَكُونُ النَّاسُ كَالْفَرَاشِ الْمَبْثُوثِ ۙ ٤
5. and mountains will be like fluffed-up wool.	5. Wa takoonul-jibaalu kal-‘ihnil-manfoosh.	وَتَكُونُ الْجِبَالُ كَالْعِهْنِ الْمَنْفُوشِ ۚ ٥
6. Those whose good deeds will weigh heavier (on the scale)	6. Fa-ammaa man saqulat mawaazeenuh.	فَأَمَّا مَنْ ثَقُلَتْ مَوَازِينُهُ ۙ ٦
7. will live a pleasant life,	7. Fahuwa fee ‘eeshatir-raaḍiyah.	فَهُوَ فِي عِيشَةٍ رَاضِيَةٍ ۚ ٧
8. but those whose good deeds will be lighter (on the scale)	8. Wa ammaa man khaffat mawaazeenuh.	وَأَمَّا مَنْ خَفَّتْ مَوَازِينُهُ ۙ ٨
9. will be thrown headlong into hawiyah.	9. Fa-ummuhoo haawiyah.	فَأُمُّهُ هَاوِيَةٌ ۚ ٩
10. What does it tell you it (hawiyah) is?	10. Wa maaa adraaka maa hiyah.	وَمَا أَدْرَاكَ مَا هِيَهْ ۚ ١٠
11. It is a burning fire.	11. Naarun ḥaamiyah.	نَارٌ حَامِيَةٌ ١١ ع ع ١١ ٢٦

Al-Takathur, Worldly Gains (102)

In the Name of Allah, the Beneficent, the Merciful.

Sûrat at-Takâsur-102

(Revealed at Makkah)

Bismillaahir Raḥmaanir Raḥeem

(١٠٢) سُورَةُ التَّكَاثُرِ مَكِّيَّةٌ (١٦)
آياتها ٨ بِسْمِ اللَّهِ الرَّحْمَٰنِ الرَّحِيمِ ركوعها ١

1. (Your) greater number has caused you to become neglectful	1. Alhaakumut-takaasur.	أَلْهَاكُمُ التَّكَاثُرُ ۙ ١
2. so you do not remember the dead.	2. Ḥattaa zurtumul-maqaabir.	حَتَّىٰ زُرْتُمُ الْمَقَابِرَ ۚ ٢
3. However, you shall know.	3. Kallaa sawfa ta‘lamoon.	كَلَّا سَوْفَ تَعْلَمُونَ ۙ ٣
4. You shall certainly know (about the consequences of your deeds).	4. Summa kallaa sawfa ta‘lamoon.	ثُمَّ كَلَّا سَوْفَ تَعْلَمُونَ ۚ ٤
5. Indeed if you had the knowledge (and faith) beyond all doubt,	5. Kallaa law ta‘lamoona ‘ilmal-yaqeen.	كَلَّا لَوْ تَعْلَمُونَ عِلْمَ الْيَقِينِ ۚ ٥
6. you would have seen (believed in the hardship of) hell.	6. Latarawunnal-Jaḥeem.	لَتَرَوُنَّ الْجَحِيمَ ۙ ٦
7. You would then (believe in it as if though you) see it with your own eyes.	7. Summa latarawunnahaa ‘aynal-yaqeen.	ثُمَّ لَتَرَوُنَّهَا عَيْنَ الْيَقِينِ ۙ ٧

8. Then, on that day, you will be questioned about the bounties (of Allah).	8. Summa latus'alunna Yawma'izin 'anin-na'eem.	ثُمَّ لَتُسْـَٔلُنَّ يَوْمَئِذٍ عَنِ النَّعِيْمِ ﴿٨﴾ ع ٨ ٢٧
Al-Asr, The Time (103) In the Name of Allah, the Beneficent, the Merciful.	**Sûrat al-'Aṣr-103** (Revealed at Makkah) **Bismillaahir Raḥmaanir Raḥeem**	(١٠٣) سُوْرَةُ الْعَصْرِ مَكِّيَّةٌ (١٣) اٰيَاتُهَا ٣ بِسْمِ اللّٰهِ الرَّحْمٰنِ الرَّحِيْمِ رُكُوْعُهَا ١
1. (I swear) by the time,	1. Wal-'Aṣr.	وَالْعَصْرِ ﴿١﴾
2. human beings are doomed to suffer loss (and fail),	2. Innal-insaana lafee khusr.	اِنَّ الْاِنْسَانَ لَفِيْ خُسْرٍ ﴿٢﴾
3. except the righteously striving believers who exhort each other to truthful purposes and to patience.	3. Illal-lazeena aamanoo wa 'amiluṣ-ṣaaliḥaati wa tawaaṣaw bilḥaqq; wa tawaaṣaw biṣṣabr.	اِلَّا الَّذِيْنَ اٰمَنُوْا وَعَمِلُوا الصّٰلِحٰتِ وَتَوَاصَوْا بِالْحَقِّ ۙ وَتَوَاصَوْا بِالصَّبْرِ ﴿٣﴾ ع ٣ ٢٨
Al-Humazah, The Slanderer (104) In the Name of Allah, the Beneficent, the Merciful.	**Sûrat al-Humazah-104** (Revealed at Makkah) **Bismillaahir Raḥmaanir Raḥeem**	(١٠٤) سُوْرَةُ الْهُمَزَةِ مَكِّيَّةٌ (٣٢) اٰيَاتُهَا ٩ بِسْمِ اللّٰهِ الرَّحْمٰنِ الرَّحِيْمِ رُكُوْعُهَا ١
1. Woe to everyone who winks with despise and shows anger at the needy,	1. Waylul-likulli humazatil-lumazah.	وَيْلٌ لِّكُلِّ هُمَزَةٍ لُّمَزَةِ ﴿١﴾
2. he who collects and hoards wealth,	2. Allazee jama'a maalañw-wa 'addadah.	الَّذِيْ جَمَعَ مَالًا وَّعَدَّدَهٗ ﴿٢﴾
3. thinking that his property will make him live forever.	3. Yaḥsabu anna maalahooo akhladah.	يَحْسَبُ اَنَّ مَالَهٗٓ اَخْلَدَهٗ ﴿٣﴾
4. Indeed, they will be thrown into Al-Hutamah.	4. Kallaa layumbazanna fil-ḥuṭamah.	كَلَّا لَيُنْۢبَذَنَّ فِي الْحُطَمَةِ ﴿٤﴾
5. What does it tell you Al-Hutamah is?	5. Wa maaa adraaka mal-ḥuṭamah.	وَمَآ اَدْرٰىكَ مَا الْحُطَمَةُ ﴿٥﴾
6. It is a fierce fire created by Allah	6. Naarul-laahil-mooqadah.	نَارُ اللّٰهِ الْمُوْقَدَةُ ﴿٦﴾
7. to penetrate into the hearts.	7. Allatee taṭṭali'u 'alal-af'idah.	الَّتِيْ تَطَّلِعُ عَلَى الْاَفْـِٕدَةِ ﴿٧﴾
8. It will engulf them	8. Innahaa 'alayhim mu'ṣadah.	اِنَّهَا عَلَيْهِمْ مُّؤْصَدَةٌ ﴿٨﴾
9. in its long columns of flames.	9. Fee 'amadim-mumaddadah.	فِيْ عَمَدٍ مُّمَدَّدَةٍ ﴿٩﴾ ع ٩ ٢٩
Al-Fil, The Elephant (105) In the Name of Allah, the Beneficent, the Merciful.	**Sûrat al-Fîl-105** (Revealed at Makkah) **Bismillaahir Raḥmaanir Raḥeem**	(١٠٥) سُوْرَةُ الْفِيْلِ مَكِّيَّةٌ (١٩) اٰيَاتُهَا ٥ بِسْمِ اللّٰهِ الرَّحْمٰنِ الرَّحِيْمِ رُكُوْعُهَا ١
1. Did you not see how your Lord dealt with the people of the elephant?	1. Alam tara kayfa fa'ala Rabbuka bi-Aṣḥaabil-Feel.	اَلَمْ تَرَ كَيْفَ فَعَلَ رَبُّكَ بِاَصْحٰبِ الْفِيْلِ ﴿١﴾
2. Did He not cause their evil plots to fail	2. Alam yaj'al kaydahum fee taḍleel.	اَلَمْ يَجْعَلْ كَيْدَهُمْ فِيْ تَضْلِيْلٍ ﴿٢﴾
3. by sending against them flocks of swallows	3. Wa arsala 'alayhim ṭayran abaabeel.	وَّاَرْسَلَ عَلَيْهِمْ طَيْرًا اَبَابِيْلَ ﴿٣﴾
4. which hit them with small pebbles of clay	4. Tarmeehim biḥijaaratim-min sijjeel.	تَرْمِيْهِمْ بِحِجَارَةٍ مِّنْ سِجِّيْلٍ ﴿٤﴾
5. to turn them into (something) like the leftover grass grazed by cattle?	5. Faja'alahum ka'aṣfim-ma-kool.	فَجَعَلَهُمْ كَعَصْفٍ مَّاْكُوْلٍ ﴿٥﴾ ع ٥ ٣٠

Al-Quraysh, Quraysh (106)

In the Name of Allah,
the Beneficent, the Merciful.

1. For Allah's favors to them during their summer and winter journeys,
2. Quraysh should worship the Lord of this House.
3. It is He who has fed them when they were hungry
4. and has made them secure from fear.

Sûrat Quraysh-106

(Revealed at Makkah)
Bismillaahir Raḥmaanir Raḥeem

1. Li-eelaafi Quraysh.
2. Eelaafihim riḥlatash-shitaaa’i waṣṣayf.
3. Falya‘budoo Rabba haaẕal-Bait.
4. Allaẕeee aṭ‘amahum min joo‘iñw-wa aamanahum min khawf.

سُوْرَةُ قُرَيْشٍ مَّكِّيَّةٌ (١٠٦) (٢٩)
بِسْمِ اللّٰهِ الرَّحْمٰنِ الرَّحِيْمِ

لِاِيْلٰفِ قُرَيْشٍ ۙ﴿١﴾
اٖلٰفِهِمْ رِحْلَةَ الشِّتَآءِ وَالصَّيْفِ ۚ﴿٢﴾
فَلْيَعْبُدُوْا رَبَّ هٰذَا الْبَيْتِ ۙ﴿٣﴾
الَّذِيْٓ اَطْعَمَهُمْ مِّنْ جُوْعٍ ۙ وَّ
اٰمَنَهُمْ مِّنْ خَوْفٍ ﴿٤﴾ ع ٤ ٣١

Al-Maun, Cooperation (107)

In the Name of Allah,
the Beneficent, the Merciful.

1. Have you seen the one who calls the religion a lie?
2. It is he who turns down the orphans
3. and never encourages the feeding of the destitute.

(Muhammad), say to the unbelievers,

4. Woe to the worshippers
5. who miss their prayers,
6. show off (their good deeds),
7. and refuse to help the needy.

Sûrat al-Mâ‘ûn-107

(Revealed at Makkah)
Bismillaahir Raḥmaanir Raḥeem

1. Ara’aytal-laẕee yukaẕẕibu-biddeen.
2. Faẕaalikal-laẕee yadu‘-‘ul-yateem.
3. Wa laa yaḥuḍḍu ‘alaa ṭa‘aamil-miskeen.
4. Fawaylul-lilmuṣalleen.
5. Allaẕeena hum ‘an Ṣalaatihim saahoon.
6. Allaẕeena hum yuraaa’oon.
7. Wa yamna‘oonal-maa‘oon.

سُوْرَةُ الْمَاعُوْنِ مَكِّيَّةٌ (١٠٧) (١٧)
بِسْمِ اللّٰهِ الرَّحْمٰنِ الرَّحِيْمِ

اَرَءَيْتَ الَّذِيْ يُكَذِّبُ بِالدِّيْنِ ؕ﴿١﴾
فَذٰلِكَ الَّذِيْ يَدُعُّ الْيَتِيْمَ ۙ﴿٢﴾
وَلَا يَحُضُّ عَلٰى طَعَامِ الْمِسْكِيْنِ ؕ﴿٣﴾
فَوَيْلٌ لِّلْمُصَلِّيْنَ ۙ﴿٤﴾
الَّذِيْنَ هُمْ عَنْ صَلَاتِهِمْ سَاهُوْنَ ۙ﴿٥﴾
الَّذِيْنَ هُمْ يُرَآءُوْنَ ۙ﴿٦﴾
وَيَمْنَعُوْنَ الْمَاعُوْنَ ﴿٧﴾ ع ١ ٣٢

Al-Kawthar, Abundant Virtue (108)

In the Name of Allah,
the Beneficent, the Merciful.

1. (Muhammad), We have granted you abundant virtue (a fountain in Paradise).
2. So worship your Lord and make sacrificial offerings.
3. Whoever has hatred toward you will himself remain childless.

Sûrat al-Kawsar-108

(Revealed at Makkah)
Bismillaahir Raḥmaanir Raḥeem

1. Innaaa a‘ṭaynaakal-Kawsar.
2. Faṣalli li-Rabbika wanḥar.
3. Inna shaani’aka huwal-abtar.

سُوْرَةُ الْكَوْثَرِ مَكِّيَّةٌ (١٠٨) (١٥)
بِسْمِ اللّٰهِ الرَّحْمٰنِ الرَّحِيْمِ

اِنَّآ اَعْطَيْنٰكَ الْكَوْثَرَ ؕ﴿١﴾
فَصَلِّ لِرَبِّكَ وَانْحَرْ ؕ﴿٢﴾
اِنَّ شَانِئَكَ هُوَ الْاَبْتَرُ ﴿٣﴾ ع ١ ٣٣

Al-Kafirun, Unbelievers (109)

In the Name of Allah,
the Beneficent, the Merciful.

1. (Muhammad), say to the unbelievers,
2. “I do not worship what you worship,
3. nor do you worship what I worship.

Sûrat al-Kâfirûn-109

(Revealed at Makkah)
Bismillaahir Raḥmaanir Raḥeem

1. Qul yaaa ayyuhal-kaafiroon.
2. Laaa a‘budu maa ta‘budoon.
3. Wa laaa antum ‘aabidoona maaa a‘bud.

سُوْرَةُ الْكٰفِرُوْنَ مَكِّيَّةٌ (١٠٩) (١٨)
بِسْمِ اللّٰهِ الرَّحْمٰنِ الرَّحِيْمِ

قُلْ يٰٓاَيُّهَا الْكٰفِرُوْنَ ۙ﴿١﴾
لَآ اَعْبُدُ مَا تَعْبُدُوْنَ ۙ﴿٢﴾
وَلَآ اَنْتُمْ عٰبِدُوْنَ مَآ اَعْبُدُ ۚ﴿٣﴾

4. I have not been worshipping what you worshipped,

4. Wa laaa anaa 'aabidum maa 'abat-tum.

وَلَآ أَنَا۠ عَابِدٌ مَّا عَبَدتُّمْ ۝٤

5. nor will you worship what I shall worship.

5. Wa laaa antum 'aabidoona maaa a'bud.

وَلَآ أَنتُمْ عَٰبِدُونَ مَآ أَعْبُدُ ۝٥

6. You follow your religion and I follow mine."

6. Lakum deenukum wa liya deen.

لَكُمْ دِينُكُمْ وَلِيَ دِينِ ۝٦

Al-Nasr, The Help (110)

In the Name of Allah,
the Beneficent, the Merciful.

Sûrat an-Naṣr-110

(Revealed at Madinah)
Bismillaahir Raḥmaanir Raḥeem

(١١٠) سُورَةُ النَّصْرِ مَدَنِيَّةٌ (١١٤)

بِسْمِ اللَّهِ الرَّحْمَٰنِ الرَّحِيمِ

1. (Muhammad), when help and victory come from Allah,

1. Izaa jaaa'a naṣrul-laahi wal-fatḥ.

إِذَا جَآءَ نَصْرُ اللَّهِ وَالْفَتْحُ ۝١

2. you will see large groups of people embracing the religion of Allah.

2. Wa ra-aytan-naasa yad-khuloona fee deenil-laahi af-waajaa.

وَرَأَيْتَ النَّاسَ يَدْخُلُونَ فِي دِينِ اللَّهِ أَفْوَاجًا ۝٢

3. Glorify your Lord with praise and ask Him for forgiveness. He accepts repentance.

3. Fasabbiḥ biḥamdi Rabbi-ka wastaghfirh; innahoo kaana Tawwaabaa.

فَسَبِّحْ بِحَمْدِ رَبِّكَ وَاسْتَغْفِرْهُ ۚ إِنَّهُ كَانَ تَوَّابًا ۝٣

Al-Masad, Condemnation (111)

In the Name of Allah,
the Beneficent, the Merciful.

Sûrat al-Lahab-111

(Revealed at Makkah)
Bismillaahir Raḥmaanir Raḥeem

(١١١) سُورَةُ اللَّهَبِ مَكِّيَّةٌ (٦)

بِسْمِ اللَّهِ الرَّحْمَٰنِ الرَّحِيمِ

1. May the hands of Abu Lahab perish!

1. Tabbat yadaaa Abee Laha-biñw-wa tabb.

تَبَّتْ يَدَآ أَبِي لَهَبٍ وَتَبَّ ۝١

2. May he also perish!

2. Maaa aghnaa 'anhu maa-luhoo wa maa kasab.

مَآ أَغْنَىٰ عَنْهُ مَالُهُ وَمَا كَسَبَ ۝٢

3. His property and worldly gains will be of no help to him.

3. Sayaṣlaa Naaran zaata lahab.

سَيَصْلَىٰ نَارًا ذَاتَ لَهَبٍ ۝٣

4. He will suffer in a blazing fire

4. Wamra-atuhoo ḥammaa-latal- ḥaṭab.

وَامْرَأَتُهُ حَمَّالَةَ الْحَطَبِ ۝٤

5. and so also will his wife who (threw thorns and firewood in the Prophet's way). Around her neck will be a rope of palm fiber.

5. Fee jeedihaa ḥablum mim masad.

فِي جِيدِهَا حَبْلٌ مِّن مَّسَدٍ ۝٥

Al-Ikhlas, The Purity (112)

In the Name of Allah,
the Beneficent, the Merciful.

Sûrat al-Ikhlâṣ-112

(Revealed at Makkah)
Bismillaahir Raḥmaanir Raḥeem

(١١٢) سُورَةُ الْإِخْلَاصِ مَكِّيَّةٌ (٢٢)

بِسْمِ اللَّهِ الرَّحْمَٰنِ الرَّحِيمِ

1. (Muhammad), say, "He is Allah, Who is One (indivisible).

1. Qul Huwal-laahu Aḥad.

قُلْ هُوَ اللَّهُ أَحَدٌ ۝١

2. Allah is Absolute (Self-sufficient).

2. Allaahuṣ-Ṣamad.

اللَّهُ الصَّمَدُ ۝٢

3. He did not have any child nor was He a child of others.

3. Lam yalid wa lam yoolad.

لَمْ يَلِدْ وَلَمْ يُولَدْ ۝٣

4. There was (and is) no one equal (similar, like, alternative, substitutive) to Him (nor will there ever be)."

4. Walam yakul-lahoo kufu-wan aḥad.

وَلَمْ يَكُن لَّهُ كُفُوًا أَحَدٌ ۝٤

Al-Falaq, The Fissure (a well in hell) (113)

In the Name of Allah,
the Beneficent, the Merciful.

Sûrat al-Falaq-113

(Revealed at Makkah)
Bismillaahir Raḥmaanir Raḥeem

(١١٣) سُورَةُ الْفَلَقِ مَكِّيَّةٌ (٢٠)

بِسْمِ اللَّهِ الرَّحْمَٰنِ الرَّحِيمِ

1. (Muhammad), say, "I seek protection of the Lord of Al-Falaq (fissure, a well in hell, a physical function)

1. Qul a'oozu bi Rabbil-falaq.

قُلْ أَعُوذُ بِرَبِّ الْفَلَقِ ۝١

2. against the evil of things He has created.
3. I seek His protection against the evil of the perpetrator's invasion,
4. and from the evil of those who practice witchcraft,
5. and from the evil of the envious ones."

2. Min sharri maa khalaq.
3. Wa min sharri ghaasiqin izaa waqab.
4. Wa min sharrin-naffaa-saati fil'uqad.
5. Wa min sharri ḥaasidin izaa ḥasad.

مِنْ شَرِّ مَا خَلَقَ ۝٢
وَمِنْ شَرِّ غَاسِقٍ إِذَا وَقَبَ ۝٣
وَمِنْ شَرِّ النَّفّٰثٰتِ فِي الْعُقَدِ ۝٤
وَمِنْ شَرِّ حَاسِدٍ إِذَا حَسَدَ ۝٥ ع ٥ ٣٨

Al-Nas, People (114)

In the Name of Allah, the Beneficent, the Merciful.

Sûrat an-Nâs-114

(Revealed at Makkah)

Bismillaahir Raḥmaanir Raḥeem

(١١٤) سُوْرَةُ النَّاسِ مَكِّيَّةٌ (٢١)

اٰيَاتُهَا ٦ بِسْمِ اللّٰهِ الرَّحْمٰنِ الرَّحِيْمِ رُكُوْعُهَا ١

1. (Muhammad), say, "I seek protection of the Cherisher of people,
2. the King of people,
3. the Lord of people
4. against the evil of the temptations of Satan,
5. who induce temptation into the hearts of people,
6. from the jinn and human beings."

1. Qul a'oozu bi-Rabbin-naas.
2. Malikin-naas.
3. Ilaahin-naas.
4. Min sharril-waswaasil-khannaas.
5. Allazee yuwaswisu fee ṣudoorin-naas.
6. Minal-jinnati wannaas.

قُلْ أَعُوْذُ بِرَبِّ النَّاسِ ۝١
مَلِكِ النَّاسِ ۝٢
إِلٰهِ النَّاسِ ۝٣
مِنْ شَرِّ الْوَسْوَاسِ ۵ الْخَنَّاسِ ۝٤
الَّذِيْ يُوَسْوِسُ فِيْ صُدُوْرِ النَّاسِ ۝٥
مِنَ الْجِنَّةِ وَالنَّاسِ ۝٦ ع ٦ ٣٩

تمّت بالخير

Prayer
(To be used after reading the Holy Qur'an)

دُعَاءُ خَتْمِ الْقُرْاٰنِ

اَللّٰهُمَّ اٰنِسْ وَحْشَتِيْ فِيْ قَبْرِيْ اَللّٰهُمَّ ارْحَمْنِيْ بِالْقُرْاٰنِ الْعَظِيْمِ وَاجْعَلْهُ لِيْ إِمَامًا وَّنُوْرًا وَّ

Allahumma aanis waḥshatee fee qabree! Allahummar-ḥamnee bil-Qur-aanil-'Aẓeemi waj'alhu leee imaamañw-wa noorañw-wa

O Allah! Change my fear in my grave into love! O Allah! Have mercy on me in the name of the Great Qur'an; and make it for me a Guide and Light and

هُدًى وَّرَحْمَةً اَللّٰهُمَّ ذَكِّرْنِيْ مِنْهُ مَا نَسِيْتُ وَعَلِّمْنِيْ مِنْهُ مَا جَهِلْتُ وَارْزُقْنِيْ تِلَاوَتَهٗ اٰنَاءَ

hudañw-wa raḥmah! Allahumma zakkirnee minhu maa naseetu wa 'allimnee minhu maa jahiltu warzuqnee tilaawatahooo aanaaa'al-

Guidance and Mercy! O Allah! Make me remember what of it I have forgotten; and make me know of it that which have become ignorant of; and make me recite it in the hours of

اللَّيْلِ وَاٰنَاءَ النَّهَارِ وَاجْعَلْهُ لِيْ حُجَّةً يَّا رَبَّ الْعٰلَمِيْنَ ۝

layli wa aanaaa'an-nahaari waj'alhu lee ḥujjatañy-yaa Rabbal-'aalameen.

the night and the day; and make it an argument for me O Thou Sustainer of (all) the worlds!
Ameen!

الحمدُ لله نحمدُهُ ، وهو المستحقُّ للحمد والثناء، نستعين به في السرّاء والضرّاءِ، ونستغفره ونستهديه لما يقرّبنا إليه، ونؤمن به، ونتوكلُ عليه، في جميع حالاتنا، ونصلي ونسلم على أفضل مبعوث للعالمين، وأوّل مشفَّع في يوم العرض والحساب سيّدنا ونبيّنا محمّد وعلىٰ آله وأصحابه ومن تبع هديه إلى يوم الدّين. اللّٰهم يا باسِطَ اليدين بالعطيّة والإجابة لعباده، ويا صاحبَ المواهبِ والعطفِ والرّأفة على خلقه، نسألكُ اللّٰهم أن تصلي وتسلم على عبدِك ورسولِك سيّدنا محمّد، كما صلّيت علىٰ إبراهيمَ وعلىٰ آلِ إبراهيم إنّك حميدٌ مجيدٌ. اللّٰهمّ إنّا عبيدك بنو عبيدك بنو إمائك، عدلٌ فينا قضاؤك، نسألك بكُلِّ اسم هو لك، سمّيتَ به نفسك، أو أنزلته في كتابك، أوعلّمته أحداً من خلقك، أو استأثرتَ به في علم الغيب عندك، نسألكَ يَا حَيّ يا قيّومُ أن تجعلَ القرآن العظيم ربيع قلوبنا ونور أبصارنا، وجلاء حزننا، وذهابَ همّنا وغمنا ياأرحم الرّاحمين ، اللّٰهُمّ يا ذاالمنِّ ولايُمَنُّ عليه، ياذاالجلال والاكرام، يا محيطا بالليالي والأيّام، نسألك يا أرحم الرّاحمين، يا جارالمستجيرين، ياأمان الخآئفينَ، أن تجعل القرآن العظيمَ ربيعَ قلوبنا ونورَ أبصارِنا، وجَلآءَ حُزنِنَا، وذَهَابَ هَمّنا وَغمّنا. اللّٰهُمّ إنّا نسألُك إيمانًا لايَرتدُّ، ونعيماً لا ينفد وقرّة عينٍ لاتنقطعُ، ولذّة النّظرِ إلى وجهك، ومرافقة نبينا مُحَمّدٍ صلى اللّٰه عليه وسلم في جنّاتِ النعيم.

اللّٰهُمّ ارحَمنا بترك المعاصي أبدًا ماأبقيتَنا، وارحمنا أن نتكلّف مالا يعنينا، وارزقنا حسن النّظرِ فيما يُرضيك عنّا. اَللّٰهُمّ بديع السّمٰوٰتِ والأرضِ ذاالجلالِ والإكرام والعزّةِ الّتي لاترام، نسألك يا اللّٰه يا رحمٰنُ يا رحيمُ بجلالك ونور وجهك أن تُلزِمَ قلوبنا حفظَ كتابك كما علّمتنا، وارزقنا أن نتلُوهُ على النّحو الّذى يرضيك عنّا. اَللّٰهُمّ بديع السّمٰوٰتِ وَالأرضِ ذاالجلال والإكرام والعزّةِ الّتى لاترام، نسألكَ يا اللّٰه يا رحمٰن بجلالك ونورِ وجهك أن تنوّر بكتابك أبصارنا وأن تُطلِقَ به ألسنتنا وأن تُفرّجَ به عن قلوبنا، وأن تشرَحَ به صدورنا، وأن تستعمل به أبداننا، فإنه لايُعينُنا على الحقِ غيرك ولا يؤتيه لنا إلاأنت ولاحول ولا قوّةَ إلّا باللّٰهِ العليّ العظم اللّٰهُمّ إنّا نسألك رَحمَةً من عِندِك تَهدِي بها قُلوبَنا، وَتجمَعُ بهَا أُمورنا وَتَلُمّ بها شعثَنا، وتُصلِحُ بهَا غَائِبَنا، وَتُزكّي بها أعمالنا، وتُلهمنَا بهَا رُشدَنَا وَتَرُدُّبهَا أُلفَتَنا وَتعصمُنا بها من كُلِّ سوءٍ. رَبّنَا لاتُؤاخِذنا إن نسينا أو أخطأنا، ربّنا ولاتحمل علينا إصراً كَمَا حملتَهُ عَلى الّذين من قبلنا، ربّنا وَلاتُحَمّلنَا ما لا طاقة لنا به واعفُ عَنّا واغفرلنا وارحَمنا. اَنت مولانا فانصرنَا على القَوْمِ الكافِرِينَ.

اللّٰهمّ فَارجَ الهَمّ، كَاشِفَ الغَمّ، مجيب دعوة المضطرّين، رحمَانَ الدُّنيا والآخرةِ ورحيمَهُما، ارحمنا برحمةٍ تغنينا بها عن رحمة من سواك. اللّٰهمّ اكفنا بحلالك عن حرامك وبطاعتك عن معصيتك وأغننا بفضلك وجودك وكرمك عمن سواك. اللّٰهمّ إنا نسألك إيمانًا يباشر قلوبنا، ويقيناً صادقاً حتى نعلم أنه لايصيبُنا إلّاماكتبْت لنا، واجعلنا راضين من الرّزق والعيش بما قسمت لنا، اللّٰهمّ إنا نسألكَ موجبات رحمتك وعزائم مغفرتك، والسّلامة من كل إثمٍ، والغنيمة من كلّ برٍّ، ونسألك الفوز بالجنة والنجاة من النار. اللّٰهمّ اقسم لنا من خشيتك ما تحول به بيننا وبين معاصيك، ومن طاعتك ما تُبلّغنا به جنّتك. ومن اليقين ماتهوّن به مصائب الدنيا ومتّعنا اللّٰهُمّ بأسماعنا وأبصارنا وقوّاتنا ماأحييتنا، واجعله الوارث منا . واجعل ثأرنا على من ظلمنا وانصرنا علىٰ من عادانا. ولاتجعل مصيبتنا في ديننا، ولا تجعل الدنيا أكبر همنا. ولا مبلغ علمنا. ولا تسلّط علينا بذنوبنا من لايخافك ولا يرحمنا. وكُفّ أيدي الظّالمين عنّا، برحمتك يا أرحم الرّاحمين. اللّٰهُمّ اجعلنا ممن سبقت لهم منك الحسنى وزيادة. اللّٰهُمّ أغننا بالعلم. وزيّنا بالحلم، وأكرمنا بالتقوىٰ وجملنا بالعافية. اللّٰهُمّ علّمنا ماينفعنا وانفعنا بما علمتنا، وزدنا علماً، الحمدللّٰه على كل حال ونعوذ باللّٰه من حال أهل النار.

اللّٰهمّ اجعل جمعنا هذا جمعاً مرحوماً، وتفرقنا من بعده تفرقاً معصوماً، ولاتجعل فينا ولامعنا شقيًّا ولا مطرودا ولامحروماً برحمتك يا أرحم الرّاحمين. يا حيّ يا قيّوم برحمتك نستغيث، ومن عذابك نستجير، أصلح لنا شأننا كله، ولا تكلنا إلى أنفسنا طرفة عين. رَبّنَا لاتُزغ قلوبنا بعد إذ هديتنا وهب لنا من لدنك رحمةً إنك أنت الوهّابُ، اللّٰهُمّ ارحمنا وارحم آباء نا وأُمّهاتنا وإخوانَنا المسلمين، الذين سبقونا بالايمان ولاتجعل في قلوبنا غِلاّ لّلذين آمنوا ربنااِنك رؤوف رحيم. اللّٰهمّ ارحمهم، وعافهم، واعف عنهم، وأكرم نُزُلَهُم و وسّع مَدخَلَهُم واغسلهُم بالماء والثلج والبَرَد. اللّٰهمّ جازهم بالحسنات إحساناً وبالسيئات عفوًا وغفراناً، ولقّهم برحمتك رضاك وقِهم فتنة القبر وعذابه. اللّٰهمّ أوصل ثواب ماقرأناه من القرآن العظيم إليهم وضاعف رحمتك ورضوانك عليهم. اللّٰهمّ حل أرواحهم في محل الأبرار وتغمدهم بالرّحمة آناء اللّيل و النّهار برحمتك يا أرحم الراحمين. اللّٰهم انقلهم من ضيق اللحود والقبورِ الى سعة الدور والقصور، في سدر مخضود، وطلح منضود، وظلّ ممدود، ومآءٍ مسكوب، وفاكهة كثيرةٍ لامقطوعةٍ ولا ممنوعةٍ مع الذين أنعمت عليهم من النبيّين والصدّيقين والشُّهدآءِ والصّالحين برحمتك يا أرحمَ الراحمين. اللّٰهم اجعلنا وإياهم من عبادك الذين تباهي بهم ملائكتك في الموقف العظيم وارزقنا حسن النظرِ إلى وجهك الكريم مع الذين أنعمت عليهم من النبيّين والصدّيقين والشهدآء والصّالحين الذين تجري من تحتهم الأنهار في جنّاتِ النعيم، دعواهم فيها سبحانك اللّٰهمّ وتحيتهم فيها سلام، وآخر دعوانا أنِ الحمد للّٰه ربّ العالمين.

جمع

مدير إدارة إحياء التراث الإسلامي

خادم القرآن الكريم

عبدالله بن ابراهيم الأنصاري

Index

(Bold numerical in the reference numbers denote
Surah Nos. while other numerical show the *Ayât* Nos.)

Betray (deceive, fraud), **2**:187; **4**:107;
5:13; **8**:27,58,71; **12**:52; **22**:38;
66:10
Birds, **2**:260; **3**:49; **5**:110; **6**:38; **12**:36,41;
16:79; **21**:79; **22**:31; **24**:41;
27:16,17,20; **34**:10; **38**:19; **56**:21;
67:19; **105**:3.
Blood-money *(Diya),* **2**:178,179; **4**:92;
17:33
Book, This word occurs more than 300 times in the Noble Qur'ân.
Mentioning every place will make the Index very big.
Booty, war, **4**:94; **8**:41; *Fai,* **59**:6-8;
Ghulul, **3**:161 (Sec spoils)
taking illegally, **3**:162
Bribery, **2**:188
Budn, **22**:36
Burden
of another, no bearer of burdens shall bear the,
35:18; **39**:7; **53**:38
disbelievers will bear also the burdens of others, **16**:25; **29**:13
evil indeed are the burdens that they will bear, **6**:31,164
Allâh burdens not a person beyond his scope,
2:286; **7**:42; **23**:62
*Burûj(*Big stars), S. **85**; **85**:1; **15**:16;
25:61
Camel, **6**:144; **7**:40; **77**:33; **88**:17
Captives, **4**:25; **8**:67,70,71; **9**:60;
33:26,27; **76**:8 (see also Prisoners of war)
Cattle, **3**:14; **4**:119; **5**:1; **6**:136,138, 139,142;
7:179; **10**:24; **16**:5-8,10,66,80; **20**:54;
22:28,30,34; **23**:21; **25**:44,49; **26**:133;
32:27; **35**:28; **36**:71-73; **39**:6; **40**:79;
42:11; **43**:12,13; **47**:12; **79**:33; **80**:32.
Cave of Thawr, **9**:40
Cave, people of the **18**:9-22,25,26
Certainty with truth, **56**:95; **69**:51;
Charity, *(Sadaqah),* **2**:196,263,264,270,
271,273; **4**:114; **9**:58,75,76-79,103,104;
57:18; **58**:12,13
objects of charity and *Zakât,* **2**:273; **9**:60
Children **2**:233; **42**:49,50
lost are they who haw killed their, from folly, without knowledge. **6**:140
Christ, (see Jesus)
Christians, This word occurs more than 600 times in the Noble Qur'ân.
Mentioning every place will make the Index very big.
Cities overthrown, **69**:9
City of security, **95**:3
Confederates, **33**:9,22 - *see Ahzâh.*
Consultation, mutual, **42**:38
Creation,
begins and repeated, **10**:4; **21**:104;
27:64; **29**:19,20
a new, **17**:49,98; **35**:16
with truth, **15**:85; **16**:3; **29**:44; **39**:5; **44**:39;
45:22; **46**:3
not for play, **21**:16,17; **24**:l15
every living thing made from, **21**:30; **24**:45;
25:54
of man, **4**:1; **6**:2; **15**:26,28,33; **16**:4
21:30; **22**:5; **23**:12-14; **25**:54; **32**:7-9;
35:11; **36**:77,78; **37**:11; **39**:6; **40**:67; **49**:13;
55:14; **56**:57-59; **75**:37-40; **76**:1,2;
77:20-23; **80**:18,19; **86**:5-8; **96**:2
the first form of **56**:62
in six Days, **7**:54; **11**:7; **32**:4; **50**:38; **57**:4
in pairs, **13**:3; **30**:8; **36**:36; **42**:11;
43:12; **51**:9,49; **53**:45
variety in, **35**:27,28
Allâh commands "Be!" and it is,
2:117; **16**:40; **36**:82; **40**:68
as the twinkling of an eye, **54**:50
night and day, sun and moon, **39**:5
of heaven and earth greater than, of mankind,
40:57; **79**:27
purpose of, **51**:56
Crow, **5**:31
Criterion, **2**:53,185; **3**:4; **8**:29,41; **21**:48; **25**:1
Dahr,(see Insân,) S. **76**; **45**:24
time, **76**:1; **103**:1
David, **4**:163; **6**:84; **21**:78-80; **5**:78; **34**:10,13;
38:17-30; **17**:55
fights Goliath, **2**:251

not a leaf falls, but He knows it, **6**:59
lost are they who have killed their children from folly, without, **6**:140
of five things, with Allâh Alone, **31**:34
with certainty, **102**:5-7
Korah (Qârûn), **28**:76-82; **29**:39; **40**:24
Kursi, **2**:255
Lahab (See *Masad),* S. **111**
Lail, S.**92**
Lamp, **25**:61; **67**:5; **71**:16; **78**:13
Languages, difference in, and colours of men, **30**:22
Lât, **53**:19
Law, prescribed, **5**:48
Laws from Allâh, **2**:219; **98**:3
Liars, **26**:221-223
Life, if anyone saved a, he saved the life of all mankind, **5**:32
Life of this world,
bought the, at the priceof Hereafter, **2**:86
is only the enjoyment of deception, **3**:185
sell the, for the Hereafter, **4**:74
is nothing but amusement and play, **6**:32; **29**:64; **47**:36; **57**:20
deceives, **6**:130
little is the enjoyment of the, than the Hereafter, **9**:38; **13**:26; **28**:60
likeness of, is as the min, **10**:24
glad tidings in the, **10**:64
whoever desires, gets therein; but then there will be no portion in the Hereafter, **11**:15,16; **17**:18; **42**:20
who love the present, and neglect the Hereafter, **75**:20,21; **76**:27
you prefer the, **87**:16
Light,
manifest, **4**:174
and darkness, **6**:1
parable of, **24**:35
goes before and with the Believers, **57**:12-15; **66**:8
given by Allâh, that the Believers may walk straight, **57**:2
Limits set by Allâh, **2**:173,187,190,230; **9**:112; **58**:4; **65**:1; **78**:22
these are the, **2**:187; 229,230; **4**:13; **58**:4; **65**:1
transgress not the, **2**:190,229
whosoever transgresses, **2**:229; **4**:14; **78**:22
but forced by necessity, nor transgressing the, **2**:173; **6**:145
do not exceed the, in your religion, **4**:171; **5**:77
when they exceeded the, (became monkeys), **7**:166
who observe the, **9**:112
Lion, **74**:51
Loan,
lend to Allâh a goodly, **2**:245; **73**:20
increased manifold, **57**:11,18
doubled, **64**:17
Loss, manifest, **39**:15
Lot, (Lût) **6**:86; **7**:80; **11**:70,74,77,81,89; **15**:59,61; **21**:71,74; **22**:43; **26**:160, 161,167; **27**:54-56; **29**:26,28,32,33; **37**:133; **38**:13; **50**:13; **54**:33,34; **66**:10
his disobedient wife, **11**:81; **15**:60; **66**:10
Lote tree, **34**:16; **53**:14-16; **56**:28
Luqmân, **31**:12-14
Luqmân, S.**31**
Ma'ârij, S.**70**
Madinah (Yathrib), **9**:120:33:13,60; **63**:8
Madyan, **7**:85-93; **11**:84-95; **20**:40; **22**:44; **28**:22,23; **29**:36,37 (see also *Aiyka*; Wood)
Mahr (bridal-money), **2**:229,236,237; **4**:4,19-21,24,25; **5**:5; **33**:50; **60**:10,11
Mâ'idah, S.**5**
Makkah (Bakkah), **3**:96; **90**:1,2; City of Security, **95**:3
Man,
generations after generations on earth, **2**:30; **6**:165;
made necessor, **35**:39
duty, **2**:83,84,88,177; **4**:1-36; **8**:41; **16**:90; **17**:23-39; **24**:22; **29**:8,9; **30**:38; **33**:33; **42**:23; **64**:14; **70**:22-35
tested by Allâh, **2**:155; **3**:186; **47**:31; **57**:25
things men covet, **3**:14

as a mercy from Allâh, **28**:46,47
close to the believers, **33**:6
good example to follow, **33**:21
last of the Prophets, **33**:40
send *Salât* on, **33**:56
sent to all mankind, **34**:28
wage is from Allâh only, **34**:47
only a human being, **41**:6
sent as a protector, **42**:48
not a new thing in the Messengers, **46**:9
witness from among the Children of Israel, **46**:10
Bai'âh (pledge) to him is *Bai'âh* (pledge) to Allâh, **48**:10,18
saw Gabriel, **53**:4-18; **81**:22-25
oppose him not, **58**:20-22
foretold by Jesus, **61**:6
to make Religion of Truth victorious overall religions, **61**:9
from the darkness to the light, **65**:11
to strive hard against disbelievers and hypocrites, **66**:9
exalted standard of character, **68**:4
not a poet or soothsayer, **69**:41,42
devoted to prayer, **73**:1-8,20; **74**:3
and the blind man, **80**:1-12
to prostrate and draw near to Allâh, **96**:19
reciting pure pages, **98**:2
Ayât regarding family of, **24**:11 -17; **33**:28-34,50-53,55,59; **66**:1,3-6; **108**:3
(see also Messengers; Prophets)

Muhammad, S,**47**

Muhsinûn (Good-doers), **2**:117,195; **4**:125,128; **10**:126; **16**:128
Allâh loves the, **3**:134,148; **5**:93
Allâh loses not the reward of the, **5**:85; **9**:120; **11**:115; **18**:30
We reward the, **12**:22; **37**:80,105,110; **39**:34; **77**:44
glad tidings to the, **22**:37; **46**:12
Allâh's Mercy is near to the, **7**:56
Allâh is with the, **29**:69
dutiful and good to parents, **2**:83
patient in performing duties to Allâh, **16**:90 (see also Good and Evil)

Mujâdilah, S,**58**

Mules, **16**:8

Mulk, S,**67**

Mu'min (see *Ghâfir*), S,**40**

Mu'minûn, S,**23**

Mumtahanah, S,**60**

Munâfiqûn, S,**63**

Murder, **2**:178,179

Mursalât, S,**77**

Muslims,
first of the, **6**:14,163; **9**:100; **39**:12
Who has named, **22**:78
forgiveness and a great reward for them who, **33**:35,36

Mutaffifin, S,**83**

Muzzammil, S,**73**

Naba', S,**78**

Nadîr, Banû-An-,(Jews), **59**:2,9,13

Nahl, S,**53**

Najas (impure) **9**:28 and its footnote.

Najm, S,**53**

Najwâ (See Secret)

Names,
to Him belong the Most Beautiful, **7**:180
to Him belong the Best, **17**:110; **20**:8; **59**:24
Naml, S,**27**
Nas, S,114
Nasr, **71**:23
Nasr, S,**110**
Nâzi'ât, S,**79**

Necessity, if one is forced by, **2**:173; **6**:145

Neighbour, **4**:36

New moons, **2**:189

News, to be tested, **4**:83

Niggards condemned, **17**:29; **47**:38; **48**:38

Night, (as a symbol), **79**:29; **92**:1; **93**:2; for rest, **10**:67
as a covering, **13**:3; **78**:10
to be of service, **14**:32
Night of *Al-Qadr* (Decree), **44**:3,4; **97**:1-5

Nisâ', S,**4**

Noah, **3**:33; **4**:163; **6**:84; **7**:59-69; **9**:70; **10**:71; **11**:25,32,36,42,45,46,48,89; **17**:3; **21**:76; **23**:23; **25**:37; **26**:105;

recite and pray, **29**:45
Truth from Allâh, **32**:3; **35**:31
on a blessed Night, **44**:3
therein is decreed every matter of ordainments, **44**:4
think deeply in the, **47**:24
warn by the, **50**:45
taught by Allâh, **55**:1
and honourable recital, well-guarded, **56**:77,78
non can touch but who are pure, **56**:79
if sent down on a mountain, **59**:21
an anguish for the disbelievers, **69**:50
an absolute truth with certainty, **69**:51
recite in a slow style, **73**:4
in Records held in honour, kept pure and holy, **80**:13-16
a Reminder to (all) the *'Âlamîn,* **81**:27
disbelievers belie, **84**:22
in Tablet preserved, **85**:22
Word that separates the truth from falsehood, **86**:13
reciting pure pages, **98**:2
(see also Book; Revelation)
Quraish, S.**106**
Quraish,
disbelievers of, **54**:43-46,51
taming of, **106**:1-4
Rabbis and monks, **9**:31,34
Race, strive as in a, in good deeds, **5**:48
Ra 'd, S.**13**
Rahmân, S.**55**
Raiment of righteousness is better, **7**:26
Rain,
Allâh's Gift, **56**:68-70
of stones, **27**:58
Ramadân, **2**:185
Ramy, **2**:200
Ransom,
no, shall be taken, **57**:15
offered by disbelievers, **3**:91; **10**:54; **13**:18
Fidyah, of fast, **2**:196; for freeing the captives, **8**:67
Rass, dwellers of the, **25**:38; **50**:12
Reality, **69**:1-3
Recompense,
the Day of, **1**:4; **37**:20; **51**:12; **56**:56; **82**:17,18; **96**:7
deniers of, **107**:1-7
of an evil is an evil like thereof, **42**:40
Reconciliation,
whoever forgives and makes, **42**:40
between man and wife, **4**:35
between believers, **49**:9,10
Record,
a Register inscribed, **83**:7-9,18-21
each nation will be called to its, **45**:28,29
written pages of deeds of every person, **81**:10
which speaks the truth, **23**:62
in right hand, **69**:19; **84**:7-9
in left hand, **69**:25
behind the back, **84**:10-15
Recording angels, **50**:17,18,23; **85**:11
Relief, with the hardship, **94**:5,6
Religion,
no compulsion in, **2**:256
is Islâm, **3**:19
of Allâh, **3**:83,84
other than Islâm, **3**:85
do not exceed the limits in, **4**:171; **5**:77
perfected, **5**:3
who take, as play and amusement, **6**:70
who divide their, and break up into sects, **6**:159; **30**:32 (see also **42**:13,14; **43**:65; **45**:17)
men have broken their, into sects, each group rejoicing in its belief, **23**:53; **30**:32
not laid in, any hardship, **22**:78
mankind created on the, **30**:30
same, for all Prophets, **42**:13-15
ancestral, **43**:22-24
Remembrance of Allâh, **63**:9
in the, hearts find rest, **13**:28
Repentance,
accepted if evil done in ignorance and repent soon afterwards, **4**:17; **6**:54
and of no effect is the, if evil deeds are continued, **4**:18
He accepts, and forgives sins, **4**:25
Respite for evil, **3**:178; **10**:11; **12**:110;